THE OXFORD ENCYCLOPEDIA OF
AMERICAN URBAN HISTORY

Editor in Chief
Timothy J. Gilfoyle
LOYOLA UNIVERSITY CHICAGO

THE OXFORD ENCYCLOPEDIA OF
AMERICAN URBAN HISTORY

Timothy J. Gilfoyle

EDITOR IN CHIEF

VOLUME 1

OXFORD

UNIVERSITY PRESS

OXFORD
UNIVERSITY PRESS

Oxford University Press is a department of the University of Oxford.
It furthers the University's objective of excellence in research, scholarship,
and education by publishing worldwide. Oxford is a registered trade mark of
Oxford University Press in the UK and certain other countries.

Published in the United States of America by Oxford University Press
198 Madison Avenue, New York, NY 10016, United States of America.

© Oxford University Press 2019

Library of Congress Cataloging-in-Publication Data
Names: Gilfoyle, Timothy J., editor.
Title: The Oxford encyclopedia of American urban history / Timothy J.
Gilfoyle, Editor in Chief.
Description: First edition. | New York, NY : Oxford University Press, 2019. |
Includes bibliographical references and index.
Identifiers: LCCN 2018041991| ISBN 9780190853860 (set) | ISBN 9780190854195
(volume 1) | ISBN 9780190854201 (volume 2)
Subjects: LCSH: Urbanization—United States—History. | Cities and
Towns—United States—History.
Classification: LCC HT384.U5 O94 2019 | DDC 307.760973—dc23
LC record available at https://lccn.loc.gov/2018041991

Printed by Sheridan Books, Inc., United States of America

To Kenneth T. Jackson

About the
Oxford Research Encyclopedias

The *Oxford Encyclopedia of American Urban History* is published as part of the *Oxford Research Encyclopedia of American History*, a dynamic and scholarly digital resource. This online collection of overview articles provides in-depth, foundational essays on both essential and emerging topics in American history. All articles are commissioned under the editorial leadership of international experts of the highest caliber and are vetted through rigorous peer review. A living reference work, the online publication is updatable and enriched with cross-linking and multimedia features. The essays are intended for scholars, practitioners, and university-level readers, including advanced undergraduates, graduate students, and researchers.

Oxford Research Encyclopedia of American History
Editor in Chief: Jon Butler, Yale University

Contents

List of Articles   xi

Preface   xv

Acknowledgments   xxiii

ARTICLES

Varieties of Urbanization
Political Economies
Informal Economies
Urban Migrations
Neighborhood, Community, and Space
Building the Metropolis
Nature and the Environment
The Social Fabric
Violence and Disorder
The Postwar and Postindustrial Metropolis

Directory of Contributors (vol. 2)   1573

Index (vol. 2)   1577

List of Articles

Varieties of Urbanization (vol. 1)

Mississippian Ancient Towns and Cities, 1000–1700
Robbie Ethridge

Seaport Cities in North America, 1600–1800
Emma Hart

Industry, Commerce, and Urbanization in the United States, 1790–1870
David Schley

Industry, Commerce, and Urbanization in the United States, 1880–1929
Jonathan Rees

Urban Exceptionalism in the American South
David Goldfield

Company Towns in the United States
Hardy Green

Globalization and the American City
Betsy A. Beasley

Political Economies (vol. 1)

Politics in Urban America before 1940
James J. Connolly

Politics in Urban America after 1945
Lily Geismer

Slavery in American Cities
Leslie M. Harris

The Central Business District in American Cities
Emily Remus

Progressives and Progressivism in an Era of Reform
Maureen A. Flanagan

The Great Depression
Erik S. Gellman and Margaret Rung

The New Deal
Wendy L. Wall

American Labor and Working-Class History, 1900–1945
Jeffrey Helgeson

Public Sector Unions in the United States
Joseph E. Hower

Public Authorities in the United States
Gail Radford

Service Economies and the American Postindustrial City, 1950–present
Patrick Vitale

Deindustrialization and the American Postindustrial City, 1950–present
Chloe E. Taft

Universities and Information Centers in US Cities
LaDale Winling

Tourism and the American City since 1800
J. Mark Souther

Professional Team Sports in the United States
Steven A. Riess

Informal Economies (vol. 1)

Gambling in Northern US Cities
Matthew Vaz

Temperance and Prohibition
H. Paul Thompson Jr.

Prostitutes and Prostitution in America
Jessica Pliley

Drug Subcultures in the American City
Chris Elcock

Urban Migrations (vol. 1)

Immigration to American Cities, 1800–1924
Hidetaka Hirota

Immigration to American Cities, 1924–2017
Charlotte Brooks

Ellis Island Immigration Station
Vincent J. Cannato

Angel Island Immigration Station
Judy Yung and Erika Lee

Immigration to the United States after 1945
Xiaojian Zhao

The Great Migration and Black Urban Life in the United States, 1914–1970
Tyina Steptoe

The Great Migration in Context: The Chicago Experience, 1916–1918
Christopher R. Reed

White Internal Migration to American Cities, 1940–1970
Chad Berry

Polish Immigration and the American Working Class
Dominic Pacyga

Irish Immigration and the American Working Class
David Brundage

Neighborhood, Community, and Space (vol. 1)

Spatial Segregation and US Neighborhoods
Carl Nightingale

Ethnicity and US Neighborhoods
Jordan Stanger-Ross

LGBTQ Politics in America since 1945
Emily K. Hobson

Native Americans and Cities
Nicolas G. Rosenthal

Latino Urbanism
A. K. Sandoval-Strausz

Puerto Ricans in the United States
Lorrin Thomas

Latino/a and African American Relations
Brian D. Behnken

The Asian American Movement
Daryl Joji Maeda

Japanese Resettlement in Postwar America:
    The Los Angeles Experience
Jean-Paul R. deGuzman

Vietnamese Americans in Little Saigon,
    California
Phuong Nguyen

Building the Metropolis (vol. 2)

Suburbanization in the United States
    before 1945
Ann Durkin Keating

Municipal Housing in America
Margaret Garb

Public Housing in Urban America
D. Bradford Hunt

Housing Policy across the United States
Kristin M. Szylvian

Urban Destruction during the American
    Civil War
Megan Kate Nelson

Skyscrapers and Tall Buildings
Elihu Rubin

The City Beautiful Movement
John D. Fairfield

Urban Planning in the United States
    since 1850
Harold L. Platt

Water and Sewers in the American City
Joel A. Tarr

Mass Transit in 19th- and 20th-Century
    America
Jay Young

Streets, Roads, and Highways in the United
    States
Peter Norton

The Automobile and the American City
David Blanke

Public Space in American Cities
Jessica Sewell

Nature and the Environment (vol. 2)

Parks in Urban America
David Schuyler

Environmental and Conservation
    Movements in Metropolitan America
Robert R. Gioielli

Environmental Pollution and the American
    City
Brian McCammack

Contagious Diseases and Public Health in
    the American City
Daniel Wilson

Climate Change and the American City
Andrew Hurley

Food in the 19th-Century American City
Cindy Lobel

Food in the 20th-Century American City
Adam Shprintzen

The Social Fabric (vol. 2)

Religion in the American City, 1600–1900
Kyle B. Roberts

Religion in the American City, 1900–2000
Christopher D. Cantwell

Poverty in the Modern American City
Ella Howard

Wars on Poverty and the Building of the American Welfare State
David Torstensson

Schools in US Cities
Ansley T. Erickson

Nightlife in the American City
Peter C. Baldwin

Jazz, Blues, and Ragtime in America, 1900–1945
Court Carney

Jazz in America after 1945
John Gennari

Rock and Roll
Eric Weisbard

Rap Music
Austin McCoy

Violence and Disorder (vol. 2)

Riots and Rioting in US Cities, 1800–2000
Alex Elkins

The Anti-Chinese Massacre in Los Angeles as a Reconstruction-Era Event
Victor Jew

Asian Americas and the 1992 Los Angeles Uprising
Shelley Sang-Hee Lee

Street Gangs in the 20th-Century American City
Andrew J. Diamond

Juvenile Justice in the United States
David S. Tanenhaus

United States Vagrancy Laws
Risa L. Goluboff and Adam Sorensen

The Postwar and Postindustrial Metropolis (vol. 2)

The Black Freedom Struggle in the Urban North
Thomas J. Sugrue

The Black Freedom Struggle in the Urban South
Claudrena N. Harold

The Sit-in Movement
Christopher W. Schmidt

The Sixties
Robert O. Self

Suburbanization in America after 1945
Becky Nicolaides and Andrew Wiese

Asian American Suburban Culture since World War II
Mark Padoongpatt

Zoning in 20th-Century American Cities
Christopher Silver

Urban Renewal
Christopher Klemek

Japantown and the San Francisco Fillmore District
Clement Lai

Gentrification in the United States
Suleiman Osman

Preface

"The United States was born in the country and has moved to the city," summarized the historian Richard Hofstadter in 1955.[1] For centuries, the populations of North America structured their lives around agriculture and rural life. In 1790, the United States populace was 95 percent agrarian. By 1920, however, more than half the citizenry lived in cities or towns; by 1990, less than three percent of all Americans were employed in agriculture. American history, Hofstadter and others argued, was best understood through the *longue durée* of urban growth. American democracy may have been nurtured on the rural frontier, as the historian Frederick Jackson Turner theorized, but modern America was a product of urbanization. Between 1800 and 2000, American metropolitan communities were transformed from "horizontal" cities of row houses, tenements, and factories to "vertical" cities of apartments and skyscrapers. From New York's Brooklyn Bridge to Chicago's Sears Tower and to San Francisco's Golden Gate Bridge, the tower and the bridge epitomized American urbanism. The transformation of the American urban landscape mirrored the equally disruptive social, cultural, environmental, and economic changes happening not only in cities but across the country.

In 1970, the historian Richard Wade complained about the dearth of research on American cities.[2] Few make such claims today. *The Oxford Encyclopedia of American Urban History* synthesizes three generations of urban

---

1 Richard Hofstadter, *The Age of Reform: From Bryan to FDR* (New York: Alfred A. Knopf, 1955), 23.
2 Richard Wade, "An Agenda for Urban History," in *The State of American History*, ed. Herbert J. Bass (Chicago: Quadrangle Books, 1970), 43–69.

historical scholarship, providing a thematic and chronological overview of American urban history from the pre-Columbian era to the first decades of the 21st century. The ninety-two articles contained in these two volumes describe and analyze the transformation of the United States from a simple agrarian and small-town society to a complex urban and suburban nation. Each article has been authored, peer-reviewed, and edited by scholars who are expert in the field, offering a reliable, historiographically informed examination of a specific subject in American urban history. The *Encyclopedia* differs from previous publications by providing semi-structured, synoptic articles ranging from 6,000 to 8,000 words each. The individual entries are divided into three parts: 1) an accessible narrative overview of a major topic in urban history; 2) a brief historiographical summary of the major writers and publications on the topic; and 3) a short introduction to important primary sources on the subject. This tripartite format allows each article to serve multiple audiences: those who simply want an informed and intelligent introduction to the topic; those interested in identifying the leading publications on a specific subject; and, finally, those interested in pursuing research on the subject at hand.

Certain recurring themes in American urban and cultural history permeate *The Oxford Encyclopedia of American Urban History*: the interaction of private commerce with cultural change; the rise of new working and middle classes; the creation and segregation of public and private spaces; the formation of new urban subcultures organized by gender, work, race, religion, ethnicity, and sexuality; problems of health and housing resulting from congestion; and blatant social divisions among wealthy, poor, native-born, immigrant, and racial groups. More broadly, the volumes attempt to comprehend the American city within the changing questions of what makes American cities distinctive. Why do American cities look the way they do? What characterizes the social and built environments of American cities? How have Americans created and adapted to those environments over time?

ORGANIZATION OF THE *OXFORD ENCYCLOPEDIA OF AMERICAN URBAN HISTORY*

The Oxford Encyclopedia of American Urban History is organized around ten broad themes. The first, "**Varieties of Urbanization**," examines the different economic and physical forms of American cities during the past millennium. Robbie Ethridge's article on "ancient" and "lost" urban settlements between 1000 and 1700 CE reconfigures North American urban history by placing the origins of the earliest settlement patterns not along the Atlantic seaboard, the borderlands of the American Southwest, or even Central America. Rather, for Ethridge, North American urban history begins in the geographic center of the continent and along the Mississippi River, exemplified by Cahokia and other pre-Columbian urban settlements before 1500. Later, the migration of European and African peoples to North America generated the first "permanent" urban settlements along the East Coast between 1600 and 1800, a development examined in Emma Hart's article on seaport cities. These cities grew slowly during the 17th and 18th centuries, but with Euro-American settlement of the interior of North America after 1790 and the rise of new industrial economies, new cities were quickly established and older coastal cities grew rapidly during the 19th and 20th centuries. This complex history is covered in articles by David Schley and Jonathan Rees. One distinctive variety of urbanization during these years was the company town, a phenomenon whose evolution is examined in Hardy Green's article. The American South was the one region that followed a different urban settlement pattern during these years, an "exceptional" process covered by David Goldfield. Finally, American cities never grew in isolation. Rather, they were influenced and affected by a multitude of global economic and migratory forces. At no point in history was the American city anything but "global." These dynamics are outlined in Betsy A. Beasley's article on globalization.

The section titled **"Political Economies"** concentrates on the relationship and intersection of urban politics with new emerging urban economies after 1800. Articles written by James J. Connolly and Lily Geismer provide overviews of the "traditional" systems of organized and party politics before and after the mid-20th century. During the Progressive Era, from 1890 to 1920, and the Great Depression and the New Deal in the 1930s, municipal politics and economies were considerably reconfigured, instigated by the urban reform movements of the first half of the 20th century. Articles by Maureen A. Flanagan, Erik S. Gellman, Margaret Rung, and Wendy L. Wall offer in-depth examinations of both national and municipal events during these years. For more detailed examinations of varied and different forms of political economy in American cities see articles on urban slavery by Leslie M. Harris, the central business district by Emily Remus, the public authority by Gail Radford, the service and post-industrial economies by Patrick Vitale and Chloe E. Taft, respectively, the university and information economies of the 20th century by LaDale Winling, urban tourism by J. Mark Souther, and 20th-century professional sports by Steven A. Riess. The impact of new economies organized around industry and "blue-collar" labor between 1850 and 1950 and those structured by service and "white-collar" workers, both of which were heavily concentrated in cities, are studied in Jeffrey Helgeson's article on industrial workers in the first half of the 20th century and Joseph E. Hower's article on public sector unionism.

As urban commerce and industry grew more complex and sophisticated after 1800,

"marginal" economic and social activity also flourished. The section **"Informal Economies"** examines the evolution of certain "criminalized" or "underground" economic and social enterprises. During the 19th and 20th centuries, the commerce related to gambling, alcohol, drug use, and sexual behavior evolved into highly developed and complex economic activities and social structures. These and related subjects are covered in the articles by Matthew Vaz on gambling in northern US cities, H. Paul Thompson Jr. on the temperance movement and Prohibition, Jessica Pliley on prostitution and related forms of commercial sex, and Chris Elcock on drug use and the emergence of related subcultures in American cities.

American cities were and are, in many ways, products of demographic revolutions that occurred in the 19th and 20th centuries. In 1800, the world's population was approximately 900 million. By 1900, the figure had increased to approximately 1.6 billion, and by 2000 to 6.1 billion.[3] The demographic transformations of the 19th and 20th centuries spurred unprecedented movements of people, many of which profoundly influenced the rise of American cities and the social structures that grew up around them. The **"Urban Migrations"** section concentrates on the three major demographic migrations to American cities: European and Asian immigrants from 1800 until 1924; European, Asian, and Latin American immigrants from 1924 until the present; and internal African American and Euro-American migrations during the twentieth century. Articles by Hidetaka Hirota, Charlotte Brooks, and Xiaojian Zhao provide broad overviews of the complicated migratory movements of foreign immigrants and refugees to the United States after 1800. David Brundage and Dominic Pacyga offer more specialized and focused examinations of

3   United Nations Populations Division, Department of Economic and Social Affairs, *The World at Six Billion* (New York: United Nations, 2002), available from http://www.un.org/en/development/desa/population/publications/pdf/newsletter/News73.pdf; United States Census Bureau, *Historical Estimates of World Population* (Washington, DC: US Census Bureau, 2018), available from https://www.census.gov/data/tables/time-series/demo/international-programs/historical-est-worldpop.html.

the immigration of Irish and Polish peoples, respectively, during these years. Many of these immigrants entered the United States through the two best-known physical ports of entry: New York City's Ellis Island on the East Coast and San Francisco's Angel Island on the West Coast. Articles by Vincent Cannato and by Judy Yung and Erika Lee, respectively, analyze the impact of these "processing centers" during their years of operation in the early 20th century. Migration, however, was never just a "foreign" phenomenon. During the 20th century, approximately six million African Americans relocated from the rural American South to southern, northern, and West Coast cities, many in search of industrial jobs. Tyina Steptoe and Christopher R. Reed examine this internal movement in their articles, Steptoe concentrating on the national phenomenon, Reed on the Chicago experience. Similarly, rural white Americans moved to cities in increasing numbers after 1940, a phenomenon treated in Chad Berry's article on the subject.

Most migrants, upon arriving in American cities, established communities in the physical spaces and neighborhoods throughout metropolitan areas in the United States. The section "**Neighborhood, Community, and Space**" explores the multiple forms and varieties of communities and spaces that various migratory and diasporic groups created or were compelled to inhabit during the 19th and 20th centuries. Carl Nightingale analyzes how "segregation" became the preferred term and practice for forcing certain city residents— especially those defined by race, skin color, or ethnic origin—to reside in separate and unequal 20th-century residential neighborhoods. Jordan Stanger-Ross considers how some specific city neighborhoods were defined by "ethnicity," a concept whereby immigrants ceased to be "foreign" while retaining traditions and networks that nevertheless connected them to their places of common origin. In the 20th century, spaces and communities defined by sexual and gender identity became more visible and politically

active, themes examined in Emily K. Hobson's article on LGBTQ politics. Native Americans, whose ancestors built some of the largest urban communities in the pre-Columbian era (previously described in Robbie Ethridge's article), migrated to metropolitan areas throughout the 20th century; by 1970, the majority of the Native American population lived in cities, an evolution examined by Nicolas G. Rosenthal. The experience of specific groups generated new ways of understanding urbanism and city spaces, themes explored in articles by A. K. Sandoval-Strausz on Latino urbanism, Lorrin Thomas on Puerto Ricans, and Brian D. Behnken on Latino/a and African American interaction. The urban experiences of Asian Americans are chronicled in articles by Daryl Joji Maeda on the Asian American movement, Jean-Paul R. deGuzman on the post-World War II Japanese resettlement in Los Angeles, and Phuong Nguyen on the creation of "Little Saigon" by Vietnamese Americans in Orange County, California.

Cities are tangible, concrete entities. The "**Building the Metropolis**" section concentrates on the history of specific physical and infrastructure elements in urban history. Ann Durkin Keating explains the long history of suburbanization prior to 1945. Various forms of shelter are covered in articles by Margaret Garb on municipal housing, D. Bradford Hunt on public housing, and Kristin M. Szylvian on federal housing policy. Megan Kate Wilson considers a counterintuitive subject: the destruction of the built environment as experienced by Southern city residents during the Civil War. Elihu Rubin documents the transformation of the horizontal city of the 19th century into the vertical city of tall buildings in the 20th. The impact and legacies of the City Beautiful movement and urban planning are analyzed in the articles by John D. Fairfield and Harold L. Platt, respectively. Physical infrastructures, in particular, are a rich and vast topic in urban history. Among the most important are sewer and water systems, examined here by Joel A. Tarr. Transportation networks and structures are explained in articles by Jay Young on mass transit, Peter Norton on streets and highways, and David Blanke on automobiles. Jessica Sewell's concluding article interprets the changing meaning of streets, parks, and other public spaces during the 19th and 20th centuries.

The urbanization of the United States during the 19th and 20th centuries not only transformed city landscapes, but created many of the environmental challenges Americans confront today. "**Nature and the Environment**" provides detailed historical coverage of some of the most pressing of those problems. David Schuyler examines one of the earliest movements to address unregulated laissez-faire urban development: the park movement in American cities. Concerns about unprecedented forms of urban pollution and conservation efforts to address those problems are covered in articles by Brian McCammack and Robert R. Gioielli. Various forms of environmental destruction and damage frequently generated contagious diseases and other threats to public health, a subject covered in Daniel Wilson's article. More recent concerns about climate change are historicized in Andrew Hurley's study of the subject. Demographic and technological change transformed food provisioning, dietary habits, and food supply systems, developments examined in articles by Cindy Lobel on the 19th century and Adam Shprintzen on the 20th.

The social impact of urbanization is examined in focused articles appearing in the section "**The Social Fabric.**" The multiple religious "revolutions" in American cities after 1600 are outlined in articles by Kyle B. Roberts and Christopher D. Cantwell. The prevalence of urban economic inequality and poverty, and reactions on the part of public and private sector actors, are examined by Ella Howard and David Torstensson. Americans often resorted to education to address such inequality and social change. Ansley T. Erickson's

article shows how American schools and the educational infrastructures were transformed by the specificities of urban life and thereby informed national questions of citizenship, economy, religion, and culture. Cities were often places and spaces of controversy because of the often unregulated social and cultural interactions enjoyed by urbanites. The changing meaning of nightlife is explored in Peter C. Baldwin's article on the subject. Much of the music that defined the 20th-century United States was born or nurtured in cities. In his article on jazz, blues, and ragtime, Court Carney argues that the United States in 1900 was a largely rural, disconnected, regionally identified nation. By the end of World War II, however, a recognized national musical culture had emerged characterized by urban sounds. John Gennari continues the story of jazz in the half-century following World War II, focusing on the intensification of jazz's long-standing relationship with African American urban life and culture. Eric Weisbard examines the history of rock and roll, which in various forms and guises became the sound of urban and suburban postwar America. The most "urban" of all forms of postwar music may have been rap—a cultural response to racism, poverty, urban renewal, deindustrialization, and inner-city violence. Austin McCoy explains how this musical practice within hip hop culture was born in the African American and Latino/a American communities of New York City and quickly spread to all regions of the United States.

The section "**Violence and Disorder**" examines some of the most extreme instances of violent urban behaviors and how municipalities reacted in various efforts to ensure order. Alex Elkins writes a broad overview of rioting in the United States from 1800 to 2000, arguing that three fundamental traditions summarize such violent behavior: a need to regulate communal morality, a desire to defend a community from perceived outside threats, and citizen protest against government abuse of power. Two articles in particular use

Los Angeles as a case study. Victor Jew argues that anti-Chinese violence in the 19th century reveals how racial violence was employed to preserve traditional social orders that were threatened by social change. Shelley Sang-Hee Lee examines the Los Angeles riots or uprisings more than a century later, in 1992, to show the multiple layers of racial and ethnic tension at the end of the 20th century, revealing little-recognized tensions in a multiracial America, the place of new immigrants, and conflicts among relatively privileged minorities and the less privileged. Andrew Diamond's article on street gangs illustrates how one group's definition of disorder was often another group's form of order. Organized street gangs emerged in the 19th-century city and remained a common fixture in American cities throughout the 20th century. Fears of "juvenile delinquency" even generated reform movements that ultimately created new institutions related to "child advocacy" and "juvenile justice," a development examined in David S. Tanenhaus's article. The most common resort to impose order and prevent perceived threats to the urban social fabric, however, were vagrancy laws. Risa L. Goluboff and Adam Sorensen explain how such laws targeted hundreds of thousands of people annually, including the poor, the homeless, labor activists, radical orators, sex workers, immigrants, religious minorities, and civil rights activists. Only in 1972 did the United States Supreme Court finally rule such statutes unconstitutional.

The "**Postwar and Postindustrial Metropolis**" section concentrates on some of the most significant urban events in the second half of the 20th and early 21st centuries. Claudrena N. Harold, Thomas J. Sugrue, and Christopher W. Schmidt explain how many of the most decisive political battles of the African American freedom struggle occurred in cities throughout the United States. Robert O. Self's article breaks down the decade of the 1960s, the period with arguably the most intense urban racial conflicts and violent riots, as well as other controversies related to the politics of suburbanization, urban renewal, the transformation of urban political machines, and the emergence of antiwar and LGBTQ movements. The postwar era was also defined by mass suburban migration. Before World War II, just 13 percent of Americans lived in suburbs; by 2010, however, more than half of the United States population resided in suburban communities. Becky Nicolaides, Andrew Wiese, and Mark Padoongpatt explain not only how the nation suburbanized, but also how suburbia became an instrumental setting for multiple and national political movements: grass-roots conservatism, meritocratic individualism, environmentalism, feminism, and social justice. By the turn of the 21st century, suburbia was home to large numbers of immigrants and their children. It was also the preferred gateway for new immigrants who broke with earlier immigration patterns and bypassed inner-city urban cores, moving directly to the suburbs upon arrival in the United States. The foundation for many physical patterns of suburbanization and racial segregation were laid with the adoption of zoning by various municipalities in the early 20th century, whose history is outlined by Christopher Silver. Municipalities throughout the United States sought to stem the migration of city residents to suburbs by "revitalizing" older, "blighted" neighborhoods with "urban renewal." Christopher Klemek explains how urban renewal— the various interlocking national and local policies, programs, and projects implemented in most American cities between 1949 and 1973— redeveloped and transformed the physical landscapes of American cities with the construction of modern housing, highway infrastructure, and new business districts. Clement Lai employs Japantown and the Fillmore District in San Francisco as case studies documenting the impact of urban renewal and how postwar urban redevelopment affected neighborhood stability and racial minorities. Such redevelopment was instrumental in the origins of gentrification. Suleiman Osman's article shows how this distinctive postwar development form dramatically reshaped cities like Seattle, San Francisco, and Boston; transformed historic districts such as the French Quarter in New Orleans, Greenwich Village in New York, and Georgetown in Washington, DC; and proved to be a major historical trend by the end of the 20th century.

The ninety-two articles that comprise *The Oxford Encyclopedia of American Urban History* encapsulate not only how the writing of urban history has changed over the past three generations; they reveal the ways in which Americans think about their cities and suburbs. Groups and subjects ignored by past generations now define urban history itself.

The essays illustrate how municipalities, urban problems, and city residents embody central themes in American history. Urban history, like cities themselves, is characterized by fragmentation and diversity, even chaos. The *Encyclopedia* addresses this historical cacophony by bringing these disparate and sometimes confusing subjects and themes together in one place. These volumes will enable teachers, students, historians, and curious readers to learn, decipher, and comprehend the most recent interpretations of American urban history. Readers of the *Encyclopedia* will learn that the sum of urban history is greater than its parts.

Acknowledgments

I have incurred numerous debts in compiling and editing *The Oxford Encyclopedia of American Urban History*. First, Kenneth T. Jackson, to whom these volumes are dedicated, changed my life by fostering my fascination in urban history when I was a confused college student with an undecided major. Since then he has been my classroom teacher, dissertation director, professional mentor, trusted friend, and surrogate parent. I know I am not alone in receiving such personal attention. His generosity of time and spirit—to say nothing of his scholarship—has left a lasting mark on the field of urban history.

I want to thank Jon Butler, editor in chief of the online *Oxford Research Encyclopedia of American History* (ORE), for inviting me to serve as the senior editor responsible for commissioning articles on urban history. I am also grateful to the sixty contributing authors with whom I worked for their patience, for meeting deadlines, for addressing my queries and edits in tracked changes, and for answering my many pesky emails. I want to extend my appreciation to the other contributing authors who wrote for the online ORE and were willing to accept my invitation to include their articles in these two volumes.

Few projects like this can be fulfilled without institutional support. I want to thank my colleagues at Loyola University Chicago, especially those in the Department of History and in particular my chairs, Robert O. Bucholz and Stephen Schloesser, SJ, for finding ways to give me free time to complete this project. I am equally grateful to Dean of the College of Arts and Sciences Thomas Regan, SJ, former President Michael Garanzini, SJ, and President Jo Ann Rooney for their ongoing support in this as well as other endeavors.

Thank you to the in-house editors at Oxford University Press in New York, all of whom did much of the tedious behind-the-scenes work that enabled me to commission and edit articles with much more speed and care. Adina Berk worked with me in the early years and first suggested that the online *Oxford Research Encyclopedia*'s urban history articles could be converted into a print publication. Carla Calandra joined the project in the later stages and was a quick study in addressing the multiple demands of the authors as well as my own. Elda Granata and Louis Gulino deserve to be singled out for special attention. For both of them, *The Oxford Encyclopedia of American Urban History* was just one of several projects for which they were responsible. Yet each gave me the illusion that I was the sole recipient of their editorial attention. They performed many roles throughout the project—commissioning peer reviewers, processing the many reader's reports, communicating with authors, sending out periodic reminders, as well as completing tasks about which I probably remain ignorant. Most importantly, they tolerated my periodic frustrations. I extend my sincere gratitude to each of them.

As always, my greatest debt of gratitude belongs to my family. Jerry Gilfoyle, Linda Pattee, Adele Alexander, John Alexander, Jimmy Carson, Paula Carson, and Reyna Cerrato supported me in this and many other endeavors. My mother and father gave me many gifts and fostered my curiosity of cities, which indirectly led to this project. I regret that neither lived long enough to read the *Encyclopedia* that resulted from their personal sacrifices. While growing up in Chicago and on vacations, my children Maria and Danielle respectfully endured the many urban adventures on which I dragged them. My wife, Mary Rose Alexander, tolerated even worse and never complained. That is true love.

Timothy J. Gilfoyle
Chicago, August 2018

Varieties of Urbanization

MISSISSIPPIAN ANCIENT TOWNS AND CITIES, 1000–1700

CHIEFDOMS

Around 1000 CE, people living along the middle Mississippi River underwent a dramatic transformation in life—they built one of the largest cities in the world, and they adopted a new world order that mandated a restructuring of their political, social, and religious lives. This new way of life lasted over 600 years, from approximately 1000 CE to 1600 CE, and spread throughout the American South and much of the Midwest. During this time period that archaeologists call the Mississippi Period, most Indians in the region became organized into a particular kind of political organization that anthropologists call "chiefdoms," or a kind of ranked political order. Our knowledge of the Mississippi Period comes mostly from archaeology, although the documents of the early Spanish explorers who encountered some of the Mississippian chiefdoms are also important sources of information. The people of the Mississippian saw numerous polities rise and fall over their 600-year history, but with European contact this world collapsed, never to rise again. It is important to remember, however, that the survivors of these fallen chiefdoms regrouped and restructured their lives and societies for living in another new world order: a colonial world on the margins of an expanding European empire.

With one important exception, most Mississippian chiefdoms were made from the same building block—the simple chiefdom. Simple chiefdoms were characterized by a two-tiered social ranking of elites and commoners, a civic and religious capital where the elite lineage lived, and five to ten affiliated farming towns in proximity up and down a river valley. The capital towns often had one or more flat-topped, pyramidal mounds situated around a large, open plaza. The towns were small, with an average population of 350 to 650 people; a simple chiefdom, as a whole, had an average population between 2,800 and 5,400 people. The mico, or chief or chieftainess, lived atop the largest mound in the capital, and lesser people of the chiefly lineage lived on the lesser mounds. Commoners lived in houses circling the mounds and plazas in the capital as well as in the farming towns. A simple chiefdom's territory usually encompassed about 20 kilometers (12 miles) of a river valley, and a chiefdom was separated from other chiefdoms by about 33 kilometers (20 miles) of uninhabited space, what archaeologists call "buffer zones."[1] In some cases, leaders elaborated on the simple chiefdom by establishing secondary mound towns a few miles away from the capital and instituting a second tier of control; archaeologists refer to this more elaborate polity as a complex chiefdom. Sometimes, simple and complex chiefdoms merged to form larger political units that archaeologists call paramount chiefdoms, which could incorporate many small and complex chiefdoms. Over the 600-year history of the Mississippian way of life, many simple, complex, and paramount chiefdoms rose and fell. This rising and falling, or cycling, was an internal dynamic common to Mississippian chiefdoms, and the life span of a typical chiefdom, no matter its size, was about 150 to 200 years.[2]

The ritual and political gear of the Mississippian people constitutes some of the most important pre-Columbian artwork in America. Craftspeople used an assortment of stone, clay, mica, copper, shell, feathers, paints, and fabric to fashion a brilliant array of ceremonial items such as headdresses, beads, cups, masks, statues, cave art, ceramic wares, ceremonial weaponry, necklaces and earrings, and figurines. Many of these ritual items are decorated with a specific repertoire of motifs, such as the hand-and-eye motif, the falcon warrior, bi-lobed arrows, severed heads, spiders, rattle-snakes, and mythical beings.[3]

War iconography, in particular, is prevalent on much Mississippian artwork, indicating that warfare was important and imbued all aspects of daily life. The palisaded towns that typically lay on a chiefdom's borders and the large buffer zones also suggest that warfare was not just important but probably endemic.[4]

This artwork represents the iconography of religious and political ideologies, and archaeologists have gone far in deciphering the meanings behind the objects. Archaeologists do not necessarily understand these objects to represent a unified religion for the Mississippian world but rather a set of basic concepts and principles used by various polities. In other words, there probably was not one religion for the whole of the Mississippian world for 600 years but rather several religions deriving from a core set of fundamental beliefs and assumptions.[5] Perhaps the most fundamental concept was that of the cosmos. The cosmos was believed to comprise three worlds: the Above World and the Below World, which were opposites, and the Middle World, or This World—the world of humans. The Above World epitomized perfect order; it was clear, with no uncertainty. The Below World was a place of inversion, ambiguity, and uncertainty. The Above and Below Worlds were complementary halves of a whole, and This World stood somewhere between the two. Like a multilayered cake, the Above World and Below World were subdivided into tiers or levels, and each level was home to specific deities and supernatural beings. Mythic warriors in particular figured prominently in Mississippian religions and underscored the reverence for warfare.[6] The boundaries between the worlds were porous, however, and deities, mythic beings, and even humans who had acquired supernatural abilities could travel among cosmic levels.

Mississippian religion also underwrote elite authority, and the elites represented the highest religious authorities as well as the political leaders. Archaeologists are uncertain about the extent and nature of a mico's authority and power. They generally agree that the chiefly elite constituted a centralized political body and that those members held permanent, inherited offices of high rank and authority, with the mico holding the highest office. But it appears that an elite's consolidation of power varied over time from one chiefdom to another and spanned the continuum from autocratic power to simply being the first among equals.

Chiefdoms operated through a mixed economy of hunting, gathering, fishing, trading, and agriculture. The chiefly elite sponsored traders who maintained far-flung trade networks through which they exchanged exotic goods such as copper, shell, mica, high-grade stones like flint, and other materials, which were then fashioned by elite-sponsored artisans into the emblems of power, prestige, and religious authority. Everyday needs came from the local environments. Although people in the South had been growing maize, or corn, and other crops for almost 2,000 years when the Mississippian world emerged, corn, in particular, came to provide the basic caloric intake and foodstuff for Mississippian people, and they began to grow it intensively.

The geographic extent of Mississippian polities conforms to the parameters of intensive corn agriculture. These polities were found from the Atlantic coast to present-day eastern Texas and eastern Oklahoma, from the Gulf coast to present-day St. Louis and into the Ohio River Valley, and up the Atlantic seaboard into present-day Virginia. Not all Mississippian chiefdoms across this vast region, however, were alike. There were polities of various sizes,

complexity, ideological convictions, centralized governances, and cultural expressions, although archaeologists have yet to map out each of these expressions. Archaeologists have come to agree that Mississippian chiefdoms, no matter how varied, were bound together in what could be called the "Mississippian world." Generally speaking, one can define a "world" as the various polities within a defined time and geographic space, and the network of political, economic, cultural, and social relationships that exist between these polities. Such a "world" is not a discrete unit; its borders are porous, and it is often connected to distant places.

CAHOKIA AND THE RISE OF THE MISSISSIPPIAN WORLD (1000–1300 CE)

The Mississippian world began around 1050 CE with the rise of a polity that does not wholly conform to the chiefdom pattern—Cahokia. Cahokia was one of the grandest cities of its time and one of the most powerful and influential polities to exist in pre-Columbian North America. Cahokia, part of which is today a state park, is located on the large floodplains of the Mississippi River, just east of present-day St. Louis in an area known as the American Bottoms. The city emerged almost overnight from a dense concentration of small-scale, village farmers in the region. People from a variety of regions and cultures had been drawn to the area undoubtedly because of the rich, alluvial floodplain soils and perhaps because it was a place of relative peace, with little of the raiding between villages that was typical of other places in the eastern woodlands at this time.[7]

Cahokia served to unify the disparate, independent farming towns of the American Bottoms, but what was the impetus for doing so? Archaeologists are not in agreement over why these farmers decided to unite; they point to a variety of ecological, economic, religious, and political factors. One thing they do agree on though is that Cahokia burst on the scene—the city was planned, quickly built, and the building of this city enacted a new world order, a new vision of how the world and the cosmos worked. The building of Cahokia, then, signaled a dramatic transformation in life—the religious, political, and social lives of these farmers and others were changed forever.[8]

At its height, the city of Cahokia spread over 14.5 (9.01 miles) square kilometers, and its influence swept up and down the Mississippi River and into the interior South and Midwest for hundreds of miles.

The city itself was composed of over 120 earthen mounds, the largest being Monks Mound, which measures 5 hectares (12.4 acres) at its base and is about 30.5 meters (100 feet) tall. Remarkably, it still stands today. The city was characterized by three ritual precincts with mounds, plazas, and elite households and had between 10,000 and 15,000 citizens, including elite artists, traders, administrators, military leaders, and priests, among others. They also built the so-called woodhenge—a large circle of upright posts aligned with celestial reckoning and most likely used for astronomical sightings. In addition, over a dozen single- and multiple-mound towns grew up around the city, and they most likely fell under Cahokia's control.[9] A cadre of local farmers provisioned the city, providing agricultural foodstuffs and perhaps other items such as wild meats, furs, forest products, and gathered plants.[10] The city of Cahokia also represented a new religious ordering, one wherein the elites were divinely ordained. The most dramatic rendering of this new religion was in the burial practices of elite Cahokians as seen at the famous Mound 72. Mound 72, located in Cahokia proper, was the burial site of elites and dozens of sacrificial victims, along with thousands of finely crafted grave goods. Mound 72 apparently was integral to a grand, staged reenactment of a sacred myth about the godly warrior Red Horn and his twin.[11] Cahokia attracted migrants from far and wide, and Cahokia's political

and religious elite devised rituals, ceremonies, and other mechanisms to integrate these outsiders into the Cahokian fold.

Cahokia reached its height around 1200 CE, and during its heyday, Cahokia's influence spread far and wide, resulting in what archaeologists call the "Mississippianization" of the American South and much of the Midwest. People living in heretofore independent farming villages blended their lives with these new ideas, institutionalizing hereditary elite leadership as well as a class of priestly elites. They also rebuilt their cities and towns to mimic Cahokia, with central elite precincts characterized by the presence of one to several large, flat-topped earthen mounds on which local elites built large homes and expansive public plazas with a central pole representing the cosmic central axis connecting the Above World, This World, and the Below World.[12] Although Cahokia could arguably be called a state, archaeologists understand the new kinds of polities that emerged from Cahokia's influence to have been chiefdoms.

While still functioning, Cahokia undoubtedly served as the center of this new world, diminishing any and all rivals. The Mississippianization of the American South, then, did not result in a fluorescence of other Cahokias. Rather, during this time (known as the Early Mississippi Period, 900 CE–1200 CE), the polities that arose reflected Cahokia but on a smaller scale: the mounds and polities were significantly smaller than those at Cahokia, and the elite control over local populations does not appear to have been as total as that at Cahokia. This is not to say that local leaders had no political and social ambitions. Rather, it appears that Cahokia's leaders managed to tamp the ambitions of elites from these distant chiefdoms either through religious ideologies, military strength or threat, or some other mechanism. Therefore, despite any ambitions of local elite rulers, during Cahokia's height, other chiefdoms throughout the region remained relatively small and fairly unimpressive, compared to Cahokia. However, Cahokia offered something no local leader could guarantee—peace. In fact, archaeologists suggest that with the rise of Cahokia, a peace settled over the land, a *pax* Cahokia, or a nonaggression pact among the true believers of the new faith. The lack of defensive palisades around most of the capital towns of these Early Mississippian chiefdoms testifies to a lack of, or at least low levels of, neighboring hostilities.[13]

Cahokia also laid the foundation for much of the history of the Mississippian world because one can discern some structures of this world that began with its rise. These are the chiefdom political order with its hereditary elite leadership, an explicit architectural grammar of mounds, plazas, and house architecture emphasizing elite order, an intensive corn agriculture mixed with the hunting and gathering, matrilineal kinship and extended kin networks of clans and moieties, a three-world belief system and associated deities, and the reverence for warfare.

Around 1250 CE, Cahokia went into a hundred-year decline. By 1350 CE, the metropole and most of the associated secondary centers were abandoned, and people scattered to parts unknown, not to return to the region until well after European contact. Archaeologists are not in agreement as to why Cahokia declined. They have pointed to factors such as climate changes and resultant decreases in agricultural outputs, depletion of wood and other environmental degradations, collapse of the religious order, political discord, and divisive ethnic factionalism.[14]

THE MIDDLE MISSISSIPPI PERIOD (1300–1475 CE)

With the fall of Cahokia, people fled from the American Bottoms, and archaeologists have not been able to determine their destination. Perhaps most puzzling is the fact that the memory of Cahokia also vanished. Later people did not tell tales of a once magnificent city in their oral traditions passed down and recorded by early Europeans, nor is Cahokia represented in later iconography.[15] As Cahokia began its decline, the mechanisms that truncated local ambitions also disappeared, and elite leaders throughout the Mississippian world took the opportunity to exert their own strength. Striking elaborations on Early Mississippian chiefdoms and the rise of new simple and grand complex chiefdoms can be seen. Archaeologists call this the Middle Mississippi Period (1200–1475 CE). Today many of these Middle Mississippian chiefdoms, considered classic Mississippian, are known only by their archaeological names—Moundville, Etowah, Spiro, Irene, Rembert, Town Creek, Bottle Creek, Lake George, and Winterville, to name but a few. These chiefdoms were still grounded in the true faith that originated from Cahokia, as evidenced in their elaborate mortuary iconography, but in time these beliefs began to take on local variations. In other words, some fundamental beliefs and ways of life persisted across chiefdoms, but varying interpretations of these beliefs and variations in life emerged.[16] Hostilities also began to rise, and the elites commanded the building of tall palisades, moats, and other defensive measures to protect their capitals and towns from enemies.

Of the Middle Mississippian chiefdoms Moundville and Etowah are perhaps the best known. Moundville, which is today an archaeological park, is located near present-day Tuscaloosa, Alabama, on the Black Warrior River.

Moundville's history is one of small beginnings, multiple transformations, and decline. Around 1120–1250 CE, local farming communities along the Black Warrior fused their local ways with Mississippian influences from Cahokia that were infiltrating the interior lower South at the time. Although retaining much about their life before these Mississippian influences, the people built a simple chiefdom and a capital town with two small mounds, instituted social ranking, and intensified their corn production, although most people still lived in the surrounding farm communities.[17]

Then, around 1200 CE, just before Cahokia began its decline, the elites at Moundville consolidated their power and elaborated their capital town. People from the surrounding countryside moved to the capital, swelling the population to around one thousand. The residents of the capital then undertook to build the 57-foot-high Mound B, the largest mound at the site, and atop of which the mico and his or her family lived. Mound B fronted a large central plaza around which were arranged an additional twenty-one smaller flat-topped mounds, each paired with a conical burial mound. These paired mounds most likely represent the households and burials of ranked elite lineages, with those most closely related to the mico closer to Mound B. An impressive wooden palisade encircled the town for defense. The rapidity with which the new capital was built indicates that it was a planned community; in addition, any vestiges of old local cultural elements gave way to pure Mississippian ones. Pottery styles changed completely, as did house construction, among other things. Archaeologists interpret this event to signal a social and political reordering at Moundville where the elites expanded their influence, consolidated their power, and invested in place. One measure of this can be seen in the affiliated secondary mound centers that were established along the Black Warrior River, probably to facilitate the flow of tribute to the elites at the capital.[18]

A century later, around 1300 CE, the people of Moundville once again underwent a radical social shift. A large portion of the residents left the capital, many of the mounds were abandoned, and the palisade was left to rot. The former residents moved into the countryside, into the extant secondary centers, and into new ones they built, indicating a dispersal of political power.

A small cadre of priestly elites stayed in the capital where they apparently oversaw the burial of those elites who had taken their residence at the other centers. Upon death, however, these elites were returned to the capital to be interred with numerous luxury and symbolic goods associated with warfare, death, and ancestors. The capital, then, had become, essentially, a cemetery for the hierarchy, or a necropolis. In short, the capital town, though the site of important mortuary rituals, was no longer the center of power. Then after about 1400 CE, people stopped burying their dead at the former capital, and they quit manufacturing the religious icons for the burials. This abrupt end to a century-long tradition may indicate that the people in the region lost faith in their religion, or in their religious and political leaders, or both. Only a few families remained at the former capital; most people now lived in simple, apparently independent, one-mound chiefdoms along the Black Warrior. The former capital had by now lost all its glory.[19]

Etowah, located in present-day northwest Georgia on the Etowah River and now a state park, was contemporaneous with Moundville. Although their histories have some similarities, the two polities were quite distinct. Around 1000 CE, this region was populated by distinct social groupings of farming towns. The towns were mostly fortified with palisades indicating a high level of raiding and warfare. Between 1100 and 1200 CE, however, a social movement centered on efforts to knit these disparate groups together into a unified polity swept through the Etowah River Valley. People came together to build a small capital town with two modest mounds (Mounds A and B). Archaeologists have also uncovered much evidence for community feasting at the site at this time, indicating that in its beginnings the capital was the center for ceremonies designed to build community solidarity and cohesion.

An elite hierarchy emerged at this time, but they focused on integrating these disparate, warring groups into a unified polity.[20] Wide acceptance of the three-worlds ideology fueled a coalescence between the groups, and elites no doubt served as proselytizing priests, promoting a new worldview that mandated leadership by those in a divine kinship line. The elites at Etowah soon established two small, secondary mound communities along the Etowah River.[21]

Curiously and for reasons unknown, around 1200 CE, people abandoned Etowah and the secondary centers as well as other sites along the Etowah River Valley. When people returned in 1250 CE, they embarked on a new social and political reordering. Over the next decades, people elaborated on the capital city of Etowah as well as the secondary centers. At the capital, citizens significantly enlarged the existing mounds and built a third mound (Mound C) as well as a large plaza and palisade. Mound A, especially, grew to tower over the town at approximately 60 feet high. Mound C served as a burial mound for the elites of the polity, who were buried with some of the most elaborate and artistic grave goods in North America.

Archaeologists interpret this elaboration of the capital with an emphasis on elites to indicate a move away from consolidating disparate groups to an intensification and solidification of elite power, prestige, and authority. These elites also expanded their influence by refurbishing the old secondary centers and building or incorporating others up and down the Etowah River.[22]

Then, sometime between 1325 and 1375 CE, the capital was abandoned, the palisades burned, and the stone statues representing the ancestry unceremoniously tossed off of Mound C. The capital was apparently raided, sacked, and desecrated, although who attacked or why is not known. The former capital remained empty for about a hundred years, with a small population returning around 1475 CE, when they put a new mantle on Mound B.[23] These new residents did no further elaborations, and the former capital of Etowah, like that of Moundville, never again reached its former glory.

That Etowah and Moundville declined around the same time is noteworthy. In fact, other grand and lesser chiefdoms throughout

the Mississippian world also fell or were diminished around this time. This upheaval in the Mississippian world may have been precipitated by a prolonged drought. Between 1375 and 1475 CE, much of North America came under a massive drought that most likely stretched across the continent. The drought would have seriously impacted Mississippian agriculture, undermining the subsistence economy. In addition, the power of the elite rested, in part, on acquiring and controlling any surplus agricultural foodstuffs for festivals, large gatherings, and emergencies such as crop failure. The drought most likely entailed successive crop failures over several years, stressing the food stores as well as the political stability of an elite lineage. Equally important, such a drought would have strained the faith of the true believers—they would have questioned the abilities of their divine elites to manage the three worlds. The lines of leadership in Mississippian politics were multiple and gave ample opportunity for contesting successions to office. This was especially so during times of stress and during succession to the chieftainship.[24] The drought, then, undoubtedly contributed to political instability through widespread famine, social discontent, and religious crisis, all of which also would have exacerbated existing tensions and hostilities between chiefdoms, which could account for the attack at Etowah that resulted in its abandonment.

THE LATE MISSISSIPPI PERIOD (1475–1600 CE)

Although chiefdoms across the South fell during the drought, this did not spell the end of the Mississippian world, and by the end of the drought, new chiefdoms were arising. This is the period of the Late Mississippi (1475–1600 CE). We have a better sense of Late Mississippian history than earlier times because early Spanish explorers such as Hernando de Soto, Tristán de Luna, and Juan Pardo, in the mid-16th century, penetrated into the interior, and the documents from these expeditions, though quite fragmentary, recorded many details about the Native world they saw.[25]

Figure 1 presents a map of the Late Mississippian world that Hernando de Soto encountered, compiled from archaeological and documentary records, featuring the known polities in existence at the time of the de Soto expedition *c.* 1540 (Figure 1). Recent estimates of the population of the Mississippian world at the time of contact put the figure at around a half million people.[26] As shown in Figure 1, these half million people were organized into dozens of chiefdoms, and some had joined together into complex and paramount chiefdoms. Although some of the Late Mississippian chiefdoms were quite impressive, none matched those of the Middle Mississippi Period in size and grandeur.

Canvassing the whole of the Late Mississippian world, one can also see differences in the chiefdoms themselves. For example, the frontiers of the Mississippian world look different from the heart of this world. The northern and western frontiers of the Mississippian world were home to small, simple chiefdoms. To the south and east, the Mississippian world is bordered by the Gulf and Atlantic oceans. Although the coastal regions could support larger chiefdoms as seen by the Middle Mississippian Bottle Creek site on the Gulf coast and the Irene site on the Atlantic coast, during the Late Mississippi Period, small chiefdoms dotted the coastlines. In the present-day Florida panhandle, however, one paramount chiefdom existed at the time of de Soto's entrada, Apalachee. South of here, in the Florida peninsula, though, the Indian polities look somewhat different—they were small, independent hierarchical chiefdoms, but they grew very little corn because of the sandy soils.[27] Those in the interior also showed much variation, ranging from simple, weakly centralized polities, to complex, strongly centralized polities, to paramount chiefdoms that integrated several polities into a single loosely organized political unit.

Combining the archaeological and documentary evidence for the mid-16th century,

we can highlight the encounters between the early Spanish explorers and two Mississippian chiefdoms—Cofitachequi, located in present-day South Carolina, and Tascalusa, located in present-day central Alabama—in order to provide a glimpse into the geopolitics of the interior South in the mid- to late 16th century. Hernando de Soto had heard about Cofitachequi soon after the expedition landed in present-day Florida, and de Soto believed he would find gold, pearls, and other wealth there. That is why he determined to move northeast from Florida, to find Cofitachequi. After departing from the province of Ocute on the Oconee River in present-day Georgia, de Soto and his expedition passed through an expansive uninhabited zone around the Savannah River for seventeen days before coming to the first towns of Cofitachequi around the beginning of May 1540.[28] Archaeologists believe that Cofitachequi was a paramount chiefdom that administered a territory of large towns and hamlets along the lower Wateree watershed, centered most likely at the Mulberry site near present-day Camden, South Carolina.[29] The uninhabited zone, which had been abandoned after the 1450 CE drought, served as a buffer zone between the chiefdom and Ocute. Cofitechequi was ruled by a woman, known today only as the "Lady of Cofitechequi." Her niece served as royal envoy, and she met de Soto at the river crossing into her town in a large canoe outfitted with a fancy awning, ladies in waiting, and a retinue of soldiers. Although the Lady of Cofitechequi proffered her hand in friendship, de Soto and his men repaid her kindness by raiding the sacred ossuary where the bones and grave goods of the elites were kept and kidnapping the chieftainess, forcing her to accompany the Spaniards to guarantee safe passage through her lands. De Soto traversed her polity, but the Lady of Cofitachequi escaped with the help of one of de Soto's African slaves, who accompanied her in her escape.[30]

About twenty years later, when Juan Pardo traveled into the lower Piedmont, he, too, encountered Cofitachequi in the same location

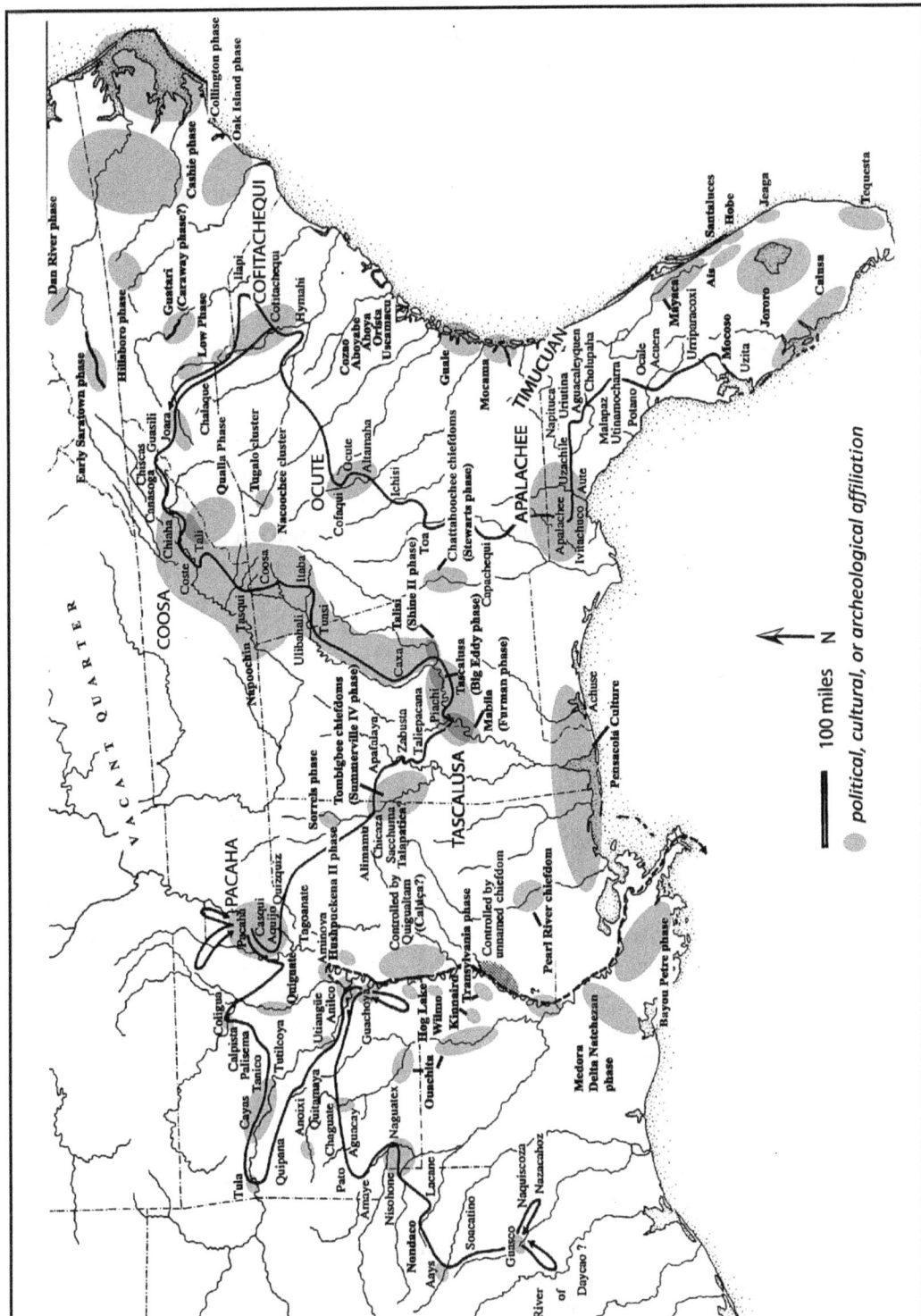

Figure 1. The Mississippian world, showing the Route of Hernando de Soto, c. 1540. Map drawn by author.

reported by members of the de Soto expedition. At the time of the Pardo expedition (1566–1568 CE), the polity was composed of the chiefdoms of Cofitachequi, Guatari (on the middle Yadkin River), and Joara (on the upper Catawba River).[31] From the Pardo accounts, it is obvious that the lower Piedmont was still densely inhabited even though some sort of political reshuffling had occurred since de Soto's visit in 1540. Cofitachequi appears to have still been intact, although in a somewhat diminished form, and perhaps no longer representing a paramount chiefdom within the region. The seat of power seems to have been shifting from Cofitachequi to the previously subordinate chiefdoms of Joara and Guatari. Archaeologists surmise that Cofitachequi's paramountcy prior to 1540 inhibited the political ambitions of chiefs along its borders. By 1567, though, Cofitachequi was significantly diminished, and Joara and Guatari were flourishing. The de Soto records hint that introduced disease was present in Cofitachequi prior to 1540, perhaps having traveled from the coast where earlier European sailors had encountered Native people and possibly transmitted lethal diseases.[32]

This development could help explain the changing political fortunes, since a deadly disease outbreak would certainly have strained chiefly authority. Nevertheless, the dense Native population in 1567 indicates that any disease episode was probably a localized event. De Soto's presence could also have precipitated such political changes in the region, especially if these challenges came directly on the heels of a major disease episode. Conversely, as we have seen, such shifts were common enough in the Mississippian world, and they may have derived purely from existing agencies and processes within Native communities.

In early October 1540, after passing through the paramount chiefdom of Coosa which stretched from present-day eastern Tennessee into central Alabama, de Soto's army crossed into the chiefdom of Tascalusa. By all accounts, Tascalusa was a powerful chief. His chiefdom, Tascalusa, was most likely on the upper Alabama River in present-day Alabama, just south of its confluence with the Coosa and Tallapoosa Rivers. The capital was likely the Charlotte Thompson mound site.[33] Tascalusa is most famous for his orchestration of a surprise attack against de Soto at the palisaded town of Mabila. Although Tascalusa and his allies did not destroy the Spanish expedition in this attack, they did succeed in doing them much harm, killing and wounding a number of the soldiers, killing several horses, and destroying many of their supplies. In hindsight, one can also see that they succeeded in pushing the Spaniards out of their provinces.[34]

Through use of archaeological evidence, the history of Tascalusa and the other polities in central Alabama can be partially reconstructed. The upper Alabama River and lower Tallapoosa River were only sparsely occupied during the Middle Mississippi Period. Instead, populations at this time were congregated in the grand Middle Mississippian sites such as Etowah, Moundville, and Bottle Creek (located in the Mobile-Tensaw delta region). However, as has been noted, all of these large Middle Mississippian polities failed sometime in the late 15th century. Groups from these fallen chiefdoms and elsewhere began to congregate in the upper Alabama and lower Tallapoosa river basins. Recent archaeological investigations indicate that the chiefdoms of Talisi, Tascalusa, Mabila, and Piachi, in present-day central Alabama, were multilingual, heterogenous polities wherein the descendants of people from various fallen Middle Mississippian chiefdoms had forged new political and social identities and lived side by side in the same towns.[35] In addition, Tascalusa may have been in the process of putting together his own paramountcy at the time of de Soto's visit by building an alliance with the adjacent polities of Mabila and perhaps Piachi to the west and by enticing the polity of Talisi, which lay on Tascalusa's eastern boundary, away from the paramount chiefdom of Coosa with whom it was aligned at the time.[36]

These examples from Tascalusa and Cofit-achequi demonstrate something of the historical dynamics and geopolitical jockeying of Mississippian chiefdoms. These chiefdoms were not isolated polities; rather, they were woven together through alliance, animosity, kinship, migration, and marriage into a distinctive, vibrant, intriguing pre-Columbian world that constituted part of the antiquity of the American South. One hundred fifty years later, with European contact, the Mississippian world that these early explorers witnessed would be in collapse, never to arise again, the polities gone and the survivors regrouping and restructuring their lives into yet another kind of new world.

CONTACT AND THE COLLAPSE OF THE LATE MISSISSIPPIAN WORLD (1540–1700 CE)

After the Spanish entradas of the 16th century, many of the interior chiefdoms in the South did not have direct contact with Europeans for over 130 years; yet those later Europeans saw something quite different than what de Soto, Luna, and Pardo had observed. Gone were the multiple chiefdoms, replaced by the more familiar large coalescent societies—the Creeks, Cherokees, Chickasaws, Choctaws, and Catawbas, among others. Between 1540 and 1700, with increasing European contact, colonialism destabilized and endangered the Native South, creating what scholars have called the Mississippian shatter zone. Certainly, de Soto's march through the Mississippian world can account for some of this instability. De Soto and his men represented a formidable military force, and in the cases of those chiefdoms that experienced intense combat, the direct military assault of the Spanish may have precipitated their collapse. In addition, de Soto's prolonged stay and ransacking of the region for food would have seriously depleted local stores and, as in the 1450 CE drought, created civil and religious unrest that could have initiated political

declines.[37] Undoubtedly, disease also played a dastardly role in shattering the Mississippian world. Most scholars agree that the introduction of Old World diseases resulted in the loss of much Native life. In recent years, the idea that disease alone was responsible for the dramatic loss of Indian life in the first hundred or so years after contact has come into question. Today, scholars agree that a demographic collapse of over 90 percent of the Indian population occurred, but they do not see disease as the sole cause. Scholars point to contributing factors such as slaving and increased warfare, and they understand this loss of life to have occurred not in a generation but over about 200 years.[38]

In addition, in present-day north Florida and south Georgia, the Spanish established St. Augustine and Catholic monks set about converting Native communities to Christianity and attempting to incorporate them into the Spanish Empire as Spanish peasants. Native communities in "La Florida" became a blend of Spanish and Indian life. Native life, however, was not rosy co-existence—harsh labor regimes, Spanish meddling in local politics, and resentments against the monks lead to periodic Indian revolts against the Spaniards for the next 150 years. Certainly, the Spanish expeditions of the 16th century, the introduction of Old World diseases, and the Spanish presence in La Florida impacted Native life, but it was the mid-17th-century introduction of a new economic system ushered in by a commercial trade in Indian slaves and guns that completed the constellation of forces that created the Mississippian shatter zone and transformed the Mississippian world. As soon as English, French, and Dutch settlers landed on North American shores, they set about the business of making money, and they brought with them strong commercial connections in a nascent global economy. The initial form of this commerce was a trade in Indian slaves and armaments. The result was the spread of militarized slaving societies across the South, who were engaged as trading partners with European slavers to capture Indian slaves to trade for guns and other European goods. Out-of-control slave raiding and intra-Indian violence that lasted for almost eighty years resulted in the widespread dislocation, migration, amalgamation, and, in some cases, extinction of Native peoples.[39]

Cofitachequi and the other lower Piedmont chiefdoms were some of the first polities to feel the effects of slavers, and by 1670 Cofitechequi and the other polities, besieged by armed Indian slave raiders working for Virginia and Carolina traders, were in a process of dispersal and coalescence. However, unlike in former times when new chiefdoms would emerge from the fall of polities, these new societies did not reconstitute the elite hierarchies and the impressive mound capitals. Instead, they were structured along more egalitarian, town-governance orders, and the people quit building mounds. By 1675, Cofitachequi was gone, and refugees from Indian slavers were pouring into the lower Catawba River Valley, where they would eventually form the Catawbas of the 18th century.[40] As slaving spread, the interior chiefdoms also came under assault. The paramount chiefdom of Coosa broke apart, with some migrating south into present-day central Alabama. In the early 18th century, they would join the Creek Confederacy as the Abihka towns.[41] Meanwhile, the chiefdoms in present-day central Alabama that had allied to defeat de Soto—Mabila, Piachi, and Tascalusa—also began to break apart. Some of the survivors moved south to the Mobile Bay area, and many moved to the northern Alabama River, where they also would become part of the Creek Confederacy as the Alabama towns. The Alabamas then began absorbing refugees from present-day Tennessee, Georgia, Alabama, and Mississippi as survivors fled slavers and their failed chiefdoms. Along the Tallapoosa River, local populations soon abandoned their chiefly ways. They, too, began taking in refugees and came to form the Tallapoosa towns of the Creek Confederacy.[42]

Refugees also fled to the functioning polities along the lower Chattahoochee River, where the local chiefdoms soon also quit building mounds and organized themselves into an egalitarian, town-centered form of governance. They became known as the Apalchicola towns of the Creek Confederacy. Some of the people from these fallen polities may have migrated west, into present-day south-central Mississippi, where they joined with other refugees from the north and south to form the Choctaws.[43]

The coalescent society known as the Chickasaws also formed during this time. The Chickasaws were the descendants of a polity on the Tombigbee River called Chicaza. De Soto spent the winter of 1540–1541 at Chicaza. After the encounter with de Soto, the people of Chicaza began a series of migrations that led them away from the Tombigbee River and eventually into the vicinity of present-day Tupelo, Mississippi, where they established several towns along nonchiefdom lines.[44] Once there, they became known as the Chickasaws, and by the early 18th century, they had entered into trade agreements with Carolina and had become militarized slavers, slaving across the lower South and destabilizing much of the region.[45]

At the time of the de Soto expeditions, the lower Mississippi River Valley was home to some of the most powerful, populous, and impressive chiefdoms through which the Spaniards had passed. About 135 years later, French explorers paddling down the Mississippi only encountered the Quapaws, the Tunicas, and the Natchez. Shockwaves from the Indian and European trade system had penetrated far beyond the Atlantic seaboard and affected Native polities on the Mississippi River, setting in motion a sequence of events, movements, opportunities, and failures that changed Indian life well before the French and their Indian allies canoed down river. The lower Mississippi Valley chiefdoms were now gone, the people apparently fleeing south and west. The Quapaws, who were relatively recent arrivals, having been forced out of the Ohio River Valley by armed Iroquois raiders, settled at the now-vacant mouth of the Arkansas River. Unlike other chiefdoms, the Natchez, in present-day Natchez, Mississippi, managed to retain their Mississippian political order through these tumultuous years, at least for a while.[46]

In addition to the Chickasaws, the other coalescent societies also sought trade agreements with Europeans, and they entered into slaving partnerships with both the English and the French. Slaving intensified across the South, impacting any remaining Mississippian polities. The simple chiefdoms along the Gulf coast suffered tremendously from slaving, with many becoming extinct and the survivors clustering into small towns close to the French. The chiefdoms in Spanish Florida, which had survived into the early 18th century, took the brunt of the slaving avalanche, and by 1710 most of Florida's Native inhabitants were enslaved, had fled—or sought refuge with the Spanish.[47] The sole remaining Mississippian chiefdom was Natchez. By 1730, however, it would be extirpated after a disastrous war with the French.[48]

When the Mississippian world collapsed, new kinds of Native polities and a new world emerged. Native South polities were now structured along lines that proved quite adaptable to the new global economic stage, and they developed a deep connection with Europeans, Africans, and the global networks they represented. Thus, the Mississippian world was transformed into the colonial world of the American South.

DISCUSSION OF THE LITERATURE

Archaeological research on the Mississippi Period is expansive and covers over a century of excavations and research, although modern archaeology can be said to have begun in the mid-20th century. Understanding of the pre-Columbian Southeast has undergone numerous paradigm shifts over this century, resulting in publications scattered in various journals, reports, anthologies, and books over decades. A good synopsis of this complicated history is Jay K. Johnson's *Development of Southeastern Archaeology*.[49] Two recent syntheses of the current state of Mississippian archaeology can serve as excellent guides to the most up-to-date literature: these are John Blitz, "New Perspectives in Mississippian Archaeology" and David G. Anderson and Kenneth E. Sassaman, "Mississippian Complexity and Contact Coalescence."[50]

Whereas earlier archaeological scholarship concentrated on material culture and processes, today archaeologists examine the material record for what it can tell us about such things as human agency, ritual, ideas, and meaning, alongside what it can tell us about ecology, economy, politics, and social organization. The resultant interpretive frame is more historical and articulates structures of the *longue durée* with the event, human agency, and meaning in exciting and innovative ways. As part of this work, several publications reconstruct the histories of Mississippian centers and sites such as Cahokia, Moundville, and Etowah. Through these works, a new major understanding of the Mississippian has arisen—namely, that Mississippian polities show both important structural similarities and a tremendous amount of diversity across space and time. These works are too numerous to mention, but some notable ones are David G. Anderson, *The Savannah River Chiefdoms*; John H. Blitz, *Ancient Chiefdoms of the Tombigbee*; David J. Hally, *King*; Adam King, *Etowah*; Vernon James Knight Jr., *Mound Excavations at Moundville*; Patrick C. Livingood, *Mississippian Polity and Politics on the Gulf Coastal Plain*; Vernon James Knight Jr. and Vincas P. Steponaitis, eds., *Archaeology of the Moundville Chiefdom*; Timothy Pauketat, *Ancient Cahokia and the Mississippians* and *Cahokia*; Amanda L. Regnier, *Reconstructing Tascalusa's Chiefdom*; Marvin T. Smith, *Coosa*; and Gregory D. Wilson, *The Archaeology of Everyday Life at Early Moundville*.[51]

Archaeologists have also developed some major breakthroughs in the interpretation of Mississippian artwork and symbolism and how religion and ideology intersected with the lived experiences of ancient people of the Southeast. This work is ongoing, but the foundations of this scholarship are in F. Kent Reilly III and James F. Garber, eds., *Ancient Objects and Sacred Realms*, and George E. Lankford, F. Kent Reilly III, and James F. Garber, eds., *Visualizing the Sacred*.[52] In 2004, the Art Institute of Chicago published a catalog for their magnificent exhibit of Southeastern Indian art, much of which was from the Mississippi Period. The catalog presents beautiful, oversized photographs of the art as well as informed essays by the leaders in Southeastern Indian iconography studies. The book is Richard F. Townsend and Robert V. Sharp, eds., *Hero, Hawk, and the Open Hand*.[53]

Finally, for diverse conceptual and methodological reasons, early scholars did not show interest in the connections between Etowah, Moundville, and the other Mississippian chiefdoms and the Creeks, Chickasaws, Cherokees, Choctaws, and Catawbas of the colonial era. Charles Hudson's *The Southeastern Indians* epitomizes this lack of historicity to the Native South. Hudson, though, later criticized this approach and insisted that archaeologists, anthropologists, and historians should appreciate the antiquity of Southern history and question the line between so-called prehistory and history. Hudson set a Mississippian benchmark for doing so in his masterpiece *Knights of Spain, Warriors of the Sun*. He then went on to formulate the basic questions that one must ask in order to stitch together the ancient South with the modern South in *Forgotten Centuries* and *The Transformation of the Southeastern Indians*.[54] Since then, some important works have explored this transformation. Patricia Galloway, in *Choctaw Genesis, 1500–1700*, was the first to attempt to make sense of collapse and coalescence.[55] Then, the contours of the commercial trade in Indian slaves in North America were revealed when Alan Gallay published *The Indian Slave Trade*, giving Native South scholars a new window onto the dramatic disturbances that occurred with contact.[56] Robbie Ethridge, in *Mapping the Mississippian Shatter Zone*, developed the concept of the Mississippian shatter zone in order to provide a framework for thinking about the collapse and restructuring of Native life in the context of widespread, destructive commercial slaving. In *From Chicaza to Chickasaw*, Ethridge examines what the slave trade meant for Native polities and the transforming effect it had on the Mississippian world.[57] More recently, Robin M. Beck published *Chiefdoms, Collapse, and Coalescence in the Early American South*, a detailed reconstruction of the early history of the lower Piedmont, the collapse of the chiefdoms, and the coalescence of the survivors into the Catawbas.[58]

PRIMARY SOURCES

Because much about the Mississippian chiefdoms comes to us from archaeology, the reader is advised to consult the endnotes and the list of suggested readings for archaeological studies. However, a few primary documents have information on Late Mississippian chiefdoms, written by Europeans who witnessed some of the chiefdoms while they were still functioning. The relations of the Hernando de Soto expedition, especially, have proven useful, and these have been collected and translated into a two-volume set. They are Hernández de Biedma, "Relation of the Island of Florida"; Rodrigo Rangel, "Account of the Northern Conquest and Discovery of Hernando de Soto"; and Garcilaso de la Vega, "La Florida."[59] In addition, two later expeditions—that of Tristán de Luna and Juan Pardo—also contain information on Late Mississippian political orders in the Native South. These papers also have been translated and published in Herbert I. Priestly, ed. and trans., *The Luna Papers*; Juan de la Bandera, "The 'Long' Bandera Relation"; and "The 'Short' Bandera Relation."[60]

In addition, the Spanish in present-day Florida lived with the Timucuan and Apalachee people, whose chiefdoms functioned into the early 18th century. Many of these records, some of which have been translated and published, contain information on the chiefdoms of northern Florida. They are John E. Worth, ed. and trans., *The Struggle for the Georgia Coast*; *Discovering Florida*; Mark F. Boyd, Hale G. Smith, and John W. Griffin, *Here They Once Stood*; Jeannette Thurbor Connor, ed. and trans., *Colonial Records of Spanish Florida* and *Colonial Records of Spanish Florida: Letters and Reports of Governors, Deliberations of the Council of the Indies, Royal Decrees, and Other Documents*; Jerald T. Milanich and William C. Sturtevant, eds., *Francisco Pareja's 1613 Confessionario*.[61] Many of the unpublished records for Spanish Florida are in the Archivo General de Indias (AGI) in Seville, Spain. However, the P. K. Yong Library of Florida History at the University of Florida in Gainesville has microfilm copies, photocopies, and some recently digitized copies of much of the material at the AGI.

Finally, the French sources on the Natchez are also quite numerous. Many of these documents have been published. The best primary source material on the Natchez is Antoine Simone Le Page du Pratz, *The History of Louisiana or of the Western Parts of Virginia and Carolina*.[62] The governmental correspondence is found in Dunbar Rowland and Albert Sanders, eds. and trans., *Mississippi Provincial Archives*.[63] Unpublished French records from the lower Mississippi Valley are found at Archives Nationales de France, Centre des Archives d'Outre Mer, Séries C11, C13, and F3/290, in Aix-en-Provence, France and at the Archives du Ministére de la Marine, Série JJ, Archives du Service Hydrographique, Paris, France.

DIGITAL MATERIALS

The major sites noted in the text can be seen today as state and national parks.

Cahokia Mounds State Historic Site. http://cahokiamounds.org/.
Moundville Archaeological Park. http://moundville.ua.edu/.
Etowah Indian Mounds Historic Site. http://gastateparks.org/EtowahMounds.
Grand Village of the Natchez Indians. http://www.nps.gov/nr/travel/mounds/gra.htm.

In addition, a series of drawings of Late Mississippians done by early colonists John White who was at Roanoke in 1585 and Jacques le Moyne who was at Fort Caroline in 1564 were later engraved by Theodore de Bry. Much of these are available online for viewing. Le Moyne's drawings can also be accessed online, as well as John White's drawings along with the De Bry engravings made from them.

FURTHER READING

Beck, Robin M. *Chiefdoms, Collapse, and Coalescence in the Early American South*. Cambridge, UK: Cambridge University Press, 2013.

Ethridge, Robbie. *From Chicaza to Chickasaw: The European Invasion and the Transformation of the Mississippian World*. Chapel Hill: University of North Carolina Press, 2010.

Ethridge, Robbie, and Sheri M. Shuck-Hall. *Mapping the Mississippian Shatter Zone: The Colonial Indian Slave Trade and Regional Instability in the American South*. Lincoln: University of Nebraska Press, 2009.

Galloway, Patricia *Choctaw Genesis, 1500–1700*. Lincoln: University of Nebraska, 1995.

Hally, David J. *King: The Social Archaeology of a Late Mississippian Town in Northwestern Georgia*. Tuscaloosa: University of Alabama Press, 2008.

Hudson, Charles. *Conversations with the High Priest of Coosa*. Chapel Hill: University of North Carolina Press, 2003.

Hudson, Charles. *Knights of Spain, Warriors of the Sun: Hernando de Soto and the South's Ancient Chiefdoms*. Athens: University of Georgia Press, 1997.

King, Adam. *Etowah: The Political History of a Chiefdom Capital*. Tuscaloosa: University of Alabama Press, 2003.

Knight, Vernon James, Jr. *Mound Excavations at Moundville: Architecture, Elites, and Social Order*. Tuscaloosa: University of Alabama Press, 2010.

Knight, Vernon James, Jr., and Vincas P. Steponaitis, eds. *Archaeology of the Moundville Chiefdom*. Washington, DC: Smithsonian Institution Press, 1998.

Lankford, George E., F. Kent Reilly III, and James F. Garber, eds. *Visualizing the Sacred: Cosmic Visions, Regionalism, and the Art of the Mississippian World*. Austin: University of Texas Press, 2011.

Pauketat, Timothy R. *Ancient Cahokia and the Mississippians*. Cambridge, UK: Cambridge University Press, 2004.

Pauketat, Timothy R. *Cahokia: Ancient America's Great City on the Mississippi*. New York: Penguin Books, 2009.

Regnier, Amanda L. *Reconstructing Tascalusa's Chiefdom: Pottery Styles and the Social Composition of Late Mississippian Communities along the Alabama River*. Tuscaloosa: University of Alabama Press, 2014.

Reilly, F. Kent, III, and James F. Garber, eds., *Ancient Objects and Sacred Realms: Interpretations of Mississippian Iconography*. Austin: University of Texas Press, 2007.

Smith, Marvin T. *Coosa: The Rise and Fall of a Southeastern Mississippian Chiefdom*. Gainesville: University Press of Florida, 2000.

Townsend, Richard F., and Robert V. Sharp, eds. *Hero, Hawk, and the Open Hand: American Indian Art of the Ancient Midwest and South*. New Haven, CT: Yale University Press for the Art Institute of Chicago, 2004.

NOTES

1. Vincas P. Steponaitis, "Contrasting Patterns of Mississippian Development," in *Chiefdoms: Power, Economy, and Ideology*, ed. Timothy K. Earle (Cambridge, UK: Cambridge University Press, 1991), 193–228; Steponaitis, "Location Theory and Complex Chiefdoms: A Mississippian Example," in *Mississippian Settlement Patterns*, ed. Bruce Smith (New York: Academic Press, 1978), 417–453; David J. Hally, "The Territorial Size of Mississippian Chiefdoms," in *Archaeology of Eastern North America: Papers in Honor of Stephen Williams*, ed. James A. Stoltman, Archeological Report, no. 25 (Jackson: Mississippi Department of Archives and History, 1993), 143–168; David G. Anderson, *Savannah River Chiefdoms: Political Change in the Late Prehistoric Southeast* (Tuscaloosa: University of Alabama Press, 1994), 4–9; David J. Hally, Marvin T. Smith, and James B. Langford Jr., "The Archaeological Reality of De Soto's Coosa," in *Columbian Consequences*, vol. 2, *Archaeological and Historical Perspectives on the Spanish Borderlands East*, ed. David Hurst Thomas (Washington, DC: Smithsonian Institution, 1990), 121–138; Patrick Livingood, "The Many Dimensions of Hally Circles, in *Archaeological Perspectives on the Southern Appalachians: A Multiscalar Approach*, eds. Ramie A. Gougeon and Maureen S. Meyers (Knoxville: University of Tennessee Press, 2015), 245–262.

2. Anderson, *Savannah River Chiefdoms*; David J. Hally, "The Nature of Mississippian Regional Systems," in *Light on the Path: The Anthropology and History of the Southeastern Indians*, eds. Thomas H. Pluckhahn and Robbie Ethridge (Tuscaloosa: University of Alabama Press, 2006), 26–42. There is some controversy over the use of the chiefdom concept as well as the paramount chiefdom; on chiefdoms see Timothy R. Pauketat, *Chiefdoms and Other Archaeological Delusions* (New York: AltaMira, 2007); Book Forum: *Chiefdoms and Other Archaeological Delusions*, ed. Robbie Ethridge and David Anderson, *Native South*, 2 (2009), 69–132. On paramount chiefdoms see Robin A. Beck, Consolidation and Hierarchy: Chiefdom Variability in the Mississippian Southeast, *American Antiquity*, 68.4 (2003), 641–661.

3. F. Kent Reilly III and James F. Garber, eds., *Ancient Objects and Sacred Realms: Interpretations of Mississippian Iconography* (Austin: University of Texas Press, 2007); George E. Lankford, F. Kent Reilly III, and James F. Garber, eds., *Visualizing the Sacred: Cosmic Visions, Regionalism, and the Art of the Mississippian World* (Austin: University of Texas Press, 2011); Richard F. Townsend and Robert V. Sharp, eds., *Hero, Hawk, and Open Hand: American Indian Art of the Ancient Midwest and South* (New Haven, CT: Yale University Press in association with the Art Institute of Chicago, 2004).

4. David H. Dye, "Art, Ritual, and Chiefly Warfare in the Mississippian World," in Townsend and Sharp, *Hero, Hawk, and Open Hand*, 191–205.

5. Vernon J. Knight Jr., "Farewell to the Southeastern Ceremonial Complex," *Southeastern Archaeology* 25 (2006): 1–5; Reilly and Garber, eds., "Introduction," in *Ancient Objects and Sacred Realms*, 4–5; James A. Brown, "Sequencing the

Braden Style within Mississippian Period Art and Iconography," in *Ancient Objects and Sacred Realms*, 213–245; Lankford, Reilly, and Garber, eds., *Visualizing the Sacred*.

6. George E. Lankford, "Some Cosmological Motifs in the Southeastern Ceremonial Complex," in *Ancient Objects and Sacred Realms*, 14–15, 21–27; R. Kent Reilly III, "People of Earth, People of Sky: Visualizing the Sacred in Native American Art of the Mississippian Period," in *Ancient Objects and Sacred Realms*, 127–129.

7. Timothy R. Pauketat, *Ancient Cahokia and the Mississippians* (Cambridge, UK: Cambridge University Press, 2004), 47–66; Susan M. Alt, "Making Mississippian at Cahokia," in *The Oxford Handbook of North American Archaeology*, ed. Timothy R. Pauketat (New York: Oxford University Press, 2012), 501–503; John E. Kelly and Jim Brown, Cahokia: The Processes and Principles of the Creation of an Early Mississippian City, 2014, in *Making Ancient Cities: Space and Place in Early Urban Societies*, ed. Andrew T. Creekmore, III, and Kevin D. Fisher (New York: Cambridge University Press, 2014), 292–323.

8. Pauketat, *Ancient Cahokia*, 67–84; *Cahokia: Ancient America's Great City on the Mississippi* (New York: Penguin Books, 2009), chapter 2; Thomas E. Emerson, "Cahokia Interaction and Ethnogenesis in the Northern Midcontinent," in *Oxford Handbook of North American Archaeology*, 400–401; Kelly and Brown, "Cahokia."

9. Emerson, "Cahokia Interaction and Ethnogenesis," 401.

10. Alt, "Making Mississippian at Cahokia," 499.

11. James A. Brown, "Where's the Power in Mound Building? An Eastern Woodlands Perspective," in *Leadership and Polity in Mississippian Society*, ed. Brian Butler and Paul D. Welch, Center for Archaeological Investigations, Occasional Paper no. 33 (Carbondale: Southern Illinois University, 2006), 197–213; Brown, "Sequencing the Braden Style." See also Pauketat, *Ancient Cahokia and the Mississippians*, 84–95; *Cahokia*, Chapters 6 and 7.

12. Pauketat, *Ancient Cahokia*, 47–66, 119–143; *Cahokia*, 11–24. In fact, Pauketat argues that Cahokia arose as religious movement when acolytes of a new religion moved from present-day Arkansas, north to the American Bottoms.

13. Pauketat, *Ancient Cahokia*, 124.

14. Recent overviews of the archaeology and reconstruction of Cahokia history are George R. Milner, *The Cahokia Chiefdom: The Archaeology of a Mississippian Society* (Washington, DC: Smithsonian Institution Press, 1998); and Pauketat, *Ancient Cahokia and the Mississippians* and *Cahokia*. On the decline of Cahokia see Thomas E. Emerson and Kristin M. Hedman, "The Dangers of Diversity: The Consolidation and Dissolution of Cahokia, Native North America's First Urban Polity," in *Beyond Collapse: Archaeological Perspectives on Resilience, Revialization, and Transformation in Complex Societies*, ed. Ronald K. Faulseit, Center for Archaeological Investigations, Occasional Paper no. 42 (Carbondale: Southern Illinois University Press, 2016), 147–175.

15. Alt, "Making Mississippian at Cahokia," 505.

16. For regional variations see the essays in Lankford, Reilly, and Garber, eds., *Visualizing the Sacred*.

17. Vernon J. Knight Jr. and Vincas P. Steponaitis, eds., *Archaeology of the Moundville Chiefdom* (Washington, DC: Smithsonian Institution Press, 1998), 10–12.

18. Knight and Steponaitis, *Archaeology of the Moundville Chiefdom*, 12–17; John H. Blitz, "Moundville in the Mississippian World," in *Oxford Handbook of North American Archaeology*, 539–541; Vernon James Knight Jr., "Moundville as a Diagrammatic Ceremonial Center," in *Archaeology of the Moundville Chiefdom*, 44–62.

19. Knight and Steponaitis, *Archaeology of the Moundville Chiefdom*, 17–24; John H. Blitz, "Moundville in the Mississippian World," in *Oxford Handbook of North American Archaeology*, 541–542.

20. Adam King, *Etowah: The Political History of a Chiefdom Capital* (Tuscaloosa: University of Alabama Press, 2003), 52–62; King, "Mississippian in the Deep South: Common Themes in Varied Histories," in *Oxford Handbook of North American Archaeology*, 516.

21. King, *Etowah*, 86–89; King, "Mississippian in the Deep South," 516.

22. King, *Etowah*, 63–81, 89–91.

23. King, *Etowah*, 78–83, 92.

24. Vernon James Knight Jr., *Mound Excavations at Moundville: Architecture, Elites, and Social Order* (Tuscaloosa: University of Alabama Press, 2010), 348–366; John E. Worth, "An Ethnohistorical

Synthesis of Southeastern Chiefdoms: How Does Coosa Compare?," 'Paper presented at the Annual Meeting of the Southeastern Archaeological Conference, Charlotte, NC, 2003; John Blitz, *Ancient Chiefdoms of the Tombigbee* (Tuscaloosa: University of Alabama Press, 1993), 12–13; Blitz, "Mississippian Chiefdoms and the Fusion-Fission Process," *American Antiquity* 64.4 (1999): 583–587; Hally, "The Territorial Size of Mississippian Chiefdoms"; "Platform Mound Construction and the Instability of Mississippian Chiefdoms," in *Political Structure and Change in the Prehistoric Southeastern United States*, ed. John Scarry (Gainesville: University Press of Florida, 1996), 92–127; Jon Bernard Marcoux, "On Reconsidering Display Goods Production and Circulation in the Moundville Chiefdom," *Southeastern Archaeology*, 26(2007): 232–245; Anderson, *Savannah River Chiefdoms*, 28–34; Mark Williams, "Paired Towns," in *Lamar Archaeology: Mississippian Chiefdoms in the Deep South*, ed. Mark Williams and Gary Shapiro (Tuscaloosa: University of Alabama Press, 1990), 163–174; John F. Scarry and Mintcy D. Maxham, "Elite Actors in the Protohistoric: Elite Identities and Interaction with Europeans in the Apalachee and Powhatan Chiefdoms," in *Between Contacts and Colonies: Archaeological Perspectives on the Protohistoric Southeast*, ed. Cameron B. Wesson and Mark A. Rees (Tuscaloosa: University of Alabama Press, 2002), 152; Hally, "Nature of Mississippian Regional Systems," 33–37; David Pollack, *Caborn-Welborn: Constructing a New Society after the Angel Chiefdom Collapse* (Tuscaloosa: University of Alabama Press, 2004), 19–24. The Mississippi Period began during the climatic event known as the Medieval Warm Period (*c.* 800–1200 CE), which may help account for the easy adoption of intensive corn agriculture across the South. Around 1300 CE, this warming trend ends with the beginning of the Little Ice Age (1300–1850 CE). The drought referred to here would have occurred within about 75 years of the onset of the Little Ice Age. For more on these climatic events and the changes in Native life, see Anderson, *Savannah River Chiefdoms*, 277–289 and David G. Anderson and Kenneth E. Sassaman, *Recent Developments in Southeastern Archaeology: From Colonization to Complexity* (Washington, DC: Society for American Archaeology, 2012), 163–165.

25. Luys Hernández de Biedma, "Relation of the Island of Florida," in *The De Soto Chronicles: The Expedition of Hernando de Soto to North America in 1539–1543*, 2 vols., ed. Lawrence A. Clayton, Vernon. J. Knight Jr., and Edward C. Moore, trans. John E. Worth (Tuscaloosa: University of Alabama Press, 1993), 1: 221–246; Rodrigo Rangel, "Account of the Northern Conquest and Discovery of Hernando de Soto," in *The De Soto Chronicles*, 1:246–306; Gentleman of Elvas, "True Relation of the Vicissitudes That Attended the Governor Don Hernando de Soto and Some Nobles of Portugal in the Discovery of the Provence of Florida," in *The De Soto Chronicles*, trans. James Robertson, 1: 25–219; Garcilaso de la Vega, the Inca, "La Florida," in *The De Soto Chronicles*, trans. Charmion Shelby, 2: 25–560; Herbert I. Priestly, ed. and trans., *The Luna Papers: Documents Relating to the Expedition of Don Tritán de Luna y Arellano for the Conquest of La Florida in 1559–1561*, 2 vols. (Deland: Florida State Historical Society, 1928); Juan de la Bandera, "The 'Long' Bandera Relation," in *The Juan Pardo Expeditions: Exploration of the Carolinas and Tennessee, 1566–1568*, Charles Hudson, trans. Paul E. Hoffman (Tuscaloosa: University of Alabama Press, 1990, reprint), 205–296; "The 'Short' Bandera Relation," in *The Juan Pardo Expeditions*, trans. Paul Hoffman, 297–316.

26. Anderson and Sassaman, *Recent Developments*, 166. Note that Mississippian polities existed farther north than de Soto went, on the Kentucky and Ohio Rivers and into present-day Virginia, which are not represented on this map.

27. Charles Hudson, *Knights of Spain, Warriors of the Sun: Hernando de Soto and the South's Ancient Chiefdoms* (Athens: University of Georgia Press, 1997), 14, 82–87, 190–203, 335–373.

28. Biedma, "Relation," 229–230; Elvas, "True Relation" 82–86, 89; Rangel, "Account," 278–280; Hudson, *Knights of Spain*, 172–184.

29. Chester DePratter, "The Chiefdom of Cofitachequi," in *The Forgotten Centuries: Indians and Europeans in the American South, 1521–1704*, ed. Charles Hudson and Carmen Chaves Tesser (Athens: University of Georgia Press, 1994), 197–226; Robin A. Beck Jr., "Catawba Coalescence and the Shattering of the Carolina

Piedmont, 1540–1675," in *Mapping the Mississippian Shatter Zone: The Colonial Indian Slave Trade and Regional Instability in the American South*, ed. Robbie Ethridge and Sheri M. Shuck-Hall (Lincoln: University of Nebraska Press, 2009), 115–116; Robbie Ethridge and Jeffrey M. Mitchem, "The Interior South at the Time of Spanish Exploration," in *Native and Spanish New Worlds: Sixteenth-Century Entradas in the American Southwest and Southeast*, ed. Clay Mathers, Jeffery M. Mitchem, and Charles M. Haecker (Tucson: University of Arizona Press, 2013), 173–174.

30. Biedma, "Relation," 229–230; Elvas, "True Relation," 82–86, 89; Rangel, "Account," 278–280; Hudson, *Knights of Spain*, 172–184.

31. Hudson, *Knights of Spain*, 68–73.

32. Robin A. Beck Jr., "Catawba Coalescence and the Shattering of the Carolina Piedmont, 1540–1675," in *Mapping the Mississippian Shatter Zone*, 115–116; Hudson, *Knights of Spain*, 421; Biedma, "Relation," 231; Elvas, "True Relation," 83; Bandera, "The 'Long' Bandera Relation."

33. Hudson, *Knights of Spain*, 229; Amanda L. Regnier, *Reconstructing Tascalusa's Chiefdom: Pottery Styles and the Social Composition of Late Mississippian Communities along the Alabama River* (Tuscaloosa: University of Alabama Press), 42–43.

34. Elvas, "True Relation," 96–105; Biedma, "Relation," 232–236; Rangel, "Account," 291–294; Hudson, *Knights of Spain*, 231. See also Robbie Ethridge, Kathryn E. Holland Braund, Lawrence A. Clayton, George E. Lankford, and Michael D. Murphey, "A Comparative Analysis of the De Soto Accounts on the Route to, and Events at, Mabila," in *The Search for Mabila: The Decisive Battle between Hernando de Soto and Chief Tascalusa*, ed. Vernon James Knight Jr. (Tuscaloosa: University of Alabama Press, 2009), 153–181.

35. Craig T. Sheldon Jr., "Introduction," in *The Southern and Central Alabama Expeditions of Clarence Bloomfield Moore*, ed. Craig T. Sheldon (Tuscaloosa: University of Alabama Press, 2001), 23; Ned Jenkins, "Tracing the Origins of the Early Creeks, 1050–1700 CE," in *Mapping the Mississippian Shatter Zone*, 200–216; Amanda R. Regnier, "A Stylistic Analysis of Burial Urns from the Protohistoric Period in Central Alabama," *Southeastern Archaeology* 25.1 (2006): 128; "What Indian Pottery of the Sixteenth-Century Central Alabama Looks Like and Why It Matters," in *The Search for Mabila*, 83–93; *Reconstructing Tascalusa's Chiefdom*, 129–139; Robbie Ethridge, *From Chicaza to Chickasaw: The European Invasion and the Transformation of the Mississippian World* (Chapel Hill: University of North Carolina Press, 2010), 66–67; Ethridge and Mitchem, "The Interior South," 176–178.

36. Hudson, *Knights of Spain*, 230–231.

37. Hudson, *Knights of Spain*, 110–115, 238–249, 266–274, 336–338; Ethridge, *From Chicaza to Chickasaw*, 60–88.

38. Robbie Ethridge, "Introduction: Mapping the Mississippian Shatter Zone," in *Mapping the Mississippian Shatter Zone*, 10–13; Ethridge, *From Chicaza to Chickasaw*, 87–88.

39. Robbie Ethridge, "Creating the Shatter Zone: The Indian Slave Trader and the Collapse of the Mississippian World," in *Light on the Path*, 207–218; "Introduction," 2010. For analysis of the Indian slave trade and slavery among Southern Indians see Alan Gallay, *The Indian Slave Trade: The Rise of the English Empire in the American South, 1670–1717* (New Haven, CT: Yale University Press, 2002) and Christina Snyder, *Slavery in Indian Country: The Changing Face of Captivity in Early America* (Cambridge, MA: Harvard University Press, 2010); On the spread of the gun trade see David J. Silverman, *Thundersticks: Firearms and the Violent Transformation of Native America* (Cambridge, MA: Harvard University Press, 2016).

40. Robin A. Beck, *Chiefdoms, Collapse, and Coalescence in the Early American South* (Cambridge, UK: Cambridge University Press, 2013); "Catawba Coalescence," 130–137; Ethridge, *From Chicaza to Chickasaw*, 104–108.

41. Marvin T. Smith, *Coosa: The Rise and Fall of a Mississippian Chiefdom* (Gainesville: University Press of Florida, 2000), 103–104, 107–109; Ethridge, *From Chicaza to Chickasaw*, 62–69.

42. Jenkins, "Tracing the Origins"; Regnier, *Reconstructing Tascalusa's Chiefdom*,135–137; Ethridge, *From Chicaza to Chicasaw*, 67–73; Gregory A. Waselkov and Marvin T. Smith, "Upper Creek Archaeology," in *Indians of the Greater Southeast: Historical Archaeology and Ethnohistory*, ed. Bonnie G. McEwan (Gainesville: University Press of Florida, 2000), 242–264.

43. John E. Worth, "The Lower Creeks: Origins and Early History," in *Indians of the Greater Southeast*, 265–298; Patricia Galloway, *Choctaw Genesis, 1500–1700* (Lincoln: University of Nebraska, 1995).

44. Johnson, "The Chickasaws," in *Indians of the Greater Southeast*, 85–121.

45. Ethridge, *From Chicaza to Chickasaw*, 149–193.

46. Marvin D. Jeter, "Shatter Zone Shock Waves along the Lower Mississippi," in *Mapping the Mississippian Shatter Zone*, 365–387; Ethridge, *From Chicaza to Chickasaw*, 116–148. The designation of the Quapaw as recent migrants from the Ohio Valley is still controversial. For a discussion of these debates, also see Marvin D. Jeter, "From Prehistory through Protohistory to Ethnohistory in and near the Northern Lower Mississippi Valley," in *The Transformation of the Southeastern Indians, 1540–1760*, ed. Robbie Ethridge and Charles Hudson (Jackson: University Press of Mississippi, 2002), 177–224.

47. Ethridge, *From Chicaza to Chickasaw*, 149–231; see also Elizabeth Ellis, "The Many Ties of the Petites Nations: Relationships, Power, and Diplomacy in the Lower Mississippi Valley 1685-1785," PhD diss., University of North Carolina, Chapel Hill, 2015.

48. James F. Barnett Jr., *The Natchez Indians: A History to 1735* (Jackson: University Press of Mississippi, 2007), 101–131.

49. Jay K. Johnson, ed., *Development of Southeastern Archaeology* (Tuscaloosa: University of Alabama Press, 1993).

50. John Blitz, "New Perspectives in Mississippian Archaeology," *Journal of Archaeological Research*, 18(2010): 1–39; and David G. Anderson and Kenneth E. Sassaman, "Mississippian Complexity and Contact Coalescence," in *Recent Developments in Southeastern Archaeology* (Washington, DC: Society for American Archaeology, 2012), 152–190.

51. Anderson, *Savannah River Chiefdoms*; Blitz, *Ancient Chiefdoms of the Tombigbee*; David J. Hally, *King: The Social Archaeology of a Late Mississippian Town in Northwestern Georgia* (Tuscaloosa: University of Alabama Press, 2008); Adam King, *Etowah*; Vernon James Knight Jr., *Mound Excavations at Moundville*; Patrick C. Livingood, *Mississippian Polity and Politics on the Gulf Coastal Plain: A View from the Pearl River, Mississippi* (Tuscaloosa: University of Alabama Press, 2011); Knight and Steponaitis, eds., *Archaeology of the Moundville Chiefdom*; Timothy Pauketat, *Ancient Cahokia and the Mississippians* and *Cahokia*; Regnier, *Reconstructing Tascalusa's Chiefdom*; Smith, *Coosa*; and Gregory D. Wilson, *The Archaeology of Everyday Life at Early Moundville* (Tuscaloosa: University of Alabama Press, 2008).

52. Reilly and Garber, eds., *Ancient Objects and Sacred Realm* and Lankford, Reilly, and Garber, eds., *Visualizing the Sacred*.

53. Townsend and Sharp, eds., *Hero, Hawk, and the Open Hand*.

54. Charles Hudson, *The Southeastern Indians* (Knoxville: University of Tennessee Press, 1976); Hudson, *Knights of Spain*; Charles Hudson and Carmen Chaves Tesser, eds., *Forgotten Centuries: Indians and Europeans in the American South* (Athens: University of Georgia Press, 1994); and Robbie Ethridge and Charles Hudson, eds., *The Transformation of the Southeastern Indians*, (Jackson: University Press of Mississippi, 2002).

55. Galloway, *Choctaw Genesis*.

56. Gallay, *The Indian Slave Trade*.

57. Ethridge, *Mapping the Mississippian Shatter Zone*; Ethridge, *From Chicaza to Chickasaw*.

58. Beck, *Chiefdoms, Collapse, and Coalescence*.

59. Biedma, "Relation;" Rangel, "Account;" Elvas, "True Relation;" Garcilaso de la Vega, "La Florida."

60. Priestly, ed. and trans., *The Luna Papers*; Bandera, "The 'Long' Bandera Relation"; and "The 'Short' Bandera Relation."

61. John E. Worth, ed. and trans., *The Struggle for the Georgia Coast: An Eighteenth-Century Spanish Retrospective on Guale and Mocama*, Anthropological Papers of the American Museum of Natural History, no. 75 (New York: American Museum of Natural History, 1995, reprinted Tuscaloosa: University of Alabama Press, 2007); Worth, *Discovering Florida: First-Contact Narratives from Spanish Expeditions along the Lower Gulf Coast* (Gainesville: University of Florida Press, 2016); Mark F. Boyd, Hale G. Smith, and John W. Griffin, *Here They Once Stood: The Tragic End of the Apalachee Missions* (Gainesville: University Press of Florida, 1951); Jeannette Thurbor Connor, ed. and trans., *Colonial Records of Spanish Florida: Letters and*

Reports of Governors and Secular Persons, Volume I, 1570–1577 (Florida State Historical Society, 1925) and *Colonial Records of Spanish Florida: Letters and Reports of Governors, Deliberations of the Council of the Indies, Royal Decrees, and other Documents, Volume II, 1577–1580* (Florida State Historical Society, 1930); and Jerald T. Milanich and William C. Sturtevant, eds., *Francisco Pareja's 1613 Confessionario: A Documentary Source for Timucuan Ethnography* (Gainesville: Florida Department of State, 1972).

62. Antoine Simone Le Page du Pratz, *The History of Louisiana or of the Western Parts of Virginia and Carolina* (Baton Rouge, LA: Claitor's Publishing Division, 1972; English translation originally published 1774).

63. Dunbar Rowland and Albert Sanders, eds. and trans., *Mississippi Provincial Archives: French Dominion.* Vols. 1–3 (Jackson: Mississippi Department of Archives and History, 1927–1932).

Robbie Ethridge

SEAPORT CITIES IN NORTH AMERICA, 1600–1800

MOTIVATIONS FOR COLONIAL CITY BUILDING

All of the Europeans who arrived in North America after 1600 came from societies in which cities fulfilled vital practical and ideological functions. Consequently, colonists transferred their urbanism with them to North America, often enhancing or adapting it to their "colonial" situation. What needed little alteration, however, was the practical purpose fulfilled by seaport cities in an age of sail. Across the early modern era, following the first sorties of Europeans across and around the Atlantic, a selection of cities enjoyed the expansion that came with the needs of merchants, mariners, and artisans who sustained trade and war. Bristol, Liverpool, Glasgow, London, Seville, Lisbon, and Bordeaux expanded

physically and economically as they absorbed the profits of these new endeavors. In London, a stupendously wealthy merchant class emerged in the late 17th century, many of whom were involved in founding the Bank of England, while also channeling vast sums into the construction of city infrastructure.[1]

With so much confirmation of the value of port cities to a growing European economy, settlers made practical plans for their recreation a key element of their colonization projects. At Jamestown, Boston, Bridgetown, Port Royal, Charleston, Philadelphia, and New Amsterdam, Europeans drew up plans for cities in what they believed to be locations well-suited to communication and connection across and around the Atlantic. Such was their desire to be close to a major body of water, they sometimes chose sites whose swamps, marshes, and sandy soil made them distinctly unsuitable for the construction of a city. Charleston's final location was on a peninsula more low-lying and swampy even than the first site selected by the colony's proprietors, while the Jamaican town of Port Royal was built on little more than a sand bar. Securely rocky, the location of Boston was fundamentally stable but was limited in scope for urban growth because of the small scale of the peninsula. But this was no matter, because access to the ocean, as well as the possibility of easily seeing off seaborne enemies, were of critical importance.

Having identified the optimal location for a secure yet accessible seaport, founding leaders then set about doing all they could to promote urban growth. Coming from a nation of city-states, the Dutch prioritized the institutional foundations of a well-governed town at New Amsterdam, as did the French at New Orleans. By creating a heavily corporatized environment that bestowed privileges on urban residents, they sought urban order through an ordered and conscientious citizenry who labored to produce a smooth-running city. At Boston, meanwhile, Puritan settlers concentrated on making a town that fostered a tightly woven community of the religious, devoting their city lives to God, and ensuring that every townsperson lived and worked according to the pronouncements of the church and its governing men. In Philadelphia and Charleston, founders looked to fix their cities in the landscape with detailed street plans, complete with plots of land and wharves, drawn out to facilitate the construction of homes and businesses by colonists. In the Caribbean islands claimed by the English during the 17th century, principally Barbados and Jamaica, seaports were viewed as vital to the projection of mercantilism in these hotly contested territories.[2]

While city-founding was very obviously propelled by ideological forces in Massachusetts, in one way or another such motivations were at the heart of most seaport-making projects of 17th-century colonial North America. Anchoring one's young colony with a town was not merely a practical concern but also a philosophical one. Among both the Dutch and the English, the belief that urban life was the key to "civilizing" a "wilderness" was a universal motivation for town-founding. William Penn's desire to see Philadelphia grow into the heart of his colonial project led him to grant each investor a lot of town land alongside a country tract. Penn then used the growth of the port city and the concentration of trade within it as evidence to the English government of the "good beginnings" of Pennsylvania. Carolina's founders likewise desired cities as civilizing vehicles as much as trading posts, attempting to make them into the centers of justice and political power that anchored the colony's orderly and hierarchical government proposed by its Fundamental Constitutions and modeled on English best practice. Such efforts were fully supported by colonial authorities based in London, including John Locke and the Board of Trade, who condemned the dearth of port cities in the Chesapeake and claimed that "if only they

had port towns" the settlers there would have been able to create a more orderly and moral society.[3]

On the ground, however, settlers themselves were frequently at odds with the goals of colonial proprietors, London authorities, and English governors. In the Chesapeake, planters determined to site tobacco trading on their rural property stymied the early success of seaport cities. Yet, some very pressing reasons explained why settlers also supported the creation of cities as a place of security and preservation of European values. In the 17th century, many colonists faced the threat of numerous and powerful Native American peoples and of competing imperial powers. Seaport cities provided protection from both groups of marauders, as they functioned for "the convenience and security of shipping" and of the colonists who wished to develop societies that were both physically and commercially secure. All of North America's colonial enterprises suffered multiple assaults by Indians and other European powers that threatened their permanence before 1720: the Pequot wars and King Philip's war in New England, and Leisler's Rebellion and Bacon's Rebellion in New York and Virginia, to name but a few. Carolinians had one early town, Port Royal, almost erased by the Yamasee War in 1715, while the fortifications in Charleston were carefully constructed to keep out Native Americans landward and the Spanish, who were poised to sail north from St. Augustine. In the Caribbean, islands regularly changed hands in imperial conflicts among the Dutch, English, French, and Spanish. On the Gulf of Mexico, New Orleans was a defense against not only Europeans but also numerous powerful Native American polities. Facing these multiple security threats, port towns acted as bulkheads of colonization. Even if inhabitants did not always agree with the goals of their imperial masters, they faced sufficient immediate peril to make retreat into the "security" of urban life a core early imperative of town creation.[4]

DRIVERS OF SUCCESS AND FAILURE

As colonists quickly learned, however, the ambition to build a seaport city and the forces at work in the colonization process—which unfolded haltingly over more than a century—often did not mutually support one another. Careful planning by a colonial proprietor or settlers looking for safety in numbers could boost a city's growth, but an array of unforeseen events and circumstances could equally bring about its demise. Port Royal, Carolina, survived the massacre of colonists during the Yamasee War of 1715, but it never managed to compete with Charleston's supremacy in the region; Jamestown failed to flourish even as Virginia grew in permanency as a site of European colonization. What determined whether a North American seaport city would succeed? And what does this reveal about the role of cities in the colonial process?

For Europeans, who came from a continent with a familiar and mostly predictable geography and climate, environmental factors proved to be the hardest to reckon with during the colonization process. Often sited on low ground near oceans and built of easily destroyed materials, young seaport cities proved especially vulnerable to the vagaries of the American weather. Perhaps the most dramatic environmental setback to their growth came in 1692, when a violent earthquake shook Jamaica, causing the sand bar on which Port Royal was built to liquefy, sending almost the entire town beneath the waves. The disaster prompted Jamaicans to lay out a new capital at Kingston, on the more secure mainland to the north. Port Royal, however, was only one of a number of circum-Caribbean towns to fall victim to epic natural disaster. Charleston was affected by a less severe late-17th-century earthquake but also endured a number of direct hits from hurricanes. One of the worst occurred in 1752, when the damage to the port and its infrastructure was so bad that the colony's newspaper, the *South Carolina Gazette*, ceased

printing for six months. Also affecting northern cities, large fires constituted a universal threat throughout the colonies and occurred with frightening regularity. Boston, New York, and Charleston all suffered conflagrations that tore through the most densely populated areas of the town, destroying valuable real estate and personal property.[5]

Many of these events killed inhabitants and flattened infrastructure, stymying urban trade and growth through sudden and large-scale destruction. In the early modern era, however, seaport cities were also brought to a standstill, or at least had their expansion checked, by the less visible (but equally dangerous) threat of disease. Disease spread easily through cities that were growing rapidly but lacked good sanitation or access to fresh water. Additionally, the unprecedented mixing of African, European, and indigenous people all facing unfamiliar disease environments, yet bringing with them their own pathogenic inheritance, created further hazards. Ships in port also regularly brought new waves of disease with them. Diseases such as malaria, spread by mosquitoes through circum-Caribbean cities built on swampy ground, checked the growth of the white population, among whom life expectancy in Charleston, Kingston, and Bridgetown remained lower even than the "urban graveyard" that was early modern London. Measles, yellow fever, and smallpox epidemics all affected America's seaports in repeated waves. During particularly acute episodes, such as Philadelphia's 1793 yellow fever outbreak and the smallpox epidemic that raged throughout the Revolutionary War, trade could cease entirely as the wealthy fled to "wholesome" countryside retreats, leaving laborers who lacked such resources out of work and fending for themselves.[6]

Epidemics brought seaport commerce to a standstill for a matter of weeks, but there was a much wider range of circumstances that may have a more profound effect on a city's ability to become economically viable. Above all, seaports needed trade to flourish—both ocean borne and from the interior—and if there was little need for them as a "hinge" of commerce they would struggle to grow. Indeed, this is what happened in both the Chesapeake and the Carolinas, where cities such as Norfolk, Annapolis, Charleston, and Wilmington had long gestations often attributable to the economic situation of the society in which they were planted. In the Chesapeake, sustained efforts to focus economic activities on seaports met with an equally enduring desire among wealthy planters to preserve the economic power and autonomy of their plantation estates, which constituted a critical agrarian powerbase. So although seaports eventually grew dramatically in the second half of the 18th century, their initial expansion was checked by the determination of the colony's rulers to starve them of the support needed for rapid growth.

Then there was the question of how one measured a city's success. In New Orleans, "les grands"—the bureaucrats, elite military men, merchants, and missionaries—viewed the port as a failure from the outset. Quickly the town became populated by métis, indigenous, and African people, as well as Europeans, who had a tendency to intermarry with one another. "Les petits" made their way by smuggling, forgery, and other forms of illegal dealing. As the city grew from its 1718 foundations, some imperial officials believed that ever-greater numbers of the chief inhabitants were becoming corrupted by this immoral and disobedient behavior, leading them even to reject the king's absolute authority within the "Vieux Carrée." Growing from a Native American crossroads to a populous town in the course of decades, New Orleans was clearly a successful city in economic terms. Yet, according to the moral and political standards of its metropolitan rulers, the failure to adhere to the norms of either absolute government or Enlightenment morality deemed it a dismal failure.[7]

Despite these setbacks, by the middle of the 18th century North America's seaports were permanent fixtures in the geography of European settlement. The largest could compete with Europe's major provincial cities, while smaller ports like Salem, Massachusetts, and Newport, Rhode Island, still had populations that matched those of its market towns. At the first United States census in 1790, five cities contained populations exceeding 10,000 people. The largest, Philadelphia, was home to more than 45,000 souls. Boston, New York, Charleston, Baltimore, and the Quaker city were big enough to compete with Britain's biggest towns of the era. Although early America's seaports endured many decades of stern tests to their existence, they ultimately survived their first two centuries to emerge as major urban places on the Atlantic stage.[8]

PORT CITIES BECOME ECONOMIC ANCHORS

Although withstanding earthquakes and smallpox was key to the survival of seaport populations, the pressing need for the economic functions a city provided in a maritime trading economy ensured that a town would not just endure but flourish. These functions were both varied and complex, leading historians frequently to argue that cities' outsize importance stemmed from their capacity as "electric transformers" for the wider economy. Everywhere, seaport cities' growth was rooted in the diverse economic roles they played in colonial societies. Often, these places were home to 10 percent or less of the overall population. Yet they thrived because of the variety of services and skills their populations provided to the wider economy. The majority of early Americans were rural-dwelling farmers, but by the 18th century they had come to be connected to and sometimes reliant on seaport cities for a whole range of everyday necessities. Some of these necessities were tangible and obvious, while some have required careful historical research to uncover them.[9]

The most obvious economic function of seaport cities was as facilitators of the exchange of material goods and people, imported from Britain, Africa, and Asia, with locally grown crops. In each and every city its wharves and waterfront streets were hives of activity in which these vital transactions took place and where goods were loaded on and off ships. Boston's Long Wharf, Gadsden's Wharf in Charleston, and New York's Cruger's Wharf were just some of the most prominent examples of these sites of feverish exchange, which were mostly owned by individual "wharfingers" or merchants, who orchestrated the dealing that took place at their portals to an Atlantic world of commerce. Christopher Gadsden's wharf was above all the single location through which the largest amount of African people arrived to be sold into a life of slavery in continental North America. As slave ships docked at the quayside, planters arrived to bid for their human cargo. These vessels were often moored alongside boats bringing European and Asian manufactures—textiles, metal wares, ceramics, and trinkets—to North America. After disgorging their cargo onto the wharf for wholesale, they would then be loaded up with rice, indigo, skins, and naval stores for the return journey to Europe.[10]

Yet this was not the only commercial activity that took place on the wharf. In a bid to maximize their profits, wharfingers populated their wharves with buildings that they then rented out to yield additional income. Most common was the construction of warehouses in which owners of imported and exported goods might be charged a fee to store their wares. Scale houses were created to weigh these products, to work out exactly what the sums owed for storage, packing, and shipping would be. Such buildings also became a place to sell wholesale goods to retailers both in and beyond the seaport, sometimes by auctions, which attracted large crowds of people whose willingness to buy was lubricated by the sale of alcohol and food. Wharfingers also built ranges of stores to rent out to men in the maritime trades as well as the likes of tailors and shoemakers, who produced goods using the

materials imported at the wharf. Although the ships that came from across the Atlantic arrived and departed according to seasonal rhythms in the spring and fall seasons, smaller watercraft appeared daily with food for sale in the local marketplace, a cut of the sale price likely going to the wharfinger who had accommodated the farmer, fisherman, or cattle keeper.[11]

In many ways, then, urban wharves were a microcosm of the layers of retailing and manufacturing activity that sustained these cities and made them so critical to the larger colonial economy. For early America's seaports were places that accommodated multiple networks of buying and making, ensuring that they were commercially critical to a majority of the population. Retail shops provided many of these goods, becoming more sophisticated as the 18th century progressed in both their physical appearance and their stock selection. Elizabeth Murray, a shopkeeper in mid-century Boston, embodied the refined shopping experience that cities could offer. Opening her dry goods store in the city during the 1750s, she ensured a superior selection of wares by personally making a trip to London to select products that would appeal to wealthy Bostonians. The cargo she assembled included the latest in fashionable textiles, haberdashery, and millinery. Although women shopkeepers were in a minority in terms of their gender, as retailers they were part of a large community— by the mid-1750s, Philadelphia had numerous households who identified themselves by this occupation.[12]

Retailing goods, but also manufacturing them, were the many artisans who flocked to these seaport cities to carry on their trades. As a place in which skilled labor was scarce but land abundant, those who decided to stick with city life and produce vital goods often enjoyed steady custom. While some Americans complained in the 17th century that their products were dear and badly made, increased competition in the 18th century spurred a refinement of their output. By the late 18th century, customers could find American-made furniture, silver, jewelry, clocks, coaches, leather wares, clothing, and books on sale. Using imported components, craftspeople produced the kind of items that could only be made-to-order in the 18th century—horse furniture, mourning rings and mementos, and clothing. Bricklayers, carpenters, wood carvers, and stonemasons also possessed important skills needed to develop colonial infrastructure more generally. To expand their businesses in an environment of free-labor scarcity, such craftsmen frequently trained enslaved African people in their trades, enabling them to expand their enterprises into complex businesses able to work multiple contracts at once.[13]

In Kingston, Bridgetown, Charleston, Newport, and New York—seaports with considerable enslaved populations—such people were also critical to the successful function of the provisioning market, the final key commercial function of these cities. These food markets drew on the city's agricultural and watery hinterlands for their produce to feed seaport inhabitants and those who lived in their suburbs. In those seaport cities situated in slave societies, enslaved and free black men and women were a mainstay of the provisioning process, catching the fish, butchering the meat, and bringing fresh fruit, vegetables, and prepared foods to the marketplace for the benefit of urban consumers. At the same time, white farmers placed close to seaport cities geared their enterprises toward growing crops that were sold in the marketplace; the Tomlinson family of Bristol, Bucks County, to the north of Philadelphia, were among the hundreds of farmers who regularly packed up their wagon with produce, arriving in the seaport late on a Friday night ready to sell at the market at dawn on a Saturday morning. Flooding into the town twice a week to market their provisions, the town relied on these farmers as much as they relied on its demand for their livings.[14]

Seaport cities, however, were economic anchors in one final, much less visible way.

Populated by traders with easy access to transatlantic networks sustained by credit and cash flow as much as tangible goods, these towns became the source of capital needed to grow enterprises in both rural and urban America. Urban merchants were linchpins because they issued credits to farmers and planters for their crops while allowing them to run up accounts for imported goods purchased in anticipation of a crop's delivery. Often planters outspent their credit or over-valued their crop, making them debtors to the city merchant. Those who operated outside of the agricultural economy were also dependent on merchants in a similar fashion. Indian traders and country storekeepers bought goods wholesale from seaport traders, fulfilling their debt obligations only when they had successfully shifted their stock. Overall, as they became custodians of reliable credit in an economy short of hard cash, urban merchants worked at the pivotal commercial nexus—the seaport city—of the colonial economy.[15]

In a multitude of ways, these towns were, by the 18th century, the conduits and the repositories of goods, capital, and wealth that greased the wheels of early North American expansion. While the economy as a whole relied on agricultural commodities, trade with Native Americans, and the export of other raw materials, such as iron ore, to power growth, seaport cities performed a central role as sites of exchange and processing. Their importance was, of course, further boosted by North America's status as a colony in a British imperial mercantilist system, which sought to keep inland areas rural and agricultural as it provided incentives to traders and planters over manufacturers, privileging seaport cities in the process.[16]

URBAN CULTURE

As seaport cities grew in the 18th century they came to be home to wealthy people and the source of an array of manufactured and imported consumer goods. In Britain itself, such processes were underway by the late 17th century, and they went hand in hand with an increasing role for towns as cultural centers. Indeed, such developments convinced Enlightenment thinkers that cities were essential to society as the motors of civility, gentility, polite manners, and sociability; in other words, the necessary attributes of a "modern" and commercial society. Colonial Americans' desire to be part of this British Atlantic world of politeness thus also became a central pillar of seaport cities' importance, and colonial elites used this exclusive culture to claim leadership and status within their respective societies. Cities facilitated the emergence of North American urbanity through three principal channels: the supply of fashionable goods, the construction of private homes and public spaces that could act as stages for polite behaviors and the display of those goods, and the hosting of social and cultural organizations and a printed public sphere to provide intellectual grist for "politeness."

Many of the wares imported and made in seaport cities were the accoutrements of a genteel lifestyle. Variously described as "polite" or "genteel," many middling and elite colonists aspired to this mode of behavior, which necessitated the consumption of a panoply of fashionable goods. Being genteel required not only the purchase of fashionable clothing but also the development of fashionable habits—such as the ritual of taking tea—and the ownership of luxury furniture and household textiles that conveyed a well-rounded "polite" character. The extent of investment in gentility certainly varied according to the particular North American seaport city. While Bostonians' Puritanism prescribed a restrained investment in such material goods until the middle of the 18th century, New Yorkers and Newporters held fewer qualms, keeping their purveyors of polite goods well patronized for most of the century. Philadelphia's Quakers, like their New England brethren, preferred a "neat and plain" gentility over a more ostentatious display. Charlestonians, on the other hand, were well renowned as the most

luxury-loving colonists on the continent. By the mid-18th century, some city dwellers had accumulated vast wealth that they eagerly spent on the material display of an increasingly anglicized elite culture.[17]

Such display involved substantial purchases not only from merchants and grocers but also from tailors, mantua makers, shoemakers, milliners, jewelers, clocksmiths, silversmiths, cabinetmakers, and upholsterers. Together these tradesmen and women clothed the genteel body and furnished the polite domestic surroundings that it inhabited. Philadelphia cabinetmaker John Head supplied mahogany tea tables, writing desks, bedsteads, mirrors, and chairs to his wealthy clientele, including John Norris, a member of an elite Quaker governing family. The Norris family also purchased coffee, brandy, lemons, silks, wig boxes, repairs to their coach, and bed linen from city suppliers. Such items represented the kind of groceries and consumer durables that were required to keep a genteel household suitably equipped to welcome and entertain fellow elites and accurately convey elite status. Genteel objects and bodies also required genteel buildings. The Norris family had a residence in Philadelphia city, but in 1742 the family patriarch, Isaac Norris Jr., moved out to a suburban retreat called Fairhill, to the north of the seaport. The Norris family townhouse, but more importantly their suburban estate house, was constructed according to fashionable English architectural styles. Specifically, the house was built on an "H-plan" footprint, with detached wings on either side of the main building adding to a pleasing classical symmetry. Finished with sash and case windows and huge marble fireplaces, and surrounded by a judiciously landscaped garden, the house was perfectly equipped to be a "polite" container for the Norris family's genteel lifestyle and a suitable platform on which they could broadcast their status to neighbors and visitors alike.[18]

Houses like the Norrisses' represented the private face of seaport gentility. Becoming a polite individual, however, was also a sociable pursuit. Gentility came not only from membership of a refined household but also from participation in a wider polite urban culture that unfolded in a city's shared spaces. Coffeehouses, inns, churches, merchant exchanges, assembly rooms, and government buildings were all constructed to reflect the same classical architectural values as the Norrisses' Fairhill mansion. For sure, not every single edifice was a perfect accomplishment of politeness, not least because many dissenting churches and inns were built and run by less wealthy colonists, who had neither the resources nor the desire to model themselves on an Anglican elite sensibility. Nevertheless, such buildings increased markedly across the 18th-century city landscape; Boston's Faneuil Hall, Philadelphia's State House (now Independence Hall), New York's Fraunces Tavern, and Charleston's Exchange building were all genteel public buildings hosting gatherings of genteel city dwellers. Outdoor spaces also provided polite leisure opportunities, and bowling greens, urban gardens, and walkways allowed for promenading and conversation among seaport elites.[19]

The grist for polite sociability—the material that provided both topics of conversation and knowledge about suitable etiquette—was the transatlantic world of letters. Here once again, 18th-century seaport cities had a vital role to play, for they were the location of the print shops that turned out books, pamphlets, and newspapers, as well as the place where imports of such materials arrived from Europe. By the 1730s, every single North American city was the home of at least one printing press and weekly newspaper. The printers, like Benjamin Franklin and his many protégées, such as Charleston's Peter Timothy, were the editors of these newspapers but also the producers of an abundance of further materials of every sort imaginable. Conduct books, novels, polemic, reading or foreign language primers, satire, and poetry all flooded out of these printers' workshops, providing urban elites with the literature necessary to engage in polite conversation and debate. By the middle of the 18th century,

seaport cities were not just centers of commercial knowledge but of scientific, political, and literary debate. Discussion unfolded in public buildings and coffeehouses, but increasingly such debates also took place in gentlemen's clubs and in subscription libraries, such as Philadelphia's Library Company and Charleston's Library Society. Seaport cities were centers of a British Atlantic Enlightenment—structurally, materially, and also intellectually.[20]

Yet these enlightened and genteel spaces were only accessible to a certain proportion of the population. Both Charleston's pleasure gardens and Philadelphia's state house were equipped with fences and walls to keep the population-at-large at a suitable distance. Genteel shops selling expensive consumer goods were off limits to those who could not master the manners or afford the fashionable clothing necessary to appear creditable to the shopkeeper. Coffeehouses and inns in large cities increasingly had a variety of rooms designed to cater to clientele of different social classes, with the most luxurious spaces reserved for elites. Even private polite spaces, like the Norrises' or Norris mansion, were constructed with back rooms, basements, and concealed staircases, in which black and white servants were supposed to remain invisible even as they did the hard work of running the household. In any case, illiteracy was often sufficient to exclude non-elites from politeness.[21]

Despite efforts by white elites to preserve urban spaces for their sole use, however, the spatial characteristics of these early modern cities made it immensely difficult for them to succeed entirely in their quest. Seaports were "walking cities" in which the absence of transport technologies meant that rich and poor, white and black, free and unfree, lived cheek by jowl with one another. By the end of the 18th century, towns possessed clearly defined elite neighborhoods; Philadelphia's Society Hill and the East Bay of Charleston were the location of a majority of large, fashionable, brick-built mansions owned by merchants and planters. Homes in the Northern Liberties and the marshy west side of the South Carolina capital's peninsula, on the other hand, were smaller and more vernacular in character. But the necessity for working people to be in proximity to their place of employment made it impossible for elites completely to remove these "lower sorts" from such areas. Enslaved and free black townspeople constantly passed through and around elite townhouses, frequented the market, and worked or socialized at the wharves. They formed interracial networks of trade and sociability with poor whites, centered on illegal grog shops, or "ordinaries," and small retail stores that often appeared around port areas. Prostitution was common in all port cities—Philadelphia's Market Street was a well-known place to find both black and white women plying this trade.[22]

During the 18th century seaports thus became places of great contrasts, a character captured by English seaman Captain Martin, whose poem about Charleston, written in 1769, recast a London rhythm that had made the same point about the English capital. Martin described "black and white all mix'd together, Inconstant, strange, unhealthful weather…

> No lamps, or lights, but streets of sand,
> Pleasant walks, if you can find 'em,
> Scandalous tounges, if any mind 'em,"
> concluding "many a bargain, if you strike it,
> This is Charles-town, how do you like it."

As Martin's emulation of the London poem suggests, American seaport cities bore comparison to the metropolis in terms of the genteel and fashionable society that resided there. However, there was also a level of racial mixing and a hard commercial edge to city life that also made these places quite distinctively American.[23]

CONFLICT AND REVOLUTION

At the end of the Seven Years War in 1763, economic conditions began to place major pressure on these cosmopolitan, rapidly growing, yet highly variegated urban societies. Now the stresses affecting them did not stem from searching for a way to grow cities, as was the case for some in the 17th century, but from the way to manage ever-faster growth. Income distribution became more uneven, with elites in all cities owning an ever-greater share of the wealth. Although middling people did enjoy some of these increased riches too, the number of city poor was rising noticeably. Urban institutions devoted to helping the destitute—church vestries, poorhouses and hospitals—were under pressure to find ever-greater amounts of money if they were to assist all who were in need. Poor taxes in all continental North American seaports were on an upward trajectory. At the same time, a postwar depression and rising prices of certain essential commodities, such as firewood, made scraping a living—"making shift" as contemporaries called it—harder and harder.[24]

Seaport cities were never oases of tranquility and social harmony up until this point. Leisler's Rebellion in 1689 and uprisings by enslaved blacks and poor whites in 1712 and 1741 meant that New York City endured at least three major flashpoints of conflict that deeply threatened the established order. In 1747 Boston was hit by the Knowles Riots when the British naval officer, Charles Knowles, ordered his men to impress colonists into service. Since Pennsylvania's colonial politics were famously factional, Philadelphia was the site of noisy protests by large crowds of commoners in the 1720s, 1742, and again in 1752. Following the Stono Rebellion in 1739, South Carolina's elites introduced a draconian slave code designed to regulate the movements and trading activities of enslaved Charlestonians. As these urban societies grew in size and complexity, so had the task that faced elites who sought to "manage" a diverse citizenry. Lacking the customary institutions of hierarchy and governance that propped up European authorities, these elites not only had to establish their own legitimacy but also devise a way to express it.[25]

Simultaneously, however, white colonial rulers were beginning the process of divesting a distant British Empire of power. The largest seaport cities were usually also the political capitals of their respective colonies. Gathered as a colonial assembly in these towns, ruling men successfully wrested authority over a wide range of critical local functions from London, including the issuance of paper money, the creation of land banks, the administration of courts, religious institutions, taxes, road construction, and the sale and survey of rural land. Such powers imbued colonial rulers with the feeling that they held the reins of authority in their polities, while colonial governors stood on the margins, frustrated at their inability to effectively implement imperial edicts. Thus, when the imperial crisis hit the colonies in the 1760s, seaport cities were epicenters of the two main clashes that drove forward the American Revolution: the dual questions of who should rule America—the British or the new Americans—and, if it was to be the Americans, which ones? The established urban elites or the democratic challengers to their leadership? Importantly, this clash was not only rooted in seaport cities because they were centers of political power and social stratification, but also because they were hubs of print production, news, and communication.[26]

Cities' revolutionary role in the conflict over these parallel issues was constant but changed subtly as the struggle evolved. During the imperial crisis between 1764 and 1775, seaports were the platform for both popular and elite resistance. Led by the Sons of Liberty, a loose association of tradesmen that existed in each continental seaport, popular patriotism was expressed in the urban streets, taverns, and green spaces, where the "liberty tree" was the most important landmark. First formed in response to the Stamp Act in 1765, the Sons persisted as a popular political force throughout the early phases of the Revolution, participating in committees that organized the non-importation protests as well as undertaking direct action against British and loyalist American officials by harrying them, damaging their property or, in the most extreme cases, tarring and feathering them. As an occasional organization, the Sons were one of a number of popular political clubs that were closely involved in a wide range of out-of-doors protests in seaport cities' streets.[27]

Throughout this first phase of the Revolution, these cities were thus hotspots of political organization and resistance. Early on in the conflict, Boston became the lead actor on the urban stage of imperial crisis; the blockade of its wharves by the British following the Tea Party of 1773, along with the heavy British military presence in the city, provoked a radical reaction among the city's patriots followed by a loud outcry across all of the continental colonies. The key to support for Boston's plight was also the second and most enduring contribution of cities to the Revolution: the urban printing press's publicization of Americans' "common cause" and its nodal role in networks of communication and correspondence. The colonial printing press, combined with the postal system established by Benjamin Franklin, placed seaports at the center of a multiplying network of committees of safety and correspondence. These committees coordinated revolutionary actions between colonies by standing in solidarity with brethren elsewhere and building unitary protest movements, such as the non-importation boycotts that constituted Americans' main response to British taxation efforts. At the same time, printers, because of the newspapers and pamphlets they produced, played a vital role in creating a patriot ideology that could unify Americans against loyalists and imperial officials. Urged on by editorials, letters, and broadsides that exhorted men and women to join the cause of American liberty and vilified those who seemed unenthusiastic about it, patriots found the strength to continue their fight, even when their cities were occupied by the British for some or all of the war that raged between 1775 and 1783.[28]

New York's occupation for the entire war era meant that patriots could accomplish little politically in that city. Their ability to develop their own governing institutions was hampered in Charleston for two years after a 1780 siege won by the British and in Philadelphia between 1777 and 1778. The Philadelphia situation was especially grievous because this, of course, was where the nascent national government, the first and second Continental Congresses, had been sitting before the war broke out. Yet, as the Revolution entered its latter phases during the 1780s, Philadelphia would assume the reins as the nation's first capital. Thus, seaport cities continued as major political centers of power in the new nation. The most obvious manifestation of this was the Constitutional Convention, held behind closed doors in the former Philadelphia state house, during the hot summer of 1787.[29]

Once again, however, the urban ruling classes were not permitted to claim pre-eminence without contest from non-elite Americans. From the 1760s onward, yeoman farmers demonstrated their displeasure with city-based leaders, first through "Regulator" movements and then as tax rebels. In the wake of the Constitutional Convention, it was rural settlers again who threatened to block ratification of the governing document drawn up in Philadelphia. While East Coast urban elites eventually succeeded in overcoming such opposition, the Revolution forced a recognition of their reliance on inland places and the growing European population who lived in them. Seaport cities never completely lost their pre-eminence, as the contemporary status of New York City, Philadelphia, Boston, and Baltimore suggests. Yet, as the 18th century drew to a close, these cities found themselves increasingly having to justify their dominance in a westward-expanding American Empire. The vast majority quickly lost their state capital status to inland towns; Lancaster, and then Harrisburg, took the crown from Philadelphia by 1799. Others lost their economic pre-eminence; Newport never recovered from revolutionary devastation, while Charleston's growth slowed as the plantation economy moved westward. As brick, stone, and wood mnemonics of the British colonization process, however, these seaport cities nevertheless endure.[30]

DISCUSSION OF THE LITERATURE

The most enduring strand of scholarship on early America's seaport cities has focused on their role in the Revolution. Carl Bridenbaugh, an early-20th-century pioneer of the topic, devoted his *Cities in the Wilderness* to the early colonial era, but in many ways the book was a prequel to *Cities in Revolt*, a study of the Revolutionary period. For a long time, Bridenbaugh's efforts and those of his doctoral supervisor, Arthur M. Schlesinger Sr., constituted the only research that treated port cities as distinctive forces in the creation of colonial society. This changed with the appearance first of Pauline Maier's study of urban popular politics, *From Resistance to Revolution*, and then of Gary Nash's magisterial study of Boston, New York, and Philadelphia, *The Urban Crucible*. Both books remain the cornerstones of the historiography. As a neo-Progressive, Nash highlighted how growing urban inequality motivated protests against both the British and local commercial elites, driving forward the Revolution as a popular movement. He was joined in this narrative by Alfred Young, whose many writings were collected together in *The Liberty Tree: Ordinary People and the American Revolution*. A more recent addition to the question of seaport cities and the Revolution is Benjamin Carp's *Rebels Rising*. Carp explains how urban space facilitated the protest and debate, locating his discussion in a variety of places in the largest cities.[31]

Nevertheless, starting with New England's seaports and moving southward, a parallel development of scholarship examined these places outside the revolutionary paradigm. Historians working in a tradition of studying

New England's towns as Puritan communities produced the earliest work on the region's seaports, mostly in a quest to understand how their commercial character related to their religious mission. Bernard Bailyn's *The New England Merchants in the Seventeenth Century* was one of the first such books to appear, while the genre was placed in a broader seaport context by Christine Leigh Heyrman with her study of Gloucester and Marblehead, *Commerce and Culture*.[32]

Since the 1990s, the variety of research on New England's seaports has been joined by a similar diversity of work first on New York and Philadelphia, and now Bridgetown, Kingston, Newport, New Orleans, and Charleston—the seaports that had previously received much less attention. Therefore we have a richer understanding of the colonial eras of all of these places than we did a generation ago. Their demography, the ethnic composition of their population, their economic functions, and their built environment are all now well known in much more than outline detail. A suitable capstone to this colonial story is Dell Upton's *Another City: Urban Life and Urban Spaces in the New American Republic*. Concentrating on Philadelphia and New Orleans, Upton explores the spatial and social dynamics that characterized Republican cities and determined how their inhabitants would relate to one another.[33]

A selection of leading themes stands out in this most recent research on early America's seaports: race, gender, material culture, and the Atlantic economy. Inquiry into the lives of seaport women and people of African descent has done much to reveal both their experiences and their centrality to all aspects of these cities. Most critically, scholars now acknowledge that African people were a vital proportion of seaport populations in almost every major town. While southern and Caribbean cities along with New Orleans of course hosted the largest enslaved and free black communities, northern cities all had black residents too. These residents were fundamental to the urban economy, as were towns' many female householders. Ellen Hartigan O'Connor's *The Ties That Buy* ably documents these issues with its focus on women's economies in Newport and Charleston. The study of slavery and freedom in Boston by Jared Hardesty reveals the importance of people of color in even the "freeist" colonial seaport.[34]

Hartigan O'Connor is also interested in the urban living arrangements of her subjects, and as such she is part of a cohort of scholars now exploring the physical and material condition of cities, their households, businesses, and their inhabitants. Work by Bernard Herman, Phyllis Whitman Hunter, Richard Bushman, and Emma Hart uncovers how these seaports functioned as early modern cities, placing their cityscapes and their environmental qualities in a broader context of city building and improving that unfolded across the pre-Revolutionary era. Much of this work is interdisciplinary, involving art historians and material culture scholars as well as historians. At the same time, as Hart has shown, urban infrastructure was also a form of capital, an issue that is linked to the abundant recent research on city economies. Cathy Matson, Thomas Doerflinger, and Christine Heyrman were among the first to lay out the dimensions of the merchant economy in New York and Philadelphia, while Max Edelson and Jennifer Goloboy have latterly anatomized the Charleston trading community.[35]

Overall, scholars have in the last two decades developed a much more even-handed approach to North America's seaports in this early modern era. While we still know much more about Boston, New York, and Philadelphia than we do about Charleston, Kingston, or New Orleans, most now acknowledge that seaports were critical to *all* of North America in this era. What is more, their importance goes far beyond their Revolutionary-era function. Additionally, most historians would now admit that differences between northern and southern seaports—in terms of levels of freedom and unfreedom, white and black inhabitants—are less stark than previously imagined. Exploring such insights in more detail, as well as placing North America's seaports in a more imaginative variety of transnational and Atlantic frameworks, will now be the work of future scholars in the field.

PRIMARY SOURCES

Materials for the study of early American seaport life fall into four main categories: quantitative sources, printed material, government documents, and private collections of manuscripts produced by urban people. The extent to which each type of document has been preserved in each city is highly variable; generally, the farther north the city, the greater the abundance of primary sources, with the documentary record in the US South and the Caribbean having suffered through war and climate.

Most city populations of the era can be measured and profiled using tax records, census material, and probate documents such as wills and inventories. The Federal Census of 1790 was the first, and, along with the second of its kind in 1800, is an invaluable guide to the free and enslaved populations of each major seaport during this era. In the colonial decades, statistical materials are harder to find. Philadelphia, Boston, Kingston, and New York all have surviving tax records—but only from occasional years or sporadic eras. Charleston has no useful tax lists at all but does have a good run of inventories and wills, as do all of the other seaports. Such records are far from perfect guides to urban wealth distributions but, as Alice Hanson Jones demonstrated in *The Wealth of a Nation to Be*, such documents can be used to make useful comparative assessments. Inventories are also great sources for finding out more about the material lives of city dwellers, as they list in exhaustive detail household goods at death. They do not, however, include real property as a matter of course; the land market and urban land's owners can instead be discovered in each colony or state's land or deed books, which recorded the purchase and sale of each lot of urban land that changed hands.[36]

Government records, such as colonial assembly minutes and financial accounts, can also be a good source for finding out more about seaport life, as they document the goings-on of a fundamentally urban institution. Usefully, they are often published and easily available. The *Pennsylvania Archives*, accessible through Fold3, incorporates council minutes and correspondence between government agents. The *Journal of the South Carolina Commons House of Assembly* is likewise widely available in paper form, and the *Journals of the House of Representatives of Massachusetts* are accessible too. City government records also survive; the *Reports of the Records Commissioners of the City of Boston* has an extensive run from 1634 all the way to 1822, while New York's city council and its mayor's office also left extensive materials, many of which are now in the state archives in Albany. However, the Philadelphia, Newport, and Charleston materials are much less comprehensive; the outline minutes of Philadelphia's Common Council survive, but in Charleston the only survival is one book of the fortification commission's accounts.

Since newspapers were published in seaport cities, they represent a major resource for research into urban life. The advertising columns alone—usually half the newspaper—contain rich material about urban businesses, social life, and governance. Now that many of these newspapers are available digitally, keyword searches open up yet more possibilities for quantitative and qualitative research using them. Likewise, the digitized *Early American Imprints* incorporates a vast amount of ephemera printed in cities before 1820—broadsides, receipts, pamphlets, and other items commissioned by urban business people and citizens that circulated in the urban environment.

The final and most complex set of sources for seaport life is the private papers of the families who populated them. Papers of some of the most prominent citizens have, of course, been published; *The Papers of Henry Laurens* represents an exhaustive view of life in Charleston during the colonial era, written by a wealthy merchant whose fortune was tied up in the seaport. Major political figures, such as John Adams, lived largely urban lives, and so their letters and diaries contain much of interest. Elite Philadelphia and New York families also left behind large collections of papers that are a window onto their city-living and dealing. The account books left by families and merchants are critical for the study of the urban economy. Much harder is accessing the experiences of the urban poor, who appear as statistics in the institutions established by elites to contain them but are rarely visible on their own terms. The chances of finding good sources reduce further for the researcher interested in urban people of color. Often, court depositions can be a useful source for commentary on the everyday life of ordinary city people, but these are not universally available— all of the criminal court records for early South Carolina have been destroyed, while survival in Philadelphia is patchy. Overall, therefore, primary sources make it easy to tell a story of an elite and middling seaport life but much harder for historians who want to construct more comprehensive histories.[37]

DIGITAL MATERIALS

Pennsylvania Archives.
https://www.fold3.com/title/450/pennsylvania
-archives.
Philadelphia's 1756 Tax List.
https://repository.upenn.edu/mead/5/.
Readex Early American Imprints.
https://www.readex.com/content/early-american
-imprints-series-i-evans-1639-1800.
Readex Early American Newspapers Series 1, 1690–1876: From Colonies to Nation.
https://www.readex.com/content/early-american
-newspapers-series.
Accessible Archives.
http://www.accessible-archives.com/.
New York Public Library Digital Collections.
https://digitalcollections.nypl.org/.

Library of Congress Map Collections.
https://www.loc.gov/maps/.
Winterthur Library Digital Collections.
http://content.winterthur.org:2011/cdm/.

FURTHER READING

Carp, Benjamin. *Rebels Rising: Cities and the American Revolution*. New York: Oxford University Press, 2007.

Choppin Roney, Jessica. *Governed by a Spirit of Opposition: The Origins of American Political Practice in Colonial Philadelphia*. Baltimore: Johns Hopkins University Press, 2014.

Dawdy, Shannon Lee. *Building the Devil's Empire: French Colonial New Orleans*. Chicago: University of Chicago Press, 2008.

Hart, Emma. *Building Charleston: Town and Society in the Eighteenth-Century British Atlantic World*. Charlottesville: University of Virginia Press, 2010.

Hartigan O'Connor, Ellen. *The Ties that Buy: Women and Commerce in Revolutionary America*. Philadelphia: University of Pennsylvania Press, 2009.

Hughes Dayton, Cornelia, and Sharon Salinger. *Robert Love's Warnings: Searching for Strangers in Colonial Boston*. Philadelphia: University of Pennsylvania Press, 2015.

Matson, Cathy. *Merchants and Empire: Trading in Colonial New York*. Baltimore: Johns Hopkins University Press, 1998.

Musselwhite, Paul. *Urban Dreams, Rural Commonwealth: The Rise of Plantation Society in the Chesapeake*. Chicago: University of Chicago Press, 2019.

Nash, Gary. *The Urban Crucible: Social Change, Political Consciousness, and the Origins of the American Revolution*. Cambridge, MA: Harvard University Press, 1979.

Robertson, James. *Gone Is the Ancient Glory: Spanish Town, Jamaica, 1534–2000*. Kingston: Ian Randle, 2005.

Roney, Jessica, ed., "Distinguishing Port Cities, 1500–1800." Special issue, *Early American Studies* 15, no. 4 (Fall 2017).

Upton, Dell. *Another City: Urban Life and Urban Spaces in the New American Republic*. New Haven, CT: Yale University Press, 2008.

Wulf, Karin. *Not All Wives: Women of Colonial Philadelphia*. Ithaca, NY: Cornell University Press, 2000.

Zabin, Serena. *Dangerous Economies: Status and Commerce in Imperial New York*. Philadelphia: University of Pennsylvania Press, 2009.

NOTES

1. Kenneth Morgan, *Bristol and the Atlantic Trade in the Eighteenth Century* (Cambridge, UK: Cambridge University Press, 2004); Nuala Zahedieh, *The Capital and the Colonies* (Cambridge, UK: Cambridge University Press, 2012); and Silvia Marzagalli, *Bordeaux et les Etats-Unis, 1776-1815: Politique et stratégies négociantes dans la genèse d'un réseau commercial* (Paris: Librairie Droz, 2015).

2. Sylvia Doughty Fries, *The Urban Idea in Colonial America* (Philadelphia: Temple University Press, 1977); Pedro L. V. Welch, *Slave Society in the City: Bridgetown, Barbados, 1680-1834* (Kingston: James Randle Publishers, 2003); James Robertson, *Gone Is the Ancient Glory: Spanish Town, Jamaica, 1534-2000* (Kingston: James Randle Publishers, 2005); Emma Hart, *Building Charleston: Town and Society in the Eighteenth-Century British Atlantic World* (Charlottesville: University of Virginia Press, 2010); and Bernard Bailyn, *The New England Merchants in the Seventeenth Century* (Cambridge, MA: Harvard University Press, 1955).

3. William Penn to Lord North, July 24, 1683, in Richard S. Dunn and Mary Maples Dunn, eds., *Papers of William Penn*, vol. 2 (Philadelphia: University of Pennsylvania Press, 1982), 414–415; Hart, *Building Charleston*, chap. 1; and Paul Musselwhite, *Urban Dreams, Rural Commonwealth: The Rise of Plantation Society in the Chesapeake* (Chicago: University of Chicago Press, forthcoming 2018).

4. Christine deLucia, *Memory Lands: King Philip's War and the Place of Violence in the Northeast* (New Haven, CT: Yale University Press, 2018); and William L. Ramsey, "'Something Cloudy in their Looks': The Origins of the Yamasee War Reconsidered," *Journal of American History* 90, no. 1 (June 2003): 44–75.

5. Matthew Mulcahy, "The Port Royal Earthquake and the World of Wonders in Seventeenth Century Jamaica," *Early American Studies* 6, no. 2 (Fall 2008): 391–421; Matthew Mulcahy, *Hurricanes and Society in the British Greater Caribbean, 1624-1783* (Baltimore: Johns Hopkins University Press, 2006); Matthew Mulcahy "The 'Great Fire' of 1740 and the Politics of Disaster Relief in Colonial Charleston," *South Carolina Historical Magazine* 99 (April 1998): 135–157; William Pencak, "Social Structure in Revolutionary Boston: Evidence from the Great Fire of 1760," *Journal of Interdisciplinary History* 10 (1979): 267–278; and Hart, *Building Charleston*, chap. 3.

6. Billy G. Smith, *Ship of Death: A Voyage that Changed the Atlantic World* (New Haven, CT, 2013); Elizabeth Fenn, *Pox Americana: The Great Smallpox Epidemic of 1775-1782* (New York: Hill & Wang, 2003); and Harry Roy Merrens and George D. Terry, "Dying in Paradise: Malaria, Mortality, and the Perceptual Environment in Colonial South Carolina," *Journal of Southern History* 50 (1984): 542–546.

7. Shannon Lee Dawdy, *Building the Devil's Empire: French Colonial New Orleans* (Chicago: University of Chicago Press, 2008), 25–62.

8. United States Bureau of the Census, *Heads of Families at the First Census of the United States, Taken in the Year 1790, South Carolina* (Washington, DC: Government Printing Office, 1908); and John Langton, "Urban Growth and Economic Change: From the Late Seventeenth Century to 1841," in *The Cambridge Urban History of Britain, Vol. 2, 1540-1840*, ed. Peter Clark (Cambridge, UK: Cambridge University Press, 2000), 453–490.

9. Fernand Braudel, *The Structures of Everyday Life: The Limits of the Possible* (New York: Harper & Row, 1981), 479.

10. Benjamin Carp, *Rebels Rising: Cities and the American Revolution* (New York: Oxford University Press, 2007), chap. 1; Paul R. Huey, "Old Slip and Cruger's Wharf at New York: An Archaeological Perspective of the Colonial American Waterfront," *Historical Archaeology* 18, no. 1 (1984): 15–37; and Gregory O'Malley, "Slavery's Converging Ground: Charleston's Slave Trade as the Black Heart of the Lowcountry," *William and Mary Quarterly* 74, no. 2 (April 2017): 271–302.

11. Cathy Matson, "Putting the *Lydia* to Sea: The Material Economy of Shipping in Colonial Philadelphia," *William and Mary Quarterly* 74, no. 2 (April 2017): 303–332; and Emma Hart and Cathy Matson, "Situating Merchants in Late Eighteenth-Century British Atlantic Port Cities," in "Special Issue on Port Cities,"

special issue, *Early American Studies* 15, no. 4 (Fall 2017): 660–682.

12. Patricia Cleary, *Elizabeth Murray: A Woman's Pursuit of Independence in Eighteenth-Century America* (Amherst: University of Massachusetts Press, 2000); and Ellen Hartigan O'Connor, *The Ties that Buy: Women and Commerce in Revolutionary America* (Philadelphia: University of Pennsylvania Press, 2009).

13. Hart, *Building Charleston*, chap. 2; Carl Bridenbaugh, *The Colonial Craftsman* (Mineola, NY: Dover Press, 1990); Jennifer van Horn, *The Power of Objects in Eighteenth-Century British America* (Chapel Hill: University of North Carolina Press, 2017); and Zara Anishanslin, *Portrait of a Woman in Silk: Hidden Histories of the British Atlantic World* (New Haven, CT: Yale University Press, 2016).

14. Philip Morgan, "Black Life in Eighteenth-Century Charleston," *Perspectives in American History* n.s. 1 (1984): 187–232; C. Clarke, *Kingston, Jamaica: Urban Development and Social Change, 1692–2002* (Kingston: Ian Randle Publishers, 2006); "Diary of George Nelson," Historical Society of Pennsylvania; and Candice Harrison, "Free Trade and Hucksters' Rights!: Envisioning Economic Democracy in the Early Republic," *Pennsylvania Magazine of History and Biography* 137 (April 2013): 147–177.

15. Cathy Matson, *Merchants and Empire: Trading in Colonial New York* (Baltimore: Johns Hopkins University Press, 1998); Thomas Doerflinger, *A Vigorous Spirit of Enterprise: Merchants and Economic Development in Revolutionary Philadelphia* (Chapel Hill: University of North Carolina Press, 1986); and Max Edelson, *Plantation Enterprise in Colonial South Carolina* (Cambridge, MA: Harvard University Press, 2006).

16. Philip Stern and Carl Wennerlind, *Mercantilism Reimagined: Political Economy in Early Modern Britain and Its Empire* (Oxford: Oxford University Press, 2013).

17. Richard L. Bushman, *The Refinement of America: Persons, Houses, Cities* (New York: Vintage, 1992); Phyllis Whitman Hunter, *Purchasing Identity in the Atlantic World: Massachusetts Merchants, 1670–1780* (Ithaca, NY: Cornell University Press, 2001); and Hart, *Building Charleston*, chap. 5; and Daniel Maudlin and Bernard L. Herman, eds., *Building the British Atlantic World: Spaces, Places, and Material Culture 1600–1850* (Chapel Hill: University of North Carolina Press, 2016).

18. Mark Reinberger and Elizabeth McLean, "Isaac Norris's Fairhill: Architecture, Landscape, and Quaker Ideals in a Philadelphia Colonial Country Seat," *Winterthur Portfolio* 32, no. 4 (Winter 1997): 243–274; and Stephen Hague, *The Gentleman's House in the British Atlantic World 1680–1780* (London: Palgrave, 2015).

19. Carl Lounsbury, *From Statehouse to Courthouse: An Architectural History of South Carolina's Colonial Capitol and Charleston County Courthouse* (Columbia University of South Carolina Press, 2001); Carp, *Rebels Rising*, chap. 5; Whitman Hunter, *Purchasing Identity*, 107–140; and Vaughn Scribner, "Cultivating 'Cities in the Wilderness': New York City's Commercial Pleasure Gardens and the British American Pursuit of Rural Urbanism," *Urban History* 45, no. 2 (May 2018): 275–305.

20. David Shields, *Civil Tongues and Polite Letters in British America* (Chapel Hill: University of North Carolina Press, 1997); James Raven, *London Booksellers and American Customers: Transatlantic Literary Community and the Charleston Library Society, 1748–1811* (Columbia, University of South Carolina Press, 2004); and Jessica Choppin Roney, *Governed by a Spirit of Opposition: The Origins of American Political Practice in Colonial Philadelphia* (Baltimore: Johns Hopkins University Press, 2014).

21. Hart, *Building Charleston*, chap. 5; Carp, *Rebels Rising*, chap. 5; and Andrea Mosterman, "Sharing Spaces in a New World Environment: African-Dutch Contributions to North American Culture, 1626–1826" (PhD diss., Boston University, 2012).

22. Bernard Herman, "Slave and Servant Housing in Charleston, 1770–1820," *Historical Archaeology* 33 (1999): 88–101; Mary M. Schweitzer, "The Spatial Organization of Federalist Philadelphia, 1790," *Journal of Interdisciplinary History* 24, no. 1 (Summer 1993): 31–57; and Serena Zabin, *Dangerous Economies: Status and Commerce in Imperial New York* (Philadelphia: University of Pennsylvania Press, 2009).

23. H. Roy Merrens, ed., *The Colonial South Carolina Scene* (Columbia University of South Carolina Press, 1977), 230–231.

24. Gary Nash, *The Urban Crucible: Social Change, Political Consciousness, and the Origins of the American Revolution* (Cambridge, MA: Harvard University Press, 1979).

25. Zabin, *Dangerous Economies*; Denver Brunsman, "The Knowles Atlantic Impressment Riots of the

1740s," *Early American Studies* 5 (Fall 2007): 324–366; and Peter Wood, *Black Majority: Negroes in Colonial South Carolina* (New York: W. W. Norton, 1979).

26. Carl L. Becker, *The History of Political Parties in the Province of New York, 1760–1776* (Madison: University of Wisconsin Press, 1968), 22; and Nash, *Urban Crucible*.

27. Nash, *Urban Crucible*; Carp, *Rebels Rising*; Edmund S. Morgan and Helen M. Morgan, *The Stamp Act Crisis: Prologue to Revolution* (Chapel Hill: University of North Carolina Press, 1953); and Hart, *Building Charleston*, chap. 6.

28. Benjamin Labaree, *The Boston Tea Party: Catalyst for Revolution* (New York: Oxford University Press, 1964); and Robert Parkinson, *The Common Cause: Creating Race and Nation in the American Revolution* (Chapel Hill: University of North Carolina Press, 2016).

29. Ruma Chopra, *Unnatural Rebellion: Loyalists in New York City During the Revolution* (Charlottesville: University of Virginia Press, 2011); and Jerome J. Nadelhaft, *The Disorders of War: The Revolution in South Carolina* (Orono: University of Maine Press, 1981).

30. Jay Gitlin, Barbara Berglund, and Adam Arenson, eds., *Frontier Cities: Encounters at the Crossroads of Empire* (Philadelphia: University of Pennsylvania Press, 2012).

31. Arthur M. Schlesinger Sr., "The City in American History," *Mississippi Valley Historical Review* 27, no. 1 (June 1940), 43–66; Carl Bridenbaugh, *Cities in the Wilderness: The First Century of Urban Life in America* (New York: Ronald Press, 1938); Carl Bridenbaugh, *Cities in Revolt: Urban Life in America, 1743–1776* (New York: Alfred A. Knopf, 1955); Pauline Maier, *From Resistance to Revolution: Colonial Radicals and the Development of Opposition to Britain, 1765–1776* (New York: Alfred A. Knopf, 1972); Nash, *Urban Crucible*; Alfred F. Young, *The Liberty Tree: Ordinary People and the American Revolution* (New York: New York University Press, 2006); and Carp, *Rebels Rising*.

32. Bailyn, *The New England Merchants*; and Christine Leigh Heyrman, *Commerce and Culture: The Maritime Communities of Colonial Massachusetts, 1690–1760* (New York: W. W. Norton, 1984).

33. Welch, *Slave Society in the City*; Cornelia Hughes Dayton and Sharon Salinger, *Robert Love's Warnings: Searching for Strangers in Colonial Boston*

(Philadelphia: University of Pennsylvania Press, 2015); and Dell Upton, *Another City: Urban Life and Urban Spaces in the New American Republic* (New Haven, CT: Yale University Press, 2008).

34. Hartigan O'Connor, *Ties that Buy*; Karin Wulf, *Not All Wives: Women of Colonial Philadelphia* (Ithaca, NY: Cornell University Press, 2000); Dawdy, *Building the Devil's Empire*; and Jared Ross Hardesty, *Unfreedom: Slavery and Dependence in Eighteenth-Century Boston* (New York: New York University Press, 2016).

35. Bernard Herman, *Town House: Architecture and Material Life in the Early American City, 1780–1830* (Chapel Hill: University of North Carolina Press, 2005); Hunter, *Purchasing Identity*; Bushman, *The Refinement of America*; Hart, *Building Charleston*; Doerflinger, *A Vigorous Spirit*; Edelson, *Plantation Enterprise*; and Jennifer Goloboy, *Charleston and the Emergence of Middle-Class Culture in the Revolutionary Era* (Athens, GA: University of Georgia, 2016).

36. Alice Hanson Jones, *Wealth of a Nation to Be: The American Colonies on the Eve of Revolution* (New York: Columbia University Press, 1980).

37. *The Papers of Henry Laurens*, ed. David Chesnutt (Columbia, University of South Carolina Press, 1968–2002).

Emma Hart

INDUSTRY, COMMERCE, AND URBANIZATION IN THE UNITED STATES, 1790–1870

The first census of the United States revealed an overwhelmingly rural nation. In 1790, a scant 5 percent of the country's 3,929,214 enumerated residents lived in urban settings (defined as communities with more than 2,500 people). The number of cities housing more than 10,000 people could be counted on one hand: Boston, New York, Philadelphia, Baltimore, and Charleston, coastal entrepôts that mediated between the worlds of Atlantic trade and hinterland agriculture. To be sure, these and other urban places exercised an influence over American commerce and culture disproportionate to their number. But few who examined the raw numbers at the start of the Washington administration would have predicted the demographic, economic, and cultural changes that unfolded over the new nation's first eighty years.

During the first four decades of the 19th century, the United States gradually but perceptibly urbanized: while the country's total population more than tripled between 1790 and 1830, its urban population expanded nearly sixfold. From 1830 to 1870, the pace of urban growth accelerated: as the total population again tripled, the urban population expanded nearly nine times more. By 1870, nearly ten million people (around a quarter of the American population) lived in cities. And while the majority of urban Americans still lived in places with fewer than 10,000 residents, the largest urban centers had grown prodigiously.

New York now housed nearly one million residents and Philadelphia stood in second place, while Baltimore and Boston held firmly to spots among the top ten by population; of the five largest cities in 1790, only Charleston failed to keep pace. Newer entries into the list of major American cities evidenced more fundamental transformations in American politics and society since the 18th century. The largest cities in 1870 included places like New Orleans, which entered US jurisdiction through diplomacy, San Francisco, gained through conquest, and still others like Chicago and Buffalo, which reflected westward trends in demography and economic shifts toward manufacturing.[1]

In short, the eight decades that separated the censuses of 1790 and 1870 saw fundamental transformations in the size, scale, and function of American cities, changes that mirrored but also precipitated shifts in American political and economic history writ large.

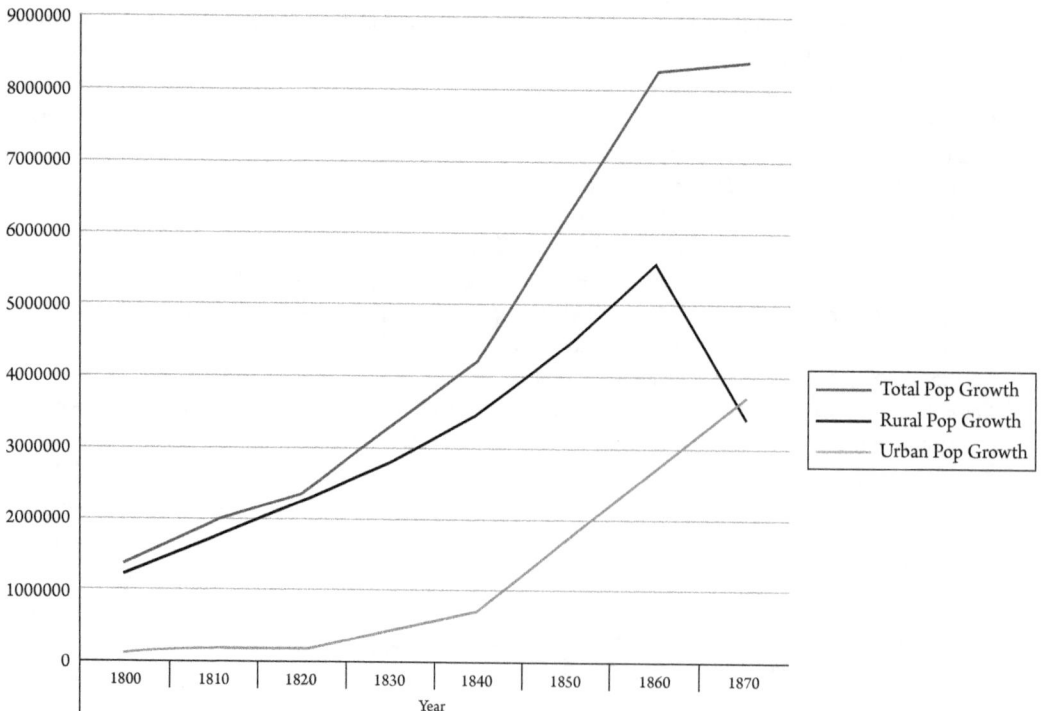

Figure 1. Increases in total, urban, and rural American population by decade.
Source: US Bureau of the Census, *Historical Statistics of the United States, Colonial Times to 1970*, Part 1 (Washington, DC: US Government Printing Office, 1975), 8, 12.

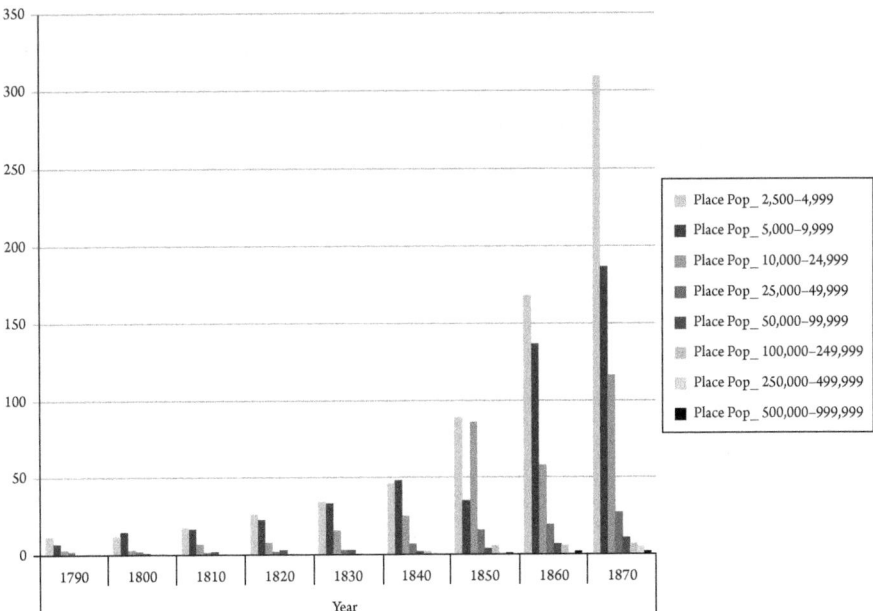

Figure 2. Total number of places classified as "urban" by the US census, sorted by population size.
Source: US Bureau of the Census, *Historical Statistics of the United States, Colonial Times to 1970*, Part 1 (Washington, DC: US Government Printing Office, 1975), 11.

Historians have offered a variety of frameworks to make sense of this period, characterizing it as an era of revolutions (market, industrial, communications), rises (of democracy, of plantation slavery, of specific cities), and downfalls (of republicanism, of artisan production).[2] The key economic changes that reordered American life and cities were the expansion of the market and its institutions across space and within society, and novel patterns of production that gave rise to large-scale wage work.

MARKET SOCIETY

The five cities strung along the coastline at the dawn of American independence shared several characteristics. All were ports that sent staple commodities to distant markets in Europe, the West Indies, or South America, receiving in return manufactured products, molasses, and lines of credit. Participation in Atlantic trading networks embedded these cities within a system of slave trading and forced labor

that had enriched European and colonial elites for centuries. Supplies and foodstuffs from the American interior enabled West Indies planters to devote nearly every acre of arable land in the Caribbean to the cultivation of sugarcane by enslaved laborers. Except for Boston, slavery had a more tangible presence in these cities as well. While only Charleston's hinterland was dominated by slave labor (Baltimore's backcountry consisted largely of free-labor wheat farms), four of these five cities housed enslaved people as of 1790. Massachusetts, New York State, and Pennsylvania each enacted gradual emancipation laws in the decades following independence, but many African Americans remained in bondage in major cities well into the 19th century. New York City in particular relied heavily on slavery, as it had since the mid-17th century. There enslaved blacks worked as day laborers, dock workers, and domestics, often alongside or in competition with free whites, until 1827 when slavery was finally eradicated in New York.[3]

Slavery remained central to the commercial economies of these and other major American cities until the Civil War. After independence, however, urban elites set their sights on new economic horizons. While some coastal merchants sent ships east to trade with China, others looked toward the agricultural lands in the American West. The Treaty of Paris, signed in 1783, assigned to the United States a territory stretching from the east coast of the continent to the Mississippi River. Subsequent treaties with European powers and war with Mexico enlarged those claims. By 1853, American borders matched those of the continental United States today. Yet while Britain, France, Spain, and Mexico ceded these regions, the United States had to wrest sovereignty of this expansive territory from the native peoples who lived in and controlled these lands. For roughly a century, starting in the 1790s, the United States waged imperial wars against various Native American groups to benefit westward-bound white settlers.[4]

To urban elites, this forcibly cleared land presented a tabula rasa: vast hinterlands primed for agricultural settlers who would soon seek an eastern market. The merchants of Boston, New York, Philadelphia, and Baltimore figured that securing privileged access to these fertile lands would position their cities at the forefront of the new nation's urban hierarchy. New Yorkers moved first by capitalizing on the results of Indian wars quite close to home. Military victories in the mid-1790s evicted the Iroquois from large swaths of upstate New York, opening this terrain to white settlers who came from New England by the tens of thousands. These newcomers filled in a valley that constitutes one of the few breaks in the mountain ranges that divide North America's eastern watershed from the Mississippi Valley, a stretch that observers had long suggested might be suitable for a canal. In 1817, construction began on the state-funded Erie Canal between Buffalo on Lake Erie and Troy on the Hudson River. When it opened in 1825, the Erie Canal changed the way freight moved through the United States. Within a year, the cost of shipping from Lake Erie to Manhattan fell by 90 percent, making New York City's commodious harbor the cheapest outlet for western merchants looking to sell nonperishable goods.[5]

Boosters in other seaboard cities took notice. Within a decade of the Erie Canal's completion, publicly funded projects in Boston, Philadelphia, and Baltimore sought to forge new ties between their ports and the western waters. Baltimore's venture, a public–private enterprise incorporated in 1827 called the Baltimore & Ohio Railroad, offered the boldest vision: an all-rail line that would span hundreds of miles of mountainous terrain in order to link the Chesapeake Bay and the Ohio River. Philadelphia's merchants invested in a more modest part-rail, part-canal system connecting their city to the western river port of Pittsburgh. Bostonians aimed to intercept the Erie Canal at Albany with a rail line of their own. These projects were part of a wave of publicly funded internal improvement projects in the 1820s and 1830s intended to develop the resources of the young nation. Many of the state-sponsored ventures failed in the Panic of 1837, and thereafter new railroads operated largely as private enterprises. Nonetheless, railroad companies continued to receive subsidies from municipalities and, in some cases, the national government until well after the Civil War.[6]

Eastern canals and railroads pointed to the West, and eastern capital followed. The Land Ordinance of 1785, by gridding western territories, rendered them readily saleable to capital-rich investors from the East or Great Britain. The rush to buy plots of land in anticipation of future development led to the rise of "paper cities" in the trans-Appalachian West. Optimistic maps promised investors well-defined streets, ready access to regional transportation networks, and a flourishing backcountry that could elevate empty lots into a leading metropolis. Every now and then these promises bore fruit. After the Black Hawk War, which forced the Potawatomis to relocate west of the Mississippi in 1833, white settlers poured into a marshy patch of land on the shore of Lake Michigan called Chicago.

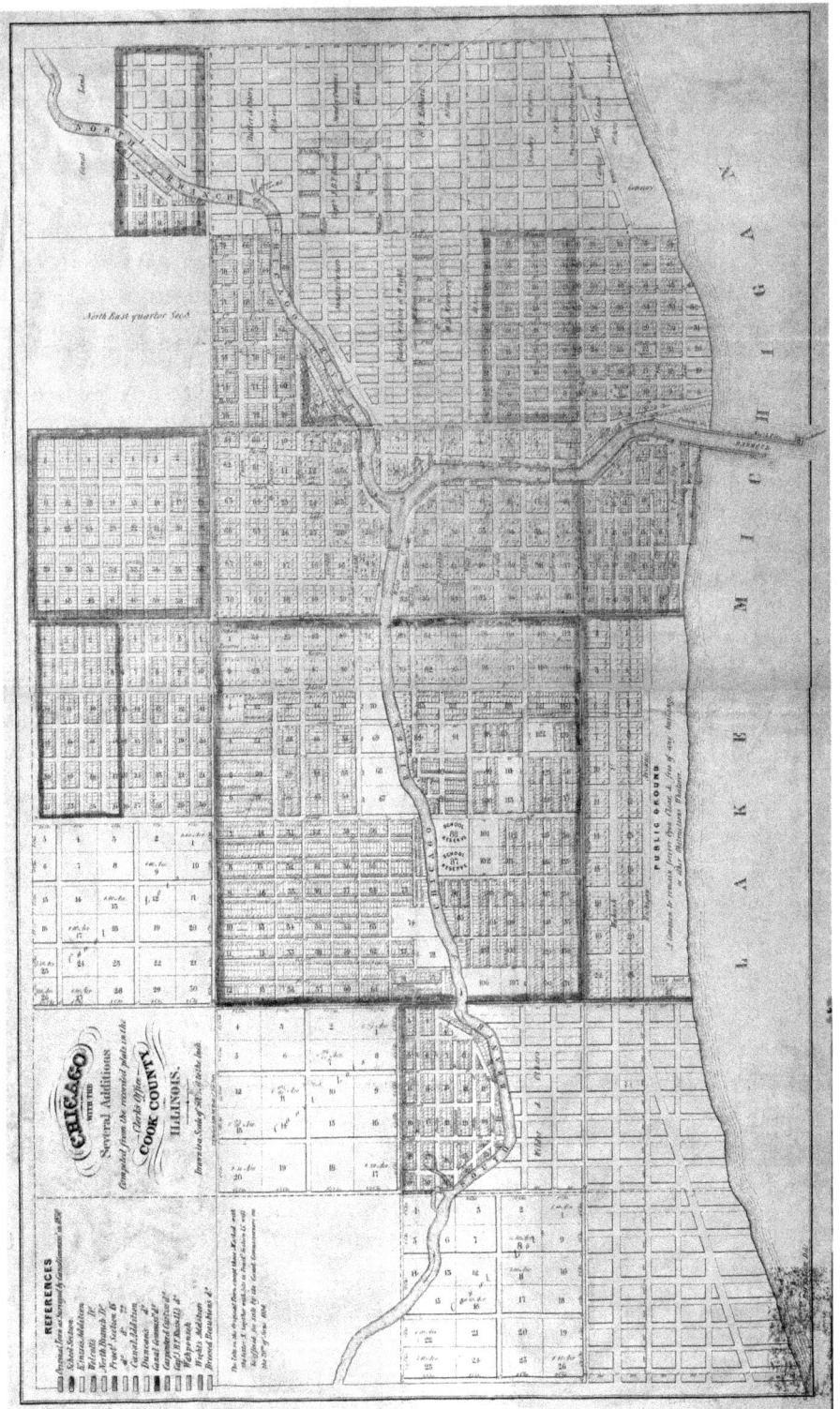

Figure 3. E. B. Talcott, *Map of Chicago Created by the Illinois and Michigan Canal Commissioners and Recorded on July 2, 1836.* Lithograph. New York: T. A. Mesier's Lith., 1836.

Courtesy of Chicago Historical Society, Creative Commons License (CC BY-SA 3.0).

By 1836, lots in Chicago sold for as much as $100,000, a figure that reflected hopes for the city's future development more than its present prospects.

New York investors saw potential in Chicago, particularly as its position on the Great Lakes could funnel goods to their waterfront via the Erie Canal. By making Chicago the western terminus of their rail lines, New Yorkers helped realize local boosters' vision of their city as the great entrepôt of the western plains.[7]

Chicago's success, however, represented the exception rather than the rule for speculative urban development. For every Chicago there were dozens of places like Cairo, located 400 miles downstate at the confluence of the Ohio and Mississippi Rivers. Cairo's undeniably central location proved beguiling for distant investors in the mid-1830s, but it and many places like it failed to sustain expectations. Charles Dickens satirized the specious appeal of these speculative ventures in *Martin Chuzzlewit* (1843–1844). The titular character, after viewing a map replete with "banks, churches, cathedrals, market-places, factories, hotels, stores, mansions, wharves," buys up fifty acres in the town of Eden—only to find "a few log-houses" waiting for him when he visits the dilapidated site.[8]

The experiences of Chicago (which in 2010 had 2.7 million residents) and Cairo (with 2,822 people in 2010) diverged sharply, but they both represented an urbanizing process oriented toward expanding market networks and reliant on capital from eastern and European investors. From 1790 to 1840, the number of places deemed "urban" by the census increased from 24 to 131. Of these communities, 46 held only 2,500 to 5,000 residents, yet even these locales served as centers of trade, movement, and exchange.

ERIE CANAL, LOCKPORT

Figure 4. *The Erie Canal, Lockport.* Lithograph (New York: Herman J. Meyer, *c.* 1855).
Creative Commons License (CC BY-SA 3.0).

Small villages often mimicked the layout of larger cities and registered their ambitions with names that harked back to imperial antiquity, such as Rome, Syracuse, or Utica. In these towns, farmers could drop off harvests to be shipped to Europe and pick up manufactured products for home consumption.[9] Market exchange and long-distance commerce had long been a feature of the North American economy, but the spread of railroads and canals and the growth of urban settlements meant that market institutions entered daily lives in new and at times unsettling ways. On the one hand, buying cloth at an urban dry goods store could free up time for family farmers to work in the wheat fields; on the other hand, wars and famines an ocean away made or broke their fortunes.[10]

Proliferating rail- and waterways bound cities and countrysides closer together, but so too did economic institutions, such as banks, that incorporated in large cities in this period. Shortly after independence, state legislatures began chartering new corporations at a rapid clip in order to facilitate political and economic development. The exclusive rights and privileges vested in corporations rankled republican sensibilities, however, and none proved more controversial than banks.[11] Banks produced the paper money that facilitated exchange in the increasingly far-flung American economic system; they also held vast stores of concentrated wealth subject to exploitation by unscrupulous operators and were prone to destabilizing crashes. During the Washington administration (1789–1797), US Treasury Secretary Alexander Hamilton successfully oversaw the incorporation of the privately run Bank of the United States (BUS). This bank (which operated from 1791 to 1811) and its successor (1816 to 1836) issued paper money, convertible into specie on request, that fueled an expanding economy. The BUS also lent money and redeemed notes received from state banks. However, both the First and Second BUS placed considerable resources in the hands of a few and insulated them from public oversight; malfeasance by some of their operatives along with a more generalized popular distrust of monopoly power rendered these institutions highly controversial. After a prolonged political struggle, Andrew Jackson allowed the charter of the Second Bank to lapse. The years from 1836 to the Civil War saw a profusion of state-chartered banks that issued their own paper currencies in its stead.[12] These monies fueled market exchange and capitalist expansion, but they assumed such a bewildering variety of forms that accepting an unfamiliar bank note became akin to an act of faith.[13]

Though the First and Second Banks of the United States were headquartered in Philadelphia, New York emerged in the 1830s as the epicenter of American commerce and finance. New York surpassed Philadelphia as an import and export center at the start of the 19th century. Even a quarter century before the opening of the Erie Canal, fully one-third of US overseas trade passed through New York's harbor. The advent of regularly scheduled packet ships to Liverpool in 1818 helped make Manhattan a convenient outlet for British manufactured goods. In turn, this gave rise to wholesale merchants or "jobbers" who bought entire cargos of imported goods at auction and then broke them up for distribution to the interior. The commercial opportunities in Manhattan encouraged banks and insurance companies to set up shop there. New York soon housed more of these institutions than any other city in the United States.[14]

The outsized influence of New York merchants over the far-flung American economy reflected the ever-quickening pace at which people, products, and information traveled in the 19th century. Both the speed and the volume of intercity traffic increased in the half-century between 1790 and 1840. One scholar has estimated that travel between New York and Philadelphia increased twentyfold in this period. A person leaving Manhattan for Washington, DC, in 1800 could expect to spend four days in transit; by 1830, travel time had been cut in half. As one moved away from the well-developed Boston-to-Baltimore corridor, travel times grew longer and less predictable, but improved nonetheless. Trips from Buffalo

Figure 5. William James Bennett, *View of South Street, from Maiden Lane, New York City.* Watercolor, *c.* 1827. From the Edward W. C. Arnold Collection of New York Prints, Maps, and Pictures (New York: Metropolitan Museum of Art). Bequest of Edward W. C. Arnold, 1954, accession number: 54.90.130. Creative Commons License (CC0 1.0).

to Detroit that might take three days in 1818 by 1834 took scarcely more than one.[15] Writers for popular publications marveled at the pace with which such changes unfolded before their eyes and celebrated what they deemed the annihilation of space and time. As influential newspaper editor Hezekiah Niles put it in 1830, "It seems as if space and gravity, though not to be wholly conquered by the ingenuity of man, are to be subjected to his dominion."[16]

Niles saw this as the fulfillment of the progressive "spirit of the age," though the spirit did not reach everyone. The cost of travel generally declined from 1790 to 1840; the six-dollar fare for travel between New York and Philadelphia in 1796 fell to between three dollars and four dollars by 1840, for example. But these tickets still remained beyond the reach of urban male laborers who by the 1830s might gross

one dollar for a day's work.[17] Working women tended to earn even less, and women of all classes had to contend with threats and condescension from their male fellow travelers when they ventured into the confined quarters of public conveyances.[18] And African Americans of both sexes and all income levels encountered restrictions and regulations that made travel experiences uncomfortable, insulting, and at times even impossible. Laws in slave states restricted black mobility, delimiting when and how African Americans could travel and forcing them to carry papers attesting to their freedom, while the expansion of transportation networks in the North precipitated some of the earliest experiments with segregation. The same modes of transit that broke down barriers for men like Hezekiah Niles erected new barriers for African Americans. Not coincidentally, racist transportation policies became the targets of some of the earliest civil rights protests in the United States.[19]

INDUSTRIALIZING PRODUCTION

The freedom to travel enjoyed by a select few, the barriers to travel experienced by many others, and the famine, enclosure, and uprisings that uprooted still more all reflected the expansion of a capitalist system with an increasingly global footprint.[20] By the second decade of the 19th century, the United States played a central role in producing the staple commodity at the center of this system: cotton.

In the 18th century, British manufacturers started to produce cotton cloth using technology copied from India, raw material grown by enslaved people in the Americas, and the labor of the dispossessed rural peasantry in England. Experiments in water-powered mechanization in Lancashire County, England, dramatically increased the productivity of the low-paid women and children who worked the looms. By the early 19th century, English manufacturers became the world's principal suppliers of cotton textiles. English manufacturers initially obtained their cotton from plantations in the West Indies and South America, but after the Haitian Revolution of 1791–1804, the center of cotton production shifted to mainland North America. Cotton was a minor crop in the United States, confined to humid coastal areas, until Eli Whitney's infamous cotton gin, designed in the 1790s, made it easier to process a varietal that grew in the drier upland regions. In 1790, before the gin, the United States produced 1.5 million pounds of cotton; by 1800, that number had shot up to 36.5 million.[21]

The tremendous demand for cotton, coupled with the newfound ability to grow it in large volumes in the American South and Southwest, had significant consequences for the American economy and the lives of millions of people. The forced relocation of the Cherokee and other southeastern Indians dovetailed with the forced relocation of hundreds of thousands of enslaved Africans and African Americans. Southeastern planters imported approximately 170,000 people from Africa prior to 1808, when the United States banned the international slave trade. Thereafter, "surplus" populations of people in bondage in the waning tobacco economies of the Upper South provided the bulk of the cotton labor force. Slave traders like Austin Woolfolk of Baltimore purchased people from Maryland and Virginia, then sold them to cotton planters, breaking up families and sending people south in chains. Ultimately, some 875,000 people were sold to the deep South between 1820 and 1860.[22]

Two cities emerged as crucial mediators between the cotton fields of the American South and the textile mills of Lancashire: New Orleans and New York. The United States acquired New Orleans in the Louisiana Purchase of 1803 after the Haitian Revolution squashed Napoleon Bonaparte's dreams of an American empire. The city's position near the mouth of the Mississippi River made it a key entrepôt for the commodities of the river valley. As the cotton trade took off, British financiers stationed representatives in New Orleans to scout opportunities and offer advice, and their investments funded the construction (often with slave labor) of the wharves and levees that made transatlantic trade possible. Financial institutions likewise centered in the city. New Orleans's four banks in 1831 mushroomed to sixteen in just six years. Though neoclassical facades advertised the banks' soundness, their vaults held more paper than gold, such as mortgages (including for enslaved persons), loans, and promissory notes. In 1820, New Orleans received almost 200 steamboats bearing 100,000 tons of freight worth around $12 million. By 1860, the port saw more than 3,500 steamboats dock and deposit 2 million tons of freight worth upward of $2 billion.[23]

A sizable portion of the cotton shipped from New Orleans passed through New York before reaching Liverpool. The same features that made New York City the preeminent commercial entrepôt in the United States also recommended it as a waypoint for southern cotton. New York saw more regular deliveries from England than any other American port; by 1835, sixteen ships a week commuted between Manhattan and Liverpool. This regularity meant better rates on transatlantic cotton shipments, and New York's financial institutions provided the loans, currency exchanges, and insurance critical to transatlantic commerce. As in New Orleans, the influx of cotton remade New York's landscape. When much of Manhattan's financial district burned in 1835, credit from England enabled merchants to remake the area on a grander scale than before. Neoclassical buildings, wider streets, and gas lighting marked much of downtown as a venue for global exchange.[24]

The vast majority of the cotton that moved through the ports of New Orleans and New York was bound for British textile mills, but about 15 percent of it went to domestic consumers, primarily in New England.[25] Starting in the mid-1810s, wealthy Bostonians funneled capital into textile manufacturing, establishing water-powered factories on greenfield sites

outside of Boston. The city of Lowell, founded in 1821, was one of the earliest and most prominent of these endeavors. Francis Cabot Lowell, the city's namesake, introduced English-style loom technology to the United States, but the Lowell mills' reorganization of labor drew as much notice as its technological innovations. The mills' workforce consisted of low-paid, unmarried women whose work was no longer needed on family farms in the region. The women lived in dormitories on site with the expectation that they would eventually return home to marry. To quiet concerns that independent living might beget moral corruption, the factory owners offered lyceum lectures and other cultural activities for those who were not too exhausted to attend after a seventy-hour workweek. Despite a transient workforce, Lowell grew quickly into a significant urban center in its own right. By 1840, the mill town's 20,000-plus residents made it the fourteenth-largest city in the United States.[26]

At the same time, villages and towns in the American northeast saw transformations in manufacturing at a smaller scale. As market-oriented agriculture and rising land prices

Figure 6. *View of Lowell, Massachusetts, c.1850* [?]. Hand-colored Engraving.
Courtesy of Library of Congress, LC-DIG-pga-07376.

altered the structure of farm life, growing numbers of people specialized in craft production. Rural artisans played a significant role in creating the American System of Manufactures in which mass production of interchangeable parts enabled the rapid assembly of intricate devices such as rifles produced in the federal armory of Springfield, Massachusetts, and clocks built in small rural shops. Each of these industries, though at different scales, deployed machine tools to create standardized components. British visitors who observed these techniques for producing weaponry and time-pieces deduced that scarcity of labor was driving American industry along a distinctly mechanized path.[27]

In large urban centers, however, a type of mass production developed in the first half of the 19th century that replicated neither the large-scale mills of Lowell nor the mechanized American System of the New England countryside. The high price of real estate and the lack of ready waterpower rendered these approaches fruitless in most established cities. Not until midcentury would steam power obviate the need to situate mechanized factories near rivers.[28] Instead, changes in production in large cities during the early republic entailed reconfiguring labor practices and the rise of a new system of wage labor.

Prior to the 19th century, most urban manufacturing took place in artisanal shops under the guidance of a master craftsman who oversaw a workforce of apprentices and journeymen, inculcating them in the secrets of the trade so that talented journeymen could eventually become masters in their own right.[29] In the late 18th and early 19th centuries, though, a few master craftsmen surveyed the changing urban landscape and surmised that organizing work in new ways could yield greater profits. Transportation improvements, by lowering shipping costs, offered the prospect of broadening the market for their goods. To do so profitably, however, required both an increase in productivity and a reduction of costs. For this they turned to the continually expanding urban labor pool. In the first half of the 19th century, American cities swelled with new arrivals, including rural Americans trying their luck in the city and immigrants from Europe, particularly Ireland and the German states, fleeing dislocations, famine, and political strife. Many of these newcomers were in desperate poverty and were willing to work long hours for substandard pay. Thus, when New York tailors began to prepare cheap ready-made clothing for sale to the cotton South in the 1810s and 1820s, they did so by sub-contracting work to women who made garments from home at a fraction of the going wage for journeymen. Cabinetmakers similarly divided work into standardized, simplified, and repetitive tasks so that journeymen performed only one step in the production process rather than seeing a single cabinet through from start to completion. In doing so, cabinetmakers bypassed the need to hire skilled labor and sped up the pace of work.[30]

Changes in the geographical scope of the market and the availability of unskilled labor signaled to many master craftsmen the rise of a new social order. The master abdicated responsibility for the professional training of his subordinates, instead hiring wageworkers to perform a specific task at a rate set by the market for labor. The master craftsmen who precipitated these changes saw them as essential accommodations to the progressive spirit of the age. The fate of the republic, they held, depended on the success of enterprising men who would generate the products needed in an expanding national market. No business could thrive if it paid higher wages than its competitors. Religious currents complemented this ideology: evangelical Christianity's emphasis on individual agency suggested that prosperous entrepreneurial craftsmen had earned their success while journeymen who failed to advance above the rank of wageworker lacked the requisite industry and virtue.[31] Yet even as craft entrepreneurs argued that the market set wages, they worked actively to keep labor costs down. Amid currency fluctuations, global commodity currents, and fickle consumer trends, the wages they paid were one of the few aspects of the market they could actually control. One way to do this was to keep the labor pool as large as possible, hiring, as needed, women, children, new immigrants, free blacks, and, in the slave states, enslaved laborers. Doing so undercut efforts by former journeymen to organize or protest wage cuts.[32]

Indiscriminate hiring practices also undermined the gendered system of household work that was the cornerstone of artisanal production. Eighteenth-century norms held that the male head of household should work in the cash economy and that his wife should supplement his income with domestic production. In practice, this ideal was beyond the reach of all but the wealthiest artisans, but it reflected an assumption that underlay women's labor as a whole: work that women did inside or outside the household was an adjunct to that performed by a male head of household. This assumption justified low wages for women and remained in place even as principles of artisanal self-sufficiency faded into memory.[33] The industrialization of tailoring, for example, entailed the expansion of "outwork" in which women sewed garments at home and received payment by the piece. In Baltimore, this amounted to wages of six and one-quarter cents per day as of 1820— far below the standard wage of one dollar per day for a male manual laborer and considerably below subsistence levels. In 1853, when the New York Times estimated that a workingman required $600 a year to support a family of four, the New York Tribune reported that a fully employed female outworker might earn at most $91. For single mothers, these were starvation wages.[34]

In the 1820s and 1830s, the men and women who engaged in wage work began to articulate their own ideas about political economy that challenged the capitalist ethos of the craft entrepreneurs. They asserted these views in public protests that represented the tentative beginnings of the modern labor movement. Male wageworkers formed trades unions in cities like New York, Philadelphia, Boston, and Baltimore. They exalted production as the root of all wealth and condemned systems of banking, credit, and paper money that allowed capitalists to control wage rates. A man's wages, unionists argued, should enable him to support a family in which his wife and daughters remained at home.[35] Women workers knew all too well the dangers of relying on male partners to provide, however. Women in industrializing cities from Baltimore to Lowell organized, protested, and struck in this period. "[I]f it is unfashionable for the men to bear oppression in silence, why should it not also become unfashionable with the women?" asked Sarah Monroe, a New York garment worker.[36]

One of the principal targets of labor activists in the 1830s was rampant inflation that drove up prices in major cities even as wages declined. Both specie and paper money poured into the United States in the early republic. Gold and credit from Britain funded cotton production and internal improvements, while silver mined in Mexico facilitated trade with China and circulated domestically as currency. The demise of the Bank of the United States in 1836 and the rise of the opium trade in China (which displaced the need for specie) pumped yet more paper and silver into the American economy. But in 1836–1837, interconnected political and economic shifts reversed the inflationary tide and catalyzed a depression that brought the nascent labor movement to a skidding halt. Moves by the Jackson administration to counter speculation by demanding specie for land purchases pulled silver from circulation even as the volume of paper money increased. Then, in 1837, a bad harvest in Britain prompted the Bank of England to raise interest rates. As British lenders began calling in debts, failures among overleveraged cotton brokers led to runs on the banks of New York and New Orleans, which ceased redeeming their notes in specie. In the prolonged depression that followed the Panic of 1837, creditors foreclosed on the enslaved people who had served as collateral for many loans. For individuals whose lives had been mortgaged, this meant years of dislocation as they were put on the auction block or as their enslavers, fleeing debts, absconded with them to the still independent Republic of Texas.[37]

In industrializing urban centers, the Panic and its aftermath marked a sea change in popular understandings of economic structures and agency. The tenets of moral economy, such as the conviction that individuals have a responsibility to transact with one another on a fair and equitable basis, had persisted even as market institutions proliferated in the 1820s and 1830s, but Americans found that the breadth of the depression in the late 1830s and early 1840s rendered it harder to blame economic crises on individual cupidity. Bankers who suspended specie payments argued that they had no choice, that conditions beyond their control led them to act as they did. Americans continued to blame high-level political figures along partisan lines, but they did not by and large blame themselves, pointing instead to systemic failures.[38] The ability to conceive of economic calamities in systematic terms reflected the degree to which urbanization, industrialization, and market integration bound places and people together. Yet individualistic explanations of *poverty*—the craft entrepreneurs' conviction that only want of individual industry and virtue kept men in wage-earning positions from achieving independence—remained a staple of political and economic thought through the 19th century and beyond.

FAULT LINES IN THE INDUSTRIALIZING CITY

Wage labor did not represent the only model for labor relations in antebellum urban America. Even as critics of the emerging industrial labor system both inside and outside the working class condemned "wage slavery," many urbanites remained in *chattel* slavery until the end

of the Civil War.[39] Though the enslaved as a percentage of southern urban populations declined in the years between 1820 and 1860 from 22 percent to 10 percent according to the census, these figures probably understate the role of enslaved people in southern cities. The boundary between urban and rural life was porous as people entered or left the city according to seasonal and economic cycles. Enslaved people from the countryside were "hired out" in the city to work in manufacturing, construction, and other trades. Slave labor built much of the commercial infrastructure of southern cities (and many northern cities besides).[40]

White laborers in the urban South lashed out violently at the indignity, as they saw it, of working alongside the enslaved. Frederick Douglass, reflecting on his time in Baltimore, observed that white mechanics took out their frustrations on free blacks rather than risk incurring the wrath of powerful slaveholders. Nonetheless, he predicted that southern white laborers would ultimately contribute to the overthrow of the slave system. "[T]he white man is robbed by the slave system, of the just results of his labor," Douglass wrote, "because he is flung into competition with a class of laborers who work without wages."[41] In the North, however, condemnations of *wage* slavery morphed into denunciations of *white* slavery by the 1840s, a formulation that signaled both white workers' acceptance of wage relations as such and their readiness to legitimize bondage for African Americans.[42] Although a number of radical working-class thinkers opposed slavery, abolitionism threatened many others who worried that the movement undermined their position. They channeled their rage into riots that targeted abolitionists and free blacks in the 1830s.[43] This violence extended to the jobsite, where white workers aggressively protected what they saw as their prerogatives in employment. Despite occasional cross-racial organization, white labor unions proved hostile to black participation. Community activism among urban free blacks in the North focused on efforts to improve their material condition, particularly by seeking middle-class employment outside of manual labor.[44] Those who sought work in manufacturing often faced violent resistance.

Violence aimed at abolitionists and free blacks represented an investment in white supremacy. Newly arrived immigrants from Europe found that laying claim to whiteness enabled them to seize political and economic power, however attenuated. Irish immigrants offer a prototypical example of this process. The millions of Irish who landed on American shores from the 1820s to the 1870s typically had few assets, little craft training, and found themselves barred from certain positions by bigoted employers. Nearly half of Boston's Irish Catholic immigrants worked in unskilled trades in 1850. Yet despite early indications that members of the Irish and African American working classes might ally against slavery and exploitation, by the 1830s Irish men sought actively, and at times violently, to wrest jobs from black men on the docks, in construction, and in service, while Irish women displaced black women as domestic servants. Moreover, the Democratic Party identified Irish immigrants as white and thus worthy of voting rights, legitimizing Irish claims on the government even as disenfranchisement rendered African Americans politically voiceless.[45]

Aside from the Chinatowns of the West Coast, however, class rather than race served as the principal sorting mechanism within urban space before the Civil War. As early as the 1790s, distinctive working-class neighborhoods took shape in major cities. The most famous of these was Five Points in New York City, a patch of unwholesome landfill in a former pond that gained notoriety as a site for vice and crime in the 19th century. In tenements owned by some of the richest families in New York, as many as fifteen people at a time lived in two-room apartments, some barely 225 square feet in area. By the 1850s, the population density in the Sixth Ward (which included Five Points) exceeded 310 people per acre; no urban neighborhoods in the United States, and scarcely any in the world, matched that figure. Yet Five Points only epitomized larger trends in working-class urban neighborhoods where dense and diverse populations lived in proximity to one another. Distinctions between public and private life blurred under such conditions. Survival strategies often hinged on pooling resources across households. Working-class women in particular moved readily between apartments and involved themselves in one another's affairs, forging domestic lives defined less by the boundaries of the home than of the neighborhood.[46]

The expansive domestic worlds of working-class urbanites stood in sharp contrast with the ideals of an emerging middle class. As wageworkers clustered into cramped neighborhoods, middling and elite urbanites developed districts of their own. In the 18th century, houses had served as both family quarters and places of business for artisans, merchants, and shopkeepers. These arrangements changed rapidly in the 19th century. From 1800 to 1810 more than 40 percent of New York's merchants and professionals separated their homes from their businesses. This process reflected a growing conviction among middle- and upper-class urbanites that the private home must stand apart from the tumult of public life. Changes in urban transportation lengthened commutes for men of means throughout the 19th century. A banker might walk to work in 1810, catch an omnibus in 1830, and ride a horse-drawn streetcar by the 1850s. Middle-class women gained authority within the household but found themselves largely excluded from the world of commercial exchange, the wages paid to domestic servants notwithstanding.[47]

The lifestyles, outlooks, and prospects of tenement dwellers and bourgeois urbanites diverged sharply, but the two populations continued to meet in the public space of the city street. For the poor, streets served as a commons, a critical site in the struggle to make a living. Parents and children scavenged in the street, looking for refuse they could repurpose or resell. Livestock, particularly hogs, consumed garbage and converted it, in effect, to food for their owners. Growing numbers of children, no longer subject to apprenticeship and not yet subject to public schooling, worked, slept, and formed communities among themselves in the streets. The street could also be a venue for the sale of newspapers, oysters, hot corn, and sex.[48] The last of these trades grew significantly in this period, as women found that stints or careers in prostitution could bring in badly needed income.[49]

Sex work was only one of the practices that alarmed genteel observers when they looked at the street. Municipal efforts to expel swine from urban thoroughfares, to regulate the movement of hucksters and peddlers, and to place unsupervised children in reformatory institutions aimed to transform the street from a commons into a site of transit and circulation. From the 1850s on, city governments and courts came down against uses of the street that obstructed traffic, practices not coincidentally associated with the habits of poor and working-class urbanites. Once prostitutes, street children, hucksters' carts, and socializing workmen were removed from the street, it could be overlaid with the water and gas pipes, railroad tracks, and telegraph wires that constituted a networked city. For elite reformers, this was modernization. For the people who saw their way of life criminalized, it was eviction.[50]

POSTBELLUM BEGINNINGS

During the Civil War, political initiatives at the state and federal levels spearheaded changes in the structure and organization of the economy. Northern state governments, eager to facilitate economic development, enlarged the scope and liberalized the terms of incorporation. The result was a dramatic spike in the number of corporations and the expansion of their operations across state lines. At the national level, Republican control of Congress and the White House, along with the party's need to finance the war, led to an array of economic measures that extended the reach of the federal government within economic affairs and encouraged further industrialization. The Republican wartime Congresses nationalized currency, raised tariffs to bolster manufacturing, and incorporated the transcontinental railroad. Most momentously, they successfully amended the Constitution to abolish slavery.[51]

The fall of slavery enshrined wage labor as a national model for economic relations. Freed people in the South found that their visions of freedom differed sharply from those of Republican politicians in Washington, who expected them to sign contracts and work for wages or as sharecroppers instead of owning land in their own names. One could not opt out of this system; vagrancy laws and other legal strictures made work compulsory. Northern states passed similar laws after the Civil War, outlawing pauperism and compelling individuals to find employment. Once on the job, wageworkers in industrial and agricultural settings alike found they had limited recourse in the event of abuse. Postbellum courts defined corporations as legal persons and contracts with employees as binding documents made by two independent individuals. Such interpretations delegitimized legislative efforts to mandate job safety requirements or set maximum hours on the grounds that such restrictions interfered with employees' rights to sell their labor. At the same time, courts defined collective action by workers as cabalism and sanctioned the use of state force to break up strikes.[52]

Large-scale mechanized factories, corporate monopolies, and unions with a national scope emerged in the late 19th century. In the 1860s, however, most employees, industrial or otherwise, still worked in small-scale workshops headed by owner-proprietors.[53] Yet even in 1865, signs of change were appearing. Any big-city urbanite who wanted an indication of what the future held for both capitalists and industrial workers could head to the nearest railroad yards. There he or she would find employees working within a bureaucratic system composed of distinct departments and layers of hierarchy, a modern, large-scale corporation with a modern, large-scale workforce. Like other industrial laborers, railroad employees worked long days, 10 to 12 hours or more, six days a week, for wages set by the employer. In many other respects, though, the size of railroad organizations and the extent of mechanization distinguished railroad work from other types of jobs. To begin with, railroads had since the 1840s separated ownership from management in response to the challenge of coordinating spatially diffused operations. As a result, workers reported to middle managers, which made for a working environment quite distinct from the small-scale manufacturing shop or even the textile mill. Trains' operating crews, for example, were expected to adhere to complex written guidelines that could stretch into the hundreds of pages. Rulebooks established a bureaucratic line of authority in which distant corporate executives stood at the top. Organizational strategies pioneered by railroad companies greatly influenced the form of the corporate enterprises that came to dominate the American economy by the end of the century.[54]

By 1860, more than 28,000 miles of track, predominantly in the North, crisscrossed the country, stitching together every major city. The Civil War proved highly lucrative for northern rail lines, and they came out of the war primed to expand. As the US Army wrested control of the Great Plains from the Sioux and the Cheyenne, western railroads, along with other western enterprises, served as principal outlets for eastern capital. Eastern railroads likewise continued their empire building, with the largest of them acquiring branch lines and expanding their economic reach. From 1860 to 1880, the track mileage in the United States more than tripled to 93,267 miles.[55]

The growing reach and power of railroad companies and other corporations took material form not only in the tracks spanning the American continent but in the spatial order of US cities. Monumental office buildings and department stores, new systems of rail tunnels and termini, and expanding transit networks changed the way people moved into, out of, and within cities. As middle- and upper-class urbanites rode streetcars ever further into the suburban fringe, poverty concentrated in the urban core. Postbellum industrial development sparked greater segregation and clustering than the antebellum city had seen, with distinct districts emerging to house particular immigrant groups or specialized economic functions.[56]

These changes led William Cullen Bryant, editor of the *New York Post*, to ask in 1868, "Can a city be planned?" The question reflected his sense that urban growth must somehow, by some agency, follow productive paths if it was to proceed efficiently in an age of industrial and commercial dynamism.[57] Bryant recognized that the United States was well on its way to becoming an urban society.

DISCUSSION OF THE LITERATURE

Economic and social historians have characterized the early years of US history as an age of market revolution. Charles Sellers's *The Market Revolution* depicts the rapid integration of capitalist institutions into American society in the early republic and recounts the social, political, and religious movements that sought to counter the ethos of unbridled competition. Subsequent work, such as books by Daniel Walker Howe and John Lauritz Larson, argue that these developments began much earlier than Sellers acknowledges and observe that many Americans actively created and welcomed these transformations, though without fully anticipating their consequences.[58]

Historians of capitalism examine similar topics from a broader chronological and geographical vantage point. Works in this field stress the ways in which capitalist ideas and practices knitted together processes and places whose histories have previously been told separately. Sven Beckert's global history of cotton, to take one example, examines inter-relationships between chattel slavery in the American South and industrial wage labor in Lancashire. By reconstructing the centrality of enslaved people to the financial and mate-rial processes of capitalist development, works by Beckert and others demonstrate that the history of industrialization and wage labor cannot be told apart from the history of slavery. Far from a premodern holdover, slav-ery emerges in these accounts as central to the formation of capitalist institutions.[59]

Urban historians have likewise reevaluated the role of slavery in the cities of both the North and the South. Richard Wade's foun-dational work in 1964 documented the forms slavery took in southern cities while arguing that slavery declined as an urban institution in the antebellum years. Later generations of scholarship have built on and challenged this thesis. Works by Shane White and Leslie Harris on African American life in New York City shift attention from the South to the North and un-cover the foundational role of slave labor and white supremacy in that city's rise. Rashauna Johnson's study of New Orleans suggests that slavery remained central to southern urban economies even as the census count of enslaved urbanites declined. In *Slavery's Metropolis*, she examines how the movement of enslaved people through and within New Orleans fa-cilitated that city's prosperity, and in turn how the Crescent City's built environment influ-enced racial formation and white suprem-acy.[60] Cities' roles as markets for the purchase and sale of human property likewise made them central to the domestic slave trade and hence to American slavery as a whole, as his-torians such as Calvin Schermerhorn, Steven Deyle, and Walter Johnson have shown.[61]

Unlike slavery, historians have recognized banking as a largely urban phenomenon, but scholars of finance in antebellum America have had little to say about urban history as such. Much of the scholarship on the eco-nomic and political travails of the 1820s and

1830s attempts to diagnose and assign blame for the Panic of 1837 and subsequent depres-sion.[62] More recent works have, consistent with trends in the history of capitalism, ex-amined the international dimensions of the an-tebellum American economy. Jessica Lepler's study of the Panic of 1837 draws, in part, on urban historical methods. She focuses on three cities—New Orleans, New York, and London—and the ties of credit and cotton that bound them together, connecting her findings to the material production of urban space.[63]

One of the factors driving urban growth in this period was the proliferation of transpor-tation lines that linked cities to one another and to distant hinterlands. Historians have ex-amined the economic and cultural effects of the new modes of transportation that re-shaped American life extensively. John Lauritz Larson's *Internal Improvement* offers insights into the political imagination that under-pinned public funding for roadways, canals, and railroads. L. Ray Gunn's book on public works in New York State and studies such as Carol Sheriff's history of the Erie Canal or Craig Miner's account of the early American railroad offer valuable insights into the social and cultural impact of these key develop-ments. Works by Amy Richter and Elizabeth Stordeur Pryor unpack the gendered and racial implications of travel within the United States.[64] For urban historians, transportation networks offer a chance to explore urban spa-tial and economic development while look-ing beyond the city limits. Perhaps the most well-known exemplar of this approach is William Cronon's *Nature's Metropolis*, which examines Chicago's growth and the trans-formative effects of city-centered capitalism on the "Great West."[65]

Though the history of industrialization is often associated with mechanization and large-scale factories, in the first half of the 19th cen-tury changes in the organization of the work-force were more widespread and just as important. The standard accounts of the decline of artisanal production and the rise of wage labor remain Sean Wilentz's *Chants Democratic* on workingmen's political and economic struggles and Christine Stansell's *City of Women* on working-class women in the same time period. Both historians examine New York, and both have been highly influential but subject to important correctives. Seth Rockman's work on Baltimore, for example, painstakingly reconstructs the lives of people whose economic position was even more precarious than that of Wilentz's bastardized journeymen.[66]

Finally, a rich tradition in urban history examines the design and uses of urban space itself. Such works shed light on the ways in which people moved through, built, and conceived of the city. Elizabeth Blackmar and Mary Ryan examine urban space as contested ground, while Dell Upton and David Scobey examine the ideological significance of urban design. Edwin Burrows and Mike Wallace's *Gotham* integrates narratives of New York's spatial, economic, and social development in an instructive way. More recently, Catherine McNeur's *Taming Manhattan* applies insights from environmental history to examine struggles over the control of streets, municipal regulation, and urban planning, highlighting the centrality of class conflict to urban development.[67]

PRIMARY SOURCES

Nineteenth-century American writers commented extensively on the economic changes unfolding in their time, leaving behind a wealth of documentary evidence for historians. Sources related to urbanization, industrialization, and the expansion of commercial networks can be found in print culture, in municipal and corporate archives, and in the built environment itself.

Print material offers a useful starting point for historical research into the 19th-century American economy. Anyone interested in the daily rhythms of urban life can find material in the newspapers. Newspapers served as bulletins for the community—places where people sought or advertised work, informed readers of goods for sale, and posted prices for travel. Moreover, newspaper editors often weighed in on critical issues of the day. Examining news stories and editorials can provide insight into how people made sense of a dynamic economy. In addition to the daily press, a few periodicals with national or regional circulation wrote at length on economic matters, including *Niles' Weekly Register* of Baltimore, *De Bow's Review* of New Orleans, and *Harper's Weekly* of New York. Newspapers may be found on microfilm in many libraries or through subscription databases like Readex's *America's Historical Newspapers* and EBSCO's *Historical Periodicals Collection*. Researchers can also find longer-form print material that sheds light on economic realities and thought. Housekeeping manuals, political economy textbooks, and both anti- and pro-slavery writings are available online and, in some cases, remain in print.

Researchers investigating a particular merchant or company can sometimes find archival material. Many historical societies hold the family papers of prominent merchants, and some corporations maintain in-house archives. For those interested in urban history particularly, municipal archives are an important resource. Though the depth and availability of materials varies from city to city, municipal archives often contain petitions from citizens whose perspectives did not make it into the newspapers. The Baltimore City Archives, to take just one example, abound with carefully indexed complaints to the City Council about obstructions to the street, letters to the mayor asking for work, and tax records down to the ward level.

Finally, scholars who live in cities that developed in this period may want to direct their attention to urban space itself. Though fires, highway construction, urban renewal, and other changes have eliminated much of the industrial landscape of the 19th century, many cities retain the form and even structures of the era. No one should confuse the urban landscape of today with that of the past, of course, but grids, infrastructure, and architecture serve as the material legacies of this period and remind us that, in a very tangible sense, the worlds people made in the 19th century condition our present realities.

FURTHER READING

Beckert, Sven. *Empire of Cotton: A Global History*. New York: Alfred A. Knopf, 2014.

Burrows, Edwin, and Mike Wallace. *Gotham: A History of New York City to 1898*. New York: Oxford University Press, 1999.

Cronon, William. *Nature's Metropolis: Chicago and the Great West*. New York: W. W. Norton, 1991.

Harris, Leslie M. *In the Shadow of Slavery: African Americans in New York City, 1626–1863*. Chicago: University of Chicago Press, 2003.

Johnson, Rashauna. *Slavery's Metropolis: Unfree Labor in New Orleans during the Age of Revolutions*. New York: Cambridge University Press, 2016.

Larson, John Lauritz. *Internal Improvement: National Public Works and the Promise of Popular Government in the Early United States*. Chapel Hill: University of North Carolina Press, 1998.

Lepler, Jessica M. *The Many Panics of 1837: People, Politics, and the Creation of a Transatlantic Financial Crisis*. New York: Cambridge University Press, 2013.

Maggor, Noam. *Brahmin Capitalism: Frontiers of Wealth and Populism in America's First Gilded Age*. Cambridge, MA: Harvard University Press, 2017.

McNeur, Catherine. *Taming Manhattan: Environmental Battles in the Antebellum City*. Cambridge, MA: Harvard University Press, 2014.

Miner, Craig. *A Most Magnificent Machine: America Adopts the Railroad, 1825–1862*. Lawrence: University Press of Kansas, 2010.

Richter, Amy G. *Home on the Rails: Women, the Railroad, and the Rise of Public Domesticity*. Chapel Hill: University of North Carolina Press, 2005.

Rockman, Seth. *Scraping By: Wage Labor, Slavery, and Survival in Early Baltimore*. Baltimore: Johns Hopkins University Press, 2007.

Roediger, David. *The Wages of Whiteness: Race and the Making of the American Working Class*, rev. ed. London: Verso, 1999.

Sellers, Charles. *The Market Revolution: Jacksonian America, 1815–1846*. New York: Oxford University Press, 1991.

Shaw, Diane. *City Building on the Eastern Frontier: Sorting the New Nineteenth-Century City*. Baltimore: Johns Hopkins University Press, 2004.

Sheriff, Carol. *The Artificial River: The Erie Canal and the Paradox of Progress, 1817–1862*. New York: Hill & Wang, 1996.

Stanstell, Christine. *City of Women: Sex and Class in New York, 1789–1860*. Urbana: University of Illinois Press, 1987.

Wade, Richard C. *Slavery in the Cities: The South, 1820–1860*. New York: Oxford University Press, 1964.

Wilentz, Sean. *Chants Democratic: New York City and the Rise of the American Working Class, 1788–1850*. New York: Oxford University Press, 1984.

NOTES

1. US Bureau of the Census. *Historical Statistics of the United States, Colonial Times to 1970*, part 1 (Washington, DC: US Government Printing Office, 1975), 8, 11–12; Richardson Dilworth, ed., *Cities in American Political History* (Los Angeles: SAGE, 2011), 9, 212.

2. Synthetic overviews along these lines include: Charles Sellers, *The Market Revolution: Jacksonian America, 1815–1846* (New York: Oxford University Press, 1991); John Lauritz Larson, *The Market Revolution in America: Liberty, Ambition, and the Eclipse of the Common Good* (New York: Cambridge University Press, 2010); Daniel Walker Howe, *What Hath God Wrought: The Transformation of America, 1815–1848* (New York: Oxford University Press, 2007); Sean Wilentz, *The Rise of American Democracy: Jefferson to Lincoln* (New York: W. W. Norton, 2005); Edward E. Baptist, *The Half Has Never Been Told: Slavery and the Making of American Capitalism* (New York: Basic Books, 2014); Sean Wilentz, *Chants Democratic: New York City and the Rise of the American Working Class, 1788–1850*, Twentieth Anniversary Edition (New York: Oxford University Press, 2004 [1984]).

3. Leslie M. Harris, *In the Shadow of Slavery: African Americans in New York City, 1626–1863* (Chicago: University of Chicago Press, 2003), 11–15, 30–33; Brooke Hunter, "Wheat, War, and the American Economy during the Age of Revolution," *William and Mary Quarterly*, 3d series, 62, no. 3 (July 2005): 505–526.

4. Steven Hahn, *A Nation Without Borders: The United States and Its World in an Age of Civil Wars, 1830–1910* (New York: Viking, 2016), 29–34 and passim; James R. Fichter, *So Great a*

Proffit: How the East Indies Trade Transformed Anglo-American Capitalism (Cambridge, MA: Harvard University Press, 2010).

5. Edwin G. Burrows and Mike Wallace, *Gotham: A History of New York City to 1898* (New York: Oxford University Press, 1999), 334–335, 429–432; Carol Sheriff, *The Artificial River: The Erie Canal and the Paradox of Progress, 1817–1862* (New York: Hill & Wang, 1996).

6. John Lauritz Larson, *Internal Improvement: National Public Works and the Promise of Popular Government in the Early United States* (Chapel Hill: University of North Carolina Press, 1998); Craig Miner, *A Most Magnificent Machine: America Adopts the Railroad, 1825–1862* (Lawrence: University Press of Kansas, 2010); David Schley, *Making the Capitalist City: Railroads and Urban Space in Baltimore, 1827–1877* (forthcoming); L. Ray Gunn, *The Decline of Authority: Public Economic Policy and Political Development in New York, 1800–1860* (Ithaca, NY: Cornell University Press, 1988). Federal support often took the form of land grants: see John F. Stover, *Iron Road to the West: American Railroads in the 1850s* (New York: Columbia University Press, 1978), esp. chap. 5.

7. D. W. Meinig, *The Shaping of America: A Geographical Perspective on 500 Years of History*, vol. 2, *Continental America, 1800–1867* (New Haven, CT: Yale University Press, 1993), 240–257; William Cronon, *Nature's Metropolis: Chicago and the Great West* (New York: W. W. Norton, 1991), 25–45, 57–62.

8. Nick Yablon, *Untimely Ruins: An Archaeology of American Urban Modernity, 1819–1919* (Chicago: University of Chicago Press, 2009), 63–79, quotes on 76–77.

9. US Bureau of the Census. *Historical Statistics of the United States*, 11; Diane Shaw, *City Building on the Eastern Frontier: Sorting the New Nineteenth-Century City* (Baltimore: Johns Hopkins University Press, 2004); Stuart M. Blumin, "The Social Implications of U.S. Economic Development," in *The Cambridge Economic History of the United States*, vol. II, *The Long Nineteenth Century*, ed. Stanley L. Engerman and Robert E. Gallman (New York: Cambridge University Press, 2000), 823–829.

10. Sellers, *The Market Revolution*, 154–157; Hahn, *A Nation Without Borders*, 83–89.

11. Pauline Maier, "The Revolutionary Origins of the American Corporation," in *William and Mary Quarterly*, 3d ser., 50, no. 1 (January 1993),

51–84; Andrew M. Schocket, *Founding Corporate Power in Early National Philadelphia* (DeKalb: Northern Illinois University Press, 2007).

12. Susan Hoffman, *Politics and Banking: Ideas, Public Policy, and the Creation of Financial Institutions* (Baltimore: Johns Hopkins University Press, 2001), chaps. 2–3; Larson, *The Market Revolution in America*, 19, 26–29; Hugh Rockoff, "Banking and Finance, 1789–1914," in *The Cambridge Economic History of the United States*, ed. Engerman and Gallman, vol. II, 646–649.

13. David M. Henkin, *City Reading: Written Words and Public Spaces in Antebellum New York* (New York: Columbia University Press, 1998), chap. 6; Stephen Mihm, *A Nation of Counterfeiters: Capitalists, Con Men, and the Making of the United States* (Cambridge, MA: Harvard University Press, 2007).

14. Burrows and Wallace, *Gotham*, 333–336, 433–436.

15. Allan R. Pred, *Urban Growth and the Circulation of Information: The United States System of Cities, 1790–1840* (Cambridge, MA: Harvard University Press, 1973), 145–165, 176–177, 183–185.

16. "Rail Road—Power and Velocity, &c. &c.," *Niles' Weekly Register*, June 26, 1830, 317–319, quote on 317.

17. Pred, *Urban Growth and the Circulation of Information*, 145–146. The one-dollar-a-day figure is a commonly reported one and can be found, among other places, in Burrows and Wallace, *Gotham*, 460. Seth Rockman notes that this figure does not account for the irregularity of work: *Scraping By: Wage Labor, Slavery, and Survival in Early Baltimore* (Baltimore: Johns Hopkins University Press, 2009), 75–76.

18. Amy G. Richter, *Home on the Rails: Women, the Railroad, and the Rise of Public Domesticity* (Chapel Hill: University of North Carolina Press, 2005); Patricia Cline Cohen, "Safety and Danger: Women on American Public Transport, 1750–1850," in *Gendered Domains: Rethinking Public and Private in Women's History*, eds. Dorothy O. Helly and Susan M. Reverby (Ithaca, NY: Cornell University Press, 1992), 109–122.

19. Elizabeth Stordeur Pryor, *Colored Travelers: Mobility and the Fight for Citizenship before the Civil War* (Chapel Hill: University of North Carolina Press, 2016), chaps. 2 and 3.

20. Eric Hobsbawm, *The Age of Capital, 1848–1875* (New York: Vintage Books, 1966 [1975]), esp. chap. 5.

21. Sven Beckert, *Empire of Cotton: A Global History* (New York: Alfred A. Knopf, 2014), 47–52, 57–69, 74–76, 84–104.

22. Beckert, *Empire of Cotton*, 104–110; Edward E. Baptist, *The Half Has Never Been Told: Slavery and the Making of American Capitalism* (New York: Basic Books, 2014), 18–22; Steven Deyle, *Carry Me Back: The Domestic Slave Trade in American Life* (New York: Oxford University Press, 2005), 247, 289; Calvin Schermerhorn, *The Business of Slavery and the Rise of American Capitalism, 1815–1860* (New Haven, CT: Yale University Press, 2015), 67–68.

23. Jessica M. Lepler, *The Many Panics of 1837: People, Politics, and the Creation of a Transatlantic Financial Crisis* (New York: Cambridge University Press, 2013), 10–16; Walter Johnson, *River of Dark Dreams: Slavery and Empire in the Cotton Kingdom* (Cambridge, MA: Harvard University Press, 2013), 256–257; Ari Kelman, *A River and Its City: The Nature of Landscape in New Orleans* (Berkeley: University of California Press, 2003), chap. 2; on mortgages and slavery, see Bonnie Martin, "Slavery's Invisible Engine: Mortgaging Human Property," *Journal of Southern History* 76, no. 4 (November 2010): 817–866; on slave labor and infrastructure, see Rashauna Johnson, *Slavery's Metropolis: Unfree Labor in New Orleans during the Age of Revolutions* (New York: Cambridge University Press, 2016), 144–146.

24. Lepler, *The Many Panics of 1837*, 33–36; Johnson, *River of Dark Dreams*, 257–258.

25. Johnson, *River of Dark Dreams*, 257.

26. Noam Maggor, *Brahmin Capitalism: Frontiers of Wealth and Populism in America's First Gilded Age* (Cambridge, MA: Harvard University Press, 2017), 22–32; Thomas Bender, *Towards an Urban Vision: Ideas and Institutions in Nineteenth-Century America* (Baltimore: Johns Hopkins University Press, 1975), 29–42; Holly Hanson, "'Mill Girls' and 'Mine Boys': The Cultural Meanings of Migrant Labor," *Social History* 21, no. 2 (May 1996): 160–179.

27. David Jaffee, *A New Nation of Goods: The Material Culture of Early America* (Philadelphia: University of Pennsylvania Press, 2010), 56–61, 174–175; Walter Licht, *Industrializing America: The Nineteenth Century* (Baltimore: Johns Hopkins University Press, 1995), 42–45.

28. Burrows and Wallace, *Gotham*, 306–307; Stanley L. Engerman and Kenneth L. Sokoloff,

"Technology and Industrialization, 1790–1914," in *The Cambridge Economic History of the United States*, ed. Engerman and Gallman, vol. II, 374–375.

29. Wilentz, *Chants Democratic*, 4–5, 53–56; Robert A. Margo, "The Labor Force in the Nineteenth Century," in *The Cambridge Economic History of the United States*, ed. Engerman and Gallman, vol. II, 232–233. For an important corrective to too-rosy views of social relations in an artisan workshop, see Robert Darnton, "Workers Revolt: The Great Cat Massacre of the Rue Saint-Severin," in *The Great Cat Massacre and Other Episodes in French Cultural History* (New York: Basic Books, 1984), 75–106, esp. 78–82.

30. Wilentz, *Chants Democratic*, 31–34; Burrows and Wallace, *Gotham*, 343–346; Tyler Anbinder, *Five Points: The 19th-Century New York City Neighborhood that Invented Tap Dance, Stole Elections, and Became the World's Most Notorious Slum* (New York: Penguin, 2001), chap. 2; Howe, *What Hath God Wrought*, 525–527.

31. Wilentz, *Chants Democratic*, 41–42, 271–286.

32. Rockman, *Scraping By*, 36–43.

33. Christine Stansell, *City of Women: Sex and Class in New York, 1789–1860* (Urbana: University of Illinois Press, 1987), 11–15, 18; Rockman, *Scraping By*, 133.

34. Stansell, *City of Women*, 105–111, numbers on 111, 262, n. 25; Rockman, *Scraping By*, 137–140.

35. Wilentz, *Chants Democratic*, 220–250; Stansell, *City of Women*, 131–133, 137–141; Rockman, *Scraping By*, 141–142.

36. Stansell, *City of Women*, 133–137, quote on 133; Rockman, *Scraping By*, 148–152; Wilentz, *Chants Democratic*, 168.

37. Howe, *What Hath God Wrought*, 502–505; Hahn, *A Nation Without Borders*, 79–83; Baptist, *The Half Has Never Been Told*, 274–297; Scott Reynolds Nelson, *A Nation of Deadbeats: An Uncommon History of America's Financial Disasters* (New York: Vintage, 2012), 117–125

38. Lepler, *The Many Panics of 1837*, 3–4, 67–70, 91–93, 191–218; Sean Patrick Adams, "How Choice Fueled Panic: Philadelphians, Consumption, and the Panic of 1837," *Enterprise & Society* 12, no. 4 (December 2011): 761–789. Ann Fabian points out that many ministers weighed in on the 1837 crisis, as they placed economic exchange within a moral framework; by the Panic of 1857, far fewer religious leaders would comment—see Fabian, "Speculation on

Distress: The Popular Discourse of the Panics of 1837 and 1857," *Yale Journal of Criticism* 3, no. 1 (Fall 1989): 127–142, esp. 132–134.

39. Jeffrey Sklansky, *The Soul's Economy: Market Society and Selfhood in American Thought, 1820–1920* (Chapel Hill: University of North Carolina Press, 2002), 2–6; David Roediger, *The Wages of Whiteness: Race and the Making of the American Working Class*, rev. ed. (London: Verso, 1999), 43–45.

40. Richard C. Wade, *Slavery in the Cities: The South, 1820–1860* (New York: Oxford University Press, 1964): numbers on 243–244; Barbara Jeanne Fields, *Slavery and Freedom on the Middle Ground: Maryland during the Nineteenth Century* (New Haven, CT: Yale University Press, 1984): esp. chap. 3; Clifton Ellis and Rebecca Ginsburg, "Introduction: Studying the Landscapes of North American Urban Slavery," in Ellis and Ginsburg, eds., *Slavery in the City: Architecture and Landscapes of Urban Slavery in North America*. (Charlottesville: University of Virginia Press, 2017), 1–17; Johnson, *Slavery's Metropolis*; Rockman, *Scraping By*, esp. chap. 8.

41. Frederick Douglass, *My Bondage and My Freedom* (1855), in Henry Louis Gates Jr., ed., *Frederick Douglass Autobiographies* (New York: Penguin, 1994), 330–335, quote on 330.

42. Roediger, *The Wages of Whiteness*, 65–77; John D. Fairfield, *The Public and Its Possibilities: Triumphs and Tragedies in the American City* (Philadelphia: Temple University Press, 2010), 39–40.

43. Roediger, *The Wages of Whiteness*, 58, 77–87, 108–109; Burrows and Wallace, *Gotham*, 552–559.

44. Harris, *In the Shadow of Slavery*, 96–100, 119–121.

45. Roediger, *The Wages of Whiteness*, 133–150; Burrows and Wallace, *Gotham*, 547–548.

46. Anbinder, *Five Points*, 72–77; Stansell, *City of Women*, 41–62; Burrows and Wallace, *Gotham*, 387–392, 475–480. On San Francisco's Chinatown, see Nayan Shah, *Contagious Divides: Epidemics and Race in San Francisco's Chinatown* (Berkeley: University of California Press, 2001): esp. 20–28.

47. Mary P. Ryan, *Cradle of the Middle Class: Family in Oneida County, New York, 1790–1865* (New York: Cambridge University Press, 1981); Ryan, *Women in Public: Between Banners and Ballots,*

1825–1880 (Baltimore: Johns Hopkins University Press, 1990), chaps. 1–2; Jeanne Boydston, *Home and Work: Housework, Wages, and the Ideology of Labor in the Early Republic* (New York: Oxford University Press, 1990), 99–108; Kenneth T. Jackson, *Crabgrass Frontier: The Suburbanization of the United States* (New York: Oxford University Press, 1985), chaps. 2–6; Shaw, *City Building on the Eastern Frontier*, 86–102; Burrows and Wallace, *Gotham*, 372; Stansell, *City of Women*, 155–163; Clay McShane and Joel A. Tarr, *The Horse in the City: Living Machines in the Nineteenth Century* (Baltimore: Johns Hopkins University Press, 2007), 63–78.

48. Mary P. Ryan, *Civic Wars: Democracy and Public Life in the American City during the Nineteenth Century* (Berkeley: University of California Press, 1997), chap. 1; Elizabeth Blackmar, *Manhattan for Rent, 1785–1850* (Ithaca, NY: Cornell University Press, 1989), 151–158, 171; Catherine McNeur, *Taming Manhattan: Environmental Battles in the Antebellum City* (Cambridge, MA: Harvard University Press, 2014), chap. 1; Timothy J. Gilfoyle, *A Pickpocket's Tale: The Underworld of Nineteenth-Century New York* (New York: W. W. Norton, 2006), chap. 2.

49. Timothy J. Gilfoyle, *City of Eros: New York City, Prostitution, and the Commercialization of Sex, 1790–1920* (New York: W. W. Norton, 1992): chaps. 2–5; Patricia Cline Cohen, *The Murder of Helen Jewett: The Life and Death of a Prostitute in Nineteenth-Century New York* (New York: Alfred A. Knopf, 1998); Stansell, *City of Women*, chap. 9; Katie M. Hemphill, "Selling Sex and Intimacy in the City: The Changing Business of Prostitution in Nineteenth-Century Baltimore," in *Capitalism by Gaslight: Illuminating the Economy of Nineteenth-Century America*, ed. Brian P. Luskey and Wendy A. Woloson (Philadelphia: University of Pennsylvania Press, 2015), 168–189.

50. Blackmar, *Manhattan for Rent*, 158–180; McNeur, *Taming Manhattan*, 23–42, 113–115; Matthew A. Crenson, *Baltimore: A Political History* (Baltimore: Johns Hopkins University Press, 2017), 197–200; Robert J. Gamble, "The Promiscuous Economy: Cultural and Commercial Geographies of Secondhand in the Antebellum City," in *Capitalism by Gaslight*, ed. Luskey and Woloson, 31–52, esp. 38–42; David M. Scobey, *Empire City: The Making and Meaning of the New York*

City Landscape (Philadelphia: Temple University Press, 2002), 174–180; Perry R. Duis, *Challenging Chicago: Coping with Everyday Life, 1837–1920* (Chicago: University of Illinois Press, 1998), 7–13; McShane and Tarr, *The Horse in the City*, 72.

51. Sean Patrick Adams, "Soulless Monsters and Iron Horses: The Civil War, Institutional Change, and American Capitalism," in *Capitalism Takes Command: The Social Transformation of Nineteenth-Century America*, ed. Michael Zakim and Gary J. Kornblith (Chicago: University of Chicago Press, 2012), 249–276; Heather Cox Richardson, *The Greatest Nation of the Earth: Republican Economic Policies during the Civil War* (Cambridge, MA: Harvard University Press, 1997).

52. Amy Dru Stanley, *From Bondage to Contract: Wage Labor, Marriage, and the Market in the Age of Slave Emancipation* (New York: Cambridge University Press, 1998), esp. chap. 3; Hahn, *A Nation Without Borders*, 325–328, 355–358.

53. Hahn, *A Nation Without Borders*, 338–346.

54. Walter Licht, *Working for the Railroad: The Organization of Work in the Nineteenth Century* (Princeton, NJ: Princeton University Press, 1983); Alfred D. Chandler Jr., *The Visible Hand: The Managerial Revolution in American Business* (Cambridge, MA: Belknap Press of Harvard University Press, 1977), esp. chap. 3; William G. Roy, *Socializing Capital: The Rise of the Large Industrial Corporation in America* (Princeton, NJ: Princeton University Press, 1997); Charles Perrow, *Organizing America: Wealth, Power, and the Origins of Corporate Capitalism* (Princeton, NJ: Princeton University Press, 2002).

55. Adams, "Soulless Monsters and Iron Horses," 267–271; Maggor, *Brahmin Capitalism*.

56. Mona Domosh, *Invented Cities: The Creation of Landscape in Nineteenth-Century New York and Boston* (New Haven, CT: Yale University Press, 1996); Thomas Bender, *The Unfinished City: New York and the Metropolitan Idea* (New York: New Press, 2002) chap. 3, esp. 35–37; Sam Bass Warner Jr., *The Private City: Philadelphia in Three Periods of Its Growth*, 2d ed. (Philadelphia: University of Pennsylvania Press, 1987 [1968]): chaps. 8–9; Carl W. Condit, *The Port of New York: A History of the Rail and Terminal System from the Beginnings to Pennsylvania Station* (Chicago: University of Chicago Press, 1980); Andrew Heath, "The Public Interest of the Private City:

The Pennsylvania Railroad, Urban Space, and Philadelphia's Economic Elite, 1846–1877," *Pennsylvania History* 79, no. 2 (Spring 2012): 177–208; Schley, *Making the Capitalist City*.

57. Scobey, *Empire City*, 1–2.

58. Sellers, *The Market Revolution*; Howe, *What Hath God Wrought*; Larson, *The Market Revolution in America*. Though these works often depict capitalist practices spreading from cities to the countryside, David Jaffee has found evidence that some market processes originated within rural communities; see his *A New Nation of Goods*.

59. Beckert, *Empire of Cotton*. See also Johnson, *River of Dark Dreams*; Baptist, *The Half Has Never Been Told*; Martin, "Slavery's Invisible Engine"; Zakim and Kornblith, eds., *Capitalism Takes Command*; Luskey and Woloson, eds., *Capitalism by Gaslight*; Hobsbawm, *The Age of Capital*; Sven Beckert and Seth Rockman, eds., *Slavery's Capitalism: A New History of American Economic Development* (Philadelphia: University of Pennsylvania Press, 2016).

60. Wade, *Slavery in the Cities*; Shane White, *Somewhat More Independent: The End of Slavery in New York City, 1770–1810* (Athens: University of Georgia Press, 1991); Harris, *In the Shadow of Slavery*; Johnson, *Slavery's Metropolis*.

61. Schermerhorn, *The Business of Slavery*; Deyle, *Carry Me Back*; Walter Johnson, *Soul by Soul: Life inside the Antebellum Slave Market* (Cambridge, MA: Harvard University Press, 1999), chap. 2.

62. Arthur M. Schlesinger, *The Age of Jackson* (Boston: Little, Brown, 1945); Peter Temin, *The Jacksonian Economy* (New York: W. W Norton, 1969); Wilentz, *The Rise of American Democracy*; Howe, *What Hath God Wrought*.

63. Lepler, *The Many Panics of 1837*; see also Nelson, *A Nation of Deadbeats*; Hahn, *A Nation Without Borders*; Robert E. Shalhope, *The Baltimore Bank Riot: Political Upheaval in Antebellum Maryland* (Urbana: University of Illinois Press, 2009).

64. Larson, *Internal Improvement*; Gunn, *The Decline of Authority*; Sheriff, *The Artificial River*; Miner, *A Most Magnificent Machine*; Richter, *Home on the Rails*; Pryor, *Colored Travelers*. Those interested in the early history of the railroad may also benefit from the works of John Stover, such as *Iron Road to the West*, and, for a postbellum perspective on law and railroad ridership, Barbara

Young Welke's *Recasting American Liberty: Gender, Race, Law, and the Railroad Revolution, 1865–1920* (New York: Cambridge University Press, 2001). George Rogers Taylor's *The Transportation Revolution, 1815–1860* (New York: Rinehart, 1951) remains worth reading.

65. Cronon, *Nature's Metropolis*. See also Maggor, *Brahmin Capitalism*; Shaw, *City Building on the Eastern Frontier*.

66. Wilentz, *Chants Democratic*; Stansell, *City of Women*; Rockman, *Scraping By*; see also Roediger, *The Wages of Whiteness*, and Harris, *In the Shadow of Slavery*.

67. Blackmar, *Manhattan for Rent*; Ryan, *Civic Wars*; Dell Upton, *Another City: Urban Life and Urban Spaces in the New American Republic* (New Haven, CT: Yale University Press, 2008); Scobey, *Empire City*; Burrows and Wallace, *Gotham*; McNeur, *Taming Manhattan*.

David Schley

INDUSTRY, COMMERCE, AND URBANIZATION IN THE UNITED STATES, 1880–1929

Industrialization and urbanization began long before the late 19th and early 20th centuries, but it accelerated greatly during this period because of technological innovations, social changes, and a political system increasingly apt to favor economic growth beyond any other concern. Before 1880, industrialization depended upon a prescribed division of labor—breaking most jobs up into smaller tasks, and assigning the same people to repeat one task indefinitely. After 1880, industrialization depended much more on mechanization—the replacement of people with machines—to increase production and maximize profits. The development of the modern electrical grid, starting in the early 1880s, facilitated such technological advances. Henry Ford's assembly line and the rise of mass production after the turn of the 20th century only strengthened this effect. As a result, the total manufacturing output of the United States was twenty-eight times greater in 1929 than it was 1859. Adjust that number for the growth in population over the same period, and it still multiplied seven times over.[1]

Cities in America date back to the beginning of the colonial period, but the tendency for new industrial factories to be located in or near urban areas meant that cities grew much faster during the late 19th century than ever before. This trend was most apparent in large cities like New York, which expanded from approximately half a million to around 3.5 million people between 1850 and 1900, and Philadelphia, which increased in size from slightly more than 100,000 inhabitants to more than 1.2 million people over the same period. During the last half of the late 19th century, Chicago proved to be the fastest growing city in the world. Overall, 15.3 percent of Americans lived in cities in 1850. By 1900, that percentage had increased to 39.7, and kept growing. The 1920 Census revealed that more Americans lived in cities than the countryside for the first time.[2]

Not every city in the country developed as fast as the largest cities did. Important regional differences existed in urbanization because of differences in the nature of industrial growth. The largest cities in the Northeast were manufacturing powerhouses that contained everything, from large factories building railroad locomotives to small shops producing textiles in people's apartments. The Northeast also gave rise to smaller cities that concentrated on particular industries, like Rochester, New York, which specialized in men's clothing, boots, and shoes. Following on a tradition of manufacturing from earlier in the century, New Bedford and Fall River, Massachusetts, increased in size because of their cotton textile factories. Other cities, like Elizabeth, New Jersey, grew as byproducts of the expansion of their larger neighbors.

Chicago, the largest city in the Midwest, made its name processing natural resources from the Western frontier before those re-sources traveled eastward as finished prod-ucts. Grain and lumber—two industries that had been crucial for Chicago's early growth—relied on Chicago for marketing and storage. With perfection of the refrigerated railroad car, meat processing became such an enor-mous industry that the vast majority of the meat that Americans ate was processed in the stockyards on that city's south side. (That ac-tivity would disperse again, after the turn of the 20th century, to other cities like Fort Worth and Kansas City.) Smaller cities in America's industrial heartland would grow around other manufacturing pursuits like steel in Youngstown, and machine tools and cash registers in Dayton, Ohio.[3]

The South had lagged behind the rest of the country since before the Civil War. As a result, many advocates for outside investment in this region expanded their activities after the war. They were somewhat successful. While the rate of industrialization (and therefore ur-banization) picked up in the South during the late 19th and early 20th centuries, it still has not fully caught up with the rest of the country. Birmingham, Alabama, for example, founded in 1871, flourished as a center for iron and steel manufacturing during the 1880s, when two railroads first linked that city to the region's mineral resources.[4] The growth of cotton mills in the "upcountry" section of the Carolinas began during the 1870s. After the turn of the 20th century, this region became an impor-tant center of activity for the textile industry, in large part because of the cheap, nonunion labor available there.

What separates this period from earlier pe-riods in urban and industrial history is that this was the first time in American history that cities had moved to the center of American life. Cities were where most of the new facto-ries got built. Waves of immigrants settled in cities because that's where the job openings in industrial factories were. Cities were also places where the effects of industrialization, especially the increased inequality of wealth, were most visible. That means that the prob-lems of cities became the problems of America.

THE ELECTRICAL GRID AND IMPROVEMENTS IN TRANSPORTATION

One of the reasons that later industrialization progressed at such a greater pace than before was the improvement in power sources. The early Industrial Revolution depended upon steam engines and waterpower. The earliest engines were large and prohibitively expen-sive for all but the largest firms. Water wheels were a possibility for smaller concerns, but they could not perform nearly as much work as later power sources could. Between 1869 and 1929, total available horsepower in the United States increased from 2.3 million to 43 million units. In factories, the greatest part of that growth came from a huge increase in the use of electricity.[5]

Although factories had grown larger and more efficient over the entire 19th century, they grew particularly large after 1880, as the power to run them became cheaper, cleaner, and more convenient to acquire. Starting in the late 1870s, Thomas Edison turned the at-tention of his extensive laboratory towards harnessing electricity to create affordable elec-tric light. This achievement depended not only upon the creation of an efficient, inex-pensive, incandescent light bulb, but also on the creation of an electrical system to power it—everything from generators, to electrical wires, to switches. Without a precedent for any of these things, the Edison Electric Company and many related subsidiaries (later gathered together under the umbrella of General Electric) had to manufacture just about every-thing to make the grid operate. "Since capital is timid, I will raise and supply it," explained Edison to one of his investors. "The issue is factories or death!"[6] Other companies soon fol-lowed, because creating the central stations and the grid that eventually powered just about everything was so obviously lucrative.

Symbolizing the importance of capital to Edison's efforts, the first person to have his home successfully wired for electricity was the banker J. P. Morgan, in 1882. Despite setbacks, his experience with electric light encouraged him to invest further in Edison's efforts. Edison built the first central generating station in New York City later that same year. The first area of Manhattan that Edison wired was a neighborhood filled with the homes and workplaces of those who operated the financial institutions he hoped to convince to invest in his enterprises, as well as two major newspapers that would publicize his achievements. By 1902, there were 2,250 electrical generating stations in the United States. By 1920, that number grew to just short of 4,000.[7] Electricity spread from large cities to small cities and eventually out into rural areas by the 1920s.

This kind of growth required substantial improvement beyond Edison's initial vision of an electrical system. The effects of a reliable electric grid on the cities where it first appeared were numerous, ranging from less coal smoke in the air to new sounds produced by various electrical creations—everything from streetcars to arc lights. Early arc lights were so bright people thought they could stop crime and vice by exposing the people who perpetrated these crimes. In smaller cities, obtaining electric light was a sign of modernization, which implied future growth. Modern light in urban workplaces made office work easier by lessening strain on the eyes. As electric light companies moved in, the much-hated urban gas companies lost a considerable amount of economic power. Since people preferred electric light to gas, it became increasingly popular, as the grid expanded and the costs dropped. Electric light even changed the way people lived inside their houses. For example, children could now be trusted to put themselves to bed since there was no longer a fire risk from the open flames that were once needed to get to bed in the dark.

Nevertheless, the growing electrical grid created new urban dangers. High voltage electrical wires strung above ground joined other wires from telephones, telegraphs—even stock tickers—posed a new urban "wire menace." Many came down in bad weather. They were a hazard for electric company employees and pedestrians alike. "The overhead system is a standing menace to health and life," reported one medical journal in 1888.[8] In 1889, a fire caused by overheated electrical wires ignited a building full of dry goods and burned down much of downtown Boston.

The most noteworthy effect of high-quality, affordable lighting was the widespread practice of running factories twenty-four hours a day—which made them much more productive without any improvements in the technology of production. Replacing putrid gas lamps also made the smell of factories better for the workmen who worked there. As the electrical grid became more reliable, electric motors gradually began to replace steam engines as the source of power in manufacturing. Using small electric motors as a source of power freed factories from having to be located near water sources to feed boilers and made it possible for them to be smaller too.

Between 1880 and 1900, factories tended to adopt electric lighting but kept using earlier sources of power for their operation. Electric power for factory operations came quickly between 1900 and 1930. Both these developments (along with the large supply of immigrant workers) contributed to the industrialization of cities. The electrification of industrial facilities of all kinds proceeded quickly during the first two decades of the 20th century. Businesses got wired for electricity much faster than cities because they could make the most use of what started out as a relatively expensive service.

Because factories were concentrated in or near cities, it was a lot cheaper to wire them than it was to wire farms or even smaller cities away from electrical generating stations. Many of the new factories built during this later period appeared outside city limits, another new development. Electrification allowed managers to automate jobs once done by hand labor, thereby eliminating inefficiency, gaining greater control over the production process, and boosting overall productivity. New devices like time clocks and even new modes of production like the assembly line also depended upon electric power.

The advent of cheap and readily available electricity had a particularly important effect upon the physical layout of American cities during this period. Frank Sprague, an electrical engineer who had once worked for Thomas Edison, designed the first electric streetcar system for Richmond, Virginia, in 1888. Such systems supplanted horse-drawn carriages, making it possible for people to travel further and faster than they would have otherwise. This gave rise to a burst of suburbanization, a spate of new towns on the outskirts of American cities where wealthy and middle-class people could move to escape from the difficulties of modern urban life but still be close enough to enjoy many of its advantages.

The new suburbanites often traveled to and from work via new electric streetcars. The electrical equipment manufacturer Westinghouse was one of the major manufacturers of vehicles powered by an overhead wire. Electric streetcars had the advantage over horses of not leaving manure or of dying in the streets. Streetcars were more popular during weekends than during the week as working class people took advantage of low fares to explore new neighborhoods or to visit amusement parks, like Coney Island, generally built at the end of these lines.

In the same way that employers and city planners depended upon streetcars to move people, manufacturers became more dependent upon railroads, after 1880, to move their finished products. Railroad track mileage grew greatly after the Civil War, connecting cities and leading to the growth of new factories in places that were convenient to the necessary resources to make marketable goods. Eventually, mass distribution was a prerequisite to benefit from all that increased productivity. For all these reasons, separating the causes and effects of industrialization and urbanization is practically impossible.

Throughout the 19th century, factories usually had to be built near shipping ports or railroad stops because these were the easiest way to get factory products out to markets around the world. As more railroad tracks were built late in the 19th century, it became easier to locate factories outside of downtowns. Streetcars helped fill up the empty space downtown where factories would have gone. They made it easier to live further away from work and still commute to the heart of downtown, thereby making it possible for other kinds of businesses to locate there. One example would be the large urban department store, a phenomenon that predates 1880, but grew into its own after that date. Such stores like Wanamaker's in Philadelphia or Marshall Field's in Chicago bought the products of industrialization in bulk and sold them at a discounted price to workers who may have had trouble getting access to them any other way.

STRUCTURAL STEEL AND SKYSCRAPERS

While retail emporiums could be blocks long and only a few stories tall, other businesses rented space in thinner buildings built much higher. By the late 1880s, structures that had once been built with iron began to be built with a structural steel—a new, stronger kind of steel. The practice had begun in Chicago, championed by the architect Louis Sullivan, who designed the first skyscrapers there. A skyscraper, Sullivan wrote, "must be every inch a tall and soaring thing, rising in sheer exultation that from bottom to top it is a unit without a single dissenting line."[9] That kind of design required a skeleton of structural steel upon which other substances like brick or granite could hang. Even then, such skyscrapers had to be tapered; otherwise, the weight from the top floors could make the whole structure collapse.

Creating structural steel for skyscrapers required entirely different production methods than had been required to make Bessemer steel (which had been used primarily for railroad rails). Quantity and speed were the main requirements of producing Bessemer steel. Structural steel required a more carefully made product. The demands of structural steel encouraged steelmakers like Andrew Carnegie to redesign entire factories, most notably replacing older Bessemer converters with the open-hearth process. This new kind of steelmaking not only produced higher quality steel, it also required fewer skilled workers. This encouraged Carnegie's company to lock out its union workforce at Homestead, Pennsylvania, in 1892, so that it could save money by employing cheap replacement workers.

The other innovation that made skyscrapers possible was the electric elevator. Elisha Graves Otis designed the first reliable elevator in 1857. With electric power, it became possible to rise sixty stories in a matter of seconds. Before the elevator, rental spaces in commercial buildings cost more on lower floors because people didn't want to have to walk up stairs to get to the top. With elevators, tenants willingly paid a premium in order to get better views out their windows. Without elevators, nobody would have bothered to erect a building taller than five stories.[10]

The construction of skyscrapers was itself a terrific example of the industrial age coordination of labor and materials distribution. Steel skeletons meant that the unornamented higher sections of a building could be worked on even before the inevitable elaborate ornamental fringes on the lower part of the building were finished. This saved both time and money. When New York got so crowded that there was no space to store raw materials, the appearance of those materials would be carefully choreographed, and they would be taken directly off of flatbed trucks and placed in

their exact positions near the tops of new buildings. Around the turn of the 20th century, a major skyscraper could be built in as little as one year. The faster a building could be built, the faster an owner could collect rents and begin to earn back construction expenses.

The great benefit of skyscrapers was the ability to compress economic activity into smaller areas. "The skyscraper," explained one New Yorker in 1897, "gathers into a single edifice an extraordinary number of activities, which otherwise would be widely separated. Each building is an almost complete city, often comprising within its walls, banks and insurance offices, post office and telegraph office, business exchanges restaurants, clubrooms and shops." These same miniature cities also included numerous retail outlets, where the products of industrialized manufacturing could be purchased.[11] Shorter distances between these locations accelerated the pace of economic activity, which promoted further economic growth. However, large projects (like the many skyscrapers associated with the building of New York's Grand Central Station) eliminated or at least obscured urban industrial areas.

Unburdened by the need to pay federal income tax, industrial titans from across the United States displayed their massive wealth by building lavish mansions along New York's Fifth Avenue during the 1890s. By the 1920s, the value of land in Manhattan grew so fast because of its possible use for skyscrapers that second generation industrial families sold their mansions, since they no longer wanted to pay huge property taxes on them. Blocks of what was known as "Vanderbilt Alley," named after the children of the steamship and railroad pioneer who had built mansions in the same area, were replaced by skyscrapers and high-end retail emporiums.

The same basic principles of skyscraper production—build it quick and large, and pack it with people—motivated the way that builders produced other kinds of urban domiciles.

"Today, three-fourths of [New York City's] people live in the tenements," wrote the reformer Jacob Riis in his 1890 classic, *How the Other Half Lives*, "and the 19th-century drift of the population to the cities is sending ever-increasing multitudes to crowd them."[12] The best-known tenement house design of this period was the dumbbell tenement of about five or six stories tall. They came about as the result of a design contest, but were generally so crowded that they did more harm than good to the people who lived in them. Four families might live on a single floor with only two bathrooms between them. Designed to let light and air into central courtyards (which explains why they were shaped like a dumbbell from above), stacked up back-to-back, one against the other they did neither. Widely copied, New York City actually outlawed this design for new buildings in 1901—but the old structures remained.

Apartment houses made it easier to pack people into small urban areas and therefore live closer to where they worked. Wealthy people could buy space and separation from one's neighbors, while those middle class people who could not afford to live in suburbs lost the space they had before urbanization accelerated. To counter these unequal tendencies, New Yorkers developed the idea of the cooperative, where many people bought a single building and managed it themselves. Lavish apartments became alternatives for mansions once Manhattan real estate became too expensive for all except those with huge fortunes.

THE ASSEMBLY LINE

The farther away that people lived from central business districts, the more they needed efficient transportation. Streetcars helped, to an extent, but passenger lines that centered on downtown neighborhoods left large areas that could be occupied with housing for a growing working population, provided that these residents had their own way to get around. "I will build a car for the great multitude," declared Henry Ford in 1908. "[I]t will be so low in price that no man making a good salary will be unable to own one."[13] That car was the Model T, and it revolutionized both auto-making and the American landscape. It also revolutionized the entire concept of American production. Ford didn't worry about whether his cars would have a market. He would make a market for his cars by producing them so cheaply that nearly every American could afford one.

Ford could achieve both quality and a low price at scale because of the assembly line. This particular conceptual breakthrough owed much to the "disassembly lines" that had been pioneered in the meatpacking industry during the previous century. In the same way that a single carcass was picked apart by men with specialized jobs as it moved along a line, mounted upon a hook, Ford arranged his new factory at Highland Park so that men with highly specialized assignments could build an automobile much faster than before. The assembly line moved work to the men rather than forcing men to move to the work, thereby saving valuable time and energy. It also extended the concept of the division of labor to its logical extreme so that workers would only perform one function in a much larger assembly process all day, every day. The applicability of these principles to the manufacturing of just about everything is what made Ford such an important figure in the history of industrialization. Mass production became possible for all kinds of things that had once seemed far removed from the automobile.

Ford built Model Ts at three different facilities over the entire history of that vehicle. He improved his production methods over time (which included introducing and improving upon the assembly line) so that he could produce them more cheaply and efficiently. Efficiency depended on speed, and speed depended upon the exact place in the factory where those machines were placed. Because Ford made only one car, he could employ single-purpose machine tools of extraordinarily high quality. The company also used lots of other automated manufacturing equipment, like gravity slides and conveyors, to get parts of the car from one place to another in its increasingly large, increasingly mechanized factories.

Because the assembly line moved the work to the men rather than the men to the work, the company could control the speed of the entire operation. Like earlier manufacturers, Ford depended upon standardized, identical parts to produce more cars for less, but the assembly line also made it possible to conserve labor—not by mechanizing jobs that had once been done by hand, but by mechanizing work processes and paying employees just to feed and tend to those machines. This was not fun work to do. "The chain system you have is a slave driver!" wrote an anonymous housewife based on her husband's experience working on the assembly line. "My God! Mr. Ford. My husband has come home and thrown himself down and won't eat his supper—so done out! Can't it be remedied?"[14] Ford instituted an unprecedented wage of $5/day to keep workers on his assembly line, but this reward did not make the work any easier.

Before Ford came along, cars were boutique goods that only rich people could afford to operate. After Ford introduced the assembly line (actually a series of assembly lines for every part of the car), labor productivity improved to such a degree that mass production became possible. Perhaps more important than mass production was mass consumption, since continual productivity improvements meant that Ford could lower the price of the Model T every year, while simultaneously making small but significant changes that steadily improved the quality of the car. Mass production eliminated choice, since Ford produced no other car, but Ford built variations of the Model T, like the runabout with the same chassis, and owners retro-fitted their Model Ts for everything from camping to farming.

The increased number of automobiles on city streets further congested already congested downtown areas. Streetcars got blocked. Pedestrians died in gruesome traffic accidents. One of the basic requirements of having so many new cars on the roads was to improve the quality and quantity of roads. Local city planners tended to attack such problems on a case-by-case basis, laying pavement on well-traveled roads and widening them when appropriate. New traffic rules, such as the first one-way streets, appeared in an effort to alleviate these kinds of problems. Traffic control towers and traffic lights—the mechanical solution to a problem inspired by industrialization—also appeared for the first time during this era.

Cities grew when industries grew during this era. Since people had to live near where they worked (and few people lived in skyscrapers), many builders built out into undeveloped areas. If a city had annexed much of the land around it previous to these economic expansions (like Detroit), those areas became parts of a larger city. If they hadn't, much of this growth occurred in new suburbs (like Philadelphia). Chicago was so confident of further growth during this period that it built streetcar lines into vacant fields. To meet rising demand for housing, homebuilders applied industrial principles to building—using standardized parts that were themselves the result of mass production techniques. By the 1920s, buying pre-cut mail order houses became big business.

THE ORIGINS OF MASS PRODUCTION

After 1880, mechanization made factories even more productive thanks to technological improvements. This can be traced back to Thomas Edison's labs in New Jersey, where he practiced systematic invention to exploit the great commercial opportunities that modern life created. The electrical and chemical industries formed the vanguard for the blending of science and the useful arts during this era. By the 1920s, engineers had been formally integrated into the management hierarchies of countless American industries.

Reorganization of production merged with technological improvement had made mass production possible long before Ford developed the assembly line. James Bonsack's cigarette rolling machine, for example, patented in 1881, could produce 70,000 cigarettes in a single ten-hour day. By the end of that decade, it could produce 120,000 cigarettes in a day.[15] When James "Buck" Duke bought exclusive rights to this machine in 1885, it became the basis of his American Tobacco Company, which quickly controlled most of the industry.

By the 1920s, mass production had arrived in industries that produced goods that were much more expensive than cigarettes. Ford's principles of mass production spread quickly throughout the manufacturing sector, to products of all kinds, because Henry Ford was so open about the way he designed his factories. Among the other manufacturers that used Fordist principles during the 1920s were the makers of home appliances, like refrigerators and radios. General Electric, for example, built an eighteen million dollar assembly line for its Monitor Top refrigerator and sold a million refrigerators just four years after its introduction in 1927.[16]

Even craft-dominated industries like furniture making came to depend upon mass production to make their products more available to the masses. People who moved from farms to cities desperately needed furniture for their new urban residences, but in industrial towns like Grand Rapids, Michigan, they could not afford pieces made by craftsmen. New mass-produced models made with minimal carving and overlays, based on stylish patterns, found a market all over the country. It helped that companies like Bassett, founded in Virginia in 1902, discouraged their workers from forming unions, just like Ford did. An unorganized workforce made it easier for industrialists to impose changes in the production process without resistance from employees.

The changeover from the Model T to the Model A, in 1927, demonstrated the limits of industrialized mass production. The Model A was incredibly expensive, and Ford had to shut his main plant for months to retool the production line for his new models. While the new car sold well initially, sales dropped precipitously as the Depression deepened. "Mass production is not simply large-scale production," wrote the department store magnate Edward Filene, in 1932. "It is large-scale production based upon a clear understanding that increased production demands increased buying."[17] Mass buying became difficult when people had little money with which to buy the products of industrialization. Urban building slowed precipitously during the Depression too. Since cities were the focal points of industrialization, urban citizens suffered disproportionately when production waned. Of course, when the United States sank into the economic downturn of the Great Depression, both urban and industrial growth decreased sharply.

DISCUSSION OF THE LITERATURE

It is difficult to cite previous scholarship on either industrialization or urbanization from precisely the 1880–1930 period because both these trends pre- and post-date this period. Equally importantly, both are so broad, in the sense that they encompass all kinds of industries and locations that they include a huge range of books and other sources. While none of the following suggestions are exact fits for these subjects during this time, they are all worth reading because they cast at least some light on industrialization and urbanization during this particular time period.

David Hounshell's *From the American System to Mass Production* is simply the best comprehensive history of industrialization available. It covers a few very important industries in detail (like automobile manufacturing), but it is at its best when dealing with the similarities in production technologies from industry to industry. My own *Industrialization and the Transformation of American Life* is a simplified introduction to these principles and a summary of their effects on many aspects of American history during this period, including urbanization.[18]

A number of excellent studies of important industries during this period show how industrialization progressed in some detail. Thomas Misa's *Nation of Steel* is the definitive work on the technology of that essential industry. Ron Chernow's *Titan*, a biography of John D. Rockefeller Sr. will teach you everything you want to know about the oil industry during this period. Richard R. John's *Network Nation* describes the intricacies of the telegraph and telephone industries. My own *Refrigeration Nation* is a close study of the American ice and refrigeration industries.[19]

Sam Bass Warner Jr.'s *The Urban Wilderness*, an important history of urbanization throughout the United States, includes discussion of many problems unique to this time period. The best works of urban history published since then tend to deal with particular cities or with the relationship between cities and surrounding suburban communities. Warner's *Streetcar Suburbs*, for example, covers the growth of Boston throughout the 19th century. Donald L. Miller's *Supreme City* masterfully handles New York during the 1920s (and before, in order to set context). Miller's *City of the Century* offers a similarly thorough treatment of Chicago during the 1890s. Perhaps the most-beloved work of urban history that covers cities around the country is Kenneth Jackson's *Crabgrass Frontier*, which takes in both the growth of suburbia and the cities they surround throughout American history, but paying special attention to the years covered in this article. *Building Suburbia* by Dolores Hayden is a detailed work that covers a similar subject over the same time period. William Cronon's *Nature's Metropolis: Chicago and the Great West* is the classic explanation of the relationship between the fastest-growing city of the late 19th century and all the natural resources that surrounded it.[20]

The turn toward social history among historians since the 1960s has made studies of broad economic forces increasingly uncommon. Early labor history, for example, was often written by economists. Therefore, it showed a tendency toward looking at the effects of technological change upon workers. Early sociologists who practiced during this period used to do fieldwork in the cities where their universities were located. While a return to this kind of study seems unlikely, more attempts to study the broader economic forces that made social change happen would likely be appreciated by scholars working in multiple disciplines.

PRIMARY SOURCES AND DIGITAL MATERIALS

The best place to start any study of the 1880–1930 period is to look at the published literature during that time. Luckily, because any book or magazine published before 1923 is in the public domain, people searching in the United States can find primary sources on just about any topic by searching on Google Books (https://books.google.com/), with their Advanced Book Search. Be sure to check the box that says "Full View Only" and narrow the publication date range to the exact years in which you are interested. A broad search will bury you in relevant material, so you may have to do a lot of reading before you find hits that match your topic exactly.

With respect to industrialization, trade journals, like *Iron Age* or *Electrical World*, are particular helpful for understanding the exact technological changes that took place during these years. Many such periodicals are available in full on Google Books, but to find articles on a particular topic can require enough patience to search inside the bound volumes of those journals one year at a time. Nevertheless, the fact that, only a few short years ago, one had to travel to a major research library in order to read them at all, demonstrates the wonders of digitization.

Chronicling America (http://chronicling america.loc.gov/), the online repository of the Library of Congress for digitized American newspapers is a particularly important resource for studying urban history during this era. Begin with their Advanced Search (http://chroniclingamerica.loc.gov/#tab=tab _advanced_search) tab, and you can limit the results to papers from the state or city of your choice. While they currently have few papers from a city as big as Chicago, they are strong on papers from New York City and Washington, DC. Anyone interested in urban history might consider perusing the digital collections of the New York Public Library before a trip there to see what isn't available online. Among the online collections focusing on urban living are *"Classic Six:" New York City Apartment Building Living, 1880s–1910s* and *Photographic Negatives of the New York City Tenement House Department, 1902–1914.*

The Encyclopedia of Chicago presents considerable materials from the online archives of the Chicago History Museum, and the *Coolidge Era and the Consumer Economy: 1921–1929* is available online from the the Chicago Historical Society.

The excellent online resources of the Library of Congress include a collection of Panoramic Maps (https://www.loc.gov/col lection/panoramic-maps/about-this-collec tion/) of cities and towns of the late 19th and early 20th centuries.Two of the best business history archives in the United States are the Hagley Museum and Library in Wilmington, Delaware, and the Baker Library of the Harvard Business School. Search these excellent online resources at Hagley Digital Exhibits and at the Harvard Library Digital Collections.

American businesses, including those that go as far back as this period, tend to restrict access to their archives by outsiders for legal reasons. Even if you can see materials that no historian has seen before, there is a good chance that these materials will not be processed, which will make using them much

harder. Therefore, many studies of industrialization on the ground during this era center on the few large companies whose records are available. These include the McCormick-International Harvester Collection (http://www.wisconsinhistory.org/Content .aspx?dsNav=N:1167) curated by the State Historical Society of Wisconsin, or the Colorado Fuel and Iron Company (http://steelworkscenter.com/) archives of the Steelworks Center of the West, Pueblo, Colorado.

FURTHER READING

Braverman, Harry. *Labor and Monopoly Capitalism: The Degradation of Work in the Twentieth Century.* New York: Monthly Review Press, 1998.

Chandler, Alfred D., Jr. *The Visible Hand: The Managerial Revolution in American Business.* Cambridge, MA: Harvard University Press, 1977.

Cronon, William. *Nature's Metropolis: Chicago and the Great West.* New York: W. W. Norton, 1991.

Hayden, Dolores. *Building Suburbia: Green Fields and Urban Growth, 1820–2000.* New York: Random House, 2003.

Hays, Samuel P. *The Response to Industrialism 1885–1914.* 2d ed. Chicago: University of Chicago Press, 1995.

Hounshell, David A. *From the American System to Mass Production, 1800–1932.* Baltimore: Johns Hopkins University Press, 1984.

Jackson, Kenneth T. *Crabgrass Frontier: The Suburbanization of the United States.* New York: Oxford University Press, 1985.

Jonnes, Jill. *Empires of Light: Edison, Westinghouse, and the Race to Electrify the World.* New York: Random House, 2003.

Misa, Thomas J. *A Nation of Steel: The Making of Modern America 1865–1925.* Baltimore: Johns Hopkins University Press, 1995.

Noble, David F. *America by Design: Science, Technology, and the Rise of Corporate Capitalism.* New York: Alfred A. Knopf, 1977.

Nye, David. *Electrifying America: Social Meaning of a New Technology, 1880–1940.* Cambridge: MIT Press, 1990.

Porter, Glenn. *The Rise of Big Business 1860–1920.* Wheeling, IL: Harlan Davidson, 1992.

Rees, Jonathan. *Industrialization and the Transformation of American Life: A Brief Introduction.* Armonk, NY: M. E. Sharpe, 2013.

Warner, Sam Bass, Jr. *The Urban Wilderness: A History of the American City.* New York: Harper & Row, 1972.

NOTES

1. Chester W. Wright, *Economic History of the United States* (New York: McGraw Hill, 1941), 707.
2. Jonathan Rees, *Industrialization and the Transformation of American* Life (Armonk, NY: M. E. Sharpe, 2013), 44.
3. On regional differences see Sam Bass Warner Jr., *The Urban Wilderness: A History of the American City* (New York: Harper & Row, 1972), 87–88.
4. Thomas J. Misa, *A Nation of Steel: The Making of Modern America, 1865–1925* (Baltimore: Johns Hopkins University Press, 1995), 41.
5. Wright, *Economic History of the United States,* 668.
6. Jill Jonnes, *Empires of Light: Edison, Tesla, Westinghouse and the Race to Electrify the World* (New York: Random House, 2003), 76.
7. Ruth Schwartz Cowan, *A Social History of American Technology* (New York: Oxford University Press, 1997), 163.
8. Ernest Freeberg, *The Age of Edison: Electric Light and the Invention of Modern America* (New York: Penguin, 2013), 81.
9. Alice Sparberg Alexiou, *The Flatiron: The New York City Landmark and the Incomparable City that Arose with It* (New York: Thomas Dunne, 2010), 50.
10. Misa, *A Nation of Steel,* 85.
11. Rees, *Industrialization and the Transformation,* 53.
12. Jacob A. Riis, *How the Other Half Lives: Studies Among the Tenements of New York* (New York: Charles Scribner's, 1914), 2.
13. Steven Watts, *The People's Tycoon: Henry Ford and the American Century* (New York: Random House, 2005), 119.
14. David A. Hounshell, *From the American System to Mass Production, 1800–1932* (Baltimore: Johns Hopkins University Press, 1984), 259.
15. Alfred D. Chandler Jr., *The Visible Hand: The Managerial Revolution in American Business* (Cambridge, MA: Belknap, 1977), 249.
16. Ruth Schwartz Cowan, *More Work for Mother* (New York: Basic Books, 1983), 136–138.
17. Hounshell, *From the American System,* 307.
18. Hounshell, *From the American System to Mass Production;* and Rees, *Industrialization and the Transformation of American Life.*
19. See Misa, *A Nation of Steel;* Ron Chernow, *Titan* (New York: Vintage, 2004); Richard R. John's *Network Nation* (Cambridge, MA: Harvard, 2010); and Rees, *Refrigeration Nation* (Baltimore: Johns Hopkins University Press, 2103).
20. See Sam Bass Warner Jr.'s *The Urban Wilderness* (New York: Harper & Row, 1972); Warner's *Streetcar Suburbs* (Cambridge, MA: Harvard University Press, 1978); Donald L. Miller's *Supreme City* (New York: Simon & Schuster, 2014); Miller's *City of the Century: The Epic of Chicago and the Making of America* (Simon & Schuster, 1997); Kenneth Jackson, *Crabgrass Frontier: The Suburbanization of the United States* (New York: Oxford University Press, 1985); Dolores Hayden, *Building Suburbia: Green Fields and Urban Growth, 1820–2000* (New York: Random House, 2003); and William Cronon, *Nature's Metropolis: Chicago and the Great West* (New York: W. W. Norton, 1991).

Jonathan Rees

URBAN EXCEPTIONALISM IN THE AMERICAN SOUTH

EUROPEAN BEGINNINGS

If Spain had settled the American South, urbanization might have turned out differently, but Spanish colonists never sustained its urban settlements in North America, most notably St. Augustine, Florida, established in 1565. Spain preferred urban settlements for much the same reasons that the Pilgrims and the Puritans favored towns in the Massachusetts Bay Colony more than seven decades later: towns offered both protection and a concentration of population to further the religious ideals of the colonists from their respective countries. For the Spanish, the duty was to convert the natives, and for the English, the responsibility was to build cities upon hills, a heaven on earth to the greater glory of God. The impact of these objectives on the local native populations was less than heavenly and, in the case of New England, religious freedom extended only to the founding sects. Spain had a second act when, in 1762, it assumed control of New Orleans from France. That legacy lives on in the lovely architecture of the ironically named French Quarter, but it otherwise failed to establish a sustainable colony in Louisiana.

The English settlement at Jamestown had no such lofty objectives. The colony was a moneymaking enterprise from the beginning in 1607, or, more precisely, an *attempted* moneymaking enterprise because the first few years were disastrous. Learning tobacco cultivation from the native population, the English colonists quickly expanded their base beyond Jamestown in favor of plantations. Tobacco

was a labor-intensive crop, and this enterprise soon led to the importation of enslaved African and Caribbean labor, placing the trajectory of Virginia, and then the Carolinas, and eventually Georgia, on a different track from the Northern colonies.

This should not imply that the colonial North was an urban society and the colonial South luxuriated in a state of nature. English colonists throughout North America were primarily tillers of the soil. The difference was that Massachusetts farmers shipped their harvests to Boston, New Yorkers to New York City, and Pennsylvanians to Philadelphia, and so on down the Atlantic coast until Virginia interrupted the farm-to-urban-market pattern.

Blessed by the deep-flowing James and Rappahannock Rivers, Virginia planters loaded their money crop on ships directly bound for Europe. The colonial capital at Williamsburg was hardly a major entrepot for goods. The exceptions were Charleston and later Savannah

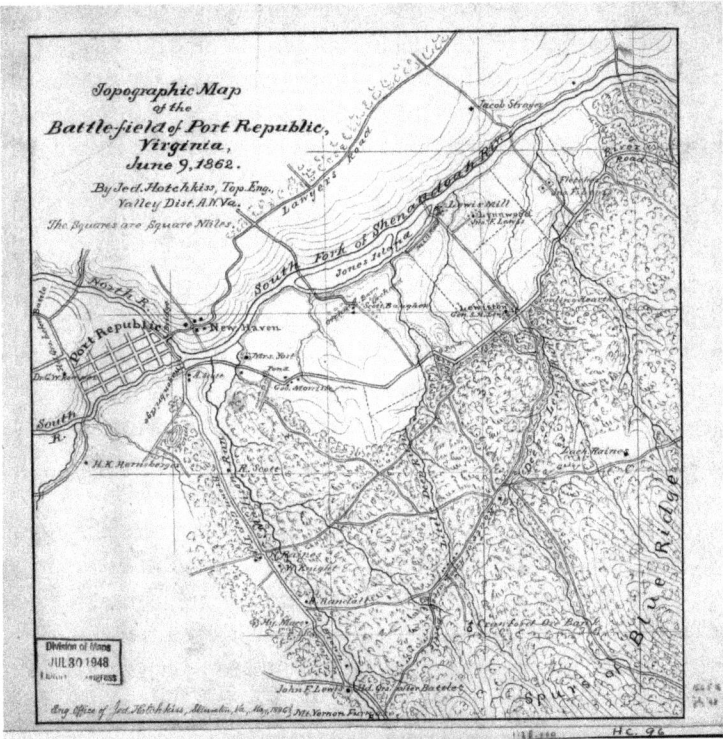

Figure 1. Small tobacco ports along rivers in Virginia, 1862.
Source: Courtesy of Library of Congress, Geography and Map Division, 99446761.

as Carolina planters frequently abandoned their farms for residences in these charming cities. The boundary between country and city became very permeable in the South, with significant political and economic consequences. The urban South from almost its inception was a creature of the planter grandees, and Southern cities assumed the culture of the countryside, from classical architecture to slavery to economic development. The industry of Charleston was rice, then cotton. While colonial Boston, New York, and Pennsylvania developed a diverse urban economy, Charleston, Savannah, and later Norfolk were handmaidens to cash crops: rice, cotton, or tobacco.[1]

THE ANTEBELLUM ERA

The staple crop trade proved lucrative for Southern city dwellers. By the early 19th century, a vibrant middle class of shopkeepers, artisans, and professionals emerged, just as in Northern cities. The dependence on agriculture and slavery in the South did not dampen urban entrepreneurs' enthusiasm for technology or industry. They advocated state subsidies for railroads, support for industries, and deepening rivers and harbors to accommodate larger vessels.

Urban boosters in Virginia were especially active in the decades prior to the Civil War. Richmond's Tredegar Iron Works rivaled similar firms in Northern cities. Both Richmond and Lynchburg sprouted tobacco manufacturing establishments, and Norfolk grew as a deepwater harbor. Elsewhere, in New Orleans, Savannah, and Charleston, a lively coastwise trade as well as international commerce lifted merchants in those cities into the wealthy class.[2]

For these reasons the debate over slavery became very personal for many antebellum Southern urban dwellers. The Southern urban economy hummed along on the foundation of slavery. Slave labor tilled the fields and harvested the crops transported to urban ports.

The institution of slavery also proved malleable in an urban environment. Enslaved people worked in the mines, tended blast furnaces in factories, stemmed tobacco, carted goods, loaded ships, maintained railroad equipment, and performed a range of semiskilled and skilled work in the urban economy.

Slavery underwent a mutation in the urban milieu that rendered it as flexible as free labor in Northern cities and connected the plantation version of the institution to its urban iteration. Southern plantation owners rented their enslaved workers to urban merchants, shipbuilders, and manufacturers, as well as to individual households for domestic work. The urban environment provided those enslaved with some latitude with respect to choice of residence, choice of companions, and even, on occasion, choice of their temporary masters. Frederick Douglass, for example, first tasted these freedoms when his master hired him out to a shipyard in Baltimore.[3]

As the Douglass example highlights, cities were not only places to become anonymous, but also to slip on ships or trains and head north. Southern states, especially in the decade prior to the Civil War, engaged in vigorous debates on how much latitude to give both free and enslaved blacks in the cities. Enslaved hires often ignored the laws and proceeded as usual, though in Charleston, a number of free blacks departed for the North during the late 1850s when restrictions became particularly onerous and the boundary between slave and free narrowed. Even so, urban slavery underscored that the institution was adaptable to a modern economy, a fact that rendered its imminent demise unlikely.

Although slave labor distinguished Southern from Northern cities before the Civil War, the influx of immigrant workers to the urban South mirrored immigration to Northern cities. Just as immigrants from Ireland and Germany crowded into Northern cities from the late 1840s to the Civil War, they made their way to the urban South as well, often stopping in Northern cities first. The rise of nativism in Northern cities found much less resonance in the urban South. The divisions in the South ran primarily along racial lines and, from the perspective of Southern urban employers, the immigrants provided a much-needed labor source in their growing economies, especially for dangerous work such as cutting through swamps to build railroads. Slaves were expensive; the Irish were expendable.[4]

As the sectional crisis worsened, white urban Southerners, like most other white Southerners, split on secession. To some degree, positions depended on individuals' connections to the national economy as opposed to the local or regional economies. The point is that there was no "urban" point of view on separation any more than there was unanimity in the countryside.

CIVIL WAR

Once the war's fury descended upon Southern cities, hardships for remaining residents— most men were off fighting—escalated. The disruption of Southern rail lines, the incursions of the invading Union armies, and the destruction of infrastructure resulted in Confederate-wide food shortages, ruinous inflation, and health crises. Women and children in the cities suffered most from these developments, especially after Confederate battlefield reverses in the summer of 1863.

Considering the weight of scholarship devoted to the Confederacy's military endeavors, it has been refreshing in recent years that the Southern home front has received increasing attention. Recent historians have highlighted not only the struggles of the urban population, but also the strides toward freedom initiated by the formerly enslaved. Cities such as New Orleans and Memphis were often spared the physical destruction that accompanied invasion, though civilians still suffered hardships. In contrast, most Northern urban residents scarcely felt what Union General William T. Sherman characterized as the "hard hand of war."[5]

THE NEW SOUTH

The war also upset traditional gender patterns in the urban South as women took over the nursing responsibilities in city hospitals, though not without remonstrance and resistance from some men. The memoirs of Kate Cumming of Mobile, Alabama, provide valuable insights into the dynamics of gender, service, and patriotism among Southern women during the Civil War. In the aftermath of the Confederate defeat, women in the cities formed memorial societies and initiated the landscape of memory. Occasionally, like Scarlett O'Hara in Gone with the Wind (1936 for the novel, 1939 for the movie), they applied themselves to business endeavors and projects in civic leadership where they could argue that urban improvements in education, prison and mental health reform, and child labor did not bend traditional gender roles, but rather complemented white Southern women's traditional role in the family. These efforts rarely crossed the color line.

The war's relatively light physical impact on the urban North portended a divergence of fates for cities in the North and in the South after the Civil War. For Southern cities such as Atlanta, Columbia, and Richmond, repair and reconstruction dominated the first years after 1865. For Southern cities relatively untouched physically by the war, such as New Orleans and Savannah, shortages in food and building materials, the presence of freed African Americans, many of whom left plantations for the urban South, and the patrols of Union soldiers disrupted normal prewar patterns of life in ways that were unknown to Northern urban residents.

For the freedmen, Southern cities meant jobs and an escape from the persistent oppressions of farms and plantations. Despite the end of slavery, rural life did not change drastically for formerly enslaved African Americans. The prospect and promise of cities drew black migration. The influx of African Americans into the urban South created tensions that

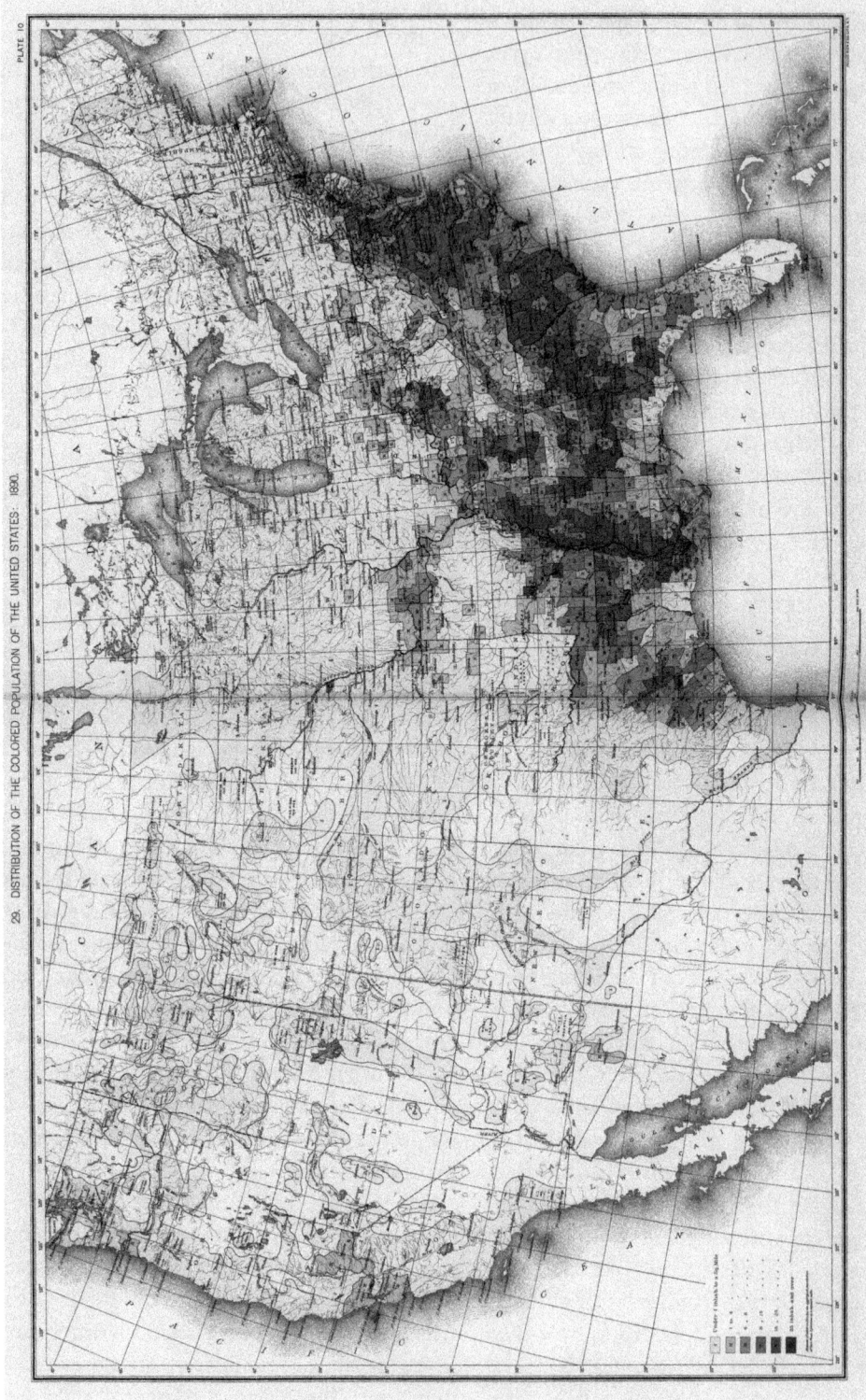

Figure 2. "Distribution of the colored population of the United States." United States Census Office, 1890.

Source: Courtesy of Library of Congress, Geography and Map Division, 07019233.

occasionally flared into violence, often because of political conflicts. White city residents were unprepared for the assertion of black civil rights with respect to voting, residence, employment, and education. These conflicts rarely appeared in Northern cities for the simple reason that, in the 1870s, more than 90 percent of the nation's African American population resided in the South. Unlike the urban North, Southern cities became biracial contested zones.

Although racial residential segregation was relatively mild—most Southern cities evinced a checkerboard pattern of racial sentiment—other aspects of urban racial life hardened in the last decades of the 19th century. The white backlash resulted from the proximity of African Americans in Southern cities and especially from the visible success of some black Southerners in building their own neighborhoods, businesses, and professional careers. These advances belied the alleged racial inferiority of African Americans. Segregation, disenfranchisement, and the increase in lynchings in the 1890s reflected the vicious white response to this contradiction, and not only in cities.

Formal racial separation—segregation by law—became commonplace in the urban South by 1910. Some of the separation resulted from technological innovations, an example of how modernization not only left white supremacy intact, but actually strengthened it. Elevators, electric trolleys, and buses threw urban residents together physically, regardless of class or color. Segregation by law emerged as a mechanism not only to sort racial categories, but also to emphasize the superiority of the white race.

Facilities were rarely equal, regardless of the Supreme Court ruling in *Plessy v. Ferguson* (1896) mandating that equality. And, in many cases, the law simply excluded black urban residents from parks, restaurants, hotels, and other public facilities. Slavery may have provided the paradigm for white supremacy before the Civil War, but racial segregation, particularly in the urban South, characterized the new and old racial order of the New South.

Segregation and discrimination existed in Northern cities as well, but, again, the relatively small black population prior to 1900 allowed African Americans to work the interstices of racial separation. The rigidity of the law in the urban South allowed for little leeway as the feeling grew that any chink in the armor of white supremacy would result in its ultimate collapse.

Still, some African Americans carved out successful lives in the urban South. The advance of the black middle class primarily serving a black clientele reflected one such avenue of upward mobility. Firms such as the North Carolina Mutual Life Insurance Company of Durham, North Carolina, took advantage of the reluctance of white companies to ensure African American residents. Also, black urban churches emerged as community institutions in addition to their primary religious functions. African American preachers often became community leaders, and churches doubled as schools, provided social services, and generally filled some of the gap between need and the unwillingness of local white-dominated governments to fund services for black neighborhoods and its residents.[6]

Middle-class African American women played expanded roles in the Jim Crow era, battling against discrimination. While black men had to tread lightly in their protests against white supremacy, African American women could be more forceful, using their social clubs to oppose racial separation while simultaneously helping less fortunate black women and children. In 1896, Mary Church Terrell of Washington, DC, founded the National Association of Colored Women, adopting the slogan "Lifting as We Climb" to inspire women across the urban South.[7]

Black teachers, many of whom were women, made the best of segregated education in Southern cities by quietly replacing the Confederate school curriculum in favor of a broader, more positive instruction. Mamie Garvin Fields taught in the segregated schools of Charlotte and Charleston during the early 20th century and recalled teaching her students "America the Beautiful" and the Pledge of Allegiance. "My school," she asserted, "was in the United States, after all, and not the Confederacy."[8]

These were measurable, though modest achievements against significant odds in the urban South. The "Atlanta Compromise," articulated by black leader Booker T. Washington at the 1895 Atlanta Exposition, capitulated to Jim Crow with the understanding that white Southerners would reciprocate by treating African Americans fairly in education and employment at the vocational level. Though it may have been the only bargain a black leader could strike in that era, it counted on white participation that never materialized. Southern cities had evolved into two separate and unequal racial spheres.

The Great Migration extracted millions of African Americans from the South to Northern cities. Typically, black families employed a staged migration where they first traveled and lived in the urban South before embarking on the big journey to the North or West. In this manner, they became accustomed to urban life and secured additional funds to assist them in setting up households in their new environments.[9]

As Southern cities modernized during the first half of the 20th century, they came to resemble more closely the residential segregation of Northern cities. The sorting out process created pockets of white privilege such as Buckhead and Druid Hills in Atlanta, and Myers Park in Charlotte. These "suburbs" mimicked the exclusiveness of similar enclaves outside the city centers of Northern cities, though the rigidity of racial segregation and exclusion in all other aspects of Southern urban life continued to separate experiences in the North and South.

The Southern urban economy provided another lingering distinction between the regions. The connections between urbanization and industrialization were more tenuous in Southern cities than in the urban North. The rapid expansion of textile manufacturing in the Southern Piedmont between the 1880s and 1920s occurred primarily in smaller communities, though major cities such as Charlotte and Atlanta benefited from the financial institutions that serviced these mills.

Aside from Birmingham, where discriminatory freight and borrowing rates hampered its steel industry, few Southern cities engaged in heavy manufacturing. The processing of crops—cotton into textiles, tobacco into cigars and cigarettes, and timber into furniture—remained the staple of Southern urban manufacturing, particularly in the Piedmont region stretching from central Virginia, through the Carolinas, Georgia, and ending at the base of the Appalachian chain in Birmingham. These activities did not create great cities or a middle-class workforce. Wages remained relatively low and skill levels required only a high school education, if that. In other words, these were not economic activities that built vibrant cities to attract capital and educated workers.

In this profile, the Southern city resembled the South at large during the first half of the 20th century: a region lumbering behind the dynamic industrial trends of the rest of the country and saddled with low-wage enterprises that did little to enhance the education or skills of the population. The great wave of immigration that washed over America in the early 20th century barely touched the South for this reason: the opportunities lay in the cities of the North and West. In the 1850s, roughly 40 percent of the white workforce in Richmond was foreign born. By the 1920s, less than 2 percent of the nation's immigrants resided in the South. Southern cities relied on migration from the countryside, both white and black, with a sizable portion of the African American population absconding to the North when they got the chance.[10]

CIVIL RIGHTS

World War II proved a bonanza for the urban South. Southern Democrats chaired key congressional committees and steered billions of dollars of defense contracts to Southern cities. Charleston received so much federal largesse that many in Washington quipped that the city might sink under all that hardware. New Orleans became a center for shipbuilding and Marietta, Georgia (an Atlanta suburb), and Dallas, Texas, served as production centers for the B-29 bombers.

The federal government not only funded war materiel, but also built the infrastructures that Northern cities had to pay for via their own bonds or tax revenues in earlier decades. Roads, sewer and water systems, and housing closed some of the gap between North and South concerning the basic amenities of urban life.

And this is when the stars began to align to dismantle white supremacy in the South, at least in its legal form. The spike in urban development whetted the appetites of Southern urban entrepreneurs for more. The postwar era was unfolding as an economic cornucopia and urban Southerners wanted to participate. Mechanization on the farm and employment opportunities in the cities promised greater consumer purchasing power to fuel economic growth. Initially, many white urban leaders believed they could sustain and extend prosperity while maintaining white supremacy, in compliance with regional culture.[11]

African Americans did not allow that to happen. The civil rights movement blossomed in Southern cities following World War II. That was natural considering the structure of white supremacy, particularly segregation and exclusion, attained its legal and proscriptive foundations in the urban South. The Montgomery bus boycott of 1955 reflected the centrality of cities in the movement. Public transportation was primarily an urban phenomenon and a flashpoint of resentment and humiliation for the black community.

African American exclusion from the basic services white citizens enjoyed in Southern cities, such as decent schools and facilities and access to public places like restaurants and parks, ultimately bred resistance. Sit-ins, usually orchestrated by black and white students in the urban South, emerged in the mid-1950s but did not spread throughout the region until four black young men from North Carolina A&T College (now University) in Greensboro sat down at a Woolworth's lunch counter in February 1960.

By that time, white urban leaders had seen the economic and public relations fallout from white intransigence to school desegregation in Little Rock and New Orleans. Racial unrest threatened postwar visions of prosperity and progress. It became apparent that the latter attributes could not exist within a system of white supremacy. Moreover, the competition between the United States and the Soviet Union in the Cold War could not abide a system of white supremacy to vitiate the American message of freedom and justice for all. So, from both the Southern urban perspective and national objectives, a solution was necessary.[12]

Some cities such as Charlotte, Nashville, and Atlanta abandoned public segregation by the early 1960s. The violence in Birmingham in the spring of 1963, however, when Martin Luther King Jr. led demonstrators in a drive to desegregate downtown facilities, proved a turning point to push the rest of the urban South toward a racial accommodation. And it inspired Washington to pass the Civil Rights Act of 1964 which, among other provisions, outlawed discrimination in public accommodations.

Voting rights remained as the last major pillar of white supremacy. Denial of voting rights for African Americans was particularly egregious in the rural Deep South, but registrars practiced exclusion in Southern cities as well. While there were examples of African Americans holding an occasional city council seat after World War II, that was rare until the passage of the Voting Rights Act of 1965.

City governments now could no longer ignore the demands of African American constituents for paved roads, upgrades in sewer and water facilities, park and recreation maintenance, and strict enforcement of building codes. Nor could employers systematically discriminate against black applicants who now had recourse to provisions of the Civil Rights Act.

By the 1970s, Southern urban school districts were, on average, more desegregated than those in Northern cities. Progressive urban administrations cropped up all over the South dedicated to economic development and racial equity, the latter exemplified by the presence of African Americans in city governments.

THE SUNBELT

These transformations moved the urban South to a more generic and positive image as part of the "Sunbelt," an amorphous region that stretched from the South to the Far West. The moderation of Southern politics as exemplified by Georgia's Jimmy Carter, Arkansas's Bill Clinton, and Florida's Reubin Askew heralded the ascendancy of a gentler, more urbane, and more cosmopolitan region. The South appeared to be following political scientist V. O. Key Jr.'s prediction in 1949 that "The growth of cities contains the seeds of political change for the South."[13]

Indeed, Sunbelt cities in the West and Southwest shared numerous characteristics between 1960 and 1990. These were sprawling places where city and countryside melted together in amorphous conglomerations of office parks, strip malls, and endless ribbons of highways. Easy annexation laws further scrambled city and suburb boundaries.

However, the predicted political change did not occur immediately. The Sunbelt was a congenial region for Republican Party growth. The Republican South found its home in these subdivisions where residents, motivated less by racial animus than by the attraction of low taxes, few regulations, and a strong national defense—the last a reflection of generous government contracts for military hardware, a legacy of World War II—endorsed a minimal federal government. This position was fine with their small town and rural white neighbors who viewed federal intrusions into regional race relations as both unnatural and dangerous.

It was not surprising that as far back as 1948, Dixiecrat vice presidential candidate Strom Thurmond, the South Carolina segregationist, found welcoming audiences in Southern California, less for his racial views than for his emphasis on states' rights. The Reagan movement blossomed two decades later in the Southern California suburbs before it moved to the suburban South. It was not that the rest of the country outside the South was becoming "southernized" as far as race was concerned. The rest of the country's racial problems were only now being discovered. They had existed all along.[14]

The regional convergence on race fit in with the larger narrative that the South, and by extension, the urban South, was losing its unique character. The Sunbelt was the shorthand description for this convergence. It was America's new place and predictions abounded that the South's distinctiveness was vanishing in these new suburban subdivisions. C. Vann Woodward, the great Southern historian, wrote of "the Bulldozer Revolution" in the metropolitan South and how it leveled "many of the old monuments of regional distinctiveness." Indeed, the metropolitan South in the 1960s and after was growing faster than any other region in the country.[15]

As if on cue, racial strife engulfed the cities of the North and West, while the urban South remained generally calm during the long hot summers from 1964 through 1967 and the riots following the assassination of Martin Luther King Jr. in April 1968. Conflicts over busing flared into ugly confrontations in Northern cities during the early 1970s, particularly in Boston, that alleged paragon of racial tolerance. As if to emphasize the changed racial landscape of America, a delegation from Boston traveled to Charlotte in order to learn how to desegregate public schools peacefully.[16]

SUBURBANIZATION

It seemed as if Southern exceptionalism on race had suddenly flipped and now Dixie was imparting lessons on racial equality to the rest of the nation. That was only the appearance, however. As in the urban North, Southern suburbs became bastions of segregated living. Combined with urban renewal policies that devastated existing black inner-city neighborhoods, residential segregation increased. And with it, so did school segregation.[17]

Suburbs from Richmond to Atlanta refused to allow cross-county busing and the US Supreme Court supported those refusals. White suburban Atlanta residents also opposed the extension of the city's subway into suburban counties. Some quipped that MARTA stood for "Moving African-Americans Rapidly Through Atlanta," and they wanted no part of that conveyance.

Urban renewal was a national policy, but its impact seemed particularly onerous in Southern cities where local administrations destroyed a higher percentage of minority housing and replaced it with fewer low-income dwellings than cities in the North. These policies appeared even in the region's most progressive cities such as Atlanta, Raleigh, and Austin. The result was more blighted neighborhoods as African Americans crowded into remaining districts. These areas became breeding grounds for crime, unemployment, and dysfunctional families which, in turn, fueled stereotypes about African Americans and their impact on neighborhoods.

Just as cities elsewhere, Southern cities ensured segregated education with zoning and planning strategies that isolated black communities. Housing and education patterns marched in lockstep. Neighborhood schools reflected their neighborhoods and property values reflected the quality of those schools,

further deepening the racial and economic divisions.[18]

The outcome of urban planning discrimination was perhaps most evident with the impact of Hurricane Katrina on the devastated black neighborhoods of New Orleans where planning policies effectively relegated African Americans to the most low-lying and exposed districts in the city. While Katrina was a natural catastrophe, its toll on New Orleans was mostly man-made.[19]

African Americans moved to the suburbs as well, but their homes were likely to be located in mostly black communities, which was also the case in Northern metropolitan areas. Southern urban exceptionalism was waning, though historical scholarship clearly demonstrated that the urban North, mostly exempt from both voting rights and school desegregation edicts, was hardly a paragon of racial equity. It was less a matter of the rest of the urban nation catching up with Southern cities than the fact that historians were exposing the unfortunate racial record of the urban North.

African Americans voted on these trends with their feet. After decades of sending its population to the rest of the nation, the South by the 1980s began to receive migrants from the North. Between the censuses of 1990 and 2010, more than ten million Americans migrated to the Southeast, most of them to the region's cities. Charlotte became the second largest banking center in the country (after New York City) with the relocation of the national headquarters of the Bank of America from San Francisco. Atlanta became the home of the nation's busiest airport. Houston and Dallas developed diversified economies, less dependent on oil and more involved in the knowledge economy. The agglomeration of Raleigh, Durham, and Chapel Hill became the Southern version of Silicon Valley. Nashville was not only Country City USA, but also a knowledge and high-tech center in its own right.[20]

Close ties to the Southern countryside have remained, however. Evangelical churches predominate the religious landscape in the urban South, even as other denominations and religions have proliferated over the past generation. NASCAR, which originated in dirt tracks in small towns and mountain counties where drivers evaded alcohol-pursuing revenue agents, became a big-time urban attraction in venues such as Richmond, Charlotte, and Atlanta. Country music, its name notwithstanding, built its brand in Southern cities, particularly in Austin and Nashville. As rural areas and small towns in the South struggled economically with the decline of industry and the mechanization of agriculture, young people moved to Southern cities and brought their cultural tastes with them. Southern cities also boasted of their barbecue brands, another small town and rural transfer.

DIVERSITY

In addition to the migration from other parts of the country, immigrants from other parts of the world have come to the urban South since the late 1980s. For a region that had very few foreign-born residents prior to the 1990s, the South has significantly increased its ethnic diversity. Most of these newcomers settled in cities because these are the places of educational and employment opportunities, just as Northern cities fulfilled those roles in the early 20th century. But they have also populated the Republican-leaning suburbs. A drive around Atlanta's suburban ring is a course in a variety of languages and cultures, a mixture of Hispanics, Indians, Pakistanis, and Vietnamese, among others. The increasing diversity of these districts has tempered Republican power and made the suburban South more competitive politically.[21]

The shops and restaurants of the urban South reflect this growing diversity. A generation ago, many Southern cities offered "a meat and three"—a meat dish of dubious origin slathered in an oily concoction of vegetables and starches. Now, the dining places in Atlanta, Houston, Dallas, Nashville, and Birmingham rival those in any other part of the country. Then there is New Orleans, the undisputed culinary capital of America, if not the Western Hemisphere, a veritable advertisement for the collision of diverse cuisines. Thank goodness the English did not settle that place.

The influence of immigrants is evident in the proliferation of ethnic restaurants, festivals, and religious institutions in the urban South. It is also notable in schools and in the workplace, especially in high-tech jobs that draw Asians in particular. Hispanic immigrants have been tending Southern fruit and vegetable farms long before the late 20th-century immigration stream. Since the 1990s, however, many Hispanics have settled in and around the major cities of the South.

Although large enclaves of immigrants are rare in the metropolitan South, an increasing number of Muslim, Indian, Latina/o, and South Asian immigrant districts are discernable. Suburban Atlanta provides a good example of these various concentrations. Immigrants have brought their educational and entrepreneurial skills to the urban South, contributing to the region's economic development.

Their presence has also generated a backlash, particularly among white supremacist groups such as the Ku Klux Klan and other organizations concerned about religious differences and the unsubstantiated charge that immigrants take away work from native-born Americans. Since Latina/o immigrants often enter the workforce at the bottom rung of the employment ladder, their competition is mainly African American, not native-born whites. But, as with immigration early in the 20th century, these newcomers typically perform jobs that neither native-born blacks nor whites are willing to perform, particularly in health care and construction. The integration of immigration into the urban South will be an interesting topic of analysis for scholars in the coming years, particularly in a region where divisions have historically formed along racial lines.[22]

URBAN-RURAL DIVISIONS

In 2012, then-presidential candidate Rick Santorum, formerly a US senator from Pennsylvania, was campaigning in Alabama prior to that state's Republican presidential primary. When a potential voter asked him how someone from Pennsylvania could understand Alabama, Santorum noted that if Philadelphia and Pittsburgh were removed from his home state, you would get Alabama. The implication was that outside Pennsylvania's two major metropolitan areas, political sentiments ran as deeply red as they did through most of Alabama.[23]

Santorum's response highlighted one of the themes of the 2016 presidential election: the divide between small-town, rural America and the major metropolitan areas, particularly along both coasts. This divide is as present now in the South as it is in Northern states. The historical correspondence between city and countryside in the South, particularly with respect to racial, economic, and political issues, is eroding in the South.

Santorum's dictum, for example, could easily be applied to North Carolina. Remove Charlotte, Greensboro, and the Triangle (Raleigh, Durham, and Chapel Hill) and North Carolina becomes deep red. Virginia offers a similar example, with the Washington, DC, suburbs, Richmond, Norfolk, and Charlottesville providing the major blue tinges in an otherwise red state. The concentration of Democrats in these metropolitan areas has been sufficient in recent presidential and off-year elections to produce Democratic majorities for presidential and senatorial candidates in the Old Dominion.

The urban–rural divide reflects the liberation of the urban South from the extractive and agricultural economy that provided its economic base for generations. Today, finance, high-tech, real estate, and legal and medical activities separate the economy of the urban South from the rest of the region. These activities have drawn diverse populations, both from other parts of the country and, especially, from other parts of the world. Their educational levels are significantly above the state norms, and the cultural and culinary supports for this new and generally younger population have been growing accordingly as well. Growing as well is the political resentment in state legislatures still dominated by rural and small-town interests.

Political division has moved lockstep with geographical distinctions in the contemporary South, with rural areas and small towns leaning Republican (the exception would be mostly black enclaves) and larger metropolitan areas typically Democratic. The political identification has hardened in recent years as the December 2017 special senatorial election in Alabama underscored. Despite a deeply flawed Republican candidate, Judge Roy Moore, an accused pedophile and mall creeper, rural and small-town Alabamians voted overwhelmingly for him. Democrat Doug Jones's margin of victory derived from a greater-than-expected turnout among African Americans, particularly black women, and from white support in the normally Republican suburbs of Birmingham, Montgomery, and Mobile. These patterns are no different from similar geographical and political divisions in states elsewhere in the country.

MEMORY

In the not-too-distant future, the exceptionalism of the urban South may exist only in the region's museums. The civil rights movement that unfolded in Southern cities is now permanently housed in several regional museums. The oldest such institution is the Birmingham Civil Rights Institute, opened in 1992 to chronicle that city's troubled racial history. Its very location, across the street from the 16th Street Baptist Church where four young black girls were murdered by a bomb one Sunday in 1963, and in front of Kelly Ingram Park where police chief Bull Connor unleashed his dogs and fire hoses on peaceful demonstrators hoping to press the city to desegregate downtown public facilities, offers a sober spatial tableau of these and related events.

The National Center for Civil and Human Rights (the distinction between the two "rights" is not clear) in Atlanta opened in 2014 and displays the civil rights movement in the 1950s and 1960s. The Center contains collections and artifacts particularly related to native son Martin Luther King Jr. In Memphis, the Lorraine Motel where Martin Luther King Jr. was assassinated in 1968 now houses the National Civil Rights Museum that includes materials and exhibits spanning most of the civil rights movement in addition to the events leading up to and including the assassination.

Greensboro, North Carolina, has transformed the Woolworth building where the formative sit-ins occurred in February 1960 into a museum commemorating that event and connecting it to the broader civil rights movement. And Montgomery, Alabama, is the site of the Rosa Parks Museum dedicated to the black seamstress and NAACP activist who defied segregation on a city bus in December 1955, touching off a wave of actions and demonstrations that formed the heart of the civil rights movement.

Other museums in the urban South are transitioning to themes that are less distinctive of the region. Of particular note here is the Levine Museum of the New South. Its core exhibit, "From Cotton Fields to Skyscrapers," relates the traditional narrative of Southern urbanization as deeply connected to the customs and values of the rural South. But, more recently, the museum, which emphasizes the history of the Southern Piedmont region, has focused on the growing ethnic diversity of the Southeast, particularly the impact of the rapidly growing Hispanic population on Southern culture.

This development is not to say that the urban South's distinctive past is, in fact, past. History is still controversial, as ongoing debates over Confederate statues and memorials attest. While Confederate monuments still

adorn courthouse squares in Southern towns, their counterparts in cities face an uncertain fate as controversies in Charlotte, Richmond, New Orleans, and, especially, Charlottesville, Virginia, attest. The urban South has gone too far down the road of diversity and development to become roiled in historical battles that expose the regional legacy of pride and prejudice, which those very cities shared and expounded.[24]

These are not new controversies. African Americans in Charleston, South Carolina, for example, have been railing against various iterations of the John C. Calhoun statue in that city since the 1880s. But now, no longer invisible politically and economically, African Americans (along with white allies) are pressing for the banishment or at least the contextual containment of these markers of white supremacy.[25]

Thus, the urban South is still connected to its region. There will always be some distinction in urban Dixie because the South's history is distinctive. However, the idea of a racially troglodyte South and a racially virtuous North is now exposed for the fiction it always was. Even so, the South's history of slavery, its peculiar and vicious application of white supremacy, and the identity between rural and urban populations and ideas are not dismissed so readily. Nonetheless, their impact on the daily life of diverse and economically vibrant cities has receded even if the denouement is much less evident in their respective states. The urban South is not particularly exceptional anymore, at least compared with cities in other parts of the country. And that is a good thing.

DISCUSSION OF THE LITERATURE

The field of Southern urban history is a relatively recent development in historical research and writing. While American urban history has enjoyed a lineage dating back to the 19th century, the urban South did not receive much scholarly attention until the 1960s.

There were at least two reasons for this gap. First, Southern historians focused primarily on the plantation, slavery, sharecropping, and the Civil War. These subjects were major influences on the divergent course of Southern history from the national narrative. Second, the civil rights movement of the 1960s and the reincarnation of the South, or at least a portion of it, as the "Sunbelt" in that decade, provided impetus for research into Southern cities.

Early studies of the urban South focused on slavery as an adjunct to the region-wide system of involuntary servitude, though with some differences.[26] By the 1970s, historians explored aspects of Southern urbanization, such as economic development and boosterism that were common to cities elsewhere. However, these works made clear that something was different, and that "something" was related to race and, in particular, to the region's history during and after the Civil War.[27]

In the early 1980s, these trends came together to present Southern urbanization as both comparable to how cities grew in other parts of the country, yet because of regional history actually reflected their region more than other cities. In other words, Southern cities were part of a rural–urban continuum rather than a break from it.[28]

But as the Southeast merged into the Sunbelt orbit in the mid-1980s, historians began to probe Southern urbanization after the civil rights movement. Some distinctive elements, particularly the avid boosterism, remained, but issues such as school desegregation, suburbanization, political change, and the implementation of federal policy at the local level mimicked experiences in other parts of the country. The very concept of "Sunbelt" implied a break from the distinctive "South" of the past. Southern urban exceptionalism is considerably weaker now as historians have demonstrated how the South's metropolitan areas reflect national trends. And the bond between Southern city and region that tied cotton fields and skyscrapers closely, if not in scale, then in ideology, has virtually dissipated.[29]

PRIMARY SOURCES

Anonymous. "Commercial and Industrial Cities of the United States: Richmond, Virginia, 1859." *Hunt's Merchants' Magazine* XL (1859): 54–66.

Anonymous. "Contests for the Trade of the Mississippi Valley." *DeBow's Review* III (1847): 98.

Anonymous. "Southern Patronage to Southern Industry." *Southern Planter* XXI (1861): 160.

Cumming, Kate. *Kate: The Journal of a Confederate Nurse.* Baton Rouge: Louisiana State University Press, 1998.

Douglass, Frederick. *Narrative of the Life of Frederick Douglass, an American Slave.* Simon & Brown, 2013; Originally published in 1845.

Du Bois, William Edward B. *Souls of Black Folk.* New York: Pocket Books, 2005; Originally published in 1903.

Fields, Mamie Garvin, and Karen Fields. *Lemon Swamp and Other Places: A Carolina Memoir.* New York: Free Press, 1985.

Garrow, David J., ed. "Jo Ann Gibson Robinson on the Montgomery Bus Boycott, 1955." In *The Montgomery Bus Boycott and the Women Who Started It: The Memoir of Jo Ann Gibson Robinson.* Knoxville: University of Tennessee Press, 1987.

White, Walter. *A Man Called White: The Autobiography of Walter White.* Athens, GA: University of Georgia Press, 1995; originally published in 1948.

Winston, George Taylor. "Speeches of D. A. Tompkins on the New South." In *A Builder of the New South, Being the Story and Life Work of Daniel Augustus Tompkins,* 84–86, 89–90, 125–126, 127–128. Garden City, NY: Doubleday, Page, 1920.

DIGITAL MATERIALS

Thomas Harriot, *A Briefe and True Report* (1588). http://docsouth.unc.edu/nc/hariot/hariot.html.

Booker T. Washington, Atlanta Exposition Speech (1895). http://historymatters.gmu.edu/d/39/.

FURTHER READING

Abbott, Carl. *The New Urban America: Growth and Politics in Sunbelt Cities.* Chapel Hill: University of North Carolina Press, 1987.

Beaupre, Lauren Elizabeth. "Saints and the 'Long Civil Rights Movement': Claiming Space in Memphis," *Journal of Urban History* 38 (November 2012): 971–1002.

Benjamin, Karen. "Suburbanizing Jim Crow: The Impact of School Policy on Residential Segregation in Raleigh," *Journal of Urban History* 38 (March 2012): 225–246.

Bernard, Richard, and Bradley R. Rice, eds. *Sunbelt Cities: Politics and Growth since World War II*. Austin: University of Texas Press, 1983.

Brownell, Blaine A. *The Urban Ethos in the South, 1920–1930*. Baton Rouge: Louisiana State University Press, 1975.

Brownell, Blaine A., and David Goldfield, eds. *The City in Southern History: The Growth of Urban Civilization in the South*. Port Washington, NY: Kennikat, 1977.

Cardon, Nathan. "The South's 'New Negroes' and African American Visions of Progress at the Atlanta and Nashville International Expositions, 1895–1897," *Journal of Southern History* LXXX (May 2014): 287–326.

Cobb, James C., and William Stueck, eds. *Globalization and the American South*. Athens, GA: University of Georgia Press, 2005.

Erickson, Ansley T. *Making the Unequal Metropolis: School Desegregation and Its Limits*. Chicago: University of Chicago Press, 2016.

Germany, Kent B. *New Orleans After the Promises: Poverty, Citizenship, and the Search for the Great Society*. Athens, GA: University of Georgia Press, 2007.

Gessler, Anne M. "Warriors for Lower Prices: The New Orleans Housewives' League and the Consumer Cooperative Movement, 1913–1921," *Journal of Southern History* LXXXIII (August 2017): 573–616.

Goldfield, David. *Urban Growth in the Age of Sectionalism: Virginia, 1846–1861*. Baton Rouge: Louisiana State University Press, 1977.

Goldfield, David. "The Urban South: A Regional Framework." *American Historical Review* 86 (December 1981): 1009–1034.

Goldfield, David. *Cotton Fields and Skyscrapers: Southern City and Region*. Baton Rouge: Louisiana State University Press, 1982.

Goldfield, David. *Black, White, and Southern: Race Relations and Southern Culture*. Baton Rouge: Louisiana State University Press, 1990.

Goldfield, David. "The Impact of Globalization on the American South: Culture, Ecology, and Economy."

In *Which "Global Village"? Societies, Cultures, and Political-Economic Systems in a Euro-Atlantic Perspective*. Edited by Valeria Gennaro Lerda, 145–154. Westport, CT: Praeger, 2002.

Goldfield, David. "A Place to Come To." In *Globalizing Charlotte*. Edited by Heather Smith and William Graves, 10–23. Athens, GA: University of Georgia Press, 2010.

Goldfield, David. *Still Fighting the Civil War: The American South and Southern History*. Baton Rouge: Louisiana State University Press, 2013.

Hill, Jeremy. *Country Comes to Town: The Music Industry and the Transformation of Nashville*. Amherst: University of Massachusetts Press, 2016.

Holliman, Irene V. "From Crackertown to Model City?: Urban Renewal and Community Building in Atlanta, 1963–1966." *Journal of Urban History* 35 (March 2009): 369–386.

Lassiter, Matthew D. *The Silent Majority: Suburban Politics in the Sunbelt South*. Princeton, NJ: Princeton University Press, 2006.

Lassiter, Matthew D., and Joseph Crespino, eds. *The Myth of Southern Exceptionalism*. New York: Oxford University Press, 2009.

Lassiter, Matthew D., and Kevin M. Kruse. "The Bulldozer Revolution: Suburb and Southern History since World War II." *Journal of Southern History* LXXV (August 2009): 691–706.

Minchin, Timothy J. "When Kia Came to Georgia: Southern Transplants and the Growth of America's 'Other' Automakers." *Journal of Southern History* LXXXII (February 2016): 889–930.

Mohl, Raymond A., ed. *Searching for the Sunbelt: Historical Perspectives on a Region*. Knoxville: University of Tennessee Press, 1990.

Nickerson, Michelle, and Darren Dochuk. *Sunbelt Rising: The Politics of Place, Space, and Region*. Philadelphia: University of Pennsylvania Press, 2011.

Odem, Mary, and Elaine Lacy, eds. *Latino Immigration and the Transformation of the U.S. South*. Athens, GA: University of Georgia Press, 2009.

Wells, Jonathan Daniel, and Jennifer R. Green, eds. *The Southern Middle Class in the Long Nineteenth Century*. Baton Rouge: Louisiana State University Press, 2011.

NOTES

1. David Goldfield, *Cotton Fields and Skyscrapers: Southern City and Region* (Baton Rouge:

Louisiana State University Press, 1982), introduction; chap. 1.

2. David Goldfield, *Urban Growth in the Age of Sectionalism: Virginia, 1846–1861* (Baton Rouge: Louisiana State University Press, 1977).

3. Frederick Douglass, *Narrative of the Life of Frederick Douglass, An American Slave*, 3d ed., ed. David Blight (Boston: Bedford/St. Martin's, 2017 [1845]), 100–103.

4. Leonard P. Curry, *The Free Black in Urban America, 1800–1950: The Shadow of the Dream* (Chicago: University of Chicago Press, 1981); Frank Towers, *The Urban South and the Coming of the Civil War* (Charlottesville: University of Virginia Press, 2004); Richard C. Wade, *Slavery in the Cities: The South, 1820–1860* (New York: Oxford University Press, 1964); and Tyler Anbinder, "Irish Origins and the Shaping of Immigrant Life in Savannah on the Eve of the Civil War," *Journal of American Ethnic History* 35 (Fall 2015): 5–37.

5. Frank Towers and Andrew L. Slap, *Confederate Cities: The Urban South During the Civil War Era* (Chicago: University of Chicago Press, 2015).

6. Howard N. Rabinowitz, *Race Relations in the Urban South, 1865–1890* (New York: Oxford University Press, 1978).

7. Mary Church Terrell, *A Colored Woman in a White World* (Amherst, NY: Humanity Books, 2005[1940]).

8. Quoted in Joan Marie Johnson, "'Drill into us . . . the Rebel Tradition': The Contest over Southern Identity in Black and White Women's Clubs, South Carolina 1898–1930," *Journal of Southern History* 66 (August 2000): 551.

9. Isabel Wilkerson, *The Warmth of Other Suns: The Epic Story of America's Great Migration* (New York: Random House, 2010).

10. James C. Cobb, *Industrialization and Southern Society, 1877–1984* (Lexington: University Press of Kentucky, 2004); see also, Cobb, *The Selling of the South: The Southern Crusade for Industrial Development, 1936–1990* (Urbana-Champaign: University of Illinois Press, 1993).

11. David Goldfield, *Black, White, and Southern: Race Relations and Southern Culture, 1940 to the Present* (Baton Rouge: Louisiana State University Press, 1990).

12. Elizabeth Jacoway and David R. Colburn, eds., *Southern Businessmen and Desegregation* (Baton Rouge: Louisiana State University Press, 1982).

13. Valdimer O. Key Jr., *Southern Politics in State and Nation* (New York: Knopf, 1949), 673.

14. Joseph Crespino, *Strom Thurmond's America* (New York: Hill & Wang, 2012).

15. C. Vann Woodward, *The Burden of Southern History* (Baton Rouge: Louisiana State University Press, 1959), 6.

16. Corinne Bermon, "Linda Lawrence papers, 1974–1975: Now open for research," August 17, 2017. http://blogs.umb.edu/archives/tag/busing/.

17. Kevin Kruse, *White Flight: Atlanta and the Making of Modern Conservatism* (Princeton, NJ: Princeton University Press, 2005).

18. Ansley T. Erickson, *Making the Unequal Metropolis: School Desegregation and Its Limits* (Chicago: University of Chicago Press, 2016); and Karen Benjamin, "Suburbanizing Jim Crow: The Impact of School Policy on Residential Segregation in Raleigh," *Journal of Urban History* 38 (March 2012): 225–246.

19. Joe W. Trotter and Johanna Fernandez, "Hurricane Katrina: Urban History from the Eye of the Storm," *Journal of Urban History* 35 (July 2009): 607–613.

20. Joel Kotkin and Mark Schill, "The Cities Creating the Most Tech Jobs, 2017," *Forbes*, March 16, 2017. https://www.forbes.com/sites/joelkotkin/2017/03/16/technology-jobs-2017-san-francisco-charlotte-detroit/#725300d038f6.

21. David Goldfield, "Unmelting the Ethnic South: The Changing Boundaries of Race and Ethnicity in the Modern South," in *The American South in the Twentieth Century*, ed. Crag S. Pascoe, Karen Trahan Leathem, and Andy Ambrose (Athens, GA: University of Georgia Press, 2007), 19–38.

22. Raymond A. Mohl, "Globalization, Latinization and the *Nuevo* New South," *Journal of American Ethnic History* 22 (Summer 2003): 31–66.

23. Santorum was paraphrasing James Carville's quote, "On one side you have Pittsburgh. On the other side Philadelphia. In the middle, you have Alabama (https://www.dailykos.com/story/2008/4/16/496768/-)."

24. David Goldfield, *Still Fighting the Civil War: The American South and Southern History* (Baton Rouge: Louisiana State University Press, 2013), chap. 12.

25. Blain Roberts and Ethan J. Kytle, "Looking the Thing in the Face: Slavery, Race, and the

Commemorative Landscape in Charleston, South Carolina, 1865–2010," *Journal of Southern History* LXXVIII (August 2012): 639–684.

26. Richard C. Wade, *Slavery in the Cities: The South, 1820–1860* (New York: Oxford University Press, 1964).

27. Blaine A. Brownell, *The Urban Ethos in the South, 1920–1930* (Baton Rouge: Louisiana State University Press, 1975); Brownell and David Goldfield, ed. *The City in Southern History: The Growth of Urban Civilization in the South* (Port Washington, NY: Kennikat Press, 1977); David Goldfield, *Urban Growth in the Age of Sectionalism: Virginia, 1846–1861* (Baton Rouge: Louisiana State University Press, 1977); and Howard N. Rabinowitz, *Race Relations in the Urban South, 1865–1890* (New York: Oxford University Press, 1978).

28. David Goldfield, *Cotton Fields and Skyscrapers: Southern City and Region* (Baton Rouge: Louisiana State University Press, 1982).

29. Matthew D. Lassiter, *The Silent Majority: Suburban Politics in the Sunbelt South* (Princeton, NJ: Princeton University Press, 2006); and Michelle Nickerson and Darren Dochuk, eds., *Sunbelt Rising: The Politics of Place, Space, and Region* (Philadelphia: University of Pennsylvania Press, 2011).

David Goldfield

COMPANY TOWNS IN THE UNITED STATES

FIRST STIRRINGS: THE NEW ENGLAND COMPANY TOWN EXPERIENCE

Company towns can be defined as communities dominated by a single company that is typically focused on one industry. Beyond that very basic definition, they varied in their essentials. Some were purpose-built by companies, often in remote areas convenient to needed natural resources. There, workers were often required to live in company-owned housing as a condition of employment. Others began as small towns with privately owned housing, usually expanding alongside a growing hometown corporation. Residences were shoddy in some company towns. In others, company-built housing may have been excellent, with indoor plumbing and central heating, and located close to such amenities as schools, libraries, perhaps even theaters.

Company towns played a key role in US economic and social development. Such places can be found across the globe, but America's vast expanse of undeveloped land, generous stock of natural resources, tradition of social experimentation, and laissez-faire attitude toward business provided singular opportunities for the emergence of such towns, large and small, in many regions of the United States. Historians have identified as many as 2,500 such places.

Questions of economics and development were much discussed from the early years of the American republic, with pro-agrarian forces, led by Thomas Jefferson, pitted against the pro-manufacturing ranks, led by Alexander Hamilton. Hamilton and his supporters wanted to establish a multi-industry hub in New Jersey, which they dubbed Paterson. This community, though, never developed as a company town. Most early US industry was isolated and small in scale. "The manufacturing operations of the United States are carried out in little hamlets," noted one late-18th-century visitor to New England, "around the water fall which serves to turn the mill wheel." Indeed, in Rhode Island, site of the country's initial textile mills, pioneer Samuel Slater's first workforce numbered only seven—all children between the ages of 7 and 12.[1]

Drawing on their experience at a small textile mill in the Boston suburb of Waltham, a group of Massachusetts businessmen determined to set up larger-scale operations. The project had three fundamental requirements: an undeveloped site, sufficient water power to run the mill, and a diligent and numerous workforce. After considering a location in New Hampshire, these capitalists, who historians later called the Boston Associates, settled upon a site near East Chelmsford, Massachusetts, along the Merrimack River. With an initial capitalization of the then-enormous sum of $600,000, three principal figures—Francis Cabot Lowell, Nathan Appleton, and Patrick Tracy Jackson—incorporated in the name of the Merrimack Manufacturing Company. By 1823, streets were laid out, mills and boardinghouses built, an existing canal enlarged, and new canals begun. Appleton decreed in 1826 that the settlement would bear the name of the figure key to the undertaking: Lowell.

The founders of the company town intended to hire the same kind of employees that they hired in Waltham: young farm women drawn from across New England. Recruiters traveled across the area, assuring the families of potential millhands that the workers would be closely supervised by female boardinghouse keepers and exposed to music, literature, and improving lectures by cultural luminaries. Whatever period of their time spent in Lowell would be far from onerous, families were promised. Employment in the town, instead, would amount to preparation for later life. Moreover, Lowell's cash wages compared well to those of other alternatives for women, including both domestic service and teaching.

A separate enterprise, the Locks and Canals Company, was placed in charge of the waterworks and town development. This company, owned by virtually the same group of capitalists as those in charge of the Merrimack Manufacturing Company, proceeded to sell land, lease water-power rights, and build new mills and boardinghouses. Soon, multiple new firms appeared, including the Hamilton Corporation (1825), the Appleton and Lowell corporations (1828), the Suffolk, Tremont, and Lawrence corporations (1830), and the Middlesex Corporation (1831). In 1845, the

Lowell Machine Shop was organized to design and build machinery for the factories.

The boards of these entities consisted of many of the same men, plus a few capital-bearing newcomers. Interlocking directorates ensured a concentration of power. The companies paid identical wages, had identical working hours, and followed similar employment policies. Marketing their popular printed calicoes via the same Boston commission houses, all were hugely profitable.

By 1850, forty mill buildings lined the river for almost a mile, their mill wheels driven by six miles of canals and a system of gates and flow-measuring devices that regulated the water. A series of belts linked mill wheels to power looms and other machinery. The population more than tripled during the 1830s, rising from 6,474 in 1830 to more than 20,000 in 1840. In 1850, Lowell's population exceeded 33,000, making it the second-largest city in Massachusetts.[2]

The early workforce was much celebrated for its intelligence and refinement. Visitors included Charles Dickens, who described how the young women not only had access to pianos and high-toned library books, but also produced their own literary periodical, the Lowell Offering, filled with original poetry, essays, and stories of millworker life.[3] The Offering received favorable notices in the Times of London and the Edinburgh Review. The women were required to observe a 10 p.m. curfew, abstain from all spirits, attend church (twenty-six of which existed by the mid-1840s), and watch their step: missteps (including drinking and dancing) could draw a reprimand from a morals police force consisting of boardinghouse keepers and co-worker snitches. Fall afoul of these watchers, and the young women risked blacklisting from employment in the region.

By the mid-1840s, the Yankee-girl workforce gave way to an employee pool made up of Irish and French-Canadian families. The farm women were drawn away by other options,

including westward migration. Sped-up machinery, lengthened workdays, wage cuts, and
boardinghouse-fee increases proved more acceptable to near-desperate immigrants. Men
and children joined women in tending the
Lowell machinery. The boardinghouse-
residency requirement ended.

Both profits and pay fell victim to increased competition. In 1839, Henry David
Thoreau observed that the Merrimack River
had evolved into "a busy colony of human
beaver around every fall." He noted that, in
addition to Lowell, factory complexes were
constructed in Newburyport, Haverhill,
Lawrence, and Concord, as well as Nashua and
Manchester in New Hampshire.[4] The grand
Lawrence, Massachusetts, development was
patterned on Lowell, but this only added to
an oversupply of textile product. Then, economic woes beginning in the late 1840s led to
failure for five of the Boston Associates' now
numerous companies. When the Civil War
(1861–1865), with its Union blockade of
Southern ports, halted the supply of Southern
cotton, many Lowell mills closed. After the
war, the new system of sharecropping that
drew largely upon the labor of former slaves

gradually rebuilt the plantation economy.
The rebound from what manufacturers had
dubbed a "cotton famine" was dramatic: By
1870, total cotton production surpassed the
previous high set in 1860.[5]

Textile production in Lowell resumed
after the war, interrupted by a series of strikes
in 1867, 1875, and, most seriously, in 1903. A
slow decline set in, with mill closings escalating after World War I. During the Great
Depression, two-thirds of the town's population were unemployed or working only part
time. By 1940, only three mills were left in
operation, and after World War II, Lowell
millwork all but disappeared. The town's
mills had become technologically obsolete,
even as mills in North Carolina and the upper
South combined modern, high-speed machinery with even cheaper labor.

In 1978, Lowell's former mill district
became the first urban national park—a sort
of Colonial Williamsburg devoted to increasingly quaint industrial practices. Tourists can
visit the still-impressive brick factories and
boardinghouses and witness the machinery in
operation. Then they can tour the canals that
once powered America's industrial revolution.

Figure 1. Lowell's Boott Cotton Mills in the late nineteenth century.
Photo courtesy of Center for Lowell History.

THE IMPETUS FOR COMPANY-TOWN DEVELOPMENT

Lowell illustrates several of the motivations and limitations associated with company-town development. Large production or extraction complexes require considerable space for initial building, and later expansion. The undeveloped area that became Lowell met that need. But like a variety of subsequent company towns, Lowell was chosen primarily for its natural resources (in this case, water power). Of secondary but still important consideration was the question of labor supply. Labor shortages were common in America during the 19th century. Lowell's masters discovered two solutions: underemployed Yankee farm girls and the increasing number of foreign immigrants, first from Ireland and Canada, then later from Greece, Poland, and forty other countries.

The more remote the location, the greater loomed the issue of transportation for the raw materials and the finished product. Lowell initially received raw cotton and sent out its finished goods via canal. After 1835, however, the Boston & Lowell Railroad assumed those tasks. Some thirty-odd miles from Lowell lay Boston itself, with its ample connections to consumer markets farther south and west.

And what of more idealistic motivations for company-town building? Profit was always an incentive to industrial development, but Alexander Hamilton was not the only figure in the young republic to concern himself with the nation's destiny. Francis Cabot Lowell visited the Lancashire mill area in Britain in 1811 and was repelled by the squalor. "Operatives in the manufacturing cities of Europe," he found, "were notoriously of the lowest character for intelligence and morals."[6] This would never do in the new republic. Hence, his town's handsome red-brick boardinghouses, absence of saloons and requirement of temperance, and the elaborate paternalistic edifice, from the churches to the improving lectures and the *Offering*.

Lowell was America's first company town, but many others exhibited similar characteristics. However, compiling a comprehensive list of US company towns is difficult, not least because of their nearly infinite variety. Does Washington, DC, with its array of federal-government operations, qualify as a company town with a federal-government overlord? Probably not. Any such large metropolitan center is simply too diversified, containing a wide array of enterprises and a power elite that transcends any single purpose. That said, any list of company towns would have to include the following places and pursuits:

- Textile towns across the Carolinas and Georgia, varying from small villages to large developments such as Kannapolis, N.C.
- Coal-mining towns in Pennsylvania, followed by more in southern Appalachia once a post–Civil War railroad building boom made the area accessible.
- Milton Hershey's model town of Hershey, Pennsylvania, erected in an area with lots of dairy farms to provide milk for his milk chocolate.
- Timber settlements, particularly in northern California, Oregon, and Washington State.
- Steelmaking towns ranging from Alabama to West Virginia and into Maryland, Pennsylvania, New York, Indiana, and Colorado.
- Midwestern manufacturing towns, ranging from those whose single companies made everything from plumbing fixtures and washing machines to Ford automobiles.
- Meatpacking towns, again notably located in the Midwest, near the supply of hogs and cattle.
- Copper and hard-rock mining towns in the West.
- Towns devoted to the production of munitions and hardware needed for World War II—notably the secret town of Oak Ridge, Tennessee.

THE COMPANY-TOWN PROBLEM

So dramatic and disruptive were two late-19th-century strikes—the bloody 1892 work stoppage at Carnegie Steel's Homestead, Pennsylvania, works; and the 1894 nationwide railroad strike kicked off by wage cuts at legendary Illinois railcar maker Pullman—that they reshaped the thinking of industry and company-town developers.

Homestead was not really a town at all, much less a company town. It was more like urban sprawl along the Monongahela River bank fourteen miles south of Pittsburgh. Carnegie Steel's awesome plant shared the area with rows of cheap frame housing erected for workers by private developers. Across the river stood another chunk of congestion known as Braddock, whose housing was characterized in Tom Bell's novel of immigrant life, *Out of This Furnace*, as "characteristic of the steel towns, long, ugly rows like cell blocks" lacking in "conveniences of any kind."[7]

In 1892, the master of the Carnegie mill, Henry Clay Frick, determined to destroy the workers' union, the Amalgamated Association of Steel and Iron Workers. After demanding pay and job cuts, Frick had the plant fortified with eleven-foot-high walls topped by barbed wire and backed by towers with searchlights. Then after a work stoppage, Frick attempted to reopen the plant, importing three hundred armed Pinkerton guards up the river by barge. Assembled on the riverbank, the strikers met the Pinkertons with a barrage of rifle and cannon fire. Nine strikers and seven Pinkertons died during a twelve-hour battle. With the aid of the state militia and more strikebreakers, Frick broke the union, but at a considerable cost to all concerned.[8]

Two years later, another labor conflagration centered on the town of Pullman, Illinois, fourteen miles outside of Chicago. In 1880, railroad sleeping-car magnate George Pullman built a model company town there, in an area that he said he considered free of all pernicious influences. His factory produced ornate sleeping cars, decked out in brocaded fabrics and polished wood. The town's residential area included many blocks of well-built, red-brick row houses and tenements, most with indoor bathrooms, natural gas, and running water. A large marketplace for meats and vegetables, a handsome hotel, an elaborate theater, retail shops, a school, parks, and playing fields provided a variety of services and amenities for residents and visitors alike.

Yet George Pullman expected his workers to pay their own way: Rents were high, and any tenant could be evicted with little notice. No town, village, or municipal government separated the community from the company. A crew of "company inspectors" maintained round-the-clock surveillance of resident-workers to make sure that their habits and opinions passed muster.

Then came the hour of reckoning. Hard times in the early 1890s led to layoffs, falling wages, unionization, and a strike, but no reduction in rents. Events continued to escalate, leading to a nationwide general strike in which mobs sabotaged tracks and trains. The president, Grover Cleveland, sent in federal troops, and thirteen railroad workers died in a confrontation in Chicago. The strike was broken, but Pullman's model town was forever tainted. The city of Chicago took over its municipal functions, and in 1904, the company began selling residential properties and other town holdings.[9]

Were company towns, no matter how plush, inherently prone to trouble and labor strife? Many wondered.

Perhaps surprisingly, the Pullman events did not mean an end to model-company-town building. In the late 1890s Apollo Iron and Steel chief George Gibson McMurtry hired the celebrated architecture firm of Olmsted, Olmsted, and Eliot to design a model steel town on the Kiskiminetas River, about thirty miles northeast of Pittsburgh. The town would be called Vandergrift, and, unusually, workers were allowed to buy property and own their own homes. Lots were offered for $750 for elite workers, $150 for lower-paid operatives, and less still for laborers. Home-owning workers would have a stake in society—and in peaceful social relations: A 1901 strike called by the Amalgamated Association of Iron and Steel Workers drew little support, as employees were "bound up by their property interests," in the words of one union observer.[10]

Similarly, in 1904, chocolate maker Milton Hershey began construction of his own model town, Hershey, Pennsylvania, in a remote area of the state convenient to lots of milk-chocolate-ready dairy products. In an echo of George Pullman's sentiments, Hershey declared that in his town, there would be "no poverty, no nuisances, no evil." In the town, laid out by local engineer Henry Herr, worker housing was once again well equipped, featuring indoor plumbing, central heating, and even electricity. Hershey constructed parks, a zoo, a public library, a medical clinic, free schools, and more. Hershey company workers received a cornucopia of benefits: insurance, medical coverage, pensions, and a tuition-free junior college. In Hershey, houses could be bought for between $1,200 and $1,500, and a hundred lots were offered to those who wanted to build their own homes. It enjoyed peaceful labor relations during most of the ensuing decades. Unions achieved little success in organizing workers until a 1937 organizing campaign, followed by 1939 recognition of the conservative Bakery and Confectionary Workers Union.[11]

But the velvet-glove approach was not the only response to the violence that seemed endemic to company towns. When the United States Steel Corporation decided in 1904 to expand its production facilities, it, too, decided that a new town was in order. That became Gary, Indiana, a megacity literally constructed from scratch on the Lake Michigan shore, just across the state line from Chicago. That company town provided plenty of space, railroad

access, and a large labor pool already nearby. US Steel went on to erect the largest steel complex in the nation, with capacity for sheet, wire, and tinplate production, a locomotive works, even a cement factory.

Like many other steelmakers, US Steel was disinclined to build worker housing. Company executives intended simply to build the works, and then arrange the city around it. No celebrated landscape-architecture firm was involved in the design of this city: Instead, the Gary Works plant engineer, A. P. Melton, provided an unforgiving grid pattern. When the private market initially failed to produce a sufficient supply of homes, the company erected a number of residences. But in time, private developers did deliver, constructing hundreds of cheap frame houses and boardinghouses.

Most important in the mind of Eugene Buffington, a key planner and president of the subsidiary Illinois Steel, was the layout of the Gary plants. The steel works stretched for eight miles along the Lake Michigan shore. On the other side of the factories was the Grand Calumet River, dividing the facilities from residential areas. In the event of a Homestead-like labor confrontation, ore and coal for steelmaking, along with guards and strikebreakers, could enter the plant from the lake side. The river served as a defensive moat against any rowdies.

US Steel did not coddle Gary workers. "Time and again the paternalistic mistakes of Pullman were given as justification for a 'do-as-little-as-you-have-to' policy in shaping town conditions," reported social reformer Graham Romeyn Taylor in his profile of the emerging Gary in 1915. Nine years after its first brick was laid, the city's population reached 50,000. Despite the company town's many faults, Taylor felt Gary was likely "the greatest single calculated achievement of America's master industry."[12] Gary factories remained productive for decades, and by 1945, the Gary Works was the largest steel plant on Earth.

Figure 2. The Illinois National Guard assembled in Pullman during the Great Railroad Strike of 1894. Courtesy of Chicago History Museum.

Figure 3. Gary, Indiana, under construction in 1907. Courtesy of Calumet Regional Archives, Indiana University Northwest.

EXPLOITATION IN THE UPPER SOUTH

At the outbreak of the Civil War, "the United States was in truth an 'undeveloped' country," according to historian Edward Chase Kirkland.[13] Thus, there was a hiatus between the establishment of New England company towns and those that followed. But after the war, industrial development took off in a host of industries. Gradually, the textile industry migrated from New England to the Carolinas and Georgia, and the postwar development of railroads in the South allowed the exploitation of the great Appalachian coal fields in Kentucky, West Virginia, and elsewhere.

Beginning in the late 19th century, the hardships of rural life prompted a multitude of Southern tenant farmers to abandon agriculture and move to one of approximately 100 mill villages that arose in the backcountry of North Carolina, South Carolina, and northern Georgia. Most such villages consisted of little more than a mill and a few rows of worker houses (each with a privy out back), and perhaps a company store, a church, and a schoolhouse. Low wages, often only 60 percent of those paid in New England, were facilitated by cheap rents, usually 25 cents a week per room. The heyday of such textile hamlets occurred between 1880 and 1930, the number of workers rose from 17,000 in 1880 to nearly 100,000 in 1900, and as many as one-quarter of the laborers were children.[14]

Housing may have been modest in Southern textile company towns. However, the Southern textile factories featured modern, labor-saving equipment that allowed workers to be little more than machine tenders. Some villages, including Burlington, North Carolina, and Greenville, South Carolina, became urban centers. Kannapolis grew into the largest nonincorporated town in North Carolina and featured seven Cannon Mills factories, the Cabarrus Memorial Hospital, hundreds of houses, and a newspaper, all owned by the Cannon family, while the Cannon company

Figure 4. Child laborers in the textile town of Kannapolis, North Carolina.
Photo by Lewis Hine, courtesy of Library of Congress, LC-DIG-nclc-02638.

handled such functions as policing, firefighting, utilities, and trash collection.

The barons of nearby coal country proved even more controlling. To hold a job in coal country, generally the worker had to live in and pay rent on a company-owned house, which was little more than a shack. No outsiders, such as peddlers, meddlers, or union organizers, were allowed into the area. Workers got paid in scrip—company-issued currency—or sometimes in cash, according to the number of tons of coal ore loaded this month. Rent and utilities were deducted from pay, often along with school fees and taxes. If a worker ran out of money, he could get food on credit at the pricey company store. But if one were injured on the job or otherwise became unable to work, he would be evicted from his house with as little as ten days' notice. The same treatment would be delivered to his family if he were killed on the job.

The living quarters in coal mining camps were among the worst in the United States, according to a 1925 report of the US Coal Commission. Only 14 percent of coal-town houses in Virginia, West Virginia, and Kentucky had running water. Most had outside privies that emptied into a nearby creek. Each little house was heated only by an open fireplace or a coal-fired, potbellied stove.

"The Man" was the law: One coal-mine operator bragged, "I was the high justice, the middle, and the low." His primary aim was keeping unions out. Private guards, blacklists, beatings, and even killings were hardly unknown. In the 1910s and 1920s, Logan County, West Virginia, sheriff Don Chafin, the personal beneficiary of largesse from mine owners, named three hundred mine guards to be his deputies. He met every train that came into the area, questioned passengers regarding what they were doing there, administered beatings to union organizers, and jailed perceived political opponents. The intimidating tactics provoked a response. In 1921, an army of thousands of miners marched on Logan to demand the release of jailed union activists.

Figure 5. The coal-mining village of Jenkins, Kentucky, founded in 1912.
Photo by Ben Shahn, courtesy of Library of Congress, LC-USF3301-006137-M5.

Chafin and his two-thousand-strong army of deputies met the marchers at Blair Mountain. The result was a war that included aerial bombings of the miners and shootouts in which thirty deputies and up to one hundred miners were killed. Intervention by federal troops resulted in a roundup, arrests, and trials of hundreds of miners, with many miners sent to prison.[15]

Similar outbreaks of violence continued well into the 20th century. In 1913, coal miners in Las Animas County, Colorado, joined in mass activity aimed at unionizing coal mines, most owned by the Rockefeller family's Colorado Fuel and Iron. The companies rejected union demands and evicted miners from their company towns. Tent cities sprung up, with the largest, housing one thousand people, set up near a railroad depot at Ludlow. Battles broke out between strikers and company guards employed by the Baldwin-Felts strikebreaking firm. A months-long siege ensued, with Colorado National Guard troops ushering strikebreakers into the mines. Finally, in April 1914, the Guard attacked the encampment at Ludlow, firing machine guns into the tents and setting fire to the site. Two women and eleven children died.

In the 1930s, violence flared in Harlan County, Kentucky. Wage cuts, walkouts, armed clashes, National Guard intervention, and strikebreakers were features of labor-relations conflict in coal country. But the New Deal's 1933 National Industrial Recovery Act, with its endorsement of the right to organize, prompted coal miners to flood into the United Mine Workers union by the thousands. Still, Harlan remained an antiunion stronghold. By the spring of 1935, bombings and shootings of union organizers were rife there. Two years later, the US Department of Justice prosecuted sixty-nine coal companies for engaging in a conspiracy to violate federal labor law. State police enforcement led to a decline in violence.

In industries where labor was plentiful, employers were sometimes generous toward workers and less hostile toward unions. But coal operators found willing workers difficult to come by during the coal-industry boom that stretched from the 1880s to the 1920s. Locals were widely aware of such risks as cave-ins, gas explosions, and less-dramatic respiratory ailments such as chronic bronchitis and pneumoconiosis, or black lung. Moreover, Appalachian workers, sometimes derided as hillbillies, were perceived by employers as prickly and unreliable, tending to gravitate back to small farming plots during planting and harvesting seasons. The companies' labor agents haunted the docks in big East Coast cities, looking for newcomers from Italy, Hungary, Poland, and Greece. Promised good pay, these penniless "transportation men" arrived via railcar in coal towns, only to find that they were already in debt for their travel expenses. Kentucky and West Virginia populations soared, but the immigrants often proved unreliable, fleeing to other jobs in other places. World War I and restrictive immigration laws also played havoc with the flow of Europeans.

Some coal towns were built as models, including Lynch, Kentucky, and Holden, West Virginia. But the little coal-mining villages, sporting such unlikely monickers as Neon, Hi-Hat, Chevrolet, and Blackey, were probably more typical. There, daily life was grim. Author Harry M. Caudill, who profiled the area in his masterful *Night Comes to the Cumberlands*, wrote of the "monstrous coal-dust genie," a black plume that rose near every town's tipple (or loading facility for railcars), infecting the towns' every nook and cranny. Moreover, there were giant refuse heaps of discarded slate that sometimes spontaneously erupted into "mountains of living fire which blazed without intermission." Polluted air peeled paint from the walls and turned every surface ashen gray.[16]

The prison-camp-like coal company town entered a period of slow decline in the 1930s. There were dramatic clashes between coal miners and the federal government during World War II and further violent strikes in the 1960s and 1980s. At the same time, the declining national demand for coal led to a rapid fall-off in the number of coal miners, along with a mass exodus to Midwestern industrial cities. The coal company town was becoming a population-free ghost town in the mode of such places as Lobo, Texas, and Bodie, California.

Federal government criticism led many Southern textile companies to abandon and sell their towns during the Depression years. By 1939, a dozen companies had sold at least thirty villages, with houses being purchased for very little by inhabitants, with another sixty villages sold during the 1940s. Larger places such as Kannapolis, however, survived and even prospered. When a *Fortune* magazine

reporter visited during the 1930s, he found the place to be "[l]ike a medieval city, [standing] aloof and self-contained in the midst of empty country, suspicious of strangers, loyal to its feudal lords."[17] The textile fiefdom lasted into the 1980s, when Cannon fell victim to corporate raiders, buyouts, bankruptcy, and finally a shutdown.

FROM COUNTRY TOWN TO COMPANY TOWN

Not every company town in the United States was built from scratch. In many cases, country towns expanded alongside a hometown corporation. Two of these serve as illustrations here: Newton, Iowa, hometown of the Maytag washing machine company; and Austin, Minnesota, home of the Spam-making Hormel Corp.

Newton, Iowa, was a coal-mining and railway hub with a population of twenty-five hundred when Frederick Maytag moved there late in the 19th century with his parents from Illinois. In 1892, the young Maytag joined with others to make and market threshing-machine accessories. Soon, several companies making hand-operated washing machines appeared in town. In 1907, Maytag and his company's mechanic began producing a washer as well—basically a wooden tub with a crank mechanism that dragged clothes against a corrugated surface. They saw this as a sideline to their farm-equipment business, but it quickly became profitable.

Within a few years, Maytag bought out his partners, renamed the company Maytag Co., and began producing both gasoline-powered and electric washers. By 1915, the company's washers were outselling its farm equipment. Its Maytag Multi-Motor became a hot seller owing to its ability to power other implements, such as a butter churn or ice-cream maker, while washing clothes.

Hundreds of manufacturers made washers during this period, but a quarter of the machines were produced by four companies in

Newton. Maytag's innovations, including the millrace washing principle, which forced hot water through tumbling clothes, spurred rapid growth. By 1920, the company had the largest factory in Iowa, with six hundred thousand square feet, two thousand employees, and a network of thousands of dealers.

In that decade, Maytag became a public corporation listed on the New York Stock Exchange. But family members remained the key executives. Chief Executive Officer Elmer Maytag and his partners purchased hundreds of vacant lots around town and built homes that they sold to employees. Mortgages were offered by a savings bank where Elmer was an officer. The family funded a local YMCA, which workers were required to join and pay dues to, and a yearly family picnic, which employees also were required to attend.

These company welfare programs, however, masked worker discontent. A 1937 union drive by the United Electrical Workers signed up fourteen hundred Maytag workers in only nine days. One year later, amid union demands for a 25 percent raise and the company's institution of a 10 percent pay cut, the workers went on a work stoppage, and the state sent in four National Guard companies equipped with tanks and machine guns. The union's strike was broken in days.

During World War II, Maytag shifted its capacity to armaments production, and when it returned to washer-making after the conflict, a raft of new competitors awaited. These included General Electric, Westinghouse, Philco, Frigidaire, Amana, and Whirlpool. But Maytag held on, its sales spurred by its successful advertising campaign featuring the "lonely Maytag repairman," underemployed thanks to the company's near-unbreakable machines. Still, during the ensuing decades, too-rapid expansion, unwise acquisitions of such lines as Jenn Air and Hoover vacuums, and finally competition from foreign makers sealed the company's fate.[18] Whirlpool took over Maytag in 2006, closed its Newton headquarters and factories in that town and

elsewhere, and laid off twenty-eight hundred Newton residents, about a fifth of the town's citizenry.

Like Newton, Austin, Minnesota, was initially a transportation and trading center. Austin, however, followed a rather different evolution. In 1891, a traveling hide-buyer out of Toledo, George A. Hormel, turned his hand to operating a retail butcher shop and packing house in Austin. During the decade, four other Hormel brothers moved to the town of thirty-nine hundred souls, where they worked in beef and pork slaughtering, sausage making, the ice harvesting necessary to keep meat refrigerated, and running the retail shop. Most meat-packing at the time was carried on in Chicago by such behemoths as Armour, Cudahy, and Swift. Small-town buyers who developed close relations with nearby farmers, however, discovered other business advantages. Before long, Hormel developed distribution centers across the Midwest and the South and perfected a means of canning ham, which proved a popular item. And in 1933, Hormel's cultivation of a national market proceeded, assisted by the construction of a new $1 million beef slaughtering plant in Austin.

Hormel also followed a different path in labor relations. Plant supervisor Frank C. Ellis and other pro-union employees, some of whom Ellis had hired and placed in strategic positions across the plant, organized mass meetings and union events. In the fall of 1933, the workers shut down the plant and escorted George's son Jay, the company president, out of the facility. Already inclined toward progressive labor relations, Hormel recognized the workers' organization, the Industrial Workers of the World–inspired Independent Union of All Workers. A number of forward-looking policies resulted, including group-incentive bonuses and profit-sharing. The speed of the work was determined by work gangs rather than by dictatorial foremen.

For more than 40 years, Hormel suffered no serious disputes between company and union. Hormel established a Hormel Foundation to support local charities and ensure "the welfare of the community in which [the company] was located." And the company's expanding line of branded products, including Dinty Moore beef stew and the spiced-ham-like product Spam, proved enormous sellers across the United States and beyond.

The company's success paid off for the town. In 1953, author Fred H. Blum reported that Austin contained no slum areas or neglected houses, and 75 percent of Austinites (a higher percentage than in any comparable US city) lived in their own homes.[19]

But by the 1980s, this cozy relationship seemed doomed. New, aggressive packers with union-busting and wage-cutting ways entered the field, and many older companies (including Wilson and Armour) were driven from the business. Recession, plant closings, union defeats, and Reagan-era pay cuts joined to bring packinghouse workers' pay down to 20 percent below the average manufacturing wage.

In 1985, Austin's Hormel workers engaged in a renowned strike against the company's demands for significant wage and benefit cuts. Led by an innovative group of young, militant workers, the strike became an inspiration for a budding anticoncessions movement. But the walkout was opposed by the local union's proconcessions national union, which imposed a trusteeship. Those who had crossed the picket line became the new union members.

By 2000, the typical meatpacking company town was a dystopia, populated by poorly paid workers, including many immigrants from Latin America. In Austin, workplace injuries and job turnover were at high levels. The hog slaughter was subcontracted to an entity called Quality Pork Producers, which paid even lower wages than Hormel. ("All of the fresh meat we process goes to the Hormel Foods Corporation," the company's website blatantly proclaimed.) Hormel ran the rest of the plant. Meanwhile, Austin's formerly pin-neat houses in many cases had been replaced by boarded-up, dilapidated hovels. The town's once-bustling shopping mall was largely vacant. And the levels of crime, drug addiction, and poverty were profound.

THE COMPANY TOWN IN THE 21ST CENTURY

Some industrial company towns lived on into the 21st century. Meatpacking is still the primary activity in Austin, Minnesota, and Fremont, Nebraska, both dominated by the Hormel Corporation, and also in Tar Heel, North Carolina, home to a huge Smithfield Packing plant.[20] The picturesque model company town of Kohler, Wisconsin, site of both the longest strike in US history and, incongruously enough, numerous top-flight golf championships, still produces Kohler plumbing fixtures. In Morenci and Bagdad, Arizona, mining company Freeport-McMoRan owns all the buildings and makes most of its money unearthing copper. Corning, New York, is still the fortunate home of Corning Inc., a world-class glassmaker, and the Corning Glass Museum, a must-stop for tourists traveling between New York City and Niagara Falls.

A new model, however, had emerged during the first half of the 20th century: the suburban corporate campus. Automobiles and improved roads encouraged companies to

Figure 6. Corning Inc.'s modern headquarters in the town of Corning, New York.
Photo by Hardy Green.

begin moving away from urban centers as early as the 1930s. One of the first was the Bell Labs division of American Telephone & Telegraph. At first, that company figured that it would erect a new headquarters and re-search laboratory in Manhattan. Instead, in 1944, Bell Labs relocated to a parklike campus near Summit, New Jersey, some twenty-five miles outside of Gotham.

The construction of Bell Labs in a New York suburban location marked the begin-ning of a substantial exodus. In 1940, fewer than thirty-five such corporate campuses ex-isted in the United States. By the early 1970s, however, more than three hundred such com-munities could be found in California alone. Numerous other examples arose in Florida, Georgia, Minnesota, Missouri, Texas, and Wisconsin. In 1957, International Business Machines (IBM) commissioned famed Finnish architect Eero Saarinen to design a scientific research center in leafy Westchester County, north of New York City. Others soon moving to the suburbs included Connecticut General Life, PepsiCo, General Electric, and Raytheon. These were not true company towns. Still, urban sociologist William H. Whyte found the new structures inhospitable and fortresslike, a triumph for the "car culture."[21]

And despite some corporate movement back into cities, the exurban trend continues today. With more than eleven thousand work-ers in the Silicon Valley town of Mountain View, California, Google owns 10 percent of the town's property. The corporation hopes to add 3.7 million square feet of new develop-ment, which could allow it to double its workforce. Was Mountain View evolving into a modern-day, one-company town? Concerned, the city council opposed Google's plans to build employee housing. Later, the company leased a thousand-acre federal airfield, where the city has no jurisdiction to prevent the housing of Google employees. Google also devel-oped plans for employee residences on the former National Aeronautics and Space Administration (NASA) base at Ames. The

Silicon Valley Mercury News estimated that housing would take up 10 percent of the base's space.[22] The ultramodern Googleplex building already offers a smorgasbord of workplace amenities, from free food to nap rooms, that give work a homey, warm-nest feeling and make employees feel that they never need to leave.

Another high-tech company town is seem-ingly being shaped by Facebook. In February 2011, Facebook announced that it was moving its headquarters to the former Sun Microsystems campus in Menlo Park, California. By 2017, the company had two campuses on either side of an expressway, a Frank Gehry–designed area that spanned 430,000 square feet and housed offices for twenty-eight hundred employees, and the "Willow Campus," reconfigured by Rem Koolhaas to include fifteen hundred units of housing and a score of merchants, from gour-met eateries to hair salons, that catered only to Facebook employees.[23]

DISCUSSION OF THE LITERATURE

A limited number of works examine the American company town as a broad topic. Among the few studies that attempt an over-view, consideration of architecture and urban planning often overshadows an examination of social or economic history. Among the most important of these is John S. Garner's *The Model Company Town: Urban Design Through Private Enterprise in Nineteenth-Century New England*, which provides a useful overview of early company towns in the Northeast. Margaret Crawford's *Building the Workingman's Paradise: The Design of American Company Towns* describes the evolution of company towns from "vernacular settlements" to impressive projects by celebrated archi-tects and planners (p. 140). Such now-forgotten sites as Phelps-Dodge Company's Tyrone, New Mexico, and the Norton Company's Indian Hill Village, Massachusetts, receive well-deserved attention.

Several works consider the company towns of particular geographical areas, such as New England or the West. And in the most common approach of all, historians have tended to examine such places individually, community by community. Such studies often provide a wealth of detail about specific places, almost as if each were developed in isolation. John Coolidge's *Mill and Mansion: A Study of Architecture and Society in Lowell, Massachusetts, 1820–1865*, shows in prose and photos how the town's buildings and its inhabitants evolved over time. Stanley Buder's *Pullman: An Experiment in Industrial Order and Community Planning* is an engrossing examination of the construction of that model town, its unfortunate role in the 1894 nationwide railroad strike, and the town and company's subsequent decline during the 20th century. *Amoskeag: Life and Work in an American Factory City*, by Tamara K. Hareven and Randolph Langenbach, provides an essential history of Manchester, New Hampshire, and, in a Studs Terkel–like section, allows the workers to give voice to their personal histories. Thomas Dublin's Bancroft Prize–winning *Women at Work: The Transformation of Work and Community in Lowell, Massachusetts, 1826–1860* is the definitive account of Lowell's early history. Finally, perhaps the most impressive of the works that concentrate on one locality is *Like a Family: The Making of a Southern Cotton Mill World*, by Jacquelyn Dowd Hall et al. This landmark effort examines a range of villages across the upper South, drawing on over two hundred interviews with textile workers to describe the transformation of agriculture, the migration to the mills, the work experience, and the sometimes-peculiar folkways of the Southern cotton mill universe.

Few writers have celebrated life in company towns. Rather, existence there has been considered grim. In his classic *The Mind of the South*, journalist W. J. Cash wrote that the model for the Southern textile village was clear: "a plantation essentially indistinguishable in organization from the familiar plantation of the cotton fields."[24] Similarly, in his landmark *Night Comes to the Cumberlands*, Harry M. Caudill writes of the "pitiful, hideous little shelters" that characterized coal-country towns.[25]

Such oppressive scenes dominate our thinking about company towns. This means that we may overlook the fact that not all towns were quite so shabby: As has been noted, some even had housing with indoor toilets, running water, and central heating. But to find accounts of life in such relatively privileged places, the reader should look for works dealing individually with such communities as Hershey, Pennsylvania; Scotia, California; and Corning, New York.

PRIMARY SOURCES

Confident of his place in the annals of history, one of the primary founders of Lowell, Massachusetts, had his recollections of the development of the town printed and bound. Nathan Appleton's *Introduction of the Power Loom and the Origin of Lowell* tells how Francis Cabot Lowell and Paul Moody perfected a loom, how the site for the new town was chosen, and how European manufacturing towns served as a negative example. *Correspondence Between Nathan Appleton and John A. Lowell in Relation to the Early History of the City of Lowell* offers further details of the town's early days.[26] There are more Appleton papers at the Massachusetts Historical Society, while various business records such as those of the Hamilton Manufacturing Company are available at the Harvard University Business School's Baker Library. The mill girls' literary magazine, *The Lowell Offering*, is available on microfilm and is excerpted frequently in anthologies.

John Brophy's *A Miner's Life* is the autobiography of a former coal miner and union officer, useful for its description of miners' work and coal towns from the 1890s through the 1920s.[27] The United States Coal Commission released a variety of reports on the industry during the 1920s, including the studies "Earnings of Anthracite Miners" and "Labor Relations in the Anthracite Industry."[28] The United Mine Workers of America maintained voluminous archives, some of which can be found at the library of the Indiana University of Pennsylvania.

In the 1930s, the Federal Writers Project of the Works Progress Administration enlisted hundreds of poor Southerners—including cotton-mill workers and villagers—to write their own life histories. The originals are at the library of the University of North Carolina at Chapel Hill. A good selection of the life histories can be found in the volume *These Are Our Lives.*[29]

The thinking behind Gary, Indiana, is revealed in Illinois Steel president Eugene Buffington's magazine article, "Making Cities for Workingmen," published in *Harper's Weekly.*[30] Graham Romeyn Taylor's studies of steel towns, including Gary, ran in several issues of *The Survey,* a journal published by the Charity Organization Society of the City of New York; these were later collected in book form.[31] The Interchurch World Movement formed a commission to study the decisive 1919 steel strike, concluding with an indictment of the labor practices of US Steel management.[32] The Russell Sage Foundation's multivolume study of living and working conditions in the Pittsburgh area, collectively known as the Pittsburgh Survey, offers a broad view of steelmaking communities. It is available online in excerpted form, and published volumes were issued by the University of Pittsburgh Press and the Russell Sage Foundation.

FURTHER READING

Allen, James. *The Company Town in the American West.* Norman: University of Oklahoma Press, 1966.

Blum, Fred H. *Toward a Democratic Work Process: The Hormel Packinghouse-Workers' Experiment.* New York: Harper, 1953.

Buder, Stanley. *Pullman: An Experiment in Industrial Order and Community Planning, 1880–1930.* New York: Oxford University Press, 1967.

Coolidge, John. *Mill and Mansion: A Study of Architecture and Society in Lowell, Massachusetts, 1820–1865.* New York: Columbia University Press, 1942.

Crawford, Margaret. *Building the Workingman's Paradise: The Design of American Company Towns.* London and New York: Verso, 1995.

D'Antonio, Michael. *Hershey: Milton S. Hershey's Extraordinary Life of Wealth, Empire, and Utopian Dreams.* New York: Simon & Schuster, 2006.

Dublin, Thomas. *Women at Work: The Transformation of Work and Community in Lowell, Massachusetts, 1826–1860.* New York: Columbia University Press, 1979.

Ely, Richard T. "Pullman: A Social Study." *Harper's New Monthly Magazine* 70 (1885): 452–466.

Garner, John S. *The Model Company Town: Urban Design Through Private Enterprise in Nineteenth-Century New England.* Amherst: University of Massachusetts Press, 1984.

Garner, John S., ed. *The Company Town: Architecture and Society in the Early Industrial Age.* New York: Oxford University Press, 1992.

Green, Hardy. *The Company Town: The Industrial Edens and Satanic Mills That Shaped the American Economy.* New York: Basic Books, 2010.

Hales, Peter Bacon. *Atomic Spaces: Living on the Manhattan Project.* Urbana: University of Illinois Press, 1997.

Hall, Jacquelyn Dowd, et al. *Like a Family: The Making of a Southern Cotton Mill World.* New York: W.W. Norton, 1987.

Hareven, Tamara K., and Randolph Langenbach. *Amoskeag: Life and Work in an American Factory City.* New York: Pantheon, 1978.

Kulik, Gary, Roger Parks, and Theodore Z. Penn, eds. *The New England Mill Village, 1790–1860.* Cambridge, MA, and London: MIT Press, 1982.

Mosher, Anne E. *Capital's Utopia: Vandergrift, Pennsylvania 1855–1916.* Baltimore: Johns Hopkins University Press, 2004.

Mozingo, Louise A. *Pastoral Capitalism: A History of Suburban Corporate Landscapes.* Cambridge, MA: MIT Press, 2011.

Reutter, Mark. *Sparrow's Point: Making Steel—the Rise and Ruin of American Industrial Might.* New York: Summit Books, 1988.

Taylor, Graham Romeyn. *Satellite Cities: A Study of Industrial Suburbs*. New York: D. Appleton, 1915.

Wilkerson, Hugh, and John van der Zee. *Life in the Peace Zone: An American Company Town*. New York: Macmillan, 1971.

Wright, Carroll D. *Fall River, Lowell, and Lawrence*. Boston: Rand, Avery, 1882.

Wright, Carroll D. *Report on the Factory System of the United States*. Washington, DC: US Congress, 47th, 2nd session: 1882–1883.

NOTES

1. Gary Kulik, Roger Parks, and Theodore Z. Penn, eds., *The New England Mill Village, 1790–1860* (Cambridge, MA, and London: MIT Press, 1982), xxiii; and Thomas Dublin, *Women at Work: The Transformation of Work and Community in Lowell, Massachusetts, 1826–1860* (New York: Columbia University Press, 1979), 15.

2. US Census Bureau, "Population of the 100 Largest Cities and Other Urban Places in the United States, 1790–1990," Washington, DC: Population Division Working Paper No. 27, June 1998. https://www.census.gov/population/www /documentation/twps0027/twps0027.html.

3. Charles Dickens, *American Notes* (London and New York: Cassell, n.d.), 55–58.

4. Henry David Thoreau, "A Week on the Concord and Merrimack Rivers," in *Walden and Other Writings of Henry David Thoreau*, ed. Brooks Atkinson (New York: Modern Library, 1937), 340–341.

5. Sven Beckert, *Empire of Cotton: A Global History* (New York: Alfred A. Knopf, 2014), 246–292.

6. Quoted in Nathan Appleton, *Introduction of the Power Loom and the Origin of Lowell* (Lowell, MA: B. H. Penhallow, 1858), 15.

7. Tom Bell, *Out of This Furnace* (Pittsburgh, PA: University of Pittsburgh Press, 1976), 122–123.

8. Paul Krause, *The Battle for Homestead 1880–1892* (Pittsburgh, PA: University of Pittsburgh Press, 1992), 12–43.

9. Stanley Buder, *Pullman: An Experiment in Industrial Order and Community Planning, 1880–1930* (New York: Oxford University Press, 1967), 97–103, 129–199.

10. Anne E. Mosher, *Capital's Utopia: Vandergrift, Pennsylvania 1855–1916* (Baltimore: Johns Hopkins University Press, 2004), 145.

11. Michael D'Antonio, *Hershey: Milton S. Hershey's Extraordinary Life of Wealth, Empire, and Utopian Dreams* (New York: Simon & Schuster, 2006), 50–51, 84–140; and Joel Glenn Brenner, *The Emperors of Chocolate: Inside the Secret World of Hershey and Mars* (New York: Random House, 1999), 75–88, 106–135.

12. Graham Romeyn Taylor, *Satellite Cities: A Study of Industrial Suburbs* (New York: D. Appleton, 1915), 10, 165.

13. Edward Chase Kirkland, *Industry Comes of Age: Business, Labor, and Public Policy, 1860–1897* (New York: Holt, Rinehart, and Winston, 1961), 1–2.

14. Jacquelyn Dowd Hall et al., *Like a Family: The Making of a Southern Cotton Mill World* (New York: W. W. Norton, 1987), 56.

15. Robert Shogan, *The Battle of Blair Mountain: The Story of America's Largest Union Uprising* (New York: Basic Books, 2006). https://books .google.com/books/about/The_Battle_of _Blair_Mountain.html?id=XyTuG5fO5E4C.

16. Harry M. Caudill, *Night Comes to the Cumberlands: A Biography of a Depressed Area* (Boston: Little, Brown, 1962), 144–145.

17. "Cannon II," *Fortune*, November 1933, 141.

18. Robert Hoover and John Hoover, *An American Quality Legend: How Maytag Saved Our Moms, Vexed the Competition, and Presaged America's Quality Revolution* (New York: McGraw-Hill, 1993), 62–156, 176–201.

19. Fred H. Blum, *Toward a Democratic Work Process: The Hormel Packinghouse-Workers' Experiment* (New York: Harper, 1953), 3.

20. Charlie LeDuff, "At a slaughterhouse, some things never die," *The New York Times on the Web*, June 16, 2000. https://partners.nytimes .com/library/national/race/061600leduff -meat.html.

21. William H. Whyte, *City: Rediscovering the Center* (New York: Doubleday, 1988), 290.

22. Sean Hollister, "Welcome to Googletown," *The Verge*, February 26, 2014, https://www.theverge .com/2014/2/26/5444030/company-town -how-google-is-taking-over-mountain-view; and Mike Swift, "Google's Growth Online re- flected by Expansion in Mountain View," *The Mercury News*, November 11, 2010.

23. Jessica Guynn, "Welcome to Zucker Burg," *Los Angeles Times*, August 10, 2012, http://articles .latimes.com/2012/aug/10/business/la-fi

-facebook-company-town-20120810; and Julianne Tveten, *The Baffler*, September 27, 2017.

24. W. J. Cash, *The Mind of the South* (New York: Alfred A. Knopf, 1941), 205.

25. Harry M. Caudill, *Night Comes to the Cumberlands*, 109.

26. Nathan Appleton, *Introduction of the Power Loom and the Origin of Lowell: Correspondence Between Nathan Appleton and John A. Lowell in Relation to the Early History of the City of Lowell* (Boston: Eastburn's Press, 1848).

27. John Brophy, *A Miner's Life* (Madison: University of Wisconsin Press, 1964).

28. The US Coal Commission, "Earnings of Anthracite Miners" and "Labor Relations in the Anthracite Industry" (Washington, DC: Government Printing Office, 1923).

29. Federal Writers Project of the Works Progress Administration, *These Are Our Lives* (New York: W. W. Norton, 1975).

30. Eugene Buffington, "Making Cities for Workingmen," *Harper's Weekly*, May 8, 1909, 15.

31. Taylor, *Satellite Cities*.

32. Commission of Inquiry, Interchurch World Movement, *Report on the Steel Strike of 1919* (New York: Harcourt, Brace, and Howe, 1920).

Hardy Green

GLOBALIZATION AND THE AMERICAN CITY

DEFINING GLOBALIZATION

Even before the nation's founding, cities were sites of global circulation. In urban ports, colonial settlers, indentured servants, and enslaved people arrived from across the Atlantic, while American crops were shipped to markets overseas. Urban dwellers bought goods manufactured far beyond the colonies, while foreign investment built American infrastructure. At no point in its history was the American city anything but "global."

Yet the relationship between American cities and the rest of the world changed dramatically during the 19th and 20th centuries.

In the second half of the 20th century, New York became not only a global cultural capital, but one of the most important financial centers in the world, making possible the economic integration that engendered the phenomenon called "globalization." Los Angeles and Silicon Valley were also crucial players in the global integration of the entertainment and technology industries, respectively. Less obvious contenders played a role as well. Houston, as the global headquarters of the international oil industry, grew from a mid-20th-century oil-producing behemoth to a white-collar headquarters of oil management, finance, and technology services, a place through which most of the world's major players in the oil industry passed. And Miami grew into the financial and cultural headquarters of Latin America.

"Globalization" is a notoriously slippery term, but commentators generally use it to refer to the process of neoliberal world economic integration that began in the mid-20th century and accelerated at the end of the Cold War. Although markets were "global" even before the United States had cities, the intense economic global integration characteristic of the 1970s through the early 2000s is a largely new phenomenon. The era of contemporary globalization was characterized by a new monetary regime with the end of the Bretton Woods system in 1971; the entrenchment of a global assembly line ushered in by increased capital mobility; new technologies that made transporting people, goods, and ideas across large distances cheap and quick; the fall of the Soviet Union; the entrance of China into the World Trade Organization; and the integration of both nations into the capitalist world economy. As historian Thomas Zeiler explains,

> globalization must be viewed as a historical phenomenon that involves the flow of goods, services, money, and people, as well as the diffusion of technology, directed toward the universal

corporate ideal of big business of a single world market in which to allocate resources, shift production, market goods, and expand financial, legal, insurance, and information services.[1]

However, the history of globalization and the American city begins much earlier than 1971. Describing the impact that late-20th-century globalization had on US cities—and the ways in which US cities shaped the process of globalization—requires tracing the longer history of how American cities have been transnational spaces. This historical context illustrates how the new era of globalization differs from earlier periods as well as how contemporary globalization grew out of older patterns in the urban past. The period of globalization can be characterized by three primary transformations in American urban life. First, a neoliberal economy dominated by the service sector supplanted the Fordist industrial economy of the early 20th century, transforming the *character of urban economies*. This transformation shaped the kinds and conditions of labor urban residents performed. Second, new patterns of investment, trade, commodity chains, and immigration *directly linked US cities to international markets*. None of these developments were entirely new, but they accelerated rapidly under neoliberal globalization. Finally, the shape of globalization that evolved resulted in hypersegregation, extreme urban wealth disparities, and new patterns of immigration, all of which have fundamentally *reshaped urban politics*.

AMERICAN CITIES AND GLOBAL EXCHANGE BEFORE THE 20TH CENTURY

Early American cities were inherently global. Colonial cities were predominantly organized around ports, which moved people and goods in and out, exporting raw materials like grain, flour, and cotton and importing manufactured commodities first from England, Europe, and the West Indies and later from South America and China. Moreover, American cities were crucial components in building the fledgling American overseas empire. US cities were, of course, crucial nodes in the brutal transatlantic slave trade, and after independence, the financial institutions in the port cities of the east financed the infrastructure for westward expansion and Indian removal. Historian Seth Rockman described the transnational character of early American cities well in his vivid description of Baltimore:

> Imagine a scene on the docks of Baltimore in 1816, as American-born stevedores loaded crates of ready-made shirts aboard a merchant ship bound for South America. Focusing in on that ship, one might see a rural miller haggling with the captain over the price of one of the indentured teenagers whom the ship had recently brought from Bremen, or a free black mariner signing articles to work the outgoing voyage as an ordinary seaman.... Along the waterfront, a middle-aged white domestic servant might be cooking breakfast in a Fells Point boardinghouse, where some of the ship's crew spent its shore leave in the company of women supporting themselves through prostitution. In the harbor, Scotch-Irish dredgers on the mudmachine were battling sedimentation to keep Baltimore's port open. From an even broader vantage, one might see the enslaved field laborers of a distant cotton plantation, whose growing market value encouraged urban slaveholders to resist liberating the men, women, and children they owned in Baltimore, or even the menial workers in Lancashire, Cap François, Ouidah, and Paramaribo— the 'Atlantic proletariat' whose labor integrated an already global economy.[2]

In the port city of New Orleans, the trade of raw materials and commercial goods was surpassed by a far larger industry: the trade and sale of enslaved people. Not far from the port, the continent's largest slave market brought together enslaved people first across the Atlantic and then from all over the South, establishing the city as one of the world's most important markets for the trade in human beings until the Civil War.[3]

After Reconstruction (1865–1877), American cities' engagement with global commerce increased. At the turn of the 20th century, the United States expanded its informal commercial empire and entered into the realm of formal, territorial, and overseas empire. These imperial ambitions produced a booming economy in American imports while also bringing new foreign imports through US ports. In the middle-class households of American cities and suburbs, white women produced a household domesticity that was explicitly global in its character. They hosted Orientalist teas, prepared around-the-world dinners, and celebrated—and exoticized—immigrants' dances and clothing.[4]

In the context of a newly robust American empire, US cities were sites where the meaning and the implications of empire were negotiated on a daily basis. In the industrial cities of the North and West, immigrants from Europe and Asia labored in the burgeoning factories of cities like New York, Chicago, and Seattle.[5] Beyond the original colonies, US cities grew through their relationships with far-flung markets. Western cities like Seattle contributed to the creation of the concept of a "Pacific world" that might allow white American boosters to reach coveted Asian markets. Meanwhile, Chinese and Japanese immigrants to the city cemented their claims to citizenship by arguing that their presence bolstered the city's cosmopolitanism—even while the West Coast remained "ground zero for . . . anti-Asian politics."[6] Immigrants themselves also reshaped the politics and urban environments of American cities. In the leisure capital of Miami, immigrants from the Caribbean gave form to the city's sexual economy, which in turn shaped

the city's spatial development. At the same time, white boosters used immigrants and the sexual economy as a framework for debating urban modernity and the relationship between Miami and US imperialism.[7]

American urban spaces were sites of global exchange, but they were also models that carried transnational resonance. Beginning in the late 19th century, white urban planners, state governments, and real estate developers in cities as disparate as Freetown, Sierra Leone; Baltimore; New Delhi; and Rio de Janeiro reached a consensus that urban segregation was necessary and desirable to preserve real estate values and maintain social order. This form of urban planning was forged through transnational conversations among urban elites. For instance, the white Baltimoreans who penned the first urban segregation ordinance in the United States in 1910 were inspired by "segregation in British India," French race theory, and "the anti-Chinese movement on the West Coast." Moreover, their ordinance carried weight far beyond Baltimore, or even the United States; Baltimore's segregationists were "besieged by letters from across the country, and even as far away as the Philippines, demanding copies of the ordinance" to be mimicked around the globe. In other words, this convergence was no accident; as historian Carl Nightengale writes, "such movements to segregate cities spread because they were interconnected."[8] The transnational development of formal segregation helped to create and sustain urban racial and class inequalities that shaped the development of the late-20th-century global city.

Not only transnational intellectual and policy connections engendered segregation in Baltimore; transnational investment literally shaped the city, too. In the 1890s, as historian Paige Glotzer argues, Baltimore's planned streetcar suburb of Roland Park became one of the first large-scale planned developments in the United States. Building an entire development at once—rather than one or two houses at a time—was made possible through international investors hailing from Egypt, India, Antigua, and the Congo. In fact, the Roland Park Company itself was a British-held concern, founded to speculate in US and colonial land. After investing in projects such as South African diamond mining, the company turned its attention to residential development in the United States. To protect its investors' money, and working off the assumption that racial integration threatened home values, the company required deed restrictions restricting home purchases in Roland Parks to whites, becoming the first such planned community in the United States.[9] This early history of urban residential segregation in the United States illustrates how American cities were interwoven in a complex network of intellectuals, policymakers, and real estate investors that spanned the globe long before the era of globalization.

THE FORDIST CITY AND THE GLOBAL ECONOMY

The industrialization of American cities continued rapidly in the early 20th century. Particularly in the Northeast and Midwest, massive industrial cities became host to skyscrapers, enormous factories, and thousands of workers, immigrant and native-born alike. Common planning wisdom coupled with the realities of energy and transportation infrastructure led to most new industrial sites being concentrated in cities. Increasingly, urban workers were employed in highly mechanized, assembly-line labor that produced manufactured goods quickly and cheaply. In 1908, Henry Ford determined to "build a car for the great multitude," affordable to a majority of American consumers. To meet this goal, Ford developed the assembly line system, in which workers performed discrete, repetitive tasks on automobile parts moving down a conveyor belt to meet the worker. This new system was quick, cheap, and efficient, driving down prices while forcing workers to speed up their production performing mind-numbing

tasks. Still, this system was extended far beyond the auto industry, making possible the mass production of a range of consumer goods. Preparation for World War I further expanded cities' industrial capacity, as industrialists rushed to build weapons and ships for the war effort. Greater rates of manufacturing brought more workers into the nation's cities. By 1920, for the first time more Americans lived in cities than in rural areas.[10]

Ford coupled the assembly line with the $5-a-day wage, a high income he offered both as a gesture of welfare capitalism and as an attempt to keep workers willing to perform such dull labor. Mass production, high wages, and the assumption that workers would eventually purchase the goods they produced—both because the assembly line drove down prices, and because the factory offered higher than standard wages—became known as the Fordist system, a set of economic assumptions about American industrial capitalism that white male workers grew to expect in the first decades of the 20th century.[11] The Great Depression shook this relationship to its core, as workers had little income for any consumer goods purchasing.

The 1930s saw the beginnings of the phenomena that ushered in contemporary globalization. In 1934, at the very beginning of the New Deal, free trade enthusiasts convinced the US Congress that the United States must replace England as the world's global marketplace. Instead of buying foreign goods from London, and allowing England to profit from the trade, the United States sought to import those goods directly. Doing so required skirting tariff and customs laws. Congress passed the Foreign-Trade Zones Act of 1934, which allowed for the creation of foreign-trade zones on US soil that were exempt from tariff charges if certain conditions were met.[12] As historian Dara Orenstein explains,

> If Ford or Toyota imports a car radio from Germany, or, more probably, from a free trade zone in Brazil, the tariff that

normally applies is suspended; if the radio leaves the zone as a radio, the tariff is charged, but if the radio exits the zone in a new form, as part of a car, voilà! The tariff vanishes. A deceptively simple legal fiction, the FTZ and its attendant perks allow state and municipal agencies in places like Ohio and Alabama to attract corporate investment by promising "the benefits of offshore, onshore."[13]

For the first time in the history of the nation, the US government "partially denationalized U.S. soil." The first FTZ was established on Staten Island in 1936.[14]

FTZs laid the groundwork for a global economy that focused not on the mass production and high wages of Fordism but on cheap, tax-free circulation, enabling and encouraging a global assembly line. In the depths of the Depression, the FTZ represented the first signs of a new economy that would emerge during the second half of the 20th century, but catalyzing that economy would necessitate a war effort.

WARFARE AND THE CITY

Just as was the case in World War I, World War II boosted industrial production in the nation's cities and helped to recuperate urban economies struggling through the Depression. But the war abroad reshaped cities back home in other ways as well. Manufacturers developed new earth-moving tools, including tractors and bulldozers, for the war effort, and new military divisions like the Naval Construction Battalions engaged in land clearance overseas. At the war's end, urban boosters, policymakers, and real estate developers fashioned the tools and the ideology of wartime land clearance for use in the nation's cities.[15] New racially segregated suburban developments dotted the postwar landscape, carrying forth both the imperialist history that had informed Baltimore's early racially restrictive housing covenants and the wartime influences that inspired urban renewal and slum clearance.

FTZs laid the early structural groundwork for contemporary globalization, but the demands of the Cold War played a crucial—and underexamined—role in creating the conditions that engendered the global cities of the late 20th century. Urban renewal was not only a means of shoring up real estate values, continuing an ideology of wartime clearance, and entrenching urban racial exclusion; it was also a Cold War imperative. In New York, historian Samuel Zipp explains, urban renewal boosters including Robert Moses "saw modern rebuilding projects as a way to make Manhattan a symbol of American power during an age of metropolitan transformation and the Cold War." Clearing slums and creating new, modernist structures contributed to the launching of New York as a "world-class city" and "an icon of global power." Becoming a postwar world-class city through urban renewal "made room in the city grid for research medicine, high culture, and higher education," and "announc[ed]...the rise of a white-collar world city" that was poised to become a global city at the end of the 20th century.[16]

This kind of white-collar city was made possible not only through urban renewal but also through federal defense spending motivated by Cold War concerns. Defense spending channeled through the Department of Defense created entire new industries and dramatically transformed the regional status quo of the nation, shoring up New England, the South, and the West and neglecting traditional industrial centers like the Mid-Atlantic and the Midwest. During the late 1940s and 1950s, defense spending created new high-tech industrial complexes in California, Texas, Massachusetts, and Florida. These high-tech centers employed highly skilled and highly educated white-collar workers, further laying the groundwork for the emergence of global cities.[17]

The Cold War emphasis on scientific research shifted urban developmental resources to a certain kind of spatial form: what historian Margaret O'Mara dubs the "city of knowledge." Federal funding transformed universities during the Cold War, in the form of grants for scientific research and GI Bill loans supporting scores of new students. The most successful grant recipients built high-tech suburban research complexes aimed at attracting highly skilled white-collar workers. Silicon Valley was the most demonstrable example. Suburban cities of knowledge were elite but also homogeneous, heralding the racial and class exclusion endemic to postwar suburban development. As O'Mara writes, the "Cold War made scientists into elites, and mass suburbanization reorganized urban space in a way that created elite places." Cold War research funding, in other words, "redefined the American city for a post-industrial Information Age."[18] If the tech-centered Silicon Valley is one archetype of the contemporary US global city (with New York and Los Angeles representing far different models of post-industrial global urbanism), it is impossible to imagine this kind of city being built without Cold War resources.

The white-collar cities that emerged during the Cold War, from New York to California, were explicitly racially exclusionary. Throughout the postwar decades, African Americans were largely barred from the prosperous suburbs and white-collar jobs. Cold War politics, however, extended suburban homeownership to some Asian Americans in San Francisco and Los Angeles, places rife with anti-Asian sentiment and discrimination before and during World War II. "As the cold war deepened," historian Charlotte Brooks writes, "a growing number of white Californians saw Asian American housing integration as a necessary price to pay for victory in the struggle," since whites understood Asian Americans to be, at root, "foreigners" who represented their countries of origin and, therefore, should be treated diplomatically if the nation's interests demanded it. This calculus allowed Asian Americans to move "to neighborhoods where blacks could not follow" during the postwar years.[19] In Houston, whites likewise embraced international students from Africa, Asia, and the Middle East while eschewing the civil rights demands of local black and Latino Houstonians, reasoning that international students represented potential business colleagues in a decentralizing global oil industry.[20] When it came to the low-income and predominantly African American neighborhoods of the nation's cities, the logic of the Cold War was deployed far differently. Under President Lyndon B. Johnson, defense intellectuals in the late 1960s turned their attention away from war and toward nation's cities, "maintaining domestic urban security by continuing to apply defense and aerospace innovations and ideas to city planning and management."[21] In other words, Cold War imperatives informed the building of white-collar suburbs while militarizing racialized urban spaces. The groundwork that the Cold War was laying for late-20th-century global cities would incorporate middle-class whites and certain middle-class nonwhites deemed sufficiently foreign to be useful in the emerging global economy, but most African Americans and Latinos were explicitly excluded.

CAPITAL FLIGHT

Part of the postwar vision for American prosperity in the Cold War heralded exporting American goods, like automobiles, abroad to showcase the strength of American labor and engineering. Prioritizing American exports was beneficial for the nation's balance of payments, but it also sent an ideological message by showcasing American prosperity and ingenuity. Highlighting the "American standard of living" was a *cause célèbre* for Cold Warriors, most notably Vice President Richard Nixon who argued with Soviet Premier Nikita Krushchev at a US Trade and Cultural Fair in Moscow in 1959. The event was immortalized as the "Kitchen Debate."[22]

This ostensible emphasis on American production notwithstanding, by the 1950s the US economy was shifting away from mass industrial production in important ways. By the late 1950s, Detroit—the birthplace of Fordism, the home of the iconic American auto industry, and the headquarters of some of the strongest labor unions in American history—was already losing much of its industrial might. Three major auto plants closed in the city between 1953 and 1957, and the city weathered four major recessions.[23] Capital flight was the primary culprit. New advances in transportation, communication, and technology enabled factories to move outside the central cities and beyond the industrial Mid-Atlantic and Midwest entirely. A federal highway system made long-distance travel more viable, and the tremendous investments the federal government had made in developing the infrastructure of the rural South and West since the New Deal made new regions of the country viable for industry. Moreover, cities outside the industrial urban core explicitly courted industrial capital, promising lucrative tax breaks and pliable workers willing to accept low wages if only the industries would relocate.[24] New automation practices also allowed employers to operate with fewer workers and threatened the power of unions.[25] Even when industries stayed in place, other employers turned to white-collar contract workers to break strikes and circumvent union agreements.[26] The impacts of these developments were devastating for the old industrial cities. In 1950, 56 percent of all automobile employment in the United States was located in Michigan; by 1960, only 40 percent remained, and the numbers kept declining.[27]

This early deindustrialization not only created the circumstances for the emergence of global cities; it served as a kind of protoglobalization in its own right. For example, the radio and television manufacturer RCA began production in New Jersey in the 1930s, moved to rural Indiana in the 1940s, relocated to Memphis in the 1960s, and finally left the United States entirely in 1968, employing workers in *maquilas* just over the Mexican border in Chihuahua. At each point of relocation, RCA sought more pliable workers willing to accept lower wages and fled powerful, unionized workers in their current location. "'Offshore' production may be a focus of political attention today," writes historian Jefferson Cowie, "but neither the causes of the transnationalization of production nor the problems it creates differ dramatically from those of the transregionalization of industry several decades earlier."[28] Union leaders and business executives celebrated a "business-labor accord" in the postwar years, a presumed shared assumption that both sides would bargain fairly and try to avoid disruptive strikes, but RCA's mobility suggests "that management may have been significantly less committed to its end of the bargain than many analysts presume."[29]

The model that these companies pursued domestically became a prototype for globalization beginning in the late 1960s. With long-distance travel more viable, and with new regulations in place that made moving offshore more attractive for employers, companies like RCA led the charge in moving beyond US borders in search of labor. With the introduction of containerization in the 1960s, transporting goods across long distances became even quicker and cheaper, further accelerating capital flight.[30]

This capital mobility encouraged labor casualization across the spectrum of work, from migrant laborers to office workers to consultants and executives. Seeking to maximize profits above all else, companies began to divest themselves of long-term workers with pensions in favor of short-term contract workers who could be hired and fired at will.[31] This insecurity became an increasingly defining characteristic of the US urban economy by the 1970s.

THE RISE OF A GLOBAL SERVICE ECONOMY

With industrial urbanism under threat, many US cities witnessed the development of robust service industries that became more powerful players in their local economies. The service sector did not emerge to fill the void left behind by deindustrialization; rather, it developed independently, growing in strength even as industrial might waned. Urban service economies included both high-wage, high-prestige industries like finance, consulting, technological services, higher education, and medicine as well as low-wage, low-prestige industries including hospitality, food service, custodial service, and care work for elders and children. These industries boomed while heavy industry declined, in part because of Cold War investment in science, technology, education, and health care.

The shift toward services was not only the effect of the unintended consequences of Cold War investment, or the inexorable logic of the market; political contestation played a tremendous role. Proponents of the service sector had long sought to remake cities in their image. In Houston during the 1940s and 1950s, for instance, boosters disagreed about whether the city's future lay in industrial development or in cementing the city as a hub of international circulation services that profited primarily through the port, banking, and import-export exchanges.[32] The early 1970s, however, represented a key turning point in the history of the US service economy. Between 1971 and 1973, the global economy faced a crisis, as the Bretton Woods agreement collapsed, oil prices skyrocketed, and the United States faced foreign industrial competition from Japan and Germany. Republicans and Democrats alike met the crisis by supporting new policies that resulted in the shoring up of finance and real estate while further harming domestic manufacturing.[33] Even more directly, when New York City was on the verge of bankruptcy in 1975,

financiers took the opportunity to shift the city's priorities—and its budget—toward supporting the financial, insurance, and real estate sectors at the expense of the city's other interests.[34] By the late 1970s, federal policymakers prioritized curbing inflation over ensuring high rates of employment and introduced reductions to capital gains taxes and other supply-side tax cuts, effectively ending the Keynesian system that had reigned since the 1930s.[35] The US economy was fundamentally transformed during the 1970s, but also transformed was the nation's political calculus, the balance of who held power and political clout. Nowhere was this transformation clearer than in the nation's cities.

By the early 21st century, global cities were *service cities*, achieving international influence and prestige through their role in providing transnational services to clients around the world. These services ranged from finance, insurance, and real estate, as in New York, to the oil engineering and management services that guided the international oil industry, as in Houston, to the technological designs developed in Silicon Valley and produced through commodity chains spanning the globe. The leading economic sectors trafficked in services, be they financial, consulting, design, or engineering services. Although banking and trade long played a crucial role in urban life, contemporary global cities represented a radically new development. As sociologist Saskia Sassen writes,

> When Max Weber analyzed medieval cities woven together in the Hanseatic League, he conceived their trade as the exchange of surplus production; it was his view that a medieval city could withdraw from external trade and continue to support itself, albeit on a reduced scale. The modern molecule of global cities is nothing like the trade among self-sufficient places in the Hanseatic League... [and] the territorial dispersal of current economic activity creates a

need for expanded central control and management.[36]

The global city is *inherently* a service city, and the service city is *inherently* global, because the global city exists to dictate and manage the operation of a global assembly line. The global city represents the economic power held by certain cities over populations in other parts of the world, demonstrating that in practice, "globalization" means, for instance, establishing Houston elites as the managers of Nigerian oil capital rather than placing Nigerian and Houstonian workers on a level transnational playing field.

The flip side of these high-end, high-prestige services lies in the low-wage service industries that support them and make the global service city possible. Global cities demand luxury services including food service, hospitality, and other care work—service labor that is generally performed by low-wage, vulnerable workers, often immigrants. As anthropologist Rachel Sherman points out,

> [i]n manufacturing, goods are sold in a market distant from the factory, which might be in Detroit or in Bangladesh, so customers who buy these products never see the workers who make them. Not so with servant clients, who are not only physically present as the interactive product is created but also, in fact, participate in its production.[37]

And just as the assembly line became globalized, so too did reproductive labor. Citizens of low-wage nations frequently sought employment elsewhere. Filipina migrants, for instance, traveled to Europe, the United States, and the Middle East in search of childcare positions that paid better than work back home—despite the fact that leaving home left them legally vulnerable.[38] The fact that low-wage service positions were generally gendered feminine and thus devalued, coupled with the fact that workers of color disproportionately

performed this work, the fact that many of these workers were immigrants, and the fact that service labor (and particularly care work) was historically omitted from US labor regulation, meant that low-wage service workers had very little leverage to advocate for higher wages or better working conditions.

Far more than in the past, the new power of finance and real estate capital reframed cities as sites of investment. Of course, urban real estate investment was long a means of profit-making, and cities have never been pure spaces of use-value. But the global service city reformulated real estate investment as an end in itself. In 1970s New York City, for instance, artists began to convert abandoned lofts, or those rented at low rates by small manufacturing concerns, into unconventional housing stock for their own use. City planners and real estate investors saw financial promise in this reuse. By the 1980s loft space—once the site of industrial production—was being converted into a space of consumption and investment at alarming rates. The gentrification of New York's SoHo district on its face appeared to be a grassroots effort at artistic urban revitalization, but soon proved to be in fact a concerted effort of real estate speculation and the revalorization of underutilized urban capital.[39] By the early 21st century, international elites were investing their excess capital into global cities' real estate, sure of a steady return. In cities like New York and Miami, scores of apartments sit unoccupied, purchased sight unseen by investors who trust that a scarcity of housing stock protects their investment. This kind of pattern has exacerbated the already spiraling split between rich and poor in the nation's global cities.[40] In response, anti-gentrification movements emerged particularly in the nation's global cities, demanding that urban space be seen primarily as a resource for urban residents rather than as a form of investment capital.[41]

The US cities that failed to become global cities were in even greater peril. The once-booming city of Detroit, for example, struggled in a contemporary economy in which manufacturing fled but high-wage service jobs concentrated in a few cities like New York and San Francisco. Although cities with high numbers of industrial jobs still exist in the United States, the broader trends toward capital mobility and the decline of unionization has made even those cities vulnerable to the same dynamics plaguing global cities and Rust Belt cities. Since 1990, the economic and legal infrastructure of globalization has continued to develop, as China aggressively began to welcome capitalist investment and as the North American Free Trade Agreement (NAFTA) eliminated trade barriers between the United States and Mexico, paving the way for the rapid expansion of *maquiladoras* across the Mexican border where Mexican workers produced manufactured goods for American companies at low wages while those companies evaded tariffs.[42]

IMMIGRATION, LABOR, AND RESISTANCE

Documented immigration into the United States accelerated rapidly after 1965. The Hart-Cellar Immigration Act of 1965 ended the national origins quota system that had been in place since the Immigration Act of 1924, which discriminated against immigrants from Africa and especially Asia in favor of Europeans. Under the new legislation, different regions of the world were ensured at least nominal equality under immigration law. During the 1970s, documented immigration was 32 percent higher than in the 1960s. During the 1980s, immigration increased 47 percent over the 1970s. The pattern continued to the end of the century as immigration in the 1990s increased 57 percent over the 1980s.[43] During the first decade of the 21st century, more than 10 million documented immigrants entered the United States, with the majority hailing from Mexico (16.5 percent), China (5.7 percent), India (5.7 percent), and the Philippines (5.3 percent).[44]

Refugees and undocumented immigration made these numbers even higher.

The 1965 Immigration Act gave special preference to immigrants of the professional class.[45] Yet many immigrants—documented and undocumented alike—entered the United States to work in low-wage positions, many of them in service fields including home health and child care.[46] Undocumented immigrants in particular are vulnerable to labor exploitation within the United States, as is the case in Los Angeles's garment industry, which became notorious for employing immigrants in sweatshop conditions and robbing them of their wages.[47] Yet Los Angeles immigrants were also the leaders of a new, robust labor movement, shocking observers who assumed immigrants were "unorganizable."[48]

The changing shape of labor and the rise of new patterns of immigration fundamentally reshaped American politics. Among white native-born Americans, vitriolic anti-immigrant sentiment increased dramatically after 1980, reaching a nativist high point during the presidential campaign of Donald Trump in 2016. At the same time, immigrants who became citizens were reshaping the electorate. At the urban level, city governments increasingly had multiethnic representation with New York, Los Angeles, and San Francisco becoming multiethnic "world cities," with tremendously diverse populations hailing from around the globe and no one ethnic or racial minority. In fact, some observers have argued that multiethnic multiculturalism is a prerequisite for achieving "global city" status.[49]

Despite the multiethnic character of contemporary global cities, power remained unevenly distributed, and extreme socioeconomic stratification has been a defining characteristic. High-income white-collar urban residents—the vast majority of them white native-born Americans—reaped the spoils of globalization while the rest of urban residents scraped by. The political options available to urban non-elites were more limited than they were in the past, as unionized labor weakened, business and finance capital strengthened, and immigration policy left immigrants vulnerable to exploitation and legal insecurity. New politics—from anti-gentrification and squatting campaigns, to the organizing of service workers and the success of the Service Employees International Union (SEIU) in organizing janitors and homecare workers—have combatted the unique conditions endemic to the contemporary global city.

DISCUSSION OF THE LITERATURE

The first scholarship on globalization and the American city emerged from the social sciences. The founding text of global cities scholarship is Saskia Sassen's *The Global City*, a book that theorizes the emergence of the global service city and its impact on urban spatial form, politics, and international relations. A robust first wave of scholarship on global cities emerged beginning in the 1990s, as the global city itself was first beginning to come to the attention of scholars, journalists, and global city residents. This scholarship tended to focus on economic and theoretical analysis.[50]

Qualitative sociologists and anthropologists in the 1990s also built a literature on the global city that focused on the phenomenological experience of workers and residents in globalized, post-industrial urban spaces. Sharon Zukin's *Loft Living* represented an early example of scholarship that brought together cultural analysis of the emerging globalized, luxury consumption oriented city with economic data that explained its emergence, a tradition built upon in Aaron Shkuda's *The Lofts of Soho*.[51] Scholars in this tradition have built a robust literature on life in the global city, although much of this work focuses more heavily on the meaning-making of laborers than on the spatial development of the global city itself.[52] A notable exception is Chloe Taft's *From Steel to Slots*, which describes how the industrial city of Bethlehem, Pennsylvania, was drawn into a global web of finance capital that remade it into a post-industrial site for leisure consumption.[53]

The first historians and geographers to address the emergence of the global city tended to focus on making sense of Los Angeles. The scholarship of Marxist urban geographer David Harvey has been—and remains—a central touchstone for this work. This body of work placed Los Angeles into a longer historical framework, tracing its transformation from an industrial to a post-industrial city and theorizing that Los Angeles represented the future of American cities as a multiethnic, decentralized, car-dependent service city.[54] More recent scholarship on the global city seeks to place the emergence of the post-industrial city and the postwar suburb into an imperial framework.[55] This scholarship suggests a relationship between postwar American global power and the rise of the post-industrial global city, though more work remains to be done to further illustrate these dynamics.

Much of the historical work on the global city remains to be written. Open questions include the role of business interests in directly building (rather than merely reaping the benefits of) the globalized city; the relationship between US foreign policy, particularly the Cold War, and the rise of the global city; the development of a feminized low-wage service economy and its relationship with the earlier history of groups excluded from labor protections; the emergence of a transnational professional white-collar class and its impact on cities; the dynamics of gentrification and real estate speculation; and the relationship between global cities and environmental change.[56]

PRIMARY SOURCES

Research on globalization and the US city could take a variety of approaches. Those interested in capital flight will likely rely on the business records of a particular company, when they are available. State and municipal records will likely also contain discussions of the threat of losing industrial capital or proposals for attracting new capital. Labor union records will likely also include meeting minutes, newspaper clippings, or statements addressing capital flight. Finally, federal records—including Congressional meeting minutes and files in presidential libraries and the National Archives—will include discussions about national policy designed either to combat capital flight or enable it, as in the case of the institution of free trade zones and NAFTA. Scholars interested in the rise of service industries might again turn to corporate records, when they are available, and the records of unions like SEIU.

Historians of gentrification and real estate speculation can turn to county and municipal government records, where they can find property records and planning documents. Newspapers, zines, and, more recently, blogs would be useful sources for tracking the progress of anti-gentrification activism. Historians interested in documenting life in the global city at the scale of the city block will likely rely on ethnographies and oral histories. The papers of key activists or business leaders, when available, would be invaluable resources.

The history of globalization and the American city draws together labor history, business history, planning history, immigration history, real estate history, and foreign relations history, while operating at scales ranging from the city block to the entire globe. Potential sources for writing this kind of history are almost infinite and depend on the scale, scope, and motivations of the individual project. The unavailability of corporate sources makes writing this kind of history a special challenge, but historians interested in this topic have a great deal of understudied ground available to cover.

FURTHER READING

Abu-Lughod, Janet. *New York, Chicago, Los Angeles: America's Global Cities*. Minneapolis: University of Minnesota Press, 2001.

Broughton, Chad. *Boom, Bust, Exodus: The Rust Belt, the Maquilas, and a Tale of Two Cities*. New York: Oxford University Press, 2016.

Cowie, Jefferson. *Capital Moves: RCA's Seventy-Year Quest for Cheap Labor*. Ithaca, NY: Cornell University Press, 1999.

Davis, Mike. *City of Quartz: Excavating the Future in Los Angeles*. New York: Verso, 1990.

Fainstein, Susan. *The Just City*. Ithaca, NY: Cornell University Press, 2010.

Friedman, Andrew. *Covert Capital: Landscapes of Denial and the Making of U.S. Empire in the Suburbs of North Virginia*. Berkeley: University of California Press, 2013.

Hackworth, Jason. *The Neoliberal City: Governance, Ideology, and Development in American Urbanism*. Ithaca, NY: Cornell University Press, 2007.

Harvey, David. *Spaces of Global Capitalism: Towards a Theory of Uneven Geographical Development*. New York: Verso, 2006.

Kwak, Nancy. *A World of Homeowners: American Power and the Politics of Housing Aid*. Chicago: University of Chicago Press, 2015.

Milkman, Ruth. *L.A. Story: Immigrant Workers and the Future of the U.S. Labor Movement*. New York: The Russell Sage Foundation, 2006.

Mitchell, Don. *The Right to the City: Social Justice and the Fight for Public Space*. New York: Guilford Press, 2003.

Nijman, Jan. *Miami: Mistress of the Americas*. Philadelphia: University of Pennsylvania Press, 2011.

O'Mara, Margaret Pugh. *Cities of Knowledge: Cold War Science and the Search for the Next Silicon Valley*. Princeton, NJ: Princeton University Press, 2005.

Parreñas, Rhacel Salazar. *Servants of Globalization: Migration and Domestic Work*. Stanford, CA: Stanford University Press, 2001.

Phillips-Fein, Kim. *Fear City: New York's Fiscal Crisis and the Rise of Austerity Politics*. New York: Metropolitan Books, 2017.

Sassen, Saskia. *The Global City: New York, London, Tokyo*. Princeton, NJ: Princeton University Press, 1991.

Sherman, Rachel. *Class Acts: Service and Inequality in Luxury Hotels*. Berkeley: University of California Press, 2007.

Shkuda, Aaron. *The Lofts of SoHo: Gentrification, Art, and Industry in New York, 1950–1980*. Chicago: University of Chicago Press, 2016.

Smith, Neil. *The New Urban Frontier: Gentrification and the Revanchist City*. New York: Routledge, 1996.

Taft, Chloe. *From Steel to Slots: Casino Capitalism in the Postindustrial City.* Cambridge, MA: Harvard University Press, 2016.

Zipp, Samuel. *Manhattan Projects: The Rise and Fall of Urban Renewal in Cold War New York.* New York: Oxford University Press, 2010.

Zukin, Sharon. *Loft Living: Culture and Capital in Urban Change.* New Brunswick, NJ: Rutgers University Press, 1989.

NOTES

1. Thomas Zeiler, "Just Do It! Globalization for Diplomatic Historians," *Diplomatic History* 25, no. 4 (Fall 2001): 530.

2. Seth Rockman, *Scraping By: Wage Labor, Slavery, and Survival in Early Baltimore* (Baltimore: Johns Hopkins University Press, 2009), 3.

3. Walter Johnson, *Soul By Soul: Life Inside the Antebellum Slave Market* (Cambridge, MA: Harvard University Press, 1999).

4. Kristin L. Hoganson, *Consumers' Imperium: The Global Production of American Domesticity, 1865–1920* (Chapel Hill: University of North Carolina Press, 2007).

5. Matthew Frye Jacobson, *Barbarian Virtues: The United States Encounters Foreign People at Home and Abroad* (New York: Hill & Wang, 2000); and Shelley Sang-Hee Lee, *Claiming the Oriental Gateway: Prewar Seattle and Japanese America* (Philadelphia: Temple University Press, 2012).

6. Lee, *Claiming the Oriental Gateway*, 4–14.

7. Julio Capó Jr., *Welcome to Fairyland: Queer Miami Before 1940* (Chapel Hill: University of North Carolina Press, 2017).

8. Carl H. Nightingale, *Segregation: A Global History of Divided Cities* (Chicago: University of Chicago Press, 2012), 2–14, 305–306.

9. Paige Glotzer, "Building Suburban Power: The Business of Exclusionary Housing Markets, 1890–1960 (http://histecon.fas.harvard.edu/visualizing/buildingsuburbanpower/index.html)," Harvard University Joint Center for History and Economics.

10. Jonathan Rees, "Industrialization and Urbanization in the United States, 1880–1920," *Oxford Research Encyclopedia of American History* (July 2016).

11. Rees, "Industrialization and Urbanization in the United States."

12. Dara Orenstein, "Foreign-Trade Zones and the Cultural Logic of Frictionless Production," *Radical History Review* 109 (Winter 2011): 36–42.

13. Orenstein, "Foreign-Trade Zones," 37.

14. Orenstein, "Foreign-Trade Zones," 37, 42.

15. Francesca Russello Ammon, *Bulldozer: Demolition and Clearance of the Postwar Landscape* (New Haven, CT: Yale University Press, 2016).

16. Samuel Zipp, *Manhattan Projects: The Rise and Fall of Urban Renewal in Cold War New York* (New York: Oxford University Press, 2010), 5, 28, 29.

17. Roger W. Lotchin, *Fortress California 1910–1961: From Warfare to Welfare* (Champaign: University of Illinois Press, 2002); and Ann Markusen, Peter Hall, Scott Campbell, and Sabina Deitrick, *The Rise of the Gunbelt: The Military Remapping of Industrial America* (New York: Oxford University Press, 1991).

18. Margaret Pugh O'Mara, *Cities of Knowledge: Cold War Science and the Search for the Next Silicon Valley* (Princeton, NJ: Princeton University Press, 2005).

19. Charlotte Brooks, *Alien Neighbors, Foreign Friends: Asian Americans, Housing, and the Transformation of Urban California* (Chicago: University of Chicago Press, 2012), 4.

20. Betsy A. Beasley, "Service Learning: Oil, International Education, and Texas' Corporate Cold War," *Diplomatic History* 42, no. 2 (April 1, 2018): 177–203.

21. Jennifer S. Light, *From Warfare to Welfare: Defense Intellectuals and Urban Problems in Cold War America* (Baltimore: Johns Hopkins University Press, 2004), 4–5.

22. Victoria DeGrazia, *Irresistible Empire: America's Advance through Twentieth-Century Europe* (Cambridge, MA: Belknap, 2005).

23. Thomas J. Sugrue, *The Origins of the Urban Crisis: Race and Inequality in Postwar Detroit* (Princeton, NJ: Princeton University Press, 1996).

24. Elizabeth Tandy Shermer, *Sunbelt Capitalism: Phoenix and the Transformation of American Politics* (Philadelphia: University of Pennsylvania Press, 2013); Robert Self, *American Babylon: Race and the Struggle for Postwar Oakland* (Princeton, NJ: Princeton University Press, 2003); Bruce J. Schulman, *From Cotton Belt to Sunbelt: Federal Policy, Economic Development,*

and the Transformation of the South, 1938–1980 (Durham, NC: Duke University Press, 1994); and James C. Cobb, *Industrialization and Southern Society, 1877–1984* (Lexington: University of Kentucky Press, 1984).

25. Sugrue, *The Origins of the Urban Crisis.*

26. Betsy A. Beasley, "White-Collar Wildcatters and Wildcat Strikes: Oil Experts, Global Contracts, and the Transformation of Labor in Postwar Houston," in *Working for Oil: Comparative Social Histories of Labor in the Global Oil Industry,* eds. Touraj Atabaki, Elisabetta Bini, and Kaveh Ehsani (London: Palgrave Macmillan, 2018), 257–284.

27. Sugrue, *The Origins of the Urban Crisis.*

28. Jefferson Cowie, *Capital Moves: RCA's Seventy-Year Quest for Cheap Labor* (Ithaca, NY: Cornell University Press, 1999), 2.

29. Cowie, *Capital Moves,* 6.

30. Marc Levinson, *The Box: How the Shipping Container Made the World Smaller and the World Economy Bigger* (Princeton, NJ: Princeton University Press, 2006).

31. Louis Hyman, *Temp: How American Work, American Business, and the American Dream Became Temporary* (New York: Viking, 2018).

32. Betsy A. Beasley, "At Your Service: Houston and the Preservation of U.S. Global Power, 1945–2008" (PhD diss., Yale University, 2016).

33. Judith Stein, *Pivotal Decade: How the United States Traded Factories for Finance in the Seventies* (New Haven, CT: Yale University Press, 2010).

34. Kim Phillips-Fein, *Fear City: New York's Fiscal Crisis and the Rise of Austerity Politics* (New York: Metropolitan Books, 2017).

35. Stein, *Pivotal Decade.*

36. Saskia Sassen, *The Global City: New York, London, Tokyo* (Princeton, NJ: Princeton University Press, 1991), 4.

37. Rachel Sherman, *Class Acts: Service and Inequality in Luxury Hotels* (Berkeley: University of California Press, 2007).

38. Rhacel Salazar Parreñas, *Servants of Globalization: Migration and Domestic Work* (Stanford, CA: Stanford University Press, 2001).

39. Sharon Zukin, *Loft Living: Culture and Capital in Urban Change* (New Brunswick, NJ: Rutgers University Press, 1989); and Aaron Shkuda, *The Lofts of Soho: Gentrification, Art, and Industry in New York, 1950–1980* (Chicago: University of Chicago Press, 2016).

40. Emily Badger, "When the (Empty) Apartment Next Door Is Owned by an Oligarch," *New York Times,* July 21, 2017. https://www.nytimes.com/2017/07/21/upshot/when-the-empty-apartment-next-door-is-owned-by-an-oligarch.html.

41. Neil Smith, *The New Urban Frontier: Gentrification and the Revanchist City* (New York: Routledge, 1996).

42. Chad Broughton, *Boom, Bust, Exodus: The Rust Belt, the Maquilas, and a Tale of Two Cities* (New York: Oxford University Press, 2016).

43. Xiaojian Zhao, "Immigration and the United States after 1945," *Oxford Research Encyclopedia of American History* (July 2016), 10.

44. Zhao, "Immigration and the United States after 1945," 10–16.

45. Zhao, "Immigration and the United States after 1945," 35.

46. Parreñas, *Servants of Globalization.*

47. Charles Davis, "'Made in America': How Sweatshops Exploit Immigrants to Make Your Cheap Clothes," *Attn:* (July 26, 2017). https://www.attn.com/stories/18483/made-america-how-sweatshops-exploit-immigrants-make-your-clothes.

48. Ruth Milkman, *L.A. Story: Immigrant Workers and the Future of the U.S. Labor Movement* (New York: The Russell Sage Foundation, 2006).

49. Scott Kurashige, *The Shifting Grounds of Race: Black and Japanese Americans in the Making of Multiethnic Los Angeles* (Princeton, NJ: University of Princeton Press, 2010), 8.

50. See, for instance, Sassen, *The Global City;* William Sites, *Remaking New York: Primitive Globalization and the Politics of Urban Community* (Minneapolis: University of Minnesota Press, 2003); Janet Abu-Lughod, *New York, Chicago, Los Angeles: America's Global Cities* (Minneapolis: University of Minnesota Press, 2001); and Jason Hackworth, *The Neoliberal City: Governance, Ideology, and Development in American Urbanism* (Ithaca, NY: Cornell University Press, 2007).

51. Zukin, *Loft Living;* and Shkuda, *The Lofts of SoHo.*

52. Broughton, *Boom, Bust, Exodus;* Parreñas, *Servants of Globalization;* Sherman, *Class Acts;* Katherine S. Newman, *No Shame in My Game: The Working Poor in the Inner City* (New York: The Russell Sage Foundation, 1999); Karen Ho,

Liquidated: An Ethnography of Wall Street (Durham, NC: Duke University Press, 2009); and Arlene M. Davila, *Barrio Dreams: Puerto Ricans, Latinos, and the Neoliberal City* (Berkeley: University of California Press, 2004).

53. Chloe Taft, *From Steel to Slots: Casino Capitalism in the Postindustrial City* (Cambridge, MA: Harvard University Press, 2016).

54. Mike Davis, *City of Quartz: Excavating the Future in Los Angeles* (New York: Verso, 1990); David Harvey, *The Condition of Postmodernity: An Enquiry into the Origins of Cultural Change* (London: Wiley-Blackwell, 1990); R. Deutsche, "Boys Town," *Environment and Planning D* 9 (1991): 5–30; Michael Dear, "The Los Angeles School of Urbanism: An Intellectual History," *Urban Geography* 24, no. 6 (2003): 493–509; and Edward Soja, *Postmodern Geographies: The Reassertion of Space in Critical Social Theory* (New York: Verso, 1989).

55. Zipp, *Manhattan Projects*; and Andrew Friedman, *Covert Capital: Landscapes of Denial and the Making of U.S. Empire in the Suburbs of North Virginia* (Berkeley: University of California Press, 2013).

56. For some emerging work in the history of US global cities, see Aaron Cavin, "The Borders of Citizenship: The Politics of Race and Metropolitan Space in Silicon Valley" (PhD diss., University of Michigan, 2012); Jeannette Estruth, "A Political History of the Silicon Valley: Social Movements, the High-Technology Industry, and the Utopia of the New Economy, 1945–1995" (PhD diss., New York University, forthcoming); Betsy A. Beasley, "At Your Service: Houston and the Preservation of U.S. Global Power, 1945–2008" (PhD diss., Yale University, 2016); and Jessica Levy, "From Black Power to Black Empowerment: Transnational Capital and Racial Integration in the United States and South Africa since 1969" (PhD diss., Johns Hopkins University, 2018).

Betsy A. Beasley

Political Economies

POLITICS IN URBAN AMERICA BEFORE 1940

The development of cities in the United States was as much a political problem as it was a social challenge. Belief in the necessity of moral consensus as the basis for politics, an expectation that leaders would possess civic virtue, and an assumption that respected gentlemen would emerge organically as communal leaders were among the ideals inherited from the colonial period. These precepts retained a purchase on the nation's political imagination well into the 19th century, but they fit poorly with the heterogeneity, conflict, and anonymity of urban life. The result was ongoing tensions that developed around the question of how democratic politics should work in big cities.

The sharpest disagreements centered upon "bosses" and "machines." By the middle of the 19th century, urban party leaders had come to rely heavily on a transactional method in which they exchanged patronage and services for electoral support. Patronage was not new, but its use and variety expanded dramatically as cities grew. The men who employed this approach were called *bosses*, and the organizations they headed came to be called *machines*. While these terms applied to American politics as a whole, they came to be most closely associated with public life in urban settings. During the final decades of the 19th century, bosses and machines faced withering attacks from business elites, as well as from labor groups, activist women, and some ethnic communities. These critics were not powerful enough to uproot the bosses or displace their machines, but they did succeed in achieving reforms that centralized the operations of municipal government and expanded the role of the state in addressing social problems.

THE RISE OF MACHINE POLITICS

By the middle of the 19th century, the largest cities in the United States were generating new forms of politics and requiring new forms of governance. Initial reservations about cities as corrupting forces—"pestilential to the morals, the health, and the liberties of man," in Thomas Jefferson's oft-quoted phrase—gave way to acknowledgement and ultimately acceptance of urbanization over the course of the 19th century.[1] Public life in these new environments assumed a different form, one that featured working-class leaders, sharp social and cultural conflict, and the open exchange of votes for favors. Although these characteristics generated substantial consternation, they nonetheless became established features of big-city politics by the latter part of the 19th century.

Significant urban growth was evident in the United States by 1840. By the end of the century the country possessed several major metropolitan centers. In 1860 New York City was home to more than 800,000 people, Philadelphia's population exceeded 500,000, and Chicago, little more than a camp in 1830, had grown to 109,000 residents. A massive surge of American productive capacity after the Civil War fueled further urbanization. By 1900 more than 30 million people lived in cities. After consolidating with neighboring Brooklyn, Queens, the Bronx, and Staten Island in 1898, New York City's population reached 3.4 million, while Philadelphia and Chicago each boasted more than a million residents as the 20th century commenced. According to official accounting, more than 50 million people lived in cities in 1920, marking the point at which a majority of the US population resided in communities that the Census Bureau classified as urban.

There were regional variations to this pattern. A mix of commerce and industry propelled the continued growth of eastern cities and Chicago, while manufacturing drove the development of Midwestern cities such as Pittsburgh, Cleveland, and Detroit, each of which boasted populations of more than 250,000 people in 1900. Trade and resource attraction fueled modest urban growth in the West before 1900, with San Francisco and Denver being the largest cities in the region. After 1900, western and southwestern urbanization would accelerated, with Los Angeles becoming the nation's fifth-largest city by 1940. City growth in the agricultural South was limited, although market centers such as Atlanta and New Orleans experienced significant population increases during the early 20th century.[2]

Urbanization produced social heterogeneity, even before the Civil War. Class gradations sharpened and took on greater significance during the early stages of American industrialization. The "mechanics interests" of the 18th and early 19th centuries became "workingmen's" parties and trade unions in many cities as early as the 1830s, making labor protests and strikes common features of the urban scene. At the same time, a surge in immigration quickly transformed eastern cities into polyglot communities. By the 1850s more than half of the residents of New York City and Boston and a third of Philadelphians were foreign-born. Urban social geography featured slum districts and ethnic enclaves. The visibility of these settings reinforced what the poet Edwin Hubbell Chapin called the "first lesson" of city life: "the diversities of human condition."[3]

Social differences generated an abundance of conflicts. Workers clashed with proprietors over wages, hours, and control of shop floors. Catholics battled Protestants, often violently, over matters of schooling, temperance, and observance of the Sabbath. Immigrants demanded civil rights in the face of nativist opposition. Business interests also pursued development opportunities, often at the expense of other portions of the community. These conflicts mattered politically in large part because of the establishment of universal white male suffrage between 1820 and 1840 in the United States. Enterprising office seekers exploited group conflicts to attract newly enfranchised voters, exacerbating social tensions in the process.

Inherited prescriptions for the conduct of public life fit poorly with this environment and quickly gave way to a plebian style of mass politics. The 18th-century ideal in which a selfless gentleman of social standing naturally assumed the role of civic leader and served the interests of a morally united community gave way to a grassroots urban ethic that celebrated working-class leadership and embraced conflict. One progenitor of this new approach was Mike Walsh, who emerged from the workingmen's movement in New York City. He headed the Spartan Association, which was part gang, part political organization, and he used the group as a springboard for his own political ambitions during the 1840s. He expressly rejected the gentlemanly style, emphasized his proletarian roots, and welcomed combat, whether verbal or physical, as a core element of politics.[4] Politicians of a similar character soon became a common feature of public life in the poor and working-class districts of large cities.

The manner in which these figures came to be called bosses underscores a key element of their method. The term *boss* is a derivation of *baas*, a Dutch word for "master." Perhaps out of a concern to avoid the use of "master" because it evoked slavery, workers in and around New York City called small-scale employers and foremen "bosses." Supervisors in the Brooklyn Navy Yard, a key source of public employment, were among those who gave this label a political meaning during the 1840s, when they began to assign jobs on the basis of partisan loyalty. "Boss" Hugh McLaughlin, who became the dominant Democrat in Brooklyn for several decades following the Civil War, used his authority over hiring in the Navy Yard to assemble a political following

and rise through the party's ranks.[5] Although these kinds of patronage practices, along with other exchanges of benefits and favors for political support, were not limited to urban environs, they came to be a characteristic element of big-city public life in 19th-century America. In the eyes of some, they represented a form of corruption.

Boss politics of this sort developed chiefly at the grassroots level before the Civil War. Men of social standing were still likely to serve as mayor, in Congress, and in other citywide offices during these years, even as plebian figures dominated lower-class districts. Prominent business leaders and men from well-regarded families, such as Richard Vaux in Philadelphia, Josiah Quincy in Boston, and New York's William Havermeyer, were among those who remained active politically, even as others of their class increasingly directed their energies to the business and philanthropic realms. Most voters, it seemed, were not ready to embrace citywide leaders who adopted the methods and style of bosses.

One exception to this pattern during the antebellum period was New York's Fernando Wood, a controversial figure whom some scholars have classified as the first citywide boss. From a poor family, Wood became wealthy through marriage and through what some observers charged were dishonest business dealings. During the 1830s, he joined Tammany Hall, at the time one of several factions within the local Democratic Party, where he expressed sympathy for working-class interests. Eventually elected mayor in 1854, re-elected in 1856, and, after a defeat, elected once more in 1860, he employed many of the patronage practices, favor trading, and cultural appeals that came to define boss politics. He defended them as necessary to govern a city as heterogeneous as New York, but he also emphasized his concern for the common good and his supposed willingness to forgo personal gain in favor of the betterment of the community. Such protestations were cover for more self-serving conduct, but they highlight the unease that greeted the emergence of an openly transactional style of politics in large cities.[6]

After the Civil War these methods of politics became pervasive, although centralized control remained uncommon. Ground-level urban politics during this period was highly competitive, with most districts subject to frequent, intense battles for supremacy among rival factions. In some instances a particular leader gained firm control of a single district. Politicians such as Martin Lomasney in Boston's West End, Jim Pendergast in Kansas City's First Ward, or Chicago's John Powers dominated their neighborhoods during the late 19th and early 20th centuries. But before the 1890s it was unusual for a single figure to emerge as a citywide boss heading an extensive organization that was capable of managing the affairs of the dominant party across an entire city. One exception was William Magear Tweed, who headed a small group within the Tammany Hall organization that gained control of New York City government during the late 1860s. The "Tweed Ring" all but looted the city treasury and soon found itself immersed in a scandal that led to its undoing and galvanized antimachine campaigns across the country. Christopher Buckley managed to ride herd on San Francisco's Democrats and control local politics for a few years during the 1880s and Tammany's John Kelly, and his successor, Richard Croker, succeeded in reviving the organization after the Tweed scandal and consolidating control of New York City's dominant Democratic Party during the same decade. Durable Republican machines emerged in Philadelphia and Pittsburgh during the Gilded Age, and George Cox became the most powerful political figure in Cincinnati by the late 1880s. Still, factional divisions, sharp intraparty competition, and coalition building were at least as common as boss rule in large cities through the final decades of the 19th century. If not as blatantly corrupt as the Tweed Ring, many, if not most, party politicians pursued opportunities for self-enrichment through the "honest graft" so colorfully described by Tammanyite George Washington Plunkitt.[7]

THE SPREAD OF MUNICIPAL REFORM

Although the laws of physics do not apply to politics, it is hardly surprising that the rise of boss politics produced a nearly equal and opposite reaction. Critics of the partisan practices of urban public life appeared almost as quickly as did bosses, and they consolidated roughly as quickly as big-city machines did. Initial responses were intermittent and ad hoc. As party organizations gained power during the late 19th century, reformers established more permanent groups of their own that aimed to end boss rule. For the most part they failed to achieve that goal, but antimachine efforts would succeed in reshaping the structure of urban politics and governance during the early 20th century.

The growth of bossism during the 1840s and 1850s elicited a good deal of grumbling but only sporadic or ineffective attempts to eliminate it. In what would become a common strategy, Whigs and Republicans challenged growing Democratic power in New York City by using their control of state government to create agencies such as the Metropolitan Police, the Metropolitan Board of Health, and the Croton Water Board. Designed to provide a counterweight to allegedly corrupt influences in New York's municipal government, these bodies spurred conflict but did not dislodge Democratic bosses. Leading New York businessmen also organized the City Reform League in 1852 to stop the "robbery" of the city's taxpayers and to ensure that "men of character" filled municipal offices. Hampered in part by connections to nativism and class resentment, as well as accusations of partisanship, this reform effort was short-lived, as were several similar campaigns in other cities before the Civil War. During that conflict, insistence on unity and the formation of cross-party Union Leagues all but eliminated party competition. Only in its wake would the state of city politics begin to attract sustained concern.[8]

The sensational scandal surrounding the Tweed Ring helped make big-city politics the subject of national debate. Tweed, a former volunteer fireman and street politician, along with a handful of colleagues, secured control of Tammany Hall; the local Democratic Party organization; and, from 1866 to 1871, City Hall. They used their power to enrich themselves, organizing kickbacks and bribes as they facilitated the city's rapid postwar development. Matters came to a head in 1871 when the *New York Times* published ledgers obtained from a disgruntled coconspirator that documented the depredations of Tweed and his confederates. Public outrage followed, the "Tweed Ring" was removed from power, and the subsequent legal proceedings lasted through most of the 1870s. The scandal's impact spread well beyond New York, earning front-page reports and stern editorializing about "Boss Tweed" in newspapers around the country. A series of powerful cartoons by *Harper's Weekly* artist Thomas Nast made "Boss Tweed" a familiar figure and the archetypally corrupt urban politician.[9]

In the wake of the Tweed Ring scandal a new term became part of the standard political vocabulary, one that captured the social dynamics of the debate over the character of urban politics. By the end of the 1870s, reformers had popularized use of the term "machine" to describe party organizations. Although it was not exclusively applied to city politics, the notion of "machine" politics, or the "political machine," became closely associated with urban party organizations. In some respects it was a misnomer, suggesting a degree of efficiency and coordination that was only rarely achieved during the late 19th century, but its symbolic properties were powerful and useful. It allowed critics to depict party politicians as lower-class factory operatives, familiar with "the wheels, shafts, and bands of the party machine," in James Bryce's suggestive phrase.[10] Implying that the men who

dominated urban party organizations were thoughtless workers, lacking the education, refinement, and respectability necessary for legitimate leadership, the term "machine" managed to provoke alarm and convey contempt.

During the Gilded Age, the desire to replace disreputable party bosses with the "best men," by which reformers generally meant prominent, native-born businessmen, animated most reform campaigns. Such efforts were generally the work of short-lived "committees." New Yorkers launched the Committee of Seventy to cleanse the city's public life in the wake of the Tweed scandal and elect honest, respectable men, but that effort faded once Tweed and his Ring lost power. Elite Philadelphians formed a Committee of Fifty-Eight for similar purposes in 1874; the same people organized a Committee of Sixty-Two the following year to pursue the same end. Committees of One Hundred became the norm during the 1880s. These ad hoc organizations worked to ensure that prominent, respectable men filled city offices. While they had occasional triumphs, such committees were short-lived, and the machine-style politics to which they objected so strongly showed no signs of abating.[11]

Faced with an increasingly entrenched system of boss politics, reformers began to establish more durable antimachine organizations with broader agendas during the final years of the 19th century. New York's City Club; Boston's Good Government Association; Chicago's Civic Federation and its offshoot, the Municipal Voters' League; and Philadelphia's City Party were examples of the new, more lasting type of reform body that became a stock element of urban public life from the 1890s until the 1930s. Dominated by middle- and upper-class men, these groups engaged in sustained efforts to weaken urban machines and bosses, both through direct electoral challenges and through structural reforms designed to weaken their hold on power. The men who organized these bodies established the National Municipal League in 1894, providing themselves with a means of exchanging ideas and coordinating reform campaigns.[12]

Journalists, most notably muckraker Lincoln Steffens, gave municipal reform efforts new momentum around the turn of the century. Most cities had experienced some form of municipal scandal, exposed by the local press, during the 1890s. A series of colorful articles Steffens published in *McClure's Magazine* during 1902 and 1903 generated national momentum for campaigns to clean up city politics. In reports on scandals and corruption in St. Louis, Minneapolis, Pittsburgh, Philadelphia, and New York as well as on reform efforts in Chicago, Steffens sought to "sound for the civic pride of an apparently shameless citizenship" in the hope of provoking greater support for reform. After republishing his essays in 1904, in a volume titled *The Shame of the Cities*, he became a sought-after expert on city government whose statements and subsequent writings galvanized political opinion in favor of significant reforms to urban civic life.[13]

Another source of support for these efforts was the emergence of municipal politics and governance as a focal point of political science research. Citing European models, scholars such as Albert Shaw and Frank Goodnow argued that cities could and should be governed by independent, empirically driven administrative methods. They criticized interference from state governments, much of it fed by partisan agendas, and sought to enlarge the capacity of municipal governments to manage the challenges associated with city life and city development, including transportation planning, the implementation of sanitation programs, the regulation and provision of housing, and other matters. Insulating the management of municipal affairs from state and national politics was essential, they argued, because the needs of urban communities did not correlate with the political concerns of major party organizations. Mechanisms that ensured public input in shaping municipal policy decisions were a vital component of proper city governance.[14]

Stoked by the energy that Steffens and other journalists created and informed by the ideas of political science, municipal reform proceeded along two lines during the Progressive Era. Some groups, most notably Chicago's Municipal Voters' League, concentrated on vetting, and even recruiting, candidates for office who met standards of honesty and probity. They used publicity campaigns to expose the wrongdoings of politicians and to promote the character and qualifications of their favored candidates. Initially, some of these groups attempted to reach across socioeconomic and ethnic lines to elicit support from working-class communities or to recruit men who might attract a following from blue-collar and immigrant voters, but attempts at cross-class coalition building largely foundered on the rocks of mutual suspicion and divergent political concerns. By the first decade of the 20th century, reformers had shifted their attention to implementing structural changes designed to limit patronage supplies, reduce or eliminate taxing powers, cut the number of elective offices, consolidate power in the mayor's office or in a commission, and shift decision-making authority to unelected experts.[15]

Most cities enacted at least some of these reforms, put through in the hope of insulating municipal rule from partisanship and parochial interest. Some cities drew upon a model city charter developed by the National Municipal League to redesign local government. It featured a small, unicameral legislative body; an increase in mayoral power; at-large, nonpartisan elections; and increased bureaucratic oversight of municipal budgets and taxation. The purpose of these changes was to reduce the influence of party agendas and neighborhood interests on municipal decisions, especially on spending matters. Boston adopted a series of reforms based upon this model in 1909, and aspects of it were taken up in other large cities. More popular in smaller and mid-sized cities was the establishment of commission governments, an arrangement in which a small board of elected or appointed commissioners, ostensibly independent from partisan control or neighborhood allegiances, ran the city. When this structure failed to deliver on its promise of boss-free governance, some reformers advocated a city manager system, which centralized power in the hands of a single appointed official, overseen by an elected council. Ultimately, the council-manager and strong-mayor systems became the prevailing municipal structures in the United States through 1940.

Municipal reform movements remained a standard element of urban public life into the 1930s, but few lasted beyond that decade. Boston's Good Government Association disbanded in 1934 after a series of elections setbacks made clear that popular appetite for its brand of reform had faded. Chicago's Municipal Voters' League persisted until 1939, at which point its operations folded into those of the Citizens Association, but its influence had waned sharply by the 1920s. New York's City Club remained active through the 20th century, but its influence never again reached the level it had during the Progressive Era.

If one reason for the decline was the movement's nominal success, another was its failure to uproot bossism. In most cities, reformers had implemented their prized structural reforms, centralizing urban governance and shifting authority from elected officials with partisan agendas to independent, expert-run agencies. Yet machine politics persisted, particularly in the nation's older, industrial cities. It was the electoral successes of partisans such as William Hale Thompson in Chicago and James Michael Curley in Boston and the resilience of organizations such as Tammany Hall that finally undercut elite-run municipal reform. Only in newer urban centers of the West and Southwest, where party organizations were not as deeply rooted, did the centralization of municipal government allow well-connected businessmen to elbow aside would-be bosses and dominate local public life.

GRASSROOTS CHALLENGES AND ALTERNATIVES TO MACHINE POLITICS

Save for a brief attempt around the turn of the 20th century, business-oriented municipal reformers usually did not seek to mobilize grassroots challenges to boss power. That failure did not mean that party machines faced no opposition from below. Workers, women, and a few democratically oriented middle-class reformers viewed bosses and machines as tools of business elites (despite the support of many well-to-do men for conventional municipal reform campaigns) or impediments to a fair and inclusive public life. These activists were no more successful than traditional municipal reformers in eliminating machine rule, but they did in some respects succeed in changing the character of American urban politics and governance.

While machines relied heavily on immigrants, their inability to generate enough patronage to accommodate a steady flow of newcomers meant that party organizations regularly faced ethnic insurgencies. Many of these challenges arose among the newer, eastern and southern Europeans whose populations increased dramatically after 1900 but who did not receive as many benefits as the Irish and other more established groups. Although these newcomers did not naturalize and become voters in great numbers before the late 1920s, they did make their presence felt in ways that troubled party politicians. Civic leaders in Boston's Jewish and Italian communities proved to be a regular thorn in the sides of bosses such as Martin Lomasney and John Fitzgerald. In New York, recent immigrants often found themselves on the receiving end of brutal treatment from the Tammany-backed city police, experiences that made them willing to back antimachine campaigns. Ethnic Catholics in Progressive Era Providence engaged in varieties of political activism that fell outside customary partisan engagement. They backed labor insurgencies, pushed for an end to suffrage restrictions, and in a few instances backed socialist campaigns. Civic activity arose from parish life as well, generally in the form of nonpartisan support for social and political reforms. When these tactics failed or were unavailable, immigrant housewives and workers turned to boycotts and street protests, some of which resulted in violence. In all of these forms, ethnically based civic action created problems for urban machines by mobilizing immigrants outside and in opposition to party structures.[16]

Probably the most common way that workers entered urban politics was through labor agitation, which intensified over the course of the 19th century. Political insurgencies by workers were a notable if sporadic element of big-city public life during the antebellum period. After the Civil War, some working-class activists advocated direct political action, but more often labor leaders such as Terrence Powderly, head of the Knights of Labor, sought to remain above the fray. Their goal was not to carry the next election but to restore a (supposedly) lost producers republic, a goal that required a more fundamental reconfiguration of the nation's economy and politics. This long-term agenda proved difficult as workers sought immediate relief in the midst of relentless industrialization. Demands for greater control over their daily lives and more influence on the shop floor mounted through the second half of the 19th century. By the 1880s, this sense of dissatisfaction boiled over, generating strikes, boycotts, and protests. When the local state intervened on the side of employers and business interests, working-class anger grew sharper and more politicized.

For a short period of time during the late 1880s, it appeared that labor would mount a serious challenge to urban party machines. The Knights of Labor experienced a surge in popularity in the wake of successful railroad strikes, and workers in many cities organized independent tickets of municipal offices in 1886. The controversy surrounding the bombing at a labor rally in Chicago that year further

energized workingmen's slates, which achieved notable successes in several cities. Victories by labor candidates in Chicago, Milwaukee, Cincinnati, and a number of smaller cities in 1886 and 1887 suggested that workers had a chance to establish a viable alternative to the major parties, one that would reform the abuses connected with boss rule. Perhaps the greatest success came not in the form of an electoral triumph, but in the strong showing of Henry George as the candidate of the Workingmen's Party in New York City in late 1886. The land reformer received sixty-eight thousand votes, which placed him second to Democrat Abraham Hewitt and ahead of Republican nominee Theodore Roosevelt.[17]

George's impressive result and successes elsewhere did not herald the arrival of a workingman's republic, but it did position organized labor as a powerful interest within urban civic life. Politicians such as Hewitt and Chicago's Carter Harrison moved quickly to meet at least some worker demands, bringing them into the Democratic Party's coalition and undercutting the logic of independent working-class parties. Labor, often in the form of Central Labor Unions representing skilled workers, became a key player in city affairs, acting as an interest group and pushing municipal governments to expand their social service and regulatory efforts in ways beneficial to the working classes. Workers' late-19th-century challenge pushed city bosses and machines to give greater weight to their concerns and laid the groundwork for the development of urban liberalism during the early 20th century.[18]

Not all workers were equally represented by labor's push for power. The most influential unions of the early 20th century, many of them connected to the American Federation of Labor and tied to Democratic machines, mainly represented the interests of the most skilled, well-established workers. Women, African-Americans, and low-skill new immigrants continued to face unfair treatment and difficult working conditions, circumstances that left them vulnerable and frustrated. Some turned to socialism, more militant organizations such as the Women's Trade Union League, and other left-wing outlets during the Progressive Era.[19] Although these tactics helped certain groups gain ground, the antiradical repression that arose in the wake of World War I undercut such efforts. Most unskilled workers would not become fully engaged with politics until the mobilization of second-generation ethnics and African Americans surrounding the presidential candidacy of Al Smith and the onset of the New Deal. While in some instances these newcomers aligned with party machines, in other cases (such as that of the coalition that supported New York City's Fiorello LaGuardia) they became key components of antiboss coalitions.

Activist women also provided a sustained challenge to boss and machine rule. Female political influence gradually expanded through the 19th century, originally through the abolitionist and temperance movements. By the Gilded Age women's clubs and settlement houses began to advocate for urban social reforms, and they soon exerted a significant influence on public policy. These efforts came to be described as "municipal housekeeping," a label that underscored the manner in which activist women relied upon the prescriptions of separate spheres ideology as a rationale for public action. Women reformers often cast their pursuit of sanitary reforms, educational measures, labor laws, juvenile court reform, and interventions into other areas of urban life as an extension of their responsibilities as wives and mothers. In many cases, they succeeded in persuading local government to take on new regulatory responsibilities through their campaigns, a development that many scholars cite as a key step in the expansion of the American welfare state.[20]

In many instances, female reformers identified bosses and machines as significant impediments to their social reform agendas. Most famously, eminent settlement worker Jane Addams pointed to South Chicago ward boss Johnny Powers as a key obstacle to achieving sanitary improvements and other reforms in her neighborhood. For a short time Addams and her Hull House colleagues spearheaded an unsuccessful campaign to unseat him.[21] There were other instances in which Progressive Era women reformers waded into the electoral arena. One such case was the 1894 formation of the Women's Municipal League in New York for the express purpose of removing Tammany from power. A women's group affiliated with the City Party in Philadelphia launched a similar initiative a few years later and eventually formed a Women's League for Good Government that remained actively engaged with electoral politics into the 1920s. These efforts were not the norm, as most women's groups focused on nonpartisan social reform activities, but they did constitute a notable element of a few antimachine campaigns during the 1890s and first decades of the 20th century.[22]

Women were also at the forefront of another important attempt to dismantle the machine. Jane Addams, Mary Parker Follett, and some women's clubs pushed for the development of institutions and practices that fostered a more inclusive, deliberative form of politics. Addams emphasized to the middle-class readers of her many essays and commentaries the necessity of taking the ideas and values of urban immigrants seriously, rather than imagining them as members of inferior groups in need of uplift. Follett, another settlement worker and later a successful theorist of business organization, became a strong advocate for social centers, which were publicly run community spaces designed to facilitate civic discussion in urban neighborhoods. She articulated these ideas in *The New State* (1918), a thorough examination of how social centers could operate and how the results of the deliberations they hosted could be translated into public policy. These ideas were not the exclusive province of women. Many male reformers, most notably Edward Ward and Frederic Howe, joined in the effort, but a number of scholars suggest that women's greater openness to cooperative action and cross-class collaboration meant that they played an outsized role in this particular brand of political reform. Although social centers and similar initiatives gained some traction during the Progressive Era, they never fully caught on and were undercut by the demand for conformity that arose after US entry into World War I.[23]

AN ERA OF CONSOLIDATION

The cumulative effect of urban reform efforts during the Progressive Era was not the end of the machine but a consolidation of civic authority. In industrial cities, party bosses often took advantage of the new resources created by the growth of state activism and the strengthening of municipal executives to solidify their power. This pattern occurred primarily in cities of the industrial belt stretching from the Northeast through the Midwest, where party organizations were well established. Although persistence never earned them full acceptance, bosses and machines responded to the criticism of reformers by justifying their methods. Such arguments helped them gain a measure of legitimacy in the minds of at least some observers during and after the Progressive Era. Further south and west, in younger cities with less entrenched party organizations, business leaders took advantage of the installation of strong-mayor and commission forms of municipal government to shape local public affairs to their ends. Both party machines and reform regimes capitalized on the consolidation of municipal government during the early 20th century to strengthen their grip on power, a development that resulted in increased attention to and support for key constituencies at the expense of less powerful groups.

Despite the best efforts of reformers, urban machines remained a standard element of urban-industrial public life through the Progressive Era and beyond. Repeated scandals and steady attacks could not dislodge Tammany Hall, which remained the dominant political force in New York City into the 1920s. Republican machines in Pittsburgh and Philadelphia endured even longer, as did Democratic organizations in Albany, Jersey City, and Kansas City. Although Boston's James Michael Curley failed to translate his personal success into a durable organization, he did use the city's strengthened mayor's office to exert significant influence over local politics into the middle of the 20th century. In each case, the centralizing reforms of the Progressive Era helped, or at least failed to hinder, bosses and machines.[24]

In a number of cities, the increased availability of federal resources through the programs of the New Deal enhanced machine power. Party organizations in Pittsburgh and Kansas City found in the Works Progress Administration and other programs a welcome source of additional patronage, which was particularly necessary at a point when many children of recent eastern and southern European immigrants were coming of age politically. Boston's Curley likewise benefited from New Deal resources. One important exception to this pattern was New York City, where Franklin Roosevelt's suspicion of Tammany and Fiorello LaGuardia's support for early New Deal programs paved the way for the Republican's eleven years as mayor, beginning in 1933, and the marginalization of the Democratic machine.[25]

Chicago's experience illustrates the significance of structural factors in shaping urban party operations. The city did not follow the lead of most other urban centers and significantly centralize its governance during the Progressive Era. Reformers pushed for charter reform but failed, which ensured that the city's government and politics remained more fragmented. As a result, neither party firmly claimed power for long, although Republican William "Big Bill" Thompson corralled enough ethnic votes during the mid-1920s to gain the upper hand for his party. The Cook County Democratic Party united competing ethnic factions under the leadership of Anton Cermak during the early 1930s. After Cermak's assassination in 1933, Irish bosses Edward Kelly and Pat Nash continued to consolidate ethnic support, firmly establishing the machine as what one scholar has described as a "House for All Peoples." Their success was in no small part a product of the abundance of patronage and other resources made available by the New Deal. Federal support thus ensured that Chicago's political structure ultimately came to be considered by many the quintessential urban political machine.[26]

Increased acceptance accompanied the persistence of machine politics. Urban bosses actively defended themselves in the face of reform criticism. Tammany boss Richard Croker was a savvy publicist who used Darwinian arguments to insist that boss rule was necessary for the management of urban affairs. He also cited the role of machines in providing welfare services and their work incorporating immigrants into the body politic. Other politicians followed suit, and by the early 20th century some observers, including journalists such as Lincoln Steffens, reformers such as Jane Addams, and popular novelists such as Paul Leicester Ford, gave credence to those claims. By the 1920s, political scientists and sociologists, particularly those associated with the Chicago school were advancing the argument that machines and bosses persisted because they delivered needed services to urban constituencies, setting the stage for a full-scale reinterpretation of urban party politics based on functionalist theory by mid-century scholars.[27]

Debates about machines mattered most in the Northeast and Midwest. As research by Amy Bridges and other scholars has shown, business-dominated reform regimes dominated southwestern and western cities. These municipal governments focused on promoting economic growth, limiting taxation, and coordinating planning efforts. Their overriding concerns were the maintenance of the civic order necessary to ensure business prosperity and the provision of services to their core upper- and middle-class supporters. City leaders sought to limit popular participation, particularly by workers and ethnic minorities, so as not to complicate their attempts to pursue this agenda. As a result, lower-class and ethnic groups (most notably Hispanics) wielded minimal influence.[28]

In this respect, southwestern and western reform regimes shared something in common with the party machines of the nation's industrial belt. As political scientist Jessica Trounstine has argued, both forms of municipal leadership and governance tended to consolidate power and reward key constituencies at the expense of other groups in the community. While urban business and civic leaders in the Sunbelt strived to limit lower-class power, party machines in industrial cities were generally reluctant to mobilize new immigrants and share scarce resources. Only through the largesse of New Deal programs such as the Works Progress Administration did urban party organizations look to broaden their electoral base. Even then, there were clear racial limits to these coalitions. When African Americans began arriving in northern and western cities in large numbers, they found local party organizations to be generally unresponsive to their concerns about housing and civil rights. The exclusionary practices of both machines and reform regimes helped set the stage for political insurgencies from below, fueled by the civil rights movement of the 1960s.[29]

DISCUSSION OF THE LITERATURE

Beginning in the middle of the 20th century, urban historians focused heavily on machines and reformers. Influenced by Robert Merton's speculative use of urban bossism as an example of latent functionalism in *Social Theory and Social Structure*, Oscar Handlin and Richard Hofstadter offered portraits of boss politics that emphasized the ways in which machine politics provided social services, coordinated fragmented urban development, and created an avenue of upward mobility for ambitious ethnics. Subsequent scholarship carried this argument further, portraying political bosses as humane and pragmatic leaders responding to the demands of urban life. These and other studies made the boss and machine seem almost natural, nearly inevitable outgrowth of ethnic working-class life in urban America, while treating reform as the expression of a native-born, Protestant, and middle-class ethos.[30]

This revisionist account of bosses and machines prevailed into the 1980s, when increased skepticism about functionalism fed challenges to the notion of the benevolent boss and the efficient machine. A number of scholars advanced structural and political explanations that rejected socially driven models of urban politics in America's industrial cities. Terence McDonald challenged the functionalist interpretation during the 1980s, insisting that political considerations outweighed social impact when explaining the rise and persistence of machines in late-19th-century and 20th-century urban America. Steven Erie's *Rainbow's End* examined the history of urban politics from the 1840s to the 1980s and emphasized the importance of connections to state and national party organizations, rather than social functions, as key determinants of machine durability. Other scholars, including David Hammack, Amy Bridges, Ira Katznelson, and Martin Shefter, also generated new explanations of the origin and evolution of urban machines that found their roots in the strategic political choices of partisans rather than in the cultural inheritances of particular ethnic groups.[31]

Another effect of the rejection of the functional interpretation of the machine was a broadening of the scholarly understanding of what constituted urban politics. Philip Ethington's *The Public City* took such an approach, drawing upon Jurgen Habermas's conception of the public sphere to examine a variety of voluntary action and public discussion in late-19th-century San Francisco. James Connolly's account of Boston politics during the Progressive Era examined a range of civic action—including neighborhood improvement groups and ethnic organizations as well conventional electioneering—that blurred distinctions between bosses and reformers. Evelyn Sterne's study of the significance of the Catholic Church to the public life of Providence, Rhode Island, brought to the fore the role of religious organizations in ethnic politics. These and other studies constituted one response to the complaints of many scholars that the traditional boss-versus-reformer framework was stale and misleading.[32]

Renewed attention to the role of class and the significance of organized labor also reinvigorated the study of urban politics in the era of industrialization. Training their sights on the political activity of workers and those who claimed to represent them, labor historians documented the central role of working-class organizations in mobilizing voters and shaping policy. In part, this body of research used close attention to grassroots public life to challenge broadly gauged studies of voting behavior that emphasized the ethnocultural determinants of party affiliation and downplayed the political salience of class identities. Sean Wilentz's *Chants Democratic* offered evidence of antebellum working-class consciousness, while a number of scholars, including Leon Fink, Richard Oestreicher, and David Scobey, traced labor's mobilization of workers amid the Great Upheaval of the late 1880s and weighed its long-term significance. Richard Schneirov's *Labor and Urban Politics* argued convincingly that the emergence of labor as a political force in Chicago during the late 19th century offers a fuller explanation of the rise of urban liberalism during the Progressive Era than do interpretations that rest chiefly upon the supposed generosity and tolerance of party bosses. Examining 1920s and 1930s Chicago, Lizabeth Cohen assigned a primary role in the mobilization of newer immigrants to the labor movement rather than the local party machine.[33]

Scholarship on women's activism has had a similarly broadening effect. Initial studies of the development and impact of the women's club movement by historians such as Estelle Freedman and Karen Blair, as well as later work by Maureen Flanagan, made the case that middle-class women assumed significant public roles well before the national adoption of woman suffrage. Focusing on clubs and settlements, much of the research in this area has demonstrated the impact of lobbying and other extra-electoral work by these groups. Activist women successfully persuaded municipal and state governments to take on new regulatory and relief responsibilities during the Progressive Era. Some scholars credit this work with laying essential groundwork for the growth of the American state in the 20th century and for expanding the definition of politics to include social welfare activism. Other research documents the ways in which some women engaged directly with electoral politics, campaigning in support of particular reformers and, usually, in opposition to machine politicians. More recent work has also pushed beyond the early focus on white middle-class women to document the ways in which working-class, African American, and immigrant women engaged in efforts to advance the interests of their communities.[34]

Pushing beyond a simplistic boss-reformer dichotomy has made urban politics an attractive context in which to analyze the evolution of American democracy. As the United States industrialized, the civic life of cities became the site of particularly intense conflict and debate. Class tensions, ethnic differences, and the multiplication and divergence of interests created new challenges, and scholars have examined the political dimensions of these developments to better understand how Americans redefined democracy in the face of the heterogeneity of modern life. Kevin Mattson and Laura Westhoff turned to Progressive Era urban reform to discover ideas and practices that represented creative responses to these challenges. A number of historians have found innovative, well-crafted approaches to remaking public life in the thought and actions of settlement workers, most notably Jane Addams. Robert Johnston located powerful and compelling demands for democratic reform in the political ideas and actions of the petit bourgeoisie of Portland, Oregon. Alan Lessoff and James Connolly returned to the study of bosses and reformers, but with a focus on the representations produced by and about these actors, to detect changing conceptions of urban democracy and pluralism. These and other studies signal the growing importance of pre–World War II urban politics as the cauldron in which Americans forged ideas and practices that might guide us as we address the challenges presented by modern American public life.[35]

PRIMARY SOURCES

Manuscript collections abundantly document reform efforts, especially those of the middle and upper classes, but only a few collections provide access to the thinking and action of urban bosses. Party leaders were famously closed-mouthed and so left few manuscript records. Some maintained scrapbooks, including Philadelphia's Israel Durham, and two Boston politicians, James Michael Curley and Martin Lomasney.[36] Helpful documentation of Tammany's history can be found in the Edwin Patrick Kilroe Papers at Columbia University.[37] Municipal reform groups were more likely to provide primary source materials, and the records of organizations such as Boston's Good Government Association and Chicago's Citizens Association (which include the papers of that city's Municipal Voters' League) are available.[38] Valuable papers and diaries of individual reformers include those of journalists E. L. Godkin and Boston's George Read Nutter.[39] Lincoln Steffens's extensive papers document his impact on popular views of urban politics.[40] While grassroots labor activism is only infrequently documented, the Henry George papers are an important exception that shed light on his insurgent campaign for mayor of New York City.[41] The papers of Jane Addams contain much information about her ideas and impact on urban civic thought.[42] Important collections documenting women's activism include the records of the Chicago Women's Club and those of Philadelphia's Anna Blakiston Day.[43] Printed materials are also an important source of information about urban politics, including major newspapers, magazines, pamphlets, and campaign materials, but there are far too many to include in a brief summary.

NOTES

1. Thomas Jefferson to Dr. Benjamin Rush, September 23, 1800, *Founders Online*, (http://founders.archives.gov/documents/Jefferson/01-32-02-0102).
2. Campbell Gibson, "Population of the 100 Largest Cities and Other Urban Places in the United States, 1790–1990" (Population Division working paper no. 27, United States Bureau of the Census, Washington, DC, 1998).
3. Edwin Hubbell Chapin, *Humanity in the City* (New York: DeWitt and Davenport, 1854), 17.
4. Sean Wilentz, *Chants Democratic: New York City and the Rise of the American Working Class* (New York: Oxford University Press, 1984), 327–335.
5. James J. Connolly, *An Elusive Unity: Urban Democracy and Machine Politics in Industrializing America* (Ithaca: Cornell University Press, 2010), 9.
6. Jerome Mushkat, *Fernando Wood: A Political Biography* (Kent, OH: Kent State University Press, 1990).
7. Jon C. Teaford, *The Unheralded Triumph: City Government in America, 1870–1920* (Baltimore: Johns Hopkins University Press, 1984), 175–187; Martin Shefter, "The Emergence of the Machine: An Alternative View," in *Theoretical Perspectives on Urban Politics*, ed. Willis D. Hawley et al. (Englewood Cliffs, NJ: Prentice Hall, 1976), 14–44; and Steven P. Erie, *Rainbow's End: Irish-Americans and the Dilemmas of Urban Machine Politics, 1840–1985* (Berkeley: University of California Press, 1988), 20.
8. Connolly, *Elusive Unity*, 23, 25–26; and Mary P. Ryan, *Civic Wars: Democracy and Public Life in the American City during the Nineteenth Century* (Berkeley: University of California Press, 1998), 161.
9. Alexander B. Callow Jr., *The Tweed Ring* (New York: Oxford University Press, 1966); and Kenneth D. Ackerman, *Boss Tweed: The Rise and Fall of the Corrupt Pol Who Conceived the Soul of Modern New York* (New York: Carroll and Graf, 2005).
10. Connolly, *Elusive Unity*, 62–65; and James Bryce, *The American Commonwealth*, 3d ed., vol. 2 (London: Macmillan, 1899), 75.
11. Teaford, *Unheralded Triumph*, 194.
12. Frank Mann Stewart, *A Half-Century of Municipal Reform: The History of the National Municipal League* (Berkeley: University of California Press, 1950).
13. Lincoln Steffens, *The Shame of the Cities* (New York: McClure, Philips, 1904), 1.
14. Alan Lessoff and James J. Connolly, "From Political Insult to Political Theory: The Boss, the Machine, and the Pluralist City," *Journal of Policy History* 25, no. 2 (2013): 151.
15. Connolly, *Elusive Unity*, 193–197.
16. James J. Connolly, *The Triumph of Ethnic Progressivism: Urban Political Culture in Boston, 1900–1925* (Cambridge, MA: Harvard University Press, 1998), 55–66; Thomas M. Henderson, *Tammany Hall and the New Immigrants* (New York: Arno Press, 1976); Steve Erie, *Rainbow's End*, 91–106; and Evelyn Savidge Sterne, *Ballots and Bibles: Ethnic Politics and the Catholic Church in Providence* (Ithaca, NY: Cornell University Press, 2004).
17. Leon Fink, *Workingmen's Democracy: The Knights of Labor and American Politics* (Urbana: University of Illinois Press, 1985); and David Scobey, "Boycotting the Politics Factory: Labor Radicalism and the New York City Mayoral Election of 1884," *Radical History Review* 28–30 (1984): 280–325.
18. Richard Schneirov, *Labor and Urban Politics: Class Conflict and the Origins of Modern Liberalism in Chicago, 1864–97* (Urbana: University of Illinois Press, 1998).
19. Gwendolyn Mink, *Old Labor and New Immigrants in American Political Development: Union, Party, and State, 1875–1920* (Ithaca, NY: Cornell University Press, 1986).

20. Karen Blair, *The Clubwoman as Feminist: True Womanhood Redefined, 1868–1914* (New York: Holmes and Meier, 1980); Maureen Flanagan, *Seeing with Their Hearts: Chicago Women and the Vision of the Good City, 1871–1933* (Princeton, NJ: Princeton University Press, 2002); and Sarah Deutsch, *Women and the City: Gender, Space, and Power, 1870–1940* (New York: Oxford University Press, 2002).

21. Harold L. Platt, "Jane Addams and the Ward Boss Revisited: Class, Politics, and Public Health in Chicago, 1890–1930," *Environmental History* 5, no. 2 (April 2000): 194–222.

22. Jo Freeman, "One Man, One Vote; One Woman, One Throat": Women in New York City Politics, 1890–1910," *American Nineteenth Century History* 1, no. 3 (Autumn 2001): 101–123; S. Sara Monoson, "The Lady and the Tiger: Women's Electoral Activism in New York City before Suffrage," *Journal of Women's History* 2 (Fall 1990): 103–135; and Drew E. VandeCreek, "Unseen Influence: Lucretia Blankenburg and the Rise of Philadelphia Reform Politics in 1911," in *We Have Come to Stay: American Women and Political Parties, 1880–1960,* ed. Melanie Gustafson, Kristie Miller, and Elisabeth Perry (Albuquerque: University of New Mexico Press, 1999).

23. Jane Addams, *Democracy and Social Ethics* (London: Macmillan, 1902), 221–279; Mary Parker Follett, *The New State: Group Organization the Solution for Popular Government* (New York: Longmans Green, 1918); Kevin Mattson, *Creating a Democratic Public: The Struggle for Urban Participatory Democracy during the Progressive Era* (University Park: Pennsylvania State University Press, 1998); and Philip J. Ethington, "The Metropolis and Multicultural Ethics: Direct Democracy versus Deliberative Democracy in the Progressive Era," in *Progressivism and the New Democracy,* ed. Sidney Milkis and Jerome Mileur (Amherst: University of Massachusetts Press, 1999).

24. Erie, *Rainbow's End,* 20; M. Craig Brown and Charles N. Halaby, "Machine Politics in America," *Journal of Interdisciplinary History* 17, no. 3 (Winter 1987): 587–612.

25. Bruce M. Stave, *The New Deal and the Last Hurrah: Pittsburgh Machine Politics* (Pittsburgh: University of Pittsburgh Press, 1970); Lyle Dorsett, *Franklin D. Roosevelt and the City Bosses* (New York: Kennikat Press, 1977); Charles H. Trout, *Boston, the Great Depression, and the New Deal* (New York: Oxford University Press, 1977); and Thomas Kessner, *Fiorello LaGuardia and the Making of Modern New York* (New York: McGraw Hill, 1989).

26. Maureen Flanagan, *Charter Reform in Chicago* (Carbondale: University of Southern Illinois Press, 1987); and John M. Allswang, *Bosses, Machines, and Urban Voters,* rev. ed. (Baltimore: Johns Hopkins University Press, 1986).

27. Lessoff and Connolly, "From Political Insult to Political Theory"; and Harold F. Gosnell, *Machine Politics: Chicago Model* (Chicago: University of Chicago Press, 1937).

28. Amy Bridges, *Morning Glories: Municipal Reform in the Southwest* (Princeton, NJ: Princeton University Press, 1997); Robert B. Fairbanks, *For the City as a Whole: Planning, Politics, and the Public Interest in Dallas, Texas, 1900–1965* (Columbus: Ohio State University Press, 1998); and Martin Shefter, "Regional Receptivity to Reform: The Legacy of the Progressive Era," *Political Science Quarterly* 98, no. 3 (Autumn 1983): 459–483.

29. Jessica Trounstine, *Political Monopolies in American Cities: The Rise and Fall of Bosses and Reformers* (Chicago: University of Chicago Press, 2008); and Diane M. Pinderhughes, *Race and Ethnicity in Chicago: A Reexamination of Pluralist Theory* (Urbana: University of Illinois Press, 1987).

30. Robert Merton, *Social Theory and Social Structure,* rev. ed. (Glencoe, IL: Free Press, 1957), 75n, 98, 80; Oscar Handlin, *The Uprooted: The Epic Story of the Great Migrations That Made the American People* (New York: Little, Brown, 1951), 187–198; Richard Hofstadter, *The Age of Reform: From Bryan to F.D.R.* (New York: Vintage, 1955), 182–186; John Allswang, *Bosses, Machines, and Urban Voters: An American Symbiosis,* rev. ed. (Baltimore: Johns Hopkins University Press, 1986); Zane Miller, *Boss Cox's Cincinnati* (Columbus: Ohio State University Press, 2000); Leo Hershkowitz's *Tweed's New York: Another Look* (New York: Anchor Books/Doubleday, 1978); and John D. Buenker, "Sovereign Individuals and Organic Networks: Political Cultures in Conflict During the Progressive Era," *American Quarterly* 40, no. 2 (June 1988): 187–204.

31. Terrence J. McDonald, "The Problem of the Political in Recent American Urban History:

Liberal Pluralism and the Rise of Functionalism," *Social History* 10, no. 3 (October 1985): 323–345; Terrence McDonald, *The Parameters of Urban Fiscal Policy. Socioeconomic Change and Political Culture in San Francisco, 1860–1906* (Berkeley: University of California Press, 1986); Erie, *Rainbow's End*; David Hammack, *Power and Society: Greater New York at the Turn of the Century* (New York: Russell Sage Foundation, 1982); Amy Bridges, *A City in the Republic: Antebellum New York and the Origins of Machine Politics* (New York: Cambridge University Press, 1984); Ira Katznelson: *City Trenches: Urban Politics and the Patterning of Class* (Chicago: University of Chicago Press, 1981); and Shefter, "Emergence of the Machine."

32. Philip J. Ethington, *The Public City: The Political Construction of Urban Life in San Francisco, 1850–1900* (New York: Cambridge University Press, 1994); Connolly, *Triumph of Ethnic Progressivism*; and Sterne, *Ballots and Bibles*.

33. Wilentz, *Chants Democratic*; Fink, *Workingmen's Democracy*; Richard Oestreicher, *Solidarity and Fragmentation: Working People and Class Consciousness in Detroit, 1875–1900* (Urbana: University of Illinois Press, 1986); Scobey, "Boycotting the Politics Factory"; Schneirov, *Labor and Urban Politics*; and Lisabeth Cohen, *Making a New Deal: Industrial Workers in Chicago, 1919–1939* (New York: Cambridge University Press, 1990).

34. Estelle Freedman, "Separatism as Strategy: Female Institution Building and American Feminism, 1870–1930," *Feminist Studies* 5, no. 3 (Autumn 1979): 512–529; Blair, *Clubwoman as Feminist*; Flanagan, *Seeing with Their Hearts*; Daphne Spain, *How Women Saved the City* (Minneapolis: University of Minnesota Press, 2002); and Freeman, "One Man, One Vote; One Woman, One Throat"; Monoson, "The Lady and the Tiger."

35. Jean Elshtain, *Jane Addams and the Dream of American Democracy* (New York: Basic Books, 2002); Louise Knight, *Jane Addams and the Struggle for Democracy* (Chicago: University of Chicago Press, 2005); Laura Westhoff, *A Fatal Drifting Apart: Democratic Social Knowledge and Chicago Reform* (Columbus: Ohio State University Press, 2007); Mattson, *Creating a Democratic Public*; Robert Johnston, *The Radical Middle Class: Populist Democracy and the Question of Capitalism in Progressive Era Portland, Oregon* (Princeton, NJ: Princeton University Press, 2002); and Lessoff and Connolly, "From Political Insult to Political Theory."

36. Israel W. Durham Scrapbooks, Historical Society of Pennsylvania, Philadelphia, PA; James Michael Curley Scrapbooks (http://crossworks.holycross.edu/curley_scrapbooks/), College of the Holy Cross Library, Worcester, MA; and Martin Lomasney Scrapbook (http://www.masshist.org/collection-guides/view/fa0167), Massachusetts Historical Society, Boston, MA.

37. Edwin Patrick Kilroe Papers (http://www.columbia.edu/cu/lweb/eresources/archives/rbml/Kilroe/), Rare Books and Manuscripts Library, Columbia University, New York.

38. Records of the Good Government Association, Massachusetts Historical Society, Boston, MA, (http://www.masshist.org/collection-guides/view/fa0403); and Citizen Association of Chicago Records, Chicago History Museum, Chicago, IL, (http://www.uic.edu/depts/lib/findingaids/MSCAC_66.html). Chicago History Museum, Chicago, IL.

39. Edwin Laurence Godkin Papers (http://oasis.lib.harvard.edu/oasis/deliver/~hou00085), 1831–1902, Houghton Library, Harvard University, Cambridge, MA; and George Read Nutter Diaries (http://www.masshist.org/collection-guides/view/fa0070), Massachusetts Historical Society, Boston, MA.

40. Lincoln Steffens Papers (http://findingaids.cul.columbia.edu/ead//nnc-rb/ldpd_4079365), Rare Books and Manuscripts Library, Columbia University, New York.

41. Henry George Scrapbooks, Selected Volumes on New York Mayoral Campaign. UCLA Libraries and Collections (microfilm), Los Angeles, CA.

42. Jane Addams Collection (https://www.swarthmore.edu/Library/peace/DG001-025/DG001JAddams/index.html), Swarthmore College Peace Collection, Swarthmore, PA.

43. Chicago Women's Club Records, 1876–1998, Chicago History Museum, Chicago, IL; and Anna Blanchard Blakiston Day Papers (http://digitallibrary.hsp.org/index.php/Detail/Collection/Show/collection_id/475), 1905–1961, Historical Society of Pennsylvania, Philadelphia, PA.

James J. Connolly

POLITICS IN URBAN AMERICA AFTER 1945

Urban politics traditionally evokes images of Tammany Hall–style machine bosses, backroom dealings, and political favors in the late 19th and early 20th century.[1] With the dissolving of the boss system and the larger decline of cities after 1945, like shuttered downtown department stores, urban politics seemed to represent a relic of a bygone era. Although urban politics undoubtedly changed from its earlier form in the second half of the 20th century, it became no less an important topic or force.

The Great Depression and World War II fundamentally expanded the scope and scale of the federal government. These events dramatically transformed urban space and governance for the next half century. In the postwar period, the federal government fueled both suburbanization and urban renewal and redevelopment, which created a new physical landscape and contributed to further racial and economic segmentation and inequity. These factors in turn shaped urban politics. In the decades after World War II, cities across the country became the home of new residents and groups such as African Americans from the South; Latinos from Mexico, Puerto Rico, and the Dominican Republic; young professionals; and queer people who altered and redefined urban politics. While white ethnic neighborhood associations, black power organizers, the middle-class members of the neighborhood movement, and gay rights activists had fundamentally different and often contrasting ideological orientations, they shared both an opposition to the liberal model of governance and a desire to forge an alternative form of urban politics emphasizing the neighborhood.

These movements produced city politicians who represented the various facets of the urban politics in the last decades of the 20th century. Figures including Coleman Young, Frank Rizzo, Harvey Milk, Ed Koch, and Tom Bradley represented the new demographic diversity of the cities in the 1970s and beyond. Yet all of these figures grappled with the larger forces of capital flight, the fiscal crisis, privatization, the contraction of the social welfare state, the war on drugs, mass incarceration, immigration, and gentrification. This confluence of factors meant that as many American cities and their political representatives became demographically more diverse they also became increasingly separated by neighborhood boundaries and divided by the forces of class and economic inequality. Residential segregation and economic restructuring, which was produced by a range of political forces, continued to define the parameters and possibilities of urban politics into the 21st century.

URBAN REDEVELOPMENT AND ITS DISCONTENTS

The postwar period marked a new era in the relationship between the federal government and American cities. The federal government had played a minimalist role in urban affairs in the early 20th century, but after World War II, new agencies and entitlements made it a key actor in shaping industry, transportation, and residency, and it was more intimately involved in urban redevelopment and municipal governance than ever before. Federal policy also subsidized the migration of millions of white families, industry, and their tax dollars into the suburban periphery while further concentrating the poor and people of color in the urban core. This sorting reinforced the segmentation of metropolitan space, creating new dilemmas for American cities.

These developments coincided with and influenced key changes in the power structure of city governments across the country. In the first decades of the 20th century, cities like Philadelphia, Boston, New York, Chicago, and Detroit had functioned on a neighborhood-based, machine-style system held together by ethnic and community attachments and the incentives of jobs and other benefits.[2] By the end of World War II, most cities had moved away from this very localized and personality-driven form of politics. Cities passed new charters that implemented at-large elections so that more city councilors represented the entire municipality rather than a single ward. The system explicitly de-emphasized the power of any single neighborhood and instead intended to elect officials who would represent "the city as a whole."[3] This innovation along with other changes led to the election and appointment of a new generation of politicians and officials committed to the principles of liberal reform and economic growth.

Urban planning and urban renewal programs became the primary mechanism through which municipal governments implemented the shared goals of reform and growth. By the end of the 1950s, all major American cities had some type of redevelopment program. From Miami to Chicago, New Haven to San Francisco, cities also boasted urban renewal coalitions composed of urban politicians, planning officials, corporate executives, and real estate developers to initiate these plans. Urban planning officials like Robert Moses of New York, Edward Logue of Boston, and Edmund Bacon of Philadelphia amassed unprecedented power in their pursuit of modernizing urban space.[4] The focus on urban planning represented the larger political and social emphasis in the postwar era, which put a heightened faith on expertise and bureaucratic efficiency.

The federal government, through legislation such as the Housing Acts of 1949 and 1954 and the Highway Act of 1956, gave cities millions of dollars and wide discretion to develop their own projects. Years of neglect had left all US cities in dire need of infrastructure investment; city governments quickly embraced the new windfall from the federal government to simultaneously modernize their city and counter the forces of mass

suburbanization. Local officials became increasingly savvy at directing urban renewal funds toward economic redevelopment, particularly enhancing central business districts.[5] Thus, rather than improving the infrastructure in older low-income areas, urban redevelopment occurred at the expense of poor, immigrant, and racially diverse communities.

Redevelopment agencies used the power of eminent domain to clear "blighted" neighborhoods and make room either for new expressways or to create parcels of private land to sell to private developers to build new skyscrapers to improve the city's tax base. The new projects often boasted a modernist architectural aesthetic that marked a clear differentiation from the previous era of city building and urban life. However, the projects imposed a new architectural uniformity among American cities and also created new tensions that captured the contradictions of modern liberalism and urban politics. Officials believed that urban renewal would bring order and stability to the cities. Instead, it generated strife and new forms of neighborhood politics. In places like Boston, urban renewal heightened the sense of neighborhood allegiance, distrust of liberal technocrats and overall alienation among blue-collar Irish and Italians who did not follow the massive migration of whites out to the suburbs.[6] The emphasis on defending turf showed the persistent importance of place and neighborhood in defining both the identity and politics of many white urban residents in the postwar era.

In other parts of the country, urban renewal, particularly highway construction, galvanized residents to protect their neighborhoods.[7] Jane Jacobs, who led a campaign to save her West Village neighborhood and other parts of lower Manhattan from highway construction, influenced this form of civic activism and offered a fierce critique of Robert Moses's style of mass clearance programs in *The Death and Life of Great American Cities* (1961).[8] Whereas Moses's vision put little value into neighborhoods, Jacobs emphasized the importance of distinctive local communities and contended that they were the most fundamental unit of civic life. She inspired a new type of urban political engagement, encouraging residents to join community boards, speak out at public hearings, and lobby their elected officials in order to fight for their neighborhoods.

The opposition to urban renewal highlighted the ways in which citizens increasingly worked within the channels of municipal politics to create change. These protests successfully convinced city officials in San Francisco, New York, Philadelphia, and Boston to abandon plans for expressway building, which facilitated a shift in urban planning politics from top-down urban renewal toward emphasis on citizen participation and input.[9] It laid the foundation for many of the urban political issues and movements that emerged in the 1970s. Yet it also revealed that this form of action benefited some residents and neighborhoods over others. The movement achieved its greatest success in saving white middle-class neighborhoods in such places as New York's Greenwich Village and Cambridge, Massachusetts.[10] The protests proved less successful in non-white and low-income neighborhoods. In Boyle Heights in East Los Angeles, neighborhood activists failed to prevent the construction of two large interchanges and six freeways from bisecting the community in the 1960s. The city also forcibly evicted residents of the nearby Chavez Ravine barrio to build a new baseball stadium for the Los Angeles Dodgers.[11] These instances exposed not only urban political power hierarchies, but also the growing and changing diversity of postwar metropolises.

NEW POPULATIONS, NEW TENSIONS

The postwar period witnessed the mass migration of new residents into cities around the country, particularly African Americans from the south and Latinos from Mexico, Puerto Rico, and the Dominican Republic, in search of job opportunities and a better quality of life. This migration produced new forms of neighborhood politics and fostered a grassroots rebellion against liberalism at the local level, particularly as residents came to realize the possibilities of both violence and municipal politics as a means to protect their neighborhood and individual rights.

Newcomers and existing residents of color bore the brunt of the urban renewal plans. Urban redevelopment agencies routinely targeted minority neighborhoods for clearance to construct new expressways and skyscrapers. These projects significantly shrank the housing supply available in most cities to underrepresented groups and created competition among African Americans, Latinos, and Japanese Americans recently returned from internment camps for the few available units. Landlords significantly overcharged for those housing options that were available, many of which were substandard.[12] The situation also led to a dramatic increase in applications for public housing. In response, city officials across the country built projects using money offered by the federal government. However, local officials confronted staunch opposition to projects in or near white sections of cities. In Chicago, and Cicero, Illinois, for example, whites rioted in opposition to the potential of public housing in their communities.[13] White residents also feared individual families, particularly African Americans, moving into their neighborhoods.

Many white working- and middle-class residents in places like Detroit, Chicago, and Miami responded to the threat of encroachment of both public housing projects and individual African American families by forming new neighborhood associations. In Detroit, residents founded almost two hundred neighborhood associations between 1943 and 1965, forming one of the largest and most power grassroots movements in Detroit's history.[14] The association members sought to protect their neighborhoods and individual property values through a combination of tactics that included pickets, arson, vandalism, and physical violence. Yet, more often, members worked within the traditional channels of politics, mobilizing residents to send letters, testify at city council meetings, and most of all to vote.[15] The movement helped to usher in mayoral candidates like Albert Cobo, who took an explicitly "pro-homeowner stance," which elevated the voice of the neighborhood groups in local political affairs and led to Detroit's retreat on its public housing plans.[16] Officials predominantly decided to place new public housing projects in already poor and minority or transitioning areas and provided far fewer units than originally planned or needed.[17] The claim by grassroots activists that public housing was a form of communism also proved an effective argument at the height of the Cold War and further justified the decisions of officials in Detroit to limit the construction of public housing. However, the cumulative effect of these policies increased patterns of racial segregation and inequality.[18]

The targets of these processes of urban renewal and homeowner politics did not stand by as passive victims. In cities in the North and West, members of underrepresented communities worked hard to achieve their own rights and protection by also working within the political system to challenge discriminatory practices, often creating alliances with white liberals sympathetic to the cause. Many urban liberal politicians in the North and West incorporated civil rights language of equal opportunity and equality under the law into their platforms and speeches and pushed for the passage of new legislation to ban forms of racial discrimination in public accommodations, employment, education, and housing at the municipal and state levels.[19] However, civil rights activists faced difficulty getting the ideals and promises of equality embedded in these laws transformed into a lived reality. This difficulty stemmed in part from the fact that very few political officials of color in municipal office were elected to represent

minority groups and their neighborhoods. The shift to a citywide election system might have diluted the power of the white ethnic machines, but it also increased the difficulty of electing local representatives from segregated neighborhoods. Even those candidates from underrepresented groups elected in the new system faced considerable obstacles.[20] Edward Roybal, a Mexican American, succeeded in a 1949 campaign for a Los Angeles city council seat representing a multiracial eastside district. He successfully built a coalition that included Mexican Americans, African Americans, Japanese Americans, and members of the left-labor movement. However, once in office, Roybal confronted the limits of his political power. He proved unable to prevent freeway construction and projects like Dodger Stadium from destroying the homes of many members of his district.[21]

Roybol's multiracial alliance was relatively rare. Many Asians and Latinos moved into deteriorating neighborhoods like Boyle Heights, the Near North Side in Chicago, and Washington Heights in New York previously occupied by lower-middle-class whites who had departed for the suburbs. These neighborhoods experienced the consequences of postwar capital flight and neglect but also became the sites of new forms of community activism and laid the foundation for later political campaigns.[22] Yet this segmentation made the forging of multiracial alliances at the city level difficult to achieve and sustain. Many Latino and Asian residents navigated the increasingly segregated landscape by positioning themselves in comparison to African Americans and each other in order to gain favor and a superior position in the changing racial and political hierarchies of American cities and the nation as a whole.[23]

In the growing metropolises of the Sunbelt south like Charlotte and Atlanta, African Americans found it easier to build alliances with municipal political leaders who came to see African Americans as potential allies in their efforts to carry out urban growth and redevelopment.[24] Residential segregation in Atlanta and Charlotte, nevertheless, actually increased during the period of this coalition as the downtown elite's emphasis on urban renewal and economic growth depended on tactics that further concentrated African Americans in distinct urban neighborhoods.[25] By the early 1960s, members of the civil rights community in Atlanta and Charlotte chafed at the asymmetrical dimensions of the alliance and grew more assertive on issues of meaningful desegregation and economic equity.[26] Civil rights activists demanded school and neighborhood desegregation and better job opportunities, thereby threatening the business elite's control over urban politics and highlighting the tenuousness of the coalition.[27] As African American leaders across the country increasingly questioned both alliances with white liberal and moderate politicians and the mechanisms of integration as a means to achieve equality, violence in the streets made racial tensions impossible to ignore.

The grassroots rebellion within the ghettoes of most major cities in the 1960s permanently changed the relationship between race and politics and propelled new forms of urban politics. The wave of urban violence began in 1963 and crested in 1967 with 163 uprisings, the most significant occurring in Los Angeles, Newark, and Detroit. The uprisings were often local in their orientation, but together represented a reaction to decades of spatial concentration of poor African Americans, Puerto Ricans, and Mexican Americans in the urban core and the failure of policymakers to establish more racial and economic equality or impose reforms on police practices.[28] Although not part of a unified political movement, the riots were above all about controlling turf and regaining control of black and Latino neighborhoods, which participants believed were controlled by political outsiders. The targets of aggression tellingly, therefore, were primarily the police and white-owned businesses.[29] Participants, nevertheless, rarely left

the ghettoes to attack city hall, corporate headquarters, or other symbols of the urban political power structure and white establishment.

Even without a physical attack on government buildings, the violence created a crisis for leadership in many major cities and challenged the liberal vision of government and urban planning. The uprisings powerfully demonstrated that the sense of cohesion and stability that postwar liberals believed their modernist concept of government would provide had not occurred. These events served as a key turning point in urban politics, but were not a nail in the coffin. As historian Heather Thompson argues, "the polarizing urban rebellions of the 1960s generated new political possibilities for America's inner cities."[30] Thus, while the riots were in part a response to the limits of political power, their legacy continued to play out politically and in response to liberalism.

NEIGHBORHOOD POWER

The late 1960s produced a series of political movements, politicians, and issues that changed the nature of urban politics. Black power, white ethnic conservatism, and the neighborhood movement were each extensions of earlier groups and causes that had opposed urban renewal. Yet each movement made that critique even more pointed and more directly sought to influence and change the political system by gaining electoral representation. While these movements had key ideological differences, they all embraced a model of neighborhood politics and sought to turn the segregation and segmentation of cities into a source of political strength.

The uprisings validated and enhanced a new generation of black power activists, who more than any group reconfigured urban electoral politics in the 1970s.[31] Black power activists sought to use the systemic segregation of African Americans into urban ghettoes as a means to gain self-determination, community control, and political power. As Eldridge

Cleaver articulated in 1969, African Americans "didn't choose to be packed into ghettos, but since that's where we are, we're not going to get any real power over our lives unless we use what have—our strength as a bloc."[32] Black power activists in several cities came to realize that representation in politics would provide a way not just to gain power, but also to channel material resources into their communities.[33]

The turn toward electoral politics by black power activists coincided with the decision by many African American candidates to embrace the ideals and rhetoric of black power, group pride, and neighborhood identity to gain the support of the African American community. This convergence contributed to a new wave of African American mayors in cities across the country. The election of Carl Stokes in Cleveland, Richard Hatcher in Gary, Coleman Young in Detroit, Maynard Jackson in Atlanta, Tom Bradley in Los Angeles, Lionel Wilson in Oakland, Wilson Goode in Philadelphia, and Harold Washington in Chicago embodied the sea change in urban political leadership. Beginning in the 1970s, thousands of African Americans gained office in cities across the country, serving on city councils and school committees and in other positions of municipal politics.[34] Thomas Sugrue observed "The surge in black political power maybe have been the most enduring consequence of the civil rights revolution."[35] Although the election of African Americans like Bradley, Goode, and Washington often depended on forging coalitions with white residents, these victories occurred primarily in cities that had black majorities or pluralities. The persistence of segregated neighborhoods, therefore, played a key role in the rise of black political representation, reinforcing the ways in which structural segregation created possibilities for social movements. Yet the persistent economic dilemmas of many low-income minority neighborhoods illustrated how African Americans, even in political office, had difficulty overcoming the pernicious forces of segregation.

The uprisings in Detroit and elsewhere bolstered and extended the antiliberal politics and defensive localism that had dominated white working-class urban neighborhoods since the 1940s. The violence also motivated many white families who could afford it to move across municipal boundaries, which made the racial ground of many major cities even more unsteady in the late 1960s and 1970s.[36] For those who stayed in the city, the uprisings reinforced the sense that their cities and neighborhoods were under attack by both African Americans and white liberal reformers. The mandatory desegregation of schools in cities across the nation in the late 1960s further fueled the anger among many urban whites who believed that they unfairly bore the burden of integration. Like the proposed public housing projects and other elements of urban renewal, these residents saw busing as something imposed by liberal bureaucrats and judges. Their opposition displayed a sense of class resentment and anti-elitism as found in earlier forms of neighborhood defense.[37] The situation proved most dramatic and fiercely violent in Boston, where white working-class residents used neighborhood-focused chants such as "Here We Go Southie." This language and slogan invoked a desire for community control similar to that of black power activists in places like Philadelphia and Oakland.

A series of white conservative politicians channeled this anger and opposition to liberalism into local politics. Racially conservative politicians seized on the riots and busing to appeal to white voters worried about the trajectory of racial and ethnic change. Frank Rizzo emerged from the ranks of the Philadelphia Police Department to become mayor by emphasizing "law-and-order," invoking inflammatory racial language, and skillfully manipulating the media. Rizzo signaled the persistence and increase of white racialist politics in many white working-class urban neighborhoods during the 1970s.[38] Similarly, in Boston a generation of politicians like Louise

Day Hicks gained seats on the city and school councils by playing on this opposition to liberal social engineering.[39] This resurgent brand of neighborhood-based politics aimed to preserve the systems of racial segregation and counter the rise of black political power. These campaigns illuminated the racial and class fragmentation of Boston, Philadelphia, Detroit, Los Angeles, and other cities throughout the 1970s, which left the future of urban politics up for grabs.[40]

The late 1960s and 1970s witnessed the rise of another variety of urban neighborhood-based political movement intent on saving local communities. Inspired and forged in part by the freeway revolts of the 1960s, a new urban-based citizens' movement emerged in places like Brooklyn that made the neighborhood a focal point of action. Like black power and urban white conservatism, neighborhood activists opposed urban renewal and growth-oriented liberalism and sought a return of political and economic power and control to the local level.[41] Many of the residents who joined the movement were disillusioned with national politics in the aftermath of the Vietnam War and Watergate. They turned to local issues over which they felt they could have more control.[42] In many cities this movement altered the structures of municipal governance. For example, in Atlanta, the neighborhood-based opposition to an expressway inspired the formation of the citywide League of Neighborhoods, which exercised increasing power in city elections. In 1974, the group pressured Atlanta to create a new charter that gave increased power and control to city neighborhoods.[43]

This movement had a powerful impact on urban politics in the 1970s even as it avoided simple political categorization as liberal, conservative, or radical.[44] Activists explained their calls of "neighborhood power" as a type of reform, but a type that was in contrast to the bureaucratic reformers who had implemented urban redevelopment.[45] The movement stood in direct opposition to the emphasis in the postwar era on large institutions, comprehensive planning, social science, cooperation between big government and business, and modernism. Instead, the neighborhood movement celebrated smallness, intimacy, voluntarism, privacy, and authenticity.[46] The movement's emphasis on individualism and self-reliance and opposition to government intervention at times put participants less in line with the new left than with the new right. Gale Cincotta, a working-class community organizer from Chicago, captured the attitude of many members of the movement, "We don't want any more government programs. It was government programs that destroyed our cities."[47] Her comment mirrored the sentiment of black power activists and white urban conservatives, showing the widespread sense of disillusionment of many urban residents following the liberal age of urban redevelopment and renewal.

The antigovernment emphasis of neighborhood activists, nevertheless, seemingly ignored the fact that many poor residents required government services like welfare assistance and public housing, revealing a larger class- and race-based tension in the movement. The most powerful and effective neighborhood activists were educated whites who purchased and renovated brownstones in places like Brooklyn. This cohort demonstrated the ways in which neighborhood activists shaped municipal politics and policy. However, their forms of political action ensured that their voices and interests were often heard over less-advantaged people and neighborhoods. The movement's ability to bring power back to the neighborhood level provided white middle-class residents a means to keep their communities even more exclusive and hostile to outsiders like low-income residents and projects like public housing, homeless shelters, and drug treatment facilities. Thus in asserting the power of the neighborhood, these activists assumed some of the same exclusionary traits as earlier antiliberal residents in places like Detroit and Chicago.

These factors made broad-based coalitions difficult to sustain and set the stage for new forms of inequity and conflicts within the local political sphere over the future direction of urban development and distribution of resources.

"THE MAYOR OF CASTRO STREET"

In the late 1960s and early 1970s, the gay rights movement also increasingly came to understand the importance of the urban neighborhood as a means to gain electoral power. The rise of the gay rights movement intersected with black power, white racial conservatism, and the neighborhood movement. It also shared features of all these groups. San Francisco led and provides the clearest example of these trends. By the late 1960s San Francisco emerged as the epicenter of the nation's gay population and activism. However, gay activists remained marginal to municipal electoral politics, as was true in most American cities. A group led by Harvey Milk believed that gay residents could not achieve full rights and privileges of citizenship and protection from harassment without electoral representation. Milk was the owner of a camera store in the Castro District of the city, a neighborhood where the forces of urban renewal and suburbanization gave birth to a burgeoning gay enclave where many young professionals started small businesses and renovated Victorian homes.[48] Although a political novice, he believed that "You're never given power, you have to take it."[49] This ethos led him to enter the race for a seat on the San Francisco Board of Supervisors.

Milk lost his first three bids for the position of supervisor, thwarted by San Francisco's citywide electoral system, but each time he gained more visibility and a following. Milk's campaigning tactics quickly earned him the nickname of "the mayor of Castro Street." The title underscored his knack for forging personal connections with local residents to build a following, which was similar to early-20th-century urban white ethnic politicians. The nickname also illustrated his understanding about the power of controlling turf as means to gain power in local electoral politics. Paralleling the black power movement, Milk used the spatial concentration of gays and lesbians to his political advantage. In the mid-1970s San Francisco switched from citywide to district elections as a means to better reflect the new diversity and identity politics of the city. The shift concentrated many middle-class, gay voters into a single precinct centered on the Castro and propelled Milk's eventual election to the Board of Supervisors in 1977. Drawing on an older model of urban pluralism, Milk also quickly realized that controlling a group and area provided a means to build coalitions. As a candidate and official, he forged alliances with representatives of other identity-based movements such as African Americans, feminists, Latinos, and the Chinese American community, as well the Teamsters and liberals like Mayor George Moscone.[50]

Throughout his career as candidate and supervisor, Milk valorized the importance of neighborhoods as a central feature of municipal politics. As president of the Castro Valley Association, he frequently railed against the ways in which city elites favored downtown at the expense of neighborhoods and small businesses, which directly echoed the sentiments of citizens' groups in Brooklyn and Atlanta. In a speech the day after he was inaugurated, he contended, "My election was not alone a question of my gayness. . . . In a very real sense, Harvey Milk represented the spirit of the neighborhoods of San Francisco. . . . my fight to make the voice of the neighborhoods of this city be heard was not unlike the fight to make the voice of the cities themselves be heard."[51] Milk, therefore, remained committed to a vision for the future of the city and queer politics that was rooted in both a neighborhood-based and pluralist past. Many residents of San Francisco, nevertheless, missed the ways in which Milk's approach drew on this older and more traditional model of ethnic politics and felt under attack by Milk and the change he represented.[52] This faction included fellow Board of Supervisor member Dan White, a former firefighter from a largely blue-collar, lower-middle class, socially conservative Catholic neighborhood. White murdered both Milk and Mayor Moscone in November 1978.

Following the death of Milk, the gay community in San Francisco continued his style of neighborhood-based coalition politics. By choosing their own elected officials, and patronizing their own businesses and bars, residents of the Castro and other gay neighborhoods across the country increasingly emulated the traditional urban ethnic political model, which gave them increased power in the fragmented landscape of municipal politics. Although gay activists remained relatively weak as an organized political force at the state and federal levels in the 1980s and 1990s, the gay vote became very effective at the municipal level in part due to the concentration of openly gay residents in particular communities that were more often than not middle-class.[53] Many African American candidates understood the importance of the gay vote in their efforts to amass a coalition to win the mayor's office. Chicago's Harold Washington reached out to gay voters in 1983, making reference to the African American and queer communities' shared history of police harassment.[54] The support of gay voters played a crucial role in Washington's victory.

These new coalitions underscored the changing demographics and power structure of many cities across the country by the 1980s. Yet the persistence of segregation and commitment to neighborhood and group identity coupled with class politics prevented these partnerships from evolving into a permanent alliance.[55] The development of new coalitions in the 1970s and new leaders represented the culmination of the previous twenty years of urban neighborhood organizing and marked a new era of city politics. Yet many wondered

if these new politicians had inherited a hollow prize, as the economic fortunes of the nation's cities took a sharp turn for the worse.

THE HOLLOW PRIZE?

The continued flight of residents and capital to the suburbs, deindustrialization, the recession of 1973, the oil crisis, increasing inflation, and unemployment hit urban areas across the country hard. The tax revolt of the late 1970s further devastated cities that depended heavily on property taxes to pay for key services. This series of cascading problems created a budgetary crisis for nearly every major American city. Some, like Cleveland, Boston, Newark, Detroit, and New York, veered toward insolvency. The fiscal crisis once again highlighted the ways in which city politics were shaped both by larger national trends beyond their control and by actions of the federal government. Federal urban policy in the 1970s and 1980s focused primarily on withdrawing funds from cities. This retrenchment revealed the continued importance of federal policy in urban politics though in a different way than in the 1950s, when it underwrote urban renewal. US president Richard Nixon initiated this shift by launching a "new federalism" that urged strengthening the power of states and municipalities by scaling back funding and programs like the Office of Economic Opportunity. Ensuing presidents pursued a similar course. In the 1980s, the Reagan administration adopted an even more aggressive version of "New Federalism," which significantly reduced assistance to cities and devolved decision making to local authorities. Coupled with the larger cuts to spending on welfare, homeless services, and low-income housing under Reagan, these budgetary restrictions were devastating. The cuts proved particularly destructive to cities with limited property tax bases and high levels of unemployment and poverty that could not make up the deficit.

The response of many cities to this federal disinvestment and economic restructuring further underscores the newfound faith in the free market and the scaling back of the social welfare state that defined American attitudes about government after 1945. No place more clearly embodied these changes and approaches than New York City. In 1975, New York teetered on the brink of bank-ruptcy as banks withdrew their lines of credit and the Ford administration refused to inter-vene, or as the *New York Daily News* inter-preted it: "Drop Dead." The city narrowly avoided that fate, after local officials imple-mented strict budget cuts that led to the laying off of over 25,000 city workers includ-ing teachers and sanitation workers, the rais-ing of tuition imposed for the first time at the City University of New York, a sharp reduc-tion in expenditures for public parks and libraries, and the creation of a non-elected fi-nancial control board with significant power over the municipal budget.[56] The garbage piled up on the streets, and graffiti-covered subway cars offered the most visible symbols of New York in the age of the fiscal crisis.

The crisis brought about a change in city leadership and initially propelled the neigh-borhood movement into political power with the election of Ed Koch in 1977. Koch had begun his career as a Democratic reformer from Greenwich Village. He won the mayor-alty through a coalition that brought together the various aspects of the neighborhood move-ments of the 1970s, including a contingent of middle-class African Americans, white working-class ethnics, middle-class profession-als, and gay voters.[57] Once inaugurated he fo-cused primarily on economic recovery, im-plementing a version of austerity politics focusing less on services to the poor and middle class and more on tax breaks for cor-porate investors and real estate developers. Encapsulating his approach of urban govern-ance, Koch declared soon after taking office that "the main job of municipal government is to create a climate in which private busi-ness can expand in the city to provide jobs and profit."[58] This statement represented a reinterpretation of the purpose of local gov-ernment that had prevailed in New York and other major cities for most of their history.

From 1977 to 1989, Koch implemented this vision of private-sector growth by pro-viding billions of dollars of incentives to economic elites. Koch facilitated office build-ing construction, encouraged corporations to keep their headquarters in Manhattan, and offered subsidies to developers who initiated a real estate boom of commercial spaces and luxury apartments. The Koch administration also initiated the redevelopment of city neigh-borhoods like SoHo and Lower Manhattan to make them more attractive to tourists and new residents. The Reagan administration's deregulation of the financial services sector led to the explosive growth of the finance in-dustry in New York.[59] Over the course of the 1980s, the city's economy gained 400,000 jobs, added almost 45 million square feet of new commercial real estate, and basked in soaring tax revenues.[60] The city once again as-sumed its position as the center of global capitalism, with new skyscrapers and a flood of new residents to work on Wall Street or an-other burgeoning industry and live in luxury apartments.[61]

Koch and other mayors proved that the emphasis on unfettered private-sector growth especially at the municipal level had become a bipartisan enterprise not solely pursued by conservative Republicans like Reagan. Many observers bemoaned Koch's style as a decline or end of the postwar liberalism. Koch's ap-proach, nevertheless, in some respects echoed the growth liberal agenda of urban mayors of the 1950s. While Koch did not initiate the aggressive decimation of low-income neigh-borhoods by eminent domain and slum clear-ance that dominated reform strategies of the 1950s, his emphasis on the private sector and austerity created comparably destructive effects. The Koch administration policies ef-fectively evicted New York's poor and low-income residents by allowing (and even en-couraging) the increase in rents and overall cost of living in the city. Moreover, the incentives for corporations generated new employment opportunities, but not for low-income residents who lacked advanced degrees and the skills required for many of the post-industrial jobs that came to New York.[62] The high overall employment numbers obscured this form of growing inequality over the course of the 1980s.

The withdrawal of federal funding and the turn toward the private sector further created winners and losers both within and among cities in the 1970s and beyond. US cities began competing with one another for corporate investment as the means to increase their tax bases. This competition put particular pressure on the wave of recently elected African American politicians, many of whom were elected in the very Rust Belt cities where the combination of deindustrialization, the recession, and the retrenchment of federal funds had the most catastrophic impact.

The economic situation produced new pressures to deliver results, which led many mayors, even those who had run on more progressive or black power–based platforms, to pursue pro-growth politics. In Detroit, Coleman Young initially tried to implement an agenda of police reform and increasing African American public- and private-sector employment. Yet, by the late 1970s, Young shifted priorities. He worked closely with the chief executives of the Big Three automobile companies in an effort to keep their investments in Detroit proper. He managed to convince a few automobile factories to move back to the city through generous tax subsidies, and oversaw the construction of the Renaissance Center, an office, hotel, and retail complex. But these projects proved inadequate to address the city's massive unemployment and drained Detroit further of its tax base. Young's efforts illuminated that the forces of economic decay and the consistent problems of racial animosity were too powerful for a single official or project to resolve.[63]

Los Angeles mayor Tom Bradley similarly symbolized the challenges for urban politicians leading in a period of rapid economic and demographic change. Bradley was first elected mayor in 1973 through a multiracial coalition of middle-class African Americans, Asian Americans, Latinos, and white liberals; he served five consecutive terms. In the 1970s and 1980s Bradley adopted a politics of austerity, refusing to institute a tax increase to raise money for social services, and instead emphasized turning Los Angeles into a "world class" city. He wooed Japanese investors to spend billions on real estate, particularly downtown.[64] At the same time the Bradley administration did little to assist residents of low-income neighborhoods of color like South LA, which was decimated by the flight of manufacturing jobs, the decline in services, and the growing drug economy.[65]

Bradley did not completely abandon public-sector spending. Rather, he coupled his pro-growth agenda with an increase in the power and budget of the Los Angeles Police Department.[66] Fueled by the larger rise of the war on drugs at the federal and state levels, the Los Angeles police arrested and eventually incarcerated thousands of low-income men for a range of infractions from gang activity and drug dealing to loitering and jaywalking.[67] Los Angeles stood at the forefront of a national trend that occurred in the aftermath of the urban violence of the 1960s as cities adopted much more aggressive policing tactics that effectively militarized urban space.[68] Politicians at the state and federal levels simultaneously embraced the issues of crime and drugs, in part to gain political favor with concerned white middle-class voters, especially those in the suburbs. The passage of new laws to penalize the use and distribution of drugs further fueled these patterns.[69] The rise of mass incarceration fundamentally changed daily life in low-income urban communities of color and showed once again the ways in which national political trends had direct impact on urban spaces.

The Bradley administration's emphasis on downtown redevelopment therefore did not help poor Angelenos but intensified the problems of inequality in the city. The politicization of issues such as growth and policing ensured that LA in the 1980s and 1990s also came to reflect the broader inequities that were characteristic of the Reagan era and beyond. The 1992 acquittal of the police officers who beat Rodney King after a traffic violation in 1991 sparked outrage and one of the largest uprisings in American history. The event illuminated the limits of the pro-growth and tough-on-crime approach to urban politics.[70] The Los Angeles uprisings also raised attention to the changing demographics of major American cities and the ways in which they had become far more multiracial since the 1960s.

"TODAY WE MARCH, TOMORROW WE VOTE"

The expansion of immigration in the late 20th century fundamentally changed the racial demographics of Los Angeles and other American cities and had a direct impact on the political landscape. The majority of the new immigrants settled in major metropolitan areas that have long served as ports of entry, such New York, Los Angeles, Miami, and San Francisco, as well new gateways like Atlanta, Seattle, Washington, DC, and Salt Lake City.[71] By 2000, immigrants and their children constituted more than half the total population of these gateway cities.[72] This wave of immigration coincided with increased racial segregation and economic restructuring that defined city politics after the 1960s and compounded these existing patterns of segregation and inequality. The shift to a post-industrial economy in places like San Francisco and New York benefited educated immigrants, who have prospered in the economy.[73] The vast majority of recent immigrants did not have such skills and entered into low-wage service positions, which further contributed to the economic and racial segregation of most major cities.

The new immigrant settlement patterns both replicated and altered existing patterns of urban neighborhood-based politics. While many educated immigrants decided to move to the suburbs or wealthy and exclusive urban areas, many members of the post-1965 wave built on the inroads made by earlier groups and clustered into ethnic neighborhoods, creating or expanding enclaves like Koreatown in Los Angeles, Pilsen in Chicago, or Gulfton in Houston. These settlement patterns created clear trade-offs. This clustering reinforced the segmentation of most Americans cities; it also served as a source of political strength for immigrant groups. Paralleling the black power and gay rights movements, many ethnic groups used population concentration in particular urban neighborhoods as a means of political power. A new generation of Latino and Asian municipal officials built their strength on new population growth and its clustering in certain neighborhoods. This group-based organizing created certain tensions, often pitting underrepresented groups against each other for resources and power.[74] Latino and Asian elected officials confronted the same difficulties of economic restructuring and the retrenchment of federal spending on cities as African Americans had.

Many immigrant rights groups, nevertheless, recognized the ways in which cities serve as sources of strength in seeking policy changes at the local, state, and national levels. The rise of new immigration fueled a backlash that echoed the fights over race and housing that occurred in the 1940s and 1950s in places like Detroit and Chicago. In response to these assertive forms of nativism, activists organized a powerful protest movement that was largely urban-based. In order to challenge the restrictive immigrant policy considered by Congress in 2006, activists organized a "national day of action" in cities around the country during the spring of that year. Between three million and five million people participated in the protests and led directly to the tabling of the legislation. Politicians clearly took to heart participants' chants of "Today we march, tomorrow we vote."[75]

Many urban mayors and local officials have realized the importance of supporting immigrant issues to gain favor with this key constituency and as a tool of economic development for their cities. Municipalities like Detroit and Baltimore have explicitly dubbed themselves "welcome cities" in order to lure immigrants and their potential tax revenue as means to expand the economy and to counter substantial population loss.[76] Latinos and other immigrant groups have also come to increasingly exert clout in state and national politics as candidates recognize the necessity of securing the votes of urban-based groups.

A NEW URBAN POLITICS

The political outreach of national political candidates to urban voters embodies a larger shift in the relationship between cities and the federal government in the 21st century. In the last few elections, urban voters helped tip the scales in several key battleground states like Ohio, Nevada, Colorado, and Pennsylvania.[77] In many traditionally Republican states there has been a growing divergence between cities and urban areas. The major cities in Texas voted Democratic in 2008 and 2012 even though the Republican Party candidate won the state. Likewise, Atlanta, Indianapolis, New Orleans, Birmingham, Tucson, Little Rock, Las Vegas, and Charleston, South Carolina, all were blue islands in red states. Moreover, many cities have received a great deal of praise for their innovative solutions to the problems of the recession in contrast to the bitter partisanship and gridlock that has paralyzed Washington and many statehouses in the 21st century.[78] Bruce Katz and Jennifer Bradley in their book *The Metropolitan Revolution* predict the "inversion of the hierarchy of power in the United States" from a federal-led to an urban and locally based system.[79]

These electoral results and endorsements reflect larger changes that have occurred in cities since the 1990s and their longer historical roots. The corporate incentives of the growth-oriented mayors coupled with the neighborhood movement's emphasis on small-scale rehabilitation have led to new job opportunities and gentrified areas for a generation of middle-class post-industrial workers. Even struggling cities like Detroit have experienced a resurgence, as members of "the creative class" have been drawn to the city's cheap rents and burgeoning artisanal movement.[80] These trends, nevertheless, did not lead to more economic equitability or racial integration but instead increased the unequal growth and segregation in cities since 1970. The efforts to make cities "safe" for the new middle-class population and corporate dollars served as a motivating factor in cities like New York to redouble the use of street-level police practices like "stop and frisk." These new tactics generated an increase in police brutality and incarceration of low-income people of color as well as a new and powerful movement to protest these practices.

The issues of police brutality and the "Black Lives Matter" campaign, gentrification, and immigration have become the dominant issues shaping both urban and national politics since the turn of the 21st century. These issues reflect the long legacy of structural segregation as well as the successes and limits of urban political movements since 1945. While their impact on local and national electoral politics remains to be seen, they demonstrate the continued centrality of urban politics to the past, present, and future of American history.

DISCUSSION OF THE LITERATURE

A review of the literature underscores the multifaceted and nuanced nature of urban politics since 1945 and how it traverses many disciplines, historical subfields, and issues. Political science spawned much of the early, traditional literature on urban politics, with a large portion of it written in the postwar era itself.[81] The fields of urban planning, sociology, and geography have also explored questions of urban politics and the political economy of cities.[82]

A rich literature on urban renewal and urban redevelopment of the postwar era exists within both political science and history. Political scientists first explored the topic of growth coalitions, which was subsequently addressed and expanded upon by urban historians.[83] Both historians and political scientists have produced extensive studies of urban renewal policy at the national and municipal levels and the role of these policies in producing inequality.[84] Scholars have also offered in-depth analysis of Robert Moses and other key postwar urban planners.[85] Historians have devoted considerable attention to Jane Jacobs as well as other critics of urban renewal and to the freeway revolts.[86] These studies are indicative of the frequent use of a biographical approach to the issue of urban politics since 1945. Scholars and journalists have written important accounts of key figures from John Lindsay and Carl Stokes to Harvey Milk and Ed Koch.[87] Several scholars have examined the riots and how urban leaders responded to the crisis.[88]

The rise of black political power in the 1970s and especially the rise of African American mayors have produced an extensive literature both in history and political science.[89] Many focus on particular figures or places.[90] Journalist Tamar Jacoby's *Someone Else's House* offers a more critical account of African American municipal power, particularly the leadership of Maynard Jackson, Andrew Young, and Coleman Young.[91] Several other political scientists and historians concentrate on the success and limits of African American coalition building in the 1970s and beyond.[92] The topic of working-class backlash since 1945 has attracted a great deal of attention by historians. In addition to looking at the attitude of white working-class urban residents toward mandatory desegregation, scholars

have studied the impact of this group on national politics, identifying this group as the quintessential "Reagan Democrats" who symbolize political realignment at the national level.[93] Suleiman Osman's work has refocused attention to the neighborhood movement, which earned a great deal of attention in the 1970s with works by many of the participants themselves, but had gained less attention from historians.[94] Many historians have challenged the traditional black-white focus of the literature and highlighted the longstanding multiracial dimensions of urban politics, particularly the role and place of Asian and Latino residents.[95] A growing literature on the urban dimensions of queer politics and the gay rights movement's impact on a variety of elements of urban politics has appeared most recently.[96]

The subfield of metropolitan history has popularized the community study model, focusing on particular cities as well as the relationship between national policy and grassroots actors. The key works in this field examine elements of municipal politics, especially its role in fostering forms of segregation and inequality.[97] Historians have also increasingly focused on questions of the fiscal crisis, privatization, and neoliberalism in cities, as part of the growing attention to 1970s and the 1980s and the history of capitalism.[98] The rise of mass incarceration and the criminalization of urban space have also gained increased attention by historians. Many have begun and will continue to examine the role of municipal and national politics and policies in shaping this important issue and the impact of the carceral state on individual urban residents and urban politics as a whole.[99]

PRIMARY SOURCES

An array of primary sources sheds light on urban politics at the national level and in many cities. The National Archives has the records of the Department of Housing and Urban Development, which provides important resources on federal urban renewal policies and programs. The papers of Edward Logue and Robert Moses provide further insight into postwar redevelopment and renewal. The papers of individual elected officials offer an excellent resource, and many have been preserved at libraries around the country. The LaGuardia and Wagner Archives at LaGuardia Community College have the records of several mayors, including John Lindsay, Ed Koch, David Dinkins, and Rudy Giuliani. The Jerome Cavanaugh, Coleman Young, and Tom Bradley papers offer important materials on the politics of Detroit and Los Angeles. Many of these figures have written useful and valuable memoirs as well.

Excellent collections on various urban-based social movements and neighborhood organizations include Northeastern University in Boston and the GLBT Historical Society in San Francisco. Northeastern University Special Collections has digitized and made available online a rich collection related to the Latino community in Boston. The Berkeley, California, neighborhood association newsletters for 1975–1976 are preserved and provide important perspective on the movement in Berkeley and around the country. The Prelinger Archives online has archival film footage related to urban politics and renewal such as *Detroit: City on the Move*. The Brookings Institution has produced several important reports on contemporary urban politics, particularly the topics of immigration and urban revitalization. The Woodrow Wilson Center has also produced several important reports on immigration and urban politics.

Documentaries address various facets of urban politics since 1945 and provide excellent visual evidence of urban politics, including *The Pruitt-Igoe Myth* (2012), *Chávez Ravine: A Los Angeles Story* (2003), *The Life and Times of Harvey Milk* (1982), *Let the Fire Burn* (2013), *Street Fight* (2005), and *Koch* (2013). The radio show *This American Life* produced a fascinating look at the mayoral career of Chicago's Harold Washington

entitled "Harold" (Episode 84, November 21, 1997). The HBO television series *The Wire* provides an outstanding fictional account of the multifaceted dimensions of urban politics at the end of the 20th century.

FURTHER READING

Avila, Eric. *Folklore of the Freeway: Race and Revolt in the Modernist City*. Minneapolis: University of Minnesota Press, 2014.

Ballon, Hilary, and Kenneth T. Jackson, eds. *Robert Moses and the Modern City: The Transformation of New York*. New York: W. W. Norton, 2007.

Banfield, Edward C., and James Q. Wilson. *City Politics*. Cambridge, MA: Harvard University Press, 1963.

Cannato, Vincent J. *The Ungovernable City: John Lindsay and His Struggle to Save New York*. New York: Basic Books, 2001.

Carmichael, Stokely, and Charles V. Hamilton. *Black Power: The Politics of Liberation in America*. New York: Random House, 1967.

Caro, Robert. *The Power Broker*. New York: Knopf 1974.

Countryman, Matthew J. *Up South: Civil Rights and Black Power in Philadelphia*. Philadelphia: University of Pennsylvania Press, 2006.

Dahl, Robert. *Who Governs?: Democracy and Power in an American City*. New Haven, CT: Yale University Press, 1961.

Fernandez, Lilia. *Brown in the Windy City: Mexicans and Puerto Ricans in Postwar Chicago*. Chicago: University of Chicago Press, 2012.

Jacobs, Jane. *The Death and Life of Great American Cities*. New York: Random House, 1961.

Judd, Dennis R., and Todd Swanstrom. *City Politics: Private Power and Public Policy*. 2d ed. New York: Longman, 1998.

Katz, Bruce, and Jennifer Bradley. *The Metropolitan Revolution: How Cities and Metros Are Fixing Our Broken Politics and Fragile Economy*. Washington, DC: Brookings Institution, 2013.

Kurashige, Scott. *The Shifting Grounds of Race: Black and Japanese Americans in the Making of Multiethnic Los Angeles*. Princeton, NJ: Princeton University Press, 2008.

Lukas, J. Anthony. *Common Ground: A Turbulent Decade in the Lives of Three American Families*. New York: Alfred A. Knopf, 1985.

Osman, Suleiman. *The Invention of Brownstone Brooklyn: Gentrification and the Search for Authenticity in Postwar New York.* New York: Oxford University Press, 2011.

Self, Robert O. *American Babylon: Race and the Struggle for Postwar Oakland.* Princeton, NJ: Princeton University Press, 2003.

Shilts, Randy. *The Mayor of Castro Street: The Life and Times of Harvey Milk.* New York: St. Martin's Press, 1982.

Soffer, Jonathan. *Ed Koch and the Rebuilding of New York City.* New York: Columbia University Press, 2010.

Stewart-Winter, Timothy. *Queer Clout: Chicago and the Rise of Gay Politics.* Philadelphia: University of Pennsylvania Press, 2016.

Stone, Clarence N. *Regime Politics: Governing Atlanta, 1946–1988.* Lawrence: University Press of Kansas, 1989.

Sugrue, Thomas J. *The Origins of the Urban Crisis: Race and Inequality in Postwar Detroit.* Princeton, NJ: Princeton University Press, 1996.

Sugrue, Thomas J. *Sweet Land of Liberty: The Forgotten Struggle for Civil Rights in the North.* New York: Random House, 2008.

Thompson, Heather Ann. *Whose Detroit?: Politics, Labor, and Race in a Modern American City.* Ithaca, NY: Cornell University Press, 2001.

Zipp, Samuel. *Manhattan Projects: The Rise and Fall of Urban Renewal in Cold War New York.* New York: Oxford University Press, 2010.

NOTES

1. For a discussion of the machine system, see Dennis R. Judd and Todd Swanstrom, *City Politics: Private Power and Public Policy,* 2d ed. (New York: Longman, 1998), 53–78.

2. Edward C. Banfield and James Q. Wilson, *City Politics* (Cambridge, MA: Harvard University Press, 1963), 51.

3. Banfield and Wilson, *City Politics,* 95.

4. Christopher Klemek, *The Transatlantic Collapse of Urban Renewal: Postwar Urbanism from New York to Berlin* (Chicago: University of Chicago Press, 2011), 48–77; and Samuel Zipp, *Manhattan Projects: The Rise and Fall of Urban Renewal in Cold War New York* (New York: Oxford University Press, 2010).

5. Alison Isenberg, *Downtown America: A History of the Place and the People Who Made It* (Chicago: University of Chicago Press, 2004), 170.

6. Ronald P. Formisano, *Boston against Busing: Race and Ethnicity in the 1960s and 1970s* (Chapel Hill, NC: University of North Carolina Press, 1991), 120–125, 165; and J. Anthony Lukas, *Common Ground: A Turbulent Decade in the Lives of Three American Families* (New York: Alfred A. Knopf, 1985), 200–201.

7. Eric Avila, *Folklore of the Freeway: Race and Revolt in the Modernist City* (Minneapolis: University of Minnesota Press, 2014).

8. Jane Jacobs, *The Death and Life of Great American Cities* (New York: Random House, 1961).

9. Klemek, *Transatlantic Collapse of Urban Renewal,* 129–142.

10. Avila, *Folklore of the Freeway,* 2–3.

11. Eric Avila, *Popular Culture in the Age of White Flight: Fear and Fantasy in Suburban Los Angeles* (Berkeley: University of California Press, 2004), 55–62, 145–184, 195–223.

12. Thomas J. Sugrue, *The Origins of the Urban Crisis: Race and Inequality in Postwar Detroit* (Princeton, NJ: Princeton University Press, 1996), 33–72.

13. Arnold R. Hirsch, *Making the Second Ghetto: Race & Housing in Chicago, 1940–1960* (New York: Cambridge University Press, 1983), 68–99, 215–219.

14. Sugrue, *Origins,* 211.

15. Sugrue, *Origins,* 211–224, 231–234.

16. Sugrue, *Origins,* 84–87, 222–225.

17. Sugrue, *Origins,* 85–88.

18. Thomas J. Sugrue, "Crabgrass-Roots Politics: Race, Rights, and the Reaction against Liberalism in the Urban North, 1940–1964," *Journal of American History* 82, no. 2 (September 1995): 568–569; and Avila, *Popular Culture in the Age of White Flight,* 38–40.

19. Heather Ann Thompson, *Whose Detroit?: Politics, Labor, and Race in a Modern American City* (Ithaca, NY: Cornell University Press, 2001), 28–44; Matthew J. Countryman, *Up South: Civil Rights and Black Power in Philadelphia* (Philadelphia: University of Pennsylvania Press, 2006), 13–79; Robert O. Self, *American Babylon: Race and the Struggle for Postwar Oakland* (Princeton, NJ: Princeton University Press, 2003), 76–95; and Scott Kurashige, *The Shifting Grounds of Race: Black and Japanese Americans in the Making of Multiethnic Los Angeles* (Princeton, NJ: Princeton University Press, 2008), 174–185.

20. Civil rights activist Charlotta Bass's quest to become the first African American elected to the Los Angeles City Council in the late 1940s symbolized the limits of black political power. Despite galvanizing many factions of the black community, she lost by two-to-one. Josh Sides, *L.A. City Limits: African American Los Angeles from the Great Depression to the Present* (Berkeley: University of California Press, 2003), 152–153.

21. Kurashige, *Shifting Grounds*, 230–232; and Sides, *L.A. City Limits*, 152–153.

22. Lilia Fernandez, *Brown in the Windy City: Mexicans and Puerto Ricans in Postwar Chicago* (Chicago: University of Chicago Press, 2012), 13–14.

23. Fernandez, *Brown in the Windy City*, 5, 81–82.

24. Kevin Kruse, *White Flight: Atlanta and the Making of Modern of Conservatism* (Princeton, NJ: Princeton University Press, 2005), 25–41.

25. Matthew D. Lassiter, *The Silent Majority: Suburban Politics in the Sunbelt South* (Princeton, NJ: Princeton University Press, 2006), 50–53, 123–131.

26. For one critique of the raw deal this coalition gave the African American community, see Stokely Carmichael and Charles V. Hamilton, *Black Power: The Politics of Liberation in America* (New York: Random House, 1967), 70–72.

27. Clarence N. Stone, *Regime Politics: Governing Atlanta, 1946–1988* (Lawrence: University Press of Kansas, 1989), 51–82.

28. Fernandez, *Brown in the Windy City*, 159–172.

29. Thomas J. Sugrue, *Sweet Land of Liberty: The Forgotten Struggle for Civil Rights in the North* (New York: Random House, 2008), 356.

30. Thompson, *Whose Detroit*, 47.

31. Self, *American Babylon*, 254.

32. Self, *American Babylon*, 254.

33. Countryman, *Up South*, 296.

34. Sugrue, *Sweet Land of Liberty*, 501–505.

35. Sugrue, *Sweet Land of Liberty*, xxii.

36. Sugrue, *Origins*, 266–267.

37. Formisano, *Boston against Busing*, 3.

38. Countryman, *Up South*, 255; Suleiman Osman, "The Decade of the Neighborhood," in *Rightward Bound: Making America Conservative in the 1970s*, ed. Bruce J. Shulman and Julian E. Zelizer (Cambridge, MA: Harvard University Press, 2008), 112.

39. Formisano, *Boston against Busing*, 44–65, 179–202; and Lukas, *Common Ground*, 115–138.

40. Thompson, *Whose Detroit*, 192–199.

41. Harry C. Boyte, *The Backyard Revolution: Understanding the New Citizen Movement* (Philadelphia: Temple University Press, 1980), 3.

42. Boyte, *Backyard Revolution* 53–54.

43. Boyte, *Backyard Revolution*, 71.

44. Osman, "Decade of the Neighborhood," 110.

45. Osman, "Decade of the Neighborhood," 114.

46. Osman, "Decade of the Neighborhood," 110.

47. Osman, "Decade of the Neighborhood," 119.

48. Clayton C. Howard, "The Closet and the Cul de Sac: Sexuality and Culture War in Postwar California" (PhD Diss., University of Michigan, 2010); and Josh Sides, *Erotic City: Sexual Revolutions and the Making of Modern San Francisco* (New York: Oxford University Press, 2009), 83–123.

49. Randy Shilts, *The Mayor of Castro Street: The Life & Times of Harvey Milk* (New York: St. Martin's Press, 1982), 74–75.

50. Shilts, *The Mayor of Castro Street*; and George C. Bailey, *Gay Politics, Urban Politics: Identity and Economics in the Urban Setting* (New York: Columbia University Press, 1998), 201.

51. Shilts, *The Mayor of Castro Street*, 323.

52. Sides, *Erotic City*, 141–173.

53. Timothy Stewart-Winter, "The Law and Order Origins of Urban Gay Politics," *Journal of Urban History* 41, no. 5 (September 2015): 825–835.

54. Timothy Stewart-Winter, "Queer Law and Order: Sex, Criminality, and Policing in the Late Twentieth-Century United States," *Journal of American History* (June 2015).

55. Stewart-Winter, "Queer Law and Order."

56. Judd and Swanstrom, *City Politics*, 346.

57. Suleiman Osman, *The Invention of Brownstone Brooklyn: Gentrification and the Search for Authenticity in Postwar New York* (New York: Oxford University Press, 2011), 274–275.

58. Judd and Swanstrom, *City Politics*, 417.

59. Vincent J. Cannato, "Bright Lights, Doomed Cities: The Rise or Fall of New York City in the 1980s?" in *Living in the Eighties*, ed. Gil Troy and Vincent J. Cannato (New York: Oxford University Press, 2009), 73–74.

60. Cannato, "Bright Lights Doomed Cities," 74–75.

61. Jonathan Soffer, *Ed Koch and the Rebuilding of New York City* (New York: Columbia University Press, 2010), 255–258.

62. Cannato, "Bright Lights, Doomed Cities," 80; and John Hull Mollenkopf and Manuel Castells, eds. *Dual City: Restructuring New York* (New York: Russell Sage Foundation, 1991).

63. Sugrue, *Sweet Land of Liberty*, 503–504; and Sugrue, *Origins*, 270–271.

64. Mike Davis, *City of Quartz: Excavating the Future in Los Angeles* (New York: Vintage Books, 1992), 136–138; and Kurashige, *Shifting Grounds of Race*, 7–8.

65. Judd and Swanstrom, *City Politics*, 397–400.

66. Davis, *City of Quartz*, 267–322; and Donna Murch, "Crack in Los Angeles: Crisis, Militarization, and Black Response to the Late Twentieth-Century War on Drugs," *Journal of American History* 102, no. 1 (2015): 162–173.

67. Judd and Swanstrom, *City Politics*, 398.

68. Heather Ann Thompson, "Why Mass Incarceration Matters: Rethinking Crisis, Decline, and Transformation in Postwar American History," *Journal of American History* (December 2010), 710–713.

69. See Michelle Alexander, *The New Jim Crow: Mass Incarceration in the Age of Colorblindness* (New York: New Press, 2010); and Dan Baum, *Smoke and Mirrors: The War on Drugs and the Politics of Failure* (Boston: Little, Brown, 1996).

70. Judd and Swantsrom, *City Politics*, 400.

71. Audrey Singer, "The Rise of New Immigrant Gateways" (Washington, DC: Brookings Institution, 2004).

72. Gary Gerstle and John Mollenkopf, *E Pluribus Unum? Contemporary and Historical Perspectives on Immigrant Political Incorporation* (New York: Russell Sage Foundation, 2001), 2.

73. Gerstle and Mollenkopf, *E Pluribus Unum*, 8; and Singer, "The Rise of New Immigrant Gateways."

74. Matt A. Barreto, Benjamin F. Gonzalez, and Gabriel R. Sanchez, "Rainbow Coalition in the Golden State: Exposing Myths, Uncovering New Realities in Latino Attitudes toward Blacks," in *Black and Brown Los Angeles: Beyond Conflict and Coalition*, ed. Laura Pulido and Josh Kun (Berkeley, CA: University of California Press, 2013), 208–232.

75. Jonathan Fox, Andrew Selee, Robert Donnelly, and Xóchitl Bada, *Context Matters: Latino Immigrant Civic Engagement in Nine U.S. Cities*, Reports on Latino Immigrant Civic Engagement (Washington, DC: Woodrow Wilson International Center for Scholars, April 2010).

76. Mike Davis, *Magical Urbanism: Latinos Reinvent the U.S. City* (New York: Verso, 2000), 1–1; and Monica Davey, "Immigrants Seen as a Way to Refill the Detroit Ranks," *New York Times*, January 24, 2014.

77. Josh Kron, "Red State, Blue City: How the Urban-Rural Divide Is Splitting America," *Atlantic Magazine*, November 30, 2012.

78. Bruce Katz and Jennifer Bradley, *The Metropolitan Revolution: How Cities and Metros Are Fixing Our Broken Politics and Fragile Economy* (Washington, DC: Brookings Institution, 2013), 1–13.

79. Katz and Bradley, *Metropolitan Revolution*, 5.

80. Richard Florida, *The Rise of the Creative Class: And How It's Transforming Work and Leisure in America* (New York: Basic Books, 2002).

81. See for example, Banfield and. Wilson, *City Politics*; and Robert Dahl, *Who Governs?: Democracy and Power in an American City* (New Haven, CT: Yale University Press, 1961). Dennis Judd and Todd Swanstrom have written the most comprehensive and widely assigned recent textbook, which highlights the themes of political economy and examines the interaction of public and private history; see Judd and Swanstrom, *City Politics*.

82. See for example, John R. Logan and Harvey L. Molotch, *Urban Fortunes: The Political Economy of Place* (Berkeley: University of California Press, 1987).

83. Paul E. Peterson, *City Limits* (Chicago: University of Chicago Press, 1981); Gregory J. Crowley, *The Politics of Place: Contentious Urban Redevelopment in Pittsburgh* (Pittsburgh, PA: University of Pittsburgh Press, 2005); and Jon C. Teaford, *The Rough Road to Renaissance: Urban Revitalization in America* (Baltimore: Johns Hopkins University Press, 1990).

84. See Martin Anderson, *The Federal Bulldozer: A Critical Analysis of Urban Renewal, 1949–1962* (Cambridge, MA: MIT Press, 1964); Jewel Bellush and Murray Hausknecht, eds., *Urban Renewal: People, Politics and Planning* (Garden City, NY: Doubleday, 1967); and John H. Mollenkopf, *The Contested City* (Princeton, NJ: Princeton University Press, 1983). For historical accounts of urban renewal and its impact on racial inequality see for example, N. D. B. Connolly, *A World More Concrete: Real Estate and the Remaking of Jim Crow South Florida* (Chicago: University of Chicago Press,

2014); Howard Gilette Jr., *Between Justice and Beauty: Race, Planning, and the Failure of Urban Policy in Washington DC* (Baltimore: Johns Hopkins University Press, 1995); Alison Isenberg, *Downtown America: A History of the Place and the People Who Made It* (Chicago: University of Chicago Press, 2004); Andrew Highsmith, *Demolition Means Progress: Flint, Michigan, and the Fate of the American Metropolis* (Chicago: University of Chicago Press, 2015); Christopher Klemek, *The Transatlantic Collapse of Urban Renewal: Postwar Urbanism from New York to Berlin* (Chicago: University of Chicago Press, 2011); Self, *American Babylon*; and Samuel Zipp, *Manhattan Projects: The Rise and Fall of Urban Renewal in Cold War New York* (New York: Oxford University Press, 2010).

85. Robert Caro's *The Power Broker* (New York: Knopf, 1974) is a highly critical account of Robert Moses's approach, while Hilary Ballon and Kenneth T. Jackson, eds. *Robert Moses and the Modern City: The Transformation of New York* (New York: W. W. Norton, 2007) offers a more sympathetic view. For more on the broader political environment in which Moses operated, see Joel Schwartz, *The New York Approach: Robert Moses, Urban Liberals and Redevelopment of the Inner City* (Columbus: Ohio State University Press, 2010). For more on planners in other cities, see, for example, Lizabeth Cohen, "Buying into Downtown Revival: The Centrality of Retail to Postwar Urban Renewal in American Cities," *The Annals of the American Academy of Political and Social Science* (May 2007): 82–95.

86. Contemporary critics of the politics and aesthetics of urban redevelopment include Jane Jacobs, *The Death and Life of Great American Cities* (New York: Random House, 1961); and Herbert Gans, *Urban Villagers: Group and Class in the Life of Italian Americans* (New York: Free Press, 1962). Historical treatments of the opposition to urban redevelopment include Klemek, *The Transatlantic Collapse of Urban Renewal*; Suleiman Osman, *The Invention of Brownstone Brooklyn: Gentrification and the Search for Authenticity in Postwar New York* (New York: Oxford University Press, 2011); and Zipp, *Manhattan Projects*. For more on the freeway revolts, see Avila, *Folklore of the Freeway*; Alan Lupo, *Rites of Way: The Politics of Transportation of Boston and the U.S. City* (New York: Doubleday, 1970); Raymond A. Mohl, "Stop

the Road: Freeway Revolts in American Cities," *Journal of Urban History* 30, no. 5 (July 2004): 674–706; and Mark H. Rose, *Interstate: Express Highway Politics, 1939–1989* (Knoxville: University of Tennessee Press, 1990).

87. Vincent J. Cannato, *The Ungovernable City: John Lindsay and His Struggle to Save New York* (New York: Basic Books, 2001); S. A. Paolantonio, *Frank Rizzo: The Last Big Man in Big City America* (Philadelphia: Camino Books, 1994); Buzz Bissinger, *A Prayer for the City* (New York: Random House, 1997); Jonathan Soffer, *Ed Koch and the Rebuilding of New York City* (New York: Columbia University Press, 2010); and John Hull Mollenkopf, *A Phoenix in the Ashes: The Rise and Fall of the Koch Coalition in New York City Politics* (Princeton, NJ: Princeton University Press, 1994).

88. See for example, Sidney Fine, *Violence in the Model City: The Cavanagh Administration, Race Relations, and the Detroit Riot of 1967* (East Lansing: Michigan State University Press, 2007); and Heather Ann Thompson, *Whose Detroit?*

89. Countryman, *Up South*; Jeffrey Hegelson, *Crucibles of Black Empowerment: Chicago's Neighborhood Politics from the New Deal to Harold Washington* (Chicago: University of Chicago Press, 2014); Adolph Reed Jr., *Stirrings in the Jug: Black Politics in the Post-Segregation Era* (Minneapolis: University of Minnesota, 1999); Self, *American Babylon*; Sugrue, *Sweet Land of Liberty*; and Thompson, *Whose Detroit?*

90. David R. Colburn and Jeffrey Adler, eds., *African-American Mayors: Race, Politics, and the American City*, New ed. (Urbana: University of Illinois, 2005). For examples of accounts of specific figures, see Leonard N. Moore, *Carl B. Stokes and the Rise of Black Political Power* (Urbana: University of Illinois Press, 2002); and Gary Rivlin, *Fire on the Prairie: Chicago's Harold Washington and the Politics of Race* (New York: Henry Holt, 1992). Wilbur C. Rich, *Coleman Young and Detroit Politics: From Social Activist to Power Broker* (Detroit: Wayne State University Press, 1999).

91. Tamar Jacoby, *Someone Else's House: America's Unfinished Struggle for Integration* (New York: Basic Books, 1998).

92. See, for example, Raphael J. Sonenshein, *Politics in Black and White: Race and Power in Los Angeles* (Princeton, NJ: Princeton University Press, 1993); and Rufus Browning, Dale Marshall, and David Tabb, *Protest Is Not Enough: The Struggle of*

Blacks and Hispanics For Equality in Urban Politics (Berkeley: University of California Press, 1986).

93. For examinations of the longstanding roots of white antiliberalism and its impact on municipal politics, see Hirsch, *Making a Second Ghetto*; Sugrue, *Origins of the Urban Crisis*; Formisano, *Boston against Busing*; Kruse, *White Flight*; and Jonathan Rieder, *Canarsie: The Jews and Italians of Brooklyn against Liberalism* (Cambridge, MA: Harvard University Press, 1985).

94. Osman, *The Invention of Brownstone Brooklyn*; Osman, "The Decade of the Neighborhood," in *Rightward Bound: Making America Conservative in the 1970s*, ed. Bruce J. Shulman and Julian E. Zelizer (Cambridge, MA: Harvard University Press, 2008); see also Rebecca Marchiel, "Neighborhoods First: The Urban Reinvestment Movement in the Era of Financial Deregulation, 1966–1989," (PhD Diss., Northwestern University, 2014); Michael Scott Foley, *Front Porch Politics: The Forgotten Heyday of American Activism in the 1970s and 1980s* (New York: Hill and Wang, 2013); and Alexander Von Hoffman, *House by House, Block by Block: The Rebirth of America's Urban Neighborhoods* (New York: Oxford University Press, 2003). For a contemporary account of this movement, see Harry C. Boyte, *The Backyard Revolution: Understanding the New Citizen Movement* (Philadelphia: Temple University Press, 1980).

95. Kurashige, *The Shifting Grounds of Race*; Mike Davis, *Magical Urbanism: Latinos Reinvent the U.S. City* (New York: Verso, 2000); Fernandez, *Brown in the Windy City*; and Jesse Hoffnung-Garskof, *A Tale of Two Cities: Santo Domingo and New York after 1950* (Princeton, NJ: Princeton University Press, 2007). See also Rufus Browning, Dale Marshall, and David Tabb, *Racial Politics in American Cities*, 3d ed. (New York: Pearson, 2002).

96. Shilts, *The Mayor of Castro Street*; Timothy Stewart-Winter, *Queer Clout: Chicago and the Rise of Gay Politics* (Philadelphia: University of Pennsylvania Press, 2016); Christina B. Hanhardt, *Safe Space: Gay Neighborhood History and the Politics of Violence* (Durham, NC: Duke University Press, 2013); and Sides, *Erotic City*.

97. See Lassiter, *The Silent Majority*; Avila, *Popular Culture in the Age of White Flight*; Hirsch, *The Making of the Second Ghetto*; Kruse, *White Flight*; Osman, *The Invention of Brownstone Brooklyn*; and Self, *American Babylon*.

98. For more on the fiscal crisis see Kim Phillips-Fein, "The Legacy of the 1970s Fiscal Crisis," *Nation* (May 6, 2013), 24–27; Ester Fuchs, *Mayors and Money: Fiscal Policy in New York and Chicago* (Chicago: University of Chicago Press, 1992); Martin Shefter, *Political Crisis/Fiscal Crisis* (New York: Columbia University Press, 1992); Peter McClellan and Alan Magdowitz, *Crisis in the Making: The Political Economy of New York State since 1945* (New York: Cambridge University Press, 1981); and Seymour P. Lachman and Robert Polner, *The Man Who Saved New York: Hugh Carey and the Fiscal Crisis of 1975* (Albany: State University of New York Press, 2010). For more on privatization particularly in New York City and Los Angeles, see, for example, Mollenkopf and Castells, *Dual City*; Mike Davis, *City of Quartz: Excavating the Future in Los Angeles* (New York: Vintage Books, 1992); Arlene Dávila, *Barrio Dreams: Puerto Ricans, Latinos, and the Neoliberal City* (Berkeley, University of California Press, 2004); and Soffer, *Ed Koch and the Rebuilding of New York City*.

99. Heather Ann Thompson, "Why Mass Incarceration Matters." See also *Journal of American History* (June 2015), which is devoted to the topic of "Historians and the Carceral State."

Lily Geismer

SLAVERY IN AMERICAN CITIES

ESTABLISHING URBAN SLAVERY IN COLONIAL NORTH AMERICA

In the United States, the prevalence historically and culturally of rural plantation slavery has obscured our knowledge of the practice of slavery in urban areas. But throughout human history slavery has been infinitely adaptable. As Europeans established North American trading and military posts and marine ports in the 17th and 18th centuries, there was little question that slave labor would be involved. By the time Europeans began establishing settlements in colonial North

America, they had used slave labor in all parts of the economy in the Americas for more than a century: both Native American and African slave labor was employed in European colonies throughout the Caribbean and Latin and South America, fueling the wealth of early capitalism through the production of sugar and the harvesting and exportation of raw materials from gold and silver to lumber. Indeed, European exploration of North America before the establishment of settlements was often conducted with racially and status-mixed crews of Europeans, Africans, and Native Americans; Africans and Native Americans might be free, enslaved, or indentured laborers, while Europeans were either indentured or free laborers. Once European colonists decided to establish a settlement, the creation of a labor force was both opportunistic and rooted in their own experiences and needs. The variations in the composition of their labor forces initially grew out of their various relationships with Native Americans: whether Natives and Europeans were at war with each other; Europeans were building on native enslavement practices; or Europeans did not have the ability to enslave native peoples or, eventually, had easier access to African slaves. British settlers in 16th- and 17th-century Virginia and New England initially relied on Native American free, indentured, and enslaved labor alongside European indentured and free labor. Before 1700, native labor was the dominant nonwhite labor force. Although the English went back and forth in terms of whether to enslave Native Americans, warfare ultimately led to decades of bound labor for native people, even if not for life, in the 17th century.[1]

Jamestown, Virginia, the first permanent British settlement in North America, was also where the first bound African settlers (as opposed to transitory explorers or free settlers of African descent) arrived, in 1619. Although it remains unclear if these "20 and odd" people of African descent eventually gained freedom or were enslaved for life,

Jamestown's function as a port city through which enslaved Africans arrived forecast the fate of most Atlantic port cities as portals between the international slave trade and the rural and urban slave labor markets. Significant numbers of Africans and Native Americans experienced port cities from Boston to Savannah as part of the Atlantic trade in slaves. From the 17th century and even as slavery became strongly associated with people of African descent in the 18th century, Native Americans were exported as slaves through northern and southern port cities to the Caribbean as punishment for crimes or as prisoners of war. In one instance, New Englanders exported at least five hundred Native American prisoners in the aftermath of King Philip's War (1675–1676) into slavery in the Atlantic, Caribbean, Mediterranean, and Indian Oceans, creating what historian Margaret Newell has termed the "second Native diaspora."[2] New Amsterdam, New York, and Providence and Newport in Rhode Island all vied to be the leading northern slave ports for the international African slave trade. The Rhode Island ports bested New York City by the mid-18th century, but New York's efforts left it with the largest urban population of African-descended slaves in the northern colonies. Laws and practices of what became 18th- and 19th-century slavery developed throughout North America, in urban as well as rural settlements. Boston is believed to be the first place where an owner attempted to force enslaved people to have children for profit, in 1638, the same year the first slave ship is recorded to have arrived there. In addition, the first known law of slavery in British North America was enacted in Massachusetts in 1641, in response to the enslavement of large numbers of Native Americans during the Pequot War.[3]

Early European settlers in New Amsterdam, which was owned and administered by the Dutch West India Company, waited more than a year for the arrival of enslaved African laborers, in 1626, to build permanent homes and the larger infrastructure of the colony. The first eleven slaves of African descent at New Amsterdam, all men, were owned by the Dutch West India Company, which was heavily involved in providing slaves to Brazil and the Caribbean, and thus had ready access to African slaves. Dutch settlers in 17th-century New Amsterdam were less likely to use enslaved Native American labor than other parts of North America, although they were just as likely to engage in brutal warfare against them.[4] Although rural slavery in the Chesapeake came to dominate the North American slave experience of the 18th century by sheer numbers, in the 17th century urban slavery in the northern colonies—New Amsterdam, Boston, and Philadelphia—outweighed southern urban and rural locations, which developed much more slowly. Charleston emerged as a leading slave trading port in the southern part of the North American British colonies.

West of the Atlantic coastal colonies, French and Spanish patterns of settlement and interactions with native peoples led to different patterns of enslavement. French settlers in 18th-century Detroit and New Orleans collaborated with free Native Americans for the purposes of trade and combined Native and African bound labor with European indentured and free labor. At Fort Detroit, established by the French in 1701 and awarded to the British by the treaty ending the Seven Years' War in 1760, enslavement of Native Americans built upon existing patterns of conflict among native nations and the need to develop fur trading relationships and utilize specific skills for processing the fur into garments, as well as the greater expense of importing African slaves. Europeans called enslaved native peoples "Panis," a perversion of Pawnees, a western Native American nation. Most enslaved natives were from western locales, although they were not necessarily all members of the Pawnee nation. The number of enslaved Africans increased only slightly after British rule was established and small numbers of British settlers moved from New York to Detroit, bringing African slaves with them.[5]

The labor roles of enslaved Native American and African people in early colonial settlements varied only slightly. Europeans in most colonial cities relied on slave labor for the establishment of infrastructure; farming for subsistence and, eventually, the provisioning of southern and Caribbean slave societies; production of trade goods; and domestic labor. In Detroit, French settlers collaborated with their native trading partners, such as the Huron and Ottawa, to enslave other native peoples, especially women. Male French settlers took native women as concubines, but as important as the enslaved women's sexual labor was their ability to process the furs which were the backbone of the early economy, a skill the women brought with them.[6] In French New Orleans, founded in 1718, the lack of a clear economic need for laborers or strong commitment by the French government meant that retaining Natives or Africans in slavery was difficult through much of the 18th century. French settlers relied on enslaved Native Americans and Africans for basic survival, such as growing food, ahead of any commercial needs, which were not well-developed in the colony.

European colonial men regularly developed intimate sexual relationships with enslaved Native and African women in the 17th century. Coerced sexual relationships for the purposes of assimilating prisoners of war and expanding households was a common practice in the aftermath of war and in societies that utilized slave labor, including Native American and African societies. Incorporation into these societies could result in a change in status. In 17th-century North America, the children of unions between Europeans and enslaved Natives and Africans did not necessarily remain enslaved, as laws of hereditary slavery were not in place in North America at the time. But neither were these concubines, as they were often called, nor their children considered the equals of those in white communities. There were few formal marriages with slave owners; religious leaders and government elites were conflicted about the status of these relationships, particularly but not only when they were not formalized in churches. Sermons and laws encouraged whites, particularly white men, not to engage in relationships with nonwhite women, but these practices were rarely halted.[7] By the 18th century the status of native people and African people diverged in British North America, as laws limiting enslavement to people of African descent spread to most Anglo-American colonies. Proof of Native ancestry became evidence of freedom in court cases to determine status, even as the children of enslaved women of African descent were compelled to remain in life-long, hereditary slavery.

The focus on African slaves led to a decline in the enslavement of Native Americans east of the Mississippi by the early 19th century. But west of the Mississippi, slavery among Native people and the enslavement of Native people by Euro-Americans continued into the early 20th century and until after the Civil War, respectively. A large portion of the enslavement of Native Americans was driven by wars and trade among native nations. Many European settlements were built on or near native towns and settlements as a way to support their own economic and political plans, but they were not able to completely harness Native slave trading to their own economic advantage. Native slave trading networks spread across the Southwest—indeed, across the continent—in ways that European settlers only dimly apprehended, even as they sometimes benefited from that trade. This was particularly true in Spanish Florida and the Spanish Southwest.[8] In northern Mexico, the Spanish created silver mines in which enslaved Native Americans labored from the 16th through the 18th centuries. After the Pueblo Revolt of 1680, Europeans were not involved in Native slavery in the region for twelve years, until the arrival of the Comanches, Utes, and

Navajos, who forced the Spanish to return to slave labor for the remainder of the 18th century. In the 19th century, the movement of Anglo-Americans west to create a variety of economic and political forms accelerated some forms of Native slavery as they bought slaves from Native allies. Mormons in Utah and missionaries throughout the Southwest once again claimed slavery as a way to civilize Natives, while cattle ranchers and other agriculturalists in California utilized their labor. Native peoples themselves saw an opportunity to create greater wealth through slave-based and other trading relationships with Europeans. Not until the early 20th century was slavery largely eradicated from the areas west of the Mississippi.[9]

Although Europeans were unable to control the Native American trade in slaves, they did control the trade in African-descended slaves in North America. The Dutch in New Amsterdam and the British in New York attempted to make the island port the center of the North American slave trade. This goal grew in urgency as the Chesapeake (Virginia and Maryland) developed the tobacco industry in the late 17th century and increased demand for African slaves. Laws passed there that limited slavery to Africans spread throughout the English colonies, gradually halting enslavement of Native Americans. Only two areas in North America attempted to avoid the enslavement of Africans before the Revolutionary War: the Georgia colony and Fort Mose in Spanish Florida. But in neither case was the exclusion of slavery a wholesale rejection of the system. James Oglethorpe hoped his colony would rehabilitate the poor of England through agricultural labor. However, he had gained his wealth in part through his leadership in the Royal African Company, which traded slaves captured on the West African coast; and he used enslaved people to build the infrastructure of Savannah, the Georgia colony's first settlement. Fort Mose was protected by the Spanish only as a way to undermine the British in North America, specifically in South Carolina: the town was part of a Spanish territory to which enslaved people could flee to live in freedom. Although fugitives created freedom there, the Spanish only (and unsuccessfully) outlawed the enslavement of Native Americans in their territories, not people of African descent.[10]

By the early 18th century, the port cities of Providence and Newport had vaulted the colony of Rhode Island to the leading slave trading locale in North America. The DeWolf family of Providence became the wealthiest slave-trading family in what became the continental United States. Charleston, South Carolina, was the leading southern port for enslaved people arriving from Africa. But even those towns and cities that did not achieve the slave trading success of the Rhode Island ports and Charleston were still influenced by slavery. Port cities up and down the East Coast welcomed slave ships from Africa and the Caribbean, and built and outfitted ships for the slave trade. They also functioned as the ports through which supplies created in urban and rural settings, such as wheat flour, butter, and other food items, were shipped to slave societies in North America, the Caribbean, and South America and received slave-produced goods from those areas in return. Slavery, slave-produced goods, and goods produced to support slave economies were central to pre-Revolutionary War urban economies.[11]

Slavery and Colonial Urban Culture.
Colonial urban communities east of the Mississippi were relatively small, multicultural, hierarchical societies, within which enslaved people, who were on the lowest rungs of the hierarchy, had highly variable access to improving their status and autonomy. The population of most colonial settlements and towns until well into the 18th century numbered from the hundreds to the low thousands. In addition, urban slave owners typically held small numbers of enslaved people, definitely fewer than ten and most often fewer than five.

Enslaved Africans and Natives were often outnumbered by European-Americans in urban settings. These demographic factors meant that enslaved urban populations frequently assimilated to European cultural norms through the 17th century and for much of the 18th century. In the 17th century, Atlantic Creoles, as historian Ira Berlin terms them, came to eastern North American cities with knowledge of European ways gained in communities off the coast of Africa, in the Atlantic World as sailors, or in Caribbean slave communities.[12] Enslaved Native Americans in the east also held knowledge of European culture, albeit more likely gained within or alongside North American European settlements. The status and possibilities for movement out of bondage for enslaved people depended on the cultural capital they brought to these settlements over the course of the colonial era, as well as the degree to which Europeans relied on slave labor.

In the early years of establishing urban communities, European settlers valued enslaved laborers who could bridge cultures as well as provide labor. Over time, however, cultural knowledge did not lead to higher status or freedom for enslaved people. At Fort Detroit, French settlers bought or traded enslaved Natives from nations with which they were aligned as a way to solidify diplomatic relations, as well as to access knowledgeable labor. Initially male settlers may have married Native women of higher status in Native communities as a way to gain knowledge and improve the potential of trading relationships. These practices were similar to those of Native enslavers, who expanded their communities by incorporating women and children acquired in war. But eventually French male settlers sought Native women for less formal sexual relationships that did not result in status beyond slavery for the women involved. Whether as wives or as concubines, and from the perspective of both Natives and Europeans, these women were at a lower social level than their husbands or than wives of the same nation, although their children might rise to a higher level. Similar practices held in New Orleans, although for most of the 18th century economically and militarily New Orleans was far less successful for the French than Detroit.[13]

In 17th-century East Coast cities participating in Native American and African slave trades, similar patterns prevailed. The small populations in colonial settlements meant that even enslaved Africans who arrived with little or no experience with European or Native cultures often quickly learned European and Native ways, depending on the makeup of the community. Labor forces in 17th-century cities included enslaved people of African and Native descent, indentured Europeans, and those who owned slaves and held the indenture contracts. These mixed labor forces worked to clear the land, build the infrastructure of the forts, ports, and towns that eventually grew into the cities we think of today, and provide military assistance. The mix of people in any city depended on the local dynamics at play. Because of their small numbers, critical role in the survival of European settlements, and knowledge and negotiating acumen, enslaved Africans gained freedom in larger numbers than would be true in the 18th and 19th centuries. In New Amsterdam in 1644, the first eleven male slaves who arrived at the settlement negotiated "half-freedom" for themselves and their wives amid the colony's war against the Lenape people, Kieft's War, a time when their military support was particularly needed. Similarly, "Antonio, A Negro," who was sold into the Virginia colony via Jamestown, gained his freedom through meritorious military service and the patronage of his owners, the Bennett family, who allowed him to work for wages and ultimately helped him, his wife, and their children to gain freedom.[14]

By the early 18th century, the East Coast slave communities in cities were embedded

in British colonies. In New Amsterdam on the eve of British takeover in 1664, the total population was about 1,575, including three hundred enslaved and seventy-five free blacks, the largest population of urban slaves in British North America. Between two hundred and three hundred enslaved blacks lived in Boston by 1700, amid a total population of about seven thousand. Philadelphia, founded in 1682, grew to a population of two thousand by 1700. The first slave ship arrived in Philadelphia in 1684; by 1710, enslaved Africans accounted for 20 percent of the city's population. In the Chesapeake, most enslaved people spent only a short time in ports or trading posts before being sent to plantation sites, a pattern that accelerated with the development of the tobacco economy in the late 17th century. "Administrative centers" such as Annapolis, Maryland, and Williamsburg, Virginia, developed into towns with the growth of planter wealth, followed by urban homes and businesses that encouraged the employment of slave labor. Norfolk (incorporated 1736) and Alexandria (1749), Virginia, and especially Baltimore, Maryland (1729), developed in response to the mid-18th century grain market, which replaced tobacco as a commercial crop. The less-demanding labor needs of grain agriculture and processing, as opposed to tobacco, provided a space for the development of slave artisans, employed first on plantations and then in cities, where the need for skilled labor grew faster than could be satisfied by white artisans. Enslaved women and men in all cities worked in a variety of domestic, market, and port jobs. Only the Georgia colony, founded in 1732, made any pretense at surviving without slave labor, but pretense it was. Savannah was built with slave labor brought in from South Carolina; and by the time the colony lifted the ban on slavery in 1751, an estimated four hundred slaves had labored in the city and surrounding countryside, illegally brought in by colonists.[15] By the time of the Revolutionary

War, slave labor was a central component of most East Coast cities.

TURNING POINT: THE REVOLUTIONARY WAR AND URBAN SLAVERY

The Revolutionary War disrupted patterns of slavery in the soon-to-be independent colonies north of Delaware. With the enactment of gradual emancipation between 1777 (Vermont) and 1804 (New Jersey), northern cities became sites of struggle between pro- and antislavery political factions down to the Civil War, embodied most dramatically through race riots against the abolitionist movement and the recapture of fugitive slaves, as well as the establishment of antislavery organizations and pro- and antislavery newspapers. In the area south of Delaware, where slavery continued, urban slavery largely experienced an expansion of 18th-century patterns. Cities in the antebellum South deepened their reliance on the slave trade and slave-produced goods as foundational to their economic success. The experience of urban slaveholding and being enslaved in cities retained forms developed in the 18th century: small holdings by slave owners, relative autonomy for enslaved people, and higher numbers of skilled slaves. As urban households expanded, enslaved women outnumbered enslaved men, perhaps because women's domestic labor was more highly prized in cities, and because enslaved men's field labor was more highly prized in rural areas.

Postrevolutionary War Expansion of Urban Slavery. The compromises in the US Constitution that facilitated the continuation of slavery in the southern states, and the development of the cotton economy in the early 19th century fed the development of urban areas and thus urban slavery in the southern states. On the East Coast, Atlantic port cities from Baltimore to Savannah expanded on colonial economic and geographic

footprints to service the expansion of the antebellum plantation economy. The differing roles the cities played in the plantation economy shaped the nature of slavery within them. Baltimore, at the center of the flailing Chesapeake tobacco plantation economy, developed a large free black community between the end of the Revolutionary War and the rise of the cotton economy. The possibility for ending slavery in the South was strongest in Maryland and Virginia after the Revolutionary War, but the rebound of slave-based agriculture to the south and west, and the closure of the international slave trade in 1807 provided a new market for the Chesapeake: the sale of excess slave labor. Over the course of the antebellum period, between 875,000 and one million enslaved men, women, and children moved south and west into the expanding plantation geography of the United States. Although some accompanied their owners who were in search of new arable land, 60 to 70 percent were sold through the domestic slave trade. Chesapeake port cities such as Baltimore, Maryland, and Alexandria, Richmond, and Norfolk, Virginia, served as locations from which enslaved people were sent overland or shipped by sea. Southern ports from Charleston and Savannah all the way to New Orleans, and interior cities such as Montgomery, Alabama; Natchez, Mississippi; St. Louis, Missouri; and Louisville, Kentucky, served as locations to which slave owners traveled from near and far to purchase slaves, and locations from which slave traders put together coffles, groups of slaves who would be marched to and through rural areas during the slave trading seasons.[16]

Thus, as tobacco-based plantation agriculture declined in the Chesapeake region, the booming cotton economy to the south and west, rice along the lower Atlantic, sugar in Louisiana, and new regions of tobacco agriculture as well as hemp and other goods in Kentucky and Tennessee provided a ready market for enslaved people between 1820 and 1860. By the 1820s and down through the Civil War, slave traders established multi-city businesses, situated to make the most of interior routes through the heart of plantation agriculture and coastal routes to New Orleans, the largest slave trading port in the South, and to smaller coastal cities as well. Austin Woolfolk began his slave trading company in Augusta, Georgia, in the 1820s but soon opened offices in Baltimore and Easton, Maryland, and in New Orleans. Isaac Franklin and John Armfield sold slaves out of Tennessee and North Carolina before meeting in the 1820s and going into business together. By the mid-1830s, Franklin & Armfield was one of the largest slavetrading businesses in the South, with offices in Alexandria, Virginia; Natchez, Mississippi; and New Orleans, as well as agents in smaller towns in Virginia and Maryland. By the 1830s, urban slave trading businesses were an essential part of the domestic slave trade. The larger interregional businesses owned storefronts and slave holding pens in southern commercial districts; smaller itinerant traders rented spaces to sell their product. All used the infrastructure of large and small cities—newspapers, banks, courts, hotels, ports, and roads—to support their businesses. The domestic slave trade in southern cities remains part of the historical iconography of antebellum slavery, particularly as exposed by radical antislavery activists, from the auction block to the slave pen.[17]

The domestic slave trade was only one element of the reality of slavery in southern cities. In the South, most whites assumed that manual labor was primarily the purview of enslaved people; white people were assumed to be looking to own slaves, not labor as they did. Thus, slave labor was often a central component of the skilled and unskilled labor force in cities. At any given time, enslaved people performing labor in cities could be residents of those cities, or laborers accompanying owners and goods from rural hinterlands for either a few hours or days, or for weeks and months. In either case, the nature of urban slavery gave enslaved people greater day-to-day

autonomy and mobility, depending on the kinds of labor they performed.

Southern cities were central economic, political, and legal nodes connected to rural areas by waterways and roads, and connecting plantations to the wider world, mostly for the sale of raw goods and the purchase of finished goods and often slave labor. Towns and cities were also the sites of legal and financial expertise necessary to slaveholders and plantation businesses—courts and lawyers to draw up and adjudicate wills, deal with contested sales, collect debts, and oversee bankruptcy claims. Banks and merchants were necessary to ordinary commerce of all kinds. Many southern cities served as centers of the trade in slaves and slave-produced goods for their region or state—New Orleans, Baltimore, Savannah, Charleston, and Memphis, for example. Wealthier slave owners might own homes in both the city and the country, avoiding disease seasons in both places, participating in urban, state or national politics, and making economic and social connections. Enslaved men, women and children, particularly those who engaged in domestic labor, circulated between rural and urban homes as their owners dictated. The sex ratio among enslaved populations in the vast majority of cities was imbalanced, with many more women than men, perhaps due to the use of enslaved women for domestic work in homes. But men also circulated between rural and urban areas, working as draymen hauling goods, on the waterways that connected rural and urban areas, loading and unloading goods on the docks and in warehouses, and as skilled workers and in factories. Richmond was the most industrial city of the antebellum South and employed the most slaves in industrial labor. But enslaved men and women throughout the South worked in various nonagricultural industries in cities. In Savannah, enslaved men were responsible for making the bricks that lined the city streets and composed numerous dwellings and municipal, religious, and business buildings within and outside the city.

Throughout the South, enslaved men and women processed raw agricultural goods—tobacco, cotton, hemp rope—for shipment. Enslaved boatmen knew the waterways better than many whites.

Urban Slave Housing.

Households, except for the wealthiest, usually owned slaves in small numbers, a pattern continued from the colonial period. Most of these slaves were used in domestic labor, with a substantial number also used in the businesses of their owners. Wealthier households held larger numbers of enslaved people as domestics, and also hired them out to other households and to businesses, with the employer often responsible for housing and feeding the hired slaves for the term of the contract. The relatively small spaces for households of whites and enslaved blacks compared to rural farms and plantations meant that enslaved people who lived with their owners and employers were more often in close quarters with whites: across the yards in rooms over the stables, in the stables themselves alongside livestock, or in the kitchens, attics, or basements of the main houses. Although large percentages of southern urban populations owned slaves, those who did not own slaves, as well as those in need of additional labor, created a market for hired slaves. For owners, hiring out was another way to make money from enslaved people, especially when they could not fully employ them in their own homes or businesses. Some enslaved people negotiated their own contracts and kept part of their earnings, but most owners themselves, or agents hired for the purpose, negotiated the terms of hiring out contracts, which might last from a few days to years. Hired-out slaves might live independently in mixed neighborhoods of free blacks and slaves or live with their employers or owners. Slave owners relied on the society's agreement on the need to control enslaved people to balance the need for a degree of autonomy in the labor force. The numbers of enslaved people in cities who were owned by

businesses rather than by individuals increased over the course of the antebellum period.[18]

The necessary autonomy of enslaved people in urban areas was balanced by the policing infrastructure on the local, state, and ultimately the national level. Although at first glance such autonomy might seem to modern viewers to provide an opportunity for escape, in fact whites in the antebellum south were more often slave owners or aspiring owners, and thus were rarely antislavery. Whites were required to and rewarded for policing enslaved people and preventing runaways. South Carolina's Colored Seamen's Acts of 1822 prevented black sailors from coming ashore after the Denmark Vesey rebellion in Charleston. Blacks were required by law to wear metal tags identifying their status or to carry passes written by their owners that indicated the specific nature of their work. These are the most well-known examples from the web of laws throughout the South that demonstrated the desire of whites to control blacks, and make sure that free blacks did not disturb or confuse the status of enslaved blacks. The punishment of urban enslaved people in the antebellum South differed from that of the plantation. On isolated plantations and farms owners and overseers could brutally whip and otherwise physically punish enslaved people in front of slave communities but out of sight and hearing of white family members and neighbors. But the close quarters of relatively small antebellum cities made such displays of power difficult, and as the radical abolitionists increased their criticism of the brutality of slave masters, owners also sought to hide their brutality. Owners used municipal prisons to lock up recalcitrant slaves; police arrested and imprisoned enslaved people out after curfew or who committed other violations of the law, and then notified their owners. Punishments included whipping by professional whippers, pillorying, work gangs, and work houses. Charleston was known for its treadmill. Slave owners supported such punishments as long as their property was returned to them able to continue work and hopefully chastened against future crimes.[19]

Urban Areas and the Politics of Slavery and Antislavery.

Nationally, the question of returning fugitive slaves to the South was an active one that most often inflamed northern cities. During the gradual emancipation era (1777 through the 1820s), as manumission societies made the end of slavery possible by lobbying for laws and constitutional amendments state by state, manumission societies were concerned that those subject to being freed by the laws were not sold south into slavery. But as the vast majority of Northern blacks gained freedom from slavery by 1830, that concern transformed into a new constellation of issues. The expansion of free black communities in cities across the Northeast and into the old Northwest inspired fear among whites who worried that they would have to compete for jobs with former slaves. Southern slaves also attempted to escape north, pursued by their owners or agents hired by their owners to be returned south. As the gradual emancipation movement wound down and the radical abolition movement began arguing for the immediate end to slavery and the racial equality of people of African descent, northern city streets bore witness to scenes of anti-abolition and anti–slave-catcher activities, from resistance to violent riots as well as race riots against black communities—and sometimes all three. In Cincinnati, Ohio, in 1829, a three-day riot by whites who feared the free black population increase (no doubt fed in part by fugitive blacks fleeing uppersouth slavery) that had occurred there drove two thousand blacks out of the city to Canada. In the 1830s and 1840s, New York, Philadelphia, and Boston, as well as smaller cities such as Alton, Illinois, and Rochester, New York, witnessed antiblack and antiabolitionist riots.

On the other end of the spectrum, as fugitives from slavery sought freedom, even temporarily, in Northern cities, Southerners and their agents seeking the return of their property roamed the streets, sometimes seizing free blacks in return for rewards or to sell them in Southern slave markets. High-profile court cases as well as struggles with whites suspected of being slave catchers inspired mob actions to rescue fugitives from slavery in Northern cities down to the Civil War. Less dramatically, antislavery activists assisted fugitives from slavery after they arrived in cities, providing legal assistance, hiding places, information on jobs, or assistance in going to a safer destination out of reach of slave catchers. In 1835, David Ruggles founded the New York Vigilance Committee, which combined the legal acumen of antislavery lawyers with the street smarts of working-class African Americans. Vigilance Committees soon emerged in other cities as a uniquely urban form of the Underground Railroad.[20]

Resistance to Slavery.

Cities provided enslaved people with unique opportunities to resist and rebel against bondage. Towns and cities were good places to make a strike for freedom, with the significant number of enslaved people located in a relatively small geographic area, concentration of governmental power, and easily accessible transportation. But these same characteristics also made it easier for individuals or groups of slave owners to bring governmental structures to bear on smaller acts of resistance, such as the capture of runaways, and larger forms of rebellion.

In the founding years of most colonial cities in North America, the ability to maintain control over a slave population, whether Native American or African in composition, depended on the degree to which the population developed relationships with neighboring Native American nations. This was most dramatically true in New Orleans, where the relative lack of a colonial governmental infrastructure and harsh living conditions led enslaved Natives and Africans to leave the city for maroon communities on the outskirts of the city that at times aligned with and utilized resources from both European and Native settlements; or to join fully with local Native nations, a transition that could be eased by providing valuable information about the European settlers' plans. More typical were individual African slaves leaving European settlements to join Native settlements, as occurred up and down the East Coast. In doing so, Africans ran the risk of being re-enslaved by Native Americans. In addition, Native nations might have their own diplomatic needs and could return runaway African or Native slaves to Europeans if they were trying to build or maintain their own safety from incursion or economic ties. Notably, the first eleven male slaves who negotiated "half-freedom" in New Amsterdam in 1644 did so in part because the colony relied on their military labor against the Lenape peoples, another indicator of the ways in which the mix of race, nation, and status within colonies and cities provided opportunities that were neither linear nor predictable.[21]

Enslaved people sometimes rose up on their own against their enslavers. In 1712, a newly arrived group of African slaves in New York set fires to outbuilding belonging to one of their owners. When the townspeople came to put out the fire, the slaves set upon them, hoping to inspire all the enslaved people in the town to rise up and either take control of the city or flee to the hinterlands to form a separate community. As with many such actions, other enslaved people failed to join. Several conspirators were killed at the scene and others were put on trial, with some executed and others sent to the Caribbean as punishment. In 1680, a more successful effort to end slavery occurred in the Pueblo rebellion in the Southwest. The widespread enslavement of Native peoples to work in the mines at Parral led to the Pueblo Revolt of 1680. Nations located in a range of pueblos, or towns, across northeastern Arizona and northwestern New Mexico—Hopi, Zuni, Acoma, Cochiti, Pueblo, and many others—rose up over two

days in August to destroy the Spanish presence among them, killing 20 percent of the Spanish population and destroying all signs of Christianity and Spanish influence. The final goal was to capture Santa Fe, the capital of the Spanish empire in the region, and demand the return of the enslaved Native people held by the Spanish. After almost two weeks of being surrounded by Native American soldiers, the Spanish governor and about one thousand settlers fled south out of the city and out of New Mexico. For twelve years, Europeans were not involved in Native slavery in the region.[22]

In both the colonial and the antebellum era, slave resistance could involve collaboration between enslaved and free people. This was true of New York's 1741 slave plot, in which a uniquely urban mix of sailors, laborers, and enslaved people gathered in the city's taverns and fomented revolution, and the 1822 Denmark Vesey revolt in Charleston, South Carolina. Vesey, a formerly enslaved sailor who purchased his freedom with his prize money from a lottery, gathered members of Charleston's African Methodist Episcopal Church and others in the city and its rural hinterlands to plan a rebellion. Both of these rebellions were ultimately unsuccessful.[23]

Cities also provided opportunities for other forms of resistance. Enslaved people frequently flouted the web of laws designed to control them. They drank and socialized with free people, went out after curfew, gathered for funerals and for religious gatherings without permission, fenced and bartered stolen goods. In addition, cities were usually established on waterways or with major thoroughfares that could provide transportation out of slavery, as was the case most famously with Frederick Douglass's and Harriet Jacobs's ship voyages from Baltimore and through Philadelphia, respectively, to New York; or William and Ellen Craft's and William "Box" Brown's voyages in disguise by train from Savannah and Richmond, respectively.[24]

TO THE CIVIL WAR

North and South, black populations enslaved and free declined after 1850. Although some scholars have seen the decline in Southern urban slave populations as indicative of a decline in the importance of slavery more generally, the fact that both enslaved and free black populations declined at the same time should perhaps push us to a different set of conclusions. Free black populations appear to have declined in the urban North in response to the 1850 Fugitive Slave Law, which strengthened the ability of Southerners to retrieve black fugitives by setting up special courts to adjudicate an individual's slave status and paying a higher bounty to the judge if he determined that a black person was a slave who should be returned south. In response, many blacks fled the cities for rural areas and a significant number left the United States for Canada, Europe, Liberia, or Haiti. With Southern slave populations, it is possible that the continued expansion of the nation westward led slave owners to increase their commitment to agriculture, and thus move their enslaved property to more rural locales. This move of slave labor from urban to rural areas may have been further supported by the increase in European migrants who came south after the 1840s. Although European immigration into the South never matched Northern numbers, a significant number of Irish and Germans came into New Orleans, Savannah, Charleston, and other Southern urban areas.[25]

DISCUSSION OF THE LITERATURE

The importance of African-descended slave labor on pre-Civil War rural plantations to the history, culture, and economy of the United States has limited the exploration of the enslavement of Native American and African-descended people in urban areas in North America. The extraordinary impact of the US Civil War further reinforced the focus on antebellum Southern plantation slavery and on people of African descent. Before and during the antebellum era, white laborers in cities argued that enslaved laborers were unsuited to skilled work in urban areas. Slave owners also expressed concerns in the press that cities were uniquely threatening to the institution. The first histories of slavery that whites wrote after the Civil War and in the early twentieth century largely aligned with the romantic vision of the rural plantation South that ruled the time. To emphasize or acknowledge the importance of Southern cities and urban slavery would have called into question the view that enslaved laborers, much less black men and women, were able to hold skilled jobs. Additionally, as Southern blacks began leaving the rural South for better pay in Northern industrial cities, such arguments about slavery aligned with attempts by Southern employers to limit their mobility. But research into the history of American slavery from the last quarter of the 20th century and the first decades of the 21st benefits from chronological and geographical comparisons and reveals a more complex understanding of the adaptability of slavery to any number of conditions.[26]

Much of the literature on urban slavery is concerned with individual cities; indeed, there is no synthetic work that examines colonial-era cities and slavery as a group. The only two books that have attempted to examine antebellum cities and slavery as a group are Richard Wade's *Slavery in the Cities, 1820–1860* (1964), which is still very useful, although some of his arguments have been challenged by Claudia Goldin's *Urban Slavery in the American South, 1820–1860: A Quantitative History* (1976). Wade's encyclopedic work brings together the most complete account of urban slavery in the antebellum South, using archival, municipal, census, and print sources to understand the "urban perimeter" of cities, the laws that grew up in cities to control enslaved labor, the varieties of labor enslaved people performed in cities, fears and realities around slave resistance and rebellion, and the late-antebellum decline in slave populations in cities. Wade's argument that urban slavery was in decline by the start of the Civil War was challenged by Goldin, an economic historian, who saw that prices and demand for urban slaves continued unabated even as the population of urban slaves dropped. Although primarily focused on free blacks, Leonard P. Curry's *The Free Black in Urban America, 1800–1850: The Shadow of the Dream* (1981) is indispensable for understanding the relationships between enslaved and free black people in cities. It contains detailed quantitative work on enslaved and free black people in cities north and south in terms of employment, property ownership, and other factors.[27]

Individual cities with the most extensive historiographical trails include, in order, New Amsterdam/New York, New Orleans, Baltimore, Charleston, and Savannah. Smaller cities such as Mobile, Natchez, Memphis, and St. Louis could withstand more investigation, although there are some recent works, particularly from legal scholars.[28]

The status of places like Boston and Philadelphia in the iconography of freedom in the United States has meant that the history of slavery in those cities has been less clearly delineated. At the same time, Philadelphia's role as the home to George Washington and Thomas Jefferson during their presidencies has refocused attention on the role of slaves brought North by Southerners. Erica Armstrong Dunbar's *Never Caught* (2017), about Ona Judge, George and Martha Washington's enslaved woman who fled Philadelphia in 1796, and Annette Gordon-Reed's *The Hemingses of Monticello* (2008), which examines in part the experiences of Jefferson's enslaved retinue in Philadelphia, as well as the interpretive work on the President's House in Philadelphia all complicate our understanding of how slavery functioned in Northern locales even after emancipation was enacted there.[29] Historians of New England have also begun to dig deeper into slavery in Boston, Providence, Newport, and other locales in the colonial period, although many books are more concerned with "New England," than

with individual cities. Two exceptions to the "New England" trend are Jared Ross Hardesty's *Unfreedom*, on 18th-century Boston, and Cristy Clark-Pujara's *Dark Work*, which is a good example of how a book focused on a state can also provide deep analysis of the unique contributions of urban areas within that geographic framework.[30] To be clear, colony- and statewide studies are needed as well, so this critique is not meant to denigrate these works, but rather to identify areas of future research.

The area most lacking in the history of urban slavery is an understanding of how the enslavement of Native Americans, by both Native peoples and by Europeans, differed in urban areas, the rise and fall of such practices, and their meaning for urban slavery after the revolutionary era. This reflects the segregation within histories of North American and US slavery of Native and African enslavement, with a few significant exceptions. The two leading historians on this topic are Tiya Miles and Daniel Usner. Miles's recent book *Dawn of Detroit* is a model for how to construct such histories for urban areas. Daniel Usner's work on Native American slavery in New Orleans, *American Indians in Early New Orleans*, promises to reset our understanding of urban enslavement of native peoples in the South, east of the Mississippi. In terms of urban slavery, there is practically no discussion of the presence of urban enslaved Native peoples. Unfortunately, this reinforces the idea that North American slavery is only inclusive of people of African descent and continues the erasure of Native American histories. Yet many works point to ways that Native American histories can be incorporated into urban histories of slavery. Historians must work a little harder at integrating these threads.[31]

PRIMARY SOURCES

Research on colonial-era urban slavery has made great use of runaway slave ads, ads for slave trades, court cases, the development of laws regulating slavery, and shipping records.

In both the colonial and the antebellum eras, using the records of families could also be fruitful. Letters, financial records, and of course wills, estate records, and taxation records could all provide a sense of the ways in which African and Native slave labor was used, the experiences of both enslaved people and their enslavers, and perhaps people's ideas about the system of slavery as it developed in North America. In addition, colonial records could be mined for information about slavery in the colonies. Metropolitan governments sometimes or often adjudicated cases involving enslaved people in the colonies or slave trading in the Atlantic world. These records have been underutilized by colonial-era historians, given how important slave trading was to these cities and to the establishment of slavery in North America, even in areas where slaves were not used for agricultural labor.

Records for the 19th century are much richer, including newspapers, abolitionists' accounts, family papers, financial records of all kinds, governmental and legal records, court cases, census records, wills, and estate and taxation records. Slave narratives, including antebellum, postbellum, and Works Progress Administration narratives, not to mention letters and other interviews from the antebellum period, can provide additional insight into urban slavery from the perspective of enslaved people. In both the pre- and post-revolutionary eras, attention to the built environment is an underutilized method of understanding the ways in which urban slavery was structured and experienced. Clifton Ellis and Rebecca Ginsburg's edited collection *Slavery in the City: Architecture and Landscapes of Urban Slavery in North America* (2017) does a great job of introducing the possibilities for such methodologies.[32]

ACKNOWLEDGMENTS

My thanks to Dawn Peterson, Timothy Gilfoyle, the anonymous reviewer, and the editors at Oxford University Press for their suggestions and assistance with this article.

Errors of fact and interpretation remain my own.

FURTHER READING

Berlin, Ira. *Many Thousands Gone: The First Two Centuries of Slavery in North America.* Cambridge, MA: Belknap Press of Harvard University, 1998.

Brownell, Blaine A., and David R. Goldfield, eds. *The City in Southern History: The Growth of Urban Civilization in the South.* Port Washington, NY: Kennikat Press, 1977.

Clark-Pujara, Christy. *Dark Work: The Business of Slavery in Rhode Island.* New York: New York University Press, 2016.

Curry, Leonard P. *The Free Black in Urban America, 1800–1850: The Shadow of the Dream.* Chicago: University of Chicago Press, 1981.

Dantas, Mariana L. R. *Black Townsmen: Urban Slavery and Freedom in the Eighteenth-Century Americas.* New York: Palgrave Macmillan, 2008.

Ellis, Clifton, and Rebecca Ginsburg, eds. *Slavery in the City: Architecture and Landscapes of Urban Slavery in North America.* Charlottesville: University of Virginia Press, 2017.

Goldin, Claudia. *Urban Slavery in the American South, 1820–1860: A Quantitative History.* Chicago: University of Chicago Press, 1976.

Powers, Bernard. *Black Charlestonians: A Social History 1822–1885.* Little Rock: University of Arkansas Press, 1994.

Takagi, Midori. *Rearing Wolves to Our Own Destruction: Slavery in Richmond, Virginia, 1782–1865.* Charlottesville: University Press of Virginia, 1999.

Tyler-McGraw, Marie, and Gregg D. Kimball. *In Bondage and Freedom: Antebellum Black Life in Richmond, Virginia.* Chapel Hill: University of North Carolina Press, 1988.

NOTES

1. Edmund Morgan, *American Slavery, American Freedom: The Ordeal of Colonial Virginia* (New York: W. W. Norton, 1975), esp. chaps. 4 and 5; Margaret Newell, "Introduction," in *Brethren by Nature: New England Indians, Colonists, and the Origins of American Slavery* (Ithaca, NY: Cornell University Press, 2015); and Wendy Warren, *New England Bound: Slavery and Colonization in Early America* (New York: W. W. Norton, 2016), chaps. 1–3.

2. Newell, *Brethren by Nature,* 159–188.
3. Ira Berlin, *Many Thousands Gone: The First Two Centuries of Slavery in North America* (Cambridge, MA: Belknap Press of Harvard University, 1998), 29; Alden T. Vaughn, "Blacks in Virginia: A Note on the First Decade," *William and Mary Quarterly* 29 (1972): 469–478; Engel Sluiter, "New Light on the '20 and Odd Negroes' Arriving in Virginia, August 1619," *William and Mary Quarterly* 54 (1997): 395–398; Leslie M. Harris, *In the Shadow of Slavery: African Americans in New York City, 1626–1863* (Chicago: University of Chicago Press, 2003), 28; Christy Clark-Pujara, *Dark Work: The Business of Slavery in Rhode Island* (New York: New York University Press, 2016); Newell, *Brethren by Nature,* 49–54; Warren, *New England Bound,* 7–8; and Warren, "'The Cause of Her Grief': The Rape of a Slave in Early New England," *Journal of American History* 93 (March 2007): 1031–1049.
4. Harris, *In the Shadow of Slavery,* 12–15; Christopher Moore, "A World of Possibilities: Slavery and Freedom in Dutch New Amsterdam," chap. 1 in *Slavery in New York,* ed. Ira Berlin and Leslie M. Harris (New York: The New Press, 2005); Thelma Wills Foote, "'To better people their land, and to bring the country to produce more abundantly': territory, trade, conquest, and the project of colony building on Manhattan Island under Dutch rule, 1624–1664," chap. 1 in *Black and White Manhattan: The History of Racial Formation in Colonial New York City* (New York: Oxford University Press, 2004).
5. Gwendolyn Midlo Hall, *Africans in Colonial Louisiana: The Development of Afro-Creole Culture in Eighteenth Century Louisiana* (Baton Rouge: Louisiana State University Press, 1992), 3, 15; and Tiya Miles, *The Dawn of Detroit: A Chronicle of Slavery and Freedom in the City of the Straits* (New York: The New Press, 2017), 21–64.
6. Miles, *The Dawn of Detroit,* 21–64
7. Midlo Hall, *Africans in Colonial Louisiana,* 3, 15; Miles, *Dawn of Detroit,* 21–64; Newell, *Brethren by Nature,* esp. chap. 3; and Jennifer Spear, *Race, Sex, and Social Order in Early New Orleans* (Baltimore: Johns Hopkins University Press, 2010), 17–51, 61–66.
8. Colin G. Calloway, *New Worlds for All: Indians, Europeans, and the Remaking of Early America* (Baltimore: Johns Hopkins University Press, 1998), 10–12, 98–99; and Andrés Reséndez, *The Other Slavery: The Uncovered Story of Indian Enslavement in America* (Boston: Houghton Mifflin Harcourt, 2016), 134–135, 196–219.
9. This paragraph is largely based on Reséndez, *The Other Slavery,* chaps. 4 through epilogue. See also Pekka Hämäläinen, *The Comanche Empire* (New Haven, CT: Yale University Press, 2008).
10. Walter J. Fraser, Jr., "James Edward Oglethorpe and the Georgia Plan," in *Slavery and Freedom in Savannah,* ed. Leslie M. Harris and Daina Ramey Berry (Athens: University of Georgia Press, 2014), 22–23; Jane Landers, "Gracia Real De Santa Teresa De Mose: A Free Black Town in Spanish Colonial Florida," *American Historical Review* 95, no. 1 (1990): 9–30; and Spanish and antislavery, see Reséndez, *The Other Slavery,* 125–148.
11. Christy Clark-Pujara, *Dark Work,* "Introduction" and chap. 1, "The Business of Slavery and the Making of Race," 1–40; Berlin, *Many Thousands Gone,* 144–145; Warren, *New England Bound,* 36–47, 52–58; Harris, In the Shadow of Slavery, 18–19, 26–30; and Gary Nash, "Slaves and Slave-owners in Colonial Philadelphia," *William and Mary Quarterly* 30 (1973): 223–256.
12. Ira Berlin, "From Creole to African: Atlantic Creoles and the Development of African-American Society in Mainland North America," *William and Mary Quarterly* 53, no. 2 (April 1995): 251–288; Many Thousands Gone, part 1: "Societies with Slaves: The Charter Generations," 15–92.
13. Miles, *Dawn of Detroit,* 16, 43–50; and Spear, *Race, Sex, and Social Order in Early New Orleans,* 17–51.
14. Harris, *In the Shadow of Slavery,* 20–26; Berlin, *Many Thousands Gone,* part 1; Antonio/Anthony Johnson, 29–34.
15. Berlin, *Many Thousands Gone,* 134–136; James A. McMillin, "The Transatlantic Slave Trade Comes to Georgia," chap. 1 in *Slavery and Freedom in Savannah,* ed. Leslie M. Harris and Daina Ramey Berry (Athens: University of Georgia Press, 2014), 21–41.
16. Ira Berlin, "Migration Generations," chap. 4 in *Generations of Captivity: A History of African American Slaves* (Cambridge, MA: Harvard University Press, 2003).

17. The best and most complete work on the domestic slave trade is Steven Deyle, *Carry Me Back: The Domestic Slave Trade in American Life* (New York: Oxford University Press, 2005); for a full exploration of the historiography of the domestic slave trade and the author's conclusions regarding the numerical estimates of those sold, see Appendix A; for cities as sites for the domestic slave trade, see chap. 4, "'CASH FOR NEGROES': Slave Traders and the Market Revolution in the South"; on Woolfolk, Franklin, and Armfield, see 98–104; on the development of urban slave trading, see 104–106; on antislavery activists and slave trading, see chap. 6, "Outside Looking In: The Domestic Slave Trade and the Abolitionist Attack on Slavery." See also Calvin Schermerhorn, *The Business of Slavery and the Rise of American Capitalism, 1815–1860* (New Haven, CT: Yale University Press, 2015); and Walter Johnson, *Soul by Soul: Life Inside the Antebellum Slave Market* (Cambridge, MA: Harvard University Press, 1999).

18. Richard C. Wade, "Bondsmen and Hirelings," chap. 2 in *Slavery in the Cities, 1820–1860* (New York: Oxford University Press, 1964); on businesses owning slaves, 22–23; Susan Eva O'Donovan, "At the Intersection of Cotton and Commerce: Antebellum Savannah and Its Slaves," chap. 3, and Harris and Berry, "Slave Life In Savannah: Geographies of Autonomy and Control," chap. 5, in *Slavery and Freedom in Savannah*. See also Robert S. Starobin, *Industrial Slavery in the Old South* (New York: Oxford University Press, 1970).

19. Richard C. Wade, "The Lash and the Law," chap. 7 in *Slavery in the Cities*; and Harris and Berry, "Slave Life in Savannah."

20. On riots against free blacks and antislavery activists, see Leonard Richards, *"Gentlemen of Property and Standing": Anti-Abolition Mobs in Jacksonian America* (New York: Oxford University Press, 1970); Paul Gilje, *The Road to Mobocracy: Popular Disorder in New York City, 1763–1834* (Chapel Hill: University of North Carolina Press, 1987), 162–170; Gary Nash, *Forging Freedom: The Formation of Philadelphia's Black Community, 1720–1840* (Cambridge, MA: Harvard University Press, 1988), 273–279; Harris, *In the Shadow of Slavery*, chap. 6; and Nikki M. Taylor, *Frontiers of Freedom: Cincinnati's Black Community, 1802–1868* (Athens: Ohio

University Press, 2004), chap. 3. On actions against slave catchers, see Harris, *In the Shadow of Slavery*, chap. 6; Gary Collison, *Shadrach Minkins: From Fugitive Slave to Citizen* (Cambridge, MA: Harvard University Press, 1998); H. Robert Baker, *The Rescue of Joshua Glover: A Fugitive Slave, the Constitution, and the Coming of the Civil War* (Athens: Ohio University Press, 2006); Graham Hodges, *David Ruggles: A Radical Black Abolitionist and the Underground Railroad in New York City* (Chapel Hill: University of North Carolina Press, 2010); and Eric Foner, *Gateway to Freedom: The Hidden History of the Underground Railroad* (New York: W. W. Norton, 2015). General histories of the antislavery and radical abolitionist movements are numerous, but the most comprehensive is Manisha Sinha, *The Slave's Cause: A History of Abolition* (New Haven, CT: Yale University Press, 2016).

21. Harris, *In the Shadow of Slavery*, 22–26; and Midlo Hall, *Africans in Colonial Louisiana*.

22. Kenneth Scott, "The Slave Insurrection in New York in 1712," *New-York Historical Society Quarterly* 45 (1961): 43–74; and Reséndez, *The Other Slavery*, chap. 6.

23. Thomas J. Davis, *A Rumor of Revolt: The "Great Negro Plot" in Colonial New York* (New York: The Free Press, 1985); Jill Lepore, *New York Burning: Liberty, Slavery and Conspiracy in Eighteenth Century Manhattan* (New York: Knopf, 2005); and Douglas Egerton, *He Shall Go Out Free: The Lives of Denmark Vesey* (Madison, WI: Madison House, 1999).

24. Frederick Douglass, *Narrative of the Life of Frederick Douglass, An American Slave. Written By Himself* (Boston: Anti-Slavery Office, 1845); Harriet Jacobs, *Incidents in the Life of a Slave Girl, Written by Herself* (Boston: Published for the Author, 1861); Richard Stearns, *Narrative of Henry Box Brown, Who Escaped from Slavery in a Box 3 Feet Long and 2 Wide, Written from a Statement of Facts Made by Himself, with Remarks Upon the Remedy for Slavery* (Boston: Brown and Stearns, 1849); and William Craft, *Running a Thousand Miles for Freedom; or, the Escape of William and Ellen Craft From Slavery* (London: William Tweedie, 1860).

25. Wade, *Slavery in the Cities*, "Introduction" and chap. 9, argues that the decline in slave populations in southern cities indicated the "disarray" of urban

slavery. This view was challenged by Claudia Goldin, *Urban Slavery in the American South, 1820–1860: A Quantitative History* (Chicago: University of Chicago Press, 1976).

26. Goldin, *Urban Slavery in the American South*, outlines the ways in which these ideas permeated the historical literature. See especially "Preface" and "Introduction."

27. Wade, *Slavery in the Cities*, "Introduction" and chap. 9; Goldin, *Urban Slavery in the American South*; and Leonard P. Curry, *The Free Black in Urban America, 1800–1850: The Shadow of the Dream* (Chicago: University of Chicago Press, 1981).

28. In addition to works already cited in this article, see: for New York: Edgar McManus, *A History of Negro Slavery in New York* (Syracuse, NY: Syracuse University Press, 1966); Shane White, *Somewhat More Independent: The End of Slavery in New York City, 1770–1810* (Athens: University of Georgia Press, 1991); Graham Hodges, *Slavery and Freedom in New York and East Jersey, 1613–1863* (Chapel Hill: University of North Carolina Press, 1999); Harris, *In the Shadow of Slavery*; Harris and Berlin, *Slavery in New York*; Jill Lepore, *New York Burning*; for New Orleans: Thomas N. Ingersoll, *Mammon and Manon in Early New Orleans: The First Slave Society in the Deep South, 1718–1819* (Knoxville: University of Tennessee Press, 1999); Judith Kelleher Schafer, *Becoming Free, Remaining Free: Manumission and Enslavement in New Orleans, 1846–1862* (Baton Rouge: Louisiana State University Press, 2003); for Baltimore: T. Stephen Whitman, *The Price of Freedom: Slavery and Manumission in Baltimore and Early National Maryland* (Lexington: University Press of Kentucky, 1997); Christopher Phillips, *Freedom's Port: The African American Community of Baltimore, 1790–1860* (Urbana: University of Illinois Press, 1997); Mariana L. R. Dantas, *Black Townsmen: Urban Slavery and Freedom in the Eighteenth-Century Americas* (New York: Palgrave Macmillan, 2008); Seth Rockman, *Scraping By: Wage Labor, Slavery and Survival in Early Baltimore* (Baltimore: Johns Hopkins University Press, 2009); Adam Malka, *The Men of Mobtown: Policing Baltimore in the Age of Slavery and Emancipation* (Chapel Hill: University of North Carolina Press, 2018); Martha S. Jones, *Birthright Citizens: A History of Race and Rights in Antebellum America* (New York: Cambridge University Press, 2018); for

St. Louis: Dale Edwyna Smith, *African American Lives in St. Louis, 1763–1865: Slavery, Freedom and the West* (Jefferson, NC: MacFarland and Co., 2017); Kelly Kennington, *In the Shadow of Dred Scott: St. Louis Freedom Suits and the Legal Culture of Slavery in Antebellum America* (Athens: University of Georgia Press, 2017); for Natchez: Ariela Gross, *Double Character: Slavery and Mastery in the Antebellum Southern Courtroom* (Princeton, NJ: Princeton University Press, 2000); and Kimberly Welch, *Black Litigants in the Antebellum American South* (Chapel Hill: University of North Carolina Press, 2018); I have limited this list to late-20th-century books, and for the most part to books that not only cover slavery predominantly, but also take the city as a unit of analysis. There are books on colonies and/or states that may have a substantial amount of material on cities within them, but there is not always an analysis of the distinctiveness of the urban environment. This is particularly true for the colonial era. In addition, a thorough reading of the journal and edited volume literature would no doubt turn up a wealth of information.

29. Erica Armstrong Dunbar, *Never Caught: Ona Judge, the Washingtons, and Their Relentless Pursuit of Their Runaway Slave* (New York: Simon and Schuster, 2017); and Annette Gordon-Reed, *The Hemingses of Monticello: An American Family* (New York: Norton, 2008). On Philadelphia's President's House, see Gary B. Nash, "For Whom Will the Liberty Bell Toll? From Controversy to Cooperation," in *Slavery and Public History: The Tough Stuff of American Memory*, ed. James O. Horton and Lois E. Horton (Chapel Hill: University of North Carolina Press, 2006), 35–36; and The President's House website.

30. Clark-Pujara, *Dark Work*; and Jared Ross Hardesty, *Unfreedom: Slavery and Dependence in Eighteenth-Century Boston* (New York: New York University Press, 2017).

31. The two leading historians on this topic are Tiya Miles and Daniel Usner. Miles's recent book *Dawn of Detroit* is a model for how to construct such histories for urban areas. Daniel Usner's book on Native American slavery in New Orleans, *American Indians in Early New Orleans* (Baton Rouge: Louisiana State University Press, 2018) resets our understanding of urban enslavement of Native peoples in the South, east of the Mississippi. In addition, the work of many of the

historians cited throughout this article (Reséndez, Newell, Midlo Hall, Spear, Calloway, and Hämäläinen) provide models and material to bring a more holistic view of North American slavery.

32. Clifton Ellis and Rebecca Ginsburg, eds., *Slavery in the City: Architecture and Landscapes of Urban Slavery in North America* (Charlottesville: University of Virginia Press, 2017).

Leslie M. Harris

THE CENTRAL BUSINESS DISTRICT IN AMERICAN CITIES

INDUSTRIAL GROWTH AND THE RISE OF THE CENTRAL BUSINESS DISTRICT

In the cities of early America, the central district was a preeminently mixed-use space.[1] Private residences stood amid workshops, stores, docks, warehouses, banks, and government buildings. Many urban dwellers, especially small business owners and artisan craftsmen, lived above or behind the very spaces where they toiled each day. Commercial and domestic life continually intersected. This lack of functional segregation was not to last, however. The growth of the industrial economy eroded the link between home and work.[2] As new factories and mills sprouted across the antebellum United States, residential space became increasingly separable from the realm of business. Families with sufficient financial resources fled the noise, fumes, and hustle of downtowns and moved into new residential areas. In New York City, for example, affluent families abandoned the crowded waterfront district of lower Manhattan in the 1830s and moved up Broadway, first settling near Washington and Union Squares.[3] Similar patterns arose in cities across the nation. By mid-century, the multifunctional downtown had given way to a business-oriented core ringed by residential neighborhoods.

The very existence, then, of the central business district owed to industrial development.

Other spatial changes accompanied capitalist growth. Chief among these was a tendency toward centralization. In an era when rising specialization ensured that commercial transactions involved ever more meetings and collaboration among separate interests, businesses reduced costly inefficiencies by operating near their trading partners and other companies on which they depended for professional services. The result was both the consolidation of commercial activity in the city center and the clustering of related businesses within particular areas of the downtown.[4] Banks, insurance companies, and brokerages, for example, were drawn together, just as wholesale merchants sought proximity to manufacturers and suppliers. By the mid-19th century, many cities had developed industry-specific streets. In Boston, for instance, all but three of fifty-four banks and insurance companies were located on State Street.[5] New York's Wall Street emerged as the host of that city's major financial institutions, eventually becoming a metonym for the nation's entire financial industry.[6]

The concentration of business in the downtown was reinforced by transportation. In the mid-19th century, the streetcar, which operated on a fixed track, supplanted the omnibus, a stagecoach-like carriage, as the primary means of mass transit. Powered first by horses and eventually electricity, streetcar lines typically radiated from the city center to residential neighborhoods. This pattern reinforced the commercial dominance of the downtown.[7] So too did the presence of railroad depots. Their location ensured that both freight and passengers coming into the region from out of town were channeled into the city center— and that businesses devoted to handling one or the other, from warehouses to hotels, tended to operate nearby.[8] Centralizing trends continued, even accelerated, as many cities established subway and elevated railway lines in the late 19th century. Although few contemporaries questioned the benefits of downtown concentration, it generated a competition for space that drove up property values. The effect was not only to eliminate any remaining residential space from America's downtowns but also to drive small businesses as well as the most land-intensive industries, such as heavy manufacturing or agricultural processing, to the periphery.[9]

The layout and use of America's city centers transformed substantially in the 19th century. Still, some crucial continuities existed. Despite rising segmentation, most areas of the central business district, even most buildings within its confines, remained multifunctional spaces, hosting everything from finance, trade, and professional services to manufacturing and processing. These varied pursuits were linked by another persistent feature of the downtown: its orientation toward men. Dominated by an industrial economy in which women played a subordinate role, the central business district was chiefly a masculine domain. Women could certainly be found there working for wages, attending public events, and running errands. Some cities, notably New York, had even developed shopping districts by the 1860s that catered to ladies.[10] Nevertheless, most of the downtown's buildings and infrastructure, no less than its cultural practices, supported the predominately male workers and capitalists who upheld the urban industrial economy. Before the late 19th century, unchaperoned women were often refused service in hotels, restaurants, and theaters, while saloons and private clubs entirely excluded female guests. Even dry goods merchants, preoccupied with their wholesale businesses, offered limited amenities to customers. To eat, rest, or simply use a bathroom, many women retreated to homes located ever farther from the downtown, in dedicated residential neighborhoods.[11]

CONSUMER CAPITALISM AND THE EVOLUTION OF THE CENTRAL BUSINESS DISTRICT

The expansion of the consumer economy challenged the masculine character of the central business district. In the final third of the 19th century, merchants and entrepreneurs established a range of new institutions that drew women consumers into city centers that had long been the preserve of men. No institution did more to drive this change than the department store. Made possible by mass concentrations of capital and new transportation networks, these retail palaces dwarfed the scale and profits of traditional dry goods houses.[12] "Such a flowering out of a modest trade principle the world had never witnessed up to that time," wrote novelist Theodore Dreiser of early department stores.[13] Emphasizing service and spectacle, retailers such as Marshall Field's in Chicago, Macy's in New York City, and Wannamaker's in Philadelphia developed new strategies of enticement that kindled customers' desires and encouraged lingering and spending.[14] These customers were primarily women—eight or nine out of every ten. Employees too were mostly women, at least below the management level. In an era, then, when most spaces in the central business district were dominated by men, the department store emerged as women's territory. It was, as Edward Filene once observed of his own Boston store, "an Adam-less Eden."[15]

But Eve did not long stay contained within the world of the department store. The success of these giant retailers soon nurtured within the central business district other consumer institutions that catered to women. By the late 19th century, new restaurants, confectionaries, tearooms, and cafés had emerged to satisfy shoppers' appetites for refreshment and pleasure. Many of these establishments offered ladies' menus and ladies' dining rooms designed to appeal to female tastes and aesthetic sensibilities.[16] Theaters too sought to boost their female patronage by expanding their matinee offerings, crafting a more luxurious atmosphere, and encouraging women to combine their shopping trips with seeing a show.[17] Even hotels attempted to capitalize on women's consumption by throwing open their banquet halls and meeting rooms to the many women's clubs and organizations that flourished during the period. All of these new consumer institutions tended to cluster together, benefiting from the pooling of potential customers.[18]

Not all women, of course, enjoyed equal access to the consumer delights newly offered in central business districts. Working-class women found their access constrained by their ability to pay.[19] Meanwhile, non-white women faced prejudice that inhibited full participation in commercial life. Such discrimination was most pronounced in the Jim Crow South, but racial minorities also faced differential treatment and outright exclusion in Northern cities where state civil rights laws were supposed to guarantee equal access to public accommodations.[20] To discourage black patronage, for example, Northern restaurateurs often provided deliberately slow or discourteous service; theater owners refused to sell choice seats to black customers; and department stores declined to assist black patrons or guided them to their bargain basements.

Despite impediments of race and class, the ranks of women who flooded downtown each day continued to grow. By the early 20th century, their public presence was unmistakable. Images from the period reveal women thronging the principal shopping thoroughfares of major American metropolises. On downtown streets, female consumers mixed with other urban inhabitants, both in retail areas and beyond. Indeed, simply to get to the local iteration of the "Ladies' Mile," a title first appended to New York's Broadway but later used in other cities, women traversed bustling downtowns.[21] They sometimes traveled by private carriage or automobile, thereby adding additional vehicles to crowded streets. But most women typically walked or took advantage of an expanding network of public transit lines. Their shopping activities augmented the crush of people on downtown sidewalks and streetcars. Even after they had reached a city's main shopping streets, women were not isolated within a bounded realm of consumption. On the contrary, in most metropolises,

department stores stood near office buildings, banks, wholesale houses, publishers, and small factories. As a result, shoppers regularly encountered the workers and businessmen who had traditionally dominated the downtown.

CONFLICTING VIEWS OF THE CENTRAL BUSINESS DISTRICT

Invited by retailers and entrepreneurs, women were found in growing numbers in central business districts at the turn of the century. Their seamless movement into these commercial spheres—where they had once been viewed as mere visitors, if not outright interlopers—has often been taken for granted. Yet there was nothing natural or inevitable about establishing women's right to occupy the downtown. Indeed, their very presence as consumers aroused profound conflict over the use and meaning of public space, as well as women's place within it. Most cities, long oriented toward the needs of industrial capitalism, were simply not prepared—physically or culturally—to accept large numbers of unaccompanied women into their downtowns. Facilitating the consumption of these women, and in turn the continued ascent of consumer capitalism, required transforming the built environment and culture of the central business district, often in unexpected and highly fraught ways.

Consider, for example, the problem of traffic. Even today, as the average urban commuter will tell you, shoppers—strolling in groups, holding packages, peering into store windows—tend to impede circulation on congested sidewalks. This effect was even more conspicuous in the late 19th and early 20th centuries, when the great department stores were still in their formative years. The luxurious interiors and convenient amenities of these retailers transformed shopping from burden to pleasure and encouraged women to spend more time in central business districts. At the same time, a new emphasis on window design induced women to linger on downtown sidewalks and street corners. The development of cast iron architecture in the mid-19th century had first permitted the use of plate glass.[22] But in the 1890s, new production methods resulting in clearer, cheaper glass spurred the proliferation of show windows and the emergence of the first professional window designers.[23] These experts crafted increasingly elaborate visual spectacles that attracted the notice of shoppers, encouraging them to linger on downtown sidewalks rather than move efficiently to their destination. By the early 20th century, as the ranks of shoppers continued to grow, their distinctive movements increasingly interfered with traffic patterns that had been established for industrial commerce.[24]

Nearly every American city was troubled by the competition of shoppers, commuters, and freight carriers for space on crowded streets in the early 20th century. Yet the traffic problem was especially acute in Chicago. The Midwestern metropolis had arisen from the ashes of the 1871 fire to experience explosive population and commercial growth. By century's end, its central business district, hemmed in by water on three sides, was nearly bursting at the seams, and traffic congestion threatened to impede continued economic development. To address the crisis, Chicago's civic and business leaders explored numerous plans for facilitating the flow of pedestrians and vehicles. The most controversial proposal called for a municipal ordinance that would prohibit shoppers from staying in the Loop, the city's central business district, after four o'clock in the afternoon, when rush hour typically began. According to its supporters, the curfew would deter shoppers, who were cast as frivolous pleasure seekers, from clogging the streets and public transit when hard-working laborers, managers, and capitalists were attempting to make their way home.[25]

From a 21st-century perspective, it seems laughable that anyone interested in the economic well-being of a city would attempt to limit shopping in the downtown. But at the turn of the 20th century, the critical role of women consumers in the urban economy was not fully established. Two models of commerce then competed for dominance in the central business district—one rooted in the older, predominately masculine realm of production; the other in a burgeoning mixed-sex world of mass consumption. Although the former emphasized efficiency, rationality, and the rapid movement of workers and freight, the latter foregrounded pleasure, indulgence, and the activity of women. The conflict between these two commercial visions, exacerbated by the congestion crisis, played out over the bodies of women shoppers—where they could be, and when. Support for the curfew was concentrated among industrialists and wholesale distributors. By contrast, retailers strenuously opposed the measure. They were joined in their opposition by Chicago clubwomen, who recognized in the shopping curfew a restriction on their freedom of movement.

Chicago did not, ultimately, adopt a shopping curfew. But the conflict shaped the city's blueprint for development—the famed *Plan of Chicago* (1909). Written by architects Daniel Burnham and Edward Bennett, the *Plan* was financed and supported by the powerful Commercial Club, which drew capitalists from across the city's industries. Unlike the proposed curfew, Burnham and Bennett's vision took into account "the convenience of both producer and consumer." Indeed, the *Plan* resolved tensions between industrial and consumer capitalists by accommodating the needs of both. Its most significant commitment was to improving circulation across the city by routing industrial traffic around—instead of through—the overburdened streets of the central business district. A new freight depot on the South Side, nearer to the major rail and shipyards, as well as better-paved, more direct roadways between outlying districts, would streamline distribution and reduce handling costs for manufacturers and industrial suppliers who vacated the city center. Meanwhile, the comfort and safety of downtown shoppers was to be enhanced by providing new pedestrian islands and crosswalks as well as ensuring that the pavement, lighting, signs, and other street accessories were aesthetically pleasing, arranged according to the "dictates of good taste."[26] Burnham's *Plan* thus affirmed the importance of consumption to the urban economy even as it addressed the circulation needs of industrial commerce.

Traffic was merely one of many points of conflict that arose as female consumers, drawn by retail and service institutions, moved into the central business districts of America's cities. To enable their consumption, civic and business leaders altered not only the built environment but also laws governing the use of public space, policing priorities, and state regulation of consumer industries. Standards of etiquette and respectability also evolved to accommodate the presence of unaccompanied women in the downtown. For better or worse, these changes worked together to promote the expansion of the consumer economy and solidify women's place in the commercial life of the metropolis. By the early 20th century, women emerged as the nation's primary "purchasing agents," and their preferences, according to advertising experts such as Christine Frederick, influenced the design, distribution, and sales of the vast majority of consumer goods.[27] Even women's foot traffic, once considered a nuisance, came to be highly prized and helped to determine the value of real estate in America's central business districts.[28]

America's downtowns evolved to accommodate retail and commercial leisure. Yet other business functions remained. Each day, hundreds of thousands of commuters poured into office buildings devoted to finance, management, government operations, and medical and professional services. For the clerks, typists, executives, bankers, policymakers, lawyers, architects, realtors, elevator operators, messengers, and insurance agents who worked downtown, no less than for consumers, the central business district remained the undisputed center of urban life. The competition for space caused real estate prices to spike and in turn promoted a parallel increase in building heights. A brand new architectural form emerged—the skyscraper. These mammoth structures, which were pioneered by builders in Chicago and New York in the late 1880s and 1890s, soon sprang up in the heart of all the nation's major cities. By the early 20th century, their presence had become a defining feature of the central business district.[29]

SUBURBAN GROWTH AND THE DECLINE OF THE CENTRAL BUSINESS DISTRICT

A century after first arising amid early industrial growth, the central business district had changed in form as well as function. Yet from approximately 1850 to 1950, its role as the sole hub for all metropolitan commerce remained undisputed. Indeed, despite rising traffic congestion and soaring rents, most Americans still believed that a healthy city required a single operational center for its commercial functions. Only in the post–World War II era, as suburban growth accelerated, did civic and business leaders begin to doubt the value of centralization and explore alternatives to the downtown business district.

Retailers first pursued decentralization in response to the growing popularity of the automobile. Before the 1920s, when automobiles belonged only to the very wealthy, workers and shoppers alike relied on public transit lines that converged in the central business district. But as automobile ownership came within reach of more Americans, public transit use declined—and downtown traffic swelled. Faced with limited parking space and increasingly frustrated consumers, many retailers looked for relief in the blossoming suburbs. Department stores opened their first suburban locations in the 1920s, and almost immediately these branch stores began siphoning customers away from downtown flagships.[30] The trend intensified mid-century as retailers developed new regional shopping centers—typically anchored by one or more department stores—which rivaled city centers in comfort and convenience. Between 1948 and 1954, despite substantial sales growth across the country, the downtown's share of retailing fell by a quarter in the largest metropolitan areas.[31] A decade later, more than half of all department store sales originated in suburban branch locations.[32] The era of the downtown shopping district's dominance had passed.

In the post-war era, as federal spending on new highways and mortgage loans for veterans enticed millions of Americans into the suburbs, the shopping center replaced the central business district as the primary focus of leisure and consumption. These new commercial spaces were constructed from scratch to reflect the priorities and desires of retailers' most sought-after customers—affluent white women. Often located in predominately white suburbs, far from public transit and accessible only by car, shopping centers segmented customers by race and class more effectively than urban retailers.[33] They also upheld the family-oriented lifestyles that defined post-war suburban culture. Parks and playgrounds were incorporated to occupy small children; restaurants and cafés for socializing with other mothers; movie theaters for entertainment; and banks, post offices, and hair salons to make life more convenient. Oversized parking spaces were intended to appeal to women who had recently learned to drive. Not least, private security forces were hired to patrol the grounds and ensure that any undesirable social elements were quickly removed.[34]

Not only retailers, however, abandoned the central business district in the post-war decades. The number of downtown hotels also fell sharply in the 1950s, as more Americans embraced the automobile for long-distance travel. New motel chains such as Holiday Inn, Ramada, and Travelodge took advantage of the expanding national highway system and established hundreds of locations. By the end of the decade, the nation's supply of motel rooms surpassed that of urban hotel rooms. Meanwhile, the emergence of suburban restaurant chains such as McDonald's, Burger King, and Kentucky Fried Chicken generated new opportunities to dine out beyond the downtown.[35]

Office functions too followed the centrifugal flow of business to the suburbs. Insurance firms, which benefited least from downtown locations, helped to spearhead the move in the late 1940s. But other industries soon joined them, a trend that accelerated in the 1960s. Between 1967 and 1974, the number of Fortune 500 companies headquartered in New York City fell by roughly 30 percent. Across the United States, office workers increasingly spent their days not in downtown skyscrapers, but in suburban office parks, where asphalt lots occupied as much space as low-rise buildings.[36] Among the most iconic illustrations of this trend occurred in 1989 when Sears Roebuck & Co., then the largest retailer in the world, decided to sell the Sears Tower, then the tallest building in the world, and move to a leafy 800-acre campus in suburban Hoffman Estates.[37] By that point, suburban office space had surpassed that of center cities.[38]

Once epicenters of economic activity, central business districts ceased to be where most Americans worked, shopped, and amused themselves in the second half of the 20th century. The shift sapped downtowns of their commercial vitality. For those left out of the suburban exodus, a majority of whom were poor and non-white, the decentralizing trend provided only dwindling job opportunities and a substantially reduced tax base.[39]

URBAN RENEWAL AND THE FUTURE OF THE CENTRAL BUSINESS DISTRICT

The drain of business, especially retail, from city centers alarmed urban leaders and conjured racialized fears that once vibrant downtowns would be swallowed whole by encroaching slums. To prevent such fates, as early as the 1950s, many cities attempted to draw shoppers back into the central business district. These efforts typically ignored working-class and poor minorities living in close proximity to city centers and instead targeted affluent, white suburbanites.[40] In pursuit of these customers, downtown leaders sought to emulate the environment of regional shopping centers. One widely used tactic was to close retail streets to automobiles. In the 1960s and 1970s, pedestrian malls were created in cities such as Fort Worth, New York, Chicago, Philadelphia, Louisville, Baltimore, Tulsa, Tampa, Little Rock, and dozens of others. The majority of these initiatives failed to reverse declining sales trends and were eventually reopened to traffic.[41]

Instead of recreating the suburbs, some cities found economic success by emphasizing their differences, their very urbanity. They sold "urban" living to a rapidly expanding market of young, childless, urban professionals—"yuppies." In the late 1970s and 1980s, these yuppies poured into downtowns, sparking redevelopment as well as clashes with long-time residents. Some metropolitan centers also leveraged their urban appeal to attract tourists and gay migrants. By century's end, the return of affluent consumers had attracted new investment in downtown stores, restaurants, theaters, and hotels. It had also promoted the displacement of minority communities. The "back to the city" movement thus revitalized central business districts while reinforcing inequalities of race and class.[42]

In the 21st century, the central business district confronts new challenges as commercial activity again relocates—this time not to the suburbs, but to the digital realm. Email, virtual chat, and other new communication tools make conducting business with parties in Berlin and Tokyo as easy as collaborating with someone down the street. Meanwhile, services such as Amazon, Netflix, and GrubHub are drawing consumption into the private sphere and causing brick-and-mortar establishments to close. The full consequences of these trends have yet to be revealed, but ecommerce is clearly impinging on downtown trade. As more spending moves online, cities will have less ability and less incentive to make their business districts—and the public transit serving them—safe and accessible. Poor residents especially stand to lose if stores and offices shutter while the costs of computing keep online shopping and employment out of reach. In short, the digital revolution, which

has expanded our world in innumerable ways, may provide a death blow to the central business district.

DISCUSSION OF THE LITERATURE

Scholars of the 19th-century city have produced substantial research on the initial growth and spatial arrangement of the central business district. The earliest work on this topic emerged in the 1920s from the Chicago School of Sociology. In 1925, Ernest Burgess published an influential essay describing his "concentric zonal" theory of urban development, which held that the city grew outward from its center in a series of concentric zones. The innermost zone, or downtown, was the hub of the city's commercial, social, and civic life.[43] Alternatives to Burgess's model of urban growth soon emerged, but the city center continued to be viewed as the locus of commercial operations for the industrial metropolis.[44]

Many historians have traced the full trajectory of the central business district's rise and fall from the late 1800s to the mid-1900s. Among the most influential accounts are Robert M. Fogelson's *Downtown: Its Rise and Fall, 1880–1950* (2001) and Alison Isenberg's *Downtown America: A History of the Place and the People Who Made It* (2004).[45] Earlier scholarship tended to present the downtown's history as a product of inexorable forces, such as economic growth, immigration, and technological advancement.[46] By contrast, Fogelson and Isenberg demonstrate that the downtown's fate was by no means inevitable, but the result of deliberate choices made by policymakers, city planners, business owners, and consumers. Although few other scholars have focused exclusively on the downtown, many have touched on aspects of its culture, politics, built environment, and social geography during its heyday.[47]

Decentralization and suburban development have attracted significant interest from historians, as have the effects of these trends on urban centers.[48] A particularly rich strain of this literature focuses on the inequalities of race and class that shaped suburban growth and ensured that middle-class whites were its principle beneficiaries.[49] Numerous studies also focus on attempts to revitalize America's downtowns in the second half of the 20th century. This scholarship was pioneered in the 1970s but has since become an especially deep and vibrant field.[50] Historians studying urban renewal have shown that its policies and practices, which were developed in response to competition from the suburbs, not only tended to fail to produce lasting economic health for most cities but also reinforced racial and class divisions.[51] In recent years, scholars have also investigated the late-20th-century return of affluent white residents to city centers and considered how this "great inversion" shaped urban culture and society.[52]

PRIMARY SOURCES

A vast number of primary materials touch in some way on the central business district. The most helpful are often local sources focused on a particular city. State and municipal archives, especially the records of planning commissions and city councils, shed light on development and revitalization strategies as well as other government actions that influenced the downtown. Local newspapers provide a unique window into the culture, politics, and everyday conflicts that shaped the central business district. Increasingly, they are available in digital format through services such as ProQuest Historical Newspapers, Newspapers.com, and the Library of Congress's free database Chronicling America. City directories, maps, and travel guides illuminate the physical landscape of the central business district and its evolution over time. Trade journals, such as the *Dry Goods Reporter* or *Hotel Monthly*, reveal the perspective of businessmen on the form and function of the city center. Many of these published sources are available through free online databases, such as Google Books, Archive.org, and HathiTrust. Photographs of urban views and streetscapes are also valuable sources for anyone studying the downtown, and many archives have their own digital image collections. The Prints and Photographs division of the Library of Congress has a particularly excellent collection, as does Explore Chicago, which brings together materials from several local archives.

FURTHER READING

Blackmar, Elizabeth. *Manhattan for Rent, 1785–1850.* Ithaca, NY: Cornell University Press, 1989.

Isenberg, Alison. *Downtown America: A History of the Place and the People Who Made It.* Chicago: University of Chicago Press, 2004.

Fogelson, Robert M. *Downtown: Its Rise and Fall, 1880–1950.* New Haven, CT: Yale University Press, 2001.

Hanchett, Thomas W. *Sorting Out the New South City: Race, Class, and Urban Development in Charlotte, 1875–1975.* Chapel Hill: University of North Carolina Press, 1998.

Howard, Vicki. *From Main Street to Mall: The Rise and Fall of the American Department Store.* Philadelphia: University of Pennsylvania Press, 2015.

Leach, William R. *Land of Desire: Merchants, Power, and the Rise of a New American Culture.* New York: Pantheon Books, 1993.

Longstreth, Richard. *City Center to Regional Mall: Architecture, the Automobile, and Retailing in Los Angeles, 1920–1950.* Cambridge, MA: MIT Press, 1997.

Murphy, Raymond E. *The Central Business District: A Study in Urban Geography.* New York: Routledge, 1971.

Park, Robert E., Ernest W. Burgess, and Roderick D. McKenzie. *The City.* Chicago: University of Chicago Press, 1925.

Remus, Emily. *A Shoppers' Paradise: How the Ladies of Chicago Claimed Power and Pleasure in the New Downtown.* Cambridge, MA: Harvard University Press, 2019.

Teaford, Jon C. *The Metropolitan Revolution: The Rise of Post-Urban America.* New York: Columbia, 2006.

NOTES

1. For Jon C. Teaford's quote, see Jon C. Teaford, *The Twentieth-Century American City: Problem, Promise, and Reality* (Baltimore: Johns Hopkins University Press, 1986), 8.

2. On the separation of home and work, see especially Jeanne Boydston, *Home and Work: Housework, Wages, and the Ideology of Labor in the Early Republic* (New York: Oxford University Press, 1990).

3. On the residential movement in Manhattan, see Sven Beckert, *Monied Metropolis: New York City and the Consolidation of the American Bourgeoisie, 1850–1896* (Cambridge: Cambridge University Press, 2001), 56–58; and Elizabeth Blackmar, *Manhattan for Rent, 1785–1850* (Ithaca, NY: Cornell University Press, 1989), 103–104.

4. Robert M. Fogelson, *Downtown: Its Rise and Fall, 1880–1950* (New Haven, CT: Yale University Press, 2001), 22–27; and Sam Bass Warner Jr., *The Private City: Philadelphia in Three Periods of Its Growth* (Philadelphia: University of Pennsylvania Press, 1968), 59–61.

5. Raymond E. Murphy, *The Central Business District: A Study in Urban Geography* (New York: Routledge, 1971), 157.

6. On the development of Wall Street, see Sarah Bradford Landau and Carl W. Condit, *Rise of the New York Skyscraper: 1865–1913* (New Haven, CT: Yale University Press, 1999), 2–7, 52–57.

7. Fogelson, *Downtown*, 44–46, 61.

8. Teaford, *Twentieth-Century American City*, 11.

9. Fogelson, *Downtown*, 46–47, 14.

10. See especially M. Christine Boyer, *Manhattan Manners: Architecture and Style, 1850–1900* (New York: Rizzoli, 1985), 43–129; and Mona Domosh, *Invented Cities: The Creation of Landscape in Nineteenth-Century New York* (New Haven, CT: Yale University Press, 1998), 35–39.

11. Emily Remus, *A Shoppers' Paradise: How the Ladies of Chicago Claimed Power and Pleasure in the New Downtown* (Cambridge, MA: Harvard University Press, 2019).

12. On the development of department stores, see especially William Leach, *Land of Desire: Merchants, Power, and the Rise of a New American Culture* (New York: Pantheon Books, 1993), xiii–xiv, 15–17; Susan Porter Benson, *Counter Cultures: Saleswomen, Managers, and Customers in American Department Stores, 1890–1940* (Urbana: University of Illinois Press, 1986), 12–30; Joseph Siry, *Carson Pirie Scott: Louis Sullivan and the Chicago Department Store* (Chicago: University of Chicago Press, 1988), 13–64; Elaine Abelson, *When Ladies Go A-Thieving: Middle-Class Shoplifters in the Victorian Department Store* (Oxford: Oxford University Press, 1989), 31–41; and Vicki Howard, *From Main Street to Mall: The Rise and Fall of the American Department Store* (Philadelphia: University of Pennsylvania Press, 2015), 9–29.

13. Theodore Dreiser, *Sister Carrie* (New York: Doubleday, Page, 1900), 17.

14. See especially Leach, "Part I: Strategies of Enticement," in *Land of Desire*, 15–152.

15. Benson, *Counter Cultures*, 76.

16. Emily A. Remus, "Tippling Ladies and the Making of Consumer Culture: Gender and Public Space in Fin-de-Siècle Chicago," *Journal of American History* (December 2014): 757–761.

17. Richard Butsch, *The Making of American Audiences: From Stage to Television, 1750–1990* (Cambridge: Cambridge University Press, 2000), 66–79; and Marlis Schweitzer, *When Broadway Was the Runway: Theater, Fashion, and American Culture* (Philadelphia: University of Pennsylvania Press, 2009), 4–5, 35–50.

18. Murphy, *Central Business District*, 157.

19. See, for example, Benson, *Counter Cultures*; Kathy Peiss, *Cheap Amusements: Working Women and Leisure in Turn-of-the-Century New York* (Philadelphia: Temple University Press, 1986); and Nan Enstad, *Ladies of Labor, Girls of Adventure: Working Women, Popular Culture, and Labor Politics at the Turn of the Twentieth Century* (New York: Columbia University Press, 1999).

20. Grace Elizabeth Hale, *Making Whiteness: The Culture of Segregation in the South, 1890–1940* (New York: Vintage Books, 1998); Robert Weems, *Desegregating the Dollar: African American Consumerism in the Twentieth Century* (New York: New York University Press, 1998); Ted Ownby, *American Dreams in Mississippi: Consumers, Poverty, & Culture, 1830–1998* (Chapel Hill: University of North Carolina Press, 1999); and Mia Bay, "Traveling Black/Buying Black: Retail and Roadside Accommodations during the Segregation Era," in *Race and Retail: Consumption across the Color Line*, ed. Mia Bay and Ann Fabian (New Brunswick, NJ: Rutgers University Press, 2015).

21. Boyer, *Manhattan Manners*, 43–44.

22. Domosh, *Invented Cities*, 57–58; and Edwin G. Burrows and Mike Wallace, *Gotham: A History of New York City to 1898* (Oxford: Oxford University Press, 1999), 68.

23. Leach, *Land of Desire*, 61–64; William R. Leach, "Transformations in a Culture of Consumption: Women and Department Stores, 1890–1925," *Journal of American History* 71 (September 1984): 325; and Peter Bacon Hales, "Grid, Regulation, Desire Line: Contests over Civic Space in

Chicago," in *Public Space and the Ideology of Place in American Culture*, ed. Miles Orvell and Jeffrey L. Meikle (Amsterdam: Rodopi, 2009), 174–175.

24. Remus, *A Shoppers' Paradise*.

25. Remus, *A Shoppers' Paradise*.

26. Daniel H. Burnham and Edward H. Bennett, *The Plan of Chicago* (Chicago: Commercial Club, 1909), 68, 83.

27. Christine Frederick, *Selling Mrs. Consumer* (New York: Business Bourse, 1929).

28. Alison Isenberg, *Downtown America: A History of the Place and the People Who Made It* (Chicago: University of Chicago Press, 2004), 78–123.

29. Joseph J. Korom, *The American Skyscraper, 1850–1940: A Celebration of Height* (Boston: Branden Books, 2008), 93–96; and Carol Willis, *Form Follows Finance: Skyscrapers and Skylines in New York and Chicago* (New York: Princeton Architectural Press, 1995), 50–51.

30. On the development of suburban retail in the 1920s, see especially Richard Longstreth, *City Center to Regional Mall: Architecture, the Automobile, and Retailing in Los Angeles, 1920–1950* (Cambridge, MA: MIT Press, 1997), 57–59, 116; and Howard, *From Main Street to Mall*, 133–138.

31. Bernard J. Frieden and Lynne B. Sagalyn, *Downtown, Inc: How America Rebuilds Cities* (Cambridge, MA: MIT Press, 1989), 13.

32. Howard, *From Main Street to Mall*, 139.

33. On the segmentation of consumption in the post-war era, see especially Lizabeth Cohen, *A Consumer's Republic: The Politics of Mass Consumption in Postwar America* (New York: Vintage Books, 2003); Eric Avila, *Popular Culture in the Age of White Flight* (Berkeley: University of California Press, 2004); and Victoria Wolcott, *Race, Riots, and Roller Coasters: The Struggle over Segregated Recreation in America* (Philadelphia: University of Pennsylvania Press, 2012).

34. Cohen, *Consumers' Republic*, 257–268, 278–283. On the architectural design of shopping centers, see David Smiley, *Pedestrian Modern: Shopping and American Architecture, 1925–1956* (Minneapolis: University of Minnesota Press, 2013).

35. Jon C. Teaford, *The Metropolitan Revolution: The Rise of Post-Urban America* (New York: Columbia, 2006), 104–107; William Kaszynski, *The American Highway: The History and Culture of Roads in the United States* (Jefferson, NC: McFarland, 2000), 152–161; and Chin Jou, *Supersizing Urban America: How Inner Cities Got*

Fast Food with Government Help (Chicago: University of Chicago Press, 2017), 51–53.

36. Teaford, *Metropolitan Revolution*, 100, 132, 190–193; and Louise A. Mozingo, *Pastoral Capitalism: A History of Suburban Corporate Landscapes* (Cambridge: MIT Press, 2011), 102–105, 146–147, 151–161.

37. Isabel Wilkerson, "New Home in Suburbs Seems Tailored to Sears," *New York Times*, July 19, 1989, p. A10.

38. Kheir Al-Kodmany, *New Suburbanism: Sustainable Tall Building Development* (New York: Routledge, 2016), 18.

39. Teaford, *Metropolitan Revolution*, 107, 130–132.

40. See especially Isenberg, *Downtown America*, 166–202.

41. On pedestrianization, see Alexander Garvin, *The American City: What Works, What Doesn't*, 2nd ed. (New York: McGraw Hill, 2002), 178–191; and Jeff Speck, *Walkable City: How Downtown Can Save America, One Step at a Time* (New York: Farrar, Straus and Giroux, 2012), 98–99.

42. Teaford, *Metropolitan Revolution*, 167–189.

43. Ernest W. Burgess, "The Growth of the City: An Introduction to a Research Project," in *The City*, ed. Robert E. Park, Ernest W. Burgess, and Roderick D. McKenzie (Chicago: University of Chicago Press, 1925), 47–62.

44. See, for example, Homer Hoyt, *The Structure and Growth of Residential Areas in American Cities* (Washington, DC: Federal Housing Administration, 1939); and David Harvey, "The Urban Process Under Capitalism: A Framework for Analysis," *International Journal of Urban and Regional Research* 2 (1978): 101–131.

45. Fogelson, *Downtown*; and Isenberg, *Downtown America*.

46. See, for example, Sam Bass Warner Jr., *Streetcar Suburbs: The Process of Growth in Boston, 1870–1900* (Cambridge, MA: Harvard University Press, 1962); Sam Bass Warner Jr., *The Urban Wilderness: A History of the American City* (New York: Harper and Row, 1972); David Ward, *Cities and Immigrants: A Geography of Change in Nineteenth-Century America* (New York: Oxford University Press, 1971); and David Ward, "The Industrial Revolution and the Emergence of Boston's Central Business District," *Economic Geography* 42 (April 1966): 152–171.

47. This literature is vast and cannot be adequately captured here. See, for example, David M. Scobey, *Empire City: The Making and Meaning of the*

New York City Landscape (Philadelphia: Temple University Press, 2002); Sarah Deutsch, *Women and the City: Gender, Space, and Power in Boston, 1870–1940* (Oxford: Oxford University Press, 2000); Maureen A. Flanagan, *Seeing With Their Hearts: Chicago Women and the Vision of the Good City, 1871–1933* (Princeton, NJ: Princeton University Press, 2002); Robin F. Bachin, *Building the South Side: Urban Space and Civic Culture in Chicago, 1890–1919* (Chicago: University of Chicago, 2004); Jessica Ellen Sewell, *Women and the Everyday City: Public Space in San Francisco, 1890–1915* (Minneapolis: University of Minnesota Press, 2011); Georgina Hickey, *Hope and Danger in the New South City: Working-Class Women and Urban Development in Atlanta, 1890–1940* (Athens: University of Georgia Press, 2003); David Goldfield, *Region, Race, and Cities: Interpreting the Urban South* (Baton Rouge: Louisiana State University Press, 1997); Thomas W. Hanchett, *Sorting Out the New South City: Race, Class, and Urban Development in Charlotte, 1875–1975* (Chapel Hill: University of North Carolina Press, 1998); and Sharon E. Wood, *The Freedom of the Streets: Work, Citizenship, and Sexuality in a Gilded Age City* (Chapel Hill: University of North Carolina Press, 2005).

48. See, for example, Kenneth T. Jackson, *Crabgrass Frontier: The Suburbanization of the United States* (New York: Oxford University Press, 1985); Rosalyn Baxandall and Elizabeth Ewen, *Picture Windows: How the Suburbs Happened* (New York: Basic Books, 2000); and Jon C. Teaford, *The American Suburb: The Basics* (New York: Routledge, 2008).

49. See, for example, Cohen, *A Consumer's Republic*; Avila, *Popular Culture in the Age of White Flight*; Matt Garcia, *A World of Its Own: Race, Labor, and Citrus in the Making of Greater Los Angeles, 1900–1970* (Chapel Hill: University of North Carolina Press, 2001); Becky M. Nicolaides, *My Blue Heaven: Life and Politics in the Working-Class Suburbs of Los Angeles, 1920–1965* (Chicago: University of Chicago Press, 2002); Andrew Wiese, *Places of Their Own: African-American Suburbanization in the Twentieth Century* (Chicago: University of Chicago Press, 2004); and David M.P. Freund, *Colored Property: State Policy and White Racial Politics in Suburban America* (Chicago: University of Chicago Press, 2007).

50. For early works in this field, see, for example, John F. Bauman, *Public Housing, Race, and Renewal:*
Urban Planning in Philadelphia, 1920–1974 (Philadelphia: University of Pennsylvania Press, 1974); Jon C. Teaford, *City and Suburb: The Political Fragmentation of Metropolitan America, 1850–1970* (1979); and Mark I. Gelfand, *Nation of Cities: The Federal Government and Urban America, 1933–1965* (Oxford: Oxford University Press, 1975).

51. See, for example, Andrew R. Highsmith, *Demolition Means Progress: Flint, Michigan, and the Fate of the American Metropolis* (Chicago: University of Chicago Press, 2015); N.D.B. Connolly, *A World More Concrete: Real Estate and the Remaking of Jim Crow South Florida* (Chicago: University of Chicago Press, 2014); Arnold Hirsch, *Making the Second Ghetto: Race and Housing in Chicago, 1940–1960* (Chicago: University of Chicago Press, 1998); Thomas Sugrue, *The Origins of the Urban Crisis: Race and Inequality in Postwar Detroit,* (Princeton, NJ: Princeton University Press, 1996); Jon C. Teaford, *The Rough Road to Renaissance: Urban Revitalization in America* (Baltimore: Johns Hopkins University Press, 1990); Steven J. McGovern, *The Politics of Downtown Development: Dynamic Political Cultures in San Francisco and Washington, DC* (Lexington: University Press of Kentucky, 1998); and David Schuyler, *A City Transformed: Redevelopment, Race, and Suburbanization in Lancaster, Pennsylvania, 1940–1980* (University Park: Penn State University Press, 2002).

52. For use of the term *great inversion*, see Alan Ehrenhalt, *The Great Inversion and the Future of the American City* (New York: Vintage Books, 2012). For historical studies of this inversion, see, for example, Teaford, *Metropolitan Revolution*; and Aaron Shkuda, *The Lofts of SoHo: Gentrification, Art, and Industry in New York, 1950–1980* (Chicago: University of Chicago Press, 2016).

Emily Remus

PROGRESSIVES AND PROGRESSIVISM IN AN ERA OF REFORM

The reform impulse of the decades from the 1890s into the 1920s did not erupt suddenly in the 1890s. Previous movements, such as the Mugwump faction of the Republican Party and the Knights of Labor, had challenged existing conditions in the 1870s and 1880s. Such earlier movements either tended to focus on the problems of a particular group or were too small to effect much change. The 1890s Populist Party's concentration on agrarian issues did not easily resonate with the expanding urban population. The Populists lost their separate identity when the Democratic Party absorbed their agenda. The reform proposals of the Progressive Era differed from those of these earlier protest movements. Progressives came from all strata of society. Progressivism aimed to implement comprehensive systemic reforms to change the direction of the country.

Political corruption, economic exploitation, mass migration and urbanization, rapid technological advancements, and social unrest challenged the rhetoric of the United States as a just and equal society. Now groups of Americans throughout the country proposed to reform the country's political, social, cultural, and economic institutions in ways that they believed would address fundamental problems that had produced the inequities of American society.

Progressives did not seek to overturn capitalism. They sought to revitalize a democratic promise of justice and equality and to move the country into a modern Progressive future by eliminating or at least ameliorating capitalism's worst excesses. They wanted to replace an individualistic, competitive society with a more cooperative, democratic one. They sought to bring a measure of social justice for all people, to eliminate political corruption, and to rebalance the relationship among business, labor, and consumers by introducing economic regulation.[1] Progressives turned to government to achieve these objectives and laid the foundation for an increasingly powerful state.

SOCIAL JUSTICE PROGRESSIVISM

Social justice Progressives wanted an activist state whose first priority was to provide for the common welfare. Jane Addams argued that real democracy must operate from a sense of social morality that would foster the greater good of all rather than protect those with wealth and power.[2] Social justice Progressivism confronted two problems to securing a democracy based on social morality. Several basic premises that currently structured the country had to be rethought, and social justice Progressivism was promoted largely by women who lacked official political power.

Legal Precedent or Social Realism. The existing legal system protected the rights of business and property over labor.[3] From 1893, when Florence Kelley secured factory legislation mandating the eight-hour workday for women and teenagers and outlawing child labor in Illinois factories, social justice Progressives faced legal obstacles as business contested such legislation. In 1895, the Supreme Court in *Ritchie v. People* ruled that such legislation violated the "freedom of contract" provision of the Fourteenth Amendment. The Court confined the police power of the state to protecting immediate health and safety, not groups of people in industries.[4] Then, in the 1905 case *Lochner v. New York*, the Court declared that the state had no interest in regulating the hours of male bakers. To circumvent these rulings, Kelley, Josephine Goldmark, and Louis Brandeis contended that law should address social realities. The Brandeis brief to the Supreme Court in 1908, in *Muller v. Oregon*, argued for upholding Oregon's eight-hour law for women working in laundries because of the debilitating physical effects of such work. When the Court agreed, social justice Progressives hoped this would be the opening wedge to extend new rights to labor. The *Muller v. Oregon* ruling had a narrow gender basis. It declared that the state had an interest in protecting the reproductive capacities of women. Henceforth, male and female workers would be unequal under the law, limiting women's economic opportunities across the decades, rather than shifting the legal landscape.

Ruling on the basis of women's reproductive capacities, the Court made women socially inferior to men in law and justified state-sponsored interference in women's control of their bodies.[5]

Role of the State to Protect and Foster.

Women organized in voluntary groups worked to identify and attack the problems caused by mass urbanization. The General Federation of Women's Clubs (1890) coordinated women's activities throughout the country. Social justice Progressives lobbied municipal governments to enact new ordinances to ameliorate existing urban conditions of poverty, disease, and inequality. Chicago women secured the nation's first juvenile court (1899).[6] Los Angeles women helped inaugurate a public health nursing program and secure pure milk regulations for their city. Women also secured municipal public baths in Boston, Chicago, Philadelphia, and other cities. Organized women in Philadelphia and Dallas were largely responsible for their cities implementing new clean water systems. Women set up pure milk stations to prevent infant diarrhea and organized infant welfare societies.[7]

Social justice Progressives sought national legislation to protect consumers from the pernicious effects of industrial production outside of their immediate control. In 1905, the General Federation of Women's Clubs initiated a letter-writing campaign to pressure Congress to pass pure food legislation. Standard accounts of the passage of the Pure Food and Drug Act and pure milk ordinances generally credit male professionals with putting in place such reforms, but female social justice Progressives were instrumental in putting this issue before the country.[8]

Social justice Progressives sought a ban on child labor and protections for children's health and education. They argued that no society could progress if it allowed child labor. In 1912 they persuaded Congress to establish a federal Children's Bureau to investigate conditions of children throughout the country.

Julia Lathrop first headed the bureau, which was thenceforth dominated by women. Nonetheless, when Congress passed the Keating-Owen Child Labor Act (1916), banning interstate commerce in products made with child labor, a North Carolina man immediately sued, arguing that it deprived him of property in his son's labor. The Supreme Court (1918) ruled the law unconstitutional because it violated state powers to regulate conditions of labor. A constitutional amendment banning child labor (1922) was attacked by manufacturers and conservative organizations protesting that it would give government power over children. Only four states ratified the amendment.[9]

Woman suffrage was crucial for social justice Progressives as both a democratic right and because they believed it essential for their agenda.[10] When suffrage left elected officials uncertain about the power of women's votes in 1921, Congress passed the Sheppard-Towner Maternity and Infant Welfare bill, which provided federal funds for maternal and infant health. The American Medical Association opposed the bill as a violation of its expertise. Businessmen and political leaders protested that the federal government should not interfere in healthcare and objected that it would raise taxes. Congress made Sheppard-Towner a "sunset" act to run for five years, after which it would decide whether to renew it. Congress temporarily extended it but ended the funding in 1929, even though the country's infant mortality rate exceeded that of six other industrial countries. The hostility of the male-dominated American Medical Association and the Public Health Service to Sheppard-Towner and to its administration by the Children's Bureau, along with attacks against the social justice network of women's organizations as a communist conspiracy to undermine American society, doomed the legislation.[11]

NEW PRACTICES OF DEMOCRACY

Women established settlement houses, voluntary associations, day nurseries, and community, neighborhood, and social centers as venues in which to practice participatory democracy. These venues intended to bring people together to learn about one another and their needs, to provide assistance for those needing help, and to lobby their governments to provide social goods to people. This was not reform from the bottom; middle-class women almost always led these venues. Most of these efforts were also racially exclusive, but African American women established venues of their own. In Atlanta, Lugenia Hope, who had spent time at Chicago's Hull House, established the Atlanta Neighborhood Union in 1908 to organize the city's African American women on a neighborhood basis. Hope urged women to investigate the problems of their neighborhoods and bring their issues to the municipal government.[12]

The National Consumers' League (NCL, 1899) practiced participatory democracy on the national level. Arising from earlier working women's societies and with Florence Kelley at its head, the NCL investigated working conditions and urged women to use their consumer-purchasing power to force manufacturers to institute new standards of production. The NCL assembled and published "white lists" of those manufacturers found to be practicing good employment standards and awarded a "white label" to factories complying with such standards. The NCL's tactics were voluntary—boycotts were against the law—and they did not convince many manufacturers to change their practices. Even so, such tactics drew more women into the social justice movement, and the NCL's continuous efforts were rewarded in New Deal legislation.[13]

A group of working women and settlement-house residents formed the National Women's Trade Union League (NWTUL, 1903) and organized local affiliates to work for unionization in female-dominated manufacturing.[14] Middle-class women walked the picket lines with striking garment workers and waitresses in New York and Chicago and helped secure concessions from manufacturers. The NWTUL

forced an official investigation into the causes of New York City's Triangle Shirtwaist factory fire (1911), in which almost 150 workers, mainly young women, died. Members of the NWTUL were organizers for the International Ladies' Garment Workers Union. Despite these participatory venues, much literature on such movements emphasizes male initiatives and fails to appreciate gender differences. The public forums movement promoted by men, such as Charles Sprague Smith and Frederic Howe, was a top-down effort in which prominent speakers addressed pressing issues of the day to teach the "rank and file" how to practice democracy.[15] In Boston, Mary Parker Follett promoted participatory democracy through neighborhood centers organized and run by residents. Chicago women's organizations fostered neighborhood centers as spaces for residents to gather and discuss neighborhood needs.[16]

Suffrage did not provide the political power women had hoped for, but female social justice Progressives occupied key offices in the New Deal administration. They helped write national anti-child labor legislation, minimum wage and maximum hour laws, aid to dependent children, and elements of the Social Security Act. Such legislation at least partially fulfilled the social justice Progressive agenda that activist government provide social goods to protect daily life against the vagaries of the capitalist marketplace.

POLITICAL PROGRESSIVISM

Political Progressivism was a structural-instrumental approach to reform the mechanisms and exercise of politics to break the hold of political parties. Its adherents sought a well-ordered government run by experts to undercut a political patronage system that favored trading votes for services. Political Progressives believed that such reforms would enhance democracy.

Mechanisms and Processes of Electoral Democracy. The Wisconsin Idea promoted by the state's three-time governor Robert La

Follette exemplified the political Progressives' approach to reform. The plan advocated state-level reforms to electoral procedures. A key proposal of the Wisconsin Idea was to replace the existing party control of all nominations with a popular direct primary. Wisconsin became the first state to require the direct primary. The plan also proposed giving voters the power to initiate legislation, hold referenda on proposed legislation, and recall elected officials. Wisconsin voters adopted these proposals by 1911,[17] although Oregon was the first state to adopt the initiative and referendum, in 1902.[18]

The political Progressives attacked a patronage politics that filled administrative offices with faithful party supporters, awarded service franchises to private business, and solicited bribes in return for contracts. Political Progressives proposed shifting to merit-based government by experts provided by theoretically nonpartisan appointed commissions or city managers systems that would apply businesslike expertise and fiscal efficiency to government. They proposed replacing city councils elected by districts (wards) with citywide at-large elections, creating strong mayor systems to undercut the machinations of city councils, and reducing the number of elective offices. They also sought new municipal charters and home-rule powers to give cities more control over their governing authority and taxing power.[19]

Political Progressives were mainly men organized into new local civic federations, city clubs, municipal reform leagues, and municipal research bureaus and into new national groups such as the National Municipal League. They attended national conferences such as the National Conference on City Planning, discussing topics of concern to political Progressives. The National Municipal League formulated a model charter to reorganize municipal government predicated on home rule and argued that its proposals would provide good tools for democracy.[20]

In general, only small cities such as Galveston, Texas, and Des Moines, Iowa, or new cities such as Phoenix, Arizona, where such political Progressives dominated elections, adopted the city-manager and commission governments.[21] Other cities elected reform mayors, such as Tom Johnson of Cleveland, Ohio, who placed the professional experts Frederic Howe and Edward W. Bemis into his administration.[22] Charter reform, home rule, and at-large election movements were more complicated in big cities. They failed in Chicago.[23] Boston switched to at-large elections, but the shift in mechanisms did lessen political party control. A new breed of politicians who appealed to interest group politics gained control rather than rule by experts.[24]

Good Government by Experts. Focus on good government reform earned these men the rather pejorative nickname of "goo-goos." These Progressives argued that only the technological expertise of professional engineers and professional bureaucrats could design rational and economically efficient ordinances for solving urban problems. When corporate interests challenged antipollution ordinances and increased government regulation as causing undue hardship for manufacturers, political Progressives countered with economic answers. Pollution was an economic problem: it caused the city to suffer economic waste and inefficiency, and it cost the city and its taxpayers money.[25] In Pittsburgh, the Mellon Institute Smoke Investigation marshaled scientific expertise to measure soot fall in the city and to calculate how costly smoke pollution might be to the city.[26] The Supreme Court in *Northwestern Laundry v. Des Moines* (1915) ruled that there were no valid constitutional objections to state power to regulate pollution.[27]

The political Progressives' cost-benefit approach to regulation clashed with the social justice idea that protecting the public health should decide pollution regulation. The Pittsburgh Ladies Health Protective Association argued that smoke pollution was a general health hazard.[28] The Chicago women's

Anti-Smoke League called smoke pollution a threat to daily life and common welfare, as coal soot fell on food and in homes and was breathed in by children. They demanded immediate strict antismoke ordinances and inspectors to vigorously inspect and enforce the ordinances. The league urged all city residents to monitor pollution in their neighborhoods.[29] The Baltimore Women's Civic League made smoke abatement a principal target for improving living and working conditions.[30] The cost-benefit argument usually won out over the health-first one.

For political Progressives, good government also meant using professional expertise to plan city growth and reorder the urban built environment. They abandoned an earlier City Beautiful movement that focused on cultural and aesthetic beautification in favor of systematic planning by architects, engineers, and city planners to secure the economic development desired by business.[31] Daniel Burnham's Chicago Plan (1909) was the work of a committee of men selected by the city's Commercial Club.[32] Experts crafted new master plans to guarantee urban functionality and profitability through "creative destruction," to build new transportation and communication networks, erect new grand civic buildings and spaces, and zone the city's functions into distinct sectors. They proposed new street configurations to facilitate the movement of goods and people.[33] As the profession of urban planning developed, cities sought out planners such as Harland Bartholomew to formulate new master plans.[34]

New York's Mary Simkhovitch contested this approach and urged planning on the neighborhood level, with professionals consulting with the people. She stressed that no plan was good if it emphasized only economy. Simkhovitch and Florence Kelley organized the first National Conference on City Planning (1909) around the theme of planning for social needs. Simkhovitch was the only woman to address the gathering. All the male speakers emphasized planning for economic

development. As architects, lawyers, and engineers, and new professional planners such as John Nolen and George Ford dominated the planning conferences, Simkhovitch and Kelley withdrew.[35]

The democratic reform theories of Frederic Howe and Mary Parker Follett reflected competing ideas about political Progressivism and urban reform. Howe believed that democracy was a political mechanism that, if properly ordered and led by experts, would restore the city to the people. The key to achieving good government and democracy was municipal home rule. Once freed from state interference, his theoretical city republic would decide in the best interests of its residents, making city life orderly and thereby more democratic.[36] For Follett, democracy was embedded in social relations, and the city was the hope of democracy because it could be organized on the neighborhood level. There people would apply democracy collectively and create an orderly society.[37] Throughout the country, municipal political reform was driven primarily by groups of men. Women and their ideas were consistently pushed to the margins of political Progressivism.[38]

Social Science Expertise. Social science expertise gave political Progressives a theoretical foundation for cautious proposals to create a more activist state. University of Wisconsin political economist Richard Ely; his former student John R. Commons; political scientist Charles McCarthy, who authored the Wisconsin Idea; and University of Michigan political economist Henry C. Adams, among others, filled the role of social science expert. Social scientists founded new disciplinary organizations, such as the American Economics Association. This association organized the American Association of Labor Legislation (AALL). Commons, University of Chicago sociology professor Charles R. Henderson, and Commons's student John B. Andrews were prominent members. The AALL focused on workers' health, compensation, and insurance, in contrast to the NCL emphasis on investigation and working conditions.[39] Frederic Howe, with a PhD in history and political science from Johns Hopkins, became a foremost theorist for municipal reform based on his social science theories. John Dewey promulgated new theories of democracy and education. Professional social scientists composed a tight circle of men who created a space between academia and government from which to advocate for reform.[40] They addressed each other, trained their students to follow their ideas, and rarely spoke to the larger public.[41]

Sophonisba Breckinridge, Frances Kellor, Edith Abbott, and Katherine Davis were trained at the University of Chicago in political economy and sociology. Abbott briefly held an academic position at Wellesley, but she resigned to join the other women in applying her training to social research and social activism. Their expertise laid the foundation for the profession of social work. As grassroots activists, they worked with settlement house residents such as Jane Addams and Mary Simkhovitch, joined women's voluntary organizations, investigated living and working conditions, and carved out careers in social welfare.[42]

Male social scientists dismissed women's expertise and eschewed grassroots work.[43] Breckinridge had earned a magna cum laude PhD in political science and economics, but she received no offers of an academic position, unlike her male colleagues. She was kept on at the university, but by 1920 the sociology department directed social sciences away from seeking practical solutions to everyday life that had linked scholarly inquiry with social responsibility. The female social scientists who had formed an intellectual core of the sociology department were put into a School of Social Services Administration and ultimately segregated into the division of social work.[44]

ECONOMIC PROGRESSIVISM

Economic Progressives identified unregulated corporate monopoly capitalism as a primary source of the country's troubles.[45] They proposed a new regulatory state to mitigate the worst aspects of the system. Reforming the banking and currency systems, pursuing some measure of antitrust (antimonopoly) legislation, shifting from a largely laissez-faire economy, and moderately restructuring property relations would produce government in the public interest.

Antimonopoly Progressivism. Antimonopoly Progressivism required rethinking the relationship between business and government, introducing new legislation, and modifying a legal system that consistently sided with business. Congress and the presidency had to take leadership roles, but below them were Progressive groups such as the National Civic Federation, the NCL, and the General Federation of Women's Clubs pushing for significant policy change. These Progressives believed collusion between a small number of capitalist industrialists and politicians had badly damaged democracy. They especially feared that the system threatened to lead to class warfare.

The Interstate Commerce Act (1887) and the Sherman Antitrust Act (1890) began to consider the problems of unregulated laissez-faire capitalism and monopoly in restraint of trade. As president, Theodore Roosevelt (1901–1909) used congressional power to regulate commerce to attack corporate monopolistic restraint of trade. The Elkins Act (1903) gave Congress the power to regulate against predatory business practices; the Hepburn Act (1906) gave it authority to regulate railroad rates; the Meat Inspection Act and the Pure Food and Drug Act (1906) did the same for those industries. Roosevelt created the Department of Commerce and Labor (1903) to oversee interstate corporate practices and in 1906 empowered the Department of Agriculture to inspect and set standards in meat production, a move that led eventually to the Food and Drug Administration.

Presidential Progressivism. Roosevelt considered the president to be the guardian of the public welfare. His approach to conservation was a primary example of how he applied this belief. He agreed with the arguments of social scientists, professional organizations of engineers, and forestry bureau chief Gifford Pinchot that careful and efficient management and administration of natural resources was necessary to guarantee the country's economic progress and preserve democratic opportunity. Roosevelt appointed a Public Lands Commission to manage public land in the West and appointed a National Conservation Commission to inventory the country's resources so that sound business practices could be implemented. The commission's three-volume report relied on scientific and social scientific methods to examine conservation issues.[46]

William Howard Taft (1909–1913) refused to support further work by the Conservation Commission. He rejected new conservation proposals as violating congressional authority and possessing no legal standing. Taft's administrative appointments, including Interior Secretary Richard Ballinger, favored opening public lands to more private development. Taft's Progressivism was the more conservative Republican approach that focused on breaking up trusts because they were bad for business.[47] Taft sided with business when he signed the Payne-Aldrich Tariff Act (1909), which kept high tariffs on many essential goods that Progressives wanted reduced to aid consumers and small manufacturers.[48]

In 1912, the Republican Party split between Roosevelt and Taft. Political, economic, and social justice Progressives, including Robert La Follette, Charles McCarthy, Jane Addams, Frances Kellor, and George Perkins, a partner at J. P. Morgan and Company, helped establish the Progressive Party. They nominated Roosevelt, who envisioned a platform of "New Nationalism," which promised to govern in the public interest and provide economic prosperity as a basic foundation of democratic citizenship.[49] Addams was unhappy with

Roosevelt's economic emphasis, but she saw him as social Progressives' best hope.

Woodrow Wilson and Roosevelt received two-thirds of the vote, while Socialist Party candidate Eugene Debs secured 6 percent of the votes. The election results indicated that the general population supported a middle way between socialism and Taft's big business Progressivism. Wilson's (1913–1921) "New Freedom" platform promised to curb the power of big business and close the growing wealth gap. As senator, La Follette helped push through Wilson's reform legislation. The Clayton Antitrust Act (1914), the Federal Trade Commission (1914), and the Federal Reserve Act (1913) each curbed the power of big business and regulated banking. The Sixteenth Amendment (1913) authorized the federal income tax. The Seventeenth Amendment (1913) provided for the direct election of state legislators, who had previously been appointed by state legislatures.

Trade Union Progressivism. Under Samuel Gompers, the American Federation of Labor (AFL) fought to secure collective bargaining rights for male trade unionists. The AFL rejected the AALL proposals for worker compensation and insurance and never supported national worker compensation laws, although local federations supported state-level legislation.[50] Gompers preferred working with businessmen and politicians to secure the right to collective bargaining, the eight-hour day, and a voice for labor in production. The AFL never tried to form a Labor Party but advocated putting a labor agenda into mainstream party politics.[51] The Clayton Antitrust Act, which acknowledged that unions had the right to peaceful and lawful actions, was a victory for trade union Progressivism. The act did not provide everything that Gompers had demanded. Only New Deal legislation would offer more extensive protections to unions.

Gompers and the AFL rejected the AALL's ideas, fearing that a more activist government might extend to regulating the labor of women and children. The AFL wanted sufficient economic security for white male workers, to move women out of the labor force.[52] Other labor Progressives sought the same end. Louis Brandeis and Father John Ryan promoted the living wage as a right of citizenship for male workers. Ryan acknowledged that unmarried women workers were entitled to a living wage, but he wanted labor reform to secure a family wage so that men would marry and families would produce children.[53] Hostile to organizing women, Gompers forced NWTUL leader Margaret Dreier Robins off the executive board of the Chicago Federation of Labor.[54]

Municipal Ownership.

On the local level, economic Progressives sought a middle way between socialism and the AFL's single-minded trade unionism. AFL affiliates and Progressive politicians such as Cleveland's Tom Johnson favored a municipal democracy that gave voters new powers. Municipal ownership of public utilities such as street railways promised the working class a way to protect their labor through the ballot.[55] Such reform would also destroy the franchise system. In Los Angeles, labor and socialists crafted a labor/socialist ticket to challenge the business/party control of the city and enact municipal ownership. A socialist administration in Milwaukee appealed to class interests to support an agenda that included municipal ownership. In Chicago, socialist Josephine Kaneko argued that she did not see much difference between socialism and women's Progressive agenda for reform to benefit the common welfare.[56] Despite such flirtations between labor and socialists, labor remained attached to the Democratic Party.

Some cities achieved a measure of municipal ownership. Most middle-class urban Progressives deemed municipal ownership too socialist. They favored state economic regulation, led by experts, rather than ownership to break the monopoly in public utilities.[57]

INTERNATIONAL PROGRESSIVISM

Progressivism fostered new international engagement. The economic imperative to secure supplies of raw materials for industrial production, a messianic approach of bringing cultural and racial civilization around the globe, and belief in an international Progressivism that focused on international cooperation all pushed Progressives to think globally.

Securing Economic Progress.

Although he was generally against Progressivism, President William McKinley annexed Hawaii (1898), saying that the country needed it even more than it had needed California.[58] The Roosevelt Corollary to the Monroe Doctrine (1904) declared that intervention in the Caribbean was necessary to secure economic stability and forestall foreign interference in the area. Progressive Herbert Croly believed that the country needed to forcibly pacify some areas in the world in order for the United States to establish an American international system.[59] The Progressive Party platform (1912) declared it imperative to the people's welfare that the country expand its foreign commerce. Between 1898 and 1941, the United States invaded Cuba, acquired the naval base at Guantanamo Bay, took possession of Puerto Rico, colonized the Philippines and several Pacific islands, encouraged Panama to rebel against Colombia so that the United States could build the Panama Canal, invaded Mexico to protect oil interests, and intervened in Haiti, Nicaragua, and the Dominican Republic. To protect its possessions in the Pacific, Roosevelt's Secretary of State Elihu Root finalized the Root-Takahira Agreement (1908), which acknowledged Japan's control of Korea in return for its noninterference in the Philippines. American imperialism based on economic and financial desires became referred to as "Dollar Diplomacy."[60]

Mission of Civilization.

Race, paternalism, and masculinity characterized elements of international Progressivism. Senator Albert

Beveridge had supported Progressive proposals to abolish child labor and had favored regulating business and granting more rights to labor, but he viewed Filipinos as too backward to understand democracy and self-government. The United States was God's chosen nation, with a divine mission to civilize the world; it should exercise its "spirit of progress" to organize the world.[61] William Jennings Bryan had previously been an anti-imperialist, but later, as Wilson's secretary of state, he advocated intervening in Latin America to tutor backward people in self-government.[62] In speeches and writings, Roosevelt stressed that new international possessions required men to accept the strenuous life of responsibility for other people in order to maintain American domination of the world.[63] Social science likened Filipino men to children lacking the vigorous manhood necessary for self-government.[64] Beveridge contended that it was government's responsibility to manufacture manhood. Empire could be the new frontier of white masculinity.[65] Roosevelt concluded a "Gentlemen's Agreement" (1907) in which Japan agreed to stop issuing passports to Japanese laborers to immigrate to the United States.

Democracy and International Cooperation.

A cadre of Progressives who had worked to extend their ideals into an international context did not welcome imperialism, dollar diplomacy, and war.[66] Addams rejected war as an anachronism that failed to produce a collective responsibility. La Follette rejoiced that failures in dollar diplomacy elevated humanity over property. Suffragists compared their lack of the vote to the plight of Filipinos. Belle Case La Follette opposed incursion into Mexico and denounced all militarism as driven by greed, suspicion, and love of power.[67]

Many Progressives opposed war as an assault on an international collective humanity. Women organized peace marches and founded a Women's Peace Party. Addams, Kelley, Frederic Howe, Lillian Wald of New York's

Henry Street Settlement, and Paul Kellogg, editor of the Progressive *Survey*, formed the American Union Against Militarism.[68] Addams, Simkhovitch, the sociologist Emily Greene Balch, and labor leader Leonora O'Reilly attended the International Women's Peace Conference at The Hague in spring 1915. Florence Kelley was denied a passport to travel.[69] The work of the American Red Cross in Europe during and after the war reflected the humanitarian collective impulse of Progressivism.[70]

Entry into World War I, President Wilson's assertion that it would make the world safe for democracy, and a growing xenophobia that demanded 100 percent loyalty produced a Progressive crisis. Addams remained firm against the war as antihumanitarian and was vilified for her pacifism.[71] La Follette voted against the declaration of war, charging that it was being promoted by business desires and that it was absurd to believe that it would make the world safe for democracy. He was accused of being pro-German, and Theodore Roosevelt said that he should be hung.[72] Labor leader Morris Hillquit and Florence Kelley formed the People's Council of America to continue to pressure for peace. Under pressure to display patriotism, Progressive opposition to the war crumbled. Paul Kellogg declared that it was time to combat European militarism. The American Union Against Militarism dissolved. Herbert Croly's *New Republic* urged the country to take a more active role in the war to create a new international league of peace and assume leadership of democratic nations. John Dewey proclaimed it a war of peoples, not armies, and stated that international reform would follow its conclusion.[73]

Other Progressives comforted themselves that once the war was won, they could recommit to democratic agendas. Kelley, Grace Abbott, Josephine Goldmark, and Julia Lathrop helped organize the home front to maintain Progressive ideals. They monitored the condition of women workers, sat on the war department's board controlling labor standards, and drafted insurance policies for military personnel. Suffrage leader Carrie Chapman Catt volunteered for the Women's Advisory Committee of the Council of National Defense. Walter Lippmann worked on government projects. City planner John Nolen designed housing communities for war workers under the newly constituted United States Housing Corporation.[74]

Suffragists protested the lack of democracy in the United States. As Wilson refused to support woman suffrage, members of the National Woman's Party, led by Alice Paul, picketed the White House in protest. Picketers were arrested, Paul was put in solitary confinement in a psychiatric ward, and several women on a hunger strike were force-fed. Wilson capitulated to public outrage over the women's treatment. The women were released, and Wilson urged passage of the suffrage amendment.[75] The Nineteenth Amendment was ratified in 1920, but Progressives' hopes that equal political rights would bring democratic equality were not fulfilled. The social justice Progressives split over whether to support the Equal Rights Amendment drawn up by the National Woman's Party, fearing that it would negate the protective labor legislation they had achieved.

RACIALIZED PROGRESSIVISM

White Progressives failed to pursue racial equality. Most of them believed the country was not yet ready for such a cultural shift. Some of them believed in theories of racial inferiority. Southern Progressive figure Rebecca Latimer Felton defended racial lynching as a means to protect white women.[76] Other Progressives, such as Sophonisba Breckinridge, fought against racial exclusion policies and promoted interracial cooperation.[77] W. E. B. Du Bois and Addams helped found the National Association for the Advancement of Colored People (1909).

African American Progressivism. African Americans believed that Progressive

ideology should lead inevitably to racial equality. Du Bois spoke at public forums.[78] He supported the social justice Progressives' agenda, attending the 1912 Progressive Party convention. Du Bois proposed a racial equality plank for the party platform. Jane Addams helped write the plank. Theodore Roosevelt rejected it, preferring the gradualist policy of Booker T. Washington. Addams objected but mused that perhaps it was not yet time for such a bold move. Racial justice would follow logically from dedication to social justice.[79] Du Bois shifted his support to Woodrow Wilson, while Ida B. Wells-Barnett backed Taft. In 1916, African American women founded Colored Women's Hughes clubs to support the Republican nominee. Hughes had reluctantly backed woman suffrage, and African American women viewed suffrage as the means to protect the race. Nannie Helen Burroughs worked through the National Association of Colored Women (1896) and the National Baptist Convention, demanding suffrage for African American women because they would use it wisely, for the benefit of the race. Burroughs lived in Washington, DC, where she witnessed the segregationist policies of the Wilson administration. She castigated African American men for having voted for him in 1912.[80] African American Progressives hoped that serving in the military and organizing on the home front during the war would result in equal citizenship when the war ended. Instead, African Americans were subjected to more prejudice and violence. Southern senators blocked the Dyer antilynching bill (1922).

Immigration Restriction. Anti-immigrant sentiment had been building in the country since passage of the Chinese Exclusion Act (1882). Several attempts to pass a literacy test bill for immigrants, supported by the Immigration Restriction League (1894), failed. The forty-one volumes of the Senate-appointed Dillingham Commission (1911) concluded that immigrants were heavily responsible for the country's problems and advocated the

literacy test. Frances Kellor believed that all immigrants could be Americanized. Randolph Bourne advocated immigration as the path to Americans becoming internationalists. The *New Republic*, however, feared that excessive immigration would overwhelm an activist state and prevent it from solving social problems. Lillian Wald, Frederic Howe, and other Progressives organized the National Committee for Constructive Immigration Legislation (1916) hoping to forestall more restrictive measures. In the midst of war fever, Congress passed a literacy test bill over Wilson's veto (1917).

100-percent Americanism. Progressives such as Kellor, Wald, and Addams believed that incorporating immigrants into a broad American culture would create a Progressive modern society. Theodore Roosevelt promoted a racialized version of American society. As president, he secured new laws (1903, 1907) to exclude certain classes of immigrants— paupers, the insane, prostitutes, and radicals who might pose a threat to American standards of labor—that he deemed incapable of becoming good Americans. He created the Bureau of Immigration to enforce these provisions. The 1907 Immigration Act also stripped citizenship from women who married noncitizens, a situation only reversed in 1922. At Roosevelt's behest, Congress tightened requirements for naturalization. Wartime fever and the 1919 Red Scare intensified the search for 100 percent Americanism and undermined the alternative Progressive ideal of a cooperative Americanism.[81]

PROGRESSIVISM BEYOND THE PROGRESSIVE ERA

The democratizing ideals of the Progressive Era lived beyond the time period. A regulatory state to eliminate the worst effects of capitalism was created, as most Americans accepted that the federal state had to take on more social responsibility. After ratification of the suffrage amendment, the National American Woman Suffrage Association reconstituted as the National League of Women Voters (1920) to continue promoting an informed, democratic electorate. The New Deal implemented a substantial social justice Progressive agenda, with the NCL, the Children's Bureau, and many women who had formed the earlier era's agenda writing the legislation banning child labor, fostering new labor standards that included minimum wage and maximum hours, and mandating social security for the elderly. The General Federation of Women's Clubs focused on environmental protection as a democratic right. A women's joint congressional committee formed to continue pressing for social justice legislation. The National Association of Colored Women joined the committee.

Progressives can be legitimately criticized for not undertaking a more radical restructuring of American society. Some of them can be criticized for believing that they possessed the best vision for a modern, Progressive future. They can be faulted for not promoting racial equality or a new internationalism that might bring about global peace rather than war. Nonetheless, they never intended to undermine capitalism, so they could never truly embrace socialism. In the context of a society that continued to exalt individualism and suspect government interference and working within their own notions of democracy, they accomplished significant changes in American government and society.[82]

DISCUSSION OF THE LITERATURE

The muckraking authors and journalists of the late 19th and early 20th centuries highlighted rapacious capitalism and characterized its wealthy beneficiaries as corrupting the country. In their exposés of the relationship between business and politics, Ida M. Tarbell, Frank Norris, and Upton Sinclair accused politicians of a corrupt bargain in pursuit of their own economic interests against the interests of the people.[83] Drawing upon these investigative writings, early analyses of Progressivism from Benjamin De Witt and Charles and Mary Beard interpreted Progressivism as a dualistic class struggle. On one side were wealthy and privileged special interests seeking to promote themselves at the expense of everyone else. On the other side was a broad public seeking to restore dignity and opportunity to the common people.[84]

By the early 1950s, George Mowry and Richard Hofstadter contended that Progressivism was a movement of an older, professional, middle class seeking to reclaim its status, deference, and power, which had been usurped by a new corporate elite and a corrupt political class.[85] In the early 1960s, Samuel Hays argued that rather than being the product of a status revolution, Progressivism was the work of an urban upper class of new and younger leading Republican business and professional men.[86] Robert Wiebe shifted the analysis to describe a broader middle-class Progressivism of new professional men who wished to reorder society by applying bureaucratic and business-oriented skills to political and economic institutions.[87] In Wiebe's organizational thesis, Progressives were modernizers with a structural-instrumentalist agenda. They rejected reliance on older values and cultural norms to order society and sought to create a modern reordered society with political and economic institutions run by men qualified to apply fiscal expertise, businesslike efficiency, and modern scientific expertise to solve problems and save democracy.[88] The emerging academic disciplines in the social sciences of economics, political economy and political science, and pragmatic education supplied the theoretical bases for this middle-class expert Progressivism.[89] Gabriel Kolko countered such analyses, arguing that Progressivism was a conservative movement promoted by business to protect itself.[90]

Professional men and their organizations kept copious records from which scholars could draw this interpretation. By the late 1960s, scholars began to examine the role of other groups in reform movements, ask different questions, and utilize different sources. John Buenker called Progressivism a pluralistic effort, an ethnocultural struggle based on religious values in which urban immigrants and their democratic politicians resisted the old-stock Protestant elites whose Progressive agenda they believed was aimed at homogenizing American culture through policies such as Prohibition and immigration restriction. Ethnic groups were not anti-Progressive but promoted a new Progressive agenda of economic regulation and rights for labor.[91] In the face of conflicting interpretations, Peter Filene questioned whether there indeed was a Progressive movement. Daniel T. Rodgers posited that Progressivism could best be understood as a shift from party politics to interest groups politics.[92]

In the last decades of the 20th century, historians began to distance themselves from the very notions of Progressivism. They criticized Progressivism as the ultimate end of a middle-class search for social control of the masses, or they focused on its class dimension.[93] Recent literature has reconsidered the meaning of the Progressive Era. Revisiting his early 1980s essay, Daniel T. Rodgers proposed that the big picture of Progressivism was a reaction to the capitalist transformation of society. Robert D. Johnston saw a revived debate concerning the democratic nature of Progressivism and its connections to the present.[94] A recent book by Robyn Muncy takes another look at the emphasis on Progressivism as a social struggle through the biography of Colorado reformer Josephine Roche and her focus on creating social welfare reforms.[95]

PRIMARY SOURCES

There is a wealth of accessible primary source material on Progressives and Progressivism. Many of these documents can now be found through electronic sources such as HathiTrust, Archive.org, and Google Books.

Consult any of the writings of Jane Addams, Louis Brandeis, John R. Commons, Herbert Croly, John Dewey, W. E. B. Du Bois, Mary Parker Follett, Frederic Howe, Florence Kelley,

Theodore Roosevelt, and Ida B. Wells-Barnett. Muckrakers Lincoln Steffens, in *The Shame of the Cities* (1904); Jacob Riis, in *How the Other Half Lives: Among the Tenements of New York* (1890); and Upton Sinclair, in *The Jungle* (1906), expose urban political corruption and social conditions. Ida M. Tarbell, in *The History of the Standard Oil Company* (1904); and Frank Norris, in *Octopus: A Story of California* (1901), expose business practices. The residents of Hull House published an investigative survey of living conditions in their neighborhood in *Hull House Maps and Papers: A Presentation of Nationalities and Wages in a Congested District of Chicago, Together with Comments and Essays on Problems Growing out of Social Conditions* (1895). Useful autobiographies are Tom Johnson, *My Story* (New York: B. W. Heubsch, 1913); Louise DeKoven Bowen, *Growing Up with a City* (New York: Macmillan, 1926); Jane Addams, *Twenty Years at Hull House* (New York: Macmillan, 1910); Ida B. Wells-Barnett, *Crusade for Justice: The Autobiography of Ida. B. Wells*, edited by Alfreda Duster (Chicago: University of Chicago Press, 1970).

Manuscript collections for national and local organizations and individuals include those of the General Federation of Women's Clubs, National Association of Colored Women, Ellen Gates Starr, Women's City Club of New York, Sophonisba Breckinridge, National Women's Trade Union League, National Consumers League, and Theodore Roosevelt. Publications of Progressive groups and organizations include *Woman Citizen's Library, Survey, Charities and Commons, New Republic*, and *National Municipal Review*. Investigative reports include the six volumes of the the *Pittsburgh Survey* (1909–1914) and *Reports of the Immigration Commission* (Dillingham Commission), in forty-one volumes (1911).

Proceedings of organization conferences include those of the National Conferences on City Planning and Congestion, National Conferences on City Planning, International Conference on Women Workers to Promote Peace, and American Federation of Labor. Supreme Court rulings include *Ritchie v. People* (1895), *Plessy v. Ferguson* (1896), *Holden v. Hardy* (1898), *Lochner v. New York* (1905), and *Muller v. Oregon* (1908).

DIGITAL MATERIALS

CORNELL UNIVERSITY, ILR SCHOOL, KHEEL CENTER

- 1911 Triangle Fire. http://trianglefire.ilr .cornell.edu/.

THE HISTORY PLACE

- Lewis Hines photos of child labor. http:// www.historyplace.com/unitedstates /childlabor.

LIBRARY OF CONGRESS

- Child labor collection. http://www.loc .gov/pictures/collection/nclc/.
- World War I posters. http://www.loc.gov /collections/world-war-i-posters/about-this -collection/.
- The National American Woman Suffrage Association. http://memory.loc.gov/ammem /naw/nawshome.html.
- The National Woman's Party and protesters. http://www.loc.gov/teachers/class roommaterials/connections/women -protest/.
- Theodore Roosevelt. https://www.loc.gov /rr/program/bib/presidents/troosevelt /memory.html.
- The Conservation Movement. http:// memory.loc.gov/ammem/amrvhtml /conshome.html.

UNIVERSITY OF ILLINOIS CHICAGO, SPECIAL COLLECTIONS

- Settlement houses in Chicago. http://www .uic.edu/depts/lib/specialcoll/exhibits /7settlements/main.htm.

HARVARD UNIVERSITY LIBRARY OPEN COLLECTIONS PROGRAM

- Immigration to the United States, 1789–1930. http://ocp.hul.harvard.edu/immigration/.

FURTHER READING

Connolly, James J. *The Triumph of Ethnic Progressivism: Urban Political Culture in Boston, 1900–1925.* Cambridge, MA: Harvard University Press, 1998.

Dawley, Alan. *Changing the World: American Progressives in War and Revolution.* Princeton, NJ: Princeton University Press, 2003.

Flanagan, Maureen A. *Seeing with Their Hearts: Chicago Women and the Vision of the Good City, 1871–1933.* Princeton, NJ: Princeton University Press, 2002.

Flanagan, Maureen A. *America Reformed: Progressives and Progressivisms, 1890s–1920s.* New York: Oxford University Press, 2007.

Greene, Julie. *The Canal Builders: Making America's Empire at the Panama Canal.* New York: Penguin, 2009.

Hofstadter, Richard. *The Age of Reform.* New York: Vintage Books, 1955.

Keller, Morton. *Regulating a New Economy: Public Policy and Economic Change in America, 1900–1933.* Cambridge, MA: Harvard University Press, 1990.

Knight, Louise W. *Citizen: Jane Addams and the Struggle for Democracy.* Chicago: University of Chicago Press, 2005.

Mattson, Kevin. *Creating a Democratic Public: The Struggle for Urban Participatory Democracy During the Progressive Era.* University Park: Pennsylvania State University Press, 1998.

McGerr, Michael. *A Fierce Discontent: The Rise and Fall of the Progressive Movement in America, 1870–1920.* New York: Free Press, 2003.

Muncy, Robyn. *Creating a Female Dominion in American Reform, 1890–1935.* New York: Oxford University Press, 1991.

Muncy, Robyn. *Relentless Reformer: Josephine Roche and Progressivism in Twentieth-Century America.* Princeton, NJ: Princeton University Press, 2015.

Piott, Steven L. *American Reformers, 1870–1920: Progressives in Word and Deed.* Lanham, MD: Rowman & Littlefield, 2006.

Rodgers, Daniel T. *Atlantic Crossings: Social Politics in a Progressive Age.* Cambridge, MA: Harvard University Press, 1998.

Salyer, Lucy. *Laws Harsh As Tigers: Chinese Immigrants and the Shaping of Modern Immigration Law.* Chapel Hill: University of North Carolina Press, 1995.

Schechter, Patricia A. *Ida B. Wells-Barnett and American Reform, 1880–1930.* Chapel Hill: University of North Carolina Press, 2001.

Sklar, Martin J. *The Corporate Reconstruction of American Capitalism, 1890–1916.* Cambridge: Cambridge University Press, 1988.

Unger, Nancy. *Fighting Bob La Follette: The Righteous Reformer.* Chapel Hill: University of North Carolina Press, 2000.

Wiebe, Robert H. *The Search for Order, 1877–1920.* New York: Hill and Wang, 1967.

NOTES

1. Maureen A. Flanagan, *America Reformed: Progressives and Progressivisms, 1890s–1920s* (New York: Oxford University Press, 2007), 10.

2. Jane Addams, *Democracy and Social Ethics* (New York: Macmillan, 1902).

3. Michael Les Benedict, "Law and Regulation in the Gilded Age and Progressive Era," in *Law as Culture and Culture as Law: Essays in Honor of John Philip Reid,* ed. Hendrick Hartog and William E. Nelson (Madison, WI: Madison House Publishers, 2000), 227–263; Christopher L. Tomlins, *The State and the Unions: Labor Relations, Law, and the Organized Labor Movement in American 1880–1960* (Cambridge: Cambridge University Press, 1985).

4. Michael Willrich, *City of Courts: Socializing Justice in Progressive Era Chicago* (Cambridge: Cambridge University Press, 2003), 100–103.

5. Nancy Woloch, *Muller v. Oregon: A Brief History with Documents* (Boston: Bedford Books, 1996).

6. Victoria Getis, *The Juvenile Court and the Progressives* (Urbana: University of Illinois Press, 2000).

7. Jennifer Koslow, *Cultivating Health: Los Angeles Women and Public Health Reform* (New Brunswick, NJ: Rutgers University Press, 2009); Daphne Spain, *How Women Saved the City* (Minneapolis: University of Minnesota Press, 2001); Anne Firor Scott, *Natural Allies: Women's Associations in American History* (Urbana: University of Illinois Press, 1992); and Judith N. McArthur, *Creating the New Woman: The Rise of Southern Women's Progressive Culture in Texas, 1893–1918* (Urbana: University of Illinois Press, 1998).

8. Nancy C. Unger, *Beyond Nature's Housekeepers: American Women in Environmental History* (New York: Oxford University Press, 2012), 86, for the General Federation of Women's Clubs. See Arthur S. Link and Richard L. McCormick, *Progressivism* (Arlington Heights, IL: Harlan Davidson, 1983), 38; Robert H. Wiebe, *The Search for Order, 1877–1920* (New York: Hill & Wang, 1967), 191; Vincent P. DeSantis, *The Shaping of Modern America, 1877–1920* (Arlington Heights, IL: Forum Press), 184; and Daniel Block, "Saving Milk through Masculinity: Public Health Officers and Pure Milk, 1880–1930," *Food and Foodways: History and Culture of Human Nourishment* 15 (January–June 2005): 115–135.

9. Kriste Lindenmeyer, *"A Right to Childhood": The U.S. Children's Bureau and Child Welfare, 1912–46* (Urbana: University of Illinois Press, 1997), 10–29 and 114–132.

10. Maureen A. Flanagan, *Seeing with Their Hearts: Chicago Women and the Vision of the Good City, 1871–1933* (Princeton, NJ: Princeton University Press, 2002); and Scott, *Natural Allies,* 159–174.

11. Robyn Muncy, *Creating a Female Dominion in American Reform, 1890–1935* (New York: Oxford University Press, 1991), 132–150, 152–154; Lindenmeyer, *"A Right to Childhood,"* chap. 4, esp. 100–103; and Lynne Curry, *Modern Mothers in the Heartland: Gender, Health, and Progress in Illinois, 1900–1930* (Columbus: Ohio State University, 1999), 120–131.

12. Scott, *Natural Allies,* 147.

13. Landon R. Y. Storrs, *Civilizing Capitalism: The National Consumers' League, Women's Activism, and Labor Standards in the New Deal* (Chapel Hill: University of North Carolina Press, 2000), chap. 1.

14. Elizabeth Payne, *Reform, Labor, and Feminism: Margaret Dreier Robins and the Women's Trade Union League* (Urbana: University of Illinois Press, 1988).

15. Kevin Mattson, *Creating a Democratic Public: The Struggle for Urban Participatory Democracy During the Progressive Era* (University Park: Pennsylvania State University Press, 1998), 45.

16. Mattson, *Creating a Democratic Public,* includes a chapter on Follett, but the rest of the book focuses on men. Alan Dawley, *Struggles for Justice: Social Responsibility and the Liberal State* (Cambridge, MA: Harvard University Press, 1991), 102, short-changes women's Progressivism, saying it "merely extended the boundaries of women's sphere to the realm of 'social housekeeping'"; Daniel T. Rodgers,

Atlantic Crossings: Social Politics in a Progressive Age (Cambridge, MA: Harvard University Press, 1998), 19–20, 239–240, calls them "social maternalists" rather than social justice Progressives and claims that they were motivated by "sentiment" and focused on protecting "women's weakness." For Chicago women's clubs, see Elizabeth Belanger, "The Neighborhood Ideal: Local Planning Practices in Progressive-Era Women's Clubs," *Journal of Planning History* 8, no. 2 (May 2009): 87–110.

17. Nancy Unger, *Fighting Bob La Follette: The Righteous Reformer* (Chapel Hill: University of North Carolina Press, 2000). Charles McCarthy, *The Wisconsin Idea* (New York: Macmillan, 1912).

18. Robert D. Johnston, *The Radical Middle Class: Populist Democracy and the Question of Capitalism in Progressive Era Portland, Oregon* (Princeton, NJ: Princeton University Press, 2003), 123.

19. Martin J. Schiesl, *The Politics of Efficiency: Municipal Administration and Reform in American, 1880–1920* (Berkeley: University of California Press, 1997), provides the clearest overall picture of these elements of this political Progressivism.

20. Committee on Municipal Program of the National Municipal League, *A Model City Charter and Municipal Home Rule* (Philadelphia: National Municipal League, 1916).

21. Amy Bridges, *Morning Glories: Municipal Reform in the Southwest* (Princeton, NJ: Princeton University Press, 1999); Bradley R. Rice, "The Galveston Plan of City Government by Commission: The Birth of a Progressive Idea," *Southwestern Historical Quarterly,* 78, no. 4 (April 1975): 365–408; and Schiesl, *The Politics of Efficiency,* 136–137 for Des Moines.

22. Kenneth Finegold, *Experts and Politicians: Reform Challenges to Machine Politics in New York, Cleveland, and Chicago* (Princeton, NJ: Princeton University Press, 1995), 82–88 for Johnson and 107–111 for charter reform in Cleveland.

23. Maureen A. Flanagan, *Charter Reform in Chicago* (Carbondale: Southern Illinois University, 1987).

24. James J. Connolly, *The Triumph of Ethnic Progressivism: Urban Political Culture in Boston, 1900–1925* (Cambridge, MA: Harvard University Press, 1998), 106–107.

25. David Stradling, *Smokestacks and Progressives: Environmentalists, Engineers, and Air Quality in America, 1881–1951* (Baltimore, MD: Johns Hopkins University Press, 1999), 21–36.

26. Angela Gugliotta, "How, When, and for Whom Was Smoke a Problem?" in *Devastation and Renewal: An Environmental History of Pittsburgh and Its Region*, ed. Joel Tarr (Pittsburgh, PA: University of Pittsburgh Press, 2003), 118–120.

27. Stradling, *Smokestacks and Progressives*, 63–67 and 108–137, provides a comprehensive overview of the political Progressivism of smoke pollution.

28. Angela Gugliotta, "Class, Gender, and Coal Smoke: Gender Ideology and Environmental Injustice in Pittsburgh, 1868–1914," *Environmental History* 6, no. 2 (April 2000): 173–176.

29. Flanagan, *Seeing with Their Hearts*, 100–102 and *America Reformed*, 173–179. See Scott, *Natural Allies*, 143–145 for more on women's health protective associations.

30. Anne-Marie Szymanski, "Regulatory Transformations in a Changing City: The Anti-Smoke Movement in Baltimore, 1895–1931," *Journal of the Gilded Age and Progressive Era* 13, no. 3 (July 2014): 364–366.

31. William H. Wilson, *The City Beautiful Movement* (Baltimore, MD: Johns Hopkins University Press, 1985); and Jon A. Peterson, *The Birth of City Planning in the United States, 1840–1917* (Baltimore, MD: Johns Hopkins University Press, 2003), Parts 2 and 3.

32. Carl A. Smith, *The Plan of Chicago: Daniel Burnham and the Remaking of the American City* (Chicago: University of Chicago Press, 2006).

33. Max Page, *The Creative Destruction of Manhattan, 1900–1940* (Chicago: University of Chicago Press, 1999); and Mel Scott, *American City Planning since 1890* (Berkeley: University of California Press, 1971), Parts 2, 3, and 4.

34. Eric Sandweiss, *St. Louis: The Evolution of an American Urban Landscape* (Philadelphia: Temple University Press, 2001).

35. Susan Marie Wirka, "The City Social Movement: Progressive Women Reformers and Early Social Planning," in *Planning the Twentieth-Century American City*, ed. Mary Corbin Sies and Christopher Silver (Baltimore, MD: Johns Hopkins University Press, 1996), 55–75; and Maureen A. Flanagan, "City Profitable, City Livable: Environmental Policy, Gender, and Power in Chicago in the 1910s," *Journal of Urban History* 22, no. 2 (January 1996): 163–190.

36. Frederic Howe, *The City: The Hope of Democracy* (New York: Charles Scribner's, 1905).

37. Mary Parker Follett, *The New State: Group Organization the Solution of Popular Government* (New York: Longmans, Green, 1918).

38. Connolly, *The Triumph of Ethnic Progressivism*.

39. Rodgers, *Atlantic Crossings*, 236–238, 251–254.

40. Rodgers, *Atlantic Crossings*, 108–109.

41. Dorothy Ross, *The Origins of American Social Science* (Cambridge: Cambridge University Press, 1991), 158–159.

42. Ellen Fitzpatrick, *Endless Crusade: Women Social Scientists and Progressive Reform* (New York: Oxford University Press, 1990).

43. Theda Skocpol, *Protecting Soldiers and Mothers: The Political Origins of Social Policy in the United States* (Cambridge, MA: Harvard University Press, 1992), 183.

44. Fitzpatrick, *Endless Crusade*, 40–44, 80, 82, and 90–91.

45. Martin J. Sklar, *The Corporate Reconstruction of American Capitalism, 1890–1916* (Cambridge: Cambridge University Press, 1988).

46. Samuel P. Hays, *Conservation and the Gospel of Efficiency: The Progressive Movement, 1890–1920* (repr., New York: Atheneum, 1969), chap. 7.

47. Hays, *Conservation and the Gospel of Efficiency*, chap. 8.

48. DeSantis, *The Shaping of Modern America*, 194–199.

49. Eric Rauchway, *Murdering McKinley: The Making of Theodore Roosevelt's America* (New York: Hill and Wang, 2003), 189–200.

50. Morton Keller, *Regulating a New Society: Public Policy and Social Change in America, 1900–1930* (Cambridge, MA: Harvard University Press, 1994), 194–196.

51. Julie Greene, *Pure and Simple Politics: The American Federation of Labor and Political Activism, 1881–1917* (Cambridg: Cambridge University Press, 1998), 219, 279; and Shelton Stromquist, *Reinventing the "People": The Progressive Movement, the Class Problem, and the Origins of Modern Liberalism* (Urbana: University of Illinois Press, 2006), 66.

52. Greene, *Pure and Simple Politics*, 9, 235.

53. Fr. John Ryan, *The Living Wage: Its Ethical and Economic Aspects* (New York: Macmillan, 1906), 283–285. Richard Ely wrote the book's introduction.

54. Payne, *Reform, Labor, and Feminism*, 95–107.

55. Shelton Stromquist, "The Crucible of Class: Cleveland Politics and the Origins of Municipal Reform in the Progressive Era," *Journal of Urban History* 23, no. 2 (January 1997): 192–220.

56. Daniel J. Johnson, "'No Make-Believe Class Struggle': The Socialist Municipal Campaign in Los Angeles, 1922," *Labor History* 41, no. 1 (February

2000): 25–45; Douglas E. Booth, "Municipal Socialism and City Government Reform: The Milwaukee Experience, 1910–1940," *Journal of Urban History* 12, no. 1 (November 1985): 51–71; and Josephine Kaneko, "What a Socialist Alderman Would Do," *Coming Nation* (March 1914).

57. Gail Radford, "From Municipal Socialism to Public Authorities: Institutional Factors in the Shaping of American Public Enterprise," *Journal of American History* 90, no. 3 (December 2003): 863–890.

58. Nell Irvin Painter, *Standing at Armageddon: The United States, 1877–1919* (New York: W. W. Norton, 1987), 150.

59. Herbert Croly, *The Promise of American Life* (New York: Macmillan, 1909).

60. Emily Rosenberg, *Financial Missionaries to the World: The Politics and Culture of Dollar Diplomacy, 1900–1930* (Cambridge, MA: Harvard University Press, 1999).

61. Matthew Frye Jacobson, *Barbarian Virtues: The United States Encounters Foreign Peoples at Home and Abroad, 1876–1917* (New York: Hill & Wang, 2000), 227.

62. Alan Dawley, *Changing the World: American Progressives in War and Revolution* (Princeton, NJ: Princeton University Press, 2003), 81.

63. Theodore Roosevelt, *The Strenuous Life: Essays and Addresses* (New York: Century, 1903).

64. George F. Becker, "Conditions Requisite to Our Success in the Philippine Islands," address to the American Geographical Society, February 20, 1901, *Bulletin of the American Geographical Society* (1901): 112–123.

65. Albert Beveridge, *The Young Man and the World* (New York: Appleton, 1905), 338; and Kristen Hoganson, *Fighting for American Manhood: How Gender Politics Provoked the Spanish-American and Philippine-American Wars* (New Haven, CT: Yale University Press, 1998).

66. Rodgers, *Atlantic Crossings*, is the most complete analysis of this internationalism.

67. Jane Addams, *Newer Ideals of Peace* (New York: Macmillan, 1907); Robert La Follette, *LaFollette's Weekly* 5.1 (March 29, 1913); Kristen Hoganson, "'As Badly-Off As the Filipinos': U.S. Women Suffragists and the Imperial Issue at the Turn of the Twentieth Century," *Journal of Women's History* 13, no. 2 (Summer 2001): 9–33; and Nancy C. Unger, *Belle La Follette: Progressive Era Reformer* (New York: Routledge, 2015).

68. David Kennedy, *Over Here: The First World War and American Society* (New York: Oxford University Press, 1980).

69. Harriet Hyman, introduction to *Women at The Hague*, by Jane Addams, Emily Greene Balch, and Alice Hamilton (repr., Urbana: University of Illinois Press, 2003); and Kathryn Kish Sklar, "'Some of Us Who Deal with the Social Fabric': Jane Addams Blends Peace and Social Justice," *Journal of the Gilded Age and Progressive Era* 2, no. 1 (January 2003): 80–96.

70. Julia F. Irwin, *Making the World Safe: The American Red Cross and a Nation's Humanitarian Awakening* (New York: Oxford University Press, 2013).

71. Jane Addams, *Peace and Bread in Time of War* (New York: Macmillan, 1922), 4–5.

72. Unger, *Fighting Bob La Follette*, chap. 14.

73. Kennedy, *Over Here*, 34; *New Republic* 10 (February 10 and 17, 1917); and Dawley, *Changing the World*, 122, 147, 165–169.

74. Walter Lippmann, "The World Conflict in Relation to American Democracy," *Annals of the American Academy of Political and Social Science* 72 (July 1917): 1–10; Rodgers, *Atlantic Crossings*, 283–285, 288–289; and Dawley, *Changing the World*, 147.

75. Christine Lunardini, *From Equal Suffrage to Equal Rights: Alice Paul and the National Woman's Party, 1910–1928* (New York: New York University Press, 1986).

76. LeeAnn Whites, "Love, Hate, Rape, and Lynching: Rebecca Latimer Fulton and the Gender Politics of Racial Violence," in *Democracy Betrayed: The Wilmington Race Riot of 1898 and Its Legacy*, ed. David Cecelski and Timothy B. Tyron (Chapel Hill: University of North Carolina Press, 1998).

77. Fitzpatrick, *Endless Crusade*, 180–181.

78. Mattson, *Creating a Democratic Public*, 44.

79. David Levering Lewis, *W. E. B. DuBois: A Biography, 1868–1963* (New York: Henry Holt, 2009), 276–277; and Gary Gerstle, *American Crucible: Race and Nation in the Twentieth Century* (Princeton, NJ: Princeton University Press, 2002), 77–78, for Addams.

80. Lisa G. Masterson, *Black Women and Electoral Politics in Illinois, 1877–1932* (Chapel Hill: University of North Carolina Press, 2009), 101–106.

81. John Higham, *Strangers in the Land: Patterns of American Nativism, 1869–1925* (1955; repr.

New York: Atheneum, 1974), 129–130, 222–224; and Gerstle, *American Crucible*, 55–56.

82. Robert D. Johnston, "Long Live Teddy/Death to Woodrow: The Polarized Politics of the Progressive Era in the 2012 Election," *Journal of the Gilded Age and Progressive Era* 13, no. 3 (July 2014): 411–443.

83. Ida M. Tarbell, *The History of the Standard Oil Company* (New York: McClure, Phillips, 1904); Frank Norris, *The Octopus: A Story of California* (New York: Doubleday, 1901); and Upton Sinclair, *The Jungle* (New York: Jungle Publishing, 1906).

84. Benjamin De Witt, *The Progressive Movement* (New York: Macmillan, 1915); and Charles A. Beard and Mary R. Beard, *The Rise of American Civilization* (New York: Macmillan, 1927).

85. George E. Mowry, *The California Progressives* (Berkeley: University of California Press, 1951); and Richard Hofstadter, *The Age of Reform* (New York: Vintage Books, 1955).

86. Samuel P. Hays, "The Politics of Reform in Municipal Government in the Progressive Era," *Pacific Historical Review* 55, no. 4 (October 1964): 157–159.

87. Robert H. Wiebe, *Businessmen and Reform: A Study of the Progressive Movement* (Cambridge, MA: Harvard University Press, 1962); and Wiebe, *The Search for Order*.

88. Schiesl, *The Politics of Efficiency*; and Finegold, *Experts and Politicians*.

89. John Louis Recchiuti, *Social Science and Progressive Era Reform in New York City* (Philadelphia: University of Pennsylvania Press, 2007); and Dorothy Ross, *The Origins of American Social Science*.

90. Gabriel Kolko, *The Triumph of Conservatism: A Reinterpretation of American History, 1900–1916* (New York: Free Press, 1963).

91. John D. Buenker, *Urban Liberalism and Progressive Reform* (New York: Charles Scribner's, 1973).

92. Peter G. Filene, "An Obituary for the Progressive Movement," *American Quarterly* 22, no. 1 (Spring 1970): 20–34; and Daniel T. Rodgers, "In Search of Progressivism," *Reviews in American History* 10.4 (December 1982): 113–132.

93. Paul Boyer, *Urban Masses and Moral Order in America, 1820–1920* (Cambridge, MA: Harvard University Press, 1978); Michael McGerr, *A Fierce Discontent: The Rise and Fall of the Progressive Movement in America, 1870–1920* (New York: Free Press, 2003); and Jackson Lears, *Rebirth of a Nation: The Making of Modern America, 1877–1920* (New York: Harper, 2009).

94. Daniel T. Rodgers, "Capitalism and Politics in the Progressive Era and in Ours," *Journal of the Gilded Age and Progressive Era* 13, no. 3 (July 2014): 379–386; Robert D. Johnston, "Long Live Teddy/Death to Woodrow, 411–443; and Stromquist, *Reinventing the "People."*

95. Robyn Muncy, *Relentless Reformer: Josephine Roche and Progressivism in Twentieth-Century America* (Princeton, NJ: Princeton University Press, 2015).

Maureen A. Flanagan

THE GREAT DEPRESSION

CAUSES

The roots of the Great Depression remain somewhat opaque, and historical considerations of causation are often entangled with efforts to explain its length and severity. A global event, it requires study from multiple national perspectives; thus, it is hardly surprising that scholars lack consensus on its causes. Some historians emphasize short-term events, others long term trends, and still others tendencies intrinsic to capitalism. Within these frameworks, historians and economists debate different factors' significance, as well as the role of policy decisions and free market forces in either triggering or exacerbating the economic crisis that lasted longer than a decade.[1]

Nevertheless, many experts ascribe some causation to World War I, crediting that conflict with destabilizing economies and polities well into the 1920s. As one study of the global Depression reflected: "Absent the war, it is impossible to imagine a Great Depression."[2] With postwar disagreements over war debt payments and reparations, as well as policies to deal with inflation, deflation, tariffs, and restoration of the gold standard, sovereign nations struggled to coordinate international stabilization efforts, inaugurating an era of economic volatility. The United States suffered a recession from 1920 to 1922, and Germany experienced hyperinflation from 1921 to 1924. Both of these disrupted domestic economies, as well as international trade, debt repayment, and currency exchange rates.[3] One economic historian, for instance, concluded that the cumulative effect of debt, bank, and currency crises in the 1920s and early 1930s meant that "people began to lose faith in money itself."[4]

By committing to the return of a gold standard long considered the benchmark of a stable and prosperous economy, postwar governments had hoped to avoid that scenario. British officials, for instance, believed that putting the pound back on the gold standard would restore its reputation as the premier currency, although they also realized that a highly valued pound threatened to make their products more expensive and less attractive as exports. In addition, a gold standard meant that governments found themselves hemmed in by their own inflexible monetary policies.[5] Debtor nations that experienced a drain on their gold reserves (which were disproportionately owed the United States as a lender nation) had to contract their money supplies, and concomitantly to tighten credit and public spending. Without ample money to spend, European nations bought fewer American goods and faced increasingly higher tariffs on their exports, which further deprived them of much-needed revenue. These developments inhibited trade and adversely affected production, making it difficult for European economies to recover from the war.[6]

The American economy was vulnerable as well. Fueled by new farm technology and lower demand in Europe, overproduction and falling prices on numerous agricultural commodities in the 1920s pinched farm income. Even though agriculture had become proportionately less important to the overall economy by the 1920s, it still employed nearly 25 percent of working adults as late as 1929, and it

remained critical to a number of regions, including the South, parts of the Midwest, and the West Coast.[7] Congress attempted to pass legislation throughout the decade to remedy the economic distress, but farm debt deepened. In some states, as many as 85 percent of the farms had mortgages.[8] When agricultural incomes fell, farmers not only faced foreclosure on their property but also pressured the industrial sector by consuming fewer manufactured goods, and they burdened banks as they missed mortgage payments and drained their savings accounts.

Industries such as automobiles and electricity expanded throughout the 1920s, but the uneven distribution of wealth strained long-term consumer demand. Across geographic regions, working-class Americans faced seasonal layoffs, an antiunion environment, and stagnant wages. Middle- and working-class Americans fortunate enough to feel secure incurred debt buying homes and durable goods, such as automobiles and appliances. Wealth became increasingly concentrated at the top of the income scale over the course of the decade, with the richest 24,000 families in 1929 earning as much as the poorest 11.5 million. These families held one-third of all savings in the country, while 80 percent of Americans had no savings at all.[9] Consequently,

Figure 1. Farm auction in Iowa after a foreclosure between 1930 and 1940.
Courtesy Library of Congress, LC-DIG-fsa-8b08252.

large parts of the population could not buy the goods being pumped out by American manufacturers. Joined together in a dangerous cycle, overproduction and underconsumption threatened to upend an economy that increasingly demanded consumption.

In addition, speculative real estate and stock market booms revealed an unregulated economy vulnerable to reckless behavior. Starting in 1926, a real estate bubble in Florida burst, erasing fortunes and crippling banks.[10] Three years later, the stock market began its steep decline. Scholars tend to downplay the stock market crash of October 1929 as a singular explanation for the Depression because it represented a shock to an already distressed economy that lacked safeguards.[11] Even so, to contemporaries and generations of Americans afterward, the event served as a convenient marker for the start of the Depression and evidence of the dangers of a finance industry free of government oversight.

In early September 1929, the Dow Jones Industrial Average peaked at 381 points, with the volume of trades rising significantly as companies speculated, sometimes in their own stock, and others bought on margin or with borrowed money leveraged against their purchased stock. The crash came in late October. Between the eight sessions spanning Wednesday, October 23, and Thursday, October 31, the Dow Jones average dropped 54 points, from 327 to 273. It rallied for a bit and then began another slide, extending into mid-November, when the average fell to 199. With 12.9 million shares trading hands (the previous record was 8.3 million) on Black Thursday, October 24, the market set another record just a few days later on Tuesday, October 29, when 16.4 million changed hands, including substantial blocks of blue-chip stocks.[12] Between September and mid-November, $26 billion of wealth disappeared from the market.[13] With little intervention by the federal government or Federal Reserve, which declined to lower interest rates and loosen credit, the crash both reflected and intensified existing weaknesses in the economy.[14]

Continuing problems with international trade, agriculture, and some other key industries converged to muffle consumption in 1930. This caused a deflationary cycle. Falling prices and profits discouraged companies from investing and encouraged them to lay off workers. Unemployed and underemployed workers stopped consuming, which then shrunk companies' incentive to invest. High interest rates also dampened a desire to borrow money to expand operations. Meanwhile, the country stayed on the gold standard, limiting options for manipulation of the money supply to spur inflation.[15] The downward cycle grew worse. The following year, as European currencies went into a tailspin and Austria's largest bank failed, it became clear that a global recession was under way. In June 1932, the Dow Jones average hit 41, reflecting the nearly nonexistent state of investment and spurring a wave of bank panics in 1930, with more than 1,350 suspending operations. In excess of 3,800 banks closed their doors in the first three months of 1933. As a result, several states ceased bank operations, and the newly elected US president Franklin D. Roosevelt declared a "Bank Holiday" that shuttered all banks within days of his March 4 inauguration.[16]

From 1933 until the end of the decade, Roosevelt and Congress devised a number of New Deal policies and programs aimed at recovery. Some of these were holdovers from President Herbert Hoover's administration, while others broke new ground in federal economic policy. These policies failed to address racial and gender inequalities, however, and given the power of Southern Democrats along with prevailing assumptions about race and gender, they made those inequalities worse over time in some cases.

Nevertheless, under Roosevelt, the federal government made an effort to improve economic conditions. While Roosevelt's economic proposals were not necessarily driven by a commitment to a specific economic theory or model, they sought to raise prices and elevate employment. According to one economic historian, Roosevelt consistently strove to combat deflation by deploying monetary mechanisms.[17] On March 6, he used emergency powers to move the United States off the gold standard. At the same time, he pursued a balanced budget by supporting a new Economy Act (the first had been signed by Hoover in 1932) that slashed government spending through cuts to veterans' benefits and civil service employment. During the first Hundred Days, Roosevelt signed into law the Agricultural Adjustment Act (AAA) and National Industrial Recovery Act (NIRA) as measures designed to raise prices on agricultural goods and manufactured products. A multitude of other statutes aimed to stabilize prices in industries beset by cutthroat competition. The Civil Aeronautics Act of 1938, for instance, created a Civil Aeronautics Authority (later Board) to oversee airline rates and route allocations.

The president also recognized the devastation wrought by high unemployment rates and firmly believed that Americans preferred work relief rather than direct payments. For example, New Deal infrastructure programs, including the Civil Works Administration, Public Works Administration, Civilian Conservation Corps (CCC), Tennessee Valley Authority, and Works Progress Administration (WPA), provided employment as well as useful products.[18] Other policies targeting banking and housing addressed immediate needs and deeper systemic problems within these sectors. The establishment of the Federal Deposit Insurance Corporation (FDIC) in 1933, for instance, protected depositors and bolstered overall confidence in banks. Government mortgage assistance through the Home Owners Loan Corporation (1933) and Federal Housing Authority (1934) similarly benefited homeowners and builders.

From the depths of the Depression in 1933, the country moved toward recovery in the mid-1930s, with a downturn from 1937 to 1938, labeled the "Roosevelt Recession."

Crediting monetary policies that increased the money supply by an average of 10 percent between 1933 and 1937, economist Christina Romer calculated that the gross national product grew 33 percent from 1933 to 1937, declined 5 percent in 1938, and then rose 49 percent from 1938 to 1942.[19] Unemployment rates also moved downward, from 22.89 percent in 1932 to 9.18 percent in 1937.[20]

Tight money policies from the Federal Reserve in 1936, along with Roosevelt's decision in the summer of 1937 to balance the budget by scaling back spending on New Deal programs such as the WPA, pushed the country back into a recession. A greater commitment to defense preparedness as well as a return to expansionary monetary and fiscal policies, championed by a group of Roosevelt's advisors, brought growth in 1939. While unemployment rates and other economic indices in the mid- to late-1930s suggest that World War II, rather than the New Deal, ended the Depression, the trend of employment and economic growth after 1933 indicates the critical role that the New Deal played in the recovery.[21]

THE GREAT DEPRESSION BY THE NUMBERS

Scholars evaluating the Great Depression have had to use data largely constructed after the fact. Until the early 1930s, the US government lacked standard mechanisms for determining national output and did not routinely collect information on unemployment or other macroeconomic indices.[22] While somewhat incomplete and problematic, this information nevertheless illuminates patterns of deep and widespread economic collapse and deprivation. The historian William E. Leuchtenburg conveyed the enormity of the data as follows: "In heavily industrialized cities the toll of the depression read, as one observer noted, like British casualty lists at the Somme—so awesome as to become in the end meaningless, for the sheer statistics numbed the mind."[23]

Across several measures—unemployment, stock market averages, gross domestic product (GDP), and farm income—the period from 1932 to 1933 was the worst year of the Depression in the United States. GDP fell from $103.7 billion in 1929 to $56.4 billion in 1933; farm income plummeted from $6.2 billion to $2 billion in the same period.[24] Meanwhile, foreclosures increased sharply, from 150,000 in 1930 to 250,000 in 1932.[25] This trough was followed by several years of incremental growth, a significant downturn in 1937–1938 due to President Roosevelt's cuts to many New Deal programs (seeing them as emergency measures no longer needed), and then slow improvement until the war ushered in substantial investment, production, and full employment.

Steep declines in investment, which fell some 79 percent between 1929 and 1933, revealed an economy unable to produce goods or jobs.[26] Durable goods industries, a major source of employment, experienced the most contraction, with national income earned by these industries falling from $11.3 billion in 1929 to $2 billion in 1932. Automobile production, an industry tied to a multitude of other businesses ranging from rubber to car dealerships, fell 66 percent, and steel production fell 60 percent from 1929 to 1933. While nondurable industries suffered less dramatic reversals (a 50 percent decline in income from 1929 to 1932), the state of American business in the early 1930s was dismal. In January 1929, 92 percent of corporations earned a profit; in January 1933, only 38.6 percent did.[27]

Unemployment rates climbed in proportion to this sharp decline, rising nationally from 2.89 percent in 1929 to 22.89 percent in 1932 and falling slightly to 20.9 percent in 1933. But those figures do not capture the problem of underemployment or the shrinking incomes of those who continued to work.[28] Neither do they reflect the uneven distribution of unemployment across region, city, ethnicity, gender, and race. For example, in Detroit, unemployment rates among African-American women reached an astounding 69 percent in 1931; in Chicago, 55 percent; and in Pittsburgh, 41 percent. The overall unemployment rate in cities such as Akron rose to 80 percent, signifying to many the collapse of capitalism.[29] With pay falling from 55–60 percent in most industries between 1929 and 1932, Americans' purchasing power evaporated. Ordinary people had little money for food, shelter, or clothing, let alone other commodities—even at the lower prices that firms were forced to adopt amid deflation.[30] As Roosevelt observed in 1937, the Depression left "one-third of a nation ill-housed, ill-clad, [and] ill-nourished."[31]

Deprivation spanned the nation, but quantitative evidence indicates that the South, with

Figure 2. Scrappers in the Black Belt, Chicago, 1941.
Courtesy Library of Congress, LC-USF33-005189-M5.

its large agricultural economy, was the most impoverished region. With the price of cotton falling from 18 cents per pound in 1928 to 6.52 cents per pound in 1932, farm income barely kept landowners afloat. Harder hit were the tenants, sharecroppers, and farm laborers, who lacked any financial resources to withstand the crushing weight of the decline. The average seasonal price of rice fell by more than half between 1928 and 1932, from $2.02 to 93 cents per one hundred pounds.[32] Between 1929 and 1933, annual per-capita income in Mississippi went from an already paltry $239 to $117.[33] Psychological depression most certainly accompanied the economic depression, with the incidence of suicide rising from 13.9 suicides per 100,000 people in 1929 to 15.9 in 1933—a 14.4 percent increase.[34]

Financial stress took an emotional toll on family life. The marriage rate fell by nearly 11 percent between 1929 and 1933 before beginning a slow climb, perhaps reflecting a faith that the New Deal would stabilize the economy. Divorce rates also fell, but this was less a result of increased marital harmony than because staying together provided a better chance of economic survival. Many couples that separated chose abandonment over the more costly process of divorce. More tellingly, the birth rate fell 13.2 percent from 1929 to 1933, and then rose only 1.6 percent from 1933 to 1937, indicating people's reluctance to have children during a period of so much economic uncertainty. Indeed, the birth rate in the United States during the 1930s was the lowest of any decade from the mid-18th century to the end of the 20th century.[35]

Although they faced labor market discrimination, especially if they were married, women entered the workforce in increasing numbers during the 1930s. This was partly because employers preferred their cheaper labor, but also because they predominated in service, clerical, and domestic service jobs, which disappeared with a lower frequency than those in manufacturing. Nevertheless, women earned an average of $525 a year in 1937, compared to men's $1,027. Newspapers reported on homelessness among women, highlighting, for example, the several hundred who slept each night in Chicago's parks.[36]

WORK AND LABOR

American workers experienced the Depression in different ways. To some, it was a continuation of long-standing economic problems; to others, a new and immediate phenomenon; and to still others, it meant a gradual decline in employment hours and income. Workers in industries such as mining and agriculture felt their economic foothold narrow in the 1920s, as mechanization and falling commodity prices led to massive layoffs well before the stock market crash of 1929. But the labor market went from bad to catastrophic between 1930 and 1933.

In the heavy industries of the Midwest, between 40 and 50 percent of the labor force was idle. Ford Motor Company, for example, shed 37,000 of its 128,000 Michigan workers in the first few years of the Depression.[37] Statistics were similarly grim nationwide, with more than 12 million unemployed by 1933.[38] Those workers who held onto their jobs were often forced to accept reduced wages, itinerant hours, and chronic insecurity. As one farm worker recalled, "I got a job cutting asparagus, 15 cents an hour, as fast as you could move. I remember standing up to rub my aching back ... [and] the straw boss yelling, 'See those men standing by the road? They're just waiting to get you fired.'"[39] The labor market for those with jobs remained tenuous, as unemployment during the decade never dropped below 14 percent of the workforce.

This poor employment situation hardly seemed like a seedbed for organized labor. In 1932, Johns Hopkins labor economist George Barnett referenced the fewer than three million organized workers nationwide in declaring

Figure 3. Filipino lettuce pickers, Imperial Valley, California, 1939.
Courtesy Library of Congress, LC-DIG-fsa-8b33136.

that unionism "was lessening [in] importance." He concluded, "I see no reason to believe trade unionism will…become in the next decade a more potent social influence."[40] But Barnett and other pundits were mistaken. Even as the Depression created a labor crisis, it also exposed the limitations of welfare capitalism. Small local employers and ethnic- and race-based private charity institutions proved ill equipped to deal with the scale of the destitution. Many neighborhood ethnic associations, retailers, and radio stations were absorbed by national institutions, chain stores, and broadcast corporations in the 1930s, which helped usher forth a more homogenous working-class identity.[41] Organized labor seized upon these new conditions, as leaders overcame some of their previous divisions to transform the structure, demographics, and power of unions during the Depression.

Workers also made legal gains during the Depression, as the federal government established new protections of their rights. A small victory came with the Norris-LaGuardia Act, a 1932 ban on "yellow dog" contracts that prohibited a worker from joining a union as a condition of his or her employment. But the two watershed pro-labor laws came after the presidential election of Franklin D. Roosevelt, who packaged them as part of the first and second New Deals. Due in part to lobbying by United Mine Workers leader John L. Lewis, President Roosevelt signed the National Industrial Recovery Act (NIRA) into law in June 1933.[42] Largely a bill to stabilize the price of consumer goods, its section 7(a) asserted workers' rights to choose their own representatives and bargain collectively with their employers. This provision proved controversial; the Supreme Court declared the NIRA unconstitutional in May 1935, but not before the law inspired over one million new workers to join the American Federation of Labor (AFL).[43]

Before this Supreme Court ruling (and perhaps anticipating it), Democratic senator Robert F. Wagner of New York authored a bill to strengthen the collective bargaining provisions of section 7(a) by adding a list of unfair labor practices, establishing a process for democratic union elections within workplaces, and forming a federal National Labor Relations Board to regulate labor-management relations.[44] This bill was signed into law on July 5, 1935, and the Supreme Court reaffirmed its legality two years later. Even though it excluded public sector, agricultural, and domestic workers (with the latter two categories an acquiescence to Southern Democrats' desire to preserve Jim Crow labor exploitation), this act helped to deliver an unprecedented period of labor organization.[45]

The organizing and strikes that preceded the law that became known as the Wagner Act of 1935 also highlighted organized labor's institutional and conceptual limitations. Formed as a federation of skilled, craft unions, the AFL struggled to accommodate new semiskilled and unskilled members, many of whom were immigrants, racial minorities, and women. The AFL had a strong record of racial exclusion, often only reluctantly acknowledging segregated locals. On matters of sex, the AFL in 1931 reaffirmed its commitment to supporting male heads of households. This stance pressured many women, especially those who were married and working in male-typed occupations, to quit and make way for men.[46] By the AFL's 1935 convention, the group of union leaders whose members did both skilled and unskilled work (principally miners, clothing, and needlepoint workers) complained about the AFL's narrow vision, but it met stiff resistance from craft unionists, such as those in the building trades. Undeterred, these unions formed the Committee for Industrial Organization (later the Congress of Industrial Organizations, or CIO) in November 1935. Formed originally as a subsection of the AFL, the CIO began to act as a renegade union body well before it broke from the AFL in late 1938. Despite mutual tension and competition, each labor body grew to around four million members by decade's end.[47]

This union growth would not have been possible without workers' grass-roots organizing and strikes that often surged ahead of national leadership. Major strikes in 1934 by auto parts workers in Ohio, dockworkers in California, teamsters in Minnesota, and textile workers in the Northeast and South led the way in exposing ordinary workers' anger and militancy. With the exception of a defeated textile workers' campaign, these strikes won employer recognition and prefigured victories to come later in the decade. But as important, they often drew violent repression that led to public sympathy, solidarity among workers in different occupations, and even citywide strikes in San Francisco and Minneapolis.

The turning point came after 1935, when the CIO organizers took on the seemingly impossible task of organizing racially and ethnically diverse workers in America's major industries. Rubber workers in Ohio, steel workers in Indiana and Illinois, and autoworkers in Michigan led the way in revealing the new CIO's resolve.[48] The workers in Flint, Michigan, who struck at a General Motors plant in late 1936 targeted the nation's largest and most profitable employer. And they did so by employing the new tactic of the sit-down strike.

Pioneered by rubber workers in 1936 in an Ohio Goodyear plant, the strategy of sitting down and occupying the factory spread across the CIO. The Flint workers' six-week sit-down

Figure 4. Sitdown strikers, Fisher body plant, Flint, Michigan, 1937.
Courtesy Library of Congress, LC-DIG-fsa-8c28669.

Figure 5. Hobo "jungle," St. Louis, Missouri, 1936.
Courtesy Library of Congress, LC-DIG-fsa-8b27090.

strike prevented strikebreakers from entering the plant and helped protect the strikers from police and other antiunion violence. When the workers emerged victorious on February 11, 1937, the Detroit *News* declared, "Sitting down has replaced baseball as a national pastime."[49] With hindsight, one historian has declared the Flint workers' victory "the most significant American labor conflict in the twentieth century."[50] Shortly thereafter, the CIO's Steel Workers Organizing Committee's strike against Republic Steel seized the nation's attention, especially after a Paramount newsreel cameraman filmed police shooting dozens of peaceful workers, and killing ten, on Memorial Day.[51] Cumulatively, workers engaged in more than 5,000 strikes in 1937 and won 80 percent of them.[52]

By the end of the Depression, millions of unskilled and semiskilled workers had organized strong industrial unions, and craft unions had expanded as well. This made organized labor a powerful broker in the New Deal coalition, reshaping politics and culture nationwide. In politics, unions had partnered with the Democratic Party to precipitate a new era of government labor market regulation. Meantime, new forms of class consciousness, citizenship, and worker identification led to a "laboring of American culture" that identified a unique national American workers' culture in art, literature, and music that was produced by and for ordinary people.[53]

HOMELESSNESS, TRANSIENCE, AND MIGRATION

For those without a steady job, the Great Depression caused alarming levels of homelessness. Early in the decade, makeshift encampments of displaced people, called "Hoovervilles" (named in rebuke of President Hoover's denial of the depth of poverty) cropped up near rail yards and in other vacant urban areas. Meantime, public and private homeless shelters in major cities reported dramatic increases in demand, from 280 percent in St. Louis, to over 400 percent in Minneapolis, to over 700 percent in Cleveland and Detroit. By January 1933, federal authorities estimated that at least 1.5 million people had no permanent home.[54]

This destitution set many Americans on the move, in search of shelter and work. But the Great Depression unfolded between two periods of the Great Migration, when many rural and Southern Americans moved to the North and West to pursue industrial jobs in cities. The Depression years were distinct because uprooted people in the 1930s were less migratory than transient. Most moved around continuously, rather than leaving one place to settle in another.[55] There were "so many ridin' the freight," one hobo recalled, that "when a train would stop in a small town and the bums got off, the population tripled."[56] Indeed, the Southern Pacific Railway ejected over 687,000 people from its trains in 1932, up from only 78,000 five years earlier.[57]

The phenomenon of the hobo or tramp was not born in the 1930s. But this prevalent figure became a symbol of the Great Depression in 1932, when more than 25,000 homeless veterans brought demands to Washington, DC. The Bonus Expeditionary Force, a group of men mostly between the ages of 35 and 40, vowed to camp out in the city and govern themselves until the government paid the bonus owed to them for their service in World War I.[58] Congress declined to authorize this payment, and President Hoover took a similarly harsh approach. He ordered army tanks and infantry cavalry to burn the camp and disperse its residents. The Bonus Expeditionary Force never got paid, but it made the homelessness and poverty of patriotic men into an emblem of the failure of the government and the American Dream.[59]

By 1933, Americans increasingly saw the problem of transients as a national crisis that required government intervention. Unlike the previous era, when hobos were generally scorned and blamed for their own poverty, the Depression's dislocation came to seem like a result of systematic economic failure. People gave money to beggars, tolerated shantytowns in cities, and set up soup kitchens and shelters in record numbers. But private efforts could hardly keep pace with the problem. The Federal Transient Service (FTS), established in 1933, funded state-level proposals to assist transient people. FTS helped to serve more than one million homeless people in the two years before government officials shifted their focus to employment relief.[60]

The Great Depression also gave rise to new types of hobos, beyond working-age white men: young people, women, and racial minorities moved about the country as never before. At the height of the Depression, at least 250,000 youth roamed the country. Officials at the federal Children's Bureau feared the long-term effects of their homelessness. In addition, estimates of women on the road rose from a negligible amount between 4 to 10 percent of the transient population, and this figure is likely too low, considering that many female hobos dressed as men and boys for protection. The sharp increase in the transient population also included many African Americans. Whether in Hoovervilles, CCC camps, or on boxcars, they interacted with whites in

Figure 6. Flood refugees, near Cache, Illinois, 1937.
Courtesy Library of Congress, LC-DIG-fsa-8b30116.

desperate yet more egalitarian environments.[61] This influx of women and men of color on the road captured national attention in 1931 when police charged nine young black men with raping two white women on a train moving through Alabama. The "Scottsboro Boys" case became an international cause célèbre for the Communist Party, which eventually exposed the charges as false and indicted the US legal and economic system as exploitive along both race and gender lines.[62]

But no group of Americans captured more attention than the victims of the Dust Bowl, which triggered a national dialogue about Americans' relationship to the natural world and its rural citizens. During the 1930s, all farmers on the plains dealt with withered crops and starving livestock, but residents on the southern plains also faced massive dust storms caused by wind erosion. These storms came as the result of shortsighted farming techniques in the 1920s, as farmers tried to make up for declining wheat prices by using one-way disc plows to break up the sod that held the land in place and cultivate more acreage. By 1934, one dust storm alone in May carried 300 million tons of fertile soil as far as the Atlantic Ocean.[63] As one farmer

Figure 7. Dust storm, Cimarron County, Oklahoma, 1936.
Courtesy Library of Congress, LC-DIG-ppmsc-00241.

recalled, "oil was in that sand" of the dust storms, which stained everything "the most awful color you ever saw."[64]

The hunger and displacement that followed exposed an extreme variant of a similar agricultural depression nationwide, sparking new ideas and demands on how to make rural America a more sustainable resource base. New ideas and projects to rectify these crises included soil preservation, tree conservation, flood control, hydropower, and electrification. Some of these programs, such as the Soil Conservation Service (SCS) project of the Department of Agriculture, helped farmers who stayed put learn how to grow more sustainable crops.[65] Meanwhile, the CCC put people to work preserving and managing America's outdoor spaces, while also purporting to restore the health of unemployed workers through hearty outdoor labor.[66] Other federal and local programs, however, prioritized agribusiness and commodities over small farmers and conservation. The AAA, for example, paid farm owners to grow fewer crops, which led them to evict tenants and sharecroppers.

Many of these dispossessed agricultural workers headed west, where economic fortunes seemed more promising.[67] By 1939, when John Steinbeck's *The Grapes of Wrath* chronicled the Joad family's belabored exodus from the Dust Bowl in Oklahoma, the media already had labeled such migrants "Okies". This caricature, which became a powerful symbol of the Depression, was of a primitive, white Southern family steering its jalopy to the West Coast.[68] "America looked at the Dust Bowl migrants," one historian concluded, "and saw itself: first finding a symbol of Depression-era failure, later an affirmation of success and deliverance," as these migrants began to find work in war industries by the end of the decade.[69]

PROTEST POLITICS

The poverty and homelessness that pervaded in the early Depression years hit the unskilled, young, minority, and foreign born especially hard. Many developed survival strategies that began in their family and neighborhood networks, but small-scale private supports soon became overwhelmed. With little government help on the horizon in 1930, radical activists began to organize employment, anti-eviction, and relief demonstrations. These included Communists, Socialists, and followers of A. J. Muste, known as "Musteites". Socialists and Communists redoubled their earlier efforts to organize the poor, with the latter organizing Unemployment Councils based on the immediate needs of urban, working-class people. These councils organized an International Employment Day, which drew over a million people nationwide into demonstrations on March 6, 1930.[70] Their focus on bread-and-butter issues led many people to respect these radicals, with cries to "Run quick and find the Reds!" when authorities threatened eviction or withdrawal of emergency food relief.[71] Meantime, Musteites had more success in smaller towns and rural areas with religious and patriotic appeals that they linked to the Bonus Expeditionary Force. They organized the poor and middle-class unemployed in mining towns in Ohio, steel mills

Figure 8. Unemployed demonstration, Columbus, Kansas, 1936.
Courtesy Library of Congress, LC-DIG-fsa-8b27577.

in Pennsylvania, and textile areas of North Carolina.[72]

This early Depression movement had drawn only about 100,000 people to its official organizations by its 1933 peak, but it reshaped protest politics. In many large cities, activist networks won moratoriums on evictions and gained more relief for people out of work. They then became less militant as they coordinated with New Deal relief and legislative efforts and helped to broker the passage of the Social Security Act of 1935. These protests convinced many Americans that poverty resulted from economic forces rather than a lack of individual merit. The experience of demonstrating in the streets opened many Americans up to radical ideas and convinced them to become activists themselves.[73]

By 1935, early relief demonstrations had given way to larger mobilization, as coalitions converged around a common determination to expand American democracy and defeat the alarming spread of fascism abroad and at home. The Communist Party adopted a new Popular Front strategy to engage in broad antifascist campaigns with liberal New Dealers and Socialists alike. Some of these activists,

particularly African Americans, protested in their neighborhoods and outside Italian consulates in major cities against Italy's invasion of Ethiopia in October 1935. Thereafter, about three thousand leftists organized the Abraham Lincoln Brigade to fight overseas against a fascist takeover of Spain from 1937 to 1939.[74] Back home, the 1935 formation of the CIO brought a wave of organizing that spawned some progressive new unions committed to civil rights—a vision that extended beyond shop-floor grievances to incorporate other forms of democratic and antiracist protest politics, mirroring the Communist Party slogan of "Negro and White: Unite and Fight."[75]

This nationwide push to organize the unorganized yielded unions that were also social movements. The Southern Tenant Farmers' Union (STFU) demanded that planters cut

Figure 9. Evicted sharecroppers, roadside demonstration, New Madrid County, Missouri, January 1939.
Courtesy Library of Congress, LC-DIG-fsa-8a10485.

agricultural workers a piece of the federal subsidies that they received to remove more than 50 percent of the region's cotton acreage from production.[76] The Socialist-led STFU and its Communist-led rival United Cannery, Agricultural, Packing and Allied Workers Union (UCAPAWA) openly challenged the racial apartheid of the Southern government and plantation system. These unions also embraced new organizing tactics—such as hiring itinerant radical preachers—in promoting social justice activism that crossed geographic, racial, and religious denominational lines.[77]

Meanwhile, in urban areas, unions such as the United Auto Workers, United Packinghouse Workers of America, and United Electrical Workers served as training grounds for working-class activists who became significant grassroots social movement leaders.[78] These included women and racial minorities, who developed feminist and antiracist class positions within and beyond the labor movement. As Depression-era unions expanded, however, they remained male dominated. The membership of the International Ladies Garment Workers Union, for example, increased by 500 percent, or 200,000 members, during the Depression. But while three-quarters of its members were women, there was only one woman on its twenty-four-member national executive board.[79]

Seeking to capitalize on these new forms of protest politics, a network of African-American intellectuals, activists, and workers developed new challenges to poverty, as well as early New Deal policies that excluded or discriminated against them. In 1935, they formed the National Negro Congress (NNC) and elected the well-known civil rights and labor champion Asa Philip Randolph as its president. Two years later, NNC activists formed the Southern Negro Youth Congress, an offshoot that dealt more explicitly with the problems of African-American youth in the South. These organizations revived a black-led and working-class dimension to the Black Freedom Movement by uniting select activists and unionists for

Figure 10. Selling Father Coughlin's *Social Justice* newspaper, New York City, 1939. Courtesy Library of Congress, LC-DIG-fsa-8b33832.

antifascist goals spanning from economic justice to protection from lynching and police brutality. While the NNC did not deliver a fatal "Death Blow to Jim Crow," it and others reoriented many communities toward a more aggressive stance on civil rights and pressured more conservative racial uplift organizations, labor unions, and New Deal liberals to embrace more militant tactics and goals.[80]

The Depression years also saw the development of regional social movements that were subsequently incorporated, coopted, or cast off by the New Deal state. When Franklin Roosevelt called for "bold, persistent experimentation" in a May 1932 speech, he inspired many interest groups to coalesce and demand reforms within the emerging broker-state that would define the New Deal during his presidency.[81] These included movements galvanized under a single leader or voice, such as governor and senator Huey Long and his Share Our Wealth Plan in Louisiana, the radio celebrity priest Charles Coughlin and his National Union for Social Justice in Michigan, the socialist Upton Sinclair and his End Poverty in California movement, and physician Francis Townsend and his Townsend

Plan for old-age insurance.[82] The Roosevelt administration drew from some of these organic movements—for example, by incorporating progressive taxation and old-age insurance into the New Deal—while eschewing others, especially when they evinced elements of fascism themselves.

DEPRESSION-ERA CULTURE

Despite their economic deprivation, Americans built a rich cultural life during the Great Depression. At times supported by the government through the WPA's Federal One projects, the US Treasury Department's art program, the Farm Security Administration's (FSA) photography program, and other initiatives, creative minds demonstrated an astounding commitment to engaging broad audiences and celebrating diverse American identities. Throughout the decade, cultural workers grappled with the same ideological currents running through the labor movement and practical realities facing those who were forced to rove around the nation. Woven into American culture, whether elite or popular, were reflections of the struggles facing ordinary people, critiques of a capitalist system that appeared broken, celebrations of American values, and utopian visions of the future. Artists sought to put a human face on the mind-numbing statistics that often defined the Depression in politics and the media.

In the end, both the creators and recipients of culture reckoned with the Depression in multiple and sometimes contradictory ways. On the one hand, audiences embraced philosophical and political themes that allowed them to wrestle with questions of power and individual agency. On the other hand, tens of millions of Americans went to the cinema, listened to radio soap operas, attended sporting events, and read comic books to escape temporarily from the pervasive anxiety of hard economic times.

Among intellectuals of the decade, the Depression encouraged explorations of the human condition pushed to its limits, as well as the marriage of art to activism. The existence of a Popular Front in cultural circles meant that working-class experiences, racial oppression, the nature of protest, and the threat of fascism appeared as topics and themes in the literature, photography, film, and music of the Great Depression. The messages varied, as a vibrant leftist perspective challenged the viability of capitalism, while liberal critics advocated for remedies within the existing system.[83]

Through searing literature, authors Richard Wright and John Steinbeck, for instance, drew attention to inequalities that challenged American narratives of upward mobility through hard work. Wright's *Uncle Tom's Children* (1938), a book of short stories, and *Native Son* (1940), a Book-of-the-Month Club selection, gave voice to racial and class oppression. Wright's characters, including Bigger Thomas of *Native Son*, face multiple injustices, yet they ultimately find a path out of alienation and toward agency. Wright probed the intersection of class and race as he highlighted the extreme violence at the foundation of racial hierarchies. Although he showcased working-class protagonists, Steinbeck often stopped short of a radical critique of the system. For instance, despite the hardships faced by the Joad family and the criticism leveled at banks and large landowners in Steinbeck's bestselling novel, *The Grapes of Wrath* (1939), the story does not advocate collective farm ownership. Instead, it aims to restore American faith in the small family farm and calls for a collective action akin to small-town community rather than Communism. At the same time, Steinbeck's realistic rendering of the Joads' trials resonated with American readers.

Frequently eliding the space between fact and fiction, writers and visual artists drew inspiration from their factual observations of

Depression-era America to craft emotional stories with a social justice message. In the tradition of social realism, Steinbeck traveled through farm communities and farm labor camps in California, penning a series of articles, "The Harvest Gypsies," for the *San Francisco News*. His research became the basis for *The Grapes of Wrath*, but he also reprinted the articles with photographs from Dorothea Lange in a pamphlet called *Their Blood Is Strong*. In turn, John Ford, the director of the film version of *The Grapes of Wrath*, which was released a year after the book's publication, modeled scenes on photographs of agricultural labor taken by Lange. Writer and anthropologist Zora Neale Hurston relied on her sensitive ear for folklore and dialect, penning fictional works that demonstrated not only the obstacles confronting poor African Americans, but also their ability to forge community and achieve self-realization.

Wright, Hurston, and Lange understood firsthand the value of public support for cultural production. For a time, Wright and Hurston found work with the WPA Federal

Figure 11. Dorothea Lange, FSA photographer, in California, 1936.
Courtesy Library of Congress, LC-DIG-fsa-8b27245.

Writers' Project, and Lange was one of the forty photographers employed by the FSA's Historical Section between 1935 and 1943 who documented the effects of the Depression on people and landscapes. Working on city and state guides for the Writers' Project in Chicago and New York by day, Wright wrote his own fiction at night. Wright and others on the project, according to one scholar, "were distilling a synthesis of fictional invention, autobiographical reflection, and urban field work" in their own writing.[84] Hurston's work collecting rural African American folklore illustrated how the New Deal fostered democratic values, with an emphasis on culture that was open to and represented all Americans, not just the privileged few.[85] Significantly, Lange's photographs of migrant farm workers, Georgia peach pickers, impoverished tenants, and others across the country brought to middle- and upper-class audiences an accounting of the Depression's ravaging effects on the poor.[86]

Photojournalism flourished during the period and challenged the boundary between journalism and art. With her husband, economist Paul Taylor, Lange published *American Exodus* (1940), showcasing her photographs accompanied by essays that sought to ground their meaning. But white authors and photographers tended to ignore or gloss over the presence and exploitation of Mexican, Filipino, and African Americans. Wright responded by publishing *Twelve Million Black Voices* (1941), featuring FSA photographs by Edwin Rosskam, which told the story of their distinct migration. Painter Jacob Lawrence visualized these experiences in his 1941 "Migration Series," calling attention to the violence and low wages that prompted African Americans to leave the South. Other painters turned to regional and historical themes, portraying characteristics that they believed would carry Americans through hard times in a genre referred to as the "American Scene." Some American Scene paintings, such as those of Thomas Hart Benton, celebrated the distinctive American values of hard work, fortitude, and thrift. Not surprisingly, Benton provided illustrations for *The Grapes of Wrath*.

In mass entertainment, producers and writers addressed class relations, but they often emphasized bridges rather than divisions. *Superman*, first published as a comic book in 1938, followed the exploits of journalist Clark Kent, an ordinary man imbued with super-human powers. In the third Action Comic of this series, *The Blakely Mine Disaster*, Superman characteristically uses his powers on behalf of the underdog. While rescuing a miner trapped in a shaft, Superman discovers that deficient safety measures caused the collapse. As Clark Kent, he confronts the mine owner, who denies any knowledge of, or responsibility for, the situation. Consequently, Superman arranges to have the owner and his wealthy friends trapped in the unsafe mine so that they understand the necessity of fixing the problem. After this harrowing experience, the enlightened mine owner pledges to adhere to the most rigid safety standards in the industry.[87]

Popular screwball comedies and dramatic films of the decade similarly reveal class divisions or political corruption but end with sanguine messages about the ultimate goodness inherent in the wealthiest capitalists.[88] In director Gregory La Cava's 1936 film, *My Man Godfrey*, rich socialite Irene Bullock (Carole Lombard) takes in a "forgotten man," Godfrey Smith (William Powell), hiring him as her family's butler. As it turns out, Godfrey, a Harvard graduate, hails from a Boston Brahmin family. He nearly committed suicide due to a failed love affair, but he was saved and taken in by the forgotten men of "the dump," a New York City Hooverville. There, he learned that "the only difference between a derelict and a man is a job." As the Bullock family butler, Godfrey helps each member of the family discover the common humanity binding together rich and poor. Consequently, in spite of their aristocratic status and frivolous lifestyle, the Bullocks are not irredeemable. In the end, Godfrey chooses to start a restaurant and open housing for the homeless on the waterfront once occupied by a Hooverville, using his inheritance as seed money for this profitable industry. No New Deal is required.

Another dramatic example was Margaret Mitchell's *Gone with the Wind*, which ends with Scarlett O'Hara optimistically declaring "Tomorrow is another day." This historical drama was the bestselling novel of 1936 and 1937 before becoming a wildly popular film in 1939. However, groups of African Americans and their allies picketed theaters to contest the book and movie's cultural depiction of docile slaves and victimized white Southern planters as false history.[89] As these films and others suggest, mainstream Hollywood did not necessarily support substantial government intervention to address inequalities, whereas the working class and minorities simultaneously created and revived new forms of culture to push for an industrial democracy.[90]

For many Americans, popular culture, such as comic books, games, and spectator sports provided much-needed escapism at little cost. But even there, the influence of contemporary politics and a depressed economy were evident. Tellingly, *Monopoly*, which had players vying for real estate, paying dreaded income taxes, and sometimes gouging other players for rent on high-end properties, was one of the most popular board games of the era. As one cultural historian remarked, in an era in which competitive capitalism had broken down, Americans seemed drawn to games that "held out the opportunity to compete and the hope of winning within a stable framework of rules."[91] Ordinary people also flocked to professional baseball games and listened to epic boxing matches on the radio, including some rife with racial and national symbolism, as when Joe Louis, the "Brown Bomber," twice fought German Max Schmeling in the 1930s. Thus, even sporting events could not always avoid political symbolism. African American track star Jessie Owens, for instance, took home four gold medals at the 1936 Berlin Olympics a year after the Nazis and Adolf

Hitler adopted the Nuremberg laws, a series of racial statutes that proclaimed the superiority of "Aryans."

Depression-era culture also displayed optimism, as Americans looked toward a better future. As the decade closed and war clouds hovered over Europe, the New York World's Fair opened with the hopes of reviving the city's lagging economy and showcasing the benefits of American democracy. Built around a theme known as the "World of Tomorrow," a team of industrial designers projected their vision of the ideal society, in which technology, democracy, and efficiency forged a seamless whole. Private corporations sponsored many of the fair's exhibits, including "Futurama," located inside the Trylon, one of two structures at the center of the fair. Spotlighting the automobile as the unifying force for the country, General Motors transported fairgoers to 1960 and a world of superhighways connecting skyscrapers and greenbelts. Absent public transportation, technology promised individuals prosperity, convenience, and order.

Next to the Trylon, the Perisphere housed "Democracity," the fair's theme exhibit, where public money and government regulation influenced urban design, with residents living in tall apartment houses, suburban garden developments, or satellite communities. In this planned community, however, people still relied upon private automobiles and highways to link its disparate parts. Unfortunately, many ordinary people could not afford the fair's average cost of $5 for a day of activities; attendance underperformed expectations, and the corporation running the fair declared bankruptcy.[92] Even so, the "World of Tomorrow" took the eyes of fairgoers off the present and the past, diverting their attention from ten long years of economic deprivation and toward visions of a thriving capitalist and more democratic nation.

DISCUSSION OF THE LITERATURE

Even as the Great Depression was unfolding, scholars sought to understand its causes and consequences. The conversation continues, and in some corners, it has intensified since the onset of the Great Recession in 2008. While the Great Depression worsened in the early 1930s, economists, social scientists, and others collected and scrutinized data in an effort to obtain clarity on why the Depression occurred, how to address it, and what it meant to the millions of Americans experiencing its ravages. In fact, in seeking to document its effects through photographs, oral history interviews, sound recordings of music, and written reports, among other works, government workers in the 1930s provided a wealth of material for future historians as they pioneered the practice of social and cultural history. Critically, that work has enriched scholarship on the decade, moving historians beyond an equation of the Great Depression with the New Deal and into studies that probe the rich tapestry of American life outside the confines of electoral politics and federal policies.

Historians and economists often have pointed to poor decision-making to explain why this economic downturn became the Great Depression. In the early years of the Depression, British economist John Maynard Keynes, a pioneer in macroeconomics, shared with government officials in Britain and the United States his theories on monetary policy and countercyclical public spending. His views offered a fundamental challenge to conventional perceptions that "market economies were naturally stable, and that the only macro-economic task of government was to maintain sound money."[93] A proponent of an active, and flexible, monetary policy to control deflation, Keynes also came to advocate for fiscal policies to stimulate growth, especially if monetary adjustments proved inadequate.

During a deflationary cycle when prices, expenditures, and employment plummeted into a death spiral, how could demand be spurred, investment increased, and employment expanded? Over the course of the 1930s, Keynes answered this question by arguing that during periods of recession and depression, governments should raise expenditures, even if it meant deficit spending. Doing so flushed money into the economy, restored consumers' purchasing power, and elevated demand, which in turn enticed businesses to increase output and hire more people. Keynes published his seminal work, *The General Theory of Employment, Interest, and Money* in 1936. While his views did not have a substantial influence on the direction that Roosevelt took economic policy in the 1930s, they gradually became accepted among many American policymakers.[94] Keynesians thus espoused a path that directly involved government in the economy, rather than a belief in a hands-off approach to business cycles. When World War II and an expanded state seemed to confirm the need for government outlays to keep unemployment relatively low and the economy stable, free market advocates lost some influence. Perhaps most important, Keynes's ideas influenced how economists and historians in the post-war era understood the causes of, and evaluated responses to, the Great Depression.

After the 1950s, a group of economists focused on a flawed monetary policy as the explanation for the deflation that defined the Great Depression. They suggested that fears of inflation in the United States and Europe may have encouraged countries to pursue deflationary policies, such as tightening of the money supply, when faced with recession. In 1963, Milton Friedman, an economist at the University of Chicago, and Anna Schwartz, an economist at the National Bureau of Economic Research, blamed American monetary policy for the Great Depression, asserting that the Federal Reserve's failure to expand the money supply led to the uncontrollable deflationary cycle.[95] Their analysis legitimated a conservative view that called for limited government intervention in the economy, thus challenging the more assertive government role called for by a Keynesian approach.[96]

In the 1980s and 1990s, Peter Temin, Charles Kindleberger, and Barry Eichengreen reframed the debate over the Great Depression's cause, as well as the appropriate cure, by pointing to the unique role that adherence to the gold standard played in instigating deflation.[97] In his work, Temin asserted that a "gold standard ideology" tied governments to a rigid money supply, preventing them from embracing policies that would have grown the money supply and inflated prices. Rising prices would have increased profits and encouraged companies to invest, expand production, and hire employees. Using their income, employees would have begun to consume again, stimulating demand and sparking a growth cycle. Data supported the idea that those countries that went off the gold standard first tended to recover first from the Great Depression.[98] Most recently, Charles R. Morris, in a less academic treatment of the Depression that applied elements from Temin and Kindleberger, emphasized the importance of global forces in pushing an economic downturn in the United States into a worldwide Great Depression.[99]

For other scholars (and contemporaries), the Great Depression was merely a reflection of the natural business cycles of boom and bust driven by capitalism. In this framework, the roots of the Depression require little investigation because busts allow the market to correct itself by purging weak firms, laying the groundwork for a new period of growth. The only lesson that it suggested for future policymakers was minimal-to-no government interference, in order to allow the market to make its own corrections. Low wages and prices, they maintained, eventually stimulated economic expansion, and therefore efforts to raise prices and wages such as the NIRA (1933), NLRA (1935), and Fair Labor Standards Act (1938) inhibited investment and recovery.[100]

At the other end of the spectrum, Marxists and other critics of capitalism saw in the Great Depression evidence of flaws built into a system based on private ownership and labor exploitation. While they perceived the solution as government control and nationalization (or collective ownership) of industries, they considered the Great Depression a consequence of large, impersonal, and somewhat uncontrollable forces that exemplified the fragility and human suffering intrinsic to capitalism. Scholars favoring a free market shared a similar view of the inevitability of booms and busts in a capitalist system; however, unlike Marxists, they understood these cycles as signs of a self-correcting system that was ultimately more beneficial than harmful to the economy and society.[101]

In conversation with conservative critics, a strong cohort of scholars who have examined why the depression ended—as opposed to why it began—have presented evidence of the New Deal's effectiveness, crediting it, rather than World War II, with stimulating the recovery. Christina Romer's 1992 article, "What Ended the Great Depression?" Gauti Eggertsson's 2008 article "Great Expectations," and Eric Rauchway's 2015 book, *The Money Makers*, explore New Deal decisions and measures that halted national economic decline and promoted economic growth.[102] At the same time, economists such as Paul Krugman and Dean Baker have reasserted Keynesian interpretations of the Depression's causes and effects. They, as well as Federal Reserve chair Ben Bernanke (2006–2014), advocated a massive government stimulus package to combat the 2008 Great Recession by taking lessons from the 1930s Great Depression.[103]

In assessing the politics of economic recovery, historians Kathryn Olmsted, Elliot Rosen, and Kim Phillips-Fein revisited the Great Depression during the 2008 recession to argue that opposition to the New Deal in the 1930s reveals the roots of modern conservatism. These scholars have analyzed the shifting Republican Party ideology with its commitment to laissez-faire economics (as elucidated in Herbert Hoover's 1934 book, *The Challenge of Liberty*), as well as the lobbying of business and especially agribusiness leaders, who allied with journalists to castigate labor as an assault of traditional gender and racial norms.[104]

Broadening the view of the Depression beyond its economic dimensions, historians have moved from top-down political narratives about the Depression and New Deal to bottom-up social and cultural perspectives.

Although there was never a rigid divide between political, social, and cultural history or a complete disregard of the lives of ordinary people, most historians at first studied the Great Depression through the lens of the New Deal. Arthur Schlesinger's three-volume study *The Age of Roosevelt* and William Leuchtenburg's *Franklin D. Roosevelt and the New Deal, 1932–1940*, framed many subsequent studies of the Depression.[105]

With the flowering of social history in the 1960s and 1970s, historical studies of the Depression era turned toward the lives of industrial workers, sharecroppers, tenants, transients, Dust Bowl migrants, and numerous other groups of ordinary people. Increasingly, historians have emphasized how regional grass-roots movements took President Roosevelt's ideas of experimentation and the broker-state seriously, as they organized to push for more robust conceptions and applications of citizenship and security. This perspective has led to a reassessment of the Dust Bowl migration, as well as a broadening of who rode the rails and why in the 1930s.[106] Historians also have focused on new forms of unionism and militancy among the working class, especially during the second half of the decade.[107] More recently, others have emphasized impactful, yet internally combative, antifascist alliances between liberals and radicals. These activists, particularly those informed by the Black Freedom struggle, linked economic justice and antiracist concerns that brought forth a "decisive first phase" of the modern civil rights movement.[108]

The study of social movements during the Depression—from the rise of industrial unionism to the growth of American radicalism—always has been a major focus of historians of the era. Early works focused on how the efforts of the forgotten men (and women) of President Roosevelt's New Deal to lobby the federal government for programs, as well as to demand existing relief, become more robust and equitable.[109] Another set of studies highlighted the activities of the Communist Party and other more radical attempts to overthrow or transform American capitalist institutions.[110]

While this give-and-take with the New Deal broker-state and its radical political alternatives certainly remains central to 1930s histories, other scholars have concentrated on grassroots social movements that operated within the broader context of the hardships and opportunities presented by the Great Depression. During the second half of the decade, many liberals and radicals joined under the umbrella of the Popular Front, responding to the global rise of fascism with protest politics that connected local campaigns to national and international ones.[111] In the meantime, African Americans and their allies fomented antiracist demands and fostered activism that represented much more than a prelude to the postwar civil rights movement.[112] While most historians agree that economic hardship alone did not necessarily inspire organized resistance, they have sought to analyze why so many Americans nonetheless worked to redress preexisting and widening inequalities and enact visions for a more participatory and egalitarian democracy, which widens the terrain of protest politics from being framed as synonymous with New Deal politics.

Related to this emphasis on ordinary Americans' experiences of the 1930s, scholars have connected protest politics to the artistic achievements of those years. Recent works have examined how an expansion of mass culture, aided by government support, was produced by and for working-class Americans. From the writings of African-American and ethnic authors, to popular music such as jazz, blues, and country, to gangster movies and *film noir*, these artists and genres defined new ideas of American cultural achievement and identity that circulated the globe in the Depression years and thereafter.[113]

PRIMARY SOURCES

Given the scope and complexity of the Great Depression, students will find no single archive or set of primary sources sufficient to master the topic. Fortunately, many primary sources on a wide variety of topics relating to the Depression have been published in books and are readily available. In addition, the proliferation of source-rich websites (see "Digital Materials") allows scholars easy access to written, visual, oral, and aural documentation of the era.

Those interested in the economic history of the period should consult *Historical Statistics of the United States*, edited by Susan B. Carter et al., which is available through many research library databases. Especially helpful are tables grouped under the heading "Great Depression Series" and accompanying essays, which explain the limitations of the data from this era. US government agencies such as the Census Bureau and Department of Labor (including the Women's Division) produced reports during the period that contain a wealth of data. Libraries designated as government document depositories are the best places to search for these reports. Frederick E. Hosen's *The Great Depression and the New Deal: Legislative Acts in Their Entirety (1932–1933) and Statistical Economic Data (1926–1946)* contains sixty-three pages of tables.[114] Data from the 1930 US Census and 1940 US Census may be fruitful as well.

A number of published books and collections provide glimpses into the hopes, fears, and desires of ordinary Americans during the Depression. Scholars have mined the papers of Franklin and Eleanor Roosevelt, publishing letters that they received during their years in the White House. See, for example, Robert McElvaine, *Down and Out in the Great Depression: Letters from the Forgotten Man*; Robert Cohen, *Dear Mrs. Roosevelt: Letters from Children of the Great Depression*; and Cathy Knepper, *Dear Mrs. Roosevelt: Letters to Eleanor Roosevelt Through Depression and War*.[115] Gerald Markowitz and David Rosner gathered letters from a variety of government archives to document the lives of the working class in *"Slaves of the Depression": Workers' Letters About Life on the Job*.[116] The multivolume *Documentary History of the Franklin D. Roosevelt Presidency* contains reports, drafts of legislation; correspondence, including letters written by ordinary Americans to Roosevelt during the Depression; and myriad primary sources on topics ranging from agriculture to social security to foreign affairs. For transcribed oral histories from people who lived through the period, see for instance, Studs Terkel, *Hard Times: An Oral History of the Great Depression,* and the oral histories of labor activists conducted by Professor Elizabeth Balanoff at Roosevelt University.[117]

During the Depression, relief administrators sent former reporter Lorena Hickok on the road to report on the lives of ordinary people. Those pieces are available in Richard Lowitt and Maurine Beasely, *One Third of a Nation: Lorena Hickok Reports on the Great Depression.*[118] Robert and Helen Lynd's two studies of Middletown, Indiana, also provide insight from the perspective of ordinary Americans: *Middletown: A Study in Modern American Culture* and *Middletown in Transition: A Study in Cultural Conflicts.*[119]

Potential archival collections are too numerous to list and depend highly upon the specific topic of interest. Even so, searches with specific terms, or for some major archives, terms as broad as "New Deal" and "Great Depression" may yield relevant sources and finding aids. Major archives with substantial holdings on the 1930s include the Franklin D. Roosevelt Presidential Library and Museum in Hyde Park, New York; the George Meany Memorial AFL-CIO Archives in College Park, Maryland; the Wayne State Archives of Labor and Urban Affairs in Detroit; the Smithsonian Institution's Archives of American Art (which has substantial manuscript and oral history collections related to New Deal artists); the Schomburg Center for Research in Black Culture in New York City; and the Library of Congress Manuscript Division in Washington, DC. Papers, maps, and photographs relating to federal agencies are housed at the National Archives and Records Administration, primarily at National Archives II in College Park, Maryland.

The National Archives also maintains regional archives throughout the country.

DIGITAL MATERIALS

America in the 1930s, American Studies at the University of Virginia. http://xroads.virginia.edu/~1930s/front.html.

American Presidency Project, University of California, Santa Barbara. http://www.presidency.ucsb.edu/.

Elizabeth Balanoff Labor Oral History Collection. http://roosevelt.edu/balanoff.

Archives of American Art, Smithsonian Institution, the New Deal and the Arts Oral History Project. https://www.aaa.si.edu/.

Eleanor Roosevelt Papers, George Washington University. https://erpapers.columbian.gwu.edu/online-documents.

Franklin D. Roosevelt Four Freedoms Digital Resources. http://fdr4freedoms.org/.

Franklin D. Roosevelt Presidential Library. https://fdrlibrary.org/.

National Archives and Records Administration. https://www.archives.gov/.

The Great Depression and New Deal, National Archives at Seattle. https://www.archives.gov/seattle/exhibit/picturing-the-century/great-depression.html.

The Great Depression and the New Deal. Picturing the Century at the National Archives. https://www.archives.gov/exhibits/picturing_the_century/galleries/greatdep.html.

Stories from the Great Depression, National Archives at Atlanta. https://www.archives.gov/atlanta/videos. Library of Congress. https://www.loc.gov/.

American Memory. https://memory.loc.gov/ammem/browse/updatedList.html.

Prosperity and Thrift: The Coolidge Era and the Consumer Economy, 1921–1929. https://memory.loc.gov/ammem/coolhtml/coolhome.html.

Lomax Family at the American Folklife Center (music). https://www.loc.gov/folklife/lomax/index.html.

Documenting America, 1935–1943: The Farm Security Administration/Office of War Information Photo Collection. http://www.loc.gov/rr/program/journey/fsa.html.

The Living New Deal. https://livingnewdeal.org/.

Mercury Theater on the Air. http://www.mercury theatre.info/.

Studs Terkel, Conversations with America, Chicago History Museum. http://studsterkel.matrix.msu .edu/.

FURTHER READING

Amenta, Edwin. *When Movements Matter: The Townsend Plan and the Rise of Social Security.* Princeton, NJ: Princeton University Press, 2006.

Brendon, Piers. *The Dark Valley: A Panorama of the 1930s.* New York: Vintage Books, 2002.

Brinkley, Alan. *Voices of Protest: Huey Long, Father Coughlin, and the Great Depression.* New York: Knopf, 1982.

Cohen, Lizabeth. *Making a New Deal: Industrial Workers in Chicago, 1919–1939.* 2nd ed. New York: Cambridge University Press, 2008.

Cooney, Terry A. *Balancing Acts: American Thought and Culture in the 1930s.* New York: Twayne Publishers, 1995.

Denning, Michael. *The Cultural Front: The Laboring of American Culture in the Twentieth Century.* New York: Verso, 1997.

Dickstein, Morris. *Dancing in the Dark: A Cultural History of the Great Depression.* New York: W. W. Norton, 2009.

Dolinar, Brian. *The Black Cultural Front: Black Writers and Artists of the Depression Generation.* Jackson: University Press of Mississippi, 2012.

Eichengreen, Barry. *Golden Fetters: The Gold Standard and the Great Depression, 1919–1939.* New York: Oxford University Press, 1992.

Fearon, Peter. *War, Prosperity, and Depression: The U.S. Economy, 1917–45.* Lawrence: University Press of Kansas, 1987.

Gellman, Erik S. *Death Blow to Jim Crow: The National Negro Congress and the Rise of Militant Civil Rights.* Chapel Hill: University of North Carolina Press, 2012.

Gordon, Linda. *Dorothea Lange: A Life Beyond Limits.* New York: Norton, 2009.

Gregory, James. *American Exodus: The Dust Bowl Migration and Okie Culture in California.* New York: Oxford University Press, 1989.

Katznelson, Ira. *Fear Itself: The New Deal and the Origins of Our Time.* New York: Liveright, 2013.

Kelley, Robin D. G. *Hammer and Hoe: Alabama Communists During the Great Depression.* Chapel Hill: University of North Carolina Press, 1990.

Kennedy, David M. *Freedom from Fear: The American People in Depression and War, 1929–1945.* Oxford: Oxford University Press, 1999.

Klein, Maury. "The Stock Market Crash of 1929: A Review Article," *Business History Review* 75, no. 2 (Summer 2001): 325–351.

Kusmer, Kenneth. "From Tramp to Transient: The Great Depression." In *Down and Out, on the Road: The Homeless in American History,* 193–220. New York: Oxford University Press, 2002.

Leuchtenburg, William. *The Perils of Prosperity, 1914–1932.* Chicago: The University of Chicago Press, 1958.

Morris, Charles. *A Rabble of Dead Money: The Great Depression and the Global Depression, 1929–1939.* New York: Public Affairs, 2017.

Pells, Richard. *Radical Visions, American Dreams: Culture and Social Thought in the Depression Years.* New York: Harper and Row, 1973.

Rauchway, Eric. *The Money Makers: How Roosevelt and Keynes Ended the Depression, Defeated Fascism, and Secured a Prosperous Peace.* New York: Basic Books, 2015.

Rosen, Elliot. *The Republican Party in the Age of Roosevelt: Sources of Anti-Government Conservatism in the United States.* Charlottesville: University of Virginia Press, 2014.

Scharf, Lois. *To Work and To Wed: Female Employment, Feminism, and the Great Depression.* Westport, CT: Greenwood Press, 1980.

Temin, Peter. *Lessons from the Great Depression.* Cambridge, MA: MIT Press, 1989.

White, Ahmad. *The Last Great Strike: Little Steel, the CIO, and the Struggle for Labor Rights in New Deal America.* Berkeley: University of California Press, 2016.

Zieger, Robert. *The CIO: 1935–1955.* Chapel Hill: University of North Carolina Press, 1995.

NOTES

1. The most significant works on the economic causes of the Great Depression include John Kenneth Galbraith, *The Great Crash, 1929* (New York: Time Inc., 1962); Milton Friedman and Anna Schwartz, *The Great Contraction, 1929–1933* (Princeton, NJ: Princeton University Press, 1964); John Garraty, *The Great Depression: An Inquiry into the Causes, Course, and Consequences of the Worldwide Depression of the Nineteen-Thirties, as Seen by Contemporaries and in the

Light of History (San Diego: Harcourt Brace Jovanovich Publishers, 1986); Charles Kindleberger, *The World in Depression, 1929–1939* (Berkeley, CA: University of California Press, 1986); Peter Fearon, *War, Prosperity, and Depression: The U.S. Economy, 1917–45* (Lawrence: University Press of Kansas, 1987); Michael A. Bernstein, *The Great Depression: Delayed Recovery and Economic Change in America, 1929–1939* (Cambridge: Cambridge University Press, 1987); Peter Temin, *Lessons from the Great Depression* (Cambridge, MA: MIT Press, 1991); Barry Eichengreen, *Golden Fetters: The Gold Standard and the Great Depression, 1919–1939* (New York: Oxford University Press, 1992); Ben Bernanke, *Essays on the Great Depression* (Princeton, NJ: Princeton University Press, 2000); and Charles R. Morris, *A Rabble of Dead Money: The Great Crash and the Global Depression, 1929–1939* (New York: Public Affairs, 2017).

2. Morris, *A Rabble of Dead Money*, 16; and Temin, *Lessons from the Great Depression*, 6, 10.

3. Temin, *Lessons from the Great Depression*, 10–38.

4. Eric Rauchway, *The Money Makers: How Roosevelt and Keynes Ended the Depression, Defeated Fascism, and Secured a Prosperous Peace* (New York: Basic Books, 2015), 18.

5. For a concise and accessible discussion of the gold standard, see Rauchway, *The Money Makers*, 19–27.

6. Temin, *Lessons from the Great Depression*, 17–25; Kim Quaile Hill, *Democracies in Crisis: Public Policy Responses to the Great Depression* (Boulder, CO: Westview Press, 1988), 65–82; and Kindleberger, *The World in Depression*, 14–41.

7. Kindleberger, *The World in Depression*, 73; and Rauchway, *The Money Makers*, 20–21. Morris tends to downplay the role that agricultural collapse played in the advent of the Depression in the United States, although he does acknowledge it as a factor. *A Rabble of Dead Money*, 103–105, 306.

8. Kindleberger, *The World in Depression*, 84.

9. Piers Brendon, *The Dark Valley: A Panorama of the 1930s* (New York: Vintage Books), 75–76.

10. Morris, *A Rabble of Dead Money*, 106–109.

11. Temin, for instance, maintains that it cut into consumer wealth and dampened individuals' and firms' economic activity. *Lessons from the Great Depression*, 45–46. See also Maury Klein, "The Stock Market Crash of 1929: A Review Article," *Business History Review* 75, no. 2 (Summer 2001): 340–348.

12. Klein, "The Stock Market Crash of 1929," 325–326; and Maury Klein, *Rainbow's End: The Crash of 1929* (New York: Oxford University Press, 2001), 214, 229.

13. David M. Kennedy, *Freedom from Fear: The American People in Depression and War, 1929–1945* (New York: Oxford University Press, 1999), 38.

14. Eichengreen, *Golden Fetters*, 12.

15. Eichengreen argues that at the time, many people perceived low interest rates and expansionist monetary policies as a cause of speculation. Consequently, the Federal Reserve responded to the boom by implementing tight monetary policies in the hope that it would squelch speculation and funnel money into tangible, productive uses. Eichengreen, *Golden Fetters*, 14.

16. Temin, *Lessons from the Great Depression*, 65. According to statistics, 1,350 banks suspended operations in 1930; 2,293 in 1931; 1,453 in 1932; and 4,000 in 1933. More than 3,400 banks closed in March 1933. Banks suspending operations during the bank holiday but reopening after its conclusion are not included in this number. Susan B. Carter et al., ed., *Historical Statistics of the United States*, Millennial Edition Online, Table Cb70: Money and Banking, Bank Suspensions (Cambridge: Cambridge University Press).

17. Rauchway, *The Money Makers*. See also Alan Brinkley, *The End of Reform: New Deal Liberalism in Recession and War* (New York: Vintage Books, 1995). Herbert Hoover and Roosevelt voiced a commitment to balanced budgets, which inhibited support for extensive government spending programs and deficit spending.

18. See, for instance, Robert D. Leighninger, Jr. *Long-Range Public Investment: The Forgotten Legacy of the New Deal* (Columbia: University of South Carolina Press, 2007); and Jason Scott Smith, *Building New Deal Liberalism: The Political Economy of Public Works, 1933–1956* (New York: Cambridge University Press, 2006). Alexander Field sees the Depression era as one of technological and organizational innovation, partially due to private-sector initiatives and partially to public-sector investment. *A Great Leap Forward: 1930s Depression and U.S. Economic Growth* (New Haven, CT: Yale University Press, 2011), especially chapter 1 and 258–276.

19. Christina Romer, "What Ended the Great Depression?" *Journal of Economic History* 52, no. 4 (December 1992): 757–761.

20. *Historical Statistics of the United States*, Table Ba475: Labor Force Employment and Unemployment: 1890–1990, Unemployment.

21. For an argument that attributes recovery to the Roosevelt administration's ability to alter expectations by dispensing with three dogmas—adherence to the ideas of a gold standard, a balanced budget, and small government—see Gauti B. Eggertsson, "Great Expectations and the End of the Great Depression," *American Economic Review* 98, no. 4 (2008): 1476–1516.

22. The US Senate requested this national data, and National Bureau of Economic Research employee Simon Kuznet led the effort to develop it. See *Historical Statistics of the United States*, "The History of National Income Accounting." Data reported in sources such as *Historical Statistics of the United States* must be used with the recognition that the figures represent the best estimation possible at the time. Moreover, the types of data and mechanisms for collecting it often shifted over time, thus complicating the comparison of one period to another, or even one year to another. Economists and economic historians have worked to revise and refine this economic data. See, for example, David R. Weir, "A Century of U.S. Unemployment, 1890–1990: Revised Estimates and Evidence for Stabilization," *Research in Economic History* 14 (1992): 301–346. Weir's work is utilized in *Historical Statistics of the United States*. For an interesting contemporary discussion of government data collection, especially by the Census Bureau, see Abraham Epstein, *Insecurity, a Challenge to America: A Study of Social Insurance in the United States and Abroad*; introduction by Frances Perkins (New York: Harrison Smith and Robert Haas, 1933), 193–194.

23. William Leuchtenburg, *The Perils of Prosperity, 1914–1932* (Chicago: University of Chicago Press, 1958), 247.

24. Unless otherwise noted, all dollars are stated in nominal terms, or unadjusted for inflation. *Historical Statistics of the United States*, Table Ca10: Gross Domestic Product, 1790–2002; Table Da1295: Farm Income.

25. Kennedy, *Freedom from Fear*, 163.

26. Gross private domestic investment fell from $14.9 billion in 1929 to $3.1 billion in 1933; see *Historical Statistics of the United States*, Table Ca98: Gross Private Domestic Investment.

27. *Historical Statistics of the United States*, Table Ca42: National Income, Durable Goods; Table Ca43: Non-Durable Goods; Table Cb55: Great Depression Series, Percentage of Corporations with Profits; Kennedy, *Freedom from Fear*, 163.

28. These figures represent rates for the civilian labor force. Rates for the private, nonfarm sector (absent government and farm workers) are higher in these years, reaching 30.02 percent in 1933. *Historical Statistics of the United States*, Table Ba475: Labor Force Employment and Unemployment: 1890–1990, Unemployment.

29. Stanley Lieberson, *A Piece of the Pie: Blacks and White Immigrants Since 1880* (Berkeley: University of California Press, 1980), 244; and Leuchtenburg, *Perils of Prosperity*, 247.

30. Epstein, *Insecurity, a Challenge to America*, 195.

31. Franklin D. Roosevelt, "Second Inaugural Address," January 20, 1937, FDR Presidential Library and Museum, https://fdrlibrary.org/documents/356632/390886/1937inauguraladdress.pdf/7d61a3fd-9d56-4bb6-989d-0fd269cdb073.

32. Frederick E. Hosen, *The Great Depression and the New Deal: Legislative Acts in Their Entirety (1932–1933) and Statistical Economic Data (1926–1946)* (Jefferson, NC: McFarland & Co., Inc., 1992), 272–273.

33. Kennedy, *Freedom from Fear*, 163.

34. Hosen, *The Great Depression and the New Deal*, 294.

35. Hosen, *The Great Depression and the New Deal*, 294. See also Kennedy, *Freedom from Fear*, 165. More women had access to birth control during the 1930s than previously. Gerald D. Nash, *The Crucial Era: The Great Depression and World War II, 1929–1945*, 2nd ed. (New York: St. Martin's Press, 1992), 78.

36. Nash, *The Crucial Era*, pp. 75–76, 84; and "Jobless Women in Parks," *The New York Times*, September 20, 1931.

37. Elizabeth Faue, *Rethinking the American Labor Movement* (New York: Routledge, 2017), 90–91; and Robert Zieger, *American Workers, American Unions* (2nd ed., Baltimore: Johns Hopkins University Press, 1994), 11.

38. Raymond Wolters, *Negroes and the Great Depression: The Problem of Economic Recovery* (Westport, CT: Greenwood Publishing, 1970), ix; and Lisa Kannenberg, "Great Depression: 1930s," in

Encyclopedia of U.S. Labor and Working-Class History, vol. 1, ed. Eric Arnesen (New York: Routledge, 2007), 542.

39. Slim Collier in Studs Terkel, *Hard Times: An Oral History of the Great Depression* (New York: Pantheon Books, 1970), 110.

40. George E. Barnett, "American Trade Unionism and Social Insurance," *American Economic Review*, cited in David Brody, *Labor Embattled: History, Power, Rights* (Chicago: University of Illinois Press, 2005), 30–31.

41. Lizabeth Cohen, *Making a New Deal: Industrial Workers in Chicago, 1919–1939* (New York: Cambridge University Press, 1990), chapters 3, 6, and 8.

42. Saul Alinsky, *John L. Lewis: An Unauthorized Biography* (New York: Vintage, 1970), 62–85; and J. Joseph Huthmacher, *Senator Robert F. Wagner and the Rise of Urban Liberalism* (New York: Atheneum, 1971), 147–151.

43. James Green, *The World of the Worker: Labor in Twentieth-Century America* (New York: Hill and Wang, 1980), 140–141.

44. Zieger, *American Workers, American Unions*, 39–41.

45. Margaret Rung, *Servants of the State: Managing Diversity and Democracy in the Federal Workforce 1933–1953* (Athens: University of Georgia Press, 2002); and Ira Katznelson, *Fear Itself: The New Deal and the Origins of Our Time* (New York: Liveright, 2013).

46. Kannenberg, "Great Depression: 1930s," 543.

47. Zieger, *American Workers, American Unions*, 60.

48. Robert Zieger, *The CIO: 1935–1955* (Chapel Hill: University of North Carolina Press, 1995).

49. Quoted from Sidney Fine, *Sit Down: the General Motors Strike of 1936–7* (Ann Arbor: University of Michigan Press, 1969), 331, 341.

50. Fine, *Sit Down*, 341.

51. Michael Dennis, *Blood on Steel: Chicago Steelworkers and the Strike of 1937* (Baltimore: Johns Hopkins University Press, 2014), vii, 50. Ahmad White, *The Last Great Strike: Little Steel, the CIO, and the Struggle for Labor Rights in New Deal America* (Berkeley: University of California Press, 2016).

52. Faue, *Rethinking the American Labor Movement*, 96.

53. Philip Dray, *There Is Power in a Union: The Epic Story of Labor in America* (New York: Doubleday, 2010), chapter 8; and quote from Michael Denning, *The Cultural Front: The Laboring of American Culture in the Twentieth* Century (New York: Verso, 1997), xvi–xvii.

54. Kenneth Kusmer, "From Tramp to Transient: The Great Depression," in *Down and Out, on the Road: The Homeless in American History* (New York: Oxford University Press, 2002), 194.

55. Todd Depastino, *Citizen Hobo: How a Century of Homelessness Shaped America* (Chicago: University of Chicago Press, 2003), 216.

56. Frank Czerwonka, quoted in Terkel, *Hard Times*, 41.

57. Errol Lincoln Uys, *Riding the Rails: Teenagers on the Move During the Great Depression* (New York: TV Books, 1999), 13.

58. Zieger, *American Workers, American Unions*, 18.

59. Kusmer, "From Tramp to Transient," 202–203; and Paul Dickson and Thomas B. Allen, *The Bonus Army: An American Epic* (New York: Walker & Company, 2004).

60. Kusmer, "From Tramp to Transient," 210–218.

61. Kusmer, "From Tramp to Transient," 204; and Uys, *Riding the Rails*, 11–32.

62. Robin D. G. Kelley, *Hammer and Hoe: Alabama Communists During the Great Depression* (Chapel Hill: University of North Carolina Press, 1990); Dan Carter, *Scottsboro: A Tragedy of the American South*, rev. ed. (Baton Rouge: Louisiana State University Press, 2007); and James Miller, Susan D. Pennybacker, and Even Rosenhaft, "Mother Ada Wright and the International Campaign to Free the Scottsboro Boys, 1931–1934," *American Historical Review* 106, no. 2 (April 2001): 387–430.

63. Sarah Phillips, *This Land, This Nation: Conservation, Rural America, and the New Deal* (Cambridge, UK: Cambridge University Press, 2007), 123 and passim.

64. Mary Owsley and Peggy Terry, quoted in Terkel, *Hard Times*, 50, 55.

65. Phillips, *This Land, This Nation*, 127, 137, 207.

66. Neil Maher, *Nature's New Deal: The Civilian Conservation Corps and the Roots of the American Environmental Movement* (New York: Oxford University Press, 2008).

67. James Gregory, *The Southern Diaspora: How the Great Migrations of Black and White Southerners Changed America* (Chapel Hill: University of North Carolina Press, 2005), 30.

68. John Steinbeck, *The Grapes of Wrath* (New York: Viking, 1939); and Gregory, *Southern Diaspora*, 64.

69. Gregory, *American Exodus*, xiv.

70. Roy Rosenzweig, "Organizing the Unemployed: the Early Years of the Great Depression,

1929–1933," *Radical America* 10, no. 4 (July–August 1976): 40–41.

71. Horace Cayton and St. Clair Drake, *Black Metropolis: A Study of Negro Life in a Northern City* (Chicago: University of Chicago Press, 1945, 1999 edition), 87.

72. Rosenzweig, "Organizing the Unemployed," 49–52.

73. Rosenzweig, "Organizing the Unemployed," 52–56; Mark Naison, "From Eviction Resistance to Rent Control: Tenant Activism in the Great Depression," in *The Tenant Movement in New York City, 1904–1984*, ed. Ronald Lawson (New Brunswick, NJ: Rutgers University Press, 1986), 94–133; and Daniel Leab, "United We Eat: The Creation and Organization of Unemployment Councils in 1930," *Labor History* 8 (Fall 1967): 300–315.

74. Penny Von Eschen, *Race Against Empire: Black Americans and Anticolonialism, 1937–1957* (Ithaca, NY: Cornell University Press, 1997), chapter 1; and Peter Carroll, *The Odyssey of the Abraham Lincoln Brigade: Americans in the Spanish Civil War* (Stanford, CA: Stanford University Press, 1994).

75. Robert Korstad, *Civil Rights Unionism: Tobacco Workers and the Struggle for Democracy in the Mid-Twentieth Century South* (Chapel Hill: University of North Carolina Press, 2003).

76. Green, *The World of the Worker*, 149; and Howard Kester and Alex Lichtenstein, *Revolt Among the Sharecroppers* (Knoxville: University of Tennessee Press, 1997).

77. Erik S. Gellman and Jarod H. Roll, *The Gospel of the Working Class: Labor's Southern Prophets in New Deal America* (Chicago: University of Illinois Press, 2011); Louis Cantor, *Prologue to the Protest Movement: The Missouri Sharecropper Roadside Demonstrations of 1939* (Durham, NC: Duke University Press, 1969); and Nan Woodruff, *American Congo: The African American Freedom Struggle in the Delta* (Cambridge, MA: Harvard University Press, 2003).

78. Robert Korstad and Nelson Lichtenstein, "Opportunities Found and Lost: Labor, Radicals, and the Early Civil Rights Movement," *Journal of American History* 75, no. 3 (December 1988): 786–811; Michael K. Honey, *Southern Labor and Black Civil Rights: Organizing Memphis Workers* (Chicago: University of Illinois Press, 1993); and Ruth Needleman, *Black Freedom Fighters in Steel: The Struggle for Democratic Unionism* (Ithaca, NY: ILR Press, 2003).

79. Green, *The World of the Worker*, 149; Lois Scharf, *To Work and To Wed: Female Employment, Feminism, and the Great Depression* (Westport, CT: Greenwood Press, 1980); and Dorothy Sue Cobble, *The Other Women's Movement: Workplace Justice and Social Rights in Modern America* (Princeton, NJ: Princeton University Press, 2004).

80. Erik S. Gellman, *Death Blow to Jim Crow: The National Negro Congress and the Rise of Militant Civil Rights* (Chapel Hill: University of North Carolina Press, 2012); Beth Tompkins Bates, "A New Crowd Challenges the Agenda of the Old Guard in the NAACP, 1933–1941," *American Historical Review* 102, no. 2 (April 1997): 340–377; and Harvard Sitkoff, *A New Deal for Blacks: The Emergence of Civil Rights as a National Issue: The Depression Decade* (New York: Oxford University Press, 1981).

81. Paul Stephen Hudson, "A Call for 'Bold Persistent Experimentation': FDR's Oglethorpe University Commencement Address, 1932," *Georgia Historical Quarterly* 78 (Summer 1994): 361–375; and William Leuchtenburg, *Franklin D. Roosevelt and the New Deal, 1932–1940* (New York: Harper and Row, 1963).

82. Alan Brinkley, *Voices of Protest: Huey Long, Father Coughlin, and the Great Depression* (New York: Knopf, 1982); Kevin Starr, *Endangered Dreams: The Great Depression in California* (New York: Oxford University Press, 1996), chapters 5–6; and Edwin Amenta, *When Movements Matter: The Townsend Plan and the Rise of Social Security* (Princeton, NJ: Princeton University Press, 2006).

83. On various aspects of Depression-era culture, see, for instance, David Peeler, *Hope Among Us Yet: Social Criticism and Social Solace in Depression America* (Athens: University of Georgia Press, 1987); Alice Goldfarb Marquis, *Hopes and Ashes: The Birth of Modern Times, 1929–1939* (New York: Free Press, 1986); Terry A. Cooney, *Balancing Acts: American Thought and Culture in the 1930s* (New York: Twayne Publishers, 1995); Bill Mullen and Sherry Lee Linkon, *Radical Revisions: Rereading 1930s Culture* (Urbana and Chicago: University of Illinois Press, 1996); and Morris Dickstein, *Dancing in the Dark: A Cultural History of the Great Depression* (New York: W. W. Norton, 2009).

84. David A. Taylor, *Soul of a People: The WPA Writers' Project Uncovers Depression America* (Hoboken, NJ, 2009), 35–37, 42–52, quote from 50.

85. Taylor, *Soul of a People*, 177–182.

86. Linda Gordon, *Dorothea Lange: A Life Beyond Limits* (New York: W. W. Norton, 2009), part 3.

87. On superheroes during the Depression, see Jeffrey K. Johnson, *Super-History: Comic Book Superheroes and American Society, 1938 to the Present* (Jefferson, NC and London: McFarland & Co., 2012), 7–20. On the Blakely Mine Disaster, see Robert S. McElvaine, *The Depression and New Deal: A History in Documents* (New York: Oxford University Press, 2000), 140–141.

88. On commercial films in general and specifically, screwball comedies, which are frequently associated with Frank Capra, see Andrew Bergman, *We're in the Money: Depression America and Its Films* (New York: New York University Press, 1971).

89. Margaret Mitchell, *Gone with the Wind* (New York: MacMillan Company, 1936); and Gellman, *Death Blow to Jim Crow*, 180–186, 261.

90. Denning, *The Cultural Front*; and Brian Dolinar, *The Black Cultural Front: Black Writers and Artists of the Depression Generation* (Jackson: University Press of Mississippi, 2012).

91. Cooney, *Balancing Acts*, 6.

92. Marquis, *Hopes and Ashes*, 202–211; and "The Iconography of Hope: The 1939–1940 New York World's Fair," America in the 1930s, American Studies at the University of Virginia, http://xroads.virginia.edu/~1930s/DISPLAY/39wf/front.htm.

93. John Maynard Keynes, *The Essential Keynes*, with an introduction and edited by Robert Skidelsky (New York: Penguin Books, 2015), xv.

94. John Maynard Keynes, *The General Theory of Employment, Interest, and Money* (New York: Harcourt, Brace & World, Inc., 1936). On the general influence of Keynes, as well as his theories of the "mature economy," see Brinkley, *The End of Reform*, especially 131–135, 232–235. In this theory, economies slowed when population rates either declined or plateaued. This situation could not sustain growth without government stimulus. For further reading on Keynes and American policy, see Rauchway, *The Money Makers*; and Herbert Stein, *The Fiscal Revolution in America* (Chicago: University of Chicago Press, 1969).

95. Friedman and Schwartz, *The Great Contraction, 1929–1933*.

96. Friedman and Schwartz, *The Great Contraction, 1929–1933*.

97. Temin, *Lessons from the Great Depression*; Kindleberger, *The World in Depression, 1929–1939*; and Eichengreen, *Golden Fetters*.

98. Temin, *Lessons from the Great Depression*, 6–9; Hill, *Democracies in Crisis*, 69; and Eichengreen, *Golden Fetters*, 12–26.

99. Morris, *A Rabble of Dead Money*.

100. Harold L. Cole and Lee E. Ohanian, "New Deal Policies and the Persistence of the Great Depression: A General Equilibrium," *Journal of Political Economy* 112, no. 4 (August 2004): 779–816. Many conservative writers adhere to theories advanced by conservative Austrian economist Friedrich Hayek, a contemporary of Keynes. Some critics have focused on the role that high tariffs, such as Smoot-Hawley, played in the Depression. See, for example, Amity Shlaes, *The Forgotten Man: A New History of the Great Depression* (New York: HarperCollins, 2007), 6–12, 95–99. Burton W. Folsom puts forth several conservative arguments regarding causation, including tariff policy, in *New Deal or Raw Deal: How FDR's Economic Legacy Has Damaged America* (New York: Threshold Editions, 2008), 30–59. For an extended discussion of Smoot-Hawley and its role as a contributor to, not a cause of, the Depression's onset, see Douglas Irwin, *Peddling Protectionism* (Princeton, NJ: Princeton University Press, 2011), especially 114–123, 142–143.

101. For overviews of various schools of thought on the roots of the Depression, see Garraty, *The Great Depression*, 2–25; Hill, *Democracies in Crisis*, 11–28; Bernstein, *The Great Depression*, 1–20; and Klein, "The Stock Market Crash of 1929," 340–348.

102. Romer, "What Ended the Great Depression?"; Eggertsson, "Great Expectations"; Rauchway, *The Money Makers*. Romer contends that an expansion of the money supply was largely responsible for economic growth in the mid- to late-1930s; Eggertsson argues that Roosevelt's primary contribution was a successful effort to undermine an unquestioning commitment to the gold standard, a balanced budget, and small government; and Rauchway demonstrates a consistent Roosevelt effort to produce inflation, especially by manipulating monetary policies.

103. See, for instance, Paul Krugman, *The Conscience of a Liberal* (New York: W. W. Norton, 2007) and *The Return of Depression Economics*

(New York: W. W. Norton, 2009). Ben S. Bernanke, *Essays on the Great Depression* (Princeton, NJ: Princeton University Press, 2000) and *The Courage to Act: A Memoir of a Crisis and Its Aftermath* (New York: W. W. Norton, 2015).

104. Kathryn Olmsted, *Right Out of California: The 1930s and the Big Business Roots of Modern Conservatism* (New York: The New Press, 2015); Elliott Rosen, *The Republican Party in the Age of Roosevelt: Sources of Anti-Government Conservatism in the United States* (Charlottesville: University of Virginia Press, 2014); Kim Phillips-Fein, *Invisible Hands: The Businessmen's Crusade Against the New Deal* (New York: W. W. Norton, 2009); and Herbert Hoover, *The Challenge to Liberty* (New York: Charles Scribner's Sons, 1934).

105. Arthur M. Schlesinger, Jr., *The Age of Roosevelt* (Boston: Houghton Mifflin, 3 vols., 1956–1960); and Leuchtenburg, *Franklin D. Roosevelt and the New Deal, 1932–1940*.

106. See Gregory, *American Exodus*; and Kusmer, "From Tramp to Transient."

107. See, for example, James Green, "Working-Class Militancy in the Depression," *Radical America* VI (Nov–Dec., 1972): 1–36; Honey, *Southern Labor and Black Civil Rights*; and Zieger, *The CIO*; but also reassessments by historians such as Bruce Nelson, *Divided We Stand: American Workers and the Struggle for Black Equality* (Princeton, NJ: Princeton University Press, 2002 edition).

108. Quote from Jacquelyn Dowd Hall, "The Long Civil Rights Movement and the Political Uses of the Past," *Journal of American History* 91, no. 4 (March 2005): 1245–1246. See also Kelley, *Hammer and Hoe*; and Korstad, *Civil Rights Unionism*. Also, for a critique of the Communist impact on these movements, see Eric Arnesen, "No 'Graver Danger': Black Anticommunism, the Communist Party, and the Race Question," *Labor: Studies in Working-Class History of the Americas* 3 (Winter 2006): 13–52.

109. Some prominent examples include Brinkley, *Voices of Protest*; Cohen, *Making a New Deal*; Sitkoff, *A New Deal for Blacks*; and Landon Storrs, *Civilizing Capitalism: The National Consumers League, Women's Activism, and Labor Standards in the New Deal Era* (Chapel Hill: University of North Carolina Press, 2000).

110. See Fraser Ottanelli, *The Communist Party of the United States from Depression to World War II* (New York: Rutgers University Press, 1991); Randi Storch, *Red Chicago: American Communist at Its Grassroots* (Chicago: University of Illinois Press, 2008); and Mark Solomon, *The Cry Was Unity: Communists and African Americans, 1917–1936* (Oxford: University Press of Mississippi, 1998).

111. See Carroll, *Odyssey of the American Lincoln Brigade*; Denning, *Cultural Front*; and Von Eschen, *Race Against Empire*.

112. Beth Bates, *Pullman Porters and the Rise of Protest Politics in Black America* (Chapel Hill: University of North Carolina Press, 2001); Gellman, *Death Blow to Jim Crow*; Kelley, *Hammer and Hoe*; Korstad, *Civil Rights Unionism*; and Patricia Sullivan, *Days of Hope: Race and Democracy in the New Deal Era* (Chapel Hill: University of North Carolina Press, 1996).

113. See Dickstein, *Dancing in the Dark*; Cohen, *Making a New Deal*; Bruce Lenthall, *Radio's America: The Great Depression and the Rise of Modern Mass Culture* (Chicago: University of Chicago Press, 2007), and especially Denning, *The Cultural Front*.

114. Hosen, *The Great Depression and the New Deal*.

115. Robert S. McElvaine, ed., *Down and Out in the Great Depression: Letters from the Forgotten Man*, 25th anniversary edition (Chapel Hill, NC: University of North Carolina Press, 2008); Robert Cohen, ed., *Dear Mrs. Roosevelt: Letters from Children of the Great Depression* (Chapel Hill, NC: University of North Carolina Press, 2002); and Cathy D. Knepper, ed. *Dear Mrs. Roosevelt: Letters to Eleanor Roosevelt Through Depression and War* (New York: Carroll & Graf, 2004).

116. Gerald Markowitz and David Rosner, eds. *"Slaves of the Depression": Workers' Letters About Life on the Job* (Ithaca, NY: Cornell University Press, 1987).

117. George McJimsey, ed. *Documentary History of the Franklin D. Roosevelt Presidency*, 43 vols. (Bethesda, MD: University Publications of America, 2001); and Terkel, *Hard Times*; Roosevelt University Elizabeth Balanoff Labor Oral History Collection (http://www.roosevelt.edu/balanoff).

118. Richard Lowitt and Maurine Beasely, eds. *One Third of a Nation: Lorena Hickok Reports on the*

Great Depression (Urbana: University of Illinois Press, 1981).

119. Robert S. Lynd and Helen Merrell Lynd, *Middletown: A Study in Modern American Culture* (New York: Harcourt Brace, 1929) and *Middletown in Transition: A Study in Cultural Conflicts* (New York: Harcourt, Brace & World, 1937).

Erik S. Gellman and Margaret Rung

THE NEW DEAL

DEFINING THE "NEW DEAL"

On July 2, 1932, Franklin Delano Roosevelt (FDR) accepted the Democratic Party's nomination for president and pledged himself to a "new deal for the American people."[1] In so doing, he gave a name not only to a set of domestic policies implemented by his administration in response to the crisis of the Great Depression but also to an era, a political coalition, and a vision of government's role in society. The New Deal has been described as a "potpourri" of sometimes-conflicting policy initiatives, and scholars and popular commentators have long debated its ideological sources, beneficiaries, and legacy.[2] Nevertheless, most agree that it marked "a pivotal moment in the making of modern American liberalism."[3] As this suggests, the New Deal cast a long shadow over the remainder of the 20th century, and it remains a touchstone for contemporary political debate.

When Roosevelt took office in March 1933, the nation was more than three years into the greatest economic cataclysm that either the United States or global capitalism had ever experienced. The stock market crash in October 1929 had led to a financial meltdown, prompting a collapse in industrial production that began in the United States but soon spread to other countries. A rise in prices for raw materials—commodities ranging from cotton and wheat to tea, silk, lumber, and steel—soon followed. This prostrated farmers, miners, and loggers,

not only in the United States but also around the globe. By the spring of 1933, the US gross national product had fallen to just half of its 1929 level. More than five thousand US banks had failed, and thousands of families across the country had already lost farms and homes to foreclosure. On the day Roosevelt was inaugurated, roughly one-quarter of the American workforce was unemployed. In cities like Chicago and Detroit, home to hard-hit industries like automobiles and steel, the unemployment rate approached 50 percent.[4]

On the campaign trail, Roosevelt had been vague about precisely how he planned to grapple with the economic crisis: he famously recommended "bold, persistent experimentation."[5] Once in office, the president turned his abundant energy to implementing this pragmatic philosophy. He surrounded himself with advisors who had strikingly different viewpoints and agendas, and set them to work tackling a troika of problems: relief, recovery, and reform.[6] The result was one of the greatest outpourings of legislation ever seen in American history. Between 1933 and 1938, Roosevelt and his New Dealers pushed through legislation that, among other things, regulated the banking and securities industries, shored up agricultural prices, established vast public works projects, repealed Prohibition, created new mortgage markets, managed watersheds, reversed a half-century of American Indian policy, bolstered the power of unions, and provided social insurance to millions of elderly, unemployed, and disabled Americans. As historian David M. Kennedy has written, "Into the five years of the New Deal was crowded more social and institutional change than into virtually any comparable compass of time in the nation's past."[7]

As Kennedy suggests, the term "New Deal" is most often used to refer to the set of domestic policies implemented by the Roosevelt administration in the 1930s in response to the Great Depression. In this narrow sense, the "New Deal" might be seen as paralleling Teddy Roosevelt's "Square Deal," Harry Truman's

"Fair Deal," or Lyndon B. Johnson's "Great Society." Scholars have also used the term more expansively to encompass later domestic legislation that seemed to be animated by the same values and impulses. Glenn Altschuler and Stuart Blumin, for instance, argue that the 1944 GI Bill built on specific New Deal policies, while reflecting FDR's broader desire to use the power of the federal government to extend a safety net to American citizens. For this reason, they dub the GI bill "a New Deal for veterans."[8] Ira Katznelson goes even further, redefining the New Deal as "the full period of Democratic rule" that stretched from Roosevelt's election in 1932 to the election of Dwight Eisenhower two decades later. Only by looking at this longer time span, he suggests, can historians understand how the New Deal "reconsidered and rebuilt the country's long-established political order."[9]

If some historians have extended the chronology of the New Deal, others have expanded its geographic scope. Scholars have most often applied the term to FDR's domestic agenda, but Elizabeth Borgwardt argues that there was also a "New Deal for the world." As World War II drew to a close, she suggests, Roosevelt administration planners translated "the New Deal's sweeping institutional approaches to intractable problems" to the international arena, establishing a framework of multilateral institutions designed to stabilize the global system and advance human rights. The International Monetary Fund, the World Bank, the United Nations, and the charter that set the parameters for the Nuremberg Trials were designed to extend economic and political security to people around the globe, she writes, "much as New Deal programs had redefined security domestically for individual American citizens."[10] In a similar vein, Kiran Klaus Patel argues that the United States "played a major role in redefining the international order by trying to project the principles of the New Deal regulatory state onto the world."[11] Sarah Phillips suggests that the success of New Deal programs like the Tennessee Valley Authority (TVA) convinced many liberals that they had "found the tools for conquering the problem of rural poverty." The postwar Point Four program of foreign assistance, she argues, drew on these lessons and attempted to "export the New Deal."[12]

Neither the domestic nor the global New Deal would have been possible had FDR not mobilized a new political coalition. From 1896 until 1932, the Republican Party dominated national politics; only in the "Solid South," which had opposed Republicans since the Civil War, did the Democratic Party consistently win elections. In 1932, Roosevelt swept into office largely because of widespread animosity toward President Herbert Hoover, who had failed to end the Depression or significantly ameliorate suffering. Over the next four years, however, Roosevelt won over Catholic and Jewish immigrants and their voting-age children, industrial workers, African Americans, and large segments of the so-called chattering classes. Together with white Southerners, these groups formed what became known as the "New Deal coalition."

The New Deal coalition brought together unlikely bedfellows—for instance, African Americans and union members with conservative white Southerners who opposed racial equality and organized labor. Nevertheless, this unwieldy political alliance endured long after Roosevelt's death, supporting the Democratic Party and a "liberal" agenda for nearly half a century. Every president elected between 1932 and 1980 was a Democrat, with the exceptions of Dwight Eisenhower and Richard Nixon. The Democratic Party also controlled both houses of Congress for all but four of those forty-eight years. When the coalition finally cracked in 1980, historians looked back on this extended epoch as reflecting a "New Deal order" with "an ideological character, a moral perspective, and a set of political relationships among policy elites, interest groups, and electoral constituencies."[13]

BATTLING THE GREAT DEPRESSION

Before scholars could reflect on a New Deal "order," there was what FDR and his contemporaries called simply the New Deal: the set of policies put in place during Roosevelt's first two presidential terms in direct response to the ravages of the Great Depression. Most of that legislation came in one of two great bursts. The first followed Roosevelt's inauguration on March 4, 1933.[14] Within days of taking office, the new president called Congress into special session. By the time Congress adjourned precisely one hundred days later, Roosevelt had signed fifteen bills into law. Taken together, they restructured vast swaths of the American economy and authorized billions of dollars in federal spending for everything from dam construction and crop subsidies to unemployment relief. Roosevelt proposed—and Congress passed—so much legislation during this first "Hundred Days" that the time frame became a benchmark for all subsequent US political leaders.

The second burst of legislation came in the first nine months of 1935. The previous November, the president's party had bucked historical trends by winning, rather than losing, seats in the midterm election. The victory was a landslide: when the new Congress convened in January 1935, Democrats held two-thirds of the seats in both the House and the Senate. The election signaled the political realignment that created the New Deal coalition, and it gave Roosevelt a mandate. This second legislative burst enabled some of the best-remembered policies of the New Deal, including the Works Progress Administration, federal support for organized labor, and the Social Security program.

Contemporary journalists called these two torrents of legislation the First and Second New Deal, and historians have generally followed their lead. For decades, both scholars and popular writers argued that the two phases of the New Deal were ideologically distinct, although they often disagreed on the precise nature of that difference.[15] In recent years, historians have suggested that any ideological shift between 1933 and 1935 was exaggerated. Many have embraced the argument made by David Kennedy that New Deal policies were designed, above all, to provide security—security not only for "vulnerable individuals" but also for capitalists, consumers, workers, farmers, homeowners, bankers, and builders. "Job security, life-cycle security, financial security, market security—however it might be defined, achieving security was the leitmotif of virtually everything the New Deal attempted," Kennedy writes.[16]

Stabilizing the Financial System. The most urgent matter that Roosevelt confronted when he took office in March 1933 was the banking crisis. The nation's banking system had been teetering on the edge of collapse since the end of 1930 as fearful domestic and foreign investors scrambled to pull their gold and currency deposits out of US institutions. A new round of panic the month before the inauguration prompted governors in state after state to close their banks to prevent runs. On the morning FDR became president, such "bank holidays" had closed all banks in thirty-two states. In six more, the vast majority of banks were closed. In the remainder, depositors could withdraw only 5 percent of their funds.[17]

Some politicians and political observers urged Roosevelt to nationalize the banking system.[18] Instead, the new president declared a national bank holiday, called Congress into emergency session, and persuaded them to pass the Emergency Banking Act. That act affirmed the temporary bank closure, authorized the Federal Reserve to issue more currency, and took other steps designed to restore the system's liquidity. With banks set to reopen on March 13, Roosevelt took to the airwaves, delivering the first of the radio addresses that would become known as "fireside chats." Using simple language and speaking in an authoritative yet avuncular voice, Roosevelt explained both the workings of the banking system and the steps that the federal government had just taken to preserve it. "I can assure you," the president told his 60 million listeners, "that it is safer to keep your money in a reopened bank than under the mattress."[19] Roosevelt's combination of quick action and calming explanation worked. As his advisor Raymond

Moley later wrote, "Capitalism was saved in eight days."[20]

New Deal efforts to shore up the banking system did not end with these emergency measures. A few months later, Congress passed the Glass-Steagall Act, which separated investment from commercial banking in an effort to insure that banks did not speculate with depositors' savings. The act also established the Federal Deposit Insurance Corporation, which guaranteed bank deposits up to an initial level of $2,500. (That figure has been raised many times since.) Although FDR initially opposed deposit insurance, it almost immediately halted bank runs. These two moves dramatically stabilized the banking system. Even during the prosperous 1920s, more than six hundred US banks had failed each year. In the early 1930s, that number climbed into the thousands. Beginning in 1934, fewer than a hundred US banks failed annually; by 1943, the number had dropped to under ten.[21]

Other New Deal financial measures were aimed at steadying the securities markets or strengthening the economy more generally. In the spring of 1933, FDR followed Britain's lead and took the United States off the gold standard, allowing the exchange value of the dollar to fall. One of the president's advisors warned that the move would spell "the end of Western civilization," but it gave New Dealers more flexibility to combat low prices by trying to stimulate inflation. Coupled with political instability in Europe, the end of the gold standard also prompted overseas investors to begin exchanging gold for dollars, further increasing the US money supply and bolstering the banks.[22] The Securities Act of 1933 sought to end insider trading in the stock market by requiring publically traded companies to disclose financial information. The following year, Congress created the Securities and Exchange Commission to guard against market manipulation. Finally, the Banking Act of 1935 put the Federal Reserve's Open Market Committee—the body that influenced the nation's money supply and thus the availability of credit—under the direct control of a Board of Governors appointed by the president. This move helped centralize the nation's banking system, and improved the Federal Reserve's ability to shape the business cycle.

Relief for the Unemployed. Having stabilized the banking system, FDR turned quickly to the problem of unemployment relief. In the spring of 1933, some 12.4 million men and 400,000 women—roughly one-quarter of the national workforce—were unemployed. Most were their families' principal breadwinners.[23] The collective need of these American families had already overwhelmed the resources of local governments and private charities, as well as family and community support networks. With millions unable to pay rent or buy food, men, women, and children lined up at soup kitchens, grubbed for scraps in garbage cans, hopped freight trains, or moved into makeshift shantytowns that sprang up in parks and open spaces on the edges of American cities.

FDR first focused on the problem posed by young men—a problem captured in a 1933 film entitled *The Wild Boys of the Road*. Teenagers and men in their twenties had fewer skills and less experience than their older counterparts; thus, they were more likely to be unemployed, to leave home, and to become hobos and vagrants. Events in Europe suggested the threat that such footloose young men might pose to the social order. Roosevelt believed that sending them to work in the countryside would not only improve the nation's rural infrastructure but also transform the young men into upstanding future citizens. He proposed a Civilian Conservation Corps (CCC) to employ those between the ages of 18 and 35 on a variety of forestry, flood control, and beautification projects. To be selected for the program, men had to be single, healthy, and US citizens and to come from families on relief. Living in military-style camps operated by the War Department, they built roads, firebreaks, trails, and campgrounds. They also planted trees, fought fires, and drained swamps. CCC workers served stints of less than two years and were required to send home $25 of the $30 they earned each month to their families. Between the program's establishment in 1933 and its expiration nine years later, the CCC put three million young men to work. It quickly became one of the New Deal's most popular initiatives, and remained popular even in conservative areas.[24]

Although the CCC kept many young men from taking to the road, it was hardly enough to relieve the distress of American families. Thus, Roosevelt urged establishment of a new agency, the Federal Emergency Relief Administration (FERA). He persuaded Congress to appropriate $500 million to FERA, and used it to provide direct relief to needy Americans who were able to pass a means test. Some FERA funds were funneled through the states. Others were passed out by Harry Hopkins, the former social worker whom FDR tapped to run the agency. Hopkins had held a similar position in New York State when Roosevelt was governor there. Both men felt great sympathy for the poor, and both also knew how to use FERA to political advantage. By enlarging the federal role in awarding relief, they helped to transfer the political allegiance of America's unemployed from local officials and political machines to Washington, DC.

FERA made life marginally easier for many, but it never had sufficient funds. As the United States headed into the fifth winter of the Depression, unemployment remained high. In November 1933, Hopkins persuaded Roosevelt to establish yet another agency to employ people directly. Drawing tools and materials from army warehouses, the Civil Works Administration (CWA) put Americans to work fixing roads, docks, and schools; laying sewer pipe; and installing outhouses for farm families. The CWA paid far more than FERA and did not subject all workers to a means test; it was soon employing more than 4 million men and women. By February 1934, the CCC, FERA, and CWA together were reaching 22 percent of the U.S. population, an all-time high for public welfare in the United States. The president,

however, worried both about the escalating costs of such programs and about relief becoming "a habit with the country." He ordered the CWA to close down at the end of March, noting that nobody would starve when the weather was warm.[25]

Americans made it through the rest of 1934, but as the new Congress convened in early 1935, the unemployment rate still hovered near 20 percent. Moreover, some 5 million Americans remained on relief. FDR and many of his advisors continued to worry about deficit spending, but they also believed that something had to be done and that only the federal government had "sufficient power and credit" to do it. Work relief cost more than direct payments, but the latter, as FDR declared in his annual message to Congress, was "a narcotic." "The lessons of history, confirmed by the evidence immediately before me," he added, "show conclusively that continued dependence upon relief induces a spiritual and moral disintegration fundamentally destructive to the national fibre." FDR proposed a massive public employment program to get 3.5 million abledbodied but jobless Americans off the relief rolls.[26]

The result was the Works Progress Administration (WPA), one of the most ambitious and best-remembered New Deal programs. Headed by Hopkins, the WPA put more than 3 million people to work in its first year. Roosevelt wanted all projects to be labor intensive and useful, and when possible to come to a natural end. He also wanted WPA to pay more than relief but less than market rates so as not to compete with private enterprise. WPA workers built highways, schools, airports, parks, and bridges. They bound books, supervised recreation areas, ran school lunch programs, and sewed garments for the needy. WPA workers even entered the arena of public health, building hospitals and clinics, conducting mass immunization campaigns, and churning out posters that promoted nutrition and warned against the dangers of tuberculosis and syphilis.

Many of those posters were produced by employees of the Federal Arts Project, part of a massive and unprecedented federal venture into the arena of culture. Both Hopkins and First Lady Eleanor Roosevelt believed that the New Deal should provide work for unemployed artists, musicians, actors, and writers, and so the WPA set up a series of cultural programs known collectively as "Federal One." The Federal Writers' Project produced dozens of state and city guidebooks, and conducted thousands of oral histories with former slaves, immigrants, stonecutters, packinghouse workers, Oklahoma pioneers, and others. It also sent folklorists to record the music and stories of Appalachian banjo pickers, southern bluesmen, Mexican American balladeers, and Okies in resettlement camps in the West. The Federal Music Project sponsored symphony orchestras and jazz groups, while the Federal Arts Project commissioned muralists and graphic artists. Both hired individuals to teach music, painting, and sculpture to schoolchildren.

If New Dealers wanted to aid unemployed artists, they also hoped to democratize culture and to generate support for New Deal programs and political values. No New Deal initiative better illustrates this goal—or the controversy it generated—than the Federal Theatre Project, which brought plays, vaudeville acts, and puppet shows to small towns across the country. It also staged controversial shows like Orson Welles's production of *Macbeth*, which featured an all-black cast. Finally, the Federal Theatre Project developed a new theatrical genre, the Living Newspaper, to dramatize current events and expose social issues. One Living Newspaper, *Power*, traced the development of the electrical power industry and urged greater support for public ownership of utilities. Other Living Newspapers dealt with agricultural policy, the shortage of affordable housing, the labor movement, and syphilis.

Not surprisingly, Federal One drew intense criticism from critics on the right: In June 1939, a more conservative Congress dissolved the Federal Theatre Project, charging that it spread New Deal propaganda and encouraged racial mixing in stage productions. Budget cuts to the other cultural programs soon followed. Conservatives warned that all WPA programs were endangering the American way of life by providing jobs for the undeserving. They also complained that the WPA was simply a Democratic Party patronage machine. (FDR did use the program to reward local power brokers who supported the New Deal, although these included progressive Republicans like New York City's Mayor Fiorello La Guardia, as well as Democratic political bosses in cities like Chicago and Memphis.)[27]

Not all criticism of the WPA came from the right. Leftist critics noted that the WPA was chronically underfunded; despite its size, it could provide jobs for only a third of those who needed them in the United States.[28] To avoid competing with the private sector, WPA jobs always paid less than the "prevailing wage" in a given community. Since that standard differed by region, gender, and race, it reinforced existing patterns of discrimination. The editors of *The Nation* complained that the program required workers to toil "at depressed wages in a federal work gang" and was "a morbid substitute for relief."[29] Nevertheless, between 1935 and its dismantling in 1943, the WPA employed some 8.5 million Americans, roughly one-fifth of the nation's workforce, at a total cost of roughly $11 billion. Many were grateful to have a job rather than a handout. "We aren't on relief anymore," the wife of one WPA worker reportedly said. "My husband is working for the Government."[30]

Aiding Farmers. Both the crisis in the banking system and the spike in unemployment were problems brought on by the Great Depression. The plight of America's farmers had deeper roots, however. Rural America had been mired in depression since shortly after the end of World War I, a situation that farmers found particularly vexing given the general economic prosperity of the 1920s.[31] The deflationary spiral of the early 1930s pushed farm income down an additional 60 percent.[32] Across the country, crops rotted in the field because prices were so low that farmers could not justify harvesting them. Western ranchers slit the throats of livestock they could afford neither to feed nor to market. Dairymen in upstate New York dumped milk into ditches, while growers in California lit mountains of oranges on fire.[33] Since taxes and mortgage payments did not fall, farmers across the country lost homes, land, and equipment to foreclosure. Many rebelled, joining "farm strikes," disrupting auctions, and nearly lynching an Iowa judge who refused to suspend foreclosure proceedings.

New Dealers believed that boosting farm incomes would help not only rural Americans but also the entire US economy. In 1933, farmers still made up roughly one-third of the nation's workforce, and their purchasing power dramatically lagged that of residents in urban areas. By restoring prosperity to the farm economy, New Dealers argued, they would increase farmers' ability to buy nonfarm goods, in turn contributing to a more general economic recovery. Such reasoning reflected not only the thought of many in the Roosevelt administration regarding the economy, but also their tendency to romanticize the nation's pastoral past and their awareness of the continuing political power of rural America.[34]

The centerpiece of the New Deal's efforts to raise farm incomes was the Agricultural Adjustment Act (AAA), passed in May 1933. The act charged the federal government with raising the price for key farm commodities in order to bring the prices that farmers received for their products into balance or "parity" with their production and living costs. It pointed to the years just before World War I as the ideal of parity. While the act was vague about the exact mechanism the government should use to achieve this end, it established a new agency and sanctioned a variety of remedies that farm advocates had been battling over for years. To prevent farmers from planting surplus crops, the AAA levied a tax on flour millers and other crop processors and used the proceeds to pay farmers for taking land out of production. At the same time, the agency tried to maintain a floor under prices by keeping harvested crops off the market when prices were low. It did this by offering farmers loans secured by their crops at above-market rates, then storing the surplus. If crop prices rose, farmers could repay the loans, redeem their crops, and sell at the higher prices. Finally, the act established a Farm Credit Administration (FCA) to provide mortgage relief to farmers.

From the beginning, the New Deal's farm policy proved controversial. Cotton and wheat farmers had already planted their crops by the time the farm bill passed. A severe drought on the plains constrained the wheat supply naturally, but AAA officials paid farmers to plow up 10 million acres of cotton. The agency also bought and slaughtered some 6 million piglets and 200,000 sows to prevent a future glut of hogs.[35] While much of this pork eventually fed hungry people, the destruction of crops and livestock angered many Americans. When journalist Lorena Hickok went on a fact-finding tour for the administration in the fall of 1933, people in Minnesota and Nebraska complained to her about the New Dealers' methods.[36] "As long as there are 25 million hungry people in this country, there's no overproduction," one Iowa farm leader declared. "For the government to destroy food and reduce crops at such a time is wicked."[37]

Considered in the aggregate, rural America benefited from New Deal farm policies. Within eighteen months of its establishment, the FCA had refinanced one-fifth of all farm mortgages.[38] Prices for crops like corn, wheat, and cotton surged, and net farm income rose by 50 percent between 1932 and 1936.[39] Yet these benefits were not evenly distributed, and AAA policies often exacerbated the plight of tenant farmers and sharecroppers. New Deal officials relied heavily on county-level committees to set production quotas, monitor acreage-reduction contracts, and dispense federal payments. Agricultural Secretary Henry Wallace considered this decentralized approach to be "economic democracy in action," but local committees were often dominated by the largest growers.[40] Large planters and landowners frequently pocketed checks for keeping acreage fallow, then pushed out the tenants and sharecroppers who were actually farming the land. In the South, many of these sharecroppers were African Americans, and so they bore the brunt of such policies. In California, where "factory farms" used migratory laborers, growers rarely restored wages to pre-Depression levels, even after prosperity returned. Tenants, sharecroppers, and farmworkers sometimes fought back—joining groups like the Southern Tenant Farmers Union and the Cannery and Agricultural Workers Industrial Union—but such efforts often provoked violent reprisals. Liberals within the Department of Agriculture who pleaded the case of the disempowered were purged.[41]

Although the Roosevelt administration did little to keep tenants and sharecroppers on their land, it did establish two agencies ostensibly designed to give impoverished farmers a fresh start. The Resettlement Administration (RA), set up in 1935, built three "greenbelt" towns, which were close to big cities and surrounded by countryside. In 1937, it was absorbed into a new agency, the Farm Security Administration (FSA), which established a chain of migrant labor camps and granted low-interest loans to enable some tenants to buy farms. Both agencies, however, faced opposition from farm corporations and southern landlords who wanted to keep their cheap labor. The RA had hoped to move half a million farm families, but ultimately resettled fewer than 5,000.[42] Photographers hired by the FSA to document America and build support for New Deal programs provided many of the most iconic pictures of the Great Depression, and the agency's migrant camps came to public attention when John Steinbeck depicted one in his epic novel *The Grapes of Wrath* in 1939. Nevertheless, the FSA's congressional opponents kept its appropriations low, limiting its ability to make a real dent in rural poverty.

Conservation and Regional Change. As FSA photographs and books like *The Grapes of Wrath* attested, the problems plaguing rural America were not limited to low commodity prices. Across the nation, uncontrolled lumbering had scarred and depleted forests, while intensive farming had ravaged the land. Meanwhile, droughts, wind, and floods depleted the soil. A massive flood on the Mississippi River in 1927 inundated thousands of square miles and displaced some 700,000 people.[43] A single dust storm on the Great Plains in May 1934 sucked 350 million tons of topsoil into the air and deposited it as far east as New York City and Boston.[44] New Dealers believed that only by developing more sustainable agriculture—and by distributing natural resources more equitably—could the living standards of Americans in rural areas be brought up to the same level as those of their urban counterparts.

To achieve this, New Dealers undertook a variety of initiatives. They retired land, sought to restore forests and soil, engaged in flood control and irrigation projects, and produced cheap hydropower to fuel farms and new industries. Historian Sarah Phillips has suggested that these projects reflected a "New Conservation," focused less on the preservation of wild areas or the efficient use of natural resources than on the welfare of rural residents.[45] Since the South and West were the most rural parts of the nation, those regions benefited disproportionately. In fact, New Deal land use and energy policies contributed to the emergence of what would eventually become known as the "Sunbelt."[46]

The first, most ambitious, and ultimately most successful of these New Deal projects was the Tennessee Valley Authority (TVA), established by Roosevelt during his first Hundred Days. Cutting across seven states in one of the most impoverished parts of the nation, the TVA brought economic progress and hope to a region that had seen little of either since the end of the Civil War. In addition to most of Tennessee, the TVA covered swaths of Kentucky, Mississippi, Alabama, Virginia, North Carolina, and Georgia. TVA dams prevented spring floods from displacing residents and washing away topsoil. They also provided ample cheap electricity, which the agency sold to rural co-ops and municipal power systems. TVA experts developed fertilizer, built model towns, upgraded schools and health facilities, planted trees, and restored fish and wildlife habitats. In 1933, 2 percent of farms in this region had electricity; by 1945, 75 percent were electrified. Cheap electricity also attracted new industries to the region, including such corporate behemoths as Monsanto and the Aluminum Company of America (ALCOA).[47] Through its generation of power, not only did the TVA help to modernize the upper South, but it also inserted the federal government more fully and permanently into the private economy than did any other New Deal agency.

The success of the TVA prompted New Dealers to dive more fully into rural electrification. Private power companies had long argued that they could not afford to provide electricity to isolated farms and small, rural communities. As a result, many Americans were still living without the benefits of running water, indoor toilets, lights, refrigeration, or labor-saving devices. In 1935, over the protests of private utilities, New Dealers convinced Congress to establish the Rural Electrification Administration (REA), a move that profoundly changed rural lives. The REA sponsored the creation of hundreds of nonprofit electric cooperatives and offered them low-cost loans for generating plants and power lines. In the early 1930s, fewer than one in ten American farms had electricity. By 1941, the number had risen to four in ten. By 1950, 90 percent of US farms were electrified.[48]

Industrial Policy. If rural electrification was one of the New Deal's greatest successes, industrial policy was one of its biggest failures. When FDR took office, both he and his advisors were convinced that the economy

needed a major stimulus, but few agreed on what form that should take. Some businessmen and New Dealers considered the Depression the result of destructive competition. They argued for suspending antitrust laws and forging industry-wide agreements that would allow businesses to stabilize prices, end overproduction, and ultimately raise wages. Others, more distrustful of the business community, argued either for stimulating competition or for engaging in national economic planning. Many advocated federal spending on publicworks projects to "prime" the economic pump; yet the president and most around him still hoped to avoid running federal deficits. This policy discord prevented FDR from taking any action until near the end of his first Hundred Days. When the Senate passed a work-sharing bill that the president opposed, he ordered staffers who favored differing plans to shut themselves in a room and develop a compromise.[49]

The resulting bill, which Roosevelt proposed in May 1933, contained what one of his advisors later called "a thorough hodge-podge of provisions."[50] Declaring a state of industrial emergency, it largely suspended antitrust laws and created the National Recovery Administration (NRA) to oversee the development of codes to regulate prices, wages, hours, and working conditions for hundreds of industries. Section 7a of the bill gave industrial workers the right "to organize and bargain collectively through representatives of their own choosing," marking a historic reversal of the federal government's traditional refusal to back unionization. Finally, the bill appropriated $3.3 billion to be spent by a new Public Works Administration (PWA). New Dealers hoped that the public works spending would jump-start the economy, buying time for the industrial codes to take effect.

This unwieldy industrial policy foundered from the start. Interior Secretary Harold Ickes, who had been charged with overseeing the PWA, moved with great caution in order to avoid accusations of misusing funds. In the agency's first six months, he spent only $110 million of the billions allocated.[51] As a result, the PWA failed to provide any short-term economic stimulus. The cotton textile millers quickly drafted an industrial code, but other industries were slow to follow. Hugh Johnson, the colorful former general appointed to head the NRA, tried to compensate for this sluggish pace by resorting to the tactics of propaganda and community pressure that had been used successfully by the United States during World War I. Employers who agreed to sign a blanket wage-and-hour code were allowed to display NRA signs picturing a stylized Blue Eagle and the slogan "We Do Our Part." The NRA's Blue Eagle soon landed in store windows and on delivery trucks, and cities across the nation held "Blue Eagle" rallies and parades. This campaign made the NRA one of the most recognized aspects of the New Deal, but it did little to boost employment or improve incomes.

The code-writing process slowly moved forward. Although Johnson and the NRA had been given formal authority over the enterprise, they had no means to enforce compliance. Thus, the largest producers in each industry tended to dominate the proceedings. Mechanisms to fix prices and control production often hurt smaller operators. Code-making panels were supposed to include labor and consumer representatives, but they rarely did. As a result, price rises tended to outpace wage increases. The law eventually produced so many overlapping industrial codes—more than five hundred—that even businessmen complained about NRA bureaucracy.[52] In October 1934, FDR finally secured Johnson's resignation. The following May a unanimous Supreme Court declared the NRA unconstitutional.

Although slow to get started, the PWA ultimately proved more successful. In contrast to other jobs programs launched by the New Deal, the PWA embodied a "trickle-down" approach. The agency paid higher wages than did other work-relief projects, hired more skilled workers, and drew fewer employees from relief rolls. By focusing on large-scale construction

projects, Ickes hoped to stimulate industries that provided materials and components, thus creating jobs indirectly. Between 1933 and 1939, PWA workers built schools, courthouses, city halls, hospitals, and sewage plants. They built the port of Brownsville, Texas; the LaGuardia and Los Angeles Airports; two aircraft carriers; and numerous cruisers, destroyers, gunboats, and planes. The PWA constructed New York City's Lincoln Tunnel, Virginia's Skyline Drive, the San Francisco–Oakland Bay Bridge, the Bonneville and Grand Coulee dams in the Pacific Northwest, and the highway that links Key West to the Florida mainland. Surveying this legacy, one scholar compared Ickes to the Egyptian pharaoh who oversaw construction of the Great Pyramid of Giza.[53]

Crafting Social Security. The PWA and the WPA both provided jobs for able-bodied Americans. They did little, however, for the sick, the disabled, or the elderly—those whom one sympathetic House member called "America's untouchables."[54] Few workers had pensions, and so most worked as long as they were able. Those considered unemployable because of age or health were forced to rely on their families or on local welfare agencies. To help these citizens, to ensure that the elderly did not take jobs away from younger compatriots, and to give all Americans the promise of future "security," the president proposed a sweeping program of unemployment and old-age insurance. The Social Security Act, which FDR signed into law in August 1935, laid the foundation for the US welfare state, reshaping the lives and futures of Americans for generations to come. One Roosevelt biographer called it "the most important single piece of social legislation in all American history, if importance be measured in terms of... direct influence upon the lives of individual Americans."[55]

Historians have argued that the Social Security Act in some ways marked a historic reversal of American political values. Politicians and political commentators had long celebrated individualism and self-help, and for most of the nation's history, the federal government provided little in the way of pensions or insurance to citizens who were not veterans of war. By contrast, the Social Security Act created a national system of old-age insurance, while using federal tax incentives to encourage states to set up their own unemployment insurance plans. The act also provided federal matching funds to states for aid to dependent mothers and children, the blind, and the physically disabled. The Social Security Act marked "a tremendous break with the inhibitions of the past," Arthur M. Schlesinger Jr., wrote in 1958. "The federal government was at last charged with the obligation to provide its citizens a measure of protection from the hazards and vicissitudes of life."[56]

If the Social Security Act was revolutionary in some respects, however, it was deeply conservative in others. New Dealers had hoped to include national health insurance in the bill, but dropped these plans in the face of intense opposition from doctors. Southern Democrats, who were key to FDR's political coalition, worried that giving African Americans too much aid would prompt them to reject backbreaking work at low wages. As a result, the bill's drafters excluded both domestic workers and agricultural laborers from old-age insurance. They also exempted both groups, plus employees of small firms, from unemployment compensation. The cost of these exclusions fell disproportionately on women and racial minorities. Administration of unemployment insurance was also left up to the states, a move that multiplied the possibilities for discriminatory treatment.

Judged by international standards, one of the most conservative aspects of the Social Security program was its funding mechanism. By the 1930s, most modern industrial nations offered some form of social insurance for the elderly that was funded out of general coffers.[57] FDR, however, insisted that the federal pension plan work like private insurance: workers would contribute to their old-age pension accounts through payroll taxes, and benefits

would be tied to the amount that workers paid in. This regressive tax system prevented Social Security from redistributing income, leading to greater levels of income inequality among the US elderly than among the aged in other industrialized nations. FDR, however, insisted that the decision to fund the program this way was political: "We put these payroll contributions there so as to give the contributors a legal, moral, and political right to collect their pensions and their unemployment benefits," he declared. "With those taxes in there, no damn politician can ever scrap my social security program."[58] In this assessment, Roosevelt proved prescient.

A New Deal for Labor. When Congress passed the National Industrial Recovery Act, United Mine Workers president John L. Lewis likened Section 7a—the section requiring management to engage in good-faith collective bargaining with workers—to Lincoln's Emancipation Proclamation. For decades, American workers had been divided along skill, race, and ethnic lines, and government at all levels had generally sided with corporations rather than unions. The 1920s had been a particularly difficult decade for organized labor as unfavorable court rulings, cautious union leadership, corporate use of welfare capitalism and government attacks on those perceived as radical all eroded union ranks. Section 7a appeared to reverse the tide, and Lewis jumped to take advantage of the new legislation. Gambling much of the mineworkers' treasury on a bold campaign, he sent organizers into the coalfields in the summer of 1933 with instructions to invoke the authority of the New Deal: "The President wants you to unionize," organizers told miners, adding that not doing so was "unpatriotic." Within months, the union's membership quadrupled.[59]

It soon became clear, however, that Section 7a was not the labor cure-all for which Lewis had hoped. Employers in many industries continued to defy the new law or to evade its requirements by installing company unions

236 • THE NEW DEAL

that they controlled. The act contained few real enforcement mechanisms, and NRA head Hugh Johnson seemed disinclined to use those that existed. As workers grew increasingly frustrated, industry after industry erupted in strikes. In 1934, a walkout by textile workers stretched across twenty states. In Toledo, Ohio, striking employees of an auto-parts company battled National Guardsmen in the streets. Strikes by Minneapolis teamsters and San Francisco longshoremen touched off general strikes in both cities.

These strikes, in and of themselves, produced only limited gains for labor, but they signaled a new militancy—and unity—on the part of America's workers. These changes in part reflected the economic strains of the Depression, but as Lizabeth Cohen has shown, they also reflected important shifts in the orientation of working-class Americans during the 1920s and 1930s. Restrictive legislation passed in the early 1920s curbed the flow of new immigrants into the United States, contributing to the maturation of ethnic communities. Mass consumption and mass culture gradually gave workers of different ethnic backgrounds common ground, creating a more unified working-class culture. Meanwhile, employers' use of welfare capitalism during the 1920s raised workers' expectations. The Depression destroyed two safety nets that workers had relied on: the wages and benefits once offered by employers, and the webs of assistance rooted in ethnic and religious institutions.[60]

The labor unrest of late 1933 and 1934 helped persuade FDR to throw his support very belatedly behind a new labor law crafted largely by New York Senator Robert Wagner. Roosevelt and his Labor Secretary Frances Perkins hoped to boost workers' purchasing power through wage-and-hour legislation and laws affecting pensions and unemployment. They were less concerned about extending workers' political power by guaranteeing their collective-bargaining rights.[61] As a result, Roosevelt initially showed little interest in closing the loopholes that weakened Section 7a.

In late May 1935, however, the Supreme Court nullified the National Industrial Recovery Act, thus limiting FDR's options. With Congress poised to pass the new labor law in any case, the president finally declared it a high priority.

Passage of the National Labor Relations Act (more commonly known as the Wagner Act) in the summer of 1935 helped set the stage for an historic organizing drive. The economy had begun to recover, making companies more vulnerable to shutdowns. Liberal Democrats allied with the New Deal and sympathetic to labor won the governorships of such key industrial states as New York, Pennsylvania, and Michigan. Lewis decided that the time was ripe to organize mass-production workers in industrial unions. In November 1935, he and a handful of allies formed what would become the Congress of Industrial Organizations (CIO).[62] In the first four months of 1937, CIO unions "conquered the two most significant outposts of the open shop in mass-production industry": General Motors and U.S. Steel. By the end of the year, organized labor had recruited some 3 million new members and unions represented almost 23 percent of the nonagricultural workforce, the largest proportion to that point in US history.[63]

Such victories were short-lived. By late 1937, the CIO's successes had sparked fierce attacks from corporate adversaries, Southern congressmen, craft unionists in the American Federation of Labor (AFL), and some New Dealers.[64] It would take World War II to again reinvigorate the labor movement. The Wagner Act did, however, help solidify labor support for the Democratic Party. Worker support, in turn, prompted New Dealers to push through the Fair Labor Standards Act (FLSA), which banned child labor and set minimum wage and maximum hour laws. (Agricultural laborers and domestic workers were exempted from the act, just as they had been from Social Security.) "For generations to come," one historian has written, "the FLSA would stand as the backbone of U.S. employment law."[65]

THE LEGACIES AND LIMITS OF THE NEW DEAL

Passage of the FLSA in June 1938 marked the end of New Deal reform. Roosevelt won a landslide reelection in 1936, but his second term proved rocky from the start. Some of the wounds were self-inflicted. Unhappy with Supreme Court decisions overturning key pieces of New Deal legislation, FDR proposed a bill allowing the president to appoint one new justice for every justice over the age of seventy who refused to retire; if passed, the bill would have enabled Roosevelt immediately to appoint six additional justices. This transparently political move drew wrath from New Deal opponents and criticism even from many of FDR's allies. Before Congress could act, the swing justice switched sides and began voting to uphold New Deal laws. His shift, together with the retirement of another justice, ushered in a new, more liberal Supreme Court era, and effectively killed the Court reform bill. Nevertheless, the backlash associated with FDR's "court-packing" scheme sapped much of the New Deal's political momentum.[66]

The president's political problems were soon compounded by an economic downturn that became known as the "Roosevelt Recession." For most of FDR's presidency, the economy had improved steadily, in part because of ample government spending. Roosevelt, however, had never abandoned his belief in a balanced budget, and in early 1937 he decided the time had come for federal belt tightening. He ordered dramatic cutbacks in both the WPA and the PWA, even as the first Social Security taxes pulled $2 billion out of the US economy. All this sent the economy into a tailspin. Stock prices began falling in October 1937 and dropped nearly 50 percent in just seven months. Industrial production cratered, and some 4 million workers lost their jobs.[67] Unemployment, which had fallen sharply throughout July 1937, moved upwards until the following June.[68]

FDR's court-packing scheme, economic duress, and a wave of sit-down strikes by industrial unionists all weakened support for the New Deal in some quarters. In the latter half of 1937, a group of conservative Democrats, mostly Southerners, joined forces with Republicans to stymie any further New Deal legislation. The FLSA squeaked through, but in the 1938 midterm elections, Republicans made big gains in both houses. In 1939, Congress began scaling back or killing off federal projects, beginning with the WPA's Federal Theater and Federal Art projects. By the end of 1943, Congress had eliminated the CCC, the WPA, the Home Owners' Loan Corporation (HOLC), and numerous other New Deal programs.[69]

So what did the New Deal do and whom did it benefit? New Deal policies did not restore the economy to pre-Depression levels—only World War II did that—but between 1933 and 1937, the nation's real gross national product grew at an annual rate of over 8 percent a year. Growth slowed during the Roosevelt Recession, but averaged over 10 percent a year between 1938 and 1941. As economist Christina Romer has written, these rates are "spectacular, even for an economy pulling out of a severe depression."[70] By strengthening the power of the federal government and extending federal regulation into entirely new areas of the economy, the New Deal helped to "devolatilize" American capitalism.[71] It stabilized the farm economy after two decades of depression, and introduced programs like crop subsidies and soil conservation that became staples of federal farm policy for decades to come. New Deal work-relief programs like the CCC, the PWA, and the WPA relieved the misery of millions of Americans, while building a vast public infrastructure that permanently changed the American landscape. Over time, Social Security dramatically reduced the number of elderly poor.

America's industrial workers helped to "make" the New Deal, and white male workers were among its prime beneficiaries. In earlier decades, many members of the working class—particularly those who were foreign born—had not bothered to vote, and their party loyalties were fickle. Many simply found national party politics irrelevant to their lives. By the end of the 1930s, all this had changed. Many workers had received federal relief checks and jobs. Even more benefited from federal bank deposit and unemployment insurance, long-term low-interest mortgages offered by the HOLC, a nationally set minimum wage, and the promise of Social Security benefits in old age. In return, millions of working-class voters became loyal Democrats, ensuring the dominance of the Democratic Party for decades to come.[72]

Not all Americans benefited equally from the New Deal, however. Women achieved important symbolic breakthroughs: FDR appointed the first female Cabinet member, Labor Secretary Frances Perkins, as well as the first woman to serve on the US Court of Appeals. Women also played an increasingly important role in the machinery of the Democratic Party. Overall, however, New Deal programs discriminated against women. Most New Dealers, including Perkins and First Lady Eleanor Roosevelt, saw men as heads of households, who were thus in greater need of work. As a result, federal work-relief programs employed women at a far lower rate than men. Of 1.6 million public-works jobs given out in 1934, only 11 percent went to women. Women held about 12 percent of WPA jobs, even though they made up at least 25 percent of the unemployed.[73] New Deal programs generally assigned women to gender-specific jobs—for instance, sewing and canning projects—and paid them a fraction of the wages given to their male counterparts. (Professional women, particularly those employed in the WPA's arts programs, fared somewhat better.)

If gender inequity was built into most New Deal programs, so too was racial inequality. White Southern Democrats played a key role in the New Deal coalition, and "Dixiecrat" politicians exercised inordinate power in both the House and the Senate.[74] As a result, FDR and his advisors went to great lengths to appease them. The CCC established segregated camps for African Americans, often far from population centers. NRA wage codes generally prescribed lower wages for blacks than for whites, while work-relief programs like the WPA often relegated African Americans to the lowest-paying jobs. Federal efforts to promote "grassroots democracy" gave control of the AAA and other New Deal programs to local authorities, who administered them in accordance with local (often racist) mores. Afraid of alienating his southern supporters, FDR refused to support antilynching legislation or a ban on the poll tax.

The New Deal's social insurance and labor protection programs also discriminated against women and racial minorities. The Social Security Act exempted domestics and agricultural laborers, as well as individuals who worked intermittently and were employed in fields like education and nursing that were heavily female. As a result, more than three-quarters of all female wage earners and at least 65 percent of African Americans were initially denied coverage.[75] These rules—together with similar exclusions in the FLSA—also hurt many other racial minorities, as well as poor, rural whites. The Wagner Act helped workers in organized industries like steel, rubber, and automobiles, which were heavily dominated by white men. It did little for agricultural laborers, those in the largely unorganized service sector, or most workers in the South—in other words, for most employed white women and racial minorities.

Despite such rampant inequities, the New Deal did more for African Americans than had any past administration since Abraham Lincoln's. As a result, African Americans switched parties en masse, setting the stage for a broader party realignment in the 1960s and beyond. African American voters put civil rights on the Democratic Party's agenda after World War II, ultimately leading to a widespread defection by white Southerners. The New Deal drew millions of immigrants from Southern and Eastern Europe into national politics for the first time, but many of these working-class ethnics eventually became "Reagan Republicans."

The industrial labor movement proved to be what Robert Zieger has called a "fragile juggernaut": unions gained members and contract rights through the 1950s, but the CIO's militancy was quickly curbed and union membership as a percentage of the American workforce fell sharply beginning in the 1970s.[76]

While many New Deal programs and institutions were killed off, others—federal deposit insurance, the Securities and Exchange Commission, the Tennessee Valley Authority, and the Fair Labor Standards Act, among them— continue to the present day. Social Security gradually expanded to include domestic workers, agricultural laborers, and other excluded groups, making it more nearly universal. All this has left scholars, politicians, and pundits arguing over how to understand the New Deal's legacy for the 20th century and beyond.

DISCUSSION OF THE LITERATURE

Few eras in modern American history have been the subject of more sustained scholarship or intense debate among both academics and popular commentators than the New Deal. Most agree that the policies of the Roosevelt administration brought new groups into the political process, laid the foundation for the welfare state, and greatly expanded both the power of the presidency and the reach of the federal government. Beyond this, however, historical judgments have differed markedly. For years, most scholars lauded President Roosevelt and cast the New Deal as a watershed in American history, albeit one consistent with American values and the nation's reform tradition. Critics on the right and left, however, portrayed Roosevelt as a political opportunist who used the New Deal either to subvert or to preserve the nation's capitalist system. In recent years, most scholars have acknowledged the New Deal's achievements, but also stressed its limitations. Many have also deemphasized the role played by Roosevelt, and some have questioned the New Deal's long-term impact.

Most New Deal scholarship has revolved around a handful of questions: how radical or conservative were Roosevelt's domestic policies? What or whom did they benefit? When and why did the political "order" created by the New Deal come to an end? And what has been the New Deal's lasting legacy for American politics, society, and culture? How historians and political scientists have answered these questions has depended on their ideological outlooks, the temper of their times, and their assessment of the possibilities and limits of American political culture. Since the New Deal itself was not always ideologically coherent and it evolved over time, historical assessments have also depended on the aspects of the New Deal that scholars have chosen to emphasize.

The first scholars to offer sustained accounts of the New Deal were those who came of age during the Great Depression. Most were liberals whose political outlooks were shaped by their own experiences during the 1930s and 1940s and by the politics of the Cold War and of McCarthyism that followed. Arthur M. Schlesinger Jr., Frank Freidel, Eric Goldman, and others focused on the commanding figure of President Franklin Delano Roosevelt, celebrating the dramatic transformation that he and his New Dealers wrought in both American policies and political culture.[77] These liberals portrayed the New Deal as a moment of democratic renewal, when the federal government intervened in the nation's political economy to protect the marginal and exploited from powerful and privileged "interests." Richard Hofstadter considered the New Deal to be "a drastic new departure."[78] Carl Degler went even further, calling it the "Third American Revolution," after the War of Independence and the Civil War.[79]

Even as these liberal historians emphasized the revolutionary nature of the New Deal, most also rooted it in a tradition of American reform. This was partly to blunt the attack of a handful of conservative commentators and scholars who argued that Roosevelt had weakened "the Constitutional system" and hurt the economy by exercising dictatorial powers on behalf of "Socialistic" and un-American objectives.[80] Such arguments originated with contemporary critics of the New Deal like Raymond Moley, a member of FDR's "Brain Trust" who eventually broke with the president and became a conservative Republican.[81] For decades, conservative critics of the New Deal were few and far between, but in recent years a new group of right-wing journalists and think-tank scholars have resurrected such arguments.[82]

By the late 1960s, the classic "liberal" interpretation of the New Deal was also drawing fire from critics in the "New Left." Scholars like Barton Bernstein, Paul Conkin, and Howard Zinn argued that the New Deal had not transformed corporate capitalism so much as "conserved and protected" it. Bernstein summarized this viewpoint in a widely read essay subtitled "The Conservative Achievements of Liberal Reform." He acknowledged that New Deal policies had helped some downtrodden Americans, but argued that Roosevelt and his advisors had spurned more substantive change. They did not question private enterprise or nationalize the banking system. They did not undertake massive public housing construction or use the tax system to fundamentally redistribute income or wealth. They failed to challenge both the southern "race system" and the power of the business class. By co-opting and incorporating the discontented, Bernstein and his allies charged, FDR and his New Dealers had blunted the possibility of more revolutionary change.[83]

Reassessing the New Deal in the Face of Conservative Resurgence. Both classic liberals and New Leftists wrote during the decades of Democratic Party dominance; thus, they assumed that "the political era ushered in by the New Deal would go on forever."[84] By the 1970s, however, that assumption seemed increasingly untenable. Richard Nixon's election to the presidency in 1968 signaled the

fraying of the New Deal coalition. In 1980, Ronald Reagan swept to victory on the Republican ticket, bringing a Republican House and Senate with him. Reagan's victory ushered in a period of conservative resurgence, which prompted scholars to conclude that the "New Deal order" had come to an end.[85] This realization helped catalyze a shift in both the dominant tone of New Deal scholarship and in the questions asked by historians. Most scholars writing in recent decades have followed the lead of William Leuchtenburg, who declared in a pioneering 1963 work that the New Deal was only a "half-way Revolution."[86] Historians have differed primarily on the relative weights they have assigned to the New Deal's achievements and limitations, and on how they have explained the demise of the "New Deal order."

No single book better exemplified this shift in tone and emphasis than the 1989 essay collection entitled *The Rise and Fall of the New Deal Order.* As editors Gary Gerstle and Steve Fraser wrote in their introduction, "The witnessing of a political era's eclipse has imparted to many of these essays a sober and ironic tone, appropriate to political analyses that stress missed opportunities, unintended consequences, and dangerous but inescapable compromises."[87] Many of those who contributed to the volume developed their arguments further in subsequent books. Steve Fraser and Nelson Lichtenstein, for instance, both argued that labor leaders entered the Depression decade with dreams of institutionalizing industrial or social democracy. They gradually gave up on this public-policy vision, however, settling instead for more generous benefits and greater job security gleaned through contracts negotiated with management.[88] In a similar vein, Alan Brinkley suggested that between 1937 and 1945, the dominant ideology among New Dealers shifted from an emphasis on regulation in the public interest to a faith in Keynesianism and economic growth as "the surest route to social progress." The result, he declared, was "the end of reform."[89]

While these historians focused broadly on issues of political economy, scholars of race and gender highlighted the limits of New Deal egalitarianism. Ira Katznelson and Mary Poole showed that many New Deal programs discriminated against African Americans, resulting in what Katznelson dubbed "affirmative action for whites."[90] The sociologist Cybelle Fox argued that European immigrants received more generous access to social welfare programs than did African Americans, and Mexican immigrants.[91] Linda Gordon, Gwendolyn Mink, Suzanne Mettler, and Alice Kessler-Harris explored what Kessler-Harris called "the gendered limits of social citizenship." They pointed out that many New Deal programs, including such landmark initiatives as Social Security and the Fair Labor Standards Act, treated men and women quite differently.[92]

Still other authors emphasized the contributions of the New Deal, even as they acknowledged its limitations. In his magisterial *Freedom from Fear*, David M. Kennedy argued that the New Deal not only provided relief and social insurance to many "vulnerable individuals," but also "erected an institutional scaffolding designed to provide unprecedented stability and predictability" to large segments of the American economy. In doing so, he suggested, the New Deal helped to catalyze postwar prosperity, while giving "countless Americans" a new "sense of security, and with it a sense of having a stake in their country."[93] Ira Katznelson struck a note of both tragedy and triumph in his monumental 2013 book, *Fear Itself*. Elaborating on a theme he had explored in earlier works, Katznelson described the way that Southern Democrats in Congress built racial inequality into the very foundation of the New Deal. This "Faustian terrible compromise" on the domestic front was the price that FDR had to pay for what Katznelson saw as the New Deal's most important achievement: its "demonstration that liberal democracy, a political system with a legislature at its heart, could govern effectively in the face of great danger." At a time when the Depression was destabilizing societies around the globe— a time when fascists and communists were on

the march—the New Deal reinvigorated democratic institutions and redefined the role of government, giving liberal democracy renewed and lasting "legitimacy and prestige" around the world.[94]

Katznelson measured the New Deal's achievements against the successes of fascism and communism abroad. I have suggested that this same context helped to derail the drive for economic justice that animated industrial unionists and their New Deal allies during the 1930s. Alarmed by the chaos of the Depression years and convinced that internal disunity had undermined democracies abroad, Americans with divergent political outlooks and agendas increasingly emphasized Americans' common ground. Against the backdrop of war and Cold War, businessmen alarmed by what they saw as the New Deal's class-based resentments sometimes made common cause with liberals eager to contain religious and ethnic hostilities. In an effort to succor social harmony, both groups sought to define a unifying and distinctive "American Way." They helped to shape a consensus ethos that privileged civility over equality, delegitimized many forms of dissent, and constrained American politics into the 1960s.[95]

Most of the authors discussed to this point either imply or explicitly argue that the ultimate demise of the "New Deal order" resulted from flaws in the New Deal's architecture or from fractures in the Democratic coalition. To paraphrase James T. Kloppenberg, they would say that the New Deal order was not pushed, but rather jumped.[96] Recently, however, several historians have focused on those who sought to speed the New Deal order on its way. Kim Phillips-Fein has shown how right-wing businessmen waged continuous and often covert war on New Deal legislation and values from the 1930s through the ascendancy of Ronald Reagan in 1980. By funding think tanks and foundations—and recruiting politicians, intellectuals, ministers, and others to their cause—these men worked "to undo the system of labor unions, federal social welfare programs, and government regulation of the economy that came into existence during and after the Great Depression of the 1930s."[97] In *One Nation Under God*, Kevin M. Kruse elaborates on the coalition of conservative businessmen and religious leaders who united to oppose the New Deal and who helped to transform both American religious and political culture.[98]

The books of both Phillips-Fein and Kruse reflect a shift in the focus of political history since the turn of the 21st century—a renewed interest in the type of conservatives that the first New Deal historians would have considered "fringe." Both books call into question the power and legacy of postwar liberalism. Recently, Jefferson Cowie has gone even further, questioning the assumption made by most prior historians that the New Deal marked a turning point in American political culture, even if only a "halfway Revolution." The New Deal was a "triumph of redistributive policy," Cowie affirms, at least for "the white, male industrial working class." Its reform of capitalism, however, could not last. Between the 1930s and the 1970s, a rare convergence of historical circumstances—"changes in the state, immigration, culture and race"—briefly enabled "a limited but powerful sense of working-class unity" that triumphed over America's long-standing ideology of individualism. When those historical factors subsided, however, the nation's commitment to overcoming economic inequality frayed. The New Deal order, Cowie argues, "marks what might be called a 'great exception'—a sustained deviation, an extended detour—from some of the main contours of American political practice, economic structure, and cultural outlook."[99]

PRIMARY SOURCES

Few eras in American history have been as well documented in words and film as the 1930s. Thus the New Deal offers scholars and students a wealth of available published and online primary sources. A number of books capture the human toll taken by the Depression, as well as the response of diverse Americans to the policies proposed by their leaders. In 1933, Harry Hopkins, who headed first the Federal Emergency Relief Administration and then the Works Progress Administration, dispatched the journalist Lorena Hickok to gather information about the day-to-day toll that the Depression was exacting on ordinary citizens. Over the course of two years, Hickok traversed thirty-two states. The reports she sent back are compiled by Richard Lowitt and Maurine Beasley in *One Third of a Nation: Lorena Hickok Reports on the Great Depression*.[100] Robert S. McElvaine's *Down and Out in the Great Depression: Letters from the Forgotten Man* collects nearly 200 letters written by ordinary men, women, and children to those who occupied or worked in the White House during the Great Depression. The letters show the personal connection many Americans felt with FDR, and they display a wide range of emotions toward both the economic cataclysm and government relief.[101] Between 1938 and 1942, the Federal Writers Project sent writers across the country to interview individuals of diverse backgrounds, occupations, and circumstances. In *First Person America*, Ann Banks offers eighty of these life stories, including those of a Polish immigrant, a Chicago jazzman, a retired Oregon prospector, a North Carolina tobacco farmer, and a Bahamian midwife living in Florida.[102] Decades after the Depression, the journalist Studs Terkel interviewed dozens of Americans who lived through the 1930s. He recorded their words in *Hard Times: An Oral History of the Great Depression*.[103]

New Dealers had a sense that they were living through and shaping history, and many produced memoirs recording their experiences. One of the first to appear was Harry Hopkins's *Spending to Save*.[104] Raymond Moley, an original member of FDR's Brain Trust who eventually became one of the New Deal's harshest critics, published *After Seven Years*.[105] The many other accounts by New Dealers include these by the only two members of Roosevelt's Cabinet who served throughout his entire presidency: Frances Perkins's *The Roosevelt I Knew* and Harold L. Ickes's *The Secret Diary of Harold L. Ickes.*[106]

Many archives have made extensive collections of New Deal materials available online and can be found in "Digital Materials." The Franklin D. Roosevelt Presidential Library and Museum has digitized major collections of FDR's papers, selected correspondence of First Lady Eleanor Roosevelt; the complete diaries of Treasury Secretary Henry Morgenthau Jr.; and other New Deal documents deemed particularly significant. The Library also provides links to videos of FDR and to online versions of two documentary films produced by the government and designed to build support for New Deal programs: Pare Lorentz's *The Plow That Broke the Plains* and *The River.* The Library of Congress has also digitized numerous collections relating to the New Deal, including photographs taken by Farm Security Administration photographers; life histories collected by members of the Federal Writers Project; ethnographic materials documenting the lives of migrants living in California work camps run by the FSA; images, posters, and scripts produced by the Federal Theatre Project; and posters designed by graphic artists working for the WPA.

DIGITAL MATERIALS

Franklin D. Roosevelt Presidential Library and Museum (http://www.fdrlibrary.marist .edu/). This link offers access to the digitized collections of the Franklin D. Roosevelt Presidential Library and Museum.

The American Presidency Project (http:// www.presidency.ucsb.edu/). This searchable document archive contains the addresses, proclamations, news conferences, executive orders, and fireside chats of Franklin Delano Roosevelt, as well as those of the presidents who preceded and followed him.

The Living New Deal (https://livingnewdeal .org/about/). The Living New Deal, developed in part by the Department of Geography at the University of California at Berkeley, is a national database of thousands of documents, photographs, and personal stories about public works made possible by the New Deal. The site contains a map, continually under construction, indicating thousands of projects undertaken by the Civilian Conservation Corps, Public Works Administration, Works Progress Administration, Tennessee Valley Authority, and other New Deal agencies. Projects are searchable by location, New Deal agency, category and artist.

The Library of Congress hosts numerous collections of primary sources related to the New Deal, including:

The New Deal Stage: Selections from the Federal Theatre Project, 1935–1939 (http:// memory.loc.gov/ammem/fedtp/fthome .html). This collection contains more than 13,000 images of stage and costume designs, still photographs, posters, scripts for productions, and other materials from the Federal Theatre Project.

Works Progress Administration Posters (http://www.loc.gov/pictures/collection /wpapos/). This collection consists of 907 digitized posters created from 1936 to 1943 by various branches of the WPA. The posters were designed to publicize health and safety programs, art exhibitions, theatrical and musical performances, travel and tourism, and educational programs in seventeen states and the District of Columbia. The states most frequently represented in the collection are California, Illinois, New York, Ohio, and Pennsylvania.

Documenting America, 1935–1943: The Farm Security Administration/Office of War Information Photo Collection (http://www .loc.gov/rr/program/journey/fsa.html). This site contains two videos introducing users to the vast collection of images taken by photographers for the FSA (and later the Office of War Information). Many of these pictures— taken by such photographers as Dorothea Lange, Walker Evans, Arthur Rothstein, and

Gordon Parks—are some of the most iconic images of the Depression era. The website also includes links to collections of these photographs digitized by the Library of Congress and to other relevant materials.

American Life Histories: Manuscripts from the Federal Writers' Project, 1936–1940 (https://www.loc.gov/collections/federal -writers-project/). This collection of life histories consists of about 2,900 documents compiled by some three hundred employees of the Federal Writers' Project working in twenty-four states. The documents include narratives, dialogues, reports, and case histories. Those interviewed recounted immigrating, undertaking grueling factory work, farming tobacco, and journeying west, among other things. The documents also include tales of meeting Billy the Kid and surviving the 1871 Chicago fire.

Voices from the Dust Bowl: The Charles L. Todd and Robert Sonkin Migrant Worker Collection, 1940 to 1941 (https://www.loc .gov/collections/todd-and-sonkin-migrant -workers-from-1940-to-1941). This website presents materials from an ethnographic field collection documenting the everyday life of residents of ten Farm Security Administration migrant work camps in central California in 1940 and 1941. Charles Todd and Robert Sonkin documented dance tunes, cowboy songs, traditional ballads, play party and square dance calls, camp council meetings, camp court proceedings, conversations, storytelling sessions, and personal experience narratives of the Dust Bowl refugees who inhabited the camps. The digitized collection includes audio recordings, graphic images, and print materials.

FURTHER READING

Badger, Anthony J. *The New Deal: The Depression Years, 1933–40.* New York: Hill and Wang, 1989.
Bernstein, Barton J. "The New Deal: The Conservative Achievements of Liberal Reform." In *Towards a New Past: Dissenting Essays in American History.* Edited by Barton J. Bernstein, 263–288. New York: Pantheon Books, 1968.
Borgwardt, Elizabeth. *A New Deal for the World: America's Vision for Human Rights.* Cambridge, MA: Harvard University Press, 2005.
Brinkley, Alan. *The End of Reform: New Deal Liberalism in Recession and War.* New York: Knopf, 1995.
Cohen, Lizabeth. *Making a New Deal: Industrial Workers in Chicago, 1919–1939.* New York: Cambridge University Press, 1990.
Cowie, Jefferson, and Nick Salvatore. "The Long Exception: Rethinking the Place of the New Deal in American History." *International Labor and Working-Class History* 74 (Fall 2008): 3–32.
Denning, Michael. *The Cultural Front: The Laboring of American Culture.* New York: Verso, 1997.
Fraser, Steve, and Gary Gerstle, eds. *The Rise and Fall of the New Deal Order, 1930–1980.* Princeton, NJ: Princeton University Press, 1989.
Hawley, Ellis W. *The New Deal and the Problem of Monopoly: A Study in Economic Ambivalence.* Princeton, NJ: Princeton University Press, 1966.
Jacobs, Meg. *Pocketbook Politics: Economic Citizenship in Twentieth Century America.* Princeton, NJ: Princeton University Press, 2005.
Katznelson, Ira. *Fear Itself: The New Deal and the Origins of Our Time.* New York: Liveright, 2013.
Kennedy, David M. *Freedom from Fear: The American People in Depression and War, 1929–1945.* New York: Oxford University Press, 1999.
Kessler-Harris, Alice. "In the Nation's Image: The Gendered Limits of Social Citizenship in the Depression Era." *Journal of American History* 86 (December 1999): 1251–1279.
Leff, Mark. *The Limits of Symbolic Reform: The New Deal and Taxation, 1933–1939.* New York: Cambridge University Press, 1984.
Leuchtenburg, William E. *Franklin D. Roosevelt and the New Deal, 1932–1940.* New York: Harper & Row, 1963.
Maher, Neil M. *Nature's New Deal: The Civilian Conservation Corps and the Roots of the American Environmental Movement.* New York: Oxford University Press, 2008.
Mettler, Suzanne. *Dividing Citizens: Gender and Federalism in New Deal Public Policy.* Ithaca, NY: Cornell University Press, 1998.
Patel, Kiran Klaus. *The New Deal: A Global History.* Princeton, NJ: Princeton University Press, 2016.
Phillips, Sarah T. *This Land, This Nation: Conservation, Rural America, and the New Deal.* New York: Cambridge University Press, 2007.

Phillips-Fein, Kim. *Invisible Hands: The Making of the Conservative Movement from the New Deal to Reagan.* New York: W. W. Norton, 2009.

Poole, Mary. *The Segregated Origins of Social Security: African Americans and the Welfare State.* Chapel Hill: University of North Carolina Press, 2006.

Schlesinger, Arthur M., Jr. *The Age of Roosevelt.* 3 vols. Boston: Houghton Mifflin, 1957–1960.

Wall, Wendy. *Inventing the "American Way": The Politics of Consensus from the New Deal to the Civil Rights Movement.* New York: Oxford University Press, 2008.

Zieger, Robert H. *The CIO, 1935–1955.* Chapel Hill: University of North Carolina Press, 1995.

NOTES

1. Franklin D. Roosevelt, "Address Accepting the Presidential Nomination at the Democratic National Convention in Chicago," July 2, 1932; available online at *The American Presidency Project*, hosted by John T. Woolley and Gerhard Peters, http://www.presidency.ucsb.edu/.

2. William H. Chafe, ed., *The Achievement of American Liberalism: The New Deal and Its Legacies* (New York: Columbia University Press, 2002), xiii.

3. Robert Westbrook, "Tragic Deal," *Reviews in American History* 43 (March 2015): 1.

4. David M. Kennedy, *Freedom from Fear: The American People in Depression and War, 1929–1945* (New York: Oxford University Press, 1999), 87, 133, 162–163. For the global causes and reach of the Great Depression, see Eric Hobsbawm, *The Age of Extremes: A History of the World, 1914–1991* (New York: Vintage Books, 1994), 85–108 and Kiran Klaus Patel, *The New Deal: A Global History* (Princeton, NJ: Princeton University Press, 2016), 10–44.

5. Franklin D. Roosevelt, "Address at Oglethorpe University in Atlanta, Georgia," May 22, 1932; available online at *The American Presidency Project.* http://www.presidency.ucsb.edu/ws /?pid=88410.

6. Roosevelt famously articulated this "3R" formula in his fireside chat of June 28, 1934, available online at *The American Presidency Project* http://www.presidency.ucsb.edu/ws/index .php?pid=14703.

7. Kennedy, *Freedom from Fear*, 363.

8. Glenn C. Altschuler and Stuart M. Blumin, *The GI Bill: A New Deal for Veterans* (New York: Oxford University Press, 2009). Altschuler and Blumin argue, for instance, that the GI Bill's provision extending low-interest home loans to veterans was built on New Deal policies that restructured the home mortgage market.

9. Ira Katznelson, *Fear Itself: The New Deal and the Origins of Our Time* (New York: Liveright, 2013), 4–5.

10. Elizabeth Borgwardt, *A New Deal for the World: America's Vision for Human Rights* (Cambridge, MA.: Harvard University Press, 2005), 7–8.

11. Patel, *The New Deal*, 274.

12. Sarah T. Phillips, *This Land, This Nation: Conservation, Rural America, and the New Deal* (New York: Cambridge University Press, 2007), 18, 242–283.

13. Steve Fraser and Gary Gerstle, "Introduction," in Steve Fraser and Gary Gerstle, eds., *The Rise and Fall of the New Deal Order, 1930–1980* (Princeton, NJ: Princeton University Press, 1989), ix–xxv, xi.

14. The Twentieth Amendment to the Constitution, which took effect in 1937, moved the presidential inauguration to January 20 of the year following the election.

15. For brief summaries of this ongoing debate from different perspectives, see William E. Leuchtenburg, *Franklin D. Roosevelt and the New Deal, 1932–1940* (New York: Harper & Row, 1963), 162–163; Morton Keller, "The New Deal: A New Look," *Polity* 31, no. 4 (1999): 657–663; Kennedy, *Freedom from Fear*, 248, n 54.

16. Kennedy, *Freedom from Fear*, 365.

17. Kennedy, *Freedom from Fear*, 132–133.

18. Arthur M. Schlesinger Jr., *The Coming of the New Deal*, vol. 2 in *The Age of Roosevelt* (Boston: Houghton Mifflin Co., 1958), 5.

19. Franklin D. Roosevelt, "Fireside Chat on Banking," March 12, 1933. Available online at *The American Presidency Project*. http://www.presidency.ucsb .edu/ws/?pid=14540.

20. Raymond Moley, *After Seven Years* (New York: Harper, 1939), 155.

21. Leuchtenburg, *Franklin D. Roosevelt and the New Deal*, 60; Milton Friedman and Anna Jacobson Schwartz, *From New Deal Banking Reform to World War II Inflation* (Princeton, NJ: Princeton University Press, 2014), 21.

22. Leuchtenburg, *Franklin D. Roosevelt and the New Deal*, 50–51; Eric Rauchway, *The Great Depression and The New Deal: A Very Short Introduction* (New York: Oxford University Press, 2008), 60–63.

23. Kennedy, *Freedom from Fear*, 163–164.

24. The best account of the CCC to date is Neil M. Maher's *Nature's New Deal: The Civilian Conservation Corps and the Roots of the American Environmental Movement* (New York: Oxford University Press, 2008).

25. James T. Patterson, *America's Struggle Against Poverty in the 20th Century*, enlarged ed. (Cambridge, MA: Harvard University Press, 2000), 56–58.

26. Franklin D. Roosevelt, "Annual Message to Congress," January 4, 1935. Available online at *The American Presidency Project*. http://www.presidency.ucsb.edu/ws/index.php?pid=14890&st=&st1=.

27. Kennedy, *Freedom from Fear*, 253–255.

28. Anthony J. Badger, *The New Deal: The Depression Years, 1933–40* (New York: Hill and Wang, 1989), 212.

29. Kennedy, *Freedom from Fear*, 253–254.

30. Harry L. Hopkins, *Spending to Save: The Complete Story of Relief* (New York: W. W. Norton, 1936), 114.

31. During World War I, crop production fell in many of the warring European powers. US farmers dramatically expanded production to meet this demand, often borrowing to buy more land and equipment. When the war ended and the demand for exported crops declined, farm production outran demand, pushing prices down.

32. Kennedy, *Freedom from Fear*, 141.

33. Leuchtenburg, *Franklin D. Roosevelt and the New Deal*, 23; "Milk Is Dumped in Rochester War," *New York Times*, March 30, 1933. John Steinbeck famously decried the burning of oranges and other crops when migrant families went hungry, see the reissue edition of *The Grapes of Wrath* (New York: Penguin Classics, 2006), 348–349.

34. Senate seats are allocated on a state-by-state basis, a method that overrepresents rural areas. Moreover, as Eric Rauchway has noted, Congress failed to adopt a redistricting scheme after the 1920 Census, the first census to show a majority of Americans living in urban areas. Rauchway, *The Great Depression and the New Deal*, 74–75.

35. Janet Poppendieck, *Breadlines Knee-Deep in Wheat: Food Assistance in the Great Depression*, updated and expanded ed. (Berkeley: University of California Press, 2014), 112.

36. Richard Lowitt and Maurine Beasley, eds., *One Third of a Nation: Lorena Hickok Reports on the Great Depression*, (Urbana: University of Illinois Press, 1981), 54, 106.

37. Schlesinger, *The Coming of the New Deal*, 65–66.

38. Leuchtenburg, *Franklin D. Roosevelt and the New Deal*, 52.

39. Kennedy, *Freedom from Fear*, 207.

40. Jess Gilbert, "Agrarian Intellectuals in an Industrializing State," in *The Countryside in the Age of the Modern State: Political Histories of Rural America*, edited by Catherine McNicol Stock and Robert D. Johnston, 213–239, 231 (Ithaca, NY: Cornell University Press, 2001).

41. Badger, *The New Deal*, 184.

42. Leuchtenburg, *Franklin D. Roosevelt and the New Deal*, 140.

43. John M. Barry, *Rising Tide: The Great Mississippi Flood of 1927 and How It Changed America* (New York: Simon & Schuster, 1997), 357.

44. Donald Worster, *Dust Bowl: The Southern Plains in the 1930s*, 25th anniversary ed. (New York: Oxford University Press, 2004), 13.

45. Sarah Philips, *This Land, This Nation*.

46. For an exploration of these issues focused on the South, see Bruce J. Schulman, *From Cotton Belt to Sunbelt: Federal Policy, Economic Development and the Transformation of the South, 1938–1980* (New York: Oxford University Press, 1991).

47. Badger, *The New Deal*, 175–176.

48. Leuchtenburg, *Franklin D. Roosevelt and the New Deal*, 157–158.

49. Kennedy, *Freedom from Fear*, 150–151.

50. Moley, *After Seven Years*, 190.

51. Badger, *The New Deal*, 73.

52. Badger, *The New Deal*, 90.

53. Leuchtenburg, *Franklin D. Roosevelt and the New Deal*, 133.

54. Leuchtenburg, *Franklin D. Roosevelt and the New Deal*, 131.

55. Kenneth S. Davis, *FDR: The New Deal Years, 1933–1937* (New York: Random House, 1986), 437.

56. Schlesinger, *The Coming of the New Deal*, 315.

57. Kennedy, *Freedom from Fear*, 260.

58. Schlesinger, *The Coming of the New Deal*, 308–309.

59. Schlesinger, *The Coming of the New Deal*, 138–140.

60. Lizabeth Cohen, *Making a New Deal: Industrial Workers in Chicago, 1919–1939* (New York: Cambridge University Press, 1990).

61. Kennedy, *Freedom from Fear*, 297.
62. Lewis initially founded the Committee for Industrial Organizations within the much older American Federation of Labor. Within a year, however, ideological differences split the two groups and the CIO unions soon formed the Congress of Industrial Organizations. The two labor federations remained bitter rivals until the 1950s. They finally merged in 1955 as the AFL-CIO.
63. Melvyn Dubofsky, *The State and Labor in Modern America* (Chapel Hill: University of North Carolina Press, 2000), 137.
64. Nelson Lichtenstein, *State of the Union: A Century of American Labor* (Princeton, NJ: Princeton University Press, 2002), 34.
65. Jefferson Cowie, *The Great Exception: The New Deal and the Limits of American Politics* (Princeton, NJ: Princeton University Press, 2016), 109.
66. Leuchtenburg, *Franklin Roosevelt and the New Deal*, 231–239.
67. Alan Brinkley, *The End of Reform: New Deal Liberalism in Recession and War* (New York: Knopf, 1995), 19, 28–29.
68. Although the Bureau of Labor Statistics collected some data on employment in the 1930s, the federal government did not track the unemployment rate as it does today. As a result, scholars have had to reconstruct unemployment rates retrospectively, a process that has been the subject of both methodological and political debate. For a brief introduction to the issues involved, see Eric Rauchway, "New Deal Denialism," *Dissent* (Winter 2010): 68–72.
69. Brinkley, *The End of Reform*, 141.
70. Christina D. Romer, "What Ended the Great Depression?" *Journal of Economic History* 52 (December 1992): 757.
71. Kennedy, *Freedom from Fear*, 372.
72. Cohen, *Making a New Deal*, 252–289.
73. Linda Gordon, "The New Deal Was a Good Idea, We Should Try It This Time," *Dissent* (Fall 2009), 33.
74. Because the white South had been "solidly" Democratic since the Civil War and most blacks were disenfranchised, the region's Democratic politicians had little competition. As a result, they achieved a seniority that gave them powerful control over many House and Senate committees. Ira Katznelson explores the racial repercussions of this Southern committee control on New Deal policy at length in *When Affirmative Action Was White: An Untold History of Racial Inequality in 20th-Century America* (New York: W. W. Norton, 2005), and in *Fear Itself: The New Deal and the Origins of Our Time*.
75. Alice Kessler-Harris, "In the Nation's Image: The Gendered Limits of Social Citizenship in the Depression Era," *Journal of American History* 86 (December 1999): 1262; Katznelson, *When Affirmative Action Was White*, 43.
76. Robert H. Zieger, *The CIO, 1935–1955* (Chapel Hill: University of North Carolina Press, 1995), 1.
77. Arthur M. Schlesinger Jr., *The Age of Roosevelt*, 3 vols. (Boston: Houghton Mifflin, 1957–1960); Frank Freidel, *Franklin D. Roosevelt*, 4 vols. (Boston: Little, Brown, 1952–1973); Eric Frederick Goldman, *Rendezvous with Destiny: A History of Modern American Reform* (New York: Knopf, 1952).
78. Richard Hofstadter, *The Age of Reform: From Bryan to FDR* (New York: Knopf, 1955), 303.
79. Carl Degler, *Out of Our Past: The Forces That Shaped Modern America* (New York: Harper, 1959), 379.
80. Edgar E. Robinson, *The Roosevelt Leadership, 1933–1945* (Philadelphia: Lippincott, 1955), 14, 263, 374, 404. See also John T. Flynn, *The Roosevelt Myth* (New York: Devin Adair, 1948).
81. Moley, *After Seven Years*.
82. The best recent example is journalist Amity Shlaes's bestseller, *The Forgotten Man: A New History of the Great Depression* (New York: HarperCollins, 2007). Shlaes argues that the policies of both Hoover and Roosevelt prolonged the Depression and that even World War II did not lead to economic recovery. Whereas most historians use the nation's gross domestic product as a measure of the economy, Shlaes bases her case on the lackluster performance of the Dow Jones Industrial Average. For a powerful critique of Shlaes's argument, see Eric Rauchway, "New Deal Denialism," 68–72.
83. Barton J. Bernstein, "The New Deal: The Conservative Achievements of Liberal Reform," in *Towards a New Past: Dissenting Essays in American History*, edited by Barton J. Bernstein, 263–288 (New York: Pantheon Books, 1968). See also Howard Zinn, ed., *New Deal Thought* (Indianapolis: Bobbs-Merrill, 1966), and Paul K.

Conkin, *The New Deal* (London: Routledge & Kegan Paul, 1968).

84. Fraser and Gerstle, eds., *The Rise and Fall of the New Deal Order*, ix.

85. Fraser and Gerstle, eds., *The Rise and Fall of the New Deal Order*.

86. Leuchtenberg, *Franklin D. Roosevelt and the New Deal*, 347.

87. Fraser and Gerstle, eds., *The Rise and Fall of the New Deal Order*, ix–x.

88. While they agreed on much, Fraser and Lichtenstein differed on whether the 1930s or the 1940s were the key conservatizing decade. In addition to Fraser and Lichtenstein's contributions to *The Rise and Fall of the New Deal Order*, see Steve Fraser, *Labor Will Rule: Sidney Hillman and the Rise of American Labor* (New York: Free Press, 1991); Nelson Lichtenstein, *The Most Dangerous Man in Detroit: Walter Reuther and the Fate of American Labor* (New York: Basic Books, 1995); and Nelson Lichtenstein, *State of the Union: A Century of American Labor* (Princeton, NJ: Princeton University Press, 2002).

89. Alan Brinkley, "The New Deal and the Idea of the State," in *The Rise and Fall of the New Deal Order: 1930–1980*, edited by Steve Fraser and Gary Gerstle, 85–121 (Princeton, NJ: Princeton University Press, 1989). See also Alan Brinkley, *The End of Reform: New Deal Liberalism in Recession and War*.

90. Katznelson, *When Affirmative Action Was White*; Mary Poole, *The Segregated Origins of Social Security: African Americans and the Welfare State* (Chapel Hill: University of North Carolina Press, 2006).

91. Cybelle Fox, *Three Worlds of Relief: Race, Immigration and the American Welfare State from the Progressive Era to the New Deal* (Princeton, NJ: Princeton University Press, 2012).

92. Alice Kessler-Harris, "In the Nation's Image: The Gendered Limits of Social Citizenship in the Depression Era"; Linda Gordon, *Pitied but Not Entitled: Single Mothers and the History of Welfare, 1890–1935* (New York: Free Press, 1994); Gwendolyn Mink, *The Wages of Motherhood: Inequality in the Welfare State, 1917–1942* (Ithaca, NY: Cornell University Press, 1995); Suzanne Mettler, *Dividing Citizens: Gender and Federalism in New Deal Public Policy* (Ithaca, NY: Cornell University Press, 1998); Alice Kessler-Harris, *In Pursuit of Equity: Women, Men, and the Quest for Economic Citizenship in 20th Century America* (New York: Oxford University Press, 2001).

93. Kennedy, *Freedom from Fear*, 365, 376, 379.

94. Katznelson, *Fear Itself*, 486, 6–7.

95. Wendy L. Wall, *Inventing the "American Way": The Politics of Consensus from the New Deal to the Civil Rights Movement* (New York: Oxford University Press, 2008).

96. James T. Kloppenberg, "Who's Afraid of the Welfare State," *Reviews in American History* 18 (1990): 398.

97. Kim Phillips-Fein, *Invisible Hands: The Making of the Conservative Movement from the New Deal to Reagan* (New York: W. W. Norton, 2009), xi–xii.

98. Kevin Kruse, *One Nation Under God: How Corporate America Invented Christian America* (New York: Basic Books, 2015).

99. Jefferson Cowie, *The Great Exception: The New Deal and the Limits of American Politics* (Princeton, NJ: Princeton University Press, 2016), 15, 24–25, 9. This book expands on an argument that Cowie and Nick Salvatore first made in "The Long Exception: Rethinking the Place of the New Deal in American History," *International Labor and Working-Class History* 74 (Fall 2008): 3–32.

100. Richard Lowitt and Maurine Beasley, eds., *One Third of a Nation: Lorena Hickok Reports on the Great Depression* (Urbana: University of Illinois Press, 1981).

101. Robert S. McElvaine, *Down and Out in the Great Depression: Letters from the Forgotten Man*, 25th anniversary ed. (Chapel Hill: University of North Carolina Press, 2008).

102. Ann Banks, *First Person America* (New York: W. W. Norton, 1991).

103. Studs Terkel, *Hard Times: An Oral History of the Great Depression* (New York: The New Press, 2005).

104. Harry Hopkins, *Spending to Save* (New York: Norton, 1936).

105. Raymond Moley, *After Seven Years* (New York: Harper, 1939).

106. Frances Perkins, *The Roosevelt I Knew* (New York: Viking, 1946); and Harold L. Ickes, *The Secret Diary of Harold L. Ickes*, 2 vols. (New York: Simon and Schuster, 1953–1954).

Wendy L. Wall

AMERICAN LABOR AND WORKING-CLASS HISTORY, 1900–1945

WORKERS AND THE RISE OF CORPORATE AMERICA

American trade unionists entered the 20th century battered by a series of savage defeats which, by 1896, brought the end of an era when millions of Americans had joined mass movements seeking alternatives to corporate-dominated, wage-labor capitalism. Labor reformers' post-Civil War dream of emancipating American laborers from the wage system and their hopes for the creation of a producers' republic based on principles of cooperation and commonwealth had been shattered in Chicago's Haymarket Square on May 4, 1886. The wind had been stolen from the spirit of unionism in the all-important steel industry at Andrew Carnegie's Homestead mill in 1892, and from industrial unionism on the nation's rail lines in the defeat of the 1894 Pullman strike and boycott. Finally, the Republican Party's defeat of the Populist-Democrat fusion in the presidential campaign in 1896 ensured that the vast majority of wage workers and farmers would not have the support of their own national political party.

Ascendant corporate leaders had been emboldened and empowered by much of the public's revulsion against the labor-related violence of the late 19th century. The forces of "law and order" at the local, state, and federal levels came to the aid of business in strikes and lockouts during the "Age of Industrial Conflict." Business also won the crucial legal conflict over the definition of "freedom" in the workplace and in employment markets. Court injunctions against labor activity were ubiquitous in the wake of the 1894 Pullman boycott, and case law privileged employers' prerogatives at all turns. In the eyes of the law, Americans generally—with the exception of married white women—had

a responsibility to work, but their sole right at work was the right to quit. Furthermore, legislators paid less attention to workers' welfare than they did to subsidizing the growth of American industry or sustaining their own political power, all too often lining their pockets with the graft that ran rampant in that period of fantastic growth. Lawmakers had taken the first steps toward regulating trusts and moderating the worst forms of corruption, but those efforts were generally weak, and the nation's courts ensured that employers' power in the workplace would be virtually unchecked.

Great changes were taking place, yet Americans generally believed that even more change was needed if the republic were to survive and thrive in the industrial era. In the workplace as much as in surrounding communities, Americans feared the implications of this new era of global economic expansion. Political and ideological violence may have been rare, but when violence broke out, it both stigmatized and divided labor groups, even as it brought swift reactions from local police, private detective firms, and state and federal officials.[1] More broadly, a general fear of the revolutionary changes taking shape in everyday life inspired both a broad-based progressive reform impulse, shared by many American workers, and a renewed American radicalism, as well as the forces of reactionary repression and business conservatism that sought to stamp out what many saw as the real possibility of mob action and socialist insurgency.

The labor violence and economic upheavals of the late 19th century had been horrific enough to convince many powerful Americans that reform was necessary. In 1898, Republican president William McKinley, who would be assassinated in 1901 by the anarchist Leon Czolgosz, appointed the United States Industrial Commission to study the causes of labor violence. At the same time, a broad group of largely middle-class and elite Americans, soon to be known as Progressives, set out to document and then ameliorate the worst forms of corruption in the economy and politics, and to soften the edges of the new industrial system by making workplaces, consumer products, and neighborhoods safer and healthier. There was no single Progressive Era social movement; rather, reformers sought everything from antitrust legislation, shorter working hours, and safer workplaces to bans on child labor, protective legislation for female workers, and reforms that would clean up manufacturing and the political process.

These top-down reform efforts—efforts that emphasized the need for greater efficiency and order in the economy and at the workplace—would be deeply ambiguous for workers. But they reflected an important move away from the commitments to Social Darwinism and laissez-faire principles that had defined the Gilded Age. Progressive reform itself could become a form of social control. Workers were subjected to intense moral campaigns, the Americanization efforts of both well-intentioned settlement house workers and less salutary anti-immigrant vigilantes, and the institution of "scientific management" regimes fostered by Frederick Winslow Taylor, Elton Mayo, and Frank and Lillian Gilbreth. One reformer's vision of order and efficiency often became a reality of social control for workers.

For most workers, the greatest fears derived from the accelerating changes at the workplace that were well underway by the turn of the century. The mechanization of industry and employers' drive for efficiency had long been forcing workers to do more specialized task work and robbing them of the control over their work many had enjoyed in systems of craft production. There were benefits as production skyrocketed across the economy. Whereas the pick miner in a coal shaft produced 2.5 tons per day on average, the fully mechanized open pit mines of the 1930s produced 16.2 tons per worker per day. In 1919, Henry Ford's assembly line produced four times the output per worker per hour

than the industry had produced in 1910. Simultaneously, the kinds of occupations Americans held and their experiences at work changed dramatically, not always for the worse. Gangs of day laborers were transformed into legions of semiskilled workers running transportation and equipment handling machines. Skilled, independent workers in iron and steel production became semiskilled machinists and repair technicians. These mechanized factories also required the development of a whole new set of tool-and-die makers. Overall, there was an upward leveling effect of mechanization. Between 1910 and 1930, the proportion of unskilled workers in industrial work fell from 36 to 30.5 percent, the semiskilled rose from 36 to 39 percent, and the skilled increased from 28 to 30.5 percent.[2] Not everyone benefited, of course. Black men, when they were not stuck in sharecropping or tenant farming, were generally relegated to the hot, heavy, hard jobs, and most black women were forced to accept the long hours and lack of independence in domestic service.

The 20th century also saw what one historian has described as the "degradation of work."[3] The dream of the United States as an independent producers republic, which had inspired Americans from Thomas Jefferson to the Knights of Labor in the 1870s and 1880s, had long been dead. As early as 1877, two-thirds of American workers were wage laborers, with little hope of opening their own shops or owning their own farms. By 1940, no more than one-fifth of the population of the United States were self-employed.[4] Wage labor—underpaid, demanding long hours, and subjecting workers to dangerous conditions (approximately 35,000 workers died in accidents annually at the turn of the century)—had become a permanent condition.[5] Not only were the benefits of the wage economy unequally distributed, but the very nature of work became both more demanding and less satisfying. A profound contradiction emerged that arguably continues to shape workers' lives in the 21st century: "The scientific-technical revolution and 'automation' requires ever higher levels of education, training, the greater exercise of intelligence and mental effort in general," which is accompanied by "a mounting dissatisfaction with the conditions of industrial and office labor."[6]

Despite their shared circumstances and some success in building a diverse labor movement in the early part of the century, American workers entered World War I perhaps more divided among themselves than at any other point in the nation's history. Nativism was on the rise, and workers were divided by skill, craft, race, gender, and region. Industrial employers took advantage of workers' fears and their internal divisions. On one hand, some corporate leaders developed systems of "welfare capitalism," voluntarily providing marginal benefits to workers in order to stifle their dissatisfaction at work. On the other hand, business leaders and their allies in politics and the press played workers of different backgrounds against one another in order to undercut the possibility of shared militancy. It would be difficult, even for the most privileged workers, to fight for a place in the system.

FIGHTING FOR A PLACE IN THE SYSTEM

With a significant economic recovery underway in 1897, American labor leaders began a new organizing push, primarily through the American Federation of Labor (AFL), railroad brotherhoods, and various unaffiliated unions. These organizations largely excluded racial minorities and women, and this model of organizing sought to come to terms with, rather than to transform, corporate dominance of the industrial economy. Nonetheless, the leaders of these unions and their largely white, male rank and file won critical victories and increased the AFL's membership from 264,000 in 1897 to 1.6 million by 1904. Moreover, as the historian Julie Greene has shown, it is easy to overstate the apolitical character of the AFL's "pure and simple unionism."

In addition to "bread-and-butter" contractual issues, the Federation actively pursued political influence in the late 19th and early 20th centuries. It is true, however, that the AFL assumed that trade unionists would speak for all American workers in the political sphere.[7]

The AFL sustained the power of craft workers in the construction and transportation trades, while also beginning to win benefits for some more skilled industrial workers. The railroad brotherhoods exerted significant, if informal, political influence through allies like Theodore Roosevelt in the Republican Party.[8] Even mineworkers—who had a reputation as the most violent and militant of unionists, and who had, indeed, fought many labor wars—had gained enough leverage to cause President Theodore Roosevelt to mediate between the workers and the mine owners in a bitter 1902 anthracite coal strike.

Many, though hardly all, employers had initially accepted the rise of the AFL, even going as far as voluntarily recognizing unions and forming the National Civic Federation, a coalition of labor and business leaders seeking cooperation in the economy. By 1904, however, employers had grown frustrated with the demands of union contracts and workers' increased militancy, and they began to hit back. They increased the use of "yellow dog contracts" to force workers to sign agreements that promised they would not join a union. Employers divided workers by national origin and regularly employed strikebreaking replacement workers. The National Association of Manufacturers embarked on a concerted "open shop" drive; the forerunner of today's "right-to-work" laws, these were campaigns by employers and their political allies to ensure that workers in a unionized shop did not have to belong to the union. This protection of workers' right to contract as individuals amounted to a thinly veiled attempt to undermine all organized labor, as unions could not afford to represent workers who were "free riders" on the backs of their union member coworkers. In 1913, the open-shop drive climaxed in an actual labor war in the Colorado coal fields, as the Rockefeller-owned Colorado Fuel and Iron Company pushed for ever greater production and at one point destroyed a workers' camp in Ludlow, Colorado, killing eleven children and two women in the attack.[9]

As a result of such attacks on organized labor, membership in unions actually dropped in 1905 and remained stagnant for the next five years. Yet the booming economy before and during World War I increased labor's power: the AFL's membership increased by approximately 800,000 between 1910 and 1917, and organized labor as a whole grew to 4 million by 1920.[10] The membership also became increasingly diverse in terms of skill level and occupations. These were important gains for workers, but they remained limited in no small part by the failure of the AFL to imagine an alliance with the vast majority of unorganized workers.

RADICAL ALTERNATIVES IN THE PROGRESSIVE ERA

Workers frustrated with the exclusionary practices and political moderation of the AFL could turn to an embattled world of labor radicalism which was going through something of a renaissance after the defeats of the 1880s and 1890s. American radicals—led by the socialist Eugene V. Debs and an eclectic band of militants that included Mother Jones (Figure 1), Elizabeth Gurley Flynn, "Big Bill" Haywood, and Lucy Parsons, among others— pushed for more radical and immediate change through the Socialist Party, insurgent industrial unions in mining and textiles, and through the Industrial Workers of the World.

Founded in 1901, the Socialist Party of America (SP) quickly emerged as a powerful political force. Within a decade the SP had built more than three thousand local branches and forty-two state organizations. Dozens of candidates affiliated with the new party won municipal and county elections in town squares stretching from Texas through Illinois to Milwaukee, Wisconsin. Meanwhile, the party's leader, Eugene V. Debs, won 897,000 votes in his run for the presidency in 1912 and more than a million votes for president in 1920, while he was in prison after being convicted of sedition during World War I.

Figure 1. "'Mother' Jones and Her Army of Striking Textile Workers." Peirce & Jones for the *New York World-Telegram & Sun*, Philadelphia, PA, 1903.
Prints and Photographs Division, Library of Congress, digital ID: LC-DIG-ds-07713.

In the 1910s, garment workers in New York City and Chicago organized unions in the industry for which the term "sweatshop" was coined. Although workers suffered oppressive conditions in sweatshops, they were isolated from the rest of the workforce, and they could not take action directly against the manufacturers. But as manufacturers moved production to larger factories in order to produce standardized clothing and to distance themselves from the increasingly negative reputation of sweatshops—spread by Progressive reformers—the larger shops also brought unskilled workers out of their relative isolation. Working conditions did not necessarily improve in larger shops, but opportunities to build worker solidarity presented themselves. Employers attempted to maintain divisions among workers, separating them by ethnicity and gender, and by offering "bonus pay" to the most productive workers.

After years of suffering, garment workers' organizing came in quick surges: the "Uprising" of 20,000 in New York City in 1909, another strike of 60,000 workers in New York City in 1910, a 1910–1911 strike of 40,000 workers in Chicago, and the movement for unionization and reform after the infamous Triangle Shirtwaist factory fire in New York in March 1911 (Figure 2). Together these actions reinvigorated the International Ladies' Garment Workers' Union and created the Amalgamated Clothing Workers of America. In one of the most dramatic moments in US labor history, the young immigrant garment worker Clara Lemlich took the stage from AFL leader Samuel Gompers, who had refused to call a strike. Speaking in Yiddish, she called her fellow garment workers to action. Within two days, approximately 20,000 workers from 500 factories were on strike. By the 1920s, the tens of thousands of members of the ACWA and the ILGWU had won the closed shop, higher wages, shorter working hours, and better working conditions. These events also revealed the politicization of immigrant women in the industry and showed that immigrant workers could be organized, contrary to much AFL commentary. Along with the United Mineworkers, the garment workers forged a new model of unionism, demonstrating that a pragmatic industrial unionism could succeed

Figure 2. "Photograph of Police Officers, Civilians and Victims on the Sidewalk during the Triangle Shirtwaist Factory Fire." March 25, 1911.
Franklin D. Roosevelt Library Photographs, 1870–2004, Franklin D. Roosevelt Library (#6040083).

as well as the more hidebound craft unionism of the AFL. In this, the new unions were important exceptions to the rule of non-socialist craft organizing of the era.[11]

The Industrial Workers of the World (IWW) created another key, if short-lived, bastion of American labor radicalism. Founded in Chicago in 1904, the IWW took inspiration from a group from the Western Federation of Miners who had been radicalized during a series of violent strikes in Idaho, Montana, and Colorado. Rallying around their shared distaste for the AFL's conservatism and exclusionary practices, the IWW sought to create "One Big Union" of all workers regardless of skill level, race, ethnicity, or gender. Emphasizing the necessity of direct action and workers' control of the workplace, they called for an end of the wage system and workers' ownership of the means of production. The "Wobblies," as the members came to be known, tapped into and inflamed the radical spirit of many of the most marginalized workers. The IWW thus backed its demands for the fulfillment of workers' needs, the bread of daily life, with the threat of a radical sensibility at least rhetorically committed to revolution.

The preamble to the IWW's 1908 constitution declared, "A struggle must go on until the workers of the world organize as a class, take possession of the earth and the machinery of production, and abolish the wage system."[12] The IWW's revolutionary vision inspired many miners, loggers, and migrant agricultural workers in the West, as well as unorganized industrial workers in the East. Together, they built a lively workers' culture with hundreds of songs collected in the *Little Red Songbook*. IWW membership peaked at 600,000 in 1916, riding a wave of important victories and broader socialist sentiment. Most famously, in the 1912 "Bread and Roses Strike" in Lawrence, Massachusetts, IWW leaders joined with local workers to strike against wage cuts and many years of low wages, long hours, dangerous working conditions, and terrible living conditions in the communities surrounding the factory. The IWW sustained a thread of American radicalism that otherwise might have been lost. The Wobblies' radical critique of capitalism, their at least rhetorical support for direct action tactics such as sabotage, and their unswerving commitment to interracial organizing among all men and women carried these principles on through the relatively conservative first three decades of the century. The IWW also sustained the idea of industrial unionism, which was a minority strain of the AFL's organizing efforts, emphasizing that workers ought to be organized across all skill levels in a given industry.

OBSTACLES TO ORGANIZING IN THE PROGRESSIVE ERA

During the Progressive Era, the American Federation of Labor claimed to speak for all American workers. Still, with few exceptions, the AFL consisted largely of skilled, white, male workers, and focused its strikes, lawsuits, and limited political activity on maintaining those workers' craft privileges.[13] Its leaders also discouraged any organizing efforts not under the banner of the AFL, treating them as "dual unions," or as enemies seeking to undermine the AFL. Furthermore, the federation's leaders refused to engage in the broad political work that would have allowed them to challenge the anti-labor decisions of the courts or the narrowness of Progressive Era reforms.[14] Such a closed, jealous, and litigious world of labor was hardly a beacon for the growing ranks of new immigrant and American migrant workers entering the deskilled factories of the North.

The limits of the Socialist Party's gains also became clear soon enough. In the electoral arena, the SP never managed to reach the status of a viable third national party. The SP may have maintained a significant base of voters—as shown in Debs's 1 million votes in the 1920 presidential election—but their efforts ran headlong into the anti-radical repression during and after World War I and the deeply conservative Republican ascendancy of the 1920s. Moreover, to the extent that Socialist politicians, such as Victor Berger and his allies in Milwaukee, made gains toward practical reform, they also distanced themselves from the more radical class politics of much of the American left. The Socialist leader Morris Hillquit denounced Berger and his allies as "sewer socialists"—sticking them for constantly bragging about how good Milwaukee's sewer system was, even as they had failed to push forward the larger class struggle. Similarly, when socialist trade unionists rose to the leadership ranks in AFL unions, their pragmatism emerged. "Time and time again," concludes the historian David Brody, "once they had acceded to office, Socialists began to act—if they did not always talk—like any other trade unionists."[15] Accommodation to established centers of power, however justifiable it may have been for Socialist activists in particular political contexts, added to the effects of internal divisions and repression of the left in limiting the SP's radical challenge to American political and economic systems.

The IWW—in part because the Wobblies had some success, and in part because they sustained an unflagging rhetorical radicalism—also became the target of government and vigilante repression. Wobbly activists leading "free speech campaigns" faced club-wielding police officers and were whipped and even tarred and feathered by vigilantes throughout the West. During World War I, 1,200 miners suspected of being aligned with the IWW in Bisbee, Arizona, were rounded up, forced onto a freight train at gunpoint, and abandoned in the desert without food or water for a day and half before a nearby military commander arranged for their extradition to New Mexico. At the same time, the federal government raided IWW offices across the country and convicted hundreds of Wobblies for anti-war speech. In the end, the IWW became one of the driving forces behind the rise of the American Civil Liberties Union and the push

for protections of free speech during and after World War I, but the Wobblies could not save themselves from this repression. By the end of the war, with many of its leaders imprisoned, deported, or having fled the country, the IWW was unable to sustain itself as an institution.

Still more obstacles stood in the way of mass labor organizing in the first decades of the 20th century. Chief among them were the racial and ethnic divisions that ran through the shop floors of American industry. Historians have examined in great detail the intraclass racism that blocked white workers from acting in ways that would have been truly class-conscious. Between the late 19th century and World War I, tens of thousands of black workers gained access to unions, some all-black but some biracial in organization. Yet unions often acted as agents of division; some included racial exclusion clauses in their constitutions, while others gave lip service to solidarity while declaring that, in practice, black workers would undercut the wages and opportunities of white workers. For their part, recent black migrants from the South, the majority of black workers in the factories, alternately feared or despised the "white man's union."[16]

White workers and union leaders used episodes of black strikebreaking as evidence that black workers were inevitably the opponents of labor progress. Whites' descriptions of black workers represented a powerful, if contradictory, mix of racist notions of black inferiority and fear of black physical superiority. Black workers, they feared, could outwork white workers, and black workers would do it on the cheap. In 1901, the AFL defended itself against accusations of racism, arguing that "the antipathy... some union workers have against the colored man is not because of his color, but because of the fact that generally he is a 'cheap man.'"[17] But by 1905, the division between white and black workers had become so pronounced that AFL chief Samuel Gompers declared, "If the colored man continues to lend himself to the work of tearing down what the white man has built up, a race hatred worse than any ever known before will result. Caucasian civilization will serve notice that its uplifting process is not to be interfered with in any such way."[18] Not surprisingly, black leaders felt differently. The black political leader Ida B. Wells praised strikebreakers as "men who proved their value by risking their lives to obtain work," and she endorsed "the constitutional right of all men to earn a living and to protect themselves in the exercise of that right."[19]

Workers and labor reformers also struggled to organize during one the most conservative eras in United States judicial history. In its 1905 decision in Lochner v. New York (198 U.S. 45), the United States Supreme Court overruled a New York law limiting hours for bakery employees. Rather than being necessary to protect the welfare of the workers, the court found that such hours legislation amounted to an unconstitutional attempt to regulate business, and "unreasonable, unnecessary and arbitrary interference with the right and liberty of the individual to contract." With this reading of the Fourteenth Amendment's due process clause, the Court would go on in subsequent years to constrain workers' rights and legislative efforts to reform the industrial system. In 1908, for instance, the Court upheld what were known as "ironclad" or "yellow dog" contracts, which forced individual workers to sign an agreement not to join a union in order to secure a job. Also in 1908, the Court found that labor boycotts of employers had been banned by the 1890 Sherman Anti-Trust Act. In fact, there were more antitrust actions brought against union activities than business combinations until the Clayton Act of 1914 attempted to exclude union activity from the regulation of commerce, declaring that "the labor of human beings is not a commodity." In 1911, the Court banned consumer boycotts, and in this period it also upheld blacklisting of union organizers, the constitutionality of company towns, and employers'

use of civil lawsuits to resist interference in their businesses. Even when the Court did support the constitutionality of reform measures, as in the 1908 Muller v. Oregon (208 U.S. 412) case allowing for limiting the number of hours women could work, the judges did so by appealing to the notion that women were the weaker sex and had special responsibilities in the home. The justices found support in the "widespread belief that woman's physical structure, and the functions she performs in consequence thereof, justify special legislation restricting or qualifying the conditions under which she should be permitted to toil."

The Supreme Court's antagonism to any limits on the individual's "liberty of contract" ran counter to legislators' gradual rewriting of state and federal law. The US Congress regulated child labor in 1919 and instituted a system of workers' compensation in 1916, while twenty-five states passed workers' compensation laws between 1911 and 1921. State and federal officials also formally began investigating workers' safety, especially after the Triangle Shirtwaist fire in New York City in 1911 created widespread outrage against the factory owners' willful refusal to protect their workers from dangerous conditions. The 1926 Railway Labor Act required railway industry employers to engage in collective bargaining and banned discrimination against unions in the railway industry (this was expanded to airlines in 1936). The 1931 Davis-Bacon Act required construction contracts with the federal government to specify a minimum or "prevailing" wage for workers under that contract. The 1932 Norris-LaGuardia Act for the first time provided protection for workers' rights to organize, banned yellow dog contracts, and outlawed the use of court injunctions in nonviolent labor disputes. By 1932, then, in the face of much judicial resistance, legislators had responded to growing public alarm by initiating a revolution in labor law that would come to fruition when the Supreme Court upheld the 1935 National Labor Relations Act.

WORLD WAR I AND THE HOPE FOR INDUSTRIAL DEMOCRACY

World War I provided an unprecedented opening for unions to make gains and for workers who had traditionally been excluded from industrial work to enter the nation's factories. The federal government spurred a national mobilization of the workforce and economic resources, while coordinating industrial planning. Although the government went so far as to take over the railroads, the federal intervention in the economy hardly represented wartime socialism. Instead, the government relied on industry leaders who acted as "dollar-a-year" men, voluntarily aiding in the planning of the wartime economy, and it ensured profits for industry with cost-plus contracts. In essence, the federal government forged a larger role in managing the economy with the primary goal of efficient war-related production. This managed economy also facilitated the private accumulation of capital for employers and benefited masses of workers.

Why was this a boon for unions and workers? In the first place, the wartime economy required labor peace. Therefore, the federal government facilitated the formation and growth of unions. At the same time, the wartime economic boom required many new workers. With the end of European immigration and the draft of white men into the military, women and African Americans found new opportunities. The long-term consequences of the war differed sharply for women and men. Women's industrial experiences proved to be a largely temporary phenomenon. The war did help to provide the necessary impetus to pass the Nineteenth Amendment to the U.S. Constitution, giving women the right to vote. But the war did not lead to major changes in gender roles; gender lines in the workforce reemerged after the war, and the popular image of the liberated "flapper" in the Roaring Twenties remained a decidedly minority experience.

For African Americans, the war sparked a major demographic, economic, and political transition. Between 1915 and 1918, nearly 500,000 African Americans migrated from the South to northern cities, with another 700,000 following in their wake during the 1920s. The Great Migration, as this movement of black southerners to industrial cities has been called, began a process that not only transformed the lives of the migrants but also fundamentally changed the populations and politics of major American cities.[20] World War I-era migrants built modern black urban communities in places like New York's Harlem, Chicago's South Side, and Detroit's Black Bottom. Out of these communities would grow civil rights organizations like the National Association for the Advancement of Colored People, black nationalist organizations like Marcus Garvey's Universal Negro Improvement Association, and the first major black labor radicals and trade unions. In the 1920s, Harlem was especially fertile ground for black working-class politics. As African American artists and writers created the Harlem Renaissance, black socialists and communists spoke on soapboxes on New York City's streetcorners and helped popularize a black class politics. Building on the longstanding activism of Hubert Harrison and others, people like A. Philip Randolph who got their start in the 1910s would help build a nationally powerful, labor-based civil rights movement in the 1930s and 1940s.

THE BUSINESS DECADE

World War I seemed to offer an opportunity for workers to improve their position in the economy. Workers, in fact, gained a great deal in real wages and political power during the brief period of nearly full employment during the war. Yet unions' efforts to institutionalize their place in an "industrial democracy" were roundly defeated in a series of strikes between 1919 and 1921. In 1919, alone, more than 4 million workers—approximately one-fifth

Figure 3. "Pittsburgh Strike [1919 Strikers Demonstrating in Car]."
Photo by Bain News Service, 1919. Prints and Photographs Division, Library of Congress (LC-B2-5005-13), digital ID: LC-DIG-ggbain-29279.

of the workforce—went on strike. A general strike of 60,000 in Seattle, Washington, a strike by nearly the entire police force in Boston, Massachusetts, and a national steel strike of 350,000 workers in Pittsburgh and beyond (Figure 3) are representative of the broad scope of the strikes by workers fearful that they would lose what they had won during the war and facing the prospect of a severe postwar recession. In each case, the workers lost, and they ended up more divided than before, and more desperate for jobs at virtually any wage. Moreover, the entrenched economic conservatism of the federal government and popular culture not only marginalized labor unions but also celebrated the spirit of innovation, speculation, and acquisitive individualism of the "business decade."

The benefits of the business decade were deeply unequal. To many Americans, the 1920s seemed to promise the unending expansion of the American economy. Consumer goods proliferated. The number of telephones doubled, by 1930 about half of Americans had indoor toilets, and Henry Ford refined assembly line production, allowing many working families to own a car. Yet the expansion of the consumer economy depended on an equal expansion of the consumer credit economy; Americans bought their radios and other modern wonders on installment plans.

Moreover, even with the greater availability of credit, full participation in the consumer economy remained a dream for most. As the economic historian W. Elliot Brownlee notes, "Only one family in six owned an automobile, only one family in five owned a fixed bathtub or had electricity in its home, and only one family in ten had a telephone."[21] As importantly, while the automobile and other manufacturing industries boomed, core American economic sectors lagged far behind. Workers in these "sick industries," including agriculture, mining, and New England textiles, were facing depression conditions well before the stock market crash in 1929.

Unions declined sharply in the 1920s under pressure from a conservative attack. Employers promoted an "American Plan" that celebrated the democracy of the open shop and that associated organized labor with un-American economic systems. Companies also promoted "welfare capitalism," providing workers with benefits such as home loans, group insurance policies, stock options, and regular sponsorship of sports teams all in the name of reducing costly labor turnover and improving industrial harmony. Perhaps most importantly, some four hundred firms created Employee Representation Plans, or company unions, which sought to promote worker allegiance to the company and to provide a kind of pressure release for workers thinking about organizing in their own interests. Welfare capitalists sought to prevent unions from ever rising again, and for a time they succeeded. The number of strikes receded dramatically, and union membership declined. The success of unregulated markets and welfare capitalism, however, was short-lived, and the mass unemployment, poverty, and insecurity of the 1930s would help spark the greatest surge in union members in US history.

THE CRASH AND ITS IMMEDIATE AFTERMATH

On October 24, 1929, "Black Tuesday," traders on the New York Stock Exchange shed

16.4 million shares of stock, causing a drastic decline in the overall value of stocks. From a high of 381 on September 3, 1929, the Dow Jones Industrial Average ultimately fell to a low of 41.22 on July 8, 1932. Approximately five thousand banks failed between 1929 and 1933. Industrial production declined by over half between the crash and the middle of 1932. By that year, unemployment soared to between one-quarter and one-third of the total labor force. Things were not much better for those who managed to hold onto employment: wages fell 50 to 75 percent in the early years of the Great Depression. Economic sectors that had been struggling in the 1920s saw conditions only worsen; farm income declined by 60 percent, and one-third of famers lost their land in the 1930s. The industries that had driven the prosperity of the 1920s were now failing; by 1932, the automobile industry was producing at only 20 percent of its capacity. The stock market crash laid bare the underlying weaknesses in the US economy and created mass unemployment, poverty, and insecurity.

President Herbert H. Hoover responded to the crash much more energetically than previous presidents had in similar crises, but his efforts were too limited to meet the depth of this one, in part because he remained steadfastly committed to voluntaristic, optimistic, Progressive-style interventions. Hoover moved to shore up public confidence while also supporting business leaders' efforts to protect their financial interests. As Secretary of Treasury Andrew Mellon advised his fellow capitalists to "liquidate labor, liquidate stocks, liquidate the farmers, liquidate real estate," Hoover assured the nation that the "fundamental business of the country was sound," and asked for voluntary cooperation from corporate managers to maintain employment and wages. As realization of the deepening crisis dawned on him, Hoover also increased federal funds for public works, moved to cut taxes, and requested private agencies, as well as state and local governments, to provide relief to the approximately 7 million unemployed by 1931.

Arguing that direct unemployment relief was a "dangerous" suggestion, Hoover instead created the Reconstruction Finance Corporation, which provided loans to businesses and banks in the hope that greater corporate stability would strengthen the economy.

President Hoover's limited, top-down response to the crisis aggravated widespread anxieties and led to a new level of popular unrest. Destitute Americans living in shantytowns, popularly known as "Hoovervilles," clearly blamed the president for their condition. Thousands of Americans joined in organizing for relief from the federal government. In unemployed organizations, spearheaded by socialist and communist organizers, Americans demanded monetary relief and reinstalled tenants in their apartments when they were evicted. The most important protests and strikes of the 1930s were still years away, but the unemployed organizing of the early 1930s played an important role in increasing popular militancy.

In 1932, a group of 22,000 World War I veterans marched on Washington, DC, to demand that the US Congress pay them the bonuses they had been promised for their service in the war. For weeks thousands of veterans camped on Anacostia Flats, within sight of the Capitol, while President Hoover and Congress refused to pay the bonuses. Finally, the president sent the US Army to break up the "Bonus Army" camps. Generals Douglas McArthur, George Patton, and Dwight Eisenhower led the operation. Photographs and newsreels showed tanks rolling through the streets of the nation's capital, and current US soldiers setting fire to tents occupied by the heroes of World War I, and they contributed to Hoover's loss of public support as the 1932 election neared.

WORKERS AND THE CHANGING STATE DURING THE NEW DEAL

By 1932, Herbert Hoover had become by all accounts the most unpopular person in the United States. In contrast, New York's governor, Franklin Delano Roosevelt, brought his optimistic paternalism to the national public, projecting confidence and campaigning on the promise that he would bring "Happy Days Again." As governor, Roosevelt had experimented with unemployment relief and public works programs that became popular among New Yorkers. Yet he came to the presidency with no immediate or comprehensive solution to the nation's economic troubles. Instead, the New Deal represented a series of experiments which, though they did not pull the nation out of the depression (only economic mobilization for World War II would do that), still dramatically transformed the American economy by creating a new welfare state, strengthening unions, and affirming the economic importance of government action as a source of both spending and business regulation.

President Roosevelt immediately took steps to address the national crisis. He initiated important banking reforms, rationalizing and regulating the banking system and providing deposit insurance. Together, these reforms arguably created the conditions for relative financial stability that helped make possible the growth of a mass middle class after World War II. Roosevelt and his allies also ended the alcohol ban of Prohibition, eliminating one cause of suffering and chaos in working-class communities. He also expanded direct relief to the poor and enlarged public works projects significantly.

President Roosevelt then embarked upon a series of legislative efforts known by historians as the "first New Deal." Congress passed the National Industrial Recovery Act (NIRA) in June 1933, which sought to create a new corporatist style of regulated and planned economy in which big government, big business, and labor would work together to achieve greater efficiency. The NIRA eliminated most antitrust restrictions and, in return, asked businesses to cooperate with the National Recovery Administration (NRA), a new federal agency which would oversee a wide range of economic activities, notably wages, the prices of consumer goods, and the cost of transportation. The Supreme Court, however, struck down the NIRA because the law amounted to unconstitutional federal intervention in interstate commerce.

Yet the NIRA had two longer-lasting and largely unforeseen consequences. First, it reinforced the federal commitment to public works programs as part of the solution to the national crisis. Second, the NIRA stipulated that "employees shall have the right to organize and bargain collectively through representatives of their own choosing," which marked the first time the federal government legally recognized workers' right to union representation. Although NIRA, and its Section 7a, were quickly found unconstitutional, the support of the federal government for labor organizing helped strengthen an already growing surge in rank-and-file labor organizing.

In the wake of the passage of Section 7a, millions of American workers acted on their desire for union representation—more than 1,800 strikes occurred in 1934 alone—while also demonstrating that the AFL would not be able to contain or take full advantage of the aspirations of American industrial workers. Mass strikes broke out in 1934 among West Coast dock workers, in auto parts factories in Toledo, Ohio, in the trucking industry in Minneapolis, Minnesota, and in the East Coast textile industry. In each case, the AFL had made initial efforts to act on the rights specified in Section 7a and to organize thousands of new workers. The AFL, however, either backed down completely or failed to address the grievances of rank-and-file workers. Tens of thousands of workers then acted without the support of the AFL. Workers battled with police, the National Guard, and citizens' committees in efforts to win their unions. In those battles, the West Coast International Longshoremen's Association, which would become the International Longshore and Warehouse Union, built its longstanding reputation for radicalism and interracial social movement unionism. In Toledo, workers at the Electro Auto Lite Company survived clashes with National Guardsmen to win union recognition, wage increases, and other gains, while creating an important piece of the foundation for what became the United Auto Workers. In Minneapolis, four workers died in citywide violence, but they also broke through in that previously hardcore anti-union city and set the stage for the national unionization of the trucking industry.

In the long term, the 1934 strikes helped organize broad sectors of the American working class, but in the short term the strikes also helped polarize domestic politics. Indeed, 1935 and 1936 were years of greatly increasing political conflict. President Roosevelt found his support from business leaders evaporating after NIRA was struck down and after the 1934 strikes demonstrated the threat, as owners saw it, of giving workers the right to unionize. At the same time, critics to the president's left argued that he had done too little to provide direct relief to the unemployed in the form of jobs, cash relief, and a safety net of welfare programs. Radical communists and socialists joined militant organizers for the unemployed to push for greater support for the unemployed. Populists such as Louisiana senator Huey Long and the Catholic radio priest Father Charles Coughlin, among others, demanded that the president do more for "the forgotten man."

In response, President Roosevelt broke with the business leaders and pushed in 1935 for a flurry of legislation that would come to be known as the "Second New Deal." The Social Security Act and Aid to Families with Dependent Children both responded directly to the populist critics by providing old age insurance and relief to poor families. In the long run, both allowed for a major reduction in poverty among young people and the elderly. In addition, the Second New Deal greatly expanded public works programs. Congress also passed the National Labor Relations Act (NLRA), which reaffirmed workers' rights to organize unions and bargain collectively, outlawed what the act called "unfair labor practices" that amounted to business efforts to prevent unionization or to break unions, and created the National Labor Relations Board to adjudicate workers' complaints against their employers.

The Second New Deal had only limited immediate effects. The first Social Security check did not go out until January 31, 1940. The public works agencies were administered by local offices and were, therefore, racially segregated in the South and everywhere tended to benefit white male workers. New Deal legislation increased the benefits that African Americans derived from the federal government, especially in northern cities, where black voters gradually shifted to the Democratic Party beginning in the late 1930s. Yet New Deal employment benefits did not apply to agricultural workers or domestic workers, which meant that most black and female workers were not covered by unemployment insurance or Social Security. At the same time, programs such as the Agricultural Adjustment Act and the Tennessee Valley Authority, among others, directly or indirectly displaced significant numbers of black farmers, tenants, and sharecroppers from the land. Conservative opposition and the Democrats' desire to scale back federal action after the flurry of legislation in 1935 and 1936 also moderated the immediate influence of the New Deal. The NLRA had to survive legal challenges, which prevented aggressive action by the NLRB during the first years of its existence. Moreover, as some of the New Deal measures began to improve economic conditions, President Roosevelt and his advisors moved to scale back federal spending in the belief that the recovery could proceed on its own, and the economy slowed down again. The resulting "Roosevelt Recession," combined with popular reaction against Roosevelt's efforts to pack the Supreme Court with New Deal-friendly justices, basically brought the New Deal to a standstill in 1938 and 1939.

THE NEW INDUSTRIAL UNION MOVEMENT

For all its limitations, the Second New Deal helped energize the US labor movement. With federal recognition of their right to organize, American workers in previously non-union industries created another surge in organizing activity. This new movement to organize the unorganized differed from the 1934 strikes because it was a coordinated and concerted drive for industrial unionism. Led by John L. Lewis of the United Mine Workers of America, Sidney Hillman of the Amalgamated Clothing Workers of America, and David Dubinsky of the International Ladies Garment Workers Union, the Committee for Industrial Organization (soon to be the Congress of Industrial Organizations, or the CIO) operated autonomously from the outset, although it was officially within the structure of the AFL, and it set out to organize industrial rather than craft unions.

Lewis, Hillman, and Dubinsky took advantage of workers' newfound rights by building unions in the mass production industries. They first formed the Steelworkers Organizing Committee (SWOC), led by Phillip Murray, to unionize steelworkers excluded from the Amalgamated Association of Iron, Steel, and Tin Workers, which had long represented only skilled steelworkers. In 1936 and 1937, the CIO broke through in the notoriously anti-union auto industry by deploying sit-in strikes at General Motors plants in Flint, Michigan. Occupying the GM factories, workers won community support and, after bitter battles in the streets (with many women on the front lines), they forced the company to recognize the CIO union. The stunning success at GM persuaded U.S. Steel, the nation's largest steel producer, to recognize Murray's steelworkers' union without a strike. The CIO faced continued, often violent resistance from Ford and from the group of steel companies collectively known as "Little Steel." Nonetheless, within months hundreds of thousands of workers joined the "house of labor," and the momentum spread among workers in packing houses, newspapers, the electrical industry, the public sector, canneries, and even white-collar workplaces.

As the CIO succeeded in organizing industrial workers, the differences between the AFL and the new unions became increasingly apparent. The CIO built unions in manufacturing centers that had been ignored by the AFL. AFL and CIO leaders also clashed over the CIO unions' willingness to work with a broad range of organizers. Between 1935 and 1939, the Communist Party of the United States (CPUSA) pursued a "popular front" strategy, allying with organizations working for broad democratic change, rather than adhering to a narrow communist ideological line. CPUSA members became perhaps the most energetic and persistent of union organizers. Dubinsky grew unhappy with the prevalence of communist organizers in CIO unions and brought the ILGWU back into the AFL fold. Finally, in November 1938, the CIO held a national convention and created an independent confederation of industrial unions, now known as the Congress of Industrial Organizations. Though the Roosevelt Recession nearly halted the CIO's growth, the industrial unions took advantage of industrial recovery during World War II to build on their gains in the 1930s. After the war, these CIO unions, along with the growing building trades and teamsters unions in the AFL, would become known as "Big Labor" and play central roles in the economy and politics.

African Americans' relationship to labor changed dramatically in the 1930s. During the first years of the decade, the CPUSA emerged as an ally for black workers and for the cause of civil rights. Communist Party organizers, for example, led many of the unemployed organizations, fighting to bring government resources to black neighborhoods and to prevent the eviction of black tenants. The party's legal arm, the International Labor Defense Fund, came to the assistance of the

"Scottsboro Boys," nine African American teenagers falsely accused of raping a white woman on a train and wrongly convicted in Scottsboro, Alabama. Black Americans pragmatically took advantage of such alliances. They were never members of the Communist Party in large numbers, but some black organizers and radicals joined the party at least for a short time, and many were generally willing to work with it to fight racial inequality through the labor movement. Party organizers energized the CIO's efforts to organize interracial unions. CIO leaders, including the important group of left-wing organizers, understood that for practical or idealistic reasons, or both, the new industrial unions could challenge the AFL and their employers only if they built a culture of interracialism. Nonetheless, as the CIO grew, according to the historian Bruce Nelson, "it was constrained by a membership majority that had little or no commitment to a broad-gauged social-democratic agenda."[22] Racial discrimination in unions and working-class racial tensions remained key factors in American workplaces, and, indeed, have yet to be fully resolved.

For all the interracial organizing of radical activists and the CIO, black workers forged their own paths into the labor movement. Most notably, the Brotherhood of Sleeping Car Porters (BSCP) became the first national African American union to win a charter from the AFL in 1935. African American men had long worked as porters for the Pullman Palace Car Company. They acted as the servants of white customers on Pullman trains, providing first-class service in return for tips. They earned meager wages, which meant that they needed to play to the racist stereotype of the subservient black man. Some historians have argued that the access to jobs as Pullman porters helped create the foundation for the black middle class, but for many workers at the time the work was degrading, required long hours, and paid far too little. In August 1925, five Pullman porters formed the BSCP in New York City. They were inspired by a growing

Figure 4. "Civil Rights March on Washington, DC [A. Philip Randolph, Organizer of the Demonstration, Veteran Labor Leader who Helped to Found the Brotherhood of Sleeping Car Porters, American Federation of Labor (AFL), and a Former Vice President of the American Federation of Labor and Congress of Industrial Organizations (AFL-CIO)]." US Information Agency, August 28, 1963. Record Group 306, Still Picture Branch, US National Archives (#542064).

labor-based black protest politics led by a "new crowd" of African American activists unsatisfied with the existing interracial, middle-class civil rights and social work groups. The porters called on New York socialist A. Philip Randolph (Figure 4) to lead their union drive. For twelve years, Randolph and the men and women organizing for the BSCP struggled to overcome resistance from the Pullman Company and skepticism toward unions in the black community. The Pullman Company bought support from black leaders, especially in its home city of Chicago, by donating money to local black organizations. The support worked, and the BSCP found that African Americans in Chicago not only distrusted unions because of their history of racial exclusions, but also saw labor protests as disreputable and perceived the Pullman Company to be the friend of the black community.[23]

The BSCP found the 1930s a much more productive period. Growing militancy of the labor and civil rights activism among the unemployed in the early 1930s, in the CIO's interracial unions, and among black railroad dining car employees and "red caps" (luggage porters at train stations) all fostered a black working-class alignment with the labor movement. In addition, New Deal labor laws created opportunities to break down resistance from the AFL and the Pullman Company. The BSCP aligned with longstanding civil rights leaders in Chicago, such as Ida B. Wells-Barnett, a famous anti-lynching activist and a member of black Chicago's political elite. Wells-Barnett brought respectability and the support of the city's thousands of black club-women to the Brotherhood. At the same time, Randolph grew in stature as the foremost black labor leader and became the first head of the National Negro Congress (NNC), a characteristic Popular Front organization that sought to forge alliances among communists, socialists, and liberals organizing against racial and economic inequality. While the BSCP reached out to black leaders and community members, the union also took advantage of the 1934 Railway Labor Act to hold successful union elections among black porters. With mass black support, a new legal foundation, and the potential competition from the emerging CIO in mind, the AFL granted a charter to the BSCP in 1935. Two long years later, the Brotherhood finally signed its first contract with the Pullman Company, the first union contract for black workers with a major corporation.

The New Deal did not bring the country out of the depression, although it did improve the lives of millions of citizens and transformed the foundations of American politics so that future battles would be fought over the nature of organized labor's place in the nation (rather than its mere right to exist) and over broad access to "security." Union membership increased dramatically from just under 3 million in 1933 to approximately 12 million by 1945. President Roosevelt also helped create a fundamentally new national political alignment; success for the Democratic Party (outside the South, where the Democrats remained a conservative party until the rise

of the southern wing of the Republican Party in the last third of the 20th century) would depend upon winning the votes of ethnic urban voters, unionized workers, and African Americans. In addition, the success of the CIO and the broad militancy of American workers led to a working-class-based cultural movement that one historian has termed "the laboring of American culture."[24] Workers and their worlds as subjects, and working-class artists, reshaped American music and the literary and visual arts, as well as popular culture on the radio, in movies, and in cartoons.

WORKERS AND WORLD WAR II

When Japan attacked the US naval base at Pearl Harbor on December 7, 1941, the rate of American manufacturing surged, and within about eighteen months the nation's economy was in a state of "full employment." World War II, therefore, marked a profound turning point because it brought the country out of the Depression, introduced thousands of women and black workers to the industrial labor force, reinforced the idea that federal government spending was essential to a healthy economy, and established unions as central permanent players in the national economy. The war also revolutionized American workers' expectations. Rather than seeking to survive in what seemed to be an economic crisis without end, American workers entered the post-war world still deeply divided by race, geography, and social class, but expecting to share in a new era of prosperity.

Labor, including the CIO, solidified its place in the nation's economy during the war. Though labor conflict continued as many workers fought for higher wartime wages, often in wildcat strikes, labor leaders gained standing by signing on to a no-strike pledge with the federal government's labor mediation agency, the National War Labor Board. Labor unions also gained thousands of new members as they convinced the NWLB to refuse employers' demands for an "open shop" in wartime industries, and they secured "maintenance of membership clauses" stipulating that workers who became union members during the war would remain members for the length of the contract.

As white men were drafted into the military by the tens of thousands, industries began to recruit white women to fill their spots. The famous images of "Rosie the Riveter" perhaps romanticize women's experiences in the workforce, but women at the time did speak to the excitement and freedom they found in working outside the home and earning their own wages. The war did not usher in a rapid change in gender norms, at least not in majority public opinion. After the war, women were expected to leave the workforce, to allow returning veterans to take their jobs back, and to return to their "rightful" duties in the home. Yet women's wartime experiences created changes that would eventually help create the modern feminist movements. First, although many women were ushered out of sectors of the workforce, women actually stayed in the labor force at higher numbers than ever before; married women, especially, worked in greater numbers than in any previous era of American history. Moreover, many women never forgot their experiences in the workforce, and their expectations for opportunities that the next generation of women should have were forever changed. Women in the labor movement who joined unions during the war also became leaders for a new labor-based feminism.[25]

Black men and women were also hired into industrial work by the tens or hundreds of thousands, but only after employers found they could not fill the jobs with white women. Mexican workers also found jobs during World War II, most notably through the federal government's Bracero Program, a guest worker program that brought tens of thousands of Mexican workers into the United States to fill labor shortages in agriculture. Although opportunity came for black workers and women later than it did for white male workers, the war brought a radical improvement in economic conditions and raised expectations for all Americans. That the raised expectations of women and racial minorities were not fulfilled after the war meant that the increased opportunity of wartime actually helped sow the seeds for the civil rights movement and other social movements to follow.[26]

The United States emerged from World War II in a position to become an economic superpower. From 1945 to 1973, American workers enjoyed higher wages, greater job security, and a steadily improving standard of living. Workers in unions made even greater gains, including not only substantially higher wages but also health insurance and pensions. Even Americans on the margins of the workforce benefited from the expansion of unemployment compensation, welfare, and job training and placement programs. Unions played a major role in improving the standard of living of their members as their gains created a "ripple effect" that raised the wages and standard of living for non-union workers.

Workers made remarkable gains between 1900 and 1945. To be sure, this was no linear narrative of inevitable upward mobility and progress. But by the end of World War II, the combined forces of top-down reform and bottom-up activism had created a federal government that legalized and protected industrial workers' right to organize and bargain collectively, as well as their right to a safe workplace with regulations for hours and wages. They had won access to a limited but growing public welfare state and a burgeoning private welfare system. Through both the AFL's trade-union-led political activism and a broad world of working-class political activism and workers' alliances with middle-class reformers and reform-minded politicians, they had made cities better places to live, banned child labor, won municipal ownership of utilities, strengthened their right of free speech, gained consumer protections, and opened new sectors of work to women and racial minorities. Moreover, industrial workers had earned a status as the virtuous "blue-collar" core of a self-consciously hard-working American society no longer divided so sharply along lines of national origin, though still deeply divided by the racism and segregation that remained the fundamental reality for African Americans, Asian Americans, Hispanic Americans, and Native Americans. With these newly won rights, protections, and status, the once marginalized and much-maligned American worker had secured a place within the consumerist industrial society and as one interest group among many in the political system.

DISCUSSION OF THE LITERATURE

The historiography of labor and working-class life and struggles in the United States originated in the labor economics movement of Progressive Era intellectuals. This was the stuff of big institutions. John R. Commons at the University of Wisconsin built on the work of earlier labor economists, including Richard T. Ely. Together, Commons and students like Selig Perlman developed a new field of institutional labor history. Taking for granted the growth of industrial production and market relations, they rather optimistically sought to understand the role that workers' self-organization had played in the rise of labor in a US context defined by American workers who were generally narrowly "job-conscious" rather than broadly "class-conscious" in their engagement with the state and industrial corporations. Emphasizing the significance of organized labor, and of trade unionism more specifically, as the key expression of American workers' economic consciousness, the Commons School of labor history necessarily underestimated the importance of the vast majority of workers who were unorganized, and particularly missed the significance of women and racial minorities in the workforce.[27]

The Commons School of institutional labor history would eventually give way to broader conceptions of the history of work and labor struggles in the context of workers' community and culture. In part, this was because some more radically minded historians did not share the Commons School's commitment to trade unionism; such scholars would recover a long history of labor radicalism in the United States. Scholars focusing on immigration history, women's history, African American history, and urban history would also revise the Commons School's arguments, seeking to understand the ways that working-class culture and economic politics manifested themselves outside of the trade union movement. By the late 1950s and early 1960s, scholars such as Melvyn Dubofsky, David Montgomery, Herbert Gutman, and David Brody had begun to examine what would be known as the "new social history" or the "new labor history."[28] Given shape by E. P. Thompson's monumental *The Making of the English Working Class* (1963),[29] this impulse to study the ways workers create, and are created by, the world around them inspired more than a generation of work that sought out the connections between work, community, and power in the United States, where a Marxist-style class-consciousness had never been predominant. The new labor history also gave rise to scholars, perhaps inspired by the black freedom struggle and other social movements of the 1960s and 1970s, who sought to recover the history of women, slaves and free blacks, Asians, Latinos, and Native Americans.[30]

Since the 1980s, there has been a persistent sense that the field of labor history has been in a crisis, even as the production of labor and working-class scholarship has hardly slowed. With the cast of characters growing and local case studies multiplying every year, some observers wondered if a synthesis of the literature was possible. Was there ever such a thing that could be defined as *the* American labor and working-class history? Moreover, post-structuralism and postmodern cultural criticism called into question whether "class" could serve as a unifying concept. As Joan Wallach

Scott would explain, it was not enough just to add women (or black workers, or immigrant workers, etc.) to the stage of history.[31] It was not even enough to recover the experiences of previously underrepresented workers as some sort of objective evidence for what it meant to be different kinds of working-class people. Historians had to give up the notion that any social category—race, class, gender, sexuality—had any content outside of its historical context in that moment. They had to focus on the ways that people constantly create and re-create their identities; it was argued that it may be all one can do to explain that process of conscious and unconscious creation of self in a world that cannot be known as a whole.

To make matters more difficult for labor historians, as poststructuralism questioned the very categories historians had used to make sense of the past, beginning in the 1980s the political world around them was destroying the very institutions—labor unions—that had given the field coherence. Given the near decimation of organized labor, the decline of manufacturing jobs, and the diversification of the politics and social positions of working-class people, historians have had to rethink the assumptions of the field. No longer could it be taken for granted that a kind of interest-group politics and "business unionism" would be part of the American political economy.

As the implications of Reaganism and Thatcherism, as well as the triangulating centrism of the "New Democrats," became clearer, historians began to explore labor and working-class history in a kind of blue mood.[32] Some have pushed to "bring the state back in" to the story of working-class history in order to highlight the persistent dominance of anti-labor law and government subsidization of finance and manufacturing, as well as the concomitant weakness of workers in the capitalist system.[33] Others have focused on why American workers have built a mode of labor so deeply intertwined with the ideologies and institutions of private property, empire, and racial and gender exclusion.[34] For many, the watchwords became hegemony, agency, infrapolitics, resistance, identity, and culture, as they sought to shed light on the power of the state, corporate leaders, and employers to bring about workers' accommodation to regimes of inequity or, alternatively, how even the most subordinated workers had managed to make their own history. This latter work, which had been initiated earlier by feminist and black historians, reshaped the investigations of all workers, bringing questions of whiteness, gender identity, and sexuality to the fore.[35]

The nearly complete triumph of anti-union politics, together with the global resurgence of economic inequality, has been so dramatic that historians have become skeptical of the value of recovering histories of workers' agency. To be sure, with the ripples of mass militancy in the early 21st century there has been some effort to recover lost traditions of radicalism.[36] But, generally speaking, the current conditions have become so reminiscent of the turn of the 20th century that historians have come to look for continuities not just of radicalism, but also of the connections among American imperialism, economic growth, and workers' positions in a persistently unequal global economy. The historian Leon Fink, for instance, has joined a growing group of scholars in arguing that the history of American workers must be understood in light of transnational economic and political dynamics, and the evolution of global capitalism.[37] In part, these histories counter notions that we live in a postracial, classless society where inequality is a sign of a healthy economy. But they are also attempts to make a clear-eyed assessment of the continuities in combined corporate and state power, whether one looks, for example, at the control of workers in the Panama Canal Zone or at the place of "unskilled" workers in a globalizing economy in the "Long Gilded Age."[38]

From this perspective, the period between 1935 and the mid-1970s—the prime years of the "New Deal Order"—when the United

States enjoyed its longest period of sustained economic growth along with the greatest equality of income in the industrial era, is really "the long exception."[39] If this is true, some argue that historians ought to look to the period between 1896 and 1945 for the most pertinent lessons on how workers have struggled to reconcile their values and traditions in an individualistic consumer society, when they have fought with or accommodated the realities of corporate dominance of the political and economic systems, and how those struggles both made great gains for American workers and left the American working class divided by race, gender, sexuality, region, skill level, and employment sector. Workers and their allies built significant, if highly problematic, reformist and radical movements that broke from the social Darwinism and laissez-faire ethos of the late 19th century, but most American workers did not directly share the more romantic experiences of such labor activism. Labor and working-class history, therefore, does not necessarily promise to offer a usable past for those seeking to build contemporary movements, but it does open the door to greater understanding and empathy with the complex lives and struggles of working people in previous eras of globalizing inequality.

PRIMARY SOURCES

The main research problems for students of labor and working-class history are, first, to sift through the nearly limitless supply of relevant sources and, second, to find ways to include the voices of working people themselves. Because the state plays such a key role in shaping law and society, labor historians regularly consult municipal, county, state, and federal records, as well as court cases.[40] Many historians of labor radicalism also make use of Freedom of Information Act requests to access the files that government agencies have collected while spying on activists.[41] Records of unions, labor leaders, and the

labor press are, of course, also critical. They are available in archives across the country, with major concentrations in New York City, Detroit, Chicago, Pittsburgh, and Los Angeles. The papers of civil rights and black nationalist organizations, as well as groups and leaders of the women's movement and immigrants' rights movements, are all essential, because the labor movement typically overlapped with other forms of social activism.[42] Labor scholars also delve deeply into oral histories, often doing interviews of their own, but also by reading the transcripts of interviews with workers completed by previous scholars, as well as by social work agencies, congressional investigations, journalists, and more. Historians interested in the culture of class, and working-class culture, examine everything from songs, plays, novels, poems, and television shows to housing, clothes, and even the sounds and smells of working people's communities in the past.

DIGITAL MATERIALS

Frank B. Gilbreth, "The Original Films of Frank B. Gilbreth," 1910–1924. Presented by James S. Perkins in Collaboration with Dr. Lillian M. Gilbreth & Dr. Ralph M. Barnes. https://archive.org/details/OriginalFilm.

FURTHER READING

Brody, David. *Workers in Industrial America: Essays on the 20th Century Struggle.* 2d ed. New York: Oxford University Press, 1993.

Commons, John R. *A History of Labor in the United States.* New York: Macmillan, 1935.

Dubofsky, Melvin. *We Shall Be All: A History of the Industrial Workers of the World.* Urbana: University of Illinois Press, 1988 [1969].

Forbath, William E. *Law and the Shaping of the American Labor Movement.* Cambridge, MA: Harvard University Press, 1991.

Kessler-Harris, Alice. *In Pursuit of Equity: Women, Men, and the Quest for Economic Citizenship in 20th-Century America.* New York: Oxford University Press, 2001.

Lichtenstein, Nelson. *Labor's War at Home: The CIO in World War II.* Philadelphia: Temple University Press, 2003 [1982].

Montgomery, David. *Worker's Control in America: Studies in the History of Work, Technology, and Labor Struggles.* Cambridge: Cambridge University Press, 1979.

Montgomery, David. *The Fall of the House of Labor: The Workplace, the State, and American Labor Activism, 1865–1925.* New York: Cambridge University Press, 1987.

Nelson, Bruce. *Divided We Stand: American Workers and the Struggle for Black Equality.* Princeton, NJ: Princeton University Press, 2001.

Tomlins, Christopher. *The State and Unions: Labor Relations, Law, and the Organized Labor Movement in America, 1880–1960.* Cambridge: Cambridge University Press, 1985.

Vargas, Zaragosa. *Proletarians of the North: A History of Mexican Industrial Workers in Detroit and the Midwest, 1917–1933.* Berkeley: University of California Press, 1993.

NOTES

1. Beverly Gage, "Why Violence Matters: Radicalism, Politics, and Class War in the Gilded Age and Progressive Era," *Journal for the Study of Radicalism* 1, no. 1 (2007): 106.

2. David Brody, *Workers in Industrial America: Essays on the 20th Century Struggle* (2d ed., New York: Oxford University Press, 1993), 6.

3. Harry Braverman, *Labor and Monopoly Capital: The Degradation of Work in the Twentieth Century* (New York: Monthly Review Press, 1974).

4. Braverman, *Labor and Monopoly Capital*, 36.

5. Gage, "Why Violence Matters," 104.

6. Braverman, *Labor and Monopoly Capital*, 3.

7. Julie Greene, *Pure and Simple Politics: The American Federation of Labor and Political Activism, 1881–1917* (Cambridge: Cambridge University Press, 2006).

8. Paul Michel Taillon, *Good, Reliable, White Men: Railroad Brotherhoods, 1877–1917* (Urbana: University of Illinois Press, 2009).

9. Thomas G. Andres, *Killing for Coal: America's Deadliest Labor War* (Cambridge, MA: Harvard University Press, 2008).

10. Melvyn Dubofsky and Foster Rhea Dulles, *Labor in America: A History, Seventh Edition* (Wheeling, IL: Harlan Davidson, 2004), 191; and Dorothy Sue Cobble, "Pure and Simple Radicalism: Putting the Progressive Era AFL in Its Time," *Labor: Studies in Working-Class History of the Americas* 10, no. 4 (2013): 67–68.

11. Youngsoo Bae, *Labor in Retreat: Class and Community among Men's Clothing Workers of Chicago, 1871–1929* (Albany: State University of New York Press, 2001); and Annelise Orleck, *Common Sense and a Little Fire: Women And Working-Class Politics in the United States, 1900–1965* (Chapel Hill: University of North Carolina Press, 1995).

12. "The Preamble to the Constitution of the Industrial Workers of the World," as amended and appeared in the *Proceedings of the 1908 IWW Convention* in the *Industrial Union Bulletin* (November 7, 1908), in Joyce L. Kornbluh, ed., *Rebel Voices: An IWW Anthology* (Ann Arbor: University of Michigan Press, 1964), 13.

13. Andrew Wender Cohen, *The Racketeer's Progress: Chicago and the Struggle for the Modern American Economy 1900–1940* (New York: Cambridge University Press, 2004).

14. Brody, *Workers*, 27–28.

15. Brody, *Workers*, 32–34.

16. Bruce Nelson, *Divided We Stand: American Workers and the Struggle for Black Equality* (Princeton, NJ: Princeton University Press, 2001), xxix.

17. Samuel Gompers, "Trade Union Attitude Toward Colored Workers," *American Federationist* 8, no. 4 (April 1901): 119.

18. Samuel Gompers, "Talks on Labor: Addresses at St. Paul and Minneapolis," *American Federationist* 12 (1905): 638.

19. Paul Moreno, *Black Americans and Organized Labor: A New History* (Baton Rouge: Louisiana State University Press, 2006).

20. James R. Grossman, *Land of Hope: Chicago, Black Southerners, and the Great Migration* (Chicago: University of Chicago Press, 1989).

21. W. Elliot Brownlee, *Dynamics of Ascent: A History of the American Economy* (New York: Knopf, 1974), 411.

22. Nelson, *Divided*, xxxiii.

23. Eric Arnesen, *Brotherhoods of Color: Black Railroad Workers and the Struggle for Equality* (Cambridge, MA: Harvard University Press, 2001); and Beth Tompkins Bates, *Pullman Porters and the Rise of Protest Politics in Black America, 1925–1945* (Chapel Hill: University of North Carolina Press, 2001).

24. Michael Denning, *The Cultural Front: The Laboring of American Culture in the Twentieth Century* (New York: Verso, 1998).

25. Dorothy Sue Cobble, *The Other Women's Movement: Workplace Justice and Social Rights in Modern America* (Princeton, NJ: Princeton University Press, 2005).

26. Glenda Elizabeth Gilmore, *Defying Dixie: The Radical Roots of Civil Rights, 1919–1950* (New York: W. W. Norton, 2009); and Zaragosa Vargas, *Labor Rights Are Civil Rights: Mexican American Workers in Twentieth-Century America* (Princeton, NJ: Princeton University Press, 2007).

27. John R. Commons, *History of Labor in the United States* (New York: Macmillan, 1918–1935); and Selig Perlman, *A Theory of the Labor Movement* (New York: Macmillan, 1928).

28. David Brody, "The Old Labor History and the New: In Search of an American Working Class," *Labor History* 20 (1979): 111–26; Brody, *Workers in Industrial America: Essays on the Twentieth-Century Struggle* (New York: Oxford University Press, 1980); Melvyn Dubofsky, *We Shall Be All: A History of the Industrial Workers of the World* (New York: Quadrangle Books, 1967); Dubofsky, *John L. Lewis: A Biography* (New York: Quadrangle Press, 1977); Herbert Gutman, *Work, Culture, and Society in Industrializing America: Essays in American Working-Class and Social History* (New York: Vintage Books, 1977); Gutman, *Power and Culture: Essays on the American Working Class,* Ira Berlin, ed., (New York: Pantheon Books, 1977); David Montgomery, *Beyond Equality: Labor and the Radical Republicans, 1862–1872* (New York: Alfred A. Knopf, 1967); Montgomery, *Workers' Control in America: Studies in the History of Work, Technology, and Labor Struggles* (New York: Cambridge University Press), 1979; and Montgomery, *Workers' Control in America: Studies in the History of Work, Technology, and Labor Struggles* (New York: Cambridge University Press, 1979.

29. E. P. Thompson, *The Making of the English Working Class* (1963, repr.; New York: Vintage Books, 1966).

30. Eric Arnesen, *Waterfront Workers of New Orleans: Race, Class and Politics, 1863–1923* (New York: Oxford University Press, 1991); Jeanne Boydston, *Home & Work: Housework, Wages, and the Ideology of Labor in the Early Republic* (New York: Oxford University Press, 1990); Barbara Fields, "Ideology and Race in American History," in *Region, Race, and Reconstruction: Essays in Honor of C. Vann Woodward,* eds. Morgan J. Koussar and James McPherson (New York: Oxford University Press, 1982), 143–177; Eugene Genovese, *Roll, Jordan, Roll: The World the Slaves Made* (New York: Pantheon Books, 1974); Grossman, *Land of Hope;* Howard Lamar, "From Bondage to Contract: Ethnic Labor in the American West, 1600–1890," in Steven Hahn and Jonathan Prude, eds., *The Countryside in the Age of Capitalist Transformation: Essays in the Social History of Rural America* (Chapel Hill: University of North Carolina Press, 1985), 293–324; Earl Lewis, *In Their Own Interests: Race, Class, and Power in Twentieth-Century Norfolk, Virginia* (Berkeley: University of California Press, 1991); Annelise Orleck, *Common Sense and a Little Fire* (Chapel Hill: University of North Carolina Press, 1985); Gunther Peck, *Reinventing Free Labor: Padrones and Immigrant Workers in the North American West, 1880–1930* (Cambridge: Cambridge University Press, 2000); Peter Rachleff, *Black Labor in the South: Richmond, Virginia, 1865–1890* (Philadelphia: Temple University Press, 1984); Alexander Saxton, *The Indispensable Enemy: Labor and the Anti-Chinese Movement in California* (Berkeley: University of California Press, 1971); and Christine Stansell, *City of Women: Sex and Class in New York, 1789–1860* (New York: Knopf, 1986).

31. Joan Wallach Scott, "Gender as a Useful Category of Analysis," *The American Historical Review* 91, no. 5 (December 1986): 1053–1075; and Scott, "The Evidence of Experience," *Critical Inquiry* 17, no. 4 (Summer 1991): 773–797.

32. Nick Salvatore, "American Labor History," in *Industrial Relations at the Dawn of the New Millennium,* ed. M. F. Neufeld and J. T. McKelvey (Ithaca, NY: Industrial Labor Relations Press, 1998), 114–123. http://digitalcommons.ilr .cornell.edu/cgi/viewcontent.cgi?article=1600 &context=articles.

33. Melvyn Dubofsky, *The State and Labor in Modern America* (Chapel Hill: University of North Carolina Press, 1994); and William E. Forbath, *Law and the Shaping of the American Labor Movement* (Cambridge, MA: Harvard University Press, 1991).

34. David Montgomery, *The Fall of the House of Labor: The Workplace, the State, and American*

Labor Activism, 1865–1925 (New York: Cambridge University Press, 1987); and Victoria Hattam, *Labor Visions and State Power: The Origins of Business Unionism in the United States* (Princeton, NJ: Princeton University Press, 1993).

35. Eric Arnesen, et al., "Scholarly Controversy: Whiteness and the Historians' Imagination," Forum in *International Labor and Working-Class History* 60 (Fall 2001): 1–92; Ava Baron, *Work Engendered: Toward New History of American Labor* (Ithaca, NY: Cornell University Press, 1991); George Chauncey, *Gay New York: Gender, Urban Culture, and the Making of the Gay Male World* (New York: BasicBooks, 1994); Robin D. G. Kelley, "'We Are Not What We Seem': Rethinking Black Working-Class Opposition in the Jim Crow South," *Journal of American History* 80, no. 1 (June 1993): 75–112; and David Roediger, *The Wages of Whiteness: Race and the Making of American Labor History* (New York: Verso, 1991).

36. Philip Dray, *There Is Power in a Union: The Epic Story of Labor in America* (New York: Anchor, 2011).

37. Leon Fink, ed., *Workers across the Americas: The Transnational Turn in Labor History* (New York: Oxford University Press, 2011).

38. Julie Greene, *The Canal Builders: Making America's Empire at the Panama Canal* (New York: Penguin, 2010); and Leon Fink, *The Long Gilded Age: American Capitalism and the Lessons of a New World Order* (Philadelphia: University of Pennsylvania Press, 2014).

39. Jefferson Cowie and Nick Salvatore, "The Long Exception: Rethinking the Place of the New Deal in American History," *International Labor and Working-Class History* 74 (2008): 1–32.

40. The local, county, and state records are often found in university government records repositories. For federal records, begin with the online site of the National Archives and Records Administration, http://www.archives.gov.

41. See Freedom of Information/Privacy Act, https://www.fbi.gov/foia/.

42. Especially helpful are the holdings of the Kheel Center at the Cornell University Library; the Southern Labor Archives at Georgia State University; the University of Wisconsin at Madison Archives; the Newberry Library in Chicago; UCLA Library Special Collections in the Charles E. Young Research Library; the Walter Reuther Library at Wayne State University in Detroit; and Taminent Library and Robert F. Wagner Archives in New York City. The papers of the National Association for the Advancement of Colored People are available in digitized format through the online database ProQuest. See also the Schomburg Center for Research in Black Culture. For a guide to researching women's history archives, see the Gateway to Library of Congress Resources for the Study of Women's History and Culture in the United States.

Jeffrey Helgeson

PUBLIC SECTOR UNIONS IN THE UNITED STATES

ORIGINS OF PUBLIC SECTOR UNIONISM IN THE 19TH CENTURY

Though often regarded as a product of the postwar era, the origins of public-sector unionism stretch back to the working-class movements of the early 19th century. In 1835, skilled craftsmen and mechanics in Philadelphia, New York, and Baltimore began lobbying the navy for reduced hours in the booming shipbuilding industry.[1] The Board of Navy Commissioners refused, and Congress declined to take action, but President Andrew Jackson ordered the navy department to implement the ten-hour day in those cities in which private shipbuilders had already granted it. In 1840, Martin Van Buren issued an executive order mandating a ten-hour day for manual laborers in the federal government.[2] Almost immediately thereafter, workmen in the federal shipbuilding industry began lobbying for the eight-hour day. In 1861, Congress passed a prevailing wage and hour law for navy projects.

These mid-century developments enshrined two critical but sometimes contradictory principles in public-sector labor relations: first, that workers employed in government enterprises should be paid according to the wages and hours prevailing in the private sector; and second, that government could serve as a model employer for private business. Over the next century and a half, government workers would strategically invoke one or the other, demanding either parity with their private-sector peers or that the state serve as a means of lifting the wages, hours, and conditions of the broader working class.

Through much of the 19th century, however, political agitation, not workplace action, proved the most effective vehicle for this agenda. This was particularly true for municipal workers, whose ranks swelled alongside urban growth in the second half of the 20th century. Though transactional hiring (trading votes for jobs or other favors) had long been a fixture of urban politics, it took on an increasingly important role as city governments expanded to meet the demands of an emerging urban-industrial society filled by a broadening range of racial, ethnic, and national identities. "If the Knights of Labor wanted to secure an advantage for any member," labor economist and pioneering labor historian John R. Commons wrote of New York City, "they went to the Tammany politician, who went to the commissioner of street cleaning, or to the mayor, and secured the desired promotion, or relaxation of discipline or release from punishment."[3]

The emergence of the urban political machine had crucial but contradictory implications for public workers. On the one hand, it delegitimized their political participation and spurred legislative and executive action to curb it. The notion that government employment was fundamentally different from private business first took hold in the late 19th century in response to political agitation in the postal service. As early as 1895, Postmaster General William Wilson issued an order that bared employees of the US Post Office from traveling to the nation's capital "for the purposes of influencing legislation before Congress."[4] President Theodore Roosevelt extended the restriction in 1902, instituting a "gag rule" that prohibited any federal employee from individually or collectively lobbying for legislation.[5] Taken to its logical conclusion, this outlook cast public employment as fundamentally different from private business. As President William Howard Taft stated in 1911, "The Government employees are a privileged class whose work is necessary to carry on the Government and upon whose entry into the Government service it is entirely reasonable to impose conditions that should not be and ought not be imposed upon those who serve private employers."[6] At its most extreme, this view prompted proposals to disfranchise government employees from municipal elections.[7]

On the other hand, fear of machine-driven political corruption encouraged some reformers to experiment with the application of elements of traditional labor relations to government employment. The first sustained experiment with an anti-machine approach to worker organization came in 1895, when New York City sanitation commissioner George E. Waring Jr. replaced a decentralized patronage network with a hierarchical employee organization empowered to bring democratically approved grievances to a joint committee of worker representatives and administration superintendents.[8] Summarizing the findings of a study of two dozen cities in Great Britain and the United States in 1913, Commons insisted that, contrary to the objections of elected officials, "a proper organization of public employees...is a protection for the service against one of the greatest evils by which public employment is menaced in democratic communities; namely, the interference of the politician."[9] Few Progressive reformers were so committed to democratizing government employment by empowering its employees, but the breakthroughs set the stage for the reemergence of public-sector labor in the 20th century.

PUBLIC-SECTOR UNIONS FROM THE PROGRESSIVE ERA TO WORLD WAR I

By even partially insulating public employment from patronage politics, civil-service protections encouraged public workers to regard their jobs as permanent, and thus to invest much more energy and activity in improving pay, hours, and conditions. This was initially clearest in the federal postal service, where a bona fide trade-union movement took root in the last decades of the 19th century. Protesting everything from low pay and long hours to employer surveillance and political manipulation of delivery routes, postal workers organized both in independent associations and with the Knights of Labor. In response, postal administrators imposed a "gag rule" that attempted to prohibit workers from lobbying Congress. When that failed to stall employee activism, the postal service attempted to bar membership in any secret society or organization. Though incompletely enforced, the anti-union moves slowed the spread of formal, open workplace organization in the postal service.[10]

The first genuine teacher organizations were born in the last decades of the 19th century in response to attempts by Progressive reformers to bring local schools under the control of a single superintendent and school board and to formalize the certification system. Classroom educators challenged these reform plans and, in so doing, formed the foundation for the first teachers' union. The Chicago Teachers' Federation (CFT), formed in 1897 and led by Margaret Haley, was the first educational association specifically designed to represent the interests of classroom teachers. It focused on three core economic issues: salary increases, pension systems, and job tenure. In the era before public-sector collective bargaining, the CFT pursued its agenda through political alliances and lobbying. After failing to transform the administrator-dominated National Education Association into a genuine teachers' organization, the CFT teamed with locals from other Midwestern cities to form the American Federation of Teachers (AFT) in 1916.[11]

The formation of the AFT reflected the broader labor movement's growing interest in and commitment to organizing in government employment. In 1905, Chicago's Electricity Department signed the first contract with a public-employee organization. The American Federation of Labor (AFL) chartered its first government union the next year, when it created the National Federation of Post Office Clerks. The Lloyd-LaFollette Act of 1912, which repealed the "gag rule" by recognizing the constitutional right of federal workers to organize and petition Congress, legitimized collective organization in the public sector and helped to inspire a wave of organizing in the years around World War I. Previously independent organizations like the National Association of Letter Carriers and Railway Mail Carriers affiliated with the AFL, while teachers, firefighters, and police flocked to AFL unions. Considering both rising union density and the growth of government at all levels, the total number of unionized public workers more than doubled between 1915 and 1921.[12]

Yet this dramatic expansion proved, in historian Joseph E. Slater's phrase, a "false dawn" for public-sector unionism. The critical turning point was the Boston police strike of September 1919. The AFL had long been suspicious of police unionism, in part because of the role police had played in violently suppressing working-class movements in the late 19th century.[13] Faced with an ever-increasing flood of applications, however, the AFL convention reversed its traditional opposition to police unions in June 1919. The response was dramatic. Over the next three months, the AFL received more than sixty applications and chartered three dozen police locals.[14] Government officials, fearing that unionized police might refuse to break stoppages by private-sector workers, fiercely resisted attempts to affiliate with the broader labor movement even when those organizations specifically renounced the right to strike.

These tensions came to a head in Boston during the late summer of 1919. Following a string of successful strikes by city firefighters and engineers and buoyed by a supportive statement from local private-sector unions, the Boston Police Union (BPU) considered affiliation with the AFL. In response, police commissioner Edwin Curtis issued Rule 102, stating his own position that "a police office cannot consistently belong to a union and perform his sworn duty" and that "his work is sharply differentiated from that of the worker in private employ."[15] Ten days later, citing low wages, long hours, arbitrary bosses, unhealthy working conditions, and the ineffectiveness of the department-sponsored Boston Social Club, the BPU filed its application. Curtis issued another order formally barring officers from membership in any organization with an outside affiliation. When the officers affiliated anyway, Curtis suspended nineteen suspected leaders for violating his personnel policy. In response, nearly three-quarters of Boston's 1,500 uniformed officers struck on September 9.[16] Substitutes failed to maintain order in the city, which descended into chaos. When Curtis proved unable to garner sufficient replacements for the striking officers, Governor Calvin Coolidge dispatched five thousand Massachusetts National Guard to quell the strike, justifying the decision in the simplest terms: "there is no right to strike against the public safety by anybody, anywhere, anytime." In the context of the First Red Scare and a wave of private-sector militancy, public sympathy swung to Coolidge, who rode his handling of the strike to the Republican Party's nomination as vice president the following year.[17]

Breaking the 1919 Boston Police Union strike was a critical moment in the history of public-sector unionism. The AFL retreated from its commitment to police unions and the thirty-seven locals it had already chartered collapsed within a few years. Though police continued to organize in the decades that followed, they remained largely outside the formal labor movement until the late 1960s. Fearing for their own future, other public-sector unions immediately adopted or reaffirmed no-strike pledges, a practice that also persisted well into the postwar era.

Though public sector union membership continued to increase through the 1920s, it barely managed to keep up with the growth of government as a whole.

More importantly, Coolidge's intervention in the strike—widely praised and supported by both the country's newspapers and political leaders—was critical in legitimizing the notion that government employees, particularly those in the protective services, were fundamentally different from private-sector workers. Though the initial reaction to the Boston strike had focused on the threat posed by police stoppages to public safety, in the decades that followed, it evolved into an objection that formal union recognition of any group of public employees constituted an illegitimate encroachment on the sovereignty of the state. Yet despite the widely held notion that, as Sterling Spero put it, public-sector unionism was "subversive of discipline and dangerous to the state" and strikes were "an act of insubordination hardly short of treason," government workers continued to organize through the age of legal uncertainty.[18]

ORGANIZING THE STATE IN AN AGE OF LEGAL UNCERTAINTY

Independent civil-service associations were the focal point of collective action in state and local government from the conclusion of the Boston police strike through the mid-1930s. Rarely challenging the marginal legal status afforded to public employees, organizations like New York City's Civil Service Forum explicitly eschewed both militant tactics and "impertinent demands" in favor of a much more modest and cooperative agenda and educational activity.[19] The economic turmoil of the 1930s strained these relationships while incubating new demands among rank-and-file workers. The Great Depression eviscerated the fiscal base of state and local governments, curtailing resources at the very moment when demand for services, particularly schools and public welfare, rose to unprecedented levels.

First evident in militant demonstrations against late and low pay, labor unrest swept through every level of government during the decade. Roosevelt triggered an outburst of militancy when he signed the Economy Act during the first hundred days. Building on a similar piece of legislation passed under Hoover, the Economy Act reduced salaries and imposed furloughs.[20] The federal-employee unions that had survived through the 1920s reacted with predictable outrage. Wrapping their critique in the language of patriotic self-sacrifice, union leaders like the National Federation of Federal Employees' (NFFE) Luther C. Steward pleaded that such acts were both counterproductive and hypocritical, given the administration's interest in putting a floor under workers' wages (and thus consumption).

Beyond simple austerity, civil-service workers chafed at the growing gap between Roosevelt's championing of private-sector labor rights and insistence on paternalism at the public workplace. The New Deal unleashed expectations for workers in government that it was unprepared to fulfill. Government employees were explicitly excluded from the National Labor Relations Act, the Fair Labor Standards Act, and, originally, the Social Security Act. While a small group within Roosevelt's inner circle favored the extension of full organizing and bargaining rights to federal workers and the creation of a public-sector counterpart to the National Labor Relations Board, the proposal was stripped out of the reorganization bill prior to its submission to Congress.[21] In a now widely cited 1937 letter, Roosevelt himself spoke to both sides of the issue. Writing to Steward, he famously declared that strikes by public workers amounted to "the paralysis of government by those who have sworn to support it" and accordingly deemed them both "unthinkable and intolerable." Yet in the very same letter, Roosevelt recognized that "the desire of Government employees for fair and adequate pay, reasonable hours of work, safe

and suitable working conditions, development of opportunities for advancement, facilities for fair and impartial consideration and review of grievances, and other objectives of a proper employee relations policy, is basically no different from that of employees in private industry."[22] The absence of either a Congressionally defined policy or a clear, singular message from Roosevelt left much of the practical working out to agency administrators and unions and gave the New Deal public-sector labor regime a chaotic, fragmented quality.

By demanding meaningful participation on matters of pay, promotions, and grievance procedures, New Deal civil servants strengthened links between government and industrial workers that had been strained by the backlash against Boston. Much of the energy came from rank-and-file workers, who showed far less caution than their leaders.[23] When the relatively conservative leadership of AFL federal employee unions refused to support a more rigorous form of bilateral negotiation, some locals defected to the United Federal Workers of America, an affiliate of the newly formed Congress of Industrial Organizations (CIO). These newer organizations proved far less willing to accept managerial prerogatives in exchange for administrative paternalism— what Rung calls a "social covenant" at the government workplace—and laid the foundation for a more militant form of unionism in the public sector.[24]

At the federal level, this was clearest in Works Progress Administration (WPA). Protesting grievances that ranged from prevailing rates of pay and hours to the failure of local governments to deliver paychecks and the removal of arbitrary supervisors and foremen, workers staged a staggering six hundred strikes between 1935 and 1937.[25] Following legal and political precedent, the Roosevelt and WPA chief Harry Hopkins initially struck a position of defiant resistance, but persistent militancy and political concerns eventually forced the administration into a much more complicated position. In November 1935, Hopkins issued an order, later codified in the official program handbook, that recognized the right of WPA workers "to organize and act collectively through representatives of their own choosing."[26] Though the order stopped short of the formal bargaining established in the Tennessee Valley Authority, it paved the way for an informal pattern of negotiation that reduced hours and weakened the power of job foremen in the later years of the program.[27]

While Depression-era militancy often focused on either short-term relief programs or the New Deal's expanding bureaucracy, it also penetrated state and local government. Organized police and firefighters, the two groups that had suffered the most direct backlash after Boston, both made modest gains during the 1930s. The International Association of Firefighters won repeal of a federal statute making it illegal for the firemen of Washington, DC, to affiliate with outside labor organizations in 1939. Police unions, which had predictably suffered the most dramatic decline after Boston, revived in the late 1930s. The American Federation of State, County and Municipal Employees (AFSCME), founded in 1932 to defend the civil service system in Wisconsin against the reinstitution of patronage politics, chartered its first local of police officers in 1937. By the end of World War II, it had at least three dozen locals organized nationally. Enduring a disastrous combination of rising unemployment, falling pay, and increased classroom enrollments, teachers launched strikes and demonstrations in cities like Chicago, sometimes joined by their pupils.[28] The economic crisis also mobilized workers in newer areas of the public sector. The Service Employees International Union (SEIU) began organizing public sector janitorial staff in 1918 and by the end of the 1930s had perhaps 25,000 members in schools, hospitals, and other government buildings.[29]

Formally, nearly every union initially retained a prohibition on strikes. Issuing a charter to the State, County and Municipal Workers

of America in 1937, CIO founder John L. Lewis declared that strikes and picketing by government employees were contrary to CIO policy and that the chief tools of public-sector unions were "legislation and education."[30] Yet by the early 1940s, even this concession began to give way to a more assertive set of demands. As AFSCME's founding president, Arnold Zander, stated in 1940, "it is one thing to state a policy against strikes, but it is quite a different thing to keep men at work when they are treated as miserably as they are in some public agencies."[31] For its part, the CIO adopted a more ambitious demand for equal rights for public- and private-sector workers because they feared that the expansion of government into previously private realms (utilities and transportation) would undermine the wages and benefits of private-sector workers.[32]

The wartime context interrupted this growing momentum toward a convergence of public- and private-sector labor law, even as it pushed administrators to adopt some of the practices of the emerging human-relations school of labor management. Wrapped in the rhetoric of a struggle for both democracy and efficiency, public administrators implemented various programs designed to promote loyalty, ensure productivity, and insulate the civil service from radical political challenges.

The new political climate was particularly stifling for African Americans and women in government, whose ranks grew as white men left the civil service for better-paying industrial jobs or military service, but who lacked the political clout to make use of traditional lobbying. Women's share of the federal workforce more than doubled between 1941 and 1944, but these gains did not coincide with widespread advancement up the civil-service hierarchy. As Margaret Rung has shown, administrators seized on "psychological paternalism" who appropriated pseudo-scientific rhetoric to blunt women's demands for promotion, claiming women were "naturally" ill prepared for greater authority or more complicated tasks.[33] Despite composing 47 percent of the DC-area federal workforce and holding 24 percent of all federal jobs by 1947, women occupied just 3 percent of managerial and policy-making positions.[34] African Americans found their advancement options similarly limited, particularly when it came to jobs that put them in a supervisory position over white women. Unrelenting pressure from civil-rights groups, labor unions, and black civil servants eventually pushed Roosevelt to issue Executive Order 8802 in 1941, creating a Fair Employment Practices Committee and charging it with policing racial discrimination in both government contractors and the federal government. However, bureaucratic structure, interagency politics, and resilient racism limited the actual effect of the new policy. In both cases, unions lobbied for a more stringent, structural correction to racial and gender discrimination at the federal workplace, but lacked the legal standing to directly challenge the practices.[35]

Faced with ideological and jurisdictional challenges, union organizers gained only limited ground in the 1940s. In the decades that followed, however, their critique of the civil service evolved into a broader challenge to managerial authority at the government workplace.[36]

POSTWAR GROWTH OF PUBLIC SECTOR UNIONS

As in the 1930s, the lack of legal rights did little to mitigate the militancy of public workers. Driven by a widening gap in both material rewards and legal rights, a diverse range of public employees challenged local and state governments during the early postwar era. The CIO's United Public Workers of America (UPWA), formed through a merger of the federal, state, and local CIO unions, launched an ambitious organizing drive among low-wage public employees in the South. Unions like AFSCME expanded their operations in Philadelphia and New York, and other northern

cities.[37] There were at least forty-three strikes by public employees in 1946 alone. By 1947, more than 600,000 public workers belonged to a labor union—approximately 10 percent of the total workforce of federal, state, and local governments. Yet these were modest gains compared to the dramatic expansion that would come over the three decades that followed.

If the wartime no-strike pledge had temporarily mitigated the most controversial aspect of public employment, the postwar strike wave reintroduced it.[38] The backlash against public worker militancy was dramatic. At the federal level, a 1946 appropriation bill required federal employees to sign an affidavit declaring their opposition to and lack of membership in any organization that asserted the right to strike, and the Taft-Hartley Act (1947) specifically extended the restriction against strikes to federal workers. In 1955, Public Law 330 simply asserted that the right to strike was made a felony offense. Nine states and many more cities adopted draconian anti-strike laws in 1946 or 1947. The restrictions transcended the strike issue. Citing the need to protect both national security and public order, public-sector union activists were targeted for expulsion from the federal workforce. The Hatch Act of 1939, which reintroduced restrictions on the political activities and affiliations of federal employees, was expansively interpreted during the early postwar era to allow for the dismissal of any worker deemed to be of dubious loyalty, and the House Committee on Un-American Activities launched investigations into some of the most progressive federal unions. In 1947, President Harry Truman issued Executive Order 9835, requiring an extensive investigation into the personal and political background of millions of federal workers.

In the short term, the backlash certainly stalled the momentum of the early postwar era. The UPWA, which had surged to more than 100,000 members nationally by end of the 1940s, came under repeated attacks for its open embrace of the Communist Party. The purges cost public-sector unions some of their most effective organizers and hastened the collapse of the UPWA, though many of the constituent locals eventually found their way into other organizations.[39] The judiciary offered little protection for public-sector activists, as courts routinely approved restrictions passed by state and local governments.[40]

Yet despite the restrictions of the early postwar era, public-sector labor relations underwent a slow but crucial transformation during the 1950s and 1960s. By culling some of the most outspoken radicals, the postwar backlash may have insulated the remaining public-sector labor movement from the worst effects of anticommunism. Though industrial-relations specialists continued to insist on the uniqueness of the government environment, they increasingly recognized that the basic concerns of public workers differed little form their private-sector counterparts.[41] The widespread adoption of routinized collective bargaining in the private sector helped insulate unionization of its more radical connotations.[42] The American Civil Liberties Union and American Bar Association both issued statements in support of labor rights for public workers during the decade, while cities like Philadelphia and New York experimented with moves to bargain with their employees. After a decade of intense lobbying by AFSCME, Wisconsin passed the country's first general statutory protections in 1959.[43] Drawing on these examples and bowing to mounting pressure from federal workers and labor allies, President John F. Kennedy issued Executive Order 10988 in 1962, extending limited bargaining rights to some federal employees.[44] Over the next decade, sixteen states followed, and by 1975, thirty-six states allowed collective bargaining for at least some groups of public workers.

In all but a few cases, public employees continued to lack some of the basic rights recognized in the private sector. Moreover, because of limits of constitutional power and political structure, public-sector unions relied on a complex combination of negotiation and lobbying to address both bread-and-butter concerns and workplace grievances. But within these limits, the legislative breakthroughs nevertheless amounted to a revolution in public-sector labor relations.

The changing legal environment both was created by and in turn propelled one of the most important yet least recognized social movements of the 1960s and 1970s, namely, the emergence of public-sector unionism as a crucial force within the labor movement and liberal politics. In cities like New York, public workers became essential parts of a coalition that pressed for a miniature social democratic society.[45] As state and local government continued to expand, it drew in increasing numbers of minority and female employees.[46] Unions like AFSCME and SEIU thrived in part because they embraced an agenda that stressed equity and dignity at the workplace as part of a broader struggle against "second class citizenship." After abandoning its earlier focus on winning civil-service protections, AFSCME became the fastest-growing union in the country by the 1970s. It fused its organizational agenda with an explicit link to the Black Freedom struggle, particularly in and after the 1968 strike by Memphis sanitation workers and the assassination of Martin Luther King Jr.[47] Left-leaning teachers unions in organizations like the New York Teachers Union pushed for an inclusive curriculum as well as bread-and-butter benefits. More broadly, public-sector unionism helped to lift the wages and benefits of minority and female public workers at a time when many cities were hemorrhaging higher-paying factory jobs, and thus mitigated, albeit to a limited degree, the impact of deindustrialization.[48] Between 1955 and 1975, the number of unionized public employees grew tenfold, to more than four million.

Though continuing to use lobbying and political activity, public-sector unions increasingly resorted to strikes to achieve their ends, despite the almost universal illegality of the practice. State and local government stoppages grew more than tenfold between 1959 and 1969.[49] Some 200,000 postal workers used an illegal strike to secure significance concessions from the postal service in 1970.[50] Weeks later, the Professional Air Traffic Controllers Organization (PATCO) followed suit. Teachers became perhaps the most militant of any group of workers, public or private, during the 1970s, pushing long-docile organizations like the NEA to embrace many of the strategies and tactics of trade unions.[51] The extension of bargaining rights reflected and in turn validated a militant mood among state and local government workers. Unions like AFSCME became increasingly aggressive in pushing for the right to strike, casting it as a central component of the negotiating process.[52] By the early 1970s, church groups, private-sector unions, labor arbiters, and a handful of jurists voiced growing support for the right of at least some public workers to strike.

This mounting militancy sometimes tested and even frayed the alliances previously forged with the Black Freedom movement. In both Ocean Hill-Brownsville (1968) and Newark (1970), mostly white teachers' demands for autonomy in the classroom proved explosively incompatible with the African American parents' insistence on greater community control.[53] Strikes also sometimes revealed class-based tensions within the African American community. In 1977, African American sanitation workers in Atlanta found little support among the city's black middle class (including Martin Luther King Sr.) in their standoff with Mayor Maynard Jackson.[54] The unionization of police and prison guards and attendant rise of the carceral state, meaning the rising numbers of Americans, especially minorities, imprisoned after criminal convictions, posed its own challenges to the public-sector brand of civil-rights unionism, particularly following the bloody uprising at Attica in 1971.[55] More generally, as Jon Shelton has

noted, strikes by public employees (and teachers in particular) served as "crisis points" that forced individuals to reevaluate their assumptions about the role of unions in a liberal-left coalition already in crisis.[56]

REACTION AND CRISIS IN THE LATE 20TH CENTURY

Public-sector union power peaked at an inopportune moment. The long postwar economic boom had slowed and then stopped in the early 1970s, but it spiraled into crisis in during the summer of 1975, when unemployment and inflation surged to 8.5 and 9.1 percent, respectively. As economists and policymakers struggled to make sense of the new phenomenon of "stagflation," state and local governments coped with growing deficits and mounting militancy from public-sector workers. Public employers took a harder line, demanding concessions, furloughing employees, leaving vacant positions unfilled, and canceling or delaying raises. Squeezed by soaring costs and lagging wages, public workers' response was predictable. The number of strikes jumped to 478 in 1975, and the wave of militancy continued through 1978.

The new fiscal climate altered the politics of taxes and public services and transformed the landscape of public-sector labor relations. It undercut a near decade-long effort to secure a federal collective bargaining law for state and local government employees, leaving public-sector labor relations under the fragmented jurisdiction of fifty states (and countless local and municipal governments), many of which never legalized bargaining.[57] Conservative critics of the public-sector labor movement, many of whom had long ties with the National Right to Work Committee and other anti-labor groups, seized on the new climate to reintroduce challenges to the basic legitimacy of public-sector collective bargaining. The near bankruptcy of New York City (averted, notably, by the willingness of the city's public unions to use retirement funds to cover the city's shortfall) seemed to validate their charges.[58] Officials in city after city took a hard line against employee raises, claiming it necessary to prevent their town from becoming "another Big Apple."[59] Declining public support emboldened employers to break strikes by hiring replacement workers, blunting the effectiveness of the direct-action tactics that had propelled the growth of the movement over the previous decade.[60] In the years that followed, activists like Howard Jarvis seized on public sector workers' pay and benefits in pushing tax-cutting proposals like California's Proposition 13.

Ronald Reagan's move to fire 11,000 highly trained air-traffic controllers participating in PATCO's illegal 1981 strike dramatically underscored the limits of public-sector labor legitimacy. It foreshadowed the way in which public and private sector labor relations grew increasingly entangled in the last decades of the 20th century. After 1981, as Joseph McCartin has shown, private employers became far more willing to hire permanent replacements for striking workers, resulting in a precipitous decline in private-sector strikes by century's end.[61] That declining militancy combined with the increasing willingness of employers to illegally fire union organizers, and the general pressures associated with automation and off-shoring decimated the private-sector labor movement in the last quarter of the 20th century.

Public employees were not fully immune to these pressures. The emergence of taxes as a crucial issue in local, state, and national politics during the 1970s encouraged elected officials to take a harder line against union demands. Privatization and contracting-out of government services became increasingly popular after the 1970s, as state and local officials sought cheaper and more pliable alternatives to unionized government workplaces. In more recent decades, reformers have touted non-union charter-school and private-voucher programs as paths to improving public education.

Yet public-sector unions proved far more resilient than their private sector counterparts, in terms of both the size of their membership and their capacity to protect hard-won gains. In a harsher political environment, unions like AFSCME pioneered new bargaining practices like comparable worth, which provided a means of boosting the pay and benefits of an increasingly feminized workforce above and beyond general raises.[62] More broadly, public-sector unions proved far more effective at protecting their traditional defined-benefit pensions from erosion to defined-contribution pension systems like 401ks.

Beyond simply holding ground, public-sector unions continued to expand the boundaries of the traditional labor movement. SEIU and AFSCME successfully supported organizing drives by home health and childcare workers, one of the fastest-growing sectors of the American economy. When more than 70,000 homecare workers in Los Angeles County captured national headlines by voting to join SEIU in early 1999, it was the largest successful union organizing drive since the Great Depression. These campaigns continued into the first decade of the 21st century, as hundreds of thousands of home, health, and childcare workers, disproportionately African American, Latina, and immigrant women, successfully overcame legal and political obstacles to form unions, often by working closely with community groups and their clients.[63] In part because of these successes, roughly half of all union members worked for federal, state, or local government by 2010.

Yet even as public-sector unions reached this newfound status, they came under fierce attack. Amid growing economic and social inequality and unprecedented power for corporate capital, organized government workers emerged as a visible, easy scapegoat for anxious taxpayers and desperate politicians. Though evident as early as the George W. Bush administration's tangle with TSA agents over unionization in the context of the War on Terror, it burst onto the national scene with the onset of the Great Recession. In the midst of the most severe economic downturn since the 1930s, public-sector unions came under political attack as overpaid and underworked from elected officials. In the name of fiscal discipline, governors like Scott Walker, John Kasich, and Chris Christie targeted pensions, benefits, and bargaining rights of public workers. Though the most visible efforts came from the political right, often with the financial and logistical support of conservative organizations with a long history of opposition to public sector unions, they gained credence and legitimacy across partisan and ideological lines. In 2015, the Supreme Court heard a case, *Friedrich vs. California Teachers Association,* which challenged the basic legitimacy of exclusive representation and agency fees in the public sector. Only the sudden death of Justice Antonin Scalia prevented the court from imposing right-to-work restrictions on every government workplace in the country.

Ironically, many of the justifications for attacks on public-sector unions turned the formative premise of parity on its head. Public-sector union activists had rooted their demands for the full range of workplace rights and protections in a rebuke of second-class citizenship. They had marched, lobbied, and even struck to secure the same rights as industrial workers. Yet to an extent that they rarely recognized in the 1960s and 1970s, these demands rested on the existence of a successful private-sector labor movement. The decline of the private-sector labor movement left government workers vulnerable because of their relative success at warding off the pressures that continue to erode the American middle class. Recognizing this, public-sector unions in recent years have gone to extraordinary lengths to broaden the scope and process of bargaining by bringing community groups (and their interests and concerns) to negotiations with their employers. This practice of "Bargaining for the Common Good" is not wholly new, but it underscores the extent to which the history of

public-sector unionism has always been tied to that of that of society at large.

DISCUSSION OF THE LITERATURE

Despite their importance to the modern American labor movement, public-sector workers received relatively little attention through most of the postwar era. Some notable exceptions notwithstanding, government employees drew far less scrutiny than their counterparts in mass-production industry, the construction trades, or even agricultural work. Despite the wealth of brilliant, innovative scholarship produced by a younger generation of labor and social historians during the last quarter of the 20th century, relatively few proved willing to treat government employees as "real" workers.[64] Prior to 1990 or so, histories of public-sector unions were few, and were generally limited to localized studies of a single union. Relatively few historians subjected government-employee organizations to the central questions of labor history: the social construction of unions, organizing drives, the often contentious relationship between workers and labor leaders, on the one hand, and unions and the broader labor movement, on the other. To the extent that they appear at all in many accounts of postwar labor history, it is as an instrument that obscured the scale of the labor movement's crisis by masking changes in overall rate of union density.[65] The result was what Joseph A. McCartin characterized as "an astonishing misallocation of scholarly interest and energy" and a significantly distorted literature on postwar American labor.[66]

In recent years, this pattern of neglect has begun to change, and the public sector has emerged as a crucial, vibrant subset within the broader field of labor and working-class history. In part, this simply reflects the new realities of the 21st-century working class, which often bear little resemblance to the industrial workers of the old Fordist order. As scholars have softened their reliance on structural conceptions of class and focused on the question of, as Michael Zweig put it, "the power and authority people have at work," they have turned their attention to those who labor for federal, state, and local governments.[67]

The result has been an astonishing shift in the literature. The last decade saw the publication of several important and pioneering works, and the trend accelerated into the early 21st century.[68] A growing number of senior scholars, junior faculty, and graduate students have challenged the traditional boundary that confined public workers to a separate, distinctive, and exceptional class. Without denying important differences, they are bringing to bear on government employees many of the crucial questions and invigorating insights of the best in the study of working-class people and their institutions.

PRIMARY SOURCES

Scholars and students of public-sector unionism may now draw on a rich and extensive array of archival sources, many of which have only begun to be examined by historians. As with many topics in American labor history, the Walter P. Reuther Library of Labor and Urban Affairs at Wayne State University in Detroit offers the most important manuscript collections relating to public-sector unionism. The official repository for the institutional papers of AFSCME, the AFT, and SEIU, the Reuther Library, also holds the personal papers of dozens of key union activists, the records of allied and related organizations, and an extensive collection of oral histories. In recent years, George Washington University has opened the institutional records of both the International Brotherhood of Teamsters and the National Education Association. The University of Maryland holds the national records of the AFL-CIO. Beyond these national collections, many unions have housed state and locality-specific records at archives and repositories. In terms of print material, the most important single source is the Government Employee Relations Report. Major magazines, including *Business Week*, *Nation's Business*, *Newsweek*, *Time*, and *U.S. News and World Report*, gave extensive coverage to the growing public-sector labor movement in the 1960s and 1970s.

The very nature of public-sector labor relations, of course, is such that the records of the "employer" are often much more freely and readily available than in the private sector—though rarely available in the same place. Federal records are spread through various agencies and across presidential libraries. The Kennedy, Johnson, Nixon, Carter, and Reagan Libraries have particular important materials relating to the policy and policy history of government labor. The Southern Labor Archives at Georgia State University have several collections relating to the history of PATCO and the PATCO strike.

For obvious reasons, it is harder to generalize about state and local government, which constitutes the majority of government employment. Government records, including the papers of mayoral and gubernatorial administrations, are often housed in official public archives and libraries, but elected officials who went on to a particularly prominent role may have their personal papers elsewhere. Among purely local collections, the Tamiment Library and Robert F. Wagner Labor Archives at New York University have an extensive range of institutional records, manuscript collections, and oral histories relating to government work in the nation's largest city. More recently, materials from several repositories relating to the Memphis Sanitation Strike have been digitized and made available through Crossroads to Freedom Project.

FURTHER READING

Freeman, Richard B. "Unionism Comes to the Public Sector." *Journal of Economic Literature* 24, no. 1 (March 1986): 41–86.

Honey, Michael J. *Going Down Jericho Road: The Memphis Strike, Martin Luther King's Last Campaign*. New York: W. W. Norton, 2008.

Johnson, Paul. *Success While Others Fail: Social Movement Unionism and the Public Workplace.* Ithaca, NY: ILR Press, 1994.

McCartin, Joseph A. "Bringing the State's Workers Back In: Time to Rectify an Imbalanced US Labor Historiography." *Labor History* 47, no. 1 (2006): 73–94.

McCartin, Joseph A. *Collision Course: Ronald Reagan, the Air Traffic Controllers, and the Strike that Changed America.* New York: Oxford University Press, 2013.

Murphy, Marjorie. *Blackboard Union: The AFT and the NEA, 1900–1980.* Ithaca, NY: Cornell University Press, 1990.

Rung, Margaret C. *Servants of the State: Managing Diversity and Democracy in the Federal Service, 1933–1953.* Athens: University of Georgia Press, 2002.

Slater, Joseph E. *Public Workers: Government Employee Unions, the Law, and the State, 1900–1962.* Ithaca, NY: ILR Press, 2004.

Spero, Sterling. *Government as Employer.* New York: Remsen Press, 1948.

Ziskind, David. *One Thousand Strikes of Government Employees.* New York: Columbia University Press, 1940.

NOTES

1. Slater, *Public Workers: Government Employee Unions, the Law, and the State, 1900–1962* (Ithaca, NY: ILR Press, 2004), 26; David Roediger and Philip S. Foner, *Our Own Time: A History of American Labor and the Working Day* (New York: Verso, 1989), 31.

2. Sterling D. Spero, *Government as Employer* (New York: Remsen Press, 1948), 77, 83–84.

3. Commons, *Labor and Administration* (New York: Macmillan, 1913), 110.

4. Quoted in Slater, *Public Workers*, 16.

5. Spero, *Government as Employer*, 117–127.

6. "Taft Against Unions of Federal Workers," *New York Times*, May 15, 1911, 4.

7. Commons, *Labor and Administration*, 173.

8. Commons, *Labor and Administration*, 109–113.

9. Commons, *Labor and Administration*, 109. In important respects, however, Commons remained wary of the full application of collective bargaining to government employment. Commons, *Labor and Administration*, 111–112.

10. Sterling D. Spero, *The Labor Movement in a Government Industry: A Study of Employee Organization in the Postal Service* (New York: George H. Doran, 1924).

11. Marjorie Murphy, *Blackboard Unions: The AFT and the NEA, 1900–1980* (Ithaca, NY: Cornell University Press, 1990).

12. Slater, *Public Workers*, 18.

13. Sam Mitrani, *The Rise of the Chicago Police Department: Class and Conflict, 1850–1894* (Urbana: University of Illinois Press, 2013).

14. Slater, *Public Workers*, 20.

15. Slater, *Public Workers*, 25.

16. Slater, *Public Workers*, 26.

17. Slater, *Public Workers*, 27–35.

18. Spero, *The Labor Movement in a Government Industry*, 9.

19. Spero, *Government as Employer*, 205–212.

20. Rung, *Servants of the State*, 54–55.

21. Rung, *Servants of the State*, 107–108.

22. Letter on the Resolution of Federation of Federal Employees Against Strikes in Federal Service, August 16, 1937. Public Papers and Addresses of Franklin D. Roosevelt, http://www.presidency.ucsb.edu/ws/?pid=15445.

23. Rung, *Servants of the State*, 62.

24. Rung, *Servants of the State*, 62.

25. David Ziskind, *One Thousand Strikes of Government Employees* (New York: Columbia University Press, 1914).

26. Ziskind, *One Thousand Strikes*, 167.

27. On labor and the TVA, see Wilson R. Hart, *Collective Bargaining in the Federal Service: A Study of Labor-Management Relations in the United States Government Employment* (New York: Harper, 1961). On the establishment of informal negotiation in the TVA, see Ziskind, *One Thousand Strikes*, 133–184.

28. Spero, *Government as Employer*, 319–324.

29. Slater, *Public Workers*, 97–124. Initially founded as the Building Service Employees International Union, SEIU officially changed its name in the late 1960s to reflect its increasingly diverse membership.

30. Qutoed in Joshua Freeman, *In Transit: The Transport Workers Union in New York City, 1933–1966* (New York: Oxford University Press, 1989), 183.

31. Quoted in Spero, *Government as Employer*, 215.

32. The Transport Workers Union (TWU) in New York was forced to grapple directly with

the difference in legal jurisdiction in the 1940s after the city took control of two previously privately owned subway systems, in a stroke converting more than 25,000 workers who had been covered under the National Labor Relations Act into public employees without legal access to collective bargaining. Eschewing both large-scale electioneering and back-room politicking, the CIO-affiliated union relied on mass demonstrations and threats of job actions to secure de facto recognition and meaningful material concessions, making it a crucial pioneer in the modern public-sector labor movement. Freeman, *In Transit*, 165–223.

33. Rung, *Servants of the State*, 137–156.

34. Landon R. Y. Storrs, "Attacking the Washington 'Femmocracy': Antifeminism in the Cold War Campaign against 'Communists in Government,'" *Feminist Studies* 33, no. 1 (Spring 2007): 121.

35. Rung, *Servants of the State*, 157–176.

36. Rung, *Servants of the State*, 176–183.

37. Francis P. Ryan, *AFSCME's Philadelphia Story: Municipal Workers and Urban Power in the Twentieth Century* (Philadelphia: Temple University Press, 2011); Jewel Bellush and Bernard Bellush, *Union Power and New York: Victor Gotbaum and District Council 37* (New York: Praeger, 1984).

38. Slater, *Public Workers*, 145.

39. This was particularly true in California, where several UPWA locals affiliated with SEIU, allowing it to carve out a dominant position in the state's non-education, non-protective workforce. In New York, remnants of the UPWA were eventually incorporated into AFSCME's District Council 37, which became the most powerful municipal union in New York City by the early 1960s.

40. Slater, *Public Workers*, 89.

41. Slater, *Public Workers*, 71–96.

42. Melvyn Dubofsky, *Labor and the State in Modern America* (Chapel Hill: University of North Carolina Press, 1994), 197–217.

43. Slater, *Public Workers*, 165–192.

44. On the drafting of Kennedy's order, see Joseph A. McCartin, *Collision Course: Ronald Reagan, the Air Traffic Controllers, and the Strike that Changed America* (New York: Oxford University Press, 2011), 36–43. On the impact of Executive Order 10988, see Richard B. Freeman, "Unionism Comes to the Public Sector," *Journal of Economic Literature* 24 (1986): 41–76; Richard C. Kearney, *Labor Relations in the Public Sector*, 5th ed. (New York, Routledge, 2014); Martin Halpern, *Unions, Radicals, and Democratic Presidents: Seeking Social Change in the Twentieth Century* (Westport, CT: Praeger, 2003), 78–103.

45. Joshua B. Freeman, *Working Class New York: Life and Labor since World War II* (New York: New Press, 2001).

46. For an interpretation of public sector unionism that stresses this convergence, see Stanley Aronowitz, *From the Ashes of the Old: American Labor and America's Future* (New York: Basic Books, 1998), 59–85.

47. Perhaps because of King's involvement, the Memphis strikes have drawn an unusual amount of attention from historians. Joan Turner Beifuss, *At the River I Stand: Memphis, the 1968 Strike, and Martin Luther King* (Brooklyn: Carlson, 1989); Steve Estes, "'I AM A MAN!': Race, Masculinity and the 1968 Memphis Sanitation Strike," *Labor History* 41, no. 2 (2000): 153–170; Michael K. Honey, *Going Down Jericho Road: The Memphis Strike, Martin Luther King's Last Campaign* (New York: W. W. Norton, 2008).

48. On race and the public sector, see Michael B. Katz and Mark J. Stern, *One National Divisible: What America Was and What It Is Becoming* (New York: Russell Sage, 2005), 86–101; Thoms B. Sugrue, "'The Largest Civil Rights Organization Today': Title VII and the Transformation of the Public Sector," *Labor: Studies in Working Class History of the Americas* 11, no. 3 (2014): 25–29.

49. *Bureau of Labor Statistics, Work Stoppages in Government* (Washington, DC: U.S. Department of Labor, 1981).

50. For the long run-up to the postal workers strike, including the crucial role played by Civil Rights activists, see Philip F. Rubio, *There's Always Work at the Post Office: African American Postal Workers and the Fight for Jobs, Justice, and Equality* (Chapel Hill: University of North Carolina Press, 2010).

51. Murphy, *Blackboard Unions*, 209–230.

52. "Policy Statement on Public Employee Unions: Rights and Responsibilities Adopted by International Executive Board, AFSCME, AFL-CIO, July 26, 1966," in *Sorry...No Government Today: Unions vs. City Hall*, ed. Robert E. Walsh (Boston: Beacon Press, 1969), 67–70.

53. Jerald Podair, *The Strike That Changed New York: Blacks, Whites, and the Ocean Hill-Brownsville Crisis* (New Haven, CT: Yale University Press, 2004); Jon Shelton, "Letters to the Essex County Penitentiary: David Selden and the Fracturing of America," *Journal of Social History* 48, no. 1 (Fall 2014): 135–155.

54. Joseph A. McCartin, "'Fire the Hell out of Them': Sanitation Workers' Struggles and the Normalization of the Striker Replacement Strategy in the 1970s," *Labor: Studies in Working Class History of the Americas* 2, no. 3 (2005): 67–92.

55. On Attica, see Heather Ann Thompson, *Blood in the Water: The Attica Prison Uprising of 1971 and Its Legacy* (New York: Pantheon, 2016). On the role played by unionized police and prison guards in the rise of the carceral state, see Ruth Wilson Gilmore, *Golden Gulag: Prisons, Surplus, Crisis, and Opposition in Globalizing California* (Berkeley: University of California Press, 2007).

56. Shelton, "David Selden and the Fracturing of America," 145.

57. Joseph A. McCartin, "'A Wagner Act for Public Employees': Labor's Deferred Dream and the Rise of Conservatism, 1970–1976," *Journal of American History* (June 2008): 123–148.

58. The literature on the New York City fiscal crisis is massive. For the particular role played by public sector unions, see Michael Spear, "A Crisis in Urban Liberalism: The New York City Municipal Unions and the 1970s Fiscal Crisis" (PhD diss., City University of New York, 2005).

59. For one example of how this played out at the local level, see Jon Shelton, "Against the Public: The Pittsburgh Teachers Strike of 1975–1976 and the Crisis of the Labor-Liberal Coalition," *Labor: Studies in Working-Class History of the Americas* 10, no. 2 (2013): 55–75.

60. McCartin, "Striker Replacement Strategy in the 1970s," 83–92.

61. Joseph A. McCartin, "Unexpected Convergence: Values, Assumptions, and the Right to Strike in Public and Private Sectors, 1945–2005," *Buffalo Law Review* 57 (2009): 727–765. From the mid-1950s to early 2000s, the average number of strikes involving at least 1,000 workers dropped from 350 annually to 25.

62. Katherine Turk, *Equality on Trial: Gender and Rights in the Modern American Workplace* (Philadelphia: University of Pennsylvania Press, 2016).

63. Eileen Boris and Jennifer Klein, *Caring for America: Home Health Workers in the Shadow of the Welfare State* (New York: Oxford University Press, 2012).

64. At root, Joseph Slater has noted, much of the negligence of historians in dealing with government workers can be traced to the intransigence of a neo-Marxist conception of class. Because public sector organization contested neither the distribution of profits nor the means of production, it has often been left out of labor history as something less than class conflict. Slater, *Public Workers*, 4–6.

65. For a prominent example of this tendency, see Michel Goldfield, *The Decline of Organized Labor in the United States* (Chicago: University of Chicago Press, 1987).

66. Joseph A. McCartin, "Bringing the State's Workers In: Time to Rectify an Imbalanced US Labor Historiography," *Labor History* 47, no. 1 (February 2006): 73. Also see Robert Shaffer, "Where Are the Organized Public Employees? The Absence of Public Employee Unionism from U.S. History Textbooks and Why It Matters," *Labor History* 43, no. 3 (August 2002): 315–334.

67. Zweig, *The Working Class Majority: America's Best Kept Secret* (Ithaca, NY: Cornell University Press, 2002), 3.

68. Two crucial early examples were Murphy, *Blackboard Unions* and Paul Johnston, *Success While Others Fail: Social Movement Unionism and the Public Workplace* (Ithaca, NY: ILR Press, 1994).

Joseph E. Hower

PUBLIC AUTHORITIES IN THE UNITED STATES

WHAT ARE PUBLIC AUTHORITIES?

Public authorities vary widely, but they tend to share three defining features that set them apart from other kinds of government agencies. First, rather than relying on legislative appropriations, they are largely (and in some cases entirely) self-funding through their own commercial activities. Second, their leaders are appointed, rather than elected. Third, they are treated by the courts as independent legal entities, distinct from the governments that created them.

The key defining feature of the public authority is the ability to fund itself, an attribute so basic that it has been called the mechanism's "heart."[1] Thus, these mechanisms can be used to provide new infrastructure or services without the necessity of asking voters to support higher taxes or bond issues. In addition, authorities are often able to circumvent statutory and constitutional limits that constrain general-purpose governments below the federal level. Initially, authorities were established to finance, build, and operate facilities, such as roads and bridges, for which users could be charged. Revenue from these charges took care of operating expenses, but it also provided collateral for loans to cover capital expenses, using financial instruments called "revenue bonds." While many public authorities still build and manage the facilities they finance, these mechanisms have been increasingly deployed simply to borrow funds in the tax-exempt municipal bond market for a variety of purposes, a practice known as conduit or back-door financing.[2]

The second defining feature of public authorities is appointed, rather than elected, leadership, which means these instrumentalities do not have the power to levy taxes. The inability to tax is what sets them apart from special districts, their close cousins within American government. In theory authorities must support themselves completely on the basis of their commercial activities. In reality, however, many do receive support from tax-supported general-purpose governments, as when the governments that create them become their customers, and courts have allowed these practices. A more indirect, but still extremely significant, form of assistance is the implicit guarantee assumed by investors that the debt of these units will be covered by the parent government should the authority encounter business setbacks.

The third defining feature of public authorities is that they are legally distinct from the governments that create them. In most cases they are formally incorporated, which is why they are often referred to as "government corporations." Their independent legal identity means they can engage in market activities more flexibly than standard government agencies. For example, they can sue and be sued like a private business enterprise. In addition, they are free of the regulations governing personnel, purchasing, and subcontracting that apply to conventional government agencies.

Public authorities come in a variety of sizes. Many are huge. For instance, the Tennessee Valley Authority (TVA), created by the federal government during the New Deal to generate electricity, among other responsibilities, posted revenues of close to $12 billion in FY 2011.[3] Another giant is the Tampa Port Authority, created by the state of Florida, which engineered the renaissance of the city's deteriorated commercial waterfront and transformed it into a profitable cargo port, a major cruise center attracting millions of passengers, and a popular entertainment destination.[4] In contrast to these behemoths, most public authorities are small- to medium-sized organizations, in charge of a single operation. A good example is the Springfield Parking Authority (SPA), in Springfield, Massachusetts. The SPA operates five garages and eight lots, generating, in 2004, $1.4 million in income.[5]

Despite the size of entities such as the TVA and the Tampa Port Authority, and the ubiquity of their smaller cousins such as the Springfield Parking Authority, even close observers of American government have been apt to overlook these kinds of institutions. Robert A. Caro, whose widely read biography of the "power broker" Robert Moses did so much to publicize the significance of self-supporting agencies that were administratively and legally independent of the elected officials and legislatures that created them, confessed that before starting the book he wondered "what a public authority was, anyway." And Caro was a journalist who specialized in politics![6]

One reason for the obscurity of these agencies is that basic information about them is hard to get. Using different definitions and hindered by lack of data, experts in public administration cannot even agree on how many there are, and estimates vary from five thousand to eighteen thousand. The difficulty in identifying and counting these bodies stems from the fact that the federal government and states create them in a bewildering variety of legal formats and do not keep track of them in any systematic way. Indeed, most states would be hard pressed even to list their authorities. In 2004, the New York State Comptroller's office conducted an investigation that initially determined that the state had 643 authorities, but after several more months of digging discovered almost 90 more.[7]

Labels do not provide a useful guide, since revenue-producing, administratively and legally independent units have been given an array of titles. They have been called boards, commissions, agencies, trusts, districts, administrations, public corporations, public benefit corporations, and government corporations—in addition to the generic name

by which they are best known: public authorities. Just to add to the confusion, some of these labels are also used to designate units within general-purpose government. At the federal level, difficulties of classification are exacerbated by the fact that Congress has created entities called "corporations," such as the Legal Services Corporation and the Corporation for Public Broadcasting, that are not primarily commercial in character, in order to provide them with more autonomy and insulate them from management rules that govern standard agencies.[8]

Even though we cannot reliably determine the precise number of public authority-type agencies, we can get a rough sense of the scale of their activities by looking at patterns in public borrowing. Most authorities fund their capital facilities by borrowing against future earnings, issuing what are called "revenue bonds" (as opposed to the "general obligation bonds," backed by taxing power, used by general purpose governments). The figure below indicates trends in the two kinds of debt. From 1949 to 2002, revenue-based debt increased fifty-six-fold (in constant dollars). General-obligation debt also increased, but only five-fold. As a result, revenue bonds, which made up only one-eighth of total sub-federal public

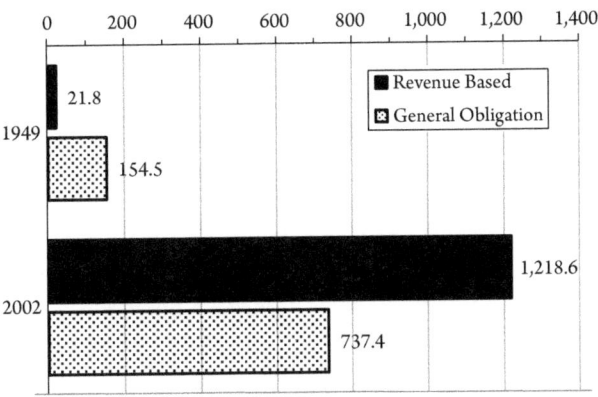

Figure 1. After 2002, the Census Bureau no longer distinguished between debt that was "guaranteed" and "non-guaranteed," so no later figures are available. Dollar value adjustments were done based on Bureau of Economic Analysis, US Department of Commerce, *National Income and Product Accounts* Tables, Table 1.1.4, Price Indexes for Gross Domestic Product (options selected: annual series and all years), available at the website for the Bureau of Economic Analysis (accessed 3/5/2011). Unpublished Census Bureau data for 1949 cited in J. Richard Aronson and John L. Hilley, *Financing State and Local Governments* (Washington, DC: Brookings Institution, 1986), 251. U.S. Department of Interior, Census Office, 2002 *Census of Governments*, vol. 4, no. 5: Government Finances (Washington, DC: GPO, 2005), Table 13, p. 15.

indebtedness fifty years earlier, constituted five-eighths of such debt by the end of the century.[9] This represents a sea change in the institutional character of public economic activity.

THE ROOTS OF THE PUBLIC AUTHORITY

Public-authority type agencies first appeared at the turn of the 20th century. This was a time when public officials began trying to create tools with which government could directly intervene in the economy in ways that were impractical or legally proscribed if pursued with existing administrative machinery. The federal government used the model extensively up through the Second World War and promoted a version that localities and states could employ to receive federal loans during the Great Depression. In the second half of the 20th century, these institutional structures lost favor at the national level, even as they became practically ubiquitous at the state and local levels.

Public authorities had antecedents in the government-chartered corporations of the early 19th century, the best known of which were the First and Second Banks of the United States. These enterprises were granted special privileges on the expectation they would pursue public purposes, in addition to private profits. Even though governments often invested in them, these companies were essentially private business operations, set up with the goal of making money for shareholders.[10] By contrast, the modern public authority is a unit of government organized on the model of a corporation, but with no private investors.

Public officials began crafting this new kind of government unit at time when industrialization and urbanization were drastically transforming the country, creating pressure for governments to furnish new kinds of infrastructure and services. The template for what became the public authority evolved through a process of trial and error, as policy entrepreneurs searched for ways to respond. The challenge was to create administrative

mechanisms that could enable governments to transcend the limitations of a legal structure that severely constricted their ability to engage in economic activities.

A variety of motives were in play. For some, it was simply an effort to find ways to finance infrastructure. Others aimed at creating public agencies that could break free of the annual funding cycle controlled by legislative bodies, in order to respond dynamically to changing market conditions and permit long-range economic planning. Still others envisioned institutions able to address issues related to social justice and economic equality in ways that unconstrained markets cannot. For many it was some mixture of all these purposes. In another context general purpose governments, perhaps using non-standard but still democratically accountable agencies, might well have been capable of meeting those goals, but the structure of government as it had developed historically in the United States made this extremely difficult.

The principal barrier to activist government at the sub-federal level in the early 20th century was the way that citizen anger over the reckless economic development schemes pursued by public officials in earlier decades had congealed into a crippling institutional legacy. During the 19th century, state and local governments had borrowed lavishly to subsidize canals, turnpikes, and especially railroads. Corruption was an issue, but even investments undertaken in good faith often failed to deliver promised benefits. Furious taxpayers who were left to pay off the debts demanded severe limitations on future government borrowing. In response, practically every state adopted rigid laws and constitutional amendments restricting the amount of debt governments could assume and prescribing cumbersome procedures for voter approval of bond issues (often requiring supermajorities). Debt caps for municipalities were set at a percentage of appraised property values within the jurisdiction (typically 5 percent). These caps were too low to finance the capital-intensive infrastructure increasingly demanded by urban residents, such as water and sewer systems, street lighting, and electric streetcars.[11] The whole framework of local public finance was inappropriate for an economically expanding, urbanizing nation, but in the short run circumvention was easier than attempting basic reforms. Two general strategies of circumvention predominated; these ultimately came together to form the public authority.

Creating new government units not bound by existing debt limits was the first strategy, because it built on a familiar approach. Urban politicians employed "special assessment" or "special taxing" districts for decades as a way to give property owners in different neighborhoods the opportunity to decide whether to incur the costs of improvements such as paved streets and sewers.[12] Special districts became increasingly popular starting in the late 19th century. Many were established to deliver services over areas that made sense functionally but that overlapped existing political jurisdictions (for example, the Boston area Metropolitan Water District, established in 1895).[13] However, many special districts were designed simply to bypass debt caps, as when the Indiana legislature, in 1917, authorized a park district and a sanitary (sewage disposal) district that covered virtually the same territory as the city of Indianapolis. The legislature bestowed independent borrowing powers on each, specifically mandating that their debts not be a legal obligation of the city. As one commentator was quick to point out at the time, Indianapolis, which already had an independent school district, had become "four separate, legally distinct municipal corporations over what is for all practical purposes the same area." The obvious effect was a substantial increase in the city's borrowing capacity, making it possible to construct infrastructure that previously was impossible to finance.[14]

In addition to providing a fiscal escape hatch, special districts possessed a variety of attributes that appealed to different constituencies. For example, state-level politicians sometimes wanted to remove control of new functions from local elected officials, either to obtain greater professionalization of management or to secure patronage possibilities for themselves. But whatever else they offered, special districts appealed because they provided an easier alternative than confronting the baroque layers of constraints on municipal finance that had accumulated over the decades in state statute books and constitutions.[15]

The second strategy for escaping the yoke of borrowing limits employed the doctrine of the "special fund," which was used to legitimate what were called "revenue bonds." Local officials argued that revenue from income-generating projects should be regarded as a separate account (i.e., a special fund), against which cities should be able to borrow, independent of laws that applied to municipal debt backed by tax revenues. Spokane is credited with pioneering the special fund concept when it convinced the Washington Supreme Court in 1895 that city bonds designated as payable exclusively from the income of its waterworks should not be considered a general obligation of the city. After the legislature explicitly authorized this method of financing, the state's largest city picked up the ball and ran with it. Seattle issued millions of dollars' worth of revenue bonds to purchase its bankrupt local street railway system and to develop the vast utility empire known as City Light.[16]

Special districts and revenue bond financing proved to be useful devices for funding public sector activities, but setting them up was laborious. Without general authority to use these mechanisms, municipalities needed to seek specific legislative approval for each one. Otherwise they could go through all the steps of putting together a complex financial arrangement, only to see it crumble in the face of a lawsuit. For example, in 1930, the Iowa Supreme Court scotched the small town of Sidney's plan to acquire an electrical plant through a method that was essentially a variant of revenue-bond financing. The town proposed to use an earmarked account, funded by charges to residents for electricity, to pay a private company to supply generating equipment. The court voided the contract, ruling that although the legislature had granted cities and towns authority to own and operate their own electric plants, no "express power" had been granted to Sidney to use revenue-based financing.[17]

THE PUBLIC AUTHORITY TEMPLATE COMES INTO WIDESPREAD USE

President Herbert Hoover during the Great Depression began the process of changing the rules for local public finance such that revenue-based financing, and ultimately the public authority, became standard practice. (This outcome seems to have been unintended, as it is likely that Hoover was unfamiliar with local public finance regulations; ironically, the changes he set in motion at the local level came about as he attempted his own end run around the existing framework of public finance at the federal level.) In 1932, under enormous political pressure for a federal public works program to provide jobs for the unemployed, but still insistent on a balanced budget, Hoover devised a revenue-neutral plan for local aid.

Hoover's plan was for the Reconstruction Finance Corporation (RFC), the newly established federal investment bank, to make loans to states and localities for "self-liquidating" public works. By this he meant projects that could generate sufficient revenue from fees and tolls to pay off the loans that had financed their construction. Clearly delighted by the cleverness of the scheme, Hoover pointed out in a letter to the American Society of Civil Engineers that the program "requires no Congressional appropriation, does not unbalance the budget, is not a drain upon the Treasury, does not involve the direct issue of government bonds, does not involve added burdens upon the taxpayer either now or in the future."[18] It was indeed an ingenious concept, and Congress cooperated by

enacting it into law in July 1932 as the main plank of the Emergency Relief and Construction Act (ERCA). There was only one hitch: the program barely functioned.[19]

Hoover hoped the ERCA program would help him in the upcoming presidential election in the fall of 1932, but that was not to be. Congress authorized the RFC to make ERCA loans totaling $1.5 billion. By the time of the election, however, less than $1 million had been approved. At the end of its eleven months of existence—it was taken over in June 1933 by the New Deal's Public Works Administration (PWA)—Hoover's initiative had spent only $30 million, a mere 2 percent of its allocated funds. Most of that went to a few large projects. Observers were livid. The *New Republic* lambasted RFC lawyers for "stick[ing] all the pins they can through every project submitted," while U.S. Senator Robert Wagner bemoaned the "mile after mile of red tape." When the RFC approved two multimillion-dollar projects in California before the election, Democrats accused the administration of trying to buy the state for Hoover.[20]

In truth, it was not finicky lawyers, too many forms, or partisan politics that prevented federal money from flowing to the local level. The main impediments were institutional—the same laws and constitutional amendments limiting debt financing of capital improvements that had hemmed in activist local officials for years. The legislation specified that the RFC make loans by buying the bonds of municipalities. But few local governments, even if they managed to write plausible proposals, could legally accept RFC loans. The Depression had pushed most municipalities close to, or over, the brink of their borrowing limits. More than three thousand municipalities went into default during the 1930s. Quite a few were reduced to meeting payrolls with scrip. This meant that general-obligation bonds were not an option, and few municipalities were already authorized to issue revenue bonds. When Congress passed Hoover's urban aid package, only nineteen states had legislation on their books that allowed revenue-bond financing, and most of those statutes designated specific projects.[21]

State legislatures failed to respond with any speed. For the most part, those bodies were not very functional. Turnover of elected officials was high and professional staffs small, and most state legislatures simply were not in session much. In 1932 more than half never convened. The debt caps written into thirty of the forty-eight state constitutions were particularly daunting barriers, as amending these documents generally involved popular and legislative elections spaced over several years.[22]

Meanwhile, the escape hatches of special districts and revenue bonds had to be individually crafted, and that took time. The two giant California projects funded by ERCA that Democrats complained about—the Bay Bridge connecting San Francisco and Oakland and the Metropolitan Aqueduct (also known as the Colorado River Aqueduct) carrying water from the Colorado River to Los Angeles—already had explicit approval from the state to borrow on the basis of their projected income streams. Preexisting borrowing authority, not partisan machinations, allowed those projects to be funded more quickly than others.[23]

Yet even as Hoover's program was stymied by the existing legal environment, it started to transform that environment. Lured by federal dollars, state legislatures began liberalizing their public finance laws. Quite promptly, considering the impediments to action, states began passing general enabling statutes that gave municipalities broad grants of power to finance projects using anticipated income as collateral for borrowing. During 1932 and 1933, fourteen states first put statutes authorizing the use of revenue bonds on their books, while many of the nineteen that had previously allowed such financing liberalized their existing laws.[24]

The New Deal's PWA, established in the summer of 1933, took over Hoover's program and made it work. That the PWA was more successful is not surprising. Its enabling legislation allowed the agency to offer easier terms (including outright grants, in addition to loans, which softened the requirement that projects pay for themselves). Even more significant, the PWA was administered by people with a greater understanding of the institutional environment in which such a program had to function. Harvey Couch, who headed ERCA for Hoover, was a brilliant Arkansas businessman who built a financial empire in telephones, electricity, and railroads from almost nothing, but he had little familiarity with the legal intricacies of local government. By contrast, Harold Ickes, the PWA administrator, was a lawyer who came to Franklin D. Roosevelt's cabinet with forty years' experience fighting for municipal reform in Chicago. Whereas Couch evidenced little awareness of the obstacles cities faced when trying to finance capital improvements, Ickes began his tenure by setting his legal staff to work helping local and state officials craft broad new statutes that simplified procedures for borrowing against future income. By 1937, PWA lawyers had drafted over five hundred bills, and forty-one states had adopted enabling legislation for revenue-bond funding.[25]

By themselves, however, revenue bonds had limitations. The biggest was that state courts sometimes balked at the premise of the special fund and insisted that any debt a municipality took on be counted against its constitutional debt limit. To avoid such problems, the PWA and President Roosevelt himself promoted new approaches. In 1934 Roosevelt sent a letter to all forty-eight governors urging them to draw on the expertise of the PWA's Legal Division to liberalize municipal finance laws so that they could take advantage of federal credit "at least for the duration of the existing emergency." The president's first recommendation was the simplification of regulations so that municipalities could borrow more freely. But where this was not feasible, he suggested state officials set up legal machinery to permit the creation of what he called "municipal improvement authorities" or "non-profit benefit corporations," which he defined as legally independent instrumentalities that could finance themselves by borrowing against future revenue.[26] In essence, Roosevelt and the PWA popularized what came to be known as the public authority, an institutional template that combined the funding strategy of revenue bonds with the organizational device of special districts.

Roosevelt was familiar with this organizational model given his association as governor with the Port of New York Authority. This agency was initially envisioned by its designer, attorney Julius Henry Cohen, as a mechanism with wide powers similar to the Port Authority of London, from which Cohen borrowed the term "authority." Cohen advocated a bi-state agency directed by a politically insulated appointed board that would coordinate transportation in the clogged New York harbor. As it ultimately emerged in 1921 after intense wrangling, the Port Authority covered a huge territory across two states, but lacked regulatory and taxing powers. It did, however, possess the ability to float bonds to build income-producing infrastructure, an ability it strikingly put to use with the construction of the George Washington Bridge spanning the Hudson River. Longer than any previous suspension bridge in the world, the bridge was an impressive engineering achievement. It also represented a significant administrative achievement, particularly in contrast to the cost overruns and delays caused by political infighting that marked the construction of the Holland Tunnel built only a few years before. At the opening ceremonies in 1931, Governor Roosevelt commended the Port Authority's management of the bridge project, calling the agency's "disinterested and capable service...a model for government agencies throughout the land."[27]

The public authority template was widely utilized while the PWA and the RFC were offering loans to states and local governments during the New Deal. Many assumed,

however, that these mechanisms would be of little use after the federal aid programs ended. Private investors were generally unfamiliar with revenue bonds, and in any case, disinclined, given the rocky finances of local governments during the Depression, to invest in municipal securities of any sort. Yet after the Second World War, municipal finances stabilized and private investors became increasingly comfortable with revenue bonds. In this environment authorities not only survived, but thrived.

The Pennsylvania Turnpike was pivotal in the transition. In 1938, when the Pennsylvania Turnpike Commission tried to raise funds for its proposed high-speed, limited-access highway with a public offering of revenue bonds, private investors looked askance. The project only went forward with federal financing. However, after the superhighway drew twice as many drivers in its first year as was projected to make it commercially successful, investors had a change of heart. After the war ended, the states that decided to construct tolled expressway systems by setting up authorities found it quite easy to market their revenue bonds in private capital markets. The New York Thruway Authority, which constructed the biggest and most expensive of these projects, the 535-mile express highway spanning the Empire State, encountered so much enthusiasm for its hundreds of millions of dollars' worth of bonds that it was able to sell them for very low interest rates. The initial offering paid only 1.1 percent.[28]

PUBLIC AUTHORITIES WHEN THERE'S NOTHING TO SELL

A large proportion of the new postwar public authorities operated along the same lines as these kinds of bodies had earlier. Although they now sold their bonds in private capital markets and sometimes provided novel services like tolled expressways and parking garages, they were organized on the same model that had crystallized during the New Deal era. Yet much of what cities and states wanted to build after the war could not readily be made to produce income. Examples include school buildings, which became a pressing necessity in the era of the baby boom, and government office buildings, which were needed to house an expanding public sector labor force. States and municipalities faced great challenges trying to provide these kinds of facilities given the fiscal limitations that had earlier impelled them toward public authorities: low debt caps and the difficulty of obtaining voter approval for incurring debt. But with regard to financing facilities for which users could not be charged, the traditional authority model was of little help.

The situation prompted increasingly creative efforts on the part of hard-pressed public officials to produce (or seem to produce) streams of income against which to borrow so that revenue bonds could be issued and building projects proceed. The new round of institutional innovation resulted in techniques by which public authorities could tap into tax-based revenues. These innovations eventually led to a new stage in the history of public authorities: the advent of the financing authority, and its junior partner, the moral authority bond. Not only did these new templates spread, they became major features of sub-federal public finance.

The first innovation was the building authority, based on techniques used in commercial lease financing. Building authorities, in the same way as traditional authorities, could borrow capital at lower cost than private businesses, because they could offer tax-free securities. At the same time, they could remain free of debt limits or requirements for voter approval. Traditional public authorities used the facilities they financed and constructed to produce goods and services to be sold to the public. These new authorities, by contrast, leased or rented what they built to the political jurisdictions that created them. Payment contracts were calculated to cover construction costs, interest, and a reserve fund over a fixed period, after which time title

would be conveyed to the commissioning unit (although in some places, to avoid judicial objections, the ultimate transfer of title was not made explicit in the contract). Thus, it was the stream of rental payments that constituted the building authority's future income, on the basis of which revenue bonds were floated.[29]

Meanwhile, public officials, searching for more ways by which to take action, were busy turning the building authority into an even more flexible and powerful tool by stripping it of any specific mission. This was the financing authority, a vehicle that functioned simply to obtain low-cost capital in the tax-free municipal bond market for any public purpose involving the construction of new facilities. Financing authorities proved to be the catalyst for yet another innovation: the so-called moral obligation bond. This financial instrument was essentially a revenue bond secured not only by income from the authority that issued it, but also by some kind of vaguely worded promise to investors that if income was at any point insufficient to make scheduled payments, the general-purpose government that had commissioned the project would make up the shortfall. Since pledging the credit of a state or municipality without voter approval was illegal in most jurisdictions, such a promise could not be enforced by courts, and the bond covenants clearly stated this fact. Therefore, any such pledge was not a legal obligation. To describe the kind of commitment actually being made to investors, the credit rating agency Moody's called it a "moral obligation."[30]

In explanations of how this elaboration of the authority concept began, much has been made of the role of John Mitchell, the nationally prominent bond attorney who advised New York governor Nelson Rockefeller. Mitchell, who later served as President Richard Nixon's attorney general and went to prison for his role in the Watergate cover-up, makes an especially good villain for those who attribute New York State's long-term fiscal problems largely to Rockefeller's enormous borrowing spree in the 1960s, which was facilitated by the moral authority device.[31]

The reality is more prosaic. As with so much of the story of the decades-long efforts to expand state capacity by evading existing statutory and constitutional controls on borrowing, this innovation occurred in an incremental, ad hoc manner, not as some conspiratorial grand plan. For example, the 1932 New York statute creating the State Bridge Authority to build the Rip Van Winkle Bridge over the Hudson specified that should any default occur, bondholders were required to wait until the end of the next legislative session before going to court. The implication was that the state might well come to the aid of the authority should it encounter financial difficulties.[32] Mitchell merely took the effort to reassure investors one step further when he inserted vague language in the 1960 statute for the Housing Finance Agency (HFA) to the effect that if the agency ran into financial troubles, the governor would urge the legislature to appropriate sufficient funds to make scheduled payments to bondholders. Created as a "public benefit corporation" (the legal term in New York State for a public authority), the HFA was set up to be the financing mechanism for the state's middle-income housing program and other construction projects that Governor Rockefeller wanted to pursue, but that the state's voters showed little interest in supporting through bond issues. Mitchell's stratagem was successful. Even though bond rating agencies had previously been unwilling even to assign ratings to nonguaranteed securities for housing construction, HFA bonds proved enormously popular. The HFA would go on to become a huge multipurpose state bank that by 1972 carried a debt load larger than that of the state itself.[33]

THE ROLE OF CAPITAL MARKETS AND COURTS

The success of public authorities with no customers outside of government has depended on the willingness of investors and courts to accept the way these entities skirt the spirit if not the letter of the law. For example, participants in the tax-exempt bond market can hardly have believed that moral obligation bonds were actually secured by ethical sentiments. As one investment banker put it to a researcher, "If one of the state corporations defaulted on debt, it would resemble an elephant dying on the state house steps—the government would have to do something about it or suffer from the stench." The suffering to which he referred would result from the impact on the government's own credit rating when the investment community perceived it would not stand behind the debts of its agencies, regardless of whether it was actually responsible in a legal sense. Thus the true nature of the obligation was perceived on all sides to be practical, not moral.[34]

Courts, too, went along with the organizational and financial innovations involved in building and financing authorities. Rather than probe whether the bonds of these new kinds of authorities conformed to the intent of their state's constitutional and statutory debt regulations, or inquire into the motives of those who set up the new kinds of authorities and issued their bonds, courts usually took a formal and procedural approach. Like other actors in this story, judges generally appeared sympathetic—and therefore gave the benefit of the doubt—to efforts to overcome the barriers that the existing legal framework placed in the way of badly needed public construction. For example, the Michigan Supreme Court made it obvious in the 1930s and again in the 1940s that it recognized that leasing served the same end as installment buying. The court justified its decision on the basis of a formal reading of the law, refusing to judge intentions, and saying explicitly that it found no illegality in using nominally legal means when the most obvious means to the same end were illegal.[35]

Courts were at times quite candid about their rationale for granting governments wide leeway in their efforts to evade legal barriers to borrowing. In 1955, New York State's highest court affirmed the right of the City of Elmira to top up the coffers of the Elmira Parking Authority in the event that financial shortfalls threatened the authority's ability to make scheduled payments to bondholders. In response to plaintiffs' complaints, the court found that even though the constitution forbade political subdivisions of the state from taking responsibility for the debts of public authorities, there were no rules against "the transfer of money or property by State or city to an authority." Thus gifts, even foreseeable ones, were declared legal. Just in case anyone missed the point, the court articulated its reasoning explicitly: "We should not strain ourselves to find illegality in such programs. The problems of a modern city can never be solved unless arrangements like these ... are upheld, unless they are patently illegal."[36]

GROWING DEPENDENCE NATIONALLY ON PUBLIC AUTHORITY FINANCING

In the same way as new ideas for evading borrowing barriers diffused throughout the country in the first half of the 20th century, New York's Housing Finance Agency became a national model. Only a decade and a half after the creation of the HFA, thirty states had established one or more institutions that floated bonds backed by some kind of a quasi-guarantee of support from general state revenues, in order to provide financing for a wide range of programs. Meanwhile, New York State made such liberal use of the HFA and other financing authorities for ambitious construction projects (including a huge expansion of the state university system) that by the time Rockefeller left the governorship in 1973, the debt of the state's public authorities had ballooned to almost four times that of the Empire State itself. As time went on, these trends only accelerated. In 2004 the New York State comptroller reported that public authority debt had climbed to nine times that of the state.[37]

Certainly New York has been a leader in the use of public authorities as tools for confronting fiscal challenges, but its story is not anomalous. Numerous states carry a heavy load of "nonguaranteed" debt—debt that is typically generated by public authority–type institutions using bonds secured against projected revenues (a good portion of which are to be derived from government payments). As of 2002, this type of debt was higher on a per capita basis in four states (Alaska, Rhode Island, Delaware, and Massachusetts) than in New York. Nine states (Colorado, Idaho, Indiana, Iowa, Kansas, Kentucky, North Dakota, South Dakota, and Wyoming) actually rely entirely on nonguaranteed debt.[38]

DIVERGENT PERSPECTIVES ON PUBLIC AUTHORITIES

Numerous controversies exist with respect to public authorities. Observers disagree about their benefits and dangers, especially with regard to their ability to borrow in the tax-exempt bond market without input from the electorate, yet with the implied backing of the governments that created them. Such disagreements lead to different opinions about when and how to employ them, as well as whether and how they should be regulated.

Supporters laud authorities for their ability "to get things done." They point to how these institutions are able to avoid the rigid budgeting, personnel, and procurement rules to which standard government agencies must conform. Most significantly, supporters highlight the ability of these agencies to generate and utilize their own sources of revenue, which liberates them from the contentious politics of taxation and public borrowing that often stymie efforts to use standard government to accomplish the task at hand. In addition, the ability to borrow against their future revenue streams for capital investments means that authorities are able to make long-range plans, which is difficult for standard agencies, funded on a yearly basis. Political scientist Jameson

W. Doig, a leading expert in the field, regards the organizational structure of the public authority as potentially very effective. Many, he says, "behave in ways not unlike the well-run private corporation." This perspective on the virtues of independence is probably most strongly held by pro-development business groups (for which, it must be noted, these structures tend to be more permeable than for other parts of civil society). In a 1986 op-ed in the *Boston Globe*, Harold Hestnes, a longtime leader of the Greater Boston Chamber of Commerce, praised public authorities for having built "many of the most significant public works in this nation," an achievement he attributed to the fact that these agencies are "removed from the vicissitudes of political interference." The basic point is that quasi-public agencies are able to accomplish tasks that their proponents take to be otherwise impossible given what they see as the American political system's tendencies toward stasis. [39]

Critics of public authorities reject these positive evaluations. They charge that the businesslike efficiency of these devices is overrated, and that whatever gains in effectiveness they do achieve come at the expense of democratic accountability. In the words of noted public administration scholar Annmarie Hauck Walsh, the public authority "involves public ownership without public policy." Another major criticism is that reliance on public authorities fragments the power of government and commercializes the public sector. Political scientist Alberta M. Sbragia charges that public authorities have "diluted the power of general purpose governments, have insulated themselves from the electorate, and have transformed taxpayers into ratepayers subject to user fees." [40] Some commentators even allege that the public authority sector is in effect an "underground" government that poses systemic risk to the economy because of its size and the fact that it is constrained neither by the electorate nor the market. [41] All the critics acknowledge that

standard government agencies are often slow moving and ineffectual at certain kinds of tasks, but they maintain that a far better solution would be "to attack the weakness in government rather than search for new forms of independence." [42]

PUBLIC AUTHORITIES AT THE FEDERAL LEVEL

Since the early 20th century, the federal government has employed public-authority type mechanisms, most often termed government or federal corporations, to administer programs. As with these kinds of agencies at the state and local levels, government corporations share core features (financial and administrative independence, plus incorporation as separate legal entities), but they vary widely one from another, reflecting the fact that they have been created on an ad hoc basis. Their history is somewhat different than that of their state and local counterparts, as the federal-level entities were originally set up to handle financial or marketing endeavors that private business seemed incapable of performing and that standard government agencies were ill-equipped to handle, rather than to circumvent legal barriers to borrowing. Also, they became less, rather than more popular in the decades after the Second World War.

Involvement with corporations was nothing new for the federal government. In the 19th century, the national government invested in private commercial corporations, such as the First and Second Banks of the United States. Also, Congress established corporate bodies to administer educational and charitable operations, such as the Smithsonian Institution. However, it was not until the early 20th century that the federal government created incorporated instrumentalities by which to engage directly in the economy. The first instance came about by accident. In 1904, when the United States purchased property in the Canal Zone from the newly formed Republic of Panama, the federal government came into possession of the Panama Railroad Company. Although owned by the government, the company was run as a self-contained enterprise. As such, it could do long-term planning, free from the uncertainty of annual congressional appropriation cycles. Nor was it subject to executive branch procurement and personnel regulations, which after all had been developed for routine administration, rather than business ventures. These conditions, combined with effective management, allowed the company to expand into a highly effective logistical support system for the building and operation of the canal. The success of the Panama Railroad Company, combined with experiments with government-owned business corporations elsewhere in the English-speaking world at this time, gave legitimacy to arguments for employing quasi-autonomous corporate agencies more widely in the United States.[43]

During the era of the First World War, a number of quasi-autonomous corporate agencies were set up from scratch. These were the Federal Farm Banks, Emergency Fleet Corporation, Grain Corporation, War Finance Corporation, Housing Corporation, Sugar Equalization Board, Spruce Production Corporation, and Russian Bureau, Inc. All except the Farm Banks, established to extend low-cost credit to farmers, were set up on a temporary basis to aid the war mobilization. As it turned out, quickly dissolving all of these mechanisms once hostilities ceased was difficult, because some acquired influential constituencies. The Emergency Fleet Corporation, with some modifications, survived until 1936. Meanwhile, the concept of the federally owned corporate agency able to directly intervene in the economy on behalf of public goals recommended itself to groups who believed themselves to be unfairly disadvantaged and deserving of government aid. Advocates of railroad nationalization, supporters of public power, residential mortgage lenders, and farmers' organizations all lobbied for corporate

agencies to resolve problems they faced. Congresses of the 1920s, unsympathetic to the idea of government activism in general, tended to be unresponsive to these calls, but attitudes changed when the economy slid into depression.[44]

To combat the deflationary slide of the Great Depression, President Hoover initiated the Federal Home Loan Banks, to make loans to residential lenders, and the Reconstruction Finance Corporation, to make loans to banks, railroads, and other businesses. These federal agencies were organized as government corporations. Many more were established during the New Deal phase of the Roosevelt administration, including a variety of credit and insurance agencies, and the most famous of all, the Tennessee Valley Authority (TVA). Most were temporary, but some have continued for decades, such as the TVA and the Federal Deposit Insurance Corporation (FDIC).[45]

The Second World War spurred a raft of new federal corporations, similar to, but more numerous than, the "war corporations" of the First World War. This period was the high-point for semiautonomous corporate agencies at the federal level, with, according to some methods of defining and counting, over one hundred in existence.[46] But at this same time, pressures crested for reining in these mechanisms.

Serious resistance to the use of this administrative form began during the 1930s. For some critics, the real issue was any expansion of the federal government, and federal corporations were merely an easy target. But even many liberals were uneasy about the rapid proliferation of these devices. One issue was their extreme heterogeneity, reflecting the ad hoc manner in which they were created—some were chartered by Congress, while others incorporated in a state on the authority of the president, an official in the administration, or even an executive of a previously existing corporate agency. Moreover, while some were formed to carry out commercial functions, others seemed to have been created primarily to evade normal executive branch regulations. Most worrisome was the general lack of oversight from either the president or Congress. As a result of these anxieties, Congress passed the Government Corporation Control Act in 1945, which called for all corporate agencies to receive yearly commercial audits by the General Accounting Office and for those with state charters to get statutory approval from Congress or else be dissolved.

Government corporations lost popularity in the years after the Second World War. One reason was that the Government Corporation Control Act established more centralized controls. But since these controls were never rigorously applied, researchers tend to emphasize other factors. Scandals during the Truman administration involving the Reconstruction Finance Corporation tarnished the reputation of this major agency, and by extension, the whole class of government corporations. In addition, management theories that prioritized a more tightly integrated executive branch came to dominate the field of public administration.[47] Most important, public officials discovered they could achieve even more autonomy and flexibility than public corporations provided by setting up contracting arrangements with private firms.

The military pioneered the contracting approach after positive experiences during the Second World War with government-owned, but contractor-managed, national laboratories, such as Oak Ridge and Los Alamos. Loath to lose top scientific talent after the war, the military services set up privately owned, nonprofit research organizations, such as the RAND Corporation, which were not subject to executive branch personnel rules and thus could pay salaries commensurate with the private sector. These Federally Funded Research and Development Centers (FFRDCs) became popular with the different branches of the military and eventually civilian agencies, as well. In many ways FFRDCs can be seen as the functional equivalents of government corporations, providing administrators with the

ability to pursue projects over multiyear periods without the uncertainties of annual congressional appropriation cycles, to hire for and manage projects without having to cope with a rigid regulatory scheme designed for more routine administrative activities, and to launch new projects without obtaining cumbersome legislative approval.[48]

Despite its decline in popularity, the government corporation organizational template remains in use at the federal level. While alternatives now exist for escaping central management rules, using FFRDCs and other kinds of contracting arrangements, the government corporation still offers policymakers certain unique advantages. This is particularly the case with regard to the new institutional environment relating to the federal budget. Congressional attempts since the 1960s to cut or slow the growth of the federal budget by setting expenditure targets means that independent corporate agencies have become convenient devices for moving spending and borrowing off-budget. A good example is the creation by the George H. W. Bush administration and Congress in 1989 of the Resolution Trust Corporation (RTC) and its financing agency, the Resolution Funding Corporation (REFCORP), to deal with the losses incurred by the widespread failures of savings and loan associations (an intervention estimated to have cost $190 billion in 2008 dollars.)[49]

The rise of the New Public Management Movement, based on theories of "entrepreneurial" public administration, has pushed the government corporation out of the shadows. Conceptions about "third way" institutions that could function between traditional public/private boundaries gained traction in Britain in the 1980s under the influence of Margaret Thatcher and were popularized in the United States by David Osborne and Ted Gaebler in their 1992 book *Reinventing Government*. From this ideological perspective, the template of the congressionally chartered agency, operating outside the normal regulatory structure of federal administration and supporting itself by charging user fees for services, took on new relevance. Proponents argued that government corporations were ideal vehicles by which to deliver social and economic services more flexibly and responsively, while costing the taxpayer less.[50]

The Clinton administration's effort to upgrade the administrative capabilities of the federal government was deeply influenced by these ideas. Indeed, the National Performance Review (NPR), led by Vice President Albert Gore, was commonly referred to as "Reinventing Government." Two of the NPR's earliest proposals were to semi-privatize the Federal Aviation Administration by creating an Air Traffic Services Corporation and to hive off the business aspects of the General Services Administration into a Real Property Management Enterprise. Other NPR suggestions for reforming specific federal agencies, while not specifying formal incorporation, called for moving them closer to the template of the government corporation in that they were to be deregulated and encouraged to generate income through commercial activities.[51] Although the National Performance Review's proposals for creating new corporate agencies did not succeed in the 1990s, the ideological climate of the early 21st century continues to favor the creation of self-funding institutions that operate outside the regulatory constraints of the executive branch. This sensibility can take surprising forms, as when the conservative Heritage Foundation adopted a trademark New Deal initiative as a desirable model with a call in 2007 "to take the [Air Traffic Control] system out of the federal budget process and make it a self-supporting entity, ... analogous to the Tennessee Valley Authority (TVA)."[52]

DISCUSSION OF THE LITERATURE

Much of the scholarly writing on public authorities has been more descriptive than analytical and has examined them exclusively at either the federal level or at the state and local levels. There are, however, exceptions that consider these mechanisms as a unified field and evaluate them in relation to other options governments could use to pursue policy objectives. In addition to those listed in the Further Reading section of this article, see: Emmette S. Redford, "The Scope of Public Enterprise," chap. 26 of Emmette Redford and Charles B. Hagan, *American Government and the Economy* (New York: Macmillan, 1968); Jamison W. Doig, "'If I See a Murderous Fellow Sharpening a Knife Cleverly ...': The Wilsonian Dichotomy and the Public Authority Tradition," *Public Administration Review* 43 (July/August 1983); and Nicholas Henry, "Privatization: Government Contracting and the Public Authority," chap. 11 of Nicholas Henry, *Public Administration and Public Affairs* (Upper Saddle River, NJ: Prentice-Hall, 1999).

Treatments of the public authority have changed over time. This organizational form attracted little attention from scholars before the 1930s, when it became widely employed at all levels of government. Important exceptions were a series of articles in *The American Political Science Review* beginning in 1914 that tracked the spread of forerunners of the public authority under the heading "Special Municipal Corporations." Harold Archer Van Dorn's *Government Owned Corporations* (New York: Knopf, 1926), described in detail the creation, organization, and operations of the authority-like entities established by the federal government during the era of First World War.

The fiscal crises of cities and the refinement and spread of the local-level public authority template by the Public Works Administration (PWA) during the Great Depression sparked an outpouring of scholarly discussion, much of it in legal journals. See especially, C. Dickerman Williams and Peter R. Nehemkis Jr., "Municipal Improvements as Affected by Constitutional Debt Limitations," *Columbia Law Review* 37 (February 1937); and articles by E. H. Foley Jr., director of the legal division of the PWA, such as "Revenue Financing of Public Enterprises," *Michigan Law Review* 35 (November 1936). For extended treatments of municipal debt and revenue bonds, see A. M. Hillhouse, *Municipal Bonds: A Century of Experience* (New York: Prentice-Hall, 1936); B. U. Ratchford, *American State Debts* (Durham, NC: Duke University Press, 1941). Comprehensive data on constitutional and statutory debt limits in effect throughout the country as of 1936 can be found in Lane W. Lancaster, "State Limitations on Local Indebtedness," *Municipal Year Book,* edited by Clarence E. Ridley and Orin F. Nolting (Washington, DC: International City Managers Association, 1936), 313–327.

Federal-level authorities, generally termed "government corporations," were discussed extensively in legal journals during the Depression era, when the Hoover and especially the Roosevelt administrations both turned to these mechanisms. These accounts were largely descriptions of how already-existing entities had come into being, how they functioned, and how courts had handled their ambiguous public-private character and vaguely defined relationship to different levels of government. However, these articles usually contained suggestions aimed at policymakers for improving the way these instrumentalities were designed and deployed. See, for example, Oliver Peter Field, "Government Corporations: A Proposal," *Harvard Law Review* 48 (March 1935). Harvey Franklin Pinney gives an enormous amount of information about the structure and legal history of government corporations in his 561-page New York University PhD dissertation of 1937: "Federal Government Corporations as Instrumentalities of Government and of Administration." For the political resistance to the increasing use of government corporations, see US Congress, Joint Committee on Reduction of Nonessential Federal Expenditures, "Report on Government Corporations," Senate Doc. 227, 78th Cong., 2nd sess. (1944); and C. Herman Pritchett,

"The Government Corporations Control Act of 1945," *American Political Science Review* 40 (June 1946).

Although early scholarly work on authorities at the state and local levels often critiqued specific aspects of design and usage, these studies almost never expressed across-the-board hostility to their use. (For an atypical denunciation, see Horace Davis, "Borrowing Machines," *National Municipal Review* 24 [June 1935]). After the Second World War, as the number of state and local agencies increased dramatically, scholarship turned more analytical and even, in some cases, sharply negative. See, for example: Joseph E. McLean, "Use and Abuse of Public Authorities," *National Municipal Review* 43 (October 1953); Jon Magnusson, "Lease-Financing by Municipal Corporations as a Way around Debt Limitations," *George Washington Law Review* 25 (March 1957); William J. Quirk and Leon E. Wein, "A Short Constitutional History of Entities Commonly Known as Authorities," *Cornell Law Review* 56 (April 1971): 521–597; and David C. Perry, "Building the City through the Back Door: The Politics of Debt, Law, and Public Infrastructure," in *Building the Public City: The Politics, Governance and Finance of Public Infrastructure,* edited by David C. Perry (Thousand Oaks, CA: SAGE, 1995). The best known and much admired critical overview is Annmarie Hauck Walsh, *The Public's Business: The Politics and Practices of Government Corporations* (Cambridge, MA: MIT Press, 1978).

Use of public authority mechanisms at the federal level in recent decades can be followed in reports by the Congressional Research Service (for example, Kevin R. Kosar, "Federal Government Corporations: An Overview," CRS Report for Congress, 2011); the Government Accountability Office (See, GAO, "Government Corporations: Profiles of Existing Government Corporations," Fact Sheet for the Ranking Minority Member, Subcommittee on Post Office and Civil Service, Committee on Government Affairs, U.S. Senate, 1995);

and A. Michael Froomkin, "Reinventing the Government Corporation," *University of Illinois Law Review*, 1995, no. 548 (1995): 543.

Examinations of the public authority as an international phenomenon can be found in: John Thurston, *Government Proprietary Corporations in English-Speaking Countries* (Cambridge, MA: Harvard University Press, 1937); Wolfgang Friedmann, *The Public Corporation: A Comparative Symposium* (Toronto: Carswell, 1954); and Wolfgang Friedmann and J. F. Garner, eds., *Government Enterprise: A Comparative Study* (New York: Columbia University Press, 1970).

PRIMARY SOURCES

Primary sources for the study of public authorities consist chiefly of public documents published either by authorities themselves or by the government entities, such as states and the federal government, that create and oversee them. Each individual authority has its own particular records of varying duration, completeness, and accessibility. As discussed in the text (see note 7), attempts to compile data on authorities as a class have been hindered by the lack of reporting requirements and enforcement of those that exist, as well as by disagreements over definitional issues. Sadly, the US Census, Census of Governments is not an authoritative source of basic information over time, as most scholars reject its classification scheme.

FURTHER READING

Abel, Albert. "The Public Corporation in the United States." In *Government Enterprise: A Comparative Study*, edited by W. G. Friedmann and J. F. Garner. New York: Columbia University Press, 1970.

Caro, Robert A. *The Power Broker: Robert Moses and the Fall of New York*. New York: Knopf, 1974.

Doig, Jameson W. *Empire on the Hudson: Entrepreneurial Vision and Political Power at the Port of New York Authority*. New York: Columbia University Press, 2001.

Mitchell, Jerry. *The American Experiment With Government Corporations*. Armonk, NY: M. E. Sharpe, 1999.

Perry, David C. "Building the City through the Back Door: The Politics of Debt, Law, and Public Infrastructure." In *Building the Public City: The Politics, Governance, and Finance of Public Infrastructure*. By David C. Perry, 202–236. Urban Affairs Annual Review 43. Thousand Oaks, CA: SAGE, 1995.

Quirk, William J., and Leon E. Wein. "A Short Constitutional History of Entities Commonly Known as Authorities." *Cornell Law Review* 56, no. 4 (April 1971): 521–597.

Radford, Gail. *The Rise of the Public Authority: State-building and Economic Development in Twentieth-Century America*. Chicago: University of Chicago Press, 2013.

Sbragia, Alberta M. *Debt Wish: Entrepreneurial Cities, U.S. Federalism, and Economic Development*. Pittsburgh, PA: University of Pittsburgh Press, 1996. 14–15.

Seidman, Harold. "Government-sponsored Enterprise in the United States." In *The New Political Economy: The Public Use of the Private Sector*. Edited by Bruce L. R. Smith. New York: Wiley, 1975.

Smith, Robert G. *Public Authorities, Special Districts and Local Government*. Washington, DC: National Association of Counties, 1964.

Walsh, Annmarie Hauck. *The Public's Business: The Politics and Practices of Government Corporations*. Cambridge, MA: MIT Press, 1980. Originally published in 1978.

NOTES

1. Robert Gerwig, "Public Authorities in the United States," *Law and Contemporary Problems* 20, no. 4 (September 1961): 602.
2. David C. Perry, "Building the City through the Back Door: The Politics of Debt, Law, and Public Infrastructure," in *Building the Public City: The Politics, Governance, and Finance of Public Infrastructure*, by David C. Perry, Urban Affairs Annual Review 43 (Thousand Oaks, CA: SAGE, 1995), 202–236; and Kenneth W. Bond, "Conduit Financing," *New York State Bar Association Government, Law and Policy Journal* 11, no. 2 (Fall 2009): 68–74.
3. Tennessee Valley Authority, *Report to SEC, Fiscal Year 2011*, 11 (accessed 5/14/2012).

http://files.shareholder.com/downloads/TVC/1868315477x0xS1376986-11-74/1376986/filing.pdf.

4. Peter Hendee Brown, *America's Waterfront Revival: Port Authorities and Urban Redevelopment* (Philadelphia: University of Pennsylvania Press, 2009), chap. 2; Hillsborough County Port District, Florida, "Comprehensive Annual Financial Report of the Tampa Port Authority, Fiscal Year Ended September 30, 2008," iv. (accessed 9/28/2009). http://www.tampaport.com/content/download/6639/28840/file/FY2008%20CAFR%20PUBLISHED.pdf.

5. Springfield Parking Authority (accessed 1/31/2010), http://www.parkspa.com/aboutus.shtml. Infrastructure Management Group, *Assessment Report on the City of Springfield Parking System* (August 2005), 9, 12, 14, 18, 43 (accessed 1/31/2010), http://www.mass.gov/Asfcb/docs/reports/parking_study.pdf.

6. Robert A. Caro, *The Power Broker: Robert Moses and the Fall of New York* (New York: Knopf, 1974); Robert A. Caro, "The City-Shaper," *New Yorker*, January 5, 1998, 40.

7. For estimates of total numbers, see Nicholas Henry, *Public Administration and Public Affairs* (Upper Saddle River, NJ: Prentice-Hall, 1999), 373. For definitional issues, see Annmarie Hauck Walsh, *The Public's Business: The Politics and Practices of Government Corporations* (Cambridge, MA: MIT Press, 1980), 5–6, 353–372, 373, n.1; and Jerry Mitchell, "The Policy Activities of Public Authorities," *Policy Studies Journal* 18 (Summer 1990), 928–942. The *U.S. Census, Census of Governments* is not a definitive source, as it lumps together special districts with public authorities. While the two share certain characteristics, such as structural independence from elected officials (plus a common history), most scholars differentiate between them—the basic distinction being that special districts are governed by elected boards and have the power to tax, whereas public authorities are governed by appointed boards and have no taxing power. For efforts to identify all public authorities in New York, see Office of the State Comptroller, *Public Authorities in New York State: Accelerating Momentum to Achieve Reform* (Albany, NY: Office of Budget and Policy Analysis, February 2005), 7.

8. Ronald C. Moe and Kevin R. Kosar, *Federal Government Corporations: An Overview*, (Washington, DC: Congressional Research Service, 2006), 6.

9. Unpublished Census Bureau data for 1949 cited in J. Richard Aronson and John L. Hilley, *Financing State and Local Governments* (Washington, DC: Brookings Institution, 1986), 251. U.S. Department of Interior, Census Office, *2002 Census of Governments*, vol. 4, no. 5: *Government Finances* (Washington, DC: GPO, 2005), Table 13, p.15. After 2002, the Census Bureau no longer distinguished between debt that was "guaranteed" and "non-guaranteed," so no later figures are available. Dollar value adjustments were done based on Bureau of Economic Analysis, U.S. Department of Commerce, *National Income and Product Accounts Tables*, Table 1.1.4, Price Indexes for Gross Domestic Product (options selected: annual series and all years), available at the website for the Bureau of Economic Analysis (accessed 3/5/2011).

10. Richard M. Abrams, "Business and Government," in Jack P. Greene, ed., *Encyclopedia of American Political History* (New York: Scribners, 1984), 1:132–133; Oliver Field, "Government Corporations: A Proposal," *Harvard Law Review* 48 (March 1935): 775–776.

11. Ballard C. Campbell, "Tax Revolts and Political Change," *Journal of Policy History* 10, no.1 (1998): 156–161; C. Dickerman Williams and Peter R. Nehemkis Jr., "Municipal Improvements as Affected by Constitutional Debt Limitations," *Columbia Law Review* 37 (February 1937), 187; A. M. Hillhouse, *Municipal Bonds: A Century of Experience* (New York: Prentice-Hall, 1936), 143–199; Lane W. Lancaster, "State Limitations on Local Indebtedness," *The Municipal Year Book*, ed. Clarence E. Ridley and Orin F. Nolting (Chicago, 1936), 319–324; and John L. Bowers Jr., "Limitations on Municipal Indebtedness," *Vanderbilt Law Review* 5 (1951–1952): 37–56.

12. Robin L. Einhorn, *Property Rules: Political Economy in Chicago, 1833–1872* (Chicago: University of Chicago Press, 1991), 15–19, 104–143; Roger D. Simon, *The City-Building Process: Housing and Services in New Milwaukee Neighborhoods, 1880–1910* (Philadelphia: American Philosophical Society, 1996), 24.

13. Sarah S. Elkind, "Building a Better Jungle: Anti-Urban Sentiment, Public Works, and Political Reform in American Cites, 1880–1930," *Journal of Urban History* 24 (November 1997): 55.

14. Frederic H. Guild, "Special Corporations," *American Political Science Review* 12 (November 1918): 681.

15. John C. Bollens, *Special District Government in the United States* (Berkeley: University of California Press, 1957); Paul Studenski, *The Government of Metropolitan Areas in the United States* (New York: National Municipal League, 1930), chap. 14; and Kathryn A. Foster, *The Political Economy of Special-Purpose Government* (Washington, DC: Georgetown University Press, 1997), 15–17.

16. *Winston v. Spokane*, 12 Wash. 524 (1895); U.S. Federal Emergency Administration of Public Works, *Revenue Bond Financing by Political Subdivisions: Its Origin, Scope, and Growth in the United States* (Washington, DC: U.S. Government Printing Office, 1936), 3–4; Lawrence L. Durisch, "Publicly Owned Utilities and the Problem of Municipal Debt Limits," *Michigan Law Review* 31 (1932–1933): 506; John F. Fowler, Jr. *Revenue Bonds: The Nature, Uses and Distribution of Fully Self-Liquidating Public Loans* (New York: Harper & Bros., 1938), 21–22; and Laurence S. Knappen, *Revenue Bonds and the Investor* (New York: Prentice-Hall, 1939), 8–10.

17. *Van Eaton v. Town of Sidney*, 211 Iowa 986, 993 (1930).

18. James Stuart Olson, *Herbert Hoover and the Reconstruction Finance Corporation* (Ames: Iowa State University Press, 1977), 62–73; quote from William Starr Myers and Walter H. Newton, *The Hoover Administration: A Documented Narrative* (New York: Scribners, 1936), 209.

19. *Emergency Relief and Construction Act*, 47 Stat. 709 (1932).

20. J. Franklin Ebersole, "One Year of the Reconstruction Finance Corporation," *Quarterly Journal of Economics* 47 (May 1933): 482; Secretary of the Treasury, *Final Report of the Reconstruction Finance Corporation* (Washington, DC: U.S. Government Printing Office, 1959), 268–269, table PA-2; Olson, *Herbert Hoover and the Reconstruction Finance Corporation*, 78; Paul Y. Anderson, "Buying California for Hoover," *Nation*, October 26, 1932, 392–393.

21. Robert G. Smith, *Ad Hoc Governments: Special Purpose Transportation Authorities in Britain and the United States* (Beverly Hills, CA: SAGE, 1974), 109; Paul Studenski and Herman E. Krooss, *Financial History of the United States: Fiscal, Monetary, Banking, and Tariff, Including Financial Administration and State and Local Finance* (New York: McGraw Hill, 1952), 433. Revenue-bond statistics computed from Lawrence S. Knappen, *Revenue Bonds and the Investor* (New York: Prentice-Hall, 1939), 279–286.

22. Ballard C. Campbell, *The Growth of American Government: Governance from the Cleveland Era to the Present* (Bloomington: Indiana University Press, 1995), 86–87; Paul Betters, *Recent Federal-City Relations* (Washington, DC: United States Conference of Mayors, 1936), 8; and Lancaster, "State Limitations on Local Indebtedness," 319–324.

23. The California Toll Bridge Authority was created in 1929 and authorized to issue revenue bonds. The Reconstruction Finance Corporation (RFC) financed the Bay Bridge project by purchasing $71 million worth of those bonds. 1929 Cal. Stat. chaps. 762 and 763; California Legislature, Joint Legislative Budget Committee, *Financial History of the San Francisco–Oakland Bay Bridge* (Sacramento, CA: Senate of the State of California, 1953), 12–16, 71–84. The Metropolitan Aqueduct was constructed by the Metropolitan Water District of Southern California, which was authorized to tax and borrow in 1927. The RFC purchased $148,500,000 worth of its bonds. 1927 Cal. Stat. chap. 429; Norris Hundley Jr., *The Great Thirst: Californians and Water, 1770s–1990s* (Berkeley: University of California Press, 1992), 215–232; Wylie Kilpatrick, "Federal Assistance to Municipal Recovery," *National Municipal Review* 26 (July 1937), 339.

24. Knappen, *Revenue Bonds and the Investor*, appendix A, 279–286; J. Kerwin Williams, *Grants-in-Aid under the Public Works Administration* (New York: Columbia University Press, 1939), 38–39. It might be argued that some of the 1933 laws were passed in response to the New Deal public works program that took over administration of the Emergency Relief and Construction Act (ERCA) in mid-June of that year. Harold Ickes, who administered the program, took a more activist approach to helping states pass laws that permitted revenue-based borrowing than Hoover's public works directors had. But considering the start-up time for a new federal agency under a new presidential administration and the fact that most state legislatures met early in the year, most of the new state laws passed in 1933 should

probably be credited primarily to the impetus of ERCA.

25. The National Industrial Recovery Act of 1933 allowed grants of 30 percent. 48 Stat. 195, Title II–Section 203(a). When the Emergency Relief and Construction Act of 1935, which continued funding for the agency, failed to specify a ceiling for grants, the president raised the limit to 45 percent. Jack F. Isakoff, *The Public Works Administration* (Urbana: University of Illinois Press, 1938), 88–93. The RFC began by setting minimum interest rates at 5.5 percent, eventually settling at 5 percent for most loans. The Public Works Administration (PWA) charged 4 percent. Olson, *Herbert Hoover and the Reconstruction Finance Corporation*, 79; U.S. Federal Emergency Administration of Public Works, *Revenue Bond Financing by Political Subdivisions*, 20; Winston P. Wilson, *Harvey Couch: The Master Builder* (Nashville: Broadman, 1947), 94; Linda J. Lear, *Harold L. Ickes: The Aggressive Progressive, 1874–1933* (New York: Garland, 1981); Harvey Couch, *Financing the Construction of Self-Liquidating Public Projects through the Reconstruction Finance Corporation* (Washington, DC: U.S. GPO, 1932); Harold L. Ickes, *Back to Work: The Story of the PWA* (New York: Macmillan, 1935), 224. The number of states that adopted enabling laws is computed from Knappen, *Revenue Bonds and the Investor*, appendix A, 279–286.

26. Quotes from Smith, *Ad Hoc Governments*, 108.

27. Jameson W. Doig, *Empire on the Hudson: Entrepreneurial Vision and Political Power at the Port of New York Authority* (New York: Columbia University Press, 2001), chapter 7. Roosevelt quote from Jameson W. Doig, "Joining New York City to the Greater Metropolis: The Port Authority as Visionary, Target of Opportunity, and Opportunist," in *Landscape of Modernity: New York City, 1900–1940*, ed. David Ward and Olivier Zunz (Baltimore: Johns Hopkins University Press, 1992), 83. Under aggressive leadership that adeptly used proceeds from projects the agency controlled to finance others, the Port Authority of New York (later renamed the Port Authority of New York and New Jersey) expanded significantly as time went on. It took over or built from scratch a large amount of the region's major infrastructure, including the Holland and Lincoln Tunnels, the region's three major airports (LaGuardia, Kennedy, and Newark), major truck terminals in the two states, and the World Trade Center. Jerry Mitchell, *The American Experiment with Government Corporations* (Armonk, NY: M. E. Sharpe), 37.

28. Dan Cupper, *The Pennsylvania Turnpike: A History* (Lebanon, PA: Applied Arts, 1990), 6–9, 22–24; Phil Patton, "A Quick Way from Here to There Was Also a Frolic," *Smithsonian* 21 (October 1990); Robert G. Smith, *Ad Hoc Governments: Special Purpose Transportation Authorities in Britain and the United States* (Beverly Hills, CA: SAGE, 1974), 121; Council of State Governments, *Public Authorities in the States: A Report to the Governors' Conference* (Chicago: Council of State Governments, 1953), 30–31; Michael R. Fein, *Paving the Way: New York Road Building and the American State, 1880–1956* (Lawrence: University Press of Kansas, 2008), 205, chap. 5; and U.S. Department of Transportation, *America's Highways, 1776–1976: A History of the Federal-Aid Program* (Washington, DC: GPO, 1976), 472–474.

29. Walsh, *The Public's Business*, 121–122; and Nathanial Stone Preston, "The Use and Control of Public Authorities in American State and Local Government" (PhD diss., Princeton University, 1960), 61.

30. Janice C. Griffith, "'Moral Obligation' Bonds: Illusion or Security?" *Urban Lawyer* 8 (1976): 54–93; and Walsh, *The Public's Business*, 132, 166.

31. "John N. Mitchell Dies at 75; Major Figure in Watergate," *New York Times*, November 10, 1988. Section titles such as "Nelson Rockefeller: The Stunting of Fiscal Viability and the Rise of Moral Obligation Bonds" make clear the viewpoint of Peter D. McClelland and Alan L. Magdovitz in *Crisis in the Making: The Political Economy of New York State Since 1945* (New York: Cambridge University Press, 1981), 225.

32. Laws of New York 1932, chap. 548, sec. 4. Moreland Act Commission on the Urban Development Corporation and Other State Financing Agencies, *Restoring Credit and Confidence* (Albany, NY: Moreland Act Commission, 1976), 86. See also, B.U. Ratchford, *American State Debts* (Durham, NC: Duke University Press, 1941), 517–521.

33. The New York State Limited Profit Housing Companies Act (1955) is commonly known as Mitchell-Lama, after its sponsors, Senator MacNeil

Mitchell and Assemblyman Alfred J. Lama. By 1972 HFA debt was $ 3.8 billion compared to the state's full-faith and credit debt of $3.4 billion. Figures from James E. Underwood and William J. Daniels, *Governor Rockefeller in New York: The Apex of Pragmatic Liberalism in the United States* (Westport, CT: Greenwood, 1982), table 6.9, p. 174, and table 6.6, p. 168. McClelland and Magdovitz, *Crisis in the Making, 156–161, 199–202, 233–234*; and William K. Reilly and S. J. Schulman, "The State Urban Development Corporation: New York's Innovation," *Urban Lawyer* 1 (1969): 135. For the section of the statute that makes this quasi guarantee: Laws of New York, 1960, chap. 671, sec. 346 (d). Walsh, *The Public's Business*, 72–77, 129–130.

34. Annmarie Hauck Walsh, "Public Authorities and the Shape of Decision Making," in *Urban Politics: New York Style*, ed. Jewel Bellush and Dick Netzer (Armonk, NY: M. E. Sharpe, 1990), 204.

35. *Bacon v. City of Detroit*, 282 Mich. 150 (1937), and *Walinske v. Detroit-Wayne Joint Bldg. Authority*, 325 Mich. 562 (1949). Joseph F. Gricar, "Municipal Corporations: Circumventing Municipal Debt Limitations," *Michigan Law Review* 48 (May 1950): 1019–1020. Also see, Eugene C. Lee, "Use of Lease-Purchase Agreements to Finance Capital Improvements," *Municipal Finance* 24 (November 1952): 78–81; and Jon Magnusson, "Lease Financing by Municipal Corporations As a Way Around Debt Limitation," *George Washington Law Review* 25 (March 1957).

36. *Comereski v. City of Elmira*, 308 NY 248 (1955), 254; and William J. Quirk and Leon E. Wein, "A Short Constitutional History of Entities Commonly Known as Authorities," *Cornell Law Review* 56 (April 1971): 583–585.

37. Walsh, *The Public's Business*, 133. In 1973 the combined debt of all New York State public authorities was $13.8 billion compared to the state's full-faith and credit debt of $3.5 billion. Figures from Underwood and Daniels, *Governor Rockefeller in New York*, table 6.5, p. 166, and table 6.6, p. 168, and Alan G. Hevesi, *Public Authority Reform: Reining in New York's Secret Government* (New York: Office of the State Comptroller, February 2004), 14.

38. Gail Radford, *The Rise of the Public Authority: Statebuilding and Economic Development in Twentieth-Century America* (Chicago: University

of Chicago Press, 2013), 150–152; Council of State Governments, *The Book of the States*, vol. 38 (Lexington, KY: Council of State Governments, 2006), 400. After 2002, the Census Bureau no longer distinguished between debt that was "guaranteed" and "non-guaranteed," so no later figures are available.

39. Henry, *Public Administration and Public Affairs*, 396; Jameson W. Doig, " 'If I See a Murderous Fellow Sharpening a Knife Cleverly…': The Wilsonian Dichotomy and the Public Authority Tradition," *Public Administration Review* 43 (July–August 1983): 295, 297; and Harold Hestnes, "Public Authorities: Should the State Take Away Their Power?" *Boston Globe*, November 7, 1986, 28, quoted in Jerry Mitchell, *The American Experiment with Government Corporations* (Armonk, NY: M. E. Sharpe, 1999), 65.

40. Walsh, *The Public's Business*, 3; and Alberta M. Sbragia, *Debt Wish: Entrepreneurial Cities, U.S. Federalism, and Economic Development* (Pittsburgh, PA: University of Pittsburgh Press, 1996), 14–15.

41. For example, James T. Bennett and Thomas J. DiLorenzo, *Underground Government: The Off-Budget Public Sector* (Washington, DC: Cato Institute, 1983); Donald Axelrod, *Shadow Government: The Hidden World of Public Authorities—And How They Control Over $1 Trillion of Your Money* (New York: John Wiley, 1992); Thomas H. Stanton, *A State of Risk: Will Government-Sponsored Enterprises Be the Next Financial Crisis?* (New York: HarperBusiness, 1991); Bert Ely, *The Farm Credit System: Reckless Past, Doubtful Future* (Alexandria, VA: Ely, 1999); Diana B. Henriques, *The Machinery of Greed: Public Authority Abuse and What to Do about It* (Lexington, MA: D.C. Heath, 1986); and Peter J. Wallison, ed., *Serving Two Masters, But Out of Control: Fannie Mae and Freddie Mac* (Washington, DC: AEI Press, 2001).

42. Emmette S. Redford and Charles B. Hagan, *American Government and the Economy* (New York: Macmillan, 1968), 623.

43. Albert Abel, "The Public Corporation in the United States," in *Government Enterprise: A Comparative Study*, ed. W. G. Friedmann (New York: Columbia University Press, 1970), 182. Harold Archer Van Dorn, *Government Owned Corporations* (New York: Knopf, 1926).

44. Radford, *The Rise of the Public Authority*, chaps. 1–2.

45. John McDiarmid, *Government Corporations and Federal Funds* (Chicago: University of Chicago Press, 1938).

46. General Accounting Office, *Reference Manual of Government Corporations, as of June 30, 1945,* Senate Doc 86, 79th Cong, 1st sess. (1945).

47. Abel, "The Public Corporation in the United States," 228.

48. Daniel Guttman, "Public Purpose and Private Service: The Twentieth Century Culture of Contracting Out and the Evolving Law of Diffused Sovereignty," *Administrative Law Review* 52 (2000): 868–872; U.S. Congress, Office of Technology Assessment, *A History of the Department of Defense Federally Funded Research and Development Centers* (Washington, June 1995), 16, 41–44; Alex Abella, *Soldiers of Reason: The RAND Corporation and the Rise of the American Empire* (Orlando, FL: Harcourt, Inc., 2008), 184–187, 202–212.

49. Harold Seidman, "The Quasi World of the Federal Government," *The Brookings Review* 6 (Summer 1988): 24; Harold Seidman, *Politics, Position and Power: The Dynamics of Federal Organization,* 5th ed. (New York: Oxford, 1998), 113–116; N. Eric Weiss, *Government Interventions in Financial Markets: Economic and Historic Analysis of Subprime Mortgage Options* (Washington, DC: Congressional Research Service, April 18, 2008), 8; Joseph Stiglitz and Bruce Greenwald, *Towards a New Paradigm in Monetary Economics* (Cambridge: Cambridge University Press, 2003), 239–244. A. Michael Froomkin refers to REFCORP as "little more than an accounting trick" in Froomkin, "Reinventing the Government Corporation," *University of Illinois Law Review* 1995, no.3: 543.

50. Ronald C. Moe, "The Emerging Federal Quasi Government: Issues of Management and Accountability," *Public Administration Review* 61 (May/June 2001): 290–293; and Nancy J. Knauer, "Reinventing Government: The Promise of Institutional Choice and Government Created Charitable Organizations," *New York School of Law Review* 42 (1997): 946, 954–958.

51. Ronald C. Moe, "The 'Reinventing Government' Exercise: Misinterpreting the Problem, Misjudging the Consequences," *Public Administration Review* 54 (March/April 1994): 111–122; Albert Gore, *From Red Tape to Results, Creating a Government That Works Better & Costs Less: Report*

of the National Performance Review (Washington, DC: The Review, 1993), 61. Other agencies identified by the National Performance Review (NPR) as appropriate for transformation into deregulated, self-funding operations include the U.S. Patent and Trademark Office, U.S. Mint, St. Lawrence Seaway Development Corporation, Department of Defense Commissary Agency, and Seafood Inspection Program. Alasdair Roberts, "Performance-Based Organizations: Assessing the Gore Plan," *Public Administration Review* 57 (November/December 1997): 465–478. U.S. General Accounting Office, *Government Corporations: Profiles of Recent Proposals,* GAO/66D-95-57FS (Washington, 1995).

52. Robert W. Poole, "The Urgent Need to Reform the FAA's Traffic Control System," *Backgrounder* #2007 (The Heritage Foundation, February 20, 2006), 6, (accessed July 6, 2011). http://www.heritage.org/Research/Reports/2007/02/The-Urgent-Need-to-Reform-the-FAAs-Air-Traffic-Control-System.

Gail Radford

SERVICE ECONOMIES AND THE AMERICAN POSTINDUSTRIAL CITY, 1950–PRESENT

FROM INDUSTRIAL TO POSTINDUSTRIAL METROPOLIS

In 1945, Manhattan's West Side was the heart of one of the world's largest industrial regions. On the streets nearest the waterfront, plants produced an array of products ranging from cookies to electrical equipment. Near Penn Station, presses printed a steady stream of catalogs and magazines. A little to the east, specialized districts devoted to apparel, fur, and hat manufacturing occupied Midtown.[1] Factories in Manhattan tended to be small, but within miles massive plants churned out ships, sugar, chemicals, and airplanes.

Manufacturing had a long presence in New York, but the plants on the West Side were recently built, when investors inundated the area with industrial lofts in the 1920s. At the same time, the Port Authority of New York and railroad companies built infrastructure to ensure the continued viability of industry in the city. These included state-of-the-art freight terminals, an elevated railroad, and the West Side Highway. Between the World Wars, private investors and city and state agencies made investments to preserve New York's viability as an industrial hub.

New York was not only a city of industry, but also of the working class. Workers in the city were among the most skilled in the United States and the most likely to be union members.[2] They helped fashion a city government devoted to liberalism. The city's public hospital and university systems; pools, beaches, and parks; and public housing all testified to a municipal government devoted to more than economic growth.[3] In the 1920s, New York's business and political leaders, the elite, and the working class often disagreed, but they agreed that manufacturing was vital to the future of the region.

Visiting the West Side of Manhattan in the early 21st century, however, it is hard to imagine the city's legacy as an industrial hub. Like most American cities, New York shifted from an industrial economy devoted to manufacturing goods to a postindustrial economy that produced services. The infrastructure built to keep industry in the city became the focal point of the postindustrial economy. Former freight terminals now house Google and clothing companies that manage globe-spanning production networks. The High Line still produces immense value; no longer by moving goods, but in the escalating prices of real estate. In the 1920s, the city's elite saw manufacturing as a vital, if annoying, aspect of the urban economy. By the 2000s, what manufacturing remained was at the periphery and under constant threat of displacement.[4]

On the 21st-century West Side, software engineers and fashion merchandisers work in former factories, couriers deliver lunches, and Amazon contractors pile packages in the shadow of former warehouses. An army of poorly paid workers, mostly immigrant women of color, polish nails, clean offices, care for children, and do a mind-boggling array of other work to keep the neighborhood functioning. If these workers make anything, it is temporary or immaterial. Their labor is often tied to manufacturing, but the production of material things usually occurs somewhere else. Like workers in the past, many of these service workers are immigrants. But unlike past workers, they often have long commutes, lack immigration status, and their primary job is to care for more privileged workers. In terms of the precarity of working-class labor and life, the postindustrial West Side is shockingly unimproved from a century earlier.

The West Side of Manhattan is an exaggerated but emblematic example of a massive change to urban economies in the United States after 1950. From New England mill towns to Sunbelt metropolises, a similar transformation has played out in cities across North America and abroad. Cities have been transformed from places for making things into places devoted to the provision of services. Manufacturing has either vanished or been pushed to the margins of the metropolis, replaced by media, entertainment, retail, tourism, personal and professional services, finance, insurance, real estate, health, education, and the administration of manufacturing that takes place somewhere else. A sharply bifurcated labor market—which operates through divisions of gender, race, and immigration status—has developed alongside these new urban economies.

The rapid remaking of the economy of North American cities raises important questions, not just for urban historians, but also for the broader field of history: how were these changes to capitalism and urban space coproduced? How did the postindustrial economy produce new or restore old social and political fractures? How did the workforce of the postindustrial city evolve and what was its class, gender, and racial composition? Who benefited from this change and how were these benefits allocated through the production of urban space?

WHAT IS THE POSTINDUSTRIAL SERVICE ECONOMY?

The postindustrialization of North American cities began at the turn of the century, accelerated rapidly after World War II, and neared its zenith in the decades after the oil shocks of 1973. Census data documents the broad shifts in employment in the postwar period. Nationally in 1950, 41 percent of workers were employed in blue-collar occupations, 37 percent in white-collar, 10 percent in services, and 12 percent in farming, fishing, and forestry.[5] By 1960, white-collar employment had surpassed blue-collar. By 1990, 58 percent of workers had white-collar occupations and 26 percent were blue-collar workers. In each decade since World War II, the growth of white-collar work far outpaced blue-collar work.

Data for workers by sector shows a similar pattern. Employment in manufacturing increased by 40 percent from 1950 to 1990. This was less than the 64 percent growth of population during this time and paled in comparison to increased employment in finance, insurance, and real estate at 317 percent and services at 274 percent. All service industries did not increase equally: employment in personal services increased by only 5 percent, whereas business and repair services increased by 295 percent and professional and related services by 478 percent.

The Census uses the term "services" for both a narrow set of occupations (household, police, firefighting, food preparation, and cleaning workers who made up 13 percent of the workforce in 1990) and a broader sector that produces services (27 percent of the workforce in 1990). This sector includes entertainment and recreation, healthcare, education, and repair, business, private household, legal, engineering, social, professional, and other services. The terms "service" and "postindustrial economy" refer to this broader sector rather than the much narrower occupational category.

Despite the growth of manufacturing in the South and West, the shift toward postindustrial employment was uniform across the United States (see table 1). In 1950, most of the twelve largest metropolitan regions in the United States had a relatively even number of white- and blue-collar workers. The exceptions were cities in the manufacturing belt where blue-collar workers outnumbered white-collar workers. In a few regions that had robust service economies or experienced early deindustrialization there were more white-collar workers than blue-collar workers.

By 1990 each of these twelve regions had significantly more white-collar than blue-collar workers. Even metropolitan regions, such as Los Angeles, which saw impressive manufacturing growth in the postwar years, were nonetheless far more white-collar cities by 1990. Each of the cities on this list either met or exceeded the national average for the percent of white-collar workers. This reflects the continued importance of manufacturing in smaller population centers that did not see the same expansion of employment in professional services and finance.

WHITHER MANUFACTURING?

Postindustrialization was the process by which finance and services replaced manufacturing as the primary form of capitalist production in North American cities. Postindustrialization was not something that happened to manufacturing firms, rather they contributed to this change. By the turn of the 20th century, manufacturing increasingly involved white-collar work. Engineers refined manufacturing processes.[6] Managers administered workforces. Advertisers created need among consumers. Most industries mechanized and experienced increased productivity. Fewer blue-collar workers produced more goods,

Table 1. Occupational Category (%) for the United States and Twelve Most Populated Metropolitan Areas in 1950 and 1990.

	1950		1990	
	White-collar %	Blue-collar %	White-collar %	Blue-collar %
United States	36.8	41.0	58.1	26.2
New York	48.0	38.9	70.4	21.7
Chicago	44.4	43.6	64.0	23.7
Los Angeles	48.7	37.7	59.9	26.6
Philadelphia	40.9	45.3	64.5	22.6
Detroit	38.4	50.1	58.8	27.6
Boston	48.4	39.0	70.2	16.9
San Francisco	50.2	35.2	66.6	20.2
Pittsburgh	38.7	49.6	61.2	23.6
St. Louis	42.1	43.6	61.6	24.1
Cleveland	43.2	45.4	61.5	25.3
Washington	57.9	25.3	73.2	14.5

but more white-collar workers were required to invent machines, induce demand, and supervise production. Large firms internalized producer services, but many also relied on outside companies for legal representation, accounting, management consulting, advertising, and research.[7] By the early 20th century, many of the largest cities in the United States were increasingly devoted to providing producer services to firms throughout the country. As services grew in importance in these cities, the fate of their economies was decoupled from local manufacturing.

The growth of the corporation and the increasing sophistication of manufacturing created an increasingly sharp division between what Harry Braverman called the execution and conceptualization of work. "Execution" refers to the physical labor of production and "conceptualization" to the administration of the labor process.[8] In the past, these two roles had taken place in close proximity to each other. For example, in the early iron industry, skilled craftsmen supervised workers and

developed new machinery and manufacturing techniques.[9] By the turn of the century, industrialists had successfully broken the control of the craftsmen and replaced them with less-skilled workers, machines, and a white-collar workforce that produced these machines. This was a seminal moment in the development of a postindustrial economy. It moved an increasingly large portion of the manufacturing workforce from industrial plants to offices where they managed the production process.[10]

This was a tremendous change to the geography of manufacturing. At first, engineers and managers might occupy a separate office building at the plant, but later, as transportation and communication technologies developed, offices moved further away. By the turn of the century corporate offices administered production networks that spanned the globe. Proximity to plants was no longer a necessary feature for corporate administration. Firms moved headquarters away from plants to Chicago or New York, because they offered easy access to finance and producer services.

The division between the conceptualization and execution of work also corresponded to a sharp divide between the middle and working classes. Middle-class, white-collar professionals, such as engineers and accountants, saw their work as different from that of manual workers. They believed they worked with their minds, rather than their hands.[11] Furthermore, they considered workers as just one of the many features of manufacturing they needed to control.[12] As companies sited new offices, proximity to industrial plants and working-class neighborhoods was not only unnecessary, it was also undesirable to white-collar workers.

The division between execution and conceptualization would set up the key feature of industrial firms in the postindustrial era: the tendency to invest in activities other than manufacturing. As firms grew larger, diversified, and moved their offices away from their plants, their economic fate was no longer tied to manufacturing. Firms could choose from reinvesting in plants or investing in real estate, stocks, or entirely different lines of work. The same applied to industrial cities, especially large ones, whose fate was now tied to their role as a center for corporate administration, finance, and producer services, rather than manufacturing.

The increased mobility of industrial capital and mechanization radically transformed the character and geography of manufacturing in the postwar period. Due to the rise of trucking, the draw of nonunionized labor, federal tax incentives, and companies' preference for flow-through design, manufacturing increasingly located away from large cities.[13] Throughout the postwar period, industrial firms moved plants to suburbs and small towns, the South and the West, and the global South. By 1990, a significant portion of white-collar workers in large cities still worked in manufacturing, but this typically involved managing dispersed production networks.

In the postwar years, industry funneled investment out of manufacturing and into other activities. Companies that had expanded production facilities rapidly during and after World War II and had increasing profits in the 1950s and 1960s, did not consider it profitable to invest further in manufacturing. Instead, they turned to investments in nonindustrial activities. In the 1960s, Alcoa became one of the largest urban developers in the country, while Weyerhaeuser, Kaiser, and other companies built suburbs. Other major players in real estate included Phillip Morris, Ford, Westinghouse, US Steel, Gulf Oil, Chevron, and Chrysler.[14] Real estate provided a "spatial fix"—an investment outlet for companies with surplus cash.[15]

Manufacturing firms did not stick to real estate. By the late 1980s, GE transitioned from manufacturing to become one of the largest financial firms in the country. Westinghouse followed suit and was bankrupted in the process. While closing its mills, US Steel developed malls and office towers and purchased Marathon Oil. The owners of private industry also got in on the action, with coal barons, plumbing supply and pet food magnates, and many an oil titan transforming themselves into developers, resort owners, venture capitalists, and leveraged buyout investors. By the late 1980s industrialists and industrial firms increasingly pursued activities other than manufacturing.

The history of postindustrialization is often written as an unfortunate calamity that befell industrial firms and the cities they called home. In fact, industrial firms cannibalized their plants in order to make the leap into the postindustrial economy. They strategically moved their investments between growing and declining regions and sectors of the economy. The strategy often had limited success, but it usually played out to the benefit of stockholders and executives. It devastated smaller industrial cities. In larger cities, local leaders and planners, who saw a need to diversify and modernize the economy, often supported this strategy.[16] They effectively transitioned cities from industrial to white-collar centers but shattered manufacturing communities on their peripheries in the process.

NEW WORK AND NEW DIVISIONS

Two broad characteristics defined the postindustrial service economy. First, it was the result of major economic shifts that increased the prevalence of workers and sectors that produced services rather than manufactured goods. Second, this radically changed the character of work and everyday life and the makeup of the workforce.

The sectors with the largest increase in employment during the postwar period were finance, insurance, and real estate and services. The growth of the real estate industry corresponded to suburbanization and the expansion of home ownership after World War II. Prior to that, real estate development had been a mostly small-scale industry. After the war, builders like William Levitt developed large tracts of land and applied the tools of mass production to home construction.[17] The growth of the finance, insurance, and real estate sectors was in part the product of the federal government subsidizing the ability of more Americans to take on debt.

By 1970 services exceeded manufacturing as the largest sector of the US economy. The service sector contained many fields. One of the biggest and fastest growing was business services, such as law, engineering, advertising, and accounting. Firms in this field not only sold services to US-based companies, but also to companies abroad. As many companies emphasized leanness and flexibility, they moved toward an increased reliance on contracts with business service firms. As fiscal crises struck local, state, and federal governments, they too contracted with these same firms.

Education and healthcare accounted for another significant portion of the growing service sector. University enrollments expanded after World War II, as university degrees became necessary credentials to work in the service sector. Hospitals also grew significantly and by the year 2000 were the largest employers in many cities. For the most part education and healthcare jobs could not be relocated offshore, and as a result they accounted for much of the employment growth in urban areas.

The federal government subsidized the growth of the education and medical sectors by steadily pumping funds into research. This exacerbated inequalities between regions. The South, the West, and southern New England tended to be the primary recipients of these lucrative contracts, which led to the explosive growth of regions such as southern California. By the 1950s, federal research funds flowed mostly to a few major universities, especially those in Boston and the San Francisco Bay Area. These funds provided a direct economic stimulus to these regions and existing firms and new spin-offs benefited from their proximity to research centers.

Between 1948 and 1990 women's participation in the labor force increased from 32 percent to 57 percent. Women made up a majority of service workers, especially those who cared for children, the sick, and the elderly. This care work was based on intimate interactions with clients, rather than the more distanced relationships that characterized work in manufacturing or business services. This work was highly gendered and employers typically paid low wages and capitalized on women's supposed natural propensity to care for others.[18] The expansion of the postindustrial economy created both demand for care workers and a labor pool to fill these difficult jobs. Deindustrialization devastated working-class communities that had relied on a sharp gendered division of labor between wage-earning men and women who did unpaid work at home. Plant shutdowns led more women to enter the service sector. The absence of women at home, where in the past they provided these services for no pay, further fueled the need for care workers.[19] Women from the Global South were another key source of labor for this growing sector.[20]

Retailing, entertainment, and tourism were also important parts of the postindustrial economy. These industries experienced significant consolidation over the postwar years with large chains replacing family-owned hotels and massive retailers replacing main street stores. Increased incomes and consumer debt fueled the growth of retailing during the postwar years. Like care work, these sectors were heavily reliant on women and people of color to do the interactive labor that was required.

Mirroring the expansion of the warfare and welfare states, government employment increased during this time period and much of it was directly tied to the postindustrial economy. A large number of government employees were on active duty in the military. Despite occasional base closings, the military was a permanent feature of the postindustrial economy and its federal appropriations rarely decreased. Defense spending stimulated growth in the southern and western United States at the expense of the manufacturing belt.[21]

One of the defining features of the early postwar years were white-collar and blue-collar workers who spent their entire careers working for one company. In a period of economic expansion, this Fordist arrangement offered workers decent wages and benefits and firms a stable workforce. In the 1970s, with the slowdown in the US economy, increased foreign competition, the decline of organized labor, and corporate firms' embrace of outsourcing and flexibility, Fordism fractured.[22] Workers increasingly moved between many positions throughout their lifetimes. Dual narratives were attached to this increasingly mobile workforce. Some celebrated precarity as the liberating potential of a free labor market. As this story went, workers were free to move between employers and regions to fully realize their potential and be rewarded

in the process.[23] In contrast to this narrative, many workers argued that the primary feature of increasingly precarious employment was firms' ability to access labor when they needed it and dispose of it when they did not. Employers increasingly relied on temporary labor, and temp firms supplied this disposable workforce. After 1970, precarious employment was not just a feature of agricultural, blue-collar, and service occupations, but was also ubiquitous in fields such as nursing, scientific research, and university teaching.

Three broad trends augmented the renormalization of precarious labor in the decades since the 1970s. First, many firms turned from a Fordist strategy that internalized all the necessary components of production to one that prioritized flexibility and relied on outsourcing in order to externalize risk. This outsourcing drove both the growth of business services and the precarity of white-collar and blue-collar work. Second, despite the efforts of unions to break into the South and white-collar professions and their successes organizing public sector and healthcare workers, union membership steadily declined after 1970. Finally, educated middle-class professionals embraced the idea that work was more than just labor and involved pursuing your passions and doing good in the world. This ideology of work as passion allowed firms to thrive in an economic system built on the valorization of mobile and disposable labor.

Another feature of the postindustrial economy was a dual labor market. In this dual labor market, a portion of the population by virtue of status, geography, gender, race, citizenship, and education gained access to well-remunerated employment in growing areas of the postindustrial economy. The same features restricted another far larger portion of the population to a narrower labor market where they largely provided services to this more affluent population.[24] Many of the most rapidly growing areas of the economy were especially marked by divisions of race and geography. For example, for decades African

Americans struggled to obtain employment in the tech industry both because of the tendency for workplaces to be located in the suburbs and structural barriers that made it more difficult for them to acquire university degrees in technical fields. The ability of whites, often aided by federal assistance, to access university education and employment in growing sectors of the economy increased racial inequality in the postwar years.[25] After 1970, the postindustrial economy led to persistent increases in income inequality in the United States. The prosperity of certain white-collar professionals in the postindustrial economy was conditioned on the exploitation of poorly compensated service workers, in particular women, immigrants, and people of color.

PLANNING POSTINDUSTRIAL SPACE

Since the beginning of the profession, planners were committed to expertise and allied themselves with "the new middle class."[26] Despite their professed objectivity, planners were fundamentally interested in working within, rather than disrupting, existing economic systems.[27] As planning developed as a profession, planners helped to reshape the city and its suburbs in the interest of postindustrial firms and white-collar professionals.

The planning profession first developed to resolve the problems of the industrial city. Planners developed parks to provide clean air and civilizing recreation, replaced "slums" with garden suburbs, and developed zoning laws to limit the locations of industry, immigrants, and African Americans. Early regional plans mapped economic activity to ensure that urban areas could function as centers of white-collar work.[28] Prior to World War II, planners' primary goal was to solve the problem of industry, often by pushing it to the margins of the city, rather than entirely removing it.

This practice shifted after World War II when federal and state governments gave planners more tools to clear neighborhoods for highways and redevelopment projects. Local governments targeted working-class, African-American, and Latino neighborhoods and industrial areas for renewal, which they saw as obsolete and inimical to their vision of the postindustrial city. They replaced these neighborhoods with stadiums, theaters, expanded university campuses and hospitals, office towers, apartment complexes, parking garages, and parks that were intended to appeal to white-collar professionals.

In the 1950s, while local governments cleared neighborhoods for redevelopment, the federal government, through tax codes and interventions in the housing market, subsidized the movement of housing, office buildings, industry, and retail into the suburbs. As is well known, the federal government provided generous but largely invisible support for white working- and middle-class people to move into the suburbs.[29] The federal government also used tax incentives, sometimes in the name of national defense, to subsidize the suburbanization of industry, office buildings, and retail centers.[30] These incentives and high corporate tax rates meant that new construction in the suburbs was highly affordable for many firms.

The federal tax code provided a financial incentive, but this was not the only reason firms moved to the suburbs. Executives and architects saw the suburbs as offering more amendable conditions for doing business. A greenfield site offered the opportunity to design a facility with fewer constraints than crowded urban areas. The suburbs also provided proximity to a desired workforce. For industries that employed large numbers of unskilled clerical workers, such as insurance, the suburbs supplied a captive feminized workforce. Department stores moved to the suburbs to capitalize on women's labor and to avoid unions.[31] Many companies built state of the art laboratories and offices in the suburbs to attract white-collar workers who were in high demand.[32] Employees, shareholders, and consumers saw modern suburban offices as indicative of a growing company. New facilities in the suburbs were a lucrative way for firms to reinvest profits and to attract investors, employees, and customers.

The movement of firms to the suburbs exacerbated cities' need to retain employers and tax dollars. This often led planners to suburbanize the urban built form. Along with clearing neighborhoods for parking, planners squeezed suburban homes onto urban lots, developed designs that emphasized defensive space, and closed commercial streets to traffic. One of the defining features of the postindustrial city in the 1960s and 1970s was the massive self-contained office center, such as the Prudential Center in Boston and Peachtree Center in Atlanta. Employees could enter these complexes in their cars and fulfill their every need without stepping outside. Planners in Calgary, Minneapolis, Montreal, and other cities took this further and created networks of quasipublic tunnels and skyways that connected entire downtowns. As cities emulated the suburbs, public space came under increasingly private control.

While cities struggled to attract business, some middle-class residents began to move into former working-class and industrial neighborhoods. Postindustrialization drove this process of gentrification. The exodus of industrial capital depreciated land values, making property in former industrial and working-class neighborhoods highly affordable for developers and new residents.[33] While industry disinvested from plants and laid off workers, firms increased the number of jobs in finance and professional services. Growing numbers of white-collar professionals sought out urban neighborhoods that offered affordable housing, shorter commutes, appealing lifestyles, and an alternative to suburban conformity.[34] Postindustrialization created both a supply of devalued property and white-collar professionals that demanded this housing.

Despite efforts by municipal leaders to imitate the suburbs and the gentrification of some neighborhoods, by the 1970s many cities were still losing population and employers. This left cities with older infrastructure and a disproportionate share of poor and elderly residents who were most reliant on public services. By the 1970s, many cities struggled to collect enough revenue to meet their annual budgets. Debt holders and state and federal government used these fiscal crises to tame the ambitions of city governments.[35] They required cities to raise taxes, sell off public assets, and reduce their payroll. This increased the perception that cities were in decline and accelerated the movement of people to the suburbs. Under the constraints of the urban crisis, increasingly indebted cities abandoned liberal agendas and began to prioritize attracting businesses and wealthy residents over all other concerns. This shift in urban governance from liberalism to neoliberalism created new opportunities for the growth of the service sector.

NEOLIBERALIZATION AND THE POSTINDUSTRIAL CITY

City governments embraced neoliberal policies in response to the urban crisis. Neoliberalism, as a philosophy and diverse set of policies, prioritizes markets and individual freedom over state intervention. Many scholars have emphasized the role of cities as sites of neoliberal policy formation.[36] One key aspect of neoliberal urban policy was the rollback of government services, layoffs of public employees, and reliance on user fees to fund the services that remained.[37] New York, under the strategy of triage, abandoned poor neighborhoods such as the South Bronx. The rationale behind this strategy was that limited budgets forced cities to be strategic about where they deployed services. Most cities informally adopted triage and concentrated services in affluent and "transitional" neighborhoods in order to retain and attract wealthy residents.

Neoliberal policies not only cut services, but also created opportunities for the private sector to replace these services. The most notable examples of these polices, what Peck and Tickell term "rollout neoliberalization," were in education, business improvement districts (BIDs), public housing, and parks. In the absence of public services, business owners formed BIDs that took on the task of cleaning sidewalks, removing graffiti, and policing. Like triage, this strategy of rolling out the market provision of public services often meant that affluent parts of the city received impeccable privately supported services while the city failed to maintain amenities in poorer neighborhoods.

Neoliberalism pitted neighborhoods against each other in a scramble for resources, but it also created an increasingly entrepreneurial style of urban governance, in which cities competed with each other for employers, sports franchises, national events, and affluent residents. The rise of urban entrepreneurialism was not simply the result of the increased mobility of capital, but also municipal debt holders' ability to dictate policy.[38] According to Harvey this shift toward entrepreneurialism had three key components. It relied on public-private partnerships in which the primary role of the public sector was to generate private development. It was speculative in nature, meaning that cities invested in amenities that they hoped would attract investment and bore the financial risk for these efforts. And finally, the goal of urban entrepreneurialism was not to address the concerns of current residents, but rather to market it to people and investment from outside.[39] Cities across the United States and around the world increasingly competed with each other to attract outside investors, tourists, and potential new residents.

In the 1970s many of these efforts became highly sophisticated. New York, which faced a growing reputation as broke, crime-ridden, and abandoned, mobilized the expertise of Madison Avenue advertisers to solve its problems. The goal of the "I Love New York" and other campaigns was to restore the image of the city and to encourage tourists, businesses,

and residents to return.[40] Pittsburgh and Cleveland imitated New York and created branding campaigns that emphasized their appeal for middle-class professionals and postindustrial enterprises, while scarcely mentioning the working class or industry.[41] Branding had several advantages: it built directly on the expertise of the service sector, spoke the language of the residents and businesses it hoped to attract, and was relatively cheap.

Neoliberal and entrepreneurial urban policy was built around the idea of attracting firms and workers who, as the story went, could freely choose where to locate. If cities succeeded then the benefits would supposedly trickle down to everyone. The firms that urban governments embraced were in the rapidly growing service sector, especially finance, corporate administration, tourism, and professional services. The desired residents were college-educated middle-class professionals. Local governments emphasized making cities "livable" for these desired residents and media and academics ranked cities on the basis of livability. Cities even used these flawed rankings as the basis for policymaking.[42]

THE FUTURE OF THE POSTINDUSTRIAL CITY

By 2015, the postindustrial economy was more significant than ever. Technology and financial firms were leading actors in many cities. These industries generated unprecedented concentrations of wealth and ever more profitable ways of immiserating people. Not content to just steal homes and neighborhoods, they also turned to transforming schools, parks, transportation systems, and social services into profit-making enterprises. The postindustrial economy valorized educated white-collar workers over all others. It offered a steady pabulum of more business and technology as the only solutions to social problems. Immigrant and racialized workers, whose labor was made hyperexploitable by this economic system, found themselves scape-goats for the economic insecurity it created.[43] The postindustrial economy intensified many of the same injustices and contradictions that had defined American cities and suburbs in the past.

DISCUSSION OF THE LITERATURE

After World War II, many commentators documented the shift to a postindustrial econ-omy. Sociologist C. Wright Mills analyzed the alienated character of white-collar work, urbanist William Whyte chronicled the rise of middle-class "organization men," and man-agement consultant Peter Drucker coined the phrase "knowledge worker."[44] The term "postindustrial" first gained currency among the New Left, who saw the shifting economy offering new sites of struggle and the possibil-ity of liberation.[45] Taking a liberal perspec-tive, Daniel Bell popularized the term in the late 1960s, arguing that the United States was entering a new technology-driven era of progress that would be led by white-collar professionals.[46]

With the exception of Whyte, most early work on postindustrialism was concerned with broad social prognosis and was disengaged with cities as sites of economic activity. In 1968, Henri Lefebvre provided a broad frame-work for understanding the capitalist produc-tion of urban space. While Lefebvre never used the term "postindustrial," he authored a theory of how the production of urban space had replaced manufacturing as the primary form of capital accumulation.[47]

Much of the historical research on postin-dustrial urban economies includes case stud-ies of metropolitan regions. Many of these studies examine how political and business leaders in industrial cities responded to the decline of manufacturing and tried to attract businesses and residents, including recent case studies of Bethlehem and Cleveland and older work on Camden and St. Louis.[48] Studies of northern industrial cities dominate the

field, but there is also significant research on Sunbelt cities. Among other topics, histori-ans explore how local boosters in the Sunbelt attempted to attract investment and popula-tion by developing environmental amenities or a business-friendly policies.[49] Other re-search examines the political culture of segre-gated white-collar suburbs and gentrifying urban neighborhoods and their effect on local and national politics.[50]

Recent scholarship has pointed to the need to understand the rise of postindustrial cities within a transnational context. Tracy Neumann shows how ideas about postindustrialism moved among North American and European cities.[51] Samuel Zipp describes how planners framed blueprints for urban renewal within the context of the Cold War.[52] Andrew Fried-man examines how intelligence agencies cre-ated conditions in Washington, DC's suburbs that allowed them to covertly exercise power abroad. Betsy Beasley traces how university and business leaders in Houston formed inti-mate relationships with international students in order to facilitate the sale of oil services. Much of this work shows how seemingly mun-dane spaces of the city, such as strip malls and pool parties, allowed for the fashioning of transnational networks that were vital to American imperialism.[53] Given that postin-dustrial cities were often command and con-trol centers, there is much potential in re-search that examines how global processes were rooted in urban space.

Not all work on postindustrial cities is built on case studies of metropolitan regions. A significant amount of research considers the importance of universities as political and economic actors in cities. Margaret Pugh O'Mara first sketched out how university re-search became central to postwar urban econo-mies, and other scholars have added to her work.[54] Recent studies also explore the grow-ing prominence of hospitals as real estate de-velopers, employers, and economic engines.[55] Other research traces the movement of re-search laboratories and office building to the suburbs and emphasizes how employers attracted white-collar employees by touting the suburban locations of these facilities.[56] Urban historians have long written on the development of suburban malls and the decline of downtown shopping districts.[57]

One glaring absence in the study of postindustrial cities is the lack of attention on labor. Few urban historians examines the lives of workers in postindustrial workplaces. Service workers, such as cleaners, security guards, and childcare workers are especially invisible in the field. This is a glaring absence given that service work was and remains vital to the functioning of the postindustrial city and central to urban historians' core interests, including segregation, suburbanization, and gentrification. There are a number of junior scholars whose work shows the potential that a focus on labor can bring to urban history.[58]

Urban historians have not devoted adequate attention to business's role in reshaping postwar cities, except for real estate. Few studies explore the role of specific firms or industries in shaping the economy and the built form of cities during the postwar period.[59] As a result, the key texts that theorize the rise of postindustrial urban economies are largely by geographers, sociologists, and other social scientists rather than urban historians.[60]

PRIMARY SOURCES

For the most part, urban historians who study postindustrial urban economies have tended to do research in local and state archives rather than the National Archives. In some regions, municipal archives have useful materials, including the Cuyahoga County Archive in Cleveland and the New York Municipal Archives. In other regions, government records are often not available, in which case universities and local archives hold the most extensive and well-cataloged collections. For example, rich Bay Area sources are located in the Bancroft Library, in Austin in the Austin History Center, and in Detroit in the Walter P.

Reuther Library. For those doing research on suburbs, local public libraries and suburban municipalities often have unprocessed records.[61] The Avery Library at Columbia University holds the architectural records of many key modern architects. Finally, extensive online archives include Historic Pittsburgh, Virtual Motor City, and Virtual Cleveland History.

Individual firms often will not provide access to their records. Some researchers have obtained permission and others rely on records donated to archives, such as the Hagley Collection. Even if one gains access to such collections they tend to be carefully curated, contain largely public relations materials, and reveal little about the day-to-day operations of firms. Most firms have public relations offices that will provide varying levels of assistance to researchers. ProQuest Historic Annual Reports are another excellent source of information about publicly traded companies.

Urban historians also do research in the National Archives and individual presidential libraries. The most visited record groups in the National Archives pertain to housing and urban renewal, including Housing and Urban Development, Department of Commerce, Home Owners' Loan Association, Economic Development Commission, and Federal Housing Administration. Urban historians who have worked in presidential libraries tend to examine a particular moment of national concern, such as the New York fiscal crisis.

Trade magazines and journals are increasingly digitized and public libraries often hold back issues. Journals such as *Architectural Forum* and *Architectural Record* are great sources of building plans and related discussions. Trade journals provide a sense of the social and professional lives of various professions ranging from nuclear engineers to social workers. Newspapers, whether on microfilm or digitized, remain key sources for urban historians.

Census records are freely available online for the post–World War II era. These records provide data about home ownership, occupations, race, and other basic demographics. Beginning in 1940 this data is usually available at the tract level for most major metropolitan areas. Working with this data over time can be highly frustrating because of changes to geographic boundaries and demographic categories. The Manufacturing Census and data from the Bureau of Labor Statistics is also helpful for getting a sense of changing economic patterns at the metropolitan, state, and national levels.

Many urban historians of postindustrial cities use oral histories. Some collect oral histories themselves and others use recordings and transcripts that are held in archives. Finally, a few urban historians use ethnographic methods, but this primarily consists of a combination of oral histories and archival research, rather than participant observation or more embedded research.

FURTHER READING

Braverman, Harry. *Labor and Monopoly Capital.* New York: Monthly Review Press, 1974.

Cummings, Alex Sayf. "'Brain Magnet': Research Triangle Park and the Origins of the Creative City, 1953–1965." *Journal of Urban History* 43, no. 3 (2017): 470–492.

Gillette, Howard, Jr. *Camden after the Fall: Decline and Renewal in a Post-Industrial City.* Philadelphia: University of Pennsylvania Press, 2006.

Greenberg, Miriam. *Branding New York: How a City in Crisis Was Sold to the World.* New York: Routledge, 2008.

Harvey, David. "From Managerialism to Entrepreneurialism: The Transformation in Urban Governance in Late Capitalism." *Geografiska Annaler I,* Series B, Human Geography, 71, no. 1 (1989): 3–17.

Heathcott, Joseph, and Maire Agnes Murphy. "Corridors of Flight, Zones of Renewal: Industry, Planning, and Policy in the Making of Metropolitan St. Louis, 1940–1980." *Journal of Urban History* 31, no. 2 (2005): 151–189.

Lefebvre, Henri. *The Urban Revolution.* Minneapolis: University of Minnesota Press, 2003.

McDowell, Linda. *Working Bodies: Interactive Service Employment and Workplace Identities.* Malden, MA: Wiley-Blackwell, 2009.

Mozingo, Louise. *Pastoral Capitalism: A History of Suburban Corporate Landscapes.* Cambridge, MA: MIT Press, 2011.

Neumann, Tracy. *Remaking the Rust Belt: The Postindustrial Transformation of North America.* Philadelphia: University of Pennsylvania Press, 2016.

Rubin, Elihu. *Insuring the City: The Prudential Center and the Postwar Urban Landscape.* New Haven: Yale University Press, 2012.

Shermer, Elizabeth Tandy. *Sunbelt Capitalism: Phoenix and the Transformation of American Politics.* Philadelphia: University of Pennsylvania Press, 2013.

Taft, Chloe E. *From Steel to Slots: Casino Capitalism in the Postindustrial City.* Cambridge, MA: Harvard University Press, 2016.

Vitale, Patrick. "Cradle of the Creative Class: Reinventing the Figure of the Scientist in Cold War Pittsburgh." *Annals of the American Association of Geographers* 106, no. 6 (2016): 1378–1396.

Winant, Gabriel. "A Place to Die: Nursing Home Abuse and the Political Economy of the 1970s." *Journal of American History* 105, no. 1 (2018): 96–120.

NOTES

1. Joshua Benjamin Freeman, *Working-Class New York: Life and Labor since World War II* (New York: New Press, 2000).
2. Freeman, *Working-Class New York.*
3. Mason B. Williams, *City of Ambition: FDR, La Guardia, and the Making of Modern New York* (New York: W. W. Norton, 2013).
4. Tom Agnotti and Sylvia Morse, *Zoned Out! Race, Displacement, and City Planning in New York City* (New York: Urban Research, 2016).
5. The Census Bureau changed the way it categorized workers in 1970. In order to track changes to occupations across the postwar period it is necessary to use the overly broad categories "white collar" and "blue collar." From 1940 to 1960, white collar included: professional, technical, and kindred workers; managers, officials, and proprietors (excluding farmers); clerical and kindred workers; and sales workers. Blue collar included: craftsmen, foremen, and kindred

workers; operatives and kindred workers; and laborers. From 1970 to 1990, white collar included: managerial and professional specialty occupations and technical, sales, and administrative support occupations. Blue collar included: precision production, craft, and repair occupations and operators, fabricators, and laborers. The Census used the category "service workers" consistently from 1940 to 1990.

6. David Hounshell, "The Evolution of Industrial Research in the United States," in *Engines of Innovation: US Industrial Research at the End of an Era*, ed. Richard Rosenbloom and William J. Spencer (Boston: Harvard Business School Press, 1996), 13–85.

7. Christopher D. McKenna, *The World's Newest Profession: Management Consulting in the Twentieth Century* (Cambridge: Cambridge University Press, 2006).

8. Harry Braverman, *Labor and Monopoly Capital* (New York: Monthly Review Press, 1974).

9. Thomas J. Misa, *A Nation of Steel: The Making of Modern America, 1865–1925* (Baltimore: Johns Hopkins University Press, 1995).

10. David Noble, *America by Design: Science, Technology, and the Rise of Corporate Capitalism* (Oxford: Oxford University Press, 1977).

11. Patrick Vitale, "Making Science Suburban: The Suburbanization of Industrial Research and the Invention of 'Research Man,'" *Environment and Planning A: Economy and Space* 49, no. 12 (2017): 2813–2834.

12. Daniel Nelson, *Managers and Workers: Origins of the Twentieth-Century Factory System in the United States, 1880–1920* (Madison: University of Wisconsin Press, 1995).

13. Jefferson Cowie, *Capital Moves: RCA's 70-Year Quest for Cheap Labor* (Ithaca, NY: Cornell University Press, 1999); and Thomas Sugrue, *The Origins of the Urban Crisis: Race and Inequality in Postwar Detroit* (Princeton, NJ: Princeton University Press, 1998).

14. Andrew Wiese, "'The Giddy Rise of the Environmentalists': Corporate Real Estate Development and Environmental Politics in San Diego, California, 1968–1973," *Environmental History* 19, no. 1 (2014): 28–54.

15. David Harvey, *The Urban Experience* (Baltimore: Johns Hopkins University Press, 1989).

16. Patrick Vitale, "Decline Is Renewal," *Journal of Urban History* 41, no. 1 (2015): 34–39.

17. Barbara Kelly, *Expanding the American Dream: Building and Rebuilding Levittown* (Albany: State University of New York Press, 1993).

18. Arlie Russell Hochschild, *The Managed Heart: Commercialization of Human Feeling* (Berkeley: University of California Press, 1983); and Linda McDowell, *Working Bodies: Interactive Service Employment and Workplace Identities* (Malden, MA: Wiley-Blackwell, 2009).

19. Gabriel Winant, "A Place to Die: Nursing Home Abuse and the Political Economy of the 1970s," *Journal of American History* 105, no. 1 (2018): 96–120.

20. Evelyn Nakano Glenn, *Forced to Care: Coercion and Caregiving in America* (Cambridge, MA: Harvard University Press, 2010).

21. Ann R. Markusen, Peter Hall, Scott Campbell, and Sabina Deitrick, *The Rise of the Gunbelt: The Military Remapping of Industrial America* (Oxford: Oxford University Press, 1991).

22. David Harvey, *The Condition of Postmodernity* (Cambridge, MA: Blackwell, 1990).

23. Richard L. Florida, *The Rise of the Creative Class: And How It's Transforming Work, Leisure, Community and Everyday Life* (New York: Basic Books, 2002).

24. John H. Mollenkopf and Manuel Castells, eds., *Dual City: Restructuring New York* (New York: Russell Sage Foundation, 1991).

25. Ira Katznelson, *When Affirmative Action Was White* (New York: W. W. Norton, 2005).

26. John D. Fairfield, "The Scientific Management of Urban Space: Professional City Planning and the Legacy of Progressive Reform," *Journal of Urban History* 20 (1994): 179–204; and Robert H. Wiebe, *The Search for Order, 1877–1920* (New York: Hill and Wang, 1967).

27. David Harvey, *The Urbanization of Capital: Studies in the History and Theory of Capitalist Urbanization* (Baltimore: John Hopkins University Press, 1985).

28. Robert Fishman, "The Regional Plan and the Transformation of the Industrial Metropolis," in *The Landscape of Modernity: Essays on New York City, 1900–1940*, ed. David Ward and Olivier Zunz (Baltimore: John Hopkins University Press, 1992), 106–125.

29. David Freund, *Colored Property: State Policy and White Racial Politics in Suburban America* (Chicago: University of Chicago Press, 2007); and Kenneth T. Jackson, *Crabgrass Frontier: The*

Suburbanization of the United States (New York: Oxford University Press, 1985).

30. Thomas W. Hanchett, "U.S. Tax Policy and the Shopping-Center Boom of the 1950s and 1960s," *American Historical Review* 101, no. 4 (1996): 1082–1110; and Jennifer S. Light, *From Warfare to Welfare: Defense Intellectuals and Urban Problems in Cold War America* (Baltimore: Johns Hopkins University Press, 2003).

31. Minna P. Ziskind, "Labor Conflict in the Suburbs: Organizing Retail in Metropolitan New York, 1954–1958," *International Labor and Working-Class History* 64 (2003): 55–73.

32. Layne Karafantis and Stuart W. Leslie, "'Suburban Warriors': The Blue-Collar and Blue-Sky Communities of Southern California's Aerospace Industry," *Journal of Planning History* (January 29, 2018): 1–24; and David Kaiser, "The Postwar Suburbanization of American Physics," *American Quarterly* 56 (2004): 851–888.

33. Neil Smith, *The New Urban Frontier: Gentrification and the Revanchist City* (New York: Routledge, 1996).

34. David Ley, *New Middle Class and the Remaking of the Central City* (Oxford: Oxford University Press, 1996); and Suleiman Osman, *The Invention of Brownstone Brooklyn: Gentrification and the Search for Authenticity in Postwar New York* (Oxford: Oxford University Press, 2011).

35. Kim Phillips-Fein, *Fear City: New York's Fiscal Crisis and the Rise of Austerity Politics* (New York: Metropolitan Books, 2017).

36. Neil Brenner and Nik Theodore, "Cities and the Geographies of 'Actually Existing Neoliberalism,'" *Antipode* 34, no. 3 (2002): 349–379; and Jason Hackworth, *The Neoliberal City: Governance, Ideology, and Development in American Urbanism* (Ithaca, NY: Cornell University Press, 2007).

37. Jamie Peck and Adam Tickell, "Neoliberalizing Space," *Antipode* 34, no. 3 (2002): 380–404.

38. Hackworth, *Neoliberal City*.

39. David Harvey, "From Managerialism to Entrepreneurialism: The Transformation in Urban Governance in Late Capitalism," *Geografiska Annaler*, Series B, Human Geography, 71, no. 1 (1989): 3–17.

40. Miriam Greenberg, *Branding New York: How a City in Crisis Was Sold to the World* (New York: Routledge, 2008).

41. Tracy Neumann, "Reforging the Steel City: Symbolism and Space in Postindustrial Pittsburgh," *Journal of Urban History* 44, no. 4 (2018): 582–602; and J. Mark Souther, *Believing in Cleveland: Managing Decline in "The Best Location in the Nation"* (Philadelphia: Temple University Press, 2017).

42. Eugene J. McCann, "'Best Places': Interurban Competition, Quality of Life and Popular Media Discourse," *Urban Studies* 41, no. 10 (2004): 1909–1929; and Ted Rutland, "Enjoyable Life: Planning, Amenity, and the Contested Terrain of Biopolitics," *Environment and Planning D: Society and Space* 33, no. 5 (2015): 850–868.

43. Llana Barber, *Latino City: Immigration and Urban Crisis in Lawrence, Massachusetts, 1945–2000* (Chapel Hill: The University of North Carolina Press, 2017).

44. C. Wright Mills, *White Collar: The American Middle Classes* (New York: Oxford University Press, 1951); William H. Whyte, *The Organization Man* (New York: Simon and Schuster, 1956); Peter F. Drucker, *Landmarks of Tomorrow* (New York: Harper & Row, 1957); and Alex Sayf Cummings, "Of Sorcerers and Thought Leaders: Marketing the Information Revolution in the 1960s," *The Sixties* 9, no. 1 (2016): 1–25.

45. Howard Brick, "Optimism of the Mind: Imagining Postindustrial Society in the 1960s and 1970s," *American Quarterly* 44, no. 3 (1992): 351.

46. Daniel Bell, "Notes on the Post-Industrial Society (I)," *Public Interest* 6 (Winter 1967): 24–35.

47. Henri Lefebvre, *The Urban Revolution* (Minneapolis: University of Minnesota Press, 2003).

48. Chloe E. Taft, *From Steel to Slots: Casino Capitalism in the Postindustrial City* (Cambridge, MA: Harvard University Press, 2016); Souther, *Believing in Cleveland*; Howard Gillette Jr., *Camden after the Fall: Decline and Renewal in a Post-Industrial City* (Philadelphia: University of Pennsylvania Press, 2006); and Joseph Heathcott and Maire Agnes Murphy, "Corridors of Flight, Zones of Renewal: Industry, Planning, and Policy in the Making of Metropolitan St. Louis, 1940–1980," *Journal of Urban History* 31, no. 2 (2005): 151–189.

49. Andrew Busch, *City in a Garden: Environmental Transformations and Racial Justice in Twentieth-Century Austin, Texas* (Chapel Hill: University of North Carolina Press, 2017); and Elizabeth

Tandy Shermer, *Sunbelt Capitalism: Phoenix and the Transformation of American Politics* (Philadelphia: University of Pennsylvania Press, 2013).

50. Lily Geismer, *Don't Blame Us: Suburban Liberals and the Transformation of the Democratic Party* (Princeton, NJ: Princeton University Press, 2014); Lisa McGirr, *Suburban Warriors: The Origins of the American Right* (Princeton: Princeton University Press, 2001); and Osman, *Invention of Brownstone Brooklyn*.

51. Tracy Neumann, *Remaking the Rust Belt: The Postindustrial Transformation of North America* (Philadelphia: University of Pennsylvania Press, 2016).

52. Samuel Zipp, *Manhattan Projects: The Rise and Fall of Urban Renewal in Cold War New York* (Oxford, UK: Oxford University Press, 2010).

53. Betsy A. Beasley, "Service Learning: Oil, International Education, and Texas's Corporate Cold War," *Diplomatic History* 42, no. 2 (2018): 177≠203; and Andrew Friedman, *Covert Capital: Landscapes of Denial and the Making of U.S. Empire in the Suburbs of Northern Virginia* (Berkeley: University of California Press, 2013).

54. Davarian L. Baldwin, "The '800-Pound Gargoyle': The Long History of Higher Education and Urban Development on Chicago's South Side," *American Quarterly* 67, no. 1 (2015): 81–103; Stuart W. Leslie and Robert H. Kargon, "Selling Silicon Valley: Frederick Terman's Model for Regional Advantage," *Business History Review* 70, no. 4 (1996): 435–472; Margaret Pugh O'Mara, *Cities of Knowledge: Cold War Science and the Search for the Next Silicon Valley* (Princeton, NJ: Princeton University Press, 2005); J. Mark Souther, "Acropolis of the Middle-West: Decay, Renewal, and Boosterism in Cleveland's University Circle," *Journal of Planning History* 10, no. 1 (2011): 30–58; and LaDale C. Winling, *Building the Ivory Tower: Universities and Metropolitan Development in the Twentieth Century* (Philadelphia: University of Pennsylvania Press, 2017).

55. Jared N. Day, "Health Care and Urban Revitalization: A Historical Overview," *Journal of Urban History* 42, no. 2 (2016): 247–258; Caitlin Henry, "Hospital Closures: The Sociospatial Restructuring of Labor and Health Care," *Annals of the Association of American Geographers* 105, no. 5 (2015): 1094–1110; Andrew T. Simpson, "Health and Renaissance: Academic Medicine and the Remaking of Modern Pittsburgh," *Journal of Urban History* 41, no. 1 (2015): 19–27.

56. Alex Sayf Cummings, "'Brain Magnet': Research Triangle Park and the Origins of the Creative City, 1953–1965," *Journal of Urban History* 43, no. 3 (2017): 470–492; Kaiser, "Postwar Suburbanization of American Physics"; Louise Mozingo, *Pastoral Capitalism: A History of Suburban Corporate Landscapes* (Cambridge, MA: MIT Press, 2011); William J. Rankin, "The Epistemology of the Suburbs: Knowledge, Production, and Corporate Laboratory Design," *Critical Inquiry* 36 (2010): 771–806; and Patrick Vitale, "Cradle of the Creative Class: Reinventing the Figure of the Scientist in Cold War Pittsburgh," *Annals of the American Association of Geographers* 106, no. 6 (2016): 1378–1396.

57. Lizabeth Cohen, *A Consumer's Republic?: The Politics of Mass Consumption in Postwar America* (New York: Knopf, 2003); and Kenneth T. Jackson, "All the World's a Mall: Reflections on the Social and Economic Consequences of the American Shopping Center," *The American Historical Review* 101, no. 4 (1996): 1111–1121.

58. Zach Schwartz-Weinstein, "Beneath the University: Service Workers and the University-Hospital City, 1964–1980" (PhD diss., New York University, 2015); and Taft, *From Steel to Slots*; Winant, "A Place to Die."

59. Exceptions include: Cowie, *Capital Moves*; Stephanie Frank, "Why a Studio without a Backlot Isn't Like a Ten-Story Building without an Elevator: Land Planning in the Postfordist Film Industry," *Journal of Planning History* 15, no. 2 (2016): 129–148; and Elihu Rubin, *Insuring the City: The Prudential Center and the Postwar Urban Landscape* (New Haven: Yale University Press, 2012).

60. Braverman, *Labor and Monopoly Capital*; Barbara Ehrenreich and John Ehrenreich, "The Professional-Managerial Class," in *Between Labor and Capital*, ed. Pat Walker (Boston: South End Press, 1979), 5–45; Ley, *New Middle Class and the Remaking of the Central City*; McDowell, *Working Bodies*; Mollenkopf and Castells, *Dual City*; and Sassen, *The Global City: New York, London, and Tokyo* (Princeton, NJ: Princeton University Press, 1992).

61. For an example see: Geismer, *Don't Blame Us*.

Patrick Vitale

DEINDUSTRIALIZATION AND THE AMERICAN POSTINDUSTRIAL CITY, 1950–PRESENT

The municipal bankruptcy of Detroit, Michigan, in 2013 punctuated what some economists called an inevitable economic transition. Many American cities had been deindustrializing for decades, but the Motor City, with $18 billion in debt, roughly 40 percent of its residents living in poverty, and nearly 80,000 abandoned and blighted properties, became a global symbol of urban decline.[1] Corrupt politicians, greedy auto corporations, and uneducated residents were variously blamed for the city's failure to transition to a new economy, while larger structures of racial segregation, disinvestment, and inequality that were germane to global capitalism received less attention. The city also became a high-profile testing ground for urban revitalization, drawing on both well-tested strategies and new interventions for rebuilding its economy, landscape, population, and image.

By 2013, the United States had lost a net of 7.3 million manufacturing jobs since peaking in the late 1970s at 19.3 million jobs. These statistics, however, fail to reveal uneven regional and local impacts and fluctuations over time. According to economist Barry Bluestone, 32 to 38 million manufacturing jobs disappeared in the 1970s alone, hitting the Northeast and Midwest especially hard.[2] Like Detroit, many cities made efforts to adapt to new economies after World War II, particularly economies based on providing services, such as healthcare, finance, or warehousing and distribution. Deindustrializing cities rebranded themselves as destinations with convention centers, stadiums, and festival marketplaces, seeking to lure tourists and new white-collar residents. Some postindustrial cities were treated as success stories of reinvention. Pittsburgh, for example, transformed from a steel hub to a center for healthcare and technology. Others struggled to recover, especially smaller cities that had been dependent on a single manufacturer. Cities entertained options to "rightsize" by shrinking their municipal footprints, adapted vacant lots for urban agriculture, or attracted "urban explorers" to gaze at their industrial ruins. Some industrial cities transformed over the course of decades; others felt the sharp blow of multiple factory closures within a few years. In either case, economic shifts and planning interventions both exacerbated existing inequalities and created new challenges.

DEINDUSTRIALIZATION

The term "deindustrialization" entered the American popular lexicon in the early 1980s amid a flurry of factory closures, downsizings, and relocations, particularly in New England, the Midwest, and the mid-Atlantic states. These regions, once known for their textile, steel, automobile, and many other industries, reached a heyday of growth during and following World War II. But within decades the moniker "the Rust Belt" signified the regions' association with a fading economic era of heavy manufacturing. As corporations locked their gates, former industrial cities were left with crumbling factory buildings, empty shipyards, abandoned mines, and expansive brownfields, often contaminated with decades of pollution from industrial chemicals and other byproducts. In Youngstown, Ohio, three major steel plants closed within five years, leading to an unemployment rate in 1982 of nearly 20 percent.[3] In Flint, Michigan, General Motors eliminated 26,000 local jobs between 1973 and 1987 and continued to downsize until more unemployed residents than autoworkers lived in the city.[4] Camden, New Jersey—once a buoyant industrial center for canning, shipbuilding, and electronics—had a poverty rate of 44 percent by 1995, the highest in the country.[5] "Shrinking cities" like Buffalo and

Detroit lost 55 percent and 61 percent of their respective populations between 1950 and 2010.[6] Journalists and scholars wrote about deindustrialization as a breaking point, a crisis for once-booming industrial cities.

But as historian Robert Self writes, deindustrialization "stands for a set of overlapping processes that vary so dramatically on every scale of analysis that the term's analytical leverage suffers."[7] In many cities, corporate disinvestment was uneven and drawn out. Although deindustrialization accelerated during the 1970s and 1980s, the process originated decades before. Much of New England's textile industry, for instance, moved south beginning in the late 19th century. By the 1920s, the South was home to more than half of US cotton textile production.[8] For electronics manufacturer RCA, the corporation's search for cheaper labor and fewer regulations began in the 1930s as it moved plants from New Jersey to Indiana, then Tennessee, and ultimately Mexico.[9] Bethlehem Steel began a long, slow decline during the 1960s, but at its headquarters in Bethlehem, Pennsylvania, the steel factory did not shut down until 1998, shortly before the corporation filed for bankruptcy. Unlike some manufacturers, Bethlehem Steel never offshored its production facilities.[10] Other industrial plants maintained their output, even as automation decimated the number of manufacturing jobs. Although the American West and South saw remarkable growth in their economies and populations during this same period, those cities in the "Sun Belt" were not entirely immune to the effects of deindustrialization either.[11] The closures of naval shipyards in California after World War II and the Cold War, for example, reshaped the economic and urban landscapes.[12]

The causes for deindustrialization and capital migration are not the inevitable effects of abstract market forces. Instead, they comprise a tangle of specific business and policy decisions that reflect manufacturers' unceasing quests to lower costs and increase profits, as well as governments' changing priorities for urban and economic development. Following the 1973 oil crisis, high unemployment combined with steep inflation—"stagflation"—led corporations to reassess and reorganize capital investments. Executives blamed union contracts that promised high wages and robust benefits to factory workers, as well as the costs of environmental regulations adopted in the 1970s, for cutting into corporate profits and shareholder value. Not only did advances in technology lead to greater productivity with fewer employees, but companies also found cheaper and more docile labor in "right-to-work" states in the American South or in other countries where unions were weaker, taxes were lower, and regulations were looser. Large integrated steelmakers in Pennsylvania, for example, lost contracts to "minimills" based in the South that used scrap steel instead of raw materials to make new products. Minimills used nonunion labor and made far lower capital investments in facilities. Meanwhile, foreign manufacturers in Japan and Germany, among other nations, received government subsidies that allowed them to "dump" products in the United States, selling them at a cost lower than production.[13]

At the community level, corporations faced additional incentives to move out of urban cores and take tens of thousands of jobs with them. Geographical and infrastructural assets that initially placed factories near canals, ports, railroad hubs, or natural resources became obsolete as the development of highways and information technology made those locations less relevant. By the second half of the 20th century, aging 19th-century factories that were surrounded by densely packed worker housing had limited space to grow. What previously seemed like fixed capital investments in multistory brick facilities and heavy machinery needed to be continuously maintained and updated. Once cars and highways made suburban greenfields more accessible, corporations built huge parking lots and sprawling facilities on cheaper land. Single-story construction made moving heavy equipment and products more efficient.[14] Tax policies, such as "accelerated depreciation," meant companies could recoup their investments in new suburban facilities or move on from failing businesses more quickly.[15] In Flint, Michigan, for example, General Motors invested in suburban facilities beginning in the 1940s. While GM initially hoped these new operations would be annexed to the city, ultimately the company's production shifted more completely beyond its bounds.[16] Elsewhere, factories moved further afield, often to other countries.

At the same time, many workers relocated. Federal subsidies made owning a home in the suburbs an attainable goal for white families after World War II. African Americans, many of whom migrated to industrial cities in the North and West between 1915 and 1970 to find work, were largely excluded from this vision, however. They and other people of color increasingly faced a "spatial mismatch" between where they lived in inner cities and where industrial jobs moved.[17] With declining property tax revenues from corporations and the "white flight" of residents to the suburbs, cities suffered both an economic and an image crisis that fueled those continuing trends. Unemployed black men standing on street corners looking for work became a potent symbol of the underclass "culture of poverty" by the 1960s.[18] The dominant association of urban decay with African American residents intensified with the riots that swept through Cleveland, Detroit, Chicago, Newark, and other major industrial cities between 1964 and 1968. While some onlookers saw the unrest as confirmation of a racial "urban crisis," many struggling residents of color saw an outlet to protest the ongoing disinvestment in inner-city housing, jobs, and other resources.[19]

POSTINDUSTRIALISM AND THE NEW ECONOMY

As cities adjusted to the reality of capital flight and shrinking populations in the second half of the 20th century, most set their sights on luring new investments. In the midst of postwar spatial and demographic transformations, policymakers, business interests, and city boosters reinvented former "smokestack cities" as part of a glistening "postindustrial" future. Cities that grew up around and depended on single industries—Akron was known for tires, Dayton for cash registers, New Haven for guns—increasingly diversified after 1950. Even more cosmopolitan centers like New York and Chicago rebranded themselves for a new era. Key to this widespread strategy was attracting new middle-class residents and white-collar jobs.

As with deindustrialization, the term "postindustrial" is contested. Most former hubs of industrial production continue to host factories at a reduced scale, often in lighter industry or more technologically advanced products. But when sociologist Daniel Bell wrote *The Coming of Post-industrial Society* in 1973, he put a finger on the pulse of a rapidly transforming economy accompanied by new expectations for urban life. Instead of making goods, Bell argued, cities would produce technology, knowledge, and services. A professional and technical class would supersede blue-collar labor.[20] Indeed, as the industrial sector became a much smaller portion of the US economy, the number of service jobs—including in healthcare, financial services, retail, hospitality, and education—quadrupled between 1950 and 2000 and continued to grow.[21]

Service economies led the growth of urban centers in the American South and West such as Houston, Raleigh-Durham, Atlanta, San Francisco, and Phoenix. Increasingly, they reshaped the postindustrial cities of the Rust Belt as part of development strategies to help the region remain relevant. Imagining a postindustrial future largely relied on rebranding urban centers in positive terms. After New York City nearly declared bankruptcy in the 1970s, for example, it launched its famous "I Love New York" campaign, which marketed a safe, harmonious, and business-friendly city and established urban marketing as a primary defense against decline.[22] A *Time Magazine* cover in 1981 featured urban planner and developer James Rouse, the creator of the "festival marketplace" strategy discussed below, declaring "Cities are Fun!" to an audience of educated suburbanites. Meanwhile, artists began moving to and transforming former industrial districts after 1950. By the early-21st century, Richard Florida's theory of the "creative class" emerged as one of the leading influences on city planning and development. Florida premised cities' economic growth and health on their abilities to attract artists, scientists, and other innovative, knowledge-based workers via cultural amenities such as sidewalk cafes, galleries, and bike paths. Jobs, Florida argued, follow where talent clusters.[23]

Together, these rebranding strategies aligned with a rebalancing of urban workforces and tax bases via a number of growing employment sectors:

Finance, Insurance, and Real Estate: The FIRE industries—finance, insurance, and real estate—exploded in the 1980s. New tax codes, reduced regulations, and other federal policies favored these sectors over manufacturing.[24] A network of what sociologist Saskia Sassen calls "global cities," including New York, emerged as highly concentrated centers for financial firms and other specialized services—such as accounting, consulting, supply chain management, legal services, insurance, and information technology—that are needed to run dispersed production facilities. As Sassen writes, instead of durable products, "the 'things' a global city makes are services and financial goods."[25] From the early 1980s to 2007, the finance industry's share of overall corporate profits in the United States rose from 10 percent to 40 percent.[26] Meanwhile, economists continued using new housing starts, or the number of new homes built in a given period, as a key indicator of the nation's economic health after 1950. Growth in

real estate markets became dependent on the financial industry's production of new lending tools and other innovations. As with residential construction, in many cities the ongoing construction of office and retail space is an economy in itself.[27]

Healthcare and Education: Hospital systems and universities—"meds and eds"—not only became the primary employers in many cities but also became dominant real estate holders and policing agents.[28] In a striking symbol of changing economic influences, for example, the University of Pittsburgh Medical Center took over US Steel Tower in downtown Pittsburgh in 2007. UPMC had become the region's largest employer with more than 40,000 employees and began to expand globally.

Likewise, universities benefited after World War II from both the GI Bill, enabling returning soldiers to attend college, and federal defense spending during the Cold War, seeding what historian Margaret O'Mara calls "cities of knowledge."[29] Beyond their economic impact, hospitals and universities were integral to strategies to counter perceptions of cities as dangerous concentrations of poverty. Reimagined as protected urban "campuses," they boasted amenities, such as coffee shops and security forces, that were attractive to educated white-collar workers and residents.[30]

Tourism, Entertainment, and Consumption: Developing urban cores as centers for tourism represents another key effort to lure visitors, suburbanites, and their consumer dollars back to cities. In addition to new office buildings and luxury condominiums, postindustrial cities invested in stadiums, convention centers, museums, and other cultural venues. Often, the buildings themselves signaled new urban identities, whether through forward-looking modern architecture, or, as with most convention centers, windowless designs that created buffers between downtown business districts and poverty-stricken neighborhoods.[31] Camden repurposed its former industrial waterfront as a tourist destination with the opening of an aquarium in 1992. Despite evidence that sports stadiums rarely return on taxpayer investments, Pittsburgh, Baltimore, Milwaukee, and Allentown represent just a handful of cities that built expensive new sports facilities after 1970, usually surrounded by massive parking lots to attract suburban fans.

Meanwhile, the 1976 opening of Faneuil Hall Marketplace at the site of a historic market in Boston marked a watershed for urban development strategies. With the help of city incentives, private developer and planner James Rouse transformed the aging Faneuil Hall and Quincy Market into a "festival marketplace," a collection of shops, restaurants, and pseudo-public spaces peppered with street performers and other entertainment. While cities had reimagined industrial districts as mixed-used space before, such as with San Francisco's Ghirardelli Square (1964), the success of Boston's experiment kicked off a nationwide trend that made festival marketplaces a leading strategy in downtown redevelopment during the 1980s, including at Baltimore's Harborplace (1980), South Street Seaport in New York (1983), and Flint, Michigan's Water Street Pavilion (1985), among other sites.[32] Rouse's model relied on cleaning up sites' industrial pasts and struggling neighborhoods' gritty images to make them amenable to middle-class consumer traffic.[33] The transformation of out-of-use railyards in the Lower West Side of Manhattan to create an elevated linear park called the High Line between 2009 and 2014 sparked another trend of reusing urban industrial infrastructure for leisure and consumption.

Other communities turned shuttered industrial facilities into heritage attractions designed to more explicitly interpret the history of the sites, such as Rivers of Steel, which offers tours of former industrial works in the Pittsburgh region, and the Sloss Furnaces in Birmingham, Alabama, where blast furnaces once used to make steel are now part of a concert venue and community center. An attempt

to lure tourists to Flint via a theme park and museum called AutoWorld, however, never reached the promised level of patronage. The attraction closed for the first time within six months of its 1984 opening. The Youngstown Historical Center for Industry and Labor, opened in 1992 to interpret the history of the area's steel industry, similarly struggled to attract the number of tourists initially projected.[34]

Industrial Parks, Warehousing, and Distribution: In place of massive steel or auto plants, new industrial parks on the urban and suburban periphery, often near highway access, focused on attracting light manufacturing, such as electronics components or medical devices. In place of solid brick structures designed to last one hundred years, aluminum sheds designed to last only as long as the tax abatements that drew them there mark new hubs for warehousing and distribution.[35] Such sites might even pop up on former factory land, capitalizing on brownfields' existing transportation infrastructure.

Other efforts to revive declining Rust Belt economies have been less concerned with improving cities' images and reflect more desperate efforts to combat severe unemployment and fiscal insolvency.

Landfills and Incinerators: While most economic development plans in postindustrial cities focused on attracting new, wealthier residents, a strategy of welcoming waste facilities, by contrast, disproportionately affected impoverished communities of color. In Chester, Pennsylvania, a former hub for shipbuilding and heavy manufacturing outside Philadelphia, several waste treatment facilities opened on vacant brownfields beginning in the late 1980s. City and county officials, eager to bring in jobs and operating fees, actively courted toxic facilities via zoning variances and promises of limited regulatory oversight, while the majority-African-American residents in the adjacent neighborhoods felt adverse effects on community health and quality of life.[36] Similarly, in the Calumet Region of Southeast Chicago, where steel manufacturers once clustered, landfills and disposal sites that drew waste from other parts of the city and country became a growth industry in the 1970s and 1980s. While pollution from manufacturing was once endured as a sign of prosperity, now waste, in addition to its toxicity, was associated with only a small number of jobs and a negative impact on proximate home values.[37]

Prisons: Some cities sought to offset shrinking populations by bringing in another type of new resident: prisoners. Between 1992 and 1997, for example, five prisons opened in and around the former steel town of Youngstown, Ohio.[38] As in other communities, many residents welcomed the jobs and spillover economic activity the prisons promised, while others worried about basing economic growth on increased criminalization.[39]

Casinos: After 1990, gambling exploded as another former "vice" industry promising a significant number of new jobs and tax revenues. Distinct from Native American casinos, commercial casinos approved through state legislatures popped up in St. Louis, Missouri, Northwest Indiana, and Cleveland, Ohio, among many other locales, as a way to offset local and state budget shortfalls. Detroit relied on its three downtown casinos as one of its most stable sources of tax income during the city's 2013 municipal bankruptcy. In Bethlehem, Pennsylvania, the Las Vegas Sands Corporation opened a profitable casino and hotel complex on Bethlehem Steel's former ore yard in 2009, even evoking the site's history with an industrial theme.

Casino corporation Wynn gained approval in 2014 to build on a former Monsanto Chemical plant in Everett, Massachusetts, which was vacant for more than thirty years. Cities like these often relied on casino operators to clean up toxic sites, build needed infrastructure, and otherwise support community institutions. But as additional states passed laws to allow commercial casinos, specifically as an economic development strategy for postindustrial regions, host communities faced the prospect of oversaturation, a fear stoked by the closure of four of twelve casinos in Atlantic City, New Jersey, in 2014.[40]

FINANCING DEVELOPMENT IN THE POSTINDUSTRIAL CITY

As the makeup of urban economies changed, the relationship between urban development, city services, and public funding also shifted dramatically in the 1970s. Beginning with the Housing Acts of 1949 and 1954, the federal government assumed a central role in remaking urban cores, providing the funds for cities to demolish aging and blighted residential and business districts. These renewal funds went disproportionately to older cities in the North and Midwest.[41] Although the urban renewal program was pitched as a way to provide improved subsidized housing, cities also used the cleared land to construct amenities including convention centers, universities, cultural centers, and condominiums. Other neighborhoods were torn down to make room for industrial expansion. The "culture of clearance" that premised urban revitalization on destruction most often displaced poor residents of color.[42] In New York, for example, the diverse, working-class neighborhood of Lincoln Square was demolished to make way for the Lincoln Center for the Performing Arts, designed to attract a wealthier clientele and signify New York's aspirational status as a city of culture.[43]

This program of top-down federal funding and authority over urban development ended by 1974. Community Development Block Grants (in effect since 1975) and Urban Development Action Grants (in effect since 1977) gave local authorities more discretion over how federal funding could be used. The government pitched these programs as providing the seeds to stimulate additional private investment.[44] Ultimately funding shrunk as it decentralized, leading cities to rely primarily on the private sector for economic development.[45] The Community Reinvestment Act, initially passed in 1977, encouraged banks to invest and provide access to credit in low- and moderate-income neighborhoods, but most private investment in American cities is not mandated in this way.

Other federal interventions in the "urban crisis" similarly shifted in the 1970s. President Lyndon Johnson's War on Poverty—launched in 1964 as a collection of social programs designed to tackle the roots of poverty by improving education, employment, and health-care services—was largely dismantled by 1973 as backlash intensified to a welfare state that was perceived to only benefit low-income minorities. New York's near bankruptcy in 1975 and President Gerald Ford's blunt refusal to intervene set the tone for a broader shift to austerity politics that cut urban social programs amid ongoing fiscal crises.[46]

Historian Tracy Neumann uses the term "postindustrialism" to represent the consequences of these interrelated shifts: a deliberate and widespread policy effort to remake cities by catering to corporate interests and appealing to middle- and upper-class suburbanite and tourist desires. A keystone of this strategy is the public-private partnership, the funding mechanism that by the 1970s eclipsed the postwar dependence on federal funding for urban redevelopment. With public-private partnerships, government entities relied on private financing to complete development projects.[47] Cities, counties, and states competed with each other for new private investments and jobs by appealing to corporate interests, offering low tax rates, tax abatements, and other "business friendly" incentives. Among other new financing mechanisms, tax increment financing (TIF) took off in the 1980s and 1990s. TIF subsidized new development in distressed areas by borrowing against future increases in property tax revenues. The additional tax revenues that resulted from the development over a set period of time were then directed toward public improvements within the defined district.

The "Pittsburgh Renaissance" serves as one of the early models of how public-private partnerships and creative financing remade former industrial cities. Beginning in the late 1940s, private corporations and public officials joined together in what was called the Allegheny Conference to harness funding for development projects to revive the city's downtown "Golden Triangle" with new skyscrapers and corporate headquarters, create a cultural district, and bolster Pittsburgh's universities, hospitals, and technology industries. As early as the 1950s and 1960s, representatives from more than seventy other cities came to Pittsburgh to learn how to replicate this model's apparent success.[48] After the 1970s, projects such as the remediation of former factory sites—J&L Steel's South Side Works became the Pittsburgh Technology Center, for example—or "rails to trails" conversions of railroad tracks to walking and biking paths trended away from large-scale government-funded programs toward smaller, market-based initiatives. As in other industrial communities, however, the transformation from a manufacturing hub to a postindustrial center was never as complete as boosters claimed. Many smaller industrial communities in Pittsburgh's hinterland struggled to replicate the Pittsburgh Renaissance model and grew increasingly isolated and impoverished.[49]

URBAN PLANNING AND OTHER APPROACHES TO DECLINE

In addition to the public and private financing of projects like condominiums, stadiums, or industrial parks, many cities sought other creative solutions to revitalize or reinvent their economies and images. For those cities most impacted by capital disinvestment, one of the primary challenges was how to address vacant and deteriorating properties.

Rightsizing: Most urban policy after 1950 focused on growth. Shrinking cities that lost large proportions of their populations with deindustrialization faced a particular quandary. Should they persist in courting large development projects and new residents, or should they accept that they may never regain their former statures? In cities confronting soaring numbers of vacant lots and public services spread thin over a dispersed population, some planners suggested that they "rightsize," or shrink their footprints to more efficiently serve those residents that remained. In these proposals, residents in neighborhoods deemed beyond hope would be asked to move to denser parts of the city. Presumably this would allow for more sustainable retail centers and cost savings for improved trash collection, transportation, and public safety services. One 2012 plan for Detroit labeled about a fifth of the city as prime land to return to nature, despite the fact that an estimated 88,000 people still resided there.[50] Youngstown adopted a new city plan in 2005 that no longer aspired to regain peak population levels or manufacturing capacity, but rather focused on diverting investments away from the most deteriorated neighborhoods and integrating the city's new economy with other regional hubs.[51] Other cities, like Philadelphia and Chicago, faced more "localized shrinkage." While certain areas of these cities were devastated, healthy parts of the cities, especially in the urban cores, gained population and housing.[52] Instead of "rightsizing" cities by abandoning certain neighborhoods or populations, planning historian Brent Ryan is among critics who called for "palliative planning" that would focus resources on the most distressed areas to prevent additional residents from leaving.[53]

Demolition: As with the postwar period of federal urban renewal, in the early 21st century cities including Buffalo and Philadelphia focused on demolishing blighted structures to improve property values, discourage arson, and otherwise beautify deteriorating neighborhoods.[54] Detroit, which since bankruptcy in 2013 attracted the special attention of planners and activists, emerged as a testing ground for innovative technological solutions to urban problems. In 2013 and 2014, a corps of residents armed with cellphones documented

the conditions of every building and lot in the city. In a process dubbed "blexting," they took cellphone pictures and classified the blight status of homes and commercial properties. A Blight Removal Task Force then used this data to propose tearing down 40,000 structures and remediating tens of thousands more.[55]

Land Banks: One result of programs focused on demolishing blighted buildings was an increase in the numbers of vacant lots without clear visions for their reuse.[56] The concept of the "land bank"—a public entity that acquires, manages, and repurposes abandoned and foreclosed properties—emerged in the 1960s, with the first land banks implemented in St. Louis in 1971 and Cleveland in 1976.[57] By removing surplus housing from the open market, they bolstered property values of the homes that remained occupied and encouraged reinvestment. Often land banks allowed homeowners to inexpensively buy vacant lots adjacent to their own. Land banks became increasingly popular and viable in the early 21st century. In Flint, the Genesee County Land Bank Authority, one of the national models for this type of initiative, owned 5,100 tax-reverted properties in 2010 and had acquired more than 10,000 properties in aggregate.[58]

Urban Exploration and Ruin Porn: The deterioration of industrial properties also spurred a trend of "urban exploration." Urban explorers sneak into shuttered factories and other urban ruins, usually at night, to take pictures and otherwise experience the thrill of transgression.[59] Some cities capitalized on this fascination with decay, establishing sanctioned tours and photography workshops for curious visitors. One popular destination for urban explorers—a church in Gary, Indiana, that was abandoned in the 1970s—received a grant in 2017 to become an official tourist destination. Instead of demolishing or renovating the church, the city planned to turn it into a "ruin garden," a public park in which urban decay is the main attraction.[60] In addition to amateur blogs and snapshots, a number of coffee-table books featuring images of decay gained notoriety in the 21st century. Critics of urban exploration call it "ruin porn," suggesting such images and accounts carry exploitative connotations and often ignore the historical contexts that led to disinvestment and decay in the first place.[61]

Urban Agriculture: Urban agriculture, whose long history includes the Victory Gardens of World War I and World War II, became a popular way to make vacant lots productive again. By the late 1980s, most large cities had not-for-profit organizations or municipal agencies to support this type of reuse. Many cities adapted zoning and city services to accommodate everything from backyard or community gardens to for-profit farming.[62] In addition to reusing blighted land, urban agriculture promoted social engagement and helped address "food deserts," the lack of access to fresh foods that often afflicts impoverished neighborhoods. Often, however, municipal officials viewed community gardens as short-term solutions until land became attractive to private development.[63] Some for-profit farms in declining neighborhoods were critiqued for employing only a limited number of local residents and producing high-end produce for restaurants and grocery stores in other parts of the city.

Adaptive Reuse: Adaptive reuse of industrial structures offered an alternative to demolition. As with San Francisco's Ghirardelli Square and the festival marketplaces mentioned above, these projects transformed old factories, warehouses, and other outworn buildings for new uses. Developers often took advantage of tax credits for historic preservation. Among the many examples of adaptive reuse in American cities, St. Louis's Union Station was redeveloped as a hotel, shopping center, and food court in 1985, while the former Winchester gun factory in New Haven, Connecticut, reopened as loft-style apartments in 2014. Other adaptive reuse projects reshaped natural landscapes. In 2009, Chicago transformed an old quarry into Palmisano Park, adding needed greenspace to the former industrial neighborhood of Bridgeport. New York's Freshkills Park opened to the public in stages beginning in 2012 on 2,200 acres of what was previously the world's largest landfill.[64]

Artist Interventions: Other urban interventions involved remaking postindustrial cities' images with art. Chicago set a precedent in 1978 with its Percent-for-Art Ordinance requiring that 1.33% of the cost of new public construction be earmarked for public art. The policy was replicated in more than two hundred other cities.[65] Beginning in 1984, Philadelphia's Mural Arts Program similarly set a national model for beautifying its neighborhoods. The mural program, which involves both community members and professional artists, initially was conceived as a way to redirect the creativity of graffiti artists. Other communities focused on attracting museums, such as North Adams, Massachusetts, which converted a former print works and electronics factory complex into the Massachusetts Museum of Contemporary Art (MassMoCA).

In some cases, artist interventions were without official sanction. The Heidelberg Project in Detroit, an installation of salvaged materials attached to homes, became a tourist attraction from 1986 to 2016 and drew connections between discarded objects and neighborhoods. Other activist art that explicitly drew attention to the conditions that led to urban disinvestment included the work of Amanda Williams in Chicago and the artist collective Object Orange in Detroit, in which the artists painted abandoned homes in the cities' poverty-ridden neighborhoods bright colors to highlight rather than obscure their presence.[66]

NEW INEQUALITIES

Despite creative efforts to remake cities that bore the brunt of capital disinvestment after 1950, the postindustrial period has in many cases exacerbated and hardened inequalities.

The industrial economy and union gains leading up to and following World War II contributed to what economists call the Great Compression; working-class earnings rose during this period to close the wealth gap with the upper classes. Although women and people of color were left out of many of these gains, economic inequality in the United States as a whole decreased. The effects of deindustrialization, deregulation, and the decimation of union protections all contributed to a reversal of this trend. Since the 1970s, income inequality has risen sharply.[67] For all the well-paid executives in the postindustrial economy, their productivity is often supported by low-wage staffers. The tourist city relies on custodial workers, waiters, reservation clerks, hotel maids, ticket scanners, casino card dealers, and line cooks, many of whom work part-time and without the robust benefits typical of the immediate postwar period.

Urban factory closures affected individuals and families, but also whole communities. With each closure, cities lost tax revenues, ancillary businesses, and charitable donations. Solutions based on attracting middle-class, white-collar workers and tourists often failed to address existing inequalities. The legacy of postwar urban renewal entrenched racial and economic divisions within the city. Highways cut through low-income neighborhoods and displaced people of color while creating new physical barriers to integration. Many postindustrial cities continued to focus their attention and resources on downtown development at the expense of neighborhood investments. Some critics of the planning approach "rightsizing"—in which impoverished, minority neighborhoods are most likely to be abandoned when cities redirect resources—have called it "whitesizing." New immigrant populations likewise often are targeted as sources of decline when in many cases they play an integral role in revitalizing urban areas.[68]

In addition to reinforcing existing inequalities, redevelopment plans often created new

ones. Richard Florida, the influential proponent of revitalizing postwar cities by catering to the "creative class" of artists and tech workers, eventually acknowledged the shortcomings of his approach. He confessed in 2017 that the rise of the creative class benefited already wealthy, educated, mostly white professionals and displaced poor and working-class residents of color.[69] Despite the surge in the so-called creative economy, cities (and suburbs) continued to lack affordable housing, investment in infrastructure, and livable wages. Cycles of gentrification, in which inexpensive real estate lured new residents or corporate investors to rehabilitate dilapidated neighborhoods and former industrial districts, ultimately priced out and displaced original residents.[70] Other neighborhoods struggled to attract any investment at all. Chicago, a city that touted its transition to a postindustrial economy, continued to lose tens of thousands of African American residents from its impoverished South and West Sides even as its downtown core of office buildings and luxury condominiums became magnets for professionals and wealthy empty-nesters in the 21st century.[71] Likewise, while urban agriculture appealed to environmentalists and sustainable food activists, others saw misdirected resources. As one African American resident of Flint said at a community meeting, "We came from sharecropping and don't want white people to turn our neighborhood into farms. That was a hard life, not a good life, and we don't want chickens in the back yard."[72]

Meanwhile, when cities based their economies on attracting suburbanites and tourists, they often constructed what Donald Judd labeled "tourist bubbles."[73] Casinos and stadiums by design discouraged patrons from leaving the complexes, despite boosters' promises that such projects brought consumer spending to adjacent neighborhoods. The images of the city marketed and presented to tourists in these enclaves were manicured and policed in ways that deliberately obscured pervasive social and economic concerns outside their bounds. Even tourist attractions that illuminated industrial decay sometimes merely aestheticized suffering. "Ruin porn" photographs of crumbling buildings often excluded the human toll of urban disinvestment and avoided confronting the economic, social, and political causes that underlie ruination.

The environmental legacies of the manufacturing economy continued to impact both urban development and community health. During the 1970s, new environmental regulations in the United States forced manufacturers to reduce pollution, even as many used the added costs of compliance to justify disinvestment. In Pittsburgh, where the soot from the steel plants regularly blotted out the sun, pollution controls had an immediate effect on beautifying the city and improving public health. But many manufacturers simply transferred their negative impacts elsewhere, leading to "sacrifice zones" in communities on the urban periphery where noxious byproducts and waste disposal sites proliferated.[74] The emergence of the environmental justice movement that began in the 1980s and 1990s focused in particular on the ways in which the negative impacts of toxic industries and other pollution disproportionately affected low-income communities of color.[75]

Even when urban factories closed, they left behind decades of waste. In East Chicago, Indiana, more than one thousand residents were evacuated from a public housing complex beginning in 2016 when government testing revealed dangerously toxic soil. The housing was built in the 1970s adjacent to a lead and copper smelter.[76] Presumably "cleaner" technology manufacturers also can have hazardous effects on surrounding communities. Residents of Endicott, New York, the original home of IBM, live over a plume of chemicals spilled during the production of computer components. Remediation efforts included venting homes to allow toxic gasses to escape, but home values in the affected area plummeted amid health concerns.[77] Despite the federal passage of the Comprehensive Environmental

Response, Compensation, and Liability Act (CERCLA) in 1980, which included the Superfund program to help pay for brownfield remediation, available federal funds have been insufficient to address all needed cleanups. Meanwhile, the lack of economic investment and tax revenue in struggling postindustrial cities led to disasters like the water crisis in Flint, Michigan, where an effort to cut costs by switching the city's water supply in 2014 led to widespread lead contamination as a result of corroded infrastructure.

DISCUSSION OF THE LITERATURE

The scholarship on deindustrialization and postindustrial development in the United States, like the cities it discusses, remains a work in progress. Historians of these trends draw from a number of disciplines, including sociology, anthropology, cultural studies, geography, ethnic studies, environmental studies, and urban planning.

Bennett Harrison and Barry Bluestone's *The Deindustrialization of America: Plant Closings, Community Abandonment, and the Dismantling of Basic Industry* (1982) emerged as a seminal work that departed from purely quantitative studies of economic change to include the social costs.[78] This study ushered in a disaster genre of anthropological case studies in the 1980s and 1990s about crises in various Rust Belt communities, generally focusing on the impact of factory closures on union workers.[79] Scholars like Kathryn Dudley (1994) and Ruth Milkman (1997) drew attention to the fact that not all residents saw factory closures as disasters; in fact, many people welcomed opportunities to escape from dangerous and difficult work in manufacturing and to improve gritty cities' images.[80]

Thomas Sugrue's *The Origins of the Urban Crisis: Race and Inequality in Postwar Detroit* (1996) extended and complicated the history of economic decline as it intersected with white flight. While the race riots of the 1960s marked the crisis moment for inner cities in many popular narratives, Sugrue placed the roots of decline in the 1940s and identified a tangle of economic, racial, and political causes. Robert Beauregard (1993) catalogued the proliferation of postwar discourse of urban decline as others began to tackle how cities actively remake their images.[81] Colin Gordon's study of decline in St. Louis (2008) presented geographic information system (GIS) mapping as a useful research tool for historians, uniquely combining archival sources with digital maps.[82] Many of these critical narratives and methodologies gained new prominence with Detroit's bankruptcy in 2013.[83]

Jefferson Cowie and Joseph Heathcott's edited collection *Beyond the Ruins: The Meanings of Deindustrialization* (2003) defined another turning point in the historical scholarship on deindustrialization. This volume emphasized the long process of economic transformation, expanding the timeline of disinvestment both before and after the 1980s. The authors' nuanced assessment of deindustrialization included diverse experiences by class, race, and gender. They set their scope beyond the Rust Belt and addressed communities that never fully industrialized in the first place, as well as those that continued to host manufacturing but with far fewer employees than before.[84]

The scholarship on deindustrialization and urban decline increasingly challenged the "declension narrative" that assumed a noncyclical trend toward decline resulting from the inevitable effects of neutral market forces.[85] Although Daniel Bell's *The Coming of Postindustrial Society* (1973) had identified the knowledge economy as a next stage in market evolution, scholars likewise began to define postindustrialism as an ongoing process rather than a breaking point.[86] Others moved beyond the case study approach to examine postindustrialism as an intellectual and cultural project. Tracy Neumann's *Remaking the Rust Belt: The Postindustrial Transformation of North America* (2016) explored postindustrialism as a

viral aspiration for postwar urban planning and development officials.

Like Saskia Sassen (1991), who identified a network of "global cities" that linked New York's economy to London and Tokyo, international approaches connected industrial decline in the Rust Belt to other parts of North America and Europe, including Germany and the United Kingdom.[87] By the 2000s, urban historians also had taken a "metropolitan turn." Scholars including Howard Gillette (2005), Andrew Highsmith (2015), and Allen Dieterich-Ward (2015) showed that urban decline and renewal did not stop at municipal borders and that suburbs face similar challenges and opportunities.[88]

Environmental historians, meanwhile, increasingly focused on urban areas in their research, including current and former industrial sites. Andrew Hurley's *Environmental Inequalities: Class, Race, and Industrial Pollution in Gary* (1995) explored the tensions between economic growth and community health in a steel town, showing how industrial pollution and environmental activism deepened class and racial divisions. The environmental justice scholarship that emerged after 1990 uncovered entrenched forms of inequality linked to industrial development, waste disposal, and environmental degradation, merging scholarship with calls for social justice.[89]

Planners and planning historians define a dominant thread in the literature on postindustrial redevelopment. Postwar urban planning and economic development strategies focused primarily on what sociologist Harvey Molotch in 1976 dubbed the "growth machine," singularly intent on attracting economic investment.[90] Bernard Frieden and Lynne Sagalyn's *Downtown Inc.: How America Rebuilds Cities* (1989) celebrated the influence of public-private partnerships in achieving these development goals in major cities across the United States, while Jon Teaford (1990) exposed a number of underlying challenges such cities continued to face after revitalization projects.[91]

Planning trends and literatures increasingly addressed shortcomings to the "growth machine" approach to revitalization. More recent scholarship acknowledges that so-called "legacy cities"—a term perceived to be less negative than "deindustrial"—may not ever regain the levels of prosperity they enjoyed during the heyday of manufacturing and rather must adapt to new realities and shrinking populations.[92] Planners continue to work in the shadow of potent critiques of the top-down approach that federal urban renewal represented in the 1950s and 1960s. In the 21st century, most emphasize community input and ground-up plans for revitalization that build on local assets and address social needs.

One of the most influential voices in 21st-century urban planning has been Richard Florida, whose *The Rise of the Creative Class* (2002) was read widely by city officials and other boosters eager to attract young professionals to their communities. Florida's work attracted broad critiques from scholars who saw his approach as reductive and favoring the elite.[93] In 2017, Florida responded to his critics with the release of *The New Urban Crisis: How Our Cities Are Increasing, Deepening Segregation, and Failing the Middle Class— and What We Can Do About It.* As the subtitle suggests, Florida shifted to the approach most urban historians already had taken to the postindustrial city, looking more critically at the mixed results and uneven impacts of revitalization projects.[94]

Critics similarly challenged representations of ruined cities that simplified and sensationalized decline. Complex portrayals of human suffering such as Latoya Ruby Frazier's *The Notion of Family* (2014), which documented the intersectional experiences of race, class, and decline in the steel community of Braddock, Pennsylvania, contrasted with books of ruin photography devoid of people, such as Yves Marchand and Romain Meffre's *The Ruins of Detroit* (2010).[95] Questions of social equity remain most pressing in the 21st century and continue to drive the newest scholarship.

PRIMARY SOURCES

For investigating particular case studies, local libraries and historical societies have a wealth of primary source materials on changing urban economies, demographics, and landscapes. Some, such as the Youngstown Historical Center of Industry and Labor or the Southeast Chicago Historical Museum, focus in particular on industrial history. University libraries in the community in question, particularly those that were built as the result of urban renewal projects, include rich archives of photographs, plans, oral histories, and documentation on redevelopment. Other archives have specialized strengths beyond their immediate locales, such as Cornell University's collection on architecture and city planning.

Development plans and renderings reveal much about how boosters imagine a city's future and residents. Contemporary plans often are available online from developers or local governments while historical plans can be located in local archives. City council minutes and public comments, which can sometimes be found online, are useful for identifying sources of conflict and support for redevelopment. State archives hold materials related to policy incentives, funding, and management for redevelopment projects. States with commercial casinos have gaming oversight boards that make applications, designs, public comments, and other relevant information on casino development available online.[96] For other types of local development projects, researchers might consider the records of municipal planning departments or metropolitan planning councils.

Researchers also can consult economic development reports from professional and research organizations such as the Urban Land Institute and the Lincoln Institute of Land Policy. Data on economic growth, unemployment, and demographics are available at the local to national scale from government agencies including the US Census Bureau and the Bureau of Labor Statistics. Federal Reserve

System branches release reports on regional economic development, decline, and revitalization. The Environmental Protection Agency documents the histories and conditions of industrial brownfields.

Finally, researchers will find that one of the richest primary sources for investigating the history of deindustrialization and postindustrial redevelopment is the built environment itself, where new construction and community priorities can be read against the material traces of the industrial past. Because these topics concern recent history in many communities, researchers also should consider interviewing longtime residents about their experiences of economic transition.

DIGITAL MATERIALS

ARCHIVAL, MAPPING, AND MULTIMEDIA SITES

Beyond Steel—Lehigh University digital archive of the Lehigh Valley, Pennsylvania's industry and culture from its origins through the present, including oral histories, images, and planning documents. http://digital.lib.lehigh.edu/beyondsteel/.

Exit Zero Project—Companion site to Christine Walley's book *Exit Zero*, including the trailer to her documentary *Exit Zero* about deindustrialization in Southeast Chicago. http://www.exitzeroproject.org/.

Latoya Ruby Frazier—Personal webpage of the artist's documentary photography and video works addressing Rust Belt revitalization, environmental justice, and community history. http://www.latoyarubyfrazier.com/.

Loveland—Parcel-by-parcel data on property in Detroit, including tax statuses, property values, photographs, and ownership. For the archive site of the original 2013–2014 land survey (not updated) see Motor City Mapping. https://detroit.makeloveland.com/.

Mapping Decline—Digital map site about St. Louis accompanying Colin Gordon's book *Mapping Decline*. http://mappingdecline.lib.uiowa.edu/map/.

Rivers of Steel National Heritage Area Online Collections—Materials on the steel industry and related work and communities in Southwestern Pennsylvania. http://riversofsteel.pastperfectonline.com/.

Social Explorer—Customizable digital mapping tool for demographic data. Many university libraries offer expanded access via subscription. https://www.socialexplorer.com/.

Youngstown State University Oral History Digital Collection—Transcripts from oral histories of Northeastern Ohioans, including about the steel, brick, and coal industries. http://www.maag.ysu.edu/oralhistory/oral_hist.html.

COVERAGE OF CONTEMPORARY ISSUES

Belt Magazine. http://beltmag.com/.
CityLab. https://www.citylab.com/.
Next City. https://nextcity.org/.
Planetizen. https://www.planetizen.com/.

FURTHER READING

Cowan, Aaron. *A Nice Place to Visit: Tourism and Urban Revitalization in the Postwar Rustbelt.* Philadelphia: Temple University Press, 2016.

Cowie, Jefferson and Joseph Heathcott, eds. *Beyond the Ruins: The Meanings of Deindustrialization.* Ithaca, NY: ILR Press, 2003.

Dieterich-Ward, Allen. *Beyond Rust: Metropolitan Pittsburgh and the Fate of Industrial America.* Philadelphia: University of Pennsylvania Press, 2015.

Frieden, Bernard J. and Lynne B. Sagalyn. *Downtown, Inc.: How America Rebuilds Cities.* Cambridge, MA: MIT Press, 1991.

Gillette, Howard, Jr. *Camden After the Fall: Decline and Renewal in a Post-Industrial City.* Philadelphia: University of Pennsylvania Press, 2005.

Gordon, Colin. *Mapping Decline: St. Louis and the Fate of the American City.* Philadelphia: University of Pennsylvania Press, 2008.

Highsmith, Andrew. *Demolition Means Progress: Flint, Michigan, and the Fate of the American Metropolis.* Chicago: University of Chicago Press, 2015.

Judd, Dennis R. and Susan S. Fainstein, eds. *The Tourist City.* New Haven, CT: Yale University Press, 1999.

Kinney, Rebecca. *Beautiful Wasteland: The Rise of Detroit as America's Postindustrial Frontier.* Minneapolis: University of Minnesota Press, 2016.

Neumann, Tracy. *Remaking the Rust Belt: The Postindustrial Transformation of North America.* Philadelphia: University of Pennsylvania Press, 2016.

Phillips-Fein, Kim. *Fear City: New York's Fiscal Crisis and the Rise of Austerity Politics.* New York: Metropolitan Books, 2017.

Ryan, Brent D. *Design after Decline: How America Rebuilds Shrinking Cities.* Philadelphia: University of Pennsylvania Press, 2012.

Sassen, Saskia. *The Global City: New York, London, Tokyo.* Princeton, NJ: Princeton University Press, 1991.

Sugrue, Thomas J. *The Origins of the Urban Crisis: Race and Inequality in Postwar Detroit.* Princeton, NJ: Princeton University Press, 1996.

Taft, Chloe E. *From Steel to Slots: Casino Capitalism in the Postindustrial City.* Cambridge, MA: Harvard University Press, 2016.

Teaford, Jon. *The Rough Road to Renaissance: Urban Revitalization in America, 1940–1985.* Baltimore: Johns Hopkins University Press, 1990.

Vergara, Camilo J. *The New American Ghetto.* New Brunswick, NJ: Rutgers University Press, 1995.

NOTES

1. Detroit Blight Removal Task Force, "Every Neighborhood Has a Future…And It Doesn't Include Blight," *Detroit Blight Removal Task Force Plan* (Detroit: Inland Press, 2014). http://jack-seanson.github.io/taskforce/.

2. Bureau of Labor Statistics, "Industries at a Glance: Manufacturing," *United States Department of Labor;* and Jefferson Cowie and Joseph Heathcott, eds., *Beyond the Ruins: The Meanings of Deindustrialization* (Ithaca, NY: ILR Press, 2003), ix.

3. Sherry Lee Linkon and John Russo, *Steeltown U.S.A.: Work and Memory in Youngstown* (Lawrence, KS: University Press of Kansas, 2002), 52.

4. Andrew Highsmith, *Demolition Means Progress: Flint, Michigan, and the Fate of the American Metropolis* (Chicago: University of Chicago Press, 2015), 4–5.

5. Howard Gillette, Jr., *Camden After the Fall: Decline and Renewal in a Post-Industrial City* (Philadelphia: University of Pennsylvania Press, 2005), 8.

6. United States Census Bureau, "Population of the 100 Largest Urban Places: 1950 (https://www.census.gov/population/www/documentation/twps0027/tab18.txt)," *U.S. Census Bureau;*

see also "QuickFacts (https://www.census.gov/quickfacts)."

7. Robert O. Self, "California's Industrial Garden: Oakland and the East Bay in the Age of Deindustrialization," in *Beyond the Ruins: The Meanings of Deindustrialization,* ed. Jefferson Cowie and Joseph Heathcott (Ithaca, NY: ILR, 2003), 160.

8. Tami J. Friedman, "'A Trail of Ghost Towns across Our Land': The Decline of Manufacturing in Yonkers, New York," in *Beyond the Ruins: The Meanings of Deindustrialization,* ed. Jefferson Cowie and Joseph Heathcott (Ithaca, NY: ILR Press, 2003), 20.

9. Jefferson Cowie, *Capital Moves: RCA's Seventy-Year Quest for Cheap Labor* (Ithaca, NY: Cornell University Press, 1999).

10. Chloe E. Taft, *From Steel to Slots: Casino Capitalism in the Postindustrial City* (Cambridge, MA: Harvard University Press, 2016).

11. For charts on Sun Belt growth see Brent D. Ryan, *Design after Decline: How America Rebuilds Shrinking Cities* (Philadelphia: University of Pennsylvania Press, 2012), 42–43. On deindustrialization in the South and West see, for example, Bill Bamberger and Cathy Davidson, *Closing: The Life and Death of an American Factory* (New York: W. W. Norton, 1998); and Robert O. Self, *American Babylon: Race and the Struggle for Postwar Oakland* (Princeton, NJ: Princeton University Press, 2005).

12. Lindsey Dillon, "Race, Waste, and Space: Brownfield Redevelopment and Environmental Justice at the Hunters Point Shipyard," *Antipode* 46, no. 5 (2014): 1205–1221.

13. Judith Stein, *Pivotal Decade: How the United States Traded Factories for Finance in the Seventies* (New Haven, CT: Yale University Press, 2010), 245–247.

14. For one example in Flint, Michigan, see Highsmith, *Demolition Means Progress,* 122–123.

15. Dolores Hayden, *Building Suburbia: Green Fields and Urban Growth, 1820–2000* (New York: Vintage, 2004), 162–164.

16. Highsmith, *Demolition Means Progress,* 122–126.

17. William Julius Wilson, *When Work Disappears: The World of the New Urban Poor* (New York: Vintage, 1997).

18. Thomas J. Sugrue, *The Origins of the Urban Crisis: Race and Inequality in Postwar Detroit* (Princeton, NJ: Princeton University Press, 1996), 120.

19. Alison Isenberg, *Downtown America: A History of the Place and the People Who Made It* (Chicago: University of Chicago Press, 2004), 203–254.

20. Daniel Bell, *The Coming of Post-industrial Society: A Venture in Social Forecasting* (New York: Basic Books, 1973).

21. United States Bureau of Labor Statistics, "BLS Data Finder (https://beta.bls.gov/labs/)," *U. S. Department of Labor*.

22. Tracy Neumann, *Remaking the Rust Belt: The Postindustrial Transformation of North America* (Philadelphia: University of Pennsylvania Press, 2016), 174–207; and Miriam Greenberg, *Branding New York: How a City in Crisis Was Sold to the World* (New York: Routledge, 2008).

23. Aaron Shkuda, *The Lofts of SoHo: Gentrification, Art, and Industry in New York, 1950–1980* (Chicago: University of Chicago Press, 2016); and Richard Florida, *The Rise of the Creative Class…and How It's Transforming Work, Leisure, Community, and Everyday Life* (New York: Basic Books, 2002).

24. Stein, *Pivotal Decade*, 288.

25. Saskia Sassen, *The Global City: New York, London, Tokyo* (Princeton, NJ: Princeton University Press, 1991), 18.

26. Stein, *Pivotal Decade*, 296.

27. For example, on Chicago, see Rachel Weber, *From Boom to Bubble: How Finance Built the New Chicago* (Chicago: University of Chicago Press, 2015).

28. Davarian L. Baldwin, "The '800-Pound Gargoyle': The Long History of Higher Education and Urban Development on Chicago's South Side," *American Quarterly* 67, no. 1 (2015): 82. See also LaDale C. Winling, *Building the Ivory Tower: Universities and Metropolitan Development in the Twentieth Century* (Philadelphia: University of Pennsylvania Press, 2017).

29. Margaret Pugh O'Mara, *Cities of Knowledge: Cold War Science and the Search for the Next Silicon Valley* (Princeton, NJ: Princeton University Press, 2004).

30. Baldwin, "The '800-Pound Gargoyle,'" 83.

31. See Aaron Cowan, *A Nice Place to Visit: Tourism and Urban Revitalization in the Postwar Rustbelt* (Philadelphia: Temple University Press, 2016).

32. See Cowan, *A Nice Place to Visit*, 127–155; Isenberg, *Downtown America*, 255–296; and Bernard J. Frieden and Lynne B. Sagalyn, *Downtown, Inc.: How America Rebuilds Cities* (Cambridge, MA: MIT Press, 1991), 171–198.

33. M. Christine Boyer, "Cities for Sale: Merchandising History at South Street Seaport," in *Variations on a Theme Park: The New American City and the End of Public Space*, ed. Michael Sorkin (New York: Hill and Wang, 1992), 181–204.

34. Ron Fonger, "'They Needed More Thrill' – Looking Back at the 25th Anniversary of Flint Legend, AutoWorld, *MLive*, July 3, 2009," http://www.mlive.com/news/flint/index.ssf/2009/07/they_needed_more_thrill_lookin.html and Youngstown Historical Center of Industry and Labor (https://www.ohiohistory.org/visit/museum-and-site-locator/youngstown-historical-center-of-industry-and-labor), *Ohio History Connection*.

35. Linkon and Russo, *Steeltown, U.S.A.*, 60.

36. Christopher Mele, "Casinos, Prisons, Incinerators, and Other Fragments of Neoliberal Urban Development," *Social Science History* 35, no. 3 (2011): 433–436.

37. Christine J. Walley, *Exit Zero: Family and Class in Postindustrial Chicago* (Chicago: University of Chicago Press, 2013), 121–122.

38. Linkon and Russo, *Steeltown, U.S.A.*, 60.

39. Linkon and Russo, *Steeltown, U.S.A.*, 60–64; and Mele, "Casinos, Prisons, Incinerators," 437–438.

40. Taft, *From Steel to Slots*; Chloe Taft, "Rust Belt Cities Gamble on Casino-Led Urban Development," *Next City*, September 15, 2016. https://nextcity.org/daily/entry/rust-belt-cities-casino-led-urban-development.

41. Ryan, *Design After Decline*, 40.

42. On "culture of clearance," see Francesca Russello Ammon, *Bulldozer: Demolition and Clearance of the Postwar Landscape* (New Haven, CT: Yale University Press, 2016).

43. Samuel Zipp, *Manhattan Projects: The Rise and Fall of Urban Renewal in Cold War New York* (Oxford: Oxford University Press, 2010), 157–252.

44. United States Government Accountability Office, "Statement of Dennis J. Dugan, Chief Economist of U.S. General Accounting Office Before the Subcommittee on Intergovernmental Relations and Human Resources, United States House Committee on Government Operations," Washington, DC: GAO, May 23, 1979, 4–7. http://www.gao.gov/assets/100/99079.pdf.

45. Neumann, *Remaking the Rust Belt*, 41–43.

46. See Kim Phillips-Fein, *Fear City: New York's Fiscal Crisis and the Rise of Austerity Politics* (New York: Metropolitan Books, 2017).

47. Neumann, *Remaking the Rust Belt*, 15–22. See also Frieden and Sagalyn, *Downtown, Inc.*

48. Neumann, *Remaking the Rust Belt*, 1.

49. See Allen Dieterich-Ward, *Beyond Rust: Metropolitan Pittsburgh and the Fate of Industrial America* (Philadelphia: University of Pennsylvania Press, 2015).

50. L. Owen Kirkpatrick, "Urban Triage, City Systems, and the Remnants of Community: Some 'Sticky' Complications in the Greening of Detroit," *Journal of Urban History* 41, no. 2 (2015): 261–278; and Detroit Future City, *2012 Detroit Strategic Framework Plan* (Detroit: Inland Press, 2012). https://detroitfuturecity.com/wp-content/uploads/2014/12/DFC_Full_2nd.pdf.

51. Margaret Dewar, Christina Kelly, and Hunter Morrison, "Planning for Better, Smaller Places After Population Loss: Lessons from Youngstown and Flint," in *The City After Abandonment*, ed. Margaret Dewar and June Manning Thomas (Philadelphia: University of Pennsylvania Press, 2012), 292; and Jason Hackworth, "Rightsizing as Spatial Austerity in the American Rust Belt," *Environment and Planning A* 47, no. 4 (2015): 766–782.

52. For example, on Philadelphia, see Ryan, *Design After Decline*, 51–61.

53. Ryan, *Design After Decline*, 205.

54. Ryan, *Design After Decline*, 179–182.

55. Motor City Mapping, https://www.motorcitymapping.org/; and Detroit Blight Removal Task Force, *Every Neighborhood Has a Future.*

56. Ryan, *Design After Decline*, 180–182, 186.

57. Frank S. Alexander, *Land Banks and Land Banking* (Flint, MI: Center for Community Progress, 2011).

58. Dewar, Kelly, and Morrison, "Planning for Better, Smaller Places," 293; and Alexander, *Land Banks and Land Banking*, 9.

59. Stephen High and David W. Lewis, *Corporate Wasteland: The Landscape and Memory of Deindustrialization* (Ithaca, NY: Cornell University Press, 2007), 41–63.

60. Kelsey Campbell-Dollaghan, "The Ruin Garden: An Old Idea That Could Help Today's Cities Fight Blight," *Co.Design*, June 16, 2017. https://www.fast-codesign.com/90129890/the-ruin-garden-an-old-idea-that-could-help-todays-cities-fight-blight.

61. High and Lewis, *Corporate Wasteland*, 41–63; Rebecca J. Kinney, *Beautiful Wasteland: The Rise*

of Detroit as America's Postindustrial Frontier (Minneapolis: University of Minnesota Press, 2016); and Dora Apel, *Beautiful Terrible Ruins: Detroit and the Anxiety of Decline* (New Brunswick, NJ: Rutgers University Press, 2015). See also Camilo J. Vergara, *The New American Ghetto* (New Brunswick, NJ: Rutgers University Press, 1995).

62. Laura Lawson and Abbilyn Miller, "Community Gardens and Urban Agriculture as Antithesis to Abandonment: Exploring a Citizenship-Land Model," in *The City After Abandonment*, ed. Margaret Dewar and June Manning Thomas (Philadelphia: University of Pennsylvania Press, 2012), 24.

63. Lawson and Miller, "Community Gardens and Urban Agriculture," 17–40.

64. St. Louis Union Station, "Past, Present and Future at St. Louis Union Station," *St. Louis Union Station*, http://www.stlouisunionstation.com/about/; Winchester Lofts, https://www.winchesterlofts.com; Chicago Park District, "Palmisano Park," http://www.chicagoparkdistrict.com/parks/Palmisano-Park/"; Freshkills Park Alliance, "Freshkills Park," http://freshkillspark.org/.

65. City of Chicago, "Chicago Public Art Program – Percent-for-Art Ordinance." https://www.cityofchicago.org/city/en/depts/dca/auto_generated/public_art_program:publandreports.html.

66. On Detroit artists, see Apel, *Beautiful Terrible Ruins*, 101–112.

67. Thomas Pikkety, *Capital in the Twenty-First Century* (Cambridge, MA: Harvard University Press, 2013), 291–303.

68. Dominic Vitello and Thomas J. Sugrue, eds., *Immigration and Metropolitan Revitalization in the United States* (Philadelphia: University of Pennsylvania Press, 2017); and Robert J. Sampson, *Great American City: Chicago and the Enduring Neighborhood Effect* (Chicago: University of Chicago Press, 2012), 251–259.

69. Richard Florida, *The New Urban Crisis: How Our Cities Are Increasing Inequality, Deepening Segregation, and Failing the Middle Class—and What We Can Do About It* (New York: Basic Books, 2017). See also Lynne M. Dearborn, "The Socioeconomic Opportunities of SynergiCity," in *SynergiCity: Reinventing the Postindustrial City*, ed. Paul Hardin Kapp and Paul J. Armstrong (Urbana: University of Illinois Press, 2012), 54–68.

70. Suleiman Osman, *The Invention of Brownstone Brooklyn: Gentrification and the Search for Authenticity in Postwar New York* (Oxford: Oxford University Press, 2011); Shkuda, *The Lofts of SoHo*; and Brian Goldstein, *The Roots of Urban Renaissance: Gentrification and the Struggle over Harlem* (Cambridge, MA: Harvard University Press, 2017).

71. Marwa Eltagouri, "Black Exodus Accelerates in Cook County, Census Shows," *Chicago Tribune*, June 22, 2017. http://www.chicagotribune.com /news/local/breaking/ct-black-population -declines-cook-county-met-20170621-story .html.

72. Dewar, Kelly, and Morrison, "Planning for Better, Smaller Places," 313.

73. Dennis R. Judd, "Constructing the Tourist Bubble," in *The Tourist City*, ed. Dennis R. Judd and Susan S. Fainstein (New Haven, CT: Yale University Press, 1999), 21–34; see also Cowan, *A Nice Place to Visit*.

74. On Pittsburgh see Dieterich-Ward, *Beyond Rust*, 125.

75. See Andrew Hurley, *Environmental Inequalities: Class, Race, and Industrial Pollution in Gary, Indiana, 1945–1980* (Chapel Hill: University of North Carolina Press, 1995); and Julie Sze, *Noxious New York: The Racial Politics of Urban Health and Environmental Justice* (Cambridge, MA: MIT Press, 2006).

76. Kevin Stark, "Behind the Scenes of East Chicago's Housing Crisis," *Pacific Standard*, October 7, 2016. https://psmag.com/news/behind-the -scenes-of-east-chicagos-housing-crisis.

77. Peter C. Little, *Toxic Town: IBM, Pollution, and Industrial Risks* (New York: New York University Press, 2014).

78. Barry Bluestone and Bennett Harrison, *The Deindustrialization of America: Plant Closings, Community Abandonment, and the Dismantling of Basic Industry* (New York: Basic Books, 1982).

79. For example Gregory Pappas, *The Magic City: Unemployment in a Working-Class Community* (Ithaca, NY: Cornell University Press, 1989); William Serrin, *Homestead: The Glory and Tragedy of an American Steel Town* (New York: Times Books, 1992); Steven P. Dandaneau, *A Town Abandoned: Flint, Michigan Confronts Deindustrialization* (Albany, NY: State University of New York Press, 1996); and *Roger and Me*,

directed by Michael Moore (1989; Burbank, CA: Warner Home Video, 2003), DVD.

80. Kathryn Marie Dudley, *End of the Line: Lost Jobs, New Lives in Postindustrial America* (Chicago: University of Chicago Press, 1994); and Ruth Milkman, *Farewell to the Factory: Auto Workers in the Late Twentieth Century* (Berkeley: University of California Press, 1997).

81. Robert A. Beauregard, *Voices of Decline: The Postwar Fate of U.S. Cities* (Cambridge, MA: Blackwell, 1993); Isenberg, *Downtown America*; and Linkon and Russo, *Steeltown, U.S.A.*

82. Colin Gordon, *Mapping Decline: St. Louis and the Fate of the American City* (Philadelphia: University of Pennsylvania Press, 2008).

83. Apel, *Beautiful Terrible Ruins*; and Kinney, *Beautiful Wasteland.*

84. Cowie and Heathcott, *Beyond the Ruins*; Cowie, *Capital Moves*; and Self, *American Babylon.*

85. See Andrew Highsmith, "Decline and Renewal in North American Cities," *Journal of Urban History* 34, no. 4 (2011): 619–626.

86. Taft, *From Steel to Slots.*

87. Sassen, *The Global City*; Neumann, *Remaking the Rust Belt*; and Steven High, *Industrial Sunset: The Making of North America's Rust Belt, 1969–1984* (Toronto: University of Toronto Press, 2003).

88. Gillette, *Camden After the Fall*; Highsmith, *Demolition Means Progress*; and Dieterich-Ward, *Beyond Rust.*

89. Sze, *Noxious New York*; and Walley, *Exit Zero.*

90. Harvey Molotch, "The City as a Growth Machine: Toward a Political Economy of Place," *American Journal of Sociology* 82, no. 2 (1976): 309–332; and John R. Logan and Harvey L. Molotch, *Urban Fortunes: The Political Economy of Place* (Berkeley: University of California Press, 1987).

91. Jon Teaford, *The Rough Road to Renaissance: Urban Revitalization in America, 1940–1985* (Baltimore: Johns Hopkins University Press, 1990).

92. Margaret E. Dewar and June Manning Thomas, eds., *The City After Abandonment* (Philadelphia: University of Pennsylvania Press, 2013); Alan Mallach and Lavea Brachman, *Regenerating America's Legacy Cities* (Cambridge, MA: Lincoln Institute of Land Policy, 2013); and Torey Hollingsworth and Alison Goebel, *Revitalizing America's Smaller Legacy Cities: Strategies for*

Postindustrial Success from Gary to Lowell (Cambridge, MA: Lincoln Institute of Land Policy, 2017).

93. For an example of Florida's influence, see Paul Hardin Kapp and Paul J. Armstrong, ed., *SynergiCity: Reinventing the Postindustrial City* (Urbana: University of Illinois Press, 2012).

94. Highsmith, *Demolition Means Progress*; Dieterich-Ward, *Beyond Rust*; Cowan, *A Nice Place to Visit*; and Cathy Stanton, *The Lowell Experiment: Public History in a Postindustrial City* (Amherst, MA: University of Massachusetts Press, 2006).

95. Yves Marchand and Romain Meffre, *The Ruins of Detroit* (Göttingen, Germany: Steidl, 2010); and Latoya Ruby Frazier, *The Notion of Family* (London: Aperture Foundation, 2014); and Vergara, *The New American Ghetto*.

96. For example, see *Pennsylvania Gaming Control Board*, http://gamingcontrolboard.pa.gov/, and *Massachusetts Gaming Commission*, http://massgaming.com/.

Chloe E. Taft

UNIVERSITIES AND INFORMATION CENTERS IN US CITIES

University-urban development and economic growth went through seven historical phases. In the first phase, colleges functioned until the early 19th century as small, religiously oriented institutions largely dedicated to the training of clergy, often removed or separated from their surrounding communities. In the second phase, throughout the first half of the 19th century, debates over religious education, universal knowledge, and colleges led to a transformation of the curriculum and opened higher education to the material world, including their nearby towns and cities. In the third phase, around the Civil War (1861–1865), scientific engagement, curricular modernization, and a growing number of public institutions made colleges and universities more central to American society, the US economy, and urban development. Cities and universities thereafter increasingly grew in tandem. In the fourth phase, Gilded Age philanthropy invested gains from American industrial growth into higher education, providing the means for major research institutions to pursue both practical education and pure research. Many leading colleges and universities became central to urban growth and development in their cities during the next century and a half.

The fifth phase commenced in the early 20th century. Progressive Era reformers and social scientists transformed colleges and universities into training grounds for various professions. The result was the creation and incorporation of normal schools, law schools, and medical schools within universities. In addition, the disciplines of history, economics, and physics emerged in part through the creation of professional academic organizations and the separation of distinct university departments. The white-collar, middle-class city became linked to higher education as a college degree became a key prerequisite for the emerging classes of urban professional workers. In the sixth phase, in the middle of the 20th century, federal support for universities to combat the crises of economic depression, global war, urban crisis, and the Cold War intensified the transformation of the American economy, urban development, and universities' role within them. The national state supported and shaped metropolitan and university growth in tandem. In the seventh and current phase, economic retrenchment and an ideological shift to embrace market forces led to increased corporate partnership and made universities, hospitals, and cities more receptive to the investment of private capital. Concurrently, however, those same institutions became less stable and predictable; notions of urban life, healthcare, communication practices, and higher education were susceptible to economic and political crises and subjected to intense debates over their purpose and practice.

ORIGINS

Universities have served as information centers and keepers of universal knowledge since their foundation. That role transformed in the 19th century to emphasize the creation of new knowledge through research and experimentation. Many of the oldest universities were in or near cities and became leaders in research, contributing to the dramatic growth of the US and global economy in the latter part of the 1800s. Daniel Patrick Moynihan put the relationship between urbanism, economic growth, and higher education most succinctly: "If you want to build a world-class city, build a great university and wait two hundred years."[1]

Debates over educational ideology and epistemology at institutions such as Yale and Harvard colleges in the middle of the 19th century moved them away from the moral and theological instruction that was the heart of higher education in the 17th and 18th centuries. In the process, colleges and universities expanded their teaching beyond the classical curriculum. This fundamentally redefined higher education. Where they had been teachers of canonical, universal knowledge, they became locales of experimentation, economic relevance, and intellectual fragmentation. This ideological change included the creation of scientific schools, led by the Lowell Scientific School (1847) at Harvard College and the Yale Scientific School (1854). In each case, patrons funded schools that trained students to study practical and experimental science, preparing them to move into industrial-related occupations. Harvard introduced an elective system of courses in the middle of the 19th century that allowed students to experiment in combining forms of knowledge—historical, artistic, scientific, moral, and professional. A secular college education became a form of elite finishing school and means of middle-class mobility as college-educated leaders took their places at the heads of corporations in the emerging urban, industrial economy. Harvard historian

Henry Adams later wrote that one of his students said, "The degree of Harvard College is worth money to me in Chicago," as he prepared to move to business opportunities in the industrial West.

INVESTMENTS IN THE AMERICAN ECONOMY

The federal Morrill Land Grant Acts of 1862 and 1890 provided resources for the creation of new state colleges and universities that emphasized engineering and agricultural education, making university instruction and research inputs into the growing US economy. The Morrill Acts and subsequent establishment of public land grant colleges in states around the country institutionalized the experimentation initiated at leading private universities at mid-century. Featuring colleges of agriculture and engineering, land grant universities were often located in small towns and rural settings. However, several important land grant universities were built in major cities, including Boston, Massachusetts; Columbus, Ohio; Madison, Wisconsin; Raleigh, North Carolina; Minneapolis, Minnesota; and Lincoln, Nebraska. Each of these cities was also the state capital, which concentrated the effects of state investment in a single city. Even large universities were modest employers in the 19th century, but by the early 21st century most of these universities were the city's largest employer, even surpassing the state government.

In Southern states, legislatures designated separate land grant institutions for white and black students. Thus, the land grant institutions were often in separate cities. The Virginia Agricultural and Mechanical College was the land grant college for white students in the rural southwest Virginia town of Blacksburg, for example, while the Hampton Institute in coastal Hampton served as the land grant for black students until the 1930s. This diluted the impact of the colleges or universities, and the Southern system of segregation meant that its higher education institutions rarely reached the capacity, prominence, or urban impact of their Northern counterparts.

PHILANTHROPIC INVESTMENT

Business leaders in the Gilded Age and the Progressive Era, including Johns Hopkins, John D. Rockefeller, Leland Stanford, Cornelius Vanderbilt, and Andrew Carnegie, collaborated with education reformers to create modern research universities. First among these were the graduate schools created at Clark University in Worcester, Massachusetts, and Johns Hopkins University in Baltimore, Maryland, each named for their key donor, businessmen Jonas Gilman Clark and Johns Hopkins, respectively. Under the direction of Daniel Coit Gilman, Johns Hopkins University emphasized the importance of graduate education and knowledge creation, making Hopkins the most prominent research institution in the country. Only a handful of universities offered medical education when donor Johns Hopkins gave $7 million to establish a hospital and university in Baltimore in 1876. The Hopkins donation, however, initiated a durable union between higher education and medical education that flourished for more than a century. The size of the Hopkins gift and prominence of the institution put it at the national vanguard of medical education and research, evidenced by the sixteen Nobel Prizes in physiology won by faculty or alumni. By the early 21st century, Johns Hopkins had a $7 billion annual budget, with more than 40,000 employees.

In Chicago, members of the American Baptist Education Society convinced oil magnate John D. Rockefeller and several prominent Chicagoans to contribute to the creation of a new university. The University of Chicago opened in 1892 almost simultaneously with the World's Columbian Exposition, which showcased an orderly neoclassical vision for urban reform in nearby Jackson Park. The university was seen as a beacon of hope for cities teeming with new immigrants and chaotic with industrial growth. University of Chicago faculty created and worked in settlement houses where social workers and researchers applied the emerging insights of sociology, economics, and other social sciences. Settlement house workers also provided services to the poor of the city, providing lessons in civics, theater, conflict negotiation, thrift, and recreation that promoted a bourgeois vision of the good life and social and economic mobility.

The philanthropic impetus followed similar lines at many universities, but the spatial and academic consequences varied. Railroad magnate and politician Leland Stanford Sr. and his wife, Jane, for example, donated $40 million to establish Stanford University in 1885 as a memorial to their son, Leland Jr., who died of typhoid fever as a teenager. The institution was explicitly coeducational, nonsectarian, and dedicated to the creation of new knowledge. At its founding, the Stanford campus, which included a farm for agricultural research, was located far from San Francisco and had no clear urban context as in Baltimore or Chicago. The low-density rural educational development at Palo Alto at the south end of the San Francisco Bay later became central to the creation of the tech ecosystem of Silicon Valley.

PROGRESSIVE REFORM

The elaboration of university disciplines and the increasingly stringent definitions of professional education during the Progressive Era created the structures of the modern university. These institutions were transformed into the training grounds for the knowledge and administrative economy. Changing standards in professional training and business administration brought the requirement of credentials and data-driven decision-making to bear on educational organizations.

The settlement house movement and urban education advocates found a willing home in the Chicago School of Civics and Philanthropy, loosely affiliated with the University of Chicago in the 1900s. In 1924, the university incorporated the School of Social Services

Administration, with professor and social worker Edith Abbott as the first dean. University leaders had once promoted direct and applied engagement with urban communities external to the university, but became less involved with practice and application in the 20th century, instead emphasizing research and the internal academic logic of a research university.[2] The university later spun off the settlement house in the Back of the Yards neighborhood near the Union Stockyards, severing enduring ties between university and community.

The emphasis on research over community-engaged practice came to characterize medicine as well. In 1910, education reformer and Johns Hopkins alumnus Abraham Flexner published a study on medical education for the Carnegie Foundation, entitled *Medical Education in the United States and Canada*. Flexner promoted the Hopkins model of research-intensive medical education and praised prevailing trends in medical education toward greater scientific laboratory research and higher standards of qualification. Flexner critiqued less prominent or prestigious institutions that had fewer resources and which emphasized practical training.

The Flexner report was part of a trend that promoted professional qualifications featuring higher education at prestigious universities.[3] This came at the expense of practical training and diminished the role of less research-intensive medical schools that trained more working-class, female, and minority physicians. One result was the closure and consolidation of many medical schools that emphasized practical training rather than scientific research. Consequently, several independent medical schools allied themselves with institutions of higher education, bringing an increasingly important form of knowledge under the umbrella of universities.

The emphasis on education at all levels in the Progressive Era led to the formation of teacher training schools, "normal schools," in order to staff the growing number of mandatory and state-supported primary and secondary schools. Many of these normal schools began modestly but grew to become colleges and universities, such as the University of California at Los Angeles, Arizona State University in Tempe, and Ball State University in Muncie, Indiana. Through the proliferation of programs and departments, these universities became community anchors for their metropolitan areas, training tens of thousands of graduates each year for the local, national, and global workforce.

Teacher training became a key element of higher education and incorporated a greater number of women, offering roles in a new profession. The growth of these programs helped accelerate the integration of women into higher education, making most institutions coeducational as a matter of course rather than as the radical act that women's attendance constituted in the latter part of the 19th century. Beyond normal schools, colleges of home economics and domestic science began to provide scientific training to women, albeit with constrained paths for employment.

MID-CENTURY LIBERALISM

After 1930, investments in higher education and defense research in the New Deal, World War II, and the Cold War intensified this transformation in American cities. The Public Works Administration (PWA) and Works Progress Administration (WPA) provided tens of millions of dollars in grants and loans to colleges and universities to construct buildings and increase their capacities for education, research, and housing.[4] At the University of Texas in Austin, the PWA funded seven buildings, including a laboratory and a library, part of the second-largest outlay in the United States. Construction at the state flagship university helped counter the economic downturn of the Great Depression in Austin and advanced the university's reputation and ambition.

In his 1944 State of the Union Address, President Franklin Roosevelt proposed a second bill of rights that was economic in nature. The proposal solidified the grounding of the New Deal welfare state and gave a forward-looking set of policy initiatives for after World War II. This bill of rights included the right to a useful and remunerative job and to a good education, both of which would be supported with federal subsidy and public policy. The Servicemen's Readjustment Act of 1944, or GI Bill, was aligned with these proposals, providing a college education and housing subsidies for veterans, both offering economic mobility, economic stimulus, and new consumer buying power.

After the conclusion of World War II, federal spending for scientific and defense research increased dramatically, largely targeted to the established universities that were leaders at the turn of the 19th to the 20th century. The federal government responded to the October, 1957, Soviet launch of *Sputnik* with the National Defense Education Act (NDEA) in 1958, providing nearly $200 million annually for graduate research in science, engineering, and mathematics, increasing enrollment in what are now known as the STEM (science, technology, engineering, mathematics) disciplines, a catalyzing investment for the postwar tech economy.

The postwar expansion of universities' agenda coincided with the growth of education infrastructure and physical plants, which, however, were troubled by rapid demographic and racial changes in metropolitan areas. During the Great Migration, millions of rural Southern African Americans moved to industrial cities, largely in northern and eastern states that also had prominent urban universities. University administrators reacted with alarm when their surrounding neighborhoods experienced racial transition, then suffered from the effects of disinvestment and white suburbanization. The University of Chicago supported segregationist neighborhood organizations that promoted the use of restrictive covenants against African Americans in real estate in an attempt to maintain racial stasis on the South Side of Chicago.[5]

Colleges and universities responded to decades of urban disinvestment and demographic transformation as enthusiastic boosters and partners of federal slum clearance and urban renewal projects. Urban renewal was often used to promote campus expansion as part of urban redevelopment. Leading private universities such as Columbia University and the University of Chicago led urban renewal efforts in their respective communities of Morningside Heights and Hyde Park. The state of Illinois and the city of Chicago collaborated to build the public University of Illinois at Chicago campus as part of a massive urban renewal project that demolished blocks of housing, built interstate expressways, and created a major public university for the city of Chicago.[6]

Universities and hospitals tied together urban renewal and the Cold War, post-*Sputnik* growth of graduate education by creating the Section 112 credits program in the federal Housing Act of 1959. This program provided matching funds to cities where university and hospital expansion coincided with urban renewal plans. Section 112 credits empowered urban universities in negotiations with city politicians who sought federal urban renewal dollars for redevelopment programs and patronage employment. Thereafter, urban universities broke out of the boundaries of their traditional campus borders and expanded into already built-up areas, often industrial neighborhoods and poorer residential communities undergoing racial transition. Julian Levi, a University of Chicago affiliate and one of the driving forces behind the legislation, testified before Congress that cities needed communities of scholars who lived near universities, not faculty commuters who lived far from the intellectual centers of campus. University of Louisville official and former Louisville mayor Charles Farnsley concurred, arguing that the "American people will keep wanting to move out of the cities and it leaves a vacuum, not only the people, but the industries and retailing." Higher education institutions, Farnsley insisted, played instrumental roles in the urban economy. "If the university is the only thing you can work for and it is respectable to live near, and if you have the professors living back down there," he believed, "that will help bring back the middle class to the city."[7] Through this program, university leaders articulated a vision in which researchers populated central cities, drawing human and investment capital back from the suburbs. At this point, universities began to explicitly remake cities into knowledge centers.

Clark Kerr, the president of the University of California, argued in the 1960s that universities and the knowledge industry were the engines of the American economy. Kerr published a series of lectures as the book *The Uses of the University* and wrote, "What the railroads did for the second half of the last century and the automobile did for the first half of this century, may be done for the second half of this century by the knowledge industry: that is, to serve as the focal point for national growth." Universities were central to the knowledge industry and allied with institutions, including federal research laboratories and major industrial corporations, that could translate research findings and improvements in corporate management and governance. He quoted scholars estimating that production, distribution, and consumption of knowledge made up 29 percent of the gross national product (GNP).

Kerr sat at the head of the multi-campus University of California and helped create the Master Plan for Higher Education and its partner legislation, the Donahoe Act of 1960. The Master Plan created a formal organization involving the state of California's community college, state colleges, and university, coordinating public efforts with the support of business leaders and elected leaders, many of whom sought the economic impact of campuses of the university and state college in their communities. The California system of higher education served as a model for several states that created statewide systems of their own in the wake of California's example.

Kerr also laid out the spatial implications of the development of the knowledge industry,

writing, "An almost ideal location for a modern university is to be sandwiched between a middle-class district on its way to becoming a slum and an ultramodern industrial park—so that the students may live in one and the faculty consult in the other."[8] Kerr singled out the Massachusetts Institute of Technology (MIT) as well situated for just such a scenario. The institute in Cambridge was located between a slum clearance site that became the Draper Laboratories at Technology Square, and a deteriorating industrial neighborhood. That east Cambridge neighborhood, through an urban renewal program, later became Cambridge Center, one of the most dynamic commercial sites for computer software and biotech development in the United States.

Austin, Texas, also illustrates the transformative effects of federal investment in the mid-century decades. For decades in the late 19th and early 20th centuries, Austin was a small city without an industrial base. The state capital of a large but impoverished state, Austin was home to an unremarkable university with the ambitions to be "a university of the first class," as specified in the state constitution.[9] The discovery of oil on state-owned lands in west Texas and the growth of the petroleum industry, largely centered in Texas, provided a massive windfall for the institution. Through oil revenues and New Deal funding, the University of Texas became a major institution with a renowned Beaux-Arts style campus and leading research and professional programs. At the conclusion of World War II, then-Congressman Lyndon Johnson arranged for the federal government to transfer a surplus magnesium plant to the university in 1946 and helped create a research park, which became the J.J. Pickle Research Center. The University of Texas received the land in direct grant from the federal government. By contrast, Stanford's research park came from the original private donation from Leland Stanford. At nearly the same time, North Carolina businessmen raised private funds for the land that would become Research Triangle Park.[10]

This expansion of the physical plant allowed hundreds, then thousands more students to enroll at the University of Texas each year. Austin rapidly transformed from a modest state capital into a leading southern metropolis, growing from a city of 53,000 in 1930 to one of 186,000 in 1960.[11] Enrollment at the University of Texas ballooned from approximately 5,700 to 25,000 in the same period, stimulated in part by the GI Bill. These developments mirrored national trends as college enrollment across the country increased from 1.1 million students in 1930 to about 4 million by 1960.[12]

The emerging technology sector in Austin was part of a broader high-tech economy in Texas, especially featuring hardware producers Compaq and Texas Instruments in Dallas, Texas. UT's Pickle Research Center was home to numerous laboratories with defense contracts and allowed the university to attract private sector technology companies and research consortia to locate at and around the research park in the 1960s, 1970s, and 1980s. The central location of Texas within the United States allowed Austin to become home to branch research and manufacturing locations of corporations such as International Business Machines (IBM), which broke ground in 1967, as well as the site for multi-institutional consortia, which included East Coast and West Coast partners. The Microelectronics and Computer Technology Corporation located in the Pickle Research Center in 1982, and SEMATECH, a partnership between the US government and fourteen semiconductor manufacturers, began operating in Austin in 1988. The number of Austin white-collar workers grew from 26,000 in 1950, or 53 percent of workers, to 250,000 in 1990, or more than 80 percent of workers, illustrating a shift from a small economy in an underdeveloped state to an intellectual, cultural, and intellectual capital with an increasingly skilled workforce.[13]

In 1984, University of Texas undergraduate Michael Dell founded the computer company that not only bore his name but soon became the world's largest personal computer (PC) manufacturer. By 2010, Dell Inc. employed 100,000 workers in metropolitan Austin. By then, the city was a technology capital. IBM and chipmakers Intel and American Micro Devices (AMD) in the computer sector located offices in Austin, building on a longer history of Texas technology enterprises, including Texas Instruments and Compaq. The University of Texas helped launch a handful of efforts, such as its master's in technology and communication (MSTC) program and semiconductor manufacturing technology (SEMATCH), but Austin was increasingly seen as a dynamic metropolitan center with a highly skilled population, first coming out of the university, then increasingly attracted from elsewhere in the state and country.

Austin's growth and wealth focused on the university, which allowed it to become a creative and artistic center beyond its technology sector. Filmmaker Richard Linklater relocated to Austin in order to make movies, and launched his career with *Slacker*, a 1991 film depicting the social lives and pastimes of Generation X Austinites. Director Robert Rodriguez also moved to Austin to be a filmmaker, attending the University of Texas and starting his film career while still an undergraduate. Austinites created the South by Southwest (SxSW) music and media festival in 1987; by 2010, it was an annual event of national scale. Tourism for events such as SxSW and the Austin City Limits festival became major features of Austin's economy, including hundreds of millions of dollars of economic impact. These events attracted new visitors to Austin and built the city's reputation as a creative capital, contributing to the city's continuing growth. By 2010, Austin was the 11th-largest city in the country by population and had doubled since 1990.[14]

Hospitals became important sources of employment and key research centers in the post-WWII era but also maintained tense relations with their local communities. In many cases, in alliance with university medical schools, research hospitals in urban areas grew into large centers of medical and pharmaceutical research as well as centers of patient care. At the Johns Hopkins University Hospital in 1951, physician and researcher George Gey took a tissue sample from Henrietta Lacks, an African American Baltimore woman suffering from cervical cancer. Johns Hopkins researchers cultivated and maintained her cancer cells, using new laboratory techniques, while Gey shared the cell line with researchers around the world under the name "HeLa" long after Lacks's death. Through this brief interaction of treatment, Johns Hopkins University researchers unsuccessfully treated a woman from working-class Baltimore, extracted her tissue, and developed the anonymous material in a manner that created new cancer therapies and intensified its own reputation as a research leader in medicine. That research success led to hospital expansion and put Johns Hopkins in greater tension with the local African American community around the hospital. The university's greatest discoveries in global science did some of the greatest damage locally.

MAKING THE MARKET UNIVERSITY

After 1970, universities incorporated market logic more explicitly in their governance and to embrace a neoliberal ideology. Within the academy, neoclassical liberal economists such as Joseph Schumpeter, Friedrich Hayek, and Ludwig von Mises were an intellectual counterweight to the prevailing logic of mid-century liberalism, embraced and reinterpreted by political leaders. The economic stagflation of the 1970s and the fragmentation of the fragile postwar liberal coalition provided academics and policy elites opportunities for advocating alternate ideas promoting economic growth. A new conservative and neoliberal coalition advocated reforming and reducing public commitments to education as part of a broader tax revolt and effort to roll back New Deal and Great Society investments. Political conservatives advocated reducing public support for higher education at both the state and federal levels, while liberals pushed universities to seek revenue from private sources, build their endowments, and partner with corporations for academic research support.[15]

Federal tax cuts and the erosion of investment returns from traditional buy-and-hold stock strategies for led university endowment management firms like the Harvard Management Company to invest more aggressively and to cultivate more donors for financial support. Capital campaigns took on far greater importance for expanding university capacity and securing academic resources for many top institutions. In the midst of a university capital campaign in 1981, for example, Harvard University administrators learned of the Reagan Administration's tax cuts and increased the fundraising campaign's goal from $259 million to $350 million.[16] In an era of federal austerity, Harvard emphasized its endowment, which grew from $1.4 billion in 1979 to $18.8 billion in 2000, the largest in the nation.[17]

With such resources, many university foundations invested their philanthropic gains in local real estate developments consistent with university growth plans. Foundations financed student housing complexes and private commercial spaces occupied by university offices and allied research centers and incubators for start-up companies, increasing the reach of university operations and shifting the emphasis of education to its commercial impact.

In the realm of research, the Bayh-Dole Act of 1980 allowed institutions to license and commercialize their federally funded discoveries to private enterprises, leading to development of new research facilities on and near university and hospital campuses. This alliance included the growth of medical research in hospitals and medical schools, the creation of affiliated institutes in university communities, and an increase in development efforts to colocate university researchers and allied employers in research parks and urban redevelopments. In numerous communities, hospitals or healthcare organizations became the largest employers.

Key in this transformation of education communities was changes in norms and expectations about research collaborations with industry.[18] In the 1970s, a group of research universities promoted the idea of technology transfer and the commercialization of research findings, and formed an organization now known as the Association of University Technology Managers (AUTM) to share practices and lobby Congress for legislation.[19] Of particular interest to technology managers was the prohibition on licensing discoveries made with federal funding. These discoveries became part of the public domain, owned by the American people. A 1968 study indicated that no pharmaceutical had ever been brought to market where the scientific discovery had been funded by the federal government and the rights were in the public domain. In effect, there was no protection and incentive for private companies to invest in a product that faced immediate competition as soon as it proved profitable in the marketplace.[20] AUTM lobbied members of Congress and found willing allies in US Senators Robert Dole (R-KS) and Birch Bayh (D-IN), who passed the Patent and Trademark Law Amendments, or Bayh-Dole Act, in 1980.

After the passage of the Bayh-Dole Act, the University of California, the University of Washington, Stanford, and MIT became the top recipients of industry licenses for the discoveries of their faculty.[21] These licensing agreements channeled hundreds of millions of dollars to local economies around universities and research parks, through scientific, engineering, and medical researchers, in an education process that created more white-collar knowledge workers for the economies each year.

By the 2010s, healthcare was not just an important sector of the American economy; it comprised 18 percent of the gross domestic product (GDP).[22] This transformation of industrial city to intellectual community was evidenced in various forms around the country. Pittsburgh may be the classic example of a city that transitioned from an industrial center to a networked information society with healthcare at its center. The city was the hub of the iron and steel industries at the turn of the 20th century and suffered job losses, decentralization, and disinvestment in the 1960s and 1970s as the American steel industry faced competition from overseas. In the midst of their urban crisis, civic leaders replanned and redesigned the metropolitan economy and built on some of the city's core institutions, such as Carnegie Mellon University and the University of Pittsburgh Medical Center. This transformed Pittsburgh into a more dynamic economic community than in prior decades, but the gains of these communities are unequally shared and in many cases exacerbated racial and economic inequality.[23]

Leaders of technology and cultural centers such as Austin also increasingly incorporated healthcare in their economic development strategies. Austin enjoyed economic and demographic growth as the University of Texas employed 14,500 in the city and claimed an economic impact of $8.2 billion.[24] The lack of a medical school concerned civic leaders and university boosters, however. The state system's medical school was located in Houston, a city with a more developed healthcare sector. University supporters affirmed the centrality of healthcare to metropolitan well-being, university robustness, and economic expansion when the university moved to create a new medical school. The Michael and Susan Dell Foundation pledged $50 million in 2013 to establish the school, which opened in 2016. One of the nation's fastest-growing cities, envied by other cities around the country, could not hope to sustain its growth without significant investments in healthcare provision, medical research, and medical education.[25]

In large cities across the country, the same employment pattern held true as universities and the healthcare sector grew over the latter half of the 20th century. In many cases, as at Harvard, the University of Pennsylvania, the University of Michigan, the University of Chicago, the University of Washington, and Stanford University, the university's medical school trained hundreds of new physicians each year and staffed the university's research hospital and network of medical centers in a large medical system reaching throughout the metropolitan area. In metropolitan Boston, Philadelphia, Chicago, Seattle, and Austin at the beginning of the 21st century, the education and health services sector employed more than one in ten workers, and in some cases as many as one in four. In Boston and Philadelphia, education and health services was the largest employment sector in the metropolitan area, giving indication of the marriage of higher education and healthcare in metropolitan economic development regimes.[26]

DISCUSSION OF THE LITERATURE

Key literature on information communities brings historical research on the origins of university and medical communities in conversation with critical examinations of the political economy of the knowledge economy. Boosteristic works also continue to dominate popular discourse and policy discussions of the future of information communities.

Historians have used universities to weave together histories of Cold War policy, science, and higher education, and recently, urban history. Clark Kerr's interpretation in *The Uses of the University* continues to shape this line of thinking. Kerr, the president of the University of California system in 1963, asserted that the knowledge industry would be to the 20th century what railroads were to the 19th century—the primary driver of economic growth. Stuart W. Leslie and Rebecca Lowen examine the work of individual research universities, MIT and Stanford University, to serve the Cold War research agenda and drive American economic development. Urban historian Roger Lotchin introduced the metropolitan region to the study of federal defense investment in studying the growth of Los Angeles, San Diego, and San Francisco.[27]

Margaret Pugh O'Mara connects the three poles of federal policy, university research, and metropolitan development in *Cities of Knowledge*.[28] O'Mara examines the spatial dynamic in the rise of Stanford University, Palo Alto, and the knowledge economy in Silicon Valley, and other communities' attempts to emulate the Stanford model, and she details the Cold War investments of the federal government and the partnership with private corporations that located in the Stanford Industrial Park. This framework places Stanford and universities more generally as a hinge between federal policy on the one hand and private economic development and metropolitan development on the other. O'Mara's examination of the development of suburban-style research campuses and subsequent attempts to adapt the Stanford model illustrates the spatial disparities and social inequalities embedded in the landscape of the new economy. In recent work, Guian McKee emphasizes the critical role of hospitals in stimulating postwar metropolitan growth. The aging of baby boomers and the economic growth of the healthcare sector translates into the increasing power of health systems and hospitals both within universities and in urban development.[29]

Annalee Saxenian's *Regional Advantage: Culture and Competition in Silicon Valley and Route 128* examined workers and employers in the two most dynamic tech regions of the 1970s and 1980s, to argue that the social and institutional dynamics of tech communities were the foundations of regional growth. The investigation of the San Francisco Bay Area and metropolitan Boston's computer-heavy ring road argued that Silicon Valley's culture of changing institutional structure and fluid social and professional networks allowed the California region to maintain its sustained economic dynamism. Metro Boston, at the same time, retained a more formal set of structures that kept people and companies from adapting to new trends in software and computing, allowing Silicon Valley to become the national leader for computer innovation by the 1990s.[30]

Richard Florida's research on economic development leads the wave of boosters promoting entrepreneurial universities and the transformative growth potential of the "meds and eds" economy. Florida argues that a "creative class" of individuals who make their living as knowledge workers emerged to make cities more economically robust. In *The Rise of the Creative Class* and *Cities and the Creative Class*, Florida uses a descriptive and analytic method to interrogate education, economic growth, and tolerance, creating a prescriptive model for economic development. Florida interprets the intellectual and cultural assets of cities such as Boston, San Francisco, Seattle, and Austin as both attractive features for workforce recruitment and as generative factors contributing to innovation and economic development. Communities with industrial legacies and traditional community values among the workforce, even those such as Pittsburgh with emerging healthcare concentrations, lag in providing young members of the creative class new outlets for their work and lifestyles.[31] Numerous policy and education leaders have followed this line of rhetoric, in line with Clark Kerr's classic *The Uses of the University*, to advocate for policy that makes universities more central to economic development and knowledge and innovation more central to city economies.[32]

Critics of these cities of intellect challenge the benefits produced by urban growth coalitions and include inquiries into gentrification, neoliberal urban development, and economic inequality. David Harvey and Henry Lefebvre led these critiques with *The Limits to Capital* and *The Production of Space*, respectively, which offer Marxist spatial considerations of architecture, city-building, and capitalist development. Subsequent scholars have applied the Marxist spatial critique to tech and finance cities, arguing that the very things that make prosperous cities desirable also undermine their inclusiveness and the material of authenticity.[33] Work such as Stephen Pitti's *The Devil in Silicon Valley* scrutinizes the labor and economic disparities around race and ethnicity in regions like Silicon Valley. There, Mexican Americans suffered displacement, and they labor, often unseen and under economic duress, in the shadows of the giants of the region's tech economy.[34]

Recently, scholars of global information communities have interrogated the development of knowledge communities overseas, especially featuring the cities of South Asia. John Stallmeyer's *Building Bangalore: Architecture and Urban Transformation in India's Silicon Valley* explores the creation of a new built environment shaped by the model of Silicon Valley and the information technology economy.[35]

PRIMARY SOURCES

University archives, municipal archives, and the archives of urban development institutions in individual cities provide the richest troves of materials for researchers, along with state archives that hold documents and archives for public redevelopment and economic development processes. In addition, the National Archives in Washington, DC, and National Archives II in College Park, MD, hold materials on federally funded planning and redevelopment projects, especially the Housing and Home Finance Agency and the Department of Housing and Urban Development in Record Group 207. The Lemelson Center for the Study of Invention and Innovation in Washington, DC, also maintains archives relevant to discoveries and economic development in the tech and service economy, as well as providing indices for local and regional archives on invention throughout the country.

FURTHER READING

Berman, Elizabeth Popp. *Creating the Market University: How Academic Science Became an Economic Engine.* Princeton, NJ: Princeton University Press, 2012.

Bernstein, Michael A. "*The Uses of the University*: After Fifty Years: Introduction." *Social Science History* 36, no. 4 (2012): 473–479. A special issue on Clark Kerr's *The Uses of the University.*

Dieterich-Ward, Allen. *Beyond Rust: Metropolitan Pittsburgh and the Fate of Industrial America.* Philadelphia: University of Pennsylvania Press, 2015.

Florida, Richard. *The Rise of the Creative Class: And How It's Transforming Work, Leisure, Community, and Everyday Life.* New York: Basic Books, 2002.

Hirsch, Arnold. *Making the Second Ghetto: Race and Housing in Chicago, 1940–1960*. Chicago: University of Chicago Press, 1983.

Jewett, Andrew. "The Politics of Knowledge in 1960s America." *Social Science History* 36, no. 4 (2012): 551–81.

Kerr, Clark. *The Uses of the University*. New York: Harper, 1963.

Lesliez, Stuart W. *The Cold War and American Science: The Military-Industrial-Academic Complex at MIT and Stanford*. New York: Columbia University Press, 1993.

Light, Jennifer S. *From Warfare to Welfare: Defense Intellectuals and Urban Problems in Cold War America*. Baltimore: Johns Hopkins University Press, 2005.

Loss, Christopher P. "From Pluralism to Diversity: Reassessing the Political Uses of 'The Uses of the University.'" *Social Science History* 36, no. 4 (2012): 525–549.

Lotchin, Rodger. *Fortress California, 1910–1961: From Warfare to Welfare*. New York: Oxford University Press, 1992.

Lowen, Rebecca. *Creating the Cold War University: The Transformation of Stanford*. Berkeley, CA: University of California Press, 1997.

Mattingly, Paul H. "Clark Kerr: The Unapologetic Pragmatist." *Social Science History* 36, no. 4 (2012): 481–497.

McKee, Guian. "The Hospital City in an Ethnic Enclave: Tufts-New England Medical Center, Boston's Chinatown, and the Urban Political Economy of Health Care." *Journal of Urban History* 42, no. 2 (March 2016): 259–283.

Mowery, David et al. *Ivory Tower and Industrial Innovation: University-Industry Technology Before and After the Bayh-Dole Act*. Stanford, CA: Stanford Business Books, 2004.

Neumann, Tracy. *Remaking the Rust Belt: The Post-Industrial Transformation of North America*. Philadelphia: University of Pennsylvania Press, 2017.

Newfield, Christopher. *Ivy and Industry: Business and the Making of the American University, 1880–1980*. Durham, NC: Duke University Press, 2004.

O'Mara, Margaret. "The Uses of the Foreign Student." *Social Science History* 36, no. 4 (2012): 583–615.

Pugh O'Mara, Margaret. *Cities of Knowledge: Cold War Science and the Search for the Next Silicon Valley*. Princeton, NJ: Princeton University Press, 2004.

Saxenian, Annalee. *Regional Advantage: Culture and Competition in Silicon Valley and Route 128*. Cambridge, MA: Harvard University Press, 1994.

Schrum, Ethan. "To 'Administer the Present': Clark Kerr and the Purpose of the Postwar American Research University." *Social Science History* 36, no. 4 (2012): 499–523.

Winling, LaDale. *Building the Ivory Tower: Universities and Metropolitan Development in the Twentieth Century*. Philadelphia: University of Pennsylvania Press, 2017.

NOTES

1. Robert Yaro, "NYU's Greenwich Village Expansion Is Necessary to Maintain World-Class Status," *New York Daily News*, July 25, 2012.
2. See Robin Bachin, *Building the South Side: Urban Space and Civic Culture in Chicago, 1890–1919* (Chicago: University of Chicago Press, 2004).
3. Paul Starr, *The Social Transformation of American Medicine: The Rise of a Sovereign Profession and the Making of a Vast Industry* (New York: Basic Books, 1983).
4. "P.W.A. Non-Federal Allotments for Colleges and Universities," 1938, Box 13 Publications, RG 135 Public Works Administration (College Park, MD: NARA II).
5. Bachin, *Building the South Side*; Wendy Plotkin, "Deeds of Mistrust: Race, Housing, and Restrictive Covenants in Chicago 1900–1953" (PhD diss., University of Illinois–Chicago, 1999).
6. Paul V. Turner, *Campus: An American Planning Tradition* (Cambridge, MA: MIT Press, 1984); and Sharon Haar, *The City As Campus: Urbanism and Higher Education in Chicago* (Minneapolis: University of Minnesota Press, 2011).
7. Housing Act of 1959: Hearings before the Committee on Banking and Currency 518–519. Committee on Banking and Currency, Housing Act of 1959. Hearings before the Subcommittee on Housing, 1959, 237.
8. Clark Kerr, *The Uses of the University* (New York: Harper, 1963), 67.
9. Texas State Constitution, Article 7 Education.
10. See Alex Sayf Cummings, *Brain Magnet: RTP and the Idea of the Idea Economy*, 2019.
11. Campbell Gibson, "Population of the 100 Largest Cities and Other Urban Places in the United States: 1790 to 1990," Population Division Working Paper No. 27, U.S. Bureau of the Census, Washington, DC, June 1998.

12. Claudia Goldin, "Enrollment in Institutions of Higher Education, by Sex, Enrollment Status, and Type of Institution: 1869–1995," in *Historical Statistics of the United States, Earliest Times to the Present: Millennial Edition,* ed. Susan B. Carter et al. (New York: Cambridge University Press, 2006), Table Bc524; "University of Texas at Austin," Texas State Historical Association; and Christopher Loss, "'The Most Wonderful Thing Has Happened to Me in the Army': Psychology, Citizenship, and American Higher Education in World War II," *Journal of American History* 92, no. 3 (December 2005): 864–891.

13. Of a total of 49,155 workers, 26,703 workers were in professional, managerial, sales, or clerical positions. U.S. Bureau of the Census, *Census of Population,* Vol. 3 (Washington, DC: Government Printing Office, 1950), Table 2. 250,125 of 302,536; and U.S. Bureau of the Census, *Census of Population,* Vol. 2, Census of Population, Social and Economic Characteristics, Texas (Washington, DC: Government Printing Office, 1950), Table 145.

14. Campbell Gibson, "Population of the 100 Largest Cities and Other Urban Places in the United States: 1790 To 1990," U.S. Census Bureau.

15. Kim Phillips-Fein, *Invisible Hands: The Businessmen's Crusade Against the New Deal* (New York: W. W. Norton, 2010); and Bruce Shulman and Julian Zelizer, *Rightward Bound: Making America Conservative in the 1970s* (Cambridge, MA: Harvard University Press, 2008).

16. Richard Eder, "Harvard's Drive for $250 Million Aims at Maintaining Standards," *New York Times,* December 3, 1979, p. 1.

17. National Center for Education Statistics, "Endowment Funds of the 120 Colleges and Universities with the Largest Amounts: 1999 and 2000." This is roughly equivalent to $5.2 billion and $28.1 billion in 2018 dollars, according to the Bureau of Labor Statistics Consumer Price Index Calculator.

18. Elizabeth Popp Berman, *Creating the Market University: How Academic Science Became an Economic Engine* (Princeton, NJ: Princeton University Press, 2012).

19. The organization was originally known as the Society for University Patent Administrators (SUPA).

20. Harbridge House, *Government Patent Policy Study: Final Report,* prepared for the Federal Council for Science and Technology, Committee on Government Patent Policy Committee On Government Patent Policy (Washington, DC: GPO, 1968).

21. David Mowery et al., *Ivory Tower and Industrial Innovation: University-Industry Technology Before and After the Bayh-Dole Act* (Stanford, CA: Stanford Business Books, 2004). In the early 2000s, MIT typically ranked within the top 10 highest recipients nationwide. INDEXP in Statistics Access for Technology Transfer (STATT) Database, Association of University Technology Managers.

22. Centers for Medicare and Medicaid Services, "National Health Expenditures 2015 Highlights."

23. Allen Dieterich-Ward, *Beyond Rust: Metropolitan Pittsburgh and the Fate of Industrial America* (Philadelphia: University of Pennsylvania Press, 2015); and Tracy Neumann, *Remaking the Rust Belt: The Post-Industrial Transformation of North America* (Philadelphia: University of Pennsylvania Press, 2017).

24. University of Texas System Administration, "Impact on Austin," University of Texas at Austin.

25. Michael and Susan Dell Foundation, "Michael & Susan Dell Foundation Invests $50M to Establish the Dell Medical School at the University of Texas-Austin," January 30, 2013.

26. United States Bureau of Labor Statistics, "Boston Area Employment," Table 1; United States Bureau of Labor Statistics "Economy at a Glance"; and United States Bureau of Labor Statistics, "Chicago Area Employment—May 2018," Table 1; Austin Chamber of Commerce, "The Central Texas Work Force".

27. Clark Kerr, *The Uses of the University* (New York: Harper, 1963); Stuart W. Leslie, *The Cold War and American Science: The Military-Industrial-Academic Complex at MIT and Stanford* (New York: Columbia University Press, 1993); Rebecca Lowen, *Creating the Cold War University: The Transformation of Stanford* (Berkeley, CA: University of California Press, 1997); and Rodger Lotchin, *Fortress California, 1910–1961: From Warfare to Welfare* (New York: Oxford University Press, 1992).

28. Margaret Pugh O'Mara, *Cities of Knowledge: Cold War Science and the Search for the Next Silicon Valley* (Princeton, NJ: Princeton University Press, 2004).

29. Guian McKee, "The Hospital City in an Ethnic Enclave: Tufts-New England Medical Center, Boston's Chinatown, and the Urban Political Economy of Health Care," *Journal of Urban History* 42, no. 2 (March 2016): 259–283.

30. Annalee Saxenian, *Regional Advantage: Culture and Competition in Silicon Valley and Route 128*

(Cambridge, MA: Harvard University Press, 1994). Florida, Saxenian, and other scholars of the post-industrial economy draw on more fundamental works that assessed the economic and policy transformations as they were happening, especially Daniel Bell's *The Coming of Post-Industrial Society: A Venture in Social Forecasting* (New York: Basic Books, 1973); and John Kenneth Galbraith's *The Affluent Society* (Boston: Houghton Mifflin, 1956).

31. Richard Florida, *The Rise of the Creative Class: And How It's Transforming Work, Leisure, Community, and Everyday Life* (New York: Basic Books, 2002). Florida has responded to critics of this framework in his new work and acknowledged the displacement and gentrification that has frequently accompanied such shifts in economic development strategies. Richard Florida, *The New Urban Crisis: How Our Cities Are Increasing Inequality, Deepening Segregation, and Failing the Middle Class—and What We Can Do About It* (New York: Basic Books, 2017).

32. See, for example, Clayton Christianson and Henry Eyring, *The Innovative University: Changing the DNA of Higher Education from the Inside Out* (New York: Jossey-Bass); and Holden Thorp and Buck Goldstein, *Engines of Innovation: The Entrepreneurial University in the Twenty-First Century* (Chapel Hill, NC: University of North Carolina Press, 2013).

33. David Harvey, *The Limits to Capital* (Chicago: University of Chicago Press, 1982); Henri Lefebvre, *The Production of Space* (London: Wiley-Blackwell, 1992); and Sharon Zukin, *The Naked City: The Death and Life of Authentic Urban Places* (New York: Oxford University Press, 2009).

34. Stephen Pitti, *The Devil in Silicon Valley: Northern California, Race, and Mexican Americans* (Princeton, NJ: Princeton University Press, 2004). A new movement in the history of technology centers the labor of maintenance as being as important as the creative genius associated with innovation. Andrew Russell and Lee Vinsel, "After Innovation, Turn to Maintenance," *Technology and Culture* 59, no. 1 (January 2018): 1–25.

35. John Stallmeyer, *Building Bangalore: Architecture and Urban Transformation in India's Silicon Valley* (New York: Routledge, 2011); M. Goldman, "Speculative Urbanism and the Making of the Next World City," *International Journal of Urban and Regional Research* 35, no. 3 (May 2011), 555–581;

and A. Roy, "Why India Cannot Plan Its Cities: Informality, Insurgence and the Idiom of Urbanization," *Planning Theory* 8, no. 1 (2009): 76–81.

LaDale Winling

TOURISM AND THE AMERICAN CITY SINCE 1800

THE EMERGENCE OF URBAN TOURISM, 1800–1870

American cities were chiefly exporters of tourists throughout most of the nineteenth century. Early in the century, no reliable, efficient, affordable means of transportation existed to facilitate travel among cities. Although the arrival of steamboat passenger service on rivers after Robert Fulton's successful run up the Hudson River in 1807 and an expanding network of canals—notably the Erie Canal that opened in 1825—delivered considerable improvements over arduous overland travel, travel still required sufficient money and leisure time, both of which were in short supply. Few but the wealthiest Americans could realistically undertake pleasure travel until late in the century. Furthermore, when most Americans contemplated traveling, they thought of excursions to see scenic natural wonders that had been popularized by elite travel accounts or by American landscape paintings by Hudson River Valley School artists, such as Albert Bierstadt, Frederic Church, and Thomas Cole; or they thought of repairing to spas or springs resorts to "take the waters" for their health. When they thought of cities, American travelers usually looked to European cities, whose longer histories and the presence of cathedrals, castles, and ruins made them more culturally appealing. The advent of railroad travel and its spectacular rise after mid-century stimulated tourism, but through the late 19th century an expanding tourist trade focused primarily on coaxing Americans to pastoral destinations and shaping their experiences in such places.

Nevertheless, it would be a mistake to conclude that urban tourism was unknown or even rare before the late 19th century. Cities exerted an undeniable pull on restless Americans. And when well-heeled travelers escaped the city, they brought their urban habits with them. The places they visited—notably Newport, Rhode Island, and Saratoga Springs, New York, but also dozens of other seaside and springs retreats—became microcosms of elite urban society each summer in the early to mid-19th century.[1] For rural dwellers, the allure of cities also encompassed a powerful social component. Historian Daniel Kilbride demonstrates that wealthy southern planters frequently found their way to Philadelphia, not simply to behold its cultural and historical attractions but also because they "looked forward to circulating in its polite society," which promised opportunities for

social advancement associated with transcending their regions. Many also longed to escape the dullness of rural life, and the potential of Philadelphia outstripped that of southern cities, such as Charleston, Savannah, Natchez, and even New Orleans.[2]

New York stood apart as the most exciting of all US cities. Richard Gassan argued that, like later tourists, those who visited the nation's largest city in the early 19th century "wanted to shop, to be entertained, to experience some urban life (but not too much), and to revel in urban novelty."[3] In New York and, to a lesser degree, in a number of cities by mid-century, visitors could attend theater, visit palatial department stores, and dine in French-style restaurants. Male travelers sometimes sought prostitutes, which contributed to the emergence of commercialized sex districts such as that of New York's Five

Figure 1. Lithograph, *c.* 1855. This print depicts prominent attractions in Philadelphia in the mid-19th century, including the Custom House, Penitentiary, Alms House, US Mint, Exchange, Hospital, Independence Hall, Insane Asylum, Navy Asylum, Fair Mount, and Girard College. [Philadelphia]: Des. eng. & pub. by Jas. Queen (P.S. Duval & Co. Lith. Phila.), *c.* 1855. Courtesy of Library of Congress, LC-DIG-ppmsca-24840.

Points in the early 19th century and, by mid-century, around Broadway above Canal Street. As Timothy J. Gilfoyle's *City of Eros* details, the striptease shows and concert saloons of Broadway fit hand in glove with the nearby concentration of upscale theaters, department stores, art galleries, "cavernous" saloons, and restaurants.[4]

It was not only the cosmopolitan amenities of cities that drew attention. As historian John F. Sears concluded, the age of reform that marked the second quarter of the 19th century produced tremendous interest, reinforced in guidebooks, in seeing prisons, mental asylums, and institutions for the deaf, dumb, and blind, many of which were located on the pastoral fringes of American cities (Figure 1).

In addition to the allure of their novelty, the orderliness and air of calm of these institutions contrasted with the dizzying sense of upheaval that seemed to mark the nation's incipient immigration and urbanization. Tourists also enjoyed visits to so-called rural cemeteries—including Boston's Mount Auburn (1831), Philadelphia's Laurel Hill (1836), Brooklyn's Green-Wood (1838), and Cleveland's Lake View (1869)—that transformed wooded knolls overlooking cities into winding lanes, monument-studded lawns, and picturesque vistas[5].

CITIES AND THE RISE OF THE TOURISM INDUSTRY, 1870–1930

The expansion of railroad passenger service, whose falling fares coincided with the growth of the middle class, hastened the emergence of a bona fide tourism industry after the Civil War by offering travelers the fastest, most reliable means of transportation to date. The advent of first-class Pullman-manufactured railcars, including sleeping, dining, parlor, club, and observation cars, beginning in the late 1860s, as well as the hiring of African American freedmen as porters, lent an air of comfort, prestige, and class-crossing racial superiority that transformed rail travel from a burden to a pleasure for the white traveling public.[6] Although

the completion of several transcontinental railroads between the 1860s and 1880s is usually mainly credited for stimulating travel to destinations such as the Grand Canyon, Yellowstone, and Glacier National Parks and the pueblos of northern New Mexico, it also increased tourism in western cities, as historian J. Philip Gruen demonstrates. Travelers bound for scenic wonders often had to spend a night in Chicago or other cities for the purpose of changing trains. However, western boosters deftly affixed the requisite picturesque and historic attributes to the cities they promoted.[7] In fact, it became common to refer to city streets flanked by tall skyscrapers as "canyons." Even more tourists flocked to the nation's largest eastern and Midwestern cities by railroad. Through the 1920s, many cities built elaborate, expansive railroad passenger terminals, such as New York's Pennsylvania Station (1910) and Grand Central Terminal (1912), Chicago's second Union Station (1925), and Cleveland's Union Terminal (1930).

Hotels in cities also changed in the later decades of the 19th century. Although Boston claimed a luxury hotel—the Tremont House—as early as 1829, the phenomenon became more pronounced after 1870 in a period of rapid wealth accumulation and growing public willingness to travel hundreds or even thousands of miles at a time. Hotels became part of a national, integrated hospitality system that offered wayfarers predictable, dependable accommodations.[8] Along with department stores, first-class "fireproof" hotels became fixtures along emerging downtown retail streets and offered luxurious lobbies, parlors, dining rooms on the "European plan," cafes, barber shops, boutiques, and hundreds of rooms featuring private baths with steam-heated water (Figure 2).

They were, as historian Catherine Cocks points out, places that "provid[ed] many Americans with their first encounter with the material expression of gentility." As demand grew, new hotels opened that were larger and more elegant. In 1897, the newly conjoined Waldorf-Astoria in New York became the first American hotel to exceed one thousand rooms.[9]

The Lobby of The New St. Charles. New Orleans.

Figure 2. Postcard of St. Charles Hotel in New Orleans, *c.* 1920. After fires claimed its two predecessors on the same site in 1851 and 1894, the third St. Charles became the first fireproof hotel in New Orleans. The hotel's grand lobby, replete with palms and plush furniture, suggested the air of opulence that luxury hotels projected by the late 19th and early 20th centuries. Postcard from author's personal collection.

Chicago reached that threshold when the LaSalle Hotel opened in the Loop in 1909, and Chicago's original Palmer House, which was rebuilt as a seven-story hotel soon after being destroyed in 1871 in the Great Chicago Fire, was replaced in 1925 by a twenty-five-story Palmer House with 2,268 rooms and a grand lobby with ornate plaster work.[10]

Railroad companies helped to fill these ever-larger hotels by promoting travel to cities through their passenger divisions. They offered special excursion rates to northern cities in the summer season and to southern ones in winter. Railroads also played a prominent role in enticing visitors by the thousands to a series of world's expositions, beginning with the Philadelphia Centennial Exposition in 1876. None achieved greater success than Chicago's World's Columbian Exposition in 1893, which became a template for subsequent fairs in Buffalo (1901), St. Louis (1904), and San Francisco (1915), among other places. The Chicago exposition also inspired much thought about how actual cities might borrow from the orderly aesthetics of the so-called "White City," as the fair was known for its ornately sculpted plaster building exteriors. Daniel Burnham, the Columbian Exposition's

lead designer, justified his coauthored Plan of Chicago (1909) in part by arguing that, once it was implemented, "the stranger will seek our gates."[11] While much of the Burnham Plan never was adopted, its influence was felt in the impressive overlaying of Grant Park atop railroad tracks along Lake Michigan, in 1919, and the subsequent additions of the Field Museum of Natural History, Buckingham Fountain, Soldier Field, Shedd Aquarium, and Adler Planetarium over the next decade[12].

Even if expositions rarely produced the "City Beautiful," they recast American cities as sights to behold, and Chicago's lakefront became the prime model shaping other cities' aspirations for waterfront transformations of their own. Although the fairs themselves may have been the initial draw, those who attended them also felt a powerful tug to see the city. As historian Chad Heap shows, Chicago's Levee district, which lay between the exposition grounds and the hotels of the Loop and very near two major railroad stations, was "uniquely situated for tourists' late-night ramblings."[13]

In addition to the promotional activities of railroad passenger divisions, tourist guidebooks prepared by chambers of commerce, newspapers, hotels, or merchant associations carefully simplified cities into selections of destinations deemed worthy of tourists' attention[14].

By 1900, tour companies were chartering electric streetcars or operating "seeing-the-city cars" that shuttled "rubberneckers" on carefully considered paths that maximized the efficiency of touring, freeing visitors from the unpredictability associated with public transit (Figure 3).

The scarcely veiled boosterism that infused tourist guidebooks and sightseeing tours steered tourists toward attractions that might produce a positive impression of the distinctiveness and progressiveness of cities. Such attractions included historic sites, harbors, bridges, skyscrapers, museums, parks, and wealthy residential sections. Downtown business districts figured prominently.[15]

Some of these publications acknowledged the presence of less respectable attractions.

Figure 3. Tourists aboard a "Seeing New York" car, ca. 1904. Detroit Publishing Company, Library of Congress, LC-DIG-det-4a11803.

"Exotic" immigrant "ghettoes," minority neighborhoods, and red-light districts were highlighted; advice was offered on how to see them.[16] Off-duty policemen and tour guides could easily be hired if one felt uneasy about peering beyond the veil where "the other half" resided.

In turn-of-the-century New York, the Lower East Side, with its many eastern and central European immigrants crowded into tenement houses, provoked a combination of curiosity and revulsion, as did Chinatown with its "oriental" air of mystery. By the 1920s, tourists might also take a tour car up the Manhattan Island to see Harlem, fast becoming a mecca of the "New Negro."[17] In San Francisco, white tour operators and guidebook writers concocted a mythic Chinatown that was inscrutable, exotic, and potentially dangerous—except on their tours. They became "theatrically adept" at staging ostensibly daring descents into "underground Chinatown," hiring Chinatown residents to stage the kinds of scenes tourists expected to encounter based on their reading of popular literature. The 1906 earthquake provided an opportunity for Chinese merchants in Chinatown, long disturbed by the racist nature of outside operators, to take the reins and to shift Chinatown's image from opium dens, gambling halls, and labyrinths to temples, restaurants, and shops.[18]

Guidebooks also created what historian William R. Taylor called a "moral geography" of the city, helping tourists navigate city streets knowingly in ways that enabled them to preserve their respectability. The demimonde, however, moved fluidly in and out of the bright and dark areas in ways that made it all but impossible to create such a tidy division of the respectable from the disreputable.[19] Elsewhere, red-light districts were carefully delineated and regulated realms that, though designed with the hope of containing vice, actually spotlighted risqué districts as destinations. New Orleans's Storyville, located next to the Southern Railroad passenger depot, the Canal Street shopping district, and the French Quarter, functioned in this manner from 1897 to 1917. Although it earned little more than passing mention in mainstream guidebooks, Storyville generated its own guide to brothels and cribs, the Blue Book, which was widely sold at railroad stations, saloons, and cafés.[20] Even after the district disappeared, "Storyville" became a widely used name that served businesses seeking to conjure one of New Orleans's most powerfully evocative images.

Just as guidebooks packaged cities as collections of attractions, a growing number of companies worked with merchants and other downtown interests by the early 20th century to produce picture postcards, which featured a myriad of idealized depictions of cities as collections of tourist attractions. As historian Alison Isenberg reveals, postcard artists embellished photographs of street scenes, removing with paintbrushes overhead electrical lines, sidewalk clutter, cobblestone pavers, and even pedestrian crowds, and also applied a simplified color palette and the "American Art" sky, which transitioned from blue with fluffy clouds to peach at the horizon.

Many postcard producers took advantage of tourist guides' characterization of emerging downtown skylines as novel, distinctively American counterparts to majestic western landscapes by offering scenes of realistic or embellished bird's-eye views of skyscraper "canyons" soaring above busy streets.[21] Seeing such vistas in print surely intensified the longing to behold them in person, and the rise of downtown skylines brought opportunities to satisfy the urge. Long before the Empire State Building's observation deck became a sensation, some proprietors of tall office buildings opened up new vistas from their roofs or upper floors. Notable among these were the seventeenth-floor observatory in Chicago's Auditorium Building (1889) and New York's twenty-story World Building (1890), which opened its iconic crowning dome to tourists.[22]

Regardless of boosters' efforts to simplify and unify the image of cities, visitors did not always encounter cities in such prescriptive ways. As Gruen has observed, tourists often continued to seek out what might be seen today as more mundane attractions: sanitariums, hospitals, asylums, waterworks, factories, and other utilitarian structures. The multiplicity of more mundane sites featured on colorful postcards created sightseeing itineraries that defied boosters' efforts to simplify them. At a time when industrial processes were novelties, some tourists in western cities chose to "follow the process of mineral extraction in the wilderness to the finished product," which took them to many sites near the urban edges. A similar desire to see the new methods of meat processing for themselves sent many tourists to Chicago's Union Stock Yards.[23] In all, these tourist pursuits reflected a desire to see the drama of modernity at close hand.

In response to the meteoric increase in fraternal, hereditary, and professional associations and the concurrent rise of railroads after the Civil War, cities vied with each other to attract their share of a rapidly growing number of conventions. Detroit created the nation's first convention and visitors bureau in 1896. Many other cities quickly followed, facilitating the growth of an emerging "industry" that in 1911, sent nearly 400,000 people to Chicago alone. Prior to World War I, conventions had usually been hold in auditoriums or civic centers. In the two decades that followed the war,

many cities, including New York, Philadelphia, San Francisco, and Boston, built their own dedicated convention and exhibition halls, although as historian Aaron Cowan notes, they filled the spaces between conventions with the civic and social events that other types of facilities had long hosted. When Cleveland completed its Public Auditorium in 1922, it was the nation's largest convention hall.[24]

CITIES IN THE AGE OF MASS TOURISM, 1930–1970

The hardships of the Great Depression provided an impetus for many American cities to invest more in tourism promotion as a way to stimulate business and entice investment. In the 1930s, Chicago, San Diego, Dallas, Cleveland, San Francisco, and New York revived the older tactic of hosting major expositions (Figure 4).

Chicago's choice to tag its 1933 exposition "A Century of Progress" was only the most explicit expression of that era's hope of "salvation from the depression."[25] The Depression years also saw significant federal investment in cities' literal and figurative infrastructures of tourism. The Works Progress Administration (WPA) public works projects went well beyond building or improving roads and bridges. WPA workers built the stone bridges, stairs, terraces, and walkways that became San Antonio's River Walk, and they made improvements to New Orleans's French Market and other historic buildings surrounding Jackson Square at a time when interest in historic preservation and tourism converged. The WPA also sponsored the Federal Writers' Project, whose workers produced more than two dozen highly detailed city guides that commented in great detail on the social, cultural, and physical attributes of cities.[26]

Very few new hotels opened in cities in the 1930s and World War II years. Existing hotels and exhibition halls generally saw a significant decline in patronage during the Depression years. The war brought a surge in hotel occupancy from soldiers en route to overseas

Figure 4. Great Lakes Exposition souvenir guide, 1936. Like a handful of other cities during the Great Depression, Cleveland hosted a major exposition on its lakefront in the hopes of bolstering the city's lagging economy. From author's personal collection.

deployment, but as Cowan argues, downtown hotels were ill-prepared to grapple with what followed. After the war, many hotels dealt with decaying surroundings and a reinforcement of the pre-Depression trend of suburban motel development, including along an emerging network of freeways.[27] In an attempt to revive the central city's place in the tourist trade in the middle decades of the century, more and more cities formed dedicated convention and tourist bureaus. By 1956, eight of the nation's eleven cities with populations of more than 500,000 had dedicated tourism promotion organizations.[28] The postwar decades also brought a second, larger wave of convention-center development in response to the professionalization of the convention industry,

corporate expansion, and the emergence of commercial jet travel.[29] Among the notable additions to the nation's roster of meeting facilities were the New York Coliseum (1956), Miami Beach Convention Center (1958), Las Vegas Convention Center (1959), Cobo Center in Detroit (1960), and McCormick Place in Chicago (1960).[30]

As downtowns reconfigured themselves to handle ever larger conventions, leisure travelers flocked in greater numbers to motor inns in the suburbs. Motels and tourist courts grew out of auto camping, originally a quirky hobby of the rather few automobile owners in the early years of the 20th century. With the advent of the Ford Model T, which drove down car prices, Americans took to the roads, availing themselves of an exponential expansion of national highways in the 1920s. Most likely more motels than hotels existed by the end of the 1930s, although hotels continued to have more total rooms through the next decade.[31] The soaring popularity of highway motels accompanied the continuing expansion of automobile ownership, especially after World War II. Car culture flourished at the expense of central cities, where business and municipal leaders raced to tear down old buildings to create parking lots and garages to accommodate cars, not understanding that the very forces that drove car culture were about to free downtown streets from the congestion they so feared. Although downtowns held their own into mid-century, the suburbs beckoned, and not simply as bedroom communities. Although its first casinos appeared along Fremont Street in downtown during the 1930s, Las Vegas reoriented its gambling-based tourism preponderantly toward "The Strip," a suburban stretch of US 91 to the south of the city, beginning in 1941 with the opening of El Rancho Vegas and accelerating with the opening of the Desert Inn, Sands, Sahara, Tropicana, and other casino resorts in the 1950s. Similarly, driving was a must to reach Disneyland, which sprang up on a former orange grove in the Los Angeles suburb of Anaheim in 1955.[32] After the opening of the much more expansive Walt Disney World in central Florida in 1971, Orlando evolved into an uneasy role as a service-sector city serving the gigantic theme park complex that came to dominate the region.[33]

As more and more attractions located outside cities, suburbia's tourism inroads exerted tremendous pressure on cities to find ways to accentuate their attractiveness to suburbanites and tourists. A handful of cities turned to their historic resources to attract visitors, setting the stage for what gradually became a widely adopted urban revitalization strategy. In the 1930s, Charleston, South Carolina, and New Orleans consolidated a decade's worth of historic preservation efforts by creating stringent standards to safeguard their distinctive cityscapes. By the 1950s, a handful of cities such as Savannah, Georgia, Winston-Salem, North Carolina, and Alexandria, Virginia, boasted historic districts as tourist attractions. A growing backlash against urban renewal and concerns about suburban decentralization, combined with a heightened awareness of the potential of tourism, prompted a tremendous increase in preservation in the 1960s. An unprecedented proliferation of historic districts ensued in the decade following the passage of the National Historic Preservation Act of 1966.[34]

A similar unease accompanied the postwar dismantling of street railways and plans for elevated freeways slicing through city centers. Under the right conditions, tourism provided a rationale for opposing such developments. In 1947, a group of San Francisco women organized to ensure that the city's famed cable cars would not entirely vanish amid transit modernization efforts that favored modern buses. Situating cable cars alongside other cities' icons like the French Quarter, Statue of Liberty, Eiffel Tower, and Big Ben, the group used cable cars as "rolling ambassadors of goodwill" to advertise San Francisco as a tourist destination.[35] Likewise, learning from the failure of activists to prevent the construction of San Francisco's Embarcadero Freeway along its waterfront in the 1950s, a concerned band of New Orleanians

waged a successful ten-year "freeway revolt" to halt a riverfront expressway that threatened to block views between historic Jackson Square and the Mississippi River, citing the tourism industry as a likely casualty of the road project.[36]

Likewise, the postwar years saw the establishment of shopping and entertainment districts in historic central-city storefronts and former industrial buildings. After World War II, New Orleans's Bourbon Street emerged as a rare example of largely unplanned coalescence of nightlife establishments that, despite their lack of coordination, inspired concerted efforts to stimulate similar excitement in other cities, some of which became models in their own right. Notable among these efforts were St. Louis's Gaslight Square, the Gaslamp Quarter in San Diego, Ghirardelli Square in San Francisco, Larimer Square in Denver, and Underground Atlanta.[37]

CONTINUITY AND CHANGE: URBAN TOURISM SINCE 1970

The marshaling of historic resources to build the tourism sector took on heightened importance in the 1970s and 1980s as the impacts of deindustrialization and suburbanization were felt more acutely in many American cities. An increasing number of cities sought to foreground what Sharon Zukin has labeled the "symbolic economy," in which cities themselves become products.[38] Mayors such as Kevin White of Boston, William Donald Schaefer of Baltimore, and Moon Landrieu of New Orleans pursued tourism-centered agendas in the 1970s that produced iconic spaces conducive to maximizing this symbolic economy. Kevin White's administration cooperated with the James Rouse Company to transform the historic Faneuil Hall and Quincy Market into the enormously popular Faneuil Hall Marketplace, whose Boston-themed specialty shops, kiosks, and eateries now shared space with traditional public market stalls. Although less national attention was accorded to it, Landrieu's tourism-focused recasting of some of the central spaces of the

French Quarter were no less impactful for New Orleans. The mayor oversaw the closure of three streets around Jackson Square to form a flagstone-paved pedestrian mall filled with artists, musicians, and fortune tellers, created a multi-terraced viewing platform and promenade along the Mississippi River levee. The French Market was transformed into what amounted to a festival marketplace in 1975, one year before Rouse's Faneuil Hall Marketplace opened. Schaefer laid the groundwork for a similar transformation of Baltimore's Inner Harbor to be realized in the 1980s, although as Aaron Cowan has argued, the mayor initially envisioned it also as a draw for locals.[39]

Such downtown transformations were only the beginning. New York's mayor Ed Koch oversaw the reinvention of seedy Times Square into a glitzy extravaganza of outsize signage, revived Broadway theaters, and eventually national-brand superstores. In Chicago, Mayor Richard M. Daley reopened State Street to vehicular traffic after nearly two decades of decline as a pedestrian mall, contributing to the revival of the street as a major retailing destination. Daley also facilitated the creation of a new driver of tourism in Chicago by spearheading the development of Millennium Park above a rail yard and parking garages along Michigan Avenue.[40] Place-making efforts to stimulate tourists and suburbanites to visit the central city were not confined to large metropolises. Some smaller cities managed to mix the same ingredients that had produced tourism-led resurgences in New York, Boston, Chicago, and Baltimore. For example, Chattanooga, Tennessee, retained the same firm that designed the National Aquarium in Baltimore to plan its Tennessee Aquarium, which opened in 1992, catalyzing the revitalization of the downtown riverfront and brightening Chattanooga's sagging image.[41] However, not all smaller cities mustered the same public enthusiasm. The AutoWorld indoor theme park and Water Street Pavilion festival marketplace promised to reinvigorate beleaguered Flint, Michigan, but both closed only a couple of years after their respective openings in 1984

and 1985. Perhaps most tourism-oriented downtown revitalization projects fell somewhere between the spectacular successes and failures. Typical of these was Augusta, Georgia's Riverwalk, which opened in 1988. After more than a decade of challenges to build upon the initial excitement that the riverfront project stirred, local officials were left to wonder if the plan had been unrealistically ambitious. Clearly there were limits to what tourism could offer cities, especially with so many of them competing for visitors.[42]

For all the hope of using downtown redevelopment to rebuild the thinning crowd, many commentators pointed to the ways in which such initiatives often segregated those they attracted by race and class. This was a new chapter in the long history of social distance as both a repelling and attracting force in tourism. In the 1990s, Dennis Judd identified what he called the "tourist bubble," an effectively cordoned-off zone in which most tourist activity was concentrated, robbing areas outside the so-called bubble from sharing in the profits and renewal generated by that activity. As Bryant Simon and others have argued, the nature of development such as that of casino hotels in Atlantic City, with their interceptor lots and garages connected to gaming venues by enclosed elevated "skywalks," effectively separated visitors from locals at street level.[43] More recently, however, Cowan called attention to the ways in which suburban and inner-city Baltimoreans appropriated space around Harborplace on the Inner Harbor in ways that challenge the simplistic notion of a tourist bubble.[44] In addition, many cities built light-rail loops in their downtowns, often with an eye to facilitating tourism. Some, like Dallas, Little Rock, New Orleans, San Diego, and Tampa, even stocked the new lines with replicas of heritage streetcars, while Philadelphia and San Francisco restored vintage mid-century streetcars to lines that ceased operation but had been dismantled.

If these tended to reinforce the tourist bubble by further delineating a geography of sightseeing, at least they did so without the physical separation of skywalks.

The tendency to channel visitors ever more efficiently to their destination, however, always existed in tension with many tourists' desire to get off the beaten path to experience a more "authentic" understanding of the places they visit. The same curiosity that sent "slummers" clambering through narrow alleys with police escorts in the late 19th century also drove more adventurous tourists in recent decades to find their own way through cities, often with the aid of alternative tourist guides or smartphone apps. Even convention and visitors bureaus began to warm to the idea of rethinking their longtime complicity in reserving most tourist activity inside the "tourist bubble." In 2012, in a city whose River Walk framed the extent of most tourists' experience, the San Antonio Convention and Visitors Bureau unveiled a tourism campaign that relied on social media campaigns to get people to submit their own photos and stories for possible inclusion in tourism marketing, thereby re-centering the production of the city's tourist image.

In 2014, Destination DC launched a similar campaign designed to get tourists off the National Mall and into the city's varied neighborhoods, which also invited visitors and locals to join the conversation about places and events worth a visit.[45]

In addition, longtime attempts by promoters to appeal to a mass market gradually relented as the nation's demographics moved toward greater diversity. No longer could they ignore the growing demand to package experiences tailored for African American or gay and lesbian audiences, to name only a couple. Black tourists, of course, had visited cities for decades, often with the aid of guides like the Green Book, but most had moved warily in mainstream tourist spaces.[46] Into the 1970s, black entrepreneurs carved out notable entertainment destinations on the margins of areas frequented by whites. For example, Louis C. Mason Jr. operated "Mason's Las Vegas Strip," a branded row of storefronts along New Orleans's South Claiborne Avenue, while Winston E. Willis ran

a block-long strip of entertainment venues in Cleveland's Euclid-105th area.[47] New Orleans and Philadelphia were national leaders in packaging tourism for black travelers in ways that pierced the tourist bubble. In 1986 the Greater New Orleans Black Tourism Center formed, followed in 1990 by the Greater New Orleans Black Tourism Network, developments that yielded new opportunities for black representation even as they failed to overturn the predominant, white-centered tourist narrative and exploitive nature of black labor in the tourism industry.[48] In 1988 the city of Philadelphia established the Multicultural Affairs Congress (MAC), which offered heritage tours, festivals, and other draws for African Americans. MAC worked to reinterpret Center City, the central tourist district in Philadelphia, more inclusively by overlaying black points of interest but also tried, with less success, to propel some of the tourist activity out to majority-black North Philadelphia.[49] The tendency of urban revitalization to occur either in areas with few African Americans or to displace them represented a continuing challenge in many cities.

The emergence of Lesbian, Gay, Bisexual, Transgender and Queer (LGBTQ) tourism promotion in cities in the late 20th and early twenty-first centuries represented a clear departure from the past even as it built upon potentials created by the social fluidity inherent in tourist spaces. In the early and mid-20th century, gay tourism was largely underground and remained relatively guarded even in more permissive places such as New Orleans's French Quarter and San Francisco's North Beach. As historian Nan Alamilla Boyd argues, in the 1930s–50s, "as sexualized entertainments became part of San Francisco's allure, tourist industry dollars cast a thin veneer of protection around the city's queer entertainments," nurturing gay bars that in later years would "shape a nascent gay movement."[50] The grassroots origins of the Southern Decadence celebration in New Orleans in the early 1970s mirrored a similar transformation in the potential for open LGBTQ tourism in San Francisco by unfolding in protective embrace of the French Quarter, where tourism had helped smooth the transgressive edge of queer life.

Following the shutdown of many gay bath-houses and clubs in the face of the AIDS epidemic in the 1980s, a number of cities' tourism bureaus embraced an LGBTQ tourism that transcended the genre of sex tourism. By the early twenty-first century, urban tourism promoters were moving "beyond images of rainbow flags and shirtless men." A wide range of special events, festivals, family activities, and even LGBTQ heritage tours reflected the growing embrace of the idea that this segment of the tourism market shared as diverse a set of interests as any other.[51]

As the end of second decade of the twenty-first century approached, it became increasingly clear that terrorism, climate change, and "culture wars" would shape the expectations and habits of those who visited cities in the future. The terror attack of September 11, 2001, destroyed the World Trade Center, one of New York City's leading tourist destinations, and subjected travelers to new fears and inconveniences even as it infused Ground Zero with new symbolic value.[52] In the ensuing years, periodic terrorist acts that involved bombs and weaponized vehicles threatened to reframe visitors' attitudes about visiting iconic urban places and spaces. Although not demonstrably a direct result of climate change, Hurricane Katrina's devastation of New Orleans in 2005 inspired a spate of "disaster tourism" much like that which lured thousands to San Francisco following that city's 1906 earthquake and fire. The event, however, also introduced a new term—"voluntourism"—into common usage as countless visitors rationalized their pilgrimages to the sodden Ninth Ward by lending a hand in rebuilding the city. This trend may have seemed novel, but it reprised an old theme so well described by historian Cindy Aron— that of infusing travel with a sense of higher purpose.[53] Nonetheless, growing public awareness of the vulnerability of America's highly popular coastal cities to sea-level rise and hurricanes suggested that tourism might remain

inseparable from advocacy for policies and efforts that might preserve many of the nation's threatened cultural and historical treasures. Finally, as they did for centuries, urban public spaces also became flashpoints in long-building tensions between rich and poor, white and black, and rural and urban Americans. In 2017, New Orleans mayor Mitch Landrieu, whose father had built a tourist-friendly pedestrian mall four decades earlier around the park whose centerpiece was a triumphal Andrew Jackson on horseback, presided over removing four monuments to the Confederacy and the "Lost Cause." In his defense of his decision, Landrieu did not omit the significance of their removal to the city's image: "If presented with the opportunity to build monuments that told our story or to curate these particular spaces, would these monuments be what we want the world to see? Is this really our story?"[54] It remained to seen how a spate of revisions to the commemorative landscape might shape the ever-shifting contours of how cities appeal to tourists.

DISCUSSION OF THE LITERATURE

Historians came rather late to the study of tourism. Anthropologists and other social scientists set the stage for a generation of scholars of tourism by affirming long-standing societal assumptions that tourism brought negative cultural and social impacts. Although historians John Kasson, Kathy Peiss, David Nasaw, and others examined the rise of commercialized leisure in the 1970s to 1990s, a direct focus on urban tourism history lagged a decade or more behind historical scholarship on seaside resorts and tourist encounters with natural scenery.[55] Notable exceptions included an essay on tourism in the 1890s in New York City by Neil Harris and Eugene P. Moehring's book on Las Vegas.[56] Even as historians turned toward the city as a locus for the study of tourism, social scientists continued to dominate urban tourism studies. In the 1990s, political scientist Dennis R. Judd coined the persuasive term "tourist bubble" to denote heavily scripted urban places that embody and often contain the tourist experience of cities.[57] Judd's term built upon earlier assumptions that tourism creates spatial and social chasms in cities, concentrating the economic benefits of the tourist trade and effectively cordoning off central urban spaces in ways that transformed their social and cultural attributes. Similar concerns about urban tourism as a contested spatial practice pervade the work of sociologist Sharon Zukin.[58] Although Hal K. Rothman was not the first historian to study urban tourism, he proved influential by affixing a provocative vocabulary to the idea of tourism as a corrosive force in Devil's Bargains (1998), a book with which historians of tourism continue to grapple.[59]

Like Rothman, Catherine Cocks's Doing the Town (2001), focuses on the production of the tourist experience, but it does so by explaining the development of an infrastructure of tourism (railroads, hotels, guidebooks, and organized tours) that built and shaped interest in visiting cities.[60] Since 2000, most historical scholarship on urban tourism, notably the work of Harvey K. Newman, J. Mark Souther, and Alicia Barber, focuses on case studies of single cities and examines how urban businessmen and municipal officials pursued tourism for profit or economic development. Souther's New Orleans on Parade (2006) was among the first books to push back against Rothman's "devil's bargain" thesis.[61]

Recent developments in the historiography of urban tourism defy generalization, except perhaps that the subfield appears to have moved past the question of whether tourism is a positive or negative force in cities. J. Philip Gruen, Reiko Hillyer, and Aaron Cowan have produced welcome and long overdue comparative studies of tourism in western cities in the 19th century, southern cities in the aftermath of Reconstruction, and Rustbelt cities in the post-1945 period, respectively. Gruen's Manifest Destinations (2014) also offers a model for balancing the producer and consumer sides of urban tourism by attempting to understand

how the tourist experience often strayed from promoters' scripted constructions of place.[62] Apart from individual articles and essays, African American agency in urban tourism remains understudied, but Lynnell Thomas's Desire and Disaster (2014) offers an important exception.[63]

PRIMARY SOURCES

Historical materials to support the study of urban tourism exist primarily on the local level. Public or university libraries (especially local history collections) and historical societies are good places to start one's search. For larger cities, such institutions increasingly provide online finding aids. Useful materials include tourist guidebooks, picture postcards, travel accounts, oral histories, promotional materials such as brochures and maps, newspaper clipping files, mayoral papers, chamber of commerce or visitor bureau records, and other government or nonprofit organization records.

Extensive collections of stereograph cards and picture postcards are available online. Examples include the Library of Congress Stereograph Cards; New York Public Library's Detroit Publishing Company Postcards, which has several thousand digitized postcards from the early 20th century; and the Tichnor Brothers Postcard Collection at Boston Public Library, which offers more than 23,000 color "linen" postcards from the 1930s and 1940s.[64] The unparalleled Curt Teich Postcard Archives Collection in the Newberry Library in Chicago contains hundreds of thousands of production files that document how the company made its cards, as well as hundreds of thousands of postcard images. Although most of the collection is not accessible electronically, some 18,000 images are online.[65] Google Books offers a wide array of fully digitized travel accounts and tourist guidebooks from the 19th and early 20th centuries. Tourist guides, maps, brochures, promotional films, and other ephemera sometimes also exist in specific library collections. Notable examples include the Anthony J. Stanonis Collection at Loyola University New Orleans and the Florida Broadsides and Ephemera Collection at the State Library and Archives of Florida.[66]

Digital page images from hundreds of newspapers from large cities to small towns are available through *Chronicling America* (Library of Congress), library subscription-based collections such as *America's Historical Newspapers* (Readex), commercial services such as GenealogyBank.com, or via individual newspapers' fee-based archives. However, with few exceptions, these collections cover only the period before 1930. Some major cities now have full runs of their daily newspapers digitized and keyword searchable but often require one to access them in a library or with a library card.

Manuscript collections often provide the deepest insights into tourism development, but pertinent collections are widely scattered, some cities having preserved and made extensive local government papers and records available and others having saved little. Collections pertaining specifically to convention and visitor bureaus are sometimes available. Examples include Austin, Texas; Los Angeles; San Diego; and Savannah, Georgia.[67]

DIGITAL MATERIALS

The Green Book (New York Public Library Digital Collections). https://digitalcollections.nypl.org/collections/the-green-book.

Travel, Tourism, and Urban Growth in Greater Miami: A Digital Archive. http://scholar.library.miami.edu/miamidigital/.

Tying and Untying the Knot (Reno Historical). http://renohistorical.org/tours/show/1.

FURTHER READING

Barber, Alicia. *Reno's Big Gamble: Image and Reputation in the Biggest Little City*. Lawrence: University Press of Kansas, 2008.

Berger, Molly W. *Hotel Dreams: Luxury, Technology, and Urban Ambition in America, 1829–1929*. Baltimore: Johns Hopkins University Press, 2011.

Blake, Angela M. *How New York Became American, 1890–1924*. Baltimore: Johns Hopkins University Press, 2006.

Cocks, Catherine. *Doing the Town: The Rise of Urban Tourism in the United States, 1850–1915*. Berkeley: University of California Press, 2001.

Cowan, Aaron. *A Nice Place to Visit: Tourism and Urban Revitalization in the Postwar Rustbelt*. Philadelphia: Temple University Press, 2016.

Culver, Lawrence. *The Frontier of Leisure: Southern California and the Shaping of Modern America*. New York: Oxford University Press, 2010.

Grant, Elizabeth. "Race, Place, and Memory: African American Tourism in the Postindustrial City." In *African American Urban History since World War II*. Edited by Kenneth L. Kusmer and Joe W. Trotter, 404–424. Chicago: University of Chicago Press, 2009.

Gruen, J. Philip. *Manifest Destinations: Cities and Tourists in the Nineteenth-Century American West*. Oklahoma City: University of Oklahoma Press, 2014.

Harris, Neil. "Urban Tourism and the Commercial City." In *Inventing Times Square: Commerce and Culture at the Crossroads of the World*. Edited by William R. Taylor, 66–82. Baltimore: Johns Hopkins University Press, 1991.).

Heap, Chad. *Slumming: Sexual and Racial Encounters in American Nightlife, 1885–1940*. Chicago: University of Chicago Press, 2009.

Hillyer, Reiko. *Designing Dixie: Tourism, Memory, and Urban Space in the New South*. Charlottesville: University of Virginia Press, 2014.

Judd, Dennis R., and Susan S. Feinstein, eds. *The Tourist City*. New Haven, CT: Yale University Press, 1999.

Kilbride, Daniel. *An American Aristocracy: Southern Planters in Antebellum Philadelphia*. Columbia: University of South Carolina Press, 2006.

Moehring, Eugene P. *Resort City in the Sunbelt: Las Vegas, 1930–2000*. 2d ed. Reno: University of Nevada Press, 2000.

Rothman, Hal K. *Devil's Bargains: Tourism in the Twentieth-Century American West*. Lawrence: University Press of Kansas, 1998.

Sandoval-Strausz, Andrew K. *Hotel: An American History*. New Haven, CT: Yale University Press, 2007.

Simon, Bryant. *Boardwalk of Dreams: Atlantic City and the Fate of Urban America*. New York: Oxford University Press, 2004.

Souther, J. Mark. *New Orleans on Parade: Tourism and the Transformation of the Crescent City.* Baton Rouge: Louisiana State University Press, 2006.

Souther, J. Mark, and Nicholas Dagen Bloom, eds. *American Tourism: Constructing a National Tradition.* Chicago: Center for American Places, 2012.

Spirou, Costas, and Dennis R. Judd. *Building the City of Spectacle: Mayor Richard M. Daley and the Remaking of Chicago.* Ithaca, NY: Cornell University Press, 2016.

Stanonis, Anthony J. *Creating the Big Easy: New Orleans and the Emergence of Modern Tourism, 1918–1945.* Athens: University of Georgia Press, 2006.

Thomas, Lynnell L. *Desire and Disaster in New Orleans: Tourism, Race, and Historical Memory.* Durham, NC: Duke University Press, 2014.

Yuhl, Stephanie E. *A Golden Haze of Memory: The Making of Historic Charleston.* Chapel Hill: University of North Carolina Press, 2005.

NOTES

1. Jon Sterngass, *First Resorts: Pursuing Pleasure at Saratoga Springs, Newport, and Coney Island* (Baltimore: Johns Hopkins University Press, 2001), 112, 118–122.

2. Daniel Kilbride, *An American Aristocracy: Southern Planters in Antebellum Philadelphia* (Columbia: University of South Carolina Press, 2006), 128–130.

3. Richard H. Gassan, "Fear, Commercialism, Reform, and Antebellum Tourism to New York City," *Journal of Urban History* 41, no. 6 (2015): 1079.

4. Gassan, "Fear, Commercialism, Reform, and Antebellum Tourism," 1081; Timothy J. Gilfoyle, *City of Eros: New York City, Prostitution, and the Commercialization of Sex, 1790–1920* (New York: W. W. Norton, 1994), 119–122.

5. John F. Sears, *Sacred Places: American Tourist Attractions in the Nineteenth Century* (Amherst: University of Massachusetts Press, 1989), 89, 92, 100.

6. Catherine Cocks, *Doing the Town: The Rise of Urban Tourism in the United States, 1850–1915* (Berkeley: University of California Press, 2001), 52–60.

7. J. Philip Gruen, *Manifest Destinations: Cities and Tourists in the Nineteenth-Century American West* (Oklahoma City: University of Oklahoma Press, 2014), 33–35, 45–69.

8. Molly W. Berger, *Hotel Dreams: Luxury, Technology, and Urban Ambition in America, 1829–1929* (Baltimore: Johns Hopkins University Press,

2011), 29; A. K. Sandoval-Strausz, *Hotel: An American History* (New Haven, CT: Yale University Press, 2007), 80, 99.

9. Cocks, *Doing the Town,* 72, 84.

10. Berger, *Hotel Dreams,* 177, 236.

11. Neil Harris, "Urban Tourism and the Commercial City," in *Inventing Times Square: Commerce and Culture at the Crossroads of the World,* ed. William R. Taylor (Baltimore: Johns Hopkins University Press, 1991), 69.

12. Timothy J. Gilfoyle, "Grant Park, Chicago, Illinois," in *American Tourism: Constructing a National Tradition,* ed. J. Mark Souther and Nicholas Dagen Bloom (Chicago: Center for American Places, 2012), 130.

13. Chad Heap, *Slumming: Sexual and Racial Encounters in American Nightlife, 1885–1940* (Chicago: University of Chicago Press, 2009), 39.

14. Cocks, *Doing the Town,* 156, 161.

15. Cocks, 167–169.

16. Cocks, 192.

17. Angela M. Blake, *How New York Became American, 1890–1924* (Baltimore: Johns Hopkins University Press, 2006), 115–120, 127–132.

18. Raymond W. Rast, "The Cultural Politics of Tourism in San Francisco's Chinatown, 1882–1917," *Pacific Historical Review* 76, no. 1 (2007): 45–47, 53–54.

19. David Nasaw, *Going Out: The Rise and Fall of Public Amusements* (New York: Basic Books, 1993), 65; Gilfoyle, *City of Eros,* 223.

20. Emily Epstein Landau, *Spectacular Wickedness: Sex, Race, and Memory in Storyville, New Orleans* (Baton Rouge: Louisiana State University Press, 2013), 1, 111–113.

21. Alison Isenberg, *Downtown America: A History of the Place and the People Who Made It* (Chicago: University of Chicago Press, 2004), 51–55, 61–62, 67–75; Harris, "Urban Tourism and the Commercial City," 71.

22. Gruen, *Manifest Destinations,* 125–126; Blake, *How New York Became American,* 52–54, 99–105.

23. Gruen, *Manifest Destinations,* 75, 102–103; Dominic A. Pacyga, *Slaughterhouse: Chicago's Union Stock Yard and the World It Made* (Chicago: University of Chicago Press, 2015), 1–2, 5–23, 100–106.

24. Aaron Cowan, *A Nice Place to Visit: Tourism and Urban Revitalization in the Postwar Rustbelt* (Philadelphia: Temple University Press, 2016), 37–38; Harris, "Urban Tourism and the Commercial City," 77–78; Eric Johannesen, *A Cleveland*

Legacy: The Architecture of Walker and Weeks (Kent, OH: Kent State University Press, 1999), 72.

25. Robert W. Rydell, *World of Fairs: The Century-of-Progress Expositions* (Chicago: University of Chicago Press, 1993), 1, 6.

26. Char Miller, "River Walk, San Antonio, Texas," in Souther and Bloom, *American Tourism*, 223; J. Mark Souther, *New Orleans on Parade: Tourism and the Transformation of the Crescent City* (Baton Rouge: Louisiana State University Press, 2006), 166; Wendy Griswold, *American Guides: The Federal Writers' Project and the Casting of American Culture* (Chicago: University of Chicago Press, 2016).

27. Cowan, *Nice Place to Visit*, 46–47.

28. Souther, *New Orleans on Parade*, 33.

29. Cowan, *Nice Place to Visit*, 38–39.

30. On the Las Vegas Convention Center's origins, see Eugene P. Moehring, *Resort City in the Sunbelt: Las Vegas, 1930–2000*, 2d ed. (Reno: University of Nevada Press, 2000), 93–96. On McCormick Place, see Roger Biles, *Richard J. Daley: Politics, Race, and the Governing of Chicago* (DeKalb: Northern Illinois University Press, 1995), 49–50.

31. Warren James Belasco, *Americans on the Road: From Autocamp to Motel, 1910–1945* (Baltimore, MD: Johns Hopkins University Press, 1979); Sandoval-Strausz, *Hotel*, 133–134.

32. Moehring, *Resort City in the Sunbelt*, 45, 256; John M. Findlay, *Magic Lands: Western Cityscapes and American Culture after 1940* (Berkeley: University of California Press, 1993), 54.

33. Richard E. Foglesong, *Married to the Mouse: Walt Disney World and Orlando* (New Haven, CT: Yale University Press, 2001).

34. Andrew Hurley, *Beyond Preservation: Using Public History to Revitalize Inner Cities* (Philadelphia: Temple University Press, 2010), 4–8.

35. Damon Scott, "When the Motorman Mayor Met the Cable Car Ladies: Engendering Transit in the City That Knows How," *Journal of Urban History* 40, no. 1 (2014): 66–67, 73, 77.

36. Souther, *New Orleans on Parade*, 64–72.

37. Richard Campanella, *Bourbon Street: A History* (Baton Rouge: Louisiana State University Press, 2014), 163–164; Isenberg, *Downtown America*, 283–292; Judy Mattivi Morley, *Historic Preservation and the Imagined West: Albuquerque, Denver, and Seattle* (Lawrence: University Press of Kansas, 2006), 50; Harvey K. Newman, "Race and the Tourist Bubble in Downtown Atlanta," *Urban Affairs Review* 37, no. 3 (2002): 309.

38. Sharon Zukin, *The Cultures of Cities* (Malden, MA: Blackwell, 1995), 3–11.

39. Nicholas Dagen Bloom, *Merchant of Illusion: James Rouse, America's Salesman of the Businessman's Utopia* (Columbus: Ohio State University Press, 2004), 152–158; Souther, *New Orleans on Parade*, 166–169; Cowan, *Nice Place to Visit*, 133–144.

40. Alexander J. Reichl, *Reconstructing Times Square: Politics and Culture in Urban Development* (Lawrence: University Press of Kansas, 1999), 16–17; Timothy J. Gilfoyle, *Millennium Park: Creating a Chicago Landmark* (Chicago: University of Chicago Press, 2006), 93–95.

41. Eric Allison and Lauren Peters, *Historic Preservation and the Livable City* (Hoboken, NJ: John Wiley, 2011), 112–115.

42. Andrew R. Highsmith, *Demolition Means Progress: Flint, Michigan, and the Fate of the American Metropolis* (Chicago: University of Chicago Press, 2015), 259–262; Meg Mirshak, "Vision for Riverwalk Is Different from Reality," *Augusta Chronicle*, July 28, 2013, http://chronicle.augusta.com/news-metro/2013-07-27/vision-riverwalk-different-reality.

43. Dennis R. Judd, "Constructing the Tourist Bubble," in *The Tourist City*, ed. Dennis R. Judd and Susan S. Fainstein (New Haven, CT: Yale University Press, 1999), 38; Bryant Simon, *Boardwalk of Dreams: Atlantic City and the Fate of Urban America* (New York: Oxford University Press, 2004), 203–205.

44. Cowan, *Nice Place to Visit*, 141–147.

45. Sara Gruber, "San Antonio Launches New Marketing Campaign to Promote Tourism," *Visit San Antonio*, March 28, 2012, http://media.visitsanantonio.com/News/English/San-Antonio-Launches-New-Marketing-Campaign-to-Pro; "Washington, DC Launches Yearlong Marketing Campaign with 'DC Cool'", *DC Press*, December 3, 2013, https://washington.org/press/Washington-DC-Launches-Yearlong-Marketing-Campaign-with-DC-Cool.

46. New York Public Library Digital Collections, *The Green Book*; Souther, *New Orleans on Parade*, 75–76.

47. Souther, *New Orleans on Parade*, 172; Adonees Sarrouh and J. Mark Souther, "Cleveland's Second Downtown," Cleveland Historical. published on Sept 19, 2010. Last updated on May 17, 2017.

48. Lynnell L. Thomas, *Desire and Disaster in New Orleans: Tourism, Race, and Historical Memory*

(Durham, NC: Duke University Press, 2014), 12–14.

49. Elizabeth Grant, "Race and Tourism in America's First City," *Journal of Urban History* 31, no. 6 (2005): 859–860, 863, 867–868.

50. Nan Alamilla Boyd, *Wide-Open Town: A History of Queer San Francisco to 1965* (Berkeley: University of California Press, 2005), 15–16, 61–62.

51. Scott S. Ellis, *Madame Vieux Carré: The French Quarter in the Twentieth Century* (Jackson: University Press of Mississippi, 2010), 142–144; Josh Sides, "Excavating the Postwar Sex District in San Francisco," *Journal of Urban History* 32, no. 3 (2006): 368–375; Stephanie Rosenbloom, "The Evolving World of Gay Travel," *New York Times*, May 30, 2014, https://www.nytimes.com/2014/06/01/travel/the-evolving-world-of-gay-travel.html.

52. Marita Sturken, *Tourists of History: Memory, Kitsch, and Consumerism from Oklahoma City to Ground Zero* (Durham, NC: Duke University Press, 2007), 165–218.

53. Kevin Fox Gotham and Miriam Greenberg, *Crisis Cities: Disaster and Redevelopment in New York and New Orleans* (New York: Oxford University Press, 2014) is just one of many works that examines disaster tourism and voluntourism; Cindy S. Aron, *Working at Play: A History of Vacations in the United States* (New York: Oxford University Press, 2001).

54. Mitch Landrieu, "'*We Can't Walk Away from This Truth*': New Orleans Mayor Mitch Landrieu Explains to His City Why Four Monuments Commemorating the Lost Cause and the Confederacy Had to Come Down," *Atlantic*, May 23, 2017, https://www.theatlantic.com/politics/archive/2017/05/we-cant-walk-away-from-this-truth/527721/.

55. John F. Kasson, *Amusing the Million: Coney Island at the Turn of the Century* (New York: Hill and Wang, 1978); Kathy Peiss, *Cheap Amusements: Working Women and Leisure in Turn-of-the-Century New York* (Philadelphia: Temple University Press, 1986); Nasaw, *Going Out*.

56. Harris, "Urban Tourism and the Commercial City," 66–82; Eugene P. Moehring, *Resort City in the Sunbelt: Las Vegas, 1930–1970* (Reno: University of Nevada Press, 1989).

57. Judd, "Constructing the Tourist Bubble."

58. Sharon Zukin, *Landscapes of Power: From Detroit to Disney World* (Berkeley: University of California Press, 1993).

59. Hal K. Rothman, *Devil's Bargains: Tourism in the Twentieth-Century American West* (Lawrence: University Press of Kansas, 1998).

60. Cocks, *Doing the Town.*

61. Harvey K. Newman, *Southern Hospitality: Tourism and the Growth of Atlanta* (Tuscaloosa: University of Alabama Press, 1999); Souther, *New Orleans on Parade*; Alicia Barber, *Reno's Big Gamble: Image and Reputation in the Biggest Little City* (Lawrence: University Press of Kansas, 2008).

62. Gruen, *Manifest Destinations*; Reiko Hillyer, *Designing Dixie: Tourism, Memory, and Urban Space in the New South* (Charlottesville: University of Virginia Press, 2014); Cowan, *Nice Place to Visit.*

63. Thomas, *Desire and Disaster in New Orleans.*

64. Stereograph Cards, Library of Congress; Detroit Publishing Company Photographs, Library of Congress; Tichnor Brothers Postcard Collection, Boston Public Library.

65. Curt Teich Postcard Archives Collection, The Newberry.

66. Anthony J. Stanonis Collection, Loyola University New Orleans; Florida Broadsides and Ephemera Collection at the State Library and Archives of Florida.

67. Austin Convention and Visitors Bureau Records, Austin History Center, Austin Public Library, Austin; Greater Los Angeles Visitors and Convention Bureau (All-Year Club of Southern California) Collection, 1900–1980, Special Collections, Oviatt Library, California State University, Northridge, Los Angeles; San Diego Convention and Visitors Bureau Collection, Special Collections and University Archives, San Diego State University, San Diego; Savannah Area Convention and Visitors Bureau Records, Georgia Historical Society, Savannah.

J. Mark Souther

PROFESSIONAL TEAM SPORTS IN THE UNITED STATES

Professional sports teams are athletic organizations composed of compensated participants hired to play, because of their talent and expertise, by club owners who profit by charging spectators admission fees. These teams typically belong to a league that schedules a championship season, although independent touring teams arranged contests against local teams in the regions where they "barnstormed."

MAJOR LEAGUE BASEBALL

The first major professional team sport emerged in baseball, a popular amateur sport that had developed in the 1830s and 1840s and by mid-century was already considered the "national pastime." In the 1860s the top amateur teams recruited top athletes to help them win championships and attract paying customers, compensating them with cash or sinecures. Approximately a dozen entirely professional teams existed by 1869, most notably the all-salaried Cincinnati Red Stockings, whose players earned from $600 to $2,000. Manager Harry Wright led them to an undefeated season (57-0-1), and then twenty-four straight wins in 1870 before losing. However, the club was unprofitable and went out of business.[1]

In 1871 the first professional league was established, the ten-team National Association of Professional Base Ball Players (NA), comprising clubs in the east and Midwest. The league struggled through five seasons because franchises paid just $10 to join, teams arranged their own schedules, and many franchises in small cities like Rockford, Illinois, came and went. Furthermore, teams were of uneven quality, and players, who earned between $1,300 and $1,600, often left their teams ("revolve") for clubs offering more lucrative salaries.[2]

The eight-team National League of Professional Baseball Clubs supplanted the NA in 1876. This business-oriented league sought to make money by putting the sport on a sound financial footing. Franchises cost $100, teams were required to represent a city with at least 75,000 residents (a rule not always followed), and the league office made up the schedule. Teams that did not complete the season were expelled. The NL drew up rules to promote a positive public image, including no Sunday baseball, no sales of alcoholic beverages, high admission prices, and "morals clauses" in contracts. Player salaries were the biggest expense, and a "reserve clause" that bound athletes to a specific team was introduced in contracts for 1879.[3]

New competing leagues immediately appeared. The main rival was the American Association, established in 1882, which catered to a working-class audience with Sunday games, 25 cent admissions, and liquor sales. High costs led the AA to ally with the NL two years later, and they completely merged in 1892. Another rival was the Players' League, established in 1890 under the sponsorship of the Brotherhood of Professional Baseball Players, the first sports union, founded in 1885 by John M. Ward to protect players from treatment as chattel.[4]

In 1901 the American League (AL) was created as a new major league. It merged with the NL in 1903, setting up the first World Series. Professional baseball flourished in the early 1900s, and by 1910 there were fifty minor leagues. The sport was heavily covered in the daily press, specialized sport weeklies, and general-interest periodicals. Baseball became a prominent topic in juvenile literature and popular music. Star players were renowned heroes, idolized for their prowess (like Ty Cobb), and their exemplary character (Christy Mathewson). The game was so popular that owners tore down the flimsy wood stadiums constructed for $30,000 to $60,000, five of which burned down in 1894, constructing larger and far more substantial stadiums. In 1909 the first fire-resistant major-league ballpark was built, Philadelphia's $500,000 Shibe Park, followed by nine more by 1916. Capacities averaged about 25,000, though the Polo Grounds in New York seated 54,000. They had idiosyncratic dimensions, often reflecting the available space in congested industrial cities. The "classic" ballpark era culminated in 1923 with the $2.5 million, 63,000-seat Yankee Stadium, the first MLB site not known as a park, field, or grounds.[5]

The popularity of baseball also spawned a short-lived Federal League (1914–1915) and a host of industrial semipro leagues. In 1915 more than 100,000 spectators viewed the national championship game between the Cleveland White Motors team and Omaha's Luxus nine, sponsored by the Krug brewery.[6]

Major League Baseball did very well in the interwar years, despite the impact of the "fixed" 1919 World Series, and remained the preeminent professional sport into the 1940s. The nature of the game on the field changed from a finesse to a power game because of slugger Babe Ruth, who hit 714 home runs. He was the era's preeminent sports hero and a model of consumption, freely spending his $80,000 salary. In the interwar era, nearly all top athletes aspired to play Major League Baseball, especially for the New York Yankees, who won eleven pennants and eight World Series in those years. The Yankees and the St. Louis Cardinals flourished by establishing extensive farm systems to produce new talent.[7]

Although the Depression undermined the prosperity that baseball enjoyed in the 1920s, producing big financial losses for both teams and players, the public demand for escapism allowed the game to fare better than most businesses. MLB adopted some marketing innovations like night games, an annual all-star game beginning in 1933, and radio broadcast of games by 1940. MLB regained its profitability by the mid-1930s.[8]

Early-20th-century professional baseball also was racially segregated. The only acknowledged African American players up to then were the Walker brothers, who played for Toledo (American Association) in 1884. Blacks were totally excluded from organized professional baseball in 1899 by an unwritten understanding, which limited them to traveling black clubs. In 1920 the Negro National League (NNL) was created by black entrepreneurs to take advantage of the potential market among the growing African American inner-city population. The league lasted until 1931, failing because of founder Rube Foster's mental illness and the economic impact of the Depression. A new NNL began in 1933, largely created by

inner-city policy bankers. The NNL became a profitable and leading community institution. The Homestead Grays became the league's top team with a roster that included Satchel Paige, Josh Gibson, and Buck Leonard, who would have been MLB stars if white.[9]

Pressure for integration grew during World War II from black and white journalists and liberal politicians pointing up the heroic accomplishments of Olympic champion Jesse Owens and heavyweight boxing champion Joe Louis, and black participation in World War II. However, strong opposition to a racially integrated baseball remained inside and outside the sport because many whites saw it as a step toward a larger racial integration of American society. The big step was taken by Dodgers president Branch Rickey, who signed Jackie Robinson on October 23, 1945, because he believed it was the right thing to do, that integration would help the Dodgers win a pennant, and that it was good for business. Robinson was not the star of the Kansas City Monarchs, but was an outstanding all-around athlete and a college-educated veteran who lived in integrated Los Angeles, was about to get married, and had a background needed to cope with life in the MLB. Despite the racism he encountered, Robinson was named rookie of the year in 1947 and helped lead the team to the World Series.

In fact, the integration of MLB was probably the single most consequential development in North American sport history because it did strongly impact broader American society. Robinson's success opened the door for other black players, but the process of integration was slow, even though African Americans like Willie Mays and Hank Aaron soon dominated the National League. Progress was slower in the American League. The last team to integrate was the Boston Red Sox in 1959. By 1965 20 percent of MLB players were black or Latino, 38 percent of the All-Stars were men of color. But by 2016, only 9 percent of MLB players were African American, compared to 70 percent in the NFL, 74.4 percent in the NBA, and 5 percent in the NHL.[10]

Professional baseball was extremely popular after World War II, with attendance doubling to an average of 16,027. Minor leagues alone numbered a record fifty-two. However, television coverage soon saturated broadcast markets, which together with television's popularity as free entertainment led to many minor leagues going out of business and MLB franchises losing money in the early 1950s.[11]

Financial woes also led to the first movement of franchises since 1903. In 1953 the Boston Braves moved to Milwaukee, where the local government refurbished County Stadium and leased it to the Braves for a nominal sum. Local boosters foresaw the team promoting their city and boosting the local economy. The Braves soon became the most profitable team in the National League, which encouraged the St. Louis Browns' move to Baltimore one year later, and in 1955 the Philadelphia Athletics moved to Kansas City. Then in 1958, the profitable Dodgers and Giants left New York City for Los Angeles and San Francisco, respectively. All these teams received considerable government assistance, although the Dodgers did finance their own ballpark in 1962. Dodger Stadium was the last new privately financed MLB park for decades. The migration to the West Coast made MLB a truly national operation.[12]

MLB introduced an expansion program to take advantage of the sport's still-increasing popularity, to counter a proposed new Continental League, and to mollify Congress after the Washington Senators moved to Minneapolis in 1960 and Congress threatened to retaliate by ending baseball's antitrust exemption. New American League teams were established in Washington and Los Angeles in 1961. One year later, the National League added the New York Mets and the Houston Colt 45s (today the Astros), who paid $1.8 million to join. In 1968 MLB added four new teams, and two more in 1976. The next expansion came in 1993, when the NL added Denver and Florida (now Miami), and in 1998 the AL added Tampa Bay, and Arizona joined the NL.[13]

Several modern publicly financed ballparks were built from 1961 to 1970 beginning with District of Columbia Stadium (later RFK Stadium) because of expansion or to attract or maintain an established franchise. They were typically multipurpose structures for baseball and football that cost $50–60 million, including Atlanta and St. Louis, and then in 1970 Cincinnati, Philadelphia, and Pittsburgh built "cookie-cutter" stadiums with very similar designs and dimensions, while in 1964 Houston constructed the most ground-breaking edifice, its Astrodome, which was the nation's first enclosed stadium.[14]

A generation later, new innovative "retro fields" were built, starting with Baltimore's $110 million (today $185 million) Oriole Park at Camden Yards (1992), seating around 45,000, which re-created the look and ambiance of the old intimate ballparks of the early 20th century. The new style was very popular, and similar fields soon followed, including Cleveland's $175 million Jacobs Field (1994), Atlanta's $209 million Turner Field (1997), and $216 million PNC Park in Pittsburgh (2001). However, these expenditures are dwarfed by the new Yankee Stadium that cost $2.3 billion (half of which was publicly subsidized).[15]

Television became a major factor in franchise profitability, although for years the revenues came mostly from local television contracts. League-wide packages were not permitted until the Sports Broadcasting Act of 1961. Total local television revenues in 1950 were $2.3 million and rose to $12.5 million in 1960, which were unevenly distributed to major market teams like the Yankees, who made $56.7 million in 2001 compared to under $6 million for Milwaukee. The first lucrative network contract came in 1972–1975, when NBC paid $72 million for Monday games. Currently MLB has contracted through 2021 with Fox Sport to pay nearly $500 million a year, and Turner pays more than $300 million annually, while ESPN is paying $700 million a year through 2020.[16]

The formation of a players' union in 1954, the Major League Baseball Players Association

(MLBPA), had a huge impact on MLB. In 1965 the then-weak union took a major step forward by hiring economist Marvin Miller of the United Steelworkers of America as its director, who secured both enhanced pension benefits and a higher minimum salary. He ran the MLBPA like a traditional trade union with a strike in 1972, the first of seven labor stoppages by 1995, and negotiated salary arbitration in 1973. Miller orchestrated an arbitration case in 1975 that led to the demise of the reserve clause, replacing it with a system based on free agency and salary arbitration. In 1981, the players held a fifty-day midseason strike over the owners' attempt to discourage free-agent signing by requiring compensation, which later led to court rulings that owners had colluded to reduce salaries and discourage free agency. The perpetual unrest culminated in the 1994–1995 strike that caused cancellation of the 1994 World Series, a huge public-relations disaster for both sides. However, the union action produced a dramatic change in player compensation. The average professional baseball-player salary in the early 1950s was approximately $11,000; it reached $19,000 in 1967 and $52,300 in 1976. Thereafter salaries skyrocketed, surpassing $1 million in 1993. Today the average MLB player salary is $4.17 million. The MLBPA succeeded because membership was unified against a divided ownership. It is today the strongest union in the United States.[17]

Although attendance growth has been pretty flat since 1997, the value of MLB teams has dramatically escalated due to higher ticket prices and increased TV revenues. The Yankees rose in value from $11.2 million in 1964 to $635 million in 2001 and $3.2 billion today, far above the average of $1.2 billion.[18]

PROFESSIONAL FOOTBALL AND THE NATIONAL FOOTBALL LEAGUE

Professional football emerged among working-class athletic clubs in the steel-manufacturing areas of Pennsylvania and Ohio, who took winning seriously and hired top players for big games. The first known pro was William "Pudge" Heffelfinger, an All-American lineman at Yale University, who in November 1892 received $500 to play for the Allegheny Athletic Association against the Pittsburgh Athletic Club. The first fully pro teams were located in Pittsburgh and its surrounding communities, drawing upward of 3,000 spectators. In 1902, journalist David Barry established the National Football League. The Philadelphia Phillies and the Pittsburgh Pirates squads included major leaguer ballplayers, and their coaches managed the local major league teams of the same names. The league lasted one year. Eight years earlier, baseball owners had organized the American League of Professional Football, a soccer league comprising six teams owned by MLB owners that also had lasted one season.[19]

In 1902 the Ohio League was organized in northeastern Ohio, but a gambling scandal in 1906 involving teams from Massillon and Canton hurt the sport. Football made a comeback by 1910, and one year later Canton returned to the league, winning championships in 1915, 1916, 1917, and 1919, led by former All-American and Olympic star Jim Thorpe. The 1916 team claimed the title of "Professional Football Champions of the World." Many top teams then were sponsored by Ohio and Pennsylvania industrialists to promote better relations with their employees.[20]

In 1920, owners of professional teams, many of which were affiliated with industrial firms, met at Canton to form a league, the American Professional Football Association, which was renamed the National Football League (NFL) in 1922. Thorpe was the initial president, replaced in 1921 by sportswriter Joe Carr. The fourteen teams of 1920 were charged a $100 membership fee, although no one paid it. The league was not well organized, and teams made their own schedules. The NFL was so unstable that it had fifty different franchises by 1933.[21]

In 1925 the Chicago Bears signed Harold "Red" Grange, considered the greatest college football player of his time, moments after he completed his last college game. His agent, C. C. "Cash and Carry" Pyle, signed a contract for Grange to immediately join the Bears and then play a nineteen-game exhibition series. Grange drew large crowds, including about 70,000 to New York's Polo Grounds, and he made about $250,000 for the season. His presence added considerable prestige to the NFL, and more collegians considered turning pro at a time when 80 percent of the players had no college background.[22]

Unlike MLB, professional football originally was not segregated, perhaps because of its lower status. The first black pro was Charles W. Follis in 1904 for Shelby of the Ohio League. A small number of African Americans played in the early NFL, most notably All-American end Paul Robeson (1920–1922), the future lawyer, singer, and radical activist, and Fritz Pollard, who coached the Akron Pros in 1921. The last blacks in the early NFL were Joe Lillard and Ray Kemp in 1933, when increased racism in the Depression and the opposition of white players, fans, and owners forced black players out of the league for over a decade.[23]

The Depression hurt the NFL, which had just eight teams in 1932. Green Bay, an original NFL franchise, was the only small town still in the league, nineteen others having dropped out. The league that year streamlined footballs to make them easier to pass and increase scoring, and staged its first post-season championship game. One year later, the College All-Star game began with the NFL's champion playing a select group of college seniors at Chicago's Soldier Field. Another important innovation was the introduction of the college draft in 1936 to improve rosters of weaker teams. By 1940, when the T-formation was widely used, the league was drawing nearly 20,000 per game.[24]

The NFL struggled during World War II, but the high expectations engendered by peace also produced three major problems: the rise of the All American Football Conference (AAFC), whose eight owners had previously tried unsuccessfully to get NFL franchises; a

betting scandal; and integration. The AAFC included franchises in San Francisco, Los Angeles, and Miami, making it a truly national league, accessible by air travel. The NFL responded by moving the Cleveland Rams to Los Angeles, where it was pressured to integrate by the Los Angeles Coliseum Commission that operated the Coliseum. The Rams signed former UCLA All-American Kenny Washington and his college teammate Woody Strode. The Cleveland Browns of the AAFC subsequently signed Marion Motley and Bill Willis of the Browns, who helped lead the team to four AAFC championships. The AAFC ended in 1950 when Cleveland, Baltimore, and San Francisco joined the NFL. The Browns maintained their dominance in the NFL with seven trips to the championship game, including three titles. NFL integration proceeded slowly, but by 1955 only the Washington Redskins had not signed a black player. Owner George Preston Marshall did not hire an African American until 1962, when he signed Bobby Mitchell, only after pressure from Attorney General Robert F. Kennedy and Secretary of the Interior Stewart Udall, who threatened to evict the team from the new, publicly owned D.C. Stadium.[25]

Teams in the 1950s and 1960s often had quotas on the number of black players, underrecruited and underpaid them, and stacked blacks in speed positions, excluding them from "intelligence" roles like middle linebacker or quarterback. This has changed, but slowly and unevenly. In 2014, nine of thirty-two NFL quarterbacks were black, but the league had only one black owner, seven general managers, and four head coaches.[26]

The most important game in the 1950s was the 1958 championship between the Baltimore Colts and the New York Giants, seen on television by 40 million fans. The Colts won the first sudden death overtime, 23-17. The game demonstrated the sport's popularity and future financial possibilities. Two years later, Pete Rozelle became commissioner and transformed the NFL into the most successful league in sports, eclipsing baseball.[27]

Roselle's biggest crisis was the rise of the American Football League in 1960, organized by wealthy businessmen previously unable to buy an NFL franchise. They sited six of eight teams in non-NFL cities, planning to survive until the NFL agreed to let them in. The NFL took up the challenge by expanding into Minneapolis-St. Paul to preempt a vacant site and into Dallas to compete with an AFL franchise there. The interlopers struggled at first, relying on a TV contract with ABC to survive. In 1964, the AFL signed a five-year, $42 million contract with NBC, which contributed to a full-scale salary war.[28]

The leagues merged in 1966 to form a single twenty-four-team league to cut costs, facilitated by congressional actions that circumvented antitrust implications. They maintained separate conferences, with the winners playing in a championship game called the "Super Bowl." The event became the preeminent single sporting contest in the United States with viewership dwarfing all other television programs. Since then the NFL has fought off other rivals: the World Football League (1974), the United States Football League (1983–1985), and the XFL (2001).[29]

The NFL Players Association (NFLPA) was founded in 1956 but was not recognized by management until 1968, when a collective bargaining agreement was signed providing minimum salaries and a pension. Football players tried to unionize, but early on, the union was so weak that the courts overturned several contracts that the union had agreed to, because the union was in an unequal bargaining position and could not negotiate a fair contract.[30]

NFLPA executive director Ed Garvey led a fifty-seven-day strike in 1982 that achieved marginal gains in the Collective Bargaining Agreement. When it expired in 1987, the executive director Gene Upshaw (1983–2008) led a strike over the free agency policy, and owners retaliated with replacement players. Once players returned to the field, they sought redress in the courts, which ruled that the owners were covered by the labor exemption

from antitrust law. The union reorganized itself into a professional organization, and individual players brought a new antitrust case against the NFL's Plan B that gave teams a right of first refusal for players seeking free agency. The owners eventually settled the case, granting free agency, and the players accepted a "hard" salary cap based on 64 percent of total team revenues. Afterward, the NFLPA reconstituted itself again as a labor union and signed a new collective bargaining agreement in 1993. In 2011, following a brief summer lockout, a new ten-year agreement got players 47 percent of revenue. A limit was placed on rookie wages, $50 million was annually funded for medical research, and owners pledged approximately $1 billion for retirees. As of 2015, the average salary was $2.11 million.[31]

Today the NFL has thirty-two teams located throughout United States in nearly all the leading television markets, reflecting the major role of its national television contract in producing huge profits. By 1990 each team made $33 million annually just from television. The current contract is worth $184.4 million a year. This helped make the average franchise worth $2 billion, led by the Dallas Cowboys at $4 billion.[32]

Perhaps the NFL's greatest current problem is the number of players who suffered concussions and other head blows leading to chronic traumatic encephalopathy (CTE), and ultimately memory loss, depression, dementia, and even suicide. In 2015, 199 players had concussions, one-third of which the NFL estimated would lead to long-term cognitive issues. Back in 2010, the NFL introduced rules to promote safer play, including banning the use of helmets against defenseless players, stopping play when a player lost his helmet, and moving kickoffs to the thirty-five-yard line to reduce the number of kickoff returns. Retired players sued the NFL in 2011, and after, some 4,500 former players and their families joined the case. The NFL settled the suit for $765 million in 2013, but the plaintiffs filed an appeal in 2016.[33]

THE NATIONAL HOCKEY LEAGUE

Ice hockey was a popular sport in Canada and select American sites in the late 19th century. Former Canadian amateur Jack "Doc" Gibson founded the Portage Lakers (Michigan) in 1903, the first professional hockey team. One year later, he established the first pro association, the International Hockey League (IPHL), with teams in the Upper Peninsula of Michigan (Calumet, Houghton, and Sault Sainte Marie), Pittsburgh, and Sault Saint Marie (Ontario). The IPHL lasted through the 1906–1907 season, playing on the first artificial ice arenas.[34]

In 1910 the National Hockey Association (NHA) was founded by railroad magnate Michael J. O'Brien and his son Ambrose, and the Pacific Coast Hockey League (PCHA) was established in 1911–1912 by Frank and Lester Patrick. The latter expanded to the United States with teams in Portland (1914), Seattle (1915), and Spokane (1916). Before the 1917–1918 season, Montreal, Ottawa, and Quebec quit the NHA to form the National Hockey League (NHL). The PCHA merged with the three-year-old Western Canadian Hockey League in 1924, to become the Western Hockey League. The WHL collapsed after the 1925–1926 season, leaving the NHL as the sport's only major league.[35]

The first American NHL franchise was the Boston Bruins in 1924. By 1926–1927, there were four Canadian and six US teams, including the Bruins, Chicago Black Hawks, Detroit Cougars (the future Red Wings), New York Rangers, New York Americans, and Pittsburgh Pirates, whose owners were associated with their city's main sports arena. The new teams paid a $15,000 fee to join the NHL. The teams played a forty-four-game season and relied mostly on gate receipts for revenue, which mainly went to the home team.[36]

The NHL enjoyed an era of great stability from 1942 through 1967 with the "Original Six" franchises—the Boston Bruins, Chicago Blackhawks, Detroit Red Wings, Montreal Canadiens, New York Rangers, and Toronto Maple Leafs. Games were broadcast over radio and on CBS-TV from 1956 through 1960.[37]

By the 1960s, several cities sought NHL franchises to promote themselves. In 1967, six new teams were added, and then six more US teams between 1970 and 1974 to fight the World Hockey Association (WHA), established in 1971 by Gary Davidson and Dennis Murphy, founders of the American Basketball Association (ABA) in 1967.[38]

WHA teams engaged in a bidding war for top talent. In 1972 Winnipeg signed Chicago Blackhawks' superstar Bobby Hull to a ten-year, $1.75 million contract plus a $1 million signing bonus. The WHA struggled to recruit experienced North Americans and turned to Finland and Sweden for talent. The costly rivalry led to a merger in 1979 with four of six WHA clubs. Thereafter, the NHL began recruiting Europeans, including eastern Europeans in 1985, who stressed skating, passing, and puck handling instead of the NHL-style of dump-and-chase that emphasized physicality and violence. In 2015, 24.2 percent of players were Americans, 49.7 percent Canadians, and 26.1 percent European. The first African American in the NHL was Willie O'Ree, who played sparingly for Boston in 1958. Five of twenty-two current players with African ancestry are US born.[39]

The NHL in the early 1970s took a very proactive role in promoting hockey internationally, particularly against the "amateur" world champion Soviet Union. The NHL was perceived as defender of the free world in competitions against the Soviet Union, beginning with the 1971 Summit Series in which the NHL All-Stars topped the Soviets by a narrow 4-3-1 margin.[40]

NHL hockey players and owners were by nature conservative, and no union was formed until 1967, when the Players' Association (NHLPA) was recognized under player agent Alan Eagleson. He tried to maintain a close, conciliatory relationship with the league, but the rank and file wanted a more aggressive leadership since their salaries, benefits, and dangerous working conditions lagged far behind other team sports. When Eagleson retired in

1991, he was replaced by Detroit lawyer and player agent Bob Goodenow, who pursued an aggressive agenda. One year later the union struck over salaries and marketing rights for players' images on merchandise. John Ziegler, the first NHL American president (1977–1992), was fired by owners dissatisfied with his negotiations. He was replaced by NHL executive Gil Stein, who gave way in 1994 to an NBA vice president Gary Bettman, appointed commissioner to promote expansion and greater network television coverage, and fight the union.[41]

The NHLPA successfully fought management in the 1990s. When the collective bargaining agreement ended in 2003, Bettman and the owners were ready for change, especially since salaries averaged $1.5 million. The owners locked out the players, blaming them for the league's financial woes. The dispute ended with the owners introducing a salary cap and pulling back on rising wages. The average NHL salary is currently $2.62 million.[42]

Commissioner Bettman promoted nationalism to enhance the NHL's profile. The league joined the Olympic Movement in 1998, and four years later Canada won its first hockey gold medal since 1952. He also pushed through expansion, adding six teams between 1993 and 2000, mainly in southern cities. Fiscal problems led to four relocations in the mid-1990s, and currently twenty-three of thirty franchises are in the United States. Bettman actively promoted network contracts, starting with a five-year, $155 million deal with Fox, and then in 1998 a five-year, $600 million agreement with ABC and ESPN. The current contract signed with Comcast in 2011 was for ten years, and worth almost $2 billion. NHL team values lag behind other sports, averaging $505 million, led by the Rangers at $1.2 billion.[43]

PROFESSIONAL BASKETBALL AND THE RISE OF THE NATIONAL BASKETBALL LEAGUE

Basketball was invented in 1891 (first game on December 21, 1891) by Dr. James Naismith at the YMCA College in Springfield, Massachusetts, to be a physically challenging indoor winter team sport. By 1898 the six-team National League of Professional Basketball was formed in metropolitan Philadelphia, and it lasted six years. At least six other eastern pro leagues soon emerged. Players earned about $5 per game, scores were very low, and play was so physical that some owners installed steel metal cages around the courts.[44]

The early dominant pro team was the Buffalo Germans, winners of the 1904 championship at the St. Louis Olympics, who toured for twenty-two years. The team disbanded in 1926 while playing as the Buffalo Bisons of the American Basketball League (ABL), founded one year earlier by NFL president Joe Carr. The ABL was the first widely located professional basketball league, comprising independent eastern and Midwestern teams. In 1926, the Brooklyn Original Celtics, the nation's top touring team, joined the ABL and captured the championship. Several top touring teams never joined, notably the SPHAs (South Philadelphia Hebrew Association) and the New York Rens, barred because its players were black. The ABL was very unstable, with nineteen teams in five seasons, and broke up in 1931. A new, heavily Jewish and exclusively eastern ABL began in 1934 and lasted until 1952–1953.[45]

In 1937 the thirteen-team National Basketball League (NBL) was established, like the early NFL, by small businessmen, local boosters, and industrial firms in small and midsized Midwestern cities who played in high school and other small arenas. Players were mostly college graduates who worked for corporate sponsors. Independent and league teams participated in the World Professional Tournament (1939–1948) sponsored by the *Chicago Herald-American*. In 1939, the New York Rens defeated the Oshkosh All Stars (34-25) to win the first championship, followed one year later by the Harlem Globetrotters, another black team.[46]

The pro game took a big step forward in 1946, when promoters who controlled the largest privately owned eastern and Midwestern sports arenas organized the eleven-team Basketball Association of America to fill open dates. The BAA, modeled after MLB, pretty much killed off the ABL, but the NBL survived with its more civic-minded owners, rabid fans, and excellent ex-collegians like center George Mikan, a future Basketball Hall of Famer. The BAA dropped down to eight teams in 1947–1948, cut back its schedule, and created a unique territorial draft that gave franchises first shot at local graduating collegians. Prior to opening day in 1948–1949, four NBL franchises joined the BAA, including the outstanding Minneapolis Lakers.[47]

THE NATIONAL BASKETBALL LEAGUE

The NBL ceased operations before the 1949–1950 season, and six of its teams joined the BAA, which renamed itself the National Basketball Association. The NBA's seventeen teams ranged from metropolises such as New York, Philadelphia, and Chicago to smaller cities like Anderson, Indiana, and Waterloo, Iowa. The league was very unstable, and six teams, mainly from smaller cities, dropped out. Gate receipts went exclusively to home teams, which was good for big cities, not good for small towns. By 1957 Syracuse was the only small city in the NBA. The Syracuse Nationals moved to Philadelphia in 1963, replacing the Warriors, who had moved to San Francisco one year earlier, joining the Lakers in California, who had moved from Minneapolis to Los Angeles in 1960. The NBA had become truly national.[48]

The early NBA game did not draw as well as top college games and often relied on doubleheaders that featured the Harlem Globetrotters to attract fans. The 1951 NCAA betting scandals severely wounded the college game, and fans began giving more attention to the pros. However, many fans were turned off by the slow pace of games because teams frequently used slow-down tactics against stronger foes. The Minneapolis Lakers, led by 6'10" George Mikan, dominated play, with

five championships between 1949 and 1954. The league also began to get more publicity through national television coverage on the Dumont network, and later on NBC.[49]

Major rule changes in 1954 tried to make the game more fan friendly by increasing scoring. The twenty-four-second shot clock was introduced to prevent teams from stalling, and new penalties were created to curtail excessive fouling by penalizing the fouling team after the seventh violation with a foul shot, plus a second if they made the first, or three chances to make two if fouled.[50]

The NBA integrated in 1950, starting with Earl Lloyd of the Syracuse Nationals, Chuck Cooper of the Celtics, and Nat "Sweetwater" Clifton of the Knicks. By the late 1950s, there were several superstar black players, including defensive stalwart Bill Russell of the Boston Celtics, Elgin Baylor of the Minneapolis Lakers, Wilt Chamberlain of the Philadelphia Warriors in 1959, and Oscar Robertson in 1960 with the Cincinnati Royals. In 1958, African Americans composed 13 percent of NBA players, rising to 49 percent of team rosters in 1975 as well as two-thirds of starting players, and three-fourths of the All-Stars. The Celtics led by Russell and Coach Red Auerbach were the dominant team, with ten NBA titles, a record unmatched in professional team sports between 1957 and 1969.[51]

The quality of play and the athleticism of players increased during these years, relying on a large pool of outstanding former collegians. There were so many talented players and so much fan interest that in 1961 Abe Saperstein, owner of the Globetrotters, set up a rival eight-team league, the American Basketball League (ABL), with franchises as far west as Hawaii. It only lasted two years.[52]

The American Basketball Association (ABA), organized in 1967 by advertising executives, was a far stronger rival. The owners believed that interest in the game extended beyond the NBA's ten cities, and their eleven-team league had many attractive young players like Julius "Dr. J" Erving, George McGinnis, David

Thompson, and Connie Hawkins; employed the three-point shot; and used a red, white, and blue ball.[53]

The rise of the ABA provided an opportunity for the National Basketball Players Association (NBPA) to fight the NBA's paternalism. Founded in 1954, the NBPA had accomplished little, and its first successful action came in 1964 when players at the All-Star Game refused to participate unless the owners agreed to concrete concessions. The outcome was a pension plan in 1965. Two years later, the union secured raises when it threatened to strike the playoffs. By 1970 they had won a minimum salary, medical insurance, severance pay, first-class air travel, and accommodations at five-star hotels. Average salaries jumped from $18,000 in 1965 to $110,000 in 1975.[54]

The NBA and ABA agreed to merge in 1970, an action the union fought, arguing that the consolidation would create a monopoly, and it secured a court injunction preventing the merger. The case was settled in February 1976, opening up player movement and including a financial settlement, and enabling Indiana, New York, San Antonio, and Denver to join the NBA. The other teams were disbanded, and their players were divided up among the remaining twenty-two teams.[55]

In 1978, the NBA signed a four-year, $74 million contract with CBS. By then the league then was more than 75 percent black, and some owners worried that their white fan base would be alienated by the black predominance. However, the NBA became more popular than ever, propelled by the rivalry between Larry Bird's Celtics and "Magic" Johnson's Lakers, who between them won eight of the nine NBA championships between 1980 and 1988.

The era of prosperity can be attributed in large measure to Commissioner David Stern (1984–2014) who took over when seventeen of twenty-three teams were losing money. He pushed for greater television coverage and convinced the Players Association to accept a salary cap and owners to accept a revenue-sharing system to maintain relative parity among teams. Stern instituted marketing campaigns that emphasized stars, particularly charismatic Michael Jordan, who led the Chicago Bulls to six NBA titles between 1991 and 1998. Stern signed television contracts with NBC in 1990 and ABC in 2002, supported importing overseas stars, and led another era of expansion to thirty teams. NBA revenue rose 500 percent during his tenure. The value of franchises rose from $114 million in 1994 to $1.1 billion in 2015, led by the Lakers at $2.6 billion. The average NBA player made $4.58 million.[56]

The most successful women's team pro sport is basketball. The first league was the eight-team the Women's Professional Basketball League (1978–1981). The Women's National Basketball Association started play in 1997 with teams all affiliated with local NBA teams. There are currently twelve teams. The games have been televised on ESPN since the league began. The current contract pays each team $1 million annually and runs to 2022. Total team salaries are currently capped at $900,000.

SOCCER IN THE UNITED STATES

The success of the four major professional team sports, supported by enthusiastic fans, powerful economic interests, and extensive television coverage, has been difficult to replicate in soccer. The North American Soccer League (1966–1984) failed, but Major League Soccer, founded in 1996, is currently profitable, playing in soccer specific stadiums, with twenty teams whose average value is $153 million. Most players are Americans, and the average salary is $282,499.[57]

DISCUSSION OF THE LITERATURE

Anyone interested in the scholarly study of sport history should begin by reviewing the literature in Steven Riess's A Companion to American Sport History (2014), which includes chapters on baseball, football, basketball, race, ethnicity, social class, business, media, stadiums, and biographies.[58]

Twenty years ago, Stephen Hardy urged historians to examine the special nature of the industry of sport and study the game form, the role of entrepreneurs in developing their product, and the types of organizations they created, namely teams that played in cartelized associations. Students of the different team sports like Benjamin Rader, Michael Oriard, and J. Andrew Ross all focus on the process of professionalization, the role of franchise owners, and explaining how leagues bureaucratized, created playing rules, and set up championship seasons. They are also concerned about recruitment of athletes and the development of quality teams, player–management relations, and the evolution of playing areas. Finally, they are concerned with components of profitability, franchise relocations, league expansion, and local and federal government relations.[59]

Historical scholarship on professional sports teams began with Harold and Dorothy Seymour's *Baseball: The Early* Years (1960), which became a model for other historians. They focused on the rise of the National League in 1876, which tried to run baseball on a money-making basis by keeping salaries low through the reserve clause, operating at modest wooden ballparks, and relying heavily on gate admissions and concessions. Then in *Baseball: The Golden Age* (1971), they examined the baseball boom of the 20th century, when it totally dominated the national sporting scene with the rise of the American League, the expansion of the minor leagues, and the construction of modern fire-resistant ballpark, which produced substantial profits.[60]

The Seymours' work influenced many scholars, including Peter Levine, whose *Albert Spalding and the Promise of American Sport* (1985) outlined the business operations of MLB's first highly profitable franchise, and Steven Riess, whose *Touching Base* (1980, rev. ed. 1999) and *City Games* (1989) emphasized the role of urbanization in the rise of professional team sports as the site of competition and as the process of urban development in the advancement

of sports. He especially stressed the connections between team sports and local politics.

Player–management relations have focused on reserve clauses that limited the negotiation opportunities of players and on unions that fought for players' rights, starting with the Brotherhood of Professional Baseball Players in 1885. Historians argue that early unions failed because of the dominant power of management and the conservatism of professional athletes who did not have a strong sense of shared class consciousness with their peers. Much of the recent scholarship examines how player unions, beginning with the Major League Baseball Players Association (MLBPA) in the mid-1960s under Marvin Miller successfully challenged management, improved working conditions, gained pensions and arbitration, and ended of the reserve clause by the mid-1970s. The MLBPA become the most powerful labor organization in the United States, yet MLB remains exempt from anti-trust law. Oriard shows how the NFL Players Union used the court system, traditionally highly pro ownership, to level the playing field between management and labor.[61]

Michael Oriard has intensely analyzed how the NFL in the 1970s became the nation's most popular spectator sport and thereafter maintained that status. Oriard attributes the considerable success to the generally astute decisions and actions taken by a series of NFL commissioners and owners to protect and enhance their bottom line, especially through television. NFL television revenues are so huge today that box-office receipts are currently of secondary importance. Scholars like Oriard, James R. Walker, and Robert V. Bellamy Jr. focus a great deal on the profitability of over-the-air and cable television to other pro team sports. A new area of study on profits is the internet's impact with through social media and the streaming of sporting events. For instance, MLB Advanced Media, launched in 2000, anticipates $1 billion in revenue in 2016.[62]

Historians are, like sports fans, intrigued by the process of creating great teams, which require recruitment of top athletes. Baseball and hockey had farm systems, and football and basketball had the player draft, and now all employ the signing of expensive free agents. Historians write biographies of prominent players on and off the field. They study their impact on team achievement, how they influenced the way the sport was played, and their heroism. Biographies of icons like Babe Ruth by Marshall Smelser and "Red" Grange by John M. Carroll go beyond their performance on the field to examine their cultural significance, while activist Curt Flood's biographer Brad Snyder emphasizes his contribution to players' rights. Scholars also examine the antiheroic Black Sox of 1919, and the impact of performance-enhancing drugs.[63]

Historians have studied the changing character of franchise owners who were originally middle-class entrepreneurs. Once pro sports became more prestigious and highly profitable, owners were increasingly very wealthy men. Scholars also study the preeminent managers and coaches like Vince Lombardi to understand their values and styles of leadership, and the important role and impact of league executives like Pete Rozelle and Judge Kenesaw M. Landis.[64]

Historians have given considerable attention to racism in professional sport, focusing primarily on African Americans. Michael Lomax has examined the black baseball business, examining the leadership role of African American entrepreneurs in addressing the entertainment needs of growing black communities, and Neil Lanctot demonstrates the profitability of black baseball in the late 1930s and early 1940. Jules Tygiel's classic study of the process of major-league integration of baseball explains the role of journalists and civil-rights activists, the impact of World War II, and the presence of star Negro Leaguers in that development. He focuses on the action of independently minded Dodger president Branch Rickey in breaking the color line, and the courage of Jackie Robinson in combating prejudice. Tygiel also demonstrates the slow process by which MLB teams integrated even

after the great success of early black pioneers. Historians Adrian Burgos and Samuel Regalado have written movingly about Latino ballplayers who encountered bigotry in a foreign land, exacerbated for many who carried the double burden as black and Latino.[65] Virtually no attention has been given to women professional team athletes, whose leagues have barely made a dent in the American sports world.

PRIMARY SOURCES

A good place to start studying the history of professional team sports are published collections of primary sources, beginning with four edited volumes of the series *Sports in America: A Documentary History*, including George B. Kirsch's *Sports in War, Revival and Expansion 1860–1880*; Gerald R. Gems's *Sports Organized, 1880–1900*; Steven A. Riess's *Sports in the Progressive Era, 1900–1920*; and Douglas O. Baldwin's *Sports in the Depression, 1930–1940*. A superb collection of documents on baseball can be found in Dean A. Sullivan's four-volume *A Documentary History of Baseball*. For documents in black sport history, see David K. Wiggins, and Patrick B. Miller, eds., *The Unlevel Playing Field: A Documentary History of the African American Experience in Sport*.[66]

There are a number of major archives that specialize in pro team sports. The most outstanding is the Giamatti Research Center of the National Baseball Hall of Fame, Cooperstown, New York, which has three million documents, including periodicals, scrapbooks, and manuscript collections, as well as over 250,000 photographic images and over 16,000 hours of recorded media. Professional football serviced by the Ralph Wilson, Jr. Pro Football Research and Preservation Center, at the Pro Football Hall of Fame in Canton, Ohio, which includes files of individual players and teams, and over 100 scrapbooks. Anyone interested in professional basketball should visit the Naismith Memorial Basketball Hall of Fame in Springfield, MA, and for hockey, the best archive is the D.K. (Doc) Seaman Hockey

Resource Centre in the MasterCard Centre for Hockey Excellence, in Toronto, Canada, home of the Hockey Hall of Fame's artifact and archival collections.

Major libraries often have valuable manuscript collections on professional sports. For example, the Library of Congress in Washington, DC, has the papers of Jackie Robinson, Dodgers president Branch Rickey, and Arthur Mann, former sportswriter and Dodgers executive. The New York Public Library has the historic A. G. Spalding Baseball Collection. The Chicago History Museum has the unpublished testimony of White Sox outfielder star Joe Jackson before the grand jury in its investigation of the Black Sox Scandal.

Digitized internet sources can be invaluable for scholars of major professional team sports. Baseball-reference.com is a definitive source of data on the statistical accomplishments of major league players, including advanced sabermetrics, and salary data. There is a lot of information on current and former major league and minor league teams. Similar sources exist for pro football, hockey and basketball. Websites maintained by individuals include considerable and valuable primary data, such as Doug Pappas, longtime SABR Business of Baseball committee chairman, who collected data on the baseball business.

The specialized periodicals *Baseball Magazine* (1908–1920) and *Sporting Life* (1885–1917) are available from the Los Angeles 84 Sports Library and Digital Collection. Additional access to baseball resources is available online to members of the Society for American Baseball Research (SABR), including the 1915 Federal League Baseball case files, Spalding Baseball Guides 1889–1939; and The Baseball Index, a database with over 240,000 records of books, articles, and other items. Members also have access to the *Sporting News* (1883–). Researchers also can avail themselves of digitized newspapers available at various local libraries whose members may access them over the internet. Many of the papers come from Proquest, which can be employed directly from the publisher. Finally, the Library of Congress has made available *Chronicling America: Historic American Newspapers* (1836–1922).

DIGITAL MATERIALS

baseball-reference.com.
basketball-reference.com.
chroniclingamerica.loc.gov.
football-reference.com.
hockey-reference.com.
LA84 Foundation.
Roadside Photos.

FURTHER READING

Bellamy, Robert V., and James R. Walker. *Center Field Shot: A History of Baseball on Television*. Lincoln: University of Nebraska Press, 2008.

Burk, Robert F. *Much More Than a Game: Players, Owners and American Baseball Since 1921*. Chapel Hill: University of North Carolina Press, 2002.

Coenen, Craig R. *From Sandlots to the Super Bowl: The National Football League, 1920–1967*. Knoxville: University of Tennessee Press, 2005.

Creapeau, Richard. *NFL Football: A History of America's New National Pastime*. Urbana: University of Illinois, 2014.

Danielson, Michael N. Home *Team: Professional Sports and the American Metropolis*. Princeton, NJ: Princeton University Press, 1997.

Davies, Richard O. *Sports in American Life: A History*. West Sussex, U.K.: Wiley-Blackwell, 2012.

Fetter, Henry. *Taking on the Yankees: Winning and Losing in the Business of Baseball, 1903–2003*. New York: W. W. Norton, 2003.

Levine, Peter. *Albert Spalding and the Promise of American Sport*. New York: Oxford University Press, 1985.

MacCambridge, Michael. *America's Game: The Epic Story of How Pro Football Captured a Nation*. New York: Random House, 2004.

Miller, James. *The Baseball Business: Pursuing Pennants and Profits in Baltimore*. Chapel Hill: University of North Carolina Press, 1990.

Nathan, Daniel A. *Saying It's So: A Cultural History of the Black Sox Scandal*. Urbana: University of Illinois Press, 2003.

Oriard, Michael. *Brand NFL: Making and Selling America's Favorite Sport*. Chapel Hill: University of North Carolina Press, 2007.

Peterson, Robert W. *Cages to Jump Shots: Pro Basketball's Early Years*. New York: Oxford University Press, 1990.

Rader, Benjamin G. *Baseball: A History of America's Game*. 3d ed. Urbana: University of Illinois Press, 2008.

Rader, Benjamin G. *American Sports: From the Age of Folk Games to the Age of Televised Sports*. 6th ed. Englewood Cliffs, NJ: Prentice Hall, 2009.

Riess, Steven A. *City Games: The Evolution of American Urban Society and the Rise of Sport*. Urbana: University of Illinois Press, 1989.

Riess, Steven A. *Touching Base: Professional Baseball and American Culture in the Progressive Era*. Rev. ed. Urbana: University of Illinois Press, 1999.

Riess, Steven A. *A Companion to American Sport History*. Chichester, West Sussex, U.K.: Wiley-Blackwell, 2014.

Ross, J. Andrew. *Joining the Clubs: The Business of the National Hockey League to 1945*. Syracuse, NY: Syracuse University Press, 2015.

Schiavone, Michael. *Sports and Labor in the United States*. Albany: State University of New York Press, 2015.

Seymour, Harold, and Dorothy Seymour. *Baseball*. 3 vols. New York: Oxford University Press, 1960–1989.

Surdam, David G. *The Rise of the National Basketball Association*. Urbana: University of Illinois Press, 2012.

Surdam, David G. *Run to Glory and Profits: The Economic Rise of the NFL during the 1950s*. Lincoln: University of Nebraska Press, 2013.

Surdam, David G. *The Big Leagues Go to Washington: Congress and Sports Anti-trust*. Urbana: University of Illinois Press, 2015.

Tygiel, Jules. *Baseball's Great Experiment: Jackie Robinson and His Legacy*. New York: Oxford University Press, 1983.

White, G. Edward. *Creating the National Pastime: Baseball Transforms Itself, 1903–1953*. Princeton, NJ: Princeton University Press, 1998.

NOTES

1. Marshall Wright, *The National Association of Base Ball Players, 1857–1870* (Jefferson, NC: McFarland 2000); and Harold Seymour, *Baseball: The Early Years* (New York: Oxford University Press, 1960), 47–58.

2. Seymour, *Baseball: The Early Years*, 59, 60, 75–80; and William J. Ryczek, *Blackguards and Red Stockings: A History of Baseball's National Association* (Jefferson, NC: McFarland, 1999).

3. Seymour, *Baseball: The Early Years*, 47–58; and Peter Levine, *Albert Spalding and the Promise of American Sport* (New York: Oxford University Press, 1985).

4. Seymour, *Baseball: The Early Years*, 148–171, 221–224, 231–249.

5. Harold Seymour, *Baseball: The Golden Age* (New York: Oxford University Press, 1971), 2–255; and Steven A. Riess, *Touching Base: Professional Baseball and American Culture in the Progressive Era*, rev. ed. (Urbana: University of Illinois Press, 1999), 99–133.

6. Daniel R. Levitt, *The Battle that Forged Modern Baseball: The Federal League Challenge and Its Legacy* (Lanham, MD: Ivan R. Dee, 2012); and Harold Seymour, *Baseball: The People's Game*, (New York: Oxford University Press, 1990), 268–269.

7. Daniel A. Nathan, *Saying It's So: A Cultural History of the Black Sox Scandal* (Urbana: University of Illinois Press, 2003); Seymour, *Baseball: The Golden Years*; Charles Fountain, *The Betrayal: The 1919 World Series and the Birth of Modern Baseball* (New York: Oxford University Press, 2016); and Marshall Smelser, *The Life that Ruth Built: A Biography* (New York: Quadrangle/New York Times Book, 1975).

8. David G. Surdam, *Wins, Losses, and Empty Seats: How Baseball Outlasted the Great Depression* (Lincoln: University of Nebraska Press, 2011); and Benjamin Rader, *Baseball: A History of America's Game* (Urbana: University of Illinois Press, 2008), 151–152.

9. William A. White, who passed as white, played in a game for Providence of the AA in 1879; Peter Morris and Stefan Fatsis, "Baseball's Secret Pioneer: William Edward White, the First Black Player in Major-League History, Lived His Life as a White Man," February 4, 2014. On black baseball, see Michael E. Lomax, *Black Baseball Entrepreneurs, 1860–1901: Operating by Any Means Necessary* (Syracuse, NY: Syracuse University Press, 2003); Lomax, *Black Baseball Entrepreneurs, 1902–1931: The Negro National and Eastern Colored Leagues* (Syracuse, NY: Syracuse University Press, 2014); and Neil Lanctot, *Negro League*

Baseball: The Rise and Ruin of a Black Institution (Philadelphia: University of Pennsylvania Press, 2004).

10. Jules Tygiel, *Baseball's Great Experiment: Jackie Robinson and His Legacy* (New York: Oxford University Press, 1983); "2015 Major League Baseball Racial and Gender Report Card"; "NFL Census: Data on Players' Race, Weight and Height," September 23, 2014; "2015 National Basketball Association Racial Gender and Report Card"; and David Sommerstein, "As First Black American NHL Player, Enforcer Was Defenseless Against Racism," February 6, 2015.

11. Rader, *Baseball*, 190; "1950 Minor Leagues Encyclopedia."

12. Steven A. Riess, *City Games: The Evolution of American Urban Society and the Rise of Sport* (Urbana: University of Illinois Press, 1989), 234–237.

13. Rader, *Baseball*, 198–202. See also the individual team histories in Steven A. Riess, ed., *The Encyclopedia of Major League Baseball Teams*, 2 vols. (Westport, CT: Greenwood Press, 2006).

14. Robert Trumpbour, *The New Cathedrals: Politics and Media in the History of Stadium Construction* (Syracuse, NY: Syracuse University Press, 2007); Michael Oriard, *Brand NFL: Making and Selling America's Favorite Sport* (Chapel Hill: University of North Carolina Press, 2010), 149–162; and Michael K. Bohne, "Cookie-Cutter Stadiums".

15. Philip Lowry, *Green Cathedrals* (New York: Walker, 2005). For a survey of data on ballpark history, see Munsey and Suppress, "Ballparks."

16. Rader, *Baseball*, 192, 194–196, 219; James R. Walker and Robert V. Bellamy Jr., *Center Field Shot: A History of Baseball on Television* (Lincoln: University of Nebraska Press, 2008); and John Ourand and Eric Fisher, "Fox, Turner To Renew MLB Packages; MLB Net Could Get LDS Games," September 19, 2012, *Street and Smith's Sport Business Daily*.

17. Michael Schiavone, *Sports and Labor in the United States* (Albany: State University of New York Press, 2015), 9–50. The average American earned about $2,786 in 1950, or around one-fourth a major league ballplayer. See Pat Sullivan, "No End in Sight as Athletes' Salaries Skyrocket," *Chicago Tribune*, January 1, 2000, 3; David Brown, "MLB Players Average Salary Tops Record $4 Million—But There's a Catch," March 31, 2015.

Cork Gaines, "The NBA Is the Highest-Paying Sports League in the World," *Business Insider*, May 20, 2015.

18. Steven A. Riess, "New York Yankees," in Riess, ed., *Encyclopedia of Major League Baseball Teams*, 730, 744; Scott Lindholm, "Major League Attendance Trends Past, Present, and Future," February 10, 2014, 2013. Kurt Badenhausen, Michael Ozanian, Christina Settimi, "MLB Worth $36B as Team Values Hit Record $1.2B Average," *Forbes*, March 25, 2015.

19. John M. Carroll, "Football, Professional," in *Sports in America: From Colonial Times to the Twenty-First Century* (Armonk, NY: York: M.E. Sharpe, 2011), 361–362; Marc S. Maltby, *The Origins and Development of Professional Football, 1890–1920* (New York: Routledge, 1997); and Steve Holroy, "The First Professional Soccer League in the United States: The American League of Professional Football (1894)."

20. Bob Braunwart and Bob Carroll, "The Ohio League," *Coffin Corner* 3.7 (1981).

21. "Franchise Encyclopedias,". Crepeau, *NFL Football*, 6–8, 20–23.

22. John M. Carroll, *Red Grange and the Rise of Pro Football* (Urbana: University of Illinois Press, 1999); and Crepeau, *NFL Football*, 9–17.

23. Charles K. Ross, *Outside the Lines: African Americans and the Integration of the National Football League* (New York: New York University Press, 1999), 12–47; and Craig R. Coenen, From *Sandlots to the Super Bowl: The National Football League, 1920–1967* (Knoxville: University of Tennessee Press, 2005), 91–92.

24. Coenen, *From Sandlots to the Super Bowl*, 69–75, 80–90; and David G. Surdam, *Run to Glory and Profits: The Economic Rise of the NFL During the 1950s* (Lincoln: University of Nebraska Press, 2013), 282–290.

25. David G. Surdam, *Run to Glory and Profits: The Economic Rise of the NFL during the 1950s* (Lincoln: University of Nebraska Press, 2013, 1–38; Richard Crepeau, *NFL Football: A History of America's New National Pastime* (Urbana: University of Illinois, 2014), 32–43; and Thomas G. Smith, *Showdown: JFK and the Integration of the Washington Redskins* (Boston: Beacon Press, 2011).

26. "In Black and White: A Racial Breakdown of the NFL." Accessed 30 March 2016.

27. Crepeau, NFL *Football*, 48–50; Oriard, *Brand NFL*, 2–14; Jerry Izenberg, *Rozelle: A Biography* (Lincoln: University of Nebraska Press, 2014); and Surdam, *Run to Profit*, 225–254.
28. Crepeau, *NFL Football*, 58–68.
29. Crepeau, *NFL Football*, 67–71, 128–129, 141; and David G. Surdam, *The Big Leagues Go to Washington: Congress and Sports Antitrust, 1951–1989* (Urbana: University of Illinois Press), 88–93, 211–222.
30. Crepeau, *NFL Football*, 135–148; and Schiavone, *Sports and Labor in the United States*, 54–66.
31. Oriard, *Brand NFL*, 109–113, 127–136, 141–149, 252–254; Schiavone, *Sports and Labor in the United States*, 66–88; Crepeau, *NFL Football*, 148–152; and Gaines, "The NBA Is the Highest-Paying Sports League in the World."
32. Crepeau, *NFL Football*, 156–157, 187–188; Oriard, *Brand Football*, 162–174; and "Forbes Announces Eighteenth Annual NFL Team Valuations," *Forbes* September 15, 2015.
33. Jason M. Breslow, "NFL Acknowledges a Link Between Football, CTE," *FRONTLINE*, March 15, 2016. Alan Schwarz, Walt Bogdanich, and Jacqueline Williams, "N.F.L.'s Flawed Concussion Research and Ties to Tobacco Industry," *New York Times*, March 24, 2016.
34. Daniel Mason, "The International Hockey League and the Professionalization of Ice Hockey, 1904–1907," *Journal of Sport History* 25 (Spring 1998): 1–17.
35. Ross, *Joining the Clubs*, 39–88.
36. Ross, *Joining the Clubs*, 89–156; and John Chi-Kit Wong, *Lords of the Rinks: The Emergence of the National Hockey League, 1875–1936* (Toronto: University of Toronto Press, 2005).
37. John Chi-Kit Wong and Morris Mott, "Ice Hockey," in Riess, *Sports in America*, 470–471.
38. Steve Rushin, "39 Gary Davidson."
39. Wong and Mott, "Ice Hockey," 472; Ed Miller, "The WHA: A Look Back Forty Years Later," May 7, 2013; and "Majority of NHL Players This Season," October 24, 2015; "List of Black NHL Players."
40. Wong and Mott, "Ice Hockey," 471–472.
41. Daniel S. Mason, "National Hockey League Players' Association," in Riess, *Sports in America*, 652–653; and Wong and Mott, "Ice Hockey," 472–473.
42. Mason, "National Hockey League Players' Association," 653–654; and "Welcome to Elite 35 Sports Institute."
43. Wong and Mott, "Ice Hockey," 473–474; and "Forbes Releases Seventeenth Annual List of NHL Team Valuations," *Forbes*, November 24, 2015.
44. Robert Peterson, *Cages to Jump Shots: Pro Basketball's Early Years* (New York: Oxford University Press, 1990), 32–34.
45. Peterson, *Cages to Jump Shots*, 56–61, 69–79, 84–101, 175; Peter Levine, *Ellis Island to Ebbets Field: Sport and the American Jewish Experience* (New York: Oxford University Press, 1992), 65–70; and Murry R. Nelson, "Basketball, Professional, Pre-NBA," in Riess, *Sports in America*, 148–150; and Murry R. Nelson, *The Originals: The New York Celtics Invent Modern Basketball* (Bowling Green, OH: Bowling Green State University Popular Press, 1999).
46. Murry R. Nelson, *The National Basketball League: A History, 1935–1949* (Jefferson: NC, McFarland, 2009); John Schleppi, *Chicago's Showcase of Basketball: The World Tournament of Professional Basketball and the College All-Star Game* (Haworth, NJ: St. Johann Press, 2008); Peterson, *Cages to Jump Shots*, 95–107, 124–141; Ben Green, *Spinning the Globe: The Rise, Fall, and Return to Greatness of the Harlem Globetrotters* (New York: Amistad, 2006); and David G. Surdam, *The Rise of the National Basketball Association* (Urbana: University of Illinois Press, 2012), 21.
47. Peterson, *Cages to Jump Shots*, 150–163; and Surdam, *Rise of the National Basketball Association*, 20–57.
48. Surdam, *Rise of the National Basketball Association*, 57–132; and Peterson, *Cages to Jump Shots*, 163–181.
49. Surdam, *Rise of the National Basketball Association*, 75, 82, 89, 104–108, 126–132, 134. The NBA had its own betting scandal surrounding Detroit Pistons' rookie Jack Molinas. Surdam, *Rise of the National Basketball Association*, 80–81.
50. Surdam, *Rise of the National Basketball Association*, 118–126.
51. Surdam, *Rise of the National Basketball Association*, 81–85; and Earl Lloyd and Sean Kirst, *Moonfixer: The Basketball Journey of Earl Lloyd* (Syracuse, NY: Syracuse University Press, 2010).
52. Murry R. Nelson, *Abe Saperstein and the American Basketball League, 1960–1963: The Upstarts Who Shot for Three and Lost to the NBA* (Jefferson, NC: McFarland, 2013).

53. Goudsouzian, "Basketball, Professional, NBA Era," 155.
54. Schiavone, *Sports and Labor in the United States*, 90–95; and Surdam, *Rise of the National Basketball Association*, 140–144.
55. Schiavone, *Sports and Labor in the United States*, 95–124; and Aram Goudsouzian, "Basketball, Professional, NBA Era," in Riess, *Sports in America*, 155–156.
56. Goudsouzian, "Basketball, Professional, NBA Era," 156–157; Kurt Badenhausen, "Lakers Top 2015 List of NBA's Most Valuable Teams; Average Franchise Is Now Worth Record $1.1 Billion," *Forbes*, January 21, 2015," *Forbes*, November 24, 2015. Forbes Releases Seventeenth Annual NBA Team Valuations," *Forbes*, January 21, 2015. Gaines, "The NBA is the Highest-Paying Sports League in the World;" Joe Dorrish, "Average Salaries in the NBA, NFL, MLB and NHL for 2015."
57. Chris Smith, "Major League Soccer's Most Valuable Teams 2015," *Forbes*, August 19, 2015; and Bobby McMahon, "MLS Is to Salary Cap What Donald Trump Is to Humility," *Forbes*, July 20, 2015.
58. Steven A. Riess, ed., *A Companion to American Sport History* (Hoboken, NJ: John Wiley & Sons, 2014).
59. Stephen Hardy, "Entrepreneurs, Organizations, and the Sport Marketplace: Subjects in Search of Historians," *Journal of Sport History* 13 (Spring 1986): 16; Rader, *Baseball*; and Oriard, *Brand NFL*; Ross, *Joining the Clubs*.
60. See also David Q. Voigt, *American Baseball: From Gentleman's Sport to the Commissioner System* (Norman: University of Oklahoma Press, 1966).
61. Schiavone, *Sports and Labor in the United States*, esp. 73–76, on the labor dispute between the NFL and the NFLPA. See also Robert F. Burk, *Never Just a Game: Players, Owners, and American Baseball to 1920* (Chapel Hill: University of North Carolina Press, 1994), and Robert F. Burk, *Much More than a Game: Players, Owners, and American Baseball Since 1921* (Chapel Hill: University of North Carolina Press, 2001); Oriard, *Brand NFL*, 135–136, 141–142; and Robert F. Burk, *Marvin Miller, Baseball Revolutionary* (Urbana: University of Illinois Press, 2015). On the internet and MLB, see Maury Brown, "The Biggest Media Company You've Never Heard Of," *Forbes*, July 7, 2014.
62. Oriard, *Brand NFL*; and Walker and Bellamy, *Center Field Shot*.
63. Smelser, *Life that Ruth Built*; Carroll, *Red Grange*; Brad Snyder, *A Well-Paid Slave: Curt Flood's Fight for Free Agency in Professional Sports* (New York: Plume, 2006); Daniel Nathan, *Saying It's So: A Cultural History of the Black Sox Scandal* (Urbana: University of Illinois Press, 2005); and Nathan M. Corzine, *Team Chemistry: The History of Drugs and Alcohol in Major League Baseball* (Urbana: University of Illinois Press, 2016).
64. Oriard, *Brand NFL*; David Maraniss, *When Pride Still Mattered: A Life of Vince Lombardi* (New York: Simon and Schuster, 1999); and David Pietrusza, *Judge and Jury: The Life and Times of Judge Kenesaw Mountain Landis* (South Bend, IN: Diamond Communications, 1998).
65. Michael Lomax, *Black Baseball Entrepreneurs: 1860–1901* (Syracuse, NY: Syracuse University Press, 2003); *Black Baseball Entrepreneurs, 1902–1931* (Syracuse, NY: Syracuse University Press, 2014); Neil Lanctot, *Negro League Baseball: The Rise and Ruin of a Black Institution* (Philadelphia: University of Pennsylvania Press, 2008); Tygiel, *Baseball's Great Experiment*; Adrian Burgos, Jr., *Playing America's Game(s): Baseball, Latinos, and the Color Line* (Berkeley: University of California Press, 2007); and Samuel Regalado, *Viva Baseball: Latin Major Leaguer and Their Special Hunger*, 2d ed. (Urbana: University of Illinois Press, 2007).
66. George B. Kirsch, ed., *Sports in War, Revival and Expansion 1860–1880* (Gulf Breeze, FL: Academic International Press, 1995); Gerald R. Gems, ed., *Sports Organized, 1880–1900* (Gulf Breeze, FL: Academic International Press, 1996); Steven A. Riess, ed., *Sports in the Progressive Era, 1900–1920* (Gulf Breeze, FL: Academic International Press, 1998); Douglas Baldwin, ed., *Sports in the Depression, 1930–1940* (Gulf Breeze, FL: Academic International Press, 2000); Dean A. Sullivan, ed., *A Documentary History of Baseball*, 4 vols. (Lincoln: University of Nebraska Press, 1995–2010); and David K. Wiggins, and Patrick B. Miller, eds., *The Unlevel Playing Field: A Documentary History of the African American Experience in Sport* (Urbana: University of Illinois Press, 2003).

Steven A. Riess

Informal Economies

GAMBLING IN NORTHERN US CITIES

Beginning in the 1830s, as urban density increased, and as the first police departments were created, a particular formulation of urban politics emerged within which popular gambling was carried on in connivance with police and machine politicians, in spite of the letter of the law. Reformers sought to curb gambling, characterizing it as sinful, a form of organized crime, and as elemental to urban machine politics and corruption of government. Various gambling forms rose and fell in popularity, and different demographic groups had distinct experiences with the gambling economy. Yet the basic contours of disputation over the status of gambling in the urban North held firm until the 1970s, when the adoption of public lotteries throughout the region supplanted criminal gambling, and severed the gambling economy from police and politics, while the introduction of new technology broke the connection between gambling and urban density.

GAMBLING IN THE 19TH-CENTURY CITY

Although gambling had deep roots in the Northern colonies, and indeed many important projects were financed through lotteries during the colonial period, state legislatures in the North took a harsh view of gambling during the years of the early Republic. Some forms of gambling such as betting on horse races and playing in high stakes card games carried aristocratic pretensions that conflicted with the political ethos of the post-revolutionary period.[1]

Furthermore, as Northern cities grew in size, the presence of gambling in large communities of strangers bore the marks of impersonal and adversarial interaction, which threatened social cohesion, while also undermining the work ethic and frugality of the working class. In this context, Northern legislatures acted to suppress gambling, with lotteries banned in New York in 1820, and across the entirety of the North by the middle of the 1840s. Nonetheless, early 19th-century urban America featured a vibrant gambling scene, with working class males in pursuit of leisure and entertainment. As historian Ann Fabian describes, "Urban artisans and mechanics gambled in grog shops, groceries and taverns. They played cards, billiards, shuffleboard, and dice, bought chances and fractions of chances in lotteries, and bet on contests between bulls, bears, cocks, badgers, horses, men, and dogs."[2] Despite the condemnation of editorialists, clergymen, and high-minded public officials, and notwithstanding the letter of the law, gambling was an undeniable feature of urban life. The most prominent forms of gambling in the 19th-century city were card and table games offered in taverns and gambling houses, lottery play, and betting on horse races. Each of these offered a variety of challenges to municipal governance.

GAMBLING HOUSES

The first successful gambling house in New York opened in 1825 near Wall Street and Water Street, and the phenomenon of houses devoted exclusively to selling gambling spread from there. By 1830 the city featured some dozen gambling houses. After Louisiana banned such establishments in 1835 and gambling in New Orleans went into decline, the growth of the New York scene accelerated. As historian David Schwartz explains, "By 1850, it was apparent that the thriving commercial hub had become the nation's new gambling capital. In that year, the New York Society for the Suppression of Gambling reckoned there were no fewer than six thousand establishments in the city that

permitted gambling." The Society estimated that these establishments employed an incredible 25,000 people.[3] The gambling houses and taverns of the period were either classed as "low dens" where the poor and working classes made their bets in bare surroundings and a rowdy atmosphere, or "first class hells" where the well-to-do gambled in style.[4] The most commonly offered games were poker, roulette, and the most popular game of the era, faro, in which gamblers bet on the turning of a card.

Chicago had not even incorporated as a city when the first gambling house opened in New York in 1825. Nonetheless, by the middle of the century it was the clear center of Western gambling.[5] As the city grew, gambling grew along with it, and gambling houses quickly dotted the landscape. Clark Street from Randolph to Monroe was known as "Gamblers Row" by the Civil War. Aside from a few saloons and brothels, gambling houses predominated on this stretch of Clark Street. In such houses, Chicagoans could easily find faro, roulette, and keno.[6] The fortunes of gambling proprietors in Chicago and New York fluctuated with changes in municipal and state government, and thus illegal gambling in those cities tended toward heavy involvement in politics, and an embrace of organization within criminal gambling to achieve protection from police raids and unfavorable legislation.

The crime syndicates that organized and operated big city gambling in the late 19th century were part of what historian Mark Haller referred to as the "Irish politics-gambling complex." Best exemplified in Chicago in a set of arrangements that prevailed until about World War I, gamblers shared their profits with Irish politicians and police in exchange for freedom to operate.[7] Most representative of this complex in Chicago was Mike McDonald, who operated an elaborate gambling house on State Street beginning in 1873. As an editorial in the *Chicago Tribune* charged, he "is synonymous with the local Democracy," and that "if one wants to know who is to be nominated Congressman or County Treasurer," by the Democrats, then he had better "consult Mike McDonald."[8] Beyond the gambling houses, the Irish syndicates of late 19th-century Chicago and New York also had a hand in the policy game and in an early form of off-track betting, operating mostly in poolrooms.

LOTTERIES AND POLICY IN THE 19TH CENTURY

Although lotteries were banned throughout the North by the 1840s, lottery play nonetheless remained popular in Northern cities, as countless people purchased tickets and fractions of ticket for lotteries conducted in other states and abroad. By the Civil War lotteries were only legal in Delaware, Missouri, and Kentucky, and drawings in Kentucky became a standard source for northern lottery play.[9] After the Civil War, depressed Southern states turned to lotteries to raise revenue, and betting in the urban North proved key to the success of these southern lottery enterprises. The most popular and the most notorious was the Louisiana Lottery, which was widely known to be fraudulent, yet persisted as a mainstay of Northern gambling into the 1880s. The prize announcements listed in the *Washington Post* invariably pointed to tickets sold in Boston, New York, Chicago, and Philadelphia.[10] The *Chicago Tribune* complained loudly of tickets for the Louisiana and Havana lotteries found easily available for purchase in the city.[11] The *New York Times* pleaded for the federal government to deny the Louisiana Lottery use of the mails, so that it may no longer take advantage of "poor, misguided, and deceived fools from other states."[12] At the behest of President Benjamin Harrison, in 1890 Congress banned the use of federal mails for dissemination of lottery tickets and promotions. When the wounded lottery relocated to Honduras, Congress responded by banning the importation and transportation of lottery material in 1895. The law was upheld by the Supreme Court in *Champion v. Ames* (1903), which maintained that such activity could be regulated as a matter of interstate commerce.[13]

The decline of the Louisiana Lottery further entrenched and formalized the game of policy, which relied on clandestine drawings in Kentucky. The term "policy" originated as a reference to a small side bet on an existing lottery. If one could not afford to purchase a lottery ticket, one might place a wager on the outcome as a kind of insurance policy. In the second half of the 19th century, northern policy play increasingly aligned with drawings held daily, at midday and in the evening, in Covington and Louisville, Kentucky, respectively. The drawings relied on the spinning of a wheel to produce 12 numbers ranging from 1 to 78 at midday, and 13 numbers in the evening. Bettors sought to anticipate a combination of three winning numbers called a gig, or two winning numbers called a saddle. Results were transmitted from Kentucky by code through the wire services, as bettors in New York, Chicago, Cleveland, and Philadelphia gathered in policy shops awaiting the day's winning results. Over time, northern policy dealers simply began spinning their own wheels to produce winning numbers.

The famed Lexow Committee of 1894 probed into policy gambling in the city and found a vast policy business deeply insinuated in city politics and policing. The final report of the committee estimated that more than one thousand policy shops operated in New York. Betting was particularly popular among the poor, and African Americans. Crusaders against this demoralizing evil also made special note of the game's significant popularity among women as evidence of the game's pernicious nature. Like the big city gambling houses, policy operations relied on collaboration with police and politicians to stay in business. As the Lexow Committee report lamented, "Not only were these violators of the law protected by police in consideration of a fixed sum of $15 a month per shop, but the area of operation of each 'king' was so clearly understood and carefully guarded, that any intruder, would be certified to the police, and would either be compelled to refrain from competition with a licensed 'policy king,' or else would be arrested."[14]

HORSE RACING

Far more public and much closer to legal than policy, yet by no means less politically connected, was gambling on horse races. Post-Civil War America featured a strong surge of interest in thoroughbred racing with New York City as the undisputed center of racing and both legal and illegal betting. The industry was also strong in Chicago, St. Louis, and Cincinnati. According to historian Steven A. Riess, by 1897, 314 tracks existed in America.[15] Although the New York State Legislature was the site of constant efforts to curtail racing in the late 19th century, tracks proliferated in Queens and Brooklyn, and the sport flourished. As Riess explains, "What kept the sport operating, despite considerable public opposition on moral grounds to the gambling, fixed races, and abuse of animals, was that the turf provided a key nexus between machine politics and organized crime."[16] And, of course, the sport endured because bettors loved betting.

Gamblers could wager at the tracks on racing days, laying their money with a bookmaker who typically rented a stall at the track. A number of tracks offered pari-mutuel betting, a system in which bets were pooled together with the winning ticket holders splitting the pool, minus a commission fee for the track. This system, first pioneered in France in 1865, held the possibility of clearing the tracks of unsavory bookmakers. Yet most bettors in New York preferred the "face to face" exchange with the bookmaker.[17] Those who could not travel to the racecourse, or those who could not afford the gate fee could nonetheless easily place a bet. Illegal off-track betting was a major enterprise in New York and Chicago. Most off-track betting unfolded in downtown or midtown betting parlors called poolrooms, or with local bookmakers in residential working class neighborhoods.[18] A typical poolroom featured a chalkboard with posted odds, and bettors could expect a narration of the on-course action delivered by an announcer who received updates via the racing wire. High end poolrooms offered food and elegant surroundings while working-class poolrooms offered nothing more than a few chairs, tables, and copies of the racing form.[19]

The poolroom business in New York was a syndicated form of criminality, with Tammany Hall machine politician Big Tim Sullivan at the head of a so-called gambling trust, which doled out police protection and determined who could operate and where. Tammany Hall boss Richard Croker, meanwhile, was heavily involved in racing, as a breeder and horse owner. Disputes divided city Democrats in New York, with Croker and track investors looking with disfavor at the sort of off-track betting available in the poolrooms. Yet, city-based Democrats uniformly supported the racing industry as upstate and rural Republicans repeatedly sought to ban the sport. In Chicago the dominant figure in off-track betting was Mike McDonald. The characters involved in horse racing and betting were frequent violators of the law, yet many of these criminal entrepreneurs sought legitimacy for their pursuits, often putting test cases through the courts and organizing for offense as well as defense in the state legislature.

ANTI-GAMBLING IN THE PROGRESSIVE ERA

Gambling operators and their political allies, as well as common bettors in the policy shops and poolrooms, continually confronted an anti-gambling politics during the late 19th and early 20th centuries. Beginning in the 1840s reformers and clergymen, including Henry Ward Beecher and William Alcott, pointed to gamblers as a pernicious social influence debasing the city environment.[20] In the late 19th century Anthony Comstock, founder of the Society for the Suppression of Vice and a US Post Office Special Agent, and the Rev. Charles Parkhurst of the City Vigilance League condemned gambling as sinful and morally degrading. Beyond the moral objections leveled against gambling, reformers also viewed widespread betting as a danger to the economic order. In particular, gambling threatened the work ethic and sobriety of the labor force, while undermining the frugality necessary to prevent dependency during hard times.[21] Anti-gambling was typically tied together with crusades against prostitution and drinking, although gambling did not tend to manifest the same degree of public horror or outrage as these other derelictions. Yet gambling was arguably the most politically embedded of the vice economies. Consequently the crusade against gambling was an important element of the progressive reform agenda that sought to neutralize corrupt urban machines. The formation of the Lexow Committee in New York in 1894 offers a prime example. The Committee was established by Republicans in the New York State Legislature seeking to unravel the alliance between the Democratic Tammany Hall political machine, the city police, and the underworld economies of vice. The reformist zeal surrounding the Lexow revelations exemplified what historian Daniel Czitrom has identified as "the deep currents of anti-urban prejudice that had long flowed—and still flow—through the nation's political and cultural life."[22]

Anti-gambling reformers also vigorously pursued legislation to suppress gambling houses, lotteries, and race-track betting. The ever-changing laws, coupled with bursts of police suppression, took a toll on track investors and their customers. State and municipal bans on betting thinned the crowds at tracks. As crowds disappeared and as the legislative environment became increasingly hostile at the turn of the century, many tracks closed never to reopen. Racing in New York halted briefly after 1910, and then limped along with a system of oral betting. Racing in Illinois struggled severely with almost no racing from 1905 until the mid-1920s. Betting in New York and Illinois concentrated ever more in the poolrooms, with information coming in from elsewhere via the racing

wire supplied by Western Union. In 1904, due to growing public disapproval, Western Union abandoned the business of supplying racing information. The Payne Telegraph Services based in Cincinnati leased wires from Western Union and quickly achieved a new monopoly on the business. The Payne franchisee in Chicago, a poolroom and handbook magnate named Mont Tennes, took the business for himself, sending collaborating police to raid his competitors. As Tennes and his confederates fixed races and fleeced bettors, the racing scene deteriorated even further.[23] Overall, the racing industry had been confronted by what historian Steven A. Riess characterizes as "a nationwide effort by moral reformers in the late 19th century to end gambling, which was adopted by the progressive movement."[24]

GAMBLING, RACE, AND ETHNICITY

A good portion of the heightened concern about gambling during the late Gilded Age and through the Progressive Era focused on betting among immigrants and people of color. Many European immigrants were pitied by reformers as dupes of unscrupulous gambling operators; other groups were written off as irredeemable gamblers. The Chinese American population, for example, was branded as inherently predisposed to gambling (see Figure 1). The gambling dens of America's Chinatowns symbolized a dangerous site at which the law, the tenets of Christianity, and the boundaries of race were all in absence. In offering an account of impoverished conditions in lower Manhattan, Jacob Riis had few kind words for the Chinese in *How the Other Half Lives* (1890). He points to gambling as the most representative Chinese behavior, declaring that the popular table game fan tan "is their ruling passion. The average Chinamen, the police will tell you, would rather gamble than eat any day."[25]

In 1894 the Lexow Committee investigated Chinese gambling in New York. A Chinese gambler named Wong Get told of a neighborhood of four or five hundred residents, which

Figure 1. A depiction of a raid of a Chinese gambling parlor, 1887.
Source: Courtesy of Library of Congress, LC-USZ62-64799.

typically swelled to three or four thousand on Sundays, as Chinese from all over the region came to lower Manhattan. The many visitors filtered in and out of the neighborhood's bustling gambling rooms, playing fan tan at the roughly sixty parlors in operation. Wong Get also described the monthly payoff regime, requiring a protection payment to the neighborhood boss, who mediated with police and politicians. In New York and beyond, gambling activity among the Chinese served as evidence of the dishonest and degraded nature of Chinese immigrants, and this stereotype served among the many excuses for the national policy of Chinese exclusion after 1882.[26]

Black urban communities were also classed as frenzied with gambling. The notion of the African American as a superstitious and wasteful gambler was a common stereotype. As the

Washington Post complained of the city's growing black population in 1893, "If a colored man finds a dime on the street or in the pocket of an old coat, he is sure to play a gig with the money ... when a groceryman or meat dealer gives a colored customer 5 or 10 cents too much change, the extra money will, in nine cases out of ten, be played in a policy shop."[27] Jacob Riis, observing the black population in lower Manhattan, writes in a similar vein, "Of all the temptations that beset him, the one that troubles him and the police most is his passion for gambling.... Between the fortune teller and the policy shop, closely allied frauds always, the wages of many a hard day's work are wasted by the negro."[28] Cultural historian Jackson Lears points out that the "coon songs" of the Gilded Age relished the stereotype of the black superstitious gambler.[29]

FROM POLICY TO NUMBERS

While a propensity for gambling was a long-standing and well-exaggerated stereotype used to limit black participation in society in any number of ways, the presence of gambling was both broad and deep in black urban life. Yet, beyond the charges of superstition and wastefulness, black gambling was a site of invention, organization, mobilization, enterprise, and social cohesion. From black gambling in the 1920s emerged perhaps the single most important innovation in gambling culture in the 20th century: the numbers game.

The exact origin of the numbers game is the stuff of legend, yet varying accounts attribute its emergence to arriving immigrants from Cuba, Puerto Rico, and the British West Indies. Other accounts specifically credit Casper Holstein, an immigrant from the Danish West Indies, as the inventor. What is beyond dispute is that a new gambling form based in Harlem emerged in the early 1920s. Historians Shane White, Stephen Garton, Stephen Robertson, and Graham White characterize the game in Harlem as "a wonderfully elegant scheme."[30] The game relied on specific digits within the published daily figures from the *New York Clearing House*, a respected financial institution, to determine the winning three-digit number. All a gambling entrepreneur had to do was simply start to take bets. At the end of 1930, the *New York Clearing House*, eager to distance itself from the game, stopped publishing its daily figures. Yet the numbers game simply turned to a new source to generate winning daily numbers. To this day, winning numbers are determined by the three digits in front of the decimal point in the published daily totals of an agreed upon area racetrack. If the Belmont Park race-track in New York takes in $54,879.22, then the winning number is 879. And to this day, a bettor who hits the winning number straight is paid $600 for a $1 bet, just as they would have been in the early 1920s. Harlem Renaissance poet Claude McKay called it "an open, simple and inexpensive game of chance."[31]

With better payouts, simpler math, and with virtually no way of fixing the outcome, the numbers game quickly supplanted the policy game in Harlem, and then subsequently in the major black urban centers on the East Coast. Numbers became the game of choice in New York, Philadelphia, Baltimore, and Washington, DC, while the older policy game held strong in Chicago. The staying power of the policy game in Chicago was linked to the strong tradition of black entrepreneurship in the game. Bettors in Chicago maintained their loyalty to black policy operators, whereas in Harlem, bettors transferred their allegiance from a white-controlled policy game to a black-run numbers game. In both cities during the 1920s and 1930s, the gambling business was a source of philanthropy, a site of capital formation to finance a wide range of business endeavors, and as the work of historian LaShawn Harris demonstrates, for the many women who worked in the numbers, the game was a means of survival.[32]

Numbers and policy gambling was also the structural basis for much black political organization. The interplay between politics and gambling was particularly well developed in Chicago. Money from the policy game financed political campaigns, and the networks of employees who worked for the policy outfits were easily converted to canvassers and get-out-the-vote teams at election time. The link between the two was best expressed in the South Side political machine of Congressman William L. Dawson, which delivered staggering vote totals from the early 1940s through the early 1960s.

The success and popularity of black gambling did not go unnoticed. During Prohibition black gambling figures temporarily evaded the attention of white-organized crime groups and grafting police. Yet with the end of Prohibition and the disappearance of profits from the illegal alcohol trade, the leaders of black gambling in Northern cities were quickly beset by white gangsters and police looking to muscle in on the game. As white-organized crime figures, most notably Dutch Schultz, entered the numbers business, they also spread the game among the white working class. Although whites gained a significant foothold in the upper echelons of the New York numbers game by the mid-1930s, black workers continued to staff the game as runners, collectors, and spot controllers. Black workers in the game continuously pursued autonomy, with many runners often selling a game known as "single action," essentially a bet on individual digits in the day's winning number, thus building up a financial base to operate independently of white backers. Yet black operators nonetheless had to reach accommodation with the police, through a payoff system mediated by the Genovese crime family, which was thoroughly imbedded by the late 1940s.[33] In Chicago, black operators maintained autonomy by relying on a degree of political protection mediated through Congressman William Dawson. These arrangements collapsed in the late 1940s, and opened the door to violent incursions by white crime groups. Nonetheless, as was the case in New York, black workers in Chicago continued to staff the game, and policy retained a central role in neighborhood employment.

Overall, the historical position of gambling in the economic history of Northern black life is difficult to assess. Numbers money undoubtedly financed a variety of more socially positive

Figure 2. Police round-up of gamblers in Washington, DC, 1925.
Source: Courtesy of Library of Congress, LC-USZ62-99829.

endeavors. Among the many cultural and economic enterprises financed by numbers gambling money were professional black sports. Gambling figures were vital to the operation of black baseball from the 1920s through the 1940s, with many numbers barons financing teams, and with others owning teams outright. Most notably, Pittsburgh gambler Gus Greenlee, whose outfit dominated numbers in the Hill District, is credited with organizing the popular East-West all-star game and establishing the second Negro National league, literally keeping black baseball alive during the difficult years of the Great Depression.[34] Greenlee also cultivated and promoted boxers, as did many other numbers men. Julian Black, a Chicago based policy operator, and John Roxborough, a Detroit numbers man, co-managed Joe Louis as he ascended to the world heavyweight championship.[35] For these black gambling impresarios, the sports world offered a path toward legitimacy and the safety of a legal endeavor. This commingling of business endeavors also spoke to the relationship between the rise of popular sports and the growth of gambling as mass entertainment in the 20th century.

BOOKMAKERS, SPORTS GAMBLING, AND THE REVIVAL OF HORSE RACING

While the numbers game spread through the working-class neighborhoods of the Northern cities, bookmaking also flourished, as horse racing revived, and as team sports grew in popularity. The relationship between gambling and sports ran strong from the 1920s through the 1950s. At no place was this more apparent than at the resurgent racetracks. Racing came back to life when northern states adopted laws to legalize pari-mutuel betting at racetracks, and the revived racing industry in turn enabled bookmakers to flourish. The legal and political change began in the Illinois legislature in 1927, as a response to unlicensed and unregulated racing going on in the state. According to the new law, tracks would pay licensing fees and a portion of gate ticket sales to the state treasury to support agricultural fairs. Legal pari-mutuel betting on horse races began in July of 1927.[36] During the first season, five tracks in the Chicago area successfully ran 172 consecutive days of racing and betting, giving over $500,000 to the state treasury.[37]

The success of the Illinois program garnered significant attention, and many other states explored legal racecourse betting as the Depression made gambling revenue increasingly attractive. Ohio Governor George White signed a bill legalizing pari-mutuel betting at tracks in 1933, and racing immediately sprang up in Cincinnati and Cleveland.[38] Massachusetts acted the same year, as voters registered their approval in a public referendum on the issue.[39] During a span of ten weeks in 1934, a construction team in

Boston turned an East Boston dump, into one of the finest tracks in the country at Suffolk Downs.[40] As the *Los Angeles Times* observed, "With new racing laws everywhere, and with new pari-mutuel tracks popping up like dandelions around the country.... Today you will find the public better informed on odds, form and chances than any self-respecting public has a right to be."[41]

In an effort driven by the political machine of Democrat Frank Hague, the Mayor of Jersey City, New Jersey voters approved a constitutional amendment to legalize pari-mutuel betting in June of 1939.[42] Legal on-track betting arrived in New York in November of 1939 when voters went to the polls to amend the state constitution. The anti-gambling New York City Mayor Fiorello La Guardia vehemently opposed the measure, and he pleaded with the public to vote it down. He complained that "the amendment will make our now difficult police problem of suppressing gambling even more difficult."[43] His pleas were ignored. New York State residents voted to legalize betting at the tracks by a substantial margin.

The boom in racing and on-track pari-mutuel betting during the Great Depression also benefitted illegal bookmakers. Despite the struggling economy, the *Chicago Tribune* reported that illegal horse bets in the city totaled more than $1,000,000 a day, and described the betting scene in the Loop with gambling available from "big fellows who operate with a large and adept staff of helpers in especially equipped offices," and sold by "neighborhood bookies, cigar stand books, the loop building lobby operators, and the newsstands."[44] With illegal gambling thriving in the city, in 1935 Chicago Mayor Ed Kelly proposed that bookmakers be permitted to operate legally. In Mayor Kelly's vision, bonded bookies would operate in particular places clear of schools and churches, and only during particular hours, and would pay a licensing fee, the revenue from which would bolster the city schools and the city police force."[45] Governor Henry Horner vetoed the enabling law passed by the Illinois legislature

in 1935. Two years later, the Mayor revived the idea and the Chicago Board of Alderman took up the ordinance on its own, passing it 43 to 4.[46] The conservative *Chicago Tribune* surprisingly supported the idea in an editorial titled "City Control of Gambling."[47] Governor Horner responded with outrage, declaring, "The Chicago City Council has no authority to take such action. The ordinance means nothing. It is anarchy."[48] The dispute was largely symbolic, as the mayor's actions did not carry the force of law. Yet the controversy marked a change in the dynamics of gambling politics, with state governments increasingly ready to accept some forms of gambling provided that revenue flowed to the state, while city governments pushed to direct gambling revenue to municipal purposes.

Just as crime figures who profited from bootlegging during Prohibition asserted themselves in the policy and numbers games, former bootleggers moved into bookmaking. In some instances they collaborated, in other situations they resorted to violence and intimidation. In New York former rum-runner Frank Costello, in addition to developing a slot machine empire, collaborated closely with city's biggest bookmaker Frank Erickson (see Figure 3). In Chicago, the remnants of the Al Capone gang, led by Jake Guzik, used violence to dominate racing information services. During the 1920s and

Figure 3. Frank Costello testifying in front of the Kefauver Committee.
Source: Courtesy of Library of Congress, LC-USZ62-120716.

1930s, the racing wire business was dominated by Moe Annenberg, beginning with his purchase of the *Daily Racing Form* in 1922. From humble beginnings on Chicago's South Side, Annenberg rose up through the newspaper circulation business, to achieve what Mark Haller describes as "a monopoly in most forms of racing and sports information." After Annenberg was convicted of tax evasion in 1939, his former business associates tried to resurrect his wire service, yet in the face of violence, they conceded a partnership interest to Guzik and the old Capone mob after 1946.[49]

Beyond racing, bookmakers also promoted heavy betting on baseball, football, and boxing. The sports betting scene hummed in New York, particularly on fight nights. Boxing clubs dotted the landscape, peaking in popularity during World War II.[50] At the center of the boxing scene was the incarnation of Madison Square Garden that stood on Eighth Avenue between Forty-ninth and Fiftieth streets in Manhattan from 1925 to 1968. The Garden lobby was a hive of betting activity, as a flurry of wagers changed hands amid the cigar smoke. Fixed fights were an aspect of the sport, with perhaps the most famous fix coming in 1947 at the Garden, when Jake LaMotta deliberately lost to Billy Fox.[51]

The reformist impulse, however, never disappeared from politics during the 1940s and 1950s. The state's anti-gambling Governor Thomas Dewey sought to purge the fight scene of its association with gamblers. Dewey and his allies broadened the statute barring the holder of a boxing license from associating with convicted felons, to include a prohibition on consorting with known gamblers.[52] Despite Dewey's efforts, boxing retained its long-standing connection to gambling and the underworld. The sport's long association with gamblers and fixes came to a head in 1957 when the Justice Department ordered the dissolution of the dominant and mob infested International Boxing Club, classing it as a monopoly in restraint of trade. Shortly after, key figures in boxing corruption, mobster Frankie Carbo and Philadelphia numbers operator

Blinky Palermo, were prosecuted and convicted for racketeering. By then, boxing was declining in popularity because the sport proved to be a poor fit for the television age.[53]

As professional team sports grew ever more popular, sports betting grew apace. Yet the commercialization of team sports involved an explicit effort to dissociate the games from gambling, beginning most notably with the Chicago "Black Sox" scandal of 1919. As historian Charles Fountain describes, "Baseball and crooked baseball had grown up together, good twin and evil twin; gambling and throwing games were as much part of early baseball as spitballs, bunts and double headers. The 1919 World Series is the moment that finally forced baseball to stop condoning impropriety."[54] After the Cincinnati Reds beat the Chicago White Sox, rumors swirled that the series was fixed. The presiding justice of the Cook County Grand Jury, Charles McDonald, directed the grand jury to investigate the matter in 1920. Information leaks from the grand jury soon fomented a national scandal.[55] Allegedly, Manhattan gambler Arnold Rothstein, with gambling intermediaries from Philadelphia and Boston, spread between $80,000 and $90,000 among a number of White Sox players to throw the series.[56] Baseball team owners, led by Charles Comiskey, sought out Chicago Federal District Court Judge Kenesaw Mountain Landis to serve as the first commissioner of baseball, charged with restoring integrity in the game. The accused players were acquitted, yet Landis sent a severe message and banned them from baseball. In the subsequent decades, the authoritative commissionership emerged as the standard of governance in most professional team sports. Significantly, those commissioners have worked strenuously to keep gambling away from their games.

Gambling on team sports nonetheless surged in popularity. Much of the popular appeal of betting on team sports originated with the development of the point spread. According to scholar Albert Figone, the point spread became a fixture in sports gambling in the early

1940s.[57] A point spread predicts the eventual point differential between the favored team and the underdog, thus allowing bettors to wager on whether teams will come within the spread or fall short. Gamblers no longer had to simply bet on winners and losers. This model was most applicable to basketball and football, while it is difficult to apply to baseball. At mid-century, baseball and horseracing were the most popular forms of sports betting.[58] Two decades later, however, football betting was dominant.[59] Undoubtedly, the point spread, together with the once-a-week pattern of engagement, and the singularity of focus on the Super Bowl beginning in 1967 greatly explain the explosion in football betting. From the moment of his appointment in 1960 and during his three decades as National Football League (NFL) Commissioner, Pete Rozelle held a hard line on gambling. Rozelle and the NFL maintained a tight security system to ward off gambling by administering lie detector tests to players and owners.[60]

The sustained opposition to sports gambling on the part of the major sports leagues culminated in 1992 when Congress passed the Professional and Amateur Sports Protection Act. The law prohibited states from authorizing sports betting. The statute stood until 2018, when the Supreme Court declared it to be unconstitutional, opening the way for states to chart their own path. During the 20th century, in the aftermath of the 1919 World Series scandal, the leagues succeeded in keeping gambling at bay. Athletes in the major sports were punished for gambling, yet the leagues remained free from the game-fixing scandals, as owners prospered from lucrative television contracts, and unionized players secured high salaries.

Such was not the case for college sports. College basketball and football both suffered from point shaving scandals, with the most prominent disgrace striking at the heart of New York City basketball. During the 1940s the gambling culture of the Madison Square Garden lobby spilled into college basketball. New York District Attorney Frank Hogan

revealed that between 1947 and 1950, 86 college basketball games in 23 cities were "fixed" through point shaving. The City College of New York, Manhattan College, New York University, and Long Island University were all implicated, with fourteen players across New York colleges admitting to collaborating with known gambler Salvatore Solazzo.[61] Most notably, several members of the legendary 1950 City College of New York team, the only team ever to win the NIT and NCAA championship in the same season, were arrested, expelled from school, and banned from the National Basketball Association (NBA). Sherman White, of Long Island University in Brooklyn, the top scorer in the nation, and widely expected to join the New York Knicks, was also arrested and sentenced to a year in prison, and banned from the NBA.[62] City College coach Nat Holman reflected on the scandal, "It wasn't just the boys' fault. It was the gamblers, and even the school for putting our games at Madison Square Garden where the gamblers could get at them."[63]

The revelations caused irreparable harm to New York City college basketball, as many schools backed away from the sport. Yet more importantly, the scandal was an important part of a moment of heightened attention to the influence of gambling in American life. Gambling in sports had gone beyond the unsavory environment at ringside and at the track, and had spread to infect young college students. The concern over gamblers corrupting college athletes folded in with a broader social and political reckoning driven by revelations of widespread police corruption in America's cities. As the scandals rolled out one after another, New York Mayor William O'Dwyer pleaded with the state legislature for a controlled legalization of sports betting. Yet Governor Thomas Dewey insisted that such a move would produce only exploitation and degradation.[64]

GAMBLING AND THE POLICE

Urban police forces were bedeviled by the issue of gambling enforcement since the formation of the earliest departments in New York, Boston, and Philadelphia before the Civil War. For several consecutive generations, from the middle of the 19th century through to the 1970s, gambling bribes proved to be a nearly intractable source of police corruption, while gambling arrests absorbed immense police energy and effort (see Figure 3). Public scandals stained the reputation of big city police forces, undermining their legitimacy and their ability to maintain order. Efforts to combat such corruption led to drastic departmental reorganizations, mass firings, and forced retirements, and endless transfers of police officers. These disruptions left American police officers demoralized and defensive.

As Daniel Czitrom explains, the Lexow Committee "inaugurated a cycle of investigations into police scandals, roughly one every twenty years over the next century."[65] (See Figure 4.) Beginning in 1930, the so-called Samuel Seabury Investigations in New York turned up widespread bribe-taking among police. In 1949 and 1950, in what was clearly becoming a repetitive pattern, a grand jury in Brooklyn uncovered a vast network of protection payoffs from gamblers to police. The scandal brought the quick retirement of New York Mayor William O'Dwyer along with his police commissioner. The burst of police reform that followed led to hundreds of hasty retirements, scores of firings, dozens of indictments, and several police suicides. The scandal of the Brooklyn grand jury was also concurrent with the Kefauver Committee hearings, which indicated police corruption in Chicago, Baltimore, Philadelphia, and other big cities.

In 1950 US Senator Estes Kefauver (Democrat, Tenn.) submitted a resolution calling for a national investigation into organized crime, particularly gambling and the use of the wire services. The Senate Committee to Investigate Organized Crime in Interstate Commerce, better known as the "Kefauver Committee," held hearings in fourteen cities between 1950 and 1952 and captivated the attention of tens of millions of Americans who listened to live

Figure 4. *Puck Magazine* illustration of police corruption as revealed by the Lexow Committee. *Source*: Courtesy of Library of Congress, LC-DIG-ppmsca-29042.

hearings on the radio or watched them on television. In fact, the Senate's effort to expose a vast criminal conspiracy led to a public consciousness about organized crime and marked the first time many Americans had ever heard the word "mafia." Furthermore, the hearings highlighted that conditions of gambling and police corruption were much the same in other big cities as they were in New York.[66] As Kefauver explained to the American Bar Association during the early days of the committee, "a $15,000,000,000 illegal gambling industry is being run in this country by the same big city gangs that were the terror of the 1920s." Pointing to "the Costello mob in New York, the Capone Gang in Chicago, the Purple Gang in Detroit," he claimed, "Crime is definitely on an organized basis in the United States. So widespread are organized criminal operations that they threaten to make a shambles of law enforcement and to create such a universal disrespect for the law that our entire system of government may be endangered."[67] Although Kefauver's assertions of a national conspiracy of crime were overblown, organized crime figures clearly exercised a degree of coordination over bookmaking across state lines through their control of the wire services and their provision of layoff services. Many high-profile crime figures scrutinized during the hearings were prosecuted by the federal government in subsequent decades. Yet for some of them one final bet paid off. After World War II, ex-bootleggers-turned-gamblers from Chicago, Cleveland, and New York invested heavily in developing casinos in Las Vegas. As Mark Haller describes, "Las Vegas became a successful culmination of the entrepreneurial endeavors," of the organized crime figures of the Northern cities.[68]

The revelations of the early 1950s showed gambling corruption to be an intractable problem. Despite the recent lessons offered by the experience of alcohol prohibition, reformers would not countenance changing the nation's gambling laws. If anything, urban police departments redoubled their efforts at suppressing gambling during the 1950s. For an ambitious generation of police professionals, maintaining a strict line on gambling became a way to demonstrate honesty and integrity in a sea of corruption. As the imperatives of administrators flowed down to the rank and file, officers often enforced the unpopular gambling laws most harshly against communities that seemed most distant from their own, and thus gambling enforcement meant heavy arrests of African Americans. Furthermore, gambling arrests were typically made without regard to probable cause or constitutional protections against unlawful search and seizure.[69]

Not surprisingly the US Supreme Court case that eventually curbed the use of warrantless searches resulted from the arrest of a black woman. Dollree Mapp was involved in the Cleveland numbers game, and in *Mapp v. Ohio* (1961), the court determined that evidence obtained in a warrantless search was not admissible in state criminal proceedings. The high court's decision touched off a revolution in the rights of the accused that substantially altered the practice of policing in the United States. In many cities, gambling arrests dropped off precipitously after *Mapp*. While some cities resumed robust enforcement after adapting to the new constitutional standards, other cities never returned to the task. Significantly police officials broadly began to reconsider the usefulness of the gambling laws. This reconsideration was further accelerated by yet another series of scandals relating to gambling corruption among police. During 1970 and 1971, the Commission to Investigate Police Corruption in New York, chaired by Whitman Knapp, revealed that a highly systemized payoff arrangement between numbers gamblers and cops known as "the pad" was thoroughly entrenched in the New York City Police Department. The Knapp Commission was followed soon after by an investigation by the Pennsylvania Crime Commission, which discovered that conditions in Philadelphia were little different.[70] The Knapp Commission's report recommended explicitly that the laws against gambling be repealed, and at the very least that police be relieved of the responsibility of enforcing them.[71] Gambling laws were never repealed, but the New York City Police Commissioner Patrick V. Murphy instituted a moratorium on gambling arrests and deemphasized gambling enforcement.[72] This shift in the emphasis in urban policing came amid a shift in state posture toward gambling.

MODERN LOTTERY GAMBLING AND LEGAL OFF-TRACK BETTING

The first modern American government lottery was approved in New Hampshire in 1963. New York State followed shortly after in 1967, engaging in a tumultuous and controversial process of lottery adoption that proved transformative to the national approach to gambling. Although officers in the New York City Police Department relentlessly chased gamblers, officially in pursuit of arrests, and unofficially in pursuit of bribes, New York Mayor Robert. F. Wagner Jr. consistently advocated for gambling reform through a process of legalization, calling for legal off-track betting during his tenure from 1954 to 1965. Yet his efforts were repeatedly stymied by the state government in Albany. The city administration achieved a small breakthrough when the state legislature allowed local governments to approve legal bingo, with city residents voting in favor of bingo in 1958. As the state explored the possibilities of further legalizations in the middle 1960s, New York City Police Commissioner Michael J. Murphy explained to the state legislature that the numbers game rather than horse race betting was the true core of the city gambling scene.[73] Horse racing had indeed slipped in popularity, and many bookmakers had turned to selling the numbers game in white working-class communities, while the numbers remained as popular as ever in black and Puerto Rican neighborhoods. Thus New York State, through a voter referendum, altered the state constitution to allow for a legal lottery to go on sale in 1968. The technical purpose of the lottery was to direct funds to the support of education in the state, while the goal of the lottery project was to take on the numbers game, dry up the source of so much police corruption, and stave off the implementation of any new taxes.[74]

Other states quickly followed New York, as New Jersey (1970), Connecticut, Pennsylvania, Massachusetts, and Michigan (1972), Maryland (1973), and Illinois and Ohio (both 1974), all entered the gambling business and established lotteries. This moment of expansion in state gambling also extended to off-track betting. In 1970, New York City Mayor John Lindsay and New York State Governor Nelson Rockefeller reached a budget deal that included the establishment of the New York City Off-Track Betting (OTB) Corporation. The state's racing law was amended to allow for the establishment of regional public benefit corporations, empowered to take bets, with the goal of relieving municipal debt and curbing illegal

bookmaking. More than 100 betting parlors in the city thrived in their first few years of operation, despite rules that prohibited them from providing food, drink, or even chairs. A surcharge tax imposed by the city upon winning bets in 1974, however, permanently stunted the growth of New York City OTB.

OTB officials explored a variety of alternative projects to bring growth, notably repeated attempts to offer sports betting. OTB founding Chairman Howard Samuels and his successor Paul Screvane dueled publicly with NFL Commissioner Pete Rozelle, who insisted that legal betting would undermine the integrity of professional sports.[75] New York OTB failed in its efforts to enter legal sports betting, and came up short in a push to purchase Madison Square Garden. Rather than emerging as an expansionist gambling entity, the agency was tethered closely to the popularity of horse-racing, which suffered decline in the face of proliferating options for gambling. OTB transformed into a site of government employment, with employees unionized by District Council 37 in pursuit of solid salaries and pensions. The growing cost of retirement benefits for employees contrasted with OTBs declining revenue stream, as statewide racing income steadily declined after 1987.[76] New York City OTB eventually collapsed, shuttering its parlors in 2010.

Illinois was slow to follow New York into the business of legal OTB. Nonetheless a de facto off-track system emerged in Chicago during the 1970s with more than 100 betting "messenger" parlors, ostensibly providing the service of carrying the customers' bets to the track for them. These operations reduced attendance at the tracks, and often booked the bets themselves, thus reducing track profitability. The Illinois legislature banned the messenger parlors in 1977, and proposed a legal off-track system. Illinois Governor James Thompson, however, rejected the idea in 1978.[77] The racing industry in the state struggled, with the overall revenue declining by 25 percent from 1979 to 1983. Legal off-track betting eventually earned the support of track operators as a potential salve.[78] In 1987, Thompson relented and signed Illinois OTB into law, making Illinois the fourth state to adopt OTB (after New York, Nevada, and Connecticut). Chicago was only the second major metropolitan area to feature legal parlors. The new law authorized each of the state's seven tracks to open two satellite parlors, tying the tracks and OTB closely together in a model meant to avoid the adversarial relationship between the tracks and OTB that had developed in New York.[79] Illinois OTB, however, failed to stop the decline in the racing industry. Two Chicago area tracks, Maywood Park and Balmoral Park, closed in 2015.[80]

In contrast to OTB, state lottery gambling eventually proved to be an ever-expanding enterprise. The lotteries of the northern states struggled at the outset as they were not selling the very same game that people were interested in playing. The lotteries of the late 1960s and early 1970s sold games comparable to raffles, within which players received a sequential ticket. This deprived urban gamblers of the practice of betting on the lucky numbers they gleaned from dreams, birthdays, baseball scores, or any other indicators of good fortune or personal attachment. Thus early lotteries failed to penetrate the urban numbers market. Lottery directors and lottery agencies were left with the technological and logistical challenge of creating statewide games that allowed bettors to pick their own numbers, and in states like New York and Illinois policy makers were left with the task of broadening the new lottery laws to allow for the offering of this very specific game.

As lotteries and lottery supporters took direct and explicit aim at the numbers game, black elected officials in New York and Illinois challenged the states. They advocated for a formulation of legal numbers that would employ the many thousands of people who were currently working as runners in the illegal trade. Despite passionate pleas not to exacerbate the employment crisis prevalent in black

neighborhoods, and dire warnings that dislocated numbers workers, unable to find new employment, would likely drift into more socially harmful categories of crime, state officials proceeded with legal numbers to be sold by a network of computer terminals, employing few while providing gambling to many. The successful replication of the numbers game brought success to the struggling lotteries of the Northeast, and by the early 1980s the illegal networks were clearly supplanted. As lotteries posted big returns, relying on their urban customers, state governments in other parts of the country took notice. During the 1980s, the modern lottery phenomenon spread to the West, and then the South. The spread of lotteries brought the standard three digit guessing game known as the numbers into rural parts of the county where the game was previously unknown. In some ways, during the late decades of the 20th century, this gambling form lost its historic connection to city life.[81]

As lottery terminals replaced numbers runners, bookmakers were increasingly replaced by online sports betting, operated through servers located offshore. In the aftermath of the Indian Gaming Regulatory Act (1988), which allowed tribal governments to establish casinos, accessible casinos popped up at a remove from urban locales, while airlines offered cheap flights to Las Vegas. By the end of the 20th century the strong link between gambling and urban density had significantly eroded. Residents of Northern cities still gambled heavily, yet few worked in gambling. Urban police departments found themselves severed from the past traditions of payoffs, while being minimally concerned with gambling enforcement. The basic urban complex of gambling, politics, and police corruption that prevailed across generations and accommodated to significant demographic change, reached its end.

DISCUSSION OF THE LITERATURE

Despite the numbers of lives gambling has impacted, the number of cities where gambling was conspicuous, and the length of time during which gambling was relevant to politics and governance, historical scholarship on gambling in American cities has been slow to develop as a full-fledged field of study. Yet many works of significance using innovative approaches have contributed greatly to assembling the history of urban gambling while offering important analysis of broader sociopolitical phenomena. In many cases, scholars exploring particular places or communities where gambling was prevalent made valuable offerings to our understanding of gambling. An early and excellent example is St. Claire Drake and Horace Cayton's *Black Metropolis: A Study of Negro Life in a Northern City* (1945). While addressing a host of topics relevant to black life in Chicago, the authors evaluate the policy game in depth, mixing the words of informants with their own analysis of policy as a kind of "informal cooperative."[82] As Drake and Cayton conducted their research in the era of flourishing black gambling in Chicago, their account stands as an excellent source and a basis for thinking about the complicated ways in which informality and illegality shaped black life in Northern cities.

The rampant gambling of the 1940s, and the heightened sense of scandal surrounding the grand jury investigations in New York and the Kefauver Committee nationally, prompted some scholars to take stock of the role of gambling in American life. The Annals of the Academy of Political and Social Science devoted an entire issue to the exploration of gambling in 1950, with several articles offering worthwhile historical background.[83] Yet the most consequential analysis that emerged from this wave of interest was undoubtedly sociologist Daniel Bell's essay "Crime as an American Way of Life" (1953). Bell placed the criminal gambler in the context of the history of American business, pointing to a continuity between the swashbuckling of earlier generations of business magnates, and the present crop of outlaw gamblers garnering so much public concern. Bell accurately predicted that the gambling

business would likely transition to some form of legitimacy, while those involved in criminal gambling could be understood as part of a process of ethnic succession in the urban underworld.[84]

Among contemporary scholars who have explored urban gambling, Ann Fabian has offered the definitive account of gambling in the 19th century with her work *Card Sharps and Bucket Shops* (1999). Her focus is by no means entirely urban, yet her attention to New York gambling culture details the manner in which gambling allowed individuals and groups to position themselves within a shifting political economic reality. David Schwarz, in his comprehensive survey of the history of gambling *Roll the Bones* (2006), also explores the centrality of New York and Chicago to American gambling history as a whole, particularly during the 19th century.[85]

The work of Mark Haller provides the foundation for the study of gambling, organized crime, and politics in the 20th century. In a series of scholarly articles Haller explores the concept of a gambling-politics complex, initially characteristic of Irish urban politics in the late 19th and early 20th centuries, and later essential to black urban politics.[86] The relationship between politics and city gambling is also examined with great depth in the work of Steven A. Riess, *The Sport of Kings and the Kings of Crime* (2011). With a focus on the interwoven histories of New York horse racing and New York politics, from the end of the Civil War through 1913, Riess elucidates the extent to which gambling drove politics both as a matter of public controversy and as an unseen structural basis.[87] Just as Riess captures horse racing, Shane White, Stephen Garton, Stephen Robertson, and Graham White capture the early history of the New York numbers game. In *Playing the Numbers* (2010) White and his coauthors emphasize the social, cultural, and economic profile of the numbers game in Harlem life. They place the numbers game at the center of a process of community formation.[88] LaShawn Hariss's *Sex Workers,*

Psychics and Numbers Runners, while not focused exclusively on gambling, highlights the
manner in which the numbers game was a
source of financial autonomy for many New
York black women. Harris's work is a genuine
breakthrough in the study of urban gambling,
situating the numbers game in our understanding of the history of black employment
and labor.[89] Taken together these works have
deepened and broadened our understanding
of the history of gambling in New York, as the
history of politics, the history of neighborhood
and community, and the history of work and
employment. Similar work of such perspective
is much needed for the history of gambling in
other cities, particularly Chicago, as the history of urban gambling continues to develop
as a field of study.

PRIMARY SOURCES

Scholars interested in urban gambling are confronted with the challenge of studying a set of
practices that were intentionally hidden from
view. Nonetheless the history of gambling
can be discovered, at least in part, in the press,
court records, the records of police agencies,
and the many thousands of pages produced by
government agencies and legislative bodies
that have conducted hearings and studies on
the problem of gambling. The transcripts of the
hearings of the Lexow Committee of 1894 have
been digitized and are available through Hathi
Trust. The transcripts of the hearings of the
Kefauver Committee are also digitized through
Hathi Trust, while the published volumes are
held in the many federal depository libraries.
The background papers of the Kefauver Committee, which are extensive and revealing, are
held at the National Archives in Washington,
DC. The papers of Thomas E. Dewey, held in
River Campus Libraries at the University of
Rochester, contain abundant correspondence
related to gambling, both from his time as a
prosecutor and his time as Governor of New
York. Papers related to the Knapp Commission
investigation into police corruption in New
York City are held in the Special Collections
at the Lloyd Sealy Library of John Jay College
of Criminal Justice. The Research Center of
the Chicago History Museum holds a collection of material on the Chicago White Sox
1919 World Series scandal. The museum also
holds the papers of Virgil Peterson, who headed
the Chicago Crime Commission from 1942
to 1969 and collected abundant material on
gambling and organized crime. The Center for
Gaming Research at the University of Nevada
Las Vegas has extensive holdings related to the
history of gambling, and has valuable original
material on the politics of lottery adoption.
The publications of police agencies are held in
fragment at various libraries, yet the Firestone
Library at Princeton University has a particularly strong concentration of annual reports
from various police departments generated
during the 20th century.

FURTHER READING

Czitrom, Daniel. *New York Exposed: The Gilded Age
    Police Scandal That Launched the Progressive Era.*
    New York: Oxford University Press, 2016.
Fabian, Ann. *Card Sharps and Bucket Shops: Gambling
    in Nineteenth-Century America.* New York, NY:
    Routledge, 1995.
Figone, Albert. *Cheating the Spread: Gamblers, Point
    Shavers, and Game Fixers in College Football and
    Basketball.* Champaign: University of Illinois
    Press, 2012
Fogelson, Robert. *Big City Police.* Cambridge, MA:
    Harvard University Press, 1977.
Harris, LaShawn. *Sex Workers, Psychics and Numbers
    Runners: Black Women in New York's Underground Eco-
    nomy.* Champaign: University of Illinois Press, 2016.
Lang, Arne K. *Sports Betting and Bookmaking: An
    American History.* Lanham, MD: Rowman and
    Littlefield, 2016.
Mason, John Lyman, and Michael Nelson. *Governing
    Gambling.* New York: The Century Foundation
    Press, 2001.
Moore, William Howard. *The Kefauver Committee and
    the Politics of Crime, 1950–52.* Columbia: University
    of Missouri Press, 1974.
Nibert, David. *Hitting the Lottery Jackpot.* New York:
    Monthly Review Press, 2000.

Riess, Steven A. *City Games: The Evolution of American Urban Society and the Rise of Sports.* Urbana: University of Illinois Press, 1989.

Riess, Steven A. *The Sport of Kings and the Kings of Crime: Horse Racing, Politics and Organized Crime in New York, 1865–1913.* Syracuse, NY: Syracuse University Press, 2011.

Schatzburg, Rufus. *Black Organized Crime in Harlem: 1920–1930.* New York: Garland, 1993.

Schwartz, David G. *Roll the Bones: The History of Gambling.* New York: Gotham Books, 2006.

White, Shane, Stephen Garton, Stephen Robertson, and Graham White. *Playing the Numbers: Gambling in Harlem Between the Wars.* Cambridge, MA: Harvard University Press, 2010.

NOTES

1. Ann Fabian, *Card Sharps and Bucket Shops: Gambling in Nineteenth-Century America* (New York: Routledge, 1995), 25.
2. Ann Fabian, *Card Sharps and Bucket Shops*, 41.
3. David G. Schwartz, *Roll the Bones: The History of Gambling* (New York: Gotham Books, 2006), 273.
4. David G. Schwartz, *Roll the Bones*, 269.
5. David G. Schwartz, *Roll the Bones*, 280.
6. David G. Schwartz, *Roll the Bones*, 282.
7. Mark Haller, "Organized Crime in Urban Society: Chicago in the Twentieth Century," *Journal of Social History* 5, no. 2 (Winter 1971–1972): 218.
8. "Mike M'Donaldism and Democracy," *Chicago Tribune*, July 20, 1890, 12; and "Mike McDonald, Famed as Gambler, Political Boss, and for his Many Marital Woes, Dies," *Detroit Free Press*, August 10, 1907, 10.
9. David Nibert, *Hitting the Lottery Jackpot* (New York: Monthly Review Press, 2000), 27.
10. As an example see "Drawings Louisiana State Lottery," *Washington Post*, June 19, 1889, 1.
11. "Public Lottery Business: Havana and Louisiana Lottery Offices Openly Violating the Law," *Chicago Daily Tribune*, September 5, 1885, 8.
12. "The Lottery in Politics: The Evil Work of the Louisiana Lottery," *New York Times*, January 28, 1884, 5.
13. G. Robert Blakey and Harold A. Kurland, "The Federal Law of Gambling," *Cornell Law Review* 63, no. 6 (August 1978): 942.
14. *Report of the Special Committee to Investigate the Police Department of the City of New York* (Albany, NY: James B. Lyon, State Printer, 1895), 37.
15. Steven A. Riess, *The Sport of Kings and the Kings of Crime: Horse Racing, Politics and Organized Crime in New York, 1865–1913* (Syracuse, NY: Syracuse University Press, 2011), xii.
16. Steven A. Riess, *The Sport of Kings and the Kings of Crime*, xiii.
17. Steven A. Riess, *The Sport of Kings and the Kings of Crime*, 35, 90.
18. Steven A. Riess, *The Sport of Kings and the Kings of Crime*, xv.
19. Schwartz, *Roll the Bones*, 335–336.
20. Fabian, *Card Sharps and Bucket Shops*, 55.
21. Fabian, *Card Sharps and Bucket Shops*, 61.
22. Daniel Czitrom, *New York Exposed: The Gilded Age Police Scandal the Launched the Progressive Era* (New York: Oxford University Press, 2016), 304.
23. Daniel Czitrom, *New York Exposed*, 336–337.
24. Riess, *Sport of Kings*, xiv.
25. Jacob A. Riis, *How the Other Half Lives: Studies Among the Tenements of New York* (New York: Dover, 1971), 78.
26. "Vice Reigns in Chinatown," *San Francisco Chronicle*, November 19, 1901, 12.
27. "The Wily Game of Policy," *Washington Post*, August 6, 1893, 13.
28. Riis, *How the Other Half Lives*, 118.
29. Jackson Lears, *Something for Nothing: Luck in America* (New York: Viking Press, 2003), 205.
30. Shane White, Stephen Garton, Stephen Robertson, and Graham White, *Playing the Numbers: Gambling in Harlem Between the Wars* (Cambridge, MA: Harvard University Press, 2010), 63.
31. Claude McKay, *Harlem: Negro Metropolis* (New York: Harcourt Brace, 1968), 107.
32. Lashawn Harris, *Sex Workers, Psychics and Numbers Runners: Black Women in New York's Underground Economy* (Champaign: University of Illinois Press, 2016).
33. Ted Poston, "Policy and Payoffs," *New York Post*, March 1, 1960, 1.
34. Neil Lanctot, *Negro League Baseball: The Rise and Ruin of a Black Institution* (Philadelphia: University of Pennsylvania Press, 2004), 9.
35. "Mich. High Court Says Roxborough Conviction Stands," *Chicago Defender*, January 8, 1944, 8.

36. "Pari-Mutuel Bill in Illinois Becomes Law, Effective July 1," *New York Times*, June 12, 1927, S6.

37. "Chicago Tracks Prosper Under Legalized Betting," *Washington Post*, November 20, 1927, 22.

38. "Ohio Racing Bill Signed," *New York Times*, April 8, 1933, 17.

39. "Massachusetts Voters Sanction Racing. Mutuels," *Chicago Daily Tribune*, November 8, 1934, 25.

40. "$2,000,000 Race Track Opens at Boston Today," *Chicago Daily Tribune*, July 10, 1935, 22.

41. John Lardner, "Wagering on Sports Booms to New High," *Los Angeles Times*, December 25, 1934, A17.

42. "Pari-Mutuels Win at Polls in New Jersey," *Daily Boston Globe*, June 21, 1939, 2.

43. "Mayor Assails Pari-Mutuel Amendment," *New York Herald Tribune*, November 6, 1939, 1A.

44. "Race Betting in Chicago Exceeds $1,000,000 Daily," *Chicago Daily Tribune*, May 20, 1932, 23.

45. "Mayor Promises Bookie Law to Protect the Public," *Chicago Daily Tribune*, June 22, 1935, 3.

46. "Vote Licensing of Bookies," *Chicago Daily Tribune*, December 23, 1937, 1.

47. "City Control of Gambling, "*Chicago Daily Tribune*, December 24, 1937, 6.

48. "'Anarchy' is Horner's Word for Betting Law," *New York Herald Tribune*, December 24, 1937, 9.

49. Mark Haller, "The Changing Structure of American Gambling in the Twentieth Century," *Journal of Social Issues* 35, no. 3 (1979).

50. Arne K. Lang, *Prizefighting: An American History* (Jefferson, NC: McFarland, 2008), 121.

51. Richard Goldstein, "Jake LaMotta, 'Raging Bull' in and out of the Ring, Dies at 95," *New York Times*, September 20, 2017.

52. Lang, *Prizefighting*, 122.

53. Mike Silver, *The Arc of Boxing: The Rise and Decline of the Sweet Science* (Jefferson, NC: McFarland, 2006), 42; and John Sugden, *Boxing and Society: An International Analysis* (Manchester, UK: Manchester University Press, 1996), 43.

54. Charles Fountain, *The Betrayal: The 1919 World Series and the Birth of Modern Baseball* (New York: Oxford University Press, 2016), 6.

55. Charles Fountain, *The Betrayal*, 152.

56. Charles Fountain, *The Betrayal*, 81.

57. Albert Figone, *Cheating the Spread: Gamblers, Point Shavers, and Game Fixers in College Football and Basketball* (Urbana: University of Illinois Press, 2012), 5.

58. "Betting a $15 Billon Industry: Plea for the Legalizing of Handbooks Here Stirs Debate," *New York Times*, January 15, 1950, E9.

59. David Smothers, "Americans Gambling at Record Rate," *Los Angeles Times*, December 16, 1973, E1.

60. Jerry Cohen, "Best for All: Pro Football: Bookies Want It Kept Clean," *Los Angeles Times*, June 27, 1969, 1.

61. "Basketball Fixing Made the Rounds," *Newsday*, September 6, 1974, 135.

62. Richard Goldstein, "Sherman White, Star Caught in a Scandal, Dies at 82," *New York Times*, August 11, 2011.

63. Doug Smith, "Ford Layne Up From Despair to Give CCNY Hope," *Newsday*, September 6, 1974, 135.

64. *The Annals of the American Academy of Political and Social Science*, "Legalized Gambling in New York?," Vol. 269 (May, 1950): 35–38.

65. Czitrom, *New York Exposed*, 293.

66. William Howard Moore, *The Kefauver Committee and the Politics of Crime, 1950–52* (Columbia: University of Missouri Press, 1977).

67. "Aid of Bar Group in Crime Wave," *Los Angeles Times*, September 20, 1950, 27.

68. Mark Haller, "The Changing Structure of American Gambling in the Twentieth Century," *Journal of Social Issues* 35, no. 3 (1979): 108.

69. "Adamowski Warning on No-Warrant Raids," *Chicago Sun Times*, April 26, 1958, 2; For race and gambling arrests see, Chicago Police Department, *Annual Report*, 1958.

70. *The Pennsylvania Crime Commission: Report on Police Corruption and the Quality of Law Enforcement in Philadelphia* (Commonwealth of Pennsylvania: Department of Justice, 1974), 191.

71. *The Knapp Commission Report on Police Corruption, Submitted to John V. Lindsay, December 26, 1972* (New York: 1972), 74–83.

72. "City Police Changing Enforcement in Gambling and Narcotics, With Purpose of Focusing on Major Dealer," *New York Times*, January 13, 1972, 33.

73. Michael J. Murphy, *The Gambling Situation 1964: A Report by Police Commissioner Michael J. Murphy on the Status of Illegal Gambling and Gambling Enforcement in New York City to The Select Legislative Committee on Off-Track Betting*, New York, February 24, 1964, 11.

74. Matthew Vaz, "We Intend to Run It: Racial Politics, Illegal Gambling and the Rise of

Government Lotteries, 1960–1984," *Journal of American History* 101, no.1 (June 2014): 71–96.

75. "Football Head Sensitive About OTB Branching Out," *Washington Post*, December 17, 1971, D7; and Anthony Ripley, "Kuhn and Rozelle Caution Against Legal Sports Bets," *New York Times*, February 20, 1975, 69.

76. *Task Force on the Future of Off-Track Betting in New York State: A Report to the Governor and the Legislature of the State of New York*, January 13, 2010, 19–21.

77. "Area Horsemen Lift Boycott: House Oks Ban on Bet Messengers," *Chicago Tribune*, June 26, 1977, 3; and John D. Moorhead, "Gambling Trend Bucked in Illinois," *Christian Science Monitor*, August 21, 1978, 1.

78. Daniel Egler, "Off-Track Betting Endorsed: OTB," *Chicago Tribune*, January 26, 1985, A1.

79. Neil Milbert, "Off-Track Betting for Illinois," *Chicago Tribune*, January 17, 1987, A1.

80. Kathy Byrne, "Horse Racing Can Thrive If States Agree to Uniform Rules," *Chicago Tribune*, November 1, 2015.

81. Vaz, "We Intend to Run It."

82. St. Clair Drake and Horace Cayton, *Black Metropolis: A Study of Negro Life in a Northern City, Volume II* (New York: Harper and Row, 1962).

83. *Annals of the American Academy of Political and Social Science*, Vol. 269, *Gambling* (May, 1950).

84. Daniel Bell, "Crime as an American Way of Life," *The Antioch Review* 13, no. 2 (Summer 1953): 131–154.

85. David G. Schwarz, *Roll the Bones*.

86. Mark Haller, "Organized Crime in Urban Society: Chicago in the Twentieth Century," *Journal of Social History* 5, no. 2 (Winter 1971–1972): 218; Mark Haller, "The Changing Structure of American Gambling in the Twentieth Century, *Journal of Social Issues* 35, no. 3 (1979); and Mark Haller, Policy Gambling, Entertainment, and the Emergence of Black Politics: Chicago 1900 to 1940," *Journal of Social History* 24, no. 4 (Summer 1991).

87. Riess, *Sport of Kings*.

88. White, Garton, Robertson, and White, *Playing the Numbers*.

89. Harris, *Sex Workers*.

Matthew Vaz

TEMPERANCE AND PROHIBITION

THE RISE OF THE TEMPERANCE MOVEMENT, 1784–1836

As with other reforms, a full understanding of temperance requires understanding its ideology, methodology, and organizational structure. All three were in constant flux and often in conflict. Temperance ideology includes what reformers meant by the term but also the panoply of rationales employed for promoting it. Temperance movement methodologies and organizations were about as varied as one's imagination can envision. However, the rise of the temperance movement, and its development over time, can be understood only when one considers alcohol consumption patterns in the context of evolving social norms and economic and demographic trends.

The colonists' consumption and regulation of alcohol replicated what was normative in 17th-century England. This meant that drinking alcoholic beverages was widely assumed to be a necessary, even healthy, practice, so "virtually everyone drank virtually all the time."[1] Equally important, drinking was embedded in specific social contexts with clearly defined customs and sanctions. Family meals were regularly accompanied by (often homemade) beer or hard cider for all ages. Farmers and master craftsmen supplied their laborers with daily rations of whiskey or rum that were enjoyed during the workday by employer and employee together. Alcohol flowed at gatherings such as weddings, funerals, ordinations, barn raisings, militia drills, corn huskings, and election days at the county courthouse. Alcoholic beverages were essential to one's diet, since many colonists did not have access to safe drinking water or milk supplies, coffee and tea were too expensive, and soft drinks and unfermented juices had yet to be invented. It was nothing for men to drink several "drams" of brandy or whiskey daily, beginning in the morning. Different kinds of ciders were often distilled into brandies; however, by the time of the Revolutionary War, rum had become the most popular distilled drink. After the war, corn and rye whiskeys soon replaced rum as the inexpensive distilled drink of choice. There were always those who drank to excess (and, of course, preachers railed against it) but most colonists pursued subsistence lifestyles on relatively isolated farms more controlled by the seasons than the clock and generally not visible to the larger community. As Americans moved west of the Appalachians in the 1800s, they found it most economical to convert their corn to whiskey before shipping it to market. This literally created a whiskey "glut" in America.

Therefore, by 21st-century standards, per capita alcohol consumption was high at the time of the revolution and continued to rise through the 1820s. Per capita consumption of distilled beverages increased from less than three, to over five gallons a year between 1800 and 1830. By comparison, current per capita consumption is only about two gallons. When cider, beer, and wine are included, the per capita intake of absolute alcohol (the amount of alcohol in beverages) rose from about three to four gallons in the same period.[2]

In the pre-industrial colonial social order people knew their "station" in life and generally acted their part. In politics and religion, the masses deferred to their "better sorts," and the better sorts willingly took the lead. Apprentices and journeymen artisans boarded with their employers, who were legally responsible for their after-work leisure. Laws that governed such matters as drinking in taverns were designed on the assumption that since people were sinners, the best the law could do was circumscribe, not eliminate, the negative effects of excessive drinking. Americans moved west into the Mohawk, Ohio, and Mississippi River valleys and into the new territories of Alabama, Mississippi, and Louisiana more rapidly than local political and religious institutions could be re-created. And people moved multiple times, constantly seeking cheaper land, new economic opportunities, or to escape

their past and begin life anew. All colonies and eastern states that had taxed residents to support churches ended the practice by 1800, except Connecticut and Massachusetts, and increasing numbers of people began living in western communities frequently lacking churches, schools, or even functioning local governments. Cities grew rapidly in both numbers and size, as young men increasingly left their family farms and families to seek their fortunes in impersonal cities as immigration exploded in the 1830s. The urban population increased an alarming 60 percent in both the 1820s and 1830s, and by 92 percent in the 1840s. In the 1820s states began to remove property and tax requirements for voting, enfranchising all white males and basically eliminating the need for deference in politics. A new generation of popular self-made preachers arose who connected rhetorically and stylistically with the masses, and sometimes even denigrated advanced theological study. Finally, unmarried journeymen craftsmen began to move out of their employers' homes into boarding houses in poorer neighborhoods, away from the oversight of their master craftsmen employers. Men increasingly drank outside the home, in taverns, during these ever-changing times. Societal transformations weakened the traditional social contexts for drinking at the same time that drinking was increasing. A general "leveling" in all areas of life made it seem to some that the nation's social order was crumbling. How could peoples' baser natures be restrained in such unsettling times? Could a republic long endure without stable, virtuous communities? It is in this context that a culture of reform and the Second Great Awakening flourished, and the temperance movement emerged as an integral part of both.[3]

Defining Temperance. Temperance reformers generally considered Philadelphia physician and signer of the Declaration of Independence, Benjamin Rush, the "father" of the movement. An active reformer in areas such as education, prisons, and medical care, Rush's ideas were all of a piece and articulated a clear republican vision for American society. In 1784 he published *An Inquiry into the Effects of Spiritous Liquors on the Human Body and Mind.* Rush attributed such vices, diseases, and punishments as idleness, swearing, epilepsy, and the gallows to drinking distilled spirits, while praising the effects of wine, beer, and cider. For over twenty years Rush's arguments fell mostly on deaf years, but once the movement began to organize, reformers found him a useful authority to cite.[4]

Even more importantly, in 1827 Reverend Lyman Beecher, father of the well-known Harriet Beecher Stowe and Henry Ward Beecher, published *Six Sermons on the Nature, Occasions, Signs, Evils, and Remedy of Intemperance.* These very influential sermons became the de facto blueprint for the temperance movement. Beecher raised the stakes by calling for abstinence from all intoxicating beverages (not just distilled drinks), national coordination of the movement, and for a public education campaign that would cause citizens to call for a ban on the liquor traffic itself. Within ten years, temperance reformers had embraced Beecher's expanded platform. Reformers gradually arrived at this teetotal position because new research had proved the presence of alcohol in beer and wine (which had previously been disputed), and because experience had proven that use of beer and wine could cause reformed drunkards to relapse. Also, because whiskey was cheap it was the drink of the working classes, so attacking only that drink created the appearance of a class-based movement, exposing reformers to all sorts of criticisms. From the 1830s onward, temperance organizations defined "temperance" to mean total abstinence from all intoxicating beverages, but they were criticized as "ultraists," and lost some of their supporters. Other organizations continued to support "temperance" in its traditional sense of meaning moderate drinking.[5]

Temperance Motivation and Rationale.

A growing number of national, regional, state, and local case studies have attributed the rise

and success of the temperance movement to causes that can be grouped into two main categories: those related to the social changes that accompanied modernization—the gender and class values associated with the rise of the middle class, the market economy, and industrialization—and those related to the ideology and worldview of the temperance reformers.

Rush, Beecher, and other northeastern reformers (who often voted with the Federalist Party), adhered to a widely held set of ideas best described as "Christian republicanism." It was a hybrid political-religious moral framework used to justify the American Revolution, and it subsequently critiqued the social, political, and economic issues of their day, prescribing the best path forward for the health of the young republic. Purely secular republicanism taught that all republics experienced a life cycle beginning with a virtuous youth, then corruption in their middle years, followed by an inevitable decline and collapse into despotism. Republics declined because their citizens lost their virtue (disinterested service for common good) to forces of corruption such as self-interest and prosperity, leading to excessive indulgence on luxuries. The most sobering aspect of classical republicanism was the presumed inevitability of a republic's decline, and America's "founding fathers" genuinely wondered how long the American "experiment" would last.

Although Christian republicanism also assumed a direct relationship between public virtue and the success of the republic, it defined virtue as hinging on one's personal morality, so a religious conversion experience would presumably lead to more virtuous behavior. Many revivalists of the Second Great Awakening, from the 1790s into the 1820s, began preaching temperance as emphatically as they did conversion and considered both to hold as much civic value as they did spiritual value. Preachers came to believe that communities with strong temperance movements tended to experience revivals of religion. Conversely, many taught that new converts should work to improve society by embracing such socially benevolent work as temperance to reduce poverty, disease, and crime.[6]

Even if people did not attend church or a revival service, they could easily be exposed to the temperance message in non-religious settings. Those who considered themselves "self-made," progressive men usually embraced abstinence as a way to improve society. As the labor of more and more men became tied to regional and national markets, success required a predictable work regimen, so entrepreneurs found a temperate lifestyle in their best economic interest. Gradually employers stopped providing the expected midday whiskey dram to their workers, became abstainers themselves, and began to lecture their workers on the need to become teetotalers and join a temperance society. During these years, the medical profession was undergoing a professionalization process, and many physicians incorporated Rush's position on distilled spirits as a part of it. Doctors such as Benjamin Richardson published research on the harmful effects of alcohol to support the movement. College presidents and professors almost unanimously supported abstinence and taught it to their students, also gaining many converts.[7]

Temperance literature (tracts, short stories, novels, and plays) also developed a thick discourse around women and alcohol that became integral to the formation of middle class gender ideology. Reformers usually portrayed women as either sympathetic victims of male drunkenness or moral exemplars who empowered men to resist temptation or restored the fallen. The realities behind these portrayals inspired many women to become active reformers. Women reformers signed petitions opposing tavern licenses, encouraged men and women to sign abstinence pledges, taught their children the evils of drink, and joined single and mixed gender temperance societies in large numbers. At its height, the Daughters of Temperance became the nation's largest antebellum woman's organization.[8]

African Americans also received strong temperance messages from various sources. Mutual aid societies were some of the most important black-controlled institutions at this time, and they had virtually no tolerance for drunken members. Using the traditional definition of temperance, their constitutions required expulsion of members known for drunkenness but not for those who used alcoholic drinks. The black convention movement, which began in 1830, regularly approved resolutions in support of the temperance movement. Richard Allen, the well-known founding bishop of the African Methodist Episcopal Church was an abstainer, and AME congregations often sponsored temperance societies for their members. African American temperance reformers often used the same arguments as did white reformers, but the extreme racism of the day lent their arguments a special urgency lacking in whites' rhetoric. Their inherited African sense of ethics inclined them to believe that every individual's behavior affected the whole community, so some blacks argued that an abstinent lifestyle would "prove" their virtuousness to white Americans, undermine racism, and thereby buttress their claims to full citizenship. Finally, black temperance reformers were particularly fond of incorporating their hatred of slavery into their temperance rhetoric, arguing that they opposed both kinds of "slavery" (dependence): slavery to another person and slavery to the bottle.[9]

Temperance Methodology and Organizations. Temperance reformers, like other reformers and revivalist preachers, held human reason in such high esteem that they believed individuals could not help but be persuaded by logically structured arguments; so until the end of this period all temperance efforts incorporated persuasive arguments. Temperance meetings bore similarities to revival services: they included prayer, songs, testimonials, and a speaker. At their conclusions, attendees were asked to make a decision and publicly sign an abstinence pledge. Signers were then encouraged to join temperance societies, where they would regularly hear encouraging speakers and where they could bring others to sign the pledge. Even in the early 20th century, when reformers committed most resources to fighting the "liquor traffic," there were always some working to get people to "sign the pledge."

Beginning in 1808, and without any national coordination, local temperance societies began springing up throughout the northeast and the Ohio Valley. The first southern temperance society was formed in North Carolina in 1822. The Massachusetts Society for the Suppression of Intemperance (MSSI), founded in 1813, was the first temperance society to create a network of affiliated local groups. It intentionally sought out the elite members of local communities, but lasted only a few years and only opposed the intemperate use of spirits, even serving wine at its meetings.[10]

In 1826, however, a group of ministers involved in various benevolent empire organizations launched the first truly national temperance organization: the American Temperance Society (ATS). It held annual conferences, published a newspaper, millions of copies of tracts, circulars, and annual reports, and financed the ministers Nathaniel Hewitt and Justin Edwards as itinerant agents to sign up existing local temperance groups and organize new ones. Unlike MSSI, the ATS pledge followed Benjamin Rush's recommendation and required total abstinence from distilled spirits. Its primary goal was not to restore drunkards but rather to make sure that sober people remained sober. Demonstrating its effective mass appeal, by 1835 the ATS had organized over 1.5 million people (about 12 percent of the population) into over eight thousand local societies in every part of the nation. But there were likely still more unaffiliated local societies. In 1833 the ATS became the United States Temperance Union, and in 1836, it became the American Temperance Union and added some Canadian societies. It was at the 1836 convention where the ATS also voted to follow the lead of many of its local and state societies and adopt the teetotal pledge.[11]

But the temperance message was also spread by other groups of the benevolent empire. The American Tract Society and local tract societies published many temperance tracts, and missionaries from such groups as the American Home Mission Society and the American Baptist Home Mission Society distributed them and organized temperance societies throughout the West. Sunday School literature often included temperance stories. Charles Finney, the most famous evangelist of the Second Great Awakening, included several temperance sermons and pledge-signing opportunities in his renowned 1830–1831 Rochester, New York, revival. Influential revivalists Asahel Nettleton and Edward Norris Kirk further tightened the revival-temperance connection by publicly questioning the sincerity of any convert who refused to also sign the abstinence pledge. Popular Methodist itinerants in the South and West, such as Peter Cartwright and James B. Finley, railed against intemperance, and not a few Baptists also castigated it. Abstinence sentiment grew slowly among Methodists and Baptists from the 1830s onward, but as the two fastest growing sects in America, their temperance efforts cannot be dismissed.[12]

EVERY WHICH WAY, 1836–1893

Temperance reformers may have agreed on their definition of temperance in 1836, but they agreed on little else. Their ranks were as notoriously divided as those of other reform movements. Some continued to persuade individuals through a flood of free and inexpensive literature, speeches, and local organizing. Others experimented with ways to use the political process to end the liquor traffic, which they now deemed intrinsically evil, just as they now argued that drinking any amount of alcohol was a sin. Some chastised the new German and Irish immigrants for their drinking customs, some worked to restore drunkards to sobriety, and some spread the temperance message through popular forms of entertainment. Rarely did any one reformer support all of these efforts. So many different things were being done in the name of temperance that one is tempted to argue that there were actually several simultaneous movements.

The Rise of New Organizations. From 1836 to 1865 the American Temperance Union (ATU) was the national voice of the movement. Although it struggled financially, its secretary, congregational minister John Marsh Jr., faithfully churned out temperance literature, annual reports, and traveled and spoke extensively. As with the ATS, the ATU's leadership unashamedly considered itself a Christian organization, even calling God himself the "supporter and director" of the movement. As the years passed, the ATU's influence declined, and its annual reports increasingly focused on overseas temperance developments.

The 1840s witnessed the rise of two dynamic new types of temperance organizations: the Washingtonians and fraternal temperance lodges. The Washingtonians originated in Baltimore in 1840 as a working-class temperance movement that used non-religious methods to reach the masses. Clergy, the middle class, and the wealthy generally criticized and avoided the movement, but by 1841 they claimed to have convinced hundreds of thousands of working men to sign the pledge and to have reformed many drunkards. They sponsored picnics, fairs, and parades. They also pioneered the use of reformed drunkard testimonials and generally re-created the camaraderie drunkards used to experience in taverns. Women formed Martha Washington auxiliaries to provide food and clothing to families in need because of an alcoholic husband. After only a few years, a variety of internal conflicts led to the fracturing and rapid decline of the Washingtonian movement, but its members had successfully popularized the movement to a mass audience in a way that the more middle class ATS and ATU never could.[13]

While difficulties arose in the Washingtonian movement, temperance lodges began appearing: Sons of Temperance (1843), Independent Order of Good Samaritans (1847), and the Independent Order of Good Templars (1852).

These groups, usually operating as secret societies, required members to sign abstinence pledges, incorporated formal rituals and regalia, held regular meetings that provided accountability, and sometimes offered the insurance benefits of a mutual aid society. They grew rapidly in the 1840s and 1850s, and although their popularity fluctuated over the years, some experienced long-term success, existing until the early 20th century. Like the Washingtonians, the Good Samaritans focused heavily on reforming drunkards. The Sons of Temperance had a strict policy of secrecy to help restore those who relapsed and to preserve the image of the movement. The Sons had an affiliate named the Daughters of Temperance that existed for about ten years. The Templars admitted men and women, spread to England and Scotland, and comprised the majority of the attendees at the organizing convention of the Prohibition Party in 1869. In the 1870s, Templars created the United Order of True Reformers, a parallel fraternity for southern blacks.[14]

There were even temperance societies for children, called Bands of Hope, which originated in England in 1847 and spread to the United States in the 1850s. Adults acted as overseers, and the membership requirements (pledge signing) and meetings were modeled after adult temperance societies. Children were taught from an official Band of Hope Catechism to abstain from all alcoholic beverages.[15]

The Move into Politics. At the 1833 convention of the American Temperance Society, radical reformer Gerrit Smith successfully sponsored a resolution that condemned the liquor traffic as morally wrong and recommended that "local communities be permitted by law to prohibit the said traffic within their respective jurisdictions." Despite its passage, many opposed government involvement, either because they believed only personal religious transformation could make someone temperate or because they thought it implied the failure of moral suasion. Supporters, however, argued that prohibition would put liquor sellers on a par with businesses such as brothels and gambling dens and that public sentiment would gradually turn against them. The focus on local political action meant it would only be attempted in locales where there was already sufficient public support for it, support presumably created through prior moral suasion. Because counties, towns, and cities had different government structures for approving retail liquor licenses, these efforts varied from place to place. While one locality might hold a referendum on granting liquor licenses (a "local option" election), in another reformers might run candidates for commissioner (or whoever granted the licenses) who promised not to grant any liquor licenses.

From the late 1840s through the 1850s, temperance reformers poured their energy into local political efforts, and they successfully "dried up" many northern and western communities. In the 1840s New York passed a law standardizing the process by which localities could prohibit the retail sale of alcohol, and within two years 728 of its 856 towns went dry. Southern attitudes toward the role of government, buttressed by the weakness of market forces in many communities and the regionally popular Protestant biblical teaching emphasizing the "spirituality of the church" (the idea that the church should not involve itself in secular matters), prevented antebellum southern reformers from experiencing nearly as much political success. In contrast, New England states often led the way in using the law to control alcohol, supported by their philosophy of governance, which assumed the right of the community to use the law to regulate individual morality for the public good. Reformers did not remain satisfied with local laws, however, and turned their efforts to the state level. In 1838 Massachusetts passed a law forbidding the sale of alcoholic beverages in the state in quantities less than 15 gallons, effectively making all sales wholesale. The opposition to this law was so strong that at the next election the Whig governor and the lawmakers who signed the bill were voted out of office, and the law was repealed.

Neal Dow, the mayor of Portland, Maine, and founder of the Maine Temperance Union, was the driving force behind the landmark 1851 Maine Liquor Law. This law made Maine the first state to ban the manufacture and the wholesale and retail sale of liquor. It inspired reformers in many other states to attempt the same thing and made Dow a temperance celebrity. Between 1852 and 1855 many states debated such a law, and twelve passed one: Massachusetts, Minnesota, Rhode Island, Vermont, Michigan, Connecticut, New York, Indiana, Delaware, Iowa, Nebraska, and New Hampshire. The nativist Know-Nothings political party was influential in state-level politics during the 1850s, and their elected officials usually supported prohibition laws. These laws produced so much backlash that courts in five states invalidated key enforcement provisions of their laws, and in four states the legislatures repealed their own laws. There were also instances of mob violence connected with enforcing these laws which tarnished the movement's image. Where the laws remained, enforcement was generally lax until after the Civil War. Despite its struggles and shortcomings, organized antebellum temperance certainly had its successes. By 1845 per capita alcohol consumption had declined to about a quarter of what it was at its peak in 1830.[16]

Temperance and Popular Culture. The temperance message entered popular culture in the 1830s and 1840s in a way that shaped both it and popular culture. Former drunkards such as John Henry Willis Hawkins and John B. Gough toured the nation giving dramatic and lurid speeches of how alcohol once controlled them but they eventually became sober. They were titillating and financially successful entertainers, but the audience always left with a temperance message. Many of these "experience speakers" had become dry through the Washingtonians, so they presented their message mostly without reference to a spiritual conversion. These speakers represented a "democratization" of the movement, for their authority rested on nothing more than their personal experience. Their stories progressed predictably from an early period of respectability, to social dislocation either in a city or on the frontier, to a decline into drunkenness, and a pledge-signing experience leading to their restoration.[17]

The temperance cause inspired a massive amount of literature, both fiction and nonfiction, and some pieces that blurred the distinction. Clergy leaders of the movement published plenty, but so too did the experience speakers, women writers, and physicians. John B. Gough published the first of several editions of his temperance-laced autobiography in 1845. Some other particularly well-known temperance writings included *Putnam and the Wolf* (1829), *Inquire at Amos Giles' Distillery* (1835), *The Distiller's Daughter: Or, The Power of Woman* (1844), and Mrs. Henry Wood's *Danesbury House* (1860). By far the most popular temperance novel was T. S. Arthur's *Ten Nights in a Bar-Room, and What I saw There* (1854), which sold over 400,000 copies. It was one of the best sellers of the 19th-century. Arthur drew the stories for his fictional work from Washingtonian testimonials he had heard. African American fiction writers also addressed temperance in their writings. Some examples include *The Two Offers*; *Clotel: or, The President's Daughter*; *The Garies and Their Friends*; and *Blake: or, The Huts of America*. African American authors spoke highly of the abstinent lifestyle, with some portraying it as a way to resist oppression by whites.[18]

Theater was growing in popularity during these years, too, and its leaders latched on to the temperance message so as to expand its appeal to the middle class, who generally avoided theaters for moral reasons. *The Drunkard: or, The Fallen Saved!*, a melodrama that opened in Boston in February 1844, was the first theater production to have over a hundred consecutive performances. It was the first of several popular shows portraying morally "respectable" temperance themes. By far the most influential temperance drama was William W. Pratt's stage adaption of T. S. Arthur's *Ten Nights*, first produced in 1857. It was produced regularly into the 20th century, during the silent film era, and as late as 1931 for the silver screen. Plays such as these enabled attendees to steep themselves "not in an ethic of restraint, frugality, and rationality but rather in the pleasures of emotional release, commercialized leisure, and compensatory fantasy, purified by evangelical trappings."[19]

Temperance and the Civil War. Although the Civil War gave temperance reformers much to fret over, such as the army's restoration of its daily spirit ration, the movement marched on. Whiskey was part of the Confederacy's daily navy ration and was authorized for use in its army "under circumstances of great exposure and protracted fatigue," as well as for medical purposes. The Confederacy's need to feed its soldiers, however, led to various prohibitions on producing spirits.[20] In 1862 the federal government began taxing distilled and malt liquors and licensing retail liquor sellers, which some reformers complained legitimized the liquor traffic. Most reformers, however, focused their attention on drinking by Union soldiers. In 1861 the Young Men's Christian Association organized the United States Christian Commission to assist army and navy chaplains in meeting the troops' spiritual and physical needs. The commission sent almost five thousand civilians behind Union Army lines to distribute Bibles, conduct prayer meetings, operate canteens, distribute medical supplies, and operate lending libraries. Promoting temperance was a commission goal, so temperance literature was included among the millions of pages of tracts its "delegates" distributed.[21]

Another way for temperance-minded men to find support was to join specifically designated "temperance regiments," such as the 13th Maine Infantry and the 24th Iowa Volunteer Infantry. Their members and officers committed themselves to abstinence. Neal Dow accepted his commission as the commanding officer of the 13th Maine Infantry Regiment only under the condition that he could select officers who were "temperate and upright men."[22]

New Postbellum Temperance Organizations.

The end of the Civil War revitalized the temperance movement. Sons of Temperance membership doubled between 1865 and 1868, and that of the Templars increased six-fold as they rapidly spread into the South. Although only four national temperance conventions were held in the thirty years before the war, five were held in the first sixteen years following the war. Reformers used these conventions to network, assess various strategies, and pass resolutions carefully articulating the "liquor problem."[23]

In addition to revitalized fraternal orders, three very different new temperance organizations emerged following the Civil War to lead the movement into the 1890s. At the Fifth National Temperance Convention in August 1865, delegates decided to close the moribund American Temperance Union and create a new organization to carry forward the vision of the ATS and the ATU. The new organization, the National Temperance Society and Publication House (NTS), intentionally perpetuated the earliest characteristics of the temperance movement, such as moral suasion, education, Christian republicanism, and clergy and church involvement. Good Templar J. N. Stearns was named its publishing agent and editor of its monthly, the *National Temperance Advocate*. The NTS committed itself to educating the public by distributing large amounts of inexpensive literature and defending every community's right to conduct local option elections.[24]

Once it became clear that the Republican Party would not adopt national prohibition as a plank in its platform, the Good Templars and Sons of Temperance called for a national convention in 1869 in Chicago to discuss the idea of creating a national Prohibition Party.

They viewed the Republican Party as key to the overthrow of slavery and thought that another party would be the best way to end the liquor traffic. Several of the more progressive reformers who had helped organize the Republican Party also attended, and together they birthed the Prohibition Party, which nominated its first presidential candidate in 1872. The party was much more than a one-issue group however, for its initial platform included a call for the direct election of senators and woman's suffrage, among other issues. The Prohibition Party did not emphasize the evangelical temperance arguments favored by the National Temperance Society, although some NTS leaders were members of the party. Prohibitionists targeted the liquor traffic, per se, stressing its high cost to society from the crime, disease, political corruption, and poverty it caused. This materialistic focus was designed to broaden its appeal to an increasingly diverse electorate. The party represented the radical fringe of the movement and highlighted its divisions because the vast majority of reformers were loath to tamper with the two party system. They preferred local option elections where people voted "yes" or "no" on prohibition, independent of any particular party, so political partisanship would not intrude on the alcohol question.[25]

The third major temperance organization was organized by veterans of the "Woman's Crusade," a movement of women who gathered in front of saloons to pray publicly for their closure. This occurred in as many as 900 towns during the winter and spring of 1873–1874 and led to saloon closures in over two hundred communities. Organization of the Woman's Christian Temperance Union followed in November 1874 at a convention in Cleveland, Ohio, with Frances Willard becoming corresponding secretary, then president in 1879. Willard became nationally famous in that role, making a much-touted tour of over fifty southern cities in 1881 that helped organize the southern temperance movement and was viewed as a major step in reunifying the nation. Although gaining prohibition was a top priority, Willard proclaimed a "do everything" motto that encouraged local chapters to engage in whatever reforms their local communities needed. She began arguing that women should be given the right to vote so that they could protect their homes by voting to close saloons. This rhetoric smartly built on middle-class gender ideology that made women responsible for the moral purity of their home and became a major turning point in the women's suffrage movement. Loyal Temperance Legion chapters were created to educate boys and girls about the dangers of alcohol, and the WCTU's Department of Scientific Temperance Instruction pressured every state legislature to implement mandatory alcohol education in its public schools. Willard welcomed both racially segregated and integrated local chapters, and although national WCTU conventions welcomed all women, the WCTU faced ongoing criticism from both blacks and whites about how it handled racial issues. Under Willard, over half of all US counties claimed a WCTU chapter, making it the first truly national voluntary organization since the end of the Civil War. In 1881 the WCTU joined a coalition of missionary groups that worked to "reach" former slaves with the temperance message. [26]

Postbellum Temperance Politics. In the 1880s the work of the NTS, WCTU, and the Prohibition Party produced the largest wave of prohibition activism since the 1850s. Republican and Democratic Party leaders knew that embracing prohibition would have easily split both of their parties, so they found ways to avoid endorsing it, to the consternation of some prohibitionists. Those who rejected the Prohibition Party, which was most temperance workers, could not work easily with the Republican or Democratic parties either. Because so many of the old 1850s state prohibition laws had been gutted when states backtracked on prohibition, the WCTU decided to work to amend state constitutions this time, presuming that such legal maneuvers would

be much more difficult to reverse. J. Ellen Foster, superintendent of WCTU legislative affairs, coordinated petition campaigns calling for statewide referenda. Although Republicans refused to add prohibition to their platform, they eventually supported the idea of holding statewide referenda so citizens could decide for themselves. Democrats, however, proudly remained the party of "personal liberty" and opposed sumptuary laws. In 1880 Kansas was the first state to successfully amend its constitution to prohibit alcohol, and nineteen more referenda were held in seventeen more states and territories. Although seven states adopted prohibition, more Republicans left for the Prohibition Party, and some African Americans even flirted with the idea of abandoning the "party of Lincoln." Prohibition Party strength peaked in the 1892 presidential election. [27]

Evangelical support for abstinence finally solidified in the postbellum South. Although Baptist, Methodist, and Presbyterian preachers proclaimed personal abstinence and their churches consistently disciplined their own intemperate members, many church members remained ambivalent about empowering state government to ban the liquor traffic. Black pastors, mostly Baptist and Methodist, also preached vigorously against alcohol and disciplined members for drunkenness. [28]

Despite conflicted evangelicals, prohibition did expand in the South during the late 1870s and 1880s, through various legal mechanisms. Georgia passed a "3 mile" law, which required all property owners within a three-mile radius to approve every proposed saloon. Tennessee's "4 mile" law created dry zones around schools outside of incorporated towns that dried up much of rural Tennessee. Some states created dry zones around every church and school. Many communities petitioned their state legislature for permission to deny liquor licenses. Ad hoc requests such as these made 80 percent of Georgia's counties dry by 1885. Then Georgia passed a general local option bill to standardize the process for the remaining counties. Virginia and Mississippi each enacted similar local option laws, which led, in Mississippi, to 80 percent of its counties using the process to close their saloons. One of the most prominent southern local option votes was Atlanta's successful 1885 vote. There was certainly plenty of opposition to prohibition, though, and in 1887 statewide referenda were defeated in Tennessee and Texas, and Atlantans later reversed their 1885 vote. These votes ended the spread of prohibition in the South for twenty years.[29]

PROHIBITION DURING THE PROGRESSIVE ERA, 1893–1933

The 1890s offered mixed successes for the largely temperance-turned-prohibition movement. Between 1890 and 1906 local option efforts dried up more than half of the nation's counties, representing about 40 percent of the population. Evangelical Protestant churches—but not most Roman Catholics, Lutherans, and Episcopalians—consistently taught personal abstinence in their Sunday Schools and their youth organizations, in their Sunday sermons, and in their denominational publications. Evangelical congregations began substituting "unfermented sacramental wine" (grape juice) for wine in Holy Communion.[30]

Although local dry politics witnessed some success, the major national temperance organizations experienced more repositioning, recalculating, and bickering than success. Frances Willard sought (with significant opposition and limited success) to ally the WCTU with the Prohibition Party while continuing to promote women's suffrage by calling it a "home protection" ballot. But talk of women's suffrage caused many southern evangelicals to distance themselves from the WCTU, and the major political parties and the Prohibition Party all were sent scrambling by the rise of Populism. In response, party Prohibitionists debated how broad or narrow their party platform should be and whether or not they should seek "fusion" with the Populists, only for both parties to fade into insignificance by the end of the

decade. The prominence of the WCTU, the Prohibition Party, and the National Temperance Society waned as key leaders died, and movement leadership gradually transitioned to the new Anti-Saloon League (ASL). Despite the organizational challenges of the 1890s, movement leaders soon found ways to successfully appropriate key aspects of their changing society to build a coalition strong enough to pass national prohibition.[31]

Just as early-19th-century social and political thought shaped the ideology and tactics of the temperance movement, Progressive Era America reshaped the movement in fundamental ways that would have made it almost unrecognizable to many earlier reformers. Over twenty million immigrants, mostly from southern and eastern Europe, industrialization, and urbanization, radically transformed the United States between the 1880s and the 1910s. Immigrants were mostly Roman Catholic and Jewish, and native-born white Protestants viewed them as inferior peoples. By 1910 almost 15 percent of Americans were foreign born, and in some cities it was close to 50 percent. They arrived with little to no education and had few opportunities to do anything but low paying factory jobs. Multigenerational families lived in cramped tenement housing, often sharing their apartment with another family. Sanitation and public health concerns abounded.

To compound matters, in the eyes of native-born white Protestants, wine and beer played central roles in the social life and cultural traditions of most immigrants. Factory workers would eat lunch in local saloons and stop by again on the way home from the factory. Between 1840 and 1910 per capita beer consumption grew over 1,000 percent, and its frequent public consumption easily caught the attention of temperance reformers. Saloons became the working man's "palace." Saloons functioned as ethnic "community centers," as well as centers of local partisan politics, as party precinct captains and ward bosses secured their constituents' votes by "taking care of" their various needs when unemployed, sick, injured, etc. Before long reformers argued that closing saloons would clean up political corruption.[32]

The desire to explore ways to ameliorate the negative side effects of industrialization and urbanization helped fuel the rise of the social sciences and social work, as various statistical and research-based urban reforms were proposed and implemented to improve the lives of city dwellers. Reformers such as Jane Addams established settlement houses to provide services such as English-language classes and childcare for immigrants and began to argue for the closing of the saloons. Supporting their efforts was a generally growing respect for science and professional expertise and a belief in its ability to solve human problems. As a result, reformers happily promoted—and exaggerated to good effect—the findings of groups such as the American Medical Association and the American Society for the study of Alcohol and Other Narcotic Drugs, which denied the health benefits of alcohol. Prominent business leaders such as John D. Rockefeller and Henry Ford supported the anti-saloon movement because they saw it as good for business efficiency and workers' health, anticipating benefits such as fewer worker absentees on "blue Mondays."

The heightened racial prejudices of the era also provided an impetus to close saloons. Many native-born white Protestants, disdainful of so many "inferior" whites in cities, began to fear such things as losing their cultural dominance and the possibility of racial "degeneracy" if the new immigrants did not assimilate quickly. Closing the saloons would help immigrants learn to live as Americans. At the same time, anti-black prejudice reached new extremes in ever tightening Jim Crow laws requiring segregation everywhere. As lynching increased, negative caricatures of black people became increasingly common, and southern white elites blamed poor whites and blacks for volatile race relations. Whiskey allegedly made black males more dangerous to white women, and southern elites who argued that the racial mixing in "low dives" was fertile soil

for race riots promoted closing saloons in the best interest of law and order. The many new turn-of-the-century socioeconomic realities provided many otherwise disparate groups of Americans reasons to support closing saloons.[33]

The Success of Prohibition in the South.

Prohibition did not become widely accepted in the South until the first decade of the 20th century. In the 1890s, "Redeemer" Democrats, fearful of losing control over state and local politics, actively undermined both Populists and Prohibitionists. At the same time, Prohibitionists had to address strong southern cultural norms that conflicted with the goals of Prohibitionists. For example, Prohibitionist rhetoric redefined the southern code of honor to mean sobriety and law-abiding orderliness, rather than hard drinking and fighting. Second, the "spirituality of the church" doctrine that prohibited church involvement in secular matters was consistently challenged until it fell out of favor. Finally, prohibitionists seized on the rising white fears of racial violence (e.g., 1898 Wilmington, North Carolina, and 1906 Atlanta race riots) and concern about white women being raped by alcohol-fueled black men. They argued that prohibition was the best way to simultaneously protect white women and stop the lawlessness of lynching. In the 1880s Prohibitionists had conveniently blamed blacks for the many defeats of local prohibition referendums while ignoring the divided white electorate. With that interpretation they came to support blacks' disfranchisement, ostensibly to reduce voting "corruption." Blacks' disfranchisement, along with prohibition and ending the convict lease system became leading causes of southern progressives. By the 1900s, because of the disfranchisement of blacks throughout the region, whites could freely debate prohibition without the risk of losing Democratic political control, and between 1907 and 1919 voters in Virginia, Texas, South Carolina, North Carolina, and Florida approved statewide prohibition referenda, while state legislatures in Georgia, Mississippi,

Alabama, Tennessee, and Arkansas approved statewide prohibition.[34]

The Anti-Saloon League and National Prohibition.

The Anti-Saloon League (ASL) had its hand in some, but not all of the southern prohibition victories. Lawyer turned Congregational minister Howard H. Russell had organized the Ohio Anti-Saloon League in 1893 based on his conviction that the model of the Prohibition Party could never succeed, but that rather narrow, pragmatic, non-partisan political action designed specifically to close saloons would be far more successful. Although Russell eschewed the larger reform agendas of the WCTU and Prohibition Party and was not explicit about his faith in his activism, this did not mean Russell rejected church support. In fact, the league claimed to be "the Church in Action Against the Saloon." It received official support from Methodists, Presbyterians, Congregationalists, and Baptists, and employed mostly ordained ministers and active laymen. Russell organized leagues in local congregations with support from pastors. In 1895 at a convention with representatives from forty-seven different temperance organizations, Russell organized the Anti-Saloon League of America, which by 1908 had branches in forty-three states. The ASL's internal structure and functioning were more akin to a corporation than a democratic grass roots social reform organization whose priorities are guided by the interests and votes of its members. State leaders were appointed, not elected, and worked in concert with the national organization's goals.

The ASL effectively pioneered several modern interest group lobbying tactics. It supported virtually any legislator who supported local option elections or the closing of saloons, even if the lawmaker was not personally abstinent. This was a significant change from the traditional temperance tactic of only electing "godly men." The ASL also, to the horror of many, disavowed loyalty to any party. Nothing mattered except its own agenda of closing saloons. It wrote "model" laws for legislators to

sponsor, kept mailing lists of dry voters, recorded and publicized legislators' voting records, organized letter writing campaigns, and printed and distributed literally tons of literature monthly. In Ohio it even successfully persuaded voters to remove a legislator and governor from office and to replace them with individuals who supported their agenda. Such tactics and successes soon gained the league the respect of elected officials from both parties. By 1908 the Ohio ASL had attracted its share of criticism, partly from its complete disregard for party loyalty; however, it had also achieved several impressive legislative victories that greatly restricted the state's liquor businesses and inspired leagues in other states to replicate its success.

Finally, in 1913 the ASL made its biggest and boldest moves. It turned its attention to the US Congress, and in a matter of weeks persuaded it to pass the Webb-Kenyon bill and override President Howard Taft's veto. The bill prohibited interstate shipment of liquor into states whose laws already prohibited possession or consumption of liquor. In the years before this victory the liquor industry had become increasingly organized and politically active and the ASL had lost some local elections. The ASL's weakness in popular votes seemed to contrast with its effective lobbying of lawmakers. At the same time, supporters of Progressivism were pushing through Congress important new laws designed to protect American citizens, such as the laws creating the Food and Drug Administration, the Meat Inspection Act, and the Federal Trade Commission. Considering urban population growth, the ASL calculated that reapportionment after the 1920 census would increase the number of congressmen from urban districts, making their work more challenging. They decided it was a favorable time to launch a campaign for a constitutional amendment creating national prohibition. Wayne Wheeler, the ASL's lead lobbyist, called the decision "the logical result of the tendency of the times toward a government under which the people may protect themselves from evil and wrong." As it turned out, the Eighteenth Amendment was one of four amendments passed between 1913 and 1919, the biggest wave of amendment writing since Reconstruction. One of those amendments established the federal income tax, which greatly reduced the federal government's dependence on liquor tax revenues. None of these changes were lost on the ASL leadership.[35]

The ASL leadership expected that it would take up to twenty years to pass their radical amendment even with marshalling all of its resources. But the beginning of the First World War rapidly transformed public opinion about patriotism, the federal government, and all things German including beer and, by implication, generally all alcohol. As the nation began to pass laws to control production in certain key industries and took control of the railroads, public opinion focused on the ways citizens could make sacrifices for the good of their nation. New laws created dry zones around army bases to ensure healthy soldiers, and required grain to be used for food, not liquor. As public opinion turned increasingly against Germans, the US Senate investigated the United States Brewers' Association for its German sympathies, and the German American National Alliance of America (which was funded by the brewers) was forced to cease operations because of its alleged sympathies with the Kaiser. In this environment, between 1914 and 1916, fourteen more states established prohibition. The 1914 Congress contained clear dry majorities but not the necessary two-thirds for approving an amendment. To bring public opinion in line with national prohibition, the ASL distributed literature in fifteen different languages, published new periodicals targeting specific demographic groups, expanded fundraising, and coordinated its efforts with other groups, such as the Federal Council of Churches and the WCTU. Ernest Cherrington, responsible for all ASL publishing, took advantage of the concern for workplace efficiency and safety by printing literature that touted the benefits of closing the saloons for the

industrial workplace. For several years, there had also been a growing body of scientific literature calling alcohol both poisonous and a narcotic, which added important gravitas to the older arguments of preachers and reformers. Citing experts and specialists, ASL literature presented the closing of America's saloons as a panacea for a widening range of American social and economic ills. As wartime needs became political priorities, Americans who might otherwise have opposed intrusive federal legislation became increasingly inclined to accept expanded federal powers.

Two-thirds of the Congress elected in 1916, in part through ASL work, were committed to a prohibition amendment. The ASL first successfully lobbied for a rider to a bill that prohibited the use of grain in distilling. Then the prohibition amendment to the US Constitution was submitted to the Senate, and passed on September 1, 1917. The House approved the amendment and sent it to the states in December. The amendment banned the manufacture, sale, and transportation of intoxicating liquor "for beverage purposes" (without defining intoxicating" liquor), and although the states had seven years to ratify it, the required two-thirds threshold was met on January 16, 1919, when Nebraska became the thirty-sixth state to ratify it. The speed of its ratification surprised everyone, including ASL leaders. It took effect one year later.

The amendment required a federal statue to implement it, and ASL lobbyist Wayne Wheeler gave representative Andrew Volstead, a Minnesota Republican, the wording for the National Prohibition Act, and Congress passed the act over Woodrow Wilson's veto on October 27, 1919. The "Volstead Act" used an IRS definition for "intoxicating beverages" that defined them as any beverage with more than .5 percent alcohol content. Further, it assigned enforcement of the law to the IRS, established usage guidelines for industrial alcohol, sacramental wine, and medicinal alcohol. The amendment also required each state to pass a law providing for enforcement of the amendment, making violation both a federal and state crime. Although every state except Maryland passed its own enforcement codes, actual state enforcement varied significantly. Eight states eventually rescinded their enforcement codes, while thirty-four states revised and strengthened their codes, but state resources and manpower seldom seemed sufficient.[36]

Prohibition and the Transformation of a Movement and a Nation.

The years of national prohibition, 1920–1933, witnessed yet another transformation of the nation's organized temperance movement. The National Temperance Society and Publication House witnessed such extreme financial challenges that by 1917, to survive, it had entered into a special "federation" with the Commission on Temperance, an arm of the Federal Council of Churches, and it remained on life support until it folded in the 1940s.

The WCTU gained tens of thousands of new members in the immediate aftermath of the passage of the Eighteenth Amendment, and its membership peaked in 1923 at almost 500,000, including its youth auxiliary membership. During the 1920s WCTU members made their motto "Education for Enforcement" and proactively supported the work of Prohibition law enforcement officials. But by 1931 the groundswell of opposition to Prohibition combined with the Depression put the WCTU on the defensive. Its claim to represent the views of all American women on alcohol was greatly undermined in 1931 when the recently organized Women's Organization for National Prohibition Reform, which supported repeal, announced that its membership exceeded that of the WCTU. Although WCTU membership began a long slow decline, the organization still exists and still has foreign chapters. Ella A. Boole, president when the Eighteenth Amendment was repealed, captured the sentiment of WCTU women when she declared, "Repeal will not change the nature of alcohol."[37]

Many members of the Prohibition Party celebrated the passage of the Eighteenth Amendment, but hardly any of them celebrated the process by which it was created. In fact, the Prohibition Party never officially endorsed the amendment. They rightly foresaw that the amendment did not have sufficient popular support to be effective but rather would breed a general contempt for the law. As one leader bemoaned, the real problem with the passage of the amendment was that the "great end" of any reform movement, the genuine "renovation of government," had not occurred. The two-party system had made things so difficult for third parties that by 1924 Prohibitionists were only on the ballot in sixteen states. The dwindling and marginalized party has continued to nominate candidates for every presidential election into the 21st century. In the 2016 election it was on the ballot in at least three states.[38]

Prohibition Party leaders were right about the nature of this reform. Missouri Senator James Reed put it this way: "The legal revolution occurred but the moral miracle did not come off according to schedule."[39] Violations of Prohibition were too numerous to track, and enforcing the law required substantial personnel commitments and challenged the traditional nature of federalism. Unfortunately for its supporters, Prohibition's uneven enforcement fell heavily on non-white and lower income communities, with elites and the middle class seldom feeling the full force of the law when they violated it. These were years when Americans and their elected officials became fixated on the "crime waves" spreading across the nation and the general disregard for law they represented. One response was a revival of the Ku Klux Klan, as it sought to use its own racist form of vigilante justice to "assist" law enforcement. The press did not miss opportunities to sensationalize every crime story. Although the murder rate had already increased more than fourfold between 1900 and 1916, something seemed different about crime in the 1920s. Although violations of the Volstead Act were a major cause, the rise in automobile use also created new categories of crime, while the "red summer" of 1919 witnessed over thirty incidences of white mobs attacking blacks as well as labor unrest and strikes. After Prohibition commenced, it quickly became obvious that selling illegal liquor would be incredibly profitable. Now, the crime trends and law enforcement challenges that dry states experienced before the First World War were being realized on a national scale and called for a national response. By the mid-1920s the nation's crime fighting apparatus was overwhelmed at every level—local, state, and federal. Prisons were overcrowded, courts were backlogged to a degree never seen before, bootleggers regularly bribed law enforcement personnel, and new constitutional and legal questions complicated court cases.

Prohibition thus "turned an entire industry over to criminal entrepreneurs"[40] and enabled them to buy off not just police but also judges and elected officials, significantly undermining Americans' confidence in their law enforcement system. This led several cities and states to establish crime "commissions" to study the problem and suggest solutions. In Herbert Hoover's 1929 inaugural speech he called crime a national problem and quickly followed up by creating the National Commission on Law Observance and Enforcement (Wickersham Commission), chaired by a former attorney general, George Wickersham, and staffed by men with experience on the earlier city and state commissions. The commission published fourteen reports that laid the foundation for federal centralization of crime fighting for many years into the future. The Prohibition Bureau was housed in the Internal Revenue Service, and at Wayne Wheeler's urging, its agents were not part of the Civil Service so he could control who was hired. When the agents were made to join the civil service later in the decade, about 40 percent could not pass the test. About one in twelve agents was accused of accepting bribes, and there were constant complaints about excessive use of force when bootleggers and still owners were killed and reportedly sometimes shot in the back. The violence

employed to enforce Prohibition became increasingly unpalatable to Americans.

The crime produced during Prohibition contributed to significant federal institutional developments. In 1924 the organization that would become the FBI began the practice of fingerprinting criminals, and in 1930 it began issuing the annual FBI Uniform Crime Report based on reports from local police departments. Serious prison overcrowding pushed the federal government to build new prisons and reorganize their administration in the Federal Bureau of Prisons that began issuing a yearly report on prisoners in state and federal prisons and reformatories. Because the court system became so backlogged with cases, the use of parole and plea bargaining became commonplace, and a Federal Parole Board was established. A 1922 law reorganized the federal judiciary, empowering the chief justice to make decisions to increase court efficiencies. New Supreme Court decisions permitted wiretapping of telephones, seizure of a vehicle if police had "reasonable and probable cause" for believing it contained bootleg liquor in transit, and allowed individuals to be prosecuted in both federal and state courts for the same crime, overturning the Fifth Amendment ban on double jeopardy.[41]

Finally, national alcohol prohibition paralleled a new "war" on narcotics and other banned substances. The 1922 Jones-Miller Act outlawed the import and export of opium, heroin, and other narcotics and established the Federal Narcotics Control Board. In 1923, Richmond Hobson, a former ASL lecturer once nicknamed the "father of Prohibition," founded the International Narcotic Education Association to persuade people of the dangers of alcohol, opium, heroin, cocaine, and morphine and end their "traffic and use." He gained support from pharmaceutical companies and later formed the World Narcotics Defense Association to end their global trade. When President Hoover created the Federal Narcotics Bureau in 1930, he appointed Henry Anslinger, former assistant commissioner of the Prohibition Bureau, to lead it. WCTU women had become enthusiastic supporters of the war on drugs by the 1930s. Put simply, all the negatives attributed to alcohol had been transferred to narcotics by the 1930s and this has continued into the 21st century. Historian Lisa McGirr notes, "The logic of alcohol Prohibition ... hardened public opinion toward substances widely judged to be more addictive and harmful than liquor," while political scientist James Morone maintains that Prohibition "constructed institutional and legal precedents for almost every aspect of the war on drugs."[42]

Opposition to this "noble experiment" was growing by the 1928 presidential election, and Al Smith, governor of New York, voiced the concerns of those wanting to revise the Volstead Act, if not rescind the Eighteenth Amendment altogether. Although Hoover easily won the election, Democratic Party leaders worked intentionally over the next four years to solidify their party as the party of repeal and to bring urban white ethnic voters who supported repeal into their coalition. Those efforts paid off in Franklin D. Roosevelt's 1932 landslide victory, and they swept a Democratic majority into Congress rooted in a coalition that remained well into the late 20th century.[43]

After national prohibition began, the ASL experienced a significant drop in financial support, and its leadership began debating the best way to use their limited resources. Wayne Wheeler wanted to leverage the league's political influence to support enforcement and use ASL literature to remind citizens to obey the law of the land. Until he died in 1927, he closely allied the league with Republicans, who were the majority party. Cherrington, on the other hand, wanted to launch an education campaign to convince Americans to embrace personal abstinence. But the ASL had never focused on personal drinking habits, and the approach fizzled. After the stock market crashed and depression spread, public opinion turned against the lackluster response of Hoover and the Republicans, while ASL claims that Prohibition enforcement was the nation's priority fell on deaf, even incredulous, ears.[44]

What H. L. Mencken had called the nation's "Noble Experiment" collapsed with the 1932 national election that repudiated Hoover and the Republican approach to both the Depression and Prohibition. The lame duck Congress passed a repeal amendment that required special state ratification conventions; it was the only amendment to ever have such a requirement. Congress wanted to verify that popular sentiment supported the repeal of Prohibition. Even though the Eighteenth Amendment had been ratified faster than anyone expected between 1917 and 1919, its repeal, occurred even more rapidly. State conventions often supported repeal with lopsided votes in the range of 65 to 70 percent, and the Eighteenth Amendment was repealed on December 5, 1933.

DISCUSSION OF THE LITERATURE

Tracing the historiography of the temperance and prohibition movement is tricky because it was such a long lasting "event" and few scholars trace its 150-year history in a single study. Most historians examine a short chronological period in a particular place and draw conclusions that others then sometimes sloppily apply to the entire time period or different places. As with most areas of study, the quantity and quality of the scholarship is unevenly distributed over time and place. For example, there are more detailed studies of the antebellum movement and the post-1890 period than the years in between, and scholarship on the African American experience with the movement is relatively thin. As the above essay has demonstrated, what was true of the movement in the 1820s was not true of the movement in the 1840s, the 1880s, or the 1910s. In popular discourse there is more awareness of the post-1890 era than earlier years, and people tend to read the traits of that era back into the earlier years. Of course, region also plays a significant role in interpreting the movement, as New England, the South, and West had different experiences with temperance and prohibition, not to mention the rural-urban contrast. To further complicate matters, not just historians have written on the topic. Sociologists, political scientists, historians, economists, cultural studies scholars, literary scholars, legal scholars, and scholars of religion have all weighed in on either the movement or factors which are, practically speaking, inseparable from it, such as theology, social customs surrounding drinking, and legal and political processes. These factors need to be taken into consideration when assessing or comparing the claims authors make about the temperance and prohibition movements. Two notable exceptions to the usually limited time frame used by temperance scholars are Lee L. Willis's *Southern Prohibition, Race, Reform, and Public Life in Middle Florida, 1821–1920* (2011) and Sabine N. Meyer's *We Are What We Drink: The Temperance Battle in Minnesota,* (2015) which covers the years 1819–1919.

Temperance and prohibition scholarship has been guided by a series of questions: What kinds of rationales were articulated to justify abstinence, and to what extent did they reflect the actual lived reality of the reformers? How were these rationales conveyed? Who was likely to become an abstainer and why? Why did the idea gain popularity where and when it did? Why was the message largely rejected, when and where it was? How did different groups respond to the abstinence message? What rationales were used to defend prohibition? What methods were successfully used to implement prohibition? Why did those methods work for some time periods and places but not others? Why did many drinkers support the Prohibition Act? How did class, race, gender, and ethnicity affect one's response to the abstinence message and to the prohibition message? What have been the lasting effects of the temperance movement, or Prohibition, on the United States? How effective was enforcement during Prohibition? Did Prohibition actually reduce the amount of drinking Americans did? Space constraints will permit only a limited exploration of the historiography on the above research questions.

One area where the scholarship is particularly thick is the antebellum era. Here the emphasis is mostly on the northeast region of the country, and scholars seek to explain why this unprecedented idea of abstinence became as popular as it did. The earliest academic attempts see the movement as closely tied to evangelical Christianity and the revivalism of the Second Great Awakening: *The Origins of Prohibition* (1925), *The Antislavery Impulse, 1830–1844* (1933) and *Freedom's Ferment: Phases of American Social History to 1860* (1944). Although the sufficiency of this approach has been vigorously challenged over the years, scholars have continued to look closely at the relationship between the temperance movement and evangelical theology, revivalist practices, and republican ideology. Some of the more recent thoughtful scholarship in this area includes *Cosmos Crumbling: American Reform and the Religious Imagination* (1994), *Bearing Witness against Sin: The Evangelical Birth of the American Social Movement* (2006), "'A Battle Not Man's But God's': Origins of the American Temperance Crusade in the Struggle for Religious Authority," by Laura A. Schmidt in *Journal of Studies on Alcohol* (January 1995), *The Politics of Benevolence: Revival Religion and American Voting Behaviors* (1979), "'Drinks He to His Own Undoing': Temperance Ideology in the Deep South," by Douglas W. Carlson in *Journal of the Early Republic* (Winter 1998), and *'A Most Stirring and Significant Episode': Religion and the Rise and Fall of Prohibition in Black Atlanta, 1865–1887* (2013).

The first major challenge to the religious/ideological school came from sociologist Joseph Gusfield, in his frequently cited 1963 book *Symbolic Crusade: Status Politics and the American Temperance Movement.* Gusfield argued that drinking customs are social status markers and that the earliest temperance reformers perceived certain changes around them as threatening their status, so "in its earliest development, Temperance was one way in which a declining social elite tried to retain some of its social power and leadership."[45] Despite the popularity of Gusfield's work,

Alcoholic Republic: An American Tradition, by William Rorabaugh, and 1970s works by Norman Clark and Jack S. Blocker Jr., have established that there was a significant increase in alcohol consumption in the early republic to which reformers were responding. Ronald G. Walters argued in *American Reformers, 1815– 1860* (1978) that evangelicals involved in the temperance movement were likely involved in other evangelical endeavors to improve society. They formed many Protestant voluntary associations with overlapping memberships that were products of their particular understanding of benevolence. These associations included, among others, the American Bible Society, American Tract Society, the American Sunday School Union, and the American Board for Commissioners of Foreign Missions. Walters called these organizations the evangelicals' "benevolent empire."[46] Probably the dominant view today is that wherever market forces were strongest, workers, professionals, and entrepreneurs were likely to embrace the benefits of an abstinent lifestyle. Two books that clearly demonstrate the links between temperance and the developing market economy and middle-class values are Paul E. Johnson's *A Shopkeeper's Millennium: Society and Revivals in Rochester, NY, 1815–1837*, 25th anniversary edition (2004), and Bruce E. Stewart's *Moonshiners and Prohibitionists: The Battle Over Alcohol in Southern Appalachia* (2011). Three useful articles that highlight the intersection of temperance, the working class, and the market economy are: "The Working Classes and the Temperance Movement in Ante-Bellum Boston," by Jill Siegel Dodd, *Labor History* (Fall 1978), "The Shuttle and the Cross: Weavers and Artisans in the Kensington Riots of 1844," by David Montgomery, *Journal of Social History* (1972), and "Cultural Aspects of the Industrial Revolution: Lynn, Massachusetts, Shoemakers and Industrial Morality, 1826–1860," by Paul Fahler, *Labor History* (Summer 1974).

There are certain state or local studies that have become classics in the field for the clarity with which they address some of the questions listed above. Some of these are Paul E. Isaac's *Prohibition and Politics: Turbulent Decades in Tennessee, 1885–1920*, Jed Dannenbaum's *Drink and Disorder: Temperance Reform in Cincinnati from the Washingtonian Revival to the WCTU*, Larry Engelmann's *Intemperance: The Lost War Against Liquor (Michigan)*, and Robert L. Hempel's *Temperance and Prohibition in Massachusetts, 1813–1852*. A recent book of this caliber is Sabine N. Meyer's *We Are What We Drink: The Temperance Battle in Minnesota*, which pays special attention to German and Irish Americans and women.

Some recent scholars of the Prohibition era have been exploring the long-term impact of Prohibition on the US government and society. Scholars have found the genesis of an increasing array of modern social, political, and economic practices, patterns, and assumptions in this era, which are rooted in patterns of law breaking, law evading, or law enforcement under prohibition. Current social customs about drinking, the relationship between the police and minorities, how the government treated criminals, and the marketing of soft drinks, among other things, were all informed by Prohibition. Three excellent works that explore the long-term impact of Prohibition on the federal government are James Morone's *Hellfire Nation: The Politics of Sin in American History* (2003), Lisa McGirr's *The War on Alcohol: Prohibition and the Rise of the American State* (2016), and Daniel Okrent's *Last Call: The Rise and Fall of Prohibition* (2010).

PRIMARY SOURCES

Probably the single largest primary source collection on this topic is the 424 microfilm reels of the "Temperance and Prohibition Papers, 1830-1933." The items in this collection are held by the Ohio Historical Society, Woman's Christian Temperance Union, Michigan Historical Collections, and the Westerville Public Library. The collection contains the records of many organizations, including the Prohibition Party, WCTU, Ohio Anti-Saloon League,

Scientific Temperance Federation, and the Anti-Saloon League of America. It also contains the papers of Ernest Cherrington, Howard Russell, Francis McBride, and Thomas Steuart. It includes the WCTU's *Union Signal* and the ASL's *American Issue*. Be aware that the *American Issue* was first published monthly, then weekly; after that, various state leagues issued their own edition. There is a useful printed finding aid that is absolutely essential for browsing this collection. The entire collection is held by the University of Michigan, the Ohio History Connection (formerly the Ohio Historical Society), and Harvard University.

The temperance related materials held at the Stephen A. Schwarzman Building of the New York Public Library are quite possibly the most extensive found anywhere. A subject search for "temperance" in the NYPL online catalog yields 573 separate subject categories, and each category lists between one and 1,678 separate items. It is the best location to find any publication of the National Temperance Society & Publication House. It holds the complete run of the *National Temperance Advocate*. The library also holds *Voice* and the *New Voice*, official organs of the Prohibition Party, the annual reports of the American Tract Society, and many of their tracts. They published much in support of temperance.

Some other libraries with extensive temperance and alcohol-related collections are the American Antiquarian Society and Brown University. A subject search for "temperance" in the Antiquarian Society's catalogue yields 1,308 items, while a keyword search reveals 4,069 results. Brown University houses the Center for Alcohol and Addiction Studies and the Chester H. Kirk Collection on Alcoholism and Alcoholics Anonymous, some of which is digitized on the Internet.

The first three annual reports of the American Temperance Society are extant and individually available. *Permanent Temperance Documents*, Volume 1, contains annual reports 4–9 of the American Temperance Society, and

Volumes 2 and 3 contain all the annual reports of the American Temperance Union. They are also microfilmed and located in many libraries. The *Journal of Humanity and Herald of the American Temperance Society* and the *Journal of the American Temperance Union* are both available on microfilm.

The Frances Willard Memorial Library and Archives (Evanston, IL) hold copies of the WCTU's first newspaper, *Our Union*, plus Frances Willard's Papers, which include her speeches, photos, eighty scrapbooks of temperance-related newspaper clippings, and many more items. Visits are by appointment only.

The records of the National Temperance Society and Publication House are held at the Presbyterian Historical Society (Philadelphia).

The Proceedings of the ten National Temperance Conventions held between 1833 and 1904 are also extant as are the annual Anti-Saloon League yearbooks, produced by Ernest Cherrington between 1909 and 1932, which are useful compendiums of Prohibition-related statistics and developments. Ernest Cherrington's six-volume *Standard Encyclopedia of the Alcohol Problem*, published between 1924 and 1930, is valuable for information on topics not covered in detail by more recent writers.

At the Rockefeller Archive Center (Tarrytown, NY) one can research the temperance-related philanthropy of the Rockefeller family members. Syracuse University holds the papers of Gerrit Smith, a philanthropist and active member of the New York Temperance Society and speaker at the 1833 National Temperance Convention. The Guy Hayler Collection (or "Temperance Collection") at the University of Wisconsin contains many microfilmed American and British temperance tracts.

The temperance activities and positions of church groups are scattered throughout their various periodicals and annual conference, convention, or association reports. Most church bodies had standing temperance committees that regularly approved resolutions from the late 1870s through the 1930s. Also, individual church congregations report church activities regarding temperance and disciplining of members for drunkenness. Some repositories include the American Baptist Historical Society (Atlanta, GA), Presbyterian Historical Society (Philadelphia), Southern Baptist Historical Society and Library (Louisville, KY), United Methodist Church General Commission on Archives and History (Madison, NJ), and the Congregational Library (Boston). The records of Georgia's African American Baptist associations and conventions are held by Mercer University's Jack Tarver Library. The annual reports and monthly publications of the various home and foreign missionary societies also contain much useful information about their missionaries' temperance activities.

Newspapers and magazines are a treasure trove of articles reporting on local option elections, temperance speeches, and activities of temperance societies. One should search whatever newspaper databases are available, using a variety of terms, such as: temperance, prohibition, alcohol, liquor traffic, and the names of various organizations and temperance speakers.

The Wickersham Commission Records are held at the Harvard Law School and the Richmond P. Hobson Papers are at the Library of Congress. The National Archives holds the records of the Bureau of Prohibition under the General Records of the Department of the Treasury.

DIGITAL MATERIALS

Anti-Saloon League Collection (Westerville, OH, Public Library). http://www.westervillelibrary.org/antisaloon.

The Dry Years: Selected Prohibition Images from the Library of Congress. https://www.loc.gov/rr/print/list/073_dry.html.

Gerrit Smith Broadside and Pamphlet Collection (Syracuse University). http://scrconline.syr.edu/.

Alcohol, Temperance & Prohibition (Brown University Library Center for Digital Scholarship). http://library.brown.edu/cds/temperance/.

Museum of Alcohol: An online Museum All About Drinking Culture. https://museumofalcohol.wordpress.com/.

Ardent Spirits: The Origins of the American Temperance Movement (Library Co. of Philadelphia). http://www.librarycompany.org/ArdentSpirits/.

P. T. Barnum's "Appeal to the Democratic Voters of Connecticut" (*New Haven Advocate*, March 26, 1852). http://lostmuseum.cuny.edu/archive/barnum-on-the-democratic-party-and-temperance.

POINTS: The Blog of the Alcohol and Drugs History Society. https://pointsadhsblog.wordpress.com/.

Sign up to receive the latest news about alcohol and drugs in your in box. https://alcoholanddrugshistorysociety.org/.

FURTHER READING

Blocker, Jack S. Jr. *American Temperance Movements: Cycles of Reform*. Boston: Twayne, 1989.

Coker, Joe L. *Liquor in the Land of the Lost Cause: Southern White Evangelicals and the Prohibition Movement*. Lexington: University Press of Kentucky, 2007.

Dannenbaum, Jed. *Drink and Disorder: Temperance Reform in Cincinnati from the Washingtonian Revival to the WCTU*. Urbana: University of Illinois Press, 1984.

Kerr, K. Austin. *Organized for Prohibition: A New History of the Anti-Saloon League*. New Haven, CT: Yale University Press, 1985.

Kyvig, David E. *Repealing National Prohibition*. 2d ed. Kent, OH: Kent State University Press, 2000.

Lewis, Michael. *The Coming of Southern Prohibition: The Dispensary System and the Battle Over Liquor in South Carolina, 1907–1915*. Baton Rouge: Louisiana State University Press, 2016.

Martin, Scott C. *Devil of the Domestic Sphere: Temperance, Gender, and Middle-Class Ideology, 1800–1860*. DeKalb: Northern Illinois University Press, 2008.

McGirr, Lisa. *The War on Alcohol: Prohibition and the Rise of the American State*. New York: W. W. Norton, 2016.

Meyer, Sabine N. *We Are What We Drink: The Temperance Battle in Minnesota*. Urbana: University of Illinois Press, 2015.

Mintz, Steven. *Moralists & Modernizers: America's Pre-Civil War Reformers*. Baltimore: Johns Hopkins University Press, 1995.

Pegram, Thomas R. *Battling Demon Rum: The Struggle for a Dry America, 1800–1933*. Chicago: Ivan R. Dee, 1998.

Rorabaugh, W. J. *The Alcoholic Republic: An American Tradition*. New York: Oxford University Press, 1979.

Tyrrell, Ian R. *Sobering Up: From Temperance to Prohibition in Antebellum America, 1800–1860.* Westport, CT: Greenwood Press, 1979.

Willis, Lee L. *Southern Prohibition: Race, Reform, and Public Life in Middle Florida, 1821–1920.* Athens, GA: University of Georgia Press, 2011.

NOTES

1. Jack S. Blocker Jr. *American Temperance Movements: Cycles of Reform* (Boston: Twayne, 1989), 3.
2. William Rorabaugh, *Alcoholic Republic: An American Tradition* (New York: Oxford University Press, 1979), 7–10.
3. Blocker, 8–10; Thomas R. Pegram, *Battling Demon Rum: The Struggle for a Dry America, 1800–1933* (Chicago: Ivan R. Dee, 1998), 9–13; William J. Rorabaugh, *The Alcoholic Republic* (New York: Oxford University Press, 1979); Steven Mintz, *Moralists & Modernizers: America's Pre-Civil War Reformers* (Baltimore: Johns Hopkins University Press, 1995), chapter 1; Ian R. Tyrrell, *Sobering Up: From Temperance to Prohibition in Antebellum America, 1800–1860* (Westport, CT: Greenwood Press, 1979), chapter 1; Mark Edward Lender and James Kirby Martin, *Drinking in America: A History*, rev. ed. (New York: The Free Press, 1987), chapter 1; and Sarah Hand Meacham, *Every Home a Distillery: Alcohol, Gender, and Technology in the Colonial Chesapeake* (Baltimore: Johns Hopkins University Press, 2009).
4. Robert H. Abzug, *Cosmos Crumbling: American Reform and the Religious Imagination* (New York: Oxford University Press, 1994), chapter 1; and John Allen Krout, *The Origins of Prohibition* (New York: Alfred A. Knopf, 1925), chapter 4.
5. H. Paul Thompson Jr., *"A Most Stirring and Significant Episode": Religion and the Rise and Fall of Prohibition in Black Atlanta, 1865–1887* (DeKalb: Northern Illinois University Press, 2013), 18–19; Abzug, chapter 2; Allan M. Winkler, "Lyman Beecher and the Temperance Crusade," *Quarterly Journal of Studies on Alcohol* 33 (1972): 939–957; Blocker, 22–24; and Krout, 155–168.
6. William Gribbin, "Republicanism, Reform, and the Sense of Sin in Ante Bellum America," *Cithara* 14 (1974): 25–41; Heman Humphrey, *The Way to Bless and Save Our Country: A Sermon* (Philadelphia: American Sunday School Union, 1831);

Albert Barnes, *The Connexion of Temperance with Republican Freedom* (Philadelphia: Boyle and Benedict, 1835); E. N. Kirk, *The Temperance Reformation Connected with the Revival of Religion and the Introduction of the Millennium* (London: J. Pasco, 1838); Lender and Martin, 35–40, 79–85; John Quist, *Restless Visionaries: The Social Roots of Antebellum Reform in Alabama and Michigan* (Baton Rouge: Louisiana State University Press, 1998), 164; and Charles C. Cole, *The Social Ideas of the Northern Evangelists, 1826–1860* (New York: Columbia University Press, 1954).
7. Blocker, 17–19; Krout, chapter 10; David Montgomery, "The Shuttle and the Cross: Weavers and Artisans in the Kensington Riots of 1844," *Journal of Social History* 5 (1972): 411–446; and Thomas S. Grimké, *Address on the Patriot Character of the Temperance Reformation* (Charleston, SC: Observer Office, 1833).
8. Scott C. Martin, *Devil of the Domestic Sphere: Temperance, Gender, and Middle-class Ideology 1800–1860* (DeKalb: Northern Illinois University Press, 2008).
9. Thompson, 124–129; Donald Yacovone, "The Transformation of the Black Temperance Movement, 1827–1854: An Interpretation," *Journal of the Early Republic* 8 (Fall 1988): 281–297; and Denise Herd, "The Paradox of Temperance: Blacks and the Alcohol Question in Nineteenth-Century America," in *Drinking: Behavior and Belief in Modern History*, eds. Susanna Barrows and Robin Room (Los Angeles: University of California Press, 1991), 354–375.
10. James R. Rohrer, "The Origins of the Temperance Movement: A Reinterpretation," *Journal of American Studies* 24 (August 1990): 228–335.
11. Blocker, 12–15, 21–25; Michael P. Young, *Bearing Witness against Sin: The Evangelical Birth of the American Social Movement* (Chicago: University of Chicago Press, 2006); Stephen Wills Murphy, "'It Is a Sacred Duty to Abstain': The Organizational, Biblical, Theological, and Practical Roots of the American Temperance Society, 1814–1830" (PhD diss., University of Virginia, 2008); and Paul R. Meyer, "The Transformation of American Temperance: The Popularization and Radicalization of a Reform Movement, 1813–1860" (PhD diss., University of Iowa, 1976), chapter 3.
12. Thompson, 21–41; Paul E. Johnson, *A Shopkeeper's Millennium: Society and Revivals in Rochester,*

N.Y., 1815–1837, 25th anniversary edition (New York: Hill and Wang, 2004); Asahel Nettleton, *Temperance and Revivals* (New York: National Temperance Society and Publication House, n.d.); Krout, chapter 6; Raymond Pierce Cowan, "From 'Noble Cordial' to Sin: Early American Methodists Confront Alcohol," *Atlanta History* 38 (Winter 1995): 5–19; Henry Wheeler, *Methodism and the Temperance Reformation* (Cincinnati: Walden and Stowe, 1882), 45–100; and John Lee Eighmy, *Churches in Cultural Captivity: A History of the Social Attitudes of Southern Baptists* (Knoxville: University of Tennessee Press, 1987), 50.

13. Krout, chapter 9; Tyrrell, chapter 7; and Blocker, 39–47.

14. Blocker, 48–51; Thompson, 141–151; David M. Fahey, *Temperance and Racism: John Bull, Johnny Reb, and the Good Templars* (Lexington: University Press of Kentucky, 1996); David M. Fahey, "How the Good Templars Began: Fraternal Temperance in New York State," *Social History of Alcohol Review* 38–39 (1999): 17–27; Lynn Dumenil, *Freemasonry and American Culture, 1880–1930* (Princeton, NJ: Princeton University Press, 1984), 75–80; and Jed Dannenbaum, *Drink and Disorder: Temperance Reform in Cincinnati from the Washingtonian Revival to the WCTU* (Urbana: University of Illinois Press, 1984), chapter 2.

15. Thompson, 20.

16. Pegram, 31–42; Tyrrell, chapter 9; Douglas W. Carlson, "Temperance Reform in the Cotton Kingdom" (PhD diss., University of Illinois at Urbana-Champaign, 1982); Joe L. Coker, *Liquor in the Land of the Lost Cause: Southern White Evangelicals and the Prohibition Movement* (Lexington: University Press of Kentucky, 2007), 25–32; Dannenbaum, chapters 3 and 4; Ian Tyrrell, "Drink and Temperance in the Antebellum South: An Overview and Interpretation," *Journal of Southern History* 48 (November 1982): 485–510; and Allen P. Tankersley, "Basil Hallam Overby: Champion of Prohibition in Ante Bellum Georgia," *Georgia Historical Quarterly* 31 (March 1947): 1–18.

17. Graham Warder, "Selling Sobriety: How Temperance Reshaped Culture in Antebellum America" (PhD diss., University of Massachusetts-Amherst, 2000), chapter 1.

18. Warder, chapters 2–5; John B. Gough, *An Autobiography* (Boston: the author, 1845); David S. Reynolds and Debra J. Rosenthal, eds., *The Serpent in the Cup: Temperance in American Literature* (Amherst: University of Massachusetts Press, 1997); Robert S. Levine, "Disturbing Boundaries: Temperance, Black Elevation, and Violence in Frank J. Webb's *The Garies and Their Friends*," *Prospects: An Annual of American Cultural Studies* 19 (1994): 349–374; and Shelley Block, "A Revolutionary Aim: The Rhetoric of Temperance in the Anglo-African Magazine," *American Periodicals* 12 (2002): 9–24.

19. Warder, chapters 6 and 7; William Gleason, "*Ten Nights in a Bar-Room* and the Visual Culture of Temperance," in *Must Read: Rediscovering American Bestsellers*, eds. Sarah Churchwell and Thomas Ruys Smith, 101–130 (New York: Continuum, 2012).

20. William M. Robinson Jr., "Prohibition in the Confederacy," *American Historical Review* 37 (October 1931): 50–58.

21. Pegram, 45–46; and Richard C. Lancaster, *Serving the U.S. Armed Forces, 1861–1986: The Story of the YMCA's Ministry to Military Personnel for 125 years* (Schaumburg, IL: Armed Forces YMCA of the USA, 1987).

22. Edwin B. Lufkin, *History of the 13th Maine Regiment from its organization in 1861 to its muster-out in 1865* (Bridgton, ME: H. A. Shorey, 1898); and Norman H. Clark, *Deliver Us from Evil: An Interpretation of American Prohibition* (New York: W. W. Norton, 1976), 4.

23. Blocker, 73.

24. Thompson, 99–107.

25. Blocker, 86–87; David Leigh Colvin, *Prohibition in the United States: A History of the Prohibition Party and of the Prohibition Movement* (New York: George H. Doran, 1926); and Lisa M. F. Andersen, *The Politics of Prohibition: American Governance and the Prohibition Party, 1869–1933* (New York: University of Cambridge Press, 2013).

26. Jack S. Blocker Jr., "*Give to the Winds Thy Fears*": *The Women's Temperance Crusade, 1873–1874* (Westport, CT: Greenwood Press, 1985); Jed Dannenbaum, "The Origins of Temperance Activism and Militancy Among American Women," *Journal of Social History* 15.2 (Winter 1981): 235–252; Frances Willard, *Woman and Temperance, or, The Work and Workers of the Woman's Christian Temperance Union* (Hartford, CT: Park Publishing, 1883); Ruth Bordin, *Woman and Temperance: The Quest for Power and Liberty, 1873–1900* (Philadelphia: Temple University Press, 1981);

Edward J. Blum, *Reforging the White Republic: Race, Religion, and American Nationalism, 1865–1898* (Baton Rouge: Louisiana State University Press, 2005), chapter 6; Ruth Bordin, *Frances Willard: A Biography* (Chapel Hill: University of North Carolina Press, 1986); James Ross Turner, "The American Prohibition Movement, 1865–1897" (PhD diss., University of Wisconsin, 1972); and Jonathan Zimmerman, *Distilling Democracy: Alcohol Education in America's Public Schools, 1880–1925* (Lawrence: University of Kansas Press, 1999): Thompson, 99–116.

27. Blocker, *American Temperance Movements*, 86–89; John M. Palmer, "An Apology for Party Prohibition," *AME Church Review* 4 (October 1887): 136–153; and J. Sampson, "The Prohibition Party," *AME Church Review* 4 (July 1887): 506–507.

28. Rufus B. Spain, *At Ease in Zion: A Social History of Southern Baptists, 1865–1900* (Tuscaloosa: University of Alabama Press, 2003); Ted Ownby, *Subduing Satan: Religion, Recreation, & Manhood in the Rural South, 1865–1920* (Chapel Hill: University of North Carolina Press, 1990); Paul Harvey, *Redeeming the South: Religious Cultures and Racial Identities among Southern Baptists, 1865–1925* (Chapel Hill: University of North Carolina Press, 1997); Hunter Dickinson Farish, *The Circuit Rider Dismounts: A Social History of Southern Methodism, 1865–1900* (Richmond, VA: Dietz Press, 1938); and Thompson, 75–81, 129–138.

29. Blocker, *American Temperance Movements*, 89–90; Thompson, 155–248; Paul E. Isaac, *Prohibition and Politics: Turbulent Decades in Tennessee, 1885–1920* (Knoxville: University of Tennessee Press, 1965); James D. Ivy, *No Saloon in the Valley: The Southern Strategy of Texas Prohibitionists in the 1880s* (Waco, TX: Baylor University Press, 2003); John Hammond Moore, "The Negro and Prohibition in Atlanta, 1885–1887," *South Atlantic Quarterly* 69 (Winter 1970): 38–57; and Gregg Cantrell, "'Dark Tactics': Black Politics in the 1887 Texas Prohibition Campaign," *Journal of American Studies* 25 (1991): 85–93.

30. Michael A. Homan and Mark A. Gstohl, "Jesus the Teetotaler: How Dr. Welch Put the Lord on the Wagon," *Bible Review* (April 2002), 28–29. Retrieved from http://www.basarchive.org/bswbBrowse.asp?PubID=BSBR&Volume=18&Issue=2&ArticleID=6.

31. Jack S. Blocker Jr., *Retreat from Reform: The Prohibition Movement in the United States, 1890–1913* (Westport, CT: Greenwood Press, 1976).

32. Perry R. Duis, *The Saloon: Public Drinking in Chicago and Boston, 1880–1920* (Urbana: University of Illinois Press, 1983); Madelon Powers, *Faces Along the Bar: Lore and Order in the Workingman's Saloon, 1870–1920* (Chicago: University of Chicago Press, 1998); and Roy Rosenzweig, *Eight Hours for What We Will: Workers and Leisure in an Industrial City, 1870–1920* (New York: Cambridge University Press, 1983).

33. James A. Morone, *Hellfire Nation: The Politics of Sin in American History* (New Haven, CT: Yale University Press, 2003), chapter 10; and Lisa McGirr, *The War on Alcohol: Prohibition and the Rise of the American State* (New York: W. W. Norton, 2016), chapter 1.

34. Coker, chapter 6; Denise A. Herd, "Prohibition, Racism and Class Politics in the Post-Reconstruction South," *Journal of Drug Issues* 13 (1983): 77–94; Haynes Walton Jr., "Another Force for Disfranchisement: Blacks and the Prohibitionists in Tennessee," *Journal of Human Relations* 18 (1970): 728–738; Haynes Walton Jr. and James E. Taylor, "Blacks and the Southern Prohibition Movement," *Phylon* 32 (1972): 247–259; Dewey Grantham, *Southern Progressivism: The Reconciliation of Progress and Tradition* (Knoxville: University of Tennessee Press, 1983); Jack Temple Kirby, *Darkness at the Dawning: Race and Reform in the Progressive South* (Philadelphia: J. P. Lippincott, 1972); and William A. Link, *The Paradox of Southern Progressivism* (Chapel Hill: University of North Carolina Press, 1992), chapters 2 and 4.

35. Blocker, *American Temperance Movement*, 112–113; and Lisa McGirr, chapter 1.

36. Pegram, 109–165; Peter H. Odegard, *Pressure Politics: The Story of the Anti-Saloon League* (New York: Columbia University Press, 1928); K. Austin Kerr, *Organized for Prohibition: A New History of the Anti-Saloon League* (New Haven, CT: Yale University Press, 1985); James H. Timberlake, *Prohibition and The Progressive Movement, 1900–1920* (Cambridge, MA: Harvard University Press, 1963), chapter 5; and McGirr, chapter 1.

37. McGirr, 125–129; Blocker, *American Temperance Movements*, 122–123; www.wctu.org; Catherine Gilbert Mudock, *Domesticating Drink: Women, Men, and Alcohol in America, 1870–1940* (Baltimore: Johns Hopkins University Press, 1998),

chapter 6; and David E. Kyvig, *Repealing National Prohibition*, 2d ed. (Kent, OH: Kent State University Press, 2000).

38. Andersen, chapter 7; www.prohibitionparty.org.
39. Morone, 328.
40. McGirr, 196.
41. McGirr, chapter 7.
42. McGirr, 212; and Morone, 343.
43. McGirr, chapters 3, 5, 6, 7; Morone, chapter 11; Daniel Okrent, *Last Call: The Rise and Fall of Prohibition* (New York: Scribner, 2010), chapters 16 and 17. For an example of problems under state prohibition before national prohibition, see Adam Krakowski, *Vermont Prohibition: Teetotalers, Bootleggers and Corruption* (Charleston, SC: The American Palate, 2016).
44. Blocker, *American Temperance Movements*, 119–127; Kerr, chapter 9; and Pegram, chapter 7.
45. Joseph Gusfield, *Symbolic Crusade: Status Politics and the American Temperance Movement* (Urbana: University of Illinois Press, 1963), 5.
46. Ronald G. Walters, *American Reformers, 1815–1860*, rev. ed. (New York: Hill and Wang, 1997), 31–33.

H. Paul Thompson Jr.

PROSTITUTES AND PROSTITUTION IN AMERICA

As the American economy moved from a local agrarian economy to a cash-based wage labor economy over the course of the long 19th century (1770–1920), prostitution became more visible in American cities, especially near American military installations and in places where large numbers of male laborers were concentrated. Women's intimate labor increasingly became monetized, used as a source of profit, as men's labor became something to be sold for wages in the labor market and more men migrated to sell their labor. Historians of women and sexual labor have noted the irony that police, moralists, and medical professionals have historically treated women who sell sex as a distinct category of women, but the data these professionals gathered revealed that the prostitute lived "very much like most other women," with the important distinction that she sold her intimate labor on the open market whereas most women reserved their intimate labor for their husbands.[1] The concept of intimate labor covers many types of care labor, ranging from keeping the home, preparing food, and caring for children and the elderly to sexual labor, and as an analytic category, intimate labor sheds important light on the history of prostitution in America.[2] As historian Susan Lee Johnson observes about male miners and laborers flocking to Gold Rush California, "men purchased proximity to women" as much as they purchased individual sex acts.[3] With this insight in mind, the flourishing of prostitution in America in the 19th century resulted from migrant men's loneliness, the sexual division of labor that kept women's wages artificially low yet also feminized care labor, and the large-scale social disruptions caused by the growth of global capitalism.

This article focuses primarily on the woman who sold sex, not because men did not sell sex, but because commentators almost always imagined the figure of the prostitute as female; the prevalence of female prostitution emerged out of the sex segregated labor market that offered women few opportunities to make money, and the policing of prostitution primarily targeted girls and women. Moreover, the historical scholarship on male prostitution remains underdeveloped.[4] In this article I use the phrases "women who worked as prostitutes," "women who sold sex," and sometimes "prostitute women" instead of "prostitute" for several reasons: to frame prostitution as an occupational category as much as a lifestyle category; to distinguish "between doing prostitution and being a prostitute"; and to highlight the choices (and sometimes coercion) women faced in the past.[5]

EMERGING SEX MARKETS DURING THE COLONIAL ERA AND THE 18TH CENTURY

During the colonial period, prostitution in the British colonies that would become the United States remained relatively rare. Crowded housing and close surveillance of family members, servants, and slaves limited the commercialization of sex in most communities. Only in seaport towns that hosted large numbers of sailors, visitors, and displaced youth have historians located a trade in sex.[6] Seaport towns such as Boston and New Amsterdam hosted some women who sold sex in the 17th century. In Massachusetts in the winter of 1671–1672 a widow named Alice Thomas faced charges of giving "frequent secret and vnseasonable [sic] Entertainment in her house to Lewd Lascivious & notorious persons of both Sexes, giving them opportunity to commit carnall wickedness, & that by common fame she is a common Bawd." The court convicted her and ordered that she be fined, whipped, and imprisoned. By October the court had released her and ordered her expelled from Boston, though the city readmitted her a year later, in 1673, after she donated a considerable amount of money for the construction of a sea wall for Boston's harbor.[7] Nevertheless, cases such as Thomas's remained rare in early colonial America—a time when marriage was almost universal and community surveillance pervasive.

The amount of colonial prostitution grew in the 1750s due to several factors: the increase in maritime trade that brought more sailors and merchants to seaport cities, the mobilization of soldiers to fight in the French and Indian Wars, and growing incidents of poverty and war refugees. In Boston and New York, female camp followers offered warm meals, laundry services, and sometimes sex to soldiers. Widows and young women refugees congregated in cities where they occupied the lower echelons of the service economy, walking the streets or selling their services in the bawdy houses of New York, Philadelphia, Boston, and Charleston. Men and women of all races gathered in the bawdy houses to celebrate "sexual license, male rowdiness and *bonhomie*" and to engage in "drinking and dancing."[8]

The widespread incidence of bastardy, adultery, fornication, and bigamy contributed to an urban culture that also tolerated commercial sex from the 1750s through the revolutionary period in Philadelphia, a city with a growing libertine reputation. Between 1759 and the start of the American Revolution in April 1775 the courts only prosecuted three women for prostitution-related crimes; all three were charged with keeping a bawdy house.[9] Surviving court records from the city only note prostitution when it was connected to other criminal offenses. Thus, from the 1760s onward prostitution flourished in the city of brotherly love.[10] Men of all classes participated in the emerging pleasure culture. Sailors had long constituted the primary customers along the waterfront, but sons of the city's leading citizens also took part in the sexual commerce of the city.[11] Samuel Coates sent a letter to William Logan, then in England, outlining the activities of twelve sons of the most prominent Quaker families. These young men purchased sexual favors, spent time gambling, and imbibed drink. One young man, he wrote, "is said to give a Girl £50 to strip Stark naked before him."[12] The growing consumer culture that encouraged young people of mid-18th-century America to value choice, taste, and personal happiness also encouraged young men—including elites—to seek their pleasure in sex markets, even as they considered the ideas that would lead to the fight for political independence.

Soldiers in the Continental Army, far from their home communities and moral watchdogs, soon encountered numerous opportunities for vice. As early as June 1775, Continental Army officials banned women who sold or bartered sex from camp. While encamped in New York City in May the following year, Colonel Alexander McDougal proclaimed, "No Woman of Ill Fame Shall be permitted to Come into the Barricks on pain of Being well Watred under a pump, and Every Officer or Soldier who Shall Bring in Any Such woman will be tryd and Punished by a Court Martial." Despite such orders, New York City hosted numerous commercial establishments where a soldier might purchase sex from "horrid Wretches."[13] Rumors of the sexual licentiousness of the army spread. John Adams noted in 1777, "The prevalence of dissipation, debauchery, gambling, profaneness, and blasphemy terrifies the best people upon the continent from trusting their sons and other relations among so many dangerous snares and temptations."[14] Chief among these temptations was the lure of female camp followers who provided a menu of what historians would later call intimate labor, selling or bartering sex even as they performed essential laundry and cooking services.[15] For example, a junior infantry officer named Benjamin Gilbert admitted in a letter that he and his fellow officers had enjoyed "the girls" in a "seraglio," or brothel, located in New Windsor, New York, near where the Continental Army wintered in 1782–1783.[16] In spite of the occasional orders barring lewd women from camp, court-martials against women who sold sex remained rare occurrences. As historian Holly A. Mayer notes, the men of the Continental Army rarely had any money to exchange for sex, and consequently women looking to earn money by selling sex were more likely to approach British officers holed up in colonial cities such as Boston, New York City, and Philadelphia.[17]

The Revolution ushered in a topsy-turvy sexual culture of license where behaviors that constituted serious crimes before the war became tolerable during and after it. The Lockean values of autonomy, independence, liberty, equality, and personal freedom that gave rise to the Revolution also encouraged the continued growth of the sexually libertine urban culture of Philadelphia. By the 1790s, foreign visitors to Philadelphia frequently commented on both the prevalence and visibility of prostitution. Moreau de Saint-Méry noted that "Houses of Ill Fame" had "multiplied in Philadelphia" and were "frequented at all hours." One young Brazilian commented, "The prostitutes of Philadelphia are so many that they flood the streets at night, in such a way that even looking at them in the streets without men you can recognize them."[18] The city's permissive sexual culture flourished as young

men flocked to the city looking for sexual adventure in its bawdy houses and taverns. As historian Clare A. Lyons argues, at this moment between the late colonial period and the 19th century, "prostitution took its most fluid and least exploitative form."[19] For example, city officials knew of women who sold sex in Philadelphia, yet they rarely incarcerated them. Similarly, bawdy houses served as public spaces where people met with associates and friends. Transactional sex, whether for money or gifts, was woven into the fabric of Philadelphia's sexually permissive recreational culture in the 1790s.

The sexual chaos of the post-Revolutionary War period, evidenced by Philadelphia's sexually libertine culture, produced anxieties among the elite, who saw the sexual independence of women as threatening to the new republic, worried about the rising numbers of bastards, and saw sexual licentiousness as undermining notions of the virtuous republican citizen. The print culture of the early national period reduced all nonmarital sex—seduction, fornication, adultery—to prostitution and then suggested that prostitution led to poverty.[20] Reducing all of the concerns about a libertine sexual culture to merely a problem of women's prostitution encouraged an association of sexual chaos with lower-class women on the one hand, and provided a rationale for city fathers to criminalize behaviors they associated with prostitution on the other hand.

In the crackdown on sexuality that occurred in some cities after the 1790s, vagrancy laws emerged as a key means to police women who sold sex. As a status crime—a crime committed by simply being a vagrant—vagrancy charges allowed for the criminalization of women who sold sex without the difficulty of proving that sex had been exchanged for money. In the late 1790s and early 1800s, Philadelphia courts described women charged with vagrancy using evocative, criminalizing phrases. Courts described Nancy Summers as "a disorderly vagrant having no means of making a living but by prostitution"; Margaret Miller as "a common and abandoned prostitute"; and Martha Patterson as "an idle dissolute person and common street walker."[21] Similarly, in Massachusetts, a 1797 grand jury indicted Elizabeth Finney, a Cambridge widow, of owning a disorderly house, "one resorted to for the purposes of Prostitution & Lewdness," and permitting individuals "to be and remain drinking[,] tippling[,] whoring[,] and misbehaving themselves[,]... to the great injury of good morals and the rules of chastity—in evil example to others to offend in like manner and against the peace and dignity of the Commonwealth aforesaid." The court issued a sixty dollar fine and sent her to a house of corrections for three months. But more significantly, her case was the first in Massachusetts to use the word "prostitution" to describe her crime.[22] By the 1810s, criminal prosecutions for prostitution began to overtake vagrancy arrests. Accompanying this development was the related trend of arresting women who ran bawdy houses and brothels, thus identifying prostitution as a specific form of criminal sex whose distribution network needed to be curbed.[23] More commonly, when city dwellers in Philadelphia or elsewhere grew weary of specific brothels, they rioted against the establishments. A mob wrecked the notorious China Factory in Philadelphia's Southwark neighborhood in 1800, pulling it down brick by brick.[24] Legal campaigns against prostitution between 1800 and 1820 functioned to mark lower-class women's sexual commerce as criminally deviant; night watchmen never dragged male customers through city streets.[25]

(SEX) MARKET REVOLUTION, 1820–1920

The era of the early republic ushered in a new bourgeois gender ideology that shaped the gender relations of women of all classes and framed the ways that prostitution would be interpreted in the 19th century. This gender ideology asserted that men and women occupied separate, yet complementary, spheres.

Men would engage in the public sphere of politics, law, commerce, and competition, while women would reign over the private sphere of domesticity, child rearing and education, and familial spiritual guidance. The ideology of separate spheres developed in tandem with the emerging market revolution that placed new emphasis on a cash-based economy and the centrality of male "breadwinning" wages to a family's survival. Yet, as Jeanne Boydston has shown, in the economically capricious times of the mid-19th century when more and more men left family farms and started working for wages, a family's survival required the unpaid labor of the wife. Nevertheless, within this ideology, women's domestic labor became reconfigured and sentimentalized. Women supposedly cared for the household and the children because that care labor was divinely sanctioned and the product of love rather than market forces. Of course, most middle-class families employed female domestic servants to aid with the household labor. These wage-earning women often came from immigrant communities and earned very low wages. They existed outside of the idealized gender system, even as their labor helped to propel this ideology. Ideal women were thought to be pious, sexually chaste before marriage and faithful after marriage, submissive to male authority, and domestic.[26] The separate spheres ideology idealized the asexual, domestic middle-class woman while simultaneously institutionalizing women's dependency on husbands and fathers. It also justified paying women low wages since women worked for "pin" money while men worked to support families.

Within this gender ideology, the figure of the prostitute stood in opposition to the ideal woman. Whereas the ideal woman was asexual, domestic (of the home), and economically dependent on male family members, the woman who sold sex seemed dangerously sexual, public (of the streets), and economically independent of male family members. Yet the figures of the ideal woman and the common prostitute remained tied together under the rubric of separate spheres by the idea of "ruin." Under the middle-class separate spheres ideology, a sexually promiscuous daughter lost her position within the marriage market (because her reputation was ruined, she would never be a suitable bride). After the crackdowns on the vibrant sexual cultures of the revolutionary era, popular understandings of prostitution promulgated by middle-class moralists functioned to collapse all forms of nonconjugal female sexuality (seduction, fornication, adultery, and often rape) into prostitution. Thus, according to middle-class commentators, "ruined" daughters had destroyed their opportunities for marriage and respectable work and would likely become prostitutes. Yet working-class families had an alternative understanding of "ruin." For them, any family or economic tragedy could and did lead their daughters to ruin—to selling sex in the city's sexual marketplaces.[27]

America's sexual marketplaces provided plenty of labor opportunities for these girls. Public, semi-tolerated prostitution expanded in the 1830s, increased further in the 1850s, peaked in the post-Civil War period, and began a slow decline in the early 20th century.[28] The growth of prostitution in the 19th century accompanied the expansion of commercialized sex within an urban, libertine sporting culture that encompassed the sporting press and pornography, bawdy houses and concert saloons, "model artists" striptease shows, picking up "harlots" on the way to the theater, as well as purchasing sex. This sporting culture developed to serve the large numbers of young men that moved to cities for work as apprentices, clerks, and laborers of all types. From the 1830s onward these young men postponed marriage but not sex, which they purchased. At the same time, more and more married men visited bawdy houses and brothels, thereby joining a "male sexual fraternity."[29] The changes that the commercialization of sex wrought were noticeable and jarring to many. William Sanger, a New York City physician, declared that prostitution "no longer confines itself to secrecy and darkness, but boldly strides through

our most thronged and elegant thoroughfares, and there, in the broad light of the sun, it jostles the pure, the virtuous, and the good. It is in your gay streets and in your quiet, home-like streets; it is in your squares…and summer resorts; it is in your theaters, your opera, your hotels."[30] By the eve of the Civil War, New Yorker George Ellington admitted that most "fashionable bloods and old fogies, known rakes, and presumably pious people, wealthy bachelors and respectable married men, fast sons and moral husbands" bought sex.[31] With the rising visibility of commercial sex, more men did seem eager to purchase sexual services.[32]

The economic precariousness of 19th-century life, characterized by dramatic booms and busts as the United States transitioned into a fully industrialized economy, combined with the gender segmentation of the labor market that paid women little for their labor, contributed to the growth of commercial sex in the United States, fueled by an expanded pool of female workers. Physician William Sanger interviewed 2,000 women arrested for prostitution and held in New York City's Blackwell Prison in 1855. The general profile that emerges from Sanger's research indicates that the New York City woman who sold sex was young, came from an impoverished working-class family, and had experienced some type of economic or personal familial upheaval.[33] He found that low wages contributed to women's participation in the sex trade. Indeed, "a large number of females," he wrote, "earn so small wages that a temporary cessation of their business or being a short time out of a situation, is sufficient to reduce them to absolute distress."[34] Of the 2,000 women he interviewed, 500 had worked in manufacturing—usually the needle trades—and 300 still had employment but had turned to the sex trade to supplement their income. Half of the women earned less than three dollars a week and a quarter of them earned a dollar or less a week.[35] The majority of Sanger's subjects had come from domestic service, the most common, most low paid, and most demanding form of female labor. Similarly, government statistician Carroll Wright, who investigated brothel-based prostitution in Boston in 1884, found that 60 percent of the inhabitants had previously worked in domestic or restaurant/hotel work as maids.[36] Put simply, laboring in the sex trade paid considerably better wages than laboring elsewhere.[37] Sanger calculated that most women who sold sex in New York City earned between ten and fifty dollars a week depending on the class of customer they serviced.[38] The sex trade often provided a temporary option for women struggling to make ends meet. Over three-quarters of Philadelphia's women who sold sex also worked jobs in manufacturing or domestic labor and casually moved in and out of the sexual marketplace until they married.[39]

Sex could be purchased in a wide array of locations within American cities, ranging from the alleys near theater districts, houses of assignation and tenement houses, bawdy houses and saloons in working-class and increasingly immigrant neighborhoods, to elegant brothels. A woman who sold sex on the street worked independently and often quite casually; she had no pimp. Frequently, these women would take their clients to houses of assignation where rooms could be rented by the hour.[40] Brothels ranged from dirty, noxious affairs to luxurious abodes, and by the mid-19th century they could be found fully integrated into many of America's urban landscapes, as indicated by the "gentleman's guides" visitors could buy to find brothels that catered to their tastes.[41]

Though brothels were integrated into their neighborhoods, they could become the target of mob violence in the form of brothel riots. As we have seen, some communities turned to mob violence to destroy brothels whose presence they opposed, often destroying all the furniture and occasionally the building. These rioters, active from the 1780s to the 1820s, typically targeted property, not people.[42] The 1830s emerged as the decade of brothel riot: 60 percent of the riots in New York City between 1830 and 1860 took place in the 1830s.[43] The targets of this violence shifted to include

assaults on madams and women who sold sex, in addition to property destruction. Young men (of whom 80 percent were laborers, 19 percent skilled artisans, and 1 percent semi-skilled workers) would get drunk and go on sprees where they would move as a gang from a saloon to a brothel to another brothel, demanding food, drinks, and generally exhibiting all sorts of obnoxious and violent behavior. Most of the men attacked brothels in their own ward, or a neighboring ward. As historian Timothy Gilfoyle contends, "the brothel riot promoted male sexual supremacy."[44] The young rioters did not make enough money to purchase sex in the tony brothels of New York, but they could invade these spaces under the ruse that they sought to buy drinks or food. The sprees and riots expressed their frustration at not having the means to access "public" women while demonstrating their superiority by forcing the women to serve them and casually deploying violence. "They were contemptuous vandals," writes historian Patricia Cline Cohen, "there to remind women of the ultimate power men have over them by sheer physical force and intimidation."[45]

Though the rising visibility of brothels and prostitution provoked some opposition, most mid-century Americans accepted the presence of prostitution as a type of inevitability, and perhaps a necessary evil—necessary because prostitution was thought to protect respectable women by drawing men's rampant sexual energy away from decent women toward the brothel, where it could be expended safely. This interpretation of prostitution harked back to the Augustinian adage that prostitution worked as a type of cesspool for the city. "The brothel in the city," wrote Francisco Farfan in 1585, "is like the stable or latrine for the house. Because just as the city keeps itself clean by providing a separate place where filth and dung are gathered, etc., so neither less nor more, assuming the dissolution of the flesh, acts the brothel: where the filth and ugliness of the flesh are gathered like the garbage and dung of the city."[46] This line of thinking, which tended to be more prominent in Catholic countries, still justified a mild toleration of prostitution in the United States in the 19th century.[47] By the end of the century, even anti-prostitution reformers such as A. Prince Morrow would still utter: "Prostitution is inherent in the human race; it cannot be annihilated, it is a necessary evil in our social system."[48]

Southern cities saw a slower rate of growth in sex markets because the region's urban development lagged behind that of the North. Before the Civil War, poor white women constituted most of the women who sold sex in underground taverns or brothels in Southern cities.[49] The systemic sexual exploitation of enslaved black women lessened the market for African American sex workers, because slave owners and others could easily coerce or demand sex from enslaved women. Courts in North Carolina sought to control prostitution rather than eradicate it. They especially sought to limit opportunities for interracial sex at taverns where blacks and whites could intermingle promiscuously. Southern courts left alone white women who sold sex to white men. These women seem to have lived on the margins of respectable town life where they resided in female-headed households, mothered illegitimate children, and ran illegal taverns. Common wisdom held that their presence protected respectable white women by drawing the lusty attentions of demanding men.[50] In Richmond, Virginia, the city that created the first police force in the United States, the police tolerated brothels and taverns in the 1830s and showed little concern about interracial mingling among free people of color and poor whites. Only crimes incidental to sites of prostitution—public drunkenness and fighting—drew the attention of the authorities.[51] Yet, as the sectional crises of the 1850s worsened, and Southern white elites grew more concerned about the Underground Railroad, abolitionists, and the presence of free blacks, Richmond city officials cracked down on interracial social spaces. In 1854, Richmond's mayor fined Jane Wright, a white woman, "for

keeping a disorderly and ill-governed house… where people of every sex and color congregate and associate by day and night."[52] After Wright refused to close her house, a mob destroyed it; but white-only spaces of sexual commerce in Southern cities thrived in the 1850s. The mayor of Savannah believed that for every thirty-nine men in his city, one white woman worked in the sex trade, and he estimated the ratio in Norfolk to be twenty-six to one.[53]

Southern cities also gave rise to sexual marketplaces that were entangled with slave markets. The system of racial slavery that structured Southern life rested on a foundation of violence and sexual exploitation of enslaved black bodies. Southern slave owners purchased some enslaved women for the explicit purpose of providing sexual companionship to their owners. John Williams, a prominent white resident of New Orleans in his forties, purchased Louisa Picquet, a mixed-race girl of fourteen years of age, for $1,500. "Mr. Williams told me what he bought me for," she wrote. "He said he was getting old, and he saw me he thought he'd buy me, and end his days with me. He said if I behave myself, he'd treat me well: but, if not, he'd whip me almost to death."[54] Cases like this one pose numerous conceptual problems for historians of sexual commerce. Unlike most cases of transactional sex, assumed to be a one-time exchange of sex for money, the purchase of enslaved women for concubinage was a relationship of a considerably greater period of time and sustained violence.[55] Yet the sexual, affective, and care labor was similar, as was the monetization of that labor, as evidenced in the high price Williams paid for Picquet.[56] Young, mixed-race, enslaved women and girls who constituted the fancy girl trade became some of the most valuable enslaved people in the South: slave traders sold young women such as Picquet, who appealed to white men's sexual desires for their sexual services in their own homes, to individuals such as John Williams. The New Orleans slave market became the premier outlet for this specialized luxury trade.[57]

Enslaved sex workers could also be found in brothels in Southern seaport cities. Fanny Hill's "house of ill fame" in Galveston, Texas, employed free white women and enslaved black women.[58] New Orleans housed numerous brothels that employed enslaved women who either sold sex to customers or managed the selling of sex within the brothel. For example, in 1851 Eliza Turner, an enslaved woman, allowed Abraham Parker entry into the brothel she managed. Parker paid Turner $2.50 so that he could visit a white woman, Eliza Philips. The fact that an enslaved woman managed the sexual labor of a free white woman seems to have gone unquestioned.[59] Enslaved women who worked in brothels sold their affective and sexual labor to white men for a limited amount of time and collected fees on behalf of their owners. Essentially, slave owners hired them out as skilled workers into the racialized sex market. Historians who seek to discover the agency exercised by enslaved people have tended to interpret enslaved women's employment in brothels as evidence of opportunity; for example, writing about brothel prostitution in Galveston, Robert Shelton asserts, "in situations where they had some authority to negotiate the sexual exploitation as a commodity exchange they perhaps were better off than enslaved women abused and raped by libidinous masters."[60] Yet it is unclear just how much negotiating power an enslaved woman would really have.[61] As Marisa J. Fuentas contends, "The brothel cannot be imagined as a space where enslaved women were empowered by the mode of (sexual) production outside the constraints of the system of slavery."[62]

The Civil War dramatically disrupted the sexual marketplaces of the South as the social disruption caused by the war concentrated soldiers in single locales and brought more desperate women into the trade. Union-occupied cities such as Norfolk, New Orleans, St. Louis, Memphis, and Nashville offered Union commanders numerous challenges to maintaining order: soldiers were flush with cash, free from the dread of the battlefield, and excited to take part in each city's recreational offerings.[63] A Union soldier stationed in occupied Richmond, Virginia, noted that the women "damnyankee us on the street in the daytime, but at night the skirts come up for the good yankee gold."[64] Both behaviors constituted a challenge to occupying Union forces. Commander Benjamin Butler grew so frustrated at the "damnyankee" and other insults that the white women of New Orleans hurled at Union soldiers that he issued General Order No. 28, known as the Woman Order, which proclaimed that any woman who insulted Union forces would be treated as a public woman (prostitute).[65] The Order equated disloyalty to the Union with the disrepute of prostitution. Women who publicly expressed political opinions became subject to the policing that women who sold sex experienced.[66] But the skirts coming up for Yankee gold presented the most serious challenge to Union commanders.

Prostitution posed a problem for occupying military forces for two reasons. Firstly, men who purchased sex often did so while engaging in a wide array of dissolute behaviors such as public drinking that harmed the reputation of Union forces occupying hostile Southern cities.[67] Secondly, prostitution facilitated the spread of venereal diseases that undermined the military readiness of troops. Union commanders approached these challenges in varying and contradictory ways. When Union troops imposed martial law in St. Louis in August 1861, Provost Marshal McKinistry instituted a policy to suppress prostitution. He aimed to do this by prohibiting the sale of hard spirits and forbidding soldiers from frequenting "low" saloons where women who sold sex could be found.[68] After enforcement proved to be predictably difficult, he expanded the order to restrict soldiers' access to saloons that also served as boardinghouses. McKinistry was trying to decouple the selling of alcohol from the selling of sex, a task bound to fail in the thriving urban metropolis of 100,000 citizens. Desperate, by September 26, 1861, he banished all women guilty of "vagrancy, lewdness, disorderly conduct and keeping brothels and houses of ill fame" from the city, solving the conundrum of how to separate the selling of alcohol from the selling of sex by simply banishing women who sold sex.[69]

When facing the same challenges, other Union commanders developed dramatically different policies. In Union-occupied Nashville, Union commanders legalized prostitution and required women who sold sex to purchase licenses, available only to women who had undergone medical exams that found them free of venereal disease. This experiment with regulated prostitution emerged out of concerns for the venereal health of Union soldiers, of whom between 6 and 9 percent sought treatment for their infections while enlisted.[70] In June 1863, Brigadier General R. S. Granger reported that he had been inundated with requests to "save the army from [venereal disease,] a fate worse...than to perish on the battlefield," by the medical professionals of Nashville.[71] Enacted in August 1863, within one year 456 white and 50 African American women had registered with Nashville officials. Officials in Memphis, in contrast, initially adopted a policy similar to the one in St. Louis after they encountered the same situation of disorderly behavior involving the entangled vices of alcohol and prostitution. One Union infantryman remembered Memphis as full of temptations: "Women and whiskey are plentiful here, and our men had been so long debarred from both that it did not take long for them to raise hell generally...[Women enter the camp] with their bodies strung round with whiskey under their clothes and sell themselves and a bottle for a dollar."[72] By the summer of 1862, Union officials were banishing lewd women from Memphis. Even so, clandestine prostitution flourished, and in the face of rising venereal disease rates Memphis officials shifted course in September 1864 and began to regulate prostitution as a strategy for gaining control of soldiers' disorderly conduct.[73] Both Nashville and Memphis ended their regulation schemes when the war ended. Both cases served as precedents for the US military turning to regulated prostitution as a solution to the problems posed by venereal disease rates. Yet the citizens of both cities decried the regulations as dangerously immoral and decadently European.[74]

After the Civil War, as American cities grew at ferocious rates, welcoming migrants from the countryside and abroad, prostitution became even more entrenched in urban landscapes. The migration and concentration of large numbers of male laborers—cowboys, miners, lumberjacks, and soldiers—in the trans-Mississippi West attracted large numbers of women willing to sell their intimate labor to the region. The mining boom towns, initiated by California's discovery of gold in 1848, produced dramatic sex imbalances. At the most extreme, in 1850 the white population of California was 90 percent male. More typically, in 1860 men made up 80 percent of the population of Walla Walla, Washington, and 59 percent of the population of Portland, Oregon.[75] In these towns, a scarcity of women—or an overpopulation of men who felt entitled to sex—combined with poorly paid jobs for women to lead to a situation in which women who sold or exchanged sex often outnumbered other women by as much as twenty-five to one in the early years.[76] The opportunities to make money in these early boom towns lured women who sold sex from all over the world to the mining towns of California, Nevada, Arizona, and so on. One man remembered, "To sit with you near the bar or a card table, a girl charges one ounce [of gold] an evening...and if you wanted anything more from these nymphs, you had to pay 15 to 20 ounces."[77]

As news of gold discoveries in California's Sacramento River spread, female sexual entrepreneurs quickly sought to get to California. Rosario Améstica boarded the *Stauelli* in Valparaiso, Chile, bound for California in December 1848. During the trip north, the "buxom and portly" woman privately entertained passengers who had known her in Concepción, Talca, and Valparaiso, sang "marvelous bawdy" songs on New Year's Eve, paraded "on deck like a ship of war in a steady tail wind," and by the time she arrived in San Francisco, "everyone on board had...dealings with her."[78] "Pretty French dancing girls" and Australian women also joined the migrant stream.[79] When San Francisco papers reported in December 1850 that two ships, carrying over 300 women, had dropped anchor, one miner scoffed, "Gads, what a rich cargo. They will be worth their weight in gold.... The imports of California are richer than the exports."[80] Japanese women migrated to the United States to sell sex to Japanese laborers and earn money to alleviate their families' poverty. Sixteen-year-old Saitō Yoshi migrated to Butte, Montana, in 1894 or 1895, to sell sex in a brothel. She regularly sent her earnings home to her father. A police investigator in her hometown of Yokohama reported that by 1896 her father "made a large fortune recently...and looks like a wealthy farmer."[81] Women also came to the towns of the booming West from the established sex markets of the United States. Mary Lee, whose real name was Mary Butler, entered the sex trade in New Orleans at Mistress Ann Wood's brothel. With news of the Gold Rush beckoning, she relocated to San Francisco, where probate court records reveal that she died in 1853, in possession of valuable clothes, jewelry, and $1,520 in cash. Another Denver madam, who came to Colorado in the 1870s and successfully ran a high-end brothel until 1919, told a newspaper reporter shortly before her death in 1929, "I went into the sporting life for business reasons and for no other. It was a way for a woman in those days to make money and I made it."[82]

The boom times faded quickly. Expensive, technologically sophisticated underground mining operations dominated by corporate or industrial concerns replaced surface mining. The timing of the shift from the self-employed to the wage-earning miner differed in each community; as early as 1852 most miners in California had become wage earners. As a result, the extravagant riches to be earned from commercial sex declined in the West, and most women who sold sex struggled economically.[83] The majority of women who sold sex in the American West were young and poor, and often women of color—Native American, Asian, Latina, and occasionally African American.[84] In 1860 in Sacramento, women of color constituted more than 75 percent of the city's prostitutes: Chinese women made up 56 percent, Latinas about 15 percent, and African Americans only 5 percent of the total.[85] The sex marketplace became stratified along racial, ethnic, and class lines, often defined by the race and class of the customer as well as the woman and reflected in the geography of individual towns.[86] At the bottom rung, measured by price of sex act, were Native American women.[87] Latino women from Mexico, Panama, and Chile, who worked in cantinas and fandango parlors, found themselves ghettoized and forced to accept lower prices than European American women. In San Francisco, city officials confined these *greaseritas* to Little Chile. Chinese and Japanese women were also geographically segregated.[88] A retired US Army major, Clarence W. Kellogg, touring California mining camps in 1854 noted that "under no circumstances were these [Chinese] women ever permitted to ply their trade except within the confines of Camp Chinatown where their domiciles were the crudest of shacks, but called 'Fancy Houses.'"[89] As elsewhere, white women who sold sex in the West enjoyed the highest status, yet contrary to popular images of prosperous madams, most failed to overcome the poverty that had driven them into prostitution in the first place.[90]

A system of transnational sex trafficking developed in the West to bring Chinese women to the United States between 1854 to 1925; most came from Hong Kong, Canton, and the surrounding areas, and most worked in the sex trades. Kellogg described the Chinese women as "the unwanted, poorest, and slave class, of the lowest valuation...dolled up as painted beauties and prostituted to all kinds of men (yellow and white alike) at a cheap price."[91] The clear majority of Chinese women in

California worked in brothels: "85 to 97 percent in 1860; 71 to 72 percent in 1870; and 21 to 50 percent in 1880."[92] Organized trafficking networks run by transnational tongs brought women to the United States through a combination of kidnapping, debt bondage, and indenture. One woman recalled in 1892, "I was kidnapped in China and brought over here [eighteen months ago]. The man who kidnapped me sold me for four hundred dollars to a San Francisco slave-dealer; and he sold me for seventeen hundred dollars. I have been a brothel slave ever since."[93] Yet traffickers only needed to find desperately poor parents in China willing to sell their daughters for as little as fifty dollars. In the 1870s, Chinese girls could be resold in California for as much as $1,000.[94] Women who came to the United States this way suffered a form of debt bondage: they had to work off either an indenture or the cost of their purchase and their maintenance. The Hip-Yee Tong conveyed 6,000 women from 1862 to 1873, which accounted for 87 percent of all Chinese women arriving in California during that period.[95] The conditions of their bondage could vary, depending on location (San Francisco or a frontier mining town) and clientele (Chinese or Chinese and white). The higher-class Chinese brothels served only Chinese clientele, whereas lower-class facilities would serve low-class Chinese laborers and whites for the low fee of twenty-five to fifty cents. Lower fees meant that a bonded laborer had to work for a longer period of time to free herself from debt.[96] The high visibility of Chinese sex trafficking and debt bondage prompted white Protestant missionaries to launch rescue societies to redeem Chinese women and fueled nativist campaigns to limit Chinese immigration to the United States.[97] By 1875, these campaigns resulted in the Page Act, which prohibited the importation of Asian women for the "purposes of prostitution." This law forged the foundation of US policy against sex trafficking and prostitution, even as it ensured that foreign-born women who sold sex would be seen as a threat to the United States.[98]

During the 19th century, cities struggled to manage flourishing commercial sex districts using a combination of suppression, regulation, and toleration. Few cities had the will to challenge the sexual fraternity of men that demanded the right to purchase sex or the power of the many vested interests that profited from the vice trade (landlords, doctors, bellboys, corrupt police and politicians), though police did try to suppress prostitution and brothels when a reform candidate took office. (Examples include the Boston police upon the election of Mayor Josiah Quincy Jr. in 1846 and New York officials after Fernando Wood won the mayoralty in 1854.)[99] Other reformers advocated regulation. Politicians who proposed peacetime regulation of prostitution in the 19th century usually faced opposition from evangelical Protestant Christians and women's rights activists. Even so, several cities did regulate prostitution, among them St. Paul, Minnesota (1865–1883), St. Louis, Missouri (1870–1874), El Paso, Texas (1882–1934), Davenport, Iowa (1893–1909), and New Orleans, Louisiana (1898–1917), whose Storyville sex district became the most infamous of all.[100] But few US communities considered official regulation of prostitution acceptable. Rather, they preferred, according to historian Lawrence M. Friedman, "covert, under-the-table recognition" by informally restricting prostitution to specific neighborhoods—variously called red-light districts, sporting districts, or segregated districts—and leaving management of the sex trade in the hands of local police.[101] This strategy of toleration suggests an attitude of public resignation toward prostitution. One 1892 newspaper editorial gave voice to this point of view toward prostitution: "Like gambling, it [prostitution] is ineradicable, yet—if handled properly, it can be curtailed. Against houses of ill fame, the *Mascot* makes no crusade, so long as they are not located in respectable neighborhoods, for they are a necessary evil."[102] Yet, within a short twenty years, American attitudes toward prostitution would shift from treating it as a "necessary evil" to coordinating a crusade against it as an eradicable "social evil."

THE PROGRESSIVE ERA: THE HEYDAY AND LAST HURRAH OF THE PUBLIC BROTHEL, 1890–1918

By 1890, the eve of the Progressive Era, urban prostitution had become highly organized throughout the country, in vice districts that hosted brothels and a new professional class of women who sold sex.[103] Vice had become immensely profitable. Reformers in Chicago estimated that men paid over fifteen million dollars each year for commercial sex, and between ten and fifteen million dollars in New Orleans. As one anti-prostitution activist noted, "a girl represents as a professional prostitute a capitalized value four times greater than she would represents as a hard working industrial worker."[104] Brothels had become sophisticated profit-generating enterprises, and they operated "much as a grocery or hardware stores … in legitimate trade."[105] Most brothels required that the worker split her earnings evenly with the madam. Additionally, the women who sold sex in brothels had to pay the madam for room and board, clothing, and beauty supplies. If a worker had a male lover, who would not have lived in the brothel, then he too would demand some of the worker's earnings. Despite these many expenses, the take-home pay earned by brothel-based workers often significantly exceeded that of their factory-employed or domestically employed peers. According to investigator George Kneeland, writing in 1913, "Lillie" earned seven dollars in six hours at a mid-level dollar house (meaning she serviced seven men) on Sixth Avenue in New York City. She paid her madam $3.50, plus a $1.50 room and board charge, and took home $2.00. If she worked five days, she would earn at minimum ten dollars beyond her rent and board, at a time when the average New York City female textile worker earned six dollars a week and still had to cover her room and board and other expenses.[106] A madam

had her own set of financial obligations, including owing a large share of her earnings to the landlord or owner of the brothel. Because brothels and prostitution remained vulnerable to reform campaigns and police harassment, landlords often charged two to three times normal rental rates on property leased "for immoral purposes."[107] Others profited from the commercial sex districts. As notorious New York City madam Polly Adler remembered, "What it comes down to is this: the grocer, the butcher, the baker, the policeman, the doctor, the city father and the politician—these are the people who make money out of prostitution, these are the real reapers of the wages of sin."[108]

Local police were among those who profited the most from the wages of sin. Putting the management of cities' red-light districts in the hands of local police resulted in direct and indirect police corruption and biased policing. Investigations into Progressive Era sex markets consistently revealed that police often demanded bribes from brothel madams. The vice commission of Chicago concluded: "it can be shown that the police have abused the discretion given to them by the people; that through their connivance, the Social Evil [prostitution] is fostered and allowed to grow through bribery and corruption."[109] The idea that police would socialize with the women who lived and worked in brothels under their purview provoked just as much concern. A vice investigator in Bridgeport, Connecticut, reported much "unbecoming familiarity" between the city police and prostitutes. After attending a ball held at a dance hall in New Haven where "practically every woman at this ball was a prostitute," he reported: "I saw five officers downstairs, eating and drinking… They did not attempt to maintain order or to interfere when fights started."[110] City officials worried that overseeing vice would infect city police with corruption, tolerance for disorder, and bad habits. Saloon keepers and brothel madams knew that their success depended on keeping the local police happy. One saloon keeper in Portland, Maine, revealed, "If you are a good fellow, set up drinks and cigars, and throw in a little [sexual] business on the side there will be no trouble with the policeman on the beat."[111] Those women who could not pay off police in money or services found themselves facing arrest for vagrancy, disturbing the peace, or similar charges. These women tended to work outside of the protections the brothel offered; they were streetwalkers or independent, casual (meaning temporary) sellers of sex. Consequently, immigrant women and women of color, especially black women, are greatly overrepresented in police records.[112]

African American women turned to casual prostitution to make ends meet because they were typically segregated into domestic service work that paid very low wages. By selling sex they could earn in one night what they earned through domestic service in a week.[113] A 1914 New York Women's Court confirmed that "meager salaries and uncongenial surroundings tend to produce a state of dissatisfaction which sometimes leads...to prostitution." Twenty-six-year-old Heather Haley admitted that she "practiced prostitution off and on since she was seventeen" to supplement the wages she earned as a cook and chambermaid.[114] As casual streetwalkers, black women could dip in and out of the sexual marketplace.

Women of all races and ethnicities sold sex in America's sex markets, but racism and racial segregation structured those markets during the Progressive Era in ways that paralleled American society at large. The extent of segregation and interracial socialization depended on the particular city, though cities typically segregated vice into neighborhoods occupied by people of color. In other words, the morally segregated city often overlapped with the racially segregated city.[115] New Orleans earned an international reputation for offering interracial sex to white-only clients in the historically black neighborhood of Storyville.[116] New York's premiere black neighborhood, Harlem, was home to the notorious black and tan clubs that offered all types of entertainment, including sexual companionship, to the white men and women who went "slumming" there.[117] The racial and ethnic composition of women who worked in brothels tended to echo that of the region in which it was located.[118] San Antonio's brothels featured Hispanic, African American, and white women in segregated brothels in the city's red-light district, located in the historically Mexican neighborhood.[119] As America's sex districts became more organized and profitable, the red-light neighborhood often came under the control of white male entrepreneurs, who pushed black brothel madams and their houses to the margins of the segregated sex district both by opening their own whites-only leisure institutions and by tasking the police to crack down in interracial spaces.[120]

The stunning visibility of red-light districts generated significant protest from a growing number of Americans. Concerns about prostitution had emerged in the United States in the 1880s among evangelical Christians, women's rights activists, and former abolitionists after several sensational reports revealed that white women were working in the brothels of the upper Midwest in conditions of debt bondage condoned by the local police.[121] These activists used the term *white slavery*, which they defined as the luring, coercing, or trapping of white women in prostitution. The term was deeply racialized, implicitly and explicitly, setting the bondage of white slavery against black chattel slavery. "There is a slave trade in this country, and it is not black folks this time, but little white girls—thirteen, fourteen, fifteen, sixteen, seventeen years of age—and they are snatched out of our arms, and from our Sabbath-schools and from our communion tables," declared one writer in 1899.[122] This common invocation of African American chattel slavery to condemn the prostitution of white women served to lessen the horrors and sexualized violence of African American slavery on the one hand, while also suggesting that the sexual exploitation of white women constituted a categorically greater offense.[123]

Stories of white slavery moved from the province of specialized purity reformers to the mainstream media in 1907 when muckraker George Kibbe Turner published his article "The City of Chicago: A Study of Great Immoralities" in *McClure's*, a magazine with national circulation. Clifford Barnes, an anti-vice reformer, recalled, "It was during the summer of 1907 that Chicago was startled out of her attitude of indifference toward commercialized vice by a series of shocking revelations, which indicated that our city was the center of a well-organized traffic in women, a very real white slave market."[124] After 1907, tales of white slavery dominated magazine exposés, providing plot points for melodramatic movies and plays, and appearing in newspapers regularly until the outbreak of World War I in 1914. These stories informed the general American public about the vicious dangers in their cities and they inspired a generation of Progressive Era reformers who sought to eradicate the conditions that seemed responsible for the brothel: the double standard of morality that excused male sexual promiscuity but condemned female sex outside of marriage, the widespread commercialization of sexuality, and women's low wages. Their campaigns against white slavery also encompassed entangled concerns about women's new roles as suffragists, individual migrants, and industrial, retail, and service employees. But to wage successful campaigns against commercial vice, reformers needed to investigate the extent of brothel-based prostitution in American cities.[125]

The celebration of social science expertise as a basis of social reform is one of the defining characteristics of the Progressive Era. Prostitution, like child labor, industrial safety, and lynching, attracted the attention of investigators sponsored by civil society groups, city governments, state legislatures, and federal agencies. Non-governmental organizations such as New York City's Committee of Fourteen, funded by corporate interests such as John D. Rockefeller's Bureau of Social Hygiene, conducted regular undercover vice investigations

from the mid-1900s to the mid-1930s. Municipal forces also probed vice conditions. Forty-three cities pursued formal investigations of prostitution and vice from 1910 to 1917.[126] The State of Illinois conducted an intensive survey into the relationship between women's wage labor and prostitution.[127] Meanwhile, the federal government's Immigration Bureau explored the relationship between foreign migration and prostitution.[128] Combined, these studies questioned the effectiveness of tolerated red-light districts managed by the police. More than forty cities blamed red-light districts for worsening the moral conditions of the city by promoting prostitution, "raising crime to the dignity of a business,... promoting the double standard of morality,... [and] debauching police morals."[129] In response to the sensational findings of municipal vice commissions, most cities quickly moved to shut down their vice districts and amend their vice laws.[130] By 1916, forty-seven cities had closed down their vice districts.[131]

These investigations into prostitution contributed to an ongoing legal trend to criminalize nonmarital sex. Since the campaigns of the 1880s to raise the age of consent and make seduction a crime, reformers had been turning toward legislatures to produce legal solutions to the social problems they documented. To address the issue of sex trafficking, Congress passed the White Slave Traffic Act in 1910, which made it illegal to transport a woman or girl over state lines for the purposes of prostitution, debauchery, or "any other immoral purpose." States followed the federal government's lead by passing state-level anti-white slavery laws, enacted by all forty-eight states by 1916.[132] The American Social Hygiene Association (ASHA), formed in 1913, took the lead in developing a model law on prostitution; it eliminated commerce as the constitutive feature of prostitution, declaring, "prostitution should be defined to include the giving or receiving of the body, for hire, or the giving and receiving of the body for indiscriminate sexual intercourse *without hire*." With this proposed law, the ASHA equated promiscuity with prostitution and erased the necessity of a commercial transaction. Between 1914 and 1916, ASHA representatives traveled to eighty cities, visiting local social hygiene societies or establishing new ones that then lobbied for legislative reform. Most state legislatures adopted ASHA's model law in part or in total.[133] Finally, to ensure that foreign women who sold sex could not migrate to the United States, Congress outlawed the immigration of people who profited from the sex trade. In addition to the aforementioned 1875 Page Act, which outlawed the importation of Asian women for "immoral purposes," the 1903 Immigration Law barred procurers (pimps) of prostitutes; a 1907 law made the practice of prostitution within three years of entry into the United States a deportable offense; a 1910 law prohibited the selling of sex for all non-naturalized women; and a 1917 law made the selling of sex a deportable offense for all non-native women regardless of their naturalization status.[134] In the United States the fight against prostitution served the purpose of national border control and established what one US attorney called "a quarantine act against the morally and physically unclean."[135]

The United States managed prostitution very differently in its newly acquired colonial territories. The Spanish American War launched the US imperial mission in 1898 when the United States gained the territories of the Philippines and Puerto Rico. Over the next thirty years US military forces would occupy territory throughout Central America and as it did so, it often encountered the vexing question of how to manage prostitution, military readiness, and discipline, which had shaped its experiences of the Civil War. In colonial spaces—tropical, far from mainland reformers, and filled with non-white women—US policy tended toward regulated prostitution. Military officials introduced regulation in Puerto Rico, the Philippines, the Panama Canal Zone, Cuba, Santo Domingo, Haiti, Nicaragua, Hawaii, and at sites near military bases along the Mexico–

US border.[136] In the Philippines, a place where US military forces fought a long war against locals in the Philippine–American War from 1898 to 1913, the US Army introduced registration in 1899 to "limit, restrict, control, and finally if possible, eliminate the unbriddled [sic] status of drunkenness, gambling, smuggling, and prostitution that prevailed."[137] Like earlier Civil War-era experiments, this regulation policy required women to undergo medical examination, register with military authorities, and carry an inspection booklet proving their compliance. News of the registration scheme reached mainland shores in 1900, prompting outrage among women's organizations and purity reformers. In response, the military temporarily suspended registration, though by 1902 it had been quietly reintroduced, yet without the accoutrement of regulation including inspection booklets and licenses.[138] Quiet regulation quickly spread throughout US colonial possessions, though these systems of prostitution control remained vulnerable to critique by organizations such as ASHA. [139]

AFTER THE BROTHEL: ABOLISHING THE BROTHEL, CLANDESTINE PROSTITUTION, AND WAR, 1918–1945

World War I. The United States' entry into World War I provided the anti-prostitution campaign, led by ASHA, with the emergency conditions to achieve their ultimate aim of shutting down the nation's brothels. In 1917, the War Department tapped the ASHA to lead the military's social hygiene agenda as a member of the Commission on Training Camp Activities (CTCA). Animated by concerns about the high rates of venereal disease among American recruits, the CTCA aimed to keep American soldiers "fit to fight." To aid in this endeavor, Congress included in the draft law a prohibition against prostitution within five miles, and later ten miles, of any military institution. Cities such as Houston, Texas, that wished to attract military investment, now had a clear justification for shutting down their red-light districts. After closing its district, the Army rewarded Houston with a National Guard training camp. Cities that valued their red-light districts, such as New Orleans, faced federal pressure to close them down. "You close the red light district," Secretary of the Navy Josephus Daniels threatened the city's mayor, "Or the armed forces will." With that order, one of the most famous red-light districts in the United States joined the other 115 red-light districts closed by the CTCA during the war.[140]

Guided by the ASHA's equating of promiscuity with prostitution, the prohibition against prostitution near military installations extended beyond the brothel and transactional sex to include women who merely had nonmarital sex with enlisted men. CTCA director Raymond Fosdick considered this measure necessary, because "we are confronted with the problem of hundreds of young girls, not yet prostitutes, who seem to have become hysterical at the sight of buttons and uniforms."[141] Military authorities arrested women accused of promiscuity and found to be infected with venereal diseases for endangering soldiers' health. Congress expanded this policy of quarantining infected women socializing with soldiers near military bases when it passed the Chamberlain–Kahn Act in July 1918, which provided one million dollars to aid states "in caring for civilian persons whose detention, isolation, quarantine, or commitment to institutions" would protect the venereal health of enlisted men.[142] The Act formed the foundation of what ASHA called "The American Plan" and freed municipalities from focusing on the "pure zones" surrounding military installations by allowing for the quarantining of putative promiscuous women with little to no due process protections by courts anywhere.[143]

Women who sold sex bore the brunt of this repression of casual and commercial sex. The close surveillance of vice districts during the preceding years meant that law enforcement officials first targeted known women who sold sex. For example, Bureau of Investigation white

slave officer Charles Braun had been stationed in Waco, Texas, prior to the war where he was tasked with investigating the vice conditions in Waco's red-light district to ensure that none of the women working in brothels had been trafficked. After Waco closed its vice district in the summer of 1917 in response to military pressure, Braun spent his time ensuring that none of the displaced prostitutes practiced prostitution near Camp MacArthur, located just outside of Waco. On Christmas night 1917, Braun and military police arrested Maggie Foster and Lillian Johnson, two African American women who worked as prostitutes, in Foster's home just outside Waco city limits. The military police charged Foster with violating the draft law by operating a bawdy house within the "pure zone" around Camp MacArthur. They handed Johnson over to local police, who charged her with vagrancy—still a catch-all charge used to police the behavior of women who sold sex. At least 30,000 women, including Foster, were incarcerated in federal facilities during the war. More commonly, courts convicted women such as Johnson under local and state laws; thirty-nine states had passed laws modeled after the Chamberlain-Kahn Act.[144] Though the federal and state laws seemed gender neutral, as legal historian Scott Stern notes, "women constituted the vast majority of those imprisoned because of venereal disease or suspected prostitution."[145] Local public health and law enforcement officials, as one law enforcement officer from Augusta, Georgia, claimed, "dealt with severely" women whom police suspected of selling sex and promiscuity.[146] The number of women incarcerated under local laws during World War I remains unknown, but was almost certainly very high.[147]

With the closing of most brothels by 1917, and of cabarets and saloons by the Prohibition Amendment in 1920, prostitution moved into the street, hotel, seedy restaurant, or apartment. One New York City investigator stopped several women who sold sex on the street in the winter of 1917: "I asked them how they were getting along now that the cabarets had to close up at midnight [due to wartime regulations] and they said it was bad for them… They said they had to go out and get them (meaning men) on the street. Several of the girls had never tried the streets they said, but it was a necessity now."[148] Displaced women who had sold sex in brothels before the war moved to the streets or left prostitution entirely. The dislocations caused by the dissolution of the brothel system opened up some opportunities for women who had been shut out by the brothel system—mostly African American women. Several historians have concluded that black women made gains in America's clandestine sex markets during the 1920s as streetwalkers, independent sexual entrepreneurs, and illegal brothel madams.[149] The increased participation of black women in the sex markets has been attributed to the growth of the black population in northern cities, the extremely limited occupational opportunities for black women, and the growth of an underground economy that paid better wages than "legitimate" work.[150]

On the street, women who sold sex encountered harassment from police and customers alike, which caused them to turn to a figure that would grow more prominent in commercial sex—the pimp. To mitigate these dangers, and to increase business, more women who worked as prostitutes began turning to pimps for protection. Pimps had long been associated with women who sold sex, but in the brothel era, a pimp was a man who had romantic relationships with women who sold sex and who lived off her earnings, much as a husband would. Pimps typically did not live in the brothels, nor did they assert total control over a woman's working conditions, number of customers, or selection of customers. Pimps in the 1920s offered women protection, but at the cost of women's control over their working conditions, wages, and autonomy.[151]

The elite sex markets shifted to anonymous but well-appointed apartments—known as call houses—after the closing of the brothels. A call house madam typically rented rooms to two to five women at any given time. She would arrange "dates" with her girls by telephone and would keep a list of young women with whom she could subcontract dates. Call houses offered customers safety and anonymity, and they offered women who sold sex independence from pimps and a steady stream of customers. Like brothel madams, call house madams charged room and board to women who lived in the house, and took an additional fee of 50 percent for arranging the dates. Madams used their earnings to bribe police to prevent raids, and to pay off the local organized crime syndicates who sought to assert control over the prostitution racket.[152]

Organized crime in the United States became more prominent and consolidated in the 1920s due to the national prohibition on alcohol, introduced just as cities shuttered America's brothels. After Prohibition came under attack in the late 1920s, some organized crime syndicates began diversifying by offering "protection," for a fee, to women who sold sex or ran call houses. In New York, mob boss Charles "Lucky" Luciano had 200 call houses and 1,000 prostitutes under his "protection." In 1935, the Women's Court arraigned over 3,000 women accused of selling sex, yet only 175 of these women worked in brothels protected by Luciano; of those, none served jail time.[153] New York prosecutor Thomas Dewey shut down Lucky Luciano's prostitution racket in 1936, but he could not prevent organized crime from continuing to profit from clandestine commercial sex.[154]

The economic devastation of the Great Depression swelled the ranks of women who sold sex, while curbing the number of men able to purchase it. "There are lots of girls who are out of work and are hustling," said twenty-six-year-old Margie Morris. "You can't tell an amateur from a professional."[155] This situation led to a drop in the prices of individual sex acts. An investigation into vice conditions in Portland, Oregon, conducted in December 1932, discovered that, although clandestine brothel owners thought they were "doing well," prices had plummeted. "Of course we used to get more money around here," divulged one madam. "I used to get $5 for the girls, then I got $3, and now they got to take $2. Occasionally, a fellow has only $1.50, so we take him, too."[156] These conditions could be found throughout the country. A New York City madam told *Time* magazine that her prices had dropped from $3 to $1.50. "'That,' she explained, 'was because of the Depression.'"[157]

World War II. The outbreak of World War II in Europe provoked anxieties about how the spread of venereal disease might undermine America's military readiness. To address this challenge, federal officials developed a preemptive policy of repressing prostitution and female promiscuity within the continental United States, while regulating prostitution abroad. Domestically, US policy was guided by the Eight-Point Agreement of 1940 and the May Act of 1941. Before the United States' entry into the war, the Eight-Point Agreement had been developed by ASHA in consultation with state health departments to set out "measures for the control of Venereal Disease in areas where armed forces or national defense employees are concentrated."[158] The plan called for repressing prostitution and tracing contacts; each infected service member was required to divulge the names of the women with whom he had had sexual contact so that public health officials could trace transmission of the disease and officials could quarantine infected women.[159] The May Act provided the tool of repression to enforce such a policy, though in many ways it served as a continuation of the American Plan established during World War I.[160] It made prostitution near any military installation or defense plant a federal offense, and it added considerable pressure for local officials to repress prostitution. In 1941 officials created the Social Protection Division within the Federal Security Agency to combat prostitution and handed leadership of the new agency to famed Prohibition agent Elliot Ness. Ness declared, "So vigorous

is the Federal attack on the prostitute that local police power in this field can be forfeited to the Federal Department of Justice if local authorities don't 'crack down.'"[161] The federal government first exercised its ability to take over local jurisdictions when it enforced the May Act in 1942 and Secretary of War Henry Stimson placed twenty-seven counties surrounding Camp Forrest in East Tennessee under federal control. Federal forces rounded up hundreds of women. Of the first hundred arrested and sentenced to the Federal Reformatory for Women at Alderson, West Virginia, sixty-eight were white, twenty were African American, and twelve were Native American. Most came from poor rural areas with limited agriculture and industry. Most surprising of all, doctors found only four of the women to be infected with a venereal disease.[162] These were hardly the hardened prostitutes that the Act ostensibly targeted.[163] Yet the May Act provided the lever for federal officials to encourage local authorities to crack down on prostitution. Faced with threats of federal forces stepping in, the mayor of Tacoma, Washington, closed down the city's twenty-four brothels. Other cities resisted federal interference. El Paso, Texas, had long been home to a thriving, profitable, and regulated vice district that provided entertainment for soldiers based at nearby Fort Bliss. City officials depended on the district's licensing revenue to fill the city coffers; in addition, the city wanted to encourage solders to spend their money in El Paso rather than in the bars, dance halls, and regulated brothels of Ciudad Juárez across the Rio Grande. In March 1941, faced with federal pressure, El Paso closed its brothels, but six months later they had reopened. Frustrated, federal forces applied more pressure to the El Paso police to conduct raids of known brothels. Any woman suspected of carrying a venereal disease faced arrest and incarceration in the city jail under the May Act.[164] After the passage of the May Act, 292 vice districts closed immediately, and by the end of the war over 700 would be closed, including the one in El Paso.[165]

Outside of the continental United States, federal and military policy shifted from repression to regulation. Hawaii's Hotel Street, long the regulated vice district of Honolulu, came under martial law after the attack on Pearl Harbor. From early 1942 until September 1944, the Army managed Hotel Street's brothels in an effort to keep the venereal disease rate under control. When the brothels, reopened after the Pearl Harbor attack, the city's madams knew that troops would pour into Honolulu. With this in mind, Honolulu's madams decided to increase their prices from three dollars for three minutes to five dollars for three minutes. Frank Steer, head of the military police, objected to the price hike, saying: "The price of meat is still three dollars."[166] He demanded that the prices be dropped to their prewar levels. With the prices set by the Army, the brothels opened for business and served 250,000 men a month, with each of the 250 registered women who sold sex seeing about one hundred men a day.[167] This scheme constituted highly efficient, regulated prostitution organized to service the largest number of customers as quickly as possible, which generated an incredible amount of profit. The average worker kept two dollars from each encounter and could earn between $30,000 and $40,000 a year.[168] The brothels recruited white women from the mainland to staff the brothels, which for the duration of the war served only white servicemen.[169] Similarly, in Liberia, where US troops protected Firestone's valuable rubber plantations, US officials established two enclosed villages—Shangri-La and Paradise—staffed with between 250 and 600 indigenous Liberian women to provide sexual services to the African American troops stationed there. White officers were prohibited from visiting the villages, though many did visit brothels in Monrovia while on leave. Army medical officers and nurses examined each woman to ensure she remained free from venereal disease. The troops in Liberia suffered a venereal infection rate of an astonishing 96.5 percent in September 1942. That rate dropped to 42 percent in December 1942 after the Army implemented regulated prostitution and by October 1943 the rate had declined to a manageable 13.6 percent.[170]

Managing militarized men's sexuality in occupied territories proved more difficult for the US military. In occupied France, US forces pursued a contradictory policy of publicly denying that they were regulating prostitution while at the same time providing the necessary prophylaxis and opportunities for commercial sex. As early as one month after D-Day, US soldiers were indirectly running brothels in Cherbourg, including one called the Corral, for US soldiers. In the words of General Charles Gerhardt's chief of staff, the Corral would "control social relations between our men and the French people rather than to allow promiscuous social relations."[171] Worried about the response of the American public back home to such support for prostitution, American forces in France engaged in a complicated communications strategy of denial, while privately affirming that "the sex act cannot be made unpopular," and thus needed to be controlled.[172] In postwar occupied Japan and Korea, the US military refined its policy of counseling sexual continence while accommodating sexual promiscuity. It set up vice zones patrolled by military police and medical officials near military camps, established prophylaxis stations for troops to use after sexual contact, and conducted contact tracing to find infected women.[173]

POSTWAR SEXUAL POLITICS

The postwar era ushered in several developments that reshaped the practice of prostitution in the United States. Corporate and government propaganda encouraged a retreat to "traditional" gender roles; popular psychologists circulated Freudian explanations for sexual development; pharmaceutical companies developed and distributed antibiotics to treat venereal disease; and popular culture celebrated heterosexual liberalism, even while severely repressing homosexuality. After World War II, American popular culture revered the nuclear family as a source of social stability, national strength, and a defense against communism. Parents, doctors, psychiatrists, government officials, magazine editors, and multitudes of others told women that their natural role lay in the home as wife and mother. Even so, more women than ever entered the paid labor force. In this context, women who violated the prescription of submissive motherhood were blamed for society's ills, and the woman who sold sex was marked as especially deviant. With women's increased employment, no longer could reformers argue that women's lack of employment opportunities drove women to prostitution—maladjustment did. Underwriting much of the gender role realignment of the decade was the popularization of Freudian ideas of sexual development that posited female promiscuity as the product of mental imbalance and social deviance. Added to this mix is the related development that prostitution no longer seemed likely to cause a public health crisis. Effective antibiotic treatments for venereal diseases had been developed in 1943 and became available to the general public after the war. Consequently, in the postwar period, women who sold sex came to be seen as dangerous to the family but not to the wider community. They were outcasts, B-girls and drug addicts living on the margins of society.[174] Yet officials remained silent about their customers, implying that they were merely exercising their healthy male libidos in an era when men's heterosexual freedom seemed to epitomize American freedom.

No publication is more emblematic of the sexual liberalism of the postwar period than *Playboy*. Hugh Hefner launched the magazine in December 1953, ushering in an era that celebrated straight men's rights to sexual freedom while laying groundwork for the sexual revolution of the 1960s. Hefner declared, "Playboy is a magazine for men—and sophisticated, city-bred men, at that."[175] Many early articles in *Playboy* focused on stories of sexual adventures with office girls, neighbors, and married women, but not prostitutes. Yet the magazine's broad support for male heterosexual freedom soon led it to publish articles that framed prostitution as a victimless crime and spoke approvingly of decriminalized commercial sex in places such as Paris, where "sex still walks her streets."[176] Hefner regularly criticized US obscenity and sex laws that infringed on commercial and consensual sex. One of the problems, for Hefner, with prostitution laws was that they frequently criminalized "indiscriminate sexual intercourse." "By this broad legal definition, a female would be guilty of prostitution if she were to engage in the same random sexual relations that many single males regularly seek without prejudice or prosecution," he wrote in 1966 in a recurring column entitled "The Playboy Philosophy."[177] Hefner declared that prostitution laws were "patently anti-female." He called for the decriminalization of prostitution so that "sexual activity of consenting adults" could be a "matter of private moral determination not to be infringed upon by the state."[178] Because prostitution involved a transaction between two consenting adults, and so lacked a complainant and did not seem to cause harm to others, it fell under the rubric developed in the mid-1960s of a victimless crime. The concept of victimless crimes had been advocated by sociologist Edwin Schur in his 1965 book *Crimes without Victims* to critique laws against abortion, homosexuality, and illegal drugs.[179] According to Schur, "it is the *combination of an exchange transaction and lack of apparent harm* to others that constitutes the core of the victimless crime."[180] Hefner in his 1966 column suggested that prostitution also constituted a victimless crime because it occurred between two consenting adults.

Feminists in the emerging second-wave women's rights movement rejected the notion that prostitution could be a victimless crime. "It is a crime, gentlemen, but it is not victimless," declared Susan Brownmiller in 1971. "There is a victim, and that is the woman."[181] Prostitution threatened to unsettle the fragile coalitions of the women's liberation movement.[182]

The feminist movement of the late 1960s and 1970s included women from a range of ideological perspectives, racial backgrounds, and class interests. Liberal feminists, typically represented by the National Organization for Women (NOW), sought to fight for women's civil rights through institutional reform using legal and political tactics. In contrast, radical feminists sought to "revolutionize consciousness and culture" in ways that would lead to the emancipation of all women by radically theorizing the history and experiences of patriarchy, especially around issues connected to sex and sexuality.[183] Liberal feminists (establishment feminists) and radical feminists (women's liberationists) frequently sparred over analysis, tactics, and priorities. Yet almost all feminists in the 1970s agreed that prostitution needed to be decriminalized because sex laws punished women for the transaction yet let male customers off without repercussions.[184] As one woman wrote to the radical feminist periodical *off our backs*, women who sold sex "are not respected or protected by society; they are used and abused."[185] For many feminists on the Left (Marxists and Socialist-Feminists), prostitution represented the clearest example that a woman's economic value remained tied to her sexual value; under capitalist patriarchy women became commodities and their economic dependence on men lay at the foundation of unequal gender relations.[186] In the eyes of many women's liberationists, prostitution was "the ultimate results of male sexism—the sale of female flesh."[187]

Despite broad feminist calls for the decriminalization of prostitution, many women in the liberal and radical feminist movements remained discomfited by actual women who sold sex. In 1971, a coalition of radical feminists held a "Conference on Prostitution" in New York City where the only woman on the program who had experience selling sex—a thirty-two-year-old former prostitute—nearly groveled: "Filled with guilt as we all were after any amount of time in 'the life,' we attempt to exorcise the guilt by shouldering the whole burden of blame, accepting the definition of 'sick' or 'deviant,' and striving to become proper." This analysis fit nicely into the current second-wave feminist theory about sex work. But on the final afternoon of the conference, a number of women still "in the life" showed up. As a reporter for the *Village Voice* wrote, "They did not fit the stereotype of prostitute.... And they were, they said, *feminist* prostitutes."[188] Living, working women who sold sex challenged feminist assumptions about the relationship between sexual commerce, shame, and oppression. As Kate Millet recalled, "the first thing they could tell us—the message coming through a burst of understandable indignation was that we were judgmental, meddlesome, and ignorant."[189]

The sex workers' rights movement emerged from the social ferment of the liberal movements of the 1960s and 1970s, especially the women's liberation movement, the gay liberation and lesbian rights movement, and the New Left.[190] It sought to decriminalize prostitution, destigmatize the selling of sex, challenge the respectability politics of mainstream liberal feminism, and counter the anti-sex message coming from radical feminism. They rejected the title of "'most oppressed' that radical [and liberal] feminists awarded them."[191] Margo St. James launched this movement as early as 1971, when she founded the San Francisco-based organization Whores, Housewives, and Others (WHO) to "expose the hypocrisy in laws that controlled female sexuality, primarily prostitution."[192] In 1973, after WHO dissolved, St. James formed Call Off Your Old Tired Ethics (COYOTE), the first and most well-known sex workers' rights organization. Within a year, COYOTE reported that it had over 1,000 members, 10 percent of whom were women who were still selling sex. St. James considered this quite an achievement "because they are a paranoid group."[193] COYOTE's activities were focused in two areas: direct assistance and public awareness campaigns. The services it offered to women who sold sex included furnishing legal assistance to prostitutes who had been arrested, providing appropriate clothing to women for their court dates, teaching in-jail classes that focused on survival skills, and running a hotline for sex workers called SLIP (Survival Line for Independent Prostitutes). In terms of raising public awareness, COYOTE's campaigns centered on five interrelated areas: firstly, calling for the decriminalization of prostitution; secondly, protesting police entrapment and harassment of prostitutes; thirdly, pointing out the discriminatory enforcement of prostitution laws, especially as related to gender and race; fourthly, drawing attention to the expense of arresting and prosecuting women for prostitution; and fifthly, trying to destigmatize prostitution.[194] Of all of these campaigns, decriminalization remained the most critical, with St. James declaring in 1973, "changing the law is, of course, the most important job."[195]

COYOTE put decriminalization, a term St. James coined, at the center of its agenda.[196] It stated that its primary goal was "Not to legalize prostitution but to decriminalize it; this is remove prostitution from any government control."[197] In COYOTE's analysis, the criminalization of prostitution led to most of the victimization that women who sold sex experienced. It led to their harassment by police, protected abusive johns who knew that law enforcement officials never believed stories of rape and abuse from known prostitutes, gave them arrest records that kept them from getting respectable employment, and drove them into the arms of pimps. COYOTE was suspicious of the state licensing of prostitution, as had taken hold in a few counties in Nevada, noting, "Making prostitution legal is NOT Coyote's position because it would still involve and enable the state to license and regulate what a woman does with her own body."[198] For COYOTE, selling sex was a service industry job, a type of work, made dangerous and deviant by the laws that victimized women who sold sex, often in especially sexist and racist ways. As part of its public awareness campaigns COYOTE pointed out that in San Francisco—a

city with laws against both the selling and buying of sex—women made up 75 percent of the 35,000 people arrested on prostitution-related charges in 1973. COYOTE highlighted such blatant sexist policing, but they also drew journalists' attention to the role that racial discrimination and class played in the enforcement of prostitution laws. *San Francisco Magazine* reported in 1973, "COYOTE is against the racism that exists with poor women of racial minorities making up a majority of those arrested while the white and higher paid call girls ply their trade in hotels and homes without arrest."[199] Supported by Del Martin of the San Francisco chapter of the NOW, COYOTE sought to raise awareness among feminists and others of the double standard by which anti-prostitution laws were enforced.[200] In this campaign, COYOTE succeeded.

COYOTE inspired the formation of a number of local sex workers' rights groups around the country, including the Los Angeles-based CAT (California Advocates for Trollops), the Seattle-based ASP (Association for Seattle Prostitutes), the Honolulu-based DOLPHIN (Dump Obsolete Laws; Prove Hypocrisy Isn't Necessary), the Boston-based PUMA (Prostitutes Union of Massachusetts), the New York City-based PONY (Prostitutes of New York), the New Orleans-based PASSION (Professional Association Seeking Sexual Identification Observant of Nature), and many others. Most of these organizations forged ties with local NOW chapters, and some of the organizations, including PROS (US PROstitutes Collective), became affiliated with transnational feminist initiatives such as the International Wages for Housework Campaign. A persistent critique of the ways that police undermined the safety, security, and sanity of women (and men) who sold sex united these organizations. Local chapters of NOW in the South, Midwest, West Coast, and Northeast, and the national NOW, endorsed decriminalization in 1973.[201]

But the coalition between mainstream liberal feminists and sex workers' rights organizations would shatter in the sex wars of the 1980s, and by the 1990s the politics of sex trafficking further divided the two groups, with many mainstream feminists supporting anti-trafficking policies that rejected sex work as an occupational choice and enshrined the victimhood of the "prostitute."[202] As early as 1980, the alliance between mainstream liberal feminists and sex workers' rights organizations began to falter on the shoals of trafficking when at the Copenhagen World Conference on Women Kathleen Barry, author of the sensational and widely read *Female Sexual Slavery*, argued that international sex trafficking posed a threat to women's rights and that immigration reform could halt the illegal flow of the traffic. Some sex workers' rights groups sounded the alarm that anti-trafficking policy could strengthen the hand of the state against sex workers. "Under the guise of catching international pimps, it is immigrant prostitutes and other women whose [cross-border] movements are going to be stopped."[203]

By the late 1990s the politics of prostitution had divided feminists. On one side of the split stood Kathleen Barry and her liberal feminist allies represented in the Coalition Against Trafficking in Women (CATW) who argued that all prostitution is exploitation and equated all prostitution with trafficking. On the other side of the split was a coalition of sex workers' rights organizations and radical sex-positive feminists represented by the Global Alliance Against the Traffic in Women (GAATW) that argued, firstly, that forced prostitution should be criminalized but that prostitution remained a meaningful occupational option for women in poverty, and secondly, that anti-trafficking law enforcement and immigration policies tend to further exploit vulnerable women. As the United Nations turned to address the issue of trafficking in the late 1990s, these two sides vied for influence over the language of the Palermo Protocol, formally known as the 2000 Protocol to Prevent, Suppress, and Punish the Trafficking in Persons, especially Women and Children. Though the debates at the UN produced

numerous compromises in language, in the realm of international policy-making and within the United States Congress Barry's CATW and her liberal feminist allies in NOW as well as the Christian religious Right ultimately wielded the most influence.[204] Since 2000, US policy at the state, national, and international level has been broadly anti-prostitute, and in the meantime, women who sell sex continue to be vulnerable to police and to customers.

DISCUSSION OF THE LITERATURE

Since 1980, there has been an explosion of literature about the history of prostitution in America by scholars who have studied the cultural significance of the image of the prostitute, social movements organized to repress prostitution, and the organization and social structure of commercial sex markets.[205] The study of prostitution offered a way to "integrate gender into political and economic history," while also allowing consideration of the role sexuality played in commercial culture and waged labor.[206] As historian Julia Laite notes, "prostitution lies at a curious intersection of broad symbolism and personal intimacy. It illuminates and is connected to enormous social realities; it is about women, men, money, sex, space, morality, labor and politics."[207]

Cultural historians have used the study of prostitution to consider how concerns about commercial sex expressed anxieties about women's changing roles, shifts in the sexual culture, increasing amounts of immigration from Southern and Eastern Europe, the influx of Southern African Americans into northern cities, the perceived foreignness of the Chinese, and the broad commercialization and industrialization of all aspects of American life.[208] These historians have mapped the ribald sporting culture by examining risqué poems and pornographic stories that were passed from one fan to another, showing the centrality of sexuality and commercial sex to urban popular cultures.[209] Conversely, they have shown how bourgeois reformers treated white fallen women as deserving of rescue, thereby castigating male lust while also motivating calls for reform.

Historians of social movements have included anti-prostitution activism in the slate of conservative progressive causes such as temperance, prohibition, gambling, and film censorship that animated anti-vice activists and religious voters during the Progressive Era. They have studied the coalition of public health officials, purity activists, and women's rights supporters who sought to eradicate prostitution entirely.[210] Social historians interested in the organization and social structure of sex markets have produced the widest array of studies. Urban historians focused on intersections between and among the development of residential real estate, red-light districts, and race have been particularly significant. Understanding the ways that vice-segregated neighborhoods interfaced with racially segregated neighborhoods has raised new questions about informal economies, community formation, and policing.[211] Considering how the informal underground economy was integrated with the formal economy has motivated a number of studies. The wages of sin flowed in many directions, and Timothy J. Gilfoyle's groundbreaking work demonstrated that even the most respectable entities in New York City's real estate market profited from prostitution.[212]

Feminist social historians have produced much of the work on women who sold sex. Instead of treating these woman as deviant, historians have interrogated how women who worked as prostitutes were situated in their working-class communities.[213] They have found that "prostitutes were 'ordinary' young females who confronted limited options and made rational and sometimes desperate choices."[214] Accordingly, women who sold sex were members of communities that offered a range of nonmarital sexual offerings.[215] These historians have endeavored to uncover the agency of women who worked as prostitutes rather than treat them as "passive victims of impersonal economic and social forces."[216] Women who sold sex were

historical actors, as Patricia Cline Cohen's brilliant case study of the life of Helen Jewett, murdered in 1836, attests.[217] The men who purchased sex from these women were also historical actors, but historians have told us less about the customers (with the important exception of Cohen). Feminist historians share a common conceptual framework when it comes to interpreting prostitution. As Judith Walkowitz notes, feminist scholars agree that "prostitution is and remains a form of sexual labor; intensified policing has negative effects on women in the sex trade; feminist interventions on behalf of their lost sisters have had a decidedly mixed outcome."[218]

Recently historians of women who sell sex have turned their attention to the ways that policing prostitution led to the growth of state power. These historians look at local policing and carceral power, how immigration law and border control read women's bodies and labor through a racialized lens, and the militarized organization of prostitution. Much of this research takes the migrating woman who sold intimate labor as its subject. This moment is critical because as a woman moved from one jurisdiction to another, she potentially posed a threat to the moral and physical health of her new nation. Conversely, in the case of state regulation of prostitution by the military, the problem is not the migrating woman but the migrating soldier, who expects to be rewarded for martial valor with sex yet remains vulnerable to venereal disease. These are the moments that produced the greatest anxiety and the clearest policy and enforcement outcomes.[219] These questions about police power, incarcerations, border control, deportation, and militarization reflect ongoing scholarly debates and anxieties about sex work, sex trafficking, and migration that are animating much of the debate in today's world.

PRIMARY SOURCES

According to historian Barbara Meil Hobson, from 1900 to 1920 around one billion pages of published material about prostitution were produced.[220] If one included the pre-1900 material and the post-1920 material, one could drown in sources. It is not a bad problem for a historian to have, but it does mean that one has to sift through a vast amount of material, much of it found in local city or regional archives.

Since city governments tended to manage prostitution, municipal records are essential sources for historians of sexuality. Court arrest and indictment records and jury trials can be very useful. Sadly, many cities have discarded their indictment records, thinking they were not important. Jury trials can be especially useful because they reveal how ordinary citizens responded to prostitution.[221] Records from mayoral offices often shed light on citizens' concerns, relations with the police, and reform campaigns. Incarceration records from penitentiaries, jails, reformatories, and other detention centers can reveal the social profiles of the women targeted by the police.

Reform organizations produced a large volume of material about prostitution. Social purity organizations from the late 19th century, such as the American Purity Alliances and the Women's Christian Temperance Union (WCTU), left records (in the WCTU's case, both chapter records hidden away in local archives and substantial records housed in Evanston, Illinois), but also published the periodicals *The Philanthropist* and *The Union Signal*, which are both housed in the Library of Congress. The Committee of Fourteen (1905–1932) conducted regular vice investigations of New York City. The New York Public Library houses its archives. Many cities had social hygiene organizations from 1905–1930, and city libraries and local archives frequently contain meeting minutes, correspondence, and materials related to lobbying efforts and public awareness campaigns. The ASHA, formed in 1913, succeeded in establishing a national anti-prostitution organization. Their records are housed at the University of Minnesota's Social Welfare Archive, and many of the ASHA papers have been digitized, including its periodical, *The*

Journal of Social Hygiene, available from the Hearth homepage at Cornell University.

Historians of prostitution often rely on materials published as primary sources. One of the most useful sources to consult is Vern Bullogh and Barrett Elcano's 1977 *A Bibliography of Prostitution*.[222] Though it is obviously dated, the bibliography is extensive and remains a useful starting point. In addition, because much of the material published about prostitution is now out of copyright, much of it can be found on the internet, particularly at Google Books, Archives.Org, and Hathi Trust.

During the Progressive Era, cities and states often conducted in-depth vice investigations into prostitution management, police corruption, and public morality. The most famous of the municipal vice reports is Chicago's, *The Social Evil in Chicago*, but the vice reports from Atlanta, Baltimore, Bay City, Boston, Bridgeport, Charlestown, Cleveland, Denver, Elmira, Grand Rapids, Hartford, Honolulu, Kansas City, Lafayette (IN), Lancaster (PA), Lexington, Los Angeles, Little Rock, Louisville, Massachusetts, Minneapolis, Newark, New York, Paducah, Philadelphia, Pittsburgh, Portland (ME), Portland (OR), Richmond, Rockland Co., St. Louis, San Francisco, Springfield, Syracuse, and Wisconsin, are also valuable resources. Howard B. Woolston published the best national overview of these reports, which he supplemented with his own significant local research, in 1921 as *Prostitution in the United States, Vol. I.*

Officials of the federal government also investigated prostitution. The Immigration Commission included the topic in its forty-one-volume investigation of immigration conducted between 1907 and 1910. Moreover, many of the "white slavery" files from the Immigration and Naturalization Service from 1900 to 1917 have been microfilmed and are available via libraries.[223] The National Archives at College Park holds numerous records related to prostitution, including the records of the Department of Justice, the case files of Mann Act investigations, the records of the Children's Bureau, and the records of Insular Affairs.

White slavery narratives are also a useful source for studying the discursive power of prostitution. Again, most of these texts can be found online. The most significant are: Theodore Bingham's *The Girl That Disappears* (1911), Clifford G. Roe's *The Prodigal Daughter: The White Slave Evil and the Remedy* and *The Great War on White Slavery* (1911), O. Edward Janney's *The White Slave Traffic in America* (1911), Reginald Wright Kaufman's *The House of Bondage*, Ernest A. Bell's *Fighting the Traffic in Young Girls* (1910), and Ernest A. Bell's *The War on the White Slave Trade* (1910). Investigative journalists also frequently published articles on prostitution in magazines including *McClure's, Collier's, Survey, Current Opinion, Forum*, and others. As always, *The Reader's Guide to Periodical Literature* is useful for locating articles, though researchers should use search terms that would be specific to the period under consideration (for example, for the Progressive Era, "vice" or "social evil" would be more useful search terms than "prostitution").

Women's rights activists frequently wrote about prostitution as a way to highlight women's economic, sexual, and political vulnerability. The most comprehensive texts are Jane Addams's 1912 *A New Conscience and an Ancient Evil* and Maude Miner's *Slavery of Prostitution: A Plea for Emancipation* from 1916. Emma Goldman's essay "Traffic in Women" from 1911 remains a classic in the fields of women's history and Marxism. The Sophia Smith Collection at Smith College Archive has a prostitution collection from between 1834 and 1983 that features many works by women's rights activists on the topic. The Harriet Laidlaw papers at the Schlesinger Library are also very useful and some have been digitized. The Schlesinger is also home to the records of COYOTE, which also includes ephemera from other sex workers' rights organizations.

Even with the millions and millions of pages of investigations, exposés, melodramatic tales, and fiery sermons, the unmitigated voices of women who sold sex remain exceedingly rare. Though many madams published memoirs, most of these were ghostwritten and are not particularly trustworthy. The only records we have that reflect the freely offered voice of a woman who sold sex are still the *Mamie Papers*, a set of correspondence between a Jewish woman who sold sex and a Bostonian philanthropist from the 1910s.[224]

DIGITAL EXHIBITS AND MATERIALS

Storyville, New Orleans (http://www.storyvilledistrictnola.com/). Includes a multitude of pictures, blue books (guides to the city's vice offerings), biographies of madams, and the jazz that was born in the brothels of New Orleans. It is a bit romanticizing, but has lovely primary sources.

Capitalism by Gaslight (http://www.librarycompany.org/shadoweconomy/). This online exhibition examines the shadow economy in 19th-century America. It has a section devoted to selling sex that includes paintings and illustrations depicting prostitution, a map of Philadelphia locating the city's brothels from 1849, numerous gentleman's guides, Dr. William Sanger's groundbreaking 1855 study of the social background of New York City's incarcerated prostitutes, and numerous other illuminating primary sources. The website is best for materials from the 1830s to the 1880s.

Digital Harlem (http://digitalharlem.org/). This site offers rich material on Harlem from 1915 to 1930. Though it features digital mapping of arrests, nightlife venues, and important events, its search function can be difficult to navigate. It is most useful for its ability to contextualize the informal and formal economies of the neighborhood.

Prostitution and Brothel Drama in the Progressive Era (https://brotheldrama.lib.miamioh.edu/). White slavery provided juicy plotlines for playwrights and early filmmakers during the Progressive Era. Dr. Katie Johnson, the foremost scholar of this phenomenon, has developed a digital humanities website that will be of interest to scholars, teachers, and students alike. It offers an analysis and some primary sources of the most riveting brothel dramas produced.

Prostitution in Philadelphia: Arrests, 1912–1918 (http://web.stanford.edu/group/spatial history/cgi-bin/site/viz.php?id=267&project _id=0). This website offers a spatial analysis of prostitution arrests in Philadelphia and shows how the policing of vice overlapped with the policing of black communities.

FURTHER READING

Blair, Cynthia M. *I've Got to Make My Livin': Black Women's Sex Work in Turn-of-the-Century Chicago.* Chicago: University of Chicago Press, 2010.

Brandt, Allan M. *No Magic Bullet: A Social History of Venereal Disease in the United States Since 1880.* New York: Oxford University Press, 1987.

Bristow, Edward J. *Prostitution and Prejudice: The Jewish Fight Against White Slavery, 1870–1939.* New York: Schocken Books, 1982.

Butler, Anne M. *Daughters of Joy, Sisters of Misery: Prostitutes in the American West, 1865–90.* Urbana-Champaign: University of Illinois Press, 1987.

Chateauvert, Melinda. *Sex Workers Unite: A History of the Movement from Stonewall to SlutWalk.* Boston: Beacon Press, 2013.

Clement, Elizabeth Alice. *Love for Sale: Courting, Treating, and Prostitution in New York City, 1900–1945.* Chapel Hill: University of North Carolina Press, 2006.

Connelly, Mark Thomas. *The Response to Prostitution in the Progressive Era.* Chapel Hill: University of North Carolina Press, 1980.

Delgado, Grace Peña. "Border Control and Sexual Policing: White Slavery and Prostitution along the U.S.–Mexico Borderlands, 1903–1910." *Western Historical Quarterly* 43, no. 2 (2012): 157–178.

D'Emilio, John, and Estelle B. Freedman. *Intimate Matters: A History of Sexuality in America* (3rd ed.). Chicago: University of Chicago Press, 2012.

Gilfoyle, Timothy J. *City of Eros: New York City, Prostitution, and the Commercialization of Sex, 1790–1920.* New York: W. W. Norton, 1994.

Godbeer, Richard. *Sexual Revolution in Early America.* Baltimore: Johns Hopkins University Press, 2002.

Harris, LaShawn. *Sex Workers, Psychics, and Numbers Runners: Black Women in New York City's Underground Economy.* Urbana-Champaign: University of Illinois Press, 2016.

Hegarty, Marilyn E. *Victory Girls, Khaki-Wackies, and Patriotutes: The Regulation of Female Sexuality During World War II.* New York: New York University Press, 2008.

Hirata, Lucie Cheng. "Free, Indentured, Enslaved: Chinese Prostitutes in Nineteenth-Century America." *Signs: Journal of Women in Culture & Society* 5, no. 1 (1979): 3–29.

Landau, Emily Epstein. *Spectacular Wickedness: Sex, Race, and Memory in Storyville, New Orleans.* Baton Rouge: Louisiana State University Press, 2013.

Luker, Kristin. "Sex, Social Hygiene, and the State: The Double-Edged Sword of Social Reform." *Theory and Society* 27, no. 5 (1998): 601–634.

Lyons, Clare A. *Sex Among the Rabble: An Intimate History of Gender and Power in the Age of Revolution, Philadelphia, 1730–1830.* Chapel Hill: University of North Carolina Press, 2012.

Mackey, Thomas C. *Pursuing Johns: Criminal Law Reform, Defending Character, and New York City's Committee of Fourteen, 1920–1930.* Columbus: Ohio State University Press, 2005.

Mackey, Thomas C. *Red Lights Out: A Legal History of Prostitution.* New York: Garland, 1987.

Mumford, Kevin J. *Interzones: Black/White Sex Districts in Chicago and New York in the Early Twentieth Century.* New York: Columbia University Press, 1997.

Oharazeki, Kazuhiro. *Japanese Prostitutes in the North American West, 1887–1920.* Seattle: University of Washington Press, 2016.

Rosas, Lilia Raquel Dueñas. "(De)sexing Prostitution: Sex Work, Reform, and Womanhood in Progressive Texas, 1889–1925." PhD dissertation, University of Texas, 2012.

Rosen, Ruth. *The Lost Sisterhood: Prostitution in America, 1900–1918.* Baltimore: Johns Hopkins University Press, 1983.

Stansell, Christine. *City of Women: Sex and Class in New York City, 1789–1860.* Urbana-Champaign: University of Illinois Press, 1987.

NOTES

1. Alain Corbin, *Women for Hire: Prostitution and Sexuality in France after 1850*, trans. Alan Sheridan (Cambridge, MA: Harvard University Press, 1990), 53. Judith Walkowitz makes the same observation in her classic study of Victorian prostitution in England. Judith R. Walkowitz, *Prostitution and Victorian Society: Women, Class, and the*

State (Cambridge: Cambridge University Press, 1980).

2. Eileen Boris and Rhacel Salazar Parreñas, "Introduction," in *Intimate Labors: Cultures, Technologies, and the Politics of Care* (Stanford, CA: Stanford University Press, 2010), 1.

3. Susan Lee Johnson, *Roaring Camp: The Social World of the California Gold Rush* (New York: W. W. Norton, 2000), 298.

4. Important exceptions are Barry Reay, *New York Hustlers: Masculinity and Sex in Modern America* (Manchester: University of Manchester Press, 2010); George Chauncey, *Gay New York: Gender, Urban Culture, and the Making of the Gay Male World, 1890–1940* (New York: Basic Books, 1994); Chad Heap, *Slumming: Sexual and Racial Encounters in American Nightlife, 1885–1940* (Chicago: University of Chicago Press, 2009); and Don Romesburg, "'Wouldn't a Boy Do?': Placing Early-Twentieth Century Male Youth Sex Work into Histories of Sexuality," *Journal of the History of Sexuality* 18, no. 3 (2009): 367–392.

5. This point I am taking from British historian Julia Laite. Julia Laite, *Common Prostitutes and Ordinary Citizens: Commercial Sex in London, 1885–1960* (New York: Palgrave Macmillan, 2012), 26.

6. Timothy J. Gilfoyle, *City of Eros: New York City, Prostitution, and the Commercialization of Sex, 1790–1920* (New York: W. W. Norton, 1992), 26. This is especially true when compared with the prevalence of prostitution in 17th- and 18th-century London. See Tony Henderson, *Disorderly Women in Eighteenth-Century London: Prostitution and Control in the Metropolis, 1730–1830* (London: Longman, 1999).

7. Quoted in Carl Bridenbaugh, *Cities in the Wilderness: The First Century of Urban Life in America, 1625–1742* (New York: Alfred A. Knopf, 1955), 72.

8. Quoted in Christine Stansell, *City of Women: Sex and Class in New York, 1789–1860* (Urbana: University of Illinois Press, 1982), 15; and John D'Emilio and Estelle B. Freedman, *Intimate Matters: A History of Sexuality in America*, 3rd ed. (Chicago: University of Chicago Press, 2012), 50.

9. Clare A. Lyons, *Sex Among the Rabble: An Intimate History of Gender and Power in the Age of Revolution, Philadelphia, 1730–1830* (Chapel Hill: University of North Carolina Press, 2006), 107.

10. Lyons, *Sex Among the Rabble*, 109–110.

11. Carl Bridenbaugh, *Cities in Revolt: Urban Life in America, 1743 – 1776* (New York: Alfred A. Knopf, 1955), 317.

12. Quoted in Lyons, *Sex Among the Rabble*, 112.

13. Quoted in Holly A. Mayer, *Belonging to the Army: Camp Followers and Community during the American Revolution* (Columbia: University of South Carolina Press, 1996), 111.

14. Quoted in Richard Godbeer, *Sexual Revolution in Early America* (Baltimore: Johns Hopkins University Press, 2002), 261.

15. John Rees, "'The Multitude Of Women': An Examination of the Number of Female Camp Followers with the Continental Army," *Minerva* 14, no. 2 (1996).

16. Godbeer, *Sexual Revolution*, 261.

17. Mayer, *Belonging to the Army*, 112.

18. Both quotes appear in Lyons, *Sex Among the Rabble*, 192.

19. Lyons, *Sex Among the Rabble*, 278.

20. Lyons, *Sex Among the Rabble*, 312.

21. Quoted in Jen Manion, *Liberty's Prisoners: Carceral Culture in Early America* (Philadelphia: University of Pennsylvania Press, 2015), 93.

22. Kelly A. Ryan, *Regulating Passion: Sexuality and Patriarchal Rule in Massachusetts, 1700–1830* (New York: Oxford University Press, 2014), 134.

23. Lyons, *Sex Among the Rabble*, 340.

24. Lyons, *Sex Among the Rabble*, 341.

25. Lyons, *Sex Among the Rabble*, 345.

26. Barbara Welter, "The Cult of True Womanhood: 1820–1860," *American Quarterly* 18, no. 2 (1966): 151–174; Jeanne Boydston, "The Woman Who Wasn't There: Women's Market Labor and the Transition to Capitalism in the United States," *Journal of the Early Republic* 16, no. 2 (1996): 183–206; and Linda K. Kerber, "Separate Spheres, Female Worlds, Woman's Place: The Rhetoric of Women's History," *Journal of American History* 75, no. 1 (1988): 9–39.

27. Christine Stansell, *City of Women: Sex and Class in New York, 1789–1860* (Urbana: University of Illinois Press, 1982), 175–176.

28. Ruth Rosen, *The Lost Sisterhood: Prostitution in America, 1900–1918* (Baltimore: Johns Hopkins University Press, 1983), 3.

29. For the most detailed exploration of the development of a male sexual fraternity, see Patricia Cline Cohen, *The Murder of Helen Jewett: The Life and Death of a Prostitute in Nineteenth-Century New York* (New York: Vintage Books, 1998), 230–247.

30. Quoted in Marilynn Wood Hill, *Their Sisters' Keepers: Prostitution in New York City, 1830–1870* (Berkeley: University of California Press, 1993), 175.

31. Gilfoyle, *City of Eros*, 102; and Helen Lefkowitz Horowitz, *Rereading Sex: Battles over Sexual Knowledge and Suppression in Nineteenth-Century America* (New York: Vintage Books, 2002).

32. Commentators offered many estimates of how many prostitutes were working in various 19th-century cities, yet almost all of these estimates pose their own interpretive challenges to historians. See Jessica R. Pliley, "Archival Trouble: Researching Sex Trafficking in Early Twentieth-Century America," in *Researching Forced Labour in the Global Economy: Methodological Challenges and Advances*, ed. Genevieve LeBaron, *Proceedings of the British Academy Series* (Oxford: Oxford University Press, 2019), chapter 11.

33. Hill, *Their Sisters' Keepers*, 47.

34. Quoted in Stansell, *City of Women*, 176.

35. Stansell, *City of Women*, 176.

36. Barbara Meil Hobson, *Uneasy Virtue: The Politics of Prostitution and the American Reform Tradition* (New York: Basic Books, 1987), 97.

37. Stansell, *City of Women*, 181.

38. Hill, *Their Sisters' Keepers*, 88. Though they earned far more than other working-class laboring women, women who sold sex frequently carried higher expenses, ranging from rent to dresses to hair dressing.

39. Hobson, *Uneasy Virtue*, 106 and 87.

40. Stansell, *City of Women*, 174.

41. Patricia Cline Cohen, Timothy J. Gilfoyle, and Helen Lefkowitz Horowitz, *The Flash Press: Sporting Male Weeklies in 1840s New York* (Chicago: University of Chicago Press, 2008); Philip Howell, "Sex and the City of Bachelors: Sporting Guidebooks and Urban Knowledge in Nineteenth-Century Britain and America," *Cultural Geographies* 8, no. 1 (2001): 20–50; and Gilfoyle, *City of Eros*, 130–135.

42. Gilfoyle, *City of Eros*, 77–78.

43. Cohen, *The Murder of Helen Jewett*, 83.

44. Gilfoyle, *City of Eros*, 81.

45. Cohen, *The Murder of Helen Jewett*, 84.

46. Quoted in Mary Elizabeth Perry, "Deviant Insiders: Legalized Prostitutes and a Consciousness of Women in Early Modern Seville," *Comparative Studies in Society and History* 27, no. 1 (1985): 138–158, quote on 143.

47. Donna J. Guy, *Sex and Danger in Buenos Aires: Prostitution, Family, and Nation in Argentina* (Lincoln: University of Nebraska Press, 1990), 13.

48. John C. Burnham, "The Progressive Era Revolution in American Attitudes toward Sex," *Journal of American History* 59, no. 4 (1973): 885–908, 894; and Mary Spongberg, *Feminizing Venereal Disease: The Body of the Prostitute in Nineteenth-Century Medical Discourse* (New York: New York University Press, 1977), 10–11.

49. Victoria E. Bynum, *Unruly Women: The Politics of Social and Sexual Control in the Old South* (Chapel Hill: University of North Carolina Press, 1992), 79.

50. Bynum, *Unruly Women*, 93–94.

51. Joshua D. Rothman, *Notorious in the Neighborhood: Sex and Families Across the Color Line in Virginia, 1787–1861* (Chapel Hill: University of North Carolina Press, 2003), 111.

52. Quoted in Rothman, *Notorious in the Neighborhood*, 123.

53. D'Emilio and Freedman, *Intimate Matters*, 134.

54. Hiram Mattison, *Louisa Picquet, the Octoroon: or Inside Views of Southern Domestic Life* (New York, 1861), 18. Louisa Picquet's mother was also a concubine. Her mixed-race status increased her value in the "fancy girl" trade. Looking at slave prices in New Orleans from 1804–1862, historian Lawrence Kotlikoff found that "light skin color added over 5.3 percent to the female's price." Quoted in Brenda E. Stevenson, "What's Love Got to Do with It? Concubinage and Enslaved Women and Girls in the Antebellum South," *Journal of African American Life and History* 98, no. 1 (2013): 99–125, quote on 105. See also Edward E. Baptist, "'Cuffy,' 'Fancy Maids,' and 'One-Eyed Men': Rape, Commodification, and the Domestic Slave Trade in the United States," *American Historical Review* 106, no. 5 (2001): 1619–1650.

55. Stevenson, "What's Love Got to Do with It?," 115.

56. In terms of the economic "value" slave owners placed on enslaved people, the young cost more than the old, skilled workers more than field laborers, and men more than women. But as Brenda Stevenson notes: "The only real exceptions to these rules of the market were the 'fancy girl' trade and 'good breeding' women, two categories of sexual commodification of enslaved females that were not mutually exclusive, particularly since many women targeted for this trade

were mixed race." Stevenson, "What's Love Got to Do with It?," 105.

57. Emily Clark, *The Strange History of the American Quadroon: Free Women of Color in the Revolutionary Atlantic World* (Chapel Hill: University of North Carolina Press, 2013), 164–165; Emily Alyssa Owens, "Fantasies of Consent: Black Women's Sexual Labor in 19th Century New Orleans" (PhD dissertation, Harvard University, 2015), 36; and Alexandra Finley, " 'Cash to Corinna': Domestic Labor and Sexual Economy in the 'Fancy Trade'," *Journal of American History* 104, no. 2 (2017): 410–430.

58. Robert S. Shelton, "Slavery in a Texas Seaport: The Peculiar Institution in Galveston," *Slavery & Abolition* 28, no. 2 (2007): 115–168, on 158.

59. Owens, "Fantasies of Consent," 1–2.

60. Shelton, "Slavery in a Texas Seaport," 159.

61. Baptist, " 'Cuffy,' 'Fancy Maids,' and 'One-Eyed Men.' "

62. Marisa J. Fuentas, *Dispossessed Women: Enslaved Lives, Violence, and the Archive* (Philadelphia: University of Pennsylvania Press, 2016), 63.

63. Jeanne Cole, " 'Upon the Stage of Disorder': Legalized Prostitution in Memphis and Nashville, 1863–1865," *Tennessee Historical Quarterly* 68, no. 1 (2009): 40–65, on 40.

64. Quoted in D'Emilio and Freedman, *Intimate Matters*, 134.

65. Alecia P. Long, "(Mis)Remembering General Order No. 28: Benjamin Butler, the Woman Order, and Historical Memory," in *Occupied Women: Gender, Military Occupation and the American Civil War*, ed. LeeAnn Whites and Alecia P. Long, 17–32 (Baton Rouge: Louisiana State University Press, 2009), 20.

66. Judith Giesberg, "Epilogue: The Fortieth Congress, Southern Women, and the Gender Politics of Postwar Occupation," in *Occupied Women*, 185–194, on 189.

67. I am focusing on Union forces because the management of prostitution is something that *occupying* forces typically face, and the Confederates did not occupy territory in the same way as the Union Army. In addition, I have not seen any research on prostitution and the Confederacy, probably due to the destruction of records of the Confederate States of America at the war's end.

68. Lee Ann Whites, *Gender Matters: Civil War, Reconstruction, and the Making of the New South* (New York: Palgrave Macmillan, 2005), 74.

69. Quoted in Whites, *Gender Matters*, 66.

70. Lawrence R. Murphy, "The Enemy among Us: Venereal Disease among Union Soldiers in the Far West, 1861–1865," *Civil War History* 31, no. 3 (1985): 257–269, on 266–269.

71. Quoted in Cole, " 'Upon the Stage of Disorder,' " 43.

72. Quoted in Cole, " 'Upon the Stage of Disorder,' " 55.

73. Cole, " 'Upon the Stage of Disorder,' " 58.

74. Licensed and regulated prostitution has its origins in wartime Napoleonic France. In 1802, Napoleon established regulated prostitution to try to control the infection rate among his soldiers. The British adopted the system in the 1830s to control the sexuality of troops stationed in India. By 1900, regulated prostitution would be the marker of modernity and public health throughout Europe and much of the colonized world, with the exception of England, which rejected regulation in 1888 in the metropole, but still periodically applied it in colonial possessions.

75. Julie Roy Jeffrey, *Frontier Women: 'Civilizing' the West? 1840–1880*, rev. ed. New York: Hill & Wang, 1998. Originally published in 1979, 133, 136.

76. Jeffrey, *Frontier Women*, 148.

77. Quoted in Judy Yung, *Unbound Feet: A Social History of Chinese Women in San Francisco* (Berkeley: University of California Press, 1995), 26–27.

78. Except the author, Vicente Pérez Rosales. Quoted in Albert L. Hurtado, *Intimate Frontiers: Sex, Gender, and Culture in Old California* (Albuquerque: University of New Mexico Press, 1999), 80.

79. Jeffrey, *Frontier Women*, 148.

80. Quoted in Hurtado, *Intimate Frontiers*, 80.

81. Kazuhiro Oharazeki, "Listening to the Voices of 'Other' Women in Japanese North America: Japanese Prostitutes and Barmaids in the American West, 1887–1920," *Journal of American Ethnic History* 32, no. 4 (2013): 5–40, quote on 9.

82. Jeffrey, *Frontier Women*, 150; and Linda Wommack, *Our Ladies of the Tenderloin: Colorado's Legends in Lace* (Caldwell, ID: Caxton Press, 2005), 50–54.

83. Jeffrey, *Frontier Women*, 133; and Anne M. Butler, *Daughters of Joy, Sisters of Misery: Prostitutes in the American West* (Urbana: University of Illinois Press, 1985), 51.

84. Butler, *Daughters of Joy, Sisters of Misery*, 1–16; and Hurtado, *Intimate Frontiers*, 79.

85. Hurtado, *Intimate Frontiers*, 93.

86. Elizabeth Jameson, *All that Glitters: Class, Conflict, and Community in Cripple Creek* (Urbana: University of Illinois Press, 1998), 127.

87. Hurtado, *Intimate Frontiers*, 87.
88. Yung, *Unbound Feet*, 31–32; and Oharazeki, "Listening to the Voices," 10.
89. Quoted in Benson Tong, *Unsubmissive Women: Chinese Prostitutes in Nineteenth-Century San Francisco* (Norman: University of Oklahoma Press, 1994), 25.
90. Butler, *Daughters of Joy, Sisters of Misery*, 1–16.
91. Tong, *Unsubmissive Women*, 25.
92. Yung, *Unbound Feet*, 29.
93. Quoted in Yung, *Unbound Feet*, 27.
94. Yung, *Unbound Feet*, 27.
95. Lucie Cheng Hirata, "Free, Indentured, Enslaved: Chinese Prostitutes in Nineteenth-Century America," *Signs: Journal of Women in Culture and Society* 5, no. 1 (1979): 3–29, on 10.
96. Hirata, "Free, Indentured, Enslaved," 13.
97. For more on "rescue homes," see Peggy Pascoe, *Relations of Rescue: The Search for Female Moral Authority in the American West, 1874–1939* (New York: Oxford University Press, 1990).
98. See Jessica R. Pliley, *Policing Sexuality: The Mann Act and the Making of the FBI* (Cambridge, MA: Harvard University Press, 2014), 16–18, 34, 205–216.
99. Hobson, *Uneasy Virtue*, 40–41; Hill, *Their Sisters' Keepers*, 109–110.
100. Joel Best, *Controlling Vice: Regulating Brothel Prostitution in St. Paul, 1865–1883* (Columbus: Ohio State University Press, 1998); John C. Burnham, "Medical Inspection of Prostitutes in America in the Nineteenth Century: The St. Louis Experiment and Its Sequel," *Bulletin of the History of Medicine* 45, no. 3 (1971): 203–218; Ann R. Gabbert, "Prostitution and Moral Reform in the Borderlands: El Paso, 1890–1920," *Journal of the History of Sexuality* 12, no. 4 (2003): 575–604; Sharon E. Wood, *The Freedom of the Streets: Work, Citizenship, and Sexuality in a Gilded Age City* (Chapel Hill: University of North Carolina Press, 2006); and Emily Epstein Landau, *Spectacular Wickedness: Sex, Race, and Memory in Storyville, New Orleans* (Baton Rouge: Louisiana State University Press, 2013).
101. Lawrence Friedman, *Crime and Punishment in American History* (New York: Basic Books, 1993), 225.
102. Quoted in Rosen, *The Lost Sisterhood*, 5.
103. Rosen, *The Lost Sisterhood*, 70.
104. Rosen, *The Lost Sisterhood*, 71–72.
105. Quoted in Rosen, *The Lost Sisterhood*, 42.
106. George Kneeland, *Commercialized Prostitution in New York City* (New York: Century, 1913), 126.
107. Rosen, *The Lost Sisterhood*, 76.
108. Polly Adler, *A House Is Not a Home* (New York: Rinehart, 1950), 309.
109. Vice Commission of Chicago, *The Social Evil in Chicago* (Chicago: Gunthorp-Warren, 1911), 145.
110. Vice Commission of Bridgeport, *The Report of the Bridgeport Vice Commission* (Bridgeport, 1916), 41.
111. Quoted in Rosen, *The Lost Sisterhood*, 74.
112. Kevin J. Mumford, *Interzones: Black/White Sex Districts in Chicago and New York in the Early Twentieth Century* (New York: Columbia University Press, 1997), 41–43; and LaShawn Harris, *Sex Workers, Psychics and Number Runners: Black Women in New York City's Underground Economy* (Urbana: University of Illinois Press, 2016), 131. Irish women were overrepresented in Sanger's investigation of 1853. See Hill, *Their Sisters' Keepers*, 53.
113. Harris, *Sex Workers, Psychics and Number Runners*, 139.
114. Quoted in Cheryl D. Hicks, *Talk with You Like a Woman: African American Women, Justice, and Reform in New York, 1890–1935* (Chapel Hill: University of North Carolina Press, 2010), 217.
115. See Cynthia M. Blair, *I've Got to Make My Livin': Black Women's Sex Work in Turn-of-the-Century Chicago* (Chicago: University of Chicago, 2010), 86–122.
116. Landau, *Spectacular Wickedness*, 110.
117. Chad Heap, *Slumming: Sexual and Racial Encounters in American Nightlife, 1885–1940* (Chicago: University of Chicago Press, 2009).
118. Rosen, *The Lost Sisterhood*, 81.
119. Lilia Raquel Dueñas Rosas, "(De)Sexing Prostitution: Sex Work, Reform, and Womanhood in Progressive Texas, 1889–1925" (PhD dissertation, University of Texas at Austin, 2012), 35.
120. Blair, *I've Got to Make My Livin'*, 141–145.
121. Pliley, *Policing Sexuality*, 23–26.
122. Charlton Edholm, *Traffic in Girls and Work of Rescue Mission* (Chicago: Charlton Edholm, 1899), 14–15.
123. Jessica R. Pliley, "Protecting the Young and the Innocent: Age and Consent in the Enforcement of the White Slavery Traffic Act," in *Child Slavery Before and After Emancipation: An Argument for Child-Centered Slavery Studies*, ed. Anna

Mae Duane (New York: Cambridge University Press, 2017), 159; and Gunther Peck, "Feminizing White Slavery in the United States: Marcus Braun and the Transnational Traffic in White Bodies, 1890–1910," in *Workers Across the Americas: The Transnational Turn in Labor History*, ed. Leon Fink, 221–244 (New York: Oxford University Press, 2011).

124. Quoted in Brian Donovan, *White Slave Crusades: Race, Gender, and Anti-Vice Activism, 1887–1917* (Urbana: University of Illinois Press, 2010), 60–61.

125. Rosen, *The Lost Sisterhood*, 112–136; Mark Thomas Connelly, *The Response to Prostitution in the Progressive Era* (Chapel Hill: University of North Carolina Press, 1980), 114–135; Gilfoyle, *City of Eros*, 270–297; Gretchen Soderlund, *Sex Trafficking, Scandal, and the Transformation of Journalism, 1885–1917* (Chicago: University of Chicago Press, 2013); and, Pliley, *Policing Sexuality*.

126. Rosen, *The Lost Sisterhood*, 14.

127. Illinois General Assembly, "Report of the Senate Vice Committee: Created under the Authority of the Senate of the Forty-Ninth General Assembly" (Chicago, 1916).

128. United States Immigration Commission (1907–1910), "Importation and Harboring Women for Immoral Purposes," *Reports of the Immigration Commission* (Washington, DC: Government Printing Office, 1911).

129. Rosen, *The Lost Sisterhood*, 17–18.

130. Rosen, *The Lost Sisterhood*, 18–19; and Peter C. Hennigan, "Property War: Prostitution, Red-Light Districts, and the Transformation of Public Nuisance Law in the Progressive Era," *Yale Journal of Law & the Humanities* 16 (2004): 123–198.

131. Rosen, *The Lost Sisterhood*, 30.

132. For more on the White Slave Traffic Act, see Pliley, *Policing Sexuality*. For more details on the increase in the number of state-level laws pertaining to sexuality and morality see: Joseph P. Mayer, *The Regulation of Commercialized Vice: An Analysis of the Transitions from Segregation to Repression in the United States* (New York: Klebold Press, 1922), 8.

133. Pliley, *Policing Sexuality*, 118, Emphasis added.

134. See Pliley, *Policing Sexuality*, 60–83; Martha Gardner, *The Qualities of a Citizen: Women, Immigration, and Citizenship, 1870–1965* (Princeton,

NJ: Princeton University Press, 2009); Eithne Luibhéid, *Entry Denied: Controlling Sexuality at the Border* (Minneapolis–St. Paul: University of Minnesota Press, 2002); and Grace Peña Delgado, "Border Control and Sexual Policing: White Slavery and Prostitution along the US–Mexico Borderlands, 1903–1910," *Western Historical Quarterly* 43, no. 2 (2012): 157–178.

135. Quoted in Pliley, *Policing Sexuality*, 104.

136. Laura Briggs, "Familiar Territory: Prostitution, Empires, and the Question of U.S. Imperialism in Puerto Rico, 1849–1916," in *Families of a New World: Gender Politics and State Development in a Global Context*, ed. Lynne Haney and Lisa Pollard, 40–63 (New York: Routledge, 2003), 50.

137. Quoted in Pliley, *Policing Sexuality*, 27.

138. Paul Kramer, "The Darkness that Enters the Home: The Politics of Prostitution during the Philippine–American War," in *Haunted by Empire: Geographies of Intimacy in North American History*, ed. Ann Laura Stoler, 366–404 (Durham, NC: Duke University Press, 2006), 394–395.

139. Briggs, "Familiar Territory," 50; Eileen J. Suárez Findlay, *Imposing Decency: The Politics of Sexuality and Race in Puerto Rico, 1870–1920* (Durham, NC: Duke University Press, 1999); José Flores Ramos, "Virgins, Whores, and Martyrs: Prostitution in the Colony, 1898–1919," in *Puerto Rican Women's History: New Perspectives*, ed. Félix V. Matmos Rodríguez and Linda C. Delgado (Armonk, NY: M. E. Sharpe, 1998), 83–104; Julie Greene, *The Canal Builders: Making America's Empire at the Panama Canal* (New York: Penguin, 2009), 289–297; Alexandra Minna Stern, "Buildings, Boundaries, and Blood: Medicalization and Nation-Building on the U.S.–Mexico Border, 1910–1930," *Hispanic American Historical Review* 79, no. 1 (1999): 41–81; and Micah Wright, " 'Protection against the Lust of Men': Progressivism, Prostitution and Rape in the Dominican Republic under US Occupation, 1916–24," *Gender & History* 28, no. 3 (2016): 623–640.

140. Pliley, *Policing Sexuality*, 120–122; Thomas C. Mackey, *Red Lights Out: A Legal History of Prostitution, Disorderly Houses, and Vice Districts, 1870–1917* (New York: Garland, 1987); and Nancy Bristow, *Making Men Moral: Social Engineering During the Great War* (New York: New York University Press, 1996).

141. Quoted in Pliley, *Policing Sexuality*, 122.

142. Quoted in Scott Wasserman Stern, "The Long American Plan: The U.S. Government's Campaign against Venereal Disease and Its Carriers," *Harvard Journal of Law & Gender* 38 (2015): 373–436, quote on 385.

143. For more on the American Plan, see David J. Pivar, *Purity and Hygiene: Women, Prostitution, and the "American Plan," 1900–1930* (Westport, CT: Greenwood Press, 2002); and Scott W. Stern, *The Trials of Nina McCall: Sex, Surveillance, and the Decades-Long Government Plan to Imprison 'Promiscuous' Women* (Boston: Beacon, 2018).

144. Stern, "The Long American Plan," 386.

145. Stern, "The Long American Plan," 395.

146. Quoted in Pliley, *Policing Sexuality*, 125–127.

147. See Stern, "The Long American Plan," 376, n. 12.

148. Quoted in Elizabeth Alice Clement, *Love for Sale: Courting, Treating, and Prostitution in New York City, 1900–1945* (Chapel Hill: University of North Carolina Press, 2006), 136.

149. Clement, *Love for Sale*, 201; Hicks, *Talk with You Like a Woman*; Harris, *Sex Workers, Psychics and Number Runners*; and Mumford, *Interzones*.

150. Clement, *Love for Sale*, 203; and Harris, *Sex Workers, Psychics and Number Runners*, 124–126.

151. Clement, *Love for Sale*, 137, 201.

152. Clement, *Love for Sale*, 199–200; and Jessica Pliley, "Vice Queens and White Slaves: The FBI's Crackdown on Elite Brothel Madams in 1930s New York City," *Journal of the History of Sexuality* 25, no. 1 (2016): 137–167.

153. Pliley, *Policing Sexuality*, 185.

154. For more on this point, see Pliley, *Policing Sexuality*, 183–206.

155. Quoted in Pliley, *Policing Sexuality*, 178.

156. Quoted in Pliley, "Vice Queens and White Slaves," 148.

157. "Bawdy Business," *Time*, May 25, 1936, 15.

158. Marilyn E. Hegarty, *Victory Girls, Khaki-Wackies, and Patriotutes: The Regulation of Female Sexuality during World War II* (New York: New York University Press, 2008), 13.

159. Hegarty, *Victory Girls*, 77–78.

160. Stern, "The Long American Plan," 411.

161. Quoted in Stern, "The Long American Plan," 412.

162. Hegarty, *Victory Girls*, 37.

163. Hegarty, *Victory Girls*, 65.

164. Hegarty, *Victory Girls*, 92–94.

165. Beth Bailey and David Farber, *The First Strange Place: Race and Sex in World War II Hawaii* (Baltimore: Johns Hopkins University Press, 1992), 99; for El Paso, see David C. Humphrey, "Prostitution in Texas: From the 1830s to the 1960s," *East Texas Historical Journal* 33, no. 1 (1995): 27–43, on 34.

166. Bailey and Farber, *The First Strange Place*, 117.

167. Bailey and Farber, *The First Strange Place*, 95, 98, 100.

168. Bailey and Farber, *The First Strange Place*, 100.

169. Bailey and Farber, *The First Strange Place*, 103.

170. Mary Murphy, "An Exceptional Endeavor: The United States Army's Industrialization of Sex Work in Liberia during World War II" (MA Thesis, Texas State University, 2017), 148, 167.

171. Mary Louise Roberts, *What Soldiers Do: Sex and the American GI in World War II France* (Chicago: University of Chicago Press, 2013), 160.

172. Roberts, *What Soldiers Do*, 167–173, quote on 167.

173. See Robert Kramm, " 'Hey, GI, Want Pretty Flower Girl?': Venereal Disease, Sanitation, and Geopolitics in US-Occupied Japan and Korea, 1945–1948," in *Global Anti-Vice Activism, 1890–1950: Fighting Drink, Drugs, and 'Immorality'*, ed. Jessica R. Pliley, Robert Kramm, and Harald Fischer-Tiné, 290–312 (Cambridge: Cambridge University Press, 2016); Grace M. Cho, "Diaspora of Camptown: The Forgotten War's Monstrous Family," *Women's Studies Quarterly* 34, no. 1/2 (2006): 309–331; Sandra Pollock Sturdevant and Brenda Stoltzfus, *Let the Good Times Roll: Prostitution and the US Military in Asia* (New York: New Press, 1992); and Robert Kramm, *Sanitized Sex: Regulating Prostitution, Venereal Disease and Intimacy in Occupied Japan, 1945–1952* (Berkeley: University of California Press, 2017).

174. See Stephanie Chalifoux, "Women on the Move: Sex Work and Sex Trafficking in the 1950s South" (PhD dissertation, University of Alabama, 2013); Angela R. Demovic, *Bourbon Street, B-Drinking, and the Sexual Economy of Tourism* (Lanham, MD: Lexington Books, 2018), 53–70; and Holly M. Karibo, *Sin City North: Sex, Drugs, and Citizenship in the Detroit–Windsor Borderland* (Durham: University of North Carolina Press, 2015).

175. "Dear Playboy: Response to Armin J. Edwards," *Playboy*, August 1, 1954, 3.

176. "Playboy Tours the Hottest Spots in Paris," *Playboy*, February 1, 1954, 37. For another

example, see Sam Baol, "The Girls of Shepherd Market," *Playboy*, January 1, 1957, 21.

177. Hugh Hefner, "The Playboy Philosophy," *Playboy*, May 1966, 159.

178. Hugh Hefner, "The Playboy Philosophy," *Playboy*, May 1966, 160.

179. Edwin Schur, *Crimes without Victims: Deviant Behavior and Public Policy: Abortion, Homosexuality, Drug Addiction* (Englewood Cliffs, NJ: Prentice-Hall, 1965); and Friedman, *Crime and Punishment*, 3.

180. Schur, *Crimes without Victims*, 171, italics in original. The list of "victimless crimes" would be extended in Robert M. Rich's 1978 follow-up to Schur's book to include: pornography and obscenity, prostitution, heterosexual deviance (statutory rape, fornication, cohabitation, and adultery), venereal diseases, euthanasia, gambling, alcoholism, and suicide. See Robert M. Rich, *Crimes without Victims: Deviance and Criminal Law* (Lanham, MD: University Press of America, 1978).

181. Susan Brownmiller, "Speaking Out on Prostitution," in *Radical Feminism*, ed. Anne Koedt, Ellen Levine, and Anita Rapone, 72–77 (New York: Quadrangle, 1973), 72.

182. Susan M. Hartmann, *The Other Feminists: Activists in the Liberal Establishment* (New Haven, CT: Yale University Press, 1998); Ruth Rosen, *The World Split Open: How the Modern Women's Movement Changed America* (New York: Viking, 2000); Sara M. Evans, *Tidal Wave: How Women Changed America at Century's End* (New York: Free Press, 2003); Dorothy Sue Cobble, *The Other Women's Movement: Workplace Justice and Social Rights in Modern America* (Princeton, NJ: Princeton University Press, 2004); Benita Roth, *Separate Roads to Feminism: Black, Chicana, and White Feminist Movements in America's Second Wave* (New York: Cambridge University Press, 2004); and Estelle B. Freedman, *No Turning Back: The History of Feminism and the Future of Women* (New York: Ballantine Books, 2002).

183. Quoted in Ellen Carol DuBois and Lynn Dumenil, *Through Women's Eyes*, Vol. 2: *Since 1865*, 3rd ed. (Boston: Bedford/St. Martin, 2012), 682.

184. Melinda Chateauvert, *Sex Workers Unite: A History of the Movement from Stonewall to SlutWalk* (Boston: Beacon Press, 2013), 24.

185. "Letter to the editor," *off our backs*, April 1983, 23.

186. There are numerous examples of this analysis, but one of the most trenchant remains Kate Millett, *The Prostitution Papers: A Candid Dialogue* (New York: Avon Books, 1973), 13.

187. Midge Lennert and Norma Wilson, eds., *A Woman's New World Dictionary* (Lomita, CA: 51% Publications, 1973), 10.

188. Quoted in Chateauvert, *Sex Workers Unite*, 36, italics in original; Robin Reisig, "Sisterhood & Prostitution," *Village Voice* 16, no. 50 (1971).

189. Quoted in Chateauvert, *Sex Workers Unite*, 38.

190. See Priscilla Alexander quote in Valerie Jenness, *Making It Work: The Prostitutes' Rights Movement in Perspective* (New York: Aldine de Gruyter, 1993), 20.

191. Chateauvert, *Sex Workers Unite*, 41.

192. Quoted in Chateauvert, *Sex Workers Unite*, 22.

193. Quoted in Jenness, *Making it Work*, 45.

194. Jenness, *Making it Work*, 47.

195. Jenness, *Making it Work*, 47.

196. Stephanie Gilmore, "Strange Bedfellows: Building Feminist Coalitions around Sex Work in the 1970s," in *No Permanent Waves: Recasting Histories of U.S. Feminism*, ed. Nancy A. Hewitt, 246–272 (New Brunswick, NJ: Rutgers University Press, 2010), 252.

197. "COYOTE Background," *COYOTE Howls* 1, no. 2 (1973/1974), 5.

198. "COYOTE Background," 5.

199. Quoted in Jenness, *Making It Work*, 54.

200. Gilmore, "Strange Bedfellows," 250.

201. Gilmore, "Strange Bedfellows."

202. Janie A. Chuang, "Rescuing Trafficking from Ideological Capture: Prostitution Reform and Anti-trafficking Law and Policy," *University of Pennsylvania Law Review* 158, no. 6 (2010): 1655–1728; Janie A. Chuang, "Exploitation Creep and the Unmaking of Human Trafficking Law," *American Journal of International Law* 108, no. 4 (2014): 609–649; Kamala Kempadoo and Jo Doezema, eds., *Global Sex Workers: Rights, Resistance, and Redefinition* (New York: Routledge, 1998); Jo Doezema, *Sex Slaves and Discourse Masters: The Construction of Trafficking* (London: Zed Books, 2013); and Elizabeth Bernstein, "Militarized Humanitarianism meets Carceral Feminism: The Politics of Sex, Rights, and Freedom in Contemporary Anti-trafficking Campaigns," *Signs: Journal of Women in Culture and Society* 36, no. 1 (2010): 45–71.

203. Coyote Records, 1962–1989, Nina Lopez-Jones, English Collective of Prostitutes to Annemiek Onstenk, March 1986. 81-M32–90-M1, folder 438. Schlesinger Library, Radcliffe Institute, Harvard University, Cambridge, MA.

204. See Kempadoo and Doezema, *Global Sex Workers*; Jo Doezema, *Sex Slaves and Discourse Masters: The Construction of Trafficking* (London: Zed Books, 2010), 145–169; Laura María Agustín, *Sex at the Margins: Migration, Labour Markets and the Rescue Industry* (London: Zed Books, 2007); Kimberly Kay Hoang and Rhacel Salazar Parreñas, eds., *Human Trafficking Reconsidered: Rethinking the Problem, Envisioning New Solutions* (New York: International Debate Educational Association, 2014); and Bernstein, "Militarized Humanitarianism Meets Carceral Feminism"; and Chuang, "Exploitation Creep and the Unmaking of Human Trafficking Law."

205. Early yet still influential work on the history of prostitution in the United States includes John C. Burnham, "The Progressive Era Revolution in American Attitudes toward Sex," *Journal of American History* 59, no. 4 (1973): 885–908; Roy Lubove, "The Progressive and the Prostitute," *Historian* 24 (1962): 308–330; Egal Feldman, "Prostitution, the Alien Woman, and the Progressive Imagination, 1910–1915," *American Quarterly* 19 (1967): 192–206; and Robert E. Riegel, "Changing American Attitudes toward Prostitution, 1900–1920," *Journal of the History of Ideas* 29 (1968): 437–452.

206. Timothy Gilfoyle, "Prostitutes in History: From Parables of Pornography to Metaphors of Modernity," *American Historical Review* 104, no. 1 (1999): 117–141, on 122.

207. Quoted in Laite, *Common Prostitutes and Ordinary Citizens*, 22.

208. Connelly, *The Response to Prostitution in the Progressive Era*; Donovan, *White Slave Crusades*; Mara Keire, *For Business or Pleasure: Red-Light Districts and the Regulation of Vice in the United States, 1890–1933* (Baltimore: Johns Hopkins University Press, 2010); and Pamela Haag, *Consent: Sexual Rights and the Transformation of American Liberalism* (Ithaca, NY: Cornell University Press, 1999).

209. Lyons, *Sex Among the Rabble*; Cohen, Gilfoyle, and Horowitz, *The Flash Press*; and Horowitz, *Rereading Sex*.

210. Paul S. Boyer, *Urban Masses and Moral Order in America, 1820–1920* (Cambridge, MA: Harvard University Press, 1992); Gaines M. Foster, *Moral Reconstruction: Christian Lobbyists and the Federal Legislation of Morality, 1865–1920* (Chapel Hill: University of North Carolina Press, 2002); David J. Pivar, *Purity Crusade: Sexual Morality and Social Control, 1868–1900* (Westport, CT: Greenwood Press, 1973); Pivar, *Purity and Hygiene*; Kristin Luker, "Sex, Social Hygiene, and the State: The Double-Edged Sword of Social Reform," *Theory and Society* 27, no. 5 (1998): 601–634; Hobson, *Uneasy Virtue*; Allan Brandt, *No Magic Bullet: A Social History of Venereal Disease in the United States since 1880* (New York: Oxford University Press, 1985); and Bristow, *Making Men Moral*.

211. Blair, *I've Got to Make My Livin'*; and Mumford, *Interzones*.

212. Gilfoyle, *City of Eros*.

213. Rosen, *The Lost Sisterhood*; Wood, *The Freedom of the Streets*; and Stansell, *City of Women*.

214. Timothy Gilfoyle, "Prostitutes in History: From Parables of Pornography to Metaphors of Modernity," *American Historical Review* 104, no. 1 (1999): 117–141, on 120.

215. Lyons, *Sex Among the Rabble*; Wood, *The Freedom of the Streets*; Clement, *Love for Sale*; Hicks, *Talk with You Like a Woman*; and Harris, *Sex Workers, Psychics and Number Runners*.

216. Ruth Rosen and Sue Davidson, eds., *The Mamie Papers* (Old Westbury, NY: Feminist Press, 1977), xxv.

217. Cohen, *The Murder of Helen Jewett*.

218. See Judith Walkowitz, "Response," *Journal of Women's History* 29, no. 4 (2017): 181–195, quote on 181.

219. Delgado, "Border Control and Sexual Policing"; Pliley, *Policing Sexuality*; Gardner, *The Qualities of a Citizen*; Luibhéid, *Entry Denied*; Kazuhiro Oharazeki, *Japanese Prostitutes in the North American West, 1887–1920* (Seattle: University of Washington Press, 2016); Roberts, *What Soldiers Do*; David J. Pivar, "The Military, Prostitution, and Colonial Peoples: India and the Philippines, 1885–1917," *Journal of Sex Research* 17, no. 3 (1981): 256–269; and Paul A. Kramer, "A Darkness Enters the Home: The Politics of Prostitution during the Philippine–American War," in *Haunted by Empire: Geographies of*

Intimacy in North American History, ed. Ann Laura Stoler, 366–404 (Durham, NC: Duke University Press, 2006).

220. Hobson, *Uneasy Virtue*, 140.
221. Timothy J. Gilfoyle, "Prostitutes in the Archives: Problems and Possibilities in Documenting the History of Sexuality," *American Archivist* 57 (1994): 514–527, on 520.
222. Vern Bullough, Barrett Elcan, Margaret Deacon, and Bonnie Bullough, eds., *A Bibliography of Prostitution* (New York: Garland, Inc., 1977).
223. Immigration and Naturalization Service, *Records of the Immigration and Naturalization Service, Series A: Subject Correspondence Files, Part 5: Prostitution and "White Slavery"*, ed. Alan Kraut (Bethesda, MD: University Publications of America, 1997).
224. Rosen and Davidson, eds., *The Mamie Papers*.

Jessica Pliley

DRUG SUBCULTURES IN THE AMERICAN CITY

NINETEENTH-CENTURY OPIATE CONSUMPTION

Although the extant literature says more about the 19th-century arrival of opiates in the medical realm, some accounts point to the existence of non-medical drug use before the end of the century. As early as 1810 reports suggested that opium was abused among prostitutes, alcoholics, and those deemed mentally disturbed. The non-medical use of opiates was far from widespread but a reality nonetheless. In the late 1840s medical and dental students were reported to take ether and chloroform at parties.[1] Toward the end of the 19th century, the United States was experiencing rapid industrialization and urbanization. In this context, and with the influence of the advertising industry, urban Americans had more time for leisure and the consumption of recreational substances. At the same time, African Americans and other minorities moved to Northern, Midwestern, and Western cities.

In new or expanding working-class neighborhoods, the consumption of alcohol and other mind-altering substances naturally increased.

In 1880 a survey in Chicago found that in the fifty drug stores that responded, 235 customers admitted they had an opiate habit.[2] A notable characteristic of pre-20th-century opiate addiction was that the majority of addicts were middle-class women, with Albany the capital of addiction. This trend continued well into the 20th century in places like Jacksonville and Memphis. They were typically housewives, but unmarried women (domestics, teachers, actresses, and especially prostitutes, whose habits interrupted menstruation) also became addicted. Nurses and doctors' wives were particularly exposed. Many physicians, dentists, and pharmacists, who could easily access opiates, became dependent.[3]

Taking morphine to relieve pain was an acceptable medical practice and subsequent addiction was deemed an unfortunate side effect. Smoking opium on the other hand was perceived as deviant. Chinese immigrants brought this practice to the United States between 1850 and 1880 and became stigmatized as a result—some of them were already addicted in their home country before they moved to the United States. They initially came to California—San Francisco's Chinatown was an important place for opium consumption—and the Far West, with some of them settling in the South and East after 1870. Hence, opium smokers were probably the first ever non-medical drug subculture in the country.[4]

Opium dens were critical places for the transplanted to escape their harsh working conditions (often close to slavery). There, they indulged in the comfort of a pipe and of a prostitute. Addiction was not the only possible side effect of this practice: sustaining a costly habit further removed the Chinese workers from the perspective of one day clearing all the debts they had incurred to move across from their country. This profited both the local underworld (the tongs), who controlled opium consumption, and merchant-creditors, who controlled the laborers' lives.[5] After 1870 the drug was no longer confined to Chinese communities. Young males in Western cities smoked it in opium dens usually controlled by the Chinese. Prostitutes, gamblers, and criminals were also reported to indulge. Some feared that opium smoking was spreading to the upper classes (the "idle" rich), even though that category was probably a minority.[6]

Chinese consumers, by virtue of their immigrant status, had little or no incentive to mix with the locals. This in turn contributed further to their exclusion from American society. In this context they were encouraged to move closer to the underworld.[7] Smoking, unlike taking morphine, was a social habit and smokers congregated in opium dens scattered in every major city, because they liked to have conversations and share jokes under the influence. As well, prospective users, who usually required a letter of introduction before they became regulars, needed the assistance of more experienced peers to prepare the drug. As in many subcultures, codes of conduct and ethics structured the behavior of smokers. They did not take advantage of or steal from others under the influence, and offenders were usually barred from coming back. Most were prepared to lie under oath to protect a den. The internal dynamics of opium-smoking subcultures were structured around a hierarchy organized according to the prestige of its smokers.[8] Those with the highest subcultural capital paid lip service to those ethics, had the ability to inhale an entire dose in a single breath, or were the most skilled "chefs" to prepare the pipes.[9]

Opium subcultures soon came under attack. As early as 1875, San Francisco passed an ordinance that prohibited smoking. The enforcements tended to be selective, and the prime targets were the dens with white patrons. Hence, white opium users were driven out of Chinatown, but they continued to smoke in small groups in nearby lodgings. The wealthier smokers had the luxury of setting up private dens, but these remained social places where most smokers congregated. Municipal and state

efforts to curtail smoking were limited but did cause several smokers to turn to other opiates as a result.[10] The trend became more obvious after 1909 with the Opium Exclusion Act that prohibited the importation of the drug. Throughout the 1910s this was clearly apparent in Philadelphia and New York City. In the following decades smoking was confined to the wealthy in New York City, Chicago, and Miami—"playboys, impresarios, show girls, high-class prostitutes, successful hustlers, and big-time gangsters," according to historian David Courtwright. Though some of them were addicted, they looked down on heroin and morphine users, whom they labeled "junkies."[11]

That did not stop many smokers from naturally turning to heroin (initially marketed as cough syrup in 1898) and morphine. Both drugs were available through licit channels and much cheaper than opium. Non-medical heroin appeared around 1910 and it was first snorted like cocaine because of fears of the needle, which was associated with painful shots. At that time heroin sniffing was prevalent in dance halls, poolrooms, and vaudeville theaters in American cities.[12] But sniffing destroyed the partition between the nasal passage and injection soon became the preferred means to administer the drug.[13]

TURN OF THE CENTURY: COCAINE MIXES WITH THE OPIATES

Meanwhile, cocaine use was gaining popularity in US cities. Cocaine was initially considered to be a promising compound in an era when scientific progress seemed to offer boundless possibilities. Cocaine was first used in the 1880s as a powerful local anesthetic, as a stimulant, to elevate the mood, and to relieve pain, even though the drug remained confined to medical research. In a context of rising opiate addiction rates, some doctors believed that cocaine might free addicts from their habits. Cocaine consumption increased during the last two decades of the 19th century and peaked in 1903.

The medical profession debated its benefits and hazards. In the mid-1890s, however, medical practitioners became concerned that it might be abused by the public. Just as in the history of opiate addiction, concerns were contingent on race and class. It was fine for the typical middle-class user to indulge in cocaine, but as the profiles changed the medical profession fought for legal control. Ironically, medical doctors were the largest group of regular cocaine users in the country, but they were regarded as unfortunate victims rather than drug fiends.[14] Reports claiming that cocaine sniffing was popular among African Americans, young people, and laborers were cause for greater concern, however. In New Orleans, the waterfront workers at the very bottom of the hierarchy—most of whom were African Americans—used it to sustain the hard and sometimes uninterrupted labor. Whereas the opiates merely relieved pain, cocaine also had a stimulant effect that made it appealing. In 1906 cocaine use among black laborers was said to be very prevalent in Louisville. Because work on the waterfronts was seasonal, the drug moved around Southern cities freely. In the Northeast it appeared in textile mills. In some instances, employers distributed it to workers to increase productivity or alleviate the pain caused by the toil. The availability of drugs like cocaine and opiates in the workplace often led to addiction and was a convenient way to force workers into submission.[15]

Coke was also used recreationally. In Fort Worth prostitutes were particularly prone to cocaine addiction and its consumption probably surpassed that of opiates at the turn of the century.[16] In New Orleans, it was prevalent in saloons and dance halls on Franklin Street, where roustabouts liked to spend their spare time. Cocaine use also appeared in the city's red-light district, Storyville, where it was commonplace among poor African Americans and prostitutes. Similar reports came from Dallas and Chattanooga, Tennessee, around the same time and connected it with blacks and crime. This occurred in a larger context of

racial tensions, and cocaine taking was seen as a manifestation of boldness among urban African Americans. In cities like Houston and Atlanta, many were alarmed by this new inner-city vice and blamed Northern liberal attitudes to race for the problem. In 1900 New Orleans passed an ordinance against cocaine.[17]

In Northern cities cocaine also became associated with the underworld. New York City's "Tenderloin," Pittsburgh's "Cocaine Street," and Chicago's "Levee" district became important hubs for consumption and trafficking. In Newark growing numbers of youth congregated in pool and billiard rooms and used the tables to snort the powder. Prostitutes were also targeted. During the Progressive Era prostitution was framed as a form of "white" slavery, and cocaine and other drugs threatened to render these unfortunate women helpless. This allowed the drug to spread to the underground: New York's Tenderloin became the city's center for illicit drug use, and in areas like the Lower East Side, young New Yorkers commonly sniffed it.[18] The average urban cocaine user also changed at the turn of the century: African Americans were overrepresented in jails and hospitals.[19]

Although cocaine had to wait until 1914 to be defined as a prohibited substance, it was far from being an over-the-counter drug that pharmacists freely supplied to their customers. One of the reasons why it was sold on the fringes of legitimate business was that the clerks had discretionary power to sell the drug to whomever they wanted, because they believed that there existed a growing drug subculture that posed a genuine threat to society. Further, a great deal of cocaine was used for non-medical purposes in every major US city, and many druggists realized that they had to shoulder the blame for it. In 1904, patrons could acquire the drug in some of Baltimore's western district drugstores, but the transaction required ordering in a coded language, indicating that the coke business was far from legitimate and that its users had formed an urban subculture with a distinct argot and codes. Clients asked for a "trip to heaven" or for "a box" or "a nail," to which the clerks would ask in turn, "how far do you want to go?" Depending on the dose, they would want one or several "blocks."[20] In Chicago's South Side, one druggist's business depended on the illicit trade, rather than his legal pharmaceuticals. One African American peddler legally obtained the drug through Knox, Greene & Company and sold it with the help of runners, who plied their trade in many prostitution houses. This scheme began in 1904 and was still ongoing in 1914. The shadow market became all the more profitable when dealers realized that they could adulterate cocaine to increase quantity.[21]

In spite of the legality of cocaine, few addicts could afford their habit and turned to theft and violence to secure their staple, the price of which dramatically increased as a result of the illicit trade. In the late 1900s boys using cocaine in Chicago became so desperate that they would "hold up and rob, smash drugstore windows, intimidate drug clerks," according to historian Joseph Spillane. But even much earlier, when the drug sold for about 3 cents a grain, regular users needed to spend a daily average of 30 cents to satisfy their habits, assuming that the drug was not adulterated and that retailers had not inflated their prices. Hence, in the early 20th century cocaine users increasingly came from poor socioeconomic backgrounds, and sustaining their habits was virtually impossible without any illegal activities to support them.[22] Some put an end to their habits, but others turned to heroin, which was much cheaper, readily available, and helped alleviate the unpleasant side effects of cocaine.[23]

At the turn of the century, cocaine snorting replaced opium smoking in the drug subcultures of the urban Northeast and West. In the Chinatown area of Philadelphia, the opium business flourished in the 1880s and 1890s, and some theatergoers liked to end their evening in one of the opium dens after a show. But at the same time, many locals believed that cocaine was just as popular as opiates, particularly in that area, which was a notorious meeting ground for gangsters who used opium and cocaine frequently. Around 1907, a young man who was employed as a houseman and a clerk in a hotel near 9th and Race Streets claimed that those drugs were available for sale and use in his hotel. Moreover, some opium users turned to a powerful and allegedly irresistible combination of cocaine and morphine (and later heroin), in alternating or combined doses. When opiates were injected, adding cocaine to the dose deadened the pain of the needle.

That many opiate users turned to cocaine can be explained by the crackdown on opium smoking that occurred in various cities and by the very nature of cocaine consumption. Long before the Opium Exclusion Act, law-enforcement agents sought to put an end to opium dens. The task was relatively easy: most of those hotspots were well known to them and the characteristic smell of smoke did not make it very hard to trace. But in San Diego, the chief of police lamented that fighting cocaine abuse was far more complicated. "Cocaine snuffing is taking the place of opium smoking here, as the dope fiends find it much more convenient to use, and the chances of detection less, the use of cocaine is increasing rapidly."[24]

DRUG USE AFTER 1914

The growing fears of a nationwide drug epidemic led to the watershed Harrison Narcotic Act of 1914 (effective in 1915) that marked a shift toward drug control and a more punitive approach to substance abuse. That was not enough, however, to curb opiate and cocaine use, which was driven underground. Cocaine temporarily faded away as a consequence of the rise of heroin consumption, but it was still consumed among musicians, entertainers, prostitutes, Bohemians, and within the underworld.[25]

In 1919, a US Supreme Court decision ruled that medical doctors could no longer prescribe opiates to stabilize addiction and prevent withdrawal symptoms. In spite of the punitive legislation and dwindling support from medical practitioners, addicts found new ways of maintaining their opiate habits by developing networks of clandestine users.[26] After the Prohibition experiment of the early 1930s, alcohol and tobacco were the two main culturally sanctioned drugs, heroin consumption rates steadily increased, and New York City became a national and international hub for heroin trafficking. By the 1920s, many drug users in New York switched from opium to heroin and morphine, and for the white underworld it was easier to smuggle in large quantities.[27] Opium smoking retained some popularity among the jet-set and prostitutes, even though it was now obscured by heroin use.[28]

Meanwhile, marijuana became popular among New Orleans jazz musicians, who soon exported its consumption to other US cities like New York. Before World War I, Harlem hustlers and entertainers gathered in "tea pads" where they listened to jazz and went through complex cannabis rituals. Under the influence musicians felt that they played better and listeners believed that it enhanced their experience of the fast-paced, improvised music. The combination of the two allowed everyone to experience something akin to transcendence. Both working-class and middle-class African Americans patronized those illicit clubs, but white users were also sometimes admitted. In any event, patrons needed a guide to gain admittance—casual weekenders were usually denied entry. To find a tea pad, users relied on porters at railroad terminals; once they were inside they usually asked the bartender or a waitress. Faced with public concerns after it was in practice prohibited in 1937 (1934 in New York City), investigators looked into the marijuana phenomenon and concluded that most users were unemployed and aged between twenty and thirty, and could not corroborate reports that the drug made them aggressive and antisocial.[29]

Around the same time amphetamines joined the battery of drugs common to urban drug subcultures. Benzedrine (originally released in 1934 to relieve nasal congestion) was the most common form and was later found to diminish appetite and favor weight loss. But it was also consumed as a powerful stimulant that could induce mild euphoria. Benzedrine was mostly used as an inhaler, which could also be cracked open in order to swallow or inject its content, or in tablets. Jazz musicians playing "bebop" in Harlem and 52nd Street clubs and in other African American cultural centers of large American cities were quite partial to it, when they were not using cannabis or cocaine.[30] Several musicians also argued that heroin helped them play or helped them relax after a set.[31]

During World War II, cannabis remained available through the underground channels, but these were tough times for heroin addicts trying to secure their materials, which then had varying levels of purity.[32] The draft led many Americans away from potential addiction in major urban centers. But addiction to opiates skyrocketed after the war, when African Americans and Hispanics moved into segregated areas and allowed the consumption and distribution to soar.[33] Young urban Americans living in poor neighborhoods were particularly vulnerable in most US cities, even if New York was the undisputed capital of "junk." Youth heroin use became commonplace in candy stores, pool halls, parks, and on rooftops and street corners.[34] In part, campaigns against the use of illicit drugs were responsible for their appeal to some of the urban young, who saw them as false propaganda and created an aura of cool deviance around these substances. Inaccurate images of adult pushers getting them "hooked" were largely the product of these campaigns. For the subcultural marijuana smokers, the fairly harmless weed was a fad that could be and ended up being substituted by heroin.[35]

Bars, dance halls, and hotels were critical places for heroin consumption, but the Times Square entertainment district and its many jazz clubs were the prime locations to get acquainted. The area was a major transportation hub that allowed white addicts to secure their materials outside Harlem, which they could find intimidating and unfriendly. Heroin consumption thrived in this favorable setting populated by musicians, fans, hustlers, dealers, and a nascent bohemian subculture that questioned the postwar consensus of conformity and consumerism. Because many of these places were venues for avant-garde music (bebop) that were open late and had a secretive aura attached to them, they favored a sense of community that allowed subcultural heroin use to blossom.[36] By the early 1950s the fad aspect of heroin consumption was on the decline, but the drug was nevertheless firmly established among young, thrill-seeking Americans looking for something better than the grim reality of the slum.[37]

Just as jazz musicians found Benzedrine (and heroin) helpful for their fast-paced and complex music, speed was just as influential for the Beats in the 1950s. For Jack Kerouac and Allen Ginsberg it became "the inspiration of a new, spontaneous way of writing that blasted the mind free of convention and communicated raw physical and emotional experience," in the words of historian Nicolas Rasmussen.[38] Speed could easily be abused with terrible consequences, however. Beat Joan Vollmer, who was later accidentally killed by William Burroughs, saw her body cover in sores as a result and developed an acute form of psychosis, which landed her in the hospital. Vollmer resumed her habit when she got pregnant: when William Burroughs Jr. was born, he appeared to be suffering from withdrawal symptoms.[39]

THE 1960S AND BEYOND

In the 1960s, drug use showed no sign of waning. Amphetamines or "speed" continued to be abused among the illicit drug subcultures of the Lower East Side and in San Francisco's Haight-Ashbury district. As well, such drugs became part of a network of celebrities who were the patients of Max Jacobson (famous

for giving his own brand of "vitamins" to President John F. Kennedy) in Manhattan. Some of them like Truman Capote and Tennessee Williams became part of an eclectic amphetamine community that revolved around Andy Warhol. The drug also reached the New York working class that did not identify with eccentric bohemians or the "speed freaks." Toward the end of the decade, amphetamine subcultures became prone to violence, including rape and murder in New York's East Village and the Haight-Ashbury.[40] In the mid-1970s speed was on the decline, but it resurfaced in the form of methamphetamines in the 1980s.[41]

The 1960s are also remembered for the rise of psychedelic drug consumption across the country. These drugs included Dimethyltryptamine (DMT), psilocybin, peyote, and the milder cannabis, but it was LSD that embodied the decade. Originally used in experimental psychotherapy to treat mental illness and alcoholism, LSD appeared in the late 1950s in New York City, and close to Hanover, New Jersey, where it was legally manufactured by the Swiss firm Sandoz. The drug soon became popular in Greenwich Village, but Bohemians were not the only New Yorkers who were taken to it. Bankers, stockbrokers, teachers, and postal clerks experimented likewise, before it reached the baby boomers on a more visible scale in the second part of the decade. The East Village and the Haight-Ashbury were the most famous psychedelic locations, but LSD also appeared in Boston, Miami, Chicago, Los Angeles, Detroit, and the capital. "Acid" use transcended race, class, gender, age, and professional barriers.

LSD and psychedelics were very different from the other typical urban drugs. They had virtually no dangerous side effects and no withdrawal symptoms, even though some users did land in mental wards for psychiatric treatment. Rather than numb the senses or create a powerful energy rush, LSD altered perception and led to colorful visions, along with moments of personal insights and reflections about the world. Stronger doses could lead to a partial disintegration of the ego, which some consumers interpreted as something akin to a mystical experience. The inherent complexity of the LSD experience also convinced some users to become active on the political stage in order to correct the flaws of their society. Others found inspiration in the powerful aesthetic experience and made a career out of it.

LSD acquired an aura that made it stand out from all the other illicit substances available in New York City. The powerful drug was dosed in micrograms and was usually purchased in a liquid form, on a saturated paper, or on a sugar cube. The experience was so strong and made such an impression on many experimenters that they created codes of conduct that users were meant to obey in order to help the psychedelic community blossom. Dealers were supposed to sell quality materials at fair prices, rather than bad, addictive drugs like heroin and speed. Imposing an "acid trip" on an unwitting friend was considered "bad form," because the outcome of an experience was largely dependent on the frame of mind of the drug takers and the environment surrounding them.

In the late 1960s, users became increasingly young and were often ill-prepared for the powerful LSD experience. Even before the drug turned into a controlled substance in New York State and on a federal level in the second part of the decade as a result of social and medical concerns, impure LSD was more readily available. Addictive drug pushers saw psychedelic drug dealers as competitors and soon cut into the new market. Eastern gurus steered many former LSD users away from drugs and into new religious movements, while from an economic standpoint, many of the subculture's distinct features were recycled and subject to a form of commercialization. However, psychedelics were still around in the following decades, although the doses were much weaker. LSD appeared to be used as a recreational drug that had lost most of its mystique.[42]

With the decline of the psychedelic culture, addictive drugs came back with a vengeance. In the 1970s and the following decades, cocaine resurfaced on an unprecedented scale partly as a result of the growing availability of methadone programs to treat heroin addiction. According to Courtwright, "At a sufficiently high maintenance dose, methadone blocked the euphoric effects of opiates while satisfying addicts' physical need for them. However, methadone patients soon discovered that nonopiate drugs, including cocaine, could still produce pleasure." After a decade of speed use, the campaigns against amphetamines also contributed to the shift, and many drug users were under the illusion that coke was harmless. American baby boomers came of age in the late 1960s and early 1970s. At a time in their lives when they were likely to want to experiment with drugs, it is not surprising that illicit-drug use rates soared around that time.[43]

The 1970s also saw heroin use reach hectic proportions in American cities. With the migration of the white middle class to suburbs and various political and economic decisions, the urban core was the home of cohorts of addicts, who were overwhelmingly working-class African Americans. The social setting in which heroin was taken, rather than the pharmacological properties of the drug, was the most important factor behind addiction—Vietnam veterans who had developed a habit in Southeast Asia rarely relapsed upon returning to their country.[44] In certain bohemian enclaves where psychedelics were plentiful, heroin consumption increased accordingly when many psychedelic drug users realized that they had yet to try the "king of drugs." Many had perceived warnings about the health hazards of comparatively more benign drugs like LSD and marijuana as government lies and turned to addictive drugs believing that more warnings were further proof of conspiracy.[45]

With the crackdown on the French distribution networks in Marseilles and with Turkey agreeing to cease its production of poppies, the traditional routes of heroin were disrupted. African Americans, Cubans, and Puerto Ricans temporarily replaced the Jewish and Italian gangsters by taking hold of the new Mexican heroin trade. When Turkey resumed cultivation in 1974, and following local scandals in the police force and its narcotics division that led to severe restrictions on law enforcement, New York City was flooded with heroin. The Lower East Side replaced Harlem as the city's heroin Mecca and the drug, along with cocaine, quaaludes, and alcohol, became part of its burgeoning punk scene.[46]

By the mid-1980s cocaine had replaced heroin, and it was once again equated with crime, poverty, and deviance. The drug was cheap and now appeared in the deadly form of "crack" that was smoked. In cities like New York, Los Angeles, Miami, Washington, DC, and the San Francisco Bay Area crack replaced heroin in some impoverished areas mostly populated by African Americans and Latinos and became a lucrative business for the underworld. With the explosion of inner-city gang violence, the crack trade migrated to second-tier cities like Kansas City, Seattle, and around the Mississippi Delta. Consumption rates were surprisingly high among urban women, who often resorted to prostitution to get their drugs. In the 1990s the uneducated were disproportionately likelier to develop a crack habit than their better-educated peers. Likewise, African Americans were overrepresented in the coke-using population.[47] This occurred in the political context of Presidents Ronald Reagan and George H. W. Bush's "war on drugs" that allocated more funding to law enforcement and less to community-based treatment like the methadone maintenance programs of the 1970s.

The 1980s also witnessed the appearance of the energizing, euphoria-inducing, and mildly psychedelic MDMA (3,4-Methylenedioxymethamphetamine)—better known as ecstasy. The drug was first synthesized some time before 1912 by the pharmaceutical company Merck, but only in the 1950s was it reconsidered

for the purpose of chemical brainwashing, in a covert Central Intelligence Agency program that was also using LSD.[48] MDMA did not enjoy the same fate as LSD, however. In the 1960s it was eclipsed by the similar MDA (3,4-Methylenedioxyamphetamine) for its ability to induce euphoria. But in the second part of the 1980s and well into the 2000s it became popular in many New York nightclubs, including the gay club scene. MDMA crossed the Atlantic courtesy of British disk jockeys. Soon after, the rave phenomenon was underway in the United Kingdom and gained a foothold in New York in 1989. In the meantime, it had become a Schedule I drug.[49]

DISCUSSION OF THE LITERATURE

The social history of illicit drug use is a relatively new field that has gathered momentum fairly recently. The history of urban drug subcultures has received less coverage. Historical discussions on inner-city drug use have indeed typically focused on addictive drug consumption from a medical and epidemiological perspective. While cocaine has received some treatment courtesy of David Courtwright and Joseph Spillane, opiates remain to date the most studied drug in the urban history of drugs scholarship, with seminal contributions coming from Courtwright and Eric Schneider.[50] A possible explanation for this coverage is that opiates and cocaine have been typically perceived as dangerous and enslaving drugs responsible for widespread addiction, violence, damage to property, and general urban decay. Scholars may have focused on this particular topic to give historical context to a social problem that has plagued inner-city life for decades and elicits strong emotional responses. Further, the lopsided coverage of opiates should not come as a surprise, because these drugs have endured a uniquely long presence in US cities (over a century), unlike cocaine use, which experienced ups and downs, and LSD, which appeared in the late 1950s and remained relatively inconspicuous after the 1970s.

By contrast, psychedelic drugs have drawn less attention, in part because their effects on human behavior differ from addictive drugs and are far less predictable. These multiple meanings, which resist easy classification, have left scholars conducting specific investigations into single aspects of the psychedelic experience: historian of medicine Erika Dyck has produced an important monograph on the use of LSD in psychiatry; journalist Ken Johnson has examined the impact of psychedelics on artistic productions; and religious scholar Morgan Shipley has more recently looked at the intertwining of politics and religion in psychedelic consciousness.[51] By contrast, many historians and commentators have dismissed positive meanings as nonsense.[52] The idea that a drug like LSD could have valid social, artistic, therapeutic, religious, and political import can seem controversial, but less so if psychedelics are treated as a unique group of illicit drugs divorced from the overarching category of illegal substances.

Because the vast majority of illicit drugs began their careers in the medical arena, only to be later framed as dangerous substances that could lead to severe physical and mental damage, it should not be a surprise that most histories of drug use have been undertaken from a medical perspective. Even though the association of drugs with spirituality remains controversial and perhaps offensive, religious scholars like Shipley and Robert Fuller, among others, have also offered important contributions that make a strong case for taking claims of chemical enlightenment seriously—albeit for the category of psychedelic drugs.[53] A handful of writers have looked at how psychedelics have influenced the arts.[54] However, the field of urban drug history would benefit from more studies examining casual or recreational drug use (as opposed to non-medical use). Whereas sociology and cultural studies pay great attention to the meaning ascribed to drug use and have produced a wealth of literature, historians, by and large, seem to balk

at this prospect and continue to examine this phenomenon from a medical perspective.

Historians seeking to write focused studies on inner-city drug use should start by consulting Schneider's *Smack*. Rather than insisting on the pharmacological causes of addiction, Schneider argues that heroin use is contingent on social setting. A good illustration of this notion is his suggestion that the shift from cannabis to heroin use in postwar New York City occurred as a result of a favorable subcultural substrate that allowed users to easily switch to a new drug. Both drugs were illegal and stigmatized and part of an underground network that was naturally inclined to disregard official public health warnings. That is not to diminish the importance of pharmacology, however—too many superficial takes on "drugs" have lumped cannabis, speed, LSD, and heroin into that category, without clearly understanding their effects on the human mind and body.

Moreover, a disproportionate number of studies on urban drug use have focused on New York City rather than other major urban centers. This is quite understandable given its sheer size and its historically widespread illicit substance use. Schneider's seminal monograph occasionally looks at other cities, but the bulk of his narrative is set in New York City.[55] Elsewhere, Jessica Neptune has examined how in 1973 Governor Nelson Rockefeller enacted a series of tough measures that targeted heroin use, which were not the product of a white backlash against drug use but the consequence of local despair with opiates, particularly among African American community leaders from Harlem.[56] As a report of the National Institute for Drug Addiction (NIDA) on drug addiction among young men in New York City indicates, the city maintains a Narcotics Register (based on reports from the police and treatment facilities) that lists opiate users, which is a unique tool to examine heroin addiction.[57]

Further studies might examine the Legalize Marijuana movement and how the various chapters in major US cities connected to further their common agenda. They could also build on existing studies that have focused on the changes in drug policies regarding the problem of addiction and the shift toward methadone-based treatment.[58] This would be a useful way of contextualizing the current wave of medicalization and decriminalization of cannabis. Additionally, the consumption of the peyote cactus among Native American Indians has been well covered in history and anthropology, but a study focusing on non-Indian use in major cities would make for a fascinating history. While the use of LSD and psychedelics in New York City has been covered, studies in Midwestern cities like Chicago and Detroit could be an interesting way of probing their relationship with the local countercultures.[59] Somewhat surprisingly, the literature lacks a scholarly treatment of the history of psychedelia in the San Francisco Bay Area, which has been mostly covered by journalists.[60] Finally, a scholarly history of inner-city MDMA (3,4-Methylenedioxymethamphetamine) use based on newspaper coverage and oral histories would make for a valuable study that would depart from the journalistic treatments of the topic.

PRIMARY SOURCES

Among the archival collections that are particularly useful for conducting research into drug use, the Ludlow-Santa Domingo Library at Harvard University is the largest collection of materials pertaining to altered states of consciousness in the entire world. The Peter G. Stafford Papers at Columbia University are the starting point for any history of drug use in the 1960s. The collection contains vast textual resources on drug use and drug subcultures. Stafford himself was passionate about LSD and psychedelics, but the documents gathered here also inform on addictive drugs, roughly from the late 1950s to the early 1970s. At the New York Public Library, historians looking to make sense of Timothy Leary's

impact on psychedelic drug subcultures in New York City and Concord, Massachusetts, would be well advised to look at his papers (http://archives.nypl.org/mss/18400), which reveal that many New Yorkers were involved in his controversial research and movement to promote the use of psychedelics. Historians interested in studying addiction in the first part of the 20th century should consult the Lawrence Kolb Papers (https://www.lib.umich.edu /database/narcotic-addiction-and-mental -health-clinical-papers-lawrence-kolb-sr) at the National Library of Medicine in Bethesda, Maryland, which have now been digitized.

For research into drug subcultures in New York City, David Courtwright has co-edited an impressive collection of oral histories that range from the early 20th century to 1965 and that usefully illustrate the lives and daily routines of addicts in New York City.[61] The classic "LaGuardia Report" on patterns of cannabis use in New York City will also be a good starting point to fill the gap in the scholarship.[62] The findings of NIDA (National Institute for Drug Addiction) research into patterns of illicit drug use in Manhattan among young men can also be a good starting point to examine drug use along race, class, and gender lines in the 1960s and 1970s.[63] Howard Lotsoff's account on the ibogaine movement in New York City is a valuable source for historians of health activism looking to study an overlooked aspect of psychedelic research after the 1960s and convergence with Act Up and the pro-marijuana movement.[64] For studies on cocaine and crack use in New York City in the 1980s, historians can look at two ethnographies by Terry Williams: *The Cocaine vpp Kids: The Inside Story of a Teenage Drug Ring* and *Crackhouse: Notes from the End of the Line*.[65]

Those interested in writing about drug use in Chicago may wish to consult Bingham Dai's *Opium Addiction in Chicago*, which looked at addiction as a social problem that was contingent on identity and the influence of peers.[66] Dai's graduate student Alfred Lindesmith also produced classic studies on opiate addicts in the late 1930s and 1940s.[67] Lindesmith in turn influenced sociologist Howard Becker, who went on to examine the way marijuana was smoked and made sense of in the 1950s.[68] The Narcotic Rehabilitation Act of 1966 contains several statements of various medical and law-enforcement figures in Chicago, Los Angeles, and New York City that can offer a glimpse of opiate and psychedelic drug use in those cities in the 1960s.[69]

DIGITAL MATERIALS

Alcohol and Drugs History Society. https://alcoholanddrugshistorysociety.org/resources/.
Erowid. https://www.erowid.org/.

FURTHER READING

Acker, Caroline Jean. "Portrait of an Addicted Family: Dynamics of Opiate Addiction in the Early Twentieth Century." In *Altering American Consciousness: The History of Alcohol and Drug Use in the United States, 1800–2000*. Edited by Caroline Jean Acker and Sarah W. Tracy, 165–181. Amherst: University of Massachusetts Press, 2004.

Acker, Caroline Jean. *Creating the American Junkie: Addiction Research in the Classic Era of Narcotic Control*. Baltimore: Johns Hopkins University Press, 2006.

Bennett, Alexander S. "The Discovery and Treatment of Juvenile Drug Use in Post-World War II Los Angeles." PhD diss., Carnegie Mellon University, 2009.

Bonnie, Richard J., and Charles H. Whitebread. *The Marijuana Conviction: A History of Marijuana Prohibition in the United States*. A Drug Policy Classic Reprint from the Lindesmith Center. New York: Lindesmith Center.

Bourgois, Philippe. *In Search of Respect: Selling Crack in El Barrio*. 2nd ed. Cambridge, UK, and New York: Cambridge University Press, 2003.

Clark, Claire. "'Chemistry Is the New Hope': Therapeutic Communities and Methadone Maintenance, 1965–71." *Social History of Alcohol and Drugs* 26, no. 2 (Summer 2012): 192–216.

Courtwright, David T. *Dark Paradise: A History of Opiate Addiction in America*. Enl. ed. Cambridge, MA: Harvard University Press, 1982, 2001.

Courtwright, David T. "The Prepared Mind: Marie Nyswander, Methadone Maintenance, and the Metabolic Theory of Addiction." *Addiction* 92, no. 3 (March 1997): 257–265.

Elcock, Chris. "High New York: The Birth of a Psychedelic Subculture in the American City." PhD diss., University of Saskatchewan, 2015.

Gabriel, Joseph M. "Gods and Monsters: Drugs, Addiction, and the Origins of Narcotic Control in the Nineteenth-Century Urban North." PhD diss., Rutgers University, 2006.

Jonnes, Jill. *Hep-Cats, Narcs, and Pipe Dreams: A History of America's Romance with Illegal Drugs*. New York: Scribner, 1996.

Lee, Martin A., and Bruce Shlain. *Acid Dreams: The Complete Social History of LSD: The CIA, the Sixties, and Beyond*. New York: Grove Weidenfeld, 1985.

Morgan, Howard Wayne. *Drugs in America: A Social History, 1800–1980*. 2nd ed. Syracuse, NY: Syracuse University Press, 1982.

Neptune, Jessica. "Harshest in the Nation: The Rockefeller Drug Laws and the Widening Embrace of Punitive Politics." *Social History of Alcohol and Drugs* 26, no. 2 (Summer 2012): 170–191.

Rasmussen, Nicolas. *On Speed: The Many Lives of Amphetamine*. New York: New York University Press, 2009.

Schneider, Eric C. *Smack: Heroin and the American City*. Philadelphia: University of Pennsylvania Press, 2008.

Spillane, Joseph F. *Cocaine: From Medical Marvel to Modern Menace in the United States, 1884–1920*. Baltimore: Johns Hopkins University Press, 2002.

NOTES

1. Howard Wayne Morgan, *Drugs in America: A Social History, 1800–1980* (Syracuse, NY: Syracuse University Press, 1982), 7–13.
2. David T. Courtwright, *Dark Paradise: A History of Opiate Addiction in America* (Cambridge, MA: Harvard University Press, 1982), 10–11.
3. Courtwright, *Dark Paradise*, 36–41.
4. Courtwright, *Dark Paradise*, 62–64.
5. Courtwright, *Dark Paradise*, 68–70.
6. Courtwright, *Dark Paradise*, 64.
7. Courtwright, *Dark Paradise*, 70–71.
8. Sarah Thornton, *Club Cultures: Music, Media, and Subcultural Capital* (Middletown, CT: Wesleyan University Press, 1996).

9. Courtwright, *Dark Paradise*, 72–74.

10. Courtwright, *Dark Paradise*, 78–79; and Caroline Jean Acker, *Creating the American Junkie: Addiction Research in the Classic Era of Narcotic Control* (Baltimore: Johns Hopkins University Press, 2006), 13–14.

11. Courtwright, *Dark Paradise*, 83–85; quotation on page 84.

12. Acker, *Creating the American Junkie*, 2.

13. David Courtwright, Herman Joseph, and Don des Jarlais, eds., *Addicts Who Survived: An Oral History of Narcotic Use in America before 1965* (Knoxville: University of Tennessee Press, 2012), 103.

14. Joseph F. Spillane, *Cocaine: From Medical Marvel to Modern Menace in the United States, 1884–1920* (Baltimore: Johns Hopkins University Press, 2002), 42.

15. Spillane, *Cocaine*, 90–93.

16. David T. Courtwright, "The Rise and Fall and Rise of Cocaine in the United States," in *Consuming Habits: Drugs in History and Anthropology*, ed. Jordan Goodman, Andrew Sherratt, and Paul E. Lovejoy (London: Routledge, 2007), 218.

17. Spillane, *Cocaine*, 93–95.

18. Spillane, *Cocaine*, 96–98; and Courtwright, "The Rise and Fall," 219.

19. Spillane, *Cocaine*, 102.

20. Spillane, *Cocaine*, 141–143; quotation on page 141.

21. Spillane, *Cocaine*, 149–153.

22. Spillane, *Cocaine*, 114–116; quotation on page 114.

23. Courtwright, "The Rise and Fall," 222.

24. Spillane, *Cocaine*, 99–100; quotation on page 100.

25. Courtwright, "The Rise and Fall," 222–223.

26. Acker, *Creating the American Junkie*, 17. The first chapter of her book offers some fascinating case studies.

27. Eric C Schneider, *Smack: Heroin and the American City* (Philadelphia: University of Pennsylvania Press, 2008), 6–9.

28. Morgan, *Drugs in America*, 128.

29. Schneider, *Smack*, 18–21.

30. Nicolas Rasmussen, *On Speed: The Many Lives of Amphetamine* (New York: New York University Press, 2009), 98.

31. Schneider, *Smack*, 28.

32. Morgan, *Drugs in America*, 144.

33. Courtwright, Joseph, and des Jarlais, *Addicts Who Survived*, 14–19.

34. Schneider, *Smack*, 35.

35. Schneider, *Smack*, 23–24.

36. Schneider, *Smack*, 24–28.

37. Schneider, *Smack*, 50.

38. Rasmussen, *On Speed*, 95.

39. Rasmussen, *On Speed*, 98.

40. Rasmussen, *On Speed*, 172–187.

41. Rasmussen, *On Speed*, 223.

42. Chris Elcock, "High New York: The Birth of a Psychedelic Subculture in the American City" (PhD diss., University of Saskatchewan, 2015).

43. Courtwright, "The Rise and Fall," 224–225; quotation on page 224.

44. Courtwright, "The Rise and Fall," 160.

45. Courtwright, "The Rise and Fall," 149–150.

46. Courtwright, "The Rise and Fall," 182–189.

47. Courtwright, "The Rise and Fall," 226–228.

48. John Marks, "Intelligence or 'Witches' Potion,'" in *The Search for the "Manchurian Candidate": The CIA and Mind Control; The Secret Story of Behavioural Sciences* (New York: W. W. Norton, 1988), 54–130.

49. Julie Holland, "The History of MDMA," in *Ecstasy: The Complete Guide*, ed. Julie Holland (Rochester, VT: Park Street, 2001), 11–17; and Elcock, "High New York," 283–284.

50. Spillane, *Cocaine*; Courtwright, "The Rise and Fall"; Courtwright, *Dark Paradise*; David T. Courtwright, "The Prepared Mind: Marie Nyswander, Methadone Maintenance, and the Metabolic Theory of Addiction," *Addiction* 92, no. 3 (March 1997): 257–265; Acker, *Creating the American Junkie*; Schneider, *Smack*; Jessica Neptune, "Harshest in the Nation: The Rockefeller Drug Laws and the Widening Embrace of Punitive Politics," *Social History of Alcohol and Drugs* 26, no. 2 (Summer 2012): 170–191; and Claire Clark, "'Chemistry Is the New Hope': Therapeutic Communities and Methadone Maintenance, 1965–71," *Social History of Alcohol and Drugs* 26, no. 2 (Summer 2012): 192–216.

51. Sarah Shortall, "Psychedelic Drugs and the Problem of Experience," *Past & Present* 222, no. 9 (January 1, 2014): 187–206. Also see Erika Dyck, *Psychedelic Psychiatry: LSD from Clinic to Campus* (Baltimore: Johns Hopkins University Press, 2008); Ken Johnson, *Are You Experienced? How Psychedelic Consciousness Transformed Modern Art* (New York: Prestel, 2011); and Morgan Shipley, *Psychedelic Mysticism: Transforming Consciousness, Religious Experiences, and Voluntary Peasants in Postwar America* (Lanham, MD: Lexington Books, 2015).

52. William O'Neill, *Coming Apart: An Informal History of America in the 1960's* (New York:

Times Books, 1971), 173; and Jill Jonnes, *Hep-cats, Narcs, and Pipe-dreams: A History of America's Romance with Illegal Drugs* (New York: Scribner, 1996). For her take on drug use in the 1960s, see "Part III: The Counterculture, 1960–1975," 203–299; as well as Camille Paglia, "Cults and Cosmic Consciousness: Religious Vision in the American 1960s," *Arion* 10, no. 3 (2003): 84; and Gerard DeGroot, *The Sixties Unplugged: A Kaleidoscopic History of a Disorderly Decade* (London: MacMillan, 2008), 214. This list of authors suggests that psychedelic drug use has been condemned by conservatives, liberals, and libertarians alike.

53. Robert C. Fuller, *Stairways to Heaven: Drugs in American Religious History* (Boulder, CO: Westview, 2000); Devin R. Lander, "Start Your Own Religion: New York State's Acid Churches," *Nova Religio: The Journal of Alternative and Emergent Religions* 14, no. 3 (February 1, 2011): 64–80; Shipley, *Psychedelic Mysticism*; Douglas Osto, *Altered States: Buddhism and Psychedelic Spirituality in America* (New York: Columbia University Press, 2016); and Mark S. Ferrara, *Sacred Bliss: A Spiritual History of Cannabis* (Lanham, MD: Rowman & Littlefield, 2016).

54. Christoph Grunenberg and Jonathan Harris, *Summer of Love: Psychedelic Art, Social Crisis and Counterculture in the 1960s* (Liverpool: Liverpool University Press, 2005); Alastair Gordon, *Spaced Out: Radical Environments of the Psychedelic Sixties* (New York: Rizzoli, 2008); and Johnson, *Are You Experienced?*

55. Schneider, *Smack.*

56. Neptune, "Harshest in the Nation."

57. John A. O'Donnell et al., *Young Men and Drugs: A Nationwide Survey* (Rockville, MD: National Institute on Drug Abuse, 1976), 2.

58. Courtwright, "The Prepared Mind"; Acker, *Creating the American Junkie*; and Clark, "Chemistry Is the New Hope."

59. Jeff A. Halde, "The White Panthers' 'Total Assault on the Culture,'" in *Imagine Nation: The American Counterculture of the 1960s and '70s,* ed. Peter Braunstein and Michael William Doyle (New York: Routledge, 2002), 125–156.

60. Martin A. Lee and Bruce Shlain, *Acid Dreams: The Complete Social History of LSD; The CIA, the Sixties, and Beyond* (New York: Grove Weidenfeld, 1985); and Jay Stevens, *Storming Heaven: LSD and the American Dream* (New York: Perennial Library, 1988).

61. Courtwright, Joseph, and des Jarlais, *Addicts Who Survived.*

62. Mayor LaGuardia's Committee on Marihuana, *The Marihuana Problem in the City of New York* (New York: The New York Academy of Medicine, 1944).

63. O'Donnell et al., *Young Men and Drugs: A Nationwide Survey.*

64. Paul De Rienzo, Dana Beal, and Staten Island Project, *Report on the Staten Island Project: The Ibogaine Story* (Brooklyn: Autonomedia, 1997).

65. Terry Williams, *The Cocaine Kids: The Inside Story of a Teenage Drug Ring* (Reading, MA: Addison-Wesley, 1989); and Terry Williams, *Crackhouse: Notes from the End of the Line* (Reading, MA: Addison-Wesley, 1992).

66. Bingham Dai, *Opium Addiction in Chicago* (Montclair, NJ: Patterson Smith, 1970).

67. Alfred R. Lindesmith, *Addiction and Opiates* (New York: Routledge, 2008).

68. Howard S. Becker, *Becoming a Marihuana User* (Chicago and London: University of Chicago Press, 2015).

69. *The Narcotic Rehabilitation Act of 1966: Hearings before a Special Subcommittee of the Committee on the Judiciary,* United States Senate, 89th Cong., 2nd Sess. (January 25–27; May 12, 13, 19, 23, and 25; June 14 and 15; and July 19, 1966) (Washington, DC: US Government Printing Office, 1966).

Chris Elcock

Urban Migrations

IMMIGRATION TO AMERICAN CITIES, 1800–1924

IMMIGRATION BEFORE THE CIVIL WAR

The early American republic was a predominantly English society. In 1790, people of English descent accounted for nearly half the US population.[1] The United States received the first significant wave of non-English immigration during the middle decades of the 19th century. Between 1820, the year when the federal government started keeping track of immigration, and the eve of the Civil War (1861–1865), about five million immigrants entered the United States, the overwhelming majority—95 percent—of whom came from northwestern Europe (Table 1). While there was a steady flow of immigration from England and Scandinavia, the principal sources of immigration during the antebellum period were Ireland and Germany. Between 1851 and 1860, for instance, the Irish and Germans made up 72 percent of all the immigrants.[2]

Immigrants made critical contributions to the social, economic, and material growth of antebellum American cities by providing labor for development and becoming residents themselves. Without solid financial bases in the United States, many of the Irish and German immigrants settled in northeastern cities, such as New York City, Boston, and Philadelphia, where various kinds of jobs were available. In 1850, when foreigners comprised about 10 percent of the US population, the proportion of immigrants to the population in New York City and Boston was 46 percent and

Table 1. Immigration to the United States, 1820–1924.

1820	8,385
1821–1830	143,439
1831–1840	599,125
1841–1850	1,713,251
1851–1860	2,598,214
1861–1870	2,314,824
1871–1880	2,812,191
1881–1890	5,246,613
1891–1900	3,687,564
1901–1910	8,795,386
1911–1920	5,735,811
1921–1924	2,344,599
Total	35,999,402

Source: US Department of Homeland Security, Yearbook of Immigration Statistics: 2016 (Washington, DC: US Department of Homeland Security, Office of Immigration Statistics, 2017), 5.

34 percent, respectively.[3] Of the estimated ten to twelve thousand domestic servants in mid-century New York City, between seven and eight thousand were reported to be Irish and another two thousand were Germans. By 1855, immigrant women accounted for two-thirds of workers in the sewing trades in the city, such as dressmakers and seamstresses, facilitating the formation of the sweating system that would flourish later in the century. Immigrant men contributed to the material development of cities as unskilled laborers, such as long-shoremen and construction workers. Between 1851 and 1855, the proportion of laborers and servants among Irish migrants remained 80–90 percent, and the Irish made up 86 percent of laborers in New York City in 1855. Germans, by contrast, were more likely to be in the skilled trades like cabinetmaking, and only about 5 percent of Germans with gainful employment belonged to the class of laborers.[4]

Antebellum European immigration enabled not only the development of northeastern cities but also the expansion of those in the west. Although the Irish tended to remain in the Northeast, some of them escaped congested seaboard cities, moving to the interior. Westward migration was a more popular option among Germans, who were more likely than the Irish to arrive with farming skills and enough capital to buy land. These Germans proceeded to the Midwest to become independent farmers. The westward migration of immigrants and Americans, when it was combined with the expansion of transportation networks, resulted in the drastic demographical and spatial growth of western cities as the crossroads of the inter-regional movement of people and goods. These cities, such as Chicago, Cincinnati, Milwaukee, and St. Louis, contained large concentrations of immigrants. In 1850, the foreign born comprised 53.4 percent of the population in Chicago (Table 2). The steady inflow of immigrants made Chicago the fourth-largest city in the United States by 1860.[5]

Irish and German immigrants in the antebellum period had two features. One of them was the increasing presence of Catholics. Irish immigrants during the 18th century tended to be Presbyterians, but the political, economic, and religious repression of the Catholic majority in Ireland under Protestant Britain's colonial rule over the first half of the 19th century provoked the mass emigration of the Catholic Irish. By 1840, 90 percent of Irish migrants to North America became Catholics. A sizable portion of German immigrants were Catholics as well, though they also included Protestants and Jews.[6] As a result of Irish and German immigration, the Catholic population in New York City grew from fifteen thousand to ninety thousand between 1815 and 1840, and Catholics accounted for half the city population by 1865. The immigration of Catholics naturally expanded the Catholic Church. New York City had only six Catholic churches in 1834, but the number of Catholic churches

Table 2. Foreign-Born Population of Largest Cities in 1850.

City	Foreign-Born Population (Percentage) (Percentage)
Eastern Cities	
New York	45.9
Philadelphia	29.8
Baltimore	21.4
Boston	34.4
Providence	23.4
Newark	31.7
Washington	11.3
Portland, ME	16.9
New Haven	18.2
Western Cities	
Cincinnati	47.4
New Orleans	49.1
St. Louis	51.2
Louisville	33.2
Chicago	53.4
Milwaukee	64.0

Source: Raymond L. Cohn, *Mass Migration under Sail: European Immigration to the Antebellum United States* (New York: Cambridge University Press, 2009), 172.

reached fifteen in 1845 and over thirty in 1860. While providing spiritual support to immigrants, the church also served as a social and cultural institution where the newcomers developed ethnic consciousness and obtained information about American life.[7]

The other important feature of antebellum European immigrants was poverty. The material conditions of immigrants to America significantly deteriorated over the first half of the 19th century. English colonialism impoverished the Irish population to the extent that a French traveler remarked in the 1830s: "An entire nation of paupers is what was never

seen until it was shown in Ireland."[8] The Irish Potato Famine during the 1840s decisively accelerated the trend of destitute Catholic immigration from Ireland. Out of the pre-famine 8.5 million population, more than one million people died during the famine between 1846 and 1855. The overwhelming magnitude of destitution, starvation, and death resulted in the exodus of people from Ireland, and it was these severely impoverished immigrants that settled in American cities. German immigrants were generally better off than their Irish counterparts, but they also included a rural population who were impoverished as a result of an uneven economic growth in the German-speaking region and economic disruption brought about by a series of revolutions in Europe in the late 1840s.[9] In search of cheap rents, poor immigrants resided in congested slums, such as Five Points in New York City and those in the North End and Fort Hill in Boston. Unable to support themselves, many of these immigrants also sought private charity and entered public charitable institutions. More than half the inmates at the Deer Island House of Industry in Boston were foreign born in 1855. In the same year, immigrants accounted for about 70 percent of the inmates in the Philadelphia almshouse, and approximately 60 percent of the paupers in the Baltimore almshouse were foreigners.[10]

THE RISE OF NATIVISM

The influx of European immigrants, many of whom were Catholics and exceptionally impoverished, provoked an outburst of nativism. Nativism was by no means an exclusively urban phenomenon, but because of the large concentrations of immigrant populations, cities became the hotbed of anti-immigrant sentiment. Above all, immigrants' Catholic faith deeply disturbed Americans, who were predominantly Protestant. The intensive arrival into the United States of Catholic immigrants, especially the Irish, frightened Protestant

Americans, who thought that these immigrants would corrupt American democratic society and replace it with despotic papism. Anti-Catholic sentiment sometimes stirred violence. On the night of August 11, 1834, a mob of forty or fifty workingmen burnt down an Ursuline convent in Charlestown, Massachusetts, where nuns ran a boarding school for girls.[11] In Philadelphia, enmity against the Catholic Irish and their determination to resist intolerance sparked a three-day riot in the Irish neighborhood of Kensington in May 1844, resulting in the destruction of more than thirty homes, two Catholic churches, and a Catholic seminary.[12]

If anti-Catholic sentiment sparked nativism, the hostility was aggravated by the poverty of immigrants. Destitute and often disease stricken, poor immigrants on the streets were already a hazard to public health. But in nativist eyes, those seeking relief and admission to charitable institutions like almshouses were even worse in that they abused welfare funds supported by Americans' taxes. Hostility to foreign pauperism crystallized into calls for the restriction of pauper immigration. In 1837, the mayor of Boston invited the mayors of New York City, Philadelphia, and Baltimore to submit a joint petition to Congress, praying for the introduction of regulatory federal immigration law "to prevent the great evils arising from the influx of paupers among us."[13] In the meantime, Eastern Seaboard states, especially New York and Massachusetts, developed their own policies for immigration control. Building upon the colonial poor law for regulating the movement of the poor, these states enacted laws for restricting the landing of destitute foreigners and those likely to become public charges. Massachusetts in particular also developed policies for deporting any immigrant pauper already resident in the state to Europe, Canada, another American state, or "any place beyond [the] sea, where he belongs." Compared to Massachusetts, New York adopted a more lenient approach to immigration. While restricting the landing of destitute foreigners upon arrival, New York's immigration officials, Commissioners of Emigration, provided the protection of admitted immigrants from exploitative practices by fraudsters such as the sale of invalid railroad tickets. In 1855, to better protect newcomers during the process of landing, the New York commissioners opened in lower Manhattan the Castle Garden Emigrant Depot, where unauthorized people were not allowed to enter and approach arriving immigrants.[14]

Antebellum nativism escalated throughout the 1840s and 1850s, reaching its peak in 1854. From 1845 to 1854, the United States received more immigrants than in the seven previous decades since independence combined. In 1854 alone, 427,833 immigrants reached the American shore, a record high that would not be superseded until the 1870s. This unprecedented influx of foreigners created intense xenophobia in northern states. In 1854, widespread nativist sentiment gave rise to nativist politicians known as Know Nothings. Emerging from secret anti-immigrant societies in New York City, the Know Nothings pledged to promote anti-Catholic and anti-foreigner legislation by running their own candidates from their official organization, the American Party. By the end of 1855, the nativist politicians captured more than one hundred seats in Congress, eight governorships, and mayor's offices in three major northern cities: Boston, Philadelphia, and Chicago.[15] To minimize the political power of immigrants by delaying their participation in American elections, the Know Nothings advocated the extension of the waiting time for naturalization from five years to twenty-one years as their primary policy goal at the national level. The Know Nothing movement collapsed in a few years due to internal divisions over slavery without achieving this goal. Nevertheless, the Know Nothings succeeded in pursuing their nativist agenda at the state level. In Massachusetts, the Know Nothing legislature required all public schools to read the Protestant King James Bible every day and banned the use of public money for sectarian schools to make Catholic children attend public schools. Also, under the initiative of the Know Nothings, the implementation of state deportation law became extremely aggressive and even some citizens of Irish descent were illegally expelled abroad from Boston.[16] Throughout the antebellum period, cities remained the sites of ethnic conflict, nativist propaganda, and immigration law enforcement.

CHINESE IMMIGRATION

The discovery of gold in 1848 provoked the rush into California of ambitious gold miners from multiple parts of the globe, leading to the rise of new cities in the West. In 1848 San Francisco was a tiny town with 1,000 residents. The Gold Rush raised the population to over 30,000 by 1850, making San Francisco one of the major American cities and the Pacific gateway to America. In 1870, San Francisco became the tenth-largest city in the nation.[17]

California attracted immigrants from Europe and South America, as well as Americans from eastern and southern states, but the discovery of gold also triggered the first substantive wave of immigration from Asia, especially China, to the United States. Only 3,491 Chinese entered California between 1848 and 1851, but as the news of gold in America spread widely in China and the Taiping Rebellion of 1850–1851 caused political unrest and economic disruption, the arrival of Chinese jumped to over twenty thousand in 1852.[18] While mining remained the major area of labor for Chinese immigrants, the Central Pacific Railroad hired ten thousand Chinese men for the construction of the transcontinental railroad during the 1860s, which facilitated the development of valley cities such as Sacramento. As Chinese increasingly left mining districts due to white hostility to them and the railroad construction came to completion by the end of the 1860s, many Chinese moved to urban areas, especially San Francisco. In San Francisco, Chinese immigrants took

jobs in manufacturing like shoe and cigar making and in washing and domestic service. Although Chinese comprised only one-twelfth of the population of San Francisco in the 1870s, they accounted for half the factory workers in the city. Chinese immigrants eventually moved beyond California, settling in cities and towns throughout the nation. By 1890, over two thousand Chinese immigrants resided in New York City as street peddlers, cigar makers, laundrymen, cooks, or owners of restaurants and grocery stores.[19]

From the period of early settlement during the Gold Rush, Chinese immigrants suffered intense racism from white Americans and European immigrants. They viewed Chinese as inferior racial others and charged them for stealing gold from America. Under the influence of racial prejudice that categorically stigmatized all Chinese immigrants as unfree, servile laborers, or coolies, whites believed that the Chinese presence was a threat to American free labor and white workers' employment, demanding the restriction of Chinese immigration. Anti-Chinese hostility became even stronger in the 1870s, when Chinese entered into industry in urban areas. The overall scale of Chinese immigration was modest at best. Between 1870 and 1880, they comprised only 4.3 percent of immigrants admitted to the United States. Nevertheless, white workers' antagonism against Chinese as inferior cheap labor led to the outbreak of the anti-Chinese movement. Under the slogan "The Chinese Must Go," labor groups like the Workingmen's Party scapegoated Chinese immigrants for white workers' sense of economic insecurity caused by rising industrial capitalism and the depression of the 1870s, advocating the expulsion of Chinese. Anti-Chinese racism was not limited to the sphere of labor but connected to various urban issues, such as prostitution and public health. White Americans believed that most Chinese women in the nation were imported prostitutes who sexually and morally endangered American society. Convinced that Chinese carried contagious diseases due to their alleged semi-barbaric living conditions, restrictionists also propagated the undesirability of Chinese on the grounds of public health. Propaganda was hardly the only way the anti-Chinese movement unfolded; physical violence played a critical part of it. From the mid-century onward, white mobs routinely expelled Chinese from mining districts or cities in the West. One of the most violent anti-Chinese race riots happened in Los Angeles in October 1871, when nineteen Chinese were murdered by a mob of five hundred, about 10 percent of the population of the city.[20]

The anti-Chinese movement culminated in the introduction of federal laws to restrict Chinese immigration. The Page Act of 1875 prohibited the entry of Asian laborers brought involuntarily and women imported for prostitution, as well as convicted criminals. In 1882, Congress passed the Chinese Exclusion Act, suspending the immigration of Chinese laborers. The Scott Act of 1888 tightened restriction by forbidding the reentry into the United States of Chinese laborers who had returned to China, including those who had secured return certificates prior to their departure. Finally, the Geary Act of 1892 required all Chinese laborers legally residing in the United States to obtain certificates of residence from the federal government within a year. Failure to register could lead to arrest and even deportation.[21] These laws were the nation's first attempt to exclude particular foreigners on the basis of race and nationality and set precedents for larger Asian exclusion policy in the early 20th century.

IMMIGRATION IN THE GILDED AGE AND PROGRESSIVE ERA

The Gilded Age and Progressive Era, broadly defined, marked a new era of American immigration. First of all, its volume expanded substantially. During the period between 1871 and 1924, more than twenty-eight million immigrants arrived in the United States, while

less than eight million entered the country during the five previous decades since 1820 combined. At the turn of the 20th century (1890 and 1910), nearly 15 percent of the US population was foreign born, the record high in American history that has not been broken (Table 3). Immigrants' presence was particularly noticeable in cities. In 1910, the foreign born accounted for 41 percent of the population in New York City; 36 percent in Chicago and Boston; 35 percent in Cleveland; 34 percent in Detroit, Providence, and San Francisco; 32 percent in Newark; 28 percent in Seattle; and 25 percent in Philadelphia.[22]

The so-called "old" immigrant groups, such as the English, Irish, and Germans, continued to come to the United States. Traditional ethnic prejudice against the Irish and Germans never disappeared, but their overall status in American society rose after the Civil War. The Irish in particular achieved significant advancement in politics. Local Democratic Irish politicians, or bosses, established personal relationships with Irish American residents in their neighborhoods by distributing patronage, services, and job contracts to them

Table 3. Proportion of the Foreign Born to the US Population (Percentage), 1850–1920.

1850	9.7
1860	13.2
1870	14.4
1880	13.3
1890	14.8
1900	13.6
1910	14.7
1920	13.2

Source: US Bureau of the Census, *Historical Census Statistics on the Foreign-Born Population of the United States: 1850 to 1990*, compiled by Campbell Gibson and Emily Lennon (Washington, DC: US Bureau of the Census, Population Division, 1999), 22.

and secured their votes in return. Taking advantage of the numerical strength of Irish American voters, Irish bosses controlled the local Democratic Party and ultimately city politics. Irish bosses dominated municipal politics in New York City between 1871 and 1924, and similar patterns of Irish rule appeared in other major cities, such as Boston, Chicago, and San Francisco.[23]

Despite the continuous arrival of immigrants from traditional sending countries, patterns of immigration fundamentally changed. Prior to the Civil War, immigrants predominantly came from northern and western Europe. At the turn of the 20th century, however, those from southern and eastern Europe who fled economic displacement, political repression, and religious persecution in their homelands, such as Italians, Slavic peoples from Austria-Hungary like Poles and Slovaks, and Russian Jews, became the major immigrant groups. Between 1901 and 1910, nearly 70 percent of immigrants to the United States came from southeastern Europe, while the proportion of those from northwestern Europe was reduced to around 20 percent (Table 4).[24] The majority of these "new" immigrants settled in urban areas, transforming the ethnic structure of the population in American cities. In New York City in 1890, Irish and German immigrants accounted for 63 percent of the city's foreign-born population, while only 13 percent of them came from Italy and Russia. By 1910, the Irish and German proportion shrank to 27 percent and that for the new immigrants expanded to 43 percent. As new immigrants settled, new ethnic neighborhoods like Little Italy emerged, enriching social, cultural, and religious diversity in American cities. The Lower East Side of New York City was particularly known for vibrant Jewish communities, which developed distinct ethnic institutions, such as Yiddish theater, literature, journalism, art, and labor unions.[25]

The arrival of new immigrants coincided with America's second industrial revolution,

Table 4. European Immigration to the United States, 1901–1910.

Country	Number	Percentage
Austria-Hungary	2,145,266	24.4
Italy	2,045,877	23.2
Russia	1,597,306	18.2
Britain	525,590	6.0
Germany	341,498	3.9
Ireland	339,065	3.9
Sweden	249,534	2.8
Norway	190,605	2.2
Greece	167,519	1.9
Other European	453,780	5.2
Total European	8,056,040	91.6
Total Immigration	8,795,386	

Source: Roger Daniels, *Coming to America: A History of Immigration and Ethnicity in American Life*, 2nd ed. (New York: HarperCollins, 2002), 188; and US Department of Homeland Security, *Yearbook of Immigration Statistics: 2016* (Washington, DC: US Department of Homeland Security, Office of Immigration Statistics, 2017), 5.

and they entered the United States as the major source of the industrial labor force. Unskilled immigrant labor sustained the mass production of iron, steel, and machinery in industrial cities such as Chicago and Pittsburgh. Of fourteen thousand laborers working at the Carnegie steel plant in Pittsburgh at the turn of the century, more than eleven thousand were southern and eastern Europeans. In some cases, the entry of new immigrants into the American labor force served as a leverage for older immigrant groups. Before the Civil War, unskilled construction work in New York City heavily relied on the Irish. By 1910, however, 20 percent of the city's construction workers were Italians. Italian laborers' participation in the construction industry pushed many Irish into foremen positions, and over 70 percent of Irish construction workers engaged in skilled jobs by 1910. Immigrants had mixed relationships with the labor movement in this period. On the one hand, German and Irish workers played critical roles in key labor events and organizations, such as the eight-hour movement, the Knights of Labor, the founding of the American Federation of Labor, and the Homestead strike of 1892. On the other hand, new immigrants were often alienated by Irish and German labor activists, who viewed them as too unruly to be included in unions. Nevertheless, more inclusive labor unionism that incorporated new immigrants, such as the Amalgamated Clothing Workers of America in Chicago, emerged in the early 20th century.[26]

New immigrants were by no means exclusively Europeans. While Chinese exclusion laws were in effect, Japanese began to migrate to the West Coast in increasing numbers from the late 19th century onward. The Japanese government's pursuit of rapid modernization and industrialization after the Meiji Restoration of 1868 economically displaced the rural population of Japan, driving impoverished farmers to emigrate abroad. Many Japanese initially went to Hawaii, but soon the mainland United States became the principal destination. While San Francisco was the major point of entry for Japanese immigrants, they also entered the United States via ports in the Canadian province of British Columbia, such as Vancouver and Victoria. Japanese immigration had an uneven impact on American society. Its overall scale was quite modest. In 1900, people of Japanese descent comprised only 0.03 percent of the US population. More Italians arrived in the United States in a single year between 1913 and 1914 than Japanese entered from the late 19th century to 1924. In Washington State, however, the Japanese population drastically expanded from 360 in 1890 to 5,617 in 1900, making Japanese the largest foreign-born group in the state. Japanese immigrants found employment in farming and railroad construction, but many also settled in urban areas such as San Francisco and Seattle.[27]

Mexicans also became part of urban America at the turn of the 20th century. Mexico experienced considerable population growth from 9.4 million in 1877 to 15.2 million in 1910. This population growth happened in the midst of the Porfirio Díaz administration's aggressive modernization policy, which opened the country to foreign capital. This policy resulted in the large-scale displacement of ordinary Mexicans, producing nine million propertyless peasants by the early 20th century. Between 1900 and 1930, the widespread impoverishment of the rural population stirred the emigration of 1.5 million Mexicans to the United States, especially the Southwest, where there was strong demand for railroad construction and agricultural labor. Mexican immigration contributed to the growth of cities in the Southwest borderlands, such as El Paso and Laredo, Texas. As a hub for railroads connecting the United States and Mexico, El Paso became the initial home for many immigrants, holding forty thousand Mexican residents in 1920. As the biggest producer of fruits and vegetables in the Southwest, California also attracted Mexicans, who constituted the largest single ethnic group among farm workers in the state by 1920. While constant migration characterized farm labor, those seeking more stable employment, better wages, and a sense of community increasingly moved to urban areas, especially Los Angeles. The reality of life in the city, however, was harsh. Employment lacked stability and wages generally remained low, making Mexican immigrants' living conditions poor. Large families often lived in overcrowded and unventilated rooms, which had a profound impact on their health. Mexicans made up less than 10 percent of the city's population, but they accounted for over one quarter of the tuberculosis patients. The infant mortality rate for Mexicans was three times higher than that for Anglo Americans. Mexicans in Los Angeles shared the same challenges with other immigrant groups in American cities.[28]

THE NATIVIST CRUSADE AND THE DEVELOPMENT OF FEDERAL IMMIGRATION POLICY

The influx of new immigrants incited intense nativist sentiment among Americans who feared that these foreigners would undermine the political, economic, and cultural fabric of American society. As was the case with antebellum nativism, religion was a primary ground of criticism. Many of the new immigrants were Catholic or Eastern Orthodox, and Jews and Asians were not even Christians. Protestant Americans viewed these immigrants as fundamentally unsuited for American democratic institutions rooted in Protestantism. The association between immigrants and urban poverty reinforced Americans' antipathy to newcomers. Urban poverty was one of the major societal problems in the Gilded Age in general, but as new immigrants settled in slums and crowded tenement houses like the ones in New York City's Lower East Side, Americans increasingly viewed poverty as part of immigrants' natural character or as an indication of their moral degeneracy.

Labor became the central subject of nativist argument in the Gilded Age and Progressive Era. America's industrial growth in this period heavily relied on cheap labor provided by new immigrants, but American organized labor regarded them as nothing but a threat to Americans' wages, employment, and ultimately freedom. Detesting the "pauper labor" of new immigrants, native-born workers protested against their entry into the American labor market. American workers held particular aversion to contract laborers imported by business owners for their supposedly servile status and docile nature, which would directly undermine American unions' cause of decent wages and the dignity of labor. Some immigrant workers incited Americans' hostility for ideological reasons. The arrest and conviction of foreign-born anarchists for throwing a bomb that killed a policeman during a labor rally in Chicago's Haymarket Square in 1886

led nativists to label immigrant workers as violent radicals who would disturb the civility and stability of American society with undemocratic principles.[29]

Intense ethnic and racial prejudice lay at the core of nativism in the Gilded Age and Progressive Era. From the perspectives of native-born Americans, especially those of Anglo descent, southern and eastern Europeans were inferior, degraded kinds of whites, whose cultural and intellectual standards were far below those of northern and western Europeans. Jewish immigrants also constantly suffered anti-Semitist harassment. Racism made Asian immigrants most vulnerable to the nativist charge that they were permanent aliens unfit for American society. The intellectual trends of the period, such as Social Darwinism, eugenics, and scientific racism, reinforced the bigoted views toward immigrants by popularizing the ideas of hierarchy among racial and ethnic groups and biological determinism that considered the seemingly inferior traits of new immigrants hereditary and permanent. Prejudice could easily inflame violence against immigrants. In New Orleans in 1891, when a jury acquitted nine Italians suspected of murdering the city's popular police chief, an angry mob broke into the jail, lynching them and killing two other Italian prisoners. In 1907, anti-Asian race riots swept the Pacific Coast of the United States and Canada. In May, white mobs in San Francisco attacked restaurants and bathhouses run by Japanese. In September, white residents in Bellingham, Washington, expelled South Asians from the city, and three days later Chinese and Japanese quarters of Vancouver were attacked by a mob of ten thousand whites.[30]

Private organizations and the government promulgated nativist sentiment. Founded in 1887, the American Protective Association promoted anti-Catholicism. By blending religious nativism with opposition to foreign labor and radicalism, the association secured 2.5 million members during the 1890s. In 1894, a group of Harvard graduates in Boston formed the Immigration Restriction League, which quickly became the major outlet for nativists. By using scientific language and analyses of immigration-related statistics, the league propagated immigration control, especially the introduction of a literacy test as a means of excluding poor immigrants from southern and eastern Europe, many of whom were illiterate. On the other side of the continent, the Japanese and Korean Exclusion League was formed in San Francisco in 1905 with the goal of extending Chinese exclusion laws to Japanese and Koreans. In 1907, Congress created a bipartisan immigration commission chaired by Senator William P. Dillingham for the purpose of investigating the causes of, and solutions to, the immigration problem. In 1911, the commission published a forty-one-volume report. Despite the guise of the objective examination of statistics and factual information, the report endorsed prejudice against new immigrants and affirmed their undesirability and unassimilability.[31]

The most crucial consequence of nativism at the turn of the 20th century was the development of federal immigration policy. While Chinese exclusion laws targeted Chinese in particular, antagonism against new immigrants catalyzed the development of general immigration law applicable to all non-Chinese immigrants, establishing a far-reaching system of immigration restriction. In 1876, the United States Supreme Court struck down state passenger laws as unconstitutional in *Henderson v. Mayor of the City of New York*. In response, officials in New York and Massachusetts started a campaign to nationalize state passenger law. The campaign resulted in the introduction of the Immigration Act of 1882, the first national law to regulate general immigration. Modelled on existing immigration laws in New York and Massachusetts, the act prohibited the landing of paupers, lunatics, and criminals.[32]

On the basis of the 1882 act, general immigration policy expanded throughout the Gilded Age and Progressive Era. In 1885, pressure from organized labor, especially the Knights

of Labor, moved Congress to pass the Foran Act, which banned the admission of contract laborers. The Immigration Act of 1891 extended the category of excludable immigrants to several more groups, such as people likely to become public charges, those with contagious diseases, and polygamists, making all excludable immigrants deportable. In New York City, Ellis Island opened in 1892 as the nation's major immigrant processing station, replacing Castle Garden. Growing concerns about immigrants' radicalism resulted in the passage in 1903 of new legislation adding anarchists to the excludable category. Congress resisted the extension of Chinese exclusion laws to Japanese for fear of offending Japan, a rising power in Asia and the Pacific, by introducing explicitly anti-Japanese immigration policy. Yet the federal government managed to establish a series of diplomatic accords with Japan in 1907–1908, known as the Gentlemen's Agreement, whereby Japan voluntarily restricted the emigration of laborers. In 1910, the Angel Island immigration station opened in the San Francisco Bay as America's Pacific gateway where regulatory immigration laws were enforced primarily against Asians. The Immigration Restriction League's long-term advocacy for a literacy test finally bore fruit when the Immigration Act of 1917 required all immigrants over sixteen years of age to be literate for entry into the United States. The same act also established an "Asiatic Barred Zone," a geographical space from which people could not immigrate to the United States. This arrangement effectively banned immigration from South and Southeast Asia.[33]

The decades-long formation of the American immigration control regime culminated in the Johnson-Reed Act of 1924. It limited the number of admissible immigrants from one country to 2 percent of the number of people from that country residing in the United States as of 1890, the year before the mass arrival of new immigrants started. This quota system significantly curtailed immigration from southern and eastern Europe, as well as the

Caribbean, Africa, and the Middle East, while giving preference to that from northern and western Europe. About two hundred thousand Italians annually arrived in the United States in the early 20th century, but the quota system set the limit of 5,800 for Italians. The United Kingdom, by contrast, received the annual quota slot of over sixty-five thousand. By prohibiting the admission of people "ineligible to citizenship," the law also virtually suspended the immigration of all Asians. By replacing traditional qualitative control with numerical limits on European immigration and shutting down Asian immigration, the Johnson-Reed Act severely reduced formal immigrant admissions but ended up stimulating illegal immigration. Due to strong business interests in Mexican labor, the act exempted from numerical limitation based on quotas immigration from the Western Hemisphere, which included Mexico. Nevertheless, the act did affect Mexicans. It introduced a new requirement of obtaining visas for all immigrants, in addition to the payment of a head tax. The charge for visas and the head tax, which amounted to $18, proved to be a significant financial burden on most Mexicans. As a result, an increasing number of Mexicans turned to illegal entry and legal Mexican admissions in turn declined from 87,648 in 1924 to 32,378 in 1925. The Johnson-Reed Act marked a new era of American immigration history and set the patterns of immigration that still continue today.[34]

DISCUSSION OF THE LITERATURE

For overviews of American immigration in the long 19th century, see Thomas J. Archdeacon, *Becoming American: An Ethnic History*; Roger Daniels, *Coming to America: A History of Immigration and Ethnicity in American Life*; Ronald Takaki, *A Different Mirror: A History of Multicultural America*; Alan M. Kraut, *The Huddled Masses: The Immigrant in American Society, 1880–1921*; Aristide R. Zolberg, *A Nation by Design: Immigration Policy in the*

Fashioning of America; Elliott Robert Barkan, *From All Points: America's Immigrant West, 1870s–1952*; Paul Spickard, *Almost All Aliens: Immigration, Race, and Colonialism in American History and Identity*; Raymond L. Cohn, *Mass Migration under Sail: European Immigration to the Antebellum United States*; Mae M. Ngai and Jon Gjerde, eds., *Major Problems in American Immigration History*; and Tyler Anbinder, *City of Dreams: The 400-Year Epic History of Immigrant New York.*[35]

Historians have extensively examined the patterns and processes of settlement, assimilation, community building, and identity formation in American cities. For classic studies on these topics, see Oscar Handlin, *Boston's Immigrants: A Study in Acculturation*; John Bodnar, *The Transplanted: A History of Immigrants in Urban America*; Robert Ernst, *Immigrant Life in New York City, 1825–1863*; Albert Camarillo, *Chicanos in a Changing Society: From Mexican Pueblos to American Barrios in Santa Barbara and Southern California, 1848–1930*; Herbert G. Gutman, *Work, Culture, and Society in Industrializing America*; Kathleen Neils Conzen et al., "The Invention of Ethnicity: A Perspective from the U.S.A."; James R. Barrett, "Americanization from the Bottom Up: Immigration and the Remaking of the Working Class in the United States, 1880–1930"; Russell A. Kazal, "Revisiting Assimilation: The Rise, Fall, and Reappraisal of a Concept in American Ethnic History"; and George J. Sánchez, *Becoming Mexican American: Ethnicity, Culture and Identity in Chicano Los Angeles, 1900–1945.*[36]

Scholarship on immigrants in cities has explored an array of subthemes such as religion, labor, gender, politics, and transnationalism. For these topics, see Jay P. Dolan, *The Immigrant Church: New York's Irish and German Catholics, 1815–1865*; Hasia R. Diner, *Erin's Daughters in America: Irish Immigrant Women in the Nineteenth Century*; James R. Barrett, *Work and Community in the Jungle: Chicago's Packing House Workers, 1894–1922*; David Montgomery, *The Fall of the House of Labor:*

The Workplace, the State, and American Labor Activism, 1865-1925; Robert A. Orsi, The Madonna of 115th Street: Faith and Community in Italian Harlem, 1880-1950; Donna Gabaccia, From the Other Side: Women, Gender, and Immigrant Life in the U.S., 1820-1990; Steven P. Erie, Rainbow's End: Irish-Americans and the Dilemmas of Urban Machine Politics, 1840-1985; Judy Yung, Unbound Feet: A Social History of Chinese Women in San Francisco; Timothy J. Meagher, Inventing Irish America: Generation, Class, and Ethnic Identity in a New England City, 1880-1928; Yong Chen, Chinese San Francisco, 1850-1943: A Transpacific Community; Tyler Anbinder, Five Points: The 19th-Century New York City Neighborhood that Invented Tap Dance, Stole Elections, and Became the World's Most Notorious Slum; Terry Golway, Machine Made: Tammany Hall and the Creation of Modern American Politics; David Samuel Torres-Rouff, Before L.A.: Race, Space, and Municipal Power in Los Angeles, 1791-1894; and Andrew Urban, Brokering Servitude: Migration and the Politics of Domestic Labor during the Long Nineteenth Century.[37]

Immigration to 19th-century American cities became the principal research field for "whiteness studies," which emerged in the 1990s. For the representative works of whiteness studies, see David Roediger, Wages of Whiteness: Race and the Making of the American Working Class and Matthew Frye Jacobson, Whiteness of a Different Color: European Immigration and the Alchemy of Race. For the critique of whiteness studies, see Thomas A. Guglielmo, White on Arrival: Italians, Race, Color, and Power in Chicago, 1890-1945; Peter Kolchin, "Whiteness Studies: The New History of Race in America"; and Eric Arnesen, "Whiteness and the Historians' Imagination."[38]

One of the major recent developments in scholarship on immigration to American cities is the growth of literature on public health, social welfare, and criminal justice. On these topics, see Alan M. Kraut, Silent Travelers: Germs, Genes, and the "Immigrant Menace"; J. Matthew Gallman, Receiving Erin's Children:

Philadelphia, Liverpool, and the Irish Famine Migration, 1845-1855; Nayan Shah, Contagious Divides: Epidemics and Race in San Francisco's Chinatown; Maureen Fitzgerald, Habits of Compassion: Irish Catholic Nuns and the Origins of New York's Welfare System, 1830-1920; Natalia Molina, Fit to Be Citizens? Public Health and Race in Los Angeles, 1879-1939; Julie Miller, Abandoned: Foundlings in Nineteenth-Century New York City; and Kelly Lytle Hernández, City of Inmates: Conquest, Rebellion, and the Rise of Human Caging in Los Angeles, 1771-1965.[39]

Scholarship on nativism has gone through significant expansion since the 1990s. The foundational studies of nativism include John Higham's Strangers in the Land: Patterns of American Nativism, 1860-1925 and Send These to Me: Jews and Other Immigrants in Urban America, as well as Alexander Saxton's The Indispensable Enemy: Labor and the Anti-Chinese Movement in California. More recent scholarship on nativism focuses on regulatory immigration law and policy and violence against immigrants. On these topics, see Lucy E. Salyer, Laws Harsh as Tigers: Chinese Immigrants and the Shaping of Modern Immigration Law; Charles J. McClain, In Search of Equality: The Chinese Struggle against Discrimination in Nineteenth-Century America; Erika Lee, At America's Gates: Chinese Immigration during the Exclusion Era, 1882-1943; Mae M. Ngai, Impossible Subjects: Illegal Aliens and the Making of Modern America; Kristofer Allerfeldt, Race, Radicalism, Religion, and Restriction: Immigration in the Pacific Northwest, 1890-1924; Jean Pfaelzer, Driven Out: The Forgotten War against Chinese Americans; Amy L. Fairchild, Science at the Borders: Immigrant Medical Inspection and the Shaping of the Modern Industrial Labor Force; Vincent J. Cannato, American Passage: The History of Ellis Island; Erika Lee and Judy Yung, Angel Island: Immigrant Gateway to America; Ronald H. Bayor, Encountering Ellis Island: How European Immigrants Entered America; Hidetaka Hirota, Expelling the Poor: Atlantic Seaboard States and the Nineteenth-Century Origins of

American Immigration Policy; and Beth Lew-Williams, *The Chinese Must Go: Violence, Exclusion, and the Making of the Alien in America.*[40]

PRIMARY SOURCES

The most useful published collections of primary sources for the study of 19th-century American immigration history are Edith Abbott's *Immigration: Select Documents and Case Records* and *Historical Aspects of the Immigration Problem: Select Documents.* The bibliography of first-person immigrant accounts in Thomas Dublin's *Immigrant Voices: New Lives in America, 1773–2000* is also helpful in locating published primary sources. Newspapers are among the best sources to obtain information about immigration into 19th-century American cities. Newspaper databases such as ProQuest and America's Historical Newspapers are particularly useful and widely available at university and public libraries. Independent scholars without affiliation will find helpful Accessible Archives, a database of 19th-century American newspapers and periodicals, for permitting individual subscription, while most databases only allow for institutional subscription.[41]

An increasing number of websites make digitized primary sources publicly accessible. Particularly useful online collections for researchers in 19th-century American immigration include "Aspiration, Acculturation, and Impact: Immigration to the United States, 1789–1930" at the Harvard University Libraries; "American Memory" at the Library of Congress; the Immigration History Research Center Archives at the University of Minnesota; and the Digital Public Library of America. Genealogists will find useful the passenger database at the website of Ellis Island and passenger records held at the National Archives and Records Administration. *A List of Books on Immigration*, compiled by the Library of Congress in 1907, can serve as a catalog of published primary documents on 19th-century American immigration for modern researchers, and many of the books listed in it are available online.[42]

For federal immigration policy, the best sources are Record Group 85: Records of the Immigration and Naturalization Service (INS) held at the National Archives and Records Administration. The INS records provide a vast amount of historical information about the enforcement of immigration laws at ports and land borders and federal immigration officers' correspondence with private citizens, business owners, and officials in state and municipal governments. Researchers can access annual reports of the Superintendent of Immigration (later Commissioner-General of Immigration), the head of the federal immigration bureau, at the website of the Historical Library section of the United States Citizenship and Immigration Services. Two government publications, *Arrivals of Alien Passengers and Immigrants in the United States from 1820 to 1892* and *Historical Statistics of the United States, Colonial Times to 1970*, contain the official historical statistics of immigration, and both are publicly available online.[43]

FURTHER READING

Anbinder, Tyler. *Five Points: The 19th-Century New York City Neighborhood that Invented Tap Dance, Stole Elections, and Became the World's Most Notorious Slum.* New York: Plume, 2002.

Anbinder, Tyler. *City of Dreams: The 400-Year Epic History of Immigrant New York.* New York: Houghton Mifflin Harcourt, 2016.

Barkan, Elliott Robert. *From All Points: America's Immigrant West, 1870s–1952.* Bloomington: Indiana University Press, 2007.

Barrett, James R. *The Irish Way: Becoming American in the Multiethnic City.* New York: Penguin, 2012.

Bayor, Ronald H. *Encountering Ellis Island: How European Immigrants Entered America.* Baltimore: Johns Hopkins University Press, 2014.

Benton-Cohen, Katherine. *Inventing the Immigration Problem: The Dillingham Commission and Its Legacy.* Cambridge, MA: Harvard University Press, 2018.

Bodnar, John. *The Transplanted: A History of Immigrants in Urban America.* Bloomington: Indiana University Press, 1985.

Cohn, Raymond L. *Mass Migration under Sail: European Immigration to the Antebellum United States.* New York: Cambridge University Press, 2009.

Cannato, Vincent J. *American Passage: The History of Ellis Island.* New York: HarperCollins, 2009.

Diner, Hasia R. *Erin's Daughters in America: Irish Immigrant Women in the Nineteenth Century.* Baltimore: Johns Hopkins University Press, 1983.

Dolan, Jay P. *The Immigrant Church: New York's Irish and German Catholics, 1815-1865.* Notre Dame, IN: University of Notre Dame Press, 1983.

Ernst, Robert. *Immigrant Life in New York City, 1825-1863.* Syracuse, NY: Syracuse University Press, 1994.

Guglielmo, Thomas A. *White on Arrival: Italians, Race, Color, and Power in Chicago, 1890-1945.* New York: Oxford University Press, 2003.

Handlin, Oscar. *Boston's Immigrants: A Study in Acculturation.* Rev. and enl. ed. Cambridge, MA: Harvard University Press, 1991.

Hernández, Kelly Lytle. *City of Inmates: Conquest, Rebellion, and the Rise of Human Caging in Los Angeles, 1771-1965.* Chapel Hill: University of North Carolina Press, 2017.

Higham, John. *Strangers in the Land: Patterns of American Nativism, 1860-1925.* New Brunswick, NJ: Rutgers University Press, 1955.

Higham, John. *Send These to Me: Jews and Other Immigrants in Urban America.* Rev. ed. Baltimore: Johns Hopkins University Press, 1984.

Hirota, Hidetaka. *Expelling the Poor: Atlantic Seaboard States and the Nineteenth-Century Origins of American Immigration Policy.* New York: Oxford University Press, 2017.

Kraut, Alan. *The Huddled Masses: The Immigrant in American Society, 1880-1921* (2nd ed.). Wheeling, IL: Harlan Davidson, 2001.

Lee, Erika, and Judy Yung. *Angel Island: Immigrant Gateway to America.* New York: Oxford University Press, 2010.

Lew-Williams, Beth. *The Chinese Must Go: Violence, Exclusion, and the Making of the Alien in America.* Cambridge, MA: Harvard University Press, 2018.

Molina, Natalia. *Fit to Be Citizens? Public Health and Race in Los Angeles, 1879-1939.* Berkeley: University of California Press, 2006.

Sánchez, George J. *Becoming Mexican American: Ethnicity, Culture and Identity in Chicano Los Angeles, 1900-1945.* New York: Oxford University Press, 1993.

Saxton, Alexander. *The Indispensable Enemy: Labor and the Anti-Chinese Movement in California.* Berkeley: University of California Press, 1971.

Zolberg, Aristide R. *A Nation by Design: Immigration Policy in the Fashioning of America.* Cambridge, MA: Harvard University Press, 2006.

NOTES

1. Thomas J. Archdeacon, *Becoming American: An Ethnic History* (New York: Free Press, 1983), 25.
2. Roger Daniels, *Coming to America: A History of Immigration and Ethnicity in American Life,* 2nd ed. (New York: Perennial, 2002), 122, 129, 146.
3. Raymond L. Cohn, *Mass Migration under Sail: European Immigration to the Antebellum United States* (New York: Cambridge University Press, 2009), 172.
4. Robert Ernst, *Immigrant Life in New York City, 1825-1863* (Syracuse: Syracuse University Press, 1994), 61–82; Kerby A. Miller, *Emigrants and Exiles: Ireland and the Irish Exodus to North America* (New York: Oxford University Press, 1985), 295; and Marion R. Casey, "Irish," in *The Encyclopedia of New York City,* 2nd ed., ed. Kenneth T. Jackson (New Haven, CT: Yale University Press, 2010), 657.
5. Cohn, *Mass Migration under Sail,* 169–173.
6. Kevin Kenny, *The American Irish: A History* (New York: Longman, 2000), 45–46; and Daniels, *Coming to America,* 146.
7. Jay P. Dolan, *The Immigrant Church: New York's Irish and German Catholics, 1815-1865* (Baltimore: Johns Hopkins University Press, 1975), 15; Jay P. Dolan, *The Irish Americans: A History* (New York: Bloomsbury Press, 2008), 55–58; and Ernst, *Immigrant Life,* 135–149.
8. Gustave de Beaumont, "Ireland: Social, Political and Religious," in *The Irish Famine,* ed. Peter Gray (New York: Harry N. Abrams, 1995), 136–137.
9. Kenny, *The American Irish,* 89–130; and Bruce Levine, *The Spirit of 1848: German Immigrants, Labor Conflict, and the Coming of the Civil War* (Urbana: University of Illinois Press, 1992), 15–34.
10. Oscar Handlin, *Boston's Immigrants: A Study of Acculturation,* rev. and enl. ed. (Cambridge, MA: Harvard University Press, 1991), 256; and US Congress, *Foreign Criminals and Paupers,* 34th Cong., 1st sess., 1856, House Rep. 359, 9–10.

11. Thomas H. O'Connor, *The Boston Irish: A Political History* (Boston: Northeastern University Press, 1995), 46–49.

12. Dolan, *The Irish Americans*, 61; and David H. Bennett, *The Party of Fear: From Nativist Movements to the New Right in American History* (New York: Vintage Books, 1995), 56–58.

13. David M. Schneider, *The History of Public Welfare in New York State, 1609–1866* (Chicago: University of Chicago Press, 1938), 298.

14. Hidetaka Hirota, *Expelling the Poor: Atlantic Seaboard States and the Nineteenth-Century Origins of American Immigration Policy* (New York: Oxford University Press, 2017); and Brendan P. O'Malley, "Protecting the Stranger: The Origins of U.S. Immigration Regulation in Nineteenth-Century New York" (PhD diss., City University of New York, 2015).

15. Tyler Anbinder, *Nativism & Slavery: The Northern Know Nothings & the Politics of the 1850s* (New York: Oxford University Press, 1992), 3, 20–102, 127–128.

16. Anbinder, *Nativism & Slavery*, 135–142; and Hirota, *Expelling the Poor*, 100–128.

17. Eric Foner, *Give Me Liberty! An American History*, 4th ed. (New York: W. W. Norton, 2014), 470.

18. Stacey L. Smith, *Freedom's Frontier: California and the Struggle over Unfree Labor, Emancipation, and Reconstruction* (Chapel Hill: University of North Carolina Press, 2013), 97–98.

19. Alexander Saxton, *The Indispensable Enemy: Labor and the Anti-Chinese Movement in California* (Berkeley: University of California Press, 1971), 3–18; and Erika Lee, *The Making of Asian America: A History* (New York: Simon & Schuster, 2015), 59, 71–79.

20. Lee, *The Making of Asian America*, 90–94; Alan M. Kraut, *Silent Travelers: Germs, Genes, and the "Immigrant Menace"* (Baltimore: Johns Hopkins University Press, 1994), 78–104; Jean Pfaelzer, *Driven Out: The Forgotten War against Chinese Americans* (Berkeley: University of California Press, 2007), 47–56; and Beth Lew-Williams, *The Chinese Must Go: Violence, Exclusion, and the Making of the Alien in America* (Cambridge, MA: Harvard University Press, 2018).

21. On Chinese exclusion laws, see Lucy E. Salyer, *Laws Harsh as Tigers: Chinese Immigrants and the Shaping of Modern Immigration Law* (Chapel Hill: University of North Carolina Press, 1995).

22. Daniels, *Coming to America*, 124–125; and Andrew R. Heinze, "The Critical Period: Ethnic Emergence and Reaction, 1901–1929," in *Race and Ethnicity in America: A Concise History*, ed. Ronald H. Bayor (New York: Columbia University Press, 2003), 142.

23. Kenny, *The American Irish*, 158–163.

24. Daniels, *Coming to America*, 188; and US Department of Homeland Security, *Yearbook of Immigration Statistics, 2016* (Washington, DC: US Department of Homeland Security, Office of Immigration Statistics, 2017), 5.

25. Michael B. Kahan, "Urban America," in *A Companion to the Gilded Age and Progressive Era*, ed. Christopher McKnight Nicholas and Nancy C. Unger (Malden, MA: Wiley Blackwell, 2017), 33–34; and James Barrett, "The World of the Immigrant Worker," in *The Oxford Handbook of American Immigration and Ethnicity*, ed. Ronald H. Bayor (New York: Oxford University Press, 2016), 264.

26. Barrett, "The World of the Immigrant Worker," 268; Julie Greene, "Race, Immigration, and Ethnicity," in *A Companion to the Gilded Age and Progressive Era*, 142; and Mae M. Ngai, "Race, Nation, and Citizenship in Late Nineteenth-Century America, 1878–1900," in *Race and Ethnicity in America: A Concise History*, ed. Ronald H. Bayor (New York: Columbia University Press, 2003), 119–123.

27. Roger Daniels, *Asian America: Chinese and Japanese in the United States since 1850* (Seattle: University of Washington Press, 1988), 100–116; Eiichiro Azuma, *Between Two Empires: Race, History, and Transnationalism in Japanese America* (New York: Oxford University Press, 2005), 17–31; and Kristofer Allerfeldt, *Race, Radicalism, Religion, and Restriction: Immigration in the Pacific Northwest, 1890–1924* (Westport, CT: Praeger, 2003), 160.

28. Archdeacon, *Becoming American*, 128–129; and George J. Sánchez, *Becoming Mexican American: Ethnicity, Culture and Identity in Chicano Los Angeles, 1900–1945* (New York: Oxford University Press, 1993), 17–83.

29. Barrett, "The World of the Immigrant Worker," 264.

30. Archdeacon, *Becoming American*, 158–162; John Higham, *Strangers in the Land: Patterns of American Nativism, 1860–1925* (New Brunswick, NJ: Rutgers University Press, 1955), 131–157; and Erika Lee,

"Hemispheric Orientalism and the 1907 Pacific Coast Race Riots," *Amerasia Journal* 33, no. 2 (2007): 19–47.

31. Archdeacon, *Becoming American*, 150–164; and Katherine Benton-Cohen, *Inventing the Immigration Problem: The Dillingham Commission and Its Legacy* (Cambridge, MA: Harvard University Press, 2018).

32. Hirota, *Expelling the Poor*, 180–204.

33. Roger Daniels, *Guarding the Golden Door: American Immigration Policy and Immigrants since 1882* (New York: Hill and Wang, 2004), 27–47.

34. Mae M. Ngai, *Impossible Subjects: Illegal Aliens and the Making of Modern America* (Princeton, NJ: Princeton University Press, 2004), 21–55; Greene, "Race, Immigration, and Ethnicity," 139–140; Sánchez, *Becoming Mexican American*, 38–62; and Daniels, *Guarding the Golden Door*, 48–58.

35. Archdeacon, *Becoming American*; Daniels, *Coming to America*; Ronald Takaki, *A Different Mirror: A History of Multicultural America* (Boston: Back Bay Books, 1993); Alan Kraut, *The Huddled Masses: The Immigrant in American Society, 1880–1921*, 2nd ed. (Wheeling, IL: Harlan Davidson, 2001); Aristide R. Zolberg, *A Nation by Design: Immigration Policy in the Fashioning of America* (Cambridge, MA: Harvard University Press, 2006); Elliott Robert Barkan, *From All Points: America's Immigrant West, 1870s–1952* (Bloomington: Indiana University Press, 2007); Paul Spickard, *Almost All Aliens: Immigration, Race, and Colonialism in American History and Identity* (New York: Routledge, 2007); Cohn, *Mass Migration under Sail*; Mae M. Ngai and Jon Gjerde, eds., *Major Problems in American Immigration History*, 2nd ed. (Boston: Wadsworth, 2013); and Tyler Anbinder, *City of Dreams: The 400-Year Epic History of Immigrant New York* (New York: Houghton Mifflin Harcourt, 2016).

36. Handlin, *Boston's Immigrants*; John Bodnar, *The Transplanted: A History of Immigrants in Urban America* (Bloomington: Indiana University Press, 1985); Ernst, *Immigrant Life*; Albert Camarillo, *Chicanos in a Changing Society: From Mexican Pueblos to American Barrios in Santa Barbara and Southern California, 1848–1930* (Cambridge, MA: Harvard University Press, 1979); Herbert G. Gutman, *Work, Culture, and Society in Industrializing America* (New York: Alfred A. Knopf,

1976); Kathleen Neils Conzen et al., "The Invention of Ethnicity: A Perspective from the U.S.A.," *Journal of American Ethnic History* 12, no. 1 (Fall 1992): 4–41; James R. Barrett, "Americanization from the Bottom Up: Immigration and the Remaking of the Working Class in the United States, 1880–1930," *Journal of American History* 79, no. 3 (December 1992): 996–1020; Russell A. Kazal, "Revisiting Assimilation: The Rise, Fall, and Reappraisal of a Concept in American Ethnic History," *American Historical Review* 100, no. 2 (April 1995): 437–471; and Sánchez, *Becoming Mexican American*.

37. Dolan, *The Immigrant Church*; Hasia R. Diner, *Erin's Daughters in America: Irish Immigrant Women in the Nineteenth Century* (Baltimore: Johns Hopkins University Press, 1983); James R. Barrett, *Work and Community in the Jungle: Chicago's Packing House Workers, 1894–1922*; David Montgomery, *The Fall of the House of Labor: The Workplace, the State, and American Labor Activism, 1865–1925* (New York: Cambridge University Press, 1987); Robert A. Orsi, *The Madonna of 115th Street: Faith and Community in Italian Harlem, 1880–1950* (New Haven, CT: Yale University Press, 1985); Donna Gabaccia, *From the Other Side: Women, Gender, and Immigrant Life in the U.S., 1820–1990* (Bloomington: Indiana University Press, 1994); Steven P. Erie, *Rainbow's End: Irish-Americans and the Dilemmas of Urban Machine Politics, 1840–1985* (Berkeley: University of California Press, 1988); Judy Yung, *Unbound Feet: A Social History of Chinese Women in San Francisco* (Berkeley: University of California Press, 1995); Timothy J. Meagher, *Inventing Irish America: Generation, Class, and Ethnic Identity in a New England City, 1880–1928* (Notre Dame, IN: University of Notre Dame Press, 2001); Yong Chen, *Chinese San Francisco, 1850–1943: A Transpacific Community* (Stanford, CA: Stanford University Press, 2000); Tyler Anbinder, *Five Points: The 19th-Century New York City Neighborhood that Invented Tap Dance, Stole Elections, and Became the World's Most Notorious Slum* (New York: Plume, 2002); Terry Golway, *Machine Made: Tammany Hall and the Creation of Modern American Politics* (New York: W. W. Norton, 2015); David Samuel Torres-Rouff, *Before L.A.: Race, Space, and Municipal Power in Los Angeles, 1791–1894* (New Haven, CT: Yale University Press, 2013); and Andrew Urban, *Brokering Servitude: Migration*

and the Politics of Domestic Labor during the Long Nineteenth Century (New York: New York University Press, 2017).

38. David Roediger, Wages of Whiteness: Race and the Making of the American Working Class (New York: Verso, 1991); Matthew Frye Jacobson, Whiteness of a Different Color: European Immigration and the Alchemy of Race (Cambridge, MA: Harvard University Press, 1998); Thomas A. Guglielmo, White on Arrival: Italians, Race, Color, and Power in Chicago, 1890–1945 (New York: Oxford University Press, 2003); Peter Kolchin, "Whiteness Studies: The New History of Race in America," Journal of American History 89, no. 1 (June 2002): 154–173; and Eric Arnesen, "Whiteness and the Historians' Imagination," International Labor and Working-Class History 60 (Fall 2001): 3–32.

39. Kraut, Silent Travelers; J. Matthew Gallman, Receiving Erin's Children: Philadelphia, Liverpool, and the Irish Famine Migration, 1845–1855 (Chapel Hill: University of North Carolina Press, 2000); Nayan Shah, Contagious Divides: Epidemics and Race in San Francisco's Chinatown (Berkeley: University of California Press, 2001); Maureen Fitzgerald, Habits of Compassion: Irish Catholic Nuns and the Origins of New York's Welfare System, 1830–1920 (Champaign: University of Illinois Press, 2006); Natalia Molina, Fit to Be Citizens? Public Health and Race in Los Angeles, 1879–1939 (Berkeley: University of California Press, 2006); Julie Miller, Abandoned: Foundlings in Nineteenth-Century New York City (New York: New York University Press, 2008); and Kelly Lytle Hernández, City of Inmates: Conquest, Rebellion, and the Rise of Human Caging in Los Angeles, 1771–1965 (Chapel Hill: University of North Carolina Press, 2017).

40. Higham, Strangers in the Land; John Higham, Send These to Me: Jews and Other Immigrants in Urban America, rev. ed. (Baltimore: Johns Hopkins University Press, 1984); Saxton, The Indispensable Enemy; Salyer, Laws Harsh as Tigers; Charles J. McClain, In Search of Equality: The Chinese Struggle against Discrimination in Nineteenth-Century America (Berkeley: University of California Press, 1994); Erika Lee, At America's Gates: Chinese Immigration during the Exclusion Era, 1882–1943 (Chapel Hill: University of North Carolina Press, 2003); Ngai, Impossible Subjects; Allerfeldt, Race, Radicalism, Religion, and Restriction; Pfaelzer,

Driven Out; Amy L. Fairchild, Science at the Borders: Immigrant Medical Inspection and the Shaping of the Modern Industrial Labor Force (Baltimore: Johns Hopkins University Press, 2003); Vincent J. Cannato, American Passage: The History of Ellis Island (New York: Harper-Collins, 2009); Erika Lee and Judy Yung, Angel Island: Immigrant Gateway to America (New York: Oxford University Press, 2010); Ronald H. Bayor, Encountering Ellis Island: How European Immigrants Entered America (Baltimore: Johns Hopkins University Press, 2014); Hirota, Expelling the Poor; and Lew-Williams, The Chinese Must Go.

41. Edith Abbott, Immigration: Select Documents and Case Records (Chicago: University of Chicago Press, 1924); Edith Abbott, Historical Aspects of the Immigration Problem: Select Documents (Chicago: University of Chicago Press, 1926); and Thomas Dublin, Immigrant Voices: New Lives in America, 1773–2000, 2nd ed. (Champaign: University of Illinois Press, 2014).

42. Library of Congress, A List of Books on Immigration (Washington, DC: Government Printing Office, 1907).

43. US Department of the Treasury, Arrivals of Alien Passengers and Immigrants in the United States from 1820 to 1892 (Washington, DC: Government Printing Office, 1893); and US Bureau of the Census, Historical Statistics of the United States, Colonial Times to 1970 (Washington, DC, 1975).

Hidetaka Hirota

IMMIGRATION TO AMERICAN CITIES, 1924–2017

OVERVIEW

Before 1924, the vast majority of the newest immigrants to the United States came from southern and eastern Europe, practiced Catholicism or Judaism, and lived in the industrial cities of the Northeast and Midwest. Congress's passage of the 1924 Immigration Act reflected the deep unease among native-born white Protestants about urban America and the racial status of the newcomers, as well as their growing role in US cultural, religious, and political life. The 1924 act placed very restrictive quotas on southern and eastern European immigration, and it ended all immigration from Asia. Although the law did not create quotas for the independent nations of the Western Hemisphere, it did require immigrants from Canada and Latin America to pay a new head tax, pass a physical examination and a literacy test, and possess a passport. Despite the 1924 law, the immigrant populations in American urban centers remained fairly stable until after World War II, when federal housing, transportation, and economic policy encouraged "white flight" to the suburbs Between the 1940s and 1970s, European immigrants and their children, whom most other Americans now saw as fully "white," slowly abandoned the central cities for suburban areas. During the same period, black migrants from the South streamed into racially segregated northern and western cities, which often deteriorated because of private disinvestment, job flight, and government policies that favored suburbs and white Americans over inner cities and people of color. The passage of the Immigration and Naturalization Act of 1965, however, changed the fortunes of a significant number of US cities. As new Asian, Latino/a, and African immigrants arrived in the United States, large numbers settled in older urban areas and often helped to revitalize them. By the 1990s, the majority of the newcomers were moving directly to suburban communities, many of which had no previous tradition of immigration. In these areas, the political and social response to the new immigration has varied tremendously, even within metropolitan areas.

THE IMMIGRATION ACT OF 1924 AND THE RURAL-URBAN DIVIDE IN AMERICA

Before the late 19th century, immigrants to the United States came primarily from northern and western Europe, who settled both in urban and rural areas and included large numbers of Protestants. By the turn of the century, however, immigrant newcomers were increasingly Jewish or Catholic or, occasionally, Eastern or Russian Orthodox Christian or Muslim. Almost all found homes in urban areas, usually in the Northeast or Midwest, and they often lived in visible ethnic enclaves, where they supported immigrant-focused businesses, worshipped at heavily immigrant churches, read foreign-language newspapers, and sometimes ran their own schools.

In 1924, the US Congress passed and President Calvin Coolidge signed the Immigration Act of 1924 (also known as the Johnson-Reed Act), which dramatically restricted southern and eastern European immigration to the United States and ended all Asian immigration. The law built on earlier restrictive measures, including the literacy tests and the Asiatic Barred Zone of the Immigration Act of 1917 and the "emergency quotas" of the Immigration Act of 1921. Over time, the 1924 act made a tremendous impact on the nation's urban areas because of the concentration of immigrants there.

The 1917, 1921, and 1924 laws all reflected the rise of nativism in the early 20th-century United States. Many native-born Protestants of northern and western European ancestry viewed the non-Protestant newcomers with growing alarm, claiming that they posed a threat to American culture, unity, and democracy. Native-born white Protestants also embraced popular eugenics and race science to argue that the new immigrants were biologically inferior to "old stock" Americans. These critics ignored the low wages and terrible working conditions many urban immigrants had to contend with and instead blamed their destitution, bad health, and poor living conditions on their alleged inferiority. During World War I, nativists even asserted that immigrants from the combatant nations were too often "hyphenated Americans" with dubious loyalties. On the Pacific Coast, European Americans of all backgrounds bemoaned the arrival of Japanese and Korean immigrants, derided the Punjabi Sikhs, and segregated the Chinese Americans.[1]

Although perceptions of racial and religious difference played the largest role in the passage of restrictive immigration laws, the arguments for these laws also reflected a growing rural-urban divide in the United States. By the turn of the century, population growth and economic dynamism were far greater in the urban areas than in the rural ones. This slowly undermined the influence and centrality of farms and small towns to the nation's cultural and political life, and the residents of these places fought back: the loudest proponents of immigration restriction included some of the most scathing critics of urban America and its growing influence on mass culture, especially the new forms of entertainment—motion pictures, radio, and jazz music. Many nativists belonged to organizations, such as the Second Ku Klux Klan, with particular strength in small-town and rural America. They also tended to live in parts of the nation with relatively few immigrants, such as the South. They abhorred the political radicalism and labor activism they associated with the heavily immigrant cities. They also supported Prohibition at far higher rates than urban residents and blamed immigrants for the wave of crime that the 18th Amendment had set in motion.[2]

These nativists celebrated the passage of the Immigration Act of 1924, which as a piece of legislation largely achieved its aims. Immigration dropped sharply beginning in the late 1920s. In 1914, the peak year of immigration, more than 1.2 million people arrived in the United States; by the late 1920s, that number had fallen to about 300,000 annually, and it had plunged to about 30,000 per year by the mid-1930s.[3] But the passage of the 1924 Act did little to repair the urban-rural cultural and political divide. This was clear in 1928, when Al Smith, New York's Catholic governor and a native of Manhattan, won the Democratic Party's nomination for president.

Across the country, Smith's opponents used widespread anti-Catholic bigotry to discredit him, and he lost the election by a wide margin. But besides the larger religious issue, Smith also grappled with the fact that many voters saw him as too representative of immigrant urban America.[4]

The post-1924 drop in immigration initially seemed to have little impact on the nation's urban centers, where the overall populations continued to rise until 1950 because of domestic migration and natural increase. But the rate of urban population growth slowed between 1930 and 1940, and the proportion of foreign-born residents in the nation's cities fell to about 12 percent in 1940, down from a high of 21 percent in 1900.[5] Before World War II, a number of different factors had preserved immigrant enclaves as second-generation residential areas, even as the actual percentage of their foreign-born populations shrank. Traditions of racial segregation prevented Asian Americans in urban California, Afro-Caribbeans in New York, and Mexican Americans in the towns and cities in the Southwest from leaving the few neighborhoods in which they could live.[6] The organization of Catholic religious, educational, and social life around geographically bounded parishes encouraged many of the children of European immigrants to remain in their home parishes.[7] The continued concentration of factories in inner cities also kept second-generation industrial workers tied to such places.

POLICY CHANGES, RACIAL SHIFTS, AND THE GREAT DEPRESSION

During the Great Depression, many of these workers became stalwart supporters of President Franklin Roosevelt, whose administration included numerous New York activists, such as Frances Perkins and Harry Hopkins, who had long experience working in the city's immigrant communities. Although Roosevelt himself romanticized rural life, his administration focused much of its attention on city dwellers, including the millions of immigrants and their children living in the industrial centers. Determined to prevent their radicalization, especially through exposure to communist or fascist movements, federal officials pushed Congress to pass the New Deal programs to create public-works jobs, low-cost housing, and health clinics and to establish unemployment insurance and old-age pension programs for salaried and mass-production workers. With the backing of the White House and the Democratic Party, the newly formed Congress of Industrial Organizations (CIO) organized millions of immigrant and second-generation industrial workers, including autoworkers and steelworkers.[8]

The CIO was able to organize successfully because it reached across ethnic and racial lines, breaking with the older unions' traditions of segregation and employers' attempts to pit different racial and national groups against each other in order to break strikes. The CIO also managed to unite urban workers because mass culture and mass consumption were reshaping the identities, politics, and economic choices of immigrants' children in cities across the country. Chain stores began to replace the pushcarts and small shops of the first generation. Second-generation Americans, whose parents had once viewed each other with suspicion, now bonded in public schools and on shop floors over their shared enjoyment of nationally syndicated radio shows, sports, and movies.[9]

But federal and local officials also used the New Deal to divide immigrant groups in ways that reshaped the cities in the decades that followed. In towns and cities in the West and Southwest, Bureau of Immigration agents rounded up destitute Mexicans and deported them, often together with their Mexican American citizen children, in a bid to create more work for "native born" people. The authorities in Los Angeles, California, with the cooperation of the Mexican consul, deported so many Mexicans and Mexican Americans that the Mexican American population dropped by almost 30 percent.[10]

New Deal housing programs essentially institutionalized patterns of racial segregation that were just a decade or so old in most urban areas. Federally funded public housing separated whites, African Americans, Latinos, and Chinese Americans and completely excluded other Asian Americans, and administrators denied Federal Housing Administration mortgage insurance to integrated neighborhoods and almost all people of color. These programs supplemented racialized aspects of other New Deal legislation, such as the exclusion of (predominantly nonwhite) agricultural and domestic workers from the old-age pension system (later known as Social Security) and from unemployment insurance, to essentially create a two-track social-welfare system in the United States for whites and people of color.[11]

In creating a stratified social-welfare state, federal officials essentially affirmed southern and eastern European immigrant and second-generation "whiteness" and helped to undercut older ways of defining race. At the turn of the century, race could refer to ethnicity, nationality, religion, or color, and immigration officials, civic leaders, and racial theorists alike frequently listed Jews, Italians, Russians, and "Negroes" as some of the many races living in the United States. Now, however, federal administrators categorized all people of wholly European ancestry as "white," regardless of their religion or national origin. This practice gave immigrants from southern and eastern Europe and their children an incentive to define themselves as "white," since this racial status allowed them access to neighborhoods and federal programs that were closed to people of color. It also encouraged some Latino immigrants and their children, especially those with lighter skin, to "pass" as Spanish or French, since doing so offered greater residential and employment opportunities in cities where "white" residents routinely racialized Latinos.[12]

WORLD WAR II

World War II deepened European immigrants' and their children's stake in whiteness. The US military largely divided soldiers based on race, placing African Americans and Japanese Americans in segregated units; Filipino and Chinese American soldiers could serve in "white" units, but only because China and the Philippine Commonwealth (an American colony slated for independence) were US allies. At the same time, the military confirmed the "whiteness" of southern and eastern European immigrants and their children by placing them in white units, which received better treatment, accommodations, food, and recreational opportunities than the nonwhite ones. Wartime mobilization and production also reshaped heavily immigrant cities. Millions of Americans, including immigrants and their children, moved to wartime boomtowns, especially on the West Coast, for work. Because of labor shortages, Mexican Americans, Chinese Americans, and other immigrants of color, many of them women, took jobs that employers had long reserved for white men. However, the racial segregation of urban America actually grew worse because of wartime housing shortages, with those on the "white" side of the divide enjoying far more housing options.

The war deeply influenced Mexican American life in the Southwest in ways that eventually reshaped the region's cities. Beginning in 1942, the US government's Bracero Program allowed thousands of Mexicans to enter the country as farmworkers to alleviate wartime labor shortages. Many of these braceros stayed on and eventually resettled in urban areas across the Southwest. (The program eventually ended in the early 1960s.) Drafted at high rates, Mexican Americans also worked in large numbers in the defense plants of overcrowded cities like Los Angeles, where wartime tensions exacerbated existing racial and ethnic antagonisms. In 1943, Anglo soldiers and sailors attacked Mexican and Mexican American residents of Los Angeles in what became known as the Zoot Suit Riot. After that, members of the Mexican American community began to organize for political power, a process that continued in the postwar era across the urban Southwest through groups such as the GI Forum and the Community Service Organization.[13]

On the West Coast, President Roosevelt's Executive Order 9066 gave the US military the authority to remove all people of Japanese ancestry, both aliens and citizens, from their homes and place them in concentration camps in remote areas. Although most of the 120,000 Japanese Americans designated for incarceration lived on farms, tens of thousands made their homes in older, heavily segregated areas of Seattle, Portland, San Francisco, and, especially, Los Angeles. African Americans migrating to the booming West Coast from the South often moved into the homes the Japanese Americans had left behind. When the US government allowed Japanese Americans to resettle to areas outside the West Coast during the war, most ended up in the cities of the Midwest and Intermountain West, Chicago being the most popular destination. Forced to give up their farms and homes in 1942, Japanese Americans who returned to the Pacific Coast after the war also faced rural vigilantism. Thousands now moved to cities, making Japanese Americans a largely urban community.[14]

POSTWAR SUBURBANIZATION

The Servicemen's Bill of Rights of 1944 (popularly known as the GI Bill), together with existing federal housing programs and postwar urban renewal and highway legislation, completed many of the transformations that the war had set in motion. Private developers used mass-production techniques to build tens of thousands of tract homes in the suburbs of cities from New York to Los Angeles. They marketed such homes to GI Bill recipients and families who qualified for Federal Housing

Administration (FHA) mortgage guarantees, almost always refusing to sell homes to people of color and, sometimes, to Jews, including veterans. Before 1948, when the Supreme Court forced the FHA to change its policies, it had openly required such racial restrictions, and the agency continued to practice covert racial discrimination until the late 1960s. The programs encouraged "white" Americans, including millions of second-generation southern and eastern European Americans, to abandon the inner cities and move to the segregated suburbs. By the 1960s, many inner-city areas were predominantly nonwhite.

These shifts did not completely undermine old immigrant neighborhoods or the second generation's sense of ethnicity. Numerous second-generation Catholics still chose to live in their home parishes, and large percentages of second-generation American Jews remained in inner-city areas. Many of the new suburbs of older, heavily immigrant cities attracted specific ethnic or religious groups, such as the heavily Jewish Scarsdale, New York, or the substantially Italian American and Irish American suburbs west of Philadelphia.[15]

In some places, the war even revived immigrant enclaves because the conflict had prompted certain adjustments to America's restrictive immigration laws. In 1943, Congress repealed the old Chinese Exclusion Act, enabling Chinese immigrants to naturalize and allowing a token number to immigrate yearly. Congress made similar allowances for South Asians and Filipinos in 1946. In 1945 and 1946, new legislation enabled Chinese American veterans and citizen men and women to bring China-born spouses to the United States, and thousands of Chinese women finally joined their husbands in America for the first time. One result was the revitalization of old Chinatown areas, many of which had become family neighborhoods by the early 1950s. Simultaneously, the US government regularized the status of thousands of Chinese students and professionals who were stranded in the United States after

the Communist takeover of the Chinese mainland in 1949.[16]

Congress also begrudgingly passed bills aimed mostly at helping war refugees from formerly Nazi-occupied areas of Europe. In 1948, one such piece of legislation allowed the admission of about two hundred thousand displaced persons, but only by mortgaging the quotas for their nations of origin well into the future. Determined to keep out Jews, anti-Semites in Congress wrote a bill that used occupational preferences, geographical definitions, and cutoff dates to prevent their entry and favored refugees from communism. Eventually Congress revised the legislation to remove some of these hurdles, and about four hundred thousand displaced persons from central, eastern, and southern Europe and China entered the United States between 1948 and 1952, with smaller numbers coming after 1953 under the new Refugee Relief Act.[17] The vast majority of these new entrants initially settled in American cities, but relatively few chose to live in the old ethnic enclaves; their aspirations, backgrounds, and occupations were often quite different from those of earlier immigrants.[18]

By the 1960s, suburbanization and the flight of industry from inner-city areas had undermined the remnants of many of the older ethnic enclaves of American cities. So did white resistance to the Second Great Migration, when hundreds of thousands of African Americans left the South annually for life in the urban North. In parts of Detroit, Chicago, Philadelphia, Los Angeles, and other older cities, white residents, many of them the children of turn-of-the-century immigrants, sometimes used violence to prevent black, Asian, and Latino integration of their neighborhoods and schools.

Eventually, many of these holdouts left for the suburbs, too. Accepted as "white," European immigrants and their children followed Cold War defense jobs along the new, federally funded highways—some of which cut through and destroyed the old enclaves—to the government-underwritten suburbs, where people of color still could not live. Those barred included Asian American, Afro-Caribbean, and Latino immigrants, who frequently shared their neighborhoods with black Americans—another group that faced tremendous discrimination in housing and employment.

Still, by the mid-1950s, middle-class, well-educated Asian Americans, including many GI Bill recipients and former "stranded students" from China, began to experience increasing residential mobility; this was tied to Cold War perceptions of them as more desirable than other groups and as "allies" in the struggle against communism—the first stirring of the "model minority myth." Yet working-class Asian Americans and recent Chinese refugees continued to live in older areas of the West Coast cities, especially in neighborhoods recently abandoned by the children of southern and eastern European immigrants. Their neighbors increasingly included not just blacks but also Mexicans and Mexican Americans, whose population grew quickly during the 1950s and 1960s because of both legal and undocumented immigration.[19] As a result of government policies and the practices of private industry, by the 1960s, what became known as the "urban crisis" was increasingly visible in the United States: inner cities were segregated, impoverished, and deprived of the benefits of a rapidly growing economy, while the almost wholly white suburbs thrived around them. People who could leave the inner cities did, despite their ties to urban ethnic and religious institutions that usually dated to the early 20th-century tide of immigration.

THE IMMIGRATION AND NATURALIZATION ACT OF 1965 AND THE "URBAN CRISIS"

The restrictionist Immigration Act of 1952 (often called the McCarran-Walter Act) reaffirmed the old national-origins basis of

American policy. But in 1965, Congress passed and President Lyndon B. Johnson signed a tremendously significant piece of legislation, the Immigration and Naturalization Act of 1965 (sometimes called the Hart-Cellar Act). The 1965 legislation eliminated the national-origins basis of US immigration policy and replaced it with a system that divided the world by hemispheres. The Eastern Hemisphere, which included Europe, Africa, Asia, and Oceania, received a 170,000-person annual quota, and no one country could use more than 20,000 slots of that quota. The slots were distributed on a first-come, first-served basis, with preferences for family reunification and for immigrants with certain professional and technical skills. Unlike earlier legislation, the new law created some limits for immigration from the Americas: the Western Hemisphere received a 120,000-person quota, without any country cap. Congress also established quotas for refugees, no longer forcing presidents to rely on executive actions and quota mortgaging.

Legislators anticipated that the 1965 bill would enable older southern and eastern European relatives to join families in the United States. In fact, the new law encouraged far more substantial immigration from Asia and Latin America than Congress had anticipated. In the 1970s alone, more immigrants entered the United States from Asia than had come in all the previous years combined. Hundreds of thousands of people from politically turbulent and economically underdeveloped parts of Latin America also arrived in large numbers, either legally, using the new law, or by circumventing it as undocumented immigrants. At the end of the Vietnam War, thousands of refugees from Southeast Asia also entered the United States under the new refugee quotas.[20]

The 1965 legislation had a substantial and fairly rapid impact on many cities across America. Rioting and disinvestment devastated scores of inner-city areas in the 1960s and 1970s, but hundreds of thousands of new immigrants flocked to many the same places in the 1970s and afterward. Some of the new arrivals replaced business owners who were leaving riot-scarred areas; others established their own small businesses, including garment factories and specialty-food manufacturing plants. Thousands of trained doctors and nurses from such places as Taiwan, the Philippines, India, Haiti, and Hong Kong took positions that had been vacated by the native-born professionals leaving inner-city hospitals for more well-funded institutions in the suburbs. Significant numbers of Jewish immigrants from the Soviet Union also settled in major cities such as New York in the 1970s, even as the native-born populations of such places fell.[21]

At the apex of the urban crisis, then, the newest immigrants were helping to slowly revitalize the crumbling cities, from the South Asians settling in northern New Jersey's industrial centers to the Mexicans and Koreans building businesses in Los Angeles. The process continued for the next two decades, as the gradual opening of the People's Republic of China and the end of the Cold War further transformed the demographics of America's foreign-born population. In the 1980s, mainland Chinese became the largest group of immigrants from Asia, and Eastern Europeans and Russians left their homelands to resettle in cities such as Chicago, Milwaukee, and New York. Legislative reforms in the 1980s and 1990s enabled more African and Afro-Caribbean immigrants to move to the United States. Thousands settled in major metropolitan areas, including New York City and Miami.[22]

Like the Europeans who had arrived in the early 20th century, the new immigrants often created visible ethnic enclaves in the cities where they settled. A few of these, such as Little Korea and Little India in Manhattan, or heavily South Asian Devon Avenue in Chicago, developed almost exclusively as business districts serving co-ethnics from across the metropolis. However, most of these neighborhoods mixed business and residential use. Some reflected the new arrivals' own styles of urbanism, such as the Oak Cliff area in Dallas, whose heavily Latino/a immigrant population created a neighborhood designed for pedestrians and small businesses and centered on a central plaza.[23] Other neighborhoods played important regional roles, including the heavily Fujianese area of Manhattan's Lower East Side, which became a transit and employment hub for Chinese restaurants across the East Coast and the South. Although these new enclaves were sometimes identified with a single ethnic group, they were frequently home to a mix of different immigrants attracted by nearby public transportation, low-cost housing, and religious or social-service institutions. East and Southeast Asians flocked to Stockton Boulevard in Sacramento; Koreans and Chinese to Flushing, Queens; Hmong, Latinos, and Somalis to Frogtown in St. Paul; and Mexicans, Central Americans, and Chinese to Los Angeles's San Gabriel Valley.

The social and political effects of the new immigration on urban America only slowly became apparent. In the 1970s and 1980s, as the economy struggled, immigrants and those in heavily immigrant ethnic groups experienced a strong backlash. Shrimping crews in New Orleans complained that Vietnamese arrivals were taking their jobs. Working-class whites in Miami charged that Cubans received preference in construction work. In Monterey Park, just outside Los Angeles, the city council in the 1980s passed one of the first "English only" laws and a slow-growth ordinance, reflections of local unease about the rapid influx of immigrants from Taiwan. Sometimes, dislike and fear of racialized immigrants exploded into violence, as in impoverished Lawrence, Massachusetts, where white residents clashed with Latinos in a two-day riot in 1984.[24]

Anti-Asian hate crimes spiked during this era, often reflecting resentment of Asians' perceived economic success or cultural difference. The most infamous crime occurred in Detroit, when two unemployed autoworkers who blamed Japanese competition for their plight murdered Chinese American Vincent Chin. Minorities, most of them native-born, also participated in some of the attacks on new immigrants. The "Dotbusters" who attacked and terrorized Indian residents of Jersey City, New Jersey, in 1987 included not just Anglo but also Latino men.

Federal disinvestment in urban areas and social-welfare programs also helped create tensions between longtime residents of color and new immigrants in American cities. In fact, both groups grappled with many of the same problems. Latino immigrants particularly struggled with police brutality, which was a factor in riots involving heavily immigrant Latino communities in Houston (1978); Perth Amboy, New Jersey (1988); Washington, DC (1991), and a number of other cities. Conservative politicians contributed to the friction by praising Asian immigrants as "model minorities" who worked hard and eschewed social-welfare programs, supposedly in contrast to native-born blacks and Latinos. Such pronouncements ignored the great diversity in the recent immigration from Asia, which included well-educated professionals and penniless refugees and working-class people who used public assistance programs.[25] The inflammatory rhetoric encouraged sometimes explosive resentment of Asian Americans by other minority groups. In some Brooklyn neighborhoods, African American and Afro-Caribbean residents boycotted Korean-owned stores after protest leaders claimed Korean businesses received US government backing in order to destroy black communities. When riots broke out in Los Angeles in 1992 after the white police officers who beat motorist Rodney King were acquitted, blacks, whites, and Latinos looted and destroyed many Korean American-owned businesses.[26]

Despite such tensions, many older urban areas eventually succeeded in incorporating the recent immigrants into local political coalitions that also included native-born people of color. In San Francisco and other Bay Area cities, people of Chinese, Korean, Japanese, Vietnamese, and Filipino ancestry built coalitions with African Americans and Latinos and became a rising political force in local and state politics. Mexican Americans and other Latinos also emerged as a major factor in Los Angeles area politics by making common cause with other people of color. Because of the entrenched political machines in New York City's heavily immigrant outer boroughs, immigrant political incorporation there has proceeded at a slower pace.[27] Either way, though many of the most successful politicians in such communities have been second-generation people, they often rely on substantial support from naturalized immigrants.

IMMIGRATION TO THE SUBURBS

After 1965, several longtime centers of urban immigrant life were once again attracting huge numbers of newcomers, especially Los Angeles, New York, and Chicago.[28] By the 1980s and 1990s, though, most of new immigrants were bypassing the older urban areas that had once been such magnets for them and moving directly to suburbs and smaller cities, which offered greater economic opportunities. Immigrants also poured into regions with little history of immigrant incorporation, especially parts of the South, such as the Atlanta, Raleigh-Durham, and Charlotte metropolitan areas. In a number of such places, the new immigration became a heated political issue, and the debates focused not only on the division of resources such as jobs and social-welfare spending but also on more ill-defined cultural and racial issues. Some suburbs of Atlanta and Dallas, two new gateways for immigrants from Asia and Latin America, crafted English-only ordinances and laws aimed at landlords who rent to undocumented immigrants. The small city of Hazleton, Pennsylvania, did the same in 2006 in a swipe at the large number of Mexican, Dominican, and other Latino immigrants moving there. But elsewhere, such as suburban areas of Washington, DC, Austin, Texas, and Minneapolis, local officials have focused on immigrant economic, educational, and social incorporation rather than exclusion.[29]

Debates about immigration in America now revolve around a host of issues, including but not limited to religion, language, culture, race, and economic impact. Fears about the relationship of immigration to national security have flared up repeatedly since the September 11, 2001 attacks on the World Trade Center and the Pentagon. Since the attacks, immigrants and native-born people perceived to be Arab or Muslim have often faced harassment even in cities with large Arab American and Muslim populations.

The diversity of immigrants in the 21st century and the distinctiveness of different regions and urban and suburban areas of the United States make generalizations about the future of both quite difficult. However, the 2016 election of President Trump undoubtedly created a climate of fear among recent immigrants, especially those living in the country unlawfully. Trump's election and his racist comments about certain immigrant groups also clarified the ways in which immigration has changed politics and attitudes in many parts of urban and suburban America. In recent years, scores of cities and suburbs have adopted "sanctuary city" laws intended to protect immigrant residents whose contributions civic leaders and ordinary citizens alike recognize and value. The Trump administration's January 2017 attempt to use an executive order to bar foreign-born Arabs and Muslims from entering the United States sparked large demonstrations in immigrant-friendly cities such as Los Angeles, New York, Chicago, and Seattle. At the same time, many pro-immigrant cities and suburbs are in conservative states such as North Carolina and Texas, where state officials with federal assistance have attacked sanctuary statutes and targeted cities for stricter immigration enforcement. The degree to which immigration will continue to contribute to the revitalization of America's urban and suburban areas is now increasingly uncertain.

DISCUSSION OF THE LITERATURE

Because different immigrant groups and specific cities vary so widely, no broad survey of immigrants in urban America really exists. The fields of 20th-century urban America and 20th-century immigration history are rich and incredibly diverse, and occasionally they overlap in a study of a specific group in a specific place. Excellent works about specific immigrant groups and their children in various cities in the first half of the 20th century include Thomas Guglielmo, *White on Arrival: Italians, Race, Color, and Power in Chicago, 1890*; Russell Kazal, *Becoming Old Stock: The Paradox of German-American Identity*; Robert Orsi, *The Madonna of 115th Street: Faith and Community in Italian Harlem, 1880–1950*; Vivek Bald, *Bengali Harlem and the Lost Histories of South Asian America*; Judy Yung, *Unbound Feet: A Social History of Chinese Women in San Francisco*; George Sánchez, *Becoming Mexican American: Ethnicity, Culture, and Identity in Chicano Los Angeles, 1900–1945*; and Shelley Sang-Hee Lee, *Claiming the Oriental Gateway: Prewar Seattle and Japanese America*.[30] On the impact of the Immigration Act of 1924, see Mae M. Ngai, *Impossible Subjects: Illegal Aliens and the Making of Modern America*.[31] An overview of immigration in New York City is Tyler Anbinder, *City of Dreams: The 400-Year Epic History of Immigrant New York*.[32]

Significant thematic works on immigrants, their children, and the way they understood race, gender, religion, sexuality, labor, and the city before World War II include Lizabeth Cohen, *Making a New Deal: Industrial Workers in Chicago, 1919–1939*; Robert A. Slayton, *Back of the Yards: The Making of a Local Democracy*; George Chauncey, *Gay New York: Gender, Urban Culture, and the Making of the Gay Male World, 1890–1940*; and Natalia

Molina, *Fit to Be Citizens? Public Health and Race in Los Angeles, 1879–1940.*[33]

Scholarship about immigrants and their children in midcentury and postwar cities and suburbs includes Charlotte Brooks, *Alien Neighbors, Foreign Friends: Asian Americans, Housing, and the Transformation of Urban California*; Lilia Fernandez, *Brown in the Windy City: Mexicans and Puerto Ricans in Postwar Chicago*; Joshua Zeitz, *White Ethnic New York: Jews, Catholics, and the Shaping of Postwar Politics*; John T. McGreevy, *Parish Boundaries: The Catholic Encounter with Race in the Twentieth-Century Urban North*; Gerald Gamm, *Urban Exodus: Why the Jews Left Boston and the Catholics Stayed*; Joshua B. Freeman, *Working-Class New York: Life and Labor since World War II*; and Maria Cristina Garcia, *Havana USA: Cuban Exiles and Cuban Americans in South Florida, 1959–1994*; and David M. Reimers, *Still the Golden Door: The Third World Comes to America.*[34]

Much of the scholarship on post-1965 immigrants and their children in American cities and suburbs is in sociology, geography, American studies, and related areas rather than in the field of history. Some notable works include Timothy Fong, *The First Suburban Chinatown: The Remaking of Monterey Park, California*; Willow Lung-Amam, *Trespassers? Asian Americans and the Battle for Suburbia*; Audrey Singer, Susan W. Hardwick, and Caroline B. Brettell, eds., *Twenty-First Century Gateways: Immigrant Incorporation in Suburban America*; Wendy Cheng, *The Changs Next Door to the Díazes: Remapping Race in Suburban California*; Warren Lehrer, *Crossing the BLVD: Strangers, Neighbors, Aliens in a New America*; Nancy Foner, *From Ellis Island to JFK: New York's Two Great Waves of Immigration*; Tarry Hum, *Making a Global Immigrant Neighborhood: Brooklyn's Sunset Park*; and Robert Vargas, *Wounded City: Violent Turf Wars in a Chicago Barrio*; and Andrew Sandoval-Strausz, "Latino Landscapes: Postwar Cities and the Transnational Origins of a New Urban America."[35]

PRIMARY SOURCES

Because of the diversity of cities, suburbs, and immigrant groups, the type and availability of primary sources about immigrant life in urban areas varies widely. The US Government's decennial Census of Population and Housing offers an invaluable overview of the foreign-born population of America's cities during the 20th century. National Archives facilities, especially at College Park, Maryland, contain detailed community maps, neighborhood surveys, and housing-project records for heavily immigrant areas. Individual community newspapers, from the Mexican American *La Opinión* of Los Angeles to the Polish-language *Dziennik Związkowy* of Chicago to the Chinese *Qiao Bao* of New York, provide insider accounts of political, social, and economic life. Many cities, especially beginning in the 1960s, undertook detailed surveys of immigrant communities in the process of developing educational and social-welfare programs for them. More recently, university-community partnerships have produced noteworthy digital collections of oral histories from local immigrant and second-generation residents.

FURTHER READING

Brooks, Charlotte. *Alien Neighbors, Foreign Friends: Asian Americans, Housing, and the Transformation of Urban California.* Chicago: University of Chicago Press, 2009.

Chauncey, George. *Gay New York: Gender, Urban Culture, and the Making of the Gay Male World, 1890–1940.* New York: Basic Books, 2008.

Cohen, Lizabeth. *Making a New Deal: Industrial Workers in Chicago, 1919–1939.* New York: Cambridge University Press, 2008.

Foner, Nancy. *From Ellis Island to JFK: New York's Two Great Waves of Immigration.* New Haven, CT: Yale University Press, 2002.

Guglielmo, Thomas A. *White on Arrival: Italians, Race, Color, and Power in Chicago, 1890–1945.* New York: Oxford University Press, 2004.

Holdaway, Jennifer, Philip Kasinitz, John H. Mollenkopf, and Mary C. Waters. *Inheriting the*

City: The Children of Immigrants Come of Age. New York: Russell Sage Foundation, 2010.

McGreevy, John T. *Parish Boundaries: The Catholic Encounter with Race in the Twentieth-Century Urban North*. Chicago: University of Chicago Press, 1996.

Sánchez, George J. *Becoming Mexican American: Ethnicity, Culture, and Identity in Chicano Los Angeles, 1900–1945*. New York: Oxford University Press, 1995.

Sugrue, Thomas. *The Origins of the Urban Crisis: Race and Inequality in Postwar Detroit*. Princeton, NJ: Princeton University Press, 1996.

Vallejo, Jody. *Barrios to Burbs: The Making of the Mexican American Middle Class*. Stanford, CA: Stanford University Press, 2013.

Waters, Mary C. *Black Identities: West Indian Immigrant Dreams and American Realities*. Cambridge, MA: Harvard University Press, 2001.

NOTES

1. Gary Gerstle, *American Crucible: Race and Nation in the Twentieth Century* (Princeton, NJ: Princeton University Press, 2001), 81–127.

2. George Chauncey, *Gay New York: Gender, Urban Culture, and the Making of the Gay Male World, 1890–1940* (New York: Basic Books, 2008), 233–234; and John Higham, *Strangers in the Land: Patterns of American Nativism, 1860–1925* (New York: Athenaeum, 1963), 286.

3. *Annual Report of the Immigration and Naturalization Service for the Fiscal Year Ended June 30, 1949* (Washington, DC: Government Printing Office, 1949), 95.

4. Matthew Avery Sutton, *American Apocalypse: A History of Modern Evangelicalism* (Cambridge, MA: Harvard University Press, 2014), 148, 202–205.

5. *Sixteenth Census of the United States, 1940, Population, Volume II: Characteristics of the Population, Part 1* (Washington, DC: Government Printing Office, 1943), 19–20.

6. Charlotte Brooks, *Alien Neighbors, Foreign Friends: Asian Americans, Housing, and the Transformation of Urban California* (Chicago: University of Chicago Press, 2009), 21–31, 60–64; Shannon King, *Whose Harlem Is This, Anyway? Community Politics and Grassroots Activism during the New Negro Era* (New York: New York University Press, 2015), 22–23; and Nestor Rodriguez, "Urban Redevelopment and Mexican American Barrios in the Socio-Spatial Order," in *Latino Urbanism: The Politics*

of Planning, Policy and Redevelopment, ed. David R. Diaz and Rodolfo D. Torres, 87–89 (New York: New York University Press, 2012).

7. John T. McGreevy, *Parish Boundaries: The Catholic Encounter with Race in the Twentieth-Century Urban North* (Chicago: University of Chicago Press, 1996), 7–28.

8. Lizabeth Cohen, *Making a New Deal: Industrial Workers in Chicago, 1919–1939* (New York: Cambridge University Press, 2008), 252–289.

9. Cohen, 100–158, 324–360.

10. George J. Sánchez, *Becoming Mexican American: Ethnicity, Culture and Identity in Chicano Los Angeles, 1900–1945* (New York: Oxford University Press, 1993), 213.

11. Brooks, *Alien Neighbors, Foreign Friends* (Chicago: University of Chicago Press), 70–111.

12. George Lipsitz, "The Possessive Investment in Whiteness: Racialized Social Democracy and the 'White' Problem in American Studies," *American Quarterly* 47, no. 3 (1995): 372–374; and Brooks, *Alien Neighbors, Foreign Friends* (Chicago: University of Chicago Press), 62–63.

13. Shana Bernstein, *Bridges of Reform: Interracial Civil Rights Activism in Twentieth-Century Los Angeles* (New York: Oxford University Press, 2011), 80–99, 138–151.

14. Brooks, *Alien Neighbors, Foreign Friends* (Chicago: University of Chicago Press), 159–170.

15. Joshua Zeitz, *White Ethnic New York: Jews, Catholics, and the Shaping of Postwar Politics* (Chapel Hill: University of North Carolina Press, 2007), 11; and James Wolfinger, *Philadelphia Divided: Race and Politics in the City of Brotherly Love* (Chapel Hill: University of North Carolina Press, 2007), 191.

16. Xiaojian Zhao, *Remaking Chinese America: Immigration, Family, and Community, 1940–1965* (New Brunswick, NJ: Rutgers University Press, 2002), 78–93; and Madeline Y. Hsu, *The Good Immigrants: How the Yellow Peril Became the Model Minority* (Princeton, NJ: Princeton University Press, 2015), 130–165.

17. Carl J. Bon Tempo, *Americans at the Gate: The United States and Refugees during the Cold War* (Princeton, NJ: Princeton University Press, 2008), 21–26, 36–50.

18. Stanislaus A. Blejwas, "Old and New Polonias: Tensions within an Ethnic Community," *Polish American Studies* 38, no. 2 (1981): 74–75; George Minton, "Integration of Displaced Persons

into U. S. Economic Life," *Monthly Labor Review* 75, no. 6 (1952): 612; and Hsu, *Good Immigrants* (Princeton, NJ: Princeton University Press), 231–233.

19. Brooks, *Alien Neighbors, Foreign Friends* (Chicago: University of Chicago Press), 194–227.

20. David M. Reimers, *Still the Golden Door: The Third World Comes to America*, 2nd ed. (New York: Columbia University Press, 1992), 89–156.

21. Reimers, 99–122.

22. Yoku Shaw-Taylor, "The Changing Face of Black America," *Contexts* 8, no. 4 (2009): 62–63.

23. Andrew K. Sandoval-Strausz, "Postwar Cities and the Transnational Origins of a New Urban America," *Journal of American History* 101, no. 3 (2014): 817–819.

24. Llana Barber, *Latino City: Immigration and Urban Crisis in Lawrence, Massachusetts, 1945–2000* (Chapel Hill: University of North Carolina Press, 2017), 121–122.

25. Ellen D. Wu, *The Color of Success: Asian Americans and the Origins of the Model Minority* (Princeton, NJ: Princeton University Press, 2014), 151–209, 242–251.

26. Helen Zia, *Asian American Dreams: The Emergence of an American People* (New York: Farrar, Straus and Giroux, 2001), 82–108; and Nancy Abelman and John Lie, *Blue Dreams: Korean Americans and the Los Angeles Riots* (Cambridge, MA: Harvard University Press, 1997), 7–8, 156–157.

27. Charlotte Brooks, *Between Mao and McCarthy: Chinese American Politics in the Cold War Years* (Chicago: University of Chicago Press, 2015), 209–242; Manuel Pastor, Juan De Lara, and Rachel Rosner, "Movements Matter: Immigrant Integration in Los Angeles," in *Unsettled Americans: Metropolitan Context and Civic Leadership for Immigrant Integration*, ed. John Mollenkopf and Manuel Pastor (Ithaca, NY: Cornell University Press, 2016), 109–111.

28. Pew Research Center, "Modern Immigration Wave Brings 59 Million to U.S., Driving Population Growth and Change through 2065." *Pew Research Center Hispanic Trends*, September 28, 2015, 73, http://www.pewhispanic.org/2015/09/28/modern-immigration-wave-brings-59-million-to-u-s-driving-population-growth-and-change-through-2065/.

29. Audrey Singer, Susan W. Hardwick, and Caroline B. Brettell, eds., *Twenty-First Century Gateways: Immigrant Incorporation in Suburban America* (Washington, DC: Brookings Institution Press, 2008).

30. Thomas Guglielmo, *White on Arrival: Italians, Race, Color, and Power in Chicago, 1890–1945* (New York: Oxford University Press, 2003); Russell Kazal, *Becoming Old Stock: The Paradox of German-American Identity* (Princeton, NJ: Princeton University Press, 2004); Robert Orsi, *The Madonna of 115th Street: Faith and Community in Italian Harlem, 1880–1950*, 3rd ed. (New Haven, CT: Yale University Press, 2010); Vivek Bald, *Bengali Harlem and the Lost Histories of South Asian America* (Cambridge, MA: Harvard University Press, 2015); Judy Yung, *Unbound Feet: A Social History of Chinese Women in San Francisco* (Berkeley: University of California Press, 1995); and Sánchez, *Becoming Mexican American*; and Shelley Sang-Hee Lee, *Claiming the Oriental Gateway: Prewar Seattle and Japanese America* (Philadelphia: Temple University Press, 2012).

31. Mae M. Ngai, *Impossible Subjects: Illegal Aliens and the Making of Modern America* (Princeton, NJ: Princeton University Press, 2004).

32. Tyler Anbinder, *City of Dreams: The 400-Year Epic History of Immigrant New York* (Boston: Houghton Mifflin Harcourt, 2016).

33. Cohen, *Making a New Deal* (New York: Cambridge University Press); Robert A. Slayton, *Back of the Yards: The Making of a Local Democracy* (Chicago: University of Chicago Press, 1988); Chauncey, *Gay New York* (New York: Basic Books); and Natalia Molina, *Fit to Be Citizens? Public Health and Race in Los Angeles, 1879–1940* (Berkeley: University of California Press, 2006).

34. Brooks, *Alien Neighbors, Foreign Friends* (Chicago: University of Chicago Press); Lilia Fernandez, *Brown in the Windy City: Mexicans and Puerto Ricans in Postwar Chicago* (Chicago: University of Chicago Press, 2012); Zeitz, *White Ethnic New York* (Chapel Hill: University of North Carolina Press); McGreevy, *Parish Boundaries* (Chicago: University of Chicago Press); Gerald Gamm, *Urban Exodus: Why the Jews Left Boston and the Catholics Stayed* (Cambridge, MA: Harvard University Press, 2001); Joshua B. Freeman, *Working-Class New York: Life and Labor since World War II* (New York: New Press, 2000); Maria Cristina Garcia, *Havana USA: Cuban Exiles and Cuban Americans in South Florida, 1959–1994*

(Berkeley: University of California Press, 1996); and Reimers, *Still the Golden Door* (New York: Columbia University Press).

35. Timothy Fong, *The First Suburban Chinatown: The Remaking of Monterey Park, California* (Philadelphia: Temple University Press, 1994); Willow Lung-Amam, *Trespassers? Asian Americans and the Battle for Suburbia* (Berkeley: University of California Press, 2017); Audrey Singer, Susan W. Hardwick, and Caroline B. Brettell, eds., *Twenty-First Century Gateways: Immigrant Incorporation in Suburban America* (Washington, DC: Brookings Institution Press, 2008); Wendy Cheng, *The Changs Next Door to the Díazes: Remapping Race in Suburban California* (Minneapolis: University of Minnesota Press, 2013); Warren Lehrer, *Crossing the BLVD: Strangers, Neighbors, Aliens in a New America* (New York: W. W. Norton, 2003); Nancy Foner, *From Ellis Island to JFK: New York's Two Great Waves of Immigration* (New Haven, CT: Yale University Press, 2003); Tarry Hum, *Making a Global Immigrant Neighborhood: Brooklyn's Sunset Park* (Philadelphia: Temple University Press, 2014); Robert Vargas, *Wounded City: Violent Turf Wars in a Chicago Barrio* (New York: Oxford University Press, 2016); and Andrew Sandoval-Strausz, "Latino Landscapes: Postwar Cities and the Transnational Origins of a New Urban America," *Journal of American History* 101, no. 3 (December 2014): 804–831, https://academic.oup.com/jah/article-abstract/101/3/804/796501.

Charlotte Brooks

ELLIS ISLAND IMMIGRATION STATION

BEGINNINGS

For much of its history, the original 2.5 acres of sandy outcropping in New York Harbor that evolved into Ellis Island was known by different names. Colonial New Yorkers called it Little Oyster Island. Ownership of the island fell into the hands of a local businessman named Samuel Ellis sometime in the late 1700s; eventually his name became permanently attached to the island. Yet in the early 19th century, most New Yorkers knew it as Gibbet Island, where the federal government executed convicted pirates by hanging.[1]

During the 1790s, the state of New York fortified the island. In 1808, the federal government assumed ownership of the island and completed the work as part of the larger fortification of New York Harbor. It remained a federal military arsenal called Fort Gibson until 1890. Another fort that was part of the city's defenses was Castle Clinton, located in Battery Park on the lower tip of Manhattan. The fort was later renamed Castle Garden and in 1855 began a new career as New York's first immigration station.[2]

Thanks in large part to the construction of the Erie Canal, New York City grew into a booming commercial emporium by the mid-19th century. Between 1810 and 1860, the city's population grew tenfold. Part of that population growth was due to immigration. During the 1840s alone, some 1.2 million immigrants entered the country through New York—although not all of them stayed. Irish and German immigrants dominated this wave of migration. With so many newcomers, some saw a chance to profit at the expense of these immigrant "greenhorns." So-called "immigrant runners" made money selling railroad tickets at inflated prices, charging exorbitant rates for rooms at boarding houses, or overcharging immigrants for their baggage by playing with the scales.[3]

In response, Irish and German immigrant aid societies lobbied New York State to create the Board of Commissioners of Emigration. At this time, immigration policy was left to individual states. In 1855, the Board chose Castle Garden as the site of the first immigration depot. The station would be jointly run by Irish and German immigrant aid societies and New York State. The goal of Castle Garden was largely to protect immigrants from being exploited and defrauded by "runners." Immigrants received reliable information about travel, jobs, and housing. They could exchange foreign money into American currency and buy railroad tickets without fear of fraud. An employment bureau helped immigrants find work around the country. The sick and disabled were provided with medical care. Immigrants' baggage was carefully handled and boarding houses were screened, licensed, and supervised by the Board. A head tax on each arriving immigrant funded Castle Garden's operations.[4]

While Castle Garden struggled with its role as an immigration processing center, evolving policies from the federal government soon meant significant changes in the way immigrants were handled. The nationalizing trends of the post–Civil War era and the challenges of industrialization slowly pushed the federal government to become more active in the regulation of commerce. One of the first areas of federal action in the late 19th century was immigration. The Supreme Court struck the first blow with *Henderson v. Mayor of New York* (1875), which declared that state laws requiring the payment of bonds and head taxes on immigrants were unconstitutional because they usurped Congress's constitutional powers to regulate immigration. In the opinion of the court: "The laws which govern the right to land passengers in the United States from other countries ought to be the same in New York, Boston, New Orleans, and San Francisco." Without funds from the head tax, officials at Castle Garden struggled to continue their work.[5]

Congress then passed laws to regulate immigration—even though it did not possess the full ability to enforce those laws. The Page Act of 1875 was the first federal immigration law, aimed mostly at Asian immigrants. The legislation banned criminals, prostitutes, and Asian laborers. In 1882, Congress passed two more laws: one expanded the exclusionary categories to include any "convict, lunatic, idiot, or person unable to take care of himself or herself without becoming a public charge." The other excluded nearly all Chinese immigrants. In 1885, Congress passed the Foran Act or Contract Labor Law, which made it illegal "to assist or encourage the importation or migration of aliens . . . under contract or agreement," thereby outlawing the recruitment of immigrants whose passages were prepaid by a third party.[6]

Meanwhile, Castle Garden was attracting unwanted attention. The old vigilance against runners had weakened and immigrants could not be guaranteed security from scams and thieves. Confusion over the enforcement of immigration laws only added to the chaos. The 1880s saw a dramatic rise in immigration to the United States, from an average of about 275,000 immigrants per year in the 1870s to an average of 525,000 a year in the 1880s. Additionally, more immigrants from southern and eastern Europe began to arrive, leading to concerns about the suitability of these new immigrants.[7]

In 1888, the US House created a committee to investigate immigration, chaired by Michigan Democrat Melbourne Ford. The following year, the committee released its report and concluded that "large numbers of persons not lawfully entitled to land in the United States are annually received at this port." The committee noted that one of the Castle Garden commissioners even called its operations "a perfect farce." The committee claimed that recent immigrants, such as the Slavs and Italians working in the coal mines of Pennsylvania, "are not such . . . as would make desirable inhabitants of the United States."[8]

In 1889, the Treasury Department conducted its own investigation and found Castle Garden inadequate to the task and the awkward arrangement between state and federal officials in the regulation of immigration unsatisfactory. The Treasury report recommended that the federal government take complete control over the regulation of immigrants, which it did in 1890. That same year, the Treasury Department ordered Castle Garden closed. In thirty-five years, some eight million immigrants had passed through Castle Garden. Now Congress chose Ellis Island as the location of a new federal immigrant depot. The island was expanded using fill from the construction of the city's subway tunnels. A channel to the island was dredged and a dock constructed. The centerpiece of the new facility was a three-story main building constructed of Georgia pine. On January, 1, 1892, the new facilities at Ellis Island opened to receive immigrants.[9]

PEAK YEARS AT ELLIS ISLAND

Fifteen-year-old Annie Moore from County Cork, Ireland, was the first official immigrant to arrive at Ellis Island on January 1, 1892. Arriving with her two younger brothers, Moore was greeted by journalists and government officials and given a ten-dollar gold piece by the new Commissioner of Ellis Island, John Weber.[10]

A month after the station's opening, government officials faced their first challenge. The ship *Massilia* arrived at Ellis Island from Marseilles with hundreds of Russian Jewish and Italian immigrants. Although some of the immigrants were sick upon arrival, nearly all of *Massilia* passengers were allowed to land. Once landed, government officials discovered that many passengers were infected with typhus. New York City public health officials, working with United Hebrew Charities, tracked down as many *Massilia* passengers as possible and put them in quarantine. A total of forty-five people died from the typhus outbreak, including thirteen of the *Massilia* passengers.[11]

Although the outbreak was contained, it cast the new operations at Ellis Island in a negative light. Should officials at the new inspection station stop the arrival of immigrants with contagious diseases? A joint House and Senate committee in Washington chaired by New Hampshire Senator William Chandler criticized what it felt was lax enforcement of the immigration laws. According to Chandler, "many undesirable immigrants" were allowed to land, "who, under a reasonable and proper construction of the laws not in force, should have been refused admission." Chandler's committee rejected expanding the categories of excluded classes but argued for tighter enforcement of current laws that would allow the continuation of immigration. A cholera outbreak later that year brought additional scrutiny of Ellis Island, but no new restrictions on immigration.[12]

In 1897, a fire broke out in the northeast tower of the main building on Ellis Island, destroying the wooden building. With some seven thousand immigrants already on ships headed for New York, the immigration service shifted inspection operations to the Barge Office on the Battery in Lower Manhattan. The chaos that ensued from the fire and the resulting move into the Barge Office left the immigration station in New York in disarray. To make matters worse, a newly elected president—William McKinley—replaced Democratic office holders in the immigration service with Republicans. Over the next four years, the New York immigration service became mired in a swamp of bureaucratic pettiness and personal vendettas that showed the limits of patronage politics.[13]

Tensions grew between Assistant Commissioner of Ellis Island Edward F. McSweeney— who ran the station—and Commissioner-General of Immigration Terence Powderly, the former labor leader appointed by President William McKinley. An investigation of the Barge Office operations by the Treasury Department detailed charges of cruelty, corruption, and abuse of immigrants "of such a pronounced and inexcusable character." Inspectors were taking money from immigrants to bypass the inspection line; one inspector was accused of harassing young female immigrants.[14]

In December 1900, work was completed on a new immigration station at Ellis Island, a steel-frame structure covered with red brick laid in Flemish bond with limestone trimmings. Four one-hundred-foot, copper-covered, bulbous towers crowned each corner, giving the building a Byzantine feel. Even with inspections moving back to the island, little was done to curb the alleged abuses by workers or the growing political feud between McSweeney and Powderly, which divided the immigration staff.[15]

Theodore Roosevelt ascended to the presidency after the 1901 assassination of McKinley. Roosevelt confided to his close friend Nicholas Murray Butler that he was "more anxious to get this office [Ellis Island] straight than almost any other." Roosevelt's statements on immigration prior to his presidency becoming president showed a restrictionist bent. In 1887, he criticized the operations at Castle Garden for admitting "moral paupers and lunatics." He castigated businessmen who demanded cheap immigrant labor, saying they were "committing a peculiarly contemptible species of treason." In 1902, Roosevelt fired Ellis Island Commissioner Thomas Fitchie, McSweeney, and Powderly.[16]

To run Ellis Island, Roosevelt tapped William Williams, a thirty-nine-year-old Wall Street lawyer, reform Republican, Yale graduate, and descendant of famed preacher Jonathan Edwards. Williams was charged with cleaning up the mess at Ellis Island and rooting out the corruption and abuse of immigrants. His reforms were largely successful and a sense of professionalism among the staff increased.[17]

Having moved swiftly to clean up the immigration service in New York, Williams proceeded to tackle what he felt was an even more vital part of his job: a rigid enforcement of the immigration laws. "Every intelligent person with whom I converse (whether engaged in charitable work or business)," Williams wrote to Roosevelt, "is of the opinion that altogether too many low-grade aliens are entering this country." Southern and eastern Europeans now dominated the immigrant wave arriving at Ellis Island. More than 857,000 immigrants arrived during Williams's first year, of whom about 60 percent were Italians, Jews, and Slavs.[18]

The German press began a steady drumbeat of criticism of Williams and his enforcement of the immigration laws, with one article calling Ellis Island "Hell on Earth." Amid the criticism, Roosevelt made the first presidential appearance at Ellis Island in 1903. The result was the appointment of a five-man commission to investigate the operations at Ellis Island, headed by German-born Arthur von Briesen, a president of the Legal Aid Society. This was the fifth investigation of Ellis Island since opening in 1892. Although the report largely exonerated Williams, it included some criticism of the sanitary conditions on the island, the money exchange, and overcrowding.[19]

A workaholic who reported for work at Ellis Island nearly every day, Williams eventually resigned his post in January 1905. Roosevelt replaced him with Robert Watchorn, a British immigrant and former coal miner who had worked his way up the ranks of the immigration service. This was the peak period of immigration during the early 20th century, with nearly 3.4 million immigrants arriving between 1905 and 1907, some 75 percent of those immigrants arriving at Ellis Island. In just one day, May 2, 1907, more than twenty-one thousand immigrants arrived in New York Harbor.[20]

At this time, the Immigration Service came under the purview of the Department of Commerce and Labor. Roosevelt had recently appointed businessman Oscar Straus as Secretary, making him the nation's first Jewish cabinet member. Straus and Watchorn took a more sympathetic view toward immigrants and marked a change in tone in the Immigration Service from the time Williams ran Ellis Island. Roosevelt himself was torn over immigration. On the one hand, he held many of the restrictionist views members of class held; however he was also a man who counted members of New York's various ethnic groups as friends and they softened his views on immigration.[21]

As ethnic groups had once criticized Williams's strict enforcement of the laws, now leaders of the Immigration Restriction League (IRL) criticized Watchorn for his leniency. Roosevelt once again ordered an investigation of Ellis Island, this time under lawyer James Reynolds, a member of the IRL. Ultimately, Reynolds's report exonerated Watchorn, but instead criticized the treatment of mentally ill immigrants in detention. Yet controversy continued to surround Watchorn and when William Howard Taft became president in 1909, he chose to replace Watchorn.[22]

Instead, Taft chose to bring William Williams back to Ellis Island for a second tour of duty. In the years since he left the job in 1905, Williams had continued to voice his concerns about the quality of the "new immigrants" arriving at Ellis Island. Returning in 1909, he was even more determined to tighten the enforcement of the immigration laws at the nation's busiest inspection station. Soon after, Williams again found himself the target of German newspapers throughout the country denouncing "Czarism at Ellis Island." Immigration exclusions increased under Williams, when compared to the Watchorn years, but were still less than 2 percent of the total immigrants who arrived at Ellis Island. Jewish groups felt that Williams's tougher enforcement singled out Jewish immigrants, and organizations such as the Hebrew Sheltering and Immigrant Aid Society stepped up their work on behalf of detained Jewish immigrants. Despite the criticism he received, Williams remained in charge at Ellis Island until June 1913.[23]

INSPECTION AND EXCLUSION

Debates over immigration in the late 1800s and early 1900s continually focused on ideas of "desirable" and "undesirable" immigrants. As Theodore Roosevelt once said: "My own feeling is that we cannot have too many of the right kind of immigrants and that, on the other hand, we should steadily and consistently endeavor to exclude the man who is physically, mentally or morally unfit to be a good citizen or to beget good citizens." Therefore, Ellis Island was created to act as a sieve to separate out and exclude those deemed "undesirable." According to Ellis Island doctor Allan J. McLaughlin: "A great system has been perfected on Ellis Island for sifting the grain from the chaff ... as a sieve fine enough in the mesh to keep out the diseased, the pauper, and the criminal while admitting the immigrant with two strong arms, a sound body, and a stout heart."[24]

With the Immigration Act of 1891, Congress set out a list of those it deemed "undesirable": "idiots, insane persons, paupers or persons likely to become public charges, persons suffering from a loathsome or a dangerous disease, persons who have been convicted of a felony or other infamous crime or misdemeanor involving moral turpitude, polygamists." Immigration officials were responsible for enforcing those laws and defining what those terms meant. Some of the categories were vague and led to debates at Ellis Island and Washington about their meaning and how to apply them to the millions of immigrants arriving in the country.[25]

To enforce these laws and weed out "undesirable" immigrants, Ellis Island officials created an inspection system that could process as many as five thousand immigrants per day. With such volume, individual exams were not possible, so immigrants were paraded through the main building in single-file lines past doctors and inspectors, who paid close attention to any possible medical or mental problem that might be present. Immigrants who were suspected of having some issue were marked with chalk and set aside for further inspection and questioning. Others continued on through the inspection process until they reached the registry clerk, who possessed a copy of the ship's manifest that included relevant information that the immigrant provided to the steamship company. Registry clerks, working through interpreters, questioned the immigrants based on that information. If everything seemed fine, the immigrant was free to land. If the clerk sensed a problem, the immigrant was detained for further questioning.[26]

More than three-quarters of immigrants passed through Ellis Island in a matter of a few hours with little controversy. The others were detained while they awaited medical exams or hearings. Detained immigrants received hearings in front of a Board of Special Inquiry, made up of Ellis Island inspectors. The board acted as an administrative court and questioned immigrants and other witnesses as to whether the immigrant should be admitted into the country. Immigrants ordered deported by the Board could appeal their case to the Commissioner and then to the immigration bureaucracy in Washington. Most remained detained at Ellis Island while their case was being appealed. Immigrants with health problems were held at the island's hospitals, while others stayed in crowded and modest dormitories. During the peak years of the early 20th century, fewer than 2 percent of immigrants who arrived at Ellis Island were ultimately sent back to their homes.[27]

This imperfect system of immigration regulation allowed for large numbers of incoming immigrants but also excluded those whom Americans had deemed, fairly or unfairly, "undesirable." Although immigrants were not required to have papers or visas prior to 1924, this era of Ellis Island immigration marked a period when the federal government made large strides in regularizing and professionalizing an immigration bureaucracy that would soon police the nation's border and make decisions as to who was worthy to enter the country and who was not.

Steamship companies, mostly foreign owned, played an important role in the migration process. Beginning in 1891, Congress made these companies liable for the immigrants they brought to America, mandating fines for steamship companies for every excluded immigrant they brought over and forcing them to pay the passage of the returned immigrants. Consequently, steamship companies had a strong financial interest in not transporting individuals they believed would not pass inspection at American ports. To that end, most steamship companies set up their own inspection process at European ports. If someone did not pass that inspection, they could not purchase a ticket. The actual number of migrants rejected at European ports is hard to come by, but Robert Watchorn estimated that some sixty-five thousand European immigrants were refused steamship tickets at European ports in 1907.[28]

More than half of all Ellis Island immigrants ordered excluded came under the category of "likely to become a public charge." The clause embodied the belief that immigrants should be able to take care of themselves. Although this was an era before the federal welfare state, persons were considered a public charge if they were being taken care of by either private charities or local government institutions like poorhouses or asylums. This differed from someone classified as a pauper who was already dependent on public funds for support.

The clause also possessed another classic characteristic of American immigration law: it was vaguely defined. As one legal scholar would write in the 1930s: "Likely to become a public charge is used as a kind of miscellaneous file into which are placed cases where the officers think the alien ought not to enter, but the facts do not come within any specific requirements of the statutes." Congress wrote the phrase into the law, but it was the responsibility of officials at stations like Ellis Island to decide which immigrants were likely to become public charges. When Commissioner William Williams wanted to more strictly enforce the law and exclude more immigrants, he focused his efforts on the "likely to become a public charge" clause. Immigrants could fall under that clause for a variety of reasons: having a hernia, which would have prevented physical labor; possessing a so-called "poor physique" or "low vitality"; as well as wives and children whose husbands and fathers were ordered excluded, in the belief that single mothers would likely end up as public charges.[29]

The medical inspection of immigrants also played a significant role in the inspection process. Although cholera and typhus outbreaks created public health scares in the 1890s, for the most part improved screening by steamships mitigated the appearance of those serious diseases. Tuberculosis remained common and was of special concern to Ellis Island doctors. The two most common medical conditions that were most likely to have an immigrant excluded, however, were trachoma, a contagious infection of the eyelid that could cause blindness, and favus, a fungal disease of the scalp. Many of the buildings at Ellis Island were medical facilities and immigrants received good-quality treatment from the public health service doctors. If the health of an immigrant improved while under their care, immigrants were allowed to enter the country. Public health service doctors, however, were torn between their professional duty to treat and heal patients with the role they played in diagnosing immigrants for possible exclusion from the country. The decision to exclude was ultimately made by inspectors, not doctors, but those decisions often relied on the diagnosis of the doctors.[30]

Going back to the 1882 Immigration Act, Congress had listed "idiots" among the categories of "undesirable" and excludable immigrants. In 1907, Congress added "imbeciles" and the "feebleminded." These terms referred to individuals with mental and intellectual disabilities. Psychologist Henry Goddard introduced Americans to the idea of intelligence testing that began in France. In 1910, Commissioner Williams invited Goddard to Ellis Island to help public health officials in identifying immigrants who appeared to be "idiots" and "imbeciles." In the end, Ellis Island doctors, mostly untrained in psychology, created their own battery of tests through trial and error to identify immigrants of low intelligence. Intelligence testing was linked with the growing ideas of eugenics at the time and

the concern was that allowing immigrants of low intelligence to enter the country would allow them to pass along their "tainted" genes to future generations of Americans. Ellis Island doctors understood some of the implicit cultural biases in intelligence testing and mostly created non-verbal tests for immigrants, many of whom never had any formal schooling and spoke no English. Many of the tests were simply jigsaw puzzles, as well as the "Cube Imitation Test," which asked immigrants to mimic the actions of a doctor in touching a series of cubes in sequential order. The use of primitive intelligence tests at Ellis Island was the first widespread use of such tests in the United States.[31]

In 1903, reacting to the assassination of President McKinley by a suspected anarchist, Congress added anarchists to the list of excluded categories. That year, British anarchist John Turner was arrested after giving a speech in Manhattan and brought to Ellis Island, where he was detained for nearly five months. Clarence Darrow represented Turner and took his case all the way to the Supreme Court, arguing that Turner's First Amendment right to free speech was being violated. In 1904, the Court unanimously rejected Darrow's argument and upheld the order of deportation. Since Turner should not have legally been allowed to enter the United States because he was an anarchist, the Court argued, the constitutional guarantees of protection of personal freedoms did not apply to him.[32]

Ellis Island officials also found themselves enforcing middle-class ideas of sexual morality under a "moral turpitude" clause. In 1907, the federal government decided that moral turpitude covered issues of private sexuality such as adultery and fornication. Unmarried men and women were forced to get married at Ellis Island before being allowed to land. Unmarried women who arrived with young children found themselves detained, as would married individuals travelling with someone other than their spouse. The enforcement of these rules most often fell upon women, but some men were also detained for these offenses. Immigration officials were also on the look-out for prostitutes and pimps and others entering the country for "immoral purposes," as set out in the Immigration Act of 1907. Concerns about so-called "white slavery" became a national issue, and Ellis Island officials were concerned about immigrants involved in trafficking and the sex trade.[33]

WORLD WAR I AND QUOTAS

Americans were determined to stay out of World War I, but in July 1916 the war arrived at Ellis Island. A few hundred yards southwest of Ellis Island was Black Tom Island. Though once a small island in New York Harbor, Black Tom had since been connected with the mainland of New Jersey by landfill, making it a peninsula that jutted out nearly a mile into the harbor. Piers and warehouses were built along its shoreline and railroad tracks connected them to points west. In July 1916, a massive explosion rocked the docks at Black Tom. The effects could be felt as far south as Maryland. The explosion turned Ellis Island into "a war-swept town." Almost every window on the island was shattered by the concussive effect of the explosion. Shrapnel and other debris were strewn across the island. The terracotta ceiling of the main hospital caved in. The iron-bound door of the main building was jammed inward, as if hit by a direct dynamite blast.[34]

The explosion was no accident, but rather was set off by a group of German agents as part of a larger plot by the German government to sabotage the Allied war effort. They had exploded train cars filled with dynamite, ammunition, shells, and other tools of war waiting to be loaded onto ships headed for Britain, Russia, and France.[35]

When President Woodrow Wilson declared war in April 1917, he set out a policy regarding "alien enemies," including all German males over the age of fourteen residing in the United States and not naturalized US citizens.

In a few weeks, some 1,500 German citizens were held at Ellis Island. Many of them were German nationals working for steamships temporarily docked in Manhattan and New Jersey. By the summer of 1917, the German detainees were sent to an internment camp in North Carolina.[36]

Wartime brought immigration from Europe to a trickle as transatlantic voyages became more dangerous thanks to submarine warfare. The US Army took over the operations of the island's hospital for wounded troops, while the Navy took over the baggage and dormitory buildings and used them to quarter sailors waiting for their assignments. At times, as many as 2,500 military men were stationed at Ellis Island, most for no longer than two weeks. At the same time, American soldiers wounded at the European front were also sent to recover at Ellis Island's hospital.[37]

In 1914, Wilson named his former Johns Hopkins graduate student, Frederic Howe, as Commissioner of Ellis Island. Howe, the author of a number of books, made a name for himself as a Progressive reformer and champion of the public ownership of railroads and utility companies. Though he had little experience with the problems of immigration, he was deeply sympathetic to the plight of immigrants and uncomfortable with his role in enforcing the immigration laws. Unhappy with Howe's work at Ellis Island, Congress launched an investigation of Howe's leadership. The hearings showed Howe to be "the most absentee commissioner" in the station's history. Howe spent a great deal of time dabbling in personal intellectual and political pursuits, few of which directly related to immigration. He remained President of the League for Municipal Ownership and Operation in New York City and was more likely to make news for his views on unemployment, the nationalization of railroads, or public ownership of utilities than on immigration policy. A disillusioned Howe left Ellis Island in 1919; before leaving, however,

516 . ELLIS ISLAND IMMIGRATION STATION

he burned all of his personal papers from his time there.[38]

Because of the war, some immigrants who were denied entry into the country could not be deported back to Europe. This meant that some unfortunate individuals were detained for the remainder of the war. In February 1916, one of those immigrants, nineteen-year-old Gemma Zitello, was refused entry on the grounds that she was an "imbecile." Unable to go back to Italy, she remained detained by the immigration service until November 1918 when she was eventually deported. Once America entered the war and Ellis Island was needed for military purposes, Zitello was transferred to a small immigration station in Gloucester City, New Jersey, until she was deported.[39]

After the war, Ellis Island became a focal point for the detention of suspected non-naturalized alien radicals during the first Red Scare. Some were brought cross country from the Pacific Northwest to Ellis Island, while others were rounded up in New York City. The most famous radicals sent to Ellis Island before their deportation were anarchists Emma Goldman and Alexander Berkman, who were eventually deported from Ellis Island to Russia in December 1919 along with 247 other suspected radical aliens on the transport ship *Buford*, which had been dubbed the "Soviet Ark." The roundups and deportations ended in 1920, but there were more changes in store for Ellis Island.[40]

Disillusionment with immigration grew after World War I and the Red Scare meant that the old way of dealing with the regulation and processing of immigrants was over. The popularity of Madison Grant's *The Passing of the Great Race* signaled a rise in anti-immigrant sentiment.[41] Supporters of eugenics found a sympathetic hearing with important members of Congress. In 1921, Congress passed the Emergency Quota Act, limiting immigration to 3 percent of the total number of foreign-born from each nationality present in the 1910 Census, with a total

ceiling of 355,000 quota immigrants per year. (Immigrant children and wives of American citizens, naturalized or native-born, could enter outside of the quotas.) The legislation was passed merely as a temporary one-year measure, but Congress reauthorized the legislation for 1922 and 1923 as well. The quotas severely restricted immigration from eastern and southern Europe; only 43 percent of immigrant slots were allotted to those regions. On a country-by-country basis, the effect of the quotas was even more startling. Although 296,414 Italians came to America in 1914, the last year in the pre-war immigration boom, under the new quotas only 40,294 were allowed to enter.[42]

In 1924, Congress moved further in the direction of restriction with the Johnson-Reed Act, which set a new quota of 2 percent of each foreign-born nationality based on the 1890 Census and further reduced the total yearly number of immigrants allowed. The rationale for moving the census estimate from 1910 to 1890 was clear: there were far fewer Italians, Greeks, Poles, Jews, and Slavs in the country then. In fact, the new quotas meant that almost 85 percent of the quota allotments would go to northern Europeans. The Italian quota went from roughly 40,000 a year to 3,845, the Russian quota from about 34,000 to just 2,248, and the Greek quota went from just over 3,000 to a negligible 100. All Asian immigrants were now barred from entering the country.[43]

Beginning in 1925, the primary authority for the inspection of immigrants moved away from stations like Ellis Island to American consulates abroad. Individuals who wanted to come to America first had to seek permission at the nearest American consulate, whose officers were tasked with inspecting the individual and making sure he or she would make a desirable immigrant. Upon successful inspection and the payment of a fee, consular officials granted the individual a visa.

By far the most important change brought by the new law did not go into effect for a few more years. Not happy with the near-complete exclusion of most southern and eastern Europeans, restrictionists saw a gross disparity in these quotas: they were based upon America's *foreign-born* population. If the goal was to maintain America as an Anglo-Saxon nation, the quotas should instead be based on the ethnic background of the entire population, both native- and foreign-born.

The new national origins plan lowered the overall immigration ceiling to 150,000 per year and granted immigrants from the United Kingdom almost half of the yearly quota. The big losers were the Germans, Irish, and Scandinavians, who saw their previous quotas cut by more than half. Ironically, although quotas were originally designed to bar southern and eastern Europeans, quotas for Italians, Greeks, and Russians all increased from the previous ones based on the 1890 Census, but their numbers were still pitifully low. Only 307 Greeks and 5,802 Italians were now admitted annually.[44]

With far fewer immigrants arriving and those who did arrive having already qualified for visas before entering the country, Ellis Island was no longer an important inspection center. Instead, for the next three decades, the station mostly survived as a detention center for those who were not approved to enter the country or who were awaiting deportation. The restrictive quotas went hand-in-hand with a rise in deportations. Deportations rose in the early 20th century, with more than two thousand immigrants being evicted from the country in 1908. However, deportations picked up in the early 1920s and continued as the nation's mood against immigrants soured. In 1921, more than 4,500 immigrants were deported and by 1930, that figure was 16,631. Increasing numbers of immigrants were stopped at the front door by quotas, but others were kicked out the back door with stepped-up enforcement of the law. Detentions and deportations defined the next stage of Ellis Island's life.[45]

DETENTION

In the months after the Japanese attack on Pearl Harbor and America's entry into World War II in December 1941, hundreds of suspected German and Italian enemy aliens were taken into custody and detained at Ellis Island. In the summer of 1942, the newly formed Office of Strategic Services (OSS), America's wartime intelligence agency, sent an undercover officer to Ellis Island to report on the activities of what the report called a "Nazi clique" detained there.[46]

The most famous wartime detainee at Ellis Island was forty-nine-year-old Italian opera singer Ezio Pinza. The leading basso at the Metropolitan Opera, Pinza was arrested at his home in suburban New York in March 1942 as an enemy alien and supporter of Mussolini's fascist Italian government. Pinza spent nearly three months in detention at Ellis Island and was released on parole thanks in part to the assistance of New York City Mayor Fiorello La Guardia.[47]

Most enemy aliens were eventually moved to internment camps in Texas and North Dakota. However, the war's end brought some of these suspected alien enemies back to Ellis Island, where they awaited deportation to Europe. While they appealed their cases, they remained at Ellis Island. At the beginning of 1947, almost a year and a half after the end of the war, more than three hundred enemy aliens still remained at Ellis Island. Not until the summer of 1948 did the US government dispose of all the cases of detained German enemy aliens at Ellis Island.[48]

By that time, the Cold War against the Soviet Union was heating up and Ellis Island began hosting non-citizens suspected of being Communists. The cases of two of these detainees garnered the attention of the press and their legal cases made their way to the Supreme Court. Ellen Knauff was born in Germany in 1915, lived in Prague, and managed to escape Nazi Germany for England before the war. After the war, she returned to her native country and worked for the American military government there. She met a recently discharged American soldier named Kurt Knauff and they married in 1948. Ellen was eligible to emigrate to America under the War Brides Act, but when she arrived in New York in August 1948, she was ordered detained at Ellis Island.[49]

She was not informed of the charges against her, but the government possessed anonymous accusations that she was working with Czech Communists while living in Germany. She was detained at Ellis Island for nine months and then released on bond while her court case made its way to the Supreme Court. In 1950, the Supreme Court narrowly ruled against Knauff, relying on the plenary power doctrine and arguing that the executive branch had tremendous latitude in its treatment of aliens, especially when it came to national security. Entry into the country, the Court argued, "is a privilege granted by the sovereign United States Government."[50]

Knauff returned to Ellis Island to await her deportation back to Europe. In the meantime, her case attracted the attention of the press and elected officials in Washington. Only in November 1951 was Knauff officially allowed to enter the country; her case had lasted more than three years and she spent twenty-seven of those months in detention at Ellis Island. The government never proved the accusations, and Knauff continued to deny the charges against her.[51]

While detained at Ellis Island, Knauff was joined by another detainee tainted by the accusation of Communist connections. Ignatz Mezei, an ethnic Hungarian who had lived in the United States since the 1920s, returned to Europe to visit his dying mother in 1948. Upon his return to the United States in 1950, Mezei was detained at Ellis Island and ordered excluded. The accusation against him was that he was a member of a Communist-affiliated group while residing in America. Mezei was born in 1897 on a ship off the Straits of Gibraltar but raised in Hungary and

Romania. In his twenty-five years in America, Mezei never become a naturalized citizen. This left his actual citizenship uncertain. France, England, Hungary, and a number of Latin American countries all refused to take in Mezei. Unable to be deported or allowed to enter the United States, Ignatz Mezei was stuck at Ellis Island, a man without a country.[52]

In March 1953, the Supreme Court ruled against Mezei in a 5–4 decision and upheld the constitutionality of his exclusion. The following year, the Justice Department re-examined Mezei's case. Although the charges against him were much stronger than in the Knauff case, the Eisenhower administration ordered him paroled and released, deeming him not a threat to national security. Mezei spent nearly three years detained at Ellis Island.[53]

By 1954, Ellis Island was tainted by its connection to the Cold War detention of aliens, which was increasingly becoming a public relations problem. Ellis Island was referred to in the press as a "concentration camp," with all of its unfortunate connotations. "Unlike the totalitarians and despots," wrote the New York Times, "we Americans abhor imprisonment by administrative officers' fiat." In this political environment, the Eisenhower administration considered closing Ellis Island for good. Publicly, it supported the move as a cost-saving measure, as the federal government would move its immigration office to Manhattan. But few historians doubt that the public attention drawn to the island by the cases of Ellen Knauff and Ignatz Mezei sealed Ellis Island's fate.[54]

ABANDONMENT AND REBIRTH

In November 1954, Attorney General Herbert Brownell announced the closing of Ellis Island. He set out a new policy on immigrant detentions. Those whose admissibility to United States was under question would now no longer be detained while their cases were decided. Only those deemed "likely to abscond" or whose freedom would be "adverse to the national security or the public safety" would be held. The high-profile detentions had given Ellis Island a bad name.[55]

The question of what to do with Ellis Island vexed the federal government, which still owned the 27.5-acre site and its nearly three dozen buildings. Some ideas for the development of Ellis Island included a clinic for alcoholics and drug addicts, a park, a "world trade center," a modern and innovative "college of the future," private apartments, homes for the elderly, and a shelter for juvenile delinquents. The Eisenhower administration attempted to sell the island to private bidders but stopped after it received little interest from bidders and scattered criticism from those opposed to the idea of selling off an important part of American history.[56]

In 1965, Lyndon Johnson signed the Immigration Act (sometimes referred to as the Hart-Celler Immigration Act, after the names of its sponsors) that ended the discriminatory quotas that had been in place since the 1920s. That same year, Johnson travelled to New York to announce that Ellis Island had been added to the Statue of Liberty National Monument and would be part of the National Park Service. Selling the island was now off the table. Architect Philip Johnson was commissioned to create a new plan for the island, but this idea also failed to gain traction.[57]

In the early 1970s, the abandoned island had attracted the attention of other groups. In 1970, a small group of American Indians attempted to set off for Ellis Island undetected before daybreak, but a gas leak foiled their plans and they were forced to give up their goal of turning Ellis Island into a center for Indian culture. In response, the Coast Guard stepped up patrols and proclaimed a zone of security around Ellis Island. Later that same year, a black neurosurgeon named Thomas Matthew and a group of some sixty fellow members of a group calling themselves NEGRO, the National Economic Growth and Reconstruction Organization, began squatting on the island. Matthew promised to restore Ellis Island and create a "rehabilitative community" for drug addicts, alcoholics, welfare recipients, and ex-cons. Government officials did not chase Matthew off the island, as it appears that he had the tacit support of a Nixon administration interested in promoting black capitalism. The experiment on Ellis Island lasted less than a year.[58]

The civil rights and Black Power movements encouraged notions of racial pride among African Americans but also helped spur white ethnic groups to more public displays of their own identity. Alex Haley's *Roots: The Saga of an American Family* and the subsequent television miniseries not only encouraged African Americans to search for their ancestors but also led to a broader popularizing of genealogical research among whites as well. This rediscovery of the immigrant past rescued Ellis Island from its state of disrepair.[59]

In the early 1980s, a private organization, the Statue of Liberty-Ellis Island Foundation, raised money to restore the Statue of Liberty in advance of its centennial anniversary in 1986. Lee Iacocca, CEO of Chrysler Corporation and the son of Italian immigrants, became the driving force behind the fundraising and restoration operations. He raised hundreds of millions of dollars from both corporate sponsors and small-scale individual donations for both the Statue of Liberty and Ellis Island. Some critics complained that Iacocca's efforts commercialized the historic sites, but his efforts paid off with the successful renovation of the Statue of Liberty in 1986 and the reopening of Ellis Island in 1990. At the cost of more than $150 million, the main building on the island's north side was opened to the public as an immigration museum.[60]

The renovated main building became a successful example of historical restoration, and combined with the new immigration museum Ellis Island became a popular tourist destination. As with during its peak time as an active immigration station, Ellis Island still retains multiple and conflicting meanings to different Americans. An estimated 40 percent of Americans can trace at least one ancestor to Ellis Island—although that number has never been verified. For those Americans, Ellis Island represents an important and personal part of their families' and nation's history. Other Americans, especially African Americans, were more ambivalent about Ellis Island. Some scholars were concerned that a focus on the idea of "a nation of immigrants" was exclusive of other groups of Americans that did not have a traditional immigrant past.[61]

To meet those criticisms, the museum changed its name in 2015 to the Ellis Island National Museum of Immigration and opened up its new "Peopling of America Center." The focus of the museum would now be the broader migration experience from the 16th century to the present and include discussion of slavery and American Indians. Yet "Ellis Island" still evokes conflicting responses among Americans grappling with the effects of the latest wave of new immigrants in the early 21st century. On the one hand, the history of Ellis Island holds out the idea of America as a welcoming nation and places the immigrant experience at the center of the national mythology. In doing so, it helps make the case for a more welcoming immigration policy. On the other hand, does the Ellis Island experience privilege those older immigrant groups over newer immigrant groups? Do current immigration policies and practices compare poorly to those of the Ellis Island era? As Americans continue to grapple with the challenges of immigration, the meanings of Ellis Island, both as a national monument and an important historical site for the enforcement of immigration, remain deeply contested.

DISCUSSION OF THE LITERATURE

The earliest historiography of American immigration dates back to the years following the imposition of the restrictive quotas of the 1920s. Scholars such as Marcus Lee Hansen,

George Stephenson, and Carl Wittke, all Americans of northern European heritage, published sweeping narratives of the early American immigration experience. In the post–World War II period, Oscar Handlin's seminal yet overly dramatic work, *The Uprooted*, began to focus scholarly attention on the immigrant experience during the Ellis Island years. John Higham's classic *Strangers in the Land* looked at the development of nativist reaction to new immigrants since the mid-19th century. Barbara Miller Solomon's study of the Immigration Restriction League looked at one of the most influential nativist groups involved in the fight for stricter immigration laws.[62]

Ellis Island itself received little or no treatment from historians at this time, as it had largely faded from the nation's collective memory. The first attempt at a comprehensive history was *Keepers of the Gate: A History of Ellis Island*, a 1975 administrative history written by National Park Service historian Thomas. M. Pitkin. In 2009, Vincent J. Cannato's *American Passage: The History of Ellis Island* was the first large-scale history of the island since Pitkin and paid particular attention to how federal immigration laws were translated into the operations at Ellis Island during its peak years. Ronald Bayor's *Encountering Ellis Island: How European Immigrants Entered America* is especially useful for describing how Ellis Island worked and how immigrants experienced it. Erika Lee and Judy Yung have written the definitive work on San Francisco's Angel Island and provide a useful comparison both in terms of how it differed from Ellis Island but also how the historical memories of these two sites differed dramatically.[63]

Scholarly inquiry into the overall development of American immigration policy is considerable. Political scientist Daniel Tichenor details the political history of how Congress molded immigration policy in the 20th century. Whereas Roger Daniels sees American immigration policy as illogical and inconsistent, Aristide Zolberg sees immigration policy as central to American nation-building. Mae Ngai looks at immigration policy during the years of the quotas and finds those laws, and the racial assumptions behind them, inadvertently leading to the rise of illegal immigration. Erika Lee has argued that exclusionary laws against the Chinese helped create the regulatory apparatus that governed the nation's immigration policies. Hidetaka Hirota has opened up research into the previously neglected aspect of 19th-century immigration policy and enforcement when it was the domain of individual states.[64]

A good deal of scholarship examines the role of health and medical issues as they relate to immigrants. Alan Kraut's *Silent Travelers: Germs, Genes, and the "Immigrant Menace"* focuses on the intersection of public health and immigration. Howard Markel continues that discussion with his monograph on the typhus and cholera outbreaks of 1892 and how public health concerns affected attitudes toward immigrants and policies at Ellis Island. His essay "'The Eyes Have It': Trachoma, the Perception of Disease, the United States Public Health Service, and the American Jewish Immigration Experience, 1897–1924" focuses on the most common disease found at Ellis Island and how perceptions of that disease stigmatized certain ethnic groups. Amy Fairchild examines the medical inspection process at stations like Ellis Island and sees it as part of the process of creating an industrial workforce. Deirdre Moloney looks at deportation policies at this time, especially as they relate to issues of gender and sexuality. Douglas Baynton links together the idea of "undesirable" immigrants with notions of disability.[65]

Intelligence testing played an important role at Ellis Island. John T. E. Richardson's biography of Howard Knox, one of the Ellis Island doctors most involved with intelligence testing, sheds light on how those tests were created and applied. Leila Zenderland's study of Henry Goddard looks at how he brought intelligence testing to the United States from France and examines his role in the testing of immigrants at Ellis Island. Daniel Kevles gives an overview of eugenics and its broader influence in society, while Ian Robert Dowbiggin's book on eugenics and psychiatry includes a discussion of Ellis Island doctor Thomas Salmon and shows how eugenics influenced immigration enforcement.[66]

As immigration scholars have paid more attention to race, some became critical of the meaning of Ellis Island. Matthew Frye Jacobson sees the memorialization of Ellis Island tied to the problematic idea of America as a "nation of immigrants," problematic especially for what it means for those like African Americans whose history is largely not rooted in the immigration experience. In a similar vein, Ellis Island appears in the title of David Roediger's book *Working toward Whiteness: How America's Immigrants Become White; The Strange Journey from Ellis Island to the Suburbs*. Apart from the title, Ellis Island barely makes an appearance in the book except to symbolize for Roediger how European immigrants allegedly bought into ideas of "whiteness."[67]

These works all demonstrate that although Ellis Island has long since had any role in processing, inspecting, or deporting immigrants, scholars will continue to debate what that history was and how the historical memory of Ellis Island fits into our national narrative.

PRIMARY SOURCES

The main body of primary sources related to the operations at Ellis Island are found in Record Group 85 of the Records of the Immigration and Naturalization Service at the National Archives in Washington, DC. This massive collection contains a wealth of material related to the immigrant inspection process at Ellis Island, including case files on immigrants and Board of Special Inquiry transcripts. Unfortunately the collection does not have a finding aid, making a systematic investigation of the records very difficult. "The Research Collections in American

Immigration, Records of the Immigration and Naturalization Service, Series A: Subject Correspondence Files," edited by Rudolph Vecoli and Alan Kraut, provides a useful service in culling through these records and pulling out documents that highlight important elements in the operations of Ellis Island and putting them on microfilm. Part 3 of this series deals with "Ellis Island, 1900–1933 (https://www.lexisnexis.com/documents /academic/upa_cis/1735_RecsINSSerAPt3 .pdf)," and is available online.

Two other resources present researchers with a wealth of information on all aspects of the operations of Ellis Island and make a good starting point for any investigation of the island's history: August C. Bolino's *The Ellis Island Source Book* and Harlan Unrau's three-volume compilation, *Ellis Island, Statue of Liberty National Monument, New York–New Jersey.*[68]

William Williams served two terms as Commissioner of Ellis Island, under both Theodore Roosevelt and William Howard Taft. His papers are found at the New York Public Library (https://www.nypl.org/sites /default/files/archivalcollections/pdf /williamsw.pdf) and Yale University. Williams was a controversial figure deeply involved in the day-to-day operations at Ellis Island and vocal in his views about immigration. Information that sheds light on Williams's attitudes toward immigrants, some of the individual cases of immigrants he handled, and the public controversies over immigration that Williams became embroiled in can be found in these papers.

Terence Powderly, the former head of the Knights of Labor, was Commissioner-General of Immigration under William McKinley. His papers at the Catholic University of America contain material dealing with his years in the immigration service and especially his battles with the staff at Ellis Island. The federal Bureau of Immigration came under the control of the Department of Commerce and Labor in the early 20th century. The papers of

two Secretaries of Commerce and Labor during the peak years of immigration contain information related to the operations at Ellis Island. The papers of Oscar Straus, who served from 1906–1909, are at the Library of Congress. The papers of Charles Nagel, who served from 1909–1913, are at Yale University.

A number of Ellis Island Commissioners from the 1890s to the 1930s published autobiographies that touch in part on their times at Ellis Island. The memoirs from John Weber, Robert Watchorn, Frederic Howe, Henry Curran, and Edward Corsi present historians with some glimpses of their experiences.[69] Howe's *Confessions of a Reformer* is an especially interesting look at his long career as a Progressive-era reformer and discusses his deep disillusionment with his tenure at Ellis Island. Staff at Ellis Island also published memoirs that discussed their time there, including doctor Victor Safford, inspector Philip Cowen, and interpreter Fiorello La Guardia.[70] Other Ellis Island doctors such as Howard Knox, Alfred C. Reed, and Alan McLaughlin wrote contemporary accounts for medical journals detailing the inspection process and intelligence testing.[71] Writers Edward Steiner and Broughton Brandenburg both made the journey with immigrants in steerage and published books that detailed the experiences of immigrants both on the journey to American and in the inspection process at Ellis Island.[72]

Oral histories are an important primary source in uncovering the history of Ellis Island. The National Park Service has created the Ellis Island Oral History Project at the Ellis Island library that has a collection of a large number of oral histories from immigrants who passed through Ellis Island. Books by Peter Morton Coan and by David M. Brownstone, Irene M. Franck, and Douglass Brownstone are useful compilations of interviews with Ellis Island immigrants.[73]

Steamship manifests listing all immigrants arriving in America during this period are a wonderful primary source for both historians and genealogists. The Statue of Liberty-Ellis

Island Foundation provides a free and easily searchable database on their website that allows anyone to access copies of these manifests. An Ellis Island Passenger Search (https://www.libertyellisfoundation.org/) is available online.

FURTHER READING

Baynton, Douglas C. *Defectives in the Land: Disability and Immigration in the Age of Eugenics*. Chicago: University of Chicago Press, 2016.

Bayor, Ronald H. *Encountering Ellis Island: How European Immigrants Entered America*. Baltimore: Johns Hopkins University Press, 2014.

Bayor, Ronald H., ed. *The Oxford Handbook of American Immigration and Ethnicity*. New York: Oxford University Press, 2016.

Cannato, Vincent J. *American Passage: The History of Ellis Island*. New York: HarperCollins, 2009.

Conway, Lorie. *Forgotten Ellis Island: The Extraordinary Story of America's Immigrant Hospital*. New York: Smithsonian Books, 2007.

Fairchild, Amy L. *Science at the Borders: Immigrant Medical Inspection and the Shaping of the Modern Industrial Labor Force*. Baltimore: Johns Hopkins University Press, 2003.

Fleegler, Robert L. *Ellis Island Nation: Immigration Policy and American Identity in the Twentieth Century*. Philadelphia: University of Pennsylvania Press, 2013.

Hirota, Hidetaka. *Expelling the Poor: Atlantic Seaboard States and the Nineteenth-Century Origins of American Immigration Policy*. New York: Oxford University Press, 2017.

Holland, F. Ross. *Idealists, Scoundrels, and the Lady: An Insider's View of the Statue of Liberty-Ellis Island Project*. Champaign: University of Illinois Press, 1993.

Kraut, Alan M. *Silent Travelers: Germs, Genes, and the "Immigrant Menace."* New York: Basic Books, 1994.

Lee, Erika, and Judy Yung. *Angel Island: Immigrant Gateway to America*. New York: Oxford University Press, 2010.

Markel, Howard. *Quarantine!: East European Jewish Immigrants and the New York City Epidemics of 1892*. Baltimore: Johns Hopkins University Press, 1999.

Mesenhöller, Peter. *Augustus F. Sherman: Ellis Island Portraits, 1905–1920*. New York: Aperture, 2005.

Moreno, Barry. *Encyclopedia of Ellis Island*. Westport, CT: Greenwood Press, 2004.

Ngai, Mae M. *Impossible Subjects: Illegal Aliens and the Making of Modern America*. Princeton, NJ: Princeton University Press, 2004.

Pegler-Gordon, Anna. *In Sight of America: Photography and the Development of U.S. Immigration Policy*. Berkeley, CA: University of California Press, 2009.

Pitkin, Thomas M. *Keepers of the Gate: A History of Ellis Island*. New York: New York University Press, 1975.

Rand, Erica. *The Ellis Island Snow Globe*. Durham, NC: Duke University Press, 2005.

Richardson, John T. E. *Howard Andrew Knox: Pioneer of Intelligence Testing at Ellis Island*. New York: Columbia University Press, 2011.

Tichenor, Daniel J. *Dividing Lines: The Politics of Immigration Control in America*. Princeton, NJ: Princeton University Press, 2002.

Yans-McLaughlin, Virginia, and Marjorie Lightman. *Ellis Island and the Peopling of America: The Official Guide*. New York: New Press, 1997.

Zolberg, Aristide R. *A Nation by Design: Immigration Policy in the Fashioning of America*. New York: Russell Sage Foundation, 2006.

NOTES

1. Vincent J. Cannato, *American Passage: The History of Ellis Island* (New York: HarperCollins, 2009), 19–23.
2. Cannato, *American Passage*, 27–29.
3. Friedrich Kapp, *Immigration and the Commissioners of Emigration of the State of New York* (New York: National Press, 1870), 62; Edwin G. Burrows and Mike Wallace, *Gotham: A History of New York City to 1898* (New York: Oxford University Press, 1999), 737–739; and Cannato, *American Passage*, 33–34.
4. Cannato, *American Passage*, 36–38. For a more detailed discussion of the history of Castle Garden, see George J. Svejda, "Castle Garden as an Immigrant Depot, 1855–1890," *National Park Service*, December 2, 1968.
5. Henderson v. Mayor of City of New York, 92 US 259 (1875).
6. Erika Lee, "The Chinese Exclusion Example: Race, Immigration, and American Gatekeeping, 1882–1924," *Journal of American Ethnic History* 21, no. 3 (Spring 2002): 36–62; Andrew Gyory, *Closing the Gate: Race, Politics, and the Chinese Exclusion*

Act (Chapel Hill: The University of North Carolina Press, 1998); and Cannato, *American Passage*, 43.

7. Cannato, *American Passage*, 44. Yearly immigration statistics can be found at United States Department of Homeland Security, *Yearbook of Immigration Statistics: 2016* (Washington, DC: U.S. Department of Homeland Security, Office of Immigration Statistics, 2017), 5.

8. The Ford Report can be found in the Congressional Record, 50th Cong., 2nd sess., 997–999.

9. Cannato, *American Passage*, 49–50.

10. Cannato, *American Passage*, 57–59.

11. On the *Massilia* incident, see Howard Markel, *Quarantine! East European Jewish Immigrants and the New York City Epidemics of 1892* (Baltimore: Johns Hopkins University Press, 1997).

12. Cannato, *American Passage*, 77–79.

13. Cannato, *American Passage*, 107–108.

14. Cannato, *American Passage*, 109–120.

15. Cannato, *American Passage*, 120–123.

16. Cannato, *American Passage*, 128–135.

17. Cannato, *American Passage*, 136–148.

18. Cannato, *American Passage*, 152–153.

19. Cannato, *American Passage*, 156–161.

20. Cannato, *American Passage*, 165–169.

21. Cannato, *American Passage*, 171–174.

22. Cannato, *American Passage*, 183–185.

23. Cannato, *American Passage*, 216–237.

24. Cannato, *American Passage*, 57, 159.

25. Immigration Act of 1891, chap. 551, 51st Cong., 2nd sess. (March 3, 1891), 1084–1086.

26. Elizabeth Yew, "Medical Inspections of Immigrants at Ellis Island, 1891–1924," *Bulletin of the New York Academy of Medicine* 56, no. 5 (June 1980): 488–510.

27. Cannato, *American Passage*, 221.

28. Cannato, *American Passage*, 221–222.

29. Cannato, *American Passage*, 195, 204–208.

30. Amy L. Fairchild, *Science at the Borders: Immigrant Medical Inspection and the Shaping of the Modern Industrial Labor Force* (Baltimore: Johns Hopkins University Press, 2003); and Howard Markel, "The Eyes Have It: Trachoma, the Perception of Disease, the United States Public Health Service, and the American Jewish Immigration Experience, 1897–1924," *Bulletin of the History of Medicine* 74 (2000): 525–560.

31. Cannato, *American Passage*, 238–259.

32. Cannato, *American Passage*, 146–148; and Turner v. Williams, 194 US 279 (1904).

33. Cannato, *American Passage*, 260–286.

34. Cannato, *American Passage*, 289–292.

35. Jules Witcover, *Sabotage at Black Tom: Imperial Germany's Secret War in America* (Chapel Hill, NC: Algonquin Books, 1989).

36. Cannato, *American Passage*, 293–296.

37. Cannato, *American Passage*, 296–297.

38. Cannato, *American Passage*, 297–300, 328–330.

39. Cannato, *American Passage*, 238–241.

40. Cannato, *American Passage*, 318–325.

41. Madison Grant, *The Passing of the Great Race* (1918; repr., New York: Arno Press, 1970).

42. Cannato, *American Passage*, 332–335.

43. Cannato, *American Passage*, 341–342.

44. Cannato, *American Passage*, 344.

45. Cannato, *American Passage*, 343.

46. Cannato, *American Passage*, 350–353.

47. Cannato, *American Passage*, 355–356; Ezio Pinza, *An Autobiography* (New York: Rinehart, 1958); and Sarah Goodyear, "When Being Italian Was a Crime," *Village Voice*, April 11, 2000.

48. Cannato, *American Passage*, 357; and Stephen Fox, *Fear Itself: Inside the FBI Roundup of German Americans During World War II* (New York: iUniverse, 2005).

49. Cannato, *American Passage*, 363–369.

50. Knauff v. Shaughnessy, 338 US 537 (1950).

51. Cannato, *American Passage*, 368–369.

52. Cannato, *American Passage*, 371–375.

53. Shaughnessy v. Mezei, 345 US 206 (1953).

54. Cannato, *American Passage*, 375.

55. Cannato, *American Passage*, 375.

56. Cannato, *American Passage*, 379–381.

57. Cannato, *American Passage*, 382–383.

58. Cannato, *American Passage*, 386–389.

59. Alex Haley, *Roots: The Saga of an American Family* (Garden City, NY: Doubleday, 1976).

60. Cannato, *American Passage*, 391–395.

61. Cannato, *American Passage*, 403–406.

62. Marcus Lee Hansen, *The Immigrant in American History* (New York: Harper & Row, 1940); George M. Stephenson, *A History of American Immigration, 1820–1924* (New York: Russell & Russell, 1964); Carl Frederick Wittke, *We Who Built America: The Saga of the Immigrant* (New York: Prentice-Hall, 1939); Oscar Handlin, *The Uprooted: The Epic Story of the Great Migrations that Made the American People* (New York: Little, Brown and Company, 1951); John Higham, *Strangers in the Land: Patterns of American Nativism, 1860–1925* (New Brunswick, NJ:

Rutgers University Press, 1955); and Barbara Miller Solomon, *Ancestors and Immigrants: A Changing New England Tradition* (New York: Wiley, 1956).

63. Thomas M. Pitkin, *Keepers of the Gate: A History of Ellis Island* (New York: New York University Press, 1975); Cannato, *American Passage*; Ronald H. Bayor, *Encountering Ellis Island: How European Immigrants Entered America* (Baltimore: Johns Hopkins University Press, 2014); and Erika Lee and Judy Yung, *Angel Island: Immigrant Gateway to America* (New York: Oxford University Press, 2010).

64. Daniel J. Tichenor, *Dividing Lines: The Politics of Immigration Control in America* (Princeton, NJ: Princeton University Press, 2002); Roger Daniels, *Guarding the Golden Door: American Immigration Policy and Immigrants since 1882* (New York: Hill and Wang, 2004); Aristide R. Zolberg, *A Nation by Design: Immigration Policy in the Fashioning of America* (New York: Russell Sage Foundation, 2006); Mae M. Ngai, *Impossible Subjects: Illegal Aliens and the Making of Modern America* (Princeton, NJ: Princeton University Press, 2004); Erika Lee, *At America's Gates: Chinese Immigration during the Exclusion Era, 1882–1943* (Chapel Hill: The University of North Carolina Press, 2003); and Hidetaka Hirota, *Expelling the Poor: Atlantic Seaboard States and the Nineteenth-Century Origins of American Immigration Policy* (New York: Oxford University Press, 2017).

65. Alan M. Kraut, *Silent Travelers: Germs, Genes, and the "Immigrant Menace"* (New York: Basic Books, 1994); Markel, *Quarantine!*; Markel, "The Eyes Have It"; Fairchild, *Science at the Borders*; Deirdre M. Moloney, *National Insecurities: Immigrants and U.S. Deportation Policy Since 1882* (Chapel Hill: North Carolina University Press, 2012); and Douglas C. Baynton, *Defectives in the Land: Disability and Immigration in the Age of Eugenics* (Chicago: University of Chicago Press, 2016).

66. John T. E. Richardson, *Howard Andrew Knox: Pioneer of Intelligence Testing at Ellis Island* (New York: Columbia University Press, 2011); Leila Zenderland, *Measuring Minds: Henry Herbert Goddard and the Origins of American Intelligence Testing* (Cambridge, UK: Cambridge University Press, 1998); Daniel J. Kevles, *In the Name of Eugenics: Genetics and the Uses of Human Heredity* (Cambridge, MA: Harvard University

Press, 1985); and Ian Robert Dowbiggin, *Keeping America Sane: Psychiatry and Eugenics in the United States and Canada, 1880–1940* (Ithaca, NY: Cornell University Press, 1997).

67. Matthew Frye Jacobson, *Roots Too: White Ethnic Revival in Post-Civil Rights America* (Cambridge, MA: Harvard University Press, 2006); and David R. Roediger, *Working toward Whiteness: How America's Immigrants Became White; The Strange Journey from Ellis Island to the Suburbs* (New York: Basic Books, 2005).

68. August C. Bolino, *The Ellis Island Source Book*, 2nd ed. (Washington, DC: Kensington Historical Press, 1990); and Harlan Unrau, *Ellis Island, Statue of Liberty National Monument, New York–New Jersey*, 3 vols. (Washington, DC: National Park Service, 1984).

69. John B. Weber, *Autobiography of John B. Weber* (Buffalo, NY: J. W. Clement Company, 1924); Robert Watchorn, *Autobiography of Robert Watchorn* (Oklahoma City: Robert Watchorn Charities, 1959); Frederic C. Howe, *The Confessions of a Reformer* (Chicago: Quadrangle Books, 1967); Henry H. Curran, *Pillar to Post* (New York: Scribner's, 1941); and Edward Corsi, *In the Shadow of Liberty: The Chronicle of Ellis Island* (New York: Macmillan, 1935).

70. Victor Safford, *Immigration Problems: Personal Experiences of an Official* (New York: Dodd, Mead, 1925); Philip Cowen, *Memories of an American Jew* (New York: International Press, 1932); and Fiorello H. La Guardia, *The Making of an Insurgent: An Autobiography, 1882–1919* (Philadelphia: Lippincott, 1948).

71. Howard A. Knox, "A Scale Based on the Work at Ellis Island for Estimating Mental Defect," *Journal of the American Medical Association* 62, no. 10 (March 7, 1914): 741–747; Alfred C. Reed, "Going through Ellis Island," *Popular Science Monthly* 82 (January 1913): 5–18; and Allan McLaughlin, "How Immigrants Are Inspected," *Popular Science Monthly* 66 (February 1905): 357–361.

72. Broughton Brandenburg, *Imported Americans: The Story of the Experience of a Disguised American and His Wife Studying the Immigration Question* (New York: F. A. Stokes, 1904); and Edward A. Steiner, *On the Trail of the Immigrant* (New York: Fleming H. Revell, 1906).

73. Peter Morton Coan, *Ellis Island Interviews: In Their Own Words* (New York: Facts on File, 1997); and David M. Brownstone, Irene M. Franck, and

Douglass L. Brownstone, *Island of Hope, Island of Tears: The Story of Those Who Entered the New World through Ellis Island: In Their Own Words* (New York: Rawson, Wade, 1979).

Vincent J. Cannato

ANGEL ISLAND IMMIGRATION STATION

The Angel Island Immigration Station, located in San Francisco Bay, was one of twenty-four ports of entry established by the US government to process and detain immigrants entering and leaving the country. From 1910 to 1940, one million people were processed through the port of San Francisco, including 341,000 aliens and 209,000 US citizens who were arriving and 483,000 aliens and 183,000 US citizens who were departing.[1] Deportees, repatriates, alien stowaways, deserting seamen, and migrants in transit also arrived and departed from San Francisco during the same time period. An estimated half a million of them were detained at the Angel Island Immigration Station for immigration inspection and while awaiting appeal decisions or deportation. Their stays could be as short as overnight or as long as two years. Which immigrants were sent to Angel Island, how long they were detained, and how they fared there depended on immigration policies that treated individuals differently according to their race, class, gender, and nationality.

It wasn't always that way. For much of its history, the United States had an open-door immigration policy. From the colonial era through the mid-19th century, foreign immigration was encouraged to help settle newly colonized lands in an expanding America. The federal government passed its first law regulating immigration in 1875, as a way to define who was fit to be admitted into the country and become an American citizen.

Responding to rising anti-Chinese sentiment, that the Chinese were taking away jobs, were posing as a moral and racial threat to the United States, and were unfit to ever become true Americans, Congress passed the 1875 Page Law to bar the entry of Chinese laborers brought to the United States involuntarily, as well as Chinese and Japanese women brought for the purpose of prostitution. It was followed by the Chinese Exclusion Act of 1882, which suspended the immigration of Chinese laborers to the United States for ten years and reaffirmed existing laws banning Chinese aliens from becoming naturalized US citizens. (The exclusion law was renewed in 1892 and not repealed until 1943.) In effect, these laws legalized the racial exclusion and deportation of immigrants considered to be threats to the United States for the first time in the country's history. Similar racist stereotypes were applied to Japanese, Koreans, South Asians, and Filipinos who followed in the footsteps of the Chinese, resulting in the passage of additional laws to exclude Asians from the United States.

Reflecting growing anti-immigrant sentiments across the country, the United States began to close its doors to a wide range of people. Beginning in 1882, a general immigration law barred criminals, prostitutes, paupers, lunatics, idiots, and those likely to become public charges (LPC) from entering the United States. The Immigration Act of 1917 enacted new provisions, including a literacy test for all adult immigrants and restrictions on suspected radicals. In response to anti-Asian sentiment, the act also denied entry to immigrants from India, Burma, Siam, the Malay States, Arabia, Afghanistan, part of Russia, and most of the Polynesian Islands.

The Quota Acts of 1921 and 1924 set quotas for each immigrant group based on national origins with the intent to limit, but not totally exclude, new arrivals from southern and eastern European countries. By adding a clause to the 1924 Act that denied admission to all aliens who were "ineligible to citizenship," a legal classification that applied only to Asians, Congress closed the door on any further Japanese immigration. Filipinos were the last Asian group to be excluded. Considered "US nationals" while the Philippine Islands was a US colony, they were not subject to US immigration laws. That changed in 1934, when Congress passed the Tydings-McDuffie Act, which gave the Philippines independence, thereby changing the status of Filipinos to "aliens," and restricted their immigration to a measly quota of fifty individuals per year.

Each of these various laws was designed to restrict and exclude Asian immigration to the United States. But they did not end it altogether. The Chinese Exclusion laws allowed for merchants, students, teachers, diplomats, and travelers to still apply for admission. Court cases brought by the Chinese eventually allowed for the wives and minor children of US citizens and merchants to do the same. Family members of Japanese and Koreans already in the United States could also continue coming, as could small numbers of Filipinos and South Asian students. More often than not, they applied for admission to the United States through the immigration station on Angel Island.

Although two-thirds of the newcomers on Angel Island were Chinese and Japanese, there were also immigrants from other parts of Asia, Europe, Latin America, and Australia. Russians and Mexicans came to America seeking refuge from the revolutionary violence and disorder ravaging their homelands; Japanese "picture brides" and Chinese "paper sons" crossed the Pacific to join their families; South Asian and Filipino laborers sought work in the fields of California's Central Valley; and Korean, Russian, and Jewish refugees hoped to find freedom from religious and political persecution. Some, like the Chinese and Japanese, crossed the Pacific Ocean directly from their homelands. Others took more circuitous routes to San Francisco: South Asians came after first working in Manila, Hong Kong, or Tokyo; Russian and Jewish refugees crossed Siberia

and Manchuria before boarding ships in Japan bound for the United States; Koreans came by way of Shanghai or Hawaii, as did Filipinos; and Spanish laborers arrived in the city after working in Panama, Mexico, Cuba, Guatemala, and Hawaii.

The Angel Island Immigration Station also played a key role in removing and deporting immigrants already in the United States on charges of prostitution, LPC, criminal offenses, radical politics, and fraudulent entry. Immigration raids became a common occurrence in certain communities as US government officials increased their efforts to track, arrest, and deport immigrants who had entered or remained in the country in violation of the law. Many Filipinos and Chinese Mexicans were also detained and deported from Angel Island during the repatriation campaigns of the 1930s. Angel Island was thus both an entry point for immigrants seeking better lives in America and a last stop on a forced journey out of the country.

BUILDING THE "ELLIS ISLAND OF THE WEST"

Although popularly called the "Ellis Island of the West," the Angel Island station was in fact quite different from its counterpart in New York. Ellis Island was built in 1892 to welcome European immigrants and to enforce immigration laws that restricted but did not exclude European immigrants. For the next sixty-two years, twelve million immigrants were processed through Ellis Island within a few hours. They were given a cursory physical exam and asked a total of twenty-nine questions to test their sound minds and ability to make a living in America. Only 2 percent were excluded and deported. The overwhelming majority went on to become US citizens and to realize their American dream. In contrast, the Angel Island Immigration Station was built in 1910, as the primary gateway for Chinese and other Asian immigrants, to better enforce discriminatory immigration policies that targeted Asians for exclusion. Chinese immigrants, in particular, were subjected to invasive physical exams, exhaustive interrogations, and were often detained for weeks and months at a time while waiting for decisions on their applications and appeals.

Before the immigration station on Angel Island opened in 1910, Chinese passengers arriving in San Francisco were kept on board ships and transferred from ship to ship until final decisions in their cases were made. The San Francisco county jail, for men, and mission homes, for women, were also used as detention facilities for those who could not post bond or who had been ordered deported. Beginning in 1898, the Pacific Mail Steamship Company converted some of its general offices on Pier 40 into a detention shed to house Chinese immigrants. The two-story ramshackle facility proved to be overcrowded, unsanitary, unsafe, and not escape-proof. After considerable protest from the Chinese community, immigration officials declared the shed beyond repair and recommended that a new immigration station be erected on Angel Island to better accommodate the growing numbers of aliens. It was thought that the island location would prevent Chinese immigrants from being coached by friends and relatives, and it would also protect Americans from contagious diseases that Asians allegedly carried. Moreover, the immigration station, like Alcatraz prison close by, would be escape-proof.

In 1904–1905, Congress appropriated $250,000 to construct the new immigration station, the War Department transferred twenty acres of land on the north side of the island for that purpose, and architect Walter J. Matthews was hired to design the new facility, patterned after the "cottage system" and campus setting on Ellis Island, where buildings devoted to specific functions, such as administration, medical services, and detention, were grouped together. After numerous delays, the immigration station finally opened on January 21, 1910, under the directorship of Commissioner of Immigration Hart Hyatt

North and over the objections of Chinatown leaders, who complained that the location was inconvenient for witnesses. By the end of that year, the Bureau of Immigration, under pressure from the Asiatic Exclusion League, had removed North from office for being too lenient with "East Indian" applicants.

The staff of thirty employees quickly grew to 137 employees by 1921, as the work of the immigration station increased in volume and complexity. That year, the station was reorganized into six divisions: law (two inspectors); files, records, accounts, and statistics (one inspector); Chinese immigration (eighteen employees); non-Chinese immigration (five inspectors); boarding and primary inspection (three inspectors); deportation and detention (one inspector). There were also seven inspectors who were stationed in the city office in San Francisco. In 1937, the "Oriental Division" replaced the Chinese division with a staff of fourteen immigrant inspectors, eight clerks, seven Chinese interpreters, and two Japanese interpreters. Reflecting the new focus on repatriation and deportation in the 1930s, there was also a "Detention and Deportation Division," which had one clerk, one telephone operator, twenty-four guards, and four matrons. Those who were needed to maintain and operate the immigration station facilities on a daily basis—engineers, gardeners, electricians, cooks, and hospital workers—lived on the island in employee cottages provided by the government. Other employees involved with the bureaucratic work of processing applications—immigrant inspectors, interpreters, and clerks—commuted from the mainland on a daily basis.

The government quickly learned that the station's insular location was far from satisfactory. Fresh water was scarce, and the station was expensive to operate since all essentials had to be shipped from the mainland. A few months after the facility opened, Surgeon Melvin Glover and Acting Commissioner of Immigration Luther Steward submitted reports highly critical of the many physical and sanitary drawbacks in the design and construction of the hospital and immigration station. Criticisms of the shoddy construction and recommendations that the immigration station be moved back to the mainland continued throughout the history of the Angel Island Immigration Station. But it was not until November of 1940, three months after a fire destroyed the administration building, that the government finally abandoned the site and moved the immigration station to San Francisco.

ENFORCING THE LAWS

The main responsibility of immigration officials on Angel Island was to enforce the nation's immigration laws. Newcomers applying for admission were subjected to a number of routine procedures that began as soon as their ships docked in San Francisco. During primary inspection, immigration and medical officials climbed aboard the ships to examine the papers and medical condition of all the passengers and crew. Nationality, race, and immigrant and economic status all played a part in determining whether further medical and immigration inspections took place on board the ship or on Angel Island. First-class cabin passengers, who were mostly white, wealthy US citizens or European visitors, received preferential treatment and were given a cursory medical inspection in the privacy of their rooms. They, along with returning residents and those traveling in second class, were usually allowed to land directly from the ship. Third-class and steerage passengers, who were mainly Asians and poor, along with sick passengers and anyone whose papers were in question, were all taken by ferry to Angel Island for a more thorough investigation. On average, 70 percent of the ship's passengers were usually required to go to Angel Island. While most non-Asians were able to avoid Angel Island altogether or had a very short stay there, all Asian newcomers were ferried to Angel Island, where many were detained for weeks and months while awaiting decisions on their applications.

When the ferry docked at Angel Island, arrivals deposited their luggage in the baggage shed at the end of the wharf and then walked to the administration building, a two-story wood-framed structure that contained inspection, examination, dining, detention, and administrative areas. The main examination room, where passenger documents were examined and where the intake process began, dominated the ground floor of the building. There were four separate waiting areas, each designated for a different class or group of individuals. Asians congregated in the largest room, which was filled with rows of wooden benches. Men and women, including husbands and wives, were separated and not allowed to see or communicate with each other again until they were admitted into the country or deported. Children under the age of twelve stayed with their mothers, while boys over twelve were detained in the male section.

Any arriving passenger who appeared ill was sent directly to the doctor's office located behind the main examination room. They then proceeded to the hospital for further treatment. Other applicants for admission were ushered up a half flight of stairs to the registry division room, which was partitioned into four large, caged areas with benches lining the two long sides and a processing desk. These areas were also segregated by race. Individuals who needed to be detained on the island were taken here to receive identification numbers and barracks assignments. Chinese and Japanese men were housed in separate sections of the detention barracks; all others were housed on the second floor of the administration building in segregated quarters. Subjected to such procedures, the new arrival's first impression of America was not one of welcome, but of imprisonment.

THE MEDICAL EXAM

The next day, new arrivals were taken to the hospital, located northeast of the administration building, for the medical exam. Medical officers on Angel Island were kept very busy, and the high number of patients and examinations sometimes stretched the hospital facility beyond its capacity. In 1910, they examined more than 11,000 immigrants. In 1920, 25,000 people were given medical examinations. Applicants could be excluded for having such "loathsome and dangerously contagious diseases" as trachoma, tuberculosis, syphilis, gonorrhea, and leprosy. Those found to be "insane," "idiots," or afflicted with a condition that would affect their ability to earn a living, such as heart disease, hernia, pregnancy, "poor physique," "nervous affections," senility, and more, could also be excluded. The medical screenings for these conditions and diseases were designed to protect Americans from diseases and to ensure that only the finest and strongest immigrants were allowed into the country.

The hospital contained patients' wards, a surgery facility, a mortuary, administrative offices, and communal spaces, including a kitchen, large dining room, small private dining room, and limited sleeping quarters for employees. A "disinfector room" was also located on the first floor, where passenger belongings were fumigated. The hospital reinforced the racial and ethnic segregation policy at the immigration station. It had separate entrances for whites and Asians and separate stairs to keep the different races apart once they were inside the building. On the second floor, separate patient wards for European men, European women, Japanese and Chinese women, Japanese men, and Chinese men were all spaced apart. Several small rooms, including dressing rooms, bathrooms, nurses' rooms, the doctor's office, the operating room, and the stairwells separated each patient ward from the next.

As was followed at Ellis Island, public health officers first conducted a line inspection to detect the presence of excludable diseases and medical defects. Eyes were particularly scrutinized for ailments that might impair the sight and lead to an inability to support oneself. Medical screenings could also involve

a physical examination of the naked body to search for abnormalities or to confirm the alleged age of an applicant who was suspected of fraudulent entry. But because scientists at the time believed that "Orientals" carried more serious strains of diseases that could be harmful to white Americans, only Asian immigrants were subjected to the indignity of blood and stool examinations to detect traces of parasitic diseases that were classified as dangerously contagious. In 1910, uncinariasis (hookworm) and filariasis (threadworm) were categorized as excludable diseases, and in 1917, clonorchiasis (liver fluke) was added to the list. The hospital on Angel Island had a state-of-the-art laboratory, and bacterial examinations of blood and waste products became a vital technique in the health screenings of Asian immigrants. During certain years, all second- and third-class passengers, including non-Asians, were also brought to the immigration station and required to take the stool examination.

Because of poor sanitation in rural parts of Asia, medical exclusions based on parasitic diseases primarily affected Asians. It became a convenient excuse to exclude South Asians before they were barred entry by the Immigration Act of 1917. Chinese and Japanese immigrants reacted strongly to what they believed were humiliating and unfair medical procedures. Community protests did result in some changes to medical policies. The US government eventually reclassified some parasitic diseases, such as hookworm and liver fluke, and lifted the penalty of exclusion for anyone with these diseases, provided they be treated and cured at the immigration hospital, and at their own expense. Asian applicants thus incurred additional expenses and delays in the process.

THE INTERROGATION

Any question about an applicant's eligibility to enter the country resulted in a hearing before the Board of Special Inquiry, which consisted of two inspectors, one of whom acted as chair, an interpreter (if necessary), and a stenographer. European applicants, such as Germans, Greeks, Spaniards, Italians, and the British were briefly interrogated about their financial situation, occupational background, and contacts in America, and were generally admitted within a day or two. The same was true of Japanese and Korean picture brides, but not of the Chinese. Because immigrant inspectors suspected that many Chinese immigrants were circumventing the Chinese exclusion laws by coming as "paper sons" or "paper daughters," falsely claiming to be family members of the exempt classes (merchants and US citizens), they subjected them to intensive interrogations that could last three or four days.

Only Chinese merchants were asked to provide detailed documentation of their business activities and volume of merchandise, a list of all partners, and two white witnesses to testify on their behalf. Chinese claiming to be wives or children of US citizens or merchants were asked detailed questions about their family history, relationships, living arrangements, and everyday life in the village:

- "What are the birth and death dates of your grandparents? Where are they buried?"
- "Who lives in the third house in the fourth row of houses in your village?"
- "Of what material is the ancestral hall built?"
- "How often did your father [or husband] write and how much money did he send home?"
- "How many guests were at your wedding? What jewelry did your husband give you as wedding presents?"

These questions, designed to confirm their identities, relationships, and immigration statuses, were also asked of their witnesses. Any significant discrepancy in the answers of an applicant and witness could mean exclusion

and deportation. So unreasonable were the questions that even true sons, daughters, and wives were known to have failed the exam. In essence, the interrogation itself exceeded its stated purpose and worked as a discriminatory practice against Chinese applicants since no other group was subjected to the same process.

In preparation for the interrogation, Chinese applicants, regardless of whether their claims for admission were legitimate or fraudulent, learned to memorize coaching information provided to them by immigration brokers months before the voyage. If their memories should fail them during an interrogation, or if wrong answers were given, a way was found to smuggle coaching information into the detention barracks, either in food and gift packages sent from San Francisco or through the Chinese kitchen staff who were willing to stop by certain stores in Chinatown on their days off to pick up coaching notes. For a small fee, they would smuggle the messages into the station and pass them at mealtimes to officers of the Self-Governing Association, a mutual aid organization that was formed by Chinese detainees in 1918.

Chinese immigrants were usually provided with Chinese interpreters. Many of the interpreters were college graduates who spoke a number of Chinese dialects and who had come highly recommended by white missionaries or trustworthy citizens. The interpreters, however, had no decision-making power on the board, and to prevent any collusion between the applicant, witness, and interpreter, the board used a different interpreter for each session of the hearing. At the end of each session, the board chairman always asked the interpreter to identify the dialect being spoken to ascertain whether the applicant and witness claiming to be members of the same family were speaking the same dialect.

Corruption in the Immigration Service was pervasive throughout the country, and it was no different at Angel Island. Immigrant inspectors were known to accept bribes to render favorable decisions. One of the biggest scandals broke in 1917, when a federal grand jury exposed a smuggling ring that was netting hundreds of thousands of dollars each year. Employees at Angel Island were caught stealing and manipulating Chinese records in connection with illegal entries. The grand jury indicted thirty people, including immigrant inspectors, lawyers, and Chinese immigration brokers. Twenty-five employees were dismissed, transferred, or forced to resign as a result of the investigation.

At the conclusion of the hearing, the board would decide whether to admit, exclude, or admit with conditions or bonds. All decisions, except for some medical conditions, could be appealed to the San Francisco commissioner of immigration, the commissioner-general of immigration in Washington, DC, and then the federal courts. Of all the immigrant groups on Angel Island, the Chinese were the most adept at taking advantage of the legal channels open to them, sparing no expense to hire the best white attorneys to represent them. According to immigration records, from 1910 to 1940, immigrant inspectors on Angel Island rejected 9 percent or 8,672 out of 95,687 Chinese applicants. Of these, 88 percent retained attorneys to appeal the decisions, and 55 percent of the appeals were successful.[2] In many cases, higher authorities found that the interrogation process at Angel Island was unfair. Only 5 percent of all Chinese applicants ended up being deported, but because of the appeal process, at least 6,000 of them languished on Angel Island for more than a year before their cases were finally decided. That is why the Chinese made up 70 percent of the detainee population on Angel Island at any time.

While immigration officials primarily used the Chinese exclusion laws to regulate Chinese immigration into the country, they used the general immigration laws to screen out non-Chinese applicants who had contagious diseases, criminal records, or were likely to become public charges. To enforce the literacy clause of the 1917 Immigration Act, which required that all immigrants aged sixteen and over be able to read in their own language, test cards in thirty-six different languages were used. Renewed xenophobia after the United States entered World War I led to increased concern about the infiltration of spies and radicals at the country's borders. Russian and German immigrants found themselves under intense scrutiny, and the Bureau of Immigration worked closely with other federal departments and local police departments to monitor, arrest, and deport alien radicals and anarchists. The passage of the 1921 Quota Act and 1924 Immigration Act required still more procedures on Angel Island and increased the already heavy staff workload. The quota law allowed 20 percent of the year's allotment for each country to be used each month. Those who arrived after the quota for their particular country had been filled were faced with longer detentions, or worse, had to turn back.

COMPARING IMMIGRANT EXPERIENCES ON ANGEL ISLAND

Immigration records show that of the half million people who were detained on Angel Island between 1910 and 1940, the largest groups were approximately 85,000 Japanese, 50,000 Chinese, 8,000 South Asians, 8,000 Russians and Jews, 1,000 Koreans, and 1,000 Filipinos. Race and nationality continued to be determining factors in the different treatment of immigrants on Angel Island—how they were scrutinized by immigration officials, the quality of food they were served, the comfortable or overcrowded conditions of their housing accommodations, and privileges such as visiting rights and exercise time that were accorded to some and not others. Most telling was the difference in detention time and deportation rates, which reflected immigration policies that privileged whites over Asians, and Japanese over other Asian groups.

Immigrants from South Asia had the hardest time getting into the country. They were primarily Sikhs and single men from the Punjab districts of present-day India and Pakistan who had left their homes to escape British colonialism and to seek a better livelihood abroad. Targeted for exclusion by anti-Asian activists and immigration restrictionists, South Asians had the highest rejection and deportation rate of all immigrants, even though there was no law that specifically excluded them until 1917. In 1910, Commissioner-General of Immigration Daniel Keefe, feeling the pressure from the Asiatic Exclusion League, ordered Angel Island inspectors to exclude "East Indians" as a whole on the basis that they were persons of poor physique and likely to become public charges (LPC) because of discrimination against them in the labor market. From 1911 to 1915, 55 percent of all South Asian applicants for admission were rejected, some because they had hookworms or some other kind of contagious disease, but most because they were deemed LPC. The majority were detained for eight to fourteen days. Very few of them had the financial resources to appeal the decisions. Moreover, there were no strong ethnic organizations of their own to assist them, and the British government, which ruled over India, was not willing to defend their rights. On the contrary, because many of the immigrants supported the Gadar Party's efforts to overthrow British colonial rule, many South Asians already in the country came under scrutiny by Angel Island officials who cooperated with US, Canadian, and British officials to arrest and deport them from the United States.

In contrast, Japanese immigrants had the shortest stay and the lowest rate of deportation (less than 1 percent) among all immigrants. Japan was a powerful nation at the time, having defeated China and Russia in two separate wars, and was able to forestall Congress from passing a Japanese exclusion law. The Japanese government negotiated the Gentlemen's Agreement of 1907–1908, in which they agreed to stop issuing passports to Japanese laborers. The agreement also permitted Japanese aliens in the United States to send for their wives and children; a privilege denied Chinese laborers under the Chinese Exclusion Act. Drawn to Hawaii and the United States by the promise of jobs and wealth, the overwhelming majority of Japanese immigrants, including ten thousand picture brides, came armed with passports and marriage and birth records proving their right to enter the country, and were admitted within a day or two of their arrival. At the worst, those found with hookworms had to stay on Angel Island for two or three weeks to undergo treatment. However, Japanese immigration came to an end with the passage of the Immigration Act of 1924, when Congress decided to add the clause barring all aliens ineligible for citizenship. From then on, only US citizens, returning residents, and temporary visitors were admitted into the country.

Overall, the treatment of Russians and Jews on Angel Island was very similar if not better than that of their counterparts on Ellis Island. Journeying east across Siberia, China, Japan, and the Pacific to reach San Francisco, this diverse group of immigrants included Jews, Baptists, Molokans, and Mennonites who were fleeing religious persecution and military service; farmers, laborers, and tradesmen seeking better economic opportunities; soldiers, aristocrats, professionals, and intellectuals escaping political persecution under the new Soviet regime; and Jewish refuges seeking a safe haven from Nazism. Those who arrived as refugees with little or no money were often barred from landing on grounds that they were LPC. Hundreds were detained for weeks at the immigration station while they appealed exclusion decisions. But with ethnic and religious organizations like the Hebrew Immigrant Aid Society to assist them, their appeals seldom failed. Many were scrutinized for their political views, but few were actually deported because of them. The average stay for Russians and Jews on Angel Island was two to three days, and less than 2 percent were deported in the end. The deportation rate for their counterparts at Ellis Island was twice as high. However, those who arrived after Congress passed the Quota Act of 1921 found their nationality to be a liability. Many were detained for months while waiting for their country's quota to open up.

Other accounts indicate that Australians and New Zealanders might have received preferential treatment and were not always subject to the restrictions of the quota laws. In July 1921, orders were passed down to San Francisco from Washington, DC, that all aliens from Australia and New Zealand should be landed expeditiously, "regardless of quota." As a result, twenty-seven Australians were landed on personal bonds of $500, while twenty-five Assyrian refugees, who had come by way of Japan after escaping slaughter by Muslims in Persia, were detained on Angel Island for over a year because their country's quota had been used up and they did not have the funds to post bonds.

The official records provide ample evidence that immigration officials looked favorably upon immigrants of all racial backgrounds who demonstrated "refinement," wealth, and status. Mexican and South Asian applicants who showed bank statements or property deeds, for example, could convince immigration officials that they were members of the middle, rather than laboring, class. Many immigrants arriving from Guatemala through Angel Island in the early 20th century were wealthy, well-connected people who were coming for vacation, education, or permanent residence. With supporting letters from the Guatemalan consul general and ample funds in their bank accounts, they were readily admitted. Temporary visitors denied admission for minor infractions under the immigration laws could also be admitted on bond, pledging to return to their home country after the time allotted for their visit had expired, but these bonds were expensive and thus available only to those with sufficient funds.

In contrast, working-class immigrants were often excluded from the country because immigration officials considered them "likely to become a public charge." The vague definition of the LPC category made it an effective tool with which to exclude a broad range of people. An LPC decision not only implied that applicants were currently unable to support themselves but also that they would not be able to support themselves in the future. Thus, immigrant inspectors routinely measured an immigrant's appearance, skill set, and work history against the current labor market, racial attitudes, and more. In this way, appearance was used as evidence of poverty in the present and in the future. Those who were aware of this class bias in America's immigration laws took precautions to disguise their economic status and to bring $50 in cash as "show money."

Immigration officials also treated female arrivals differently from males. Immigration policies like the Chinese Exclusion Act and the Gentlemen's Agreement explicitly allowed Chinese and Japanese women to enter the country only as dependents of a husband or father. All female applicants were subjected to gender-based policies that favored the admission of valuable laborers (mostly men) and "respectable" women who conformed to middle-class standards of domesticity. Working-class women were at a clear disadvantage under these terms. Those traveling alone were routinely excluded as LPC. Those traveling with husbands who were suspected of not being able to support their families were also excluded. Whether a woman was capable of supporting herself and her family was irrelevant.

Women from all countries encountered a gendered immigration inspection process, whereby immigration officials held them to higher moral standards than their male counterparts. Female applicants were subjected to interrogations that included personal, invasive questioning about their moral behavior and sexual activities. In contrast, the same type of questioning or level of invasiveness was rarely applied to male applicants. Immigrant women were especially vulnerable to exclusions based on crimes of moral turpitude, which had been defined by a federal district court in 1913 as an "act of baseness, vileness, or depravity." The Bureau of Immigration included a wide range of behaviors as immoral, including perjury, indictment for murder, and conviction of criminal libel. But the realm of immigrants' private sexuality came under the most scrutiny. Fornication, premarital sex, adultery, and homosexuality were all listed as cause for exclusion. Women suspected of having premarital or extra-marital sexual relations with men prior to their arrival in the United States were commonly excluded as committing crimes of moral turpitude, whereas the sexual behaviors of male immigrants was largely irrelevant in the eyes of the government.

IN DETENTION

Life in detention tended to follow a mundane routine of endless waiting that was occasionally interrupted by periods of anxiety, even terror. But again, detainees' experiences on Angel Island differed. Non-Asian detainees described the conditions at the station as tolerable when the barracks were not overcrowded. A group of Russian students, who were stuck on Angel Island for three months in 1923 because of the quota laws, wrote home about their spacious quarters, the good food, visits with friends, and the musical concerts and plays they were allowed to perform at the immigration station. Smaller rooms for "special cases" and first-class female passengers were also available, at least for some years. One Canadian family looked upon their four-month detention in 1930 as a welcome respite from the harsh Canadian winter and the usual toil of work.

In contrast, Chinese detainees, who faced both higher rates of exclusion and longer detention periods than other groups, chafed at the injustices they experienced. In interviews conducted decades after their detention on Angel Island, detainees recalled, often emotionally

and angrily, the feelings of frustration and hopelessness that characterized their time on the island. They were confined to the barracks except for meals and two exercise periods daily. Only the women could go for walks under guard. In addition to the discomfort of confinement, the dormitories themselves were extremely crowded and unsanitary, and posed fire hazards. Rows of rods supporting three tiers of metal bunks lined the rooms. When fully occupied, there was hardly any room to move.

One of the detainees' biggest sources of complaint concerned the poor quality and lack of variety of food served in the dining facilities. Meals took place in the dining rooms located in the administration building and connected to the detention barracks by a covered stairway. Like other aspects of the immigration station, food service was also strictly regulated by racial segregation. Four dining rooms occupied the entire south wing of the administration building's second floor. One public dining room, one officers' dining room, a European dining room, and the Chinese and Japanese dining room separated detainees from immigration officials and visitors and also segregated the detainees by race. Amenities also differed. The European dining room had tablecloths; the Asian dining room did not.

Both immigrants and immigration officials agreed that the quality of the food offered to the detainees was generally poor all around. European detainees complained that their food was served cold and had no variety. Seventeen Russian Jews refused to eat the non-kosher food during Passover week. In 1915, Japanese women detainees cried when they told a visiting social worker about the food served to them on the island. Chinese detainees flatly called the food inedible, and two food riots erupted over food, in 1919 and 1925. Moreover, the dining rooms were unsanitary. The tables, chairs, and dishes were dirty, often with caked-on food from many previous meals.

The poor food quality, especially for Asian detainees, was a result of racial inequality at the immigration station. The government required that the private firms hired to prepare all meals for the immigration station staff and detainees spend less on meals for Asian detainees than for Europeans or staff members. In 1909, concessionaires were allotted 14 cents per meal for Asian detainees, 15 cents per meal for European detainees, and 25 cents for employee meals. There was also a vast difference in the variety of food offered to detainees. This was partly to accommodate different palates and diet preferences, but the specific menus and cost requirements set by the government resulted in a disparity in the quality and variety of food. The fact that the kitchen was equipped with steamers instead of woks did not help matters. "They just steamed the food till it was a like a soupy stew," recalled one Chinese detainee. "After looking at it, you'd lose your appetite."[3] The lucky ones had relatives in San Francisco who sent them tasty deli food, sausages, dim sum, and fresh fruits. Those with a little cash could also buy snacks at the small concession in the dining room.

With such poor quality meals and little distractions, the monotonous routine and the endless waiting took its toll, especially on the Chinese, who had the longest detentions and highest rate of suicides (at least half a dozen reported cases). Many Chinese male detainees found ways to occupy their time gambling, reading newspapers, and listening to phonograph records. Some expressed their frustrations through poetry written or carved into the barracks walls. Recreation time in the small, fenced, outdoor yards allowed them to enjoy some sunlight and fresh air. Once a week, detainees were escorted down to the storehouse on the dock to retrieve personal items from their luggage. In contrast, the women passed the time sewing, knitting, reading, attending English classes, and going for walks under guard. Non-Chinese detainees were allowed to see friends and attorneys on Saturdays and relatives on Sundays, whereas Chinese immigrants were not granted visiting rights until after their cases had been settled.

Other visitors to Angel Island included missionaries and representatives of immigrant and social service organizations who provided religious services, occasional cultural programs, and comfort and assistance to distressed immigrants. Missionaries from the mainland began to visit the station soon after it opened. The most influential missionary at the immigration station was Methodist deaconess Katharine Maurer, who was known as the "Angel of Angel Island." For twenty-eight years, she took the ferry every day from San Francisco to the immigration station to distribute religious teachings, hold English classes and Christmas parties, and visit both men and women in the barracks and in the hospital. In addition, she served as interpreter for German speakers during the interrogations and as witness in the American weddings required of Japanese picture brides until 1917.

Other organizations, such as the Daughters of the American Revolution (DAR), the Young Men's Christian Association (YMCA), and the Young Women's Christian Association (YWCA), assisted Katharine Maurer in her work at the station. The DAR established an emergency fund and contributed boxes of clothing, books, toys, wool and knitting needles, fabric to make clothes, and a radio. The YMCA and YWCA sent staff and volunteers to the station to teach detainees about American customs; provide reading materials, movies, games, and recreational equipment; and perform small services for the detainees. Ethnic organizations and religious institutions such as the Chinese Six Companies, Japanese Association of America, Korean National Association, Hebrew Immigrant Aid Society, Mennonite Church, and Sikh Temple were all instrumental in advocating for improved conditions at the immigration station and providing material and legal assistance to shorten the detainees' stay on Angel Island. The combined efforts of these outside groups helped to alleviate the monotony of detention, provided an important connection to life off the island, and for those who were eventually admitted into the country, helped immigrants make the transition to America.

It could take several hours or several months for the US government to make a final decision about whether to admit or exclude an applicant for admission. For those who were admitted, Angel Island became the gateway that opened up to new lives in America. For those who were excluded, the island represented an impenetrable wall barring them from families, work, and the promise of riches or freedom on the other side. Whether admitted or deported, the time on Angel Island was memorable for many. Over the years, detainees, social workers, immigration officials, and visitors recorded their recollections in interviews, personal collections, autobiographies, and official documentation. Many of these stories can be found in Yung and Lee's book, *Angel Island: Immigrant Gateway to America* or online at the Angel Island Immigration Station Foundation (http://www.aiisf.org/).

Some detainees expressed themselves by writing or carving their names, the dates of their detention, or other thoughts and feelings onto the walls of the immigration station itself. Hundreds of Chinese poems bear witness to the harsh treatment suffered by Chinese detainees, but they are also evidence of resistance, perseverance, and nationalist sentiments in the face of adversity. Carved into the barracks walls of the detention building is one poem written by a Chinese detainee on the eve of his deportation back to China. He expressed his hopes that fellow detainees from his native village would remember their time together. But the poem also stands as a testament to how close the author came to a new life in the United States:

> For half a year on Island, we experienced both the bitter and the sweet
> We only part now as I am being deported
> I leave words to my fellow villagers that when they land,
> I expect them to always remember the time they spent here.[4]

ANGEL ISLAND'S LEGACY

In 1940, a fire destroyed the administration building, and the immigration station was moved back to the mainland. The island site reverted to the US Army, and during World War II, it was used for processing and housing American troops, German and Japanese prisoners of war, and enemy aliens bound for inland camps. In 1963, Angel Island formally became part of the state park system, and the abandoned and dilapidated buildings were slated for demotion. Fortunately in 1970, park ranger Alexander Weiss came upon hundreds of Chinese poems on the walls of the detention building and had the foresight to alert the Asian American community to his discovery.

Over the next forty years, community activists and descendants of Angel Island detainees recovered the poetry and history of immigration through Angel Island, successfully lobbied for National Historic Landmark status, secured funds to restore the site, and embarked on a massive preservation project to transform the site into a museum that would call attention to Angel Island as a symbol of America's history of racial exclusion and as a site of conscience and reconciliation for the nation.

In 1943, Congress repealed the Chinese Exclusion Act as a good-will gesture to China, an ally to the United States in World War II. Chinese aliens were finally able to become US citizens, but only 105 Chinese were admitted into the country each year. Other Asian immigrants were not granted the same privilege until after World War II. It was not until Congress passed the Immigration Act of 1965 that the last vestige of racism was removed from our immigration laws and thousands upon thousands of Asian immigrants were admitted based on a preference system that favored family reunification and skilled and professional labor. The broken immigration system was finally fixed. In 2012, on the 130th anniversary of the Chinese Exclusion Act, Congress saw fit to pass a resolution expressing regret for the discriminatory laws that had resulted in the persecution and political alienation of persons of Chinese descent.

From its founding, the United States has benefited from the skills, ideas, capital, labor, creativity, and values that immigrants have brought to this country. Immigration is critical to our economy, families, and communities. It is also a central component of our national identity. As we continue to debate the role of immigration in 21st-century America, we would do well to heed the lessons of Angel Island—of what can go wrong when a nation's immigration policies do not live up to its democratic ideals of liberty and justice for all.

DISCUSSION OF THE LITERATURE

Very little was known or written about the Angel Island Immigration Station until park ranger Alexander Weiss called attention to the Chinese poems on the walls of the detention barracks in 1970. In an effort to save the poetry and restore the immigration site, Asian American community activists, descendants of former detainees, scholars, and preservationists began researching its history and lobbying for its preservation. Some of the earliest articles on the subject were written by Him Mark Lai and Connie Young Yu and published in *East West Chinese American Journal, San Francisco Journal, Bridge Magazine, California History,* and *Amerasia.*

In 1980, Him Mark Lai, Genny Lim, and Judy Yung teamed up to write and self-publish *Island: Poetry and History of Chinese Immigrants on Angel Island, 1910-1940.* The book includes a historical introduction, 135 poems in Chinese and English translation, excerpts from 39 oral history interviews, and 22 photographs of the period. Many of the poems, which are no longer legible on the walls, came from the notebooks of Tet Yee and Smiley Jann, who were detained on Angel Island in the early 1930s. The second edition of *Island* was published by the University of Washington Press,

in 2014. In addition to the original 135 poems, it includes Chinese poems that had been found on the walls of the immigration stations at Ellis Island and Victoria, BC, an expanded historical introduction based on new research, twenty full profiles of former detainees and employees, and over one hundred photographs of the immigration station and the people associated with the place.

During the years between the two editions of *Island,* there have been much new research and many publications about the Angel Island immigration story. Of particular importance are the following: Erika Lee's *At America's Gates: Chinese Immigration during the Exclusion Era, 1882-1943,* which is based on the Chinese exclusion files and immigration records at the National Archives; Nayah Shah's *Contagious Divides: Epidemics and Race in San Francisco's Chinatown,* which includes a chapter on public health issues and medical practices at Angel Island; Estelle Lau's *Paper Families: Identity, Immigration, Administration, and Chinese Exclusion,* an expose on the paper son immigration strategy and the Confession Program; Robert Barde's *Immigration at the Golden Gate: Passenger Ships, Exclusion, and Angel Island;* Mae M. Ngai's *Impossible Subjects: Illegal Aliens and the Making of Modern America,* which focuses on the legal regime of restriction in the 1920s; John Soennichsen's *Miwoks to Missiles: A History of Angel Island,* including the immigration station; Erika Lee and Judy Yung's comprehensive history, *Angel Island: Immigrant Gateway to America;* and Roger Daniels's article, "No Lamps Were Lit for Them: Angel Island and the Historiography of Asian American Immigration." Two noteworthy studies on Chinese American literature that include an analysis of the Angel Island poems are: Steven Yao's *Foreign Accents: Chinese American Verse from Exclusion to Postethnicity* and Yin Xiao-huang's *Chinese American Literature since the 1850s.*

Major Master's theses and PhD dissertations about Angel Island immigration include: Chen Wen-hsien's dissertation, "Chinese under

Both Exclusion and Immigration Laws" (University of Chicago, 1940); Jennifer Gee's dissertation, "Sifting the Arrivals: Asian Immigrants and the Angel Island Immigration Station, San Francisco, 1910-1940" (Stanford University, 1999); Tom Nishi's thesis, "Actions and Attitudes of the United States Public Health Service on Angel Island, San Francisco Bay, California, 1891–1920" (University of Hawaii, 1982); and Maria Sakovich's thesis, "Angel Island Immigration Station Reconsidered: Non-Asian Encounters with the Immigration Laws, 1910-1940" (Sonoma State University, 2002).

Moreover, in their efforts to restore the immigration station as a National Historic Landmark and museum of Pacific immigration, the Angel Island Immigration Station Foundation and the California Department of Parks and Recreation commissioned Daniel Quan Designs and the Architectural Resources Group to conduct major feasibility studies on the immigration station's buildings, cultural artifacts, history, and grounds. They also hired a team of Chinese scholars to do a comprehensive study of all the poems and inscriptions on the walls: "Poetry and Inscriptions: Translation and Analysis." The various reports from these studies provide new and extensive information about the history and wall inscriptions of the Angel Island Immigration Station.

PRIMARY SOURCES

The National Archives at San Francisco hold the largest collection of immigration records related to the history and operation of the Angel Island Immigration Station. Of particular importance are the following Record Groups:

- *RG 21, Records of the District Courts of the United States*: contains court records of admiralty, civil, and criminal case files. Of special interest are the thousands of case files relating to habeas corpus actions that contested the Chinese exclusion actions of Federal immigration officials.

- *RG 36, Records of the U.S. Customs Service*: contains correspondence received and sent by the Secretary of the Treasury pertaining to the enforcement of the Chinese Exclusion Acts.

- *RG 85, Records of the Immigration and Naturalization Service*: contains arrival investigation case files; Chinese partnership case files; case files of investigations involving deportation; return certificate application case files of Chinese departing; and administrative records, including general correspondence, historical files, and construction and maintenance files; and microfilmed records of Chinese mortuary records, certificates of identity for Chinese residents, registrar of Chinese departure case files, passenger lists of Chinese, daily records of applications for return certificates, indexes of Chinese partnership case files, minutes of Boards of Special Inquiry, passenger lists of vessels arriving in San Francisco, registers of Chinese laborers returning, lists of Chinese passengers arriving in San Francisco, and lists of Chinese applying for admission. (Some of these microfilmed records have been indexed, scanned, and made available at Ancestry.com). A few annual reports of the San Francisco Commissioner of Immigration and all annual reports of the Commissioner-General of Immigration are available at the San Francisco branch.

- *RG 90, Records of the Public Health Service*: contains correspondence and general administrative files of the Angel Island Quarantine Station relating to fumigation and disinfection of vessels and cargo, immigration hospital operations, medical examinations of immigrant aliens, quarantine procedures, and administrative matters.

The National Archives in Washington, DC, hold additional records and photographs relating to the Angel Island Immigration Station: general correspondence files (RG 85), central office subject correspondence and case files (RG 85, Entry 9), administrative files of the Public Health Service (RG 90), and subject correspondence files relating to Asian immigration and exclusion (Series A), which are also available on microfilm at the San Francisco branch.

The Ethnic Studies Library at the University of California, Berkeley, has the largest Chinese American archival collection in the country. Primary sources about Angel Island include transcripts of interviews with former Chinese detainees that were conducted in the 1970s and 1980s (Angel Island Oral History Project) (http://eslibrary.berkeley.edu/); research materials used by Him Mark Lai in his publications about Angel Island (Him Mark Lai Papers); and major Chinese language newspapers on microfilm. For finding aids and online digitalized items, go to Online Archives of California (http://www.oac.cdlib.org/).

The Bancroft Library at the University of California, Berkeley, has the following research materials about the Angel Island Immigration Station: Angel Island interviews with former detainees, Hart Hyatt North Papers, John Birge Sawyer Diaries, and photographs. For finding aids and online digitalized items, go to Online Archives of California (http://www.oac.cdlib.org/).

The Angel Island Immigration Station Foundation (AIISF), founded in 1983 to preserve and restore the immigration station and educate others about its history, has the following research materials in their collection: past and current feasibility studies and interpretive plans by the Angel Island Immigration Station Historical Advisory Committee, California Department of Parks and Recreation, and Architectural Resources Group; oral history recordings and transcripts of interviews conducted by volunteers for AIISF and by the authors of both *Island* and *Angel Island*; and historical and contemporary photographs. Its website has a link, Immigrant Voices to numerous stories, oral histories, and videos created by staff or submitted by volunteers and relatives of former detainees (http://www.aiisf.org/).

The California Department of Parks and Recreation is the primary source for a number of feasibility studies and interpretive plans past and present; transcripts of interviews with former Chinese detainees that were conducted in the 1970s and 1980s; and many historical photographs of the Angel Island Immigration Station.

The San Francisco Public Library (http://sfpl.org/) has the largest collection of San Francisco newspapers in the country; the annual reports of the Commissioner-General of Immigration and the annual reports of the Surgeon-General of the Public Health Services; and newspaper clippings and photographs of the Angel Island Immigration Station in its San Francisco History Center.

FURTHER READING

Barde, Robert. *Immigration at the Golden Gate: Passenger Ships, Exclusion, and Angel Island.* Westport, CT: Praeger, 2008.

Daniels, Roger. "No Lamps Were Lit for Them: Angel Island and the Historiography of Asian American Immigration." *Journal of American Ethnic History* 17.1 (Fall 1997): 3–18.

Lai, Him Mark. "Island of the Immortals: Angel Island Immigration Station and the Chinese Immigrants." *California History* 57.1 (Spring 1978): 88–103.

Lai, Him Mark, Genny Lim, and Judy Yung, *Island: Poetry and History of Chinese Immigrants on Angel Island, 1910–1940.* 2d ed. Seattle: University of Washington Press, 2014.

Lau, Estelle. *Paper Families: Identity, Immigration Administration, and Chinese Exclusion.* Durham, NC: Duke University Press, 2007.

Lee, Erika. *At America's Gates: Chinese Immigration during the Exclusion Era, 1882–1943.* Chapel Hill: University of North Carolina Press, 2003.

Lee, Erika, and Judy Yung. *Angel Island: Immigrant Gateway to America.* New York: Oxford University Press, 2010.

Shah, Nayan. *Contagious Divides: Epidemics and Race in San Francisco Chinatown.* Berkeley: University of California Press, 2001.

Soennichsen, John. *Miwoks to Missiles: A History of Angel Island*. Tiburon, CA: Angel Island Association, 2005.

Yu, Connie Young. "Rediscovered Voices: Chinese Immigrants and Angel Island." *Amerasia Journal* 4.2 (1977): 123–139.

NOTES

1. See Table 1 in the Appendix of Lee and Yung, *Angel Island*, 327–328.
2. See Tables 1 and 2 in the Appendix of Lai, Lim, and Yung, *Island*, 2d ed., 341–342.
3. Interview with Mrs. Wong by Genny Lim and Judy Yung, August 15, 1976, San Francisco. Interview 3 (Mrs. Jew), Angel Island Oral History Project, Ethnic Studies Library, University of California, Berkeley.
4. Translation from Lai, Lim, and Yung, *Island*, 2d ed., 154.

Judy Yung and Erika Lee

IMMIGRATION TO THE UNITED STATES AFTER 1945

OVERVIEW

The vast majority of the immigrants who came to the United States in the late 19th and early 20th centuries arrived from Europe, especially western Europe. The enactment of the 1882 Chinese Exclusion Act ended free immigration. Through legal measures and diplomatic agreements, the government also found ways to exclude Japanese (and Koreans), Indians, and Filipinos. The national origins quota system enacted in 1924 narrowed the entryway for eastern and southern Europeans. Although territorial annexation and the need for Mexican labor for industrial and agricultural developments drove Mexican immigration to the United States since the late 19th century, deportation of Mexican workers had prevented many Mexicans from attaining permanent residency in the United States. After 1945, however, sources of immigration became more diverse. As issues concerning the US economy, World War II, and America's role in international affairs became increasingly important, government regulations also became less restrictive. The result is that 21st-century trends in US immigration have their roots in the important developments during and after World War II, especially in programs and policies designed to import agricultural workers from Mexico, end Asian exclusion, admit refugees, and abolish the national origins quota system. As streams of newcomers arrived from the western hemisphere, Asia, and Africa, immigration from Europe declined, and many European nations also began to shift from sources of US immigration to destinations of international migration. These changes have affected the American population and American society in profound ways. Today, in 2018, European immigrants and their descendants represent less than two-thirds of the American population, as the growth of immigrants from the western hemisphere, Asia, and Africa and their US-born descendants has continued.

THE BRACERO PROGRAM

The most important source of US immigration since 1945 is Mexico. Mexico occupies a unique position in US immigration history due to its political and economic ties with the United States and geographical proximity of the two nations. Some Mexicans were longtime residents of the southern and western regions of North America. In the 1848 Treaty of Guadalupe-Hidalgo ending the Mexican-American War, the United States annexed northern Mexico, making some fifty thousand Mexicans living in that region American residents. For several decades after the annexation, residents of both nations crossed the border frequently to join their family members and relatives; the nearly two thousand miles of national border that separates the southwestern states and Mexico made the crossing relatively easy. High demands in southwestern states for low-wage labor provided economic incentives for US-bound migration. Around 1900, the United States began to recruit impoverished rural workers from west-central Mexican states. Recruitment intensified after World War I. After the 1924 immigration law restricted the entry of southern and eastern Europeans, more than six hundred thousand Mexicans arrived in the 1920s.[1] But during the Great Depression, the government deported as many as 453,000 Mexicans to reduce domestic unemployment pressure.[2]

Compared to these early efforts, the recruitment of Mexican farm workers that began in World War II was larger in scale and had a more lasting impact. Immediately after the Pearl Harbor incident, severe shortages of domestic labor compelled the United States to seek labor once again from its next-door neighbor. Initiated in 1942 with the collaboration of the Mexican government, the Bracero Program arranged for the importation of young male Mexicans to southwestern US farms as guest workers (some also contracted to work on the railroad). These workers entered on a temporary immigration status; their six-month visas were renewable upon approval of their employers. Between 1942 and 1964, as many as 4.6 million Mexicans came to work under the Bracero Program; many workers renewed their visas or entered the program multiple times.

By using guest workers, the Bracero Program enabled the US government to solve the problem of labor shortages while maintaining control over immigration. Nevertheless, the program enhanced a mutual dependency between Mexican workers and American growers. To many Mexican peasants, seasonal work in the United States became an economic strategy, as small savings from temporary employment away from home provided a much needed financial supplement. When the demand for manual labor in the United States outstripped the supply, Mexicans moved across the border in increasing numbers without documentation. Some braceros who were dissatisfied with the terms and conditions of their contracts also found employment elsewhere. In 1954, the US Border Patrol launched the "Operation

Wetback" program to massively deport undocumented migrants, but the number of undocumented Mexican workers increased again after the Bracero Program ended.

The Bracero Program recruited only male workers and required them to leave after fulfilling their contracts. Some women and children crossed the border without inspection to live with their families; many women lived in bracero camps and worked alongside male workers in the fields. Domestic labor was another form of employment for these immigrant women. Workers with families tended to stay in the United States longer. In the 1950s and early 1960s, some bracero families gained legal status to settle permanently.[3] After the program ended in 1964, many former braceros adjusted their legal status and eventually gained citizenship. They played an important role in the growth of Mexican American population.[4]

THE REPEAL OF ASIAN EXCLUSION

The United States has actively engaged in trade and commerce with Asian nations since the mid-19th century. Two years after Great Britain forced China to open its ports for trade in the Treaty of Nanjing (1842) following the Opium War, the United States secured concessions from the Qing government through the Treaty of Wanghia (Wangxia). In 1852, Commodore Matthew C. Perry was dispatched to open the doors of Japan to American trade. His mission was accomplished in the 1854 Treaty of Kanagawa. The United States also took military action against Korea in 1871 and imposed the Treaty of Amity and Commerce on the kingdom in 1882.

Trade and commerce with Asia led to the movement of people. The Chinese started to arrive during the California Gold Rush (1848–1855), along with tens of thousands of migrants from Latin America, Europe, and Australia. The Japanese came next, followed by the Koreans. Indians also arrived from the British colony. Once the United States incorporated the Philippines as a territory after the Spanish-American War, Filipinos could enter freely. The Asian population in the United States, however, remained small (about a quarter million) before World War II. An 1882 law and its amendments, known as the Chinese Exclusion Acts, barred the entry of Chinese laborers for sixty-one years. Diplomatic negotiations between the United States and Japan excluded Japanese laborers in 1907. A 1917 immigration law denied entry to those from the British colony in India. Meanwhile, Asian immigrants were categorized as "alien ineligible for citizenship" by law or court decisions. And finally, the 1924 Immigration Act created an "Asia-Pacific Triangle" to bar immigrants from all Asian countries. Sentiment against Filipino migration played a crucial role in the ideological and moral debate over American Empire, leading to the enactment of the 1934 Tydings-McDuffie Act. Granting independence to the Philippines in ten years, the new law changed the status of Filipinos from nationals to aliens and reduced Filipino immigration to fifty per year. These laws prevented Asian immigration and effectively limited the growth of the Asian American population.

Asian exclusion began to end during World War II. The end of Chinese exclusion in 1943 was hardly a genuine measure of immigration reform. Instead, the government used this goodwill gesture to boost China's resistance against Japanese military aggression in the Pacific. The campaign to abrogate exclusion was led by the Citizen's Committee to Repeal Chinese Exclusion, organized by a group of "friends of China." As a political strategy, the Committee kept a distance from Chinese Americans and downplayed the impact of the repeal on Chinese immigration. Endorsed by Congress and signed into law by President Franklin D. Roosevelt, the Magnuson Act, named for Representative Warren G. Magnuson (D-WA), repealed all the Chinese exclusion acts, provided an annual quota of 105 for Chinese immigration, and granted Chinese immigrants naturalization rights. Magnuson argued that "the quota system amply puts brakes and complete

control over any migrant labor," and the "purpose of the bill is not in any sense to allow migrant labor, merely to put Chinese, our allies, on equal basis with other countries."[5] Responding to questions from those who feared a Chinese influx, President Roosevelt assured the Congress that the small Chinese quota would prevent that from happening, and that "there can be no reasonable apprehension that any such number of immigrants will cause unemployment or provide competition in the search of jobs."[6]

The repeal of Chinese exclusion opened the door for other Asian groups almost immediately. In 1946, the government ended exclusion of Filipinos and Indians, providing the Philippines and India each a quota of one hundred. Pakistan received the same quota after it gained independence in 1947. Because Japan was the wartime enemy, Japanese exclusion continued for several more years, until 1952. The McCarran-Walter Act brought Asian exclusion to an end. Adopting the "Asia-Pacific Triangle" concept, it granted each Asian nation an annual quota of one hundred, with a cap of two thousand for the entire continent. The law also made all Asian immigrants eligible for naturalization.

Some scholars view the McCarran-Walter Act as a product of nativism, because it perpetuated the national origins quota system established in the 1924 Immigration Act. Others, however, see it as progressive. Recognizing the limitations of the legislation, Roger Daniels argues that it was the "liberalizing elements in the 1952 act, part of the Cold War transformation of American immigration policy that helped lay the demographic basis for the multiculturalism that emerged in the United States at the end of the twentieth century."[7]

The repeal of exclusion laws indeed laid the demographic basis for the expansion of Asian immigration. Although the number of quota immigrants granted to Asian nations was small, once classified as "admissible," some Asians were able to come using non-quota status under general immigration laws. Two years after the repeal of Chinese exclusion, the 1945 War Brides Act granted admissions to spouses and children of US military personnel, allowing Chinese American war veterans to bring over their family members. In 1946 this privilege was extended to alien fiancées and fiancés. And in 1946, another act allowed Chinese wives of American citizens to enter as non-quota immigrants. More than seven thousand Chinese women arrived as spouses or fiancées of war veterans, and many of them came with children.[8] The 1947 amendment of the War Brides Act removed exclusion restrictions, giving admission to spouses and children of American military personnel regardless of their race and nationality. More Asian women arrived in the 1950s and 1960s under the McCarran-Walter Act, which provided non-quota status for spouses and minor children of US citizens. As a byproduct of the postwar US military presence in Asia, thousands of women from Japan, Korean, and the Philippines gained entry to the United States because of their marriage to US military personnel. For the first time, the majority of Asian newcomers were female, which helped balance the sex ratio of Asian populations in the United States. The male-to-female ratio among Chinese Americans, for example, went from 2.9 to 1 in 1940 to 1.9 to 1 in 1950 and 1.3 to 1 in 1960.[9]

FORMULATING REFUGEE POLICIES

During and after World War II, the United States emerged as the world's leading power, which required not only its involvement in international affairs but also new directions for domestic and foreign policy. Refugee policies formulated during this period reflected this change. Pressure to accommodate refugees began during the war. In 1940, the government used administrative measures to accept thousands of individuals who escaped from Germany and German-occupied Europe. Established in 1944, the War Refugee Board facilitated the entry of European refugees, the majority of whom were Jewish. Later, the government also developed ways to enable these refugees to become permanent immigrants.[10] The number of refugees admitted during the war was relatively small, but the measures and creative ways to accommodate them and the public debate involved had a lasting impact on US immigration policies.

Immediately after the war, the United States was pressured to deal with the over thirty million dislocated Europeans, including a million displaced persons (DPs) who had been forced from their homelands during the war. President Harry S. Truman issued a directive in 1946 to allocate half of the European quotas for refugee admissions. Enacted in 1948 and amended in 1950, the displaced persons acts authorized the admission of 202,000 individuals in two years. These measures were developed within the framework of the existing immigration law by allowing nations to mortgage their future quotas. The DP acts eventually admitted four hundred thousand Europeans; 16 percent of them were Jewish.[11] From 1949 to 1952, almost half of the new immigrants were admitted as refugees; most of them had no connections with American citizens. In the 1952 McCarran-Walter Act, refugee policies were incorporated into immigration regulation. Because many of the newcomers had no connections in the United States, assistance was provided through voluntary social service networks (VOLAGS). As this practice continued, the VOLAGS and the religious and ethnic groups involved in them also began to influence American immigration policy.[12]

International politics during the Cold War led to more lenient immigration policies for those who claimed to be political refugees from communist nations. The increasing pressure to accept more and more political refugees and allow them to adjust their legal status made immigration reform inevitable. The 1953 Refugee Relief Act abandoned the mortgaging practices of the DP acts, admitting 214,000 refugees as non-quota immigrants.[13] Most of those entered as political refugees after World War II were from eastern Europe, and a relatively smaller number admitted were from Asia. The 1950s and 1960s saw an influx of Hungarian refugees who rebelled against the communist government and Cuban refugees after communists took over during the Cuban Revolution. Coming from a western hemisphere nation, the Cubans were not subject to quota restrictions. In 1957, Congress defined refugees to be those persons fleeing persecution in communist countries or nations in the Middle East. The 1965 Immigration Act included refugees in the preference system and provided a quota of up to 10,200. Although the 1965 Immigration Act imposed a numerical ceiling for western hemisphere nations, President Lyndon B. Johnson introduced an open-door policy for Cuba, promising to admit every refugee from there.

Most successful asylum petitions were filed by individuals from communist countries. In 1987 alone a total of 7,318 immigrants from the Soviet Union, Poland, and Romania adjusted their status through asylum. In the years since 1990 political asylum was a major means for undocumented individuals or temporary visa holders from China to adjust legal status. A 1989 act provided admissions to three hundred thousand Soviet Jews, Pentecostal Christians, and Armenians. Between 1992 and 2007, more than 131,000 individuals from war-torn Bosnia and Herzegovina were granted asylum. Like those who came with refugee status, immigrants who were granted asylum could work and receive government assistance.

Cold War politics also brought the United States into the war in Vietnam in the late 1950s. More than half a million US troops were sent to Vietnam fighting against the Northern communist forces in the 1960s. After the gradual withdrawal of American troops, North Vietnamese forces took control of the country. Thousands of Vietnamese fled with the assistance of the American embassy after the fall of Saigon in April 1975; among them were former South Vietnamese officials, military personnel, and individuals who had close ties with Americans. More individuals left by their own means for other nations. This refugee crisis caught the US government unprepared, for the numerical cap provided in the 1965 Immigration Act was far from adequate. Between 1975 and 1979, Presidents Gerald Ford and Jimmy Carter used their executive power to create one refugee program after another, allocating more slots each time. Some four hundred thousand refugees were admitted, including not only Vietnamese but also Cambodians and Laotians who fled after communists took power in their countries. The exodus continued throughout the 1980s and early 1990s, as large groups of Southeast Asians crossed the borders to refugee camps in Thailand. Most of those who left after 1978 had little education and could not speak English, and the United States had no choice but to accept most of them. To organize the situation, the 1980 Refugee Act set a cap of fifty thousand refugees each year. Adopting the criteria of the United Nations, the law defined refugees as "any person" who, owing to "a well-founded fear of persecution, on account of race, religion, nationality, membership of a particular social group or political opinion," seeks refuge outside of his country.[14] The 1987 Amerasian Homecoming Act also admitted children fathered by American soldiers with Asian women as well as these children's parents and siblings. Among the one million refugees arriving in the 1980s were some 581,000 from Vietnam, Laos, and Cambodia. For the first time after World War II, more than 70 percent of the refugees admitted were from Asia. The Southeast Asia refugee exodus continued into the early years of 1990s, until the normalization of diplomatic relations with Laos, Cambodia, and Vietnam. By 2000 more than a million Vietnamese had been admitted.

ABOLISHING NATIONAL ORIGINS QUOTAS

The most important piece of immigration legislation, one that would change the pattern of immigration more profoundly than any other measures, was enacted on October 3, 1965.

Known as the 1965 Immigration and Nationality Act (or Hart-Celler Act), the new law abolished the discriminatory national origins quota system established in the 1924 Immigration Act.[15] Whereas the 1952 McCarran-Walter Act allocated a quota of 2,990 for Asia, 1,400 for Africa, and 149,667 for Europe, the new legislation provided each nation an equal annual number of twenty thousand slots. The cap for the total quota for the eastern hemisphere was set at 170,000. The law also imposed a ceiling of 120,000 for the western hemisphere, with no limit for individual nations. A new preference system was introduced, as well as a labor certification program.

The new law was applauded for its emphasis on family unification. It gave non-quota status to immediate family members, including spouses, unmarried minor children, and parents of US citizens. A new preference system also reserved 74 percent of the eastern hemisphere quota for four categories of family members and relatives of US citizens and permanent residents, including unmarried children age twenty-one or older of US citizens, spouses and unmarried children age twenty-one or older of permanent residents, married children age 21 or older of US citizens, and siblings of US citizens. Two of the three remaining categories of the preference system included occupations needed in the United States, such as professionals, scientists, or artists of exceptional ability, as well as skilled and unskilled workers. The last preference provided 6 percent of the total quota for refugees. Western hemisphere immigrants, although not limited by the new preference system, were subject to labor clearance.

Although the Hart-Celler bill was endorsed by the majority of both the House of Representatives and the Senate, some scholars argue that few politicians had anticipated that the new law would change the structure of US immigration. The populations of Asian and African Americans were small in the mid-1960s, which suggested that they would be unlikely to take full advantage of the preference system. In other words, European immigration would continue to be the dominant force.[16] At the signing ceremony in front of the Statue of Liberty, President Lyndon Johnson reassured the public, announcing, "This bill that we will sign today is not a revolutionary bill. It does not affect the lives of millions. It will not reshape the structure of our daily lives." Right after the ceremony, however, the president admitted to his press secretary, Bill Moyers, in private, "If this was not a revolutionary law, what the blank did we go all the way to New York to sign it for?"[17]

Amendments to the 1965 Immigration Act adjusted the proportion of professionals and family members allowed under the quota. In the late 1970s Congress reduced the number of professionals and other workers. Immigrants admitted in these categories were required to have job offers in hand, and their employers were responsible for filing the application for alien employment certificates. In 1986, the Immigration Reform and Control Act imposed civil and criminal penalties on employers who knowingly hired illegal aliens. The quota number for siblings of citizens was reduced significantly. The Immigration Act of 1990 re-endorsed the family preference system, increased the number of visas for priority workers and professionals with US job offers, and encouraged the immigration of investors. It also created a "diversity visas" program to benefit immigrants from underrepresented countries.[18]

POST-WORLD WAR II IMMIGRATION

Changes in US immigration policies during and after World War II had a great impact on contemporary immigration. A major shift was the sources of immigration. In the first three decades of the 20th century, 80 percent of the roughly 28 million immigrants originated from Europe. Deportations of Mexican laborers and implementation of Asian exclusion limited the growth of immigrants from the western hemisphere and Asia. The number of immigrants dropped significantly during the Great Depression and World War II. Although Europeans continued to dominate the immigration statistics in the first two decades after the war, a new pattern began to emerge. In the 1950s over half of the total immigrants came from Europe, and the majority of them arrived from western European countries. In the 1960s, however, immigrants from the western hemisphere would replace those from Europe to become a dominant source.

Europe. Western Europeans dominated US immigration statistics until 1890. Although the number of immigrants from southern and eastern Europe began to rise between 1890 and 1920, their entry was limited by the national origins quota system created in the 1924 Immigration Act. The 1952 McCarran-Walter Act reaffirmed this policy, providing large quota allotment to Great Britain (65,000), Germany (26,000), and the Republic of Ireland (18,000) out of the 149,667 total for all European immigrants. In contrast, the numbers allotted for Asia and Africa stood at 2,990 and 1,400, respectively. In addition, a large number of Europeans also came as refugees or displaced persons (Table 1).

The dominance of western European immigration ended in the 1960s when the number of immigrants from other regions began to rise. By the time the 1965 Immigration Act became effective, several southern European communities in the United States were large enough to utilize the new law for family unification. Greek and Italian populations in the United States grew rapidly, followed by the Portuguese and other groups. During the Cold War era, many eastern Europeans, especially those from Hungary, the Soviet Union, Poland, and Romania, gained admissions as refugees (Table 1). At the same time, economic recovery in western European countries provided local opportunities, giving less incentive for people to migrate. Moreover, as the pace of economic growth quickened, Germany, France, Britain, Belgium, and the Netherlands also became destinations of international migration, attracting large numbers of immigrants from southern Europe, the Balkans, Turkey, and Asia. These changes significantly changed the pattern of US immigration.

Most contemporary European immigrants arrived through family unification. A large number of them, especially eastern European immigrants, also came as professionals. Some students who came to seek advanced degrees were able to adjust their legal status upon graduating and receiving US-based job offers. An increasing number of well-educated European professionals came with job-sponsored visas, but many others also came for agricultural and manual work. Poverty rates are high among several eastern European immigrant groups, especially those from Albania, Belarus, Bosnia and Herzegovina, Moldova, and Yugoslavia.[19]

Since the late 20th century, European immigration to the United States has been heavily affected by the pace of globalization. The development of the European Union in the 1990s, with the creation of European citizenship, enabled free movements of goods, services, and capital, as well as people. This means that Europeans have many options if they want to relocate. Migrants who gained entry to one European country could also relocate to another. The United States is still attracting European immigrants, especially those with family connections and marketable skills. European workers seeking better employment opportunities, however, could find alternatives in closer destinations, especially when demand for manual labor and agricultural workers increased in Germany, Italy, and Spain. Western Europe itself has become a magnet for immigration.

Western Hemisphere. Historical and geographical ties with the United States shaped some of the unique features of western hemisphere immigration. The Monroe Doctrine of 1820 declared the United States had a special interest in the Americas. Although during the 1930s Franklin D. Roosevelt's Good Neighbor policy seemed to suggest that the United States might stay out of Latin American affairs, this

Table 1. Sources of Immigration to the United States, 1950–2009. Yearbooks of Immigration Statistics, US Department of Homeland Security.

Region of Origin	1950–1959	1960–1969	1970–1979	1980–1989	1990–1999	2000–2009
Total (000s)	2,499	3,214	4,248	6,244	9,775	10,229
Europe(%)	**56.2**	**35.3**	**19.4**	**10.7**	**13.8**	**13.1**
Austria	3.3	.5	.3	.2	.2	.2
Belgium	.8	.3	.1	.1	.1	.1
Bosnia-Herzegovina	–	–	–	–	.3	1.0
Czechoslovakia	.1	.1	.1	.1	.1	.2
Denmark	.4	.3	.1	.1	.1	.1
France	2.0	.5	.6	.5	.4	.4
Germany	23.1	6.5	1.8	1.4	.9	1.2
Greece	1.8	2.3	2.4	.6	.3	.2
Hungary	1.3	.3	.1	.1	.1	.1
Ireland	1.9	1.2	.3	.4	.7	.2
Italy	7.4	6.2	3.5	.9	.8	.3
Netherlands	1.9	1.2	.2	.2	.1	.2
Norway	.9	.5	.1	.1	.1	.0
Poland	.3	1.7	.8	1.0	1.8	1.1
Portugal	.6	2.2	2.5	.7	.3	.1
Romania	.0	.1	.3	.4	.5	.5
Russia[1]	.0	.1	.7	.5	4.4	1.6
Spain	.3	1.3	1.0	.4	.2	.2
Sweden	.9	.6	.1	.2	.1	.1
Switzerland	.7	.6	.2	.1	.1	.1
Ukraine	–	–	–	–	1.3	1.5
United Kingdom	7.8	6.9	3.1	2.5	1.6	1.7
Yugoslavia[2]	.3	.6	.8	.3	.6	1.3
Others	.5	.2	.1	.1	.0	.3
Asia(%)	**5.4**	**11.2**	**33.1**	**38.3**	**29.3**	**33.7**
Bangladesh	–	–	.1	.2	.6	1.0
Cambodia	–	–	.1	1.8	.2	.3

Asia(%)	5.4	11.2	33.1	38.3	29.3	33.7
China	.4	.4	.4	2.7	3.5	5.7
Hong Kong	.6	2.1	2.8	1.8	1.2	.6
India	.1	.6	3.5	3.7	3.6	5.7
Iran	.1	.3	.8	1.6	.8	.7
Israel	.9	1.0	.9	.7	.4	.5
Japan	1.6	1.3	1.2	.7	.7	.8
Jordan	.2	.3	.6	.5	.4	.5
Korea, South	.2	.8	5.7	5.2	1.8	2.0
Laos	–	–	.2	2.4	.5	.2
Pakistan	–	–	.6	.9	1.2	1.5
Philippines	.7	2.2	7.9	8.0	5.5	5.3
Syria	.0	.1	.2	.2	.2	.3
Taiwan	.0	.5	2.0	1.9	1.4	.9
Thailand	–	–	.9	1.0	.5	.6
Turkey	.1	.3	.3	.3	.4	.5
Vietnam	.0	.1	2.9	3.2	2.8	2.8
Others	.6	1.3	2.1	1.4	3.3	3.6
West Hemisphere(%)	**36.9**	**52.1**	**44.8**	**43.2**	**52.6**	**43.1**
Argentina	.7	1.5	.7	.4	.3	.5
Brazil	.5	.9	.4	.4	.5	1.1
Canada	14.1	13.5	4.2	2.5	2.0	2.3
Colombia	.6	2.1	1.7	1.7	1.4	2.3
Cuba	2.9	6.3	6.0	2.1	1.6	2.6
Dominican Republic	.4	2.6	3.3	3.5	3.7	2.8
Ecuador	.3	1.1	1.1	.8	.8	1.0
El Salvador	.2	.4	.7	2.2	2.8	2.4
Guatemala	.2	.4	.6	.9	1.3	1.5
Guyana	.0	.1	.9	1.4	.8	.7

(*Continued*)

Table 1. Continued

West Hemisphere(%)	36.9	52.1	44.8	43.2	52.6	43.1
Haiti	.2	.9	1.3	1.9	1.8	2.0
Honduras	.2	.5	.4	.6	.7	.6
Jamaica	.3	1.9	3.1	3.1	1.8	2.0
Mexico	11.0	13.7	14.6	16.2	28.2	16.5
Nicaragua	.3	.3	.3	.5	.8	.7
Peru	.2	.6	.6	.8	1.1	1.3
Venezuela	.4	.6	.3	.4	.4	.8
Others	2.4	.7	.0	.0	.0	.0
Africa(%)	**.5**	**.7**	**1.7**	**2.3**	**3.5**	**7.4**
Egypt	.1	.2	.6	.4	.5	.8
Ethiopia	.0	.0	.1	.2	.4	.8
Liberia	.0	.0	.1	.1	.1	.2
Morocco	.1	.1	.0	.1	.2	.4
South Africa	.1	.1	.2	.2	.2	.3
Others	.2	.3	.7	1.2	2.2	4.8
Oceania(%)	**.5**	**.7**	**.9**	**.7**	**.6**	**.6**
Australia	.3	.5	.4	.3	.2	.3
Fiji	–	–	.1	.1	.1	.1
New Zealand	.1	.1	.1	.1	.1	.1
Others	.1	.2	.3	.2	.1	.1

[1] Data between 1950 and 1990 refer to the Soviet Union. From 1991 to 1999, data refer to Russia, Armenia, Azerbaijan, Belarus, Georgia, Kazakhstan, Kyrgyzstan, Moldova, Tajikistan, Turkmenistan, Ukraine, and Uzbekistan. Beginning in 2000, data refer to Russia only.

[2] Data include Bosnia and Herzegovina, Croatia, Kosovo, Macedonia, Montenegro, Serbia, Slovenia, and Serbia and Montenegro.

policy was reversed during the Cold War. Interventions by the United States in the affairs of Latin American countries played an important role in shaping immigration policies toward these countries. Demand for low-wage labor in the United States and poverty at home created economic incentives for US-bound migration from Latin American countries, especially in times of war, civil unrest, and violence. According to the US Census Bureau, a total of fifty-four million Hispanics lived in the United States in 2013, representing 17 percent of the population. More than half of the Hispanic population were Mexicans (64 percent). As Table 1 and Table 2 indicate, immigration from western hemisphere nations grew at a

Table 2. Top Ten Sources of US Immigration, 1950–2009. Yearbooks of Immigration Statistics, US Department of Homeland Security.

1950–1959	1960–1969	1970–1979	1980–1989	1990–1999	2000–2009
Germany	Mexico	Mexico	Mexico	Mexico	Mexico
Canada	Canada	Philippines	Philippines	Philippines	China
Mexico	UK	Cuba	South Korea	Russia	India
UK	Germany	Korea	India	Dominican Rep.	Philippines
Italy	Cuba	Canada	Dominican Rep.	India	Dominican Rep.
Austria	Italy	Italy	Vietnam	China	Vietnam
Cuba	Dominican Rep.	India	Jamaica	Vietnam	Cuba
France	Greece	Dominican Rep.	China	El Salvador	El Salvador
Ireland	Philippines	UK	Canada	Canada	Colombia
Netherlands	Portugal	Jamaica	UK	South Korea	Canada

fast pace in the second half of the 20th century, and since the 1960s Mexico has been the most important source of US immigration.

Canada was a major western hemisphere source of immigration in the 1950s, but it could not hold its place a decade later, as an increasing number of the immigrants also began to return to their homeland. The 1960s also witnessed a significant increase of immigrants from other western hemisphere nations, including some 200,000 Cubans, 100,000 Dominicans, and 70,000 Colombians. As indicated in Figure 1, immigrants from the western hemisphere replaced those from Europe to become the driving force of US immigration in the 1960s.

The importance of Mexico in US immigration reflects the close relationship between the two nations. The Bracero Program initiated in 1942 recruited 4.6 million Mexican agricultural workers over a period of twenty-two years. Although the program required the workers to return to Mexico after their contracts ended, some bracero wives and children found ways to come and eventually adjusted their legal status. Many of those remaining in the United States in 1964 also became permanent US residents and later were eligible to send for their families and relatives. Without quota

limitation, the number of Mexican immigrants rose quickly, from 61,000 in the 1940s to 300,000 in the 1950s, and to 454,000 during the 1960s. After a ceiling of 120,000 entries per year for western hemisphere immigration was imposed by legislation in 1965, no national quota limit was set. This allowed Mexican immigrants to take a large share of the hemisphere quota. A 1976 law provided each western hemisphere country with an annual quota of 20,000 and established a preference system.[20] In 1978, a new law set a worldwide ceiling of 290,000 and established a universal preference system.[21] Because immediate family members of US citizens are not counted, some 680,000 Mexicans gained entry in the 1970s. In the 1990s, Mexico's share of immigration was 28.2 percent, slightly smaller than the share from all Asian nations (29.3 percent) but significantly larger than that of all European nations (13.8 percent).

Since the Bracero Program, the number of unauthorized immigrants from Mexico has increased, as many migrants adopted a pattern of back-and-forth movement across the border. The dependence of American growers on the supply of low-wage labor from Mexico also bound the countries together. In the 1980s, a

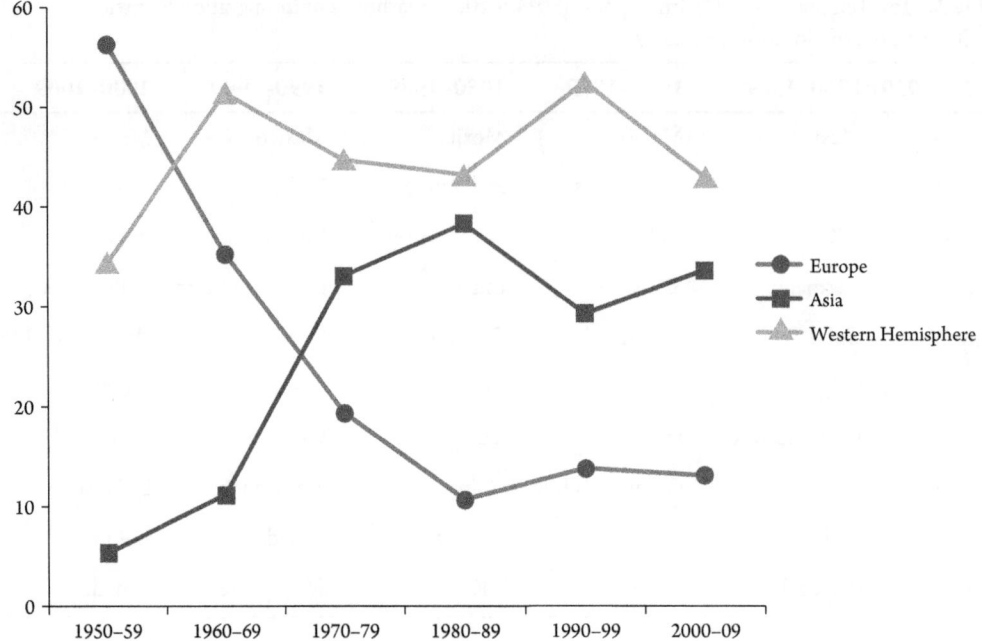

Figure 1. Percentage of Total Immigrants to the United States by Region, 1950–2009. Yearbooks of Immigration Statistics, US Department of Homeland Security.

record high of three million Mexicans gained entry, including 2.3 million undocumented individuals under the 1986 Immigration Reform and Control Act (IRCA). The new law also tightened border patrols and imposed penalties for hiring undocumented immigrants, but several million more still arrived between 1990 and 2010. Of an estimated 11.3 million undocumented immigrants in the United States in 2012, about 59 percent were from Mexico.

The Cuban exodus to the United States reflected deteriorating relations between the two countries. From 1959 and the Cuban missile crisis in 1962, more than one hundred thousand refugees were admitted to the United States; many of them were educated or had professional skills. Those that came between 1965 and 1973 were more numerous but less well-to-do. In the chaotic exodus of the Mariel boatlift in 1980, which lasted for 162 days, the United States Coast Guard assisted more than one thousand vessels carrying refugees from the small fishing port of Mariel west of Havana to South Florida, bringing 125,000 individuals, including a large number of blacks and

unskilled workers. That year alone, some 350,000 Cubans gained entry, which was more than the annual total allotted for all immigrants. Although there were no formal diplomatic relations between the two countries, the United States reached an agreement with Cuba in 1996 and granted the country an annual quota of 20,000.[22] By 2000, some 900,000 Cubans were admitted as refugees. An annual average of more than 30,000 individuals gained entry since then. A program administered by the Department of Homeland Security in 2006 also brought six thousand medical professionals from Cuba. Cuban immigrants built a large ethnic community in Miami, which became the most desirable destination for newcomers.

Increasing numbers of immigrants also arrived from several other western hemisphere nations. The Dominican Republic, which had a historical tie with the United States (US troops occupied the island nation for eight years from 1916 to 1924), began to send large numbers in the 1960s. In the years after 1970, an annual average of twenty-five thousand Dominicans have been admitted, and those who came as tourists and overstayed their visas or who arrived in the United States via Puerto Rico were largely uncounted. Many Dominican immigrants could enjoy dual citizenship after 1994, which further encouraged migration. War, violence, poverty, and natural disasters also encouraged immigration from Nicaragua, Guatemala, El Salvador, and other Central American nations. The Nicaraguans began to arrive in large numbers in the 1960s and joined Cuban immigrants in Florida, especially Miami. Most immigrants from Guatemala and El Salvador were from rural backgrounds. In 1997, the Nicaraguan Adjustment and Central American Relief Act granted amnesty to tens of thousands of Central Americans (Nicaraguans, Salvadorans, Guatemalans, etc.) who had arrived by that year. Asylum was rarely granted for undocumented immigrants who arrived after 1997. South America, especially Brazil, Colombia, Ecuador, Argentina, and Venezuela, began to send large numbers of immigrants in the 1970s. From that continent about one half million migrants arrived in the 1990s, and an average of seventy-five thousand arrived annually in the first decade of the 21st century.

Jamaica and Haiti are two major Caribbean sending nations. Jamaica was the tenth-largest source of immigration in the 1970s and climbed to seventh in the following decade. Although most Haitians came as refugees, the United States did not treat them the same as they did Cubans. Several thousand Haitians fled from the increasingly authoritarian government before 1960. Most of the ninety thousand Haitians who came between 1961 and 1980 were poor and had little education; they left to escape poverty, violence, and political turmoil. After 1980, more Haitians landing on American soil were undocumented. Fleeing from right-wing tyrants instead of communism, Haitians were often classified as economic migrants rather than political refugees, which led to frequent rejection of their petitions for asylum. Those who arrived before 1982 were eligible for amnesty under IRCA.

In 1990, the Haitian Fairness Refugee Act provided a means for over twenty thousand individuals to adjust their legal status. As many Haitians became American citizens, they could sponsor family members, but undocumented immigrants continued to arrive. As members of the poorest immigrant group, many Haitians could not find decent jobs due to their limited education levels, lack of English proficiency, and in some cases poor health.

Asia. After several decades of exclusion, the Asian American population began to grow slowly in the postwar years. The majority of the early immigrants from Asia were male in the late 19th and early 20th centuries. The repeal of exclusion laws, though with a small quota for each country, made it possible for women and children to gain admission outside the quota system. After World War II, family-centered Asian American communities began to develop.

The 1965 Immigration Act had a profound impact on Asian immigration. For the first time, Asian countries were placed on the same basis as European countries. The law increased the quota for each Asian country more than one hundredfold, making large-scale immigration from the continent possible. The new law also opened the door for professional labor, allowing Asians with occupational qualifications to come.

Whereas the 1965 Immigration Act opened the door wide to Asian immigration, not all countries took the full quota allotment. Most Asian countries did not have large population bases in the United States at the time. Among the five established Asian American communities— Chinese, Japanese, Filipino, Korean, and Indian, only three were able to benefit from the new law within a relatively short time. Filipino Americans took the lead. By then, there was a large population of Filipinos living in the United States. Political instability and economic problems in the Philippines were the major incentives for emigration. Due to the US colonization of the Philippines in the first half of the 20th century (1900–1946), Filipinos were quite familiar with American culture and society. Educated in an American-style school system, most young Filipinos could speak English, which made the United States the most desirable destination for prospective migrants. Those trained in the medical profession, especially nurses, were welcomed by American hospitals. With established family networks in this country and marketable skills, it was relatively easy for Filipino immigrants to adjust their lives in America. In the decade of the 1960s, the Philippines emerged as one of the top ten immigrant-sending countries. It ranked second, behind Mexico, for the three decades between 1970 and 2000 (see Table 2).

The Korean immigrant population in the United States was relatively small before 1945. After the Korean War, however, many Korean wives of American servicemen gained entry under the McCarran-Walter Act as wives of US citizens. Small groups of students also gained entry during this period. These military brides and some established students were among the first to sponsor their family members and relatives after 1965. In the 1960s and 1970s the South Korean government encouraged emigration to reduce the pressure of its growing population. By then, the presence of American troops in Korea after the Korean War and frequent exchanges between the two nations had exposed South Koreans to the material advantages of the American way of life. Streams of emigration to the United States began almost immediately after the 1965 Immigration Act became effective. Regardless of their skills and educational background, many Korean immigrants became self-employed, because it was difficult for them to find employment. During the three decades between 1970 and 1999, Korea was one of the top ten immigrant-sending countries.

The South Asian immigrant population was small before 1945. In the two decades after World War II, some Indian students came to study science, engineering, medicine, and business. Once these students settled in the United

States, they became the core node of the immigration network for family unification. Since 1970, India has made the list of the top ten sending nations every decade. In addition to family members and students, Indian immigration to the United States was facilitated by the employment-based preference. In the 2014 fiscal year, Indians accounted for 70 percent of the 316,000 H1-B petitions.[23] As indicated in Table 1, the Indian share of total immigrants increased steadily from 3.5 percent in the years 1970–1979 to 5.7 percent in 2000–2009. The partition of Pakistan from India in 1948 and the creation of Bangladesh in 1971 also affected the immigration from South Asia. Once they were independent, the two nations received separate quotas. Pakistani immigrants began to increase significantly in the 1980s. After a slow start, Bangladesh also emerged as an important source of immigration in the 21st century.

The Japanese and Chinese were the two largest Asian immigrant groups in 1960, but neither Japan nor China was a major source of immigration in the 1960s and 1970s. After World War II, Japan built close ties with the United States. In addition to the existing ethnic Japanese population, thousands of Japanese women arrived as wives of US servicemen. Like the Koreans, citizens of Japan were familiar with American culture and society. But unlike in the postwar years, by the late 1960s, Japan had emerged as an industrial country, and its economy was able to provide good employment opportunities to its own citizens. Enjoying a relatively high standard of living during the economic boom, the Japanese had little incentive to move abroad. As a result, Japan has not filled the immigration quota provided by the 1965 law.

Immigration from China has been shaped by contemporary Chinese history and US-China relations. Although the Chinese were the second-largest Asian immigrant group in 1960, most Chinese living in the United States could not sponsor their family members or relatives in China from 1949 to 1979 because of the lack of diplomatic relations between the United States and the People's Republic of China. Most of the Chinese who came in the 1960s and 1970s were from either Taiwan or Hong Kong; the latter was then a British colony. Most of those from Taiwan in the 1960s and 1970s were students, and they later were able to sponsor their family members. Not until 1979, when the United States normalized diplomatic relationship with the People's Republic of China, did the number of Chinese admitted begin to rise. Many of those sponsored by their relatives in the United States were from China's southern coastal province of Guangdong. Beginning in the 1980s, China also sent large numbers of students each year; many of them later settled in the United States. During the first decade of the 21st century, China replaced the Philippines as the second-largest source of immigration after Mexico. Immigration from Taiwan also continued, as the United States granted it the same quota numbers as China. In the mid-1990s, the United States also set aside sixty thousand annual slots for Hong Kong immigrants, before the British returned the colony to China in 1997. These slots were not filled, however, for relatively few in Hong Kong took the opportunity. The combined sources of immigrants from China, Taiwan, and Hong Kong, along with those from the Chinese diaspora, have made the Chinese the largest Asian American population group in the United States.

Asian immigration expanded significantly after 1975, when streams of refugees from Southeast Asia began to arrive. Before 1945, the United States showed little interest in Southeast Asia. Even after the United States entered the war in Vietnam, the presence of Southeast Asians in this country was very small. Only 335 Vietnamese entered in the 1950s, and some 4,300 more came in the 1960s. The collapse of the US-backed governments in Southeast Asia triggered an international refugee crisis. Because of its two-decade-long military involvement in Indochina and for political and humanitarian reasons, the United States had to take the lead in admitting and accommodating these refugees. In the 1980s, Vietnam suddenly became a major source of immigration, ahead of China. By the time the United States normalized diplomatic relations with Vietnam, Cambodia, and Laos in the 1990s, most newcomers from Southeast Asia came under the family unification system. By 2000, 1.1 million Vietnamese had been admitted, along with 170,000 Cambodians and 340,000 Laotians. About half of the refugees and immigrants from Laos are ethnic Hmong.

The expansion of Asian immigration after 1945 added a new dimension to US immigration history. In the 1950s, Asia's share of immigration was rather insignificant compared to that of Europe. As European immigration declined, Asian immigration rose. In the 1970s, immigrants from Asia surpassed those from Europe. By the 1980s, the vast majority of immigrants to the United States were from Asian and western hemisphere countries (see Figure 1).

Africa. For almost a century after the slave trade, Africa sent relatively few immigrants to the United States. In the 1950s and 1960s, the number of arrivals from Africa accounted for less than 1 percent of all immigrants. Africa's share of immigrants increased consistently every decade since then, however. The 2000 census counted one million African-born persons in the United States. Beginning in 2008, more Africans have been admitted than Europeans every single year (Table 3) This change indicates a new trend in US immigration.

Egypt was the largest sending country in Africa until the end of the 20th century, followed by Ethiopia, Morocco, South Africa, and Liberia. Ethiopia began to take the lead in 2002, followed by Egypt, Liberia, Morocco, and South Africa. Other than South Africa, sub-Saharan African countries had not sent many people to the United States. Wars, violence, poverty, natural disasters, and lack of adequate education and health care were responsible for an African exodus to Europe and the United States. Some Africans left their

Table 3. Sources of Immigration to the United States, 2001–2013 (in thousands). Yearbooks of Immigration Statistics, Department of Homeland Security.

Region of Origin	2001	2002	2003	2004	2005	2006	2007	2008	2009	2010	2011	2012	2013	2001–2013
Total	1,059	1,059	703	958	1,122	1,266	1,052	1,107	1,131	1,043	1,062	1,031	991	13,585
Europe	166	164	94	125	165	146	107	104	105	89	84	82	87	1,517
Germany	9.8	8.9	5.1	7.1	9.3	8.4	7.6	7.1	7.6	6.9	6.1	5.8	6.0	96
Poland	11.8	12.7	10.5	14.3	15.4	17.1	10.4	8.4	8.8	7.6	6.9	6.3	6.4	136
Russia	20.3	20.8	13.9	17.4	18.1	13.2	9.4	11.7	8.2	6.7	7.9	10.0	9.8	167
Ukraine	20.9	21.2	11.6	14.2	22.7	17.1	11.0	10.8	11.2	8.5	8.3	7.6	8.2	173
U.K.	18.3	16.3	9.5	14.9	19.8	17.2	14.5	14.3	15.7	12.8	11.6	12.0	13.0	190
Others	84.4	84.4	43.2	57.0	79.8	73.3	53.7	51.5	53.9	46.3	43.1	39.9	43.2	754
Asia	357	350	250	343	412	440	398	399	413	422	452	430	401	5,066
China	56.3	61.1	40.6	55.5	69.9	87.3	76.7	80.3	64.2	70.9	87.0	81.8	71.8	903
India	70.0	70.8	50.2	70.2	84.7	61.4	65.4	63.4	57.3	69.2	69.0	66.4	68.5	866
Korea, South	20.5	20.7	12.4	19.8	26.6	24.4	22.4	26.7	25.9	22.2	22.8	20.8	23.2	288
Philippines	53.0	51.0	45.3	57.8	60.7	74.6	72.6	54.0	60.0	58.2	57.0	57.3	54.4	756
Vietnam	35.4	33.6	22.1	31.5	32.8	30.7	28.7	31.5	29.2	30.6	31.2	28.3	27.1	396
Others	122.0	112.5	79.9	108.1	137.0	162.0	132.1	143.2	176.6	171.0	181.6	174.9	155.6	1,857

West Hemisphere	474	477	305	414	449	552	446	492	478	424	420	407	397	5,734
Cuba	27.5	28.2	9.3	20.5	36.3	45.6	29.1	49.5	39.0	33.6	36.5	32.8	32.2	420
Dominican Rep.	21.2	22.5	26.2	30.5	27.5	38.1	28.0	31.9	49.4	53.9	46.1	41.6	41.3	458
El Salvador	31.1	31.1	28.2	29.8	21.4	31.8	21.2	19.7	19.9	18.8	18.7	16.3	18.3	306
Colombia	16.6	18.8	14.7	18.8	25.6	43.1	33.2	30.2	27.8	22.4	22.6	20.9	21.1	316
Mexico	205.6	218.8	115.6	175	161.4	173.7	148.6	190.0	164.9	139.1	143.4	146.4	135.0	2,118
Others	172.2	157.8	111.0	139.4	179.5	219.6	185.7	170.5	177.0	156.0	152.7	149.2	148.7	2,116
Africa	54	60	49	66	85	117	95	106	127	101	100	107	98	1,166
Egypt	5.2	4.9	3.3	5.5	7.9	10.5	9.3	8.7	8.8	9.0	7.8	9.0	10.3	100.1
Ethiopia	5.1	7.6	6.6	8.3	10.6	16.2	12.8	12.9	15.5	14.3	13.8	14.5	13.1	151.2
Liberia	2.3	2.9	1.8	2.8	4.9	6.9	4.1	7.2	7.6	4.8	4.2	4.1	3.3	56.8
Morocco	5.0	3.4	3.1	4.1	4.4	4.9	4.5	4.4	5.4	5.0	4.4	3.7	3.3	55.8
South Africa	4.1	3.9	2.2	3.4	4.5	3.2	3.0	2.7	3.2	2.8	2.6	2.8	2.6	41.0
Others	32.2	37.6	31.5	42.4	52.8	75.7	61.1	69.9	86.5	65.5	67.6	73.2	65.6	761.5
Oceania	6	6	4	6	7	7	6	5	6	5	5	5	5	73

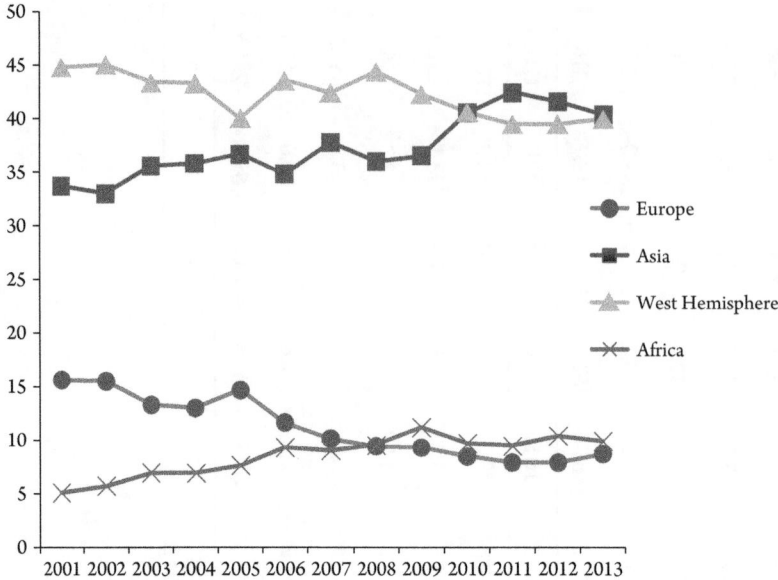

Figure 2. Percentage of Total Immigrants to the United States, 2001–2013. Yearbooks of Immigration Statistics, Department of Homeland Security.

homeland because they rejected the apartheid policies of South Africa. Although the majority of African immigrants were black, a significant number of them were white and Asian. The latter group included descendants of Indian laborers who came to Africa in the 19th century for railroad construction.

Students from Africa often adjusted their status after the completion of their programs. The number of African-born professors, doctors, and engineers has increased significantly since the late 20th century. Among the new immigrants were well-educated professionals and people with special skills. Female African immigrants with medical training often found work in hospitals.

The arrival of immigrants from the western hemisphere, Asia, and Africa changed US immigration history in profound ways. Countries in the western hemisphere emerged as a leading source in the 1960s, whereas Europeans and Asians reversed their positions in immigration statistics: Between 1950 and 1959, more than half (56.2 percent) of the immigrants admitted were Europeans, and only a fraction (5.4 percent) were Asians. Two decades later,

between 1970 and 1979, only 19.4 percent of the immigrants came from Europe, when Asian immigrants increased to 33.1 percent. The gap has widened in recent decades, as Europe's share of all immigrants declined further, to 13.1 percent from 2000 to 2009. Meanwhile, African immigrants began rising: once amounting to less than 1 percent of the statistics, they represented more than 7 percent of all immigrants during the first decades of the 21st century. More recent immigration statistics provided yet another sharp contrast. Beginning in 2008, as the actual number of Europeans admitted continued to decline, more Africans arrived every single year (Figure 2). This trend would continue in the years to come.

IMMIGRANT NATION

Diverse sources of immigration have changed the face of America. Of the 312 million Americans in 2011, about 13 percent were foreign-born. About 67.2 percent of Asian Americans were foreign-born, followed by 36.2 percent among Hispanics. In comparison, only 3.9 percent of white Americans were foreign-born, which was lower than that of black Americans (8.2 percent) and other American population groups (9.1 percent).

New immigrants have changed the nation's urban landscape. Mexican immigrants, who first arrived in the West and Southwest, gradually moved to every region of the nation in pursuit of employment opportunities. Their Asian counterparts first settled in California and other Pacific states, but now they have dispersed to every state. The immigrants built communities in urban areas, expanding ethnic networks throughout the country with businesses and markets. Providing shelter, assistance, and employment opportunities to newcomers, these communities have served as magnets for new immigrants. The availability of new immigrant labor also facilitated the growth of ethnic economies. There are large Mexican communities in Houston, Los Angeles, San Diego, Chicago, and New York, as well as communities of Cubans in Miami, Chinese in New York and Los Angeles, Koreans in Los Angeles, and Vietnamese in Orange County. Professional immigrants, such as engineers and technicians from India and doctors, nurses, and domestic care providers from the Philippines have been able to find employment in different regions throughout the country. Although the Indian and Filipino ethnic economies are not as big as those established by the Mexicans, Cubans, Chinese, Koreans, and Vietnamese, their US-bound immigration set examples for later arrivals.[24]

Jobs provided by ethnic enclaves are especially important to newcomers without marketable skills, English proficiency, or work permits. Relatively few immigrant women could afford the luxury of staying at home; many worked in the garment industry, restaurants, domestic care, and other service industries. Three-generation households are common among Latino and Asian immigrants, with grandparents providing childcare. Mutual support from extended family members, relatives, and fellow immigrants are crucial for newcomers to adjust to their new lives in the United States.

The influx of new immigrants from different parts of the world also led to heated debate on issues concerning acculturation and assimilation. Although foreign-born immigrants were under the pressure to learn English and abandon their native languages, more and more immigrants were able to preserve their linguistic and cultural heritage. Whereas ESL (English as a second language) courses are offered in schools and colleges, there is also an increasing demand for Spanish- and Asian-language classes in high school and college. In large cities bilingual or multilingual business signs can be seen everywhere. Several metropolitan areas are home to Spanish- or Asian-language television networks, entertaining newcomers with films, soap opera, and music programs produced in Latin America or Asia.

The presence of a large immigrant population has had a great impact on American domestic politics. As was the case before World War II, policies concerning immigration and border control are of great importance in state and national politics. In addition to more relaxed admission policies, the federal government provided comprehensive assistances to Cuban, Southeast Asian, and other refugee groups with temporary cash assistance, food distribution, medical care, English classes, and job training. The American attitude toward most ethnic groups has also become more tolerant, increasing the effectiveness of assistance through religious charities and other organizations.

This does not mean anti-immigration sentiment has disappeared. A growing foreign presence can cause discomfort among the general public, and opponents of immigration continue to try to instill fear in the native population of the foreign invasion. Immigration has become a central theme in local and national politics. After the terrorist attack of September 11, 2001, immigration policy was often debated in the context of national security. Muslim immigrants were immediately under harsh scrutiny. More significant was the creation of a new immigration enforcement machinery to screen individuals and place immigrant agencies under the direction of the new Department of Homeland Security (DHS) in 2003. With highly effective tools and sophisticated data-bases, the government could also track, apprehend, and remove unauthorized immigrants who posed no security threat.[25] The government also tied border patrol to national security, adding traffic checkpoints along the borders. The number of deportations has gone up. Between 2008 and 2010, the Immigration and Customs Enforcement of the DHS conducted a national campaign against undocumented immigrants. In 2009 alone, nearly four hundred thousands undocumented workers, including families and US-born children, were forced to leave.[26] The terrorist attacks in Paris on November 13, 2015, seem to have provided critics of immigration with another opportunity to tie immigration issues to national security.

At the same time, however, Hispanic Americans and Asian American citizens are registering to vote in increasing numbers, making anti-immigration measures more difficult to enforce. California's Proposition 187, for example, led to a massive political mobilization of the Hispanic population, which made it far more difficult for the Republican Party to win statewide elections.[27] In 2011, the federal government reformed the campaign against undocumented immigrants, limiting deportation enforcement to those who have been "convicted of serious crimes" and are "threats to public safety." The vast majority of undocumented immigrants would be entitled to a certain degree of protection to remain in the United States.[28] Many states also created scholarship programs to assist undocumented students obtain a college education.

THE UNITED STATES IN INTERNATIONAL MIGRATION

The scope of this essay does not allow a lengthy analysis of every sending nation, but it is a safe bet that future sources of immigration will be more diverse. The Immigration Act of 1990 mandated fifty-five thousand "diversity visas" to promote immigration from underrepresented countries. Individuals from eligible countries not related to citizens or permanent residents in the United States could obtain a diversity visa through a lottery. This program boosted immigration from many underrepresented countries, including some of the world's most populous countries, such as Brazil, Pakistan, and Bangladesh. Although no longer eligible, each of these countries was able to use the program to establish a large population base in the United States to take advantage of the family preference system. Immigrants from these countries will increase in the years to come. Indonesia, the world's fourth most populous nation, is still underrepresented, but it has the potential to send more immigrants. Other more populous nations, such as Ethiopia, Egypt, Iran, and the Democratic Republic of Congo, are among the heaviest users of the lottery; their shares of immigration numbers are likely to increase in the near future.

The United States has been the leading destination of international migration since the 1970s and will probably continue to hold this position for many years to come. More relaxed immigration policies played an important role in shaping the patterns of immigration, but government policy alone is not sufficient to control the flows of immigration completely. The 1965 Immigration Act, which opened the door to migrants from different parts of the world, had relatively little impact on western European countries and Japan. Many underdeveloped countries were not affected by the law because of their lack of contact with the United States. The United States also failed to prevent the growth of undocumented immigration. Since the late 20th century large streams of immigrants from Mexico and elsewhere have found ways to bypass border checkpoints despite tough border enforcement. The 1986 Immigration Reform and Control Act allowed 3.3 million undocumented individuals to legalize but could not solve the problem. There is no indication that the inflow of unauthorized immigrants will diminish soon. Although exclusion acts and the 1924 Immigration Act did reduce immigration from Asia and East Europe, the impact of these laws was rather limited compared to that of the two world wars, the Great Depression, the Cold War, and the Vietnam War. As indicated in Table 4, the top destinations of international migration have changed from time to time. More important than the economic development, immigration policies, and foreign relations of the United States are events that took place elsewhere, as war, revolution, and economic developments around the world all play a big part in international migration.

As the world's largest economy, the United States will continue to be a leading receiving country as long as the demand for newcomers to fill low-paying jobs exists. This also means that the inflow of immigration will fluctuate based on the strength of the US economy in the years to come. In addition to wage-earning workers, a stable economy has attracted investors. An increasing number of immigrants who arrived in recent decades came with capital. In 1990, Congress created the Immigration Investor Program to stimulate the US economy through job creation and capital investment by foreign investors. Known as the EB-5 program, it required individual applicants to invest one million dollars in new commercial enterprises that would create at least ten full-time jobs for US citizens.[29] Although the number of individuals admitted through the EB-5 program is relatively small, they indicated a new immigration pattern in US immigration history.

Provisions in the 1965 Immigration Act created opportunities for professionals to immigrate, causing "brain drain" in the countries of origin. As the world's leader in higher education and high-tech industry, the United States has been the most important destination for students seeking advanced degrees. It has also been the most important destination for well-educated professionals to seek research and employment opportunities.[30] Highly trained medical professionals from the Philippines, for example, can be found in hospitals throughout the United States. The H-1B visa program, initiated in the 1990 Immigration Act, enabled US employers to sponsor professional immigrants. In most years in the 21st century, the H-1B program admitted more than a quarter

Table 4. Top Ten Destinations of International Migration, 1960–2013. Department of Economic and Social Affairs, *Trends in International Migrant Stock: The 2013 Revision–Migrants by Destination and Origin* (United Nations database).

1960–1970	1970–1980	1980–1990	1990–2000	2000–2010	2010–2013
France	US	US	US	US	US
UK	W. Germany	Iran	Germany	UAE	Italy
US	Somalia	Saudi Arabia	UAE	Spain	UK
W. Germany	Saudi Arabia	Pakistan	UK	Saudi Arabia	Saudi Arabia
Australia	Nigeria	Australia	Canada	Italy	UAE
Malaysia	France	Malawi	Spain	UK	Thailand
Canada	UAE	Ethiopia	Jordan	Thailand	Australia
Cote d'Ivoire	Canada	Netherlands	Serbia	Australia	South Africa
DR Congo	Kuwait	Canada	Thailand	Canada	Canada
Italy	Iran	Sudan	Italy	South Africa	South Korea

million immigrants.[31] Since the late 20th century, the number of international students enrolled in US institutions has also increased substantially. Whereas 48,486 international students were enrolled in US colleges and universities in 1960, the number climbed to 819,644 in 2012.[32]

A wide range of developments in countries around the world has made the subject of migration far more complex than it was before. Many European countries, for example, were sources of US immigration not too long ago, but they have become destinations of worldwide migration. The European Union, with its lengthy land and sea borders involving so many countries, provides opportunities for border crossing from multiple directions. Whereas large numbers of migrants from Syria, Iraq, Libya, and Afghanistan crossed the Mediterranean to Italy and Greece, those from Asia and Africa reached the continent via land through Turkey. Many migrants also crossed borders through Bulgaria, Hungary, and Russia. It is relatively easy for the migrants to move

around and resettle within the European Union. Several European countries, such as Germany, Britain, France, Italy, and Sweden have become destinations for both European migrants and international migrants.

Moreover, migration means different things to different people. Developing countries that exported large numbers of laborers seeking higher wages abroad may also attract professionals, entrepreneurs, and investors for more ambitious projects. This has become more evident as the world has grown more and more integrated. In the context of international migration, Figure 3 shows that the United States has become one of many destinations for migrants. In the 1990s, 57 out of every 100 international migrants came to the United States, but fewer than 15 did between 2010 and 2013.

Unlike most post–World War II immigrants who came to the United States with one-way tickets, an increasing number of permanent residents and US citizens have returned to their ancestral homeland or resettled to other countries in more recent decades. Studies on

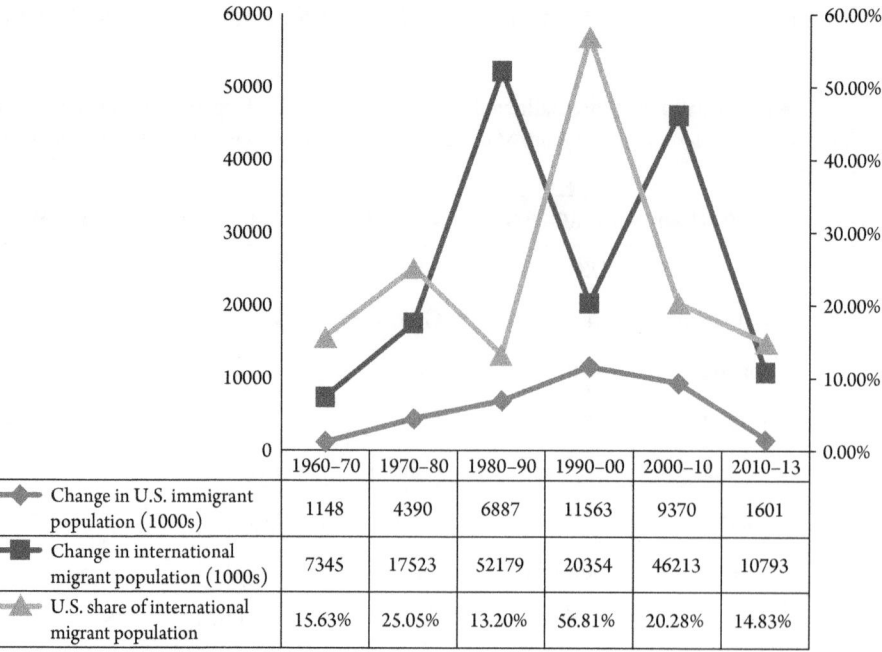

	1960–70	1970–80	1980–90	1990–00	2000–10	2010–13
Change in U.S. immigrant population (1000s)	1148	4390	6887	11563	9370	1601
Change in international migrant population (1000s)	7345	17523	52179	20354	46213	10793
U.S. share of international migrant population	15.63%	25.05%	13.20%	56.81%	20.28%	14.83%

Figure 3. US Share of International Migrant Population, 1960–2013. Department of Economic and Social Affairs (2013), *Trends in International Migrant Stock: The 2013 Revision–Migrants by Destination and Origin* (United Nations database).

Mexican immigration, which utilized data from both the United States and Mexico, offer a deeper understanding of human migration involving borders and borderlands. In *Return to Aztlan: The Social Process of International Migration from Western Mexico*, published in 1987, Douglas Massey, Rafael Alarcón, Jorge Durand, and Humberto González highlighted a complex historical process that fostered the interdependence between western Mexico and the southwestern United States and the people who lived on both sides of the borders and moved back and forth.[33] Mexican immigrants are most numerous, but the Pew Research Center reported that the movement of Mexicans went in both directions. Between 2005 and 2010, Mexico sent a total of 1.4 million immigrants to the United States. In the same period, an equal number of immigrants returned to Mexico, including three hundred thousand US-born children.[34] From 2009 to 2014, one million Mexicans returned to their country of origin, but the number of Mexicans admitted during the same period was significantly smaller, at 879,000. The economic recession and its slow recovery may have made the United States less attractive to prospective migrants. Opportunities in their country of origin may become attractive to those who have left. Deportation is another factor, although only about 14 percent of the returning migrants were deported.[35] Whereas US immigration statistics provide the most reliable data on arrivals, migrants who left for other destinations are difficult to track. Besides Mexico, we know very little about migration outflow from the United States.

As different parts of the world experience rapid economic growth, ideas, capital, and goods move across national borders frequently. More and more migrants have been participants in a wide range of transnational activities, especially those with the means to do so, and they have preserved ties to their country of origin. The advancement of telecommunication and transportation, the expanded volume of international trade and transnational business transactions, and the emergence of international corporations have all worked to blur national borders, posing new challenges to migration studies. Many male braceros and Asian immigrants could not see their wives and children for months and years (if not decades) due to immigration restrictions in the past. Today, many families and individuals maintain residences in more than one location but still stay close to one another using telecommunication and modern transportation. Residing in multiple locations, the family can enjoy benefits offered by more than one country. Studies of dual citizenship or flexible citizenship reveal the complex characteristics of contemporary migrants, but US immigration statistics have not provided ways to measure the size of these international commuters. Understanding the magnitude and trend of migration flows requires not only statistics from the United States but also data compiled in related countries.

DISCUSSION OF THE LITERATURE

Several books provide general accounts of immigration after 1945, including David M. Reimers, *Still the Golden Door: The Third World Comes to America*; Leonard Dinnerstein and David M. Reimers, *The World Comes to America: Immigration to the United States Since 1945*; and Susan A. Martin, *A Nation of Immigrants*. Roger Daniels's *Guarding the Golden Door: American Immigration Policy and Immigration since 1882* provides an overview of immigration policy since 1882.[36]

The fourth edition of *Immigrant America: A Portrait* by Alejandro Portes and Rubén G. Rumbaut addresses important questions concerning ethnicity, assimilation, education, religion, and politics.[37] It helps explain the formulation of various public policies that helped immigrants to adjust to life in the United States.

Tracing the origins of undocumented immigrants, Mae M. Ngai's *Impossible Subjects: Illegal Aliens and the Making of Modern America* shows how the categories of "legal" and "illegal" immigrant were constructed by the government to render Mexicans and Asians as perpetual aliens. Most of the discussions on pre-1965 policies are still relevant to contemporary immigration issues.[38]

For European immigration, see Leo Lucassen, *The Immigrant Threat: The Integration of Old and New Migrants in Western Europe Since 1850.* Martin A. Schain's *The Politics of Immigration in France, Britain, and the United States* offers a comparative perspective. Several studies focus on specific groups of European immigrants, including Linda Almeida, *Irish Immigrants in New York City, 1945–1995*; Annelise Orleck, *The Soviet Jewish Americans*; Helena Zaiecka Lopata, *Polish Americans*; Carl J. Bon Tempo, *Americans at the Gate: The United States and Refugees during the Cold War*; and Beth B. Cohen, *Case Closed: Holocaust Survivors in Postwar America.*[39]

For general accounts of Asian immigration, see Sucheng Chan, *Asian Americans: An Interpretive History*; Uma A. Segal, *A Framework for Immigration: Asians in the United States*; Erika Lee, *The Making of Asian America: A History*; and John S. Park, *Elusive Citizenship: Immigration, Asian Americans, and the Paradox of Civil Rights.* There are many books on specific Asian immigrant groups: Xiaojian Zhao, *Remaking Chinese America: Immigration, Family and Community, 1940–1965* and *The New Chinese America: Class, Economy, and Social Hierarchy*; Barbara Posada, *Filipino Americans*; Ji-Yeon Yuh, *Beyond the Shadow of Camptown: Korean Military Brides in America*; Nancy Abelmann and John Lie, *Blue Dreams: Korean Americans and the Los Angeles Riots*; Madhullika S. Khandelwal, *Becoming American, Being India*; Min Zhou and Carl Bankston, *Growing Up American: How Vietnamese Children Adapt to Life in the United States*; and Sucheng Chan, *Survivors: Cambodian Refugees in the United States.*[40]

Mary Waters's *Black Identities: West Indian Immigrant Dreams and American Realities* and John A. Arthur's *Invisible Sojourners: African Immigrant Diaspora in the United States* provide valuable information on the patterns and characteristics of African immigrant communities in the United States. Anny Bakalian and Mehdi

Bozorgmehr's *Backlash 9/11: Middle Eastern and Muslim Americans Respond* provides general information on Middle Eastern and Muslim Americans.[41]

There is a relatively large body of literature on Latino immigrants. For general accounts and statistical analyses, see Roberto Suro, *Strangers Among Us: How Latino Immigration Is Transforming America*, and Laird W. Bergad and Herbert S. Klein, *Hispanics in the United States: A Demographic, Social, and Economic History, 1980–2005.* Scholars on Mexican immigration often take transnational approaches, considering circumstances in both sending and receiving countries. They are also successful in utilizing statistics and other primary sources compiled outside the United States. Deborah Colen's *Braceros: Migrant Citizens and Transnational Subjects in the Postwar United States and Mexico* is a good example. Douglas Massey, Rafael Alarcón, Jorge Durand, and Humberto González, *Return to Aztlan: The Social Process of International Migration from Western Mexico,* has become a classic. Also see Douglas Massey, Jorge Durant, and Noland J. Malone, *Beyond Smoke and Mirrors: Mexican Immigration in an Era of Economic Integration.* For accounts on other Latino immigration, see Maria Cristina Garcia, *Havana USA: Cuban Exiles and Cuban Americans in South Florida, 1959–1994*; Silvia Pedraza, *Political Disaffection in Cuba's Revolution and Exodus*; Leon Fink, *The Maya of Morgantown: Work and Community in the Nuevo New South*; Maxine L. Margolis: *Little Brazil: An Ethnography of Brazilian Immigrants in New York City*; Jesse Hoffnung-Garskof, *A Tale of Two Cities: Santo Domingo and New York After 1950*; and Sherri Grasmuck and Patricia R. Pessar, *Between Two Islands: Dominican International Migration.*[42]

PRIMARY SOURCES

Annual immigration statistics compiled by the US Citizenship and Immigration Services (USCIS, 2003–) and Immigration and Naturalization Service (INS, 1933–2003) are the most important primary source for the study of immigration after 1945. The *Yearbook of Immigration Statistics*, published annually by the Department of Homeland Security, is available online, and hard copies of INS publications are available in most public and research university libraries. Special reports published by the DHS and INS provide additional details and interpretations. The US census, which provides information regarding the racial, ethnic, and national origins of the US population, is another important source. Released US Census data as well as publications of the Census Bureau could be found in the government document section of research libraries, and also at the US Census Bureau's website. Several Internet sites also provide immigration data, including the Center for Immigration Studies, the Pew Hispanic Center, and the American Community Survey. The Migration Information Source, an online journal of the Migration Policy Institute, is also useful for sources on recent immigrants.

FURTHER READING

Daniels, Roger. *Guarding the Golden Door: American Immigration Policy and Immigration Since 1882*. New York: Hill and & Wang, 2004.

Massey, Douglas S. "The New Immigration and Ethnicity in the United States." *Population and Development Review* 21.3 (September 1995): 631–652.

Motel, Seth, and Eileen Pattern. "Statistical Portrait of the Foreign-Born Population in the United States, 2011." *Pew Research Hispanic Trends Project*, January 29, 2013.

Passel, Jeffrey S., D'vera Cohn, and Ana Gonzalez-Barrera. "Net Migration from Mexico Falls to Zero—and Perhaps Less." Pew Research Center, April 23, 2012. http://www.pewhispanic.org/2012/04/23/net-migration-from-mexico-falls-to-zero-and-perhaps-less/.

Reimers, David M. *Still the Golden Door: The Third World Comes to America*. New York: Columbia University Press, 1992.

Robila, Mihaela. "Characteristics of Eastern European Immigration in the United States." *Journal of Comparative Family Studies* 39.4 (2008): 545–556.

NOTES

1. Lawrence Cardoso, *Mexican Emigration to the United States, 1897–1931* (Tucson: University of Arizona Press, 1980).
2. Abraham Hoffman, *Unwanted Mexican Americans in the Great Depression: Repatriation Pressures, 1929–1939* (Tucson: University of Arizona Press, 1974).
3. Douglas Massey, Rafael Alarcón, Jorge Durand, and Humberto González, *Return to Aztlan: The Social Process of International Migration from Western Mexico* (Berkeley: University of California Press 1987), 55–76; and Rachael Frances DeLaCruz, "Bracero Families: Mexican Women and Children in the United States, 1942–64," M.A. thesis, Old Dominion University, 2014.
4. Douglas S. Massey and Kathleen M. Schnabel, "Recent Trends in Hispanic Immigration to the United States," *International Migration Review* 17.2 (1983): 212–244.
5. Warren G. Magnuson to William Green, September 28, 1943, Magnuson Papers, University of Washington Libraries.
6. Franklin D. Roosevelt, "Message to Congress on Repeal of the Chinese Exclusion," October 11, 1943, available online at *The American Presidency Project*. http://www.presidency.ucsb.edu/ws/?pid=16325.
7. Roger Daniels, *Guarding the Golden Door: American Immigration Policy and Immigrants since 1882* (New York: Hill & Wang, 2005), 113.
8. Xiaojian Zhao, *Remaking Chinese America: Immigration, Family, and Community, 1940–1965* (New Brunswick, NJ: University of Rutgers Press, 2002), 78–93.
9. US Census Bureau publications.
10. Daniels, *Guarding the Golden Door*, 84–85.
11. Daniels, *Guarding the Golden Door*, 110–112.
12. David M. Reimers, *Still the Golden Door: The Third World Comes to America* (New York: Columbia University Press, 1992), 12.
13. 57 Stat. 600, Act of July 19, 1953.
14. 94 Stat. 102.
15. 79 Stat. 911.
16. Reimers, *Still the Golden Door*, 63–90.
17. Transcript, *Becoming American: The Chinese Experience*, 2003, program 3, http://www-tc.pbs.org/becomingamerican/program3_transcript.pdf.
18. 104 Stat. 4978.
19. Mihaela Robila, "Characteristics of Eastern European Immigration in the United States," *Journal of Comparative Family Studies* 39.4 (2008): 545–556.

20. 90 Stat. 2703, Act of October 20, 1976.

21. 90 Stat. 90, Act of October 5, 1978.

22. Matias F. Travieso-Diaz, "Immigration Challenges and Opportunities in a Post-Transition Cuba," *Berkeley Journal of International Law* 16.2 (1998): 234–266.

23. US Citizenship and Immigration Services, *Characters of H-1B Specialty Occupation Workers Report for Fiscal Year 2014.*

24. Alejandro Portes and Rubén G. Rumbaut, *Immigrant America: A Portrait* (Berkeley: University of California Press, 2014), 83–106.

25. Muzaffar Chishti and Claire Bergeron, "Post-9/11 Policies Dramatically Alter the U.S. Immigration Landscape," *Migration Policy Institute*, September 8, 2011.

26. Portes and Rumbaut, *Immigrant America*, 33.

27. Matt Barreto, "The Prop 187 Effect: How the California GOP Lost Their Way and Implications for 2014 and Beyond," *Latino Decisions* (blog), October 17, 2013. http://www.latinodecisions .com/blog/2013/10/17/prop187effect/.

28. Marc R. Rosenblum, *Understanding the Potential Impact of Executive Action on Immigration Enforcement*, Migration Policy Institute, July 2015.

29. US Citizenship and Immigration Services, "EB-5 Immigrant Investor (http://www.uscis .gov/eb-5)."

30. Lucie Cheng and Philip Q. Yang, "Global Interaction, Global Inequality, and Migration of the Highly Trained to the United States," *International Migration Review* 32.3 (Autumn 1998): 626–653.

31. US Citizenship and Immigration Services, *Characters of H-1B Specialty Occupation Workers Report for Fiscal Year 2014.*

32. Data from the Institution of International Education.

33. Massey et al., *Return to Aztlan.*

34. Jeffrey S. Passel, D'vera Cohn, and Ana Gonzalez-Barrera, Net Migration from Mexico Falls to Zero—and Perhaps Less, Pew Research Center, April 23, 2012. http://www.pewhispanic.org/2012 /04/23/net-migration-from-mexico-falls-to-zero -and-perhaps-less/.

35. Ana Gonzalez-Barrera, "More Mexicans Leaving Than Coming to the U.S," Pew Research Center, November 19, 2015.

36. Reimers, *Still the Golden Door*; Leonard Dinnerstein and David M. Reimers, *The World Comes to America: Immigration to the United States Since 1945* (New York: Oxford University Press, 2014); Susan A. Martin, *A Nation of Immigrants* (New York: Cambridge University Press, 2010); and Daniels, *Guarding the Golden Door.*

37. Portes and Rumbaut *Immigrant America.*

38. Mae M. Ngai, *Impossible Subjects: Illegal Aliens and the Making of Modern America* (Princeton, NJ: Princeton University Press, 2004).

39. Leo Lucassen, *The Immigrant Threat: The Integration of Old and New Migrants in Western Europe Since 1850* (Urbana: University of Illinois Press, 2005); Martin A. Schain, *The Politics of Immigration in France, Britain, and the United States* (New York: Palgrave Macmillan, 2008); Linda Almeida, *Irish Immigrants in New York City, 1945–1995* (Bloomington: University of Indiana Press, 2001); Annelise Orleck, *The Soviet Jewish Americans* (Westport, CT: Greenwood, 1999); Helena Zaiecka Lopata, *Polish Americans* (New Brunswick, NJ: Rutgers University Press, 1994); Carl J. Bon Tempo, *Americans at the Gate: The United States and Refugees during the Cold War* (Princeton, NJ: Princeton University Press, 2008); and Beth B. Cohen, *Case Closed: Holocaust Survivors in Postwar America* (New Brunswick, NJ: Rutgers University Press, 2007).

40. Sucheng Chan, *Asian Americans: An Interpretive History* (New York: Twayne, 1991); Uma A. Segal, *A Framework for Immigration: Asians in the United States* (New York: Columbia University Press, 2002); Erika Lee, *The Making of Asian America: A History* (New York: Simon & Schuster, 2015); John S. Park, *Elusive Citizenship: Immigration, Asian Americans, and the Paradox of Civil Rights* (New York: New York University Press, 2004); Zhao, *Remaking Chinese America*; Xiaojian Zhao, *The New Chinese America: Class, Economy, and Social Hierarchy* (New Brunswick, NJ: Rutgers University Press, 2010); Barbara Posada, *Filipino Americans* (Westport, CT: Greenwood, 1999); Ji-Yeon Yuh, *Beyond the Shadow of Camptown: Korean Military Brides in America* (New York: New York University Press, 2002); Nancy Abelmann and John Lie, *Blue Dreams: Korean Americans and the Los Angeles Riots* (Cambridge, MA: Harvard University Press, 1995); Madhullika S. Khandelwal, *Becoming American, Being India* (Ithaca, NY: Cornell University Press, 2002); Min Zhou and Carl Bankston, *Growing Up American: How*

Vietnamese Children Adapt to Life in the United States (New York: Russell Sage, 1998); and Sucheng Chan, *Survivors: Cambodian Refugees in the United States* (Urbana: University of Illinois Press, 2004).

41. Mary Waters, *Black Identities: West Indian Immigrant Dreams and American Realities* (Cambridge, MA: Harvard University Press, 1999); John A. Arthur, *Invisible Sojourners: African Immigrant Diaspora in the United States* (Westport, CT: Praeger, 2000); and Anny Bakalian and Mehdi Bozorgmehr, *Backlash 9/11: Middle Eastern and Muslim Americans Respond* (Berkeley: University of California Press, 2009).

42. Roberto Suro, *Strangers Among Us: How Latino Immigration Is Transforming America* (New York: Alfred A. Knopf, 1998); Laird W. Bergad and Herbert S. Klein, *Hispanics in the United States: A Demographic, Social, and Economic History, 1980–2005* (New York: Cambridge University Press, 2010); Deborah Colen, *Braceros: Migrant Citizens and Transnational Subjects in the Postwar United States and Mexico* (Chapel Hill: University of North Carolina Press, 2011); Massey et al., *Return to Aztlan: The Social Process of International Migration from Western Mexico* (Berkeley: University of California Press, 1987); Douglas Massey, Jorge Durant, and Noland J. Malone, *Beyond Smoke and Mirrors: Mexican Immigration in an Era of Economic Integration* (New York: Russell Sage, 2002); Maria Cristina Garcia, *Havana USA: Cuban Exiles and Cuban Americans in South Florida, 1959–1994* (Berkeley: University of California Press, 1996); Silvia Pedraza, *Political Disaffection in Cuba's Revolution and Exodus* (New York: Cambridge University Press, 2006); Leon Fink, *The Maya of Morgantown: Work and Community in the Nuevo New South* (Chapel Hill: University of North Carolina Press, 2003); Maxine L. Margolis, *Little Brazil: An Ethnography of Brazilian Immigrants in New York City* (Princeton, NJ: Princeton University Press, 1994); Jesse Hoffnung-Garskof, *A Tale of Two Cities: Santo Domingo and New York After 1950* (Princeton, NJ: Princeton University Press, 2008); and Sherri Grasmuck and Patricia R. Pessar, *Between Two Islands: Dominican International Migration* (Berkeley: University of California Press, 1991).

Xiaojian Zhao

THE GREAT MIGRATION AND BLACK URBAN LIFE IN THE UNITED STATES, 1914–1970

WAR, ECONOMIC CHANGE, AND BLACK MIGRATION

The First Great Migration began during World War I, when African Americans began relocating to southern cities and urban centers in the Midwest and Northeast. Wage labor in US cities especially appealed to African Americans living in the rural South. Since the end of the Civil War, white southern landowners strove to drive black people back into agricultural labor. Beginning in the Reconstruction period, former slaveowners issued labor contracts to freed people, which bound them to a particular parcel of land for a set term. The exploitative labor system known as sharecropping grew from these labor arrangements. Theoretically sharecroppers kept a fraction of the crop they raised. They often described the terms of their contract using expressions like "working on quarters" (or even "thirds" or "halves," if they were more fortunate), indicating what percentage of the crop they could keep at the end of the growing season. Yet sharecropping families typically faced an endless cycle of debt because they acquired the items they needed to work and survive—from farm tools to cornmeal—through credit extended to them by the landowner. At "settling time," landowners calculated how much the sharecroppers had borrowed on credit. Sharecroppers often learned that, rather than receive payment for the crop they had grown, they actually owed money to the landowner. To settle their debts they signed another contract for the next year. The system of sharecropping metaphorically locked African Americans to the land, ensuring that southern landowners maintained a cheap labor force.[1]

Natural disaster exacerbated an already dire situation for rural black farmers. The boll weevil, a bug that feeds on cotton buds, infested the Cotton South at the turn of the century.

Swarms of the insect from Mexico appeared in Texas in the 1890s. By the 1920s, the boll weevil had infested the entire South, devastating cotton production in a region that thrived on that the crop. The Great Mississippi Flood of 1927 also influenced rural black southerners' decision to relocate. Beginning in August 1926, record-setting rainfall in the Mississippi River Valley caused the river to overflow. Flooding eventually affected some 27,000 miles of land, mostly in the South, by the summer of 1927. Thousands of rural black farmers in Arkansas, Mississippi, and Louisiana relocated in response to the disaster.[2]

In the face of such unrelenting debt, flooding, and boll weevil infestations, millions of rural black southerners abandoned agricultural labor in favor of industrial labor in cities. Industrial production in urban America accelerated when World War I erupted in Europe in 1914, and the availability of labor especially encouraged rural black southerners to migrate. Trade between the United States and the Allied Powers (including Britain, France, Russia, and Italy) increased fourfold during the war. As a result, the United States transformed from a debtor nation to a creditor nation, lending money and goods to European nations like England and France. Americans supplied the Allies with material they needed to fight the war, like cotton and oil. In 1917, the United States exported 65.4 million barrels of oil, mainly to Great Britain and France.[3]

The majority of African Americans who left the countryside during World War I decided to remain in the South. Cities like Houston, Texas, a growing center of the cotton and oil industries, recruited African American men from East Texas and Louisiana to load and unload ships at the port and work on railroad lines during the war. The black population of Houston increased from just under 24,000 in 1920 to more than 63,000 in 1930.[4] Meanwhile, the black population of Birmingham, Alabama, increased by 89 percent between 1910 and 1930, while black Atlanta grew by 74 percent in those two decades.

While southern cities swelled with migrants from the rural countryside, new black communities also emerged in the urban North. Between 1917 and 1930, approximately one million black southerners moved to the Midwest and Northeast during the First Great Migration. Northern cities experienced a labor shortage during and after the war. The US economy accelerated at the same time the federal government restricted the number of European immigrants who could come to the United States. By World War I, a growing sense of resentment against immigrants had emerged in US politics. Anti-immigrant sentiment fueled the passage of the Immigration Act of 1917, which banned anyone with a disability, excluded illiterate immigrants over the age of sixteen, and required immigrants to pay a head tax of eight dollars in order to enter the country. The act also restricted anyone from the "Asiatic Barred Zone" from entering the country. Seven years later the Johnson-Reed Act of 1924 excluded most immigrants from Asia and restricted the number of southern and eastern Europeans who could enter the country. These restrictions on foreign immigration affected labor and economics within the United States. Factory owners had relied on immigrant labor since the 1880s, but the immigration acts of 1917 and 1924 left them with significantly fewer workers. Southern migrants helped fill that void. For example, Chicago's meatpacking factories employed approximately 11,000 African American men and women by 1919.[5]

Southern migrants relocated in response to economic opportunity in the North, but they also sought to escape disfranchisement, legal segregation, and racial violence. By 1910 every state in the former Confederacy had established laws to segregate African Americans and strip black men of the right to vote. Furthermore, lynching had reached an all-time high in the South in the late 19th and early 20th centuries. Sociologists Stewart Emory Tolnay and E. M. Beck found that white lynch mobs murdered approximately 2,500 African Americans in the Deep South and Border South between

1882 and 1930.[6] For countless black southerners, leaving the South was a form of protest against Jim Crow and racial violence. In "Jim Crow Blues," singer Maggie Jones cites segregation laws as her main reason for trading Dixie for New York City:

> Got my trunk and grip all packed
> Goodbye, I ain't coming back
> Going to leave this Jim Crow town
> Lord, sweet pape, New York bound
> Got my ticket in my hand
> And I'm leaving dixieland
> Going north child, where I can be free
> Going north child, where I can be free
> Where there's no hardships, like in Tennessee
> Going where they don't have Jim Crow laws
> Going where they don't have Jim Crow laws
> Don't have to work there, like in Arkansas[7]

The black southern exodus had altered the demographics of the urban North by 1930. The black population of New York City more than tripled, from 91,709 to 327,706, between 1910 and 1930.[8] The Midwest transitioned from a region with a small African American population to one with multiple black urban centers. Between 1910 and 1920, approximately 65,000 African Americans moved to Chicago. In total, the black population of the city grew by 430 percent in the years between 1910 and 1930. Most dramatically, the black population of Detroit increased by a factor of 20 in that twenty-year period, growing from 6,000 to 120,000.

Economic change during World War II motivated a new wave of black migration. Beginning in 1940 and continuing through the 1960s, approximately five million black southerners participated in the Second Great Migration. Many black migrants found work in the newly desegregated defense industry. Facing mounting pressure from black activists like A. Phillip Randolph, who threatened a march on Washington to protest discrimination in the military and national defense industry in 1941, President Franklin D. Roosevelt signed Executive Order 8802. This federal act desegregated the national defense industry by prohibiting discrimination based on race, creed, color, or national origin. Executive Order 8802 opened jobs to African Americans across the nation. Detroit, which became known as the "Arsenal of Democracy" due to its central role in the defense industry, experienced another influx of black migrants during World War II. In the two years between 1941 and 1943, more than 100,000 African Americans migrated to the Motor City.[9]

Cities in the Midwest and Northeast remained popular destinations for southerners, but African Americans who participated in the Second Great Migration also moved to the West Coast to take jobs in the defense industry. While industrial employers had primarily recruited black men during World War I, companies also hired black women during World War II. Boeing, an aircraft company in Seattle that produced B-17 and B-29 bombers during the war, hired large numbers of African American women. Shipbuilders in California also recruited black workers from the South during the war. Spurred by the availability of labor, black Los Angeles grew by 168.5 percent in the 1940s. In 1943, twelve thousand African Americans moved to the city in the month of June alone.[10]

FACILITATING MIGRATION

Black southerners frequently participated in "chain migration"—migrants from the same town or region relocated to a new place en masse. For example, Detroit primarily attracted migrants from Georgia during the First Great Migration, while most of the black migrants who settled in Los Angeles—and the West Coast in general—hailed from Texas, Louisiana, Arkansas, and Oklahoma during the Second Great Migration.[11] As early recruiters of black laborers, railroads facilitated chain migration. Some companies gave workers free railroad passes and paid for travel expenses. For example, the Pennsylvania Railroad funded the travel of 12,000 workers between 1916 and 1918. The Southern Pacific

Railroad similarly recruited approximately 500 French-speaking Afro-Creole families from southwest Louisiana to move to Houston, Texas, where they established a community called Frenchtown in the 1920s.

The location of railroad lines influenced where migrants settled. Most of the African Americans who migrated to Chicago hailed from the Mississippi Delta region, and the Illinois Central Railroad, which ran from Chicago toward New Orleans, inspired that movement. The Southern Pacific Railroad connected the Gulf Coast to the West Coast, running from New Orleans through most of California. African Americans from Louisiana and Texas used the Southern Pacific to travel west to cities like Los Angeles and Oakland.

Social networks also influenced where migrants moved. Black migrants were attracted to places where their family and friends were already settled. As historian Earl Lewis notes in his study of black migration from rural Virginia to Norfolk, "Family members often facilitated the move from Norfolk County into the city by providing the new migrants with living quarters and financial assistance during the initial adjustment period."[12]

Black-owned newspapers also facilitated the migration process, often encouraging rural African Americans to relocate. The Chicago *Defender*, founded by Robert Abbott in 1905, emerged as the most influential black newspaper in the nation during the First Great Migration. Abbott's publication featured articles that discussed racial atrocities across the country, while also providing local news for black Chicagoans. Meanwhile, the Houston *Informer* made migration a central feature of the Texas-based publication. Edited by Clifton F. Richardson, who also migrated to Houston from East Texas, the *Informer* encouraged other rural blacks to relocate. In 1919, the first year of publication, the newspaper ran advertisements that touted the city as "Heavenly Houston." The ad campaign appealed to prospective migrants by listing economic opportunities, boasting that the city offered "unexcelled

industrial opportunities to the colored man," but also pointed to socials benefits, like that fact that Houston was home to sixteen black elementary schools and two black hospitals.[13] By providing local information and discussing national issues like racial violence and segregation, newspapers like the *Defender* and *Informer* played a vital role in easing the migration and community-building processes during the Great Migrations.

Founded in New York in 1910 as the Committee on Urban Conditions Among Negroes, the National Urban League worked to assimilate black southerners into city life. The Urban League often encouraged migration by heralding northern cities. In 1921 co-founder George Edmund Haynes said of New York, "the cosmopolitan atmosphere knows less of color prejudice than probably any other city in the United States."[14] League employees also helped migrants find employment. The Detroit Urban League assisted men in obtaining industrial work and assisted women in securing domestic employment during the First Great Migration. The Urban League also worked to shape the migrant's behavior through programs that promoted "cleanliness, thrift, domesticity, and sexual chastity." The Urban League believed that migrants who exhibited those values would attract white employers. Forrester B. Washington, Detroit's first Urban League director, described the organization's goals in 1916: "You cannot do much for a man spiritually until you have given him a healthy and wholesome physical environment. In other words, 'You cannot grow lilies in ash barrels.'" Some of the Urban League's programs were based on stereotypes of black southerners as "backwards" and "uncouth." Washington, for example, created the Dress Well Club in 1917 to discourage southern black women in Detroit from wearing aprons and head wraps in public. The Urban League also organized dances and basketball games in order to steer youth away from pursuits like gambling.[15]

Membership in urban churches, social groups, and fraternal organizations increased as migrants poured into cities. Previously established churches gained new members, while working-class congregations often created storefront churches in urban communities. Southerners living in New York established associations like the Sons and Daughters of Virginia and the Sons and Daughters of Florida in the 1920s. These groups sponsored cultural events, held educational forums, and offered financial assistance to members and their families during emergencies. Additionally, fraternal organizations like the Masons, Pythians, and Odd Fellows recruited new members as black urban communities expanded.[16] Membership in churches and social organizations helped migrants establish new social ties and gain a sense of belonging in their new environs.

BUILDING BLACK URBAN COMMUNITIES

The steady influx of African Americans to US cities led to the growth and development of black urban neighborhoods. Black migrants often lived close to one another because of segregationist housing practices. Through the practice of "redlining" and restrictive housing covenants, cities created and maintained racially segregated residential areas. Banks often refused to extend mortgage loans to African Americans who wished to purchase property in white-majority areas. The Fair Housing Administration (FHA) contributed to housing segregation through the practice of redlining, which denied or limited the availability of financial services in certain neighborhoods based on racial or ethnic demographics, regardless of residents' qualifications. In the Los Angeles metropolitan area, the city of Compton excluded black residents by establishing racially restrictive housing covenants in the 1920s. Real estate brokers' licenses could be revoked for selling property to African Americans. The Supreme Court decisions *Shelley v. Kraemer* (1948) and *Barrows v. Jackson* (1953) ruled the practice of racially restrictive housing covenants unconstitutional.[17]

Excluded from certain parts of their adopted cities, black migrants quickly established neighborhoods. Cities that previously had small African American populations became home to thriving black communities. New enclaves developed in cities like Chicago, where a "black belt" emerged on the city's South Side. In New York City, the Harlem neighborhood in northern Manhattan transitioned from a largely Jewish and Italian settlement into the largest and most celebrated black community in the United States.

Every migration city had its own center for business and leisure. Harlem's 125th Street developed into that neighborhood's commercial hub. Residents of Pittsburgh's major black district, the Hill, could stroll Wylie Avenue when they wanted entertainment. In the Detroit neighborhood called "Paradise Valley," which became the heart of the city's black community in the 1930s, residents could hear live music, find a dentist, or shop for groceries.[18] Black Houstonians found similar amusements on West Dallas Street, which housed 95 percent of the city's black-owned businesses by 1920.[19]

As newcomers in migration cities, African Americans often did not own the majority of businesses in their neighborhoods, especially in the early years of the Great Migration. They often lacked the capital to launch businesses or were denied loans from banks with discriminatory practices. Black migrants who rented houses or apartments typically paid rent to white landlords. And while the local Urban League promoted New York as a type of black Promised Land, Harlem was not free of discrimination. "Blacks regularly endured unfair treatment and segregation in Harlem, especially in the chain stores along 125th Street that were less dependent upon local black patronage throughout the late 1920s," asserts historian Shannon King.[20]

Yet black entrepreneurship developed and took various forms in migration cities. Black newspapers urged African Americans to patronize establishments owned by members of their own race, especially since black business owners were more likely to live in the neighborhood where their businesses were located.

The New York *Age* stated in 1916 that white business owners only employed black workers in menial positions, while African Americans could obtain positions of leadership in companies owned by other black people.[21] In the 1920s, the Houston *Informer* promoted the development of black enterprise as a way to avoid segregation in white-owned movie theaters, restaurants, and stores.[22] Regardless of region, African Americans saw the development of black business as a grassroots effort to improve their economic standing in migration cities.

The beauty culture industry established by black women during the First Great Migration provides one of the most successful examples of black economic autonomy in the Jim Crow era. The Madam C. J. Walker Manufacturing Company was the most prosperous of these enterprises. Born Sarah Breedlove in Delta, Louisiana, Walker began selling hair care products for black entrepreneur Annie M. Turnbo-Malone's company, Poro, in St. Louis in the early 1900s. She eventually developed her own products and created the Madam C. J. Walker Manufacturing Company, which was headquartered in Indianapolis by 1910. Walker hired and trained women to become "beauty culturists" who used her system of hair treatments. The success of the Madam C. J. Walker Manufacturing Company led Walker to become one of the wealthiest black people in the United States by the time she died in New York in 1919. Other black women attained financial security through the beauty business. Nobia A. Franklin began creating and selling hair care products when she moved from the small town of Cuero, Texas, to San Antonio as a young woman. She established the Franklin Beauty School in Houston during World War I, and eventually opened another school and salon in Chicago. Beauty companies like these gave black women labor opportunities outside of domestic work in white homes while also cultivating black women's economic autonomy.[23]

Black female domestic laborers played a crucial role in migration cities. About 40 percent of all black workers in Houston between World Wars I and II were women.[24] Most worked as cooks, maids, and washerwomen. The labor of black cooks and maids was so significant to white Houstonians that when Juneteenth (the June 19th holiday that celebrates the emancipation of slaves in Texas) occurred on a Friday in 1917, a local hotel held a "rescue party" for families whose black employees had taken the day off from work.[25] Washerwomen often preferred that form of labor to other types of domestic employment because it gave them more independence. They performed laundry service in their own homes and neighborhoods, so they worked without white supervision.[26]

Black workers who spent their wages on recreational pursuits stimulated the growth of establishments devoted to commercial leisure in migration cities. "Migrants were lured to cities not only by jobs but also by promises of the 'high life'," writes historian Victoria Wolcott. "With higher wages and more leisure time came the ability to purchase luxuries such as clothes, liquor, and even a Ford automobile."[27] Black urban communities also developed informal economies, economic practices that lay outside of governmental regulation. During the era of Prohibition (1920–1933) establishments like "blind pigs" sold illegal alcohol. Through the numbers game, working-class African Americans gambled in urban communities.[28] A migrant from South Carolina named Ellsworth Raymond Johnson, known as "Bumpy," became the most well-known crime boss in Harlem through the numbers game in the 1930s. Some black women became sex workers after moving to cities, either to escape the drudgery of domestic labor or because other forms of labor were unavailable. Blues songs like Gertrude "Ma" Rainey's "Hustlin' Blues" frankly addressed the situation of black prostitutes:

> It's rainin' out here and tricks ain't walkin'
>   tonight
> It's rainin' out here and tricks ain't walkin'
>   tonight
> I'm goin' home, I know I've got to fight[29]

Black middle-class reformers and religious groups disdained these extralegal practices, but some African Americans turned to them for entertainment and economic necessity.

CULTURE AND THE GREAT MIGRATIONS

Artistic expressions flourished during the Great Migration as African Americans adapted older cultural practices to their new environs and developed new ones. Literary arts and musical forms—from blues to jazz to zydeco—especially thrived and proliferated.

New York City, which had become the center of American commercial music and theater by the early 20th century, was a logical choice for black musicians migrating to cities. The musical *Shuffle Along* opened in May of 1921 and became the first successful show with a black cast to appear on Broadway in twelve years. Written by comedians Flournoy Miller and Aubrey Lyles and composers/singers Eubie Blake and Noble Sissle, the musical helped inaugurate a new era of interest in black arts in New York. Edward "Duke" Ellington, who became one of the nation's most prominent jazz musicians, expressed his love for the city he chose in 1923: "New York is a dream of a song, a feeling of aliveness, a rush and flow of vitality that pulses like the giant heartbeat of humanity. The whole world revolves around New York, especially my world."[30]

Black musicians found work in clubs that served an African American clientele as well as segregated whites-only venues. Harlem attracted curious white people who wanted to visit the black community for entertainment and/or vice. The Cotton Club, which opened in 1923, provided a space for both. Gangster Owney Madden established the club as a whites-only venue where patrons could eat, consume illegal alcohol, and dance to the sounds of music played by African Americans. As historian Kevin Mumford asserts, the Cotton Club "represented a sort of flagship nightclub of white slumming."[31] The club decor reminded visitors of pervasive black stereotypes. Murals depicted African jungles and southern cotton fields. White patrons could watch "exotic" black performance without interacting with African Americans as equals.

The house band at the Cotton Club became one of the most influential jazz outfits in the United States during the interwar years. Georgia-born Fletcher Henderson led the first house band in 1923, and Ellington took over in 1927. Both men's work at the Cotton Club helped create the form of jazz known as "big band swing," which dominated American popular music from the mid-1930s through World War II. As his band drew national acclaim (partly due to the radio show broadcast performances from the club), Ellington pushed Madden to gradually allow some black patrons to enter the establishment. Other noted bandleaders from the Cotton Club include Cab Calloway and Jimmie Lunceford.

The decade of the 1920s is often called the "Jazz Age" because of the proliferation of that genre of music. Jazz especially thrived during the Great Migrations. Cultural historian Burton Peretti argues, "This migration, more than any other historical event, defined the social and intellectual significance of jazz for African Americans." Peretti estimates that of all black musicians born in the South before 1915, more than 63 percent migrated to the North, Midwest, or West by 1930.[32] Jazz flourished in dance halls, theaters, and nightclubs that hired black talent. High schools in migration cities helped the proliferation of jazz through music programs. Black public high schools across the country offered music instruction, so students could access instruments and learn to read music. Students from music programs at Jefferson and Jordan high schools in Detroit were crucial to the development of jazz in that city. Segregated schools in the urban South also offered music programs. Three black high schools in Memphis—Booker T. Washington, Manassas, and Douglass—provided instruction in music. In the 1930s students from the music programs at Houston's Jack Yates High

and Phillis Wheatley High played profession-
ally at venues across the city before they graduated. On the West Coast, a young Quincy Jones
learned to arrange music while attending Seattle's
James Garfield High in the 1940s.[33]

The music of black southerners changed in
urban contexts. By 1930 blues and jazz musicians preferred guitars to the banjoes that had
been central to southern music since the 1600s.
Arkansas native Sister Rosetta Tharpe performed
gospel music using an electric guitar, thrilling
secular audiences at places like the Cotton Club,
where she first performed in 1938. In the place
commemorated in blues songs as "Sweet Home
Chicago," music from the Mississippi Delta grew
louder and more raucous. During and after
World War II, blues musicians like Muddy
Waters, Howlin' Wolf, and Jimmie Reed also
"plugged in" by amplifying their guitars in order
to be heard above the din in urban nightclubs.
In Los Angeles, the electric blues of Dallas-born
T-Bone Walker contributed to the rollicking
music scene that developed in clubs on Central
Avenue. The genres of rhythm and blues and
rock 'n' roll grew, in part, from those sonic explorations of the 1940s and 1950s.

New genres of music emerged in migration
cities. In Houston, blues played by black migrants from East Texas mingled with la-la, a
style of music Afro-Creole migrants played using
accordions and washboards. By World War II,
Creoles living in Houston's Frenchtown called
that combination of blues and la-la *zarico* or
zologo—anglicized pronunciations of the French
word for beans, "les haricots." ("Les haricots
sont pas sales" was the name of a popular la-la
tune.) When music collector and folklorist
Robert McCormick visited Frenchtown in
1949, he standardized the spelling as *zydeco*.
The new genre was the musical outgrowth of
the Great Migrations, which brought French-
speaking Creoles from Louisiana and black
East Texans into the same Houston spaces.[34]

The mix of diverse people of African descent
who made contact in New York contributed
to the cultural movement known as the Harlem Renaissance. As black southern migrants

poured into Harlem, they made contact with
migrants from Caribbean islands like Cuba,
Jamaica, and Puerto Rico. By 1930, 160,340
black people resided in Harlem, and Caribbean
migrants comprised approximately 25 percent
of that population.[35] Jamaican Marcus Garvey
made Harlem the base for his Universal Negro
Improvement Association, which attracted
members from the Caribbean and United
States.

Journals like *The Crisis*, edited by W. E. B.
Du Bois, and *Survey Graphic*, edited by Paul
Kellogg, showed an early interest in the literary
products emerging from Harlem residents.
Writers from different parts of the United States
and the Caribbean explored themes that
linked the groups to a common African diaspora, celebrated black cultures, and protested
racial injustice. US-born Langston Hughes
wrote poems like "Brothers" that emphasized
shared African ancestry among migrants, regardless of national origins. Arturo Alfonso
Schomburg, a Puerto Rican who moved to
Harlem, collected items for the New York Public
Library and curated exhibits that pertained
to people of African descent from around the
world.[36]

The Harlem Renaissance was also notable
for its literary and musical explorations of gender
and sexuality. Writers like Jessie Fauset, Nella
Larsen, and Zora Neale Hurston produced works
that centered on black women's experiences—
and sometimes drew backlash from their black
male peers (e.g., in the case of Hurston). A visible
queer subculture emerged in Jazz Age Harlem,
a neighborhood that "provided a degree of
tolerance for lesbians and gay men," according to historian James Wilson.[37] Drag queen
balls (sometimes called "freak balls") included
female impersonation, dancing contests, and
costume contests.[38] Entertainer Gladys Bentley
made gender ambiguity part of her stage persona and personal life. Bentley, who began playing the piano and singing the blues in Harlem
in 1928, performed in a tuxedo and top hat, and
she flaunted multiple taboos by reportedly
marrying a white woman in a civil ceremony.

Bentley sometimes performed under the stage name "Bobbie Minton."[39]

While the Harlem Renaissance was certainly the most recognized and celebrated black arts movement, it was not the only one to develop during the Great Migrations. Black artists in cities like Atlanta and Chicago authored poems, stories, and plays. Atlanta emerged as a significant space for the cultivation of black southern music. Bailey's 81 Theatre hired black performers who migrated to the growing city in Georgia. After leaving Macon, a young Richard "Little Richard" Penniman played at the 81 Theatre as a member of a traveling theater troupe in the 1940s.[40] Whether they remained in the South or moved to a city in a different region of the country, black migrants significantly contributed to the literary and musical development of urban America.

BLACK POLITICS IN MIGRATION CITIES

The migration of black southerners to the North and West influenced electoral politics in the United States and led to political party realignment. Northern and western states did not disfranchise African Americans, so black migrants in those regions could vote. Black voters on Chicago's South Side reshaped local politics during World War I. In 1914 Republican Oscar De Priest became the first black alderman elected to the Chicago city council. Born in Alabama and raised in Kansas, De Priest entered politics when he moved to Chicago. He received the support of Mayor William Hale "Big Bill" Thompson, who dominated the local Republican Party machine. After resigning from the city council in 1917, De Priest founded a political organization called the People's Movement Club to organize black voters in Chicago.

In 1928 De Priest became the first black politician to serve in Congress in the 20th century when voters on the South Side of Chicago elected him to the House of Representatives. De Priest represented the 1st Congressional District of Illinois for three terms. When he went to Washington, DC, for his first session as a congressman, De Priest was the only African American member of the House.

African Americans shifted their political loyalties from Republican to Democrat during the First Great Migration. The party realignment began in the 1920s, when African Americans increasingly questioned their loyalty to a Republican Party that did little to combat lynching or segregation at the national level. In 1934 De Priest lost his seat in the House to the Democratic candidate Arthur Mitchell, who became the first black Democrat ever to serve in Congress. Mitchell's victory over De Priest can be attributed to his ability to mobilize black voters who supported the New Deal and Franklin D. Roosevelt. New Deal programs often discriminated against African Americans. Nevertheless, Roosevelt made inroads with black voters through actions like appointing black educator Mary McLeod Bethune as director of the Division of Negro Affairs in the National Youth Administration, an agency within his Works Progress Administration. African Americans also noted First Lady Eleanor Roosevelt's outspokenness against racial segregation, especially the well-publicized examples of her ignoring Jim Crow laws in the South. When 75 percent of African Americans voted for Roosevelt in the election of 1936, he became the first Democratic presidential candidate in US history to receive the majority of the African American vote. Democrats increasingly courted black voters in migration cities in the North and West.

A new wave of African American politicians entered the House of Representatives after World War II. Black voters in New York City began sending representatives to Congress in the 1940s. Adam Clayton Powell Jr. represented Harlem in the House of Representatives from 1945 to 1971. Charles Diggs of Detroit represented Michigan's 13th Congressional District from 1955 to 1980. Robert N. C. Nix Sr., the first black congressman to represent Pennsylvania, served in the House of Representatives from 1958 to 1979. When Los Angeles voters sent Augustus F. Hawkins to the House in 1963, he became the first black congressman in California and the first black representative elected west of the Mississippi River. These politicians often promoted civil rights legislation and worked toward racial equality. Congressman Hawkins authored Title VII of the 1964 Civil Rights Act, which prohibits employers from discriminating on the basis of race, color, religion, sex, or national origin.[41]

Black women from migration families increasingly entered state and national politics in the 1960s. Born in New York in 1924 to Caribbean migrants, Shirley Chisholm was the first black woman elected to the US House of Representatives in 1968. She represented New York as a congresswoman for seven terms. In 1972 Chisholm became the first major-party black candidate to seek the Democratic nomination during a presidential election. Barbara Jordan, whose parents migrated to Houston before she was born, ran successfully for the Texas Senate in 1966, which made her the first black woman to ever hold that office and the first African American since the 19th century. She was elected to the House of Representatives in 1972, becoming the first black woman from the former Confederacy to serve in Congress.

BACKLASH AND URBAN VIOLENCE

The rapid influx of black migrants into urban America elicited fear and suspicion among some white Americans In East St. Louis, Illinois, a riot erupted over labor tensions in July 1917. When white workers at the Aluminum Ore Company went on strike that year, the company responded by replacing the strikers with African American workers who were pouring into East St. Louis and nearby St. Louis, Missouri. Fear over interracial sex exacerbated economic tensions. Rumors that local white women were dating black male workers, who made up the majority of black migrants in East St. Louis, circulated that spring and summer. On the evening of July 2, 1917, groups of armed whites began shooting at African Americans and

setting fire to black residences. White mobs lynched African Americans, while other rioters attacked black passengers on streetcars. To protest the violence in East St. Louis, approximately ten thousand black people marched down Fifth Avenue in New York in a Silent Parade. The *Crisis* also published a detailed investigation of the violent event.[42]

The violence continued after the end of World War I. Beginning in May of 1919, and continuing through September, twenty-six race riots occurred across the United States during "Red Summer." One of the most notorious riots occurred in Chicago. On July 27 a black youth named Eugene Williams was swimming with friends in Lake Michigan when he drifted into an area informally reserved for white people. A group of white men began throwing stones at Williams as he swam, and the boy drowned. When the police showed up at the scene, they made no arrests. They ignored eyewitness accounts of the event and refused to arrest those responsible for the boy's death. Crowds of angry black people gathered. Quickly, the scene escalated into a riot. Over the next week, black and white Chicagoans engaged in open warfare, especially on the city's South Side. The state militia entered the scene on the fourth day of the fighting, but they could not restore order. Ultimately thirty-eight Chicagoans died—twenty-three blacks and fifteen whites.

While reading news about Chicago and other sites of violence during Red Summer, African Americans noticed that the character of the violence had changed. Across the nation, African Americans armed themselves against white aggression. Black writers applauded these acts of self-defense, arguing that by protecting their communities African American men had proven their manhood. The fact that fifteen white people died during the Chicago Riot of 1919 showed that a fair number of black people were taking up arms and fighting back. Claude McKay, a Jamaican poet who migrated to the United States, recalled, "Our Negro newspapers were morbid, full of details of clashes between colored and white, murderous shootings and hangings."[43] In response to Red Summer, McKay penned the poem "If We Must Die," to celebrate black armed self-defense:

> If we must die—let it not be like hogs
> Hunted and penned in an inglorious spot,
> While round us bark the mad and hungry dogs,
> Making their mock at our accursed lot.
> If we must die—oh, let us nobly die,
> So that our precious blood may not be shed
> In vain; then even the monsters we defy
> Shall be constrained to honor us though dead!
> Oh, Kinsmen!
> We must meet the common foe;
> Though far outnumbered, let us show us brave,
> And for their thousand blows deal one deathblow!
> What though before us lies the open grave?
> Like men we'll face the murderous, cowardly pack,
> Pressed to the wall, dying, but fighting back!

As they created urban communities, black migrants—regardless of region—often referred to themselves as "New Negroes." Some writers promoted armed self-defense as a central aspect of New Negro identity. Additionally, black consumerism and the emergence of literary and cultural movements contributed to the idea that black Americans who participated in the Great Migrations had emerged with a new sense of self.

DISCUSSION OF THE LITERATURE

Scholarly interest in the Great Migrations can be traced to two phenomena that affected the study of the African American history—the emergence of African American studies as a field after the civil rights and Black Power movements and the increasing interest in cultural and social history in the 1970s. Social histories that examine individual black urban communities began to appear during that era. Joe Trotters's trailblazing *Black Milwaukee* (1985) highlights industrial labor and the development of a black ghetto in Wisconsin's largest city.

The 1990s were a watershed moment for the study of black migration and urbanization. Most historical works focused on migration to one specific city. James Grossman's *Land of Hope* (1991) offers a rich analysis of the factors that motivated black migration to Chicago and the circumstances migrants encountered in the city. During that decade, Albert Broussard and Quintard Taylor shifted the focus to the Pacific Coast with *Black San Francisco* (1993) and *The Forging of a Black Community* (1994), which looks at the development of black Seattle. Nearly a decade later, Shirley Ann Wilson Moore (2001) examines the smaller West Coast city of Richmond, California.

As the largest and most well-documented Great Migration community, Harlem has received perhaps the most scholarly attention. David Levering Lewis's *When Harlem Was in Vogue* (1981) and Cary D. Wintz's *Black Culture and the Harlem Renaissance* (1988) have surveyed the history of the Harlem Renaissance. Shannon King's *Whose Harlem Is This, Anyway?* (2015) offers an excellent analysis of grassroots organization and community politics in Harlem through 1930.

Isabel Wilkerson's *The Warmth of Other Suns* (2010) offers one of the most comprehensive studies of African Americans who left the South. Wilkerson reads the Great Migration experience through the journeys of three African Americans from different parts of the South who moved to Chicago, New York, and Los Angeles, respectively. By focusing on these cities, she shows how black urban communities developed in the West, Midwest, and Northeast.

Historian Earl Lewis was one of the first historians to produce a lengthy study of a southern city during the Great Migration. *In Their Own Interests* (1991) examines the development of black communities in Norfolk, Virginia, in the 20th century. In the last decade, more historians have focused on black migrants who remained in the South. Luther Adams focuses on Kentucky in *Way Up North in Louisville* (2010). Black Houston takes center stage in Bernadette Pruitt's *The Other Great Migration* (2013).

Comparative studies that examine the Great Migration alongside the migration of other groups have emerged since the turn of the 21st century. As James Gregory points out, more white southerners moved north during the Great Migrations. Gregory's *The Southern Diaspora* (2007) shows how the migration of black and white southerners affected culture, society, and politics in the North and West. In the last decade, a growing number of studies have examined interactions between African Americans and Latina/os in migration cities. In *Forging Diaspora*, Frank Guridy (2010) identifies multiple sites of Afro-Cuban and African American interaction. A few migration histories compare the development of black and Latina/o communities in the same cities. Gaye Theresa Johnson's *Spaces of Conflict, Sounds of Solidarity* (2012) shows how African Americans who established communities in Los Angeles engaged with the city's Mexican American residents. Tyina Steptoe offers a comparative study of how black East Texans, Louisiana Creoles, and ethnic Mexicans from Texas and Mexico built communities in *Houston Bound* (2016).

A growing number of writers have examined the Great Migrations through the lens of culture. While highlighting the experiences of black women who moved to Detroit, gender historian Victoria Wolcott (2001) interprets cultural practices that emerged during the First Great Migration. In *Chicago's New Negroes* (2007), Davarian Baldwin builds on the work of historians like Grossman by focusing on the development of beauty culture, sports, music, and film in black Chicago. Steptoe's book highlights the development of diverse musical cultures in Houston, while Johnson surveys musical styles that emerged from multiethnic Los Angeles.

PRIMARY SOURCES

Black newspapers from major cities, such as the New York *Age*, the California *Eagle* (Los Angeles), the Chicago *Defender*, and the Houston *Informer*, can be found on microfilm in university libraries and in public libraries in those cities. The Chicago *Defender* has been digitized and is available online through many university libraries. Additionally, the Library of Congress website Chronicling America offers digitized African American periodicals from the 1910s. The Wisconsin Historical Society, located on the campus of the University of Wisconsin–Madison, houses one of the nation's most comprehensive collections of microfilmed black newspapers in the United States.

Libraries and historical societies in migration cities offer the most resources for archival research. The Schomburg Center for Research in Black Culture at the New York Public Library is the best archive available for the study of the Harlem Renaissance. The Chicago History Museum holds materials related to black migration and urban life. The Houston Public Library's Gregory School and Houston Metropolitan Research Center hold collections related to the Great Migrations to that city.

A significant number of universities, research libraries, and online collections have digitized collections related to the Great Migrations. Some notable examples are the Digital Public Library's Great Migration Primary Source Set, which includes materials like photographs and maps, the Newberry Library's Chicago and the Great Migration, 1915–1950, and The Great Migration: Letters of Negro Migrants of 1916–1918, a collection of letters that appeared in *The Journal of Negro History* in 1919. The site "History Matters" provides a similar online resource, "Sir I Will Thank You with All My Heart": Seven Letters from the Great Migration. The National Humanities Center's The Making of African American Identity: Volume III, 1917–1968 contains primary sources and discussion questions that may be useful to professional historians, students, and researchers. A website sponsored by Humanities Texas offers online access to writings by Langston Hughes and contemporary reviews of the writer's work. The Houston Public Library's digitized collections highlight influential migrants, such as Celebrating the Life of C. F. Richardson Sr., as well as dozens of digitized oral histories.

DIGITAL MATERIALS

The Blues and the Great Migration (http://teachrock.org/lesson/the-blues-and-the-great-migration/).

In Motion: The African-American Migration Experience (http://www.inmotionaame.org/home.cfm;jsessionid=f8302002091506858896005?bhcp=1).

LIBRARY OF CONGRESS

A Guide to Harlem Renaissance Materials (http://www.loc.gov/rr/program/bib/harlem/harlem.html).

The African-American Mosaic: Migration (https://www.loc.gov/exhibits/african/afam008.html).

The African-American Mosaic: Chicago: Destination for the Great Migration (https://www.loc.gov/exhibits/african/afam011.html).

The African American Odyssey: A Quest for Full Citizenship: World War I and Postwar Society (https://www.loc.gov/exhibits/african-american-odyssey/world-war-i-and-postwar-society.html).

SCHOMBURG CENTER FOR RESEARCH IN BLACK CULTURE

African Americans and World War I (Africana Age) (http://exhibitions.nypl.org/africanaage/essay-world-war-i.html).

The New Negro Renaissance (Africana Age) (http://exhibitions.nypl.org/africanaage/essay-renaissance.html).

SPECIFIC BLACK URBAN COMMUNITIES

African Americans in Atlanta: Adrienne Herndon, an Uncommon Woman (https://southernspaces.org/2004/african-americans-atlanta-adrienne-herndon-uncommon-woman).

Auburn Avenue (Atlanta and the 1910s) (http://www.georgiaencyclopedia.org/articles/counties-cities-neighborhoods/auburn-avenue-sweet-auburn).

Black Chicago Renaissance (http://www.chicagohistoryfair.org/for-teachers/curriculum/black-chicago-renaissance.html).

DuSable to Obama: Chicago's Black Metropolis (http://interactive.wttw.com/a/main.taf-p=76,3.html).

Goin' to Chicago and African American "Great Migrations" (https://southernspaces.org/2010/goin-chicago-and-african-american-great-migrations).

The Great Migration: A City Transformed (Philadelphia and the Great Migration) (https://greatmigrationphl.org/).

FURTHER READING

Adams, Luther. *Way Up North in Louisville: African American Migration in the Urban South, 1930–1970.* Chapel Hill: University of North Carolina Press, 2010.

Baldwin, Davarian L. *Chicago's New Negroes: Modernity, the Great Migration, and Black Urban Life.* Chapel Hill: University of North Carolina Press, 2007.

Chatelain, Marcia. *South Side Girls: Growing Up in the Great Migration.* Durham, NC: Duke University Press, 2015.

Gregory, James N. *The Southern Diaspora: How the Great Migrations of Black and White Southerners Transformed America.* Chapel Hill: University of North Carolina Press, 2007.

Grossman, James. *Land of Hope: Chicago, Black Southerners, and the Great Migration.* Chicago: University of Chicago Press, 1991.

Guridy, Frank Andre. *Forging Diaspora: Afro-Cubans and African Americans in a World of Empire and Jim Crow.* Chapel Hill: University of North Carolina Press, 2010.

King, Shannon. *Whose Harlem Is This, Anyway?: Community Politics and Grassroots Activism During the New Negro Era.* New York: New York University Press, 2015.

Lewis, David Levering. *When Harlem Was in Vogue.* New York: Penguin Books, 1997.

Lewis, Earl. *In Their Own Interests: Race, Class, and Power in Twentieth-Century Norfolk, Virginia*. Berkeley: University of California Press, 1991.

Peretti, Burton. *The Creation of Jazz: Music, Race, and Culture in Urban America*. Champaign: University of Illinois Press, 1992.

Steptoe, Tyina. *Houston Bound: Culture and Color in a Jim Crow City*. Oakland: University of California Press, 2016.

Trotter, Joe. *Black Milwaukee: The Making of an Industrial Proletariat, 1915–45*. Champaign: University of Illinois Press, 1985.

Wilkerson, Isabel. *The Warmth of Other Suns: The Epic Story of America's Great Migration*. New York: Random House, 2010.

Wilson, James F. *Bulldaggers, Pansies, and Chocolate Babies: Performance, Race, and Sexuality in the Harlem Renaissance*. Ann Arbor: University of Michigan Press, 2011.

Wolcott, Victoria W. *Remaking Respectability: African American Women in Interwar Detroit*. Chapel Hill: University of North Carolina Press, 2001.

NOTES

1. Pete R. Daniel, *Breaking the Land: The Transformation of Cotton, Tobacco, and Rice Cultures Since 1880* (Champaign: University of Illinois Press, 1986).

2. Richard M. Mizelle Jr., *Backwater Blues: The Mississippi Flood of 1927 in the African American Imagination* (Minneapolis: University of Minnesota Press, 2014).

3. Bruce Andre Beauboeuf, "War and Change: Houston's Economic Ascendancy During World War I," *The Houston Review* 14, no. 2 (1992): 89–112.

4. Howard Beeth and Cary D. Wintz, eds., *Black Dixie: Afro-Texan History and Culture in Houston* (College Station: Texas A&M Press, 1992); Bernadette Pruitt, *The Other Great Migration: The Movement of Rural African Americans to Houston, 1900–1941* (College Station: Texas A&M University Press, 2013); Tyina Steptoe, *Houston Bound: Culture and Color in a Jim Crow City* (Oakland: University of California Press, 2016).

5. James Grossman, *Land of Hope: Chicago, Black Southerners, and the Great Migration* (Chicago: University of Chicago Press, 1991); Burton Peretti, *The Creation of Jazz: Music, Race, and Culture in Urban America* (Champaign: University of Illinois Press, 1992), 45.

6. These statistics do not include Texas or Virginia. Stewart Emory Tolnay and E. M. Beck, *A Festival of Violence: An Analysis of the Lynching of African-Americans in the American South, 1882–1930* (Urbana: University of Illinois Press, 1995).

7. Maggie Jones, "Jim Crow Blues," Uncensored History of the Blues, September 18, 2009 (http://uncensoredhistoryoftheblues.purplebeech.com/2009/09/show-43-jim-crow-blues.html).

8. Shannon King, *Whose Harlem Is This, Anyway?: Community Politics and Grassroots Activism During the New Negro Era* (New York: New York University Press, 2015), 23.

9. Anthony Macías, "'Detroit Was Heavy': Modern Jazz, Bebop, and African American Expressive Culture," *Journal of African American History* 95, no. 1 (Winter 2010): 47.

10. Quintard Taylor, *In Search of the Racial Frontier: African Americans in the West, 1528–1990* (New York: W. W. Norton, 1999), 254–256.

11. Taylor, *In Search of the Racial Frontier*, 254–256.

12. Earl Lewis, *In Their Own Interests: Race, Class and Power in Twentieth-Century Norfolk, Virginia* (Berkeley: University of California Press), 31.

13. Steptoe, *Houston Bound*, 35.

14. King, *Whose Harlem Is This, Anyway?*, 13.

15. Victoria W. Wolcott, *Remaking Respectability: African American Women in Interwar Detroit* (Chapel Hill: University of North Carolina Press, 2001), 54–55.

16. King, *Whose Harlem Is This, Anyway?*, 24.

17. Josh Sides, "Straight into Compton: American Dreams, Urban Nightmares, and the Metamorphosis of a Black Suburb," *American Quarterly* 56, no. 3 (September 2004): 585–586.

18. Macías, "'Detroit Was Heavy'," 47.

19. Beth Anne Shelton, Nestor Rodriguez, Joe R. Feagin, Robert D. Bullard, and Robert D. Thomas, *Houston: Growth and Decline in a Sunbelt Boomtown* (Philadelphia: Temple University Press, 1989), 71.

20. King, *Whose Harlem Is This, Anyway?*, 16.

21. King, *Whose Harlem Is This, Anyway?*, 26.

22. Steptoe, *Houston Bound*, 56.

23. Tiffany M. Gill, *Beauty Shop Politics: African American Women's Activism in the Beauty Industry* (Champaign: University of Illinois Press, 2010); Davarian L. Baldwin, *Chicago's New Negroes: Modernity, the Great Migration, and Black Urban Life* (Chapel Hill: University of North Carolina Press, 2007).

24. Bernadette Pruitt, "For the Advancement of the Race: The Great Migrations to Houston, Texas, 1914–1941," *Journal of Urban History* 31, no. 4 (May 2005): 435–478.

25. Robert V. Haynes, *A Night of Violence: The Houston Riot of 1917* (Baton Rouge: Louisiana State University Press, 1977), 28; Steptoe, *Houston Bound*, 37.

26. See Tera W. Hunter, *To 'Joy My Freedom: Southern Black Women's Lives and Labors After the Civil War* (Cambridge, MA: Harvard University Press, 1997).

27. Wolcott, *Remaking Respectability*, 53.

28. Wolcott, *Remaking Respectability*, 85–114.

29. Angela Y. Davis, *Blues Legacies and Black Feminism: Gertrude Ma Rainey, Bessie Smith, and Billie Holiday* (New York: Vintage Books, 1999), 222–223.

30. Peretti, "Therefore, I Got to Go," 43.

31. Kevin J. Mumford, *Interzones: Black/White Sex Districts in Chicago and New York in the Early Twentieth Century* (New York: Columbia University Press, 1997), 143.

32. Peretti, "Therefore, I Got to Go," 43.

33. Macías, "Detroit Was Heavy"; Steptoe, *Houston Bound*. On jazz in black Seattle, see Quintard Taylor, *The Forging of a Black Community: Seattle's Central District from 1870 Through the Civil Rights Era* (Seattle: University of Washington Press, 1994).

34. Steptoe, *Houston Bound*, 197–199.

35. King, *Whose Harlem Is This, Anyway?*, 23.

36. Cary D. Wintz, *Black Culture and the Harlem Renaissance* (Houston, TX: Rice University Press, 1988); Frank Andre Guridy, *Forging Diaspora: Afro-Cubans and African Americans in a World of Empire and Jim Crow* (Chapel Hill: University of North Carolina Press, 2010).

37. James F. Wilson, *Bulldaggers, Pansies, and Chocolate Babies: Performance, Race, and Sexuality in the Harlem Renaissance* (Ann Arbor: University of Michigan Press, 2011), 39.

38. Mumford, *Interzones*, 81; Wilson, *Bulldaggers, Pansies, and Chocolate Babies*, 13–14.

39. Wilson, *Bulldaggers, Pansies, and Chocolate Babies*, 172; Eric Garber, "Gladys Bentley: The Bulldagger Who Sang the Blues," *Out/Look* 1, no. 1 (Spring 1988): 52–61.

40. Charles White, *The Life and Times of Little Richard: The Authorized Biography* (1984; reprint, London: Omnibus Press, 2003).

41. Rita Werner Gordon, "The Change in the Political Alignment of Chicago's Negroes During the New Deal," *Journal of American History* 56 (1969): 586–588; Harvard Sitkoff, *A New Deal for Blacks: The Emergence of Civil Rights as a National Issue: The Depression Decade* (New York: Oxford University Press, 1981); Nancy Weiss, *Farewell to the Party of Lincoln: Black Politics in the Age of FDR* (Princeton, NJ: Princeton University Press, 1983). See also "Keeping the Faith: African Americans Return to Congress, 1929–1970," *History, Arts and Archives: The United States House of Representatives*, http://history.house.gov/Exhibitions-and-Publications/BAIC/Historical-Essays/Keeping-the-Faith/Introduction/.

42. Elliott M. Rudwick, *Race Riot at East St. Louis* (Carbondale: Southern Illinois University Press, 1964).

43. Quoted in Claude McKay, *A Long Way Home*, (1937; New Brunswick, NJ: Rutgers University Press, 2007), 29.

Tyina Steptoe

THE GREAT MIGRATION IN CONTEXT: THE CHICAGO EXPERIENCE, 1916–1918

The voluntary migration of blacks abandoning the South between the years 1916 and 1918 represented a pivotal point in both American and African American history, ranking at the time as secondary in socially transformative significance only to the Emancipation. Labeled as the "Great Migration" for generations among academicics and laypersons, the movement of blacks in succeeding decades, from the 1920s through the 1960s, has led to both an intellectual reappraisal and relabeling, with titles such as the "Great Black Migration" or the "Second Great Migration."[1] This unprecedented phenomenon during the early 20th century proved to be the ultimate African American resistance to southern oppression, manifested through nonviolent yet assertive mass movement.

In the 19th century, the fight for freedom was manifested in "running away" to the North or to Canada before and during the Civil

War—often in a small, continuous wave—or moving to Kansas and farther westward during the Reconstruction Era. In both instances, migration reflected dissatisfaction with the enforced subordinate status for blacks as slaves, accompanied by the intolerable conditions of place. Viewing black migration northward convinced the Harvard-trained historian Carter G. Woodson in 1918 that he was witnessing a portion of a century of migration that had begun in the previous century. He penned *A Century of Negro Migration* to explain the event as an amazing episode in the transformation of the human condition.[2]

In the case of Chicago, the city's strategic spatial presence as the nation's major economic transfer center, along with its reputation as a humanitarian anchorage, were magnetic forces. The city appeared to be a haven for those seeking to attain greater freedom and enjoy material betterment in a diversified economic setting. On the cusp of the Great Migration, W. E. B. Du Bois wrote a paean in *The Crisis* that praised life in a viable black community exhibiting both growth and development. It clearly placed the extant black population of some 50,000 persons as already progressing along a path that was notable for its dynamism and triumph over adversities.[3] Joining this resident population as a result of the impending Great Migration would be approximately 50,000 energized newcomers. They were a portion of the migration northward represented within a mass of approximately 500,000 people *in toto* journeying from the oppressive South to the alluring prosperous and democratic North, with approximately one-tenth of the aggregate settling in Chicago. Linked to the advent of the First World War, this trend did not end with the cessation of hostilities in Europe. It continued into the 1920s and onward, with more than six to seven million persons migrating to the North and West, with 500,000 arriving in Chicago over a fifty-year period.

The contemporary sense of the phenomenon's significance was uncontestable. It represented dual responses to a persistent dehumanizing existence in the South and hope for immediate remediation of attendant racial problems in the North. Contemporaries traditionally categorized this anticipation and reaction as expressed by two influences, one being centrifugal or "push," and the other, centripetal or "pull." Perhaps there is a need for an addition to the traditional "p's"—the element of personality. On an individual basis, a person's reasons for any distinct action might just be explainable by the character of one's being, especially with the recognition today that black agency has been overlooked in the past. Historian Leon F. Litwack has described this proclivity toward individual and group assertiveness in his 1998 *Trouble in Mind: Black Southerners in The Age of Jim Crow*. Litwack wrote about persons who would have filled the migrant ranks who felt an immediate need for greater control over and competency in life's endeavors. This was a direct legacy of the release of pent-up assertiveness following emancipation.[4]

The southern migrants' origins, experiences, motivations, and goals often proved complicated to comprehend. Although they were southerners by custom and had inclinations toward work, religious worship, and family organization, they never constituted a homogeneous amalgam. Females migrated as well as males, with the latter being numerically predominant. They traveled not only alone but also in families, in unrelated groups, and even as whole church congregations. Circumstances of habitation had them emerging from plantations as well as villages, towns, and cities. As evidenced in their varied physiognomy, their racial ancestry could be traced to Europe, Africa, and the diverse indigenous peoples of North America. This factor of mixed racial backgrounds shaped their outlooks of a possible future in the South as well as hopes for a better life in the North, where economic competition overshadowed secondary concerns such as skin complexion and lack of an industrial background. Numerous cases of blacks obtaining employment while "passing for white," as part of the "invisible migration," prove this point.

That there were inherent, as well as acquired, adaptive differences among the migrants was discernible to contemporaries Julius Rosenwald, Ida B. Wells-Barnett, and Charles S. Johnson. Africans' tendency to adjust to changing circumstances once in America demonstrated an acute skill at adaptation.[5] Chicago philanthropist Rosenwald observed the transformative influences of life in a northern city on migrants as well. The milieu that pervaded black Chicago was one that released individual assertiveness, leading to competitiveness. As assessed by Julius Rosenwald to A. Clement McNeal of the Chicago NAACP, "under Northern freedom, a Southern Negro *does* change."[6] On the occasion of Wells-Barnett's death, a eulogizer reflected that she had assessed a variation in migrant thought and behavior, with some being able to break free from their acquiescence to previous southern norms, while others could not. Wells-Barnett "was a profound [student] of sociology. She knew that there were many who were doubtful of the natural equality of their race; that many were ashamed [of their origins and very being]....She knew that only a few people knew the Negro's part in world history and culture and [their pursuit of] freedom & emancipation."[7] To correct these attitudes, she set about on her mission as a social activist and civic leader to convert them into proactive and responsible citizens, as noted sociologist Charles S. Johnson wrote, interested in assimilation and becoming "city Negroes."[8]

Historian Lerone Bennett Jr. succinctly described their varied motivations. "They moved because the sheriff was mean, because the planters were mean, because life was mean. They were pushed by drought, boll weevils and tyranny, and they were pulled by the lure of employment in burgeoning wartime industries."[9] They had experienced hard, unrelenting work as a requirement for survival in a slave-driven society, one that was transformed after 1865 into a labor-intensive, peonage-dominated environment. They were rural workers for the most part, but with some industrial workers from

Birmingham, New Orleans, Mobile, and elsewhere who were to be fully transformed into an industrial proletariat in Chicago's modern, urbanized, industrial environment.[10] For certain southern females with family values that prevented work outside the home, they managed to adjust to the new drudgeries, albeit seen as opportunities, offered in the service and domestic sectors.[11]

To the benefit of scholarship and posterity, and to understand the migration's significance to the nation, the Carnegie Institute for Peace engaged Emmett J. Scott, the erudite former secretary to Booker T. Washington, to conduct research on this phenomenon. Scott assembled a research team composed of future notable African American scholars to conduct a major study on motivations and impact. Their significant and influential study helps to explain the continuity, causes, stimulation, and effects of the migration that took place during the First World War.[12]

ORIGINS OF THE GREAT MIGRATION

The precipitating cause of the "Great Migration" was a need to fill a labor shortage during time of war in order that America could maintain a high level of production of war materials for the Allies at war in Europe. This shortage of workers resulted in the expedience of inducing black workers to shift from their region of provenance in the South to a region of wartime labor needs in the North. One rarely cited incentive was that which involved the federal government initially through the Department of Labor, which lasted only for a very short period because of white southern resistance. Individual northern firms proved more persistent in pursuit of black labor, especially from Chicago's vast stockyards, which sent agents into the South seeking workers, sometimes with free rail passes. This factor among others, along with the desire to work for reasonable wages, propelled economically exploited southern labor northward. Accordingly, the employers' success was to be manifested in a changed stockyards workforce that by 1920 was near predominantly African American.

Even without a central leadership that marked the 1878 exodus to the West, an indigenous set of leaders and collective efforts spurred and directed movement away from the economic and social oppression of the South.[13] At the same time, the crusading *Chicago Defender* newspaper, with its national circulation, played a major part in fomenting sensitivity among southern blacks to the need for racial liberation. Centripetally, the paper's influence served as a major pull factor attracting African Americans to a land of hope and promise. Its basic attitude toward life in the South found that region totally inhospitable and unsuitable for raising a family, aspiring and achieving goals, or to experiencing any sense of personal freedom. In its attitudes toward life in the North, particularly in Chicago, the newspaper communicated an admiration that added to the region's attractiveness. Personally, Abbott had enjoyed his first trip to the North during the World's Columbian Exposition held in 1893, and he was so mesmerized by the city he returned almost immediately. He translated this affection toward the nation's blacks. They, in turn, corresponded about their innermost aspirations, fears, and perceptions, providing an excellent pool of data in their letters from which to extrapolate what W. E. B. Du Bois described as the meanings of "their daily lives and longings...their homely joys and sorrows... [and] their real shortcomings."[14] Abbott's enthusiasm grew to a point that led him to declare May 15, 1917, as an anointed day for a mass exodus, the day of the "Great Northern Drive."[15]

The centrifugal or push factors of southern discrimination, segregation, and overt terrorism that included lynchings, beatings, rapes, and other public humiliations, along with economic deprivation, provided more than enough in the way of disincentives to prompt individual and mass departures. The combination of significant push-and-pull factors, along with the agency accompanying a personality model emanating from a collective consciousness,

contributed as the *necessary conditions* to spur a migration of this magnitude that occurred during this short period of time.

THE GREAT MIGRATION TO CHICAGO

The Great Migration dramatically affected the character of life in Chicago's several black enclaves dramatically. These transformative features were evidenced in several areas, first in race relations, next in labor relations, and then in housing or a hegemonic neighborhood stratagem. According to St. Clair Drake and Horace R. Cayton, the Great Migration ended the supposed "golden age of [inter]race relations."[16] At the same time, the Great Migration extended a "golden age of *intra-racial* relations" among members of a variegated migrant mass, including Old Settlers and the *newest* newcomers of 1916–1918. While much of the anecdotal testimony in support of the former belief represented retrospective myth to Drake and Cayton, an expanding black population did profoundly alter relationships between blacks and the whites, dramatically changing the basic economic and social structure of the black community. In 1910 Negroes formed a small, almost insignificant, part of the city's life. By 1920 there were enough to attract attention as the black population grew to 4.1 percent of the city's total, and the rapidity of the influx merely exacerbated white racial apprehensions.[17]

The epochal Great Migration that took place, according to Drake, "represented the transfer of a large population from participation in a caste-system to participation in a social order characterized by greater social mobility, less economic subordination, and a system of ideas which did not sanction the 'fixing' of the Negroes' status. Such as system reconditioned them, and they, in turn, modified it (in tandem with the exiting, residential black population)."[18]

Indeed, the dynamic impact of this newest wave of migrants overshadowed the forgotten phenomenon of *melding*, or their internal assimilation, into the African American population already there.

What transpired in this melding between older and newer components was a process of commingling of blood and of communal, experiential, and religious ties. Its first manifestation appeared in the high level of racial consciousness noted by contemporary academic and lay observers in abundance.[19] As to intraracial relations, the ability of African Americans to coalesce into a kind of highly conscious whole, based on shared cultural proclivities, produced a level of collaboration in reaching a collective goal of racial progress so that by the 1920s, great progress in political, business, and cultural matters resulted in the emergence of Chicago's Black Metropolis. It is nowadays a historical model used to examine and understand all large urban concentrations.

It has been written that the bulk of the migrants came to the city from the Africanized folk culture of the rural South where the daily round was timed by what one eminent anthropologist has called "the great clocks of the sky," and where the yearly rhythm of life was set by the cultivation of cotton and sugarcane. Their first task was to adjust themselves to a modern industrial city, in which they substituted the clock for the sun and the discipline of the factory for that of the agricultural cycle. It meant, too, an adjustment to a complex world with a wide variety of associations and churches, and a multitude of recreational outlets and new opportunities in industry, business, and politics.

Fortunately for later generations, the character of this ever-expanding mass of humanity was explored in the exhaustive 1927–1928 work of renowned sociologist E. Franklin Frazier who examined all dimensions of group life through data for the census year 1920, along with acute observation and interpersonal contacts. Frazier's contribution on family life as it existed in its various dimensions of class, occupation, age, residence, and marital status throughout the city resulted in his first tome, *The Negro Family in Chicago*, published shortly after the decade ended.[20] Decades later, historian Herbert G. Gutman, in his study of the

black family in slavery and freedom, established that the social integrity overall of the migrating family to the North possessed the needed resiliency to remain intact and functional.[21]

The Great Migration significantly provided the key components of demographic mass, melding all segments of the latter into a unified group, and group consciousness, qualifying as *necessary conditions* for and collectively establishing the foundation for the emergence of Chicago's black-controlled enclave, the Black Metropolis. The arrival of the migrants supplied the potential to provide the synergy needed to propel black Chicago along toward its dream of black control over and independence within its own residential and commercial district. That confluence depended on a high level of cooperation and amiability between different groups of African Americans with varying degrees of cultural affinity and within variegated stages of assimilation into American mainstream life.

Previously in Chicago, in the sphere of employment, opportunities were always limited. Not unexpectedly, African Americans predominated in domestic and personal service. Old Settlers, with a tendency to romanticize the premigration period, consistently minimized the extent of the job discrimination before the war. That it was a reality, however, is evident from examination of the few careful studies that are available for that period, including an investigation in 1913 by the Juvenile Protective Association. In its *The Colored People of Chicago*, there is the reference to "the tendency of the employers who use colored persons at all in their business to assign them to the most menial labor." It was asserted that "the colored laborer is continually driven to lower kinds of occupation which are gradually being discarded by the white man." Likewise, the larger corporations were accused of refusing to employ African Americans.

Noted sociologist Charles S. Johnson noted a difference in attitudes among African Americans toward these employment restrictions. "The Negroes who had come to Chicago [during the period of the Great Migration] as a rule were satisfied with conditions at work, including hours, wages, and treatment. Among the Negroes who had lived in Chicago for a longer period the most insistent complaint was lack of opportunities for advancement or promotion."[22]

Some migrants were to be found among the ranks of the Pullman porters, joining black Chicagoans of longer residency now as one of the two largest labor groups among blacks. According to the first formal account of the porters, written by historian Brailsford R. Brazeal, the passage of time had already phased out the first wave of workers along with their thinking about work and their externally as-signed status. Through the following years, the ranks of the Pullman porters absorbed a new wave of workers who were more assertive and willing to challenge authority and their status. Such a generational difference implied a vari-ance in mindset toward both work and race relations. In the white mind, especially in the eyes of the transnational railroad-riding public, where sometimes the only interracial contact most whites had with blacks existed, the white perception served as the only valid image of these workers and of all African Americans. While the original generation of porters might have acquiesced emphatically to the racist whims of a manipulative company as well as the white public in general, this new breed in the early 20th century accepted the demands of their employment status more begrudgingly and with a steady eye to self-transformation.[23] Where the newest migrants stood in terms of acquiescence or assertiveness is conjectural, but by the 1920s they would encounter the aggres-sive recruiting campaign of the militant Brotherhood of Sleeping Car Porters with Chicago as a hub of that union's activism.

Beyond the thousands of Pullman porters and other workers in the service field, within the new industrial-labor sphere, the southern migrants reacted enthusiastically to the eco-nomic opportunities and the freer atmosphere of the North. Circumstantially, Carter G. Woodson observed that "the present migra-tion differs from others in that the Negro has opportunity awaiting him…whereas formerly it was necessary for him to make a place for himself upon arriving among enemies." As Chicago resident and journalistic observer Claude A. Barnett wrote specifically of Chicago, "[the Great Migration] *brought* Colored work-ers north in large numbers to invade fields that were new to them" (emphasis added).[24]

It was stated that while most labor unions did not refuse to accept African American members, some consistently denied work oppor-tunities to African Americans after they had accepted their initiation fees and dues. These charges were thoroughly documented, and the conclusion was drawn that African Americans were gradually being "crowded into undesira-ble and underpaid occupations."[25] Historian James R. Grossman has explained that this refusal by whites to accept blacks into union brotherhood led to marked black resistance.[26]

If ever a limited span of time warranted labeling as an epoch, it was the years 1916 through 1918 and up to the end of 1919. Significantly, the occupational as well as social statuses of African American men and women underwent transformation as they moved from the do-mestic and service spheres into the industrial domain. In becoming an industrial proletariat for the first time of their lengthy settlement in Chicago, their demographic invisibility faded into competitive notoriety. Chicago, city of "Big Shoulders, Hog Butcher for The World," now included more African Americans among its ranks than ever before in its short history. Racial consciousness and a thirst for a change in status grew among these black Chicagoans who quickly acclimated themselves to their new environment, the transformed attitudes of their kin, and the invigorating New Negro thinking.

While the city's first black industrial prole-tariat was composed mainly of the rural un-skilled, their ranks also contained a smattering of urbanized, skilled, and professional groups, along with some children. Previously Pullman porters in the service sector constituted 20 percent of the male workforce and proved a dominant social force in black Chicago. Now in this succeeding period, packinghouse workers constituted 25 percent of that labor constituency in that industrial arena. Also, the Great Migration not only provided northern factories with needed labor, but also germinated animosities that led to increased racial tension between whites and blacks as job placement, housing, recreational space, and political choice became flashpoints for conflict. However, it also provided the races an opportunity to work together in a milieu in which labor peace produced a larger black union membership than ever before as well as economic advancement. Residential areas where racial harmony existed, it was due to the minimal residential footprint left by blacks. An awareness also existed on the part of city government, especially in the Health and Police Departments, indicating that policy changes were underway that would improve the lives of all of the city's citizenry. Recognition that such policies had to be developed and implemented was a positive step forward. While blacks and whites conflicted over recreational space, both races enjoyed the spectacle of baseball as produced by the all-black Chicago American Giants, and high school sports still pitted skilled athletes of both races in competition. For the litmus test of interracial harmony and progress to be met in Chicago, the city would have to experience a cessation in residential bombings, school-level tensions, personal assaults, clashes at military training camps, and job conflicts.

Competition over housing led to tensions between the races, but also the development of a sense of territorial prerogative among blacks that produced the Black Metropolis of the 1920s. Just as other non–Anglo-Saxon newcomers to the city sought solace and revitalization of their familiar cultural moorings by establishing their enclaves—Polonia for the Poles, Little Italy, the Maxwell Street colony for eastern European Jews, Chinatown, the Irish in Bridgeport, the Swedes in Andersonville. The Chicago

Race Riot of 1919 was one consequence of ethnic and racial jockeying for desirable space with violence and tragic deaths serving as a combined means to protect one's turf. This major racial confrontation resulted in thirty-eight fatalities (twenty-five were black; thirteen were white), hundreds of injuries, and thousands of dollars of property damage. A maladministration of justice followed until the black community asserted itself, bringing both white and black perpetrators of mayhem and violence forward to account for their offenses. As devastating as the event was, it established among blacks a sense of worth in having protected themselves against white assault in a manner found to be impossible in the South, while solidifying a higher level of group solidarity that was manifested in politics, business, and purpose.[27]

The migrants' entry into the Black Belt within a period of ten years swelled the membership of all existing organizations to the bursting point. Olivet Baptist Church could claim a membership of 10,000 members, making it perhaps the largest Protestant church in the nation. As groups of migrants found their congenial intellectual and social levels, old organizations accepted new members; additional units of older associations and churches were formed; and new types of organizations came into being. Old social patterns, too, were often modified by the migrants who brought their southern customs. Leaders sometimes had to shift their appeals and techniques to deal with the newcomers. New leaders poured up from the South to both challenge and supplement or attempt to supplant the indigenous leadership. The migrants found a functioning political machine in the Black Belt that welcomed their participation as well. From the South, where they were disfranchised, they came to a community where the African American vote was not only permitted but actually cultivated as the First Congressional District of Illinois soon gained a reputation as the most effectively run Republican political unit in the nation.[28]

THE CONSEQUENCES OF THE GREAT MIGRATION

The remarkable demographic increase in the African American population of Chicago in 1910–1920 of 148.5 percent and 1916–1919 of 86 percent was matched in significance by the increase in population from 109,458 persons in 1920 to 233,903 persons in 1930. In and of itself, Jazz Age migration represented an increase of 114 percent over the 1920s. Whenever a demographic milepost was reached during the 20th century, it now indicated an almost automatic increase. Reductions in the labor force added to a national recession at the war's end, affecting the employment status of black workers adversely, but not demographic increase.

In 1921, the population had climbed to 121,902 as the magnetism of life in Chicago continued to beckon black southerners. By 1923, the increase resulted in 146,791 of old and new black residents. Some black newcomers expressed the sentiment that Chicago offered them a hope not found elsewhere or under any other circumstances. One man responded resolutely when confronted with high joblessness in Chicago, "I also know that there is no work in Mississippi, and I had rather be out of work in Chicago than out of work in Mississippi."[29]

The Great Migration was highly consequential in that it returned the American problem of race to a national scale, the first since the nation relieved itself of the burden of slavery during the post-Revolutionary period. It produced a major transformation within the national labor force in that the newly formed industrial proletariat of post–Civil War days took on diverse color tones for the first time. The Great Migration established the foundation of Chicago's African American industrial working class as well. The comments of Chicago communist spokesman Harry Haywood during the Depression emphasized the character of the workforce "Chicago is one of most industrial cities for blacks."[30] Thousands of black workers, some with industrial experience, had entered a sector of Chicago's economy that had been virtually closed to blacks previously.

And, contrary to popular belief that supposed that all migrants arrived penniless, the Great Migration brought some persons with disposable income, along with their furniture and other household belongings. Their presence increased the business base, aiding in the emergence of Black Wall Street and expanding the level of consumerism at a time of reported national prosperity.[31] In Chicago it heightened political participation to a level where the black electorate became an important cog in Republican Party politics, and in later days, within the Democratic Party, laying the groundwork for the election of the first black congressman in the 20th century, along with the first black female senator and first African American president.

DISCUSSION OF THE LITERATURE

The literature of the period 1935–1950 influenced perspectives on what had been a signal event in the nation's history. Writers within the Chicago School of Sociology at the University of Chicago took the lead in examining the impact of migration and subsequently influenced other forms of scholarship, and even literature. The late Robert Bone noted that this was significant because literary figures "wrote repeatedly of the Great Migration, and of the transformation that it wrought in the black community. They wrote of the pathology that was too often the price of adjustment to the urban scene. And they celebrated the common folk of Bronzeville as they accommodated to the conditions of urban life."[32] Most notable among the scholarship was St. Clair Drake and Horace R. Cayton's *Black Metropolis*, published in 1945. It assumed the status of a tome, and its influence is still cited as the model of urban life.[33]

While the 1960s had witnessed the fascination of social scientists and lay writers with the black community emerging as one big "Negro Ghetto," an environment lacking solutions to its problems, a different view was presented through new research by St. Clair Drake. Many of the Great Migration's sojourners had produced families that constituted the core of black Chicago's expanding middle class and elite. The renowned scholar was able to show another side of black life as he updated *Black Metropolis* beginning in 1961, and again in 1969.[34]

Additional historiographical influences from the 1960s, and extending into the 1990s, made a dramatic impact as well. Under the influences of the literary and scholarly discovery of the "Negro Ghetto," coupled with the continued migration northward of black southerners and the widespread urban rebellions, the "Great Migration" was now repositioned as part of the "Great Black Migration" or the "Second Great Migration" extending from World War II until the Vietnam War era.[35] Emanating from the print and electronic media as well as scholarly circles, a process of remolding unfolded, at times challenging the relevance of the existential accounts of the World War I exodus. With the nation's awareness of the formally recognized "ghetto," lay writers imagined it in their unfolding answer to change in the racial demographics of their day. This was the case, particularly in the North's large urban centers. What had been a short yet explosive burst of demographic transformation during the First World War among one of the nation's most noticed, yet maligned, ethnic/racial groups now was envisioned as a continuous surge covering roughly five decades.

Among scholars, historian James R. Grossman explored the features of pre–Great Migration migrants and those of the First World War-time flood in terms that explained more clearly changed circumstances, indigenous southern motivations, and localized initiatives.[36]

And, although 1992 brought the most incisive scholarly treatment of migration to Chicago, detailed in Grossman's *Land of Hope*, journalists likewise developed a new take on the migratory urge. They expanded it past World War II into the 1960s. Beginning with *Atlantic Monthly* writer Nicholas Lemann's *The Promised Land: The Great Black Migration and How It Changed America* (1992) and subsequently with Isabell Wilkerson's *The Warmth of Other Suns*, the Great Migration now became a half-century phenomenon.

Lemann's *The Promised Land* focused on the mechanization of the South's economy that acted as a major push factor, propelling blacks northward. Although newer and more efficient mechanization partially explained the migratory urge, the resurgent pull factor of global war likewise acted to produce greater job opportunities and better pay in the North. This increase in economic advantages continued until globalization resulted in de-industrialization during the 1960s. In combination, centripetal and centrifugal forces accounted for the migration of six and a half million black people from the South to the North between 1910 and 1970, with five million migrating after the mechanization of cotton production and global conflict.

Another comprehensive as well as salutary treatment followed with Isabel Wilkerson's *The Warmth of Other Suns*, appearing in print in 2014. This insightful, alternative view resulted from her research into her family's quest for identity as former migrants. Wilkerson added a more humanizing dimension to the story of World War II migration up to the present, in which both the horrors of the South and the disappointments and challenges found in the North were illuminated.

PRIMARY SOURCES

Binder, Carroll. *Chicago and the New Negro*. Chicago: The Chicago Daily News, 1927.

Du Bois, W. E. B. "Colored Chicago." *The Crisis* 10 (September 1915): 234–242.

De Koven Bowen, Louise. *The Colored People of Chicago*. Chicago: The Juvenile Protective Association 1913.

E. Franklin Frazier, "Chicago: A Cross-Section of Negro Life." *Opportunity* 7 (March 1929): 70–73.

Johnson, Charles S., and Chicago Commission on Race Relations. *The Negro in Chicago*. Chicago: University of Chicago Press, 1922.

Johnson, Charles S. "These Colored United States, Illinois: Home of the Migrant Mob." *Messenger* 5 (1923): 926–928, 933.

Sandburg, Carl. *The Chicago Race Riots*. New York: Harcourt, Brace and Howe, 1919.

Scott, Emmett J. "Letters of Negro Migrants of 1916–1918." *Journal of Negro History* 4 (July 1919): 290–340.

Scott, Emmett J. "More Letters of Negro Migrants of 1916–1918." *Journal of Negro History* 4 (October 1919): 412–465.

Scott, Emmett J. *Negro Migration during the War*. New York: Oxford University Press, 1920.

Woodson, Carter G. *A Century of Negro Migration*. Washington, DC: The Association for the Study of Negro Life and History, Inc., 1918.

SUPPLEMENTARY SOURCES

Drake, St. Clair. *Churches and Voluntary Associations in the Chicago Negro Community*. Chicago: Work Projects Administration, 1940.

Drake, St. Clair, and Horace R. Cayton. *Black Metropolis: A Study of Negro Life in a Northern City*. New York: Harcourt, Brace and World, 1945.

Frazier, E. Franklin. *The Negro Family in Chicago*. Chicago: University of Chicago Press, 1932.

Henri, Florette. *Black Migration, 1900–1920*. Garden City, NY: Anchor Press, 1975. http://dcc.newberry.org/collections/chicago-and-the-great-migration.

Lemann, Nicholas. *The Promised Land: The Great Black Migration and How It Changed America*. New York: Alfred A. Knopf, 1991.

Marks, Carol. *Farewell—We're Good and Gone: The Great Black Migration*. Bloomington: Indiana University Press, 1989.

Reed, Christopher Robert. *The Rise of Chicago's Black Metropolis, 1920–1929*. Urbana: University of Illinois Press, 2011.

Sernett, Milton C. *Bound for the Promised Land: African American Religion and the Great Migration*. Durham, NC: Duke University Press, 1997.

Strickland, Arvarh E. *History of The Chicago Urban League*. Urbana: University of Illinois Press, 1967.

Trotter Joe William, Jr., ed. *The Great Migration in Historical Perspective*. Bloomington: Indiana University Press, 1991.

Tuttle, William M., Jr. *Race Riot: Chicago in the Red Summer of 1919*. New York: Atheneum, 1972.

Wilkerson, Isabel. *The Warmth of Other Suns: The Epic Story of America's Great Migration*. New York: Random House, 2011.

FURTHER READING

Baldwin, Davarian L. *Chicago's New Negroes: Modernity, the Great Migration, and Black Urban Life*. Chapel Hill: University of North Carolina Press, 2007.

Bone, Robert. "Richard Wright and the Chicago Renaissance." *Callaloo* Issue 28 (Special summer issue 1986): 452.

Chatelain, Marcia. *South Side Girls: Growing Up in the Great Migration*. Durham, NC: Duke University Press, 2016.

Binder, Carroll. *Chicago and the New Negro*. Chicago: The Chicago Daily News, 1927.

Du Bois, William Edward Burghardt. "Colored Chicago." *The Crisis* 10 (September 1915): 234–242.

De Koven Bowen, Louise. *The Colored People of Chicago*. Chicago: The Juvenile Protective Association 1913.

Drake, St. Clair. *Churches and Voluntary Associations in the Chicago Negro Community*. Chicago: Work Projects Administration, 1940.

Drake, St. Clair, and Horace R. Cayton. *Black Metropolis: A Study of Negro Life in a Northern City*. New York: Harcourt, Brace and World, 1945.

Frazier, E. Franklin. *The Negro Family in Chicago*. Chicago: University of Chicago Press, 1932.

Frazier, E. Franklin. "Chicago: A Cross-section of Negro Life." *Opportunity* 7 (March 1929): 70–73.

Gregory, James N. "The Second Great Migration: An Overview." In *Africa American Urban History Since World War II*. Edited by Kenneth L. Kusmer and Joe Trotter, 19–38. Chicago: University of Chicago Press, 2009.

Gregory, James N. *The Southern Diaspora: How the Great Migration of Black and White Southerners Transformed America*. Chapel Hill: University of North Carolina Press, 2005.

Grossman, James R. *Land of Hope: Chicago, Black Southerners, and the Great Migration*. Chicago: University of Chicago Press, 1989.

Gutman, Herbert G. *The Black Family in Slavery and Freedom, 1750–1925*. New York: Pantheon Books, 1975.

Johnson, Charles S., and Chicago Commission on Race Relations. *The Negro in Chicago*. Chicago: University of Chicago Press, 1922.

Johnson, Charles S. "These Colored United States, Illinois: Home of the Migrant Mob." *Messenger* 5 (1923): 926–928, 933.

Lemann, Nicholas. *The Promised Land: The Great Black Migration and How It Changed America*. New York: Alfred A. Knopf, 1991.

Litwack, Leon F. *Trouble in Mind: Black Southerners in The Age of Jim Crow.* New York: Alfred A. Knopf, 1998.

Reed, Christopher Robert. *Knock at the Door of Opportunity: Black Migration to Chicago, 1900–1919.* Carbondale: Southern Illinois University Press, 2014.

Scott, Emmett J. "Letters of Negro Migrants of 1916–1918." *Journal of Negro History* 4 (July 1919): 290–340.

Scott, Emmett J. "More Letters of Negro Migrants of 1916–1918." *Journal of Negro History* 4 (October 1919): 412–465.

Scott, Emmett J. *Negro Migration during the War.* New York: Oxford University Press, 1920.

Spear, Allan H. *Black Chicago: The Making of a Negro Ghetto.* Chicago: University of Chicago Press, 1967.

Strickland, Arvarh E. *History of the Chicago Urban League.* Urbana: University of Illinois Press, 1967.

Wilkerson, Isabel. *The Warmth of Other Suns: The Epic Story of America's Great Migration.* New York: Random House, 2011.

Woodson, Carter G. *A Century of Negro Migration.* Washington, DC: The Association for the Study of Negro Life and History, Inc., 1918.

NOTES

1. Noted historian David Levering Lewis refers to the phenomenon as "The Great Black Migration" in the endorsements section for Isabel Wilkerson, *The Warmth of Other Suns: The Epic Story of America's Great Migration* (New York: Random House, 2011), n.p. To James N. Gregory, it is "The Second Great Migration," in *Africa American Urban History Since World War II*, eds. Kenneth L. Kusmer and Joe Trotter (Chicago: University of Chicago Press, 2009), 19.

2. Carter G. Woodson, *A Century of Negro Migration* (Washington, DC: The Association for the Study of Negro Life and History, Inc., 1918), 174; and Claude A. Barnett, "We Win a Place in Industry," *Opportunity* 6 (March 1929): 82.

3. W. E. B. Du Bois, "Colored Chicago," *The Crisis,* September 1915: 234–242.

4. Leon F. Litwack, *Trouble in Mind: Black Southerners in The Age of Jim Crow* (New York: Alfred A. Knopf, 1998), esp. 149–116.

5. Herbert Gutman, *The Black Family in Slavery and Freedom, 1775–1925* (New York: Pantheon, 1974), xxi, 465.

6. Julius Rosenwald to A. Clement McNeal, December 26, 1919, Julius Rosenwald Papers, Special Collections and Archives, Regenstein Library, University of Chicago.

7. "Tribute," March 30, 1931, Irene McCoy Gaines Papers, Special Collections, Chicago History Museum.

8. Charles S. Johnson, "The Frontage on American Life," in *The New Negro*, ed. Alain Locke (New York: Boni and Sons, 1925), 285.

9. Leone Bennett Jr., *Before the Mayflower: A History of Black America* (Chicago: Johnson, 1982), 344.

10. See contemporary documentation found in Emmett J. Scott, "Letters of Negro Migrants of 1916–1918," *Journal of Negro History* 4 (July 1919): 290–340; and Scott, "More Letters of Negro Migrants of 1916–1918," *Journal of Negro History* 4 (October 1919): 412–465.

11. Sylvia Woods, "If I Had Known Then What I Know Now," in *The Black Women in the Middle West Project: A Comprehensive Resource Guide*, eds. Darlene Clark Hine et al. (Indianapolis: The Black Women in the Middle West Project, 1985), 21.

12. Emmett C. Scott, *Negro Migration during the War* (New York: Oxford University Press, 1920).

13. See Scott, *Negro Migration during the War*, 6; and James R. Grossman, *Land of Hope: Chicago, Black Southerners, and the Great Migration* (Chicago: University of Chicago Press, 1989).

14. Du Bois, *The Souls of Black Folk* (New York: Alfred A. Knopf, 1976), 110. Had Du Bois been writing about Chicago's Black Belt and its satellite communities instead of Georgia's Black Belt, he well might have added their many achievements, despite adversity. Major, contemporary, highly informative documentation is to be found in Scott, "Letters of Negro Migrants of 1916–1918" and "More Letters of Negro Migrants of 1916–1918," along with Scott, *Negro Migration during The War*.

15. Christopher Robert Reed, *Knock at the Door of Opportunity: Black Migration to Chicago, 1910–1919* (Carbondale: Southern Illinois University press, 2014), 224.

16. St. Clair Drake and Horace R. Cayton, *Black Metropolis: A Study of Negro Life in a Northern City* (New York: Harcourt, Brace and World, 1945), 825, and reference to the 1953 Mayor's Commission on Human Relations, 24.

17. Drake and Cayton, *Black Metropolis*, 75.

18. St. Clair Drake, *Churches and Voluntary Associations in the Chicago Negro Community* (Chicago: Work

Projects Administration, 1940), 136, 137. See also E. Franklin Frazier, "Chicago: A Cross-Section of Negro Life," *Opportunity* 7 (March 1929): 70–73.

19. Charles S. Johnson, E. Franklin Frazier, Carroll Binder, Frederick H. H. Robb, Ralph J. Bunche, and George F. Robinson Jr. were all impressed with this phenomenon, to echo its relevance and influence throughout the decade of the 1920s. While a University of Chicago doctoral candidate, E. Franklin Frazier was completing his 1929 study entitled *The Negro Family in Chicago* (later appearing in book form as *The Negro Family in Chicago* [Chicago: University of Chicago Press, 1932]), *Chicago Daily News* journalist Carroll Binder published a pamphlet exploring black life in the city as *The Negro in Chicago* (Chicago: Chicago Daily News, 1927). A decade later, Frazier continued his examination of the nexus between occupation and class in "Occupational Classes of Negroes in Cities," *American Journal of Sociology* 35 (March 1930): 718–738.

20. Frazier further expanded his work beyond Chicago into other northern cities and published *The Negro Family in the United States* in 1939. Both as a detached scholar mingling freely among the populace and as a participant-observer, Frazier matched the abilities of University of Chicago scholars who preceded him—Monroe Nathan Work, Richard R. Wright Jr., and Charles S. Johnson. While studying the history of the formation of the black community with its many complexities, a valuable and more accurate history of a socially and economically differentiated group within a *community* was being uncovered, although its internal dynamics were generally overlooked in the latter part of the 20th century.

21. Gutman, *The Black Family in Slavery and Freedom*, xxi, 465.

22. Charles S. Johnson and Chicago Commission on Race Relations, *The Negro in Chicago* (Chicago: University of Chicago Press, 1922), 387.

23. See Litwack, *Trouble in Mind: Black Southerners in The Age of Jim Crow*, esp. 149–163.

24. Woodson, *A Century of Negro Migration*, 174; and Barnett, "We Win a Place in Industry," 82.

25. De Koven Bowen, *The Colored People of Chicago* (Chicago: The Juvenile Protective Association 1913), n.p.

26. James R. Grossman, "The White Man's Union: The Great Migration and the Resonance of Race and Class in Chicago," in *The Great Migration in*

Historical Perspective, ed. Joe William Trotter Jr. (Bloomington: Indiana University Press, 1991), 85.

27. See Johnson and Chicago Commission on Race Relations, *The Negro in Chicago*; Carl Sandburg, *The Chicago Race Riots* (New York: Harcourt, Brace and Howe, 1919); Drake and Cayton, *Black Metropolis*; William M. Tuttle Jr., *Race Riot: Chicago in the Red Summer of 1919* (New York: Atheneum, 1972); and Reed, *Knock at the Door of Opportunity* and *The Chicago NAACP and the Rise of Black Professional Leadership, 1910–1966* (Bloomington: Indiana University Press, 1997).

28. Reed, *Knock at the Door of Opportunity: Black Migration to Chicago*, 190.

29. Arvarh E. Strickland, *History of the Chicago Urban League* (Urbana: University of Illinois Press, 1967), 72.

30. Harry Haywood, *Black Bolshevik: Autobiography of an Afro-American Communist* (Chicago: Liberator Press, 1978), 442.

31. Binder, *Chicago and the New Negro* (Chicago: The Chicago Daily News, 1927), 11.

32. Robert Bone, "Richard Wright," *Callaloo* (Summer 1986): 452.

33. There are limits to the interpretations and presentation of Black Metropolis that stem from its being written from a sociological perspective; a contradictory and much more detailed perspective is offered from the historical ranks. See Christopher Robert Reed, *The Rise of Chicago's Black Metropolis, 1920–1929* (Urbana: University of Illinois Press, 2011).

34. See the new preface, postscript, and appendix of the Harper Torchbook editions (1962 and 1969) of Drake and Cayton, *Black Metropolis*. As valuable as the original data in the 1945 edition are, the information from the 1960s is of immense scholarly value to see the changes wrought by both time and African American agency.

35. See note 1.

36. Grossman, *Land of Hope*. See also Binder, *Chicago and the New Negro*; De Koven Bowen, *The Colored People of Chicago*; Johnson and Chicago Commission on Race Relations, *The Negro in Chicago*; Drake and Cayton, *Black Metropolis*; Frazier, "Chicago: A Cross-Section of Negro Life," 70–73, and *The Negro Family in the United States* (Chicago: University of Chicago, 1939).

Christopher R. Reed

WHITE INTERNAL MIGRATION TO AMERICAN CITIES, 1940–1970

"Migration," historian James N. Gregory writes,

> is one of the great forces of history. When people move in large numbers, they sometimes rearrange not only their own lives but also the places they leave and the places they settle. Migration can rebalance economies, reorganize politics, transform cultures. Migrations across oceans and borders have continually reshaped the United States. Internal migrations have been at times nearly as significant.

Gregory identifies the period between 1930 and 1970, roughly corresponding with the time focus of this essay, as "the golden age of migration research."[1]

And so it is with the millions of white Americans who contemplated, and then acted upon, a move to urban areas between 1940 and 1980. Although this article focuses on white Americans, Euro-American internal migration often involved similarities with other Americans who made the United States during this time increasingly urban and decreasingly rural. African Americans, for example, continued to move out of the South during the mid-20th century, for reasons and directions that typified both their own experiences, desires, and agency.[2]

MORE URBAN, MORE SUBURBAN, AND EVENTUALLY MORE UNEQUAL AND WESTERN AND SOUTHERN

Any high-altitude view of internal migration during this period begins with rural people becoming urban people, as rural dwellers were long kept in place by chronic implicit and explicit systemic forces—from low wages to disfranchisement to low mobility through education. The Great Depression was but the last impediment to people who lived in rural places in the South,

the Southwest, and the Plains leaving those places. And as World War II mobilization sent soldiers abroad, the war simultaneously attracted women as well as men to defense areas that produced unprecedented war matériel. Beginning in the 1950s, white Americans were still becoming less rural, but rather than increasingly urban, it was more correct to label them suburban—all, of course, due to the way race in America was playing out mid-century.[3] All kinds of discriminatory mechanisms ensured that suburbia became home to white people, with people of color increasingly confined, upon their own internal migrations, to cities. The result was incredible growth in suburbia: from 22 million living in those areas in 1940 to triple that number in 1970.[4] And when paired with stagnant wage growth after 1980, such migrations in the mid-20th century only portended the rising inequality in the 21st century.

Sheer numbers tell this story. In 1910, 28 percent of the American population was metropolitan; by 2000, it was at 80 percent. But after mid-century, suburbs, not urban parts of metropolitan areas, were the real areas of growth. And by the dawn of the 21st century, half of the American population resided in suburbs. Rural states overall, including North Dakota, Arkansas, Mississippi, Oklahoma, West Virginia, and South Dakota, lost the most population between 1940 and 1980.[5]

The second image from this vista involves the increasing migration to the West. The Census Bureau, making sense of the century's population change at the millennium, noted that the West grew faster than the Northeast, Midwest, and South in every decade of the 20th century. Nine western states, plus Florida, were the ten fastest-growing states in the first half of the 20th century, and eight western states, plus Florida and Texas, were the ten fastest in the last half. California was the fastest-growing state in the first half of the century; Nevada outpaced it in the second half.[6] Spurred by development strategies, federal investment in infrastructure, and defense and military bases, the West during this time exploded with population.

With the continued oxidation and decline of the Rust Belt, a surprising reversal occurred, constituting the third trend: the ascendancy of what came to be known as the Sunbelt. "The Sunbelt reversal caught demographers by surprise in the 1970s," Gregory writes, "but it should not have. Demographers seemed more interested in the out-migrations from the South rather than the ways southern areas were making investments that stood ready to recruit industries and of course people."[7] By the 1980s, the South was the new place to move to, replacing the West for that title for the first time. By century's end, the country went from 62 percent of the population living in the Northeast and Midwest in 1900 to 58 percent living in the South and the West in 2000.[8] Truly, Americans during this period kept population analysts busy, and in the process they remade American rural, urban, and suburban spaces.

Take, for example, the University of Wisconsin's fascinating website that visually and interactively makes meaning from internal migrations in the United States, all based on net migration (http://www.netmigration.wisc .edu/). Regarding the white net migration rate for 1950 nationally, for example, one overwhelmingly sees vast sections of the country, from coast to coast, exhibit negative net migration rates. Many of these are rural areas. On the other end of the spectrum, however, are areas where rates are positive, anywhere from 5 to 20 or more net migrants per 100 people. These appear in interesting trends. First is the Southwest, in which large areas of California, Arizona, and Nevada see influxes of people. Southern California mushroomed with people during this time, as did Clark County, Nevada. A second area of significance is virtually all of Florida, especially south of a line between Tampa and Jacksonville. A third area is the mid-Atlantic corridor, which extends up from Maryland and throughout New Jersey. Finally, there is the regional destination of midwestern states, especially urban industrial areas: Milwaukee; Chicago; northern Indiana and Indianapolis; Cincinnati, Columbus, and Cleveland; and southwestern Michigan and Detroit. The data suggest how the urban and industrial Midwest was a prime area for rural people looking for work, though it did not remain so for long. Finally, metropolitan areas throughout the country, from Seattle to St. Louis to Houston to Boston, increased their populations.[9]

The 1980s map still reveals that large areas of the country—centered in rural areas— suffered population declines. And significant areas of positive net migration continue in and around San Francisco and Los Angeles, Arizona, and Nevada. Metropolitan areas of Seattle and Denver figure prominently, along with the Texas triangle of San Antonio/Austin, Dallas–Fort Worth, and Houston. Florida—almost the entire state—is a growth area, along with Nashville, Atlanta, Raleigh, and northern Virginia. By the 1980s, the Sunbelt migration was clearly visible.[10]

These big trends, however, ignore some of the more nuanced stories of internal migration of white people between 1940 and 1980. The Sunbelt indeed arose late in this era and was an enormous attraction to internal migrants. But between 1940 and 1970, before the rise of the region, 8 million whites left the South for other areas.[11] And while demography often seems to involve horse-racing metaphors of the fastest and the slowest in terms of growth, it should be noted that fastest is not always unquestionably good. Environmental impacts were costly in places such as Phoenix and Houston—indeed, in every large urban area at mid-century. And in former agricultural and in deindustrialized areas, too, there were impacts from shrinking populations—environmental, economic, political, for sure, but also social. What did it mean to individual and community psyches to remain in an area that saw people leaving?[12]

Jim Gregory reminds us that while economic motives for migration were prime, other incentives encouraged movement to a new place. College degree attainment uprooted people throughout the country. World War II brought new mobility options for women as well as men initiated by World War II that continued throughout the period. Increasing transportation options appeared with an expanding car culture that created highways and, ultimately, suburbs. By 1980, 39 percent of Americans lived outside the state of their birth.[13]

WORLD WAR II AND THE LOOSENING OF PLACE

As with most large-scale wars, tremendous social change resulted, and World War II was exemplary for the changes it prompted, especially in migration. The war induced hordes of people to enlist in the armed forces or to travel to manufacturing centers where myriad products supported the Allied cause abroad. Although plenty of destinations were in the traditional industrial centers in the Midwest and East, new destinations emerged in the West and laid the foundation for things migratory to come. Millions of men and women left home to move to areas of labor shortage during the war. And, of course, millions were sent to Europe, Africa, and the Pacific to fight. If lucky enough to survive, many soldiers saw life differently, for the war and its aftermath—notably the GI Bill that made them attractive to universities and employers—introduced them to a new life filled with many more places in which to live and work.

This period was classic economic opportunity joined with patriotic cause. For those unable to enlist, great money was to be made, and many reasoned they would answer the call of industry, working temporarily and then returning home with their savings, perhaps making a down payment on some land for those still hopeful of an agrarian future. Other migrants during this time looked forward and rarely backward at the places of residence left behind.

If new arrivals failed to obtain assembly line or other manufacturing jobs, they often found work in construction—building new factories, housing, and roads. The mammoth Willow Run plant near Detroit, for example, with a projected employment of sixty thousand, attracted many job seekers. Even by 1941, estimates placed the in-migration rate in Detroit at more than seventy-five thousand, prompting housing shortages.[14]

A Works Progress Administration (WPA) student of predominantly white workers and their dependents in Detroit found a large number from "Appalachia" during this time. The statistics painted a picture of the migrant job seeker to Detroit: average distance traveled was 340 miles; 41 percent were from rural areas; 21 percent were last involved in agriculture; 68 percent were in Detroit for the first time; 10 percent were unemployed; more than 50 percent were alone (and thus not yet a burden on local schools); and approximately 33 percent lived in a separate dwelling, more than 50 percent doubled up with others, and 10 percent resided in trailers and motels.[15]

Because the South was especially an area of labor surplus, manufacturers advertised in southern newspapers to lure whites away from home. "ASSIST THE WAR EFFORT! TO WIN THE WAR OUR BOYS NEED EQUIPMENT," a Michigan employer advertised in the *Nashville Tennessean*. Melvin Proffitt, himself a migrant during the time, recalled that "in World War II the works picked up in Dayton, Cincinnati, and everywhere, and people just moved off and left this country."[16]

Jim Hammittee, the oldest of thirteen children, was born on Christmas Day in 1916 in eastern Kentucky's Bell County and was one of thousands who answered such calls. He went to work in a coal mine at age sixteen to help support the large family. "I worked in a coal mine until nineteen and forty-two," he said. "At that time World War II had broken out," and "Detroit, Michigan, was calling for help in the war plants. I left the hills of Kentucky to try working in war plants." He continued, summarizing a classic wartime experience of many white southerners if not white migrants nationwide:

I arrived in Detroit in July of forty-two and found employment in the east side of Detroit in a roller bearing plant. My wife went with me. At that time we had two small children which we left with my mother. . . . We found employment and a place to live, then we brought the two kids along. I immediately like my work, decided I'd stay till the war was over.

When I first came there, we only planned to stay till the war was over and then we's moving back South, back home—cause it was hard to adjust to living in Detroit, living in the big city after being used to a mountain life, and a small town was such a drastic change, it was hard to adjust to. So to make ourselves feel comfortable, well, we'll go back home as soon as the war's over. So it was either work there or go into the service. We decided to stay with it. But by the time the war's over in 1945, we had pretty well decided to stay with it. We had pretty well adjusted and accepted that way of life as the way we wanted to live. So we settled down in the city for another five years. Then we decided it was time we bought a home, so we went out in the suburbs (at that time if was farm section) bought property, and started building a home.[17]

Packing up and moving is never easy. Many encountered hostility, as Hammittee recalled, touching on the racialization that was a part of white migration.

Surprisingly, in the North, I don't think public opinion was like this, but the southern whites working in the northern plants with southern blacks, I should say at that time, there was very little problem. In my opinion, it was the northern people prejudiced to the blacks. In my honest opinion, the southern white was only just one step ahead of the blacks as far as the northern people was concerned when I went there, and I felt this real deep, because we suffered a lot by being from the South. I'm talking about for the schools and in public places where you spoke with a Southern accent; I never felt comfortable for a lot of years. I worked hard at overcoming it and ignoring the slurs or gigs. . . . The schools were overcrowded. I felt that our kids were going to a good school but all at once they were overcrowded so they wanted to put kids in another school which they had to go by bus, and it upset a whole lot of people. But the only kids that had to transfer and go to another school by bus was southern people. I spoke my piece to the school principal, but she let it roll right over; she didn't do anything about it. Such licks as this hurt real deep, took a long time to get over.

Others disagreed with Hammittee about southern white attitudes toward African Americans. On June 20, 1943, in Detroit, a two-day race riot began, and ultimately twenty African Americans were killed. After the calm ensued, southern white migrants were linked to the cause of the riot that began at Belle Isle Park.[18]

Hammittee often got jobs in Detroit for his siblings, which fueled further out-migration. Bringing family northward had the effect of easing the dislocation of migrating.

This seemed to be one of the worst things of southern people going north. We's so close in our relation with each other; it was just hard to separate yourself from the family, and going north was one of the worst difficulties you can imagine. Pulling yourself away from the family, you know, church on Sundays, Sunday dinner at one of the houses, and visits two or three times a week, or doing it all the time. I lived in a mining community where I could see my grandmother daily, half-dozen uncles, aunts, and when you move out away from that, moving to a strange city, it was really hard to adjust to.[19]

Emma Martin left for Nashville, Tennessee, to be a domestic while her fiancé was abroad. Before long, she quit her seven-day-a-week babysitting job to work at a nearby Du Pont rayon plant in 1943. She said she was given a "man's job" because she was so strong. "In the spinning room," she said, "I had to do cake wrapping, they called it. But before that I was in the room [that] was really hot and really steamy and stinky. And I would lift like fifty pounds at a time all day long. This was a man's work—a man's job. Men's jobs is what I did." Eventually, she and her husband settled in Indianapolis.[20]

The historical record is peppered with such revealing responses because of this massive internal migration. For example, by the mid-1950s, nearly three thousand people born in Cocke County, Tennessee, deep in the Smoky Mountains, had settled in Cleveland, Ohio. Jack Shepherd, who edited Cocke County's *Plain-Talk Tribune*, said that he had more than four hundred subscribers who were living in Cleveland who "pass the paper around for other Cocke families up there." One Lorain Avenue furniture store in Cleveland ran advertisements in the Tennessee paper simply to reach migrants in Ohio.[21]

THE POSTWAR INTERNAL MIGRATION

If internal migration during World War II helped win the war effort, that same internal migration after the war stimulated unprecedented economic expansion. Take Adolph Lacy, for example, who was born and raised in Cleburne County, Arkansas, in the north-central part of the state. During the war, he and his siblings moved with their parents to southwestern Michigan to pick fruit there. The migratory push came from Arkansas's diminishing timber stock, and along with farming, these were the only options to earn money. In Michigan, the Lacys were housed in little "huts"; chicken coops and cow pens were common homes for the workers. Seven years later, Adolph, now married with two children, went back to Michigan, to Benton Harbor, lured by the giant Whirlpool plant there. "This is the God's truth," he said, "I had thirty-seven dollars and a half in my pocket. I had two pairs of blue overalls, two blue denim shirts, and my

underwear." His wife Jemae Lacy had made them out of "VC Fertilizer" sacks. "It had the *V.C.* still on the hip back there," he said. After a two-and-a-half-day journey to Michigan, he had a job by week's end making venetian blinds and making $1.04 an hour. It was his first factory job. In the evening, he picked fruit with his parents, who had returned, for 75 cents an hour. Even with parents nearby, he said, "I got so homesick I thought I couldn't stay there. But I didn't have no other choice." Later in the year, his wife and children joined him. After a layoff and several frustrated factory stints, he finally got his dream job at Whirlpool a year later.[22]

Vast areas of the Great Plains, like most regions of the country during the 1950s and 1960s, were involved in this great migration. Along with the rest of the country, population densities declined in rural areas and increased in urban ones. Since at least the 1920s, if not before in some areas, life had been difficult for rural people scattered across the Plains, a combination of both economics—particularly low prices—and the environment—periods of hot, dry weather. These two factors were always a push to leave. Only in the 1940s, however, did people begin moving due to the pull of prosperity beyond, particularly in defense plants. After the war, though, researchers noted that people continued to abandon rural areas for urban areas in or near the region. Visualizations of migration during the mid-century show the losses and gains in this region. Rural areas emptied, while urban areas grew, sometimes by massive numbers, such as in Denver and Houston.[23]

Census data complement these visualizations. The population of twelve Plains states (Montana, Wyoming, the Dakotas, Minnesota, Iowa, Nebraska, Kansas, Colorado, Oklahoma, Texas, and New Mexico) grew by 16 percent during the 1950s, but nearly all of this growth was concentrated in metropolitan areas, which grew by 33 percent. Rural counties lost more than 128,000 people. "The exodus of young adults was particularly severe," one source noted. "Rural areas lost more than 229,000 twenty- to twenty-nine-year-olds between 1950 and 1960, or 44 percent of the age group. Because this age group produces most of the children, the out-migration had significant demographic implications and represented a substantial loss of human capital."[24]

By 1960, a little more than four in ten people lived in rural areas; by 2000, that figure dropped to 28 percent. Colorado grew by more than 400,000 people in the 1950s, mostly in and around Denver, while eastern counties lost population. "While the rural population declined by 231,000 in the 1960s," Kenneth Johnson noted, "the urban population grew by 668,000. . . . By the end of the 1960s the population residing in metropolitan areas of the Great Plains exceeded that in rural areas for the first time in history."[25]

By the 1960s, some of the migration signals were sufficiently strong that they would foreshadow the continued trends well into the 21st century. White population growth was significant in all regions except the North Central states (Dakotas, Nebraska, Kansas, Minnesota, Iowa, Missouri, Wisconsin, Illinois, Michigan, Indiana, and Ohio) and New England. In fact, all twelve North Central states experienced more white out-migration than in-migration, which was significant, and the East North Central states (Wisconsin, Illinois, Michigan, Indiana, and Ohio) had the greatest losses. Apparently, such population declines were the early signs of economic problems in the Midwest.[26] Meanwhile, California was the major recipient of white migrants, experiencing almost a net million increase between 1960 and 1963 alone. Florida was a distant second with a 410,000 net increase. A study during this time noted that "the direction of white migration has also been reversed in a number of southern and southwestern States, from relatively heavy losses during the 1950s to modest gains in the early 1960s."[27]

Florida, along with California, had plenty of mid-century migration manifestations. In 1900, Florida had one of the smallest populations east of the Mississippi. By 2000, however, the state had a population of 16 million, making it the fourth largest in the nation. Compared to decadal growth rates averaging 10–20 percent for the United States, during the 20th century Florida had growth rates between 20 and 80 percent each decade. Only California outpaced Florida in net migration growth during the forty years of this essay.[28]

Amid all the quantitative data and the metaphors of gain and loss, there are the human stories of difficult decisions about whether to stay or go, second-guessing after a decision was made, the difficulty of packing up and starting over in a new place, and, later in life, reflections about achievements, regrets, and what the home of origin might be like decades later. Amid many of these narratives is a feeling of satisfaction in finding the economic opportunity one was seeking.

Lucille Clardy, for example, was born and raised in Waterloo, Alabama, on the Tennessee River. The daughter of farmers, she decided to leave behind her boyfriend, Joe, and light out for new territory in northern Indiana, where her older sister had moved. Ostensibly, Lucille moved to babysit her nieces and nephews, but she soon grew weary of no wages and found a paid job babysitting for seven dollars a week. "I thought I was getting rich," she said. Then she found a car hop job at a local drive-in and was making fifteen cents an hour plus tips—well more than $15 a week. After marrying Joe, she worked at a factory that employed a number of women, many of whom were migrants from the South, and she more than doubled her salary again. Eventually, she worked at Studebaker and began at $1.15 an hour.[29]

Will Pennington had a similar story of being amazed at economic success through migration. He was raised in Clay County, in Appalachian Kentucky, and remembered his citified relative returning home to Kentucky as a youngster.

When they left they left with nothing. They left with a bag with practically nothing in it, they caught a bus to the city, and when they came back he was driving his own car, he had a nice suit on, and he had *money*. That's the thing about it: he had money. He would pull out money, give it to his mom [and say], Go down and get you this. And surely the other people were envious of him to an extent. They'd say, Well, if he can do it, I can do it; he's got more than I've got. Like I say, it was a treat to go out with him, because he'd stop at a store and buy you an ice cream. You just didn't have money to buy ice cream. When I was coming up I remember the most money I ever had until I was twelve years old. I used to trap animals and sell the hides, and that's where I used to make my money, because I never got any money from the tobacco, we never got any money from that. The kids didn't. You'd get a pair of shoes or some clothing, or one little toy for Christmas or something like that, an apple or an orange, or something like that, but you never got any money. I liked to hunt so I trapped, and I trapped a big old opossum. This guy gave me a dollar and a quarter for it. I will never forget that, I kept that dollar for a long, long time. Spent the quarter, but kept the dollar. That was the most money I ever had in my life. It's things like that. Then one person goes and another person went and like I said, finally six out of eight of the members of the family are in the city [Cincinnati] now.[30]

UPSIDE DOWN: WEST, SOUTH, AND METROPOLITAN

For decades, at least since the 1920s when immigration was curtailed by Congress, the South and the West were akin to "colonies" that supplied excess population to fuel industry and manufacturing in the North and the East.[31] In the second half of the 20th century, this trend turned upside down, trending more and more toward the South and the West, which continued well after 1980.[32] A second trend during this time was what the Census Bureau termed the "metropolitanization" of the country. Before 1940, the Bureau noted,

80 percent of Americans lived outside metropolitan areas; by 2000, the rate flipped, with 80 percent living in metro areas. To be even more specific, the metropolitan growth during the postwar era was a suburban growth—that is, the metropolitan population living outside of central cities.[33]

Major metropolitan areas such as Atlanta, Austin, Charlotte, Dallas–Fort Worth, Denver, Houston, Las Vegas, Los Angeles, Miami, Phoenix, Raleigh-Durham, northern Virginia, San Diego, and San Jose come to mind as 21st-century economic opportunity magnets that attract millennials and other internal migrants, not to mention those from beyond US borders. These areas, however, were not "born" as innovation hubs; rather, they were made. Elizabeth Tandy Shermer argues that what came to be the Sunbelt was "once a distinct region, which included those southern and southwestern metropolises that transcended their region's old commodity-based economies and traditional power structures." This transcendence, she notes, along with industrial flight, "transformed the entire country." The Steelbelt rusted while the Sunbelt grew.[34]

Even amid growing metropolitan centers firing economic growth, however, the same unevenness in terms of equality from earlier periods of internal migration continued to typify later migration. "Over the past twenty-five years," one scholar wrote in the late 1980s, "industrial recruiters, politicians, and businessmen have sung the praises of the South as a region of bountiful opportunity. They have pointed with pride to the number of new manufacturing and service jobs that have led the South to the forefront of industrial development. Cheap land, tax abatements of one kind or another, a low wage structure, an unorganized labor force, and a host of other state- and locally sponsored incentives are part and parcel of the 'good business climate' that is deemed necessary and sufficient to develop the South." Per capita income in the South was growing fast, to be sure. In 1960, it was 60 percent of the national average, and almost 90 percent by 1980. And while poverty declined, still almost 11 million southerners, according to Thomas A. Lyson, were living in poverty, making up more than 40 percent of poor people nationwide.[35]

Low incomes, persistent poverty, low educational attainment, and racial inequality continued to characterize the Sunbelt even amid such explosive growth. Thomas Lyson wrote eloquently to remind readers of reality versus marketing in the South:

The South as portrayed in the mass media and hyped by assorted industrial recruiters and frontmen, however, is neither as homogeneous nor as prosperous as it is made out to be. Below the veneer of aggregate statistics and projections and away from the gleeming [sic] and growing sunbelt cities, there is another South. It is a South checkered with places that are best characterized by their slow growth, declining industries, and static or falling standard of living. And it is a South populated by persons who have remained relatively untouched by the growth and prosperity that improved the quality of life for many, but not all, of the region's residents. It is found in the "black belt" counties that divide the Piedmont from the Atlantic Coast, that line the Gulf Coast and that cluster along both banks of the Mississippi River. It exists in the mountain counties of Appalachia. It can be found in the remote nonmetropolitan counties of the Ozarks.

It is, he says, the "other side of the sunbelt." This story has only grown more acute since. One of the most important challenges has been incentives, which Lyson writes "have been offered to any and all comers to the region without any regard for the long-term consequences of an industrial mix that could in fact impede the ability of the South finally to close the longstanding social and economic gaps with the rest of the nation."[36]

Phoenix and Las Vegas in many ways typified Sunbelt growth, made possible by widespread air conditioning to comfort newcomers and interstate highways that made migration even easier. More than 700 firms moved to or opened in and around Phoenix, for example, in the two decades following World War II, laying the groundwork for population growth well beyond the 1960s. Local elites transformed Phoenix's traditional economy into one focused on "high-tech consumer electronics, defense production, and research and development, new investment that sparked a population increase from 65,000 in 1940 to 440,000 in 1960." By 2015, Phoenix was the nation's fifth-largest city.[37] In Las Vegas, a combination of tourism and defense work attracted internal migrants beginning in the 1950s, but by the late 1960s, the Las Vegas metropolitan area was gaining more than 1,000 new residents each month. Again, such development often overlooked, for example, the underside of poverty and struggle, even in boomtowns. Not to be forgotten, for example, were "the day labor collection points that daily take over the parking lots of the many home improvement megastores" throughout Phoenix.[38]

By the end of the period in discussion, internal migration slowed. Why is up to debate, but James Gregory points to several potential reasons, from dual-wage households that make it more difficult to leave for another area and the decline of manufacturing. "One argument," he notes,

is that migration has become less necessary precisely because of the great migrations of the twentieth century. Regions are more alike now in social, cultural, and also economic dimensions. Metropolitan areas often have reasonably similar economies and occupational distributions, so that opportunities that once required a long-distance move can now be found within commuting distance of home.[39]

Regardless, the period between 1940 and 1980 resulted in dislocation and relocation of white Americans, as well as many others, such as people of color, on a vast scale. An appropriate metaphor seems to be *tectonic*.

DISCUSSION OF THE LITERATURE

Internal migration in the 20th century is an excellent topic to incorporate a variety of historical methods and sources for synthetic understanding. For example, quantitative historians and demographers have long used census data to interpret population changes. More recently, though, the Integrated Public Use Microdata Samples (IPUMS) reveal new insight into social and economic history. Data now are now available from all decennial censuses between 1790 and 2010. For more information, see the IPUMS USA website (https://usa.ipums.org/usa/). James N. Gregory was one of the early users of IPUMS data in an article published in the *Journal of American History*.[40]

Quantitative data, however, can come to life when complemented by qualitative research, particularly oral history. Chad Berry used both archival oral histories and new interviews for *Southern Migrants, Northern Exiles*. And rich oral history collections exist nationwide, particularly at collections from coast to coast. Together, quantitative and qualitative sources are giving a more complete understanding of the challenges and opportunities involved in internal migration.

FURTHER READING

Berry, Chad. *Southern Migrants, Northern Exiles*. Urbana: University of Illinois Press, 2000.

Cobb, James C. *The Selling of the South: The Southern Crusade for Industrial Development, 1936–90*. 2nd ed. Urbana: University of Illinois Press, 1993.

Ferrie, Joseph P. "Internal Migration." In *Historical Statistics of the United States, Earliest Times to the Present*, Millennial Edition, Vol. 1, Part A. Edited by Susan B. Carter et al., 1-489–1-494. New York: Cambridge University Press, 2006.

Gregory, James N. *The Southern Diaspora: How the Great Migrations of Black and White Southerners Transformed America*. Chapel Hill: University of North Carolina Press, 2005.

Klein, Herbert S. *A Population History of the United States*. 2nd ed. New York: Cambridge University Press, 2013.

Ruggles, Steven, Katie Genadek, Ronald Goeken, Josiah Grover, and Matthew Sobek. Integrated Public Use Microdata Series: Version 7.0 [dataset]. Minneapolis: University of Minnesota, 2017. https://dx.doi.org/10.18128/D010.V7.0.

Shermer, Elizabeth Tandy. *Sunbelt Capitalism: Phoenix and the Transformation of American Politics*. Philadelphia: University of Pennsylvania Press, 2013.

NOTES

1. James N. Gregory, "Internal Migration: Twentieth Century and Beyond," in *Oxford Encyclopedia of American Social History*, ed. Lynn Dumenil (New York: Oxord University Press, 2012), 540; James N. Gregory, "Paying Attention to Moving Americans: Migration Knowledge in the Age of Internal Migration," in *Migrants and Migration in Modern North America: Cross-Border Lives, Labor Markets, and Politics in Canada, the Caribbean, Mexico, and the United States*, ed. Dirk Hoerder and Nora Faires (Durham, NC: Duke University Press, 2011), 277; and see also Herbert S. Klein, *A Population History of the United States*, 2nd ed. (New York: Cambridge University Press, 2013).

2. James. N. Gregory, *The Southern Diaspora: How the Great Migrations of Black and White Southerners Transformed America* (Chapel Hill: University of North Carolina Press, 2005), 5; and Isabel Wilkerson, *The Warmth of Other Suns: The Epic Story of America's Great Migration* (New York: Random House, 2010).

3. See, for example, Thomas J. Sugrue, *The Origins of the Urban Crisis: Race and Inequality in Postwar Detroit* (Princeton, NJ: Princeton University Press, 1996); and Kevin M. Kruse and Thomas J. Sugrue, eds., *The New Suburban History* (Chicago: University of Chicago Press, 2006). See also Joseph P. Ferrie, "Internal Migration," in *Historical Statistics of the United States, Earliest Times to the Present*, Millennial Edition, Vol. 1, Part A, ed. Susan B. Carter et al. (New York: Cambridge University Press, 2006), 1-489–1-521.

4. Gregory, "Internal Migration," 541.
5. Frank Hobbs and Nicole Stoops, *Demographic Trends in the 20th Century: Census 2000 Special Reports* (Washington, DC: U.S. Census Bureau, 2002), 7, 25.
6. Hobbs and Stoops, *Demographic Trends.*
7. Gregory, "Internal Migration," 542.
8. Hobbs and Stoops, *Demographic Trends,* 7.
9. See "Net Migration Patterns for US Counties (http://www.netmigration.wisc.edu/)."
10. "Net Migration Patterns."
11. Gregory, "Internal Migration," 542; and Chad Berry, *Southern Migrants, Northern Exiles* (Urbana: University of Illinois Press, 2000).
12. See Ferrie, "Internal Migration," 489.
13. Gregory, "Internal Migration," 544, 540–541.
14. US Congress, House, Select Committee Investigating National Defense Migration, *National Defense Migration: Hearings,* 27:10290; US Congress, Senate, Special Committee Investigating the National Defense Program, *Investigation of the National Defense Program,* 22:5253–5254, 5270.
15. Amos H. Hawley, *The Population of Michigan, 1840 to 1960: An Analysis of Growth, Distribution, and Composition* (Ann Arbor: University of Michigan Press, 1949), 73–88, esp. 82.
16. *Nashville Tennessean,* July 18, June 22, 1942; Melvin Proffitt Interview, by Laurel Anderson, Hazel Green, KY, May 30, 1975, 18, Appalachian Oral History Project. For an example of the migration to the West, see Margaret Louise Cathey, "A Wartime Journey: From Ottumwa, Iowa, to the Richmond Shipyards, 1942," an oral history conducted in 1985 by Judith K. Dunning, Regional Oral History Office, the Bancroft Library, University of California, Berkeley, 1990.
17. Jim Hammittee, interview by Mary Thompson, November 23, 1974, Special Collections, Samford University Library, Birmingham, AL, 1.
18. Hammittee, interview by Thompson, 2–4; Alfred McClung Lee and Norman D. Humphrey, *Race Riot (Detroit, 1943)* (New York: Dryden, 1943), 91, 89.
19. Hammittee, interview by Thompson, 4.
20. Jesse and Emma Martin, interview by Chad Berry, Indianapolis, IN, December 7, 1993.
21. "Cocke County Boasts Scenery and Moonshine," clipping (from *Harlan Daily Enterprise*), Urban Migrant Project, folder 3, box 278, Records of the Council of the Southern Mountains, Southern Appalachian Archives, Hutchins Library, Berea College.
22. Adolph and Jemae Lacy, interview by Chad Berry, Mishawaka, IN, December 21, 1989.
23. Stephen J. Lavin, Fred M. Shelley, and J. Clark Archer, *Atlas of the Great Plains* (Lincoln: University of Nebraska Press, 2011), 90–91, 92–96.
24. Kenneth M. Johnson, "Rural-Urban Population Change," in *Encyclopedia of the Great Plains,* ed. David J. Wishart (Lincoln: University of Nebraska Press), 182.
25. Lavin, Shelley, and Archer, *Atlas of the Great Plains,* 91, 97; Johnson, "Rural-Urban Population Change," 182.
26. "Recent Patterns of Internal Migration in the United States," *International Migration Digest* 3, no. 1 (1966): 92.
27. "Recent Patterns."
28. Stanley K. Smith, "Florida Population Growth: Past, Present and Future," Bureau of Economic and Business Research, University of Florida, June 2005, 6. https://www.bebr.ufl.edu/sites/default/files/FloridaPop2005_0.pdf.
29. Joe and Lucille Clardy, interview by Chad Berry, South Bend, IN, December 22, 1989.
30. Will Pennington, interview by Laurel Anderson, Cincinnati, OH, September 27, 1975, Appalachia Oral History Project.
31. See Berry, *Southern Migrants, Northern Exiles.*
32. See Elizabeth Tandy Shermer, *Sunbelt Capitalism: Phoenix and the Transformation of American Politics* (Philadelphia: University of Pennsylvania Press, 2013), 9; and Hobbs and Stoops, *Demographic Trends in the 20th Century,* 9.
33. Hobbs and Stoops, *Demographic Trends in the 20th Century,* 9, 32.
34. Shermer, *Sunbelt Capitalism,* 10, 226.
35. Thomas A. Lyson, *Two Sides to the Sunbelt: The Growing Divergence Between the Rural and Urban South* (New York: Praeger, 1989), 1–2.
36. Lyson, *Two Sides,* 2, 5. See also Shirley Abbott, *Womenfolks: Growing Up Down South* (Boston: Mariner Books, 1983); Eve S. Weinbaum, *To Move a Mountain: Fighting the Global Economy in Appalachia* (New York: New Press, 2004); James C. Cobb, *The Selling of the South: The Southern Crusade for Industrial Development, 1936–90,* 2nd ed. (Urbana: University of Illinois Press, 1993); Bruce J. Schulman, *From Cotton Belt to Sunbelt: Federal Policy, Economic Development, and the Transformation of the South, 1938–1980* (Durham, NC: Duke University Press, 1994); and "State of the

South Archives (http://stateofthesouth.org/sos-archives/)" published by MDC.

37. Shermer, *Sunbelt Capitalism*, 2.

38. Eugene P. Moehring, *Resort City in the Sunbelt: Las Vegas, 1930–2000*, 2nd ed. (Reno: University of Nevada Press, 2000), 73, 107; Shermer, *Sunbelt Capitalism*, 2.

39. Gregory, "Internal Migration," 544.

40. James N. Gregory, "The Southern Diaspora and the Urban Dispossessed: Demonstrating the Census Public Use Microdata Samples," *Journal of American History* 82 (June 1995): 111–134.

Chad Berry

POLISH IMMIGRATION AND THE AMERICAN WORKING CLASS

The Polish American working-class community arrived in several waves on the shores of the United States. Working-class history is best understood when positioned within the wider social framework in which workers found themselves. Thus, working-class ethnic communities, including Polish working-class communities, were indeed amalgams of various social classes that nonetheless forged a sense of solidarity crucial to the working-class experience. What is the class difference between a store or tavern keeper or even an ethnic journalist and his or her neighbors? In America all knew that they were part of a working-class immigrant community. Even the Polish American clergy understood this reality. Events on both the shop floor and in Poland deeply impacted Polish American workers. Polish immigrants and their children knew that many unions originally discriminated against them and others from eastern and southern Europe, but nevertheless called for communal actions to defend their economic position. The history of Polonia—the Polish American community—is filled with examples of solidarity and communal action. This was rooted first in the Polish rural experience and transplanted to the industrial American milieu. These were not straw men and women, but active participants in their history. Despite assimilation and suburbanization, they created a working-class ethnic culture that still persists in many urban centers.

ORIGINS

Polish workers appeared in the British colonies as early as 1608, when several Polish skilled artisans arrived in Jamestown to help establish the glass, pitch and tar, and soap-making trades. Supposedly these Poles struck the colony in 1619 because they had been denied the same rights as Englishmen and could not vote for the House of Burgesses. This is supposedly the first labor action in American history. While the sources are not clear, a few Polish craftsmen were among the earliest colonists in British North America, and spotty evidence locates Polish inhabitants in colonial and early national America from the 18th century into the 1840s. However, the major arrival of Polish immigrants does not occur until just before the American Civil War. This largely economic migration, called in Polish *Za Chlebem* or "For Bread," shaped the Polish community, commonly referred to as Polonia, in the years before World War I. The great majority of immigrants from the Polish lands were peasants who fit into the category of unskilled workers in the United States. But the immigration also contained intellectuals, political exiles, and others who joined together with the majority in forming viable communities.[1]

Poles settled in rural areas as well as in industrial cities and coal towns. But the vast majority (estimates run up to 80 percent) of Polish workers lived in America's urban areas and mining centers. Chicago was home to the largest Polonia, but large communities gathered in Detroit, Cleveland, Pittsburgh, Buffalo, Milwaukee, and the New York–New Jersey area, among others. As the Industrial Revolution transformed America, its pull was felt throughout the Polish lands. These immigrants largely filled unskilled positions, although some worked as skilled workers or at small businesses. Poland, divided among three partitioning powers, Germany (Prussia), Austria-Hungary, and Russia, also went through changes as industrial capitalism expanded across Eastern Europe and the growing market economy changed longstanding historical relationships.

Beginning as early as 1854, Polish immigrants traveling from the German-occupied province of Silesia established the first permanent Polish settlement in Panna Maria, Texas. Shortly thereafter Poles began to arrive in the Midwest. The economic migration to America quickly expanded across Silesia, Poznania, and other parts of the German Partition. Many of these Poles spoke at least a little German, and they settled near German colonies in the United States. Between 1870 and 1900, more than two million Poles had permanently left the Polish lands in both a continental and overseas migration. As the migration to the United States progressed, Polish immigrants also arrived from the other two partitions. In the streets of industrial America, these sojourners met not only Poles from other parts of the Polish lands, but immigrants from across Europe and eventually those from other parts of the world as American industry's veracious appetite for workers transformed not only the United States but also Europe as well as parts of Asia in the 19th century. Although the numerical calculation of Polish immigration to the United States can be difficult to assess, both because Poles were often counted as citizens of Germany, Austria-Hungry, or Russia and because immigrants from Polish lands included large numbers of Lithuanians, Ukrainians, Germans, Jews, and others. Still, most historians argue that by 1910 some 3,000,000 Polish-speaking immigrants had arrived in the United States, most of them concentrated in the northern industrial states skirting the Great Lakes between the Atlantic coast and the Mississippi River.[2]

THE COMMUNAL RESPONSE/ EXTRA-COMMUNAL RESPONSE

The initial response of Polish immigrants to the new industrial-urban milieu in which they found themselves was inward. This communal response was vital to the creation of a sense of safety in the United States. Central to this was the formation of a Roman Catholic parish, which had played an essential role in Polish villages. It provided a pivotal institution around which others could revolve or respond to. It was thus natural that the formation of a parish proved to be essential in the new American settlements. The erection of a church gave Poles a sense of stability. Much more than simply a place of worship for Polonia, it provided social space and was thus indispensable for the eventual creation of a working-class public sphere in which various important economic, political, and ideological issues could be discussed and acted upon. Polish immigrants brought with them a fervent personal faith, yet with a strong sense of anticlericalism, especially if the church seemed to be opposed to what they saw as their economic interests.[3]

From the beginning, the erection of a Catholic parish was seen as an important although somewhat divisive affair. What did it mean to be a Pole in America? Even the question of who was a Pole revolved around the idea of parish. The old Polish-Lithuanian Commonwealth had included many different ethnicities. It also contained various religious groups besides Catholics. Protestants, Orthodox Christians, Jews, and even atheists all called Poland home. Before the rise of nationalism, these were all considered to be simply subjects of the Polish crown. By the end of the 19th century, they began to see themselves in another light. The growth of nationalism along with the introduction of industrial capitalism greatly altered the cultural and social landscape of the Polish lands. Emigration meant that these people even more than before began to define themselves as separate ethnic entities. What did it mean to be a Polish Jew in America? What did it mean to be a Polish-speaking socialist? All of this led to a bitter argument within the diaspora.

The question of *Polskość* or Polishness quickly manifested itself. The majority of the Catholic clerical leadership saw being Catholic as central to Polishness. Catholicism remained important for more secular leaders, but what really mattered was a devotion to the resurrection of the Polish state. For the secular group it did not matter if an immigrant was a Protestant, an Orthodox Christian, or a Jew, as long he or she believed in the idea of Poland. Thus, from the very beginning the immigrant community saw itself divided, and outsiders often saw the Polish diaspora as quarrelsome and hopelessly split into various warring factions.[4]

Perhaps surprisingly, given the potential religious tensions with the immigrant Polish community, the most immediate division occurred within the Catholic community, producing an independent parish movement that, in turn, eventually resulted in a schism within the Roman Catholic Church and the creation of the Polish National Catholic Church (PNCC). While the PNCC is usually traced to the Anthracite coal fields of Pennsylvania, its origins really lay across the entire Polish American community. The Independent Church Movement emerged after the Civil War in Polish Chicago and other Polonia centers largely over the issue of who actually owned the physical parish plant, the people or the diocese. It turned into a struggle between some Polish clerics and the Irish-dominated American hierarchy. The American Catholic Church was established in a way unfamiliar to many immigrants. This caused problems in various ethnic communities beyond Polonia, especially German Catholic parishes. Bishop Franciszek Hodur brought the issue to a head in 1898, resulting in the PNCC. Hodur had various connections to the socialist movement, and the PNCC has long been identified with the working class.

In many cases Polish American women played major roles in parishes and therefore were deeply involved in these conflicts. Women were seen as the keepers of tradition, especially of those traditions revolving around religious practices. While coming from a rural patriarchal society and entering an industrial patriarchal society, they still saw their roles expanded in the new urban setting. This gave them a good deal of power in the immigrant community and expanded their functions in Polish American society.[5]

Various female religious orders played an important role in the creation of this communal response. Nearly every Polish parish in the United States included a parochial school. Run largely by Polish sisterhoods, the schools faced a formidable task. When large-scale immigration to the United States took off in the 1890s, illiteracy still ruled much of the Polish countryside. As late as 1890, roughly 70 percent of the rural population in Russian-occupied Poland was illiterate. Among Polish immigrants to the United States arriving between 1901 and 1904, 27.4 percent were illiterate, a figure that rose to more than 32 percent by 1908. Sources estimated that roughly 35 percent of all members of the Polish American community were illiterate in 1900. Education would prove crucial to the children of these immigrants. Estimates saw the rate of illiteracy in Polonia drop to 3 percent in 1924 largely because of the Polish parochial school system. The schools passed on Polish history, culture, and traditions as well, even as they provided bridges to the larger American society. By 1918 the Polish Catholic community maintained 511 schools nationwide and taught 214,000 students.[6]

The immigrant drive to define Polishness also brought about the formation of competing fraternal groups. In 1873 clerical leaders and their allies formed the Polish Roman Catholic Union of America (PRCUA). Seven years later those espousing a more secular and nationalistic approach formed the Polish National Alliance (PNA). Both fraternals quickly spread to all of the Polish communities in the United States, joined by the Polish Women's Alliance (1898), the Polish Falcons (1887), and many others.

The Polish Women's Alliance (PWA) emerged in response to the refusal of the PNA and the PRCUA to accept women members or allow women to buy life insurance except through their husbands. Many Polish immigrant women arrived as young single women, and while many married shortly after their arrival, the purchase of death benefits was problematic. Born at the same time that the Progressive Movement emerged as a major social, political, and cultural force in society, the PWA embraced many of the goals of the reformers, especially those that revolved around women and children. Organizers saw the PWA as a feminist institution, and it vigorously supported such measures as women's rights and the education and protection of children. It campaigned against abusive husbands and also played an important role in the emerging Polish independence movement. The PWA and its newspaper, *Głos Polek* (*The Voice of Polish Women*), combined nationalism, ethnic solidarity, and the emancipation of women as its main goals. The organization also supported the labor movement and campaigned against the abuse of alcohol in the community, which it saw as a major influence on the abuse of women and children by men.[7]

These organizations provided a firm base for the diaspora and also provided valuable ties with the homeland. In addition, they attracted immigrant intellectuals, many of whom were interested in promoting Poland's resurrection as an independent state. This emphasis on Europe often gave the impression that the Polish community in the United States was a temporary one and that immigrants would return to the new Poland once independence was accomplished. Indeed, this was the view of the first leaders of the PNA. The PRCUA, on the other hand, felt that the immigration was largely permanent, and while the leadership hoped to promote a love and respect for Polish culture, the PRCUA emphasized maintaining Catholicism in the face of assimilation into a Protestant-dominated America. For the leadership of the PRCUA, only a Roman Catholic could be a Pole, whether in America or Europe. These different views sometimes resulted in violent conflict within the community, especially when it came to the organization of the primal institution in Polonia, a Catholic parish, arguments particularly common between the Civil War and the outbreak of the First World War.[8]

While the community seemed to be more concerned with internal issues and the fate of Poland than larger issues in the United States, the reality of living in America meant that the communal response was insufficient even when important and beneficial. Emigrating to the United States thrust Poles into a new urban-industrial milieu. This impacted gender roles, family life, and institutional life. Polish immigrant women usually arrived at a young age and found themselves free of the restriction of rural communal life. In Poland spouses were often picked by parents, especially fathers, and often through matchmakers. In the new American milieu, women found their choices expanded and could chose more freely with less familial interference. These young women therefore found they had more control over their own lives. Also once married they took on more responsibilities than at home in rural Poland. For one, the village tradition had a bride moving into her husband's family home and being subservient to his parents. In the United States, the married couple generally established their own households. Also in the new setting, men most likely worked away from home and were removed from the home for long periods of time. This meant that the tasks of dealing with financial matters and the discipline of children fell solely upon women. Suddenly, through immigration, women found themselves in a more independent position. Married women in America were also more aware of their rights. Unlike traditional practice in Poland, women in America who were abused by their husbands turned more quickly to the police and courts for aid. In turn women set up networks that aided them in the migration as traditional family resources such as grandparents, aunts, and cousins were no longer available. By surrounding themselves with other Polish women, they were able to navigate the new industrial state of affairs.[9]

Before 1914 the vast majority of unmarried Polish women in America worked outside the home. Roughly 20 percent continued to work after marriage. This to a degree resulted from the types of industry located in the various Polish American communities. It also resulted from working-class realities at the time. Often men did not earn enough wages to support their families. This resulted in women continuing to work and/or children working at an early age. Joseph Parot found that by 1900, 38.7 percent of Polish women employed in Chicago worked in the garment trades, 7.3 percent labored in laundries, and only 1.9 percent held professional positions, patterns that appear to have been common in other cities. Women made up roughly 20 percent of the labor force in Chicago's packinghouses around 1920, many of them Polish immigrant women.

The family remained an important economic unit in the United States as it had in rural Poland. Each member was to contribute to the family's survival. Often after marriage wives helped with finances by taking in boarders. These were often family members or *rodacy*, people from the same village or region. Many Poles considered themselves "birds of passage" who intended to return to the rural homeland and expand their family holdings. These single men often sought out places where they could board with a family member or neighbor from Poland. An estimated 50 percent of Polish households in Johnstown, Pennsylvania, took in boarders during the height of immigration. This number was repeated all across Polish America before World War I. The fact that all family members contributed to its survival also meant that children often went to work at an early age, as they had on Polish farms. The difference was, of course, that in America children often joined the industrial labor force.[10]

This environment, so different from the rural villages from which most Polish immigrants came, also meant that they were thrown into a modern multi-ethnic society. Polish peasants, now Polish American workers, labored along with people from somewhat European backgrounds and with large groups of people they did not know. The proliferation of immigrant groups from other parts of Europe, Asia, and Latin America as well as African American migrants from the American South complicated the picture. Industrial American cities proved to be hodgepodges of different and often rival ethnic and racial groups. This eventually called for an extra-communal response to working, living, and political conditions to establish control over the immigrants' own destiny.

The attempt to obtain agency took various forms, from labor unions and political parties to neighborhood organizations. Due to the realities of American urban industrial society, this meant reaching out beyond ethnic boundaries to other groups. Polish American workers found themselves immersed in multicultural settings. In Chicago's Stock Yard District, the Polish community, while large, was hardly dominant. In Brooklyn's Greenpoint neighborhood, Poles made up a large portion of the community, but they shared it with European immigrants including Irish, Germans, Jews, and others. This ethnic diversity proved, at first, to be a barrier to working-class solidarity, but eventually differences were overcome across industrial America. The same would be true for coal-mining towns like Lattimer, Pennsylvania, and small industrial areas such as New York Mills, in upstate New York.[11]

On September 10, 1897, striking workers marched on the mines in Lattimer and nearby Harwood. These company towns were like many others in the Anthracite district of Pennsylvania. Coal-mine owners brought in Polish, Italian, Slovak, and Lithuanian workers to diversify the predominantly English-speaking Irish, Welsh, and English workforce and fragment the union movement. Nevertheless, union miners organized the district. Polish women in particular played an important role in both instigating and sustaining the Lattimer strike. When a major confrontation led to the deaths of eighteen Lattimer miners, eleven were Polish, the remaining Slovak and Lithuanian.[12]

Such events reproduced themselves across industrial American in the 19th and early 20th centuries. Polish American workers often provided the most active strikers in labor actions across the country. They took part in the 1877 Railroad Strike, especially in Chicago. In both 1882 and 1885, they participated in the Cleveland Rolling Mill Strikes. Polish and Slavic strikers were directly involved in the Anthracite Strike of 1902, which firmly established the United Mine Workers in the nation's coal industry. They were active participants in the large strikes at McKees Rock, Pennsylvania, against the Pressed Steel Car Company (1909), and the 1912 Lawrence, Massachusetts, Textile Strike led by the radical Industrial Workers of the World (IWW). Polish Americans took part in the Paterson, New Jersey, silk strike (1913), also led by the IWW. In Bayonne, New Jersey, Polish workers predominated in the refinery industry. The 1915 strike met with violence, but the following year another strike brought higher wages and better benefits to the workers at Standard Oil. In Chicago Polish immigrants joined strikes in the stockyards and provided the backbone for the 1919 Steel Strike. All of these were multi-ethnic confrontations.

Poles and other immigrant workers were not the passive pawns of industrial capitalism as they were portrayed by many contemporary unionists, journalists, and academic observers. John R. Commons, the pro-union economist and labor historian at the University of Wisconsin at Madison, saw Slavs as too passive on the one hand and as too radical on the other, making them a threat to the American labor movement. Many American Federation of Labor (AFL) unions promoted anti-immigrant measures despite being led by Samuel Gompers, himself an English immigrant of Dutch Jewish descent. Gompers, of course, represented an older strain of immigrants whose unions saw the newer immigrants as competition for jobs and as undercutting wages.

Despite being stereotyped as un-organizable, Poles and other new immigrants flocked to unions. The Amalgamated Meat Cutters and Butcher Workmen eventually embraced the unskilled and in 1904 struck to increase their wages, thus breaking with previous AFL policies to primarily organize the skilled crafts. The United Mine Workers were among the first to recognize their importance. In 1912 the coal miners began publication of the weekly, *Gornik Polski* (The Polish Miner), to reach out to the Polish community.

Chicago, as the unofficial capital of the American Polonia, proved also to be a hotbed for labor organizations and confrontations. In 1919 the city and northwest Indiana became the focal point of the steel strike in which Polish workers played a crucial role. The strike had been preceded by a violent race riot the summer before, and both events helped to shape race relations in the city. Polish workers for the most part avoided the race riot, but as Polonia became more assimilated in the following years, America's racial hierarchy would shape its views.

During the 1921–1922 Packinghouse Strike, Polish American workers took part in what could only be called a communal strike enforcing loyalty to the union on the streets of the Back of the Yards neighborhood. By World War I, Chicago's Polish packinghouse workers had organized six Catholic parishes near the stockyards. These parishes provided a solid institutional base for the Stockyard Polonia. In addition, they provided a home for the fraternal organizations to further expand the institutional base. A December 1921 strike proved especially violent. Women played critical roles in these communal strikes. On December 8, mounted police confronted Polish women with babies in their arms at 44th and Marshfield Streets in Back of the Yards, beating them with batons. Striker supporters fired on police and pelted them with bricks as they made their way through the neighborhood.

Led largely by women, the entire neighborhood seemed to back the strikers and enforce loyalty to the union. Priests and local ethnic businessmen showed their support as did the families of strikers. When a strike breaker broke ranks with the union, mobs often gathered in front of their homes chanting "scab" and then attacking the building. Strike breakers and their families were often shunned by the community. Despite this solidarity, the realities of political and economic power doomed the strike, and unions disappeared from Chicago's meat industry for more than fifteen years. The fiercely activist roles played by women in these confrontations should not be underestimated.[13]

Often stereotyped as conservative peasants, Polish Americans actually played a large role in several radical organizations. Hardly passive workers, they joined unions and various socialist organizations especially in the period before World War I. Polish Chicagoans joined the International Working People's Association (IPWA), an anarchist group that advocated direct action in bringing about the collapse of the capitalist system. Poles, as well as their German and Czech neighbors, were often portrayed as communists in Chicago's English-language press. In Milwaukee Polish immigrants joined the Knights of Labor, and during Milwaukee's 1886 General Strike, the Wisconsin State Militia fired upon a predominantly Polish group of strikers at the Bay View steel rolling mill, killing seven strikers and injuring more.

In New York City, Polish radicals organized the *Związek Oddiallow Polskich* (ZOP) associated with the Socialist Labor Party. These Polish radicals convinced the Polish National Alliance to allow socialists to join the fraternal. In 1900 some Polish socialists left ZOP and started the Polish Socialist Alliance. After the Russian Revolution of 1905, others broke again from this group and in 1907 began publishing the Chicago socialist newspaper, *Dziennik Ludowy*. The next year they began the Polish Section within the Socialist Party

of America. By 1914 there were Polish socialist papers in five cities. Again events in Poland drew the attention of the Polish American left as Józef Pilsudski began his struggle for Polish independence, which was finally successful in November 1918.[14]

WORLD WAR I AND ITS AFTERMATH

The important focus on labor was not the only concern of the American Polonia. Many felt that the power maneuvers of the massive European empires would inevitably produce war in the new 20th century. Three of those empires, Russia, Germany, and Austria-Hungary, occupied the Polish lands. That war came in 1914, and the Polish American working class played a crucial role in the independence movement that resulted in the restoration of the Polish state. At first Polish American support came as funds to be raised for Polish Relief. After the American entrance into the war, however, Polish Americans raised a Polish Army to fight alongside the Allies on the Western Front. More than 24,000 Polish Americans joined the Blue Army, or Haller's Army, named for General Józef Haller von Hallenburg. The American Polonia also organized a group of nurses, the Gray Samaritans, who arrived in Poland to help deal with the postwar famine ravaging that country. Of course the Polish American working class also took part in the American Armed Forces during the war. Polish Americans volunteered and were drafted in numbers far exceeding those who joined the Polish Army. They also purchased Liberty Bonds at a very high rate in support of the war effort. So while the Polish American working class fought for its rights as labor unionists, it also supported both the ancestral homeland and the United States during the global conflict.[15]

After the war the nativist movement gained traction and in the 1920s Polonia found itself under political, social, and cultural attack. This assault on the community was part of the larger societal attack against immigrants in general. The publication of the US Congress's Dillingham Commission report in 1911 criticizing recently arrived immigrants and Madison Grant's 1916 book *The Passing of the Great Race*, which argued for "Nordic" racial superiority, set the parameters of the attack. Together, they facilitated the movement to restrict immigration resulting in the 1924 Immigration Act that greatly restricted immigration from eastern and southern Europe and Africa and banned immigration from Asia.[16]

These developments produced a protective stance within the American Polish community. In addition, those Polish Americans who returned to the newly established Polish state found themselves not as welcome as they had expected. They were often ignored or treated as outsiders. In turn the emigration began to use the phrase *Wychodźstwo dla Wychodźstwo* or "the Emigration for the Emigration" and to focus on its American setting. The pressures to assimilate or at least acculturate seemed to increase as a result of World War I as the community's sense of *Polskość* or Polishness seemed under attack.[17]

These questions haunted the community in the years between 1920 and the Great Depression. In fact, the institutional network of Polish parishes and parochial schools had hardly prevented acculturation into the larger American society. Traditionalists complained that the Polish language had been watered down with American words. This had been an old complaint, but it seemed more urgent now that immigration had been cut off by congressional fiat. Were Polish Americans in danger of losing their cultural heritage? Working-class Catholic parishes also felt pressure from the Irish-dominated Catholic hierarchy to become more American and to introduce English into schools and sermons. Almost ironically, the parochial schools acted as a means of assimilation for working-class children. The various orders of nuns, led by the Felician Sisters, an order founded in Poland and sent to the United States to aid the Polish immigrant population, acted as bridges to American society. The curriculum advanced assimilation in a nuanced way even while holding on to Polish Catholic cultural values.[18]

In addition, the American Polonia felt that it was being stereotyped by American intellectuals. William I. Thomas and Florian Znaniecki's monumental study *The Polish Peasant in Europe and America* caused consternation among ethnic leaders. While they were proud of Znaniecki's achievement, they worried about the two sociologists' conclusions concerning Polish American society. Thomas and Znaniecki pointed to the disruption caused in traditional Polish culture by the onset of capitalism in general and industrial capitalism in particular. Polish American families were portrayed as disintegrating and dysfunctional given the new urban industrial milieu in which they found themselves. Further sociological studies in the 1920s and early 1930s portrayed Polonia as a hotbed of juvenile delinquency and social disorder. Frederic M. Thrasher's *The Gang* (1927) and Clifford R. Shaw's *The Jack-Roller* (1930) further exposed the problem of out-of-control youth in Polonia. While neither Thrasher nor Shaw blamed juvenile delinquency on any ethnic culture, but instead on American urban social and economic realities, Polish Americans felt that they were being singled out. Polish American girls and young women as well as working-class males seemed to be pulling away from traditional mores. *Flaperki* (Flappers) became a concern as young Polish American women attended urban dance clubs and halls, many of which were of a mixed ethnic and even racial character.[19]

There could be no denying the problem of juvenile delinquency and street gangs in Polonia. It did not take a close reading of either the daily newspapers or the sociological literature to know that crime disturbed Polish immigrant settlements. Polish Americans played active roles in the street life of the city, adjusting to the gang cultures that had long developed in American working-class neighborhoods. Increasingly these children of immigrants became known as part of the city's underworld. Poles played important roles in the world of organized crime in the 1920s. Gangsters who had risen through the ranks of street gangs were problematic, but the fate of young boys and girls who often looked to these men as heroes was of even more concern. The outside world closely identified the Polish community with a high crime rate and juvenile gangs. In fact, as Thrasher and others noted, these areas had long harbored such activities even before large Polish populations had settled in them. The native born, Irish, German, and other Western European immigrant groups had all been involved in criminal activity.[20]

One response was the creation of Polish American welfare agencies designed to deal with juvenile delinquency, alcoholism, and domestic abuse. The organization of *Harcerstwo* groups (Polish Boy Scouts) and sports leagues by the large fraternal organizations also aimed at the youth problem. In a nod to the growing number of youth who did not have good Polish language skills, Polish American newspapers began to print sports sections in English. The Polish community looked inward to deal with what actually were multi-ethnic issues revolving around urban living and poverty. But the coming economic storm would force Polonia to look beyond its borders.

The economic crises triggered by the 1929 stock market crash decimated America's industrial immigrant and ethnic communities. Like other working-class Americans, Polish workers in America saw their savings and, in many cases, jobs disappear during the 1930s. In that decade an urge to organize swept all across the American Polonia and throughout much of the American working class. This organizational spirit took many forms, but the most important resulted in the revival of the American labor movement. Polish immigrants and their American-born children remained an important part of the industrial workforce. In addition, the Polish community had a large and intricate institutional base that could again be utilized to gain political and economic power. In particular, the urban

Democratic machines that dominated northern industrial cities saw Poles as important members of a growing Democratic coalition resulting from the Great Depression and the rise of Franklin Delano Roosevelt. This would prove to be true in Chicago, Detroit, Milwaukee, Cleveland, Pittsburgh, New York, and other cities, as well as in the coal towns across Pennsylvania, Illinois, and West Virginia. The Congress of Industrial Organizations (CIO) reached out to these communities as the labor movement strove to establish itself in the mass-production industries of auto making, meat packing, coal, and steel. Some 600,000 Polish Americans joined CIO unions in the 1930s, providing a large amount of working-class support in the Industrial Belt for this new organization.

In Detroit, Polish auto workers joined the CIO-led United Auto Workers (UAW) in droves, and Detroit's Polonia displayed substantial militancy. Polish radical leaders such as Stanley Nowak and Leo Krzycki played important roles in organizing workers for the CIO.[21] Polish American women, led by Mary Zuk, organized the Detroit Meat Strike in 1935. The strike spread across Detroit and even to other urban centers in the Midwest. It was the brainchild of the Committee Against the High Cost of Living, which began in the Polish-dominated suburb of Hamtramck. As the strike waned, its supporters organized a political movement, the People's League, which elected Zuk to the Hamtramck city council. Many of the other women in the league became union activists.[22] Polish Americans, now the children and grandchildren of immigrants, flocked to the unions in the 1930s and supported the Democratic Party. These two loyalties would last for at least three decades and in many cases longer. Everywhere Polonia responded to the call to organize labor during the Great Depression.

WORLD WAR II AND POLONIA

On September 1, 1939, just twenty years after regaining its independence, the Nazi German army invaded the Polish Republic. The American Polonia was shocked by the quick German advance and by the Soviet invasion of September 17, which basically ensured Poland's defeat. The eyes of Polonia again turned toward the homeland. Now Poland suffered yet another occupation, and Polonia felt it had to come to its aid. National Polish organizations immediately donated money for Polish war relief. The PNA offered $250,000 ($4,391,310 in 2016 dollars) immediately to help the beleaguered Poles. The largely working-class membership of the Polish fraternals happily donated funds to the national cause. A new organization, the Polish American Council (Rada Polonii Amerykanskiej or RPA), emerged to provide funds and clothing for the suffering Polish people. In 1942 the RPA was made eligible for funds coming through an agency of the US government. This furthered the work of the RPA to provide aid to Poles fighting in the West, Polish prisoners of war in Nazi-held territories, and Poles deported to Siberia by the Soviets. After the war the RPA gave aid to Polish displaced persons in Allied occupied Europe. It continued into the 1970s, providing assistance to Poles in Poland and to immigrants in the United States.

The Polish government in exile, first in France and then in London, hoped to raise an army in the United States as Polonia had during World War I. Polish Americans overwhelmingly turned away from this effort, and only about 1,000 volunteered to join the Polish army in the west. The failure of Polonia to recruit a second army was not surprising. While the Polish American working class, now largely American-born children of immigrants, would not fight for Poland, they would provide millions of dollars in relief to Poland's citizens impacted by the Nazi invasion.[23]

While the war brought Poland back to the center of the attention of Polonia, once the Japanese bombed Pearl Harbor, Polish Americans saw themselves caught up in the war effort of their adopted country. Polish American young men joined the United States Armed

Forces or were drafted in large numbers. Again the Polish American working class bought bonds and sent their children to war. Cities with large Polish populations led the war effort. Polish American workers labored in Detroit, Chicago, Milwaukee, Cleveland, Pittsburgh, and the Greater New York area to build the Arsenal of Democracy. Polish American servicemen found themselves fighting under the American flag across Europe, Africa, and the Pacific. Back home Polish American women, many who had always worked in industries vital to the war effort, now saw themselves as part of a greater struggle. Like all working-class communities, they took up the brunt of the fighting and work of creating a response to the war.[24]

The Soviet Union had been one of the invading powers in 1939, but Germany attacked Russia in the summer of 1941, and the USSR joined Poland's allies against the Nazis. This complicated the response both of the Polish government in exile and of Polish Americans. Radicals such as Nowak and Krzycki supported those who saw the Russians as valuable allies and postwar friends. Others, especially the leaders of the national fraternals, were leery of Russian objectives. In 1944 all of the major Polish organizations in the United States formed the Polish American Congress (PAC) to pursue the hope of a noncommunist, free, and independent Poland. The largest fraternal, the Polish National Alliance, dominated this umbrella organization, but it represented the voice of all of Polonia. In the postwar era PAC proved to be a loud voice of opposition to the communist regime imposed by the Soviets after 1945. The 1945 Yalta agreement between the allies recognized Poland and Eastern Europe as within the Soviet sphere of influence. Polish Americans saw this as a major betrayal, but military realities offered few alternatives.[25]

Polish American working-class men and women returning from the war had been part of a large movement of people, leading to further assimilation. The postwar years proved to be transformative for America's working class.

For the Polish American working class, it would be a period of change that would bring both positive and negative effects. The old neighborhoods would change under the pressures of a new urban American system that saw resources flow away from the traditional Industrial Belt to cities in the South and West.

THE POST–WORLD WAR II ERA

When Polish American GIs returned from Europe and the Pacific, they reentered their old neighborhoods with different attitudes. For one, they saw themselves as more American. The wartime experience had lessened their attachment to the old neighborhood and its institutions. Many veterans did return to live near their parents and families. But others joined the march to suburbia or migrated to cities in the West even if most remained in the working class.

The American city underwent rapid economic, racial, and social change in the thirty-year period following 1945. The urban centers of the 1960s were vastly different from those of the 1930s, and the history of Polonia reflected this change. Hispanics and blacks succeeded Polish Americans in inner-city neighborhoods. Large, once ethnically stable districts such as south Milwaukee, large swaths of Detroit and Buffalo, and even Chicago's "Polish Downtown" changed quickly and forever in the 1950s and 1960s. By the 1980s many old Polish churches offered Mass and other services in Spanish as well as Polish and English. Ethnic walls crumbled as the 1960s progressed. The question of how high these walls actually were to begin with is crucial in determining how great the fall was. Whether progress or trauma, the decline of inner-city Polish neighborhoods was real. The changes were not, however, simply racial or ethnic or even a matter of assimilation or acculturation. They were part of technological and economic transformations of the American city and the American working class, transformations that also changed the concept of ethnicity in American life.

The neighborhood system that seemed to stand so solidly in the 1950s had a long history. It was a creation of the technology that had made the American industrial city possible. To a large extent it was a system limited by the technology of 19th-century transportation, communication, and manufacturing. The industrial revolution that created the stockyards, steel mills, tanneries, and factories that provided the economic foundation for the working-class Polonia revolved around rails, telegraph lines, and steam engines. This technology created a very special kind of urban neighborhood that built on the traditions of the immediate pre-industrial past. Polonia grew up in this kind of neighborhood. The urban Polish community could gather its resources in time of strife because of its vivid rural village past. This communalism, when combined with the institutional wealth of the immigrant-ethnic community, led to neighborhood organizations, labor unions, and political power.

When the technological and therefore the economic base of these neighborhoods changed, the whole structure came tumbling down and gave birth to a new era. Polish and other ethnic Americans faced this painful transition first in the 1950s but then especially in the 1960s and 1970s. Jobs, housing, and schools had all revolved around this communal world. Blood and ethnic relations were the important connections. Polish peasant and other immigrants actively participated in change, but with a strong connection to their past. Ironically the system began to decay just as it provided a better life for Polonia's residents. As Poles reached out to form neighborhood organizations and labor unions during the 1930s, the seeds of change had been planted. Chicago's Hispanic and black minorities had already settled near Polish Americans, and Poles had already begun to move out along the major streets to secondary settlements. Second-generation Polish Americans started to buy single-family homes in outlying neighborhoods and suburbs. Chicago's Polish families left the Milwaukee-Division-Ashland area where they had lived since the turn of the century and made their way to Avondale and Jefferson Park. Polish families in Back of the Yards began moving west to the neighborhoods of Brighton Park, Gage Park, and beyond. Suburbanization was simply the logical outcome of these earlier movements.

While the automobile had long been a familiar sight on urban streets, it did not destroy the "walking-city" character of working-class neighborhoods until after World War II. The widespread introduction of automobiles in the 1950s ushered in the seeds of changes that undermined the traditional industrial city neighborhood. The car provided working-class families with mobility. They did not have to live near their places of employment. If they did, they no longer necessarily found it more convenient to work in nearby industrial plants. The automobile revolutionized the entire neighborhood system. The old communal system crumbled once postwar "boom" times allowed an unprecedented swath of consumers to purchase cars and suburban homes. Working-class Polish Americans, like other American ethnic groups, saw their options broadened by their newfound prosperity.

Technological change also came to the industries that Polish Americans had long relied on for employment. Deindustrialization transformed the core of cities such as Chicago, Detroit, Pittsburgh, Cleveland, and Milwaukee. Industries fled these cities for the suburbs or for the Sunbelt, and some eventually moved overseas. Polish Americans felt abandoned in their inner-city enclaves. Many also felt abandoned by the Democratic Party and began to support the Republican Party, as Reagan Democrats. The bond between the Democratic Party and Polonia, while not totally severed, began unraveling. Much of this was a result of the Civil Rights Movement in the 1950s and 1960s, and white working-class communities often felt these victories at their own expense. The Vietnam War also proved to be a tragic and divisive issue. Polish Americans, like other white ethnic working-class communities, felt that their concerns were ignored during the turbulent 1960s. Culturally this resulted in the revival of ethnic feeling in the 1970s and early 1980s. The "New Ethnicity" was largely driven by white ethnic elites. This largely conservative and reactionary movement saw Polish Americans and other white ethnic groups question their allegiances to the Democratic Party and the so-called liberal consensus established by Roosevelt's New Deal. More importantly, however, the era's disruptions led much of Polonia to vote first for Richard Nixon and then Ronald Reagan as the Republican Party began to make inroads in working-class white ethnic communities. As many as 53 percent of Polish Americans probably voted for Nixon in 1972. This trend continued for both Reagan and, later, George H. W. Bush.

Polonia itself was changing in many ways. The democratization of American higher education after 1945 had an impact on the Polish American working class. While college attendance by Polish Americans was rare before 1940, thirty years later the offspring of that generation attended universities in larger and larger numbers. Polish American attendance at Chicago-area medical, dental, and law schools jumped in the 1970 and 1980s. Sociologist Andrew Greeley pointed out that Polish Americans had made considerable gains in higher education in the postwar period. These new college and professional-school students often were children of second-generation working class Poles, and the overwhelming majority were first-generation college students. Polonia could no longer be called simply a working-class community. Yet despite these advances, that stereotype remained. The 1960s and 1970s also impacted on the growing number of Polish Americans attending graduate schools and saw the increased interest in the study of their ethnic group. [26]

The Polish American working class developed over time from an immigrant to an ethnic community. The various waves that transformed it over a more than 150-year history also reflected changes in Poland. The last two decades of the 20th century would see the election of a

Polish Pope, the rise of the Solidarity labor movement in Poland, and the fall of communism throughout Eastern Europe. For many Polish Americans, this meant the restoration of Polish independence. Yet more Polish immigrants came to the United States, although the great majority came from Poland's cities and were more educated than their predecessors. They would bring yet a different concept of Polishness to the American Polonia, sometimes entering the ranks of the working class, but eventually moving beyond it. They also would also clash with the older Polonia leadership, many of whom feared that the new arrivals were not "real" Poles, but Poles raised under the specter of communism, once again raising the question of Polishness.

For those immigrants and native-born Polish Americans who remained in the working class, the continued disruption by globalism of the industrial economy moved them deeper into the ranks of the Republican Party, and many supported the election of Donald J. Trump as president in 2016. William Ciosek, who had worked on the Reagan campaign, helped arrange a meeting with Donald Trump and the Polish National Alliance as well as the Polish American Congress during his presidential campaign. He stated that Trump "wouldn't win" without Polish American votes. Ciosek cited the popularity of Trump among Polish Americans in Michigan, Ohio, and Wisconsin, states Trump won narrowly with the help of the Polish American vote. Ciosek claimed that 15 percent of voters in Wisconsin were Polish-Americans and made up 10 percent of Michigan and Pennsylvania voters. Furthermore, Ciosek pointed out that even in Chicago most Polish Americans voted for Trump. By 2016, then, Polonia mirrored the fears of the American working and middle classes across the country.[27]

DISCUSSION OF THE LITERATURE

Much has been written on the Polish immigration to the United States and its peasant and working-class origins. This literature ranges from studies such as those done by the early 20th-century Polish American priest, historian, and activist Wacław Kruszka, to less formal but informative parish yearbooks, almanacs, and memoirs. Much of this early work must be considered filiopietistic in its celebration of the Polish accomplishment in the United States. These were often authored by amateur historians interested in the development of their ethnic group and its early struggles. Members of the large fraternal organizations as well as members of the Roman Catholic clergy, brotherhoods, and sisterhoods played an important role in this early historiography.[28]

The sociologists W. I. Thomas and Florian Znaniecki also contributed to the development of Polonia Studies with their monumental five-volume study, *The Polish Peasant in Europe and America* (1918–1921). This work helped to establish the Chicago School of Sociology and led to other such studies in the field. While sociologists looked at the Polish community in a scholarly manner, Polonia continued to put out various studies celebrating its growth. Many of these continued to be written by amateur historians and activists.[29]

Even as amateur historians continued to play an important role, the professionalization of the field took a giant leap with the arrival of Polish-born Miecislaus Haiman, who came to the United States in 1913. Haiman began as a journalist, but by the 1930s his interest in history dominated his writing, and he embarked on a study of Polish immigrants during the American Civil War. He would be the founding director of the Polish Museum and Archives of America (1937) and among the founders of the Polish American Historical Association in 1942. Haiman laid the groundwork for the study of Polonia through the medium of primary sources. Others, such as Detroit's Joseph A. Wytrwal, expanded the work of Haiman and contributed to the resurgence of Polonia studies in the 1960s and 1970s.[30]

At that time young scholars were drawn to Polonia studies. Many of these were first-generation college graduates who found their way into graduate school. Victor Greene's publication of *The Slavic Community on Strike* in 1968 proved to be an important turning point in the historiography of the Polish community in America. Many others followed including Edward Kantowicz's study of Polish politics in Chicago, Joseph Parot's work on Polish Catholics in that same city, and Greene's ongoing study of the immigrant experience and the Polish experience in particular. Major contributions were made to the field by a group of scholars connected with the Polish American Historical Association (PAHA) and its journal, *Polish American Studies* (*PAS*). These include M. B. Biskupski, Ewa Morawska, John Bukowczyk, Thaddeus and John Radziłowski, Mary Patrice Erdmans, Anna D. Jaroszyńska-Kirchmann, and many others The journal is a major source of information regarding Polonia studies. For years it was edited by James S. Pula, who besides writing many books on Polish American topics also edited the *Polish American Encyclopedia*, which appeared in 2011.[31]

Polonia studies has left its filiopietistic past behind and today is a major part of American immigration history. It is also a large field of study in Polish universities. Poland's oldest university, the Jagiellonian in Kraków, regularly publishes a journal, *Studya Migracyjne— Przegląd Polonynich,* which includes both Polish-language and English-language scholarship. It along with *PAS* and *The Polish Review*, a journal put out by the Polish Institute of Arts and Sciences in America, continues to add to the growing field. Jagiellonian scholars such as Adam Walaszek, Gregorz Babiński, and Dorota Praszałowicz have contributed mightily to the field. Historians from other universities such as Andrzej Brożek, Marcin Kula, Anna Mazurkiewicz, and Joanna Wojdon have made a major impact on the historiography of Polonia. Studies of the working class, institutions, and communities, and the importance of Polish Americans to the political and economic life of the United States play a considerable role in the historiography. Today the study of Polish immigration is a well-recognized field in both American and Polish history.[32]

PRIMARY SOURCES

There is a vast amount of resources available for the study of the Polish diaspora in the United States. The most obvious collection is located at the Polish Museum and Archives in Chicago. Other Chicago depositories also hold valuable collections concerning Polonia. The best way to see a list of these is through the Chicago Collections Consortium Website. This site lists major academic collections in the Chicago area. The website maintained by the Polish Institute of Arts and Sciences in America is also a valuable resource for searching nationally. Other important collections are located at the Immigration History Research Center at the University of Minnesota in Minneapolis, which holds the Polish American Collection including over 4,000 monographs written by Polish immigrants, 500 newspaper and serial titles published by Polish organizations, and roughly 650 linear feet of unpublished records and documents from Polish American organizations and private papers. The Connecticut Polish American Archives located at Central Connecticut State University in New Britain, CT, hold a vast amount of material. The Center for Research Libraries in Chicago has many Polish American publications. The Orchard Lake Schools just outside of Detroit maintain a large archive of material. The Bentley Historical Library at the University of Michigan also holds a substantial amount of resources regarding the Michigan Polonia. The University of Wisconsin at Milwaukee has a very large Polish American Collection including a rich photographic collection of some 32,000 images. Buffalo State University also has a large collection. The Fronczak Room Collection is a repository of primary sources and other materials related to the Polish American community in western New York. It includes papers, manuscripts, publications, flyers, official documents, photos, paintings, World War II memorabilia, and other items. The Polish Room, Lockwood Library, SUNY Buffalo, North Campus, Amherst, NY, also contains information on the New York Polonia. The Polish collection was begun in 1955 and includes books, periodicals, newspapers, films and artifacts covering the numerous contributions of the Poles in the humanities, science and US history. Over 9,000 volumes, over thirty video recordings, and a small collection of rare books and documents have been collected. The University of Pittsburgh has a collection dealing with the Polish communities of western Pennsylvania. The Polish National Catholic Church History and Archives Commission in Scranton, PA, maintains the archives of the church. The Balch Institute for Ethnic Studies in Philadelphia is a treasure throve of material including the records of various Polish American organizations, Polish churches, and private papers from the 19th and 20th centuries. There are records of Polish American ethnic societies in Maryland, Pennsylvania, and Ohio; political records of the Polish American Congress (PA) and the Polish National Alliance in the United States; and records regarding the newspaper *Gwiazda* and the Polish Publishing Press Co. The archives include the papers of Adam de Gorowski (1805–1866), Henry Dende (publisher), and Zygmunt Nagorski (member of the Polish government in exile). There are many valuable photograph collections as well. For those unable to read Polish, the Chicago Foreign Language Press Survey contains articles translated from Chicago's Polish newspapers up until the 1930s. It can be accessed through the Newberry Library website.

FURTHER READING

Babiński, Gregorz. *Polonia W USA: Na tle Przemian Amerykańskiej Etniczności*. Kraków: AFM, 2009.

Brożek, Andrzej. *Polish Americans, 1854–1939*. Warsaw: Interpress, 1985.

Bukowczyk, John J. *And My Children Did Not Know Me: A History of Polish-Americans*. Indianapolis Indiana University Press, 1987.

Bukowczyk, John J., editor. *Polish Americans and Their History, Community, Cuture, and Politics*. Pittsburgh, PA: University of Pittsburgh Press, 1996.

Erdmans, Mary Patrice. *Opposite Poles: Immigrants and Ethnics in Polish Chicago, 1976–1990*. University Park: Pennsylvania State University Press, 1998.

Erdmans, Mary Patrice. *The Grasinski Girls: The Choices They Had and the Choices They Made*. Athens, OH: Ohio University Press, 2004.

Greene, Victor R. *The Slavic Community on Strike*. Notre Dame, IN: University of Notre Dame Press, 1968.

Lopata, Helena Znaniecka. *Polish Americans*. New Brunswick, NJ: Transaction Publishers 1994.

Pacyga, Dominic A. *Polish Immigrants and Industrial Chicago*. Chicago: University of Chicago Press, 2003.

Praszałowicz, Dorota. *Stosunki Polsko-Niemiecki na Obczyźnie: Polscy i Niemieccy Imigranci w Milwaukee, Wisconsin (USA), 1860–1920*. Kraków: Universitas, 1999.

Pula, James S. *Polish Americans: An Ethnic Community*. New York: Twayne, 1995.

Pula, James S., editor. *The Polish American Encyclopedia*. Jefferson, NC: McFarland, 2011.

Pula, James S., and Eugene E. Dziedzic. *United We Stand; The Role of Polish Workers in the New York Mills Textile Strike, 1912 and 1916*. Boulder, CO: East European Monographs, 1990.

Walaszek, Adam. *Światy Imigrantów: Tworzenie Polonijnego Cleveland, 1880–1930*. Kraków: Nomos, 1994.

Wylie, Jeanie. *Poletown: Community Betrayed*. Urbana: University of Illinois Press, 1989.

NOTES

1. John J. Bukowczyk, *And My Children Did Not Know Me: A History of Polish-Americans* (Indianapolis: Indiana University Press 1987), ch. 1; James S. Pula, *Polish Americans: An Ethnic Community* (New York: Twayne, 1995), 22–23, Andrzej Brożek, *Polish Americans, 1854–1939* (Warsaw: Interpress, 1985), ch. 2, 11.

2. Julian Korski Grove, "The Polish Group in the United States," *The Annals of the American Academy of Political and Social Science* 93 (January 1921): 153–156; Ewa Morwaska, "Labor Migrations of Poles in the Atlantic World Economy, 1880–1914," *Comparative Studies in Society and History* 31.2 (April 1989): 237–272; Brożek, *Polish Americans*, 34–42.

3. For a discussion of the communal and extracommunal responses, see Dominic A. Pacyga, *Polish Immigrants and Industrial Chicago, Workers on the South Side, 1880–1922* (Chicago: University of Chicago Press, 2003), chs. 4 and 5.

4. Victor R. Greene, *For God and Country: The Rise of Polish and Lithuanian Ethnic Consciousness in America, 1860–1910* (Madison: Wisconsin Historical Society Press, 1975); Joseph Parot, *Polish Catholics in Chicago, 1850–1920* (DeKalb: Northern Illinois University Press, 1981).

5. Pier Versteegh, "A League of Their Own: Strategic Networks of Polish Women as a Female Response to Male Dominated Networks," in *Irish and Polish Migration in Comparative Perspective*, eds. John Belchem and Klaus Tenfelde (Essen, Germany: Klartext-Verlag, 2003), 201–220.

6. James S. Pula, "Polish American Women," in *The Polish American Encyclopedia*, ed. James S. Pula (Jefferson, NC: McFarland, 2011), 552; Thaddeus C. Radzilowski, "Family, Women, and Gender: The Polish Experience," in *Polish Americans and Their History: Community, Culture, and Politics*, ed. John J. Bukowczyk (Pittsburgh, PA: University of Pittsburgh Press, 1996), 58–79.

7. Maria Anna Knothe, "Recent Arrivals: Polish Immigrant Women's Response to the City," in *Peasant Maids—City Women: From the European Countryside to Urban America*, ed. Christine Harzig (Ithaca, NY: Cornell University Press, 1997), 299–338; Versteegh, " A League of Their Own," 212.

8. Donald E. Pienkos, *PNA: A Centennial History of the Polish National Alliance of the United States of North America* (Boulder, CO: East European Monographs, 1984), 51–63; John Radziłowski, *The Eagle and the Cross: A History of the Polish Roman Catholic Union of America* (Boulder, CO: East European Monographs, 2003), 43–51, 89–90; Edward R. Kantowicz, *Polish-American Politics in Chicago, 1888–1940* (Chicago: University of Chicago Press, 1975), 40.

9. Knothe, "Recent Arrivals," 311; Versteegh, "A League of Their Own," 202–204; Radzilowski, "Family, Women, and Gender," 61–62, 70.

10. Radzilowski "Family, Women, and Gender," 61, 75; Pula, "Polish American Women," 548.

11. Dominic A. Pacyga, "To Live Amongst Others: Poles and Their Neighbors in Industrial Chicago, 1865–1930," *Journal of American Ethnic History* (Autumn 1996): 55–74.

12. Edward Pinkowski, *Lattimer Massacre* (Philadelphia: Sunshine Press, 1950).

13. Pula, *Polish Americans*, 46–51; Pacyga, *Polish Immigrants and Industrial Chicago*, 250–257; James R. Barrett, *Work and Community in the Jungle: Chicago's Packinghouse Workers, 1894–1922* (Urbana: University of Illinois Press, 2002), 255–263.

14. Mary Krane Dryer, "Polish American Socialists," in *The Polish American Encyclopedia*, ed. James S. Pula (New Brunswick, NJ, 2011), 491.

15. Joseph T. Hapak, "Prelude to Arms: Polonia and the Struggle for Polish Independence in World War I," *The Polish Review* 61.1 (2016), 81–89; Robert Szymczak, "An Act of Devotion: The Polish Grey Samaritans and the American Relief Effort in Poland, 1919–1921," *Polish American Studies* 43.1 (Spring 1986): 13–36.

16. James S. Pula, "American Immigration Policy and the Dillingham Commission," *Polish American Studies* (1980): 5–31; Madison Grant, *The Passing of the Great Race* (New York, 1916); Roger Daniels, *Guarding the Golden Door: American Immigration Policy and Immigrants since 1882* (New York: Farrar, Straus and Giroux, 2005), 45–48.

17. For a discussion of remigration to Poland from the United States, see Adam Walaszak, *Reemigracja ze Stanów Zjednoczonych do Polski po I wojnie światowej, 1919–1924* (Kraków, 1983).

18. Dorota Praszałowicz, "Polish American Sisterhoods: The Americanization Process," *U.S. Catholic Historian* 27.3 (Summer 2009), 45–57; Thaddeus C. Radzialowski, " Reflections on the History of the Felicians in America," *Polish American Studies* 32.1 (Spring 1975): 19–28; Edward R. Kantowicz, *Corporation Sole: Cardinal Mundelein and Chicago Catholicism* (Notre Dame, IN: Notre Dame University Press, 1983).

19. William I. Thomas and Florian Znaniecki, *The Polish Peasant in Europe and America*, 5 vols. (Chicago: University of Chicago Press, 1918–1920); Paul G. Cressey, *The Taxi-Dance Hall* (Chicago: University of Chicago Press, 1932), 37–44.

20. Frederic M. Thrasher, *The Gang: A Study of 1,313 Gangs in Chicago* (Chicago: University of Chicago Press, 1927); Clifford R. Shaw, *The Jack-Roller: A Delinquent Boy's Own Story* (Chicago: University of Chicago Press, 1930).

21. Eugene Miller, "Leo Krzycki: Polish American Labor Leader," *Polish American Studies* 33.2 (Autumn 1976): 52–64; Margaret Collingwood Nowak, *Two Who Were There: A Biography of Stanley Nowak* (Detroit, 1989).

22. Georg Schrode, "Mary Zuk and the Detroit Meat Strike of 1935," *Polish American Studies* (Autumn 1986): 5–39.

23. Donald E. Pienkos, *Yesterday, Today, Tomorrow: The Story of the Polish National Alliance* (Chicago: Alliance Printers and Publishers, 2008), 15–16.

24. A. J. Baime, *The Arsenal of Democracy: FDR, Detroit, and an Epic Quest to Arm an America at War* (Boston: Mariner Books, Houghton Mifflin Harcourt, 2015).

25. Donald E. Pienkos, *For Your Freedom Through Ours: Polish American Efforts on Poland's Behalf, 1863–1991* (Boulder, CO: East European Monographs, 1991); Joanna Wojdon, *White and Red Umbrella: The Polish American Congress in the Cold War Era 1944–1988* (St. Helena, CA: Helena History Press, 2015), 54–57.

26. Dominic A. Pacyga, "Polish America in Transition: Social Change and the Chicago Polonia, 1945–1980," *Polish American Studies* 44.1 (Spring 1987): 38–55.

27. Dziennik Zwiazkowy, *Polish Daily News*, November 21, 2016, http://dziennikzwiazkowy .com/news-in-english/trump-wouldnt-win -without-polish-americans-an-interview-with -william-bill-ciosek/.

28. The most valuable of these early studies includes Wacław Kruszka's monumental thirteen-volume study *Historya Polska w Ameryce* (Milwaukee, WI: Drukiem Spółki Wydawniczej Kuryera, 1905–1908). Much of this study was later translated and reissued as *A History of the Poles in America to 1908* (Washington, DC: The Catholic University of America Press, 1993–2001) under the editorship of James S. Pula. See also James S. Pula, "Wacław Kruszka: A Polonia Historian in Perspective," *Polish American Studies* 44.2 (Autumn 1987): 57–69.

29. Thomas and Znaniecki, *The Polish Peasant*; Thrasher, *The Gang*; Shaw, *The Jack-Roller*.

30. For a discussion of Haiman's impact, see Bonnie Troka, "Miecislaus Haiman: Polish American Historian," *Polish American Studies* 20.2 (July–December 1963): 93–96

31. Victor Greene, *The Slavic Community on Strike*; Edward R. Kantowicz, *Polish-American Politics in Chicago*; Joseph Parot, *Polish Catholics in Chicago*; M. B. B. Biskupski, *The United States and the Rebirth of Poland* (Dordrecht, The Netherlands: Republic of Letters Publishing, 2012); Ewa Morawska, *For Bread with Butter: The Life-Worlds of East Central Europeans in Johnstown, Pennsylvania, 1890–1940* (Cambridge: Cambridge University Press, 1986); John J. Bukowczyk, *A History of the Polish Americans* (New York: Routledge, 2007); Radziłowski, *The Eagle and the Cross*; Mary Patrice Erdmans, *Opposite Poles: Immigrants and Ethnic in Polish Chicago, 1976–1990* (University Park: Pennsylvania, 1998); Anna D. Jaroszyńska-Kirchmann, *The Exile Mission: The Polish Political Diaspora and Polish Americans, 1939–1956* (Athens, OH: Ohio University Press, 2004; James S. Pula, ed., *The Polish American Encyclopedia* (Jefferson, NC: McFarland, 2011).

32. Adam Walaszek, *Światy Imigrantów: Tworzenie Polonijnego Cleveland, 1880–1930* (Kraków: Nomos, 1994); Gregorz Babiński, *Polonia W USA: na tle przemian amerykańskiej etniczności* (Kraków: AFM, 2009); Dorota Praszałowicz, *Stosunki Polsko-Niemiecki Na Obczyźnie: Polscy I Niemieccy Imigranci w Milwaukee, Wisconsin (USA), 1860–1920* (Kraków: Universitas, 1999); Andrzej Brożek, *Polish Americans, 1854–1939* (Warsaw: Interpress, 1985); Witold Kula, Nina Assorodobraj-Kula, and Marcin Kula, *Listy Emigrantów z Brazylii i Stanów Zjednoczonych* (Warsaw: Ludowa Spółdzielnia Wydawnicza, 1973)—an English-language translation of the book edited and translated by Josephine Wtulich appeared under the title *Writing Home: Immigrants in Brazil and the United States, 1890–1891* (Boulder, CO: East European Monographs, 1986); Anna Mazurkiewicz, ed., *East Central Europe in Exile: Transatlantic Migrations* and *East Central Europe in Exile: Transatlantic Identities* (Newcastle upon Tyne, UK: Cambridge Scholars Publishing, 2013); Joanna Wojdon, *W Imieniu Sześciu Milionów: Kongres Polonii Amerykańskiej w Latach 1944–1968* (Torún, Poland: Adam Marszalek, 2005) and *W Jedności Siła: Kongress-Polonii Amerykańskiej w Latach, 1968–1988* (Torún, Poland: Adam Marszalek, 2008).

Dominic Pacyga

IRISH IMMIGRATION AND THE AMERICAN WORKING CLASS

BEFORE THE GREAT IRISH FAMINE, 1790–1845

From the 1790s through the early 1840s, the Irish in America were employed mainly as unskilled workers. This was a period when the nascent labor movement was dominated by a minority of highly skilled artisans and mechanics, especially printers and shoemakers, but also carpenters and other building trades workers, coopers, tailors, cabinet makers, shipwrights, and handloom weavers. Such workers responded to the new manufacturing processes that were eroding their crafts and to the widening social gulf between themselves and their employers by engaging in strikes and by building a set of institutions that included trade societies (as early trade unions were called), cooperatives, adult educational bodies, so-called working men's political parties, and pro-labor newspapers. Demanding higher wages, shorter hours, free public schools, and (in states like Rhode Island that still lacked it) white adult male suffrage, this labor movement, which had taken hold in many American cities and smaller industrial communities by the mid-1830s, was shaped by notions of republican citizenship, the customs of the craft workshop, and an ethos of "manly" independence that derived from the preindustrial era. American labor historians have sometimes conceptualized this period as the initial stage of working-class formation in the United States, a process comparable to what the British historian Edward Thompson called "the making of the English working class."[1]

Although approximately 1.5 million Irish people immigrated to the United States before the onset of the Great Famine, Irish immigrants and their descendants participated to only a limited degree in the formation of the early working class. A handful of Irish-born male workers—mainly handloom weavers (the one skilled craft in which Irish men predominated),

those with some previous industrial experience in Britain, and/or Protestants (a religious group that still made up the largest share of emigrants from Ireland as late as 1830)—emerged as important labor activists. In Philadelphia, for example, one of the nation's strongest labor centers in the 1830s, a charismatic Irish-born handloom weaver named John Ferrall joined a mainly English- and native-born local labor leadership, while his fellow Irish Catholic handloom weavers waged a series of successful strikes against their employers and helped build the citywide General Trades Union, one of a number of central labor bodies that appeared in these years.[2]

Some of the mainly middle-class and Protestant United Irishmen who had arrived in America in the years before or after their defeat in Ireland's bloody 1798 Rebellion against Britain also played a kind of supporting role in this emerging labor movement. Philadelphia's William Duane, a veteran of both Irish republican and English plebeian radical movements, used the pages of his influential Jeffersonian Republican newspaper, the *Aurora*, to voice the aspirations of the city's artisans, while the New York attorney William Sampson, who had spent several years in a British prison for his support of the Society of United Irishmen, played an important role in defending the leaders of that city's striking shoemakers in their 1809–1810 trial, one of several important conspiracy cases in this period that grew out of employers' efforts to prosecute unions and strikers under English common law. In his defense of the workers, Sampson drew on his understanding of Irish history to denounce "the specter of the common law" as an oppressive British relic that deserved no place in a republic. In so doing, he provided later generations of US labor leaders with intellectual ammunition for their argument that the right to strike was central to the worker's liberty. Generally, however, Irish participants in America's early labor movement were few and far between.[3]

Moreover, as the number of Catholic emigrants from Ireland to the United States began to grow after 1815, religious tensions between Catholic and Protestant workers increasingly undermined the unity of the early labor movement. Between the end of the Napoleonic Wars in 1815 and the onset of the Great Famine in 1845, between 800,000 and one million Irish men and women arrived in North America, twice as many as in the entire previous two centuries. Facing economic depression, growing competition from England, and increasing mechanization that hindered the ability of men and women to earn wages by spinning textiles or weaving cloth at home, along with staggering population growth (Ireland's population doubled from 4 million in 1780 to 8 million in 1841), many Irish people opted for transatlantic migration. Between 1815 and 1845, the Irish accounted for a full third of all immigrants to the United States. As Irish migration increased, the social, regional, and religious backgrounds of the migrants gradually changed. Poorer farmers and workers began to emigrate in larger numbers in these years. By 1836, for example, nearly two-thirds of all Irish immigrants arriving in New York were servants or laborers, up from under a third just a decade earlier. Equally important, though Protestants from Ulster continued to emigrate through the 1830s, they were increasingly joined by Catholics from that province and from Ireland's three more heavily Catholic southern provinces, Leinster, Munster, and Connacht. In the 1830s, Irish Catholic immigrants to America outnumbered Irish Protestants for the first time since 1700.[4]

Settlement patterns in the United States began to shift as well, as the demand for labor stimulated by American industrialization and urbanization drew more and more Irish immigrants to the cities, canal towns, and industrial mill villages of the Northeast and Mid-Atlantic States. Unskilled and low-paid occupations in which Irish Catholic men typically found employment in this period included work on the docks, carting and hauling goods, street paving, and ditch digging, occupations often summed up by the all-encompassing term "common labor," while Irish Catholic women, in addition to performing indispensable labor in the maintenance of working-class families, often worked in their own apartments as seamstresses, laundresses, or shoe binders. These recently arrived Irish-born men and women formed an important segment of a larger social grouping, the urban laboring poor, whose ranks also included African American slaves and freed people and who, vulnerable and chronically impoverished, spent more energy in a daily struggle to make ends meet than in building labor organizations.[5]

The growing population of Catholic Irish in the United States had significant ramifications for the American Catholic Church, which was increasingly dominated by men of Irish birth or ancestry. Historians estimate that in the two decades after 1830, American Catholics increased from approximately 3 to 8 percent of the total population—making theirs the largest religious denomination in the country. In addition, the Irish made up a majority of the nation's approximately 1.6 million Catholics in 1850. The composition of the church hierarchy reflected this changing religious demography: as late as 1829, only one American bishop was Irish-born, but by the mid-1840s, Irish bishops led the dioceses of Boston, Chicago, Cincinnati, Pittsburgh, and, most notably, New York, where an outspoken Ulsterman named John Hughes was named bishop in 1842. The Catholic Church would remain a central institution within Irish American urban working-class life up through the present time.[6]

A new style of urban working-class Democratic Party politics also began to emerge in this period, one with a distinctively Irish flavor and most visible in the larger cities. Mike Walsh, the Protestant son of a United Irishman who became the leader of the "shirtless" or "subterranean" Democrats in New York, epitomized the new style. A vocal supporter of trade unions and of labor's fight to end Rhode Island's property restrictions on the suffrage, Walsh also helped link Irish immigrant voters in the North to southern slaveholders in a national

Democratic Party that became the leading political voice for white supremacy in this period.[7] Meanwhile, Bishop Hughes, the most influential Catholic prelate in America, was vehement in his opposition to abolitionism. Though the Irish and African American laboring poor often had a great deal of contact with each other in their day-to-day lives—sometimes even marrying—the political developments of this period (along with ongoing competition between Irish and African Americans over access to low-wage jobs in many locales) made the Irish as a group a principal opponent of black advancement. The legacy of this development for the American working class as a whole would be profound.[8]

As the numbers and political influence of the Catholic Irish grew, so too did anti-Catholicism and anti-Irish nativism. Fomented by Protestant religious revivals and popular writings that portrayed Irish Catholics as superstitious, ignorant, and priest-ridden—and thus intrinsically antirepublican—this development led to bitter local conflicts between Catholics and Protestants over public school policies like the use of the Protestant King James Bible in classrooms and, by the early 1840s, to the emergence of new nativist political parties that actively contested elections. These developments, along with perennial competition between native-born Americans and immigrants over low-wage jobs, pitted worker against worker in a number of cities, disrupting local labor movements that were also badly damaged by the economic downturn that began in 1837. In Boston, for example, unskilled Protestant laborers burned down an Ursuline convent in the Charlestown district in 1834, and, in 1837, a Protestant volunteer fire company attacked an Irish Catholic funeral procession, leading to the destruction of many homes in what was called the "Broad Street riot." Nativism rose to a crescendo in 1844 when the anti-immigrant American Republicans elected six congressmen and dozens of local officials in Boston, New York, and Philadelphia and when bloody and destructive anti-Catholic riots erupted over the school Bible issue in the Kensington and Southwark districts of the latter city.[9]

Violence was also part of the experience of the Irish immigrant laborers who helped construct the nation's extensive system of canals, though in this case they were more often the instigators than the victims of riots. As early as 1830, a majority of the nation's 35,000 canal diggers were Irish, constituting the largest concentration of workers in this era by far. They did not organize trade unions, but they did form short-lived organizations based on their county of origin and engaged in numerous strikes and riots in the 1830s, with the Chesapeake and Ohio Canal experiencing a particularly high level of unrest. Though their violent attacks were often directed against fellow canal diggers (German immigrants, for instance, or men with origins in other Irish counties, in what were called "faction fights"), these were sometimes directed against employers as well. One such attack, on the Chesapeake and Ohio in 1834, triggered the first intervention of federal troops in a labor dispute in American history.[10]

THE GREAT IRISH FAMINE AND US INDUSTRIAL GROWTH, 1845–1880

With the onset of the Great Famine in 1845, emigration from Ireland to the United States increased dramatically, peaking in 1851, when more than 221,000 Irish men and women arrived in the country. An estimated 1.5 million people left Ireland for North America in the famine decade of 1846–1855, and it was in this period that Irish Catholics became the most urbanized immigrant group in the nation. Meanwhile, the rapid pace of industrialization in this period opened up unskilled jobs for Irish men and women in a wide variety of manufacturing industries. To take one example, the locus of textile manufacturing in the 1820s and 1830s had been New England, most famously Lowell, Massachusetts, where employers recruited local unmarried farm women to work in the factories and live in adjacent boarding houses. Their stated goal was to create a clean, healthy, and controlled environment, avoiding the widespread distress caused by Britain's industrial revolution (Figure 1).

However, this model was already collapsing by the 1840s, when workers began to express dissatisfaction in a variety of ways, including going on strike. The arrival of the new Irish famine immigrants, along with growing numbers of German immigrants in the same period, was a boon to the mill owners. Irish families, and Irish women in particular, took jobs at pay and under conditions that the Yankee mill women were rejecting. Irish women found employment tending machines in New England's myriad shoe factories in this period as well.[11]

After the decline of handloom weaving in the 1850s, no single occupation had a majority of Irish workers. Since most of the famine migrants arrived without marketable skills, common labor remained the most important area of male employment. As late as 1870, 40 percent of Irish-born men were unskilled laborers. Meanwhile, Irish women began to find work as domestic servants in this period, an occupation they dominated through the remainder of the century. Though African American, German, and Scandinavian women also worked as domestics in these years,

the association of Irish women ("Bridget" or "Biddy") with domestic service became a staple of American popular culture.[12] By the 1850s and 1860s, Irish men and women comprised a significant section of the working class, not only in the northeastern cities and mill towns, but in the mining counties of Pennsylvania, midwestern cities, and even in the urban South, where, in New Orleans, for instance, Irish and African American men competed for jobs on the city's docks.

Nonetheless, skilled work became increasingly common for Irish men in these years, particularly in the cities of the Midwest and Far West, where rapid urban growth translated into more occupational opportunities, as detailed quantitative studies of cities like Detroit and San Francisco have made clear.[13] Coal mining and transportation also attracted significant numbers of Irish-born men and their sons. With this movement into the skilled trades came a more complete entry of Irish men (and some women as well) into the ranks of the American labor movement, which grew fitfully in the 1850s but then revived dramatically in the northern states in the years during and after the Civil War.

The emergence of a national labor movement in the towns and cities of the northern states was one of the most important developments of this era, culminating in the birth

Figure 1. Irish American child textile workers in Lowell, Massachusetts, photographed by Lewis Hine, early 20th century.
Courtesy Library of Congress, Prints and Photographs Division, Washington, DC, LC-DIG-nclc-02394.

of the National Labor Union in 1866 and the first major struggle for an 8-hour day. The Irish contributed in significant ways to these developments. Irish immigrant miners, for example, played the key role in founding the American Miners' Union in 1861. In 1868, John Siney, who had been born in Ireland but was raised in an industrial town in Lancashire, where he developed a familiarity with the traditions of British trade unionism, founded the Workingmen's Benevolent Association (renamed the Miners' and Laborers' Benevolent Association in 1870), which organized over 30,000 miners and mine laborers in Pennsylvania's anthracite districts, making it the largest labor union of its day.[14] In Boston, the scene of violent conflict between Irish and non-Irish workers in earlier years, the 8-hour day struggle of the later 1860s brought them together. Irish immigrants, along with their sons and daughters, emerged as leaders of New England unions, notably the two shoemakers' organizations, the Knights of St. Crispin (the second-largest union of the era), and the Daughters of St. Crispin.

Somewhat paradoxically, interethnic unity was also furthered by the emergence of the Fenian Brotherhood, an oath-bound organization dedicated to winning an independent Irish republic by force of arms, at the end of the 1850s. The Fenians counted many native-born workers and labor leaders among their supporters. In Boston, for instance, the labor newspaper, the *Daily Evening Voice*, enthusiastically endorsed the struggle for Irish independence, and the city's labor movement nominated the Irish nationalist and Civil War veteran, General Patrick Guiney, as an independent candidate for Congress in 1866.[15] In Civil War-era Chicago, where labor's growth was especially impressive, native-, German-, and Irish-born workers organized a dozen new trade unions, established a citywide central labor assembly and weekly labor newspaper, engaged in numerous strikes, and began waging a political campaign for the 8-hour day. Chicago's trade unionists participated enthusiastically in an 1864 Irish nationalist fundraiser, the "Fenian Fair," with the city's Typographical Union, Horseshoers' Association, and Tailors' Union all marching in the opening parade and the Iron Molders' Union presenting the Fenians with a McCormick reaper to be carried in the procession. Such deep connections between Fenians and trade unionists were common throughout the industrializing East and Midwest in the Civil War and immediate postwar period.[16]

Violence remained a part of Irish American working-class life, however. Even before the defeat of Siney's miners' union in the so-called Long Strike of 1875, some of Pennsylvania's Irish miners turned to a secret society called the "Molly Maguires," which engaged in violent acts of retribution that drew on traditional strategies of Irish rural protest and led eventually to the conviction and hanging of twenty miners for murder.[17] Irish racial violence continued in this period as well, most famously in the New York City Draft Rots of July 1863, in which a now-entrenched anti-black racism, intensified by the inequities of the 1863 Conscription Act, led to an explosion of violence, with mobs of mainly Irish workers beating and lynching African Americans and burning the city's Colored Orphan Asylum to the ground.[18] A similar mix of white racism and class resentments was apparent in California, where Irish American workers figured prominently in the often-violent anti-Chinese movement of the late 1870s. The Belfast-born Frank Roney, a key figure in San Francisco's labor movement, combined Irish nationalism with an embrace of the anti-Chinese movement, while Denis Kearney, the Irish immigrant leader of California's Workingmen's Party, ended every speech with the party's slogan, "The Chinese Must Go!"[19]

IRISH AMERICAN WORKERS IN THE MULTIETHNIC CITY, 1880–1925

By the turn of the 20th century, the occupational structure of Irish America had been transformed. As studies of the 1900 Federal

Census have demonstrated, Irish-born men had achieved near occupational parity with native-born white males and stood well above immigrants from eastern and southern Europe, whose numbers grew significantly after 1890. Although there continued to be significant regional variations, at the national level, only 15 percent of Irish men worked as unskilled manual laborers in 1900; they were now to be found disproportionately in trades that were skilled, unionized, and relatively high paid. A majority of Irish-born women in the paid workforce still labored as domestic servants, but for second-generation American-born women there was a clear trend toward employment in clerical jobs, nursing, and school teaching.[20]

Irish Americans increasingly took on leadership roles in the American labor movement. The typical Irish labor leader of this period was not an immigrant, but rather a second- or even third-generation man or woman who had grown up entirely in urban-industrial America.

Thus, the Knights of Labor (KOL), the most important national labor organization of the 19th century, which advanced a broad program of social and political reform and peaked with a membership of over 750,000 in 1886, enrolled large numbers of Irish Americans. It was led by Terence V. Powderly, an American-born Irish Catholic machinist and the one-time mayor of Scranton, Pennsylvania (Figure 2).[21]

The KOL went into decline in the later 1880s, but Irish Americans were equally prominent in the leadership of the national craft unions affiliated with the American Federation of Labor (AFL). AFL President Samuel Gompers was not Irish in background, having been born in London into a Jewish family of Dutch origins. But in the trade union world that he inhabited, the Irish were everywhere, occupying the presidencies of more than 50 of the 110 unions affiliated with the AFL in the first decade of the 20th century. So too, at the local level, Irish Americans could be found leading central labor councils and building trades councils in cities from Chicago to San Francisco.

Figure 2. Terence V. Powderly, Irish American leader of the Knights of Labor.
Courtesy of Library of Congress, Prints and Photographs Division, Washington, DC, LC-DIG-pga-01926.

Like Powderly, the typical union leader of this later period had been born and raised in an American industrial town or city. Daniel Keefe, a founder and first president of the International Longshoremen's Association, for example, had been born in Illinois, while James O'Connell, head of the International Association of Machinists, had been born in Pennsylvania. Such leaders generally supported Gompers's vision of "pure and simple unionism" and his ongoing struggle against radical labor activists in the Socialist Party and the Industrial Workers of the World (IWW).[22]

Nonetheless, the "labor left" did attract some notable Irish American figures, despite the Catholic Church's vehemently antisocialist stance. At the opening of the 20th century, Massachusetts shoe workers' leaders John Tobin and James Carey were vigorous supporters of the American socialist movement, and the radical Western Federation of Miners included

Edward Boyce, John O'Neill, and several other Irish Americans among its officers. The revolutionary IWW attracted few Irish American supporters, despite the tireless efforts of the radical activist Elizabeth Gurley Flynn, who was descended from a long line of Irish nationalists going back to the United Irishmen.[23]

Irish American women took on leadership positions in a wide range of labor organizations in this period. Leonora Barry headed the Knights of Labor's Department of Women's Work, and Elizabeth Rogers led a KOL assembly in Chicago with over 50,000 members.

Early 20th-century leaders included Leonora O'Reilly, a key figure in the Women's Trade Union League; Margaret Haley, who led the Chicago Teachers' Federation; and, perhaps most famously, the Cork-born labor organizer, Mary Harris ("Mother") Jones (Figure 3). Indeed, until the emergence of the Jewish garment unions, after a dramatic series of strikes in 1909, nearly every prominent woman labor leader was of Irish birth or ancestry.[24]

Even more than in the 1860s, Irish nationalism constituted an important influence in the American labor movement. In the wake of a nationwide tour by the Irish Home Rule leader Charles Stewart Parnell in 1880, an organization called the Land League sprang up in towns and cities across the nation to provide support for the Home Rule and agrarian reform movements in Ireland. Though most Land League leaders were middle class, a radical working-class wing of the organization, represented by Patrick Ford's weekly newspaper, the *Irish World and American Industrial Liberator*, sought to draw connections between the land struggle in Ireland and the labor struggle in the United States, emphasizing the problems of monopoly common to both settings. In some areas of the country, working-class branches of the Land League emerged that adhered closely to Ford's views, sometimes virtually merging with the Knights of Labor. Organized workers (Irish and non-Irish alike) also widely adopted the boycott, a tactic popularized in the Irish agrarian struggle, and rallied to the unsuccessful but impressive 1886 campaign of economic reformer and Land League supporter Henry George for mayor of New York. This deep connection between Irish nationalism and the American labor movement grew weaker in the later 1880s but resurfaced in the five years after the 1916 Dublin Easter Rising, when local labor councils in Chicago, San Francisco, and other cities voiced support for Irish independence and when workers on New York's docks staged a dramatic walkout in 1920 in support of an Irish republican hunger striker.[25]

The leadership position of Irish Americans in the labor movement was paralleled by their leadership in urban politics and culture, even as Irish immigration slowed and the working-class residents of large cities grew increasingly diverse. In the 1840s, for example, about half of all immigrants to the United States had been Irish, but by the 1890s that figure had dropped to just 10 percent. Only in atypical settings, like the copper mining and smelting town of Butte, Montana, did the Irish numerically dominate an urban center and its workforce. Irish immigrants and their children remained numerically significant in large cities, of course—they still represented a quarter of the population of New York in 1890—but that percentage was steadily dropping, as the number of "new immigrants" from eastern and southern Europe

Figure 3. Cork-born Mary Harris "Mother" Jones, labor leader.
Courtesy Library of Congress, Prints and Photographs Division, Washington, DC, LC-USZ62-50377.

grew dramatically. Thus, the influence they wielded was less a matter of numerical superiority than of "knowing the ropes" of urban-industrial life. For all the tensions between new immigrants and Irish Americans, the two groups interacted constantly, especially in the larger cities. As the social reformer Emily Balch noted in 1910, "the newcomers, encountering Irish policemen, Irish politicians, Irish bureaucrats, Irish saloon keepers, Irish contractors, and Irish teachers could be excused for thinking that 'Irish' equaled 'American.'" Historian James Barrett has described this interaction as a kind of "Americanization from the bottom up."[26]

IRISH AMERICAN WORKERS AFTER THE 1920s

After the mid-1920s, the situation of the Irish American working class changed in profound ways. The combination of new quotas for immigrants under the 1924 National Origins Act and—much more importantly for the Irish—the collapse of the American job market in the 1930s brought migration from Ireland to the United States to a virtual halt. The perils of an Atlantic crossing during World War II solidified the pattern, and when immigration to the United States began to revive again at the end of the war, it was at a significantly lower level. Britain, not the United States, was the primary destination for Irish emigrants in the postwar period. To be sure, Irish immigration never ceased entirely, and there were significant upticks in the number of migrants in the 1950s and the 1980s. But the days of mass migration were over.[27]

Irish Americans continued to improve their material conditions, a trend that was temporarily reversed in the 1930s but reasserted itself during the long economic expansion after the war. By 1950, 24 percent of Irish-born men held white-collar jobs (the professions, managers, clerks, and salesmen), while nearly 42 percent of second-generation men could be found in such occupations. Professional jobs, especially as accountants, clergymen, and lawyers, were particularly important in the occupational profile of second-generation men, while second-generation women were heavily represented in law, teaching, engineering, and clerical work. Irish immigrants—and particularly their children and grandchildren—were slowly moving up America's occupational ladder. This was not a "rags to riches" story by any means, and even the second generation remained mainly working class in the early 1950s, but the upward trend was clear enough.[28]

Postwar federal policies that encouraged highway construction, home ownership, and affordable mortgage financing for white Americans led to increasing suburbanization for many Irish Americans, especially in the second generation and beyond. Suburban Irish Americans often became strong opponents of the African American freedom movement when that movement turned to efforts to desegregate their neighborhoods or schools. But urban working-class Irish enclaves could be bitterly arrayed against desegregation as well, most famously in the Boston school busing crisis of 1974–1975.[29]

Irish American men and women continued to occupy an important place in the American labor movement in the 20th century, playing an especially important part in the industrial union upsurge of the 1930s, which brought millions of new mass production workers into the labor movement and culminated in the founding of the Congress of Industrial Organizations (CIO) in 1938. The experience of CIO organizing marked a political "coming of age" for immigrant workers from a variety of backgrounds and places: Jews and Italians in the East, Poles and Slavs in the Midwest, Mexicans in southern California. But it was frequently the Irish, industrial pioneers with the deepest experience in the labor movement in America or abroad, who emerged as leaders of the new unions.[30]

John Brophy, for example, who had been a leading progressive figure in the United Mine Workers in Pennsylvania in the 1920s, served as national director of the CIO. He went on to play a critical role in the strikes and organizing drives of some of the most important of the new industrial unions, including the United Auto Workers, the United Rubber Workers, and the United Steel Workers. Other important Irish American labor leaders of the 1930s included James Carey and Albert Fitzgerald of the United Electrical Workers; National Maritime Union leader Joseph Curran; New York City's Transport Workers Union leader Mike Quill; and Philip Murray, Vincent Sweeney, and Joseph P. Molony of the United Steel Workers. Murray, who had been born in Scotland to Irish immigrant parents, would become president of the CIO in 1940. Experienced in the traditions, tactics, and ideals of organized labor, Irish American labor activists like these often became, as Carey and autoworkers' leader Walter Reuther later put it, "missionaries of industrial unionism."[31]

A variety of intellectual and political influences were at work on such individuals, inspiring them in some cases to devote their entire lives to work in the labor movement. For some, including Carey and Murray, Catholic social thinking played an important role, especially Pope Pius XI's 1931 encyclical calling on Catholics to build corporate associations in industries and professions for the common good, a stance that many working-class American Catholics interpreted as a mandate for industrial unionism. This period also saw the emergence of the so-called labor priests, many of whom were Irish in background. Thus, Father (later Bishop) Joseph Donnelly, the son of Irish immigrants, told Connecticut brass workers at a 1941 CIO rally that unions "were not only American" but "Christian," urging them to "recognize your dignity as men of God [and to] recognize your dignity as workingmen." But Donnelly also expressed concerns about communist labor organizers with "un-American political theories and social teachings," concerns that eventually led him into anticommunist efforts in the postwar era.[32]

For other CIO leaders, an early exposure to Irish nationalism (in either Ireland or the wider diaspora) played a more important role than Catholicism in their political formation. Brophy, for example, who had been born in industrial Lancashire, was strongly affected by the political outlook of his Irish immigrant father, a coal miner and enthusiastic supporter of the Irish Land League. The influence was even more direct in the case of New York transit workers' leader Mike Quill, who had been born to a strongly nationalist family in County Kerry and who had fought with the Irish Republican Army before immigrating to New York in the 1920s. In the following decade, Quill emerged as the key union organizer among the largely Irish workforce on New York's subway system. The Transport Workers Union was founded in 1934 with Quill as president. Heading a union with 30,000 members and with a series of successfully negotiated union contracts behind him, Quill became an important political figure in New York and was elected to the New York City Council from the Bronx in November 1937. Although Quill consistently denied being a member of the Communist Party, he remained ideologically close to the party into the postwar years.[33]

Irish American labor leaders could be found on both sides of the fight over communism that tore the CIO apart after the war and led to the expulsion of nine allegedly "communist-dominated" unions in 1948. West Coast longshore leader Harry Bridges, born in Australia to an Irish mother, was expelled that year, along with his union. Quill moved in a different direction, breaking with the communists in 1948 and (working closely with CIO president Philip Murray) defeating an opposing group of TWU officials who fought to retain their communist connections. Quill went on to become a CIO national vice president in 1950, though he soon moved to the left again, criticizing (Irish American) Joe McCarthy's anticommunist crusade and calling for the founding of an American labor party.

A more representative Irish American labor leader than either Bridges or Quill was probably Murray himself, who supported Harry

Truman's foreign and domestic policies and helped engineer the 1955 merger with the American Federation of Labor. Another representative figure was the leader of the new AFL-CIO, a third-generation Irish American named George Meany, who combined a kind of working-class Keyneseanism with a vigorous Cold War anticommunism that he championed well into the years of the Vietnam War, making the labor federation a byword for political conformism in an era of dramatic social change.[34]

Labor union corruption, though far from a new problem, received increasing scrutiny from the public and federal authorities in the postwar era and was particularly prevalent in unions representing building trades workers, truck drivers, laundry workers, and longshoremen. While Irish American labor leaders had no monopoly on union corruption, much attention focused on the New York–New Jersey waterfront, where a distinctly Irish ethos that included a deeply ingrained code of silence, deference to authority, and hostility toward outsiders, prevailed among the dock workers, making corruption in the International Longshoremen's Association (ILA) a particularly intractable problem. Dramatized in the Hollywood film, *On the Waterfront* the situation led to the ILA's expulsion from the AFL in 1953.[35]

George Meany remained at the head of the AFL-CIO for nearly a quarter of a century, stepping down only in 1979, the year before his death. Over that time, the American union movement continued to lose members and at the same time became increasingly diverse, with immigrants from Asia, Central America, and Mexico becoming more and more active in unions, especially those in the service sector. Yet it was indicative of the long-lasting Irish American influence that when the AFL-CIO held its first ever contested election for president in 1995, both of the candidates, John J. Sweeney and Thomas R. Donahue, were Irish Americans.

A similar situation could be seen in the urban wing of the Democratic Party: even as its core constituencies grew more diverse, Irish Americans continued to occupy a prominent place in its leadership. The urban political machine, with which the Irish had been so strongly identified since the 19th century, went into decline in the postwar era, with, for example, Tammany Hall losing its last election in New York City in 1961. At the same time, however, Irish Americans continued to exercise leadership in the party at the national level, with the election of the Irish Catholic John F. Kennedy (the great-grandson of a famine immigrant) to the presidency in 1960 serving as a symbol of their ascent. Kennedy's younger brother, Edward, was a powerful liberal US senator from Massachusetts for nearly five decades, though his death in 2009 and the retirement of the AFL-CIO's John Sweeney the same year was seen by some observers as marking the end to the long Irish American ascendancy in both Democratic and labor circles.[36]

So, too, Irish American dominance of the Catholic Church persisted even as the Irish share of American Catholics continued to decline. By 1970, for example, less than 20 percent of Catholics were of Irish descent; yet over half of American bishops and a third of its priests had an Irish background. There was a range of political views among the Church's hierarchy, from deeply conservative anticommunists like New York's Cardinal Francis J. Spellman (1939–1967) to the Irish-born Cardinal Timothy Manning of Los Angeles (1970–1985), who provided important clerical support for the effort to organize Mexican American and Filipino agricultural workers in the United Farm Workers (UFW) during the 1960s and 1970s.[37]

Images of ethnic groups in American popular culture are often slow to change. Although Irish America had grown increasingly diverse in socioeconomic terms by the 1990s and although voting patterns among Irish Americans had also been shifting toward the Republican Party, for many the "typical" Irish American remained a Catholic, an urban dweller, a Democrat, and a labor union member. The persistence of such images is itself a topic worthy of further study.[38]

DISCUSSION OF THE LITERATURE

The scholarly study of the Irish American working class can be said to begin in 1941, with Oscar Handlin's *Boston's Immigrants*. A bleak, if sympathetic, analysis of the pre-famine and famine Catholic Irish in a city dominated by an entrenched, anti-Catholic upper class, Handlin's book shaped understanding of the Irish Catholic urban immigrant experience for decades. Elegantly written and deeply researched—in Boston, if not Irish, sources—the revised edition of the book, which took the story up to 1880, concluded that the Irish remained even then overwhelmingly "proletarian." Prefiguring *The Uprooted*, his later account of the European immigrant experience as a whole, Handlin portrayed the Boston Irish as a people buffeted by forces they could barely understand and were powerless to control.[39]

Over the course of the 1960s and 1970s, immigration and labor historians began to chip away at different parts of Handlin's interpretation. Local studies employing quantitative methods revealed a far less dire situation for those Irish migrants who ended up in cities outside of New England; outside of this region, opportunities were significantly greater and anti-Catholic sentiments sometimes less salient than in Boston. David Doyle, who has emphasized regional differences in the Irish American experience, also relied on national-level census data to conclude that by 1900, the Irish-born had achieved rough occupational parity with native-born whites.[40]

Labor historians, meanwhile, were challenging Handlin's portrait of the Irish as a totally powerless group, lacking (to use a term frequently employed by historians in the 1970s) *agency*. Some of their work focused on what Eric Foner memorably termed the "symbiotic relationship between class-conscious unionism and Irish national consciousness" in the late 19th century. Other scholars took up this theme and extended it to the high point of Irish American nationalism in the years from 1916 to 1923, with Joshua Freeman even finding echoes of this symbiotic relationship in the organizing drives among heavily Irish American New York transit workers as late as the 1930s.[41]

Two path-breaking books moved the discussion in new directions during the 1980s. The first was Hasia Diner's *Erin's Daughters in America*, which provided a model for the analysis of other groups of immigrant women while stimulating research into one of the distinctive features of the Irish American experience, the large number of single women among the migrants. The second was Kerby Miller's *Emigrants and Exiles*, the most influential work in Irish migration studies since *Boston's Immigrants*. Miller's sustained attention to class tensions in both Ireland and the United States was salutary, and the book was also notable for spurring transnational approaches to the study of Irish American history. The 1990s saw the emergence of critical whiteness studies, an early focus of which was the shifting racial identity of Irish American workers in the mid-19th century.[42]

The Irish American experience in the 20th century remains relatively uncharted in comparison with that of the 19th, and this is particularly true for Irish American working people. The noted labor historian David Montgomery pointed to a paradox that became increasingly salient over the course of the 20th century: "The importance of Irish Americans in both workplace and political organizations of labor rose as their share of the total working-class and immigrant population declined." In his recent book, *The Irish Way*, James Barrett has produced the most satisfying treatment of this paradox for the first few decades of the century, demonstrating how urban working-class Irish men and women helped "Americanize" later waves of newcomers in the multi-ethnic city. How this process developed after the 1920s, however, is a history that still needs to be written.[43]

PRIMARY SOURCES

Relevant primary sources are scattered around the country, in a variety of different archives. Libraries and archives with strong collections in US labor history include the Walter P. Reuther Library of Labor and Urban Affairs at Wayne State University; the Wisconsin Historical Society; the Tamiment Library and Robert F. Wagner Labor Archives at New York University (location of the Transport Workers Union of America Records); and the American Catholic History Research Center at Catholic University (where the voluminous Terence V. Powderly Papers are held). The Chicago Federation of Labor Records at the Chicago History Museum and the Frank P. Walsh Papers at the New York Public Library are especially valuable for research on both Irish American labor and the history of Irish American nationalism.[44] Published primary sources, such as the multivolume *Samuel Gompers Papers*, are filled with letters from Irish American labor leaders and Irish-related issues of concern to the American Federation of Labor president.[45] Labor newspapers (far too many to list here) are a critical primary source as well.

There are also numerous archives with materials relevant to urban Irish American working-class life and culture beyond the labor movement, but the University of Notre Dame Archives and the growing collections at the Archives of Irish America, Bobst Library, New York University, merit special mention.[46] Autobiographies and memoirs of Irish American workers offer significant insights, though naturally these privilege activists and leaders rather than rank-and-file working people.[47]

FURTHER READING

Barrett, James R. *The Irish Way: Becoming American in the Multi-Ethnic City*. New York: Penguin, 2012.

Brundage, David. *Irish Nationalists in America: The Politics of Exile, 1798–1998*. New York: Oxford University Press, 2016.

Diner, Hasia R. *Erin's Daughters in America: Irish Immigrant Women in the Nineteenth Century*. Baltimore: Johns Hopkins University Press, 1983.

Emmons, David, *Butte's Irish: Class and Community in an American Mining Town, 1875–1925*. Urbana: University of Illinois Press, 1989.

Fisher, James T. *On the Irish Waterfront: The Crusader, the Movie, and the Soul of the Port of New York*. Ithaca, NY: Cornell University Press, 2009.

Freeman, Joshua B. *In Transit: The Transport Workers Union in New York City, 1933–1966*. New York: Oxford University Press, 1989.

Kenny, Kevin. *Making Sense of the Molly Maguires*. New York: Oxford University Press, 1998.

Lee, J. J., and Marion R. Casey, eds. *Making the Irish American: History and Heritage of the Irish in the United States*. New York: New York: University Press, 2006.

Miller, Kerby A. *Emigrants and Exiles: Ireland and the Irish Exodus to North America*. New York: Oxford University Press, 1985.

Montgomery, David. "The Irish and the American Labor Movement." In *America and Ireland, 1776–1976: The American Identity and the Irish Connection*, edited by David Noel Doyle and Owen Dudley Edwards, 205–218. Westport, CT: Greenwood, 1980.

Montgomery, David. *The Fall of the House of Labor: The Workplace, the State, and American Labor Activism, 1865–1925*. New York: Cambridge University Press, 1987.

Way, Peter. *Common Labor Workers and the Digging of North American Canals, 1780–1860*. New York: Cambridge University Press, 1993.

NOTES

1. E. P Thompson, *The Making of the English Working Class* (New York: Vintage, 1963). For a good example of this approach to the study of early American working-class formation, see Bruce Laurie, *Artisans into Workers: Labor in Nineteenth-Century America* (New York: Hill and Wang, 1989).

2. David Montgomery, "The Shuttle and the Cross: Weavers and Artisans in the Kensington Riots of 1844," *Journal of Social History* 5.4 (Summer 1972): 411–446.

3. David Brundage, *Irish Nationalists in America: The Politics of Exile, 1798–1998* (New York: Oxford University Press, 2016), 40–41, 44–45.

4. For overviews of Irish migration patterns in the pre-famine era, see Kerby A. Miller, *Emigrants and Exiles: Ireland and the Irish Exodus to North America* (New York: Oxford University Press, 1985), 193–240; Kevin Kenny, *The American Irish: A History* (Harlow, UK: Longman, 2000), 45–87; Timothy J. Meagher, *The Columbia Guide to Irish American History* (New York: Columbia University Press, 2005), 42–59; and David Noel Doyle, "The Irish in North America, 1776–1845," in *Making the Irish American: History and Heritage of the Irish in the United States*, ed. J. J. Lee and Marion R. Casey (New York: New York University Press, 2006), 171–212.

5. David Montgomery, "The Working Classes of the Pre-Industrial American City, 1780–1830," *Labor History* 9.1 (Winter 1968), 3–22. For an exemplary recent study, see Seth Rockman, *Scraping By: Wage Labor, Slavery and Survival in Early Baltimore* (Baltimore: Johns Hopkins University Press, 2009).

6. Kenny, *The American Irish*, 75; Doyle, "The Irish in North America," 194–195.

7. Sean Wilentz, *Chants Democratic: New York City and the Rise of the American Working Class, 1788–1850* (New York: Oxford University Press, 1984), 326–335.

8. David R. Roediger, *The Wages of Whiteness: Race and the Making of the American Working Class* (London: Verso, 1991), 133–163; Graham Hodges, "'Desirable Companions and Lovers': Irish and African Americans in the Sixth Ward, 1830–1870," in *The New York Irish*, ed. Ronald H. Bayor and Timothy J. Meagher (Baltimore: Johns Hopkins University Press, 1996), 107–124; John T. McGreevy, *Catholicism and American Freedom: A History* (New York: W. W. Norton, 2003), 43–67.

9. Doyle, "The Irish in North America," 197–200; James R. Green and Hugh Carter Donahue, *Boston's Workers: A Labor History* (Boston: Boston Public Library, 1979), 29; Montgomery, "The Shuttle and the Cross," 422–439; David Emmons, *Beyond the American Pale: Irish Outlanders and the American West, 1845–1910* (Norman: University of Oklahoma Press, 2010), 44–75.

10. Peter Way, *Common Labor: Workers and the Digging of North American Canals, 1780–1860* (New York: Cambridge University Press, 1993), 200–28.

11. Thomas Dublin, *Women at Work: The Transformation of Work and Community in Lowell, Massachusetts, 1826–1860* (New York: Columbia University Press, 1979).

12. Hasia R. Diner, *Erin's Daughters in America: Irish Immigrant Women in the Nineteenth Century* (Baltimore: Johns Hopkins University Press, 1983); Maureen Murphy, "Bridget and Biddy: Images of the Irish Servant Girl in Puck Cartoons, 1880–1890," in *New Perspectives of the Irish Diaspora*, ed. Charles Fanning (Carbondale: Southern Illinois University Press, 2000), 152–175; Margaret Lynch-Brennan, "The Ubiquitous Bridget: Irish Immigrant Women in Domestic Service in America, 1840–1930," in *Making the Irish American*, 332–353.

13. Jo Ellen Vinyard, *The Irish on the Urban Frontier: Nineteenth Century Detroit, 1850–1880* (New York: Arno Press, 1976); R. A. Burchell, *The San Francisco Irish, 1848–1880* (Berkeley: University of California Press, 1980).

14. Kevin Kenny, "Labor and Labor Organizations," in *Making the Irish American*, 357–358.

15. Green and Donahue, *Boston's Workers*, 30.

16. John B. Jentz and Richard Schneirov, "Chicago's Fenian Fair: A Window into the Civil War as a Popular Awakening," *Labor's Heritage* 6.3 (Winter 1995): 4–19. David Montgomery, *Beyond Equality: Labor and the Radical Republicans, 1862–1872* (New York: Alfred A. Knopf, 1967) remains the best study of the labor movement in this period.

17. Kevin Kenny, *Making Sense of the Molly Maguires* (New York: Oxford University Press, 1998).

18. Iver Bernstein, *The New York City Draft Riots: Their Significance for American Society and Politics in the Age of the Civil War* (New York: Oxford University Press, 1991).

19. Alexander Saxton, *The Indispensable Enemy: Labor and the Anti-Chinese Movement in California* (Berkeley: University of California Press, 1971).

20. David Noel Doyle, *Irish Americans, Native Rights and National Empires: The Structure, Divisions and Attitudes of the Catholic Minority in the Decade of Expansion, 1890–1901* (New York: Arno, 1976).

21. Craig Phelan, *Grand Master Workman: Terence Powderly and the Knights of Labor* (Westport, CT: Greenwood, 2000).

22. David Montgomery, "Labor Movement," in *The Encyclopedia of the Irish in America*, ed. Michael Glazier (Notre Dame, IN: University of Notre Dame Press, 1999), 525–531, provides an excellent overview, building on the more detailed picture in his book, *The Fall of the House of Labor: The*

Workplace, the State, and American Labor Activism, 1865–1925 (New York: Cambridge University Press, 1987). For Chicago and San Francisco, see Elizabeth McKillen, *Chicago Labor and the Quest for a Democratic Diplomacy, 1914–1924* (Ithaca, NY: Cornell University Press, 1995) and Michael Kazin, *Barons of Labor: The San Francisco Building Trades and Union Power in the Progressive Era* (Urbana: University of Illinois Press, 1987).

23. John H. M. Laslett, *Labor and the Left: A Study of Socialist and Radical Influences in the American Labor Movement, 1881–1924* (New York: Basic, 1970). For a good introduction to Flynn's life, see Lara Vapnek, *Elizabeth Gurley Flynn: Modern American Revolutionary* (Boulder, CO: Westview, 2015).

24. Marjorie Murphy, *Blackboard Unions: The AFT and the NEA, 1900–1980* (Ithaca, NY: Cornell University Press, 1990); Janet Nolan, *Servants of the Poor: Teachers and Mobility in Ireland and Irish America* (Notre Dame, IN: University of Notre Dame Press, 2004); Elliott J. Gorn, *Mother Jones: The Most Dangerous Woman in America* (New York: Hill and Wang, 2001).

25. Eric Foner, "Class, Ethnicity, and Radicalism in the Gilded Age: The Land League and Irish-America," in his *Politics and Ideology in the Age of the Civil War* (New York: Oxford University Press, 1980), 150–200; Michael A. Gordon, "The Labor Boycott in New York City, 1880–1886," *Labor History* 16.2 (Spring 1975): 184–229; Edward T. O'Donnell, *Henry George and the Crisis of Inequality: Progress and Poverty in the Gilded Age* (New York: Columbia University Press, 2015); Brundage, *Irish Nationalists in America*, 111–119, 156–160.

26. David Emmons, *Butte's Irish: Class and Community in an American Mining Town, 1875–1925* (Urbana: University of Illinois Press, 1989); Balch quoted in James R. Barrett, *The Irish Way: Becoming American in the Multi-Ethnic City* (New York: Penguin, 2012), 2.

27. See J. J. Lee, "Emigration: 1922–1998," in *The Encyclopedia of the Irish in America*, 263–266.

28. Kenny, *The American Irish*, 226–267.

29. Ronald P. Formasiano, *Boston Against Busing: Race, Class, and Ethnicity in the 1960s and 1970s* (Chapel Hill: University of North Carolina Press, 1991).

30. The literature on the CIO as an Americanizing force among immigrants is vast. See Thomas Göbel, "Becoming American: Ethnic Workers and the Rise of the CIO," *Labor History* 29.2 (Spring 1988): 173–198, for a good overview.

31. Montgomery, "Labor Movement," 530; Walter P. Reuther and James B. Carey, "Forward" to John Brophy, *A Miner's Life*, ed. John O. P. Hall (Madison: University of Wisconsin Press, 1964), v.

32. Ronald W. Schatz, "Phillip Murray and the Subordination of the Industrial Unions to the United States Government," in *Labor Leaders in America*, ed. Melvyn Dubofsky and Warren van Tine (Urbana: University of Illinois Press, 1987), 35–36, 246; Ronald W. Schatz, "'I Know My Way Around a Little Bit': Bishop Joseph Donnelly and American Labor, 1941–1977," *Labor: Studies in Working-Class History of the Americas* 12.2 (May 2016): 35, 37.

33. Brophy, *A Miner's Life*, 3, 7, 10, 31, 78; Shirley Quill, *Mike Quill, Himself: A Memoir* (Greenwich, CT: Devin-Adair, 1985), 13–14; Joshua B. Freeman, *In Transit: The Transport Workers Union in New York City, 1933–1966* (New York: Oxford University Press, 1989), 137.

34. Freeman, *In Transit*, 267–285.

35. See James T. Fisher, *On the Irish Waterfront: The Crusader, the Movie, and the Soul of the Port of New York* (Ithaca, NY: Cornell University Press, 2009).

36. Kenny, *The American Irish*, 242–246; Stephen P. Erie, *Rainbow's End: Irish Americans and the Dilemmas of Urban Machine Politics, 1840–1985* (Berkeley: University of California Press, 1988); Harold Meyerson, "The Age of the Irish: What Ted Kennedy and John Sweeney Built On," *Washington Post*, August 28, 2009.

37. Kenny, *The American Irish*, 233–235.

38. For two insightful discussions of these and other relevant issues, see Timothy J. Meagher, "The Fireman on the Stairs: Communal Loyalties in the Making of Irish America," in *Making the Irish American*, 609–648, and Peter Quinn, *Looking for Jimmy: A Search for Irish America* (New York: Overlook, 2008).

39. Oscar Handlin, *Boston's Immigrants, 1790–1880: A Study in Acculturation* (1941; rev. and enl. ed., New York: Atheneum, 1969); Handlin, *The Uprooted* (1953: 2d ed., Boston: Little, Brown, 1973).

40. David Noel Doyle, "The Regional Bibliography of Irish America, 1800–1930," *Irish Historical Studies* 23.91 (May 1983): 254–283; Doyle, *Irish Americans, Native Rights*.

41. Foner, "Class, Ethnicity, and Radicalism," 176; Freeman, *In Transit*.
42. Diner, *Erin's Daughters in America*; Miller, *Emigrants and Exiles*; Roediger, *The Wages of Whiteness*.
43. Montgomery, "Labor Movement," 525; Barrett, *The Irish Way*.
44. For an excellent detailed discussion of the holdings at a number of labor history archives, see Daniel J., Leab and Philip P. Mason, eds., *Labor History Archives in the United States: A Guide for Researching and Teaching* (Detroit, MI: Wayne State University Press, 1992).
45. Stuart Bruce Kaufman et al., eds., *The Samuel Gompers Papers*, 13 vols. (Urbana: University of Illinois Press, 1986–2013).
46. Patrick J. Blessing, *The Irish in America: A Guide to the Literature and the Manuscript Collections* (Washington, DC: Catholic University of America Press, 1992) lists numerous archives, organized by state.
47. See, for example, Frank Roney, *Frank Roney, Irish Rebel and California Labor Leader: An Autobiography*, ed. Ira B. Cross (1931; New York: AMS Press, 1977); Mother Jones, *Autobiography of Mother Jones* (New York: Arno, 1969); Elizabeth Gurley *The Rebel Girl: An Autobiography, My First Life (1906–1926)*, reprint ed. (New York: International Publishers, 1973); Brophy, *A Miner's Life*.

David Brundage

Neighborhood, Community, and Space

SPATIAL SEGREGATION AND US NEIGHBORHOODS

DIVIDED CITIES ARE STUNTED CITIES

To begin, it is worth clarifying the nature of segregation as a form of social inequity and injustice. This can be done in several ways. One is to focus on separation itself and to obstacles segregation creates to beneficial communication between racial or socioeconomic groups with urban space. Sociologists have measured this lack of proximity using a wide array of segregation indices, whose sophistication has increased markedly since the 1990s. For the United States, in the 1950s and 1960s, these indices reached levels close to those of contemporary South African cities under apartheid. Since then, they have tended to show a

mild decrease in segregation between most groups in recent years, but they still remain very high. Though whites, blacks, and other people of color interact in limited ways in other institutions and on many downtown city streets, few question that most still return home to vastly separate worlds.[1]

Housing discrimination and a lack of enforcement of civil rights laws offer another way to conceptualize segregation. Most of the world's governments, including the US federal government since 1968, have declared housing discrimination illegal. Yet, largely because of continued push-back against fair housing laws, the US government has failed to allocate sufficient resources for the enormous task of bringing violators to justice, let alone that of compensating victims. This situation was confirmed in 2008 by a bipartisan federal commission on housing equity, which found that in the United States only about twenty thousand out of an estimated four million acts of housing discrimination receive any official attention in any given year.[2]

A more comprehensive historical view of segregation begins with the idea that dividing urban residential space is a way of controlling the process by which urban newcomers discover livable niches in cities and gradually claim access to superior opportunities for livelihoods available there. Those who are targeted by segregation face obstacles to the kind of geographic mobility and dispersal throughout the urban fabric that is necessary to gain access to the full range of social and economic opportunities. In this way, urban race and class zoning work similarly to immigration restriction along national borders, which likewise prohibits mobility toward spaces of greater privilege and promise. Perceived from this vantage, segregation can also be seen as a fundamental violation of the "right to the city," that is, the right to access advantages that are by their very nature primarily found in urban areas.

Very often, groups of newcomers to cities cluster in so-called vestibule neighborhoods reception areas, or ports of entry with people of the same place of origin, language, or culture. Because they have served as powerful magnets for immigrants, many American cities have had several or even dozens of these neighborhoods. This process of clustering is often misleadingly called "voluntary segregation" or even "good segregation"—to distinguish it from "forced" or "bad" segregation. The distinction is misleading for several reasons. First, "forced" segregation is itself the most "voluntary" of all forms of segregation. Racist segregationists have the will, the clear purpose, and the actual power both to live together and to exclude others from their neighborhoods. Thus, they go about their business in the fullest sense of the word "voluntary." Immigrant groups, by contrast, may wish to cluster together, but they rarely have the

institutional power to exclude others from their reception areas, whether or not they had the collective will to do so. Though some "ethnic neighborhoods" contained a clustering of businesses, places of worship, and ethnically based associations of one group, they were almost always multiethnic and even in some cases multicolored. In the United States, only when elite white segregationists made the Chicago-inspired segregationist policies of government and private institutions available to groups of immigrants deemed "white" did those groups actively participate in excluding "non-whites," including African Americans, Latino Americans, and occasionally Asian Americans. Indeed, the jury is out on exactly how "good" clustering really is for newcomers. For most, access to superior prospects means the ability to move freely to neighborhoods that are closer to the employment and educational opportunities that best suit individual households. Because of the system of racial segregation that came to rule US cities, the right to seek out greater opportunity eventually meant the ability to disperse "voluntarily" into suburban areas. This was the path followed by virtually all immigrant groups who achieved "white" status. Yet, that right was precisely what the same segregationist system denied to most people of color.[3]

The bleak consequences of neighborhood racial segregation for African Americans and Hispanic Americans (especially those with darker-skin color) are well documented. These include poor access to those areas of the city with the most dynamic job growth because of the distances involved, physical barriers, discriminatory law enforcement techniques such as racial profiling in traffic stops, or the lack of transport. Obstacles to accruing wealth through the housing market have included low housing appreciation rates, higher home mortgage and insurance costs, and lack of access to maintenance capital. Barriers to high-quality education stemmed from systems of school financing based on local property tax receipts.

Draconian law enforcement campaigns, such as the War on Crime and the War on Drugs, have singled out segregated neighborhoods of color resulting in a massive outflow of their residents to prisons, and a greater risk of violent death at the hands of police officers. Other consequences include relative absence of healthy food due to lower local investment in full-service food markets, poorer water quality, greater exposure to household and industrial toxins, and inadequate health-care facilities. All of these factors resulted in poorer health and lower life expectancy. In many African American neighborhoods in the United States residents live shorter lives than residents of some of the least-developed countries of the world.[4]

Once segregationists put residential color boundaries in place, they can rely upon the very fabric of urban space to help them hoard resources and power in their favored neighborhoods and to enable early death in neighborhoods they marginalize. Initially an act of political will, segregation thus also becomes an exemplary instance of the "agency" of the city itself—one that weakens cities' vaunted capacity to deliver general improvement to the masses of humanity that have become urban residents during our own era.

THE SEGREGATION PARADOXES

Cities, by their very nature, amass people. They bring us close together, cheek by jowl, in teeming crowds; they bless our yearnings for the social. Yet one of the oldest impulses in city design is to drive people apart: to rend the urban fabric into separate and unequal zones, to indulge our equally human penchant for distinguishing the "we" from the "them." Though the word *segregation* is a recent invention, and though the concept of race is not much older, the impetus to divide cities is as old as cities themselves—we could call it our "original urban sin." Eridu, known as Mesopotamia's "urban Eden," was founded seventy centuries ago. The ziggurats that came

into being there and elsewhere in the region, constituted nothing less than a separate, monumental urban neighborhood for the gods, set above and apart from the mortals who thronged the dustier wards below. The Mesopotamian version of the divine-human boundary likely took thousands of years to solidify as the region's urban palace-temple districts became more foreboding. But the Sumerian ziggurat—and its later analogs the Chinese Forbidden City, the Mesoamerican *teocalli*, the royal citadel, the acropolis, the Palatine Hill—have cast a shadow upon all cities since. From the outset, city-splitting was intrinsic to domination and hierarchy.[5]

It is a long stretch, of course, from Eridu to the "chocolate cities" and "vanilla suburbs" of the present-day United States. Only through another of segregation's paradoxes can we adequately ponder the connection. If city-splitting impulses can make any claim to universality, they can do so only because of their enormous variability. As urban civilizations rose, fell, and rose again across the millennia, so did the basic formulas determining who belonged in the elect districts and who did not. The outer walls of cities put in place one aspect of segregationism: they divided the urban and the urbane from the rural and the rustic. Within cities themselves, local residents marked themselves as "from here" by corralling their city's foreigners—those "from there"—into separate compounds. Whether strangers were locked in or given control of their own district, they became especially useful to local leaders as scapegoats, partly too because so many were rich merchants or financiers and thus vulnerable to charges of parasitism and greediness. The many iterations of this nasty trick include the invention of the Jewish ghetto in Europe during the Middle Ages. Elsewhere and in other times, creed, class, caste, clan, craft, and even sex could determine urban boundary lines to greater or lesser degrees. Dividing lines were also more penetrable in some places than others. Sometimes—paradoxically again—the porosity of the boundaries was essential to their operation as a tool of domination. How could local elites maintain their aloof status, for example, if they did not enroll hundreds of shanty-dwellers as domestic servants and provide them quarters in the very heart of the palace?

Segregationists embraced urban dividing lines because segregation gave them a tool of enhanced power. Divine-right monarchs were the first city-splitters; they were helped by court intellectuals or priests, and, in other ways, by landowning elites. Divided cities enabled such power-brokers to establish authoritarian governments, to disseminate official state ideologies, and to stockpile wealth. But as a political tool segregation has always been paradoxical in its own right. No matter how powerful, segregationists also have to *expend* large quantities of power to put the boundary lines in place. Splitting a city requires huge effort and expense, and it demands specialized tools of its own, designed explicitly for making, unmaking, and remaking urban space. Over the millennia these tools have included monumental architecture (as in the ziggurat), walls, palisades, battlements, bastions, fences, gates, guard shacks, checkpoints, booms, railroad tracks, highways, tunnels, rivers, inlets, mountainsides and ridges, buffer zones, free-fire zones, demilitarized zones, *cordon sanitaires*, screens of trees, road blocks, violent mobs, terrorism, the police, armies, curfews, quarantines, pass laws, labor compounds, building clearances, forced removals, restrictive covenants, zoning ordinances, racial steering practices, race-infused economic incentives, segregated private and public housing developments, exclusive residential compounds, gated communities, separate municipal governments and fiscal systems, discriminatory access to land ownership and credit, complementary rural holding zones, influx control laws, and restrictions against overseas immigration. In great part, segregation persisted because city-splitters adapted to changing circumstances by varying the combinations of these tools in seemingly countless ways.[6]

THE RISE OF URBAN COLOR LINES

In the modern era, a new notion of human difference arose: race. By fusing scientific universality and political malleability, race gave Western city builders license to do something unprecedented: to stamp a single civilization's segregationist style on cities spread across every inhabited continent—in the process reinforcing the West's global hegemony. In a series of five wide-reaching historical lurches during the 18th and 19th centuries, Europeans spread racially divided colonial cities across Asia, the Pacific Rim, Africa, and parts of the Americas. In the process the signature spaces of the new form of city-splitting proliferated: white towns, black towns, "Asiatic" bazaars, Chinatowns, native locations, black townships, and black ghettos. All of the tools used by earlier segregationists were brought to bear. New enhanced techniques of class segregation were developed in Europe and shipped across oceans and empires to become tools of racial control.

Governments, as in premodern times, were the biggest segregationists in the era of race. The British, French, and American Empires account for most of the new urban color lines, though the Spanish, Dutch, Belgians, Germans, Italians, and even the Portuguese were active as well. Segregation enhanced the prestige and "manifest destiny" of these empires' "ruling races." More practical imperial administrators, such as Stamford Raffles in Singapore or Lord Lugard in Nigeria, also averred that racially divided cities minimized disputes between subject peoples with differing legal systems.

A new group of modern-era, globe-trotting, semi-independent professional intellectuals also played crucial roles in the spread of segregation. Race theorists helped justify Western imperialism as well as the split cities needed to sustain it. Successive generations of peripatetic urban reformers promoted it as well. Public health officials, for example, thought segregation necessary to minimize health threats posed to whites by the inferior races and their supposedly inherently poor sanitary habits. Later, housing reformers allowed their slum clearance and public housing schemes to serve segregationist ends. Professionalized urban planners also incorporated segregation into what they called "comprehensive" blueprints for ever more lavish colonial cities.

Another, somewhat more anarchic institution also spread through the colonies at the same time: the global capitalist real estate industry. The new tools that it pioneered, such as London's land-use covenants in property deeds, were adapted to solidify color lines. But the expanded property rights upon which the industry was based also weakened race boundaries in many colonial capitals. There, wealthy Asians or Africans could afford to buy and live in the white town. Because empires depended on allies among local elites, colonial officials sometimes balked at legislating or enforcing racial zoning. [7]

Segregation's variability, backed by the power of empires and their roving experts, nonetheless won out. Urban segregation was central to the earliest big undertaking of modern Western empire-building, the British conquest of India. The first surge of racial segregation began with the original "White Town" and "Black Town" at the British East India Company's principal outpost at Madras (today's Chennai), which later helped inspire the less successfully divided capital at Calcutta (Kolkata). As the conquest proceeded, practices of segregation by color further diversified among the one hundred seventy five segregated military and civil "stations" of the British Raj. In Asia—scattered from Afghanistan to the Malay Peninsula, from the hot military outposts in the Indian plains, such as Canpore, Mian Mir (near Lahore), or Secunderabad (near Hyderabad), to the cool "hill stations" in the uplands, such as Simla, Darjeeling, or Ootacamund—racial segregation proved enormously adaptable in diverse political, social, economic, religious, and geographical terrains. [8]

The second surge, associated with the European "opening" of China, brought segregation to places as diverse as Singapore, Shanghai, Hong Kong, and Yokohama. From there the concept of the Chinatown spread across the Pacific, following the emigration of millions of Chinese people to the Americas and Australasia. In these places, urban segregation adapted for the first time to the rawer racial politics of white settler colonies, such as those headquartered in San Francisco, Vancouver, Melbourne, and Honolulu. [9]

The year 1894 marked the debut of the word *segregation* as a global political slogan. The occasion was the global plague pandemic that began in Hong Kong, and, two years later, in Bombay. There, panicked public health officials evicted Asian plague victims wholesale from their homes, often to redeposit them in "segregation camps." Their actions sparked the third and, to date, most widespread surge in implementation of segregation at the turn of the 20th century, namely segregation mania. This mania for splitting cities travelled across much of the colonial world, as calls for segregation multiplied everywhere ship-born rats carried plague-infested fleas—eastward to Hawaii and California and westward to African cities from Nairobi to Cape Town to Accra and Dakar. In West Africa, the mania was strengthened by fervent campaigns targeting urban Africans (especially their children), suspected as the prime source of *malaria plasmodia* carried by the mosquitoes that sent so many white men to their tropical graves. [10]

Professional city planners also entered the business of city-splitting during the period of segregation mania. Backed by lavish imperial investment and power, they initiated the fourth surge of racial segregation by resurrecting the city-dividing capacities of monumental architecture in their designs for colonial capitals. Exemplified above all by Edwin Lutyens's New Delhi and Henri Prost's Rabat, the capital of French Morocco, the broad avenues, looming palaces, and elaborate racial zoning systems called for in their plans were intended to function as arrogant disquisitions on the contrast between the timeless but backward splendor of the East and the cutting-edge progressivism of the West.[11]

As these third and fourth surges crested in a worldwide frenzy of racial city-splitting, they coincided—paradoxically again—with the rise of the most important global adversaries of race segregationism. In the early 20th century, people of color everywhere began joining the giant tide of loosely interconnected anticolonial, national liberation, civil rights, and black freedom movements that would later launch an unprecedented revolution against white supremacy and Western imperialism. While interwar and postwar decolonization did not end urban segregation—for class boundaries grew more acute in cities everywhere, including in former colonies—it did terminate the tradition of separate white towns and black towns that had been in place for two hundred-fifty years.

ARCHSEGREGATION

The story did not end there, though, for the era of segregation mania also gave birth to a fifth surge, exemplified by two much more robust and radical forms of racial city-splitting—in South Africa and the United States. In these two countries, the practice of urban racial segregation actually gained ground amid the great mid-20th-century calls for race equality. For that reason I call the systems in both places "archsegregation."

South Africa and the United States were white settler societies where the settlers themselves held unusually commanding positions in politics. They were places where a screaming pitch of white supremacy was sharpened by an opposing sense that white power was especially vulnerable to a "rising tide of color"—whether arising from the perceived threat of the black majority in South Africa or that of the "Great Migration" of blacks to US cities. The two countries were

both directly connected to British and other European networks of reformers as well as the many actors of the transnational urban real estate industry. That meant that local segregationists found it relatively easy to import a wide range of urban reform legislation and planning practices useful in dividing cities by race, including slum clearance and public housing legislation, state-guaranteed mortgage protections for first-time homebuyers, racist public health ideologies, restrictive covenants in title deeds, British jurisprudence that clarified how these functioned, and zoning laws. Both societies were also major importers of British capital, courtesy of transnational development and construction companies. Both also welcomed British-style organizational instruments such as title registries and property courts; professional associations of real estate agents, appraisers, lawyers, and surveyors; and homeowners' or ratepayers' associations. Finally, urban whites in South Africa and the United States also possessed a permanent stake in local real estate markets, unlike the peripatetic communities of imperial officials who formed the majority of whites in most colonial white towns. They were thus susceptible to the self-serving myth that black neighbors brought down the value of nearby property. This myth linked segregation tightly to racially infused economic incentives that completely transformed the role of the real estate industry in the politics of city-splitting. It also gave a new logic to the policies and practices that both societies imported from abroad. From a source of irritation for government-led segregationist planning, the business of buying and selling land became a nearly unstoppable force of urban racial division.[12]

Comparing the two archsegregationist societies reveals another paradox. South Africa, the society that most publicly, unrepentantly, and viciously harnessed city-splitting to the power of formal discriminatory legislation, also took the longest to be successful. Then it expired the quickest; apartheid is, after all, no longer with us. The American system, which by contrast was designed to operate as much as possible outside the fray of politics, not only divided cities earlier and with almost as much efficiency as apartheid at its height, but it also remains alive and well.[13]

This paradox highlights the sharp differences in the two systems, which are as important as the elements they shared. The explanation largely lies in striking contrasts in the historical contexts of black-white politics in each society. In South Africa, black-white politics arose from a matrix of imperial conquest and land dispossession. Under the law of conquest that followed, blacks, coloreds, and Indians had severely limited civil, political, and property rights. White racial fears notwithstanding, the resistance movements of color wielded relatively little leverage during the era of segregation mania, even when Indians organized under the aegis of Mohandas Gandhi. As a result the British Empire, and the whites-only Union of South Africa it helped found in 1910, created legislated racial segregation instruments—such as Native Location laws, labor compound policies, pass laws, and rural reserves—early in the period of segregation mania. From there, the notoriously strident politics of "black peril" in places such as Johannesburg, combined with vicious anti-Asian sentiment, propelled national discussions toward state-legislated segregation. But the state precedents themselves, virtually unchecked by any liberal constitutional authority, also channeled South African segregationist movements' priorities toward the same goals. Their victories, such as the Native (Urban Areas) Act of 1923, the Slums Act of 1935, and the apartheid-era Group Areas Act of 1950, all built upon the political precedents of earlier laws.[14]

In the United States, by contrast, black-white politics proceeded from the regional conflict over slavery and emancipation. The victory of the North in the Civil War and the period of Reconstruction that followed gave the victorious Republican Party, based largely in the North, overwhelming political incentives to give largely Southern black men a wider range of rights, including property, civil, and voting rights. These newfound rights proved fragile, and the US Supreme Court whittled away at these nearly continuously throughout the late 19th century and beyond—most notably in its decision in *Plessy v. Ferguson* (1896), which gave the green light to segregationist Jim Crow laws. But even at the "nadir" of post-emancipation black history, amid Southern disfranchisement of blacks and terrible waves of racist lynchings, African Americans still possessed far more organizational and political power than blacks in South Africa or, for that matter, coloreds or Indians there.

Under these circumstances a group of failed white disfranchisement activists in Maryland passed the closest equivalent to South Africa's Native Location Laws in the United States: the Baltimore Segregation Ordinance of 1910. The ordinance divided every street in Baltimore into "white blocks" and "colored blocks" based on the race of the majority of the inhabitants at the time of the ordinance's passage. It set a penalty of one hundred dollars and up to a year in the Baltimore city jail for anyone who moved to a block set aside for the "opposite race." The only exception was for black servants who lived in the houses of their white employers. The US version of segregation mania spread from there, as city councils and mayors in dozens of cities in the South and the Midwest passed or considered copy-cat legislation. In 1917, a group of aldermen in Chicago nearly followed suit, but they were too late. In November of that year the otherwise largely white-supremacist Supreme Court passed down its decision in *Buchanan v. Warley* that declared Baltimore-style laws unconstitutional. Deftly using a property-rights argument, the multiracial team of lawyers from the NAACP had demonstrated just how much power the organized African American community could wield.[15]

In the absence of state power—and in the face of an unprecedented wave of migration of African Americans from the South to cities in the North, which quickly filled existing black districts and burst their boundaries— American whites in many places turned to their longstanding practice of enforcing neighborhood color lines by mob violence and house bombings. These actions stood in sharp contrast to South Africa, where street riots were rare because whites could more plausibly put their faith in government. During World War I and in the years immediately after, violence spiraled out of control in a wave of race riots across the United States, capped by a bloody week in Chicago in 1919 in which more than thirty-five people were killed, most of them black. An alliance of segregationist urban reformers and real estate agents in that city went back to the drawing board to lay out neighborhood-splitting schemes that operated as far as possible outside the political limelight.[16]

THE CHICAGO SYSTEM

The Chicago-based alliance had many leaders, but two stand out: Nathan William MacChesney, lead council of the National Association of Real Estate Boards (NAREB), and the great reform economist Richard T. Ely, founder of the Institute for Research on Land Economics and Public Utilities. In 1925, MacChesney arranged the transfer of Ely's institute from the University of Wisconsin Madison to the Chicago campus of Northwestern University. Together, they drafted a series of textbooks for real estate agents that consistently taught the racist theory of property values as a scientific fact. From there, they and other Chicago-based realtors and self-described "progressive" intellectuals devised an ingenious and many-headed hydra of a segregation system. One of the system's set of teeth was provided by the model racial restrictive covenant drawn up by MacChesney. Another consisted of his "Realtor's Code of Ethics" for the NAREB, which borrowed language from

the mission statement of Ely's institute and made it a badge of professional responsibility for true "realtors" to steer blacks away from white or transitioning neighborhoods. Another was promotion by both of their organizations of a federally coordinated model zoning code that, most importantly, allowed new suburban municipalities to prohibit apartment buildings. The US Supreme Court gave its blessing to such measures in 1926 despite the fact that they were widely seen as (among other things) an effective means to keep black renters out of town.[17]

The "redlining" policies of the New Deal's mortgage insurance program constituted the most important "head" of the new hydra. These policies were also the brainchild of economists at Ely's institute, though the developer and economist Homer Hoyt at the University of Chicago also played an important independent role. Once again they imported British models for long-term mortgages and government subsidies for first-time homebuyers and rearranged them to suit American racial contexts at just about the time that South Africans were doing the very same thing (and in the process putting in place another often overlooked precedent for apartheid). To save defaulting homeowners during the Great Depression, and then to promote home buying as a way out of the crisis, Presidents Herbert Hoover and Franklin Roosevelt called upon Hoyt and a half-dozen other Chicagoans to staff several federal housing agencies, most notably the New Deal's Home Owner's Loan Corporation (HOLC) and the Federal Housing Administration (FHA). The real estate appraiser and amateur economist Frederick Babcock left Ely's institute for the FHA in Washington, where he wrote the agency's *Underwriting Manual*, thus using the relatively obscure rule-making power of the FHA to transform the agency's formally nonracial legal mandate into a discriminatory program. The *Manual* explicitly called for an expansion of restrictive covenants and directed FHA valuators to avoid insuring mortgages in transitional neighborhoods. Along with HOLC, the FHA drafted the famous red-lining maps, using model surveys originally developed by Ely and Hoyt that highlighted the race and ethnicity of the population as a factor in property values. In neighborhood-by-neighborhood interviews with realtors and mortgage providers nationwide, the agencies documented, among other things, the commonplace acceptance of already existing private practices of racial steering and discriminatory lending. Red areas on the maps, which designated high-risk areas to be avoided by federal insurance, largely coincided with African American neighborhoods, including those whose residents were deemed relatively affluent. The FHA maps and reports effectively gave the federal stamp of approval to private racist practices. Thus, as a HOLC report on Chicago put it—shedding few tears in the process—the government's main housing agencies helped guarantee that "mortgage lending institutions will continue to withhold mortgage funds at reasonable terms from deteriorating neighborhoods," especially those inhabited by African Americans.[18]

Other technically nonracial legislation provided further sets of government-sharpened teeth to the American urban color line, at the same time that the FHA program, combined with a similar initiative at the Veteran's Administration, went into full effect after World War II. Federally funded "urban renewal" and slum-clearance programs, for example, were placed under the control of local governments and downtown business interests, which prioritized projects that leveled black neighborhoods located near many American downtowns and consigned their former residents into public housing projects largely sited in the heart of what African American activists now pointedly called the "ghetto." The massive postwar highway building programs added further swaths of destruction, often leveling promising black business districts, to create the right-of-way for superhighway spurs that quickened commutes from the outskirts to downtown. Even

so, none of these practices guaranteed fixed color lines like the contemporary Group Areas Act in apartheid South Africa. As the number of African American migrants to cities rose during the 1950s and 1960s, they moved into previously white neighborhoods—expanding the "ghetto" across urban space. Still, the many-headed Chicago system provided all the necessary enabling amenities for whites to flee racially changing urban neighborhoods, purchase mortgages for houses in the wider and more lucrative reaches of the suburbs, and commute back to downtown or to jobs in the rapidly expanding economy of the suburbs themselves. In this way the US policy also fatally linked segregation with both higher black unemployment rates and automobile-driven, gasoline-dependent sprawl.[19]

CHALLENGES TO SEGREGATION

By most measures, the Civil Rights movement in the United States launched the most elaborate of all the world's assaults on urban residential color lines. At its broadest base, the revolution against urban segregation in the United States was a movement of ordinary, courageous people seeking housing in neighborhoods where they were not welcomed. Tens of thousands of largely anonymous pioneering black home-seekers willingly walked into the teeth of white violence because available housing in black neighborhoods was hard to find, overcrowded, unsanitary, dangerous, and outrageously expensive. Beyond the ever-moving American color line lay ever-elusive spaces of urban opportunity, where better deals on housing also came with higher-quality amenities for the whole family: schools, parks, public health infrastructure, a less polluted environment, transport, and easier access to jobs.

To help these ordinary African Americans, the NAACP opened up a second front of activism within the law: Moorfield Storey's brilliant maneuvers in *Buchanan v. Worley* in 1917 against racial zoning ordinances was one legendary victory in the US Supreme Court. In 1948, Thurgood Marshall returned to the Court to defeat racially restrictive covenants in *Shelley v. Kraemer*. Marshall also exposed the FHA's proprietary *Underwriting Manual* in 1938, though he had to repeatedly badger a local FHA official from the Long Island suburbs to give him a copy. Now at least partly uncovered, the federal government's complicity in segregation, along with that of municipal public housing authorities, became the target of yet another tactic: persistent petitions and protests in the name of open housing.[20]

From the 1940s through the 1960s, open-housing activists put sufficient pressure on state legislatures to pass a raft of fair housing laws that explicitly prohibited racial steering and redlining. Large numbers of liberal white suburban homeowners also entered the fray, some by signing so-called covenants of open occupancy, typically declaring they would "welcome into their neighborhood any residents of good character, regardless of race, color, religion, or national origin." Others went door to door in efforts to persuade their white neighbors to ignore blockbusting real estate swindlers. Still others joined with blacks to persuade real estate agents and bankers to help keep racially changing liberal neighborhoods—like Chicago's Oak Park, Cleveland's Shaker Heights, and Philadelphia's West Mount Airy—permanently integrated. In 1960, open-housing activists pressured the Democratic Party presidential candidate John F. Kennedy to promise he would end federal housing discrimination "with the stroke of the pen"—a pledge he belatedly fulfilled two years later.[21]

The next step belonged to Martin Luther King Jr. In 1966, fresh from his historic victories in the South, he plunged straight into the maul of American urban archsegregationism by turning his favorite weapon, Gandhian nonviolent resistance, against the color line in Chicago. From his headquarters in a Black Belt housing project he alternately sent black

and white testers to white real estate offices to verify the wide spread of racial steering. Then he deployed pickets outside offending real estate agents' offices and personally led a wave of mass marches into the surrounding neighborhoods. There, he ran headlong into the white violence that had long sustained American urban color lines. Crowds of white counter-demonstrators shouted racist epithets, brandished swastika flags, and launched volleys of bricks. After a face-saving truce with Chicago mayor Richard J. Daley, King left town to nurse his realization that peaceful protest had done little to dislodge divisions deeply rooted in racialized economic interest.

Two years later, King fell to an assassin's bullet in Memphis. In response, the poorest African American residents of US cities added their own version of mass action to the movement. For five previous "long hot summers," anger and violence had engulfed places such as Harlem, North Philadelphia, Watts, Newark, and Detroit. This time, in 1968, the fire once again raged in more than one hundred black "ghettos." As before, the most immediate results were scores of people killed and injured and new swaths of burned-out buildings and businesses. But the din of a hundred riots also gave President Lyndon Johnson the leverage to persuade Senate minority leader Everett Dirksen (R-IL) to release the votes necessary for the open-housing movement's long-delayed federal Fair Housing Act. Discrimination of all kinds in the housing market was now against the law.[22]

In the years following this bitterly won victory, the Civil Rights movement championed creative solutions to the problems of the residential color line in an increasingly conservative age. In Chicago, activists filed a lawsuit against segregationist practices in public housing. In *Hills v. Gautreaux* (1976), they won another landmark victory: the justices ordered the Chicago Housing Authority to offer thousands of housing vouchers to allow poor African American families to relocate to the suburbs. Though their numbers were comparatively small, the families who were selected for the program did demonstrably better than their counterparts in the ghetto. Meanwhile, a movement also gained steam in a handful of cities for inclusionary zoning laws, which typically require new developments to include substantial shares of affordable housing. The Home Mortgage Disclosure Act (1976) and the Community Reinvestment Act (1977) were perhaps even more promising. These were federal laws that required private redliners to reveal information about the location of their mortgage lending and to assume an "affirmative obligation" to lend money in all neighborhoods where they took deposits. Meanwhile, other policies, including the federal Community Development Block Grants and the various state-initiated Enterprise Zones, unleashed government funds and tax breaks for the development of neglected areas. Grassroots efforts to channel federal, corporate, and private foundation money into community development corporations (CDCs) or neighborhood-based direct-action organizations have had notable successes across the country.[23]

HOW "COLOR BLIND" POLITICS RESCUED RACIAL SEGREGATION

By 1970, America's sprawling suburbs had outgrown the cities they surrounded. While suburban areas did began to diversify in terms of class, immigration status, and race, they also remained home to the single largest and most influential uniracial white voting bloc in the country (and perhaps the world). Forsaking the balder white supremacist rhetoric of Jim Crow, suburban whites voiced their support for longstanding privileges tied to residential segregation by tapping into traditions of camouflaged racial demands that went back to the work of the NAREB and Ely's institute. Already in the late 1940s, for example, suburbanites outside Atlanta, Los Angeles, Detroit, and Chicago articulated their defense of homogeneous neighborhoods in terms of a defense of property rights and the

"civil right" to choose one's neighbors. Others fought fair housing laws by appealing to the right of free association or the freedom from unwarranted government interference.[24]

The idea of refashioning white privilege as a defense of rights and liberty proved appealing to politicians such as George Wallace, Richard Nixon, and Ronald Reagan. Such rhetoric allowed leaders to combine promises of support for middle-class white privileges with revived "free-market" attacks on welfare states, labor unions, government regulations, and progressive taxation systems. Meanwhile, a language of racial resentment also lured at least some white working-class voters away from traditional left-leaning parties and toward those favored by their employers.

Several feats of political conjury were involved in these campaigns. One was an insistence upon an upside-down narrative of social history in which the black and brown civil rights revolution and its liberal white allies had succeeded in seizing enormous power—thus transforming white people into the true victims of racial inequality. Accusing civil rights activists of demanding "special rights" for black and brown people, including fair housing enforcement, so-called New Right leaders proposed an attractive-sounding "color-blind" and ostensibly meritocratic society—thus effectively perpetuating segregation and black subordination by denying its existence. While repeatedly disavowing racist intent, New Right leaders could simultaneously channel racial hatred through code words such as "welfare," "taxes," "quotas," "immigrants," "values," "social pathology," "inner cities," "the underclass," "ghettos," and, most of all, "crime." Three kinds of policy tools helped to drive urban segregation forward and even to give it new forms: authoritarian anticrime and anti-immigration policies disproportionately directed at urban people of color; a willful neglect of fair housing laws that encouraged a variety of segregationist dynamics to persist in land markets; and a campaign to deregulate the financial industry, which gave it an enormous new sway over both global and urban politics.

The New Right's mania for "tough" criminal justice policies created new possibilities for government coercion in the drawing of color lines. Since the Nixon years, successive "wars" on crime and drugs, waged against largely urban, black, low-level drug dealers, transformed a medium-sized (if already racially unequal) prison system into a massive archipelago of what some sociologists call "carceral ghettos." Now holding more than 2.3 million people, the majority of them black and brown city dwellers, these prison ghettos have multiplied across the American countryside, festooning the outskirts of hundreds of nearly all-white small towns with watch towers and barbed-wire enclosures. Meanwhile, problems with police misconduct in neighborhoods of color, as revealed by the incidents in the multiracial suburbs of Sanford, Florida, in 2012, and Ferguson, Missouri, in 2014, also persist across the United States and in many other Western countries. Instances of police abuse repeatedly provide the trigger for urban rioting.[25]

Race-tinged authoritarianism has also crept into New Right–era immigration policy. In 1965, the United States repealed racist immigration restrictions. Since the 1980s, federal and state governments have put increasingly militarized influx-control efforts in place and have combined these efforts with massive deportations. In the context of widening desperation in many parts of the global South and increased demand for migrant labor in the global North, such border-interdiction measures do much more than control influxes. They intensify the bureaucratic nightmares involved in acquiring passes and other documentation, promote racial profiling of both legal and illegal migrants, make it more difficult for migrant workers to protest low pay and bad working conditions, encourage criminal enterprises that exploit migrants, increase the numbers of potentially productive

people behind bars, and put migrants at greater risk of death crossing oceans and deserts. All of these discriminatory side effects of the ever-more fortress-like "global color line" resonate deeply in the segregated black and brown urban communities of the United States and other Western societies.[26]

In the "color-blind" era, increased government coercion of people of color is mirrored by the willful retreat of governments from their legal obligations to control segregationist actions by real estate agents, developers, bankers, and privileged white homeowners in the housing market. The racial theory of real estate values is thus left free to continue driving practices of racial steering, redlining, and white flight. Meanwhile, these same real estate market dynamics, helped by big developers and sometimes by governments, have created new forces of coercive segregation, such as gated communities and gentrification.[27]

Surveys of white attitudes in the United States show repeatedly that whites are more willing than before to consider black neighbors— as long as they are not too numerous and as long as they meet certain class thresholds. White mob violence against black home-seekers decreased once the postwar black migration to cities ended and reversed after 1970. Indexes of segregation in the United States have declined somewhat since. Immigrants continue to arrive in large numbers despite restrictions, and many settle in and around the moving color line, often creating much more complex borders and even some integrated checkerboard neighborhoods, including some in the suburbs. In some cities, most notably Chicago and Detroit, the number of people impacted by extreme segregation may be diminishing simply because thousands of ghetto residents have reversed the Great Migration by moving to the comparatively less segregated cities of the US South. Despite all of these changes, though, segregation measures remain extremely high, especially in the largest cities. In Chicago almost

80 percent of the population would still have to move for all of the city's neighborhoods to have the same racial composition (down from about 90 percent in 1960). Ghetto neighborhoods have always been segregated internally by class, but rates of spatial concentration of poor black people have risen in many cities, including Chicago. Blacks who move to the suburbs are still largely steered to older, inner-ring, "hand-me-down" municipalities with declining property values. White flight from those areas continues, if now financed by whites' generally higher personal wealth more than by federal subsidies. In many suburban rings, racial segregation indexes are higher than in neighboring cities. Meanwhile, some of the outright aggression of whites toward unwanted outsiders and their fear of crime have been rechanneled into the fortified gated communities that private developers began scattering across the suburbs of Los Angeles, Miami, Chicago, and New York after 1970.[28]

Gentrification is another potentially coercive form of market-based segregation that has increased after 1970. In the global North it usually involves well-to-do and often younger people buying up promising old real estate in poorer neighborhoods near downtown that seem more sophisticated, "edgier," or simply more convenient to work and play. When gentrification gains momentum, it can work like a market-driven form of slum clearance. Renovations push up property values and taxes, forcing poorer residents nearby to relocate elsewhere. Gentrifiers, like the worst of government slum-clearance programs, are under no obligation to provide affordable rehousing. The government plays a role as well. Local housing authorities' ever more zealous efforts to raze long-neglected public housing projects have in some cases had the effect of opening new areas for gentrification; in any case, the decline of American public housing in general gives poor people fewer anchors of affordable housing that would otherwise allow them to remain in gentrifying districts. Other urban authorities organize "business improvement districts" that offer special services to elite downtown residents. District officials sometimes replicate the fortified feel of suburban gated communities by hiring private security patrols, authorizing periodic roundups of homeless people, and installing bristling networks of surveillance cameras.[29]

Persistent segregation at once reflects and encourages the sharply increasing economic inequalities that are a hallmark of the supposed era of color blindness. One of the most important causes of this increasing inequality was the free-market-driven deregulation of finance. For people of color in American cities, the deregulation of the global economy went hand in hand with the New Right's neglect of fair-housing enforcement to create new disadvantages in segregated land markets and thus new obstacles to accruing wealth. Surveys of mortgage lending repeatedly demonstrate tremendous disparities in the willingness of banks to lend to whites and blacks all along the spectra of income and education—even as New Right politicians and Wall Street lobby strongly to weaken the antiredlining Community Reinvestment Act.

Paradoxically, though, big finance's practice of "reverse redlining"—selective targeting of poor people and ghetto residents with predatory loans—sowed almost as much destruction as redlining itself. This practice, just as paradoxically, first became widespread in the United States precisely because of legislation accompanying the 1968 Fair Housing Act. That legislation directed the FHA to guarantee mortgages in areas it had previously redlined. Unscrupulous realtors, appraisers, and mortgage lenders took advantage of the new mandate by colluding in schemes to overassess the value of structurally unsound houses, then sell them fraudulently to desperate ghetto residents with financing fully ensured by the US Treasury. Once the new homeowners ran into insurmountable repair and repayment problems, the predatory sting drew quickly to a close: the banks recouped the unpaid loan from the FHA and walked away, leaving it up to the federal government to bulldoze the house. This explains why large tracts of the South Side of Chicago and other "Rust Belt" ghettos first acquired their contemporary bombed-out look, with scores of spectral, abandoned houses dotting large swaths of vacant land that is now returning to its former state of open prairie.[30]

The most devastating of all of the regulatory concessions to big finance occurred in 1998 when US president Bill Clinton joined conservative congressmen in support of legislation allowing high-risk investment banks to enter the housing finance business. Wall Street money artists quickly devised or expanded three types of speculative financial instruments: predatory "subprime" loans to poor people; mortgage-backed securities consisting of predatory loans bundled with other loans and re-sliced into highly lucrative "tranches"; and so-called credit default swaps meant to insure the mortgage-backed securities. The market success of these "designer" assets pushed piratical mortgage companies, some of them subsidiaries of big banks, to lure ever-larger numbers of poor people into mortgages. The loans they peddled, again often using grossly fraudulent practices, virtually guaranteed default. Most contained "adjustable" interest rates that soon increased the size of monthly payments beyond most borrowers' means.

Across the United States, black people were more than twice as likely as white people of the same income—and over three times as likely in Chicago—to be steered into subprime loans, even though two-thirds were eligible for standard mortgages that on average cost $100,000 less over the life of the loan. Racial segregation, noted the sociologists Jacob S. Rugh and Douglas S. Massey, "created a unique niche of minority clients who were differentially marketed risky subprime loans." The resulting racial disparities in housing foreclosures widened the large inequalities in wealth on either side of the American color line. After 2000, Barack Obama parlayed his career as a community organizer on Chicago's South Side to become an Illinois state senator, then a US senator, then the country's first black president, inaugurating renewed talk of a "post-racial age." In 2008, as the American mortgage bubble burst, bringing on a global recession, US whites possessed a staggering ten times more wealth on average than blacks of equal income, largely because of segregation in the American housing market. Four years later, as Obama finished his first term, the black-white wealth gap had doubled to twenty to one.[31]

In these many ways, American segregationists have kept their creation alive, letting new heads grow on the monster as others get chopped off. No law forbids white flight or the often equally segregationist undertow of gentrification. No legislation can outlaw the idea that black neighbors bring white people's property values down. Such racially inflected dynamics in the private housing market—coupled with ongoing steering, redlining, and devastating bouts of discriminatory predatory lending—continue to quietly guarantee unequal and separate racial spaces in American cities to our day. So quietly does segregation work that many Americans are tempted to think of it as a "de facto" phenomenon. It just is—it was never made, let alone planned. Thus the jagged color lines that run right through most American cities seem to fade out of our collective consciousness, never coming close to the top of the country's or the world's political priorities. In this way American-style segregation has outlived its arch-segregationist cousin, South African apartheid, whose reliance on explicit state action ultimately rendered it more vulnerable to local and global anti-segregationist forces. [32]

A BITTERSWEET PARADOX

Segregationists continue to occupy the commanding heights of urban spatial politics not only in the United States, but also many other societies the world over. The exact nature of urban dividing lines has been blurred. Race, class, ethnicity, culture, and (most toxically) religion all play interconnected roles, depending on the place. With some notorious exceptions, explicitly segregationist government legislation is no longer the principal coercive force behind the sundering of cities. Instead, most city-dividers today use tools that resemble those at work in the many-headed system of the United States. Far from "informal" or "voluntary" (let alone "de facto"), such tools, embedded above all in the real estate and financial industries, pack plenty of coercive institutional force. They also benefit from an aura of plausible deniability that probably even more crucially explains their political longevity.

That said, there is a final, bittersweet paradox to the global history of urban segregation. As powerful as these forces are, our age is also blessed with more knowledge about the devastating effects of segregation than any other era in human history. We also have more knowledge than ever about ways to create open, egalitarian, and empowering urban spaces and communities. This knowledge had been put into action in many places: in the scrappy anti-segregationist grassroots community organizations of the United States, which seek to redirect whatever capital flows they can toward impoverished neighborhoods; in the French "anti-ghetto" laws, which mandate that 20 percent of the housing stock of all towns be owned by the public; in the shanty-and-shack-dwellers associations of the global South, which mobilize to take control over World Bank and NGO policies; and in the vibrant interchanges of the UN Global Urban Forum. In all of these places can be found conversations all city-lovers and city-planners should listen to carefully. Only by helping to elaborate such visions can we wean ourselves from our seventy-century-old habit of dividing—and impoverishing—our species' most promising form of habitat.[33]

DISCUSSION OF THE LITERATURE

Racial segregation in the United States has long been a central topic in the fields of urban sociology and urban history. Sociologists have given much energy to measuring and modeling "processes" of segregation, and we are indebted to them for multiple indices that give

varying perspectives on the spatial of segregationist practices on the ground. The classic work is by Douglas Massey and Nancy A. Denton.[34] They have also extensively documented the consequences of segregation.[35]

Urban historians have focused their energies on the politics, policies, and practices that bring segregation into being, both in classical national level studies[36] and in dozens of local studies.[37] Another recent historiographical breakthrough centers on "metropolitan" approaches to segregation that trace the connection between the politics of the inner city and the suburbs.[38] Segregation has also long been a central theme in the history of South Africa and of colonial cities.[39]

PRIMARY SOURCES

The famous "redlining" maps generated by the HOLC's city surveys can be found in the City Survey file (CSF), record group 195 (Federal Home Loan Bank Board), National Archives II, in College Park, Maryland. Note that these files also contain extensive, valuable, and damning documentation about the ways these surveys were conducted and the people involved. The Area Description forms contain enormous numbers of reams of information about how some of the city's elites perceived the city's neighborhoods and the people who lived in them. The reports show repeatedly that the valuators knew full well what the consequences of their actions would be. Some of these maps and documents are available online, notably those for a half dozen cities in California and North Carolina that have been digitally archived at the T-RACES website (see visual materials, above).

Copies of Fredrick Babcock's *FHA Underwriting Manual* can be found in many university libraries.

The papers of Richard T. Ely's Institute for Land Economics and Public Utilities and his vast personal papers, all of which shed light on his activities during the 1920s in Chicago, can be found at the Wisconsin Historical Society in Madison.

Documentation about the Baltimore West Segregation Ordinance and its influence on lawmakers elsewhere in the United States can be found at the Baltimore City Archives, most notably in the mayoral files of J. Barry Mahool and James Preston. Leads to other sources can be found in, among other places, Carl H. Nightingale, "The Transnational Contexts of Early-Twentieth-Century American Urban Segregationism," *Journal of Social History* 39 (Spring 2006): 668–702.

The Texts of the Supreme Court's opinions in *Buchanan v. Warley*, *Shelley v. Kraemer*, and *Hills v. Gautreaux* can all be found by searches under the parties' names.

DIGITAL AND VISUAL MATERIALS

- Sheila Bernard and Sam Pollard, "Tale of Two Societies," program from series 2 of *Eyes on the Prize: American at the Racial Crossroads* (Blackside Productions, 1989). The first segment of this program is about Martin Luther King Jr.'s efforts to desegregate Chicago.
- Tim Cole, Alberto Giordano, and Erik Steiner, "Mapping Mobility in the Budapest Ghetto" (http://web.stanford .edu/group/spatialhistory/cgi-bin/site /viz.php?id=411&project_id=#swf)
- Eric Fisher, "Race and Ethnicity 2010" (https://www.flickr.com/photos /walkingsf/sets/72157626354149574/) (the "dot-maps")
- Colin Gordon, "Mapping Decline: St. Louis and the American City" (http:// mappingdecline.lib.uiowa.edu/map/)
- Brian Milbrand, Squeaky Wheel, Erie Country Fair Housing Partnership, "*This Doesn't Happen Here*" (http://www .homeny.org/pages/resources/this -doesnt-happen-here), video about segregation in Buffalo, NY.
- Carl H. Nightingale, "A World Atlas of Urban Segregation in Zoom-Maps" (http://www.globalsegregation.com/)

- Stephen Roberston, "Digital Harlem" (http://digitalharlemblog.wordpress .com/digital-harlem-the-site/)
- Robert Sampson, "Chicago Mapping Project" (http://worldmap.harvard.edu /chicago/)
- Testbed for the Redlining Archives of California's Exclusionary Spaces (http:// salt.unc.edu/T-RACES/) (T-RACES)

FURTHER READING

Boyle, Kevin. *Arc of Justice: A Saga of Race, Civil Rights, and Murder in the Jazz Age.* New York: Henry Holt, 2004.

Freund, David M. P. *Colored Property: State Policy and White Racial Politics in Suburban America.* Chicago: University of Chicago Press, 2007.

Hirsch, Arnold R. *Making the Second Ghetto: Race and Housing in Chicago, 1940–1960.* Cambridge: Cambridge University Press, 1983.

Jackson, Kenneth. *Crabgrass Frontier: The Suburbanization of the United States.* New York: Oxford University Press, 1985.

Katz, Alyssa. *Our Lot: How Real Estate Came to Own Us.* New York: Bloomsbury, 2009. See pp. 1–26.

Katz, Michael B. *Why Don't American Cities Burn?* Philadelphia: University of Pennsylvania Press, 2013.

Kruse, Kevin. *White Flight: Atlanta and the Making of Modern Conservatism.* Princeton, NJ: Princeton University Press, 2007.

Kusmer, Kenneth. *A Ghetto Takes Shape: Black Cleveland, 1870–1930.* Urbana: University of Illinois Press, 1976.

Lassiter, Matthew. *The Silent Majority: Suburban Politics in the Sunbelt South.* Princeton, NJ: Princeton University Press, 2006.

Light, Jennifer. "Nationality and Neighborhood Risk at the Origins of the FHA Underwriting." *Journal of Urban History* 36 (2010): 634–653.

Logan, John R., and Brian Stults. "Separate and Unequal: The Neighborhood Gap for Blacks, Hispanics and Asians in Metropolitan America." Report on urban segregation based on the 2010 US Census. Available at http://www.s4.brown .edu/us2010/projects/authors_su.htm (accessed October 7, 2014).

Massey, Douglas, and Nancy A. Denton. *American Apartheid: Segregation and the Making of the Underclass.* Cambridge, MA: Harvard University Press, 1993.

National Commission on Fair Housing and Equal Opportunity (NCFHEO). *Report: The Future of Fair Housing.* Washington, DC: NCFHEO, 2008.

Nicolaides, Becky M. *My Blue Heaven: Life and Politics in the Working-Class Suburbs of Los Angeles, 1920–1965.* Chicago: University of Chicago Press, 2002.

Nightingale, Carl H. *Segregation: A Global History of Divided Cities.* Chicago: University of Chicago Press, 2012.

Oliver, Melvin, and Thomas M. Shapiro. *White Wealth/Black Wealth: A New Perspective on Racial Inequality.* New York: Routledge, 2006.

Sampson, Robert J. *Great American City: Chicago and the Enduring Neighborhood Effect.* Chicago: University of Chicago Press, 2012.

Satter, Beryl. *Family Properties: How the Struggle over Race and Real Estate Transformed Chicago and Urban America.* New York: Picador, 2010.

Schneider, Eric. *Smack: Heroin and the American City.* Philadelphia: University of Pennsylvania Press, 2008.

Self, Robert O. *American Babylon: Race and the Struggle for Postwar Oakland.* Princeton, NJ: Princeton University Press, 2003.

Silverman, Robert Mark, and Kelly L. Patterson. "The Four Horsemen of the Fair Housing Apocalypse: A Critique of Fair Housing Policy in the USA." *Critical Sociology* 38.1 (2012): 123–140.

Squires, Gregory D., ed. *From Redlining to Reinvestment: Community Responses to Urban Disinvestment.* Philadelphia: Temple University Press, 1992.

Stanger-Ross, Jordan. *Staying Italian: Urban Change and Ethnic Life in Postwar Toronto and Philadelphia.* Chicago: University of Chicago Press, 2009.

Sugrue, Thomas J. *Origins of the Urban Crisis: Race and Inequality in Postwar Detroit.* Princeton, NJ: Princeton University Press, 1996.

Sugrue, Thomas J. *Sweet Land of Liberty: The Forgotten Struggle for Civil Rights in the North.* New York: Random House, 2008.

Taub, Jennifer. *Other People's Houses: How Decades of Bailouts, Captive Regulators, and Toxic Bankers Made Home Mortgages a Thrilling Business.* New Haven, CT: Yale University Press, 2014.

Wiese, Andrew. *Places of Their Own: African American Suburbanization in the Twentieth Century.* Chicago: University of Chicago Press, 2004.

NOTES

1. For segregation indexes in the 1950s and 1960s, and comparisons with contemporary South African cities, see Karl E. Taeuber and Alma F. Taeuber, *Negroes in Cities: Residential Segregation and Neighborhood Change* (Chicago: Aldine, 1965), 39–40; Anthony Lemon, "The Apartheid City," in *Homes Apart: South Africa's Segregated Cities,* edited by Anthony Lemon (Bloomington: Indiana University Press, 1991), 8, 13; A. J. Christopher, "Port Elizabeth," in Lemon, *Homes Apart,* 51; R. J. Davies, "Durban," in Lemon, *Homes Apart,* 79, 82. For present-day research, the best place to begin is John R. Logan and Brian Stults, "Separate and Unequal: The Neighborhood Gap for Blacks, Hispanics and Asians in Metropolitan America," report on urban segregation based on the 2010 US Census, at http://www.s4.brown.edu/us2010/projects/authors_su.htm.

2. National Commission on Fair Housing and Equal Opportunity (NCFHEO), *Report: The Future of Fair Housing* (Washington, DC: NCFHEO, 2008), 13.

3. Ceri Peach, "Good Segregation, Bad Segregation," *Planning Perspectives* 11 (1996): 379–398; Carl H. Nightingale, "Is There Such a Thing as Voluntary Segregation?" (http://globalsegregation.com/is-there-such-a-thing-as-voluntary-segregation/). Also, David Roediger, *Working Towards Whiteness: How America's Immigrants Became White* (New York: Basic Books, 2005). Jordan Stanger-Ross gives an example of how Italians did use the practices of local real estate agents to keep the Italian neighborhood in South Philadelphia relatively exclusive. In Toronto, Italians did no such thing, however. More of this kind of research will be helpful in determining whether, as I suspect, the Philadelphia example is an exception that proves the rule. See Jordan Stanger-Ross, *Staying Italian: Urban Change and Ethnic Life in Postwar Toronto and Philadelphia* (Chicago: University of Chicago Press), 33–58.

4. Melvin Oliver and Thomas M. Shapiro, *White Wealth/Black Wealth: A New Perspective on Racial Inequality* (New York: Routledge, 2006); Robert J. Sampson, *Great American City: Chicago and the Enduring Neighborhood Effect* (Chicago: University of Chicago Press, 2012); Michelle Alexander, *The New Jim Crow: Mass Incarceration in the Age of*

Colorblindness (New York: New Press, 2010); Eric Schneider, *Smack: Heroin and the American City* (Philadelphia: University of Pennsylvania Press, 2008); Food and Nutrition Board, Board on Agriculture and Natural Resources, Board on Population Health and Public Health Practice, Institute of Medicine, National Research Council, *The Public Health Effects of Food Deserts: Workshop Summary* (Washington, DC: Academies Press, 2009); Luke W. Cole and Sheila R. Foster, *From the Ground Up; Environmental Racism and the Rise of the Environmental Justice Movement* (New York: New York University Press, 2001).

5. Carl H. Nightingale, *Segregation: A Global History of Divided Cities* (Chicago: University of Chicago Press: 2012), 19–45.

6. Nightingale, *Segregation*, 12.

7. Nightingale, *Segregation*, 4–8.

8. Nightingale, *Segregation*, 47–134.

9. Nightingale, *Segregation*, 135–158.

10. Nightingale, *Segregation*, 159–192.

11. Nightingale, *Segregation*, 193–226.

12. Nightingale, *Segregation*, 262, 275–284, 300–317.

13. Nightingale, *Segregation*, 379–380.

14. Nightingale, *Segregation*, 264, 290–294; 358–380.

15. Nightingale, *Segregation*, 295–307.

16. Nightingale, *Segregation*, 307–317.

17. Nightingale, *Segregation*, 317–331. David M. P. Freund, *Colored Property: State Policy and White Racial Politics in Suburban America* (Chicago: University of Chicago Press, 2007).

18. Nightingale, *Segregation*, 341–349. Quotation from Federal Home Loan Bank Board, "Metropolitan Chicago: Summary of Economic, Real Estate, and Mortgage Finance Survey" (1940), City Survey File, Box 84, Record Group 195, National Archives II, College Park, Maryland, 15.

19. Nightingale, *Segregation*, 349–358. Arnold R. Hirsch, *Making the Second Ghetto: Race and Housing in Chicago, 1940–1960* (Cambridge: Cambridge University Press, 1983); Mark A. Rose and Raymond A. Mohl, *Interstate: Highway Politics and Policy since 1939* (Knoxville: University of Tennessee Press, 2012).

20. "Reveal Rigid Policy of Segregation at FHA," *New York Amsterdam News*, December 31, 1938.

21. Thomas J. Sugrue, *Sweet Land of Liberty: The Forgotten Struggle for Civil Rights in the North* (New York: Random House, 2008), 200–250.

22. Sugrue, *Sweet Land*, 400–448.

23. Nightingale, *Segregation*, 387–389; Sugrue, *Sweet Land*, 433–444; Alexander Polikoff, *Waiting for Gautreaux: A Story of Segregation, Housing, and the Black Ghetto* (Evanston, IL: Northwestern University Press, 2006); Mary Patillo, *Black on the Block: The Politics of Race and Class in the City* (Chicago: University of Chicago Press, 2007), 181–258; Gregory D. Squires, ed., *From Redlining to Reinvestment: Community Responses to Urban Disinvestment* (Philadelphia: Temple University Press, 1992), 1–37.

24. Becky M. Nicolaides, *My Blue Heaven: Life and Politics in the Working-Class Suburbs of Los Angeles, 1920–1965* (Chicago: University of Chicago Press, 2002), 120–182; Robert O. Self, *American Babylon: Race and the Struggle for Postwar Oakland* (Princeton, NJ: Princeton University Press, 2003), 256–290; Matthew Lassiter, *The Silent Majority: Suburban Politics in the Sunbelt South* (Princeton, NJ: Princeton University Press, 2006), 1–20, 69–93, 148–174; Kevin Kruse, *White Flight: Atlanta and the Making of Modern Conservatism*, 3–18, 78–104, 161–179 (Princeton, NJ: Princeton University Press, 2007).

25. Michelle Alexander, *The New Jim Crow: Mass Incarceration in the Age of Colorblindness* (New York: New Press, 2010); Ruth Wilson Gilmore, *Golden Gulag: Prisons, Surplus, Crisis, and Opposition in Globalizing California* (Berkeley: University of California Press, 2007); Loïc Wacquant, *Deadly Symbiosis: Race and the Rise of the Penal State* (Cambridge, Polity Press, 2008); Mike Davis, *City of Quartz: Excavating the Future in Los Angeles* (London: Verso, 1990).

26. Joseph Nevins, *Operation Gatekeeper: The Rise of the "Illegal Alien" and the Making of the U.S.-Mexico Boundary* (New York: Routledge, 2002).

27. National Commission on Fair Housing and Equal Opportunity (NCFHEO), *Report: The Future of Fair Housing* (Washington DC: NCFHEO, 2008), 13; Robert Mark Silverman and Kelly L. Patterson, "The Four Horsemen of the Apocalypse: A Critique of Fair Housing Policy in the USA," *Critical Sociology* (2011): 1–18.

28. Logan and Stults, "Separate and Unequal"; Edward J. Blakeley and Mary Gail Snyder, *Fortress America: Gated Communities in the United States* (Washington, DC: Brookings Institution, 1997); Setha Low, "How Private Interests Take over Public Space: Zoning, Taxes, and Incorporation

of Gated Communities," in *The Politics of Urban Space*, edited by Setha Low and Neil Smith (New York: Routledge, 2006), 81–104.

29. Neil Smith, *The New Urban Frontier: Gentrification and the Revanchist City* (London: Routledge, 1996); Chris Mele, *Selling the Lower East Side* (Minneapolis: University of Minnesota Press, 2000).

30. Alyssa Katz, *Our Lot: How Real Estate Came to Own Us* (New York: Bloomsbury, 2009), 1–26; Jill Quadagno, *The Color of Welfare: How Racism Undermined the War on Poverty* (New York: Oxford University Press, 1994), 89–116; Simon Johnson and James Kwak, *13 Bankers: The Wall Street Takeover and the Next Financial Meltdown* (New York: Pantheon, 2010), 120–153; Jennifer Taub, *Other People's Houses: How Decades of Bailouts, Captive Regulators, and Toxic Bankers Made Home Mortgages a Thrilling Business* (New Haven, CT: Yale University Press, 2014).

31. Jacob S. Rugh and Douglas S. Massey, "Racial Segregation and the American Foreclosure Crisis," *American Sociological Review* 75 (2010): 629–651, quotation from p. 629.

32. Nightingale, *Segregation*, 394–402.

33. Nightingale, *Segregation*, 421–430.

34. Douglas Massey and Nancy A. Denton, *American Apartheid: Segregation and the Making of the Underclass* (Cambridge, MA: Harvard University Press, 1993).

35. Melvin Oliver and Thomas M. Shapiro, *White Wealth/Black Wealth: A New Perspective on Racial Equality* (New York: Routledge, 2006); Robert J. Sampson, *Great American City: Chicago and the Enduring Neighborhood* (Chicago: University of Chicago Press, 2012).

36. Kenneth Jackson, *Crabgrass Frontiers: The Suburbanization of the United States* (New York: Oxford University Press, 1985); David M. P. Freund, *Colored Property: State Policy and White Racial Politics in Suburban America* (Chicago: University of Chicago Press, 2007).

37. Kenneth Kusmer, *A Ghetto Takes Shape: Black Cleveland, 1870–1930* (Urbana: University of Illinois Press, 1976); Arnold Hirsch, *Making the Second Ghetto: Race and Housing in Chicago, 1940–1960* (Cambridge: Cambridge University Press, 1983); Thomas Sugrue, *The Origins of the Urban Crisis: Race and Inequality in Postwar Detroit* (New York: Random House, 2008).

38. Robert O. Self, *American Babylon: Race and Struggle for Postwar Oakland* (Princeton, NJ: Princeton University Press, 2003).

39. These literatures in combination with American materials in comparative and world historical contexts are addressed in Carl H. Nightingale, *A Global History of Divided Cities* (Chicago: University of Chicago Press, 2012).

Carl Nightingale

ETHNICITY AND US NEIGHBORHOODS

HOW SHOULD WE THINK ABOUT ETHNICITY?

Ethnicity is a concept employed to understand the experiences of immigrants and their children in relation to the wider mainstream of American society. Academic study of ethnicity has often focused on processes of integration, assimilation, or adaptation whereby newcomers ceased to be "foreign" and yet retained practices and networks that connected them, at least imaginatively, with their places of origin, even over multiple generations in the United States.

From an early juncture, discussion of immigrant adaptation to American life was interwoven with the study of cities. Sociologists at the University of Chicago in the 1920s, founders of the "Chicago school," pioneered analyses that articulated immigrant integration in relation to urban ecology, a theorization of city life using metaphors of organic and environmental processes of competition, cooperation, and selection.[1] Ernest W. Burgess, in his contribution to an influential compendium of Chicago sociology in *The City* (1925), described immigrant neighborhoods as providing newcomers "a place and a rôle in the total organization of the city." Sketching a stylized model of urban life that included a "Little Sicily" and a "Chinatown," where new immigrants inhabited a "slum" alongside African Americans in the inner-city "Black Belt," Burgess envisioned that second-generation immigrants would "escape" to neighborhoods of "skilled and thrifty" workers as typified by an enclave he called "*Deutschland*."[2] This theorization of the relations among immigrant neighborhoods, mobility, and assimilation continues to exert influence in the study of immigrant adaptation to American life.[3]

The widespread conception of such matters in terms of "ethnicity" emerged in the second half of the 20th century, as decades of immigration restriction after 1920 brought the descendants of immigrants, rather than newcomers themselves, into increased focus. In their influential book *Beyond the Melting Pot* (1963), Nathan Glazer and Daniel P. Moynihan declared that "*the ethnic group*" could no longer be thought of as a mere remnant of mass immigration. Rather, enduring ethnic collectivities were, in their view, a characteristic American "*social form*."[4]

During the same era, and in the context of the civil rights movement, spokespeople for an "ethnic revival" defended the positions of "ethnics," descendants of European immigrants who never entirely integrated, revivalists felt, into the American mainstream and often stood in the foreground of high-profile urban conflicts over schooling, work, and neighborhoods.[5] In *The Rise of the Unmeltable Ethnics*, for example, Michael Novak spoke for the descendants of immigrants who, criticized as part of the white power structure, instead saw themselves as victims of discrimination and marginalization on the basis of their origins.[6] While this position subsequently came under criticism for its failure to appreciate the privilege afforded to "white ethnics" by enduring structures of racial inequality (for example housing covenants and employment practices that discriminated against African Americans), Novak's work, and the wider "revival" of which it was a part, heightened awareness of ethnicity as a political and sociological category.[7]

Scholars now use the concept of ethnicity to refer to collective practices, rather than individual attributes. A competing view—which tied ethnicity to instincts, feelings, and innate patterns of behavior—has largely given way to interpretations that see ethnicity as dynamic and socially constructed.[8] Ethnicity is widely analyzed as a process of invention and adaptation, whereby preexisting commonalities (such as birth, or deeper ancestral origins, in Ireland, for example) are adapted, amplified, and organized within social, political, and cultural life.[9] Ethnicity is thus a practice—people *do* ethnicity.[10] As they organize communal events, political constituencies, family holidays, and so on, people choose to re-create, reinvent, and make relevant today past or perceived commonalities of origin and tradition. Ethnicity as a social practice is intermittent, uneven, and context dependent. It requires leadership and is often politicized. It is linked, as a dynamic historical process, to other facets of American history, including economic inequality and the politics of race and gender. Rather, therefore, than talking about "ethnic" people, ethnicity is examined in terms of processes of "ethnicization," which may be present or absent, pronounced or muted, relevant or irrelevant, depending on historical circumstances.

ETHNICITY AND URBAN NEIGHBORHOODS

Ethnic neighborhoods in American cities were generated by migratory networks. Historically, very few migrants to America were mythological "pioneers," plunging into the unknown in a strange land, an ocean away from all friends and family. Instead, the vast majority of migrants followed others: they moved within networks, benefited from the capital and knowledge of prior migrants, and were met by familiar faces at their places of debarkation.[11] Vast chains of people—linked by families, friends, hometowns, languages, churches, agents, and labor—have carried millions of migrants to the United States. Historians have long referred to this process as chain migration. Once in America, networks continued to matter. The boardinghouses, sidewalks, corner stores, ball parks, union halls, and religious institutions of North American cities—along with many other local sites—continued to draw people of common origins together.

Gatherings of people within city neighborhoods were constitutive of ethnicity. Networks among people with shared histories of migration connected newcomers and their children with people speaking their languages, enabled them to purchase products from back home, and helped to determine among whom they worshiped, played, and worked. These networks were never entirely harmonious: families, workplaces, and churches were all sites of exploitation and conflict as well as sources of connection.[12] Further, urban ethnic neighborhoods endured over time in part due to discrimination and inequality.[13] In turn they also served as mechanisms of exclusion, as immigrants and their descendants mobilized communal networks to bar other prospective residents from their neighborhoods, particularly African Americans.[14] Emerging from the constraints faced and choices made by their inhabitants, ethnic neighborhoods also varied over time. Many residents moved away when given the choice, others stayed put and defended their turf. Neighborhoods varied by time and place, and in relation to the particular traditions and practices of their inhabitants.[15] In all their complexity and variety, urban neighborhoods have often been places where ethnicity was made.

URBAN ETHNICITY IN EARLY AMERICA

From an early juncture in American history, cities served as incubators of ethnicity. The "middle" colonies of early America (New York, New Jersey, Delaware, and Pennsylvania) were especially diverse, with English settlers constituting a minority, 30 to 45 percent of all residents in 1760. Most inhabitants of the colonies were German, Dutch, African, Scottish, Scots-Irish, and Irish, many among them newcomers. While most lived rurally, cities were important in shaping ethnicity even at this juncture: in Philadelphia, Scots developed urban institutions that, according to historian Jon Butler, helped to constitute Scottishness as a "modern ethnic identity."[16] Even more so than Scots, Germans in 18th-century Philadelphia foreshadowed the urban enclaves of subsequent centuries, settling together in concentrated and institutionally complex neighborhoods and socializing predominantly with other Germans (as exemplified by in-marriage rates of some 80 percent). While views of Germans in the surrounding society varied (and Germans and non-Germans connected in commerce and other facets of civic life) virulent prejudice was also evident in this period, as, for example, Benjamin Franklin decried the "swarm" of "Palatine boors" who "by herding together, establish their language and manners to the exclusion of ours."[17] Such views were likely, as they would be in the following centuries, both a cause and an effect of the concentration in neighborhoods of people with shared foreign origins.

ETHNICITY IN AMERICA'S GROWING CITIES: 1850–1920

In 1850, the large majority of Americans—immigrant and not—continued to live rurally. Nonetheless, cities were growing, and large immigrant neighborhoods were visible. Newcomers from Ireland and the German states of central Europe, in particular, concentrated in various central city districts. In Boston and New York, several wards were more than 40 percent Irish. The most conspicuous ethnic neighborhoods in the country were German. In the First Ward of St. Louis, Missouri, for example, almost 9,000 people reported birth origins in German-speaking places, constituting more than 65 percent of the local population, even without counting their American-born children.[18]

In Cincinnati, Ohio, at the same date, a majority in the 10th and 11th wards. reported German birth origins. Such urban neighborhoods were the forerunners of immigrant enclaves that characterized American cities during the following half-century. As the German visitor Max Oertel observed in 1851, "A part of Cincinnati is almost entirely German, there it swarms with German faces and one hears the dialects of Baden, Austria, Frankfurt, low German, and even some Yiddish."[19] Within such urban enclaves, a German-speaker might walk for blocks hearing only her own language; shops, restaurants, and public houses advertised familiar fare on signs posted in German; German boardinghouses, barbershops, and banks—service providers of all kinds—created the institutional framework of an urban community.[20]

As Oertel's portrait suggests, however, German America (like Irish America) was internally diverse. Germans divided by regional and political differences, dialects, faiths, and class. In St. Louis, Heinrich Boernstein, one of thousands of refugees from the factious German revolutions of 1848, gained editorial control of the *Anzeiger des Westens* newspaper in 1850, using it, in particular, to express anticlericalism. By the middle of the decade, Catholic Germans had an answer in *Tages-Chronik*, and Lutherans produced *Volksblatt*; the community, reflecting the realities of its European origins, was both internally connected and deeply divided.[21] The ethnicity of Germans in urban America was not one common attribute, but rather a complex social practice that led German speakers down varied, but often interconnected, paths.[22]

The decades that followed saw the simultaneous and rapid growth of the urban population of the United States, as well as of the number of foreign born. In 1850, the census counted 237 "places" with at least 2,500 inhabitants, together housing a population of just under 3.6 million people. The remaining 20 million people lived in the countryside. By 1880, almost 1,000 urban places housed

14 million Americans (28 percent of the total population) and in 1920, urban places, with more than 54 million inhabitants, were home, for the first time, to a majority of Americans. Meanwhile, immigrants poured into the country. In 1850, according to the census, 2.2 million first-generation immigrants constituted just under 10 percent of the total population. By 1880, 6.7 million immigrants represented 13 percent of Americans; in 1890, immigrants reached their historical peak within the national population at 15 percent, a figure replicated in 1910 before the start of a long-term decline. Thus, by the first decades of the 20th century, America was a considerably more urban place, and home to considerably more immigrants, than ever before.

ETHNIC URBAN NEIGHBORHOODS AT THE TURN OF THE 20TH CENTURY

The turn of the 20th century saw a significant change in the sources of immigration to the United States. In 1850, Northern and Western Europeans constituted the great majority, 90 percent, of immigrants, with Irish, Germans, and British Islanders dominating. By 1910, Southern and Eastern Europeans (especially Italians, Poles, and Russians) represented a third of all newcomers, and by 1920 more than 40 percent. Among the Eastern Europeans, many were Yiddish speakers. For the first time in American history, Jewish people represented a demographically significant category. They also settled some of the country's most distinctive urban enclaves. Subjected to anti-Semitism and mobilizing robust communal and associational networks, Jewish Americans were more segregated in 1910 than any national (or indeed racial) category recorded in the census. In cities as diverse as New York, Chicago, San Francisco, Baltimore, St. Louis, and Detroit, Jews lived in neighborhoods composed of other Yiddish speakers.[23]

No Jewish neighborhood in America was more conspicuous than that of New York's Lower East Side. In 1910, an estimated 861,980

Figure 1. Life on the Lower East Side, cor. Pitt and Rivington Streets, North, NY.
Courtesy of Library of Congress, LC-DIG-stereo-1s07674.

Yiddish-speaking New Yorkers constituted 20 percent of the population; remarkably, at the same date, Jewish children represented some 40 percent of students in the city's public schools. According to census statistics from Demographia, in the crowded tenements of the Lower East Side's 7th, 10th, and 13th Wards, Yiddish speakers represented as much as 70 percent of the population.[24] Together, they built a diverse and robust neighborhood life, sustained in the streets and apartments they shared, as well as by mutual aid associations, religious schools and institutions, labor unions, theaters, and a thriving Yiddish press.[25] One former resident, born into a Yiddish-speaking family in the Lower East Side in 1935, remembered most vividly the density of Jewish commerce near his tenement home, where a pushcart market went on for blocks, with vendors occupying every part of the street, hawking their wares and yelling out their sales:

That's where I was introduced to seeing a chicken having its neck slit, which is the Jewish way of slaughtering a chicken,

and the blood come out and I remember being horrified…and you'd see all these things, you'd see live fish being taken out of this large container…and it was jumping around and a man came over with a hacksaw and he would chop it in half…the sights and sounds of that street, I still remember them in the background of my mind.

Years later, having moved to Brooklyn, the Lower East Side of his youth gone forever, he reflected on the Jewish enclosure that it represented; his mother, at whose side he visited the pushcart stalls of neighborhood, "didn't know from non-Jews."[26]

Although New York also had an important "Chinatown" (and indeed a long history of commercial and political engagement with China), the largest and most symbolically important Chinese immigrant neighborhood at the turn of the 20th century was a continent away, in San Francisco.[27] The neighborhood, like other urban ethnic enclaves, stemmed from migratory networks that preserved ties to China and was organized around shared local institutions:

boardinghouses, language schools, and Chinese-language newspapers. More than any European immigrant neighborhood, it was also shaped by far-reaching, deeply held, and legally entrenched racism, which banned virtually all Chinese immigration after 1882, outlawed marriages between people defined in law as Chinese and those defined as white, and prevented Chinese immigrants from owning land.[28] Targeted by boycotts and ruined by the cataclysmic 1906 earthquake (after which it was rebuilt), San Francisco's Chinatown proved remarkably durable.

San Francisco's Chinatown, like other ethnic enclaves, was internally diverse and divided. Residents nevertheless maintained practices that reinforced bonds among co-ethnics and rooted them in place. Distinctive among these was the "Miss Chinatown Pageant," which survived a controversial inaugural season in 1915 to become an enduring local tradition. Accompanied by a parade, with floats representing local organizations, schools, and stores, as well as a raffle—and attended by neighborhood residents as well as notable outsiders, including, in 1927, San Francisco's mayor—the event creatively reinforced the culture of neighborhood by adapting an American tradition to a Chinese immigrant community, and raised funds for such local institutions as a Chinese hospital.[29]

The enclaves of the early 20th century exemplified a common form of ethnic neighborhood life in early-20th-century America, when immigrants, as well as African Americans, lived in high levels of residential isolation in the country's largest cities.[30] Yet, ethnicity was also lived in contact—sometimes harmonious, sometimes conflict ridden—across and among people of varied origins. In Los Angeles at the turn of the 20th century, migrants of diverse national and racial origins found common cause in a broad alliance of workers, sharing also church pews, school classrooms, playgrounds, and parks.[31] In Detroit between 1880 and 1920, the bond of ethnic community loosened, as social life became increasingly structured by class, rather than national origins.[32] In Washington Heights and the South Bronx, Irish and Jewish New Yorkers struggled to control neighborhood turf in the 1930s and 1940s, before interfaith alliances and residential succession quieted their conflicts.[33] Although sites of contact and conflict among immigrant groups and their descendants have generated less interest than large, homogenous communities, the boundaries of neighborhood and ethnicity in America were often porous, and the relations among neighbors of diverse backgrounds likely as important, especially in the long run, as the self-sufficiency of people from common origins.

DECLINING IMMIGRATION AND RISING SUBURBANIZATION, 1920–1970

The middle decades of the 20th century saw significant declines in the foreign-born population in the United States, as well as changes to metropolitan America. The Depression of the 1930s, World War II, and legislative restrictions on immigration, which continued into the 1960s, meant that America was increasingly a country of the native born. Indeed, from 1910 to 1970, the immigrant percentage of the total population declined in every census, falling in total from 15 to just 5 percent of Americans. This change was felt acutely in the country's largest cities. The census shows that in 1910, 41 percent of New Yorkers, 36 percent of Chicagoans, and 25 percent of Philadelphians had been born outside the country. By 1970, these figures were 18, 11, and 7 percent, respectively. With communities of common origin no longer replenished by newcomers, many observers concluded that, despite the "ethnic revival," the assimilation of ethnic groups into the American mainstream was under way. With the children and grandchildren of immigrants attending American schools, attaining economic mobility, departing from ethnically isolated neighborhoods, and marrying people of other backgrounds, the structural sources of European ethnicity, in particular, had entered their "twilight" in the United States.[34]

At the same time, cities were changing, as white Americans moved en masse to suburbia. Before World War II, only 13 percent of Americans lived in the suburbs, but by the first decade of the 21st century, more than half did so. Suburbanization undermined the urban neighborhoods that long served as foundations for ethnic community. In 1980, when the census asked Americans their "ancestry," it found people of German, Italian, Irish, Polish, and other European origins highly integrated across urban America. The neighborhood isolation of ethnic groups 70 years prior was gone; in 1980, unlike in the heyday of immigration, African Americans stood out as singularly isolated in urban America.[35] Cities divided along racial lines, and the children and grandchildren of immigrants streamed to the suburbs. It is harder to say for certain whether Judaism in America remained neighborhood-based. With Yiddish-speaking no longer a suitable proxy for Judaism and religion absent from the census, analysis on a national level is impossible.[36] Anecdotal evidence suggests that the larger pattern held for Jews as well: Jewish residents of North Philadelphia, for example, dispersed to the suburbs, disbanding a neighborhood that at its peak had included some fifty thousand of their co-religionists, two Jewish colleges, several major and historic synagogues, the Jewish Publication Society, and hundreds of small businesses.[37] The Jewish neighborhood of the Lower East Side disappeared in the same period. In the era of suburbanization, urban racial division, and immigration restriction, the older urban neighborhoods where immigrants made their lives withered or disappeared entirely.

Yet, some older ethnic neighborhoods persisted. In 1980, 4 million people of German ancestry lived in census tracts—small urban areas of several thousand people—in which they constituted a majority. At the same date, 570,000 people of Italian ancestry lived in

majority-Italian neighborhoods; 125,000 people of Irish ancestry lived where they predominated, as did 134,000 Poles.[38] Reflecting on dating and marriage, residents of one such Italian neighborhood described the social ties that persisted among its residents, despite the loss of thousands of others to the suburbs: "I lived on this corner," remembered one, "and if you walked to the next corner was my husband, and we got to know each other and we went out." Another explained: "[Y]ou all knew their mothers and fathers and aunts and uncles, you didn't have to be introduced." A third met her husband at her family store: "His mother used to come in and buy the groceries, and he would come in once and awhile…we started going to skating parties and the dances and all, and that was that."[39] With high rates of ethnic endogamy and close relations among neighbors, such urban places continued to function as they had in the past—as social structural settings for the making of ethnicity—long after they had ceased to be the norm within American urban life.

NEW IMMIGRANTS, NEW NEIGHBORHOODS, AND ETHNOBURBIA

The decline of older ethnic neighborhoods did not mean that American cities ceased to sustain ethnic community. Instead, as older immigrant neighborhoods withered, new ones appeared. The Immigration and Nationality Act of 1965 (sometimes referred to as the Hart-Celler Act after its prime sponsors) abolished discriminatory national quotas and opened the doors for a renewed era of mass immigration to the United States. The results over the next several decades were unanticipated and dramatic. Whereas more than 3 million immigrants arrived in the decade of the 1960s, by the 1990s this number had increased to 10 million. By 2000, according to Migration Policy Institute statistics, the 30 million foreign born in the United States were two times as numerous as their counterparts of a century prior; they constituted 10 percent of the total population in the country, two times the figure in 1970. In the first decades of the 21st century, these numbers continued to rise. By 2016, nearly 44 million foreign-born Americans constituted 14 percent of the population, Migration Policy Institute statistics indicate. During the same period, the sources of immigration were transformed. In 1960, 1.3 million Italian-born Americans were the largest immigrant group in the country, according to Migration Policy Institute statistics. Canada, Germany, Poland, the Soviet Union, and the United Kingdom remained major sources of newcomers, contributing almost 50 percent of all arrivals between 1960 and 1969. In the decades that followed, the sources of immigration to the United States shifted markedly. By the first decade of the 21st century, 17 percent of all newcomers came from Mexico, while China, India, and the Philippines were also major contributors. In the early 2000s, the Americas and Asia, taken together, were the source of more than 75 percent of all newcomers, Europe only 13 percent.

As in the previous era of mass immigration to the United States, turn of the 21st century immigrants concentrated in urban America. By 1990, cities from coast to coast teemed with newcomers. The census indicates that a remarkable 60 percent of Miami residents, 38 percent of the population of Los Angeles, and 28 percent of New Yorkers reported birth origins outside of the country. Further, large contiguous neighborhoods emerged as a result of the new immigration. In New York in 1990, for example, 63 percent of Dominicans lived in areas heavily populated by other Dominicans. At the same time, 51 percent of Afro-Caribbeans lived in concentrated central city enclaves, as did 48 percent of Chinese, and 39 percent of Koreans. In Los Angeles at the same date, Salvadorans were particularly likely (51 percent) to live in central city ethnic neighborhoods, followed by Guatemalans (43 percent), and Koreans and Filipinos (22 percent each).[40]

In the Los Angeles suburbs, a new kind of ethnic neighborhood emerged: the ethnic suburb. In different parts of the metropolitan area, 38 percent of Chinese, 35 percent of Vietnamese, 26 percent of Mexicans, and 24 percent of Japanese lived in suburban ethnic neighborhoods.[41] For the most part, residents of these neighborhoods were not isolated within the urban environment. In the neighborhoods where Chinese Americans concentrated in suburban Los Angeles, for example, they remained a minority—only 23 percent of the local population was Chinese. Dominicans in New York were highly concentrated in neighborhoods, but within those neighborhoods only 31 percent of residents were Dominican. Such neighborhoods still sustained the institutional frameworks of ethnic life; as they had in the past, churches, stores, clubs, and restaurants catered to migrants of common origin. Neighborhoods remained places where ethnicity was re-created, where institutional life emerged from and sustained ethnic networks. However, such neighborhoods were not exclusive: bonds among Dominicans, for example, necessarily coexisted alongside and in relation to those of other neighborhood residents. An exception to this rule was Mexican American Los Angeles. In their neighborhoods, both suburban and central city, Mexicans constituted approximately 70 percent of the local population, a figure akin to the Jewish Lower East Side of New York a century prior.[42]

The emergence of ethnic enclaves in suburban America clearly demonstrates that older understandings of ethnicity and urban ecology no longer describe the relation between urban space and ethnicity in America. The inner city is no longer the exclusive site of immigrant arrival. Settlement in, or movement to, suburbia does not require assimilation into the mainstream. Instead, suburbs—whose historical diversity is also increasingly well understood—are the sites of varied immigrant experience, including what can be understood as neighborhood life. Some suburban ethnic communities, emerging on the outskirts of cities such as Los Angeles, are the product of immigrant affluence. Skilled immigrants, able to choose where they live, established affluent suburban enclaves as they seized the opportunities available in the metropolitan areas of "world cities" as a result of global economic restructuring and growth. Establishing businesses (that seek less well-paid employees) and demanding consumer services (restaurants, nail salons, grocers, etc.), these immigrants also drew less wealthy co-ethnics into nearby residence, creating economically diverse suburban neighborhoods.[43] Meanwhile, some "inner-ring" suburbs became the sites of concentrated disadvantage, where less privileged immigrants and their children concentrated—often alongside African Americans—in sites of less opportunity and affluence, despite their suburban location.[44] These developments demand some reconsideration of how "ethnic neighborhood" and "suburb" have each been traditionally understood.

DISCUSSION OF THE LITERATURE

Immigrant neighborhoods in the United States received early and influential scholarly attention from "Chicago school" sociologists. In a 1925 compendium of this work interpreting urban industrial America, *The City*, Ernest Burgess's "The Growth of the City," diagramed the urban life in concentric circles, describing the movement of second- and third-generation immigrants out of center-city slums to better organized outer rings of the city. This vision of neighborhood success and immigrant assimilation continues to influence scholarship in multiple fields.[45]

Study of immigration flourished in the post–World War II era, particularly after the publication of Oscar Handlin's Pulitzer Prize–winning monograph *The Uprooted* (1951), which described immigrant neighborhoods and the trials of immigrant adaptation to industrial America.[46] This argument ultimately

encouraged an enduring counter-argument within the historiography, spurred by Rudolph Vecoli's 1964 rebuttal, which gave more careful attention to the origins of immigrants, stressed the networks among them, the complexity and specificity of their experiences, and the importance of their neighborhoods as sites of connection.[47] As a result, ethnic neighborhoods received sustained scholarly attention as part of the new social history that blossomed from the 1960s through the 1980s. A useful discussion of the scholarship in that period, as well as a theorization of ethnicity, can be found in the *Journal of American Ethnic History* article entitled "The Invention of Ethnicity."[48]

In the 1960s and 1970s, influential scholars observed that ethnic identity remained a powerful aspect of American life, despite decades in which immigration was minimal and the descendants of immigrants learned English, acquired American educations, and, often, left their parents' old neighborhoods. In 1963's *Beyond the Melting Pot*, Nathan Glazer and Daniel P. Moynihan argued that ethnicity was a permanent feature of American life.[49] A year later, Milton Gordon's influential analysis of assimilation suggested that although second- and third-generation immigrants "acculturated" to American life, deeper, structural assimilation remained elusive.[50]

Since the 1990s, fewer scholars have undertaken close studies of previously studied ethnic neighborhoods, but research continues to convey urban and space-specific expressions of ethnicity. Gerald Gamm, for example, demonstrates that the local institutions of ethnic and religious life shaped the responses of Jews and Catholics to postwar transformations of urban America.[51] Russell Kazal's *Becoming Old Stock* (2004) analyzes the differing trajectories of middle-class Lutheran and working-class Catholic Germans in their movements from German immigrant neighborhoods to the American mainstream.[52] Thomas Guglielmo chronicles the changing place of Italian immigrants within the shifting racial structures of Chicago.[53] Jordan Stanger-Ross compares an ethnic neighborhood in Canada with one in the United States, arguing that the local politics and economy of cities continued to shape ethnic communal life long after World War II.[54] Meanwhile, a rapidly growing scholarship on "ethnoburbia" points toward a new area of place-based scholarship on ethnicity, in particular in relation to Asian Americans.[55]

PRIMARY SOURCES

Diverse social historical sources serve as a foundation for studies of ethnic American neighborhoods. Generally, the resources available will vary significantly by location and by the chosen research subject. Researchers might begin with local newspapers, especially community-based publications. For demographic or statistical analyses, census data (those working with populations after 1940 may find tract-level data especially helpful) can be supplemented with local sources such as tax assessments, city directories, and marriage registers. Some of the most useful sources—organizational minutes and membership lists, various community-based publications, personal letters, photographs, and ephemera—can be found in local institutional repositories, as well as in university, municipal, and archdiocesan archives. Researchers may find oral histories especially useful; some exist in archival and digital repositories, but, depending on the time period being studied, it may be advisable (and enjoyable) to conduct interviews.

FURTHER READING

Bayor, Ronald, ed. *The Oxford Handbook of American Immigration and Ethnicity*. New York: Oxford University Press, 2016.

Bodnar, John. *The Transplanted: A History of Immigrants in Urban America*. Bloomington: Indiana University Press, 1987.

Brubaker, Rogers. *Ethnicity without Groups*. Cambridge, MA: Harvard University Press, 2006.

Chen, Yong. *Chinese San Francisco, 1850–1943*. Stanford, CA: Stanford University Press, 2000.

Conzen, Kathleen Neils, David A. Gerber, Ewa Morawska, George E. Pozzetta, and Rudolph J. Vecoli. "The Invention of Ethnicity: A Perspective from the U.S.A." *Journal of American Ethnic History* 12, no. 1 (1992): 3–48.

Howe, Irving. *World of Our Fathers: The Journey of the East European Jews to America and the Life They Found and Made*, Anniversary ed. New York: NYU Press, 2005.

Jacobson, Matthew Frey. *Roots Too: White Ethnic Revival in Post–Civil Rights America*. Cambridge, MA: Harvard University Press, 2008.

Kazal, Russell A. *Becoming Old Stock: The Paradox of German-American Identity*. Princeton, NJ: Princeton University Press, 2004.

Orsi, Robert. *The Madonna of 115th Street: Faith and Community in Italian Harlem*. New Haven, CT: Yale University Press, 1985.

Park, Robert E., Ernest W. Burgess, and Roderick D. McKenzie. *The City*. Chicago: University of Chicago Press, 1925.

Sanchez, George. *Becoming Mexican American: Ethnicity, Culture, and Identity in Chicano Los Angeles, 1900–1945*. New York: Oxford University Press, 1993.

Stanger-Ross, Jordan. *Staying Italian: Urban Change and Ethnic Life in Postwar Toronto and Philadelphia*. Chicago: University of Chicago Press, 2009.

Vecoli, Rudolph J. "Contadini in Chicago: A Critique of the Uprooted." *Journal of American History* 51, no. 3 (1964): 404–417.

Wild, Mark. *Street Meeting: Multiethnic Neighborhoods in Early Twentieth-Century Los Angeles*. Los Angeles: University of California Press, 2005.

Zunz, Olivier. *The Changing Face of Inequality: Urbanization, Industrial Development, and Immigrants in Detroit, 1880–1920*. Chicago: University of Chicago Press, 1982.

For a wide array of further sources in the area of immigration history more broadly (both primary and secondary sources), researchers and students might consult the Immigration Syllabus recently published by the University of Minnesota.

NOTES

1. Emanuel Gaziano, "Ecological Metaphors as Scientific Boundary Work: Innovation and Authority in Interwar Sociology and Biology," *American Journal of Sociology* 101, no. 4 (1996): 882. On the Chicago school more generally, see Andrew Abbott, *Department and Discipline: Chicago Sociology at One Hundred* (Chicago: University of Chicago Press, 1999).

2. Ernest W. Burgess, "The Growth of the City: An Introduction to a Research Project," in *The City*, ed. Robert Park, Ernest W. Burgess, and Roderick D. McKenzie (Chicago: University of Chicago Press, 1925), 54–57.

3. See, for example, Richard Alba and Victor Nee, *Remaking the American Mainstream: Assimilation and Contemporary Immigration* (Cambridge, MA: Harvard University Press, 2003), 19–23.

4. Nathan Glazer and Daniel P. Moynihan, *Beyond the Melting Pot: The Negroes, Puerto Ricans, Jews, Italians, and Irish of New York City*, 2nd ed. (Cambridge, MA: MIT Press, 1970), 16, emphasis in original.

5. Jonathan Rieder, *Canarsie: The Jews and Italians of Brooklyn against Liberalism* (Cambridge, MA: Harvard University Press, 1987); Thomas Sugrue, *The Origins of the Urban Crisis: Race and Inequality in Postwar Detroit* (Princeton, NJ: Princeton University Press, 1996); Arnold R. Hirsch, *Making the Second Ghetto: Race and Housing in Chicago, 1940–1960* (Chicago: University of Chicago Press, 1998); Ronald P. Formisano, *Boston against Busing: Race, Class, and Ethnicity in the 1960s and 1970s* (Chapel Hill: University of North Carolina Press, 2004); and Jordan Stanger-Ross, *Staying Italian: Urban Change and Ethnic Life in Postwar Toronto and Philadelphia* (Chicago: University of Chicago Press, 2009).

6. Michael Novak, *The Rise of the Unmeltable Ethnics: Politics and Culture in the Seventies* (New York: Macmillan, 1973).

7. Matthew Frey Jacobson, *Roots Too: White Ethnic Revival in Post–Civil Rights America* (Cambridge, MA: Harvard University Press, 2008); and David Roediger, *Working toward Whiteness: How America's Immigrants Became White* (New York: Basic Books, 2006).

8. Rogers Brubaker, *Ethnicity without Groups* (Cambridge, MA: Harvard University Press, 2006), and *Grounds for Difference* (Cambridge, MA: Harvard University Press, 2015).

9. Kathleen Neils Conzen et al., "The Invention of Ethnicity: A Perspective from the U.S.A.," *Journal of American Ethnic History* 12, no. 1 (1992): 3–48.

10. Brubaker, *Ethnicity without Groups*.

11. Rudolph J. Vecoli, "Contadini in Chicago: A Critique of the Uprooted," *Journal of American History* 51, no. 3 (1964): 404–417; John Bodnar, *The Transplanted: A History of Immigrants in Urban America* (Bloomington: Indiana University Press, 1987); Dirk Hoerder and Horst Rossler, eds., *Distant Magnets: Expectations and Realities in the Immigrant Experience, 1840–1930* (New York: Holmes & Meier, 1993); George Sanchez, *Becoming Mexican American: Ethnicity, Culture, and Identity in Chicano Los Angeles, 1900–1945* (Oxford: Oxford University Press, 1993); and Kornel S. Chang, *Pacific Connections: The Making of the U.S.-Canadian Borderlands* (Berkeley: University of California Press, 2012).

12. See Donna Gabaccia, *From the Other Side: Women, Gender, and Immigrant Life in the U.S., 1820–1990* (Bloomington: Indiana University Press, 1995); Gunther Peck, *Reinventing Free Labor: Padrones and Immigrant Workers in the North American West, 1880–1930* (Cambridge: Cambridge University Press, 2000); Daniel Bender, *Sweated Work, Weak Bodies: Anti-Sweatshop Campaigns and the Languages of Labor* (New Brunswick, NJ: Rutgers University Press, 2004); Robert Orsi, *The Madonna of 115th Street: Faith and Community in Italian Harlem, 1885–1950*, 3rd ed. (New Haven, CT: Yale University Press, 2010); Andrea Geiger, *Subverting Exclusion: Transpacific Encounters with Race, Caste, and Borders 1885–1928* (New Haven, CT: Yale University Press, 2011); and Chang, *Pacific Connections*.

13. Leonard Dinnerstein, *Antisemitism in America* (New York: Oxford University Press, 1995); Roger Daniels, *Asian America: Chinese and Japanese in the United States since 1850* (Seattle: University of Washington Press, 1988); Erika Lee, *At America's Gates: Chinese Immigration during the Exclusion Era, 1882–1943* (Chapel Hill: University of North Carolina Press, 2004); and Donna Gabaccia, "Global Geography of 'Little Italy': Italian Neighbourhoods in Comparative Perspective," *Modern Italy* 11, no. 1 (2006): 9–24.

14. Jordan Stanger-Ross, *Staying Italian*, chap. 2.

15. See Gerald Gamm, *Urban Exodus: Why the Jews Left Boston and the Catholics Stayed* (Cambridge, MA: Harvard University Press, 2001).

16. Jon Butler, *Becoming America* (Cambridge, MA: Harvard University Press, 2000), 25.

17. Butler, *Becoming America*, 30–36; and Stephanie Grauman Wolf, *Urban Village: Population, Community, and Family Structure in Germantown Pennsylvania 1683–1800* (Princeton, NJ: Princeton University Press, 1976). Franklin quoted in Wolf at 138–139, in Butler at 32

18. These figures do not include Austrian immigrants.

19. Maximilian Oertel quoted in Joseph M. White, "Cincinnati's German Catholic Life: A Heritage of Lay Participation," *U.S. Catholic Historian* 12, no. 3 (Summer 1994): 1.

20. James M. Bergquist, "German Communities in American Cities: An Interpretation of the Nineteenth-Century Experience," *Journal of American Ethnic History* 4, no. 1 (Fall 1984): 9.

21. Bergquist, "German Communities in American Cities," 15.

22. Russell A. Kazal, *Becoming Old Stock: The Paradox of German-American Identity* (Princeton, NJ: Princeton University Press, 2004).

23. Dinnerstein, *Antisemitism in America*; and Michael J. White, Robert F. Dymowski, and Shilian Wang, "Ethnic Neighbors and Ethnic Myths: Residential Segregation in 1910," in *After Ellis Island: Newcomers and Natives in the 1910 Census*, ed. Susan Cotts Watkins (New York: Russell Sage Foundation, 1994), 196–197.

24. Jeffrey S. Gurock, *When Harlem Was Jewish, 1870–1930* (New York: Columbia University Press, 1979), 17–18.

25. Irving Howe, *World of Our Fathers: The Journey of the East European Jews to America and the Life They Found and Made*, Anniversary ed. (New York: NYU Press, 2005).

26. Melvin Stanger, interviewed by the author, February 2010, Brooklyn, New York.

27. John Kuo Wei Tchen, *New York before Chinatown: Orientalism and the Shaping of American Culture, 1776–1882* (Baltimore: Johns Hopkins University Press, 1999).

28. Yong Chen, *Chinese San Francisco, 1850–1943: A Transpacific Community* (Palo Alto, CA: Stanford University Press, 2000); Lee, *At America's Gates*; and Mae M. Ngai, *Impossible Subjects: Illegal Aliens and the Making of Modern America* (Princeton, NJ: Princeton University Press, 2004).

29. Chen, *Chinese San Francisco*, 192–193.

30. Michael J. White, Robert F. Dymowski, and Shilian Wang, "Ethnic Neighbors and Ethnic Myths: Residential Segregation in 1910," in *After Ellis Island*, ed. Cotts Watkins, 196–197.

31. Mark Wild, *Street Meeting: Multiethnic Neighborhoods in Early Twentieth-Century Los Angeles* (Berkeley: University of California Press, 2005).

32. Olivier Zunz, *The Changing Face of Inequality* (Chicago: University of Chicago Press, 1982).

33. Ronald Bayor, *Neighbors in Conflict: The Irish, Germans, Jews, and Italians of New York, 1929–1941* (Baltimore: Johns Hopkins University Press, 1978), chap. 8.

34. Richard D. Alba, *Italian Americans: Into to the Twilight of Ethnicity* (Englewood Cliffs, NJ: Prentice-Hall, 1985).

35. Michael J. White, *American Neighborhoods and Residential Differentiation* (New York: Russell Sage Foundation, 1987), 97; and Douglas S. Massey and Nancy A. Denton, *American Apartheid: Segregation and the Making of the Underclass* (Cambridge, MA: Harvard University Press, 1998).

36. In Canada, which includes religion on the census, Jews remained the most segregated urbanites. See Jordan Stanger-Ross, "Citystats and the History of Community and Segregation in Post-WWII Urban Canada," *Journal of the Canadian Historical Association* 19, no. 2 (2008): 3–22.

37. Jordan Stanger-Ross, "Neither Fight nor Flight: Urban Synagogues in Postwar Philadelphia," *Journal of Urban History* 32, no. 6 (2006): 791–812. See also Gamm, *Urban Exodus*.

38. Stanger-Ross, *Staying Italian*, 146.

39. Stanger-Ross, *Staying Italian*, 1.

40. John R Logan, Wenquan Zhang, and Richard D Alba, "Immigrant Enclaves and Ethnic Communities in New York and Los Angeles," *American Sociological Review* 67, no. 2 (2002): 309–310. Note that this study used a mix of racial, origins, and ancestry variables to identify groups for analysis (303 n. 3).

41. Logan, Zhang, and Alba, "Immigrant Enclaves and Ethnic Communities," 309–310.

42. Logan, Zhang, and Alba, "Immigrant Enclaves and Ethnic Communities."

43. Wei Li, *Ethnoburb: The New Ethnic Community in Urban America* (Honolulu: University of Hawai'i Press, 2009).

44. Bernadette Hanlon, "A Typology of Inner-Ring Suburbs: Class, Race, and Ethnicity in U.S. Suburbia,"

City and Community 8, no. 3 (September 2009): 221–246. Michael B. Katz et al., "Immigration and the New Metropolitan Geography," *Journal of Urban Affairs* 32, no. 5 (2010): 523–547.

45. Burgess, "The Growth of the City."
46. Oscar Handlin, *The Uprooted* (Boston: Little, Brown, 1951).
47. Vecoli, "Contadini in Chicago."
48. Conzen et al., "Invention of Ethnicity."
49. Glazer and Moynihan, *Beyond the Melting Pot*.
50. Milton Gordon, *Assimilation in American Life: The Role of Race, Religion, and National Origins* (New York: Oxford University Press, 1964). Russell Kazal, "Revisiting Assimilation: The Rise, Fall, and Reappraisal of a Concept in American Ethnic History," *American Historical Review* 100, no. 2 (1995): 437–471.
51. Gamm, *Urban Exodus*.
52. Kazal, *Becoming Old Stock*.
53. Thomas Guglielmo, *White on Arrival: Italians, Race, Color, and Power in Chicago, 1890–1945* (New York: Oxford University Press, 2004).
54. Stanger-Ross, *Staying Italian*.
55. For a recent summary of this scholarship, see also Becky M. Nicolaides, "Introduction: Asian American Suburban History," *Journal of American Ethnic History* 34, no. 2 (2015): 5–17.

Jordan Stanger-Ross

LGBTQ POLITICS IN AMERICA SINCE 1945

CONTEXTS FOR POSTWAR LGBTQ POLITICS

Across the postwar era, urbanization and consumerism have propelled the growth of sexual communities; they have also embedded racial and class inequality as structuring problems of LGBTQ politics. Rights to sexual privacy and marriage have been won amid the loss of a social-welfare state and the containment of public sexual cultures. Advocates have disentangled gay and lesbian identities from criminality and illness, yet in the early 21st century many LGBTQ people—particularly people of color and transgender people—

remain disproportionately policed and imprisoned.

These contradictions run alongside and help to explain the multiple visions of change that have structured LGBTQ politics. Major divergences in LGBTQ politics include liberal versus leftist agendas of sexual freedom; minoritarian versus universalist conceptions of sexuality; and strategies distinguished by race, gender, gender expression, and class.[1] Liberal agendas for LGBTQ politics have prioritized civil rights and inclusion in the US nation-state. Activists in this tradition have most often relied on a minoritarian rhetoric of distinct sexual identities—advocating for the rights of people designated as homosexual, gay, lesbian, bisexual, or transgender—though they have at times pursued universalist claims of sexual privacy and free expression. By contrast, leftist LGBTQ activists have sought possibilities beyond the norms of national citizenship, connecting sexual freedom to antimilitarist, anticapitalist, and antiracist goals. Leftist activists have used minoritarian rhetoric to call for radical solidarity, but at the same time, they have made universalist claims about everyone's capacity for same-sex desire. Leftists have also argued that because "deviance" is regulated via race and class, as well as sexuality, organizing on the basis of sexual identity alone is insufficient to win freedom. Although liberal and leftist debates have defined themselves in relationship to the politics of race and class, differences of ideology have not been equivalent to differences of identity per se. People of color, transgender people, and working-class people have taken up both leftist and liberal goals, often organizing autonomously to counter the greater visibility of white, middle-class, and gender-conforming LGBTQ people.

THE STRAIGHT STATE AND HOMOPHILE RESPONSES

Across the postwar era, LGBTQ life was structured in significant part by what Margot

Canaday calls the "straight state."[2] The term describes the institutionalization of heteronormativity through law and policy, particularly at the federal level, and in multiple areas of governance, including the military, social-welfare policy, and immigration. Although the straight state began developing in the early 20th century, it cohered most strongly during World War II and the early years of the Cold War. Its construction designated homosexuals outside the boundaries of normative citizenship and influenced LGBTQ activism for years to come.

In the military, the straight state was produced not only through surveillance and the prosecution of sexual acts, but also through the institutionalization of "blue" or "other than honorable" discharges for those designated homosexuals.[3] Military exclusion overlapped with social-welfare policy when those discharged veterans were denied the benefits of the GI Bill. An estimated nine thousand people were discharged from the military during World War II on the basis of homosexuality, and five thousand people who wanted to join the military were rejected for the same reason. The pattern continued in the 1950s and 1960s and resulted in nine hundred to eighteen hundred discharges a year.[4] The earliest gay rights groups were formed partly in response to these exclusions, and civil rights groups, including the National Association for the Advancement of Colored People and the Civil Rights Congress, voiced concern over them, as well.

The straight state became entrenched in the early 1950s, through restrictions on homosexual employees in the federal government and the exclusion of homosexual immigrants. The mass expulsion of federal workers in what is now known as the Lavender Scare was linked to anticommunism: homosexuals were designated as security threats, not only because homosexuality was considered a personality disorder, but also because it was thought that the anti-gay stigma made employees vulnerable to blackmail by foreign agents. Between 1947 and 1950, more than four hundred federal employees resigned or were dismissed on the basis of homosexuality, and an estimated seventeen hundred applicants for government jobs were denied.[5] The pattern of dismissals led to congressional hearings and sparked a national debate over the threat posed by gay people lurking unnoticed in public life. In 1953, President Eisenhower signed Executive Order 10450, which listed "sexual perversion" among a list of character defects that could flag a federal employee as a potential "security risk." The logic of the Lavender Scare was further reflected in the Immigration and Nationality Act of 1952 (McCarran-Walter Act), which denied entry to both communist and homosexual immigrants. In 1967, the Supreme Court affirmed the exclusion of homosexual immigrants in its ruling in *Boutilier v. INS*.[6]

State regulation took shape at the local level in response to a moral panic over sexual crimes against children and through ties between anti-gay policing and racial control. Sexual assaults against children had not grown numerically, but they were newly perceived as an epidemic and generated waves of arrests, as well as sensationalistic media coverage.[7] Sources ranging from FBI reports to Hollywood films conflated pedophilia with consensual adult homosexuality. In Boise, Idaho, between 1955 to 1957, some fifteen hundred people were questioned in an investigation purporting to uncover the exploitation of adolescent boys; ultimately fifteen men were sentenced, the large majority only accused of contact with other adults. In Florida, between 1956 and 1965, a right-wing legislative committee purged dozens of gay and lesbian teachers from the public schools.[8] Meanwhile, the policies of the Los Angeles Police Department carried national influence by systematizing anti-gay entrapment, surveillance, and raids, and by disproportionately concentrating these tactics in multiracial neighborhoods and gathering sites.[9] Such policing caused lasting harm, including by constraining the recognition of gay and lesbian leaders in other movements. Civil rights organizer Bayard Rustin, arrested on anti-gay charges in 1953, found that the fallout from the scandal lingered for years, and resulted in the marginalization of his central role in organizing the March on Washington for Jobs and Freedom in 1963.[10]

Despite the severity of state regulations, the early postwar years saw growing gay and lesbian communities, and spaces for positive recognition of homosexuality could be glimpsed in venues ranging from the Kinsey Reports, to coverage of drag balls in the African American press, to the Beat counterculture.[11] Yet organized LGBTQ activism—typically treated by historians as the central expression of LGBTQ politics—was far more contained in the 1950s and early 1960s than it would be in later years. The "homophile," or early gay rights, movement was deeply shaped by the Cold War exclusions from citizenship. Homophiles on the left drew on Marxist thought to argue that gayness could be a basis of group politics, and liberal homophiles relied especially on Americanist rhetoric of privacy and freedom of expression to argue for their rights. Intriguingly, this pattern in the homophile era stood in contrast to the late 1960s and 1970s, when leftist gay radicals turned to a universalist language of liberation, and liberals invested in a minoritarian language of rights.

The first major (though not the earliest) homophile organization was the Mattachine Society, founded in 1950 in Los Angeles. One of its key originators was Harry Hay, earlier a member of the Communist Party, though he had recently resigned because of the Party's prohibition of openly homosexual members. Hay's Marxism shaped Mattachine's initial conception that "homosexuality" was analogous to "nation" or "race" and the broader view that homosexuality was a group identity that could be politicized.[12] By 1953, thousands of people were participating in Mattachine discussion groups across California. However, amid the Lavender Scare and with Mattachine coming under investigation by the FBI and local media, moderates in Mattachine wrested control from Hay.[13] From then on, the dominant voices in the homophile movement were those of the liberal, libertarian, and anticommunist left. Homophile activists were largely white, middle-class, and distanced from the experiences of working class queer people and queer people of color; their strategies emphasized rights of privacy and nondiscrimination in employment and the military, though they also pushed back against censorship and advocated for the protection of bars and cruising spots.

Propelled in part by federal exclusions, homophile activists won their biggest victories by challenging regulation at the state and local levels, particularly in the courts. In a number of cases in the 1950s, judges and juries affirmed the rights of businesses to serve a gay and lesbian clientele; rejected the censorship of homophile publications; and lessened the severity of police practices. In 1951, the California Supreme Court declared, in *Stoumen v. Reilly*, that the state could not revoke the licenses of bars that had a solely homosexual clientele; in the 1959, in *Vallerga v. Department of Alcoholic Beverage Control*, the same court upheld the rights of homosexuals to congregate in bars. In 1958, in *One, Inc. v. Olesen*, the US Supreme Court affirmed the right of the homophile organization ONE to distribute its magazine—thereby agreeing that a publication was not obscene simply because it discussed gay and lesbian identities and politics. Beginning in 1952, activists won local challenges to police entrapment, as in the Dale Jennings case in Los Angeles and the Edward Kelly case in Washington, DC.[14]

Homophile responses to police practices reflected the movement's efforts to politicize gay identity, and they also shaped the movement's racial and class limits. The Mattachine Society was the lead organization behind the Jennings case, in which a gay man won acquittal on charges of solicitation of a police officer after testifying that he had been the target of police harassment and entrapment. Immediately before the trial, Mattachine had also backed five teenagers, four of them Mexican American, who had stated that although they were not gay, they too had been arrested and brutalized during an anti-gay entrapment operation.[15] Mattachine initially sought to end entrapment regardless of its targets, and the group worked briefly with the Civil Rights Congress, a multiracial left organization that supported the teenagers' case. However, they soon dropped this alliance and concentrated on Jennings, a white man who identified himself publicly as gay and who could argue for the distinction between gay identity and lewd behavior.[16]

Homophile activists also built change through publications. The Mattachine Society published the magazine *Mattachine Review*; ONE, Inc. produced *One*; and the lesbian feminist Daughters of Bilitis, founded in 1955, published *The Ladder*. All three publications, later joined by others, circulated nationally and transnationally (especially in Western Europe).[17] These publications allowed homophile activists to report on many events and debates outside their own organizational circles, and so tracked a diversity of opinions, strategies, and approaches to sexuality. For example, *The Ladder* bridged literature and activism, while *Drum* (published by the Philadelphia-based Janus Society) combined physique images with editorials and articles on homophile politics.[18]

Activists helped to further advance new ways of thinking about homosexuality by reaching out to sympathetic psychiatrists and, by the mid-1960s, liberal members of the clergy. They organized educational events and collaborated with such figures as psychologist Evelyn Hooker, at times volunteering as subjects in research that demonstrated the psychological health of gay and lesbian people. In 1965 and 1966, the Daughters of Bilitis worked with antipoverty organizations and a progressive church to develop

programs to serve gay youth and "street queens" in San Francisco's Tenderloin neighborhood.[19] Such efforts built on the rebellion expressed in the Compton's Cafeteria Riot of 1966.

By the 1960s, the homophile movement was growing but fracturing as a new, increasingly militant politics began to emerge. The Mattachine Society split into distinct groups with varying agendas; for example, the Mattachine Society of Washington, DC, led by Frank Kameny, embraced the tactic of public protest.

Other homophile groups began to speak out more forcefully on the right to sexual expression, and efforts to develop community services grew. A rising countercultural and radical sexual politics would soon declare itself with the label "gay liberation."

GAY LIBERATION, LESBIAN FEMINISM, AND THE GAY AND LESBIAN LEFT

Although the Stonewall riots of 1969 mark a key event in queer history, gay liberation did not begin with that rebellion. In fact, a gay liberation movement was growing in the late 1960s as the activism of the New Left converged with everyday queer life and the counterculture to generate a new sexual politics. The vocabulary of gay radicalism developed among a generation that was prompted by the Black Power movement, anticolonialism, and the antiwar movement to embrace the term "liberation" as a rhetoric of sexual and gender freedom—a way to reimagine sexuality and to declare solidarity with freedom struggles around the world.

One way to mark the emergence of gay liberation is by tracking its opposition to police. Increasingly, political demands were voiced in acts of rebellion. In August 1966, trans women and drag queens in San Francisco's Tenderloin district fought back against routine police harassment; their rebellion became known as the Compton's Cafeteria Riot.[20]

Figure 1. Stonewall Veteran and Trans Activist Miss Major Griffin-Gracy Honored in the San Francisco Pride March, 2014.
Photo by Quinn Dombrowski, Creative Commons License, CC BY-SA 2.0.

In the weeks and months that followed, trans people increasingly organized and built ties with homophile and New Left groups. Six months later, in the early hours of New Year's Day, 1967, Los Angeles police raided two gay bars in the city's Silver Lake neighborhood. The patrons fought back and, in February, held the city's first gay protest by picketing in front of the Black Cat bar. Marking a trend, these activists connected gay politics to the hippie, Chicano, and black radical movements.[21] In spring 1969, Carl Wittman's "A Gay Manifesto" observed "an awakening of gay liberation ideas and energy," and tracked the shift to 1968 when "Amerika in all its ugliness... surfaced with the [Vietnam] war and our national leaders."[22]

Perceived in this context, the Stonewall riots were ordinary: a multiracial and gender-diverse assembly of patrons fought a police raid at the Stonewall Inn, a New York City bar. But the scale of that rebellion soon outpaced past events. Begun on June 28, 1969, in Greenwich Village, the Stonewall riots occupied Christopher Street for two nights and attracted the attention of straight news outlets, including the *Village Voice*. Transgender people and gay youth, including the trans women of color Sylvia Rivera, Marsha P. Johnson, and Miss Major Griffin-Gracy (see Figure 1), led the fight.[23]

Within a month, neighborhood activists had founded the Gay Liberation Front (GLF), and in June 1970, they entrenched Stonewall's significance with an anniversary march—the first of many commemorations to come.

Although Stonewall was not an origin point, it served as a further catalyst of gay liberation. Gay, lesbian, bisexual, and transgender radicals around the country soon adopted the name of the Gay Liberation Front, creating dozens of GLFs from Philadelphia and Los Angeles to Tucson and Detroit. Within months, activists in multiple cities were protesting to win such changes as the right to same-sex affection in gay bars, and they built countercultural alternatives through collective living and by holding public gatherings, termed "gay-ins," in public parks.

Gay liberation groups distinguished themselves from homophile organizations by opposing the Vietnam War, supporting Black Power, and critiquing the traditional political establishment. In San Francisco, the GLF broke with the homophile group SIR (Society for Individual Rights) over military inclusion: SIR advocated for gay men to be accepted as soldiers, and by contrast, the GLF opposed the Vietnam War and the draft. GLFs across the country urged activists to "come out against the war" and propelled gay contingents in antiwar marches.[24] Gay caucuses developed inside GI antiwar groups and Vietnam Veterans Against the War, and gay critiques of military masculinity found a welcome audience among many GIs and vets.[25] Gay liberationists also built ties to black radicalism through a shared challenge to police abuse and by forging alliances with the Black Panther Party. These links accelerated after August 1970, when the Black Panther Huey Newton made statements in support of gay liberation and when gay radicals participated in public defense of Panther chapters. Gay, and to a lesser extent lesbian, radicals participated in the Panthers' Revolutionary People's Constitutional Convention meetings held in fall 1970 in Philadelphia, Washington, DC, and Berkeley. These links proved strongest in Philadelphia, in part because the city's GLF was majority people of color.[26]

At the outset of gay liberation, "gay" referred not just to gay men but also to lesbians and trans people; increasingly, however, those groups operated in parallel instead of under one umbrella. Lesbian feminists pursued autonomy from multiple forces, including the state, men, and straight feminists. In May 1970 in New York, lesbian feminists at the Second Congress to Unite Women organized the Lavender Menace action to challenge fears about their presence in the women's movement. The Radicalesbians, formed in the aftermath of this event, argued that desire between women would subvert patriarchal norms.[27] Meanwhile, through groups including Street Transvestite Action Revolutionaries (STAR, in New York) and Radical Queens (in Philadelphia), trans activists challenged not only the exploitation

they faced in broader society but also the hostility they met from many gay and lesbian radicals. Although gay liberation prized gender transgression, some gay and lesbian activists perceived trans people as upholding gender norms rather than transforming them.[28]

By 1972, GLFs around the country had dissolved, for reasons that were a combination of their internal differences and the broader downturn of radical activity in a climate of state repression. Yet this did not spell an end to radical sexual politics; rather, it marked a transition into a gay and lesbian left that persisted throughout the 1970s and 1980s. The gay and lesbian left developed after the height of the Vietnam War but during a continuation of Cold War foreign policy. Its activists saw radical solidarity and sexual liberation as interwoven goals. They engaged especially with socialist feminism and antimilitarism, and by the 1980s, they had fused those agendas through participation in the Central American solidarity movement. Explicitly antiracist and anti-imperialist, the gay and lesbian left often overlapped with organizing among gay and lesbian people of color. Broadly, the gay and lesbian left warrants attention as an important driver of mobilizations between Stonewall and AIDS.

Beginning in the early 1970s, gay and lesbian leftists drew on socialist feminism to critique discrimination against gay and lesbian workers and to explain how homophobia was intertwined with inequality in the capitalist nuclear family. By mid-decade, activists were forging alliances with organized labor. In San Francisco, the Gay Teachers Campaign laid groundwork for the 1978 defeat of California's ballot initiative Proposition 6. Known as the Briggs Initiative for its author, state senator John Briggs, Proposition 6 sought to ban anyone who was gay, lesbian, or who supported gay and lesbian rights from working in the public schools.[29] Gay and lesbian leftists of the 1970s also organized in support of the radical underground, the Chilean solidarity movement, the antinuclear movement, and struggles around housing and police, and against racism and anti-effeminate bias in gay bars.[30] Lesbian leftists crafted a politics of collective defense against both gendered and state violence, linking the two concerns in national campaigns to defend Susan Saxe, a white lesbian being prosecuted for radical activism, and Inez Garcia and Joanne Little, women of color fighting murder charges for their acts of self-defense against rapists.[31]

In the 1980s, the gay and lesbian left coalesced around the Central American solidarity movement. In addition to participating in larger, visibly straight solidarity groups, activists formed specifically gay and lesbian solidarity organizations and travel brigades, particularly in support of Nicaragua's Sandinista Revolution.[32] These efforts began at the end of the 1970s as the Sandinistas seized power, and they flourished in the 1980s as US intervention in Central America grew. Gay and lesbian leftists saw themselves as sharing common enemies with the Nicaraguans who were fighting against the global New Right, and they were inspired by the presence of Sandinista women leaders to hope for gay and lesbian inclusion in the country's socialist revolution. Central American solidarity furthered multiracial queer organizing, especially in California and other sites with large Central American and Latinx communities.[33] It also fostered transnational links because some gay and lesbian radicals in the United States collaborated directly with gay, lesbian, and AIDS activists in Nicaragua. Finally, lesbian and gay solidarity with Central America shaped the organizing for the Second National March on Washington for Lesbian and Gay Rights, in 1987, and the related day of civil disobedience at the Supreme Court.[34]

GAY AND LESBIAN LIBERALISM: AT THE GRASS ROOTS, IN THE BALLOT BOX, AND IN THE COURTS

Gay and lesbian liberals of the 1970s and 1980s worked through legislation, electoral politics, and the courts. Early in the 1970s, some liberal groups were formed by splitting off from radical groups. This could be seen in the Gay Activists Alliance (GAA), a splinter group of New York's GLF founded in December 1969, and then in the National Gay Task Force (now the National Gay and Lesbian Task Force), which was formed in 1973 in a separation from the GAA. The first of these splits occurred because the GAA opposed the GLF's support of the Black Panther Party. The GAA membership was predominantly white, middle class, male, and gender normative, though it continued to employ militant protest tactics against the media and other targets and by the end of 1973 had succeeded in getting homosexuality removed from the American Psychiatric Association's *Diagnostic and Statistical Manual of Mental Disorders-II*. The National Gay Task Force's split from the GAA reflected a turn to the tactics of lobbying rather than protest. The ranks of national advocacy groups continued to grow with the founding of the Gay Rights National Lobby in 1976, the Human Rights Campaign Fund in 1980, and Gay and Lesbian Alliance Against Defamation (GLAAD) in 1978.

Gay and lesbian liberalism also gained grassroots strength in the 1970s (see Figure 2).

Working at local and state levels, activists pressured candidates and developed voting blocs, including by creating Democratic Party clubs. In the 1970s, over forty cities and counties passed laws banning anti-gay discrimination on the job, in housing, and in public accommodation; in the 1980s these gains reached the state level in twelve states.[35] Police entrapment operations and raids began to diminish; some courts struck down laws against cross-dressing and cruising; and by 1981, twenty-four states had overturned sodomy laws. Courts began to grant rights to parents who sought to retain custody of their children after having come out as gay or lesbian and having divorced heterosexual spouses. However, many of the early rulings awarded

Figure 2. Gay and Lesbian Political Buttons, 1970s and 1980s, Collected by the National Museum of American History.
Photo by Erinblasco, Creative Commons License, CC BY-SA 4.0.

custody that was contingent on discriminatory conditions, such as prohibiting gay or lesbian parents from dating or from living with same-sex partners.[36]

In the electoral arena, gay and lesbian activists consolidated power at urban scales. The first openly gay or lesbian elected officials were Nancy Wechsler and Jerry DeGriek, in Michigan, who came out soon after being elected to the Ann Arbor city council in 1972. In 1974, lesbian Elaine Noble was elected to the Massachusetts House of Representatives. In 1977, Harvey Milk, a gay activist representing the Castro District, won his third bid for San Francisco supervisor; in 1978, Milk and the city's mayor, George Moscone, were assassinated by Dan White, a former police officer who had recently resigned his own supervisor post. In Chicago, gay and lesbian activists formed a voting bloc inside the urban political machine and eventually gained influence by embracing urban-development goals.[37] Patterns of gentrification became interwoven with gay political power in Chicago, San Francisco, New York, and other sites.[38]

By the late 1970s, gains in gay and lesbian freedoms were being constrained by the rising New Right, which had won power at state and local levels and would soon dominate the White House and the Supreme Court. The New Right fused populist and elite conservatism into a powerful coalition that opposed shifts toward civil rights, feminism, and sexual freedom and embraced privatization and cuts in social spending. Although gay and lesbian rights were not the New Right's sole concern, these issues proved an effective target for mobilizing opposition, particularly among conservative Christians and through the rhetoric of child protection. Some states began to enact specifically anti-gay sodomy laws, and in 1986, the Supreme Court's ruling in *Bowers v. Hardwick* upheld bans on sodomy. In 1977, a minor celebrity named Anita Bryant mobilized opposition to gay and lesbian rights with the slogan "Save Our Children"; her efforts rolled back a gay and lesbian rights ordinance in Dade County, Florida, and helped achieve similar reversals in Boulder, Colorado; Eugene, Oregon; St.

Paul, Minnesota; Wichita, Kansas; and San Jose, California. The interruption to this sweep came in California when liberals and leftists forged a successful coalition to defeat Proposition 6.[39]

At the federal level, gay and lesbian advocates won a hint of recognition under President Carter. The National Gay Task Force was granted the first White House meeting on gay and lesbian issues in 1977, and the National Coalition of Black Gays followed with their own White House meeting in 1979.[40] In 1980, the Democratic Party convention passed a gay and lesbian rights plank, whereas the Republican platform supported the Family Protection Act—proposing to deny federal funding to people or groups that presented homosexuality as an "acceptable lifestyle." The act died in Congress, but its impulses shaped the federal responses to the AIDS crisis. Less well-recognized shifts that took place under Carter concerned immigration and the military. In 1980, three advocates for military inclusion—Leonard Matlovich, Vernon Berg, and Miriam Ben-Shalom— contested their discharges from the armed forces in the federal courts and won. The same year, immigration authorities revised existing policy to only exclude homosexuals if they explicitly stated their sexual identities. Yet this shift continued to meet Cold War prerogatives: authorities applied the change almost exclusively to the Cuban refugees arriving through the Mariel boatlift and continued to exclude many other LGBTQ immigrants.[41]

LITANIES OF SURVIVAL AND DIFFERENCE: RACE, CLASS, AND GENDER

Differences in LGBTQ politics have not only entailed splits between leftist and liberal points of view; they have also included differences of race, class, gender expression, and sexual nonconformity. Transgender people, queer people of color, working-class queer people, bisexual people, and sex radicals have often found themselves pushed to the margins of LGBTQ activism, and they have responded to such marginalization with distinct forms of political rhetoric and organizing practices.

LGBTQ people of color have often been compelled to respond to the pervasive comparisons drawn between sexuality and race— comparisons that have obscured the intersections of racism and heterosexism and constrained work to challenge inequality. Starting in the late 19th century, eugenic and sexological discourses cited homosexuality and gender transgression as forms of racial degeneracy.[42] By the 1950s, homophile activists were drawing on Marxist and liberal thought to define themselves as a minority group akin to African Americans and other people of color. Through such rhetoric—and despite regulations that tied communities of color to sexual "vice"—many activists imagined sexuality and race as being parallel but dichotomous.[43] Gay liberationists and lesbian feminists at times imagined that, as Carl Wittman ingenuously put it, "Chick equals nigger equals queer. Think it over."[44] Meanwhile, racial and anticolonial nationalisms often mobilized heterosexist norms of reproduction and family. In the 1980s, the Christian right worked to undermine African American support for gay and lesbian issues by accusing gay and lesbian activists of falsely assuming the legacy of the civil rights movement and seeking "special rights."[45] Yet queer people of color also sharply contested the equation of LGBTQ freedom with racial justice, noting that analogies between sexuality and race were not only inaccurate but also failed to address racism in gay and lesbian life.

Responding to these contexts, LGBTQ people of color crafted independent narratives of their concerns and used them to network with one another and to mobilize for political change. At the emergence of gay liberation, they had asserted the interdependence of sexual and racial politics, forming groups such as Third World Gay Revolution (two formations, in New York and Chicago) and Third World Gay People (Berkeley). The term "Third World" signaled a conception of racial inequality as a system of "internal colonialism" and defined people of color, gay or straight, in anti-imperialist terms.

By the mid-1970s, organizing among lesbian and gay people of color was growing dramatically. Examples include the lesbian groups Gente (Oakland), Salsa Soul Sisters (New York), and the Combahee River Collective (Boston); the primarily gay men's Gay Latino Alliance (San Francisco) and the national network Black and White Men Together (also formed in San Francisco, in 1981); and the National Black Gay Caucus (later, the National Coalition of Black Lesbians and Gays, based in Washington, DC).[46] These activists challenged racist policies at gay bars and gentrification in urban "gayborhoods," and they worked to develop gay and lesbian coalitions that would center racial justice and people of color. For example, in 1978, San Francisco's Third World Gay Caucus organized to defeat both Proposition 6 and another California ballot initiative authored by John Briggs: Proposition 7, which reinstated the death penalty. The group's call for solidarity stood in contrast to the broader gay and lesbian movement, which defeated Proposition 6 but did almost nothing to oppose Proposition 7.[47] The following year, the first National Third World Lesbian and Gay Conference— held in Washington, DC, organized by the National Coalition of Black Gays, and timed to coincide with the first March on Washington for Lesbian and Gay Rights—engaged a language of breaking silence and enabling survival.

Activism by LGBTQ people of color expanded the boundaries of LGBTQ politics to more assertively include intellectual and cultural expressions as sites of struggle and tools of organizing. Queer and feminist bookstores, newspapers, film festivals, and conferences became increasingly important venues for antiracist critique and networking.[48] By the 1980s and 1990s, a growing number of lesbian and gay people of color, among them Cherríe Moraga, Gloria Anzaldúa, Joseph Beam, Essex Hemphill, Marlon Riggs, June Jordan, and Audre Lorde (whose poem "A Litany for Survival" inspired the title of this section), advanced LGBTQ cultural politics as writers, filmmakers, and theorists.[49]

Other sites for the expansion of LGBTQ politics lay in transgender and bisexual organizing and in debates over sex radicalism. Trans people, bi activists, and sex radicals shared experiences of being marginalized outside the boundaries of respectability and authenticity. In 1973, Sylvia Rivera was sharply challenged when she spoke at the Stonewall anniversary in New York, known as the Christopher Street Liberation Day, while participants at the West Coast Lesbian Conference divided over the presence of Beth Elliott, a white trans woman and singer. Fellow activist Robin Morgan termed Elliott "an opportunist, an infiltrator, and a destroyer— with the mentality of a rapist."[50] The hostility apparent in this language resonated for years, though a number of others at the conference defended Elliott's presence.

Questions over trans and bi existence were interwoven with lesbian and feminist debates over butch-femme expression, sadomasochism, and pornography, as well as to a lesser extent with gay men's debates over commercialized sexuality and masculinism. Such debates did not align neatly along left versus liberal divides, but the fact of conservative opposition to sex radicalism raised the stakes of activist responses.[51] By 1989 and 1990, conservative politicians had mobilized controversies over the public funding of queer artists Robert Mapplethorpe, Andres Serrano, and the "NEA 4" (performance artists Tim Miller, Karen Finley, John Fleck, and Holly Hughes, whose grant applications to the National Endowment for the Arts were denied). In response to these battles, which were often termed the "culture wars," a queer politics emerged that was invested in oppositional aesthetics and that rejected strict boundaries around sexual or gender identity.[52] The category of "queer" also helped to open space for, and was influenced by, bisexual and transgender organizing. In 1990, activists held the First National Bisexual Conference and formed the organization BiNet USA. Others founded Queer Nation in 1990; the Lesbian Avengers in 1992; Transgender Nation in 1992; and Transsexual Menace in 1994.

MOURNING AND MILITANCY: AIDS ACTIVISM, AIDS CARE, AND QUEER POLITICS

AIDS transformed LGBTQ politics in the 1980s and 1990s, catalyzing new modes of grassroots activism and radicalism even as the scale of the deaths from the illness cut younger people off from an older generation's political history. The epidemic brought the complexity of sexuality—especially its intersections with race, class, and global inequality—to the forefront of LGBTQ politics. It highlighted the gaps between sexual identity and practice, revealing the limits of strictly identitarian conceptions of gay and lesbian life, and fostered the rise of queer theory and queer activism. AIDS was also a site of intense mourning and of battles over memory, dynamics that persist today not only in scholarship on the history of HIV/AIDS, but also in contemporary activism aimed at reasserting the epidemic as a core issue in health care and in LGBTQ politics.[53]

Although it is now understood that HIV/AIDS was affecting large numbers of people by the 1970s (including intravenous drug users, sometimes then described as dying from "junkie pneumonia"), the first cases of AIDS illness were identified in the United States in 1981 and associated with gay men. In the first years of the epidemic a virus had yet to be identified, and the details of sexual transmission remained unclear. However, a gay men's health movement had begun to develop in late 1970s, and this network initiated practices of community care and prevention, as well as efforts to establish what would come to be known as AIDS service organizations.

Fierce debates developed among gay activists over the sources of risk. Some held that bathhouses, commercialized sex, or gay men's leather culture must be the problems; others viewed that argument as homophobic and argued, accurately, that the transmission of semen or blood was of greater concern than the number of partners. (Such debates also shaped reception of Randy Shilts's *And the Band Played On*, which popularized the now-disproven myth of a highly promiscuous "Patient Zero."[54]) In 1982, Michael Callen and Richard Berkowitz's pamphlet "How to Have Sex in an Epidemic" extended an ethos of friendship to casual sex; in 1983, New York's People with AIDS Coalition and the Gay Men's Health Crisis crafted the first prevention messages; and by 1984, the discovery of the HIV virus condensed safe sex debates into an emphasis on condom use.[55] Jennifer Brier argues that, for the majority of activists, "gay liberation and the sexual revolution were not the cause of AIDS but rather an answer to it."[56]

Both sexual and racial politics were implicated in debates surrounding the origins of HIV. Although the dominant representations of people with AIDS and of AIDS activists centered on white men, blame for the source of the epidemic highlighted Central Africa and Haiti.[57] In 1983, when the Centers for Disease Control designated those at high risk of HIV infection, Haitians were the only ethnic group identified (joined by homosexuals, heroin or intravenous drug users, and hemophiliacs to make up a so-called 4-H club). Meanwhile, safe sex messages tended to reify the splits between the categories "gay men" and "people of color." Activists of color contested not only the rhetoric of these splits but also the broader health and economic inequalities that fueled HIV infection and disease.[58] By the mid-1980s the range of AIDS service organizations had expanded to include such groups as the Minority AIDS Project (Los Angeles) and Blacks Educating Blacks about Sexual Health Issues (Philadelphia).

AIDS catalyzed energetic resistance to conservatism as the Reagan administration privileged moralism and nationalism over the arguments of science and public health. Although the surgeon general during the Reagan presidency, C. Everett Koop, proved to be an important supporter of HIV/AIDS education, research, and social spending, he represented an unusual voice in the administration as a whole. Many other conservatives took punitive approaches; some even argued that victims should be quarantined. Gay and lesbian anxieties accelerated in 1986 when the Supreme Court upheld Georgia's sodomy law in *Bowers v. Hardwick* and the Justice Department issued a ruling that allowed AIDS discrimination on the job.[59] Reagan did not give a speech addressing AIDS until 1987, and when he did, he called for mandatory testing instead of prevention and treatment. He did form an AIDS commission, but it included several anti-gay conservatives, only one gay man (Dr. Frank Lilly), and no people with AIDS or AIDS activists. The same year, US senator Jesse Helms pushed through amendments that barred immigrants with HIV/AIDS from entering the country and that banned the granting of federal funds to any AIDS programs that appeared to condone homosexuality or drug use.[60]

Street protests demanding that government authorities confront the AIDS crisis grew out of networks fostered in the gay and lesbian left, but the AIDS movement also greatly altered the meanings of gay, lesbian, and queer radicalism. The first two AIDS direct-action organizations, Citizens for Medical Justice and the AIDS Action Pledge, formed in 1986 in San Francisco and were strongly shaped by gay and lesbian involvement in the Central American solidarity movement. These influences could be seen in the slogan "money for AIDS, not war," which blended a critique of militarism with the view that the epidemic reflected unmet needs in housing, welfare, and health care.[61]

By March 1987, activists in New York had founded the AIDS Coalition to Unleash Power, or ACT UP, which became one of the most influential radical organizations of the late 20th century. ACT UP combined powerful art and graphics with militant direct action against targets that included Wall Street, public health agencies, and the Catholic Church. It demanded lower drug costs, massive public education, and a national AIDS policy built on the needs and input of people with AIDS; it also forged strong ties to reproductive rights organizing, demands for universal health care, and the harm reduction movement (which argued for safety in intravenous drug use). ACT UP's Treatment and Data Committee brought nonexperts into research and drug policy, and the Change the Definition campaign fought hard—and ultimately successfully—to expand the government's definition of AIDS to better account for the presence of the epidemic among women, poor people, and people of color. By 1990 and 1991, ACT UP was splitting between two approaches to organizing, one that centered on a "treatment" approach and the other that prioritized a "social" approach to AIDS. The first emphasized drug research and access, while the second sought to address poverty, homelessness, incarceration, and racism as agents in the disease. The split was also demographic; treatment activists were typically white, middle class gay men, whereas social activists included greater numbers of people of color and women. Yet despite its internal debates, ACT UP mobilized thousands of people and greatly accelerated research and treatment, including the development of the antiretroviral drug therapies that were made available in 1996 and pre-exposure prophylaxis (PrEP), approved in 2012. In the early 21st century, HIV/AIDS activists remain prominent in health care debates, helping to lead organizing to preserve the Affordable Care Act and Medicaid.

NORMATIVITY AND ITS CRITICS: MARRIAGE, THE MILITARY, AND BEYOND

Since the early 1990s, LGBTQ politics has come to occupy an important place in neo-liberal agendas and debates.[62] Reflecting broad patterns across the postwar era, this shift has been both acclaimed and critiqued within LGBTQ communities. The LGBTQ demands that have, however unevenly, gained traction—corporate antidiscrimination, marriage equality, hate crime legislation, and military inclusion—are those that align with the loss of a social welfare state, the growth of incarceration, and post–Cold War and post-9/11 nationalisms. Many LGBT activists have used human rights discourse to pressure the US and international governments, whereas queer radicals have critiqued the alignment of rights discourse with neocolonialism and the war on terror. It remains as important to recognize the tensions that exist in LGBTQ politics as it is to note the changes that have been achieved.

After the Reagan–George H. W. Bush years, advocates began to win important though uneven inroads during the presidency of Bill Clinton; these were interrupted under George W. Bush, expanded under President Obama, and are being contested under Trump. Although many of the victories were won in the courts rather than through legislation, presidents have carried significant weight through their appointment of judges, public statements, and directives for State Department and Department of Justice policy. Military and immigration policy, sodomy law, and marriage have been the most significant areas of change, while employment nondiscrimination has met significant challenges at the federal level.

In 1993, the March on Washington for Gay, Lesbian, and Bi Equal Rights for Inclusion centered the call to "Lift the Ban" on gay and lesbian people in the military—a goal that many queer radicals strongly opposed. By the end of the year, President Clinton had issued the compromise policy Don't Ask, Don't Tell, which barred openly gay, lesbian, and bisexual people from military service, resulted in an increase of expulsions (these dropped after 9/11), and fueled patterns of sexual harassment and rape.[63] Don't Ask, Don't Tell was ended in 2011. In 2016 the military ended a ban on transgender service members, though this has been challenged under President Trump. The exclusion of homosexual immigrants was ended in 1990, and in 1994, Attorney General Janet Reno added homosexuality to the list of reasons migrants might petition for asylum.[64] In 1996, in the precedent-setting *Romer v. Evans*, the Supreme Court ruled that a Colorado state measure banning the inclusion of gay, lesbian, and bisexual people in antidiscrimination law failed the Equal Protection Clause of the Fourteenth Amendment. In 2003, in *Lawrence v. Texas*, the Supreme Court declared bans on sodomy to be unconstitutional.[65] Finally, in what arguably reflected the greatest shift in mainstream views, advocates for marriage equality moved from contestations over domestic partnerships and civil unions to the Defense of Marriage Act (1996) to the cascade of rulings in *United States v. Windsor* (2013), *Hollingsworth v. Perry* (2013), and the granting of the right to marry in *Obergefell v. Hodges* (2015).[66]

Queer critics of marriage have voiced concern over the ways marriage has remained predicated on the perpetuation rather than transformation of the nuclear family—validating its role as a vehicle for the allocation of social resources. In 2006, the collectively authored document "Beyond Same-Sex Marriage" called for recognition of "diverse kinds of partnerships, households, kinship relationships and families" as a means to access not only love, but also "economic benefits and options."[67] Many activists, working through community groups such as FIERCE, the Sylvia Rivera Law Project, and Queers for Economic Justice, have defined welfare reform, criminalization, and poverty as important concerns of queer politics.[68] Queer radicalism has also been developed through opposition to "homonationalism" and "pinkwashing." The first of these terms, popularized by Jasbir Puar, criticizes the mobilization of LGBT rights as justification for Islamophobia and the war on terror.[69] The second censures corporations and governments, particularly in the United States and Israel, for using a rhetoric of LGBT inclusion to draw attention away from state violence and inequality.

Today, a number of important LGBTQ issues remain situated at the margins of recognition in LGBTQ politics, and some have become sites of conservative retrenchment under President Trump. These include treatment on the job. The Employment Non-Discrimination Act (ENDA) has repeatedly failed to advance in Congress, and in the 2000s, the best-funded gay and lesbian advocacy group, the Human Rights Campaign, repeatedly supported a version of ENDA that excluded trans people from coverage. Though a federal court has ruled that the 1964 Civil Rights Act can be extended to gay and lesbian workers, the Trump administration's Justice Department contests this finding.[70] Restrictions on LGBTQ recognition have also been tied to health care and education. President Trump justified his proposal to end trans inclusion in the military by citing medical costs. Further, within the first six months of his presidency, he expanded the global gag rule and proposed cuts to health care that greatly threaten HIV/AIDS treatment and policy.[71] Trump's appointment of Betsy DeVos as secretary of education reflects the neoconservative investments in both privatizing schools and restricting the civil rights of LGBTQ, especially trans, students. Other important concerns have been less visible, but they affect large numbers of people. LGBTQ youth make up a large portion of the homeless population, an issue

generally not addressed by antibullying campaigns or the growth of Gay-Straight Alliances in schools. LGBTQ people remain disproportionately arrested and incarcerated, especially when they are transgender, gender nonconforming, or people of color—and in part because many are profiled as engaging in public sex and prostitution.[72] Some thirty-six states criminalize HIV transmission, including in acts that pose very low risk; these penalties have especially affected African Americans and other people of color. All these contemporary concerns underscore the point that, across the postwar era, LGBTQ politics has proven complex in ideological content, uneven in recognition, and unstable in material gains.

DISCUSSION OF THE LITERATURE

Work in LGBTQ history began in the 1970s and initially developed outside traditional academic venues, crafted by independent scholars or by individuals who were trained in historical research but did not hold traditional academic appointments. Activism to gain recognition in professional organizations and academic curricula soon constituted an important facet of LGBTQ politics. Meanwhile, the field of LGBTQ history became enriched by the presence of community scholars, independent archives, and oral history projects. In the 1980s and 1990s, LGBTQ history emphasized local and community histories that blended ethnography or oral history with archival research. Rooted primarily in social history, these projects situated politics and activism alongside geography and the construction of identity-based communities. Starting in the 2000s, LGBTQ history expanded to place a stronger focus on histories of law and state regulation. Studies centering the intersections of race and class became more common, as did those that pursued the histories of LGBTQ people of color, transgender history, and transnational analyses of citizenship and activism. These shifts reflect the growing recognition of the field and a greater attention to sexuality within legal and political history. Going forward, LGBTQ history might benefit from more narratives that bridge accounts of activism with histories of the arts and artistic subcultures, including writing, performance, and visual expression.

The leading professional organization in the field is the Committee on LGBT History (CLGBTH), an affiliate society of the American Historical Association. The CLGBTH sponsors scholarly presentations at the AHA, awards book and article prizes, publishes a regular newsletter containing book and archive reviews, and serves as a network for both senior and rising scholars.

PRIMARY SOURCES

LGBTQ materials are contained in a wide variety of venues, including university libraries, independent archives, oral-history collections, and online. Periodicals provide one of the most accessible and useful entry points for historical research; such publications were central sites of political organizing and discussion across the homophile movement during the growth of gay liberation and lesbian feminism and throughout the 1970s and the 1990s. Many important periodicals are held in university repositories or by independent archives. A significant number of these periodicals, as well as of unpublished primary sources, are also available online through the digital Archives of Human Sexuality and Identity, hosted by Gale/Cengage Learning. The first part of the archive, "LGBTQ History and Culture since 1940, Part I," covers the post-1940 period and includes roughly 1.5 million pages of fully searchable content, ranging from newsletters and government documents to pamphlets and organizational papers. Additional online venues of note include Outhistory.org; the searchable online repository of the AIDS Memorial Quilt; the ACT UP Oral History Project; the Voices of Feminism Oral History Project, at Smith College;

and the African American AIDS History Project, organized by the scholar Dan Royles.

Among the many LGBTQ archival collections in the United States, standouts include the ONE National Gay and Lesbian Archives (Los Angeles), the GLBT Historical Society (San Francisco), the Cornell University Library Human Sexuality Collection (Ithaca, NY), the Lesbian Herstory Archives (Brooklyn, NY), and the Gerber/Hart Library and Archives (Chicago). The New York Public Library (International Gay Information Center), San Francisco Public Library (Hormel Center), and San Francisco History Center) hold important collections, as do a number of smaller, more localized archives, ranging from the Lambda Archives (San Diego) and Colorado LGBT History Project (Denver) to the Wilcox GLBT Archives (Philadelphia) and the LGBT collections of the Rose Library (Emory University, Atlanta). Researchers working in California should take note of the Online Archive of California, a searchable database that describes collections throughout the state in both independent and university holdings.

FURTHER READING

Brier, Jennifer. *Infectious Ideas: U.S. Political Responses to the AIDS Crisis.* Chapel Hill: University of North Carolina Press, 2011.

Bronski, Michael. *A Queer History of the United States.* Boston: Beacon Press, 2012.

Canaday, Margot. *The Straight State: Sexuality and Citizenship in Twentieth-Century America.* Princeton, NJ: Princeton University Press, 2011.

Duggan, Lisa. *The Twilight of Equality? Neoliberalism, Cultural Politics, and the Attack on Democracy.* Boston: Beacon Press, 2003.

Eaklor, Vicki L. *Queer America: A People's GLBT History of the United States.* New York: New Press, 2008.

Frank, Miriam. *Out in the Union: A Labor History of Queer America.* Philadelphia: Temple University Press, 2015.

Gould, Deborah B. *Moving Politics: Emotion and ACT UP's Fight against AIDS.* Chicago: University of Chicago Press, 2009.

Hanhardt, Christina B. *Safe Space: Gay Neighborhood History and the Politics of Violence*. Durham, NC: Duke University Press, 2013.

Hobson, Emily K. *Lavender and Red: Liberation and Solidarity in the Gay and Lesbian Left*. Oakland: University of California Press, 2016.

Johnson, David K. *The Lavender Scare: The Cold War Persecution of Gays and Lesbians in Federal Government*. Chicago: University of Chicago Press, 2004.

Luibhéid, Eithne, and Lionel Cantú Jr., eds. *Queer Migrations: Sexuality, US Citizenship, and Border Crossings*. Minneapolis: University of Minnesota Press, 2005.

Mumford, Kevin J. *Not Straight, Not White: Black Gay Men from the March on Washington to the AIDS Crisis*. Chapel Hill: University of North Carolina Press, 2016.

Rivers, Daniel Winuwe. *Radical Relations: Lesbian Mothers, Gay Fathers, and Their Children in the United States since World War II*. Chapel Hill: University of North Carolina Press, 2015.

Rupp, Leila J., and Susan K. Freeman, eds. *Understanding and Teaching U.S. Lesbian, Gay, Bisexual, and Transgender History*. Madison: University of Wisconsin Press, 2014.

Stein, Marc. *Rethinking the Gay and Lesbian Movement*. New York: Routledge, 2012.

Stein, Marc. *Sexual Injustice: Supreme Court Decisions from Griswold to Roe*. Chapel Hill: University of North Carolina Press, 2010.

Stewart-Winter, Timothy. *Queer Clout: Chicago and the Rise of Gay Politics*. Philadelphia: University of Pennsylvania Press, 2016.

Stryker, Susan. *Transgender History*. Berkeley: Seal Press, 2008.

NOTES

1. On minoritarian versus universalist conceptions, see Eve Sedgwick, *Epistemology of the Closet* (Berkeley: University of California Press, 1990); and Marc Stein, *City of Sisterly and Brotherly Loves: Lesbian and Gay Philadelphia, 1945–1972* (Philadelphia: Temple University Press, 2004).

2. Margot Canaday, *The Straight State: Sexuality and Citizenship in Twentieth-Century America* (Princeton, NJ: Princeton University Press, 2011).

3. When the American Psychiatric Association issued its first diagnostic manual in 1952, it built on the systems of classification enacted by the military and termed homosexuality a "sociopathic personality disorder." Multiple government agencies relied on the APA definition. Eithne Luibhéid, *Entry Denied: Controlling Sexuality at the Border* (Minneapolis: University of Minnesota Press, 2002), 87.

4. Canaday, *Straight State*; and Marc Stein, *Rethinking the Gay and Lesbian Movement* (New York: Routledge, 2012), 42.

5. David K. Johnson, *The Lavender Scare: The Cold War Persecution of Gays and Lesbians in Federal Government* (Chicago: University of Chicago Press, 2004); see also Stein, *Rethinking*, 43, 65.

6. Marc Stein, "All the Immigrants Are Straight, All the Homosexuals Are Citizens, but Some of Us Are Queer Aliens: Genealogies of Legal Strategy in *Boutilier v. INS*," *Journal of American Ethnic History* 29.4 (Summer 2010): 45–77.

7. George Chauncey Jr., "The Postwar Sex Crime Panic," *True Stories from the American Past*, ed. William Graebner (New York: McGraw-Hill, 1993), 160–178.

8. Karen L. Graves, *And They Were Wonderful Teachers: Florida's Purge of Gay and Lesbian Teachers* (Urbana: University of Illinois Press, 2009); and Stacy Braukman, *Communists and Perverts under the Palms: The Johns Committee in Florida, 1956–1965* (Gainesville: University Press of Florida, 2012).

9. Emily K. Hobson, "Policing Gay LA: Mapping Racial Divides in the Homophile Era, 1950–1967," in *The Rising Tide of Color: Race, State Violence, and Radical Movements across the Pacific*, ed. Moon-Ho Jung (Seattle: University of Washington Press), 188–212.

10. John D'Emilio, *Lost Prophet: The Life and Times of Bayard Rustin* (Chicago: University of Chicago Press, 2003); Mumford, *Not Straight, Not White*.

11. On coverage in the black press, see Kevin J. Mumford, *Not Straight, Not White: Black Gay Men from the March on Washington to the AIDS Crisis* (Chapel Hill: University of North Carolina Press, 2016); and Allen Drexel, "Before Paris Burned: Race, Class, and Male Homosexuality on the Chicago South Side, 1935–1960," in Brett [Genny]Beemyn, ed., *Creating a Place for Ourselves: Lesbian, Gay, and Bisexual Community Histories* (New York: Routledge, 1997), 119–144.

12. Hobson, "Policing Gay LA"; Daniel Hurewitz, *Bohemian Los Angeles and the Making of Modern Politics* (Berkeley: University of California Press,

2007). The foundational work on the homophile movement is John D'Emilio, *Sexual Politics, Sexual Communities: The Making of a Homosexual Minority in the United States, 1940–1970* (Chicago: University of Chicago Press, 1983).

13. Martin Meeker, "Behind the Mask of Respectability: Reconsidering the Mattachine Society and Male Homophile Practice, 1950s and 1960s," *Journal of the History of Sexuality* 10.1 (2001): 78–116.

14 Stein, *Rethinking*, 48, 61. See also Marc Stein, *Sexual Injustice: Supreme Court Decisions from Griswold to Roe* (Chapel Hill: University of North Carolina Press, 2010).

15. Hobson, "Policing Gay LA."

16. Hobson, "Policing Gay LA."

17. David Churchill, "Transnationalism and Homophile Political Culture in the Postwar Decades," *GLQ* 15.1 (2009), 31–65. See also "U.S. Homophile Internationalism," special issue, *Journal of Homosexuality* 64 (2017): 843–990.

18. Marcia M. Gallo, *Different Daughters: A History of Daughters of Bilitis and the Rise of the Lesbian Rights Movement* (New York: Seal Press, 2006); and Marc Stein, "Canonizing Homophile Respectability: Archives, History, and Memory," *Radical History Review* 120 (2014): 53–73. On the homophile press, see Martin Meeker, *Contacts Desired: Gay and Lesbian Communications and Community, 1940s–1970s* (Chicago: University of Chicago Press, 2005); Craig M. Loftin, *Masked Voices: Gay Men and Lesbians in Cold War America* (Albany: State University of New York Press, 2012); and Craig M. Loftin, ed., *Letters to ONE: Gay and Lesbian Voices from the 1950s and 1960s* (Albany: State University of New York Press, 2012).

19. Christina B. Hanhardt, *Safe Space: Gay Neighborhood History and the Politics of Violence* (Durham, NC: Duke University Press, 2013).

20. Susan Stryker and Victor Silverman, dirs., *Screaming Queens: The Riot at Compton's Cafeteria* (San Francisco: Independent Television Service, 2005), DVD; and Susan Stryker, *Transgender History* (Berkeley: Seal Press, 2008).

21. Mike Davis, "Riot Nights on Sunset Strip," in *In Praise of Barbarians: Essays against Empire*, ed. Mike Davis (Chicago: Haymarket, 2007).

22. Carl Wittman, "A Gay Manifesto" (1969)," in *We Are Everywhere: A Historical Sourcebook of Gay and Lesbian Politics*, eds. Mark Blasius and Shane Phelan (New York: Routledge, 1997), 380–390.

23. Annalise Ophellian, *Major!* (Floating Ophelia Productions, 2015), DVD; Arthur Dong, *The Question of Equality: Outrage '69* (San Francisco: Independent Television Service, 1995), VHS; and Martin Duberman, *Stonewall* (New York: Penguin, 1994).

24. Justin David Suran, "Coming Out against the War: Antimilitarism and the Politicization of Homosexuality in the Era of Vietnam," *American Quarterly* 53.3 (2001): 452–488.

25. Emily K. Hobson, *Lavender and Red: Liberation and Solidarity in the Gay and Lesbian Left* (Oakland: University of California Press, 2016), 39–40.

26. Amy Abugo Onigiri, "Prisoner of Love: Affiliation, Sexuality, and the Black Panther Party," *Journal of African American History* 94.1 (2009): 69–86; Marc Stein, "'Birthplace of the Nation': Imagining Lesbian and Gay Communities in Philadelphia, 1969–70," in *Creating a Place for Ourselves*, ed. Beemyn, 253–288; and Hobson, *Lavender and Red*, 31–34, 51–53. On the question of gay support for Cuba, see Ian Lekus, "Queer Harvests: Homosexuality, the U.S. New Left, and the Venceremos Brigades to Cuba," *Radical History Review* 89 (Spring 2004): 57–91.

27. Anne M. Valk, "Living a Feminist Lifestyle: The Intersection of Theory and Action in a Lesbian Feminist Collective," *Feminist Studies* 28.2 (Summer 2002): 303–332; and Alice Echols, *Daring to Be Bad: Radical Feminism in America, 1967–75* (Minneapolis: University of Minnesota Press, 1989).

28. Stryker, *Transgender History*; Betty Luther Hillman, "'The Most Profoundly Revolutionary Act a Homosexual Can Engage In': Drag and the Politics of Gender Presentation in the San Francisco Gay Liberation Movement, 1964–72," *Journal of the History of Sexuality* 20.1 (2011): 153–181.

29. See especially Miriam Frank, *Out in the Union: A Labor History of Queer America* (Philadelphia: Temple University Press, 2015). Other important works on LGBTQ labor include Ryan Patrick Murphy, *Deregulating Desire: Flight Attendant Activism, Family Politics, and Workplace Justice* (Philadelphia: Temple University Press, 2016); and Phil Tiemeyer, *Plane Queer: Labor, Sexuality, and AIDS in the History of Male Flight Attendants* (Berkeley: University of California Press, 2013).

30. Hanhardt, *Safe Space*; Tamara Lea Spira, "Intimate Internationalisms: 1970s 'Third World' Queer Feminist Solidarity with Chile," *Feminist Theory* 15.2 (2014): 119–140.
31. Emily Thuma, "Lessons in Self Defense: Gender Violence, Racial Criminalization, and Anti-carceral Feminism," *WSQ: Women's Studies Quarterly* 43.3–4 (2015): 52–71; Judy Grahn, *A Simple Revolution: The Making of an Activist Poet* (San Francisco: Aunt Lute, 2012); and Hobson, *Lavender and Red*.
32. Important groups included Gay People for the Nicaraguan Revolution, Lesbians and Gays against Intervention, the Victoria Mercado Brigade, and the Philadelphia Lesbian and Gay Work Brigade. Several gay and lesbian newspaper, including the Boston-based *Gay Community News*, covered the issue.
33. *Latinx* has become adopted as a gender-neutral term to refer to Latina and Latino people and communities.
34. Hobson, *Lavender and Red*, 155–185.
35. Stein, *Rethinking*, 103–105, 114, 167; see also Vicki L. Eaklor, *Queer America: A People's GLBT History of the United States* (New York: New Press, 2008), 155–156.
36. Daniel Winuwe Rivers, *Radical Relations: Lesbian Mothers, Gay Fathers, and Their Children in the United States since World War II* (Chapel Hill: University of North Carolina Press, 2015).
37. Timothy Stewart-Winter, *Queer Clout: Chicago and the Rise of Gay Politics* (Philadelphia: University of Pennsylvania Press, 2016).
38. Hanhardt, *Safe Space*.
39. Fred Fejes, *Gay Rights and Moral Panic: The Origins of America's Debate on Homosexuality* New York: Palgrave Macmillan, 2008). On impacts among gay and lesbian activists, see Heather Murray, *Not in This Family: Gays and the Meaning of Kinship in Postwar America* (Philadelphia: University of Pennsylvania Press, 2010); and Rivers, *Radical Relations*.
40. Eaklor, *Queer America*, 149; Stein, *Rethinking*, 134; and Mumford, *Not Straight, Not White*.
41. Julio Capó Jr., "Queering Mariel: Mediating Cold War Foreign Policy and US Citizenship among Cuba's Homosexual Exile Community, 1978–1994," *Journal of American Ethnic History* 29.4 (2010): 78–106. See also Susan Peña, *¡Oye Loca! From the Mariel Boatlift to Gay Cuban Miami* (Minneapolis: University of Minnesota Press, 2013).
42. See, for example, Siobhan Somerville, "Scientific Racism and the Emergence of the Homosexual Body," *Queering the Color Line: Race and the Invention of Homosexuality in American Culture* (Durham, NC: Duke University Press, 2000), 15–38.
43. On links to vice, see Kevin J. Mumford, *Interzones: Black/White Sex Districts in Chicago and New York in the Early Twentieth Century* (New York: Columbia University Press, 1997); and Kwame Holmes, "Beyond the Flames: Queering the History of the 1968 D.C. Riot," in *No Tea, No Shade: New Writings in Black Queer Studies*, ed. E. Patrick Johnson (Durham, NC: Duke University Press, 2016), 304–322.
44. Wittman, "Gay Manifesto."
45. A vehicle of this argument was the documentary *Gay Rights, Special Rights* (Hemet, CA: Jeremiah Films, 1993), VHS. On LGBTQ responses at the time, see Mab Segrest, *Memoir of a Race Traitor* (Boston: South End Press, 1999).
46. Horacio N. Roque Ramírez, "'That's My Place!': Negotiating Racial, Sexual, and Gender Politics in San Francisco's Gay Latino Alliance, 1975–1983," *Journal of the History of Sexuality* 12.2 (2003): 224–258; and Mumford, *Not Straight, Not White*.
47. Hobson, *Lavender and Red*, 91–92.
48. Kristen Hogan, *The Feminist Bookstore Movement: Lesbian Antiracism and Feminist Accountability* (Durham, NC: Duke University Press, 2016).
49. Key primers include Gloria Anzaldúa and Cherríe Moraga, eds., *This Bridge Called My Back: Writings by Radical Women of Color*, 4th ed. (Albany: State University of New York Press, 2015). Anzaldúa and Moraga originally published their work in 1981 and it was quickly followed by a second edition in 1983. See also David L. Eng and Alice Y. Hom, eds., *Q&A: Queer in Asian America* (Philadelphia: Temple University Press, 1998); E. Patrick Johnson and Mae J. Henderson, eds., *Black Queer Studies: A Critical Anthology* (Durham, NC: Duke University Press, 2005); and Michael Hames-García and Ernesto Javier Martínez, eds., *Gay Latino Studies: A Critical Reader* (Durham, NC: Duke University Press, 2011).
50. Emma Heaney, "Women-Identified Women: Trans Women in 1970s Lesbian Feminist Organizing," *TSQ: Transgender Studies Quarterly* 3.1–2 (2016): 137–145.
51. Whitney Strub, *Perversion for Profit: The Politics of Pornography and the Rise of the New Right*

(New York: Columbia University Press, 2011); and Lisa Duggan and Nan D. Hunter, *Sex Wars: Sexual Dissent and Political Culture*, 10th anniversary edition (New York: Routledge, 2006).

52. The term "culture wars" refers to the political conflicts over obscenity, sexuality, and the arts in the 1980s and 1990s. It is also used more broadly to describe battles over traditionalist versus progressive, liberal, or secular points of view, or to chart neoconservatism in general; see Andrew Hartman, *A War for the Soul of America: A History of the Culture Wars* (Chicago: University of Chicago Press, 2015).

53. Jonathan Bell et al., "Interchange: HIV/AIDS and U.S. History," *Journal of American History* 104 (September 2017): 426–455.

54. Randy Shilts, *And the Band Played On: People, Politics, and the AIDS Epidemic* (New York: St. Martin's Press, 1987).

55. Jennifer Brier, *Infectious Ideas: U.S. Political Responses to the AIDS Crisis* (Chapel Hill: University of North Carolina Press, 2011), 35–44.

56. Jennifer Brier, "How to Teach AIDS in a U.S. History Survey," in *Understanding and Teaching U.S. Lesbian, Gay, Bisexual, and Transgender History*, eds. Leila J. Rupp and Susan K. Freeman (Madison: University of Wisconsin Press, 2014), 282.

57. Among the best histories of the origins are Jacques Pepin, *The Origins of AIDS* (Cambridge: Cambridge University Press, 2011); and Paul Farmer, *AIDS and Accusation: Haiti and the Geography of Blame* (Berkeley: University of California Press, 2006). Farmer's book was originally published in 1992.

58. Cathy J. Cohen, *The Boundaries of Blackness: AIDS and the Breakdown of Black Politics* (Chicago: University of Chicago Press, 1999); and Adam Geary, *Antiblack Racism and the AIDS Epidemic* (New York: Palgrave Macmillan, 2014).

59. Deborah B. Gould, *Moving Politics: Emotion and ACT UP's Fight against AIDS* (Chicago: University of Chicago Press, 2009), 138.

60. Stein, *Rethinking*, 157–158; Jennifer Brier, "The Immigrant Infection: Images of Race, Nation, and Contagion in Public Debates on AIDS and Immigration," in *Modern American Queer History*, ed. Allida Black (Philadelphia: Temple University Press, 2001): 253–270. See also Anthony M. Petro, *After the Wrath of God: AIDS, Sexuality, and American Religion* (New York: Oxford University Press, 2016).

61. Hobson, *Lavender and Red*, 155–185.

62. Lisa Duggan, *The Twilight of Equality? Neoliberalism, Cultural Politics, and the Attack on Democracy* (Boston: Beacon Press, 2003); and Dean Spade, *Normal Life: Administrative Politics, Critical Trans Politics, and the Limits of the Law*, rev. ed (Durham, NC: Duke University Press, 2015).

63. Tim McFeeley, "Getting It Straight: A Review of the 'Gays in the Military' Debate," in *Creating Change: Sexuality, Public Policy, and Civil Rights*, eds. John D'Emilio, William B. Turner, and Urvashi Vaid (New York: St. Martin's Press, 2000), 236–250; Allan Bérubé, "How Gay Becomes White and What Kind of White It Stays," *My Desire for History: Essays in Gay, Community, and Labor History*, eds. John D'Emilio and Estelle B. Freedman (Chapel Hill: University of North Carolina Press, 2011), 202–230; Aaron Belkin, *Bring Me Men: Military Masculinity and the Benign Façade of American Empire, 1892–2001* (New York: Oxford University Press, 2012); and Doug Ireland, "Gay-Baiting under Don't Ask, Don't Tell," *The Nation*, July 3, 2000.

64. Alissa Solomon, "Trans/Migrant: Christina Madrazo's All-American Story," in *Queer Migrations: Sexuality, US Citizenship, and Border Crossings*, eds. by Eithne Luibhéid and Lionel Cantú Jr. (Minneapolis: University of Minnesota Press, 2005), 3–29.

65. George Chauncey, "What Gay Studies Taught the Court: The Historians' Amicus Brief in *Lawrence v. Texas*," *GLQ: A Journal of Lesbian and Gay Studies* 10.3 (2004): 509–538.

66. For primary sources and firsthand accounts, see Kevin M. Cathcart and Leslie J. Gabel-Brett, *Love Unites Us: Winning the Freedom to Marry in America* (New York: New Press, 2016).

67. "Beyond Same-Sex Marriage: A New Strategic Vision for All Our Families and Relationships," *Monthly Review*, August 8, 2006. Available online (https://mronline.org/2006/08/08/beyond-same-sex-marriage-a-new-strategic-vision-for-all-our-families-relationships/).

68. Scholarly arguments in this regard include Cathy Cohen, "Punks, Bulldaggers, and Welfare Queens: The Radical Potential of Queer Politics?" in *Black Queer Studies: A Critical Anthology*, eds. E. Patrick Johnson and Mae J. Henderson (Durham, NC: Duke University Press, 2005), 21–51; and Laura Briggs, *How All Politics Became Reproductive Politics: From Welfare Reform to*

Foreclosure to Trump (Berkeley: University of California Press, 2017).

69. Jasbir K. Puar, *Terrorist Assemblages: Homonationalism in Queer Times* (Durham, NC: Duke University Press, 2007).

70. Matthew Haag and Niraj Choksi, "Civil Rights Act Protects Gay Workers, Court Rules," *New York Times*, April 4, 2017; and Alan Feuer, "Justice Dept. Weighs in against Protections for Gays in the Workplace," *New York Times*, July 27, 2017.

71. On trans military service, see Phil McCausland, "Trump Claims Transgender Service Members Cost Too Much: But Is That True?," *NBC News*, July 27, 2017. http://www.nbcnews.com/news/us-news/trump-claims-transgender-service-members-cost-too-much-true-n786891. On HIV criminalization, see Center for HIV Law and Policy, *Ending and Defending against HIV Criminalization*, 2d ed. (New York: Center for HIV Law and Policy, 2015); and the Centers for Disease Control and Prevention, "HIV-Specific Criminal Laws (http://www.cdc.gov/hiv/policies/law/states/exposure.html)." On the impact of the global gag rule under Trump, see Jerome A. Singh and Salim S. Abdool Karim, "Trump's 'Global Gag Rule': Implications for Human Rights and Global Health," *The Lancet* 5.4 (2017): 387–389.

72. Mitch Kellaway, "Phoenix Drops 'Walking While Trans' Charge against Monica Jones," *The Advocate*, February 27, 2015; Joey L. Mogul, Andrea J. Ritchie, and Kay Whitlock, *Queer (In) Justice: The Criminalization of LGBT People in the United States* (Boston: Beacon Press, 2012); and Regina Kunzel, *Criminal Intimacy: Prison and the Uneven History of Modern American Sexuality* (Chicago: University of Chicago Press, 2003).

Emily K. Hobson

NATIVE AMERICANS AND CITIES

An important relationship has existed between Native Americans and cities from pre-Columbian times to the present day. Long before Europeans arrived in the Americas, indigenous peoples developed societies characterized by dense populations, large-scale agriculture, monumental architecture, and complex social hierarchies. Following European and American conquest and colonization, Native Americans played a crucial role in the development of towns and cities throughout North America, often on the site of indigenous settlements. Beginning in the early 20th century, Native Americans began migrating from reservations to US cities in large numbers and formed new intertribal communities. By 1970, the majority of the Native American population lived in cities and the numbers of urban American Indians have been growing ever since. Indian Country today continues to be influenced by the complex and evolving ties between Native Americans and Cities.

PRE-COLUMBIAN NORTH AMERICAN CITIES

Highly complex and sophisticated societies existed in the Americas for thousands of years before Europeans arrived in the late 15th century, including dense population centers that we can refer to as cities. These civilizations indigenous to the Americas developed social hierarchies, irrigated agriculture, specialized tools, arts and crafts, religion, public works projects, and monumental architecture, among many other characteristics of urban areas.

Mesoamerica, for example, saw the rise of the city of Teotihuacán between 200 and 900 CE. During its height the city was the largest in the world and home to as many as 250,000 people. It was a multiethnic city, ruled at times by various groups that included the Zapotec, Mixtec, Mayan, and Nahuat cultures, who maintained political and economic control over the region. Much of the great architecture associated with Mesoamerica and that remains a major tourist attraction today (often referred to popularly as "Mayan") comes from Teotihuacán. Travelers to and residents of the city followed the broadly built and linear Avenue of the Dead for three miles from the outskirts to the heart of the city, passing courtyards, temples, staircases, and large platforms capped by tall towers, until reaching the massive Pyramid of the Moon, situated in a dramatic setting with the looming mountain and extinct volcano, Cerro Gordo, in the background. Teotihuacán went into decline after 900 and by 1300 another city, Tenochtitlan, rose. Located farther to the south, it served as the center of empire for the Mexica, a group commonly known as the Aztecs. The population of 200,000 lived in an urban space characterized by a complex system of streets, canals, aqueducts, and sanitation such that one scholar has called Tenochtitlan "perhaps the greatest planned city ever created by human beings." Hernán Cortés, who led the Spanish conquest of Tenochtitlan in 1521, described the Templo Mayor (one of the main temples in the city) as having

"as many as forty towers, all of which are so high that in the case of the largest there are fifty steps leading up to the main part of it; and the most important of these towers is higher than that of the cathedral of Seville. They are so well constructed both their stone and woodwork that there can be none better in any place."

Seventy-eight additional buildings surrounded the Templo Mayor, including schools, jails, armories, and altars used for tens of thousands of human sacrifices. After the destruction of Tenochtitlan by the Spanish (which included the razing of the Templo Mayor), it was rebuilt and renamed Mexico City.

In the Eastern Woodlands region of North America, another major civilization developed during the pre-Columbian period. Sometimes referred to as the Mound Builders for their construction of massive earthworks, these groups thrived largely because of the advanced farming techniques that they developed in the fertile river valleys of the present-day northeastern, southeastern, and midwestern United States. The largest Eastern Woodlands population center was Cahokia, located at the confluence of the Mississippi and Missouri Rivers just outside of what is now St. Louis, Missouri. Between 700 and 1250 CE, Cahokia covered about 400 acres and had a population of 10,000 to 16,000 people, making it larger than London, England. It included defined neighborhoods representing a class-based social organization, roads linking the city center to suburbs and other nearby towns, water reservoirs, recreational courts, and temple complexes. Cahokia also maintained eighty-five massive earthwork mounds that were used for burial, astronomical, and religious and ceremonial purposes. The largest of these, Monk's Mound, covered sixteen acres and was 1,037 feet long and approximately 100 feet high. Items found in the mounds, such as jewelry and weapons made from obsidian, copper, and mica, showed that the Woodland cultures were involved in long-distance trading networks that ranged a thousand miles from Cahokia. Pottery was also widely used and potters forged carefully carved and etched pieces for special occasions, in addition to making jars, bowls, beakers, plates, and cups for everyday purposes.

Farther west, in the region that became the southwestern United States, another major population center was built by the Anasazi people around 850 CE. Twelve planned towns and up to 350 villages, housed a population of about 15,000 people dispersed over a twelve-mile stretch of Chaco Canyon, which, in turn, was connected by roads to an extensive network of settlements up to sixty miles away. Chaco Canyon relied on an extensive irrigation system that supported agriculture and provided drinking water in the arid environment. Intricately constructed stone buildings of aboveground living quarters and underground kivas (ceremonial chambers) ranged in size from rather small in the villages to a complex of more than 800 rooms at Pueblo Bonito, the largest town. One scholar has calculated that at the town of Chetro Ketl the walls were built from fifty million stones, all individually cut and shaped. The Anasazi's skill in stonework extended to tools and jewelry, made from both local materials and those obtained through trade. Turquoise, for example, was used for ornaments, beads, and jewelry, all of which were exchanged with other groups. The soft sandstone that lined the walls of Chaco Canyon also became a medium for the Anasazi to communicate, to record important events, and to express their cultural and spiritual beliefs through petroglyphs. Carved directly into the stone, Anasazi rock art included clan symbols, depictions of ceremonies, records of migrations, human and animal motifs, and commemorative displays of annual solstices and equinoxes. Chaco Canyon was occupied until about 1150, when the Anasazi moved to nearby cliff dwellings, probably for protection from other groups.

Hundreds of additional cities existed throughout the Americas in this period. The decline of the great pre-Columbian cultures—and the cities that they built and inhabited—was once considered a mystery, but scholars now point to such explanatory factors as warfare and the vulnerability of large population centers, political instability, climatic changes, overpopulation, disease, and the straining of environmental resources. Contrary to earlier beliefs, the people of these civilizations did not simply disappear; rather they had a profound impact on the shaping of the new societies and population centers that developed in North America after the arrival of Europeans. The Mexica were the people who first met the Spanish in Mesoamerica and remained a vital part of Mexico City through the period of colonization. The Pueblo peoples, who the Spanish encountered in present-day New Mexico, were the direct descendants of the Anasazi. Up and down the Atlantic seaboard, the tribes that met Spanish, British, Dutch, and French colonizers were descended from the Eastern Woodlands peoples. All of these groups bore social and cultural characteristics developed over thousands of years in North America, including the experiences of living in cities. They continued to influence the population centers of North America well into the post-contact period.

NATIVE AMERICANS AND THE GROWTH OF NORTH AMERICAN TOWNS AND CITIES

Many towns and cities in North America were founded on the site of indigenous settlements. This meant that the massive dispossession of Native American land and resources stretched from the first days of colonization to the growth of modern cities in the late 19th to early 20th centuries. Nonetheless, Native peoples maintained a significant presence and played important roles as these places were transformed into towns and cities controlled, first, by European arrivals and, later, by succeeding generations of European Americans.

One example of the continuing presence of Native people through the period of European colonization can be found in southern New England. By the 1670s, as English settlers seized Indians lands throughout the region, Native peoples found it difficult to sustain their traditional economy of agriculture, fishing, hunting, and gathering. Small towns founded by missionaries, known as "praying towns," attracted Native peoples looking for refuge. In places such as Natick, Massachusetts, Native residents converted to Christianity, adopted English-style farming and livestock raising, engaged in wage labor, entered the whaling industry, served in the military, sold baskets and brooms, and became indentured servants. They also traveled to bigger towns, such as Cambridge and Boston, where they bought and sold items in the marketplace, had access to the courts and other workings of the legal system, and participated in the expanding labor market. Over time, by the mid-18th century, the pressures on these newly titled lands grew more intense and English colonists made increasing efforts to displace the region's Indian residents. Nonetheless, Native people survived and maintained a presence in the towns and cities of southern

New England through the period of the American Revolution and American statehood, if not as landowners, then as wage laborers, domestic servants, and seafarers.

Such a pattern is illustrated in the nearby British colony, and later US state, of Rhode Island, where between 1750 and 1800, Narragansett people survived both on their reservation and in nearby towns. After more than a century of colonial encounter, Narragansett residents tended to live on the margins of town life in Rhode Island, rarely holding property, struggling with debt and forced bondage, and grouped among the poor of society. Narragansett children, in particular, were subject to indentured servitude and educated in town schools. Despite efforts by town officials to classify them in ways that erased their legal status as Indians (perhaps to eliminate future land claims), Narragansett town-dwellers nonetheless maintained a strong sense of Indian identity. They continued to refer to themselves in official records as Indians, lived in extended families, took in and cared for other Native people, and persisted in traditional patterns of hunting and gathering on a seasonal basis.

Towns and cities that were founded and developed later as part of the United States also maintained and even relied upon a Native American presence. After the establishment of Seattle, Washington, in 1851, Native people traded for goods, forged political alliances, and participated in the labor market, in addition to partaking in many of the new city's opportunities for leisure and entertainment. Indeed, Seattle would hardly have survived through its first decades without Native people to work in the mills, provide food for sale, haul mail and goods by canoe, clear the land, build houses, and work in the city's brothels. Native people also resettled in small enclaves around the city, working as domestic servants, living as members of mixed-race families, and residing in tribal communities alongside the expanding suburbs. These close connections between Indian and non-Indian residents of

the city are illustrated by an anecdote from the 1870s, in which a municipal judge required a Chinese American man who appeared before him to prove his residency by answering a query in Chinook jargon (a local Indian dialect; he did so, successfully). From 1880 to the 1930s Seattle emerged as a major metropolitan area. During this period of explosive growth, Native people suffered massive losses of land as the city carried out major engineering projects and private developers constructed new housing divisions. Nonetheless, Native people remained in the city, living in working-class neighborhoods and on Skid Row, in addition to making regular trips from nearby reservations to experience urban life, sell goods, and work.

While the Native American population of, first, European and, then, US towns and cities throughout North America remained relatively small in relation to the increasing numbers of non-Indians, Native people did not simply vanish quietly into the past, as many popular accounts would have us believe. On the contrary, despite suffering terrible hardships and the massive loss of lands and resources, Indian people continued to maintain a presence in the territories that had come under the control of Euro-American settlers, but they did so often on very different terms. This movement of Indians back to the growing cities and towns of North America set the stage for a more dramatic rise in urban Indian populations as the United States itself came to be defined as a predominantly urban nation in the 20th century.

NATIVE AMERICANS AND CITIES IN THE FIRST HALF OF THE 20TH CENTURY

Throughout the first half of the 20th century, the Native American population of urban areas throughout the United States steadily increased as American Indians traveled to cities and their surrounding areas for thousands of new jobs in the agricultural, industrial, and service sectors.

This migration was often regional, since Native people were most likely to take advantage of economic opportunities in the towns and cities closest to their established communities, but significant American Indian migration also took place to cities farther away from tribal homelands. During World War II, even larger numbers of Indian people traveled to urban areas for defense work and military service.

Many Native Americans first experienced towns and cities through migratory labor. This work could provide Indian people with crucial sources of income and also presented possibilities for integrating wage labor into social, cultural, and economic strategies rooted in tribal lands and communities. Tohono O'odham Indians in southern Arizona, for instance, engaged in cotton-picking, mining, domestic service, and railroad work to complement their seasonal subsistence patterns. Navajos in the Four Corners area of the Southwest similarly absorbed wage labor on and near the reservation into a diverse, household-centered economy that included domestic production and sheepherding. During the 1920s, in Needles, California, on the Arizona border, about three hundred Mojave Indians from nearby Fort Mojave Reservation found jobs as casual laborers for the Santa Fe Railway, alongside European Americans, African Americans, and immigrants from Mexico and Japan. Mojave Indians also worked paving streets, building roads, constructing houses, and working on area farms. Apache Indians from the San Carlos Reservation in Arizona spent part of the year in the nearby towns of Globe and Miami employed in mining, road construction, railroad work, domestic service, and the production of Native crafts. Members of the Hualapai tribe similarly worked for wages in Kingman, Arizona, just outside the reservation's western boundary. Throughout British Columbia and Alaska, Indians served as loggers, longshoremen, teamsters, cowboys, miners, fishermen, and cannery workers. In the Northern Plains and Upper Midwest regions, Menominee Indians were employed in the forests and sawmills, while Ho-Chunk Indians picked strawberries, cranberries, cherries, corn, peas, and potatoes. Outside the Pine Ridge Reservation in South Dakota, the town of Rapid City maintained a population of about 3,000 Sioux Indians who worked largely in cutting timber. In northern Maine, Mi'kmaw, Passamaquoddy, Penobscot, and Maliseet Indians were recruited as migratory laborers in the 1920s on the region's growing potato farms. During the same period, Indians from reservations throughout Southern California could be found seasonally in the vicinity of Riverside, outside Los Angeles, where the orange groves provided months of steady work. These patterns of migratory work were replicated by Native Americans in many other parts of the United States.

Indian people also sought better jobs and living conditions in the burgeoning cities of the United States, even if it meant moving farther away from tribal communities. Urban areas around the country experienced a period of tremendous expansion at the turn of the 20th century, and Native Americans were among the groups who traveled to these locales to fill hundreds of thousands of new jobs. Railroads and commercial ships hired Indians as traveling laborers, so that places such as Chicago, the San Francisco Bay area, and other regional transportation centers became familiar places to Native people. Indians took a variety of mill, construction, and factory jobs in expanding industrial areas that included Minneapolis–St. Paul, Milwaukee, Detroit, Phoenix, Seattle-Tacoma, and Los Angeles. Mohawk Indians from reservations in New York State and Canada worked in New York City's steel industry beginning in the 1920s, constructing many of the high-rise office buildings that came to dominate the city's skyline, while shuttling between reservations and an Indian neighborhood in Brooklyn. Laguna Pueblo people worked for the Santa Fe Railway building and maintaining the tracks all the way from their lands in New Mexico through the American Southwest to the East San Francisco Bay area city of Richmond, where they established an enclave. Some cities were home to small communities or populations of Native people who were alumni of nearby Office of Indian Affairs boarding schools. A 1928 government survey in Phoenix, Arizona, for instance, found about forty Indian families and thirty single Indian women who were either graduates of or current students in a work program from Phoenix Indian School. More broadly, Indian women who attended federal boarding schools found jobs as domestic servants in non-Indian homes throughout the cities of the American West.

Drawn to the city by new jobs, many Native people settle into the multiethnic, working-class neighborhoods that could be found there. In Los Angeles, for example, Native people moved through the industrial, commercial, and residential spaces developing in the central city and South Bay areas. A few examples from the 1920s can illustrate larger patterns. Joseph and Ethel Mills, two Indians born in Oklahoma, lived with their nine-year old son in a predominantly white, middle-class neighborhood while Joseph worked as an auto mechanic. Several streets over in a white and Latino working-class neighborhood, two families of California Indians worked as railroad machinists and shared a house with their children, their landlady, a second-generation Russian street laborer, and a Russian immigrant couple. Etta Sarracino, a single, forty-two-year-old Indian born in New Mexico, shared a house with three other single women while working as a nurse in a local hospital. Carlos McPherson, a veteran of World War I and a driller for Standard Oil Company, headed a home in a neighborhood populated by white, working-class, and middle-class residents.

While small, a growing middle-class American Indian community could also be found in some American cities. Graduates of Indian boarding schools and missionary colleges moved to urban areas and viewed the city as a place from which they could improve conditions for Native peoples both in the city and across the country, often while working as professionals. Chicago, for instance, due to its place as a transportation hub with ready access to both the eastern and western United States, drew an especially large number of Indians who became local and national leaders. They advocated for the rights of their relatives back in their reservation and rural homelands, participated in national policy discussions, and established social networks throughout the city. These efforts in activism and community organization became the foundation for the support structure and urban Indian community that developed in a later period of increasing Indian migration to the cities.

Thousands of American Indians also traveled to cities throughout the United States and Europe in the late 19th and early 20th centuries for careers as entertainers and performers, taking advantage of nostalgia for the nation's western past and a fascination with the "disappearing" cultures of American Indians. Touring "Wild West" shows, first organized by William "Buffalo Bill" Cody, gave Native people the chance to earn relatively good wages, travel around the world, and engage in the singing, dancing, and other cultural activities that were discouraged on federally administered reservations. American Indians also took jobs as performers for international expositions, such as the Kwakwaka'wakw from Vancouver Island, British Columbia, who lived in a reconstructed Northwest Coast village during the 1893 Columbian Exposition in Chicago, where they engaged in dancing and exhibiting Native skills that included wood carving and basket weaving. Smaller entertainment venues also featured American Indian performers. Miccosukee Indians worked in "Indian villages" alongside state highways that catered to Florida's increasing tourist trade and Seminole Indians marketed Native culture through tourist villages in Ft. Lauderdale that combined demonstrations of older cultural practices with new tourist-oriented activities such as alligator wrestling. By the 1910s and 1920s, the Hollywood film industry became another source of employment for Indian performers and hundreds participated in the first decades of the film industry as actors, stunt persons, and technical advisers. Many Indian entertainers also built careers that combined different displays and performances of Indian culture. Molly Spotted Elk, for example, from the Penobscot Indian Reserve in Maine, played an Indian character for vaudeville shows, worked as an "Indian dancer" at cabarets and nightclubs, acted in Hollywood films, and toured Europe as a member of an Indian jazz band. Similarly, Richard Davis Thunderbird, a Cheyenne Indian born in 1867, worked as an anthropological informant, traveled with Wild West shows, appeared in vaudeville, led a troupe of Cheyenne dancers, lectured on Indian history and lore, wrote a manuscript on Cheyenne religion, and worked steadily as an actor and technical adviser in Hollywood until his death in 1946.

During World War II, urban populations throughout the United States again experienced an upsurge as individuals of all backgrounds migrated from rural areas to urban locales in support of the war effort through military service and work in the defense industries. American Indians were no exception, with about 25,000 Indians entering the armed forces and approximately 40,000 working in plants producing armaments. Practically all Native people involved in the war effort experienced life in an urban area, whether laboring in a factory, training for the military, or deploying oversees. Indian migration was particularly acute in places with war industries and military installations, such as Portland, Oregon, where a relatively small prewar Indian population expanded following the arrival of newcomers to work in the shipyards. A few individual cases help to illustrate the wider patterns at work. Helen and George Reifel were Indians from Oklahoma who were teaching on the Navajo Reservation when the United States entered World War II. So many of their students left to join the armed forces that they decided to take their two sons to Portland,

where Helen found work as a welder and George became a shipwright. Lewis Tomahkera, a Comanche Indian, arrived from Lawton, Oklahoma, to work at the Kaiser Shipyards. Inspired by a contest for new recruits, he convinced seven tribal members, six of them women, to come to Portland as welder trainees. Ernest Peters, aged sixty-three years, found work as a swing shift worker at Kaiser's Swan Island shipyards and settled down in southeast Portland, where he lived in a five-room house with ten family members. Joe Bergie came to Kaiser via the Carlisle Indian School in Pennsylvania and Stanford University, where he was a football star, to work at the Vancouver yards across the Columbia River from Portland. Similar patterns of Indian urbanization occurred at other centers of wartime mobilization, such as Seattle, the San Francisco Bay area, Los Angeles, Detroit, Milwaukee, and Chicago.

A substantial portion of Indian migrants to US cities and servicewomen and men went back to their reservations and rural communities after the war, especially as the troops returned home and defense plants reverted to peacetime production. Yet World War II changed Indians who traveled to cities in the United States and to places overseas in profound ways that would continue to resonate in the postwar years. Purcell Rainwater, a Sioux Indian living on the Rosebud Reservation, recalled what happened when his daughter came home after serving in the US military for three years: "She went, come back and stayed for, I don't know, a week or two. Then she says, Dad, there's nothing around for me. Well, I said, that's all right, I said, I know it's hard for you. And so we helped her get ready and she left." After stints in Indiana and Chicago, Rainwater's daughter settled in Los Angeles, where she worked and started a family. While wartime experiences influenced these subsequent migrations, American Indian postwar urbanization was also predicated upon decades of earlier experiences in the urban areas of the United States. Throughout the first half of the 20th century, cities throughout the country were places where Indian people participated in the expansion and development of urban America.

NATIVE AMERICANS AND CITIES IN THE SECOND HALF OF THE 20TH CENTURY

American Indians continued to move to cities in increasing numbers during the decades that followed World War II for many reasons. Native people served in the military, the federal government promoted Indian urbanization through the "relocation program," better roads connected reservations and urban areas, and the Civil Rights movement led to greater opportunities for American Indians to attend college. Most importantly, vibrant urban American Indian communities welcomed newcomers and nurtured generations of Native people born and raised in the city. Indeed, a majority of American Indians resided in cities by 1970 and urban Indian populations have continued to rise ever since.

Shortly following World War II, the federal government became an active promoter of American Indian migration to cities through the Relocation Program. Primarily, relocation worked as a corollary to the "termination" policy, or an effort by the federal government to absolve itself of responsibility for managing American Indian affairs. With relocation, federal officials hoped to move Native peoples to cities where they would become self-sufficient and assimilate into American society. By the mid-1950s, the federal Bureau of Indian Affairs had set up relocation field offices in Chicago, Denver, Salt Lake City, Los Angeles, San Francisco, Oakland, San Jose, Portland (Oregon), Dallas, Oklahoma City, Tulsa, St. Louis, Cincinnati, Cleveland, and Joliet and Waukegan, Illinois. Indians "on relocation" arrived in their destination city, either by themselves or with their families, and were provided help in finding employment and housing, along with limited aid that included subsistence funds, counseling, and basic

health care. After intense criticism that the federal government was simply "dumping" Indians in the cities, the program was expanded to include tuition and living stipends for two-year vocational courses. About 155,000 Indians participated in relocation until it was discontinued in the 1970s.

Despite the intentions of the federal government, American Indian identity did not disappear in the city; rather, it developed in complex ways that combined elements of tribal culture, a broader sense of "being Indian," and the experiences of urban life. "Indian Centers," Indian churches, powwow groups, and other tribal and intertribal organizations were formed by Indians in cities to address a wide range of social and cultural needs. Bars, parks, individual homes, churches, and city streets also served as places where Native people met more informally. The most inclusive urban Indian activity was the powwow, an intertribal gathering where Native people could express tribal culture and learn about other groups through tribal dances, dress, and songs, while reinforcing the idea that they were all to some extent "urban Indians." In Los Angeles, the city with the largest American Indian population, known as the "urban Indian capital of the United States," a powwow was held every Sunday for nine months of the year. Urban Indian organizations also sponsored all-Indian sports leagues and holiday parties, held classes in Indian language and culture, collected clothing and food for the Indian poor, and maintained youth and elder groups, among many other activities. Most importantly perhaps, they simply provided an open and comfortable place for Indian people of all backgrounds to get together— Jack Forbes (Powhatan/Delaware) was attending college and graduate school in Los Angeles during the 1950s, and he remembered the city's Indian Center as a place to meet other Indians and listen to records.

Indeed, the need for such organizations stemmed from the considerable challenges that many Native people faced in making the transition from reservations to cities throughout the postwar period. Urban American Indians often struggled to find solid ground in the city after arriving with few job skills, little education, and limited experiences with urban life. The city could be an alienating place for American Indians, full of unfamiliar bureaucracies and multiple pressures to assimilate into the dominant society. Consequently, urban Indians, who concentrated in the poorest and most dilapidated neighborhoods, faced high rates of unemployment, drug and alcohol abuse, suicide, domestic violence, incarceration, and preventable disease. Yet many other Indians established more comfortable and secure places in the urban working and middle classes by finding good jobs in the urban industrial economy, starting their own businesses, buying homes in suburban neighborhoods, and raising families in the city. By the 1970s, minority recruitment programs at some colleges and universities and the growth of tribal colleges meant that a small but significant number of American Indians were able to earn degrees that qualified them for work in government, business, law, social services, and other professions. The Tafoya family, for example, moved to Los Angeles from Santa Clara Pueblo through the relocation program in the 1950s, and they eventually settled in the coastal community of Hermosa Beach. Joseph, the family patriarch and a veteran of World War II, worked in the aerospace industry while playing a leading role in the city's Indian organizations with his wife, Trudy. The couple's five children grew up working with their father as "Indian dancers" at Disneyland and for civic groups, public events, and private parties, in addition to dancing on the city's intertribal powwow circuit. Dennis, who was five years old when the family moved to the city, remembered growing up in several overlapping communities that nurtured his tribal background and broader identity as an American Indian, citizen of the United States, and member of the larger world. He attended the University of California, Los Angeles (UCLA), did graduate work at California State University, Long Beach,

and went to work for city government, eventually becoming the director of Affirmative Action Compliance for the City and County of Los Angeles, the highest rank achieved by an American Indian employee in the history of Los Angeles.

The transformation of the Indian Centers and other urban Indian organizations from self-help organizations supported by charitable fundraising into more institutionalized social service providers operating on multimillion dollar grants constituted one factor in this type of social mobility. By the early 1970s, new sources of state and federal funding flooded into urban Indian communities to be used to finance job training, health care, education, drug and alcohol counseling, cultural forums, and a host of additional services targeting the specific needs of American Indians in the city. In large part, this effort marked an extension of the federal government's "War on Poverty" to urban American Indian populations, but the issue was brought to the forefront by the "Red Power" movement, or the rise of American Indian activism. High-profile, public protests, such as the occupation of Alcatraz Island and the activities of the American Indian Movement, popularized Indian causes, leading to enhanced support for urban American Indian populations. Activists on the local level, already working through urban American Indian organizations, harnessed these new funds with renewed energy. Often younger and college-educated, this generation of Indian activists proclaimed that previous efforts to address Indian issues had woefully neglected Indian culture and identity, and they were forceful in keeping the pressure on public officials to support their activities. Raymond Sprang, for example, a Northern Cheyenne Indian from Montana, served on the council of the American Indian Student Association at UCLA. In response to a reporter's question about the rising numbers of American Indian students enrolled in higher education and their role at the university, he stated: "[Native American students are] bucking the administration for more recognition and we want an Indian studies department. We're also working for changes in our [American Indian recruit program], we want more student input of ideas and dynamics."

Education, in fact, was one long-neglected area that garnered sustained attention from urban Indian activists in the early 1970s. Studies during the period found that urban American Indians consistently ranked at the bottom of performance testing and maintained some of the highest dropout rates of any racial or ethnic group in American cities. A rise in Indian advocacy and increased funding led to a rethinking of the ways that Indians in cities experienced the educational system from preschool through higher education, specifically placing importance on the foregrounding of Indian identity and culture. State and federal grants led to the establishment of new schools for Indian students in cities such as Milwaukee, Minneapolis, and Chicago, where Native instructors were hired who taught Indian history, language, arts and crafts, dancing, storytelling and music, in addition to other aspects of Indian culture and heritage. These "Indian community" schools were supplemented by commissions of American Indian educators and parents who advised public school districts on a variety of issues, such as defending the rights of Indian students, representing Indian parents in school disputes, assisting Indian teachers in personnel matters, and training non-Indian school personnel on how to work with Indian students and respect Indian culture and values in the classroom. While local school districts sometimes undervalued these collaborations, they did provide Indian input in urban pubic school curriculums and decision making. Major colleges and universities throughout the country increased funding for recruiting and retaining American Indian students and for the development of American Indian Studies programs. At UCLA, for example, American Indian enrollment reached 195 students by fall 1973 and included thirty-two graduate students, while the American Indian Student Association provided peer counseling, sponsored Indian speakers and musicians, and organized

an annual Indian Culture Week. The American Indian Cultural Center (later renamed the American Indian Studies Center) offered fourteen courses in American Indian Studies and maintained a library of 6,000 volumes. Such programs helped Native students "be Indian" socially, culturally, and intellectually while earning their degrees, a substantial shift from their past educational experiences. James Monroe, a Blackfeet and Yakama Indian, noted: "[When I enrolled as a student at UCLA, it was] the first time that I really can remember relating to Indians, as something that, I don't know how you would say it... as an identity."

Funding for urban Indian organizations and activities and other efforts to serve American Indian populations declined dramatically during the 1980s, but cities remained vital centers of Indian activity and home to the majority of the Indian population. Social service networks for urban Indians persevered, as Native professionals who came of age in the 1970s regrouped to find new ways of funding services. Cultural groups continued to hold urban powwows and Native American student groups at colleges and universities remained particularly active. At the same time, Native people in cities maintained and further developed links to reservations through regular visits, intermarriage with Indians of other tribes, and careers that required travel between reservations and cities. Beginning in the 1990s, the boom in Indian gaming further blurred the boundaries between urban and reservation Indians, as some tribes took advantage of their newfound wealth and influence to play a more active role in the political, cultural, and social life of the urban areas in their states and regions. The Seminole tribe of Florida, for example, by 2014 employed over 2,000 non-Indians and purchased more than $24 million in goods and service annually through its various enterprises, including the iconic Hard Rock Café chain, which the tribe bought for $965 million. Other gaming tribes, from the Mississippi Choctaw to the Mashantucket Pequots in Connecticut to the Ho-Chunk Nation of Wisconsin have contributed billions of dollars to dozens of local, state, and national elections and political campaigns while also sponsoring numerous events and annual festivals, donating to major universities, and advertising on television and billboards. Thus, by the end of the 20th century, it was becoming increasingly clear that "Indian Country" included not just the reservations and rural areas of the American West, but also the cities of the United States. For American Indians, this was something that was already well understood—their urban traditions stretch back hundreds of years and remain a major feature of Native America today.

DISCUSSION OF THE LITERATURE

Although it constitutes one of the most defining trends in Native American history, scholars have paid relatively little attention to the relationships between Native Americans and cities. Recently, however, interest has grown in the topic and studies are now emerging to help define both the broad parameters and the particularities of American Indian urban experience. Many questions remain open and urbanization promises to be a vibrant subfield of Native American studies well into the future.

The first wave of scholarship on Native Americans and cities occurred in the 1960s and 1970s, when anthropologists and sociologists noticed the swelling of urban Indian populations and saw an opportunity to examine the process by which people they understood as culturally differentiated functioned within the urban milieu. These studies often reinforced popular notions of Indians as perpetually marginalized from the mainstreams of American life, arguing that the persistence of "traditional culture" in the city explained the "failure" of Indians to "adjust," resulting in high rates of unemployment, alcoholism, and other social problems. Nonetheless, this work identified populations of urban American Indians and occasionally revealed Native American voices and perspectives. Over time, anthropologists

emerging from this school developed more complex and less deterministic modes of analysis that allowed for cultural adaptation. Studies of Native people in Los Angeles published in the 1990s, for example, examined how tribal practices and beliefs influenced new forms of ethnicity and cultural identity, and the relationships between urban American Indian organizations and community. More recently, innovative work on California's Silicon Valley highlighted the complex networks that have developed throughout Native America by showing how indigenous peoples of various backgrounds come together in cities while remaining connected to tribal homelands.

Since the 1990s historians have also begun to seriously investigate urban American Indian experiences. Place-based studies of urban Indian populations in cities such as Albuquerque, Chicago, Los Angeles, Phoenix, and Seattle have addressed a variety of topics (many of which are mentioned previously in this article), including reasons for migration, employment patterns, civil rights activism, urban Indian organizations, shifting notions of identity, and other aspects of Indian life in the city, while other scholars have attempted to synthesize past scholarly literature on American Indians and cities into broader and more generalized studies of the "urban Indian experience." This recent period has also seen disciplines such as sociology, literature, and communications address the topic of Native Americans and cities, often within the frameworks and institutions provided by American Indian studies. By keeping track of the field's conferences, top journals, and major university press lists, scholars can see the slow but steady development of urban studies as an important subfield.

Much work remains to be done so that the relationships between Native Americans and cities can be better understood by scholars, policymakers, and the general public. Scores of cities and urban regions that existed in the Americas before European contact have yet to be studied. Very limited attention has been given to the presence of indigenous peoples in the towns and developing cities during the period of European colonization and American settlement. Much of the work on American Indian and cities in the 20th century begins with World War II, thus neglecting the patterns by which Native people took part in the massive urbanization of the United States during the first half of the 20th century. Studies of developments in the 20th century have also focused on the largest cities and urban regions in the country, neglecting smaller cities and towns, especially those close to Indian reservations. Even so, the last seventy-five years of urban American Indian experiences have only begun to be addressed, with much room still for additional studies of particular cities and research that compares multiple urban populations. More broadly, scholars need to grapple with the patterns that link the different places throughout Native America, so that a more complex portrait might emerge of an Indian Country that has long been composed of reservations and rural areas, towns, and cities, with American Indians regularly traveling the networks that connect them. American Indians have long been involved in the process of "reimagining Indian Country" as they have adapted to changing circumstances and conditions—it is long past time for others to adopt this inclusive vision of Native Americans and cities.

PRIMARY SOURCES

Primary sources related to Native Americans and cities are located in the following archives and special collections: the Richard Davis Thunderbird Collection (MS 641) at the Southwest Museum of the American Indian, Autry National Center, Los Angeles, California; the Indian Urbanization Project, Center for Oral and Public History, Pollak Library, California State University Fullerton; the Chicago American Indian Oral History Project, Newberry Library, Chicago; and Record Group 75, Bureau of Indian Affairs, Branch of Relocation Services, at various regional branches of the National Archives and Records Administration.

Relevant books and printed materials include Susan Lobo, ed., *Urban Voices: The Bay Area American Indian Community* (Tucson: University of Arizona Press, 2002); L. Lawney Reyes, *Bernie Whitebear: An Urban Indian's Quest for Justice* (Tucson: University of Arizona Press, 2006); and *Talking Leaf*, a publication of the Los Angeles Indian Center (1951–1978).

Articles on Native Americans and cities can also be found in various searchable newspaper databases and online news archives (e.g., *New York Times, Los Angeles Times*).

FURTHER READING

Amerman, Stephen Kent. *Urban Indians in Phoenix Schools, 1940–2000.* Lincoln: University of Nebraska Press, 2010.

Carpio, Myla Vicenti. *Indigenous Albuquerque.* Lubbock: Texas Tech University Press, 2011.

Calloway, Colin, ed. *After King Philip's War: Presence and Persistence in Indian New England.* Hanover, NH: University Press of New England, 1997.

Fixico, Donald L. *The Urban Indian Experience in America.* Albuquerque: University of New Mexico Press, 2000.

Forbes, Jack D. "The Urban Tradition among Native Americans." *American Indian Culture and Research Journal* 22 (1998): 15–42.

Herndon, Ruth Wallis, and Ella Wilcox Sekatau. "The Right to a Name: The Narragansett People and Rhode Island Officials in the Revolutionary Era." In *After King Philip's War: Presence and Persistence in Indian New England.* Edited by Colin Calloway, 114–143. Hanover, NH: University Press of New England, 1997.

Hosmer, Brian, and Colleen O'Neill, eds. *Native Pathways: American Indian Culture and Economic Development in the Twentieth Century.* Boulder: University of Colorado Press, 2004.

LaGrand, James B. *Indian Metropolis: Native Americans in Chicago, 1945–1975.* Urbana: University of Illinois Press, 2002.

LaPier, Rosalyn R., and David R. M. Beck. *City Indian: Native American Activism in Chicago, 1893–1934.* Lincoln: University of Nebraska Press, 2015.

Lobo, Susan, and Kurt Peters, eds. *American Indians and the Urban Experience.* Walnut Creek, CA: AltaMira, 2001.

O'Brien, Jean. *Dispossession by Degrees: Indian Land and Identity in Natick, Massachusetts, 1650–1790.* Cambridge: Cambridge University Press, 1997.

Ramirez, Renya K. *Native Hubs: Culture, Community, and Belonging in Silicon Valley and Beyond.* Durham, NC: Duke University Press, 2007.

Rosenthal, Nicolas G. *Reimagining Indian Country: Native American Migration and Identity in Twentieth-Century Los Angeles.* Chapel Hill: University of North Carolina Press, 2012.

Shoemaker, Nancy. "Urban Indians and Ethnic Choices: American Indian Organizations in Minneapolis, 1920–1950." *Western Historical Quarterly* 19 (1988): 431–448.

Thrush, Coll-Peter. *Native Seattle: Histories from the Crossing-Over Place.* Seattle: University of Washington Press, 2007.

Weibel-Orlando, Joan. *Indian Country L.A.: Maintaining Ethnic Community in Complex Society.* Urbana: University of Illinois Press, 1991.

Nicolas G. Rosenthal

LATINO URBANISM

LANDSCAPES OF COLONIZATION

Latino urbanism originated in the encounter between the people and plans of Spain's emergent overseas empire and the indigenous civilizations and landscapes of the Americas. Both of these regions included large and complex cities. Spain had been an urban civilization since the Roman period, and the Iberian Peninsula became a major political and cultural center by the 2nd century CE. It was home to numerous cities in which tens of thousands of people lived in landscapes that were a palimpsest of Roman, Visigothic, Muslim, and Christian architectural styles. Indigenous America was just as impressively urban, boasting a number of substantial cities and other population centers with large and elaborate buildings that required extraordinary technical ability in stone construction and exceptional creativity in ornamentation. This included, of course, the Aztec capital of Tenochtitlán, its population of hundreds of thousands making it one of the world's leading cities in the 15th century.

The Spanish advanced into the Americas in the 16th century with a developing set of landscape plans designed to facilitate the conquest and settlement of their newly explored and claimed territories. Their hope was to simply impose those plans upon the hemisphere, but they were limited by Native Americans' existing human geography and infrastructure, which also benefited their colonial project. In most cases the Spaniards built on lands where Indians already lived, since such settlements had the wealth they sought, not to mention the people whose labor they exploited and whom they were determined to convert to their religion. In what is today Mexico, for example, the Spanish established their headquarters at the center of the Aztec capital; and there and elsewhere, particularly in the city of Puebla, they demolished indigenous temples and built churches in their place.

As they expanded their area of settlement northward, the colonizers made use of three key features of Spanish urbanism in the Americas: the mission, the presidio, and, most importantly, the three ranks of civil settlements—*pueblo, villa,* and *ciudad.* Missions were built near existing Indian villages in order to concentrate their populations, control their labor, and impose Catholicism on them—by force if necessary. The basic mission form was a church, an attached courtyard with dwellings for clergy and assistants, an *atrio* forecourt surrounded by a waist-high wall, and often a corral. Missions were constructed in various architectural styles.

Among the most durable and famous were those that combined elements of Spanish and Puebloan adobe and timber construction; many are still standing in New Mexico, for example. But it is important to remember that missions were situated across a vast area: throughout

Figure 1. San Xavier del Bac, a mission church originally completed at the end of the 18th century, Tohono O'odham Nation, Arizona.
Photograph by Daniel Ramirez, Creative Commons License (CC BY 2.0).

Figure 2. Aerial view of the Pueblo of Acoma, Cibola County, New Mexico, showing mission church and Indigenous and Spanish plazas.
Courtesy Historic American Buildings Survey, Library of Congress.

present-day Mexico and the US Southwest from California to Texas, as well as northward from the Caribbean into Florida and Georgia.

Alongside the missions, the Spanish built structures known as presidios. These were fortified military garrisons intended to hold territory against those who resisted Spain's claims on North America: both the Native peoples the colonizers were dispossessing and other European powers hoping to control part of the continent. The usual form of the presidio was a quadrangle of inward-facing rooms with bastions at opposite corners, but numerous variants were constructed in locations from coastal California to the Atlantic littoral, particularly in a cordon along what later became the US-Mexico border.[1]

But the major work of colonization in Spanish North America was accomplished subsequently through *pueblos*, or villages, as well as larger settlements classified as *villas* (towns) and *ciudades* (cities). In 1573 King Philip II of Spain promulgated the *Laws of the Indies*, a manual for colonizing the New World that contained detailed rules for locating, planning, and populating urban places. The basic plan was quite simple. Each town or city would be built around a rectangular central plaza, with a church occupying one side and the municipal headquarters another; this basic architectural

arrangement thus manifested the primacy of religious faith and civil authority. The remaining lots on the central plaza and along surrounding streets would be awarded to its first settlers as their reward for holding the territory for Spain. They would enjoy the prestige (and greater safety) of living at the center of the settlement, and the merchants among them would have immediate access to the plaza on market days. These founders would also receive the royal title of *hijodalgo* or *hidalgo*, a rank of nobility they could pass down to their descendants. In sum, the *Laws of the Indies* was an urbanizing project—one intended to transplant basic elements of Spanish city planning into the Americas so that their people and places would become reflections in miniature of imperial Spain itself.[2]

The work of town building was rarely so straightforward, however, since the Spanish had to contend with Indigenous people and geographies already in place for centuries or millennia. The colonizers learned, for example, that they were hardly alone in planning their settlements around central gathering places. Puebloan peoples, for example, had long constructed villages around ceremonial spaces that were architectural manifestations of their cosmology, symbolizing their place at the center of creation while also orienting them to the four cardinal directions. Various existing patterns of habitation, along with the vagaries of topography and the limitations of materials and labor, shaped the resultant towns, which often included irregular or unsanctioned forms. In some, the plaza might be oddly shaped or incompletely bounded; in others, the church could be located well off the plaza; elsewhere, streets might not form a proper grid, or dwellings could be sited at odd angles.[3]

These places were the first iteration of Latino urbanism, their plazas serving as centers of community life, loci of face-to-face interaction in shared public space. Whatever the individual quirks of their planning and construction, they formed a cultural area extending across the southern part of North America, one that was home to thousands of communities over hundreds of years. These settlements were always both hybrids and palimpsests: a combination of landscape traditions in which subsequent arrivals to a place overlaid new design principles and everyday behaviors upon an already-occupied terrain.

BORDERS CROSSING PEOPLE

When the United States instigated a war with Mexico in 1846 and annexed its northern half two years later, the region's Spanish-Indigenous landscapes became part of the US Southwest. In some areas, most notably northern California in the era of the Gold Rush, Anglos began to arrive in large numbers and heavily outnumbered the Hispanic population within a few years. In other parts of the region with a larger settled population and fewer immediately exploitable natural resources, most notably New Mexico, it was decades before the numerical preponderance of *hispanos* was seriously challenged.

Among the ways that Anglos altered urban landscapes was by shifting the population centers of cities away from the plazas of the Indigenous, Spanish, and Mexican eras and toward other features. In the case of Californian cities, this typically involved a westward move toward increasingly busy Pacific Ocean harbors that became the leading foci of Anglo settlement. Farther inland, the arrival of railway links with the East often meant that the plaza-centered urbanism of earlier centuries was challenged by separate urban grids oriented to the railroad tracks. In Albuquerque, New Mexico, for example, an Anglo settlement characterized by wood-frame Queen Anne, Colonial Revival, and bungalow dwellings surrounding a commercial district consisting of brick business blocks grew up around the Atchison, Topeka, and Santa Fe Railroad line; this "New Town" was located about a mile to the east of the *hispano* "Old Town" situated closer to the Rio Grande.[4]

The human geography of the Mexican borderlands was also shaped by another key part of the continent's railway network: the one running from south to north. Over the last quarter of the 19th century and right up to the Revolution of 1910, the Mexican government worked to expand railroad connections between their North and the US Southwest in a drive for economic development. This fostered population growth in numerous border towns and cities where Mexican urban forms and Anglo landscapes abutted each other directly and where there was sustained daily contact between Anglos and Mexicans. One common type of border settlement comprised small cities that grew quickly as resource-extraction and transportation centers—places such as El Paso, Texas, with its railroad, lead mining, and smelting facilities, and copper towns such as Bisbee, Arizona—where a substantial proportion of the working class were ethnic Mexicans. Also typical of the region were the river towns at crossings along the Rio Grande: places where both Mexican and Anglo workers, labor recruiters, entrepreneurs, consumers, and tourists crossed paths as they looked for employment, business opportunities, and entertainment on the other side of the border.[5]

The era's other major move of consequence for Latino urbanism was the Spanish-American War of 1898 and the transfer of Puerto Rico and Cuba from Spanish to US possession. This had no immediate effect on US Latino landscapes, but it established the basis for subsequent migrations from the Caribbean that would populate cities decades later.

PEOPLE CROSSING BORDERS

By the turn of the century, the urbanistic confluence of Latin America and the United States had already been growing strongly, fueled on the one hand by US companies searching for profits along the border and on the other by the simple fact that Mexican laborers could earn far higher wages in the United States than at home. This process was jolted in the 1910s by the Mexican Revolution. The violence and disorder of the conflict drove huge numbers of people to flee areas with intense fighting, with as many as one and a half million finding their way to the United States. These dynamics resulted in the augmentation of the ethnic Mexican population as well as the elaboration of new kinds and regions of settlement.

Early in the 20th century, the United States remained predominantly rural—even in 1920 half the people still lived in small towns— and the nation's Hispanic population was even more so. Most were involved in agricultural work, whether in long-standing towns in the borderlands or as migrant laborers in the fast-growing farm sector. In California, for example, the dramatic expansion in citrus and other crops depended upon a greatly expanded work-force. Ethnic Mexicans were its largest contingent, which drove their pattern of settlement. Many lived in rural towns, but an increasing number made homes in *colonias*: small semiformal settlements on undeveloped land that lay between farms and cities. While such places offered inexpensive housing, their lack of basic infrastructure took a toll on the health of their residents.[6]

Over time, tens of thousands of ethnic Mexicans who worked on farms and lived in rural and peripheral areas began to migrate to cities. For most, it was the draw of better-paid urban employment in industrial, commercial, and service jobs that proved decisive, though many new city dwellers continued to do seasonal agricultural labor on farms not far beyond the city limits. Easily the most important example of this phenomenon was the rise of Los Angeles as the nation's preeminent concentration of urban Latinos. From a population of between 3,000 and 5,000 in 1900, ethnic Mexican Angelenos grew to an estimated 97,000 to 190,000 people by 1930, likely comprising about 10 percent or more of the city's residents.

Notably, this growth propelled a reclaiming of Latino urban space as Mexicans became the predominant population around the old plaza area of Los Angeles. La Placita, as it was often called, which had been declining in importance since annexation in 1848, gradually grew into the focus of religious, social, entertainment, and business life for much of the growing community, especially male migrants.[7]

In other cities in or near the US-Mexico borderlands, similar factors motivated many ethnic Mexicans to move from rural areas to urban centers, driving the expansion of Latino neighborhoods. Some "Little Mexicos" expanded in areas with a long-standing Hispanic presence; others sprang up in new places of settlement. In San Antonio, for example, the existing Mexican population grew to 41,500 by 1920; in Dallas, the same years saw the area just northwest of downtown fill with several thousand Mexican migrants and refugees, who soon remade Pike Park into a plaza that served as the center of community life.

The early 20th century also saw the spread of Mexican urban residents beyond the Southwest, particularly to the cities of the Midwest. This was the origin of Latino settlement in places such as Chicago, Detroit, Milwaukee, and Kansas City. The dramatic expansion of heavy industry in these cities generated a massive appetite for workers, one that was mainly fed by ongoing immigration from central, eastern, and southern Europe. But with the outbreak of World War I and the decline in European migrant flows, Mexico supplied a growing share of the needed labor. The integration of US and Mexican railroad networks in previous decades had created a fast, direct route for workers from south of the Rio Grande, and northern companies sent a constant flow of labor recruiters to the border along the same tracks. As a result, by the end of the 1920s, communities of many thousands of Mexican workers had grown up, especially around the region's factories and railway workshops.[8]

In whatever region they settled, ethnic Mexicans quickly set about creating the kinds of basic institutions and spatial forms that would serve their communities; these were the key elements of Latino urbanism in the United States. New Hispanic city dwellers were keen to do business in a familiar language, and entrepreneurs saw the opportunity to earn a living providing their co-ethnics with essential goods and services. It was in these circumstances that one sees the origins of the basic urban neighborhood infrastructure of Spanish-language business districts— restaurants, groceries, various kinds of shops, entertainment venues, a few professional offices, and the like—and of dwelling forms and everyday street-side conviviality around them. Ethnic Mexicans and other Hispanics were also eager to gather in welcoming church parishes and to establish schools and community centers—institutions that manifested their identity in physical space and became mainstays of neighborhood life.[9]

Notably, however, Mexicans in major cities typically did not live in homogeneous neighborhoods in this era. Rather, they were more likely to share urban space with immigrants of other nationalities: for example, even the plaza district in Los Angeles was 40 percent non-Hispanic, and in the industrial neighborhoods

where Mexicans lived in Chicago, they were easily outnumbered by European immigrants— concentrated Hispanic neighborhoods in big cities would not come about until later. In the meantime, during the Great Depression Mexican migration and settlement were severely impaired by racial hostility and ruthless repatriation and deportation campaigns; though in many cases the neighborhoods that remained would eventually serve as centers of subsequent Latino urban settlement.[10]

FROM WARTIME RECRUITMENT TO URBAN RENEWAL

Although the first third of the 20th century had witnessed significant urbanization among the nation's Hispanic population and the establishment or expansion of their settlement in a number of larger cities, the extent of Latino urbanism was still comparatively modest. Nationally, as of 1940 Hispanics only comprised between 1 and 2 percent of the national population, the overwhelming majority of them ethnically Mexican. And only in a few large cities were they able to shape substantial parts of the urban landscape; the clearest examples of US Latino urbanism were still in the borderlands, in places of long-standing Hispanic settlement such as the plaza-centered towns of South Texas, southern Arizona, and northern New Mexico.

This began to change during and after World War II as an expansion of agricultural labor recruitment fostered Latino migrations that eventually fed urban growth. The first and most important example was the Bracero Program, initiated between the United States and Mexico in 1942 to remedy the wartime labor shortage. Mexican farmworkers became an indispensable part of the war effort by supplying the armed forces with necessary foodstuffs. (The program was renewed for nearly two decades after the war's end to satisfy the nation's persistent demand for farm labor.) Also beginning in the 1940s, officials and employers in the United States and Puerto Rico made agreements to bring agricultural workers to the mainland. These programs were firmly focused on farm labor, but their participants were often cheated of their wages and otherwise mistreated, and they had little recourse in isolated rural areas. Many therefore quit their jobs and sought work in cities, where wages were higher in industrial and other occupations; they were also attracted by the opportunity for sociability and support in larger Spanish-speaking communities.[11]

The resultant growth in urban barrios followed two distinct paths. People of Mexican ancestry were drawn to many of the same cities and neighborhoods where their co-ethnics had already established areas of settlement. The Southwest predominated as before, but there was also some growth in the Midwest. Notably, the Bracero Program included a railroad division that moved many workers through and to industrial areas, strengthening migration flows from Mexico. Among Puerto Ricans, New York City became the preeminent destination for migrants, who settled throughout the city, with concentrations in northern and southern Manhattan and Brooklyn.

Philadelphia was also home to a growing community of *puertorriqueños*. In both cases, it became more common for Latinos to live in neighborhoods in which a single group predominated.

Even as they grew, these barrios faced a new threat in the form of urban renewal and highway construction. Beginning in the late 1940s, city officials grew concerned about the spread of "urban blight," which they defined as decaying city districts with dilapidated housing and shabby storefronts that threatened to expand into "healthy" parts of the city. These officials also believed that cities needed better highway access to outlying areas and other cities. Municipal governments eagerly applied for federal funding, especially through the Housing Acts of 1949 and 1954 and the Interstate Highway Act of 1956, which would allow them to clear and renew some neighborhoods and cut through others to make way for highways. But because of these officials' preconceptions about poverty and race, such projects disproportionately affected poor neighborhoods, especially ones where people of color lived. Black neighborhoods were most commonly targeted, but Hispanic areas were also repeatedly razed. One example of this was Chávez Ravine, a Mexican American neighborhood in Los Angeles area that was cleared in the early 1950s and ultimately given over for the construction of Dodger Stadium; another was the Puerto Rican neighborhood on Manhattan's Upper West Side that was destroyed to make way for Lincoln Center for the Performing Arts. While these kinds of clearance strategies had largely fallen out of favor by the late 1960s, the damage had by then already been done in the form of dozens of Latino settlements cleared, their homeowners forced out, their businesspeople deprived of stores and clienteles, entire communities divided or scattered.[12]

As they struggled to maintain a place for their communities in fast-changing cities, many Latinos and Latinas turned to public art to express themselves collectively. Mexican American artists in the Southwest led the way through muralism. Mexico had emerged in the early 20th century as the global leader in this medium, and eminent proponents of *muralismo* such as Diego Rivera, José Clemente Orozco, and David Alfaro Siqueiros completed works throughout Mexico in the 1920s and received commissions in the United States, especially at the height of the public art movement of the 1930s. In subsequent decades Chicano artists, inspired by the aesthetic quality and political commitments of *muralismo*, adapted the form as a means of social protest and place making. For example, Chicano Park in San Diego originated in the late 1960s after many years of demolition, displacement, and highway construction in the surrounding Barrio Logan. As the community mobilized to preserve key parts of the neighborhood, local artists began to paint murals on the highway overpass stanchions. In the years that followed, they created dozens of scenes depicting centuries of Aztec, Spanish, Mexican, and Mexican American history and social struggle.

Muralismo soon spread to cities across the nation and was adopted by artists from many backgrounds, becoming arguably the most distinctive visual signature of Latino urban places.

THE ERA OF MASS MIGRATION BEGINS

Beginning in the 1960s, the Latino demography and geography of the United States changed dramatically. At the most basic level, the number of Hispanic-origin people skyrocketed, rising far beyond the few percent of the national population that they had comprised previously. Immigration increased rapidly, and what had been an overwhelmingly Mexican American population of Latinos grew more diverse, especially due to a greater influx of people from the Caribbean. This period is often called the "post-1965" era of immigration, referring to the Hart-Celler Act of 1965, which abolished the racist quotas of the National Origins Act of 1924 but also introduced the first-ever limits upon migration within the Americas. This, in effect, criminalized many previously legal migrants, especially those from Mexico. But other contemporaneous events were at least as influential, including the cancellation of the Bracero Program, the agricultural crisis in Mexico, the Cuban Revolution, and the political instability in the Dominican Republic.[13]

This era's Latino migration to cities was also linked to the emergent urban crisis in the United States. As millions of predominantly white city dwellers fled to suburbia in response to desegregation and other urban social changes, they left behind a large amount of older housing stock that was relatively affordable due to its condition and location. In many cases declining neighborhoods were repopulated by Hispanic migrants and immigrants who continued to move out of the agricultural

sector and into cities seeking better jobs and more welcoming communities. As they did so, they gradually transformed entire city districts by supporting housing values, opening neighborhood businesses, and filling local institutions such as churches and schools.[14]

Neighborhood institutions such as these became important centers of community organizing and protest for Latino social movements. In mid-1960s New York City, for example, Puerto Rican activists joined their African American neighbors in demanding equality and accountability from a public school system that kept students of color segregated and underfunded; there and in other city school systems they launched campaigns for more community control of their children's education. Mexican Americans also demonstrated in and around schools: among the most important episodes in the Chicano movement were a series of massive "blowouts" that began in 1968 in East Los Angeles, where thousands of high school students protested against the district's discriminatory policies and near-complete neglect of their history and culture by walking out of their classrooms and assembling around nearby parks, monuments, and other public property. Similar demonstrations were launched in the years that followed in ethnically Mexican communities nationwide, including Denver, Chicago, and Crystal City, Texas. In subsequent decades, the public space of schools and universities and the sacred space of churches were indispensable sources of protest on other issues of importance to Latino communities, including labor organizing, police misconduct, and immigrant rights.

The existing elements of Latino urbanism expanded greatly in this period as newcomers occupied and modified the preexisting building stock, often importing physical forms and cultural norms common in Latin America and adapting them to the spaces of US cities. The Mexican American hybrid homescape was one example. Homes were sometimes repainted in brighter colors than the previous staid palette, and many included shrines to Catholic saints, especially La Virgen de Guadalupe. But the most prominent and important feature was perimeter fencing around the property line of what was usually a freestanding house in the center of the lot. This homescape has been interpreted as a combination of the Anglo-style detached dwelling and the Mexican courtyard house composed of a series of rooms arrayed around the periphery of its property. Functionally, these houses created an active front area, sometimes called by the Spanish neologism *la yarda*, that extended the space of the home out onto porches, stoops, and front lawns. Not infrequently these areas were further equipped with furniture and playsets, which allowed parents and grandparents to keep an eye on children as they played safely inside the fence, away from cars passing on the street.

In neighborhoods with a heavy ethnic Mexican presence, one could often see block after block in which virtually every house corresponded to this typology. Another important type of Latino space that gained prominence in this period was the Puerto Rican *casita*. These were small houses built in the same architectural styles seen on the island. A *casita*, often sited on a vacant or abandoned lot, remade the empty space into a community center, often featuring productive gardening and social events.[15]

Another key feature of Latino urbanism in this period was its distinctive commercial landscape. Many barrios gave rise to bustling shopping districts with numerous small businesses serving a Spanish-speaking clientele who lived on nearby residential streets. These were certainly not the first of their kind, as many had existed since the Latino immigrant influx of the early 20th century. Rather, they were more extensive iterations of these, some in existing locations, others in new ones due to earlier demolitions of Hispanic barrios. As with housing, these business districts often emerged in parts of cities where whites were moving out and where their small mom-and-pop stores were being shuttered due to competition from peripheral malls and big-box stores. For Spanish-speaking entrepreneurs, older commercial spaces were well suited to their kinds of businesses—small, local, and often family-run and lightly capitalized. By the early 1980s, there were dozens of cities with Spanish-language commercial districts in which people could access a wide variety of goods and services—from restaurants, clothing stores, and shops selling devotional items to banking, legal services, and medical care—all in their own language.

Moreover, in the aggregate, these commercial districts led to an upsurge in business activity in central cities with growing Hispanic

Figure 3. Three residences showing characteristic features of the Mexican American homescape, Little Village neighborhood, Chicago, 2014.
Photograph by A. K. Sandoval-Strausz.

Figure 4. A single block along the Twenty-sixth Street commercial corridor in Chicago's overwhelmingly Latino Little Village neighborhood, 2014.
Photograph by A. K. Sandoval-Strausz.

populations, and within a decade or two such barrios became essential sources of sales tax revenue for municipal governments in dire fiscal straits after the departure of many businesses for the suburbs.

The Little Village neighborhood in Chicago offers an excellent example. In the early 1960s, the area's longtime ethnically Czech and Polish residents were increasingly moving out to the suburbs. A local real estate broker recalled that "single-family homes were selling for $12,000 and half-blocks were selling for $50,000" and that there were scores of empty storefronts along the Twenty-sixth Street shopping corridor. Indeed, the local chamber of commerce reportedly offered to pay to wash the windows of vacant stores so that the commercial district would not look so rundown. Only the arrival of mostly Mexican and some Puerto Rican families stabilized the neighborhood, which had become more than one-third Hispanic by 1970 and almost four-fifths Hispanic by 1980. Without these newcomers, Little Village would have lost residents at an even faster rate than Detroit in its worst-ever decade of depopulation. In the years that followed, the neighborhood became the most important shopping destination for ethnic Mexicans from around the Midwest. As business boomed, local Latino and Latina entrepreneurs teamed up with the City of Chicago to build an arch over Twenty-sixth Street in the Spanish Colonial style, emblazoned with the words "BIENVENIDOS A LITTLE VILLAGE." By the turn of the millennium *Crain's Chicago Business* was reporting that the Little Village shopping district had become the second most active in the city, behind only the Magnificent Mile along Michigan Avenue.[16]

This and other Latino neighborhoods that appeared or expanded in this period were more culturally homogeneous than before, with high percentages of Spanish-speaking or Spanish-heritage residents. While this could provide advantages to local businesses and create cohesive communities, the increased separation also entailed disparities in political representation and municipal spending. In many cities, older non-Hispanic residents were reluctant to share power with the newcomers and worked to limit officeholding among them. In some cities, Chicago among them, this was accomplished through gerrymandering and secret deals with city hall; other municipalities, including San José and Dallas, relied upon older modes of de facto disfranchisement such as at-large elections. In all cases, however, it meant that these fast-growing barrios did not benefit from a level of spending commensurate with their population and economic importance. They therefore suffered from overcrowded and underfunded schools and were forced to take direct action to pressure city officials into belatedly building new ones. Much the same happened with other kinds of spending such as for road repair, fire stations, and policing: it was an early sign of official disinvestment even in neighborhoods that Latino newcomers were saving from abandonment.

URBANISM ACROSS THE AMERICAS

Latino neighborhoods expanded and diversified due to a new wave of immigration that began in the early 1980s and continued for a quarter-century. This period saw the acceleration of arrivals from established sending countries and also brought newcomers from a wider variety of nations in the hemisphere. The causes of this were various and included strong growth in the US economy that attracted workers, the eruption of US-backed civil wars in Central America, sudden changes in Cuban emigration policy, and especially the neoliberal restructuring of governments and economies across a number of Latin American nations. This led to cuts in urban employment and shifts in agricultural production, leading many Latin American city dwellers to seek opportunity in US metropolitan areas and also redirecting much preexisting rural-to-urban migration from within the region toward the United States.[17]

As a result, the overall population of Latinos in the United States surged from 14.6 million (6.4 percent of the national population) in 1980 to 22.4 million (9 percent) in 1990 to 35.3 million (13 percent) in 2000 to 50.5 million (16 percent) in 2010. This new influx was also discernible on the streets of Latino America: Salvadoran *pupuserías* and Peruvian *ceviche* restaurants joined the existing offerings of Mexican *taquerías* and Caribbean *cocina criolla* restaurants, and the sounds of Central American *punta* and especially Colombian *cumbia* were heard on the sidewalks of increasingly multinational Hispanic barrios.

The rising number and diversity of Hispanics added impetus to another key feature of Latino urbanism—the active use of a variety of public spaces. In Latin America, public sociability on plazas and in parks and the streets had long been a cultural norm, and the arrival of millions of Latino newcomers (as well as the many other groups that were also creating thriving immigrant neighborhoods) repopulated and repurposed countless urban spaces. *Ambulantes,* street vendors who offered everything from popsicles to empanadas to horchata from their pushcarts, roamed barrio streets, prefiguring the subsequent mainstream popularity of food trucks. Immigrants from the many Latin American nations where *fútbol* was the national pastime quickly organized soccer clubs that packed players and spectators into public fields on weekends. And Latino children and their parents and grandparents thronged city parks, restoring life and vitality to areas that had often been abandoned during the long crime wave that helped define the urban crisis years. This aspect of Latino urbanism often restored the kind of street-side sociability that Jane Jacobs had celebrated in her 1961 classic *The Death and Life of Great American Cities.* Many observers had bemoaned the decline of the public realm, correctly noting the gradual but pervasive privatization of space in which middle-class people withdrew from front stoops and sidewalks into sheltered backyards, from public natatoriums to private pools, and from movie theaters to home entertainment centers. But they often overlooked the way that Latinos were reclaiming and revitalizing public spaces across the country.[18]

Among the most important influences on Latino urbanism in this period was the Immigration Reform and Control Act (IRCA) of 1986. Two major provisions in the law—border reinforcement and immigrant amnesty—crucially shaped Latin American immigrant life in US cities. The militarization of the US-Mexico border made it more difficult, more expensive, and more dangerous for undocumented people to move between countries. In response, migrants who previously had only sojourned in the United States instead stayed; they also brought their families with them rather than suffer long-term separation from their loved ones. In addition, their search for year-round rather than seasonal work brought more of them from rural areas to cities. Meanwhile, the law's amnesty provision allowed about three million undocumented people nationwide to regularize their legal status. With security of residence and no fear of deportation, these immigrants were free to come out of the shadows, purchase more property, and open additional businesses—and thus even more effectively revitalize the city neighborhoods where they lived.[19]

These legalizations augmented an earlier trend in which Latinos established a wider variety of city-based transnational business links. In Miami, for example, the Cuban community had organized banking operations that served a substantial clientele from Latin America, and the city soon became the nation's second most popular location for such banks; these customers also became major purchasers of real estate, contributing to a construction boom in the city.

Meanwhile, the rising number of Latinos nationwide with citizenship or permanent resident status fostered an upsurge in businesses serving people who traveled back and forth between the United States and their home countries, especially Mexico. In the nation's barrios, import-export firms, transportation companies, travel agencies, and associated service firms flourished. For example, a study of Dallas-based bus companies operating between Mexico and the United States found that virtually all of them had been incorporated after the IRCA. More generally, the rise in entrepreneurialism could also be seen clearly in the aggregate: the Kaufman Index, an established measure of entrepreneurial activity, showed that in almost every year from 1996 through 2008, Latinos were more likely than any other demographic group to open their own businesses.[20]

One of the most intriguing aspects of this phase of Latino urbanism was the way it began to link the United States with Latin America in new ways. The flows of people, money, and goods across the Americas intensified significantly in the 1980s and beyond. But distant places were also tied together in the most concrete way possible: through the built environment. The clearest example was seen in Mexico, where returning migrants began to build houses in their hometowns in American architectural styles. The pitched roofs, columned porticoes, and modern kitchens that often went into such homes were US vernaculars transposed back to Mexico in a sign of the cultural cachet that they carried. Over time, other aspects of the Anglo-American landscape were reproduced throughout Latin America.

Among the most notable was peripheral development. Suburban-style, automobile-dependent neighborhoods had been attempted in Mexico around the mid-20th century, but with limited success. That began to change near century's end. In a notable departure from the previous expectation that the wealthy would seek out the prestige of the center city while the poor would occupy informal housing at the periphery, developers and prosperous elites in places such as Mexico, Argentina, and Brazil began to build homes and patronize stores located at the edges of their cities.

The adaptation of culturally specific urbanisms across the border between Latin and Anglo America was thus becoming fully reciprocal.[21]

INTO THE PRESENT

Since the late 1990s, Latino urbanism has become an important category of inquiry and practice in a number of fields, including planning, architecture, governance, and real estate. A number of city planners have emphasized how key features of most barrios—especially their density, walkability, mixed uses, public orientation, and small carbon footprint—exemplify the kind of urbanism essential to a future threatened by wasteful sprawl, fraying social fabric, and dangerous climate change. They often point out that Latino urbanism, which is already existing, non-elite, and participatory, is a more feasible alternative to New Urbanism, which shares the goal of smarter, more sustainable cities and suburbs but has been criticized as elitist and over-reliant on the built environment to modify people's behavior. Some architects and planners, meanwhile, have deployed Latino-inspired plazas, shopping areas, and parks in order to show how well they function as parts of new developments and infill projects. Others have adapted vernacular uses from Latino and Latin American homes and workplaces as they design spaces to better accommodate and serve the fast-growing Hispanic population of US metropolitan areas. They have been joined by municipal officials and local boosters who have sponsored initiatives to attract and integrate Latinos and other immigrants to their cities, foster growth and stability in their neighborhoods, and shield them from arbitrary and counterproductive forms of enforcement.[22]

Notably, the years of the most rapid US Latino population growth have coincided with a period of dramatic decline in the nation's crime rate, especially in cities with large numbers of immigrants. Urban sociologists have investigated what the relationship could be between these phenomena using sophisticated geodata techniques—essentially by mapping where and when crimes take place, where foreign-born people live and work, and their respective demographic characteristics. These studies have clearly demonstrated that the presence of immigrants has corresponded to significantly lower rates of many crimes; in addition, this protective effect is not limited to immigrants themselves but also to those who live in or adjacent to their neighborhoods (by far the largest contingent among these immigrants have been from Latin America, but the findings are similar for those from elsewhere in the world). Another line of research using incarceration records yielded similar findings, for example that American-born men were five times more likely to be imprisoned than men born in Mexico, and seven times more likely than men from El Salvador and Guatemala. Researchers have yet to settle on the causes behind these findings, but some have proposed that Latino urbanism may have played a role, since other studies have found that the spatial and social organization of Hispanic neighborhoods have offered protection against heatstroke fatalities, mental illness, childhood asthma, and other conditions.[23]

In a number of cities, Latino urbanism has been threatened by gentrification. Over the course of decades of immigration and migration, millions of Latino city dwellers have turned once-dying neighborhoods into viable urban communities, thereby preserving numerous historic districts. However, these very neighborhoods have become appealing to well-to-do people, the great majority of them non-Hispanic whites, who want to live in places with "character." In many cases, real estate developers have exploited barrios through marketing campaigns that commodify Latino cultures and aesthetics as amenities in upscale real estate products—the effect of which is to push up the cost of living, making it difficult for working-class Latino families to stay in the communities they created. Among the best-known examples are found in the Mission District in San Francisco, Los Angeles's Boyle Heights, and New York City's Washington Heights, the heavily Dominican American neighborhood that served as the setting for Lin-Manuel Miranda's first musical, *In The Heights* (2005), in which gentrification was a central theme. While the population and extent of Latino neighborhoods in US cities have grown more quickly than the incursions of gentrifiers, the prospect of displacement in some of the most vital barrios in the nation has generated a great deal of local organizing around issues of affordable housing and community sustainability.[24]

Cities have been the most important sites of Latino urbanism, but its influence has gradually extended throughout metropolitan areas and even to exurban and rural places across the country. Late in the 20th century, the outward migration of US-born Latinos combined with a growing number of Latin American newcomers who immigrated directly to suburbia, resulting in fast-growing populations around major cities. For example, Westchester County, the closest suburban area north of New York City, is now about one-quarter Hispanic. And while suburbs are typically much less dense than cities, they include older satellite cities that have been resettled and revitalized by Latinos: the Westchester town of Port Chester, which includes a high-density industrial downtown that grew up around a harbor and a railway line, is now nearly half Latino, about the same percentage as Los Angeles itself. Another vector of migration has taken migrants from countries such as Mexico and Guatemala to towns on the Great Plains and hamlets in the rural Southeast, where they have found work in food processing and light manufacturing and where they have opened businesses on tiny main streets and set their children to play on courthouse squares—giving nearly extinct communities a new lease on life. In sum, Latino urbanism has grown into a nationwide phenomenon and a national resource—one that can be cultivated to our shared benefit, or squandered to our ultimate detriment.[25]

DISCUSSION OF THE LITERATURE

The historical study of Latino urbanism has involved scholars in a number of fields, each with its own intellectual trajectory and major questions. These literatures have often drawn on common sources and assumptions, however, and working together their authors have greatly improved our understanding of the subject.

The clearest historical genealogy for Latino urbanism originates with some of the founding texts of Chicano and Mexican American history. In *Occupied America* (1972), Rodolfo Acuña demonstrated that conflicts over territory were central to the history of the US Southwest, emphasizing the struggles of ethnically Mexican communities as their lands were overrun by Anglos; in *A Community Under Siege* (1984), he showed how such struggles played out in the urban space of Los Angeles. Albert Camarillo's *Chicanos in a Changing Society* (1979) paid close attention to the way power relations were manifested in the spatial reorganization of towns and cities following the US invasion and annexation of northern Mexico. (Notably, these approaches to land and identity in the West became foundational parts of a new Western history that defined the "frontier" as a territory of violent conquest rather than a place of freedom and opportunity.) In addition to the way that borders crossed people, another line of research emphasized how people crossed borders, focusing on migration and immigration from Mexico and the ways that newcomers formed identity and constructed communities in physical space. These histories often focused on the origins and meaning of the barrio, documenting the way it was created by aggressive expropriation and segregation perpetrated against ethnic Mexicans. But these histories also considered how they used this disadvantaged space to create neighborhood institutions and movements that could help them make their way in a hostile society. Other key works on Latinos, such as Virginia Sánchez Korrol's *From Colonia to Community* and María Cristina García's *Havana U.S.A.*, also emphasized community and place identity, though with less emphasis on the urban fabric, since Puerto Ricans and Cubans largely arrived in already-existing Anglo cities rather than defending long-standing Hispanic landscapes.

The idea of Latino urbanism as a distinct and identifiable set of spaces and behaviors that develop over time also has origins in cultural landscape studies, historical geography, and vernacular architecture. Scholars in these fields have defined cultural regions, catalogued their particular architectural and other material-culture characteristics, and debated what this has revealed about the people who created and recreated them. One early example was J. B. Jackson's "Chihuahua as We Might Have Been" (1951), which surveyed the different built environments on either side of the US-Mexico border and the reasons why these landscapes diverged even though they shared the same ecological and geological space. Other scholars, including Daniel Arreola and Chris Wilson, have done fieldwork in South Texas and New Mexico to identify and record landscapes built along mixed Spanish, Indigenous, and Mexican lines. They have shown how these landscapes have both persisted and eroded—combining with Anglo forms and also being reinvented or reintroduced by Anglos migrating westward and Mexicans migrating northward. Most recently, Sarah Lynn Lopez's *The Remittance Landscape* has shown how the migration of rural Mexicans to the United States has created new transnational vernaculars, with Anglo-American design elements and enacted spatial behaviors being re-exported back to small-town Mexico.

City planning scholars and practitioners have focused more intently on Latino urbanism than people in any other discipline, using the term most consistently and regularly applying it to their design work. This is mainly because planners have been clearly oriented to the present and future: they look to the past to establish the lineage of Latino urbanism, but the majority of their collective energies are devoted to planning and architectural solutions. Key works in the field laid the groundwork by criticizing the majority of planners and planning programs for their Eurocentrism and consequent narrowness of vision when it came to professional practice. This was accompanied by the even more important task of looking around cities (especially Los Angeles, the unofficial capital of Latino America), identifying actually existing elements of Latino urbanism—plazas, portales, murals, parks, ambulatory vendors, walkability, and density, among others—and showing how they have met people's practical needs. These Latino urbanistic resources were then available for use in actual projects in cities and suburbs, whether in existing barrios or in places with few Latinos but a need to densify the urban fabric, promote pedestrian use, enliven the streetscape, and create opportunities for entrepreneurship. Often such projects become the subject of additional publications, since the evaluation of Latino urbanism-derived planning solutions is an expected part of the cycle of study, planning, construction, and critique.

With the recent growth of a specialized subfield of Latino urban history has come greater attention to the broader historical processes within which Latinos have created their landscapes. In some cases this has been studied in US-Mexico borderlands cities in places such as California, Texas, and Arizona, where local place identity and spatial inequality have been shaped by long-standing crossborder flows of workers, capital, and culture, as with William Deverell's *Whitewashed Adobe,* Monica Perales's *Smeltertown,* and Geraldo Cadava's *Standing on Common Ground.* In others, Latinos have had to create neighborhoods and negotiate their identities in places where most people understood race in terms of black or white, as with the Puerto Ricans and Mexicans of Chicago in Lilia Fernández's *Brown in the Windy City.* The transnational dynamics that connect distant municipalities together has also been an area of rising interest; Jesse

Hoffnung-Garskof's *A Tale of Two Cities* demonstrates how Dominican neighborhoods in New York City and those in the capital of Santo Domingo have for decades been engaged in a multifaceted process of mutual influence. Other works in progress feature Latino communities in smaller cities and other less widely recognized destinations for Latin American migrants.

PRIMARY SOURCES

The sheer geographic and chronological extent of Latino urbanism is so vast that any account of the sources used to study it is necessarily partial. The study of urbanism is much more visual and architectural than most other fields of conventional history: purely textual sources are only part of the record and must be supplemented with images and, whenever possible, actual site visits. For an online introduction, there are about two hundred Hispanic sites documented in the Library of Congress by the Historic American Buildings Survey/ Historic American Engineering Record/ Historic American Landscapes Survey of the National Park Service.

The Native American planning and architectural legacy that form part of Latino urbanism are still visible in pre-Columbian sites across Latin America and the United States and ranging in size from the pyramid complex at Teotihuacán, Mexico, to the Pueblo structures at places such as Acoma and Taos, New Mexico. Spanish city planning in the Americas is detailed in text in the *Recopilación de Leyes de Indias* and shown visually in maps and drawings from the colonial period such as José Urrutia's 1766 plan of Santa Fe in what eventually became New Mexico. The missions, presidios, and pueblos that facilitated the colonizing project are well documented historically, and many still remain in some form in places across the US Southwest; in addition, there are scores of extant plaza-centered towns in the region. These sites also show how the preexisting palimpsest of

Indigenous and subsequent Spanish urban landscapes were once again overlaid by the human geography of Anglo America.

In the post-1848 period, documentation from US sources comes into play. As its statistical categories became more detailed and the manuscript census more complete, the Census Bureau increasingly compiled information on the geographic distribution of Latinos. Spanish surnames are apparent on the original enumerators' forms in the manuscript census, showing a great deal about Hispanic settlement, family structure, type of residence, and occupation. Starting in the mid-20th century, the statistical tables begin to categorize the population using ethnic or national markers— Spanish language, Spanish heritage, foreign-born by nation of birth, Puerto Rican, Hispanic, and the like—that make it increasingly easy to identify the concentration, persistence, and growth of Latino populations down to the level of census tracts containing thousands of people. For further details, see the data available online through the United States Census Bureau.

Having located a substantial Latino presence, a researcher can then use some of the basic sources in the field to learn more about the community: parish records; community organization archives; reportage from newspapers and magazines, whether the "mainstream" variety or the Spanish or English work of Latino publishers; reports by municipal authorities; and immigration and naturalization records. Because people who were workingclass or immigrants (or both) often had little opportunity to author conventional written sources, oral histories have become a regular feature of work on Latino history. In some cases historians have recorded their own interviews, and in others have depended on archival holdings of oral histories such as those at UCLA, the University of Texas, and the University of Florida.

The urbanistic aspects of Latino communities are also recorded in visual sources. State archives and local historical societies typically have photographic collections organized by subject and neighborhood, sometimes including by ethnicity. Local organizations such as the Dallas Mexican American Historical League have undertaken efforts to digitize photographs from community members' personal and family collections, creating the possibility of a much more detailed visual record of Latino life. City planning agencies often commissioned reports on neighborhoods that included maps of ethnoracial settlement areas combined with surveys or statistical reports. And some municipalities systematically photographed properties by block or neighborhood, adding to the available visual evidence. Online resources related to Latina and Latino studies continue to grow; the Yale University Library maintains a guide to some of these, and the Smithsonian Latino Center maintains a Virtual Museum. For the most up-to-date visual information on Latino urbanism, however, there is no substitute for walking around the barrio oneself.

FURTHER READING

Acuña, Rodolfo. *A Community Under Siege: The Chronicle of Chicanos East of the Los Angeles River, 1945–1975*. Los Angeles: Chicano Research Study Center Publications, 1984.

Arreola, Daniel. *Tejano South Texas: A Mexican American Cultural Province*. Austin: University of Texas Press, 2002.

Cadava, Geraldo L. *Standing on Common Ground*. Cambridge, MA: Harvard University Press, 2013.

Camarillo, Albert. *Chicanos in a Changing Society: From Mexican Pueblos to American Barrios, 1850–1930*. Cambridge, MA: Harvard University Press, 1979.

Dávila, Arlene R. *Barrio Dreams: Puerto Ricans, Latinos, and the Neoliberal City*. Berkeley: University of California Press, 2004.

Davis, Mike. *Magical Urbanism: Latinos Reinvent the U.S. Big City*. London: Verso, 2000.

Deverell, William. *Whitewashed Adobe: The Rise of Los Angeles and the Remaking of Its Mexican Past*. Berkeley: University of California Press, 2004.

Diaz, David R. *Barrio Urbanism: Chicanos, Planning, and American Cities*. New York: Routledge, 2005.

Diaz, David R., and Rodolfo D. Torres. *Latino Urbanism: The Politics of Planning, Policy and Redevelopment.* New York: New York University Press, 2012.

Fernández, Lilia. *Brown in the Windy City: Mexicans and Puerto Ricans in Postwar Chicago.* Chicago: University of Chicago Press, 2012.

García, Matt. *A World of Its Own: Race, Labor, and Citrus in the Making of Greater Los Angeles.* Chapel Hill: University of North Carolina Press, 2001.

Hoffnung-Garskof, Jesse: *A Tale of Two Cities: Santo Domingo and New York after 1950.* Princeton, NJ: Princeton University Press, 2010.

Jackson, J. B. "Chihuahua as We Might Have Been." In *Landscape in Sight: Looking at America,* edited by Helen Horowitz. New Haven, CT: Yale University Press, 2000.

Leclerc, Gustavo, Raúl Villa, and Michael J. Dear, eds. *Latino Urban Cultures: La Vida Latina en L.A.* Thousand Oaks, CA: Russell Sage Foundation, 1999.

Londoño, Johana. "Barrio Affinities: Transnational Inspiration and the Geopolitics of Latina/o Design." *American Quarterly* 66 (2014).

Lopez, Sarah Lynn. *The Remittance Landscape: Spaces of Migration in Rural Mexico and Urban USA.* Chicago: University of Chicago Press, 2015.

Mendez, Michael. "Latino New Urbanism: Building on Cultural Preferences." *Opolis* 1 (2005).

Perales, Monica. *Smeltertown: Making and Remembering a Southwest Border Community.* Chapel Hill: University of North Carolina Press, 2010.

Portes, Alejandro, and Alex Stepick. *City on the Edge: The Transformation of Miami.* Berkeley: University of California Press, 1993.

Rios, Michael, Leonardo Vazquez, and Lucrezia Miranda, eds. *Diálogos: Placemaking in Latino Communities.* New York: Routledge, 2012.

Rojas, James. "The Enacted Environment: The Creation of 'Place' by Mexicans and Mexican Americans in Los Angeles." Master's thesis, Massachusetts Institute of Technology, 1991.

Sánchez, George J. *Becoming Mexican American: Ethnicity, Culture and Identity in Chicano Los Angeles, 1900–1945.* New York: Oxford University Press, 1993.

Sandoval-Strausz, A. K., "Latino Landscapes: Postwar Cities and the Transnational Origins of a New Urban America." *Journal of American History* 101 (December 2014).

Valle, Victor M., and Rodolfo D. Torres. *Latino Metropolis.* Minneapolis: University of Minnesota Press, 2000.

Wilson, Chris. *The Myth of Santa Fe: Creating a Modern Regional Tradition.* Albuquerque: University of New Mexico Press, 1997.

NOTES

1. Michael P. Conzen, ed., *The Making of the American Landscape,* 2d ed. (New York: Routledge, 2010).

2. Dora P. Crouch, Daniel J. Garr, and Axel I. Mundigo, *Spanish City Planning in North America* (Cambridge, MA: MIT Press, 1982).

3. Chris Wilson and Stefanos Polyzoides, eds., *The Plazas of New Mexico* (San Antonio: Trinity University Press, 2011); and Setha M. Low, *On the Plaza: The Politics of Public Space and Culture* (Austin: University of Texas Press, 2000).

4. William Deverell, *Whitewashed Adobe: The Rise of Los Angeles and the Remaking of Its Mexican Past* (Berkeley: University of California Press, 2004).

5. Samuel Truett, *Fugitive Landscapes: The Forgotten History of the U.S.-Mexico Borderlands* (New Haven, CT: Yale University Press, 2006); and Daniel D. Arreola, *Postcards from the Rio Bravo Border: Picturing the Place, Placing the Picture, 1900s–1950s* (Austin: University of Texas Press, 2013).

6. Matt García, *A World of Its Own: Race, Labor, and Citrus in the Making of Greater Los Angeles* (Chapel Hill: University of North Carolina Press, 2001).

7. George J. Sánchez, *Becoming Mexican American: Ethnicity, Culture and Identity in Chicano Los Angeles, 1900–1945* (New York: Oxford University Press, 1993).

8. Zaragoza Vargas, *Proletarians of the North: Mexican Industrial Workers in Detroit and the Midwest, 1917–1933* (Berkeley: University of California Press, 1993); and Gabriela Arredondo, *Mexican Chicago: Race, identity and Nation, 1916–39* (Urbana: University of Illinois Press, 2008).

9. Sánchez, *Becoming Mexican American*; Michael Innis-Jiménez, *Steel Barrio: The Great Mexican Migration to South Chicago, 1915–1920* (New York: New York University Press, 2013).

10. Sánchez, *Becoming Mexican American.*

11. Deborah Cohen, *Braceros: Migrant Citizens and Transnational Subjects in the Postwar United States and Mexico* (Chapel Hill: University of

North Carolina Press, 2011); and Carmen Teresa Whalen, *From Puerto Rico to Philadelphia: Puerto Rican Workers and Postwar Economies* (Philadelphia: Temple University Press, 2001).

12. Eric Avila, *The Folklore of the Freeway: Race and Revolt in the Modernist City* (Minneapolis: University of Minnesota Press, 2014).

13. Mae Ngai, *Impossible Subjects: Illegal Aliens and the Making of Modern America* (Princeton, NJ: Princeton University Press, 2004).

14. A. K. Sandoval-Strausz, "Latino Landscapes: Postwar Cities and the Transnational Origins of a New Urban America," *Journal of American History* 101 (December 2014): 804–831.

15. Daniel Arreola, "Mexican American Housescapes," *Geographical Review* 78.3 (1988): 300–301; and James Rojas, "The Enacted Environment: The Creation of 'Place' by Mexicans and Mexican Americans in Los Angeles" (Master's thesis, Massachusetts Institute of Technology, 1991).

16. A. K. Sandoval-Strausz, *Migrantes, Negocios*, and *Infraestructura*: Transnational Urban Revitalization in Chicago," in *Immigration and Metropolitan Revitalization*, eds. Thomas J. Sugrue and Domenic Vitiello (Philadelphia University of Pennsylvania Press, 2017).

17. Alejandro Portes and Kelly Hoffman, "Latin American Class Structures," *Latin American Research Review* 38 (2003): 41–82.

18. Sandoval-Strausz, "Latino Landscapes."

19. Jorge Durand, Douglas S. Massey, and Emilio A. Parrado, "The New Era of Mexican Migration to the United States," *Journal of American History* 86 (1999), 518–536; and Sandoval-Strausz, "Latino Landscapes."

20. Alejandro Portes and Alex Stepick, *City on the Edge: The Transformation of Miami* (Berkeley: University of California Press, 1993); Robert Kemper et al., "From Undocumented *Camionetas* (Mini-Vans) to Federally Regulated Motor Carriers," *Urban Anthropology* 36 (2007); and Richard T. Herman and Robert L. Smith, *Immigrant, Inc.: Why Immigrant Entrepreneurs Are Driving the New Economy* (New York: Wiley, 2010).

21. Sarah Lynn Lopez, *The Remittance Landscape: Spaces of Migration in Rural Mexico and Urban USA* (Chicago: University of Chicago Press, 2015); and Lawrence A. Herzog, *Global Suburbs: Urban Sprawl from the Rio Grande to Rio de Janeiro* (New York: Routledge, 2015).

22. Gustavo Leclerc, Raúl Villa, and Michael J. Dear, eds., *Latino Urban Cultures: La Vida Latina en L.A.* (Thousand Oaks, CA: Russell Sage Foundation, 1999); Victor Valle and Rodolfo Torres, *Latino Metropolis* (Minneapolis: University of Minnesota Press, 2000); David R. Díaz, *Barrio Urbanism: Chicanos, Planning, and American Cities* (New York: Routledge, 2005); Michael Mendez, "Latino New Urbanism: Building on Cultural Preferences." *Opolis* 1 (2005); and Michael Rios, Leonardo Vazquez, and Lucrezia Miranda, eds., *Diálogos: Placemaking in Latino Communities* (New York: Routledge, 2012). Available online (http://www.globalclevelandinitiative.com;%20 neweconomyinitiative.cfsem.org/resources /research-library/global-detroit-study).

23. Robert Sampson, "Rethinking Crime and Immigration," *Contexts* 7 (2008), 28–33; Rubén G. Rumbaut and Walter A. Ewing, "The Myth of Immigrant Criminality and the Paradox of Assimilation: Incarceration Rates among Native and Foreign-Born Men," Immigration Policy Center Special Report (Washington DC: American Immigration Law Foundation, 2007); Eric Klinenberg, *Heat Wave: A Social Autopsy of Disaster in Chicago* (Chicago: University of Chicago Press, 2002); and Kyriakos Markides and Jeannine Coreil, "The Health of Hispanics in the Southwestern United States: An Epidemiologic Paradox," *Public Health Reports* 101.3 (1986): 253–265.

24. Arlene Dávila, *Barrio Dreams: Puerto Ricans, Latinos, and the Neoliberal City* (Berkeley: University of California Press, 2004); and Johana Londoño, "Barrio Affinities: Transnational Inspiration and the Geopolitics of Latina/o Design," *American Quarterly* 66 (2014).

25. Audrey Singer, Susan W. Hardwick, and Caroline B. Brettell, eds., *Twenty-First Century Gateways: Immigrant Incorporation in Suburban America* (Washington, DC: Brookings Institution, 2008); Daniel Arreola, ed., *Hispanic Spaces, Latino Places: Community and Cultural Diversity in Contemporary America* (Austin: University of Texas Press, 2004); and Owen J. Furuseth and Heather A. Smith, eds., *Latinos in the New South: Transformations of Place* (New York: Routledge, 2006).

A. K. Sandoval-Strausz

PUERTO RICANS IN THE UNITED STATES

INTRODUCTION

Puerto Ricans have resided in the United States since before the Spanish-Cuban-American War of 1898, when the United States took possession of the island of Puerto Rico as part of the Treaty of Paris. After the war, groups of Puerto Ricans began migrating to the United States as contract laborers, first to sugar-cane plantations in Hawaii, and then to other destinations on the mainland. After Puerto Ricans became US citizens in 1917, with the passage of the Jones Act, a migrant population grew rapidly in New York City, where a strong post–World War I economy attracted thousands of Puerto Rican workers each year. Until World War II, New York remained the center of the lively and heterogeneous Puerto Rican diaspora in the United States. With the "great migration" of Puerto Ricans from the island beginning in the late 1940s, New York's Puerto Rican population remained the largest, but many migrants dispersed, settling in Chicago and other midwesterns cities, in Philadelphia, Hartford, and various New Jersey cities, as well as in rural communities in the Midwest and mid-Atlantic that attracted migrant farmworkers.

Since the 1980s, with the old manufacturing centers in steep decline and the nation's economic growth shifting to the Sun Belt, some of the fastest-growing Puerto Rican communities have emerged in Texas, California, Georgia, and, most notably, Florida—where Puerto Rican voters' impact on the presidential election of 2012 was widely noted. Throughout the 20th century, Puerto Ricans in the United States were often marginalized, first as a racially suspect and unskilled migrant population and later as a group presumed to comprise a politically apathetic "underclass." A review of Puerto Ricans' history in the United States—their deep roots, social heterogeneity,

and political activism—helps rectify such distortions. It also enables us to see historical patterns in the demographic, socioeconomic, and political changes that have emerged among Puerto Rican communities in the United States in the 21st century.

EARLY MIGRANTS IN NEW YORK CITY: 1890–1930

The first community of Puerto Rican migrants developed in New York City in the late 19th century, part of a larger settlement of exiled Antillean nationalists who supported the overthrow of Spanish colonial rule in its last colonies in the Americas, Cuba and Puerto Rico. Many of these Cuban and Puerto Rican transplants were *tabaqueros*, skilled immigrant artisans who dominated the growing business of cigar making in New York. Whatever their occupations, these early migrants tended to be well educated and very active in homeland politics, especially as Cuba's second independence war with Spain began in 1895, and they drew the United States into the conflict by 1898. One member of this early *colonia*, Arturo Schomburg, would become a renowned bibliophile, collector, and intellectual—although after his marriage to an African American woman in the 1890s, he left the Spanish-speaking community for "black Harlem," and spent the rest of his adult life culturally separate from his compatriots.

Having allegedly entered the war with Spain to support the independence goals of the Antillean *independentistas*, the United States won possession of Puerto Rico as part of the spoils of war following its quick victory over Spain in 1898. In 1900, the US legislature passed the Foraker Act, creating a US-controlled civilian government in the island. Still, Puerto Ricans entering the United States after that point were considered "aliens." The exact status of Puerto Ricans in relation to the United States—alien or national, subject or citizen—would preoccupy members of

Congress and legal scholars for over a decade. Those who favored the extension of citizenship argued that the US Constitution, and the protections of citizenship, must "follow the flag" into the territories it now controlled; those opposed to the extension of citizenship to inhabitants of the new territories made a racist case for their "incapacity for self-government."

In 1917, when the Jones Act finally was passed and Puerto Ricans finally did become citizens of the United States, there were several thousand Puerto Ricans living in New York. After 1917, with citizenship in hand and drawn by a wartime economic boom, a steady stream of Puerto Rican migrants found work in skilled trades and the service sector. Jesús Colón, an early migrant who would become a lifelong political activist in his community, described the heterogeneous Spanish speaking world into which Puerto Rican migrants settled, including "Puerto Ricans who are poor, middle class, white like some inhabitant of a Nordic forest, *trigueños* like good descendants of Chief Aguaybana [sic], black like a shining citizen of old Ethiopia."[1] Along with the other mostly working-class members of the multiethnic communities they settled in, Puerto Ricans spent their days working at factory jobs or in kitchens or doing piecework in their small apartments. "We work our fingers to the bone, but why complain? We all have to work to improve our situation," wrote one woman to *La Prensa* about her work as a seamstress in a small Manhattan garment factory.[2]

The young and middle aged Puerto Rican workers who migrated to New York in the 1920s had come of age in Puerto Rico in a period of intense labor struggles. Dock workers, agricultural laborers, and urban artisans like carpenters, shoemakers, and *tabaqueros* engaged in strikes countered by violent repression from both employers and the island government. Conflicts between workers and bosses played out in a context of widespread tension over the transformation of the island's economy. US-based corporations bought up huge tracts of mixed-use agricultural land to convert into profitable sugar plantations, causing disruption in the agricultural sector. Socialists and workers began organizing the Federación Libre de Trabajadores, a craft-based labor union, which by the early 1920s had forged close ties with the American Federation of Labor.

Among Puerto Rican workers in New York, it was the *colonia*'s cigar makers who engaged most intensively in cross-national labor organizing in this period, motivated in part by the challenges they faced from the mechanization of their industry in the mid-1920s. By 1925, following the lead of their *compañeros* in Puerto Rico and Tampa, Puerto Rican and other immigrant cigar makers in New York had begun to organize to improve working conditions.

The conflict generated by the rapid evolution of island politics increasingly divided the New York *colonia*. After the 1900 Foraker Act established a US-dominated government on the island (with a legislature elected by Puerto Rican voters, and a governor appointed by the US president), political parties in Puerto Rico formed around various positions on the "status question"—the unsettled relationship between Puerto Rico and the United States. The Union Party supported independence; the Republican Party (with no ties to the US Republican Party) advocated the full integration of the island into the United States via statehood; the Socialist Party vacillated on the issue of independence, but ultimately allied with the pro-statehood Republicans; and the Nationalist Party advocated full independence. Because migrants retained close ties to their homeland, and because its political fate remained in flux, changes and developments in island party politics reverberated deeply in New York's Puerto Rican communities.

On the other hand, as the 1920s progressed, most politicized New York Puerto Ricans became equally preoccupied by the question of their community's survival in New York City. Some migrants were drawn to the local Republican Party, but most followed the pattern of earlier European immigrants, seeking an alliance with the city's Democratic machine as the most effective means to represent the interests of Puerto Rican migrants. Neighborhood Democratic clubs, often tied to hometown organizations, proliferated in the *colonia*, competing for members and vying for attention from the representatives of New York's Democratic machine.

While many Puerto Ricans "pioneers" who were interviewed about their lives in the 1920s recalled their New York communities in the early 1920s as peaceful places where neighbors of different nationalities got along well, others noted that conflicts between ethnic groups sometimes arose, both in their workplaces and in the streets surrounding their homes. In the East Harlem *barrio*, inter-ethnic tensions exploded in the summer of 1926 in a series of street fights, or *choques*. Most observers said that the trouble originated between Jewish shopkeepers (many of whom no longer lived in Harlem) and Puerto Rican migrants, whose population there was growing quickly. By the time the neighborhood settled down after two weeks of "disturbances," as the Spanish-language newspaper called them, fifteen people were estimated to be seriously injured, and business owners on both sides suffered untotaled losses in sales, merchandise, and property damage.

Leaders of the Puerto Rican community saw the *choques* as a wake-up call, and formed new community self-defense organizations. One observer of the *choques* told a *New York Times* reporter that the real problem was "that people do not realize that we Porto Ricans are American citizens in the fullest sense of the word. ... We believe that we have readily adapted ourselves to American standards and ideals and there is no reason why we should be looked upon with suspicion."[3] Even before the financial crash of 1929, Puerto Ricans in New York knew that the next decade would present new challenges.

SURVIVING THE GREAT DEPRESSION

When the Great Depression hit, Puerto Ricans were the fastest-growing group of foreign workers in New York, and they felt the

deprivations of the Depression earlier and more keenly than most. "When we say in an employment office that we are from Puerto Rico, they frankly reject us," declared one migrant in a letter to the editor of *La Prensa*, in spite of the fact that "we are as American as they are."[4] Puerto Ricans a decade earlier had expected to be identified much like earlier immigrants, as outsiders only temporarily. The social strains of the early 1930s seemed to intensify inter-ethnic hostilities, particularly in the job market.[5]

The Depression also exacerbated racial prejudice, an increasing concern for Puerto Ricans in New York. Several articles emphasizing migrants' low status and racial inferiority appeared in widely circulating magazines in the early 1930s. Nationalists in particular rejected this ascription, since they tended to identify with the white elite on the island. Working-class Socialists took a broader view, although they saw the danger to Puerto Ricans of being positioned low down in the US racial hierarchy. There were also the native racisms of various groups in the Spanish-speaking *colonia*. It was not uncommon for announcements for some social events, like a charity dance sponsored by the Mexican Club Azteca in support of victims of a hurricane in Puerto Rico in 1932, to specify "for whites only."[6]

After the passage in 1933 of the National Industrial Recovery Act and its wages and working hours protections, unions grew in size and power during the 1930s and helped improve the lives of a growing number of working-class Americans. Nevertheless, Puerto Ricans were consistently excluded from mainstream labor organizations, including the racially progressive AFL-CIO. Even the International Ladies Garment Workers Union (ILGWU), which successfully organized Chicana women in the Los Angeles garment industry starting in 1933, made uneven efforts to organize the many Puerto Rican migrant women garment workers in New York, and rebuffed several efforts by Puerto Rican migrant workers to create a Spanish-speaking local in the 1930s.[7]

In this context, the New Deal seemed to promise some payoffs of political participation at the local level. In addition to the scores of hometown clubs, employees' unions, and various community defense groups that Puerto Ricans organized in this era to serve the unmet needs of Puerto Ricans in New York, *colonia* leaders and voters also began to intensify their focus on gaining the recognition of the major political parties.[8] If residents of the Puerto Rican districts could convince political bosses of their importance as an ethnic voting bloc, they would be in a position to demand their rights to the benefits of patronage and city services. One migrant, writing to *La Prensa* in 1936, reminded his compatriots in Harlem that after the "racial disturbances" in East Harlem a decade earlier, "it was our ability to vote that saved us from being driven out of this district, that induced political leaders to defend us for the interest of gaining our votes."[9]

Even if local party leaders were beginning to notice their growing Puerto Rican constituencies, New York's political terrain was undergoing dramatic ruptures and realignments in the 1930s that cast a shadow over Puerto Ricans' hopeful vision of political advancement. An extensive reform movement in the early 1930s hurt the city's Democratic machine, and the impact of national-level New Deal policies reduced the power of some local politicians. Inclusion in the city's new liberal order proved problematic for Puerto Ricans for reasons beyond their relatively small numbers (in 1940, the US Bureau of the Census counted just over 61,000 Puerto Ricans living in New York City, while African Americans numbered over 450,000) or the faltering support of the political machines.[10] In the mid-1930s, intensifying agitation for independence in Puerto Rico, and several incidents of high-profile political violence, brought the question of the island's still-indeterminate status back to the center of *colonia* political culture. Migrants' calls for the end of US colonialism in Puerto Rico further spurred the radicalization of the *colonia*, and some accused

even New Deal liberals of adopting imperialist policies regarding Puerto Rico. This nationalist agenda for Puerto Rico was beyond the tolerance of mainstream liberals in the United States. The Puerto Rican status issue had become a political hot potato that very few US lawmakers were willing to touch.

Many Puerto Ricans leaned further left by decade's end, and invested even more faith in their stalwart advocate, Vito Marcantonio, first elected to represent East Harlem in Congress in 1934. Earlier in the Depression, many of these activists had begun to embrace "the politics of here," initiating their first focused efforts at making demands of the state on the basis of their citizenship. Now, they framed their expectations of their US citizenship around a new set of political claims, combining demands for local rights and island sovereignty. It was their own version of a New Deal language of rights, but it complicated their effort to create a niche for Puerto Ricans in mainstream city politics. One Puerto Rican, Oscar García Rivera, was elected on the Republican ticket in 1937 to represent the East Harlem district in the New York State Assembly, but he was defeated in 1940 by Hulan Jack, a popular black leader born in Saint Lucia. Puerto Rican migrants made few concrete political gains during this decade-long push for recognition by the major parties in the United States, leaving them more marginalized—if somewhat more visible—than they had been in 1930.[11]

THE GREAT MIGRATION AND COLD WAR POLITICS

During World War II, members of Congress quietly addressed what a few commentators were beginning to call "the Puerto Rican problem": the question of the island's status, now revived as a political dilemma for the United States amid the growing tide of decolonization movements during a war fought in the name of freedom and democracy. Due to a persistent lack of interest in the island's affairs—beyond support for US business interests in the island—Congress was unable to achieve any kind of resolution to its colonial problem at this moment of great visibility. (The 1948 triumph of island leader Luis Muñoz Marín's Popular Democratic Party, with its developmentalist agenda that won strong support from US policymakers, would pave the way for joint support for the island's new Commonwealth status.)

Meanwhile, a postwar economic boom in the United States provided a favorable context for a process of government-sponsored migration that nearly doubled New York City's Puerto Rican population in two years. By the late 1940s, the "Puerto Rican problem" was popularly understood to be one created by the island's people rather than its unresolved political situation. New York's daily papers published countless stories and photographs of Puerto Rican migrants who crowded four and five to a room in shabby apartments, often without coats or blankets to protect them from New York winters. Within a few years, the Puerto Rican Department of Labor created a comprehensive service agency for migrants, the Migration Division, designed to help migrants with housing, employment, education, health, and all other issues related to "adjustment." A second office of the Migration Division opened in Chicago in 1949 to draw Puerto Ricans (both from the island and from New York) to msidwestern industrial centers. Together, the two offices created scores of programs for adults throughout the early 1950s, including English classes and vocational training but also "housekeeping" and "budgets and finances."[12]

During this "great migration" from Puerto Rico, progressive civic leaders and social service professionals argued that New Yorkers should welcome the newcomers, whose difficulties and differences would soon fade, just as they had for the earlier generation of eastern and southern European immigrants. A number of Puerto Rican community leaders, too, asserted that Puerto Ricans' poor image

in New York would improve if the public would recognize that they were "just like other immigrants." One problem with this argument, though, was that Puerto Ricans' mixed-race heritage made them very unlike European immigrants. As psychologist Kenneth Clark (who would soon be the key expert witness in the *Brown v. Board of Education* case) told a reporter for the New York Amsterdam News, "'we are a nation of immigrants, and all immigrants have been stereotyped and discriminated against... every minority has had the privilege of moving upward—if it is white.... The reality of the United States is that assimilation is blocked by skin color.'"[13]

The second flaw in the argument that Puerto Ricans were just like other immigrants in the United States was that their status as colonial citizens of the United States set them apart. And while Puerto Ricans' US citizenship was widely misunderstood or unknown by the public and even many officials in the United States, some of those who did know about migrants' status feared its impact: because they were citizens, they could not be deported, even if they committed a crime; and they could vote, giving their growing communities the potential to exert political power. Exacerbating this concern about political empowerment, McCarthy-era assumptions about radical foreigners made life very hard for left-leaning migrants in the 1950s.

As pervasive as the vilification of Puerto Ricans was in New York, the situation in Chicago during the early postwar years was quite different. There, newspapers touted Puerto Ricans as model migrants, representing the best of the hardworking new workers in Chicago's industries. The context was very different, of course. Puerto Ricans joined a population of Mexican migrants that had begun arriving in the city in the 1920s; and postwar city boosters portrayed the newcomers as more industrious and less impoverished than their Mexican neighbors. Also, whereas New York was receiving around fifty thousand Puerto Ricans per year during the peak years of the postwar migration, Chicago's Puerto Rican population was still only thirty-two thousand total by 1960. The demographic situation was similar in Philadelphia, whose Puerto Rican population grew from two thousand in 1950 to about twelve thousand in 1960. Although there was one notable instance of inter-ethnic tension there in 1953, when hostile white neighbors instigated an episode of street fighting in the Spring Garden neighborhood, city officials, noting how the migration had affected New York, asserted in 1959 that a "Puerto Rican problem...has not yet arisen"—although things could "easily change for the worse."[14]

An additional challenge for those seeking to protect Puerto Rican migrants' group image stemmed from two high-profile attacks on the US government by Nationalist migrants in the early 1950s. In 1950, Nationalists in Puerto Rico had initiated an armed rebellion on the island in response to the passage of Public Law 600, the first step in transition for the island from an "unincorporated territory" of the United States to an "Associated Free State" or "Commonwealth." Supporters of independence derided the new arrangement as "perfumed colonialism." In November 1950, two Nationalist migrants attempted to assassinate President Harry S. Truman who was unharmed—in Washington, DC. Few Americans had any idea of the nature of the United States' relationship with Puerto Rico, or of the contentious politics surrounding that relationship, but the assassination attempt tarnished the image of Puerto Ricans in the United States, making them seem politically volatile and "un-American."

Then, on the 1954 anniversary of the signing of the Jones Act and the extension of US citizenship to Puerto Ricans, four armed Puerto Rican Nationalists entered the gallery of the United States House of Representatives and opened fire, wounding five congressmen. The Nationalist Party in Puerto Rico, and its branch in the United States, continued to protest vehemently the island's new Commonwealth status, instituted in 1952. Nationalists begged

to differ—violently—with the popular governor, Muñoz Marín, who pronounced that, with the status change, "the United States of America ends every trace and vestige of the colonial system in Puerto Rico."

In this highly charged moment, Puerto Rican leaders in New York sought to make a renewed push for political empowerment. By 1956 there was still only one elected Puerto Rican representative in the city, Felipe Torres, of the Bronx 4th Assembly District—the first Puerto Rican in the state government since the end of García Rivera's two-year term in the state assembly in 1940. No Puerto Rican was appointed to any municipal post until Mayor Robert Wagner named Manuel Gómez a municipal magistrate in 1957. Many *colonia* leaders expressed deep pessimism about the prospect of improvements for Puerto Ricans in housing, employment, schooling, and health without political representation.

Puerto Rican leaders argued that low voter registration among Puerto Ricans had less to do with "apathy"—an increasingly common accusation—and more to do with the hindrance created by the English-only literacy test, which remained in place until outlawed by the 1965 Voting Rights Act. They also accused the Republican state legislature of gerrymandering the districts in which most Puerto Ricans lived in East Harlem and the Bronx so that only one out of approximately eight such districts actually obtained a Puerto Rican majority, hindering both their traditional support of Democratic candidates and their ability to lobby for backing for Puerto Rican candidates from the Democratic party.[15] The much smaller Puerto Rican communities in Chicago and Philadelphia, and those more recently established in in other midwestern and mid-Atlantic cities, were still some years away from attempting political influence.

DEINDUSTRIALIZATION AND THE SECOND GENERATION

A study published in 1957 by a group at New York University (NYU) concluded that, ten years after the first "influx" of migrants to New York, Puerto Ricans as a group were continuing to struggle with poor health and limited access to health care, dilapidated housing and discrimination in the housing market, inadequate English instruction in the schools, and a heavy reliance on welfare services. The researchers warned that "the problems of serving these new New Yorkers and of integrating them into the community are likely to increase in the near future."[16] Puerto Rican community leaders and activists did not need an NYU study to tell them this.

Based on the reporting of its clients, the Migration Division identified exploitation by landlords as the most urgent problem for newly arriving Puerto Ricans. This was a widely reported problem not just in New York but in other cities with smaller—but now rapidly growing—Puerto Rican populations. The Migration Division office in Chicago systematically aided Puerto Rican families in their search for housing. Settling in some of that city's more heterogeneous neighborhoods in the 1950s, Puerto Ricans "learned that being ambiguous about their ethnoracial origins worked to their advantage," writes historian Lilia Fernández. "When landlords mistook Puerto Ricans for Italians or Greeks, they did not correct them."[17] In Philadelphia, where migrants lacked the benefit of any organized social services, Puerto Ricans also recalled pervasive discrimination by landlords. In the neighborhoods where migrants first settled in the 1950s, "For Rent" signs increasingly noted "whites only."

Aside from housing, the other top concern for Puerto Ricans in their new urban environments was access to decent schooling for their children. In New York, where the Puerto Rican community had the deepest roots, a small number of progressive educators had worked to help Puerto Rican children's adjustment in city schools since the 1930s, and parents had worked with the school district officials to make their needs known. The education department of the Migration Division produced a variety of short films and pamphlets for distribution in schools, intended to familiarize teachers and other students with both the struggles of migrant children, and the richness of their culture.

Puerto Rican young adults and adolescent members of the "second generation" emerged as important community activists in this era, especially on issues related to education. The first formally organized, youth-led Puerto Rican organization in New York, the Hispanic Young Adult Association (HYAA), formed in the early 1950s out of a collective of young activists including Manuel "Manny" Díaz and Antonia Pantoja. Over the next several years, members of this group collaborated with other community leaders to create the Puerto Rican Association for Community Affairs (PRACA) and the Puerto Rican Forum, which would be instrumental in fostering further community activism among young Puerto Ricans.

This rising generation of young leaders in the 1950s was interested not just in increasing educational opportunities for Puerto Ricans; they also wanted to challenge the image of young Puerto Ricans as susceptible to juvenile delinquency and gang participation. *West Side Story*, which appeared on Broadway in 1957, played on these hardening stereotypes of Puerto Rican youth. Two years later, in 1959, a high-profile murder by a young Puerto Rican gang member dubbed the "Capeman" brought the preoccupation with delinquency and gang violence to a head. Two weeks after the Capeman incident, the murder in Chicago of an Italian man randomly targeted by two young Puerto Rican men sparked the same kind of hysteria about Puerto Ricans and crime.

It was in this climate of fear and prejudice that Antonia Pantoja and other members of the Puerto Rican Forum—most notably Frank Bonilla, who would become one of the early leaders of the push to create programs in Puerto Rican studies at the university level—formed a youth leadership organization that focused on educational opportunity. They named the organization ASPIRA, "to aspire," which Pantoja described as a movement, not a service agency, to be structured around "clubs" that would allow youth to set their own agendas and designate their own leadership. ASPIRA, which still exists as a national organization after more than fifty years, represented precisely the goals articulated by a group of college-bound Puerto Rican youth in 1960 at their second annual Puerto Rican Youth Conference: "We must set a positive image...to show the Puerto Rican as ambitious, with a desire and increasing ability to climb upwards, as have all past newcomers to the city."[18]

THE LONG 1960S

Although some Puerto Rican youth nurtured a combination of hopefulness and aspiration by the early 1960s, most Puerto Rican children still lived in households in which poverty and insecurity outweighed opportunity. If their parents worked in the garment industry they made, on average, 30 percent (men) to 50 percent (women) less than their white male counterparts. And their prospects worsened over the course of the 1960s: Puerto Ricans' small socioeconomic gains over the 1950s faded with a growing trend in "deindustrialization," the moving of manufacturing plants to locations cheaper than their original urban base, which hit the garment industry, with its high concentration of Puerto Rican workers, earlier than most. Virtually every US urban area in which Puerto Ricans had settled—New York, Chicago, Philadelphia, Hartford—was affected. Nationwide, Puerto Ricans' family earnings dropped from 71 percent of the national average in 1959 to 59 percent by 1974.[19] In 1967, 33 percent of Puerto Ricans were receiving welfare benefits, up from 29.5 percent in 1959. By the late 1960s, Puerto Ricans—including a substantial number of young activists under the age of twenty-five—would confront these problems in their communities head on.

Many young adult activists got involved in promoting civil rights for Puerto Ricans during the early 1960s, working with organizations like the National Association of Puerto Rican Civil Rights (NAPRCR), which focused on equity issues specific to Puerto Ricans.[20] One of the first major events NAPRCR was involved in was a massive school boycott in New York City in 1964, organized by African American and Puerto Rican leaders to protest the Board of Education's failure to take adequate steps toward integrating New York City schools.[21] The boycott was considered a major success, and the participation of nearly half the city's public school children called attention to the failures of city officials to meet the needs of black and Puerto Rican students.

Another important moment in education-related activism was the "community control" movement of the late 1960s. In 1966, half the students in New York's schools were African American (30 percent) or Puerto Rican (20 percent), but they only comprised a tiny proportion (3.6 percent and 1.6 percent, respectively) of those graduating from academic high schools.[22] These statistics showed, said those who protested Board of Education policies, the impact of inequality: black and Puerto Rican students were not being adequately supported in their schools. Protesters demanded a new governance structure for the local school boards, with substantial representation from parents and community members. The Board of Education ultimately consented to the creation of several "experimental" school districts. Although each of these experimental or "community controlled" districts only lasted a few years, they left an enduring legacy: residents of poor communities forced the city to give them more than a token say in the way institutions operated in their neighborhoods.

The battle for self-determination—ensuring that the institutions serving the people in poor neighborhoods were managed and led by those people—was also being waged with force by many of the increasingly radical social work and community development organizations that Puerto Rican activists founded in

every city with a notable Puerto Rican population. Especially after major riots exploded
in the Puerto Rican communities of both
Chicago and New York (in 1966 and 1967,
respectively), activists made real the idea of
"maximum feasible participation of the poor."
They also saw the momentum and energy
they gained when they also aimed for the
maximum feasible participation of the young.
A radical social work organization based in
New York's Lower East Side, called the Real
Great Society, gained prominence in the late
1960s when it started a program called the
"University of the Streets," which offered free
classes to thousands of people in poor communities, on subjects ranging from karate
to photography to Puerto Rican and African
American history.[23]

A similar motivation to dramatically expand opportunities in his impoverished community led José "Cha Cha" Jiménez, head of
the Chicago street gang the Young Lords, to
turn the gang into a radical community service organization in the late 1960s.[24] The
founders of the New York Young Lords Organization (YLO) were inspired by Cha Cha
Jiménez, although their organizations were not
formally affiliated. Most founding members
of the New York YLO were college students,
active in one or more of the many political organizations that thrived on City University
campuses in the 1960s. Activist Iris Morales,
who became one of the first women leaders in
the YLO, recalled what motivated her cohort
at City University of New York (CUNY)—
almost all of them the first in their families to
attend college—in the late 1960s: "we were
marginalized, and we tended to stick together
united by common experiences of poverty and
racial oppression."[25]

Structurally, both the Chicago and the
New York Young Lords—and the branches
that formed in Philadelphia, in Newark, in
Camden, New Jersey, and in Hartford, Connecticut—modeled themselves after the Black
Panther Party, relying on a central committee
composed of various "ministers," and an

organizational platform that emphasized the
group's commitment to self-determination,
racial justice, and a socialist society. Many
people who joined the Young Lords had attended Student Nonviolent Coordinating
Committee (SNCC) or Black Panther meetings as high school students, in some cases
because they were unaware of activist Puerto
Rican groups, and in other cases because they
already identified as Afro-Puerto Rican. A
powerful influence for many of these activists
was the intersection of Black Power and
Puerto Rican nationalist ideology. For example, SNCC leader Stokely Carmichael had
joined Puerto Rico's Movimiento Pro-
Independencia leader Juan Mari Bras in a
massive anti-war demonstration Puerto Rico
in 1967, reportedly ten thousand strong, at
which Carmichael told the crowd, "Our
people is a colony within the United States, in
the same form that Puerto Ricans are a colony
outside the continental United States."[26]

Around the time the Young Lords were organizing in Chicago and New York, black and
Puerto Rican student leaders had shut down
New York's City College campus in April, demanding a more inclusive admissions policy
that would provide more open access for
Puerto Rican and African American students
to a university education. They wanted a more
equitable representation of students of color
admitted to the CUNY colleges. The student
activists also lobbied for the creation of Black
and Puerto Rican studies programs on their
campuses. The idea was not simply to provide
minority students with the opportunity to
"study themselves," as one critic complained
during the takeover in 1969. Their larger goal
was to create a new visibility for the silenced
histories of Puerto Ricans and African
Americans. The Puerto Rican studies programs
developed at CUNY starting in 1969 were part
of a larger national trend—programs in Black,
Third World, Chicano, and Puerto Rican studies emerged at universities around the country
in the early 1970s, transforming campus protests into a durable legacy of academic impact.

CHALLENGES OF THE 1970s–1990s

By the mid-1970s, urban fiscal crises—fueled by inflation, deindustrialization, and the declining incomes and unemployment these forces produced for blue collar workers—had dealt a heavy blow to most Puerto Rican communities in the United States. By 1975, a federal report found that Puerto Rican households in the United States had a lower per capita income than any other group, and they suffered unemployment rates roughly 300 percent higher than white workers. Puerto Rican neighborhoods in a handful of cities in the United States experienced some version of the New York Puerto Ricans' trauma of that era: "The Bronx was burning," recalled one community activist about the 1970s, "and nobody cared to try to stop it."[27]

After several decades of struggling to secure decent housing and stabilize their impoverished communities, Puerto Ricans faced the accumulated pressures of what social scientists were beginning to call "the underclass," a label that only added to the stigma of their communities. No longer were Puerto Rican migrants and their US-born children hoping to make good on the promises of life in a "nation of immigrants"; the paucity of both basic material stability and social equality in their communities was now a hardened reality. In response, during the 1970s, for the first time, more Puerto Ricans were returning to the island than arriving in the United States

On the other hand, the 1970s was also the decade when many Puerto Rican communities managed to elect their own political officials (New York Puerto Ricans had won some important political gains beginning in the early 1960s, with the election of several State Assembly representatives). Much of the political energy of Puerto Rican leaders in this era focused on addressing the community's problems; but they were also creating a permanent place in local, state, and (on a smaller scale) national politics. Herman Badillo, for example, after two successful terms in the US

Congress, became deputy mayor of New York in 1978. One reason for these electoral successes—beginning in the 1960s in New York and in the 1970s and 1980s in other cities with notable Puerto Rican populations—was the simple math of larger constituencies and more powerful voting blocs in predominantly Puerto Rican districts. But another key reason was the resilience of existing community organizations, and the growth of new ones, that nurtured a growing Puerto Rican leadership.

The most powerful and durable Puerto Ricans organizations of this era were those that litigated and lobbied for Puerto Ricans' civil rights. ASPIRA had continued, since its founding in 1961, to be a substantial supporter of Puerto Rican youth, especially those who aspired to graduate from high school or go to college. After the federal Office of Civil Rights issued a memo in 1970 that gave powerful support to the idea of bilingual programs (asserting that failure to provide such programming by school districts may constitute a violation of Title VI of the Civil Rights Act), ASPIRA collaborated with the newly formed Puerto Rican Legal Defense and Education Fund (PRLDEF) to initiate a class action lawsuit against the New York City Board of Education. The major result of this suit was a consent decree, in 1974, stipulating that New York City schools would implement transitional bilingual instruction to children who needed it. Similar cases were mounted—and won—by the PRLDEF in Philadelphia, Long Island, and Connecticut.

Another other area of civil rights litigation pursued by the PRLDEF was voting rights, ensuring that non-English speakers (linguistic minorities) had fair access to the ballot. During the early 1970s, the organization won cases to establish bilingual election systems in New York City, Philadelphia, New York State, and New Jersey. In 1975, largely as a result of this body of case law, the 1965 Voting Rights Act was amended to ensure federal protection of voting rights for linguistic minorities. The other key dimensions of Puerto

Ricans' battle for civil rights in this era dealt with equity in employment and in government benefits. Through cases targeting discrimination in civil service exams and other employment requirements, and highlighting the need for bilingual access to information about government benefits ranging from Aid to Families with Dependant Children (AFDC) to unemployment insurance, the PRLDEF waged a rapid and successful campaign to secure a range of civil rights for Puerto Ricans—at a moment when a stagnant economy and mounting prejudice challenged the group's social standing.

Even as many young Puerto Rican leaders focused their efforts on expanding educational opportunity and civil rights in the United States, others continued the Nationalist struggle. The detention of the Puerto Rican Nationalists responsible for the 1950 attack on Truman (one of the two assailants was killed) and for the 1954 attack on Congress remained a powerful symbol for Nationalists. Some radical factions of the Puerto Rican independence struggle embraced increasingly violent tactics, and persisted through the 1970s and 1980s. Most prominent among these was a group called the Armed Forces of National Liberation (FALN), which claimed responsibility for over one hundred bombings in several US cities between 1974 and 1983 that resulted in five deaths and $3 million in damage. A less contentious but high-profile action, by a group formed to lobby for the release of Puerto Rican political prisoners in the United States, was the mounting of the Puerto Rican flag on the crown of the Statue of Liberty in 1977. The symbolic power of the Puerto Rican flag adorning this icon of American inclusion won the support of many Puerto Ricans, even those who did not endorse the Nationalist cause. As more members of armed nationalist groups went to prison or went into hiding throughout the 1980s, campaigns to sever the political relationship between the island and the United States by force dwindled.

The "underclass debate"—concerning the perception of a set of seemingly self-reinforcing disadvantages that kept Puerto Ricans locked in extreme poverty—emerged with new force in the 1980s, when the impact of two decades of economic hardship had seriously destabilized the poor urban neighborhoods where the majority of US Puerto Ricans lived. In 1991, President Reagan's former director of the US Commission on Civil Rights, Linda Chávez, published a book titled *Out of the Barrio*, which labeled Puerto Ricans as a "tragic and curious exception" to the growing successes of Latinos as a group nationwide. Citing statistics about welfare dependency and low marriage rates (and making a fuzzy case for a causal relationship between them), Chávez posited that it was Puerto Ricans' access to the full range of social benefits, rather than the structural disadvantages they encountered in the areas in which they settled, that caused their suffering. "Puerto Ricans have been smothered by entitlements," she asserted, "which should serve notice as a warning to other Hispanics."[28]

Since the publication of Chávez's controversial cautionary tale, the population of other Hispanics—immigrants from the Dominican Republic, Mexico, Central America, and elsewhere—has continued to grow rapidly, including in the eastern and midwestern cities where most Puerto Ricans in the United States live. While it is impossible to generalize accurately about the relationships of these newer immigrant groups to the older Puerto Rican communities, some observations are instructive. First, while poverty rates of Puerto Ricans nationwide may remain higher overall than those of other Hispanics, comparisons of demographic data within most cities where Puerto Ricans live point to improvements. Second, many of the "pioneer" organizations started by Puerto Ricans in the 1960s or 1970s have made a transition to adopting Latino-inclusive agendas and names, symbolizing not just the possibilities for a shared agenda of Latinos of different national origins, but also the strength of Puerto Ricans' history of effective community organizing. By the late 20th century, Puerto Ricans as a group began to shed at least some of the stigma of the "failed immigrant" identity that followed them since the 1940s.

PROSPECTS IN THE NEW MILLENNIUM

The new millennium has shown that warnings about the alleged intractability of Puerto Ricans' socioeconomic failings were off the mark. As the long decades of economic suffering between the 1960s and 1980s turned into a more hopeful horizon by the mid-1990s, the Puerto Rican middle class—always part of the diaspora—has become increasingly visible, forcing the reconsideration of presumptions of Puerto Ricans' intractable socioeconomic failures.

At least as important, the political salience of Puerto Ricans as a group has begun to shift since 2000. Although the number of those who support outright independence has remained small, nationalist activism animated many Puerto Ricans, on the island and in the United States during the successful movement to force the US Navy to abandon its base and bombing targets at Vieques, off Puerto Rico's eastern coast. The Navy gave up its holdings on the island between 2001 and 2003. On the other hand, the question of statehood for Puerto Rico has continued to attract many supporters—particularly among those on the island: in a two-part plebiscite in 2012, a plurality voted in favor of US statehood as a solution to the island's problematic relationship to the United States.[29] Although statehood remains an unlikely final outcome, the plebiscite in 2012 showed the continuing importance of the question of the island's political status in relation to the United States.

Even more important in the new millennium is the growing significance of Puerto Rican voters in the United States. For the better part of the last century, Puerto Ricans in the United States have been considered numerically insignificant or politically impotent, or both. In the last two presidential elections, however, their growing populations in the South, especially in Florida, have drawn attention to their demographic impact and to their political sensibilities. After nearly a century of residing in this country as citizens, Puerto Ricans in the United States may at last be recognized as an important constituency.

DISCUSSION OF THE LITERATURE

The history of Puerto Ricans in the United States received very little attention from scholars before the 1980s, and most of what was published about Puerto Ricans focused on their "adjustment problems" and other pathologies. A few historically minded social scientists diverged from this pattern: Lawrence Chenault, who taught economics at the University of Puerto Rico, published *The Puerto Rican Migrant in New York City* in 1938; the renowned sociologist C. Wright Mills was the primary author of a study that resulted in a book, *The Puerto Rican Journey*, in 1950; and Mills's student Elena Padilla published *Up From Puerto Rico* in 1958. Between the 1940s and the end of the 1970s, even researchers who took an interest in Puerto Ricans as subjects of social science in their own right had to address the predominant approaches that objectified Puerto Ricans' problems and dramatized their alleged deficits.[30]

With the development of academic programs in Puerto Rican studies by the mid-1970s, this trend began to change. Scholars from a variety of disciplines now collaborated on the goal of framing serious intellectual questions about Puerto Ricans' lives and history that would be acknowledged in the academy. A growing group of scholars, including members of History Task Force at the Center for Puerto Rican studies, confronted the impoverishment of old ideas; this collective published *Labor Migration Under Capitalism: The Puerto Rican Experience* in 1979. Such work challenged the assumptions of liberal luminaries like Nathan Glazer and Daniel Patrick Moynihan, whose 1963 book *Beyond the Melting Pot* (updated in 1970 to address the social and political upheaval of the late 1960s) represented Puerto Ricans as insignificant historical actors incapable of developing their own political analysis. Since 1987, the *CENTRO Journal*, connected to the Centro de Estudios Puertorriqueños, has published a wide variety of scholarship on Puerto Ricans, from a full range of humanities and social science disciplines.[31]

One of the most central set of questions embraced by scholars of the 1970s—addressing the impact of the colonial relationship of the island to the United States—was rooted in the political culture of Puerto Ricans in the United States dating back to the 1920s, and remains relevant to both activists and scholars today. Legal theorist and federal judge José Cabranes published a definitive review of Puerto Rican's legal status, *Citizenship and the American Empire: Notes on the Legislative History of the United States Citizenship of Puerto Ricans*, in 1979. Subsequently, scholars have examined historical details of that status, and its origins and impact, in works like Cristina Duffy Burnett and Burke Marshall, eds., *Foreign in a Domestic Sense: Puerto Rico, American Expansion, and the Constitution*, and Charles Venator Santiago, *Puerto Rico and the Origins of U.S. Global Empire*. Literary, cultural, and anthropological perspectives add dimension to the political issues in books like *Puerto Rican Jam*, edited by Frances Negrón Muntaner and Ramón Grosfoguel and *National Performances* by Ana Ramos-Zayas.[32]

Scholarship on the social history of Puerto Ricans in the United States accumulated slowly after the 1970s, picking up increasing momentum by the late 1990s. Virginia Sanchez-Korrol was the first US historian to publish a book-length study of Puerto Ricans there; *From Colonia to Community*, published in 1983, has served as the starting point for several generations of scholars already. Historians

following in her footsteps have approached that social history from various angles. Ruth Glasser, focusing on the music traditions of early Puerto Rican migrants in her book *My Music Is My Flag*, also provided a foundation for the cultural history of the New York community before World War II. Carmen Whalen's study of Philadelphia's Puerto Rican migrants focused on labor history and the industrial economy that attracted migrants to the city in the postwar period. Lorrin Thomas's work on New York Puerto Rican communities before and after World War II emphasized evolving political identities in the changing historical contexts.[33]

Given the continuously fraught political relationship of the island to the United States, as well as the political dynamism of many Puerto Rican communities throughout the 20th century (which has been often overlooked by observers), it is not surprising that political scientists and political historians have produced varied and dynamic scholarship on Puerto Ricans in the United States José Cruz's study of Puerto Rican politics in Hartford, Connecticut, *Identity and Power: Puerto Rican Politics and the Challenge of Ethnicity*, asked important new questions about the relationship between ethnic identity and political empowerment, at the same time pushing forward the diversification of scholarship beyond New York City. In their powerful edited volume, *The Puerto Rican Movement: Voices from the Diaspora*, Andrés Torres and José Velázquez offered an impressive range of perspectives on and analysis of the politics that motivated the period known as the Puerto Rican movement, spanning the mid-1960s to the mid-1970s. Reflecting the spirit of the era, radical leftist politics comprise much of the focus of the book, but not the whole story. Johanna Fernández's and Darrel Wanzer-Serrano's work on the Young Lords and their connections to other politically engaged groups of their era carry forward the questions about the enduring legacies of Puerto Rican radicalism.[34]

The scope of contemporary studies that broaden both geographic and disciplinary perspectives in the study of Puerto Ricans has been expanded by *Adios Borinquen Querida: The Puerto Rican Diaspora, Its History and Contributions*, by Edna Acosta-Belen et al.; Carmen Teresa Whalen and Victor Vazquez-Hernandez's *The Puerto Rican Diaspora, Historical Perspectives*; Edna Acosta Belen and Carlos E. Santiago's *Puerto Ricans in the United States: A Contemporary Portrait*; and Mérida Rúa's *A Grounded Identidad: Making New Lives in Chicago's Puerto Rican Neighborhoods*.[35]

Last but certainly not least among recent scholarly trends is the examination of Puerto Rican history in close relationship to other social groups. This is not a new approach—sociologist Felix Padilla wrote *Latino Ethnic Consciousness: The Case of Mexican Americans and Puerto Ricans in Chicago* in 1985—but it is gaining momentum as scholars continue to make the case that, in a number of major US cities, the history of postwar urban politics simply cannot be written without analyzing Puerto Ricans' relationship to other groups and how they remade social, economic, and political life together. Historian Lilia Fernández's book *Brown in the Windy City* presents the separate and converging development of Mexican and Puerto Rican communities in Chicago, and analyzes their shared as well as their distinctive preoccupations over time. The most recent additions to this area of historical scholarship include Sonia Lee's *Building a Latino Civil Rights Movement* and Frederick Douglass Opie's *Upsetting the Apple Cart: Black-Latino Coalitions in New York City from Protest to Public Office*, both of which examine how Puerto Rican activists and leaders interacted with African Americans—and learned from their strategies—as they sought to make their own claims to equal rights in the United States.[36]

Scholarship on Puerto Ricans in the United States has reached a new level of growth and dynamism in the past decade, in each of the areas of research described above. The genre of personal memoir, pioneered by early 20th- / 20th-century leaders century leaders Bernardo Vega and Jesús Colón, has provided an indispensable complement to scholarly writing, with important recent examples including Antonia Pantoja's *Memoir of a Visionary* and Gilberto Gerena Valentin's *Gilberto Gerena Valentin: My Life as a Community Activist, Labor Organizer, and Progressive Politician in New York City*. The momentum created by this diverse body of work will have an increasingly visible impact, bringing the study of Puerto Ricans closer to the center of urban, labor, social, and political history in the United States.[37]

PRIMARY SOURCES

Much of the primary source research conducted on Puerto Ricans in the United States in the past four decades has begun with materials from the Centro de Estudios Puertorriqueños Library and Archive, housed at Hunter College in New York City. The Centro archive consists of 240 collections, most of them personal or organizational papers, although the archive also contains collections of photographs, political posters, and other visual materials. Most of the collections document Puerto Ricans in New York City and the mid-Atlantic region, but there are also collections that deal with the migration to Hawaii and California. The largest of the Centro archive's collections (fourteen hundred of the archive's five thousand feet of archival materials) is the Offices of the Government of Puerto Rico in the United States, including the papers of the Migration Division, which served migrants in the United States from 1948 to 1989. Also important at the Centro Archive, and at nearly all the archives discussed below, are the holdings of microfilmed local and community newspapers that contain abundant information on Puerto Ricans' lives in each of the places they settled.

Other important sources on Puerto Ricans in New York City are located at the New York Public Library (NYPL) Manuscripts and Archives Division, especially the papers of longtime East Harlem congressman Vito Marcantonio; the Rare Book and Manuscript Library at Columbia University, which holds the records of several major New York settlement houses and community centers that served Puerto Rican populations; the Fordham University Archives and Special Collections, especially the Joseph Fitzpatrick papers there; and at the Municipal Archive of the New York City Department of Records, with valuable materials in the Works Progress Administration Writers' Project collection, mayor's papers, and the published and unpublished records of various city agencies. A variety of holdings and collections related to Puerto Ricans can be found at the Schomburg Center for Research in Black Culture, part of the NYPL; the Oral History Archives at Columbia University; the Tamiment Library and Robert F. Wagner Labor Archives at New York University; the Laguardia and Wagner archives at Laguardia Community College; the Brooklyn Collection at the Brooklyn Public Library; the Brooklyn Historical Society; and La Casa de la Herencia Cultural Puertorriqueña. The Puerto Rican Records of the National Archives of New York City primarily contain materials related to the island, although some materials deal with Puerto Ricans in the United States.

Elsewhere in the mid-Atlantic, the Puerto Rican Community Archives, part of the New Jersey Hispanic Research and Information Center, is housed at the Newark Public Library and contains several dozen collections of personal papers and organizational records. At the Historical Society of Pennsylvania (HSP), the extensive papers of East Harlem (New York City) educator and community organizer Leonard Covello contain a substantial amount of material on Puerto Ricans in New York. HSP also houses significant archival materials on Puerto Ricans in other collections, organized as the Hispanic/Latino Collections. The Temple University Urban Archives houses a number of collections that deal with Puerto Ricans in Philadelphia, as well as microfilmed runs of many local and community

newspapers. At the University of Connecticut's main campus at Storrs, El Instituto: Institute of Latina/o, Caribbean, and Latin American Studies houses archives that include the Puerto Rican Collections.

The US city with the second-largest Puerto Rican population, Chicago, also offers significant archival holdings on the history of Puerto Ricans in the United States, especially in the Midwest. The Illinois Regional Archives Depository at Northern Illinois University houses municipal government records, many of which are relevant to Puerto Ricans in Chicago. The Archives and Manuscripts collections of the Chicago History Museum, and the Special Collections of the University of Illinois at Chicago, include personal papers and many organizational records with materials related to Puerto Ricans. Finally, DePaul University houses the papers of several Puerto Rican community organizations in Chicago, including the Young Lords Organization.

FURTHER READING

Fernández, Lilia. *Brown in the Windy City: Mexicans and Puerto Ricans in Postwar Chicago*. Chicago: University of Chicago Press, 2012.

García, Gervasio Luis. "I Am the Other: Puerto Rico in the Eyes of North Americans, 1898." *Journal of American History* 87 (2000): 39–64.

Hoffnung-Garskof, Jesse. "The Migrations of Arturo Schomburg: On Being Antillano, Negro, and Puerto Rican in New York." *Journal of American Ethnic History* 21 (2001): 3–49.

Iglesias, César Andreu, ed. *Memoirs of Bernardo Vega: A Contribution to the History of the Puerto Rican Community in New York*. New York: Monthly Review Press, 1984.

Lee, Sonia. *Building a Latino Civil Rights Movement: Puerto Ricans, African Americans, and the Pursuit of Racial Justice in New York City*. Chapel Hill: University of North Carolina Press, 2014.

Rodríguez, Clara E., and Virginia Sánchez-Korrol, eds. *Historical Perspectives on Puerto Rican Survival in the U.S.* Princeton, NJ: Markus Wiener, 1996.

Sánchez-Korrol, Virginia. *From Colonia to Community: The History of Puerto Ricans in New York City, 1917–1948*. Westport, CT: Greenwood, 1983.

Thomas, Lorrin. *Puerto Rican Citizen: History and Political Identity in Twentieth Century New York City.* Chicago: University of Chicago Press, 2010.

Torres, Andrés. *Between Melting Pot and Mosaic: African Americans and Puerto Ricans in the New York Political Economy.* Philadelphia: Temple University Press, 1995.

Whalen, Carmen. *From Puerto Rico to Philadelphia: Puerto Rican Workers and Postwar Economies.* Philadelphia: Temple University Press, 2001.

NOTES

1. *"Trigueño"* means "wheat-colored," a description for light-skinned mulattos. Chief Agüeybaná was a leader of the Taínos, the native people of Puerto Rico. Jesús Colón, "La unica manera—A los puertorriqueños en NY," March 30, 1923, Colón papers, series III, box 5, folder 8.

2. Interview with Juan Ramos, conducted by Mayda Cortiella, October 21, 1974, *Pioneros* Project, LIHS; Mercedes Hernández, "De Nuestros Lectores," *La Prensa*, December 2, 1924, 4. On migrant women's work in the needle trades in this era, see Altagracia Ortiz, *"En la aguja y el pedal eché la hiel*: Puerto Rican Women in the Garment Industry in New York City, 1920–1980," 55–81; and Virginia Sánchez-Korrol, "Survival of Puerto Rican Women in New York Before World War II," *Puerto Rican Women and Work: Bridges in Transnational Labor*, ed. Altagracia Ortiz (Philadelphia: Temple University Press, 1996), 59–60, 64–66.

3. "Harlem Porto Ricans Unite to Prove Faith," *New York Times*, August 16, 1926, 8.

4. José C. González, "De Nuestros Lectores," *La Prensa*, August 22, 1930, 4. González later became active in the Democratic Party in Brooklyn.

5. Puerto Ricans were not counted separately in census figures on unemployment for this decade; the categories were Negro, Native white, Foreign-born white, and Other races. Census takers made their own judgements about the categories in which Puerto Ricans should be placed, which means that they were scattered throughout the aforementioned categories. See Cheryl Greenberg, *Or Does It Explode?* (New York: Oxford University Press, 1991), Appendix II, for a thorough review of statistics on unemployment in the 1930s, tabulated by race.

6. Club Azteca flyer, "Gran Baile ...," October 15, 1932, Colón papers, reprinted [image no. 8] in *My Music Is My Flag: Puerto Rican Musicians and their New York Communities, 1917–1940*, by Ruth Glasser (Berkeley: University of California Press, 1995).

7. Altagracia Ortiz, "Puerto Rican Women in the Garment Industry," in *Puerto Rican Women and Work*, ed. Ortiz, 58–59. See also various interview transcripts in the *Costureras* collection, Centro de Estudios Puertorriqueños.

8. The "Organizations" sections of the WPA "Spanish Book" lists or describes scores of organizations—fraternal, political, labor, social, and cultural—that were founded by Puerto Ricans (and other Hispanics) during the 1930s. See WPA Federal Writers Project, "Organizations," 1938, Spanish Book, WPA Files, reel 269.

9. Enrique C. Rosario, "De Nuestros Lectores," *La Prensa*, October 19, 1936, 8.

10. Ira Rosenwaike, *Population History of New York City* (Syracuse, NY: Syracuse University Press, 1972), 121.

11. Historical sociologist Margaret Somers has written extensively on the idea of citizenship not as a status but as "a set of institutionally embedded social practices," framed by expressions of expectations of the state. See, for example, Somers, "Citizenship and the Public Sphere: Law, Community, and Political Culture in the Transition to Democracy," *American Sociological Review* 58 (October 1993), 587–620.

12. Leonard Covello, notes on Hilliard's 1949 report on "The Puerto Rican Problem..." [nd], Covello papers, box 110, folder 1.

13. "Confab to Strengthen Puerto Rican Unity; Same Bias Snags Both Groups," December 13, 1952, *New York Amsterdam News*, 36.

14. Philadelphia Commission on Human Rights, *Puerto Ricans in Philadelphia* (1959), quoted in Carmen Whalen, *From Puerto Rico to Philadelphia: Puerto Rican Workers and Postwar Economies* (Philadelphia: Temple University Press, 2001), 198.

15. Colón, "The Growing Puerto Rican Minority in New York City," Colón papers, series III, box 2, folder 1. See various other statements by Puerto Rican candidates: "Nuestros Candidatos," *Vida Hispana*, November 2, 1952, 2; "Meet Two of Your Neighbors [Jesús Colón and José Giboyeaux

for City Council on the American Labor Party ticket]," 1953, Colón papers, series IV, box, 1 folder 1.

16. Graduate School of Public Administration and Social Service, New York University, *The Impact of Puerto Rican Migration on Governmental Services in New York City* (New York: New York University Press, 1957), 63 and *passim*.

17. Lilia Fernández, *Brown in the Windy City: Mexicans and Puerto Ricans in Postwar Chicago* (Chicago: University of Chicago Press, 2012), 103.

18. Second Puerto Rican Youth Conference, "We the New Yorkers Contribute," 1960, Covello papers, series X, box 102, folder 10.

19. US Commission on Civil Rights, *Puerto Ricans in the Continental United States: An Uncertain Future* (A report of the US Commission on Civil Rights October, 1976), 47.

20. On the school boycott issue see, for instance, "Dr. Theobald Writes Letter to Parents," *New York Amsterdam News*, September 10, 1960, 1; and J. Fitzpatrick, "Puerto Ricans in Perspective: The Meaning of Migration to the Mainland," *International Migration Review* 2 (Spring 1968), 7–20, 11.

21. Counting the number of total participants—those who marched and those who stayed home—Bayard Rustin called it the largest civil rights protest in the nation's history. (The 1963 March on Washington, which Rustin had also played a key role in organizing, had drawn 200,000, who, unlike school boycotters, all convened in one place.) "Boycott Cripples City Schools; Absences 360,000 Above Normal; Negroes and Puerto Ricans Unite," *New York Times*, February 4, 1964, 1. The *Times* clarified that the figures for both students and teachers who did not attend classes should be adjusted to account for the typical daily absentee rate: 10 percent for students, 3 percent for teachers.

22. "Negro and Puerto Rican Pupils in Majority Here for First Time," March 15, 1967, *New York Times*, 1.

23. "A 'University' Is Opened by Former Street Fighters," *New York Times*, June 27, 1967, 23; "Ex-Gang Leaders Obtain U.S. Funds," *New York Times*, February 27, 1968, 53.

24. After spending time in prison in 1967 and reading about Martin Luther King Jr., Malcolm X, and Puerto Rico's famous nationalist Pedro

Albizu Campos, Jiménez slowly transformed his former gang into the Young Lords Organization. Fernandez, *Brown in the Windy City*, 182.

25. Iris Morales, interview with Ron Grele, November 19, 1984, Columbia Oral History archive, 19–20.

26. "'Poder Negro' y MPI Firman Pacto para Acciones Conjuntas," *El Tiempo Nueva York*, August 3, 1967, 16–17.

27. José Morales, interview with author, December 13, 2007, New York City.

28. Linda Chávez, *Out of the Barrio: Toward a New Politics of Hispanic Assimilation* (New York: Basic Books, 1992), 152.

29. There is much debate about how to read the results of the plebiscite, given its confusing two-part strucuture, the alleged abstention by many voters who support the current Commonwealth status, and given the defeat, on the same day, of the incumbent pro-statehood governor in favor of a governor who supports some form of Commonwealth status. One thing is clear, though: a majority of Puerto Ricans voted against the colonial status quo. See Charles Venator-Santiago, "Constitutional Questions Incident to President Obama's Puerto Rico Status Plebiscite," *New England Law Review On Remand* 48 (2013), 61.

30. Lawrence Chenault, *The Puerto Rican Migrant in New York City* (New York: Columbia University Press, 1938); C. Wright Mills, Clarence Senior, and Rose Kohn Goldsen, *The Puerto Rican Journey: New York's Newest Migrants* (New York: Harper, 1950); Elena Padilla, *Up from Puerto Rico* (New York: Columbia University Press), 1958.

31. History Task Force, *Labor Migration Under Capitalism* (New York: Monthly Review Press), 1979; Nathan Glazer and Daniel Patrick Moynihan, *Beyond the Melting Pot: The Negroes, Puerto Ricans, Jews, Italians, and Irish of New York City* (Cambridge, MA: MIT Press, 1970 [1963]).

32. José A. Cabranes in *Citizenship and the American Empire: Notes on the Legislative History of the United States Citizenship of Puerto Ricans* (New Haven, CT: Yale University Press, 1979); Christina Duffy Burnett and Burke Marshall, "Between the Foreign and the Domestic," in Burnett and Marshall, eds., *Foreign in a Domestic Sense: Puerto Rico, American Expansion, and the Constitution* (Durham, NC: Duke University Press, 2001); Charles Venator Santiago, *Puerto Rico and the*

Origins of U.S. Global Empire (New York: Routledge, 2015); Ramón Grosfoguel and Frances Negron Muntaner, eds., *Puerto Rican Jam: Rethinking Colonialism and Nationalism* (Minneapolis: University of Minnesota Press, 1997); Ana Ramos Zayas, *National Performances: The Politics of Class, Race, and Space in Puerto Rican Chicago* (Chicago: University of Chicago Press, 2003).

33. Virginia Sánchez-Korrol's *From Colonia to Community: The History of Puerto Ricans in New York City, 1917–1948* (Westport, CT: Greenwood, 1983); Ruth Glasser, *My Music Is My Flag: Puerto Rican Musicians and Their New York Communities, 1917–1940* (Berkeley: University of California Press, 1995); Carmen Whalen, *From Puerto Rico to Philadelphia: Puerto Rican Workers and Postwar Economies* (Philadelphia: Temple University Press, 2001); Lorrin Thomas, *Puerto Rican Citizen: History and Political Identity in Twentieth Century New York City* (Chicago: University of Chicago Press, 2010).

34. José Cruz, *Identity and Power: Puerto Rican Politics and the Challenge of Ethnicity* (Philadelphia: Temple University Press, 1998); Andrés Torres and José E. Velázquez, eds., *The Puerto Rican Movement: Voices from the Diaspora* (Philadelphia: Temple University Press, 1998); Johanna Fernández, "The Young Lords and the Postwar City," in *African American Urban History Since World War II*, eds. Kenneth Kusmer and Joe Trotter (Chicago: University of Chicago Press, 2009); Darrel Wanzer-Serrano, *The New York Young Lords and the Struggle for Liberation* (Philadelphia: Temple University Press, 2015).

35. Edna Acosta-Belen et al., *Adios Borinquen Querida: The Puerto Rican Diaspora, Its History and Contributions* (Albany, NY: CELAC Publications, 2000); Carmen Teresa Whalen and Victor Vazquez-Hernandez, *The Puerto Rican Diaspora, Historical Perspectives* (Philadelphia: Temple University Press, 2005); Edna Acosta Belen and Carlos E. Santiago, *Puerto Ricans in the United States: A Contemporary Portrait* (Boulder, CO: Lynne Rienner, 2006); Mérida Rúa, *A Grounded Identidad: Making New Lives in Chicago's Puerto Rican Neighborhoods* (New York: Oxford University Press, 2012).

36. Felix Padilla, *Latino Ethnic Consciousness: The Case of Mexican Americans and Puerto Ricans in Chicago* (Notre Dame, IN: University of Notre Dame Press, 1985); Lilia Fernández, *Brown in the Windy City: Mexicans and Puerto Ricans in Postwar Chicago* (University of Chicago Press, 2012); Sonia Lee, *Building a Latino Civil Rights Movement: Puerto Ricans, African Americans, and the Pursuit of Racial Justice in New York City* (Chapel Hill: University of North Carolina Press, 2014); Frederick Douglass Opie's *Upsetting the Apple Cart: Black-Latino Coalitions in New York City from Protest to Public Office* (New York: Columbia University Press, 2014).

37. César Andreu Iglesias, ed., *Memoirs of Bernardo Vega: A Contribution to the History of the Puerto Rican Community in New York* (New York: Monthly Review Press, 1984); Jesús Colón, *The Way It Was and Other Writings* (Houston: Arte Público, 1993); Antonia Pantoja, *Memoir of a Visionary* (Houston: Arte Publico, 2002); Carlos Rodriguez-Fraticelli, ed., *Gilberto Gerena Valentin: My Life as a Community Activist, Labor Organizer, and Progressive Politician in New York City* (New York: Center for Puerto Rican Studies, 2013).

Lorrin Thomas

LATINO/A AND AFRICAN AMERICAN RELATIONS

African American and Latino/a relations during the civil rights era is a complicated topic, made more so by differences in community interactions and the geography of black and Latino/a peoples. Relations tended to differ by city and state, and especially by the national origins of various Latino/a groups. Race relations also differed based on the relative potency of Jim Crow segregation. In a southern state like Texas, for instance, Jim Crow pitted blacks and Latino/as against each other. In other states with a less rigid, more de facto type of segregation, blacks and Latino/as had more room to maneuver in their respective struggle for rights. Relations also tended to differ from state to state and city to city, depending on the relative populations of these groups.

The racial histories of various colonies or nations in Latin America also affected black–Latino/a relations in the United States. For example, the racial history of Mexico differed from that of Puerto Rico. Mexico had a racial hierarchy not dissimilar to that of the United States, with white Mexicans at the top of the social and political hierarchy, and nonwhites below. Mexico also had a smaller black slave population during its colonial period, and thus a smaller black population in the postcolonial era. Spain's Caribbean colonies had much larger slave populations, which made their postcolonial populations more ethnoracially diverse. As such, Mexicans who came to the United States had an understanding of black people not altogether different from understandings common among white Americans, while Puerto Ricans who migrated there often came with a more inclusive understanding of race. That understanding could, and often did, work to open dialogues and cross-ethnic collaborations between African Americans and Puerto Ricans.

Collectively known as the "Big Three," Mexican Americans, Puerto Ricans, and Cuban Americans comprise the largest population group of all Latino/a people in the United States (76 percent of the nation's total Latino/a population). That percentage was similar in the civil rights period. As such, if black Americans were to encounter Latino/as, they typically encountered Mexican Americans, Puerto Ricans, and Cuban Americans.

The civil rights activism of these groups reflects the obstacles they sought to eliminate, especially racial segregation. Racial acrimony, especially between blacks and Mexican Americans and between blacks and Cuban Americans, often stymied common civil rights efforts. But coalitions were also possible, and African Americans and Mexican Americans, and especially African Americans and Puerto Ricans, could generate sustained cooperative efforts, particularly the cross-ethnic coalition that was the Poor People's Campaign (PPC). Looking at Latino/a–African American relations

across multiple regions and ethnic groups reveals the diversity of the experiences of the groups across the United States. A "one size fits all" analysis simply does not fit black–brown relations. Rather, an ever-shifting and sweeping number of relationships between Latino/as and blacks, often dependent on shared and competing economic, political, and social conditions, characterized black–brown relations in the United States. Ultimately the civil rights movement represented a moment of coalitional possibility between African Americans and Latino/as which had moments of great success amid some notable failures.

JIM CROW SEGREGATION AND RACIAL DISCRIMINATION

Many Americans think of Jim Crow segregation as a distinctly southern phenomenon. While the bulk of de jure segregation laws were certainly crafted in the US South, the broader patterns of racial and ethnic segregation were national, not regional. Neighborhood segregation in southern cities such as Houston, San Antonio, or Miami were only marginally different from non-southern cities such as Los Angeles, Chicago, or New York City. While many southern states and their cities enacted laws and ordinances that segregated businesses, it was common for blacks and Latino/as to encounter segregation signs in businesses that read "We Cater to White Trade Only" or "No Spanish or Mexicans" in Phoenix, Arizona, Los Angeles, or elsewhere.[1] Schools were also segregated across the United States. Numerous communities developed a tripartite type of school segregation, with schools for whites, blacks, and Latino/as.[2]

In their day-to-day lives, African Americans and Latino/as experienced many commonalities with the regimes of segregation they encountered. Public places, neighborhoods, schools, and city facilities were all segregated by race and ethnicity. Many states prohibited or strongly discouraged interracial or interethnic marriage. Political rights were not extended to blacks and Latino/as, and voting and jury service, especially, were prohibited or proscribed. Popular culture mocked and vilified blacks and Latino/as. Most egregiously, African Americans and Latino/as suffered from very real threats to their lives: lynching afflicted both groups in the 19th and early 20th centuries, and throughout this period heavy-handed law enforcement tactics and police brutality also served to control blacks and Latino/as.

Beyond the basic and ugly racism evident in the system itself, segregation hid the problems of African Americans and Latino/as from one another and often worked to establish a framework of antagonism between these groups. For example, San Antonio drew its segregation lines both ethno-racially and geographically. The African American population of the city was segregated on the east side of town, while the Mexican-origin population was segregated on the west side. Each part of town had its own segregated schools. When protesting school segregation, each community tended to fight for itself because of the education system's racial lines.[3] School desegregation battles also developed based on different legal issues. For black people, racial segregation in schools was a matter of state law, and thus black activists had a distinctly racist body of laws they could challenge in court. For Mexican Americans segregation was less well codified, and if they used the courts they first had to prove that segregation existed, and then find remedies to it. Thus, the legal battles and methods of legal redress differed.[4]

Segregation could not prevent all cross-ethnic contact, such as the intimate relationships of blacks and browns. Miscegenation, a pejorative term for interracial marriage of blacks and whites, was banned in many states, but relationships between blacks and Latino/as were legally, if not always socially, permissible. In California, state law banned intermarriage between whites, blacks, Indians, and Asians, but said nothing of Latinos. The

decision signaling the demise of a ban on white–Latino intermarriage, *Perez v. Sharp*, occurred in 1948. The Los Angeles county clerk, W. G. Sharp, had refused to grant a marriage license to Sylvester Davis, who was black, and Andrea Perez, a Mexican American, because Perez had identified herself as "white" on their application, a claim that threatened traditional understandings of white supremacy. The California Supreme Court in a vote of 4–3 declared California's anti-miscegenation law was unconstitutional—the first state supreme court to do so, and a predecessor to *Loving v. Virginia*, in which the US Supreme Court invalidated all anti-miscegenation laws.[5]

Shared grievances could also generate coalitions. Police brutality is a good example of this phenomenon. For generations, blacks and Latino/as suffered abuses from law enforcement. When one group suffered from police brutality, those in another group could relate to it. In numerous examples across the United States, blacks and Latino/as came together to protest police abuse and brutality. While these protests occurred primarily after the 1960s, there are also a number of examples from earlier eras.

Segregation and racism could, then, act as barriers to close relations and coalition building. But the racism inherent in segregation could also lead to cross-racial unity, especially if the abuses blacks and Latino/as suffered came from a similar source, such as police brutality, or if the instance of racism and segregation stemmed from a more personal space, as in the example of Perez and Davis.

AFRICAN AMERICAN AND MEXICAN AMERICAN ACTIVISM AND RELATIONS

Mexican Americans and African Americans across the US Southwest had a long history of interactions and civil rights activism. In some cases these interactions were beneficial and positive, but in others they were negative or harmful to collaboration. Some Mexicans came to the United States with a preconceived notion of white supremacy, or they quickly learned its power once there. The US racial binary presented some Mexican Americans with a strategy to eradicate the segregation they experienced; they could argue that Mexican-origin people were white. Since the alternative to whiteness in the racial binary was to be considered black, and since black people were legally segregated and second-class citizens, whiteness made sense to some Mexican American leaders.[6]

The ferocity with which some Mexican Americans fought for inclusion in the white race was frequently intense. In newspaper articles, letters of protest to government officials, lawsuits, and public protests, Mexican Americans demanded recognition as white people throughout the early 20th century. In some parts of the Southwest, this was more a simplistic battle about what Mexican-origin people should be called. For example, in New Mexico and Arizona, Mexican Americans preferred and occasionally demanded to be called Spanish Americans, Iberian Americans, or Hispanos, which connoted European ancestry.[7] In other cases, the battles were more intense. In Texas, for example, Mexican American leaders vigorously fought for and in many instances won recognition as white. They then had to fight to maintain that status.[8]

In other instances, Mexican Americans won important legal decisions by arguing for whiteness. A number of school desegregation cases bear this out. Similarly, and most importantly, *Hernandez v. Texas* (1954) cogently made an argument for including Mexican-origin people in the white race for the purpose of jury selection. In that case, Pete Hernandez was convicted of killing Joe Espinosa in 1951. Hernandez's lawyers appealed. That appeal went to the Supreme Court where, two weeks before the more famous *Brown v. Board of Education* decision, the court acknowledged that Mexican Americans were a recognized class of white people, and that their exclusion from Hernandez's jury pool was discriminatory.[9]

The problem with whiteness was that it complicated Mexican American relations with black people. African Americans generally interpreted whiteness negatively, viewing it as, at best, an attempt by Mexican Americans to curry favor with whites and, at worst, a fabricated identity that may have lifted some Mexican-origin people out of Jim Crow but left black people firmly segregated. Not all black people were offended by Mexican American white racialization, but such positioning could lead to hurt feelings that impeded collaboration. As one black Texan explained, Mexican American whiteness "didn't make us [African Americans] feel very good."[10]

Other instances of white racialization also marred collaborative efforts during the 1960s. For example, the Student Nonviolent Coordinating Committee (SNCC) originally welcomed the participation of whites, and by extension Mexican Americans. Several Mexican Americans joined the group in the South, especially the now well-known activists Elizabeth Martínez and María Varela. But in 1967 leaders in SNCC dismissed all whites, and SNCC became a major Black Power organization. Unfortunately, in dismissing whites the group also dismissed its Mexican American collaborators and severed ties with Mexican American civil rights groups.[11]

In fact, SNCC's earlier history illustrates its beginnings as a multiethnic group that welcomed all allies, white, black, and Mexican American. California's Bay Area chapter of SNCC not only had some Mexican American members but also pioneered a coalition with Cesar Chavez's National Farm Workers Association. SNCC activists in California not only joined forces with the farm workers, they in many cases trained the farm workers in nonviolent resistance, and provided technical assistance in the form of walkie-talkies so the farm workers could maintain communication during their protests; SNCC also promoted the NFWA's national boycott of grape products.[12] The presence of Mexican Americans in SNCC and the SNCC-NFWA alliance proved short-lived and ended when SNCC expelled all whites.

Other instances of cooperation are equally important. In California, blacks and Mexican Americans had since the 1930s joined in a number of efforts to battle the racism of the period. Some organizations assumed a more confrontational stance. For example, El Congreso de Pueblos de Habla Española (El Congreso, Congress of Spanish-speaking Peoples) developed in the 1930s. Founded by the labor organizer Luisa Moreno and led by the activists Eduardo Quevedo and Josefina Fierro de Bright, the group pushed an aggressive civil rights agenda. While often thought of as a Mexican American organization, El Congreso had a much bolder agenda of encouraging unity with all groups—Mexican American, African American, white liberal—interested in the uplift of under-represented people. The group therefore downplayed ethnic-racial differences in support of civil rights. Because of the anticommunist sentiment of the era, El Congreso was "red-baited" and folded in 1942.

It is also important to remember that while some Mexican Americans fought for whiteness through the courts, others employed different strategies that won the support of African American allies. In the 1948 *Mendez v. Westminster* school desegregation case, Mexican American families sued to integrate an Orange County, California, school district. Unlike the *Hernandez* case, *Mendez* did not rely on an argument that posited Mexican American whiteness as a reason for desegregation. Instead, the lawsuit argued that segregation violated the Fourteenth Amendment rights of Mexican Americans. The NAACP (National Association for the Advancement of Colored People) supported the case, and Thurgood Marshall coauthored an *amicus curiae* (friend of the court) brief. With this support, Mexican Americans won the case.

This type of coalition building continued into the activist phase of the civil rights period, with the alliances developed by members of the Chicano (a term then used by activists for Mexican American) Brown Berets and the Black Panther Party. The Panthers originated in 1966 in Oakland and quickly spread to other cities, such as Los Angeles. The Brown Berets were founded in 1968. Like the Panthers, they were a self-defense group aimed at protecting the Mexican American community from police brutality and other forms of state violence. Like its focus, the Brown Berets borrowed its structural organization from the Panthers. Additionally, similar to the Panthers, the Brown Berets promoted Chicano cultural nationalism, demanded strict discipline, and emphasized a particular notion of masculinity among its members, which not surprisingly resulted in a vast majority of its leadership being male.

The Brown Berets first major outing began in 1968 with the "LA Blowouts," massive protests of high school youths who decried the substandard education they received in Los Angeles. The Berets assisted in the organization of the Blowouts and protected the students from the police. In subsequent protests, especially anti-Vietnam War demonstrations, the Berets joined forces with the Panthers in Los Angeles. Numerous Brown Berets also participated in major protests the Panthers planned. While never a named coalition, many of the Berets and Panthers saw themselves as parallel organizations.[13]

Other radical groups also joined forces. The Black Panther Party, for instance, worked closely with Cesar Chavez and the United Farm Workers (UFW, formerly the NFWA). This was especially evident when BPP founder Bobby Seale became a candidate for mayor of Oakland in 1973. The BPP had previously supported the farm workers' opposition to California's Proposition 22, an initiative by California's agribusinesses designed to undercut the ability of farm workers to protest and strike. The BPP sided with the UFW and issued a number of statements encouraging black voters to reject the proposition in 1972. These efforts were successful, and the proposition was soundly voted down. This success encouraged more collaboration, and when Seale decided to run for mayor of Oakland, the UFW supported his candidacy. Bobby Seale openly courted the Mexican American vote, published campaign material in English and Spanish, and included African Americans and Mexican Americans equally in his campaign. The BPP also won the endorsement of Cesar Chavez. Despite this flurry of activism, Seale lost the election.[14]

For African Americans and Mexican Americans, race relations and cross-ethnic civil rights efforts proved somewhat of a mixed bag. While in the 1940s and 1950s these groups frequently had difficulty working together, by the 1960s and 1970s avenues for more cooperative efforts presented themselves. Part of the increase in cooperation is attributable to the civil rights reforms of the 1960s and the diminishing ideological power of whiteness at this time. More importantly, as both groups grew in relative numbers and strength, many activists recognized the power that came with cooperation. While their efforts were not always successful, coalition building became a far more potent tactic than more divisive strategies, such as white racial positioning or attempting to fight battles alone.

AFRICAN AMERICANS AND PUERTO RICANS

Puerto Ricans and African Americans have generally lived close to one another, in the United States and on the island, and have typically shared a closer relationship than blacks and Mexican Americans. Puerto Rican settlement in New York City is a good example of this. El Barrio, Manhattan's neighborhood of Puerto Rican settlement, is directly adjacent to Harlem, historically the neighborhood with the highest concentration of African Americans in the city. Puerto Rico's multiethnic population had already facilitated a more collaborative dialogue between the two groups in places as diverse as New York City and Chicago. Puerto Rico's African-origin

population certainly gave some nonblack Puerto Ricans a vantage point through which to view African Americans. The many writings of Jesús Cólon, such as *A Puerto Rican in New York* (1961), detailed life in New York City from both black and Latino/a positions. For their part, African American civil rights activists tended also to welcome Puerto Rican allies.[15]

There are numerous instances of cooperative relations and civil rights activism shared by blacks and Puerto Ricans. One good way to see this is by exploring the history of labor unions. In New York City, the International Ladies Garment Workers' Union (ILGWU) had for decades had a large percentage of Latina and African American women. By the 1950s and 1960s, women of color predominated in at least six of the major locals of the ILGWU. Despite their numbers, almost all of these women were rank-and-file union members who held the lowest-paying jobs in the workforce and had no real presence in the union's, or their local's, leadership. They had also experienced a great deal of discrimination from management as well as union leaders. By the 1960s they were no longer willing to accept this abuse.[16]

African American and Puerto Rican workers began constructing strategic alliances within labor movements after a series of congressional investigations in the early 1960s. There was initially some give and take regarding the supposed similarities and differences of black and Puerto Rican experiences in the unions. While some saw hope for unity, others saw a long history of conflict. But within the union they learned from one another, and via the ILGWU's Training Institute some blacks and Puerto Ricans were able to craft their own positions of authority and leadership. Moreover, a Puerto Rican sense of being an oppressed minority group similar to African Americans facilitated greater unity in the unions. That greater sense of unity also helped cross-ethnic alliances develop outside of the unions.[17]

These cross-ethnic alliances were particularly visible in settlement house work and
education. One leader, Manny Diaz, had
gained an education in leadership via the
unions, and later became involved in settlement work. Diaz, for instance, found white
settlement workers much more amenable to
ethnic leadership and programs specifically
for members of ethno-racial communities
than were the unions. The same was also true
for those interested in improving black and
Puerto Rican access to education. Diaz found
great unity in a group called Mobilization for
Youth (MFY), which began as a settlement
house initiative designed to combat juvenile
delinquency. Blacks and Puerto Ricans also
developed a similar united group called the
United Bronx Parents (UBP). This group used
a community control model to fight against
the marginalization of minority schoolchildren, who in the Bronx made up the vast majority of students. The UBP aimed to unite
marginalized people and their school-age children in a multiethnic coalition that would
utilize the distinct sense of cultural nationalism (itself a product of 1960s activism) to
promote expanded and culturally sensitive
educational reforms for black and Puerto
Rican youths.[18]

Perhaps nothing better illustrates the collaborative mission of Puerto Ricans and African
Americans than the militant organizations of
the period, especially Chicago's Black Panther
Party and the Young Lords. The charismatic
Fred Hampton first organized the Chicago
chapter of the BPP in 1968. The Young Lords,
led by Jose "Cha Cha" Jimenez, were initially
a territorial gang that morphed into a civil
rights group in 1968. Hampton and Jimenez
worked closely together, and the foundational
documents of both groups, particularly their
programs, mirrored one another. The BPP's
ten-point program called for full employment
for black people, opposed military service
(then compulsory for US men) for blacks,
and advocated community control and armed
self-defense, an end to police brutality, and

the creation of a socialist society, among other
points. The Young Lords' thirteen-point program included self-determination for Puerto
Ricans, community control of institutions and
land, bilingual and bicultural education, opposition to military service, armed self-defense
and armed struggle, and a socialist society,
among other points. Thus the two groups
mirrored each other, and in Chicago the two
organizations were quickly spliced into the
broader Rainbow Coalition.[19]

The original Rainbow Coalition established
by Hampton was a multiethnic group that
had broad goals, which included greater political representation for under-represented
groups, an end to police brutality, and access
to programs of the federal War on Poverty established in the mid-1960s. One of the group's
most noteworthy achievements had to do
with gang violence. Jimenez, Hampton, and
other leaders rightly believed that gang warfare diminished the strength of ethnic communities and was a tool used by local white
politicians for political gain. So the Rainbow
Coalition successfully brokered a number of
treaties between various gangs to end this violence. Such treaties also helped to facilitate
another goal of the Rainbow Coalition, ending
police brutality. With an easing of tension and
violence between rival gangs, police involvement, they hoped, would be lessened in the
various ethnic neighborhoods in Chicago.[20]

African American and Puerto Rican coalitions also proved significant in other areas
where the Young Lords operated chapters.
While the New York City branch did not
work as closely with black activists as did the
Chicago branch, the New York Young Lords
maintained ties with Black Power leaders. In
other locales where there were no established
BPP or Young Lords chapters, the two communities worked in tandem. In Camden,
New Jersey, for example, black and Puerto
Rican activists came together after police killed
an unarmed Puerto Rican man in 1971. Instead
of the established civil rights groups, blacks
and Puerto Ricans joined forces in a grassroots

effort to demand changes in how the police treated minority suspects. They also participated in a massive rally to convince the city government to alter police procedures. The city's inaction ultimately led to a riot in Camden, a multiethnic upheaval that forcefully demanded rights denied to local communities of color. While not much changed with the city government or police, the riot did cement relations with black and Puerto Rican activists, who found great strength in collaborative activism.[21]

African Americans and Puerto Ricans, then, tended to have a more cooperative type of race relations. Their unity, of course, took work, but the coalitions pioneered by labor leaders, parents interested in better education, or activist groups such as the Young Lords and the Black Panthers represented a spirit of cooperation that was often harder to establish where blacks and Mexican Americans battled for rights. Such coalitions also proved difficult between African Americans and Cuban/Cuban Americans.

BLACK AND CUBAN AMERICAN RELATIONS

The black freedom struggle in Miami, Florida, had been going on for many years when large numbers of Cuban exiles began settling in the city after Fidel Castro's successful revolution in Cuba in 1959. Numerous Cubans, especially those with the means to leave or those with jobs in American corporations, fled Cuba after Castro took over. They experienced significant hardships and were often forced to leave with nothing more than the clothes they were wearing. The US government, as well as Florida and Miami-Dade County governments, all responded with a variety of social aid programs designed to assist the Cuban exiles. And therein lay the tension for local black people.[22]

The aid Cubans received ranged from access to social welfare programs to increased enrollment in local universities. Cubans also

eventually received expedited citizenship and access to federal home and business loans, to name just a few of the benefits offered by the US government. Moreover, politicians and Americans more generally tended to visualize and valorize Cubans as Cold War allies who deserved these benefits.[23] In contrast, African Americans had for generations been a part of what many in government viewed as the undeserving poor. As American citizens, black people felt entitled to such aid, but they could really only watch as the various levels of government bestowed social aid on noncitizens. This increased tension not only with Cuban exiles, but also with the various levels of government that seemed willing to empower Cuban immigrants while disempowering black Americans.[24]

For blacks in Miami, perhaps nothing better illustrated the unfairness of this situation than the battle to integrate local schools. For years after the 1954 *Brown* decision, black residents had attempted to enroll their children in segregated white schools. When local schools did begin admitting a few black children, the response of white people was to withdraw their children from the schools, resulting in massive white flight from Miami-area schools. When Cubans began arriving, the district willingly admitted Cuban children and began offering an extensive program designed to help these children adjust to life in the United States, including an accelerated English language instruction program. As such, local government responses facilitated Cuban integration into the school system while continuing to deny black people access to quality education.[25]

The situation in Miami, and in other communities where Cuban migrants settled, exacerbated tensions between African Americans and Cubans. Some Cubans readily accepted this situation, adopting a distinctly conservative political outlook that, as they saw it, would help protect the benefits bestowed by federal, state, and local governments. Other Cubans, however, were really being used as pawns by

US anticommunists. They had no distinct animus toward black people and were perhaps ignorant of how black people might have felt about the situation. To put this differently, the tension between Cubans and African Americans was not solely the fault of the Cuban exiles. Instead, government practices in distributing aid and the competition for government assistance created a tense environment that prevented Cuban–African American cooperation.

MULTIETHNIC COALITIONS: THE POOR PEOPLE'S CAMPAIGN

African Americans and Latino/as had pioneered coalitions locally in cities as diverse as Chicago, New York City, Houston, or Los Angeles, but a nationally focused coalition was a major task of the various civil rights struggles in the mid-1960s. Of the attempts at coalition building, none proved more important than the Poor People's Campaign (PPC). The PPC was the brainchild of Martin Luther King Jr., who viewed combating poverty as the second phase of the civil rights movement. King sent out a call for activists to meet in Atlanta in 1968 at a gathering that came to be called the Minority Group Conference. The conference was attended by representatives of almost every major ethnic group in the country, including Mexican Americans, Puerto Ricans, Native Americans, and poor whites.[26] King was, however, ignorant of the specific issues of his nonblack allies, which convinced some Latino/as that the PPC was not a worthwhile venture. For example, José Angel Gutiérrez, an important activist Mexican American from Texas, had asked King, "Is this another black-white thing or are we involved?"[27] Gutiérrez was evidently dissatisfied with King's response; he and others from Texas did not participate in the campaign. Similarly, Cesar Chavez did not attend the Minority Group Conference, even though he had been invited. Chavez saw the PPC as having little chance of success, and he worried that joining the campaign might weaken his union work in California.[28]

Others, however, chose to attempt to work out their differences with King and the other activists involved in the PPC. As opposed to simply seeing ignorance, some leaders, such as the New Mexican land reform activist Reies López Tijerina, chose to educate King about Mexican American land issues. Colorado's Rodolfo "Corky" Gonzales made it clear that he and other activists in his Crusade for Justice would participate, but on an equal footing with King and the other black leaders. Thus Gonzales stressed the equal leadership role that all the groups would share, instead of simply presuming that the PPC would be led by King or other African American leaders. A spirit of cooperation was established, therefore, when Latino/a leaders demanded an equal place at the table.[29]

King was assassinated only a few months after the Minority Group Conference. The activists involved in the conference wondered if the PPC would go forward after his death. Ralph David Abernathy, King's hand-picked successor, made the PPC a memorial to King, telling the other groups involved in the campaign that King's death, which came during a sanitation workers' strike in Memphis, Tennesee, was demonstrative of the deleterious effects of poverty in the United States. The PPC went forward.[30]

After King's assassination, Abernathy organized a massive gathering in Washington, DC., to protest the nation's treatment of poor people and expand the attention given them by the federal government. The nation's capital offered an excellent venue for this goal. Activists constructed a tent city at the National Mall. Resurrection City, as it came to be called, would house the activists who traveled to Washington, DC. From Resurrection City, volunteers could march through the capital, picket the Supreme Court, and demand that Congress pass legislation that addressed the needs of the nation's poor.[31]

The protest brought thousands of activists from across the county to Washington, DC. These included African Americans, Mexican Americans, Puerto Ricans, whites, and Native

Americans. But the protests in the capital quickly spun out of control. The Federal Bureau of Investigation (FBI) disrupted the campaign. The FBI's actions including spreading misinformation about the campaign, infiltrating PPC protests and meetings, and using paid informants to report on the campaign's activities. Moreover, Resurrection City experienced numerous problems. Several days of rain left the camp a muddy, flooded mess. Some of the groups involved in the campaign also had trouble working together. Black leaders did not treat the Latino/a and Native American participants particularly well, and some of the latter felt excluded from leadership. Tijerina commented that "the black militants seem to have taken over out here and nobody gets a chance to talk."[32] He and other Mexican Americans threatened to leave the protest. Mexican Americans eventually abandoned Resurrection City and relocated to the Hawthorne School, a private experimental academy.

In the end, the PPC did not generate the kind of response from government, nor the long-lasting unity between different peoples of color, that the campaign's organizers had hoped it would. While the Poor People's Campaign was for many years decried as a failure, it did produce some results. First, although cross-ethnic alliances generated by the campaign did not last long, their occurrence remains important. Second, the campaign taught leaders from a variety of communities important lessons about coalition building. Third, although the coalition itself fell apart, it strengthened bonds within at least some of the groups involved. This was particularly true for Mexican American activists, who found via the campaign an increased sense of awareness about the Mexican-origin community across the United States as well as greater unity among the various state-level Mexican American activist groups.[33]

Thus, African American and Latino/a relations illustrate a long, complex history in a nation where race consciousness remained strong throughout the 20th century. For many years before the civil rights era, blacks and Latino/as were often distant from one another, separated by the segregation of the era or by perceived ideological and philosophical differences. The racial dynamics at work in the United States also often inhibited close relationship. In particular, the racial binary in numerous American cities and towns, with its distinct black-white dichotomy, tended to fracture close relationships. This was especially true when Latino/a people positioned themselves as members of the "white race." Blacks did not tend to look favorably upon this racial positioning, or they tended to ignore Latino/as because of it.

During the civil rights era, however, more chances for interaction presented themselves. The activism of the period often necessitated a close working relationship between these groups. This was especially true during the more militant phases of the movement, when Black Power and Brown Power or Puerto Rican Power activists came together to discuss coalitions, borrow ideas and tactics, and generate new campaigns. This proved true when blacks and Latino/as shared similar problems, especially police brutality and poverty. As such, the civil rights era represented a unique moment when these groups actively worked to improve their own race relations in order to more effectively combat the racism(s) that they encountered.

DISCUSSION OF THE LITERATURE

A growing body of scholarship on black/Latino/a relations has emerged within the past decade or so. This scholarship has generally fallen into several different methods or modes of discussion. Some studies compare the various communities and their civil rights movements, discussing the protests of the groups in relation to one another. Others tend to explore relations by examining the coalitions that blacks and Latino/as forged. Still other works treat specific groups, their organizations, and their histories in distinct chapters. Much of this literature focuses on a regional, state, or city level. Finally, there is a growing body of literature on relations viewed from the perspective of culture.

Generally speaking, the comparative type of scholarship has tended to be the most popular way of writing about blacks and Latino/as. Neil Foley's *Quest for Equality* (2010) and Brian Behnken's *Fighting Their Own Battles* (2011) are good examples. Foley examines Mexican American and African American efforts to end employment discrimination in the defense industries during World War II and to integrate schools after the war. He shows that differences in group power, class level, and ideology made strategic alliances for African Americans and Mexican Americans difficult. Behnken has a similar approach, but one more specifically focused on the civil rights activism of the 1950s to 1970s. He explores well-known types of protest activism such as sit-ins or boycotts, and periods such as the Black Power and Brown Power eras.

One state-focused volume, looking at different communities in different chapters, is Mark Brilliant's excellent study *The Color of America Has Changed* (2010). Brilliant's overall goal is to present a multiethnic account of what he calls California's "wide civil rights movement." His ultimate conclusions mirror those of other scholars who have analyzed the gains and pitfalls of multiracial civil rights struggles. In a similar approach, Lauren Araiza in *To March for Others* (2013) concentrates on coalition building among African American and Mexican American activists in the San Francisco Bay area in the late 1960s and early 1970s. That chronology is important to her focus, as Araiza is able to bypass the earlier, tenser moments in California's civil rights history. She notes that activists in SNCC assisted Cesar Chavez's National Farm Workers Association. Araiza also shows how the Black Panther Party worked with the farm workers well into the 1970s. Shana Bernstein also provides a unique perspective on Los Angeles in *Bridges of Reform* (2011). She explores the cooperative activism generated by the

anticommunism of the 1940s. In fact, she asserts that the Cold War climate, which has usually been seen as destructive to civil-rights efforts, actually facilitated coalition building, as blacks and browns battled not only for civil rights but also for protection in an unwelcoming political environment.

Sonia Lee's *Building a Latino Civil Rights Movement* (2014) is an excellent account of Puerto Rican–African American activism and relations in the New York City area. She joins a host of scholars, from Lorrin Thomas to Brian Purnell, to explore race and civil rights in that city. Lee pays particular attention to how black activism spurred Puerto Rican activism. She demonstrates how Puerto Ricans initially looked to black activism hesitantly, but over time they came to see the many connections between the Puerto Rican community and the African American community. Jakobi Williams takes a similar approach in *From the Bullet to the Ballot* (2015), which focuses on Chicago. He shows how the original Rainbow Coalition was conceived by Fred Hampton to bring together activists there. In 1969, Cha Cha Jimenez and the Young Lords organization joined forces with the BPP in the Rainbow Coalition. The two groups had many similarities, especially their focus on community control and their own experiences in the city of Chicago. Frederick Douglass Opie's *Upsetting the Apple Cart* (2014) concentrates on black and Latino civil rights efforts in both New York City and Chicago, and he also focuses on Puerto Ricans and Cuban Americans, as well as a few other Latino/a groups. This makes his book more inclusive as to the cast of Latino/a characters.

Gordon Mantler's *Power to the Poor* (2013) is a wide-ranging account of the Poor People's Campaign. Mantler's focus is more national in scope and demonstrates that the PPC was one of the key moments in African American and Latino/a coalition building. He documents the long history of antipoverty activism in the United States, noting that multiple strands of it existed long before the PPC.

He also shows that while the campaign itself ultimately failed and the connections made by various activists of color rarely lasted beyond the campaign, the PPC produced numerous intraracial benefits, especially for the burgeoning Chicano movement.

Other scholars examine relations though the lens of culture. Danny Widener, Luis Alvarez, and Gaye Theresa Johnson have explored ethnic relations via the impact of music on black-Latino/a interactions. Widener and Alvarez's work (2012) on "brown-eyed soul" music is particularly relevant given that they focus on music as well as night life, highlighting the ways blacks and Mexican Americans/Latinos came together for recreation and social protest. Johnson's work (2013) is similarly important. She explores how the racial geography of Los Angeles and the cultural, especially musical, alliances of blacks and browns led to a social activism built around solidarity and sound.

Finally, there is a growing body of literature that positions African American–Latino/a relations within an international framework. Laura Pulido (2006) and Cynthia Young (2006) have explored interactions from a discursive, Third World Internationalism viewpoint. Frank Guridy (2010) and Jesse Hoffnung-Garskof (2010) push international analysis further, exploring racial issues at multiple transnational sites. Hoffnung-Garskoff, for example, examines African American, Dominican, and Afro-Latino interaction in both Santo Domingo and New York City. Guridy's *Forging Diaspora* (2010) is an excellent account of the transnational relationships developed by African Americans and Afro-Cubans that reinforced, and united, both groups in a shared battle against racism and oppression.

PRIMARY SOURCES

Primary sources that examine black and Latino/a relations and civil rights are often difficult to discover because archivists tend to catalog these items within a particular ethno-racial framework. The papers of a well-known individual who pioneered cross-ethnic alliances, such as those of Rodolfo "Corky" Gonzales are found under keywords like "Mexican American Leadership – Colorado" or "Mexican Americans – Civil Rights – West (U.S.)." There is no subject keyword that indicates Gonzales's involvement in collaborative civil rights activism with African Americans, and therefore to discover his involvement historians must search within the collection itself. Primary sources that detail black/Latino relations are thus difficult to locate and often involve exploring multiple collections from individuals and organizations.

There are numerous collections pertaining to individual black and Latino/a leaders. For some important collections pertaining to prominent black and Latino/a leaders, researchers should explore the voluminous papers of Martin Luther King Jr., at the King Center for Peace and Nonviolent Social Change; the Cesar Chavez papers at Wayne State University; the papers of Rodolfo "Corky" Gonzales at the Denver Public Library; the Reies López Tijerina papers at the University of New Mexico, Albuquerque; and the José Angel Gutiérrez papers at the University of Texas, San Antonio. Researchers should also consider exploring the various organizations these individuals, and others like them, were associated with. This would include the papers of the Southern Christian Leadership Conference at the King Center; the United Farm Workers papers at Wayne State; the Alianza Federal de Pueblos Libres collection at the University of New Mexico; and the Raza Unida Party papers at the University of Texas.

There also exists a host of organizational archival collections across the United States. The University of Texas has a massive collection relating to the League of United Latin American Citizens. The papers of the National Association for the Advancement of Colored People, the Student Nonviolent Coordinating

Committee, and the Congress of Racial Equality were microfilmed and are available at many libraries. The Young Lords Collection is housed at DePaul University.

A number of universities and public libraries house collections relating to local and statewide figures and groups. For examples of a few libraries and a few collections, see the Eldridge Cleaver papers at the University of California, Berkeley; the George I. Sánchez papers at the University of Texas; the Bayard Rustin papers at Duke University; the Ella Baker papers at the Schomburg Center of the New York Public Library; the Mario G. Obledo papers at the University of California, Davis; or the Ernesto Galarza Papers at Stanford University.

Additional primary materials such as legal cases and oral history interviews are available in many of the archival collections mentioned above. Some legal records are also available digitally on open-access sites such as findlaw .com and on subscription sites such as lexisnexis.com or westlaw.com. Some government documents are available at the Library of Congress and the National Archives and Records Administration. State governments also collect voluminous archival material, most of which is available at libraries in state capitals.

DIGITAL MATERIAL

Relatively little of the material on African American and Latino/a civil rights and relations has been digitized. For a few examples, see the following.

Herman Baca Collection, University of California, San Diego. http://library.ucsd.edu/dc/collection /bb03768122.

Civil Rights in Black and Brown. https://crbb.tcu .edu/.

FURTHER READING

Alvarez, Luis, and Danny Widener. "Brown-Eyed Soul: Popular Music and Cultural Politics in Los Angeles." In *The Struggle in Black and Brown*, edited by Brian D. Behnken, 211–236. Lincoln: University of Nebraska Press, 2012.

Araiza, Lauren. *To March for Others: The Black Freedom Struggle and the United Farm Workers.* Philadelphia: University of Pennsylvania Press, 2013.

Behnken, Brian D. *Fighting Their Own Battles: Mexican Americans, African Americans, and the Struggle for Civil Rights in Texas.* Chapel Hill: University of North Carolina Press, 2011.

Behnken, Brian D., ed. *The Struggle in Black and Brown: African American and Mexican American Relations during the Civil Rights Era.* Lincoln: University of Nebraska Press, 2012.

Bernstein, Shana. *Bridges of Reform: Interracial Civil Rights Activism in Twentieth-Century Los Angeles.* New York: Oxford University Press, 2011.

Brilliant, Mark. *The Color of America Has Changed: How Racial Diversity Shaped Civil Rights Reform in California, 1941–1978.* New York: Oxford University Press, 2010.

Foley, Neil. *Quest for Equality: The Failed Promise of Black-Brown Solidarity.* Cambridge, MA: Harvard University Press, 2010.

Hoffnung-Garskof, Jesse. *A Tale of Two Cities: Santo Domingo and New York after 1950.* Princeton, NJ: Princeton University Press, 2010.

Guridy, Frank Andre. *Forging Diaspora: Afro-Cubans and African Americans in a World of Empire and Jim Crow.* Chapel Hill: University of North Carolina Press, 2010.

Johnson, Gaye Theresa. *Spaces of Conflict, Sounds of Solidarity: Music, Race, and Spatial Entitlement in Los Angeles.* Los Angeles: University of California Press, 2013.

Kun, Josh. *Audiotopia: Music, Race, and America.* Los Angeles: University of California Press, 2005.

Lee, Sonia Song-Ha. *Building a Latino Civil Rights Movement: Puerto Ricans, African Americans, and the Pursuit of Racial Justice in New York City.* Chapel Hill: University of North Carolina Press, 2014.

Mantler, Gordon K. *Power to the Poor: Black-Brown Coalition and the Fight for Economic Justice, 1960– 1974.* Chapel Hill: University of North Carolina Press, 2013.

Opie, Frederick Douglass. *Upsetting the Apple Cart: Black-Latino Coalitions in New York City from Protest to Public Office.* New York: Columbia University Press, 2014.

Pulido, Laura. *Black, Brown, Yellow, and Left: Radical Activism in Los Angeles.* Berkeley: University of California Press, 2006.

Purnell, Brian. *Fighting Jim Crow in the County of Kings: The Congress of Racial Equality in Brooklyn.* Lexington: University Press of Kentucky, 2013.

Reitan, Ruth. *The Rise and Decline of an Alliance: Cuba and African American Leaders in the 1960s.* East Lansing: Michigan State University Press, 1999.

Rose, Chanelle N. *The Struggle for Black Freedom in Miami: Civil Rights and America's Tourist Paradise 1896–1968.* Baton Rouge: Louisiana State University Press, 2015.

Sánchez-Korrol, Virginia E. *From Colonia to Community: The History of Puerto Ricans in New York City.* Berkeley: University of California Press, 1994.

Thomas, Lorrin. *Puerto Rican Citizen: History and Political Identity in Twentieth-Century New York.* Chicago: University of Chicago Press, 2014.

Williams, Jakobi. *From the Bullet to the Ballot: The Illinois Chapter of the Black Panther Party and Racial Coalition Politics in Chicago.* Chapel Hill: University of North Carolina Press, 2015.

Young, Cynthia A. *Soul Power: Culture, Radicalism, and the Making of a U.S. Third World Left.* Durham, NC: Duke University Press, 2006.

NOTES

1. Arnoldo De León, *They Called Them Greasers: Anglo Attitudes toward Mexicans in Texas, 1821–1900* (Austin: University of Texas Press, 1983).
2. Rubén Donato, *The Other Struggle for Equal Schools: Mexican Americans During the Civil Rights Movement* (New York: State University of New York Press, 1997).
3. Brian D. Behnken, *Fighting Their Own Battles: Mexican Americans, African Americans, and the Struggle for Civil Rights in Texas* (Chapel Hill: University of North Carolina Press, 2011).
4. Lisa Y. Ramos, "Not Similar Enough: Mexican American and African American Civil Rights Struggles in the 1940s," in *The Struggle in Black and Brown: African American and Mexican American Relations during the Civil Rights Era*, ed. by Brian D. Behnken (Lincoln: University of Nebraska Press, 2012).
5. Peggy Pascoe, *What Comes Naturally: Miscegenation Law and the Making of Race in America*

(New York: Oxford University Press, 2010), 205–230.
6. Neil Foley, *The White Scourge: Mexicans, Blacks, and Poor Whites in Texas Cotton Culture* (Berkeley: University of California Press, 1999).
7. Laura E. Gómez, *Manifest Destinies: The Making of the Mexican American Race* (New York: New York University Press, 2007).
8. Behnken, *Fighting Their Own Battles*, 62–63.
9. Ignacio M. García, *White But Not Equal: Mexican Americans, Jury Discrimination, and the Supreme Court* (Tucson: University of Arizona Press, 2009).
10. Behnken, *Fighting Their Own Battles*, 215.
11. Lauren Araiza, *To March for Others: The Black Freedom Struggle and the United Farm Workers* (Philadelphia: University of Pennsylvania Press, 2013).
12. Lauren Araiza, "Complicating the Beloved Community: The Student Nonviolent Coordinating Committee and the National Farm Workers Association," in *The Struggle in Black and Brown*, ed. Brian D. Behnken (Lincoln: University of Nebraska Press, 2012).
13. Laura Pulido, *Black, Brown, Yellow, and Left: Radical Activism in Los Angeles* (Berkeley: University of California Press, 2006).
14. Araiza, *To March for Others*.
15. Virginia E. Sánchez-Korrol, *From Colonia to Community: The History of Puerto Ricans in New York City* (Berkeley: University of California Press, 1994); Miguel "Mickey" Melendez, *We Took the Streets: Fighting for Latino Rights with the Young Lords* (New Brunswick, NJ: Rutgers University Press, 2005).
16. Sonia Song-Ha Lee, *Building a Latino Civil Rights Movement: Puerto Ricans, African Americans, and the Pursuit of Racial Justice in New York City* (Chapel Hill: University of North Carolina Press, 2014).
17. Lee, *Building a Latino Civil Rights Movement*.
18. Lee, *Building a Latino Civil Rights Movement*.
19. Jakobi Williams, *From the Bullet to the Ballot: The Illinois Chapter of the Black Panther Party and Racial Coalition Politics in Chicago* (Chapel Hill: University of North Carolina Press, 2015).
20. Williams, *From the Bullet to the Ballot*.
21. Lauri Lahey, "'Justice Now!, ¡Justicia Ahora!' African American-Puerto Rican Radicalism in Camden, New Jersey," in *Civil Rights and Beyond:*

African American and Latino/a Activism in the Twentieth-Century United States, ed. Brian D. Behnken (Athens: University of Georgia Press, 2016).

22. María Cristina García, *Havana USA: Cuban Exiles and Cuban Americans in South Florida, 1959–1994* (Los Angeles: University of California Press, 1997).

23. García, *Havana USA.*

24. Chanelle Nyree Rose, *The Struggle for Black Freedom in Miami: Civil Rights and America's Tourist Paradise, 1896–1968* (Baton Rouge: Louisiana State University Press, 2015).

25. Rose, *The Struggle for Black Freedom in Miami.* Chanelle Nyree Rose, "Beyond 1959: Cuban Exiles, Race, and Miami's Black Freedom Struggle," in *Civil Rights and Beyond,* ed. Brian D. Behnken (Athens: University of Georgia Press, 2016).

26. Gordon K. Mantler, *Power to the Poor: Black-Brown Coalition and the Fight for Economic Justice, 1960–1974* (Chapel Hill: University of North Carolina Press, 2013).

27. Gordon K. Mantler, "Black, Brown, and Poor: Civil Rights and the Making of the Chicano Movement," in *The Struggle in Black and Brown,* ed. Brian D. Behnken (Lincoln: University of Nebraska Press, 2012), 165.

28. Mantler, "Black, Brown, and Poor."

29. Mantler, *Power to the Poor.*

30. Mantler, *Power to the Poor.*

31. Mantler, *Power to the Poor.*

32. Behnken, *Fighting Their Own Battles,* 151.

33. Mantler, *Power to the Poor.*

Brian D. Behnken

THE ASIAN AMERICAN MOVEMENT

By 1968, Asian immigrants and their descendants had been in the United States for over a century and had engaged in various forms of resistance to racism for many decades. However, the particular ideologies and forms of activism that characterized the "Asian American movement" only emerged with the dawn of Third World movements for power and self-determination in the late 1960s. Previously, Chinese, Japanese, Filipino, Korean, and Asian Indians participated in divergent forms of political organizing. Class-based politics aimed to gain better wages and working conditions; homeland politics attempted to bolster the international standings of their nations of origins or free them from colonial rule; assimilationist politics attempted to demonstrate that Asians were worthy of the rights and privileges of citizenship. None of these forms built a sense of common cause among Asian immigrants of different ethnicities, and homeland politics even exacerbated tensions. In the early to mid-1960s, a number of Asian Americans participated individually in various New Left movements—including the Free Speech Movement, Civil Rights movement, and anti-Vietnam War movement—that did not directly address Asian American issues. In contrast to these earlier forms of political activism, the Asian American movement emphasized Asian collectivity, arguing that Asians of all ethnicities in the United States shared a common position of subjugation due to anti-Asian racism, and furthermore, that Asians in the United States should oppose US imperialism abroad, especially in Asia. Drawing influences from the Black Power and antiwar movements, the Asian American movement forged a coalitional politics that united Asians of varying ethnicities and declared solidarity with other Third World people in the United States and abroad. Segments of the movement struggled for community control of education, provided social services and defended affordable housing in Asian ghettos / [predominant style in article], organized exploited workers, protested against US imperialism, and built new multiethnic cultural institutions. By the end of the 1970s, the contours of the movement shifted dramatically enough to mark an end to the Asian American movement per se, though certainly not an end to Asian American activism.[1]

ORIGINS

The Asian American movement grew out of two of the most significant social movements of the 1960s: the Black Power and anti-Vietnam War movements. Unsatisfied with insistence on inclusion and civil rights, the Asian American movement demanded self-determination and power both for Asians in the United States and in Asia. The Red Guard Party of San Francisco provides the clearest example of how engaging with Black Power helped Asian Americans build an understanding of their own racial positioning in the United States. The Black Panther Party for Self-Defense, established in 1966 by Huey Newton and Bobby Seale, rose to prominence as the vanguard organization among radicals of color by the late 1960s. The Panthers melded radical politics with racial pride, advocating community control over institutions such as education and law enforcement in black ghettos and demanding fair housing and employment, while celebrating the aesthetics of black people, black bodies, and black culture. This powerful mélange of ideas impacted Chinese Americans in the ghetto of San Francisco Chinatown, which suffered from substandard education, housing, social services, and employment opportunities, but an overabundance of police brutality. When a group of young people who congregated regularly at the Legitimate Ways pool hall on Jackson Street began to discuss how to address these conditions, the Panthers took notice, visiting the pool hall, inviting the Chinatown youth to study sessions on political theory, and urging them to form an organization. The Red Guard Party that arose was named after Mao's youth cadre and largely mirrored the Panthers' ideology and language, but with key adaptations. Where the Panthers advocated power for "black" people, the Red Guards demanded it for "yellow" people, a sign that the largely Chinese American Red Guards had adopted a racial, rather than ethnic rubric.

Minister of Information Alex Hing articulated the commonalities shared by blacks and Asian Americans, who both experienced racism and exploitation in the United States, and argued that the Panthers' example of directly providing social services (such as the free breakfast program) provided a viable model for Chinatown.

Across the Bay, in Berkeley, a graduate student named Yuji Ichioka, who would go on to be an influential historian, coined the term "Asian American" when he co-founded the Asian American Political Alliance (AAPA) as an explicitly pan-Asian organization in 1968. Seeking Asian Americans with progressive leanings, Ichioka and co-founder Emma Gee pored over / [usage] the roster of the antiwar Peace and Freedom Party, identifying all individuals with Asian last names and inviting them to join the new organization. AAPA thus included Chinese, Japanese, and Filipino Americans, both American-born and immigrants, from the mainland and Hawaii. AAPA advocated for Asian American solidarity to counter racism and imperialism and declared its camaraderie with other people of color in the United States and abroad. Richard Aoki, undoubtedly the most colorful member of the group, served as a Field Marshal of the Black Panther Party prior to helping to form AAPA.

On the East Coast, the formation of Asian Americans for Action (AAA), in 1969, demonstrated again how the Asian American movement drew together the influences of Black Power and the antiwar movement. Two long-time leftist Nisei (second generation Japanese American) women, Kazu Iijima and Minn Masuda, noted approvingly that the anti-racist and anti-imperialist politics preached by Black Power advocates like H. Rap Brown were also accompanied by a strong dose of racial pride. They saw Black Power as an antidote to the pro-assimilationist fever that had struck many Japanese Americans after their experiences in concentration camps during

World War II. They sought ways to convey this sense of pride to the next generation in their own community. Significantly, Iijima's son Chris urged them to reach out to all Asians, regardless of ethnicity. Iijima and Masuda's recruitment strategy resembled Ichioka's in that they organized within the antiwar movement by approaching every individual Asian they spotted at Vietnam protests. The best-known AAA member was Yuri Kochiyama, whose legendary radicalism formed through her relationship with Malcolm X, whom she counted as a personal friend.

Because it arose from encounters with Black Power and antiwar protests, the Asian American movement eschewed the Civil Rights framework in favor of pursuing self-determination for Asian Americans and all other Third World people in the United States, and opposing what it deemed to be a genocidal, anti-Asian war in Indochina.

ACTIVISM ON CAMPUS

A radical coalitional impulse characterized the Asian American movement from its inception onward, driving it to create multiethnic Asian organizations and pursue alliances with other people of color. The movement's actions aimed at revolutionizing higher education, clearly displayed this emphasis on building solidarity. Asian Americans participated in student strikes at San Francisco State College (1968–1969) and Cal Berkeley (1969), in both cases as members of Third World Liberation Fronts (TWLF) (although the Berkeley version was inspired by its counterpart at SF State and shared its ideals, there were no organizational ties between the two).[2] Students at the largely commuter campus of San Francisco State were politically active throughout the 1960s, protesting against the war, capital punishment, government repression, and racial discrimination. Perhaps most importantly, students operated tutoring and recruitment programs for youth in neighborhoods such as the predominantly black

Fillmore, the Mission, and Chinatown. In the spring semester of 1968, three Asian American organizations—AAPA (discussed above), Intercollegiate Chinese for Social Action (ICSA), and Pilipino American Collegiate Endeavor (PACE)—joined the Black Student Union, Latin American Student Organization (LASO), and Mexican American Student Confederation (MASC) to form the TWLF. The largely Japanese American members of the San Francisco chapter of AAPA, which shared the anti-racist and anti-imperialist politics of the original Berkeley chapter, worked on community issues such as opposing urban redevelopment in Japantown / [as elsewhere]. At the ICSA office on Clay Street, members tutored Chinatown youth and recruited them to apply for college. PACE members located their office in the Mission district, where they recruited Filipino high school students and community members to State and organized within the community. Like the other members of the TWLF coalition, all three of the Asian American groups sought to connect the college to the community, increase access for their community members, and transform the meaning of a college education.

The strike at San Francisco State began on November 6, 1968, with the TWLF issuing fifteen non-negotiable demands that collectively promised to revolutionize the college by according Third World people authority over the production and dissemination of knowledge about their communities, in terms of both curriculum and institutional control, and granting Third World applicants much greater access to admission and financial aid. TWLF members picketed campus, held large rallies and marches on campus, and fought running battles with police. At times class attendance dropped by 50 percent as the strike brought the campus to a near standstill. Acting President S. I. Hayakawa gleefully repressed the strikers, calling the San Francisco Police Department's Tactical Squad onto campus and having hundreds arrested over the course of the strike. Hayakawa, a Japanese American who had emigrated from Canada, presented a particular problem for Asian American strikers, as he positioned himself as a neutral arbiter between blacks and whites, in stark contrast to the strikers who understood Asian Americans to be a racially subjugated group positioned alongside other people of color. Thus, Asian Americans condemned Hayakawa as a "bootlicker" of California Governor Ronald Reagan and decidedly not a spokesman for their communities. After nearly five months of back-and-forth action and repressive police action, the TWLF signed a settlement on March 21, 1969, that ended the strike and created the first ever School of Ethnic Studies in the United States, composed of departments of American Indian studies, Asian American studies, Black studies, and La Raza studies.

Students at the prestigious University of California, Berkeley—where blacks, Chicana/os, and Native Americans made up only 1.5 percent of the student body—drew inspiration from their compatriots at SF State. The Afro-American Student Union (AASU), Asian American Political Alliance (AAPA), Mexican American Student Confederation (MASC), and Native American Student Union (NASU) formed the Berkeley version of the Third World Liberation Front. Student activists negotiated with administrators for months, suggesting reforms that would make the university more accessible, relevant, and responsive to their communities. Dissatisfied with the scope of institutional concessions and the pace of implementation, the TWLF called a strike on January 22, 1969. They demanded the establishment of a Third World College with departments of Asian studies, Black Studies, and Chicano studies subject only to community control, recruitment of Third World people in positions ranging from administrators to custodians, and full access to financial aid for Third World applicants. Unsurprisingly, the TWLF strike at Berkeley, famous as a roiling political cauldron from which

arose the Free Speech Movement and antiwar protests, featured impassioned picketers and demonstrators, along with violent police repression. The strike ended after three months, when, on March 19, the chancellor announced the formation of a department addressing the experiences of black, Mexican, Asian, and Native Americans. Both TWLF strikes concluded successfully, in the sense that they forced the establishment of academic units dedicated to ethnic studies; however, in neither case did the administrations grant oversight over the units to students and community members, nor did they cede control over financial aid.

Asian American students at the University of Hawai'i at Manoa and Seattle Central Community College also struggled to force their institutions to respond to the needs of their communities. In response to a 1969 proposal by students and community members for an Ethnic Studies unit that would address the histories and cultures of Native Hawaiian people and ethnic immigrants, the University of Hawai'i administration cannily agreed to create it, but only as an experimental program. Over the next eight years, Ethnic Studies was threatened repeatedly with dissolution, only to be rescued by student and community protests. The Board of Regents finally made the program permanent in 1977, but it did not become a degree-granting department until 1995. In Seattle, Alan Sugiyama and Mike Tagawa, who had been a member of the Black Panther Party, founded the Oriental Student Union in 1970. OSU picketed and occupied the Seattle Central administration building, demanding the hiring Asian American administrators, which echoed the calls for educational self-determination in San Francisco, Berkeley, and Honolulu. Today, the fact that Asian American Studies and Ethnic Studies are taught at innumerable colleges and universities across the nation provides a testament to the lasting impact of Asian American student activists who collaborated with like-minded allies.

SELF-DETERMINATION FOR COMMUNITIES

From Honolulu to New York, and many points in between, Asian American movement organizations sought to improve living and working conditions in urban ghettos and rural areas by operating "Serve the People" programs that provided badly needed social services, fighting against the displacement of poor people by urban redevelopment, and organizing workers.

In Hawai'i, Japanese, Chinese, and Filipino "locals" joined Native Hawaiians in 1970 and 1971 in their quest to preserve the then-rural Kalama Valley, located east of Honolulu. The powerful Bishop Estate that owned the land planned to evict the poor families and farmers who lived in the valley in order to build hotels, high-rise buildings, and a golf course. University of Hawai'i and antiwar activists formed the Kokua Kalama Committee (KKC) to support the residents. Members moved into the valley, erected tents, planted vegetable gardens, and did chores for farmers. Despite these efforts, the residents were eventually evicted. KKC transformed into Kokua Hawai'i, which fought for Native Hawaiian sovereignty from an anti-colonialist perspective, which enabled them to form relationships with other peoples colonized by the United States, including Puerto Ricans and Inuits, and also with Asian American radicals. Urban renewal also threatened Honolulu's Chinatown, where elderly Asian men lived in cheap residential hotels. A group called People Against Chinatown Evictions (PACE) opposed the destruction of the hotels and succeeded in forcing the city to construct replacement housing.

Asian American activists in Seattle struggled to preserve the International District (known fondly as "the ID"), the traditional home of Asian immigrant communities. Groups like Inter*Im, the International District Youth Council, and International District Drop-In Center vigorously opposed the construction of the Kingdome, a sports stadium that threatened to demolish affordable housing and destroy the character of the neighborhood. Seattle activists, who showed a greater willingness to work with city and federal officials than radicals in other locales, obtained funding from the Department of Housing and Urban Development to rehabilitate low-income apartments. Three hundred volunteers spent three years cleaning, repairing, and renovating the Milwaukee Hotel, one of the largest residential hotels in the ID. Asian American activists also provided food to the elderly, opened centers that provided counseling and legal services, and obtained state and local funding to establish a multilingual health clinic.

In San Francisco, the Red Guard Party took a cue from the Black Panther Party and started a Free Breakfast for kids program, but transitioned to a Free Sunday Brunch for elders to better meet the needs of Chinatown residents. Following the TWLF strike at Berkeley, in 1970 some AAPA members formed the Asian Community Center (ACC), which ran a drop-in center for elders, operated Everybody's Bookstore, provided food and health care, and screened films. ACC transitioned into the explicitly anti-imperialist Wei Min She ("Organization for the People") in 1971–1972. The struggle to save the International Hotel is one of the best-known sagas in Asian American movement history. The elderly Filipino men who lived in the decrepit hotel first received eviction notices in 1968, when the owner threatened to raze the building to build a parking lot. Numerous Asian American students, volunteers, and members of organizations including the I-Hotel Tenant's Association, KDP, Wei Min She, and I Wor Kuen repaired the hotel's decaying infrastructure, communed with the aging "manongs" who lived there, rented office space in the capacious basement, and managed to forestall the evictions until 1977. Similarly, the Committee Against Nihonmachi Eviction

(CANE) and the J-Town Collective unsuccessfully opposed the redevelopment of Japantown. Both IWK and WMS organized workers in the Chinatown garment industry, most visibly in the fractious Jung Sai strike of 1974–1975, which exposed contradictions within the movement around how various groups understood the relationships among race, class, and nation.[3]

Los Angeles was another critical site of Asian American struggle in the 1970s. The Little Tokyo People's Rights Organization and the Anti-Eviction Taskforce defended the historically Japanese American enclave of Little Tokyo against redevelopment, which threatened to displace affordable housing units and small ethnic businesses. Yellow Brotherhood and Asian American Hardcore organized among Asian male youth, while Asian Sisters fought drug abuse among young women. The East Wind collective, composed primarily of Japanese Americans, worked assiduously to develop relationships with other people of color. The UCLA Asian American Studies Center functioned as a hub for activists; several UCLA students created *Gidra*, the monthly newspaper published from 1969 to 1974, which became the unofficial newspaper of record for the Asian American movement. California's Central Valley saw the formation of the Yellow Seed organization in Stockton, and Asian American volunteers helped to build Agbayani Village, a United Farm Workers retirement home for elderly Chicano and Filipino laborers in Delano.

Although the West Coast—home of the majority of Asian Americans—produced the largest movement organizations, critical activism occurred on the East Coast as well. Beginning in 1971, the Philadelphia organization Yellow Seeds (unrelated to the Stockton Yellow Seed) fought to preserve the city's small Chinatown, provided translation services, job training, draft counseling, and advice on health care. From 1972 to 1977, its newspaper, *Yellow Seeds*, publicized the plight of elderly immigrants,

exposed the role of the Chinese Benevolent Association as a slumlord, and decried the exploitation of Chinatown workers. New York City spawned I Wor Kuen ("Righteous Harmonious Fists"), which took its name from the Chinese martial artists who took on British imperialism in the unsuccessful Boxer Rebellions. IWK aligned with the People's Republic of China, admired Mao, and argued for Asian American solidarity with other people of color. In Chinatown, IWK screened pro-Chinese films and faced physical repression from goons hired by the Chinese Consolidated Benevolent Association (CCBA), Chinatown's anti-communist power elite. On the affordable housing front, IWK supported Chinese and Italian American families facing eviction due to expansion by New York Telephone. The construction of Confucius Plaza, an enormous housing project in Chinatown, provided an opportunity for Asian American groups to demand employment for Asian American workers. In 1974, the radical group Asian Study Group (ASG) and its affiliate, Asian Americans for Equal Employment (AAFEE), protested against discriminatory hiring practices and also the CCBA's lackluster advocacy for the community. The police beating, in 1975, of a Chinese American architectural engineer named Peter Yew served as another lightning rod, drawing over 10,000 marchers to City Hall and sparking a sit-down in the middle of Broadway.

Asian American activism in these diverse locations centered on similar issues: land, housing, social services, and employment. Although the various movement organizations did not always agree with each other, and in fact disagreed vociferously at times, they shared commitments to safeguarding the character of traditionally Asian American neighborhoods, defending affordable housing, and preserving small ethnic businesses. Their "Serve the People" programs directly provided health care, food, legal and counseling services. Finally, they sought to increase access to jobs and organized for better wages and working conditions for Asian American workers.

INTERNATIONALISM AND INTERRACIALISM

A critical internationalism deeply shaped the Asian American movement. The nations of left Asia—the People's Republic of China, North Vietnam, and North Korea—provided exemplars that the movement admired; in some cases, Asian political activists played key roles in mobilizing Asian American movement organizations. Tracing the development of the Kalayaan collective and Katipunan ng mga Demokratikong Pilipino (KDP, or the Union of Democratic Filipinos) illustrates one case of how the melding of Asian leftists with US Third World activists produced a new, transnational formation. Philippine student activists associated with the Communist Party of the Philippines (CPP), who fled the country in the face of political repression, found common cause with Filipino Americans who had cut their teeth in Third World movements in the United States. The *Kalayaan* collective published a newspaper in 1971 and 1972, and its members formalized their organization as KDP in 1973, following President Ferdinand Marcos's declaration of martial law in the Philippines. KDP held a dual focus, advocating revolution in the Philippines and socialism in the United States. It mustered opposition to martial law, mobilized Filipino American youth by building a sense of Filipino ethnic pride, participated in the I-Hotel struggle, and defended two Filipina nurses, Narciso and Perez, in a famous trial for murder.[4]

Although most Asian American movement groups did not share KDP's direct tie to Asian activists, they were nevertheless deeply influenced by and admired Asian radicalism and performed solidarity work on Asian issues, particularly those linked to US militarism. The Vietnam War loomed as the largest international issue confronted by the Asian American movement. Although groups like AAPA and

AAA had arisen in part out of the antiwar movement, the Asian American movement adopted a distinctive line against the war. Whereas various antiwar groups opposed warfare in general, the disproportionate killing of black and brown soldiers, or the capitalist and imperialist aspects of the war, Asian Americans protesters objected specifically to its anti-Asian nature. In rallies, demonstrations, leaflets, flyers, newsletters, and newspapers, they criticized the war as genocidal against the Vietnamese people, whom they embraced as fellow Asians. Asian American contingents marched as cohesive groups within larger antiwar protests, flying the flags of left Asia and endorsing self-determination for the peoples of Indochina, whom they characterized as uniformly opposed to US intervention. Demonstrating against the war together created alliances among various movement organizations and enhanced their sense of Asian American identity as a shared multiethnic collective.

The Asian American movement's line against the war extended to its stance on many other international issues and its interpretation of the history of the Pacific. Every August, commemorations of the atomic bombings of Hiroshima and Nagasaki emphasized the US military's wanton disregard for Asian lives and situated the bombings within the long history of US militarism in Asia, noting the brutality of the US-Philippines War of 1898 and the occupations of the Philippines, Okinawa, Japan, and Korea. Movement groups, even those composed mostly of Japanese Americans, understood Japan to be a "running dog" of US imperialism and thus opposed the renewal of the US-Japan Security Pact, port visits by Japanese naval ships, and the expansion of Narita Airport outside of Tokyo. They also viewed Marcos as an instrument of US imperialism and opposed his dictatorship of the Philippines.

In contrast to its opposition to US militarism, the movement admired Asian nations that had thrown off the yoke of western imperialism, viewing mainland China as a shining example of the possibilities of Asian socialism. (Given what is now known about the human toll of the Cultural Revolution and the repressive nature of North Korea, we can say in retrospect that this perspective was based in part upon a lack of plausible information on communist Asia and also required a certain level of overly romantic political naïveté.) Several individuals, including Alex Hing of the Red Guard Party, antiwar activist Pat Sumi, and *Gidra* writer Evelyn Yoshimura traveled to places such as the People's Republic of China, North Vietnam, and North Korea. Their letters and testimonies praising the leaders of these nations and lauding the equality and lack of racism they found demonstrate the intensity of the desire among Asian American radicals to find alternatives to capitalism and imperialism. These longings were shared with radicals of all races during this period, and indeed, Hing and Sumi journeyed to Asia as members of Eldridge Cleaver's 1970 US People's Anti-Imperialist Delegation.[5]

The Asian American movement's support for anti-imperialist mobilizations abroad reflected its domestic agenda, which linked it closely to social movements for liberation among people of color in the United States. As discussed above, the Asian American movement emerged from engagements with Black Power advocates, and its campus activism proceeded in alliance with black, Chicano, and Native American students. In Los Angeles, Asian American activists lived and worked in multiracial neighborhoods with African Americans and Chicana/os; in New York, they collaborated with Puerto Ricans; in Honolulu, their efforts supported Native Hawaiians. *Gidra* covered the Black Panthers, Los Siete de la Raza (seven Latino youth charged with murder in San Francisco), the United Farm Workers, which combined Filipino and Mexican workers, the Chicano Moratorium against the war, the Young Lords Party, and Native American occupations of Alcatraz and Wounded Knee. As the 1970s wore on, various

Asian American organizations consolidated with a number of black, Chicano, and Latino radical groups to form multiracial parties, including the League of Revolutionary Struggle-Marxist Leninist, Line of March, and Revolutionary Union.[6]

GENDER AND WOMEN'S LIBERATION

The Asian American movement compiled an uneven record on gender equality. On the one hand, the movement generally admired Mao, who famously stated, "Women hold up half the sky." It tended to advocate for women's liberation, took up many women's issues, and featured women as prominent leaders of key organizations. On the other hand, however, its practices did not always live up to its ideological and rhetorical support for women's equality, as women often found themselves marginalized to support roles and subjected to sexual objectification. Asian American women caught in this contradiction linked racial justice to women's liberation, arguing that neither could be achieved without the other. They formed women's organizations, but located them within the larger Asian American movement rather than breaking away from it.

The Asian American movement addressed gender and women's issues in both its domestic and international agendas. Many local "Serve the People" programs attended to the needs of women and families, including provision of food, clothing, and health care. Asian American women's organizing has been best studied in Los Angeles, where the Asian Women's Center offered child care, counseling, and education and Asian Sisters identified the dual causes of drug abuse among young Japanese American women as racism, which made them feel inferior by enforcing white norms, and sexism, which devalued them within their own communities.[7] IWK and WMS stressed in their community work that traditional Asian gender roles oppressed women by subjugating them to fathers and husbands, but criticized in equally vociferous terms the system of capitalism that exploited women as wage workers and unpaid domestic laborers.

On the international front, the Asian American movement's critique of the Vietnam War took on a decidedly gendered perspective. The war's effect on women numbered among the movement's chief objections, as it noted that the war encouraged American GIs to view all Vietnamese women, and by extension all Asian women, as prostitutes. Conversely, the movement developed a great admiration for Vietnamese women, who personified principled resistance to US imperialism. A drawing published in *Gidra*, of a peasant woman with a baby in one hand and a rifle in the other, emblematized the belief that women could be revolutionary fighters as well as nurturers. Asian American women also drew inspiration from Vietnamese women whom they met in person at two conferences held in Canada in 1971, at which the Vietnamese women enthralled North American audiences with their explanation of their struggle for self-determination and their staunch resolution to achieve victory.[8]

Like their sisters in nearly all of the New Left and Power movements of the 1960s and 1970s, Asian American women battled sexism and male chauvinism, which sought to pigeonhole them as caretakers and support workers rather than recognizing them as leaders, public speakers, and intellectually talented theorists. However, women founded or co-founded AAPA and AAA and rose to leadership positions in KDP and IWK. Even when critiquing the sexism of the Asian American movement, women remained firmly entrenched within it because they understood the interlocking nature of racism and sexism. Even when carving out women-only spaces, they urged their brothers in the movement to reform their attitudes and practices and join in a shared fight to eliminate the overarching formation of racism, sexism, and class exploitation. For example, the International Hotel Women's Collective, formed by women participating in the I-Hotel struggle as parts of other organizations, called out men who sexualized and patronized women and sought to build both women's consciousness and leadership skills. In a missive explaining the collective's purpose, its members invited men to "support us in our goals by building relationships of mutual respect," which they signed, "With love, your sisters."[9] Thus, despite its significant flaws, the Asian American movement served as an arena in which women developed as activists and honed their abilities as leaders.

CULTURE

One of the signal achievements of the Asian American movement was to create the category of "Asian American" as a political identity that encompassed all Asian ethnicities in the United States. The power of this amalgamation can be seen in the emergence of Asian American art, literature, music, and cultural institutions during the movement period. During the movement period, the folk trio "A Grain of Sand" performed and recorded music that celebrated Asian American struggles for justice and expressed solidarity with black, Latino, Native American, and Vietnamese people. Asian American jazz emerged in the 1970s and 1980s, performed by artists including the jazz-fusion group "Hiroshima," saxophonist and political activist Fred Ho, and the musicians associated with AsianImprov Records, all of whom sought to articulate Asian American aesthetics, culture, and politics, though with varying emphases.[10]

Community-based arts organizations fostered artistic expressions that documented and celebrated Asian American history, experiences, and cultures and used art as a way to mobilize and empower communities. Basement Workshop (BW), the most important Asian American cultural institution on the East Coast, began in 1970, in New York City's Chinatown, but soon incorporated other Asian American writers and artists. Its Creative Arts Program introduced community members to creative writing, music, and visual arts including photography and silk screening, and its Chinatown cleanup program painted street murals. In addition, BW published *Bridge*, a bimonthly magazine covering Asian cultural and political issues in the United States and abroad, from 1971 to 1978. San Francisco's Kearny Street Workshop (KSW) began in 1972, in the basement of the I-Hotel. Like its East Coast counterpart, KSW soon blossomed into a multiethnic organization that integrated arts education and community empowerment. KSW offered workshops in crafts such as making jewelry and stained glass, photography, silk screening, and creative writing. KSW artists painted a block-long mural depicting Asian workers on the I-Hotel and produced the images that became the visual icons of the struggle to save the hotel.

Asian American theater also thrived during the movement period.[11] The most significant theater companies included East West Players in Los Angeles, Pan Asian Repertory Theater in New York City, Asian American Theater Workshop in San Francisco, and Asian Exclusion Act in Seattle. Each of these organizations produced works by playwrights of varying ethnicities and assembled multiethnic casts and audiences. EWP, founded in 1965, fostered Asian American drama with its playwriting contest, produced important plays such as Frank Chin's *Chickencoop Chinaman* and Wakako Yamauchi's *And the Soul Shall Dance*, and afforded Asian American actors opportunities to act in canonical plays by authors including Shakespeare and Chekhov.[12] AATW began in 1973, as a summer training program for the American Conservatory Theater, intended to develop Asian American talent in writing, acting, directing, and production. Director Frank Chin encouraged fledgling writers and actors to create scripts and performances based upon oral histories collected from community members, reflecting his aim to have Asian American theater speak from and reflect the cultures that ordinary Asian immigrants and their descendants built in the United States.

Visual Communications (VC), founded by Asian American movement participants in Los Angeles, fused filmmaking with the movement's radical politics of interracialism, internationalism, and community empowerment. Its early productions examined the lives of poor Asian American workers and sought to counter racist media stereotypes of Asians as exotic and passive. The cultural institutions built by the Asian American movement stand as some of its most lasting legacies, as Asian Improv Records (now Asian Improv aRts), Kearny Street Workshop, East West Players, AATW (now Asian American Theater Company), Pan-Asian Repertory Theater, and Visual Communications continue to foster and provide venues for Asian American creative expression.

OUTLOOK

The Asian American movement began in the heyday of Black Power and antiwar activism and flourished throughout the early to mid-1970s. By the late 1970s, however, many of the movement's organizations shifted focus. A number of groups consolidated with non-Asian American counterparts to form multiracial radical parties, while other fruits of the movement became institutionalized as artistic organizations, academic units, and nonprofit social service agencies. These alterations marked an inflection point at which the Asian American movement moved away from its signature characteristics of grassroots, community-oriented radicalism. However, even today new forms of action, new issues, and new actors continue to emerge that recall the Asian American movement's dedication to bettering the lives and working conditions of people of Asian ancestry in the United States and allying with other people of color in the United States and abroad.

DISCUSSION OF THE LITERATURE

In her enormously useful historiographical overview of the Asian American movement,

Diane C. Fujino periodizes writings about the movement into the 1960s and 1970s, dominated by activists writing in the moment; the 1980s, characterized by an absence of work; the 1990s, typified by civil rights interpretations; and the 2000s, in which scholars emphasize the radical roots of the movement.[13] Her categorization rings true. For example, two anthologies published by the UCLA Asian American Studies Center, *Roots* and *Counterpoint*, contained reprints from Asian American movement publications and analytical essays covering the history of Asian migration and labor, contemporary community struggles, education, US imperialism (especially in Asia), and Asian American political organizing. The key anthology, *Asian Women*, published by UC Berkeley Asian American Studies, connected racism and patriarchy to capitalism and imperialism, arguing that they represented interlocking systems of oppression. During the third period, William Wei published *The Asian American Movement*, in which he characterized the movement as an outgrowth of the Civil Rights movement and divided it into reformist and revolutionary wings, valorizing the former and demonizing the latter. Since 2000, numerous works have countered this interpretation, locating the Asian American movement as an outgrowth of the Black Power and anti-Vietnam War movements. These works emphasize the movement's advocacy of self-determination rather than civil rights, preference for grassroots politics instead of lobbying, and opposition to US militarism in Asia and elsewhere. In *The Snake Dance of Asian American Activism: Community, Vision, and Power*, Michael Liu, Kim Geron, and Tracy Lai analyze the movement using social movement theory. Daryl Joji Maeda's *Rethinking the Asian American Movement* argues that the movement exhibited a radically coalitional impulse that united Asians across ethnic divides, sought to ally with other people of color in the United States, and declared solidarity with Asians in Asia.

This extended on his analysis in *Chains of Babylon: The Rise of Asian America*, a cultural history in which he explained the movement's twin goals of confronting racism at home and imperialism abroad.[14]

Alongside these general overviews, several monographs examine particular topics within the Asian American movement. Diane Fujino's closely collaborative biographies of Yuri Kochiyama (*Heartbeat of Struggle: The Revolutionary Life of Yuri Kochiyama*) and Richard Aoki (*Samurai Among Panthers: Richard Aoki on Race, Resistance, and a Paradoxical Life*), reveal the complexities of the lives of two legendary activists, both of whom journeyed from naïve patriotism to critical internationalism and were deeply influenced by Black Power. Estella Habal's *San Francisco's International Hotel: Mobilizing the Filipino American Community in the Anti-Eviction Movement* provides a concentrated look at one of the most important and best-known chapters of the movement, explaining both coalitions and contradictions within the struggle to save the hotel. In *Radicals on the Road: Third World Internationalism and American Orientalism during the Vietnam Era*, Judy Tzu-Chun Wu shows how travels to and encounters with Left Asia impacted not only Asian American activists, but more generally, the Third World left in the United States.[15]

Both Max Elbaum and Laura Pulido discuss the multiracial movements for power and justice during the 1960s and 1970s and include Asian American activism within this context. Elbaum's *Revolution in the Air: Sixties Radicals Turn to Lenin, Mao and Che* examines the transition from related but distinct Third World movements in the United States to what he calls the New Communist Movement, a process in which several Asian American groups played integral roles. In *Black, Brown, Yellow, and Left: Radical Activism in Los Angeles*, Pulido concentrates on Los Angeles, a hotbed of radicalism by African American, Chicano, and Asian American activists. She concludes that Asian American organizations were the most self-consciously and consistently dedicated to solidarity work among all of the groups she studies.[16]

The historiography on the Asian American movement remains relatively sparse, as many topics—including organizational histories of key groups, examinations of activism in localities other than the San Francisco Bay Area and Los Angeles, and thematic explorations of issues such as labor and health care—remain to be fully explored. Elsewhere I discuss the historiographical terrain more fully, explain why the periodization of the movement should be demarcated roughly as 1968 to 1980, and argue that studies incorporating gender, sexuality and internationalism should form the next wave of scholarship.[17]

PRIMARY SOURCES

Primary sources on the Asian American movement are available in published anthologies and archival collections. These include the contemporary anthologies, *Roots, Asian Women,* and *Counterpoint,*[18] along with more recent publications such as Louie and Omatsu, *Asian Americans: The Movement and the Moment,* Fred Ho et al., *Legacy to Liberation,* and Asian Community Center, *Stand Up.*[19] Useful archival collections include the Steve Louie Asian American Movement Collection in Special Collections of the Charles E. Young Research Library at the University of California, Los Angeles; the UCLA Asian American Studies Center Reading Room; the Social Protest Collection in the Bancroft Library, University of California, Berkeley; the Asian American Studies Collection in the UC Berkeley Ethnic Studies Library; and the California Ethnic and Multicultural Archives at UC Santa Barbara, which holds papers of the Asian American Theater Company, Kearny Street Workshop, and several Asian American artists and writers, including Frank Chin.

In conjunction with the wealth of extant written primary sources, oral histories can provide unparalleled levels of detail, explanations of particulars not reflected in the written record, and a sense of the sights, sounds, and feelings that infused the Asian American movement. Researchers should collect oral histories with as many movement participants as possible to capture these data. The standard caveats about oral history apply: memories are partial and tend to be sketchy on specifics such as particular dates; recollections are often tailored to support specific perspectives; and oral histories should be understood as meaning-making narratives rather than as transcriptions of events.

DIGITAL MATERIALS

- Steve Louie Asian American Movement Collection (http://www.oac.cdlib.org/findaid/ark:/13030/kt338nd7wf/) at UCLA.
- Asian American Studies Center Reading Room and Library (http://www.aasc.ucla.edu/library/) at UCLA.
- Social Protest Collection at Berkeley (http://vm136.lib.berkeley.edu/BANC/collections/socialprotest.html).
- Asian American Studies Collection at UC Berkeley (http://eslibrary.berkeley.edu/asian-american-studies-collection).
- Asian/Pacific American Collections at the California Ethnic and Multicultural Archives at UC Santa Barbara (http://www.library.ucsb.edu/special-collections/cema/asian-pacific-american-collections).
- Asian American Movement Blog (https://asianamericanmovement.wordpress.com/).

FURTHER READING

Elbaum, Max. *Revolution in the Air: Sixties Radicals Turn to Lenin, Mao, and Che.* London: Verso, 2002.

Fujino, Diane C. *Heartbeat of Struggle: The Revolutionary Life of Yuri Kochiyama.* Minneapolis: University of Minnesota Press, 2005.

Fujino, Diane C. *Samurai among Panthers: Richard Aoki on Race, Resistance, and a Paradoxical Life.* Minneapolis: University of Minnesota Press, 2012.

Habal, Estella. *San Francisco's International Hotel: Mobilizing the Filipino American Community in the Anti-Eviction Movement*. Philadelphia: Temple University Press, 2007.

Liu, Michael, Kim Geron, and Tracy Lai. *The Snake Dance of Asian American Activism: Community, Vision, and Power*. Lanham, MD: Lexington Books, 2008.

Maeda, Daryl J. *Chains of Babylon: The Rise of Asian America*. Minneapolis: University of Minnesota Press, 2009.

Maeda, Daryl Joji. *Rethinking the Asian American Movement*. New York: Routledge, 2012.

Pulido, Laura. *Black, Brown, Yellow, and Left: Radical Activism in Los Angeles*. Berkeley: University of California Press, 2006.

Wei, William. *The Asian American Movement*. Philadelphia: Temple University Press, 1993.

Wu, Judy Tzu-Chun. *Radicals on the Road: Third World Internationalism and American Orientalism during the Vietnam Era*. Ithaca, NY: Cornell University Press, 2013.

NOTES

1. For more elaborate overviews of the Asian American movement, see Daryl Joji Maeda, *Rethinking the Asian American Movement* (New York: Routledge, 2012); and Michael Liu, Kim Geron, and Tracy Lai, *The Snake Dance of Asian American Activism: Community, Vision, and Power* (Lanham, MD: Lexington Books, 2008).

2. On the TWLF strike at San Francisco State, see Karen Umemoto, "'On Strike!' San Francisco State College Strike, 1968–69: The Role of Asian American Students," *Amerasia Journal* 15.1 (1989): 3–41; and Jason Michael Ferreira, "All Power to the People: A Comparative History of Third World Radicalism in San Francisco, 1968–1974" (PhD Diss., University of California, Berkeley, 2003). For information on the TWLF strike at Berkeley, see Harvey C. Dong, "The Origins and Trajectory of Asian American Political Activism in the San Francisco Bay Area, 1968–1978" (PhD Diss., University of California, Berkeley, 2002).

3. An invaluable collection of documents chronicling WMS/Asian Community Center programs has been published as Asian Community Center Archive Group, *Stand Up: An Archive Collection of*

the Bay Area Asian American Movement, 1968–1974 (Berkeley, CA: Eastwind Books, 2009).

4. Estella Habal, *San Francisco's International Hotel: Mobilizing the Filipino American Community in the Anti-Eviction Movement* (Philadelphia: Temple University Press, 2007), discusses the I-Hotel struggle and provides valuable perspective on KDP.

5. Judy Tzu-Chun Wu, *Radicals on the Road: Third World Internationalism and American Orientalism during the Vietnam Era* (Ithaca, NY: Cornell University Press, 2013).

6. Max Elbaum, *Revolution in the Air: Sixties Radicals turn to Lenin, Mao and Che* (London: Verso, 2002).

7. May Fu, "'Serve the People and You Help Yourself': Japanese-American Anti-Drug Organizing in Los Angeles, 1969 to 1972," *Social Justice* 35.2 (2008): 80–99; Susie Ling, "The Mountain Movers: Asian American Women's Movement in Los Angeles," *Amerasia Journal* 15.1 (1989): 51–67; and Mary Uyematsu Kao, "Three Step Boogie in Los Angeles: Sansei Women in the Asian American Movement," *Amerasia Journal* 35.1 (2009): 112–138.

8. See Wu, *Radicals on the Road*, chapters 8 and 9.

9. International Hotel Women's Collective, "Sisterhood Is Powerful," in *Asian Women* (Berkeley, CA, 1971), 122–124.

10. On Fred Ho and Asian American jazz, see Diane C. Fujino, "Introduction: Revolutionary Dreaming and New Dawns," in Fred Wei-han Ho and Diane C. Fujino, eds., *Wicked Theory, Naked Practice: A Fred Ho Reader* (Minneapolis: University of Minnesota Press, 2009), 7–38.

11. See Esther Lee, *A History of Asian American Theatre* (Cambridge: Cambridge University Press 2006).

12. Yuko Kurahashi, *Asian American Culture on Stage: The History of the East West Players* (New York: Garland, 1999).

13. Diane C. Fujino, "Who Studies the Asian American Movement? A Historiographical Analysis," *Journal of Asian American Studies* 11.2 (June 2008): 127–169.

14. Amy Tachiki, Eddie Wong, and Franklin Odo, eds., Roots: An Asian American Reader (Los Angeles: UCLA Asian American Studies Center Press, 1971); International Hotel Women's Collective, "Sisterhood Is Powerful," in Asian

Women (Berkeley, CA, 1971), 122–124.); Emma Gee, ed., *Counterpoint: Perspectives on Asian America* (Los Angeles: UCLA Asian American Studies Center Press, 1976); William Wei, *The Asian American Movement* (Philadelphia: Temple University Press, 1993); Michael Liu, Kim Geron, and Tracy Lai, *The Snake Dance of Asian American Activism: Community, Vision, and Power* (Lanham, MD: Lexington Books, 2008); Daryl Joji Maeda, *Rethinking the Asian American Movement* (New York: Routledge, 2012); and Daryl J. Maeda, *Chains of Babylon: The Rise of Asian America* (Minneapolis: University of Minnesota Press, 2009).

15. Diane C. Fujino, *Heartbeat of Struggle: The Revolutionary Life of Yuri Kochiyama* (Minneapolis: University of Minnesota Press, 2005); Diane C. Fujino, *Samurai among Panthers: Richard Aoki on Race, Resistance, and a Paradoxical Life* (Minneapolis: University of Minnesota Press, 2012); Habal, *San Francisco's International Hotel*; and Wu, *Radicals on the Road*.

16. Elbaum, *Revolution in the Air*; and Pulido, Laura. *Black, Brown, Yellow, and Left: Radical Activism in Los Angeles* (Berkeley: University of California Press, 2006).

17. Daryl Joji Maeda, "The Asian American Movement," in *Oxford Handbook of Asian American History*, ed. David Yoo and Eiichiro Azuma (New York: Oxford University Press, 2016).

18. Tachiki, Wong, and Odo, *Roots: An Asian American Reader*; International Hotel Women's Collective, "Sisterhood Is Powerful"; and Gee, ed., *Counterpoint: Perspectives on Asian America*.

19. Steve Louie and Glenn Omatsu, eds., *Asian Americans: The Movement and the Moment* (Los Angeles: UCLA Asian American Studies Center Press, 2001); Fred Ho, Carolyn Antonio, Diane Fujino, and Steve Yip, eds., *Legacy to Liberation: Politics and Culture of Revolutionary Asian/Pacific America* (San Francisco: AK Press, 2000); and Asian Community Center Archive Group, ed., *Stand Up: An Archive Collection of the Bay Area Asian American Movement, 1968–1974* (Berkeley, CA: Eastwind Books, 2009).

Daryl Joji Maeda

JAPANESE RESETTLEMENT IN POSTWAR AMERICA: THE LOS ANGELES EXPERIENCE

NIKKEI LOS ANGELES: THE CONTEXT OF MASS INCARCERATION

For several generations, Los Angeles has been a major center of Japanese and Japanese American life, culture, and politics. In the midst of vast social, economic, and political upheavals in Meji Era Japan, and lured by the economic opportunities in US West Coast agriculture, Japanese immigrants first began to settle in the greater Los Angeles area in the mid-1880s. Their migration took place within the dual contexts of the rapid expansion of agribusiness in the peripheral areas of Los Angeles as well as the passage of the Chinese Exclusion Act in 1882. Although men comprised the initial cohort of immigrants, Japan's imperialist agenda encouraged the settler migration of women and families and soon thereafter, the Nisei, or second generation was born.

In the face of various forms of state-sanctioned discrimination such as Alien Land Laws, as well as interpersonal racism, Japanese Americans in the greater Los Angeles region created networks for a bustling community. Although that community was anchored in the downtown enclave of Little Tokyo near various business districts and markets, Nikkei settlement stretched southward to Terminal Island, up to the San Fernando Valley in the north, and Pasadena in the east. Issei men and women forged institutions that included farmer's associations, language schools, martial arts dojos, markets and small businesses, and a vibrant ethnic media that included the *Rafu Shimpo*, which is still published today. Devout immigrants facilitated the growth of a diverse religious landscape, as they founded various Buddhist (Jōdo Shinshū, Jōdo Shū, Nichiren, Shingon, and Zen), Shinto (Konko), Tenrikyo, Catholic, and Protestant (Methodist,

Congregational, and Presbyterian) temples and churches. Women specifically created various *fujinkai*, or women's clubs, in religious organizations that provided an important space for fellowship and community building. By the 1920s, the Nisei, through an eclectic network of clubs, dances, and other social spaces, began to fashion their own hybrid cultural identities that melded together the world of their immigrant parents as well as American mass culture.

This lively community, however, came crashing down after Japan's Imperial Military bombed US Navy installations at Pu'uloa (Pearl Harbor) in the Territory of Hawai'i on December 7, 1941. Long targeted as a racial Other through discriminatory laws or Orientalist stereotypes, the bombing of Pu'uloa crystallized long-simmering anti-Japanese prejudice across the nation, but particularly the West Coast. Within a day, the Federal Bureau of Investigation swept through Los Angeles detaining various Issei community leaders such as language school teachers, the officers of ethnic organizations, and Buddhist and Shinto priests. Government agencies including the Immigration and Naturalization Service commandeered erstwhile Civilian Conservation Corps camps in places such as Sunland-Tujunga or Griffith Park and transformed them into detention stations for so-called "enemy aliens" of Japanese, as well as German and Italian descent. Government agents subjected Japanese American families to contraband searches for anything that might be construed as subversive, such as a radio. Various individuals remember family members hastily destroying any item with a connection to Japan.

Following the initial roundups of Issei leaders, the federal government hastened the entire liquidation of Japanese and Japanese American communities across the West Coast under the banner of national security. After President Franklin Delano Roosevelt signed Executive Order 9066 in February 1942, which set into motion the exclusion of Japanese and Japanese

Americans from the West Coast military zone, the government forcibly removed 120,000 individuals, the majority of whom were citizens.

The government claimed that the mass incarceration of Japanese Americans from the West Coast was a matter of military necessity, a specious argument given that Japanese Americans in the Territory of Hawai'i were not imprisoned on the same mass scale as those in the states of California, Oregon, and Washington. Rather, a dangerous combination of wartime hysteria, deep-seated racism, and a failure of political leadership informed the decision to incarcerate Japanese Americans.[1]

While some families with enough financial or social capital were able to move to the Midwest or East Coast, the vast majority of Japanese Americans remained subject to the exclusion orders. These people, whether they were Issei, Nisei, or Kibei (Japan-educated Nisei), left behind their homes, businesses, possessions, and other assets as the military oversaw their "evacuation" to temporary processing centers and subsequent removal to desolate concentration camps in rural areas of California, Idaho, Utah, Wyoming, Colorado, Arizona, and Arkansas.

Japanese Americans in Los Angeles, as elsewhere, abandoned their property or entrusted it to an assortment of neighbors, employees, attorneys, or others. Oftentimes, social institutions such as churches or temples served as storehouses for various possessions. Fortuitously, one of the ministers of the Los Angeles Hompa Hongwanji Buddhist Temple, the Reverend Julius Goldwater, was a European American convert to Buddhism and during the war took great pains to safeguard the possessions of the temple's *sangha* (congregation) and watch over their homes to ensure they were not sold.[2]

The center of Nikkei life in greater Los Angeles, Little Tokyo, underwent a curious transformation as scores of African Americans moved to the enclave in the absence of Japanese Americans. Renamed Bronzeville, the new community became an important destination or temporary stop for scores of African Americans who migrated from the South to participate in Los Angeles's wartime defense industries or head to war in the Pacific Theater. As these new black migrants created a new space for themselves in Bronzeville, Japanese Americans imprisoned behind barbed wire wondered about their prospects of returning home.

THE ARCHITECTURE OF RETURN AND RESETTLEMENT

In 1943 the War Relocation Authority (WRA) admitted there was no military need for the mass incarceration of Japanese Americans and the War Department soon thereafter sought to release "loyal" detainees. However, the camps remained open due to pressure from racist politicians and at the insistence of the Western Defense Command (WDC), led by General John De Witt who famously remarked, "A Jap's a Jap. There is no way to determine their loyalty."[3] However, when De Witt stepped down from his post, replaced by General Delos Emmons, the former military governor of Hawai'i, the WDC along with the WRA allowed small numbers of Japanese Americans to leave the camps.

The first re-settlers included university students and agricultural workers who went to the Interior West, the Midwest, or the East Coast. California and the rest of the West Coast, however, remained off limits. The process to leave camp was often extensive: applicants had to provide evidence of their employment or university status to ensure they would not rely on public assistance. Further, they had to successfully pass the notorious "loyalty questionnaire"—which asked all Japanese and Japanese Americans if they would foreswear allegiance to Japan and fight for the United States—and sign an oath that they would not congregate with other Nikkei outside of camp. The slightest infraction on one's record could halt the process. Overtime though, the migration of Japanese Americans

to places beyond the West Coast helped establish small Nikkei populations in places such as the Twin Cities, Chicago, Detroit, New York City, and even Seabrook, New Jersey, where Seabrook Farms eagerly recruited Japanese American workers for their vegetable cannery and packing plant. Overall, government authorities sought to disperse Japanese Americans to ideally diffuse racial tensions. According to Lane Hirabayashi, WRA director Dillon Myer "believed that if resettlers eschewed living in 'Little Tokyos,' they could assimilate into mainstream society more fully and be more accepted in and by members of the larger society."[4] Despite such aspirations, Japanese Americans sought to return to what was most familiar: the West Coast.

A series of events in the judicial and executive branches of the federal government in 1944 helped open the doors to the West Coast. At that time, when the Supreme Court of the United States ruled, in *Ex Parte Endo*, that the government could not continue to detain a "decidedly loyal" citizen, the WDC decided to lift the exclusion orders that applied to the West Coast. After the presidential election of 1944 President Roosevelt revisited the possibility of closing the camps and on December 17, 1944, issued Public Proclamation Number 21, which rescinded the exclusion orders.

Soon thereafter, Japanese Americans began to return to Los Angeles.[5] The initial cohort to return to Los Angeles included individuals or families with enough capital and resources to settle back into their homes or businesses. This group entrusted their property to scrupulous real estate agents, friends, neighbors, employees, or others who maintained their farms, homes, or businesses. This group was by far the minority. Therefore, another handful of Nikkei known as the "scouts" returned to the city to explore the racial climate, assess the possibilities of finding homes and employment, and report their findings back to those still in the concentration camps.[6] Regardless of their financial resources, or lack thereof, Japanese Americans returned to Los Angeles with a great sense of anxiety, fearful of what they might encounter.

The return to Los Angeles and the West Coast more generally was fraught with economic insecurity and lingering anti-Japanese prejudice. The Federal Reserve estimated Japanese Americans suffered losses upward of $400 million, a rather conservative number.[7] Moreover, Japanese American–owned property was often defaced or destroyed during the war. As Japanese American families slowly made their way home, social scientist Charles Spaulding found that they "had difficulty returning to the rural areas, because the antagonisms seemed more virulent there and the land was being operated by others."[8] His observation, however, belied the racism Japanese Americans faced in the city's urban areas as well as its new suburban neighborhoods. In October 1946, for example, two Nikkei-owned homes were completely razed due to arson in the East Los Angeles neighborhood of Belvedere and Japanese Americans soon thereafter reported over thirty-five other instances of vandalism, gunfire, or other harassment.[9]

Furthermore, organizations such as the Native Sons of the Golden West or the Remember Pearl Harbor League continued to fan the flames of anti-Japanese hatred and preach exclusion. Despite overall support from a sympathetic student body, staff, and faculty, in the mid-1940s the Pasadena Chamber of Commerce, the Daughters of the American Revolution, and others fought mightily to prevent Nisei Esther Takei from enrolling at Pasadena Junior College. Due to a concerted effort by a diverse group of supporters that ranged from churches to veterans to California Technological Institute scientist Linus Pauling, Takei eventually enrolled.[10] Yet, the virulence with which her detractors fought to keep her out of the college spoke to the enduring prejudice that still existed. A "citizens' group" in Orange County, located to the south of Los Angeles County went as far as to harass a white farmer who had rented the property of a Japanese American family during the war.

Moreover, as erstwhile rural spots became popular suburbs, residents of towns such as Burbank mobilized petitions that called on the government to ban the Nikkei resettlement in their neighborhoods. This agitation blended both old pre-war racism as well as newer postwar anxieties that Japanese Americans would threaten property values. The text of the petition by Burbank residents read, for example, "It is unthinkable that any progressive group of educated people or government agencies should establish a slum even temporarily."[11] Indeed in a 1943 poll, the Los Angeles Times found that of 10,845 respondents, 91 percent wanted the wholesale exclusion of Japanese Americans from the West Coast.[12]

Local news media, such as the Los Angeles Examiner, and unscrupulous civic leaders compounded the precariousness of resettlement. For example, they circulated rumors that the return of Japanese Americans to Little Tokyo—which became an African American enclave known as Bronzeville during the war—would hasten an entire race war. To be sure interpersonal and larger racial tensions did occur during the transition. In one well-known instance, the Los Angeles Hompa Hongwanji Buddhist Temple and the Providence Baptist Association, the African American church that occupied the temple during the war, briefly found themselves embroiled in a legal battle over the property. Despite this, the overall prognostications of massive racial strife between African Americans and Nikkei never came to fruition. The brief operation of Pilgrim House, a social welfare agency, illustrated how many Little Tokyo constituents intentionally tried to cultivate cross-racial harmony. If anything, such rumors did more to burnish arguments in support of the exclusion of Japanese Americans than to reveal outright violence. In 1946 Ebony ran an article, for example, that described the transitions in Little Tokyo entitled "The Race War That Flopped" and spoke to a larger sentiment that the two groups found common ground as victims of racial oppression.[13] However, the construction of Parker Center, the new headquarters for the Los Angeles Police Department, cut away at Little Tokyo and accelerated the destruction of Bronzeville.[14] Indeed, "Bronzeville ceased to exist," according to historian Hillary Jenks, "less from disputes between African and Japanese Americans than as a result of racist spatial practices by a local state that continued to view property associated with *either* community as less valuable, and thus easier to manipulate than Anglo-occupied real estate."[15]

HOUSING, EMPLOYMENT, AND THE SOCIAL WORLD OF RESETTLEMENT

In addition to the transitions that took place in Little Tokyo, housing was perhaps the most pressing issue for Nikkei as they resettled into or ventured for the first time to Los Angeles. Before the war, redlining, racially restrictive covenants, and other discriminatory practices circumscribed where Japanese Americans and other People of Color could live in the city. Within these spaces, they often lived in poor living conditions as well: a 1939 study by the Housing Authority of the City of Los Angeles found that 28.6 percent of African Americans, 47.2 percent of Asian Americans, and 59.6 percent of Mexican Americans in the city lived in "substandard housing."[16] The large influx of defense workers, military personnel, and their families exacerbated an already precarious housing situation during and after the war.

Despite the lacuna of housing, Nikkei continued to return to Los Angeles in droves. Only two years after the end of the war, the Japanese American population in Los Angeles County swelled to 28,000 (where there had been 37,000 individuals before the war).[17] Families with enough resources moved to multiethnic neighborhoods such as Boyle Heights, which had a sizeable pre-war Nikkei community, North Broadway (near Chinatown), Jefferson Park, Crenshaw, or Watts, which

laid the groundwork for postwar coalition building and civil rights activism in African Americans. Families with very little financial stability settled into cheap apartments in slum conditions in and around downtown. For example, the popular actor George Takei, who was only nine years old when his family returned to Los Angeles, recalled that his family settled in Skid Row after his father found a job as a dishwasher in Chinatown.[18]

Hostels provided temporary shelter for individuals and families who could not return to their pre-war homes or move into private housing. Christian and Buddhist churches, which served as storehouses for the possessions of Japanese Americans during the war, became some of the best-known hostels where residents could also receive assistance with tasks such as finding a job or applying for a driver's license. Senshin Gakuin, a South Central Los Angeles Japanese language school affiliated with the Los Angeles Hompa Hongwanji Buddhist Temple, became a hostel run by Rev. Goldwater and Nisei college student Arthur Takemoto.[19] Just down the street from Senshin, a Methodist group also opened a hostel. In Boyle Heights, the Japanese Union Church operated the Evergreen Hostel. A Nisei woman who lived there after she returned from Heart Mountain Relocation Center in Wyoming recalled that it "was almost like camp in that all we had was a bed and a little stand where we kept our personal belongings, and it was more or less the honor system for everyone.... There were some house rules about what time you had to be in by and things like that."[20] Hostels received no support from the WRA; residents paid a minimal daily fee (between $1 to $2) and assisted with the daily operations.

For particularly distressed Nikkei families and those who were the last to leave the concentration camps, especially those with small children, the impoverished, or the elderly, WRA oversaw the haphazard construction of temporary camps throughout Los Angeles County. In the years immediately after the government lifted the West Coast exclusion orders, the WRA built camps in locations that included Hawthorne, Santa Monica, El Segundo, Long Beach, Lomita, Sun Valley, and Burbank. Residents lived in trailers or old army barracks fashioned from wood and tarpaper. Nikkei re-settlers shared stories of substandard living conditions such as a lack of electricity or sanitary bathrooms and kitchens. Although the WRA and FPHA closed most of the camps by 1946, when the WRA ceased to exist, they kept the Burbank and Sun Valley camps open. The Burbank camp, filled with families and individuals with no resources and fearful of readjustment to mainstream society, stayed open until 1956, which indicates the extent of their hardships.

In a reflection on the state of resettlement for Japanese Americans forced from the WRA/FPHA camps, one Nisei journalist opined, "The failure of the government to provide for the return of these people in peacetime in the same efficient, clockwork manner in which they were torn from their homes is an indictment of a nation."[21] His words certainly resonated with harried Japanese Americans, particularly as the government's apathy grew. A pithy WRA pamphlet entitled *When You Leave the Relocation Center* encapsulated that view as it instructed Nikkei that "No government or private agency...can relieve you of the major responsibilities that every person must assume for himself and for members of his family.... The decision to relocate rests with you and you must accept the initiative in adjusting yourself into the community where you plan to reside."[22]

Even when Nikkei could find a place to live, employment remained an obstacle in the early resettlement years. Often armed with little personal finances and/or unable to return to their pre-war farms or businesses, many Nikkei experienced downward economic mobility. Both the civil service and private sectors largely barred Japanese Americans from their ranks after the war. Furthermore, Japanese Americans, along with previously employed African Americans, Mexican Americans, and women of all races, were shut out of the region's lucrative defense industry: when the war ended the factories turned jobs over to white male veterans. To remedy this, Japanese Americans took on a variety of jobs. Nikkei created a new ethnic niche in gardening and estimates suggest that after the war one out of every four gardeners was a Japanese American.[23] Meanwhile Japanese American nursery workers reestablished their pre-war Flower Market in Montebello in the autumn of 1946.[24] By 1955 Nikkei gardeners created the Southern California Gardener's Federation to support their industry and provide a co-op for members. Those who lived in the slowly diminishing agricultural parts of greater Los Angeles worked as farm laborers. Meanwhile, others found employment in domestic labor or service work, often hired by other Asian Americans. In her study of gender in the history of Nisei Los Angeles, Valerie Matsumoto found that "within the ethnic community, women found work in beauty salons, one of the avenues for female entrepreneurship and employment before the war."[25] Nisei women became employed in the garment industry. In response to anti–Japanese American discrimination, some individuals used aliases in an attempt to get hired.[26]

Furthermore, Japanese Americans reestablished or created entirely new social networks during the resettlement period. According to one social scientist who observed the Nikkei community in the late 1940s, "resettled Japanese Americans have developed an increased feeling of 'social belonging' to the community as a whole. This is particularly true of urban districts and in connection with political and social activities."[27] The Japanese American Citizens League (JACL), which was formed by Nisei businessmen in 1929, was Japanese America's best known organization before and during the war and played a decisive role in the community's wartime history. Its leaders urged cooperation with the government and military service, which angered many Japanese Americans who felt unjustly persecuted. Despite this enmity, as the largest organization of its kind, JACL chapters across the nation and throughout Los Angeles "reactivated," to use the organization's parlance. At a local level, JACL chapters, that stretched from the San Fernando Valley to West Los Angeles to Little Tokyo to Pasadena, sponsored social activities for the Nisei and their families as well as political advocacy, as outlined below. In addition to the JACL, athletic and social clubs that had once flourished before the war, resumed their activities.[28]

CHANGING RACE RELATIONS AND NEW SETTLEMENT PATTERNS IN THE 1950S AND 1960S

In the midst of these various hardships, race relations began to realign in Los Angeles, driven by the Cold War and the growth of homeowner politics. Although reviled upon their initial return, various global and local factors that took place within a shifting framework of white privilege, helped shift the patterns of settlement and integration for Japanese Americans.

First, organizations such as the JACL and Nisei veterans groups embarked on a public relations campaign to arrest and reverse patterns of anti-Japanese prejudice. Specifically, they highlighted the wartime valor of the all–Japanese American 442nd Regimental Combat Team as a means to claim various forms of social citizenship and belonging. This appeal to wartime service fell into a larger civil rights strategy deployed by several veterans of color organizations, which emphasized wartime sacrifice to challenge domestic racism. Such activism helped veterans and other Japanese Americans slowly gain entry into occupations such as teaching, the civil service, and the corporate world. While Nikkei veterans (like other Japanese Americans and People of Color) continued to face examples of housing

discrimination, the JACL readily defended them in court and used such cases to expose the hypocrisy of American democracy.

Due in part to this rearticulation of race and the place of Japanese Americans in US society, groups such as the JACL led the different forms of political advocacy that assisted the immigrant Issei generation, particularly in California. The JACL helped spearhead the campaign against Proposition 15 in 1946, a nativist statewide ballot measure that would have enshrined old Alien Land Laws (from 1913 and 1920) into the Constitution of California. The courts also upheld the constitutionality of Issei land purchased in the names of Nisei children and then lifted the ban against Issei commercial fishing along the coast. One of JACL's crowning achievements was the passage of the 1952 McCarran-Walter Act that granted citizenship to the Issei. A less well known, but just as politically active group, the Nisei Progressives, however, critiqued that legislation for its exclusionary immigration provisions against anyone deemed "subversive."

Indeed, all of these changes took place within the political landscape of the Cold War, and while ostensibly positive, court decisions, new legislation, and changes in cultural attitudes were not the complete result of moral altruism. In the shadow of political realignments in Asia as US foreign policymakers scrambled to assemble solid American allies, the federal government, civic leaders, and others sought to reiterate America's place as a model of democracy. These imperatives played out in the battlefield of housing and employment where white attitudes toward Asian Americans gradually changed. "With Japan remade as America's junior partner," according to Scott Kurashige, "whites no longer saw industrious Nisei engineers as a threat to national security but rather as contributors to American global hegemony."[29] As historian Charlotte Brooks has pointed out, whites began to see Chinese Americans and Japanese Americans less as "alien neighbors" and more as "foreign friends." In other words, while main-stream society may not have been able to completely interpret Asians as Americans, begrudging acceptance, particularly through housing integration, represented the promise of American ideology. Furthermore, white homeowners, realtors, and developers inter-preted Japanese Americans as less of a threat to property values than African Americans. This "racial triangulation" would shape the legacy of resettlement and race relations for several years to come.

Nevertheless, aside from the cultural changes in attitudes toward Asian Americans, either in relation to Asian nation-states or to African Americans, various structural forces shaped the contours of Nikkei settlement in greater Los Angeles. One of the most important do-mestic legal decisions during this time period was the US Supreme Court's ruling in *Shelley v. Kraemer* in 1948. The justices struck down the constitutionality of racially restrictive covenants in housing. To be sure, discrimina-tory lending practices continued to restrict Nikkei (as well as black and Mexican American) integration so, for example, places such as much of the San Fernando Valley remained off limits until the 1960s.

In addition to federal legal changes that fa-cilitated housing integration, such as *Shelley v. Kraemer*, several local issues related to Southern California's housing markets also shaped Nikkei suburbanization. Due to the lacuna of hous-ing for the mass migration of employees in greater Los Angeles's military-industrial com-plex (whether they were rank-and-file factory workers or middle managers or highly edu-cated researchers), developers quickly subdi-vided plots of land to create the vast sub-urban sprawl that quickly defined postwar Los Angeles. These spaces were generally off limits to People of Color, including Japanese Americans. Thus, the earliest types of Nikkei housing integration took place within multi-ethnic spaces, those neighborhoods that had traditionally welcomed Mexican Americans, blacks, and Asian Americans before World

War II. As such, Japanese Americans were able to settle alongside Latinos in East Los Angeles or Pacoima and with African Americans in Crenshaw.

Whereas savvy developers catered to up-wardly mobile African Americans and built subdivisions, such as the Joe Louis Homes, for that community, Japanese Americans had realtors such as Kazuo K. Inouye. Inouye, a fierce Boyle Heights–born Nisei veteran of the 442nd Regimental Combat Team, established Kashu Realty in the primarily black neigh-borhood of Crenshaw in 1947. He worked to aggressively sell homes in Crenshaw to both African American and Japanese American buyers, and helped blockbust large portions of the neighborhood. During the 1950s and 1960s, Crenshaw became home to a large Nikkei community that boasted a variety of businesses such as restaurants, groceries, and other services. Meanwhile, Nisei profession-als such as doctors and dentists also opened their practices in the neighborhood.[30]

Beyond Crenshaw other modest suburban Nikkei enclaves grew throughout the South-land as Japanese Americans experienced greater upward mobility as they took on middle-class positions as teachers, physicians, or engineers, working in the region's sprawling and lucra-tive military industrial complex. Vibrant neighborhoods grew in areas that had once been home to working-class or agricultural Nikkei communities before World War II, in-cluding, but not limited to, the Gardena Valley in the South Bay, Sawtelle in West Los Angeles, and Pacoima in the East San Fernando Valley. By the 1970s, Kazuo Inouye estab-lished other branches of Kashu Realty and helped facilitate the growth of Nikkei, Chinese American, black, and Mexican American set-tlement in the San Gabriel Valley, located east of downtown Los Angeles. Owing to the gains of the Civil Rights Movement, the legal sup-port of organizations such as the JACL, and changing views of the Nisei (relative to African Americans), some Japanese Americans were able to move to generally white areas without incident by the 1960s and 1970s. Nevertheless, the community did not simply assimilate into the fabric of mainstream society.

As the locus of community leadership shifted to the Nisei, the Japanese American community engaged in a concerted campaign to build new institutions or structures for organizations that had existed even before the war. With attention to the Nisei baby boom that began in the camps, community leaders oversaw the building of a large federation of Japanese American Community Centers, with member organizations located from Pasadena to Little Tokyo to West Covina. These centers hosted athletics leagues, language schools, chapters of the Veterans of Foreign Wars and the Japanese American Citizens League, and other assorted cultural activities from *taiko* drumming to *ikebana* (flower arranging). Even as the concentration of Japanese Americans in various neighborhoods became more diffuse, due to greater opportunities for mobility, particularly after the 1960s and 1970s, their institutions remained strong centers of social networks and cultural bonding. For example, even though the northeast San Fernando Valley is now overwhelmingly a Latino region, it is still home to two Nikkei community centers, two Japanese language schools, two Jōdo Shinshū temples and a Christian church with roots that go back to the pre-war Issei. As the Issei began to age, Japanese American communities in Gardena, Little Tokyo, East Los Angeles, and Pacoima also built Nikkei-oriented retirement homes.

THE LEGACY OF RESETTLEMENT

Lest these gains suggest that the resettlement period was a linear process from deprivation to success, it is important to acknowledge the deep psychological imprint on Japanese Americans. Although many Nikkei did eventually enjoy opportunities for upward mobility by the 1960s, sociologist Tetsuden Kashima cautions, "An analysis of this period will show that a smooth 'transition' image is accurate only if one overlooks the many problems and pitfalls suffered by this group."[31] While the experiences of property loss and racist violence may have been documented, Kashima states that Japanese Americans also had to endure a type of "social amnesia." While the camp experience traumatized individuals, this "social amnesia" represented "a group phenomenon in which attempts are made to suppress feelings and memories of particular moments or extended time periods." The weight of this silence and collective "hazukashi," or shame, shaped community discourse.

Thus, the complex afterlives of the wartime and resettlement experiences were often manifested in conflicts between the Nisei and their third generation, or Sansei, children. As filmmaker Janice Tanaka captured in her 1999 documentary, *When You're Smiling: The Deadly Legacy of Internment*, the outward successes of the Japanese American community—entry into the suburbs, acceptance to prestigious schools, or professional occupations a far cry from the pre-war farms—masked the struggles that took place in Nikkei homes.

Unable to mentally process the camp experience and return to mainstream society, many Nisei refused to speak about their wartime years. Often, many turned to alcohol to ease the pain. Meanwhile, the Sansei grew up often with no knowledge of what happened to their parents or grandparents, and were met with silence when they would ask. They grew up with stifling pressure, both from mainstream society and parents traumatized by war, to fit in at any cost. As a result, many Los Angeles Sansei battled with substance abuse, participation in gang violence, and prison incarceration. Swept up in the frenetic landscape of racial activism around the black and Chicana/o Power Movements in the city in the late 1960s, many Sansei activists formed organizations such as Yellow Brotherhood (in Crenshaw) and Storefront (in West Los Angeles) to abate drug abuse by fellow Sansei as they returned from prison. More generally, these activists helped foment a radical "Asian American" identity that forged political ties with other Third World people. The shared histories of housing discrimination that led to black and Nikkei or Mexican American and Nikkei settlements after World War II helped contribute to this new political movement and moment.

Taken together, the history of Japanese American resettlement in Los Angeles and elsewhere was a complex affair structured around race and the traumas of war. In retrospect, that history is an important chapter that provides a corrective to specious narratives that uphold Nikkei as "model minorities." This account, popularized by social scientists, journalists, and sometimes Japanese Americans themselves in the midst of the Black Freedom Struggle of the 1960s, suggested that through cultural values of perseverance, Nikkei pulled themselves up by the proverbial bootstraps after the tragedies of World War II to (allegedly) enjoy high educational rates, economic upward mobility, and acceptance into the mainstream. As critics have long noted, even going back to the days of the Sansei solidarity with Black Power, this myth did more to blunt the calls for racial and economic justice by other People of Color, than to benefit Japanese Americans themselves. "The superficial compliment paid to Japanese Americans for successfully integrating into the American mainstream," according to Scott Kurashige, "would be used to cast a deeper aspersion on the much larger and still growing numbers of African Americans living increasingly isolated and impoverished in places like South Central Los Angeles. If in the eyes of many whites, moderate measures had solved the 'Japanese problem,' there was scant legitimacy to black demands for greater state and civil action."[32] Therefore, the history of resettlement illustrates the political and economic complexities that Japanese Americans faced.

DISCUSSION OF THE LITERATURE

The literature on Japanese American resettlement in general has undergone significant changes since the 1960s. It has been bound up in ideological battles over the place of Japanese Americans in the United States' racial order in the shadow of the Civil Rights Movement. The first scholars and government social scientists to write about the experiences of Japanese Americans after their camp experiences captured the demographics and economics of resettlement. They provided important snapshots into issues such as the dearth of housing that Nikkei endured and early instances of racism the returnees faced. Instructive texts include Charles Spaulding's "Housing Problems of Minority Groups in Los Angeles" (1946), which focuses specifically on the city, as well as multi-sited studies such as the War Agency Liquidation Unit's *People in Motion: The Postwar Adjustment of the Evacuated Japanese Americans* (1947) and Elmer Smith's "Resettlement of Japanese Americans" (1949).[33] Leonard Broom and Ruther Reimer's *Removal and Return: The Socio-Economic Effects of the War on Japanese Americans* (1949) provides some data on the economic losses and subsequent difficulties Nikkei endured.[34] Thus, these studies tended to view Japanese Americans as statistics and focus on individual instances of racism.

By the 1960s, scholarship on the resettlement period took a different turn. In a conservative response to the Civil Rights Movement, journalists and other observers began to craft a narrative of Japanese Americans as a "model minority." Pieces such as "Success Story: Japanese American Style" (1966) by sociologist William Peterson glossed over the racism, poverty, and other deprivations that Japanese Americans faced immediately after World War II to point to their economic successes and integration into the larger fabric of American society.[35] Furthermore, this argument became a weaponized narrative used to quell critiques against structural inequality and calls for racial and economic justice by other People of Color. The arc of scholarship such as Peterson's article positioned Japanese Americans as the racial foil to African

Americans' alleged "ghetto culture," a concept popularized in Daniel Patrick Moynihan's *The Negro Family: The Case for National Action* (1965).[36]

The concerted Third World activism of the 1960s led to the birth of Ethnic Studies. Guided by intertwined commitments to social justice and foregrounding the long buried histories of People of Color, Ethnic Studies, including Asian American Studies, sought to retell the past from the bottom up. By the 1970s, the growth of Asian American Studies coincided with the on-the-ground movement to secure redress and reparations and scholars began to produce important works on the wartime incarceration, yet few looked specifically at resettlement. Tetsuden Kashima's "Japanese American Internees Return, 1945–1955: Readjustment and Social Amnesia" is an important exception, however, and helped shaped future studies.[37] Even by 2000, Valerie Matsumoto remarked, "how Japanese Americans rebuilt their lives and communities after World War II is a vastly understudied subject."[38]

However, in the past few years, three new books that draw on an array of unpublished sources, ethnic media, oral histories, and government documents have painstakingly recreated the world of the resettlers. They include Lane Hirabayashi and Kenichiro Shimada's analysis of WRA photographs in *Japanese American Resettlement Through the Lens* (2011); Greg Robinson's collection of essays on the geography, politics, and identities of the resettlers, *After Camp: Portraits in Midcentury Japanese American Life and Politics* (2012); and Matsumoto's *City Girls: The Nisei Social World in Los Angeles, 1920–1950* (2014), a study of gender and social networks that were forged before the war and survived after.[39] Charlotte Brooks's *Alien Neighbors, Foreign Friends: Asian Americans, Housing, and the Transformation of Urban California* (2009) provides the best overview of Japanese Americans and housing politics in Cold War California.[40]

Meanwhile, the general maturation of historical writing about Japanese Americans and other People of Color helped shape new comparative race studies of the urban west. The growth of multiethnic histories of Los Angeles and California at midcentury provide additional windows into the resettlement period, especially in regards to racial formation in a multiethnic setting. Hillary Jenks's article, "Bronzeville, Little Tokyo, and the Unstable Geography of Race in Post-World War II Los Angeles," provides an important account of how resettlement took place within the contexts of black migration to Los Angeles as well as state power.[41] Scott Kurashige's *The Shifting Grounds of Race: Black and Japanese Americans and the Making of Multiethnic Los Angeles* (2008) is the best example, joined with Mark Brilliant's *The Color of America Has Changed: How Racial Diversity Shaped Civil Rights Reform in California, 1941–1978* (2010), among others.[42]

PRIMARY SOURCES

NEWSPAPERS

The most comprehensive source for information on resettlement from the postwar period itself is the Japanese American ethnic press, including the *Rafu Shimpo*. The Japanese American Citizen's League's national newspaper, the *Pacific Citizen* provides some of the most detailed accounts of the travails of returnees, instances of vandalism, and life in the resettlement camps. Both papers are available at the Japanese American National Museum (JANM) in Los Angeles's Little Tokyo, while the *Rafu Shimpo* is available on microfilm in various university libraries such as UCLA's Charles E. Young Research Library. The African American press in Los Angeles, such as the *California Eagle* and the *Los Angeles Sentinel*, mindful of midcentury race politics that went beyond black and white also covered Japanese American resettlement in Little Tokyo/Bronzeville and beyond. The *Eagle* is available on microfilm at UCLA and the *Sentinel* is available through ProQuest Historical Newspapers.

ARCHIVAL COLLECTIONS

One of the most extensive archival collections that houses materials on the wartime and postwar experiences of Japanese Americans is UCLA's Japanese American Research Project. This expansive holding primarily includes the private papers of individuals as well as the records of the Japanese American Citizens League. Additional information on the JACL is available at the Japanese American National Library in San Francisco. Harry Honda, the previous editor of the *Pacific Citizen* left behind an extensive collection at JANM in Los Angeles that includes both clippings from his paper as well as other assorted articles, government documents, and ephemera.

ORAL HISTORIES AND DIGITAL REPOSITORIES

Oral histories have provided the best source to paint a fully textured portrait of the resettlement period. The popular anthology series *Nanka Nikkei Voices*, published by the Japanese American Historical Society of Southern California, includes one collection that profiles several brief memoirs and recollections about the resettlement experience. In the late 1990s, JANM spearheaded the REgenerations Oral History Project, which focused on the resettlement of Japanese Americans in cities such as Los Angeles, Chicago, and San Jose. The full text is available online through the University of California's Digital Library's Calisphere website (http://www.calisphere .universityofcalifornia.edu). WRA photographs of the resettlement are also available at Calisphere. Discover Nikkei and Densho also hold comprehensive databases of visual and aural resources that range from government documents to photography to oral history interviews. Densho has a particularly rich trove of sources that capture how the federal government framed resettlement and the responsibilities of Japanese Americans upon their return.

DIGITAL MATERIALS

- Discover Nikkei (http://www .discovernikkei.org).
- REgenerations Oral History Project: Los Angeles Region (http://texts.cdlib.org /view?docId=ft358003z1&doc. view=entire_text).
- UC Digital Library's Calisphere (http:// www.calisphere.universityofcalifornia.edu) and the Japanese American Relocation Digital Archive (http://www.calisphere .universityofcalifornia.edu/jarda).

FURTHER READING

Bloom, Leonard, and Ruth Riemer. *Removal and Return*. Berkeley: University of California Press, 1949.

Brooks, Charlotte. *Alien Neighbors, Foreign Friends: Asian Americans, Housing, and the Transformation of Urban California*. Chicago: University of Chicago Press, 2009.

Hirabayahi, Lane Ryo, with Kenichiro Shimada. *Japanese American Resettlement Through the Lens: Hikaru Carl Iwasaki and the WRA's Photographic Section, 1943–1945*. Boulder: University of Colorado Press, 2009.

Japanese American Historical Society of Southern California. *Nanka Nikkei Voices: Resettlement Years, 1945–1955*. Torrance: Japanese American Historical Society of Southern California, 1998.

Japanese American National Museum. *REgenerations Oral History Project: Rebuilding Japanese American Families, Communities, and Civil Rights in the Resettlement Era*. Los Angeles Region: Volume II. Los Angeles: Japanese American National Museum, 2000.

Kashima, Tetsuden. "Japanese American Internees Return, 1945 to 1955: Readjustment and Social Amnesia." *Phylon* 41.2 (June 1980): 107–115.

Kurashige, Scott. *The Shifting Grounds of Race: Black and Japanese Americans in the Making of Multiethnic Los Angeles*. Princeton, NJ: Princeton University Press, 2010.

Matsumoto, Valerie. *City Girls: The Nisei Social World in Los Angeles, 1920–1950*. New York: Oxford University Press, 2014.

Robinson, Greg. *After Camp: Portraits in Midcentury Japanese American Life and Politics*. Berkeley: University of California Press, 2012.

NOTES

1. The Commission on the Wartime Relocation and Internment of Citizens found that the forced removal and mass incarceration of Japanese Americans was the result of wartime hysteria, deep-seated racial prejudice, and a failure of political leadership. See Commission on the Wartime Relocation and Internment of Citizens, *Personal Justice Denied Report of the Commission on Wartime Relocation and Internment of Civilians* (Seattle: University of Washington Press, 1997).

2. Elaine Woo, "Rev. Julius Goldwater; Convert to Buddhism Aided WWII Internees," *Los Angeles Times*, June 23, 2011. Rev. Goldwater's well-known cousin was Senator Barry Goldwater.

3. Brian Niiya, "Introduction," Japanese American Historical Society of Southern California, *Nanka Nikkei Voices: Resettlement Years, 1945–1955* (Torrance, CA: Japanese American Historical Society of Southern California, 1998).

4. Lane Hirabayashi with Kenichiro Shimada, *Japanese American Resettlement through the Lens: Hikaru Carl Iwasaki and the WRA's Photographic Section, 1943–1945* (Boulder: University of Colorado Press, 2009), 4.

5. Lon Kurashige, *Japanese American Celebration and Conflict: A History of Ethnic Identity and Festival, 1934–1990* (Berkeley and Los Angeles: University of California Press, 2002); and Valerie Matsumoto, *City Girls: The Nisei Social World in Los Angeles, 1920–1950* (New York: Oxford University Press, 2014).

6. Brian Niiya, "Return to West Coast" *Densho Encyclopedia*. March 3, 2015, http://encyclopedia.densho.org/Return%20to%20West%20Coast.

7. Tetsuden Kashima, "Japanese American Internees Return, 1945 to 1955: Readjustment and Social Amnesia," *Phylon* 41.2 (June 1980): 110.

8. Charles B. Spaulding, "Housing Problems of Minority Groups in Los Angeles County," *Annals of the American Academy of Political and Social Science* 248 (November 1946): 225.

9. *Pacific Citizen*, October 6, 1946.

10. Matsumoto, *City Girls*, 177.

11. *Pacific Citizen*, November 3, 1945, 2.

12. Niiya, "Return to the West Coast."

13. "The Race War That Flopped," *Ebony* (July 1946): 3–9.

14. Hillary Jenks, "Bronzeville, Little Tokyo, and the Unstable Geography of Race in Post-World War II Los Angeles," *Southern California Quarterly* 93.2 (Summer 2011): 201–235.

15. Hillary Jenks, "Bronzeville, Little Tokyo, and the Unstable Geography of Race in Post-World War II Los Angeles," 232.

16. Spaulding, "Housing Problems of Minority Groups in Los Angeles County," 220–221.

17. Greg Robinson, *After Camp: Portraits in Midcentury Japanese American Life and Politics* (Berkeley: University of California Press, 2012), 60.

18. George Takei, interviewed by Terry Gross, "From 'Star Trek' To LGBT Spokesman, What It Takes 'To Be Takei'" *Fresh Air*, National Public Radio, July 28, 2014, http://www.npr.org/2014/07/28/335945625/whats-it-like-to-be-takei-george-takei-offers-a-glimpse.

19. Rev. Goldwater, a descendant of German Jewish immigrants, converted to Buddhism. During World War II he oversaw the possessions of Japanese American Buddhists held at the Hompa Hongwanji Buddhist Temple, "Senshin Buddhist Temple History (http://www.senshintemple.org/Senshin.html)" n.d.; and the Reverend Arthur Takemoto, interviewed by James V. Gatewood in *REgenerations Oral History Project: Rebuilding Japanese American Families, Communites, and Civil Rights in the Resettlement Era* (Los Angeles Region: Volume II. Los Angeles: Japanese American National Museum, 2000). http://texts.cdlib.org/view?docId=ft358003z1&doc.view=entire_text.

20. Quoted in Matsumoto, *City Girls*, 187.

21. *Pacific Citizen*, May 25, 1946, 5.

22. *When You Leave the Relocation Center* (http://encyclopedia.densho.org/sources/en-ddr-densho-274-15-1/) (War Relocation Authority, n.d.)

23. Corina Knoll, "Japanese Gardener One of the Last of a Disappearing Breed," *Los Angeles Times*, September 25, 2012; and Naomi Hirahara, *A Scent of Flowers: The History of the Southern California Flower Market, 1912–2004* (Pasadena, CA: Midori Books, 2004).

24. Hirahara, *Scent of Flowers*, 24

25. Matsumoto, *City Girls*, 192.

26. Matsumoto, *City Girls*.

27. Elmer Smith, "Resettlement of Japanese Americans," *Far Eastern Survey* 18.10 (May 1949): 118.

28. Matsumoto, *City Girls*.

29. Scott Kurashige, *The Shifting Grounds of Race: Black and Japanese Americans and the Making of*

Multiethnic Los Angeles (Princeton, NJ: Princeton University Press, 2008), 250, 252.

30. Kurashige, *The Shifting Grounds of Race*, 245.

31. Kashima, "Japanese American Internees Return, 1945 to 1955," 108.

32. Kurashige, "Crenshaw and the Rise of Multiethnic Los Angeles," *Afro-Hispanic Review* 27.1 (Spring 2008): 51.

33. Spaulding, "Housing Problems of Minority Groups in Los Angeles County"; US Department of the Interior, War Agency Liquidation Unit (formerly the War Relocation Authority), *People in Motion: The Postwar Adjustment of the Evacuated Japanese Americans* (Washington, DC: US Government Printing Office, 1947); and Smith, "Resettlement of Japanese Americans."

34. Leonard Bloom and Ruth Riemer, *Removal and Return* (Berkeley: University of California Press, 1949).

35. William Petersen, "Success Story: Japanese American Style," *New York Times Magazine*, January 6, 1966.

36. Daniel Patrick Moynihan, *The Negro Family: The Case for National Action* (Washington, DC: US Department of Labor, 1965).

37. Kashima, "Japanese American Internees Return, 1945 to 1955."

38. Valerie Matsumoto, "Los Angeles: Postwar Snapshots," *REgenerations Oral History Project: Rebuilding Japanese American Families, Communities, and Civil Rights in the Resettlement Era* (Los Angeles: Japanese American National Museum, 2000), xxix.

39. Hirabayashi with Shimada, *Resettlement Through the Lens*; Robinson, *After Camp*; and Matsumoto, *City Girls*.

40. Charlotte Brooks, *Alien Neighbors, Foreign Friends: Asian Americans, Housing, and the Transformation of Urban California* (Chicago: University of Chicago Press, 2009).

41. Jenks, "Bronzeville, Little Tokyo, and the Unstable Geography of Race in Post-World War II Los Angeles."

42. Kurashige, *The Shifting Grounds of Race*; and Mark Brilliant, *The Color of America Has Changed: How Racial Diversity Shaped Civil Rights Reform in California, 1941–1978* (New York: Oxford University Press, 2010).

Jean-Paul R. deGuzman

VIETNAMESE AMERICANS IN LITTLE SAIGON, CALIFORNIA

Little Saigon in Orange County, California, is the largest diasporic community of Vietnamese, and home to nearly 200,000 Vietnamese, or 10 percent of the entire Vietnamese American population. It is also the cultural and political nucleus of the overseas Vietnamese population, which, in the West, has historically been a refugee-oriented and anti-communist demographic. The name Saigon holds tremendous nostalgic significance for overseas Vietnamese as a signifier for the country and capital city that ceased to exist under communist rule. Little Saigon's business presence spans a multitude of adjacent small cities such as Santa Ana, Garden Grove, Fountain Valley, and Westminster. The sheer size of Little Saigon has allowed it to sustain longstanding and culturally influential businesses and institutions at the local level, which has translated into greater visibility at the global level. As a result, Vietnamese throughout the world know of Little Saigon, sometimes via alternative references such as the town of Westminster or Bolsa Avenue. Spatially, Little Saigon follows a contemporary model of suburban ethnic enclave formation, which started with Asian-owned businesses occupying what used to be white-owned shopping centers and establishments.

Vietnamese enclaves in San Francisco, San Jose, San Diego and other towns have chosen, sometimes after acrimonious debate, to adopt the moniker "Little Saigon," which is generally reserved for Orange County, California, home to nearly 200,000 Vietnamese. The business presence of Little Saigon in Orange County spans a multitude of adjacent small cities such as Santa Ana, Garden Grove, and Fountain Valley, but its historically central thoroughfare—and Lunar New Year parade route—runs along the 9000 strip of Bolsa Avenue in Westminster. The sheer size of Little Saigon has allowed it to sustain longstanding and culturally influential businesses and institutions at the local level, which has translated into greater visibility at the global level. As a result, Vietnamese throughout the world know of Little Saigon, sometimes via alternative references such as Bolsa Avenue or the neighboring city of Santa Ana. Spatially, Little Saigon follows a contemporary model of suburban ethnic enclave formation, which started with Asian-owned businesses occupying what used to be white-owned shopping centers and establishments. Despite the turnover in the commercial sector, the residential makeup in and around Little Saigon is a little more diverse, consisting primarily of whites, Latinos, and Asians.

Unlike most immigrants, Vietnamese Americans, as refugees, have gained entry into the United States on moral, rather than legal, grounds. Their presence in the United States, once viewed as a melancholy reminder of an unfortunate war that Americans would rather forget, eventually served to portray America, as the receiving nation for half a million Indochinese refugees, in a far more positive light than the war ever could. Consistent with that logic, charitable and guilt-ridden white Americans have felt morally obligated to support the formation and preservation of a South Vietnamese refugee community as a way to atone for America's failure to protect its wartime allies from communism.

ORIGINS

Little Saigon first came into existence after the end of the Vietnam War—what Vietnamese history books refer to as the Second Indochina War or American War—in 1975. Prior to that time, only a small number of Vietnamese, mostly those possessing a student or marriage visa, lived in the United States. The defeat of the American-backed Saigon regime after a ten-year civil war created an exodus of refugees fearful of persecution under the new Soviet-backed communist government.

Washington, fearing the worst, arranged for the evacuation of 130,000 select individuals from Saigon prior to April 30, 1975. On this list were high officials of the regime, relatives of American citizens, and US government employees, most of whom were of Vietnamese origin. The chaotic nature of a hastily arranged evacuation, in which family and friends would be forever separated, resulted in many missed flights out of Vietnam while many unauthorized and undocumented individuals found their way into military custody. This cohort of 130,000 would become the first of many waves of refugee migration. Despite the inclusion of rural fishing families with no college education and poor English skills, this wave of exiles was collectively far more educated, urbanized, and Christian than the rest of the country. Prior to resettlement as civilians in the United States, they were housed by the US military in makeshift tent cities at Camp Pendleton in California, Fort Chaffee in Arkansas, Fort Indiantown Gap in Pennsylvania, and Eglin Air Force Base in Florida. Even in these transient surroundings, the Vietnamese managed to create the semblance of an ethnic enclave by organizing religious services, publishing poetry, attending music concerts, and scheduling dozens of weddings. According to one camp volunteer, the staff at Camp Pendleton journeyed approximately sixty miles "all the way to Chinatown in Los Angeles to get fish sauce and rice noodles" for the refugees because "those things weren't available in Orange County or San Diego County at that time."[1] Journalists of the period, borrowing from naming conventions of past American ethnic enclaves, referred to the military camps as "Little Saigon," not realizing it would become the preferred title for most refugee Vietnamese communities.

Few Americans expected Little Saigon to survive beyond the refugee camps. It was the intention of the United States government to disperse 130,000 Southeast Asian refugees across every stretch of the country, mostly for the sake of easing the economic burden on local communities, but also based on the assumption that less exposure to co-ethnics would encourage refugees, most of whom spoke very limited English, to more quickly become self-sufficient. Camp newsletters and refugee pamphlets with names like *New Life* and *New Horizon* provided lessons on "American Ways" of body language, conversation, and customs. They stated that the best way to express gratitude for America's generosity was to assimilate into the new society. Churches sponsored refugees in large numbers and often encouraged them to attend English-language Sunday services and convert to Christianity. Without any formalized diplomatic relationship between Washington and Hanoi, most observers assumed that all human traffic between Vietnam and the United States would cease after 1975.

Orange County in the 1970s was still a suburban metropolis in the making, as much of its semirural acreage had yet to be converted to valuable real estate beyond Disneyland. It was situated just north of Camp Pendleton Marine Base and in 1970 had a population of 1,421,233, almost all white. Like most rural whites of the 20th century, Orange Countians voted overwhelmingly Republican, to the chagrin of Democratic presidential candidates since Franklin Roosevelt. Despite the region's ultra conservative political leanings, the editorial board of the local newspaper, the *Orange County Register*, made an impassioned case for admitting Vietnamese refugees during a time of economic uncertainty. "We have to accommodate them, absolutely must," despite their anticipated burden on a sluggish job market. "We'll think about those practical matters later," they continued. "Right now we must think of the moral imperative."[2] For them, saving 130,000 was the least America could do to an ally it had abandoned. The area that would become Little Saigon consisted of postwar suburban formations that had never outgrown their semirural status while emerging suburban utopias such as Costa Mesa and Irvine, located strategically along the San Diego Freeway and close to a new University of California campus, hoped to fulfill that dream. The *Los Angeles Times* once described Westminster as a city "lined with bean fields and half-empty shopping centers." Suburbs promised a refuge from the bustling city, but without economic growth, suburbs constantly flirted with bankruptcy for lack of sufficient tax revenue. Ed Bynon, former publisher of the *Westminster Journal*, once quipped that "if it were not for the Westminster Mall, there would be no Westminster."[3]

What Orange County lacked in economic stability it made up for with generous churches willing to house and care for Southeast Asian refugees. Overall, faith-based organizations in the United States found sponsors for almost 75 percent of the refugee caseload in 1975.[4] As one sponsor observed, "the church structure guaranteed a kind of built-in conscience which would guard against mistreatment."[5] This was important because sponsors were under no legal obligation to care for refugees, only a moral one. The United States Catholic Conference sponsored over fifty thousand while the American Lutheran Church exceeded their pledge to sponsor ten thousand refugees.[6] The Reverend Lester Kim of Los Angeles asked Asian American Christians to welcome their "sisters and brothers from Southeast Asia."[7]

The ability of Southern California churches to absorb so many refugees allowed more families to stay intact, an early harbinger of things to come in terms of community building.[8] According to Alicia Cooper of the International Rescue Committee, the Catholic and Episcopalian churches in Orange County outdid the rest when it came to accepting refugees. As she recalled, "it was nothing for a church in Orange County to take twelve or thirteen families." By that standard, St. Anselm's in Garden Grove acquired legendary status among Vietnamese Americans. It reportedly "never said no" to any of the refugees. "It did not matter if there were two people in that family or twenty people in that family," said Cooper. "If you called Father Habibi and said, 'I have this family, Father, and I have to get them out of here by five o'clock tonight or there's to be serious trouble,' he would say, 'OK.'"[9] Several bilingual Vietnamese who already served as volunteers in Camp Pendleton, most notably Mai Cong and Nam Lộc Nguyễn, became social workers who served as valuable cultural brokers for their co-ethnics in need of immigration services, job assistance, and public benefits. Because of generous churches and California's desirable climate, Camp Pendleton's refugee center was the first to close its doors on October 31, 1975, despite receiving over 40 percent of the first wave of refugees. By the end of 1975, approximately twenty thousand Vietnamese refugees found themselves resettled all over Southern California. With its proximity to Camp Pendleton and its abundance of altruistic Christian sponsors, Orange County received twelve thousand of them. By the end of 1976, up to seven hundred low-income refugees had crammed themselves into seventy-five units at the Villa Park apartment complex in Garden Grove, forming an early building block of the largest overseas Vietnamese community.[10]

EARLY COMMUNITY SPACES

The refugee dimension of Little Saigon, and the politics of rescue associated with refugees, differentiates it from traditional immigrant ethnic enclaves. Refugees cannot simply rely on their country of origin in navigating strange new lands. The fact Vietnamese were scattered across all fifty states meant they barely interacted with Asians on a regular basis. The fact most lived beneath the poverty line meant that few had time for pursuits beyond individual and family survival. Places like Villa Park were the exception rather than the rule. It is thus not surprising that the first signs of ethnic community mostly took shape in existing spaces staffed by exceptionally charitable individuals. Little Saigon's formation was

wrapped in a discourse and history of American goodwill, with refugees conditioned to be grateful for every American intervention, from war to resettlement to a place of their own. At the same time, American goodwill was borne of a profound sense of guilt and obligation for the failure to secure a more favorable outcome to the Vietnam War. It is only within this nexus of guilt and gratitude that we can properly grasp the Vietnamese American experience.

The Vietnamese Catholic community in Orange County started out with three thousand would-be parishioners, and by October 1975 approximately two hundred of them attended their first post-camp Vietnamese mass at the auxiliary hall of St. Boniface Church in Anaheim. From the onset, diocese officials organized mixers for the refugees, who "cherished every opportunity to see each other."[11] Carpooling from as far as Norwalk and El Monte, often with the help of diocese volunteers, the Vietnamese soon convinced Monsignor John C. Keenan to grant them the 9:00 AM time slot every Sunday at St. Catherine's Military School. Initially, there was only one priest, Father Vũ Tuấn Tú, to serve the Vietnamese community. By the end of 1977, the Roman Catholic Diocese of Orange had three Vietnamese priests—as a result of secondary migration from colder climates in the United States—leading prayers in the vernacular at five different parishes.[12] Attendance at St. Barbara's in Santa Ana routinely exceeded its twelve-hundred-seat capacity despite the 6:30 AM start time every Sunday. The concentration of Vietnamese Catholic services in Orange County gave a quarter of the Vietnamese population there, especially the elderly and poor, a prime incentive to live as close as possible to these churches.[13]

Vietnamese in their twenties and thirties took advantage of Southern California's affordable and plentiful public higher education system to build small but significant social networks. Gayle Morrison, a guidance counselor at Santa Ana College in the 1970s, took a particular interest in the new influx of Southeast Asian students at her school by co-founding the New Horizons program and advising the Vietnamese Student Association. With her assistance, the VSA successfully staged one of the first refugee Tết lunar new year festivals at Santa Ana College on February 7, 1978.[14] Knowing her students could not get far without financial assistance, Morrison petitioned the federal government to grant fee waivers for hundreds of Vietnamese community college students in Southern California who would take the Test of English as a Foreign Language exam (TOEFL) in order to successfully transfer to a four-year college.[15] New Horizons also published a list of forty-five subsidized child-care centers in Orange County so that Vietnamese parents had no excuse to forgo a college education.[16]

Early on, it was necessary to travel all the way to Chinatown in Los Angeles to secure ethnic foodstuffs, pick up a newspaper, go dancing, and converse with people from the old country. As social worker Mai Cong recalls, "I rarely saw Asian people [in Orange County.] I only ran across whites. Therefore, I dreamed of seeing Asian people when I went to the markets…I felt so happy when meeting with any Asian because I was actually homesick."[17] As future politician Tony Lâm explained, "We either met each other in Chinatown or we called every Vietnamese name in the phone book."[18] Social worker Nam Lộc Nguyễn stated it even more emphatically: "Every weekend, people from Orange County drove to Chinatown or Hollywood. That was their treat…after a hardworking week, go to Chinatown, go to Hollywood. There was a Vietnamese nightclub and Vietnamese restaurants on Hollywood Boulevard."[19] One could also shop at Man Wah Company, just off College Street, for bootlegged Vietnamese music cassettes, Chinese herbal medicine, Vietnamese periodicals and books, fish sauce from Thailand, shrimp paste from the Philippines, Chinese sausage from Canada, pickled scallions from Japan, and instant noodles

from Taiwan.[20] Also among the first refugee markets in Chinatown was Ai Hoa, which continues to operate at 860 North Hill Street. Many businesses catering to Vietnamese, especially grocery stores, jewelry, and commercial real estate, were owned by Vietnamese of Chinese ancestry, many of whom worked as merchants in pre-1975 Saigon. Even those with little to no business background were better positioned than their Southeast Asian peers to become ethnic entrepreneurs right away. Their ethnic background and fluency in Cantonese enabled them to potentially link up with Chinese businesspeople across North America and in Asian countries not embargoed by the United States. Just as importantly, it gave them access to a larger customer base as Chinese have always outnumbered Vietnamese in the United States. Potential access to longstanding import/export networks gave Sino-Vietnamese (and other refugees) of Chinese descent a twenty-year head start on the rest of Little Saigon.

GROWTH IN ORANGE COUNTY

Upon his arrival in 1979, newspaper publisher Yến Đỗ remembered "only 12 businesses in Orange County," which included places like Saigon Market, which opened its doors on 2329 West First Street in the summer of 1976, as well as Hoa Bình Market, which did the same on Bolsa Ave in 1978. Danh's Pharmacy opened virtually next door, and has remained there to this day. Scanning the rest of the business district, one took notice of bean fields, strawberry patches, and Anglo-owned family businesses. But by 1980, over one hundred Indochinese businesses had sprung up all over Orange County, and in the process transformed a majority-white suburb just as Chinese entrepreneurs were doing in the suburban Los Angeles to the north.[21] On the supply side, entrepreneurs like Roger Chen, the owner of Man Wah Market in Chinatown, joined forces in 1981 with Frank Jao, then a fledgling entrepreneur, to buy up properties on the 9000 block of Bolsa Avenue in Westminster.[22] That same year, Duong Huu Chuong, a pharmacist from Vietnam, opened up Wai-Wai, the largest Asian supermarket in Orange County at the time.[23] Back in 1979, he had just opened up his first grocery store with $5000 he had managed to smuggle out of Vietnam. By 1984, he, along with Chinese friends in Taiwan, Thailand, and the United States operated an import-export business that stocked over one hundred grocery stores in Southern California.[24] From 1975 to 1984, developers from Taiwan and Hong Kong had invested $10 million along Bolsa Avenue alone.[25] Frank Jao would go on to dominate Little Saigon's commercial real estate market, becoming by far the wealthiest Vietnamese American.

This growth occurred in Westminster in particular because of affordable real estate and local politicians who proved far more accommodating to Vietnamese refugees. In 1981, Westminster's new mayor Kathy Buchoz championed Little Saigon's growth despite the outcry of angry white residents who had gathered 170 signatures opposing further Indochinese business expansion. After walking away outraged from meetings with them she likened to "being with the Ku Klux Klan," Buchoz convinced the city council to continue issuing business licenses, to the delight of Vietnamese Americans. During the 1980s, Vietnamese businesses in Orange County generated $300 million per year in annual sales. Buchoz's successor, Chuck Smith, followed the same course. US Census data indicated that between 1982 and 1987, the number of Vietnamese-owned businesses increased from 4,989 to 25,671, an astronomical 415 percent rate that far exceeded the 135 percent increase in their population during the same period. No other Asian American group saw such a dramatic rise in their business sector.[26] Under Smith's watch, Little Saigon became an officially recognized and designated Special Tourist Zone. At a June 17, 1988, ceremony held at Frank Jao's Asian Garden Mall, Governor George Deukmejian formally unveiled the "Little Saigon" freeway sign to an audience of nearly four hundred awed spectators. "Each year, Little Saigon attracts thousands of tourists, shoppers and business people," said the governor to enthusiastic applause. "The dedication of this new freeway sign is further recognition of the importance of Little Saigon as a major cultural, social and commercial center." For a people whose home country literally erased the name "Saigon" from the map, seeing "Saigon" back on the map thirteen years later brought forth tears of joy, affirmation, and gratitude. "Only in America is Saigon being resurrected," said future politician Văn Thái Trần, who was in attendance.[27]

On the demand side, Little Saigon's population grew by leaps and bounds since the 1970s, providing businesses with thousands of paying customers. Some of it was the result of secondary migration as first-wave refugees across the United States packed their bags for Southern California. Many more came directly from Southeast Asia as the boat people crisis of the late 1970s convinced much of the non-communist world that hundreds of thousands would not risk death at the open sea or in the Cambodian jungles unless life in communist Vietnam was much worse. When the United States in 1979 agreed to admit over ten thousand Indochinese refugees per month, California's relatively robust social welfare system provided thousands of Southeast Asians with the means necessary to pay for food, shelter, and medical care. This fact enabled supermarkets and physicians to profit despite widespread poverty in Little Saigon. During the 1980s, Vietnamese Americans very infamously exploited welfare benefits to help themselves and their loved ones. As publisher Yến Đỗ admitted, "For health [care], some people overused Medi-Cal vouchers to buy drugs for relatives back home [while] some people applied for housing [assistance] in more than one place while the rules say every citizen should apply for housing in only one city. Some refugees applied for their relatives even before the relatives arrived. It may look like fraud, but that's the way they survived."[28] Many outside observers, unaware of these extenuating circumstances, hastily labeled Vietnamese as model minorities who went from rags to riches with minimal government assistance. The residents of Little Saigon, under extreme pressure to assimilate, refute new stereotypes of themselves as thugs, and justify an unpopular war that cost 58,000 lives, billions of dollars, and a great deal of American prestige, were all too willing to play along with the model minority stereotype.

CULTURAL AND BUSINESS INSTITUTIONS

Little Saigon is home to many culturally influential businesses and institutions of the Vietnamese diaspora such as newspapers, radio, television, and music production. Yến Đỗ, a former newspaperman in Saigon, arrived in Orange County in 1979 determined to combine his old trade with the new skills he had acquired as a social worker in Texas. He started *Người Việt News* and filled it with articles on, "how to get jobs, how to apply for welfare, how to apply for a driver's license, even how to buy insurance."[29] Within a few years, it became the most successful Vietnamese newspaper in America. Over the years it has competed with dozens of publications as a part of an ethnic media niche that has managed to remain strong in the early 21st century even while mainstream newspaper readership has declined. Beside providing readers valuable updates about life in post-1975 Vietnam, *Người Việt News* and its competitors once served as the unofficial "yellow pages" of Little Saigon via ad copy. Accompanying ads for restaurants and doctors were those for brand new tract housing starting at $40,000 and new shopping centers in need of tenants, which reflected a growth potential in Orange County not possible in Los Angeles.[30]

Music is the dominant form of entertainment produced by the Vietnamese American community, all by companies based in Orange County. This particular industry is unique because many of its world-famous—within the diaspora—artists specialize in music created during the short-lived Saigon regime that lasted from 1954 to 1975. These songs range from dance tunes and love songs about soldiers and spouses to the antiwar music of Trịnh Công Sơn. Through new arrangements and new voices, music producers have breathed new life into old covers, and maximized profits without having to invest in a new generation of songwriters. The first wave of refugee artists like Phạm Duy, Khánh Ly, Hoàng Oanh, and Thanh Tuyền sold analog copies of whatever music tapes they carried with them, charging $5 per tape. The arrival of later waves of refugees reunited established stars with their old profession and created opportunities for new talent like emcee Nguyễn Ngộc Ngàn and vocalist Như Quỳnh. During the early 1990s, music companies began selling epic-length concert videos under brands like Hollywood Nights, Paris by Night, Asia, and Vân Sơn. Because of Cold War barriers that banned pre-1975 Saigon music in post-1975 Vietnam, these songs were especially meaningful to new refugees who could finally enjoy this music without fear of persecution.

The continuing growth and competition in Little Saigon often pits these businesses and institutions against each other. During the 1990s, as many as three lunar new year's festivals competed against each other, often diluting the quality of each. Historically, the onset of external threats led these competing interests to find common ground.

POLITICS OF LITTLE SAIGON

Vietnamese Americans have traditionally been politically active on issues related to their Asian homeland. During the Cold War, they campaigned on two major issues: reuniting with family members still in Vietnam and regime change in Hanoi. The former issue energized much of Little Saigon prior to the 1990s. When the boat people crisis saw tens of thousands of Indochinese languishing in refugee camps across Southeast Asia, hoping to be granted asylum, community members rallied in downtown Los Angeles, carrying signs that read "Sending the Refugees Back Is Murder" or "Please do not send Vietnamese refugees back to Vietnam." Fourteen Vietnamese refugees in Santa Ana participated in a hunger strike to protest human rights violations in Vietnam while hundreds marched in front of the White House. Events like these inaugurated a tradition of protest urging America not to turn its back on old allies in need. The State Department reached a series of agreements with Hanoi to grant exit visas to people with special ties to the United States such as relatives of Vietnamese Americans, Amerasian children, and former political prisoners. Having largely succeeded in their efforts to win asylum for the boat people and ensure that Vietnamese Americans were reunited with family members, this coalition often appears at community functions with signs reading, "Thank you, America."

The coalition agitating for regime change in Vietnam is better known, but has enjoyed far less success. Whereas the cause of family reunification attracted broad nonpartisan support, the cause of regime change has appealed primarily to American conservatives. During the Reagan years—when the United States secretly funded anti-communist insurgents throughout the world—various diasporic Vietnamese groups raised money to ostensibly build their own army of insurgents to reclaim the lost homeland. Organizations like the National United Front for the Liberation of Vietnam raised millions of dollars through grassroots fundraising and a chain of restaurants, but never recruited an army of ten thousand men as they often claimed. Nevertheless, the resistance movement created a climate of fear and paranoia in which those who dared to question its motives

and methods would be branded as communist sympathizers, a crime for which the fortunate received only death threats. Five not-so-lucky Vietnamese American journalists paid with their lives. Consequently, Yến Đỗ publisher of Little Saigon's largest newspaper, *Người Việt News*, mastered the art of pretending to outsource news from the *Los Angeles Times* and *Orange County Register*, quoting from stories his own reporters leaked to the English-language papers, in order to avoid charges of pro-communist bias. Mainstream observers hoped that this negative component of Little Saigon would fade away over time as the younger American-born generation replaced the refugee generation.

Orange County was home to many firsts in Vietnamese American electoral politics. In 1992, businessman Tony Lâm ran for one of the vacant seats in the Westminster City Council. Having lived in Orange County since the late 1970s, where he ran the Viễn Đông restaurant and co-founded the Vietnamese American Chamber of Commerce, Lâm had built a wealth of contacts and allies all the way up to Mayor Chuck Smith. His victory garnered national headlines as he became America's first elected official of Vietnamese descent. In 2004, attorney Vân Thái Trần, a protégé of State Senator Ed Royce and US Representative Bob Dornan, became the first Vietnamese to serve in a state assembly, where he represented the 68th district. In 2007, Janet Nguyễn became the first Vietnamese to be elected as county supervisor. In 2012, Trí Ta of Westminster became the first Vietnamese to win a mayoral election in the United States. All four politicians ran as Republicans based partly on their own conservative and anti-communist values, but it was also the only realistic way to move up the power structure in a region dominated by Republicans. In addition, Republicans were among the white politicians speaking in defense of Vietnamese Americans in times of need. Mayor Pete Wilson of San Diego was among the first to welcome Vietnamese in

1975 when 54 percent of Americans felt otherwise. Westminster Mayor Kathy Buchoz defended the Vietnamese against white nativists. Her successor, Chuck Smith, helped get Little Saigon designated as a Special Tourist Zone. State Senator Ed Royce reminded locals that the arrest of twenty-four Vietnamese for health insurance fraud should not reflect on Little Saigon as a whole. And Congressman Bob Dornan tirelessly advocated for the two major political constituencies within Little Saigon. Despite the Republican Party's general insensitivity toward blacks, women, immigrants, and other minorities, there emerged a cozy relationship between them and Vietnamese (as well as Cuban) refugees, partly because the accelerated rags to riches journey of the refugees provided a morally uplifting conclusion to the Vietnam War, an ending that portrays America in a very positive light, an ending conservatives would like to see more of in US textbooks and collective memory.

In November 2014, Bảo Nguyễn became the first ever Vietnamese mayor of Garden Grove, California, defeating incumbent Bruce Broadwater by fifteen votes. Nguyen is best known in the community as the University of California, Irvine, student who in 2000 protested against Senator John McCain for his casual and problematic distinction between "good" Vietnamese Americans and the "gooks" who tortured him for six years in a communist prison. Elders in the refugee community, seeing McCain as a rare political ally they could not afford to alienate, attacked Bảo Nguyen and his comrades. After graduating from UCI with a degree in political science, Nguyen eventually joined the Garden Grove Unified School District Board of Trustees. A Democrat who is fluent in English, Spanish, and Vietnamese, Nguyen's success will likely serve as a template for future candidates and coalitions that speak on behalf of constituents not as well served by the traditional Vietnamese-Republican alliance.

POST–COLD WAR ERA AND SAVING LITTLE SAIGON

The post–Cold War reconciliation between Washington and Hanoi carried significant ramifications for Little Saigon. Neoliberals like President Bill Clinton embraced normalization between former enemies as a victory for US capitalism while decades of modernity in Asian republics convinced Hanoi's communist leadership that capitalism could be treated as an inevitable outgrowth of Eastern society. Vietnamese Americans in Little Saigon felt more ambivalent about lifting the American embargo in the absence of mandatory political reforms. Normalization effectively killed the possibility of regime change in the near term and introduced the possibility that the free flow of pro-Hanoi immigrants to America would, in the long term, transform Little Saigon into Little Ho Chi Minh City, and that refugees would lose one of the few spaces left for them to enjoy their version of Vietnamese culture, history, and identity, a version banned in the homeland. The arrival of over 200,000 former political prisoners during the 1990s—known informally as the H.O. people—intensified anti-communist sentiment in Little Saigon, for these families had endured the worst brutalities under the post-1975 regime and thus had the greatest incentive to see that it never gained a foothold in the United States.

The H.O. people were among the thousands who gathered for nearly two months outside a video store displaying the current Vietnamese flag and a portrait of communist hero Hồ Chí Minh. The problems began in January 1999 when the owner of the Hi-Tek video store, Trần Văn Trường, decided after a winter trip to Ho Chi Minh City that he would proudly display these communist symbols at his Bolsa Avenue store in order to "further the dialogue" on how much Vietnam had progressed for the better. He was eventually arrested and evicted from his property for selling pirated videos, but mainstream media treated him as a champion of free speech and the protestors as the champions of intolerance. Westminster city council member Margie Rice, exasperated from Anglo complaints, confessed that, "I feel like [the Vietnamese] are taking over our city, plain and simple. I would think that after 20 years or so of being here and being given the freedoms that they want, they would calm down. By God, how long can you go on fighting this war?"[31] In a 2004 documentary entitled *Saigon USA*, filmmakers Lindsey Jang and Robert Winn explored what they saw as a widening generation gap between anti-communist—that is to say, *paranoid*—parents and their Americanized— that is to say, *normal*—children.[32]

Mainstream media, by refusing to view the incident through a transnational lens, left the impression that protestors were ignorant of American laws and customs—such as free speech—when in fact the protesters were fully aware that only in America could they engage in dissent against the government of Vietnam and have it heard around the world. When viewed through a transnational lens, refugees were not refusing to become American, but rather taking full advantage of their status as Americans. The high concentration of Vietnamese in Orange County gives them the political leverage at the local level necessary to maintain the types of "Cold War refuge" that is not possible in communities with a smaller percentage of Vietnamese Americans.[33]

The political priorities of the H.O. people in the midst of normalization helped to frame the transformation of Frank Fry from local bête noire to populist friend of the South Vietnamese. Starting in 1996, Mayor Fry supported the construction of a Vietnam War Memorial that also honored America's allies, telling his constituents, "It's the only place in the world where you'll see an American and a [South] Vietnamese standing side by side on the battlefield."[34] Indeed, the memorial displayed a level of American respect and admiration the for South Vietnamese that hardly

existed during the actual war. But when an official from communist Vietnam demanded that the statue instead depict American and North Vietnamese soldiers standing side-by-side in a show of friendship, the entire community of Westminster rallied behind the refugee statue. The memorial was finally unveiled on April 2003 to a packed audience at Freedom Park in Westminster.

Following the Hi-Tek protests of 1999, community members took more preemptive, yet controversial, measures to save Little Saigon from extinction. The majority-white city leaders of Westminster and Garden Grove, wanting no repeat of the costly and embarrassing Hi-Tek protests, were happy to have their towns declared Communist Free Zones. Little Saigon led the way in city councils passing resolutions recognizing the yellow flag of the defunct Republic of Vietnam as the official flag of the overseas Vietnamese community, fixing a refugee identity on a population in flux. Beginning in 2000, local refugee newspapers published oral histories from the older generation. Cal State Fullerton University did the same in 2000, while the Southeast Asian Archive at UC Irvine followed suit in 2011. Vietnamese now make up over 40 percent of Westminster, the largest concentration in any American city, giving this Asian American group tremendous potential political clout, assuming they can reach consensus on issues. When asked if Little Saigon would survive the double onslaught of cultural assimilation and immigration from post–Cold War Vietnam, one prominent community member postulated, "The day you see democracy in Vietnam is the day Little Saigon is no longer needed." Whether they succeed in preserving Little Saigon will also depend on how committed the younger generation remains to refugee identity, how morally obligated the rest of American society feels about keeping Little Saigon intact, and how new migrants from Vietnam feel about maintaining a community whose ethnic history and identity, though claiming to be authentic, is not currently allowed to exist in the homeland.

DISCUSSION OF THE LITERATURE

The literature on Vietnamese Americans has primarily focused on the question of assimilation. Social scientists of the 1970s and 1980s used case studies of Vietnamese Americans to determine whether the particularly traumatic experiences and memories of refugees put them on a different trajectory of structural adaptation than that of regular immigrants. These studies by concerned liberal scholars treated the refugee experience, one borne of war and trauma and the desire to return home, as something inherently problematic with unforeseen effects on mental health and economic well-being. They wondered whether refugees could become American. Representative studies of that period include Gail Paradise Kelly's *From Vietnam to America: A Chronicle of the Vietnamese Immigration to the United States* (Boulder, CO: Westview, 1977); Darrel Montero's *Vietnamese Americans: Patterns of Resettlement and Socioeconomic Adaptation in the United States* (Boulder, CO: Westview, 1979); and Walter Liu's *Transition to Nowhere: Vietnamese Refugees in America* (Nashville, TN: Charter House, 1979).

Early ethnic studies scholars, who had posed an alternative model of Americanization whereby immigrants become racialized in the United States, wondered aloud if Vietnamese Americans' apparent obsession with the past and returning to the homeland functioned as a form of false consciousness that obscured their ability to collectively mobilize against social issues in their midst. In other words, they wondered if Vietnamese refugees could assume the sociohistorical / identity known as Asian American, as people aware and equipped to deal with racism and economic inequality. A few studies attempted to awaken an Asian American panethnic consciousness within Vietnamese Americans. These include Ronald Takaki's *Strangers from a Different Shore* (Boston: Penguin, 1989); Nazli Kibria's *A Family Tightrope: The Changing Lives of Vietnamese Americans* (Princeton, NJ: Princeton University Press, 1995); and Min Zhou and Carl Bankston's *Growing Up American: How Vietnamese Children Adapt to Life in the United States* (New York: Russell Sage Foundation, 1999); and Sucheng Chan's, *The Vietnamese American 1.5 Generation: Stories of War, Revolution, Flight and New Beginnings* (Philadelphia: Temple University Press, 2006).

A new generation of ethnic studies scholars, influenced to a certain degree by cultural studies, has not treated refugee identity as simply false consciousness, but as a social reality shaped by historical, material, social, and cultural forces in and outside the United States. Such works highlight the contingent and contextual nature of social identities, particularly the structural conditions that encourage refugee gratitude toward the United States. Studies in this mold include Karin Aguilar-San Juan's *Little Saigons: Staying Vietnamese in America* (Minneapolis: University of Minnesota Press, 2009); Nhi T. Lieu's *The American Dream in Vietnamese* (Minneapolis: University of Minnesota Press, 2011); Mimi Nguyen's *The Gift of Freedom: War, Debt, and Other Refugee Passages* (Durham, NC: Duke University Press, 2012); Kieu-Linh Valverde's *Transnationalizing Vietnam: Community, Culture, and Politics in the Diaspora* (Philadelphia: Temple University Press, 2013); Yen Le Espiritu's *Body Counts: The Vietnam War and Militarized Refuge(es)* (Berkeley: University of California Press, 2014); and Phuong Nguyen's forthcoming social and cultural history of Little Saigon, *Becoming Refugee American*.

PRIMARY SOURCES

The Southeast Asian Archive (http://seaa .lib.uci.edu/) at the University of California, Irvine, is the single largest repository of primary sources on the Vietnamese in America. There one can locate archived periodicals in English and Vietnamese such as the *Orange County Register*, *Người Việt Daily News*, *Viet Weekly*, and *Viet Tide*. In 2011, the Archive embarked on an ambitious oral history project to collect stories from hundreds of local Vietnamese Americans. Their offices house a variety of State Department reports related to Vietnamese refugees from 1975 onward. The Special Collections Department contains a variety of rare documents such as the records of Washington, DC's, Southeast Asia Resource Center (1975–2003); photographs from refugee camps in Southeast Asia; the Gayle Morrison Files on Southeast Asian Refugees in Community Colleges; interviews and clippings by scholar Sucheng Chan; and photographs from a variety of locations from 1975 to the present.

The Hoover Institution (http://www.hoover.org/library-archives) at Stanford University has an extensive collection of refugee case files from 1946 to 1989, a time span that includes refugees from Europe after World War II, from Hungary after 1956, from Cuba after 1959, and Vietnam after 1975. These documents will be in English. Both the SEAA and Hoover materials, along with other primary sources, can be located on the Online Archive of California (http://www.oac.cdlib.org/).

The Vietnam Center and Archive (VNCA) at Texas Tech University in Lubbock, Texas, focuses mainly, but not exclusively, on the US military involvement in Southeast Asia. As such, most of the documents are in English and can be easily located through their online search engine. The Center promotes all points of view about the Vietnam War and administers scholarships, outreach programs, conferences, and symposiums to bring people together to better understand this important period of history. The VNCA website can be found here (http://www.vietnam.ttu.edu).

Cornell University, in Ithaca, New York, is home to a vast collection of newspapers and periodicals, such as the newspapers from the 1975 US based refugee camps and those of diasporic communities in Los Angeles, New York, Paris, Berkeley, Washington, DC, Quebec, Tokyo, and Portland. They also have publications from post-1975 Vietnam and pro-Hanoi publications in the United States such as *Thái Bình*. They have several copies of the newspaper *Kháng Chiến*, published by the National United Front for the Liberation of Vietnam, a major anti-communist organization from the early 1980s. Most of these documents will be in Vietnamese.

FURTHER READING

Aguilar-San Juan, Karin. *Little Saigons: Staying Vietnamese in America*. Minneapolis: University of Minnesota Press, 2009.

Chan, Sucheng. *The Vietnamese American 1.5 Generation: Stories of War, Revolution, Flight and New Beginnings*. Philadelphia: Temple University Press, 2006.

Do, Yen, and Jeffrey Brody. *Yen Do and the Story of Nguoi Viet Daily News*. Fullerton, CA: Jeffrey Brody, 2003.

Espiritu, Yen Le. *Body Counts: The Vietnam War and Militarized Refuge(es)*. Berkeley: University of California Press, 2014.

Kibria, Nazli. *Family Tightrope: The Changing Lives of Vietnamese Americans*. Princeton, NJ: Princeton University Press, 1995.

Lieu, Nhi T. *The American Dream in Vietnamese*. Minneapolis: University of Minnesota Press, 2011.

Nguyen, Mimi. *The Gift of Freedom: War, Debt, and Other Refugee Passages*. Durham, NC: Duke University Press, 2012.

Valverde, Kieu-Linh Caroline. *Transnationalizing Vietnam: Community, Culture, and Politics in the Diaspora*. Philadelphia: Temple University Press, 2013.

The Vietnamese Community in Orange County: An Oral History. 4 vols. Santa Ana, CA: Newhope Library, 1991–1992.

Zhou, Min, and Carl Bankston, III. *Growing up American: How Vietnamese Children Adapt to Life in the United States*. New York: Russell Sage Foundation, 1999.

NOTES

1. Interview with Alicia Cooper, *The Vietnamese Community in Orange County: An Oral History III: Refugee Service Programs and Mutual Assistance Associations* (Santa Ana, CA: Newhope Library, 1992), 117.

2. "The Evacuees," *Orange County Register,* April 25, 1975, C6.

3. Andy Rose, "Down on Its Luck: Westminster's Saddled with a Corrupt Past and an Uncertain Future," *Los Angeles Times,* October 19, 1986, OC-A1.

4. The combined total of the US Catholic Conference (52,100), Church World Service (17,864), the Lutheran Immigration and Refugee Service (15,897), and United Hebrew Immigrant Aid Society (3,531), amounted to 74.7 percent of 119,591 total 1975 refugees resettled in the United States. Gail Paradise Kelly, *From Vietnam to America: A Chronicle of the Vietnamese Immigration to the United States* (Boulder, CO: Westview, 1977), 152. For more on the role of churches in receiving refugees see Helen Fein, *Congregational Sponsors of Indochinese Refugees in the United States, 1979–1981: Helping Beyond Borders* (Rutherford, NJ: Fairleigh Dickinson University Press, 1987); Ann Crittenden, *Sanctuary: A Story of American Conscience and the Law in Collision* (New York: Weidenfeld & Nicolson, 1988); and William E. Nawyn, *American Protestantism's Response to Germany's Jews and Refugees, 1933–1941* (Ann Arbor, MI: UMI Research Press, 1981).

5. Ellen Matthews, *Culture Clash* (Chicago: Intercultural Press, 1983), x.

6. "Lutherans to Care for 10,000 Viet Refugees," *Los Angeles Times,* May 4, 1975, A7.

7. John Dart, "Southland Churches Gear Up to Aid Asian Refugees," *Los Angeles Times,* May 10, 1975, A26.

8. Out of 24,522 families surveyed at Camp Pendleton, approximately 37 percent of families—including extended families—had five or more members. Walter Liu, *Transition to Nowhere: Vietnamese Refugees in America* (Nashville, TN: Charter House, 1979), 45.

9. Interview with Alicia Cooper, *The Vietnamese Community in Orange County: An Oral History III: Refugee Service Programs and Mutual Assistance Associations* (Santa Ana, CA: Newhope Library, 1992), 119.

10. Howard Seelye, "Agencies Take Steps to Ease Overcrowding," *Los Angeles Times,* November 16, 1976, OC1.

11. Phạm Văn Phố, "A Lot Changes in 20 Years," *Hiệp Nhất* 28 (April 1995), 17.

12. Monsignor Nguyễn Duc Tien, "The Vietnamese Catholic Community at 20 (1975–1995)" *Hiệp Nhất* 28 (April 1995), 5.

13. For more on Vietnamese Catholicism and religion in general, see Paul James Rutledge, *The Role of Religion in Ethnic Self-Identity: A Vietnamese Community* (Lanham, MD: University Press of America, 1985); *The Vietnamese Community in Orange County: An Oral History II: Religion and Resettlement of Vietnamese Refugees in Orange County* (Santa Ana, CA: Newhope Public Library, 1991); Jesse W. Nash, *Vietnamese Catholicism* (Harvey, LA: Art Review Press, 1992); and Douglas M. Padgett, *Religion, Memory, and Imagination in Vietnamese California* (PhD diss., Indiana University, 2007).

14. Letter from Vietnamese Friends Club, Santa Ana College, to Community Business Managers, January 12, 1978; Program for Tet Santa Ana College, February 7, 1978; Gayle Morrison Collection, University of California at Irvine.

15. Letter to HEW Refugee Task Force, June 27, 1978, Gayle Morrison Collection, University of California at Irvine.

16. Santa Ana College, New Horizons, *Orange County Child Care Resource Guide,* October 1979, Gayle Morrison Collection, University of California at Irvine.

17. Interview with Mai Cong, *The Vietnamese Community in Orange County: An Oral History III: Refugee Service Programs and Mutual Assistance Associations* (Santa Ana, CA: Newhope Library, 1992), 73–74.

18. Interview with Tony Lam, Westminster, CA, April 2007.

19. Interview with Nam Loc, April 2007.

20. *Trang Den* magazine, advertisement for Man Wah, March 6, 1976, 1:1, 42.

21. For more on the San Gabriel Valley's transformation, mostly by sociologists, see Leland Saito, *Race and Politics: Asian Americans, Latinos, and Whites in a Los Angeles Suburb* (Urbana and Champaign: University of Illinois Press, 1998); John Horton, *The Politics of Diversity: Immigration, Resistance, and Change in Monterey Park, California* (Philadelphia: Temple University Press, 1995); Timothy Fong, *The First Suburban Chinatown: The Remaking of Monterey Park, California* (Philadelphia: Temple University Press, 1994); and Wei Li, "Building Ethnoburbia: The Emergence and Manifestation of the Chinese

Ethnoburb in Los Angeles' San Gabriel Valley," *Journal of Asian American Studies* 2, no. 1 (February 1999), 1–28.

22. Jeffrey Brody, "Frank Jao: Real-Estate and Power Broker," *Orange County Register*, January 11, 1987, C01.

23. Rev. Nguyễn Xuan Bao, the founder of Vietnamese Christian Reformed Church, remembers upon his arrival to Orange County in 1982 that "the biggest market among many others was Wai-Wai [which was owned by Duong Huu Chuong]." *The Vietnamese Community in Orange County, An Oral History, vol. 2: Religion & Resttlement of Vietnamese Refugees in Orange County* (Santa Ana, CA: Newhope Library, 1991), 46.

24. Holley, David, "Orange County's 'Little Saigon': Chinese, Vietnamese Feel Tension, But They Coexist," *Los Angeles Times*, OC edition, October 3, 1984, 1.

25. Holley, "Orange County's 'Little Saigon."

26. Associated Press, "Businesses Up 415% Among Vietnamese," *Sun-Sentinel*, August 5, 1991, 33; Ronald Campbell, *"Vietnamese-Americans Make Business Their Life,"* Orange County Register, August 2, 1991, A1.

27. Paddock, Richard, "Governor Courts 'Little Saigon' Votes," *Los Angeles Times*, 18 June 1988, 1.

28. Do, Yen, with Jeff Brody, *Yen Do and the Story of Nguoi Viet Daily News* (Fullerton, CA: Jeffrey Brody, 2003), 45–46.

29. Do and Brody, *Yen and the Story*, 15.

30. The ad for Kingsplace tract homes appeared in the April 24,1980, issue of *Người Việt Ca Li*. The ad for the Saigon Shopping Center at the corner of Bolsa and Magnolia, complete with 20,000 square feet of retail space and 60,000 square feet of parking space, appeared in the Tết 1982 edition (nos. 41 and 42) of *Người Việt*.

31. Schmidt, Steve, "Little Saigon still reeling from Ho Chi Minh Poster," *San Diego Union-Tribune*, May 3, 1999, A1.

32. The protests in front of the Hi-Tek video store also brought out clear divisions among Vietnamese Americans. Most conspicuously, it revealed the growing voice of younger, American-raised ethnics who had no memories of suffering under the Communists or any interest in Vietnam whatsoever. More likely than their parents or grandparents to identify as American, this generation did not suffer from refugee nationalism's deference to the host country. Therefore they found it easier to not vote Republican without feeling vulnerable to conservative attacks questioning their loyalty to America.

33. Maureen Feeney, *Freedom to Speak: Vietnamese Reeducation and the Search for Cold War Refuge* (PhD diss., University of Michigan, 2002).

34. Gail Schiller, "Vietnam War Dead Saluted," *San Jose Mercury News*, April 28, 2003.

Phuong Nguyen

THE OXFORD ENCYCLOPEDIA OF
AMERICAN URBAN HISTORY

Editor in Chief
Timothy J. Gilfoyle
LOYOLA UNIVERSITY CHICAGO

THE OXFORD ENCYCLOPEDIA OF
AMERICAN URBAN HISTORY

Timothy J. Gilfoyle

EDITOR IN CHIEF

VOLUME 2

OXFORD

UNIVERSITY PRESS

OXFORD
UNIVERSITY PRESS

Oxford University Press is a department of the University of Oxford.
It furthers the University's objective of excellence in research, scholarship,
and education by publishing worldwide. Oxford is a registered trade mark of
Oxford University Press in the UK and certain other countries.

Published in the United States of America by Oxford University Press
198 Madison Avenue, New York, NY 10016, United States of America.

Library of Congress Cataloging-in-Publication Data
Names: Gilfoyle, Timothy J., editor.
Title: The Oxford encyclopedia of American urban history / Timothy J.
Gilfoyle, Editor in Chief.
Description: First edition. | New York, NY : Oxford University Press, 2019. |
Includes bibliographical references and index.
Identifiers: LCCN 2018041991| ISBN 9780190853860 (set) | ISBN 9780190854195
(volume 1) | ISBN 9780190854201 (volume 2)
Subjects: LCSH: Urbanization—United States—History. | Cities and
Towns—United States—History.
Classification: LCC HT384.U5 O94 2019 | DDC 307.760973—dc23
LC record available at https://lccn.loc.gov/2018041991

1 3 5 7 9 8 6 4 2
Printed by Sheridan Books, Inc., United States of America

To Kenneth T. Jackson

About the
Oxford Research Encyclopedias

The Oxford Encyclopedia of American Urban History is published as part of the *Oxford Research Encyclopedia of American History,* a dynamic and scholarly digital resource. This online collection of overview articles provides in-depth, foundational essays on both essential and emerging topics in American history. All articles are commissioned under the editorial leadership of international experts of the highest caliber and are vetted through rigorous peer review. A living reference work, the online publication is updatable and enriched with cross-linking and multimedia features. The essays are intended for scholars, practitioners, and university-level readers, including advanced undergraduates, graduate students, and researchers.

Oxford Research Encyclopedia of American History
Editor in Chief: Jon Butler, Yale University

Contents

List of Articles   xi

Preface (vol. 1)   xv

Acknowledgments (vol. 1)   xxiii

ARTICLES

Varieties of Urbanization
Political Economies
Informal Economies
Urban Migrations
Neighborhood, Community, and Space
Building the Metropolis
Nature and the Environment
The Social Fabric
Violence and Disorder
The Postwar and Postindustrial Metropolis

Directory of Contributors   1573

Index   1577

List of Articles

Varieties of Urbanization (vol. 1)

Mississippian Ancient Towns and Cities,
1000–1700
Robbie Ethridge

Seaport Cities in North America,
1600–1800
Emma Hart

Industry, Commerce, and Urbanization in
the United States, 1790–1870
David Schley

Industry, Commerce, and Urbanization in
the United States, 1880–1929
Jonathan Rees

Urban Exceptionalism in the American
South
David Goldfield

Company Towns in the United States
Hardy Green

Globalization and the American City
Betsy A. Beasley

Political Economies (vol. 1)

Politics in Urban America before 1940
James J. Connolly

Politics in Urban America after 1945
Lily Geismer

Slavery in American Cities
Leslie M. Harris

The Central Business District in American
Cities
Emily Remus

Progressives and Progressivism in an Era
of Reform
Maureen A. Flanagan

The Great Depression
Erik S. Gellman and Margaret Rung

The New Deal
Wendy L. Wall

American Labor and Working-Class History,
1900–1945
Jeffrey Helgeson

Public Sector Unions in the United States
Joseph E. Hower

Public Authorities in the United States
Gail Radford

Service Economies and the American
Postindustrial City, 1950–present
Patrick Vitale

Deindustrialization and the American
Postindustrial City, 1950–present
Chloe E. Taft

Universities and Information Centers
in US Cities
LaDale Winling

Tourism and the American City since 1800
J. Mark Souther

Professional Team Sports in the United States
Steven A. Riess

Informal Economies (vol. 1)

Gambling in Northern US Cities
Matthew Vaz

Temperance and Prohibition
H. Paul Thompson Jr.

Prostitutes and Prostitution in America
Jessica Pliley

Drug Subcultures in the American City
Chris Elcock

Urban Migrations (vol. 1)

Immigration to American Cities,
1800–1924
Hidetaka Hirota

Immigration to American Cities, 1924–2017
Charlotte Brooks

Ellis Island Immigration Station
Vincent J. Cannato

Angel Island Immigration Station
Judy Yung and Erika Lee

Immigration to the United States after 1945
Xiaojian Zhao

The Great Migration and Black Urban Life in
the United States, 1914–1970
Tyina Steptoe

The Great Migration in Context:
The Chicago Experience, 1916–1918
Christopher R. Reed

White Internal Migration to American
Cities, 1940–1970
Chad Berry

Polish Immigration and the American
Working Class
Dominic Pacyga

Irish Immigration and the American
Working Class
David Brundage

Neighborhood, Community, and Space (vol. 1)

Spatial Segregation and US
Neighborhoods
Carl Nightingale

Ethnicity and US Neighborhoods
Jordan Stanger-Ross

LGBTQ Politics in America since 1945
Emily K. Hobson

Native Americans and Cities
Nicolas G. Rosenthal

Latino Urbanism
A. K. Sandoval-Strausz

Puerto Ricans in the United States
Lorrin Thomas

Latino/a and African American Relations
Brian D. Behnken

The Asian American Movement
Daryl Joji Maeda

Japanese Resettlement in Postwar America:
The Los Angeles Experience
Jean-Paul R. deGuzman

Vietnamese Americans in Little Saigon,
California
Phuong Nguyen

Building the Metropolis (vol. 2)

Suburbanization in the United States
before 1945
Ann Durkin Keating

Municipal Housing in America
Margaret Garb

Public Housing in Urban America
D. Bradford Hunt

Housing Policy across the United States
Kristin M. Szylvian

Urban Destruction during the American
Civil War
Megan Kate Nelson

Skyscrapers and Tall Buildings
Elihu Rubin

The City Beautiful Movement
John D. Fairfield

Urban Planning in the United States
since 1850
Harold L. Platt

Water and Sewers in the American City
Joel A. Tarr

Mass Transit in 19th- and 20th-Century
America
Jay Young

Streets, Roads, and Highways in the United
States
Peter Norton

The Automobile and the American City
David Blanke

Public Space in American Cities
Jessica Sewell

Nature and the Environment (vol. 2)

Parks in Urban America
David Schuyler

Environmental and Conservation
Movements in Metropolitan America
Robert R. Gioielli

Environmental Pollution and the American
City
Brian McCammack

Contagious Diseases and Public Health in
the American City
Daniel Wilson

Climate Change and the American City
Andrew Hurley

Food in the 19th-Century American City
Cindy Lobel

Food in the 20th-Century American City
Adam Shprintzen

The Social Fabric (vol. 2)

Religion in the American City, 1600–1900
Kyle B. Roberts

Religion in the American City, 1900–2000
Christopher D. Cantwell

Poverty in the Modern American City
Ella Howard

Wars on Poverty and the Building of
the American Welfare State
David Torstensson

Schools in US Cities
Ansley T. Erickson

Nightlife in the American City
Peter C. Baldwin

Jazz, Blues, and Ragtime in America,
1900–1945
Court Carney

Jazz in America after 1945
John Gennari

Rock and Roll
Eric Weisbard

Rap Music
Austin McCoy

Violence and Disorder (vol. 2)

Riots and Rioting in US Cities, 1800–2000
Alex Elkins

The Anti-Chinese Massacre in Los
Angeles as a Reconstruction-Era Event
Victor Jew

Asian Americas and the 1992 Los Angeles
Uprising
Shelley Sang-Hee Lee

Street Gangs in the 20th-Century American
City
Andrew J. Diamond

Juvenile Justice in the United States
David S. Tanenhaus

United States Vagrancy Laws
Risa L. Goluboff and Adam Sorensen

The Postwar and Postindustrial Metropolis (vol. 2)

The Black Freedom Struggle in the Urban
North
Thomas J. Sugrue

The Black Freedom Struggle in the Urban
South
Claudrena N. Harold

The Sit-in Movement
Christopher W. Schmidt

The Sixties
Robert O. Self

Suburbanization in America after 1945
Becky Nicolaides and Andrew Wiese

Asian American Suburban Culture since
World War II
Mark Padoongpatt

Zoning in 20th-Century American Cities
Christopher Silver

Urban Renewal
Christopher Klemek

Japantown and the San Francisco Fillmore
District
Clement Lai

Gentrification in the United States
Suleiman Osman

Building the Metropolis

SUBURBANIZATION IN THE UNITED STATES BEFORE 1945

Since the foundations of US cities, fringe areas have been home to a variety of settlements and enterprises with close links to urban centers. All in some way or another can be considered suburbs in a broad definition that includes exurban or periurban territory. In addition, the rise of industrialization fostered new forms of suburban development. Beginning in the early 19th century, the increasing scale of business and industrial enterprises separated workplaces from residences. This allowed some urban dwellers to live at a distance from their place of employment and commute to work. Others lived in the shadow of factories located at some distance from the city center. Still others provided food or raw materials for urban residents and businesses. While industrialization and mass transportation fostered an intense concentration and density of people and land uses in city centers, they also allowed other people and uses to deconcentrate along transportation lines.

Suburbanization in the industrial age was often planned, fostered homogeneity, and led to the expansion of local government. It was tied to the intense urbanization that accompanied the industrial era and rested on the growing separation of formal work and the private home. By the late 19th century, metropolitan areas across the United States included outlying farm centers, industrial towns, residential rail (or streetcar) suburbs, and recreational/institutional centers. Changing intracity transportation, including railroads, interurbans, streetcars and cable cars, enabled people and businesses to locate beyond the limits of a walking city. With suburbs generally located along rail or ferry lines into the early 20th century, the physical development of metropolitan areas often resembled a hub and spokes. With the advent of automobile commutation and the growing use of trucks to haul freight, suburban development took place between transportation lines (generally railroads), filling in the earlier star pattern into a more ubiquitous built-up area.

SUBURBANIZATION

Working from a basic definition of suburbanization "as a process of decentralization, with all the functional and social diversity it encompassed," it is clear that the process was at work in American cities even before the United States came into being.[1] For much of history, a clear distinction has existed between urban and rural ways of life. Indeed, across the world walls often surrounded cities, clearly distinguishing urban from rural. In 17th-century Manhattan under the Dutch, Wall Street was indeed the divide between urban and rural. South of Wall Street was a small urban settlement protected from attack from the north. As Manhattan grew, though, development spilled out beyond the designated urban area: gardens, retreats, noxious industries like slaughterhouses, poor squatters, and more. Eventually this once suburban area became part of lower Manhattan, now one of the most intensively urban places in the world. Suburban is not necessarily, or even usually, a permanent distinction.

This form of suburbanization is indistinguishable from sprawl that Robert Bruegmann defines as "as low-density, scattered, urban development without systematic large-scale or regional public land-use planning."[2] Sprawl is characteristic of growing cities across history, as this form of suburbanization results from pressure to find places for new development.

It could be tremendously heterogeneous, as hundreds (and sometimes thousands) of individuals chose among widely varying development paths. Country villas could sit close to quarries, garbage dumps, or a poorhouse.

Sprawl as a form of suburbanization remains a constant part of the fringe development in US cities across history. The particular uses and scales have changed over time, but their heterogeneity has not. In late 20th-century suburban Sacramento, scrap metal yards stood close to homes on large acreage as well as warehouses. Physical, economic, and social diversity characterize this development whenever and wherever it has evolved.[3]

From this heterogeneous landscape, groups of suburban residents emerged who came together to create communities of various kinds. As Henry Binford notes, "long before mass transportation or regular contact, the suburban economy was more diverse, the suburban population far more varied than the economy of society of any country area." These communities were "larger, denser, more diverse, more urbane, and faster growing than small towns of the country, but smaller, more specialized, and less wealthy than the adjacent city."[4] Binford finds that these "first suburbs" emerged in Cambridge and Somerville on the outskirts of Boston between the 1790s and the 1840s. Residents had jobs that oriented them toward the city (and often brought them into Boston): wagonmen, omnibus drivers, land hustlers, food brokers, and artisan manufacturers. Others were engaged in activities that could only take place on the urban fringe: building transportation routes or supplying food and other goods for consumption in Boston.[5]

These suburban communities were a precursor to a new form of suburbanization that flourished in the industrial age. However, this was not a progression, a replacement of one landscape for another. Instead, it was a layering of new forms born of the industrial era, onto older traditional suburban forms. Rather than replacing an older suburban form, new residential commuter suburbs joined older fringe development (alongside other new forms) by the mid-19th century in cities across the United States.

SUBURBANIZATION IN THE INDUSTRIAL AGE

Industrialization made possible new choices for urban residents. Two changes were especially important: the separation of work and home and daily commuting. These two changes fostered a shift from a preindustrial walking city to a city with a growing number of commuters. Until the early 19th century, most people either resided and worked in the same location, or in proximity. The increasing scale of business and industrial enterprises separated workplace from home, fostering the advent of strictly residential areas. Transportation advances—the railroad and the streetcar in particular—made it possible for people to live farther than walking distance from their place of work.

Robert Fishman locates the models of the homogeneous middle- and upper-class residential suburbs that evolved in the industrial era in 18th-century England in places like Clapham five miles outside the City of London. There evolved a "prototypical suburban community" that united "the country house, the villa, and the picturesque traditions." From Clapham, Fishman traces a line to John Nash's Park Village (1824) to the railroad suburb of Riverside, Illinois (1868), and all the way to the automobile suburb of Radburn, New Jersey (1928).[6]

Kenneth T. Jackson argues that the origins of these elite residential suburbs in the United States lie in the years after the War of 1812. He notes that a low residential density, high levels of homeownership, the absence of low-income families, and long commutes (journeys to work), characterized these suburbs.[7] Ferry commuters traveling between jobs in Manhattan and homes in Brooklyn created the first of these residential suburbs in the United States. But commuter railroads quickly became the mode of transportation that underlay this kind of suburban development. By the late 1840s, daily trains used seven depots in Boston, a rail line connected Westchester County with Manhattan, and Chicago had its first railroad. Commuter suburbs followed in cities across the country along the main rail lines.

Men and women experienced these spaces quite differently. Men were usually the commuters, taking the train into the bustle of the city and retreating each night. Women were homemakers who tended to house, garden, and family, spending their days in the suburb itself. So midday, these residential suburbs were largely women's space, interrupted only by sight of a Protestant minister, shopkeeper, or butcher.

But it would be wrong to assign these commuter suburbs simply to a woman's sphere. In many ways, the 19th-century suburb was a landscape designed and supported by men who wanted to escape the ills of urban life. Still, women exerted considerable influence on home, garden, and community. As John Stilgoe suggests, many women "looked not *up* to the city, but down upon it."[8]

Riverside is one of the most famous of these commuter suburbs, in large part because it was designed by Frederick Law Olmsted and Calvert Vaux. Located about ten miles west of the Loop along the Chicago, Burlington, and Quincy Railroad, Riverside has been studied by urbanists and landscape architects since they devised their 1869 plan for curvilinear streets, large lots, and a 160-acre reserve along the Des Plaines River.

In promotional material for the Riverside Improvement Company, in Olmsted's written descriptions and in the later work of scholars, Riverside is described as a retreat from urban life: "For years it was somewhat remote from Chicago, a village of winding roads and lovely parks inhabited by a small number of well-to-do residents of old stock."[9] But by the early 20th century Riverside was surrounded by suburban neighbors as well as the winding Des Plaines River.

Riverside's putative isolation was belied by its location only a few miles north of the Illinois and Michigan Canal Corridor, which also included a railroad and eventually the Sanitary and Ship Canal. The Argo Corn Starch Company anchored a new industrial town, known today as Summit, south of Riverside after 1910. The area drew other employers as well as hundreds of resident workers. To the east, Berwyn developed quickly with worker housing after Western Electric built the Hawthorne Works to the east. Directly west of Riverside, Samuel E. Gross subdivided a new railroad suburb in 1889 along the same line as Riverside. Initially known as Grossdale (now Brookfield), the area offered smaller lots and more modest improvements than Riverside. North of Riverside, leisure activities dominated development along the Des Plaines River. The Chicago city treasurer in the 1860s developed a country estate, while the Riverside Holiness Association developed a colony of summer cottages along the river near to a canoe club and an outdoor ballroom. To the south of Riverside, Lyons was home to picnic groves, a beer garden, and an amusement park.

While Riverside's neighbors were diverse, they were not unusual in suburban Chicago or in suburban areas across the United States by the early 20th century. Residents of commuter suburbs found a rich diversity of neighbors, especially as development filled in between rail stops. To focus only on the residential commuter suburbs is to miss their often disparate neighbors that also emerged in response to industrialization, including: industrial suburbs, farming communities, institutional and leisure centers. Temperance, zoning, incorporation, and annexation have all been employed as a response to interactions between groups. Suburbanization includes not just individuals and communities, but also layers upon layers of relationships between individuals, institutions, businesses, and communities across metropolitan areas.

INDUSTRIAL SUBURBS, FARMING COMMUNITIES, INSTITUTIONAL AND LEISURE CENTERS

With the arrival of regular rail service in many US cities in the 1840s and 1850s, train stops spurred suburbanization at a distance from the city center. Not just commuter suburbs, but other kinds of suburbs evolved during these years. Farmers, industrialists, and residents seeking leisure-time activities all took advantage of the speed and ease of rail travel. The railroad provided farmers with access to city centers as daily "milk runs" brought dairy products and farm produce into the city from across the metropolitan area. Residents of railroad settlements also shipped the raw materials of city building into urban centers, and suburbs often evolved around these train stations. In many cities, stockyards developed along the rail lines. Agricultural processing industries also located near the rails, including mills and creameries.

Heavy industries also located along the railroad lines, where raw materials and finished products could be easily transported. In many cities, industrialists found large undeveloped sites along rail lines, in proximity to (but not necessarily adjacent to) city centers, to be ideal locations for their operations. Unlike commuter suburbs, where people traveled back and forth into the city, in industrial suburbs, workers lived and worked nearby while the products of their labor were shipped along the railroad. For instance, in Chicago the massive car works at Pullman were built south of the city alongside a planned worker town.

Leisure opportunities drew these workers from the suburb or neighborhood where they lived and worked. Sunday excursions to ballparks, cemeteries, picnic groves, and music halls were found in many industrial cities in suburban areas developed along rail lines. Workers who seldom left their neighborhood or industrial suburb were drawn by leisure opportunities found along rail lines. While they could not afford the park-like residential commuter suburbs of more affluent metropolitan residents, they found ways to enjoy the borderland between urban and rural.

Metropolitan and urban development during the railroad age was characterized by a star pattern of rail lines in and out of downtown. Urban regions in the 19th century (and by extension those in the present) came to have two parts: settlements that hugged the rail lines, and the areas between them. Places near rail stations with regular train service into Chicago, for example, could be closer in actual commuting time to the city center than inner-city neighborhoods. Not until the 20th century would in-filling result in a contiguous built-up region spreading out from the city center. In areas beyond easy reach of rail stations, intensive development languished. Farmers were less able to serve the urban market, the distance from raw materials and consumers precluded factories, idyllic spots were not worth developing as recreational sites, and commuters had no hope of reaching Chicago within a day from places between rail lines.[10]

TECHNOLOGY AND LOCAL GOVERNANCE

Technological change and resident demands for new and improving services also affected the shape of suburban development. By the 1850s, the major cities in the United States grappled with water supply and sewerage issues, as well as new gas lines. Urban government, which had heretofore concerned itself primarily with issues of trade and transportation, now was responsible for creating infrastructure that transformed the daily lives of urbanities with indoor plumbing and gas lighting. Pipes for running water, sewer hookups for indoor plumbing, gas (and later electric) fittings for lighting and appliances, as well as telephones for direct communication beyond the home revolutionized both domestic life and its connections to the outside world. Homes became physically attached to the communities around them largely through these new utility networks. Outside central cities, however, rural government continued along a traditional limited path of collecting taxes, supervising elections, operating courts and schools, and maintaining roads and bridges. Perhaps at no time before or after was the contrast between urban and rural living so dramatic.

Suburbanites entered the void between these contrasting worlds. Since many suburban dwellers, drawn outward along new transportation lines, originated from city centers where new basic services were available, these residents demanded infrastructure and other improvements in outlying districts. Among the first to recognize these demands were real-estate developers. They understood that they could use outlying residential subdivisions as a means of directing growth, cutting short the years of waiting for rising real-estate values. To attract settlement to their subdivisions, some speculators made use of the dramatic changes taking place within homes and provided new kinds of service connections necessary to have indoor plumbing and lighting. Others simply laid out streets and built rail depots. This range reflected both the amount of capital various speculators were willing to risk and the variety of conveniences that potential residents wanted or could afford. What emerged was a range of internally homogeneous suburban subdivisions that provided varying levels of services and costs. These subdivisions fostered class (as well as ethnic and racial) segregation which, while crude in its early stages, is still characteristic of suburban areas today.

Suburban government emerged as a new form by the end of the 19th century, providing many of the services and functions of chartered urban governments while also being shaped by existing traditions of rural government. This new form of governance developed over the course of the 19th century in response to the demands placed on it by new suburban communities. Suburban governments emerged to meet the calls of residents and real-estate developers for services and amenities.[11]

In many states, permissive incorporation laws stimulated an explosion of suburban government. By 1880, Michigan had 229 incorporated cities and village; by 1910 there were 459. Cook County, which included Chicago, had at least 73 incorporated villages, towns, and cities by 1910, while suburban Pittsburgh had 65 incorporated settlements. At the same time, there were 242 municipalities in New Jersey, 32 incorporated places within a ten-mile radius of Boston, and 32 incorporated towns and cities in Westchester County outside of New York City.[12] As Jon Teaford notes:

> by 1910 suburban America was a segregated collection of divergent interest, industrial and residential, Protestant and Catholic, truck farmer and commuter, saloon habitué and abstainer. Each group had its own particular goals and desires, its distinctive views on taxation, pollution, morality, planning and ethnicity. Some segments sought a taxation policy that would benefit industry or a lenient attitude toward industrial pollution. Others sought ordinances that would safeguard local purity from the threats of saloons and wicked women, whereas still other segments worked to sustain human iniquities…resulting in political fragmentation.[13]

Countering this move toward fragmentation were campaigns for annexation and consolidation of metropolitan areas. Suburban communities could become part of the city center in order to access better services. In fact, into the 20th century, many central city governments offered better services at lower costs than were possible with suburban government. A wide range of factors had to be considered: the economics of scale involved in public improvements; the value of real estate inside and outside city limits; the cost of taxes and special assessments; the differential expenses involved with schools, fire, and police forces and other services; the level of corruption and graft; and the level of political representation desired by residents. One by-product was municipal annexation of adjoining suburban settlements. In 1854, Philadelphia annexed 127 square miles (from 2 square miles), Chicago added 133 square miles in 1889 (from 43 square miles) and New York City grew from 40 to 300 square miles as a result of its 1898 consolidation.

Between 1915 and 1925, Los Angeles increased from 108 to 415 square miles.[14]

While annexations brought in large swathes of suburban territory into central cities, the movement also saw significant defeats beginning in 1873 in Boston and 1894 in Chicago. This correlated with the increasing efficacy of smaller suburban governments in providing services at competitive rates. As Jon Teaford explains,

> By the 1920s voters were no longer sanctioning consolidation schemes as readily as in earlier decades, for the central cities no longer enjoyed such an advantage in municipal services. Special districts and counties were providing services formerly reserved to major cities, and the suburban municipality had expanded its range of responsibilities and raised its level of performance.[15]

Among the suburban territory particularly targeted by annexation campaigns were those along streetcar lines. Horse-drawn streetcars were first introduced in US cities in the decades before the Civil War. But their effect on suburbanization increased dramatically with electrification in the last decade of the 19th century. Within a decade, the vast majority of streetcars in the nation's cities were electrified. These streetcars and trolleys spurred suburban residential development in what Sam Bass Warner Jr. has coined "streetcar suburbs." Warner suggests that

> streetcar suburbs stand as a monument to a society which wished to keep the rewards of capitalist competition. … Middle-class families were free to choose among hundreds of possible locations, free to find a neighborhood that suited both their ethnic feelings and their progress up the economic ladder.[16]

Warner found that some streetcar suburbs, including Brookline outside Boston in 1873, voted against annexation. Warner explained that the "sudden and permanent collapse of the annexation movement had two causes: the first concerned municipal services; the second, the idea of community."[17]

Regardless, the line between city center and suburbs has remained contested. Therefore, the history of suburbanization in any metropolitan region across the country must include areas that are now part of the central city, but once were outside its political boundaries. Many urban neighborhoods started as suburbs of one kind or another. These neighborhoods include places that began as residential commuter suburbs, but also places that began as industrial suburbs, leisure sites, farming communities and more.[18]

Implications of These Patterns for Race, Class, and Ethnicity.

The great diversity that characterized suburbanization in the industrial era was juxtaposed by the homogeneity of specific subdivisions and communities. The fragmentation of local government in many metropolitan areas often allowed for homogeneous constituencies even in starkly diverse regions. Sam Bass Warner describes this broad suburbanization process as the result "of hundreds of thousands of separate decisions."[19] Suburban residents sorted themselves principally and with considerable care by ethnicity, class, and race, but also on less obvious grounds to early 21st-century eyes.

The ability to pay for certain services (or the choice about which to support) points to class divisions that were a fundamental part of suburbanization in the 19th century. For some urban workers, purchasing land was of preeminent importance. The lower prices of suburban property propelled some workers to suburbanize to accomplish this dream. They often built their own houses in unincorporated areas with few services or taxes. These owner-built homes often did not have expensive services and plumbing.[20]

Workers with strong religious or ethnic ties often chose suburban locations that were not only close to work, but also close to those with similar ethnic or religious ties. Olivier Zunz found that in Detroit, working-class families led the way in home ownership (much of it on the periphery of the city center). Zunz also found that in Detroit, early 20th-century immigrants, even those with very limited means, found "a freedom of choice as to where they would live."[21] Ethnic workers could choose to live in inner city neighborhoods or move to outlying subdivisions, depending on work, family, institutional affiliations, or other preferences.

Likewise, Joseph Bigott found that Polish Catholic workers in Chicago sought home ownership in suburban areas that offered less expensive land and proximity to industrial work. Bigott found that alongside the corporate capitalism of industrial America, a strong strain of local capitalism, often supported by ethnic buyers, fueled the development of many suburbs. At least part of this local capitalism was shaped by the desire of immigrant workers to own their own homes. Middle-class ethnic real-estate developers platted outlying subdivisions, often offering land to ethnic churches or institutions as a way to attract interest in their property. In the case of West Hammond, Indiana, the land syndicate that developed property in the 1890s donated one city block as the site for a Catholic church for Poles, particularly those then living near St. Stanislaus Kostka on Chicago's near north side. The syndicate employed agents to sell property in West Hammond and in other Polish neighborhoods. Then workers either built their own homes or built and sold homes to other Poles. With this sort of local capitalism, the land syndicate was successful in selling land and fostering suburban development.[22]

Planned worker suburban communities like Pullman stand in sharp relief to nearby West Hammond. George Pullman envisioned a suburb that was the antithesis of places like West Hammond, where ethnicity played a crucial choice in where workers lived. Instead Pullman wanted a town without the presence of ethnicity. Pullman's architect Solon S. Beman designed a town for five thousand residents with a single church—a community church in which all residents, regardless of religion, could worship. Pullman had water and sewers connected to all the housing, but workers could only rent and not own their homes. Alongside worker housing, the town included an arcade structure that housed stores, offices, a library, and meeting rooms. Beman designed a round market building in an Italian style, where workers could buy food and other goods. Pullman rented space in the market for small vendors. Little room was available for local capitalism (and especially ethnic capitalism) in this shrine to corporate capitalism.[23]

Pullman also decided that the only place to buy liquor in his town would be at the hotel that was off-limits to his workers. Across the rest of the Chicago area, and the nation, residents of individual neighborhoods and suburbs generally made decisions about liquor and its regulation. Temperance served as an issue that divided suburbanites across the 19th and into the early 20th centuries. On Chicago's North Shore, elite commuter suburbs like Wilmette, Kenilworth, and Evanston prohibited the sale of liquor within their boundaries. This was a way to attract like-minded neighbors and ward off imbibers. Among those who opposed prohibitions on alcohol were immigrant farmers living in farming centers like Gross Pointe. They organized as a separate suburb to protect their right to support local saloons. Religion and ethnicity played a role in this debate, with the largely Protestant commuter suburbs supporting temperance against their often Catholic and immigrant neighbors.[24]

In contrast to the late 20th century, where public schools and taxes often served as key choices for potential suburban locations, schools were less important in the 19th or early 20th century. One of the earliest examples of public schools shaping suburban development appeared in an outlying neighborhood of Chicago. Organized in 1896, Edison Park was a suburb thirteen miles northwest of Chicago's downtown along the Chicago and Northwestern Railroad. The suburban government

supported a park, a small water system, improved streets, and electricity, but with roughly three hundred residents, they could not support a high school. Students had to travel to the small high school supported by the largely agricultural township. In 1910, Edison Park residents eyed the newly constructed, state-of-the-art high school built by the City of Chicago just three train stops toward the city center. Edison Park residents, wanting the best for their children, decided to annex with Chicago in 1911, largely so their children could attend the newer, bigger high school in the city. By the 1920s, Clarence Perry's notion of a "neighborhood unit," reflected the emergence of schools as a central institution, alongside infrastructure, parks, and local shopping.

If race did not play a major role in suburban development in northern cities before World War I, the reason was not beneficent: the number of African Americans living in northern cities was small. In the south, Andrew Wiese finds patterns for black residents similar to those of white ethnic workers. African Americans in the south moved into suburban lands in subdivisions marketed to black purchasers "scattered among white neighborhoods, farms, and millworks on the margins of town." They lived together creating a homogeneous pocket within a wider white landscape.[25]

WORLD WAR I AND AFTER

Suburbanization began to change in crucial ways with World War I. The end of large-scale European immigration led to shifting notions of ethnicity within American metropolitan areas. The first wave of the Great Migration led to the growing populations of African American residents in northern cities and changes in suburbanization. As well, the growing importance of the automobile shifted development patterns across the United States. The building boom in the 1920s and the Great Depression that followed helped set policy and patterns that remain today. Finally, the increased involvement of government, at all levels, in planning and regulating suburban development, changed the relationship between public and private responsibilities and space.

The number of Americans who owned automobiles grew rapidly in the 1920s. In 1920, there were eight million vehicles registered in the United States; by 1927, the figure reached twenty-six million. That same year, almost sixteen million Model Ts were sold by Henry Ford, many of them driven by residents of metropolitan areas. Federal and state legislations supported highway construction, both between and within cities. Gasoline taxes were introduced as a way to provide revenues for road building.

At the same time, the streetcar systems that had fueled suburban development in the 19th century receded. Private companies found it difficult to remain profitable and continue low fares (a nickel in many metropolitan areas). Buses replaced trolleys and streetcars. Private companies suffered bankruptcy. While commuter rail lines grew in the 1920s, other forms of mass transportation either slowly disappeared (as with streetcars) or increasingly became the responsibilities of local government authorities.

With these transportation changes, new areas of metropolitan regions opened up for development. Outlying city neighborhoods and new suburbs emerged as cars could reach new places in a region. The housing boom of the 1920s was largely a suburban boom. As Kenneth Jackson notes "the suburbs of the nation's 96 largest cities grew twice as fast as the core communities."[26]

The form of this suburbanization remained as varied as it was in the 19th and early 20th centuries. Into the 1920s, many families across the country built their own suburban homes in fringe areas with few restrictions. By the 1920s, white-collar workers and professionals, who had previously been "largely indifferent to home ownership," came to see it as essential to the American Dream.[27] As well the rising prosperity of America's working class was seen not only in the explosion of families who owned automobiles, but also in the growing number of families who could afford to buy homes with modern kitchens, bathrooms,

and heating. In cities like Chicago, the development of the "bungalow belt" in the 1920s was predicated on the affordability of automobiles and new homes for a growing group of the region's inhabitants.

As well as building more homes, some real-estate developers built suburbs from start to finish. Mark Weiss called them community builders who "designs, engineers, finances, develops, and sells an urban environment using as the primary raw material rural, undeveloped land."[28] While California led the way in real-estate regulation, the most famous community builder in the 1920s was Jesse Clyde (J. C.) Nichols, who built numerous communities in and around Kansas City. His most famous community development was the Country Club District that he began in 1922 that included a planned shopping district with parking. Likewise, some urbanists, including Lewis Mumford, conceived of planned communities within metropolitan areas that incorporated the best design thinking of the day. Clarence Stein and Henry Wright's plans for Radburn, New Jersey, west of Manhattan, were among the most famous.

J. C. Nichols and other real-estate developers supported the creation of the National Association of Real Estate Boards that worked in tandem with the new professionals of city planning. They understood that large residential subdividers needed municipal assistance through infrastructure, zoning, and planning regulations. During these same years, city and regional planning grew prominent in cities across the country. Regional planning flourished in New York City, Chicago, and Los Angeles, working particularly with traffic and highway construction to meet the needs of the growing number of car owners (and real-estate developers). Robert Fogelson suggested that regional planning in Los Angeles during the 1920s had "an overriding concern for automobile transport."[29]

Planners and suburban governments also increasingly adopted zoning as a way to foster and maintain specific kinds of development. Zoning was predicated on the notion that land uses should be segregated to utilize real estate more rationally. The first zoning ordinance was adopted in 1916 in New York City, while the first comprehensive zoning ordinance was adopted in Los Angeles in 1925. By 1936, 1,322 US cities had zoning ordinances that embraced these notions of separation of land uses. As Marc Weiss notes "suburban governments, smaller and more responsive to local demands than big-city officials, experimented with restrictive land-use planning: zoning and subdivision regulations, health and safety ordinances, and building codes governing the cost of new construction and the uses to which it could be put."[30]

Most zoning ordinances set minimum lot sizes, setback requirements, separation of single family and multi-family residences, and residences from industry and commercial uses. Therefore, zoning became a way of further sorting metropolitan regions into homogeneous parcels. This was a process begun long before zoning, but zoning regulations affirmed the perceived value of homogeneity.

Euclid, a suburb of Cleveland, illustrates the ways in which zoning excluded many land uses and people. Euclid prohibited the construction of multiple-family residents anywhere within its bounds through its zoning ordinances. Taken to court over this restriction on the property rights of individuals in the suburb, the US Supreme Court sustained Euclid's right to prohibit all but single-family residences within its borders (*Euclid v. Ambler*, 1926).

Zoning extended to racial, religious, and ethnic exclusion. That is, zoning was used to foster (or maintain) racial segregation. In 1916, the US Supreme Court, in *Buchanan v. Warley*, ruled racial zoning was unconstitutional. Nevertheless, many real-estate developers utilized restrictive covenants to maintain racial exclusion. During the suburban building boom of the 1920s, developers used deed restrictions to govern future land uses without zoning. Restrictions were placed on deeds within a new subdivision, often determining the "cost, size, location, and style of housing that could be constructed, its occupancy by single or multiple families, and the race and ethnicity of

inhabitants." Racial restrictive covenants excluded certain groups of people (most often African Americans, but also Jews, Catholics, and other groups depending on the locale) from ever owning or renting the property.[31]

The rising popularity of racial restrictive covenants came in response to the Great Migration, with millions of rural African Americans moving to northern cities after 1915. While many African Americans went to urban neighborhoods creating crowded ghettos, other migrants moved directly to suburban areas in major northern cities. Andrew Wiese found 200,000 African Americans living in suburban areas across the United States in 1910. That number grew to more than one million on the eve of World War II, as African Americans urbanized in the first wave of the Great Migration. Many lived in unincorporated suburbs, built their own homes, and maintained gardens and orchards. Others moved close to suburban work in industrial towns or to domestic service work in commuter suburbs. Like the immigrants and mainly white migrants who came to northern cities before World War I, African Americans made residential and work choices circumscribed by class, religion, and outlook. However, the added layer of racial discrimination, particularly in real estate, led to even starker segregation than in earlier generations.[32]

The Great Depression halted the suburban expansion of the 1920s. The foundation of the Home Owners Loan Corporation (HOLC) in 1933 and the passage of the National Housing Act the following year, brought the federal government more directly into home financing and so indirectly into suburban development. The Federal Housing Authority (FHA) fostered minimum design standards for the design of subdivisions. Taking their cue from the work of groups like the National Board of Realtors and professional planners, the FHA developed templates for assessing the value of existing and proposed housing. The FHA made a link between homogeneity (of all kinds, including race) and value that shaped the direction of post–World War II suburbanization. After 1945, FHA practices that had been developed during the Great Depression promoted the development of white middle-income single-family suburban subdivisions. Much of the urban development of US cities took place during the long industrial era. After World War II, the decline of industrial work, federal policy, and the automobile reshaped the landscape, both urban and suburban, that developed from the 1810s to the 1930s.

DISCUSSION OF THE LITERATURE

The study of suburbanization before 1945 has been fundamentally shaped by attitudes toward suburbs after 1945. That is to say, the disdain for the bland, cookie-cutter quality of postwar suburban development for a broad middle class coupled with the racism that underlay real estate and federal guidelines have made it difficult to study pre-1945 suburbanization dispassionately.

Suburbanization did not go unnoticed by a first generation of professional social scientists. One of the first to describe the modern suburb was Adna Ferrin Weber in his 1899 study of city growth. According to Weber, a suburb "combined at once the open air and spaciousness of the country with the sanitary improvements, comforts and associated life of the city." Weber's suburb was an area with lower population density than the city, and was distinguished from the surrounding countryside by the existence of city improvements, comforts, and society.[33] Other early observers of suburbs included Graham Taylor in his 1915 *Satellite Suburbs: A Study of Industrial Suburbs* and Harlan Paul Douglass in his 1925 *The Suburban Trend*.

Suburbs were seen by many early social scientists and reformers as a means to humanize the city. Ebenezer Howard's garden city idea was essentially a plan for moving individuals, as well as industry, away from the city center in order to provide a more healthful environment. Like Weber, Howard called for further suburbanization (deconcentration), in order that more metropolitan residents could take advantage of the benefits of suburban living.[34]

In contrast to this positive reaction to suburbs themselves, few heralded the arrival of suburban government as a stunning achievement for modern American society. Instead, critics such as Roderick D. McKenzie in 1925 viewed it as "little short of disastrous," because "every great city now has around it a metropolitan area, one with it economically and socially, but without political unity." Critics blamed political fragmentation both for the inadequate provision of basic services to protect the health and safety across entire metropolitan regions, and for widely varying tax rates.[35]

While sociologists like Herbert Gans focused on post–World War II developments, historians and geographers began exploring suburbanization in earnest during the 1960s and 1970s. In the 1960s, Sam Bass Warner Jr. made a groundbreaking study of Boston's streetcar suburbs, while Roy Lubove contributed an overview of the urbanization process that still provides a broad framework for considering suburbs and their metropolitan regions.[36] In the 1980s, studies by Kenneth Jackson and Robert Fishman emphasized the importance of the middle and upper classes in suburban development. Jackson defined a suburb as "an area of non-farm residential development for the middle and upper class."[37] Fishman identified suburbs as middle-class residential communities with "a distinctive low density environment defined by the primacy of a single family house set in a greenery of an open, parklike setting."[38]

Henry Binford, writing in 1985, suggested that the residential suburb that emerged in the United States between 1815 and 1860 was so important that "it permanently changed the meaning of the word 'suburbs.'" Binford noted that although the term had for centuries "denoted an undifferentiated zone outside the city limits," that by the 1850s, suburbs "meant a collection of separate communities housing many city workers, linked to the city through commuting, but often defiantly independent in government." Several decades later, Robert Bruegmann challenged the demise of this undifferentiated development on the outskirts of cities by describing it as sprawl, not suburban development.[39]

Since the 1980s, historians and geographers have expanded our knowledge of suburbanization with studies of metropolitan areas across the United States and Canada. Case studies by Michael Ebner, Zane Miller, and Robert Fogelson enriched our understanding of specific places, while Margaret Marsh brought gender more directly into focus.[40] Geographers Robert Lewis and Richard Harris moved discussion to working-class and industrial suburbs, alongside historians like Joseph Bigott. Andrew Wiese, LeeAnn Lands, and Becky Nicolaides have skillfully explored the role of race and class in early 20th-century suburbs, again expanding the lens of suburban history.[41] Work, like that by Jon Teaford and Ann Durkin Keating, focused on the role of local, state, and federal government policies and initiatives makes clear the great importance of public policy to what is in many other ways private development.[42] Overall, researchers have considered more carefully the place of gender, class, ethnicity, and race in our understanding of suburbanization before World War II.

PRIMARY SOURCES

Primary source materials on suburban history are located in local and state historical societies and archives across the country, as well as local public libraries. These materials can include oral histories, historical maps, photographs, community organization records, and historical materials. While traditionally access was limited to actual visits to facilities with limited hours and staff, digitization and web access have expanded accessibility.

For the period 1850–1945, local newspapers offer a rich resource for suburban historians. As with other archival material, more local newspapers are available electronically. However, suburban papers often remain available only in paper formats.

Government archives at the local and state level are also excellent sources for relevant materials for suburban history before 1945, if sometimes difficult to access. Some of these local public documents have been turned over to state archives, where efforts for their digitization continue. As well, there are valuable federal records in the Library of Congress and the National Archives, including Sanborn Insurance Atlases (some now online), as well as records of the Department of Commerce, the Home Owners Loan Corporation, and the Federal Housing Authority.

Finally, suburban history also relies on material culture, in particular on buildings still extant in the landscape. Many residences, buildings, and streetscapes of historical significance remain in use. Local and state historical societies also maintain some of these buildings because of local significance, and they can be useful for a broader history.

DIGITAL MATERIALS

Advertisement for D. S. Taylor Property, c. 1873. http://www.encyclopedia.chicagohistory.org/pages/10996.html.

Annexations and Additions to the City of Chicago. http://www.encyclopedia.chicagohistory.org/pages/3716.html.

Map Chicago and Suburbs, 1921. http://www.encyclopedia.chicagohistory.org/pages/10345.html.

Chicago Tribune, Map of Chicago and Century of Progress, 1934. http://www.encyclopedia.chicagohistory.org/pages/10346.html.

Chicago's Street Railways in 1890. http://www.encyclopedia.chicagohistory.org/pages/1772.html.

Electronic Encyclopedia of Chicago. http://www.encyclopedia.chicagohistory.org/.

FURTHER READING

Bigott, Joseph C. From Cottage to Bungalow: Houses and the Working Class in Metropolitan Chicago, 1869–1929. Chicago: University of Chicago Press, 2001.

Binford, Henry C. The First Suburbs: Residential Communities on Boston's Periphery, 1815–1860. Chicago: University of Chicago Press, 1985.

Bruegmann, Robert. Sprawl: A Compact History. Chicago: University of Chicago Press, 2005.

Cronon, William. *Nature's Metropolis: Chicago and the Great West*. New York: W. W. Norton, 1991.

Ebner, Michael H. *Creating Chicago's North Shore*. Chicago: University of Chicago Press, 1988.

Fishman, Robert. *Bourgeois Utopias: The Rise and Fall of Suburbia*. New York: Basic Books, 1987.

Harris, Richard. *Unplanned Suburbs: Toronto's American Tragedy, 1900–1950*. Baltimore: Johns Hopkins University Press, 1996.

Hayden, Dolores. *Building Suburbia: Green Fields and Urban Growth, 1820–2000*. New York: Vintage, 2003.

Jackson, Kenneth T. *Crabgrass Frontier: The Suburbanization of the United States*. New York: Oxford University Press, 1985.

Keating, Ann Durkin. *Chicagoland: City and Suburb of the Railroad Age*. Chicago: University of Chicago Press, 2005.

Lewis, Robert. *Chicago Made: Factory Networks in the Industrial Metopolis*. Chicago: University of Chicago, 2008.

Marsh, Margaret. *Suburban Lives*. New Brunswick, NJ: Rutgers University Press, 1990.

Nicolaides, Becky M. *My Blue Heaven: Life and Politics in the Working-Class Suburbs of Los Angeles, 1920–1965*. Chicago: University of Chicago Press, 2002.

Stilgoe, John R. *Borderland: Origins of the American Suburb, 1820–1939*. New Haven, CT: Yale University Press, 1988.

Teaford, Jon C. *City and Suburb: The Political Fragmentation of Metropolitan America, 1850–1970*. Baltimore: Johns Hopkins University Press, 1979.

Warner, Sam Bass, Jr. *Streetcar Suburbs: The Process of Growth in Boston, 1870–1900*. Cambridge, MA: Harvard University Press, 1978.

Wiese, Andrew. *Places of Their Own: African-American Suburbanization in the Twentieth Century*. Chicago: University of Chicago Press, 2004.

NOTES

1. Becky M. Nicolaides and Andrew Wiese, "Introduction," *The Suburb Reader* (New York: Routledge, 2006), 8.

2. Robert Bruegmann, *Sprawl: A Compact History* (Chicago: University of Chicago Press, 2005), 14.

3. See Dolores Hayden, *Building Suburbia: Green Fields and Urban Growth, 1820–2000* (New York: Vintage, 2003), 12.

4. Henry C. Binford, *The First Suburbs: Residential Communities on Boston's Periphery, 1815–1860* (Chicago: University of Chicago Press, 1985), 2

5. Binford, *The First Suburbs*, 8–9.

6. Robert Fishman, *Bourgeois Utopias: The Rise and Fall of Suburbia* (New York: Basic Books, 1987), 49.

7. Kenneth T. Jackson, *Crabgrass Frontier: The Suburbanization of the United States* (New York: Oxford University Press, 1985), 6–11.

8. John R. Stilgoe, *Borderland: Origins of the American Suburb, 1820–1939* (New Haven, CT: Yale University Press, 1988), 26. Margaret Marsh points out the critical role of men in defining these suburbs. See *Suburban Lives* (New Brunswick, NJ: Rutgers University Press, 1990). See also Gwendolyn Wright, *Building the Dream: A Social History of Housing in American* (New York: Pantheon, 1981), p. xx, and *Moralism, and the Model Home: Domestic Architecture and Cultural Conflict in Chicago, 1873–1913* (Chicago: University of Chicago Press, 1980) for more on the suburban house.

9. Harold M. Mayer and Richard C. Wade, *Chicago: Growth of a Metropolis* (Chicago: University of Chicago Press, 1969), 330–332.

10. See Ann Durkin Keating, *Chicagoland: City and Suburb of the Railroad Age* (Chicago: University of Chicago Press, 2005) for a more detailed discussion on these suburban types. See also Robert Lewis, ed., *Manufacturing Suburbs: Building Work and Home on the Metropolitan Fringe* (Philadelphia: Temple University Press, 2004).

11. For more discussion on the evolution of suburban government, see Ann Durkin Keating, *Building Chicago: Suburban Developers and the Creation of a Divided Metropolis* (Columbus: Ohio State University Press, 1988). On neighborhoods and suburbs, see Zane L. Miller, *Neighborhood and Community in Park Forest, Ohio, 1935–1976* (Knoxville: University of Tennessee Press, 1981).

12. Jon C. Teaford, *City and Suburb: The Political Fragmentation of Metropolitan America, 1850–1970* (Baltimore: Johns Hopkins University Press, 1979), 9.

13. Teaford, *City and Suburb*, 12.

14. Robert M. Fogelson, *The Fragmented Metropolis, Los Angeles, 1850–1930* (Berkeley: University of California Press, 1993), 223.

15. Teaford, *City and Suburb*, 5.

16. Sam Bass Warner Jr., *Streetcar Suburbs, The Process of Growth in Boston, 1870–1900* (Cambridge, MA: Harvard University Press, 1978), 160–161.
17. Warner, *Streetcar Suburbs*, 163. In contrast, John Stilgoe has gone so far as to suggest that streetcar "suburbs" were not suburbs "except in fitful pipedreams." Instead, these were developments predestined "to become urban residential neighborhoods." See Stilgoe, *Borderland*, 152.
18. Richard Harris and Robert Lewis argue that city and suburb are not useful constructs, because of the heterogeneity on either side of the city limits. See Richard Harris andRobert Lewis, "North American Cities and Suburbs, 1900–1950: A New Synthesis," *Journal of Urban History* 27 (March 2001): 262–292.
19. Warner, *Streetcar Suburbs*, 3.
20. See Richard Harris, *Unplanned Suburbs: Toronto's American Tragedy, 1900–1950* (Baltimore: Johns Hopkins University Press, 1996), esp. 16, 167.
21. Quoted in Joseph C. Bigott, *From Cottage to Bungalow: Houses and the Working Class in Metropolitan Chicago, 1869–1929* (Chicago: University of Chicago Press, 2001), 8.
22. Bigott, *From Cottage to Bungalow*, esp. 7–12.
23. Keating, *Chicagoland*, 81–85.
24. For more on diversity on Chicago's North Shore, see Michael H. Ebner, *Creating Chicago's North Shore* (Chicago: University of Chicago Press, 1988), 133–160.
25. Andrew Wiese, *Places of Their Own: African-American Suburbanization in the Twentieth Century* (Chicago: University of Chicago Press, 2004), 18. More recently Elaine Lewinnek has suggested early roots for white racism regarding African American neighbors rooted in "the mortgages of whiteness." See *The Working Man's Reward: Chicago's Early Suburbs and the Roots of American Sprawl* (New York: Oxford University Press, 2014).
26. Jackson, *Crabgrass Frontier*, 175.
27. Richard Harris, *Building a Market: The Rise of the Home Improvement Industry, 1914–1960* (Chicago: University of Chicago Press, 2012), 9. See also LeeAnn Lands, "Be a Patriot, Buy a Home: Re-imaging Home Owners and Home Ownership in Early 20th Century Atlanta," *Journal of Social History* 41.4 (Summer 2008): 943–965.
28. Marc A. Weiss, *The Rise of the Community Builders: The American Real Estate Industry and Urban Land Planning* (New York: Columbia University Press, 1987), 1.
29. Fogelson, *Fragmented Metropolis*, 252.
30. Weiss, *Rise of the Community Builders*, 42.
31. Wiese, *Places of Their Own*, 42.
32. Wiese, *Rise of the Community Builders*, 27, 43, 54.
33. Adna Ferrin Weber, *The Growth of Cities in the Nineteenth Century* (Ithaca, NY: Cornell University Press, 1899), 459.
34. Ebenezer Howard, *Garden Cities of Tomorrow* (Cambridge, MA: MIT Press, 1965).
35. Roderick D. McKenzie, *The Metropolitan Community* (New York: McGraw Hill, 1933), 307. This monograph was part of the series Recent Social Trends in the United States, prepared in the 1920s under the auspices of the President's Research Committee on Social Trends.
36. Roy Lubove, "The Urbanization Process: An Approach to Historical Research" *Journal of the American Institute of Planners* 33 (January 1967): 33–39.
37. Jackson, 45.
38. Fishman, *Bourgeois Utopias*, 5.
39. Binford, *The First Suburbs*, 1; and Bruegmann, *Sprawl*, esp. 21–32.
40. Ebner, *Creating Chicago's North Shore*; Miller, *Neighborhood and Community in Park Forest, Ohio*; Fogelson, *Fragmented Metropolis*, and Margaret Marsh, *Suburban Lives*.
41. Lewis, *Manufacturing Suburbs*; Harris, *Unplanned Suburb*; Bigott, *From Cottage to Bungalow*; Wiese, *Places of Their Own*; LeeAnn Lands, *The Culture of Property: Race, Class, and Housing Landscapes in Atlanta, 1880–1950* (Atlanta: University of Georgia Press, 2008); and Becky M. Nicolaides, *My Blue Heaven: Life and Politics in the Working-Class Suburbs of Los Angeles, 1920–1965* (Chicago: University of Chicago Press, 2002).
42. Teaford, *City and Suburb*; and Keating, *Building Chicago: Suburban Developers and the Creation of a Divided Metropolis* (Urbana: University of Illinois Press, 2002).

Ann Durkin Keating

MUNICIPAL HOUSING IN AMERICA

Housing in America has long stood as a symbol of the nation's political values and a measure of its economic health. In the 18th century, a farmhouse represented Thomas Jefferson's ideal of a nation of independent property owners; in the mid-20th century, the suburban house was seen as an emblem of an expanding middle class. Alongside those well-known symbols were a host of other housing forms—tenements, slave quarters, row houses, French flats, loft condos, and public housing towers—which revealed much about American social order and the material conditions of life for many people.

Housing markets since the 19th century have been fundamental forces driving the nation's economy and a major focus of government policies. Home construction provided jobs for skilled and unskilled laborers. Land speculation, housing development, and the home mortgage industry absorbed billions of dollars in investment capital, while ups and downs in housing markets have been considered signals of major changes in the economy. Since the New Deal of the 1930s, the federal government has buttressed the home construction industry and offered economic incentives for home buyers, giving the United States the highest home ownership rate in the world. The housing market crash of 2008 slashed property values and sparked a rapid increase in home foreclosures, especially in places like Southern California and northeastern US suburbs, where housing prices had ballooned over the previous two decades. The real estate crisis led to government efforts to prop up the mortgage banking industry and to assist struggling homeowners. The crisis led, as well, to a drop in home ownership rates, an increase in rental housing, and a growth in homelessness.

Home ownership remains a goal for many Americans and an ideal long associated with the American dream. The owner-occupied home—whether single-family or multi-family dwelling—is typically the largest investment made by an American family. Through much of the 18th and 19th centuries, housing designs varied from region to region. In the mid-20th century, mass production techniques and national building codes tended to standardize design, especially in new suburban housing. In the 18th century, the family home was a site of waged and unwaged work; it was the center of a farm, plantation, or craftsman's workshop. Two and a half centuries later, a house was generally defined as a consumer good: its size, location, and decor marked the family's status and wealth.

Even as home ownership rates rose steadily in the 20th century—plateauing above 60 percent in the 21st century—there were regular spikes in homelessness and in the number of people living in inadequate and poorly maintained shelter. At the height of the Great Depression, hundreds of thousands of people lacked housing. That number fell in the postwar years, then jumped again in the 1980s, a result of a drop in urban manufacturing jobs and major cuts in federal housing programs. Even as much of the nation's real estate recovered from the housing crash of 2008, more than 600,000 Americans remained homeless or living in transitional shelters.

MAKING REAL ESTATE

Europeans arriving in North America in the 17th century saw an abundance of land, some of which was occupied by native peoples. The European vision of housing and property ownership differed from that of American Indians. Whether as farmers or nomadic hunters, Indians generally conceived of land ownership as an active practice. Several groups could claim ownership of a single piece of land if all were using it for different and complementary purposes. English settlers, by contrast, drawing on English common law, believed that holding title to property meant exclusive and permanent rights to the uses and benefits of the property. While an Iroquois community that farmed a plot of land might allow others to travel across it, Europeans saw the travelers as trespassers. Early English settlers treated land and housing as resources necessary for survival. Yet, Europeans almost immediately moved to make land and housing into saleable commodities, establishing a system of private property ownership. In the 17th century, Europeans set to work creating scarcity out of abundance.

Grants of land to corporations and to friends of European monarchs allowed a few large landholders to begin to form real estate markets in port cities. In New York, the Dutch West India Company, chartered in 1621, secured land rights from American Indians, built a fort and trading post, and distributed town lots to settlers and absentee investors. Colonial administrators under the Dutch and English governments granted larger and multiple town lots, and farm tracts, to themselves, to military and church officials, and to influential merchant stockholders or their agents. Early proprietors sold or rented land to new arrivals, using their property in housing to generate profits, often for investment in more land or trade. Historian Elizabeth Blackmar writes that several of New York's early merchant families started with large land grants.

Housing markets formed in Williamsburg, Virginia, and other southern towns, following the expansion of tobacco cultivation and the hugely profitable sales of tobacco in European markets in the mid-17th century. Early landowners turned their profits in agriculture to the acquisition of larger farms and the purchase of enslaved people to work the land. By the early 18th century, rice and cotton production, driven by an expanding slave trade, shaped speculative markets in land and housing in coastal cities and rural areas. While New York, Philadelphia, Baltimore, and Boston relied on artisans, unskilled laborers, and merchant traders to fuel urban housing markets, in Jamestown, Williamsburg, and Charleston it was agricultural goods, moving through the cities to European markets, and the vast wealth of slaveholding rural families that spurred house construction.

In many colonial towns, land surveyors mapping town lots and agricultural land sped the formation of housing markets. Town plans, which on paper at least erased topographical features, rendered urban spaces as rows of neat blocks, evenly divided into rectangular lots. William Penn, who was granted approximately 2,000 square acres by Charles II, in 1681, hired a surveyor to sketch a plan for Philadelphia. In the drawings, a grid suspended between the Delaware and Schuylkill Rivers provided for a series of town lots, which were advertised for sale to artisans, investors, and friends of the Penn family. In St. Louis, settled initially by French fur traders, house lots drawn across the bluff overlooking the Mississippi River were marketed with long, narrow plots of farmland just beyond the settlement, giving each town resident a piece of land to cultivate. In 1811, New York officials hired a team of surveyors to draw a grid across Manhattan Island, to promote development of the farmland north of the settlement.

The grid was the most common urban plan. A few city designs, like those for Washington, DC. and Williamsburg, Virginia, relied on Baroque plans with diagonal boulevards to create grand vistas of civic buildings and to copy the design ideals of European cities. The grid pattern, which gave order to what had been haphazard real estate development, made property values more stable and predictable, and aimed to establish a rational and reliable housing market.

THE DOMESTICATION OF THE FAMILY HOME

Property rights in land and housing have long held a primary place in American political theory and society. In the agrarian republic, property owners claimed rights and independence based on their ownership of productive property and control over household labor. Republican political theory, which shaped revolutionary-era political debates, contended that a man who owned property could support his household and was, in theory at least, free from the control of a patron landlord, an employer, or market forces. Paradoxically, the home owner's claim to economic and political independence rested on the labor of his wife, children, servants, and slaves, the politically and economically dependent members of his household. This yeoman farmer, in the vision of republican theorists like Thomas Jefferson, was the ideal citizen for the new republic. When he participated in politics, the farmer, with his assertion of economic independence, could claim to act out of a concern for the common good, rather than self-interest. Early 19th-century urban craftsmen asserted similar rights to political independence founded on their ownership of workshops, tools, and skills as well as their control of the labor of the apprentices, journeymen, and family members who lived under the same roof. Until the 1820s, most states set property requirements for the vote, affirming the republican theory that a man who owned property and controlled the labor of his household would cast his vote according to the best interests of the nation.

In the years after the Revolution, writers and public lecturers repeatedly sought a housing style that would reflect the republican values of the new nation. Uniformity of design was believed to represent social equality, the hallmark of the new republic and a sharp contrast to the rigid hierarchies of European society. Inequality did not disappear; indeed, it was institutionalized in urban plans and in different sizes, styles, and locations of housing. Moreover, critics and commentators could hardly agree on what constituted republican design. The architect Charles Bulfinch, who promoted row house designs, wrote several treatises urging simplicity and uniformity in urban housing. Yet, on a visit to the United States, Frances Trollope, the English writer, objected to the dull consistency of Philadelphia houses. By the time of the Civil War, the pursuit of republican design gave way to new, more elaborate houses, especially as regional housing styles emerged. For the new urban middle class, simplicity was replaced by peaked roofs, turrets, and intricately adorned cottages, while laboring people struggling to get by on low wages turned to multi-family dwellings.

From the American Revolution to the early 19th century, small houses of one or two stories were the common dwelling for urban skilled workers, shopkeepers, and merchants. Artisans and other laborers often built or purchased houses of wood frame. In New York and Chicago, homeowners often built their houses on a rented lot. Land speculators, then, could generate income without risking capital in constructing houses; even small-time investors, such as prosperous artisans, might invest in a couple of town lots, which they rented to other laborers. The lot renter could own a house without the added expense of purchasing the land. And, if land prices increased and lot rents went up, or if lots became available in a more attractive area, the homeowner might move his house to a new lot. House moving was a lively business in the first half of the 19th century. On May 1, the common moving day, streets of New York and Chicago might be jammed by carts carrying frame houses as well as tenants moving their household possession.

Industrialization and the introduction of mass production techniques gradually transformed the meaning and economic functions of housing. Under the craft system, apprentices and journeymen lived within the craftsman's home, exchanging their labor for room, board, and training. In the early 19th century, master craftsmen, responding to competition or seeking greater profits, aimed to produce more goods at lower cost. Some separated their workshops from their houses and, without new technology, subdivided the tasks of producing goods like boots, barrels, clothing, and furniture. This shift, called the "deskilling of labor," eroded the older craft system and sped production of goods for local and global markets. It also gave rise to a growing class of laborers who worked for cash wages and no longer lived with their employer's family. Instead, wage workers boarded or rented rooms in older houses or sometimes cottages. The breakdown of the craft system and the expansion of waged labor gave rise to rental housing markets in port cities, to a growing number of landlords who generated income from renting housing and tenants who used their wages to pay rent.

In the antebellum era, no ideal better illustrated the reorganization of work and urban life than the family home. In scores of books, magazine articles, and advice manuals dedicated to guiding young people through the rigors of courtship and marriage, writers defined the home as a pastoral refuge removed from the competitive worlds of commerce and politics. Many families employed servants or owned slaves, and both waged and unwaged labor was needed to maintain a household. Yet the ideology that dominated much of American culture distinguished between men's world of work and women's world of domesticity. The "cult of domesticity" invested the family home with priceless emotional value. Writers like Sarah Josepha Hale defined the home as a seat of virtue and piety, where children were trained to be good citizens. Landscape architect Andrew Jackson Downing similarly claimed the single-family house, surrounded by well-tended nature, would generate physical health and strong character. By the mid-19th century, the family home, whether rented or owned, represented an idealized refuge from market relations, a feminine domain separate from men's world of work and politics.

The rise of waged labor and the decline of household economies, or broadly, the shift from an agricultural to an urban industrial economy transformed the social meaning of housing in America. Though wives, daughters, servants, and slaves continued to prepare food, scrub floors, wash clothes, and generally maintain domestic space, the house was set, in the dominant ideology, as the opposite of work. Production in an industrial society was associated with manufacturing enterprises and transportation networks; work was increasingly defined as labor remunerated with cash. Cities with streets lined with cottages and brick two- or three-flat buildings a short walk or trolley ride from factories, shops, and offices appeared to strip the family home of its productive activities. The economic value of a house set on a tiny lot on an urban street was obscured by the sentimentalization of the family home. The separate spheres ideology set the middle-class home with a male breadwinner and a wife devoting her unwaged labor to the family as the emblem of the American house, an ideal that persisted through the 20th century.

ANTEBELLUM HOUSES IN TOWNS AND CITIES

Home construction was a leading industry in 19th-century cities. Building tradesmen were among the first urban laborers to form "workingmen's associations" in the 1830s. The early labor organizations largely disappeared, under pressure from the economic depression of 1837 and from expanding immigration from Europe. Though some tradesmen built their own houses, most urban housing was built by speculators in land and home construction. A land speculator typically sold several lots to a house wright or to an independent tradesman, usually a carpenter, who put up one or two new houses in a year, then sold the houses, using his profits to invest in materials for new houses. Only a few carpenters built houses on commission for particular clients. Larger land investors contracted with professional row house builders who hired crews of skilled and unskilled laborers to build three or four row houses in a year, or whole block fronts.

By the 1820s, the row house was the most common form of housing in Providence, Baltimore, Annapolis, Philadelphia, and many other cities. The typical row house, generally three or four dwellings, was narrow, usually just fifteen to twenty feet wide, and thirty to forty feet deep. In most row houses, the kitchen was moved to the lowest level of the house—what would become a basement—to keep the smells, sounds, and work of cooking separate from the parlor floor upstairs. The parlor, with ever more elaborate furnishings as the century wore on, was where the family visited with friends or, in more affluent homes, where a merchant might demonstrate his wealth and status to prospective business partners. Baltimore's prestigious Waterloo Row (1815) was a terrace of twelve houses. Elite New Yorkers could purchase houses in Colonnade Row (1832–1833) on LaGrange Terrace (now Lafayette Street), a four-story edifice with a marble facade and elaborate colonnade. The row house proved popular with the less affluent as well. Smaller versions of the dwellings, often with wooden colonnades, appeared in some neighborhoods.

House designs were fairly similar, though style and construction materials varied from city to city. Houses in Philadelphia tended to be smaller, often just two rooms deep. Architectural historian Gwendolyn Wright notes the New York row house had a distinctive high front stoop, which derived from the Dutch "stoep," a flight of stairs designed to keep the dwelling above Holland's recurring flood waters. In some districts of St. Louis, houses were set sideways to the street with a narrow passage between houses leading to the entrance. Charleston, too, often featured side porches and entrances. The freestanding wood cottage was common in midwestern cities in the mid-19th century, often built from Wisconsin pine. In Boston, Philadelphia, Chicago, and St. Louis deep red pressed brick was widely used; much of the brick was produced in St. Louis's clay pits. Even as social critics and commentators promoted a republican design for urban residences, houses took distinctive form depending on available materials and local history.

PUBLIC HEALTH AND HOUSING

Through much of the 19th century, significant labor was required to maintain city homes. Most families kept a garden, a few chickens, and sometimes a pig or cow in the space behind their house. Individual homeowners and tenants were responsible for their household's waste and water needs. Many urban families obtained water from a backyard pump attached to a well dug ten to twelve feet into the bottom soil. Some purchased water from peddlers who went door to door with a horse-drawn cart. In some cities private companies sold water to residents. The Chicago Hydraulic Company received a charter from the state legislature in 1836 to provide Chicago with water, but its services were limited and inadequate. New York, Philadelphia, and Detroit began construction of water systems before the Civil War, but most houses lacked running water, leaving the work of carrying buckets of water for drinking, bathing, and cleaning to wives, daughters, servants, and slaves.

Elimination of household waste was similarly a householder's responsibility. Garbage was often dumped directly into the street or rear lot. Private companies hired scavengers by the day to remove dead animals from the streets and pick up household garbage. Most families used a privy in the backyard as few urban houses had indoor plumbing before the 1870s. In poorer neighborhoods, several families shared one privy. Privy vaults were sunk into the soil, often right next to the backyard well. The vaults were seldom tight, sometimes leaking into the nearby water supply. Regular outbreaks of dysentery, typhoid, and cholera suggest that city water often was tainted by waste. A national cholera outbreak, in the early 1850s, prompted several cities to build or expand existing sewer and water systems to improve the water supply. Disease, a consequence of a lack of infrastructure in rapidly expanding cities, was widely feared and became a force in urban housing markets.

By the 1830s, worries about contagious diseases and growing concerns about the chaos and disreputable characters on the docks prompted growing numbers of merchants and well-to-do shopkeepers and artisans to move their family dwellings away from the business districts in Baltimore, New York, Philadelphia, and Boston. Outbreaks of disease were associated with life along the docks, though it is likely only cholera arrived on sailing ships.

But sailors, dockworkers, and immigrants were seen as threats to respectable family life. Health and respectability were increasingly linked to the design and location of the family home, attributes that could be acquired with the purchase of a house in a more expensive residential district. New neighborhoods, upholding the separate spheres ideology, appeared in rural areas edging built-up districts, as affluent and middling families increasingly detached their dwellings from sites of waged labor and business.

In 1869, Catherine Beecher and her sister, Harriet Beecher Stowe, published a new guide to middle-class housing, arguing that family health was directly related to the design, location, and organization of the family home. *The American Family Home: Principles of Domestic Science* (Bedford, MA: Applewood Books, 1869), was a best seller. (It did not sell nearly as well as Harriet Beecher Stowe's anti-slavery novel, *Uncle Tom's Cabin*.) Pictured on the cover was the ideal house, a suburban dwelling with a turret, sun porch, and intricate woodwork set on a lawn landscaped with trees and flowers. The Beecher sisters believed housing served a wider political purpose. The properly organized family home would, they contended, raise virtuous citizens; standardized childrearing and household order would unite a nation divided by Civil War. The book guided readers through the organization of the kitchen and the design of children's bedrooms, as well as advice on how best to scrub floors, clean sheets, and discipline servants. The authors' most widely repeated advice had to do with household health; they urged women to make sure the house had plenty of light and fresh air, which were considered nature's cleansers. Light and air were available only in a semi-suburban location, a place surrounded by trees and plants, on enough land to feel a fresh breeze. The Beechers' book heralded the fashionable Victorian "cottage" for middle-class families.

Poorer families who could not afford lots or houses in newer districts typically crowded into existing dwellings, subdividing houses into multiple flats. Between 1840 and 1860, 4.5 million immigrants arrived in the United States. Many originated from Ireland, arriving with poor health, few skills, and no jobs. In addition, gradual emancipation of enslaved people in New York and Pennsylvania led to growing numbers of impoverished and homeless African Americans in northern cities. The poorest families crowded into dirt-floored basements or tiny attics. In many cities, rear yards were filled with wooden shacks, which were rented to impoverished laborers. Working-class families often shared dwellings, and unmarried workers found shelter in boarding houses run by widows or single women. A concentration of subdivided rental dwellings, boarding houses, and low-wage tenants led to a drop in property values and in neighborhood respectability.

In the 1840s, builders began constructing multi-family dwellings for working class tenants. Tenements, initially defined (under New York law) as any building housing three or more independent households, were a new sector for real estate investment, a strategy for generating profit from low-cost housing with a high density of residents. Some tenements, like those in Manhattan, were four or five story buildings. To maximize profits, builders filled the entire lot with the building, leaving little space between buildings and almost no light or air circulating in interior rooms. In Baltimore, the poor and laboring classes congregated in subdivided two-story dwellings, and often in shacks set along the alleys. Rental dwellings built for two or three families often were subdivided into housing for six families, or more. The crowded tenement or subdivided house stood in stark contrast to the Beechers' domestic ideal.

In the mid-19th century, physicians and public health reformers, known as sanitarians, led campaigns to improve housing conditions through building codes and inspections. In 1872, these physicians, joined by engineers, professors, architects, and others, formed the American Public Health Association. The sanitarians were inspired by new knowledge about disease causation, a devotion to science, and a determination to ameliorate the dangerous effects of industrialization. Their most significant project was the promotion of sewer and water lines to provide urban residents with clean water. As one municipal engineer stated, in the "modern" era, cities had "been transformed from loose aggregates" of scattered houses "into well-organized systems." It was, the sanitarians argued, the responsibility of municipal governments to provide the urban infrastructure that protected the health of its citizens. Though many tenements lacked indoor plumbing well into the 20th century, the sanitarians effectively linked urban housing to household health and made the issue of inadequate housing for the urban poor a subject of political debate.

In the 1880s and 1890s, as cities expanded sewer and water lines, indoor plumbing increased housing prices, leading to growing distinctions between those urban residents able to acquire housing and health and those who could not. The home became a showplace for the latest pumping technology. Readers of Harriet Plunkett's popular and exhaustive guide to household sanitation, *Women, Plumbers, and Doctors* (New York: Appleton, 1885) were told that openness and simplicity of design were the keys to proper household sanitation. "The bath tubs standing up on feet, the lavatory slabs are supported by metallic brackets, and the whole arrangement leaves no dark corners to become filthy," Plunkett wrote.[1] Yet, even when the city paid to lay the pipes, poorer households often lacked the financial resources to pay a one-time hook-up fee; some landlords rejected sewer connections, since it would have required them to install indoor plumbing fixtures in rented dwellings; others refused to pay for repairs when plumbing fixtures fell into disrepair. An 1893 US Commissioner of Labor study found that 73 percent of Chicagoans had access only to an outdoor privy.

Between 1890 and 1920, millions of immigrants arrived in the United States from Europe, moving into tenements in New York's Lower East Side, Chicago's West Side, and Boston's West End. A new generation of reformers—including middle-class college-educated women born just after the Civil War—sought to improve living conditions in urban neighborhoods. Reformers like New York's Lawrence Veiller and Chicago's Jane Addams and Robert Hunter urged government regulation of tenement housing to force landlords to maintain their properties. Veiller, founder of the National Housing Association, published *The Model Tenement House Law* in 1910 (New York: Charities Publication), a manual of proposed housing codes. Though many cities adopted building codes, the regulations, rarely enforced, seemed inadequate to the reformers, spurring a growing movement to improve urban housing.

While some reformers drew attention to housing for the poor, other late 19th-century reformers critiqued the private single-family house. Writer and lecturer Charlotte Perkins Gilman promoted the "kitchenless" house, arguing that women, freed from the burden of household labor, would benefit from a stronger education and could become full and active citizens. Instead of working in private kitchens, women could pool their labor in communal kitchens. Around the turn of the 20th century, women in at least thirty towns organized communal eating clubs to share the burdens of cooking for their families. Though kitchenless houses never caught on, about 50 communities in New York, Wisconsin, and California were designed with shared facilities.

In the late 19th century, some well-to-do households, rejecting single-family houses, sought the fashionable "French flats" or apartments in the city center. Rental dwellings for upper income families appeared in New York, Philadelphia, Boston, and Chicago. The architect Richard Morris Hunt designed some of the earliest apartments for investor Rutherford Stuyvesant on 18th Street in Manhattan. The buildings featured a full-time concierge. Possibly the most luxurious apartment building in the United States was the Dakota (1884), a richly ornamented building with separate servant's entrance and service stairways. Located at the corner of 72nd Street and Central Park West, the Dakota was so-named because it was so far from the city center that some New Yorkers said it might as well be in the Dakotas.

Working-class neighborhoods, often communities of European immigrants, were built within walking distance of factories, slaughterhouses, lumber mills, and steelworks. In smaller industrial towns and midwestern cities, workers lived in a range of housing types, including frame three-decker rental buildings, wood cottages, and brick bungalows. Workers in New Orleans and Louisville often lived in single-story shotgun houses. In some urban neighborhoods, nearly all the residents, especially men, worked in local factories. Homestead, southwest of Pittsburgh, Hegewisch in Chicago, and Gary, Indiana, housed workers in nearby steel plants, while thousands of auto workers lived in "vehicle cities" like Flint, Michigan. The companies—which set working hours, provided employee services, and sparked industrial labor unions—shaped community culture and residents' daily lives.

The rise of the tenement and the movement of more affluent families to residential districts away from wharves and manufacturing sites marked the rise of class-segregated real estate markets. By the final decades of the 19th century, infrastructure improvements funded by municipal governments—sewers, water lines, paved streets, and sidewalks—enhanced property values in housing for some urban residents, especially those living in "fashionable sections," leaving others—those in tenement districts or working-class neighborhoods—to struggle to acquire health for their families. In rapidly expanding industrial cities, the health of household members was increasingly linked to the location and material conditions of the family home.

HOME OWNERSHIP

The American ideal of home ownership, promoted by builders, real estate developers, and federal housing programs, is, in many ways, rooted in the massive social and economic shifts in late 19th-century America. In the decades after the Civil War, as the nation moved from an agrarian to an industrialized urban society, as immigrants from abroad and migrants from rural regions arrived in American cities, and as reformers sought to improve dangerous living conditions in impoverished neighborhoods, ownership of a single-family house was conceived as an "American standard" of living. Ownership of single-family houses in urban and suburban areas grew in the late 19th and early 20th centuries and rapidly increased after the New Deal.

Yet, expanding home ownership rates did not catapult all homeowners into the middle class. Some Americans, including nearly two generations of black families, were denied home loans under discriminatory mortgage programs and generally were barred from white-only suburban communities. Indeed, the promotion of home ownership by builders and federal officials quickly left cities sharply segregated by race and class, and ultimately contributed to the mid-20th-century devastation of many urban neighborhoods.

Working people who did not earn enough to purchase houses often moved into boarding houses and, by the 1920s, single-room occupancy hotels. Boarding houses, sometimes owned or managed by widows or single women, provided dwelling spaces and generally a meal for a low weekly fee. Residents typically included single adults, young people recently arrived in the city, or older tenants who fell on hard times and lacked family support. The boarding house provided the services of a low-priced hotel in a family-style home.

Well into the 20th century, some laboring families built their own houses, using purchased and scavenged materials. Self-built housing was usually valued at less than $2,000 in 1900. Geographer Richard Harris estimates that as much as 16 percent of American housing was self-built up to 1950.[2] Working-class self-built suburbs could be found on the edge of Detroit, in southern California, and other American cities. Some families purchased prefabricated houses. Sears, Roebuck and Co. published its first housing catalogue in 1908, marketing house plans and kits for build-your-own houses. Three years later, the firm entered the mortgage business, lending up to 75 percent of the cost of the lot, house, and labor. From about 1910 and into the 1920s, Sears's offerings ranged from a one-bedroom shack without indoor plumbing for a couple hundred dollars to a four-bedroom, Colonial-style house marketed for $7,960, in 1919. Architectural historian Dolores Hayden estimates that Sears had sold about 50,000 homes by 1934, when Sears closed down its Modern Homes division.[3] Self-built communities, while freeing working class families from rent paying, often lacked sewer lines, water pipes, electricity, and paved streets.

The home construction industry changed dramatically in the years between the Civil War and the New Deal. In the 1880s, a new type of businessman-builder merged three separate businesses: subdividing large tracts of land into individual lots, constructing houses, and providing loans to home buyers. Businessmen gradually replaced carpenter-contractors who had controlled home construction through much of the 19th century. Businessmen turned what had been immigrant-controlled enterprises run by skilled craftsmen into regional industries that hired skilled laborers as waged workers to mass-produce housing.

The businessmen lowered construction costs by using factory-produced materials. The move allowed them in turn to hire less skilled workers at lower wages on construction sites, undercutting the wages of skilled carpenters and other craftsmen. By the 1870s, new technology enabled factories to use semiskilled labor to mass-produce moldings, doors, window sashes, and standard-sized lumber. In Cook County, Illinois, for example, there were 51 planing mills and sash, door, and blind factories employing 2,288 workers in 1870; twenty years later, 116 woodworking factories employed more than 8,000 workers. The new industry could build and sell as many as 35 to

40 houses per year, often on newly subdivided land edging the built-up sections of the city.

Businessmen-builders transformed the process of home buying. Until the 1880s, wealthy and middle-class families paid for their homes with inherited money or savings. Most had down payments of more than 50 percent, and they paid off the loans at two-year intervals within six to eight years. Poorer and working-class families, particularly immigrant families, acquired home loans through immigrant savings and loans, or building associations or local organizations, often of people from the same village or region in Europe. The new businessmen-builders used large construction loans from commercial banks and insurance companies to purchase land, subdivide, build houses, and provide credit for homebuyers. Samuel Eberly Gross, a Chicago builder, was among the first to introduce the "easy payment plan," through which buyers could put as little as $50 dollars down and make monthly payments of $15 to $40. In the 1880s, Gross's "workingman's cottages" were priced from $1,000 to $2,000 for a four- to six-room house. The payment system was immensely popular among skilled workers and was quickly copied by other builders.

From the 1890s through the 1920s, housing developers produced whole suburban communities in St. Louis, Los Angeles, Chicago, and other cities. Using the construction and financing techniques pioneered by late 19th-century builders, developers—like Edward H. Bouton in Baltimore, Hugh Potter in Houston, and J. C. Nichols in Kansas City, MO—built suburbs designed for affluent families. They used landscaping, park spaces, and contoured streets to market their developments. Nichols, in his Country Club Hills development, introduced a shopping district to his community, as an added attraction to homebuyers. Palos Verdes, CA, designed by Fredrick Law Olmsted Jr., was a community of Spanish colonial houses on rolling hills overlooking the Pacific Ocean, featuring a golf course and nursery school. The community builders maintained control of the entire process of development from land acquisition through street design, housing, landscaping, marketing, financing, and the location of commercial services.

New suburban communities were racially segregated, a form of social engineering promoted by real estate interests seeking to boost property values in white neighborhoods and enforced by state and municipal legislation. Southern state legislatures, aiming to crush biracial labor organizing, began in the 1890s to pass laws designed to separate black and white citizens, establishing segregated schools, public transportation, and neighborhoods. Municipalities in California, reacting to Chinese immigration, adopted segregation ordinances. Northern cities used zoning regulations, a legal instrument introduced in 1910 to 1920, to enforce racial segregation in real estate markets. In St. Louis in 1916, the city's realtors association, the Real Estate Exchange, campaigned for a ballot referendum to prohibit black buyers from moving onto blocks where at least 75 percent of the residents were white. Baltimore and Louisville passed similar ordinances. Some social reformers argued that segregation laws would secure social harmony by separating black from white citizens and, thus, preventing white mobs from lynching and terrorizing black Americans. In the 1917 *Buchanan v. Warley* case, the Supreme Court ruled unconstitutional a Louisville ordinance designed to prevent "conflict and ill-feeling between white and colored races in city of Louisville and to preserve the public peace..."[4] by requiring separate blocks of residence for black and white people. Some municipalities simply ignored the court ruling. Other towns and cities used zoning laws to restrict industry, saloons, and even brothels to largely African American neighborhoods, leading to a further drop in property values by linking black communities to crime, vice and industry.

In the wake of the *Buchanan* decision, white home owners and developers also used racial covenants, addendums attached to the house title, that barred the sale of the house to African Americans, and sometimes Jews, Japanese, or "Mongolian" buyers. Harland Bartholomew, the St. Louis urban planner and leader in the national planning movement, wrote that the city's zoning was designed to "preserv(e) the more desirable residential neighborhoods" and prevent movement into "finer residential districts ... by colored people."[5] Racial segregation in housing, rooted in early 20th-century law and real estate policies, was neither accidental nor inevitable.

Developers in the 1920s also introduced a series of regulations designed to enhance property values. Most draconian were rules restricting sales to white, native-born, and middle-class buyers. Houses in Palos Verdes included deed restrictions prohibiting Mexican Americans from buying houses there. Regulations set design features for the houses, required owners to maintain their lawns, and banned amenities like clotheslines, which were associated with immigrant tenement neighborhoods. The regulations, later challenged in the courts, functioned to create well-to-do, racially homogenous communities.

The developers' strategies for attracting affluent buyers to suburban locales and for linking property values to the race and class of the residents would influence federal housing policies and the home construction industry for much of the 20th century. Despite the builders' efforts, real estate markets stalled in the mid-1920s. Developers, seeing little profit in housing for working-class families, had saturated the market for high-end housing. The 1929 stock market crash simply clinched an already steep decline in home building, spurring policymakers to look for new ways to buttress the industry and to subsidize the lower-priced housing markets.

HOUSING AND FEDERAL POLICY

The federal government entered the nation's housing markets in the 1930s, during the Great Depression, when house construction came to a near halt and large numbers of homeowners, desperate and unemployed, faced foreclosure. The New Deal programs were not the first federal housing programs. In 1918, a year after the United States entered World War I, Congress appropriated $110 million for housing war workers. The effort was designed for the wartime emergency and resulted in just a few developments: Yorkshire Village in Camden, New Jersey; Atlantic Heights in Portsmouth, New Hampshire, and several other subdivisions. The crisis of the Depression spurred large, direct, and enduring federal action on housing. The federal government provided generous subsidies to builders and middle-class buyers of suburban houses while simultaneously funding the clearance of urban townhouses and the construction of large, multi-family housing developments for the urban poor. With suburban developers largely rejecting black buyers, African Americans were left out of the postwar housing boom. In the 1970s, federal officials moved to eliminate racial segregation in housing.

President Herbert Hoover, widely reviled for presiding over the onset of the Depression in 1929, introduced the first major national housing legislation. Hoover, who was secretary of commerce in the 1920s, was a bold proponent of home ownership. His Department of Commerce had issued a series of pamphlets that urged Americans to buy houses and guided homebuyers through the rigors of purchasing and decorating a house. The Depression demonstrated that housing depended on wages and, without government intervention, savings banks and insurance companies, which had provided home mortgages, and the home construction industry would fail. Between 1928 and 1933, construction of residential property fell by 95 percent, and spending on home repairs fell by 90 percent. In 1931, when foreclosures hit nearly one thousand per day, Hoover convened the President's National Conference on Home Building and Home Ownership and pushed through the Federal Home Loan Bank Act. The law proved limited and was replaced in 1933 by President Franklin Roosevelt's Home Owners Loan Corporation (HOLC).

The HOLC refinanced tens of thousands of mortgages in danger of default. More importantly, the agency introduced the long-term, self-amortizing mortgage that became a model for the banking industry. The HOLC systematized appraisal methods across the nation, creating what later became a set of highly controversial maps that determined the relative risk of providing home loans in varied communities. HOLC appraisers were charged with determining whether the government should refinance mortgages. They set out across the country, dividing cities into neighborhoods and using elaborate questionnaires relating to the occupation, income, and ethnicity of inhabitants and the age, type of construction, price range, sales demand, and general state of repair of housing stock. The HOLC devised a rating system that undervalued older neighborhoods of multi-family housing, and depreciated communities that were racially integrated or predominantly African American. Using four categories of quality, which were color-coded, HOLC appraisers mapped the nation's cities using green for communities described as new, homogenous, and low-risk for housing loans. Homogenous, as historian Kenneth Jackson writes, meant "American business and professional men," excluding neighborhoods with an "infiltration of Jews" or immigrant or black residents. The second grade was colored in blue for communities that were "still desirable;" yellow neighborhoods were typically described as "definitely declining," while the fourth grade, circled in red, was defined as fully deteriorated.[6] The HOLC saved thousands of families from foreclosure. It also introduced the practice of redlining, which devastated many urban neighborhoods and racially divided American cities and suburbs.

The Federal Housing Administration (FHA), established under the National Housing Act of 1934, had a long-term and profound impact on housing in America. Initially, the law was designed to alleviate unemployment by putting laborers to work in construction projects. The FHA quickly became the leading force behind the construction of single-family housing in American suburbs. It was supplemented by the Servicemen's Readjustment Act of 1944, known as the GI Bill, which created a Veterans Administration (VA) program to help the sixteen million returning soldiers and sailors of World War II purchase a home. Under the FHA and VA programs, the federal government insured long-term mortgages made by private creditors. The government essentially eliminated the risk of providing home loans, encouraging lenders to free money for investment in residential construction and home ownership. The FHA, following the HOLC, extended the loan period of its insured mortgages from twenty-five to thirty years. Additionally, it required down payments of 10 percent or less of the value of the home, in contrast to the 1920s, when buyers were required to put down one-third to one-half of the price. With the FHA and VA insuring long-term mortgages with low down payments, home ownership was finally within the reach of a broad section of the American public.

The FHA and VA programs also re-enforced and legitimized racial segregation in housing markets. To determine the risk of insuring mortgages—and whether to insure the mortgages at all—the FHA turned to the HOLC maps and pamphlets, putting into broad practice the redlining initiated by the HOLC. With the federal government refusing to insure mortgages in dense urban neighborhoods and in low-income black communities, many city neighborhoods were left starved for investment capital, while the construction of white suburbs was largely subsidized by federally insured construction loans and home mortgages.

Many urban residents simply could not afford to purchase new single-family houses. American policymakers influenced by social reformers, looked to European efforts to eliminate run-down tenements in American cities. Catherine Bauer's *Modern Housing* published in 1934 (New York: Houghton Mifflin), compared housing programs in the United States and Western Europe. She advocated European models of large-scale, state-funded housing on vacant urban land. Low-rise apartment buildings clustered around small parks would follow the modernist Bauhaus designs used in Germany. Bauer's plan included childcare centers, playgrounds, and neighborhood organizations. The first major public housing came from the Public Works Administration (PWA), a New Deal agency established in 1933, under the National Industrial Recovery Act. The PWA financed the construction of fifty-two developments in the United States, Puerto Rico, and the Virgin Islands. Atlanta's Techwood Homes, completed in August 1936, included a kindergarten, communal laundry facilities, and a library. Similarly, the Carl Mackley Houses in Philadelphia, opened in 1935, featured five four-story buildings clustered around landscaped parks and a swimming pool. The apartment complexes could be made affordable for American workers priced out of the for-profit housing market.

To speed production of low-income housing, the Wagner-Steagall 1937 Housing Act, proposed by New York Senator Robert Wagner and largely written by Bauer, provided an initial $10 million for public housing. The new program represented policy compromises among reformers, real estate entrepreneurs, builders and bankers. Administration of the program was left to local officials; communities that did not want public housing could reject it. Local housing authorities determined the size and location of the housing developments, and set rents, managed tenants, and oversaw maintenance. An "equivalent elimination" provision required the clearance of one slum unit for each new public housing unit; public housing would not add to the cities' overall supply of housing. The bill set maximum construction costs. The program was pushed forward with the passage in 1949 of the Taft-Ellender-Wagner Housing Act, which provided for the construction of 810,000 additional units of public housing over the following six years.

In the late 1940s and early 1950s, public housing tenants were a mix of poor and working-class families, white and black residents. Moving from run-down housing—tenants often were recent arrivals from the rural south—many residents enjoyed the sleek modern apartments. Some low-rise row house-style apartments in Philadelphia and Brooklyn were, for over a decade, stable communities with social services for lower-income families. Some of New York City's high-rise public housing proved a long-term practical alternative to the city's high-priced market-rate housing. But in many places, mismanagement and corruption by local officials charged with administering public housing led to the rapid deterioration of the buildings. Public housing, though intended to solve the problem of over-crowded tenements, was under-funded and poorly maintained; in some cases, it deteriorated into communities plagued by crime and poverty.

Most public housing built after World War II was high-rises, the "tower in the park" design promoted by the Swiss architect Le Corbusier in the 1920s. Federal urban renewal funds were used to tear down older working-class neighborhoods, which were replaced by high-rise developments of 150 to more than 4,000 apartments. The massive buildings often were built on super-blocks, eliminating the neighborhood street grid. In some, like the notorious Pruitt-Igoe in St. Louis, contractors saved construction costs by installing elevators that stopped on every other floor, leaving mothers to carry babies and groceries up and down dirty stairwells. Cutting costs meant cheaply built and easily broken bathroom sinks and toilets, and few of the once-touted playgrounds.

Public housing came to signal racially segregated cities and the cruel marginalization of impoverished black families. Residents in Baltimore, San Francisco, and Chicago responded by establishing community groups and pressuring officials to fund improvements in public housing. The efforts of residents, though significant, largely failed. By the late 20th century, most cities were tearing down

high-rise buildings. Some municipalities used a new stream of federal housing funds under the HOPE VI program to build mixed-income communities and renovate low-rise public housing developments.

By the early 1960s, shoddy construction, poor maintenance of public housing, and the use of federal funds to subsidize suburban development, combined with rising unemployment among the black working class, led to rapid deterioration of living conditions in American cities. In 1960, more than 11 million units of urban housing were considered substandard; these units—some public housing, some run-down privately owned tenements—were occupied almost exclusively by African Americans. In 1968, in the aftermath of half a decade of urban riots and President Lyndon Johnson's massive anti-poverty program, Congress passed the Fair Housing Act, which banned redlining and promoted home ownership for the urban poor. Johnson also pushed through the 1968 Housing and Urban Development Act, often called "Model Cities," which called for the federal government to partner with real estate and banking industries to create new home owners in American cities. After a decade of protest, Model Cities finally emphasized the rehabilitation of housing and neighborhoods rather than clearance.

The 1968 housing program was, however, riddled with fraud and incompetence. In some cities, real estate brokers, recognizing black buyers as a lucrative new market, engaged in the longstanding practice of "block-busting," frightening working-class white home owners with the threat of black neighbors who, brokers claimed, would pull down property values. White owners quickly sold to speculators who could then raise housing prices when they sold to desperate black buyers. Neighborhoods rapidly flipped from white to black residents with real estate entrepreneurs reaping great profits. Even worse, in some cities, real estate brokers hid housing defects and glossed the cost of taxes and maintenance, pushing bankers to provide FHA-insured mortgages on run-down houses to low-income buyers. A rash of new foreclosures followed as the new buyers realized they could not afford repairs. In some cases, banks rushed to foreclose so the agencies could resell and refinance the house, illegally pushing black homeowners out of their homes. In 1975, the *Chicago Tribune* published an investigation of the HUD programs in Chicago, reporting more than 7,000 defaults, 4,000 actual foreclosures, and more than 12,000 abandoned homes owned by HUD. Bankers continued to profit as the federal government insured all the mortgages, while struggling families lost their houses.

But the federal model of public-private partnerships proved useful to a new generation of reformers seeking to revive low-income urban communities in the 1970s and 1980s. Working with local officials, housing activists formed community development corporations (CDC), non-profit corporations designed to provide grants for housing repairs and low-interest loans to homebuyers in low-income communities. The CDCs typically were launched with federal or state grants and were buttressed by funds from private philanthropies, like the Ford Foundation. Among the most successful CDCs was the New Community Corporation, which was started in Newark, New Jersey, in 1968. Over the following two decades, it built more than 2,500 houses for low-income people, a childcare center, and housing and services for people with HIV and AIDS. In the 1980s, community efforts were supported by national funds; the two most prominent national housing organizations were Neighborhood Housing Services and the Local Initiatives Support Corporation, which raised millions of dollars to support construction and renovation of low-income housing, and commercial development in hundreds of urban neighborhoods.

In addition, housing activists used the courts to challenge racial segregation in housing. In a series of decisions across the 20th century, the Supreme Court ruled that laws segregating housing by race or wealth were unconstitutional. In *Shelley v. Kraemer* (1948), the court ruled racial covenants were "unenforceable as law and contrary to public policy." Nearly thirty years later, the NAACP in Mount Laurel Township, New Jersey, challenged the use of land use ordinances to effectively exclude low and moderate-income households. In major opinions issued in 1975 and 1983, the New Jersey Supreme Court ruled unconstitutional the use of zoning regulations that required, for example, such large lot sizes that all single-family houses were prohibitively expensive. Municipalities, the court ruled, must plan for and make available opportunities for the construction of low-income housing, and accept a share of the state's low-income residents. The Court rulings never eliminated the practices of racial steering by real estate sales people, racially tainted lending practices, or the class-segregation of housing markets.

New Deal housing programs dramatically expanded home ownership rates in the United States. Some New Deal programs sought to surmount racial and class divisions in residential communities. The Greenbelt towns, like Greenbelt, Maryland, included a mix of rental apartments and single-family houses with cooperatively owned commercial spaces. Similarly, the Public Works Administration built several apartment buildings, like the Hosiery Workers Housing in Philadelphia and the Harlem River Houses, which, while promoted to black New Yorkers, aimed for households of varied incomes. Yet, federal intervention created what historian Gail Radford calls a "two-tiered" housing market. The federal government built multi-family dwellings for the urban poor while subsidizing the construction of largely white single-family suburban houses.

SUBURBS AND CITIES

Affluent Americans began moving to semi-rural enclaves in the 19th century. Some, like Llewellyn Haskell, the developer of Llewellyn Park in Bloomfield, New Jersey, in the 1850s, sought a spiritual retreat outside the city. After the Civil War, the construction of new streetcar lines spurred construction of "street-car sub-urbs," like the frame houses built in Dorchester and Roxbury outside of Boston in the 1890s. But it was only in the years after World War II that suburban housing came to typify the white working- and middle-class home. Demand for housing skyrocketed at the end of World War II. Home construction came to a near halt during the Depression and, during the war years, most builders were diverted to military projects. As veterans returned from Europe and the Pacific theaters, many young couples jammed into their parents' city row houses and apartments.

Developers responded to the pent-up de-mand for housing by making use of federal programs and by mass-producing suburban dwellings. The most widely known of the new generation of builders was the Levitt Com-pany, which provided custom-built housing on Long Island in the 1920s. A contract with the War Department to produce houses for mil-itary personnel during the war led the firm's owners, brothers William J. and Alfred Levitt, to develop a system to build houses quickly and efficiently. After the war, the firm bought up 4,000 acres of potato fields on Long Island and applied their system to suburban Cape Cod-style single-family houses. The Levitts treated home building like an assembly line with teams of workers moving from lot to lot, each adding a portion of the house. The firm rejected labor unions, under-cutting the wages of local trades-men. With their system, the Levitts constructed about 35 houses per week and charged as little as $6,999 for an 800-square-foot house. Ranch houses sold for $9,500. Veterans, using VA-insured loans, lined up for hours to purchase Levittown houses. William Levitt appeared on the cover of *Time* magazine in July 1950.

Developers throughout the United States followed Levitt's model. Joseph Kelly in Boston, Fritz Burns in Los Angeles, and Del Webb in Phoenix were among the leading developers of the nation's suburbs in the postwar years.

New techniques of home construction, com-bined with the expansion of interstate highways, produced a variety of new fringe communities.

Sociologist William M. Dobriner used the term "reluctant suburbs" for the subdivisions appearing on farmland surrounding older rural towns. Dobriner was writing about a Connecticut coastal community outside of New Haven, opened for development by the construction of Interstate 95. Fringe housing included inex-pensive communities of trailers or manufac-tured houses. Trailers made up 10 to 20 percent of new housing units in 2000. Retirement communities of mixed multi-family and single-family dwellings appeared in semi-rural dis-tricts. In the 1990s, affluent fringe suburbs saw ever-larger houses, "McMansions" with multi-car garages, expansive family rooms and home offices. In 1999, the average new house was 2,250 square feet, sited on a 12,910 square foot lot. Whether living in a trailer or a McMan-sion, residents of fringe communities relied on their cars to travel to work, shopping, and entertainment.

Even as growing numbers of Americans purchased single-family houses, a lack of safe, affordable housing remained a serious problem for many. In the 19th century, impoverished adults might move into crowded tenements or turn to the "poorhouse," state-run institu-tions that might house dozens of impoverished or ill adults. Police stations were also used to shelter the homeless, especially during cold winter nights. The Great Depression led to new forms of housing for the homeless. Hoovervilles, rows of run-down shacks named for the pres-ident, could be found on the edges of many cities. Seattle's Hooverville was among the larg-est, covering nine acres and housing as many as 1,200 people. Impoverished men and women also found shelter in single-room occupancy hotels (SROs), four- and five-story buildings along what became known in many cities as "skid row." In districts like Pioneer Square in Seattle or San Francisco's Tenderloin district, men and women rented tiny rooms. In the 1980s, developers began purchasing and tear-ing down SROs as many skid row districts, like the Bowery in New York and Uptown in Chicago, were gradually gentrified. Homeless shelters, funded by non-profit organizations and municipalities, became the housing of last resort for homeless single adults and families.

In the final decades of the 20th century, gentrification transformed urban neighborhoods, replacing older communities of working-class families living in row houses with, in many cases, modern high-rise buildings and brownstones rehabilitated into single-family dwellings. Older manufacturing buildings were transformed into loft apartments. Artists and young people who initially remade urban industrial spaces into housing were, by the 1990s, replaced by more affluent households buying million-dollar loft condominiums in San Francisco, New York, and Chicago.

Co-owned multi-family housing—the condominium and the co-op apartments, which originated in New York in the 1880s—allowed owners to share costs of maintaining large apartment buildings while also gaining the tax benefits of home ownership. Centralized management of condominium communities, whether high-rise buildings or townhouse communities, meant that owners turned over maintenance and governance to an elected board of residents. Streets in townhouse communities, like atriums in high-rises, were considered the community's private property, policed by private security guards and maintained by private companies. Condominium development allowed developers to generate quick profits from new construction or gut renovation of older manufacturing or rental buildings. Developers in Chicago, Atlanta, and Dallas, aiming to attract middle-class and elite households, fitted condominium buildings with a host of amenities like gyms, pools, and indoor shopping centers. By 2000, as many as one-fifth of urban dwellers were living in condominiums or co-operative buildings.

Booming real estate markets in some urban centers put new pressure on housing markets in residential neighborhoods and inner-ring suburbs. In Manhattan, the growth of investment banking and a finance-driven economy, attracted very wealthy families and pushed middle-class families into working-class neighborhoods, forcing up housing prices in Harlem, Brooklyn, and Washington Heights. Similarly, the Silicon Valley boom sent housing prices in San Francisco to dramatic heights, transforming the working-class Tenderloin into a high-priced district. Poorer and working-class residents were forced ever further away from jobs in business districts.

Some communities fought gentrification. Renters in West Hollywood, feeling the pressure of rising property prices, incorporated the city in 1984, and then imposed rigid rent controls to protect housing for lower-income residents. Tenants in Oakland, California, similarly sought to control skyrocketing housing costs with municipal regulation of rents. Most cities in the late 20th century experienced uneven development as housing prices climbed in commercial centers, while some neighborhoods and edge suburbs, often of African American or Latino residents, were stuck with deteriorated housing, poorly performing schools, and few decent-paying jobs.

In the final decades of the 20th century, a gradual movement of middle-class people to city houses, apartments, and condominiums, following the historical preservation and home rehabbing movements, helped to gentrify urban neighborhoods. Expanding concerns for the environment spurred some Americans to seek housing within walking (or biking) distance of jobs, schools, and work. At the turn of the 21st century, while some cities, like Detroit and St. Louis continued to struggle with declining populations and decaying housing stock; others, like San Francisco, Atlanta, and Seattle faced soaring housing prices and expanding affluent communities.

DISCUSSION OF THE LITERATURE

The history of housing in America, often combining advocacy with empirical research, derives from both academic scholarship and social reform literature of the early 20th century. The earliest housing studies came from tenement reformers determined to document housing conditions in rapidly industrializing cities at the turn of the 20th century. Housing advocates like Edith Elmer Wood and Laurence Villier in New York, W. E. B. Du Bois working in Philadelphia, and Sophonisba Breckinridge in Chicago toured the homes of the urban poor—generally European immigrants and African Americans—and wrote detailed reports on housing conditions. They aimed to draw public attention to run-down and overcrowded living conditions, and to urge municipal officials to regulate urban housing. Reports published with *Hull-House Maps and Papers* (New York: Thomas Y. Crowell, 1895) or Du Bois's *Philadelphia Negro* (Philadelphia: University of Pennsylvania, 1899) have been widely used by scholars of urban housing.

Housing studies entered the university in the 1920s. The University of Chicago's new sociology department, under the leadership of Robert Park and Ernest Burgess, launched a series of studies of urban residential patterns. Park's *The City* (Chicago: University of Chicago Press, 1925) introduced the ecological theory, which, though largely discredited today, powerfully influenced research on immigrant life in American cities for much of the 20th century. At the University of Wisconsin, economist Richard T. Ely and his students produced a series of studies of real estate markets and housing finance. Several of Ely's students, including Helen Munchow, later went to Washington to work with the Roosevelt administration in developing housing policies. Scholars of urban housing in the 1920s and 1930s often moved from academic to government jobs, and back again.

In the late 1960s and 1970s, scholars, influenced by the political movements of the 1960s, published a series of studies on working-class housing, middle-class domesticity, household labor, and urban real estate. Among the first histories of the homes of ordinary people were Carl Bridenbaugh's voluminous studies of colonial American cities. Stephen Thernstrom's pathbreaking book on Irish

immigrants in Newburyport, MA, was an early history of the American ideal of home ownership. Thernstrom demonstrated that Irish immigrants in the late 19th century often put their children to work for wages, sacrificing education, to purchase a house. Elizabeth Blackmar's remarkable study of rental housing markets in Manhattan traced the emergence of class-segregated neighborhoods and vividly linked wages to housing conditions and public health. Feminist historians like Christine Stansell and Jeanne Boydston, along with legal scholars like Jan Lewis and Norma Basch, highlighted the connections between prescriptive gender order and housing forms, property law, and housework. Architectural historians, most prominently Delores Hayden and Gwendolyn Wright, published studies of housing design history. The urban home, and the family relations it contained, was, in these late 20th-century studies, a product of a host of intersecting social forces concerning relations between men and women, black and white, rich and poor Americans.

Sociologist Nels Anderson's Depression-era studies of homeless men made the lack of housing or inadequate housing a significant piece of urban social science. Research on homelessness was revived in the 1980s, as homeless people became a common site in American cities. Scholars tracked the tramps and hoboes of the late 19th century, the rise and decline of single-room occupancy hotels and skid rows, and the shifting demographics of America's homeless across the 20th century. These studies, some by sociologists engaged in ethnographic research, traced populations who slipped in and out of homelessness and called attention to instabilities in urban housing markets in the late 20th century.

Expanding anger over the deterioration of high-rise public housing and massive mid-century urban renewal programs prompted new studies of federal housing policies and postwar deindustrialization. Arnold Hirsch's, *Making the Second Ghetto* (Chicago: University of Chicago Press, 1983) proved a devastating critique of urban renewal on Chicago's South Side and launched a reconsideration of postwar urban housing. It was followed by studies of Detroit, Oakland, Philadelphia, Los Angeles, and Miami. Historians, sociologists and journalists took on public housing, offering powerful indictments of federal policies, while also highlighting the resilience of households headed largely by women living in urban public housing. In the early 21st century, new technology spurred new efforts to document the impact of urban renewal. Colin Gordon's *Mapping Decline* (Philadelphia: University of Pennsylvania Press, 2008), a study of St. Louis, was among the first to use geographic information systems (GIS) mapping techniques to provide a nearly block-level analysis of federal land clearance programs.

Histories of suburbia appeared alongside studies of declining urban centers. Sam Bass Warner's *Streetcar Suburbs* (Cambridge, MA: Harvard University Press, 1962), Robert Fishman's *Bourgeois Utopias* (New York: Basic Books, 1987), and Kenneth Jackson's *Crabgrass Frontier* (New York: Oxford University Press, 1985), among others, emphasized the uniformity of housing styles and homogeneity of white, middle-class suburbs. A new suburban history emerged in the 1990s, highlighting working-class suburbs, self-built suburban housing, African American suburbs and, generally, the wide variety among housing forms and residents in American suburbs. Much of this scholarship noted the racial segregation in suburban communities, and continued to emphasize the unequal distribution of public resources, with suburban developments gaining significantly more federal housing subsidies.

FURTHER READING

Baum, John F., Roger Biles, and Kristin M. Szylvian, eds. *From Tenements to Taylor Homes: In Search of Urban Housing Policy in America.* University Park: Pennsylvania State University Press, 2000.

Blackmar, Elizabeth. *Manhattan for Rent, 1785–1850.* Ithaca, NY: Cornell University Press, 1991.

Boydston, Jeanne. *Home and Work: Housework, Wages and the Ideology of Labor in the Early Republic.* New York: Oxford University Press, 1994.

Connolly, N. B. D. *A World More Concrete: Real Estate and the Remaking of Jim Crow South Florida.* Chicago: University of Chicago Press, 2014.

Countryman, Matthew J. *Up South: Civil Rights and Black Power in Philadelphia.* Philadelphia: University of Pennsylvania Press, 2006.

Cromley, Elizabeth Collins. *Alone Together: A History of New York's Early Apartments.* Ithaca, NY: Cornell University Press, 1990.

Dunbar, Erica Armstrong. *A Fragile Freedom.* New Haven, CT: Yale University Press, 2011.

Freund, David M. P. *Colored Property: State Policy and White Racial Politics in Suburban America.* Chicago: University of Chicago Press, 2007.

Garb, Margaret. *City of American Dreams: A History of Home Ownership and Housing Reform in Chicago, 1871–1919.* Chicago: University of Chicago Press, 2005.

Goldfield, David R. *Region, Race and Cities: Interpreting the Urban South.* Baton Rouge: Louisiana State University Press, 1997.

Gordon, Colin. *Mapping Decline: St. Louis and the Fate of the Modern American City.* Philadelphia: University of Pennsylvania Press, 2008.

Grossman, James. *Land of Hope: Chicago, Black Southerners, and the Great Migration.* Chicago: University of Chicago Press, 1991.

Groth, Paul. *Living Downtown: The History of Residential Hotels in the United States.* Berkeley: University of California Press, 1999.

Harris, Leslie. *In the Shadow of Slavery: African Americans in New York City, 1626–1863.* Chicago: University of Chicago Press, 2003.

Harris, Richard. *Unplanned Suburbs: Toronto's American Tragedy, 1900–1950.* Baltimore: Johns Hopkins University Press, 1999.

Hayden, Dolores. *The Grand Domestic Revolution: A History of Feminist Designs for American Homes, Neighborhoods and Cities.* Cambridge, MA: MIT Press, 1982.

Hayden, Dolores. *Building Suburbia: Green Fields and Urban Growth, 1820–2000.* New York: Vintage, 2004.

Hirsch, Arnold. *Making the Second Ghetto: Race and Housing in Chicago, 1940–1960.* Chicago: University of Chicago Press, 1998.

Hise, Greg. *Magnetic Los Angeles: Planning the Twentieth-Century Metropolis.* Baltimore: Johns Hopkins University Press, 1999.

Jackson, Kenneth T. *Crabgrass Frontier: The Suburbanization of the United States.* New York: Oxford University Press, 1985.

Kerr, Daniel R. *Derelict Paradise: Homelessness and Urban Development in Cleveland, Ohio.* Amherst: University of Massachusetts Press, 2011.

Lewis, Earl. *In Their Own Interests: Race, Class and Power in Twentieth-Century Norfolk, Virginia.* Berkeley: University of California Press, 1993.

Loeb, Carolyn S. *Entrepreneurial Vernacular: Developers' Subdivisions in the 1920s.* Baltimore: Johns Hopkins University Press, 2001.

Melosi, Martin. *The Sanitary City: Urban Infrastructure in America from Colonial Times to the Present.* Baltimore: Johns Hopkins University Press, 2000.

Nickerson, Michelle, and Darren Dochuk, eds. *Sunbelt Rising: The Politics of Place, Space and Region.* Philadelphia: University of Pennsylvania Press, 2011.

Nicolaides, Becky. *My Blue Heaven: Life and Politics in the Working-Class Suburbs of Los Angeles, 1920–1965.* Chicago: University of Chicago Press, 2002.

Page, Max. *The Creative Destruction of Manhattan, 1900–1940.* Chicago: University of Chicago Press, 2001.

Radford, Gail. *Modern Housing for America: Policy Struggles in the New Deal Era.* Chicago: University of Chicago Press, 1997.

Rockman, Seth. *Scraping By: Wage Labor, Slavery and Survival in Early Baltimore.* Baltimore: Johns Hopkins University Press, 2009.

Self, Robert. *American Babylon: Race and the Struggle for Postwar Oakland.* Princeton, NJ: Princeton University Press, 2005.

Stansell, Christine. *City of Women: Sex and Class in New York, 1789–1860.* Urbana: University of Illinois Press, 1987.

Sugrue, Thomas. *The Origins of the Urban Crisis: Race and Inequality in Post-War Detroit.* Princeton, NJ: Princeton University Press, 1996.

Williams, Rhonda. *The Politics of Public Housing: Black Women's Struggles Against Urban Inequality.* New York: Oxford University Press, 2004.

Wright, Gwendolyn. *Building the Dream: A Social History of Housing in America.* Cambridge, MA: MIT Press, 1998.

NOTES

1. Harriet Plunkett, *Women, Plumbers and Doctors: Household Sanitation* (New York: D. Appleton, 1885), 109–110.

2. Richard Harris, *Unplanned Suburbs: Toronto's American Tragedy, 1900–1950* (Baltimore: Johns Hopkins University Press, 1999).

3. Dolores Hayden, *Building Suburbia: Green Fields and Urban Growth, 1820–2000* (New York: Vintage, 2004), 105.

4. Colin Gordon, *Mapping Decline: St. Louis and the Fate of the Modern American City* (Philadelphia: University of Pennsylvania Press, 2008), 70–71.

5. Gordon, *Mapping Decline,* 70.

6. Kenneth T. Jackson, *Crabgrass Frontier: The Suburbanization of the United States* (New York: Oxford University Press, 1985), 196–197.

Margaret Garb

PUBLIC HOUSING IN URBAN AMERICA

Public housing in the United States began with great promise and the best of intentions during President Franklin Roosevelt's New Deal in the 1930s. Progressive reformers, after decades of frustration with the private housing market, pushed Congress to enact a federal-local partnership to clear slums and construct modern, large-scale housing intended for the utopian uplift of the working poor. But by the 1970s, many projects began a downward spiral characterized by deferred maintenance, broken infrastructures, and increasing poverty of residents. By the 1990s, public housing was the nation's most problematic social welfare program. Overt and structural racism, misguided policy choices, and the politics of the US welfare state deeply undermined projects, turning them into underfunded, badly maintained warehouses for the urban poor. With their often bleak architecture and disproportionately African American tenancy, "the projects" became racialized shorthand for urban poverty, imprinted on the built environment in concrete form.

But generalizations about public housing are often misleading. The program evolved considerably over time and produced a wide range of outcomes. Cities large and small built projects in all shapes and sizes, from sprawling agglomerations of high-rise towers to modest single-family developments. Southern states like Alabama and Georgia and conservative cities like Dallas actively participated in the program in its first decades, but Los Angeles largely shunned it after World War II. While many fled public housing as conditions deteriorated, others stayed and sank deep roots in their communities, fighting for resources and community-centered solutions. Several cities, including Chicago, Atlanta, Baltimore, and New Orleans, eventually dismantled the bulk of their projects, but New York City—the largest housing authority in the United States—tore down none of its high-rise developments. Many stereotypes suggest public housing serves only African Americans, but in 2017 the public housing population was 40 percent black, 34 percent white, 22 percent Latino, and 4 percent Asian and other; senior citizens amounted to 30 percent of residents that year.[1] Today, housing vouchers, which provide federal subsidies for families to rent privately owned housing, and the Low-Income Housing Tax Credit (LIHTC), which finances construction of privately owned affordable housing developments, have supplanted and surpassed the original New Deal program. "Public housing" is no longer a single program of government-owned housing and has evolved—often painfully and still insufficiently—into a patchwork of affordable housing programs that support low-income families.[2]

Still, a history of public housing must confront the fact that the program as conceived in the New Deal and widely implemented in the 1950s and 1960s proved unsustainable. Projects like Pruitt-Igoe in St. Louis, Cabrini-Green in Chicago, Tasker Homes in Philadelphia, Techwood Homes in Atlanta, and Jordan Downs Homes in Los Angeles became infamous for their dysfunction and violence, giving public housing—and the welfare state in general—a bad name. Exploding the stereotypes surrounding public housing is important, but unpacking the failures of the past is also critical, as the demise of the New Deal program had major repercussions for cities and urban politics in the 20th century.

PUBLIC HOUSING LAUNCHES, 1933–1945

Public housing became politically viable only after other housing reforms proved ineffective at dealing with the problems of poverty and slum housing. Progressive-era reformers convinced cities to enact building codes to regulate private housing, but few cities enforced them rigorously, as landlords chafed at inspections while tenants feared rental increases triggered by city-mandated improvements. The real estate industry argued that new construction for the middle class could improve conditions, with older housing "filtering down" to lower-income families over time. But impoverished districts with predominantly unsanitary and dilapidated housing—what progressive reformers and conservative civic interests alike labeled "slums"—continued to be profitable as a steady stream of poor migrants desperately sought urban shelter.[3]

The Great Depression of the 1930s and the New Deal state changed the calculus for housing reform. High unemployment, the continued presence of slums, and the collapse of new housing construction opened the door to state action. Progressives looked to Europe for policy ideas, made the case for direct government construction of housing, and lobbied Congress, with women playing central roles in the effort. Edith Elmer Wood developed a market failure argument that the housing problem was "insoluble ... under the ordinary laws of supply and demand" for the "bottom third" of the population, a theme picked up by President Franklin Roosevelt, whose second inaugural address saw "one-third of a nation ill-housed."[4] Mary Kingsbury Simkhovitch, a longtime New York settlement house leader and founder of the National Public Housing Conference, rallied political support among urban reformers across the country. Housing reformer Catherine

Bauer wrote *Modern Housing* (1934), a call to action based on European precedents, and won the admiration of Senator Robert Wagner (D-NY), a crucial ally.[5] But Simkhovitch and Bauer did not always see eye-to-eye. The former wanted to rebuild slums with the goal of cleaning up the city and uplifting its poor residents; the latter was willing to let such neighborhoods further decay and instead wanted to design affordable modernist apartment complexes on vacant land using interwar German models. Importantly, both sought direct federal subsidies for the construction of large-scale projects at below-market rents; both believed that governments could build better communities than private developers driven by profit.[6]

Of the two visions, "slum clearance," as it was known, had greater political appeal. In 1933, Simkhovitch successfully lobbied Congress to authorize the Public Works Administration (PWA) to undertake slum clearance and public housing construction. Over five years, the PWA built fifty-one projects with 21,000 units, using row house and walk-up designs. But housing reformers viewed the PWA experiment as a disappointment. A federal court case in 1936 rejected the federal government's use of eminent domain to obtain land for public housing; as a result, roughly half of PWA projects ended up on vacant sites. Further, the high cost of construction pushed rents out of the reach of the working poor. Reformers blamed inadequate subsidies, federal micromanagement, and excessive designs for this outcome. Few, however, openly criticized the PWA's racial policies, including its "neighborhood composition" rule, which deferred to local norms and blocked new projects from changing the racial makeup of an area, thereby preventing racial integration at projects in all-white neighborhoods.[7]

Learning from the PWA effort, housing reformers produced the Housing Act of 1937, which established the basic parameters of public housing for the next several decades. Bauer and Leon Keyserling, an aide to Senator Wagner, wrote much of the legislation and allowed for the development of modern housing on vacant land, but the act's deep subsidies and greater local control also made slum clearance attractive. Under its terms, a new United States Housing Authority (USHA) agreed to pay 90 percent of the capital costs to build public housing, including buying and clearing slum land, designing new projects, and constructing them. Local housing authorities (charted by cities under state housing laws) would contribute 10 percent of capital costs, select sites, clear them, contract for construction, manage finished projects, charge sufficient rents to pay for their maintenance, and build up a reserve fund for periodic renovations. The 10 percent local contribution could be met in part by exempting projects from property taxation; in this way, cities could clear slums and build new public housing without significant cash outlay. In essence, public housing was nearly "free" to cities, at least initially. Deep subsidies would mean low rents, but in deference to real estate interests who hoped to limit public housing to the poor, the 1937 Housing Act included restrictions on tenant incomes. The law said nothing about race or racial integration, though local control over site selection and tenant selection meant deference to local customs.[8]

The Housing Act of 1937, coupled with other New Deal housing legislation, created what historian Gail Radford calls a "two-tiered" policy. The first tier centered on homeownership, with laws reorganizing and insuring the private mortgage market while also codifying discriminatory real estate practices in order to help whites achieve higher rates of ownership in racially exclusive communities. This vast but largely invisible set of politically popular supports and subsidies dwarfed the second tier—a limited, circumscribed, highly visible, and ultimately unsustainable public housing program intended for the working poor.[9]

Implementation of the 1937 Housing Act got off to a rocky start. President Roosevelt appointed New York developer Nathan Straus to lead the new USHA, but he proved to be a weak leader with a fixation on driving down costs and an inability to get along with legislators or local officials. In 1939, Congress stopped authorizations for additional public housing, but not before Straus set dangerous precedents by forcing local housing authorities to design projects with monotonous layouts and small room sizes—all to reduce costs in a misguided effort to demonstrate public housing's frugality. Further, the law allowed local housing authorities to choose between vacant land and slum clearance; most chose the latter over Bauer's vision of modern housing for the working class in the nascent suburbs.[10]

Early public housing projects were, nevertheless, highly sought after by eligible families, especially the "submerged" middle class devastated by the Great Depression. New apartments amounted to a major step up from poverty, with modern amenities like electric refrigerators, full plumbing, reliable heat, and private bedrooms. Most projects included park facilities, health clinics, and other public space. Public housing, writes historian Lawrence Vale, "was more than an attempt to destroy the slums; it was also a concomitant effort to rebuild the village." Local housing authorities published "before" and "after" images to demonstrate public housing's remarkable transformation of the built environment. Rents were set significantly below those in the private sector, resulting in long waiting lists, especially among projects open to African Americans who faced discrimination in housing and job markets. When the Ida B. Wells Homes opened on Chicago's South Side in 1939, more than 18,000 families applied for 1,600 apartments.[11]

But the 1937 Housing Act was barely under way when World War II intervened, and public housing's mission quickly shifted. President Roosevelt, disdainful of Straus, reorganized the USHA out of existence in 1942, pressed many projects into service to house essential war workers, and developed new bureaucracies to meet wartime housing needs. By the end of the war, more than 625,000 public housing units had been built across the country, mostly in temporary structures including Quonset huts, trailers, and dormitories, and much of it constructed quickly on marginal sites. Enormous projects were built near the nation's costal shipbuilding cities and airplane factories. The Planeview project near Boeing's Wichita, Kansas, plant included 4,382 housing units, while the entirely new community of Vanport, Oregon, had 10,400 units of temporary housing, finished in a mere 110 days. Vanport lay near Portland's shipyards on low-lying land, and on May 30, 1948, a flood destroyed the community, displacing 18,000 people, one-third of them African American. Other temporary projects survived into the 1950s, deteriorating into blighted communities. Racial tensions flared as whites resented the housing of African Americans in new locations; in 1942, more than two thousand police and national guardsmen protected the first six black families to integrate the all-white Sojourner Truth project in Detroit. While the massive construction of shelter supported the war effort, it did little to generate political support for the public housing program.[12]

POSTWAR STRUGGLES, 1945–1960

Liberals had every expectation after World War II that public housing construction would resume, especially given severe housing shortages across the country. Depression and war in the previous fifteen years meant little new private housing had been built, while returning veterans created considerable demand. But public housing faced an uphill battle in Congress throughout the postwar period, as charges of socialism from real estate interests and localized battles over race put supporters on the defensive. The Housing Act of 1949, passed after four years of stalemate, authorized 135,000 units of public housing per year for five years with nearly the same terms as in 1937, potentially a massive expansion. But the program never came close to this figure, as first the Korean War and then Republican control of Congress and the presidency sharply limited construction throughout the 1950s. Public housing survived in large part because it played an important supporting role to the federal urban renewal program (initiated in 1949 and expanded in 1954) by taking in low-income dwellers to make way for private redevelopment.[13]

Congressional debates reflected the deep opposition of real estate interests to public housing, which tarred the program as socialist and, more to the point, as direct governmental competition in the rental market. The National Association of Real Estate Boards (NAREB) organized anti-public housing campaigns across the country asking, rhetorically, "Who is going to pay YOUR rent?"—a message to voters that a select few in public housing received a rent subsidy while most did not. NAREB's lobbying gained traction nationwide and had its greatest success in California, which passed a state referendum in 1950 requiring city voters to directly approve the location of housing projects. Further, in a three-year battle that roiled Los Angeles politics, conservative activists forced that city to back out of a 1949 agreement on a slate of public housing projects.[14]

Public housing also faced backlashes over its potential for racial integration. The migration of African Americans to the urban North during the war continued in the 1950s, and where they would live preoccupied whites. In Chicago, Detroit, Philadelphia, Seattle, and St. Louis, city leaders directed public housing into existing black neighborhoods in a not-so-subtle effort to avoid integration. Historian Arnold Hirsch argues these site decisions amounted to a "domestic containment policy," analogous to the Cold War's effort to contain communism in Europe, that would rebuild a "second ghetto" on top of the old one. Other cities sought to use public housing to reclaim black neighborhoods for white occupancy; Miami, for example, relocated African Americans to public housing on outlying lands so areas near downtown could be cleared. In nearly all cases, white voters placed racial considerations front and center when influencing site

selection policy. Progressives fought back but often lost: Chicago officials engineered the ouster of its longtime housing leader Elizabeth Wood in 1954 when she publicly championed integration.[15]

In the American South, small cities and even towns embraced public housing as long as racial integration could be avoided. Local housing authorities (LHAs) sprang up across the South, and by 1958 Georgia (118 LHAs), Texas (111) and Alabama (84) led the nation in participation. As with other New Deal programs like the Tennessee Valley Authority, southern states eagerly sought federal dollars, and many cities feared slums more than socialized housing. Southern communities often constructed separate but nearly equal projects, one for whites and one for blacks, building *Plessy v Ferguson* onto the landscape. For example, San Antonio's first four projects included one built one for whites, two for African Americans, and one for Mexican Americans. Meanwhile, midwestern states such as Minnesota (9 LHAs in 1958), Wisconsin (4), Nebraska (1), and Kansas (0) viewed public housing through ideological lenses, with real estate interests and political conservatism resisting participation.[16]

Southern enthusiasm for public housing remained strong until the issue of racial segregation reached the US Supreme Court in 1954. One week after the *Brown v Board of Education* decision, the Court let stand a California Supreme Court ruling that declared unconstitutional San Francisco's segregation of public housing by race. In the decade that followed, many public housing projects racially transitioned rather than racially integrated, as the admission of African Americans led to high turnover among whites. Without policies to intentionally sustain integration (which would have required some form of quotas), public housing in many cities became predominantly African American. Black residents, who faced discriminatory housing and job markets, sought out—and remained—in public housing far longer than whites.[17]

By the late 1950s, liberals began to sour on public housing. In 1957, Bauer wrote a weary critique of the program to date, bemoaning that it had not "taken off" politically, creating "excessive caution, administrative rigidity, and lack of creative initiative" that resulted in designs amounting to "watered-down modernism." Urban critic Jane Jacobs railed against the scale of public housing in her influential *The Death and Life of Great American Cities* (1961), saying the removal of streets to create "superblocks" of housing contributed to anonymous communities without "eyes on the street," thereby inviting disorder.[18] These critiques, however, had little impact on public debate, at least initially. In the deepening urban crisis of the 1960s, desperate policymakers hoped more public housing might placate African American unrest. In 1965, in response to the Watts riots in Los Angeles the year before, President Lyndon Johnson reorganized housing and selected social programs into a cabinet-level agency, the Department of Housing and Urban Development (HUD). In the wake of Martin Luther King Jr.'s assassination, the Housing and Redevelopment Act of 1968 authorized a surge of new public housing construction, though many cities chose to build housing for senior citizens—politically far less controversial than family units.

HIGH-RISE DESIGNS AND PUBLIC HOUSING DECLINE: 1950–1972

Even as Congress doubled-down on public housing, the 1968 Housing Act discouraged the use of tall buildings in future public housing (except for senior housing), as it became clear that elevator buildings for families were an albatross in cities that used the form. Since the 1920s, European modernists had argued that the future of the city lay in its clearance and rebuilding with forests of tall buildings in park-like settings, and several of the largest housing authorities adopted the model for early postwar projects. But high-rises, when translated through the constraints of the public

housing program, did not fare well in cities except New York. Design restrictions, driven by the federal government's continued obsession with cost, produced monotonous, drab complexes easily stigmatized as housing for the poor. Further, some cities planned elevator buildings with a large proportion of multi-bedroom apartments to serve low-income families with several children, as such families faced the most difficulties in the private market. The resulting youth density—unprecedented demographically—exacerbated wear and tear and created problems of social order unanticipated by planners. Elevators became play spaces for children, and their constant breakdown strained high-rise living.[19]

The Pruitt-Igoe project in St. Louis showed the problems of cost-constrained, youth-filled, high-rise public housing in the extreme. Constructed in 1954 and designed by highly regarded architect Minoru Yamasaki (who later designed the World Trade Center in New York City), the project contained 2,870 apartments in eleven-story buildings at high densities. Federal cost restrictions led to unusual choices, including the use of "skip-stop" elevators that stopped at every third floor; residents on adjoining floors had to walk up or down one flight to reach an elevator. Within a decade, the project faced serious maintenance issues due to shoddy construction and large proportions of youth. Management became overwhelmed. Disarray triggered a tenant rent strike in 1964, followed by an exodus of those with options; within a year, vacancies rose to one-third of units and the project soon became housing of last resort. Physical conditions deteriorated further, and in 1968 negotiations over the fate of the project shifted toward demolition. In 1972, the first buildings were imploded with dynamite, creating an indelible image of public housing failure. While Pruitt-Igoe was something of an anomaly—widespread demolition of public housing did not begin until the 1990s—the project represented the leading edge of deeper systemic problems that threatened the entire program.[20]

Public housing's unsustainable fiscal structure contributed to its slow unraveling. The 1937 Housing Act aimed federal subsidies only at capital costs and required housing authorities to collect enough rent to pay for ongoing maintenance. In a progressive effort to keep apartments affordable for the poor, many housing authorities set rent at 25 percent of a tenant's income. If a family's income fell, rent would be adjusted downward; conversely, a pay raise would trigger a rent increase. While seemingly fair-minded, income-based rents created incentives for the upwardly mobile to leave and for those without steady employment to stay, often for lengthy periods. As a result, public housing projects increasingly concentrated poverty over the course of the 1960s, thereby diminishing resources available for maintenance.[21]

To counteract negative trend lines, housing authorities sought to attract working-class residents and extract more rental income. But tenants complained, and beginning in 1969, Congress passed the Brooke Amendments, named after Senator Edward Brooke (R-MA), to protect low-income tenants from rental increases. In 1972, Congress belatedly recognized the fiscal crisis and authorized new federal operating subsidies to support maintenance. But the formula for distributing subsidies was left to HUD, which allocated funds based on measures of housing authority efficiency. Many big-city housing authorities scored poorly and were penalized, and thus starved of much needed resources. Meanwhile, costs exploded in the 1970s, as boilers, roofs, cabinets, and elevators reached life expectancies and needed replacement, while high youth densities required repeated repair of windows, doors, and lights. The energy crises of the 1970s sent utility costs skyrocketing, a cost absorbed by local housing authorities and not tenants. By the 1980s, the federal-local partnership had evolved into a dependent relationship, with local housing authorities entirely reliant on penurious congressional funding for basic operations.[22]

While other cities struggled, public housing largely thrived in New York City. That city's experience remains a vital riposte to narratives of universal public housing failure. Between 1934 and 1965, the New York City Housing Authority (NYCHA) constructed 154 projects with 153,000 units, volumes that dwarfed the next-closest city, Chicago (31,000 units). Of these, 69 projects used elevator buildings in large-scale developments of more than 1,000 apartments. Unlike elsewhere, public housing in New York had strong political support, was well-managed, and sustained working-class tenancy due to careful tenant selection and the city's chronically tight private housing market. Further, residents had strong relations with NYCHA's own police force to sustain social order. With more revenue, smaller family sizes, and less concentrated poverty—relative to other housing authorities—New York weathered public housing's fiscal and social crises of the 1970s and 1980s. While projects experienced typical urban ills and were far from utopian, NYCHA projects nonetheless provided an enormous stock of affordable housing. Only in the 21st century, after decades of federal underfunding resulting in deferred maintenance, did the NYCHA enter its own crisis, all the more harrowing as its projects sheltered one in fourteen New Yorkers in 2017.[23]

THE NEOLIBERAL TURN: 1965–1992

As public housing slipped, Congress began experimenting with public-private partnerships during the 1960s in a shift that amounted to a neoliberal turn. The Housing and Community Development Act of 1974 consolidated this turn by expanding trial programs for private developers to build or rehabilitate—and now own and manage—complexes designated for low-income tenancy. Even more significantly, the 1974 legislation made permanent a housing voucher experiment dating back to 1965 to subsidize low-income families in existing privately-owned housing. Collectively, these programs became known as "Section 8" housing, after the section of the 1974 act that created them. Crucially, Section 8 subsidies were more generous than the public housing program, as they guaranteed private owners a federally determined "fair market rent," regardless of a tenant's income. (Tenants still paid an income-based rent that offset the government's fair market rent payment to the landlord.)

While Section 8 programs amounted to a vast expansion of affordable housing opportunities, they did little for the 1.4 million public housing units struggling to stay afloat. Many residents—especially women of color—valiantly organized to resist the profound neglect of their communities. In Baltimore, historian Rhonda Williams documents how African American women became politicized, challenged housing authority officials, and organized to demand action, with some success. Baltimore women were not alone, and by the 1980s a groundswell of resident organizations demanded greater power, taking head-on the Reagan administration's hostility to public housing and the welfare state. Jack Kemp, HUD secretary under President George H. W. Bush, championed resident management of public housing as an empowerment technique, though his ultimate goal was to sell off projects. A small number of public housing residents did form resident management corporations, but the movement still faced the same maintenance and resource challenges that bedeviled housing authorities. While a handful of resident management corporations invested enormous effort to repair and maintain their developments, often preventing their demise, most found themselves at odds with housing authorities, and the commitment of time and effort proved unsustainable.[24]

Another radical idea emerged in the 1970s and came to fruition in the 1990s, one that rejected cities and project living altogether. As part of a lengthy and complex lawsuit brought in Chicago in 1966 and eventually decided in the 1976 Supreme Court decision *Hills v. Gautreaux*, legal activists won a court order for a new program to actively move African American public housing residents to white suburban areas using Section 8 vouchers. The idea was that an intentional "opportunity move" would

improve social outcomes for families and begin desegregation. From 1976 until 1998, counselors carefully relocated more than 7,000 Chicago public housing families to scattered suburbs and tracked their experiences. In the near-term, researchers found mixed results: participants reported decreased fear of crime but increased fear of racial harassment in their new communities. Still, the *Gautreaux* experiment led Congress in 1992 to authorize a federally managed demonstration effort called "Moving to Opportunity for Fair Housing," that similarly moved 4,600 public housing residents to middle-class areas around Baltimore, Boston, Chicago, Los Angeles, and New York. But a federal program, as opposed to a court-ordered one, proved vulnerable to voices objecting to government-led social engineering; Congress cut off further funding for the program after three years.[25]

The neoliberal turn continued in the 1980s with the creation of a program entirely separate from HUD that soon became the primary engine for affordable housing development in the United States. The Low Income Housing Tax Credit (LIHTC), enacted in 1986 and run by the Department of the Treasury, supported production or preservation of 2.3 million affordable housing units between 1987 and 2015. The Treasury Department allocated tax credits to state housing agencies, which awarded the credits to approved projects proposed by private developers or housing authorities, who then sold the credits to private corporations to raise cash for construction, and then the corporation reduced its federal taxes dollar-for-dollar. Regulations on tenant incomes for admission varied from state to state and project to project; most required policies that avoided concentrations of poverty. In essence, LIHTC was and is a way to attract private capital to affordable housing without direct federal outlay (the program, however, was a substantial "tax expenditure," amounting to $7.8 billion in 2016, but one dwarfed by the $62.4 billion mortgage interest deduction). While critics point to high overhead on complex

LIHTC deals, the program nonetheless produced large quantities of sustainable affordable housing that elicited less resistance from whites than did public housing or Section 8.[26]

HOPE VI AND BEYOND, 1992–PRESENT

The neoliberal turn eventually reached the traditional public housing program in the 1990s. By then, a subset of projects—neglected throughout the Reagan administration—were in deep crisis and no longer viable, with housing authorities practicing triage to save some units but abandoning others, a practice activists labeled "de-facto demolition." The proportion of destitute public housing families—those with incomes below 10 percent of the local median—rose from 3 percent in 1981 to nearly 20 percent a decade later. In 1992, the National Commission on Severely Distressed Public Housing, whose commissioners consisted largely of local housing authority leaders, argued that only 6 percent of the nation's public housing units (86,000 apartments) could be labeled "severely distressed"—a surprisingly low figure—though it called the situation a "national disgrace." The Commission asked for dramatically more funding, more regulatory flexibility, more social services, and more resident control in public housing.[27]

But rather than investing heavily in renovation of existing projects, Congress instead created the "HOPE VI" program (one of a series of "Homeownership and Opportunity for People Everywhere" programs intended to expand affordable housing). Over two decades HOPE VI offered $6 billion to local housing authorities to rebuild severely distressed projects in new modes. The Clinton administration, under HUD Secretary and former San Antonio Major Henry Cisneros, encouraged housing authorities to create public-private partnerships to undertake redevelopment, manage properties, and deconcentrate poverty using "mixed-income" strategies that blended public housing tenants with families paying market rates. In design, HUD wanted HOPE VI redevelopments to follow the tenets of the "New Urbanist" movement of the 1990s, which called for architecture that respected local traditions; no longer would public housing's aesthetic create stigmas.

Responses varied greatly by city. Atlanta led the way, aggressively using HOPE VI to tear down over 12,000 public housing units and rebuild approximately 4,000 affordable units under private management; in the process, 10,000 families were relocated using Section 8 vouchers (renamed Housing Choice Vouchers in 2001). Baltimore and Chicago soon followed much of the "Atlanta Blueprint," though on a larger scale and with extensive acrimony; critics called Chicago's displacement and demolition in advance of replacement housing a form of "urban cleansing." Within a decade, nearly all of Baltimore and Chicago's high-rise public housing came down, though the promised mixed-income communities materialized only years later. Housing Choice Vouchers kept total affordable opportunities nearly neutral, but the demolition and slow rebuilding dramatically altered the physical and demographic landscapes of these cities, and residents often took the brunt of change.[28]

Other cities prioritized tenants over clearance and avoided a net loss of "hard" (i.e., government-owned) public housing units. For example, in San Francisco, activists and tenants organized at North Beach Place to win full replacement of the project's 229 public housing units as part of a 341-unit, HOPE VI–funded redevelopment. Overall, the "mix" of incomes also ranged widely among the 260 HOPE VI grants awarded between 1993 and 2010. Some thirty HOPE VI projects remained completely targeted to low-income families, while roughly 12 percent skewed toward high-income residents, as in Atlanta and Chicago. Still, just over half supported a predominantly low-income tenant mix.[29]

The mixed-income solution for public housing gained traction mostly because it promised to remove unsightly buildings and problematic concentrations of poverty—especially African American poverty. To justify its radical reshaping of communities, HOPE VI advocates suggested that mixing incomes was good for low-income families because proximity to middle-class and affluent families would—somehow vaguely and certainly condescendingly—rub off on the poor and improve life opportunities. Research in the last decade has consistently failed to demonstrate these "proximity" effects but did find improved security and city services in rebuilt communities.[30]

CONCLUSION

Public housing's historical balance sheet remains a contested space. On the one hand, projects constructed in the first few decades replaced slums and provided modern housing at affordable rents for low-income families—a godsend for many. But those same projects displaced many, were often located for segregationist ends, and reinforced race and class divides. While the majority of projects continue to perform reasonably well and remain an asset, a portion failed spectacularly, stigmatizing residents and dragging down the program. Still, residents formed tight-knit communities out of these struggles and were often reluctant to leave, even as media coverage and popular culture presented public housing in stark terms as dangerous and deviant. The neoliberal turn marked a rejection of government-owned and government-managed public housing but has nonetheless resulted in a vast expansion of affordable housing opportunities.

Despite these contradictions, public housing is far from dead, but its delivery has radically changed. Of 1.4 million public housing units built nationwide under the terms of the 1937 Housing Act, roughly 1.0 million remain in operation in 2017. Hope VI redevelopments, while drawing much attention, remain a small fraction of this universe—less than 5 percent of units were redeveloped. Public-private partnerships surpassed conventional public housing: the Housing Choice Voucher program served 2.2 million households and HUD provided project-based subsidies to another 1.2 million units in 2017. All told, HUD supported five million households that year with deep federal subsidies, a figure that rose dramatically in the 1970s but plateaued after 2000. Still, another eight million households in 2017 remained unserved with "worst-case" housing needs, paying more than 50 percent of their income toward rent or living in severely inadequate housing, or both.[31] Public housing in the United States still leaves many behind.

The neoliberal turn had the effect of decoupling "public" from "housing." While HUD's programs from the 1970s made subsidies largely invisible, they also removed a strong public presence in housing policy. During two centuries, governments in the United States produced, managed, and controlled a wide range of public goods, including public schools, public roads, public parks, public hospitals, and municipally owned water systems, to name a few. But the question of a public commitment to providing housing for citizens has proved far more contentious. Unlike in many European countries, which embraced a strong state role in developing housing for the working poor, the United States never considered housing to be a human right, let alone an entitlement program like Social Security. This failure of the state, however, came from the painful experience of seeing a New Deal program sink under the weight of structural racism, misguided policies, inadequate subsidies, and little political support. The neoliberal turn in housing, then, is a historical artifact more than an ideological one.

DISCUSSION OF THE LITERATURE

The experience of Chicago dominates much of the literature of public housing, starting with Arnold Hirsch's *Making the Second Ghetto: Race and Housing in Chicago, 1940–1960*. His pathbreaking study presents public housing and urban renewal programs as powerful governmental tools in the hands of the city's white power structure who hoped to contain African Americans. Site selection and tenant practices served segregationist ends and, by implication, doomed public housing to failure. Monographs on other cities, including Philadelphia, Atlanta, Miami, Detroit, Cincinnati, and Oakland, confirm similar site selection patterns and collectively form a "second ghetto thesis" on postwar urban policy. Still, site selection was only one of many variables influencing public housing outcomes, and the link between location and failure remains tenuous.[32]

A recent stream in the literature moves away from "second ghetto" studies to more directly recover tenant agency, especially among African American women. In these presentations, residents are beneficiaries and defenders of public housing, not simply victims, and their stories offer a counterpoint to state-centered perspectives focused on the white power structure. The recovery efforts by Roberta Feldman and Susan Stall, Rhonda Williams, Lisa Levenstein, Amy Howard, and Sudhir Venkatesh use oral history and careful cultivation of sources to tell the story of residents who demanded landlord accountability and who created significant community assets despite obvious hardships.[33]

Lawrence Vale's work on Boston, Chicago, Atlanta, New Orleans, San Francisco, and Tucson blends both policy history and tenant empathy into careful explorations of public housing's implementation at the local level. Boston city leaders moralized to limit public housing to the "worthy" poor in its early years, but tenant leadership proved decisive in the 1980s and 1990s when the city went to redevelop several of its earliest projects. Atlanta, Chicago, and New Orleans took a harsher turn, as the "design politics" of public housing pushed for clearance—both in the 1930s and the 1990s—to wipe away perceived blight, with tenants struggling against a powerful state. San Francisco and Tucson offer somewhat more hopeful stories. For Vale, the lack of resident input in decisions affecting their communities is a critical mistake of housing policy.[34]

In recent years, historians have challenged the "failure" narrative that stereotypes all public housing by its worst outcomes and thereby undermines governmental action to house the poor. This approach can be traced to 1991 with Katharine Bristol's article, "The Pruitt-Igoe Myth," which explained the forces arrayed against the St. Louis project. A subsequent documentary of the same title in 2011 used a tragic narrative arc to amplify the point that neither architecture nor tenants are wholly responsible for that project's demise. Nicholas Dagen Bloom, Fritz Umbach, and Lawrence J. Vale's edited volume *Public Housing Myths: Perception, Reality, and Social Policy* fleshes out these arguments considerably, adding tenant agency and policing as areas of strength, not weakness. Finally, Bloom's work on New York City remains the most important rebuttal to a monolithic failure narrative.[35]

The field of public housing history continues to have fertile opportunities. Most works are highly city-centric in nature, and few national-level synthesis or international-level comparisons been written. The broader experience in the rural South remains under-developed, as does the LIHTC story. Nor has public housing policy been well-integrated into larger histories of the welfare state, with few exceptions.[36] Public housing's failures remain better understood than its successes.

PRIMARY SOURCES

Despite its origins as a federal-local partnership, finding official public housing records can be difficult. Local housing authorities are most often state-chartered, semi-independent agencies, with often spotty archival practices compared to other state or local agencies and widely varying accessibility. As with other aspects of public housing, the New York City Housing Authority is an outlier, with deep archival holdings maintained at the La Guardia and Wagner Archives (http://www.laguardiawagnerarchive .lagcc.cuny.edu/) at La Guardia Community College in New York. Elsewhere, local public libraries often hold annual reports and other published material of housing authorities, but these rarely offer insight into the political battles that surrounded the program.

Federal records are in somewhat better shape, though large volumes and limited finding aids mean that research is highly labor intensive. The National Archives' Record Group 196 (https://www.archives.gov/research/guide-fed-records/groups/196.html) holds the records of the Public Housing Administration and its predecessor agencies, covering the period 1933–1965, while Record Group 207 (https://www.archives.gov/research/guide-fed-records/groups/207.html) includes the Department of Housing and Urban Development, formed in 1965.

Unlike federal records, the papers of many nongovernmental actors in public housing policy are well organized with rich finding aids. Cornell University's Special Collections library, particularly its collection on architecture and planning (http://rmc.library.cornell.edu/EAD/browselists/plan.html), holds the papers of numerous New Deal and early postwar planners who conceived and administered public housing programs. The papers of Warren J. Vinton are especially rich in public housing policy history. Women played seminal roles in initiating the program, as seen in the papers of Catherine Bauer Wurster at the Bancroft Library (https://oac.cdlib.org/findaid/ark:/13030/tf487003tj/) at the University of California Berkeley and the papers of the National Housing Conference, founded by Mary K. Simkhovitch, at the University of Minnesota. In other cities, citizen-led housing advocacy organizations produced reports and covered policy debates in detail; for example, Arnold Hirsch's study of Chicago relied heavily on the Metropolitan Planning and Housing Council, whose papers are held at the University of Illinois at Chicago. While oral history collections are scarce and much-needed, the Library of Congress produced the "Pioneers in Housing (https://lccn.loc.gov/mm2002084909)" series, which includes transcribed interviews of twenty-three leaders in mid-20th-century

housing policy and advocacy. Finally, the widely held monthly *Journal of Housing*, published by the National Association of Housing and Redevelopment Officials since 1944 (and now the *Journal of Housing and Redevelopment*), covers public housing news from a practitioner perspective at a national level.

FURTHER READING

Bauman, John F., Roger Biles, and Kristin M. Szylvian, eds. *From Tenements to the Taylor Homes: In Search of an Urban Housing Policy in Twentieth-Century America*. University Park: Pennsylvania State University Press, 2000.

Bloom, Nicholas Dagen. *Public Housing That Worked: New York in the Twentieth Century*. Philadelphia: University of Pennsylvania Press, 2008.

Bloom, Nicholas Dagen, Fritz Umbach, and Lawrence J. Vale, eds. *Public Housing Myths: Perception, Reality, and Social Policy*. Ithaca, NY: Cornell University Press, 2015.

Cisneros, Henry G., and Lora Engdahl, eds. *From Despair to Hope: Hope VI and the New Promise of Public Housing in America's Cities*. Washington, DC: Brookings Institution Press, 2009.

Fairbanks, Robert B. *The War on Slums in the Southwest: Public Housing and Slum Clearance in Texas, Arizona, and New Mexico, 1935–1965*. Philadelphia: Temple University Press, 2014.

Goetz, Edward G. *New Deal Ruins: Race, Economic Justice and Public Housing Policy*. Ithaca, NY: Cornell University Press, 2013.

Hirsch, Arnold. *Making the Second Ghetto: Race and Housing in Chicago, 1940–1960*. New York: Oxford University Press, 1983.

Hunt, D. Bradford. *Blueprint for Disaster: The Unraveling of Chicago Public Housing*. Chicago: University of Chicago Press, 2009.

Radford, Gail. *Modern Housing for America*. Chicago: University of Chicago Press, 1996.

Vale, Lawrence J. *From the Puritans to the Projects: Public Housing and Public Neighbors*. Cambridge, MA: Harvard University Press, 2000.

Vale, Lawrence J. *Purging the Poorest: Public Housing and the Design Politics of Twice-Cleared Communities*. Chicago: University of Chicago Press, 2013.

Williams, Rhonda Y. *The Politics of Public Housing: Black Women's Struggles against Urban Inequality*. New York: Oxford University Press, 2004.

NOTES

1. US Department of Housing and Urban Development (HUD), "Picture of Subsidized Households."
2. Nicholas Dagen Bloom, Fritz Umbach, and Lawrence J. Vale, eds., *Public Housing Myths: Perception, Reality, and Social Policy* (Ithaca, NY: Cornell University Press, 2015); and Lawrence J. Vale and Yonah Freemark, "From Public Housing to Public-Private Housing: 75 Years of Social Experimentation," *Journal of the American Planning Association* 78, no. 4 (2012): 379–402.
3. Lawrence M. Friedman, *Government and Slum Housing: A Century of Frustration* (Chicago: Rand McNally, 1968).
4. Edith Elmer Wood, *Recent Trends in American Housing* (New York: Macmillan, 1931), 1.
5. Catherine Bauer, *Modern Housing* (Boston: Houghton Mifflin, 1934); and Daniel Rodgers, *Atlantic Crossings: Social Politics in a Progressive Age* (Cambridge, MA: Harvard University Press, 1999), 477–478.
6. D. Bradford Hunt, "Was the 1937 Housing Act a Pyrrhic Victory?" *Journal of Planning History* 4, no. 3 (2005): 195–222; and John F. Bauman, *Public Housing, Race, and Renewal: Urban Planning in Philadelphia* (Philadelphia: Temple University Press, 1987), chap. 1.
7. Lyle Woodyatt, "The Origins and Evolution of the New Deal Public Housing Program" (PhD diss., Washington University, 1968); and Wendell Pritchett, *Robert Clifton Weaver and the American City* (Chicago: University of Chicago Press, 2008), 82–83.
8. Public Law 412, 75th Congress; and Robert Moore Fisher, *Twenty Years of Public Housing: Economic Aspects of the Federal Program* (New York: Harper and Brothers, 1959). Many housing authorities agreed to make modest "payments-in-lieu-of-taxes" to cities amounting to 10 percent of their rental income, a practice put into law in 1949.
9. Gail Radford, *Modern Housing for America* (Chicago: University of Chicago Press, 1996).
10. Hunt, "Was the 1937 Housing Act a Pyrrhic Victory?"; and Nathan Straus, *Seven Myths of Housing* (New York: Holt, 1944),
11. Lawrence Vale, *From the Puritans to the Projects: Public Housing and Public Neighbors* (Cambridge, MA: Harvard University Press, 2000), 223; and J. S. Fuerst, *When Public Housing Was Paradise* (Urbana: University of Illinois Press, 2005).
12. Sarah Jo Peterson, *Planning the Home Front: Building Bombers and Communities at Willow Run* (Chicago: University of Chicago Press, 2013); Phillip J. Funigiello, *The Challenge to Urban Liberalism: Federal-City Relations during World War II* (Knoxville: University of Tennessee Press, 1978); and Manly Maben, *Vanport* (Portland, OR: Western Imprints, 1987).
13. Richard O. Davies, *Housing Reform during the Truman Administration* (Columbia: University of Missouri Press, 1966); and D. Bradford Hunt, "How Did Public Housing Survive the 1950s?" *Journal of Policy History* 17, no. 2 (2005): 193–216.
14. *Winning the Fight to Clear Slums by Building Low-rent Public Housing* (Washington, DC: National Housing Conference, 1950; and Don Parson, *Making a Better World: Public Housing, the Red Scare, and the Direction of Modern Los Angeles* (Minneapolis: University of Minnesota Press, 2005).
15. Arnold Hirsch, *Making the Second Ghetto: Race and Housing in Chicago, 1940–1960* (New York: Oxford University Press, 1983); and N. D. B. Connolly, *A World More Concrete: Real Estate and the Remaking of Jim Crow South Florida* (Chicago: University of Chicago Press, 2014).
16. Fisher, *Twenty Years of Public Housing*; and Robert B. Fairbanks, *The War on Slums in the Southwest: Public Housing and Slum Clearance in Texas, Arizona, and New Mexico, 1935–1965* (Philadelphia: Temple University Press, 2014).
17. *Journal of Housing*, June 1954, p. 197; Charles Abrams, *Forbidden Neighbors: A Study of Prejudice in Housing* (New York: Harper and Brothers, 1955); and D. Bradford Hunt, *Blueprint for Disaster: The Unraveling of Chicago Public Housing* (Chicago: University of Chicago Press, 2009).
18. Catherine Bauer, "The Dreary Deadlock of Public Housing," *Architectural Forum*, May 1957, 140–142; and Jane Jacobs, *The Death and Life of Great American Cities* (New York: Vintage, 1961).
19. Hunt, *Blueprint for Disaster*, chaps. 5–7.
20. Joseph Heathcott, "Public Housing Stands Alone," in *Public Housing Myths: Perception, Reality, and Social Policy*, ed. Nicholas Dagen Bloom, Fritz Umbach, and Lawrence J. Vale (Ithaca, NY: Cornell University Press, 2015), 31–46.
21. Frank de Leeuw, "Operating Costs in Public Housing: A Financial Crisis" (Washington, DC: The Urban Institute, 1968); and Hunt, *Blueprint for Disaster*.

22. Robert Schafer, *Operating Subsidies for Public Housing: A Critical Appraisal of the Formula Approach* (Boston: Citizens Housing and Planning Association of Metropolitan Boston, 1975).

23. Nicholas Dagen Bloom, *Public Housing That Worked: New York in the Twentieth Century* (Philadelphia: University of Pennsylvania Press, 2008); Fritz Umbach, *The Last Neighborhood Cops: The Rise and Fall of Community Policing in New York Public Housing* (New Brunswick, NJ: Rutgers University Press, 2011); and NYCHA 2017 Fact Sheet. It should be noted that the Puerto Rico Housing Authority is the second largest housing authority in the nation, peaking at around 57,000 public housing units.

24. Rhonda Y. Williams, *The Politics of Public Housing: Black Women's Struggles against Urban Inequality* (New York: Oxford University Press, 2004); and William Peterman, *Neighborhood Planning and Community-Based Development* (Thousand Oaks, CA: SAGE, 2000).

25. Leonard S. Rubinowitz and James E. Rosenbaum, *Crossing the Class and Color Lines: From Public Housing to White Suburbia* (Chicago: University of Chicago Press, 2000); and Raj Chetty, Nathaniel Hendren, and Lawrence Katz, "The Effects of Exposure to Better Neighborhoods on Children: New Evidence from the Moving to Opportunity Project," *American Economic Review* 106, no. 4 (2016): 855–902.

26. Department of Housing and Urban Development, "Low Income Housing Tax Credits"; Budget of the United States Government, Analytical Perspectives, Fiscal Year 2017, Table 14-1; and David Erickson, *The Housing Policy Revolution: Networks and Neighborhoods* (Lanham, MD: Rowman & Littlefield, 2009).

27. *Final Report of the National Commission on Severely Distressed Public Housing* (1992), 47–48; and Lawrence J. Vale, "Beyond the Problem Projects Paradigm: Defining and Revitalizing 'Severely Distressed' Public Housing," *Housing Policy Debate* 4, no. 2 (1993): 147–174.

28. Lawrence J. Vale, *Purging the Poorest: Public Housing and the Design Politics of Twice-Cleared Communities* (Chicago: University of Chicago Press, 2013); Reneé Lewis Glover, "The Atlanta Blueprint: Transforming Public Housing Citywide," in *From Despair to Hope: Hope VI and the New Promise of Public Housing in America's Cities*, ed. Henry G. Cisneros and Lora Engdahl

(Washington, DC: Brookings Institution Press, 2009), 145–167; and Edward G. Goetz, *New Deal Ruins: Race, Economic Justice and Public Housing Policy* (Ithaca, NY: Cornell University Press, 2013).

29. Amy L. Howard, *More than Shelter: Activism and Community in San Francisco Public Housing* (Minneapolis: University of Minnesota Press, 2014). Lawrence J. Vale and Shomon Shamsuddin, "All Mixed Up: Making Sense of Mixed-Income Housing Developments," *Journal of the American Planning Association* 83, no. 1 (2017): 56–67.

30. Robert J. Chaskin and Mark L. Joseph, *Integrating the Inner City: The Promise and Perils of Mixed-Income Public Housing Transformation* (Chicago: University of Chicago Press, 2015); and Susan Popkin, *No Simple Solutions: Transforming Public Housing in Chicago* (Lanham, MD: Rowman & Littlefield, 2016).

31. Kent Colton, *Housing in the 21st Century* (Cambridge, MA: Harvard University Press, 2003), 3–33; and HUD, Office of Policy Development and Research, "Picture of Subsidized Households"; and HUD, "Worst Case Housing Needs," August 2017.

32. Hirsch, *Making the Second Ghetto*; Timothy J. Gilfoyle, "Urban History, Arnold Hirsch, and the Second Ghetto Thesis," *Journal of Urban History* 29, no. 3 (2003): 233–237; and Hunt, *Blueprint for Disaster*.

33. Roberta M. Feldman and Susan Stall, *The Dignity of Resistance: Women Residents' Activism in Chicago Public Housing* (New York: Cambridge University Press, 2004); Williams, *The Politics of Public Housing*; Lisa Levenstein, *A Movement without Marches: African American Women and the Politics of Poverty in Postwar Philadelphia* (Chapel Hill: University of North Carolina Press, 2009); Howard, *More than Shelter*; and Sudhir Venkatesh, *American Project: The Rise and Fall of a Modern Ghetto* (Cambridge, MA: Harvard University Press, 2002).

34. Vale, *From the Puritans to the Projects*; Lawrence J. Vale, *Reclaiming Public Housing: A Half Century of Struggle in Three Public Neighborhoods* (Cambridge, MA: Harvard University Press, 2002); Vale, *Purging the Poorest*; and Lawrence J. Vale, *After the Projects: Public Housing Redevelopment and the Governance of the Poorest Americans* (New York: Oxford University Press, 2018).

35. Howard Husock, *America's Trillion-Dollar Housing Mistake: The Failure of American Housing Policy*

(Chicago: Ivan Dee, 2003); Katherine G. Bristol, "The Pruitt- Igoe Myth," *Journal of Architectural Education* 44, no. 3 (1991): 163–171; Nicholas Dagen Bloom, Fritz Umbach, and Lawrence J. Vale, eds., *Public Housing Myths: Perception, Reality, and Social Policy* (Ithaca, NY: Cornell University Press, 2015); and Bloom, *Public Housing That Worked.*

36. Goetz, *New Deal Ruins*; Douglas Massey and Nancy Denton, *American Apartheid: Segregation and the Making of the Underclass* (Cambridge, MA: Harvard University Press, 1998); Carl Nightingale, *Segregation: A Global History of Divided Cities* (Chicago: University of Chicago Press, 2012); Erickson, *The Housing Policy Revolution*; and Florian Urban, *Tower and Slab: Histories of Global Mass Housing* (Abingdon, UK: Routledge, 2012).

D. Bradford Hunt

HOUSING POLICY ACROSS THE UNITED STATES

US cities have both benefited and suffered from federal housing laws and policies adopted since the inauguration of President Franklin D. Roosevelt in 1933. His program of "relief, recovery, and reform," known as the New Deal, brought permanent federal government involvement in practically every facet of the urban and suburban housing market, including architecture and design, land use planning, financing, construction, marketing, and management. Federal intervention functioned in five important ways. First, the national state valorized the private commercial market. Second, the federal government created, expanded, and reinforced various types of segregation and market inequities, sometimes deliberately, other times inadvertently. Third, federal authorities transformed and promoted single-family homeownership with new forms of commercial market financing. Fourth, government policies functioned to keep the noncommercial market in a subordinate role throughout the 20th century. Finally, national

policies designed to promote the "American Dream" of homeownership served as an international model on a global basis.

After World War II, housing conditions improved dramatically in US metropolitan areas. The rate of homeownership increased during the 1950s and 1960s to become one of the highest in the world, peaking in 2004 at 69 percent.[1] The following offers a largely chronological discussion of federal housing policy since 1933. Several themes, including the creation of a regulatory framework for identification and remediation of the effects of racism and discrimination in the real estate market, and the federal response to the 2007 home mortgage crisis, will be examined in greater detail.

THE ROOSEVELT YEARS ESTABLISH KEY PRECEDENTS

More than a dozen so-called "alphabet agencies" were created under the New Deal to restore profitability to the urban housing market and save the "American Dream" of homeownership for low- and middle-income families. Taken together, their programs stabilized and expanded the real estate market, household finance, house building, and building supplies industries, and laid the groundwork for the fixed-rate, long-term mortgage. The Home Owners Loan Bank (created under the 1932 Federal Home Loan Bank Act) formed a secondary market for banks to sell their mortgages. In June 1933, Congress offered relief to households facing mortgage foreclosure and eviction by passing the Home Owners' Loan Act, creating the Home Owners' Loan Corporation (HOLC). The HOLC spent roughly $3 billion to purchase and refinance mortgages for roughly one million homeowners.[2] The National Housing Act of 1934 authorized the Federal Housing Administration (FHA) to provide mortgage guarantees to house buyers and home builders. The criteria developed for mortgage insurance was widely accepted and became the standard for household finance providers and residential contractors. The HOLC, the FHA, and federal agencies that regulate the secondary mortgage market, such as the Federal Home Loan Bank Board, helped make housing production a leading indicator of the health of the national economy. Homeownership became the centerpiece of a regressive policy that extends the most generous income tax and other financial benefits to households that can best afford to commercially finance the purchase of a dwelling.

The HOLC, the FHA, and other agencies that served commercial market interests were generally favored by Congress, the press, and the private sector. Roosevelt administration agencies, including the Tennessee Valley Authority, the National Resources Planning Board, and the Resettlement Administration (RA), approached residential development as part of regional and metropolitan planning. But some regarded them as a threat to commercial real estate market interests. The RA, led by Columbia University economist Rexford G. Tugwell, became a lightning rod for criticism for promoting centralized community planning that introduced the 19th-century Garden Cities concept into the automobile age. Roosevelt administration "boondoggling," critics charged, reached a new height with the construction of the three "Greenbelt Towns" the RA constructed for white, white-collar, middle-income commuters on the urban periphery of Washington, DC, in suburban Maryland; in Cincinnati, Ohio; and in Milwaukee, Wisconsin.[3]

The Federal Emergency Relief Administration of the Public Works Administration (PWA) began offering long-term, low-interest loans in 1934 to limited-dividend housing corporations to build affordable dwellings. Philadelphia's Carl Mackley Houses, sponsored by the American Federation of Full-Fashioned Hosiery Workers, was among the most admired of these projects. The PWA's limited-dividend loan program was barely underway when it was replaced with a program offering funds to state and local housing authorities for the construction of rental housing for low-income families.

In 1937, Congress made the low-income public housing program permanent with the passage of the United States Housing Act, also known as the Wagner-Steagall Act. The United States Housing Authority (USHA) was established to provide subsidies to qualified local and state housing bodies to offset the cost of building, operating, and maintaining residential communities for low-income families. Prior to World War II, most public housing authorities were modest operations that owned and operated several hundred units of public housing in a single municipality or county; only a few, such as Akron, Ohio, had a metropolitan service area. The PWA's Division of Housing and the USHA were held in contempt by real estate interests and congressional budget committees that regarded the agencies as a "socialist" threat to the commercial market.

Despite the efforts undertaken by the New Deal in its early days, the United States remained a "nation one-third ill housed" in 1937 when President Roosevelt gave his Second Inaugural Address.[4] In 1942, President Roosevelt ordered the consolidation of the housing activities of more than a dozen federal agencies into the National Housing Agency. Five years later, during the administration of President Harry S. Truman, the Housing and Home Finance Agency became the nation's first permanent federal housing agency.[5]

EMBEDDED RACISM AND DISCRIMINATION

New Deal housing and urban development legislation were devised to protect and promote speculative real estate development and commercial market lending. But those very policies reinforced and extended private sector segregation by race, class, ethnicity, and religion. The HOLC's practice of "redlining" and other discriminatory policies were replicated in various forms by the FHA, the Veterans Administration, and other agencies, with the effect of sealing certain neighborhoods or districts off from new investment. Much to the disappointment of 1940s civil rights leaders, the Roosevelt administration did not treat the critical shortage of housing precipitated by mobilization for World War II as an opportunity to begin nationwide desegregation with the publicly funded defense housing program.[6] The nearly 1 million units of temporary and permanent housing provided for civilian defense workers under the National Defense Housing Act (widely known as the Lanham Act) expanded segregation by race and income. Few state or local housing authorities followed the precedent of the Housing Authority of the City of Los Angeles, which began voluntarily desegregating low-income and defense housing developments in 1942.[7] Although the US Supreme Court–ruled racial real estate covenants were unenforceable in *Shelley v. Kraemer* (1948), neither legislation nor a policy framework was in place to ensure its enforcement. More importantly, public officials lacked any political will to desegregate housing. President Truman allowed the FHA to underwrite mortgages on property with restrictive racial covenants until February 1950. Albert Cole, the former Republican Congressman appointed by President Dwight D. Eisenhower as head of the Housing and Home Finance Agency, announced a four-point program in 1954 that included a voluntary program to make an "unprecedented production of new homes available to minority buyers."[8] As historian Nancy Kwak notes, at the same time that federal agencies and departments were resisting calls to end residential segregation at home, housing aid was being sent abroad to nations in the developing world that the United States hoped to secure as Cold War allies.[9]

POSTWAR HOUSING POLICY PROMOTES SPECULATIVE DEVELOPMENT

Popular movies such as the Academy Award–winning, *The Best Years of Our Lives* (1946) fed consumer hopes that the colossal wartime industrial infrastructure would be retooled to make "machines for living"—houses.[10] Richard J. Neutra, Walter Gropius, and other architects who fled Europe before or during World War II eagerly collaborated with their new American colleagues in rebuilding US cities worn out from years of economic depression and war. They experimented with prefabricated housing as part of a larger effort to integrate new wartime fabrication methods and materials into home production. In the end, however, the emergency housing funds appropriated by Congress as part of the Truman administration's Veterans Emergency Housing Program were not used to build new, architect-designed planned residential communities as starting points for urban revitalization. Homebuilders, realtors, and home finance providers encouraged veterans to use their benefits under the Serviceman's Readjustment Act of 1944 (GI Bill of Rights) and other postwar housing bills to obtain conventional market mortgages to buy single-family dwellings in speculatively built subdivisions located on the urban periphery.

Partisan politics fueled speculative residential construction on the urban periphery and undermined noncommercial housing initiatives. The bipartisan Wagner-Ellender-Taft (W-E-T) bill was introduced in 1945 to provide aid to veterans, aspiring homeowners, and renters. The W-E-T bill secured the approval of the US Senate, but Republicans and southern Democrats in the House of Representatives blocked the bill's passage for four years because it proposed constructing 810,000 dwelling units of low-income public housing over a six-year period. Reconstituted and passed as the Taft-Ellender-Wagner [T-E-W) bill, the legislation authorized funding for a program of urban revitalization to help cities tear down slums, fix up their downtown commercial districts, and keep their core neighborhoods from losing further population to the suburbs. Also known as the Housing Act of 1949, the law was a cornerstone of federal housing policy for roughly half a century.[11]

When the Eisenhower administration proposed its first major piece of housing legislation in 1954, it antagonized civil rights, labor, and urban leaders by downplaying the need for public housing to resettle residents, often minorities, displaced by the construction of public housing, highways, airports, and other infrastructure projects. Consistent with the earlier trend established under the 1937 Wagner-Stegall Act and the 1949 Taft-Ellender-Wagner Act, the rehabilitation of structurally sound but dated urban dwellings authorized under the Housing Act of 1954 was downplayed in favor of new construction. Urban renewal funds helped cities tear down substandard "slum" housing, with the goal of restoring economic and social vitality to downtown areas, but the economic and social cost of the federal "bulldozer" or wrecking ball approach favored by real estate developers and investors was high. Urban renewal was especially detrimental in older neighborhoods, where residents or local business proprietors lacked the economic means or political clout to challenge private sector developers and their public sector allies. Jane Jacobs's national bestseller *The Death and Life of Great American Cities* (1961) criticized neighborhood destruction under the impact of publicly subsidized highway building and urban renewal.[12]

During the 1950s, new residential development shifted to developing suburban areas as a result of many factors, including changes to the federal income tax code, interstate highway construction, and the lack of environmental review and regulation. In 1954, Congress shortened the amount of time the owners of new commercial building owners (including multi-unit dwellings) had to wait before they could deduct their depreciation on their taxes. Apartment buildings eligible for "accelerated depreciation" were often located in developing suburban areas, where they functioned as a buffer between commercial and single-family residential development. The Federal-Aid Highway Act, signed into law by President Eisenhower in 1956, hastened the decline of US cities and the rise of the suburbs as centers of production and commerce. Environmental attitudes and practices also encouraged single-family and multi-unit residential development outside the city limits. Local and state governments seldom compelled private developers to shoulder or contribute to the cost of extending publicly owned water, sewerage, and waste disposal systems to developing suburban areas. Humorist Erma Bombeck's satirical look at life in suburbia, *The Grass Is Always Greener Over the Septic Tank* (1976), did little to inspire a nationwide effort to protect groundwater quality.[13]

TURNING THE CORNER: URBAN HOUSING AND THE GREAT SOCIETY

In 1965, the cabinet-level Department of Housing and Urban Development (HUD) was established, and economist Robert Weaver was appointed as the first HUD Secretary by President Lyndon B. Johnson. Johnson proposed rent subsidies for qualified low- and middle-income families residing in privately owned dwellings, but by the time he signed the Housing Act of 1965 into law in August, Congress favored only the former. The law also called for a new approach to public housing construction. Under the "turnkey" program, public housing authorities were given the option of using federal subsidies to purchase rental housing developments built by private developers. In 1966, President Johnson proposed a $2.3 billion Demonstration Cities program that emphasized the development of low- and middle-income housing in large, medium, and small cities to serve as models to help guide decision-making by other municipalities that shared the same problems. The president secured the passage of the Demonstration Cities and Metropolitan Development Act of 1966, but Congress remained reluctant to fund the program. Even after the program name was changed to Model Cities, housing did not receive adequate funding. During the Richard Nixon administration in the 1970s, the program was merged into the block grant program.[14]

A serious effort to extend federal oversight over issues of equity in the private housing market was made in 1968, six years after President John F. Kennedy's November 10, 1962, Executive Order 11063, prohibiting discrimination in publicly assisted housing. The Civil Rights Act of 1968 was passed in the aftermath of the assassination of civil rights leader Martin Luther King Jr. Title VIII, known as the Fair Housing Act of 1968, mandated equal opportunity housing and targeted realtors and residential developers who engaged in the practices and behaviors that served as a foundation of a vast, voluntary effort to economically and socially engineer exclusionary neighborhoods.[15] HUD's enforcement mechanisms proved to be too weak for the enormity of the task of desegregating the nation's housing. In 1988, the Fair Housing Amendments Act was passed to facilitate the investigation of charges of discrimination. Earlier, in 1975, Congress began requiring household finance corporations to report information about their loaning and loan service practices with the passage of the Home Mortgage Disclosure Act. The Community Reinvestment Act of 1977 compelled household finance providers to provide access to information about their lending practices to ensure that they offer mortgages and financial services across the entire geographical area where they receive deposits.[16]

The Housing and Urban Development Act of 1968—the "Magna Charta to liberate our cities," in the words of President Johnson—marked the zenith of federal housing innovation and activism. The bill introduced a number of new policy initiatives, including home mortgage interest subsidies for low- and middle-income homeowners, experimentation in new building materials and construction techniques, the creation of public–private initiatives such as the National Corporation for Housing Partnerships, and a renewed commitment to new communities. The New Communities program was inspired in part by the earlier New Deal community program and produced a small handful of new communities nationwide.[17]

The impact of Johnson's Great Society programs on federal housing policy was second only to the New Deal. Between 1960 and 1980, the rate of homeownership continued to rise, although at a slower rate than in earlier decades.[18] During that same period, substandard urban housing—characterized by structural deficiencies or the lack of complete plumbing or utility systems—declined. Nevertheless, inner-city "blight" and growth took place at the same time within increasingly segmented cities. As investment and job growth became concentrated on the urban edge, abandonment and decay engulfed former commercial, manufacturing, and residential districts in central cities and inner ring suburbs. Pockets of prosperity were found in certain city neighborhoods and industrial and commercial districts. College Hill in Providence, Rhode Island, for example, was typical of urban neighborhoods that utilized their location and the quality of the housing stock to attract investors interested in restoration and adaptive reuse.[19] The federal tax incentives encouraging historic preservation during the 1960s were short-lived, forcing developers to rely on limited state and local programs. Historic preservation and other gentrification programs fell under increasing scrutiny for their tendency to contribute to increased real estate values for property owners, rising rents for tenants, and the displacement of minorities and older-term residents.

THE PRIVATIZATION OF PUBLIC HOUSING

During the 1950s, the federal government retreated from its commitment to the public housing program. Republican President Eisenhower favored private sector production of affordable housing and did little to help the United States realize the national goal of 810,000 units of public housing over a six-year period established under the Housing Act of 1949. Eisenhower's successor, President John

F. Kennedy, a Democrat, was more empathetic toward the public housing program but at the same time encouraged private sector production of affordable housing. The Housing Act of 1961 offered subsidies to limited-dividend corporations, cooperatives, and other non-profit low- and moderate-income housing developers. Under Republican President Richard M. Nixon, public housing construction slowed to a trickle. The Housing and Urban Development Act of 1969 reduced funding for public housing but committed the federal government to replace every unit of affordable housing torn down as part of a federal urban renewal project. An amendment sponsored by US Senator Edward Brooke, a Massachusetts Republican, mandated that public housing residents could not be required to pay more than 25 percent of household income for rent.

During the 1970s, administrative indifference, the inadequacy of federal subsidies, and the collective weight of decades of policy-making driven by racial and class bias helped make many public housing developments places of violence and entrenched poverty. The television program *Good Times* (1974–1979) used humor to expose the shortcomings of federal housing policy and show how African Americans—as represented by characters James and Florida Evans and their three children—depended on self-reliance and family cohesiveness for their survival. State and local housing bodies that retreated from constructing residential communities for low-income families often pursued funding from HUD programs that restricted occupation to the elderly, disabled, or later, the homeless.[20]

In keeping with the Nixon administration's efforts to roll back urban expenditures, a revenue-sharing approach was introduced under the Better Communities Act of 1972. The Housing and Community Development Act, signed into law by President Gerald R. Ford in August 1974, created two potential sources for affordable housing. The first was Title I, which created the Community Development Block Grant (CDBG) program to provide "stable urban communities," and replaced Urban Renewal, Model Cities, New Communities, and a half dozen other federal programs that required cities and states to compete for federal funding for specific projects. [21] The CDBG program adopted a funding formula and offered grant recipients more leeway in deciding how their federal aid would be spent. Later, a second block grant program—one directed exclusively at low- and moderate-income housing—was created under the Cranston-Gonzalez National Affordable Housing Act of 1990. Taken together, these policies contributed to a gradual increase in the percentage of minorities residing in the suburbs. Under the administration of President Jimmy Carter, the Urban Regional Policy Group (URPG) gave special attention to the desegregation of the suburbs.

The 1974 law also created the Section 8 Existing Housing program authorizing subsidies that paid renters of existing or rehabilitated housing the difference between the adjusted "fair market rent" and 25 percent (later 30%) of household income. In 1983, the Existing Housing program was supplemented by the Freestanding Voucher program, which allowed more flexibility in the use of rental subsidies. The Housing Choice Voucher (HCV) program was created in 1998, during the administration of President William J. Clinton, with the passage of the Quality Housing and Work Responsibility Act. Qualified participants were entitled to use their rent vouchers anywhere in the nation they wished, and property owners were allowed to lease to multiple voucher holders. The law also imposed an eight-hour-per-month community service requirement for public housing residents who were not economically self-sufficient. Debate over the demise of the public housing program and increased reliance on the private sector for affordable housing revealed how fragmented housing advocacy had become since the Roosevelt-Truman years.[22]

HUD shrank in size and political power during the Clinton and George W. Bush administrations. Any hopes that HUD's mission might be clarified and its administrative structure reorganized were dashed in 2007 when financial disaster struck the residential housing and household finance markets. For both President Bush and his successor, President Barack Obama, the scope of the home mortgage crisis was so great that the prospect of solving HUD's larger structural problems became increasingly remote.

THE SEARCH FOR FAIR LENDING PRACTICES

Congress recognized that discriminatory practices were pervasive in home finance, forcing increased federal oversight of the primary and secondary mortgage markets. In 1968, Congress converted the Federal National Mortgage Association (known as Fannie Mae), founded 50 years earlier, into a federally regulated private corporation known as a "government-sponsored enterprise." Congress also authorized the Government National Mortgage Association (known as Ginnie Mae) to buy the FHA– and Veterans Administration–backed mortgages formerly acquired by Fannie Mae. Two years later, Congress created the Federal Home Loan Mortgage Corporation (known as Freddie Mac) to assist Fannie Mae in purchasing the non-government-backed, conventional mortgages issued by savings and loan banks and mutual saving banks called "thrifts." Millions of US wage earners utilized such local or neighborhood banks to deposit their paychecks in anticipation of the day when they would apply for a fixed-rate, 30-year mortgage to purchase a house in a nearby community.

During the 1960s and 1970s, the ability of thrift banks to profit from the conventional home mortgage business declined due to rising mortgage interest rates, a loss of consumer interest in traditional savings accounts, and other factors. The Reagan administration supported the deregulation of thrift banks to solve the problem; instead, it grew worse during the 1980s. The "savings and loan crisis" from 1986 to 1995

resulted in the bankruptcy of more than 1,000 savings and loan banks and ultimately required a $157 billion federal bailout under the Financial Institutions Reform, Recovery, and Enforcement Act of 1989.[23] The law established new regulations for home lending by thrift saving banks and liquidated the assets of failed banks. The law did not halt the percentage of single-family home mortgages held in the secondary mortgage market from increasing from 17 percent in 1980 to 59 percent in 2000. Mortgage underwriting regulations and standards changed under the impact of what one leading analyst described as "a combination of deregulation, heightened competition, technological innovation, and securitization."[24] Household finance providers began offering variable rate, prime, or sub-prime loans to borrowers who could not meet the credit rating and down payment requirements commonly associated with conventional fixed-rate lending. In some markets, borrowers were given "exotic" or boutique mortgages resembling the "balloon," or lump-sum, mortgages that had largely disappeared after 1933 with the emergence of federal oversight of home lending. Roughly a century earlier, Upton Sinclair's novel The Jungle exposed how immigrants and other urban newcomers to Chicago's meat-packing district fell victim to predatory lenders and realtors.[25]

Even before the onset of the home mortgage crisis in 2007–2008, certain nefarious household finance practices targeted racial and ethnic minorities whose access to fair credit had historically been limited. Between 1997 and 2007, mortgages extended to minorities grew at a dramatically faster rate than those for non-minority households.[26] The increase in sub-prime mortgages should have caused alarm in Congress, but Congress required only improved procedures to ensure that borrowers fully understood the terms of the loans they were offered.

The rate of mortgage default rose sharply in 2007 and 2008, and peaked nationally in 2009. Congress passed the Housing and

Economic Recovery Act to provide loan and grant funds in 2008, but did not require overhauling the home finance system until 2010. By 2012, more than 12 percent of all mortgaged houses in Florida were in foreclosure; the foreclosure rate in New Jersey, Illinois, and Nevada hovered around 5 percent.[27] The Dodd-Frank Wall Street Reform and Consumer Protection Act authorized the establishment of the Consumer Financial Protection Bureau to develop a new set of regulations for home lending that prohibited most forms of sub-prime lending. Even though an estimated seven million homeowners suffered the economic and social distress of mortgage foreclosure during the crisis, in 2018, the Trump administration and the president's supporters in Congress began identifying ways to roll back Dodd-Frank regulations. The scale of the financial disaster and its impact on wage earners was quickly forgotten on Wall Street and Capitol Hill.

THE DEBATE OVER FEDERAL AID FOR AFFORDABLE HOUSING

During the 1970s and 1980s, HUD's budgetary allocations shrank as Republican Presidents Richard M. Nixon, Gerald R. Ford, and Ronald Reagan favored shifting fiscal and administrative responsibility for housing and other domestic policy issues to state and local governments. Proponents of the "New Federalism" blocked efforts by Democrats and moderate Republicans to obtain the budgetary allocations needed by HUD and the local public housing authorities to meet the demand and maintain their housing stock. President Reagan's support of the Budget Reconciliation Act of 1981 resulted in a roughly 40 percent reduction in the amount of money available for the public housing and Section 8 programs over the last Carter administration allocation. The Urban-Rural Recovery Act of 1983 was one of the few measures authorizing new public housing construction passed during the Reagan years. It also appropriated

funds for 15,000 housing vouchers, far fewer than the number proposed by the nation's mayors. The Housing and Community Development Act of 1987 encouraged public housing residents to buy their public housing dwellings, although few such sales took place. Overall, the Reagan years brought declining support for public housing. According to one calculation, in the six-year period from 1981 to 1987, federal funding for housing was reduced by about two-thirds. The lack of funds for maintenance and upkeep would have serious short- and long-term consequences for the health and safety of residents.[28]

During the administration of George H. W. Bush, HUD Secretary Jack Kemp favored the concentration of federal housing aid in a series of enterprise zones that would attract private investment. Title IV of the Cranston-Gonzalez National Affordable Housing Act of 1990 created the Home Ownership and Opportunity for People Everywhere (HOPE) program. Between 1993 and 2010, 98,592 units of public housing were torn down under the Urban Revitalization Demonstration program known as the HOPE VI program for "severely distressed public housing." The new or newly refurbished dwelling units at the first 260 targeted communities were larger and better appointed than the original ones, but a sizeable percentage of those displaced by HOPE VI became permanently displaced from the neighborhood. The rate of return to the revitalized units was 20.7 percent.[29]

Scandals and mismanagement in the 1990s brought HUD's influence and prestige to the point where Republican members of the 104th Congress proposed its elimination as part of the Contract with America platform. Secretary Henry Cisneros, appointed by President William J. Clinton, successfully fought for HUD's survival but was unable to realize his "Reinvention Blueprint," which called for the gradual elimination of federal operating subsidies to state and local housing bodies as authorized in the Wagner-Steagall Act. The likelihood that public housing authorities, particularly those in large cities, would be able to offer dwellings to compete with private sector housing as Secretary Cisneros envisioned seemed dim considering the enormous sums required to make long-neglected repairs and keep up routine maintenance. Earlier, in 1987, New York City committed itself to a $4 billion, multi-year plan to help the New York City Housing Authority build new affordable housing and rehabilitate existing apartment buildings. During the 2000s, Mayor Michael Bloomberg threw his political weight behind continuing the plan, pledging another $7.5 billion. Despite this investment, the New York City Housing Authority suffered from considerable infrastructure and managerial problems. In early 2018, Democrat Mayor Bill De Blasio, Bloomberg's successor, faced questions about the Housing Authority's ability to function when it was revealed that residents in several public housing towers were forced to endure winter weather without heat.[30]

Dr. Ben Carson, appointed by President Donald Trump in 2017, recommended reducing the amount of federal funds allocated for housing vouchers for low-income families. The Housing Choice Mobility Demonstration Act, proposed in 2018, was an indication of congressional support for continued federal assistance for cities seeking to improve access to fair and affordable housing.[31] At the request of President Trump, in 2018, Congress limited the mortgage interest deduction that homeowners may take when filing their annual federal income tax returns. Despite this unpopular policy shift, homeowners—particularly those residing in single-family dwellings—have remained the major beneficiaries of direct and indirect public subsidies since 1933. In 2012, more than 34 million homeowners took advantage of tax benefits and claimed over $220 billion in mortgage interest deductions. During the same period, $47.9 billion was used to provide direct subsidies for roughly seven million low-income renters.[32] The disparity between the subsidies provided to home renters and homeowners had long been codified and normalized.

DISCUSSION OF THE LITERATURE

Students and scholars can be easily overwhelmed by the size and diversity of the body of scholarship pertaining to US housing policy since 1933. Historians are not alone in their interest in describing and analyzing how federal housing policy has and has not changed since the Great Depression. Architects, anthropologists, city planners, economists, lawyers, political scientists, sociologists, and others have also published extensively in this area. Their political and economic perspectives need to be considered in assessing readings in housing policy. Housing policy researchers should begin their work by consulting the two-volume *The Encyclopedia of Housing*, edited by Andrew T. Carswell.[33] Alex Schwartz's *Housing Policy in the United States* and *Housing in America: An Introduction* by Marijoan Bull and Alina Gross provide a broad overview of housing past and present.[34] Older classics include Gwendolyn Wright's engaging and highly readable *Building the Dream*.[35] Several collections of essays offer a good starting point for understanding federal housing policy.[36]

Several federal housing policy officials, including Nathan Straus of the United States Housing Authority; Nathaniel Keith of the Housing and Home Finance Agency; and Henry Cisneros, HUD Secretary, published accounts of their work and ideas.[37] There are a number of recent biographies of public and private sector housing leaders, including Charles Abrams, Catherine Bauer, US Senator Paul H. Douglas, and Robert Weaver.[38] A handful of works offer insight into public housing policy from the residents' perspective. Rhonda Y. Williams provides a perspective on gender and family issues in *The Politics of Public Housing: Black Women's Struggles Against Urban Inequality*.[39] Perceptions of Chicago's public housing, for example, are found in J. S. Fuerst and D. Brad Hunt's *When Public Housing was Paradise* and Audrey Petty's *High Rise Stories: Voices from Chicago Public Housing*.[40]

Drawing upon methods borrowed from the social sciences, urban historians have energetically documented and analyzed the role the federal government played in reinforcing and expanding segregation and efforts made to create a federal system of oversight to end housing discrimination. Many, if not most, of these works have an urban renewal or suburban focus.[41] Numerous scholars have an interest in the relationship between housing, architecture, and planning.[42] With the important exception of the work of Marc Weiss, until the publication of *Building a Market: The Rise of the Home Improvement Industry, 1914–1960* by Richard Harris and *Houses for a New World: Builders and Buyers in American Suburbs, 1945–1965* by Barbara Miller Lane, little attention had been given to the history of residential real estate development and marketing, building suppliers, household finance, and home building and renovations, especially in Native American and ethnic and racial minority communities.[43]

PRIMARY SOURCES

Students and scholars of federal housing policy need to pay careful attention to the names and operating dates of each federal housing agency and program as their research proceeds; name changes and administrative realignments were frequent and sometimes resulted in errors. Before delving into the unpublished records, researchers should first familiarize themselves with the annual reports typically mandated by Congress, as well as other published reports and studies. Many of the Roosevelt era agencies responsible for urban development produced newsletters, magazines, and reports aimed at the general public. The USHA, for example, sent copies of its lavishly illustrated newsletter, *Public Housing Weekly* (later known as *Public Housing*), to public and private housing organizations throughout the United States. The agency also made and distributed posters, motion pictures, and other visual aids to help the public understand its mission and relationship with state and local governments.

Among the most important published sources for understanding the shifting priorities of the federal housing program are the special reports and studies commissioned by the president, Congress, or the agencies. During the "urban crisis" years of the 1960s, reports prepared by blue-ribbon commissions made up of housing and public policy experts include the National Commission on Urban Problems (chaired by former US senator Paul Douglas), the President's Committee on Urban Housing (chaired by industrialist Henry F. Kaiser), and the Kerner National Advisory Commission on Civil Disorders (chaired by former Illinois governor Otto Kerner). Later reports, including the July 1982 *President's National Policy Report*, "Enterprise Zones in America: A Selected Resource Guide II," prepared for HUD at the request of Secretary Kemp, and the report of the National Commission on Severely Distressed Public Housing show how public policy priorities at HUD shifted in response to larger economic, political, and social issues. In *Interwoven Destinies: Cities and the Nation*, Secretary Cisneros presented his ideas for changing HUD and the racial and class imbalance in federal housing policy.

Thousands of cubic feet of records created by HUD and its predecessor agencies are available to researchers who visit the National Archives. Accurate finding aids exist for each record group. The volume of records can make it difficult for researchers to locate files pertaining to particular programs, properties, and individuals. Patience, persistence, and luck are needed when seeking specific documents. Researchers relying on digital access to research resources will find that the National Archives, the presidential libraries, and the Library of Congress offer little of what they need; only the key laws, documents, and reports have been digitized. Digital access to working files of federal housing agencies is unlikely. Digitalized photographs of federally aided housing can be readily found in major research collections.

Public and private state and local housing organizations can also provide research resources. State and municipal libraries, archives, and historical societies should be consulted. Few local public housing or redevelopment authorities retain inactive records, and they can seldom provide researchers with assistance; those researchers who gain access to a few clippings, published reports, and an envelope or two of old pictures should consider themselves fortunate. Records relating to the functions of private banks, residential developers, and real estate firms are exceedingly difficult to locate.

Further insight into federal housing policy can be obtained through private organizations and institutions. The Congressional Quarterly Service, the National Association of Housing and Redevelopment Officials, the United States Conference of Mayors, the National Public Housing Conference (later the National Housing Conference), the Low-Income Housing Coalition, and the Brookings Institution are reliable sources. The National Association of Home Builders and the National Association of Realtors were involved in most legislative and public policy debates pertaining to housing. The National Association for the Advancement of Colored People (NAACP) and the Urban League are examples of privately funded groups that played an active role in the desegregation of housing and the provision of affordable housing.

The American Federation of Labor, the Congress of Industrial Organizations, and the combined AFL-CIO maintained standing housing committees that issued regular reports and other publications, particularly on federal housing legislation. Certain unions such as the Amalgamated Textile Workers Union and the United Automobile Workers Union acquainted their members with housing problems, legislation, and public policy options through newspapers, pamphlets, and reports.

Few, if any systematic efforts have been undertaken to conduct oral history interviews with housing activists, law and policymakers, architects and planners, realtors, and residential developers. A few interviews with New Deal era housers and architects are available online. For example, see the Oral History Center, Bancroft Library, University of California, Berkeley (http://bancroft.berkeley.edu/ROHO).

FURTHER READING

Anderson, Martin. *The Federal Bulldozer: A Critical Analysis of Urban Renewal, 1949–1962.* Cambridge, MA: MIT Press, 1964.

Archer, John, Paul J. P. Sandal, and Katherine Solomonson, eds. *Making Suburbia: New Histories of Everyday America.* Minneapolis and London: University of Minnesota Press, 2015.

Hayden, Dolores. *Building Suburbia: Green Fields and Urban Growth.* New York: Pantheon Books, 2003.

Hunt, D. Bradford. *Blueprint for Disaster: The Unraveling of Chicago Public Housing.* Chicago: University of Chicago Press, 2009.

Immergluck, Daniel. *Foreclosed: High-Risk Lending, Deregulation, and the Undermining of America's Home Mortgage Market.* Ithaca, NY: Cornell University Press, 2009.

Jacobs, James A. *Detached America: Building Houses in Postwar Suburbia.* Charlottesville: University of Virginia Press, 2015.

Keets, John. *The Crack in the Picture Window.* Boston: Houghton Mifflin, 1957.

Lasner, Matthew. *High Life: Condo Living in the Suburban Century.* New Haven, CT: Yale University Press, 2012.

Perrin, Constance. *Everything in Its Place: Social Order and Land Use in America.* Princeton, NJ: Princeton University Press, 1977.

Radford, Gail. *Modern Housing in America: Policy Struggles in the New Deal Era.* Chicago: University of Chicago Press, 1996.

Rome, Adam. *The Bulldozer in the Countryside: Urban Sprawl and the Rise of American Environmentalism* New York: Cambridge University Press, 2001.

Sander, Richard Henry, Yana A. Kucheva, and Jonathan M. Zasloff. *Moving Toward Integration: The Past and Future of Fair Housing.* Cambridge, MA: Harvard University Press, 2018.

Squires, Gregory D. *The Fight for Fair Housing: Causes, Consequences, and Future Implications of the Federal Fair Housing Act of 1968.* New York: Routledge Press, 2018.

Sugrue, Thomas. *The Origins of the Urban Crisis: Race and Inequality in Postwar Detroit.* Princeton, NJ: Princeton University Press, 2005.

Thurston, Chloe N. *At the Boundaries of Homeownership: Credit, Discrimination, and the American State.* Cambridge, UK, and New York: Cambridge University Press, 2018.

Vale, Lawrence. *From the Puritans to the Projects: Public Housing and Public Neighbors.* Cambridge, MA: Harvard University Press, 2000.

Vale, Lawrence. *After the Projects: Public Housing Redevelopment and the Governance of the Poorest Americans.* New York: Oxford University Press, 2018.

NOTES

1. Alex Schwartz, *Housing Policy in the United States,* 3rd ed. (New York and London: Routledge Press, 2015), 25.

2. Kenneth T. Jackson, *Crabgrass Frontier: The Suburbanization of the United States* (New York: Oxford University Press, 1985), 186.

3. Paul K. Conkin, *Tomorrow a New World: The New Deal Community Program* (Ithaca, NY: Cornell University Press for the American Historical Association, 1959).

4. "Roosevelt in Inaugural Urges That Nation 'Hold to Progress' in Spite of Returning Prosperity; Says Self-Interest Reappears," *Wall Street Journal,* January 21, 1937: 4.

5. Arthur Krock, "President Speaks," *New York Times,* January 21, 1937: 1.

6. "Negroes Are Called to Form '2nd' Party," *New York Times,* November 18, 1940, p. 2; and Byron Darnton, "Housing Shortage in Major Centers Impedes Defense," *New York Times,* December 22, 1940, p. 1.

7. Turner Cartledge, "Our Greatest Social Problem," *New York Times,* December 9, 1943, p. SM10.

8. "U.S. Housing Chief Wars on Race Bias," *New York Times,* October 30, 1954, p. 15.

9. Nancy Kwak, *A World of Homeowners: American Power and the Politics of Housing Aid* (Chicago: University of Chicago Press, 2015).

10. "The Best Years of Our Lives," directed by William Wyler and produced by Samuel Goldwyn, won seven Academy Awards in 1946.

11. Richard O. Davies, *Housing Reform During the Truman Administration* (Columbia: University of Missouri Press, 1966).

12. Jane Jacobs, *The Death and Life of Great American Cities* (New York: Random House, 1961).

13. Erma Bombeck, *The Grass Is Always Greener Over the Septic Tank* (New York: McGraw-Hill, 1976).

14. "Demonstration for the Cities," *Washington Post,* November 6, 1966, p. E6.

15. "President Signs Civil Rights Bill," *New York Times,* April 12, 1968, p. 1.

16. "Maximizing Mortgages, Minimizing Risks," *New York Times,* November 27, 1977, p. 186.

17. "Transcript of Johnson's News Conference," *New York Times,* April 11, 1968, p. 18; and Alexander von Hoffman, "Calling Upon the Genius of Private Enterprise: The Housing and Urban Development Act of 1968 and the Liberal Turn to Public–private Partnerships," *Studies in American Political Development* 27, no. 2 (October 2013): 165–194.

18. Schwartz, *Housing Policy in the United States,* 24–25.

19. Briann Greenfield, "Marketing the Past: Historic Preservation in Providence, Rhode Island," in *Giving Preservation a History: Histories of Historic Preservation in the United States,* ed. Max Page and Randall Mason, 117–132 (New York: Routledge Press, 2004), 117–132.

20. Aid for the construction of elderly housing was available under the Section 202 program created in 1959.

21. Edward C. Burks, "Ford Signs Bill to Aid Housing," *New York Times,* August 23, 1974, p. 9.

22. "Clinton Seeks Funds to Expand Housing Vouchers," *Wall Street Journal,* December 29, 1999, p. A16; and Roger K. Lewis, "Apathy, Solid Economy Keep Slamming Doors on Affordable Housing," *Washington Post,* May 16, 1998, p. MG12.

23. Robert M. Garson, "President's Pen Ends Era of Deregulation For Thrift Industry," *American Banker,* August 10, 1989, p. 1.

24. Schwartz, *Housing Policy in the United States,* 89.

25. Upton Sinclair, *The Jungle* (New York: Doubleday, 1906).

26. Barbara Ehrenreich and Dedrick Muhammad, "The Recession's Racial Divide," *New York Times,* September 13, 2009, p. WK17; and "Another Kind of Crisis," *New York Times,* October 9, 2009, p. A30.

27. Schwartz, *Housing Policy in the United States,* 414–417.

28. Roger Biles, *The Fate of Cities: Urban America and the Federal Government, 1945–2000* (Lawrence:

University of Kansas Press, 2011), 256, 264–267.

29. HOPE VI Data Compilation and Analysis.

30. Alan Finder, "$4.2 Billion Housing Program Moves Off Ground Floor," *New York Times*, April 28, 1988, p. B1; "Mayor Bloomberg Brings Housing Home," *New York Times*, December 27, 2002, p. A20; and William Neuman, "As 4 in 5 Public Housing Lost Heat, a Demand for an Apology is Unfulfilled," *New York Times*, February 6, 2018, p. 12.

31. "Fair Housing's New Champions," *New York Times*, June 8, 2018, p. A24.

32. Schwartz, *Housing Policy in the United States*, 7.

33. Andrew T. Caswell, ed., *The Encyclopedia of Housing*, 2 vols. (Thousand Oaks, CA: SAGE, 2012).

34. Schwartz, *Housing Policy in the United States*; and Marijoan Bull and Alina Gross, *Housing in America: An Introduction* (New York: Routledge, 2018). See also Roger Biles, *The Fate of Cities*; Kent W. Colton, *Housing in the Twenty-First Century: Achieving Common Ground* (Cambridge, MA: Harvard University Press, 2003); R. Allen Hays, *The Federal Government and Urban Housing: Ideology and Change in Public Policy* (Albany: State University of New York, 1995); and David C. Schwartz, Richard C. Ferlauto, and Daniel N. Hoffman, *A New Housing Policy for America: Recapturing the American Dream* (Philadelphia: Temple University Press, 1988).

35. Gwendolyn Wright, *Building the Dream: A Social History of Housing in America* (New York: Pantheon Books, 1981). See also Lawrence M. Friedman, *Government and Slum Housing: A Century of Frustration* (Chicago: Rand McNally, 1968); and Mark I. Gelfand, *A Nation of Cities: The Federal Government and Urban America, 1934–1975* (New York: Oxford University Press, 1975).

36. Nicholas D. Bloom, Fritz Umbach, and Lawrence J. Vale, eds., *Public Housing Myths: Perception, Reality, and Social Policy* (Ithaca, NY, and London: Cornell University Press, 2015); Becky M. Nicolaides and Andrew Weiss, eds., *The Suburb Reader* (New York: Routledge, Taylor & Francis Group, 2006); and John F. Bauman, Roger Biles, and Kristin M. Szylvian, eds., *From Tenements to Taylor Homes: In Search of an Urban Housing Policy in Twentieth Century America* (University Park: Pennsylvania State University Press, 2000);

37. Nathan Straus, *The Seven Myths of Housing* (New York: Alfred A. Knopf, 1944); Nathaniel S. Keith, *Politics and the Housing Crisis Since 1930* (New York: Universe Books, 1973); and Henry Cisneros, *From Despair to Hope: HOPE VI and the New Promise of Public Housing in America's Cities* (Washington, DC: Brookings Institution Press, 2009).

38. W. Roger Biles, *Crusading Liberal: Paul H. Douglas of Illinois* (DeKalb: Northern Illinois University Press, 2002); A. Scott Henderson, *Housing & the Democratic Ideal: The Life and Thought of Charles Abrams* (New York: Columbia University Press, 2000); H. Peter Oberlander and Eva Newbrun, *Houser: The Life and Work of Catherine Bauer* (Vancouver: University of British Columbia Press, 1999); and Wendell E. Pritchett, *Robert Clifton Weaver and the American City: The Life and Times of an Urban Reformer* (Chicago: University of Chicago Press, 2008).

39. Rhonda Y. Williams, *The Politics of Public Housing: Black Women's Struggles Against Urban Inequality* (New York: Oxford University Press, 2004).

40. J. S. Fuerst and D. Bradford Hunt, *When Public Housing Was Paradise* (Westport, CT: Praeger, 2003); and Audrey Petty, *High Rise Stories: Voices from Chicago Public Housing*, New Voice of Witness series (San Francisco: McSweeney's, 2013).

41. See Christopher Bonastia, *Knocking on the Door: The Federal Government's Attempt to Desegregate the Suburbs* (Princeton, NJ: Princeton University Press, 2008); David M. P. Freund, *Colored Property: State Policy and White Racial Politics in America* (Chicago: University of Chicago Press, 2007); Arnold Hirsch, *Making the Second Ghetto: Race and Housing in Chicago, 1940–1960* (Chicago: University of Chicago Press, 1983); Douglas S. Massey and Nancy A. Denton, *American Apartheid: Segregation and the Making of the Underclass* (Cambridge, MA: Harvard University Press, 1993); Richard Rothstein, *The Color of Law: A Forgotten History of How Our Government Segregated America* (London: Liveright, 2018); and Robert Mark Silverman and Kelly L. Patterson, *Fair and Affordable Housing in the U.S.: Trends, Outcomes, and Future Directions* (Leiden and Boston: Brill, 2011).

42. Andres Duany, Elizabeth Plater-Zyberk, and Jeff Speck, *Suburban Nation: The Rise of Sprawl and the Decline of the American Dream* (New York: North Point Press, 2000); and Lawrence Vale, *Purging the Poorest: Public Housing and the Design*

Politics of Twice-Cleared Communities (Chicago: University of Chicago Press, 2013.)

43. Marc A. Weiss, "Planning Subdivisions: Community Builders and Urban Planners in the Twentieth Century," *Essays in Public Works History* 15 (1987): 21–37; Richard Harris, *Building a Market: The Rise of the Home Improvement Industry, 1914–1960* (Chicago: University of Chicago Press, 2012); and Barbara Miller Lane, *Houses for a New World: Builders and Buyers in American Suburbs, 1945–1965* (Princeton, NJ: Princeton University Press, 2015).

Kristin M. Szylvian

URBAN DESTRUCTION DURING THE AMERICAN CIVIL WAR

CITIES AS MILITARY TARGETS

The antebellum era was a time of rapid urbanization in the United States. Large, densely populated cities and towns had proliferated on both sides of the Mason-Dixon Line by 1861. During the Civil War, Union and Confederate commanders made the capture or destruction of enemy cities a central feature of their campaigns. Why?

First, all acts of warfare involve both battles between armies and attempts to gain control over the enemy's territory—its cities, towns, agricultural fields, and infrastructure.[1] By advancing into and occupying enemy territory, armies destroyed the geographic integrity of their adversaries, a major step in destroying their will to fight.[2] Second, most Americans assumed that the fall of capital cities—Washington, DC, and Richmond, Virginia—would mean victory for one side and defeat for the other. How could the body politic function without its nerve center? Third, because antebellum cities had manufacturing and storage centers within their borders, bombarding and setting fire to cities also destroyed factories, foundries, supply depots, and warehouses. Interrupt or incapacitate the enemy's ability to arm, feed, and clothe themselves and the war ends.[3] Fourth, burning cities damaged

civilian morale, "bringing the enemy to the point where it can go no further physically, emotionally, or ideologically."[4]

Both Union and Confederate armies bombarded and burned cities with all of these goals in mind. Sometimes Union troops fought battles on city streets but more often, they initiated long-term sieges in order to capture Confederate cities. Vengeance motivated some soldiers to destroy cities while self-defense drove others—throughout the war, Confederate soldiers deliberately set fire to their own urban centers in an attempt to keep valuable war materiel out of the enemy's hands. Cities were vital assets and targets for both armies during the American Civil War; whoever controlled them determined the outcome of the conflict.

DESTROYED IN BATTLE: FREDERICKSBURG

From Jackson, Mississippi, to Gettysburg, Pennsylvania, battles and skirmishes carried over into the streets of small towns. But as important as urban centers were to campaign strategies, generals on both sides tried to avoid long-term battles in cities. The urban landscape was not conducive to fights between large armies, and the presence of civilians was problematic for the development of battle strategy. Fredericksburg, Virginia, was the only southern city to host a major battle between the Civil War's largest armies. For several days in early December 1862, the Union's Army of the Potomac and the Confederacy's Army of Northern Virginia clashed in a battle that ruined many of the city's central neighborhoods.

Fredericksburg's location—midway between the major urban centers of Richmond and Washington, DC—made it a strategic target, and way station for Union troops under General Ambrose Burnside marching southward in an attempt to take the Confederate capital. The city was also a manufacturing center, producing guns and ammunition for Confederate forces. Burnside's troops gathered across the Rappahannock from Fredericksburg in late

Figure 1. "Bombardment of Fredericksburg, Va., by the Army of the Potomac, Commanded by General Burnside, Thursday, December 11, 1862." *Frank Leslie's Famous Leaders and Battle Scenes of the Civil War* (New York: Mrs. Frank Leslie, 1896).
Courtesy of the private collection of Roy Winkelman.

November 1862 but could not cross; the bridges were burned and Burnside's pontoon boats were late arriving. The delay gave Confederate general Robert E. Lee's soldiers time to march to the city and establish battle lines. By early December both Union and Confederate artillery and infantry were posted on high hills, with the city in-between.

In the foggy, early morning hours of December 11, the Union army (which had finally received the pontoon boats) began to assemble their bridge. When the fog lifted, "suddenly, Crack! crack! crack! From a hundred muskets tells us the ball is opened."[5] General Lee had posted three Confederate regiments within the city and on the bank in front of Fredericksburg to contest the crossing. These soldiers fired upon Union engineers assembling the pontoon boats and then upon federals streaming across the completed bridge.[6] These actions provoked

Burnside to order the bombardment of the city. Union general Edwin Vose Sumner, whom Burnside had tapped to command the bombardment, gave notice to the mayor on December 11, and the next day civilians began to stream out of Fredericksburg, making their way behind Confederate lines, Union batteries then turned upon the town, rendering it "untenable by any considerable body."[7]

By mid-afternoon, most of the central business district along Princess Anne Street was on fire. A "huge column of dense black smoke tower[ed] like a monument above the livid flames, that leap and hiss and crackle, licking up the snow upon the roofs with lambent tongues, and stretching like a giant."[8] As Union troops began to pour through the city, the streets divided their ranks and discipline broke down; they wandered down thoroughfares and clambered over rubble, losing their regiments in the growing dark and drifting smoke. The bombardment had knocked many buildings to pieces, revealing their contents to soldiers who almost immediately set to work looting them.

The accepted laws of warfare condemned the sacking of captured cities.[9] But as was often the case during the American Civil War, the "confusion and excitement" of warfare undermined traditional modes of behavior and belief.[10] For close to twenty-four hours, Union soldiers—tempted by the chaos and seeking revenge for the attack on their engineers at the pontoon bridge—broke into businesses and homes alike, smashing furniture, mirrors, and crockery and dragging chairs, couches, desks, and pianos out into the streets.[11] After this melee, Union forces moved across the city and formed battle lines at its western edge, at the bottom of Marye's Heights. The next day, several successive charges against this strong Confederate position failed, and the defeated Federals retreated back through the town and across the Rappahannock.

Confederate soldiers retaking Fredericksburg on December 15 were astonished at the level of destruction in the city. Four days of bombardment, battle, and looting had brought stunning changes to Fredericksburg. "Oh! what a ruined town," Confederate soldier Francis Coker lamented. "It is a nice old place, nearly as large as Macon. It is now battered to pieces & parlors & furniture destroyed."[12] For Southerners, the ruins were evidence of Confederate sacrifice and Yankee barbarism. For Northerners like New Hampshire soldier Napoleon Perkins, the city's ruins seemed a "terrible sight." But military necessity dictated its destruction; "such is war," Perkins lamented.[13] The rubble of Fredericksburg represented the significance of Southern cities in Civil War campaigns, and the violent destructiveness of urban warfare that both armies sought to avoid for the remainder of the war.

UNDER SIEGE: CIVILIANS IN CITIES

The shelling of Fredericksburg was brief and occurred before the battle. However, most sieges during the Civil War included long-term, regular bombardment and blockading, and they were initiated after battles failed to force the capitulation of the soldiers who defended urban centers. Beginning in 1863, the Union army increasingly used siege tactics against Southern cities. Soldiers established positions around their targets and cut off their communication and supply lines; then they began throwing shells into protective fortifications (and often, city streets) multiple times a day.

The sieges of Vicksburg, Mississippi (May–July 1863), and Atlanta, Georgia (July–September 1864), were the Union's most successful assaults on Confederate cities. The former secured control of the Mississippi River while the latter brought a vital center of railroad traffic and war production under Union occupation; Atlanta then became the staging ground for Union general William Tecumseh Sherman's March to the Sea. The extended sieges of Charleston, South Carolina (August 1863–February 1865), and Petersburg, Virginia (August 1864–April 1865), put great stress on soldiers and civilians alike, but these cities, defended by strong works and intact supply lines, resisted until the last months of the war, when Confederate soldiers abandoned them in the face of oncoming Union soldiers.

During all of these sieges, bombardment destroyed significant portions of the urban landscape. The inability of artillerists to hit precise targets from more than two miles away meant that shells aimed at military targets often struck houses and churches instead. In August 1864, after the Army of the Potomac had settled into the siege of Petersburg, for example, a correspondent for the *Richmond Enquirer* reported that the steady shelling of the city had not injured many residents, but it had done considerable damage to their property. Shot and shell plunged down through roofs and into parlors and bedrooms. "Pantries have been invaded," he wrote, "and unmerciful crashes sent breaking and ringing through piles of crockery and rows of jars, whose precious contents still swim or stick in sweet ruin upon the indented floors

Figure 2. Adalbert John Volck, "Cave Life In Vicksburg" (1864). Courtesy of Library of Congress, Prints and Photographs Division, Washington, DC Illus. in E468.7.V65 1863 Stern Coll (Rare Book RR).

and caved in shelves that mark the scenes of the disaster."[14]

In cities under siege, civilians who could not afford to evacuate lived in a constant state of anxiety, never knowing when and where the bombs would fall. The more than 22,000 shells that rained down on Vicksburg over the course of two months forced residents to take refuge in churches, cellars, or in caves that they paid workers anywhere from $20 to $50 to dig into the city's many steep hillsides.

Some families decorated their caves with carpets, tables, and beds. Despite these comforts and the novelty of "cave life," the siege took its toll. One anonymous woman who detailed her experiences in Vicksburg in her diary, for example, was chagrined to note that after more than a month of artillery barrages, she had lost her nerve. Several shells had exploded around her house and as she retreated to her cave, "for the first time I quailed. ... [I] seemed to realize that something worse than death might come; I might be crippled, and not killed." She resolved to "summon that higher kind of courage—moral bravery—to subdue my fears of possible mutilation."[15]

Carrie Berry and her family experienced a similar sense of terror under siege. Berry, who was ten years old and living in Atlanta when Sherman's troops arrived outside the city in

July 1864, wrote in her diary that, "We can hear the canons [sic] and muskets very plane [sic], but the shells we dread. One has busted under the dining room which frightened us very much." Almost every day, she and her family heard the shells whistling into the city and then ran in a panic to their cellar. But even here they did not feel safe, as the shells "fell so thick and fast." The Berry family moved several times during the siege of Atlanta, looking not for large houses to live in but large cellars.[16] The constant threat of injury or death and the dislocations of multiple moves profoundly affected the Berrys and other Atlanta residents living under siege in the fall of 1864.

This was one of the goals of siege warfare: to demoralize the enemy's civilians and thereby undermine their support for the war effort. Constant shelling was effective in achieving these ends, as was cutting the city off from supply routes. As General Ulysses S. Grant shut down all access to Vicksburg in the early summer of 1863, civilians increasing feared they would starve. The Vicksburg diarist noted that she "never understood before the full force of those questions—What shall we eat? What shall we drink? And wherewithal shall we be clothed?" In the decades before the war, the industrial and transportation revolutions had brought an increasingly diverse range of foodstuffs and material goods to urban markets. Wartime sieges, however, almost immediately created a provisioning crisis. The Vicksburg diarist sent her enslaved woman Martha to "run the gauntlet to buy the meat and milk once a day," a terrifying experience for Martha that produced very little in the way of food or drink. "I send five dollars to market each morning and it buys a small piece of mule-meat," she wrote. She could not bring herself to eat it, so she subsisted on cornbread and a mixture of rice and milk for weeks.[17]

After months of living under siege, most civilians greeted the capitulation of their cities with relief. The residents of Vicksburg were eating white bread and reveling in quiet evenings by July 4, 1863. Carrie Berry's family went back to work with "glad spirits" in early September 1864 after Union troops moved in to occupy Atlanta.[18] But the end of a siege also meant the end of slavery: the entrance of Union soldiers into fallen cities functionally emancipated urban slaves. White residents were chagrined by these developments; emancipation was another form of destruction that took from them their wealth in slaves. And although sieges were harrowing experiences for enslaved people and free blacks as well (they suffered alongside their white masters and mistresses, starving and thirsty and in constant fear for their lives—imagine Martha, having to dodge shells on her daily run to the market in Vicksburg), the capitulation of Southern cities brought freedom, so they welcomed Union soldiers with open arms.[19]

But Union occupation did not mean the end of civilian suffering. In many cities, including Vicksburg, Union officials "expelled citizens who refused to renounce their loyalty to the rebellion or to comply with Federal regulations."[20] Less than a week after the siege of Atlanta ended, Carrie Berry's family heard about Sherman's order requiring all of Atlanta's civilians, both white and black, to evacuate the city. "Every one I see seems sad," Berry wrote in her diary. "The citizens all think that it is the most cruel thing to drive us from our home. ... Mama seems so troubled she can't do any thing. Papa says he don't know where on earth to go."[21] Her father was ultimately able to secure a job that allowed the family to stay, but many of the young girl's family and friends, and many formerly enslaved men and women, left Atlanta for points northward in late September 1864.[22]

As civilians abandoned their homes in the wake of sieges they joined hundreds of thousands of other refugees on the road. These large populations of black and white refugees lived lives of constant instability as they moved to places unknown to them, seeking aid from strangers. Some of them ended up in other Southern cities; many refugees from Charleston, South Carolina, who had left when the artillery barrages began in the summer of 1863, moved to Columbia—which was then destroyed in a massive conflagration after Sherman's troops arrived there in February 1865. The refugee situation put stress on individuals, and on rural and urban communities. It "radically reshaped customary relations of power in the realm of spatial mobility," creating new kinds of social conflict on the road that remade southern culture after the war.[23]

Northerners generally accepted the validity of the siege as a military tactic, but Southerners deplored the destruction, terror, starvation, and forced evacuations that sieges brought to urban communities. The Southern press especially excoriated Sherman for attacking Atlanta, a city he knew to be filled with women and children. Confederate general John Bell Hood was outraged by Sherman's evacuation order, which he thought transcended "in studied and ingenious cruelty, all acts ever before brought to my attention in the dark history of war."[24] Despite the scorn heaped upon him for his actions in Atlanta, Sherman did not regret them. In his view, the siege was a military necessity; it was a tool that armies had to use in order to win. "War is cruelty," he famously wrote, "and you cannot refine it."[25] But white civilians across the South neither forgave nor forgot the ways that sieges destroyed their dignity and their wealth, and victimized women and children. They called for revenge, for retaliation in kind. Some military commanders answered that call.

SOLDIERS AND THE RUINS OF REVENGE

Vengeance is a powerful emotion and impetus to action. For Civil War–era military officials, the practice of retaliation moved beyond passion and became a legitimate military tactic. Retaliation was understood as an official, compensatory response to "barbarous outrages" on the part of the enemy; it was an act of "protective retribution" that would conceivably prevent the enemy from executing "barbarous outrages" in the future.[26] Both Union and Confederate soldiers used these justifications to explain their destruction of enemy homes and outbuildings across the South and in parts of the North and West. But the most spectacular moment of urban destruction as a punishment occurred during the summer of 1864 in southern Pennsylvania, at the hands of Confederate soldiers under orders from General Jubal Early.

With the Army of Northern Virginia pinned at Petersburg and Union general David Hunter attempting to occupy the Shenandoah Valley, General Lee sent Jubal Early's corps to the valley. In July Early learned that Hunter had been engaging in "his favorite mode of warfare" in the Shenandoah: burning the homes of prominent Confederates. As he noted in his *Memoir*, Early quickly "came to the conclusion that we had stood this mode of warfare long enough" and on July 26, 1864, he dispatched two brigades and a battery of artillery under John McCausland to Chambersburg, Pennsylvania. He instructed McCausland to "demand of the municipal authorities the sum of $100,000 in gold, or $500,000 in United States currency, as a compensation for the destruction of the houses and their contents." Early had previously wrested money and supplies from a number of towns in Maryland using this strategy.

Early informed McCausland that if he was unsuccessful in securing the ransom he was "to lay the town in ashes, in retaliation for the burning of those houses and others in Virginia, as well as for the towns which had been burned in Southern States."[27] McCausland and his men reached Chambersburg on July 30, converging at the town square. As residents came to meet them, McCausland read Early's order aloud and asked the City Council to collect the money. Chambersburg's leaders had sent their capital northward already, but they pretended this was not the case in order to stall for time, hoping for Union forces in the area to come to their aid.

McCausland soon lost patience, however, and within a few hours he ordered his men to set fire to the town at different locations.[28] The flames spread quickly despite the relatively calm day. The Confederates were impressed with the conflagration, which was "one of surpassing grandeur and terror." The tall columns of black smoke "rose up to the very skies; around it were wrapped long streams of flames, writhing and twisting themselves into a thousand fantastic shapes." Many observers noted how the fire seemed to create its own kind of weather. "Whirlwinds" of fire lifted clothing, wood, bricks, and furniture into the air and hurled them across the city.[29]

A civilian committee later determined that more than 500 of Chambersburg's 800 buildings were destroyed: 278 residences and places of business, 98 barns and stables, and 173 outbuildings of various kinds.[30] General Early and other Confederates believed—or rather, hoped—that the burning of Chambersburg would "open the eyes of the people of other towns at the North, to the necessity of urging upon their government the adoption of a different policy."[31] As the editors of the *Richmond Enquirer* crowed ecstatically, "We have lit in Chambersburg a blaze that will arrest the view of the Northern people, and illustrate the destruction of villages, homesteads, and towns in every Southern state."[32]

Of course, many Northerners—and especially the inhabitants of Chambersburg—protested against the burning as a legitimate war tactic. Technically, this order was not justified militarily as retaliation, for it did not directly punish David Hunter, who had fired Confederate houses.[33] In addition, Early's destruction of an *entire* Northern city as retribution for the destruction of a handful of Southern homes seemed like a punishment way out of proportion to the crime, an excessive and "monstrous" act of violence. However, as military theorist (and Union general) Henry Halleck argued in 1864, "in times of war, it might not be possible to punish the individual responsible for egregious acts," and in those cases a larger body could be held responsible. In wartime, Halleck reasoned, "a city, an army, or an entire community, is sometimes punished for the illegal acts of its rulers or individual members."[34] Chambersburg in particular proved that wartime retaliation was inherently contradictory: it subverted its own stated goal of preemptive violence and provoked additional acts of vengeance. For example, Union soldier Allen Campbell, who took part in the destruction of Atlanta's business district several months later considered that "*Chambersburg* is dearly paid for."[35]

John T. Trowbridge, a Northern journalist who toured Chambersburg in the fall of 1865, was initially shocked to see the "skeletons of houses burned by the Rebels," the "empty eye-sockets" of their windows staring at him and yawning with "their fanged and jagged jaws." But he quickly overcame his aversion to the ruins and saw them as a sign of future strength. "There is no loss without gain," he wrote. "Chambersburg will in the end be greatly benefited by the fire" and so "let it be with our country; fearful as our loss has been, we shall build better anew."[36] With state funds and philanthropic donations, the residents of Chambersburg did in fact rebuild their town. Architects and carpenters set to work almost immediately and reconstructed most of the Diamond by 1870.[37] City residents put up several memorials to the burning—a memorial slab and a fountain—and today they annually reenact its destruction on July 30. Chambersburg's ruins may no longer exist in reality, but they do exist in collective memory, reminding residents and visitors of the costs of vengeance enacted in the name of war.

DEFENSIVE BURNING AS A MILITARY TACTIC

Retaliation was a controversial wartime tactic that military theorists spent considerable time debating. But one element of urban warfare that was not much discussed in military codes or army regulations was the deliberate annihilation of one's own cities. Confederate troops stationed in several large urban centers—Charleston,

Columbia, Atlanta, and Richmond—burned arsenals, warehouses, and factories before they withdrew in the face of the Union army's overwhelming numbers. One of the only Southern cities *entirely* destroyed using defensive burning was Hampton, Virginia. It was the first large-scale urban ruin of the conflict, and it revealed the various and important roles that cities—and emancipation—played in the American Civil War.

In May 1861, after Virginia's residents had voted to secede, Union general Winfield Scott transferred two regiments of Massachusetts soldiers to Fortress Monroe (a large military installation in the Virginia Peninsula), increasing the size of its garrison to 12,000 men. Confederate commanders determined that they could not hold the town of Hampton—which sat across Mill Creek from the fort—against these Union "invaders." They advised its white residents to evacuate the town and to take all of their moveable property—including slaves—with them.[38]

When preparations for an evacuation began, however, many of Hampton's enslaved people did not accept their own removal; instead, they fled to Fortress Monroe. On May 24, 1861, three enslaved men named Shepard Mallory, Frank Baker, and James Townshend, all of whom belonged to Colonel Charles Mallory, arrived at the fort, appealing for sanctuary. When Confederate major John Cary of the Virginia Artillery appeared the next day and demanded the return of these three men under the Fugitive Slave Act of 1850, Union major-general Benjamin Butler denied the request, informing Cary that because Virginia had seceded, its slaveholders no longer had claims under federal policies like the Fugitive Slave Act. This led to Butler's famous decree that slaves, because they could be employed to dig fortifications and engage in other acts of hostility against the Union, would be considered "contraband of war" and subject to confiscation at will.

By late July 1861 almost 1,000 fugitive slaves who had confiscated themselves gathered around Fortress Monroe, and Butler wrote a series of letters and reports to Secretary of War Simon Cameron asking for orders regarding their housing and care.[39] Several of these letters and reports were published in the Northern papers, one of which found its way into the hands of General John B. Magruder, who was in command of Confederate forces on the Peninsula. After reading one of Butler's reports on August 6, Magruder concluded that the Union general considered slaves to be free and "would colonize them at Hampton, the home of most of their owners." Therefore, Magruder later wrote, "I determined to burn it at once."[40]

Just before midnight on August 7, 1861, four companies of men, many of whom lived in the vicinity, ran through the streets of Hampton with torches, setting fire to the business district and the houses that fanned out from the core of the town.[41] A correspondent for the Associated Press posted at the fort reported that "the glare of the conflagration was so brilliant that I was enabled to write by it" and that a strong south wind fanned the flames. The fire raged all night, he noted, and "a more sublime and awful spectacle has never yet been witnessed." Observers reported that around 500 buildings had been reduced to piles of rubble, and that only seven or eight were left standing. The next morning, nothing was left "to mark the once beautiful Hampton but the charred, towering chimneys" while "smoke ascending from the ruins" wafted lazily in the air.[42]

Virginians viewed this act of urban destruction as a civilian "sacrifice" rather than a military strategy, a patriotic act of devotion to the Confederacy on the part of its citizens. The fire would keep the town's buildings out of Northern hands, they reasoned, and the smoking heaps of rubble would stand as a permanent monument to their defiance of Union authority. Northerners, on the other hand, argued that, "a more wanton and unnecessary act than the burning, . . . could not have been committed."[43] For Union

commanders and many Northern civilians, Hampton's ruins became evidence of what they believed to be the typically rash and violent nature of Confederate soldiers, and the victimization of Southern civilians by their own protectors. Thus, quite early in the war, Northerners and Southerners were using urban ruins to dispute the nature of "civilized warfare," and the role of emancipation in waging it.

By April 1862, the ruins of Hampton had begun to disappear, their brick and stone fragments taken and used to build shelters for Union soldiers and for the fugitive slaves who flocked to the area in escalating numbers. This is the irony of Hampton's destruction: Magruder had burned the town in August 1861 in part because he feared its use as a camp for runaway slaves. By the time that John Trowbridge visited Hampton (after his visit to Chambersburg) in 1865, he "found it a thrifty village, occupied chiefly by freedmen."[44] Magruder's fears had come to pass and yet it was he (not Butler) who had made it so.

The burning of Hampton, like the destruction of Fredericksburg, Vicksburg, Atlanta, and Chambersburg, reveals that cities that came under fire during the Civil War provoked disputes about battles and sieges, and acts of retaliation and defense as military tactics. The presence of civilians in cities complicated these discussions, and helped to shape critiques of urban destruction as a military tactic.

THE AESTHETICS OF RUINED CITIES AND THE LOST CAUSE

Photographs and illustrations also influenced this wartime discourse of destruction. Ruins photograph beautifully: their sharp edges and empty spaces make them ideal aesthetic subjects. Northern wartime photographers like Alexander Gardner, Timothy O'Sullivan, and George N. Barnard, all of whom worked for New York City photographic studio owner Mathew Brady, created spectacular images of urban ruins, mostly in 1865. Photographers could not yet capture motion, so it was left to newspaper illustrators and lithograph production companies like Currier and Ives to depict the leaping flames and roiling smoke of cities on fire.

During the 1860s, image production and reproduction technologies advanced rapidly and therefore images of burning and ruined cities—Harpers Ferry, Hampton, Fredericksburg, Vicksburg, Chambersburg, Atlanta, Columbia, Charleston, and Richmond—were increasingly accessible and affordable. Due to the dominance of northern printing and photographic establishments before and during the war, the bulk of the images were produced by Northerners and for Northern audiences. Thus, images of destroyed cities usually narrated Union military conquests and victories, suggesting that urban destruction was integral to the ultimate Union victory.

For Confederates, these images conveyed tragedy and suffering. The South's urban ruins—in photographs and illustrations, and in novels and later, films—became bedrock symbols within the narrative of the Lost Cause, a popular Southern memory of the war that depicted Union soldiers as rapacious, evil invaders intent on annihilating all vestiges of the "Old South," including its architecture and its genteel white womenfolk. One popular novel published in the postwar period, William Henry Peck's *The M'Donalds; or, the Ashes of Southern Homes: A Tale of Sherman's March* (1867), for example, used urban destruction as both a thematic and a plot device. Throughout the novel, Union troops pursue Mrs. Preston M'Donald and her daughter Myrtis from Atlanta to Columbia. As these cities burn down around them, the M'Donald women have their moments of fear and anxiety, but they survive these conflagrations and remain staunch believers in the Confederacy and its purpose. Thus, Southerners dismissed one of the central justifications of urban destruction during the war: the demoralization of Southern civilians. In Southern popular culture after the war, white women in burning cities became embodiments of the Lost Cause and of the increasingly popular adage that "The South Shall Rise Again."[45]

The visual and narrative power of urban ruins meant that the extent of the damage done to Southern cities was often exaggerated. Photographers tightly focused their images, using a block or two of rubble to stand in for the entire city; they also emphasized destroyed cities in their collections of "war views." Sometimes they deliberately misled viewers regarding the cause of urban destruction. George N. Barnard, for example, took many photographs of the ruins of Charleston, South Carolina, in the year after it fell to Union troops. He did not distinguish between his images of the sections of the city damaged in the siege of 1863–1865, and the sections of the city leveled by a fire that swept through the business district in December 1861—before any Union troops had set foot in the city.[46]

Northern photographers were invested in shaping a triumphant narrative using urban ruins; the Southern press, on the other hand, saw such images as a way to critique Northern military tactics as "uncivilized" and "barbaric."

Figure 3. George N. Barnard, "Charleston, S.C. View of ruined buildings through porch of the Circular Church (150 Meeting Street)" (1865). Courtesy of Library of Congress, Prints and Photographs Division, Washington, DC LC-B811-3448 [P&P] LOT 4163.

The emphasis that both sides placed on destroyed cities and the profusion of images of them in the pages of photographic albums and magazines created the impression that many Southern cities were entirely annihilated during the Civil War. But in most cases, "ruined" cities experienced the loss of only about one-third of their buildings, concentrated in the business districts that were producing war materiel.

But these ruins still existed. Their material reality speaks to the centrality of cities in Civil War military strategy; to the many ways in which soldiers turned buildings into rubble; to the suffering of black and white civilians enduring these acts; and to the diverse meanings all Americans found in the urban ruins of war.

DISCUSSION OF THE LITERATURE

Just as urban centers were attractive targets for Union and Confederate armies in the 1860s, cities have become an increasingly popular topic in Civil War history. Since the late 20th century studies of Northern and Southern cities in wartime have proliferated. Some, such as George Rable's *Fredericksburg! Fredericksburg!* (2002), are military histories of cities under siege and in battle that determine the role they played in Civil War campaigns.[47]

However, as J. Matthew Gallman has noted in his article "Urban History and the American Civil War" (2006) many recent Civil War "city biographies" relate homefront stories of "recruiting and conscription, emancipation and racial tensions, voluntarism and fund raising, inflation and labor strife, politics and dissent."[48] Civil War cities need not be southern to capture historians' attention. Many recent histories focus on urban centers north and west of the Mason-Dixon Line: Boston, Chicago, New York City. Adam Arenson's *The Great Heart of the Republic: St. Louis and the Cultural Civil War* (2011), for example, reveals how St. Louis—which was northern, southern, and western—endured all manner of attacks and counterattacks during the war, remaining in contention until 1865.[49]

Those historians interested in the Southern cities have many urban centers to choose from—and these cities represent a wide range of wartime experiences. Not every Southern city was targeted for destruction, or assaulted. As William Warren Rogers's *Confederate Home Front: Montgomery during the Civil War* (1999) suggests, many Southern cities survived relatively unscathed, far away from the major theaters of the war. Scholars like Chester Hearn, in *When the Devil Came Down to Dixie: Ben Butler in New Orleans* (1997), and those whose essays are gathered in LeeAnn Whites's and Alecia P. Long's edited collection *Occupied Women: Gender, Military Occupation, and the American Civil War* (2009), focus on the experiences of white and black civilians in Confederate cities occupied by Union forces. These cities were fertile ground for political, gendered, and racial conflicts that interest social historians of the Civil War.[50]

Cities surrendered without any shots fired were rarely destroyed afterward. But those that were positioned between armies or were located at vital transportation junctions were often partially or wholly destroyed. These urban centers have attracted a great deal of attention from scholars. Some, such as Nelson Lankford (*Richmond Burning: The Last Days of the Confederate Capital* [2002]) and Marion Brunson Lucas (*Sherman and the Burning of Columbia* [2000]), have written detailed local histories of the several days before and after a city's destruction while others such as A. Wilson Greene, in *Civil War Petersburg: Confederate City in the Crucible of War* (2006) and Wendy Hamand Venet, in *A Changing Wind: Commerce and Conflict in Civil War Atlanta* (2014), discuss destruction as part of longer chronologies of wartime urban development.[51]

Cities have sometimes entered the narratives of scholars interested in the emergence of "hard war" strategies (deliberate acts of violence against civilians), especially on the part of the Union Army. Charles Royster's *The Destructive War: William Tecumseh Sherman, Stonewall Jackson, and the Americans* (1991) opens with a vivid chapter on the burning of Columbia, South Carolina, and Mark Grimsley's *The Hard Hand of War: Union Military Policy toward Southern Civilians, 1861–1865* (1995) examines hard war policies as they applied to both urban and rural residents of the Confederacy. More recently, Megan Kate Nelson studies the burnings of Hampton, Chambersburg, and Columbia to exemplify one of four kinds of wartime destruction in *Ruin Nation: Destruction and the American Civil War* (2012).[52]

Despite this recent upsurge in urban studies of warfare, there is clearly more work to be done in this field. More comparative studies of Southern cities under fire are needed in order to assess the commonalities and explain the differences in their experiences. Most important is the need for more studies of destroyed cities during Reconstruction. Historians have examined many facets of racial and political Reconstruction in the postwar period (necessarily and much to our benefit) but they do not often address the issue of actual reconstruction—the rebuilding of cities partially destroyed in the war. Even the wartime city biographies and texts that address destruction more broadly mention Reconstruction only in passing, or in final chapters or epilogues. William A. Link's *Atlanta, Cradle of the New South: Race and Remembering in the Civil War's Aftermath* (2013) has begun to answer important questions that historians need to ask in other locations: How was urban rebuilding financed? How long did it take? Did these projects provide work for freedpeople? Did some cities take longer to rebuild than others? How did wartime destruction shape the racial and political histories of Reconstruction, and the broader sweep of the history of American capitalism?[53]

Studies of Civil War cities—destroyed or left intact—have and can continue to illuminate local circumstances *and* speak to broader military, social, and cultural narratives of the conflict. They suggest the diversity of wartime experiences across the nation, and the important roles that cities played in American life in the 19th century.

PRIMARY SOURCES

The historical researcher can find evidence of urban destruction in tens of thousands of military records and Civil War–era letters and diaries, penned by Union and Confederate soldiers and civilians, and in hundreds of photographs, illustrations, lithographs, and engravings.

Military records, particularly those orders and reports compiled in the US War Department's *The War of the Rebellion: A Compilation of the Union and Confederate Armies* (commonly referred to as the *OR*) provide information about the timing and extent of urban destruction. They can also offer insights into individual and collective motivation, circumstances that drove most of the discussions about the burning of cities in wartime. In these documents, military officials explain and justify their actions, often in reference to another set of texts: laws of warfare. Union general Henry W. Halleck was one of the most prominent military theorists in the antebellum period, and his *Elements of International Law and Laws of War* (1866), building on a long history of military law, argued for the destruction of enemy property as a justifiable tactic; both Union and Confederate military and government officials used these laws to shape and defend their actions. Northern officials found the need to clarify some matters, however, in the context of a civil war. In 1863, the Union Adjutant General's office published *General Orders No. 100. Instructions for the Government of Armies of the United States in the Field*, written by Francis Lieber.

Military leaders were not the only Americans who thought and wrote about urban destruction. Civil War diaries, letters, and reminiscences abound with descriptions of wartime bombardments and fires, and the ruins they produced. Soldiers also wrote about the cities they shelled, laid siege to, pillaged, and burned. Massachusetts officer Charles Fessenden Morse's descriptions of the burning of Atlanta in his letters to his brother and sister are remarkably candid about the Union army's plans for "that devoted city," and Morse's qualms about the siege of Atlanta during the battles of July and August 1864.

Many of the most vivid accounts of Civil War urban destruction come from the pens of civilians (especially women) living in urban areas on fire. In Columbia, South Carolina, for example, Emma LeConte, Mary Whilden, Grace Brown Elmore, and Robert Gibbes wrote detailed accounts of the defensive burning of cotton on the streets as Confederate forces evacuated, the entrance of General Sherman's troops into the city, and the subsequent conflagration that consumed most of Columbia's business district in February 1865. After Sherman's troops departed, William Gilmore Simms collected the accounts of city residents and took a survey of the destruction. His *The Capture, Sack, and Destruction of the City of Columbia* (1865) contains a wealth of information about the progress of the fire and the property destruction that resulted.

As Simms roamed the streets of Columbia in the days and months after the fire, recording the words of city residents, the photographer Richard Wearn documented the destruction of the city in a series of images he later published as cartes de visite (small images printed on paper cards) (http://library.sc.edu/digital/collections/civilwar.html). These photographs show the extent of the city's ruins, and they informed the vociferous debate about who exactly was to blame for the fire (a debate that continues today). One must examine both print and visual primary sources with a careful eye, of course. Union and Confederate Army records often emphasized military necessity and ignored wanton destruction. In their shock and dismay, civilians living in besieged and destroyed cities regularly exaggerated the extent of the damage. Soldiers wielding torches alternately crowed about it, blamed others, or downplayed their participation. Visual images—even photographs, which many people tend to

assume convey "the truth" in ways that illustrations do not—are the work of artists who shaped their images to suit aesthetic preference or political ideologies. But if we read these primary documents with this in mind, we can see them as evidence of wartime urban destruction and also as signs of popular belief and emotional investments in these acts in Civil War America.

FURTHER READING

Gallman, J. Matthew. "Urban History and the American Civil War." *Journal of Urban History* 32.4 (May 2006): 631–642.

Greene, A. Wilson. *Civil War Petersburg: Confederate City in the Crucible of War.* Charlottesville: University of Virginia Press, 2006.

Grimsley, Mark. *The Hard Hand of War: Union Military Policy toward Southern Civilians, 1861–1865.* Cambridge: Cambridge University Press, 1995.

Lankford, Nelson. *Richmond Burning: The Last Days of the Confederate Capital.* New York: Penguin, 2002.

Link, William A. *Atlanta, Cradle of the New South: Race and Remembering in the Civil War's Aftermath.* Chapel Hill: University of North Carolina Press, 2013.

Lucas, Marion Brunson. *Sherman and the Burning of Columbia.* Columbia: University of South Carolina Press, 2000.

Nelson, Megan Kate. *Ruin Nation: Destruction and the American Civil War.* Athens, GA: University of Georgia Press, 2012.

Rable, George C. *Fredericksburg! Fredericksburg!* Chapel Hill: University of North Carolina Press, 2002.

Royster, Charles. *The Destructive War: William Tecumseh Sherman, Stonewall Jackson, and the Americans.* New York: Vintage, 1991.

Sheehan-Dean, Aaron. "*Lex Talionis* in the U.S. Civil War: Retaliation and the Limits of Atrocity." In *The Civil War as Global Conflict: Transnational Meanings of the American Civil War,* edited by David T. Gleeson and Simon Lewis, 172–189. Columbia: University of South Carolina Press, 2014.

Sternhell, Yael. *Routes of War: The World of Movement in the Confederate South.* Cambridge, MA: Harvard University Press, 2012.

Venet, Wendy Hamand. *A Changing Wind: Commerce and Conflict in Civil War Atlanta.* New Haven, CT: Yale University Press, 2014.

Whites, LeeAnn, and Alecia P. Long, eds. *Occupied Women: Gender, Military Occupation, and the American Civil War*. Baton Rouge: Louisiana State University Press, 2009.

NOTES

1. Brian Burrell, *Damn the Torpedoes! Fighting Words, Rallying Cries, and the Hidden History of Warfare* (New York: McGraw-Hill, 1999), 153.
2. Archer Jones, *The Art of War in the Western World* (Urbana: University of Illinois Press, 1987), 417–418.
3. Jones, *The Art of War in the Western World*, 418; and G. J. Ashworth, *War and the City* (London: Routledge, 1991), 8, 13, 19.
4. Ashworth, *War and the City*, 113–114; and Bruce Allen Watson, *Sieges: A Comparative Study* (Westport, CT: Praeger, 1993), 129.
5. "The Bombardment of Fredericksburg," originally published in the *New York Herald*, reprinted in *Harper's Weekly* (27 December 1862): 830.
6. George Rable, *Fredericksburg! Fredericksburg!* (Chapel Hill: University of North Carolina Press, 2002), 160. Robert E. Lee, Report of the Battle of Fredericksburg [to General S. Cooper], 10 April 1863, in United States War Department, *The War of the Rebellion: A Compilation of the Official Records of the Union and Confederate Armies* (Washington, DC: Washington Printing Office, 1880–1901) [hereafter *OR*], ser. I, vol. 21, chap. 33, p. 552.
7. Report of Brigadier General Henry J. Hunt, Chief of Artillery, 10 January 1863, *OR* ser. I, vol. 21, chap. 33, p. 183.
8. "The Bombardment of Fredericksburg," originally published in the *New York Herald*, reprinted in *Harper's Weekly* (27 December 1862): 831.
9. Henry W. Halleck, *Elements of International Law and Laws of War* (Philadelphia: J. B. Lippincott, 1885), 198–199. Originally published 1866.
10. Lauren Chauncey Mills to Fred Humphrey from near Fredericksburg, 24 December 1862, Lauren Chauncey Mills Letter (1862), Connecticut Historical Society [hereafter CHS].
11. Rable, *Fredericksburg! Fredericksburg!* 177.
12. Francis Marion Coker to his wife, Sarah (Sallie) Alice Reid Coker from camp five miles west of Fredericksburg, 16 December 1862, Francis Marion Coker Papers (1861–1866), Folder 4, Box 1, Florence Hodson Heidler Collection, Hargrett Library, University of Georgia [hereafter HL, UGA].

13. Napoleon Perkins, "The Memoirs of N. B. Perkins," New Hampshire Historical Society [hereafter NHHS].
14. A. Wilson Greene, *Civil War Petersburg: Confederate City in the Crucible of War* (Charlottesville: University of Virginia Press, 2006), 221; and "From Petersburg," *Richmond Enquirer* 37.61 (6 August 1864): 1, CC, BA.
15. "A Woman's Diary of the Siege of Vicksburg," *Century Illustrated Magazine* 8 (1885), as quoted in *The Civil War and Reconstruction: A Documentary Collection*, ed. William E. Gienapp (New York: W. W. Norton, 2001), 159.
16. Carrie Berry Diary, July [20], 5 August, 22 August 1864, Carrie Berry Papers, Kenan Research Center, Atlanta History Center, Atlanta, Georgia.
17. "A Woman's Diary of the Siege of Vicksburg," as quoted in *The Civil War and Reconstruction*, 160–161.
18. "A Woman's Diary of the Siege of Vicksburg," as quoted in *The Civil War and Reconstruction*, 162; and Carrie Berry Diary, 8 September 1864, Carrie Berry Papers, Kenan Research Center, Atlanta History Center, Atlanta, Georgia.
19. Yael A. Sternhell, *Routes of War: The World of Movement in the Confederate South* (Cambridge, MA: Harvard University Press, 2012), 100–102.
20. Sternhell, *Routes of War*, 139.
21. Carrie Berry Diary, 10 September 1864, Carrie Berry Papers, Kenan Research Center, Atlanta History Center, Atlanta, Georgia.
22. Carrie Berry Diary, 26 September 1864, Carrie Berry Papers, Kenan Research Center, Atlanta History Center, Atlanta, Georgia.
23. Sternhell, *Routes of War*, 152.
24. John Bell Hood to William Tecumseh Sherman, 9 September 1864, as quoted in Brian Craig Miller, *John Bell Hood and the Fight for Civil War Memory* (Knoxville: University of Tennessee Press, 2010), 141.
25. William Tecumseh Sherman to Mayor James M. Calhoun and S. C. Wells, 12 September 1864, reprinted in Sherman, *Memoirs of General William T. Sherman*, vol. 2 (New York: D. Appleton, 1875), as quoted in *The Civil War and Reconstruction*, 254.
26. Aaron Sheehan-Dean, "*Lex Talionis* in the U.S. Civil War: Retaliation and the Limits of Atrocity," in *The Civil War as Global Conflict: Transnational Meanings of the American Civil War*, ed. David T. Gleeson and Simon Lewis (Columbia: University of South Carolina Press, 2014); and

Francis Lieber, *General Articles No. 100 (Lieber Code)*, The Avalon Project, http://avalon.law.yale.edu/19th_century/lieber.asp#sec1.

27. Jubal Anderson Early, *A Memoir of the Last Year of the War for Independence in the Confederate States of America* (New Orleans, LA: Blelock, 1867), 57.

28. Scott C. Patchan, *Shenandoah Summer: The 1864 Valley Campaign* (Lincoln: University of Nebraska Press, 2007), 281.

29. J. Scott Moore, "Unwritten History: A Southern Account of the Burning of Chambersburg," *Richmond Dispatch* (5 February 1899), ed. R.A. Brock, *Southern Historical Society Papers* 27 (January–December 1898): 318–319.

30. B. S. Schneck, "Buildings Burned," in *The Burning of Chambersburg, Pennsylvania*, 4th ed. (Philadelphia: Lindsay and Blakiston, 1865), 74.

31. Henry Gilmor, *Four Years in the Saddle* (New York: Harper and Brothers, 1866), 209; and Early, *A Memoir*, 57.

32. "The Burning of Chambersburg," *National Intelligencer*, reprinted in the *Richmond Enquirer* 37.60 (5 August 1864): 1, CC, BA; and "Retaliation" [editorial], *Richmond Enquirer* 37.60 (5 August 1864): 2, CC, BA.

33. Sheehan-Dean, "*Lex Talionis* in the U.S. Civil War."

34. Henry W. Halleck, "Retaliation in War," *The American Journal of International Law* 6.1 (January 1912): 110, 111.

35. Allen Campbell to his father, 21 December 1864, Campbell Family Papers, Michigan State University, as quoted in Joseph T. Glatthaar, *The March to the Sea and Beyond: Sherman's Troops in the Savannah and Carolinas Campaigns* (New York: New York University Press, 1985), 139.

36. John T. Trowbridge, *The South: A Tour of Its Battle-Fields and Ruined Cities* (New York: Arno Press, 1969), 34, 38–39. Originally published 1866.

37. National Register of Historic Places Inventory Nomination Form: Chambersburg Historic District; and Chambersburg Walking Tour pamphlet, http://www.explorefranklincountypa.com.

38. Shelby Foote, *The Civil War: Fort Sumter to Perryville, a Narrative* (New York: Random House, 1958), 54; and Robert F. Engs, *Freedom's First Generation: Black Hampton, Va., 1861–1890* (New York: Fordham University Press, 2004), 13–14. Originally published 1979.

39. Edward H. Bonekemper III, "Negro Ownership of Real Property in Hampton and Elizabeth City County, Virginia, 1860–1870," *Journal of Negro History* 55.3 (July 1970): 170; and James McPherson, *Battle Cry of Freedom: The Civil War Era* (New York: Oxford University Press, 1988), 355.

40. Brigadier-General John B. Magruder, Report to Colonel George Deas, from Bethel, 9 August 1861, *OR* ser. I, vol. 4, chap. 13, p. 571.

41. Magruder Report to Deas, 9 August 1861, *OR* ser. I, vol. 4, chap. 13, p. 571; and S. H. Stringham, Report to Gideon Welles from the *U.S.S. Minnesota*, 8 August 1861, *OR* ser. I, vol. 6, p. 66.

42. "The Burning of Hampton," *Harper's Weekly* (31 August 1861): 554; Rev. James Julius Marks, *The Peninsular Campaign in Virginia, or Incidents and Scenes on the Battle-fields and in Richmond* (Philadelphia: J. B. Lippincott, 1864), 130, Albert and Shirley Small Special Collections Library, University of Virginia [hereafter SSCL, UVA]; and S. H. Stringham, Report to Gideon Welles from the *U.S.S. Minnesota*, 8 August 1861, *OR* ser. I, vol. 6, p. 66.

43. Benjamin Butler to Winfield Scott, 8 August 1861, *OR* I, vol. 4, chap. 13, p. 567.

44. Trowbridge, *The South*, 220.

45. William Henry Peck, *The M'Donalds; or, the Ashes of Southern Homes. A Tale of Sherman's March* (New York: Metropolitan Record Office, 1867), 7, Georgia Room, Hargrett Library, University of Georgia; and Megan Kate Nelson, *Ruin Nation: Destruction and the American Civil War* (Athens, GA: University of Georgia Press, 2012).

46. Megan Kate Nelson, "George N. Barnard, 'Charleston, S.C. View of Ruined Buildings through a Porch of the Circular Church (150 Meeting Street), 1865,'" in *Lens of War: Exploring Iconic Photographs of the Civil War*, ed. J. Matthew Gallman and Gary W. Gallagher (Athens, GA: University of Georgia Press, 2015).

47. Rable, *Fredericksburg! Fredericksburg!*

48. J. Matthew Gallman, "Urban History and the American Civil War," *Journal of Urban History* 32.4 (May 2006): 634.

49. Adam Arenson, *The Great Heart of the Republic: St. Louis and the Cultural Civil War* (Cambridge, MA: Harvard University Press, 2011).

50. William Warren Rogers Jr., *Confederate Home Front: Montgomery during the Civil War* (Tuscaloosa: University of Alabama Press, 1999); Chester G. Hearn, *When the Devil Came Down to Dixie: Ben Butler in New Orleans* (Baton Rouge: Louisiana State University Press, 1997); and

LeeAnn Whites and Alecia P. Long, eds., *Occupied Women: Gender, Military Occupation, and the American Civil War* (Baton Rouge: Louisiana State University Press, 2009).

51. Nelson Lankford, *Richmond Burning: The Last Days of the Confederate Capital* (New York: Viking, 2002); Marion Brunson Lucas, *Sherman and the Burning of Columbia* (Columbia: University of South Carolina Press, 2000); A. Wilson Greene, in *Civil War Petersburg: Confederate City in the Crucible of War* (Charlottesville: University of Virginia Press, 2006); and Wendy Hamand Venet, in *A Changing Wind: Commerce and Conflict in Civil War Atlanta* (New Haven, CT: Yale University Press, 2014).

52. Charles Royster, *The Destructive War: William Tecumseh Sherman, Stonewall Jackson, and the Americans* (New York: Alfred A. Knopf, 1991); Mark Grimsley, *The Hard Hand of War: Union Military Policy toward Southern Civilians, 1861–1865* (London: Cambridge University Press, 1995); and Megan Kate Nelson, *Ruin Nation: Destruction and the American Civil War* (Athens, GA: University of Georgia Press, 2012).

53. William A. Link, *Atlanta, Cradle of the New South: Race and Remembering in the Civil War's Aftermath* (Chapel Hill: University of North Carolina Press, 2015).

Megan Kate Nelson

SKYSCRAPERS AND TALL BUILDINGS

TECHNICS AND CIVICS: THE FIRST TALL BUILDINGS

Tall office buildings were the most conspicuous expressions of American economic expansion after the American Civil War (1861–1865). The growth of industrial cities, the separation of administrative functions from the sites of industrial production, the growing volume and specialization of clerical work, the growth of financial and communications firms, and the consolidation of a dedicated business district in the rapid, if uneven, spatial sorting of the 19th-century city all set the stage for this new building type.

The cast iron facades of antebellum commercial buildings anticipated tall office buildings in New York, where advances in iron framing, fireproofing (with terra cotta and cement), plate glass, and hollow-tile floor arches that bridged iron floor joists coalesced to form the requisite technical conditions. Improvements in heating, ventilation, and plumbing systems were also salient; but the key feature was the advent of safe and effective passenger elevators that made the upper floors of office buildings attractive to the tenants who ultimately paid for them. New York's Equitable Building (1868–1870) boasted the first hydraulic-gravity elevator to be installed in an office building that, at ten stories, towered over its urban context: the emerging downtown financial district that the building itself signaled (Figure 1).[1]

Vying for prestige, clients, and (ultimately) tenants, rivalry among insurance companies provided that additional element so critical to the rise of tall buildings: corporate self-consciousness. Patrons were keenly aware of the impact an imposing building generated as

Figure 1. Equitable Building, New York City, Gilman and Kendall and George Post, architects, 1868–1870.

Courtesy of Library of Congress, LC-USZ62-100550.

an advertisement for the company's financial security and benevolent public image. Architects for the Equitable borrowed motifs from the "Second Empire" style, modeled on Napoleon III's additions to the Louvre in Paris, which featured steep mansard roofs and baroque neoclassical detailing. The style was already employed in large public buildings, and insurance companies were likewise drawn to the civic iconography. The façade was organized as a stack of attached columns, in ascending order, each stretching two floors to frame double-height windows that flooded interior spaces with light and culminated in a steep roof studded with rounded dormers. A capacious, galleried business hall was provided for the insurance company on the second and third floors. Above the building's entrance, which led to a vaulted arcade, perched a statuary grouping called "Protection," featuring a Guardian Angel of Life, the company's emblem, protecting a widow and orphan. "Second Empire" style insurance company buildings such as this one became common features in the fledgling business districts of burgeoning industrial cities in the years after the Civil War.[2]

Newspaper companies, also vying for the public's trust, were early patrons of tall buildings. The Tribune Building (1873–1875), designed by the École des Beaux Arts–trained architect Richard Morris Hunt, culminated with a projection based on a medieval clock tower. In the same year, architect George Post—who worked on the Equitable Building and later emerged as one of the most prolific and influential designers of his day—capped his Western Union building with a campanile in the same vein. Both set precedents for the picturesque towers that adorned buildings for aspirational clients, and by extension (literally), the habit of reaching for higher official heights with a symbolic appendage, mast, or spire that could be seen from all directions. The Tribune was joined by competitors—including Joseph Pulitzer's World Building (1890) designed by George Post with a great billowing dome—on what became known as Newspaper Row facing New York's City Hall Plaza.

This conveniently served as a viewing platform for an opulent architectural fashion show.

Again, and again, insurance companies translated the liquid capital amassed from the premiums collected by their many policyholders into lucrative real estate deals that housed their growing operations and served as corporate brands. In Newark, New Jersey, the Prudential Life Insurance Company called on George Post to design an eleven-story office tower, completed in 1892. The iron frame building was clad in rough-hewn stone and featured heavy, rounded arches that borrowed from the Romanesque style made popular by Henry Hobson Richardson. The roof was adorned with turrets, conical towers, and elaborate dormers. The building's fortress-like quality was intended to emphasize the strength and security of its patron; just a few years later Prudential adopted the Rock of Gibraltar as its emblem. Nostalgic on the outside, the building was a modern marvel on the inside, with hydraulic piston-driven elevators, steam heat, running hot and cold water, gas and electric lighting, and telephones in every office— a model of the networked office that came to characterize the tall office building. Most of the space was devoted to large, open floors where the clerical staff processed and filed insurance policies that were printed on site.[3]

The elevator soon migrated to other building programs and by the 1880s hotels, apartment buildings, and even loft manufacturing and warehouse buildings reached ten stories and taller. The twelve-story Chelsea Apartments (later the Chelsea Hotel) opened in 1885, built as cooperative apartments sold to multiple owners, with cast-iron balconies and Victorian Gothic styling, including a sequence of picturesque dormers. When the second phase of the Waldorf Astoria was completed in 1897, the sixteen-story hotel was one of the world's largest and most luxurious hotels.[4]

SKYSCRAPER SPECULATIONS

The term "skyscraper" was in common usage by the 1890s, especially in Chicago where tall commercial blocks were an increasingly common building type. Chicago emerged as the leading metropolis of the West by the mid-19th century, the center of a great inland empire connected to New York by the Great Lakes, the Erie Canal, and a far-flung railroad network. Lumber, grain, and livestock at great scale were all processed in "nature's metropolis." Tall buildings in "The Loop," framed first by streetcar lines and then the elevated railroad (1892), called "the el" for short, signaled brisk demand for space to house the offices of railroad companies and other industrial concerns, as well as the legal, financial, and real estate firms that served them. Outside capital joined with local enterprise to push buildings to unprecedented height and scale.[5]

A major fire in 1871 set the stage for the rebuilding of Chicago with tall buildings. The first generation of post-fire building in the 1870s and 1880s combined masonry construction and load-bearing walls with internal metal cages. The ten-story Home Insurance Building (1883–1885), designed by William Le Baron Jenney, who was trained as an engineer, has often been credited as the first of "skeleton frame" buildings in which the metal frame supported the structure, freeing the exterior walls from load-bearing responsibilities to be attached as "curtains" to the frame. Subsequent analysis (carried out when the building was demolished in 1932) revealed that the dead load was not carried exclusively by the metal skeleton members, which were encased in masonry; certainly, it was another critical step in a collective pattern of innovation. In any event, architects continued to use masonry to brace metal-framed structures, at least until the turn of the century when the steel frame came into common practice. Masonry buildings (with stone or brick bearing walls) could be very tall, but at sixteen stories, the Monadnock (1891) in Chicago achieved the limits of that structural technology. With advances in the production of Bessemer-process steel, large plate glass, and foundation techniques, including the use of isolated footings, architects and builders soon mastered the skeleton frame and the light, "curtain" walls that could be attached to them, eliminating the need for thick, load-bearing walls that eroded rentable space, especially at the lower floors.[6]

Advances in communications technology facilitating the exchange of information between dispersed locations were equally important to the viability of tall office buildings. Telegraph and telephone connections became ubiquitous and required features. Nonetheless, the profit motive, not the technologies themselves, hastened the development of speculative office blocks in Chicago. The Home Insurance Building included office space for rent but was financed by the insurance company itself. By contrast, the speculative office building was financed by individuals or stock subscription companies that raised the capital and took the risks required to erect tall buildings that would be marketed to tenants. In this milieu, real estate logics prevailed in the emergence of best practices and skyscrapers were designed "from the inside out: from the smallest cell, to the full-floor plan, to the three-dimensional form," according to historian Carol Willis.[7] Large businesses with many clerks and secretaries required wide open-floor plans. But the majority of tenants in speculative office buildings were small firms and required offices of less than a thousand square feet; this appealed to owners because smaller offices could be rented for a higher rate per square foot. Small tenants were also less likely to create large and sudden vacancies or to clog up the elevators en masse. To suit these tenants, the "T"-office—allowing for two private rooms, each with their own window, and a reception area that served both of them— prevailed as the norm. Though electrical light was available by the 1890s, it was relatively weak and access to natural light circumscribed an "economic depth" of each floor plate. Large windows and high ceilings maximized this resource and, for wider sites, light courts were designed to bring light to the interior units.

In one example of a speculative tall office building, Chicago attorney and property owner Wirt Walker financed the fourteen-story Tacoma Building (1886–1889), built by George A. Fuller and designed by Holabird & Roche, one of the large architectural firms that emerged to handle design needs for a range of clients in the booming city. The metal frame was braced for wind with internal masonry walls, and the external, street-facing walls were composed of horizontal strips of windows arranged in canted bays and separated by terra cotta brick. The builders created a public spectacle by hanging the terra cotta and glass wall to the metal frame simultaneously at the second, sixth, and tenth floors, flaunting its non-load-bearing, "curtain"-like attributes.[8] At ground level, an entrance passage connected LaSalle and Madison Streets, leaving more room for rent-paying storefronts than a lobby, which was minimal. The building was equipped with electricity, gas, and steam radiators for heat. Sanitary facilities (bathrooms and plumbing) were also an important selling point. Law firms, insurance company branch offices, lawyers, and insurance and real estate dealers made up the majority of tenants, which also included vendors of other products and trades. Not named for a company, the building was given a whimsical name, Tacoma, which was a romantic allusion to the American West (it was the original name of Mount Rainier in Washington State) and the rapidly subjugated American Indian, linking the skyscraper to a majestic natural landscape and to manifest destiny.[9]

Each skyscraper was conceived, designed, planned, and constructed over a period of time, and the act of building represented its own economic activity. Large building contractors such as George A. Fuller (b. 1851–d. 1900) became experts in steel-framed construction and built up national operations. Fuller was an effective organizer of labor and materials; his efforts augmented the role of the builder by serving as a general contractor that encompassed all of the sub-trades. His Chicago-based company was responsible for the construction of many of the key structures of the time, including the Rookery Building (1888) and the Monadnock Building (1891). The demands of constructing large office buildings also hastened the emergence of the architectural firm as a large organization in its own right, equipped to handle large and complicated design and engineering projects. Examples included Holabird & Roche, Adler & Sullivan, and Burnham & Root—the first name usually given to the business partner and the second to the design partner. Like any other modern business firm, architects were also in the market for office space. Burnham & Root kept their offices in the Rookery Building—which they designed for speculative builders Peter and Shepherd Brooks—where they oversaw a small army of draftsmen producing drawings on an assembly line for a national practice in architecture and city planning.[10]

The most impressive of the new skyscrapers transcended the building itself to encompass "a City under one Roof." With commercial arcades and skylighted lobbies, the architectural interiors competed with facades for visual and emotional impact.[11] When completed in 1892, Chicago's Masonic Temple (Figure 2), designed by Burnham & Root, was the tallest commercial building in the world at 302 feet (twenty stories) and combined elaborate meeting halls for the fraternal organization with speculative office space.[12] The internal light court ascended the full height of the building that included six stories of retail and services. The basement housed a two-thousand-seat restaurant. Environments such as this one folded the social functions of the street into the building itself and fused public and commercial life.[13] Henry B. Fuller may have been thinking of the Tacoma, the Rookery, or the Masonic Temple in his 1893 novel *The Cliff Dwellers* that satirized daily life in a large Chicago office building, when he described the "Clifton," which aimed to be "complete within itself." The structure both contributed to the life of the street and served as its retreat.[14]

Figure 2. Masonic Temple, Chicago, Burnham and Root, architects, 1892 (demolished 1933). Courtesy of Library of Congress, LC-DIG-det-4a09124.

DESIGN, REGULATION, AND URBAN MORPHOLOGY

Daniel Burnham emerged in the 19th century as the great organizer of large projects, including the World's Columbian Exposition (1893), which established a Beaux-Arts neoclassical architectural language as the de facto style to govern a unified assemblage of buildings. The Columbian Exposition also inspired City Beautiful planning exercises in cities across the United States, starting with the McMillan Plan for Washington, DC, in 1901, with Burnham himself frequently at the helm. These plans called for new boulevards cutting through existing urban grids terminating in plazas that anchored a collection of public and institutional buildings in a "civic center," along with new local and regional parks, and modernized industrial, railroad, and port facilities. City Beautiful planners expressed a broad disenchantment with the uncoordinated, congested, inefficient, and ugly spaces of the industrial city and, by extension, the laissez faire politics and

corruption that lay at its root. Images produced by Jules Guerin in *Plan of Chicago* (1909), written by Burnham and Edward Bennett, made these ideals especially vivid in pastel-hued watercolors of epic new boulevards stretching horizontally across the landscape, lined with mid-rise blocks unified by an even cornice line. Not surprisingly, the skyscraper itself became a focal point of these debates—admired by some as an expression of progressive, civic values and bemoaned by others as greedy, self-interested parasites.[15]

In 1903, leading architectural critic Montgomery Schuyler identified a "skyscraper problem" in New York. A cacophonous and uncoordinated profusion of tall buildings had "turned the sky-line of New York into a horribly jagged sierra," Schuyler complained, "and converted the commercial quarters of all our chief commercial cities into gloomy and windy canyons."[16] New skyscrapers grabbed light and air for themselves at the expense of their neighbors. Architect Ernest Flagg, who designed the Singer Tower (1908) in New York, also worried about a city of canyons and ravines and lamented the "wild-Western appearance" of the skyscraper city. He called for even cornice lines with towers, not exceeding one quarter of the total site, set back from the street.[17] The human density implied by the skyscraper created its own set of problems, exacerbating traffic congestion—already central to planners' critique of the central city—and presenting public health concerns, as well. In the 1890s, city governments in Baltimore, Boston, and Chicago, among many others, enacted building height ordinances to curb the most aggressive efforts to concentrate office space at a single site. Supporters included existing property owners, who hoped that new buildings would not overshadow older stock, as well as large landowners at the edges of the business district who believed that height limits would spread out land values across a broader swath of the urban landscape.[18]

In some cases, the cacophony was located within a single façade. Despite the refinement of some of the metal-framed, curtain-wall structures of 1880s Chicago, the World's Columbian Exposition refueled a tendency toward historicist pastiche. At least one architect of tall buildings took a stand against this impulse. Louis Sullivan insisted that the "the tall office building should not, must not, be made a field for the display of architectural knowledge in the encyclopedic sense... that the sixteen-story building must not consist of sixteen separate, distinct, and unrelated buildings piled one upon the other until the top of the pile is reached." In "The Tall Building Artistically Considered" (1896), Sullivan succinctly analyzed the economic and social forces that gave rise to the tall building, including the growth of urban populations, the increase of land values, the steel frame, and high-speed elevators. "How shall we impart to this sterile pile, this crude harsh brutal agglomeration, this stark, staring exclamation of external strife, the graciousness of those higher forms of sensibility and culture that rest on the lower and fiercer passions?" As opposed to giving up on the aesthetic possibilities of the tall building, as some architects had, Sullivan offered a solution that accentuated its "loftiness": "It must be every inch a proud and soaring thing, rising in sheer exultation that from bottom to top it is a unit without a single dissenting line."[19]

Sullivan modeled his ideal attributes for the skyscraper five years prior with the Wainwright Building (1890–1891) in St. Louis, commissioned by a brewery magnate. The building was organized around a two-story base containing storefronts and a lobby; a continuously extruded shaft with recessed spandrels that accentuated the lift of its vertical piers; identical windows for each office, plainly expressing their repetitive nature; and a thick, protruding cornice to resolve the figure and to contain the building's attic and mechanical functions. Interwoven into this exquisitely proportioned composition, Sullivan interlaced ornamental foliating motifs along the frieze of the cornice and gracing each window spandrel. The piers themselves terminated in abstracted reliefs

of Corinthian capitals, a subtle reference to neoclassicism. Blending the naturalistic and the formal, Sullivan rebutted the critique of modern capitalism to convey a "benign image of modern commerce."[20]

For the Schlesinger and Mayer department store in Chicago (later Carson, Pirie Scott, and now the Sullivan Center), Louis Sullivan asserted the mercantile emporium as a civic presence by wrapping the "World's Busiest Corner" with ornate wrought-iron ornament in his signature organic patterns and carrying the decoration across the top of the second floor, a private endowment to the public street and a lure to potential consumers. Meanwhile, above, a crisp white grid of uniform "Chicago windows"—a large, fixed pane in the center with two operable double sash windows on each side—would later inspire avatars of modernism such as Sigfried Giedion. The Swiss art historian dismissed Sullivan's ornament as a concession to his clients. If, however, as Sullivan claimed, "form ever follows function," certainly there were merchandising functions to eye-catching ornament.[21]

Sullivan expressed an elegant if dissenting note to the national trend toward a baroque and bombastic neoclassicism, heavy and ponderous, as the United States lumbered into the 20th century as its heir apparent. In Chicago, where height limits were established in 1893—perfectly timed with the vision of order advanced by the Columbian Exposition and reasserted in the *Plan of Chicago*, and also aligned with acceptance of the skeleton steel-frame, reducing technical limitations to achieving great height—tall buildings took the form of a "massive palazzo type" organized as a hollow square on a large block reaching either sixteen or twenty stories, depending on the prevailing ordinance, with offices on the perimeter and again lining the internal court. Many were designed by Daniel Burnham's firm and its successor, Graham, Anderson, Probst, and White. In New York, where there were no height limits, architects adapted to narrow lots to form tall, slim towers. Daniel Burnham & Co. designed

Figure 3. Flatiron Building, New York City, Daniel Burnham and Co., architect, 1903.
Courtesy of Library of Congress, LC-USZ62-107693.

Figure 4. Metropolitan Life Insurance Co., New York City, Napoleon LeBrun and Sons, architect, 1909–1915.
Courtesy of Library of Congress, LC-DIG-det-4a19543.

the steel-framed Fuller Building (1903), named for the builder, which became known as the "Flatiron" for its wedge-shaped site at the intersection of Broadway and Fifth Avenue. Wrapped in neoclassical detailing and topped with a colonnade and jutting cornice, the structure was instantly an icon of the city (Figure 3).

The Flatiron's location at Twenty-Third Street and Broadway, across from Madison Square Park, staked out a "midtown" district distinct from the downtown financial core. Neighbors included the Metropolitan Life Insurance Company, which built a palatial eleven-story office block facing the Park in 1893. Growing rapidly, the insurance company acquired adjacent lots and made plans to surpass the Singer Building (1908) as the world's tallest. Metropolitan Life Tower (1909), modeled on the Campanile in Venice, became the company's great symbol: the "light that never fails."[22] Met Life Vice President Haley Fiske called the tower "an advertisement that didn't cost the company a cent because the tenants footed the bill" (Figure 4).[23]

Beaux-Arts neoclassical towers proliferated and the most ambitious patrons built protruding towers that vied for public attention, often drawing from picturesque European models. Ernest Flagg's Singer Building for the sewing machine manufacturer culminated in a bulbous crown that resembled an over-scaled French *hôtel de ville*. Madison Square Garden, an indoor arena designed by McKim, Mead & White (1890), featured a tower inspired by the Giralda, the bell tower of Seville, Spain. The forty-story New York Municipal Building (1910–1914, also designed by McKim, Mead & White), also borrowed this motif and the Giralda was echoed again in Chicago's Wrigley Building (1920, Graham, Anderson, Probst & White). Richard Schmidt designed a Venetian-style tower building for Montgomery Ward in Chicago (1899) and in Seattle, typewriter magnate L. C. Smith built the tallest tower in the West along the same lines—it was also part of Smith's effort to prevent the northward flow of the business district. Universities with

Beaux-Arts campus plans, like the University of California at Berkeley and the University of Texas at Austin, also installed picturesque bell towers to anchor the composition. In the 1920s, public buildings increasingly took skyscraper form, from the Los Angeles City Hall (1928) to the Nebraska State Capitol (1922–1932) designed by Bertram Goodhue and known as the "Tower on the Plains."

The ultimate model of the convergence of private and civic architecture was the tower built by Frank Woolworth as the headquarters of his far-flung empire of five-and-dime stores. Designed by Cass Gilbert with French Gothic styling and soaring 792 feet, the Woolworth Building (1910–1913) was marketed as the "Cathedral of Commerce" and epitomized skyscraper ideals: a great icon, an administrative center, and a corporate advertisement paid for by the provision of office space for lease. The model embodied by the Woolworth Building was that enlightened private interest would produce beautiful and functional urban environments, aggrandizing their patrons and, by extension, the city at large.[24]

The Chicago Tribune Tower competition, launched in 1922 for a site across Michigan Avenue from the Wrigley Building, exposed a range of alternatives that influenced later skyscraper development. With the intention of creating "the most beautiful building in the world," *Tribune* co-editors Joseph Patterson and Robert McCormick embarked on a self-promotional campaign. The event marked a high tide in the role of newspapers in shaping the city's skyline and was itself a terrific publicity gambit.[25] Judges considered more than 263 submissions, including some from European modernists soon to make their presence felt on the American scene, before settling on a neogothic tower with flying buttresses at its crown designed by John Mead Howells and Raymond Hood. Aesthetically conservative— at least compared to the avant-garde, functionalist designs submitted to the competition— Sigfried Giedion later dismissed the Tribune Tower as "Woolworth Gothic."[26]

The second-place design by Eliel Saarinen, featuring vertical piers and tapered, stepped-back massing, probably had more influence in giving architectural form to the soaring towers of the 1920s building boom, including Raymond Hood's design for the American Radiator Building (Hood & Fouilhoux, 1924) facing Bryant Park in New York and clad in dark brick accented with gold details that introduced the possibilities of color schemes for tall buildings.[27]

SKYSCRAPER ZONING AND THE ADVENT OF ART DECO

Tall buildings had long raised concerns that unchecked building practices would leave the business district shrouded in darkness. In New York, the lack of flat height restrictions allowed a number of flagrant offenders, like the 1915 Equitable Building at 120 Broadway with thirty-eight stories that rose like sheer cliffs from the edges of narrow streets. It was one factor hastening the city's 1916 comprehensive zoning ordinance intended to limit the height and bulk of large buildings by mandating setbacks based on street width and forming an allowable building envelope. The new regulations inspired similar zoning laws in cities across the country and ended the national norm of flat height restrictions. Set-back massing was joined with the emergence of art deco styling to produce one of the most widespread and recognizable skyscraper typologies. These buildings were characterized by soaring verticality achieved by recessed window mullions that emphasized vertical piers, decorative crowns, rich detailing in chrome and glazed terra cotta brick, and often lush sculptural programs.[28]

Art deco became the de facto language of tall buildings in the 1920s across the United States, in time for a building boom where even small and medium-sized cities began to develop a "skyline" closely linked to the dominant financial, industrial, and social institutions of the town. The art deco skyscrapers of

Houston and Tulsa, for example, represented the ascendancy of oil and gas corporations that headquartered there in the 1920s. In 1926, the tallest building in Missouri was the twenty-eight-story Bell Telephone Building in St. Louis, designed by Mauran, Russell & Crowell, which featured elaborate massing with neogothic crenellations punctuating each of the seventeen different roof levels and a civic arcade at ground level. Reynolds Tobacco Company (1929) hired future Empire State architects Shreve, Lamb and Harmon to design a set-back skyscraper in Winston-Salem, North Carolina. In Detroit, the Greater Penobscot Building (1928), designed by Wirt C. Rowland, blended native American and art deco motifs in its ornament (Figure 5). At forty-seven stories, it was the tallest building outside of New York and Chicago. Architect

Figure 5. Penobscot Building, Detroit. Wirt C. Rowland, architect, 1928.
Courtesy of the author's private collection.

Albert Kahn, already famous for his factory buildings, designed the Fisher Building (1928) in Detroit's emerging midtown location (later known as New Center) for the company that sold automobile chassis to General Motors and other car builders. Kahn's building (the lead designer was Joseph Nathaniel French) included elaborate frescoes and ceiling paintings in the three-story lobby and also featured a 3,500-seat theater with Aztec- and Mayan-revival motifs.

In New York, art deco skyscrapers became a vernacular as well as an exceptional building type. Architects such as Ely Jacques Kahn specialized in tall buildings in this fashion, varying in color scheme and degree of decorative program.[29] Ralph Walker, whose design for the Barclay Vesey Building (1923–1927) in downtown New York was among the first to respond to the 1916 zoning law, also came to the fore. A cluster of set-back, art deco towers vied to dominate the city's downtown financial district, including structures for Cities Services, Irving Trust, City Bank Farmers Trust, and 40 Wall Street.[30] At the decadent tail end of the 1920s boom, boasts of the world's tallest came one after the other. At midtown, close to Grand Central Terminal, the Chrysler Building (1931), designed by William Van Alen, soared to 1,046 feet, seventy-seven-stories and quickly became an icon; its four gargoyle-like eagles were frequent photographic subjects and the public was dazzled by its spire, a sequence of radiating chrome chevrons.

More than fashion statements, the art deco skyscrapers of the 1920s and early 1930s were also finely tuned financial products. The massing of a skyscraper's steel framework was the result of intricate calculations with factors that included land value, cost of labor and materials, projected rentable area, office planning, and expected demand. Real estate consultants wrote treatises on the topic, concluding that the "economic height" of a modern office building was not always the limit of what the site could legally accommodate.[31] In other words, as skyscraper historian Carol Willis has coined it: "form follows finance." One issue addressed the size of the building's core and how many elevator banks it had to house in order to serve its upper floors without sacrificing too much rentable floor space. Over-speculation became a risk. The Empire State Building, for example, became the tallest structure of its age and the epitome of set-back massing and art deco detailing. It occupied half of a city block, 427 feet long, and the entire frontage of Fifth Avenue between Thirty-Third and Thirty-Fourth Streets, which was assiduously gathered by the developers. The construction, by Starrett Brothers and Eken, was its own well-documented feat of engineering prowess and human daring. But the gargantuan structure was located neither in midtown nor downtown, demand could not meet supply, and it was years before the building was profitable.[32]

THE SKYSCRAPER AND REGIONAL PLANNING

In his manifesto, *Metropolis of Tomorrow* (1929), architectural illustrator Hugh Ferriss rendered a catalogue of leading art deco skyscrapers before generating his own speculative images of the future city, an orderly composition of tall buildings with multileveled transport connections. Ferriss identified the Chanin Building, the Chrysler Building, and the Bank of Manhattan Company Building in New York; and the Penobscot, Fisher and David Stott buildings in Detroit.[33] He imagined a city of broadly spaced skyscrapers that marked distinct zones for business, science, and arts, for example. In the 1920s, the tall building was frequently mobilized as a key aspect of regional planning. Inspired in part by the rash of new skyscraper buildings, the Regional Plan Association published the *Regional Plan of New York and Its Environs* (published in two volumes, 1929 and 1931) calling for the planned development of tall buildings in the business district to relieve congestion and to redistribute industry and manufacturing to the urban fringe.

Swiss architect Le Corbusier critiqued the New York skyline after his 1935 trip, lamenting the jumble of buildings, the lack of planning, and the absence of visual clarity. He believed that skyscrapers should be bigger and spaced farther apart. In polemics such as *Toward a New Architecture* (1923) and *The City of Tomorrow and Its Planning* (1929), diagrammatic schemes for a *Ville Radieuse* [Radiant city] (1924) and the Plan Voisin for Paris (1925), commissioned by a car company, Le Corbusier presented an image for the dramatic rebuilding of cities with massive cruciform-plan towers straddling the ground plane laced with new limited-access highways. The buildings should be lifted off the ground on stilts, recovering the ground plane for human activities and ensuring the circulation of light and air.[34]

Frank Lloyd Wright also imagined urban and regional planning with the skyscraper, mostly in unrealized projects such as his proposal for a St. Mark's-in-the-Bouwerie Towers project for New York (1927–1931). Wright was intrigued by the limitations placed on building by the 1923 Chicago building code that mandated set-backs, and he created a "Skyscraper Regulation Project" in 1926 that conceived a multileveled block of grouped towers. In 1940, Wright proposed Crystal City for a site in Washington, DC, a skyscraper ensemble organized on a massive plinth for car parking and other services. His concept for a pinwheeling skyscraper eventually migrated to Bartlesville, Oklahoma, where the Price Tower was built for a local oil company. In his 1935 proposal for Broadacre City, Wright imagined the lone skyscraper in the midst of his prairie subdivision.[35]

Meanwhile, large hotel complexes anchored downtown development in a number of secondary American cities, reflecting planners' ambitions for coordinated skyscraper ensembles. The forty-nine-story Carew Tower-Netherland Plaza in Cincinnati was completed in 1930 on land assembled by Cincinnati industrialist and real estate developer John J. Emery and built by the prolific Starrett Brothers and Eken.

Hailed as a prototype for the next generation of the mixed-use "city-within-a-city," the group included a hotel, department store, theater, office space, and parking garage tower for 750 cars all linked by infrastructure and circulatory systems.[36] Even more ambitious was the Cleveland Union Terminal project that marked the culmination of efforts by the Van Swearingen brothers to unify the city's streetcar and passenger railroad facilities while linking their suburban Shaker Heights development to the central city with inter-urban rail, a fact that highlighted the emerging tensions of decentralization. Designed by Graham, Anderson, Probst and White, successors to the Burnham firm, the Cleveland Terminal complex included a hotel, department store, medical buildings, as well as a soaring fifty-two-story tower—briefly the second tallest in the world—which appropriated civic imagery in the form of a crowning tempietto reminiscent of the New York Municipal Building.

Rockefeller Center (1931–1939) was the best-known and most influential of the "city-within-a-city" projects. The development set the standard for a successful grouping of commercial buildings that persuasively claimed the mantle of civic space. Developed by a private consortium led by John D. Rockefeller Jr., on seventeen acres in midtown Manhattan owned by Columbia University, the ensemble included towers for US Rubber Company, Eastern Airlines, and the Associated Press. An elegant sequence of low pavilions facing Fifth Avenue framed a retail promenade and the central open space featured a skating rink. Presiding over it all was the slim, cliff-like, seventy-story tower named for its chief tenant, the Radio Corporation of America, a strong statement of confidence in the midst of the Great Depression. Rockefeller Center's design is usually attributed to Raymond Hood who worked with Wallace K. Harrison and a group of associated architects. The complex integrated underground concourses, roof gardens, and art deco design in the statuary and public art. Unified yet varied, self-contained yet porous

to the street grid, Rockefeller Center also included an underground parking garage and access for truck deliveries.[37]

MODERNISM: FROM SKYSCRAPER TO CITY

By mid-20th century, the influence of European modernism was felt in American skyscraper design, as émigré architects began to work at American schools of architecture and accept important building commissions. In this way, the first inklings of what became known as the "International Style" made its way to the American city. The Philadelphia Savings Fund Society Building (1932) was designed by American George Howe with Swiss architect William Lescaze. Here the architects arranged the skyscraper's spaces as legible, asymmetrical masses and relieved the building of conventional ornament save for the large letters "PSFS" at the top.[38] The PSFS building in Philadelphia was among the first to feature a fully air-conditioned and climate-controlled interior. Operable windows nearly disappeared from tall office buildings in the postwar boom, though window blinds have prevailed (Figure 6). The Equitable Insurance Company building in Portland, Oregon, designed by Italian émigré Pietro Belluschi, produced a new image for a concrete-framed building with aluminum window frames and large plate glass windows pushed flush to the frame, giving the appearance of a flat, unornamented slab and a wall full of windows.[39] The building included all the modern amenities of what architectural historian Reyner Banham calls the "well-tempered environment."[40] Le Corbusier contributed to the design of the Secretariat Building, an elegant glass and marble slab that anchored the United Nations campus on the East Side of Manhattan on land assembled by developer William Zeckendorf, purchased and donated by the Rockefeller family, and cleared by the City of New York.[41]

The neoclassical decorative flourishes of the Beaux-Arts skyscraper gave way to the reliefs,

Figure 6. Philadelphia Savings Fund Society Building (PSFS Building), Philadelphia, George Howe and William Lescaze, architects, 1932. Courtesy of Library of Congress, HABS PA,51-PHILA, 584–5.

murals, and metal detailing of art deco towers; by mid-century, emerging design conventions tended to strip all of that away in favor of a more strict expression of the tall building's steel frame without applied decoration. Urbanistically, the new towers increasingly eschewed the traditional street frontages and retail arcades that marked previous eras in favor of open plazas and austere lobbies, often creating the sensation of lifting the entire building off the ground plane on stilts, as Le Corbusier prescribed. In this way, the postwar slabs were detached objects that created their own contexts.

One of the first and most influential of these new designs was built on Park Avenue in New York for Lever Brothers, the American division of a global soap company. Chief executive Charles Luckman was trained as an architect and went on to a second career at the helm of a large architectural design firm;

he claimed it was his idea to lift the building off the ground plane of this choice site, forgoing retail storefronts, and to turn the width of the office block perpendicular to the flow of the street, creating a porous, pedestrian plaza. Credit usually goes to Natalie DeBlois and Gordon Bunshaft of Skidmore, Owings & Merrill (SOM), who gave Lever House (1952) the form of a slab of aquamarine-tinted glass pulled taut across the steel frame. A stunning statement, the building opened up a void in the once-solid frontage of Park Avenue, dismaying some critics who saw it as the beginning of an erosion of the once-tangible solidity of the traditional street.[42]

In the postwar era, American corporations picked up the modernist aesthetic with gusto, and SOM emerged as the go-to national firm for office slabs of steel and glass. In their permutations on the tall office building, designers experimented with the disposition of the services and elevator core to open up as much of the office floor plan as possible, a technique anticipated by the PSFS building. Window cleaning became its own choreographed ritual and interiors designed by Florence Knoll and others set a modern tone for the open office landscape. Though driven by functionalist aesthetics, many of the postwar corporate towers were luxury affairs, including the Seagram Building, across the street from Lever House on Park Avenue, which cemented the reputation of German émigré Ludwig Mies van der Rohe as a guru and avatar of a cool minimalism. Mies came from the Bauhaus to the Illinois Institute of Technology where he designed a campus of steel and glass pavilions in the 1940s. Working on the Seagram Building with Philip Johnson, Mies set the bronze, "whiskey-colored" tower back on its lot to create a now-iconic plaza and indulged in a peculiarly modern form of ornamentation: thin steel I-beams that were attached to the vertical piers to simulate a guileless expression of the building's structure. Also included in the building was the Four Seasons restaurant, a restrained composition of rich materials.[43]

POSTWAR DECENTRALIZATION AND RENEWAL

Despite a number of high-profile investments, the "specter of decentralization" haunted cities in postwar America as some corporations moved their headquarters to the suburbs where they commissioned low-rise campuses.[44] Even as they sponsored many of the emerging sub-urban landscapes, insurance companies were also among the first to invest in urban real estate in the postwar era, erecting tall buildings to house headquarters and branch offices. Between 1948 and 1955, Newark-based Pru-dential built a series of regional home offices as part of a comprehensive plan for corporate decentralization. In Los Angeles, Jacksonville, Houston, Minneapolis, and Chicago, each office complex was guided by a consistent strat-egy to retain the iconic tower—always with PRUDENTIAL spelled across the top. But the complexes were located on a large site outside of downtown where Prudential built a mid-town campus that set the stage for a multinu-cleated urban structure.

Prudential sparked a postwar building boom in Chicago, opening the forty-one-story Mid-Western Home Office in 1952. The structure was the first air-rights project over the Illinois Central Railroad yards and terminal, new ter-ritory for the business district, and initiated the broader redevelopment of the "Illinois Center" buildings. In Boston, Prudential spon-sored a sprawling mixed-used redevelopment of another railyard site. The fifty-two-story Prudential tower, then the tallest in Boston, along with a hotel, shopping plaza, and public auditorium, was dedicated in 1965 with resi-dential towers and additional office towers to follow, anchoring a midtown office district in the Back Bay (Figure 7).[45]

Insurance companies proved reliable finan-ciers of large central city redevelopment projects. In Pittsburgh, Equitable backed the Gateway Center, a trio of cruciform-plan towers that resembled a Le Corbusier model, in the "Golden Triangle" at the confluence of the

Figure 7. Prudential Center, Boston, Charles Luckman and Associates, architects, 1965.
Courtesy of Library of Congress, LC-DIG-ppmsca-51018.

Allegheny and Monongahela Rivers where a cleared Point Park was threaded with new highways. In postwar Pittsburgh, the Aluminum Corporation of America (Alcoa) and US Steel both built new skyscrapers that reaffirmed their faith in Pittsburgh as a headquarters city, encouraged by financier and philanthropist Richard King Mellon and his advocacy of the "Pittsburgh Renaissance." Seizing the oppor-tunity to advertise their products, Alcoa con-structed an all-aluminum tower and US Steel showcased an exposed grid of steel trusses.

Influential and sometimes flamboyant real estate developers took center stage as impre-sarios of large redevelopment projects, such as William Zeckendorf of the Webb & Knapp Co.[46] Frequently working with architect I. M. Pei, Zeckendorf advanced a series of projects like the Mile High Center in Denver and Society Hill Towers in Philadelphia. Tall apartment buildings were constructed in New York and Chicago in the early 20th century; but it was not until the postwar period that developers began to experiment with very tall residential structures, advancing new visions for urban living. With Marina City, Bertrand Goldberg attempted to lure middle-class suburbanites back to the city in a condominium development with first-rate amenities, another mixed used "city-within-a-city." The twin "corn-cob"-shaped towers, each sixty-five-stories tall with the first nineteen-story spiral ramp given over to car parking and wedge-shaped residential units arrayed around its core.[47]

Pairing with real estate developer Herbert Greenwald, Ludwig Mies van der Rohe designed a pair of Lake Shore Drive towers (1951), an extension of the "Gold Coast" area of prewar tall apartment buildings. Greenwald again hired Mies, with urban planner Ludwig Hilberseimer, to design Lafayette Place for an urban renewal site adjacent to downtown Detroit, where towering apartment slabs mixed with an ensemble of low-rise garden apartments. By the late 1950s, less well-funded residential towers were built as segregated housing estates by local authorities across the country, places like Pruitt-Igoe (1954) in St. Louis and Cabrini Green Homes (1942–1962) in Chicago. In the following generation, planners came to rue these projects and the concentrations of poverty they implied. The demolition of Pruitt-Igoe began as early as 1972, and it was taken as a strong indication that the spatial tactics of modernist urbanism had run their course. In New York, a number of Title I slum clearance projects resulted in high-rise public housing estates, a trend that many other cities followed in the 1950s and 1960s.[48]

The public sector also sponsored urban redevelopment projects for their own administrative purposes, frequently organized around skyscrapers. Mies van der Rohe, for example, designed the Federal Center in Chicago as two black slabs framing a plaza with a low-slung post office building, also made of black steel and massive sheets of glass: it also featured

a high-arching sculpture of a "flamingo" made of bright red steel and designed by Alexander Calder. Walter Gropius and The Architects Collaborative (TAC) designed the John F. Kennedy Federal Building in Boston (1966), two offset twenty-six-story towers made of pre-cast concrete panels, as part of a broader Government Center urban redevelopment project. Perhaps the most impressive of these public estates was built in Albany by Governor Nelson Rockefeller and the State of New York as an urban redevelopment project: The Empire State Center comprised a suite of reinforced concrete towers, clad in stone, including the forty-four-story Corning Tower, arranged on a massive plaza and designed by Wallace K. Harrison.

The Rockefeller family was also responsible for key investments in New York City, including a 1960s expansion of Rockefeller Center with new towers on Sixth Avenue and an effort to rejuvenate lower Manhattan as a premier banking and financial district with the Chase Manhattan Bank (1961, sixty stories, Skidmore, Owings & Merrill), which featured a large sculpture by Jean Dubuffet and a sunken plaza designed by Isamu Noguchi. After a new zoning law in 1961, New York builders took advantage of floor bonuses in exchange for the provision of public plazas; some were useful, others willfully alienating. Through the Downtown Lower Manhattan Association, David Rockefeller was also involved as an advocate for the World Trade Center (1973), twin 110-story towers built by the Port Authority of New York and New Jersey on a sixteen-acre urban redevelopment site in what had been "Radio Row" but dismissed as a "commercial slum."[49]

By the middle of the 1960s, the public reception of modernist towers could be ambiguous as popular taste confronted modernist aesthetics and its implications for urban form. Working with Pietro Belluschi and the Architects Collaborative, Walter Gropius produced a tower for the New York Central Railroad that sought to capitalize on its midtown properties during a downturn for the railroad business. The fifty-nine-story Pan-Am Building (since renamed Met Life) opened in 1963. Despite its canted, "lozenge"-shaped plan, an effort to deflect its massiveness, the building, clad in pre-cast concrete panels, accentuated a kind of brutalism that was tough and dismissive to the street and insensitive to its own urban dynamics.[50]

NEW URBAN FORMS

With the harbinger of the Pan-Am Building in the late 1960s, austerity in skyscraper design gave way to bolder forms like the Knights of Columbus building in New Haven (1969), designed for the international headquarters of a Catholic fraternal organization-cum-insurance company, with exposed corten steel girders bridging monumental, cylindrical concrete towers clad in a rust-colored tile. Architect Kevin Roche achieved large open floor spaces by distributing service functions to the four corner towers, reducing the bulk of the central elevator core.

Skyscrapers in the 1970s could be glamorous. There was the trapezoidal, mirrored John Hancock Tower in Boston (1976), built to rival the Prudential Center. And the epic Sears Tower was built in Chicago (1973, now the Willis Tower), a bold, asymmetrical composition of bundled square "tubes." At 110 stories and 1,450 feet high, it was the tallest building in the world for nearly twenty-five years and the tallest in the Western Hemisphere until 2014—for what was in 1969 the largest retailer in the world. The Transamerica Building burst on the San Francisco skyline as a tapering pyramid with flared "wings" astride a web of diagonal concrete trusses (Figure 8). In the hot climates of booming sunbelt cities, sealed environments were even more important. The thirty-six-story Pennzoil Place (1975) in

Figure 8. Transamerica Building, San Francisco, William Pereira, architect, 1972.
Courtesy of Library of Congress, LC-DIG-highsm-13780.

Houston, orchestrated by developer Gerald Hines and designed by the Philip Johnson and John Burgee firm, built up the oil company's image as a pair of twin, pyramidal towers in dark, opaque glass, whose bases were enclosed by a glass atrium (Figure 9). Only with Philip Johnson's much publicized 1979 design for the AT&T building in New York did "postmodernism" claim the scene as a new design paradigm for tall buildings drawing on historical motifs, but now often oversized and almost cartoon-like. At AT&T, Johnson crowned the structure with a massive broken pediment that resembled a piece of Federalist-period furniture, a graphic rebuttal to the austerity of International Style "slabs" and heralding a new era in corporate branding. Architect Michael Graves set the tone for this aesthetic with a tower for Humana (1985), the insurance company, in Louisville, Kentucky, that featured bold colors and abstracted, playful forms.

Updates on the city-within-a-city concept turned ever more inward and focused on interiorized environments that almost entirely

Figure 9. Pennzoil Place, Houston, Philip Johnson and John Burgee, architects, 1975.
Courtesy of Library of Congress, LC-DIG-highsm-11857.

severed a connection to the street that had made Rockefeller Center so effective and urbane. Atlanta-based architect and developer John Portman designed colossal hotel, office, and shopping facilities that were worlds unto themselves with elaborate internal circulation systems and linked to highways and parking structures. Literary critic Fredric Jameson pointed to the Bonaventure Hotel in Los Angeles as a paradigm of the disorienting and self-referential condition of postmodernism in "late capitalism."[51] Portman designed major redevelopment projects such as the Renaissance Center in Detroit for patrons Ford and General Motors. His design for Atlanta's Peachtree Center included a Hyatt Hotel with a vertiginous atrium space that ran the height of the building and exposed, glass-encased elevators that theatrically bobbed up and down.[52] Developers felt that to attract capital back to the city in the 1970s, the architectural and urban spaces had to take an ambiguous, if not entirely rejecting, attitude to their surroundings, with plenty of parking to ensure that suburban commuters could limit and control their interactions with the city at large.

A building boom in the 1980s was spurred in part by real estate speculation and skyscrapers such as Trump Tower (1983), designed by Der Scutt, stood for the excess of the period. Privately owned public spaces became even more common, and glassy futurism mingled with postmodern form making in the architecture of Helmut Jahn and Cesar Pelli, for example, who called for three mirrored towers with set-back forms at the World Financial Center in Lower Manhattan—designers whose future influence was heralded by the competition for the Humana Building won by Michael Graves as well as a competition for Times Square in New York.[53]

The tragedy of September 11, 2001, and the struggle to rebuild New York's World Trade Center led to a planning competition at Ground Zero in which the symbolic function of replacing tall buildings was put front and center. Daniel Libeskind's winning entry used shard-like forms to focus on the outlines of the twin towers, which would become a memorial. By the early 21st century, an expressive techno-futurism that emphasized structural technology came to the fore, including the New York Times building (2007, fifty-two stories) designed by Renzo Piano, and Norman Foster's Hearst Tower (2006), a forty-six-story tower sprouting from the company's 1928 building as a futuristic diagonal grid. The latter was also the first major "green" high-rise building and New York's first LEED Gold skyscraper, introducing another measure of prestige for tall office buildings.

New York continues to lead in tall buildings, and Hudson Yards promises to create a new skyscraper city on the city's West Side on the air rights of the Pennsylvania Railroad yards. Recent developments have shifted toward high-profile residential developments, like the Frank Gehry-designed Beekman Tower at 8 Spruce Street, developed by Forest City Ratner (2011, seventy-six stories) and including a five-story kindergarten as well as commercial space. The undulating form resonates with the Aqua Tower in Chicago, an eighty-two-story mixed-used residential skyscraper designed by Studio Gang Architects that marks the ascendance of computer-aided, parametric design. In sunbelt cities such as Miami, Florida, and Austin, Texas, speculative high-rise apartment towers now spike the new skyline. And New York has seen the rise of super-tall and super-slender luxury residential high rises. On Fifty-Seventh Street in Manhattan, critics bemoan a "Billionaire's Row," where skinny towers leap skyward to get views for their elite inhabitants. Building on narrow sites, developers max out the allowable floor-area ratio (FAR) and take advantage of the purchase and transfer of adjacent air-rights to generate these new icons of New York's uneven affluence.[54]

While some cities thrive, others have suffered. At the end of the 20th century, Detroit became famous as a site of abandoned tall buildings downtown. In 1999, photographer and social commenter Camilo José Vergara made the controversial argument to preserve

some of those buildings as a "ruins park" that would form an "American Acropolis," a monument to the failure of speculative capitalism. By the second decade of the 21st century, however, some of those towers were being renovated and Detroit mortgage-mogul Dan Gilbert proposed constructing the city's tallest skyscraper on the former site of the Hudson's, once the tallest department store in the world that was demolished in 1998 after twenty years of vacancy.[55]

THE SKYSCRAPER'S CULTURAL AFTERLIVES

The towers of Zenith aspired above the morning mist; austere towers of steel and cement and limestone, sturdy as cliffs and delicate as silver rods. They were neither citadels nor churches, but frankly and beautifully office-buildings.
—Sinclair Lewis, *Babbitt*, 1922

The tall building plays a special role in American history as both a functional and symbolic element, central to economic life and urban development as well as an icon for urbanity that has embedded itself in the public imagination as technological and cultural marvels. From the start, a sense of the sublime was attached to the American skyscraper, a thing both inspiring and terrifying. From their viewing platforms, tall buildings offered new perspectives on the metropolis; and from afar, the skyline symbolized a heroic, cosmopolitan modernity that stood in for the life of the city itself.[56] Builders of skyscrapers have always competed with one another for prominence, often producing height comparison illustrations to show how a proposed structure would rank in a pantheon of impressive structures.

No wonder that artists have so frequently taken the tall building as their subject. Indeed, tall buildings have alternate lives as visual and literary artifacts. Works of art, poetry, literature, postcards, and advertisements have been central to public perception and efforts to grasp the monumentality, verticality, and symbolic implications of the skyscraper. Exceptional structures were represented over and over again. The Flatiron in New York captivated American impressionist painters such as Colin Campbell Cooper and Childe Hassam, as well as Edward Steichen, whose 1903 photograph of the skyscraper helped advance his claims for the art form. The Empire State Building riveted photographers such as Margaret Bourke-White, who created soaring, disorienting images of the tower and its construction workers; Berenice Abbott, for whom the building was central to her rendering of a "changing New York"; and Lewis Hine, who also focused on the human labor that lay behind the tower.[57] Georgia O'Keeffe made a series of paintings of New York skyscrapers in the 1920s that suggested their mysterious and seductive auras.

Indeed, tall buildings captured both the excitement of the growing city as well as fears of its vulnerability. The Metropolitan Life Tower in New York figured prominently in apocalyptic visions of the future and inevitable ruin of city. Filmic representations have frequently used the skyscraper as the site of potential disasters, such as *The Towering Inferno* (1974), which revolves around a fire in a fictitious 138-story "Glass Tower" in San Francisco; or *The Hunter* (1980) in which a car plummets into the Chicago River from the spiral parking ramp of Marina City.[58] The presence of King Kong at the top of the Empire State Building in 1933 galvanized the skyscraper's presence in the public consciousness.

DISCUSSION OF THE LITERATURE AND PRIMARY SOURCES

A significant part of skyscraper literature originates from professional critics, from Montgomery Schuyler at the turn of the last century, to Ada Louise Huxtable, in the late 20th century, who both assessed the search for a "skyscraper style." A strong tradition among architectural historians emphasizes formal analysis—consider William Jordy's reflections

on the "laconic splendor of the metal frame" with respect to the Seagram Building and other modernist towers—and urbanistic critique—such as Vincent Scully's discourse on Lever House and the Pan Am Tower as "The Death of the Street."[59]

Early skyscraper historians often focused on materials and technology, sometimes identifying in the Chicago skyscrapers the seeds of a modern architecture.[60] A range of popular books marvels at the construction and operation of tall buildings, often amounting to celebrations of the building type. Along similar lines are the popular histories of individual buildings, the competition between builders, and the race for the tallest; these books reveal more about the personalities and politics behind skyscraper building.[61]

Scholarship has moved from debates over "firsts" and discussions around material and technology to rich explorations of the financial, geographical, and cultural dimensions of skyscrapers, demystifying these buildings as products of hard-nosed financial speculation. Architectural historians have also focused on specific buildings in efforts to generate broader analyses of architectural culture, the politics of patronage, and the changing city.[62] The literature on postwar urban renewal has begun to take tall buildings seriously, along with the formative role of real estate developers.[63]

Leading architects such as Louis Sullivan have attracted a wide range of scholarly interest and key buildings such as the Empire State Building continue to fascinate professional historians and the public at large. More than sixty years after it was completed, the *Notes on Construction of Empire State Building* surfaced, written and compiled in the office of the builders Starrett Brothers and Eken.[64] Both Paul Starrett and William A. Starrett wrote autobiographies that chronicled their building triumphs.[65]

Recent scholarship has demonstrated a sensitivity to the life cycles of tall buildings, from the symbolic politics of dedication ceremonies to physical and economic obsolescence.[66] Social historians have examined the social world of the tall building as gendered work-place.[67] Literary studies of the skyscraper have greatly enriched the sense that these buildings played in popular culture, and scholars continue to push the frontier of cultural studies of the tall building. In *The Black Skyscraper* (2017), for example, literary critic Adrienne Brown exposes another dimension of the skyscraper as part and parcel of the production of race in America.[68]

Skyscrapers have always played an even larger role than the already substantial facts of its production, and the most persuasive skyscraper narratives will work to place them in a suite of contexts.[69] Many resources for scholars of skyscrapers and tall buildings exist, including the archives and drawings of individual architects and architectural firms; the corporate archive of patrons, builders, real estate developers, and public agencies, like urban redevelopment agencies in the 1950s and 1960s. Reports, reactions, and reviews, and perceptions of tall buildings are documented in newspapers, magazines, and journals, including a range of materials searchable through the Avery Index, which includes architectural periodicals. There is at least one museum dedicated entirely to the tall building; in 1997, the Skyscraper Museum was founded in in a temporary space in Lower Manhattan and since 2004 has a permanent home in Battery Park City in the ground-floor of a thirty-eight-story condominium tower.[70]

DIGITAL MATERIALS

The Skyscraper Museum. https://www.skyscraper.org/.

Ten & Taller, 1874-1900. https://www.skyscraper.org/tenandtaller/index.php.

FURTHER READING

Abramson, Daniel. *Skyscraper Rivals: The AIG Building and the Architecture of Wall Street.* New York: Princeton Architectural Press, 2001.

Brown, Adrienne. *The Black Skyscraper: Architecture and the Perception of Race.* Baltimore: Johns Hopkins University Press, 2017.

Clausen, Meredith. *The Pan Am Building and the Shattering of the Modernist Dream.* Cambridge, MA: MIT Press, 2004.

Condit, Carl. *The Chicago School of Architecture: A History of Commercial and Public Buildings in the Chicago Area, 1875-1925.* Chicago: University of Chicago Press, 1964.

Fenske, Gail. *The Skyscraper and the City: The Woolworth Building and the Making of Modern New York.* Chicago: University of Chicago Press, 2008.

Fine, Lisa M. *The Souls of the Skyscraper: Female Clerical Workers in Chicago, 1870-1930.* Philadelphia: Temple University Press, 1990.

Flowers, Benjamin. *Skyscraper: Politics and Power of Building New York City in the Twentieth Century.* Philadelphia: University of Pennsylvania Press, 2009.

Gibbs, Kenneth Tunney. *Business Architectural Imagery in America, 1870-1930.* Ann Arbor, MI: UMI Research Press, 1984.

Huxtable, Ada Louise. *The Tall Building Artistically Reconsidered: The Search for a Skyscraper Style.* Berkeley: University of California Press, 1984.

Landau, Sarah Bradford, and Carl W. Condit. *Rise of the New York Skyscraper, 1865-1913.* New Haven, CT: Yale University Press, 1996.

Leslie, Thomas. *Chicago Skyscrapers, 1871-1934.* Urbana: University of Illinois Press, 2013.

Moudry, Roberta, ed., *The American Skyscraper: Cultural Histories.* New York: Cambridge University Press, 2005.

Rubin, Elihu. *Insuring the City: The Prudential Center and the Postwar Urban Landscape.* New Haven, CT: Yale University Press, 2012.

Solomonson, Katherine. *The Chicago Tribune Tower Competition.* New York: Cambridge University Press, 2010.

Willis, Carol. *Form Follows Finance: Skyscrapers and Skylines in New York and Chicago.* New York: Princeton Architectural Press, 1995.

NOTES

1. Sarah Bradford Landau and Carl W. Condit, *Rise of the New York Skyscraper, 1865-1913* (New Haven, CT: Yale University Press, 1996).

2. Kenneth Tunney Gibbs, *Business Architectural Imagery in America, 1870–1930* (Ann Arbor, MI: UMI Research Press, 1984); and Winston Weisman, "A New View of Skyscraper History," *The Rise of An American Architecture*, ed. Edward Kaufmann Jr. (New York: Praeger, 1970), 125.

3. Sarah Bradford Landau, *George B. Post, Architect: Picturesque Designer and Determined Realist* (New York: Monacelli Press, 1998).

4. See Ten and Taller; Elizabeth C. Cromley, *Alone Together: A History of New York's Early Apartments* (Ithaca, NY: Cornell University Press, 1989); and Paul Groth, *Living Downtown: The History of Residential Hotels in the United States* (Berkeley: University of California Press, 1994).

5. William Cronon, *Nature's Metropolis: Chicago and the Great West*; Harold M. Mayer and Richard C. Wade, *Chicago: Growth of a Metropolis* (Chicago: University of Chicago Press, 1969); and Daniel Bluestone, *Constructing Chicago* (New Haven, CT: Yale University Press, 1991), 114.

6. Thomas Leslie, *Chicago Skyscrapers, 1871–1934* (Urbana: University of Illinois Press, 2013); Carl Condit, *The Chicago School of Architecture* (Chicago: University of Chicago Press, 1964); "The Father of All Skyscrapers," *Scientific American* (May 1932), 291; Rosemarie Haag Bletter, "Invention of the Skyscraper: Notes on Its Diverse Histories," *Assemblage*, no. 2 (February 1987): 110–117; and Donald Friedman, "Hidden Intricacies: The Development of Modern Building Skeletons," *APT Bulletin: The Journal of Preservation Technology* 43, no. 4 (2012): 13–21.

7. Carol Willis, *Form Follows Finance: Skyscrapers and Skylines in New York and Chicago* (New York: Princeton Architectural Press, 1995), 24.

8. Robert Bruegmann, *The Architects and the City, Holabird & Roche of Chicago, 1880–1918* (Chicago: University of Chicago Press, 1997), 83.

9. Bruegmann, *The Architects and the City*, 65; and Robert Bruegmann, "The Marquette Building and the Myth of the Chicago School," *Threshold* (Fall 1991): 6023.

10. Thomas Hines, *Burnham of Chicago: Architect and Planner* (Chicago: University of Chicago Press, 2009).

11. "A City Under One Roof," *Scientific American*, February 10, 1894; and Bluestone, *Constructing Chicago*, 105.

12. Edward W. Wolner, "Chicago's Fraternity Temples: The Origins of Skyscraper Rhetoric and the First

of the World's Tallest Office Buildings," *The American Skyscraper: Cultural Histories*, ed. Roberta Moudry (Cambridge: Cambridge University Press, 2005): 98–119.

13. The Masonic Building was in competition with the Independent Order of Odd Fellows, which planned an even taller structure designed by the firm of Adler and Sullivan; Weisman, "A New View of Skyscraper History."

14. Bruegmann, *The Architects and the City*, 99; and Henry Blake Fuller, *The Cliff Dwellers* (New York: Harper and Brothers, 1893).

15. Wilson, *The City Beautiful*; Hines, *Burnham of Chicago*.

16. Montgomery Schuyler, *American Architecture and Other Writings*, ed. William H. Jordy and Ralph Coe (Cambridge, MA: The Belknap Press of Harvard University Press, 1961), 446.

17. Ernest Flagg, "Is New York Becoming a City of Canyons and Ravines?" *New York Times*, December 29, 1907.

18. Robert Fogelson, *Downtown: Its Rise and Fall, 1880–1950* (New Haven, CT: Yale University Press, 2001), 114; Mona Domosh, *Invented Cities: The Creation of Landscape in Nineteenth-Century New York and Boston* (New Haven, CT: Yale University Press, 1996); and Michael Holleran and Robert Fogelson, "'The Sacred Skyline': Boston's Opposition to the Skyscraper," Working Paper 9 (Cambridge, MA: Center for Real Estate Development, Massachusetts Institute of Technology, 1987).

19. Louis Sullivan, "The Tall Office Buildings Artistically Considered," *Lippincott's Monthly Magazine* 339 (March 1896): 403–409.

20. Bluestone, *Constructing Chicago*, 143.

21. Louis Sullivan, "The Tall Office Buildings Artistically Considered"; and Sigfried Giedion, *Space, Time, and Architecture: The Growth of a New Tradition* (Cambridge, MA: Harvard University Press, 1947), 388.

22. Roberta Moudry, "The Corporate and the Civic: Metropolitan Life's Home Office Building," *The American Skyscraper: Cultural Histories*, ed. Roberta Moudry (Cambridge: Cambridge University Press, 2005), 120–146.

23. Marquis James, *The Metropolitan: A Study in Business Growth* (New York: Viking, 1947), 174.

24. Gail Fenske, *The Skyscraper and the City: The Woolworth Building and the Making of Modern*

New York (Chicago: University of Chicago Press, 2008); and Willis, *Form Follows Finance*, 147.

25. Sally A. Kitt Chappell, *Architecture and Planning of Graham, Anderson, Probst and White, 1912–1936: Transforming Tradition* (Chicago: University of Chicago Press, 1992).

26. Giedion, *Space, Time and Architecture*, 391.

27. Katherine Solomonson, *The Chicago Tribune Tower Competition* (Cambridge: Cambridge University Press, 2010); and Harvey Wiley Corbett, "The American Radiator Building," *Architectural Record* 55, no. 5 (1924): 473–477.

28. Keith D. Revell, "Regulating the Landscape: Real Estate Values, City Planning, and the 1916 Zoning Ordinance," in *The Landscape of Modernity: New York City, 1900–1940*, ed. David Ward and Olivier Zunz (Baltimore: Johns Hopkins University Press, 1997); and Norbert Messler, *The Art Deco Skyscraper in New York* (New York: Peter Lang, 1986).

29. Jewel Stern and John A. Stuart, *Ely Jacques Kahn, Architect: Beaux-Arts to Modernism in New York* (New York: W. W. Norton, 2006).

30. Daniel Abramson, *Skyscraper Rivals: The AIG Building and the Architecture of Wall Street* (New York: Princeton Architectural Press, 2001).

31. W. C. Clark and J. L. Kingston, *The Skyscraper: A Study in the Economic Eight of Modern Office Buildings* (New York: American Institute of Steel Construction, 1930); and Ely Jacques Kahn, "Economics of the Skyscraper," *Architectural Record* 63, no. 4 (April, 1928): 298–301.

32. Willis, *Form Follows Finance*.

33. Hugh Ferriss, *The Metropolis of Tomorrow* (New York: Ives Washburn), 1929.

34. Robert Fishman, *Urban Utopias of Twentieth Century: Ebenezer Howard, Frank Lloyd Wright, and Le Corbusier* (New York: Basic Books, 1977).

35. Neil Levine, *The Urbanism of Frank Lloyd Wright* (Princeton, NJ: Princeton University Press, 2016).

36. Edward W. Wolner, "Design and Civic Identity in Cincinnati's Carew Tower Complex," *Journal of the Society of Architectural Historians* 51, no. 1 (March 1992): 35–47.

37. L. Andrew Reinhard, "What Is the Rockefeller Radio City?" *Architectural Record* 69, no. 4 (1931) 276–281; James Marston Fitch and Diana S. Waite, *Grand Central Terminal and Rockefeller Center: A Historic-Critical Estimate of Their Significance* (New York: New York State Parks and Recreation, 1974); and Carol Herselle Krinsky, *Rockefeller Center* (New York: Oxford University Press, 1978).

38. William Jordy, *American Buildings and Their Architects: The Impact of European Modernism in the Mid-Twentieth Century* (Garden City, NY: Doubleday & Company, Inc., 1972), 87–164.

39. Meredith Clausen, "Belluschi and the Equitable Building in History," *Journal of the Society of Architectural Historians*, 50, no. 2 (June 1991): 109–129.

40. Banham, *Architecture of the Well-Tempered Environment* (Chicago: University of Chicago Press, 1969).

41. Samuel Zipp, *Manhattan Projects: The Rise and Fall of Urban Renewal in Cold War New York* (New York: Oxford University Press, 2010).

42. Vincent Scully, "Death of the Street." *Perspecta* 8 (1963): 91–96.

43. Benjamin Flowers, *Skyscraper: The Politics and Power of Building New York City in the Twentieth Century* (Philadelphia: University of Pennsylvania Press, 2009); Phyllis Lambert, *Building Seagram* (New Haven, CT: Yale University Press, 2013); William Jordy, *American Buildings and Their Architects*, 221–278; and William H. White, *The Social Life of Small Urban Spaces* (Washington, DC: Conservation Foundation, 1980).

44. Louise Mozingo, *Pastoral Capitalism: A History of Suburban Corporate Landscapes* (Cambridge, MA: MIT Press, 2011).

45. Elihu Rubin, *Insuring the City: The Prudential Center and the Postwar Urban Landscape* (New Haven, CT: Yale University Press, 2012).

46. Sara Stevens, *Developing Expertise: Architecture and Real Estate in Metropolitan America* (New Haven, CT: Yale University Press, 2016).

47. Igor Marjanović and Katerina Rüedi Ray, *Marina City: Bertrand Goldberg's Urban Vision* (New York: Princeton Architectural Press, 2010).

48. Katharine G. Bristol, "The Pruitt-Igoe Myth," *Journal of Architectural Education* 44, no. 3 (May 1991): 163–171; and Arnold R. Hirsch, *Making the Second Ghetto: Race and Housing in Chicago, 1940–1960* (Chicago: University of Chicago Press, 1998). Samuel Zipp, *Manhattan Projects: The Rise and Fall of Urban Renewal in Cold War New York* (New York: Oxford University Press, 2010); Nicholas Dagen Bloom, *Public Housing That Worked: New York in the Twentieth Century*

(Philadelphia: University of Pennsylvania Press, 2008); and Lawrence Vale, *Purging the Poorest: Public Housing and the Design Politics of Twice-Cleared Communities* (Chicago: University of Chicago Press, 2013).

49. Victoria Newhouse, *Wallace K. Harrison, Architect* (New York: Rizzoli, 1989); Jerold S. Kayden, *Privately Owned Public Space: The New York City Experience* (New York: John Wiley, 2000); Flowers, *Skyscraper*; Eric Darton, *Divided We Fall: A Biography of New York's World Trade Center* (New York: Basic Books, 1999); and Danny Lyon, *Destruction of Lower Manhattan* (New York: Macmillan, 1969).

50. Meredith Clausen, *The Pan Am Building and the Shattering of the Modernist Dream* (Cambridge, MA: MIT Press, 2004).

51. Fredric Jameson, *Postmodern: Cultural Logic of Late Capitalism* (Durham, NC: Duke University Press, 1998).

52. Charles Rice, *Interior Urbanism: Architecture, John Portman and Downtown America* (London: Bloomsbury Academic, 2016).

53. Ada Louise Huxtable, *The Tall Building Artistically Reconsidered: The Search for a Skyscraper Style* (Berkeley: University of California Press, 1984).

54. In 2013–2014, the Skyscraper Museum created the exhibit "Sky High: The Logic of Luxury," which addressed this emerging phenomenon and has continued to follow the evolution of New York's "Super-Slenders"; "Why 57th Street Is the Supertall Tower Mecca of New York," *Curbed*, September 25, 2014. For a critique, see Kevin Baker, "The Death of a Once Great City: The Fall of New York and the Urban Crisis of Affluence," *Harper's Magazine* (July 2018).

55. Camilo José Vergara, *American Ruins*; and John Gallagher, "Gilbert, Duggan, Snyder Headline Groundbreaking for Detroit's New Tallest Skyscraper," *Detroit Free Press*, December 14, 2017.

56. David E. Nye, "The Sublime and the Skyline: The New York Skyscraper," *The American Skyscraper: Cultural Histories*, ed. Roberta Moudry (Cambridge: Cambridge University Press, 2005): 255–270.

57. Berenice Abbott, *Changing New York* (New York: E. P. Dutton, 1939).

58. Nick Yablon, *Untimely Ruins: An Archaeology of American Urban Modernity, 1819–1919* (Chicago: University of Chicago Press, 2009); and

Max Page, *The City's End: Two Centuries of Fantasies, Fears and Premonitions of New York's Destruction* (New Haven, CT: Yale University Press, 2010).

59. Ada Louise Huxtable, *The Tall Building Artistically Reconsidered*; Schuyler, *American Architecture*; Paul Goldberger, *The Skyscraper* (New York: Knopf, 1983); Jordy, *American Buildings and Their Architects*; and Scully, "Death of the Street."

60. Condit, *The Chicago School of Architecture*.

61. Didier Cornille, *Who Built That? Skyscrapers: An Introduction and Their Architects* (New York: Princeton Architectural Press, 2014); Kate Ascher, *The Heights: Anatomy of a Skyscraper* (New York: Penguin, 2011); Judith Dupré and Adrian Smith, *Skyscrapers: A History of the World's Most Extraordinary Buildings* (New York: Black Dog & Leventhal, 2013); John Hill, *How to Build a Skyscraper* (London: Quarto, 2017); Neal Bascomb, *Higher: A Historic Race to the Sky and the Making of a City* (New York: Doubleday, 2003); Alice Sparberg Alexiou, *The Flatiron: The New York Landmark and the Incomparable City That Arose with It* (New York: St. Martin's Press, 2010); and Jim Rasenberger, *High Steel: The Daring Men Who Built the World's Greatest Skyline, 1881 to the Present* (New York: HarperCollins, 2004).

62. Gail Fenske, *The Skyscraper and the City: The Woolworth Building and the Making of Modern New York* (Chicago: University of Chicago Press, 2008).

63. Rubin, *Insuring the City*; Stevens, *Developing Expertise*; and Zipp, *Manhattan Projects*.

64. David S. Andrew, *Louis Sullivan and the Polemics of Modern Architecture: The Present Against the Past* (Urbana: University of Illinois Press, 1985); and Carol Willis, ed., *Building the Empire State* (New York: W. W. Norton, 1998).

65. William Aiken Starrett, *Skyscrapers and the Men Who Build Them* (New York: Scribner, 1928); and Paul Starrett, *Changing the Skyline: An Autobiography* (New York: McGraw-Hill, 1938).

66. Daniel M. Abramson, *Obsolescence: An Architectural History* (Chicago: University of Chicago Press, 2016); and Neil Harris, *Building Lives: Constructing Rites and Passages* (New Haven, CT: Yale University Press, 1999).

67. Lisa M. Fine, *The Souls of the Skyscraper: Female Clerical Workers in Chicago, 1870–1930* (Philadelphia: Temple University Press, 1990); and

Angel Kwolek-Folland, *Engendering Business: Men and Women in the Corporate Office, 1870–1930* (Baltimore: Johns Hopkins University Press, 1994).

68. Adrienne Brown, *The Black Skyscraper: Architecture and the Perception of Race* (Baltimore: Johns Hopkins University Press, 2017).

69. Roberta Moudry, ed., *The American Skyscraper: Cultural Histories* (New York: Cambridge University Press, 2005).

70. The Skyscraper Museum.

Elihu Rubin

Figure 1. Carcasses from the three and a half million horses that worked in city streets added to the squalor of urban America.
Courtesy of the Library of Congress, LC-DIG-det-4a09038.

THE CITY BEAUTIFUL MOVEMENT

UGLY, DIRTY, AND UNHEALTHY CITIES GENERATE UTOPIAN VISIONS

American cities grew rapidly during the 19th century and became centers of industrial production. Only sixteen cities exceeded 50,000 in population in 1860; by 1910, more than one hundred did. Poverty and social unrest, crime and overcrowding, and uncontrolled growth overburdened these cities. Uncollected garbage, human and animal excrement, and industrial by-products filled the streets, compromised water supplies, and emitted a pervasive stench. Cholera, typhoid, and diphtheria ravaged urban populations. Coal smoke and other pollutants fouled city air and led to respiratory ailments. Solid wastes, buried underground or dumped in huge slag heaps, further compromised both health and quality of life. The clang and grind of machinery, snarls of traffic, networks of overhead wires, construction sites, vacant lots, and decaying buildings further blighted the landscape. In the last decade of the century, an avalanche of commercial advertising added to the clutter and chaos of city streets.[1]

Over the course of the 19th century, sanitarians and physicians, landscape architects and civil engineers, and business leaders and citizen activists clamored for new municipal powers and services to address environmental threats. In the middle decades of the 19th century, the courts expanded municipal powers to take property for a public purpose under eminent domain, regulate private and public nuisances, and wield police power to protect the safety, health, and convenience of citizens. Such legal innovations made possible the construction of waterworks, sewers, and the paving of streets. Municipal governments also regulated building practices and offensive trades, demolished buildings and removed obstructions, seized property through eminent domain, and constructed public parks. New public agencies took over from private agencies the responsibility for providing clean water, removing waste, protecting air quality, and improving conditions in the slums.[2]

A series of terrifying epidemics in the 1870s revealed that much still had to be done. Improved waterworks and the spread of the flush toilet added vast quantities of wastewater to city streets. The filth or miasma theory of disease held decaying organic wastes and stagnant water responsible for disease. Beset by the highest death rate in the nation, Chicago pioneered the comprehensive sanitary sewer system in the 1850s. But widespread adoption of sewers only came in the 1880s, driven by continuing epidemics and increasing acceptance of the germ theory of disease. By 1910, virtually every city had a sewer system. Improved standards of street cleaning supplemented sewer construction, especially after George Waring's spectacular success in New York City beginning in 1894.[3]

The City Beautiful movement emerged against this backdrop of environmental reforms. City Beautiful activists embraced a strategy of positive environmentalism, believing that the improvement of individual character and civic life depended on improved environments rather than rigid behavioral standards and coercive measures. Social progress, as the philosopher John Dewey summed up the new consensus, depended on "the intelligent selection and determination of the environments in which we act." A moral environmentalism had long shaped efforts at sanitation, under the assumption that the poor and working class could not possibly lead upright lives surrounded by dirt and disorder. But now the strategy focused less on deficiencies of individual character and more on the inadequacies of the physical city. Extended to the wider city, positive environmentalism demanded not just sanitation, but parks and playgrounds, uplifting civic spaces, art, and pageants, urban transit and lighting, and unified railway stations.[4]

Over the course of the 19th century, the successes of sanitarians and engineers in constructing urban systems raised expectations about technological solutions to urban problems. Over the same period, communitarians built and utopians wrote about settlements that combined the benefits of the machine with the qualities of a garden. As one utopian novelist put it in 1902, the city should be "treated as the canvas of a painter or the marble of a sculptor"; everything should be done "to enhance the beauty of any part of the growing city, or to increase its convenience or the comfort or welfare of its inhabitants." A city of convenience and beauty promised to reconcile the machine and the garden.[5]

By the end of the century, public opinion, literary utopias, and the aspirations of environmental reformers coalesced around the ideal of a technologically sophisticated city set within and attuned to the rhythms of nature. The authors of urban utopians built on the accomplishments of 19th-century reformers and anticipated the vision of the City Beautiful. Perfect sewage and water distribution, cooling and heating, rapid transit, and instantaneous communication turned these imagined cities into what another utopian novelist called "immense palaces nicely intermingled with fragrant gardens and luxuriant parks—there being no dirty streets or unsightly habitations of any description." The utopians' civic centers, parks, parkways, and boulevards fit into many of the City Beautiful plans to come.[6]

FEARS OF URBAN DESTRUCTION AND A PHILOSOPHY OF PUBLIC PARKS

The City Beautiful vision originated out of 19th-century accomplishments, including piped water and underground sewers, paved and lighted streets, street cleaning and trash collection, zoning laws and public health regulations, and parks and playgrounds. But the City Beautiful also responded to darker fears of urban destruction. As American cities filled with immigrants and migrants who were unprepared for urban life, the middle classes fled to outlying suburbs. Overcrowding, physical deterioration, and inadequate municipal services turned neighborhoods into slums. Crime punctuated everyday life and occasionally escalated into large-scale violence. "If the club of the policeman, knocking out the brains of the rioter will answer," a religious weekly editorialized in 1877, "then all well and good; but if it does not . . ., then bullets and bayonets, canister and grape . . . constitute the one remedy." Such visions isolated the volatile city as a threat to civilization.[7]

Sensational newspapers, crime magazines, and dime novels added to the image of the urban menace. With advances in flash photography, exposés like Jacob Riis's *How the Other Half Lives* (1890) provided the affluent with glimpses of places into which they rarely ventured. A suburbanizing middle class, increasingly unfamiliar with the actual slums, devoured the dystopian novels of urban destruction that arose alongside the utopian literature of the period. Ignatius Donnelly's fictional destruction of New York City, *Caesar's Columns* (1890), depicted a nightmare of violence between greedy capitalists and the debased poor; by 1906, it had sold half a million copies. Nightmare images of urban life even appeared within the utopian literature. Julian West, the fictional hero of Edward Bellamy's influential novel *Looking Backward, 1888–2000*, awoke in 2000 to find that Boston had become a city of "large open squares filled with trees, along which statues glistened and fountains flashed in the late-afternoon sun." But West also recalled in a dream that Boston had once reeked "with the effluvia of a slave ship's between decks" and been infested with "half-clad brutalized children," like "starving bands of mongrel curs" fighting over garbage.[8]

Labor unrest lent a hard edge to urban disorder, exploding in massive waves of strikes and armed encounters. Living close to their work in polluting factories and overcrowded into substandard housing, industrial workers harbored grievances related to both urban workplace and neighborhood. When Riis explored "the foul core of New York's slums," he described the city's poor as "shiftless, destructive, and stupid," just "what the tenements have made them." The "sea of a mighty population, held in galling fetters, heaves uneasily in the tenements," Riis wrote; the city had already "felt the swell of its resistless flood. If it rises once more, no human power may avail to check it." Riis was referring to New York City's 1863 draft riots, but economic depression and labor unrest intensified such fears in the 1890s.[9]

Political corruption, especially at the municipal level, appeared to paralyze public efforts to address urban ills. Although modern historians point to the unheralded triumph of municipal governance, middle-class reformers at the time focused on corrupt bosses collecting bribes and herding ignorant and immigrant voters to the polls. Public service corporations, the agencies upon which improved environments depended, stood at the center of municipal corruption, distributing bribes to secure franchises to supply transit, electricity, and other utilities. While reformers wished for a spirit of civic loyalty to redeem the city, they also knew that American cities lacked the landmarks, symbols, and traditions that might kindle such loyalty. Little in these cities engaged the emotions, the senses, or the imagination—"no magic to stir men's blood," in the phrase attributed to Daniel Burnham by his editor and biographer Charles Moore.[10]

At the core of the City Beautiful impulse lay a belief that a more attractive and inspiring urban environment would inspire a surge of civic loyalty. The advocates of public parks had already pointed the way. In the 1840s, the landscape architect Andrew Jackson Downing called for public parks to bring the benefits of a middle landscape—neither urban grid nor wilderness, but nature ordered and improved by human effort—into the heart of the city. Downing extolled the public park as "republican in its very idea and tendency," as it "raises up the man of the working men to the same level of enjoyment with the man of leisure and accomplishment." The park, Downing added, "would soften and humanize the rude, educate and enlighten the ignorant, and give continual enjoyment to the educated." In mixing affluent urbanites and the lower classes, the public park provided one affirmation of an organic, interdependent society in an otherwise competitive urban environment.[11]

Public parks proved popular, both among real estate speculators, who recognized their impact on surrounding land values, and the citizenry at large that flocked to them. But no one did more to advance the cause of parks and articulate their larger public purpose than the landscape architect Frederick Law Olmsted.

Alarmed by the pace of urbanization and the attendant coarsening of individual character and degradation of the physical environment, Olmsted argued that "the further progress of civilization is to depend mainly upon the influences by which men's minds and characters will be affected while living in large towns." The city promoted "a peculiarly hard sort of selfishness," but the park provided a positive environment that brought people together so that each contributed to "the pleasure of the others, all helping to the greater happiness of each." The park also would exert a "harmonizing and refining influence" on the urban masses, Olmsted believed, "favorable to courtesy, self-control, and temperance."[12]

The designer of public parks in thirty US cities including Boston, Buffalo, Chicago, Montreal, New York City, and San Francisco, Olmsted left a multifaceted legacy that City Beautiful advocates built upon. Aside from his contributions to positive environmentalism, Olmsted championed massive public works that required heavy municipal expense, encouraged the collaboration of artists and professionals, and experimented with strategies for the control of crowds and traffic—all hallmarks of the City Beautiful movement. Extending his vision to include systems of parks, parkways, and boulevards designed to guide and direct urban development, Olmsted pioneered the organic understanding of the city that informed this movement. Olmsted's consulting practice also trained and nurtured many of the planning consultants of the City Beautiful period.[13]

THE WHITE CITY

Near the end of his career, Olmsted designed the grounds of "the White City" at the heart of the World's Columbian Exposition in Chicago in 1893. Although he later expressed dismay over the neoclassical design and architecture of the White City, he had used such elements in his parks, adding one more item to his legacy. But Olmsted's desire to keep park design in the hands of experts and park management in the hands of professional administrators may best explain his participation in the exposition planning. He had long chafed under his association with what he saw as venal politicians, and he defended his profession as a means for men of intellect and vision to exert an influence usually denied them in municipal affairs. Tapped to recommend a site by a public commission of appointed officials, Olmsted expressed pleasure at the acceptance of his recommendations. The commissioners, he wrote, "could not be led to believe that we should have given this advice without having, as experts, sound reasons for doing it.... Comparing this experience with some in my earlier professional life, I can but think that it manifests an advance in civilization." Olmsted must have valued this deference to his professional expertise.[14]

As Olmsted recognized, the World's Columbian Exposition provided a model not only of what a city should look like, but how it should be governed. Authorized by an act of Congress in celebration of the 400th anniversary of Columbus's voyage to America and ostensibly overseen by a public commission, the project actually answered to a private corporation directed by Chicago capitalists. Winning the trust of the corporate directors, the prominent Chicago architect Daniel H. Burnham quickly became the undisputed manager of the exposition. Burnham oversaw the transformation of nearly 700 acres of swampy land on Chicago's southern lakeshore, managing scores of architects and other professionals. Dredged and filled according to Olmsted's plan, the site accommodated four hundred buildings. At its center stood the Court of Honor, a collection of neoclassical buildings fronting Olmsted's reflecting pool and dubbed "the White City." Burnham's benevolent autocracy ensured the elimination of billboards, the strict control of signage and other communications, and the discrete isolation of deliveries. The exposition's Columbian Guard kept the peace without interference from corrupt or partisan politicians.[15]

In terms of physical appearance and function, the White City represented a culmination of advances in urban design, aesthetics, and engineering, as well as in sanitation, transportation, illumination, and public safety. Filtered drinking water, sewage treatment, convenient toilets, and nightly sweeping and cleaning of streets and sidewalks made the White City a wonder. The landscaping and the design of buildings, arising from the collaboration of architects, sculptors, mural painters, and landscape architects, also built on the experiments of the past twenty years. The Court of Honor reflected the principles of the Parisian Écoles des Beaux-Arts and its emphasis on proportion, scale, and the balanced arrangement of forms. Although composed of temporary structures faced with a white plaster called "staff," the White City left a lasting impression.[16]

For all its advances in urban utilities, the White City made its greatest contribution in showing that cities could be beautiful. Both the architecture and Olmsted's landscapes united functionality with visual pleasure. Above all,

Figure 2. The White City's Grand Court, pictured here during the twenty-second anniversary of the Chicago Fire, inspired visitors to believe that cities could be beautiful.
Photo by C. D. Arnold, Creative Commons license (public domain).

the White City invoked an emotional response, akin to religious awe, that American cities so conspicuously lacked. Like many future members of the City Beautiful movement, Burnham retained a Protestant religiosity, even a mystical strain, that expressed itself in an effort to inculcate higher ideals of civic spirit in elites, and especially in the masses. Commentators marveled on the good behavior of the "obscure and anonymous myriads of unknown laborers" who attended the fair. "It seemed as though the beauty of the place," a Protestant minister wrote, "brought gentleness, happiness, and self-respect to its visitors." Whether order and decorum amounted to civic spirit, the White City heartened those who would redeem the American city.[17]

The designers of the White City failed to articulate a strategy of comprehensive planning, or even suggest how its successes might be applied to transform actual cities. But they did encourage the belief that an improved urban environment might lead to an improved city and citizenry. The White City demonstrated the potential of combining environmental reforms focused on sanitation and parks to those related to civic art and design. The effect stunned and inspired visitors who saw an ideal image of a future city. The White City energized new and existing municipal improvement associations to clean up and beautify cities across the nation. Writing in 1899, when the term *City Beautiful* first came into common usage, Charles Mulford Robinson rejected the claim that the White City "created the subsequent aesthetic effort in municipal life." But he agreed that it "immensely strengthened, quickened, and encouraged" those efforts.[18]

THE CITY BEAUTIFUL MOVEMENT TAKES SHAPE IN A PLAN FOR THE NATION'S CAPITAL

The City Beautiful movement arose during the decade following the Chicago exposition. Improved economic conditions and a lessening of social conflicts in the final years of the

1890s gave the movement an optimistic tenor. As park planning and civic art coalesced, they also combined with a campaign for municipal improvement. Before the Civil War, village improvement societies encouraged civic pride and a sense of community by beautifying entire communities; these organizations provided a foundation for later municipal improvement programs. Engaging citizens (especially middle-class women), village improvement went beyond sanitation and parks to include tree-lined streets and walks, attractive shops and railroad stations, and trim and well-maintained residential districts. In the 1890s, municipal improvement extended this union of beauty and utility to larger cities and added the additional goals of promoting civic responsibility and efficiency in government.[19]

As municipal improvers pursued comprehensive beautification and political renewal, landscape architects felt their influence waning. The American Park and Outdoor Art Association (APOAA), founded in 1897, sought to reverse that decline. After a brief resistance, the organization embraced active recreation and urban beauty as part of its goals. By 1902, the APOAA sought federation with other civic associations, especially the National League of Improvement Associations (NLIA). Founded in 1900, the NLIA changed its name to the American League for Civic Improvement (ALCI) in 1901. The change in name and shift of its headquarters from Springfield, Illinois, to Chicago signaled its enlarged ambitions. In 1903, the APOAA and the ALCI, both headed by informed laypeople respectful of professional expertise, united to form the American Civic Association (ACA). As the major organizational expression of the City Beautiful movement, the ACA united citizen activists and professionals and raised hopes for a comprehensive remaking of American cities.[20]

An essential element of urban beautification, civic art depended on the collaboration of architects, sculptors, and painters in adorning public parks and the facades and interior spaces of public buildings. New York City artists, building on the fame of the White City that many of them had helped to create, established their city's Municipal Art Society in 1893. Under the motto "to make us love our city, we must make our city lovely," and inspired as much by European urbanism as the White City, civic art advocates made war on crass commercialism and heedless destruction and spread their ideas nationwide. Moving from piecemeal efforts to more expansive plans and embracing the catchphrase *City Beautiful*, the drive for civic art spread the idea of ensemble design and the grouping of public buildings to San Francisco, Cleveland, Chicago, and beyond.[21]

Municipal improvement and civic art articulated an urban conception of beauty and, when combined with park planning, suggested the potential for comprehensive city planning. In 1901, Robinson published his influential codification of the municipal improvement and civic art credos, *The Improvement of Towns and Cities*, in the hope that "civic art's transforming touch" would be "carried into every portion of the community." Only a year later, the 1902 McMillan Plan for Washington, DC, provided a dramatic example of Robinson's hopes by combining civic art and park planning into a scheme of municipal improvement that also engaged transit, slum clearance, playgrounds, and scenic preservation.[22]

Even as Washington became the center of a more assertive federal government in the new century, Pierre L'Enfant's 1791 plan for a great capital city lay in tatters. L'Enfant's grand Mall, designed as a unified space, was broken up by gardens, intruded upon by a railroad station, and crossed by a railroad itself. But the centennial celebration of the removal of the nation's capital to the Potomac provided an opportunity to resurrect L'Enfant's plan. Initially, however, nothing of the sort was contemplated. As chairman of the Senate Committee on the District of Columbia, the powerful Republican senator James McMillan simply hoped to eliminate grade crossings in the city. McMillan proposed to allow the

Baltimore and Potomac Railroad to build a new terminal on the Mall and to cross the Mall above grade on a twenty-foot-high structure. When the Army Corps of Engineers opposed the new terminal, McMillan asked Chicago architect Henry Ives Cobb to devise a plan consistent with L'Enfant's vision for the Mall and favorable to the new terminal.[23]

The new plan, revealed in February 1900, called for a diagonal Centennial Avenue to cross the length of the Mall and provide frontage for the new terminal. This initiated a battle of plans, including one from the Army Corps of Engineers, to move the terminal off the Mall. Some business leaders also opposed the new avenue, fearing that it would attract the government buildings that they needed elsewhere to upgrade "Murder Bay," the slumlike wedge of land between Pennsylvania Avenue and the Mall (now known as the Federal Triangle). Centennial Avenue also interfered with the vision of park advocates on the Washington Board of Trade for a grand "ring street" connecting (and upgrading) various parks in the district. Starting from the Mall, the ring street would connect a variety of green spaces, including the undeveloped Potomac Park southwest of the Washington Monument and the National Zoological Park in the northwest suburbs.[24]

In May 1900, McMillan hoped to placate all sides by introducing legislation to establish a panel of art professionals to devise a plan for the Mall–Triangle area and develop a connection to Potomac Park and the zoo. But officials in the Army Corps of Engineers secured a change in the legislation that left them in charge. In December, the American Institute of Architects entered the fray. Having rescheduled their conference to meet in Washington, Glenn Brown, secretary of the American Institute of Architects, established the conference theme as the "grouping of public buildings" (a code word for the professionals' conception of civic art). A partisan of the L'Enfant plan, Brown hoped to usurp the engineers who, he said, had "never been accused of being artistic." The conference focused on the civic core but in ignoring the parks and transit issues, it failed to rally sufficient support.[25]

McMillan, also eager to elbow the engineers out, succeeded in uniting architects and park advocates on a special commission to advise the Senate Committee on the District of Columbia. The new US Senate Park Commission, also known as the McMillan Commission, reassembled a version of the World's Columbian Exposition team. Its members included Burnham and Charles McKim, a New York architect who had worked with Burnham on the White City, as well as Frederick Law Olmsted Jr. (son of the pioneer park planner). McMillan urged them to proceed cautiously in the hope that he could maneuver the new plan through various congressional committees. But Burnham convinced the commission to exceed its mandate and produce a grand, authoritative plan, including a resolution of the controversial issue of the terminal (which the Pennsylvania Railroad hired Burnham to design). To Burnham's good fortune, the Pennsylvania Railroad wanted to construct a new union station northeast of the Mall. Burnham also secured additional funds to build three-dimensional models of central Washington before and after implementation of the proposed plan.[26]

First exhibited in January 1902, the McMillan plan offered the most comprehensive plan of civic improvement and beautification to date. With a redesigned Mall at the center, it employed ensemble design to group buildings and set them off with gardens to maximum effect (much of this was McKim's work). McMillan's plan also provided for the new union station, a memorial bridge over the Potomac, and a gradual clearing of the slums in the Triangle. It included a system of parkways, connecting green spaces on both sides of the Potomac, and preserved the Chesapeake and Ohio Canal as a scenic and recreational resource. Suggestions for a new system of neighborhood parks and playgrounds, an enhanced Georgetown waterfront, a Great Falls of the Potomac national park, and a reclamation of the

Anacostia flats as a waterfront park rounded out the McMillan plan, which profoundly shaped the future development of the capital, as well as planning practices in the United States.[27]

MOTIVATIONS AND STRATEGIES IN THE FORMATIVE AND TRANSITIONAL ART OF CITY BEAUTIFICATION

With city coffers filling and the new US president Theodore Roosevelt championing an expansive public interest, the McMillan plan sparked interest in comprehensive planning in cities across the nation. Robinson, once content with piecemeal efforts, now argued in *Modern Civic Art; or, The City Made Beautiful* (1903) that "in the effort for civic improvement…the first step is to secure a comprehensive plan." Harrisburg, Pennsylvania, already engaged in three separate planning efforts involving park planning, sewers and sanitation, and street paving, claimed for itself the mantle of comprehensive planning. A host of giant civic schemes followed, focused on civic centers, gateway railroad stations, processional boulevards, belt parkways, outer park systems, and public playgrounds. Although still piecemeal and separate, such projects made comprehensive planning easier to envision and trained many who would later engage in it.[28]

A wide variety of motivations shaped these efforts, ranging from a desire to attract investors and customers and repair or enhance a city's reputation to the determination to impose social control on unruly urban masses and construct a cohesive moral order. But for the middle-class business and professional leaders who drove the movement, a faith in organic, evolutionary progress, a belief in the civic duty of all to work for the good of their city, and a conviction that expertise could identify and secure the public interest justified their efforts. City Beautiful proponents surely showed too much faith in experts and their supposed ability to identify the public good and transcend conflicting interests. City

Beautiful advocates' deference to vested interests and their narrow and homogenized conception of moral order compromised their efforts. One of the most popular of City Beautiful developments, the playground, most overtly embraced top-down social control. But City Beautiful proponents also acted from a genuine desire for civic improvement and the good of the whole society.[29]

Civic improvement organizations and plans sprouted in large, medium, and small cities. Burnham continued to be a central figure, particularly in the larger cities. He served on the commission that designed Cleveland's civic center in 1902, contributed to plans for Manila and Baguio in the Philippines and for San Francisco in 1905, and took the lead role in the construction of Union Station in Washington, DC, between 1903 and 1907. The consolidation of the railroad industry freed private capital for facility upgrades and union operations, making the gateway railroad station one of the movement's more common successes. The huge expense of civic centers and their disruption of downtown real estate markets meant that more plans were made than centers constructed. But, where successful, they energized the movement.[30]

Robinson worked with some larger cities, including Detroit, Los Angeles, and Denver, with little success. His genius came not in grand, monumental plans, but in turning small parcels of land into civic vignettes that brought out the individuality of a place and expressed civic pride. Both directly and indirectly, he shaped the landscapes of scores of small and medium-sized cities and towns. Placing civic buildings, usually columned and white, on river bluffs and other prominent sites and attending to the width and appearance of "parked" boulevards (i.e., with grassy medians) and tidy, unfenced, tree-lined residential streets, Robinson sought to inspire his clients rather than overwhelm them with unachievable plans. The siting, neoclassical design, and surrounding plazas of countless public buildings, from libraries to city halls to state capitols, can be traced to Robinson and his articulation of City Beautiful principles.[31]

Among the most common City Beautiful projects, processional boulevards punctured the gridiron of streets and belt parkways linked parks and increased access to open spaces. Boulevards attracted and protected grand residences, discouraging suburban escape and promoting compact settlement. Invoking utility and beauty (the watchwords of the movement), Robinson explained that boulevards provided "shortcuts to traffic" and provided "variety in street intersection, revealing pleasant vistas, and making easy the provision of little open spaces." The promise of easing traffic congestion supposedly justified the expense of boulevards. But while the boulevards achieved some success, the assumption of a radial-center pattern of traffic did not age well in the automotive era, when city centers no longer served as focal points. Wide, diagonal boulevards also created barriers to pedestrians and stranded parcels of land.[32]

But the diagonal boulevards, some of which are still in use today, reflected creative thinking about urban circulation and lent grace and beauty to many cities. Belt parkways had greater success in easing congestion and sometimes served as spines to direct new development. Parkways, Robinson added, linked parks and extended the benefits of natural beauty into "busy, workaday sections of the town." At their best, the parkways respected the natural contours of land and provided access to outer park systems and forest preservers.[33]

Without legal tools or an established discipline of city planning, City Beautiful proponents engaged in a formative art. No one knew exactly what to expect and new concerns and issues emerged over time. Private groups, usually business or civic associations with occasional labor support, initiated most plans; the federal government commissioned the plans for Manila and Baguio, executed by Burnham, which were the only plans fully implemented. Architects and landscape architects predominated among the professionals; engineers

played almost no part. Promotion and deference to business remained key; only billboards and utility wires, roundly opposed by the greater public, justified the danger of taking on vested interests. Housing, the placement of industry, and sanitation were largely ignored or left to other experts.[34]

The City Beautiful movement's emphasis on civic life, education, and culture did challenge the view of the city as an economic machine, however. Burnham's ambitious plan for San Francisco included an inner ring street lined with cultural institutions, parks on every hilltop, and an outer beltway featuring spectacular views of the region. His grand civic plaza, with converging boulevards, would have been enormously expensive and difficult at best for traffic patterns. Opponents of such improvements saw the city as simply an economic machine. Grand improvements also required centralized control, and yet Robinson counseled against the minor uses of regulatory power for the enemies that it made. City Beautiful projects thus depended on the political skill of their proponents. They considered excess condemnation as a means of financing improvements, but judged it too radical. The courts never endorsed this extension of eminent domain, so the movement relied largely on the public mood. Unlike Burnham's "make no little plans," Robinson advocated small, cost-conscious acts of beautification, finding opportunities in the cityscape to emphasize the individuality of a place.[35]

As they encountered new legal and physical challenges, City Beautiful advocates also practiced a transitional art. While the movement maintained an emphasis on volunteerism, improvement required some governmental role and pointed toward the value of an official planning commission. After Hartford, Connecticut, created the first planning commission in 1907, the official planning commission became a key element of City Beautiful plans. But even the creation of a commission did not resolve all legal issues, as the editor Herbert Croly made clear in his critique of the report of the New York City Improvement Commission in 1907. The city, Croly argued, lacked the borrowing capacity and the power of excess condemnation to overcome the resistance of landowners and real estate speculators. City Beautiful plans in St. Louis and Chicago stressed the financial benefits of beauty in trying to secure greater power to issue bonds to pay for improvements. In Chicago, a team of lawyers even explored a consolidated regional government to increase bonding power. But such efforts never overcame the limited public powers at the disposal of the movement.[36]

"MAKE NO LITTLE PLANS": *PLAN OF CHICAGO* (1909)

The boldest plans of the City Beautiful era broke free of the aesthetic framework and limited public powers and offered a comprehensive and expansive vision of the urban future. None did so more than *Plan of Chicago* (1909). Devised by Burnham and his young, Beaux-Arts–trained assistant Edward H. Bennett, *Plan of Chicago* is the best known and arguably the most successful of City Beautiful plans. The plan relied on the money and talent of hundreds of Chicagoans and a host of expert-led committees. Much of this came from the ranks of the Merchants Club, which commissioned and sponsored the plan, and the Commercial Club (the two clubs merged in 1906 under the latter name). Although *Plan of Chicago* asserted that rapid growth made it previously "impossible to plan," the project also built on a host of established and long-simmering plans stretching back to the transportation and sanitary improvements that made Chicago's marshy site productive and inhabitable. More recent contributions included plans for park systems along the disheveled lakefront (to which Burnham had contributed), an outer park system, the union of five major railroad terminals, and transit expert Bion J. Arnold's scheme for restructuring Chicago's elevated, surface, and subsurface transit lines.[37]

The most distinctive element in *Plan of Chicago* was a strategy for solidifying and enhancing Chicago's commercial dominance of its region, facilitating movement into and around the urban core. Chicago's growth had increased the value of downtown real estate many times over during the previous thirty years, but congestion now threatened that value. Reflecting the ambitions of the commercial and financial elite that commissioned it, the plan treated Chicago as a place "without bounds or limits," surrounded by "illimitable space now occupied by a population capable of illimitable expansion." To secure that expansion, however, Burnham sought to ease congestion that seemed bound to "increase in geometrical ratio" to the city's reach. The plan envisioned regional highways, both radial and concentric, reaching sixty miles into the hinterland. On the city's far southwest side, a new freight handling center would work as a "perfect machine" serving the twenty-two railroads entering the city. In the central city, complementary freight distribution and passenger routing systems utilized existing underground tunnels and linked the railroad terminals to the city's transit system. Taken together, these improvements would enable Chicago to accommodate "many times" its current traffic.[38]

Even beauty served the cause of commercial dominance and economic efficiency. "Beauty has always paid better than any other commodity," Burnham told the Commercial Club in 1897, "and always will." If the city would "put on a charming dress," he told a confidant in the same year, it will serve "to keep our rich people and their money here, and to bring others." Beauty would also make Chicago "a good labor market," according to *Plan of Chicago*, "in the sense that labor is sufficiently comfortable to be efficient and content." Lakefront parks and wooded preserves encouraged wage-earners to "take up the burden of life in our crowded streets and endless stretches of buildings with renewed vigor and hopefulness."[39]

Plan of Chicago's blueprint for commercial dominance was embedded, however, into a much more expansive vision of city life. "Make no little plans," Burnham is supposed to have said, "they have no magic to stir men's blood." There was nothing little about *Plan of Chicago*. Believing that "good citizenship is the prime object of good city planning," Burnham and his associates embraced the positive environmentalism and the faith in the harmonizing influence of civic art that the City Beautiful movement had done so much to spread. Their plan endeavored to turn the city into "an efficient instrument for providing all its people with the best possible conditions of living." A plan for a well-ordered and convenient city, they believed, would win over public sentiment and improve life for all.[40]

But a lingering fear also shaped *Plan of Chicago*. The very first page invoked a fear of chaos that rapid growth and "the influx of people of many nationalities without common traditions or habits of life" created. Burnham and Bennett knew that the "frequent outbreaks against law and order" troubling Chicago expressed grievances stemming "from narrow and pleasureless lives." But they hoped that the grand civic center (which was never built), the boulevards and parks, and above all, the

CXXXI. CHICAGO. VIEW, LOOKING WEST, OF THE PROPOSED CIVIC CENTER PLAZA AND BUILDINGS, SHOWING IT AS THE CENTER OF THE SYSTEM OF ARTERIES OF CIRCULATION AND OF THE SURROUNDING COUNTRY. Painted for the Commercial Club by Jules Guerin.

Figure 3. Jules Guerin's painting of Burnham's proposed civic center (which was never built) captures the expansive ambitions of *Plan of Chicago*. Painted by Jules Guerin, Creative Commons license (public domain).

lakefront (which "by right belongs to the people") still might create an organic unity. Burnham always emphasized the importance of Lake Michigan as a civic and recreational resource that might promote unity and contentment; he struggled against plans to make it a working harbor. He often ended his speeches by invoking the lake as a means toward the City Beautiful movement's animating vision of a technologically sophisticated city, attuned to the rhythms of nature. It seemed, Burnham declaimed, "as if the lake has been singing to us all those years." We had finally taken notice, so that in the future, we would be "merged into nature and become part of her."[41]

As much as *Plan of Chicago* imagined the city of the future, it was nevertheless rooted in an analysis of the city of 1909. Accurately describing and assessing the contemporary city helped to establish the plan's credibility. In surveying the noise, filth, congestion, and general inefficiency of the city, the analysis emphasized the costs of a lack of planning. Substandard housing, unpaved streets, illogical location of transit and other facilities, and railroad crossing at grade all wasted the time and taxed the health and well-being of Chicagoans and exacerbated labor troubles. State-imposed limitations on the borrowing capacity of the city, overlapping local governments and boards, and a corrupt political culture sapped the ability of the city to address these challenges. "The public authorities," Burnham told business leaders in the Commercial Club, "do not do their duty and they must be made to." Ensuring that elected officials did their duty comprised a significant element of Burnham's strategy for the plan.[42]

In Chicago, as elsewhere, the success of the City Beautiful movement depended on its political strategy. Burnham and the various committees established advisory boards that engaged state and local officials, from the governor of Illinois down to the Chicago Board of Education and park commissioners. In the fall of 1907, Chicago voters rejected a charter reform that would have consolidated many local governing bodies and strengthened the hand of elite reformers. In the wake of that defeat, the plan's proponents redoubled their efforts to court local officials and build public support. They cultivated alliances with everyone, ranging from such unsavory politicians as Mike "Hinky Dink" Kenna and "Bathhouse" John Coughlin to the outspoken settlement house leader Jane Addams. The plan's proponents also worked closely with propertied interests and the Army Corps of Engineers to secure support for lakefront parks. Their proposal for a new bridge across the main stem of the Chicago River at Michigan Avenue (easing a bottleneck and extending that avenue north of the river in what is now known as "the Magnificent Mile") required diplomacy with propertied interests, various governing bodies, and local legislators.[43]

THE CITY BEAUTIFUL MOVEMENT AND THE DEMOCRATIC PROCESS

Plan of Chicago established city planning as a powerful force in municipal politics, creating a stirring expression of the City Beautiful movement's optimism about the city and its plasticity. The city's challenges could be overcome, *Plan of Chicago* promised, and "a unified city, wherein each portion will have organic relations to all other portions," could be created. The publication of the plan on July 4 reflected this optimism, as did the physical artifact itself. Burnham learned of the power of visual effects from his work on the McMillan plan, so he secured the services of Jules Guerin (who had worked on the Washington project) to head a group of seven gifted artists who produced the drawings for *Plan of Chicago*. That tome, with a midnight-green cover, the title and cipher of the Commercial Club impressed in gold upon it, and weighing more than five pounds, appealed first and foremost to the senses. The publication offered the reader/ viewer a vision of a future Chicago, invoking wonder at the urbane beauty of a serenely civilized place. In arguing that the "cities that

truly exercise dominion rule by reason of their appeal to the highest emotions of the human mind," *Plan of Chicago* announced its own ambitions.[44]

But while every significant public official received a copy of *Plan of Chicago*, the $25 price put it out of reach of most Chicagoans. To win over machine politicians, secure enabling legislation from the state, create an official city planning commission, and defeat the Army Corps of Engineers over lakefront planning, the backers of *Plan of Chicago* needed the general public as an ally. To secure public support for implementation of the plan, Chicago mayor Fred Busse appointed 328 men to the Chicago Plan Commission in November 1909. Chaired by Charles Wacker, the Commission hired the master salesman Walter D. Mooney to head a publicity effort. Cultivating newspaper editors and reporters, Mooney blanketed the city with five hundred lantern-slide lectures, reaching 150,000 people. He also produced several short publications, including *Chicago's Greatest Issue: An Official Plan* (1911), provided free to property owners and those who paid more than $25 rent a month. In addition, Moody negotiated an agreement to make another of his publications, *Wacker's Manual of the Plan of Chicago* (1911), the civics textbook for eighth graders in Chicago. Moody's film, *A Tale of Our City*, reached sixty theaters and 175,000 viewers. In part due to Moody's efforts, Chicagoans approved $234 million in eighty-six *Plan*-related bond issues between 1912 and 1931.[45]

But the success of such publicity campaigns signaled the eclipse of the City Beautiful movement. The top-down effort to lobby key decision-makers while overawing the public with a media blitz belied the most promising methods and the most alluring vision of the movement. At its best, the City Beautiful movement relied on a civic-spirited citizenry energized by a vision of the city as an organism designed to enhance people's lives, rather than merely an economic machine for the accumulation of wealth. The logical product of that vision would be an enlarged public realm as a barrier against the encroachments of crass commercialism. Philadelphia's Benjamin Franklin Parkway, connecting City Hall with the Philadelphia Museum of Art, demonstrated the potential of linking the center of democratic power with the institutions of a public culture. The project made a start in asserting the claims of a shared public realm and setting limits to dominance of private interest. The Boston Public Library off Copley Square, the Detroit Public Library and Institute of Arts, the Denver Public Library and Art Museum, and Cleveland's six-building Group Plan anchor similar spaces. But the full realization of that public and democratic vision required an engaged and active citizenry as a counterweight to commercial interests.[46]

The City Beautiful movement's encounter with the explosion of commercial billboards revealed the limits of its democratic vision. City Beautiful advocates had long complained about commercial billboards that obtruded, as Frederick Law Olmsted, Jr., put it, into public space with "all sorts of sordid ideas." The billboard menace, however, called forth their suspicions of mass democracy, as they equated the "din" of visual salesmanship with "a riot" of "the mob." But the billboard industry proved adept at—indeed, had pioneered—the same sort of public relations that the Chicago Plan Commission employed. Industry spokesmen insisted that the billboards offered color, amusement, and companionship to harried urbanites, providing relief from the dreary and monotonous industrial cityscape. Some even asserted the billboard's public service, calling it a more genuinely public art than the elitist civic monuments that City Beautiful activists favored. Monumental architecture spoke in authoritarian idiom, demanding obedience, it seemed, while the billboards spoke in favor of freedom over self-denial.[47]

The difference between an elite culture imposed upon the masses and a mass culture offered by commercial agencies did not necessarily favor the City Beautiful concept. The use of civic monuments to produce a unified and loyal citizenry, moreover, too closely resembled the advertisers' effort to mold mass markets. Both sides seemed to think of the urban populace as spectators; neither envisioned an active, deliberating public. Moody's use of the advertisers' techniques of public relations had already blurred any distinction between the two sides. Worse, the trends in city life favored billboards over civic monuments. Civic identity depended on "permanent, unimpeachable" architectural forms, The Architectural Record opined in 1915, which billboards defiled. But the accelerating pace of city life, particularly with the spread of the automobile, overwhelmed the unimpeachable monument with the fleeting, transitory billboard. Then, during World War I, Plan of Chicago's Guerin volunteered for George Creel's Committee on Public Information, using the same public relations techniques to build support for the war effort. The City Beautiful movement's faith in public space as the source of a unifying vision had begun to give way to a new model of the public, associated with the mass consumption of goods and ideas and signaling a move toward mass-mediated forms of civic and mass culture.[48]

Even as the City Beautiful movement found itself squeezed by an expansive capitalism, it also suffered assault from the champions of participatory democracy. Some in the movement saw civic art as a means to "soothe... popular discontent" or advertise the benevolence of a philanthropic elite. Robinson called for imposing civic centers that would "visibly dominate" the city. "To them," he wrote, "the community would look up, seeing them lording over it at every turn, as, in fact, the government ought to do." But others thought that civic spaces should promote a "spirit of liberalism and equality," encourage interaction among diverse peoples, and "arouse in the individual a keen sense of proprietary pride." Charles Zueblin, an academic sociologist who rose to the presidency of the American League for Civic Improvement, initially saw the movement as ultimately a matter of citizenship and "the idea of striving for a purification of politics." He stood with those who wanted public spaces that served as "open-air clubs at which political affairs and questions of art and literature were discussed from varied, individual points of view." But Zueblin eventually left a movement that he found deficient in democratic credentials to search for better ways of promoting a deliberating public, including university extension and the forum movement.[49]

Women stood at the forefront of those who tried to lead the City Beautiful movement in more democratic directions. Believing that the improvement of city life depended on the actions of every citizen, women's clubs set out "to promote by education and active cooperation a higher public spirit and a better social order." A more inclusive civic life, they argued, would reveal that citizens could become experts when they focused on local conditions. By building a parallel movement for municipal housekeeping (applying the domestic skills of women to the city as a whole), they enlarged their own role in civic life. Caroline Crane spoke on municipal housekeeping in more than sixty cities, always renting the largest possible hall. The "people will come," she argued, "when the selection of a large and popular auditorium makes it plain that they are really *expected* to come." To secure a higher level of municipal service, municipal housekeepers published popular books, articles, and pamphlets; held public meetings; conducted surveys; held protests; ran political candidates; accepted official positions; and even submitted a bid for a garbage removal contract. No one struggled more consistently to make political reform an integral part of the City Beautiful movement than women.[50]

WOMEN AND THE PATH FROM THE CITY BEAUTIFUL/LIVABLE TO THE CITY PRACTICAL/PROFITABLE

Municipal housekeepers broadened the agenda of the City Beautiful movement to include cleaner streets and improved sanitation, pure water and smoke abatement, careful disposal of wastes, inspection of public markets and supplies of milk and meat, and regulation of buildings to ensure adequate light and ventilation. The effort led to new legislation and new municipal responsibilities regarding littering, the placement of noxious industries, new methods of garbage disposal, restrictions on dumping, and the regulation of public markets. The interest in public markets challenged the prejudices of some in the movement. An inveterate foe of clutter, Robinson treated public markets, generating litter, congestion, and odor, as antithetical to clean and efficient cities and regularly recommended their removal. But women defended the importance of access to clean and healthful markets, recommending regulation and upgrading rather than removal.[51]

As part of the effort to broaden the agenda of the City Beautiful movement, women agitated for social as well as physical planning. The movement tended to avoid housing reform, land-use regulation, and other issues that required greater public control over private interests. The movement avoided the social issues surrounding poverty altogether. About "such details—sociologically pressing though they are—as sunless bedrooms, dark halls and stairs, foul cellars, dangerous employments, and an absence of bathrooms," Robinson wrote, "civic art has no responsibility, however earnestly it deplores them." *Plan of Chicago* warned of the eventual necessity of providing public housing for low-income Chicagoans who had become "so degraded by long life in the slums that they have lost all power of caring for themselves." But housing and poverty and other social issues remained off the City Beautiful agenda.[52]

Male reformers tended to look to private enterprise to address social issues. Women more commonly demanded an expansion of municipal responsibilities, in the belief that there is "a common dependency from which there is no escape." In dealing with pollution and urban cleanliness, women wanted immediate action and municipal regulation rather than a cautious, cost-benefit approach. The gender differences boiled down to a choice between the city profitable or the city livable. Women sought a new attitude about—and within—municipal government, holding that "the welfare of human beings is the chief business of a city government." The struggle over Chicago's lakefront illustrates the point. Whether focused on the lakefront in terms of industrial and harbor development or recreational and commercial opportunities, men thought in terms of profit. Faced with the male City Club's lakefront plan for a commercial development with restaurants, boardwalks, and plenty of parking, the Women's City Club advocated for a public lakefront, accessible by streetcar extension and open to all in "a broad and democratic spirit."[53]

Women played key roles on the Committee on Congestion of Population (CCP) in New York, which launched a public exhibition on poverty and housing in 1908 and laid the groundwork for the first national conference on city planning, held in 1909. The settlement house leader Mary Kingsbury Simkhovitch chaired the committee, and activist (and Addams associate) Florence Kelley organized the exhibition. As Simkhovitch explained, the exhibition "pictured graphically what overcrowding meant in New York's tenements." Well acquainted with the challenges of immigrant and working-class neighborhoods, settlement leaders pushed for a bottom-up form of city planning that included such issues as child care, education, recreation, and health care.[54]

The National Conference on City Planning convened in Washington, DC, in May. The only woman to address the conference, Simkhovitch pushed for neighborhood self-determination and community organization. Speaking for the city livable, she insisted that "no matter how good a plan looks from the point of view of a sound economy, it is not a good plan unless the people like it." Inspired by the example of European planning efforts in

land-use controls and the construction of new towns and garden cities for the working classes, Simkhovitch nonetheless knew that her neighbors did not want to lose "the social advantages which a city affords." Any solution of the housing problem would have to take the needs and desires of the poor into account.[55]

The impassioned arguments of the social reformers for a fight for "sunlight and pure air against greed" captured the imagination of some City Beautiful practitioners at the first National Conference on City Planning. But most attendees saw physical and social planning as two distinct, if related, issues. As the struggle to control future national conferences ensued, veterans of the City Beautiful movement seized the opportunity to think through exactly what planning might become. Some stood with the insurgents in seeking to make city planning "a social and democratic movement," but most found the insurgents too radical and impractical, likely to frighten ordinary citizens and alienate powerful interests.[56]

Future conferences and the emerging profession of city planning narrowed rather than broadened the scope of city planning. Downplaying the democratic and popular dimensions of its activity, the new profession appealed to more powerful and conservative groups. Where the City Beautiful movement once had welcomed women's contributions, the profession found the emphasis on beauty to be effeminate. As male professionals embraced "the city practical," they also closed the doors to women. "There is nothing effeminate and sentimental about it," one male professional said of city planning, "—like tying tidies on telephone poles and putting doilies on cross-walks,—it is vigorous, virile, sane." The purview of planning and environmental reform narrowed, leaving off such supposedly female concerns as beauty, sympathy, and social justice.[57]

At the same time, the emerging profession redefined planning as a dynamic process of constant monitoring, revision, and guidance of the city's growth, rather than the publication of a single dramatic plan geared toward enlisting public support. More process than result, city planning might have enlisted the entire citizenry in the creation, implementation, monitoring, and constant revision of a plan. Moreover, it might have followed the City Beautiful movement's emphasis on the city as an organism and treated planning as an aspect of human ecology. Olmsted Jr., pointed the way in 1911, defining comprehensive planning as "a single complex subject" focused on "the intelligent control and guidance of the entire physical growth and alteration of cities." A comprehensive city planning outline for Pittsburgh, published in 1910, illustrated the potential of this approach. Addressing transportation, water and sewage, public control over private development, flood control, and smoke abatement, it focused on the essential elements of the city as an ecosystem.[58]

Like the City Beautiful movement, both the science of ecology and the city planning profession emerged against the backdrop of successful environmental reform. As water and sewer systems dramatically extended life expectancies, success excited greater ambitions. Ellen Richards, a municipal housekeeper and sanitary chemist, introduced ecology to the American public in 1892 and worked to popularize it for much of her life. To preserve the physical environment that was our home, Richards wrote in 1910, "there must be inculcated habits of using the material things in daily life in such a way as to promote and not to diminish health." It was of the "greatest importance that every one should acquire such habits of belief," she concluded, and that ecological knowledge be directed to "inculcating right and safe ways in daily life." Worried about the growing specialization of scientific and technical knowledge, Richards understood ecology as an integrative science aimed at the transformation of daily life.[59]

In contrast, the city planning profession remained focused on cultivating a narrow, professional expertise. Trends toward specialization, professionalization, and bureaucratization undercut the efforts of citizen activists and generalists. Architects, landscape architects, housing reformers, and playground advocates all went their separate ways. Alumni of the CCP effort began meeting as a separate National Housing Association in 1911. Competing with other professions, municipal engineers established exclusive control of matters of sanitation, street construction, and drainage. Among the new specialized commissions proliferating in municipal government, city planning commissions empowered professions and excluded lay activists.[60]

A short-lived and in many ways unsuccessful effort, the City Beautiful movement nevertheless left behind an impressive and useful legacy. Across the United States, many beloved urban spaces and ensembles of buildings from the City Beautiful movement remain. Chicago's lakefront parks, Washington, DC's, monumental core, Cleveland's downtown mall and cluster of civic and governmental buildings, Denver's partially realized civic center and formal gardens, grand railroad stations in Kansas City, Los Angeles, and Washington, university campuses such as Columbia University in New York City and Yale University in New Haven, and boulevards, public buildings, parks, and parkways in numerous cities, large and small, all testify to the enduring value of the City Beautiful movement. The movement's emphasis on civic architecture, landscaped parks, and generous public spaces influenced the Congress for the New Urbanism and interest in form-based zoning codes. In perhaps its most important contribution, the City Beautiful movement remains a source of insight and inspiration for those who believe that cities are organisms that can be both efficient and beautiful.

DISCUSSION OF THE LITERATURE

The history of the City Beautiful movement intersects with architectural history, the history of technology, and urban and political history, and sources in these fields can be consulted usefully. But the movement is centrally located in the history of city planning, the serious study of which began with John W. Reps, *The Making of Urban America* and Mel Scott, *American City Planning Since 1890*.[61] Each provides a broad survey of planning history, paying considerable attention to the City Beautiful movement.

William H. Wilson spent more than a quarter-century studying the City Beautiful movement, beginning with *The City Beautiful Movement in Kansas City*.[62] His many books and articles, and especially his later and more synthetic book-length study, *The City Beautiful Movement*, provide a useful starting point for a more in-depth investigation. [63] So, too, does the work of Jon A. Peterson, whose article "The City Beautiful Movement: Forgotten Origins and Lost Meanings" stimulated greater interest in the movement. [64] While focused on the eventual emergence of the city planning profession, Peterson's *The Birth of City Planning in the United States 1840–1917* is full of insights on the City Beautiful movement.[65] Michelle H. Bogart's *Public Sculpture and the Civic Ideal in New York City, 1890–1930* focuses on a group of public arts advocates who first popularized the term *City Beautiful*.[66]

Feminist scholars have deepened our understanding of a movement that relied so heavily on women. Suellen M. Hoy's "'Municipal Housekeeping': The Role of Women in Improving Urban Sanitation Practices, 1880–1917" documents the crucial role that women played in the effort to sanitize and beautify American cities.[67] Maureen Flanagan's "The City Profitable, the City Livable: Environmental Policy, Gender, and Power in Chicago in the 1910s," investigates the different agendas of male and female reformers while casting the City Beautiful movement as an environmental reform.[68] Susan Marie Wirka's "The City Social Movement: Progressive Women Reformers and Early Social Planning" details the role of women in trying to broaden the

agenda of the City Beautiful and City Efficient movements.[69]

Several studies place the City Beautiful movement in broader contexts. Paul S. Boyer's *Urban Masses and Moral Order* locates the City Beautiful movement in a long history of elite efforts to reform the urban masses morally, a view that has been both influential and challenged.[70] Stanley K. Schultz's *Constructing Urban Culture: American Cities and City Planning, 1800–1920* traces the 19th-century development of many of the legal tools that City Beautiful activists employed, as well of the vision of a technologically sophisticated city set in a garden that animated their efforts.[71] M. Christine Boyer's *Dreaming the Rational City: The Myth of American City Planning* places the City Beautiful movement in a structuralist account of planning discourses.[72] John D. Fairfield's *The Mysteries of the Great City: The Politics of Urban Design, 1877–1937* examines the City Beautiful movement in the context of social and political conflicts in the turn-of-the-century American city.[73]

The Chicago story is carefully examined in Carl Smith's *Plan of Chicago: Daniel Burnham and the Remaking of the American City*.[74] Burnham's career receives a fuller treatment in Thomas S. Hines's *Burnham of Chicago*.[75] The international dimensions of the City Beautiful have been comparatively neglected, but for a start, see Mario Manieri-Elia, "Toward an 'Imperial City': Daniel H. Burnham and the City Beautiful Movement," in Giorgio Ciucci, Francesco Dal Co, Mario Manien-Ella, and Manfredo Tafuri, *The American City: From the Civil War to the New Deal* (Barbara Luigia LaPenta, trans.), 1–142; and the "City of Monuments" chapter in *Cities of Tomorrow; An Intellectual History of Urban Planning and Design Since 1880*, by Peter Hall.[76]

PRIMARY SOURCES

The City Beautiful movement can be tracked in the rich periodical literature published during the Progressive era. A useful research guide for these publications is *The Readers' Guide to Periodical Literature.* Although it only reaches back to the later years of the movement, *The International Index: A Guide to Periodical Literature in the Social Sciences and Humanities* is also useful. Both are widely available through college libraries. One of the lay leaders of the movement, J. Horace McFarland, edited a "Beautiful America" section of the *Ladies Home Journal* between 1904 and 1907.

The papers of several leaders on the movement are available as well. Materials by and related to Frederick Law Olmsted can be found at the Frederick Law Olmsted National Historical Site and the Frederick Law Olmsted Papers, Manuscript Division, Library of Congress, Washington, DC. The professional and personal papers of Daniel H. Burnham, along with other archival material, are available at the Ryerson and Burnham Libraries at the Art Institute of Chicago. The University of Pennsylvania's Kislak Center for Special Collections houses the Charles Mulford Robinson Papers The J. Horace McFarland's papers are housed at the Pennsylvania State Archives.

The most important publications of the City Beautiful movement are available digitally, including Charles Mulford Robinson, *The Improvement of Towns and Cities* and *Modern Civic Art; or, The City Made Beautiful* and Burnham and Bennett, *Plan of Chicago.*

DIGITAL MATERIALS

"Architecture: The City Beautiful Movement," *Encyclopedia of Chicago.* http://www.encyclopedia.chicagohistory.org/pages/61.html.

The Burnham Plan Centennial. http://chicagocarto.com/burnham/index.html.

City Beautiful Movement The New York Preservation Archive Project. http://www.nypap.org/preservation-history/city-beautiful-movement/.

City Beautiful; The 1901 Plan for Washington DC University of Virginia Xroads. http://xroads.virginia.edu/~CAP/CITYBEAUTIFUL/dchome.html.

The City Beautiful Movement and Harrisburg's Old 8th Ward. http://www.old8thward.com/citybeautiful.htm.

FURTHER READING

Baker, Laura E. "Public Sites Versus Public Sights: The Progressive Response to Outdoor Advertising and the Commercialization of Public Space." *American Quarterly* 59 (December 2007): 1187–1213.

Bogart, Michelle H. *Public Sculpture and the Civic Ideal in New York City, 1890–1930.* Chicago: University of Chicago Press, 1989.

Boyer, Paul S. *Urban Masses and Moral Order.* Cambridge, MA: Harvard University Press, 1978.

Brownlee, David B. *Building the City Beautiful: The Benjamin Franklin Parkway and the Philadelphia Museum of Art.* Philadelphia: The Museum: Distributed by the University of Pennsylvania Press, 1989.

Burnham, Daniel H., and Edward H. Bennett. *Plan of Chicago.* Chicago: Commercial Club, 1909.

Fairfield, John D. *The Mysteries of the Great City: The Politics of Urban Design, 1877–1937.* Columbus: Ohio State University Press, 1993.

Flanagan, Maureen A. "The City Profitable, the City Livable: Environmental Policy, Gender, and Power in Chicago in the 1910s." *Journal of Urban History* 22 (January 1996): 163–190.

Hines, Thomas S. *Burnham of Chicago: Architect and Planner.* New York: Oxford University Press, 1974.

Hoy, Suellen M. "'Municipal Housekeeping': The Role of Women in Improving Urban Sanitation Practices, 1880–1917." In *Pollution and Reform in American Cities, 1870–1930.* Edited by Martin V. Melosi, 173–198. Austin: University of Texas Press, 1980.

Mattson, Kevin. *Creating a Democratic Public: The Struggle for Urban Participatory Democracy in the Progressive Era.* University Park: Pennsylvania State University Press, 1998.

Peterson, Jon A. *The Birth of City Planning in the United States, 1840–1917.* Baltimore: Johns Hopkins University Press, 2003.

Schultz, Stanley K. *Constructing Urban Culture: American Cities and City Planning, 1800–1920.* Philadelphia: Temple University Press, 1989.

Smith, Carl. *Plan of Chicago: Daniel Burnham and the Remaking of the American City.* Chicago: University of Chicago Press, 2006.

Wilson, William H. *The City Beautiful Movement.* Baltimore: Johns Hopkins University Press, 1989.

NOTES

1. Suellen Hoy, *Chasing Dirt: The American Pursuit of Cleanliness* (New York: Oxford University Press, 1996); Martin V. Melosi, *Effluent America: Cities, Industry, Energy, and the Environment* (Pittsburgh: University of Pittsburgh Press, 2001); Joel Tarr, *The Search for the Ultimate Sink: Urban Pollution in Historical Perspective* (Akron, OH: University of Akron Press, 1996); Laura E. Baker, "Public Sites Versus Public Sights: The Progressive Response to Outdoor Advertising and the Commercialization of Public Space," *American Quarterly* 59 (December 2007), 1187–1213; and, on urban population, US Census Bureau, " Population of the 100 Largest Cities and other Urban Places in the United States: 1790 to 1990, https://www.census.gov/population/www/documentation/twps0027/twps0027.html.

2. Stanley K. Schultz, *Constructing Urban Culture: American Cities and City Planning, 1800–1920* (Philadelphia: Temple University Press, 1989); Harold Platt, *Shock Cities: The Environmental Transformation and Reform of Manchester and Chicago* (Chicago: University of Chicago Press, 2005); Stanley K. Schultz and Clay McShane, "To Engineer the Metropolis: Sewers, Sanitation, and City Planning in Late-Nineteenth-Century America," *Journal of American History* 65 (September 1978), 389–411; Martin V. Melosi, *The Sanitary City* (Pittsburgh, PA: University of Pittsburgh Press, 2008).

3. Melosi, *The Sanitary City*, 71–112; and Hoy, *Chasing Dirt*, 59–86.

4. Paul S. Boyer, *Urban Masses and Moral Order* (Cambridge, MA: Harvard University Press, 1978), 220–232, 261–278; Dewey quoted on 225; and Jon A. Peterson, *The Birth of City Planning in the United States, 1840–1917* (Baltimore: Johns Hopkins University Press, 2003), 98–104.

5. Schultz, *Constructing Urban Culture*, 3–32; novelist quoted on 21; and Leo Marx, *The Machine in the Garden: Technology and the Pastoral Ideal in America* (New York: Oxford University Press, 1964).

6. Schultz, *Constructing Urban Culture*, 3–32, novelist quoted on 25.

7. Boyer, *Urban Masses and Moral Order*, 123–131.

8. Boyer, *Urban Masses and Moral Order in America*, 123–131; Edward Bellamy, *Looking Backward* (New York: Ticknor and Co., 1888; reissued, New York, New American Library, 1960), quoted passage on 213; and Schulz, *Constructing Urban Culture*, 3–4.

9. Jacob Riis, *How the Other Half Lives* (New York: Scribners, 1890), passim; quoted passages on 55, 273, 296; and Boyer, *Urban Masses and Moral Order*, 123–131.

10. Jon C. Teaford, *The Unheralded Triumph: City Government in America, 1870–1900* (Baltimore: Johns Hopkins Press, 1984); Boyer, *Urban Masses and Moral Order*, 261–265; Kevin Mattson, *Creating a Democratic Public: The Struggle for Urban Participatory Democracy in the Progressive Era* (University Park: Pennsylvania State University Press, 1998), 14–20; Charles Moore, *Daniel H. Burnham, Architect, Planner of Cities* (New York: Houghton Mifflin Co., 1921), "magic," vol. 2, 147; and Carl Smith, *Plan of Chicago: Daniel Burnham and the Remaking of the American City* (Chicago: University of Chicago Press, 2006), on Moore's attribution of the phrase to Burnham, 98.

11. William H. Wilson, *The City Beautiful Movement* (Baltimore: Johns Hopkins Press, 1989), 13–14; and Peterson, *The Birth of City Planning*, 98–108.

12. Peterson, *The Birth of City Planning*, 39–54; Wilson, *The City Beautiful Movement*, 14–22, "progress" on 19; "hard" on 20; Boyer, *Urban Masses and Moral Order*, 236–240; "pleasure" on 239; "harmonizing" on 238.

13. Wilson, *The City Beautiful Movement*, 22–33; and Peterson, *The Birth of City Planning*, 29–73.

14. John D. Fairfield, *The Mysteries of the Great City: The Politics of Urban Design, 1877–1937* (Columbus: Ohio State University Press, 1993), 41–49; Olmsted quoted on 42; Geoffrey Blodgett, "Frederick Law Olmsted: Landscape Architecture as Conservative Reform," *Journal of American History* 62 (March 1976), 869–889; Roy Rosenzweig and Elizabeth Blackmar, *The Park and the People: A History of Central Park* (Ithaca, NY: Cornell University Press, 1992).

15. Alan Trachtenberg, *The Incorporation of America: Culture and Society in the Gilded Age* (New York: Hill and Wang, 1982), 208–234.

16. Trachtenberg, *The Incorporation of America*; Wilson, *The City Beautiful Movement*, 56–60; and Schultz, *Constructing Urban Culture*, 209–217.

17. Thomas S. Hines, *Burnham of Chicago: Architect and Planner* (New York: Oxford University Press, 1974), 4–6. passim; Carl Smith, *Plan of Chicago: Daniel Burnham and the Remaking of the American City* (Chicago: University of Chicago Press, 2006), 19–22, 32–33; and Boyer, *Urban Masses and Moral Order*, 182–184, 269–271; quotations on 183.

18. Peterson, *The Birth of City Planning*, 69–102; Wilson, *City Beautiful Movement*, 56–64; and Robinson quoted on 60.

19. Peterson, *The Birth of City Planning*, 98–122; and Wilson, *The City Beautiful Movement*, 35–45.

20. Wilson, *The City Beautiful Movement*, 35–47; and Peterson, *The Birth of City Planning*, 98–122.

21. Peterson, *The Birth of City Planning*, 102–108; motto quoted on 103; Michele H. Bogart, *Public Sculpture and the Civic Ideal in New York City, 1890–1930* (Chicago: University of Chicago Press, 1989); and Wilson, *The City Beautiful Movement*, 35–47.

22. Peterson, *The Birth of City Planning*, 69–102; Wilson, *The City Beautiful Movement*, 35–47; and Robinson quoted on 46.

23. John W. Reps, *The Making of Urban America: A History of City Planning in the United States* (Princeton. NJ: Princeton University Press, 1965), 240–262, 502–508; and Peterson, *The Birth of City Planning*, 77–81.

24. Peterson, *The Birth of City Planning*, 80–85.

25. Peterson, *The Birth of City Planning*, 85–88; and Brown quoted on 86.

26. Peterson, *The Birth of City Planning*, 88–95; and Reps, *The Making of Urban America*, 502–508.

27. Reps, *The Making of Urban America*, 508; and Peterson, *The Birth of City Planning*, 94–97.

28. Charles Mulford Robinson, *Modern Civic Art; or, The City Made Beautiful* (New York, G. P. Putnam's Sons, 1903), 32; and Peterson, *The Birth of City Planning*, 98–138.

29. Boyer, *Urban Masses and Moral Order*, 261–276; Wilson, *The City Beautiful Movement*, 75–95; Peterson, *The Birth of City Planning*, 139–150, 166–170; Mario Manieri-Elia, "Toward an 'Imperial City': Daniel H. Burnham and the City Beautiful Movement," in Giorgio Ciucci, Francesco Dal Co, Mario Manien-Ella, and Manfredo Tafuri, *The American City: From the Civil War to the New Deal*, Barbara Luigia LaPenta, trans. (Cambridge MA: MIT Press, 1979), 1–142.

30. Peterson, *The Birth of City Planning*, 151–162; and Manieri-Elia, "Toward an 'Imperial City.'"

31. Peterson, *The Birth of City Planning*, 146–149, 190–197; and Wilson, *The City Beautiful Movement*, 46–47, 234–238.

32. Peterson, *The Birth of City Planning*, 162–172; Wilson, *The City Beautiful Movement*, 108–112; Daniel Baldwin Hess, "Transportation Beautiful: Did the City Beautiful Improve Urban Transportation?" *Journal of Urban History* 32 (May 2006), 511–545; and Robinson quoted on 523.

33. Peterson, *The Birth of City Planning*, 162–172; Wilson, *The City Beautiful Movement*, 108–112; Hess, "Transportation Beautiful," 511–545; and Robinson quoted on 524.

34. Peterson, *The Birth of City Planning*, 175–181.

35. Peterson, *The Birth of City Planning*, 181–192; and Wilson, *The City Beautiful Movement*, 99–278.

36. Peterson, *The Birth of City Planning*, 202–206; and Wilson, *The City Beautiful Movement*, 99–278.

37. Peterson, *The Birth of City Planning*, 213–222; Smith, *Plan of Chicago*, 1–10, 23–25, 64–78; Daniel H. Burnham and Edward H. Bennett, *Plan of Chicago*, ed. Charles Moore (New York: Princeton Architectural Press, 1993), "impossible" on 32; Hines, *Burnham of Chicago*, 319–325. On who actually wrote *Plan of Chicago*, see Smith's useful discussion on 103–110; following the work of architectural historian Kristen Schaffer, Smith argues that Charles Moore, the *Plan's* editor, whom Burnham first met during the McMillan Commission effort, crafted the prose from Burnham's extensive notes.

38. Burnham, *Plan of Chicago*, quotations on 66, 74, 80, and 99; Peterson, *The Birth of City Planning*, 213–222; Fairfield, *The Mysteries of the Great City*, 119–124.

39. Hines, *Burnham of Chicago*, 314–317, "Beauty" on 316; Smith, *Plan of Chicago*, 31–33, "charming" on 32; Burnham, *Plan of Chicago*, "labor market" on 32; "burden" on 53;

40. Burnham, *Plan of Chicago*, "citizenship" on 123; "efficient" on 1; "Make no little plans" is often attributed to Burnham, but there is no definitive source; see Smith, *Plan of Chicago*, 98.

41. Burnham, *Plan of Chicago*, "frequent" and "narrow" on 32; "influx" on 1; "Lake front" on 50; Smith, *Plan of Chicago*, 11–37, 99–103; Burnham's musing on the lake quoted on 33; Fairfield, *The Mysteries of the Great City*, 119–124.

42. Smith, *Plan of Chicago*, 34–53; and Burnham quoted on 52.

43. Wilson, *The City Beautiful Movement*, 99–278; Smith, *Plan of Chicago*, 71–84; and Hines, *Burnham of Chicago*, 312–331.

44. Smith, *Plan of Chicago*, 80–117; "serenely civilized place" is Smith's elegant phrase on 91; Burnham, *Plan of Chicago*, "unified" on 100; "dominion" on 30.

45. Smith, *Plan of Chicago*, 116–125, 132–133; and Thomas J. Schlereth, "Burnham's *Plan* and Moody's *Manual*: City Planning as Progressive Reform," *Journal of the American Planning Association* 47 (January 1981), 70–82.

46. Wilson, *The City Beautiful Movement*, 99–278; David B. Brownlee, *Building the City Beautiful: The Benjamin Franklin Parkway and the Philadelphia Museum of Art* (Philadelphia: Philadelphia Museum of Art, 1989).

47. Baker, "Public Sites Versus Public Sights," 1187–1205, Olmsted on 1194; and *Architectural Record* on 1199.

48. Baker, "Public Sites Versus Public Sights," 1199–1209; Smith, *Plan of Chicago*, 118–121.

49. Mattson, *Creating a Democratic Public*, 14–30; "soothe" on 17; "spirit" on 18; "proprietary" on 19; "open-air" on 21; Robinson, *Modern Civic Art*, "visibly" on 91; Peterson, *The Birth of City Planning*, "striving" on 113; John D. Fairfield, *The Public and Its Possibilities: Triumphs and Tragedies in the American City* (Philadelphia: Temple University Press, 2010), 149–151; Smith, *Plan of Chicago*, 126–129.

50. Suellen M. Hoy, "'Municipal Housekeeping': The Role of Women in Improving Urban Sanitation Practices, 1880–1917," in Martin V. Melosi, ed., *Pollution and Reform in American Cities, 1870–1930* (Austin: University of Texas Press, 1980), 173–198; "promote" on 174; Crane on 187; Harold L. Platt, "Jane Addams and the Ward Boss Revisited: Class, Politics, and Public Health in Chicago, 1890–1930," *Environmental History* 5 (April 2000), 194–222.

51. Peterson, *The Birth of City Planning*, 192–194; Gregory Alexander Donofrio, "Feeding the City," *Gastronomica: The Journal of Food and Culture* 7 (Fall 2007), 30–41; Hoy, "'Municipal Housekeeping'"; and Platt, "Jane Addams and the Ward Boss Revisited."

52. Susan Marie Wirka, "The City Social Movement: Progressive Women Reformers and Early Social Planning," in Mary Corbin Sies and Christopher Silver, eds., *Planning the Twentieth Century City* (Baltimore: Johns Hopkins University Press,

1996), 55–75; Robinson, *Modern Civic Art*, "details" on 257–258; Burnham, *Plan of Chicago*, "degraded" on 109; Peterson, *The Birth of City Planning*, 229–232; and Robinson quoted on 230.

53. Wirka, "The City Social Movement,"; Maureen A. Flanagan, "The City Profitable, the City Livable: Environmental Policy, Gender, and Power in Chicago in the 1910s," *Journal of Urban History* 22 (January 1996), 163–190; "common" and "broad are from Chicago Women's City Club member Anne E. Nicholes, quoted on 172 and 175; and Platt, "Jane Addams and the Ward Boss Revisited."

54. Wirka, "The City Social Movement," "pictured" on 69; Peterson, *The Birth of City Planning*, 227–245; and Fairfield, *Mysteries of the Great City*, 119–157.

55. Wirka, "The City Social Movement"; Simkhovitch quoted on 72–73.

56. Peterson, *The Birth of City Planning*, 240–259, "sunlight" on 242; "social" on 253; and Fairfield, *Mysteries of the Great City*, 119–157.

57. Peterson, *The Birth of City Planning*, 255–259; Adam Rome, "'Political Hermaphrodites': Gender and Environmental Reform in Progressive America," *Environmental Reform* 11 (July 2006): 440–463; "effeminate" on 431.

58. Peterson, *The Birth of City Planning*, 246–259; Frederick Law Olmsted Jr., quoted on 256; Pittsburgh plan on 257–258; John D. Fairfield, "A Populism for the Cities: Henry George, John Dewey, and the City Planning Movement," *Urban Design Studies* 8 (2002) 19–27; for a later elaboration of this potential, see Lewis Mumford, *The Culture of Cities* (New York: Harcourt, Brace, and Co., 1938) and Ben A. Minteer, *The Landscape of Reform: Civic Pragmatism and Environmental Thought in America* (Cambridge, MA: MIT Press, 2006).

59. Peterson, *The Birth of City Planning*, 29–73; Schultz, *Constructing Urban Culture*, 209–217; Hoy, "Municipal Housekeeping"; Ellen H. Richards, *Sanitation in Daily Life* (Boston: Whitcomb & Barrows, 1910), vii–viii; and Robert Clarke, *Ellen Swallow: The Woman Who Founded Ecology* (Chicago: Follett, 1973)

60. Wilson, *The City Beautiful Movement*, 285–290; Wirka, "The City Social Movement"; and Rome, "'Political Hermaphrodites.'"

61. Reps, *The Making of Urban America*; Mel Scott, *American City Planning Since 1890* (Chicago: American Planning Association, 1969).

62. Wilson, *The City Beautiful Movement in Kansas City* (Columbia: University of Missouri Press, 1964).

63. Wilson, *The City Beautiful Movement.*

64. Jon A. Peterson, "The City Beautiful Movement: Forgotten Origins and Lost Meanings," *Journal of Urban History* 2 (August 1976), 415–434.

65. Peterson, *The Birth of City Planning in the United States 1840–1917.*

66. Bogart, *Public Sculpture and the Civic Ideal in New York City, 1890–1930.*

67. Suellen M. Hoy, "'Municipal Housekeeping': The Role of Women in Improving Urban Sanitation Practices, 1880–1917," in Martin V. Melosi, ed., *Pollution and Reform in American Cities, 1870–1930* (Austin: University of Texas Press, 1980), 173–198.

68. Flanagan, "The City Profitable, the City Livable."

69. Wirka, "The City Social Movement."

70. Boyer, *Urban Masses and Moral Order.*

71. Schultz, *Constructing Urban Culture.*

72. M. Christine Boyer, *Dreaming the Rational City: The Myth of American City Planning* (Cambridge, MA: MIT Press, 1983).

73. Fairfield, *Mysteries of the Great City.*

74. Smith, *Plan of Chicago.*

75. Hines, *Burnham of Chicago.*

76. Manieri-Elia, "Toward an 'Imperial City'"; and Peter Hall, *Cities of Tomorrow; An Intellectual History of Urban Planning and Design Since 1880* (Chichester, UK: Wiley-Blackwell, 2014).

John D. Fairfield

URBAN PLANNING IN THE UNITED STATES SINCE 1850

In 1900, a new generation of reformers called "Progressives" coined the term "city planning" to define something different from previous conscious efforts to build the urban environment. Since ancient times, every place of dense habitation has required some coordinated and collective action. City residents had to design and construct large-scale projects to provide basic necessities of water supplies and drainage, roads and bridges, and harbors and markets. They have also engaged in laying out utopian and realistic street grids of land use for new townsites.

But these plans were piecemeal compared to the Progressives' conception of the city in holistic terms that turned space and society into a living organism. Believing that physical conditions shaped society and culture, these reformers conceived of grand metropolitan plans of beauty, efficiency, and order. This modern, comprehensive approach to planning remains the ideal of professional experts, although it has rarely been achieved. Parallel to the conscious creation of formal plans there have always been informal approaches to city building. From designing domestic architecture to laying out entire shantytowns, marginalized people produced urban space at the center as well as in the suburbs. City planning in the United States since 1850, then, has been marked by the historic watershed of the Progressive Era and the inexorable contestation between top-down and bottom-up approaches. It has also been a part of a much larger, transatlantic conversation on the urban ideal.

THE STATE OF THE ART: 1850

By the 1850s, metropolitan New York City was fast approaching one million residents. Immigration and industrialization fueled the rise of many other urban places along the Eastern seaboard and inland across the Great Lakes to Chicago and St. Louis. City building in the United States and Europe was not only a topic of constant political debate, but also the focus of a growing field of expertise in engineering, sanitation, architecture, and landscaping. The sheer scale and pace of urban growth created immense, collective problems of epidemics, slums, gridlock, pollution, crime, and disorder.

The experts proposed plans on a piecemeal, incremental basis to address each specific physical shortcoming and moral evil of city life. A fearful series of cholera outbreaks put sanitation and public health at the top of civic agendas. Prior to the ascendency of germ theories of disease in the 1890s, doctors relied on miasma theories of putrefaction, or bad smells. Their common sense prescription was to cleanup the stenches and filth. Led by London's scientists, sanitary officials also linked the spread of cholera to water supplies contaminated by human wastes. Engineers in European and American cities including New York, Boston, and Chicago presented plans to construct drinking supply and sewer systems of water management. Their blueprints mapped reservoirs, aqueducts, pumping stations, and pipes and drains on an unprecedented scale. At the same time, policymakers expanded the power of the state over daily life in the name of the public welfare. City governments, for instance, required property owners to hook up their homes and buildings to the water and sewer systems. They also took the first steps toward the professionalization of public administration by establishing fire, police, and public works departments. In most cases, however, the provision of essential urban services was left to privately owned utility companies operating under special franchise contracts with municipal governments. In addition to offering gas lighting, streetcars, and telegrams to middle-class consumers, private firms built and operated the waterworks in many places.

Landscape artists and architects, moreover, started meeting the demands of city dwellers for open, green space and outdoor recreation by drawing plans for public parks in the center and exclusive enclaves in the suburbs. The work of New York City's Frederick Law Olmsted and Calvert Vaux trace one of the taproots of comprehensive city planning. In 1858, they won a design competition for a 780 acre/316 hectare site just north of the fast-moving expansion of the built-up area from the bottom of the island. The "Greensward Plan" embodied a pastoral ideal of nature and an equally formal order of decorum. The construction of Central Park over the next several years also illustrated the clash between formal and informal planning because the site was occupied by several thousand residents living in rural-like communities with colorful names like Seneca Village and Nanny Goat Hill. Portrayed in pejorative terms as "filthy shantytowns" by the park's promoters, their residents were poor but hard-working immigrants and African Americans. They built their own houses and planted garden plots on what was previously farmland. These so-called squatters were evicted in the name of civic progress and social order.[1]

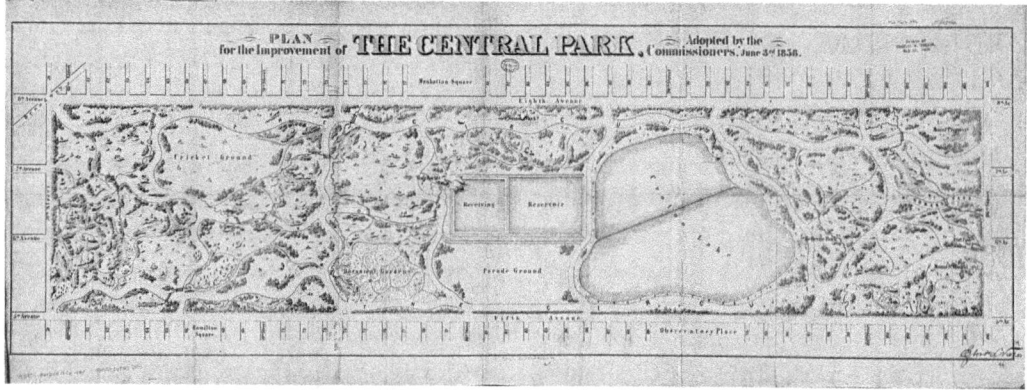

Figure 1. Plan for the improvement of the Central Park, adopted by the Commissioners, June 3rd, 1856. Boston Public Library, Norman B. Leventhal Map Center Collection, 06_01_010785.

THE EVOLUTION FROM GILDED AGE HISTORICISM TO PROGRESSIVE ERA MODERNISM: 1850s–1909

From the 1850s into the 1900s, local governments and private companies operating as public utilities built a "networked city" of infrastructure technologies.[2] Formal planning was often large-scale, albeit disjointed, as each street railway company, municipal sewer department, and state health board worked independently of each other. During the Gilded Age, nonetheless, the search for better ways to resolve the industrial city's problems engendered innovation and opportunity in technology, science, public administration, and business management. City building became a wellspring of invention, including electric lighting to replace fire-prone gas and kerosene lamps; cable and trolley cars to replace horses; and telephones to replace telegraph messenger boys. Big national manufacturing companies emerged that specialized in supplying the hardware and know-how for these urban services as well as spinning off complete home systems of central heating, plumbing fixtures, and kitchen equipment.

During this period of step-by-step planning to meet the needs of cities exploding in population and size, the professionals, businessmen, and tradesmen engaged in this evolutionary process underwent their own metamorphoses. Led by engineers, they became more college-educated and organized into associations that increased the transatlantic flow of information and best practice. Awe-inspiring public works created a fascination in popular culture with the technological sublime of mastering the environment. Taking fourteen years to construct, the Brooklyn Bridge was hailed as a wonder of the world when it opened on May 24, 1883, to great fanfare. The well-deserved hero-of-the-day was its chief engineer, Washington Roebling, the son of its German immigrant designer, John Augustus Roebling, who died in 1869 from injuries suffered on the construction site. The unsung hero was the chief engineers'

wife, Emily Warren Roebling, who did the math to make sure the inventive cable-style suspension bridge could hold the expected traffic loads.[3] Many other cities boasted about their big technology projects: sanitation and ship canals, railroad terminals, maritime dock facilities, waterworks pumping stations, and underground subway tunnels.

In 1869, speculators hired Olmsted and Vaux to plan Riverside, Illinois, a model suburb near Chicago on land along the heavily wooded Des Plaines River. Since it had been recently crossed by a railroad, commuting times were cut to a half-hour ride in comfort. Riverside's developers planned to lure well-to-do families to the countryside by providing them with all the modern amenities of the networked city. In addition to the famous planners' park-like townsite map, Riverside had a shopping arcade, gaslights, water mains, and paved streets and sidewalks.[4] Such examples from the top down of virtually utopian residential and industrial communities were rare compared to much more common, vernacular architecture from the bottom up. Local subdividers, homebuilders, craftsmen, and do-it-yourselfers were responsible for constructing most of the neighborhoods in the cities' outer rings and in the railroad and the streetcar suburbs. Homeowners' front yards and shopkeepers' storefront facades along commercial strips added to the preponderance of informal planning in the production and experience of urban space. These landscapes reflected the infinite variety of individual creativity, while their formal architectural structures expressed the era's fashion of historic revivals such as Romanesque and Gothic. Outward sprawl was matched by new levels of concentration at the center, where experts used new materials such as steel I-beams and large plate-glass windows to erect ever taller skyscrapers.

Although germ theories of disease had revolutionary implications, they initially reinforced traditional miasma theories and their emphasis on cleanliness. The American medical community took thirty years to recognize Louis Pasteur's pioneering work in the 1860s and establish new public health institutions based on the life sciences of bacteriology and organic chemistry. During this long transitional period, water management planning in the cities remained fragmented and incremental. The job of laying mains and pipes usually lagged behind the pace of development at their outer edges. Like other networked technologies, urban water supply and sewer systems became standardized in their equipment and management.

The transformation of these critical necessities of city life, moreover, illuminates how the integration of science and technology helped foster the birth of comprehensive planning. Armed with microscopes and petri dishes, researchers identified bacteria that not only caused disease but also ones that rendered them harmless. Engineers started building a new generation of water purification and sewage treatment plants based on biotechnologies that dramatically cut death rates. To reduce the toll from the 19th century's most infectious germ, *Mycobacterium tuberculosis*, they devised an ad hoc array of plans ranging from power plants and railroad engines to eliminate smoke, to suburban sanitariums to isolate the sick, homes redesigned to maximize air and light, and publicity campaigns to prohibit spitting.[5]

Public discourse on the city's problems also generated novel ideas about metropolitan areas and the ways that these sprawling, urbanizing environments influenced society and culture. A second taproot of modern planning grew out of the parks and recreation movements to get back-to-nature, spawning civic improvement groups that lobbied for their favorite municipal monuments and outdoor art projects. They tended to emphasize the social, as opposed to the spatial, benefits of their plans to reform the urban environment, especially for children living in the slums of the inner city and the industrial suburbs. Middle-class women's and men's clubs, religious organizations, trade unions, and social settlement workers became spearheads of reform to upgrade the

quality of daily life. In 1893, experts wove many strands of Gilded Age planning together in the creation of the Chicago's World's Fair. Visited by one out of every five Americans, the imperial splendor of the formal Court of Honor in this make-believe "White City" impressed them as much as its dazzling displays of electricity, cornucopia of consumer goods, and titillations of popular amusements along the Midway Plaisance. The fairgrounds were exclusively for affluent whites to enjoy because Jim Crow policies barred African Americans from entering its gates and an admission ticket they could not afford kept poor people out.[6]

THE MACHINE AGE AND THE ORGANIC CITY: 1909–1945

Fed by the success of the World's Fair as a prototype of a future utopia, a notion gained momentum that the physical conditions and the social functions of real urban areas were interdependent parts of a natural system, an "Organic City." A leading spirit of this reform idea and chief architect of the fair was Daniel H. Burnham. He and many other experts involved in making it a model of beauty, efficiency, and order concluded that comprehensive approaches to planning were needed to gain control of the physical metabolism and the social health of the urban ecology. They gradually included more and more civic improvements in blueprints of their urban ideal. Sixteen years later in 1909, a revolutionary breakthrough occurred when Burnham and his collaborator, Edward H. Bennett, published the monumental *Plan of Chicago*. With visionary color illustrations, Burnham and Bennett imagined the Chicago metropolis fifty years in the future. *Plan of Chicago* appeared the same year as the first National Conference on City Planning in Washington, DC; a year later a similar international meeting was held in London. In the wake of these seminal watersheds, comprehensive city planning by professional experts became institutionalized in university degree programs, city departments, and blue-ribbon commissions. Over the next thirty-five years, the formal role of the planner expanded over not only what academic theorists cast as the Organic City, but also the nature conservation and the social geography of entire metropolitan regions.[7]

Burnham's formal hierarchy of special purpose zones for the fairgrounds, and Olmsted's landscape architecture for the parks surrounding it, inspired a ferment of reform to rebuild the cities. Progressives gained official approval to draw grand plans in a lengthening list of places stretching from Washington, DC, to San Francisco, California, and beyond to the capital of the Philippines, Manila, which the United States had colonized after the Spanish-American War in 1898. Local politicians learned that they could build patronage armies and electoral majorities by sponsoring the construction of pieces of these visionary schemes. Real estate developers, moreover, learned that beauty paid, becoming lobbyists for more public parks because adjacent land values always went up. By the coming of World War I and the machine age of mass production, the new profession's identity and goals were well established. "The new and significant fact for which this new term 'city planning' stands," stated Frederick Law Olmsted Jr., in 1916, "is a growing perception of a city's

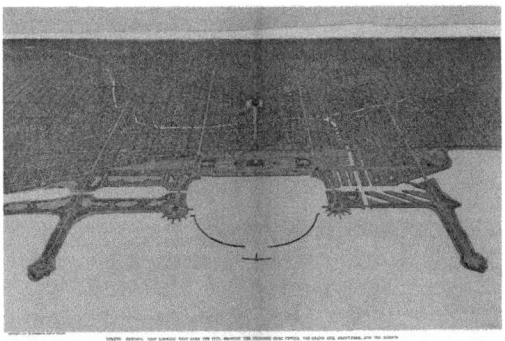

Figure 2. The 1909 Plan of Chicago, commonly referred to as the "Burnham Plan." Daniel H. Burnham and Edward H. Bennett. *Plan of Chicago.* Illustrator Jules Guérin.
Chicago: Commercial Club of Chicago, 1909.

organic unity.... The ideal of a unified, intelligent, and purposeful control of the city's entire development follows obviously and logically from the conception of the city as a social unity with its fate in its own hands."[8]

In spite of the crescendo of appeals from this planner and his colleagues to put the fate of urban society in the hands of experts like themselves, few places implemented more than fragments of their grand designs. The examples were found in Cleveland, Denver, and Harrisburg, all of which redeveloped significant parts of their municipal and civic downtown areas. Perhaps their greatest achievement was the widespread enactment of municipal zoning codes that divided urban real estate into a hierarchy of residential, commercial, and industrial zones. The first zoning law was passed in Los Angeles in 1908, identifying certain parts of the city as residential and industrial districts. New York adopted the first comprehensive zoning law in 1916. Some southern cities, including Baltimore, Richmond, Atlanta, Louisville, and New Orleans passed racially restrictive zoning codes between 1910 and 1918. Such Jim Crow statutes were eventually ruled unconstitutional in *Buchanan v. Warley* (1917). But zoning as a form of planning grew more popular, especially in the wake of *Euclid v. Ambler* (1926), which upheld the constitutionality of zoning.

The near universal demand of city residents and suburbanites alike to get back to nature also led to the fulfillment of many of their proposals for metropolitan-scale networks of recreational parks, nature preserves, and greenbelts. The Progressives' conservation and planning ideas fused into a novel concept of the Organic City as a regional-scale ecology of natural resource and social demographic flows of energy. Advocates of regional planning, for example, envisioned high-voltage lines literally and figuratively linking remote hydroelectric dams, rural farms, and urban areas in bonds of mutual benefit. During the 1920s, however, a conservative majority put political brakes on civic improvement projects; the Great Depression of the 1930s restricted local funding of these public works; and World War II brought them to a virtual standstill.

In contrast, individual philanthropists, real estate developers, and trade unions funded plans to build models of the Anglo-American, suburban ideal during the interwar years. Housing reformers contributed to the construction of physical space that was designed to foster family unity, and community. To rekindle these traditional values, planners teamed up with social workers to create a modern solution to what they perceived as the city's primary pathology: overcrowding in the city center. The Regional Planning Association of America (1923–1933), led by Clarence Stein, Benton MacKaye, Lewis Mumford, Frederick Ackerman, and Henry Wright, was among the leading proponents of deconcentration. In 1924, Stein, Wright, and Ackerman completed Sunnyside Gardens, a "garden city" planned community in Queens, New York. In 1929, Wright and Stein founded Radburn, New Jersey, as a suburban, garden city prototype for the motor age. These planners generally adopted a top-down, formal approach called the "neighborhood unit plan," best exemplified by the *Regional Plan of New York* developed during the 1920s.[9] The cell of the Organic City was structured around the neighborhood elementary school. It was the geographic and social nucleus of the community, surrounded by a ring of green space, a shopping mall, and single-family homes. Limited access roads into the cell protected its homogenous communities from invasive cancers of members of undesirable racial, ethnic, and religious groups. Private ownership and governance of this early example of a master-planned community ensured strict conformity to architectural guidelines and social segregation.[10]

The New Deal, moreover, ushered in the heyday of regional and national planning. From

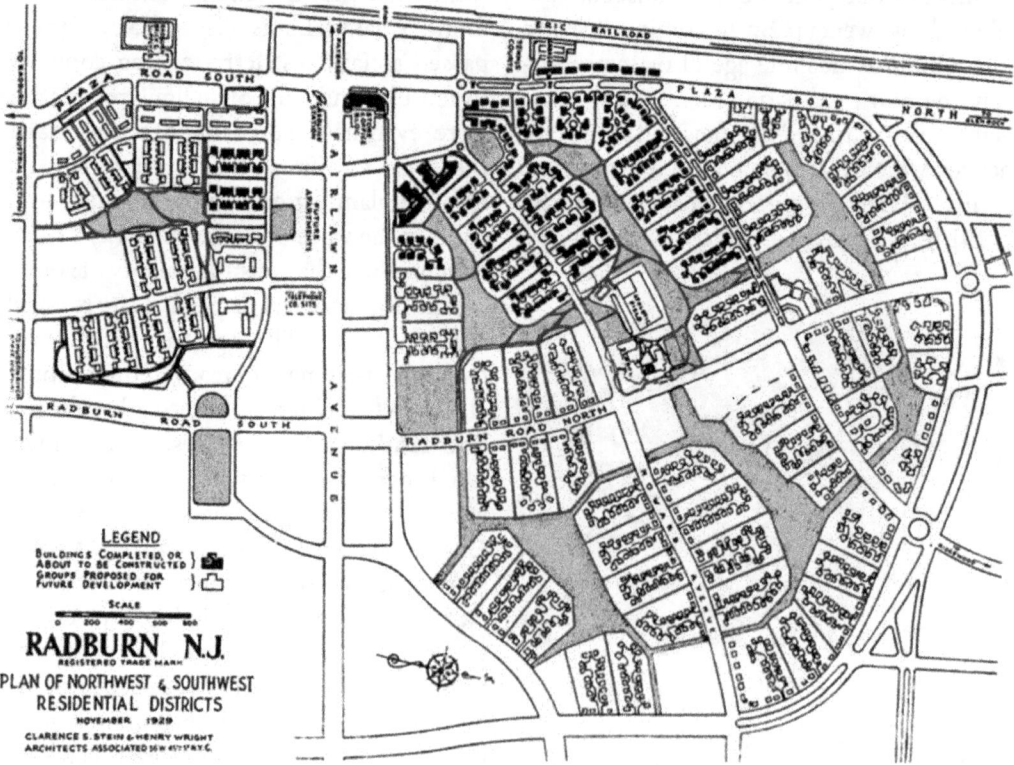

Figure 3. Plan of Radburn, New Jersey. Clarence Stein and Henry Wright, 1929.
Courtesy of Regional Plan Association.

1933 to 1945, the federal government became a seedbed of experiments in engineering the environment and society on an unprecedented scale. Regionalists, for example, were put in charge of the Tennessee Valley Authority, while conservationists made long-term projections of the country's use of natural resources. A few city planners, furthermore, were given the opportunity to oversee the construction of complete "New Towns," suburban subdivisions and rural villages. For example, the US Resettlement Administration under Rexford Guy Tugwell developed several "greenbelt" towns, the most famous being Greenbelt, Maryland (1937). Planners were also empowered for the first time to build public housing on a large scale. First Houses (1935) in New York City and Techwood Homes (1936) in Atlanta were the first public housing projects completed in the United States. Their success contributed to passage of the federal Housing Act of 1937 (sometimes called the Wagner Housing Act after US Senator Robert Wagner of New York), which initiated the construction of public housing in urban areas throughout the United States. Planners, however, were constrained by a 1935 Supreme Court ruling declaring that the federal government had no right to condemn private land for low-cost housing because such programs were not considered a "public purpose." Only states and municipalities enjoyed that right. The Public Works Administration proceeded to establish local housing authorities throughout the country. Thus after 1937, the federal government did not build one unit of housing, but simply supplied funds to communities with housing authorities which applied for funding.

At the same time, armies of the unemployed built shantytowns called "Hoovervilles," which sprang up across the country in city parks, railroad yards, and on abandoned suburban land. Money from the federal government also poured into city halls to fund a laundry list of infrastructure improvement projects to put some of the unemployed back to work, ranging from laying sewers in the streets to planting trees in the forest preserves. Although the wartime emergency stymied most of their projects, planners looked forward to a coming era of peace and prosperity.

THE GOLDEN ERA OF FORMAL, CLEAN-SWEEP PLANNING: 1945–1965

For twenty years following the end of World War II, city planners enjoyed more power to influence the building of the urban environment than before or since. Academically trained experts played central roles in the modernization of the inner cities and the sprawl of the suburbs. A transatlantic consensus persuaded policymakers that overcrowding in the slums was the root cause of social disorder and crime. Their professional unity amplified their call for clean-sweep demolition in the center and mass resettlement in healthy homes in the periphery. Fueled by federal funding, highway engineers took the lead in creating computer simulations of future traffic patterns to justify bulldozing historic neighborhoods in the name of national defense. New Deal experiments in housing became major programs to underwrite "urban renewal" projects, beginning with the Housing Act of 1949. The federal government expanded home mortgage subsidy programs with the passage of the Servicemen's Adjustment Act of 1944 (better known as the GI Bill), which facilitated record-setting home ownership in the United States, especially for white male veterans. Buying a house in the suburbs became a better deal than renting an apartment in the city. While the older, railroad cities in the "Rustbelt" of the Northeast and the Midwest gave top priority to remaking their downtowns into international business centers, the newer, automobile cities of the "Sunbelt" in the West and the South put their emphasis on constructing freeways to the city's expanding outer rings of settlement.

Pent-up demand for housing to accommodate a historic baby boom generated a wellspring of opportunity for planners to design complete communities on the "crabgrass frontier" of suburbia.[11] Many of them incorporated the model suburban ideals of Riverside and the neighborhood unit plan of Radburn. They helped the community builders apply industrial-scale, assembly line methods to building this suburban ideal, complete with front yard landscaping and cul-de-sac streets. William Levitt was the leading pioneer of these new suburban communities. His family business constructed "Levittowns" in Long Island (1947), Pennsylvania (1952), and New Jersey (1958). These and other similar projects, such as Los Angeles County's Lakewood (1954)—constructed by Louis Boyer, Mark Taper, and Ben Weingart—were mass-produced in a frenzy of construction, shifting the population by 1970 from an urban to a suburban majority. Lakewood was also the nation's first community to "contract out" for all of its municipal services when it incorporated, making it the nation's first "contract city." The "Lakewood Plan" became a low-tax model for postwar suburban planners. The original goal of comprehensive city planning to create a dispersed metropolis had triumphed.

The two postwar decades may have been a golden era for city planners, but those years represented a dark period of despair for the hundreds of thousands of people displaced by their clean-sweep approach to urban renewal. The neighborhoods of mostly poor African American and other nonwhite ethnic groups were specifically targeted for so-called slum clearance. Official experts and private mortgage lenders had already doomed these community areas as patches of land at the end of their life cycles. They were "red-lined" as unworthy of any further financial investments or conservation efforts. To accommodate some families bulldozed out of their homes, the planners designed clusters of public housing tower blocks that became "second ghettos" of class and racial and ethnic segregation.[12] Many others displaced by the wrecking ball and discrimination had to cram into substandard housing in other red-lined neighborhoods, disrupting their social order, accelerating their physical decline, and fueling the rise of violent youth gangs. Under the reign of top-down, formal approaches to city planning, the geographic and the social distance between the haves and the have-nots kept widening over sprawling metropolitan regions.

Largely unnoticed at the time, some neighborhoods in the city and inner ring of historic suburbs experienced revivals with thriving districts of restored housing, trendy shops, and nightlife attractions. In these parishes and neighborhoods, a core group of homeowners, shopkeepers, and local leaders, according to the most influential critic of the official planners, Jane Jacobs, came together to save their communities from the wrecking ball of urban renewal. In *The Death and Life of Great American Cities* (1962), Jacobs praised their informal, bottoms-up approaches to planning because they were restoring a vibrant culture of city life in the streets, parks, and other public spaces between the buildings.[13] She also condemned the concept of the Organic City as a cruel myth that kept planners and policymakers hidden behind an academic façade of the autonomous, natural life cycle of cities. In addition to highlighting the vitality of such inner-city districts as North End in Boston and Back-of-the-Yards in Chicago, Jacobs could have also named a growing list of ethnoburbs, where various immigrant groups remade their neighborhoods into comfort zones. In metropolitan Los Angeles, for example, a majority of Monterey Park/San Gabriel became Asian, while nine out of ten residents of once white, working-class South Gate were Latino by the end of the 20th century. The immigrants established their own churches, social clubs, business owners associations, restaurants, food markets, and so on that nurtured a sense of community solidarity and cultural identity in their new homeland.[14]

THE REVOLT AGAINST THE PLANNERS: 1965–1980s

A revolt against the planners began in the Watts district of Los Angeles in 1965, escalating over the next three years into a national (and an international) crisis of civil disorder, racial inequality, and environmental injustice. These mass uprisings demanded answers to questions about the city planners' value-laden assumptions about society, and their undemocratic, top-down process of decision making. Other, more peaceful forms of protest sprang up to stop the highway builders from destroying any more historic neighborhoods. These class-bridging, coalition movements raised questions about the profession's blind faith in technological modernization as the only way to bring about a utopian, Organic City. The revolt triggered an internal crisis among the experts that resulted in fundamental changes in the theory and practice of formal city planning over the next twenty years.

During this period of energy transitions and related economic stagflation, advocates of new approaches contested the postwar consensus. Some called for professional experts to assume different roles as advocates of citizen participation from the bottom up in the formation of public policy. Others called for private institutions and business corporations to take greater roles in partnership with government in the production of urban space. Defenders of technological modernization doubled down by designing much more sophisticated computer simulations of the Organic City as an autonomous, metabolic system of flows. The planner became a manager, according to the influential textbook, *Urban and Regional Planning: A System Approach*, whose role was "the deliberate control or regulation of this system

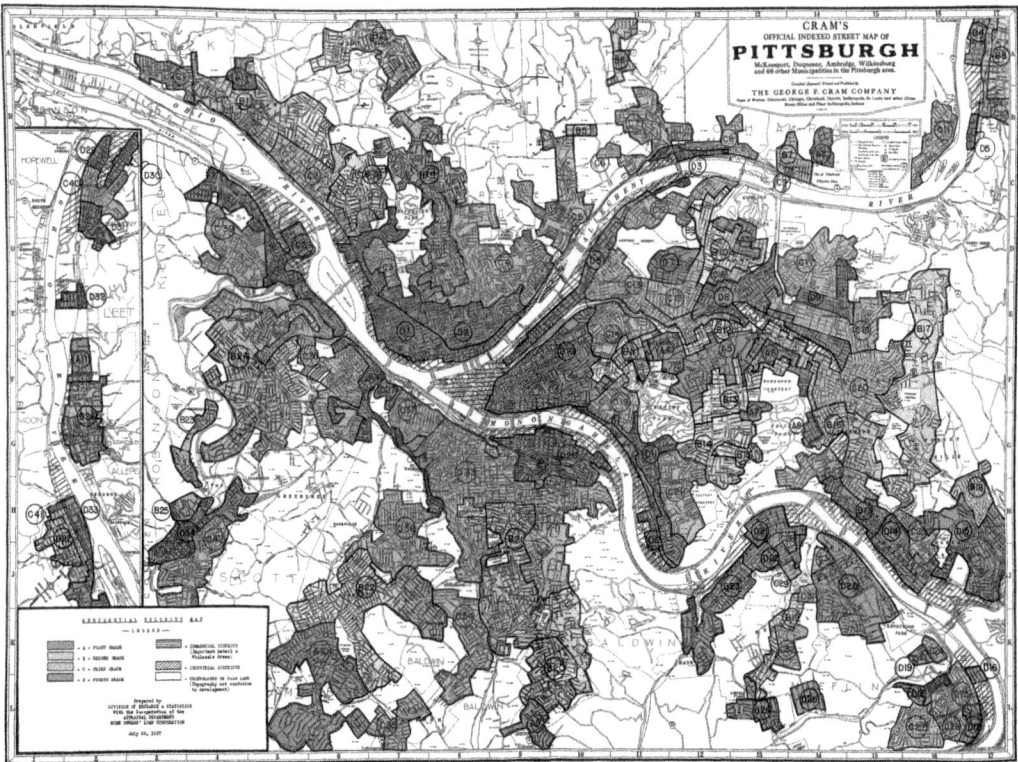

Figure 4. HOLC Redlining map of Pittsburgh, PA. Courtesy of Mapping Inequality.
Creative Commons License (CC BY-NC-SA 4.0).

so that the physical environment shall yield the greater social benefit in relation to cost."[15]

Voiceless were the growing ranks of the city's homeless, unemployed victims of deindustrialization, globalization, and deconcentration of jobs to the car-accessible-only periphery. Rising into the tens of thousands in several metropolitan areas, they often found relative safety and mutual aid by clustering together in makeshift campsites and shantytowns. Their daily presence on city streets and in public spaces, however, heightened fears of violence and crime among middle-class residents, setting off a panic appropriately called white flight to fortified, gated communities in new style, "edge cities."[16]

From the Watts riots to the Battle of Chicago at the 1968 Democratic Party National Convention, the nation was rocked by civil uprisings in city after city by African Americans and other nonwhite racial and ethnic groups. Although these outbursts of bloodshed, looting, and arson usually started with a police confrontation, they forced the larger issue of institutional racism into the public arena. The ensuing political debate exposed the central role of formal city planning in slum clearance and urban renewal projects that resulted in segregated and inferior public housing, education, healthcare, recreation, and other essential urban facilities and services. The real estate industry's systematic practice of racial and ethnic prejudice also came to light during this frightening period of so-called hot summers. In addition, the critics of modernism like Jacobs, who were previously dismissed out-of-hand, now became prominent spokespersons of alternative approaches to city building. In 1968, for example, these avatars of reform helped write the Fair Housing Act, which made discrimination a federal offense. Congress also passed legislation that empowered community groups in the formation of plans for local improvement projects that accepted federal funding. At the same time, the collapse of the postwar consensus of clean-sweep planning exiled the professional experts from the centers of power at city hall.

During these lean years of intense infighting, some planning practioners found work helping private developers build complete mini or edge cities on the crabgrass frontier of metropolitan regions. They followed a formula that located a mix of corporate headquarters set in college campus-like settings, ever-bigger shopping malls, and commercial/professional office space near a superhighway. Adjacent to these economic anchors, developers morphed the neighborhood unit into the gated community. The limited access feature of the original design was ready-made for adaptation to consumer demand for security as a top priority in deciding where to live. Planners also appealed to homebuyers' special interests by fashioning homogenous communities for retirees, golfers, artists, and those seeking the exclusivity of class from million-dollar-plus price tags. Urban areas became multicentered and commuting patterns reversed as city residents in the center followed the diffusion of jobs into the periphery.

In 1968, the revolt against the planners became international, when the largest protest movements in the postwar era erupted in cities throughout Europe and Latin America. The rejection of technological modernism was a common cause bringing diverse groups into the streets, including trade unionists, college students, political activists, and counterculture radicals such as Betty Friedan, Abbie Hoffman, and Andy Warhol. They now echoed critics who had earlier decried the planners' creation of a dystopian "technological society" that was reducing human consciousness to a robotic "one-dimensional man."[17] New voices called for advocacy and participatory approaches to institutionalize democratic planning at the neighborhood level. Building on this political ideal of the city as a landscape of self-governing villages, the infusion of modern environmentalism further blurred the lines between formal and informal planning. Denouncing grand plans, they applauded the reconstruction of Watts by Mexican Americans into a neighborhood, where the front yards and streets were alive with hot music, mural art, religious ritual, low-riders, spicy food, and pride in the community.[18] The appearance of a profusion of alternative visions of the city generated a permanent state of contestation over planning proposals for makeovers of inner city and suburban districts.

THE AGE OF THE MULTICENTERED METROPOLIS: 1980s–PRESENT

During the recovery of the US economy in the mid-1980s, planners enjoyed a revival of their personal fortunes and professional influence in building the urban environment. But the theory and practice of planning remained fractured, challenged by opposing factions from within as well as outside critics from all sides of the debate over the future of the city. Reflecting the growing divisions in contemporary society, perhaps, formal approaches to planning expressed an equally widening gap between competing urban ideals. In a similar way, city hall's response to the problem of homelessness ranged from criminalization and imprisonment to expansion of social welfare and public housing programs.

On the one hand, the top-down proponents of technological modernization envisioned smart cities, where computers coordinate the flow of people, information, and goods in real time. Like some of today's high-tech buildings that automatically adjust the window shades to maximize interior light and temperature, the cyborg City of Flows will have digital feedback loops to control environmental conditions and maintain social order. On the other hand, the bottom-up champions of participatory planning foresee a democratic future embedded in multicentered metropolitan regions. The accretion of government jurisdictions has devolved power from city hall and corporate boardrooms into the hands of local communities. In a populist City of Citizens, residents will take primary responsibility for the production and experience of urban space in their home districts.[19] While system planners called for

administrative consolidations like the ten-county Atlanta Regional Commission (ARC), participatory advocates worked to give a seat at the table of policymakers to groups such as homeowners associations, ward advisory councils, and environmental protection organizations.[20]

Over the next quarter century, a wide spectrum of formal plans was implemented with varying degrees of success. Local politicians and business leaders led the effort to restart "the city as growth machine," returning to incremental, piecemeal approaches to planning from the top down.[21] Relinquishing comprehensive plans, experts designed projects at a middle-range scale to kickstart the urban economy: convention centers, tourist attractions, trendy districts, and environmental modernization projects for public parks and nature preserves. Downtown regeneration plans, for instance, included San Antonio's Riverwalk, Chicago's Millennium Park, and New York's High Line. The highway engineers restored their reputations as leaders of the profession by creating the most sophisticated system approaches. For example, the planners of Atlanta's ARC presented computer simulations of the city's future patterns of growth as all-but-inevitable projections of spatial and demographic trends. They facilitated a political process that confounded value-laden, software scenarios and physical reality. They became partners with civic elites, who used their reports to justify not only funneling increasingly limited funds into their city boosting schemes but also cutting off investment in other districts, turning them into "ghettos of exclusion."[22]

Adopting the real estate developers' age-old law of land values, formal approaches to planning gave special emphasis to bringing about greater physical intensification of people and activity in both the center and the periphery. Revitalization of the inner ring of suburbs, for instance, involved government-business partnerships to pay for improving the streetscapes of their Main Streets with public funds and upgrading their storefront facades with private money. The plans also typically recommended rezoning these commercial districts to permit high-density, multifamily housing in new apartment and condominium buildings as well as in units converted from old shops and warehouses. Plans for intensification of select patches of urban space depended on a second common assumption of top-down approaches: the need to weave metropolitan areas seamlessly into an emerging global infrastructure of interconnectivity. One exemplar of transnational urbanism was the Club of Rome. Founded in 1968, its supercomputers have quantified flows of geophysical, economic, and social data on a global scale. Another was post-Watts Los Angeles's Silver Book Plan and its successors, designed to attract investment capital from other countries and forming a Pacific Rim of economic markets. To stay competitive as a vital node in this flow of trade, the planners drew maps to integrate seaports and airports, highway networks, transit systems, innovation centers, and Internet capacities. Initially designed to subsidize the rebuilding of the downtown district, the plan was modified in the late 1980s to spread the benefits to commercial office centers throughout the metropolitan region.[23] To create a global city of suburbs, the planners also responded to a continuing intensification of a psychological state of fear of crime and violence among some city residents by offering blueprints of fortified tower blocks in the center and high-security, mini-cities of walls in the periphery.[24]

In the follow-up to the first Earth Day in 1970, environmental reform movements sprang up to save the planet, or at least patches of it. In the city, the highway revolt often became an early source of political demands from the bottom up to participate in the planning process. Since the proposed routes of the bulldozer tore through many neighborhoods, these top-down schemes also served as coalition builders that cut across social divisions of race and ethnicity, gender, and class. Sometimes with the help of the new breed of university-trained, advocacy planners, the grassroots no longer

accepted the lame role offered by city hall to voice feedback on, but to make no significant changes in its finished plans.[25] Like the conservation movement during the Progressive Era, more and more people formed place-based groups to save nature from the city as growth machine that was paving over the land, polluting the air and the water, and killing off the native wildlife. To reclaim urban and suburban natures from overdevelopment, reformers proposed solutions that ranged from more technology to dismantling it in favor of replacing brownfields with open lands, invasive species with indigenous plants and animals, and sanitation channels with restored waterways.[26]

In the post-consensus age, planners were liberated from the orthodoxy of modernism to create hybrids that combined various mixes of technological, environmental, civic, and ethnocultural values. A visionary of socially and economically balanced communities, master builder James Rouse personified the evolution of planning on an ever-larger scale by the private sector. During the thirty years following World War II, he moved up from a mortgage loan broker to a pioneer developer of shopping malls as suburban town centers, to designer of the master-planned community of Cross Keys (1965) outside of Baltimore, Maryland, to the planner of a complete new city, Columbia, Maryland (1967). Around a town square, Rouse arranged twelve, neighborhood unit-like villages that provided a range of housing stock, industrial parks, commercial zones, recreational spaces, and all the other facilities and conveniences of modern life. Rouse went on to develop Boston's Faneuil Hall/Quincy Market (1976), Baltimore's HarborPlace (1980), and New York's South Street Seaport (1983) into major tourist destinations. Six years after opening, HarborPlace had tripled the number of tourists in the Inner Harbor area of Baltimore. Boston's Faneuil Hall attracted twelve million tourists in 1995.[27]

While inner-city neighborhoods were undergoing makeovers with suburban strip malls and big-box stores, Rouse's comprehensive planning inspired the rise of a "New Urbanism" in the utopian tradition of city building.[28] To create the master-planned community of Celebration, Florida, for example, the Walt Disney Company employed professional firms and famous architects. They reimagined, circa 1900, an affluent railroad suburb, a village green surrounded by single-family houses set back on large front lawns. Governed as private space, the company required homebuyers to sign an agreement to obey a thick bible of restrictive property rules and social prohibitions. Other New Urbanism designs devoid of public space included enclosed shopping malls and commercial buildings equipped with elevators without push-buttons and entry only by personal keycard, permission from a security guard, or remote-control surveillance camera. In the postmodern era of pluralism, premodern models of urban commons, civic centers, and residential enclaves were also reinvented on patches of built-up areas.

The current state of urban planning in the United States remains highly contested between formal and informal, top-down and bottom-up approaches. Returning to piecemeal and small- and middle-scale projects, the intensification of the New Urbanism has transformed declining downtown cores and railroad suburbs into upscale hubs of cosmopolitan life. These conscious efforts have been matched by community activists, rehabbers, and speculators, who applied ad hoc methods of gentrification to neighborhoods throughout the metropolitan region. Some of them have been reborn as not only ethnocentric districts but class-exclusive ones as well. Against the benefits of these projects to modernize the urban environment must be weighed the costs in terms of human displacement and loss of the city's architectural heritage. Equally problematic has been the rise of place-based groups, which rally behind a banner of Not-In-My-Backyard (NIMBY) to defeat reforms aimed at narrowing social and environmental gaps of inequality. The politics of planning remains at the center of the ongoing civic debate about the ideal American city of the future.

DISCUSSION OF THE LITERATURE

The history of planning history is relatively brief. Its origins paralleled and eventually converged with two other budding fields of scholarly interest in the post–World War II era, cities and technology. At first, all three fields took a biographical approach to tell heroic stories of leading pioneers, metropolitan growth, and revolutionary inventions, respectively. By the mid-1960s, they each had adopted sociological concepts that created a methodological framework of political culture and economy. Formal planning became seen as playing an instrumental role in much larger processes of urbanization and modernization. Planning history expanded in terms of the number, type, and organization of actors, as well as the range of research topics. Some scholars, moreover, traced the ideological roots of urban planning back into the 19th century.

By the mid-1980s, interdisciplinary approaches more or less morphed into multidisciplinary ones that wove planning into the socioeconomic, political, and cultural fabric of the city. Planning history broadened its perspectives by drawing insight from emerging fields of study, including the environment, suburbanization, transnational urbanism, and globalization. Since then, it has continued to become more enmeshed in postmodernist models of an increasingly complex web of society and culture. In a similar way, the American experience is being intertwined into larger comparative and international frameworks of research.

An antiurban, pastoral bias left the city a long-neglected subject of study by American historians compared to traditional topics such as the westward conquest of a continent, and the Civil War. With the official birth of "city planning" in 1900, and a majority of the population living in urban areas two decades later, a nation in denial could not persist forever. Yet, it took another twenty years to reach a

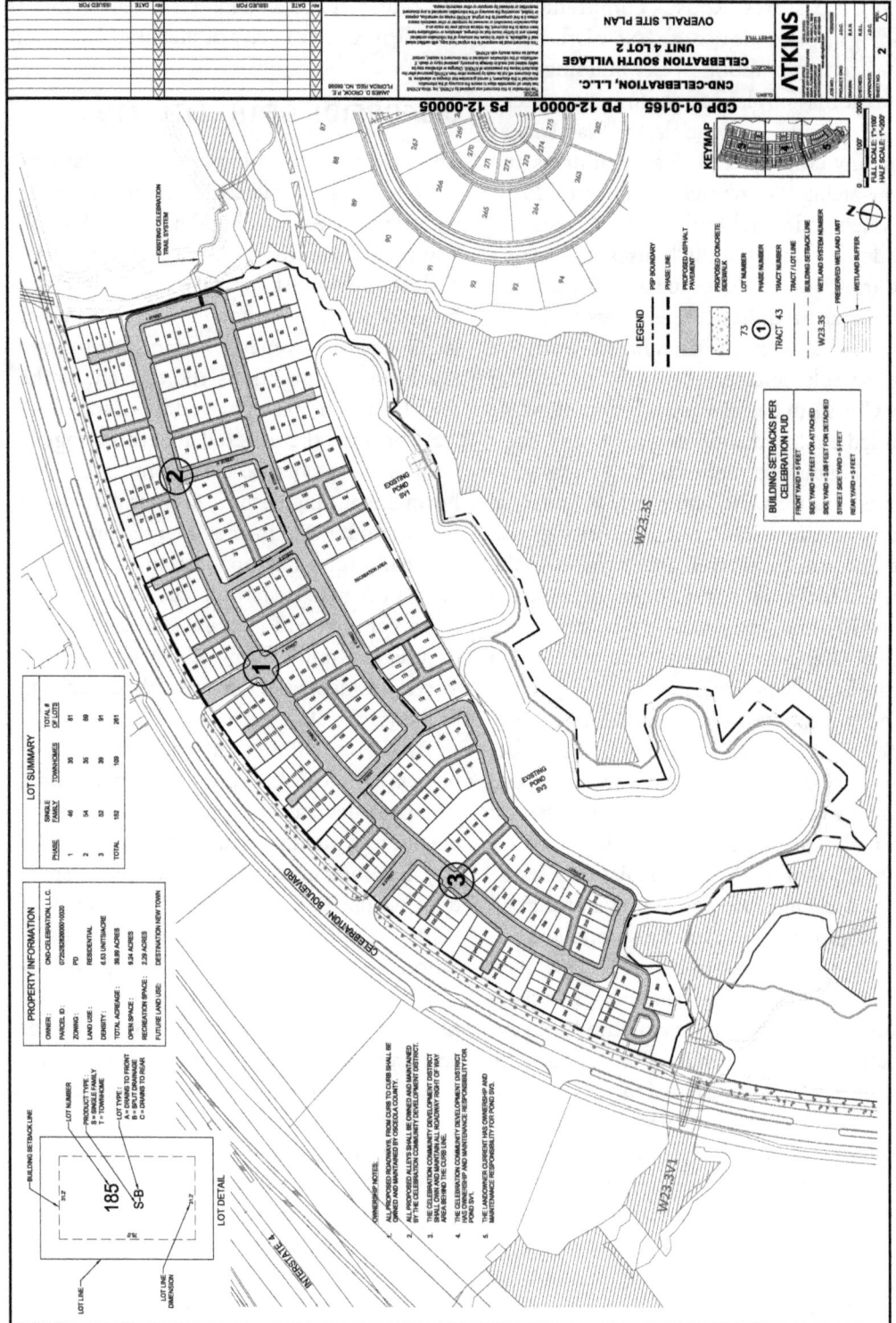

Figure 5. Plan of Celebration, FL, 2012.
From public records.

tipping point with the publication of Arthur Schlesinger Sr.'s influential essay, "The City in American History."[29] After 1945, peace and returning veterans brought prosperity to colleges and universities, including their social science and humanities departments. The first serious history of planning, however, did not appear until 1969, when Mel Scott produced *American City Planning since 1890*.[30] Before this important study of the institutionalization of planning, the field was occupied by biographies of its first generation of founding heroes, who were now fast passing away. The American Institute of Planner's journal sponsored a series of them as well as Scott's celebratory history of the profession and its milestones.[31]

During the twenty years after the mass uprising of the Watts section of Los Angeles in 1965, scholars created a widening spectrum of urban studies that focused attention on class, gender, race and ethnicity. In giving agency to previously ignored place-based communities and special interest groups, historians shed light on the multitude of ways that they had contributed to making the urban environment. The researchers not only gave credit to informal methods of city building, but also gave voice to protests from the bottom up against planning from the top down. Paralleling the revolt against the planners in the streets, scholars applied postmodernist techniques of deconstruction to dissect the ideological roots and literary classics of the profession. For example, they linked the ideas behind Fredrick Law Olmsted's park and suburban plans in the 1850s to the birth of comprehensive planning and Organic City concepts during the Progressive Era. Historians, moreover, traced the anti-urban bias of the profession to its postwar plans of clean-sweep slum clearance, urban renewal, and high-speed freeways to middle-class, white suburbs.[32]

Although slow in gaining traction, the architectural critic Jane Jacobs's *The Death and Life of Great American Cities* (1961) was an intellectual bulldozer that demolished the planner's postwar consensus of value-laden, albeit unspoken assumptions about urban society and its political economy.[33] Historians followed in her footsteps to reexamine the long-term causes and consequences of metropolitan sprawl and technological modernization that by 1970 had created a suburban majority. Planning history evolved to work within multidimensional, socioeconomic frameworks and methodologies. Furthermore, it continued to expand the chronological and spatial boundaries of the impacts of planning theory and practice on American cities. The garden city plan of England's Ebenezer Howard, for instance, was reframed from a suburban blueprint of metropolitan growth to a utopian ideal of social cooperation. Following his antiurban, pastoral ideas through literary texts, Raymond Williams illuminated their genesis in 17th-to-18th-century London, when it became a "monster," the western world's first big city.[34] At the other end of the timeline, historians gave modern planners a makeover from their Progressive Era self-image as social reformers to neoliberal agents of the business class that helped rationalize and construct the "Capitalist City."[35]

Over the last quarter century, historians have been pushing the frontiers of urban and planning history in all directions from the local to the regional, transnational, and global. On these multiple geographic scales, they have been investigating the flow of planning ideas among the grassroots, professional elites, and policymakers. Equally important, they have been examining the process of turning plans into shapes on the ground. Individual and comparative case studies remain the basic approach to research projects. Some of them are exploring planning theory and practice at the micro-neighborhood level while others are putting the local in larger international contexts. For example, ethnographic perspectives from inside exploding shantytowns in the global South inform scholarship on America's big city ghettos of despair. In contrast, historians are producing studies that show how the worldwide spread of American-style gated communities and edge-cities are creating global suburbs.[36] Taken together, these investigations are spawning new ways of seeing the planning cultures of different ethnic and national groups. This scholarship also invites self-reflection on America's cultural shifts from conservation to environmentalism, Levittown subdivisions to New Urbanism, and bricks-and-mortar stores to wireless interconnectivity.[37]

PRIMARY SOURCES

Planning history is embedded in larger social and cultural frameworks of urban studies. The geographical scale of the research project will direct attention toward specific sources. The official records of planning, public works, public health, and parks and recreation departments, and special commission reports exist at every level of the federal system from city hall to the national capital. Private organizations and advisory groups often provide a parallel set of sources of formal planning from the local to the national and beyond, to a global level of computer simulations. Metropolitan and regional scale agencies offer additional documents. The published works of academic theorists and working practitioners can be consulted in their books and essays in professional journals and conference proceedings. Researchers can also seek access to the archives of individual planners, as well as to their architectural, engineering, and consulting firms.

Literary and artistic sources are another depository of the social and cultural history of planning when they reveal visions of life in futuristic utopian and dystopian cities. And, of course, material culture, in the form of patches of the built environment, can be interrogated by scholars to evaluate the successes and failures of specific plans in the production of urban space. Historic photographs, films, and videos can also help provide a way to examine over time the planners' intended uses of their city building projects in comparison to their actual uses.

A different basic set of primary sources exists for formal and informal planning at the neighborhood and parish levels of community organization. Hopefully, these groups and their leading spokespersons have kept a collection of their records, or have given them to a historical archive. Daily newspapers and monthly local magazines, especially in digital form, can prove invaluable in recreating timelines and agendas of planning activism from the bottom up. These accounts supply the raw materials of the politics of planning. In the period before the institutionalization of city planning during the Progressive Age, the bigger cities often had several newspapers that represented the viewpoint of different political factions and ethnic groups. A reading of these documents—some in foreign languages—can uncover each of their plans and proposals for building the city of the future.

DIGITAL MATERIALS

Citylab.
https://www.citylab.com/.
Cornell University Library, Rare and Manuscript Collections, Architecture and City Planning. https://rare.library.cornell.edu/collections/archandplanning.
Next City.
https://nextcity.org/.
Streetsblog USA.
https://usa.streetsblog.org/.

FURTHER READING

Abbott, Carl. "Urban History for Planners." *Journal of Planning History* 5 (November 2006): 301–313.

Arnold, Joseph L. *The New Deal in the Suburbs: A History of the Greenbelt Town Program, 1935–1954*. Columbus: Ohio State University Press, 1971.

Blackmar, Elizabeth, and Roy Rosenzweig. *The Park and the People: A History of Central Park*. Ithaca, NY: Cornell University Press, 1998.

Buder, Stanley. *Visionaries and Planners: The Garden City Movement and the Modern Community*. New York: Oxford University Press, 1990.

Davis, Mike. *The City of Quartz*. New York: Vintage, 1990.

Gillette, Howard, and Zane L. Miller, eds. *American Urbanism: A Historiographical Review.* New York: Greenwood Press, 1987.

Hirsch, Arnold R. *Making the Second Ghetto: Race and Housing in Chicago, 1940–1960.* New York: Cambridge University Press, 1987.

Jackson, Kenneth T. *Crabgrass Frontier—the Suburbanization of the United States.* New York: Oxford University Press, 1985.

Jacobs, Jane. *The Death and Life of Great American Cities.* New York: Random House, 1961.

Kruse, Kevin Michael, and Thomas J. Sugrue, eds. *The New Suburban History.* Chicago: University of Chicago Press, 2006.

Light, Jennifer S. *The Nature of Cities: Ecological Visions and the American Urban Professions, 1920–1960.* Baltimore: Johns Hopkins University Press, 2009.

Marcuse, Peter. "The Ghetto of Exclusion and the Fortified Enclave: New Patterns in the United States." *American Behavioral Scientist* 41, no. 3 (1997): 311–326.

Melosi, Martin V. *The Sanitary City—Urban Infrastructure in America from Colonial Times to the Present.* Baltimore: Johns Hopkins University Press, 2000.

Mohl, Raymond A. "The Expressway Teardown Movement in American Cities: Rethinking Postwar Highway Polity in the Post-Interstate Era." *Journal of Planning History* 11, no. 1 (2012): 89–103.

Peterson, Jon A. *The Birth of City Planning in the United States, 1840–1917.* Baltimore: Johns Hopkins University Press, 2003.

Radford, Gail. *Modern Housing for America.* Chicago: University of Chicago Press, 1995.

Rome, Adam. *The Bulldozer in the Countryside—Suburban Sprawl and the Rise of American Environmentalism.* New York: Cambridge University Press, 2001.

Schaffer, Daniel, ed. *Two Centuries of American Planning.* Baltimore: Johns Hopkins University Press, 1988.

Sies, Mary Corbin, and Christopher Silver, eds. *Planning the Twentieth-Century American City.* Baltimore: Johns Hopkins University Press, 1996.

Scott, Allen John, and Edward W. Soja, eds. *The City: Los Angeles and Urban Theory at the End of the Twentieth Century.* Berkeley: University of California Press, 1996.

Scott, James C. *Seeing Like a State: How Certain Schemes to Improve the Human Condition Have Failed.* New Haven, CT: Yale University Press, 1998.

Scott, Mel. *American City Planning since 1890.* Berkeley and Los Angeles: University of California Press, 1969.

Smith, Carl S. *The Plan of Chicago: Daniel Burnham and the Remaking of the American City.* Chicago: University of Chicago Press, 2006.

Tomes, Nancy. *The Gospel of Germs: Men, Women, and the Microbe in American Life.* Cambridge, MA: Harvard University Press, 1998.

Warner, Sam Bass, Jr. *Streetcar Suburbs: The Progress of Growth in Boston, 1870–1900.* Cambridge, MA: Harvard University Press, 1962.

NOTES

1. Roy Rosenzweig and Elizabeth Blackmar, *The Park and the People: A History of Central Park* (Ithaca, NY: Cornell University Press, 1998).

2. Joel A. Tarr and Gabriel DuPuy, eds., *Technology and the Rise of the Networked City in Europe and America* (Philadelphia: Temple University Press, 1988).

3. David G. McCullough, *The Great Bridge* (New York: Simon and Schuster, 1972).

4. David Schuyler, *The New Urban Landscape: The Redefinition of City Form in Nineteenth-Century America* (Baltimore: Johns Hopkins University Press, 1986), 162–167.

5. Nancy Tomes, *The Gospel of Germs: Men, Women, and the Microbe in American Life* (Cambridge, MA: Harvard University Press, 1998); and Martin V. Melosi, *The Sanitary City—Urban Infrastructure in America from Colonial Times to the Present* (Baltimore: Johns Hopkins University Press, 2000).

6. Carl S. Smith, *The Plan of Chicago: Daniel Burnham and the Remaking of the American City* (Chicago: University of Chicago Press, 2006).

7. Harold L. Platt, *Building the Urban Environment: Visions of the Organic City in the United States, Europe, and Latin America, Urban Life, Landscape, and Policy* (Philadelphia: Temple University Press, 2015).

8. Frederick Law Olmsted Jr., "Introduction," in *City Planning,* ed. John Nolen ([New York: D. Appleton, 1916] as quoted in Jon A. Peterson, *The Birth of City Planning in the United States, 1840–1917* [Baltimore: Johns Hopkins University Press, 2003]), 2.

9. New York, *Regional Plan of New York and Its Environs.* 10 vols. (New York: Regional Plan of New York and Its Environs, 1927).

10. Robert Fishman, "The American Garden City: Still Relevant?" in *The Garden City: Past, Present*

and Future, ed. Stephen V. Ward (London: Spon, 1992), 146–164.

11. Kenneth T. Jackson, *Crabgrass Frontier: The Suburbanization of the United States* (New York: Oxford University Press, 1985).

12. Arnold R. Hirsch, *Making the Second Ghetto: Race and Housing in Chicago, 1940–1960* (New York: Cambridge University Press, 1983); and Mindy Thompson Fullilove, *Root Shock: How Tearing Up City Neighborhoods Hurts America, and What We Can Do About It* (New York: Ballantine, 2004).

13. Jane Jacobs, *The Death and Life of Great American Cities* (New York: Random House, 1961).

14. Mike Davis, *Magical Urbanism: Latinos Reinvent the U.S. City* (New York: Verso, 2000); and Becky M. Nicolaides and James Zarsadiaz, "Design Assimilation in Suburbia: Asian Americans, Built Landscapes, and Suburban Advantage in Los Angeles's San Gabriel Valley since 1910," *Journal of Urban History* 43, no. 2 (2017): 332–371.

15. Quoted in H. W. E. Davies, "Brian McLoughlin and the Systems Approach to Planning," *European Planning Studies* 5, no. 6 (1997): 719–729. Also see J. Brian McLoughlin, *Urban and Regional Planning: A Systems Approach* (New York: Praeger, 1969).

16. Joel Garreau, *Edge City: Life on the Frontier* (New York: Doubleday, 1991); and Edward James Blakely and Mary Gail Snyder, *Fortress America: Gated Communities in the United States* (Washington, DC: Brookings Institution Press, 1997).

17. Jacques Ellul, *The Technological Society* (New York: Alfred A. Knopf, 1964 [1954]); and Herbert Marcuse, *One-Dimensional Man: Studies in the Ideology of Advanced Industrial Society* (Boston: Beacon Press, 1964).

18. Ricardo Romo, *East Los Angeles: History of a Barrio* (Austin: University of Texas Press, 1983); and Davis, *Magical Urbanism*.

19. Erik Swyngedouw, "The City as Hybrid: On Nature, Society and Cyborg Urbanization," *Capitalism, Nature, Socialism* 7, no. 2 (June 1996): 65–80; and European Council of Town Planners, *Towards the New Charter of Athens: From the Organic City to the City of Citizens* (Greece: European Council of Town Planners, 1998).

20. Carlton Wade Basmajian, *Atlanta Unbound: Enabling Sprawl through Policy and Planning* (Philadelphia: Temple University Press, 2013). Also see Harold L. Platt, *Building the Urban Environment: Visions of the Organic City in the United States, Europe, and Latin America* (Philadelphia: Temple University Press, 2015).

21. Harvey Molotch, "The City as Growth Machine: Toward a Political Economy of Place," *American Journal of Sociology* 82 (September 1976): 309–332.

22. Peter Marcuse, "The Ghetto of Exclusion and the Fortified Enclave: New Patterns in the United States," *American Behavioral Scientist* 41, no. 3 (November/December 1997): 311–326; and Basmajian, *Atlanta Unbound*.

23. Manuel Castells, *The Rise of the Network Society* (Malden, MA: Blackwell, 1996); Allen J. Scott, "Resurgent Metropolis: Economy, Society and Urbanization in an Interconnected World," *International Journal of Urban and Regional Research* 32 (September 2008); Donella H. Meadows, Jørgen Randers, and Dennis L. Meadows, *The Limits to Growth: The 30-Year Update* (White River Junction, VT: Chelsea Green, 2004); and Mike Davis, *The City of Quartz* (New York: Vintage, 1990).

24. Mike Davis, "Fortress Los Angeles: The Militarization of Urban Space," in *Variations on a Theme Park—the New American City and the End of Public Space*, ed. Michael Sorkin (New York: Noonday, 1992), 154–180; Raphael Sonenshein, *The City at Stake: Secession, Reform, and Battle for Los Angeles* (Princeton, NJ: Princeton University Press, 2004); William Sites, "Global City, American City: Theories of Globalization and Approaches to Urban History," *Journal of Urban History* 29 (March 2003): 222–246; William I. Robinson, "Globalization and the Sociology of Immanuel Wallerstein: A Critical Appraisal," *International Sociology* 26, no. 6 (October 2011): 723–745; and Nicolas Kenny and Rebecca Madgin, eds., *Cities Beyond Borders: Comparative and Transnational Approaches to Urban History* (Farnham, UK: Ashgate, 2015).

25. Barbara Ferman, *Challenging the Growth Machine: Neighborhood Politics in Chicago and Pittsburgh* (Lawrence: University Press of Kansas, 1996).

26. Rutherford H. Platt, Rowan A. Rowntree, and Pamela C. Muick, eds., *The Ecological City: Preserving and Restoring Urban Biodiversity* (Amherst: University of Massachusetts Press, 1994).

27. Nicholas Dagen Bloom, *Merchant of Illusion: James Rouse, America's Salesman of the Businessman's Utopia* (Columbus: Ohio State University Press, 2004)

28. Andres Duany, Elizabeth Plater-Zyberk, and Jeff Speck, *Suburban Nation: The Rise of Sprawl and the Decline of the American Dream* (New York: North Point Press, 2000); and Sonia A. Hirt, "Premodern, Modern, Postmodern? Placing New Urbanism into a Historical Perspective," *Journal of Planning History* 8, no. 3 (August 2009): 248–273.

29. Arthur Schlesinger Sr. "The City in American History," *Mississippi Valley Historical Review*, 27 (June 1940): 43–66. For the half century following World War II, this essay draws heavily upon Mary Corbin Sies, and Christopher Silver, "The History of Planning History," in *Planning the Twentieth-Century City*, eds. Mary Corbin Sies and Christopher Silver (Baltimore: Johns Hopkins University Press, 1996), 1–36. It provides a much more comprehensive analysis and bibliography than this short historiographical note.

30. Mel Scott, *American City Planning since 1890* (Berkeley and Los Angeles: University of California Press, 1969).

31. See Donald A. Krueckeberg, ed., *The American Planner: Biographies and Recollections* (New York: Methuen, 1983), for a collection of these essays. See also Robert Fishman, *Urban Utopias in the Twentieth Century: Ebenezer Howard, Frank Lloyd Wright, Le Corbusier* (New York: Basic Books, 1977).

32. See Peter J. Schmitt, *Back to Nature: The Arcadian Myth in Urban America, 1900–1930* (New York: Oxford University Press, 1969); William H. Wilson, *The City Beautiful Movement* (Baltimore and London: Johns Hopkins University Press, 1989); Blackmar and Rosenzweig, *The Park and the People*; Peterson, *The Birth of City Planning in the United States, 1840–1917*; Christopher Klemek, *The Transatlantic Collapse of Urban Renewal: Postwar Urbanism from New York to Berlin* (Chicago: University of Chicago Press, 2011); and Christopher C. Sellers, *Crabgrass Crucible: Suburban Nature and the Rise of Environmentalism in Twentieth-Century America* (Chapel Hill: University of North Carolina Press, 2012).

33. Jacobs, *The Death and Life of Great American Cities*. See also the equally devastating, early postwar critique of social life in a new suburban subdivision, William Hollingsworth Whyte, *The Organization Man* (New York: Simon and Schuster, 1956). Significantly, he was the editor of the financial elite's *Fortune* magazine.

34. Raymond Williams, *The Country and the City* (New York: Oxford University Press, 1973), 145–148. On the garden city, see Peter Hall, *Cities of Tomorrow: An Intellectual History of Urban Planning and Design in the Twentieth Century* (London: Blackwell, 1988); and Stanley Buder, *Visionaries and Planners: The Garden City Movement and the Modern Community* (New York: Oxford University Press, 1990)

35. Richard E. Foglesong, *Planning the Capitalist City: The Colonial Era to the 1920s* (Princeton, NJ: Princeton University Press, 1986); and M. Christine Boyer, *Dreaming the Rational City: The Myth of American City Planning* (Cambridge, MA: MIT Press, 1983).

36. Robert Fishman, "Global Suburbs," a paper presented at the First Biennial Conference of the Urban History Association (Pittsburgh, September 2002). See also Garreau, *Edge City*; William Sites, "Global City, American City": 222-246; Kristen Hill Maher, "Borders and Social Distinction in the Global Suburb," *American Quarterly* 56, no. 3 (2004): 781–806; Justin A. Read, "Obverse Colonization: Sao Paulo, Global Urbanization and the Poetics of the Latin American City," *Journal of Latin American Cultural Studies* 15 (December 2006): 281–300; and Platt, *Building the Urban Environment*.

37. Christopher Silver, "New Urbanism and Planning History: Back to the Future," in *Culture, Urbanism and Planning, Heritage, Culture, and Identity*, eds. F. J. Monclús and Manuel Guàrdia i Bassols (Aldershot, UK: Ashgate, 2006), 179–193; Sellers, *Crabgrass Crucible*; Manuel Castells, *The Informational City: Information Technology, Economic Restructuring and the Urban-Regional Process* (Oxford: Blackwell, 1989); and Nicolas Kenny and Rebecca Madgin, eds., *Cities Beyond Borders: Comparative and Transnational Approaches to Urban History* (Farnham, UK, and Burlington, VT: Ashgate, 2015).

Harold L. Platt

WATER AND SEWERS IN THE AMERICAN CITY

Urban infrastructure includes the technological framework for the operations of a city: water supply and sewer lines; roads, bridges, and transit networks; and power and communications systems. These facilities allow cities and their metropolitan areas to function as centers of commerce, industry, entertainment, and residence. Of these infrastructure systems, none is more important for the urban quality of life and the quality of its environment than those relating to water supply, wastewater removal, and storm water disposal.

Cities cannot exist without adequate supplies of water. Vital functions require water: drinking, cooking, sanitation, commercial and industrial needs, firefighting, and street cleansing. The disposal of wastewater, including both sewage and storm water, is a second and related critical function. US water and sewer infrastructure followed a five-stage evolution during different and often overlapping periods. These stages were:

1. Development and use of piped-in water
2. Sewage system construction
3. Sewage pollution and water treatment
4. Sewage treatment
5. Storm water and the development of green infrastructure

WATER SUPPLY

Water supply systems were the earliest centralized infrastructure systems provided by cities. Throughout the 19th century increasingly large numbers of city residents shifted from dependence on local water sources such as wells, ponds, cisterns, or vendors to piped-in water to fill their needs. The shift to centralized water systems, according to historian Carl Smith, raised four vital questions: How was the "public good" to be defined at a time of rapid urban change; how did city or "manufactured" water blur the line between nature and the built environment; how did acquiring city water connect "one's human body" to the "body of the city" but separate it from the non-connected population; and how did urbanites cope with the issue of raising funds for a capital-intensive waterworks when it meant encumbering the future through bonds?[1]

These issues dominated the discussions that ensued as 19th-century cities constructed capital-intensive and centralized water systems. Local sources of water became increasingly contaminated, compelling urbanites to seek other sources of supply. The initial motivation for centralized water systems originating from non-local sources of supply involved a desire for more copious and less-polluted water supplies, concern over threats to the public health from epidemics generated by decaying organic materials, inadequate water to flush filthy streets, and the insufficiency of supplies to control the fires that frequently raged through antebellum cities. In addition, as cities became more industrialized, industrialists demanded a pure and abundant supply of water for their various processes.[2]

Starting with Philadelphia in 1799, coalitions of commercial elites, industrialists, and sanitarians in different cities pushed for the construction of public and private waterworks. Progress was relatively slow because of the complexity of technical, social, and financial issues involved and by 1850 only about 36 percent of cities (eighty-four in total) possessed waterworks.[3] Cincinnati and Pittsburgh, for instance, built waterworks in the 1820s drawing from local rivers. New York City and Boston, after prolonged debate, elected to draw their supplies from upcountry sources—New York in 1842 via the Croton Aqueduct and Boston in 1848 via the Cochituate Aqueduct.[4] These systems used combinations of steam pumps, gravity, reservoirs, and water towers to draw water from various sources, store it, and distribute it through the city.

Many of the initial waterworks were privately owned. By 1860, however, the sixteen largest cities had municipally owned systems, as private companies failed to provide the water resources for various urban needs such as firefighting and protecting the public health. By 1880 the number of public and private water supply systems were approximately equal, but private providers tended to be located in smaller cities, as an increasingly large percentage of the urban population was served by municipal waterworks. The increase in public rather than private provision of water highlights the widespread belief that water was too important to city life to be left to the private profit-making sector.[5]

Piped-in water was usually provided first to commercial and elite living areas that could pay for the service. Working-class neighborhoods were supplied, if at all, through street corner spigots or wells. In cities with private companies, such as Baltimore up to 1854, water supply was class structured. The affluent residential districts and the central business district received the piped water of a private corporation for an annual fee while the poor districts depended on shallow polluted wells supplied by city pumps. Historian Robin L. Einhorn calls this a "segmented system"—a system that provided benefits to those who paid for them but that also "made the American urban landscape a physical expression of political inequality."[6] The absence of meters, the use of annual flat charges, and the presence of free hydrants, as well as technological factors such as leaky pipes, faulty pumps, and bad connections, drove high rates of water wastage.

Over time, expansion of water supply systems and their increasing public ownership, in spite of inequities in provision, improved the quality of urban life as water gradually spread to previously underserved neighborhoods. The number of waterworks in the nation increased from 1,878 in 1890 to 9,850 in 1924. Most works drew on local sources such as groundwater, lakes, and rivers and distant sources such as protected watersheds. As water use increased, cities such as New York (Catskills), Los Angeles (Owens Valley) and San Francisco (Hetch Hetchy Valley) sought water from more and more distant sources. By extending their ecological footprints, such cities disrupted local ecologies, communities, and economies.[7]

The provision of running water to households increased the use of domestic water-using appliances such as sinks, baths, and showers, providing conveniences and improved

domestic sanitation. Such water-using appliances, however, also increased the flows of gray and black wastewater that needed disposal. The water closet, which discharged water contaminated with fecal matter, was a major polluting technology. Flows from water closets were often discharged into inadequately maintained privies and cesspools; these proved simply inadequate to handle the larger wastewater flows.[8] Even when sewers were available, householders often failed to connect them to their water closets because of the expense. In Pittsburgh in 1881, for instance, only about 1,500 of the city's 6,500 water closets were connected to street sewers; the remainder flowed into privies and cesspools. By 1880, although the data are imprecise, approximately one-quarter of urban households had water closets (usually of the pan or hopper type), while the remainder still depended on privy vaults.[9]

Wastewater from overcharged privies and cesspools produced nuisance problems and sanitary hazards. Soils became saturated, cellars flooded with stagnant and offensive fluids, and cesspools and privies had to be frequently emptied. Wastes often leaked into groundwater, polluting wells and streams. Overwhelmed by the nuisances, cities desperately sought other solutions for wastewater disposal. Among the different approaches were the earth closet as a substitute for the water closet, the odorless excavator, a vacuum pump to empty the contents of cesspools and privies into a horse-drawn tank truck for removal, and sewage farms. Scavengers often collected wastes and sold them to farmers for fertilizer.[10] None of these approaches proved fully successful, as the technology of wastewater disposal lagged behind that of water supply.

SEWER SYSTEMS

Water supply and sewer systems should ideally have been linked as critical urban hydraulic systems. Because of financial constraints and underestimates regarding future water use, however, cities almost never constructed sewer systems when they built waterworks.[11] While some private and public underground sewers existed in larger cities in the 19th century, they were largely intended for storm water drainage from streets rather than human waste removal. In New York, for instance, the existing sewers were unplanned—some were circular while others were elliptical; some were constructed of stone and others of brick. A number of streets had private sewers that made their own path to the river. The absence of maps or system records meant that maintenance was impossible, even if municipal authorities were so inclined. These sewers usually lacked self-cleansing characteristics and became "sewers of deposit," rather than of removal. Many cities passed ordinances forbidding the placing of human wastes in them, although after 1845 the New York City Council permitted householders to connect their drains to them.[12]

The majority of 19th-century cities, however, had no underground drains. Street gutters of wood or stone, either on the side or in the middle of the roadway, provided for surface storm water. Private householders often constructed drains to the street gutters to remove storm water from cellars. The focus on storm water removal from streets reflected the difficulty of maintaining commerce in flooded streets, the threat of flooded basements, and the belief that health hazards (the "filth theory") could arise from decaying stagnant wastes in streets.

Overflowing cesspools and privies created both nuisances and public health concerns. During most of the 19th century, physicians generally divided into two groups: contagionists and anticontagionists. The former maintained that epidemic disease was transmitted by contact with a diseased person or carrier, a belief that often led to quarantines to prevent diseased individuals from entering the city. Anticontagionists held that vitiated or impure air ("miasmas") arising from conditions such as putrefying organic matters, feces, exhalations from swamps, and stagnant pools, or human and animal crowding, resulted in sickness and epidemics. By the latter half of the 19th century the majority of physicians and sanitarians were anticontagionists who believed that filth conditions accelerated the spread of contagious disease, thus underscoring demands by the sanitary movement for urban environmental improvements.[13]

Increasingly urban public figures realized that the only solution to the wastewater problem was construction of a self-cleansing underground system of pipes or sewers that used household water supply to transport human wastes to a point of disposal—the water carriage system. This approach was modeled on the work of the British sanitarian Edwin Chadwick in the 1840s. He believed that odors from decaying organic matter caused the spread of many fatal diseases. Fecal matter in particular needed to be swiftly transported from the vicinity of the household.[14] While considerable opposition to Chadwick's theories existed in Great Britain, they strongly influenced American sanitarians concerning the benefits of systematic sewerage. Throughout the remainder of the 19th century, visits to sewerage works in cities in Great Britain and Europe were almost mandatory for American engineers involved in planning new sewerage systems. Water-carriage technology provides a good example of the international interchange and transfer of ideas and experience concerning urban infrastructure.[15]

Before cities could embark on major centralized sewer-building projects, however, they had to confront issues similar to those when they constructed water supply systems: how to pay for them and what technology to adopt. In addition, with wastewater, cities had to address the disposal issue. Brooklyn, Chicago, and Jersey City constructed sewer systems in the 1850s, but the great burst of sewer construction occurred after 1890, as engineers and sanitarians formulated fuller answers to key questions of technology choice and disposal. The construction of planned sewage systems, argued their promoters, would substitute a systematic, sanitary, and self-acting technological system for a set of haphazard, inefficient, and unhealthful methods for dealing with the problems of human wastes, wastewater, and storm water.

The debate focused on technology choice— should the sewer system be a separate, small pipe system that carried only domestic and industrial wastes, the technology advocated by the famous sanitarian Col. George E. Waring Jr.? Or should it be a larger, combined system that could accommodate both wastewater and storm water, as sanitary engineer Rudolf Hering advocated?[16] Many physicians, believers in the filth theory of disease, preferred the separate system because they argued it would protect health by removing wastes from the household before they had begun to generate disease-causing miasmas. Storm water, they maintained, was a secondary matter and could be handled by surface conduits. Engineers from the new profession of sanitary engineering, however, largely took a different position. They argued that sanitary wastes and storm water were equally important and that a large pipe system that accommodated both was more economical. In addition, they maintained that the separate system had no health advantages over the combined.[17]

Large cities, faced with the need to control storm water in commercial districts as well as domestic wastes, elected to build combined sewers. Smaller cities, on the other hand, in order to lower costs, installed small-pipe separate sewers for domestic wastes, usually leaving storm water to run off on the surface. Between 1890 and 1909, the total miles of sewers in the nation's cities increased from approximately 6,000 to about 25,000 miles; sewers served more than 70 percent of the residents in cities of over 50,000 population. In 1909 cities with more than 300,000 residents had almost 10,000 miles of combined sewers and less than a thousand miles of separate sewers; cities with populations between 30,000 and 50,000 had about 1,200 miles of sanitary sewers and just more than 1,500 miles of combined.[18] This immense construction was facilitated by the growth of investment banking, which made supplies of capital more accessible to municipal borrowers. Systems of piped sewerage in the United States were generally funded by a combination of user fees, assessments on abutting property holders, bonds, and general tax revenues.[19]

SEWAGE POLLUTION AND WATER TREATMENT

The use of combined rather than separate sewers, given the available treatment technology in the late 19th and early 20th century, increased the costs of both wastewater treatment and resource recovery. In addition, the decision had large consequences in regard to water quality in the future because combined sewer overflows on rainy days bypassed sewage treatment plants and discharged raw sewage into rivers. Before sewerage treatment plants were available, however, most urban policymakers and engineers believed that dumping raw sewage into streams was adequate treatment because of the self-purifying nature of running water. By the 1890s, however, biologists, chemists, and sanitary engineers seriously questioned this hypothesis. Nevertheless, as late as 1909, municipalities discharged 88 percent of the wastewater of the sewered population in waterways without treatment.[20] Where treatment was utilized at the beginning of the 20th century, it was only to prevent nuisance rather than to avoid contamination of drinking water downstream.

The disposal of untreated sewage in streams and lakes from which other cities drew their water supplies caused large increases in mortality and morbidity from typhoid fever and other infectious waterborne diseases. Bacterial researchers, following the seminal work of Louis Pasteur and Robert Koch, identified the processes involved in such waterborne disease as germ theory gradually replaced the filth theory in public health considerations.

In the early 1890s, biologist William T. Sedgwick and an interdisciplinary team at the Massachusetts Board of Health's Lawrence Experiment Station clarified the etiology of typhoid fever and confirmed its relationship to sewage-polluted waterways.[21] The irony was clear: cities had adopted water-carriage technology because they expected local health benefits, but disposal practices produced serious health problems for downstream users. This increased morbidity and mortality was an unanticipated impact of sewerage technology— a rise in health costs where health benefits had been predicted. Because these costs were often borne by downstream users, in the absence of alternatives, cities continued to build sewer systems and to dispose of untreated wastes in adjacent waterways.

Sanitarians and progressive reformers advocated laws and institutions to address the threats to health from urban sewage-disposal practices. One result was the creation of state boards of health (beginning with Massachusetts in 1869) and the passage of legislation to protect water quality. In 1905, the US Geological Survey published its *Review of the Laws Forbidding Pollution of Inland Waters in the United States*, listing thirty-six states with some legislation protecting drinking water. Eight states had "unusual and stringent" laws, usually passed in response to severe typhoid epidemics. State boards of health, whether through merely advisory powers or through stricter enforcement provisions, were usually responsible for protecting water quality.[22]

In 1909, the raw sewage of 88 percent of the urban population was discharged into neighboring water bodies from which they often drew their water supplies or into which upstream cities discharged their sewage. Cities that drew their water supplies from neighboring rivers and lakes often experienced high death rates from typhoid fever. In 1900, for instance, Pittsburgh had a typhoid fever mortality rate of 144 per 100,000, Richmond 104, and Washington, DC, 80. In contrast, cities that drew their water supplies from protected upstream watersheds, such as Boston and New York, had much lower rates.[23]

Sanitary engineers had originally justified the discharge of sewage into streams on the basis of the concept of the self-purifying nature of running water, later further elaborated as the theory of dilution—that stream flow would disperse the sewage before it created problems. Rivers were conceptualized as "a kind of 'organic machine' for the processing of human waste," the social utility of which rested upon changing concepts of health risks and other water resource uses.[24] As the *Engineering Record* noted in 1909, "it is often more equitable to all concerned for an upper riparian city to discharge its sewage into a stream and a lower riparian city to filter the water of the same stream for a domestic supply, than for the former city to be forced to put in sewage treatment works."[25]

In the late 19th century and the initial decades of the 20th century, the options for dealing with sewage pollution of drinking water supplies were relatively limited. Among them were sewage treatment through sewage farming (mainly in the West) and intermittent filtration (mainly in New England), but both were land-intensive and impractical with sewage output from combined systems used by the majority of cities. Another was to shift the municipal water supply from a local to a distant and protected watershed, a course followed by Jersey City and Newark. In the late 1890s, however, another option appeared for cities drawing their water supplies from sewage-polluted rivers. This was water filtration by either slow sand or mechanical filtration. Many inland cities installed mechanical or sand filters in the years after 1897, resulting in sharp declines in morbidity and mortality rates from typhoid fever as well as other diseases. In addition, beginning in 1908, the use of chlorination to disinfect water supplies became increasingly common, driving down typhoid rates even further.[26]

Water filtration, however, did not remove the sewage from the rivers and lakes. Some health authorities argued that cities should both filter their water *and* treat their sewage in order to protect both their own water supply and that of downstream cities. Most sanitary engineers took an opposite position, arguing, as did Allen Hazen in, *Clean Water and How to Get It* (1907), that "the discharge of crude sewage from the great majority of cities is not locally objectionable in any way to justify the cost of sewage purification." Hazen maintained that downstream cities should filter their water to protect the public health, and sewage purification should be utilized only to prevent nuisances such as odors and floating solids.[27]

SEWAGE TREATMENT

By the beginning of World War I, the perspective of sanitary engineers on the question of the disposal of raw sewage into streams had triumphed over that of the "sentimentalists and medical authorities" (sanitary engineer George W. Fuller's characterization) who opposed the use of streams for disposal. Essentially, the engineering position was that the dilution power of streams should be utilized to its fullest for sewage disposal, as long as no danger was posed to the public health or to property rights and no nuisance created. Water filtration and chlorination could protect the public from waterborne disease.[28]

The practical consequences of this position was that in the period from 1910 to 1930, while the population newly served by sewers rose by over 25 million, the number whose sewage was treated rose by only 13.5 million. At the same time, the increase in the population receiving treated water was approximately 33 million. In 1930, not only did the great majority of urban populations dispose of their untreated sewage by dilution in waterways, but also their numbers were actually increasing over those who were treating their sewage before discharge. Because of water filtration and chlorination, however, waterborne infectious disease had greatly diminished and the

earlier crisis atmosphere that had led to the first state legislation had disappeared.[29]

Waterway pollution, however, worsened, as industrial discharges increasingly joined untreated municipal discharges in water bodies. Raw sewage and industrial wastes overwhelmed the oxidation capacity of rivers, creating offensive sights and smells. Water treatment had sharply reduced typhoid deaths, but diarrhea and enteritis death rates remained elevated. Fish were absent from long dead stretches of the rivers, and chemical pollution fouled the taste of many drinking water supplies as waste disposal in waterways created an ecological footprint that threatened the health of downstream cities.[30]

Filtration and chlorination had provided one safety net in regard to drinking water quality, but many sanitarians and public health physicians believed that it was necessary to treat urban sewage for maximum protection. Professional, business, and medical groups protested against sewage disposal by dilution only, concerned that further safeguards against bacterial pollution were necessary. They demanded that municipalities treat their sewage and agitated for state laws against stream pollution.

In the years after the turn of the century, Connecticut, Massachusetts, Minnesota, New Hampshire, New Jersey, New York, Ohio, Pennsylvania, and Vermont, responding to a series of severe typhoid epidemics, authorized state boards of health to control sewage disposal in streams. In addition, the federal government became involved through the work of the US Public Health Service (USPHS). In 1914, the USPHS established the first federal drinking water standards.[31] While these applied only to water served on interstate carriers, it became widely accepted as a relevant standard. Regulatory authority over pollution, however, remained limited, and experimentation with various methods of sewage treatment accelerated.

The various technologies developed included sewage farming, intermittent filtration, contact filters and trickling filters (biologically based), septic and Imhoff tanks, and sewage disinfection. The most effective treatment technology, however, was the activated sludge process developed in Great Britain in 1913. This process involved the introduction of oxygen into a mixture of screened treated wastewater combined with organisms to develop a biological floc or sludge, reducing the organic content of sewage into carbon dioxide, water, and other inorganic compounds. Experimentation with the process proceeded in a number of major cities in the 1920s, with more widespread adoption in the 1930s. In 1939 Chicago operated the world's largest activated sludge plant.[32]

The 1920s and 1930s also witnessed an increasing concern with industrial wastes and their contribution to total pollution load in streams. Initially waterworks laboratories focused on biological concerns and neglected possible impacts by industrial wastes on drinking water supplies. In 1922, however, the Committee on Industrial Wastes in Relation to Water Supply of the American Water Works Association reported that industrial pollutants had damaged at least 248 water supplies in the United States and Canada. Phenols, petroleum wastes, and mine acid drainage were matters of special concern. Still, USPHS leaders were reluctant to act against industrial pollutants because they believed that the organization's charter limited them to studying the effects of pollution on the public health.[33]

A marked change regarding the relationship of different governmental bodies to infrastructure development in water supply and sewers emerged after 1930. Previously, all water supply and sewer construction was the responsibility of municipalities, which used a variety of financial instruments such as bonds, assessments, and user fees to pay for them. President Franklin D. Roosevelt's New Deal, however, brought about a revolution in terms of the involvement of the federal government in public works and infrastructure provision. The Civil Works Administration (CWA) employed over four million workers in tasks such as road building and construction of sewer lines, while its

successor, the Works Progress Administration (WPA), was also involved in many public works programs.[34]

The foremost contributor to the domains of water supply, sewage, and sewage treatment construction was the Public Works Administration (PWA). PWA funds accounted for 35 to 50 percent of all new sewer and water supply construction during the 1930s. These projects generated a variety of benefits to local communities. New water supply systems, for instance, provided a return by providing improved water supplies and sharply reducing fire insurance premiums. Sewer construction not only provided unemployment relief but also addressed the problems of water pollution control. The administration accelerated investment for sewage treatment facilities by approving only PWA sewer projects that provided for waste treatment. Similarly, the WPA could not construct sanitary sewers unless they were designed to be compatible with treatment works. By 1938, federal financing had contributed to the construction of 1,165 of the 1,310 new municipal sewage treatment plants built in the decade. The population served by sewage treatment increased from 21.5 million in 1932 to more than 39 million by 1939. In 1945, 62.7 percent of people living in sewered communities had treated sewage, although 37.3 percent still disposed of raw sewage into waterways.[35]

The decades following World War II were marked by extensive metropolitan growth and by recognition that, in spite of New Deal construction, urban water and sewer infrastructure was in need of renewal. Total spending on new construction for sewer and water systems did not actually reach the 1930 level in constant dollars until 1951. Questions of adequacy of supply were often accompanied by issues of water quality, especially in the face of new concerns over the possible health effects of industrial wastes.

Congress, riven by partisan differences, reacted in a hesitant fashion. In 1948 it approved the Water Pollution Control Act

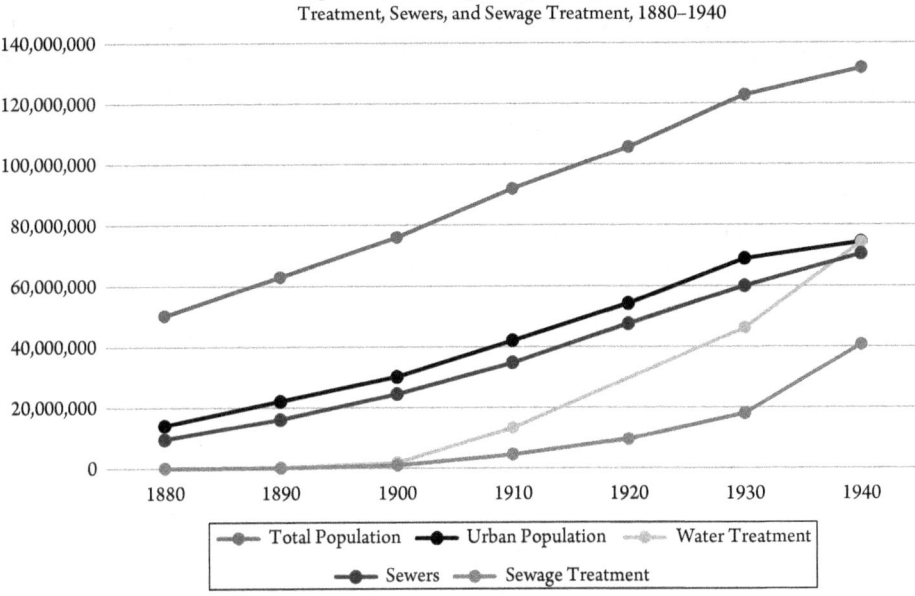

US Population, Urban Population, and Population with Water Treatment, Sewers, and Sewage Treatment, 1880–1940

Figure 1. Joel A. Tarr, with James McCurley III, Francis C. McMichael, and Terry Yosie, "Water and Wastes: A Retrospective Assessment of Wastewater Technology in the United States, 1800–1932," *Technology and Culture* (April 1984) 25: 245.

containing limited provisions to abate interstate water pollution and provided financial assistance to municipalities, interstate agencies, and the state for construction of facilities reducing water pollution. The Federal Water Pollution Control Act of 1956 extended these provisions and provided a loan program for construction of sewage treatment facilities. Amendments in 1961 to this act increased the funds available for construction. Still, water and sewer construction did not keep up with metropolitan growth; as new suburban neighborhoods expanded they often depended on home sewage-disposal systems such as septic tanks rather than sewers.[36]

The decades of the 1960s and 1970s were marked by an increase in environmental consciousness and the rise of the environmental movement. Water pollution was a major concern. Congressional environmentalists, led by Edmund Muskie (D, Maine), pushed for stronger water quality standards, resulting in the Water Quality Act of 1965. This controversial legislation provided for the creation of the Federal Water Pollution Control Administration

to enforce higher standards of water quality, taking the responsibility away from the USPHS.

Urban wastewater infrastructure increasingly benefited from federal programs, as the environmental movement stimulated concern about water quality. In 1970 the Nixon administration created the Environmental Protection Agency; one of its main functions was the reduction of water pollution. Congressional passage of the Clean Water Act of 1972 was a major step forward. The law set a number of goals: to attain water quality in navigable waters suitable for fisheries and for swimming by 1983, secondary treatment in all wastewater-treatment plants by 1988, and zero pollutant discharge by 1995. Federal dollars poured into sewer, sewage treatment, and water facilities, especially new construction. Between 1967 and 1977, Federal expenditures for sewer systems increased from $150 million to $4.052 billion. Localities also increased their spending on wastewater systems, although the nation's expanding suburbs often lacked centralized wastewater systems.

The 1980 election of Ronald Reagan to the presidency resulted in a new federal attitude toward infrastructure spending. Government "disinvestment" resulted in sharp cuts in funding for new infrastructure and maintenance of old, causing the deterioration of many systems.[37] Engineers and public officials became increasingly concerned over infrastructure decay and its economic and public health implications. At the same time the nation became increasingly aware of new threats to water quality, especially groundwater pollution and nonpoint source pollution. As federal dollars for infrastructure evaporated, states and localities sought to fill the gap.[38]

During these decades suburbanization increased at a rapid rate, consuming greenfields, increasing erosion, and altering hydrologic patterns, leading to flooding and pollution of rivers and lakes. Many suburban developments were inadequately served by wastewater disposal systems and depended on septic tanks for domestic wastes, threatening groundwater pollution. Suburbs often lacked storm water sewers and rainwater ran off on street surfaces, absorbing pollutants such as oil and salt. Inadequate facilities for storm water disposal increased the pollution load of receiving streams.[39] Central cities also suffered greatly from combined and separate sewer overflow problems. Most combined sewers in the nation were constructed in the late 19th and early 20th centuries in larger cities and were designed to discharge untreated sewage into receiving water bodies. They were concentrated in the Northeast, the Great Lakes region, and the Ohio River basin although some West Coast cities were also involved. As sewers were connected to sewage treatment facilities they were increasingly required to construct overflow facilities to protect the sewage treatment plants from being flooded with excess flows. At these overflow points, raw sewage often entered rivers and lakes, causing nuisances and health hazards and violating the Clean Water Act. In the Water Quality Act of 1987, Congress responded to the storm water problem by requiring that industrial dischargers and municipal systems obtain a National Pollutant Discharge Permit by a specific deadline. In 1994, the US Environmental Protection Agency (EPA) issued the CSO Control Policy, the national framework for control of CSOs, through the National Pollutant Discharge Elimination System permitting program. Even so, the storm water pollution problem persists in many cities, especially in regard to combined sewer overflows.[40]

Although water pollution remains a pressing concern for metropolitan areas because of infrastructure and policy limitations, the United States has made major progress since 1950 in terms of providing basic water supply and sewer services to its population. In 1950, for instance, 56 percent of the rural population and 11 percent of the urban population lacked full plumbing services. By 2000, only 1 percent of the rural population and 0.5 percent of urban residents lived without them. Those without access to these services tend to be poor minority populations, often living in scattered rural areas.[41]

CITIES AND GREEN INFRASTRUCTURE

None of the major goals set forth in the Clean Water Act of 1972 were reached by 2000, although the number of people whose wastes are provided with secondary or more advanced wastewater treatment has increased by about 30 percent since 1950. The focus on different sources of pollution, however, has shifted since the 1970s. Much of the emphasis of pollution control from the 1950s–1980s was on point source pollution. The last several decades have been marked, however, by increasing attempts to cope with the threats to water quality from non–point source pollution and combined and separate sewer overflows. These issues largely stemmed from past decisions regarding wastewater collection and disposal practices in regard to both sewage and storm water, especially combined sewers.

Engineers had originally sought to deal with these issues with traditional gray infrastructure such as large collection facilities and storage pipes. After 2000, environmentalists and a new breed of environmental engineers increasingly gave enhanced consideration to green infrastructure in dealing with storm water issues as well as other urban environmental concerns such as heat island effects. Water and sewer systems, therefore, were ideally to be considered as an integrated part of the urban ecology rather than as elements of the built environment imposed upon the city's ecology.

Green infrastructure is an approach to water management that protects, restores, or mimics the natural hydrological cycle by absorbing water through approaches such as bio-retention systems, permeable pavements, tree planting, and green roofs. In this manner storm water is directed away from sewers, reducing the amount of raw sewage directed into receiving bodies of water. In a sense the pattern regarding storm water has gone full cycle: viewed by engineers for many years as something to be eliminated from the city as a nuisance and flooding threat, it is now to be retained, as much as possible, on site. In this manner sewage flows into rivers are reduced, sewage treatment facilities less burdened, and receiving water bodies cleaner.[42]

CONCLUSION

For a period of more than two hundred years, American cities and metropolitan areas have struggled to construct infrastructure to provide sanitary drinking water to their populations and to dispose of wastewater in a manner that did not create nuisances and endanger the public health. In most cases engineers imposed their technological infrastructures on the urban ecology rather than attempting to integrate them into the environment, frequently burying streams in pipes and changing hydrological patterns. Due to financial and technological limitations, cities constructed additions to their water and wastewater systems incrementally, often resulting in poor systems integration. Thus, water systems were constructed without adequate consideration of wastewater disposal; sewage was disposed in neighboring water bodies without full consideration of its impact on downstream cities; and drinking water but not sewage was treated. When sewage treatment plants were constructed, they were often inadequate to address enlarged storm water flows. Raw sewage continued to enter and pollute receiving water bodies.

From the late 19th century and into the 20th century sanitary engineers made major gains in pollution control and significantly improved the public health. They continued to believe in the efficacy of traditional gray infrastructure, however—large concrete and brick pipes, for instance—even when its limitations were becoming obvious. They constructed sewer systems that emphasized sewer sheds based on population locations rather than as elements to be integrated into natural watersheds. Since the launching of the environmental movement, environmental engineering has supplanted sanitary engineering. Gradually the benefits of green infrastructure, in coordination with existing gray infrastructures, are coming to be accepted. In the face of global climate change, with drought in some regions and torrential rains in others, environmental engineers must be constantly alert to the necessity of designing water supply and wastewater systems that are integrated into the environment and adaptable in the face of changing conditions.

DISCUSSION OF THE LITERATURE

The subject of urban infrastructure, the urban environment, and more specifically water supply, sewers, and sewage treatment has received increasing attention in the literature in recent decades. This is especially so since the development of the environmental history of cities as a major subsection of environmental history. However, although earlier engineering texts often contained extensive discussions of the history of both water supply and sewers, historians largely neglected it as a specialized topic until Nelson Blake's *Water for the*

Cities: A History of the Urban Water Supply Problem in the United States.[43] Further publication by historians on the topic, however, did not appear until the 1980s.

Several compilations of articles and chapters on urban infrastructure from the 1980s are still useful.[44] All include essays on water and wastewater issues.

The 1980s and 1990s witnessed an increase in publications regarding water supply decisions and conflict.[45] The water supply of the cities of Allegheny City, Atlanta, Fresno, Milwaukee, New Orleans, Philadelphia, Pittsburgh, Shreveport, and Wilmington are dealt with in specialized articles in the historical literature.

More recently, Carl Smith's *City Water, City Life: Water and the Infrastructure of Ideas in Urbanizing Philadelphia, Boston, and Chicago*[46] provides a comparative discussion of water supply decision making in these cities in the 19th century with a particular cultural focus. Michael Rawson's *Eden on the Charles* discusses Boston's early water supply issues in depth.[47] Gerald T. Koeppel's *Water for Gotham: A History* addresses the 19th-century conflict over the provision of water to New York City while David Soll's *Empire of Water: An Environmental and Political History of the New York City Water Supply* provides a comprehensive study of New York water supply decisions in the 20th century.[48]

Finally, water supply issues in a multitude of settings are dealt with in Martin V. Melosi's compilation, *Precious Commodity: Providing Water for America's Cities* and his prizewinning study, *The Sanitary City: Urban Infrastructure in America from Colonial Times to the Present.*[49]

Students interested in wastewater systems should begin with the publications of Melosi and Joel Tarr. *Sanitary City* extensively examines the evolution of these systems. Melosi's work on both water and wastewater systems must be the starting point for any investigation of these topics. Many comprehensive articles are included in Tarr's volume *The Search for the Ultimate Sink: Urban Pollution in Historical Perspective* and *Devastation and Renewal: An*

Environmental History of Pittsburgh and Its Region.[50] Early methods of dealing with household plumbing issues are insightfully analyzed in Maureen Ogle's *All the Modern Conveniences: American Household Plumbing, 1840–1890.*[51] In addition, on wastewater systems see Joanne Abel Goldman's *Building New York's Sewers: Developing Mechanism of Urban Management* and Louis P. Cain's *Sanitation Strategy for a Lakefront Metropolis: The Case of Chicago.*[52] Studies of sewage treatment technology are even fewer, but see Daniel Schneider's *Hybrid Nature Sewage Treatment and the Contradictions of the Industrial Ecosystem*, which brings the history of science to bear on this question.[53]

Green infrastructure is a recent topic for historical investigation, but see Andrew Karvonen's *Politics of Urban Runoff: Nature, Technology and the Sustainable City* and Rutherford H. Platt's *Reclaiming American Cities: The Struggle for People, Place, and Nature since 1900.*[54] Discussion of water supply and wastewater issues must include a public health perspective because this issue is so woven into the history of the subject. A useful starting point is John Duffy's *History of Public Health in New York City, 1860–1966* and *The Sanitarians: A History of American Public Health.*[55] See also Barbara Gutmann Rosenkrantz's *Public Health and the State: Changing Views in Massachusetts, 1842–1936.*[56]

PRIMARY SOURCES

The amount of information available on issues of water supply and sewage systems is immense because every city, large and small, provides water and sewage services. Many of these systems originated in the 18th century. Record keeping, however, may be very sporadic, and archives are often inadequate to understand fully how decisions were made. For instance, engineers trying to cope with the repair and maintenance of systems in older cities today are constantly frustrated by a lack of adequate maps of the sewers. A good starting point for information regarding the major issues, aside from engineering texts on water and sewage and secondary historical works, is the technical literature of the times such as *Engineering News* and *Engineering News Record*. These journals and proceedings are increasingly available online, although not all materials have been scanned. Local histories and newspapers are also a valuable source because water and sewer issues often dominated discussions of city affairs while memoirs and biographical accounts of principal actors often contain insightful material. In addition, various governmental reports, on both the state and later the federal level, contain much valuable information.

Archival materials of principal figures in water and sewers affairs are available in some cases, especially if the actors were involved in discussions on the national level. For instance, there are important collections of water- and sewer-related materials in the archives of MIT, Harvard, Yale, and Johns Hopkins University relating especially to public health issues. In addition, the US National Archives contain valuable records concerning water and sewer issues in the collections relating to the Public Health Service. Records on the state level can also be valuable as they relate to public health issues but also for spending on water and sewers.

NOTES

1. Carl Smith, *City Water, City Life: Water and Infrastructure of Ideas in Urbanizing Philadelphia, Boston, and Chicago* (Chicago: University of Chicago Press, 2013), 4–7.
2. Nelson M. Blake, *Water for the Cities* (Syracuse, NY: University of Syracuse Press, 1956).
3. Joel A. Tarr, "The Evolution of the Urban Infrastructure in the Nineteenth and Twentieth Centuries," in *Perspectives on Urban Infrasructure*, ed. Royce Hanson (Washington, DC: National Academy Press, 1984), 13.
4. Gerard T. Koeppel, *Water for Gotham: A History* (Princeton, NJ: Princeton University Press, 2000), 201–284; and Michael Rawson, *Eden on the Charles: The Making of Boston* (Cambridge, MA: Harvard University Press, 2010), 75–128.
5. Martin V. Melosi, *Precious Commodity: Providing Water for America's Cities* (Pittsburgh: University of Pittsburgh Press, 2011), 45–46, 51.
6. Robin Einhorn, *Property Rules: Political Economy in Chicago, 1833–72* (Chicago: University of Chicago Press, 1991), 104.
7. Norris Hundley Jr., *The Great Thirst: Californians and Water: A History* (Berkeley: University of California Press, 2001, rev. ed.); David Soll, *An Environmental and Political History of the New York City Water Supply* (Ithaca, NY: Cornell University Press, 2013), 1–148; and Martin V. Melosi, *The Sanitary City: Urban Infrastructure from Colonial Times to the Present* (Baltimore: Johns Hopkins University Press, 2000), 117–148.
8. Joel A. Tarr, *The Search for the Ultimate Sink: Urban Pollution in Historical Perspective* (Akron, OH: University of Akron Press, 1996), 112–117; and Maureen Ogle, *All the Modern Conveniences: American Household Plumbing, 1840–1890* (Baltimore: Johns Hopkins University Press, 1996), 61–84.
9. Joel A. Tarr and Terry F. Yosie, "Critical Decisions in Pittsburgh Water and Wastewater Treatment," in *Devastation and Renewal: An Environmental History of Pittsburgh and Its Region*, ed. Joel A. Tarr (Pittsburgh, PA: University of Pittsburgh Press, 2003), 67–70.
10. Tarr, *Search for the Ultimate Sink*, 293–308.
11. Melosi, *Precious Commodity*, 55.
12. Joanne Abel Goldman, *Building New York's Sewers: Developing Mechanisms of Urban Management* (West Lafayette, IN: Purdue University Press, 1997), 76–98.
13. John Duffy, *The Sanitarians: A History of American Public Health* (Urbana: University of Illinois Press, 1990).
14. Christopher Hamlin, *Public Health and Social Justice in the Age of Chadwick* (New York: Cambridge University Press, 2009).
15. Tarr, *Search for the Ultimate Sink*, 159–178.
16. Tarr, *Search for the Ultimate Sink*, 131–152.
17. Melosi, *The Sanitary City*, 158–174.
18. Tarr, *Search for the Ultimate Sink*, 159–170.
19. Joel A. Tarr, "The City as an Artifact of Technology and the Environment," in *The Illusory Boundary: Environment and Technology in History*, eds. Martin Reuss and Stephen H. Cutcliffe (Charlottesville: University of Virginia Press, 2010), 153–154.
20. Tarr, *Search for the Ultimate Sink*, 120–128.

21. Tarr, *Search for the Ultimate Sink*, 164–176.

22. Tarr, *Search for the Ultimate Sink*, 192–195.

23. Melosi, *The Sanitary City*, 128–130.

24. Arn Keeling, "Urban Wastes as a Natural Resource: The Case of the Frazer River," *Urban History Review* 34 (2005): 58–70.

25. Tarr, *Search for the Ultimate Sink*, 159–178.

26. Melosi, *The Sanitary City*, 134–148.

27. Tarr, *Search for the Ultimate Sink*, 170–176.

28. John T. Cumbler, *Reasonable Use: The People, the Environment, and the State, New England, 1790–1930* (New York: Oxford University Press, 2001), 49–62, 131–160.

29. Tarr, *Search for the Ultimate Sink*, 126–128.

30. Timothy M. Collins, Edward K. Muller, and Joel A. Tarr, "Pittsburgh's Three Rivers: From Industrial Infrastructure to Environmental Asset," in *Rivers in History: Perspectives on Waterways in Europe and North America*, eds. Christof Mauch and Thomas Zeller (Pittsburgh, PA: University of Pittsburgh Press, 2008), 53.

31. Patrick L. Gurian and Joel A. Tarr, "The Origin of Federal Drinking Water Quality Standards," *Engineering History and Heritage: Proceedings of the Institution of Civil Engineers* (February 2011) 164: 17–26.

32. Daniel Schneider, *Hybrid Nature: Sewage Treatment and the Contradictions of the Industrial Ecosystem* (Cambridge, MA: MIT Press, 2011).

33. Joel A. Tarr, "Industrial Waste Disposal in the United States as a Historical Problem," *Ambix: The Journal of the Society for the History of Alchemy and Chemistry*, 49 (March 2002): 4–20; and Tarr, *Search for the Ultimate Sink*, 354–384.

34. Tarr, *Search for the Ultimate Sink*, 376–778.

35. Mark A. Gelfand, *A Nation of Cities: The Federal Government and Urban America, 1933–1965* (New York: Oxford University Press, 1975), 23–105; and Melosi, *Sanitary City*, 205–338.

36. Adam Rome, *Bulldozer in the Countryside: Suburban Spread and the Rise of American Environmentalism* (New York: Cambridge University Press, 2001), 15–152.

37. Samuel P. Hays, *Beauty, Health, and Permanence: Environmental Politics in the United States, 1955–1985* (New York: Cambridge University Press, 1987), 351–356.

38. Richard N. L. Andrews, *Managing the Environment, Managing Ourselves: A History of American Environmental Policy* (New Haven, CT: Yale University Press, 1999), 227–254.

39. Rome, *Bulldozer in the Countryside*, 15–152.

40. "Clean Water Act," Wikipedia, (https://en.wikipedia.org/wiki/Clean_Water_Act#Nonpoint_sources).

41. Rural Community Assistance Partnership, *Still Living without the Basics in the 21st Century: Analyzing the Availability of Water and Sanitation Services in the United States*, http://www.win-water.org/reports/RCAP_full_final.pdf.

42. Andrew Karvonen, *Politics of Urban Runoff: Nature, Technology and the Sustainable City* (Cambridge, MA: MIT, 2011); and Melosi, *The Sanitary City*, 32.

43. Nelson Blake, *Water for the Cities: A History of the Urban Water Supply Problem in the United States* (Syracuse, NY: Syracuse University Press, 1956).

44. These include Ellis Armstrong, Michael Robinson, and Suellen Hoy, eds., *History of Public Works in the United States, 1776–1976* (Chicago: APWA, 1976); Martin V. Melosi, ed., *Pollution and Reform in American Cities, 1870–1930* (Austin: University of Texas Press, 1980); and Joel A. Tarr and Gabriel Dupuy, eds., *Technology and the Rise of the Networked City in Europe and America* (Philadelphia: Temple University Press, 1988).

45. See, for instance, Abraham Hoffman, *Vision or Villainy: Origins of the Owens Valley–Los Angeles Water Controversy* (College Station: Texas A&M Press, 1981); William L. Kahrl, *Water and Power: The Conflict over Los Angeles' Water Supply in the Owens Valley* (Berkeley: University of California Press, 1982); and Norris Hundley, *The Great Thirst: Californians and Water: A History* (Berkeley: University of California Press, 1992). Fern L. Nesson, Great Waters: *A History of Boston's Water Supply* (Hanover NH: University Press of New England, 1983) provides an introduction to that city's water supply issues, while Sarah S. Elkind, *Bay Cities and Water Politics: The Battle for Resources in Boston and Oakland* (Lawrence: University Press of Kansas, 1998) provides a comparative framework. Kate Foss-Mollan, *Hard Water Politics and Water Supply in Milwaukee, 1870–1995* (West Lafayette, IN: Purdue University Press, 2001) is useful.

46. Carl Smith, *City Water, City Life: Water and the Infrastructure of Ideas in Urbanizing Philadelphia, Boston, and Chicago* (Chicago: University of Chicago Press, 2013).

47. Michael Rawson, *Eden on the Charles* (Cambridge, MA: Harvard University Press, 2010).

48. Gerald T. Koeppel, *Water for Gotham: A History* (Princeton, NJ: Princeton University Press, 2000); and David Soll, *Empire of Water: An Environmental and Political History of the New York City Water Supply* (Ithaca, NY: Cornell University Press, 2013).

49. Martin V. Melosi, *Precious Commodity: Providing Water for America's Cities* (Pittsburgh, NY: University of Pittsburgh Press, 2011) and *The Sanitary City: Urban Infrastructure in America from Colonial Times to the Present* (Baltimore: Johns Hopkins University Press, 2000; revised University of Pittsburgh Press, 2008).

50. Tarr, *Search for the Ultimate Sink and Devastation and Renewal: An Environmental History of Pittsburgh and Its Region* (Pittsburgh, PA: University of Pittsburgh Press, 2003).

51. Maureen Ogle, *All the Modern Conveniences: American Household Plumbing, 1840–1890* (Baltimore: Johns Hopkins University Press, 1996).

52. Joanne Abel Goldman, *Building New York's Sewers: Developing Mechanism of Urban Management* (West Lafayette, IN: Purdue University Press, 1997); and Louis P. Cain, *Sanitation Strategy for a Lakefront Metropolis: The Case of Chicago* (Chicago: Northern Illinois Press, 1978).

53. Daniel Schneider, *Hybrid Nature Sewage Treatment and the Contradictions of the Industrial Ecosystem* (Cambridge, MA: MIT, 2011).

54. Andrew Karvonen, *Politics of Urban Runoff: Nature, Technology and the Sustainable City* (Cambridge, MA: MIT Press, 2011); and Rutherford H. Platt, *Reclaiming American Cities: The Struggle for People, Place, and Nature since 1900* (Amherst: University of Massachusetts Press, 2013).

55. John Duffy, *History of Public Health in New York City, 1860–1966* (New York: Russell Sage Foundation, 1974) and *The Sanitarians: A History of American Public Health* (Urbana: University of Illinois Press, 1990).

56. Barbara Gutmann Rosenkrantz, *Public Health and the State: Changing Views in Massachusetts, 1842–1936* (Cambridge, MA: Harvard University Press, 1972).

Joel A. Tarr

MASS TRANSIT IN 19TH- AND 20TH-CENTURY AMERICA

Mass transit—streetcars, elevated and commuter rail, subways, buses, ferries, and other transportation vehicles serving large numbers of passengers and operating on fixed routes and schedules—has been part of the urban scene in the United States since the early 19th century. Regular steam ferry service connected Brooklyn and New Jersey to Manhattan in the early 1810s and horse-drawn omnibuses plied city streets starting in the late 1820s. Expanding networks of horse railways emerged by the mid-19th century. A half century later, technological innovation and urban industrialization enabled the electric streetcar to become the dominant mass transit vehicle. During this era, mass transit had a significant impact on American urban development, suburbanization, the rise of technological networks, consumerism, and even race and gender relations. Mass transit's importance in the lives of most Americans started to decline with the growth of automobile ownership in the 1920s, except for a temporary rise in transit ridership during World War II. In the 1960s, when congressional subsidies began to reinvigorate mass transit, heavy-rail systems opened in cities such as San Francisco and Washington DC, followed by light rail systems in San Diego, Portland, and other cities in the next decades. As the 21st century approached, concern about environmental sustainability and urban revitalization stimulated renewed interest in the benefits of mass transit.

The history of urban mass transit in the United States is more complex than a simple progression of improved public transportation modes before the rise of the automobile ultimately replaced transit's dominance by the mid-20th century. Transit history in American cities is rooted in different phases of urbanization, the rise of large corporate entities during the industrial era, the relationship between technology and society, and other broad themes within American history. At the same time, mass transit history shows the value of emphasizing local contexts, as the details of urban transit unfolded differently across the United States based on municipal traditions, environments, economies, and phases of growth.

FERRY BOATS, OMNIBUSES, AND THE BEGINNINGS OF MASS TRANSIT IN THE EARLY 19TH CENTURY

The ferry boats that regularly crossed the waters of a few American cities in the early 19th century provided an important precedent to the mass transit industry that emerged later in the century. Before the age of industrialization, the cities of the American merchant economy were primarily sites of commercial exchange of goods and services. Boston, New York, Philadelphia, and most other urban centers were dense, port cities located along rivers, bays, and other bodies of water. And while this geography facilitated the transshipment of goods, it also impeded the expansion of urban settlement. During the early 1810s, Robert Fulton, an engineer and inventor, established a regular ferry service using steam power. The service linked lower Manhattan with Jersey City over the Hudson River, as well as the village of Brooklyn, at the time a small suburban settlement across the East River. The early development of regular ferry service illustrates the dominant role that New York City would play in American urban mass transit—not surprising considering the city's rapid demographic and physical growth and dominant position in the hierarchy of American cities during the 19th century. Ferries also demonstrate the early connections between transit and urban expansion, as the service allowed commuters living in areas such as the newly subdivided Brooklyn Heights neighborhood to overcome obstacles for continuous settlement posed by bodies of water. Typically, regular users of this service enjoyed above-average

incomes and social positions. Unlike most working people, they could afford the expense of a daily fare.[1] By the 1860s, the annual ridership of New York's ferry industry had expanded to more than thirty-two million people. Thirteen companies employed seventy steamboats for more than twenty different ferry routes.[2] Similar service had also spread to other northeastern cities, such as Philadelphia, Pittsburgh, and Cincinnati. Ferry service is still an integral part of daily commuting in some cities today. Despite its success, however, ferry boat service could do little to improve transportation over land.[3]

By the late 1820s, New York also became home to the first significant form of land-based mass transit: the omnibus. This operation—a large horse-drawn wheeled carriage similar to a stagecoach yet open for service to the general public at a set fare—originated in Nantes, France, in 1826. Omnibus service spread to Paris two years later and to other French cities as well as London by 1832.[4] Abraham Brower brought the service to New York in 1828 when he launched a route running a mile and a quarter along Broadway. Brower's original vehicles, *Accommodation* and *Sociable*, held approximately twelve passengers.[5] Three years after Brower inaugurated service, more than one hundred omnibuses traveled on New York streets.[6] By the 1840s, Boston, Philadelphia, Baltimore, and other American cities had omnibus service. It spread from larger to smaller cities in subsequent decades.[7]

The omnibus had weaknesses. Since most vehicles featured unpadded seats and typically travelled on uneven cobblestone roads (if paved at all), passengers experienced an uncomfortable ride.[8] The fare—generally 12 cents—was too expensive for most urban dwellers. Nonetheless, the omnibus initiated a "riding habit" of regular transit use within its main segment of users: members of the urban middle class. This growing demographic found private stagecoaches too expensive, but they had the affluence and desire to commute to work instead of walking.[9] Although getting around by foot remained the main source of mobility for most urban dwellers, the "walking city" was slowly eroding.

HORSECARS: THE "AMERICAN RAILWAY"

A vehicle with less surface friction could reduce the shortcomings that had plagued the omnibus. Horse streetcars—commonly known as horsecars—traveled on rail instead of road, and had numerous advantages over the omnibus. The use of rails provided a faster, quieter, more comfortable ride, while enabling a more efficient use of horse power. This fact allowed for larger cars that carried approximately three times as many riders as the omnibus. Importantly, the horsecar's lower operating cost per passenger mile translated to a cheaper fare for users (typically 5 cents compared to the 12-cent omnibus fare) and a growing "riding habit" within the American urban population.[10] Horsecars reduced the time and cost of commuting to and from the central core, and, thus, they expanded the area of development along the urban fringe. Following a slow start, other American cities adopted horsecars by the 1850s, part of the wider context of rampant urbanization during the second half of the 19th century. Typically, a private company ran lines under a franchise awarded by the municipality that outlined the public roads on which the company could build rails and operate routes, along with other stipulations. By the end of the 1850s, New York, New Orleans, Brooklyn, Boston, Philadelphia, Baltimore, Pittsburgh, Chicago, and Cincinnati provided horsecar service. Further expansion developed during the 1860s.[11] Two decades later, almost twenty thousand horsecars traveled on more than thirty thousand miles of street railway across the United States. Such expansion was particularly notable in contrast to comparatively slower growth in Europe (where people called the technology "American Railways").[12]

The horsecar's initial development in the United States, and its early spread across the country, exemplified how the country was often at the forefront of transit use and technological innovation during the second half of the 19th century and the early 20th century.

The world's first horsecar line began service in 1832, when the New York and Harlem Railroad Company inaugurated a horse-powered rail car route along Fourth Avenue. The franchise owners, including banker John Mason, intended the line to serve as the first stage of a passenger steam railway linking lower Manhattan to Harlem. However, fears of noise, smoke, and boiler explosions from those living along the right-of-way prompted the city to prohibit the railroad from operating steam engines within the built-up area south of Twenty-Seventh Street, so the company relied upon horse power within the restricted area.[13] Despite the operating advantages of horsecars, its "technology transfer" to other American cities was slow until the early 1850s. This phenomenon reinforced the value of local contexts, as horsecar lines developed differently in each city based on factors such as local politics, geography, and population density. Horsecars—and the rails upon which they travelled—began a process of redefining the meaning of city streets that continued with electric streetcars and automobiles. The street became more a place for mobility, diminishing the centrality of sociability, recreation, and other traditional street uses. Initially, popular sentiment opposed the placement of rails along streets, especially since rails were not flush with the street surface and impeded cross movement until the invention of grooved rails in 1852. That same year, New York saw its first horsecar operation distinct from steam railroads, and the service soon spread to many other American locales.[14]

Historians Joel Tarr and Clay McShane demonstrate that horsecars exemplify how the rise of industrialization and urbanization during the 19th century led to a growing exploitation of horse power. Ironically, steam power, an essential component of the first Industrial Revolution, created a greater demand for this older form of energy in industrial cities.[15] Yet the horsecar's reliance on these "living machines" presented the greatest weakness of the technology, especially as cities sought to expand their systems once easily commutable distances from the urban fringe via horsecar were reached. Horses were expensive to maintain. They ate their value in feed each year, required large stables and care from veterinarians, stablehands, and blacksmiths, and their average work life lasted less than five years.[16] In terms of social costs, horses produced massive amounts of pollution as their manure and urine fell on city streets. And once horses met their ultimate fate, their bodies had to be removed. New York alone disposed of fifteen thousand horse carcasses annually.[17] Sudden disease outbreaks were common. The most dramatic occurred in 1872, when an equine influenza epidemic—the "Great Epizootic"— hit North America (especially Eastern Seaboard cities). Thousands of horses died during the epidemic, which created operational upheaval for the horsecar industry. Not surprisingly, the event further reinforced the need for cheaper, more reliable forms of transit power.[18]

Steam was one alternative source of power. It had provided power for ferry services since the 1810s and passenger railways two decades later. By the mid-19th century, commuter railways using steam locomotives (essentially short-haul passenger rail) connected affluent residents living in small suburban areas to places of work and entertainment in large cities. For example, upper-middle-class towns, such as New Rochelle and Scarsdale in Westchester County, New York, grew with commuter rail service to New York City, while Evanston, Highland Park, Lake Forest, and other commuter towns emerged around Chicago.[19] Yet steam power presented challenges for urban transit. Many city dwellers living along crowded streets considered the noise, pollution, and other dangers associated with the technology to be nuisances. Steam operation also generally cost more than horse power until the 1870s. A few New York companies gambled on steam-powered conveyances during the 1860s, but they all soon ceased their experiments.[20] Nonetheless, transit companies in greater New York and Chicago began building elevated railroads using steam power above urban thoroughfares. This proved to be among the earliest forms of rapid transit, since vehicles operated on their own right-of-way, not in mixed traffic. By 1893, Jay Gould's New York Elevated Railroad Company carried half a million daily passengers from lower Manhattan to the Bronx, while Chicago saw the first line of its "L" system open in 1892. Although short-lived "elevateds" existed in the smaller cities of Sioux City, Iowa, and Kansas City, Missouri, high capital costs made them mostly a big city phenomenon unlikely to become a dominant mode of transit across the United States.[21] Elevateds also darkened the street below. Once electricity became a possible power source by the 1890s, city dwellers clamored for rapid transit to burrow underground.

Power generated from a stationary central source—rather than within a moving locomotive—offered another alternative. Cable cars traveled on rail, similar to horsecars and steam railways, but these vehicles clasped on a moving cable within a street conduit. This feature eliminated much of the noise, smoke, and danger of boiler explosions that plagued urban steam locomotives (although such nuisances were still present at the stationary power source). Cable car operation began in San Francisco in 1873, when Andrew Hallidie began his service on Clay Street. San Francisco's hilly terrain required four horse teams to pull a single omnibus, with some hills too steep for any kind of horse service.[22] Since various transit experiments in steam, compressed air, chemical engines, and electricity failed to produce an inexpensive method of propulsion, cable cars seemed the best alternative to horse power by the 1870s. Following Hallidie's successful operation, most large cities across the United States built cable car networks.[23]

With hindsight, the cable car emerged as a temporary solution for the transit industry until the refinement of a more efficient power distribution method. Cables had advantages over horse power, but they also carried particular weaknesses. Cables were always under the threat of snapping. Maintenance and replacement constituted a complex, expensive process that negatively affected service. Ice buildup produced issues in colder cities. The cable had to run at the same capacity no matter the service level, which meant power generation could not diminish at off-peak times. Twenty years after Hallidie's first run on Clay Street, more than three hundred miles of cable car tracks had been laid across the United States. But numbers declined soon after electric streetcar operation became practical in the 1890s. By 1913, only twenty miles of cable car track were still in use.[24] Electric streetcars and other electric transit technologies exacerbated the changes in urban life that horsecars and cable cars had unleashed.

TRANSIT BECOMES ELECTRIC

Technological innovations, demand from the transit industry for improved operations, and a desire for mobility enabled the electric streetcar to become the dominant mass transit vehicle in the United States by the turn of the 20th century. The streetcar's use of electricity makes it a key technology of the second Industrial Revolution. "[N]o invention," urban historian Kenneth Jackson has argued, "had greater impact on the American city between the Civil War and World War I than the visible and noisy streetcar and the tracks that snaked down the broad avenues into undeveloped land."[25] The idea of transmitting electrical current to move vehicles had existed since the 1840s, but no practical technique could generate sufficient electrical power. Experiments with battery power also failed in terms of feasible, everyday operation.[26] Early streetcar pioneers such as Leo Daft and Charles van Depoele made significant advances to the technology;

however, Frank Sprague (1857–1934) is most commonly associated with the vehicle's development. Similar to names associated with other critical technologies, Sprague was not the sole "inventor" of the electric streetcar. Rather, as transit historian Brian J. Cudahy explains, Sprague's success derived from "his ability to blend aspects of previous experiments with his own developments into a fully orchestrated whole."[27] A former Edison employee, his key technical contribution was a trolley poll and wheel design that overcame previous flaws whereby overhead electrical wires detached from vehicles (and thus the power source). Sprague's system also demonstrated operational reliability and financial feasibility when it was put to the test along twelve miles of track for the Union Passenger Railway in Richmond, Virginia, in 1888. Twelve years later, 90 percent of all streetcars in the United States relied on his patents, and few horsecars were still in operation.[28]

Street railway companies quickly adopted electricity. Often, they used existing rails and even former horsecar vehicles.[29] Electric streetcars transformed the transit industry. New forms of expertise related to electricity replaced veterinarians, blacksmiths, and other horse-related professions. The new technology also generated mergers with large companies swallowing up smaller enterprises, monopolizing service in urban areas, and employing corporate business forms in order to raise capital needed for investment in electricity infrastructure (in some cases, electrical utility companies were also transit providers). Transit remained within the private market in most American cities until the second half of the 20th century, but the organizational structure of the industry became more complex.[30]

Electric streetcars rapidly spread across the country. Like horsecars decades earlier, electric streetcars accommodated heavier passenger loads compared to predecessors. This reduced passenger cost per mile, lowered fares, and stimulated greater transit use by wider segments of society. Two years after Sprague's Richmond success, the vehicle carried twice the number of passengers in the United States compared to the rest of the world, with thirty-two thousand electric streetcars traversing American streets from small towns to major metropolises—a number that nearly doubled by the turn of the century.[31]

Electric traction also removed an obstacle for underground transit. The London Underground had operated steam-powered trains when it opened in 1863, but most commentators believed Americans would avoid smoke-filled subway tunnels. The massive construction cost also impeded subway building. In 1894, the Massachusetts legislature authorized Boston to build the first subway in the United States. The line, which was completed four years later, buried 1.5 miles of a busy streetcar under Tremont Street's retail district. The Boston Transit Commission, a public body, financed construction, while the private West End Street Railway operated the line and serviced its debt.[32] Public money was also required to build the country's largest subway network in New York—foreshadowing the growing role of the state in mass transit in the second half of the 20th century. In 1904, the Interborough Rapid Transit Company's service began connecting the Bronx to Manhattan, followed by the construction of hundreds of more miles of subway in New York during subsequent decades.[33]

THE EFFECTS OF ELECTRIC STREETCARS ON URBAN LIFE

Streetcars and other forms of electric traction had a tremendous influence on the shapes and sensations of urban life during the late 19th and early 20th centuries. In many cases, the technology exacerbated trends that began with the horsecar. Streetcars continued the horsecar's role in enabling the seemingly contradictory yet related forces of centralization and dispersal in American cities. In essence, this entailed the general separation between major commercial activities in the downtown and districts of residence and other activities, such as manufacturing, in less dense areas surrounding

the core and along the urban fringe. The American walking city—in which the dominant mode for the journey to work was by foot—came to an end, although many workers still walked to their places of employment.

The many streetcar lines that radiated from central business districts across the United States increased accessibility to and from downtown. The shapes, spectacles, and symbols of what is still associated today with "downtown"— business skyscrapers and other tall buildings as well as large theaters, department stores, hotels, and other palaces of consumption— emerged with the arrival of horsecars, but they reached a new scale with electric streetcars. Electric traction had a centralizing effect by increasing land values in the core and creating the economy of large buildings and places of entertainment during the late 19th and early 20th centuries. These attractions relied upon other technologies such as the elevator, telephone, and electric light, yet the rise of skyscrapers and other iconic elements of the modern urban landscape would have been unlikely without streetcars.[34]

Streetcars played a dramatic role in suburbanization. Unlike the natural limits of horsecars, electric streetcars could journey well beyond the existing city once trackage was laid. In Boston, for example, the area of urban settlement expanded from two miles outside the old walking city core during the horsecar era to four miles during the first decade of electric streetcar service.[35] Suburban living was more readily available to Americans of the growing middle class and in the skilled trades from cities as varied as New York City to Milwaukee. Those who worked within the older city but could not afford the daily ten-cent round trip fare were forced to stay (or walk long distances from the urban fringe).[36] The characteristics of "streetcar suburbs" differed across and within cities, yet they also shared similarities. For example, accessible, cheap land enabled suburban residential developments of semi-detached or detached dwellings set back from the street and surrounded by a yard (apartments also existed). Walkability remained important for at least some daily tasks and, of course, for the journey to the nearby streetcar stop. Thus, on the whole, streetcar suburbs had fairly compact forms and high population densities compared to the automobile-centric suburbs that developed later in the 20th century, although such forms and densities varied based on local influences, levels of affluence, and other factors. Real estate speculators knew the value of streetcar service to their developments. In many cases, transit companies held real estate interests along the urban fringe, which they connected via streetcar to spur development, even if the line itself was unprofitable. Yet the many streetcar suburbs that still dot the American landscape today were not simply the result of ambitious developers, but also the desires and actions of many people, from local politicians to the varied residents who made such places home.

Various social factors joined the development and expansion of the electric streetcar to create the new scale of suburbanization at the turn of the 20th century. The streetcar did not solely create the suburbs; the relationship was more complex. The experience of suburbanization in the United States evolved differently from that in Europe, where dense row housing continued to develop along the urban fringe. Demand existed for suburbanization—and its distinct shapes and forms—as well as the technologies that made it possible. Scholars have often explained such demand through the value placed by Americans on private property ownership and the 19th-century belief in the "rural ideal." To these factors, historian Clay McShane has added popular ideas about public health that emerged during the second half of the 19th century. The miasmic theory of disease contended that vapors emanating from rotting organic matter caused illness. To counter these miasmic threats, Americans sought suburban environments filled with grass, trees, and fresh air.[37] Ironically, the new scale of suburbanization generated by electric streetcars created new social issues, such as the growing geographic division of wealth and political fragmentation within the American metropolis.[38]

Transit also enabled new social experiences associated with the modern age. Whereas streetcars linked people to department stores, theaters, and other attractions of downtown, the technology also connected riders to attractions at the end of the line. Amusement parks were the most prominent. Transit companies often owned such parks as a means to generate more passenger traffic in outer areas and on off-peak times: weekends and holidays. For example, Atlanta's Ponce de Leon Park originated as a natural springs attraction served by omnibus service and became a large amusement park after the Atlanta Street Railway assumed control of it by the turn of the 20th century. Even one of the greatest attractions at amusement parks—the rollercoaster—had a connection to transit technology; it turned apprehensions about new transit technology (such as the fear of accidents) into a sensorial thrill. According to David Nye, destinations at both ends of the streetcar line—the downtown department store and the amusement park along the urban fringe—promoted a consumerist, mass society that "subverted the Victorian moral code" of thrift and self-restraint.[39]

Electric streetcars, along with subways and elevated railroads, allowed for new ways of seeing the city and its inhabitants. Riding within a swift, enclosed transit vehicle emphasized a visual understanding of the urban landscape. In particular, elevateds allowed for a comprehensive, panoramic view of the city that was unattainable by walking on the ground. The interiors of transit vehicles also became essential public spaces by forcing face-to-face contact between people of varying racial, class, and gender identities. Crowded rush-hour cars such as those of the New York elevateds and subways made social contact particularly common.[40] Ironically, transit interiors became points of intimate contact at the same time that the American city, through suburbanization via transit technology, was becoming more residentially segregated by race and class.[41]

Yet streetcars or other forms of transit also reinforced social differences. They were "moving theaters" of racial conflict, according to historian Robin Kelley.[42] In antebellum America, omnibus companies in New York and Philadelphia forbade African Americans from riding in their vehicles, while slaves sometimes rode with their white owners or in separate conveyances in southern cities.[43] Segregated transit was at the center of Jim Crow–era discrimination in the South. Although the Montgomery Bus Boycott in 1956—sparked by the refusal of Rosa Parks to give up her bus seat to a white passenger—is rightly remembered as a major moment in the Civil Rights movement, African Americans participated in failed protests in at least twenty-five southern cities against the injustice of Jim Crow laws during the first decade of the 20th century. These laws, following the US Supreme Court case *Plessy v. Ferguson* (1896), dictated black riders sit in the back of transit vehicles and give up their seat to white riders if they sat in the middle section.[44] Women had mixed experiences using transit. Spaces within a transit vehicle were common sites of sexual harassment, especially after streetcar companies switched to one-man operations by eliminating guards and ticket collectors who used to watch over passengers in the early 20th century. Such harassment led Julia D. Longfellow of the Women's Municipal League in 1909 to request the operator of New York's Interborough Rapid Transit to provide a female-only car during rush hours (higher operating costs motivated the private company to reject her request).[45] Nevertheless, streetcars and other forms of mass transit allowed for opportunities for greater freedom, through urban mobility, for women, who constituted a high percentage of transit users. A ride on a streetcar embodied the complex contradictions of American urban life during the age of modern technology.

THE DECLINE OF MASS TRANSIT IN 20TH-CENTURY AMERICA

Mass transit's importance in the lives of city dwellers decreased by the 1920s. This decline lasted until the 1970s, and, in many ways, it has continued to the present. The roots of this trend emerged during the early 20th century. From 1890 to 1905, annual streetcar ridership across the country more than doubled from two billion to five billion passenger trips. However, over the next two decades ridership grew at a slower rate. From 1917 to 1923, the industry added only one billion more annual trips. Annual transit ridership (all modes including subway, streetcar, and bus) peaked in 1926 (excluding exceptional war-related conditions during the 1940s and early 1950s), with more than seventeen billion passenger trips—a figure since unmatched. The slowdown in transit ridership growth coincided with an explosion of automobile ownership and use: in 1910, Americans owned less than half a million automobiles, a figure that rose to eight million vehicles in 1920.[46] Mass transit's fall in prominence is more complicated than simply the invention and popularity of the private automobile, for as historians of technology remind us, no technology is innately superior to another. Rather, social values and practices influence the acceptance of technologies based on complex factors. Multiple reasons within and outside of the transit industry explain declining passenger numbers during the 20th century.

Starting in the 1910s, inflation imposed pressure on the overwhelmingly private-owned transit industry. Transit companies began to reduce investment in their capital stock before World War I.[47] Inflation led to increased prices for materials (the value of steel rails rose by 50 percent after the war) and other costs. Labor, the largest part of the industry's operating costs, also became more expensive as more workers unionized.[48] Greater demand for better service from interest groups—not only users who protested against any hike to the common five-cent fare, but also politicians and business groups—compounded these economic forces by making more difficult the implementation of positive reforms that could have improved the competitiveness of transit against the automobile.

Another challenge originated with jitneys: privately owned automobiles operated by entrepreneurs who cruised streets (typically those with transit routes) in search of possible customers. Passengers enjoyed the jitney's flexibility, especially its ability to drop off riders closer to their destination compared to the same cost as a streetcar. Unlike transit companies, jitneys usually were unlicensed and paid no municipal fees or taxes. Transit operators saw jitneys as unfair competition and pressured local governments to prohibit the service in many cities. The jitney enjoyed only short-lived success, but it provided but one example of how the automobile threatened the transit industry.[49]

The popular perception that transit was a private business, rather than a public service deserving government aid, added to the industry's woes. Years of negative sentiment from passengers, politicians, and other interest groups about poor service, corruption, and large profits hindered the industry. Historian Paul Barrett argues that municipal ordinances passed in Chicago in 1907 enforced levels of service on the city's private transit provider, but they failed to provide a subsidy that would make such service financially feasible. Instead, either complete municipal ownership or minimal regulation constituted better alternatives. San Francisco had municipalized transit in 1912, but few cities followed suit until the 1950s.[50] Transit was not alone in suffering from negative opinion; the automobile did too, despite its relative newness. Historian Peter Norton has shown that a consensus of politicians, city planners, and most citizens believed automobile use on city streets should be highly regulated to ensure not only the safety for other road users (especially pedestrians), but also the efficient flow of traffic. The young automobile industry countered such sentiment by branding its product as the symbol of individual freedom. It also lobbied policymakers. This strategy allowed "motordom" to gain policy concessions for items such as parking restrictions, often at the expense of the transit industry and other street users.[51] The private nature of the automobile also may have influenced transit users to drive

cars, especially women. The automobile created its own problems, but many ex-transit passengers believed it offered a better alternative to the mixed company in a crowded streetcar, often filled with cigarette smoke and other harassing passengers.[52]

The bus, a vehicle on wheels employing an internal combustion engine, also illustrates the changing tide of transit between 1920 and 1940. Bus service emerged during the first decade of the 20th century and its use grew during the 1920s, when enterprising companies decided to service new suburban developments located past the termini of streetcar lines. Although most streetcar companies initially feared the bus, they increasingly saw it as a flexible vehicle with low capital costs that competed with the automobile and served areas with lower ridership levels. A survey in 1924 revealed that little more than one thousand buses plied American streets, but this figure jumped to at least twenty thousand buses eight years later.[53] Buses slowly replaced streetcar lines across the country. While more than seventy thousand streetcars operated in 370 cities in 1912, only 1,200 vehicles serviced seven cities five decades later.[54]

Scholars and other analysts offer varied explanations for the replacement of streetcars by buses across the United States. One interpretation claims that the phenomenon emerged as part of a conspiracy by General Motors. This argument became popular in the early 1970s, when lawyer Bradford Snell testified in front of a US Senate subcommittee. He contended that General Motors, under its National Coach Lines subsidiary, purchased a number of transit companies during the 1930s and 1940s in order to convert streetcar lines to bus operation, with the purpose of weakening or eliminating transit service so that disgruntled passengers would purchase automobiles. The theory even entered popular culture as inspiration for a plotline in the 1988 film *Who Framed Roger Rabbit*. Although the investigation ultimately found that GM broke antitrust laws, the central conspiratorial charge— the provision of poor transit service in order to increase automobile sales—was not the basis of the investigation. In fact, most transit historians and other scholars generally disregard the conspiracy theory. National Coach Lines controlled approximately 10 percent of the country's urban transit systems, yet a majority of the remaining 90 percent of companies also switched to buses. Moreover, a consensus within the transit industry believed that buses—operating without the capital concerns of rails—possessed economic and operational benefits compared to streetcars, especially on lower density systems and lines.[55] The case of bus substitution in New York City during the 1920s and 1930s suggests politics played a role in the shift rather than rational cost-benefit considerations of each mode of transport. Historian Zachary Schrag argues that the streetcar-bus debate served as a "proxy" for other issues such as public ownership, regulation, and fare prices.[56] Technological novelty also played a part; to most passengers, a new bus seemed more modern in comparison to streetcars, which many passengers saw as the antique relics of corrupt private transit companies.[57] Regardless, buses likely saved the mass transit industry during the post–World War II era, when ridership numbers continued to plummet. Implementation of diesel engines and automatic transmissions in buses by the 1940s also reduced energy costs even as these innovations led to noise, pollution, and other negative consequences on the urban environment.[58]

World War II saw a steep but temporary rise in ridership—in fact the highest in the mass transit industry's history. The booming war economy created a strong demand from passengers requiring transit for work trips, especially compared to the rampant unemployment and declining rider figures during the Great Depression. Wartime gasoline and rubber rationing, and an automobile production ban, also led to increased ridership. Yet the boom failed to solve the transit industry's larger issues, which were evident before the war. In fact, the wartime riding experience hurt transit in

the long run. Passengers in Detroit and other industrial cities crowded into packed, often dilapidated transit vehicles, which created uncomfortable riding situations and even racial conflict. These memories surely remained with former riders who decided to purchase automobiles once the conflict ended.[59]

After the war, the longer trajectory of declining passenger numbers resumed. Numerous transit companies faced financial ruin, which led to public ownership in Chicago, Los Angeles, and other larger cities in the immediate postwar era. In smaller towns, transit often ceased operation. Despite the wave of public takeovers during the late 1940s and 1950s, the popular conception of transit as a service run on a cost-recovery basis remained unchanged. Service failed to improve significantly enough to curtail declining ridership.[60] At the same time, the postwar years marked the growth of automobile-dependent suburbs and car ownership as well as a rapid push for road building. In 1956, President Dwight Eisenhower signed the Federal Aid Highway Act, which dedicated twenty-five billion dollars to build more than forty thousand miles of limited-access roadways across the country.[61] Although transit's decline began decades before the federal government constructed new highways in the postwar era, the interstate program—which funded 90 percent of urban expressway costs—demonstrated the federal government's enthusiasm for automobility. By the 1950s, the United States had become "car country," according to Christopher Wells.[62] Meanwhile, the transit industry suffered. But change was around the corner.

FEDERAL FUNDING AND A RETURN TO RIDERSHIP STABILITY

Mass transit has made a modest comeback since the 1960s, when the federal government began to subsidize transit expansion on a broad scale. The push for federal funding originated from a coalition of railroad executives and big city mayors. In the late 1950s, rail companies with major freight operations cut many of their unprofitable commuter rail services that served large metropolitan areas. Together, the mayors and rail companies fought for a national transportation policy from the federal government that recognized the importance of mass transit, not just highways and automobiles. Older cities worried that further decline of transit would diminish the competitive advantages of their central cores over more peripheral areas in terms of business services and manufacturing. And middle-class suburbanites who relied on commuter rail worried about the loss of a service that connected them to places of work, consumption, and leisure. A few precedents for capital funding from government existed, for example, municipal funds for subways in Boston and New York City, and federal funding for the Chicago subway during the Great Depression and World War II.[63]

These lobbying efforts came to fruition in 1964 when President Lyndon Johnson signed the Urban Mass Transportation Act (UMTA). The legislation enabled capital grants from the federal government to cover a maximum of two-thirds the capital costs of equipment and facilities for transit systems.[64] Over the next decade, Washington provided more than three billion dollars, which cities used to purchase private systems, improve existing vehicles and infrastructure, and build new systems. From 1965 to 1974, the number of publicly owned transit systems rose from less than sixty to more than three hundred. Yet federal funding alone did not solve transit's woes, as ridership across the country continued to decline in the years following the passage of the act in 1964.[65]

More dramatically, a few cities used new federal funding to construct rapid transit systems. The idea that transit operating in its own right-of-way could best compete with the automobile and the nation's growing expressway network constituted a major impetus for such large-scale, expensive transit systems. Postwar rapid transit was often debated within the wider context of desires for regional government

and planning. San Francisco's Bay Area Rapid Transit (BART), approved by area residents in a municipal referendum in 1962, took advantage of federal funding after 1964. Although the original push for BART came from downtown business interests, it was also supported by politicians, the media, and residents, who believed that rapid transit could improve the growing region's traffic congestion, especially following the end of streetcar service across the Bay Bridge between San Francisco and Oakland during the mid-1950s. When BART opened in 1972, it made use of unproven, space-age technology designed by aerospace firms in an attempt to create a more modern transit riding experience. This reliance on unproven technology led to cost overruns and technical problems, but BART quickly became a key part of the San Francisco Bay area's distinctive urban landscape.[66]

The other new major system developed in the nation's capital. The Washington Metro originated from ideas within planning circles during the 1950s to build a small rapid transit system in conjunction with a larger network of automobile freeways. Inner-city residents feared the damage that the controversial Three Sisters Bridge over the Potomac River as well as other freeway plans would have on their communities and the local environment. They pushed for a larger rapid transit system as an alternative to the expressway web. The eventual 100-mile Metro system faced challenges, including a period of stalled capital funding from expressway proponents before a congressional vote stopped the logjam. The first leg of the system opened in 1976 with subsequent sections opening during the next three decades. Despite initial ridership numbers that were lower than originally projected, Metro historian Zachary Schrag argues that the project embodied admirable goals of Great Society–era liberalism: the value of the public realm and the belief in the ability of government to improve the daily lives of its citizens.[67]

Federal funding since the 1960s has had a mixed legacy. Both contemporary scholars and historians looking back at the program are critical. For example, they question UTMA's endorsement of rapid transit systems, which often had ridership numbers far lower than initial projections that were used to promote such networks. An early articulation of this argument came from John Meyer, John Kain, and Martin Wohl in their *The Urban Transportation Problem* (1965). Published soon after President Johnson signed UTMA and based on quantitative analysis, the study criticized transit funding from an economic perspective.[68] Promoters of the Washington Metro had naively argued that ambitious ridership projections would mean that fares alone could cover all operating and even some capital expenses, a belief that became untenable with inflation during the 1970s. But others, such as Schrag, believe that quantitative critiques overlook the more qualitative benefits that public funding for transit in general—and rapid transit more specifically—has given cities. Schrag cites the positive impact of the Metro on Washington, where rapid transit has reduced the city's reliance on cars, freeways, and gasoline, created more sustainable developments, and improved the mobility of residents—especially those who choose or are unable to own a car because of personal finances, age, or disability.[69]

The 1970s marked a turning point for transit in the United States. Transit historian Brian Cudahy has even suggested that the decade saw the beginning of a "transit renaissance" in the United States.[70] In statistical terms, the long decline of annual passengers since the late 1920s (with the exception of World War II) ended in 1973, although per capita rides continued to decline. This resurgence arose from many factors: growing ecological consciousness from the environmental movement of the late 1960s and 1970s, revolts by citizens against the negative consequences of urban freeways, energy crises, and general disillusionment with the dominant car culture and other problems in American cities. To those searching for an alternative to the automobile, transit seemed like a viable solution to various urban issues, from redevelopment to social equity. Federal subsidies also influenced transit's reversal of fortunes. By the 1970s, funding from Capitol Hill that began in the previous decade started to make its mark. Major rapid transit systems in San Francisco, Washington, and Atlanta opened for use.[71] In 1973, Congress listened to expressway protesters and authorized cities to use funds for transit projects that had been earmarked for the Interstate Highway System. These funds failed to go as far as expressway dollars. Whereas federal funds covered 90 percent of expressway projects, Washington provided only four dollars for every dollar spent by local authorities for transit.[72] Federal funds also began to provide operating subsidies for transit the following year, with passage of the National Mass Transportation Assistance Act.[73]

Since the 1980s, numerous cities have built light rail transit (LRT) systems. With LRT, vehicles operate on lines with dedicated rights-of-way but power is supplied by overhead wires instead of a third rail. LRT requires lower capital costs and ridership levels compared to heavy rail systems, and LRT projects have become more common than capital-intensive heavy rapid transit systems such as BART and the Washington Metro. Escalating construction costs and a more restrictive environment of federal funding for capital projects is one motivation for LRT's rise, which began in the early 1980s.[74] In a development that has proved fascinating to the historian, nostalgia and heritage have also contributed to the popularity of rail transit developments since the 1980s. Cities have kept or built "heritage" streetcar lines (or cable cars in San Francisco) along downtown streets with tourist dollars in mind. When the first LRT line in the United States opened in 1981, it was called the "San Diego Trolley," despite little similarity between the new line and the trolleys that served the city until the late 1940s. Most passengers today have no personal memory of riding streetcars, and so LRT and heritage lines are commonly associated with a vibrant urbanism of the early-20th-century American city rather than the more negative streetcar sentiments and experiences held by many people at the time.[75] The place of the past within current transit branding demonstrates just one example of why the history of mass transit matters today.

DISCUSSION OF THE LITERATURE

Urban mass transit has been a focus of academic historical research since the 1960s. Sam Bass Warner Jr. produced the first major academic work on the subject.[76] He examined the connections between changing forms of transit technology (namely horsecars and electric streetcars) and residential growth in the Boston suburbs of Roxbury, West Roxbury, and Dorchester. Relying on sources such as censuses, land deeds, government reports, and local histories, Warner focused on the impact street railways and other institutions—as well as the choices of individual builders and residents—had on the metropolitan landscape. He also paid attention to the relationship between commuting and the geography of class, as he noted the overwhelmingly middle-class nature of the new suburbs in contrast to the higher proportion of poorer residents concentrated in the inner city. Warner, writing during the era of suburban "white flight" and the transformation of the inner city through urban renewal, defined this process of suburban–inner city segregation by class as "the central event of the 1870s–1900 era."

Historical research on mass transit history continued during subsequent decades. Such interest developed as part of the growth of urban history during this time, as scholars sought to uncover the historical roots and wider contexts of housing issues, racial segregation, and economic inequality that came to the surface in American cities during the postwar "urban crisis." In the wake of rising concern over air pollution, energy use, and the impact of automobiles on the urban fabric, several works focused on the historical factors that had led to the rise and fall of mass transit (and related, the rise of urban automobile use). Increased attention to transit also followed federal funding starting in the 1960s.[77] Brian J. Cudahy has looked at the issue from a national perspective. Other authors have selected single cities—Scott Bottles on Los Angeles or Paul Barrett on Chicago, for example—as their case studies or took a comparative approach in order to emphasize how such processes unfolded in different locales. A common thread running through much of this work emphasized the technological choices behind various transit forms and the political relationships among private transit providers, local governments, and various interest groups.

A growing body of work by urban historians surveys the impact of suburbanization on American life since the 19th century.[78] The connections between suburbanization and mass transit, along with the growth in automobility and road building, serve as major aspects of the work. Clay McShane used an innovative approach to examine the impact of transportation patterns on urban life.[79] He argued that the rising popularity of the automobile in the early 20th century derived from changing social perceptions of the street as traffic corridors rather than public spaces, a trend that had begun with the railway and mass transit in the 19th century. Peter Norton built on this approach to uncover the highly contested nature of the street in American cities as different interest groups, including mass transit operators and users, fought for or against its transformation via the automobile.[80]

More recently, the influences of environmental history and cultural history have made their mark on the study of mass transit. Clay McShane and Joel Tarr have focused on an integral part of the horsecar that historians had previously ignored: the animal that powered the vehicle. They show the essential role that horses had on not only mass transit, but also the wider processes of change in the industrial American city. David Nye's work on electricity has emphasized the need to consider the creation of social meaning as key in understanding the influence of the electric streetcar and other transit technologies. To Nye, the electric streetcar emerged as part of a constellation of technologies at the turn of the 20th century that influenced the transition to the modern American city based on consumerism and spectacle. Recent scholarship has also focused less on the elite decisions made within corporate boardrooms and political offices and more on the daily experiences of transit passengers. Robin Kelley and others have conceptualized the transit vehicle as a contested public space in which the practices of racial and gender inequality in everyday life were reinforced and challenged. Others, influenced by a growing emphasis on the user within the history of technology and mobility studies, have examined how unfavorable experiences of transit may have influenced former passengers to purchase automobiles.

While the dynamics of mass transit during the 19th and early 20th centuries has received a fair amount of attention from scholars, the subject's more recent history has received far less attention. For instance, broad histories of mass transit in the United States rightly emphasize earlier eras when more Americans used transit per capita, while giving much shorter accounts of transit since the mid-20th century. To give one example, no extensive study examines San Francisco's BART—one of the largest megaprojects of the 1960s and 1970s—from a historical perspective. Fortunately, historians are beginning to focus more attention on mass transit during the eras after World War II. Leading this trend is Zachary Schrag's fine work on the Washington Metro, which has brought a postwar perspective to the literature on subways by Clifton Hood and other historians.[81] Public concern about environmental sustainability, alternative transportation forms and energy sources, and the consequences of an automobile-based lifestyle suggest that research on more recent transit history will continue to grow.

PRIMARY SOURCES

Historians of mass transit use a variety of primary sources to understand issues related to the topic. Such breadth reflects the fact that the study of mass transit requires knowledge of both technical matters and social dynamics, since both elements are interconnected. The voices of elites—politicians, company executives, and technical experts—are often found in reports, trade publications, government records, and other official documents. Uncovering the thoughts and behaviors of ordinary people (whether they be users, observers, or workers) is more challenging but can be gleaned from newspaper reports, literature, and photographs and other forms of visual art as well as the census and other quantitative sources. Scale is a further consideration in the study of mass transit, as transit may be approached from a national to a local perspective. Depending on the research question, scale influences the types of sources used by the historian.

Historical Tables presented in the American Public Transportation Association's (APTA) annual *Public Transportation Fact Book* is a good place to begin research on general statistical trends. Information dates to 1890 for some categories and draws from the census and APTA records. George Mason University is home to the American Public Transportation Association records. The collection, featuring materials related to APTA, its predecessor organizations, and the Institute for Rapid Transit, is arranged in seven thematic series from meetings and publications to local transit files. Industry trade publications are also excellent sources for understanding mass transit developments. These magazines are usually devoted to a specific transport mode or the industry more generally. A short list of publications includes: *Street Railway Journal* (published

1884–1908); *Electric Railway Journal* (published 1908–1931); *Bus Transportation; Bus World; Motor Coach Age/Motor Coach Today* (published 1950–2003); *Mass Transit; Passenger Transport; Metro; Headlights; National Railway Bulletin; Railway Age* (published 1856–present).

Several institutions contain historical information on mass transit at a national level. The National Transportation Library of the Department of Transportation features digitized sources with an emphasis on statistical, technical, or policy documents. The collection is more useful for the study of the recent past since a majority of its documents date from the late 20th century to the present. The Transportation Research Board operates TRID, a massive search database that covers more than one billion transportation documents, including conference proceedings, technical reports, books, and journal articles related to transit. More than thirty institutions across the United States form the University Transportation Centers program. These centers often feature strong transportation libraries, such as the Harmer E. Davis Transportation Library of Berkeley's Institute of Transportation Studies.

Local collections—archives, museums, libraries, and other repositories—are essential for historical research on mass transit in a specific city or region. These collections often feature reports, meeting minutes, and other documents related to local transit activities. For example, the New York Transit Museum houses an extensive collection of materials related to the transit history of the New York metropolitan area. The Dorothy Peyton Gray Transportation Library and Archive—operated by the Los Angeles Metro transit authority—caters to research devoted to Southern California's transportation history. Since transit held a prominent place in public debates and daily life during the 19th and 20th centuries, local newspapers are also excellent sources for research on significant developments as well as more quotidian matters related to local transit history.

FURTHER READING

Barrett, Paul. *The Automobile and Urban Transit: The Formation of Public Policy in Chicago, 1900–1930.* Philadelphia: Temple University Press, 1983.

Cudahy, Brian. *Cash, Tokens, and Transfers: A History of Urban Mass Transit in North America.* New York: Fordham University Press, 1990.

Hood, Clifton. *722 Miles: The Building of the Subways and How They Transformed New York.* Baltimore: Johns Hopkins University Press, 2004.

Jackson, Kenneth T. *Crabgrass Frontier: The Suburbanization of the United States.* New York: Oxford University Press, 1985.

McShane, Clay. *Down the Asphalt Path: The Automobile and the American City.* New York: Columbia University Press, 1994.

Norton, Peter. *Fighting Traffic: The Dawn of the Motor Age in the American City.* Cambridge, MA: MIT Press, 2008.

Nye, David E. *Electrifying America: Social Meanings of a New Technology, 1880–1940.* Cambridge, MA: MIT Press, 1992.

Post, Robert C. *Urban Mass Transit: The Life Story of a Technology.* Westport, CT: Greenwood, 2007.

Schrag, Zachary M. *The Great Society Subway: A History of the Washington Metro.* Baltimore: Johns Hopkins University Press, 2006.

Warner, Sam Bass. *Streetcar Suburbs: The Process of Growth in Boston, 1870–1900.* Cambridge, MA: Harvard University Press, 1962.

NOTES

1. Kenneth T. Jackson, *Crabgrass Frontier: The Suburbanization of the United States* (New York: Oxford University Press, 1985), 31, 28.
2. Brian Cudahy, *Cash, Tokens, and Transfers: A History of Urban Mass Transit in North America* (New York: Fordham University Press, 1990), 60–61.
3. Jackson, *Crabgrass Frontier*, 33.
4. Jackson, *Crabgrass Frontier*, 34.
5. Cudahy, *Cash, Tokens, and Transfers*, 8–10.
6. Glen E. Holt, "The Changing Perception of Urban Pathology: An Essay on the Development of Mass Transit in the United States," in *Cities in American History*, edited by Kenneth T. Jackson and Stanley K. Schultz (New York: Alfred A. Knopf, 1972), 325.

7. Robert C. Post, *Urban Mass Transit: The Life Story of a Technology* (Westport, CT: Greenwood, 2007), 14–15.

8. Jackson, *Crabgrass Frontier*, 35.

9. Joel A. Tarr and Clay McShane, *The Horse in the City: Living Machines in the Nineteenth Century* (Baltimore: Johns Hopkins University Press, 2007), 61–62.

10. Tarr and McShane, *Horse in the City*, 64–65.

11. Cudahy, *Cash, Tokens, and Transfers*, 13.

12. Post, *Urban Mass Transit*, 19, 14.

13. Tarr and McShane, *Horse in the City*, 63; Jackson, *Crabgrass Frontier*, 39.

14. Tarr and McShane, *Horse in the City*, 70–71; Clay McShane, *Down the Asphalt Path: The Automobile and the American City* (New York: Columbia University Press, 1994), 14.

15. Tarr and McShane, *Horse in the City*, 1, 14.

16. David E. Nye, *Electrifying America: Social Meanings of a New Technology, 1880–1940* (Cambridge, MA: MIT Press, 1992), 89.

17. Post, *Urban Mass Transit*, 22; Jackson, *Crabgrass Frontier*, 106.

18. Cudahy, *Cash, Tokens, and Transfers*, 14–15.

19. Jackson, *Crabgrass Frontier*, 92–94.

20. Tarr and McShane, *Horse in the City*, 5.

21. Cudahy, *Cash, Tokens, and Transfers*, 64–71.

22. Post, *Urban Mass Transit*, 24.

23. Cudahy, *Cash, Tokens, and Transfers*, 27–33.

24. Post, *Urban Mass Transit*, 27–31.

25. Jackson, *Crabgrass Frontier*, 103.

26. Nye, *Electrifying America*, 86.

27. Cudahy, *Cash, Tokens, and Transfers*, 41, 48.

28. Jackson, *Crabgrass Frontier*, 108.

29. Cudahy, *Cash, Tokens, and Transfers*, 48.

30. Nye, *Electrifying America*, 90–91.

31. Robert Fogelson, *Downtown: Its Rise and Fall, 1880–1950* (New Haven, CT: Yale University Press, 2001), 16; Cudahy, *Cash, Tokens, and Transfers*, 48.

32. Fogelson, *Downtown*, 55–60; Cudahy, *Cash, Tokens, and Transfers*, 84–87.

33. Clifton Hood, *722 Miles: The Building of the Subways and How They Transformed New York*. Centennial Edition (Baltimore: Johns Hopkins University Press, 2004).

34. Fogelson, *Downtown*, 20; Nye, *Electrifying America*, 112; Jackson, *Crabgrass Frontier*, 113.

35. Sam Bass Warner Jr., *Streetcar Suburbs: The Process of Growth in Boston, 1870–1900* (Cambridge, MA: Harvard University Press, 1962), 22.

36. Nye, *Electrifying America*, 96–97.

37. McShane, *Asphalt Path*, 23–25.

38. Warner, *Streetcar Suburbs*, 3.

39. Nye, *Electrifying America*, 132.

40. Clifton Hood, "Changing Perceptions of Public Space on the New York Rapid Transit System," *Journal of Urban History* 22, no. 3 (March 1996): 308.

41. Nye, *Electrifying America*, 137.

42. Robin D. G. Kelley, "'We Are Not What We Seem': Rethinking Black Working Class Opposition in the Jim Crow South," *Journal of American History* 80 (1993): 103.

43. Tarr and McShane, *Horse in the City*, 79.

44. Blair L. M. Kelley, *Right to Ride: Streetcar Boycotts and African American Citizenship in the Era of Plessy V. Ferguson* (Chapel Hill: University of North Carolina Press, 2010).

45. Hood, "Changing Perceptions," 319–321; Donald F. Davis, "North American Urban Transit, 1890–1950: What If We Thought about It as a Type of Technology?" *History and Technology* 12 (1995): 318–320.

46. Cudahy, *Cash, Tokens, and Transfers*, 152.

47. David W. Jones, *Mass Motorization + Mass Transit: An American History and Policy Analysis* (Bloomington: Indiana University Press, 2008), 33.

48. Post, *Urban Mass Transit*, 67.

49. Post, *Urban Mass Transit*, 66–67.

50. Paul Barrett, *The Automobile and Urban Transit: The Formation of Public Policy in Chicago, 1900–1930* (Philadelphia: Temple University Press, 1983), 96–105, 221.

51. Peter Norton, *Fighting Traffic: The Dawn of the Motor Age in the American City* (Cambridge, MA: MIT Press, 2008), 8–11.

52. Post, *Urban Mass Transit*, 69–70.

53. Cudahy, *Cash, Tokens, and Transfers*, 98; Post, *Urban Mass Transit*, 68, 83.

54. Post, *Urban Mass Transit*, 4.

55. Post, *Urban Mass Transit*, 151–153; Cudahy, *Cash, Tokens, and Transfers*, 188–190.

56. Zachary M. Schrag, "'The Bus Is Young and Honest': Transportation Politics, Technical Choice, and the Motorization of Manhattan Surface Transit, 1919–1936," *Technology and Culture* 41 (January 2000): 51–79.

57. Davis, "North American Urban Transit," 315.

58. Post, *Urban Mass Transit*, 119; Cudahy, *Cash, Tokens, and Transfers*, 163.

59. Sarah K. Frohardt-Lane, "Race, Public Transit, and Automobility in World War II Detroit," PhD diss., University of Illinois at Urbana-Champaign, 2011.

60. David W. Jones Jr., *Urban Transit Policy: An Economic and Political History* (Englewood Cliffs, NJ: Prentice Hall, 1985), 80.

61. Richard F. Weingroff, "Federal-Aid Highway Act of 1956: Creating the Interstate System," *Public Roads* 60.1 (Summer 1996), http://www.fhwa.dot.gov/publications/publicroads/96summer/p96su10.cfm.

62. Christopher Wells, *Car Country: An Environmental History* (Seattle: University of Washington Press, 2012).

63. Jones, *Urban Transit Policy*, 81, 116; Cuhady, *Cash, Tokens, and Transfers*, 221; Post, *Urban Mass Transit*, 135.

64. Edward Weiner, *Urban Transportation Planning in the United States: An Historical Overview*, rev. ed. (Westport, CT: Praeger, 1999), 42–43.

65. Jones, *Urban Transit Policy*, 83.

66. Peter Hall, *Great Planning Disasters* (Berkeley: University of California Press, 1982), 109–137.

67. Zachary M. Schrag, *The Great Society Subway: A History of the Washington Metro* (Baltimore: Johns Hopkins University Press, 2006).

68. J. R. Meyer, J. F. Kain, and M. Wohl, *The Urban Transportation Problem* (Cambridge, MA: Harvard University Press, 1965).

69. Schrag, *Great Society Subway*, 3.

70. Cudahy, *Cash, Tokens, and Transfers*, 196.

71. Cudahy, *Cash, Tokens, and Transfers*, 196–197; Post, *Urban Mass Transit*, 147.

72. Schrag, *Great Society Subway*, 180–181.

73. Weiner, *Urban Transportation*, 84.

74. Weiner, *Urban Transportation*, 99.

75. Post, *Urban Mass Transit*, 5–6.

76. Warner, *Streetcar Suburbs*.

77. Cudahy, *Cash, Tokens, and Transfers*.

78. Jackson, *Crabgrass Frontier*.

79. McShane, *Down the Asphalt Path*.

80. Norton, *Fighting Traffic*.

81. Schrag, *The Great Society Subway*.

Jay Young

STREETS, ROADS, AND HIGHWAYS IN THE UNITED STATES

The social processes of which history is made depend on roads, streets, and other infrastructure. They sustain trade and travel, and their development imperfectly reflects and shapes the growth of the society that builds them. Yet roads and streets also disrupt balances of power and favor some at the expense of others, and thereby divide as well as unite the societies they serve. In these respects, the study of roads and streets sheds light on social groups and forces too often overlooked in national-scale histories.

NATIVE, COLONIAL, AND EARLY US ROADS AND STREETS

Roads and trails predate the arrival of Europeans and Africans in North America. Systems of trails connected native traders; some of these routes, such as the famous Natchez Trace, were later adapted by the continent's newcomers as early roads. For long-distance travel, however, such roads were poor alternatives to coastal and river traffic, then the real sinews of commerce. But roads could reach where waterways could not, and postal and military needs justified roads that commerce could not. Some roads, such as the Natchez Trace, served traffic returning upriver. In Spanish California, El Camino Real evolved as a link between missions.

After the Revolutionary War, vast public lands north and west of the Ohio River gave the US government a revenue opportunity. Through the Land Ordinance of 1785 and the Northwest Ordinance of 1787, Congress applied a grid to the land (see Figure 1), so that it could then be parceled out and sold to speculators and settlers.[1] To make the Northwest more accessible, in 1805 Congress committed funds from western land sales for a road from Cumberland, Maryland, into Ohio. By the 1830s the National Road reached central Ohio. Most roads, however, remained local or state affairs; by 1840, even the so-called National Road was no longer federally funded.[2]

Yet local and state governments lacked the means to build sufficient roads, leaving an opportunity for entrepreneurs. Chartered turnpikes (toll roads) in Britain and toll bridges in America established the example for later

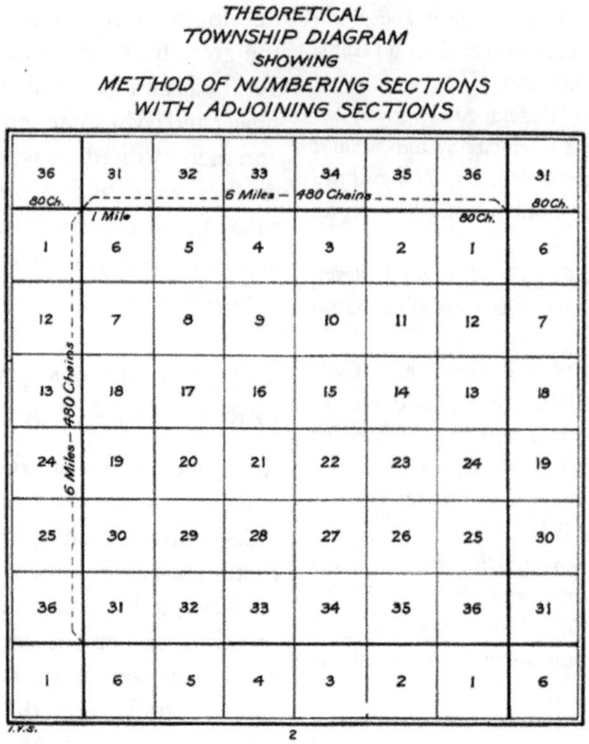

THEORETICAL
TOWNSHIP DIAGRAM
SHOWING
METHOD OF NUMBERING SECTIONS
WITH ADJOINING SECTIONS

36	31	32	33	34	35	36	31
80 Ch.			6 Miles – 480 Chains			80 Ch.	80 Ch.
1	6	5	4	3	2	1	6
12	7	8	9	10	11	12	7
13	18	17	16	15	14	13	18
24	19	20	21	22	23	24	19
25	30	29	28	27	26	25	30
36	31	32	33	34	35	36	31
1	6	5	4	3	2	1	6

Figure 1. The Land Ordinance of 1785 imposed a grid on the Old Northwest; it later extended into most of the West. The grid established parcel and township borders, and determined the locations of most roads. The diagram shows one township of 36 sections plus adjoining sections in neighboring townships. Courtesy of the US Interior Bureau of Land Management.

American toll roads. In 1794, the first American turnpike linked Lancaster, Pennsylvania, to Philadelphia, 62 miles away. Turnpike companies soon proliferated.[3]

Canals and, after 1840, railroads did not so much deter road building as reorient it. Where canals and railways did not reach, roads were needed. In lumber-producing states, especially New York, Pennsylvania, Ohio, Michigan, and Wisconsin, entrepreneurs laid private plank roads to feed toll-paying traffic to canals and railroads. In just seven years, 3,500 miles of plank roads were laid in New York, until the boom ended in 1853. Such roads were expensive and degraded quickly, but they could manage heavy freight (such as milk).[4]

NINETEENTH-CENTURY STREETS

The distinction between roads and streets has come to seem minor; streets might even now be defined, almost correctly, as urban roads. Yet the words are distinct because they once defined quite distinct things. Like roads, 19th-century streets were transportation conduits, but they were much more besides. Streets were public spaces, markets, promenades, playgrounds, and parade grounds. They were at least as much like city parks as they were like rural roads. Their users were regulated far more by social norms than by formal rules.[5]

Most American towns, particularly in the Midwest, are laid out at least partly on a gridiron street plan. Such grids reversed the typical European plan in which construction shapes the streets; on American grids, the streets usually came first. Indeed, streets were often planned and named long before anything resembling an actual street existed. Philadelphia's 1682 street plan (see Figure 2) was a pioneer in this respect. In 1811 such planning reached its most ambitious form in the Commissioners'

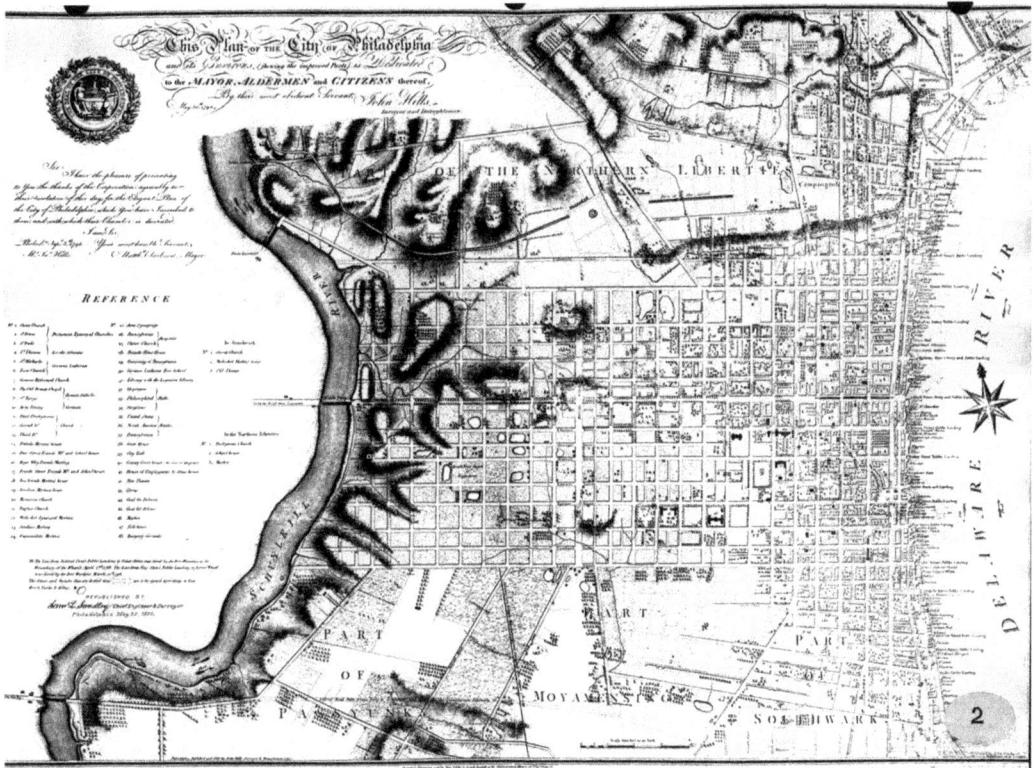

Figure 2. Philadelphia's plan of 1682 was an early model for the typical American urban street grid. This map by John Hills shows Philadelphia in 1796.
Courtesy of Library of Congress, Geography and Map Division, 2007625050.

Plan of New York, which laid out 2,000 city blocks of what was then still rural land.[6]

Streets' transportation functions grew more important as they linked the steam railway depots to their greater regions.[7] Especially before the 1880s and in the largest cities, wherever nearby property owners could not support high assessments, streets could be squalid.[8] In the second half of the 19th century, however, a sanitation movement improved some conditions, and streets accommodated a lengthening list of city services: storm water and sewer drainage, fresh water supply, telegraph and telephone service, street railways, and finally "light" (electric power).[9]

TRANSFORMATION: 1890–1910

Beginning about 1890, several related trends accelerated the transformation of American roads and streets, even before automobiles appeared

in numbers. These included rural free delivery, mass bicycling, the "good roads" movement, the proliferation of electric railways, and the City Beautiful movement.

Horse-drawn streetcars were common in the densest cities by the mid-19th century.[10] While New York was the leader in urban rail transportation, introducing elevated steam railroads (1868) and subways (1904), practical electric street railways were introduced first in Richmond, Virginia, in 1888. In the 1890s such railways proliferated, promoting radial urbanization even in small cities. Line extensions, fueled by land speculation, often preceded and stimulated real estate development, leaving a lasting legacy in the form of "streetcar suburbs."[11]

Unusual in 1890, bicycling was ubiquitous by the middle of the decade. Bicyclists, many of them well-to-do, promoted paved streets and rural "good roads." They even achieved some

Figure 3. A typical main thoroughfare of the mid-19th century, in this case Louisville's Main Street in 1846. Courtesy of the National Archives Catalog, ID 513346.

dedicated, high-grade bicycle paths. Organized as the League of American Wheelmen, bicyclists were influential. In rural areas, the good roads movement was also promoted by postal service demands, and particularly by rural free delivery. By 1900, however, bicycling was already in sharp decline. The reasons for the retreat are contested. Automobiles apparently did not displace bicycles; they were still very scarce when the cycling boom was in decline. Electric streetcars surely account for some of the decline.[12]

Taking their inspiration from European examples, and especially from Baron Haussmann's Parisian boulevards, elites in American cities rebuilt segments of them in grand fashion. The first great American example was Chicago's temporary "White City," built for the World's Columbian Exposition of 1893. Its revivalist architectural styles, straight vistas, and broad avenues found imitators in American cities large and small. Washington, DC's McMillan Plan (1901) was also an influential early example. Broad streets, already common in most American cities, were modified. New boulevards were cut or planned.[13] Such streets, generally commodious and well paved, were relatively welcoming to automobiles as they appeared in city streets in 1900. Nevertheless, with their frequent intersections and streetcar tracks, they were not designed as motor thoroughfares, and were creatures more of the 19th century than of the 20th.

The 1890s were thus years of rapid change. Rural roads were extended and improved, typically with macadam pavements. Urban streets were better paved as well, often widened, with provision for diverse new city services and sanitation. Nevertheless, by 1900 neither urban streets nor rural roads were well suited to the automobile traffic that would soon arrive. In the next decade, in the era of expensive "pleasure cars," automobiles were scarce. The problem of adjustment to the new vehicles was generally understood not as a matter of adapting streets to new motor cars, but of making the new vehicles conform to streets as they were. Though a few automobile "scorchers" and "joy drivers" menaced the streets, most well-to-do motorists conformed to prevailing speeds. In some large cities, especially New York, fleets of slow electric motor cars served as taxis and delivery vehicles.[14]

On rural roads as in cities, cars had to accommodate conditions as they were. Nearly every motorist carried one or more spare tires. Utilitarian driving was mostly a rural affair. The Ford Model T succeeded not only for its economy, but also because it was designed for poor rural roads. Its large wheel diameter, high clearance, and high torque suited it not for speed but for ruts.[15]

Though in 1910 motor cars were no longer rare, roads and streets were still pre-automotive routes. Motorists and their vehicles had to adapt to them. Rural motorists who refused to adapt found themselves stranded, looking for a farmer willing to hitch a team to the motor car. City motorists who refused to drive slowly menaced less themselves or each other than the non-motoring majority in the streets, earning them widespread hostility.[16]

The financing of roads and streets constrained what they could be. As private toll roads declined, rural roads were paid for primarily through state and local bond issues, which yielded variable and often limited funds. In cities, most funds for streets came from property assessments, which could be ample only in the "best" neighborhoods.

CITY STREETS AND THE AUTOMOBILE

In cities, however, financing was by no means the major constraint on automobiles. By the prevailing norms of street use, autos were ill suited to streets. Neither by law nor by custom were streets primarily for cars. To the contrary, as the newcomers, motorists' claim to street space was tenuous and vulnerable. Streets were public, shared spaces. Though pedestrians preferred the cleaner sidewalks, they roamed streets at will, and in so doing they had the law on their side. Local and state statutes, common law traditions, and customs favored no class of user over another. In general, users kept to the right and were expected to avoid obstructing or endangering others. The location of streetcar tracks both promoted and legitimized pedestrians' use of the full width and length of streets. Because tracks followed the centerlines of streets, streetcar riders crossed streets wherever they could. While judges and other authorities typically favored movement over stasis in streets, they did not value speed. Motorists driving much faster than other vehicles were not only violating the very low speed limits of the era, they were also the objects of general disapproval. In the conventional wisdom of the era, because motorists were operators of inherently dangerous and space-hungry machines, they bore a responsibility to drive them prudently. When motorists failed these responsibilities—in official courts or in those of public opinion—they were judged harshly. While motorists met some hostility in rural areas as well, typically they were more immediately accepted there.[17]

American police departments responded to proliferation of motor cars by trying to make them conform to the status quo. States imposed low speed limits in city streets, and often permitted local authorities to set them still lower, especially at intersections. A limit of ten miles per hour was typical. Though enforcement of such limits was impractical, police had other ways to slow cars down. A favorite practice was to require left-turning vehicles to pass a "silent policeman" (a post or column) or other object at the center point of an intersection before turning. Hence left turners, compelled to make a very sharp turn, almost had to come to a stop. The consequent slowing of traffic was, to police, a plus.[18]

Nothing earned cars enmity in cities as much as the injuries and deaths attributed to them. Especially in the early years, automobiles were dangerous. By 1923, annual fatalities attributable to motor vehicles were at about 15,000, even though most American families still owned no car. In cities, most of the fatalities were not drivers or their passengers, but pedestrians; in the larger cities, about three-fourths of the people cars killed were on foot. Among pedestrians killed, about half were eighteen or younger. While later generations, raised to regard streets as places primarily for cars, would have assigned parents and pedestrians much of the blame, in the early 1920s blame was overwhelmingly directed at cars and their drivers. The conventional wisdom of 1920, reflected in newspapers and in popular fiction, treated speed as inherently dangerous; automobiles, as fast vehicles, were menaces to safety. Safety publicity, newspaper columns and cartoons, letters to editors, and judges' lectures from the bench tended to agree in this condemnation. Instead of objecting, automobile clubs, the voice of their motorist members, tended to urge cautious driving so as to limit the damage. Such perceptions were barriers to the urban future of the automobile and to the automotive street.[19]

By the norms of the 1920s, cars were also prodigal hoarders of scarce street space. Moving and parked cars congested streets. Many among the first generation of traffic engineers, whose diverse backgrounds included municipal engineering and electric railways, regarded cars as poorly suited to dense cities, preferring to discourage driving in cities—for example, through curb parking bans—than to accommodate cities to cars. Pedestrians and streetcar riders complained that automobiles were depriving them of their rights to the street.[20]

THE STRUGGLE FOR THE CAR'S FUTURE, 1920–1940

Hence, in the conventional wisdom of the teens and early 1920s, automobiles took the brunt of the blame for both traffic casualties and traffic congestion. To clear their own names, automotive interest groups joined in efforts to prevent accidents and relieve congestion. Local auto clubs, dealers, taxicab companies, and other motor fleet operators supported and joined in public safety campaigns, and participated in coalitions of local interest groups seeking ways to promote efficient traffic flow. For example, local automotive interest groups urged motorists to drive with caution, and they might back curb parking bans if these promised to improve traffic capacity. In both efforts, however, automotive interest groups risked lending their support to those who blamed cars and who wanted to restrict them. By the early 1920s, many in businesses related to the auto industry perceived a threat in these efforts.[21]

In 1923 and 1924, fearing for the future of their business in cities, automotive interest groups withdrew their support from mainstream efforts to prevent accidents and relieve congestion, seeking instead to redefine both problems in ways that were more consistent with a bright future for cars in cities. The change in course arose from several causes, but from two in particular. First, disappointing sales in cities in 1923 and 1924, despite a strong economy, convinced manufacturers and dealers that traffic jams were making cars unattractive in cities, and that the popular version of the safety problem was giving cars a bad image. More specifically, many cities threatened drastic restriction of cars to protect pedestrians (especially children). In many cities there were calls to equip automobiles with speed governors that would limit them to 20 or 25 miles per hour (mph). In Cincinnati this threat took the form of a petition drive in favor of a speed governor ordinance on the ballot; 42,000 Cincinnatians joined in the demand. If approved by voters, the initiative would limit cars by law to 25 mph; enforcement would be automatic because the cars would have to be equipped with a mechanical speed governor. Local automotive interest groups and their allies quickly organized a massive "Vote No" effort, securing backing from the National Automobile Chamber of Commerce (NACC), the trade association representing major manufacturers except for Ford. The ordinance was crushed at the polls.[22]

Facing common threats, automotive interest groups thereafter remained more united, better organized, and better led. They more often used an old term in the industry as a name for their united effort. At the American Automobile Association (AAA), president Thomas P. Henry spoke of "organized motordom"; to others in the coalition, "motordom" was sufficient. Motordom's leaders were AAA and NACC, but they worked closely with many other organizations. Their common cause was to redefine the problems of safety and congestion. By the conventional wisdom, speed and therefore automobiles were inherently dangerous; pedestrians were victims, and therefore not guilty. In 1923 and 1924, NACC developed a plan to shift blame for traffic casualties from speed to recklessness. By redirecting blame at a minority of reckless drivers, they hoped to exonerate the prudent majority and to reconcile safety with speed. Unlike speed, recklessness was a fault of which even pedestrians could be guilty, and NACC, through a new traffic safety department, developed a national campaign to shift blame to jaywalking pedestrians. By redefining congestion as insufficient road capacity, they hoped to shift blame from excessive cars to insufficient roads. The AAA and its member clubs made themselves leaders in school safety education, teaching a generation of children that "streets are for autos."[23]

Thus motordom's strategy was to seek to redirect blame for accidents from speed to recklessness (among both motorists and pedestrians), and congestion as insufficient road capacity. Given the strength of the status quo, however, both components of the strategy were long shots. But in the 1920s, motordom struck a rich reserve of funds that strengthened its cause. Proposed in the teens and first implemented in Oregon in 1919, gasoline taxes could yield prodigious revenues. For a few years, most automotive interest groups resisted gas tax proposals as a grab for the motorist's wallet. but as motordom united in common cause, it saw advantages in gas taxes. In state after state, motordom agreed to gas taxes in return for guarantees that the revenues would be committed to road construction and maintenance. With motordom's backing, by 1924 most states had a gas tax; by the end of 1929, all 48 states, plus the District of Columbia, had one. Despite widespread "diversion" (expenditure of gas tax revenues on anything except roads), gas taxes yielded a flood of state road funds. As roads were ostensibly bought and paid for by motorists, they could be designed primarily with motorists in mind. While local streets remained local problems, state highways funded by gas taxes were entering America cities by the late 1920s. Symbolic of the new motor age, New Jersey opened the "Clover Leaf," the first completely grade-separated interchange for motor traffic, at Woodbridge, just outside Staten Island, in 1929. It represented a triumph of motordom's precepts that speed can be safe and that high-capacity road design can relieve congestion.[24]

In the 1930s, motordom formed networks of alliances with contractors, shippers, and state and federal agencies to secure its versions of traffic flow and traffic safety. While particular congestion problems might be relieved in many ways, the prevailing assumption was that congestion meant insufficient road capacity warranting new construction; accidents demanded new capacity designed to prevent accidents through grade separations, median strips, shoulders, and wider curves. In the federal Bureau of Public Roads, engineers developed the standards of the motor age. Through the American Association of State Highway Officials, state highway departments worked closely with motordom to formalize such standards.[25]

As for safety, with help from motordom an entirely new way to prevent traffic casualties took hold. Into the 1920s, speed on roads was typically regarded as inherently dangerous; efforts to prevent crashes were almost one and the same with efforts to curtail speed. In the mid-1920s, motordom took this version of traffic safety head on, proposing instead that recklessness, not speed, was the real culprit, and that modern road design could make speed safe. In the 1930s, engineers, often working on projects funded by gasoline taxes intended to serve motorists, promised "highway safety": accident prevention through the design of motor roads. Forgiving curves, grade separations, shoulders, and median strips would prevent collisions and make speed safe. Meanwhile, the automobile industry took the lead in highway safety; in 1937 it combined smaller efforts in the Automotive Safety Foundation. The ASF was the leading authority on highway safety into the 1960s and helped to define an approach to safety that prevented accidents by targeting reckless drivers and by designing roads for safe driving at speed.[26]

In the 1930s, gas taxes, fees, and federal and state relief funds supported more construction of motor highways than ever before, particularly near the major cities of the Northeast, the upper Midwest, and southern California.[27] Nevertheless, the projects were very modest by the standards of later generations. The Great Depression suppressed driving, gas tax revenues, and the market for automobiles. Some

Figure 4. Before the Interstate Highway Act of 1956, some toll roads served long-distance motor traffic. This is the Pennsylvania Turnpike in 1942, two years after it opened. Courtesy of Library of Congress, LC-DIG-fsa-8d06851.

new toll roads—in particular the Pennsylvania Turnpike (Figure 4), which opened in 1940—suggested what was possible where traffic would pay.[28] Especially in the late 1930s, however, automotive interest groups were planning for a much more ambitious future. Shell Oil commissioned the theater designer Norman Bel Geddes to design a model of the "city to tomorrow"—a motor age city that drivers could cross at speed without ever encountering a red light. General Motors saw an opportunity for something much greater and put Bel Geddes to work on a gargantuan model of the "World of Tomorrow", beginning with what he had made for Shell. This became the most popular exhibit at the New York World's Fair of 1939–1940.[29]

Motordom's influence was also felt in more official channels. The National Highway Users Conference, a coalition of pro-highway interest groups led by General Motors and the American Automobile Association, was organized in 1932 to promote ample, toll-free, long-range motor highways. NHUC championed toll-free roads funded by tax dollars, and found a willing partner in this endeavor in the Bureau of Public Roads (BPR). The success of NHUC and other highway promoters in casting taxpayer-funded motor highways as "free roads" was attested by a major report BPR submitted to Congress in 1939. *Toll Roads and Free Roads* recommended a system of toll-free, federally supported "free roads," to be preferred over toll roads, to cross the length and breadth of the 48 states.[30]

TOWARD THE INTERSTATE HIGHWAYS

For a decade following World War II, federal expenditures on roads were modest; roads remained overwhelmingly a state and local responsibility. Among the most commodious highways, many were toll roads. The National Highway Users Conference worked with interest groups in the construction industry to depict toll roads as a threat to "free roads." Meanwhile, General Motors, Ford, and others with a stake in toll-free roads produced films, booklets, and other publicity to sell a major national highway program to the general public, mainly on grounds of congestion relief.[31]

The Eisenhower administration worked with interest groups to propose a program they would support. President Eisenhower personally promoted the program both as a means to relieve congestion and as a way to save lives through safe road design. In 1954 he said that "metropolitan area congestion" could be "solved" by "a grand plan for a properly articulated highway system."[32] Later, using an Automotive Safety Foundation claim, he announced that interstate highways would "save four thousand American lives a year."[33] In this effort, Eisenhower followed the advice of economist Noobar Danielian, who told the president that the program must be designed so as "to hold together the natural friends of an expanded federal highway program." With "concessions to proponents of highways," the "strength of pro-highway forces" would negate the "opposition of the railroads."[34] Eisenhower put a personal friend, general Lucius Clay, at the head of a committee of businessmen and charged them with proposing a federal highway program. Over the following year the committee built a foundation of support among industries "interested in highway development."[35] Getting their support entailed forgoing toll roads in favor of a mostly toll-free interstate highway system, except that those segments of the system that already charged tolls would be permitted to retain them. Most of the system, however, would be funded by a new federal Highway Trust Fund, sustained by gasoline and other motor excises and committed to right-of-way acquisition and road construction. With this fund the federal government would bear 90 percent of the construction costs of the new interstate highway system. The consequent Federal-Aid Highway Act of 1956, allocating $25 billion over ten years for a 41,000-mile interstate highway system, passed with bipartisan support.[36]

The Highway Act of 1956, in combination with state highway projects, transformed American social geography.[37] Low gasoline prices, massive highway projects, and suburbanization helped make driving most Americans' primary mode of transportation. They supported social trends such as shopping malls, school district consolidation, and "white flight" from cities. Unlike other highway programs in other countries, where the major through roads tended to skirt the fringes of cities, the interstate highways entered American cities, often going right through them. Ample roads poured cars into cities, where parking was scarce. Taking advantage of the opportunity, property owners quickly demolished buildings to replace them with surface parking lots. Aerial photography captures a proliferation of surface lots in the 1950s and 1960s. The scale of destruction drew harsh criticism almost immediately. Citizens' groups fought some projects. Critics such as William H. Whyte, Jane Jacobs, and Lewis Mumford decried the destruction.[38] In response, pro-highway groups characterized the demand for roads as the free choice of a free people, and the critics as distrustful of democracy. To them, "Americans' love affair with the automobile" justified the projects; elitist critics would have to get used to it.[39]

In the 1960s, however, resistance to urban segments of the interstate highways grew into a "freeway revolt." Highways were typically routed through poorer and blacker districts. Many neighborhoods, such as Overtown (Miami), Paradise Valley (Detroit), and the Inner Core (Milwaukee), were virtually destroyed. Segments of urban interstates were also planned through more affluent neighborhoods, but there, local opposition more often stopped them.[40]

Less spectacular, but at least as important, local roads and streets changed as well. Beginning in the 1930s, but especially after World War II, engineering standards adapted roads and streets to the governing assumption that moving motor vehicles was their primary purpose, that speed was desirable, and that roads could be designed to make speed safe for the occupants of vehicles. On postwar roads and streets, the consequence was less frequent intersections, lanes of ample width, and multiple lanes even for local roads. Local zoning ordinances typically contributed to the trend by making off-street parking provision a responsibility of retailers and employers. The consequent "free" parking incentivized driving.[41] Meanwhile, other means of mobility generally grew more difficult. Busy streets with faster vehicles, infrequent intersections, and the greater distances between stores separated by large parking lots made walking and bicycling less convenient and sometimes hazardous. For some, such as children and the frail, walking as a means of getting around became a practical impossibility. Low-density development also made bus service less cost-effective.[42]

Both safety and congestion relief were elusive targets. For decades, the Automotive Safety Foundation took the position that safe road design and the exclusion of reckless drivers would make roads safe. The vehicles themselves, ASF experts held, were already safe. But as driving—and driving more—became the norm, casualties rose. Annual fatalities passed 40,000 in 1963, then exceeded 50,000 in 1966. Consequent pressures compelled change. If collisions could not be prevented, "crashworthy" cars would have to be designed. In such vehicles, passengers wearing seat belts could hope to survive crashes that would otherwise have been fatal. Since then, while total annual casualties (about 33,000 in 2014) remained disturbingly high, the risk per vehicle mile has fallen sharply.[43]

In the 1950s, highway projects were often sold as ways to "solve" congestion. Except on the few toll roads, however, drivers paid no direct charge to use a road, and thus any additional capacity invited additional demand. And as public policy neglected alternatives to driving, for many the choice to use the additional capacity became more a compulsion. Capacity expansions stimulated more driving and diverted more travelers from alternatives. In short, the more public policy attempted to relieve congestion, the more it stimulated driving.[44]

Capacity expansion through construction has remained the predominant response to congestion. Since the 1970s, however, US transportation policy has experimented, but with limited success. High-occupancy vehicle lanes and carpooling programs were generally disappointing. Digital electronics have simplified tolling and enabled innovations such as "high-occupancy toll" (HOT). Using mobile phones, commuters in suburban Washington, DC, devised their own ride-sharing system called "slugging." Self-driving and shared vehicles may yield greater spatial efficiencies. Nevertheless, toll-free access to taxpayer-funded roads remains by far the predominant model.

Since 2000, transportation officials' hold on transportation planning has been steadily challenged from within and without. The World Wide Web has empowered advocates of alternative transportation, and transportation officials have begun, in modest and piecemeal ways, to adapt. New York City set an example. Under Mayor Michael Bloomberg, Janette Sadik-Khan led the New York City Department of Transportation onto an independent path that welcomed pedestrian districts and protected bicycle lanes, and that introduced bus rapid transit. Under Mayor Bill de Blasio the trend continued; in 2014 the city introduced a citywide 25 mph default speed limit to make the streets safer for pedestrians and bicyclists. In these respects New York was breaking from decades of design that favored drivers and that sought to make speed safe. Other US cities have been watching and learning.

Elsewhere, street railways, with the assistance of public subsidies, have staged a remarkable comeback since the late 1980s; by 2010 about thirty-five US cities had light rail systems, and more have been implemented since. Their cost efficacy is a matter of controversy. Critics charge that they do not pay their own way; defenders reply that they cannot because they compete against drivers who do not pay their own way either.

Perhaps the most fitting symbol of the changing direction of road infrastructure is a new bridge in Portland, Oregon. Tilikum Crossing, opened in 2015, carries pedestrians, bicyclists, buses, and light rail—but not motorists. A decade or more ago, a $135-million bridge that would serve the traveling public but carry no cars was scarcely conceivable. Tilikum Crossing may someday be recognized as a turning point in the history of road infrastructure in the United States.

DISCUSSION OF THE LITERATURE

Scholars of American history have taken much more interest in 20th-century roads and streets than in their colonial and 19th-century predecessors. A useful overview of the social-geographical expansion of European colonial powers and of the early United States into North America, which depended in part upon roads, is found in the first two volumes of D. W. Meinig's *The Shaping of America*.[45] Apart from specialized studies,[46] much of the scholarship is embedded in larger works on government and commerce, such as in books by Peter Onuf on the Northwest Ordinance and by Brian Balogh on government support for roads and other internal improvements.[47] For work on the National Road and on turnpikes, readers should consult the anthology edited by Karl Raitz,[48] and an article by Daniel Klein and John Majewski.[49] Together with Christopher Baer, Klein and Majewski have also examined plank roads.[50] William Cronon's pathbreaking environmental history of Chicago and its vast hinterland, *Nature's Metropolis,* documents the transformative power of waterways, roads, and railroads in the Midwest.[51]

For 19th-century streets, *The Horse in the City* by Clay McShane and Joel Tarr is an indispensable book.[52] A collection edited by Hilary Ballon offers diverse work on New York's influential grid plan.[53] Suburbanization, in the 19th century and later, is thoroughly examined in Kenneth Jackson's classic *Crabgrass Frontier*.[54] Peter Baldwin captures the social and cultural life of streets in a study of Hartford.[55] The transformation of city streets in the late 19th century is evident in books by John Duffy on the history of public health, and by Thomas P. Hughes and Mark Rose on electric power.[56]

For the transformational decades of the late 19th and early 20th centuries, work on roads and streets proliferates. James Flink's 1970 book *America Adopts the Automobile* was long a standard work.[57] By the time Flink followed it up with *The Automobile Age* (1988), his generally straightforward account of a gradual welcoming of the car was contested.[58] Some, such as Scott Bottles, continued to emphasize the automobile's attractions, attributing its proliferation to consumer demand among a population chafing under the limitations of the alternatives.[59] Others, such as Clay McShane, presented a messier account, in which some welcomed the automobile while many others resented and resisted it as an intruder.

Particularly divisive was the question of streetcars' demise. To Bottles and others, their decline was clearly the product of mass preference for the automobile. Other historians, such as Mark Foster, Paul Barrett, and John Fairfield, attributed streetcars' decline to other factors, such as trends in city planning, city politics, and strategizing among automotive interest groups.[60] Some have seen streetcars as casualties in a larger, implacable competition between rail and road.[61] Other works trace the rise of the motor age city in America to a competition over the legitimate uses of streets. By the norms prevailing in 1910, pedestrians belonged in streets and automobiles were tolerated intruders. Following a contentious struggle among social groups, by 1930 streets were motor thoroughfares where cars unquestionably belonged. Thereafter, streets and urban roads would welcome cars and the American cities would ultimately be reconstructed to make room for them.[62]

For the development of the motor highway in America, Christopher Wells offers a broad, synthetic environmental history in *Car Country*.[63] Related but more particular perspectives are available from Warren Belasco, who connects early motor roads to new kinds of recreation, and from Paul Sutter, who links roads to the popularization of notions of wilderness.[64] In *Republic of Driving*, Cotten Seiler examines the incorporation of automobility into American notions of citizenship and freedom.[65] For an in-depth study of the pioneering Lincoln Highway, readers should see Drake Hokanson's book.[66] Early motor toll roads get close study in Dan Cupper's book on the Pennsylvania

Turnpike and Bruce Radde's on the Merritt Parkway.[67]

As the greatest public works project in American history, the interstate highway system has attracted extensive attention among historians. In *Building the American Highway System*, Bruce Seely offers the essential background on Thomas MacDonald's Bureau of Public Roads.[68] The indispensable work on the political origins and development of the interstates is Mark Rose's *Interstate*.[69] Other historians, indebted to Seely and Rose, have brought the politics and engineering of the interstates to more popular audiences.[70] By examining three cases in depth (Syracuse, Los Angeles, and Memphis), Joseph DiMento and Cliff Ellis have recently offered an in-depth, long-range study in *Changing Lanes*.[71] Interstates' devastation of cities still has received less attention than the subject's importance deserves. Readers should in particular see the work of Raymond Mohl, Zachary Schrag, and Eric Avila.[72]

FURTHER READING

19TH-CENTURY ROADS

Cronon, William. *Nature's Metropolis: Chicago and the Great West*. New York: W. W. Norton, 1991.

Klein, Daniel, and John Majewski. "Turnpikes and Toll Roads in Nineteenth-Century America." In *Encyclopedia of Economic and Business History*. Edited by Robert Whaples. EH.Net, 2008. https://eh.net/encyclopedia-2/.

Majewski, John, Christopher Baer, and Daniel B. Klein. "Responding to Relative Decline: The Plank Road Boom of Antebellum New York." *Journal of Economic History* 53.1 (1993): 106–122.

Raitz, Karl, ed. *The National Road*. Baltimore: Johns Hopkins University Press, 1996.

19TH-CENTURY STREETS

Baldwin, Peter C. *Domesticating the Street: The Reform of Public Space in Hartford, 1850–1930*. Columbus: Ohio State University Press, 1999.

Ballon, Hilary, ed. *The Greatest Grid: The Master Plan of Manhattan, 1811–2011*. New York: Columbia University Press, 2012.

Duffy, John. *The Sanitarians: A History of American Public Health*. Urbana-Champaign: University of Illinois Press, 1992.

McShane, Clay, and Joel Tarr. *The Horse in the City: Living Machines in the Nineteenth Century*. Baltimore: Johns Hopkins University Press, 2007.

Warner, Sam Bass. *Streetcar Suburbs: The Process of Growth in Boston, 1870–1900*. Cambridge, MA: Harvard University Press, 1962.

THE 20TH CENTURY

Norton, Peter. "Four Paradigms: Traffic Safety in the Twentieth-Century United States." *Technology and Culture* 56.2 (2015): 319–334.

Wells, Christopher. *Car Country: An Environmental History*. Seattle: University of Washington Press, 2013.

STREETS, 1900–1945

Barrett, Paul. *The Automobile and Urban Transit: The Formation of Public Policy in Chicago, 1900–1930*. Philadelphia: Temple University Press, 1983.

Bottles, Scott L. *Los Angeles and the Automobile: The Making of the Modern City*. Berkeley: University of California Press, 1987.

Foster, Mark. *From Streetcar to Superhighway: American City Planners and Urban Transportation, 1900–1940*. Philadelphia: Temple University Press, 1981.

McShane, Clay. *Down the Asphalt Path: American Cities and the Coming of the Automobile*. New York: Columbia University Press, 1994.

Norton, Peter. *Fighting Traffic: The Dawn of the Motor Age in the American City*. Cambridge, MA: MIT Press, 2008.

ROADS, 1900–1945

Belasco, Warren J. *Americans on the Road: From Autocamp to Motel, 1910–1945*. Cambridge, MA: MIT Press, 1979.

Berger, Michael L. *The Devil Wagon in God's Country: The Automobile and Social Change in Rural America, 1893–1929*. Hamden, CT: Archon, 1980.

Hokanson, Drake. *The Lincoln Highway: Main Street across America*. Iowa City: University of Iowa Press, 1988.

Seely, Bruce E. *Building the American Highway System: Engineers as Policy Makers*. Philadelphia: Temple University Press, 1987.

Sutter, Paul. *Driven Wild: How the Fight Against Automobiles Launched the Modern Wilderness Movement.* Seattle: University of Washington Press, 2005.

ROADS AND STREETS SINCE 1945

Avila, Eric. *The Folklore of the Freeway: Race and Revolt in the Modernist City.* Minneapolis: University of Minnesota Press, 2014.

DiMento, Joseph F. C., and Cliff Ellis. *Changing Lanes: Visions and Histories of Urban Freeways.* Cambridge, MA: MIT Press, 2013.

Mohl, Raymond A. "The Interstates and the Cities: The U.S. Department of Transportation and the Freeway Revolt, 1966–1973." *Journal of Policy History* 20.2 (2008): 193–226.

Rose, Mark. *Interstate: Express Highway Politics 1941–1989.* Rev. ed. Knoxville: University of Tennessee Press, 1990.

NOTES

1. Peter S. Onuf, *Statehood and Union: A History of the Northwest Ordinance* (Bloomington: Indiana University Press, 1987); and Frederick D. Williams, ed., *The Northwest Ordinance: Essays on Its Formulation, Provisions, and Legacy,* (East Lansing: Michigan State University Press, 1989).

2. Merritt Ierly, *Traveling the National Road: Across the Centuries on America's First Highway* (Woodstock, NY: Overlook, 1990); and Karl Raitz, ed., *The National Road* (Baltimore: Johns Hopkins University Press, 1996).

3. Daniel Klein and John Majewski, "Turnpikes and Toll Roads in Nineteenth-Century America," in *Encyclopedia of Economic and Business History,* 2008, https://eh.net/encyclopedia-2/.

4. John Majewski, Christopher Baer, and Daniel B. Klein, "Responding to Relative Decline: The Plank Road Boom of Antebellum New York," *Journal of Economic History* 53.1 (1993): 106.

5. Mona Domosh, "Those 'Gorgeous Incongruities': Polite Politics and Public Space on the Streets of Nineteenth-Century New York City," *Annals of the Association of American Geographers* 88.2 (1998): 209–226; and Peter Baldwin, *Domesticating the Street: The Reform of Public Space in Hartford, 1850–1930* (Columbus: Ohio State University Press, 1999).

6. Hilary Ballon, ed., *The Greatest Grid: The Master Plan of Manhattan, 1811–2011* (New York: Columbia University Press, 2012).

7. William Cronon, *Nature's Metropolis: Chicago and the Great West* (New York: W. W. Norton, 1991).

8. Lawrence H. Larsen, "Nineteenth-Century Street Sanitation: A Study in Filth and Frustration," *Wisconsin Magazine of History* 52.3 (1969): 239–247.

9. John Duffy, *The Sanitarians: A History of American Public Health* (Urbana-Champaign: University of Illinois Press, 1992); Thomas P. Hughes, *Networks of Power: Electrification in Western Society, 1880–1930* (Baltimore: Johns Hopkins University Press, 1983); and Mark H. Rose, *Cities of Light and Heat: Domesticating Gas and Electricity in Urban America* (University Park: Pennsylvania State University Press, 1995).

10. Clay McShane and Joel Tarr, *The Horse in the City: Living Machines in the Nineteenth Century* (Baltimore: Johns Hopkins University Press, 2007).

11. Charles W. Cheape, *Moving the Masses: Urban Public Transit in New York, Boston, and Philadelphia, 1880–1912* (Cambridge, MA: Harvard University Press, 1980); Clifton Hood, *722 Miles: The Building of the Subways and How They Transformed New York* (New York: Simon & Schuster, 1993); Brian J. Cudahy, *Cash, Tokens, and Transfers: A History of Urban Mass Transit in North America* (New York: Fordham University Press, 1990); and Sam Bass Warner, *Streetcar Suburbs: The Process of Growth in Boston, 1870–1900* (Cambridge, MA: Harvard University Press, 1962).

12. Evan Friss, *The Cycling City: Bicycles and Urban America in the 1890s* (Chicago: University of Chicago Press, 2015); Evan Friss, "Writing Bicycles: The Historiography of Cycling in the United States," in *Mobility in History: Yearbook of the International Association for the History of Transport, Traffic, and Mobility* 6 (New York: Berghahn, 2015); Wayne E. Fuller, *RFD: The Changing Face of Rural America* (Bloomington: Indiana University Press, 1964); and Carlton Reid, *Roads Were Not Built for Cars: How Cyclists Were the First to Push for Good Roads and Became the Pioneers of Motoring* (Washington, DC: Island, 2015).

13. William H. Wilson, *The City Beautiful Movement* (Baltimore: Johns Hopkins University Press, 1994); and Jan Cigliano and Sarah Bradford Landau, eds., *The Grand American Avenue, 1850–1920* (San Francisco: Pomegranate Artbooks, 1994).

14. Clay McShane, *Down the Asphalt Path: American Cities and the Coming of the Automobile* (New York: Columbia University Press, 1994); and Gijs Mom, *The Electric Vehicle: Technology and Expectations*

in the Automobile Age (Baltimore: Johns Hopkins University Press, 2004).

15. Robert Casey, *The Model T: A Centennial History* (Baltimore: Johns Hopkins University Press, 2008).

16. McShane, *Down the Asphalt Path.*

17. Peter Norton, *Fighting Traffic: The Dawn of the Motor Age in the American City* (Cambridge, MA: MIT Press, 2008); Michael L. Berger, *The Devil Wagon in God's Country: The Automobile and Social Change in Rural America, 1893–1929* (Hamden, CT: Archon, 1980).

18. McShane, *Down the Asphalt Path*; Norton, *Fighting Traffic.*

19. Norton, *Fighting Traffic.*

20. Norton, *Fighting Traffic.*

21. Norton, *Fighting Traffic.*

22. Norton, *Fighting Traffic.*

23. Norton, *Fighting Traffic.*

24. John Chynoweth Burnham, "The Gasoline Tax and the Automobile Revolution," *Mississippi Valley Historical Review* 48.3 (1961): 435–459; Norton, *Fighting Traffic*; Christopher Wells, "Fuelling the Boom: Gasoline Taxes, Invisibility, and the Growth of American Highway Infrastructure, 1919–1956," *Journal of American History* 99 (2012): 72–81; and Christopher Wells, *Car Country: An Environmental History* (Seattle: University of Washington Press, 2012).

25. Norton, *Fighting Traffic*; and Bruce E. Seely, *Building the American Highway System: Engineers As Policy Makers* (Philadelphia: Temple University Press, 1987).

26. Peter Norton, "Four Paradigms: Traffic Safety in the Twentieth-Century United States," *Technology and Culture* 56.2 (2015): 319–334.

27. Mark Foster, *From Streetcar to Superhighway: American City Planners and Urban Transportation, 1900–1940* (Philadelphia: Temple University Press, 1981).

28. Dan Cupper, *The Pennsylvania Turnpike: A History* (Lebanon, PA: Applied Arts, 1990); and Bruce Radde, *The Merritt Parkway* (New Haven, CT: Yale University Press, 1996).

29. Roland Marchand, "Designers Go to the Fair II: Norman Bel Geddes, the General Motors 'Futurama,' and the Visit to the Factory Transformed," *Design Issues* 8 (1992): 22–40.

30. US Department of Agriculture, Bureau of Public Roads, *Toll Roads and Free Roads* (Washington, DC: Government Printing Office, 1939); and Seely, *Building the American Highway System.*

31. Mark Rose, *Interstate: Express Highway Politics 1941–1989* (rev. ed.; Knoxville: University of Tennessee Press, 1990); Peter Norton, "Fighting Traffic: U.S. Transportation Policy and Urban Congestion, 1955–1970," *Essays in History* 38 (1996), http://www.essaysinhistory.com/articles /2012/164.

32. US Congress, House, *National Highway Program*, 84th Congress, 1st Session, 1955, House Document No. 93, as quoted in *The Eisenhower Administration, 1953–1961: A Documentary History*, ed. Robert L. Branyan and Lawrence H. Larsen (New York: Random House, 1971), vol. 1, 538.

33. In *Public Papers of the Presidents of the United States: Dwight D. Eisenhower*, vol. 8 (Washington, DC: National Archives and Records Service, 1961), see "Remarks at the Dedication of the Hiawatha Bridge," Red Wing, Minn., October 18, 1960, 780–781 (781: "… will save 4,000 lives every year"), and "Address in Philadelphia at a Rally of the Nixon for President Committee of Pennsylvania," October 28, 1960, 815–816 (815: "…will save four thousand American lives a year").

34. Danielian to Eisenhower, August 16, 1955, in *Eisenhower Administration*, vol. 1, 550–551.

35. President's Advisory Committee on a National Highway Program, *A Ten-Year National Highway Program: A Report to the President* (Washington, DC: Government Printing Office, 1955), 2, 32.

36. Rose, *Interstate.*

37. Joseph F. C. DiMento and Cliff Ellis, *Changing Lanes: Visions and Histories of Urban Freeways* (Cambridge, MA: MIT Press, 2013); and Tom Lewis, *Divided Highways: Building the Interstate Highways, Transforming American Life* (Ithaca, NY: Cornell University Press, 2013).

38. William H. Whyte, "Are Cities Un-American?" *Fortune* 55 (September 1957): 123–125, 213–214, 218; Jane Jacobs, "Downtown Is for People," *Fortune* 57 (April 1958): 133–140, 236, 238, 240–242; and Lewis Mumford, "The Highway and the City," *Architectural Record* 123 (April 1958): 179–186.

39. Peter Norton, "Of Love Affairs and Other Stories," in *Incomplete Streets: Processes, Practices, and Possibilities*, eds. Stephen Zavestoski and Julian Agyeman (London: Routledge, 2015), 17–35.

40. Raymond A. Mohl, "The Interstates and the Cities: The U.S. Department of Transportation and the Freeway Revolt, 1966–1973," *Journal of Policy History* 20.2 (2008): 193–226; and Zachary

M. Schrag, "The Freeway Fight in Washington, D.C.: The Three Sisters Bridge in Three Administrations," *Journal of Urban History* 30 (2004): 648–673.

41. Donald C. Shoup, *The High Cost of Free Parking* (Chicago: Planners Press, 2005).

42. Owen D. Gutfreund, *Twentieth-Century Sprawl: Highways and the Reshaping of the American Landscape* (New York: Oxford University Press, 2004).

43. Norton, "Four Paradigms."

44. Michelle J. White, "Housing and the Journey to Work in U.S. Cities (1991), in National Bureau of Economic Research," in *Housing Markets in the United States and Japan,* eds. Yukio Noguchi and James M. Poterba (Chicago: University of Chicago Press, 1994), 133–159.

45. D. W. Meinig, *The Shaping of America: A Geographical Perspective of 500 Years of American History* (New Haven, CT: Yale University Press), vol. 1, *Atlantic America, 1492–1800* (1988), and vol. 2, *Continental America, 1800–1867* (1995).

46. E.g., Richard Pillsbury, "The Urban Street Pattern As a Culture Indicator: Pennsylvania, 1682–1815," *Annals of the Association of American Geographers* 70 (1970): 428–446.

47. Onuf, *Statehood and Union*; Brian Balogh, *A Government Out of Sight: The Mystery of National Authority in Nineteenth-Century America* (New York: Cambridge University Press, 2009).

48. Raitz, *National Road.*

49. Klein and Majewski, "Turnpikes and Toll Roads."

50. Majewski, Baer and Klein, "Plank Road Boom."

51. Cronon, *Nature's Metropolis.*

52. McShane and Tarr, *The Horse in the City.*

53. Ballon, *The Greatest Grid.*

54. Kenneth T. Jackson, *Crabgrass Frontier: The Suburbanization of the United States* (New York: Oxford University Press, 1985).

55. Baldwin, *Domesticating the Street.*

56. Duffy, *The Sanitarians*; Hughes, *Networks of Power*; Rose, *Cities of Light and Heat.*

57. James J. Flink, *America Adopts the Automobile, 1895–1910* (Cambridge, MA: MIT Press, 1970).

58. James J. Flink, *The Automobile Age* (Cambridge, MA: MIT Press, 1988).

59. Scott L. Bottles, *Los Angeles and the Automobile: The Making of the Modern City* (Berkeley, CA: University of California Press, 1987); and McShane, *Down the Asphalt Path.*

60. Foster, *From Streetcar to Superhighway*; Paul Barrett, *The Automobile and Urban Transit: The Formation of Public Policy in Chicago, 1900–1930* (Philadelphia: Temple University Press, 1983); and John D. Fairfield, *The Mysteries of the Great City: The Politics of Urban Design, 1877–1937* (Columbus: Ohio State University Press, 1993)

61. Stephen B. Goddard, *Getting There: The Epic Struggle between Road and Rail in the American Century* (Chicago: University of Chicago Press, 1996).

62. Peter Norton, "Street Rivals: Jaywalking and the Invention of the Motor Age Street," *Technology and Culture* 48.2 (2007): 331–359; and Norton, *Fighting Traffic.*

63. Wells, *Car Country.*

64. Warren J. Belasco, *Americans on the Road: From Autocamp to Motel, 1910–1945* (Cambridge, MA: MIT Press, 1979); and Paul Sutter, *Driven Wild: How the Fight Against Automobiles Launched the Modern Wilderness Movement* (Seattle: University of Washington Press, 2005).

65. Cotton Seiler, *Republic of Driving: A Cultural History of Automobility in America* (Chicago: University of Chicago Press, 2008).

66. Drake Hokanson, *The Lincoln Highway: Main Street across America* (Iowa City: University of Iowa Press, 1988).

67. Cupper, *Pennsylvania Turnpike*; and Radde, *Merritt Parkway.*

68. Bruce E. Seely, *Building the American Highway System: Engineers as Policy Makers* (Philadelphia: Temple University Press, 1987).

69. Rose, *Interstate.*

70. Earl Swift, *The Big Roads: The Untold Story of the Engineers, Visionaries, and Trailblazers Who Created the American Superhighways* (New York: Houghton Mifflin Harcourt, 2011); and Tom Lewis, *Divided Highways: Building the Interstate Highways, Transforming American Life* (Ithaca, NY: Cornell University Press, 2013).

71. Joseph F. C. DiMento and Cliff Ellis, *Changing Lanes: Visions and Histories of Urban Freeways* (Cambridge, MA: MIT Press, 2013).

72. Mohl, "Interstates and the Cities"; Schrag, "Freeway Fight in Washington, D.C."; and Eric Avila, *The Folklore of the Freeway: Race and Revolt in the Modernist City* (Minneapolis: University of Minnesota Press, 2014).

Peter Norton

THE AUTOMOBILE AND THE AMERICAN CITY

DEFINING THE RELATIONSHIP BETWEEN THE CAR AND THE CITY

Take a casual drive through any American city and, inevitably, some common questions arise: why do the streets and highways seem incapable of reducing traffic congestion? Why are there so many cars and so few suitable alternatives to access the city? Why do urban residents tolerate the many inconveniences to their daily lives caused by the automobile? These issues form the backbone of the scholarly inquiry into the historical relationship between cars and the city, highlighting the conflicting perspectives that provide some answers. From the vantage of the *lived* urban experience, drivers, pedestrians, bicyclists, and mass-transit commuters appreciate the automobile through a subjective lens of personal mobility, safety, ease of access, and a host of other impressions related to a desired quality of life. By contrast, commercial interests—from auto manufacturers and mass-transit providers to land developers, employers, and other urban businesses—perceive the car primarily as a tool to achieve more material ends. Between them stands a wide array of transit specialists and public advocates—like city planners, highway engineers, landscape architects, preservationists, and environmentalists—hoping to reconcile these contradictory impulses to achieve, in the words of automotive historian James J. Flink, "a social order based upon technical efficiency in which traditional cultural values would be preserved and enhanced."[1]

This awkward mixture of the subjective, lived experience and utilitarian efficiency led to the somewhat paradoxical relationship between the car and the city. On the one hand, Americans eagerly embraced the freedom and personal mobility offered by the passenger car. Ownership climbed sharply—from less than one million registered automobiles in 1912 to more than two hundred million in

Figure 1. Americans' frustration with "Crowded Highways" and their growing dependency upon the personal passenger car for urban transit were widely shared by mid-century.
Cartoon by Hy Rosen.
Courtesy of Library of Congress, 2016684046.

2018—as vehicles became more affordable, easier and (when measured by miles driven) far safer to operate. For their part, transit planners successfully identified the bottlenecks and other inefficiencies that produced the most bothersome congestion, opening new opportunities in both the city and its hinterland.[2]

Yet these pleasures, opportunities, and efficiencies remain rooted within the context of their times. The decisions by millions to leave the city for America's growing automotive suburbs, from the 1920s to the 1960s, prodded transit planners to rethink the urban form in ways that often ignored or even harmed those who remained. Spread out over more than a century, the accumulated result produced a vicious cycle of growth, road expansion, sprawl, automotive dependency, and a proportional increase in congestion and waste. The problems facing today's car country, as historian Christopher Wells argues, are particularly vexing because "car dependency is [now] woven into the basic fabric of the landscape" of American life. This recurring dialectic, where short-term solutions privileged fewer transit options and reduced the long-term flexibility of future societies, remains the most compelling lesson drawn from the twinned histories of the car and the city.[3]

THREE CHRONOLOGICAL PHASES OF THE CAR AND THE CITY

The periodization of the car and the city was influenced by the social and cultural experiences of the citizenry. Falling into three broad phases, the first lasted roughly until the onset of the Great Depression and witnessed the rise and fall of the "streetcar city." Here, transit planning remained largely a local phenomenon that served proximate needs for mobility, geographic expansion, and the displacement of the "ugly" remainders of the premodern past. The automobile gained its ascendency during the second phase, spanning from the late 1920s until the late 1960s. During these decades, the desire for transit efficiency, economic growth, and suburbanization surpassed those of urban aesthetics and were increasingly directed by state or federal authorities. Earlier planners in Chicago, New York, and Detroit, for example, struggled to balance these new urban priorities with established patterns of living while later planners and city officials, particularly in Los Angeles, generally accepted the needs of the driver over those of the urban resident. The interstate system—enacted and built from 1956 to 1970—revealed a national commitment to the car and suburb. While the city was not wholly abandoned—and many raised concerns about the new urban form which the car had spawned—nondrivers were largely ignored. In the final phase the limits and "hidden costs" of these policies became more apparent. Armed with new regulatory powers to stop or delay highway construction, citizens challenged the assumption that regional or national economic growth superseded the desires of local residents who experienced life in the city on a daily basis.

UNDERSTANDING THE CITY, URBAN PLANNING, AND DRIVERS

The shifting interpretations of the city, drivers, and urban planning play an influential role in the historical assessment of change. For example, recent urban scholars have moved away from understanding the city merely in terms of population densities within municipal boundaries to seeing their subject as a unique physical space offering a distinct, rapidly changing, and often highly subjective use value to those who reside there. Here, density is linked to human volition and transit systems evaluated for how well they maximize the public's access to desired housing, work, commerce, and leisure. Two generic yet crucially distinct forms of urban congestion emerged over time. The first was caused by traffic *to-and-from* a city, in the form of working commuters or cultural tourists. The second was that produced *within* a city's functional spaces. Density alone did not produce a transit crisis (or, said another way, congestion was always accompanied by the concentration of people within a specific physical space). Rather, the time-dependent concentration of street *activity* and its relationship to commuting drew the ire of citizens and the attention of planners.[4]

Transit planning has also embodied a variety of meanings. Viewing automobiles as part of a diffuse yet logical transit "technology system," scholars examine policymakers within the material realities of modernization—like mass production, skyscrapers, suburbanization, and various forms of geographic segregation. These and other realities drove the concerns of transit planners who sought to anticipate and maximize the *efficiencies* of each alternative. Ironically, successful plans often generated more congestion, thereby sowing the seeds of their own obsolescence. The automobile did not create the desire to suburbanize, for example, but "solved" the problem of how this might be most easily achieved. Seeking to maximize the car's advantage, planners widened city streets, provided street-level parking, mandated auto-friendly traffic patterns, and encouraged suburban growth in areas underserved by existing traction companies. Such reforms, and the popularity of the car, then produced congestion that rapidly overwhelmed the limited resources available. A dynamic common to many modern technologies—from the television to the Internet—the difference here was the profound material cost weighing on Americans who had grown dependent upon the car. Property values, personal income, and the price of essential consumer items rose and fell in response to these decisions, just as perceptions about the quality of life, ease of access, and community within a city assayed the efficiency of the resulting material reality. Planners' emphasis on "rational behavior" appeared justified—given the strict calculus of material change—and most reforms did ameliorate the inefficiencies of *existing* problems.[5]

But the concept of rational behavior—isolated through material metrics—breaks down when viewed through the perspective of drivers over an extended historical arc. For people of color, for example, individual automobility allowed them to avoid the humiliating experiences of mass transit segregation. Women drivers participated in the public sphere as equals behind the wheel decades before the right to vote. Before World War II, American drivers from all regions and walks of life expressed a set of shared positive values toward driving that can loosely (hence, problematically) be termed an automotive "love affair." While evident through numerous letters, essays, and other popular formats, these values—including a pride in mastering modern technology, equal access to the public sphere, and an embrace of the experiential thrills of driving—remained indeterminate and highly contingent upon the times. That these values failed to persist into the modern era or are often seen today as self-defeating or hypocritical does not undermine their presence or profound influence over American drivers. As historian Clay McShane writes, "the importance here is not whether or not cars really did these things, but that motorists believed they did. . . . More than any

other consumer good the motor car provided fantasies of status, freedom, and escape from the constraints of a highly disciplined urban, industrial order."[6]

PHASE I: ADOPTING AND ADAPTING TO MASS AUTOMOBILITY

The need for mechanized mass transit emerged as the country outgrew the "walking city." Confined to the distance an average resident could reasonably walk each day from home to work, most cities exhibited high population densities (far greater than today) where property values rose the closer one lived to the central business district. The streets were narrow and chaotic, surfaced, if at all, by cobbles or loose gravel, and provided for a variety of uses. Only the wealthy could afford horses or cabs for regular or extended urban travel. Since most street improvements were then paid by owners whose property directly abutted the road, little incentive existed for citywide upgrades to the transit system. Proximity to open spaces near the center of town including markets, parade grounds, and public greens was highly prized while the distant periphery housed the poorest citizens and most offensive commercial endeavors, such as tanneries and slaughterhouses.[7]

Beginning in the early 19th century, the geographic separation of the urban population by class began to put pressure upon the limited transit options of the walking city. The concentration of low-skill factory labor and overall rising populations produced undesirable living conditions for those without the economic means to avoid them. While central business districts retained their commercial exclusivity, the suburban ideal of quiet, healthy, open spaces drew many, including skilled artisans, the emerging middle class, and merchant capitalists, to the unincorporated periphery. Heavy rail saw little profit in servicing the core (and was often legally barred from doing so), but emerging main line suburbs surrounding cities like New York and Boston handled thousands of daily commuters (regular riders could purchase discounted monthly passes, thus "commuting" a portion of their expenses) producing a familiar "star" density pattern radiating from the center. Within the city, lighter, privately owned transit options like the horse-drawn omnibus and cable cars emerged as the primary form of intraurban traffic. While affordable, these conveyances were slow, crowded, and did little to ease congestion over the obsolete streets.[8]

The well-chronicled travails of urban light rail, which first appeared in the 1850s, are only fully understood within this context of early urban geographic migration. Congestion was not new, but *commuter* congestion to and from the city posed unique problems for planners. After developing low-profile rails that did not prohibit cross-traffic (as the tie-and-rail system did in the countryside), the success and growth of private traction companies turned the walking city inside-out. Steam and cable cars appeared first, after the Civil War, only to be replaced by electric vehicles during the last decade of the 19th century. Many progressive reformers in cities like Detroit, Cleveland, and Toledo viewed low-fare streetcars as the best means by which the working poor might leave urban tenements for the suburbs. But service often proved intermittent, with delays caused by overextended lines, missed transfers, strikes, accidents, and the fiscal needs of the increasingly despised "trolley rings." In Philadelphia, for example, public frustration with the corrupt practices of boss Jim McManes (stoked by the writing of Lincoln Steffens) left the city "in no mood to seek municipal rapid transit." Moreover, the privatized sensibilities of the emerging middle class—concerned with male status as professionals, the cult of female domesticity, and a growing segregation between the private home and the public sphere—rankled commuters forced to share straps with recent immigrants and the working class. The timing of suburbanization also mattered greatly to the long-term structure and automotive dependency of most major cities. Those with well-established downtowns before automobility

tended to retain the function and allure of the core, while those lacking these roots diffused their economic and cultural functions far more readily.[9]

The bicycle craze gave the first hint that Americans would trade their reliance on the rails for a new form of personal transportation. Peaking in the 1890s, enthusiasts promoted the notion of a "Cycling City." According to historian Evan Friss, cycling offered city residents "a new way to understand their environment" through individual mobility. Early cycling advocates formed a lobby, the League of American Wheelmen, to push for better roads and sing the praises of individual travel for commerce and pleasure. Progressive urban reformers, concerned by deteriorating sanitary conditions, joined with the League to press for the formation of the Office of Road Inquiry (ORI; later the Bureau of Public Roads) within the Department of Agriculture, in 1893. The ORI gave legitimacy to the search for transportation alternatives to fixed rail and spotlighted the "need" for municipalities to pay for significant road improvements. By 1900, well before the adoption of the car, municipalities spent more than $850 million on street improvements. The *experience* of biking was also critical to its popularity. Gone were the inconveniences and boredom of mass transit, replaced by an apparatus that easily changed speed, maneuvered, and went wherever one desired. As Flink writes, the bicycle "created an enormous demand for individualized, long-distance transportation that could only be satisfied by the mass adoption of motor vehicles." The bicycle craze gave way to auto-mania, Friss adds, not because it represented a "fading technology rendered obsolete" but due to the "interplay among people, bicycles, and cities."[10]

The Automotive Revolution. European innovators far outpaced those in the United States in the development of automobile technology. As a result, early adopters of the car were typically the very wealthy with means of enjoying their purchases beyond the city limits. In 1901, Ransom Olds began selling a dependable, low-cost automobile with interchangeable parts. This revolutionary "Oldsmobile" opened the car market to Americans of more modest means. Henry Ford's Model T (1907) and General Motors' (GM) Model 20 (1908) were both the product of managerial skills that harnessed the immense scale of mass production that lowered the cost of owning a reliable car to less than a year's wages for the average American worker.[11]

The eventual dominance of internal combustion engines—rather than steam or battery power—was not the result of mass production, however. The United States boasted more than 4,000 cars by 1900, but less than 1,000 used internal combustion. These devices were loud, caused noticeable vibrations, emitted noxious fumes, and proved quite dangerous when cranking them to life. Steam offered more power and was familiar to most Americans (and could easily be fueled by cheap petroleum products) while electric cars offered the advantages of being quiet, producing no exhaust, and driven without the need for manual shifting. Yet both foundered on the marketplace due to limits related to their use by consumers. Steam-engine car drivers needed to monitor the boiler pressure (or face a catastrophic explosion). Electric-powered vehicles suffered from the limited capacity of their batteries (allowing for little more than twenty miles of service, in 1900, and roughly twice that by 1910). The fear of boiler explosions and early association of the electric vehicle as a "lady's car" drained both products of their mass market appeal and, with it, venture capital. Regardless of the power plant, Americans proved eager consumers of automobiles. By 1907, American manufacturers outpaced their European rivals. Less than a decade later half of all cars owned in the United States were made by Ford.[12]

The earliest car owners were overwhelmingly urban. By 1910, city residents were four times more likely to purchase a car than their rural counterparts. While most city roads remained substandard, they far exceeded the rutted and muddy traces found in the countryside. Moreover, urban residents relied on at least minimal service and repair facilities. This balance shifted with Ford's manufacturing success (the Model T's simplicity and low cost tapped a vast opportunity with rural consumers) and the mass market exploded. From less than a half a million vehicles on the streets (or 5 vehicles per 1,000 persons) in 1910, ownership mushroomed to 26.7 million (or 190 vehicles per 1,000 persons) by 1929.[13]

The rapid growth of American automobility radically shifted planners' conception of the city. Ironically, most of the infrastructure needed for mass automobile use—particularly improved roads arranged in a grid-like pattern— was in place well before the rise in car ownership. Early urban planners, like Frederick Law Olmsted of Boston and Daniel Burnham of Chicago, promoted landscape designs that accentuated civic beauty, pride, and uncluttered green space. This "City Beautiful" movement, which by 1908 included more than 2,500 civic improvement societies, also advocated manicured boulevards and parkways as a means to decrease crime, disease, and overcrowding— that is, to improve the lived experience of urban residents. But as historians Joseph F. C. DiMento and Cliff Ellis show, by the 1920s traffic engineers, state highway officials, and pro-highway urban growth coalitions succeeded in shifting planning from city beautification to transit efficiency. "City Efficient" planners, they write, "downplayed . . . aesthetic and moral concerns" to advance "the scientific analysis of street patterns in order to move traffic." By the 1920s, architects like Raymond Hood, Harvey Wiley Corbett, Fritz Malcher, and Hugh Ferriss drafted plans for idealized future cities featuring limited access parkways that included "elaborate road hierarchies and turning lanes required to accommodate the uninterrupted movement of the motorized vehicle." Planning for Detroit's "Super Highway" (1924), Chicago's split-level street designs (1928), and New York City's "Regional Plan of New York and Its

Environs" (1928)—which included the Henry Hudson Parkway, the Gowanus Parkway, and the West Side Highway—revealed the shifting ambitions of planners seeking to integrate high-volume auto traffic into the existing city.[14]

The priority given to traffic throughput by these municipal planners—now also pursued in Baltimore, Boston, Los Angeles, and scores of smaller cities—not only encouraged more drivers to rely on personal means to access the city but also limited the range of transit options available to future designs. The influence of state highway engineers and federal officials also increased. In 1896, the ORI counted 2,151,570 miles of road in the United States, but only 153,662 (or 7 percent) of these were improved. After more than a decade of reform, less than 9 percent of the nation's streets were surfaced. The Federal Aid Road Act of 1916 authorized $75 million to, in effect, match state funds for local road construction. In 1921 the US Congress strengthened the 1916 legislation by providing $75 million *per year*. Nine years later more than 90,000 miles of roadway were improved because of these two statutes. By the 1930s, the funds went into projects that more typically bypassed existing neighborhoods and street traffic, creating "a kind of moat around the downtown, separating the office and retail uses of the CBD from the blighted areas of the core frame." As historian Christopher Wells argues, the shifts led transit reformers to consider roads not as a public realm but rather "as technologies that government agencies—staffed by experts—could use to overcome what earlier generations had always seen as fundamental environmental limits on private transportation. " These were changes "that slowly but permanently transformed the relationships that Americans had with their roads and streets, with one another, and with the natural world."[15]

PHASE II: THE AUTOMOTIVE CITY

The second phase in the relationship between the car and the city, spanning from the late 1920s until the early 1970s, proved to be particularly damaging to many urban residents. Clearly, this was not the intent of planners nor were these changes seen in a negative light by those leaving the city for the suburbs. During the Great Depression new road and home construction served as a means of national economic recovery, not urban renewal, and while highway designs retained their focus on the centers of traffic congestion, "planners did not perceive that the motor vehicle," as historian Mark S. Foster writes, "permitted both the concentration and the outward movement of households and business firms."[16]

Public financing for road construction increased dramatically. Federal legislation in 1944, 1947, and, most famously, the Highway Act of 1956 pumped billions of dollars into the road construction industry. The Housing Acts of 1949 and 1954 tied suburban home ownership and property development to these new highways. By 1966, more than half of the $25 billion allocated to improve, widen, and create high-speed thoroughfares was devoted to expressways flowing into and out of the central business districts of most American cities. Unlike the requirement placed upon transit companies to pay for their own infrastructure, the Highway Trust Fund tapped user fees (on gasoline, tires, and new car sales) to pay for 90 percent of these physical improvements. Urban renewal projects designed to clear away slums and abandoned industrial sectors also championed new highway construction as a means to facilitate transit *around* these troubled regions.[17]

Robert Moses and Thomas MacDonald.

The projects initiated by Robert Moses of New York and Thomas MacDonald of Washington, DC serve as useful examples of this trend. Moses bridged the "City Beautiful" versus "City Efficient" divide, but saw his public works projects as opportunities to grant urban residents easier access to residential and recreational hinterlands. The Henry Hudson Parkway, completed in 1937 for the then-staggering price of $109 million, allowed for much faster transit along the western shore of Manhattan yet also undermined the vitality of existing neighborhoods, replaced the city's last freshwater marsh with acres of concrete, and introduced new and permanent sources of noise and air pollution.[18]

Representing the growing influence of federal authorities, Bureau of Public Roads (BPR) chief Thomas H. MacDonald used the revenues supplied by the Highway Act of 1938 to radically reconceptualize automotive transit. Rather than treat roads and highways as means of local efficiencies, MacDonald spearheaded the move toward a national interstate system that drove radial freeways deep into the city. The BPR's *Interregional Highways* report (1944) was sensitive to the needs of local communities. The report noted how *rapid* decentralization would harm existing urban neighborhoods and called for greater cooperation with local officials. In operational terms their highest priority remained "the efficient movement of high volumes of traffic through the cities," historians DiMento and Ellis report, "with other city planning concerns such as land use and coordination with mass transit pushed into the background."[19]

Yet their support failed to account for the ancillary damage done to otherwise healthy residential and commercial regions existing within the city. Coupled with widespread racial and economic discrimination, the work of Moses and MacDonald divided and isolated traditional urban neighborhoods, introduced unwelcome noise and unsightly vistas from congested multilane highways, reduced existing property values held by home owners (just as clearance projects removed residential inventory and increased rental costs), and hastened the flight of white-collar taxpaers from the city. Early skeptics, like St. Paul's George Herrold, doubted whether these thoroughfares would even lower congestion and viewed them as introducing a new "disrupting force to all the factors of good living." By the late 1950s, the urbanist and social critic Lewis Mumford offered data to back up these claims. Watching the hidden costs of the automotive city reveal

themselves, he lamented how "the current American way of life is founded not just on motor transportation but on the religion of the motorcar, and the sacrifices people are prepared to make for this religion stand outside the realm of rational criticism."[20]

A significant role in the crisis can be ascribed to the periodic instability and short-term profit motives of American automakers. The late 1920s saw a saturation point in the market—where nearly three-fourths of new car sales *replaced* existing vehicles rather than serving a new driver—and a growing public concern over the "motor menace" responsible for rising casualty figures. In response, the industry followed a two-pronged marketing approach that featured technical innovations, greater personal comfort and power, as well as a heightened differentiation of their product lines through styling. The war years limited drivers far more than Detroit (which received $29 billion in military contracts, or nearly a fifth of all war production funds). By 1945 the industry constricted into a small yet stable oligarchy that prevented the entry of new and innovative providers (like Preston Tucker) which, in the words of James Flink, set a pattern of complacency "that would characterize automobile manufacturing in the United States into the 1970s with only minor variations." Perhaps justifying their smugness, by 1950 the "Big Three" automobile manufacturers (GM, Ford, and Chrysler) controlled 82 percent of the world market and 94 percent of the massive American niche. Their reliance upon styling and consumer comfort to spur new car sales produced heavy, over-powered, expensive, and spatially large products that far exceeded the needs of most motorists (who, on an average trip, typically carried a payload of one or two people traveling less than fifteen miles over congested streets). By 1958, again facing slow sales, manufacturers sought to differentiate their product lines by adapting existing designs to produce smaller, more affordable cars. The results, such as the AMC Rambler, Ford Falcon, and Chevy Corvair, suffered from handling and safety concerns.

The twin shocks produced by foreign oil embargoes (in 1973 and 1979) and the appearance of low-cost, high-quality Japanese and European imports broke the grip of domestic suppliers and added to the deindustrialization experienced in many northern and midwestern cities.[21]

Inefficiencies of Time and Space. The growing awareness of the limits to an urban mass transit system tied to individual automobility emerged along three tracks. The first involved the inefficient use of time and space. Cars did not create urban congestion, sprawl, or inner city economic decline. But unlike the fixed pathways offered by mass transit, the flexibility of the automobile gave transportation planners and officials the ability to address transit delays for *all* commuters. Indeed, the public's willing embrace of this approach soon overwhelmed transit planners and created a vicious cycle of street expansion, geographic dispersal, and increased congestion. These delays then spread from the core to the periphery. By 1956, the number of cars in the United States (more than 65 million) far exceeded the number of total households (49 million). Carmakers were thus encouraged to target young people and suburban women for the purchase of a family's second car. One of the many signals that urban transit now *required* the personal passenger car appeared that same year, as Ford Motor Company began its campaign warning homemakers to avoid being "stranded in suburbia." The suburban station wagon served as the most fitting icon of 1950s automobility, designed for multistop, short-haul uses yet packaged to meet the suburban cultural dream of the postwar generation, much as the sport utility vehicle (SUV) aspired to do at the turn of the 21st century. While the additional local transit added only a minor load to urban commuter thoroughfares, the *randomness* of traffic stymied transit planners and produced "rush hour" conditions in many older bedroom communities.[22]

The growth in suburban car ownership also pointed to the greater spatial demands that these automobiles made on the city. By the 1960s, more than half of all urban acreage was devoted exclusively to cars, including streets, parking, and auto-related services. This number varied based on the maturity of various downtowns. Los Angeles, for example, devoted nearly 60 percent of its central space to cars while in Chicago the number was closer to 40 percent. What was shared across the country, however, was the significant decrease in space devoted to pedestrians and bicycle traffic. Given that a car is parked for more than 90 percent of its useful service, the ceding of such large chunks of limited urban space prohibited other, more varied uses of land from developing to offset the dispersal of the population.[23]

The result of these inefficiencies was the inevitable spatial reorganization of the urban environment. By 1970 a majority of Americans now lived within a Metropolitan Statistical Area (MSA). These inhabitants, however, were spread out over significantly larger space. Retail businesses seeking patrons (increasingly frustrated by the lack of parking) and manufacturers frustrated by the delays caused by automotive congestion moved their activities to the fringe. The suburbanization of commerce redefined the very notion of a "bedroom community" and abandoned those without the means to afford an automobile to the shrinking services remaining within the core. This spatial mismatch, where job growth appeared in areas largely unserved by public transit, was only exacerbated by the financial advantages enjoyed through Federal Housing Administration (FHA) loans and other federal initiatives designed to decentralize the city. In 1954, federal tax code changes, for example, allowed for the accelerated depreciation of new commercial construction in the suburbs. Responding to the incentive, developers added more than 10 million square feet of new suburban retail space per year from 1957 to 1962.[24]

Pollution. Environment and health concerns linked to mass automobility attracted greater public attention after 1970. Some of these were localized, emerging from the massive infrastructure built to oblige car owners. The additional roadways, for example, served as collectors of refuse and, accentuated by run-off, conduits for toxic chemicals deposited far from their source of origin. In 1956, a result of the steel industry's discontinued use of open-hearth furnaces, demand for scrap iron fell by half. Lacking the economic incentive to collect and ship derelict cars for recycling, American cities saw a rapid rise in the number of abandoned vehicles. In New York City alone the number grew from 2,500 hulks left on the streets in 1960 to more than 70,000 by 1969. Isolated within the automotive city, poorer and often minority communities viewed the resulting waste as a sign of political neglect. Maggie Landron, a journalist and advocate for the Mexican American community living in heavily industrialized East Houston, asserted in 1970 that residents were "fed up choking on our own exhaust fumes; fed up looking at cement ribbons crisscrossing our cities; fed up with homes and people being destroyed to build more and more freeways; and fed up with others determining what is good for us."[25]

The gaseous byproducts of internal combustion were less discriminating. Air pollution affected all citizens, not merely those who used the car. By the 1950s, photochemical smog, which generated air with a brownish-gray tint and irritated air passages in the body, led to major health crises in Baltimore, Houston, Philadelphia, and Washington. The predicament in Los Angeles, which suffered through air quality emergencies in 1953, 1955, and 1958, compelled the federal government to begin research on automotive air pollutants and their effects on the populace. Researchers discovered that half of all hydrocarbons—produced from the incomplete combustion of gasoline and primarily in the form of carbon monoxide and carbon dioxide—and nearly two-thirds of all airborne pollutants (the remainder in the form of ozone, nitrogen oxides, and lead) were derived from the automobile. California first mandated, in 1959, stricter emission

Figure 2. Photochemical smog, caused by the incomplete combustion of petroleum products, led to major health crises in cities like Los Angeles, Baltimore, Houston, Philadelphia, and Washington DC. Courtesy of Library of Congress, LC-USZ62-114346.

standards for all cars sold and licensed in the state. Pressed to install technologies—such as Positive Crankcase Ventilation (PCV), fuel-injection, catalytic converters, and electronic timing systems—designed to cut down on incomplete combustion and capture nitrogen oxides, the automobile industry's obvious delays and foot-dragging convinced many of Detroit's willing complicity with these ills. The Motor Vehicle Air Pollution Act of 1965 and Clean Air Act of 1970 set national emission standards that domestic suppliers claimed were impossible to meet. Foreign imports like Honda, however, quickly achieved the new standards.[26]

Safety. Driver and passenger safety brought about a third crisis in urban automobile use. By the 1930s, manufacturers had greatly simplified the operation and experience of driving a car (thus reducing distractions that often caused accidents), but their design choices and consumers' fixation on speed resulted in more than 50,000 traffic fatalities in 1966 alone. While these numbers—when considered in relation to the total miles driven or number of cars owned—remained well within the statistical range of other industrialized countries, the lack of transit options in American metropolitan areas and the open hostility shown by the industry to design critics like John Keats and Ralph Nader (who, it was learned, was placed under surveillance by GM) created conditions that compelled Congress to act.[27] Federal legislators, using the power of their budget—which purchased a massive number of vehicles each year—passed the National Traffic and Motor Vehicle Safety Act of 1966 and formed the National Highway Traffic and Safety Administration in 1967 to set design standards, demand crash performance data from manufacturers, and require mandatory recalls for cars known to possess defective parts.

The recognition of the hidden costs buried within mass automobility signaled the end of this second phase of the city's relationship with the car and presaged the rise of a postmodern urban environment. While most scholars no longer hold that the car caused the massive exodus from the inner cities it remains true that commuter suburbs made automobile ownership essential for most Americans. This transit enslavement, driven by planners seeking to increase land values in the periphery, penalized existing nonautomotive functions and effectively trapped those without the means to drive within an environment where work disappeared. As the urbanist Jane Jacobs concluded, "swiftly or slowly, greater accessibility by car is inexorably accompanied both by less convenience and efficiency of public transportation, and by thinning-down and smearing-out of uses, and hence by more need for cars." Detroit, which once promised to solve the problems of fixed transit schedules and widespread suburbanization, appeared to be equally trapped by the irresistible momentum of mass automobility. In the words of industry critic John Keats, by the 1970s the public's

"marriage to the American automobile [was] at an end" and "only a matter of minutes to the final pistol shot, although who pulls the trigger [had] yet to be determined."[28]

PHASE III: THE POSTMODERN QUANDARY

The rapid rise in the cost of living, led by the instability of foreign oil markets, served as that pistol shot. As many critics noted, most of the hidden costs of America's car-based transit system were found to be external to the purchase and operation of the vehicle itself. Seeing the car as a more flexible option, automobile consumers proved willing to pay for their own transit "system." But the obvious environmental degradation, threat of accidents, and growing awareness of our dependency on limited resources produced a fundamental reevaluation of both the practical and theoretical arrangement of the urban environment. Accordingly, the third and final phase of the car-city relationship was clouded by both the postmodern sensibility that emerged following the collapse of the industrial city as well as a tendency to scapegoat the automobile as the source of all the city's ills.[29]

In response to the "urban crisis" of the 1960s and 1970s, planners reassessed the primacy of economic growth, demanded by land developers, when conceptualizing the new field of "urban design." As the planner Edward Relph concludes, "The planning equivalent of postmodernism is urban design, just as the planning equivalent of modernism" in the 1940s and 1950s "was the institutional practice of planning by the [fiscal] numbers." For urban designers, a city required mixed-used zoning that reenvisioned access to the public amenities offered by high-density living. Where planners once sought to guide economic growth through social controls that favored underdeveloped land, designers now hoped to engage with the expressed needs of local citizens who already lived and worked in urban neighborhoods. In many ways, this renewed emphasis on place and the character of a city echoes the much earlier works of planners like Camillo Sitte, Raymond Unwin, and Frederick Law Olmsted who looked to the interrelation between objects of the built environment and their linkages and discontinuities, rather than a fixation on the object itself.[30]

Both Universal and Subjective Trend Lines.

True to the times, this sensibility resulted in diverse yet often reinforcing trends. Building upon the linkages exposed through the study of ecology, a new universalism infused urban design to consider how the built environment worked with the natural one, rather than each standing in opposition to the other. Experiments, like those of architect Paolo Soleri, building outside of Phoenix in 1970, embraced the unique local conditions to construct a "solar-powered mini-city" that combined housing, work, and leisure activities and made the car unnecessary. The interdisciplinary nature of these endeavors involved community-based planning that encouraged the formation of groups like the Institute for Architecture and Urban Planning (1972).[31]

A second trend, by contrast, responded to a rising subjectivity in the minds of many urban residents toward the automobile. Faced with external risks they were unable to control—from pollution to auto accidents—and with little confidence in elected officials to mitigate these threats, many turned to a "reflexive modernization" that measured well-being through more personal and less material means. Scholars like Ulrich Beck theorized a "risk society" where citizens expressed greater concern over the abuses within the existing transit system than past planning failures that they could not avoid. A host of initiatives, including zero-tolerance laws for convicted drunk drivers; zero-emission requirements compelling laggard automakers; and mandatory seat-belt, child restraints, emission inspections, and liability insurance shifted attention from those poorly served by the automobile to those who should be prevented from driving altogether.[32]

Post-Suburbia and Edge Cities.

The loss of a clear consensus, past failures of centralized planners, and the breakdown of traditional distinctions between urban, suburban, and rural cultures also shattered the strict dualism between the core and periphery. In its stead emerged a focus on borders, edges, and multicentered urban living. Notably, the shift here was in the reconception of space and the cultural fusion produced from the merger of suburbs and white-collar work, and not on the form of transit, which remained almost exclusively automotive. The result, popularized by the writer Joel Garreau and historian Robert Fishman, preserved the suburban ideal by bringing the amenities of the core nearer to the intersection of high-volume automotive transit. Edge cities may have cut down on the distance of one's daily commute, and perhaps offered cultural pursuits that could rival the core, but they elided all efforts to address the inefficiencies, economic segregation, and pollution that accompanied mass automobility. Garreau left unanswered the problems of sprawl, social isolation, and the cultural uniformity typically found amid these indistinguishable interchanges. His quaint reference to fax machines as an example of the "dematerializing technologies" that rendered transit moot presaged the as yet unknown, yet clearly significant shifts that resulted from the Internet and mobile cell phone use.[33]

City residents also appeared intent on dematerializing the aging urban highways built to achieve the dream of the automotive city. Beginning in the late-1970s and gaining momentum in the 1990s, communities in Portland (OR), Chattanooga, Milwaukee, and San Francisco removed whole segments of their highway systems in the hope of urban redevelopment. In Boston the "Big Dig" literally buried the elevated Central Artery highway while in New York City the West Side Highway redesigned the Henry Hudson Parkway to allow for more mixed use. Both projects reopened these cities to their waterfronts and reclaimed hundreds of acres of land. Many other municipalities,

Figure 3. A growing network of urban highways encouraged businesses to develop property far from traditional commercial hubs, further accelerating the post-suburban sprawl.
Courtesy of Library of Congress, LC-DIG-highsm-15949.

such as Los Angeles, Dallas, St. Louis, and Cincinnati, are well along the path to repurposing similarly reclaimed urban space.[34]

CONCLUSION

Transportation and environmental reforms adopted after 1960 mitigated some of the inefficiencies of mass automobility. While still a leading polluter, hydrocarbon and nitrogen oxide emissions were reduced 96 and 76 percent, respectively from 1960 to 2000. The number of ozone "alert days" in Southern California declined from 208 in 1977 to 36 by 2001; "first-stage" smog episodes fell from 121 to 0 during the same years. Measured by statistical averages, the fatality rate per vehicle miles of travel (VMT) declined between 1970 and 2000 by more than 68 percent.

Manufacturers, too, have responded to changing consumer tastes. The development of electric cars (like GM's ill-fated EV1, which was leased then decommissioned, to the outrage of users, in 2003); those powered by hydrogen fuel cells (which, like cars running on natural gas, show great improvements on emissions yet limited savings in total energy costs); and particularly the introduction of hybrids—like the Honda Insight and Toyota Prius, which combine internal combustion and electric power—suggest as well that consumers retain some agency in demanding low-cost and environmentally sound alternatives.[35]

A more substantive problem was the political will of the driving majority. The lack of early public funding for light rail and then the improvement and expansion of streets and highways did significant damage to existing mass transit systems before the 1960s. Since then, federal law attempted to rectify this historical oversight. Beginning in 1973 and then institutionalized in 1982, highway funding mandated that 20 percent of all gas tax revenues be set aside for public transit. By 1992, more than $3.7 billion had been spent by federal authorities and $18.7 billion by state and local agencies on such projects. Yet many of those not living within easy distance to mass transit remain unwilling to restructure their transit or consumer behaviors around these utilities. Within the city's core, reliance by women, people of color, and those at or near the poverty level on public modes of transit further "others" them from the car-owning majority. While only 9 percent of households today do not own a car, they represent more than 25 percent of the overall population. In many ways, the problem cycles back to where the relationship between the car and city first began: with economic expediency and consumer-based expressions of individuality. The booming markets for light trucks and SUVs, which surged in the 1990s and remain the most profitable products sold by American automobile manufacturers, offer consumers end-runs that avoid strict emission, mileage, and safety standards. Crashes involving both trucks and SUVs are also far more deadly, particularly for those they hit, and result in nearly twice the number of fatal "roll-over" accidents than passenger cars. Like the initial success enjoyed by cars, the popularity of both trucks and SUVs appears to rest on perceptions of how consumers might avoid the problems of urban mass automobility reality rather than an efficient management strategy to deal with the realities of congestion.[36]

The dependency of Americans on the automobile, the petroleum products that keep them in motion, and the physical infrastructure required to maintain this technology as the primary means of transit are difficult to overstate. In 1995, citizens saw for the first time the number of vehicles equal the number of licensed drivers. Only eight years later, the average number of cars per household exceeded the average number of drivers per household. Cities at the dawn of the age of automobile once offered choices to its residents, but it was the affordability, flexibility, and invigorating culture of driving that, ironically, curtailed these options for future generations. The hidden costs of these decisions—and the economic limits reached by many American consumers—forced both planners and everyday citizens to reexamine the shrinking cost-benefit ratio derived from the car. While the city thrived throughout this period of reimagining the urban and suburban environments, the nation's continued dependency on the car suggested that only a significant external crisis will compel the country to resuscitate viable transit alternatives for the hundreds of millions trapped in "car country." The response will not occur quickly. As DiMento and Ellis caution, "It has taken us more than half a century to build our way into this predicament. It may take nearly as long to find a way out." That this transition will occur within the expected lifetimes of the majority of Americans living today and that this shift will likely carry a significant economic, social, and cultural cost to the nation is no longer in doubt.[37]

DISCUSSION OF THE LITERATURE

The scholarship on the car and the city is vast. Those dealing with the rise to prominence of the automobile and American automotive industry serve as the essential starting point from which to access modern transit technology. The work by John B. Rae and James J. Flink remains the best starting point in understanding the contingencies of this development and the many paths not taken.[38] Rudi Volti offers a more condensed narrative of the life of the internal combustion automobile as a consumer technology. More recent interest in electric-powered vehicles, by David A. Kirsch and Gijs Mom, show both the limits of early electrics and the cultural burdens they carried when compared to their gas-powered rivals.[39]

The relationship between mass transit, the car, and changes to the American city is best approached first through the work of Joseph F. C. DiMento and Cliff Ellis, Kenneth T. Jackson, and Clay McShane and Joel Tarr. They show the contextual struggles faced by light rail in the light of early automobility. While there exist a number of fascinating case studies, Paul Barrett's work on Chicago, Kyle Shelton on Houston, and Peter Derrick on New York demonstrate the value of nuanced, case-specific histories of urban planning within the broader rise of American automobility.[40] The role of federal funding for road improvement and, particularly, the interstate highway system—as discussed by DiMento and Ellis, Mark S. Foster, Bruce E. Seely, Tom Lewis, and Raymond A. Mohl—prove essential in wedding the narrative of suburbanization to the automobile.[41] Finally, the focus on the growing frustrations of motorists offers an important bridge between the unchallenged rise of America as a car country and more recent concerns over its hidden costs. Works by Robert Fishman, Joel Garreau, Jon Teaford, Dolores Hayden, William T. Bogart, and Peter S. Norton are necessary starting points in understanding these continuities.[42]

The social and cultural adaptation by urban drivers to the automobile plays an important role in the early success and often illogical persistence of mass automobility. Beginning with Warren Belasco and continuing through several volumes written by John A. Jackle and Keith A. Sculle, scholars have looked to the changes in the built and consumed environments of a motorized citizenry.[43] The experiences behind the wheel by women and people of color differed significantly from those of white men, as shown by Virginia Scharff, Andrew Weise, and Georgine Clarson.[44] David Blanke and Brian Ladd explore the conflicted love-hate relationship expressed by Americans for driving and how these affected critical debates surrounding auto safety and suburbanization.[45] Cotton Seiler's more recent work summarizes this diverse literature and points to ways

that the culture of driving shapes and is shaped by the broader historical forces of the 20th century.[46]

Building upon the groundbreaking work of Martin Melosi, recent environmental histories of the automobile by Tom McCarthy, Christopher W. Wells, and David B. Lucsko offer convincing arguments for how rising health and environmental concerns, coupled with a new emphasis on material sustainability, have fundamentally restructured the historical interpretation of mass automobility. The sweeping scope of Wells's work, in particular, offers a model for others to follow and remains the best place today for students to begin to understand the paradoxical relationship between urban Americans, the environment, and cars.[47]

PRIMARY SOURCES

Given its importance to urban transit, a wide range of readily available primary sources exists on the car and the city. Even a cursory glance at most municipal, state, and federal archives will reveal scores of traffic and transit studies exploring the source of urban congestion and the growing auto-centered worldview of most public officials. A sampling of examples includes:

- Detroit Rapid Transit Commission. *Proposed Super-Highway Plan for Greater Detroit*, 1924. https://babel.hathitrust .org/cgi/pt?id=uc1.5014895;view=1up; seq=3.
- Works Progress Administration. *A Survey of Traffic Conditions in the City of Dallas Texas with Checks of Obedience to Traffic Laws*. Project No. 1065, Sponsored by the Dallas Police Department, Field Work, 1933–1937 (Dallas: WPA, 1937).
- New York City Planning Commission. *Selected Measures for the Partial Relief of Traffic Congestion in New York City 1946*. http://worldcat.org/identities /lccn-n50074724/.
- San Francisco, Department of Public Works and Department of City Planning.

Trafficways in San Francisco—A Reappraisal (San Francisco: Department of City Planning, 1960). https://archive.org/details/trafficways-reappraisal.

State highway and municipal and county road departments provide detailed physical specifications for transit bottlenecks and other perceived problems. Their annual reports, most found in hard copy form in state historical archives, detail significant road improvements, budgets, revenues, and contractors. Examples include:

- Texas Department of Public Safety, *Records* (1935–1995).
- State of Texas, State Highway Department. *First Biennial Report of the State Highway Commission* (issued biennially).
- State of California, Department of Public Works, Division of Highways. *Reports* (annual).
- New York State Engineer and Surveyor. *Record of Contracts Awarded for Improvement of Public Highways* (1898–1908).
- New York State Highway Commission. *Report of the Commission of Highways* (annual).

The US federal government provides official summary data on the material nature of our driving infrastructure, often with extensive details on numerous locales. The most relevant, showing examples of selected digital archive reports, include:

- US Bureau of Public Roads (https://www.archives.gov/research/guide-fed-records/groups/030.html).
  - *Report of a Study of Highway Traffic and the Highway System of Cook County, Illinois* (1925).
  - *Report of a Survey of Transportation on the State Highway of Pennsylvania* (1928).
  - *Highway Statistics: Summary to 1945* (1947).
  - *General Locations of National System of Interstate Highways* (1955).
  - *Highways and Economic and Social Change* (1964).
  - *Literature References to Highways and Their Environmental Considerations* (1969).
  - *Highway Joint Development and Multiple Use* (1970).
- US Department of Commerce (https://www.commerce.gov/).
  - *A City Planning Primer: By the Advisory Committee on City Planning and Zoning* (1924).
  - *Freeways to Urban Development* (1966).
  - US Department of Transportation, Federal Highway Administration (https://www.fhwa.dot.gov/).
  - *Highway Statistics* (published each decade).
  - *The Freeway in the City: Principles of Planning and Design* (1968).
  - *Social and Economic Effects of Highways* (1976).
  - *Urban System Study* (1977).
  - *Highway History* (including links to the work of Thomas H. MacDonald) (https://www.fhwa.dot.gov/highwayhistory/history_fhwa.cfm).
- US Federal Housing Administration, *Successful Subdivision: Principles of Planning for Economy and Protection against Neighborhood Blight* (Washington, DC: Federal Housing Administration, 1940).
- US Bureau of the Census (https://www.census.gov).

Periodical literature and newspapers remain quite useful in gauging the public's response to automotive congestion yet need to be read with caution in terms of the assumptions they make about their subscribers. The same is true for professional organizations, which are numerous and led by groups like the American

Automobile Association, the Automobile Manufacturers Association, and numerous civil engineering groups.

- *American Auto News*
- *American City*
- *American Society of Civil Engineers: Journal of Professional Practice*
- *Automotive Industries*
- *City Manager Magazine*
- *Environment and Planning*
- *Highway Research Bulletin Board*
- *Horseless Age*
- *Journal of the American Institute of Planners*
- *Journal of the American Planning Association*
- *Landscape Architecture*
- *Motor*
- *Motor Age*
- *Motor Life*
- *Motor Travel*
- *Motor World*
- *Planning*
- *Proceedings of the Institute of Traffic Engineers*
- *Public Interest*
- *The American Magazine*
- *The American Motorist*
- *The Chauffeur*
- *Traffic Digest*
- *Traffic Quarterly*

Many early "traffic engineers" found success publishing their work as guides for others. Notables include:

WILLIAM PHELPS ENO

- *Street Traffic Regulation* (Chicago: National Safety Council, 1909).
- *Fundamentals of Highway Traffic Regulation* (Washington, DC: Eno Foundation, 1926).
- *Setting Forth How Traffic Regulation May Be Improved in Town and Country: A Supplement to Simplification of Highway Traffic* (Saugatuck, CT: Eno Foundation, 1936).

- *The Story of Highway Traffic Control, 1899–1939* (Saugatuck, CT: Eno Foundation, 1939).

ALBERT RUSSEL ERSKINE BUREAU

- *A Report on the Street Traffic Control Problem of the City of Boston* (Boston: N.p., 1928).
- *A Traffic Control Plan for Kansas City* (Kansas City: N.p., 1930).

MILLER MCCLINTOCK

- *Report and Recommendations of the Metropolitan Street Traffic Survey* (Chicago: Chicago Association of Commerce, 1926).
- *A Report on the Street Traffic Control Problem of San Francisco* (San Francisco: Traffic Survey Committee, 1927).
- *The Street Traffic Control Problem of the City of New Orleans* (New Orleans: N.p., 1928).
- *A Report of the Parking and Garage Problem of Central Business District of Washington, D.C.* (Washington, DC: N.p., 1930).
- *The Greater Chicago Traffic Area: A Preliminary Report on the Major Traffic Facts of the City of Chicago and Surrounding Region* (Chicago: Illinois Commission on Future Road Program, 1932).

FURTHER READING

Blanke, David. *Hell on Wheels: The Promise and Peril of America's Car Culture, 1900–1940*. Lawrence: University Press of Kansas, 2007.
Clarson, Georgine. *Eat My Dust: Early Women Motorists*. Baltimore: Johns Hopkins University Press, 2008.
DiMento, Joseph F. C., and Cliff Ellis. *Changing Lanes: Visions and Histories of Urban Freeways*. Cambridge, MA: MIT Press, 2013.
Flink, James J. *America Adopts the Automobile, 1895–1910*. Cambridge, MA: MIT Press, 1970.
Flink, James J. *The Automobile Age*. Cambridge, MA: The MIT Press, 1988; 2001.

Foster, Mark S. *From Streetcar to Superhighway: American City Planners and Urban Transportation, 1900–1940.* Philadelphia: Temple University Press, 1982.

Hayden, Dolores. *Building Suburbia: Green Fields and Urban Growth, 1820–2000.* New York: Vintage, 2004.

Jackle, John A., and Keith A. Sculle. *Lots of Parking: Land Use in a Car Culture.* Charlottesville: University of Virginia Press, 2004.

Jackson, Kenneth T. *Crabgrass Frontier: The Suburbanization of the United States.* New York: Oxford University Press, 1985.

Jacobs, Jane. *The Death and Life of Great American Cities.* New York: Vintage, 1961. Reprint 1992.

McCarthy, Tom. *Auto Mania: Cars, Consumers, and the Environment.* New Haven, CT: Yale University Press, 2007.

McShane, Clay. *Down the Asphalt Path: The Automobile and the American City.* New York: Columbia University Press, 1994.

McShane, Clay, and Joel Tarr. *The Horse in the City: Living Machines in the Nineteenth Century.* Baltimore: Johns Hopkins University Press, 2007.

Melosi, Martin V. "The Automobile Shapes the City." *Automobile in American Life and Society,* 2018. http://www.autolife.umd.umich.edu/Environment/E_Casestudy/E_casestudy1.htm.

Mom, Gijs. *Electric Vehicle: Technology and Expectations in the Automobile Age.* Baltimore: Johns Hopkins University Press, 2004.

Norton, Peter D. *Fighting Traffic: The Dawn of the Motor Age in the American City.* Cambridge, MA: MIT Press, 2008.

Rae, John B. *The Road and Car in American Life.* Cambridge, MA: MIT Press, 1971.

Wells, Christopher W. *Car Country: An Environmental History.* Seattle: University of Washington Press, 2012.

NOTES

1. This article will use specific job titles when appropriate to clarify the shifting power relations among the professions. Elsewhere, the idea of transit planners is treated generically to include everyone working to revise or reform street and highway usage to best suit contemporary and anticipated conditions. For a discussion of the various forms of planners affecting automotive transit, see Joseph F. C. DiMento and Cliff Ellis, *Changing Lanes: Visions and Histories of Urban Freeways* (Cambridge, MA: MIT Press, 2013), xi–10. James J. Flink, "Three Stages of American Automobile Consciousness," *American Quarterly* 4, no. 4 (1972), 457.

2. US Census Bureau, Statistical Abstract of the United States: 2003 (No. HS-41, Transportation Indicators for Motor Vehicles and Airlines, 1900 to 2001), 77–78, https://www2.census.gov/library/publications/2004/compendia/statab/123ed/hist/hs-41.pdf.

3. Christopher W. Wells, *Car Country: An Environmental History* (Seattle: University of Washington Press, 2012), xxx–xxxi.

4. For examples of how transit flow influences street design, see Jonathan Barrett, *Redesigning Cities: Principles, Practice, Implementation* (Chicago: American Planning Association, 2003); and Galina Tachieva, *The Sprawl Repair Manual* (Washington: Island Press, 2010).

5. For two noteworthy examples of "rational behavior" planning, see Miller McClintock, *Report and Recommendations of the Metropolitan Street Survey* (Chicago: Chicago Association of Commerce, 1926); and William Phelps Eno, *Fundamentals of Highway Traffic Regulation* (Washington: Eno Foundation for Highway Traffic Regulation, 1926).

6. Clay McShane, *Down the Asphalt Path: The Automobile and the American City* (New York: Columbia University Press, 1994), 147–148. For a complete account of the cultural expression comprising the early automotive "love affair" and its role in the rising accident crisis, see David Blanke, *Hell on Wheels: The Promise and Peril of America's Car Culture, 1900–1940* (Lawrence: University Press of Kansas, 2007), 63–89.

7. Kenneth T. Jackson, *Crabgrass Frontier: The Suburbanization of the United States* (New York: Oxford University Press, 1985), 14–20. See also Elizabeth Blackmar, "Re-Walking the 'Walking City': Housing and Property Relations in New York City, 1780–1840," *Radical History Review* 21 (Fall 1979): 131–148; Patricia Mooney-Melvin, "The Neighborhood-City Relationship," in *American Urbanism: A Historiographical Review,* ed. Zane Miller and Howard Gillette (New York: Praeger, 1987), 257–270; and Thomas W. Hanchett, *Sorting Out the New South City: Race, Class, and Urban Development in Charlotte, 1875–1975* (Chapel Hill: University of North Carolina Press, 1998).

8. The foundational work remains Sam Bass Warner Jr., *Streetcar Suburbs: The Process of Growth in Boston, 1870–1900* (Cambridge, MA: Harvard University Press, 1962). For the ways that the streetcar influenced later urban transit design, see Mark S. Foster, *From Streetcar to Superhighway: American City Planners and Urban Transportation, 1900–1940* (Philadelphia: Temple University Press, 1981); Paul Barrett, *The Automobile and Urban Transit: The Formation of Public Policy in Chicago, 1900–1930* (Philadelphia: Temple University Press, 1983); Peter C. Baldwin, *Domesticating the Streets: The Reform of Public Space in Hartford, 1850–1930* (Columbus: Ohio State University Press, 1999); Clay McShane and Joel Tarr, *The Horse in the City: Living Machines in the Nineteenth Century* (Baltimore: Johns Hopkins University Press, 2007); and Robert C. Post, *Urban Mass Transit: The Life Story of a Technology* (Westport, CT: Greenwood, 2007).

9. Foster, *From Streetcar to Superhighway*, 16–23. For Philadelphia, quoting Charles W. Cheape, *Moving the Masses: Urban Public Transit in New York, Boston, and Philadelphia, 1880–1912* (Cambridge, MA: Harvard University Press, 1980), 177.

10. James J. Flink, *The Automobile Age* (Cambridge, MA: MIT Press, 2001), 6. Evan Friss, *The Cycling City: Bicycles and Urban America in the 1890s* (Chicago: University of Chicago Press, 2015), 3, 9. See also David Herlihy, *Bicycle: The History* (New Haven, CT: Yale University Press, 2004); Zach Furness, *One Less Car: Bicycling and the Politics of Automobility* (Philadelphia: Temple University Press, 2010); and Lorenz J. Finison, *Boston's Cycling Craze, 1880–1900: A Story of Race, Sport, and Society* (Amherst: University of Massachusetts Press, 2014).

11. Flink, *The Automobile Age*, 27–40.

12. Rudi Volti, *Cars and Culture: The Life Story of a Technology* (Westport, CT: Greenwood, 2004), 7–14.

13. US Census Bureau, *Statistical Abstract of the United States: 2003* (No. HS-41, Transportation Indicators for Motor Vehicles and Airlines, 1900 to 2001); US Bureau of the Census, *Historical Statistics of the United States, Colonial Times to 1957* (Washington, DC, 1960), 462.

14. Joseph F. C. DiMento and Cliff Ellis, *Changing Lanes: Visions and Histories of Urban Freeways* (Cambridge, MA: MIT Press, 2013), 1–20. This text serves as an essential starting point for those

interested in the subtle shifts in power and authority of transit planners throughout the 20th century.

15. John B. Rae, *The Road and Car in American Life* (Cambridge, MA: MIT Press, 1971), 32. Wells, *Car Country*, 8. Assessing the effect of two major highways traversing through the heart of Syracuse, New York, and displacing numerous neighborhoods, DiMento and Ellis, concluded that future residents "paid a steep price in quality of life for this experiment in urban reconstruction." DiMento and Ellis, *Changing Lanes*, 65, 211.

16. Foster, *From Streetcars to Superhighways*, 44.

17. For a concise summary and useful timeline of "Major Urban Freeway Decision-Making Events," see DiMento and Ellis, *Changing Lanes*, 133–142.

18. For Moses's complex and controversial career, see Robert Caro, *The Power Broker: Robert Moses and the Fall of New York* (New York: Alfred A. Knopf, 1974); and DiMento and Ellis, *Changing Lanes*, 38–41.

19. DiMento and Ellis, *Changing Lanes*, 68.

20. DiMento and Ellis, *Changing Lanes*, 38–41, 55, 68, 76–78, 103–104. For Herrold see Alan Altshuler, *The City Planning Process: A Political Analysis* (Ithaca, NY: Cornell University Press, 1965), 52–57. Lewis Mumford, "The Highways and the City," *Architectural Record* 123 (April 1958): 179–182; and Mumford, *The Highway and the City* (New York: Harcourt, Brace, and World, 1963), 244–248.

21. Flink, *The Automobile Age*, 277–278.

22. For Ford's campaign, see Tom McCarthy, *Auto Mania: Cars, Consumers, and the Environment* (New Haven, CT: Yale University Press, 2007), 148–149.

23. Melosi, "Automobile in American Life and Society," 2018. See also John A. Jackle and Keith A. Sculle, *Lots of Parking: Land Use in a Car Culture* (Charlottesville: University of Virginia Press, 2004).

24. Wells, *Car Country*, 262–269.

25. For the problems of physical waste linked to the automobile, see David B. Lucsko, *Junkyards, Gearheads, and Rust: Salvaging the Automotive Past* (Baltimore: Johns Hopkins University Press, 2016). Landron quoted in Kyle Shelton, *Power Moves: Transportation, Politics, and Development in Houston* (Austin: University of Texas Press, 2017), 107.

26. Volti, *Cars and Culture*, 120.

27. Volti, *Cars and Culture*, 116–119.

28. Jane Jacobs, *The Death and Life of Great American Cities* (New York: Vintage, 1992), 351. Keats quoted in Flink, *The Automobile Age*, 281.

29. An example of American's unwillingness to accept the problems caused by modern automotive dependency is seen in Holtz, *Asphalt Nation*. She concludes the book's introduction with a distillation of these sentiments: "A nation in gridlock for its auto-bred lifestyle, an environment choking from its auto exhausts, a landscape sacked by its highways has distressed Americans so much that even this go-for-it nation is posting 'No Growth' signs on development from shore to shore." Jane Holtz Kay, *Asphalt Nation: How the Automobile Took Over America and How We Can Take It Back* (Berkeley: University of California Press, 1997), 9.

30. Edward Relph, *The Modern Urban Landscape* (Baltimore: Johns Hopkins University Press, 1987), 229.

31. Nan Ellin, *Postmodern Urbanism* (Princeton, NJ: Princeton University Press, 1996), 67.

32. Ulrich Beck, *Risk Society: Towards a New Modernity* (London: SAGE, 1992), 49.

33. Garreau defines an "edge city" as possessing at least 5 million square feet of office space and 600,000 square feet of retail space, as being an employment location rather than a residential location, as being perceived as a separate place in itself, and as having been once wholly residential or rural as recently as thirty years ago; see Joel Garreau, *Edge City: Life on the New Frontier* (New York: Doubleday, 1991), 425. As part of a widespread reassessment of urban form, often associated with the "Los Angeles School of Urbanism," recent scholars have significantly qualified Garreau's observations. For example, see Robert Fishman, *Bourgeois Utopias: The Rise and Fall of Suburbia* (New York: Basic Books, 1987); John R. Stilgoe, *Borderland: Origins of the American Suburb, 1820–1939* (New Haven, CT: Yale University Press, 1988); Jon Teaford, *Post-Suburbia: Government and Politics in the Edge Cities* (Baltimore: Johns Hopkins University Press, 1997); William T. Bogart, *Don't Call It Sprawl: Metropolitan Structure in the 21st Century* (New York: Cambridge University Press, 2006); Michael Dear and Nicholas Dahmann, "Urban Politics and the Los Angeles School of Urbanism," *Urban Affairs Review*, 44, no. 2 (November 2008): 266–279; Robert E. Lang, Thomas W. Sanchez, and Asli Ceylan Oner, "Beyond Edge City: Office Geography in the New Metropolis," *Urban Geography* 30, no. 7 (October 2009): 726–755; and Nicholas A. Phelps, Andrew M. Wood, David C. Valler, "A Postsuburban World? An Outline of a Research Agenda," *Economy and Space*, 42, no. 2 (February 2010): 366–383.

34. For a list of such projects, see DiMento and Ellis, *Changing Lanes*, 220–229.

35. Volti, *Cars and Culture*, 149–153.

36. McCarthy, *Auto Mania*, 239–243; and Volti, *Cars and Culture*, 143–145.

37. DiMento and Ellis, *Changing Lanes*, 230.

38. John B. Rae, *The American Automobile Industry* (Boston: Twayne, 1984); and James J. Flink, *America Adopts the Automobile, 1895–1910* (Cambridge, MA: MIT Press, 1970).

39. David A. Kirsch, *The Electric Vehicle and the Burden of History* (New Brunswick, NJ: Rutgers University Press, 2000); and Gijs Mom, *Electric Vehicle: Technology and Expectations in the Automobile Age* (Baltimore: Johns Hopkins University Press, 2004).

40. Paul Barrett, *The Automobile and Urban Transit: The Formation of Public Policy in Chicago, 1900–1930* (Philadelphia: Temple University Press, 1983); Peter Derrick, *Tunneling to the Future: The Story of the Great Suburban Expansion That Saved New York* (New York: New York University Press, 2001); and Kyle Shelton, *Power Moves: Transportation, Politics, and Development in Houston* (Austin: University of Texas Press, 2017).

41. Bruce E. Seely, *Building The American Highway System: Engineers as Policy Makers* (Philadelphia: Temple University Press, 1987); Tom Lewis, *Divided Highways: Building the Interstate Highways, Transforming American Life* (New York: Penguin, 1997); and Raymond A. Mohl, *The Interstates and the Cities: Highways, Housing, and the Freeway Revolt* (Washington, DC: Poverty and Race Research Action Council, 2002). See also numerous essays by Mohl in the *Journal of Urban History*.

42. Dolores Hayden, *Building Suburbia: Green Fields and Urban Growth, 1820–2000* (New York: Vintage, 2004); Peter D. Norton, *Fighting Traffic: The Dawn of the Motor Age in the American City* (Cambridge, MA: MIT Press, 2008); Jon Teaford, *Post-Suburbia: Government and Politics in the Edge Cities* (Baltimore: Johns Hopkins University Press, 1997); and Bogart, *Don't Call It Sprawl*.

43. Warren J. Belasco, *Americans on the Road: From Autocamp to Motel: 1910–1945* (Cambridge, MA: MIT Press, 1979). For a sample of their diverse catalog, see John A. Jackle and Keith A. Sculle, *Lots of Parking: Land Use in a Car Culture* (Charlottesville: University of Virginia Press, 2004).

44. Virginia Scharff, *Taking the Wheel: Women and the Coming of the Motor Age* (New York: Free Press, 1991); Andrew Weise, *Places of Their Own: African American Suburbanization in the Twentieth Century* (Chicago: University of Chicago Press, 2004); and Georgine Clarson, *Eat My Dust: Early Women Motorists* (Baltimore: Johns Hopkins University Press, 2008).

45. Brian Ladd, *Autophobia: Love and Hate in the Automotive Age* (Chicago: University of Chicago Press, 2008).

46. Cotton Seiler, *Republic of Drivers: A Cultural History of Automobility in America* (Chicago: University of Chicago Press, 2008).

47. Martin Melosi, *Coping With Abundance: Energy and Environment in Industrial America* (Philadelphia: Temple University Press, 1984); and Martin Melosi, *The Sanitary City: Urban Infrastructure in America from Colonial Times to the Present* (Baltimore: Johns Hopkins University Press, 2000).

David Blanke

PUBLIC SPACE IN AMERICAN CITIES

STREETS AND SIDEWALKS

The street is the most fundamental public space of the city, a space of circulation, commerce, politics, and sociability open to all. The "man in the street" is a metaphor for a member of the public; the street is also where residents perform as a collective through celebratory parades and political marches. The streets of North American cities were repeatedly remade and reimagined to accommodate changing understandings of the urban public and the appropriate uses and users of the space of the street. The street was often made up of two distinct spaces—the street itself, focused in large part on circulation by horse, cart, and eventually car and streetcar, and the sidewalk, a more ambiguous space that was and remains variably defined as a space of commerce, sociability, and pedestrian movement.

By the first part of the 19th century the major streets in large North American cities had curbs and either gravel or wooden sidewalks that separated the muddy and crowded space of the street and vehicles from a raised and often gaslit sidewalk space for pedestrians and commerce. Over the course of the century, sidewalks were increasingly constructed with permanent materials, with cement becoming common by the 1890s and concrete by the 1910s.[1] Sidewalks were often cleaner and less crowded than the streets, which in the first part of the 19th century were congested, unpaved, muddy, and full of human and animal refuse.[2] The growth of urban population and commerce in the later 19th century only increased the number of horses and people using dirty streets. New understandings of disease led to new sewage and drainage systems and improved the cleanliness of streets. However, only after bicycles and automobiles became common in the early 20th century were streets regularly paved. As automobiles and electric streetcars gradually replaced horse-drawn vehicles, the problem of horse dung was eradicated. With increased traffic, automobiles, and the growth of modernist ideas about the specialized use of space in the 20th century, streets were increasingly designed and managed purely as spaces of vehicular movement, rather than as spaces of a more varied public interaction, including commerce and play.

In the 19th century improvements in both streets and sidewalks were typically paid for not by the municipality, but rather by abutting property owners. Sidewalks especially were seen not primarily as a public good, but rather as a means of increasing the value of a property. Because there were multiple business owners on any given block, the improvement of street and sidewalk paving and the installation of sidewalks were typically overseen by city government, although segments were sometimes built individually by property owners. Often property owners petitioned the government and arranged for the physical improvements at their own expense. In the early 20th century, with the growing use of automobiles and concerns with health and safety tied to urban infrastructure, streets gradually became a municipal concern; paving, drainage, and maintenance was increasingly organized and paid for through local government. While sidewalks were also seen as a city concern, their uses were increasingly subject to regulation. Nevertheless, in many cities cleaning and clearing the sidewalks remained the duty of the abutting landowners, reflecting the continuing power of the idea of the sidewalk as a benefit to individuals rather than purely a public good.[3]

STREETS AND SIDEWALKS AS COMMERCIAL SPACE

Sidewalks were claimed as an extension of the interior space of shops and stores by the shopkeepers who paid for such physical improvements. However, this was in conflict with city officials and other forces of order, who saw the goods displayed on sidewalks as clutter that inhibited movement and also interpreted shopkeepers' use of the sidewalk as an inappropriate taking of public space. Shopkeepers, in turn, were frustrated by the use of the streets and sidewalks by street peddlers, who made commercial use of the streets and sidewalks without having paid for them and whose activities restricted shopkeepers' access to potential customers. Between the commercial activities of abutting landowners and street peddlers, narrow streets and sidewalks in major cities like New York were often blocked by goods, carts making deliveries, signage, construction, and any number of street entrepreneurs. In response, many cities passed ordinances in the late 19th century to control the commercial use of streets and sidewalks, as well as

used vagrancy laws and restricted licenses to attempt to control and remove peddlers. Cities also passed statutes to curtail the perceived visual clutter of commercial signage, in part because of a belief that the spatial and visual disorder of commercial streets threatened the sense of order necessary to maintain civilized behavior. Rules controlling the nature of the commercial use of streets and sidewalks and who could use them have rarely been entirely successful, however. Historian Elizabeth Blackmar argues that peddlers' continued use of the streets and sidewalks as commercial space in the 19th century constituted a claim of common property, a demand for the right to make a living in public space, one that was echoed in the late 20th century by the New York City sidewalk book vendors discussed by anthropologist Mitchell Duneier.[4]

The rise of commercial downtowns in the late 19th century was characterized by the spatial agglomeration of spaces for new managerial and white-collar work and new forms of mass consumption and amusement. Popular theaters, eating places, and most notably department stores selling ready-made clothing and other household goods were available to a growing consumer public. Downtown shopping districts typically coalesced around several blocks of a main street, such as State Street in Chicago, Broadway in New York, and Market Street in San Francisco. The wide sidewalks of these main streets were lined with commercial show windows tempting window shoppers. Shopping districts were typically next to and even overlapping with office districts and centered on a central street well-served by public transportation. Such districts attracted both male and female pedestrians, workers and shoppers alike. To some, they served as symbols of democratic cosmopolitanism, places where the varied classes and races of the city came together. However, this cosmopolitanism was often more symbolic than real. The shops along downtown main streets were typically aimed exclusively at a middle-class and elite white, native-born female shopper.

Different times of day saw main street dominated by different groups, with office workers in the morning, shopping women midday, and workers promenading and window shopping in the evening.[5]

Beginning in the 1890s the downtown sidewalk became a focus of beautification efforts aimed at strengthening both civic pride and the urban economy. Women's clubs took up the cause of cleaning and beautifying the sidewalks of the downtown under the banner of "municipal housekeeping," arguing that their improvements lifted the civic morality of the whole community through their shared stewardship of the public realm. By the 1910s businessmen's associations, professional planners, and city officials also advocated improving the beauty and order of main streets through improved pavement, street furniture, zoning, and a host of regulations on signage and the uses of the sidewalk.[6] The push to keep main streets appealing through beautification continued well into the 1930s, when the US government's response to the pressures on downtown retail districts from the Great Depression (1929–1939) and the growth of suburban shopping strips included New Deal funding for the modernization of main street store facades.[7]

Suburbanization after 1950, tied in part to the expansion of inner-city African American populations during and after World War II and associated "white flight," caused an enormous anxiety among urban boosters about the fate of the downtown. Suburban shopping malls, many with branches of downtown department stores, were significant competition for the white middle-class female shoppers whom downtown planners saw as most important. Strategies to attempt to strengthen the downtown included a new wave of beautification and facade renovation, as well as urban renewal projects that destroyed nearby "blighted" areas, intending to make the downtown more orderly and create new parking spaces. Urban renewal also targeted many neighborhood main streets in poor and black neighborhoods, particularly those adjacent to the downtown.[8] In the early 1960s,

African American civil rights activists demanded the right to be treated as equal consumers on main street, picketing segregated and racist shops and demanding counter service at downtown lunch counters. The violence of white resistance to these moves toward integration and the urban riots of the late 1960s further stressed downtown main streets by marking them as "dangerous" and "violent" rather than family-friendly shopping destinations.[9]

Main streets were remade again in the final quarter of the 20th century to appeal to shoppers and leisure seekers bored or unhappy with suburban conformity. Beginning in the late 1950s, and becoming common in the 1970s, the pedestrianization of main streets aimed in part to make the experience of shopping downtown more like the experience in a shopping mall. Pedestrianized main streets replaced traffic lanes with landscaped areas that included seating to encourage lingering, hoping to create a pleasant destination for shopping as leisure. Unlike suburban malls, pedestrianized downtown main streets also appealed to nostalgia, learning from festival marketplaces such as Faneuil Hall in Boston, South Street Seaport in New York, and Ghirardelli Square in San Francisco, which used historical quaintness and a focus on experience as the basis of their appeal.[10] Unlike the shopping malls they evoked, pedestrianized main streets also remained public, unable to restrict speech, uses, and users. Less successful main streets (particularly in smaller cities) were often reclaimed by the growing homeless population of the 1980s.

In the late 20th century, with the gentrification of larger cities, a new affluent and largely white population breathed a new life into many neighborhood main streets, where a cleaned up streetscape, historical touches, and plentiful eateries provided a safe urban experience. Older main streets were imitated in shopping malls and New Urbanist developments, and many already existing local and downtown main streets were renovated to match their simulacra. Some shopping streets like Chicago's

"Magnificent Mile" of North Michigan Avenue were reinvigorated by the addition of urban vertical shopping malls beginning in the mid-1970s, which brought mall shoppers downtown. Both urban malls and the renovation of main streets worked to create a safe, elite shopping experience that capitalized on history and revitalized the street and sidewalk as a public space, but defined the public as leisurely consumers.

STREETS AND SIDEWALKS AS SOCIAL SPACE

Streets and sidewalks were a primary space of urban sociability in the early 19th century. Unlike the masculine commercial public haunts of restaurants, theaters, and coffee shops, selected streets and sidewalks were open to and appropriate for respectable women as well as men as a place to take exercise, meet both old and new acquaintances, and show off stylish clothing and carriages, although only at particular times and when following strict rules of conduct. Streets such as the Battery in New York City and the Levee in New Orleans, as well as the streets of elite neighborhoods, were frequented by members of polite society, who scrupulously followed formal codes of propriety. However, even these select streets and sidewalks were never purely spaces of elite sociability; they were also peopled by a wide range of the populace and were a center of commerce of all sorts, from peddling to polite recreation. Elite promenaders were often accosted by cabbies, street peddlers, and beggars. Sometimes the pavement was taken over by working-class men. The commerce, tobacco smoke, and presence of common people, many of whom ignored polite rules on the treatment of elite women, resulted in social elites choosing to largely abandon mixed streets as promenade grounds. They moved instead first to newly redesigned and highly regulated park-like squares, then in the 1850s and after to picturesque parks and to the commercial spaces of newly genteel public amusements.[11]

Even as the streets and sidewalks became less central to the lives of elites, they nevertheless continued as spaces of sociability for a larger public. Major streets in increasingly segregated working-class neighborhoods assumed greater importance. For example, the Bowery was the "main street" for working-class New Yorkers in the 19th century. By the 1840s, the street was the haunt of "Bowery B'hoys" and "Bowery Gals," working-class young people with their own flashy styles. The Bowery was home to horse races, fights, and young men and women promenading, showing off their distinctive bright and colorful clothing and walking with a swagger. While the rules of decorum for the middle class and elite required women to wear dull colors and generally make themselves as invisible as possible, Bowery Gals wore vivid and bright colors with elaborate hats without veils, emphasizing their bare faces and freedom of vision.[12]

Taking possession of the streets and sidewalks served as a way of asserting one's rights and presence as a member of the public. Promenading, whether by elites or by working-class youths, was a mode of asserting possession of public spaces, as well as a pleasurable pastime. Parades, public celebrations, protests, and riots were more explicit means of taking possession of the city through its streets. The particular nature of the street as public space made it the prime site of these symbolic actions. The street was a neutral or common ground, a shared space more fully public than any other space in the city. Historian Dell Upton argues therefore "that any ritual that took place there was an image of a unified citizenry and its values."[13] The unified citizenry was embodied not only by the people marching in a parade, but also by the spectators, or in the case of public celebrations like the raucous New Year's Eve celebrations on Market Street in San Francisco and Times Square in New York City, by all of the celebrants. Nineteenth- and early-20th-century parades typically featured mostly white men, representing well-organized groups such as trade unions, ethnic fraternal organizations, and voluntary societies, but the spectators and celebrants included women and nonwhites.[14]

In addition to large, official parades, which performed the city and the nation on the main streets of the city, smaller parades were organized by political parties, occupational groups, and ethnic and racial organizations. Smaller parades often parodied the elite official parades, implicitly or explicitly critiquing the image of the public they embodied. Through their physical presence on the streets and the noise and commotion of their parades, working-class and African American paraders in the 19th century made a claim to their membership in the public. In the 20th century, Gay Pride parades, beginning in 1970 in Chicago, Los Angeles, and New York, similarly took over the streets of cities to argue for the social and political rights of LGBTQ members of the public and to assert their presence within the city.[15]

Parades and public celebrations not only made use of the street, but they also remade it. In preparation for a parade, streets were often decorated and (by the early 20th century) lit. During the parade, no ordinary uses of the street were possible—traffic of all sorts was replaced by walkers moving at a slow pace; the sidewalks filled with spectators, blocking both through pedestrian traffic and the regular activities of commerce. By remaking a street in a performance of the polity, parades re-inscribed the importance of the street as a public space and particularly of the downtown main street as the symbolic heart of its city.

PUBLIC SQUARES

The public square is a common urban public space in North American cities, although the origins of these squares lie in differing urban traditions. The many Spanish settlements in North America followed the Law of the Indies plan, in which both government and church buildings sat on a central square. Some French settlements, such as New Orleans, adopted a similar planning tradition. Other French settlements like Quebec and fort settlements

like Detroit were based on fortress architecture and engineering conceived in France. Pennsylvania towns were influenced by William Penn's design for Philadelphia, which in turn mimicked the residential squares of London. New England town "commons," typically part of the original meetinghouse lot, reflected the "commonwealth" ideals of 17th-century Puritan settlers in which community members shared grazing land "in common." In the early 19th century this often disorderly public space was made over into a more formal cleared, grassy landscaped common, often used as a training green for the militia. Each of these models then influenced the founding of new cities and towns as populations spread westward.[16]

Important buildings, especially town halls and courthouses, were built in the early 19th century facing or within town squares, which served as a symbolic center for the city and a location for municipal celebrations, including the parading of the military. By the 1830s, town squares in major cities were transformed through fencing and landscaping into civilian recreation sites rather than spaces for military parades and other civic celebrations. Bowling Green in New York City, Washington Square in Philadelphia, and similar public squares were planted with rows of trees along gravel walks intended for genteel promenading, while new regulations banned working-class activities including lying on the grass, climbing trees, smoking, and bringing in carts or wheelbarrows. In poorer neighborhoods, areas of undeveloped land such as Congo Square in New Orleans were used as gathering spaces for commerce and recreation. In more elite neighborhoods, a network of squares designed after 1820 were intended for genteel recreational use. Some, like New York's Gramercy Park (1831–1832), were not open to the public, and accessible only to abutting homeowners.[17]

As cities grew rapidly after the Civil War (1861–1865), old central city squares were increasingly marginal to the city. Many were neglected as elites spent their leisure time in new picturesque parks, shopping on downtown main streets, and with new commercial amusements.[18] Some squares, such as Union Square in San Francisco and Copley Square in Boston, remained popular because of their proximity to shopping districts. In order to try to keep them lively and fitting symbols of their cities, downtown squares throughout America were redesigned repeatedly, particularly during the heyday of the City Beautiful movement in the early 20th century. New squares such as City Hall Plaza in Boston and Embarcadero Plaza (formerly Justin Herman Plaza) in San Francisco were also created in many cities as part of urban renewal in the 1960s and 1970s. Both new and old downtown squares have largely remained marginal in the 20th century. By the 1980s and 1990s, they were more often used as homeless encampments than as lively public parks. However, the civic history of public squares, particularly those adjacent to city halls, meant that they have a political salience that was repeatedly demonstrated when used for protests and political speech. Both the suffragists who used San Francisco's Union Square as the site of a rally in 1911 and the white anti-busing activists who rallied on Boston's City Hall Plaza in the mid-1970s chose these squares because of their importance to the image of the city.[19]

PICTURESQUE PARKS

In the second half of the 19th century, city officials across North America created large, picturesque parks. These parks provided immense new public spaces in cities and were expressive of a new interest in spaces that served the public as a collectivity. Unlike public squares and streets, parks did not directly serve private economic purposes; rather, these parks were envisioned as noncommercial—even anticommercial—spaces. The public use of these large parks and the structuring of activities within them excluded many previously accepted public activities, including politics, commerce, and various class-specific behaviors.

The first and grandest of North American urban parks was the 843-acre Central Park in New York City, designed by Frederick Law Olmsted and Calvert Vaux in 1858. Central Park was built on a site at the northern edge of the built-up area of Manhattan, in a rocky, largely treeless area occupied by villages of free blacks and Irish immigrants. The site required significant reworking and planting to be turned into an urban park, inspired in part by earlier parks in France and England. Central Park encompassed a variety of areas, from the wooded wilderness of the Ramble, to bucolic fields like the Sheep Meadow, to the Central Park Mall, a formal allée leading to Bethesda Fountain. The location distant from the densest part of the city not only provided affordable land, but also had significant social and economic effects. The presence of the park created new desirable real estate along its edges, helping to boost the development of expensive new housing.

Other major urban parks were typically sited on undesirable land at the edges of urban growth. For example, Chicago's Lincoln Park was created in 1860 on land next to the city's burial grounds to the north of the city. The park was later expanded to include the same burial grounds and other nearby areas. Jackson Park on Chicago's South Side was constructed on marshy land prone to flooding. Similarly, in 1871, San Francisco's Golden Gate Park was founded on top of sand dunes in an area west of the city known as the "Outside Lands." The creation of a picturesque wooded park in the western portion of the San Francisco peninsula fueled development in the Richmond District to Golden Gate Park's north and the Sunset District to the south, just as other parks throughout North America gave new real estate value to underdeveloped land at the borders of previous urban growth.

Picturesque parks expressed a rural ideal. They were conceptualized as antidotes to the evils of the city. In the context of rapid urban growth and industrialization, such parks were designed to re-create the experience of nature separate from the city around them, reflecting the transcendentalist idealization of the contemplation of nature as a spiritual experience.

They were designed in the picturesque tradition, in which asymmetrical and varied landscape plantings created a pleasant, surprising experience that sat between the awesome terrors of the sublime and the gentle calmness of the beautiful. Picturesque parks included areas of designed wilderness, like the Ramble in Central Park, and large bucolic fields sheltered from the city by plantings of trees, which created an opportunity for visitors to experience an explicitly nonurban space, with curving paths and asymmetrical greenery that contrasted sharply with the rational grid, pavement, and hard surfaces of the city beyond.

The types of activities allowed in Central Park and other picturesque parks were carefully controlled. As these parks functioned as antidotes to the city, certain aspects of urban life, including commercial activity, politics, alcohol, and working-class amusements, were prohibited. In an era when ads were posted on every fence and wall, advertising was banned entirely within the parks. Not only were commercial signs banned, but even noncommercial signs announcing the activities of athletic associations were banned in San Francisco's Golden Gate Park. Similarly, the park served as an escape from commercial activity, such as the public markets that commonly filled public squares. Early regulations for Central Park banned gambling, gaming, fortune-telling, hawking, peddling, and any unlicensed commercial activity. An exception was sometimes made for a limited number of commercial services that served park visitors, such as restaurants.[20]

The boosters of large parks described them as serving the public as a whole. In fact they were designed for and initially primarily used by the elite and middle classes. In the 1860s and 1870s, no more than 12 percent of the visitors to Central Park and 7 percent of visitors to Golden Gate Park were working class.[21] Parks were frequently located far from low-income or immigrant neighborhoods, making them difficult for poorer residents to visit because of both their limited leisure hours and the cost of transportation. In addition, working-class city dwellers often opted to spend their time and money at commercial amusements, where drinking, German bands, and other amusements banned within public parks were available.[22]

Large urban parks were initially created as naturalistic counterparts to the artificial city, but transformations in their design and use in the later 19th century and after expanded their uses and users. One significant modification was the addition of cultural institutions, particularly zoos and museums, within park grounds in the later 19th century. These increased visitorship to parks while also increasing the status of the city. For many cities, hosting a world's fair created an impetus to create or improve a large park and to add new institutions to it. Parks, fairs, and museums alike served as symbols of the importance of a city and tools for boosters who wanted to attract residents and businesses. Golden Gate Park (1871) hosted San Francisco's Midwinter Fair in 1896; Forest Park (1876) in St. Louis played host to the Louisiana Purchase Exposition in 1904; and Balboa Park (1868) in San Diego was the site of both the Panama-California Exposition in 1915–1916 and the California Pacific International Exposition in 1935–1936. Chicago's Jackson Park, designed by Olmsted and Vaux, was created specifically as the site of the World's Columbian Exposition in 1893. Each of these fairs left behind new institutions, including the Saint Louis Art Museum in the Palace of the Arts from the 1904 Fair in Forest Park; the De Young Museum in Golden Gate Park, originally housed in the Fine Arts Building from the 1896 Fair; the San Diego Zoo in Balboa Park, created from animal exhibitions in the 1915–1916 Fair; and Chicago's Museum of Science and Industry in the Fine Arts Building from the 1893 Columbian Exposition.

With changing ideas about the purposes of parks in the 20th century, parks were modified to allow a wider range of uses in addition to the new civic attractions. In Central Park, more playing fields and playgrounds created new spaces for activities that welcomed users from a broader range of classes, while new vendors facilitated picnicking and playing in the park. Festivals, group picnics, pageants, and other popular but noncommercial entertainments began to be permitted in the early 20th century. The population of park users shifted to become more inclusive as the nature of available activities changed, the city grew up around the park, and improved public transportation made parks more accessible. Even as Central Park and other large picturesque parks were adjusted to meet changing demands, their essential identity as naturalistic antidotes to the built-up city and as places of pleasure and contemplation set up against the commercialization of the city has remained constant.

Like other parts of major cities, picturesque parks were increasingly neglected in the post–World War II period. Older cities lost occupants and business to the suburbs and to sprawling Sun Belt cities. One response was to turn over many elements of parks, such as zoos and skating rinks, to private for-profit managements. Central Park was particularly badly hit by the combined stresses of its large size, a focus on programming rather than maintenance in the 1960s, and the fiscal crisis that left New York City nearly bankrupt in 1975. In 1980, much of the financing and administration of Central Park was handed over to the Central Park Conservancy, a private-public partnership dominated by corporate executives. The Conservancy raised funds and restored the park to great acclaim, but questions were later raised about both the public accountability of the Conservancy and its tendency to make decisions that favor the elites and surrounding property rather than the public as a whole.[23]

PLAYGROUNDS, NEIGHBORHOOD PARKS, AND PLAZAS

Picturesque parks in the 19th century served a largely middle-class and elite public as a nature-filled space conceived as an antidote to the city. As a result, by the early 20th century working-class urbanites were served by small neighborhood parks offering opportunities for organized play. The playground movement was started by female settlement house reformers seeking to provide children a healthy and educational alternative to the evils of the working-class street. By the 1890s playgrounds, often in public schoolyards or attached to settlement houses, were started by philanthropists in Chicago, New York, Boston, and other cities. By the early 20th century these same cities also built publicly funded small parks that included playgrounds.[24] These small parks were conceptualized as a significantly different kind of public space from either squares or large picturesque parks. While squares were sites of polite recreation, civic performance, and public action, including political speech, and picturesque parks were the home of civilized leisure and the enjoyment of nature, small neighborhood parks were educational, focused on orderly physical activity and education.

In the early 20th century neighborhood parks offered programmed activities including social dances, classes, gardening, and sporting competitions that were anathema to earlier promoters of picturesque parks. Neighborhood park administrators, however, also banned political assemblies, commercial amusements, and peddling. The focus on programmed activities declined in the 1930s, and was replaced with an emphasis on leisurely recreation.[25] This interest in recreation also characterized the next wave of park building both as part of the New Deal and after World War II. Many of these recreational parks were quite small and shared playground facilities with new public schools. Other larger parks provided public recreation facilities including swimming pools, beaches, and golf courses, while basketball courts and playgrounds were part of parks of all sizes.[26] Not only did these new ideas about the purposes of parks lead to the creation of new parks, they also affected the large picturesque parks. After 1930, many of them incorporated playgrounds, tennis courts, and other recreational spaces. By the 1960s, some even sponsored large public concerts.[27]

Park maintenance and use declined during the 1960s and 1970s. The postwar era had seen a gradual abandonment of cities by not only middle-class white residents, but also by their retail dollars, increasingly spent at suburban malls, and by their employers, many of whom moved to suburban office parks. The racial unrest and urban riots of the late 1960s exacerbated this trend, leaving many cities financially stretched, a situation that was made worse by decreasing federal funding for cities. Beginning in the late 1960s, vacant lots in some cities were transformed into "vest pocket parks," including playgrounds and adventure playgrounds in residential neighborhoods and tiny, mostly paved parks downtown serving workers and shoppers. In the late 1960s and 1970s in many cities, community activists sometimes took over abandoned lots and created gardens and other informal public spaces in neglected neighborhoods, including People's Park in Berkeley and the many community gardens of the Lower East Side in New York. The New York City community gardens were formalized in the late 1970s, but remained only semi-public, often requiring membership and a key to enter. Downtown, new public policies, notably the 1961 Zoning Resolution in New York City, created an incentive for the creation of new public spaces with private money. This resolution, which gave builders bonus floor space for the creation of a public plaza, resulted in a wave of new privately owned public spaces (POPS) in New York and in other cities that followed its lead. Under further financial pressure in the 1970s and 1980s, cities provided tax abatements and other incentives that accelerated the creation of POPS.[28]

Pocket parks, POPS, and other small parks in downtown cities, particularly New York, became the focus of the sociologist William Whyte's book and film *The Social Life of Small Urban Spaces* (1980). Whyte argued for a number of amenities, including food, moveable and plentiful seating, and water that could be touched, influencing the design and programming of these and later POPS and small parks.[29] White solidified an idea of these plazas and small parks as a place of leisure and collective amusement, without politics, conflict, or "undesirables." The corporate management and ownership of POPS reinforced this narrow definition of publicness, even as many cities turned increasingly to POPS and public-private conservancies to provide and improve public spaces in the late 20th century.[30]

DISCUSSION OF THE LITERATURE

Historians have taken a typological approach to the study of urban public space, focusing on one particular element of public space in the city and exploring it in depth. These works often deal only tangentially with the concept of the public, but provide enormous depth on how these public spaces in the city were conceptualized, shaped, managed, and experienced. Alison Isenberg's *Downtown America* examines main streets across the United States throughout the 20th century. Galen Cranz's *The Politics of Park Design* similarly explores American urban parks from the mid-19th century through 1980.[31] Other studies explore the semipublic realms of commercial public amusements and shopping spaces and deal tangentially with the public space of the street.[32] More commonly, historians have explored public space in one particular city as one element (often a single chapter) of a larger study, many of which focus on the experience of marginalized groups including the working classes, homosexuals, and women.[33] The majority of the works are on New York City, which has been studied significantly more than any other American city. The particularity of New York does raise questions about the extent to which one can generalize from their findings.

Since 1990, urban historians have focused more explicitly and critically on urban public space. The public sphere became a subject of increased academic interest in the early 1990s in the wake of the translation into English of

Jurgen Habermas's *The Structural Transformation of the Public Sphere*.[34] Michael Sorkin's collection *Variations on a Theme Park: The New American City and the End of Public Space* was among works that examined the perceived threats to public space and the public sphere from neoliberal policies and privatization of public space.[35] This broader discussion about both public space and the public sphere influenced urban historians including Mary Ryan, David Henkin, Jessica Sewell, and Dell Upton to critically explore the history of urban public space, its historical relationship with the public sphere, and the history of the idea of the public.[36]

PRIMARY SOURCES

A wide range of historical documents including newspapers, letters, diaries, and etiquette books, can be read for information on the experience of and debates about urban public spaces. Government records and laws can tell detailed stories of the process of creating and regulating specific public spaces. Guidebooks and historical travel accounts provide detailed descriptions of urban space and how it was understood. The American Guide Series created by the Federal Writers Project during the Great Depression is a particularly rich source for the late 1930s.

One of the most important sources is the physical spaces themselves. Historical prints, paintings, photographs, and postcards provide information about the nature of urban public spaces and how they were popularly portrayed. The Library of Congress has an extensive collection of photographs and postcards of American cities, and archives in city and university libraries and historical societies contain rich imagery of the cities where they are located.[37] Maps also provide essential information about urban public space in context. The Library of Congress has extensive collections of city maps, urban panoramas, and Sanborn Fire Insurance maps.[38] The Perry-Casteñeda Library Map Collection at the University of

Texas and the David Rumsey Collection also have many historical maps of American cities.[39]

FURTHER READING

Cranz, Galen. *The Politics of Park Design: A History of Urban Parks in America*. Cambridge, MA: MIT Press, 1982.

Davis, Susan G. *Parades and Power: Street Theater in Nineteenth-Century Philadelphia*. Philadelphia: Temple University Press, 1986.

Henkin, David. *City Reading: Written Words and Public Spaces in Antebellum New York*. New York: Columbia University Press, 1998.

Isenberg, Alison. *Downtown America: A History of the Place and the People Who Made It*. Chicago: University of Chicago Press, 2004.

Loukaitou-Sideris, Anastasia, and Renia Ehrenfeucht. *Sidewalks: Conflict and Negotiation over Public Space*. Cambridge, MA: MIT Press, 2009.

Mitchell, Don. *The Right to the City: Social Justice and the Fight for Public Space*. New York: Guilford Press, 2003.

Rosenzweig, Roy, and Elizabeth Blackmar. *The Park and the People: A History of Central Park*. Ithaca, NY: Cornell University Press, 1992.

Ryan, Mary. *Civic Wars: Democracy and Public Life in the American City during the Nineteenth Century*. Berkeley: University of California Press, 1998.

Scobey, David. *Empire City: The Making and Meaning of the New York City Landscape*. Philadelphia: Temple University Press, 2002.

Sewell, Jessica Ellen. *Women and the Everyday City: Public Space in San Francisco, 1890–1915*. Minneapolis: University of Minnesota Press, 2011.

Upton, Dell. *Another City: Urban Life and Urban Spaces in the New American Republic*. New Haven, CT: Yale University Press, 2008.

Zaitevsky, Cynthia. *Frederick Law Olmsted and the Boston Park System*. Cambridge, MA: Harvard University Press, 1982.

NOTES

1. Anastasia Loukaitou-Sideris and Renia Ehrenfeucht, *Sidewalks: Conflict and Negotiation over Public Space* (Cambridge, MA: MIT Press, 2009), 18.
2. Mary Ryan, *Civic Wars: Democracy and Public Life in the American City during the Nineteenth Century* (Berkeley: University of California Press, 1998),

40–41; and David Scobey, *Empire City: The Making and Meaning of the New York City Landscape* (Philadelphia: Temple University Press, 2002), 140.

3. Loukaitou-Sideris and Ehrenfeucht, *Sidewalks*, 18–20, 26–29. Elizabeth Blackmar, *Manhattan for Rent, 1785–1850* (Ithaca, NY, and London: Cornell University Press, 1989), 159.

4. Loukaitou-Sideris and Ehrenfeucht, *Sidewalks*, 23–25; Scobey, *Empire City*, 140–141, 148; David Henkin, *City Reading: Written Words and Public Spaces in Antebellum New York* (New York: Columbia University Press, 1998), 39–70; Blackmar, *Manhattan for Rent*, 171–172, 180; and Mitchell Duneier, *Sidewalk* (New York: Farrar, Straus and Giroux, 2000).

5. Jessica Ellen Sewell, *Women and the Everyday City: Public Space in San Francisco, 1890–1915* (Minneapolis: University of Minnesota Press, 2011), xii; and Alison Isenberg, *Downtown America: A History of the Place and the People Who Made It* (Chicago: University of Chicago Press, 2004), 5–6.

6. Isenberg, *Downtown America*, 13–77.

7. Gabrielle Esperdy, *Modernizing Main Street: Architecture and Consumer Culture in the New Deal* (Chicago: University of Chicago Press, 2008).

8. Isenberg, *Downtown America*, 166–202, 207.

9. Isenberg, *Downtown America*, 203–254.

10. Isenberg, *Downtown America*, 255–296.

11. Dell Upton, *Another City: Urban Life and Urban Spaces in the New American Republic* (New Haven, CT: Yale University Press, 2008), 322–333.

12. Christine Stansell, *City of Women: Sex and Class in New York, 1789–1860* (Urbana and Chicago: University of Illinois Press, 1986), 89–101.

13. Upton, *Another City*, 313.

14. Ryan, *Civic Wars*, 58–93; and Sewell, *Women and the Everyday City*, 115–126.

15. Upton, *Another City*, 315; and Katherine McFarland Bruce, *Pride Parades: How a Parade Changed the World* (New York: New York University Press, 2016).

16. John W. Reps, *The Making of Urban America: A History of City Planning in the United States* (Princeton, NJ: Princeton University Press, 1965); and Joseph S. Wood, *The New England Village* (Baltimore: Johns Hopkins University Press, 1997).

17. Ryan, *Civic Wars*, 26–35; Upton, *Another City*, 329–330; and Blackmar, *Manhattan for Rent*, 150–151, 160–167.

18. Ryan, *Civic Wars*, 198–202.

19. Sewell, *Women and the Everyday City*, 155.

20. Cranz, *Politics of Park Design*, 13–14, 21, 23; and Roy Rosenzweig and Elizabeth Blackmar, *The Park and the People: A History of Central Park* (Ithaca, NY: Cornell University Press, 1992), 243–246.

21. Rosenzweig and Blackmar, *The Park and the People*, 232; and Ryan, *Civic Wars*, 208–209.

22. Rosenzweig and Blackmar, *The Park and the People*, 233–237.

23. Rosenzweig and Blackmar, *The Park and the People*, 499–504, 507–525.

24. Cranz, *The Politics of Park Design*, 61–65; and Marta Gutman, *A City for Children: Women, Architecture, and the Charitable Landscapes of Oakland, 1850–1950* (Chicago: University of Chicago Press, 2014), 217–219.

25. Cranz, *The Politics of Park Design*, 68–78, 101–117.

26. Cranz, *The Politics of Park Design*, 119–123; and New York City Parks, "Robert Moses and the Modern Park System, 1929–1965."

27. Cranz, *The Politics of Park Design*, 138–142.

28. Rosenzweig and Blackmar, *The Park and the People*, 507–508; Cranz, *The Politics of Park Design*, 143–151; and New York City Parks, "History of the Community Garden Movement."

29. William Whyte, *The Social Life of Small Urban Spaces* (Washington, DC: Conservation Foundation, 1980).

30. Don Mitchell, "The End of Public Space? People's Park, Definitions of the Public, and Democracy," *Annals of the Association of American Geographers* 85, no. 1 (March 1995): 108–133.

31. Isenberg, *Downtown America*; and Cranz, *The Politics of Park Design*.

32. See, for example, Kathy Peiss, *Cheap Amusements: Working Women and Leisure in Turn-of-the-Century New York* (Philadelphia: Temple University Press, 1986); and David Nasaw, *Going Out: The Rise and Fall of Public Amusements* (New York: Basic Books, 1993).

33. See, for example, Stansell, *City of Women*; and George Chauncey, *Gay New York: Gender, Urban Culture, and the Making of the Gay Male World, 1890–1940* (New York: Basic Books, 1994).

34. Jurgen Habermas, *The Structural Transformation of the Public Sphere: An Inquiry into a Category of Bourgeois Society* (Cambridge, MA: MIT Press, 1989). Books inspired by Habermas include Craig Calhoun, ed., *Habermas and the Public Sphere* (Cambridge, MA: MIT Press, 1993), and Michael

Warner, *Publics and Counterpublics* (Brooklyn, NY: Zone Books, 2005).

35. Michael Sorkin, ed., *Variations on a Theme Park: The New American City and the End of Public Space* (New York: Hill and Wang, 1992).

36. Ryan, *Civic Wars*; Henkin, *City Reading*; Sewell, *Women and the Everyday City*; and Upton, *Another City.*

37. Library of Congress, "Prints and Photographs Online Catalog." Examples of collections for major cities include San Francisco Public Library, "San Francisco Historical Photograph Collection"; New York Heritage Digital Collections and Chicago History Museum Collection Online.

38. Library of Congress, "Cities and Towns" Library of Congress, "Panoramic Maps" and Library of Congress, "Sanborn Maps."

39. University of Texas Libraries, University of Texas at Austin, "Perry-Casteñeda Library Map Collection"; and David Rumsey Map Collection.

Jessica Sewell

Nature and the Environment

PARKS IN URBAN AMERICA

EARLY PARKS

William Penn's 1682 plan for Philadelphia reserved five squares as neighborhood breathing spaces, and James Oglethorpe's 1733 plan for Savannah established a ward system, with each neighborhood organized around a public square. Other urban spaces evolved from more prosaic uses to become parks: the Boston Common, for example, was originally a pasture for cows and became the location for military musters in the 18th century; only in the 19th century did it become a handsome park surrounded by four wide, planted malls for promenading. Similarly, the Battery, at the southern tip of Manhattan Island, started out as a fortification, but after the War of 1812, it became a

place of resort for the fashionable. Washington Square had been the city's potter's field from 1797 to 1826; in the following year, New York acquired the land and began its transformation for park use. Gramercy Park, located between 18th and 23rd Streets and Third Avenue and Park Avenue South, was created as (and remains) a private park owned by residents of buildings on nearby streets.[1]

The first urban park was undoubtedly Fairmount Gardens, in Philadelphia, created in 1812, when the city constructed its waterworks at the Schuylkill River. Originally a 5-acre tract surrounding the neoclassical buildings of the waterworks, the park proved so popular that by 1828 it had been enlarged to 24 acres. In the 1850s two large estates, Lemon Hill and Sedgley, were added to Fairmount, forming the nucleus of what became Fairmount Park.

In Brooklyn, Walt Whitman, then the editor of the *Daily Eagle*, championed the creation of Washington Park (the modern Fort Greene Park) in 1847, in what was a working-class neighborhood close to the Brooklyn Navy Yard, but it was apparently chosen as a park site because its hilly topography made it prohibitively expensive to grade into rectangular streets.[2]

The poet and editor William Cullen Bryant and the landscape gardener Andrew Jackson Downing became the most articulate spokespersons for a large public park for New York City. After visiting London in 1844, Bryant found the parks there essential to the "public health and happiness of the people" and expressed regret "that in laying out New York, no preparation was made, while it was yet practicable, for a range of parks and public gardens along the central part of the island." In his influential essay "The New-York Park," Downing dismissed the city's squares as woefully inadequate: "What have been called parks in New-York are not even apologies for the things; they are only squares, or paddocks." Numerous other Americans, especially after returning from London's Crystal Palace exhibition of 1851 or visits to other European capitals, echoed the pressing need for large parks in the nation's cities.[3]

The most important park plan undertaken prior to the construction of Central Park was Downing's design for the public grounds in Washington, DC. This area, extending west from the Capitol Grounds, to the site of the Washington Monument, and then north, to the President's House, was the centerpiece of Pierre Charles L'Enfant's 1791 plan for the new capital, but it was largely undeveloped in the first half of the 19th century. Indeed, one contemporary described it as "a large common... presenting a surface of yellow or white clay, cut into by deep gullies, and without trees except one or two scraggy and dying sycamores." Smithsonian Institution Secretary Joseph Henry and financier W. W. Corcoran convinced President Millard Fillmore to invite Downing "to examine the grounds and report a plan of improvement." Downing visited Washington in November 1850 and during the next two months worked on a plan that, he hoped, would transform the site into an extended landscape garden that would be an "ornament to the capital of the United States." Work began on Downing's plan in the spring of 1851, but his death in the burning of the Hudson River steamboat *Henry Clay*, in July 1852, halted development. Downing had hoped that the public grounds would become the first great urban park in the country and inspire other cities to create similar places of public resort and recreation, but the project remained incomplete and never proved as influential as he intended.[4]

CENTRAL PARK

Downing's advocacy of a large park for New York City, along with that of Bryant and others, convinced city leaders to begin the process of obtaining land and establishing a park. After a prolonged debate over whether the park should be in the Jones Wood section of Manhattan, along the East River, between 66th and 77th Streets, or in the central part of the island, New York City began acquiring the land for Central Park, in 1853. The park site extended from 59th Street to 106th Street and from Fifth to Eighth Avenues, an area of 778 acres (in 1863 it was extended to 110th Street, as Olmsted and Vaux urged, and reached its modern dimension of 843 acres). Mayor Fernando Wood and Street Commissioner Joseph S. Taylor, the first Central Park commissioners, hired engineer Egbert L. Viele and, in 1856, adopted a plan for the park he had prepared. However, in what Olmsted termed a "storm of reform," in 1857 the state legislature adopted a new city charter that replaced the Wood commission with the state-appointed Board of Commissioners of the Central Park. In one of their first acts, the new commissioners set aside Viele's plan and announced a public competition to determine the park's design. Thirty-three entries were submitted, and, on

April 28, 1858, the commissioners awarded first place to Olmsted and Vaux's Greensward plan. Olmsted, who had been the superintendent of labor under Viele, was named architect in chief and superintendent on May 17, 1858, and Vaux was named consulting architect.[5]

The site chosen for Central Park was distant from the built area of the city: the cost of Manhattan real estate precluded buying land for a large park in the densely built lower part of the island, and this would be true in other cities as they acquired land for parks throughout the remainder of the century. Still, the process of assembling land for park purposes was a visionary accomplishment, removing 9,792 standard 25 × 100 foot Manhattan building lots and reserving them for public use. Anticipating continued urban growth, Olmsted and Vaux recognized that within a generation "the town will have enclosed the Central Park." The land was acquired at the cost of $5,029,000.[6]

However, the park site—a largely treeless, scarred landscape—was anything but park-like. Olmsted described the site as "filthy, squalid and disgusting," and during his initial tour of the property, he was often knee-deep in mud. Major structures on the site included the Arsenal, near Fifth Avenue; the old, rectangular receiving reservoir of the Croton system; and the convent of the Sisters of Charity, at Mount St. Vincent. The new Croton receiving reservoir was under construction. A small community of African Americans and Irish immigrants, Seneca Village, stood on the park's west side, near 86th Street. As many as sixteen hundred people resided within the boundaries of the park. During the fall of 1857, workers demolished or removed three hundred dwellings as well as a number of factories to make way for improvements to the park.[7]

Central Park was a massive public works project. As many as thirty-eight hundred men were employed at the height of construction. Olmsted calculated that workers used 260 tons of gunpowder to blast rock on the site and handled 4,825,000 cubic yards of stone and earth, "or nearly ten million ordinary city one-horse cart-loads, which, in single file, would make a procession thirty thousand … miles in length"—that is, extending from New York to San Francisco and back again, five times. During construction, workers used more than 46,000 cubic yards of manure and compost to prepare the ground for planting approximately 270,000 trees and shrubs. The elm trees along the Mall, or Pedestrian Promenade, were dug up in the Bronx and carted to the park for replanting. Workers built miles of drives, walks, and bridle paths, and more than twenty bridges and underpasses, to create a complete separation of ways as well as a number of buildings to serve the visiting public. The cost of construction was enormous. The state legislation establishing the park had authorized spending a maximum of $1.5 million in building the park. By 1859, costs totaled $1,765,000, at which time only part of the lower park had been completed and opened to the public. In 1861 the legislature authorized an additional $2 million for construction, bringing the total amount appropriated for building the park to $4 million. By 1870, Olmsted estimated that constructing Central Park had cost New York City approximately $8.9 million.[8]

Building the park was so expensive because of the rockiness of the site and the transformations Olmsted and Vaux made in reshaping the landscape. Swampy lowlands were excavated to become lakes, and so much rock was carted off the site, and soil brought in, that Olmsted estimated a change in the grade of the park's 843 acres of 4 feet. The result of all that work—blasting, construction, soil preparation, and planting—proved to be a marvel to New Yorkers, who first encountered the finished parts of the lower park in 1859. Horace Greeley, for one, was pleased that the designers had preserved the existing landscape more than he anticipated. As is true of many visitors in the early 21st century, Greeley did not realize the degree to which Central Park is a humanly created landscape, one that, in its meadows, its picturesque areas, and its water, provides a welcome relief from the cityscape beyond its borders.[9]

Perhaps inevitably, the park was drawn into the maelstrom of city politics from its very inception. The Charter of 1857, which created the Board of Commissioners of the Central Park, was a patently undemocratic document that attempted to remove control of park construction from the city's Democratic leaders. Construction was halted by strikes, as a fractious workforce, beset by the deskilling that accompanied industrialization and by competition for jobs from immigrants, resisted Olmsted's efforts to establish a strong work discipline among employees. Park commissioners of every political affiliation sought patronage appointments on the park's workforce, which led Olmsted, in the 1870s, to maintain a journal recording his travails at the hands of city politicians. Moreover, opponents of the park's administration and cost launched several administrative reviews of operations, each of which concluded that the management of Central Park was efficient, even exemplary.[10]

Despite the enormous difficulties and extravagant cost, Olmsted, Vaux, and their associates created, with Central Park, an urban landscape that delighted residents. Shortly after the park opened to the public, skating on the park's lake and ponds became a favorite pastime, as was carriage driving and strolling on the park's paths, though Olmsted fought to keep competitive sports, such as baseball, out of the park. Visitors wrote about their enjoyment of the park, publishers issued guides to its landscape, and photographers recorded its scenery and the public's appreciation of its many features. Central Park remains one of the best investments New York City has ever made. Indeed, it is hard to imagine life in Manhattan without it.

THE INFLUENCE OF CENTRAL PARK

Central Park's example would transform US cities. In 1859, the year the lower park was first opened to the public, the editor of the *Horticulturist* observed, with regard to parks, that Central Park had "given the initiative, and awakened inquiry and conviction of their importance." Philadelphia, then the nation's second-largest city, began the process of enlarging Fairmount Gardens in the 1850s and in 1859 held a competition to determine the park's design. In 1868 the city began acquiring a much larger property on the west side of the Schuylkill River, which, two years later, totaled 2,648 acres, at the time by far the largest urban park in the nation. Baltimore's civic leaders began their quest for a park in 1859, and the city used a penny tax on streetcar fares to finance the acquisition of what became Druid Hill Park, in 1860. The park was designed by Howard Daniels, perhaps best known for his work on rural cemeteries. Brooklyn sought approval from the state legislature in 1859 to acquire a park, and by 1860 the new park commission, headed by James S. T. Stranahan, had assembled a tract of land embracing Mount Prospect that became part of the modern Prospect Park.[11]

Central Park, like the grid street system that surrounded it, was a rectangular box two-and-a-half miles long and half a mile wide. The land acquired for Prospect Park was more irregular in outline, but the original site was bisected by Flatbush Avenue, a major north-south artery linking Brooklyn with southern Kings County. At Vaux's recommendation, the park commission added land to the south and west of the original park site, with Flatbush Avenue becoming its eastern boundary. This realignment enabled the designers to create the Long Meadow, perhaps the most dramatic example of pastoral scenery in an urban park, as well as much of the Ravine and Lake areas. Pastoral scenery, exemplified by the Long Meadow, was key to Olmsted's conception of an urban park. He described pastoral scenery as consisting of "combinations of trees, standing singly or in groups, and casting their shadows over broad stretches of turf, or repeating their beauty by reflection upon the calm surface of pools, and the predominant associations are in the highest degree tranquilizing and grateful, as expressed by the Hebrew poet: 'He maketh me to lie down in green pastures; He leadeth me beside the still waters.'"[12]

In Brooklyn, Olmsted and Vaux looked beyond the park to see its relationship to the rest of the city. Thus, they proposed construction of two parkways, Eastern and Ocean, which would be linear extensions of the park and provide recreational space in distant areas of the city. In 1866, Olmsted and Vaux described the parkway as a "shaded pleasure drive" and anticipated that Eastern Parkway would extend to the East River, where, by bridge or ferry, it would link with Central Park and the new system of boulevards the Central Park commission envisioned building in northern Manhattan; "such an arrangement," they explained, "would enable a carriage to be driven on the half of a summer's day, through the most interesting parts both of the cities of Brooklyn and New York, through their most attractive and characteristic suburbs, and through both their great parks." Two years later, Olmsted and Vaux presented a fuller description of the parkway, a 260-foot-wide strip with a central roadway for pleasure driving, flanked by service roads and pedestrian paths separated by plots of grass and six rows of trees.[13]

Construction of Prospect Park began in the summer of 1866. At the height of construction, as many as eighteen hundred men were employed by the park. Even as construction proceeded, Olmsted and Vaux successfully urged the park commissioners to acquire land for a parade ground across the street from the southern end of the park, which they believed would be used for military musters and active recreation, and Vaux designed a lodge and shelter for users and spectators. The partners also prepared revised plans for Washington Park, which they intended to be the site for civic events, public meetings, and a memorial to the prison ship martyrs, as well as Carroll Park and Tompkins Square. In Brooklyn, then, Olmsted and Vaux moved beyond the design of a single large park and, through parkways and smaller parks, began to plan holistically for the city's recreational needs.[14]

Olmsted visited Buffalo, New York, in mid-August 1868 and examined potential sites for that city's parks. When he returned to the city on August 23, he was the featured speaker at a public meeting called to promote park development. According to the *Commercial Advertiser*, Olmsted

suggested that, commencing at the base ball lot and grounds in the vicinity, a small auxiliary Park might be constructed, giving a beautiful river front; from this a Boulevard could be laid out, with roads for business and pleasure travel, leading to the land on either side of Delaware street north of the cemetery, where the Central Park would be located. Thence by another roadway or Boulevard similar to the first one mentioned, to the elevated land in the neighborhood of High and Jefferson streets, where another small Park of thirty acres, more or less, for the accommodation of citizens in that vicinity, might be established, and in which, if the city carries out the plan of enlarging the Water Works, the tower could be erected.

The park and parkway development Olmsted proposed at this initial meeting became the Front, the Park (the modern Delaware Park), and the Parade (the modern Martin Luther King Jr. Park) as well as Lincoln Parkway and Humboldt Parkway. Here was the first American park system: three park spaces devoted to different uses. The Front, overlooking the Niagara River and Lake Erie, would be the site for civic events; the Park, the large, naturalistic area Olmsted considered essential to any city, a place for passive recreation; and the Parade, an area devoted to military musters and active recreation— all linked by broad, tree-lined parkways.[15]

Because of a parochial attitude shared by homeowners and other real estate holders, who viewed parks as a neighborhood matter rather than as part of an interconnected system,

Chicago established three separate park commissions in 1869. For this reason, Olmsted believed that the city's ambitious park system was not as successful as it otherwise would have been. The Parisian-trained engineer William Le Baron Jenney designed the west parks, and Olmsted and Vaux designed the South Park, a 1,000-acre expanse that consisted of an Upper Division (later known as Washington Park) and a Lower Division (later named Jackson Park), which were connected by a mile-long, 600-foot-wide strip, the Midway. Much of Olmsted and Vaux's plan for Washington Park was carried out under the superintendence of Horace William Shaler Cleveland, in the 1870s, but only the northern part of Jackson Park had been improved at the beginning of planning for the World's Columbian Exposition, in 1890.[16]

The phenomenon Downing termed "parkomania" was sweeping the nation. Smaller cities, such as Albany, New York, and New Britain, Connecticut, began taking steps to incorporate large parks in their midst. Olmsted also presented plans for Mount Royal, in Montreal, in 1881, and for Belle Isle Park, in Detroit, in March 1883.[17]

In the mid-1870s, Boston hired Olmsted to prepare a design for the Back Bay Fens, a sewage-filled tidal basin that was a noisome affront to residents' sensibilities. The Fens was an area of approximately 106 acres, consisting largely of marsh, mud, and water, that carried sewage from homes along the Muddy River and Stony Brook, which drained into the Charles River. Creating a plan for the Fens involved sanitary engineering to address pollution, as well as the tidal inflows from the Charles River, and the use of water-tolerant plantings that could survive the fluctuations in the water level. The result was not a park, as Olmsted conceived the term, but an urban waterway reclamation project that could offer opportunities for passive recreation.[18]

The Back Bay Fens launched Olmsted's career in Boston, and he would relocate to an old farmhouse on Warren Street, in nearby Brookline, in 1883. He then designed a park in West Roxbury (Franklin Park) and began conceiving the system of interconnected parks and parkways subsequently known as the Emerald Necklace. These included the Muddy River Improvement—like the Back Bay Fens, a creative combination of sanitary engineering and landscape architecture that linked the Fens with Jamaica Park, the Arnold Arboretum, and other parkways throughout the city.[19]

The most distinctive aspect of Olmsted's work in Boston, in the last decade of his professional career, was his attention to the need for facilities for active recreation. As early as his "Notes on the Plan of Franklin Park and Related Matters," Olmsted had drawn attention to a significant number of small parcels of land, already owned by the city, that were "well situated for playgrounds for school children" and "for open air gymnasiums." He argued that the park commission should obtain the use of these properties, especially in densely populated and working-class areas of the city, to afford opportunities for different forms of recreation. The first important success in developing these kinds of spaces was the Charlesbank, a relatively narrow property adjacent to the Charles River, for which Olmsted, together with the Harvard physical fitness expert Dudley Sargent, designed gymnasiums and turf fields, for women and girls at one end of the site and for men and boys at the other. He was pleased that the Charlesbank proved immediately popular with Boston's poorer and working-class residents. He pointed with some satisfaction to the women's gymnasium there, especially its child-care services and the educational potential of the facility, which could have "the character of an out-of-door kindergarten" and teach children how to play. The success of the Charlesbank was an example he used in arguing for an expanded program of facilities designed "expressly for the physical training of *school children*." In the 1890s, Olmsted and his partners prepared designs for Wood Island Park, in East Boston; Marine Park, in South Boston; a playground in Charlestown;

Dorchester Park; Charlestown Heights; and Copp's Hill Terrace, many of which contained facilities for small children. The Charlesbank is especially important because it established a template for incorporating gymnasiums and facilities for active recreation in parks in other cities, including Genesee Valley Park, in Rochester; the Front, in Buffalo (the undeveloped plan for its expansion); and Jackson Park, in Chicago (1895 redesign after the World's Columbian Exposition). Olmsted and his partners' efforts to accommodate recreational facilities within park systems and, when necessary, within rural parks, is a significant if long underappreciated part of the history of urban public parks.[20]

Olmsted's was not the only voice arguing for accommodations for active recreation. The Progressive journalist and housing reformer Jacob Riis did so as well, and organized play for children became a rallying cry for Progressive reformers. New York City adopted the Small Parks Act in 1887, and one of the first major accomplishments of the new law was the demolition of tenement housing along the Bend, on Mulberry Street, the heart of the Italian immigrant community, and the creation of Columbus Park. In his 1895 design for the park, Vaux proposed transforming a warren of streets and substandard housing into an expansive lawn, trees, walks, and benches. Witnessing the tenements being demolished, Riis wrote, was "little less than a revolution," and all the better that what replaced substandard housing was an oasis of green space and fresh air. The creation of smaller parks in densely crowded areas of cities would remain a major focus of Progressive reformers well into the 20th century.[21]

Other landscape architects or engineers who designed public parks in the second half of the 19th century included H. J. Schwarzmann, who laid out Fairmount Park; William Hammond Hall, who created Golden Gate Park, in San Francisco, which contained what Olmsted considered the finest children's playground in the country; and Maxmilian G. Kern, who

directed construction of Forest Park, an expanse of more than 1,000 acres in St. Louis. Given the importance of *turnverein* (which emphasized gymnastic exercise) in German culture, Forest Park included significant opportunities for active recreation more than a decade before Olmsted began incorporating gymnasiums in the parks he designed. Although the Olmsted firm consulted with officials in Kansas City on a park for that city, the park system there would be designed by George Kessler, a German immigrant who turned to Olmsted for advice when he began his career as a landscape architect in the United States. Olmsted's friend and frequent correspondent H. W. S. Cleveland designed a comprehensive park system for Minneapolis that included the preservation of Minnehaha Falls and other distinctive attributes of natural scenery in the metropolitan area. In 1889, Cleveland also prepared a plan for a park and boulevard system in Omaha, Nebraska. Charles Eliot, who apprenticed with Olmsted before becoming his partner, brought to the Olmsted firm the design of the Cambridge, Massachusetts, park system as well as his work with the Metropolitan Park Commission. Eliot linked Boston's impressive park and parkway system to the new parks and reservations then being created beyond the city through a system of parkways and pleasure drives. Although the Olmsted firm dominated the nation's park planning in the second half of the 19th century, it was not the sole voice for what a park should be.[22]

FREDERICK LAW OLMSTED JR. AND THE WASHINGTON, DC, PARK SYSTEM

Beginning in 1894, when his firm was appointed landscape architects advisory to the Brooklyn park commission, Olmsted fought to defend the pastoral qualities of Prospect Park that he and Vaux designed. Commissioner Frank Squier wanted to add neoclassical buildings and statuary to the natural landscape and replace the original rustic shelters and structures with more formal elements. Squier worked with the architect Stanford White, who apparently refused to meet with Olmsted. Squier also replaced the Vaux-designed fountain at the oval entrance plaza (Grand Army Plaza) with John H. Duncan's Soldiers and Sailors Memorial Arch and hoped to add horticultural variety to the park by planting numerous species of ornamental trees and shrubs that Olmsted believed were inappropriate in a large, naturalistic park. Olmsted also feared that Richard Morris Hunt's design for a monumental entrance at the Fifth Avenue and 59th Street entrance to Central Park, originally proposed in 1864, would finally be adopted in 1895. The battle over the proper design of parks for the 20th century was underway, and the most important new park and civic spaces created at the dawn of the new century, in Washington, DC, would reflect both the continuity of the Olmstedian tradition and the introduction of more formal plazas, terraces, and statuary.[23]

Olmsted had been involved in planning in Washington since the mid-1870s, when he began designing the grounds and west terrace of the US Capitol. During the 1890s his firm was engaged to plan the National Zoo; consulted on the layout of a subdivision in northwest DC and adjacent Montgomery County, Maryland, for the Chevy Chase Land Company; and created a street system for areas of the city beyond the original L'Enfant plan as well as the campus of American University. Other than the Capitol Grounds, these projects were not realized before the end of Olmsted's professional career. The greater impact on the park system of the nation's capital was the work of his son and namesake, Frederick Law Olmsted Jr. He joined his father's firm in late 1895, after graduating from Harvard in 1894 and completing a thirteen-month apprenticeship at the Biltmore estate.[24]

Frederick Law Olmsted Jr. came to the forefront of the landscape architecture and urban planning professions when he was selected as a member of the Senate Park Commission panel of experts to advise on the planning of Washington. He joined his father's collaborators from the World's Columbian Exposition, the architects Daniel H. Burnham and Charles Follen McKim and the sculptor Augustus St. Gaudens. The goal of the Senate Park Commission, led by Senator James McMillan, was to restore L'Enfant's plan for the District of Columbia, and over the course of decades, guided by the Commission of Fine Arts, on which Frederick Law Olmsted Jr. served for almost a decade, the commission achieved much.[25]

The Senate Park Commission has rightly been credited with reviving L'Enfant's plan for the monumental core of the capital and with launching the City Beautiful movement in American city and regional planning, though, as Olmsted's battles over architecture and sculpture in Prospect Park and Hunt's monumental gateways in Central Park demonstrate, it is more accurate to state that the Senate Park Commission plan gave impetus to a new direction in urban design already underway. The proposals for the areas surrounding the Capitol; the Mall; and the new land reclaimed from the Potomac, which became the sites of the Lincoln Memorial and the Jefferson Memorial, have been well documented. Perhaps surprisingly, given that it was a document prepared for the Senate Park Commission, the crucial role that Frederick Law Olmsted Jr. played in creating a modern park system for the capital has received far less attention.[26]

Washington had experienced significant growth during the Civil War, which continued in succeeding decades, and Alexander ("Boss") Shepherd and the Board of Public Works had initiated an ambitious program of infrastructure construction for the fast-expanding city. Moreover, Congress approved the acquisition of land for a large park in the valley along Rock Creek in September 1890, but because of protests against the assessment of benefits—that is, the financing of the park's construction by raising property taxes on adjacent land (as had been done for Central

Park), the rationale being that the owners of that land would especially benefit from the park—little development took place until the first decade of the 20th century. The rapid increase in population, and the extension of streets beyond the original extent of L'Enfant's plan, left the city poorly prepared to meet the challenges of urban growth. The Senate Park Commission plan addressed the redesign of the monumental core, the reclaimed land along the Potomac Flats, and proposed an ambitious park system for the district.[27]

At the heart of the park system was the Mall, long divided by railroad tracks that crossed it, and the grounds around the President's House, which, during hot, wet summer months sometimes became a malarial swamp. The Senate Park Commission called for the removal of the railroad tracks from the Mall and the relocation of a passenger station to a new Union Station, north of the Capitol, and the restoration of the sweeping "grand avenue" of grass and trees L'Enfant had proposed in 1791, which would be lined by Beaux Arts classical buildings (for governmental purposes, on the south side of the mall, for national museums, on the north). The plan designated the construction of Union Square at the foot of Capitol Hill, a plaza with terraces and fountains organized around an equestrian statue of Ulysses S. Grant, as well as additional terraces to demarcate the site, just west of the Washington Monument, at the intersection of the north-south axis from the White House and the east-west axis along the center of the Mall, which L'Enfant had originally intended as the site for a statue of George Washington. The Senate Park Commission proposed a large memorial to Abraham Lincoln at the western terminus of the Mall and a site for another monument (eventually the Jefferson Memorial) on newly reclaimed land directly south of the White House.[28]

Beyond the Beaux Arts classicizing of the Mall, the Senate Park Commission report drew on much of the Olmsted firm's recent work

on the Boston park system and its proposals for the redesign of Jackson Park after the Columbian Exposition. The report called for the creation of hundreds of smaller parks, often in conjunction with sites reserved for schools; facilities for active recreation of adults as well as children; and a series of boulevards linking parks on hilltops formerly used as fortifications during the Civil War. Illustrated with photographs of the Charlesbank, in Boston, and other Olmsted firm projects, the report was clearly deeply influenced by Olmsted's legacy. Rock Creek Park, of course, would be the city's large, naturalistic park, but, as his father had done, Frederick Law Olmsted Jr. also advocated the acquisition of land at key scenic destinations, most notably the Great Falls of the Potomac, which he proposed be linked to the city's park system by a parkway.[29]

The most important example of how the Senate Park Commission plan built on the Olmsted firm's work of the preceding decades was the proposal for a water park along the Anacostia River. The commission's report decried the "outrageous condition of the Anacostia River," a freshwater estuary that suffered from tidal inflows from the Potomac and that was severely polluted. Land adjacent to the river was periodically flooded or left to bake in the hot summer sun. As was true of the designs Olmsted had prepared for the Back Bay Fens and the Muddy River Improvement, in Boston, the Anacostia Water Park was first and foremost a work of sanitary engineering. Frederick Law Olmsted Jr. called for construction of a dam at the confluence with the Potomac, which would regulate the water level, thereby eliminating much of the pollution that flowed into the Anacostia and that fouled the adjacent meadows, and the dredging of mud flats to the depth of 12 feet to create a large lake. As the report explained:

the result of the proposed treatment would be a great lake, deep enough to be clean and free from vegetation, refreshed by a sufficient flow of water, kept free from mosquitoes and malaria by its depth, by the unobstructed sweep of the wind, and by its clean shores, and surrounded by natural meadows and groves that need only to be cultivated and protected from inundation to become a charming park.

As his father had done in plans for the Boston parks, Chicago's South Park, and the World's Columbian Exposition, Frederick Law Olmsted Jr. suggested that the lake would "provide opportunities for boating, such as are eagerly seized upon where they exist near other great cities." Frederick Law Olmsted Jr. and the firm remained deeply involved in the development of the park system in the capital, preparing 113 plans for Rock Creek Park and 42 plans for McMillan Park, both beginning in 1907, but his visionary proposal for the water park along the Anacostia River was never implemented.[30]

MODERN PARKS FOR MODERN LIFE

At the turn of the 20th century, most northeastern and midwestern cities had large parks, and several had ambitious park systems. Seattle had established several parks and boulevards prior to 1903, when John Charles Olmsted first visited the city and proposed an ambitious program of park and parkway construction. Olmsted conceded that Seattle's exceptional scenery made a large landscaped park unnecessary, and as a result he proposed a series of smaller parks in each of the city's neighborhoods as well as a system of playgrounds. The park commission, however, had limited authority to raise money, and only the city council could approve the acquisition of land for park use. This fragmentation of authority impeded the development of Seattle's parks, and many of the improvements Olmsted recommended were never implemented. Another early-20th-century park, Balboa Park, in San Diego, had its origins years earlier, but its improvement was largely the result of efforts by Kate Olivia

Sessions, who operated a local nursery in the park and who planted one hundred trees annually to beautify it. Sessions invited Olmsted to visit San Diego in 1891 and prepare a plan for the park, but his firm was already overcommitted to other major projects and could not do so. Balboa Park was developed slowly and later became the site of the Panama-California Exposition (1915–1916) and the California Pacific International Exposition (1935–1936) as well as numerous museums and cultural institutions.[31]

Perhaps the most important park plan proposed in the early 20th century was embedded in Burnham and Edward H. Bennett's 1909 Plan of Chicago. This marked the apogee of City Beautiful park planning, in which the landscape was defined by formal spaces, architectural design, and sculpture—really an elaboration of the Beaux Arts tradition first demonstrated on a large scale at the Columbian Exposition. Nevertheless, Burnham and Bennett pointed to the success of the Metropolitan Park Commission, in Boston, and to the work of the Senate Park Commission, in the capital, as examples for Chicago to follow. They advocated the reservation of the shoreline of Lake Michigan for an extended park, along with interior lagoons that would offer boating opportunities for residents. Burnham and Bennett also urged the acquisition and improvement of forests as well as large parks throughout the city that were "accessible to all citizens," and an "encircling system of forest parks and park connections" that extended beyond the municipal boundaries. Significant, too, was the preservation of marshes and wooded ridges. Much of the park system proposed in the 1909 plan came to fruition in succeeding years.[32]

In the 19th century, parks were not designed for many of the changes the new century wrought, particularly the rise of the automobile. Park drives were designed for carriages, with grades and curves appropriate for leisure travel. But, as automobiles increasingly clogged city streets, drivers veered into parks and introduced new levels of noise, pollution, and speed in what had formerly been serene landscapes. The first automobile fatalities in Central Park occurred in 1906, when three people died in a crash. As the number of motorized vehicles grew, road surfaces were widened; graceful curves straightened; and the roadbeds paved with asphalt. Traffic engineers even installed stoplights and posted speed limits. In Central Park, road widening necessitated the destruction of the Marble Arch, which had enabled pedestrians entering the park at 59th Street to pass beneath a drive and reach the Mall and the interior of the park without crossing a line of traffic at grade. Ironically, to accommodate the automobile, park administrators eliminated important elements of the separation of ways at the very time when the greater volume and speed of traffic made the park more dangerous to pedestrians.[33]

Most of the large parks created in the second half of the 19th century also became the locations of municipal zoos, museums, and other cultural institutions. Olmsted fought the expansion of the Central Park Menagerie into a larger zoo throughout his career, and the Metropolitan Museum of Art was located in Central Park in 1880. Other cities followed suit: a zoo in Franklin Park (West Roxbury); a zoo and the Albright-Knox Art Gallery in Delaware Park (Buffalo); a zoo and the St. Louis Art Museum in Forest Park; a zoo and concert pavilion in Fairmount Park (Philadelphia); a zoo in Druid Hill Park (Baltimore); a zoo in Lincoln Park (Chicago); and so many institutions in Grant Park that it had become the cultural center of Chicago. There are numerous similar examples throughout the nation. Many cities also constructed large conservatories in their parks. Like the expansive parking lots necessitated by the rise of the automobile, these cultural institutions consumed considerable park space.

The enlargement or redesign of older park systems was a major theme of the early 20th century. Louisville, Kentucky, for example, where Olmsted and his partners had designed Iroquois, Cherokee, and Shawnee parks in

the 1890s, added two large parks in the 1920s, Chickasaw Park (1923) and Seneca Park (1928), as well as a number of smaller neighborhood parks, all designed by the Olmsted firm. After Louisville's parks were segregated, in 1924, Chickasaw, not completed until the early 1930s, was the only large park accessible to African Americans. Jens Jensen redesigned Chicago's west parks in the early decades of the 20th century and helped popularize a new style of landscape planning, the prairie style, which, inspired especially by the landscape of the Midwest, emphasized horizontality in plant materials.[34]

Major park development in the 1920s took place not in cities, but in suburbs and on the metropolitan fringe. Robert Moses developed Jones Beach and other Long Island parks in the 1920s, but these were state parks and were accessible only by automobile. The Bronx River Parkway was a waterway reclamation project. When it opened in 1923, the parkway provided motorists with a smooth ride and handsome scenery as well as places to picnic and play. The parkway also presented a new way to commute between central Westchester County and New York City, which made possible a new wave of suburban development. Moses's work and the Bronx River Parkway were imitated in other places but did not add to the recreational opportunities available to most residents of the nation's cities.[35]

The stock market crash of 1929 and the onset of the Great Depression created enormous personal hardship throughout the nation, but New Deal federal funds for combating unemployment and stimulating the economy made possible the renovation of many existing parks and the creation of new parks in urban America. Moses used Civil Works Administration funding to put men to work in New York City's parks. According to the Moses biographer Robert Caro, by May 1934:

> every structure in every park in the city had been repainted. Every tennis court had been resurfaced. Every lawn had

been reseeded. Eight antiquated golf courses had been reshaped, eleven miles of bridle paths rebuilt, thirty-eight miles of walks replaced, 145 comfort stations renovated, 284 statues refurbished, 678 drinking fountains repaired, 7,000 wastepaper baskets replaced, 22,500 benches reslatted, 7,000 dead trees removed, 11,000 new ones planted in their place and 62,000 others pruned, eighty-six miles of fencing, most of it unnecessary, torn down and nineteen miles of new fencing installed in its place.

It was a remarkable accomplishment, one warmly greeted by residents. Moses also oversaw the construction of new golf courses and tennis courts and fifty-one baseball diamonds in 1933 and 1934 and introduced a much heightened level of active recreation to the large parks Olmsted had long defended as places of passive recreation. Throughout his long tenure as park commissioner, Moses continued to add facilities for active recreation and playgrounds, demolished historic structures (the Casino, Mineral Springs Pavilion), and erected buildings not in keeping with Central Park's historic landscape. For all his achievements in the early 1930s, Moses's ultimate legacy was to transform the city's historic parks into his own vision. Lewis Mumford described Moses's improvements to the city's parks as "damnably neat," but his overall assessment was that "wide, asphalted paths and stone embankments completely counteract the natural loveliness of the landscape." New Deal–supported projects in parks in other cities were dwarfed by the money Moses received in New York but were nonetheless important in maintaining and upgrading parks throughout the nation.[36]

The outbreak of World War II ended New Deal funding, and the postwar years were not kind to the nation's cities. Suburbanization took its toll, as did deindustrialization, which shrank the tax base of cities, even as the percentage of poor and minority residents rose.

Crime went up as well, leading to increased migration to the urban periphery. As municipal revenues decreased, at least relative to demands on resources, many cities cut expenditures for parks and recreation, with the result that maintenance and the proper stewardship of public landscapes declined dramatically. When New York City endured a fiscal crisis in the mid-1970s, the condition of its public parks became deplorable. In Central Park, graffiti was omnipresent, buildings were in disrepair, benches were left with missing slats, litter was everywhere, and once lush greensward had been ground into dust. With the city unable to maintain the park, the private sector responded. Several wealthy individuals organized the Central Park Community Fund, and a citizen's group organized the Central Park Task Force to prepare a strategy for returning the park to its former glory. In 1979, park commissioner Gordon Davis appointed Elisabeth Barlow Rogers the first Central Park Administrator, and under her guidance, the Community Fund and Task Force merged the following year to become the Central Park Conservancy. Since 1980 the Conservancy has raised hundreds of millions of dollars to restore the park, maintain its facilities, and improve visitors' experience. The Conservancy has led a remarkable effort to revitalize the park. The Conservancy's success led other parks, in New York and other cities, to establish conservancies or friends groups to lobby for the parks, to raise money for restoration, and to articulate to the public the importance of these historic parks to the quality of life in cities.[37]

NEW PARKS FOR THE NEW MILLENNIUM

Three projects demonstrate different strategies for urban park creation in the 21st century. Each involves different strategies for financing improvements as well as innovative solutions to different problems.

In 1997 the Illinois Central Railroad donated its lakefront land to the city of Chicago, and in March 1998, Mayor Richard M. Daley announced a major new project on the Grant Park lakefront, Millennium Park. Planning began with a relatively modest set of goals—linking the new space to Grant Park; constructing an intermodal transportation center and a new parking garage; and, as a civic amenity, building a small park atop the garage. Under the leadership of John H. Bryan, who raised an enormous amount of money from private, foundation, and corporate donors, the park became the newest and most modernist icon of the city. Frank Gehry's Pritzker Pavilion and BP Bridge; Anish Kapoor's sculpture *Cloud Gate*; a small theater for music and dance; Crown Fountain; Lurie Garden; and other elements of the park constitute a modernist statement that integrates the park with the 19th- and 20th-century skyscrapers reflected in Kapoor's sculpture and also reconnects Chicago with Lake Michigan. Millennium Park in some ways harkens back to Downing's conception of the urban park as an omnibus cultural center, yet it is also the most powerful statement of the role of the park and public-private initiatives in urban planning and revitalization in the 21st century.[38]

Boston confronted a different challenge. Instead of railroad tracks, what divided its downtown was the elevated Central Artery, completed in 1959, which became a wall that separated the central business district from southern parts of the city. As planners studied ways to replace this misguided link in the Eisenhower Interstate System, and proposed a tunnel instead (the Big Dig), they realized that they had the opportunity to knit together a city long fragmented by a superhighway. In place of the highway, Boston constructed a greenway, named in honor of Rose Fitzgerald Kennedy; a 15-acre trail that follows the route of the elevated highway, linking downtown Boston with South Boston and the harbor. Small parks along the route of the greenway provide recreational amenities to residents. Boston's greenway is certainly one of the most important remedies to the tragic construction

of interstates in urban areas, if not the most important, and has returned much of central Boston to a walkable city, though it still lacks the density and activity that its promoters surely hoped to achieve. A greenway conservancy joined with the city in a fifty-fifty funding program to construct and maintain the park.[39]

A third example of a new park for a new millennium is Brooklyn Bridge Park. This 85-acre park extends for 1.3 miles along the East River, in the shadow of the Brooklyn Bridge, opposite Lower Manhattan. Although this was once among the busiest ports in the world, the shipping industry had changed with the shift to containerized transport, which even the finest natural port in the eastern United States could not accommodate. With piers decaying and the once thriving riverfront's economic future grim, the city and state collaborated in creating a public-private partnership, the Brooklyn Bridge Park Development Corporation, which hired Michael Van Valkenburgh and partners to prepare a plan for a site. Van Valkenburgh's plan called for adaptive commercial and recreational use of the piers (the commercial uses are to generate revenue to pay for the maintenance of the park), and a sweeping greensward along the riverfront, with spectacular views of the Manhattan skyline. The park combines active and passive recreation, hotels and shopping, and breathtaking scenery. Brooklyn Bridge Park has quickly become a destination for residents and tourists alike, contributing to the borough's renaissance, and, most important, reconnecting the city with its waterfront.[40]

CONCLUSION

The history of urban parks in the United States is long and continues to evolve. This history illuminates key themes in the American experience. The great parks created in the second half of the 19th century were constructed by cities, though often under limitations imposed by state legislatures. As immigrants crowded the nation's cities, and density increased to intolerable levels, park planners and public officials added new places for active recreation for children and adults, especially in the most congested areas of the city. Cycles of decline and renewal followed, and in the closing decades of the 20th century, a new model emerged, a public-private partnership in which philanthropic giving largely replaced public expenditures for park maintenance and improvement.

Public-private partnership has a long history in the United States, extending back at least as far as the incorporation of the Metropolitan Museum of Art and the American Museum of Natural History, in 1870. In each case, New York City agreed to erect the building and provide certain services, such as security and maintenance, while a private board of trustees assumed responsibility for assembling the collections and paying professional staff. But, with parks there is a fundamental difference. The creation of Central Park was an assertion that parks are important to the physical health and psychological well-being of residents— that parks are not amenities but essential public services. In the early 21st century, unfortunately, city governments seeking to balance budgets without raising taxes have cut funds for parks, thus increasing the need for support from other sources. Through the efforts of private sector conservancies, Central Park and some other parks have thrived in this new economic environment, but many, if not most, parks in midsize and smaller cities have not fared as well. Downing Park, in Newburgh, New York, for example, has seen its public sector dollars decline precipitously, and this poor city cannot call on the wealthy corporations and individuals that surround Central Park for support. Downing Park, whose 1889 design by Olmsted and Vaux was their last collaboration, is probably more representative of the future of urban parks than Central Park, with the wonderful accomplishments of the Central Park Conservancy, or Millennium Park, made such an icon of the modern city by Chicago's civic and corporate leaders. Residents

of poorer cities and small towns desperately need a place to walk amid grass and trees or for active recreation, as a respite from everyday life. That is the great challenge facing urban parks in the early 21st century—to maintain Olmsted's vision of the park as the one essential space in a modern city. As he wrote in 1870, Central Park, in New York, and Prospect Park, in Brooklyn, were

the only places in those associated cities where, in this eighteen hundred and seventieth year after Christ, you will find a body of Christians coming together, and with an evident glee in the prospect of coming together, all classes largely represented, with a common purpose, not at all intellectual, competitive with none, disposing to jealousy and spiritual or intellectual pride toward none, each individual adding by his mere presence to the pleasure of all others, all helping to the greater happiness of each. You may thus often see vast numbers of persons brought closely together, poor and rich, young and old, Jew and Gentile.

This is a vision of the park as civic space, the one common ground shared by all residents of a city, and it is as relevant in the early 21st century as it was when Olmsted spoke these words in 1870.[41]

DISCUSSION OF THE LITERATURE

The subject of urban parks in the United States has received considerable attention in the late 20th and early 21st centuries, but it, too, has a long history. Gherardi Davis published the pamphlet "The Establishment of Public Parks in the City of New York" in 1897. Frederick Law Olmsted Jr. and Theodora Kimball devoted the second volume of *Frederick Law Olmsted, Landscape Architect, 1822–1903* (2 vols., New York: Putnam's, 1922–1928) to documents detailing the creation of Central Park.

Of all urban parks in America, Central Park has received the most attention. Important studies include Sara Cedar Miller, *Central Park: An American Masterpiece* (New York: Abrams, 2003); Roy Rosenzweig and Elizabeth Blackmar, *The Park and the People: A History of Central Park* (Ithaca, NY: Cornell University Press, 1992); and Charles E. Beveridge and David Schuyler, eds., *The Papers of Frederick Law Olmsted, Vol. 3: Creating Central Park, 1857–1861* (Baltimore: Johns Hopkins University Press, 1983). Other New York City parks have not gotten the attention they deserve. Prospect Park, which *Garden and Forest*, in 1888, described as "one of the great artistic creations of modern times," is the subject of Clay Lancaster's brief, unannotated, and dated *Prospect Park Handbook* (New York: Long Island University Press, 1972), but the park desperately needs a comprehensive history. Other parks have been almost completely neglected, including the massive Bronx parks the city added in the 1880s, including Van Cortlandt Park and Pelham Bay Park, each more than 1,000 acres, as well as smaller parks and three parkways in what was then the Twenty-Third and Twenty-Fourth wards of New York, frequently referred to, before the 1898 consolidation of Greater New York, as the annexed district. Parks created in Queens and Staten Island in the 20th century also deserve attention.

Cynthia Zaitzevsky's *Frederick Law Olmsted and the Boston Park System* (Cambridge, MA: Belknap, 1982) is an important work, as is Francis R. Kowsky's *The Best Planned City in the World: Olmsted, Vaux, and the Buffalo Park System* (Amherst: University of Massachusetts Press, 2013). Two chapters in Daniel Bluestone's *Constructing Chicago* (New Haven, CT: Yale University Press, 1991) analyze that city's 19th-century parks, and Terence Young's *Building San Francisco's Parks, 1850–1930* (Baltimore: Johns Hopkins University Press, 2008) traces the evolution of that city's parks. Elizabeth Milroy's *The Grid and the River: Philadelphia's Green Places, 1682–1876* (University Park: Pennsylvania State University Press, 2016) adds significantly to our knowledge of parks in that city.

As significant as these writings are, save for Rosenzweig and Blackmar's *The Park and the People*, much work remains in documenting the evolution of parks and park systems in the 20th century. Moreover, major 19th-century park systems require comprehensive study. Blake McKelvey long ago published "An Historical View of Rochester's Parks and Playgrounds," *Rochester History* 11 (January 1949): 1–24, but Rochester's parks call for a full, modern history. The same is true of Louisville, the site of the most important new park system undertaken by Olmsted and his partners in the 1890s and where the firm continued to design public spaces into the third decade of the 20th century. New studies should focus on changing conceptions of recreation in the late 19th and early 20th centuries and how these ideas affected both historic parks and the design of new ones. Crucial, too, is careful analysis of public sector funding and the role that private conservancies have been playing in the early 21st century as cities have faced budgetary shortfalls.

In addition, much work remains to be done on the individuals who designed urban parks. Olmsted's partners John Charles Olmsted, Henry Sargent Codman, and Charles Eliot deserve full biographies, as does Frederick Law Olmsted Jr. Other park makers who are worthy of study include such 19th-century figures as Horace William Shaler Cleveland, William Hammond Hall, and George Kessler, and in the 20th century, Gilmore Clark, among many others. Parks in smaller cities, especially those not designed by significant figures in landscape architecture or planning, are also deserving of scholarly attention.

The history of urban parks in the United States is a rich, exciting field. Long dominated by study of Olmsted, the field must move beyond his towering shadow and especially investigate how historic parks evolved in the 20th century and how new parks have been created to meet modern recreational needs.

PRIMARY SOURCES

Primary source materials are located online and in archives at the Frederick Law Olmsted National Historic Site; the Frederick Law Olmsted Papers, Manuscript Division, Library of Congress, Washington, DC; the John Charles Olmstead Papers, Frances Loeb Library, Graduate School of Design, Harvard University, Cambridge, MA; the Charles William Eliot Papers, Harvard University Archives, Cambridge, MA; the Annual Reports and Minutes of the New York City Department of Parks; the Olmsted Associates Records, Manuscript Division, Library of Congress, Washington, DC; and the Olmsted Research Guide Online.

FURTHER READING

Beveridge, Charles, and Paul Rocheleau. *Frederick Law Olmsted: Designing the American Landscape.* New York: Rizzoli, 1995.

Cranz, Galen. *The Politics of Park Design: A History of Urban Parks in America.* Cambridge: Massachusetts Institute of Technology Press, 1982.

Kowsky, Francis R. *The Best Planned City in the World: Olmsted, Vaux, and the Buffalo Park System.* Amherst: University of Massachusetts Press, 2013.

McLaughlin, Charles Capen, et al., eds. *The Papers of Frederick Law Olmsted.* 11 vols. Baltimore: Johns Hopkins University Press, 1977–.

Miller, Sara Cedar. *Central Park, an American Masterpiece.* New York: Abrams, 2003.

Rosenzweig, Roy, and Elizabeth Blackmar. *The Park and the People: A History of Central Park.* Ithaca, NY: Cornell University Press, 1992.

Schuyler, David. *The New Urban Landscape: The Redefinition of City Form in Nineteenth-Century America.* Baltimore: Johns Hopkins University Press, 1986.

Zaitzevsky, Cynthia. *Frederick Law Olmsted and the Boston Park System.* Cambridge, MA: Belknap, 1982.

NOTES

1. For an overview, see John W. Reps, *The Making of Urban America: A History of City Planning in the United States* (Princeton, NJ: Princeton University Press, 1965). See also M. A. DeWolfe Howe, *Boston Common: Scenes from Four Centuries* (Boston: Houghton Mifflin, 1921), 41–42, and Kenneth T. Jackson, ed., *The Encyclopedia of New York City*, 2d ed. (New Haven, CT: Yale University Press, 2010), 102–103, 541–542, 1243.

2. David Schuyler, *The New Urban Landscape: The Redefinition of City Form in Nineteenth-Century America* (Baltimore: Johns Hopkins University Press, 1986), 67, 101–103.

3. Schuyler, *New Urban Landscape*, 59–66.

4. David Schuyler, "The Washington Park and Downing's Legacy to Public Landscape Design," in *Prophet with Honor: The Career of Andrew Jackson Downing, 1815–1852*, ed. George B. Tatum and Elisabeth Blair MacDougall (Washington, DC: Dumbarton Oaks—Trustees for Harvard University and the Athenaeum of Philadelphia, 1989), 291–311; David Schuyler, *Apostle of Taste: Andrew Jackson Downing, 1815–1852* (Baltimore: Johns Hopkins University Press, 1996), 191–203.

5. Roy Rosenzweig and Elizabeth Blackmar, *The Park and the People: A History of Central Park* (Ithaca: Cornell University Press, 1992), 37–58; Charles E. Beveridge and David Schuyler, eds., *The Papers of Frederick Law Olmsted, Vol. 3: Creating Central Park, 1857–1861* (Baltimore: Johns Hopkins University Press, 1983), 14.

6. Frederick Law Olmsted and Calvert Vaux, "Description of a Plan for the Improvement of the Central Park: Greensward," in Beveridge and Schuyler, *Creating Central Park*, 120.

7. Frederick Law Olmsted, "Passages in the Life of an Unpractical Man," in Beveridge and Schuyler, *Creating Central Park*, 84–94; Rosenzweig and Blackmar, *Park and the People*, 59–91.

8. Frederick Law Olmsted, "Statistical Report of the Landscape Architects, 31st December, 1873, Forming Part of Appendix L of the Third General Report of the Department," in New York City, Department of Public Parks, *Third Annual Report* (New York, 1875), 46–47; Frederick Law Olmsted to William R. Ware, May 31, 1893, Columbia University Archives; New York City, Board of Commissioners of the Central Park, *Fourth Annual Report* (New York, 1861), 24.

9. Olmsted, "Statistical Report," 46–47; Greeley is quoted in Clarence C. Cook, *A Description of the Central Park* (1869; New York: B. Blom, 1972), 110; Frederick Law Olmsted, "Patronage Journal," in Beveridge and Hoffman, *Supplementary Series 1*, 653–704.

10. Edward K. Spann, *The New Metropolis: New York City, 1840–1857* (New York: Columbia University Press, 1981), 384–397; Rosenzweig and Blackmar, *Park and the People*, 150–170; J. M. Murphy et al., "Report of Special Committee Appointed to Examine into Condition, Affairs, and Progress of the New York Central Park," Board of Commissioners of the Central Park, *Fourth Annual Report*, 121–122.

11. Schuyler, *New Urban Landscape*, 102–116.

12. David Schuyler and Jane Turner Censer, eds., *The Papers of Frederick Law Olmsted, Vol. 6: The Years of Olmsted, Vaux and Company, 1865–1874* (Baltimore: Johns Hopkins University Press, 1992), 19–22; Olmsted, Vaux and Company to the Board of Commissioners (of Prospect Park), January 24, 1866, Beveridge and Hoffman, *Supplementary Series 1*, 90–91.

13. Beveridge and Hoffman, *Supplementary Series 1*, 105–106; Olmsted, Vaux and Company, "Report of the Landscape Architects and Superintendents," in Beveridge and Hoffman, *Supplementary Series 1*, 134–141.

14. Schuyler and Censer, *Years of Olmsted, Vaux*, 23–25, 202–208, 309–312.

15. Frederick Law Olmsted to Mary Perkins Olmsted, August 23, 1868, and August 25, 1868, Schuyler and Censer, *Years of Olmsted, Vaux*, 266–273; *Buffalo Commercial Advertiser*, August 26, 1868, 3; Olmsted, Vaux & Company to William Dorsheimer, October 1, 1868, Beveridge and Hoffman, *Supplementary Series 1*, 158–170. See also Francis R. Kowsky, *The Best Planned City in the World: Olmsted, Vaux, and the Buffalo Park System* (Amherst: University of Massachusetts Press, 2013).

16. Daniel Bluestone, *Constructing Chicago* (New Haven, CT: Yale University Press, 1991), 7–61.

17. A. J. Downing to J. J. Smith, n.d. (probably 1847) and March 17, 1850, *Horticulturist*, n.s., 6 (April 1856), 160. For Olmsted's reports on Mount Royal and Belle Isle Park, see Beveridge and Hoffman, *Supplementary Series 1*, 350–436.

18. Frederick Law Olmsted, "Paper on the (Back Bay) Problem and Its Solution Read before the Boston Society of Architects," in Beveridge and Hoffman, *Supplementary Series 1*, 437–459; Frederick Law Olmsted to the Board of Commissioners of the Department of Parks (Boston), December 29, 1880.

19. See Cynthia Zaitzevsky, *Frederick Law Olmsted and the Boston Park System* (Cambridge, MA: Harvard University Press, 1982).

20. Frederick Law Olmsted, "Notes on the Plan of Franklin Park and Related Matters," in Beveridge and Hoffman, *Supplementary Series 1*, 467–472; Zaitzevsky, *Boston Park System*; John Charles Olmsted to William A. Stiles, February 15, 1896, Olmsted Associates Records, A series, Vol. 45, 580–580; William A. Stiles, "The Revised Plan for Jackson Park, Chicago," *Garden and Forest* 9 (May 20, 1896), 201–202.

21. Francis R. Kowsky, *Country, Park, and City: The Architecture and Life of Calvert Vaux* (New York: Oxford University Press, 1998), 308–309.

22. For Schwartzmann and Fairmount Park, see John Maass, *The Glorious Enterprise: The Centennial Exhibition of 1876 and H. J. Schwartzmann, Architect-in-Chief* (Watkins Glen, NY: American Life Foundation, 1973); for Hall and Golden Gate Park, see Terence Young, *Building San Francisco's Parks 1850–1930* (Baltimore: Johns Hopkins University Park, 2004); for Kern and Forest Park, see Caroline Loughlin and Catherine Anderson, *Forest Park* (Columbia: University of Missouri Press, 1986); the most comprehensive assessment of Cleveland's significance is Aaron Sachs, *Arcadian America: The Death and Life of an Environmental Tradition* (New Haven, CT: Yale University Press, 2013), pp. 241–251; for Eliot, see Keith N. Morgan's introduction to the reprint edition of Charles W. Eliot, *Charles Eliot: Landscape Architect* (Amherst: University of Massachusetts Press for the Library of American Landscape History, 1999).

23. Clay Lancaster, *Prospect Park Handbook* (New York: Long Island University Press, 1972), 70–74; Rudolph Ulrich to Olmsted, Olmsted and Eliot, September 11, 1894, Olmsted Associates Records, Manuscript Division, Library of Congress, B series, microfilm reel 25, frame 500; Frederick Law Olmsted to Calvert Vaux, late August 1894, Olmsted Papers.

24. Frederick Law Olmsted to Frank Baker, late 1890, Olmsted Papers; Frederick Law Olmsted to Francis G. Newlands, November 16, 1891, Olmsted Papers; DC Streets Memorandum, December 30, 1891, Olmsted Papers; Frederick Law Olmsted to Samuel Beiler, Department 28, 1894, Olmsted Associates Records, A series, reel 19, frame 784.

25. Jon A. Peterson, "The Senate Park Commission's Plan for Washington, D.C.: A New Vision for the Capital and the Nation," in *Designing the Nation's Capital: The 1901 Plan for Washington, D.C.*, ed. Sue Kohler and Pamela Scott (Washington, DC: U.S. Commission of Fine Arts, 2006), 1–46; on the Commission of Fine Arts, see Sue Kohler, "The Commission of Fine Arts: Implementing the Senate Park Commission's Vision," in Kohler and Scott, *Designing the Nation's Capital*, 245–273.

26. Timothy Davis has provided the fullest account of the Senate Park Commission's park planning, but while he points to the Olmsted firm's work in Boston and to Charles Eliot's 1893 report to the Metropolitan Park Commission, he does not identify specific projects that are direct antecedents of the 1901 plan. Timothy Davis, "Beyond the Mall: The Senate Park Commission's Plans for Washington's Park System," in Kohler and Scott, *Designing the Nation's Capital*, 137–180.

27. Alan Lessoff, *The Nation and Its City: Politics, "Corruption," and Progress in Washington, D.C., 1861–1902* (Baltimore: Johns Hopkins University Press, 1992), 233–234.

28. Daniel H. Burnham et al., "Report of the Park Commission," in *The Improvement of the Park System of the District of Columbia*, ed. Charles Moore (Washington, DC: U.S. Government Printing Office, 1902), 23–53.

29. Burnham et al., "Park Commission," 83–89, 96.

30. Burnham et al., "Park Commission," 105–109.

31. William H. Wilson, *The City Beautiful Movement* (Baltimore: Johns Hopkins University Press, 1989), 147–167; Kate O. Sessions to Frederick Law Olmsted, October 14, 1891, Olmsted Associates Records, C series, box 4, folder 1; Writers Program, California, *Balboa Park, San Diego, California; A Comprehensive Guide to the City's Cultural and Recreational Center* (San Diego: Neyenesch Printers, 1941).

32. Daniel H. Burnham and Edward H. Bennett, *Plan of Chicago*, ed. Charles Moore (New York: Princeton Architectural Press, 1993), 43–60.

33. Roseenzweig and Blackmar, *Park and the People*, 400–401.

34. For Louisville, see the Our Parks section of the Frederick Law Olmsted Parks website (http://www.olmstedparks.org/our-parks/); Robert E. Grese, *Jens Jensen: Maker of Natural Parks and Gardens* (Baltimore: Johns Hopkins University Press, 1992), 62–93.

35. Robert A. Caro, *The Power Broker: Robert Moses and the Fall of New York* (New York: Knopf, 1974), 221–240; on the Bronx River Parkway, see Randall Mason, *The Once and Future New York: Historic Preservation and the Modern City* (Minneapolis: University of Minnesota Press, 2009).

36. Caro, *Power Broker*, 372 passim; Lewis Mumford, "The Sky Line: Artful Blight," *New Yorker*, May 5, 1951, 85.

37. Information provided by Elizabeth Barlow Rogers.

38. See Timothy J. Gilfoyle, *Millennium Park: Creating a Chicago Landmark* (Chicago: University of Chicago Press, 2006).

39. Tom Lewis, *Divided Highways: Building the Interstate Highways, Transforming American Life* (Ithaca: Cornell University Press, 2013), 307–308.

40. See the Brooklyn Bridge Park website (http://www.brooklynbridgepark.org/park).

41. Frederick Law Olmsted, "Public Parks and the Enlargement of Towns," Beveridge and Hoffman, *Supplementary Series 1*, 186.

David Schuyler

ENVIRONMENTAL AND CONSERVATION MOVEMENTS IN METROPOLITAN AMERICA

By the late 19th century, American cities like Chicago and New York were marvels of the industrializing world, with sprawling, integrated factories, the first skyscrapers, and majestic suspension bridges tying the metropolis together. The shock urbanization of the previous quarter century, however, brought on a host of environmental problems. "The sickening stench on the branch of the river known as "Bubbly Creek" at times make that section of the city unbearable," Jane Addams wrote about the Chicago packinghouse district's urban stream in 1904. Although particularly infamous, Bubbly Creek was not unusual. Most cities had "mill creeks" and other small rivers that became universal sinks for all matter of personal and industrial waste. "All night we can hear the cinders falling like hail on the roof. Nothing will grow here. My trees and flowers are dead," a Cleveland resident told the local newspaper about living in the shadow of a local steel mill. Most cities were powered and heated by coal, the burning of which spewed soot and ash into the urban sky non-stop. "A fairly large part of the working classes is compelled to use toilet accommodations in a condition of which the rest of the world would be unwilling to hear in full," a Philadelphia reformer wrote in 1904. Housing conditions, particularly for the urban poor and working classes, were often not only unsanitary but also hazardous, with skyrocketing disease and mortality rates.[1]

Industrialization introduced a host of metropolitan environmental issues and challenges. Various groups of urban residents responded to them with a series of activist movements to reform public and private policies and practices, from the 1890s until the turn of the 21st century. Three themes regarding this environmental and conservation activism stand out. First, urban activism and environmental reform efforts were at the center of the American environmentalist movement. These activities were at least as important as rural conservation, saving the wilderness, or global population and wildlife concerns, when it came to driving the movement during the 20th century. Second, environmental activism and reform was frequently undermined by social division, particularly over race and class, at least in terms of stated goals of creating healthy, just, and sustainable cities. These divisions and conflicts occurred both within and between movements themselves, but also on a broader, spatial level, as urban inequalities created different types of environmental issues, hazards, and challenges. Third, the primary strains of the "environmentalism of the poor" in the United States are urban in nature. From activism by Jane Addams against the "ward bosses" of turn-of-the-century Chicago to groups marching against the siting of incinerators in 1990s Los Angeles, the primary voices against

environmental injustice in modern America originated from the city.[2]

THE ENVIRONMENTAL CRISIS

The American cities of the late 19th century were some of the first to present the great contradictions of the capitalist, industrial metropolis. Alongside great wealth existed grinding poverty. Gorgeous, immaculate office towers were often just a few blocks away from tenements teeming with vermin and disease, which constantly appeared to be on the verge of collapse. Streetcars and elevated railways shuttled thousands of passengers an hour from one end of the city to another, but much of the heavy hauling was still done by teams of horses (that dumped millions of pounds of excrement on city streets every week), and walking was still the primary form of conveyance for most people. On one street a person could see the type of hope and optimism that was on display in the White City at the 1893 World's Columbian Exposition in Chicago. But a block or two away was another street emblematic of the despair that ran through the pages of Jacob Riis's *How the Other Half Lives*.[3]

One of the primary reasons for these incongruities was the speed at which American cities had expanded in the second half of the 19th century. Chicago is the most well-known "shock city," going from 30,000 to 1 million inhabitants from 1850 to 1890, but Philadelphia grew by almost 800 percent in the same period and Boston 300 percent. Western cities like Denver, Seattle, and Portland also exploded, albeit a bit later, each going from a few thousand residents in the late 1800s to more than 200,000 by 1920. These great booms, however, never included a concomitant upgrade in infrastructure, especially when it came to water, sanitation, and housing. The crush of new urban residents overwhelmed privy and cistern systems designed for much smaller populations. These inadequate sanitary systems and lack of fresh water contributed to frequent disease outbreaks, such as cholera, and, in southern cities, yellow fever and malaria. In 1878, four thousand people were killed in the New Orleans yellow fever epidemic. Apartment buildings designed for three or four families were subdivided into tenements with more than a dozen units.

The scale of industrial production also had a major impact on the urban environment. Take Cincinnati, for example. In 1850, the "Queen City of the West" was also known as "Porkopolis." Every year about 400,000 hogs were slaughtered, packed into pork products and byproducts, like soap and candles, and sold all over the world. But during the antebellum decades, a lack of refrigeration and dependence on river transport had limited the slaughtering and packing season to the winter months—November to February. But by the end of the century, railroads allowed Cincinnati's packers, along with those of its more successful rival, Chicago, to slaughter and process animals year round, overwhelming local creeks and rivers with blood, offal, and other byproducts. Similar examples exist for scores of other industries, as the railroads brought access to national and international markets for manufacturers in all of America's largest cities and in many of its smaller ones.

This rapid influx of people and expansion of production, all on top of infrastructure built for much smaller cities, created a significant environmental crisis. Many cities had implemented a series of environmental reforms over the course of the 19th century, such as the creation of water and sewer systems and urban parks. These improved sanitation but also provided needed recreational and leisure space. New York's Central Park, constructed during the 1860s and 1870s and designed by Frederick Law Olmsted and Calvert Vaux, would be tremendously influential, with Olmsted going on to design a number of significant park systems in the United States, including Louisville and Milwaukee. Despite these improvements, however, by the end of the 19th century the environment in American cities continued to

degrade. A strong, effective response to these conditions would not come until the turn of the 20th century, when middle-class urbanites, and their sponsors and patrons among the wealthy and politically powerful, spawned what was known as Progressivism.[4]

Progressives have received credit for much of America's environmental reform efforts during the early 20th century, but this has primarily been focused on policies and programs that shaped rural landscapes, particularly the establishment of the National Forest and National Park systems, as well as state-level resource conservation efforts. But Progressivism was primarily an urban movement, both in terms of the location of most of the reformers and the places they were hoping to address. Recently, historians have re-examined that activism and found that a significant amount of it was oriented toward the urban environmental crisis. Urban progressives, particularly women, worked to regulate water and smoke pollution in cities, establish parks and other metropolitan green spaces, and address issues more closely related to environmental inequality and public health, such as housing, clean water and sanitation, and refuse collection.[5]

Progressive-Era urban activism was America's first grassroots, wide-scale environmental movement. It was diffuse, with no major national figures, organizations, or institutions, but local adherents in almost every major city in the country. This lack of structure was arguably a source of strength, as it allowed easy entry points for local activists, particularly women. In most cities the primary outside agitators, complaining about lack of proper trash disposal and the dangers of smoke pollution, were women, organized through various clubs, societies, and other civic associations. They were predominantly married, middle-class and above, which gave them the means and time to join and become active in these clubs, where they looked to push the boundaries of what was considered legitimate political activism for women. Urban environmental issues allowed an entry point for these critiques through the general framework of "municipal housekeeping." Significant cultural and social (if not economic and political) power over the domestic sphere had been ceded by middle-class men to middle-class women in the 19th century. So when confronted with the challenges of rapid urbanization and industrialization, women claimed that "the city was a home and that what went on in individual homes was public business," giving municipal reformers the right to regulate private action.[6]

Municipal housekeeping was a powerful organizing framework and rhetorical device that women used to become involved in a wide variety of reform efforts. Their institutional support mattered as well. The term "clubwomen" may conjure up images of a few dozen ladies drinking tea, eating finger sandwiches, and tsk-tsking at the problems of the day. But these were powerful civic organizations, with the largest having thousands of members, sophisticated research, communication, and political action committees, and well-developed platforms and positions. For example, the Woman's City Club of Chicago had almost three thousand members by the end of the 1910s; they actively sparred with men's organizations over the proper route toward municipal trash reform. Whereas their male counterparts in the Civic Club argued that fiscal matters should be the sole concern when deciding on trash removal policy, the Woman's City Club argued that health and sanitation should be given priority. After sponsoring one of their members, Mary McDowell, an experienced settlement house worker, on a research expedition to Europe, they proposed not only municipal ownership of the system, which was more fiscally responsible, but also the use of incinerators, which more efficiently disposed of all waste.[7]

This clash highlights the gendered politics of urban environmentalism during the Progressive Era. In general, no matter the issue, female activists adopted positions similar to the Chicago Woman's City Club: that urban pollution caused problems related to cleanliness and aesthetics, morality, and public health. Of these, claims about public health were the most powerful, as the argument that a dirty environment led to unhealthy morals made women's groups vulnerable to attacks of sentimentality. These claims were also becoming more suspect as germ theory began to take hold within the scientific establishment. Male politicians and men's groups, even those that considered themselves Progressives, usually emphasized efficiency over healthfulness, contending, for example, that excess coal smoke was primarily a problem because of the waste of resources versus its detrimental impact on the health of the city's residents. Men controlled municipal governments, as well as the newly emerging regulatory bureaucracies and engineering professions responsible for developing, enacting, and enforcing new practices, policies, and regulations. As insider reformers (as opposed to women, who were usually outsider activists), they redefined urban environmental issues primarily as technical hurdles that could be overcome by better and more efficient systems and not necessarily wholesale adjustment of the existing system.[8]

This technocratic impulse points to the class politics of urban environmentalism in the Progressive Era. Although historians long ago gave up trying to find a cohesive political ideology among Progressives, the middle-class nature of most activist and reform efforts during this period is important. These were individuals and groups who had largely benefited, some significantly, from the urban industrial growth of the previous half-century. Thus, their desires were primarily to preserve the existing system while correcting some of its excesses. This was one of the conundrums of Progressivism—its marriage to the existing system and the inability of its adherents to understand how their own power and privilege often exacerbated issues they were trying to solve. This was especially true of environmental concerns, where the desire of the urban middle class to separate their residential neighborhoods in the early suburbs from the rest of the city helped lay the groundwork for later metropolitan inequalities.[9]

THE CREATION OF METROPOLITAN INEQUALITY

Some, however, sought to correct the environmental injustices of the Gilded Age city. In Chicago, for example, Jane Addams led a campaign for housing reform in Chicago at the turn of the century. Drawing on the "municipal housekeeping" framework of women as protectors of the overall health and cleanliness of the city, as well as the robust research power of Hull House social workers and scientists such as a young Alice Hamilton, Addams demonstrated that a local typhoid epidemic was in large part caused by corrupt politicians who did not enforce local sanitary regulations (particularly regarding indoor plumbing) and recalcitrant landlords who refused to update their properties.[10]

Some historians have labeled this activism, often conducted by well-educated, middle-class professionals such as social workers and doctors, as a nascent form of environmental justice. Although this connotation is problematic, because it flattens the specific political and institutional context for the emergence of the American environmental justice movement in the 1980s, the conceptual goal of showing that activists, organizers, and writers recognized and mobilized around environmental inequalities around the turn of the century is valid. What is needed is more research in this vein, going beyond traditional Progressive voices, such as Addams, who were often blinded by middle-class conceptualizations of class, ethnicity, immigration status, and especially race, that examines immigrant and minority communities and explores their experiences of the Gilded Age city to see if they engaged in any forms of formal and informal protest, organizing, and activism concerning sanitation, public

health, parks and recreation, and other urban environmental issues.[11]

Most middle-class Progressives were focused on general reform efforts that, when successful, provided significant improvements for the poor, working class, and people of color because they enhanced the environment of the entire city. Even if they lived in leafy streetcar neighborhoods on the hilltops, outside of polluted industrial districts, Progressives were usually municipal residents and thus committed to the proper functioning of the city. From the early 1900s onward, they worked for the development of transparent and professional water and sanitation, trash and refuse systems and agencies, and housing and fire divisions that enforced basic health and safety codes. Progressives also provided key support for the City Beautiful movement. Inspired by Daniel Burnham's plan for Chicago and work on the 1893 World's Columbian Exposition, City Beautiful had a significant impact in not only creating grander public spaces but also improving environments. This movement was especially effective in newer, western cities like Denver, where Mayor Robert Speer's work led to not only the construction of the Denver Civic Center but also the paving of hundreds of miles of streets and roads and new water and sewer systems.

By the time of the New Deal, cities like Denver, New York, and Memphis had vastly more advanced bureaucracies staffed by professional civil servants that provided basic services and managed modern infrastructure that addressed public health and environmental issues on a scale that would have been unimaginable just a few decades before. Yet environmental issues persisted in American cities, especially in the poorest neighborhoods, in industrial districts, and in minority communities, areas that more often than not overlapped. There are a number of reasons for this, all of which shaped the environmental experience and activism in cities for the rest of the 20th century. The first is that although they were in large part committed to the city,

Progressive activists and reformers did not, in general, posit a vision that looked to fundamentally deal with the pollution issues caused by modern industry. Manufacturing was not only considered the backbone of most urban economies but also something that middle-class reformers benefited from, either directly as white-collar employees of industrial firms or indirectly as attorneys, research-focused university professors, or owners of smaller supply firms. The primary way to deal with pollution was to segregate it from the rest of the city in specifically designated industrial districts. Although market practices and infrastructure led to the ad hoc centralization of specific types of industries in the late 19th and early 20th centuries, this became systematized in the 1920s with the adoption of single-use, "Euclidean" zoning, which hived off the most intensive heavy industries into specific areas of the city, usually those that already had a significant number of factories. Pioneered in many western cities, like Los Angeles, zoning rarely included any sort of regulation of emissions but did solve issues for middle-class residential and commercial property owners, who were looking to protect their existing investments but also guarantee that any future homes or properties in which they invested their savings or capital would be protected from a chemical-spewing plant popping up next door.[12]

By making sure that polluting industries only operated in certain sections of the metropolis, zoning ensured that middle-class residents could safely invest in single-family homes. This was the first of a suite of policies and programs, developed from the 1930s to the 1950s at the local, state, and national levels, which distended the American city into a sprawling metropolis where spatial divisions hardened around class and race. The first wave of this was the federal reconstruction of the American residential housing market in the 1930s. Agencies such as the Home Owners Loan Corporation (HOLC), the Federal Housing Administration (FHA), and the Federal Home

Mortgage Guarantor Association (Fannie Mae) nationalized, systemized, and incentivized practices that had been going on ad hoc at the local level for years. In aggregate these policies had three effects. First, they divided the city (and later the larger metropolis) into neighborhoods that were worthy of housing investment and those that were not. The worthy areas were almost always whiter and more affluent, whereas the unworthy areas were either a mix of different racial and ethnic groups or a homogeneous minority. Neighborhoods that were majority black were considered virtually off-limits to regular forms of investment capital, a policy that had devastating impact in the decades to come. Second, these investment policies also overwhelmingly privileged single-family homes and new construction. This meant that capital much more easily flowed to newer suburban areas rather than older urban ones. Finally, all of these policies were enforced with tremendous financial subsidies and incentives. During the immediate postwar decade, the FHA and Veteran's Administration (VA), which also followed these regulations, only originated about 10 percent of residential mortgages. But much of the private market was directly subsidized by Fannie Mae, which purchased millions of mortgages from private banks and savings and loans, freeing up private capital to originate more loans. And in general, Fannie Mae required that new loans only be given to homes in areas of sound investment, which were overwhelmingly considered to be white, suburban single-family residential communities.[13]

These policies and practices had a tremendous decentralizing impact on the American city. Combined with the rapid shift to mass automobile transport, the American metropolis exploded across the landscape in the 1950s and 1960s, with new single-family housing developments popping up seemingly every week in cities large and small. To millions of Americans these new, modern homes were the physical manifestation of the postwar promise of a mass consumer society, as well as representing the superiority of the democratic-capitalist system versus Soviet state socialism. But because most builders, banks, and mortgage agents still followed the policies laid out by federal housing administrators in the 1930s, they were also thoroughly racialized spaces. Up until the late 1960s, it was virtually impossible for an African American family to get a mortgage or purchase a home in one of these new suburbs, and, when they attempted to, they were met with fierce resistance by current residents, many of whom were in the process of creating new identities as whites, shedding their former identities as Irish, Italian, or Jewish.[14]

This new racialized, rapidly suburbanizing metropolis was the structural core to postwar metropolitan environmental movements. These proved to be fundamentally divided by space, race, and class, with different groups responding to the disturbances, destructions, and hazards in their own part of the metropolis. This activism, local at first, also fed into the larger national environmental movement as it emerged during the late 1960s and 1970s. Although by the time of the first Earth Day in 1970 activists employed a more global framing for their arguments and adopted a language of universal concern, the modern American environmental movement was significantly rooted in local, and particularly metropolitan, issues and activism.

FIGHTING SPRAWL

To look upon Levittown on Long Island was to see a wonder. Three years before it had been potato fields, but now it was home to more than 40,000 people, many of them young families. A few years before they lived in cramped apartments in New York City, often with other family and friends. But now they could afford their own modest, but brand-new, single-family homes. The genius behind this, *Time* magazine proclaimed by putting him on its cover in July 1950, was William Levitt. Fueled by the access to capital provided by government-backed mortgage programs

(including from the new VA), the Levitts led a homebuilding revolution across the United States. What once had been a small-time business, with developers and builders putting up, at most, fifteen to twenty houses in a given neighborhood, Levitt's mass-production techniques led to the creation of large, tract-home developments in cities across the country. This was a boon for America's late 1940s housing crisis, when returning GIs and their families jockeyed for space with former war workers in crowded cities; it also played a key role in driving the postwar consumer boom.[15]

Only a few years after Levitt was celebrated by America's most important magazine, critics emerged. Some were cultural, lamenting the aesthetic and social homogeneity of the "little boxes made of ticky-tacky," but a significant number were environmental. One of the fundamental issues was that many Americans moved to the suburbs not just because it offered inexpensive access to single-family home ownership, a key site for material consumption, and an important source of economic security, but also because it was perceived as "the country." Postwar developments at the metropolitan edge abutted farmland, forests, rivers, and marshes. Even if the greenspace was not readily accessible, new residents valued the general pastoral landscape of their new communities. Thus, when it was bulldozed for new communities, they became concerned. Not necessarily seeing the irony of how their own developments also destroyed local rural landscapes, by the 1960s they were vigorously organizing and advocating for land use controls, open space planning, and regulation.[16]

This anxiety about preserving open space makes the issue seem aesthetic (as well as sociological—the desire to live in a semirural community), but it was also ecological. Postwar suburbs were edge communities and thus caused particular sets of environmental problems. Many were not connected to metropolitan water and sewer systems and so depended on septic tanks for wastewater disposal. This worked fine in sparsely populated rural areas, but new developments were often built at high densities without adequate drainfields or an understanding of local water table or aquifer dynamics. The patchwork nature of different tracts not only gave residents the aesthetic benefits of butting up against forests, fields, and waterways but significantly broke up animal habitats. Homebuilders often developed projects on low-lying or marginal land, increasing the chances of flooding, which was also exacerbated in some areas by the clear-cutting of local forests. In Sunbelt states, edge communities were (and still are) at a significantly higher risk for being damaged by forest fires.

The experience of the suburbs—a place that promised pastoral nature but often delivered disturbed and polluted environments—mobilized activism in two specific ways. First, it engaged suburbanites to become involved locally, pushing for land use regulations, more open space, and better water and sewer systems. This was often more reformist activity, not requiring much in the way of traditional social movement organizing, since middle-class suburbanites were often well-educated professionals who usually had ready access to the halls of power at the local and state levels. The second and perhaps more significant result of suburbanization was that it helped motivate residents for environmental engagement at the national level. The experience of desiring and purchasing access to particular environmental amenities but then seeing how a lack of regulation and irresponsible building practices harmed those amenities helped suburban residents see that America's modern industrial and consumer system could be destructive of the environment and thus made them more receptive to other arguments swirling around in the 1960s about the dangers of pesticides and nuclear power, the threat of overpopulation and resource depletion, and the value of saving wilderness landscapes and endangered species on a national scale.

Most historians agree that the suburban experience shaped environmentalism. Much of their work, however, ignores how the residents of those white middle-class suburbs shaped the class, racial, and spatial politics of the postwar environmentalism movement. Postwar suburbanites wanted to preserve environmental amenities, particularly clean air and water, natural areas and open land, which they had hoped to gain access to by moving to the metropolitan fringe. When these were threatened, they protested and organized, leading many to connect the suburban experience to the broader critiques of modern technology and ecological thinking emanating from Barry Commoner, Rachel Carson, and other national environmental thinkers and organizations.

But what those critiques usually ignored was that residents only had access to these amenities because of particular class, and especially racial, privileges that were built into American housing policy. The suburbs were built on specific racialized policies, but one key part of those policies was to forcefully argue that the government was not playing a role in subsidizing and shaping the market, especially when it came to suburban, single-family homes, which led to the belief by most suburbanites that the ability to live in the suburbs was based solely on the invisible hand of the market and individual initiative and success. This hid, in plain sight, the profound environmental inequalities that federal housing policy constructed. They were also further reinforced by the emerging suburban environmentalism. In their attempts to contain sprawl and preserve open space, metropolitan activists made the suburbs less accessible to poor, working class, and minority urbanites. Minimum lot sizes, restrictions on multifamily construction, and suburban conservation districts (which bought up land for open space preservation) improved the quality of life for existing suburbanites but also inflated property values and severely limited new development.[17]

THE URBAN CRISIS

While the suburbs became more exclusionary, the urban land-use regimes of the mid-20th century did virtually nothing to regulate what was coming out of industrial smokestacks and water outflow pipes in American cities.

This meant that when suburbanites left the city, they did not solve the problem of pollution but left it behind for urban residents—the growing percentage of whom were working class, poor, and minority—to deal with. Some of these were legacy issues, such as factories that were decades old, with only the most rudimentary pollution control technology, and corporate owners with no interest in upgrading or remodeling them. Other issues were newer. American streets became clogged with cars after 1920. But since the newer postwar suburbs were almost completely dependent on automobile transportation, every city now had thousands of more commuters clogging central city streets every day. Urban planners responded to the attendant traffic by redesigning streets completely for automobile use (which only increased traffic), and most cities switched their remaining mass transit from streetcars to busses. This increased the amount of exhaust being spewed onto city streets and caused a significant spike in blood lead levels, since most automobiles were running on gasoline that had been reformulated with tetraethyl lead. Suburbanization also increased blood lead levels because it drained people, resources, and capital from the city. This lack of investment, plus the highly segregated nature of postwar neighborhoods, led to a significant deterioration of central city housing stock, which exposed children to ever-increasing amounts of lead from peeling paint and plaster from poorly maintained rental housing. The deterioration of urban housing stock also led to significantly higher rat populations, with the rodents thriving in the edge communities of empty, trash-strewn lots neglected by both absentee landlords and cash-strapped municipal governments.[18]

These environmental problems were largely a result of the centrifugal force of the suburbs and American urban policy, which pulled people, resources, and investment capital away from older industrial cities. This led to a deterioration of older infrastructure but also left cash-strapped governments with fewer

and fewer resources to engage in preventive maintenance and provide general urban services, like trash and waste pickup, especially in working-class and minority communities. But the other source of this environmental decline was active efforts to try to reconstruct and redevelop parts of cities that suffered significant economic, social, and environmental problems, replacing them with what were seen as more productive uses, more desirable residents, or needed forms of infrastructure. Broadly, the name for these efforts was urban renewal, but they encompassed activities as diverse as constructing new industrial districts and middle-class housing complexes, university buildings and sports arenas, and multilane interstate highways. And almost always the communities being "renewed" were poor and working-class districts close to the city center, the populations of which were mostly African American. For these residents renewal usually meant being evicted from their apartments, having their homes condemned, and being "relocated," often without any assistance, to another neighborhood far outside of the original community. For those who stayed, renewal often meant the community might be cut in half by a new highway, blocks and blocks bulldozed for a new government office complex, or empty lots and abandoned buildings from cratering housing values and land that sat empty while government officials shopped around for private redevelopment proposals.

During the Progressive Era, poor and working-class urbanites rarely had vehicles to voice their concern about urban environmental issues. Most community organizations were based on ethnic, racial, or religious ties, not spatial connections, and much of urban industrial pollution was seen as a sign of prosperity, and property rights, and thus the right to befoul the air and water, were seen as absolute. Moreover, the sciences of environmental and public health were just then emerging, and many urbanites had virtually no way to access this knowledge or make claims based on scientific or medical concerns. But the 1960s was a different moment. The civil rights movement sparked a wave of energy for community organizing that spread throughout minority communities in cities across the United States. Although many of these local movements focused on more traditional civil rights concerns such as improving education and increasing political power, others sought to address urban environmental and public health inequalities. Much of this activism focused around substandard housing, which was concentrated in minority neighborhoods. In New York, the Young Lords protested against childhood lead poisoning caused by substandard housing conditions and even occupied the local hospital for a day to protest substandard medical and public health services in the South Bronx. In many cities a key part of this activism was the support of institutions, many of them associated with the federal War on Poverty that provided access to scientific and technical expertise, as well as a certain amount of legitimacy. In Seattle, the local Model Cities agency supported rat control and neighborhood cleanup efforts. In St. Louis, the local housing agency worked with scientists from Washington University to pass a citywide childhood lead poisoning ordinance and then mobilized the community to force the city government to enforce it.[19]

Much of this organizing was focused around particular environmental threats and so appears to be very similar to environmental justice activism rather than the traditional conservation or emerging environmental movements. Certain activists and commentators even put a sharp point on this. "The causes and solutions to ecological problems are fundamentally different in the suburbs and the ghetto," psychiatrist Nathan Hare wrote in his essay "Black Ecology" in 1971. Nevertheless, it would be incorrect to argue that marginalized minority groups were only concerned about exposure to environmental hazards. For example, in southern California, Chicana

community organizer Pat Herrera-Duran helped lead a coalition of other community groups and local activists to protect Cabrillo Beach. Long used by a diverse group of residents as a free and accessible public recreation space, in 1968 the LA Harbor Commission announced plans to replace the beach with a yacht marina. This was similar to what was occurring with urban renewal and highway construction, where local governments and monied private interests were eyeing what had been treasured and publicly accessible spaces for development that would primarily be used by the middle class or wealthier suburban residents. After six years of fighting, community groups forced the Habor Commission to accept a compromise plan that ensured public access.[20]

Although they focused on urban environmental inequalities and access to natural recreation and leisure spaces, many of these activists did not consider themselves environmentalists. This is partially because the idea of environmental activism was quite new in the late 1960s. Not until the first Earth Day and the quick institutionalization of a new set of "green" activist groups at the local and national levels did environmentalism emerge as a coherent movement with which one could identify. But it is also reflective of the racial, spatial, and class divide within that emerging movement. Efforts, starting with the protests on and around the first Earth Day in 1970, to create an expansive definition of environmentalism left room for the concerns of poor, working-class, and minority groups, the majority of them from urban areas. These reformers were concerned with issues related to environmental inequalities and injustices. But even so, many of the social, economic, and political forces that defined environmentalism as a politics of the more powerful and privileged, particularly middle class and elites, were already baked in and emerged to drive the green movement in the remaining decades of the 20th century. Some of these had to do with the technical and scientific nature of the environmental-regulatory state that was erected within the federal and state governments in the 1960s and 1970s. In order to successfully make claims of harm or injury (to human communities or the natural world), citizens needed access to scientific and legal expertise that was often in short supply in less well-off communities.

This was not just a class concern, however. Because the majority of middle-class and wealthier Americans lived in the suburbs, or exclusively residential neighborhoods within city boundaries, they were afforded a spatial privilege that shaped their approach to activism. Without immediate threats, they saw environmental issues as universalist concerns that affected all Americans relatively equally and were not necessarily place-specific. Although they were not immune to a language and politics of crisis, especially during the 1970s, suburban American environmentalists primarily opted for a more moderate, reformist approach to activism that privileged institutions and organizations that were focused on the management of existing systems rather than radical change. This led to the growth of what would become known as the "Group of Ten" environmental organizations, most of which were not focused on grassroots activism but instead depended on large, well-educated professional staffers to conduct research and lobby legislative and regulatory bodies. Direct action rarely took the form of protests, marches, or mass mobilization campaigns. It was usually a lawsuit that was highly technical and complex and often dragged on for years.[21]

URBAN ENVIRONMENTAL JUSTICE

This more moderate, almost bureaucratic approach shaped environmentalism in the United States until well into the 20th century. But in the 1980s "mainstream environmentalism" was challenged by another movement identified as "environmental justice." Although many histories focus on rural activism, particularly in Warren County, North Carolina, and other parts of the American South at the beginning of this new movement, on the whole it was primarily urban in orientation. Robert Bullard, who helped define and legitimize the movement through his early scholarship, wrote about the discriminatory siting of toxic waste dumps and factories in and around metropolitan Houston, and other early hotspots of activism were in New York and Los Angeles, where African American and Latinx organizations protested efforts by local authorities to place trash and waste incinerators almost exclusively in their communities.[22]

Because the environmental justice movement was the first large-scale effort to consciously merge claims of environmental harm and social justice, this form of activism was legitimately something new in American history. But it was part of a long history of these types of claims being made indirectly by working-class and minority peoples and organizations that were concerned about environmental issues but just did not specifically claim or develop an environmentalist language. This is not only an American phenomenon but part of a larger global movement that environmentalists Juan Martinez Alier and Ramachandra Guha dubbed "the environmentalism of the poor." All over the world, marginalized and subaltern groups have developed their own, predominantly local environmental critiques and movements that seek to address immediate needs, injustices, and hazards. They were just not dubbed "environmentalism" because they did not follow traditional definitions or come out of more mainstream environmental institutions.[23]

Globally, many of these struggles were in rural areas over access to water, timber and forests, and farmland. In the United States, much of environmental justice was connected to the spatial critiques about metropolitan inequality that urban environmental activists had developed twenty years before. As the writer Laura Pulido and others have argued, looking for a "smoking gun" in siting decisions for toxic dumps and chemical factories—that officials and executives consciously choose minority neighborhoods because of outright racism—misses the point. One of the primary reasons that toxic hazards are primarily in poor and minority communities is because they are not in white middle-class and wealthy communities. Race and class privilege allowed whites to develop and access communities that were devoid of toxic uses and had lower overall pollution loads. Those groups used their political and economic power to maintain the environmental quality of those communities over time. Since the regulatory regimes of most cities never really focused on reducing emissions, only sequestering noxious and toxic uses into certain zones and communities, this meant that poor, minority, and working-class communities bore a higher burden of the direct harm from the effluent of industrial America.[24]

Continuing into the new millennium, urban environmental justice organizing has developed into some of the most dynamic grassroots activism in the United States. Evolving from the original focus on incinerator siting, groups like the Little Village Environmental Justice Organization in Chicago worked to build local parks and recreation spaces and community gardens and improve public transit connections, all while also continuing to fight the pollution loads that inordinately burden their communities. The Hattie Carthan Community Garden in New York envisioned community gardening not just as a way to "green" vacant lots and educate schoolchildren about agriculture but as important parts of the larger food justice movement, providing robust and healthy food options for the local community.[25]

From the late 19th to the early 21st centuryies, some of the most vibrant and important environmental activism and organizing in the United States emerged out of cities and suburbs. Because much of it has been primarily local—focused on issues and problems that are often unique to a particular place—it does not lend itself to the creation of national institutions and thus has generally not been considered a significant part of the broader American environmental and conservation movements. This is unfortunate, because not only have most people who consider themselves environmentalists been actively looking to address issues at the grassroots level, urban movements are where it is possible to see some of the greatest promise for this type of organizing, and some of the most important conflicts, especially over class and race, in the American movement.

DISCUSSION OF THE LITERATURE

The literature on urban conservation and environmental movements in the United States was virtually nonexistent twenty-five years ago, but recently the field has picked up steam, and now the city, and its attendant conservation and environmental movements, is one of the primary foci of a younger generation of urban and environmental historians. As in most explorations of American environmental politics, Samuel Hays's two books, *Conservation and the Gospel of Efficiency* and, with Barbara Hays, *Beauty, Health, and Permanence* stand as the premier works that influenced scholars well into the 21st century. Both are not particularly place-based but discuss activists and movements that were obviously responding to environmental issues and problems in urban and metropolitan landscapes. *Beauty, Health, and Permanence*'s specific claim that environmental consciousness and activism was new in the post–World War II decades also sparked numerous scholars to go looking for activism in other times and contexts, and some found it in the city. David Stradling's *Smokestacks and Progressives* pushed the timeline back to the turn of the century and examines vigorous activism against air pollution by middle-class men and women across the county, and numerous scholars continue to explore the pollution and public health campaigns of the Progressive Era. Some, such as Harold Platt and Dolores Greenberg, even argue that environmental justice first emerged in the battles over Progressive-Era urban inequalities.[26]

After the Progressives, the next era and place that sparked significant exploration has been the postwar suburbs. Adam Rome's *Bulldozer in the Countryside* redirected the study of both postwar and urban environmentalism by showing how, far from being just "not-in-my-backyard" concerns, suburban environmentalism helped kickstart the broader movement. Despite its problems, particularly a universalism that ignores issues of racial and class inequality within suburbia and the broader metropolis, *Bulldozer* remains the standard text on the subject. Christopher Sellers explores similar landscapes in *Crabgrass Crucible*, focusing on suburban Los Angeles and New York. These case studies tell the story of specific activists and explore how tract home construction disturbed the ecosystems of "edge communities" in ways that Rome, with a national study, simply could not. Sellers also addresses inequality by bringing the experiences of working-class and minority suburbanites into the story, although the effectiveness of these arguments is somewhat limited because of the lack of a metropolitan framework. Sellers and Rome also do not really place this activism within broader suburban political developments, which is the strength of Lily Geismer's *Don't Blame Us*.[27] Although primarily a political history, the focus on liberals allowed Geismer to explore how suburban environmentalism offered opportunities for metropolitan coalition building, particularly in opposition to highway projects, while also reinforcing inequality. Although there are a number of works that solely consider antisprawl activism as a primarily exclusionary politics, there is a need for more critical examinations of suburban environmentalism that explore the broader race, class, and political context.[28]

On the other side of the metropolitan coin sits the central city. Postwar urban activism has never been completely hidden, but it was often considered part of the long civil rights movement or examined in a broader public health framework. The breakthrough work here is Andrew Hurley's *Environmental Inequalities*. Although primarily an examination of how certain groups in industrial cities like Gary, Indiana, gain greater access to environmental amenities, and others greater exposure to pollution and toxics hazards, Hurley shows how urban leaders attempted to come to terms with the unequal impact of urban pollution in the 1970s. This perspective is reinforced by David and Richard Stradling's *Where the River Burned: Carl Stokes and the Struggle to Save Cleveland*, which shows how Stokes, America's first elected black big-city mayor, dealt with the environmental crisis of how to turn a pollution-ridden industrial city into a more verdant and healthful industrial one. Other work, particularly my *Environmental Activism and the Urban Crisis* and Jeffrey Craig Sanders's *Seattle and the Roots of Urban Sustainability*, examine grassroots activism, particularly by working-class, poor, and minority communities, that attempted to deal with the environmental problems caused by suburbanization, deindustrialization, and urban renewal. On a similar track, in *Pests in the City: Flies, Bedbugs, Cockroaches and Rats*, Dawn Biehler explores how city residents responded to, and took action against, the specific ecologies of urban poverty that caused greater exposure to and risk from urban pests.[29]

All of these authors show how the activism of the1960s and early 1970s portended the later environmental justice movement, whose urban context is examined most cogently in Julia Sze's *Noxious New York*. Although a useful study of recent activism, Sze approaches the topic from an interdisciplinary framework, and so the historical and historiographical context of the work is somewhat lacking. This is also true for other works, such as Dorceta Taylor's *The Environment and the People in American Cities* and Robert Gottlieb's *Forcing the Spring*. Although environmental and urban historians should find their work useful, their sociological perspective either leads to the construction of quite cumbersome social science frameworks (Taylor) or is episodic and lacking full historical context (Gottlieb).[30]

Despite the growth of scholarship on urban environmental activism over the past quarter-century, there is still much work to be done. Although not activist histories per se, Brian McCammack's *Landscapes of Hope* and Eric Avila's *Folklore of the Freeway* show how minority and marginalized groups understood, experienced, and shaped the urban environment and deal with environmental inequalities. More work that takes the experiences of urban residents at face value is necessary. There is also room for more social movement and activist histories, especially of the postwar era, particularly case studies of major cities that could help flesh out the broader narrative of American environmentalism. Perhaps the greatest need is for work that bridges the metropolitan divide, looking at not only how suburban and central city environments helped produce each other but the interaction of ideas, activists, and movements. In addition to providing a more complete picture of urban and suburban environmentalism, it could also show the promises and pitfalls of cross-class, interracial environmental coalitions.[31]

PRIMARY SOURCES

Sources for urban environmental and conservation movements are relatively easy to find, although they are almost all available locally in municipal archives and record collections located in the city in which the movement occurred or was active. Researchers should consider three primary types of collections for local movements. The most desirable are collected papers of actual organizations. These can be the papers of a group that was specifically focused on environmental issues or a subset of papers of a larger civic organization involved in some type of environmental campaign or project. Also useful are organizations that advocated for planning and housing reform or were engaged in community organizing, including settlement houses and social work organizations and churches. Especially when examining the 1960s, records for local agencies connected to the federal Great Society (War on Poverty, Model Cities, etc.) can be rich sources because these groups often built campaigns around urban environmental issues. The second type of useful cache is personal papers of leaders or organizers, which contain their correspondence and reflections on the issue but also may indirectly include organizational records. The third are official municipal records, including papers of mayoral and city council administrations, which show not only how politicians and local officials were responding to activism but also the general structure and tenor of campaigns that had an impact. For environmental issues, researchers should also be sure to peruse the papers of local and regional planning agencies, water and sanitation districts, solid waste departments, and park systems. More recently (since the 1970s) many cities have official departments of environmental affairs or sustainability, and their records would be useful.

Researchers should also make sure they get a full picture of the urban environment and landscape and as objective a picture as possible of the issue that activists were attempting to address. For example, if air pollution was the issue, track down any available municipal regulator's records, as well as air quality research and surveying done by local doctors or hospitals, or associated nonprofit organizations, such as the American Lung Association. Municipal and political records should also be examined to understand the broader political and social context of the city at the time. Newspapers are especially helpful for this, of course, although using them to explore environmental issues can be tricky. Most metropolitan dailies did not have anything close to an "environmental beat" until the late 1960s.

What is often particularly helpful are newspaper morgues or clip files. Usually housed in the central branches of municipal libraries, these are clippings of physical newspapers organized by name, topic, or event. Make sure to be creative, since a topic like air pollution can be filed away under "pollution," "smoke," "smog," "dust," etc. Local and regional magazines and alternative weekly newspapers can also be helpful, especially for the postwar period. More and more newspapers' archival collections are becoming fully searchable online. Some of these databases can be accessed through university libraries, but also via pay subscriptions to websites like newspapers.com.

When searching for records, it pays to be creative, going beyond the local historical society to university and college archives, religious organizations, public libraries, small museums, and historic sites. For more recent movements, it is helpful to get in touch with former or current activists and municipal officials, not only for oral history interviews but also to see if they have personal records that have never been formally deposited in a publicly accessible archive. Depending on the movement or topic, certain national archives can be helpful. If an activist was active locally but prominent nationally, their papers might be at the Library of Congress, New York Public Library, a major university archive, or similar institution. Governmental records, especially federal and state housing, public health, and environmental agencies, can also be helpful and are usually in more centralized archives. Finally, a few archives have particular collections that are of national interest. These include the Department of Archives and Special Collections at the University of Pittsburgh, which has Samuel Hays's papers, a treasure trove of documentation on local environmental movements all across the country. The Walter Reuther Library of Labor and Urban Affairs has the records of the Urban Environment Conference, a small but influential national organizing group from the 1970s, as well as scores of labor union records, many of which were involved in various sorts of urban and public health activism.

DIGITAL MATERIALS

Walter Reuther Library of Labor and Urban Affairs (http://reuther.wayne.edu/).

University of Pittsburgh Archives and Special Collections (https://www.library.pitt.edu/archives-special-collections).

Mapping Inequality: Redlining in New Deal America, 1935–1940 (https://dsl.richmond.edu/panorama/redlining).

Renewing Inequality: Urban Renewal, Family Displacements, and Race: 1955–1966 (https://dsl.richmond.edu/panorama/renewal/).

Project Toxicdocs (https://www.toxicdocs.org/).

FURTHER READING

Biehler, Dawn. *Pests in the City: Flies, Bedbugs, Cockroaches, and Rats.* Weyerhaeuser Environmental Book. Seattle: University of Washington Press, 2015.

Bullard, Robert D. *Dumping in Dixie: Race, Class, and Environmental Quality.* 3rd ed. Boulder, CO: Westview Press, 2000.

Fingal, Sara. *Turning the Tide: The Politics of Coastal Land and Leisure During the Age of Environmentalism.* Seattle: University of Washington Press, forthcoming.

Freund, David M. P. *Colored Property: State Policy and White Racial Politics in Suburban America.* Historical Studies of Urban America. Chicago: University of Chicago Press, 2010.

Geismer, Lily. *Don't Blame Us: Suburban Liberals and the Transformation of the Democratic Party.* Politics and Society in Twentieth-Century America. Princeton, NJ: Princeton University Press, 2015.

Gioielli, Robert. *Environmental Activism and the Urban Crisis: Baltimore, St. Louis, Chicago.* Urban Life, Landscape and Policy. Philadelphia: Temple University Press, 2014.

Guha, Ramachandra, and Juan Martínez Alier. *Varieties of Environmentalism: Essays North and South.* London: Earthscan, 1997.

Hurley, Andrew. *Environmental Inequalities: Class, Race, and Industrial Pollution in Gary, Indiana, 1945–1980*. Chapel Hill: University of North Carolina Press, 1995.

Jackson, Kenneth T. *Crabgrass Frontier: The Suburbanization of America*. New York: Oxford University Press, 1985.

Johnson, Benjamin Heber. *Escaping the Dark, Gray City: Fear and Hope in Progressive-Era Conservation*. New Haven, CT: Yale University Press, 2017.

Leif, Fredrickson. "The Age of Lead: Metropolitan Change, Environmental Health, and Inner City Underdevelopment in Baltimore." PhD dissertation, University of Virginia, 2017.

Longhurst, James Lewis. *Citizen Environmentalists. Civil Society: Historical and Contemporary Perspectives*. Medford, MA: Tufts University Press, 2010.

McCammack, Brian. *Landscapes of Hope: Nature and the Great Migration in Chicago*. Cambridge, MA: Harvard University Press, 2017.

Platt, Harold L. *Shock Cities: The Environmental Transformation and Reform of Manchester and Chicago*. Chicago: University of Chicago Press, 2005.

Pulido, Laura. "Rethinking Environmental Racism: White Privilege and Urban Development in Southern California." *Annals of the American Association of Geographers* 90 (2000): 12–40.

Rome, Adam Ward. *The Bulldozer in the Countryside: Suburban Sprawl and the Rise of American Environmentalism*. Studies in Environment and History. Cambridge, UK: Cambridge University Press, 2001.

Sanders, Jeffrey C. *Seattle and the Roots of Urban Sustainability: Inventing Ecotopia*. History of the Urban Environment. Pittsburgh, PA: University of Pittsburgh Press, 2010.

Sellers, Christopher C. *Crabgrass Crucible: Suburban Nature and the Rise of Environmentalism in Twentieth-Century America*. Chapel Hill: University of North Carolina Press, 2012.

Stradling, David. *Smokestacks and Progressives: Environmentalists, Engineers and Air Quality in America, 1881–1951*. Baltimore: Johns Hopkins University Press, 1999.

Sze, Julie. *Noxious New York: The Racial Politics of Urban Health and Environmental Justice*. Urban and Industrial Environments. Cambridge, MA: MIT Press, 2007.

NOTES

1. Jane Addams, *Newer Ideals of Peace: The Moral Substitutes for War* (New York: MacMillan, 1907), 63; David Stradling, *Smokestacks and Progressives: Environmentalists, Engineers and Air Quality in America, 1881–1951* (Baltimore: Johns Hopkins University Press, 1999), 86; and Emily Dinwiddie, *Housing Conditions in Philadelphia* (Philadelphia: The Octavia Hill Association, 1904), 11.

2. Ramachandra Guha and Juan Martínez Alier, *Varieties of Environmentalism: Essays North and South* (London: Earthscan, 1997).

3. Richard White, *The Republic for Which It Stands: The United States During Reconstruction and the Gilded Age, 1865–1896* (New York: Oxford University Press, 2017).

4. Elizabeth Blackmar and Roy Rosenweig, *The Park and the People: A History of Central Park* (Ithaca, NY: Cornell University Press, 1998).

5. Samuel P. Hays, *Conservation and the Gospel of Efficiency: The Progressive Conservation Movement, 1890–1920* (Cambridge, MA: Harvard University Press, 1959).

6. Angela Gugliotta, "Class, Gender, and Coal Smoke: Gender Ideology and Environmental Injustice in Pittsburgh, 1868–1914," *Environmental History* 5, no. 2 (2000): 165–193; and Nancy C. Unger, *Beyond Nature's Housekeepers: American Women in Environmental History* (Oxford: Oxford University Press, 2012).

7. Maureen A. Flanagan, "Gender and Urban Political Reform: The City Club and the Woman's City Club of Chicago in the Progressive Era," *The American Historical Review* 95, no. 4 (1990): 1032–1050.

8. Gugliotta, "Class, Gender, and Coal Smoke"; Adam Rome, "'Political Hermaphrodites': Gender and Environmental Reform in Progressive America," *Environmental History* 11, no. 3 (2006): 440–463; and Stradling, *Smokestacks and Progressives*.

9. Robert M. Fogelson, *Bourgeois Nightmares: Suburbia, 1870–1930* (New Haven, CT: Yale University Press, 2005); and Daniel T. Rodgers, "In Search of Progressivism," *Reviews in American History* 10, no. 4 (1982): 113–132.

10. Chad Montrie, *The Myth of Silent Spring: Rethinking the Origins of American Environmentalism* (Berkeley: University of California Press, 2018); and Harold L. Platt, *Shock Cities: The Environmental Transformation and Reform of Manchester*

and Chicago (Chicago: University of Chicago Press, 2005).

11. Colin Fisher, *Urban Green: Nature, Recreation, and the Working Class in Industrial Chicago* (Chapel Hill: University of North Carolina Press, 2015); Dolores Greenberg, "Reconstructing Race and Protest: Environmental Justice in New York City," *Environmental History* 5, no. 2 (2000): 223–250; Brian McCammack, *Landscapes of Hope: Nature and the Great Migration in Chicago* (Cambridge, MA: Harvard University Press, 2017); Martin V. Melosi, *The Sanitary City: Environmental Services in Urban America from Colonial Times to the Present* (Pittsburgh, PA: University of Pittsburgh Press, 2008); and Montrie, *The Myth of Silent Spring*.

12. Melosi, *The Sanitary City*; Mary Corbin Sies and Christopher Silver, eds., *Planning the Twentieth-Century American City* (Baltimore: Johns Hopkins University Press, 1996).

13. David M. P. Freund, *Colored Property: State Policy and White Racial Politics in Suburban America* (Chicago: University of Chicago Press, 2010); and Kenneth T. Jackson, *Crabgrass Frontier: The Suburbanization of America* (New York: Oxford University Press, 1985).

14. Adam Ward Rome, *The Bulldozer in the Countryside: Suburban Sprawl and the Rise of American Environmentalism* (Cambridge, UK: Cambridge University Press, 2001).

15. Rome, *The Bulldozer in the Countryside*.

16. Monica Prasad, *The Land of Too Much: American Abundance and the Paradox of Poverty* (Cambridge, MA: Harvard University Press, 2012); Rome, *The Bulldozer in the Countryside*; and Christopher C. Sellers, *Crabgrass Crucible: Suburban Nature and the Rise of Environmentalism in Twentieth-Century America* (Chapel Hill: University of North Carolina Press, 2012).

17. Mike Davis, *City of Quartz: Excavating the Future in Los Angeles* (New York: Verson, 2006); and Lily Geismer, *Don't Blame Us: Suburban Liberals and the Transformation of the Democratic Party* (Princeton, NJ: Princeton University Press, 2015).

18. Dawn Biehler, *Pests in the City: Flies, Bedbugs, Cockroaches, and Rats*, Weyerhaeuser Environmental Book (Seattle: University Of Washington Press, 2015); Robert Gioielli, *Environmental Activism and the Urban Crisis: Baltimore, St. Louis, Chicago*, Urban Life, Landscape and Policy (Philadelphia: Temple University Press, 2014); Leif Frederickson, "The Age of Lead: Metropolitan Change, Environmental Health, and Inner City Underdevelopment in Baltimore" (PhD dissertation, University of Virginia, 2017); James Longhurst, *Citizen Environmentalists* (Medford, MA: Tufts University Press, 2010); and Gioielli, *Environmental Activism and the Urban Crisis*.

19. Jeffrey C. Sanders, *Seattle and the Roots of Urban Sustainability: Inventing Ecotopia*, History of the Urban Environment (Pittsburgh, PA: University of Pittsburgh Press, 2010); Matthew Gandy, "Between Borinquen and the Barrio: Environmental Justice and New York City's Puerto Rican Community, 1969–1972," *Antipode* 34, no. 4 (September 2002): 730–761; and Laura Fingal, "Latinx Environmentalism," *Oxford Research Encyclopedia of American History*.

20. Nathan Hare, "Black Ecology," *The Black Scholar* 1, no. 6 (April 1970): 2; and Sara Fingal, *Turning the Tide: The Politics of Land and Leisure During the Age of Environmentalism*, forthcoming.

21. Paul Sabin, "Environmental Law and the End of the New Deal Order," *Law and History Review* 33, no. 4 (November 2015): 965–1003.

22. Robert D. Bullard, *Dumping in Dixie: Race, Class, and Environmental Quality*, 3rd ed. (Boulder, CO: Westview, 2000); and Julie Sze, *Noxious New York: The Racial Politics of Urban Health and Environmental Justice* (Cambridge, MA: MIT Press, 2007).

23. Guha and Martínez Alier, *Varieties of Environmentalism*.

24. Laura Pulido, "Geographies of Race and Ethnicity 1: White Supremacy vs White Privilege in Environmental Racism Research," *Progress in Human Geography* 39, no. 6 (December 1, 2015): 809–817.

25. Kristin Reynolds and Nevin Cohen, *Beyond the Kale: Urban Agriculture and Social Justice Activism in New York City* (Athens: University of Georgia Press, 2016); and Mariela Fernandez, "Utilizing the Non-Profit Sector to Advance Social and Environmental Justice" (PhD dissertation, University of Illinois at Urbana-Champaign, 2015).

26. Greenberg, "Reconstructing Race and Protest"; Samuel P. Hays and Barbara D. Hays, *Beauty, Health, and Permanence: Environmental Politics in the United States, 1955–1985*, Studies in Environment and History (New York: Cambridge University Press, 1987); Melosi, *The Sanitary City*; Platt, *Shock Cities*; and Stradling, *Smokestacks and Progressives*.

27. Geismer, *Don't Blame Us*; Rome, *The Bulldozer in the Countryside*; and Sellers, *Crabgrass Crucible*.

28. Davis, *City of Quartz*; Andrew Hurley, *Environmental Inequalities: Class, Race, and Industrial Pollution in Gary, Indiana, 1945–1980* (Chapel Hill: University of North Carolina Press, 1995); and Matthew W. Klingle, *Emerald City: An Environmental History of Seattle* (New Haven, CT: Yale University Press, 2008).

29. Gioielli, *Environmental Activism and the Urban Crisis*; Hurley, *Environmental Inequalities*; Sanders, *Seattle and the Roots of Urban Sustainability*; David Stradling and Richard Stradling, *Where the River Burned: Carl Stokes and the Struggle to Save Cleveland* (Ithaca, NY: Cornell University Press, 2015); and Sze, *Noxious New York*.

30. Robert Gottlieb, *Forcing the Spring: The Transformation of the American Environmental Movement* (Washington, DC: Island Press, 2005); Sze, *Noxious New York*; and Dorceta E. Taylor, *The Environment and the People in American Cities, 1600s–1900s: Disorder, Inequality, and Social Change* (Durham, NC: Duke University Press Books, 2009).

31. Eric Avila, *The Folklore of the Freeway: Race and Revolt in the Modernist City*, A Quadrant Book (Minneapolis: University of Minnesota Press, 2014); and McCammack, *Landscapes of Hope*.

Robert R. Gioielli

ENVIRONMENTAL POLLUTION AND THE AMERICAN CITY

URBAN POLLUTANTS AND MIASMA THEORY IN EARLY AMERICA

In small early American cities prior to industrialization, water polluted by human and animal waste was the primary concern because of the ways it contributed to the spread of diseases such as yellow fever, typhoid fever, and cholera. In this era, pollution was mitigated on an individual, ad hoc basis, rather than coordinated by municipalities. Cesspools and privy vaults kept human and household wastes close to their sources until they were emptied; solid wastes were merely tossed to the street, where scavengers recycled and pigs foraged. A great deal of food waste and offal was also refined for use in other industries or as hog feed, primarily by the poorer classes in neighborhoods where organized refuse collection was virtually nonexistent. Cities such as New York and Boston recycled horse manure and human waste, converting it into fertilizer for use on nearby farmlands, but the practice was never widespread. Industrial sources of pollution were relatively minimal, but operations such as tanneries and slaughterhouses generated animal wastes that were simply discharged onto adjacent lands and into nearby waterways, eventually leading to growing "tragedy of the commons" problems that led Americans to look toward Europe for solutions.[1]

Growing urban density contributed to these problems. New York, the most populous American city with more than 60,000 inhabitants in 1800 (a population that would not even place in the top 300 in 2010) arguably faced the worst of these pollution problems—and hence was the vanguard of developing solutions—but no city was safe. In 1793 and 1798, yellow fever outbreaks killed scores in Philadelphia, then the nation's second-largest city. In the midst of the latter outbreak, the early sanitary engineer Benjamin Latrobe observed that Philadelphia's polluted water was "worst in the most crowded neighborhoods," where residents regularly fell victim to "all kinds of putrid and putrifying animal substances" that gave off noxious gases.[2] Latrobe gave voice to the predominant theory of disease transmission through the late 19th century: miasma. A word derived from the Greek for pollution, miasma denoted foul-smelling, filthy air or water associated with decomposing organic matter. Miasma theory led many Americans to perceive New Orleans' swampy environment as especially unhealthy. When yellow fever broke out in New York City in 1822, miasma theory drove residents to attempt to purify the air with coal smoke.[3]

In major cities, miasma theory also drove the adoption of municipal sanitary systems by the 1840s—primarily with respect to delivering potable water, and secondarily for the removal of sewerage. New York City and Boston built storm water sewers in the late 18th century. It was not until the 1850s, however, that cities such as Chicago (led by sanitary engineer Ellis Chesbrough) began constructing the first combined sewerage systems, which carried off household and industrial wastes along with storm water in a single large pipe. Sanitary (or separate) sewer systems, by contrast, used smaller pipes to handle only domestic and, increasingly, industrial wastes; storm water was handled with a larger pipe or simply not dealt with at all. Sanitary sewer systems became more common later in the 19th century and into the early 20th century, after combined systems were already widespread. Memphis and Baltimore both eventually built sanitary systems, but they were more commonly built by even smaller, lower-density cities. While those technological developments addressed polluted water and soil at the source, they merely shifted the burden elsewhere rather than treating disease-causing pollutants. Sewers, for instance, relied on the creation of sewage—mixing solid and liquid waste with 200 times its weight in water—and because its sheer volume was unmanageable for most cities, it was simply dumped into nearby rivers and lakes. Additionally, heavy rainfalls regularly overwhelmed combined systems, leading to uncontrolled overflows of storm water and sewage into waterways. Even these small marks of progress were much slower to come to many cities across the South, and a critical lack of sanitation in cities such as Atlanta and New Orleans persisted well beyond the Reconstruction era.[4]

Along with these technological advances, miasma theory was also a driving force behind many social and political trends in this period. The New York Metropolitan Board of Health was created in 1866, and other cities including Chicago, Milwaukee, Louisville, Indianapolis, and Boston followed suit in the next decade. A national board of health was founded in 1879, but public health remained primarily a local concern through the early 20th century as each city responded to its own unique set of pollutants. The desire to escape urban pollutants also contributed to the push for city parks as breathing spaces for urban residents and suburbanization as early as the mid-19th century. As suburbs grew, often those residents were soon forced to grapple with the same sorts of pollution problems that plagued urban dwellers, however, necessitating the same sorts of infrastructure cities were building. For many of the wealthier industrialists and businessmen who had a disproportionate role in creating urban pollution, a move to the suburbs was an attempt to escape both pollution *and* the poor, who were themselves seen as a sort of social pollutant.[5]

Unequal exposure to these pollutants characterized urban life from the very beginning, as occupational and residential discrimination meant that people of color, the working classes, and women were disproportionately subject to polluting industries and less apt to see the benefits of technological solutions. Latrobe observed that those who fell victim to Philadelphia's 1798 yellow fever epidemic "very frequently happened to [be] the lower class of people," for instance, while Atlanta's lack of sewerage meant that urban minorities were more likely to suffer from pollution-borne diseases such as cholera and typhoid fever.[6] Slavery and the ideology of white supremacy foisted perhaps the worst environmental burdens onto African Americans, in part because many, including Thomas Jefferson, saw miscegenation as racial pollution. That racist conflation of genetic pollution and environmental pollution, of nature and nurture, became a self-fulfilling prophecy that justified blaming the victims. Because African Americans and other racial and ethnic minorities were deemed inferior, even subhuman—and, by contrast, white people were seen as clean—it naturalized the unequal extent to which they suffered from urban pollutants. Prejudices many also harbored against ethnic immigrants fed into perceptions that environmental pollution was linked to immorality.[7]

POLLUTION IN INDUSTRIALIZING AND URBANIZING AMERICA

In the half-century between 1820 and 1870, American cities grew at a rate three times that of the nation as a whole. Immigration and internal migration accelerated urban growth in the next half-century, the period that environmental historian Robert Gottlieb contends "can be seen as laying in place the contemporary environmental hazards of daily life in urbanized and industrialized America."[8] By 1920 more than half of Americans (more than 54 million people) lived in urban areas. These thriving urban centers grew thanks to centralized factories whose economies of scale required large labor forces and well-developed transportation networks, both for the raw goods transported from surrounding hinterlands—iron ore, coal, livestock, lumber, and the like—and for the distribution of manufactured finished goods. The myriad pollutants generated by rapid industrial growth and emerging technologies, increasing population densities, as well as the sheer geographical footprint of the built environment simultaneously posed daunting challenges for urban sanitation. This had a detrimental impact on the air, water, and soil of rural areas where raw materials were extracted. Until pollution reached a crisis point, many urban and suburban dwellers—particularly those who benefited most from industrialization—saw pollution as a necessary evil, the price to be paid for progress.[9]

The price of that progress was not borne equitably by all urban dwellers. Populated almost exclusively by ethnic working-class whites (Irish American, Italian American, Polish American, and the like), the Back of the Yards neighborhood adjacent to Chicago's Union Stockyards is a good example of how pollution was more likely to affect working-class racial and ethnic minorities in cities nationwide. Bubbly Creek—a stagnant, polluted branch of the Chicago River in which the stockyards disposed of assorted animal wastes—and the stockyards themselves bordered the neighborhood on one side; on another was vacant land where stockyards waste rotted; on another was the city's open-pit garbage dumps. Rather than attributing the neighborhood's high mortality and illness rates to these environmental hazards, many instead blamed the victims' poor morality and hygiene. Rationalizing these groups' disproportionate exposure to material pollutants built on earlier prejudices and dovetailed with more metaphorical understandings of pollution in the Progressive Era such as eugenicist fears of race pollution and even more widespread fears of moral pollution (stemming from supposed "vices" such as alcohol and sex).[10]

As the Progressive Era drew to a close, the demographics of cities that absorbed millions of ethnic immigrants changed profoundly. Nearly two million African Americans left the South for northern industrial cities including Chicago, New York, Detroit, and Pittsburgh in what became known as the Great Migration; many also abandoned agricultural lives for the growing urban industries of Southern cities such as Birmingham and Atlanta. Chicago's black population, for instance, more than sextupled between 1910 and 1940, rising from roughly 44,000 to more than 275,000; their share of the city's overall population quadrupled, growing from less than 2 percent to more than 8 percent. To an even greater extent than the ethnic working-class whites who suffered the worst of the city's pollution in neighborhoods such as the Back of the Yards, racial violence and discriminatory policies largely confined black Chicagoans to occupations and residential districts that suffered disproportionate exposure to polluted air, water, and soil. The same story was repeated in cities across the country, North and South, from the steel mills of Gary, Indiana, to the steel mills of Birmingham, Alabama.[11]

Although considerable regional variation existed, cities generally dealt with urban pollutants in two main ways, both of which consigned people of color and ethnic whites to dirty work and polluted neighborhoods in close proximity to industry. The first solution was to draft nuisance and zoning laws that effectively quarantined polluting industries in certain areas of the city. Smoke and other pollutants emanating from industries such as slaughterhouses and tanneries were legally limited on the basis of nuisance laws by the early 20th century in many cities. By the same token, New York City (1916) and St. Louis (1918) were the first two American cities to enact zoning laws in the early 20th century that prohibited industry from locating in residential areas. Crucially, however, zoning laws did not restrict homes from being built in industrial areas. This effectively perpetuated inequalities as working-class homes were built in close proximity to polluting industries where land values were low. Middle- and upper-class neighborhoods, by contrast, remained relatively safe—and far, as suburbs continued to grow—from pollution sources. Other residential policies such as restrictive covenants and redlining similarly became tools that legally backed racial segregation and led communities of color to disproportionately bear the social and environmental costs of industrialization, reinforcing racist ideas.[12]

Progressive Era social reformers, many of them women such as Jane Addams and Alice Hamilton in Chicago, led movements to curb urban pollution. Those reformers focused more on the unequal pollution burdens facing the working classes. Sanitarians—experts including engineers and public health officials—rather quickly dominated the conversation, however, promoting the second main approach to urban pollution: the search for technological fixes. Improving sewer infrastructure, treating water with chemicals, and constructing sanitary landfills were common technological fixes that rarely attempted to eliminate pollutants at their source. Instead, they merely mitigated negative public health impacts (with little to no regard for the impacts on non-human life

or the environment) stemming from what many saw as the inevitable byproducts of industrialization. In so doing, they merely shifted pollution from one area of the metropolis to another (in some cases, out of the city to rural or suburban areas) or to a different sink (from water to air, for instance). Inevitably, the least politically powerful communities—predominantly working-class racial and ethnic minorities—found themselves on the receiving ends of those shifts.[13]

Water Pollution. By the late 19th century, industries added a range of new pollutants—heavy metals and chemicals in particular—to the human and animal waste streams that had long fouled waterways. Factories were often situated adjacent to lakes or rivers to take advantage of the water for steam and cooling, but these bodies of water were also convenient because dumping in them was an easy and low- or no-cost waste disposal method. Already by 1900, industry alone—overwhelmingly situated in cities—accounted for 40 percent of the nation's river pollution. Virtually every city had its version of Chicago's Bubbly Creek, rendered unrecognizable by pollution: in New York, Newtown Creek and Kill Van Kull were heavily polluted by industrial wastes. Raw sewage dumped into Manhattan's watershed and harbor polluted and then destroyed the region's fertile oyster beds.[14]

Bacteriological theory supplanted miasma theory in the 1880s, leaving less room for the layman to identify potential disease sources via smell and helping drive the emergence of the professional class of sanitarians. Municipal sanitary engineers designed water delivery systems and sewers, added chlorine to water sources, and later pioneered filtration systems to mitigate water-borne diseases. Mostly, though, engineers simply attempted to dilute pollution in waterways to mitigate negative public health impacts rather than treating it or reducing pollution outflows; there was little to no regard for the impact water pollution had on non-human life or the environment more broadly. Many cities developed fairly extensive water delivery and sewerage networks by the early 20th century that carried pollutants away from densely populated residential areas and dramatically cut disease rates. Perhaps most notably, engineers reversed the flow of the Chicago River in 1900 so that the city's sewage flowed toward the Mississippi River (and St. Louis and New Orleans) rather than toward Lake Michigan, from which the city drew its fresh water. Cities' capacity for adopting technological fixes that simply displaced pollution problems downstream eventually led states—rather than municipalities—to take the lead in legislating water pollution controls. Despite these advances, cities such as Atlanta grew so fast in the early 20th century that officials struggled to build sewers and waterworks quickly enough, exposing citizens—typically working-class communities of color—to water polluted with human and animal waste and, hence, the possibility of diseases such as typhoid fever.[15]

Solid Waste and Soil Pollution. Pollution stemming from inadequate solid waste disposal methods was problematic for decades. This issue, however, failed to arouse many concerns until the end of the 19th century, when the sheer volume of urban waste generated by burgeoning populations—more than half a ton of refuse per capita—became difficult to manage and finally compelled cities to take action. Animal waste alone posed a profound challenge for many municipalities: approximately 3.5 million urban horses nationwide each produced up to thirty pounds of manure daily. Streets and alleys were filthy as many citizens simply dumped waste there. To the extent that cities collected and disposed of wastes, they did so in unsanitary ways on nearby vacant lands or bodies of water. The latter method was especially hazardous to human health, but New York dumped garbage in the ocean while Chicago dumped solid waste, like its sewage prior to the river reversal, in Lake Michigan.[16]

Across the country, civic-minded urban residents—especially middle-class women acting on Victorian notions of cleanliness, aesthetics, and moral reform associated with the City Beautiful movement—mobilized to change these practices. Foremost among these was the Ladies' Health Protective Association (LHPA), founded in New York City in 1884, and similar activist groups sprung up in many cities and often involved children in clean-up campaigns. Although the LHPA was instrumental in the city's decision to begin incinerating garbage (New York began operating the country's first incinerator in 1885, and many cities followed suit), these social movements gave way to expert-driven bureaucracies founded on Progressive Era ideals of efficiency. George Waring, who began serving as New York's Street-Cleaning Commissioner in 1894, is perhaps the most famous sanitarian of the era. Waring took a comprehensive approach to solid waste sanitation—initiating a range of measures including waste separation, street cleaning, ocean dumping, and beginning a reduction plant—that pushed New York to the vanguard of pollution remediation strategies. More than three-quarters of cities with populations larger than 25,000 required solid waste separation, and even though they did not become widespread until the 1920s, sanitary landfills relied on that separation, interspersing layers of decaying garbage with ashes and other rubbish or dirt. Waring and other sanitarians had made such great strides by the early 20th century that many began to view the city—despite all the pollutants generated there—as a healthier place than the country.[17]

Urban dwellers rightfully did not regard all parts of the city as equally healthy, however. Sanitarians' technological solutions mitigated disease transmission from rotting garbage, but as Hull House settlement worker Jane Addams noted in Chicago, while "the system of garbage collecting was inadequate throughout the city [...] It is easy for even the most conscientious citizen of Chicago to forget the foul smells of the stockyards and the garbage dumps, when he is living so far from them that he is only occasionally made conscious of their existence."[18] Not only did working-class racial and ethnic minorities live closer to pollution sources, they were more likely to have jobs that exposed them to a wide variety of urban pollutants. Mostly that increased the health hazards of urban life, but there was also ample entrepreneurial possibility in industries such as garbage hauling, junk peddling, and recycling that others avoided; Jews and Italians constituted a large proportion of these trades. Indeed, when sanitarians began more strictly regulating these spaces, some of those opportunities disappeared.[19]

Atmospheric Pollution.   While water and land pollution tended to differ in degree from problems urbanites encountered in early America, widespread fossil fuel burning marked the first time air pollution seriously impacted cities. Intensifying industrialization pushed that issue to a crisis point by the late 19th century. Air pollution's severity was largely linked to a city's mix of industries as well as the type of fuel they burned: the anthracite coal from Pennsylvania that New Yorkers burned was cleaner, relatively speaking, than the bituminous coal burned in Pittsburgh and midwestern cities such as Cincinnati, Chicago, and St. Louis. Coal smoke came from factories and, to a lesser extent, homes, but trains also burned coal in great quantities, accounting for one-fifth to one-half of all smoke in cities such as Chicago and Pittsburgh; in 1880, more than 90 percent of railroad fuel was the smokier bituminous variety. Although major metropolises with higher concentrations of industry suffered the most, even smaller cities such as Albany, New York, choked on the soot from locomotives and industry.[20] Already by 1861, for instance, the smoke primarily from iron foundries in Wheeling, West Virginia, led one resident to remark that it "settles down in black, slimy pools on the muddy streets. Smoke on the wharves, smoke on the dingy boats, on

the yellow river,—clinging in a coating of greasy soot to the house-front, the two faded poplars, the faces of the passers-by. [...] Smoke everywhere!"[21] While smoke's atmospheric dispersal meant that a wider swath of urban residents were likely exposed to it than more hyper-localized water and soil pollutants, its costs were not borne equally, either. In Cincinnati, for example, sootfall was heaviest in tenement districts located nearest the main industrial sources of air pollution. The working classes were also more likely to face additional health risks from laboring in those polluting industries, and those occupational hazards led to some of the first attempts to regulate air quality in the early 20th century.[22]

Cities attempted to address air pollution, but progress on mitigating the problem was incremental at best. As with protests against inadequate solid waste removal, the early phase of this social activism against smoke at the turn of the century was led by women and played on middle-class Victorian ideals of beauty, health, and civilization. Rather quickly, those social movements were followed by a second phase in the 1910s that searched for technological fixes and relied much more heavily on the scientific expertise of engineers and doctors. Chicago's severe smoke problem inspired the nation's first pollution control ordinance in 1881, and more than 80 percent of the country's largest cities had enacted similar ordinances by 1912. Most of them used a fairly rudimentary visual test of smoke density (employing the Ringlemann Chart) to determine if polluters were in violation of the ordinance.[23] On the whole, however, smoke control ordinances proved largely toothless because polluting industries were successful in framing air pollution as progress. Unlike water pollution, air pollution was not strongly associated with ill health despite the prominence of respiratory illnesses' contribution to high urban mortality rates. Polluters also held significant sway over municipal government and the legal system. St. Louis, for instance, passed a smoke control ordinance in 1893, but it was quickly challenged by industry and declared unconstitutional. In Chicago, the railroads led similarly successful campaigns to limit smoke control efforts. In Birmingham, Alabama, industry was even more aggressive and regulation attempts were even weaker. Smoke problems also continued because urban populations grew ever larger and denser, new energy-intensive industries added to the tragedy of the atmospheric commons, and consumption rates accelerated. Chicago gained more than one million residents between 1900 and 1920, for example, when residents' per capita coal consumption more than doubled. Unlike clean water, clean air was seen more as a luxury that could be sacrificed in the name of economic progress.[24]

The same held true for peace and quiet. Anti-noise campaigns lagged behind efforts to mitigate water, soil, and air pollution, but they appeared in cities large and small as early as the 1890s and persisted well into the 1930s. Many cities including New York, Chicago, Louisville, and Atlanta founded committees and commissions to investigate noise pollution—like smoke, mainly emanating from factories and trains—and adopted anti-noise zones around hospitals and schools by the early 20th century. Despite those efforts, cities did not get any quieter thanks in part to new technologies: automobile traffic, skyscraper construction, and businesses' advertising loudspeakers all contributed to the cacophony. New York City was generally acknowledged as the noisiest city in the world by the 1920s. The increased prevalence of air travel in the post-World War II era only further contributed to noise pollution in all cities, especially major metropolises which began building large international airports.[25]

THE POST-WORLD WAR II ERA: MODERN ENVIRONMENTALISM AND NATIONAL REGULATION

As was true of turn-of-the-century industrialization, technological developments were the primary contributors to urban pollution levels, which reached a crisis point by the 1960s. Ecologist and environmentalist Barry Commoner identified technology as the primary culprit behind pollution levels he calculated had at least tripled in the quarter-century following World War II. Added to industrial smoke and effluent was an entirely new set of pollutants generated as wartime production transitioned into producing consumer goods. Most notable were radioactive isotopes and a wide array of toxic chemicals. The aboveground detonation of atomic bombs released radioactive isotopes such as strontium-90 into the atmosphere, with little understanding of its human or environmental health impacts. At the same time, more than 80 percent of untreated chemical wastes—nearly six million tons of hazardous material including polychlorinated biphenyl (PCB), phenol, benzene, toluene, naphtha, lead, arsenic, sulfite, and a variety of acids—was simply dumped into the nation's waterways, skies, and soil even prior to World War II. The problem only grew worse in the postwar years as industry continued to frame pollution as necessary for economic growth, even inevitable.[26]

Technology was not the only factor to blame for cities' growing pollution problems, however. The postwar baby boom ballooned the nation's population, which was increasingly affluent and suburban. Rising affluence contributed to demand for the industrially produced consumer goods that generated pollutants. Suburbanization—under way since the 19th century but greatly accelerated after World War II—made cities less densely populated and expanded their geographical footprint, necessitating massive infrastructural investments on pollution-control projects such as sewage treatment plants. They also made Americans ever more dependent on fossil fuel-intensive transportation methods that added to the air pollution produced by factories. Many factories still relied on coal, but increasingly oil and gas accounted for the lion's share of Americans' energy consumption and, in turn, raised a different set of pollution concerns than those that occupied urban dwellers at the turn of the century. Rapid and energy-intensive metropolitan growth was most notable in southern "Sunbelt" cities such as Dallas, Houston, Atlanta, and Charlotte, which sprawled over vast expanses of land and grew nearly twice as fast as Rust Belt cities such as Chicago, Detroit, and Pittsburgh, which had been destinations for migrants in an earlier era. Metropolitan areas' spatial distribution of population changed greatly from the interwar era: by 1980, the suburbs of the nation's largest cities were larger than the city centers themselves.[27]

Suburban affluence also somewhat paradoxically spurred the social movements that led to landmark legislation regulating pollutants on a national rather than municipal or state level. Modern environmentalism challenged the long-standing notion that pollution was necessary for progress, and late 1960s environmental disasters built on the legacy of Rachel Carson's *Silent Spring* (1962), awakening the nation—especially white middle-class suburban dwellers—to the toxic risks of their postwar society. In particular, growing scientific knowledge in ecology and toxicology contributed to Americans' consciousness about the myriad human health and environmental hazards that air, water, and soil pollution posed. By the first Earth Day in 1970, when an estimated 20 million Americans took to the streets, many saw pollution as a threat to planetary survival. Cities and suburbs were ground zero for the nascent environmental movement as well as this question of survival: in a speech delivered at the first Earth Day, US Senator Gaylord Nelson of Wisconsin pleaded for money to be spent "on our decaying, crowded, congested, polluted urban areas that are inhuman traps for millions of people. If our cities don't work, America won't work."[28]

The popular outcry led the US Congress to pass landmark environmental legislation that mandated air, water, and soil quality standards to be enforced by the Environmental Protection Agency (EPA), established in 1970.

Although the EPA was hampered by a lack of funding and scientific uncertainty that hamstrung enforcement, metropolitan areas—and the nation more broadly—enjoyed substantially less polluted air, water, and soil in the wake of these laws. Carson had warned Americans about the cancer-causing potential of chemicals such as DDT, and as the 1970s wore on, mounting concern about the health impacts of industrial pollutants led to another wave of environmental legislation aimed at limiting exposure to toxics. Nevertheless, the partial ban of DDT in 1972 was an exception to the more general rule: these laws mostly continued to emphasize technological fixes rather than curtail or outright ban industry's production of pollutants. Scientific uncertainty surrounding specific pollutant–disease causality and pathways hobbled activists' grassroots efforts to limit exposure despite the identification of many chemicals as known carcinogens, and the sheer array of new pollutants generated by industry added further complexity. But toxicological science—which supplanted bacteriological science as the predominant way of understanding how pollutants lead to adverse health outcomes—largely backed up Carson's broader concerns about chemical pollutants and increasingly found that even low-dose exposure was unsafe.[29]

Rapidly changing urban demographics compounded and reinforced the long-standing environmental inequalities working-class communities of color faced as the overall pollution problem mounted. African Americans migrated to cities in the North and West at rates that far outpaced the first wave of the Great Migration, while middle-class whites fled urban cores for the suburbs, driven by racial fear and underwritten by discriminatory real estate policies that built on early 20th-century policies and reinforced economic anxieties. Fairly representative of cities that were previously migration destinations, Chicago's black population nearly quadrupled between World War II and 1970 while the city's overall population remained virtually unchanged and its suburbs grew by leaps and bounds. The resulting "urban crisis" left predominantly minority populations in cities with the decades-long legacy of industrial pollution as well as diminished job opportunities and tax bases (which in turn hobbled cities' ability to clean up pollutants). Like earlier social movements that battled urban pollutants, the grassroots environmental justice movement that emerged in the 1980s focused on the human health hazards posed by pollution from sites such as power plants, toxic waste dumps, incinerators, solid waste facilities, and sewage treatment plants. But the environmental justice movement contested the racial inequalities of pollution exposure more than ever before. Activists mobilized to protest pollution hazards on Chicago's far South Side in the 1990s, for instance, where the area's overwhelmingly African American residents lived amid the greatest concentration of landfills anywhere in the nation and breathed air fouled daily with more than 100,000 pounds of pollutants. Despite many local victories and a robust movement that continues, numerous studies found that these inequities persisted more than three decades later, suggesting that, as environmental justice activists claim, national pollution control legislation was and is inequitably and inconsistently enforced.[30]

Water Pollution. Although many problems remained with untreated sewage and other organic effluent, the primary threat to waterways shifted to a vast array and enormous volume of toxic chemical wastes that industry commonly discharged into adjacent rivers, lakes, and municipal sewer systems in order to avoid treatment and remediation costs. Combined sewers that handled both storm water runoff and sewage were particularly vulnerable to heavy storm events and sewage treatment plants failed more often, discharging chemical pollutants and untreated sewage into waterways. Suburban sprawl that paved over permeable surfaces with little regard for watershed hydrology further

exacerbated these problems. Detergents from both domestic and industrial sources contributed to a sevenfold increase in phosphates discharged in municipal sewers between 1940 and 1970. Fish kills, foul-tasting and -smelling water, and rivers and lakes foaming with phosphate suds all elicited public pressure to more stringently regulate water pollution. Cleveland's Cuyahoga River fire and adjacent Lake Erie rendered unswimmable were the most iconic examples of these problems. But metropolitan areas of all sizes and in all regions suffered growing water pollution loads; even the suburbs were vulnerable to polluted groundwater from septic tank failures. In a vivid illustration of how rural and urban areas are inextricably connected through ecosystems and economies, even tiny Decatur, Illinois's water supply was polluted in the early 1970s by nitrogen fertilizer that had run off from surrounding farmland. Some of the monocropped, fertilizer-reliant food produced from those fields— characteristic of industrial agriculture in the post–World War II era—no doubt fed upstate Chicagoans and urban dwellers well beyond.[31]

National legislation such as the Water Quality Act (1965) and Safe Drinking Water Act (1974) regulated water pollutants, but the most important water pollution law that emerged in this era was the Clean Water Act (CWA) (1972). In part the CWA mandated that sewage plants reduce the pollution they received by 85 percent, but its primary approach was to allocate massive subsidies for municipalities to upgrade and build wastewater treatment plants. Although a significant portion of cities remained out of compliance with the law, in just a decade many types of industrial water pollution were cut in half. In fact, the most dramatic improvements were seen in metropolitan rather than rural areas because the Clean Water Act was much more effective at regulating point source pollution (mostly industrial and domestic in nature) rather than non-point pollution sources (mostly agricultural in nature). Storm water runoff that carried a wide range of pollutants from city streets and other impermeable surfaces into waterways was a troublesome non-point source pollution that many metropolitan areas began to address with infrastructural solutions such as bioswales and porous pavements. The EPA employed growing toxicological and ecological knowledge about what pollution levels are harmful, but sometimes government officials themselves endangered public health. In Flint, Michigan, public officials unwittingly initiated a water crisis in 2014 when they switched to a water source that corroded lead pipes' protective lining and leached high levels of lead and other contaminants into residents' water supply. A majority-black city, Flint was representative of the unequal pollution burdens facing communities of color. New technologies also continued to create new water pollution sources. Hydraulic fracking threatened to contaminate urban and rural water supplies, for instance, while pharmaceutical wastes and microplastics dumped into the sewage stream further challenged municipal wastewater treatment.[32]

Toxic Waste and Soil Pollution.

Rising affluence contributed to per capita solid waste production doubling in the quarter-century following World War II. Although paper constituted the largest single category of municipal waste, a much wider array of pollutants that carried their own disposal challenges—chemicals and plastics chief among them—also entered the solid waste stream. After a resurgence motivated by Depression-era and wartime scarcity, refuse recycling and repurposing declined in the more affluent throwaway culture; the widespread use of plastic garbage bags deposited directly into trash compactor trucks further hindered such efforts. Recycling did not gain renewed interest until the modern environmental movement's heyday in the 1970s led to volunteer-led recycling centers opening in cities such as Chicago, Ann Arbor, Berkeley, and Boulder; only in the 1980s did recycling grow more widespread. By the 21st century, cities such as San Francisco

increasingly turned to curbside organic waste composting programs, harkening back to earlier, prewar waste separation practices. While both San Francisco and New York (which also continued its practice of dumping solid waste in the ocean) pioneered ambitious sanitary landfill projects in the 1930s, most larger cities turned to solid waste incineration with little regard for their contribution to air pollution. When more stringent air and water pollution regulations were passed in the early 1970s, those wastes were displaced onto urban soils, lacing them with high levels of trace metals and toxic chemicals that persist for hundreds or even thousands of years. Hazards abounded, even in people's homes: disproportionately minority children in substandard urban housing were especially vulnerable to poisoning from lead paint, for example. Accumulating radioactive waste generated from the nuclear plants that powered cities' growing energy needs presented arguably the steepest long-term disposal problems and remain largely unresolved.[33]

National legislation addressing polluted soils lagged behind air and water regulations. Passed in 1976, the Resource Conservation and Recovery Act (RCRA) curtailed garbage burning and ocean dumping within a decade. New York finally halted ocean dumping in 1991 when Congress refused to grant it further extensions. The Comprehensive Environmental Response, Compensation, and Liability Act (CERCLA, more popularly known as Superfund) was passed in 1980 to remediate the worst toxic waste sites. Superfund was motivated primarily by the outcry over the human health impacts of toxic chemicals buried in the Love Canal neighborhood of Niagara Falls, New York, but it was just one of literally thousands of cities with neighborhoods that the EPA identified as similarly vulnerable to the toxic legacy of urban industrial development. The EPA's "brownfields" program expanded Superfund's purview in the mid-1990s, aiming to redevelop industrial and commercial sites whose soil had been more lightly contaminated by toxic pollutants, many of them located in suburban or exurban areas. Because these contamination sites—many of which escaped regulatory review—remained ill-suited to residential and other non-industrial uses, they were commonly redeveloped to process garbage and other wastes. Some working-class communities of color were so desperate for economic development that they welcomed such projects, effectively doubling down on long-standing environmental inequalities.[34]

Love Canal spurred countless grassroots social movements that fought urban pollutants, sometimes disparagingly called "Not in My Backyard" (NIMBY) protests. These local protests tended to emphasize the human health hazards resulting from a community's proximity to common pollution sources such as toxic waste dumps, industrial facilities, and power plants. Environmental justice activists built on that legacy, explicitly arguing that the costs of pollution tended to be disproportionately borne across lines of race, ethnicity, and class. Although protests against the siting of a toxic waste dump in predominantly African American Warren County, North Carolina, are typically regarded as the genesis of the environmental justice movement, even that rural locale illustrated connections to the Sunbelt's metropolitan industrial patterns: the toxic PCBs were produced in Raleigh, North Carolina, at a factory that was itself later remediated via Superfund. One of the first comprehensive environmental justice studies found that racial and ethnic minorities were disproportionately likely to live in close proximity to toxic waste sites in cities nationwide, Rust Belt and Sunbelt alike. African Americans were most likely to live near such sites in Memphis, St. Louis, Houston, Cleveland, Chicago, and Atlanta, while Los Angeles had the most Hispanic Americans living near them; subsequent research revealed that racial disparities were greatest in metropolitan areas in the Midwest and West. Similar disparities were just as evident in the South. Home to the petrochemical industry that discharged toxic

chemicals into the air, water, and soil, the stretch of the Mississippi River corridor between Baton Rouge and New Orleans, Louisiana—populated largely by people of color—was dubbed "cancer alley." Indeed, toxic chemical exposure was far from limited to large industrial cities; even residents of small towns such as Anniston, Alabama, were forced to confront soils contaminated with probable human carcinogens including PCBs.[35]

Atmospheric Pollution. The industrial air pollution sources urban dwellers faced at the turn of the century grew worse in the postwar era. They were joined by two new especially problematic pollutants: smog from tailpipe exhaust and radioactive fallout from above-ground nuclear bomb detonations. While above-ground nuclear testing was not conducted near urban areas, downwind cities (especially in the West) felt the impacts of such testing as atmospheric radiation dispersed, and many were concerned that agricultural products such as milk and meat had been contaminated. The Limited Nuclear Test Ban Treaty in 1963 curtailed the further accumulation of fallout, but radioactive isotopes such as strontium-90 persisted in the atmosphere. Author and essayist E. B. White mused from his Turtle Bay, New York, neighborhood in 1956, "This section of Manhattan boasts the heaviest sootfall in town, and the United States of America boasts the heaviest fallout in the world, and when you take the sootfall and the [nuclear] fallout and bring smog in on top of them, I feel I am in a perfect position to discuss the problem of universal pollution."[36] Many felt that pollution was universal in this era, and White's New York was far from alone in the problems it faced. In Detroit, air pollution was so bad that airplanes could not land, and in Pittsburgh, activists warned that particulate matter and sulfur dioxide made the air more dangerous to breathe than when soot had blocked out the sun in the early 20th century. Small cities were vulnerable, too: in 1948, just south of Pittsburgh, twenty people died when smog became trapped over Donora, Pennsylvania. Seen primarily as a local problem, industries often just built taller smokestacks to carry pollutants further away, dispersing them over downwind rural skies. Like sewers and sanitary landfills, tall smokestacks—some up to the height of a sixty-five-story building—simply transferred pollutants elsewhere rather than mitigating them.[37]

Oil and natural gas increasingly supplied the nation's energy after World War II, and while those fuels burned cleaner than coal (which had choked cities with smoke for a century), they created a different set of pollution problems that were most evident in Sunbelt cities such as Los Angeles, Houston, and Dallas. Those cities' suburban sprawl tended to disperse metropolitan air pollution sources, but sprawl also made those cities especially dependent on automobiles that generated a wide array of pollutants including smog, ozone, and lead (before the EPA began phasing out leaded gasoline in the 1970s). Situated in a basin that traps air pollutants, Los Angeles epitomized the hazards of car culture and suburban sprawl in the postwar era.[38] As Barry Commoner put it in 1971, "There are few cities in the world with climates so richly endowed by nature and now so disastrously polluted by man."[39] The costs of America's car culture and suburban sprawl were not borne equally, however. Children and the elderly were most vulnerable to the human health impacts of these air pollutants, and urban-dwelling people of color battled the worst environmental assaults from white suburban commuters' tailpipe exhaust as highway construction gutted minority neighborhoods. The same year Commoner lamented Los Angeles's dire air quality, for instance, the Black Panthers protested a proposed highway through Boston's African American neighborhood because automobile emissions posed myriad health hazards to the community.[40]

Concern about air pollution's human health hazards led to the Clean Air Act of 1970, which adhered to the "polluter pays principle" requiring industry to mitigate air pollution regardless of cost (different from the federal subsidy approach to water pollution). Despite those costly regulatory changes, some industries welcomed national regulations that were less restrictive than those that some especially polluted cities such as Los Angeles were eager to impose. The EPA set air quality standards for major pollutants and was broadly successful; some cities cut their air pollution in half. Despite those improvements, working-class communities of color continued to suffer poorer air quality than middle-class white communities: cities as diverse as Denver, Los Angeles, San Francisco, Chicago, New York, and Washington, DC, exhibited these inequalities in the 1980s. These communities under assault have mounted countless grassroots campaigns protesting their exposure to pollutants, and have achieved many victories. Race remains a stronger predictor of pollutant exposure than class, however: urban African Americans continue to have the highest exposure to major air pollutants such as small particulate matter, putting them at higher risk for a range of respiratory and cardiovascular ailments.[41]

Growing metropolitan energy consumption in tandem with technological development has far-ranging consequences that can negatively impact even rural minority communities. When extra-high-voltage, low-loss, economically feasible long-distance power lines allowed Phoenix to rely on distantly burned coal rather than more locally burned natural gas, indigenous peoples nearly 400 miles away—rather than the (overwhelmingly white) city residents themselves—bore the brunt of air pollutants such as fly ash and heavy metals. Air pollution was generally regarded as a local problem until the Clean Air Act Amendments of 1990 recognized at least one iteration of these regional connections: sulfur dioxide emissions, mainly from coal-fired power plants in midwestern cities, were restricted in an effort to mitigate acid rain in downwind states.[42]

In the 21st century, long-standing byproducts of fossil fuel burning—light and greenhouse gas emissions, both of which have regional and even global impacts—came under new scrutiny and began to change how the very idea of pollution was defined. Another effect of car culture, light pollution originated mainly from urban parking lots and streetlights; the lights of Las Vegas, perhaps the world's brightest city, were visible from far-off national parks. While much less was known about light pollution's adverse health effects compared with the cardiovascular and respiratory ailments caused by air pollutants, scientific research increasingly demonstrated that light pollution disrupts humans' and animals' circadian rhythms, linking it to an array of maladies including obesity, depression, and even cancer.[43] More notable was the changing perception and regulatory framework surrounding greenhouse gas emissions from fossil fuel burning that dated back to the 19th century but had risen dramatically in the post-World War II era. In *Massachusetts vs. EPA* (2007), the Supreme Court narrowly ruled that the EPA must regulate carbon dioxide emitted from new motor vehicles as an air pollutant under the Clean Air Act (1970) because of its endangerment of public health. The new motor vehicle provisions of the Clean Air Act had been developed in response to the smog that cities such as Los Angeles confronted in the 1950s and 1960s (and were, in turn, influenced by the way air quality was degraded by soot and regulated at the turn of the century). But the state of Massachusetts—joined by coastal cities including New York, Baltimore, and Washington, DC—convinced the court that carbon dioxide endangered public health in a different way: primarily by contributing to rising sea levels.[44]

DISCUSSION OF THE LITERATURE

The first wave of urban environmental history concerning pollution was stimulated by scholars such as Martin Melosi and Joel Tarr. They and others focused on the period of intense industrialization in the late 19th and early 20th centuries that was most dramatically observed in large cities in the East and Midwest such as New York, Pittsburgh, and Chicago. Indebted to science and technology studies, those histories tended toward top-down analyses of the technological and public health implications of urban pollution, chronicling the accomplishments and motivations of sanitarians—the expert class of engineers, public health officials, and the like—who worked to mitigate urban pollution problems. Legal and political history also informed these earliest approaches, and those perspectives on turn-of-the-century urban pollution were augmented by works such as David Stradling's *Smokestacks and Progressives* that addressed the bottom-up social movements (many led by women) that contested urban pollution.

The lived experiences of those most vulnerable to cities' polluted air, water, and soil—working-class racial and ethnic minorities—were present in those earliest accounts, but they have moved from the margins to the center in social and cultural histories such as Catherine McNeur's *Taming Manhattan*, David Pellow's *Garbage Wars*, Matthew Klingle's *Emerald City*, and Craig Colten's *Unnatural Metropolis*. Beyond showing how working-class racial and ethnic minorities suffered the worst effects of urban pollution, each of those monographs also interrogates the extent to which sanitarians' and municipal officials' efforts actually created and reinforced those environmental inequalities. Whereas earlier histories relied on published documents and archival sources produced by public officials and the professional class of experts who worked to solve pollution problems, newer histories employ different sources altogether—newspapers, popular periodicals, oral histories, and the like—to narrate their stories from the bottom up. The commitment to understanding the lived experience of pollution has also translated into works such as Melanie Kiechle's sensory history of 19th-century cities,

Smell Detectives, as well as histories such as Christopher Sellers' *Crabgrass Crucible* and Ellen Griffith Spears' *Baptized in PCBs*, both of which employ oral history methodologies. Many monographs, including Spears' *Baptized in PCBs* and Nancy Langston's *Toxic Bodies*, interrogate the bodily consequences of toxic chemicals that proliferated in the postwar era, and they increasingly use scientific data to bolster their arguments.

While the earliest urban environmental histories spent relatively little time on pollution in the post-World War II era, it was mainly examined in the context of how those problems and the rising affluence among middle-class suburban whites animated modern environmentalism. More recently, the environmental justice movement itself, along with developments in fields such as sociology and critical race studies, has led historians to increasingly analyze the contours of urban environmental inequalities in this era (and to unpack those inequalities in earlier periods); on the whole, urban historians have become ever more attentive to race and ethnicity, class, and gender. Andrew Hurley's *Environmental Inequalities* is perhaps the earliest example of this work, and more recent contributions, such as Dorceta Taylor's *Toxic Communities*, abound. These works increasingly interrogate the ways that policies undergirding racial segregation—restrictive covenants, redlining, and the like—contribute to the disproportionate exposure of people of color to urban pollutants, hence connecting urban environmental history to broader historiographies. Until recently, however, relatively little work attempted to understand these postwar pollution inequalities in the context of historical trends such as the emerging "urban crisis" in the 1960s; Robert Gioielli's *Environmental Activism and the Urban Crisis* and David and Richard Stradling's *Where the River Burned* are outstanding early examples of these efforts.

Histories of urban pollution continue to diversify, in a multitude of ways beyond the attentiveness to vastly disparate urban experiences along lines of space and place, race and ethnicity, class, and gender. Perhaps most notably, a wealth of suburban histories have shown how pollutants—and the social movements that arose to fight them—were generated in cities' wider metropolitan areas. Among these are Adam Rome's *The Bulldozer in the Countryside* and Sellers' *Crabgrass Crucible*. Taking those insights a step further (and following William Cronon's insights in *Nature's Metropolis* concerning the inextricable connections between cities and their hinterlands), historians are also examining how urban patterns of consumption, particularly of fossil fuels, have generated pollution far outside the city. Outstanding examples of these energy histories include Christopher Jones' *Routes of Power* and Andrew Needham's *Power Lines*. Histories examining metropolitan pollution still tend toward local case studies, but Needham's study of Phoenix along with Klingle's study of Seattle, *Emerald City*, are characteristic of a move beyond the industrial Rust Belt cities of the East and Midwest toward more complete analyses of the Sunbelt and West. Spears' *Baptized in PCBs*, a case study of Anniston, Alabama, is representative not only of this growing environmental scholarship on the South (driven partly by the rise of Sunbelt history more generally), but also of an increasing attention to smaller cities and towns.

PRIMARY SOURCES

Although one can make general claims about the pollutants city dwellers faced in a given time period, because the particulars of a given city's pollution problems often varied widely, one should begin research with local municipal primary sources. Official municipal records (of boards of health, engineering departments, courts, and the like) as well as the papers of activist groups (such as the Ladies' Health Protective Association) and key figures concerned with urban pollution (for example Jane Addams) make local municipal archives indispensable. These records generally can be found in large cities such as New York (at the New York Public Library and the New York City Municipal Archives, among other repositories) and Chicago (at the Chicago History Museum and the Municipal Reference Collection at the Harold Washington branch of the Chicago Public Library, among other repositories), but cities of all sizes and in all regions have similar resources. Local archives on the East Coast and in the South are strong in antebellum material, and Cornell University Library's Making of America Collection is a good online resource with primary sources documenting all aspects of the nation's development from colonial America through Reconstruction.

Anti-pollution activism and growing expert-driven concern with pollution during the Progressive Era makes local collections especially rich in late 19th- and early 20th-century sources, and extensive bibliographical essays in Martin Melosi's *The Sanitary City* and David Stradling's *Smokestacks and Progressives* are especially useful for locating them. They reference, for example, comprehensive Progressive Era local studies including Pittsburgh's *Mellon Institute of Industrial Research Smoke Investigation* (1912–1922) and the Chicago Association of Commerce's *Smoke Abatement and Electrification of Railway Terminals in Chicago* (1915), both of which have been digitized and are accessible via HathiTrust, a vast online archive of primary sources. Sanitarians' perspectives can also be found in professional journals such as *Sanitary Engineer* as well as *American Journal of Public Health* which, after more than a century, continues to publish peer-reviewed research on public health hazards from urban pollutants. Industry's perspective on the pollution it produced can be found in municipal records as well as industry and trade publications; *Industrial World* (later *Steel and Iron*) was the steel industry's publication, for example.

For social and cultural histories, local newspapers and other periodicals—increasingly digitized—are crucial. Major urban newspapers including the *New York Times*, *Chicago Tribune*,

Atlanta Constitution, and *Los Angeles Times* are digitized and keyword searchable via databases such as ProQuest Historical Newspapers, as are African American newspapers including the *Pittsburgh Courier*, *Baltimore Afro-American*, and *Chicago Defender*. Although many of these digital archives are behind paywalls, the Chronicling America: Historic American Newspapers collection via the Library of Congress is openly accessible and incredibly vast. Ranging from the 18th century to the mid-20th century, it includes a wide array of publications from small and mid-size cities in virtually every state as well as many racial and ethnic publications. Many historians are increasingly incorporating oral histories into their research to help reconstruct the lived experience of urban pollution—sometimes conducting their own interviews, and sometimes relying on audio and transcribed oral histories often in the possession of local archives. Local archives also possess documents concerning that particular city's racial segregation linked to environmental inequalities—zoning laws, restrictive covenants, redlining, and the like—and many are also available online; a national collection of urban redlining maps is available through the *Mapping Inequality* project. Similar place-based insights can be achieved with readily available US Census data and Geographic Information Systems (GIS) software, some of which is free and open-source.

The rich photographic record of urban pollution can be found at both local and national levels, and much of it is digitized. The Farm Security Administration–Office of War Information archives available through the Library of Congress website boasts thousands of images of urban and suburban America in the 1930s and 1940s (and Yale's Photogrammar map makes those urban images easy to locate), the Environmental Protection Agency's Documerica Project photographed environmental hazards in the 1970s (and is easily accessible through the National Archives website), and local collections—such as the New York City Municipal Archives Online Gallery and the

Chicago Sewers Collection at the Chicago Public Library—are increasingly accessible online. Social and cultural histories of urban pollution could be further enriched with the use of sources such as novels, narrative nonfiction, plays, and songs. To name just two of countless such sources, William Attaway's novel *Blood on the Forge* dramatizes the African American experience of Pittsburgh's early 20th-century pollution, while Richard Wright's book *12 Million Black Voices* pairs photographs with nonfiction prose to depict the urban environmental hazards African Americans faced in Chicago and similar Great Migration destinations.

A proliferation of primary source material accompanied the modern environmental movement in the post-World War II era, driven both by a growing federal bureaucracy that documented urban pollution problems and environmentalist non-governmental organizations that fought for tougher regulations. The full text of key national environmental policies in the postwar era is easily accessible, as is a wealth of documentation from all branches of government: the Congressional Record, Supreme Court decisions, presidential statements and executive orders, Council on Environmental Quality reports, and the like. Vast amounts of the Environmental Protection Agency's documentation are available online (in addition to their National Library Network with regional outposts), and significant portions of the voluminous records of non-governmental organizations such as the Sierra Club (at the University of California, Berkeley) and the National Resources Defense Council (at Yale University) deal with urban pollution.

DIGITAL MATERIALS

Chicago Sewers Collection (https://cdm16818 .contentdm.oclc.org/customizations/global /pages/content.php?id=dtd).

Chronicling America: Historic American Newspapers (https://chroniclingamerica.loc.gov/).

Cornell Making of America (https://babel.hathitrust .org/cgi/mb?a=listis&c=1930843488).

Council on Environmental Quality, Annual Environmental Quality Reports (https://ceq.doe .gov/ceq-reports/annual_environmental_quality _reports.html).

Encyclopedia of Chicago (http://www.encyclopedia .chicagohistory.org/).

Environmental Studies: Documerica Highlights (https://www.archives.gov/research/environment /documerica-highlights.html).

Farm Security Administration/Office of War Information Black-and-White Negatives (http:// www.loc.gov/pictures/collection/fsa/).

Mapping Inequality: Redlining in New Deal America (https://dsl.richmond.edu/panorama /redlining).

National Service Center for Environmental Publications (https://www.epa.gov/nscep).

New York City Municipal Archives Online Gallery (http://nycma.lunaimaging.com/luna/servlet).

The New York Public Library Digital Collections (https://digitalcollections.nypl.org/).

Photogrammar (http://photogrammar.yale.edu/map/).

US Environmental Protection Agency Publications (https://babel.hathitrust.org/cgi/ls?c=6593885 70;a=srchls;q1=*).

FURTHER READING

Andrews, Richard, N. L. *Managing the Environment, Managing Ourselves*, 2nd ed. New Haven, CT: Yale University Press, 2006.

Bullard, Robert. *Dumping in Dixie: Race, Class, and Environmental Quality*. Boulder, CO: Westview Press, 1990.

Colten, Craig E. "Cities and Water Pollution: An Historical and Geographic Perspective." *Urban Geography* 26, no. 5 (2005): 435–458.

Colten, Craig E. *An Unnatural Metropolis: Wresting New Orleans from Nature*. Baton Rouge: Louisiana State University Press, 2005.

Gioielli, Robert R. *Environmental Activism and the Urban Crisis: Baltimore, St. Louis, Chicago*. Philadelphia: Temple University Press, 2014.

Hays, Samuel P. "The Urban Environment." In *Beauty, Health, and Permanence: Environmental Politics in the United States, 1955–1985*. Cambridge: Cambridge University Press, 1987.

Hurley, Andrew. *Environmental Inequalities: Class, Race, and Industrial Pollution in Gary, Indiana, 1945–1980*. Chapel Hill: University of North Carolina Press, 1995.

Kiechle, Melanie. *Smell Detectives: An Olfactory History of Nineteenth-Century Urban America*. Seattle: University of Washington Press, 2017.

Langston, Nancy. *Toxic Bodies: Hormone Disruptors and the Legacy of DES*. New Haven, CT: Yale University Press, 2010.

McNeur, Catherine. *Taming Manhattan: Environmental Battles in the Antebellum City*. Cambridge, MA: Harvard University Press, 2014.

Melosi, Martin. *The Sanitary City: Urban Infrastructure in America from Colonial Times to the Present*. Baltimore: Johns Hopkins University Press, 2000.

Melosi, Martin. *Effluent America: Cities, Industry, Energy, and the Environment*. Pittsburgh, PA: University of Pittsburgh Press, 2001.

Pellow, David Naguib. *Garbage Wars: The Struggle for Environmental Justice in Chicago*. Cambridge, MA: MIT Press, 2002.

Rawson, Michael. *Eden on the Charles: The Making of Boston*. Cambridge, MA: Harvard University Press, 2010.

Roberts, Jody A., and Nancy Langston. "Toxic Bodies/ Toxic Environments: An Interdisciplinary Forum." *Environmental History* 13, no. 4 (2008): 629–703.

Rome, Adam. *The Bulldozer in the Countryside: Suburban Sprawl and the Rise of American Environmentalism*. New York: Cambridge University Press, 2001.

Ross, Benjamin, and Steven Amter. *The Polluters: The Making of Our Chemically Altered Environment*. New York: Oxford University Press, 2010.

Schneider, Daniel. *Hybrid Nature: Sewage Treatment and the Contradictions of the Industrial Ecosystem*. Cambridge, MA: MIT Press, 2011.

Sellers, Christopher. *Crabgrass Crucible: Suburban Nature and the Rise of Environmentalism in Twentieth-Century America*. Chapel Hill: University of North Carolina Press, 2012.

Smith, Carl. *City Water, City Life: Water and the Infrastructure of Ideas in Urbanizing Philadelphia, Boston, and Chicago*. Chicago: University of Chicago Press, 2013.

Spears, Ellen Griffith. *Baptized in PCBs: Race, Pollution, and Justice in an All-American Town*. Chapel Hill: University of North Carolina Press, 2014.

Stradling, David. *Smokestacks and Progressives: Environmentalists, Engineers and Air Quality in America, 1881–1951*. Baltimore: Johns Hopkins University Press, 1999.

Stradling, David, and Richard Stradling. *Where the River Burned: Carl Stokes and the Struggle to Save Cleveland*. Ithaca, NY: Cornell University Press, 2015.

Sze, Julie. *Noxious New York: The Racial Politics of Urban Health and Environmental Justice*. Cambridge, MA: MIT Press, 2007.

Tarr, Joel. *The Search for the Ultimate Sink: Urban Pollution in Historical Perspective*. Akron, OH: University of Akron Press, 1996.

Tarr, Joel., ed. *Devastation and Renewal: An Environmental History of Pittsburgh and Its Region*. Pittsburgh, PA: University of Pittsburgh Press, 2003.

Taylor, Dorceta. *Toxic Communities: Environmental Racism, Industrial Pollution, and Residential Mobility*. New York: New York University Press, 2014.

Zimring, Carl. *Clean and White: A History of Environmental Racism in the United States*. New York: New York University Press, 2015.

NOTES

1. Martin Melosi, *The Sanitary City: Urban Infrastructure in America from Colonial Times to the Present* (Baltimore: Johns Hopkins University Press, 2000), 19, 41; and Catherine McNeur, *Taming Manhattan: Environmental Battles in the Antebellum City* (Cambridge, MA: Harvard University Press, 2014), 27–28, 102–106, 120–121, 137–140, 188–192. On sewage farms, see also Daniel Schneider, *Hybrid Nature: Sewage Treatment and the Contradictions of the Industrial Ecosystem* (Cambridge, MA: MIT Press, 2011), 140–164.

2. Benjamin Henry Latrobe, *The Journal of Latrobe: Being the Notes and Sketches of an Architect, Naturalist and Traveler in the United Sates from 1796 to 1820* (New York: D. Appleton, 1905), 96.

3. Melanie Kiechle, *Smell Detectives: An Olfactory History of Nineteenth-Century Urban America* (Seattle: University of Washington Press, 2017), 4, 33–39; and David Stradling, *The Nature of New York: An Environmental History of the Empire State* (Ithaca, NY: Cornell University Press, 2010), 40.

4. Joel Tarr, *The Search for the Ultimate Sink: Urban Pollution in Historical Perspective* (Akron, OH: University of Akron Press, 1996), 154; Schneider, *Hybrid Nature*, xxi–xxiii; Melosi, *The Sanitary City*, 17–18, 80, 92–93, 153–159; Craig Colten, *An Unnatural Metropolis: Wresting New*

Orleans from Nature (Baton Rouge: Louisiana State University Press, 2005), 77–107; and Carl Smith, *City Water, City Life: Water and the Infrastructure of Ideas in Urbanizing Philadelphia, Boston, and Chicago* (Chicago: University of Chicago Press, 2013).

5. Melosi, *The Sanitary City*, 68–69; Stradling, *The Nature of New York*, 133; Kiechle, *Smell Detectives*, 75–77; Martin Melosi, *Effluent America: Cities, Industry, Energy, and the Environment* (Pittsburgh, PA: University of Pittsburgh Press, 2001), 37; and Michael Rawson, *Eden on the Charles: The Making of Boston* (Cambridge, MA: Harvard University Press, 2010), 131, 145–157. For the definitive account of suburbanization, see Kenneth Jackson, *Crabgrass Frontier: The Suburbanization of the United States* (New York: Oxford University Press, 1985).

6. Latrobe, *The Journal of Latrobe*, 96. See also Stradling, *The Nature of New York*, 117; and Melosi, *The Sanitary City*, 60, 80.

7. Carl Zimring, *Clean and White: A History of Environmental Racism in the United States* (New York: New York University Press, 2015), 3, 10–14, 19.

8. Robert Gottlieb, *Forcing the Spring: The Transformation of the American Environmental Movement* (Washington, DC: Island Press, 1993), 52. See also Melosi, *The Sanitary City*, 59; and Martin Melosi, *Garbage in the Cities: Refuse, Reform, and the Environment, 1880–1980* (College Station: Texas A&M University Press, 1981), 16.

9. Martin Melosi, "Environmental Crisis in the City: The Relationship between Industrialization and Urban Pollution," in *Pollution and Reform in American Cities, 1870–1930*, ed. Martin Melosi (Austin: University of Texas Press, 1980), 6. On the environmental pollutants generated by these city–hinterland connections in the 19th century, see Christopher Jones, *Routes of Power: Energy and Modern America* (Cambridge, MA: Harvard University Press, 2014); and William Cronon, *Nature's Metropolis: Chicago and the Great West* (New York: W. W. Norton, 1991).

10. Sylvia Hood Washington, *Packing Them In: An Archaeology of Environmental Racism in Chicago, 1865–1954* (Lanham, MD: Lexington Books, 2004), 75–125; Dorceta Taylor, *The Environment and the People in American Cities, 1600–1900s: Disorder, Inequality, and Social Change* (Durham, NC: Duke University Press), 202–207; Gottlieb,

Forcing the Spring, 54, 64; Harold Platt, *Shock Cities: The Environmental Transformation and Reform of Manchester and Chicago* (Chicago: University of Chicago Press, 2005), 20–21; Ian Tyrrell, *Crisis of the Wasteful Nation: Empire and Conservation in Theodore Roosevelt's America* (Chicago: University of Chicago Press, 2015), 186–187; and Zimring, *Clean and White*, 32–33.

11. Brian McCammack, *Landscapes of Hope: Nature and the Great Migration in Chicago* (Cambridge, MA: Harvard University Press, 2017), 1–4; Andrew Hurley, *Environmental Inequalities: Class, Race, and Industrial Pollution in Gary, Indiana, 1945–1980* (Chapel Hill: University of North Carolina Press, 1995), 2–6; Dorceta Taylor, *Toxic Communities: Environmental Racism, Industrial Pollution, and Residential Mobility* (New York: New York University Press, 2014), 172–173; and Zimring, *Clean and White*, 82.

12. Craig E. Colten, "Cities and Water Pollution: An Historical and Geographic Perspective," *Urban Geography* 26, no. 5 (2005): 435–436; Craig E. Colten, "Environmental Justice in the American Bottom: The Legal Response to Pollution, 1900–1950," in *Common Fields: An Environmental History of St. Louis*, ed. Andrew Hurley (St. Louis: Missouri Historical Society Press, 1997), 167–168; Samuel Hays, *Beauty, Health, and Permanence: Environmental Politics in the United States, 1955–1985* (New York: Cambridge University Press, 1987), 83–84; Taylor, *Toxic Communities*, 149–184; Andrew Hurley, "Busby's Stink Boat and the Regulation of Nuisance Trades, 1865–1918," in *Common Fields*, 147, 160–161; and McNeur, *Taming Manhattan*, 96–97, 136. On environmental injustice and land values, see Laura Pulido, "Rethinking Environmental Racism: White Privilege and Urban Development in Southern California," in *American Studies: An Anthology*, ed. Janice Radway (Malden, MA: Wiley-Blackwell, 2009), 468.

13. Gottlieb, *Forcing the Spring*, 59; Tarr, *The Search for the Ultimate Sink*, 8, 104; and Melosi, *Effluent America*, 43.

14. Tarr, *The Search for the Ultimate Sink*, 8; Gottlieb, *Forcing the Spring*, 54; Melosi, *Effluent America*, 27; and Stradling, *The Nature of New York*, 127.

15. Melosi, *The Sanitary City*, 114, 144–145, 163–167; Gottlieb, *Forcing the Spring*, 58–59; Platt, *Shock Cities*, 140; Kiechle, *Smell Detectives*, 5; J. R. McNeill, *Something New Under the Sun: An Environmental History of the Twentieth-Century*

World (New York: W. W. Norton, 2000), 126; Tarr, *The Search for the Ultimate Sink*, 208–209; Stuart Galishoff, "Triumph and Failure: The American Response to the Urban Water Supply Problem, 1860–1923," in *Pollution and Reform in American Cities*, 49–51; and Colten, *Unnatural Metropolis*, 77–107.

16. Melosi, *Garbage in the Cities*, 3, 21, 23, 42; and Melosi, *The Sanitary City*, 177–180.

17. Melosi, *Garbage in the Cities*, 42–65, 111–112, 129–132; Melosi, *The Sanitary City*, 200, 271–272; Zimring, *Clean and White*, 63; Julie Sze, *Noxious New York: The Racial Politics of Urban Health and Environmental Justice* (Cambridge, MA: MIT Press, 2007), 58, 137; and Linda Nash, *Inescapable Ecologies: A History of Environment, Disease, and Knowledge* (Berkeley: University of California Press, 2006), 95.

18. Jane Addams, *Twenty Years at Hull-House* (New York: Macmillan, 1930 [1910]), 281, 283. See also David Pellow, *Garbage Wars: The Struggle for Environmental Justice in Chicago* (Cambridge, MA: MIT Press, 2002), 21–22.

19. Pellow, *Garbage Wars*, 35; McNeur, *Taming Manhattan*, 3, 188–192; and Zimring, *Clean and White*, 116–126.

20. McNeill, *Something New Under the Sun*, 55–58; Stradling, *The Nature of New York*, 55, 113; David Stradling, *Smokestacks and Progressives: Environmentalists, Engineers and Air Quality in America, 1881–1951* (Baltimore: Johns Hopkins University Press, 1999), 8–11; Melosi, *Effluent America*, 52; and Zimring, *Clean and White*, 56.

21. Rebecca Harding Davis, "Life in the Iron Mills," *Atlantic Monthly*, April 1861, 430. On the myriad impacts of omnipresent smoke, see Stradling, *Smokestacks and Progressives*, 29–31.

22. Platt, *Shock Cities*, 13; Tyrrell, *Crisis of the Wasteful Nation*, 92–93; Stradling, *Smokestacks and Progressives*, 23; and Linda Nash, "Purity and Danger: Historical Reflections on the Regulation of Environmental Pollutants," *Environmental History* 13, no. 4 (2008): 653.

23. Stradling, *Smokestacks and Progressives*, 49–51, 72; Gottlieb, *Forcing the Spring*, 57; Kiechle, *Smell Detectives*, 19–20; Tarr, *The Search for the Ultimate Sink*, 15; and Pellow, *Garbage Wars*, 24.

24. Hurley in *Common Fields*, 153–154; Platt, *Shock Cities*, 474, 484; Stradling, *Smokestacks and Progressives*, 25, 34, 63, 130–131, 150; and Tarr, *The Search for the Ultimate Sink*, 15.

25. Melosi, *Effluent America*, 28; Stradling, *The Nature of New York*, 113; Raymond W. Smilor, "Toward an Environmental Perspective: The Anti-Noise Campaign, 1893–1932," in *Pollution and Reform in American Cities*, 135–151, at 135–137, 141–144; David Hendy, *Noise: A Human History of Sound and Listening* (London: Profile Books, 2013), 304–307; Mike Goldsmith, *Discord: The Story of Noise* (Oxford: Oxford University Press, 2012), 135–150; and Hays, *Beauty, Health, and Permanence*, 85.

26. Barry Commoner, *The Closing Circle: Nature, Man, and Technology* (New York: Knopf, 1971), 140; Richard Andrews, *Managing the Environment, Managing Ourselves: A History of American Environmental Policy* (New Haven, CT: Yale University Press, 2006), 188–189; McNeill, *Something New Under the Sun*, 28–29; Benjamin Ross and Steven Amter, *The Polluters: The Making of Our Chemically Altered Environment* (New York: Oxford University Press, 2010); Melosi, *Effluent America*, 101–102; Melosi, *The Sanitary City*, 228; and Sarah A. Vogel, "From 'The Dose Makes the Poison' to 'The Timing Makes the Poison': Conceptualizing Risk in the Synthetic Age," *Environmental History* 13, no. 4 (2008): 668.

27. Robert Bullard, *Dumping in Dixie: Race, Class, and Environmental Quality* (Boulder, CO: Westview Press, 1990), 23–26; Andrew Needham, *Power Lines: Phoenix and the Making of the Modern Southwest* (Princeton, NJ: Princeton University Press, 2014), 7; and Jackson, *Crabgrass Frontier*, 283–284.

28. Nelson's remarks as delivered varied slightly from the notes. "Partial Text for Senator Gaylord Nelson, Denver, Colo., April 22," Gaylord Nelson and Earth Day: The Making of the Modern Environmental Movement. See also Gottlieb, *Forcing the Spring*, 77; Hays, *Beauty, Health, and Permanence*, 71–73; Adam Rome, "Give Earth a Chance: The Environmental Movement and the Sixties," *Journal of American History* 90, no. 2 (2003); Adam Rome, *The Bulldozer in the Countryside: Suburban Sprawl and the Rise of American Environmentalism* (New York: Cambridge University Press, 2001); and Christopher Sellers, *Crabgrass Crucible: Suburban Nature and the Rise of Environmentalism in Twentieth-Century America* (Chapel Hill: University of North Carolina Press, 2012).

29. Andrews, *Managing the Environment, Managing Ourselves*, 203–254, 265; Chapter 2 in Judith Layzer, *The Environmental Case: Translating Values Into Policy* (Washington, DC: CQ Press, 2016), 31–62; Vogel, "From 'The Dose Makes the Poison,'" 667–670; and Nancy Langston, *Toxic Bodies: Hormone Disruptors and the Legacy of DES* (New Haven, CT: Yale University Press, 2010).

30. Robert Gioielli, *Environmental Activism and the Urban Crisis: Baltimore, St. Louis, Chicago* (Philadelphia, PA: Temple University Press, 2014), 1–10; Pellow, *Garbage Wars*, 68; and Sze, *Noxious New York*, 2–3.

31. Melosi, *The Sanitary City*, 162, 226, 311; Andrews, *Managing the Environment, Managing Ourselves*, 188; Schneider, *Hybrid Nature*, 164–167; Harold Platt, *Sinking Chicago: Climate Change and the Remaking of a Flood-Prone Environment* (Philadelphia: Temple University Press, 2018); David Stradling and Richard Stradling, *Where the River Burned: Carl Stokes and the Struggle to Save Cleveland* (Ithaca, NY: Cornell University Press, 2015); Matthew Klingle, *Emerald City: An Environmental History of Seattle* (New Haven, CT: Yale University Press, 2007), 203–229; Rome, *The Bulldozer in the Countryside*, 87–118; and Commoner, *The Closing Circle*, 91.

32. Sze, *Noxious New York*, 60; Andrews, *Managing the Environment, Managing Ourselves*, 236–237; Hays, *Beauty, Health, and Permanence*, 76–80; Schneider, *Hybrid Nature*, 203; and Andrew Karvonen, *Politics of Urban Runoff: Nature, Technology, and the Sustainable City* (Cambridge, MA: MIT Press, 2011), 1–16.

33. Melosi, *The Sanitary City*, 276–278, 340–348, 411–415; Andrew Hurley, "From Factory Town to Metropolitan Junkyard: Postindustrial Transitions on the Urban Periphery," *Environmental History* 21, no. 1 (2016): 21–22; Pellow, *Garbage Wars*, 44, 51–52; Melosi, *Garbage in the Cities*, 171–172, 193–194; Tarr, *The Search for the Ultimate Sink*, 20; Andrews, *Managing the Environment, Managing Ourselves*, 247; McNeill, *Something New Under the Sun*, 27; Jody A. Roberts and Nancy Langston, "Toxic Bodies/Toxic Environments: An Interdisciplinary Forum," *Environmental History* 13, no. 4 (2008): 629; Gioielli, *Environmental Activism and the Urban Crisis*, 38–72; and David Rosner and Gerald Markowitz, "Building the World That Kills Us: The Politics of Lead, Science,

and Polluted Homes, 1970 to 2000," *Journal of Urban History* 42, no. 2 (2016): 323–345.

34. Andrews, *Managing the Environment, Managing Ourselves*, 248; Hays, *Beauty, Health, and Permanence*, 80–83; Sze, *Noxious New York*, 61; Richard Newman, *Love Canal: A Toxic History from Colonial Times to the Present* (New York: Oxford University Press, 2016), 3, 84, 176–177; Zimring, *Clean and White*, 195–212; Hurley, "From Factory Town to Metropolitan Junkyard," 3–4; James R. Elliott and Scott Frickel, "Environmental Dimensions of Urban Change: Uncovering Relict Industrial Waste Sites and Subsequent Land Use Conversions in Portland and New Orleans," *Journal of Urban Affairs* 33, no.1 (2011): 61–82; and Pellow, *Garbage Wars*, 1–2, 90–91.

35. United Church of Christ, *Toxic Wastes and Race at Twenty, 1987–2007*, xii; United Church of Christ, *Toxic Wastes and Race in the United States*, xiv; Bullard, *Dumping in Dixie*, 42; Paul Mohai et al., "Racial and Socioeconomic Disparities in Residential Proximity to Polluting Industrial Facilities: Evidence from the Americans' Changing Lives Study," *American Journal of Public Health* 99, no. S3 (2009): S653–S654; and Ellen Griffith Spears, *Baptized in PCBs: Race, Pollution, and Justice in an all-American Town* (Chapel Hill: University of North Carolina Press, 2014).

36. E. B. White, "Sootfall and Fallout," in *Essays of E. B. White* (New York: Harper & Row, 1977), 91. Earlier he had quipped that "Soot is the topsoil of New York." Quoted in Stradling, *The Nature of New York*, 182.

37. Kate Brown, *Plutopia: Nuclear Families, Atomic Cities, and the Great Soviet and American Plutonium Disasters* (Oxford: Oxford University Press, 2013), 166; Andrews, *Managing the Environment, Managing Ourselves*, 207–208; David Stradling, ed., *The Environmental Moment: 1968–1972* (Seattle: University of Washington Press, 2012), 52, 101; Ross and Amter, *The Polluters*, 86–97; and Tarr, *The Search for the Ultimate Sink*, 18, 29.

38. McNeill, *Something New Under the Sun*, 61–62; Stradling, *Smokestacks and Progressives*, 182–188; Chapter 7 in Sellers, *Crabgrass Crucible*; and Ross and Amter, *The Polluters*, 73–85.

39. Commoner, *The Closing Circle*, 66.

40. "People Before Highways," *Black Panther*, August 21, 1971, 7, 19. See also Gioielli, *Environmental Activism and the Urban Crisis*, 73–103.

41. Tarr, *The Search for the Ultimate Sink*, 18; Andrews, *Managing the Environment, Managing Ourselves*, 209, 233–234; Hays, *Beauty, Health, and Permanence*, 73–76; United Church of Christ, *Toxic Wastes and Race in the United States*, 2; Ihab Mikati et al., "Disparities in Distribution of Particulate Matter Emission Sources by Race and Poverty Status," *American Journal of Public Health* 108, no. 4 (2018): 480, 483. See also Sze, *Noxious New York*, 92–99; and Gregg Mitman, *Breathing Space: How Allergies Shape Our Lives and Landscapes* (New Haven, CT: Yale University Press, 2007), 130–166.

42. Needham, *Power Lines*, 10–11.

43. Paul Bogard, *The End of Night: Searching for Natural Darkness in an Age of Artificial Light* (New York: Little, Brown, and Company, 2013), 3, 103–104.

44. Supreme Court of the United States, "Syllabus: Massachusetts et al. v. Environmental Protection Agency et al.," October Term, 2006.

Brian McCammack

CONTAGIOUS DISEASE AND PUBLIC HEALTH IN THE AMERICAN CITY

CONTAGIOUS DISEASE AND PUBLIC HEALTH IN THE AMERICAN CITY

From the first appearance of cities, contagious diseases posed a serious challenge to public health. Most of the early cities in European colonies were seaports and centers of trade and commerce. Ships brought people and cargo as well as contagious diseases including smallpox, yellow fever, and cholera. City health authorities responded in different ways as the cities grew, as medical understanding of contagious disease improved, and as medical science provided new weapons in the effort to prevent and cure infectious disease. Three broad approaches to the problem of contagious disease have marked the urban response to contagion. Quarantines to prevent the spread of disease dominated public health from the early colonial period until the early 20th century. Quarantines were never completely effective, although they often delayed an epidemic or limited its damage. Although earlier efforts at cleaning streets and removing garbage were successful, the sanitary era developed in the late 19th century as a result of increased medical knowledge and the effectiveness of sanitary reform during the Civil War (1861–1865). The sanitary era arose with the recognition that clean water supplies, unadulterated food sources, and proper removal of human and animal waste significantly reduced the incidence of contagious disease. Next, the bacteriological revolution of the late 19th century identified the microscopic sources of many of the infectious diseases that fostered sanitary reform. The final significant development was the vaccine and antibiotic era that began in the 1940s and continues. Although a vaccine for smallpox was developed in the early 1800s, the creation of a broad range of vaccines and antibiotics followed the bacteriological revolution and the recognition of specific microorganisms as the cause of specific diseases. Antibiotics such as sulfa drugs and penicillin and the development of vaccines against such viral diseases as influenza and polio at mid-century gave public health officials powerful new weapons to cure bacterial diseases and prevent contagious viral diseases. By the late 20th century, public health authorities used all three approaches—quarantine, sanitary reform, and vaccines and antibiotics—to significantly limit the spread of infectious disease and to maintain the health of urban America.

THE QUARANTINE ERA, 1700–1920

Quarantines against contagious disease have an ancient lineage. Ancient Greek and Roman physicians recognized that the spread of contagious diseases could be limited if healthy individuals were kept from close contact with the sick. Later, the spread of plague led to restrictions and isolation of sailors and travelers from plague-infested regions. The term *quarantine* originates from the Italian words *quarantina* and *quaranta giorni*. Quarantines in Venice isolated incoming ships for forty days during plague epidemics in the Middle Ages. "From medieval times on," writes historian Howard Markel, "shutting the gates of a city or port to all those suspected of being ill and isolating those sick people discovered to have entered represented the best, and often the only, means available for stemming the tide of an epidemic."[1]

Eighteenth-Century Quarantines. Civil authorities in colonial American seaports early recognized that quarantine was key to keeping a city healthy. Smallpox and yellow fever most often triggered quarantine in early America. Ships suspected of carrying infected crew or passengers were held at isolated locations in the harbor. However, quarantines disrupted the bustling trade of seaports with severe economic consequences. Thus, the imposition of a quarantine was usually a source of tension between the business community and the public health authorities. Since many believed disease was God's punishment for sin, community and church leaders often proclaimed days of prayer and fasting to placate an angry God. Colonial cites were also noted for the garbage and human and animal waste that typically littered the yards and streets. So public authorities typically ordered the streets and docks cleaned. In the 18th century, however, these public health initiatives did not prevent epidemics from sweeping through ports and cities.[2]

The appearance of smallpox in Boston, Massachusetts, in 1721 illustrates the limits of quarantine as well as the introduction of a new method of protecting citizens from the disease. Smallpox is an acute viral disease that produces characteristic skin lesions—the pox—and is often fatal. When smallpox appeared in Boston, guards were stationed at the house where the disease first appeared, isolating those inside. The ship that brought the disease was sent to isolation at Bird Island in the harbor. But smallpox was in the city, and by mid-June there were so many cases that city officials ceased individual quarantines.[3]

With quarantines ineffective in stopping the spread of smallpox, Cotton Mather, a prominent Puritan minister, and Zabdiel Boylston, a local physician, turned to inoculation to try to protect residents. Inoculation involved taking pus from an individual with an active case of smallpox and introducing it under the skin of the individual being inoculated. In most cases, this process resulted in a mild case of smallpox that protected the individual from a more serious case. Mather convinced Boylston to employ the new and controversial process. Boylston and a few associates inoculated 286 patients with only six deaths (about 2% fatality rate). Some 6,000 Bostonians came down with smallpox during the epidemic, and 844 died (about a 14% fatality rate).[4] In spite of its success, inoculation was opposed by many, including physicians, on the grounds that it was unsafe. However, in subsequent smallpox epidemics, inoculation became an increasingly common practice.

Eighteenth-century public health officials also tried to prevent yellow fever through quarantine. Yellow fever is a viral disease spread by the bite of an infected *Aedes aegypti* mosquito. The disease produces a high fever, liver failure, jaundice, and hemorrhaging from nose, mouth, and stomach. Fatality rates range from 10 to 60 percent of those infected. The disease was recognized as contagious, but not until the late 19th century did doctors determine that the disease was spread by the bite of an infected *Aedes aegypti* mosquito. Quarantine was largely ineffective because mosquitoes easily evaded quarantined ships and homes. Yellow fever appeared frequently in the 1690s but became less common during the 18th century. However, in 1793, Philadelphia experienced a major epidemic, and the disease then circulated widely for the next decade.[5]

Yellow fever arrived in Philadelphia in 1793, probably coming on ships from the

West Indies, where the disease was endemic. By the end of August, Philadelphia was in the midst of a major yellow fever epidemic. The city had a public health officer and quarantine regulations, but lacking funding, the regulations were unenforced. Mayor Matthew Clarkson led the fight against yellow fever. Quarantines of houses where the disease appeared were ineffective in stopping its spread, as were efforts to clean the streets of manure and garbage. The epidemic paralyzed Philadelphia and ultimately killed more than 5,000 residents in the four months it stalked the city.[6]

The reports of the epidemic coming from Philadelphia convinced other ports to revive their quarantine regulations and to establish new ones. For example, both Baltimore and New York tried to bar Philadelphians. Health officials in New York set up a quarantine, increased inspections of arriving ships, established an isolation hospital for sick individuals, and sought volunteers to guard the city entrances. These measures lasted until cold weather ended the threat of the disease by killing the mosquitoes.[7]

Nineteenth-Century Quarantines. For much of the 19th century, yellow fever epidemics were common in southern port cities. Southern legislatures and public health officials tried to keep ships from bringing diseases from foreign ports. Once an epidemic disease appeared, authorities tried to keep it from spreading without substantially impairing business and trade. Quarantines were very controversial because of their negative impact on trade and commerce.[8]

Cholera posed the next challenge to the ports and cities of the eastern United States. Cholera is an acute bacterial disease of the intestines, usually acquired from water or food contaminated with the bacterium *Vibrio cholerae*. The disease causes a watery diarrhea that can result in dehydration and death. Asiatic cholera originated in the Indian subcontinent and began to spread into Europe in the early 1830s. The disease contaminates water supplies by the discharge of infected fecal material from sick individuals. In the unsanitary cities of the 19th century, cholera spread quickly and killed thousands.[9] The United States experienced three waves of cholera in 1832, 1849, and 1866.

In the early 1830s, Americans feared the spread of cholera through Europe. In response, Canadian and American ports established quarantines against ships sailing from Europe, but they were ineffective.[10] Cholera made its first appearance in North America in Quebec and Montreal in 1832, and shortly thereafter in New York City. A special medical committee organized to combat the epidemic urged residents to clean up the city and to lead moral lives. Like the quarantine, these measures proved ineffective. The epidemic in New York lasted six weeks, with a death toll of about 3,000, mostly among the poor. From New York, cholera spread along canals and roads to much of the eastern United States. As in New York, quarantines failed to stem the spread of the disease. The cholera epidemic of 1832 did not lead to a significant improvement in either sanitation or public health.[11]

America's experience with cholera in 1832 was largely repeated when the disease again swept across the Atlantic in 1849. As historian Charles Rosenberg writes, "America's greatest port possessed no facilities adequate to quarantine fifty, let alone three hundred, immigrants." By 1849, "New York's quarantine had become little more than an administrative gesture." Individuals in quarantine escaped, and the disease soon appeared in the city. New York's epidemic was halted by the cold temperatures of January 1849, but the disease found a more favorable climate in southern cities such as New Orleans and along the rivers leading to the interior of the United States. As before, quarantines did not prevent or stop the epidemic.[12]

When cholera returned in 1866, states and municipalities focused their energies on sanitary measures rather than ineffective quarantines. New York was particularly successful under the authority of the newly established Metropolitan Board of Health, the first public health department to effectively apply sanitary measures against an epidemic disease. When cholera cases appeared in 1866, the board emphasized its cleanliness approach, opened hospitals and dispensaries dedicated to cholera victims, and set up a scientific laboratory. The cholera epidemic proved to be mild, and the Metropolitan Board of Health received credit for containing the disease.[13] "Quarantines had never succeeded in containing cholera," Charles Rosenberg observes. "Only an efficient and thoroughgoing sanitary reform could, it seemed, guarantee relative immunity."[14]

In spite of its failures, quarantine remained in the arsenal of public health officials in the late 19th century. Historian Howard Markel argues that as "bacteriology's powerful tenets began to dominate public health and medicine, the process of quarantine was fine-tuned to the natural histories of specific, living, etiologic agents called germs." By the 1890s, New York had an effective system to medically inspect incoming ships and to detain sailors and passengers with infectious diseases. All ships entering the port were required to stop at a distant spot off Staten Island for inspection. Individuals with an infectious disease were admitted to the quarantine station isolation hospital. When one of these diseases developed in the city, the public health authorities ordered the removal of the patient to the contagious disease hospital. These more effective quarantine measures were aided by the growing knowledge of bacteriology and the improved and more powerful Metropolitan Board of Health.[15]

At the end of the 19th century, plague, the disease that had inspired the institution of quarantines in the Middle Ages, returned to the United States. Plague is an infectious bacterial disease caused by the bacterium *Yersinia pestes*. Humans most often catch the disease from the bite of an infected flea. Untreated, plague is often fatal. Plague was identified in the Chinatown of Honolulu in December 1899

and in San Francisco's Chinatown in March 1900. Following the diagnosis of plague in a Chinese resident, the Board of Health of Honolulu instituted travel restrictions in and out of the city and imposed a quarantine of Chinatown. National guardsmen patrolled the streets to enforce the quarantine, but individuals evaded the quarantine and blended into the Asian populations outside of Chinatown. The quarantine severely disrupted business and was enforced mainly against Chinese residents. Economic activity came to a halt, and food supplies ran short. When no new deaths had occurred for five days, the Board of Health lifted the quarantine. When plague deaths resumed, the Board reinstated the quarantine on December 27.[16]

In addition to quarantine, the Board of Health adopted a policy of burning homes and businesses where a case of the plague occurred. This decision failed disastrously. On January 20, 1900, the wind suddenly shifted and increased in intensity. The fire quickly spread and the inferno burned through the quarantined area. Ultimately, one-fifth of Honolulu's buildings were destroyed, and 5,000 people lost their homes, businesses, and possessions. Residents who were quarantined in the quarter were moved to detention camps so they could not spread the plague into the unburned part of the city.[17]

Twentieth-Century Quarantines. Three months later, plague was discovered in San Francisco's Chinatown. The city health department quickly imposed a complete quarantine of Chinatown. Two days later they lifted the quarantine after it met strong resistance from the Chinese community. Authorities turned instead to disinfection of residences and businesses where plague victims were found, and for a while this policy seemed to work. However, four new cases appeared in early May, at which point the US Surgeon General Walter Wyman ordered a "complete cordon sanitaire around Chinatown." The quarantine was less than complete; it applied only to the Chinese, whereas whites were granted easy access to Chinatown. Chinese authorities strenuously protested the quarantine and the unequal treatment. The quarantine ended in June 1900 when court-ordered injunctions agreed that the quarantine was unequally and unfairly enforced. A later federal study concluded that the most effective measures against the disease were targeted efforts to clean and disinfect residences and businesses where plague appeared. Plague returned to San Francisco in 1907, but in the meantime, scientists had uncovered the role of rats and lice in spreading the disease. The campaign against plague in 1907–1908 emphasized reducing or eliminating rats, fleas, and the dirty places where they lurked, rather than quarantining Chinese.[18] Once again, quarantine had proved both costly and ineffective against contagious disease.

In the early 20th century, quarantines were applied to a new disease: poliomyelitis, or infantile paralysis, as it was known at the time. Polio is an old disease, but the improving sanitation of the late 19th century transformed it into an epidemic disease. Polio is transmitted through patients' infected fecal material that contaminates water supplies or food. Three to 5 percent of infected individuals will develop paralysis when the poliovirus destroys nerve cells in the spinal cord. In many cases, the paralysis is permanent and sometimes fatal.

The first substantial polio epidemic in the United States occurred in Rutland, Vermont, in 1894, but the 1916 epidemic in New York and twenty-five other states attracted significant national attention. Overall, 27,000 cases were identified, resulting in 6,000 deaths. New York City alone had some 8,000 cases and 2,400 deaths. As the number of cases rose that summer, the public, particularly parents with children, grew frightened. As historian Naomi Rogers writes, "Public health officials and private physicians responded with traditional measures of epidemic control—quarantine and sanitation—and also methods of the new scientific medicine." As the epidemic spread, many wealthier parents tried to flee the city.

Public health officials attempted to lessen the panic by identifying sick children and moving many to isolation hospitals. However, most of the public health measures to limit the polio epidemic were directed at immigrant families, who were thought most likely to spread the disease. Neighboring communities and states implemented quarantines barring the entry of children from New York. New York and several other cities, along with the US Public Health Service, issued certificates certifying that a child did not have polio, but neighboring states and communities often rejected these certificates.[19]

Families with a sick child were quarantined by public health authorities restricting who could enter and leave. Families preferred to treat children at home, but strict quarantine regulations meant that many immigrant homes were unsuitable. No tenement had a private toilet for the patient or separate dining rooms, and immigrant families could not afford to pay for private nurses. Consequently, many immigrant children were sent to isolation hospitals over the strenuous objections of their parents. Rogers noted that "immigrant communities were special targets for official action," such as shutting down popular "immigrant festivals, working-class block parties, and public playgrounds." As the epidemic continued, opposition to the quarantines mounted among businessmen, who argued that the restrictions were bad for the economy. Summer tourist and vacation sites such as Coney Island were especially hard hit by declines in attendance.[20]

Quarantines were not particularly effective in preventing the spread of polio in 1916. Medical science knew little about the disease and could not offer much effective advice to public health officials. Some 90 percent of individuals with polio had a mild intestinal disease with no paralysis. However, they could shed the virus in their fecal material and thus spread the disease. Quarantine works only if doctors and public health officials can reliably identify infected and sick individuals. That simply was not the case with polio in 1916.

Two years later a more familiar disease, influenza, in a particularly virulent variety, struck New York and much of the world. Some estimate that the flu killed more than 650,000 in the United States and another 50 million worldwide. The epidemic occurred during the last year of World War I, and the movement of troops and the disruptions of war likely contributed to the spread and severity of the disease. Although public health officials used quarantines in the flu epidemic, they were ineffective. Historian Nancy Bristow observes that "the first hope was to limit the severity of the epidemic by hindering its entry from overseas, an effort likely doomed from the start." In August 1918, the surgeon general of the United States, Rupert Blue, imposed an inspection of all ships coming from Europe. Infected ships were quarantined. Even as the Public Health Service called for additional measures, influenza spread throughout the eastern United States, especially in army camps and major cities.[21] Various local officials tried to establish quarantines, but they were no more successful in limiting the spread of the disease. Public health authorities also tried to limit public gatherings and other places where crowds could be found. These measures, however, met significant resistance from affected businesses and institutions as well as from citizens who did not want to be barred from their accustomed habits. Thus, the regulations were often quickly rescinded.[22] Because this respiratory disease spread so easily, and because so many citizens resisted quarantines and closures, neither quarantines nor closures were effective in limiting or ending this epidemic.

The limitations of quarantine were perhaps best illustrated in the case of Mary Mallon, an Irish immigrant and New York cook better known as "Typhoid Mary." Mallon was a healthy carrier of typhoid, which is a bacterial infection found in contaminated water and food. Typhoid was a major problem for the urban public in the late 19th and early 20th centuries. Healthy carriers, like Mallon, carried the bacteria and could infect others but did not themselves come down with typhoid fever. Mallon was identified after deaths occurred in families where she was a cook. Mallon was first apprehended in 1907. When she refused to cooperate with public health officials, she was kept in a hospital on North Brother Island in the East River. She was released in 1910. Authorities rearrested Mallon in 1915 after they traced a hospital outbreak of typhoid to her work in the hospital kitchen. They then confined her in isolation on North Brother Island until she died in 1938. Mallon was the first and only person to suffer such a lengthy isolation as a healthy carrier of typhoid. She likely suffered this fate because she was both female and an Irish immigrant. Public health officials turned to other means to address the problem of healthy carriers because of the large numbers involved. In 1919, one authority estimated that 25,000 healthy carriers resided in the city. Two were in isolation (one of them was Mallon); three others had disappeared; and sixty-two lived under conditions and regulations set by the health department. The cost to quarantine 25,000 healthy carriers scattered across New York City would have been prohibitive. Instead, they concluded it was unnecessary to quarantine healthy carriers.[23] Other public health initiatives in working with healthy carriers protected the public as effectively as quarantines, making Mary Mallon the great exception.

SANITARY REFORM

If quarantines were the first response to the appearance of contagious disease, sanitary reform was a close second. Sanitary reform included cleaning cities during an epidemic of contagious disease and long-term infrastructure improvements such as providing clean water and adequate sewage removal. Doctors and public health authorities had long recognized a link between dirt, human and animal waste, and infectious disease. The bacteriological revolution of the late 19th century revealed that microorganisms in the filth caused disease, but even without that knowledge, cleaning up a city usually meant a healthier city. From colonial times onward, city authorities urged cleanliness upon their residents, especially when confronted with an epidemic, but only in the 20th century did sanitary reform have a significant impact on contagious disease.

Eighteenth-Century Sanitary Reform.

As colonial towns grew in population, sanitary reform became a frequent concern of public officials. By the 18th century, most large towns relied on scavengers to remove all sorts of garbage, human and animal waste, and dead animals from city streets. Laws required homeowners and businesses to clean streets in front of their buildings. Drainage was a problem in many places, and the sewers constructed soon became filthy. Clean water was another issue. Increased population both increased demand for clean water and fouled nearby supplies. Historian John Duffy notes that "compared to modern cities, colonial towns were odorous and lacked effective water, sewer, and street-cleaning systems."[24]

Little changed in the decades immediately following the Revolution. As American cities and towns grew in the decades after the Revolution, so did their sanitary problems.[25] The yellow fever epidemics of the 1790s gave impetus to sanitary improvements in many cities. These summer epidemics intensified concerns about rotting and smelly garbage and human and animal waste. Doctors also linked unclean water to the prevalence of intestinal complaints. Some epidemics did provide the impetus to the construction of municipal systems to provide clean water. Sanitary reform met opposition because of the cost and the unwillingness of many citizens to cooperate with sanitary initiatives, especially once the immediate threat of an epidemic had passed.[26]

Nineteenth-Century Sanitary Reform.

Sanitary reform gained strength in the early 19th century. Many cities appointed health boards, but they typically functioned only during epidemics. Their main purpose was to establish and enforce quarantines, but they also had some authority to establish sanitary reforms. However, these boards were typically weak and ineffective, and had little impact on public health. The continued growth of cities and the rise of industries meant deteriorating public health.[27] According to Duffy, "The American sanitary movement arose, at least in part, from efforts to account for the omnipresent epidemics that periodically scourged the population."[28] By the 1830s, most cities had taken some steps to clean streets and to remove human and animal waste. Cities also began improving existing water supplies or creating new systems to provide clean water. Municipal water systems, however, often generated drainage problems. As late as 1830, few cities had established sewer systems to drain wastewater.[29] These systems provided engineering challenges, and they were costly, which reduced their appeal to city officials.

Thirty years before the Civil War, city officials gave increasing emphasis to public health. Some municipalities collected vital statistics in a systematic way that for the first time outlined the dimensions of the problems. In addition, a number of important public health reformers rose to prominence during these decades.[30] These reformers produced a number of reports that highlighted the key issues. This early movement culminated in several national sanitary conventions between 1857 and 1860, which marked the beginnings of an American sanitary revolution. The conventions led to a reform of quarantine regulations, but significantly they began to shift the focus from quarantines to sanitary and environmental components of public health.[31]

The American Civil War (1861–1865) strengthened the nascent sanitary reform efforts. The activities of the US Sanitary Commission during the war demonstrated the effectiveness of the sanitary disposal of human waste; that scurvy could be prevented by providing fruits and vegetables; and that isolation worked in cases of contagious disease.

The success of the Sanitary Commission strengthened the campaigns for sanitary reform.[32] During the war years, the sanitary challenges facing New York City provided the incentive to find a more effective response. In 1866, the New York state legislature passed the New York Metropolitan Health Act that created the first modern and effective urban department of public health. Once its success was demonstrated, it became a model for other cities.[33] When cholera hit New York in 1866, the response of the Board of Health kept cases to a minimum and demonstrated the benefits of an effective and permanent board of health.[34] As historian Charles Rosenberg notes, "For the first time, an American community had successfully organized itself to conquer an epidemic. The tools and concepts of an urban industrial society were beginning to be used in solving this new society's problems."[35]

Following the success of the Metropolitan Board of Health, cities and states across the nation created new, more effective health boards to clean up cities and improve residents' health. This shifted emphasis from the alleged moral failures of the poor to improving the physical environment in which they lived and worked.[36] By the 1890s, urban health departments provided sites where children could be vaccinated and where clean milk and untainted meat were available. In addition, they began to operate in the schools and to provide doctors for immigrant communities and tenement dwellers They also developed sanitary engineering as a profession, and urban centers improved existing water supplies and waste sewers or built new ones[37] Still, the rapid expansion of urban populations and industrialization often outpaced reformers' efforts to clean up the city and improve the health of residents. Despite progress by 1900, many of the urban poor lived in housing and sanitary conditions that contributed to high rates of contagious disease. Infectious diseases such as tuberculosis, diphtheria, scarlet fever, typhoid, and smallpox still sickened and killed many.[38]

Twentieth-Century Sanitary Reform.

At the beginning of the 20th century, sanitary reform had improved urban living. The morbidity and mortality rates from contagious diseases began, in many cases, to decline. Infectious diseases remained a serious threat, but a higher standard of living for many improved urban health. Provisions for clean water, adequate sewage removal, and inspections of milk and food all had an impact. In large cities the education programs of health departments helped improve public cooperation with health initiatives.[39]

The sanitary reforms of the late 19th and early 20th centuries were significantly aided by the bacteriological revolution that began in the 1870s. The work of Robert Koch, Louis Pasteur, and many others identified the specific microorganisms that caused many of the contagious diseases.[40] These discoveries made it possible to discover how an organism was transmitted and how to interrupt that transmission, thus preventing the spread of the disease. The first public health laboratory for investigating disease-causing organisms was established in New York City in 1887 and won praise for its identification of the cholera vibrio, which helped limit its spread. By 1895, 10 other cities had followed New York's lead and had established diagnostic laboratories. The ability to identify disease organisms as well as disease vectors and carriers, along with the development of antitoxins and vaccines, gave public health new tools to prevent and cure contagious disease. As John Duffy observes, "Science rather than sanitation now seemed to be the solution to sickness and disease."[41]

The medical implications of the bacteriological revolution did not completely supplant sanitary reform after 1900. Cities continued to expand both their population and their geography. That meant that clean water supplies and proper sewage removal needed to keep pace. Water supplies were cleaned initially with a filtration system and later with chemicals. Engineers began realizing that simply dumping sewage into the nearest body of water created dangerous contamination. Environmental and health concerns led to the development of sewage treatment facilities in many cities. Beginning in the 1940s, some cities adopted the controversial practice of adding fluoride to the water supply to prevent tooth decay.[42] Thus, if sanitary reform no longer dominated urban public health the way it had in the late 19th century, it remained an essential component of a healthy urban population and a key element in the prevention of contagious disease.

VACCINES AND ANTIBIOTICS

The bacteriological revolution and the rise of scientific medicine in the late 19th century provided public health with two new weapons against contagious disease: vaccines and antibiotics. Vaccines prepared the immune system so that, when infected by a wild virus, the system could respond vigorously and prevent illness. Antibiotics are ineffective against viruses but were very effective in curing bacterial diseases. Smallpox vaccination was developed at the end of the 18th century, and the later bacteriological revolution led to the development of numerous new vaccines in the 19th and 20th centuries. The sulfa drugs developed in the 1930s were the first effective antibiotics, followed by penicillin in the 1940s. Other antibiotics soon came along. Although sanitary reform reduced the incidence of several contagious diseases, vaccines and antibiotics quickly proved effective in reducing incidence to minimal levels. In spite of their success, these scientific advances, especially vaccines, produced a vigorous anti-vaccination movement that sometimes threatened public health. Nonetheless, they represented a major achievement in reducing the morbidity and mortality from contagious diseases in urban America.

Vaccination. Smallpox was the first disease to be attacked using vaccination. In Boston in 1721, Dr. Zabiel Boylston, with the encouragement of the prominent Puritan minister Cotton Mather, inoculated some 300 individuals during a smallpox epidemic. Inoculation worked, but it was dangerous. In late 18th-century England, Dr. Edward Jenner discovered that inoculation with cowpox, a mild disease in humans, conveyed immunity to smallpox. He called the procedure vaccination. Dr. Benjamin Waterhouse introduced vaccination to Boston in 1802, and other American doctors soon adopted the procedure. Vaccination significantly reduced the incidence of smallpox in the first several decades of the 19th century.[43]

The bacteriological revolution and the ability to identify disease-specific organisms led ultimately to new vaccines and antitoxins to prevent disease. However, the success of the smallpox vaccine in particular also led to the rise of an anti-vaccine movement in the late 19th century. The movement was led by "irregular" and largely untrained physicians, and endorsed by those skeptical of modern science and compulsory vaccination. The result was an increase in smallpox. By 1900, scientists knew how to develop vaccines, but vaccines for specific diseases were only slowly created.[44] Doctors developed a diphtheria toxin-antitoxin in the late 19th century that helped reduce significantly the toll from this disease among the urban poor.[45] A typhoid vaccine was developed in time to vaccinate 97 percent of American troops in World War I. Though effective, the vaccine was slow to win acceptance among civilians where clean water and milk had significantly reduced the disease.[46] With the arrival of World War II, the military was anxious to avoid repeating the devastating 1918 flu epidemic. Their concerns would lead to an increased study of viruses during and following the war, and eventually to new vaccines.[47]

The development of the polio vaccines by Dr. Jonas Salk and Dr. Albert Sabin in the 1950s provided a major boost to vaccination as a central means of eliminating contagious disease in urban America. Following World

War II, polio increased in both incidence and severity. The attack on polio was led by the National Foundation for Infantile Paralysis and its fundraising arm, the March of Dimes, both supported by President Franklin D. Roosevelt, who contracted the disease in 1921. The March of Dimes raised millions of dollars to support polio research and to develop a vaccine. Salk succeeded first with his killed virus vaccine. After a massive field trial in 1954 demonstrated its safety and efficacy, the US government approved the vaccine in 1955. Sabin's live virus vaccine, which was easier to administer, was approved in the early 1960s and gradually replaced the Salk vaccine. Both vaccines effectively eliminated polio in the United States by the early 1960s.[48] In ensuing years, virology continued to develop, and doctors created vaccines against many of the contagious diseases that had previously devastated urban populations for centuries.[49] However, the success of vaccines generated a vigorous anti-vaccine movement that has seen the return of diseases once thought eliminated from the United States.

Antibiotics. Although virology and vaccines led to dramatic decreases in viral diseases, especially in the second half of the 20th century, antibiotics had much the same effect on infectious bacterial diseases. Where vaccines aimed to prevent disease, antibiotics were most often used to cure diseases resulting from bacterial infections, including pneumonia, rheumatic fever, syphilis, and tuberculosis. The first of these new antibiotics was sulfonamide, which became available in limited supplies beginning in 1935. This sulfa drug was particularly effective against streptococcal infections, including some types of pneumonia. Sulfa drugs gained widespread use during World War II, when they were regarded as miracle drugs.[50]

Alexander Fleming discovered penicillin, a type of mold and the second effective class of antibiotic, in England in the late 1920s, although it was not developed into an effective antibiotic until the 1940s. Once researchers demonstrated the effectiveness of penicillin, other scientists developed methods of growing large quantities of the mold to produce the drug. The supply, initially restricted to military use, was occasionally used on civilian cases. Publicity about this new miracle drug created a huge demand among the civilian population. Sufficient supplies gradually became available for civilian use by 1943 and by 1945 met both military and civilian needs. Antibacterial research continued, and in the late 1940s and the 1950s numerous new antibiotics were developed every year. The sulfa drugs and penicillin ushered in a new world of medicine; doctors could now cure many of the infectious diseases they encountered.[51]

CONTAGIOUS DISEASES AND PUBLIC HEALTH IN THE EARLY TWENTY-FIRST CENTURY

By the mid-20th century public health had three types of weapons to deploy against contagious disease: quarantine, sanitary reform, and vaccines and antibiotics. Working together, they significantly reduced the incidence of most of the contagious diseases that had for centuries threatened urban America. However, this triumph over infectious disease was short-lived. Doctors soon discovered that bacteria evolved resistance to commonly used antibiotics, rendering them ineffective. Second, new viral diseases appeared, such as SARS (Sudden Acute Respiratory Syndrome) and HIV/AIDS (Human Immunodeficiency Virus/Acquired Immunodeficiency Syndrome), against which medicine had no preventive and no cure. HIV/AIDS was particularly devastating because the virus destroyed the patient's immune system, leaving him or her vulnerable to a variety of serious infectious diseases, including tuberculosis and pneumonia. Although HIV/AIDS was found to be partially controlled by a multidrug cocktail, it remains a serious problem in many cities. The public health battle against contagious disease will never end.

Bacteria evolve resistance to antibiotics requiring new drugs. New viral diseases emerge for which there are no vaccines. To keep contagious diseases in American cities at low levels, public health officials need to continue to employ all of the weapons at their disposal, but especially quarantines, sanitary measures, and, when available, vaccines and antibiotics.

DISCUSSION OF THE LITERATURE

The historians of urban public health in the United States have produced a growing body of literature. Good places to begin are general histories of public health. George Rosen's classic *A History of Public Health* takes the story from the ancient world to the mid-20th century. John Duffy's *The Sanitarians: A History of American Public Health* is more recent and focused on the United States. A recent history of medicine in America, John Burnham's *Healthcare in America: A History*, contains much information pertaining to urban public health.[52]

Historians have given considerable attention to particular diseases and their impact on urban populations. The 1721 smallpox epidemic in Boston is the subject of Stephen Coss's *The Fever of 1721: The Epidemic That Revolutionized Medicine and American Politics*; and Michael Willrich, in *Pox: An American History*, focuses on the early 20th century.[53] Charles Rosenberg's classic study of cholera, *The Cholera Years: The United States in 1832, 1849, and 1866*, focuses on New York but discusses other cities as well.[54] Margaret Humphreys studies yellow fever in New Orleans and the 19th-century South in *Yellow Fever and the South*.[55] Howard Markel discusses the public health impact of several contagious diseases in both *Quarantine! East European Jewish Immigrants and the New York City Epidemics of 1892* and *When Germs Travel: Six Major Epidemics That Have Invaded America and the Fears They Have Unleashed*.[56] Plague is addressed in both James C. Mohr's *Plague and Fire: Battling the Black Death and the 1900 Burning of Honolulu's Chinatown* and

Howard Markel's *When Germs Travel*.[57] The challenges of typhoid fever in an urban setting are explored in Judith Walzer Leavitt's *Typhoid Mary: Captive to the Public's Health*.[58] Two recent studies of the 1918 influenza epidemic are John M. Barry, *The Great Influenza: The Story of the Deadliest Pandemic in History*, and Nancy K. Bristow, *American Pandemic: The Lost Worlds of the 1918 Influenza Epidemic*.[59] Tuberculosis was a major cause of death in American cities down to the 20th century. Sheila M. Rothman's *Living in the Shadow of Death: Tuberculosis and the Social Experience of Illness in America* and Emily K. Abel's *Tuberculosis and the Politics of Exclusion: A History of Public Health and Migration to Los Angeles* explore this history.[60] Two studies of the urban impact of the polio epidemics are Naomi Rogers' *Dirt and Disease: Polio Before FDR*, which is focused on the 1916 epidemic in New York, and David Oshinsky's *Polio: An American Story*, which covers the subject more broadly, including the development of the Salk and Sabin vaccines.[61] The AIDS epidemic in the United States began in cities including New York and San Francisco. Recent studies include Victoria A. Harden's *AIDS at 30: A History* and David France's *How to Survive a Plague: The Inside Story of How Citizens and Science Tamed AIDS*.[62] These titles by no means exhaust the histories of particular diseases, but they provide good examples and are a good starting point.

An important development in urban public history is an emphasis on ways in which environmental factors cause disease. These diseases are not necessarily contagious, as they were in the 19th century, but they are important. Lead poisoning in urban environments is the subject of Christian Warren's *Brush with Death: A Social History of Lead Poisoning*. Samuel Kelton Roberts Jr. explores the impact of racial segregation on tuberculosis in Baltimore in *Infectious Fear: Politics, Disease, and the Health Effects of Segregation*. Disease-bearing animal and insect pests are the focus of Dawn Day Biehler's *Pests in the City: Flies,*

Bedbugs, Cockroaches, and Rats. And Devra Davis examines the cost of air pollution in *When Smoke Ran Like Water: Tales of Environmental Deception and the Battle Against Pollution.*[63]

Many scholars have focused on the public health of individual cities, such as Roberts's study of tuberculosis in Baltimore or Abel's study of the same disease in Los Angeles, previously cited. New York, not surprisingly, has attracted considerable attention, as was noted in Rosenberg's work on cholera, Rogers's study of polio, and Markel's examination of quarantine and immigration. Other examples include David Rosner, *Hives of Sickness: Public Health and Epidemics in New York City*; James Colgrove, *Epidemic City: The Politics of Public Health in New York*; and Bruce F. Berg, *Healing Gotham: New York City's Public Health Policies for the Twenty-First Century.*[64]

Several historians have explored the role of vaccination and antibiotics in curbing contagious diseases. Arthur Allen, in *Vaccine: The Controversial Story of Medicine's Greatest Lifesaver*, and Meredith Wadman, in *The Vaccine Race: Science, Politics, and the Human Costs of Defeating Disease*, discuss the rise of vaccination as an effective preventive for many contagious diseases beyond smallpox. In spite of the many successful vaccines, a significant anti-vaccination movement has impeded the elimination of some diseases. Michael Willrich's *Pox: An American History* explores the opposition to smallpox vaccination in the early 20th century, and Paul A. Offit's *Deadly Choices: How the Anti-Vaccine Movement Threatens Us All* looks at the broader history of the movement. William Rosen's *Miracle Cure: The Creation of Antibiotics and the Birth of Modern Medicine* and Scott H. Podolsky's *The Antibiotic Era: Reform, Resistance, and the Pursuit of a Rational Therapeutics* trace the 20th-century development of antibiotics as effective cures for bacterial diseases.[65]

Finally, hospitals increasingly became the place where individuals with contagious diseases were treated and sometimes cured.

A good history of the rise of the urban hospital is Charles E. Rosenberg's *The Care of Strangers: The Rise of America's Hospital System.* Studies of particular urban hospitals include Sydney Lewis's *Hospital: An Oral History of Cook County Hospital*, Chicago's public hospital, and David Oshinsky's *Bellevue: Three Centuries of Medicine and Mayhem at America's Most Storied Hospital*, New York's public hospital.[66]

PRIMARY SOURCES

Primary sources for the history of public health and contagious disease are numerous and increasingly available in digital formats. Because public health has long been a function of government, most bureaus of public health produced regular, often annual, reports as well as documents and reports concerning particular epidemics and diseases. The records of the United States Public Health Service are available at the National Archives in College Park, Maryland, and several other locations. The National Library of Medicine in Bethesda, Maryland, also has archival material related to public health and contagious diseases.[67] Some states and larger cities will have archival collections and/or collections of official reports. For New York City, "The Living City," a digital archive of public health covering 1860 to 1920, developed by the Mailman School of Public Health at Columbia University, provides a wealth of material related to the health of that city.[68]

Medical libraries associated with major medical schools, such as Johns Hopkins University, Harvard University, Yale University, Columbia University, and the University of Michigan, often contain archival material related to particular contagious diseases and public health. Several of these schools have launched digitization projects of selected primary sources such as "The Living City" at Columbia University. The Center for the History of Medicine at the University of Michigan provides the "1918 Influenza Escape Communities," primary source documents from communities that had low rates of influenza, and "The American Influenza Epidemic of 1918–1919: A Digital Encyclopedia," articles on how fifty cities dealt with the epidemic.[69] "The AIDS History Project" at the University of California, San Francisco contains both primary documents and oral histories of the epidemic.[70]

FURTHER READING

GENERAL STUDIES

Burnham, John. *Healthcare in America: A History.* Baltimore: The Johns Hopkins University Press, 2015.

Duffy, John. *The Sanitarians: A History of American Public Health.* Urbana: University of Illinois Press, 1990.

PARTICULAR DISEASES

Bristow, Nancy K. *American Pandemic: The Lost Worlds of the 1918 Influenza Epidemic.* New York: Oxford University Press, 2012.

Harden, Victoria A. *AIDS at 30: A History.* Washington, DC: Potomac Books, 2012.

Humphreys, Margaret. *Yellow Fever and the South.* Baltimore: The Johns Hopkins University Press, 1992.

Leavitt, Judith Walzer. *Typhoid Mary: Captive to the Public's Health.* Boston: Beacon Press, 1996.

Markel, Howard. *When Germs Travel: Six Major Epidemics That Have Invaded America and the Fears They Have Unleashed.* New York: Vintage Books, 2005.

Roberts, Samuel Kelton, Jr. *Infectious Fear: Politics, Disease, and the Health Effects of Segregation.* Chapel Hill: University of North Carolina Press, 2009.

Rogers, Naomi. *Dirt and Disease: Polio Before FDR.* New Brunswick, NJ: Rutgers University Press, 1992.

Rosenberg, Charles E. *The Cholera Years: The United States in 1832, 1849, and 1866.* Chicago: University of Chicago Press, 1987.

NEW YORK CITY

Colgrove, James. *Epidemic City: The Politics of Public Health in New York.* New York: Russell Sage Foundation, 2011.

Rosner, David, ed. *Hives of Sickness: Public Health and Epidemics in New York City.* New Brunswick, NJ: Rutgers University Press, 1995.

NOTES

1. Howard Markel, *Quarantine! East European Jewish Immigration and the New York City Epidemics of 1892* (Baltimore: The Johns Hopkins University Press, 1997), 3.

2. John C. Burnham, *Healthcare in America: A History* (Baltimore: The Johns Hopkins University Press, 2015), 28–30.

3. Burnham, *Healthcare in America*, 40–41.

4. Burnham, *Healthcare in America*, 41.

5. John Duffy, *The Sanitarians: A History of American Public Health* (Urbana: University of Illinois Press, 1990), 38.

6. Duffy, *The Sanitarians*, 39.

7. Duffy, *The Sanitarians*, 39–41.

8. Margaret Humphreys, *Yellow Fever and the South* (Baltimore: The Johns Hopkins University Press, 1992), 2, 8.

9. Duffy, *The Sanitarians*, 79–81.

10. Duffy, *The Sanitarians*, 80; see also Charles Rosenberg, *The Cholera Years: The United States in 1832, 1849, and 1866* (Chicago: University of Chicago Press, 1962), 14, 24.

11. Duffy, *The Sanitarians*, 81–82, 91; see also Rosenberg, *Cholera Years*, 98.

12. Rosenberg, *Cholera Years*, 104–105.

13. Duffy, *The Sanitarians*, 120–121.

14. Rosenberg, *Cholera Years*, 185–186.

15. Markel, *Quarantine*, 7.

16. James C. Mohr, *Plague and Fire: Battling Black Death and the 1900 Burning of Honolulu's Chinatown* (New York: Oxford University Press, 2005), 57, 64–65, 80.

17. Mohr, *Plague and Fire*, 89, 2–5.

18. Howard Markel, *When Germs Travel: Six Major Epidemics That Have Invaded America and the Fears They Have Unleashed* (New York: Vintage Books, 2005), 58, 65–68, 73–74, 76.

19. Naomi Rogers, *Dirt and Disease: Polio Before FDR* (New Brunswick, NJ: Rutgers University Press, 1990), 30, 33, 37–39.

20. Rogers, *Dirt and Disease*, 40–44.

21. Nancy K. Bristow, *American Pandemic: The Lost Worlds of the 1918 Influenza Epidemic* (New York: Oxford University Press, 2012), 88.

22. Nancy Tomes, " 'Destroyer and Teacher': Managing the Masses During the 1918–1919 Influenza Epidemic," *Public Health Reports* 45, Suppl. 3 (April 2010): 50–51; and Bristow, 112–116.

23. Judith Walzer Leavitt, *Typhoid Mary: Captive to the Public's Health* (Boston: Beacon Press, 1996), 27, 61.

24. Duffy, *The Sanitarians*, 28–30, 33.

25. Duffy, *The Sanitarians*, 37.

26. Duffy, *The Sanitarians*, 48–50.

27. Duffy, *The Sanitarians*, 62.

28. Duffy, *The Sanitarians*, 67.

29. Duffy, *The Sanitarians*, 75–77.

30. Duffy, *The Sanitarians*, 93.

31. Duffy, *The Sanitarians*, 102, 107–108.

32. Duffy, *The Sanitarians*, 113.

33. Duffy, *The Sanitarians*, 120; and Rosenberg, *Cholera Years*, 193.

34. Duffy, *The Sanitarians*, 121.

35. Rosenberg, *Cholera Years*, 193.

36. Duffy, *The Sanitarians*, 128.

37. Duffy, *The Sanitarians*, 142, 147.

38. Duffy, *The Sanitarians*, 174, 179.

39. Duffy, *The Sanitarians*, 190.

40. Duffy, *The Sanitarians*, 193.

41. Duffy, *The Sanitarians*, 194–196.

42. Duffy, *The Sanitarians*, 288–290.

43. Duffy, *The Sanitarians*, 27–28, 54, 56.

44. Duffy, *The Sanitarians*, 200–201.

45. Arthur Allen, *Vaccine: The Controversial Story of Medicine's Greatest Lifesaver* (New York: W. W. Norton, 2007), 123–126.

46. Duffy, *The Sanitarians*, 134–137.

47. Duffy, *The Sanitarians*, 137

48. Duffy, *The Sanitarians*, 160–214.

49. Burnham, *Healthcare in America*, 307–308.

50. Burnham, *Healthcare in America*, 270–271.

51. Burnham, *Healthcare in America*, 272–274; and William Rosen, *Miracle Cure: The Creation of Antibiotics and the Birth of Modern Medicine* (New York: Viking, 2017), 120–150.

52. George Rosen, *A History of Public Health: Expanded Edition* (Baltimore: The Johns Hopkins University Press, 1993); Duffy, *The Sanitarians*; and Burnham, *Healthcare in America*.

53. Stephen Coss, *The Fever of 1721: The Epidemic that Revolutionized Medicine and American Politics* (New York: Simon & Schuster, 2019); and Michael Willrich, *Pox: An American History* (New York: Penguin Press, 2011).

54. Rosenberg, *Cholera Years*.

55. Humphreys, *Yellow Fever and the South*.

56. Markel, *Quarantine!* and Markel, *When Germs Travel*.

57. Mohr, *Plague and Fire*.

58. Leavitt, *Typhoid Mary*.

59. John M. Barry, *The Great Influenza: The Story of the Deadliest Pandemic in History* (New York: Penguin Books, 2005); and Bristow, *American Pandemic*.

60. Sheila M. Rothman, *Living in the Shadow of Death: Tuberculosis and the Social Experience of Illness in America* (New York: Basic Books, 1994); and Emily K. Abel, *Tuberculosis and the Politics of Exclusion: A History of Public Health and Migration to Los Angeles* (New Brunswick, NJ: Rutgers University Press, 2007).

61. Rogers, *Dirt and Disease*; and David Oshinsky, *Polio: An American Story* (New York: Oxford University Press, 2005).

62. Victoria A. Harden, *AIDS at 30: A History* (Washington, DC: Potomac Books, 2012); and David France, *How to Survive a Plague: The Inside Story of How Citizens and Science Tamed AIDS* (New York: Knopf, 2016).

63. Christian Warren, *Brush with Death: A Social History of Lead Poisoning* (Baltimore: The Johns Hopkins University Press, 2000); Samuel Kelton Roberts Jr., *Infectious Fear: Politics, Disease, and the Health Effects of Segregation* (Chapel Hill: University of North Carolina Press, 2009); Dawn Day Biehler, *Pests in the City: Flies, Bedbugs, Cockroaches, and Rats* (Seattle: University of Washington Press, 2013); and Devra Davis, *When Smoke Ran Like Water: Tales of Environmental Deception and the Battle Against Pollution* (New York: Basic Books, 2002).

64. David Rosner, ed., *Hives of Sickness: Public Health and Epidemics in New York City* (New Brunswick, NJ: Rutgers University Press, 1995); James Colgrove, *Epidemic City: The Politics of Public Health in New York* (New York: Russell Sage Foundation, 2011); and Bruce F. Berg, *Healing Gotham: New York City's Public Health Policies for the Twenty-First Century* (Baltimore: The Johns Hopkins University Press, 2015).

65. Arthur Allen, *Vaccine: The Controversial Story of Medicine's Greatest Lifesaver* (New York: W.W. Norton, 2007); Meredith Wadman, *The Vaccine Race: Science, Politics, and the Human Costs of*

Defeating Disease (New York: Viking, 2017); Paul A. Offit, *Deadly Choices: How the Anti-Vaccine Movement Threatens Us All* (New York: Basic Books, 2011); William Rosen, *Miracle Cure: The Creation of Antibiotics and the Birth of Modern Medicine* (New York: Viking, 2017); and Scott H. Podolsky, *The Antibiotic Era: Reform, Resistance, and the Pursuit of a Rational Therapeutics* (Baltimore: The Johns Hopkins University Press, 2015).

66. Charles E. Rosenberg, *The Care of Strangers: The Rise of America's Hospital System* (New York: Basic Books, 1987); Sydney Lewis, *Hospital: An Oral History of Cook County Hospital* (New York: New Press, 1994); and David Oshinsky, *Bellevue: Three Centuries of Medicine and Mayhem at America's Most Storied Hospital* (New York: Doubleday, 2016).

67. National Archives, Records of the Public Health Service (PHS), 1912–1968; U.S. National Library of Medicine.

68. The Living City, Columbia University, Mailman School of Public Health.

69. Center for the History of Medicine, "1918 Influenza Escape Communities" and "The 1918 Influenza Digital Archive," The University of Michigan.

70. "AIDS History Project," University of California San Francisco.

Daniel Wilson

CLIMATE CHANGE AND THE AMERICAN CITY

AMERICAN CITIES AND CLIMATE CHANGE

Early American urbanization occurred at the tail end of the Little Ice Age, a period of planetary cooling stretching from 1350 to 1850 in which average temperatures in North America fell by about 3.5 degrees Fahrenheit. Thereafter, the North American climate warmed, a phenomenon that most scientists attribute, in part, to the burning of fossil fuels. Since 1901, the average temperature in the continental United States has increased about 1.6 Fahrenheit degrees. During this period, the United States experienced a 5 percent increase in precipitation along with an uptick in heavy rain events.[1] These continental trends unfolded across dramatic regional variations in climate, making human adaptation to meteorological conditions a highly localized endeavor. Furthermore, for people living in cities, what mattered was not so much the overarching characteristics of climate but rather the daily and seasonal circumstances of weather, manifested as highly variable fluctuations in rain, wind, and temperature.

Changes in the social organization and physical form of US cities over the course of two centuries profoundly altered the urban impact of these weather fluctuations and propelled a process of continuous adaptation. As the increasingly complex and interlocked networks that underlay critical urban functions interacted with the nonlinear dynamics of weather, cities faced novel hazards and magnified risks. Ultimately, urban ecosystems, in which climate and weather played crucial roles, proved far more complex and unpredictable than 19th- and 20th-century developers, policymakers, and planners imagined.

CLIMATE AND URBAN SETTLEMENT

Euro-Americans were highly attuned to climate and weather as they sought to replicate Old World urban patterns amid the more volatile and extreme environments they encountered on the western side of the Atlantic Ocean. Prevailing temperatures, moisture levels, and air circulation patterns were not simply assessed in terms of familiarity and comfort; they were understood as critical determinants of bodily health. Through much of the 19th century, settlers staking claim to unfamiliar territory relied on reigning medical theories to distinguish the relative advantages of both regional and highly localized environments as defined by wind vectors, heat, and humidity.[2] Appealing climatic attributes were publicized relentlessly by urban boosters to attract migrants, especially in the nation's interior where speculative competition for urban primacy was fierce.

Climatological considerations, however, were at best secondary in determining the location of towns or the internal form of growing cities. For one thing, no medical consensus existed regarding the health implications of specific meteorological conditions. Moreover, geographic factors related to economic potential such as the quality of harbors, proximity to transportation routes, and access to raw materials and markets generally overrode concerns about environmental salubrity.[3] Within cities, the presence of refreshing breezes propelled the formation of elite enclaves on high ground as urban terrain became more segregated by socioeconomic status in the early 19th century. On the other hand, plans to relieve urban dwellers from excessive heat through the generous placement of parks fell victim to a voracious real estate market that maximized profit through the construction of a denser (and hotter) built environment. After 1850, business interests became more inclined to advocate for large parks, recognizing the profits to be made through adjacent property sales.[4]

Nowhere was climatological urban boosterism employed more aggressively or to greater effect than in the American Southwest where real estate and business interests marketed aridity and warmth as consumer amenities. Plentiful sunshine, mild temperatures, and ocean breezes figured prominently in the gush of promotional literature emanating from southern California following the arrival of railroads in the 1870s and 1880s. Vividly illustrated brochures and magazines, initially aimed at convalescents and tourists, fueled the growth of many fledgling communities that eventually formed parts of greater Los Angeles and San Diego. By the 1920s, southern California's pleasant weather had coaxed the permanent relocation of over a million Americans from eastern portions of the country. Los Angeles' newfound status as a booming metropolis was assisted by the westward migration of weather-dependent industries such as aviation and filmmaking.[5] Urban boosters in Phoenix followed a similar script in the 1930s, rebranding their city as the "Valley of the Sun" to lure seasonal seekers of health and leisure.[6] Scorching desert heat in summertime, however, posed an obstacle to year-round habitation. Civic leaders thus seized on incremental advancements in mechanical air cooling over the next several decades to counteract negative perceptions of its weather. As early as 1940, Phoenix proclaimed itself the "air-conditioned capital of the world." Only with the widespread adoption of household units cooled with chemical refrigerants in the 1960s and 1970s, however, did meteoric population growth vault Phoenix into the ranks of the nation's top ten cities.[7] Yet even where climate boosterism and weather considerations seemed to matter most, a multiplicity of unrelated factors including cheap land; accessibility of suburban-style private homes for middle-class households; and low-tax, pro-business, anti-union politics proved equally instrumental in fueling Sunbelt urbanization in the 20th century. Although not inconsequential, the connection between urban settlement patterns and climate in American history can best be described as tenuous.

Likewise, climatic influences on early American urban architecture were overshadowed by the strong inclination to follow European precedent. A tight connection between climate and design can be found in the example of the raised Creole cottage with open-air passageways that became popular in 18th-century New Orleans on account of the region's warm temperatures and soggy soils. More typically, however, European designs underwent selective modification to accommodate environmental particularities. In northern colonies, the substitution of roof shingles for thatch was most likely a concession to harsher winters, as were the construction of larger fireplaces and more generous use of weatherboarding for insulation. More comprehensive attempts to design homes in concert with nature persisted, perhaps best exemplified by Frank Lloyd Wright's prairie-style houses of the early 20th century, which integrated indoor and outdoor elements to maximize energy efficiency and comfort during the steamy summers and hard winters of the American Midwest. The more general trend, however, especially pronounced after World War II, was toward a uniformity of national styles that defied environmental distinctions. Especially after World War II, when central heating and air conditioning became widespread, the demise of regional architecture included the gradual disappearance of features—shutters, large porches, vestibules, thick walls—that once afforded passive climate control.[8]

STORMS AND THE CITY

If weather played a secondary role in determining where cities appeared and how they were built, the process of urbanization profoundly influenced the ways in which Americans experienced the effects of weather. Population growth combined with the outward spatial expansion of cities in the 19th century turned predictable rainfall irregularities into damaging floods. Rising demand for fresh water for drinking, bathing, street cleaning, firefighting, and flushing human waste frequently outstripped the ability of cities to capture local rainfall, especially during dry seasons. Chronic water shortages became endemic in east-coast cities and towns by the mid-19th century, prompting the construction of engineered hydraulic systems that enlarged catchment basins and stored excess capacity in reservoirs. Some of the worst instances of urban flooding, such as the notorious calamity afflicting Johnstown, Pennsylvania, in 1889, resulted from the collapse of poorly constructed reservoir dams in the aftermath of heavy rain.[9]

Further west, cities located along the nation's great interior rivers benefited from reliable freshwater supplies but faced increasing threats of inundation as settlement spread from well-protected high ground to low-lying floodplains. Between the American Civil War (1861–1865) and World War I (1914–1919), periodic bouts of intense precipitation caused rising waters of the Mississippi, Missouri, and Ohio Rivers to spill over their banks onto recently settled terrain. Urban settlement in flood-prone districts was typically initiated by railroads that preferred to stretch their routes across flat bottom lands due to the ease of construction. Factories gravitated to these transportation corridors, thereby encouraging surrounding settlement by laborers and their families. In this manner, industrial geography and topography conspired against working-class families, immigrants, and people of color, who bore the disproportionate burden of river inundation.

The damage incurred by flooding was particularly devastating when key nodes in urban infrastructure—bridges, water pumping stations, electrical generators—were rendered inoperable, as was the case in Kansas City after more than ten inches of rain fell in late May of 1903 and caused rivers to overflow their banks. Although the tens of thousands of African Americans and European immigrants who occupied the packing house districts adjacent to the surging Kansas River suffered the greatest losses, a near-total breakdown in municipal services produced calamity throughout the bi-state metropolis. For nearly a week, residents were without electrical power, telephone communication, piped gas, and most dangerously, potable water. Indeed, the most lethal consequence of the flood may have been the outbreak of typhoid fever that was estimated to have sickened approximately 1,500 people and killed another 135 along the flooded river corridor between Topeka and Kansas City. Damage to transportation systems magnified losses and delayed recovery. Six feet of water at Union Depot halted incoming and outgoing trains, thereby stalling the delivery of needed provisions, including coal and meat. Deprived of electrical power, streetcars remained out of commission for nearly two weeks. Of the seventeen bridges connecting the Kansas and Missouri sides of the metropolis, only one remained in operation. Blocked routes and immobilized vehicles hindered rescue efforts and permitted the spread of uncontained fires.[10]

As municipal governments turned to professional planners for guidance during the Progressive Era, destructive storms, like the one that crippled Kansas City in 1903, prompted the formulation of comprehensively engineered urban hydrological systems. Based on extensive measurements of rainfall, runoff, and stream flow, these plans reconciled the appetite for developable land with the need to protect fixed investment by directing storm water through subterranean sewers and barricading major rivers with artificial barriers. In New Orleans, for example, a drenching rain on August 13, 1894 dumped more than a billion gallons of water on New Orleans and gave Progressive reformers the ammunition they needed to authorize a plan for draining the city's swampy terrain by way of street gutters, branch drains, canals, and a central outflow channel that pumped rainwater to peripheral lakes. By 1908, New Orleans had constructed more than forty miles of canals assisted by seven pumping stations.[11]

Likewise, Pittsburgh encountered disastrous flooding in 1907, prompting its Chamber of Commerce to commission a study for regional watershed management. The resulting report, issued four years later, recommended an ambitious program of environmental intervention that included the obligatory flood walls in the downtown area, urban land reclamation through the filling of river back channels, impoundment of reservoirs upstream, and the creation of forest reserves in headwater areas.[12] Three straight days of heavy rainfall in the midst of a wet El Nino cycle had a similar effect in Los Angeles County in February 1914,

providing the impetus for a comprehensive flood-control plan that called for fortified embankments along a straightened Los Angeles River, dams and reservoirs on tributary streams, and a relocated outlet to the sea.[13] In each of these cases, financial stringency delayed full implementation until the federal government was more forthcoming with funds during and after the New Deal.

Once in place, engineered hydraulic systems proved no panacea and worked less to eliminate floods than to alter the scale and geography of risk. Too often, physical protections against flooding emboldened developers to build in precarious zones that were among the first to go under water when rain exceeded expectations or when flood-control infrastructure malfunctioned. A 1958 study conducted by a University of Chicago research team concluded that twenty years after the federal government had committed to huge flood-control expenditures, financial losses attributable to flood damage had actually increased.[14] Even when physical protections worked as intended, they merely shifted the burden of flooding from one location to another. While safeguarding downtown districts and other critical nodes from rising rivers, pumping stations and levees displaced excess flow to low-lying areas where unprotected streams overflowed and overburdened sewers backed up into basements and streets. Sewer overflows became especially hazardous in older northeastern and midwestern cities where storm water with raw sewage travelled through the same pipes. Moreover, when urban expansion entailed the drainage of wetlands, cities lost an important ecological buffer that had previously mitigated floods by storing and slowly releasing large volumes of rainwater.

The Great Mississippi River Flood of 1993 exposed the inequities and shortcomings of engineering solutions as it rolled across metropolitan St. Louis in late July. Heavy rains throughout the Upper Mississippi watershed earlier that summer swelled the river as it charged southward toward the confluence of a cresting Missouri River. Although the maximum discharge at St. Louis, just below this conjuncture, was significantly lower than it had been in previous periods of high water, artificial confinements along the river banks pushed the Mississippi to record heights. Yet, most of St. Louis City remained secure behind a fifty-two-foot flood wall that was authorized to receive federal funds in 1949 due to the high value of commercial and industrial properties along eleven miles of waterfront. Predominantly white working-class residential districts situated further downstream, however, had not met federal cost-benefit thresholds and faced the full force of the gushing Mississippi as it backed up through smaller tributary streams and damaged hundreds of homes.[15]

As urban populations became increasingly dependent on interconnected or "tightly coupled" infrastructural networks in the late 19th and 20th centuries, weather-related malfunctions scaled toward the catastrophic. The advent of the wired and piped city in the late 19th century created new opportunities for storm-related disruption and calamity. Snowfalls that minimally hampered the mobility of horse-drawn vehicles thoroughly disrupted urban transportation systems dependent on steam power and electricity, as New York City residents first discovered during the Great Blizzard of 1888.[16] High winds from hurricanes, nor'easters, and tornadoes wrought havoc with overhead lines and cables critical to the functioning of telegraph, telephone, and electrical services. By September 1938, when hundred-mile-per-hour gales swept across New England, its cities and towns were fully electrified. The hurricane downed twenty thousand miles of hanging wires, knocking out power throughout the region for weeks.[17] Exposed power lines were also vulnerable to snow and ice accumulation as well as nearby trees that became unstable when their limbs were covered in ice or their roots were loosened by rain-saturated soil. Even cities like New York City and Chicago that buried wires underground were not immune from the cascading effects of weather-induced malfunctions. In 1977, a lightning strike on two 345-kilovolt power lines in Westchester County triggered a cascade of mechanical breakdowns and human errors that quickly plunged most of New York City into darkness, quiet, and stillness. The "blackout" also generated arson and looting sprees in several neighborhoods, revealing the extent to which the power networks that connected city dwellers also played a role in the maintenance of social order.[18]

EXTREME TEMPERATURES IN THE CITY

Urban growth and increased interconnectivity also complicated efforts to mitigate the impact of temperature extremes. In northern latitudes, city dwellers met the challenge of cold winters with incremental advancements in interior heating; over the course of the 18th and 19th centuries, inefficient open fireplaces gave way to closed stoves and furnace-based central heating. These technological leaps made freezing temperatures survivable and improved thermal comfort but at the price of increased carbon emissions from fossil fuel combustion. The grave dangers associated with excessive heat, on the other hand, persisted well into the 20th century.

For much of the 19th century, summer mortality exceeded that of other seasons, primarily due to illnesses related to food spoilage and the proliferation of water-borne bacteria. Sanitation reforms and public regulation of food and milk supplies in the early 20th century reduced this peril, but city dwellers continued to suffer from the direct impact of excessive heat, especially when it descended on cities for prolonged periods.[19]

The heatwave of 1901 killed approximately ten thousand people in the Northeast and Midwest, and large cities were hit hard. Deaths attributed to heat exhaustion topped four hundred in New York City and 250 in St. Louis. Horses, still vital to urban transportation systems at the turn of the century, also fell victim to heat stroke, although some cities reported that they were better cared for than people due to their high investment value. An even more severe heatwave swept much of the nation in the 1930s. Although the unusually hot and dry weather of this period is normally associated with the plight of farmers on the Great Plains, the impact on cities was significant due to both the influx of Dust Bowl refugees and extraordinarily high death rates. The summer of 1936 was particularly hot due to a high-pressure system that stalled over the continental United States for six weeks, sending temperatures soaring above the one-hundred-degree -Fahrenheit mark in forty-six states. More than five thousand deaths were recorded with high mortality rates affecting all of the nation's large cities. Among the adaptive legacies of this brutal spell was the switch from incandescent to fluorescent lighting in urban schools and hospitals.[20]

Summer mortality, morbidity, and discomfort in cities were aggravated by the growing density of the human-constructed environment, which raised temperatures between five and nine degrees Fahrenheit over surrounding rural areas where natural vegetation utilized solar radiation in the cooling process of evapotranspiration. Unlike natural vegetation, the primary building materials of American cities—asphalt, concrete, glass, tile—absorbed solar radiation during the daytime and emitted it as heat overnight. Emissions from factories, power plants, cars, trucks, and by the latter part of the 20th century, air conditioners, raised temperatures further.[21] In the mid-20th century, the term "urban heat island" was coined to describe the temperature discrepancy between urban and rural areas.

In the face of searing summertime heat, urban populations adopted coping strategies that varied in use according to one's financial means. Long before the term "urban heat island" was popularized, city dwellers recognized the temperature differential between built-up areas and surrounding forests, prompting the flight of wealthy families to country estates and seaside retreats during hot summer months. Those who remained in the city took advantage of the cooling functions of water and vegetation as best they could. Through the 19th century, many cities contained an abundance of water features—streams, ponds, springs—to which lower-income populations had free and easy access. Abandoned quarries created by the extraction of clay and stone provided another source of accumulated water that functioned as swimming holes. As comprehensive urban drainage and landfilling eliminated many of these unregulated water features from the urban landscape, Progressive-Era reformers established recreation centers with public swimming pools that teemed with supervised bathers on hot summer days. In the latter half of the 20th century, however, resistance among white families to racially integrated leisure spaces and budgetary constraints led to the closure of many public swimming pools.[22]

Natural vegetation offered another widely sought source of heat relief. Large landscaped parks with shaded foliage, grassy fields, and water features became regular features of big cities in the latter half of the 19th century and were supplemented by scattered patches of designated greenery. As historian Colin Fisher demonstrated in his study of Chicago, these city parks were widely used and enjoyed by the urban masses, and they became important cultivators of ethnic and racial identity.[23] On warm summer days, they provided a pleasant setting for festivals, athletic events, and informal leisure. During the hottest of summer nights, they were converted to open-air dormitories, where drowsy families with sheets and pillows in tow reaped the cooling benefits of evapotranspiration. Cities periodically prohibited overnight sleeping in public parks, however, sending those in search of cooling breezes to less comfortable tenement rooftops and fire escapes.[24]

Widespread household adoption of mechanical air conditioning toward the end of the

20th century reduced the discomfort and peril of excessive heat considerably, but its salutary effects were not distributed equally. Technology for refrigerating and dehumidifying interior space was pioneered by industrial engineer Willis Haviland Carrier in 1902, but for more than fifty years its application was confined to factories, movie palaces, and department stores.[25] By the early 1970s, however, most new homes constructed in US cities included centralized cooling systems, and by the mid-1980s about two-thirds of American households enjoyed some form of mechanical air conditioning in their homes. Remaining households, disproportionately comprised of the poor, the elderly, and people of color, had fewer cooling options at their disposal. With sharp reductions in the number of people seeking nighttime relief in city parks, outdoor spaces lacked the critical mass of people to assure public safety, thereby inducing many to take their chances inside their baking homes. The resulting social skew in mortality rates was dramatically exposed during the Chicago heatwave of 1995 when more than seven hundred people, many of them elderly and poor, perished during a week of above-average temperatures. In his retrospective social autopsy of this calamity, sociologist Eric Klinenberg discovered that well-to-do and middle-class households made it through the episode by turning on their air conditioners or fleeing the city for cooler climes. Deaths occurred disproportionately in neighborhoods characterized by limited social services, social isolation, and concentrated poverty.[26]

UNDERSTANDING THE WEATHER AND DISASTER PLANNING

If infrastructural and mechanical interventions did not eliminate weather disasters, there was much that could be achieved to better prepare urban populations for them and reduce losses in their aftermath. Enhanced capabilities for anticipating extreme weather ultimately saved thousands of lives in American cities but advancements in meteorological knowledge came slowly. Only after the Civil War did public opinion begin to break away from the perception of violent storms as inscrutable acts of God and begin to see weather as a puzzle to be unlocked through empirical research. Meteorological study received an important boost in the 1870s when the federal government, under the auspices of the US Army Signal Corps, assumed responsibility for collecting weather data and issuing forecasts. In 1890, those duties were transferred to the newly created US Weather Bureau. With the science of meteorology still in its infancy, however, weather predictions remained unreliable well into the early 20th century. As late as 1900, few local newspapers provided readers with daily forecasts, and those that did were often ridiculed for their erroneous prognostications.[27] Some of the worst weather catastrophes of this era, including the Great New York City Blizzard of 1888 and the Galveston Hurricane of 1900, caught victimized populations unaware and off guard.

During the 1930s, new techniques for analyzing air masses and fronts improved forecasting capabilities and made it possible in the postwar years to issue advance warnings of impending storms. Simultaneously, Cold War anxieties about thermonuclear attacks on civilian populations provided the impetus for federally funded research on disaster preparedness and the rise of a disaster-planning profession. Insights gleaned from this new field of study also found application in natural disaster planning, as reflected in the proliferation of underground shelters, the implementation of radio and siren-based warning systems, and the development of mass evacuation protocols.[28]

Significantly, the federal government became more directly involved in disaster relief and recovery during the Cold War era. Prior to World War II, the task of picking up after natural disasters primarily fell to local communities and specialized volunteer organizations such as the American Red Cross. Although the Red Cross was not specifically urban in its mandate, the agency was instrumental in dispensing medical care and provisions in many cities, beginning with a series of floods in cities and towns along the Ohio and Mississippi Rivers in the early 1880s.[29] The Federal Disaster Relief Act of 1950 was the first in a series of laws authorizing the president to issue disaster declarations and disperse direct financial assistance to disaster victims. The emergence of an "all-hazards" emergency planning and response paradigm in the 1960s and 1970s culminated in the establishment of the Federal Emergency Management Agency (FEMA) in 1979.[30]

Improved emergency management techniques heightened expectations for efficient recovery operations and also produced widespread frustration when those expectations were not met. Botched responses to weather disasters had especially severe repercussions for local office holders, as Mayor Michael Bilandic learned after it took weeks for Chicago to dig out of a January 1979 blizzard. Popular exasperation about the slow pace of street plowing took its toll on Bilandic, a protégé of longtime political boss Richard Daley, and contributed to the electoral defeat of the Democratic Party machine in that year's mayoral election.[31]

Improvements in weather forecasting, warning communication systems, and disaster planning had a decisive effect on human casualty rates but did little to reduce the amount of property damaged by hurricanes, tornadoes, and floods. Indeed, losses from property damage measured in constant dollars continued to rise dramatically into the 21st century.[32] Some of these losses were offset through the expansion of insurance coverage. Localized disasters typically produced upticks in the purchase of insurance policies as specialized coverage became available for tornadoes and wind storms in the late 19th century. Private insurers were reluctant to insure against water damage, however. The large numbers of uninsured losses from Hurricane Betsy in 1965 prompted passage of the National Flood Insurance Act in 1968, with the dual purpose of making flood insurance more affordable and reducing floodplain development. Under its provisions, the federal government subsidized flood insurance premiums in jurisdictions where local governments discouraged new construction or rebuilding in flood-prone areas. In 1973 the program became mandatory for all federally guaranteed mortgages sold in flood hazard zones.[33] Insurance coverage had a minimal effect on reducing property destruction, however; indeed, it often worked in conjunction with the extension of protective public infrastructure to embolden urban expansion into perilous areas. In the case of the National Flood Insurance Program, its intended effects were undermined by a combination of relaxed provisions and local governments bent on development granting waivers. One indication of the program's limited effectiveness was the high percentage of repeat claims, roughly 50% percent, filed by policy holders between 1978 and 1994.[34]

TWENTY-FIRST-CENTURY STORMS AND RESILIENCE PLANNING FOR CITIES

A series of deadly and costly tropical storms in the early decades of the 21st century highlighted the continuing vulnerability of cities to extreme weather and propelled more systematic consideration of climate change in resiliency planning for cities. During the 20th century, dozens of easterly tropical storms that assumed hurricane proportions in the Caribbean Sea and Gulf of Mexico wrought havoc on American coastal cities. The Galveston Hurricane of 1900 remains the deadliest in the nation's history, claiming over six thousand casualties. Subsequent tropical cyclones, including the Great Miami Hurricane of 1926, Hurricane Betsy in 1965, Hurricane Camille in 1969, and Hurricane Andrew in 1992, resulted in less death but more destruction due to the penchant of Sunbelt migrants to build near the water. What was different about Hurricane Katrina in 2005, Superstorm Sandy in 2012, and the one-two punch of Hurricanes Harvey and Maria in 2017 was their occurrence in the midst of growing scientific certainty and rising public awareness of human-induced global warming. Each of these tropical storms highlighted different aspects of the urban predicament. Together they exposed deep flaws in the structural forces that drove urban growth and allocated catastrophic risk. Several initiatives in the 2010s sought to address these deficiencies within a more holistic and flexible planning paradigm that went beyond technical solutions by addressing social conditions and urban design.

By any measure, Hurricane Katrina ranked as one of the worst natural disasters in the nation's history. The body count of 1,833 was the highest for a domestic natural disaster since the 1928 Okeechobee Hurricane, and the death toll of nearly 1,500 in New Orleans was the highest for any United States city since the 1906 San Francisco earthquake. Hurricane Katrina was also the most expensive in the nation's history. Much of the death and destruction in New Orleans was due to the failures of an elaborate internal levee system that was undermaintained and underfunded for years. The stress on the city's flood-control infrastructure, however, was exacerbated by a century of wetland drainage that had removed natural buffers for storm water absorption and further sank the elevation of settled districts. Levee construction along the Mississippi River also contributed to the loss of surrounding wetland buffers by preventing natural sediment deposition along the alluvial floodplain.

Above all, Katrina exposed glaring racial disparities in social impacts. The concentration of poor African Americans in the lowest elevations of the city assured that they would bear the brunt of any failure to contain an incoming storm surge, and that is precisely what

occurred. Those most vulnerable to flooding were also least equipped to follow an evacuation plan that relied on private automobile transportation. In the nightmarish week after the storm, tens of thousands of predominantly poor and black survivors struggled without food, water, or shelter. Twenty thousand refugees were penned into the fetid and sweltering Superdome while others slogged through flooded streets searching for escape routes and waited on rooftops for airborne rescue. A highly militarized relief operation (the Federal Emergency Management Agency [FEMA] had recently been rehoused under the Department of Homeland Security) criminalized stranded and homeless populations. As geographer Neil Smith noted, "we see, that one's chances of surviving a disaster are more than anything dependent on one's race, ethnicity and social class."[35]

If New Orleans's uniquely susceptible topography and gross political ineptitude made Katrina a weak indicator of more generalized urban failures, a series of devastating storms in the following decade spoke more forcefully to a pervasive critique of two centuries of American urban development. Although Hurricane Sandy was recategorized as a post-tropical cyclone by the time it made landfall south of New York City on October 29, 2012, its high winds and storm surge assaulted the metropolitan area with enough force and fury to destroy more than nine hundred buildings, claim at least seventy-three fatalities, and inundate fifty-one square miles of coastline in New York City alone, earning it the informal moniker of "superstorm." In the subsequent mayhem, more than four million households remained without electrical power for days, subways were idled, bridges and tunnels were impassable, and a shortage of gasoline created chaos and long lines at filling stations. The storm's repercussions were felt far beyond New York City as approximately twenty thousand flights were cancelled, and for the first time since the Great Blizzard of 1888, the New York Stock Exchange suspended operations for two straight days.[36] Five years later, in one of the

Atlantic Ocean's most active storm seasons, Hurricane Harvey soaked Houston with an unprecedented 120 billion gallons of rain. Overtopped bayous and reservoirs forced thousands of people from their homes and caused more property damage than any storm besides Katrina. Post-mortems on both Sandy and Harvey blamed the extent of damage and misery on what had become the usual set of historical suspects—the destruction of protective wetlands, the expansion of urban development into high-risk flood zones, and the tight coupling of transportation, power, and provisioning systems.[37] One notable element of the post-Harvey analysis was the conclusion drawn by generally cautious climatologists that global warming was a likely contributor to the storm's severity.[38]

Katrina, Sandy, and Harvey along with slightly less notorious 21st-century accomplices—Rita, Ike, Irma, Wilma, Maria— compelled urban planners and policymakers to take the threat of climate change more seriously and think more systematically about adaptive practices. Previously, climate change operated within the more static framework of sustainability planning, where it argued for reducing carbon footprints through stricter energy efficiency standards in new construction, transit-oriented development, greater use of renewable energy sources, and more parks, trees, and green spaces. The enormous disruption caused by Katrina, Sandy, and Harvey suggested that mitigation efforts alone were unlikely to shield cities from environmental adversity. Resilience emerged as a conceptual basis for policies and plans that aimed to improve capacities for recovery and constructive transformation in the aftermath of unforeseeable external shocks, especially those precipitated by global warming. Informed by the precepts of tactical urbanism, resilience planning moved beyond technocratic solutions by encouraging grass-roots participation in the pursuit of more flexible and creative synergies between natural and human systems, including social and governmental structures.[39]

Resilience planning was embraced most fervently by coastal cities that had the most to lose as global warming raised sea levels. New York City already stood in the vanguard of sustainability planning when Superstorm Sandy arrived. But in its wake, the Rockefeller Foundation and the US Department of Housing and Urban Development nudged the city toward a resilience paradigm by funding six projects under the auspices of the Rebuild New York campaign that employed participatory design practices to better prepare it for future shocks. Among the funded projects were the Big-U, a proposed ten-mile berm surrounding lower Manhattan that simultaneously defended settled land against storm surges and provided neighborhood amenities such as parks and bicycle paths. Building on this concept, the Rockefeller Foundation launched its 100 Resilient Cities initiative in 2013 to further propagate resilience planning through competitive awards that included technical assistance and funds for personnel. New Orleans and New York City were among the eleven US cities selected in 2013 to join the initial cohort of thirty-two. For all its attention, resilience planning did not garner universal praise. New York City's Rebuild By Design, for instance, was criticized for not going far enough to reform urban politics and address social conditions. Indeed, some critics derided resilience planning as a cover for the perpetuation of neoliberal political economies.[40]

DISCUSSION OF THE LITERATURE

A well-defined body of literature about the history of American cities and climate does not exist. Indeed, the study of climate and historical change remains in its infancy, and most scholarly research in this area probes long-term change at regional scales. Among the relatively small number of works that examine weather impacts on urbanization, two overlapping historical subfields inform scholarly analysis: environmental history and the history of technology. Whereas environmental historians are more likely to assign agency to the intricacies of weather dynamics, historians of technology emphasize the adaptive responses to meteorological events. A burgeoning social science literature about urbanism and climate focuses in its historical treatments on the social and political aspects of recent hurricanes, floods, and heat waves.

Since the 1990s, American historians have published several works that take weather as the primary focus of inquiry. Among them, Blake McKelvey's *Snow in the Cities: A History of America's Urban Response* lies squarely in the history of technology tradition, approaching the interaction between winter precipitation and urbanization through a lens of transportation systems and snow removal devices. William Meyer's *Americans and Their Weather* offers the most comprehensive treatment of how cultural perceptions, social arrangements, and adaptive technologies interacted with weather conditions in the United States, although his coverage is not specifically urban.[41] Meyer's fierce stand against weather determinism places him in line with prevailing scholarly opinion. Bernard Mergen's *Weather Matters: An American Cultural History since 1900* probes shifting popular understandings of weather in the 20th century and reflects a decisive cultural turn in the recent literature.[42]

A larger body of work encompasses case studies of weather-induced natural disasters. David McCullough's narrative of the Johnstown Flood, published in 1968, provided a template for such studies by combining dramatic narrative with a sharp critique of human landscape interventions.[43] As this genre of analysis evolved, historians devoted more attention to the ethnic, racial, and class divisions that shaped social impact of floods, tornadoes, hurricanes, and heat waves.[44] Few, if any, domestic natural disasters have spawned as much scholarship across humanities and social science disciplines as Hurricane Katrina. Although most accounts of Katrina expose the folly of past environmental decisions, authors generally assign culpability for human suffering to the incompetence of public officials charged

with emergency management responsibilities.[45] Social science literature on the calamity often couches the disaster within an indictment of neoliberal politics.[46]

In the 1990s, several historians began moving beyond case studies toward a more comprehensive examination of natural disasters. Approaching the topic from the perspective of environmental history, Ted Steinberg showed how power hierarchies were perpetuated through the "naturalizing" of human-induced social catastrophes such as hurricanes, floods, tornadoes, and earthquakes.[47] Scott Knowles' study of disaster experts reflected a growing interest among historians of technology in the social and cultural formulations of innovation and risk.[48] Kevin Rozario added a valuable cultural dimension to the historiography of disaster by elaborating on America's morbid fascination with calamity and its inclination to view tragic events optimistically, as agents of progress.[49]

The unnatural underpinnings of natural disaster also received illumination in studies of particular cities, most notably Los Angeles. For Mike Davis, human meddling on behalf of the wealthy and powerful magnified the volatility of Southern California's natural environment, producing an urban "ecology of fear."[50] Focusing more narrowly on the magnification of flood hazards in the Los Angeles basin, Jared Orsi castigated bureaucratic rigidity for a series of ill-informed engineering decisions.[51] The shortcomings of human hydraulic engineering also looms large as a theme in environmental histories of New Orleans, as exemplified by the scholarship of Craig Colten, Ari Kelman, and others.[52] Phoenix and Tucson, on the other hand, have emerged as exemplars of cities that owed their explosive growth to the emergence of weather as an amenity in the 20th century.[53] Andrew Needham's study of Phoenix also demonstrates the metropolis's contribution to climate change through its dependence on coal production.[54]

Another strand in the historiography of urban weather consists of scholarship on technologies that have developed to overcome climate constraints and weather hazards. Joel Tarr and Martin Melosi pioneered historical studies of urban sewerage in the 1970s, a topic that touched on the challenge of excess rainwater. Their work on urban infrastructure continued well into the 21st century.[55] Since the 1990s, the topics of air-conditioning and refrigeration have captured increasing notice from historians, with emphasis shifting from an engineering perspective to a more nuanced social and cultural analysis.[56]

PRIMARY SOURCES

The major source of climate data in the United States is the National Oceanic and Atmospheric Administration (NOAA). Raw weather data from National Weather Service monitoring stations, including temperature and precipitation readings, is available for American cities and towns going back to the 1870s, in many cases. This data, which can be accessed through the NOAA's online data portal (https://www.ncdc.noaa.gov/cdo-web/), can be used to identify extreme weather events and to reconstruct long-term climatic trends. In addition, researchers can access regional and statewide publications dating to the late 19th century that provide descriptive overviews of weather conditions. Beginning in 1959, NOAA's monthly publication, *Storm Data* (https://www.ncdc.noaa.gov/IPS/sd/sd.html), provided qualitative assessments of storm occurrences and unusual weather phenomena. These reports, arranged chronologically by state, contain information on storm paths, deaths, injuries, and property damage, and can be accessed online.

Investigating the impacts of weather and climate on urban society requires a more decentralized approach, although records of the American Red Cross and the Federal Emergency Management Agency housed at the National Archives permit a national overview of natural disasters. In the aftermath of major storms, state legislatures sometimes commissioned reviews of relief and recovery efforts.

Genealogical records such as death certificates are valuable for assessing mortality risks associated with extreme weather events. For the more mundane challenges posed by fluctuations in rainfall, wind, and temperature, the best sources are reports issued by city agencies, particularly sewer boards, health commissions, and parks departments. Finally, local newspapers should not be overlooked as a rich source of information about individualized and informal adaptations to a variety of weather conditions. Only recently has climate figured prominently in city planning; plans developed under the auspices of the Rockefeller Foundation's 100 Resilient Cities (https://www.100resilientcities.org/) initiatives can be accessed online.

FURTHER READING

Ackerman, Marsha. *Cool Comfort: America's Romance with Air-Conditioning*. Washington, DC: Smithsonian Institution Press, 2002.

Davis, Mike. *Ecology of Fear: Los Angeles and the Imagination of Disaster*. New York: Metropolitan Books, 1998.

Knowles, Scott Gabriel. *The Disaster Experts: Mastering Risk in Modern America*. Philadelphia: University of Pennsylvania Press, 2011.

Kohn, Edward P. *Hot Time in the Old Town: The Great Heat Wave of 1896 and the Making of Theodore Roosevelt*. New York: Basic Books, 2010.

McKelvey, Blake. *Snow in the Cities: A History of America's Urban Response*. Rochester: University of Rochester Press, 1995.

Mergen, Bernard. *Snow in America*. Washington, DC: Smithsonian Institution Press, 1997.

Mergen, Bernard. *Weather Matters: An American Cultural History since 1900*. Lawrence: University of Kansas Press, 2008.

Needham, Andrew. *Power Lines: Phoenix and the Making of the Modern Southwest*. Princeton, NJ: Princeton University Press, 2014.

Orsi, Jared. *Hazardous Metropolis: Flooding and Urban Ecology in Los Angeles*. Berkeley, CA: University of California Press, 2004.

Platt, Harold L. *Sinking Chicago: Climate Change and the Remaking of a Flood-Prone Environment*. Philadelphia: Temple University Press, 2018.

Smith, Carl S. *City Water, City Life: Water and the Infrastructure of Ideas in Urbanizing Philadelphia, Boston, and Chicago*. Chicago: University of Chicago Press, 2013.

Steinberg, Ted. *Acts of God: The Unnatural History of Natural Disaster in America*. Oxford: Oxford University Press, 2000.

Valencius, Conevery Bolton. *The Health of the Country: How American Settlers Understood Themselves and Their Land*. New York: Basic Books, 2002.

NOTES

1. Jerry M. Melillo, Terese Richmond, and Gary W. Yohe, eds., *Climate Change Impacts in the United States: The Third National Climate Assessment* (Washington, DC: US Global Change Research Program, 2014), 28–37.

2. Conevery Bolton Valencius, *The Health of the Country: How American Settlers Understood Themselves and Their Land* (New York: Basic Books, 2002).

3. Timothy R. Mahoney, *River Towns in the Great West: The Structure of Provincial Urbanization in the American Midwest, 1820–1870* (New York: Cambridge University Press, 1990); and William Cronon, *Nature's Metropolis: Chicago and the Great West* (New York: Norton, 1991), 36–39.

4. Catherine McNeur, *Taming Manhattan: Environmental Battles in the Antebellum City* (Cambridge, MA: Harvard University Press, 2014); Roy Rosenzweig and Elizabeth Blackmar, *The Park and the People: A History of Central Park* (Ithaca, NY: Cornell University Press, 1998); Robin Faith Bachin, *Building the South Side: Urban Space and Civic Culture in Chicago, 1890–1919* (Chicago: University of Chicago Press, 2004); and Carl S. Smith, *The Plan of Chicago: Daniel Burnham and the Remaking of the American City* (Chicago: University of Chicago Press, 2006).

5. Carey McWilliams, *Southern California: An Island on the Land* (Santa Barbara: Peregrine Smith, 1979), 96–112, 331; and Roger D. Launius and Jessie L. Embry, "Fledgling Wings: Aviation Comes to the Southwest, 1910–1930," *New Mexico Historical Review* 70 (January 1995): 1–27.

6. Andrew Needham, *Power Lines: Phoenix and the Making of the Modern Southwest* (Princeton, NJ: Princeton University Press, 2014), 60–61.

7. Michael F. Logan, *Desert Cities: The Environmental History of Phoenix and Tucson* (Pittsburgh: University of Pittsburgh Press, 2006), 137–157.

8. Jay D. Edwards, "The Origins of Creole Architecture," *Winterthur Portfolio* 29 (Summer–Autumn 1994): 155–189; Reyner Banham, *The Architecture of the Well-Tempered Environment* (Chicago: University of Chicago Press, 1969), 104–121; and William B. Meyer, *Americans and Their Weather* (New York: Oxford University Press, 2000), 28–32, 179–180.

9. Michael Rawson, *Eden on the Charles: The Making of Boston* (Cambridge, MA: Harvard University Press, 2010), 75–128; Matthew Gandy, *Concrete and Clay: Reworking Nature in New York City* (Cambridge, MA: The MIT Press, 2002), 19–51; and David McCullough, *The Johnstown Flood* (New York: Simon and Schuster, 1968), 54–56.

10. Amahia Mallea, *A River in the City of Fountains: An Environmental History of Kansas City and the Missouri River* (Lawrence: University Press of Kansas, 2018).

11. Ari Kelman, "'The Catfish Became the Companion of the Crawfish': Struggling to Reclaim New Orleans' Wetlands," *Human Geography* 32 (2004): 157–180.

12. Timothy M. Collins, Edward K. Muller, and Joel A. Tarr, "Pittsburgh's Three Rivers: From Industrial Infrastructure to Environmental Asset," in *Rivers in History: Perspectives on Waterways in Europe and North America*, ed. Christof Mauch and Thomas Zeller (Pittsburgh: University of Pittsburgh Press, 2008), 41–62.

13. Jared Orsi, *Hazardous Metropolis: Flooding and Urban Ecology in Los Angeles* (Berkeley, CA: University of California Press, 2004), 11–54; and Blake Gumprecht, *The Los Angeles River: Its Life, Death, and Possible Rebirth* (Baltimore: John Hopkins University Press, 1999), 167–191.

14. Gilbert F. White et al., *Changes in Urban Occupance of Flood Plains in the United States* Department of Geography Research Paper No. 57 (Chicago: University of Chicago, 1958).

15. Stanley A. Chagnon, ed., *The Great Flood of 1993: Causes, Impacts, and Responses* (New York: Westview, 1996); and Andrew Hurley, "Floods, Rats, and Toxic Waste: Allocating Environmental Hazards Since World War II," in *Common Fields: An Environmental History of St. Louis*, ed. Andrew Hurley (St. Louis: Missouri Historical Society Press, 1997), 242–262.

16. Blake McKelvey, *Snow in the Cities: A History of America's Urban Response* (Rochester: University of Rochester Press, 1995), xiv–xviii, 57–64.

17. William B. Meyer, *Americans and Their Weather* (New York: Oxford University Press, 2000), 166–167.

18. David E. Nye, *When the Lights Went Out: A History of Blackouts in America* (Cambridge, MA: MIT Press, 2010), 105–136.

19. Meyer, *Americans and Their Weather*, 125–126.

20. Philip J. Hutchinson, "Journalism and the Perfect Heat Wave: Assessing the Reporting of North America's Worst Heat Wave, July–August 1936," *American Journalism* 25 (Winter 2008): 31–54.

21. Anne Whiston Spirn, *The Granite Garden: Urban Nature and Human Design* (New York: Basic Books, 1984), 52–55.

22. Jeff Wiltse, *Contested Waters: A Social History of Swimming Pools in America* (Chapel Hill: University of North Carolina Press, 2007).

23. Colin Fisher, *Urban Green: Nature, Recreation, and the Working Class in Industrial Chicago* (Chapel Hill: University of North Carolina Press, 2015).

24. Edward P. Kohl, *Hot Time in the Old Town: The Great Heat Wave of 1896 and the Making of Theodore Roosevelt* (New York: Basic Books, 2010).

25. Marsha Ackerman, *Cool Comfort: America's Romance with Air-Conditioning* (Washington, DC: Smithsonian Institution Press, 2002).

26. Eric Klinenberg, *Heat Wave: A Social Autopsy of Disaster* (Chicago: University of Chicago Press, 2002).

27. Bernard Mergen, *Weather Matters: An American Cultural History since 1900* (Lawrence: University of Kansas Press, 2008), 12.

28. Mergen, *Weather Matters*, 275–285; and Scott Gabriel Knowles, *The Disaster Experts: Mastering Risk in Modern America* (Philadelphia: University of Pennsylvania Press, 2011), 250–279.

29. Marian Moser Jones, *The American Red Cross: From Clara Barton to the New Deal* (Baltimore: Johns Hopkins University Press, 2013), 37–60.

30. Mergen, *Weather Matters*, 275–285; and Knowles, *The Disaster Experts*, 250–279.

31. Stephan Benzkofer, "1979 Blizzard Was Debacle," *Chicago Tribune*, January 5, 2014, 19.

32. Mergen, *Weather Matters*, 188; and Dennis S. Mileti, *Disasters By Design: A Reassessment of Natural Hazards in the United States* (Washington, DC: Joseph Henry Press, 1999), 65–104.

33. Knowles, *The Disaster Experts*, 256.

34. Ted Steinberg, *Acts of God: The Unnatural History of Natural Disaster in America* (New York: Oxford University Press, 2000), 173–195; Meyer, *Americans and Their Weather*, 203; and Mileti, *Disasters By Design*, 73.

35. Neil Smith, "There's No Such Thing as a Natural Disaster," *Understanding Katrina: Perspectives from the Social Sciences*, Social Science Research Council, 2006.

36. Adam Sobel, *Storm Surge: Hurricane Sandy, Our Changing Climate, and Extreme Weather of the Past and Future* (New York: HarperCollins, 2014).

37. Ted Steinberg, *Gotham Unbound: The Ecological History of Greater New York* (New York: Simon and Schuster, 2014), 326–352; Ashley Dawson, *Extreme Cities: The Peril and Promise of Urban Life in the Age of Climate Change* (New York: Verso, 2017), 1–6; and Devanandham Henry and Jose Emmanuel Ramirez, "On the Impacts of Power Outages during Hurricane Sandy—A Resilience-Based Analysis," *Systems Engineering* 19 (January 2016): 59–75.

38. Mark D. Risser and Michael F. Wehner, "Attributable Human-Induced Changes in the Likelihood and Magnitude of Extreme Precipitation During Hurricane Harvey," *Geophysical Research Letters* 44 (December 2017): 457–464.

39. Adriana X. Sanchez, Jeroen van der Heijden, and Paul Osmond, "The City Politics of an Urban Age: Urban Resilience, Conceptualisations, and Policies," *Palgrave Communications* 4, no. 25 (2018): 1–12; and Judith Rodin, *The Resilience Dividend: Being Strong in a World Where Things Go Wrong* (New York: Public Affairs, 2014).

40. Ashley Dawson, *Extreme Cities*, 157–187.

41. McKelvey, *Snow in the Cities*; and Meyer, *Americans and Their Weather*.

42. Mergen, *Weather Matters*.

43. McCullough, *The Johnstown Flood*.

44. Kohl, *Hot Time*.

45. Douglas Brinkley, *The Great Deluge: Hurricane Katrina, New Orleans, and the Mississippi Gulf Coast* (New York: HarperCollins, 2006); and John McQuaid and Mark Schleifstein, *Path of Destruction: The Devastation of New Orleans and the Coming Age of Superstorms* (New York: Little, Brown and Company, 2006).

46. For example, Cedric Johnson, *The Neoliberal Deluge: Hurricane Katrina, Late Capitalism, and the Remaking of New Orleans* (Minneapolis: The University of Minnesota Press, 2012).

47. Steinberg, *Acts of God.*
48. Knowles, *The Disaster Experts.*
49. Kevin Rozario, *The Culture of Calamity: Disaster and the Making of Modern America* (Chicago: University of Chicago Press, 2007).
50. Mike Davis, *Ecology of Fear: Los Angeles and the Imagination of Disaster* (New York: Metropolitan Books, 1998).
51. Orsi, *Hazardous Metropolis.*
52. Craig Colten, ed., *Transforming New Orleans and its Environs: Centuries of Change* (Pittsburgh: University of Pittsburgh Press, 2001); Ari Kelman, *A River and Its City: The Nature of Landscape in New Orleans* (Berkeley, CA: University of California Press, 2003); Craig E. Colten, *Unnatural Metropolis: Wresting New Orleans from Nature* (Baton Rouge: Louisiana State University Press, 2004); and Craig E. Colten, *Perilous Place, Powerful Storms: Hurricane Protection in Coastal Louisiana* (Jackson: University of Mississippi Press, 2009).
53. Michael F. Logan, *Desert Cities.*
54. Needham, *Power Lines.*
55. Joel A. Tarr, *Search for the Ultimate Sink* (Akron: University of Akron Press, 1996); and Martin V. Melosi, *The Sanitary City: Urban Infrastructure in America from Colonial Times to the Present* (Baltimore: Johns Hopkins University Press, 1999).
56. For example, Gail Cooper, *Air-Conditioning America: Engineers and the Controlled Environment, 1900–1960* (Baltimore: Johns Hopkins University Press, 1998); Ackerman, *Cool Comfort*; and Jonathan Rees, *Refrigeration Nation: A History of Ice, Appliances, and Enterprise in America* (Baltimore: Johns Hopkins University Press, 2013).

Andrew Hurley

FOOD IN THE 19TH-CENTURY AMERICAN CITY

With the growth of American cities in the 19th century, urban foodways became increasingly complex. Among the developments that occurred were the shift from public markets to retail food shops as the main suppliers of urbanites' daily necessities, the emergence of restaurants, the increasing immigrant influence on urban foodways, industrialization of the food system, and the development of certain cities as food-processing centers. Food history is a burgeoning field, and historians are just beginning to explore the intersections between urban growth and foodways, seeing food as a lens for understanding the growth of cities and vice versa.

TECHNOLOGICAL DEVELOPMENTS

A host of technological developments—from canal and railroad building to the manufacturing of ice and the creation of refrigerated railcars—indelibly altered urban American foodways during the 19th century. The most crucial of these developments involved new forms of transportation that eased and cheapened the carriage of foodstuffs from rural to urban areas. The opening of the Erie Canal heralded an era of canal building throughout the country and revolutionized shipping, allowing for the vast expansion of domestic agricultural markets. Before the artificial river opened in 1825, the cost to transport agricultural goods overland trebled their value. The canal reduced these costs by almost 100 percent and contributed to the overnight growth of cities along its route, including Buffalo, Troy, Utica, Syracuse, and Rochester, New York.

The waterway also transformed agriculture in New York State, extending New York City's hinterlands to the Midwest via the Great Lakes. Upstate and western farms turned to production of durable agricultural goods—especially wheat and other grains—while areas closer to the city that had previously produced wheat turned to dairy production. The city's immediate hinterlands—Long Island, New Jersey, Staten Island—abandoned grain and livestock and switched from extensive to intensive agriculture, focusing on the most delicate and perishable fruits and vegetables for the New York market. On the whole, more goods came into the city than ever before and at a far cheaper cost to the consumer.

The Erie Canal's impact reached far beyond New York State. Manufacturers and farmers from the Philadelphia area used the canal route to ship goods to and from western Pennsylvania. Cities as far away as Savannah, Georgia, availed themselves of northeastern and midwestern farm products for far less money than it cost to transport the bulky grain from within the state. Other states, including Ohio, Pennsylvania, and Maryland, also rushed to compete with the lucrative Erie Canal, building their own canal systems in the 1830s and 1840s. A canal completed in 1848 connected Chicago to the Illinois River, paving the way for that city's tremendous expansion in the second half of the 19th century.

The canal era, while crucial in its impact, was nonetheless short-lived. An even quicker, cheaper, and more expansive transportation system emerged in the 1840s. By 1860 the railroad supplanted the canal as the primary system of transport for agricultural goods around the country. Like canals, railroads considerably cheapened the cost of carrying agricultural goods across long distances. The speedy form of transit so shortened the distances between rural areas and cities that locations far afield were able to service one another's market needs. Thus, southern cities like Norfolk, Virginia, became major suppliers of the produce needs of cities up north. Railroads carried peas from New Orleans to Chicago and peaches from the inland Carolinas and Georgia to the southern seaports from whence they were shipped to the cities of the Northeast and beyond. Another transportation improvement—steam-powered ships—brought fruit from Cuba, the Caribbean, and even Central America to the markets of eastern cities.

The new transportation networks also improved the quality of food entering American cities. Cattle that rode to market on railcars were fed a regular diet en route rather than grazing along the way. These cows thus yielded more tender and tastier meat than those that had walked hundreds of miles. Similarly, pigs that were bred for taste rather than for ability to walk to market offered better meat after slaughter. Foods that previously had perished during travel along rudimentary roads now endured long distances without spoiling. Railroads carried milk from rural areas to far-off cities, oysters from New York City to Buffalo, wild game from Iowa to Baltimore, salmon from Maine to Philadelphia, even lobster from the East Coast to Chicago.

Finally, the canals and railroads made food-processing centers out of small towns at their termini. Cincinnati, Chicago, Minneapolis, Louisville, Milwaukee, and Kansas City emerged as important suppliers and processors of agricultural products thanks in part to their location on transportation routes. From there, they grew into important cities.

Technologies related directly to food storage, preservation, and processing also contributed to the transformation of urban food habits. Among the most important were those involved in the commercial production and storage of ice. American commercial ice production can be traced to the 1820s, with two important technological advances—an improved ice cutter that allowed ice companies to harvest ice from lakes and improvements to the icehouse that vastly reduced waste from melting. The horse-drawn ice cutter was a grooved saw, dragged across a lake to create a groove pattern. Large ice blocks were then floated to shore, briefly stored in icehouses, and then broken up and shipped in coolers via horse cart to nearby cities. There, icemen delivered them door to door to subscribers. The ice industry was confined to the North in the 19th century and serviced cities such as Boston, New York, and Philadelphia.

The earliest customers for commercial ice were breweries, restaurants, markets, and grocery stores. By the mid-19th century, however, the iceman—delivering ice to individual homes—was a fixture on northern city streets. Householders posted a note in their windows stipulating how much ice they required, and the iceman would deposit a block in that amount in the box placed in front of the house. Inside the urban home—particularly those belonging to the middle class—iceboxes (which contemporaries called refrigerators) became a fixture. Eventually, the refrigerator lessened the need for daily marketing, affecting the patterns of household life in the 19th-century city. The device also required maintenance, cleaning, and ice delivery, so in some ways it added to the work of homemakers and their servants.

Ice also allowed for refrigeration of railcars. This development was crucial to shifts in the urban food chain. Refrigeration enabled certain cities to emerge as central processing centers of perishable food. Chicago, in particular, grew into the nation's central meat-processing center at this time. The city enjoyed a reputation for meat processing even before the Civil War, but it faced limits. Once the refrigerated railcar was implemented and perfected, largely at the behest of Chicago meat barons Gustavus Swift and Philip Danforth Armour, the city quickly became the nation's preeminent meat-packing center. Meatpacking factories were mechanized as well; slaughtering, processing, and packing took place along assembly lines, operated by immigrant laborers. The packing and transport of meat was horizontally and vertically integrated. Butchered cows and pigs traveled directly from refrigerated factories to refrigerated railcars and from there along rail lines to markets throughout the country.

Other food industries also consolidated in the late 19th century, forming horizontally and vertically integrated conglomerates based in US cities. Along with Chicago's National Packing Company, or beef trust (a cooperative created by meat packing giants Armour, Morris, and Swift) Brooklyn's American Sugar Refining Company (commonly called the Sugar Trust) and New York City's National Biscuit Company (Nabisco) cornered their respective markets. Large food brands such as Borden's Milk (New York), Campbell's Soup (Camden), Heinz (Pittsburgh), Pillsbury (Minneapolis), and Zatarain's (New Orleans) also emerged during this period.

Food-safety issues arose periodically over the course of the 19th century because of the absence of any regulation of large conglomerates or small, food-related businesses. The milk supply was of particular concern, as distilleries in places like New York, Chicago, and Cincinnati paired with dairies within the city limits. The cows at these dairies often fed on the leftover grain that was discarded during the distillery process. These cows produced "swill milk," a thinned-down, alcohol-laden variety that medical professionals and reformers decried throughout the 19th century. These pundits blamed swill milk for sickening and even killing city residents, especially poor children whose families could not afford to import milk from the countryside. The cows themselves were sickened—penned into cramped stables and subject to inhumane conditions. In some cases, when these cows died, their meat found its way to the markets of the cities to be sold as cheap cuts. Despite outcry against these practices, pure milk reform succeeded only at the turn of the 20th century, and even then only at the local level. Likewise, unsanitary practices in the meat industry, exposed in the early 20th century with Upton Sinclair's novel The Jungle, led to federal laws regulating food-based industries.

By the end of the 19th century, more Americans than ever before lived in large towns and cities and relied on industrialized, centralized food-distribution networks rather than providing for their own dietary needs or patronizing local producers. Giant corporations supplied Americans with bread and wheat, which was replacing corn, oats, and barley as the primary grain consumed by Americans. Large, industrializing farms produced livestock, which were slaughtered and packed in centralized stockyards in Chicago and Cincinnati. Local fruits and vegetables shared space in the markets with tropical fruits from far afield, such as lemons and limes from Italy and pineapples from the Caribbean. Meats, vegetables, fruits, condensed milk, and soup were canned and bottled in factories and shipped to grocery stores around the country. Agricultural crossroads emerged into metropolises, central processing and distribution centers for the nation's foodstuffs.

PUBLIC MARKETS AND PRIVATE FOOD SHOPS

With increasingly vast and complex supply systems, the distribution of foodstuffs to and within American cities changed significantly as well. The highly regulated public market system inherited from the colonial period was complemented—and in most cases replaced by—a system of private food shops and markets that served the retail food needs of urban Americans.

The governments of older cities had established public markets during the colonial era. Initially, specific days were designated for nearby farmers, hunters, dairymen, fishermen, and artisans to sell their goods to city dwellers on the town commons. By the 19th century, these public market days were codified into market systems with multiple market houses and functions regulated by the city to protect the public health and pocketbook as well as the prerogatives of fee-paying market vendors. Some market houses gained fame within and beyond their cities—Boston's Faneuil Hall; New York's Washington, Fulton, and Jefferson Markets; and the French Market in New Orleans.

In the antebellum period, market vendors usually were also the producers of the meats, produce, fish, and game they sold. Every day except Sunday, farmers carried their goods via horse cart and in some cases ferryboat; hunters and fishermen carted overland and sailed to shore with their catch; drovers walked cattle, sheep, and pigs from Ohio and Connecticut to Philadelphia, New York, Baltimore, and other eastern cities.

Within the cities, food-related artisans enjoyed strong guilds and important craft traditions. Most prominent among these artisans were bakers and butchers. Members of these trades marched proudly at the front of the line in early national processions, protested loudly when their prerogatives were violated (for example, market regulations protecting butchers' exclusive right to sell meat in New York's antebellum markets), and sat at the center of a raucous, bawdy workingmen's culture as their working conditions deteriorated with the decline of the artisan tradition in the middle decades of the 19th century.

In addition to providing foodstuffs to antebellum urbanites, public markets also served as important civic institutions, as historian Helen Tangires argues.[1] Municipal offices, the night watch, and the police force might be located in the top floors of urban market houses, expanding the function of these buildings beyond food provisioning. The public markets also served as central gathering places for people from varying backgrounds.

A variety of private food shops complemented the antebellum market system. Primary among these shops were grocery stores, which traced their history to the early colonial period. Colonial grocers imported and sold wines, liquors, spices, teas, coffee, and prepared preserved foods such as salted fish, olives, catsups, and pickles from Europe and the West Indies. Grocery stores often were located near the docks or near the public markets, contributing to the establishment of proto-shopping districts even in the colonial seaports. Other types of private food shops included bakeries, pastry shops, and confectioners. In many cases, the latter were established by French immigrants to the United States.

In the days before refrigeration, daily shopping was a necessity, and the season shaped the market offerings. The summer months were most abundant and diverse, with stone fruits, berries, apples, tomatoes, watermelons, lettuces, and other warm-weather produce crowding the tables under the market-house roofs. Food also spoiled quickest in these months, and observers noted the rapidity with which meat spoiled and vegetables wilted. Even milk had to be consumed or turned into butter or cheese within a few hours of exiting the cow. Market meats also were seasonal: veal appeared in the spring, lamb in the summer, and pork in the fall. Beef was available year-round.

By necessity, market provisioners were local, so region influenced what was available. In the case of New York, shoppers could find nearby produce such as root vegetables in the winter; melons, berries, and stone fruits in the summer months; and apples year-round. Gotham's location near the sea meant that its fish markets were well stocked with offerings such as shad, trout, salmon, shrimp, lobster, and oysters, which became emblematic of New York City in the 19th century. New Orleans' French Market had more tropical merchandise, including bananas (very rare in northeastern cities until the 20th century), pineapples, coconuts, oranges, and limes as well as an amazing variety of shellfish, including crab, lobster, shrimps, and "enormous oysters, many of which it would certainly be of necessity to cut up into four mouthfuls, before eating," according to a description that Charles Dickens reprinted in his 1874 *All the Year Round*.[2]

Newer cities set up marketing networks quickly and in an ad hoc fashion. For example, in San Francisco, which rapidly urbanized following the 1849 gold rush, few commercial farmers existed to provision the city. The winter months offered little in terms of fresh fruits and vegetables until farmers in nearby Santa Cruz began to grow peas, beans, squashes, turnips, carrots, quinces, pears, plums, and other fresh produce for San Francisco's residents. Meat, game and fish also began to appear on the city's market tables. By the 1850s, farmers from Southern California and Oregon were provisioning the city by the bay, and imported goods found their way to the markets as well. Wholesale food provisioning became centralized along Sansome Street and Colombo Market, in businesses dominated by Italian immigrants. Along the commercial wharves, fishmongers sold fresh and prepared fish—especially crabs—from boats and shacks along the docks.

While the public markets held sway in the antebellum period, private shops began to take over retail functions by the mid-19th century. Meanwhile, the large public markets shifted primarily to offering wholesale services. This development was certainly true of New York, whose municipal government deregulated the public markets in 1843, allowing private butchers and grocers to sell fresh meats, previously limited to public markets. Here, regulation followed practice; since the 1830s, the city had grown geographically, but the municipal government built no public markets in its newer neighborhoods. By the 1850s, most New Yorkers obtained their daily necessities from private food shops, which were provisioned by the public markets on a wholesale basis.

In Philadelphia, on the other hand, the markets themselves were privatized in the 1800s, twenty private markets opening in the second half of the century. The private markets that began to proliferate in the cities of Pennsylvania, like the private food shops catering to middle- and upper-class New Yorkers, were well appointed and hygienic and incorporated the latest technologies for refrigeration, ventilation, and transportation.

While privatization and the move away from public retail markets happened in the 20th century only in cities such as New Orleans, the trend was set toward private groceries for retail needs. Newer cities, like those in the Midwest, established and built public markets in the 1860s and therefore were more interested in protecting their municipal investments. The public markets of St. Louis, Dubuque, Pittsburgh, and Cincinnati thus remained predominant over private food shops even as their East Coast counterparts waned in importance (in terms of retail function) in eastern cities.

STREET VENDORS

In addition to the public markets and brick-and-mortar food shops, itinerant food vendors were iconic figures in most 19th-century cities.

In the beginning of the century, the trade was dominated by single-item vendors, often poor women selling goods to support their families. By the end of the century, pushcart vendors predominated, selling items from sturdy carts in the immigrant wards of the city.

In the early republican city, huckstering—selling market goods outside of the market houses from baskets and bins, sometimes door to door—served as a form of welfare work. Poor women dominated the huckstering trade, which offered a meager and scant subsistence and often involved scavenging merchandise from city streets, docks, and wharves.

Most street vendors focused on an individual food item—strawberries, radishes, peanuts, or the most famous item in antebellum New York: hot corn. The hot corn vendor, invariably a poor woman, walked the streets of Gotham selling ears of corn on the cob to a familiar cry: "Hot corn, hot corn, here's your lily white hot corn!" These cries were compiled into children's books bearing such names as New York Street Cries in Rhyme and Cries of Philadelphia.[3] Iconic street vendors in Philadelphia included the pepper-pot vendor, who sold a highly seasoned meat soup. Like the hot corn girls of New York, pepper-pot vendors were usually African American women. In New Orleans black women sold pralines through the streets of the Crescent City well into the 20th century.

In Charleston, South Carolina, the street cries "offered an African twist on an Old World Theme," explains culinary historian Jessica B. Harris.[4] Hucksters in the southern city sold produce they raised themselves in gardens behind the slave quarters or cooked on stoves inside—cake, milk, fruit, vegetables, and grains—throughout the streets of the city. Enslaved persons selling goods from their gardens had to be registered with the city by their owners. The vendors were required to purchase and carry a badge asserting their right to sell foodstuffs on the city streets. Other cities with enslaved populations, including Baltimore, New Orleans, and New York City

(until 1827), had similar systems for overseeing food-based economic transactions on the part of enslaved workers.

As the cities' market systems grew more complex, the numbers and kinds of street vendors expanded, incorporating pushcarts where all manner of foodstuffs was sold—produce, milk, oysters, clams, and root beer, among other offerings. By the mid-19th century immigrant men who sold goods from carts increasingly replaced the itinerant female hucksters. They sold old standbys as well as some newer items that reflected the increasing ethnic diversity of American cities—German vendors offered pretzels and sausages; Chinese salesmen peddled rock candy; Italian peddlers hawked fruits and vegetables. Regional variations determined the iconic street foods of different cities. For example, by the 1880s, San Francisco's most famous street food was the tamale. The San Francisco Chronicle explained in 1884 that "the tamale is eaten in a small way by persons of all classes in the city, though," the paper admitted, "in many instances the first eating has been purely experimental."[5] Meanwhile in the second half of the 19th century, the term huckster came to denote not a desperate woman supporting her family but rather a duplicitous middleman seeking to undercut market prices while avoiding licensing and leasing fees.

RESTAURANTS AND PUBLIC DINING

The restaurant was a purely urban phenomenon in the 19th century. Small towns and rural areas contained taverns and hotels that served travelers and might entertain locals on an occasional basis. But the freestanding restaurant was found, at this point, only in cities. Restaurants emerged to suit the needs particular to expanding cities—places to serve hot lunches to male workers whose offices, workshops, and factories were newly at a distance from their homes; venues for travelers and tourists who hoped to eat meals away from their hotels; refectories for boardinghouse dwellers; and social centers for newly arrived immigrants. A new phenomenon on the urban scene in 1800, restaurants had become a central part of the fabric of cities by the end of the 19th century. A vast range of restaurants existed, catering to urbanites of various economic levels and social backgrounds.

As the 19th century opened, American cities offered few public dining options. Among them were taverns and hotels, where meals were included in the price of lodgings, and food businesses that had tables where patrons could eat food purchased on premises (for example, confectionery shops). The geographic growth of the cities in the antebellum period, however, necessitated new institutions to cater to commuters and travelers who either worked too far from home to return there for meals or who sought dining options outside of their hotels and taverns.

New York City led the way in new forms of public dining. While Gotham did not pioneer the restaurant (that distinction goes to Paris), New York did create a template that other cities soon replicated. Furthermore, many successful restaurateurs in cities throughout the country trained in the kitchens of New York City restaurants. The first freestanding restaurants in New York followed two tracks—high-end restaurants that emerged from the city's luxury hotels and low-end, short-order houses that catered to men commuting down to the city's financial district from newer residential neighborhoods on the city's outskirts. Delmonico's was by far the most famous elite restaurant. Operated by the Swiss-born Delmonico brothers, the restaurant opened in 1827 as a simple confectionery shop on William Street in Lower Manhattan. In 1830, the brothers expanded their operation into a full-service restaurant. Delmonico's distinguished itself by its food and service and truly introduced fine dining to the United States. Delmonico's employed a French chef and pioneered such dishes as Lobster Newburg and Baked Alaska.

Over the course of the 19th century, Delmonico's developed into a minichain, opening several outposts in Manhattan, each more opulent than the previous one. Memoirist Abram Dayton raved about one Delmonico branch's "frescoed ceilings, mirrored halls, and sumptuous appointments," proclaiming: "One cannot fail to be impressed by the absence of bustle and confusion, no boisterous commands are heard, and the waiters glide about as noiselessly as ghosts. An air of luxury surrounds you as the attentive *garcon* stands motionless before you, and respectfully awaits your wishes."[6] Delmonico's served as a model for restaurants in other cities and several (including those in Louisville, New Orleans, and even London) borrowed its imprimatur, either by declaring themselves to be the Delmonico's of that city or by adopting the Delmonico's name itself.

Far more common than the luxury fine-dining restaurant was the downtown short-order restaurant. Also known as "sixpenny houses" because individual dishes cost six pence, these restaurants, such as Sweeney's, Dunlop's, and Sweet's, opened in the 1820s and catered to men commuting down to the city's financial district from newer residential neighborhoods on the city's peripheries. So connected were these early restaurants to the development of the commuter city that the *New-York Daily Times*—later the *New York Times*—subtitled a feature article in the 1850s about the city's restaurants, "The Eating Houses—How New Yorkers Sleep Up Town and Eat Down Town."[7] The atmosphere of the sixpenny houses was a far cry from the hushed, refined tones of Delmonico's. At Sweeney's and establishments of its ilk, the cacophony of clattering dishes and waiters bawling out orders offered the soundscape for the rush of customers whose entire meal from entry to departure lasted an average of twenty minutes. The food was notoriously bad—tough meat, lukewarm vegetables, and weak coffee. Journalist George Foster wryly summed up the gastronomical environment: "It is really wonderful how men of refined tastes and pampered habits ... find it in their hearts—or stomachs either—to gorge such disgusting masses of stringy meat and tepid vegetables, and to go about their business again under the fond delusion that they have dined."[8]

Indeed, on the whole, Americans fast developed a reputation for poor eating habits. English visitor Frances Trollope remarked with disgust upon dining habits she witnessed on a steamboat, where she observed "the total want of all the usual courtesies of the table." She decried "the voracious rapidity with which the viands were seized and devoured ... the loathsome spitting ... the frightful manner of feeding with their knives, till the whole blade seemed to enter into the mouth; and the still more frightful manner of cleaning the teeth afterwards with a pocket knife."[9] New Yorkers' eating habits came up for special derision, so busy were Gothamites making money that they had no time to focus on culinary matters.

Beginning in the 1830s, restaurants emerged in New York and other cities that specifically sought the ladies' trade. These establishments provided a "safe" space where women who were concerned about their reputations could dine in public, usually among other ladies. Ladies' eateries distinguished themselves by their interiors, which were richly furnished and decorated and replicated the private, middle-class parlor. The emergence of the ladies' restaurants reflected the somewhat salacious reputation that restaurants earned in the 19th century, related as they were to other commercial entertainments, including theater and prostitution.

The only 19th-century city that challenged New York in terms of the extent and sophistication of its restaurant culture was New Orleans. Like Gotham, the Crescent City was home to some of the nation's most famous and well-regarded early restaurants, some still extant—including the legendary Antoine's and Commander's Palace. In 1840, the French immigrant Antoine Alciatore opened Antoine's—the first known restaurant in New Orleans. The institution has served French Creole food ever since and is still run by descendants of Alciatore. In the 1850s, Antoine's was joined by butcher shop turned Creole restaurant Begue's and by

Tujague's and Bruning's. Tujague's later moved to the Begue's site when the latter closed in 1914. The seafood restaurant Bruning's operated continuously from 1859 until damage from Hurricane Katrina forced it to close down permanently. The legendary Café du Monde also traces its history to the 19th century, when it opened as a coffeehouse in the French Market in 1862.

As the nation's cities grew, each developed its own distinct restaurant culture, offering up regional variations. Chinese proprietors dominated San Francisco's restaurants. Many of these restaurants served a Euro-focused menu, but a few high-end Chinese restaurants in the city catered exclusively to white patrons. In 1890s San Antonio, Texas, diners could order tacos and enchiladas alongside rice and beans, a nod both to the culinary traditions of Native Americans and Spanish settlers as well as to the tastes of more recent Anglo arrivals. This Tex-Mex food was featured alongside other "ethnic" cuisines at the 1893 Columbian Exhibition in Chicago. Mexican influence on local cuisine was evident in San Francisco as well, where restaurants served tamales and "tortillas and frijoles." Not surprisingly, Washington, DC had a very cosmopolitan dining scene, featuring German, Italian, Chinese, and Tex-Mex dishes.

By the second half of the 19th century, respectable restaurants that catered to middle-class urbanites, including families, opened. Known as tables d'hote, these establishments offered a prix-fixe menu, serving five- to seven-course meals for a set price. In New York, tables d'hote were dominated by French, Italian, and Hungarian proprietors serving an Americanized version of these European cuisines; in San Francisco, most tables d'hote were French. Buffalo, Detroit, and Milwaukee had several German tables d'hote.

Restaurants became part and parcel of city life throughout the 19th century. Restaurant hierarchies emerged in every city with a significant restaurant sector—high-end restaurants catering to the elite, middle-class tables d'hotes, and working-class coffee and cake shops. Street vendors selling prepared foods complemented these public dining offerings. By the end of the 19th century, all but the poorest urban dwellers could—and did—participate in some form of public dining in the nation's cities.

THE DAILY DIET OF 19TH-CENTURY URBANITES

The changes in the urban food supply during the 19th century transformed the daily diet of city dwellers as well. By the end of the 19th century, urban Americans had access to a more diverse and cheaper diet than had their parents and grandparents. At the same time, however, class differences significantly shaped access to foodstuffs and determined the quality of available food. As cities grew larger and more spatially stratified along class lines, those who lived in more expensive neighborhoods enjoyed access to food shops of higher quality with more expensive food. The reverse was true for the poor. As the standard of living rose for wealthy and middle-class Americans over the course of the 19th century, it declined for the working classes and low-income groups. Foodways were a central part of this standard of living.

Before refrigeration and reliable transportation, perishable foods were scant in the diet of most urbanites. Even the wealthiest were accustomed to eating spoiled or rancid food or forgoing fresh produce in the colder months. In the winter, only the wealthy had the space and disposable cash to be able to lay in provisions. A paradox characterized the urban food supply—those urbanites with money had a more diverse diet than their rural counterparts, whereas those without money had a less diverse diet than the rural poor because they had no space to grow their own food.

Thanks to abundant grazing land, meat was available even to poorer urban Americans, relative to their European counterparts. Indeed, access to meat on a regular basis was an important symbol of economic mobility for immigrant laborers. While pork was the most widely eaten meat in the United States in the

19th century and also the most common one found on rural tables, in the cities beef was the most popular fresh meat. Urban Americans also ate considerable chicken and pork (often smoked or salted), and smaller amounts of veal, sheep, and lamb.

Coastal city residents availed themselves of local fisheries, and locals ate fish and shellfish as the market allowed. Common offerings included shad, salmon, sturgeon, halibut, mackerel, cod, trout, lobster, clams, and oysters. New Orleanians partook of local delicacies such as shrimp and crawfish. Freshwater fish such as trout, pike, perch, bass, and catfish were most commonly found on the tables of denizens of urban midwesterners.

The 19th century was the era of the oyster. The bivalves were abundant in cities near the coast, which housed oyster cellars, oyster stands, and oyster markets. New York City was a particularly important oystering center, the national wholesale distributor for pickled and preserved oysters sent to ports domestic and foreign. A brisk trade existed within the city for fresh oysters as well. According to an 1890 estimate, New Yorkers consumed "over a million dozens of oysters every day."[10] While New York was the largest market and consumer of oysters, each city had an oyster culture, replete with oyster cellars offering "all you can eat" oysters shucked on the half shell as well as oysters prepared in a variety of ways— scalloped, baked, fricasseed, baked in pies, simmered in soups, and folded into stuffings.

As for fresh vegetables, they were not commonly consumed in the 1800s, though the diet expanded to incorporate them by the second half of the century. Tomatoes, peas, lettuces, celery, squashes, and other fresh vegetables became increasingly available in the markets and grew in popularity, along with more exotic varieties like artichokes, broccoli, and asparagus. Fruits also were more commonly eaten in stewed and dessert forms rather than fresh.

Throughout the 19th century, urban Americans had access to an abundant and diverse diet through the public markets and private retail food shops dotting their cities. Access, however, was increasingly shaped by geography and social class. As more middlemen stepped in and as the patrician market regulations of the early republic fell away, the cost of food rose. Moreover, the spatial stratification of cities according to class coincided with the proliferation of neighborhood retail food stores. Not surprisingly, the wealthiest neighborhoods were serviced by the highest-quality and most expensive food shops; poorer neighborhoods developed into what we might now call food deserts. Wealthy and middle-class urbanites enjoyed fresh meats, fish, cheeses, and a bounty of fruits and vegetables throughout the year. Meanwhile, laborers subsisted on bread, potatoes, and molasses for sweetener (in place of sugar, which was expensive). Blood pudding (pig's or cow's blood mixed with ground pork and seasoning and stuffed into a casing), paired with butter crackers, was a common meal.

FOOD SERVICE

As urban food systems became increasingly complex, a host of food-service employment categories opened up. For much of the 19th century, these job sectors were dominated by African Americans and Irish immigrants. In the antebellum city, food preparation and service was one of the few occupational areas open to African Americans. The niching of African Americans in food service was rooted in slavery, where African Americans served as cooks, waiters, and gardeners both on large plantations and in urban townhouses. In both slave and free cities, African Americans dominated domestic service and waitering both in private homes and public spaces such as clubs, hotels, and restaurants, although Irish immigrant laborers subsumed and displaced them as they arrived in large numbers after 1830.

Catering and restaurant work offered a rare route to entrepreneurship and mobility to African Americans, for whom so many occupational areas were closed owing to racism. Black entrepreneurs like New York oysterman Thomas Downing and his son George Downing,

who served as manager of the congressional dining room in Washington, DC; Philadelphia caterer Robert Bogle; and San Francisco boardinghouse keeper Mary Ellen Pleasant were but three examples of black individuals who parlayed their positions in food service into wealth and some measure of influence within the racist strictures of their time.

FOOD IN THE IMMIGRANT CITY

As urban populations became predominantly foreign-born, immigrants made an indelible impact on the foodways of US cities. Immigrants helped to change the tenor of daily urban life in many ways, including their contributions to an increasingly cosmopolitan food landscape. Restaurants, groceries, and other food-based ventures provided an entrepreneurial wedge for immigrants and contributed to their economic mobility as well as easing their settlement. These businesses also served as mitigating institutions for their patrons, offering reminders of home as well as a variety of services connecting them to each other and their countries of origin.

Food-related businesses provided entrepreneurial opportunities to many 19th-century immigrants. Ethnic groceries, operated by German, Chinese, Italian, and Mexican migrants and immigrants were important social institutions in immigrant neighborhoods throughout the United States. These shops sold foods imported from the "old country," such as sharks' fins from China and olive oil and pasta from Italy, and became informal gathering spaces for locals. Ethnic groceries also offered news from home and served as informal post offices, banks, and job offices.

Upon their respective arrivals, 19th-century immigrants dominated certain niches in terms of food businesses. Irish newcomers played an important role in shaping antebellum foodways primarily as servants in private homes and waiters in public hotels and restaurants. German immigrants controlled the baking and grocery trades, which they later ceded to the

Italians who arrived in large numbers in the 1870s and 1880s. Most notably, Germans also invented the American beer industry, opening hundreds of breweries in cities where they settled, some of which—Pabst, Schlitz, Anheuser-Busch, Piel's—grew into national brands. Meanwhile, in German delicatessens customers could purchase prepared dishes like meat pies and potato salad as well as smoked, pickled, and cured meats and vegetables. These establishments were concentrated in primarily German neighborhoods in cities with large German populations like New York, Milwaukee, and Chicago. In New York, the center of American Jewish immigration, kosher delicatessens appeared at the end of the 19th century.

Chinese immigrants dominated food service in San Francisco, running many of the city's restaurants (which offered steak and potatoes over Chinese cuisine). Chinese San Franciscans also opened groceries from which they sold goods imported from China, such as sharks' fins, cuttlefish, Chinese pickles, dried ducks, soybeans, bean sprouts, ginger, and various teas. Chinese grocers also sold prepared dishes—mainly to Chinatown locals—such as stir-fried vegetables and meats or fish. Like other borderlands, San Francisco enjoyed the influence of the Mexican, or "Californio," population that had long lived in the area, operating ranches on the land. Enchiladas, tortillas, pozole, and rice and beans were found in *fondas* around the city in the 1850s, including Pascual Estrada's Fonda Mejicana on Jackson Street and the Restaurante Mejicano on Dupont Street.

Other examples of immigrant-run restaurants included the cafés of Little Italy, the tortillerias of Little Mexico, and the tea parlors of Chinatown. At first, these "ethnic restaurants" did not attract a native-born clientele. Only the most adventurous native-born eaters sought meals in the exotic restaurants of the immigrant wards in the 19th century, and even these cosmopolitan diners were likely to view their escapades into the restaurants of Chinatown or Little Italy as a foray into the exotic. The chop suey craze was a product of the 20th century city, not the 19th century. As historian Andrew Haley explains, "'Cosmopolitan' described the diner, not the restaurateur, and embracing the label did not eliminate intolerance."[11] But by the end of the 19th century, some immigrant entrepreneurs branched out into the nonimmigrant wards of the nation's cities, serving a hybrid cuisine that included some elements of their home country, adapted to the American palate.

The United States offered an abundant food landscape to late-19th-century immigrants in comparison with that available in their homelands. Italian immigrants serve as a prime example. This group, who immigrated primarily to cities like New York, Boston, and Philadelphia and in lesser numbers to Pittsburgh, Chicago, and San Francisco created an indelible cuisine in the United States that blended traditions of various regions in Italy. Foods that were previously accessible only to wealthy landowners in Italy, like pasta and olive oil, became staples of the Italian American pantry. Meanwhile, meat—a treat that Italian peasants might enjoy on an annual basis—was eaten weekly or even daily in the United States. Abundant family meals, once relegated to feast days, became weekly Sunday dinners in the homes of urban Italians and Italian Americans.

Italian American food is just one example of a fusion cuisine created in American cities out of various cultural traditions from within Italy. In other cases, fusions emerged from different ethnic communities living close to each other in urban neighborhoods, such as New York's Lower East Side, where Eastern European Jewish immigrants embraced the Chinese food served in nearby Chinatown as "safe treyf." While it may contain pork, shellfish, and other non-kosher ingredients, these foods were chopped so finely as to be indistinguishable and thus appealed particularly to Jews who were willing to thwart dietary rules out of willful ignorance.[12]

In terms of foodstuffs, urban immigrants introduced new kinds of foods to the American diet, some of which "crossed the boundaries of taste," into the mainstream diet as historian Donna Gabbaccia has phrased it.[13] German hamburger, sausages, pickles, and the famous lager beer; Italian sandwiches and spaghetti; Jewish egg creams; and Tex-Mex nachos and chili made their way into the diets of native-born Americans.

DISCUSSION OF THE LITERATURE

The subfield of food history is relatively new. Anthropologists, sociologists, folklorists, and culinary historians have long examined the topics of food and rituals of eating, but historians only recently began to take food seriously as a subject of study.[14] With the emphasis on social and cultural history since the 1960s, historians have examined food and foodways as a lens onto social, cultural, economic, and political processes. Recent monographs examine food and urban development, urban public markets and food distribution, and individual food items such as meat.[15] This literature does not focus exclusively on 19th-century urban foodways but also examines urban infrastructure, economics, social and cultural life, food distribution networks, food retailing, and the role of restaurants in the entertainment life of cities.[16]

Studies of 19th-century African American urban life include information on black entrepreneurship, which necessarily touches on food service.[17] The literature on urban immigration also often discusses food and food-related businesses in the life of immigrant communities. Again, while many of these projects focus on the 20th-century city, some important works address 19th-century urban development.[18]

PRIMARY SOURCES

Nineteenth-century newspapers and periodicals such as *Harper's Weekly* offer invaluable information about urban foodways, including market reports, grocers' and housewares'

advertisements, and descriptions of restaurants. Magazines geared toward middle-class women included recipes and domestic advice that provide a sense of the range of possibilities in terms of urban foodways in the 19th century. Many of these newspapers and periodicals are digitized, including *Harper's Weekly* and the *New York Times*, which dates back to 1851. The American Antiquarian Society's *Early American Newspaper Series, American Periodical Series,* and *Early American Imprints* series (all digital collections available through subscription at research libraries) as well as Cornell's *Making of America* digital collection of American periodicals are searchable databases with a trove of primary source materials that relate to 19th-century urban foodways.

Published travel literature, exposés of urban life (such as the "sunshine and shadows" genre) and—in the second half of the 19th century—travel guides to the city include discussions of restaurants, food markets, and other food-related businesses.

Archives at the New York Public Library (NYPL) and the New-York Historical Society (NYHS) include collections of menus from restaurants, hotels, and banquets. The NYHS holds the Bella C. Landauer Collection, a large collection of business papers and ephemera, including items referencing many food-related businesses and industries both local and national. Many of the NYPL's menus are digitized and available at "What's on the Menu? [menus.nypl.org]." Published diaries and letters also shed light on urban foodways in the 19th century, though in some cases a researcher needs to go to the source, especially for older edited collections whose editors viewed food references as trivial.

Important cookbooks collections—both published and manuscript—exist at Radcliffe's Schlesinger Library, the American Antiquarian Society, and the Fales Collection at New York University. Michigan State University has an excellent digital cookbook collection entitled "Feeding America."

FURTHER READING

Anderson, Heather Arndt. *Portland: A Food Biography.* Lanham, MD: Rowman and Littlefield, 2014.

Baics, Gergely. "Is Access to Food a Public Good? Meat Provisioning in Early New York City, 1790–1820." *Journal of Urban History* 39, no. 4 (2013): 643–668.

Block, Daniel R. *Chicago: A Food Biography.* Lanham, MD: Rowman and Littlefield, 2015.

Carroll, Abigail. *Three Squares: The Invention of the American Meal.* New York: Basic Books, 2013.

Diner, Hasia. *Hungering for America: Italian, Irish, and Jewish Foodways in the Age of Migration.* Cambridge, MA: Harvard University Press, 2003.

Gabaccia, Donna. *We Are What We Eat: Ethnic Food and the Making of Americans.* Cambridge, MA: Harvard University Press, 1998.

Haley, Andrew. *Turning the Tables: Restaurants and the Rise of the American Middle Class, 1880–1920.* Chapel Hill: University of North Carolina Press, 2011.

Harris, Jessica B. *High on the Hog: A Culinary Journey from Africa to America.* New York: Bloomsbury, 2012.

Hauck-Lawson, Annie, and Jonathan Deutsch, eds. *Gastropolis: Food and New York City.* New York: Columbia University Press, 2010.

Horowitz, Roger. *Putting Meat on the American Table: Taste, Technology, Transformation.* Baltimore: Johns Hopkins University Press, 2005.

Horowitz, Roger, Jeffrey Pilcher, and Sidney Watts. "Meat for the Multitudes: Market Culture in Paris, New York City, and Mexico City over the Long Nineteenth Century." *American Historical Review* 109, no. 4 (2004): 1055–1083.

Kurlansky, Mark. *The Big Oyster: History on the Half Shell.* New York: Ballantine Books, 2006.

Lobel, Cindy R. *Urban Appetites: Food and Culture in Nineteenth-Century New York.* Chicago: University of Chicago Press, 2014.

Peters, Erica J. *San Francisco: A Food Biography.* Lanham, MD: Rowman and Littlefield, 2013.

Rees, Jonathan. *Refrigeration Nation: A History of Ice, Appliances, and Enterprise in America.* Baltimore: Johns Hopkins University Press, 2013.

Smith, Andrew F. *New York: A Food Biography.* Lanham, MD: Rowman and Littlefield, 2013.

Tangires, Helen. *Public Markets and Civic Culture in Nineteenth-Century America.* Baltimore: Johns Hopkins University Press, 2003.

Wallach, Jennifer. *How America Eats: A Social History of U.S. Food and Culture.* Lanham, MD: Rowman and Littlefield, 2015.

Ziegelman, Jane. *97 Orchard: An Edible History of Five Immigrant Families in One Tenement.* New York: Harper, 2011.

NOTES

1. Helen Tangires, *Public Markets and Civic Culture in Nineteenth-Century America* (Baltimore: Johns Hopkins University Press, 2003).

2. "The French Market at New Orleans," *All the Year Round: A Weekly Journal Conducted by Charles Dickens* 13 (October 17, 1874–March 27, 1875): 261.

3. Mahlon Day, *New York Street Cries in Rhyme* (1825; repr., New York: Dover Publications, 1977); and John Bouvier, *Cries of Philadelphia* (Johnson and Warnerin, 1810).

4. Jessica B. Harris, *High on the Hog: A Culinary Journey from Africa to America* (New York: Bloomsbury, 2012), 127.

5. Erica J. Peters, *San Francisco: A Food Biography* (Lanham, MD: Rowman and Littlefield, 2013), 32.

6. Abram Dayton, *Last Days of Knickerbocker Life in New York* (New York and London: G. P. Putnam's, 1897), 145.

7. "The Eating Houses—How New Yorkers Sleep Up Town and Eat Down Town," *New-York Daily Times*, November 6, 1852.

8. George Foster, *New York in Slices, by an Experienced Carver* (New York: Garrett, 1852), 67.

9. Frances Trollope, *Domestic Manners of the Americans*, ed. Donald Smalley (New York: Vintage, 1949), 18–19.

10. "How the City Is Fed," *Christian Union* 42, no. 14 (October 2, 1890): 428.

11. Andrew Haley, *Turning the Tables: Restaurants and the Rise of the American Middle Class, 1880–1920* (Chapel Hill: University of North Carolina Press, 2011), 116.

12. Jennifer Wallach, *How America Eats: A Social History of U.S. Food and Culture* (Lanham, MD: Rowman and Littlefield, 2015), 83.

13. Donna R. Gabaccia, *We Are What We Eat: Ethnic Food and the Making of Americans.* (Cambridge, MA: Harvard University Press, 1998), 93–121.

14. Two notable exceptions to the dearth of academic food histories until recent years are

Arthur M. Schlesinger, "A Dietary Interpretation of American History," *Massachusetts Historical Society Proceedings* 68 (1944–1947): 199–227; and Richard Osborn Cummings, *The American and His Food: A History of Food Habits in the United States* (1941; rprt., New York: Arno Press, 1970), which includes a chapter on urban food-ways in the 19th century. Popular food histories, written by journalists and culinary historians, are useful to academic historians seeking to gain a sense of the texture of foodways in the American city. These include Waverley Lewis Root and Richard de Rochemont, *Eating in America: A History* (New York: William Morrow, 1976); Richard Hooker, *Food and Drink in America: A History* (Indianapolis: Bobbs-Merrill, 1981); P. G. Kittler and K. Sucher, *Food and Culture in America* (New York: Van Nostrand Reinhold, 1989); Michael and Ariane Batterberry, *On the Town in New York from 1776 to the Present* (New York: Charles Scribner's, 1973), revised and republished in 1999 as *On the Town in New York: The Landmark History of Eating, Drinking, and Entertainments from the American Revolution to the Food Revolution*; John Mariani, *America Eats Out: An Illustrated History of Restaurants, Taverns, Coffee Shops, Speakeasies, and Other Establishments That Have Fed Us for 350 Years* (New York: William Morrow, 1991); William Grimes, *Appetite City: A Culinary History of New York* (New York: North Point Press, 2010); and Mark Kurlansky, *The Big Oyster: History on the Half Shell* (New York: Ballantine Books, 2006). Rowman and Littlefield is publishing a series called "Big City Food Biographies," aimed at a popular audience. These works offer narrative histories of foodways in American cities. Recent titles include Elizabeth M. Williams, *New Orleans: A Food Biography* (Lanham, MD: Rowman and Littlefield, 2012); Andrew F. Smith, *New York: A Food Biography* (Lanham, MD: Rowman and Littlefield, 2013); Erica J. Peters, *San Francisco: A Food Biography* (Lanham, MD: Rowman and Littlefield, 2013); Heather Arndt Anderson, *Portland: A Food Biography* (Lanham, MD: Rowman and Littlefield, 2014); and Daniel R. Block, *Chicago: A Food Biography* (Lanham, MD: Rowman and Littlefield, 2015). Scholars outside of history, including anthropologists, geographers, sociologists and folklorists, have contributed to our understanding of foodways in general, and in some cases these works touch on the 19th-century city. Geographer Richard Pillsbury, for example, offered a relatively early history of restaurants, *From Boarding House to Bistro: The American Restaurant Then and Now* (Boston: Unwin Hyman, 1990). A valuable collection that focuses on New York City is Annie Hauck-Lawson and Jonathan Deutsch, eds., *Gastropolis: Food and New York City* (New York: Columbia University Press, 2010).

15. Among the published works that focus specifically on 19th-century urban food history are Cindy R. Lobel, *Urban Appetites: Food and Culture in Nineteenth-Century New York* (Chicago: University of Chicago Press, 2014); Helen Tangires, *Public Markets and Civic Culture in Nineteenth-Century America* (Baltimore: Johns Hopkins University Press, 2003); Marc Linder and Lawrence S. Zacharias, *Of Cabbages and Kings County: Agriculture and the Formation of Modern Brooklyn* (Iowa City: University of Iowa Press, 1999); and Erica J. Peters, "A Path to Acceptance: Promoting Chinese Restaurants in San Francisco, 1849–1919," *Southern California Quarterly* 97.1 (2015): 5–28. Recent surveys of US food history that include some sections and chapters on 19th-century urban foodways include Elaine McIntosh, *American Food Habits in Historical Perspective* (Westport, CT: Praeger, 1995); Susan Williams, *Food in the United States, 1830–1890* (Santa Barbara, CA: Greenwood, 2006); Megan J. Elias, *Food in the United States, 1890–1945* (Santa Barbara, CA: Greenwood, 2009); and Jennifer Jensen Wallach, *How America Eats: A Social History of U.S. Food and Culture* (Lanham, MD: Rowman and Littlefield, 2012). Meanwhile, an important history of 19th-century foodways that includes discussions of urban patterns is Andrew Haley, *Turning the Tables: Restaurants and the Rise of the American Middle Class, 1880–1920* (Chapel Hill: University of North Carolina Press, 2011). For histories of meat provisioning, see Roger Horowitz, *Putting Meat on the American Table: Taste, Technology, Transformation* (Baltimore: Johns Hopkins University Press, 2005); Roger Horowitz, Jeffrey Pilcher, and Sidney Watts, "Meat for the Multitudes: Market Culture in Paris, New York City, and Mexico City over the Long Nineteenth Century," *American Historical Review* 109, no. 4 (2004): 1055–1083; Paula Young Lee, ed., *Meat, Modernity and the Rise of the Slaughterhouse* (Durham: University of New

Hampshire Press, 2008); and Gergely Baics, "Is Access to Food a Public Good? Meat Provisioning in Early New York City, 1790–1820," *Journal of Urban History* 39, no. 4 (2013): 643–668.

16. Monographs on urban nightlife and consumer culture include some information on restaurants and other venues of public dining. See, for example, Timothy Gilfoyle, *City of Eros: New York City, Prostitution and the Commercialization of Sex, 1790–1920* (New York: W. W. Norton, 1992); Patricia Cline Cohen, *The Murder of Helen Jewett: The Life and Death of a Prostitute in Nineteenth-Century New York* (New York: Vintage, 1998); Amy Gilman Srebnick, *The Mysterious Death of Mary Rogers: Sex and Culture in Nineteenth-Century New York* (New York: Oxford University Press, 1997); Tyler Anbinder, *Five Points: The 19th-Century Neighborhood That Invented Tap Dance, Stole Elections, and Became the World's Most Notorious Slum* (New York: Free Press, 2001); David Nasaw, *Going Out: The Rise and Fall of Public Amusements* (New York: Basic Books, 1993); Stephen Nissenbaum, *The Battle for Christmas: A Cultural History of America's Most Cherished Holiday.* (New York: Vintage, 1996); and Kathy Peiss, *Cheap Amusements: Working Women and Leisure in Turn-of-the-Century New York* (Philadelphia: Temple University Press, 1986). Studies of urban development and infrastructure include important information on food distribution networks in the 19th-century city. Two of the most notable are Edward Spann, *The New Metropolis: New York City, 1840–1857* (New York: Columbia University Press, 1981); and William Cronon, *Nature's Metropolis: Chicago and the Great West* (New York: W. W. Norton, 1991). Likewise, studies of urban public culture and consumer culture address issues such as the role of food-related consumer goods in middle-class formation and the development of "safe" spaces for middle-class women in public. See, for example, Stuart Blumin, *The Emergence of the Middle Class: Social Experience in the American City, 1760–1900* (Cambridge, U.K., and New York: Cambridge University Press, 1989); Mary Ryan, *Women in Public: Between Banners and Ballots, 1825–1880* (Baltimore: Johns Hopkins University Press, 1990); and Mona Domosh, "Those 'Gorgeous Incongruities': Polite Politics and Public Space on the Streets of 19th-Century New York," *Annals of the Association of American Geographers* 88, no. 2

(1998): 209–226. Histories of the urban working class include discussions of food-related artisans and the role of food in working-class entertainments. See, for example, Howard Rock, *Artisans of the New Republic: The Tradesmen of New York City in the Age of Jefferson* (New York: New York University Press, 1979); Richard B. Stott, *Workers in the Metropolis: Class, Ethnicity, and Youth in Antebellum New York* (Ithaca, NY, and London: Cornell University Press, 1990); Sean Wilentz, *Chants Democratic: New York City and the Rise of the American Working Class, 1788–1850* (New York: Oxford University Press, 1984); and Christine Stansell, *City of Women: Sex and Class in New York, 1789–1860* (New York: Alfred A. Knopf, 1986). On domestic servants and food, see Faye E. Dudden, *Serving Women: Household Service in Nineteenth-Century America* (Middletown, CT: Wesleyan University Press, 1983). On waiters' strikes, see Margaret Garb, "The Great Chicago Waiters' Strike: Producing Urban Space, Organizing Labor, Challenging Racial Divides in 1890s Chicago," *Journal of Urban History* 40.6 (2014): 1079–1098. On hotels and boardinghouses, including discussion of food habits in these spaces, see Andrew Sandoval-Strausz, *Hotel: An American History* (New Haven, CT: Yale University Press, 2008); and Wendy Gamber, *The Boardinghouse in Nineteenth-Century America* (Baltimore: Johns Hopkins University Press, 2007). On urban tourism, see Catherine Cocks, *Doing the Town: The Rise of Urban Tourism in the United States, 1850–1915* (Berkeley: University of California Press, 2003).

17. See, for example, Leonard P. Curry, *The Free Black in Urban America 1800–1850* (Chicago and London: University of Chicago Press, 1981); Leslie Harris, *In the Shadow of Slavery: African Americans in New York City, 1626–1863* (Chicago: University of Chicago Press, 2003); John H. Hewitt, "Mr. Downing and His Oyster House: The Life and Good Works of an African-American Entrepreneur," *New York History* 74 (1993): 229–252; and Graham Hodges, *Root & Branch: African Americans in New York & East Jersey, 1613–1863* (Chapel Hill: University of North Carolina Press, 1999). See also Psyche Forson-Williams, *Building Houses out of Chicken Legs: Black Women, Food and Power* (Chapel Hill: University of North Carolina Press, 2006).

18. On immigrant foodways, see Donna Gabbaccia, *We Are What We Eat: Food and the Making of Americans* (Cambridge, MA: Harvard University Press, 1998); and Hasia Diner, *Hungering for America: Italian, Irish, and Jewish Foodways in the Age of Migration* (Cambridge, MA: Harvard University Press, 2003). See also Robert Ernst, *Immigrant Life in New York City, 1825–1863* (1949; rprt., Port Washington, NY: Ira J. Friedman 1965); Stanley Nadel, *Little Germany: Ethnicity, Religion, and Class in New York City, 1845–1860* (Urbana: University of Illinois Press, 1990); Jane Ziegelman, *97 Orchard: An Edible History of Five Immigrant Families in One Tenement* (New York: Harper, 2011); and Andrew Heinze, *Adapting to Abundance: Jewish Immigrants, Mass Consumption, and the Search for American Identity* (New York: Columbia University Press, 1990).

Cindy Lobel

FOOD IN THE 20TH-CENTURY AMERICAN CITY

TECHNOLOGICAL CHANGES AND MODERN FOOD

Rapid industrial growth in the early decades of the 20th century changed the nature of food production, consumption, and transportation to American cities. Urban populations skyrocketed thanks to the dual forces of industrialization and immigration, as the United States became a predominantly urban nation by 1920.[1] The movement of individuals from rural areas into cities, waves of migrants from abroad, and the Great Migration of African Americans from the South into the urban North all ensured that food cultures, consumption, and economics would change in urban America. Mechanical refrigeration, which first became available in the home in the 1920s, ensured that food remained fresh longer and provided more efficient and convenient access to food in the home. Mass electricity—widely available in urban American homes by the mid-1920s—allowed for the use of important

kitchen appliances, including the refrigerator. Electrification also changed the nature of food processing, improving producers' ability to manufacture, store, and handle food, ensuring less spoilage in the process.[2]

Entrance into urban areas fundamentally changed migratory groups and their relationships with food. Individuals who previously produced their own food on farms became consumers of purchased food products. New relationships with food products resulted. People who previously ate only local foods now enjoyed access to national and even transnational food products. The use of steamships and refrigerated rail cars ensured that perishable goods were transported effectively and safely through the 19th century and into the early years of the 20th century. During the 20th century, shipping of food products shifted from the primary domain of the railroads to trucking by the 1970s, reflecting the expansion of the interstate highway system that linked major cities throughout the United States.[3] In 1924, quick freezing emerged as a viable method of food preservation and transportation, further lowering the costs of food for consumers. Frozen foods grew in popularity during the 1940s as Americans were encouraged to support the war cause and sought alternatives to canned goods that were sent abroad to soldiers serving overseas.

IMMIGRATION

Constant waves of immigration throughout urban America irrespective of geography served as a powerful force dictating changes to foodways in cities throughout the United States. The 20th century began with the mass entrance of so-called "new immigrant" groups, mostly from eastern and southern Europe, arriving on America's shores escaping a variety of harsh conditions in their home countries, including religious persecution, natural disasters, lack of economic opportunity, and public health crises. Indeed, food availability was one reason that immigrants sought refuge in the

United States. Italian immigrants (primarily from southern Italy) came to the United States in pursuit of food security that was not available at home. For the Italian peasant class, food was basic and limited—hard bread with a sardine was a common meal. In contrast, the Italian upper class enjoyed a variety of foods including meats, cheeses, pasta, and wine. Stories of food abundance motivated numerous Italian peasants to seek refuge in the United States, with promises of food that was similar to that of the Italian upper class.

Once in America, Italian immigrants—while remaining part of the urban underclass—had access to foods previously unavailable in Italy. Meat became a staple part of the Italian American diet in the early years of the 20th century. For the first time, cheeses, pasta, olive oils, and other specialty foods became attainable on a worker's wage by 1910. In the process, Italian immigrants in America—coming in direct contact with people from throughout the country irrespective of region—helped "invent" a new Italian food and singular identity in the United States, moving away from the regional foodways and identities that were found in Italy.[4]

Food as business offered opportunities for new immigrants to advance economically in the United States while maintaining many of the food traditions of their home countries. The Jewish delicatessen—with its roots in America dating to New York City in the late 1860s—became an iconic institution of Ashkenazi Jewish food culture in the United States. In the 19th century, the American Jewish delicatessen catered toward the foods of German Jews. However, the influx of Eastern European Jewish immigrants that began at the end of the 19th century significantly altered the nature of these restaurants. German-style delicatessens offered a variety of meats, poultry, fish, olive oils, caviar, and other imported canned goods. Eastern European–influenced delicatessens shifted the menu toward smoked meats, gefilte fish, and knishes. Delicatessens helped spread the notoriety of Eastern

European breads such as bagels, rye bread, and pumpernickel. These establishments also offered in-house dining, particularly drawing lively lunch crowds at such famed delicatessens as Katz's on New York City's Lower East Side, Manny's Coffee Shop and Deli on Maxwell Street in Chicago, Canter's on Fairfax Avenue in Los Angeles, and Mazo's in Charleston, South Carolina.[5]

Chinese food—a staple of American cities from the turn of the 20th century forward—also shifted during the time period. The earliest importation of Chinese cooking into the United States in the 19th century was primarily from Guangdong Province in southern China, known more frequently as Canton. As a result, early Chinese-American food was highly influenced by Cantonese methods such as stir-frying, often using more meat in recipes to fit American tastes and reflect the availability of flesh foods. The end of the Chinese Exclusion Act in 1943 coupled with expanded immigration from China after 1965 ensured that new food cultures would arrive in American cities. Spicier dishes influenced by northern Chinese, Szechuan cooking found their ways to restaurant menus, emphasizing the use of dried, hot peppers. This diversification also led to the rise of more expensive Chinese restaurants in the 1960s, starting with Shun Lee Dynasty in midtown Manhattan. In 1969, the restaurant—with its newly expanded Szechuan menu—received four stars from the *New York Times Guide to Dining*. These restaurants appealed to American diners based on the perception of authenticity of flavors and ingredients, as well as a cultural fascination that only grew with the opening of diplomatic relations with China in the early years of the 1970s.[6]

Food offered commercial and social opportunities, but also social tensions. Battles over immigrant foods in the early decades of the 20th century represented tensions surrounding ideas of Americanization and fears among urban reformers about the speed or effectiveness of assimilation into a narrowly defined American identity. Mexicans migrated to

American cities outside of the Southwest in the 1920s drawn by the promise of industrial jobs—meat-packing plants in Chicago, the automobile industry in Detroit, and garment factories in Los Angeles. Cultural conflicts soon arose. Settlement house workers, domestic scientists, and others concerned about assimilation offered advice steeped in cultural stereotypes, ethnic assumptions, and native paternalism. As one domestic guide aimed at acculturating Mexican immigrants in Los Angeles explained, "Mexican families are malnourished, not so much from a lack of food as from not having the right varieties of foods containing constituents favorable to growth and development." The guide proclaimed that young, Mexican elementary school girls did not have the capability to understand "chemical terms" but could be taught to remember what foods to prepare for both thrift and nutrition. The recipes included in the domestic guide illustrate the limitations on its authors own knowledge of healthy foods and what was considered "healthy": eleven out of fifteen recipes for salads featured mayonnaise as a main component.[7]

The experience of the so-called "chili queens" of San Antonio—Mexican American women who sold chili con carne to the expanding numbers of tourists visiting the city—provide an important example of the limits that cities placed on the food expressions of immigrants. The chili queens sold their foods to locals in public plazas as early as the 1860s and businesses expanded to meet the demand of eager visitors to San Antonio's plazas dating back to the 1880s. The plazas became locations of racial and socioeconomic mixing, while providing these women with enough money to support families. However, by the 1930s, city officials began pushing the chili queens out of the plazas, under the guise of a public health crusade, and filled the spaces with landscaping. By 1943, the celebrated chili queens of San Antonio were no longer found in the city's plazas, relegated into indoor cooking spaces to satisfy the queries of health inspectors or drawn to other, World War II–era job opportunities.[8]

Similar battles over urban space and the buying and selling of food occurred in the same time period in New York City. In the late 1930s, Mayor Fiorello La Guardia began speaking publically against the sanitary conditions of pushcarts—a staple of the city dating back to the 1880s. La Guardia's crusade gained momentum with the opening of the indoor Essex Street Market on the Lower East Side, forcing peddlers to apply for licenses and stalls in order to sell their products.[9] In both instances the closing of outdoor food service was sold under the banner of cleaner cities, the process of professionalization, and Americanization for sellers.

Yet the popular embrace of ethnic foods by native-born Americans and the dominant culture over time also presented the opportunity to reflect America's reputation as a cultural melting pot. By 1991, salsa—whose roots date as far back as the Aztec Empire—had replaced ketchup as the highest selling condiment in the United States, just forty-three years after it had begun to be mass produced by Pace Foods, based out of San Antonio.[10] This major shift was not without its ironies that formed because of new relationships born out of cultural exchange. The founder of Pace Foods, David Pace, was a Louisiana native who claimed no Mexican ancestry.[11]

FOOD AND PROTEST

While food and food service had the power to unite across ethnic lines, it also had the potential to divide along racial lines. In the urban South, civil rights activists focused on segregated lunch counters as a locale of political participation. While white Southerners had no problem eating meals prepared by African American cooks, they fought viciously against the idea of sitting next to black patrons while consuming these foods. Thus, food service contrasted with food consumption—one built on a relationship of subordination, and the other imbued with the possibility of social equality. Ideas of racial purity dictated white responses to the notion of integrated dining spaces, often dictated by paranoia that interracial dining would lead to interracial sex. By the 1960s, civil rights advocates focused on access to integrated lunch counters as a consumer right provided by citizenship, while white supremacists considered these segregated locations as a property right protected by both law and biblical tradition.[12]

Food also represented potential social change and opportunity for black Southerners migrating north for economic opportunity and to escape the oppression of Jim Crow laws, physical violence, and political repression. As migrants escaped the South, the group desired the familiar foods from the South. Some opened cafes and restaurants in the North that served what was later called "soul food." Use of the word "soul" was part of a larger attempt to emphasize black cultural traditions and contributions, started by black jazz musicians as early as the 1940s. The term "soul food" implied not just food from the South, but foods specifically prepared by African American cooks born out of food traditions dating to enslavement, and gained wide use in the 1960s. In 1962, Sylvia Woods opened her namesake restaurant in Harlem, Sylvia's. She eventually earned the popular nickname, "the queen of soul food." Restaurants such as Soul Queen in Chicago and Pascal's in Atlanta helped expand popular use of the label while continuing a tradition of connecting the food with pride in culture and identity.[13] By the late 1960s, cookbooks utilizing the term "soul food" further spread the use of the phrase across the United States.[14]

Food was also utilized as a form of grassroots political protest throughout American cities in the 20th century. Consumer groups organized by women fought for financial stability, protesting the rising prices of food in urban areas. Consumer activists utilized a variety of methods to utilize their proscribed social roles as housewives to express themselves politically. Throughout the 1930s housewives in Detroit, Los Angeles, and New York protested the high price of meat created by the Agricultural Adjustment Act (AAA). In Detroit,

white and black working-class women worked together to build a national movement against the financial burden that the AAA placed on consumers. Local protests coalesced into larger, national movements, as the New Deal years offered housewives the opportunity to gain leadership and organizing experience through consumer coalitions and labor union auxiliary ranks associated with the Congress of Industrial Organization. Consumer protests from the mid-1960s through the mid-1970s created significant change in locations like Long Island, Denver, and the Chicago suburbs, with changes in supermarket labeling and a federal response to the growing price of meat.[15]

The 20th century ended with attempts to bring the process of food production back to America's cities, particularly as a way to fight food insecurity. The 20th-century history of growing food in cities represents a threaded continuity despite larger trends toward the city as a place of consumption. With the kitchen gardens of World War I fresh in the public's mind, local community organizations in New York City began offering garden plots for the unemployed during the Great Depression, growing vegetables such as tomatoes, corn, beets, and turnips. The World War II years, filled with food shortages and mandatory rationing, saw urban gardens continue to be associated with times of sacrifice and crisis, a temporary solution to a finite problem. Programs that began in the late 20th and early 21st centuries sought to reframe the need for city gardens. Efforts in places like Chicago, Detroit, Milwaukee, and New York City attempted to present city gardens as a necessary resource to provide healthy food and a natural part of a city's landscape, rather than a response to a specific crisis.[16]

PURCHASING AND SELLING FOOD

The early decades of the 20th century marked a significant change in the ways that some urbanites acquired their food. Small, often family-run grocery stores were a staple of early 20th-century American cities. While these stores often had higher prices, the lack of ability to travel because of expense and convenience ensured that the working classes patronized these stores. Local groceries often appealed to a neighborhood's predominant ethnicity, providing not only familiar foods but also the ability to converse with a grocer in the same language.

For the working classes living throughout urban America in the first half of the 20th century, food choice was often dictated by labor conditions, economics, and availability. These limitations ensured that working-class diets remained not only limited but also expensive. Working-class Americans spent nearly half of their earned income on food. And yet for this group—unlike the upper classes and growing middle classes—food was infrequently a source of pleasure; more often, it was a challenge. Workers in cities often suffered from unpredictable meal hours given the length of the workday. Extensive hours at industrial work sites and small apartment kitchens ensured that food preparation time was limited and difficult. Ironically, these limitations brought working- and middle-class diets closer together. The lower prices of processed foods ensured that these products were more easily available while providing convenience and calories to industrial laborers. Middle-class households simultaneously desired these food products thanks to promotion from both dietary advice and popular culture. Processed and frozen foods became an acceptable American diet by the mid-20th century.[17]

By the 1930s, the suburban middle classes began flocking to nearby chain grocery stores located outside the center of cities. Large, self-service grocery stores offered convenience, lower prices, and shopper autonomy at the expense of interpersonal interactions with grocers.[18] The rise of the automobile made shopping trips outside of a neighborhood more convenient. A new institution—the supermarket—drew customers with the promise of abundant parking, lower prices, and the convenience of one-stop shopping for a week's worth of groceries. Conglomerate chains such as A&P, Piggly Wiggly (founded in Memphis), and Kroger (based out of Cincinnati) changed the nature of food acquisition and the relationship between consumers and the social process of purchasing food. By 1925, A&P was the world's largest retailer, with sales exceeding $420 million.[19] The Great Depression eliminated many of the small, family-owned grocery stores, ensuring that national chains would dominate the landscape in the post-Depression era. Grocery stores' rise to dominance did not occur without challenge. Food co-ops—rooted in antebellum American buying clubs—saw a resurgence in response to the proliferation of grocery stores. The years from the Great Depression through the 1950s saw a rise in the number of food co-ops in northeastern and midwestern cities, supported primarily by radical labor groups and recent immigrant communities. However, the challenge was short-lived as many of these cooperatives transformed into grocery stores themselves in the 1960s and 1970s.[20]

The changes in cooperatives did not mark the end of alternative food movements in American cities. In the late 1960s and 1970s, a series of activist entrepreneurs opened natural foods stores—some of which were cooperatives—that challenged the urban grocery status quo, illustrating that social justice could be advanced as part of the economic marketplace. These stores emphasized shared ownership and workplace democracy, turning their backs on the profit-driven models that drove the conventional marketplace. Nearly 700 activist natural food stores existed in the United States through the 1970s, many in urban areas, promoting organic foods, vegetarianism, environmentalism, and animal rights. The most well known of these businesses, Whole Foods—which began in Austin, Texas, under the satirical name Saferway—embraced corporate capitalism in the 1980s, eventually expanding nationwide and internationally. However, the natural markets found in cities in the 1970s not only promoted the notion of ethical food consumption but also created a new vernacular about food ethics that connected the buying and selling of food with social activism that continues to remain in the 21st century. The legacy of these businesses was ultimately mixed: simultaneously co-opted by American food culture while building an appreciation for ethical food purchasing practices.[21]

Public markets—a staple of 19th-century American cities—became less important as they moved from bustling outdoor markets to indoor, closed markets housed inside buildings by the 1940s. Recently arrived immigrants in cities, however, continued to largely buy food from specialized shops (butchers, bakers, and greengrocers), as well as pushcarts through the 1930s. Technological developments as well as public health crusades ended the food pushcarts by the 1940s as the merchants were coaxed into selling their goods from trucks, thanks to both automobile traffic and anti-pushcart legislation.

The expansion of American cities also further moved residents away from food preparation at home. In the early 20th century local, neighborhood bakers provided a majority of cities' bread. Technological change eventually transformed the relationship between consumer and bread, as well. Truck transportation ensured that commercial baking would predominate as the delivery areas for large bakers expanded and commercially produced bread founds its way to the shelves of grocers and eventually supermarkets.

RESTAURANT CULTURE

Restaurants in American cities in the early years of the 20th century were intricately tied to the process of creating a distinctive middle-class culture in the United States that served as a model of good living. By the 1920s, the middle classes, rather than the upper classes, were the dictators of taste in American restaurant dining. Expansive, multi-course meals, French gastronomy, and extravagant dining rooms were replaced by urban restaurants with less formal service, more ethnically diverse cuisine, and an emphasis on American rather than continental foods. The middle classes in these nascent decades of the century served as agents of culinary change that represented a larger cultural change toward consumer, consumptive culture.[22] The shift represented a more egalitarian restaurant scene throughout American cities, one that expanded further over the century.

Women participated in more visible ways in the restaurant industry in the early 20th century. This shift began slowly in the latter years of the 19th century, with women serving more visible roles in restaurants rather than the "back-of-the-house," unseen professions of the past, such as dishwashers and cooks. The case of Mary Mallon, a typhoid carrier twice apprehended and arrested for infecting diners because of her work as a cook, sparked a public panic that reflected fears of the role of immigrant women in professional kitchens. Still, during the opening decades of the 20th century women became more visibly prominent in the restaurant industry, working as servers, owners, and managers. Two dining locations—the cafeteria and the tea room—became particularly associated with women managers and workers. Tea rooms in large cities like New York, Philadelphia, and Chicago remained largely sex-segregated, not by rule but by informal practice. The locations were geared toward socially prominent and economically prominent women, but these small businesses also offered economic and social opportunity, primarily for middle-class, native-born white American women. Some tea rooms, however, were operated by African American owners and staff in Chicago's Bronzeville neighborhood and Harlem, New York.[23] The rooms were popular through the early years of the 1930s and declined in numbers following the World War II years.[24]

Simultaneously, the development of business districts filled with shopping destinations led to another form of public dining. The growth of department stores—paeans to consumption—became connected to dining culture as lunch rooms opened that were located inside of urban shopping palaces to keep shoppers from leaving the building. Department stores like Wanamaker's (located in both New York and Philadelphia), R. H. Macy and Co. in New York, Bullock's in Los Angeles, and Mandel Brothers and Marshall Field's in Chicago all opened lunch rooms to ensure that hungry shoppers would not leave the department stores in search of nourishment. Meals tended to be small, in part to support middle-class cultural norms of women not eating overly indulgent meals in public.[25]

As urban Americans continued eating outside of the home, the desire for speed, convenience, and quality assurance led to the rise of a new dining environment and experience that was particularly geared toward office workers. The automat—borrowing heavily from the methods of a successful, late 19th-century German restaurant chain—offered urban eaters a dining experience that in many ways reflected the scientific planning that shaped the work days of both industrial laborers and white-collar office workers. Automats allowed consumers the opportunity to choose freshly prepared, cheap, filling food (macaroni and cheese, mashed potatoes, a variety of sandwiches) by simply dropping a nickel into a coin slot, opening a compartment, and pulling out their meal. The Horn & Hardart chain of automats proliferated throughout the United States, beginning with its first location in Philadelphia in 1902. By 1912, automats arrived in New York City, with a two-story, marble-floored building located in the middle of Times Square. At the height of the automat's popularity in New York, more than forty locales operated simultaneously. The demise of the automat in American cities began by the 1950s with the growth of suburbanization, office building cafeterias, and rising food costs. New forms of cheap, fast, convenience foods frequently replaced the automats.[26]

The rise of fast food restaurants in urban areas—particularly in low-income and working-class neighborhoods—did not always reflect food choice but rather was influenced by a concerted effort by the federal government to encourage minorities to open fast food franchises. In response to growing urban unrest driven by segregation and lack of economic opportunity in the post–World War II years, the federal government encouraged the Small Business Association to provide Equal Opportunity loans to minority entrepreneurs, many of whom invested in opening fast food franchises. Fast food corporations such as McDonald's and Kentucky Fried Chicken—whose businesses originally began in suburbs and along well-traveled roadways in the 1950s—viewed cities as a necessary location to expand franchise profits. As a result, these companies began marketing geared specifically toward African Americans and other minority groups. The long-term results were profound, ensuring that fast food would remain abundant and easy to access in poor neighborhoods, while fresh food and grocery stores often remained difficult to find in these urban food deserts.[27]

DISCUSSION OF THE LITERATURE

Food history's foray into 20th-century cities is a growing subfield for both urban historians and food historians. Historians of American food history have focused somewhat disproportionately on the early development of American food culture in the 18th and 19th centuries. However, recent works have emphasized the importance of food in the broader history of American cities in the 20th century. Rowman & Littlefield's "Big City Food Biographies" series is the first large-scale attempt to center food production, consumption, and the economics of food at the center of urban history. *New Orleans* explores food as building the city's Creole and Cajun cultural identity. *Chicago* emphasizes the connections between the city's population boom in the late 19th century, immigration, and its role as a center of industrial food production in the

20th century. *Kansas City* traces the city's role as a crossroads and the food culture that was born out of its location as a conduit into the west. *Portland* explains the city's modern transformation from a pioneer town of fur traders and lumberjacks into a center of the modern, 21st-century American fine dining scene. *New York City* delves into the city's place in creating and sustaining national food trends and iconic dishes. Lastly, *San Francisco* looks at the role of immigrant groups in shaping the city's culinary culture, including Chinese, Italian, French, and Latin American influences. [28]

Additionally, the growth of the discipline of food history has led to the publishing of comprehensive, broad food histories where cities serve as important historical backdrops. Andrew W. Smith's *30 Turning Points in the Making of American Cuisine* includes sections that consider the impact of Upton Sinclair and *The Jungle* on the meat-packing industry and food reform, the opening of the first King Kullen grocery store in Jamaica Estates, Queens, and the opening of Chez Panisse in Berkeley, California, and its effects on the locavore food movement. Jennifer Wallach utilizes urbanization as a lens of inquiry in her social history, *How America Eats: A Social History of U.S. Food and Culture*. Chapters covering immigration, industrial food production, and food politics are particularly relevant to 20th-century urban America and food. Similarly, Megan Elias's cultural history of American food, *Food in the United States, 1890–1945*, provides a broad overview of the relationship between cities and food. The book's organization is thematic, including sections on ingredients, preparation, eating habits, and dietary reform. Each chapter includes a chronological exploration with cities often emphasized. Jeffrey Pilcher's *Food in World History* explores American cities within a larger, global historical analysis, including considerations of industrialization, immigration, and changing food cultures.[29]

Books related to the immigrant experience in 20th century America are a common source for information about the changing dynamics of food and food cultures in cities. Hasia Diner's *Hungering for America* illustrates how food was a driving factor for Irish, Eastern European Jewish, and Italian immigrant groups in the late 19th and early 20th centuries. The book also explores how these groups' food traditions changed because of their arrival in America, while simultaneously changing American foods. Simone Cincotto's *The Italian American Table* expands on Diner's analysis of Italian immigrant groups by focusing on the lives of Italian Americans in East Harlem in the 1920s and 1930s. Cincotto shows how food played a central role in Italian American life, a means to negotiate challenges facing the community, as well as a path toward social and economic mobility. In *We Are What We Eat*, Donna Gabaccia illustrates the complex relationship between ethnic identity and food in the United States. Food traditions have allowed ethnic groups the opportunity to define identity, while simultaneously flattening these identities by experimenting with the foods, traditions, and methods of other groups in America, a similar theme emphasized by Cara De Silva in an article that proclaims New York to be "Fusion City." Andrew Coe highlights the ways that interaction with the world abroad has shaped food preferences in the United States in his cultural history of American interactions with Chinese food, *Chop Suey: A Cultural History of Chinese Food in the United States*. The transformation of foods from throughout Asia in the United States has led Robert Ji-Song Ku to label dishes such as California rolls and SPAM "dubious food," mimicking American prevailing cultural views of Asians in America as either inauthentically Asian or not sufficiently American.[30]

Works that have explored gender roles in 20th-century America have often focused on the domestic responsibilities of women in urban areas, including food purchasing and preparation. Ruth Schwartz Cohen's *More Work for Mother* explains how household technologies, including those in the kitchen, that first appeared to provide convenience actually ensured that middle-class women became responsible for domestic work previously done by men, children, and domestic servants. Laura Shapiro's *Perfection Salad* traces the development of the domestic sciences in America at the turn of the 20th century. The work of reformers such as Fanny Farmer set the precedence for a culture that emphasized convenience, precise measurement, and rational cooking. The long-term results helped create a culture that connected women with consumer culture, in the process tethering middle-class women as domestic experts and limiting other social and labor opportunities. Megan Elias expands on this view in *Stir it Up*, charting the domestic sciences' evolution into staunch gender roles of the 1950s, resulting in the movement's rejection by 1960s feminists.[31]

PRIMARY SOURCES

The growth in interest about food and culinary history has been reflected by an increase in the number of publicly available, digitized primary sources. Researchers interested in 20th-century cities and food will benefit particularly from digital resources that have made cookbooks, restaurant menus, and advertisements available.

Digitized 20th-century cookbooks can be found via Michigan State University's "Feeding America," the New York Public Library's General Research Division of the Humanities and Social Sciences Library, the Cookbook and Home Economics Collection from the Young Research Library Department of Special Collections at UCLA, the Bancroft Library at The University of California, Berkeley, and the Prelinger Library in San Francisco. Other collections can be found at the Fales Collection at New York University, the Schlesinger Library at the Radcliffe Institute for Advanced Study at Harvard University, and the Culinary Institute of America's Conrad N. Hilton Library in Hyde Park, New York.

Menus provide researchers with a sense of food trends, differences in food availability, and preferences based on demographics and class. A large-scale collection of 20th-century city restaurant menus can be found at the New York Public Library's Rare Books Division, online through the "What's on the Menu?" crowdsourcing transcription project. Additional menu collections that include establishments include Cornell University Library's Menu Collection and the National Restaurant Association Collection at Johnson & Wales University. The vast majority of menu holdings in repositories around the United States are composed of urban restaurants. Major collections of food advertisements can be found at Duke University Library's John W. Hartman Center for Sales, Advertising & Marketing History and the Smithsonian National Museum of American History.

FURTHER READING

Anderson, Heather Arndt. *Portland: A Food Biography*. Lanham, MD: Rowman & Littlefield, 2014.

Block, Daniel R. *Chicago: A Food Biography*. Lanham, MD: Rowman & Littlefield, 2015.

Coe, Andrew. *Chop Suey: A Cultural History of Chinese Food in the United States*. New York: Oxford University Press, 2009.

Cooley, Angela Jill. *To Live and Dine in Dixie: The Evolution of Urban Food Culture in the Jim Crow South*. Athens: University of Georgia Press, 2015.

Davis, Joshua Clark. *From Head Shops to Whole Foods: The Rise and Fall of Activist Entrepreneurs*. New York: Columbia University Press, 2017.

Diner, Hasia. *Hungering for America: Italian, Irish, and Jewish Foodways in the Age of Migration*. Cambridge, MA: Harvard University Press, 2003.

Elias, Megan J. *Food in the United States, 1890–1945*. Santa Barbara, CA: ABC Clio, 2009.

Gabaccia, Donna. *We Are What We Eat: Ethnic Food and the Making of Americans*. Cambridge, MA: Harvard University Press, 1998.

Haley, Andrew. *Turning the Tables: Restaurants and the Rise of the American Middle Class, 1880–1920*. Chapel Hill: University of North Carolina Press, 2011.

Hauck-Lawson, Annie, and Jonathan Deutsch, eds. *Gastropolis: Food and New York City*. New York: Columbia University Press, 2010.

Imbert, Dorthée, ed. *Food and the City: Histories of Culture and Cultivation*. Cambridge, MA: Harvard University Press, 2015.

Jou, Chin. *Supersizing Urban America: How Inner Cities Got Fast Food With Government Help*. Chicago: University of Chicago Press, 2017.

Levenstein, Harvey. *Revolution at the Table: The Transformation of the American Diet*. Berkeley: University of California Press, 2003.

Nye, David. *Electrifying America: Social Meanings of a New Technology, 1880–1940*. Cambridge, MA: MIT Press, 1992.

Opie, Frederick Douglass. *Hog and Hominy: Soul Food from Africa to America*. New York: Columbia University Press, 2008.

Peters, Erica J. *San Francisco: A Food Biography*. Lanham, MD: Rowman & Littlefield, 2013.

Rees, Jonathan. *Refrigeration Nation: A History of Ice, Appliances, and Enterprise in America*. Baltimore: Johns Hopkins University Press, 2013.

Shprintzen, Adam. *The Vegetarian Crusade: The Rise of an American Reform Movement, 1817–1921*. Chapel Hill: University of North Carolina Press, 2011.

Smith, Andrew F. *New York: A Food Biography*. Lanham, MD: Rowman & Littlefield, 2013.

Turner, Katharine Leonard. *How the Other Half Ate: A History of Working-Class Meals at the Turn of the Century*. Berkeley: University of California Press, 2014.

Twarog, Emily E. LB. *Politics of the Pantry: Housewives, Food, and Consumer Protest in Twentieth-Century America*. New York: Oxford University Press, 2017.

Wallach, Jennifer. *How America Eats: A Social History of U.S. Food and Culture*. Lanham, MD: Rowman & Littlefield, 2015.

Whitaker, Jan. *Tea at the Blue Lantern Inn: A Social History of the Tea Room Craze in America*. New York: St. Martin's Press, 2002.

Ziegelman, Jane. *97 Orchard: An Edible History of Five Immigrant Families in One Tenement* New York: Harper, 2011.

NOTES

1. Carl Abbott, *Urban America in the Modern Age, 1920 to the Present* (Hoboken, NJ: Wiley-Blackwell, 2006), 138.

2. Jonathan Rees, *Refrigeration Nation: A History of Ice, Appliances, and Enterprise in America* (Baltimore: Johns Hopkins University Press, 2013); and David Nye, *Electrifying America: Social Meanings of a New Technology, 1880–1940* (Cambridge, MA: MIT Press, 1992).

3. Shane Hamilton, *Trucking Country: The Road to America's Wal-Mart Economy* (Princeton, NJ: Princeton University Press, 2008), especially chapters 2, 3, and 4.

4. Hasia Diner, *Hungering for America: Italian, Irish, and Jewish Foodways in the Age of Migration* (Cambridge, MA: Harvard University Press, 2002).

5. Ted Merwin, *Pastrami on Rye: An Overstuffed History of the Jewish Deli* (New York: New York University Press, 2015).

6. Andrew Coe, *Chop Suey: A Cultural History of Chinese Food in the United States* (New York: Oxford University Press, 2009), 222–225.

7. Pearl Ellis, *Americanization Through Homemaking* (Los Angeles: Wetzel, 1929), 27–28.

8. Jeffrey M. Pilcher, "Who Chased Out the 'Chili Queens'? Gender, Race, and Urban Reform in San Antonio, Texas, 1880–1943," *Food and Foodways* 16, no. 3 (July 2008): 173–200.

9. Suzanne Wasserman, "Hawkers and Gawkers: Peddling and Markets in New York City," in *Gastropolis: Food and New York City*, ed. Annie Hauck-Lawson and Jonathan Deutsch (Columbia University Press, 2009), 160–162.

10. Donna R. Gabaccia, *We Are What We Eat: Ethnic Food and the Making of Americans* (Cambridge, MA: Harvard University Press, 2000), 219.

11. *Obituary: David E. Pace, Picante Sauce Producer, 79. The New York Times*, December 30, 1993.

12. Angela Jill Cooley, *To Live and Dine in Dixie: The Evolution of Urban Food Culture in the Jim Crow South* (Athens: University of Georgia Press, 2015).

13. Frederick Douglass Opie, *Hog & Hominy: Soul Food from Africa to America* (New York: Columbia University Press, 2008), 108–110.

14. Adrian Miller, *Soul Food: The Surprising Story of an American Cuisine, One Plate at a Time* (Chapel Hill: University of North Carolina Press, 2013), 29–47.

15. Emily E. LB. Twarog, *Politics of the Pantry: House-wives, Food, and Consumer Protest in Twentieth-Century America* (New York: Oxford University Press, 2017).

16. Laura Lawson and Luke Drake, "From Beets in the Bronx to Chard in Chicago: The Discourse and Practice of Growing Food in the American City," in *Food and the City: Histories of Culture and Cultivation* ed. Dorthée Imbert (Cambridge, MA: Harvard University Press, 2015), 143–162.

17. Katharine Leonard Turner, *How the Other Half Ate: A History of Working-Class Meals at the Turn of the Century* (Berkeley: University of California Press, 2014).

18. Tracy Deutsch, *Building a Housewife's Paradise: Gender, Politics, and American Grocery Stores in the Twentieth Century* (Chapel Hill: University of North Carolina Press, 2010).

19. Marc Levinson, *The Great A&P and the Struggle for Small Business in America* (New York: Hill & Wang, 2011), 101.

20. Anne Meis Knupfer, *Food Co-ops in America* (Ithaca, NY: Cornell University Press, 2013).

21. Joshua Clark Davis, *From Head Shops to Whole Foods: The Rise and Fall of Activist Entrepreneurs* (New York: Columbia University Press, 2017), 176–222.

22. Andrew P. Haley, *Turning the Tables: Restaurants and the Rise of the American Middle Class, 1880–1920* (Chapel Hill: University of North Carolina Press, 2011).

23. See, for example, Schomburg Center for Research in Black Culture, Jean Blackwell Hutson Research and Reference Division, The New York Public Library, "The Ideal Tea Room at 3344 South Michigan Avenue; Mrs. Mayme Lee Clinkscale, proprietress (http://digitalcollections.nypl.org /items/510d47de-4d68-a3d9-e040-e00a18064a99)," New York Public Library Digital Collections.

24. Jan Whitaker, *Tea at the Blue Lantern Inn: A Social History of the Tea Room Craze in America* (New York: St. Martin's Press, 2002), 17–36.

25. Megan Elias, *Food in the United States, 1890–1945* (Santa Barbara, CA: Greenwood Press, 2009), 83–84.

26. Elias, *Food*, 82–83.

27. Chin Jou, *Supersizing Urban America: How Inner Cities Got Fast Food With Government Help* (Chicago: University of Chicago Press, 2017).

28. Many of these works have been singular, focused monographs on the development of food cultures in prominent American cities. Titles in Rowman & Littlefield's "Big City Food Biographies" are important contributions to the development of city-specific food histories. These books provide a full arc of historical development, though include an exploration of the 20th century for each of the locations. Books in this series that discuss the 20th century include: Heather Arndt Anderson, *Portland: A Food Biography* (Lanham, MD: Rowman & Littlefield, 2014); Daniel R. Block, *Chicago: A Food Biography* (Lanham, MD: Rowman & Littlefield, 2015); Andrea L. Bloomfield, *Kansas City: A Food Biography* (Lanham, MD: Rowman & Littlefield, 2016); Erica J. Peters, *San Francisco: A Food Biography* (Lanham, MD: Rowman & Littlefield, 2013); Andrew F. Smith, *New York: A Food Biography* (Lanham, MD: Rowman & Littlefield, 2013); and Elizabeth M. Williams, *New Orleans: A Food Biography* (Lanham, MD: Rowman & Littlefield, 2012).

29. Andrew W. Smith, *30 Turning Points in the Making of American Cuisine* (New York: Columbia University Press, 2009); Elias, *Food in the United States*; Jennifer Wallach, *How America Eats: A Social History of U.S. Food and Culture* (Lanham, MD: Rowman & Littlefield, 2015); and Jeffrey M. Pilcher, *Food in World History* (New York: Routledge, 2017).

30. Diner, *Hungering for America*; Simone Cincotto, *The Italian American Table: Food, Family, and Community in New York City* (Urbana: University of Illinois Press, 2013); Gabaccia, *We Are What We* Jane Ziegelman, *97 Orchard: An Edible History of Five Immigrant Families in One New York Tenement* (New York: Harper Collins, 2010); Harvey Levenstein, *Revolution at the Table: The Transformation of the American Diet* (Berkeley: University of California Press, 2003); Cara De Silva, "Fusion City: From Mt. Olympus Bagels to Puerto Rican Lasagna and Beyond," in *Gastropolis: Food and New York City*, ed. Annie Hauck-Lawson and Jonathan Deutsch (New York: Columbia University Press, 2009), 1–14; Andrew Coe, *Chop Suey: A Cultural History of*

Chinese Food in the United States (New York: Oxford University Press, 2009); and Robert Ji-Song Ku, *Dubious Gastronomy: The Cultural Politics of Eating Asian in the USA* (Honolulu: University of Hawai'i Press, 2013).

31. Ruth Schwartz Cohen, *More Work for Mother: The Ironies of Household Technology from the Open Hearth to the Microwave* (New York: Basic Books, 1983); Laura Shaprio, *Perfection Salad: Women and Cooking at the Turn of the Twentieth Century* (Berkeley: University of California Press, 1986); and Megan J. Elias, *Stir It Up: Home Economics in American Culture* (Philadelphia: University of Pennsylvania Press, 2008).

Adam Shprintzen

The Social Fabric

RELIGION IN THE AMERICAN CITY, 1600–1900

"The truth is, the city of today, the modern city, whether in the East or in the West, is a hell, in which the manhood of the nation is daily being consumed," Thomas Dixon Jr. lamented in 1896, in *The Failure of Protestantism in New York and Its Causes*. The Social Gospel minister, better known today as the author, in 1905, of *The Clansman*, argued that Protestant New Yorkers had abandoned the field in the face of a familiar catalogue of urban sins (and the expansion of their Roman Catholic and Jewish competitors); they had uprooted churches from neighborhoods most needful of them, privileged the wealthy over the working-class, and preached outdated theologies unsuited to present circumstances. Dixon celebrated the democratic impulse that guaranteed religious freedom but disparaged the sectarianism that distracted the urban religious with petty squabbles about "small differences." He held out hope for what might still be accomplished through united effort. "The city is the heart of modern civilization. It is the key to the century. It is the key to the future."[1]

By the end of the 19th century, American cities had well earned their reputations for temptation and vice, but the discursive focus of Thomas Dixon and other Social Gospel reformers on the city as a threat to the moral health of individuals and the nation obscures the innovative ways in which the urban religious lived in and through their urban environments. "'Urban religion' does not refer simply to religious beliefs and practices that happen to take place in cities (and that might as well take place elsewhere)," historian Robert Orsi explains. Urban religion is what arises from the dynamic engagement of religious traditions with the conditions of urban life. "The results are distinctly and specifically urban forms of religious practice, experience, and understanding."[2] In early American cities, that meant engaging with the hallmarks of an emerging modern society: heterogeneous populations, integrated economies, large-scale participatory politics, technological advancements, and religious pluralism. Rather than shying away, the urban religious embraced the materials the city offered as the basis for religious expression and community building.

As the city shaped religion, religion shaped the city and the nation. Americans have long entertained Dixon's idealized vision of the moral city. John Davenport attempted to recreate the heavenly city in his 1638 plan for New Haven. Early 19th-century merchant Divine Bethune saw New York as the heavenly city that saved him from the "den of iniquity" in the slave plantations of Tobago. The Azusa Street revivalists proclaimed Los Angeles the New Jerusalem in 1906. Such visions, however, had to be reconciled with the reality of a competitive urban spiritual marketplace. In America, the Celestial City bore an uncanny resemblance to Vanity Fair. Despite—or perhaps because of this—it was in America's pueblos, seaports, manufacturing centers, and along the urban frontier that some of the most distinctive elements of American culture—freedom of choice, toleration, reform, and even the welfare state— arose through the efforts of the religious. Where Dixon saw declension, others found opportunities for innovation, adaptation, and negotiation.

NATIVE AND COLONIAL CITIES, 1050–1780

Indigenous peoples, European settlers, and African slaves alike knew the value of religious communities in urban settlements for providing opportunities for emotional support, moral discipline, social networking, economic assistance, and political participation. They fought hard to establish and preserve them, sometimes at the expense of others' efforts. In time, exposure to a diverse range of faiths within colonial cities paved the way for the acceptance of the pluralism characteristic of modern America.

Long before the arrival of European colonizers, Native Americans formed communities with many of the hallmarks associated with urban life. Densely populated permanent settlements at Cahokia, near present-day East St. Louis, and the Ácoma and Abó Pueblos, in modern New Mexico, arose between the 10th and 15th centuries at the crossroads of economic, political, and religious networks. Cahokia's giant mounds, still visible today, and the rich archaeological remains within, speak to the site's role as a religious, political, and commercial center. Realizing the symbolic significance (and pragmatic value) of native settlements, Spanish colonizers built St. Augustine, Santa Fe, and San Antonio on their foundations as imperial outposts. Some Roman Catholic missionary orders saw the replication of a European built environment as essential to effecting native conversions. A minority of the population, Spaniards relied as much on evangelization as military might to maintain order over large native populations.

Living in densely settled communities with Franciscan missionaries, Spanish colonial authorities, and an increasing population of mestizo settlers, Pueblo Indians exploited the tensions between these factions. The Pueblos kept their traditional religious culture alive under a veneer of observance, rather than simply submitting to the Catholicism promulgated by European missionaries. After several decades of hardship brought on by famine, disease, oppressive tribute demands, and raiding parties, they found strength through their covertly preserved faith to accomplish what no other indigenous people achieved before or after: the complete setback of European expansion in the New World. But, native religious unity proved no less impervious to factionalism than their European colonizers following the Great Pueblo Revolt of 1680. The Pueblos were reconquered by the turn of the 18th century.

Seventeenth-century Dutch, French, and English colonizers shared with their Spanish competitors an appreciation for the utility of urbanized settlements on North American shores for production, trade, defense, rule, and worship. Old World religious beliefs and practices mingled with New World commercial ambitions as much for the spiritual benefit of colonizers as a justification and means for establishing state authority. Colonial established churches, funded with public monies and supported by civil authority, stood as one arm of a larger effort to replicate European political, cultural, and economic structures in a North American context. They aimed to provide broad, inclusive unity by bringing together people of all ranks and backgrounds. To promote community cohesion while enforcing social discipline, these churches were erected adjacent to government buildings and marketplaces (oftentimes inside a military fort). Here colonizers and their subjects performed complex rituals of incorporation into Christianity, mercantilism, and empire.

Yet as Atlantic World ports, these cities welcomed heterogeneous populations of sailors and slaves, merchants and artisans, laborers and refugees, who brought with them their own ideas of religion (and irreligion), undercutting efforts to unify them around a single established church. Charleston, Newport, New York, and Philadelphia each had congregations of at least eight different religious traditions by the mid-18th century—as well as adherents of an unknowable number of faiths celebrated informally or under cover of darkness. Even John Winthrop's "City on a Hill," which came closest to the established church ideal in the 17th century, faced the continual need to suppress those who believed and worshipped differently: dissenting Puritans, Baptists, and Quakers. Not surprisingly, Baptist and Quaker influence in Newport, and later Philadelphia,

influenced the outright rejection of establishment in those colonies. Religious difference at times bred fear and hostility in colonial cities. The assumption that two Catholic priests were behind the 1741 "Great Negro Plot" in New York was widely held by the overwhelmingly Protestant urban community despite little credible evidence.

Religion provided a key component of urban identity formation and the cornerstone for the emergence of a genuinely pluralistic society. For New York's Dutch population, after the English conquered the colony in the mid-17th century, the arrival of new rulers with their own established religious culture did not catalyze a process of assimilation, but rather of ethnicization. Dutch Reformed churches became a focal point around which the children of Dutch residents formed themselves into a self-conscious ethnic group unified by religion, language, and architecture. The process of ethnicization around British identity proved slower in contrast, stymied by divisions between Anglicans, Quakers, Baptists, and Presbyterians. Decades passed before ties of ethnicity gave way to personal predilection, social class, family, and education in shaping religious preferences.

Houses of worship in a diversity of shapes, forms, and styles could be found throughout colonial seaports by the mid-18th century. Their design reflected the diverse origins of their congregations, embodied their theology, and stated their place within colonial society. Heavenward soaring steeples of established churches, often copied from or modeled on structures in the metropolis, marked their location on land and signaled their dominance to those viewing from the sea. Storefront churches, like the Rigging Loft on William Street in New York, accommodated poor, dissenting congregations before modest, unassuming meetinghouses could be erected on the back of lots on side streets.

Judaism did not require a synagogue for prayer, so the act of establishing a congregation and building a synagogue represented a significant financial and psychic investment. Sephardic Jews expelled from Curacao landed in several North American seaports in the late 17th century. In Newport, they completed the Touro Synagogue in 1763, today the oldest synagogue in America. The structure's unassuming architecture resonates with surrounding domestic residences, a choice that reflected the congregation's modesty and limited financial means, but also its desire to avoid offending the predominantly Christian community.

In time, the conjunction of people, leadership, and events in colonial seaports provided the necessary conditions for rebellion; religion provided a moral sanction, occasions for protest, grounds for united action, but also a source of disagreement. Jonathan Mayhew of Boston's West Church served as a patriotic lightning rod during the Stamp Act Crisis, while Anglican ministers at King's Chapel a few blocks away offered loyalist views. Traditional rituals with religious significance, like Pope's Day celebrations, took on new meaning as protests against imperial authority. With its emphasis on individualism and its challenge to the power of the clergy, evangelicalism provided a language and a forum in which the laboring classes of Boston, New York, and Philadelphia expressed discontent with imperial politics. But in Newport, suspicions of sectarian motives proved a barrier to the formation of political coalitions among the city's evangelical congregations. Philadelphia Quakers, known for their pacifism, faced a wrenching schism when a group of "Free Quakers" separated in order to take up arms against the British. Anglican ministers in every city had a difficult decision to make: stay true to the Church headed by the British King or make the potentially treasonous decision to support the American cause.

The outbreak of war proved traumatic. The violent conflict led to the dispersal of congregations, the desecration of meetinghouses, and the anxiety of wondering whether Providence had really foreordained a war that stretched on for far longer than either side expected.

In the midst of this upheaval, state constitutions created new governments with a radical approach to toleration and freedom of choice. Surrounded as they were by numerous religious traditions, revolutionary city dwellers could not avoid questioning the exclusive claim of theirs being the one true church, the fate of religious truth if all beliefs were free to compete, and the likelihood of organized religion's continued existence without state support. Such thinking unified an unlikely coalition of urban evangelicals and deists to secure disestablishment and religious equality for all. The result of their efforts marked an important transition in American religion.

EARLY NATIONAL UNITED STATES, 1780–1830

The First Amendment to the Federal Constitution declared, "Congress shall make no law respecting an establishment of religion, or prohibiting the free exercise thereof." Freedom of religious choice was theoretically guaranteed across the young nation, laying the foundation for a vibrant post-revolutionary urban spiritual marketplace. Many states had already provided such a right in their constitutions. Previously marginalized groups—evangelicals, African Americans, Roman Catholics, and Jews—embraced this new spirit of toleration (and the legal rights of incorporation also granted at this time) to emerge as active participants in the religious life of 19th-century cities.

America quickly became more urban over the half-century following the Revolution. In 1790, the United States had five cities with more than 10,000 residents, and only one in twenty Americans lived in them; by 1830, that number rose to twenty-three cities, in which resided almost one in eleven. As East Coast seaports grew, so too, did new cities along the Ohio and Mississippi River valleys. Pittsburgh, Cincinnati, Louisville, and Lexington formed what has been called the urban frontier, cities that preceded and facilitated the establishment of farms in the hinterland. In these frontier cities, counting houses and warehouses stood alongside churches representing a wide range of faith. The Louisiana Purchase, in 1803, brought a new accent to American urbanization as cities with French and Spanish ancestry, like New Orleans and St. Louis, were integrated into the nation.

The post-revolutionary urban spiritual marketplace encouraged individuals to let personal choice, rather than family tradition, determine church membership. To survive, faiths that stayed loyal, like Anglicans and Methodists, severed their connection to the British Crown and reformed themselves as American denominations. Churches discovered they had to actively court new members. Competition among Presbyterians, Methodists, Baptists, and Unitarian churches for the patronage of new residents in 1830s St. Louis, for example, compelled Roman Catholics to rebuild their colonial French chapel into a grand new cathedral. Historians posit this period represented nothing less than the democratization of American Christianity, the rise of a new individualistic and disestablishmentarian style of religious culture. Too often they treat this development as a rural phenomenon—of camp meetings and itinerant preachers spread out across the hinterland—but anyone walking the streets of an early 19th-century city would have run into women and men attending worship at multiple churches (colloquially known as "sermon gadding"), disputing the authority of ministers, or choosing to attend no church at all.

Broadly inclusive churches gave way to a landscape fragmented by denomination, ethnicity, and class. In older cities like Albany, traditional ethnic cultural influences increasingly competed with new political (republican, mechanic) and religious (Calvinist, Methodist, evangelical) ideologies. In Providence, manufacturers and workers both turned to evangelical denominations in times of social ferment, but chose to worship in separate congregations. Decisions about faith had far-reaching ramifications. Privileging individual choice in the spiritual realm reinforced resolutions made in the economic, political, and social realms. No two cities were identical: religion shaped social change in different ways in major commercial centers such as New York and Philadelphia, new industrial cities such as Lowell and Utica, and the urban frontier of Cincinnati and Louisville.

Evangelical denominations enjoyed the greatest success in the post-revolutionary urban spiritual marketplace. Their decision to make conversion—the assurance of salvation revealed through the creation of a personal relationship with God—their primary criterion for membership resonated with the individualistic ethos of the time. In New York City, by 1830, fully half of the city's houses of worship belonged to evangelical congregations. In Baltimore, the number was even higher. The nation's most prominent evangelical denominations—Baptists, Methodists, and Presbyterians—emerged from the margins of colonial society to become dominant denominations across American cities and throughout the nation by the middle of the 19th century. This national ascendancy could not have been accomplished without the organizational, technological, financial, and distributional resources provided by cities.

Urban African Americans did not achieve many of the legal, economic, and political liberties for which they fought in the Revolution, but they did gain the right to found separate congregations and legally incorporate them. Fed up with being consigned to marginal seats in meetinghouses they helped build, African Americans formed their own congregations. First African Baptist in Savannah (1773), Mother Bethel in Philadelphia (1794), and the African Meetinghouse in Boston (1806) stood as community centers providing opportunities not only for worship, but also for education, economic advancement, socializing, and political activism. At first they remained autonomous, but not independent of white-led denominations. That changed when Richard Allen, a freed slave from rural Virginia who moved to Philadelphia, founded the African

Methodist Episcopal (AME) Church in 1816. Unity remained as elusive among black urban churches as among white ones: the AME aggressively competed with the New York-based African Methodist Episcopal Zion (AMEZ) Church as well as other independent congregations. By and large, African Americans embraced evangelicalism, but the urban milieu accommodated High Church Protestant Episcopal and Dutch Reformed African American congregations as well.

The prevailing spirit of republicanism sparked a flurry of church constitution writing and championing of the authority of American laity over European clergy among Roman Catholics and Jews. Post-Revolutionary American Catholics, many of English origins, democratized local church government through the adoption of a system of lay trustees annually elected by pew renters to oversee temporal affairs of the church. Jews also put lay committees in charge of church finances, clerical invitations, and disciplinary cases. The scarcity of priests and rabbis in the colonial period had already forced lay leaders to take charge of the operation of their congregations, but this was a significant departure from European tradition. This new model of governance, known as trusteeism, created significant tensions between foreign-born clerics, who expected to run these churches, and powerful lay trustees, unwilling to cede their authority. The influx of Irish and German Catholics with much different views and expectations ensured it did not last longer than a generation among Catholics in Baltimore, New York, or Philadelphia. A few more decades passed before powerful rabbis arrived in the United States and demanded a similar change in Jewish congregations.

Urban religion found a home in churches, meetinghouses, and synagogues of America's growing cities, but it also was actively performed in the public square. Baptisms happened in the waters of the rivers that ran around and through these cities (often to the delight of pious and profane alike), rioters stormed the homes of upstart radical preachers, and funerals processed through city streets to urban cemeteries (many long since disappeared, although some, like the African Burial Ground in New York, have been rediscovered). Religious belief, practices, and worldviews were created, negotiated, adapted, and modified in and through all the spaces of the city.

ANTEBELLUM AND CIVIL WAR, 1830–1870

Antebellum urbanization transformed seaports into metropolises and materialized new cities at the inland junctures of important transportation routes. Cities at this time produced great wealth for some but reduced others to poverty. In response to the proliferation of intemperance, prostitution, and other urban social problems, pious individuals dedicated vast amounts of time, energy, and resources to campaigns for the moral perfection of American cities and their inhabitants. As Protestant reformers went about their work, they confronted an increasing number of Roman Catholic and Jewish immigrants engaged in their own forms of urban community building. Throughout this period, unity remained elusive, especially when most needed on the eve of the Civil War.

By 1860, one hundred and one cities with more than ten thousand inhabitants stretched from coast to coast. Approximately one in five Americans made their homes there. Urban religious communities arose through the efforts of people as diverse as Jewish peddlers, evangelical Protestant merchants, and Irish Catholic nuns. Initial optimism was often tempered by significant hardship. In 1854, eight Irish Sisters of Mercy and five Presentation Sisters discovered firsthand the realities of these new American cities. Five died in Pittsburgh as a result of the change in climate, long hours of work, and poor living conditions. The remaining sisters ventured on to San Francisco, but the mining-camp mentality there quickly unsettled them. One became mentally ill, another physically unwell. Within two years both groups returned to Ireland, but not before first laying the foundation of institutions essential to the needs of the new city.

Protestant men and women—many, but not all evangelical—formed a variety of benevolent, reform, and missionary associations that actively drew on the financial, organizational, and technological resources of the city. Following British precedent, they founded local, and later national, tract and Bible societies. The American Bible Society and the American Tract Society, headquartered in New York, coordinated the printing of millions of publications on the most technologically advanced presses of the time and distributed them across the city, throughout the nation, and around the world. Denominational publishing houses, like the Methodist Book Concern in New York and the American Baptist Publishing House in Philadelphia, produced some of the earliest national newspapers to knit together believers from coast to coast. Protestants also initiated Sabbath schools, another British import, to provide religious education for poor children feared to be falling through the cracks as a result of accelerating industrialization. The American Sunday School Union, headquartered in Philadelphia, and several denominational societies supported these schools evolve from missionary endeavors to fixtures of middle-class congregations.

Innovative urban missions targeted women and men in the spaces of their work and play—parlors, ballrooms, and boardinghouses—and transformed them into places for worship and prayer. Missionary societies run by Protestant laity sponsored enterprising young college graduates who sought the excitement of missionary work without the dangers (and often early death sentence) of the foreign field. They held Bethel meetings nightly on the decks of ships along the waterfront. They opened missions in rented storefronts and other secular structures, like the Old Brewery in New York's Five Points, one of the most dangerous and overcrowded tenements in the city. The Ladies' Home Missionary Society of the Methodist Episcopal Church tore down the latter in 1853

and replaced it with a mission house that combined chapel, classrooms, accommodations for the hired missionary, and housing for the worthy poor. Orphan houses, work rooms, Magdalen asylums, Old Sailor's Homes, lying-in hospitals, and medical dispensaries were just a few of the many institutions initiated, funded, and operated by the religious to provide essential services to urban communities.

Reform also occurred in the streets, squares, and halls of the city. Some crusaded for temperance pledges, while others sponsored rallies, concerts, and lectures series. A General Distribution scheme put a tract in the hands of every family in New York once a month in the mid-1830s. Reformers solicited signatures on petitions, crossing over the line into political activism in hopes of ending delivery of the mail on the Sabbath, curtailing the granting of liquor licenses, and abolishing slavery. From Sunday school parades to Anniversary Week meetings, the spaces of the city became the stage for enacting a new, moral vision of America. Reform's prejudicial sister, nativism, also reared her ugly head with increasing frequency. Rioting mobs burned down a Roman Catholic convent on the outskirts of Boston in 1834 and a church in Philadelphia in 1844. Urban African Americans also found themselves a target for reasons ranging from their competition for scarce jobs to their support of abolition.

Historians have long debated the motivations of urban reformers. Some argue reform reflected an unprecedented optimism in the perfectibility of the individual and society, while others interpret it as a form of middle-class social control. There is an element of truth in both. During Charles Grandison Finney's 1831 Rochester revival, for example, middle-class manufacturers sought to restore their moral authority over workingmen lost in the separation of the home from the shop, an important contemporary workplace transformation. They deployed implicit and explicit coercion to chasten workingmen who did not attend revivals or join reform organizations. But workingmen found in the evangelicalism that their employers allegedly used to control them a rich vocabulary and set of symbols to justify their labor protests. It provided them with the foundation for a powerful critique of prevailing social conditions. Reform offered an important means of challenging not only class, but also gender and racial norms.

Most early 19th-century cities had a single Jewish "synagogue-community," where Sephardim and Ashkenazi from places around the Atlantic World attempted to coexist. Out of these emerged a new "community of synagogues" split along lines of ethnicity in the second quarter of the 19th century. Once they reached a critical mass (and a sufficient level of frustration with their Sephardic congregants), Ashkenazi often opened the second synagogue in a city. Here they could devise their own worship practice and community order. Increasing immigration from Germany and Eastern Europe ensured that several more synagogues followed in quick succession.

Even more significant was the rise of new confessional divides within American Judaism. The advent of Reform Judaism in the United States is often attributed to the efforts of Rabbi Isaac Mayer Wise, in Cincinnati in the 1850s, but a generation earlier, the native-born children of Charleston's Kahal Kadosh Beth Elohim synagogue came under the diverse influences of American political reform, evangelical associationalism, and German calls for prayer reform. They established their community as an early Reform society, rather than a synagogue, worshipped in a Masonic Hall, and offered services in English as well as Hebrew. The convergence of a diverse range of influences in America's cities allowed young Jews and those of other faiths the chance to re-imagine religious traditions in new ways.

Large-scale immigration of Irish and German Catholics, beginning in the 1830s, brought the republican period of trusteeism to an end and marked a decided shift toward more autocratic and hierarchical clerical control. Powerful bishops, many of them European born, refused to contend with lay trustees. The presence of ethnic populations who spoke different languages, preferred various forms of liturgy, and disagreed about the relationship between religion and society led to the creation of national, over terrestrial, urban parishes. By the eve of the great fire of 1871, Chicago had twenty-eight parishes, which included English, Irish, German, French, and Polish Catholics. Irish clergy disproportionately dominated the hierarchy of the immigrant Catholic Church, as historians have referred to it, and continued to do so well into the 20th century.

Roman Catholic religious orders, especially those run by women, embraced urban institution building with all the fervor of Protestant laity. In East Coast cities, these institutions provided crucial support for impoverished and vulnerable Catholic immigrants and their dependent children as well as a key means of countering the designs of Protestant reformers. Irish Catholic nuns in New York, for example, were remarkably successful in securing public support for their orphan asylums, creating what one historian argues was the foundation of the American welfare state. In the new cities of the Great Lakes region—Detroit, Chicago, and Milwaukee—Protestants and Catholics arrived at the same time and in comparable numbers. Catholic schools, academies, asylums, and hospitals were thus among the earliest public institutions in these cities and served mixed-religious audiences. That changed over time, but such an early civic presence mitigated the intensity of nativism that scarred other cities in the 1850s.

The antebellum urban spiritual marketplace also accommodated a range of faiths beyond the dominant evangelical Protestant, Roman Catholic, and Jewish religious traditions. Many remain invisible to us today because they were never listed in city directories, although that anonymity is likely what allowed them to exist in the first place. For example, the Prophet Matthias (also known as Robert Matthews) preached an eccentric theology influenced by Scotch Presbyterianism, African American

Methodism, and Judaism that garnered him an equally diverse congregation in New York in the 1830s, including wealthy evangelical merchants, working- and middle-class wives, and a freed slave who later earned fame as an abolitionist. The modernizing city offered Matthias financial wealth, organizational resources, and, in the midst of his sensational murder trial, a communications network to disseminate his decidedly anti-modern ministry.

The specter of fragmentation over slavery and a desire for unity and peace pervaded urban religious communities at mid-century. Each national evangelical Protestant denomination split along sectional lines in the 1830s and 1840s, presaging later political divide. A massive awakening in 1857–1858, known as the Businessman's Revival, developed into the first truly national Protestant urban revival and tried to stem the divide. Confronting economic depression and simmering political divisions over slavery, an unlikely alliance of conservative clergy and secular newspaper editors presented an exaggerated image of cross-denominational unity and overplayed the prominence of men as converts within the revival. Their accounts influenced how the revival was understood across the country. As radical evangelicals abandoned the religious realm for the political arena to advance anti-slavery, conservative evangelicals sought to use revivals and the press in an ultimately unsuccessful bid to promote national unity.

By the eve of the Civil War, religious values provided the underpinning for the country's reform movements, determined the political party to which one belonged, justified an expansionist ideology that pushed American settlement all the way to the Pacific, and shaped sectional understandings of free labor and republican virtue. Religion supplied the language and imagery people used to understand the war and consolation in the face of unprecedented loss. Cities served as centers of political mobilization, military recruiting and production, financing, and benevolent organizing. Urban ministers, priests, and rabbis gave religious

sanction to war in their pulpit addresses; Roman Catholic men demonstrated their patriotism and allegiance to the nation by enlisting, and women of all faiths drew on their deep experience with voluntary associations to fundraise and gather needed supplies, or, in the case of the Quakers, to protect their fellow Friends from conscription. But cities also turned out to be social and cultural battlegrounds. Devastating draft riots over four hot July days in New York, in 1863, revealed a terror in the heart of the city just as fearsome as on the battlefield.

The exigencies of wartime catalyzed new religious beliefs and practices. Southern religion had long privileged a single-minded interest in personal salvation, without the corporate sense of responsibility for the social order that pervaded the North. Yet in the midst of war, urban Southerners invented a civil religion and national identity around the much older, and Northern, genre of the "jeremiad." Confederates in Richmond politically sanctioned fast days and Thanksgiving Day, previously unknown in a city that rigidly preserved a division between church and state. They sought to bind urban residents in a public ritual that reinforced their sense of being a singular people, a uniquely Christian nation favored by God. As defeats and losses mounted, Richmond's secular press openly questioned the jeremiad's strategy of public humiliation and moral reformation to gain God's favor. In response, the religious press pushed a revitalized model of southern spirituality that tied an emphasis on individual salvation with the sanctification of being a chosen nation. Out of this mix emerged the curious hybrid known as the Lost Cause, a set of religiously undergirded beliefs that shaped the self-perceptions of white southerners, urban and rural, as a chosen people long after the war had ended.

LOOKING TO THE GILDED AGE AND BEYOND, 1870–1900

As the postwar urban South retreated into the consolation of a retrospective faith, the urban North, fresh off its victory, built larger and more lavish houses of worship. As pious reformers devoted significant time, labor, and wealth to the search for religious remedies to mounting social and economic problems, others found in religion the more mundane, but no less important, means to comprehend the vast city around them, to create communities, and to understand their place in the urban order.

The number of cities and the percentage of Americans living in them grew steadily in the decades following the Civil War. By 1900, fifty cities had more than one hundred thousand inhabitants. Even more impressive was the growth of smaller cities with populations between ten thousand and one hundred thousand. They swelled from 84 in 1860, to 587 in 1900, a more than sixfold increase. This growth was the result, in part, of the ongoing influx of foreign immigrants and expanding opportunities for industrial labor. The completion of transcontinental railroads facilitated the spread of urbanization. El Paso and Butte, Seattle and Omaha, and most other major cities in the West arose as important nodes in this national network. These cities not only provided for the economic and social needs of their new residents, but also their spiritual concerns.

Urban spiritual marketplaces only grew more diversified in the decades following the American Civil War. The monolithic categories of Protestant, Catholic, and Jew do not do justice to the diversity of forms found within them. Evangelical Protestants saw their dominance erode, a reflection of changing urban demographics rather than simple evidence of declension. Black Protestant churches enjoyed a resurgence of membership with the exodus of formerly enslaved African Americans from the Southern countryside. Ethnic Roman Catholic parishes proliferated as Italian, Polish, French Canadian, Mexican, and eastern European immigrants formed national parishes alongside Irish and German ones from before the war. Conservative Jewish congregations also

began to appear alongside Orthodox and Reform ones. But the real story of diversification can be found in the section labeled "Miscellaneous" at the end of the "Churches" section in city directories. Residents of turn-of-the-century New York could attend the Aryan Lotus Circle at 144 Madison Avenue, the Christian Israelites' Sanctuary at 108 First Street, and perhaps fittingly, the Strangers' Church at 123 W. 12th Street. Other cities exhibited a similar diversity.

Across the urban landscape, an eclectic array of cathedrals, churches, and synagogues served as visible reminders of diversified urban congregations and their efforts to compete with one another. Gone were the sedate days of the Touro Synagogue and Mother Bethel. Congregations employed an ever-expanding array of architectural styles in the design and ornamentation of their houses of worship. Seeing the church as an enclave in which to preserve the culture of the mother country and to ease immigrants groups into the mainstream of American life, Roman Catholics built large ecclesiastical complexes (often including rectories, schools, and convents) adorned in such a way as to cultivate an explicit ethnic identity well beyond what immigrants would have known in the home country. Evangelical denominations, on the other hand, built structurally innovative auditorium sanctuaries that drew on contemporary advances in secular theater design to accommodate larger crowds, improve acoustics, and give their minister greater freedom of movement. Jews shifted from blending into the urban environment to standing out from it by adopting dramatic Moorish-style architecture. The Plum Street Temple in Cincinnati (1866) exemplified this new style and located itself in the heart of the city across from City Hall and around the corner from leading Protestant and Roman Catholic churches.

From the efforts of Protestant Episcopalians to express High Church ceremonialism through the ecclesiastical Gothic, to the desire of Eastern Orthodox to replicate provincial

Russian churches, the last three decades of the 19th century marked an unprecedented period of experimentation. Yet by the early 20th century, the ongoing assimilation of future generations of immigrants into American life constricted this creative outpouring and led to a greater conformity in architectural styles, although it did not catalyze a comparable unity among the churches. The fruits of this architectural revival were not equally shared or enjoyed. In the constricted urban real estate market, for every grand religious edifice there were an even larger number of congregations that could only afford to worship in basements, storefronts, and rented halls.

Postwar urbanization also exacerbated social and economic problems associated with the city. The widening chasm between the slum-dwelling poor and the suburb-fleeing middle- and upper-classes created a volatile mix that led to rising poverty, crime rates, and occasional labor strikes and nativist riots. Reformers aggressively sought to address these problems, but their inability (or unwillingness) to confront their source—industrialization and capitalism—has led many modern historians to find their efforts wanting. A new generation of professional reformers traded their work bringing women and men to conversion for a more humanitarian response to the social and economic concerns of the working class through institutional churches, settlement houses, non-sectarian missions, and cooperative efforts with other denominations. Yet 19th-century critics feared these initiatives subordinated piety to charity, spiritual guidance to temporal relief, an age-old tension. Only in the early 20th century, when the number of Americans living in cities surpassed 50 percent, did reformers significantly rethink their strategy and trade a focus on individuals and families for a fundamental restructuring of urban environments.

Gilded Age reformers, however, were anything but anti-modern in their efforts. They displayed a sophisticated understanding of how secular resources offered by the modernizing city could forward their religious agendas. From 1875 to 1877, urban revivalists Dwight Moody and Ira Sankey led an evangelistic campaign stretching from Boston to Chicago that successfully harnessed the power and reach of modern mass media. They formed strategic alliances with secular newspaper editors to drum up interest before they arrived in town and to provide daily coverage as their work progressed. The Salvation Army, another English import, enjoyed success by embracing an urban culture driven by commerce and fueled by consumption. Through pageants, parades, and distinctive uniforms, the Salvation Army sought to saturate the secular with the sacred and pioneered a new way of doing religion. Alert to changing trends within popular culture, it pitched its message and medium to the tenor of the times. The Salvation Army eventually attracted public support disproportionate to its actual membership, at the cost of transforming from an evangelical faith to a philanthropic organization.

Despite the fragmentation brought by pluralism and ongoing secularization, faith not only persisted but also flourished among postwar urban residents. Social Gospel reformer and minister Walter Laidlaw, who worked under the aegis of the New York Federation of Churches, gathered data that revealed remarkable rates of identification with institutional religion by urban middle-class whites at the end of the 19th century. Laidlaw's findings correlate with Census Bureau data that showed the religious affiliation of adults in principal cities increasing from 37.9 percent to 46.9 percent between 1890 and 1906, as compared to a rise from 31.2 percent and 39.1 percent in rural areas.

To understand the appeal of the faith that Laidlaw uncovered, one need only look farther north up Manhattan Island. Religion helped Roman Catholic residents of Italian Harlem make sense of the problems inherent in their urban experience: persistent poverty; the crime and filth that contaminated the streets; economic, social, and geographic isolation from the larger city; and degradation in the eyes of their neighbors. In the annual Festa of the Madonna of Mount Carmel, they saw their own experience reflected and refracted through the symbol of the Madonna, linking the rural past with the urban present, the individual with the community. The history of this community reminds us that urban religion is as much about what reformers did for poor immigrants as the world immigrants created for themselves in cities: the spiritual topographies they carved out of a landscape designed by others, the rituals they observed that simultaneously offered connection with the old world and the new, and the urban selves they fashioned in response to their surroundings. Their rituals of the streets were enacted in many forms by a variety of faiths across the nation's cities.

By century's end, a spirit of optimism animated the urban religious. The World's Columbian Exposition of 1893, in Chicago, offered an ideal of urban harmony for cities reeling from labor unrest, immigration, and crime. As crowds flocked to the utopian White City, liberal and conservative Protestant urban clergy saw an opportunity to promote religious unity out of the fragmentation of faiths that surrounded them, albeit in different ways. A Parliament of World Religions organized by liberal Protestant ministers drew religious leaders from around the world for an unprecedented international summit, while an enormous evangelistic campaign spearheaded by the hometown favorites, Moody and Sankey, targeted evangelical fairgoers. The most dramatic response to the spirit of the fair came in 1894, with the publication of reporter and reformer William T. Stead's sensational and scathing indictment of the city, *If Christ Came to Chicago!*[3] Imagining Christ's response to modern day Chicago in a critique that spared few, Stead looked to the 20th century in his final chapter, returning to a familiar theme in urban religious thought. A great civic revival would turn Chicago of the future into an ideal city, a New Jerusalem, in which all denominations and sects subsumed their differences as branches of a single Church of Chicago and functioned as moral arbiters of the city. Copies of Stead's vision flew off the shelves of booksellers. His vision, however, has yet to materialize.

DISCUSSION OF THE LITERATURE

Historians have produced much of the literature on urban religion since the 1980s. Before that point, urban history and religious history typically were treated as separate fields of study. Urban historians generally avoided engaging with religion as a component of urban experience or growth other than in the context of ethnicity, specific institutions, or, like Thomas Dixon, as evidence of Protestant declension. Religious historians tended to focus on denominational or congregational histories and did not take into account the larger urban context. They also did not distinguish between the history of congregational leaders and the lived experience of the laboring and middle-class men and women in the pews. More recent work takes institutions and practice equally seriously, but tends to be micro-historical, overly focused on a single congregation, denomination, or city. As the field continues to develop, more expansive books will surely be published.

Several excellent overviews explicitly, and more often implicitly, deal with the urban context of their faiths. On Jews, see Hasia Diner, *The Jews of the United States, 1654–2000*; Jonathan Sarna, *American Judaism: A History*; and Deborah Dash Moore, *Urban Origins of American Judaism*. On Roman Catholics, see Jay Dolan, *The American Catholic Experience: A History from Colonial Times to the Present*; John McGreevy, *Catholicism and American Freedom*; and James O'Toole, *The Faithful: A History of Catholics in America*.[4] For an illuminating discussion of the theoretical underpinnings of urban religion, see Robert A. Orsi, ed., *Gods of the City: Religion and the American Urban Landscape*; and Jon Butler's article, "Religion in New York City: Faith That Could Not Be."

For a helpful overview of American urban history, see *The Evolution of American Urban Society*.[5]

Historians influenced by 19th- and 20th-century urbanism continue to debate what constitutes an urban settlement in pre-19th-century North America. On early Native American urban religion, see Andrew Knaut, *The Pueblo Revolt of 1680: Conquest and Resistance in Seventeenth-Century New Mexico*. A classic overview of the development of colonial seaports in British North America can be found in Carl Bridenbaugh's *Cities in the Wilderness: The First Century of Urban Life in America, 1625–1742*; and in *Cities in Revolt: Urban Life in America, 1743–1776*. Valuable studies of religion in particular cities include Joyce Goodfriend, *Before the Melting Pot: Society and Culture in Colonial New York City, 1664–1730*; David G. Hackett, *The Rude Hand of Innovation: Religion and Social Order in Albany, New York, 1652–1836*; and Darrett B. Rutman, *Winthrop's Boston: A Portrait of a Puritan Town, 1630–1649*.[6]

Works that discuss the role of religion in cities during Revolutionary upheaval and war include Gary Nash, *The Urban Crucible: Social Change, Political Consciousness, and the Origins of the American Revolution*; Benjamin L. Carp, *Rebels Rising: Cities and the American Revolution*; and Alfred Young, *Liberty Tree: Ordinary People and the American Revolution*.[7]

The period between 1780 and 1830 witnessed disestablishment, the foundation of the spiritual marketplace, and the ascendancy of evangelical denominations. On pluralism and toleration, see Richard Pointer, *Protestant Pluralism and the New York Experience: A Study of Eighteenth-Century Diversity*. On Methodists, see Dee Andrews, *The Methodists and Revolutionary America: The Shaping of an Evangelical Culture*. On the African American church, see Gary Nash, *Forging Freedom: The Formation of Philadelphia's Black Community, 1720–1840*; Kyle Bulthius, *Four Steeples Over the City Streets: Religion and Society in New York's Early Republic Congregations*; and Craig Townsend,

Faith in Their Own Color: Black Episcopalians in Antebellum New York City. On constitution writing and trusteeism among Roman Catholics, see Patrick Carey, *People, Priests and Prelates: Ecclesiastical Democracy and the Tensions of Trusteeism*.[8]

Urban reform movements in the period between 1830 and 1870 have especially captured the attention of historians. Early works argued for reform as social control, most influentially in Carroll Smith-Rosenberg, *Religion and the Rise of the American City: The New York City Mission Movement, 1812–1870*; and Paul Boyer, *Urban Masses and Moral Order in America, 1820–1920*. On revivalism and reform, see Paul Johnson, *A Shopkeeper's Millennium: Society and Revivals in Rochester, New York, 1815–1837*; and Terry Bilhartz, *Urban Religion and the Second Great Awakening: Church and Society in Early National Baltimore*. On the importance of class, Mark S. Schantz, *Piety in Providence: Class Dimensions of Religious Experience in Antebellum Rhode Island*; and Jama Lazerow, *Religion and the Working Class in Antebellum America*. On the importance of gender in reform, see Nancy Hewitt, *Women's Activism and Social Change: Rochester, New York, 1822–1872*; and Bruce Dorsey, *Reforming Men and Women: Gender in the Antebellum City*. On the Businessman's Revival, see Timothy L. Smith, *Revivalism and Social Reform in Mid-Nineteenth-Century America*; and Kathryn Long, *The Revival of 1857–1858: Interpreting an American Religious Awakening*.[9]

There is a small but growing literature on antebellum urban Catholics and Jews. For Catholics, the place to start is Jay Dolan, *The Immigrant Church: New York's Irish and German Catholics, 1815–1865*. On the contributions of women religious to cities, see Maureen Fitzgerald, *Habits of Compassion: Irish Catholic Nuns and the Origins of New York's Welfare System, 1830–1920*; and Mary Beth Fraser Connolly, *Women of Faith: The Chicago Sisters of Mercy and the Evolution of a Religious Community*.[10] On the shift from a "synagogue-community" to a "community of synagogues" see Jonathan Sarna, *American Judaism: A History*; and Howard Rock, *Haven of Liberty: New York Jews in the New World, 1654–1865*.[11]

For a religious leader who defies simple categorization, see Paul E. Johnson and Sean Wilentz, *The Kingdom of Matthias: A Story of Sex and Salvation in Nineteenth-Century America*.[12]

Pathbreaking works by J. Matthew Gallman, *Mastering Wartime: A Social History of Philadelphia During the Civil War*; and Thomas O'Connor, *Civil War Boston: Home Front and Battlefield*, interweave religion into a much broader analysis of urban wartime experience. For an excellent study of Confederate Richmond during wartime, see Harry S. Stout and Christopher Grasso, "Civil War, Religion, and Communications: The Case of Richmond," in *Religion and the American Civil War*.[13]

Literature on urban religion in the half-century following the Civil War is even more voluminous than the periods before. Late 19th-century accounts of urban Protestant declension include Thomas Dixon Jr. *The Failure of Protestantism in New York and Its Causes*; and William T. Stead, *If Christ Came to Chicago! A Plea for the Union of All Who Love in the Service of All Who Suffer*. Highlights of more recent histories include: on Protestant evangelicals, Bruce Evensen, *God's Man for the Gilded Age: D. L. Moody and the Rise of Mass Evangelism* (2003); and Mathew Bowman, *The Urban Pulpit: New York City and the Fate of Liberal Evangelicalism*. On mainline Protestants, Jon Butler, "Protestant Success in the New American City, 1870–1920: The Anxious Secrets of Rev. Walter Laidlaw, Ph.D.," in *New Directions in American Religious History*. On reformers, Aaron Abell, *The Urban Impact on American Protestantism, 1865–1900*. On religion and the working classes, Herbert Gutman, "Protestantism in the American Labor Movement: The Christian Spirit in the Gilded Age," *American Historical Review*; and Heath Carter, *Union Made: Working People and the Rise of Social Christianity in Chicago*. On the Salvation Army, Diane Winston, *Red-Hot and Righteous: The Urban Religion of the Salvation Army*. On Roman Catholics, see Robert A. Orsi, *The Madonna of 115th Street: Faith and Community in Italian Harlem, 1880–1950*. On Jews, see Annie Pollard and Daniel Soyer, *Emerging Metropolis: New York Jews in the Age of Immigration*.[14]

PRIMARY SOURCES

A vast array of primary source material survives in many different repositories for the study of urban religion in cities before the 20th century.

- *Individuals.* Manuscript journals, diaries, and correspondence for the urban religious can be found in city, state, and national historical societies and libraries. The popular interest in biographies in the 19th century ensured that the papers of many leading religious figures, clerical and lay, were published as memoirs or collected letters. For example, Isabella Marshall Graham, an evangelical Presbyterian who lived in New York City and was active in benevolent causes, is documented in three publications: *The Power of Faith, Exemplified in the Life and Writings of the Late Mrs. Isabella Graham*; *The Unpublished Letters and Correspondence of Mrs. Isabella Graham*; and *The Life of Mrs. Isabella Graham*.[15]

- *Churches.* Manuscript materials, such as membership records; vital records; trustee, elder, and deacon's minutes; financial accounts; Sunday school lists, Torah rolls, and a host of other information related to urban congregations survive to varying degrees. Some can still be found in the safes and cupboards of those churches today, while others have been gathered into local historical societies or denominational archives. Printed materials include hymnbooks, psalters, Bibles, church manuals, sermons, congregational and denominational histories, and broadsides. The Presbyterian Historical Society, in Philadelphia; the American Baptist

Historical Society, at Mercer University, in Macon, Georgia; and the United Methodist Archives and History Center, at Drew University, Madison, NJ, are just a few of the leading denominational repositories. Records for Roman Catholic churches survive in diocesan and archdiocesan archives in cities across the country. For a good overview of church records in general, see United States Church Records. Urban development has claimed many pre-20th-century urban houses of worship, but a number still survive, allowing for the study of their style, form, and layout. Also surviving are many material artifacts—communion vessels, vestments, paintings, and relics—which provide insight into religious beliefs and practices not recorded in printed sources.

- *Institutions and Organizations.* Non-denominational and denominational voluntary associations produced a range of documentary material. Printed materials include tracts and books, annual reports, and newspapers. Manuscript materials include constitutions, meeting notes, registers of beneficiaries of assistance, and more. Some archives of major organizations are still held by them, while others have been deposited with historical societies and archives. The archives of the American Sunday School Union Collection at the Free Library of Philadelphia, for example, has a wealth of materials related to 19th-century evangelical print culture. Occasionally, the physical structures of these institutions survive, but many were torn down after they were no longer useful.
- *The City.* Because urban religion occurred not just in churches and synagogues, but in all spaces of the city, there is a broad range of materials in which evidence of it can be found. Most cities published annual directories that listed houses of worship, benevolent organizations, and other relevant information. City maps were not published with the same frequency, but

they can be used to chart the locations and movement of the religious over time. Council minutes and court records reveal when the religious requested government support (or were called in to defend themselves). City histories often include a chapter or section on religious life. Census records in the second half of the 19th century record more information about religious adherence.

DIGITAL AND VISUAL MATERIALS

- Layout of New Haven, 1641 (http://i1.wp .com/hylbom.com/family/wp-content /uploads/2014/02/New_Haven_1641.jpg)
- Paul Revere, engraver, "A View of Part of the Town of Boston in New-England and British Shops of War Landing their Troops 1768" (http://upload.wikimedia.org/wikipedia /commons/a/a6/Boston_1768.jpg)
- "The Rigging House" (New York, 1846) (http://www.loc.gov/exhibits/religion /images/00264us.jpg)
- Touro Synagogue (Newport, 1763) (https://upload.wikimedia.org/wikipedia /commons/thumb/b/ba/Touro _Synagogue_Newport_Rhode_Island_3 .jpg/1280px-Touro_Synagogue _Newport_Rhode_Island_3.jpg)
- Mother Bethel, African Methodist Episcopal (AME) Church (http://images .nypl.org/index.php?id=1231517&t=w)
- "Representation of the Old Brewery, at the Five Points, in New York" (http://www .anthropologyinpractice.com/2010/04 /five-points-then-and-now-landmarks .html) (c. 1853)
- Destruction of the St. Augustine's Church (https://en.wikipedia.org/wiki /Philadelphia_nativist_riots#/media /File:Riots1844staugestine.jpg) in nativist riots (Philadelphia, 1844)
- The Prophet! A Full and Accurate Report of the Judicial Proceedings in the

Extraordinary and Highly Interesting Case of Matthews, alias Matthias (http://4.bp .blogspot.com/_RHk5fP6iA9w /TFRW6rzXnSI/AAAAAAAAAks /_xVYHcAdbPE/s1600/TheProphet .png) (New York, 1834)

- Plum Street Temple (http://digital.libraries .uc.edu/exhibits/arb/sacredSpaces /EighthandPlumStSynagogue.jpg) (Cincinnati, 1866)
- Salvation Army Band and War Chariot (http://s3.amazonaws.com/use-cache .salvationarmy.org/d2eca9b5-294d-47 af-9850-0b4848ad3146_mas_his_band _chariot_710.jpg) (Boston, late 19th century)
- "An Actual Scene at One of the Sessions of the Parliament" (http://publications .newberry.org/outofmany/files/original /e06289ee29afe8b35df627eadd9a5d67 .jpg) (World Parliament of Religions, Chicago, 1893)

DIGITAL RESOURCES

Scholars are increasingly creating new digital resources with primary and secondary material related to urban religion in urban America. To get a sense of the range of work being done, see:

- *Houses of Worship* (https:// housesofworship.umn.edu/items): documents the congregations and houses of worship that developed in the Twin Cities between 1849 and 1924
- *Issac Mayer Wise Digital Archive* (http:// americanjewisharchives.org/collections /wise/home.php): electronic edition of the correspondence and published writings of the organizational genius behind the rise of American Reform Judaism in the late 19th century
- *Jesuit Libraries Provenance Project* (http:// jesuitlibrariesprovenanceproject.com/): a reconstruction of a 19th-century urban Catholic college library

- *Out of Many: Religious Pluralism in America* (http://publications.newberry.org /outofmany/): a digital archive of primary sources from the Newberry Library related to the diversity of American faiths

FURTHER READING

Bilhartz, Terry D. *Urban Religion and the Second Great Awakening: Church and Society in Early National Baltimore*. Rutherford, NJ: Fairleigh Dickinson University Press, 1986.

Boyer, Paul S. *Urban Masses and Moral Order in America, 1820–1920*. Cambridge, MA: Harvard University Press, 1978.

Dixon, Thomas, Jr. *The Failure of Protestantism in New York and Its Causes*. New York : Strauss and Rehn, 1896.

Dolan, Jay. *The Immigrant Church: New York's Irish and German Catholics, 1815–1865*. Baltimore: Johns Hopkins University Press, 1975.

Dorsey, Bruce. *Reforming Men and Women: Gender in the Antebellum City*. Ithaca, NY: Cornell University Press, 2002.

Goodfriend, Joyce. *Before the Melting Pot: Society and Culture in Colonial New York City, 1664–1730*. Princeton, NJ: Princeton University Press, 1992.

Knaut, Andrew. *The Pueblo Revolt of 1680: Conquest and Resistance in Seventeenth-Century New Mexico*. Norman: University of Oklahoma Press, 1995.

Moore, Deborah Dash. *Urban Origins of American Judaism*. Athens, GA: University of Georgia Press, 2014.

Orsi, Robert A. *Gods of the City: Religion and the American Urban Landscape*. Bloomington: Indiana University Press, 1999.

Winston, Diane. *Red-Hot and Righteous: The Urban Religion of the Salvation Army*. Cambridge, MA: Harvard University Press, 1999.

NOTES

1. Thomas Dixon Jr., *The Failure of Protestantism in New York and Its Causes* (New York: Strauss and Rehn, 1896), 112, 110; also by Dixon, *The Clansman: An Historical Romance of the Ku Klux Klan* (New York: Grosset and Dunlap, 1905).
2. Robert A. Orsi, ed. *Gods of the City: Religion and the American Urban Landscape* (Burlington: Indiana University Press, 1999), 43.

3. The image of rioting is from J. B. Perry, *A Full and Complete Account of the Late Awful Riots in Philadelphia* (Philadelphia: Nafis and Cornish, 1844), opposite page 6.

4. F. W. Brown, *Cincinnati and Vicinity: An Alphabetically Arranged Index and Descriptive Guide to Places, Institutions, Societies, Amusements, Resorts, Etc., In and About the City of Cincinnati* (Cincinnati, OH: Press of C. J. Krehbiel, 1898), opposite page 46.

5. W. T. Stead, *General Booth, a Biographical Sketch* (London: Isbister, 1891), 79.

6. William T. Stead, *If Christ Came to Chicago! A Plea for the Union of All Who Love in the Service of All Who Suffer* (Chicago: Laird & Lee, 1894).

7. See Hasia Diner, *The Jews of the United States, 1654–2000* (Berkeley: University of California Press, 2004); Jonathan Sarna, *American Judaism: A History* (New Haven, CT: Yale University Press, 2004); and Deborah Dash Moore, *Urban Origins of American Judaism* (Athens, GA: University of Georgia Press, 2014). On Roman Catholics, see Jay Dolan, *The American Catholic Experience: A History from Colonial Times to the Present* (Garden City, NY: Doubleday, 1985); John McGreevy, *Catholicism and American Freedom: A History* (New York: Norton, 2003); and James O'Toole, *The Faithful: A History of Catholics in America* (Cambridge, MA: Belknap, 2008).

8. Orsi, *Gods of the City*; and Jon Butler, "Religion in the City: Faith That Could Not Be," *U.S. Catholic Historian* 22 (Spring 2004), 51–61. Howard P. Chudacoff and Judith E. Smith cover urban history in *The Evolution of American Urban Society* (Boston: Pearson, 2015).

9. Andrew Knaut, *The Pueblo Revolt of 1680: Conquest and Resistance in Seventeenth-Century New Mexico* (Norman: University of Oklahoma Press, 1995); Carl Bridenbaugh, *Cities in the Wilderness: The First Century of Urban Life in America, 1625–1742* (New York: Oxford University Press, 1971); and in *Cities in Revolt: Urban Life in America, 1743–1776* (New York: Alfred A. Knopf, 1955). See also Joyce Goodfriend, *Before the Melting Pot: Society and Culture in Colonial New York City, 1664–1730* (Princeton, NJ: Princeton University Press, 1992); David G. Hackett, *The Rude Hand of Innovation: Religion and Social Order in Albany, New York, 1652–1836* (New York: Oxford University Press, 1991); and Darrett B. Rutman, *Winthrop's Boston: A Portrait of a Puritan Town, 1630–1649* (New York: W. W. Norton, 1965).

10. Gary Nash, *The Urban Crucible: Social Change, Political Consciousness, and the Origins of the American Revolution* (Cambridge, MA: Harvard University Press, 1979); Benjamin L. Carp, *Rebels Rising: Cities and the American Revolution* (Oxford: Oxford University Press, 2007); and Alfred Young, *Liberty Tree: Ordinary People and the American Revolution* (New York: New York University Press, 2006).

11. Richard Pointer, *Protestant Pluralism and the New York Experience: A Study of Eighteenth-Century Diversity* (Bloomington: Indiana University Press, 1998). On Methodists, see Dee Andrews, *The Methodists and Revolutionary America: The Shaping of an Evangelical Culture* (Princeton, NJ: Princeton University Press, 2000). On the African American church, see Gary Nash, *Forging Freedom: The Formation of Philadelphia's Black Community, 1720–1840* (Cambridge, MA: Harvard University Press, 1988); Kyle Bulthius, *Four Steeples Over the City Streets: Religion and Society in New York's Early Republic Congregations* (New York: New York University Press, 2014); and Craig Townsend, *Faith in Their Own Color: Black Episcopalians in Antebellum New York City* (New York: Columbia University Press, 2005). On constitution writing and trusteeism among Roman Catholics, see Patrick Carey, *People, Priests and Prelates: Ecclesiastical Democracy and the Tensions of Trusteeism* (Notre Dame, IN: University of Notre Dame, 1987).

12. Carroll Smith-Rosenberg, *Religion and the Rise of the American City: The New York City Mission Movement, 1812–1870* (Ithaca, NY: Cornell University Press, 1971); and Paul Boyer, *Urban Masses and Moral Order in America, 1820–1920* (Cambridge, MA: Harvard University Press, 1978). On revivalism and reform, see Paul Johnson, *A Shopkeeper's Millennium: Society and Revivals in Rochester, New York, 1815–1837* (New York: Hill and Wang, 1979); and Terry Bilhartz, *Urban Religion and the Second Great Awakening: Church and Society in Early National Baltimore* (Rutherford, NJ: Fairleigh Dickinson University Press, 1986). On the importance of class, Mark S. Schantz, *Piety in Providence: Class Dimensions of Religious Experience in Antebellum Rhode Island* (Ithaca, NY: Cornell University Press, 2000); and Jama Lazerow, *Religion and the Working Class in Antebellum America* (Washington: Smithsonian Institution Press, 1995). On gender

in reform, see Nancy Hewitt, *Women's Activism and Social Change: Rochester, New York, 1822–1872* (Ithaca, NY: Cornell University Press, 1984); and Bruce Dorsey, *Reforming Men and Women: Gender in the Antebellum City* (Ithaca, NY: Cornell University Press, 2002). On the Businessman's Revival, see Timothy L. Smith, *Revivalism and Social Reform in Mid-Nineteenth-Century America* (New York: Abingdon, 1957); and Kathryn Long, *The Revival of 1857–58: Interpreting an American Religious Awakening* (New York: Oxford University Press, 1998).

13. Jay Dolan, *The Immigrant Church: New York's Irish and German Catholics, 1815–1865* (Baltimore: Johns Hopkins University Press, 1975). On women's contributions, see Maureen Fitzgerald, *Habits of Compassion: Irish Catholic Nuns and the Origins of New York's Welfare System, 1830–1920* (Urbana: University of Illinois Press, 2006); and Mary Beth Fraser Connolly, *Women of Faith: The Chicago Sisters of Mercy and the Evolution of a Religious Community* (New York: Fordham University Press, 2014).

14. For synagogues in community, see Jonathan Sarna, *American Judaism: A History* (New Haven, CT: Yale University Press, 2004); and Howard Rock and Deborah Moore, *Haven of Liberty: New York Jews in the New World, 1654–1865* (New York: New York University Press, 2012).

15. Paul E. Johnson and Sean Wilentz, *The Kingdom of Matthias: A Story of Sex and Salvation in Nineteenth-Century America* (New York: Oxford University Press, 1994).

Kyle B. Roberts

RELIGION IN THE AMERICAN CITY, 1900–2000

THE MINARET AND THE FERRIS WHEEL

The first mosques constructed in America were intended to be sideshows more than places of worship, but the religious histories of urban landscapes are rarely what they seem. Built on Chicago's Midway Plaisance by organizers of the World's Columbian Exposition of 1893, the mosques were the centerpieces of elaborate re-creations of notable Islamic sites intended to transport visitors to a "typical" Tunisian village, Ottoman palace, or Cairo street. Indeed, planners placed such a premium on the authenticity of these sites that they paid foreign nationals from Egypt, Tunisia, Syria, and other regions to work as actors at these and other international pavilions. Although fairgoers looked upon these mosques only as attractions, the Middle Eastern workers, many of whom were Muslim, used them for genuine religious purposes. As one newspaper reported, "every detail of Mohammedan worship" could be found in the mosques, from special services to the daily calls to prayer. Nor did Islam's presence in the United States end after these faux houses of worship came down. By 1900 a sizeable portion of the nearly one thousand Syrians who called Chicago home had come to the United States by way of the Midway Plaisance.[1]

In addition to Islam, the Columbian Exposition introduced American visitors to many other faith traditions. Alongside the Plaisance's attractions, the fair hosted a World's Parliament of Religions in September, which hosted more than two hundred delegates from religions across the globe for two weeks of interfaith dialogue. Organizers claimed that the Parliament offered the country's first public lectures by a Hindu swami, Buddhist monk, and Jain priest. Though these and other non-Christian faiths enjoyed a long presence in America through Asian immigrations on the West Coast as well as through the Atlantic slave trade, the Parliament for the first time brought together religious leaders who gave these religions institutional support. The Hindu Swami Vivekananda, for example, followed his widely reported visit to the Parliament with a nationwide speaking tour. Before he returned to India, Vivekananda organized dozens of Vedanta societies in cities big and small, where communities of largely white converts practiced yoga. The Japanese Buddhist Shaku Soyen and the Zen monk Anagarika Dharmapala of Ceylon (modern Sri Lanka) similarly stayed in or returned to

America after the Exposition in order to organize new centers of meditation.

The Columbian Exposition heralded a number of themes that would define the religious history of American cities throughout the 20th century. The first was growing religious diversity. By the century's end, nearly every religious tradition had found a place in America's cities as changes in US immigration policy shifted the flow of immigrants from largely Catholic and Jewish centers throughout Europe to religiously diverse regions across Asia, Africa, and Latin America. At the same time, these established faiths were joined by a number of homegrown religious movements born of the city's diverse milieu. Second, the Exposition highlights how the spiritual lives of cities increasingly found expression in consumer culture. In the same way that Muslims prayed in a carnival attraction and visitors witnessed Islam while riding the Ferris wheel, citydwellers increasingly encountered new faiths or performed their own either in or in reaction to the marketplace. Urban religious institutions frequently arose in order to help their members navigate or protest the industrial economy as more and more city dwellers suffered under its excesses. Finally, the history, use, and eventual destruction of the Exposition's mosques illustrate the relationship between religious communities and the built environment. Much as Muslims at the Exposition repurposed a carnival attraction for their own use, the religious histories of American cities often reflect adaptation and reuse. Urban religious communities often made even the most secular sites into sacred spaces, worshiping in storefronts, on the airwaves, and even in sports leagues. But as the mosques' ultimate destruction also conveys, the urban devout often lived their lives amid political and economic forces beyond their control.

Studying the religious life of American cities involves more than simply documenting the activities of religious communities who happen to find themselves in urban spaces. It also requires attending to the impact city life had on

religious expression, as well as how religious communities shaped the social life of cities. "Urban religion," the historian Robert A. Orsi suggests, "is what comes from the dynamic engagement of religious traditions . . . with specific features of the industrial and post-industrial cityscapes and with the social conditions of city life."[2] This interplay has not only yielded distinctly urban religious forms and subjectivities, but has also imprinted religious life onto the American city. The remainder of this article surveys the history of urban religion throughout the 20th century, moving through four overlapping phases of religious and urban development. Beginning with the Protestant response to the influx of Catholic immigrants into the city, the article also considers the dynamic rise of new religious movements driven in part by the religious creativity of African Americans who migrated to cities throughout the century, the religious history of suburbanization in the postwar era, and the remarkable religious diversity of the contemporary city made possible by changes in US immigration law.

CATHOLIC CITY, PROTESTANT RESPONSE, 1900s–1920s

Before the calendar even officially flipped over to 1901, many observers had already concluded that the 20th century would be the century of the city. "We must face the inevitable," the Social Gospel minister Josiah Strong proclaimed in 1898. "The new civilization is certain to be urban; and the problem of the twentieth century will be the city." Statistics certainly supported Strong's contention. Where the United States had only six cities of more than one hundred thousand residents in 1850, the 1900 census counted thirty-eight. Within twenty years' time, more than half the nation would call cities home. But Strong's portrayal of the city as a "problem" was a far more loaded and subjective assessment; it reflected his particularly Anglo-Protestant fears over specific conditions of urban living that posed a threat to Protestantism's cultural dominance. Such concerns would animate the era's religious developments.[3]

This is not to say that life in the early 20th-century city was not without its challenges. The rapid, largely unregulated industrialization that fueled urban growth throughout the 19th century generated numerous social problems. Industrial slums, tenement districts, and other concentrated sites of poverty plagued nearly every American city, from established industrial metropolises like New York and Chicago to emerging New South cities like Atlanta and Charlotte, as well as West Coast hubs like Seattle and San Francisco. The lack of sanitation, adequate housing, and city services that defined these areas not only subjected their residents to horrendous living conditions but also shocked many middle-class observers. Equally as troubling, however, were the residents who came to populate these areas. From New York City's Five Points neighborhood, where Irish Catholics lived, to San Francisco's Chinatown, immigrants had long called these industrial districts home. The first decades of the 20th century, however, saw a decisive shift in both the origin and scale of immigration to the United States. In contrast to the 19th century, when a majority of immigrants originated from northern European regions such as Ireland, Germany, and Britain, by 1900 immigration shifted dramatically to people from southern and eastern Europe. By then, a handful of American cities were home to some of the world's largest concentrations of Jews, Poles, Italians, and certain other nationalities.

For white, middle-class, Anglo-Protestant observers like Josiah Strong, then, the "problem" of the city was as much about the threat it posed to Protestantism's longstanding hold on America's moral order as it was about the conditions under which Jews, Catholics, and other religious communities lived. For Strong, the deplorable living conditions produced by industrial capitalism signaled the declining influence of Christian benevolence in the country, while the scale of European immigration raised the specter of foreign rule. Reestablishing Protestantism's moral and cultural authority over the city therefore became a central concern of many ecclesiastical and interdenominational associations in this era, inspiring several developments that contributed to the growing divide among Protestantism's major theological camps. More liberal Protestants, for example, turned from the moral reform campaigns that had defined 19th-century urban evangelism and embraced more academic and professional methods that could alleviate the inequalities of industrial capitalism. Long-established settlement houses and institutional churches like Chicago's Hull House (1889) or New York City's Henry Street Settlement (1893) increasingly incorporated the practices of social workers and the survey methods of social scientists into their work. For these exemplars of the Social Gospel, the city's spiritual redemption was dependent upon first addressing citydwellers' material needs.

In contrast, a growing network of evangelical Protestants argued that the city could be redeemed only by vigorously recommitting to personal piety and social morality. The first two decades of the 20th century witnessed a series of large-scale urban revivals led by evangelists who preached an "old-time" religion while also promoting numerous moral reforms. The famed evangelist Billy Sunday, for example, preached the gospel of both Jesus and Prohibition on the revival circuit, using his stops in cities big and small to promote the passage of local option laws and, eventually, the Eighteenth Amendment. While liberal Protestants decried these efforts as regressive, evangelicals were anything but antimodern. Many were among the most cosmopolitan innovators of their time, repurposing consumer culture for religious ends. Sunday effectively employed secular advertising methods in his campaigns, while the founder of the International Church of the Foursquare Gospel, Aimee Semple McPherson, built radio towers instead of church steeples atop her Angelus

Temple in Los Angeles in order to broadcast her sermons across the country. Nor did the evangelical emphasis on personal conversion necessitate a rejection of social welfare. Though founded in mid-19th-century London, the Salvation Army continued to thrive in American cities through a series of spectacular urban welfare campaigns like the "Christmas kettle" fund drives. Other evangelical leaders established a number of alternative urban missionary training centers, such as the Moody Bible Institute (1886), the Bible Institute of Los Angeles (1908), and Northwestern Bible and Missionary Training School in Minneapolis (1902), which became headquarters of the fundamentalist movement in their battles with theological modernists throughout the early 20th century.

While native-born Protestants of every theological stripe attempted to claim control over the urban landscape, the immigrant Catholics and Jews who were the target of these efforts busied themselves with creating safe havens of their own within the city. Churches and synagogues proved vital in this regard, proclaiming in stone their sense of ownership over portions of the city. These houses of worship were not only the seats of religious communities but also the anchors of entire social worlds which helped immigrant families navigate the industrial economy while reinforcing their ethnic identity. The concentration of some forty Orthodox Jewish shuls, or synagogues, along Chicago's Maxwell Street, for instance, also allowed for the growth of a an open-air market where eastern European Jews could buy and sell religious and ethnic wares. Roman Catholic parishes similarly became sites of ethnic identity and social mobility where religious practices connected immigrants to the old world while helping them thrive in the new. Following practices established in the 19th century, most dioceses created "national" parishes that allowed particular immigrant groups to express the particularities of their ethnic faith through architectural styles or religious practices. The *festa* to Our Lady of

Mt. Carmel in Harlem, for example, allowed Italians to create a cultural connection to home which the experience of immigration had severed, while devotions to Our Lady of Guadalupe in San Antonio helped Mexican Americans celebrate their ethnic identity amid a growing Anglo population hostile to it. Despite their diversity, however, virtually every national parish hosted numerous sodalities, benevolent organizations, and clubs that provided the church's working-class parishioners not only with religious instruction but also with important social and professional networks. They organized athletic leagues, employment agencies, and even some labor unions, all of which helped immigrant Catholics thrive in the urban world.

The influence that immigrant Catholics and Jews exercised over the urban landscape was profound. In most cities they overlaid a sacred topography atop the city streets that for many residents ordered the urban world. Catholics, for example, often described their place in the city not by what neighborhood they lived in but by what parish they were from, while official city names like Chicago's Maxwell Street or New York's Lower East Side came to refer to the Jewish communities who lived there more than their geographic location. In many cities these overlapping ethnic and religious identifications persisted even well after immigrant families left the area. And by 1920, the ethnic composition of many industrial cities did begin to change. World War I and the passage of restrictive immigration laws in 1924 effectively closed America's borders to European immigration, cutting off the arrival of newcomers who had regularly bolstered ethnic communities. The nationalism and nativism that lay behind these events also prompted a number of concerted Americanization campaigns intended to shear immigrants of their old-world traditions. Federal agencies, Protestant organizations like the YMCA, and even a number of influential Catholic and Jewish leaders conspired to assimilate the nation's immigrants. Major urban bishops such as

Minneapolis's John Ireland and Chicago's George Mundelein blocked the formation of national parishes and mandated the use of English in parochial schools, while established Jewish communities contributed extensively to the formation of Jewish settlement houses in order to bring more Orthodox Jews arriving from southern and eastern Europe under Reformed Judaism's influence. The biggest change in the religious history of American cities, however, came in the arrival of an entirely new community of residents who would transform not only urban spaces but the whole nation.

NEW PEOPLES, NEW FAITHS, 1920s–1940s

Though immigrants and their children comprised a large portion of the urban population throughout the 20th century, the demographics of American cities shifted significantly in the decades after World War I. African Americans from the rural South migrated to northern cities in massive numbers throughout this era, drawn by economic opportunities and the chance to flee Jim Crow segregation. Nearly 2 million black southerners migrated northward before 1930, many of them settling in industrial centers such as New York, Pittsburgh, Cleveland, and Chicago. Those who settled along the nation's Eastern Seaboard also joined some 140,000 Afro-Caribbeans who immigrated to America's cities in search of greater opportunity in the decade before the nation's strict immigration laws went into effect. These urban newcomers not only transformed many preexisting religious communities but yielded a host of new ones as well.

Many historic African American congregations attempted to incorporate the rapidly arriving southerners through direct outreach or expanded social services, but encounters between established black communities and southern migrants were often fraught affairs. In addition to being relatively small, most northern African American churches at the start of the 20th century tended to be largely middle-class congregations who supported longstanding denominations such as the African Methodist Episcopal Church or the National Baptist Association. In contrast, most southern migrants were unskilled laborers with a broader set of religious affiliations, including Holiness and Pentecostal associations that originated in the South. Some migrants bristled at the expectation of religious leaders that they adopt the middle-class sensibilities of their northern neighbors in order to join their churches and opted to organize their own congregations instead. The rapid proliferation of the Church of God in Christ, Pentecostal Holiness Associations and even unaffiliated charismatic or apostolic assemblies in black neighborhoods reflected the religious transformations brought on by this demographic and cultural change.

Ever since the journalist H. L. Mencken, while covering the Scopes Monkey Trial in 1925, had depicted Pentecostals as culturally backward "holy rollers" whose home was in the countryside, observers and scholars alike have characterized Pentecostalism as an antimodern reaction to the traumas and excesses of contemporary life.[4] Yet southern Pentecostal migrants proved remarkably adept at successfully navigating the urban environment. Indeed, Pentecostalism's emergence on the national stage was on Los Angeles's Azusa Street, where a massive, nearly decade-long revival began in 1906. Led by William J. Seymour, a Louisiana-born son of former slaves who migrated to Los Angeles by way of Kansas, the revivalists deftly repurposed urban spaces for their own purposes. Seymour himself held revival services in a former stable, while his followers occupied homes, business, and abandoned warehouses. This became a hallmark of many urban Pentecostal and Holiness denominations. Many assumed ownership of formerly white churches and synagogues whose members had fled the city. Even more formed in old storefronts, where the only cost associated with starting a church was a month's rent.

By the 1930s, a distinct African American sacred topography had developed in most cities, where businesses and religious associations mingled along the main streets of every "Black Belt" or segregated neighborhood.

Such unconventional congregations in part reflected the limited means of the individuals who founded them, but they also conveyed Pentecostalism's entrepreneurial ethos. In contrast to most historic denominations, which located religious authority in the ordination conferred by ecclesiastical bodies, Pentecostals argued that the Holy Spirit's calling would be proved in the success of their efforts. In addition to making space for several female preachers and religious leaders, this belief also privileged innovative approaches to religious expression that allowed Pentecostalism to thrive. Nowhere is this more clearly seen in than in the development of gospel music. Like fellow Pentecostal Aimee Semple McPherson, many southern migrants took to the airwaves to broadcast their services. But alongside their messages ministers also showcased the new, urban sound of their choir directors. Mixing the rhythms of jazz and blues with messages from the Bible, gospel music directly reflected the tastes and experiences of southern migrants. It also became a musical genre that reached beyond black communities. Many gospel innovators, such as Chicago's Thomas A. Dorsey and New Orleans's native Mahalia Jackson, whom Dorsey mentored, went on to become internationally recognized recording artists for such hits as "Precious Lord, Take My Hand." For these and many other gospel musicians, commercial culture became not only an outlet to spread the good news but also an avenue toward a livelihood. Gospel music also became a fount that influenced American culture more broadly. Even secular musicians like Ray Charles and Aretha Franklin, a southern migrant and a child of one, respectively, honed their talents performing in black churches.

The Great Migration's movement of people also gave rise to a number of new religious movements that departed even further from the dominant Protestant culture. The Barbadian immigrant Arnold Josiah Ford, for example, abandoned Christianity altogether and founded an African American Jewish congregation in 1924. An early advocate for the United Negro Improvement Association founder Marcus Garvey's black nationalist vision that people of African descent should unite and build self-sustaining communities, Ford determined that only a reclaimed Jewish identity could promote black self-determination. Similarly, the southern migrant Thomas (or Timothy) Drew determined that "Negro" was an artificial construction imposed upon blacks by white slaveholders. After founding the Moorish Science Temple in Chicago in 1925, Drew called upon African Americans to return to what he claimed was their rightful Islamic heritage as descendants of the Moors. To emphasize this break, Drew encouraged followers to forsake their Christian names for more holy designations. Drew himself took the name Noble Drew Ali, and by the time of his death in 1929 he had helped found dozens of temples with thousands of members. The movement fractured after his death, however, and in the absence of a clear leader the most prominent Islamic group to emerge was Wallace Fard's Nation of Islam (NOI). Fard, who may have been a member of Drew Ali's Moorish Science Temple, founded the NOI in Detroit sometime in the early 1930s and quickly amassed a following. After Fard's disappearance in 1934, a former Baptist minister from Georgia named Elijah Poole succeeded him as NOI's leader. An early convert of Fard, Poole eventually took the name Elijah Poole Muhammad, declared himself to be the Messenger of Allah, and taught that Fard had been God in the flesh. Like Fard and Garvey, Muhammad advocated the reestablishment of black communities. But alongside self-determination Muhammad injected an antagonistic cosmology that predicted the United States' ultimate destruction and called upon African Americans to secure not only their cultural independence but also political and territorial autonomy.

While the Nation of Islam, the Moorish Science Temple, and numerous other new religious movements accounted for a relatively small portion of the Great Migration's urban religious landscape when compared to the number of African Americans who remained in established churches, their cultural impact extended well beyond mere membership. Their existence afforded African American communities the opportunity to reimagine their identity in a new urban environment. The collective emphasis of these movements on the importance of self-determination also contributed to the social and commercial infrastructure of many black communities. While not every southern migrant agreed with the NOI's rejection of Christianity, many still appreciated and frequented the black-owned businesses and community centers NOI temples helped support and that Elijah Poole Muhammad claimed were crucial to the race's survival.

SOULS AND THE SUBURBS, 1940s–1960s

Southern migrants repurposed many storefronts because their previous owners were increasingly abandoning the city as the 20th century progressed. Streetcars and other forms of mass transit had facilitated the outward migration of well-to-do congregations since the late 19th century, but the process increased dramatically in the decades after World War II. Driven by federal housing policies and a sustained postwar economic boom, fully 80 percent of US population growth between 1950 and 1970 occurred in suburban areas. Planned communities of single-family homes like the pioneering Levittown, which opened outside New York City in 1946, encircled established cities throughout the north, while Sunbelt cities such as Miami, Dallas, and Los Angeles developed as a network of residential subdivisions. Connected to urban centers by a recently developed federal highway system, these new communities transformed the American urban landscape from a series of dense industrial districts into sprawling regional metropolises composed of inner cities, the surrounding suburbs, and a number of "edge cities," or exurban business districts, where growing numbers of suburbanites shopped and worked.

Suburban development also transformed America's religious landscape. A sizable portion of families who moved to the suburbs after World War II included second- and third-generation Catholic and Jewish immigrants who had recently joined the middle class by way of high union wages and programs in the Servicemen's Readjustment Act of 1944, better known as the GI Bill. While their predecessors had built the tight-knit ethnic enclaves that defined the 19th-century city, these new suburbanites settled in religiously integrated spaces defined more by class. To some observers, such interfaith residential patterns heralded a new spiritual watershed. As the sociologist Will Herberg argued in his widely popular survey of postwar religious life *Protestant, Catholic, Jew* (1955), the commercial amenities of suburban life had stripped away the ethnic or cultural differences that had divided America's religions and revealed the "spiritual values" they all shared. Buying a house, going to church, and participating in politics were all ritual expressions of a civil religion whose creed was "the American way of life." While differences between religions would certainly persist, it now mattered less to what religion an individual belonged, so long as they were religious. "By and large, to be an American today means to be either a Protestant, a Catholic, or a Jew," Herberg wrote of this suburban reality. "Not to be a Catholic, a Protestant, or a Jew today is not to be anything, not to have a *name.*"[5]

Herberg's assessment of suburban religious life was apt. The Cold War demonization of the Soviet Union placed a premium on America's constitutional commitment to religious liberty, which supported a pluralistic conception of the nation as one built on "Judeo-Christian" values. Americans also reported a greater appreciation of religious life after World War II, as survey after survey found that the nation's religious membership had reached historic highs. As one 1959 poll determined, fully 60 percent of the population claimed to belong to some religious denomination—the highest such number in American history. And as Herberg hypothesized, the religious sensibilities of middle-class Catholics, Protestants, and Jews mirrored one another in crucial ways. This was especially seen in the explosion in church construction that accompanied suburban development. Unlike their inner-city forebears, where the built environment proclaimed in stone the congregation's ethnic or theological distinctiveness, the churches and synagogues constructed in America's suburbs largely embraced modernist architectural styles whose abstract designs and technological triumphalism reflected their collective embrace of consumer culture.

Beneath the surface of this interfaith veneer, however, were numerous fault lines. Poets, writers, and other figures of the Beat Generation argued that while postwar Americans might have found religion, the oppressive uniformity of suburbia revealed that they had no soul. Reclaiming urban spaces abandoned by suburbanites, such as Haight-Ashbury in San Francisco and Greenwich Village in New York City, these countercultural prophets offered up an urban religious vision that eschewed tradition and reveled in the city's diversity. From their bohemian enclaves, Jack Kerouac and Allen Ginsberg embraced not only Asian spirituality but also the revelatory power of urban commercial staples such as art galleries and the theater. Nor were the Beats the only figures concerned about the effects suburban culture had on the nation's soul. While more conservative, straitlaced figures like the evangelical minister Billy Graham never embraced the intemperance of beatnik spirituality, they nonetheless shared their concern that America's postwar consumer culture was a sign of its moral decline. A North Carolina Southern Baptist minister educated at Wheaton College in Illinois, Graham became a national figure in 1947 after

hosting a successful revival campaign in Los Angeles. Calling upon Americans to forgo both the hedonism of the Beats and the shallow spirituality of the suburbs, Graham helped revive conservative evangelicals through an ongoing series of urban crusades that laid the groundwork for the rise of the "religious right."

Even in the suburbs, however, the portrayal of suburbia as peaceful, homogenous, and uneventful ultimately broke down. Surveys of suburban life found that Catholics and Jews continued to feel excluded by their Protestant neighbors despite their shared economic status. Levittown, for example, saw tensions emerge over a youth sports league after Protestant residents complained that their working-class Catholic neighbors taught their children to compete too roughly. As a result, suburban Catholics and Jews across the country continued to place a premium on organizing their own social and recreational associations. When matters turned to questions of schooling, zoning, or municipal governance, tensions sometimes erupted into open conflict. School board elections in particular were often tense as Protestant, Catholic, and Jewish families variously accused one another either of injecting religion into or removing religion from public education. The suburban hamlet of Rutherford, New Jersey, for example, became the site of contentious legal battles in 1951 after the local school board voted to allow the Gideons society to distribute Protestant Bibles to students. Despite the board's requirement that the Gideons give Bibles only to students whose parents signed a waiver, Catholic and Jewish families successfully argued that the board's approval amounted to religious establishment. Though the case never made it beyond the New Jersey Supreme Court, it was indicative of the religious currents of suburban communities across the country. Indeed, many of the US Supreme Court's landmark cases on religion in public education began as suburban school conflicts.

The religious integration of suburban America, however, was based on its complete racial segregation. While postwar suburbs were home to Protestants, Catholics, and Jews, race-based housing practices at both the federal and local levels ensured that they remained exclusively white. Indeed, white families fleeing the city's growing African American population had propelled suburban development. Some 5 million black southerners migrated to cities across the north between 1940 and 1970, a process some historians refer to as the Great Migration's second wave. The process decreased the overall population of many cities while simultaneously increasing African Americans' demographic prominence. The result proved disastrous for urban African American communities. In addition to relocating a sizable portion of the urban tax base, the federal highway system also demolished viable working-class communities as the roads were laid. Historic black communities like New York's Harlem and Chicago's Bronzeville quickly became overcrowded, while the decline in municipal services led to rapid neighborhood decay. What federal money cities did see after World War II often came in the form of poorly planned public housing projects whose construction only demolished more potential residential areas. Designed by reformers who, like their Protestant forebears, believed urban life stunted community growth, these projects, under the ironic label of "urban renewal," leveled the churches, homes, and storefronts of vibrant African American communities.

In the same way that religious institutions facilitated the growth of black communities during the Great Migration, prominent ministers, local congregations, and religious rituals and symbols helped African Americans challenge social injustice in the postwar city. Religious communities catalyzed local efforts to combat Jim Crow, while ministers stood at the forefront of many campaigns for civil rights as respected, and connected, community leaders. The famed Montgomery bus boycott in 1955, for example, began as a one-day protest over the city's segregated transit system. But after thousands of members of the African American community met in local churches and organized the Montgomery Improvement Association, the boycott carried on for a year, led by a then largely unknown minister, Martin Luther King Jr., who had become the association's president at the community's insistence. This pattern was repeated in cities across the South, as urban ministers like Birmingham's Fred Shuttlesworth and Tallahassee's C. K. Steele became the public faces not only of local campaigns for justice but also of the national civil rights movement through the Southern Christian Leadership Conference (SCLC), which they helped found.

Although substantial differences existed between the religious histories of urban and suburban developments in this era, campaigns to address injustices were also marked by growing interfaith efforts. King especially made religious collaboration a central part of his leadership, claiming that every faith shared a commitment to justice and nonviolence. The struggle for civil rights in America's cities more broadly was defined by its religious diversity. An influential Nation of Islam member, Malcom X, disagreed with the SCLC's willingness to work with white religious leaders and politicians. But Malcolm's advocacy for African American self-determination by "any means necessary" was rooted in NOI teachings, to which this Omaha, Nebraska native, born Malcolm Little, had converted in the late 1940s.

Other urban religious activists used the civil rights movement as an opportunity to address the racial injustices of their own institutions. After northern Catholic churches found themselves faced with declining membership due to suburbanization, a number of parish priests began concerted efforts to aid black communities. Following what came to be called "the Chicago plan" after a number of South Side Catholic churches transitioned from being the home of white ethnics to vibrant African American parishes, a handful of priests in northern cities opened churches and schools as resources for their new neighbors. In the process, some came to criticize the Roman Catholic Church's implication in the decline of American cities. Milwaukee's Father James Groppi became both a civil rights activist and a vocal critic of the church's racial biases. The son of Italian immigrants, Groppi criticized not only his white brethren for engaging in racist housing practices, but also the church for divesting in urban spaces by shuttering city churches in order to follow white parishioners to the suburbs. The suburb and the city, then, were never as disconnected from each other as the spaces between them might imply.

GLOBAL CITIES, GLOBAL FAITHS, 1970s–2000s

The strains placed upon cities by suburbanization only increased at the end of the 20th century. Manufacturing firms soon joined white middle-class families in leaving the city, relocating to non-union sectors of the Sunbelt South or abroad. This flight of capital affected the entire US economy as manufacturing went from comprising fully one-third of the nation's economic output to just over 10 percent at the turn of the millennium. Deindustrialization particularly affected northern cities born of the Industrial Revolution. Detroit, for example, had already lost half of its manufacturing jobs by 1977 and would see most of the rest leave by the century's end. The process amplified the decline in central business districts already underway since the end of World War II, as the newly rechristened "Rust Belt" became subject to staggering rates of unemployment, crime, and poverty. Entire tracts of many inner cities became filled with shuttered factories, abandoned businesses, and boarded-up homes, leading to the widespread perception that the American city was in crisis.

Decline, however, is always a relative register, an interpretation of change rooted in presumptions about what constitutes normalcy. Despite their many challenges, cities witnessed something of a revival at the turn of the 21st century. First, America's rate of urbanization

had continued unabated throughout the entire 20th century. Much of this growth took place in cities throughout the Sunbelt, which benefited from the Rust Belt's economic decline. But metropolitan regions as a whole also saw their numbers continue to climb. According to the 2010 Census, more than 80 percent of the US population then lived in metropolitan statistical areas, the highest such number in American history.

The kinds of people moving to America's cities in the final third of the 20th century also changed dramatically. Amendments to the Immigration and Naturalization Act in 1965 reopened America's borders for the first time in nearly half a century and quickly transformed the nation's demographic landscape. European immigration dropped precipitously, while the number of immigrants coming from Asia, Africa, and Latin America rose rapidly. Many of these settled in and around metropolitan regions. Distinct local histories always shaped patterns of settlement: Laotian Hmong settled around Minneapolis as refugees from the Vietnam War, for instance, while California welcomed the "Silicon Sikhs" whom Silicon Valley tech firms recruited from India in the 1990s. In fact, nearly every major city witnessed the growth of new immigrant communities by the century's end.

These new immigrants reshaped the urban religious landscape. Buddhist and Hindu temples, Sikh gurdwárás, and Muslim mosques soon emerged alongside churches and synagogues in cities across the country. Even more dramatic was the effect these newcomers had on the rhythms of neighborhood life. Santería shrines, Buddhist prayer flags, and murals to Our Lady of Guadalupe soon filled front porches and alleyways in many cities and were joined by public processions or religious festivals. While the growth in Asian, Arab, and Latino populations often contributed to popular portrayals of the city as alien or "other" throughout this era, these newcomers often revitalized urban spaces. The eastern European immigrants who had settled in Chicago's

Pilsen neighborhood, for example, migrated out of the area after 1950 as the city's stock-yards declined. By 2000, however, Pilsen was a thriving Mexican American community whose members resuscitated not only the neighborhood but also a number of once struggling Catholic parishes. Similarly, Chicago's Devon Avenue was once home to Orthodox Jews until most fled to the suburbs after World War II. After a period of decline, Devon was transformed into the arterial hub of the city's South Asian community, filled with Asian groceries, Indian restaurants, and Hindu shrines.

The 21st-century city, then, is in many ways a profound departure from the White City of the 1893 World's Fair in Chicago. Where cities of largely white residents struggled to combat the excesses of industrial capitalism at the start of the 20th century, cities today cast themselves as "global cities" that are home primarily to communities of color striving to fill the void left by the departure of major industries. Despite these major changes, however, those themes that defined the industrial city continue to shape the religious history of the post-industrial metropolis. First is the continued religious vitality born of the city's diversity. In addition to adherents from the world's major religious traditions, American cities continue to be crucibles in which new religious movements and domestic revitalizations are born. The Calcutta native A. C. Bhaktivedanta, for instance, arrived in New York City the same year the United States reopened its borders to immigration. A former manager at a chemical firm in India, Bhaktivedanta came in 1965 to spread a devotional brand of Hinduism that quickly attracted thousands of largely white converts and followers. Within a decade the International Society for Krishna Consciousness (ISKCON) had established some thirty temples with thousands of devotees across the country in what became one of the first distinctly American—and urban—varieties of Hinduism. As Hindus from throughout Asia immigrated to the United States in growing numbers, ISKCON temples were often the only temples available, leading to a uniquely urban amalgam of several sects occupying the same house of worship.

Urban religious communities also continue to develop in relationship to the urban marketplace. The increasing number of evangelical churches that intentionally locate themselves in blighted areas claim they are motivated in part by correcting the injustices of deindustrialization and white flight. Through targeted church plants and "urban immersion" missionary programs, these "emergent evangelicals" represent an urban blend of Social Gospel activism and conservative theology that arose in response to the city's economic plight. Yet the relationship between urban religion and the urban economy operates at much more subtle, but no less profound, levels as well. The Latino Catholic who attends Bikram yoga classes or the evangelical Christian who encounters a shrine to the Buddha in a Thai restaurant also traffic in religion while they consume other wares.

Finally, the contours of the city's religious history continue to develop in relationship to the built environment. In contrast to densely packed 19th-century cities built around a central business district, today's cities are fractured, composite landscapes defined by varying levels of decline and development that often overlap municipal, county, or state lines. Connecting these widely dispersed locales are an ever-increasing number of highways and interchanges, so that religious communities no longer have to be within walking distance of their houses of worship or other important sites. This is why so many Hindu temples and evangelical megachurches are situated near suburban interchanges. As a result, cities are now crisscrossed by a variety of different, and occasionally competing, sacred routes, as today's urban religious sometimes travel great distances in order to practice or pray. Devotees to Our Lady of Guadalupe in Chicago, for example, initially established their shrine to the Virgin in the suburban town of Des Plaines because city parishes refused to accept a statue of the Virgin commissioned by a Mexican American layperson as a gift. After church officials in Mexico blessed the shrine in 2001 as the "Second Tepeyac in North America," it became a site of pilgrimage for Mexicans from across Chicagoland who similarly felt neglected by the Roman Catholic Church.

Historians might not be able to predict how the religious history of American cities will unfold throughout the coming century. But if the previous century is any indication, religion and the city will continue to form and shape each other as diverse peoples continue to live in, with, and through the built environment.

DISCUSSION OF THE LITERATURE

The earliest scholarly works that considered the religious lives of cities as a distinct object of study appeared alongside the rapid growth of American cities themselves in the first decades of the 20th century. Based on social scientific surveys and extensive interviews, these early works in what would become the sociology of religion often read like primary sources in their detailed documentation of urban religious life. H. Paul Douglass's *1000 City Churches* (1926), for example, surveyed how urban conditions and Social Gospel theology changed local congregations, while Louis Wirth's 1928 classic *The Ghetto* surveyed the community eastern European Jews formed around Chicago's Maxwell Street.[6] In addition to archiving the religious lives of urban communities, these texts also forged a lasting interpretation of urban religion that cast city living as a challenge to faiths. The Chicago School of sociology proved particularly influential in this regard. Without exception, the works published by sociologists such as Robert Park, Ernest Burgess, and their students—who included Wirth—portrayed city life as, at best, a challenge to faith, and more often a detriment to it.[7] This conclusion—that the city's social diversity, population density, and economic inequality threatened religious faith—was more a value judgment than an empirical reality. It rested on a particular conception of religious life as institutionally stable, ethically progressive, and culturally modern which mirrored the social worlds of researchers more than the people they studied; but it would haunt the study of urban religion throughout the century.

The legacy of this early work can be seen in the earliest histories of urban religious life. Works like Charles Howard Hopkins's *The Rise of the Social Gospel in the Progressive Era, 1900–1920* (1940), Aaron I. Abell's *The Urban Impact on American Protestantism, 1865–1900* (1943), and Henry F. May's *Protestant Churches and Industrial America* (1949), for example, were in their time pathbreaking works of religious history. Unlike older church histories that focused on a single denomination or emphasized theological developments, these authors considered how urbanization and industrialization spurred developments that transcended denominational lines. Their work surveyed the myriad institutional, ecclesiastical, and political efforts Protestant bodies undertook to address urban problems, often focusing on the history of a particular institutional church or rescue mission over denominational efforts at church planting or evangelizing. But in their focus on educated, ordained, and, principally, Protestant leaders, these first histories perpetuated older themes of the city's threat to spirituality. The focus on the efforts of settlement house workers and urban evangelists came at the expense of those who attended, or were the target of, these institutions and perpetuated the notion that their religious lives were somehow lacking or deficient.

The rise of social history in the second half of the 20th century challenged these assumptions by incorporating overlooked voices in the history of cities. The interest among many historians in the experiences of women, immigrants, and working people also inspired scholars of religion to make Catholics, Jews, and African Americans a part of the historical narrative as well. Given the immigration patterns of many Catholic and Jewish communities, much of this new work was urban religion by default—particularly works that focused on the first half of the 20th century. James W. Sanders's *The Education of an Urban Minority* (1977) and Leslie Woodcock Tentler's *Seasons of Grace* (1990), for example, homed in on a particular archdiocese in order to explore the impact immigration had on the development of the Roman Catholic Church in America.[8] Works on 20th-century Judaism, such as Susan A. Glenn's *Daughters of the Shtetl* (1990) and Ruth Gay's *Unfinished People* (1996), similarly placed the arc of American Jewish history in the cities where many eastern European Jews first settled.[9] For African American Protestantism, Milton C. Sernett's foundational *Bound for the Promised Land* (1997) was one of the first texts to cast the Great Migration of black southerners to northern cities as a distinctly religious phenomenon.[10] For Sernett, the scale of the Great Migration was made possible only by religious idioms that framed the flight from the Jim Crow South as a new exodus for a chosen people.

Work on the second half of the 20th century has similarly sought to include a diversity of voices. In contrast to many studies of the early 20th century, which have tended to focus on a single religious tradition or community, works on the postwar period often explore the histories of a city's religious communities in tandem. Works like John T. McGreevy's celebrated *Parish Boundaries* (1996), Gerald Gamm's *Urban Exodus* (1999), and Etan Diamond's *Souls of the City* (2003) variously consider how Catholic parishes, Jewish communities, and African American churches participated in the suburbanization of American culture or navigated the onset of urban decline.[11] Works on the rise of Sunbelt cities also tend to see the rapid development of places like Los Angeles and Miami as interfaith affairs. For example, even though Deborah Dash Moore's *To the Golden Cities* (1994) and Darren Dochuk's *From Bible Belt to Sunbelt* (2011) focus on a particular religious community, they both see the Sunbelt's social and religious diversity as important factors in

the development of postwar American Jewish culture and evangelical social conservatism, respectively.[12]

While the rise of social history increased the cast of characters that appeared in urban religious histories, the city often remained cast as the stage upon which religious histories took place or as a force effecting change. Only recently have scholars begun to challenge longstanding assumptions that the religious creativity of city dwellers was merely a curious departure from established traditions. The publication of Robert A. Orsi's *The Madonna of 115th Street* (1985) and Karen McCarthy Brown's *Mama Lola* (1991) are groundbreaking in this regard.[13] Together these books stimulated two fundamental changes in the study of urban religion. First, both books became a part of a larger reassessment of urban religion that saw the city less as a threat to religious life and more as an idiom that could be utilized in fashioning distinctly urban religious formulations. Brown's textured ethnography of a Haitian Vodou priestess's practices destigmatized Vodou worship by highlighting its personal and communal efficacy. Both she and Orsi challenged portrayals of urban religious practices as eccentric or superstitious by attending to the meanings they had for their participants.

Orsi's and Brown's work has led to a reevaluation of several established traditions in the field. Works such as Wallace Best's *Passionately Human, No Less Divine* (2005), Jacob Dorman's *Chosen People* (2013), and Judith Weisenfeld's *New World A-Coming* (2016) have recentered the religious history of the Great Migration away from Sernett's focus on established black denominations and toward the new religious movements that became a hallmark of African American communities throughout the urban north.[14] Lila Corwin Berman's *Metropolitan Jews* (2015) and Deborah Dash Moore's *Urban Origins of American Judaism* (2014) similarly reconceived the role of the city in American Jewish history.[15] For Berman, Moore, and others, urbanity is as much a component of American Jewish identity as it is a reflection of the spaces where many Jews once lived.

In addition to rethinking the "urban" in urban religious histories, Orsi's and Brown's pioneering work also popularized the use of ethnography alongside archival research in the study of lived religion. The ethnographic investigation of contemporary religious practices has helped scholars read printed sources against the grain. Through participant observation, scholars could contrast the perspectives of religious leaders with the cultural practices of the non-elite. But in a return to the study of urban religion's very origins, ethnography has also facilitated the documentation of today's diverse religious communities. For Thomas Tweed's *Our Lady of Exile* (1997), Timothy Matovina's *Guadalupe and Her Faithful* (2005), Zain Abdullah's *Black Mecca* (2010), and Jeff Wilson's *Dixie Dharma* (2012), for example, participant observation proved crucial in simply uncovering the histories of Miami's Cuban Catholics, San Antonio's Mexican Catholics, African Muslims in New York, and Richmond's Chinese and American Buddhists, as well as interpreting them.[16]

PRIMARY SOURCES

Historians of religion in the modern city have a multitude of primary sources available to them. Such abundance stems from the fact that most histories of religion in the city require scholars to account for a topic's urban and religious contexts. Following these interwoven threads will often lead researchers to sources at both the national and local level. The papers and publications of denominations or other large ecclesiastical institutions typically contain the voices of the elite, while local church records provide insight into the beliefs and practices of ordinary people. Despite their disparate locations, however, national and local sources often speak to each other and are frequently explored in tandem.

This interplay between the local and the national is most clearly seen in the records left by individuals that historians utilize in writing about urban religion. The journals, correspondence, and other manuscript sources of

prominent individuals have long outlined the impact urban religious life has had on American history. The papers of the urban minister and social welfare activist Graham Taylor (http://mms.newberry.org/xml/xml_files /Taylor.xml), for example, touch on multiple topics of inquiry simultaneously. Since he was pastor of Tabernacle Congregational Church and founder of the Chicago Commons settlement house, Taylor's papers provide insight into the intimate details of the neighborhood in which he worked. However, his faculty position at the Chicago Theological Seminary and role in support of national reform campaigns also placed Taylor at the center of numerous theological and political conversations about the fate of American cities more broadly. The same is true for the papers of other ministers, religious leaders, activist, and laypeople. These collections can be found in multiple locations, in archives both religious and secular, at the local, state, and national levels.

Beyond ministers, the papers and publications of those seminarians and social scientists who first studied urban phenomena often provide a wealth of raw data on urban religious communities. Publications on religion such as the aforementioned H. Paul Douglass's *1000 City Churches* (1925) and Louis Wirth's *The Ghetto* (1928) are obvious places to start. The papers of researchers or activists like University of Chicago sociologist Ernest Burgess (https://www.lib.uchicago.edu/e/scrc /findingaids/view.php?eadid=ICU.SPCL .BURGESSADDENDA) or New York social reformer Leonardo Covello (http://www2.hsp .org/collections/Balch%20manuscript_guide /html/covello.html) are also filled with primary source material on the religious lives of cities. The dissertations of students whom these early social scientists trained also provide first-hand accounts of urban religious communities.

In addition to the collections of individuals, the organizational records of institutions and houses of worship are important primary source material. Churches, synagogues, and other houses of worship in particular constitute the foundation for many people's religious life, and their surviving records can provide important insights into the religious lives of cities. Membership records often contain vital records such as births, baptisms, marriages, deaths, and transfers that illuminate the social and ethnic composition of a congregation. The minutes of church and synagogue committees reveal the activities and worldviews of dedicated laypeople. Published material such as church histories, congregational directories, manuals, weekly bulletins, broadsides, hymnbooks, services, and special service programs often survive and can contain information on the devotional and aesthetic worlds of local church life. Sometimes this material can still be found in the attics and basements of congregations that are still active. Often, however, churches donate older material to a variety of local and denominational archives. The Presbyterian Historical Society in Philadelphia, the American Baptist Historical Society at Mercer University in Macon, Georgia, the Southern Baptist Historical Society in Nashville, the United Methodist Archives and History Center at Drew University in Madison, New Jersey, the Archives of the Evangelical Lutheran Church in America in Elk Grove Village, Illinois, and the American Jewish Archives in New York, and the American Jewish Historical Society's collections in Cincinnati are national repositories that collect such historic congregational material. Again, local libraries and archives should also be consulted. The ecclesiastical structure of the Roman Catholic Church, meanwhile, often ensures that local church records remain in diocesan and archdiocesan repositories.

While local churches often anchored the religious life of America's cities, a hallmark of urban religion has been how experiences and perceptions of the city spurred broader forms of institutional growth, interdenominational cooperation, and, eventually, interfaith dialogue. These voluntary, denominational, or parachurch organizations produced diverse source material. For example, the published material and organizational records of denominational hospitals, orphanages, asylums, settlement houses, and community centers, as well as the records of denominational offices focused on particularly urban issues such as labor, immigration, and social welfare, often provide insight into the ecclesiastical perceptions of a city as well as the living conditions of citydwellers. Found in local or denominational archives, these collections occasionally have restrictions on their use for privacy reasons. Many urban locales also had city church unions, ministerial associations, Sunday school societies, and other denominational or ecumenical gatherings whose published and unpublished collections shed light on the religious life of a particular locale as well as trends in urban religion more broadly. The records of Chicago's Community Renewal Society (http://www .congregationallibrary.org/finding-aids /CommunityRenewalSociety5061), for example, not only demonstrate ways specific religious communities engaged with the civil rights movement, but also the rise of interfaith activism and reconciliation theology more broadly.

Yet the history of urban religion is more than just the history of ecclesiastical institutions. Because the urban religious lived in, with, and through the city, municipal records are valuable sources for documenting the religious history of cities. In the absence of robust denominational records, urban sources are sometimes the only outlet for documenting small and short-lived new religious movements. For example, city directories or service announcements in city newspapers often provide clues to the existence of even the most eccentric religious communities. City council minutes and municipal court papers also provide insight into moments of conflict and cooperation among religious communities. Noise ordinances and zoning debates can be particularly revealing sources, as established religious communities complained about the worship styles or church plants of more recent religious communities.

Finally, ethnography has also become an important resource for scholars documenting topics in urban religion. Observing and analyzing contemporary religious communities not only uncovers devotional practices or cultural meanings that official sources might leave out, but also helps interpret printed sources from the recent past. Researchers interested in undertaking ethnographic research can consult examples mentioned in the discussion of the literature above, as well as primers in the ethnographic study of religion, such as James R. Bowen's *Religions in Practice: An Approach to the Anthropology of Religion* (2014), James Spickard, J. Shawn Landres, and Meredith B. McGuire's edited collection *Personal Knowledge and Beyond: Reshaping the Ethnography of Religion* (2002), and Penny Edgell Becker and Nancy L. Eiesland's text *Contemporary American Religion: An Ethnographic Reader* (1997).[17]

DIGITAL PROJECTS AND MATERIALS

Bodenhamer, David et al. *Digital Atlas of American Religion*. Polis Center, Indiana University-Purdue University Indianapolis. http://religionatlas.org/.

Cantwell, Christopher D. *Faith in the City: Chicago's Religious Diversity in the Era of the World's Fair*. Newberry Library. http://publications.newberry.org/faith/.

Chiat, Marilyn D., and Jeanne Halgren Kilde. *Houses of Worship*. University of Minnesota. http://www.housesofworship.umn.edu/.

Eck, Diana. *World Religions in Greater Boston*. Pluralism Project, Harvard University. http://pluralism.org/wrgb.

Howell, Sally, and Andrew J. Shyrock. *Building Islam in Detroit*. University of Michigan. http://biid.lsa.umich.edu/.

Jews in America: A Portal to American Jewish History. http://www.jewsinamerica.org/.

A Journey through NYC Religions. http://www.nycreligion.info/.

Mapping Jewish L.A. Alan D. Leve Center for Jewish Studies, University of California, Los Angeles. http://www.mappingjewishla.org/.

FURTHER READING

Berman, Lila Corwin. *Metropolitan Jews: Politics, Race, and Religion in Postwar Detroit*. Chicago: University of Chicago Press, 2015.

Best, Wallace D. *Passionately Human, No Less Divine: Religion and Culture in Black Chicago, 1915–1952*. Princeton, NJ: Princeton University Press, 2005.

Dochuk, Darren. *From Bible Belt to Sunbelt: Plain-Folk Religion, Grassroots Politics, and the Rise of Evangelical Conservatism*. New York: W. W. Norton, 2011.

Eck, Diane L. *A New Religious America: How a "Christian Country" Has Now Become the World's Most Religiously Diverse Nation*. San Francisco: HarperSanFrancisco, 2001.

Giggie, John M., and Diane Winston, eds. *Faith in the Market: Religion and the Rise of Urban Commercial Culture*. New Brunswick, NJ: Rutgers University Press, 2002.

Gamm, Gerald. *Urban Exodus: Why the Jews Left Boston and the Catholics Stayed*. Cambridge, MA: Harvard University Press, 1999.

Livezey, Lowell W., ed. *Public Religion and Urban Transformation: Faith in the City*. New York: New York University Press, 2000.

McGreevy, John T. *Parish Boundaries: The Catholic Encounter with Race in the Twentieth-Century Urban North*. Chicago: University of Chicago Press, 1998.

Moore, Deborah Dash. *Urban Origins of American Judaism*. Athens, GA: University of Georgia Press, 2014.

Numrich, Paul D., and Elfriede Wedam. *Religion and Community in the New Urban America*. Chicago: University of Chicago Press, 2015.

Orsi, Robert A., ed. *Gods of the City: Religion and the American Urban Landscape*. Bloomington: Indiana University Press, 1999.

Wilson, Jeff. *Dixie Dharma: Inside a Buddhist Temple in the American South*. Chapel Hill: University of North Carolina Press, 2012.

NOTES

1. Quote from *Olean Democrat* (Olean, New York), May 12, 1893. I wish to thank Peter Manseau for alerting me to this quote. While some of Chicago's Syrians were Muslims, the majority of this first wave of settlers were Melkites, or Greek Catholic Christians. On Chicago's Syrian population see Sarah Gualtieri, "Syrians," in *Encyclopedia of Chicago*, ed. James R. Grossman, Ann Durkin Keating, and Janice L. Rife (Chicago: University of Chicago Press, 2004), 808.

2. Robert A. Orsi, "Introduction: Crossing the City Line," in *Gods of the City: Religion and the American Urban Landscape*, ed. Robert A.

Orsi (Bloomington: Indiana University Press, 1999), 43.

3. Josiah Strong, *The Twentieth Century City* (New York: Baker and Taylor, 1898), 54. The above statistics, as well as the quote from Strong, are cited in Jon C. Teaford, *The Twentieth-Century American City* (Baltimore: Johns Hopkins University Press, 1993), which remains one of the best surveys of urban history across the 20th century. All statistics cited here are derived from Teaford's text.

4. Mencken's coverage of the Scopes trial is gathered in H. L. Mencken, *H. L. Mencken on Religion*, edited by S. T. Joshi (New York: Prometheus, 2002), 180, 183.

5. Will Herberg, *Protestant, Catholic, Jew: An Essay in American Religious Sociology* (Chicago: University of Chicago Press, 1983 [1955]), 40.

6. H. Paul Douglass, *1000 City Churches: Phases of Adaptation to Urban Environment* (New York: George H. Doran, 1926); Louis Wirth, *The Ghetto* (Chicago: University of Chicago Press, 1956).

7. See Robert E. Park, Ernest Burgess, and R. D. McKenzie, *The City: Suggestions for the Study of Human Nature in the Urban Environment* (Chicago: University of Chicago Press, 1925).

8. James W, Sanders, *The Education of an Urban Minority: Catholics in Chicago, 1833-1965* (New York: Oxford University Press, 1977); Leslie Woodcock Tentler, *Seasons of Grace: A History of the Catholic Archdiocese of Detroit* (Detroit, MI: Wayne State University Press, 1990).

9. Susan A. Glenn, *Daughters of the Shtetl: Life and Labor in the Immigrant Generation* (Ithaca, NY: Cornell University Press, 1990; Ruth Gay, *Unfinished People: Eastern European Jews Encounter America* (New York: W. W. Norton, 1996).

10. Milton C. Sernett, *Bound for the Promised Land: African American Religion and the Great Migration* (Durham, NC: Duke University Press, 1997).

11. John T. McGreevy, *Parish Boundaries: The Catholic Encounter with Race in the Twentieth-Century Urban North* (Chicago: University of Chicago Press, 1998); Gerald H. Gamm, *Urban Exodus: Why the Jews Left Boston and the Catholics Stayed* (Cambridge, MA: Harvard University Press, 1999); Etan Diamond, *Souls of the City: Religion and the Search for Community in Postwar America* (Bloomington: Indiana University Press, 2003).

12. Deborah Dash Moore, *To the Golden Cities: Pursuing the American Jewish Dream in Miami and L.A.* (New York: Free Press, 1994); Darren Dochuk, *From Bible Belt to Sunbelt: Plain-folk Religion, Grassroots Politics, and the Rise of Evangelical Conservatism* (New York: W. W. Norton, 2011).

13. Robert A. Orsi, *The Madonna of 115th Street: Faith and Community in Italian Harlem, 1880-1950* (New Haven, CT: Yale University Press, 1985); Karen McCarthy Brown, *Mama Lola: A Vodou Priestess in Brooklyn* (Berkeley: University of California Press, 1991).

14. Wallace D. Best, *Passionately Human, No Less Divine: Religion and Culture in Black Chicago, 1915-1952* (Princeton, NJ: Princeton University Press, 2005); Jacob S. Dorman, *Chosen People: The Rise of American Black Israelite Religions* (New York: Oxford University Press, 2013); Judith Weisenfeld, *New World A-coming: Black Religion and Racial Identity During The Great Migration* (New York: New York University Press, 2016).

15. Lila Corwin Berman, *Metropolitan Jews: Politics, Race, and Religion in Postwar Detroit* (Chicago: University of Chicago Press, 2015); Deborah Dash Moore, *Urban Origins of American Judaism* (Athens: University of Georgia Press, 2014).

16. Thomas A. Tweed, *Our Lady of Exile: Diasporic Religion at a Cuban Catholic Shrine in Miami* (New York: Oxford University Press, 1997); Timothy M. Matovina, *Guadalupe and Her Faithful: Latino Catholics in San Antonio, from Colonial Origins to the Present* (Baltimore: Johns Hopkins University Press, 2005); Zain Abdullah, *Black Mecca: The African Muslims of Harlem* (New York: Oxford University Press, 2010); Jeff Wilson, *Dixie Dharma: Inside a Buddhist Temple in the American South* (Chapel Hill: University of North Carolina Press, 2012).

17. James R. Bowen, *Religions in Practice: An Approach to the Anthropology of Religion* (6th edn.; Boston: Prentice Hall, 2014); James V. Spickard, J. Shawn Landres, and Meredith B. McGuire, *Personal Knowledge and Beyond: Reshaping the Ethnography of Religion* (New York: New York University Press, 2002); Penny Edgell Becker and Nancy L. Eiesland, eds., *Contemporary American Religion: An Ethnographic Reader* (Walnut Creek, CA: AltaMira, 1997).

Christopher D. Cantwell

POVERTY IN THE MODERN AMERICAN CITY

American cities are often celebrated as sites of financial growth, where towering skyscrapers house thriving corporations and the successful executives who manage them. Yet cities are complex networks in which the wealthy and the poor coexist. Multimillion-dollar Manhattan penthouses and condos are situated across the street from housing projects. Prestigious Boston law firms similarly abut parks occupied by transients. Such tensions between socioeconomic classes vying for city space emerged early in the nation's history but became pronounced as urbanization increased during the 19th century. The major issues in urban poverty since the late 19th century address developments in housing policy, interventions by social reformers, and shifting perceptions of the poor, their social conditions, and impact on the built environment.

DEFINING POVERTY

Defining poverty is never straightforward, especially in the realm of history. Poverty has been variously classified through absolute measures such as household income, relative measures such as standard of living, and cultural perceptions of socioeconomic class. Each of these approaches is incomplete, capturing only a partial snapshot of lived experience. More perplexing still, each measure shifts over time and place. Ownership of refrigerators and other appliances once signified middle-class living but no longer conveys much distinction, for example, while the threshold for an adequate living space in New York City does not translate easily to South Dakota.

The federal government uses two primary poverty measures. The poverty thresholds were developed by economist Mollie Orshansky in 1963–1964, when she worked for the Social Security Administration.[1] The thresholds continue to be used by the Census Bureau for statistical analysis of poverty. A simplified version of this data, known as the "poverty guidelines," are used by the Department of Health and Human Services to determine program eligibility. They are also useful for students of postwar American history. Historian James T. Patterson drew upon the thresholds to estimate that around the turn of the 20th century, 40 percent of Americans were poor. During the Great Depression, the poverty rate fluctuated between 33 percent and 40 percent. In the mid-1950s, amid the booming postwar economy, 25 percent of Americans remained poor. By the 1970s, that number shrank to between 6 percent and 15 percent.[2] Patterson cautioned readers, however, that all measures of poverty are subjective and politically constructed, designed to ignore the "millions of people whose incomes place them barely above whatever lines may be used."[3]

As the American economy rose and fell over the course of the century, perceptions of poor people changed as well. Overall, poverty was more commonly seen as aberrant during periods of national prosperity. The approaches taken to address poverty were also profoundly shaped by the values and priorities of government officials, charity administrators, and reformers. At its core, modern American poverty policy owes much to the English Poor Laws, which separated the deserving from the undeserving poor. If one was not willing to work, under this logic, that individual did not deserve support and generosity. To be worthy of assistance, it was not enough simply to be poor. One was also expected to have fallen into poverty accidentally and continued to maintain a positive, rugged individualistic attitude. Time and again, this philosophy surfaced in modern American poverty programs, limiting aid available to recipients and guiding their behavior.[4]

Such 19th-century American attitudes influenced emerging public assistance programs. The Association to Improve the Condition of the Poor, founded in 1843, set out to reform the moral character of the poor and discouraged unregulated charitable assistance. The Charity Organization Society, established in London in 1869 and rooted in Christian moralism, similarly researched whether or not applicants for assistance were deserving of aid, exploring their home life, activities, and work history. The two organizations merged in 1939, forming the Community Service Society of New York. The Methodist Five Points Mission, opened in 1853 to provide religious instruction as well as poverty assistance, was joined in New York by several other missions and by The Salvation Army in 1880. Such organizations typically required poor individuals to participate in religious services in order to receive aid, defining their primary deficit as spiritual rather than economic. These skeptical attitudes toward the poor, undergirded by religious morality, predominated during the 19th century and held sway until the rise of the Progressive Era.[5]

By the late 19th century, the dire conditions of American poverty were attracting headlines. Robert Hunter's *Poverty* (1904) described 10 million impoverished Americans and was one of the first social scientific examinations of the problem. Hunter contrasted poverty in the urban North with that of the South, finding northern poverty more severe. He identified industrialization and unemployment as the driving factors in urban poverty, estimating that 20 percent of the northern population lived in poverty. He concluded that only 10 percent of Southerners lived in poverty. Later scholars, however, argue that Hunter underestimated the devastation of rural and southern poverty.[6]

Hunter described the poor in lurid and demeaning terms:

This distinction between the poor and paupers may be seen everywhere. There are in all large cities in America and abroad, streets and courts and alleys where a class of people live who have lost all self-respect and ambition, who rarely, if ever, work, who are aimless and drifting, who like drink, who have no thought for their children, and who live more or less contentedly on rubbish and alms.[7]

Historians have discredited Hunter's descriptions, arguing instead that most impoverished individuals at the turn of the century were not dependent paupers, but in 21st-century terms, the working poor.[8]

URBAN GROWTH PROMPTS PROGRESSIVE REFORM

The Progressive Era, characterized by forward-looking reformers committed to social progress, witnessed advancements in the regulatory powers of the government. American cities changed dramatically during the 19th century, as the nation was swept by the interlocking waves of industrialization, immigration, and urbanization. Manufacturing and other industries flourished, increasing the profits flowing to the members of the upper classes. New business models developed, as corporations merged and consolidated smaller firms, shutting out competition and paving the way for unprecedented growth.

In this rapidly changing climate, the Rockefellers, Morgans, and other elites reaped new profits and needed large numbers of workers to perform necessary labor and carry out the tasks of lower management. To meet these needs, Americans increasingly moved to the cities, abandoning family farms and their accompanying routines for exciting, sometimes dangerous city life. Joining these domestic migrants were multiple waves of immigrants, who converged upon American cities in search of employment, housing, and entertainment. Urban immigrants in the 19th century included the Irish, Italians, Chinese, and eastern Europeans. Such communities struggled to survive and then to prosper, eventually moving out of the city centers to more affluent neighborhoods. As each successive group of immigrants arrived, they took up residence in the cheap rooming houses and tenement apartments abandoned by many of the previous groups.

Designed to generate maximum profits for building owners, tenements were densely packed. Families crowded into small rooms, sometimes also operating businesses or completing piecework sewing tasks or rolling cigars in the space as well.[9] These structures lacked adequate ventilation and light and fostered the spread of disease. Most Americans, even those who lived in cities, had little reason to venture into immigrant districts such as New York's Lower East Side or Boston's North End. The stark living conditions of the poor went largely unremarked by the middle and upper classes until the Progressive Era.

Since the 1860s, New York reformers had tried to improve the health and sanitation of tenement life, with some success. Their actions had brought about the "dumbbell" tenements after 1879, whose expanded airshaft between structures gave the floor plans the outline of a dumbbell. These became the standard for newly constructed tenements. As the Progressive movement grew in strength, such reforms expanded. The 1901 Tenement Act required indoor flush toilets to be shared by no more than two families.[10]

Jacob Riis provided some of the impetus for these turn-of-the-century reforms. An immigrant himself, Riis came to America from Denmark as a young man, following a broken engagement. Riis worked as a crime reporter for the *New York Tribune*, venturing into the most dangerous areas of the Lower East Side. He was also a pioneer of photojournalism. Working with a team of assistants, Riis captured photos of the poor on the streets, in schoolhouses, and in their homes. His indoor work was especially innovative, as he was one of the first to use flash photography to take clear indoor photographs. Riis's *How the Other Half Lives* (1890) presented these photographs beside descriptive texts. Although Riis was critical of his subjects, often indulging in racist stereotypes, he achieved his goal of making the middle and upper classes aware of the suffering of the urban poor.[11]

The settlement house movement reflected a similarly complex blend of empathy and criticism toward the poor. The American settlement house movement owed its roots to the English movement, started by Arthur Toynbee, who moved into the London slums to aid the poor. In the United States, the Neighborhood Guild (later the University Settlement) was founded on the Lower East Side in 1886. Three years later Jane Addams and Ellen Gates Starr established Hull House in Chicago. By 1910, more than a hundred American settlement houses existed throughout the United States.[12]

The specific purpose of settlement houses varied, with some taking a heavy-handed approach to the Americanization of immigrants. Overall, the houses offered services ranging from language instruction to vocational training to well-baby care and cooking classes. The staff often included women college graduates who sought a useful outlet for their training and skills.

The settlement house movement embodied the spirit and methods of the Progressive Era. Educated activists identified social problems and then used research to try to solve them. The staff pursued change through privately funded organizations but had long-range impact on the development of public programs as well such as social work. The settlement house movement reflected the discomfort many middle- and upper-class city residents felt due to mounting urban poverty and their efforts to improve the lives of the poor.

EARLY-20TH-CENTURY SEGREGATION AND REDLINING

During the 20th century, cities typically became more segregated by race and class. Due to racism's role in perpetuating social inequality, class differences were often reflected in racial divisions. Racial segregation was created and maintained in distinct ways in different regions of the country. In the Jim Crow South, the separation of the races was often crude and openly displayed through signs, city directories, and other means. Segregation was more subtly implemented in other times and places.

In 1917, the Supreme Court declared in *Buchanan v. Warley* that racial zoning was unconstitutional. The ruling applied to government actions rather than those of private citizens, however, many of whom continued to create discriminatory agreements, including restrictive covenants that blocked African Americans (and sometimes Jews and Catholics) from purchasing or renting homes in many predominantly white, middle-class neighborhoods.[13]

Historically, southern cities had varied greatly in their rates of racial integration. Old South cities such as Savannah and New Orleans maintained traditionally racially integrated residential areas, with African Americans occupying small houses along the alleyways, while prosperous whites owned large homes facing the streets. The cities of the New South, such as Atlanta and Birmingham, by contrast, developed after the Civil War, with zones of racial segregation embedded in their very structure.[14]

In the early 20th century, African Americans began migrating from the southern rural farms to southern cities and then northern ones such as Chicago and New York. While most African Americans continued to live in the South, many migrants hoped to escape the blatant racism of the Reconstruction and the South's Jim Crow laws. They arrived in the North, however, only to find similar patterns of prejudice and emerging trends of spatial segregation. African Americans were allowed to live primarily in specific neighborhoods within northern cities. As late as the 1940s, for instance, 70 percent of African American New Yorkers lived in Harlem.[15]

The New Deal policy of redlining exacerbated racial segregation. As part of the effort to rationalize and stabilize the nation's economy, the Franklin Roosevelt administration established the Home Owners' Loan Corporation. This federal agency was tasked with cooperating with local authorities to create area-specific security grade reports. Using standardized survey forms, teams comprising realtors and others knowledgeable about neighborhood housing markets collected data about each area. They noted the demographics of the residents, the conditions of the structures, and key features of the neighborhood such as proximity to transit, and natural features. The central factor that was used to determine the rating of a neighborhood, though, was the race and ethnicity of its residents. Areas that were home to a large number of African Americans or Jewish people were routinely downgraded, regardless of the physical conditions of the buildings or area amenities. Grades ranged from green (A), favorable for lending, to red (D), hazardous. The resulting brightly colored maps were intended for circulation to banks and lending institutions in order to prevent mortgage lending and investment in downgraded zones. Historians have struggled to trace the specific distribution patterns of the maps. In many cases, however, the areas that were "redlined" were subject to underinvestment in the postwar period and remained dilapidated and unstable.[16]

POSTWAR DIVISIONS: URBAN RENEWAL, PUBLIC HOUSING, AND SUBURBANIZATION

Racial segregation was also fueled by urban renewal, another reform effort of the New Deal. Originally tied to slum clearance, urban renewal was a federal initiative designed to reinvigorate city centers. Initial plans called for clearing poor and minority populations from designated areas, in some cases moving them into public housing facilities. These areas were then sold to developers and used for more profitable mixed-income and mixed-use developments.

Urban renewal projects changed city centers in dramatic ways. In Boston, the West End was destroyed to build the Government Center and the Charles River park developments. In Manhattan, Lincoln Center, Stuyvesant Town, and the United Nations appeared in place of earlier neighborhoods. Such renewal projects frequently dislocated impoverished and minority populations, devastating communities and disrupting neighborhoods. The resulting developments, however, housed middle- and upper-income residents, thus lowering poverty in such areas. Urban renewal contributed to a postwar trend away from inclusion, as city officials seeking to retain and entice potential suburbanites marginalized the working classes in city centers.[17]

The Housing Act of 1937, which launched the urban renewal program, also sparked the nation's public housing program, providing federal funds to local housing authorities. During World War II, temporary communities were built to house wartime employees. After the war, the Housing Act of 1949 called for decent housing for even the poorest Americans, tying the program to slum clearance and urban renewal.[18]

Public housing took varied forms. Early developments were often built as low-rise structures complete with amenities, while later ones were more densely populated and lacking in greenspace and playgrounds. Public housing projects were later and justly criticized for their role in concentrating poverty. Early public housing required a substantial minimum income for most applicants, drawing primarily working-class residents, but later generations of public housing became home to a city's most destitute families. In *Making the Second Ghetto*, historian Arnold Hirsch documented the ways in which public housing programs created and maintained racial segregation.[19]

Funded only after political negotiation and compromise, public housing projects were constructed with federal funding. Maintenance costs, however, were to be drawn largely from tenant rents. By the 1960s, public housing residents were increasingly drawn from the poorest families, rather than the working-class residents who first occupied many facilities. As tenant incomes and subsequent rents fell, maintenance services declined as well. Some public housing facilities, having fallen into dramatic disrepair, were demolished relatively shortly after they were built. Most famously, the Wendell O. Pruitt Homes and William Igoe Apartments (known simply as Pruitt-Igoe) in St. Louis lasted only twenty years; the Cabrini-Green Homes in Chicago met a similar fate.[20]

By the 1970s, as many families struggled to pay rising rents, housing officials sought a flexible method of providing housing support. The Housing and Community Development Act of 1974 created the Section 8 program, which was rooted in the Housing Act of 1937. The program allowed for flexible housing for the poor through a means-tested voucher program. Recipients redeemed the vouchers within designated buildings or in participating private residences. Program guidelines limited rents to 30 percent of the recipients' adjusted gross income.[21]

The racial segregation patterns of American cities have also been inextricably tied to the growth of their suburbs. American suburbs grew during the first wave of late-19th-century streetcar suburbs, expanding in the 1920s and more drastically during the 1950s and 1960s. This postwar suburban growth stemmed from the New Deal housing reform legislation as low-interest mortgages as well as advantageous mortgages for military veterans through the Servicemen's Readjustment Act of 1944 (better known as the GI Bill) encouraged more Americans to leave the cities for suburban life. The suburbs were also supported by highway construction, which reflected a federal and local emphasis not on cities but on their outlying areas.[22]

As the suburban population grew, the racial demographics of their residents remained overwhelmingly white. In some cases, such as the well-known developments constructed by Levitt & Sons, racial segregation was enforced and codified through restrictive covenants. Deemed unenforceable by the Supreme Court in 1948 in *Shelley v. Kraemer*, such agreements continued to be practiced informally. Whether written or verbal, binding or informal, such practices limited minority access to suburban housing.[23]

Urban centers became, across the nation, home to a higher proportion of African Americans and impoverished people as a result of the "white flight" prompted by these policies. These demographic shifts had devastating effects on urban institutions and life. As the tax base shifted to the suburbs with higher earning residents, urban public services as well as public schools struggled to obtain funding. The character of inner cities shifted as a result of these trends, as the poorest of whites remained alongside minority residents unable to relocate. This pattern defined the period of postwar urban poverty, which inspired a massive federal response.[24]

THE 1960s AND WAR ON POVERTY

During the early 1960s, debate swirled around the "culture of poverty." First articulated by the anthropologist Oscar Lewis, culture of poverty theorists argued that poverty resulted not only from economic structures and conditions but also from individual mindsets, patterns of living, and ways of approaching problems. Such cultural explanations were often used to describe the behavior of minority groups. Oscar Lewis intended for his work to foster better understanding of and assistance to the poor, but the culture of poverty theory fueled much of the criticism the postwar poor. Opposing Lewis on these issues was Gunnar Myrdal, whose pivotal work *An American Dilemma: The Negro Problem and Modern Democracy* (1944) argued that structural economic factors, rather than individual and cultural ones, shaped the lives of the poor.[25]

Michael Harrington's landmark book *The Other America* surveyed the national poverty situation. Harrington estimated poverty at 25 percent, according to government guidelines. Harrington's work addressed the nearly invisible poor of American cities. In the past, he noted, middle-class and wealthy Americans directly confronted their neighbors' poverty, routinely crossing paths with beggars, vagrants, and slum dwellers. Through the evolution of the postwar city and its suburbs, however, the poor became increasingly physically segregated, leaving them visible only to each other. Many of the poor were also either youths or elderly, rendering them even less visible. While in the past, one's clothing may have revealed one's socioeconomic status, Harrington noted that the widespread availability of inexpensive clothing left many impoverished individuals indistinguishable on the streets: "Clothes make the poor invisible too: America has the best dressed poverty the world has ever known."[26] Harrington criticized the modern welfare state, which was forged in response to the Great Depression and benefitted primarily the middle and upper classes rather than the poor. He noted that Social Security was not available to all workers and was also quite limited in scope, proving a better secondary than primary source of retirement income. Harrington reminded readers that the Minimum-Wage Law of 1961 had excluded over 16 million domestic workers, restaurant staff, and hotel personnel. Such workers were vulnerable to exploitation from both management and corrupt unions. Historically, Harrington observed, poverty was a widespread phenomenon; as a result, while many Americans had endured harsh living conditions due to poverty, they had not suffered the additional burden of social stigma. As most Americans had advanced up the social ladder, however, many poor were left behind, branded as failures and blamed for their status.[27]

President Lyndon B. Johnson's Great Society programs attempted to address "the other America" and marked the first real expansion of the American welfare state since the New

Deal. A schoolteacher in rural Texas early in his career, Johnson brought to politics a desire to improve the lot of working-class Americans.[28] In March 1964, Johnson announced a new War on Poverty, which focused on providing "opportunity" rather than expanding relief rolls or facilitating job creation. In part, this philosophical distinction stemmed from the starkly different historical contexts. Facing the devastating financial turmoil of the Great Depression, the Roosevelt administration had struggled to preserve capitalism and maintain the economy. To achieve those goals, they employed a wide array of experimental tactics, including transfer payments and job creation programs. The Johnson administration, by contrast, was operating in a climate of economic prosperity. They saw no reason why the strong American economy could not eliminate poverty by simply expanding opportunity in higher education and facilitating community programs.[29]

Between 1964 and 1966, Great Society legislation was enacted, shaping the future of generations of Americans. The Economic Opportunity Act established programs including Head Start, which provided vital early childhood education opportunities to economically vulnerable students, and VISTA, through which youth served the nation by working on service projects. The Food Stamp Act increased low-income families' access to nutritional meals. The Social Security Acts of 1965 launched Medicare and Medicaid, which provided health insurance for the elderly and poor. The Department of Housing and Urban Development Act established "HUD" as a Cabinet-level agency, overseeing federal housing programs. The "Model Cities" program, established in 1966, funded urban improvement projects in impoverished neighborhoods. Rather than being direct transfer payments, many of these programs were growth opportunities. The programs were also built around the principles of community participation, acknowledging the rising pressure from community activists seeking a role in program design and oversight.

WOMEN AND WELFARE

Public assistance programs were heavily shaped by understandings of gender roles. The modern welfare state, forged during the New Deal, drew much of its inspiration from the mothers' pensions developed by Progressive reformers. Settlement house workers, social workers, and pioneers of the Children's Bureau had persuaded nearly all states to establish Mothers' Aid by 1930. Single mothers, half of whom were widows, received this assistance in order to care for their children. Motherhood was a valued activity worthy of state financial support. Political compromises left these initiatives only partially funded, however, as some opposed providing full support to female heads of households.[30]

New Deal administrators drew upon this model in establishing Aid to Dependent Children, which became the centerpiece of public assistance programs. The Great Depression destabilized many families, leaving women seeking assistance. Women's needs were tied to those of their children, and their eligibility for aid hinged on the number of children for whom they were responsible.[31]

During the Johnson years, welfare programs expanded, amid pressure from welfare activists for better funding as well as recipient and community participation in program development and oversight. Many women were frustrated by the heavy-handed and invasive controls that were placed on their behavior. Residents of public housing, for instance, were subjected to nighttime inspections to ensure no man was present in their home. In response to such treatment, the National Welfare Rights Organization pressed for more respectful treatment of clients as well as adequate support.[32]

As the Welfare Rights and Civil Rights movements grew in the early 1960s, conservative voices escalated as well, claiming that

African Americans and other minorities were asking for unearned and undeserved benefits. Two government reports had a tremendous influence on this debate and continue to draw attention today. In 1965, Assistant Secretary of Labor Daniel Patrick Moynihan attempted to draw attention to the systemic inequality facing African Americans. In "The Negro Family: The Case for National Action," he argued that civil rights legislation alone would not be enough to foster racial equality: "A national effort is required that will give a unity of purpose to the many activities of the Federal government in this area, directed to a new kind of national goal: the establishment of a stable Negro family structure."[33] Conservative politicians seized upon this opportunity to blame African American families for their own poverty. By the late 1960s, American cities were exploding in unrest, as protests turned violent and riots escalated. President Johnson assembled the Kerner Commission to analyze the situation. Their ensuing report blamed the riots primarily on systemic racism and the lack of economic opportunity for inner-city minority residents. Poverty, in their analysis, was causing urban violence.[34]

Images of single mothers as undeserving, and lazy "welfare queens" frequently appeared in the political discourse of the 1970s and especially the 1980s. Ronald Reagan, when campaigning for the presidency in 1976, had described this character: "She used 80 names, 30 addresses, 15 telephone numbers to collect food stamps, Social Security, veterans' benefits for four nonexistent deceased veteran husbands, as well as welfare. Her tax-free cash income alone has been running $150,000 a year."[35] Neoconservative authors such as Charles Murray argued that the largesse of the Johnson-era social welfare programs inadvertently created a culture of dependence in which the poor had little incentive to support themselves through labor.[36] In this climate, little public outcry met the dramatic reductions in public services and assistance programs promoted by the Reagan administration.

Cuts to food support programs, subsidized housing and mental health services among many others, exacerbated existing poverty and pushed more Americans out of the working class.[37]

The Personal Responsibility and Work Opportunity Reconciliation Act of 1996 was fueled by the criticism of welfare recipients that permeated political discourse during the Reagan years and continued into the 1990s. Welfare reform carried out in Wisconsin by Republican Governor Thomas Thompson also proved influential to the act. While campaigning, President Bill Clinton promised to reform the welfare system. Once in office, his administration initially focused on health care and other domestic issues. The Republican-controlled Congress pressed for change, however, emboldened by their "Contract with America," which called for denying increased Aid to Families with Dependent Children (AFDC) to program participants whose families expanded. Clinton signed their proposal into law, despite reservations about its severity. The law ended the AFDC program, replacing it with Temporary Assistance for Needy Families (TANF). This program limited the time individuals and families could receive assistance. Highly publicized "workfare" requirements ensured recipients would perform labor in order to receive assistance. In subsequent years, recipient rolls declined, but analysts struggled to distinguish the effects of the program from the broader impact of the era's booming economy. Also, many families who left the program remained in poverty.[38]

Throughout the 20th century, women's fertility, their relationships with men, and with their own children were thus subject to surveillance and control by administrators of assistance programs. Recipients of public assistance were frequently accused of laziness and greed, particularly during periods of relative economic prosperity. Women who received welfare faced added criticism of their sexual behavior and morality, leading to highly regulated assistance programs.

HOMELESSNESS

At any historical moment, some Americans have been homeless. During the late 19th and 20th centuries, urban homelessness changed dramatically. The shifts reflected not only changing demographics of poverty but also changing attitudes toward the poor and their relationship to city life.

Earlier in American history, the limited assistance offered to homeless individuals in the urban environment came from the police force, who sometimes offered transient lodgings. Religious missions also provided services to the poor, often in exchange for attendance at sermons and other religious services. Well known among these agencies was the Salvation Army, a conservative Christian organization founded in England during the late 19th century. The Salvation Army employed a rigid organizational structure including militaristic uniforms. Establishing transient shelters in major cities, Salvationists insisted that clients not consume alcohol if they sought shelter. The Charity Organization Society also provided services to the poor but did so through programs like their New York City Woodyard. City residents purchased tickets they distributed to beggars, which entitled the bearers to chop wood in exchange for food and lodging. Such initiatives were designed to prevent anyone from receiving unearned benefits. In this manner, with a patchwork of public, private, and religious initiatives, American cities addressed the needs of the homeless. Aid was local, varied, and subjective, shaped by the principles and priorities of administrators.[39]

The Great Depression dramatically changed all existing poverty programs, including these addressing homelessness. As the Dust Bowl compounded the economic upheaval in the Midwest, farmers lost their properties to foreclosure and eviction. Local relief agencies, including those in major cities, felt no obligation to provide assistance to vagrants, who were left to fend for themselves.[40] To address these concerns, from 1933 to 1935 the Roosevelt administration ran the Federal Transient Program (FTP), which provided funding for relief facilities designed for uprooted individuals and families.[41]

As the economic crisis continued, the Roosevelt administration's approach to poverty shifted starkly, in a series of moves that would have lasting effects on American cities. During the early years of the New Deal, the administration embraced programs that provided emergency assistance to those in need, while also stabilizing the economic climate for corporations and financial institutions. In 1935, the administration launched a new series of programs, centered on labor.

The "Second New Deal" passed the Social Security Act of 1935, the massive program of social insurance that remains the greatest legacy of the New Deal. The program rewarded those who were either able or willing to work. Those with disabilities or enduring temporary unemployment would be provided for under this program, as would those in eligible, full-time jobs. The second wing of this vision centered on the Works Progress Administration (WPA). Roosevelt and Harry Hopkins saw the WPA as a vehicle toward full employment, when deployed alongside the Social Security program. Those able to find employment within the corporate sector would do so, while those who were able and willing to work yet unemployed might find government-sponsored jobs through the WPA. Those unable to work due to age or disability might find assistance through the Social Security program.

Single men who were homeless and unwilling to work were largely excluded from this model of the modern welfare state. Those men who were heavy drinkers or drug users, as well as those who were simply uninterested in working, did not have a place within this model. As a result, postwar homelessness reverted to being a localized, frequently urban problem.

Accompanying this shift in welfare policy were broader cultural attitudes toward the homeless themselves. During the 1940s, the theory of alcoholism as a progressive disease was actively promoted by the Yale School of Alcohol Studies. This model aligned closely with that promoted by the popular organization Alcoholics Anonymous and helped to define national discourse. Homelessness was seen as end-stage alcoholism. Its victims were sick and perhaps worthy of help, but the nature of assistance they received focused narrowly on substance use.[42]

During the 1960s the "Culture of Poverty" debates subjected homeless people to more critical scrutiny. Researchers affiliated with the Columbia University Bureau of Applied Social Research, as well as other academic research institutions, approached homeless individuals as broken, lost, and disaffiliated. Waves of research carefully probed the social, familial, and organizational attachments maintained by the homeless. Influenced by sociological theories such as Emile Durkheim's work on anomie, they concluded that homeless people led lives with low rates of attachment. Instead, they found that the homeless were united by their extreme poverty.[43]

From the late 19th century through the late 20th century, America's urban homeless largely congregated on skid rows. Seedy areas fitted with missions, single-resident occupancy hotels, and inexpensive restaurants, these districts served as a form of homeless policy. Homeless people were not merely welcomed in these spaces: at times, they were compelled to remain there. This flexible arrangement kept the homeless out of the line of sight of the general public, allowing middle- and upper-class city dwellers to remain uninformed about the dire conditions of the city's poor.

In the 1970s, the homeless demographic of the population in many cities started to shift. The deinstitutionalization of the mentally ill, policies that began under the Kennedy administration, led to the release of large numbers of mentally ill people from healthcare facilities in cities throughout the United States without the funding necessary to support adequate therapies and assistance. Many

became homeless. Women also increasingly appeared among the homeless. Sometimes such individuals were fleeing domestic violence. Others were divorced or widowed, unable to provide for themselves. As a result of all of these factors, the homeless population grew.[44]

The homeless also became far more visible. With the skid row districts mostly gone, the homeless instead appeared in parks, transit stations, and on the streets in large numbers, prompting public outcry over "the new homeless." Composed of fewer elderly white men and more people of color, women, veterans, and youth, the homeless population of the 1980s and beyond required different types of services than had previous generations. Pioneering "right to shelter" legislation in New York City, instituted under *Callahan v. Carey* (1981), and later emulated in Massachusetts, committed the city to providing temporary shelter on demand.

Skid rows no longer exist in many American cities, having changed with the dramatic effects of urban renewal at mid-century in cities such as Boston and St. Louis, as well as of gentrification in congested, high-cost real estate markets such as New York City.[45] Many business owners and residents objected both to the sight of homeless individuals and shelters and housing for formerly homeless individuals in their neighborhoods. Some cities, however, saw a marked growth of the size and population of skid row in the early 21st century—most notably, Los Angeles, where homelessness reached a crisis point. In the postwar decades, many of the dilapidated residential hotels on Los Angeles' Skid Row were demolished, sending many homeless individuals to the streets. In 2016, Los Angeles County claimed 47,000 individuals were without homes, 30,000 of whom were unsheltered. The Skid Row area alone was home to over 17,000 individuals. County residents authorized funding for increased residential facilities, but solutions proved difficult in the face of such overwhelming need.[46]

DISCUSSION OF THE LITERATURE

The history of urban poverty has been analyzed from a variety of angles, including policy reform, welfare, housing, and homelessness. Useful information can also be drawn from studies of segregation due to the persistence of racism and social inequality. Current trends in income inequality and social outlooks are captured by the work of sociologists as well as journalists.

Any student of American poverty will do well to begin with James T. Patterson's classic influential *America's Struggle Against Poverty in the Twentieth Century*.[47] Packed with specific data yet interpreted with nuance and situated within the broader thematic history, the book is extremely useful as a survey of poverty and the responses it inspired.

The history of programs assisting the poor also offers several key sources. Joel Schwartz's *Fighting Poverty with Virtue: Moral Reform and America's Urban Poor, 1825-2000*, surveys the history of reformers' efforts to change the behaviors of the poor.[48] Walter I. Trattner's *From Poor Law to Welfare State: A History of Social Welfare in America* provides a useful overview of the development of public assistance programs throughout American history.[49]

A number of authors have addressed the rising trends of social inequality. David Shipler's *The Working Poor: Invisible in America* explores the struggles faced by the contemporary working class.[50] Barbara Ehrenreich's *Nickel and Dimed: On (Not) Getting By in America*, also provides insights into the challenges faced by the working poor.[51] William Julius Wilson has continued to write critical sociological analyses of poverty. His study *When Work Disappears: The World of the New Urban Poor* analyzed the limiting situations faced by the inner-city poor.[52]

The history of racial segregation has yielded a rich literature, spanning many academic disciplines. *American Apartheid: Segregation and the Making of the Underclass* by Douglas N. Massey and Nancy A. Denton offers clear analysis of the driving trends of segregation by race and class.[53] More recently, Richard Rothstein's *The Color of Law: A Forgotten History of How Our Government Segregated America* explores the history of policy-funded segregation throughout the 20th century.[54]

Impoverished women have been analyzed through the lens of welfare policy and reform. Linda Gordon's important *Pitied but Not Entitled: Single Mothers and the History of Welfare, 1890–1935* surveys the history of welfare from mothers' pensions through Social Security.[55] Paula W. Dail's *Women and Poverty in 21st Century America* examines contemporary issues such as crime, health, education, and labor.[56]

National studies provide useful analysis and framing of the history of homelessness. Kenneth Kusmer's *Down and Out, on the Road: The Homeless in American History* surveys the plight of the homeless, focusing on the period from the late 19th century through the New Deal.[57] *Citizen Hobo: How a Century of Homelessness Shaped America* by Todd DePastino explores homelessness as it shaped policy, arguing that responses to poverty often stemmed from fear of the poor.[58]

PRIMARY SOURCES

Studying urban poverty necessitates an interdisciplinary approach to research. Valuable information can be found in sources ranging from government documents, historical newspaper collections, and digital history projects, as well as memoirs of both the poor and their advocates. Finally, analyses of poverty become primary sources over time, capturing the perspectives of their authors.

Historical federal census records provide a wealth of data on not only income but also other markers of socioeconomic status, such as education levels, family composition, housing conditions, rents, plumbing conditions, electricity status, and appliances owned. Data on racial demographics can also be used to track the effects on an area of programs such as redlining, urban renewal, and public housing.

The Oxford University Press Social Explorer website can be used to quickly generate maps based on historical census data dating back to the first census in 1790.[59] Much of the basic information on racial demographics and income remains available in the open access areas of the site; some other census data queries will require a paid subscription. Users willing to map the data themselves can do so in a straightforward manner. All historical census data is available from the IPUMS NHGIS collections.[60] It can then be mapped using GIS software such as QGIS or ESRI ArcGIS, or visualized in other ways with tools such as Tableau or Microsoft Excel.

Redlining reports are also useful for the study of urban development. Two projects created by the Digital Scholarship Lab at the University of Richmond have made it possible for anyone to access detailed redlining and urban renewal reports without having to travel to the National Archives and Research Administration in College Park, Maryland, to see the original documents. In "Mapping Inequality: Redlining in New Deal America: 1905–2016," the infamous Home Owners' Loan Corporation redlining maps have been digitized and georectified, so that site users can see the areas overlaid onto a contemporary map.[61] In "Renewing Inequality: Family Displacements Through Urban Renewal: 1955–1966," this project has been extended through the addition of data drawn from various urban renewal reports.[62] Many urban renewal reports are also available through the aggregate sites hosted by the Internet Archive and the Digital Public Library of America.

Also useful to the study of poverty are social reformers' narratives from the Progressive Era. Jane Addams's *Twenty Years at Hull House* (1910) lends insight into not only the work done in the settlement houses but also the motivations and experiences of the reformers.[63] Jacob Riis's *How the Other Half Lives*, now infamous for its racist and inappropriate tone, is also invaluable to the study of tenements, immigrant life, and the reform movements they sparked.[64]

Several historic studies of poverty now serve as primary sources in their own right. Robert Hunter's *Poverty* presented detailed observations on national trends at the turn of the 20th century.[65] Michael Harrington's *The Other America* remains a classic primary source, capturing the enthusiastic "discovery" of poverty in the postwar period.[66] The debates over structuralism versus the culture of poverty are encapsulated in Gunner Myrdal's *An American Dilemma* and Oscar Lewis's *Five Families: Mexican Case Studies in the Culture of Poverty* and *La Vida*.[67] Charles Murray's *Losing Ground* reflects much of the opposition to the continuation of public welfare programs during the 1980s.[68]

FURTHER READING

Addams, Jane. *Twenty Years at Hull House, with Autobiographical Notes.* New York: Macmillan Press, 1910.

Bloom, Nicholas Dagen. *Public Housing That Worked: New York in the Twentieth Century.* Philadelphia: University of Pennsylvania Press, 2008.

Bullard, Robert D., Eugene Grigsby III, and Charles Lee, eds. *Residential Apartheid: The American Legacy.* Los Angeles: University of California Press, 1994.

Carr, James H., and Nandinee K. Kutty, eds. *Segregation: The Rising Costs for America.* New York: Routledge, 2008.

Dáil, Paula W. *Women and Poverty in 21st Century America.* Jefferson, NC: McFarland, 2011.

Davis, Allen F. *Spearheads for Reform: The Social Settlements and the Progressive Movement, 1890–1914.* New Brunswick, NJ: Rutgers University Press, 1984.

DePastino, Todd. *Citizen Hobo: How a Century of Homelessness Changed America.* Chicago: University of Chicago Press, 2003.

Duneier, Mitchell. *Ghetto: The Invention of a Place, The History of an Idea.* New York: Farrar, Straus and Giroux, 2016.

Ehrenreich, Barbara. *Nickel and Dimed: On (Not) Getting By in America.* New York: Henry Holt, 2001.

Goetz, Edward G. *New Deal Ruins: Race, Economic Justice, & Public Housing Policy.* Ithaca, NY: Cornell University Press, 2013.

Gordon, Linda. *Pitied But Not Entitled: Single Mothers and the History of Welfare, 1890–1935*. New York: The Free Press, 1994.

Greenberg, Cheryl. *Or Does It Explode? Black Harlem in the Great Depression*. New York: Oxford University Press, 1991.

Harrington, Michael. *The New American Poverty*. New York: Holt, Rinehart and Winston, 1984.

Harrington, Michael. *The Other America: Poverty in the United States*. New York: Touchstone, 1997.

Hirsch, Arnold R. *Making a Second Ghetto: Race and Housing in Chicago, 1940–1960*. Chicago: University of Chicago Press, 1983.

Howard, Ella. *Homeless: Poverty and Place*. Philadelphia: University of Pennsylvania Press, 2013.

Hunter, Robert. *Poverty*. New York: Macmillan Press, 1912.

Jackson, Kenneth T. *Crabgrass Frontier: The Suburbanization of the United States*. New York: Oxford University Press, 1985.

Johnston, David Cay. *Divided: The Perils of Our Growing Inequality*. New York: New Press, 2014.

Kornbluh, Felicia. *The Battle for Welfare Rights: Politics and Poverty in Modern America*. Philadelphia: University of Pennsylvania Press, 2007.

Kruse, Kevin M. *White Flight: Atlanta and the Making of Modern Conservatism*. Princeton, NJ: Princeton University Press, 2005.

Kusmer, Kenneth L. *Down and Out, on the Road: The Homeless in American History*. New York: Oxford University Press, 2001.

Lewis, Oscar. *La Vida: A Puerto Rican Family in the Culture of Poverty—San Juan and New York*. New York: Vintage, 1968.

Lissak, Rivka Shpak. *Pluralism and Progressives: Hull House and the New Immigrants, 1890–1919*. Chicago: University of Chicago Press, 1989.

Massey, Douglas S., and Nancy A. Denton. *American Apartheid: Segregation and the Making of the Underclass*. Cambridge, MA: Harvard University Press, 1993.

Mink, Gwendolyn, and Rickie Solinger, eds. *Welfare: A Documentary History of U.S. Policy and Politics*. New York: New York University Press, 2003.

Myrdal, Gunnar. *An American Dilemma: The Negro Problem and Modern Democracy*. New Brunswick, NJ: Transaction Publishers, 1996.

O'Connor, Thomas H. *Building a New Boston: Politics and Urban Renewal, 1950–1970*. Boston: Northeastern University Press, 1993.

Patterson, James T. *America's Struggle Against Poverty in the Twentieth Century*. Cambridge, MA: Harvard University Press, 2000.

Pimpare, Stephen. *A People's History of Poverty in America*. New York: New Press, 2008.

Plunz, Richard, and Kenneth T. Jackson. *A History of Housing in New York City*. New York: Columbia University Press, 2016.

Riis, Jacob. *How the Other Half Lives: Studies Among the Tenements of New York*. New York: Charles Scribner's Sons, 1890.

Rothstein, Richard. *The Color of Law: A Forgotten History of How Our Government Segregated America*. New York: W.W. Norton, 2017.

Schwartz, Joel. *Fighting Poverty with Virtue: Moral Reform and America's Urban Poor, 1825–2000*. Bloomington: Indiana University Press, 2000.

Shipler, David K. *The Working Poor: Invisible in America*. New York: Alfred A. Knopf, 2004.

Sugrue, Thomas J. *The Origins of the Urban Crisis: Race and Inequality in Postwar Detroit*. Princeton, NJ: Princeton University Press, 1996.

Teaford, Jon C. *The Rough Road to Renaissance: Urban Revitalization in America, 1940–1985*. Baltimore: Johns Hopkins University Press, 1990.

Thomas, June Manning, and Marsha Ritzdorf, eds. *Urban Planning and the African American Community: In the Shadows*. Thousand Oaks, CA: SAGE, 1996.

Trattner, Walter I. *From Poor Law to Welfare State: A History of Social Welfare in America* (4th ed.). New York: Free Press, 1974.

Vale, Lawrence J. *Reclaiming Public Housing: A Half Century of Struggle in Three Public Neighborhoods*. Cambridge, MA: Harvard University Press, 2002.

Wilson, William Julius. *When Work Disappears: The World of the New Urban Poor*. New York: Alfred A. Knopf, 1996.

Zipp, Samuel. *Manhattan Projects: The Rise and Fall of Urban Renewal in Cold War New York*. New York: Oxford University Press, 2010.

NOTES

1. Gordon M. Fisher, "The Development and History of The Poverty Thresholds," *Social Security Bulletin* 55, no. 4 (1992): 3–14.
2. James T. Patterson, *America's Struggle Against Poverty in the Twentieth Century* (Cambridge, MA: Harvard University Press, 2000), 12–13.
3. Patterson, *America's Struggle*, 243.

4. Patterson, *America's Struggle*, 19.
5. Joel Schwartz, *Fighting Poverty with Virtue: Moral Reform and America's Urban Poor, 1825–2000* (Bloomington: Indiana University Press, 2000).
6. Robert Hunter, *Poverty* (New York: Macmillan Press, 1912).
7. Hunter, *Poverty*, 3.
8. Patterson, *America's Struggle*, 6–14.
9. These conditions can be seen firsthand at the Lower East Side Tenement Museum.
10. Richard Plunz and Kenneth T. Jackson, *A History of Housing in New York City* (New York: Columbia University Press, 2016), 21–49.
11. Jacob Riis, *How the Other Half Lives: Studies Among the Tenements of New York* (New York: Charles Scribner's Sons, 1890).
12. Rivka Shpak Lissak, *Pluralism and Progressives: Hull House and the New Immigrants, 1890–1919* (Chicago: University of Chicago Press, 1989). Allen F. Davis, *Spearheads for Reform: The Social Settlements and the Progressive Movement, 1890–1914* (New Brunswick, NJ: Rutgers University Press, 1984).
13. Christopher Silver, "The Racial Origins of Zoning in American Cities," in *Urban Planning and the African American Community: In the Shadows*, ed. June Manning Thomas and Marsha Ritzdorf (Thousand Oaks, CA: SAGE, 1997), 23–42.
14. Ella Howard, "Redlining Georgia," in *Reassessing the 1930s South*, ed. Karen Cox and Sarah Gardner (Baton Rouge: Louisiana State University Press, 2018).
15. Cheryl Greenberg, *Or Does It Explode? Black Harlem in the Great Depression* (New York: Oxford University Press, 1997), 3–12.
16. Louis Lee Woods, "The Federal Home Loan Bank Board, Redlining, and the National Proliferation of Racial Lending Discrimination, 1921–1950," *Journal Of Urban History* 38 (2012): 1036–1059.
17. Thomas H. O'Connor, *Building a New Boston: Politics and Urban Renewal, 1950–1970* (Boston: Northeastern University Press, 1995), xi–xvi; and Samuel Zipp, *Manhattan Projects: the Rise and Fall of Urban Renewal in Cold War New York* (New York: Oxford University Press, 2012), 3–32.
18. Richard Rothstein, *The Color of Law: A Forgotten History of How Our Government Segregated America* (New York: W. W. Norton, 2017), 30–32.
19. Arnold R. Hirsch, *Making a Second Ghetto: Race and Housing in Chicago, 1940–1960* (Chicago: University of Chicago Press, 1998); and Nicholas Dagen Bloom, *Public Housing that Worked: New York in the Twentieth Century* (Philadelphia: University of Pennsylvania Press, 2008).
20. Chad Freidrichs, dir., *The Pruitt-Igoe Myth* (Columbia, MO: First Run Features, 2011).
21. Howard Husock, *America's Trillion-Dollar Housing Mistake: The Failure of American Housing Policy* (Chicago: Ivan R. Dee, 2003), 45–60.
22. Kenneth T. Jackson, *Crabgrass Frontier: The Suburbanization of the United States* (New York: Oxford University Press, 1985), 3–11.
23. Douglas S. Massey and Nancy A. Denton, *American Apartheid: Segregation and the Making of the Underclass* (Cambridge, MA: Harvard University Press, 1998).
24. Jackson, *Crabgrass Frontier*, 231–245. Kevin M. Kruse, *White Flight: Atlanta and the Making of Modern Conservatism* (Princeton, NJ: Princeton University Press, 2007).
25. Oscar Lewis, *La Vida: A Puerto Rican Family in the Culture of Poverty—San Juan and New York* (New York: Vintage, 1968); and Gunnar Myrdal, *An American Dilemma: The Negro Problem and Modern Democracy* (New Brunswick, NJ: Transaction Publishers, 1996).
26. Michael Harrington, *The Other America: Poverty in the United States* (New York: Touchstone, 1997), 5.
27. Harrington, *The Other America*, 1–18.
28. Robert A. Caro, *The Path to Power: The Years of Lyndon Johnson, Volume 1* (New York: Vintage, 1990).
29. Patterson, *America's Struggle*, 122–137.
30. Linda Gordon, *Pitied but Not Entitled: Single Mothers and the History of Welfare, 1890–1935* (New York: Free Press, 1994), 37–66.
31. Gordon, *Pitied but Not Entitled*, 209–252.
32. Felicia Kornbluh, *The Battle for Welfare Rights: Politics and Poverty in Modern America* (Philadelphia: University of Pennsylvania Press, 2007).
33. "The Negro Family: The Case for National Action," US Government Printing Office, 1965.
34. Report of the National Advisory Commission on Civil Disorders, Summary of Report.
35. Rachel Black and Aleta Sprague, "The 'Welfare Queen' Is a Lie," *The Atlantic*, September 28, 2016.

36. Charles Murray, *Losing Ground: American Social Policy, 1950–1980* (New York: Basic Books, 2015).

37. Walter I. Trattner, *From Poor Law to Welfare State: A History of Social Welfare in America*, 4th ed. (New York: Free Press, 1974), 327–342.

38. Vann R. Newkirk II, "The Real Lessons From Bill Clinton's Welfare Reform," *The Atlantic*, February 5, 2018.

39. Ella Howard, *Homeless: Poverty and Place* (Philadelphia: University of Pennsylvania Press, 2013), 1–21.

40. Howard, *Homeless*, 22–59.

41. Howard, *Homeless*, 60–87.

42. Howard, *Homeless*, 88–115.

43. Howard, *Homeless*, 138–178.

44. Howard, *Homeless*, 179–209.

45. Howard, *Homeless*, 210–222.

46. Gale Holland, "L.A. Tallies Homeless Population amid Concern about Rising Encampments," *Los Angeles Times*, January 27, 2017; and Doug Smith, Scott Harrison, and Shelby Grady, "Homelessness Became a Crisis in L.A. During the 1980s, but the City Struggled to Act," *Los Angeles Times*, October 28, 2016.

47. Patterson, *America's Struggle*.

48. Schwartz, *Fighting Poverty with Virtue*.

49. Trattner, *From Poor Law to Welfare State*.

50. David K. Shipler, *The Working Poor: Invisible in America* (New York: Alfred A. Knopf, 2004).

51. Barbara Ehrenreich, *Nickel and Dimed: On (Not) Getting By in America* (New York: Henry Holt, 2001).

52. William Julius Wilson, *When Work Disappears: The World of the New Urban Poor* (New York: Alfred A. Knopf, 1996).

53. Massey and Denton, *American Apartheid*.

54. Rothstein, *The Color of Law*.

55. Gordon, *Pitied But Not Entitled* (1994).

56. Paula W. Dáil, *Women and Poverty in 21st Century America* (Jefferson, NC: McFarland, 2011).

57. Kenneth L. Kusmer, *Down and Out, On the Road: The Homeless in American History* (New York: Oxford University Press, 2001).

58. Todd DePastino, *Citizen Hobo: How a Century of Homelessness Changed America* (Chicago: University of Chicago Press, 2003).

59. Social Explorer

60. IPUMS

61. Mapping Inequality: Redlining in New Deal America 1905–2016

62. Renewing Inequality: Mapping Displacements Through Urban Renewal 1955–1966

63. Jane Addams, *Twenty Years at Hull House, with Autobiographical Notes* (New York: Macmillan, 1910).

64. Riis, *How the Other Half Lives*.

65. Hunter, *Poverty*.

66. Harrington, *The Other America*.

67. Gunnar Myrdal, *An American Dilemma*; and Oscar Lewis, *Five Families: Mexican Case Studies in the Culture of Poverty; La Vida: A Puerto Rican Family in the Culture of Poverty—San Juan and New York* (New York: Vintage, 1968).

68. Murray, *Losing Ground*.

Ella Howard

WARS ON POVERTY AND THE BUILDING OF THE AMERICAN WELFARE STATE

Since President Lyndon B. Johnson left office in 1969 competition between America's two major political parties has in many ways centered on their relationship to the conflicts of the late 1960s. On most major issues, whether it is how the United States is governed, what role the federal government should play vis-à-vis the states, how minorities—ethnic or sexual—should be treated, or the role of the Supreme Court in interpreting the Constitution, the real and imaginary divisions the 1960s spawned continue to profoundly shape American politics. By and large these divisions have discredited American liberalism, making the 1960s known as the decade of "liberal overreach."[1] American conservatives have for decades argued that the expansion of government through the Great Society programs was a mistake and often failed to help its intended recipients, the poor and underprivileged.[2] Charles Murray in his mid-1980s social policy blockbuster *Losing Ground* flatly stated that: "We tried to provide more for the poor and produced more poor instead. We tried to remove the barriers to escape from poverty, and inadvertently built a trap."[3]

While historians and social scientists have generally been more nuanced in their assessment of the Great Society, there is still a distinct sense in the literature that if not outright failures, the Johnson administration's social programs did not live up to their expectations and were, at the very least, a missed opportunity.[4] Indeed, in one of the leading textbooks on American postwar history William Chafe has argued that the antipoverty effort was fundamentally flawed because policy makers never realized that what was really needed to fight poverty was a massive jobs program and redistribution of income. Other historians have agreed. They have argued that a massive program of employment and/or large-scale income redistribution would have been much more successful and desirable than the War on Poverty.[5]

This broadly negative judgment on the Great Society (and in particular the War on Poverty) has become part of the wider narrative on the American welfare state. Ramshackle and largely ineffective, it is often accused of and criticized for not living up to the size and standards set by other developed countries, most notably in Europe. The manner in which the United States fights (or doesn't fight) poverty is an important example often referred to as illustrating this broader point. Negative pronouncements are made every year in conjunction with the Census Bureau's publication of the official poverty rates. The perennial questions asked are variations on if America needs a new war on poverty or why decades on (since the original 1964 launch) the war is still being lost.[6] Indeed, critics of varying political colors point to how rates of poverty have barely budged since the mid-1960s and that compared to European countries the United States is far behind and spends ever less on the poor.[7] In the late 1950s and early 1960s the poverty rate stood at over 20 percent.[8] By the early 1970s this had fallen to close to 10 percent and the US Census

Bureau's latest (2013) estimated rate is 14.5 percent.[9] For example, noted economist and public policy doyen Jeffrey Sachs in 2006 argued in *Scientific American* that the United States (and other "Anglo Saxon" modeled countries) had fallen behind the high-tax and high-spend Nordic region on most indicators of economic performance.[10] He claimed that "the US spends less than almost all rich countries on social services for the poor and disabled, and it gets what it pays for: the highest poverty rate among the rich countries and an exploding prison population."[11] Others have argued a similar point. In 2001 a National Bureau of Economic Research paper argued that the United States was indeed much less generous to its poor and did not fight poverty as well as many European countries.[12] The authors argued that this was primarily a result of a political system that by and large was geared against income redistribution and a concomitant lack of broad public support for income redistribution primarily due to racism.

The Great Society and War on Poverty programs offer a fascinating prism for understanding the evolution of the 20th-century American welfare state. Its postwar development is not only a story about a number of "wars" or individual political initiatives against poverty, but also about the growth of institutions within and outside government to address, alleviate, and eliminate poverty and its concomitant social ills. From the New Deal to modern-day reform efforts including the Personal Responsibility and Work Opportunity Reconciliation Act of 1996, the expansion of Medicare and Medicaid coverage through Medicare Part D and the most recent Patient Protection and Affordable Care Act, one of the key characteristics of the American welfare state is its piecemeal and gradual evolution. While there have been a number of "big bang" reform efforts, overall the story of the postwar period is the incremental development of a welfare state that has evolved and changed as part of other major political and socioeconomic changes and processes. This development has not been driven only by a policy or reform initiative's perception of success; more intriguingly, policies and reforms considered as grave political errors or failures in a particular era have over time become staples of American social policy. In this respect the Johnson administration's War on Poverty initiative is instructive. It was largely discredited at the time and since, and few would argue that the Great Society and War on Poverty have an enviable reputation—political or otherwise. Yet the fate of its biggest and most maligned component—the Community Action Program—illustrates how a social policy can fail politically and by reputation, yet survive. Over the long-term the program itself and the ideas underpinning it have become an institutionalized and elemental part of the American welfare state.

"FIGHTING MAN'S ANCIENT ENEMIES": THE WAR ON POVERTY AND LYNDON JOHNSON'S GREAT SOCIETY

I want to be the President who educated young children to the wonders of their world. I want to be the President who helped feed the hungry and to prepare them to be taxpayers instead of taxeaters. I want to be the President who helped the poor to find their own way and who protected the right of every citizen to vote in every election.... This great, rich, restless country can offer opportunity and education and hope to all: black and white, North and South, sharecropper and city dweller. These are the enemies: poverty, ignorance, disease. They are the enemies and not our fellow man, not our neighbor. And these enemies too, poverty, disease, and ignorance, we shall overcome.[13]

— *Lyndon Johnson, Special Message to the Congress, March 15, 1965*

Johnson's cause—the thing for which he hoped to be remembered—was the Great Society, his effort to outpace the New Deal, outflank group conflict, override class structure, and improve the lot of everybody in America.[14]

— *Richard Neustadt, in* Presidential Power, *1976 edition*

When he spoke about poverty, Lyndon Johnson spoke with passion. Whether it be from his childhood growing up in rural Texas, his experience from a year out from college teaching destitute Mexican schoolchildren in Cotulla, south Texas, or in his first major political assignment during the mid to late 1930s managing the Texas National Youth Administration, the 36th president of the United States had a deeply personal relationship with poverty. Throughout his years in public office, in speeches and on the campaign trail, Johnson would frequently—no matter what the topic—revert back to images of the poor and of the basic needs and wants of all peoples, regardless of their color or background. In his public and private remarks the president expressed his belief that most people had the same basic wants and desire for education, medical care, and an opportunity to lift themselves out of poverty. Because this conviction was absolutely central to his presidential program, Johnson never saw the War on Poverty and poverty itself as being discrete policy issues isolated from his overall domestic program. On the contrary, most of the Great Society's legislative goals and victories—the extension of civil rights, voting rights legislation, setting federal standards and providing funding for elementary and secondary education, funding health care for the elderly and poor through Medicare and Medicaid—were part of the same idea of building on the New Deal to provide and extend equality of opportunity to all.[15]

But poverty was never defeated. Instead of leading the fight on poverty, the President's Office of Economic Opportunity (OEO) and its local staff were accused of playing an active part in the Newark riots of 1967, funding criminal gangs in Chicago, supporting the staging of racist theater performances in New York City, and embezzling federal money in Mississippi. Such key War on Poverty components as Community Action, the Job Corps, Legal Services, Upward Bound, and even the popular Head Start, were often mentioned in sensational news stories of violence, corruption, and financial mismanagement. Almost as quickly as it had risen to the top of the national policy agenda, the War on Poverty and its programs became one of the topics the president and White House least wanted to discuss. By the end of LBJ's presidential term when poverty as an issue did present itself, it was in the context of the growing welfare rights movement and the newfound militancy of the poor. Revealingly, for these the president did not have much sympathy. For example, during the summer of 1968 the Poor People's Campaign—originally a campaign idea by Martin Luther King Jr.—marched and set up a camp in Washington, DC. Giving speeches and meeting with administration officials, the campaign demanded that the federal government and Congress do more for minorities and the poor. But the president was not moved. Illustrating just how much the times had changed from four years earlier, when the antipoverty campaign had been launched and Johnson had laid out his Great Society vision, LBJ complained to Agriculture Orville Freeman: "the very people we are seeking to help in Medicare and education and welfare and Food Stamps are protesting louder and louder and giving no recognition or allowance for what's been done."[16] In a remarkable glimpse of the subsequent staple conservative criticism that was to define the Great Society in a post-LBJ world, the president lamented the undesirable social consequences that his programs seemed to have resulted in: "Our efforts seem only to have resulted in anarchy.... The women no longer bother to get married, they just keep breeding. The men go their way and the women get relief—why should they work?"[17] If Vietnam became LBJ's foreign policy albatross, the War on Poverty was viewed by many as his

domestic one. Indeed, *Time* magazine in 1966 wrote that "next to the shooting war in Viet Nam, the spending war against home-front poverty is perhaps the most applauded, criticized, and calumniated issue in the U.S."[18]

Not much has changed since the 1960s. Ronald Reagan's famous 1987 sound bite—"we had a war on poverty—poverty won"[19]—if not a wholly accepted verdict, still rings true to a lot of subsequent observers and the American public. Indeed, the chief political legacy of the Great Society and War on Poverty programs can best be understood through this prism of chaotic failure. Politically the results have been stark and largely negative for the Democratic Party. Drained by the war in Vietnam and the general perception that although government programs were not directly responsible for urban rioting and student militancy, they were not doing enough to discourage them, the Johnsonian brand of consensus politics that had so dominated the Democratic Party for nearly two decades fell apart. Beginning in 1968 Democrats in a post-Johnson world embraced what many voters deemed social and political radicalism and abandoned the center ground. Indeed, presidential elections since have often been fought on the issues and perception of the issues permeating from the 1960s. In the words of former presidential speech writer to George W. Bush David Frum, Republicans have been "reprising Nixon's 1972 campaign against McGovern for a third of a century."[20] The results have been profound: since 1968 virtually no Democratic presidential candidate either running as a self-described liberal or labeled as one by his Republican opponent has won an election. In fact, those who have run as outspoken liberals—George McGovern in 1972 and Walter Mondale in 1984—lost forty-nine states each and were beaten in some of the biggest landslides in American electoral history.

For the American welfare state the political legacy and poor reputation of the Great Society programs have meant that it has often found itself facing criticism of not doing enough for its intended recipients while maintaining a deep unpopularity with the general public. As sociologist John Myles has put it, there is a general perception that "for middle-aged, middle-income Americans, the welfare state is virtually all cost and no benefit."[21] Yet while critical in contributing to these negative perceptions of the welfare state, the negative political history and legacy of the Great Society is only half of the story. Paradoxically, many of the most heavily criticized anti-poverty programs are the most misunderstood, as they have had, and continue to have, a long-lasting impact on social and welfare services in the United States.

MAXIMUM FEASIBLE MISUNDERSTANDING: THE COMMUNITY ACTION PROGRAM AND THE DIVISIONS OF THE 1960s

While more famous programs, such as Project Head Start and Legal Services, have achieved higher levels of visible success and entrenchment within the American social policy framework, it is arguable whether any of the War on Poverty programs have been more influential on American social policy than the Community Action Program (CAP).

When it was launched in the mid-1960s, Community Action was meant to be a way of funneling federal support directly to local communities and involving these communities in the design and implementation of local anti-poverty action programs. It was in many ways intended to bypass conventional interest groups and involve a multitude of stakeholders. Indeed, communities consisting of the poor, local government, and business and labor interests would come together and form not-for-profit Community Action Agencies (CAAs) to coordinate, engage, and devise plans for tackling the problems of local poverty. The CAP designers believed that locally planned and implemented programs would stand a better chance of successfully fighting poverty and coordinating existing federal, state, and local efforts than any program that was centrally designed and managed through existing federal departments. In particular this was a view supported and promulgated by the president's economic counselors including Walter Heller and Charles Schultze of the Council of Economic Advisors (CEA) and Bureau of the Budget (BOB), respectively. Yet the CAP quickly became one of the Johnson administration's most heavily criticized and maligned programs. At root was a basic and unresolved disagreement over what Community Action actually meant.

To some the idea of Community Action was simply a management vehicle, a way of coordinating the many disparate and overlapping anti-poverty programs existing within the federal, state, and local bureaucracies. Community Action was in this light viewed as a deliverer and coordinator of services to combat poverty. Certainly, consultation with the poor and participation of the poor were elemental parts of this approach, but this version of Community Action was not about political or social empowerment. It was simply a new way of more efficiently coordinating programs and engaging the poor in an effort to help them help themselves.[22] Bypassing state government and distributing federal funds directly to the CAAs was administratively a relatively new approach,[23] but one based on what the White House and administration viewed as the "traditional and time-tested American methods of organized community effort to help individuals, families and whole communities to help themselves."[24] This was also the view held by many in Congress. For example, Republican congressman Albert Quie was a staunch supporter of the Community Action concept, if harsh critic of the OEO, arguing that the Community Action concept devolved power locally.[25] Similarly, Carl Perkins, a member of the House Education and Labor Committee to which the poverty bill was referred in March 1964, supported the idea of local community involvement and participation of the poor.[26]

But to others, Community Action translated into direct political empowerment—a way of forcefully confronting political and economic power structures. It was a way of taking, and giving, power to the poor by means of confrontation. This type of Community Action was closely associated with the thinking of Saul Alinsky, a former Chicago academic and community organizer who ran several independent community organizations around the country and later became associated with some of the more radical OEO-funded programs in Syracuse and Chicago. Crucially, this brand of Community Action became the popularized perception of the program and was extensively covered by major news outlets and in Congress throughout the 1960s.[27]

President Johnson's views on what Community Action would do to shake up social policy and local government appear to be very different and certainly a lot less radical than those of other proponents of Community Action. As he would later reveal in his memoirs: "This plan [community action] had the sound of something brand new and even faintly radical. Actually, it was based on one of the oldest ideas of our democracy, as old as the New England town meeting—self determination at the local level."[28] The tragedy of Community Action, the OEO, and the War on Poverty is that these efforts never had the type of leadership and clarity of purpose that could have made this vision a political reality and from the beginning effectively sidelined the noisy minority of radicals both within the OEO and on the ground. The anti-poverty director Sargent Shriver was never wholeheartedly committed to the Johnsonian view of the War on Poverty and Community Action. While this does not mean that he was committed to a more radical view of Community Action, Shriver's political ambitions and willingness to cater to some of his more radical constituents and own staff meant that the fundamental confusion about the purpose of Community Action and the War on Poverty—highlighted in management survey after management survey of the agency—was never resolved.[29]

When the anti-poverty director finally attempted to grapple with this fundamental problem in 1967 by amending the anti-poverty legislation to include more representation of local government, the OEO had already reached a political endgame. Once the ghettos started burning and conflict and militancy firmly replaced consensus and peaceful civil rights, neither the OEO director nor the White House were in any position to stem the tide.

When CAP was launched, Shriver expressed the sentiment that it relied "on the traditional and time-tested American methods of organized community effort to help individuals, families and whole communities to help themselves."[30] While this was certainly the view that the president took, Shriver never consistently or convincingly maintained this position. Norbert Schlei, Department of Justice lawyer and drafter of the original Economic Opportunity Act in 1964, has argued that relatively early on there was a real shift in the emphasis of the poverty program, a shift that came from the anti-poverty director himself:

> I think the whole concept [of maximum feasible participation and Community Action] began to evolve and it got to be much more this matter of putting the target population in charge, putting the local people in charge of the federal money.... I really hadn't understood that that was part of it....I think that even while it was not yet passed [the EOA] there appeared some drift in the whole thinking about community action.... Some of it came out of Shriver. I would hear Shriver say things that made me feel that there had been some evolution in thinking since I was directly involved... the idea of putting the target population in a power position and the idea of putting the local government people in a power position seemed to me to be talked about like they were much more integral to the whole idea than I had understood originally.[31]

Other OEO insiders have supported this view. For example, Eric Tolmach, who worked on CAP in the OEO, has also described Shriver as sending very mixed messages to those within the agency who supported radical Community Action. Tolmach argued that Shriver felt that by supporting radical CAPs "it separated him from the average bureaucrat in town, and it gained him some credibility on the one hand with large groups of people who were for doing this kind of thing, and with the poor."[32] This is an important aspect of the history of the War on Poverty as it ties in with the bigger narrative of the changing politics of poverty and the Democratic Party during the mid to late 1960s.

Ambitious Democratic politicians such as Sargent Shriver and Bobby Kennedy—and even some Republicans like New York mayor John Lindsay[33]—saw the radicalization of the political discourse that permeated this period as an opportunity as well as a shift in how future elections and voters would be won. For Shriver, building up and maintaining a natural constituency through the poverty programs was a way of connecting with this new type of politics and its new constituents. Indeed, some have argued that this was in fact Shriver's raison d'être for staying on as OEO director. In his oral history interview for the Johnson Library, Ben Heinemann (chairman of one of the internal White House policy task forces) described Shriver's and the president's working relationship as "terrible" and commented that the only reason Shriver stayed on was "ambition" and a desire to "remain in the public view."[34] The anti-poverty director, Heinemann said, "didn't have a good alternative [to the War on Poverty] that would still have been in the public eye."[35] That he was intent on running for office was clear to Heinemann, who described Shriver in 1967 as being "anxious to talk…about the possibilities of his running for Governor in Illinois in '68."[36]

But Shriver's constituency and brand of New Politics did not have the kind of national electoral impact for which he had hoped. In 1968 the Democratic presidential coalition fell apart with Richard Nixon and George Wallace combining to shave off almost 20 percentage points from LBJ's 1964 margin of victory over Goldwater. The New Politics never emerged as a winning electoral force; instead, it created the bedrock for the success of the Republican coalition. In no small measure this was caused by the perceived radicalism of the New Politics constituents: younger voters, Vietnam protesters, and radical civil rights and welfare activists. Many of these groups took their roots in the poverty programs and the type of militancy that became the public image of the OEO. These groups contributed to splitting the Democratic Party by pushing white blue-collar voters into the GOP and shaping subsequent winning Republican presidential coalitions. When Shriver finally ran as George McGovern's vice presidential candidate in 1972, Richard Nixon leaned heavily on his opposition to this New Politics coalition and scored a historic victory on par with Johnson's eight years earlier. Similarly, in 1976 when Shriver was a candidate for the Democratic presidential nomination, he did not win a single primary; his best showing was in Vermont, where he came in second, gaining 28 percent of the vote and losing to the eventual nominee, Jimmy Carter.

In many ways, the history of Community Action represents a microcosm for the wider War on Poverty and Great Society effort. Maligned at the time, both the very nature of the program and its achievements tell a different story. Now lost in the broader fireworks of the 1960s, the Community Action Program at the time became the prime example of everything that had gone wrong with the anti-poverty effort and a symbol of the Johnson administrations' and "big government's" overreach. The most famous and scathing criticism came from former White House and executive branch insider Daniel Patrick Moynihan, whose negative assessment of the War on Poverty set the tone for both contemporary understanding and subsequent analysis.[37] In 1968 he went as far as to claim that intended or not, Community Action had contributed to the past summers' rioting:[38] Although vehemently denied in government press release after press release, this image of the OEO and Community Action Agencies as playing a prominent part in the tearing up of the American social fabric persisted in the popular as well as the political mind.

Yet for all the bad press and brouhaha it is not clear that a majority, or even a large minority, of Community Action Agencies were engaged in the types of activities as depicted in the media. Certainly, there were many instances in which a local agency got into political trouble and hit the front pages of the national newspapers for all the wrong reasons, but these instances are not representative of the policy directions taken by all, or even a majority, of the agencies that had been established by the mid-1960s. By 1967 there were almost 1,100 Community Action Agencies in operation, and only a handful of these can be described as having been marked by the type of radicalism and conflict that has come to define the entire program. And, as accurately noted by historian Alice O'Connor, these grants were primarily from the CAP's experimental demonstration programs.[39] These facts were noted and understood at the time within the White House. Internal memoranda and research suggests that there was broad support and understanding for the real achievements of Community Action within the War on Poverty.[40] For example, in the recommendations to President Johnson of the 1966 Taskforce on Government Organization it was argued that "community action agencies remain the best available instrument for integrating and focusing government and private social service programs at the local neighborhood and community level" and that "at their best, community action agencies reflect a thoroughly American, solidly conservative approach to social problems: they are locally inspired and controlled, and responsive to the disadvantaged people whom they seek to serve."[41] Even President Johnson himself lent the program his vocal support in the 1967 State of the Union address, which dealt in some detail with the War on Poverty and, if anything, reaffirmed the president's commitment to fighting poverty through localized Community Action.[42] Yet, these messages never reached the broader public or, until recently, the scholarship.[43] But for all the negative press, Community Action has lived on and continued to shape American social policy.

While the OEO was finally disbanded by President Gerald Ford in 1976, Community Action has survived as a federally funded program. Today there are over 1,000 Community Action Agencies.[44] The latest data from the National Association for State Community Services Programs shows that in 2013 Community Action Agencies served close to 16 million individuals (part of 6.7 million families) of which over 70 percent were at or below the federal poverty line.[45]

But in contrast to its role set out in the original Economic Opportunity Act of 1964, the federal government now plays a reduced part in the funding and monitoring of national Community Action. Instead, much of the responsibility has since the 1990s been transferred to the state level.

Created as a new federal agency by Congress in December 1974, the Community Services Administration (CSA) replaced the disbanded OEO. Never part of the Executive Office of the President, the CSA remained a separate independent agency outside the established federal bureaucracy until its own subsequent closure in 1981. That year President Ronald Reagan replaced, and Congress approved, the CSA with a small Office of Community Services lodged in the Department of Health and Human Services. This office remains in operation and is today responsible for the government-supported Community Action effort. But under the Omnibus Reconciliation Act of 1981 the federal government's direct role in funding local CAPs was replaced by Community Service Block Grants (CSBG). No longer do federal grants go directly to local Action Agencies. Instead CSBGs are distributed to the states, which then in turn administer them to organizations that are officially designated Community Action Agencies under the CSBG Act.[46] These block grants are applied for by individual states and approved on an annual basis by the Office of Community Services. Outside of government, Community Action is represented by the National Association of Community Action Agencies, a group formed in 1971 to provide a national voice for Community Action. This association professes to be a "national forum for policy on poverty and to strengthen, promote, represent, and serve its network of member agencies to assure that the issues of the poor are effectively heard and addressed."[47]

It would seem that if longevity is any measure of success, there is a strong argument to be made that Community Action has been anything but a failure. Although the CAAs of today are different from those of the 1960s, the requirement that Community Action boards should be made up of a combination of the poor, local and state government, and the private sector is still there.[48] Outlasting the Office of Economic Opportunity, the continued existence of these CAAs suggests that while the centralized operational arm of President Johnson's War on Poverty could not survive on its own, the local organization, run for and by local communities, could, and has. This is a powerful testament to the idea that decentralized policymaking in social and welfare policy involving all relevant stakeholders is an enduring part of American social policy. Remarkably, this belief has since the late 20th century crossed party and ideological lines, becoming a defining characteristic of modern American conservatism.

FROM COMMUNITY ACTION TO COMPASSIONATE CONSERVATISM

In the mid-1990s *compassionate conservatism* became part of the mainstream political lexicon. Pioneered by Texas academic Marvin Olasky in his 1992 *The Tragedy of American Compassion*, compassionate conservatism was embraced by a number of influential Republican thinkers, politicians, and strategists. Indeed, during this time many Republican think tanks and grassroots organizations acutely felt the need for the Republican Party to redefine itself, and move away from the popularized image of the party with a cold heart, dead-set against helping the poor and needy. John Ashcroft, Ralph Reed, Bob Dole, Bill Bennett, Jack Kemp, Dan Coats, and Jim Talent all became part of this burgeoning compassion movement. Loudest of the voices calling for a new direction was freshly appointed Speaker of the House, Newt Gingrich, who pleaded for more compassion in the GOP. During his first session as Speaker he repeatedly made reference to Olasky's work when outlining the need for Republicans to adopt a new conservative agenda.[49]

But it was not only in Washington that Republicans were talking about compassion. While George W. Bush had shown an interest in the founding ideas of compassionate conservatism as early as 1993—even meeting with Professor Olasky—and had during his first term as governor made it easier under Texas state law for private and religious charities to operate, Bush would not become compassionate conservatism's national face until his 1998 gubernatorial re-election. On victory night of his landslide win he declared that he had big plans for the future, wanting to give the Republican Party a new look, that of compassionate conservatism.[50]

During the following primary campaign for the Republican 2000 presidential nomination, Governor Bush set out his vision and philosophy for what compassionate conservatism meant to him and a future Bush administration. In a defining speech summing up the work of a task force of policy analysts and academics he had appointed in February, Bush in July 1999 outlined what compassionate conservatism meant and what as president he could do for America's poor. Central to this speech, and the governor's conception of compassionate conservatism, was the idea that anti-poverty initiatives should be local and as far as possible designed and run by third-sector agencies. He argued that local communities, religious organizations, and other nongovernmental groups should together with local, state, and the federal government fight poverty and provide opportunity for the poor, homeless, and needy:

> We will make a determined attack on need, by promoting the compassionate acts of others. We will rally the armies of compassion in our communities to fight a very different war against poverty and hopelessness, a daily battle waged house to house and heart by heart. This will not be the failed compassion of towering bureaucracies. On the contrary, it will be government that serves those who are serving their neighbors. It will be government that directs help to the inspired and the effective. It will be government that both knows its limits and shows its heart. And it will be government truly by the people and for the people.[51]

To Governor Bush, such a plan to fight poverty stood in stark contrast to the efforts of the War on Poverty and the Great Society, which he accused of being too bureaucratic, government-centered, and lacking in true compassion:

> In the past, presidents have declared wars on poverty and promised to create a great society. But these grand gestures and honorable aims were frustrated. They have become a warning, not an example. We found that government can spend money, but it can't put hope in our hearts or a sense of purpose in our lives.[52]

The ideas of fighting poverty through local charities and religious organizations became a defining feature of Bush's successful presidential campaign. Compassionate conservatism and the belief that faith-based organizations could revolutionize the way in which the federal government delivered its social welfare programs became one of the campaign's core selling points on domestic policy. Indeed, as early as June 1999 political correspondent Adam Nagourney of the New York Times was writing about compassionate conservatism as being Governor's Bush's defining political slogan.[53] Once he took office, the president's Faith-Based Initiative was at the center of his compassionate agenda. While the actual legislation put forward for the initiative was primarily about the federal government not discriminating against religious groups when providing funding for local anti-poverty and social welfare services, at its heart the initiative was as much about local action being the best remedy for social problems like poverty, drug addiction, and single parenthood.[54] Yet what Governor and then President Bush failed to at least publicly acknowledge was that the influence of the War on Poverty and Community Action had already extended and heavily influenced the manner in which America's welfare state actually provides and delivers its public services. The Great Society's, War on Poverty's, and Community Action's most important social policy legacy is perhaps the contribution it made toward the outsourcing of service provision to the third sector and nonprofits.

COMMUNITY ACTION AND MODERN AMERICAN SOCIAL POLICY

Local, decentralized, usually not-for-profit and nongovernmental—in all but a few instances, these are the defining characteristics of the providers of many of the public services Americans receive today. Since the 1960s and the launch of the Great Society programs, the growth in the provision of governmental services through the third sector has been astonishing. Although in sheer numbers the

Social Security program is still the number one social welfare program today, many public services are not provided through or by the American government. Instead, government services are now largely provided by nongovernment entities and nonprofits in particular. This is especially pronounced with regard to social services and human services, where nonprofit organizations actually deliver a larger share of the services government finances than do government agencies themselves.[55] Through some of the biggest federal welfare and human services programs such as Medicare, Medicaid, student aid, and food stamps, the American state at all levels—federal, state, and local—serves mainly as the ultimate payer and regulator, but not provider of public services.

Similarly, and while conceptually different, the expansion of the use of grants-in-aid programs since the 1960s has also significantly bolstered the use of nonprofits and nongovernmental entities in the provision of public services. Through grants-in-aid the federal government provides block grants to state and local governments with relatively few programmatic requirements on how services should be provided. These grants are then used and distributed by state and local governments, which contract out the provision of services to nonprofits and the private sector.[56]

In 2011 it was estimated that over 30 percent of the federal government's budget went to the direct purchasing of public services or grants to provide such services.[57] For nonprofits in particular the growth has been significant both for direct purchases and grants, growing by an estimated 195 percent for the former between 1977 and 1997 and over 330 percent for the latter in the two decades between 1982 and 2002.[58]

While the seeds of the use of nonprofits and nongovernmental entities existed prior to the 1960s, the Johnson administration's anti-poverty and welfare programs greatly expanded and institutionalized the use of the third sector in the provision of public services, primarily through the War on Poverty programs and

the use of Community Action. Indeed, political scientist and noted historian of the third sector Peter Hall saw the War on Poverty as central to the growth of the postwar nonprofit sector:

> if the political right supplied the rhetoric for efforts to down-size government, liberals and progressives could take credit for actually implementing large-scale privatization, first through local nonprofit organizations—many of them faith-based—subsidized by Lyndon Johnson's War on Poverty, and later through deinstitutionalization of the mentally disabled and the subsequent creation of a vast system of community-based treatment and care provided by nonprofits operating under contract with state and local government.[59]

CONCLUSION: AMERICA'S WARS ON POVERTY AND WELFARE STATE

In his classic 1990 dissection of the welfare state, Danish sociologist Gøsta Esping-Andersen outlined three welfare state regimes: liberal, corporatist, and social democratic.[60] With its traditional reliance on the power of the market, strict entitlement rules and means-testing, low social welfare benefits, and a culture of individualism the United States was described as the archetypal liberal regime standing in stark contrast to most European nations.[61] While Esping-Andersen's work has been much criticized since—and revised by the author—the idea that the American welfare state is fundamentally different (indeed even exceptional) in size, purpose, and function from other developed Organisation for Economic Co-operation and Development (OECD) economies lives on both inside and outside academia. But what does the evidence actually show?

Traditionally, measures of welfare states and social protection look at the availability of social insurance (e.g., unemployment and health insurance) and availability of welfare and assistance programs, as well as labor market policies.[62] More often than not these are measures of total public and government expenditure. Using these traditional measures of social spending as an initial gauge of the size of the welfare state it is clear that the United States has historically spent less than other developed countries on social and welfare services. For instance, OECD data from 2014 show public social expenditure in the United States totaled just over 19 percent of GDP.[63] This is in comparison to an average of between 28 and 32 percent in France, Finland, Belgium, Italy, Sweden, and others. Clearly the United States is behind these countries. And for this year the United States was also below the OECD average of 21.62 percent but ahead of both Canada and Australia. But levels of public spending do not necessarily tell the whole picture.

Less attention has been paid to private or third-sector spending and activities and indirect variables such as the impact of tax laws. Regarding the latter, instead of authorizing direct social spending, American lawmakers have long used the federal tax code as a social policy tool. The most notable example in which the tax code works as a government subsidy by tax exempting certain types of benefits is the employer-based health insurance benefit, which is exempt from income and payroll taxation. While this benefit has been in place since the 1940s it was formalized into law in the 1954 Revenue Act.[64] The growth and development of this benefit has profoundly shaped the American welfare state and while nominally in the nonpublic sphere of spending it is nevertheless a significant de facto concession of tax revenue for the federal government. In 2013 this was estimated to amount to a loss of revenue to the federal government of $250 billion or roughly 7 percent of the total 2013 federal budget.[65] Moreover, if one looks beyond levels of public social expenditure and also include spending outside of

government the US position changes dramatically. Looking at the latest total public and *private* spending estimates by the OECD the United States actually has one of the highest rates of social expenditure—and biggest welfare states—in the world at close to 29 percent of GDP in 2011, behind only France.[66] Table 1 shows this data for the United States and other OECD countries.

By comparison the country and welfare model the American welfare state is most often contrasted with, Sweden, is quite far behind with a rate of 24.6 percent of GDP net social expenditure in 2011. Furthermore, if one looks at the trajectory of public social expenditure over a longer time-frame it is not at all clear that the American postwar experience is any different from that of other developed countries or the EU. OECD data going back to 1960 suggest that while always lagging behind average public spending levels in the EU (which is explained by the higher levels of nonpublic spending) US government expenditure has since the 1960s followed an almost identical trajectory. Table 2 shows public social expenditure from 1960 to 2014 comparing levels in the United States, Japan, EU21, and OECD.

As Table 2 shows, the spending patterns and trajectory are very similar across all countries and regions. Interestingly, the data in the table also suggest that social spending has over the long term, by and large, been immune to changes in government and political affiliation. For example, except for the Reagan years, social expenditure in the United States grew quite markedly during periods of Republican administrations particularly in the 1970s and 2000s under presidents Richard Nixon and George W. Bush. Indeed, the period in which the biggest difference between levels of social expenditure between the EU 21 and the United States can be seen is between the mid-1970s and early 1980s. During this time social spending continued to grow in the EU21 while in the United States it actually decreased under President Jimmy Carter.

Table 1. Net total social expenditure (public and private), % of GDP, OECD countries 2011. [67]

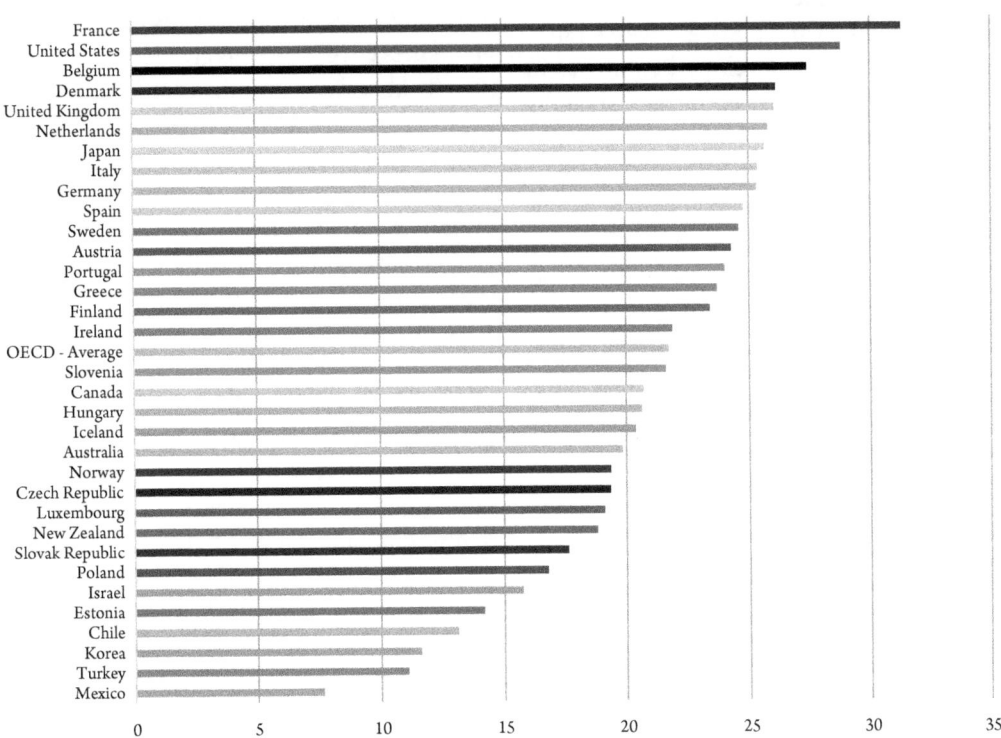

Table 2. Public social expenditure, % of GDP, United States, Japan, EU-21, and OECD, 1960–2014. [68]

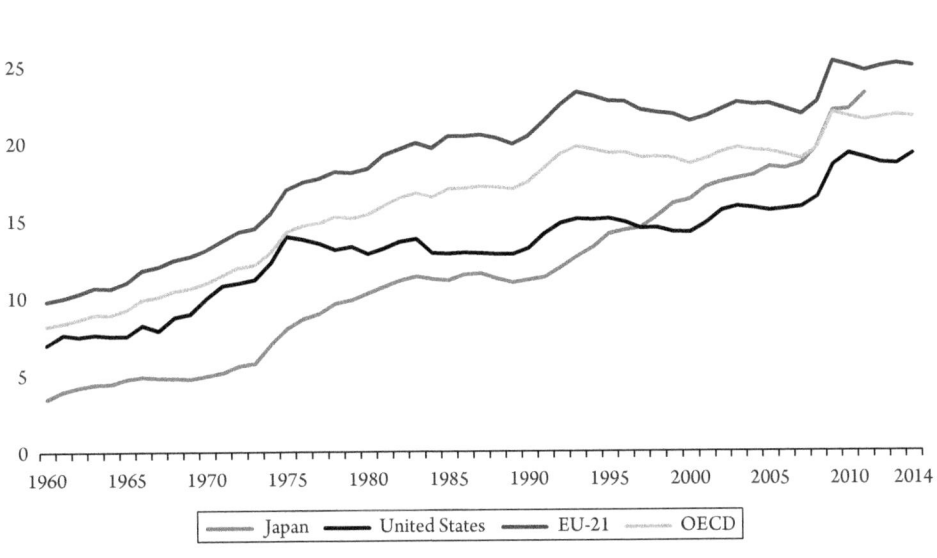

The above statistics and data from the OECD show that measured as a share of economic output the United States invests a similar amount to other developed countries in social spending. They also show how since the 1960s and throughout most of the postwar period the trajectory of American public social expenditure has not been markedly different from other developed economies. Instead, the difference between the United States and other countries has been the presence of nonpublic entities. One of the key findings by political scientist Jacob Hacker in his 2002 *The Divided Welfare State* was that in the United States a large portion of social spending and the make-up of the American welfare state is nonpublic.[69] Looking at the history of the American welfare state, there was no Beveridge report or equivalent starting point for a complete overhaul and introduction of a welfare model. The closest the United States came to this was during the New Deal era and World War II. Some have indeed argued that US policy planners during the latter stages of the New Deal (and particularly during the course of World War II) were intent on moving America toward a Beveridge-style full-employment welfare state.[70]

The War on Poverty and the Great Society illustrate the development of the postwar American welfare state. The Community Action Program specifically offers an instructive historical example of the ways in which the modern American welfare state—the provision of public services through nonprofits—gradually and paradoxically developed over decades out of what was and has been widely regarded as a prime example of a failed social policy. Mirroring the broader organization of the American political system, with a relatively weak center of power and delegated authority and decision-making in fifty states, the welfare model has developed and grown over decades. Policies such as Community Action viewed in one era as unmitigated failures have instead over time evolved and become part of the fabric of the welfare state.

DISCUSSION OF THE LITERATURE

There is no distinct unitary historiography of all themes covered in this article, that is, Great Society liberalism, President Johnson, the War on Poverty, Community Action, and the American welfare state. Instead, broadly speaking, scholars have focused on various aspects within these topics, which, while although often overlapping, are often best viewed and understood as coming from discrete research silos. For example, studying the American welfare state has often been the purview of social scientists. Perspectives have ranged from the quantitative to sociological to political institutional to a more traditional history narrative.[71] Looking at the Great Society, the Johnson administration, and the War on Poverty programs, this literature can roughly be divided into two categories: that which looks specifically at, say, the War on Poverty (or specific programs or components of the War on Poverty including Community Action, Legal Services, etc.), and that which looks at either of these within the context of bigger themes like the 1960s, Great Society liberalism, the Johnson presidency, or the evolution of the American welfare state. Since the 1970s more has been published on the latter than the former; consequently, books on these broader themes make up the larger and more well-established literature. They include textbook accounts and more traditional sweeping narratives, including biographies. Because Community Action and the War on Poverty never lived up to their political or policy expectations—neither vanquished poverty or revolutionized the way federal, state, and local anti-poverty efforts were coordinated—much of the general historiography about the two tends to emphasize failure—failure to fight poverty, failure to adequately plan programs, failure to foresee the conflict that the War on Poverty programs (in particular Community Action) are viewed as invariably leading to. There is also a strong tendency to view Community Action and the War on Poverty as targeting black poverty.

These ideas are as common in specialist studies as in general surveys of American history and the 1960s. Examples where one or more of these perceptions are prominent include William Chafe's *The Unfinished Journey*, Walter Trattner's *From Poor Law to Welfare State*, Irving Bernstein's *Guns or Butter*, and Judith Russell's *Economics, Bureaucracy, and Race: How Keynesians Misguided the War on Poverty*. There are a few exceptions to this negativism, including Robert F. Clark's 2002 *The War on Poverty: History, Selected Programs and Ongoing Impact*, Michael Katz's *The Undeserving Poor: From the War on Poverty to the War on Welfare*, and John E. Schwarz's *America's Hidden Success: A Reassessment of Public Policy from Kennedy to Reagan*. However, these have had a relatively limited influence on public or academic perceptions of the poverty programs.

Recently, a new generation of scholars have been examining the War on Poverty and local programs, often from a grass-roots perspective. Examples of these include Kent B. Germany's 2007 *New Orleans after the Promises*, Robert Bauman's 2007 *Journal of Urban History* article "The Black Power and Chicano Movements in the Poverty Wars in Los Angeles," Noel Cazenave's 2007 *Impossible Democracy: The Unlikely Success of the War on Poverty Community Action Programs*, Susan Youngblood Ashmore's 2008 *Carry It On: The War on Poverty and the Civil Rights Movement in Alabama*, and Guian McKee's 2008 *The Problem of Jobs: Liberalism, Race, and Deindustrialization in Philadelphia*.[72] These studies are all of real importance, as they form part of a new historiography that in many respects challenges established perceptions about the War on Poverty. They provide an often detailed and rich account of a particular local anti-poverty effort and real insight into the local politics of a program. While many of these studies still focus on urban areas, there has also emerged a new sub-field in the study of anti-poverty programs that examines its rural component.[73] Just as with their urban counterparts these studies are adding nuance and much needed detail to the War on Poverty scholarship. They are showing how rural anti-poverty efforts functioned and were part of wider historical processes that were changing the complexion of American society, in particular the advance of civil rights in the South and Southwest.

PRIMARY SOURCES

The National Archives, College Park, Maryland, and Lyndon Johnson presidential library in Austin, Texas, house the most important primary sources with regard to the federal and presidential aspects of the War on Poverty, Johnson administration, and Community Action Program. For the Community Action Program the most relevant archival records and record groups are: National Archives, College Park, Maryland, Records of the Community Services Administration, Record Group 381, Headquarters Records of the Office of Economic Opportunity 1963–1981. For the War on Poverty and administration of the OEO the most relevant files in the Johnson Library archives are organized around the President's key staffers.[74] The Johnson Library also houses a number of important oral history interviews of the key figures in the War on Poverty. The Miller Center of Public Affairs, University of Virginia, Scripps Library and Multimedia Archive, houses a significant collection of oral history interviews and tape recordings from a number of postwar presidencies including the Johnson administration.[75] Significantly, these collections are digital and housed in an online library accessible to all anywhere in the world.

FURTHER READING

Brauer, Carl M. "Kennedy, Johnson and the War on Poverty." *Journal of American History* 69.1 (June 1982): 98–119.

Danziger, Sheldon, and Daniel H. Weinberg, eds. *Fighting Poverty: What Works and What Doesn't*. Cambridge, MA: Harvard University Press, 1986.

Davies, Gareth. *From Opportunity to Entitlement: The Transformation and Decline of Great Society*

Liberalism. Lawrence: University Press of Kansas, 1996.

Davies, Gareth. *See Government Grow: Education Politics from Johnson to Reagan*. Lawrence: University Press of Kansas, 2007.

Gillette, Michael L. *Launching the War on Poverty: An Oral History*. New York: Twayne, 1996.

Heale, M. J. *The Sixties in America: History, Politics and Protest*. Edinburgh: Edinburgh University Press, 2001.

Heale, M. J. "The Sixties as History: A Review of the Political Historiography." *Reviews in American History* 33.1 (March 2005): 133–152.

Hecker, J. *The Divided Welfare State: The Battle over Public and Private Social Benefits in the United States*. Washington, DC: New America Foundation, 2002.

Heidenhammer, Arnold J., Hugh Heclo, and Carolyn Teich Adams. *Comparative Public Policy: The Politics of Social Choice in America, Europe, and Japan*. Basingstoke, UK: Macmillan, 1990.

Hodgson, Godfrey. *America in Our Time: From World War II to Nixon*. Princeton, NJ: Princeton University Press, 2005.

Johnson, Lyndon. *The Vantage Point: Perspectives of the Presidency 1963–1969*. New York: Holt, Rinehart and Winston, 1971.

Jorgenson, Dale W. "Did We Lose the War on Poverty?" *Journal of Economic Perspectives* 12.1 (Winter 1998): 79–96.

Katz, Michael. *The Undeserving Poor: From the War on Poverty to the War on Welfare*. New York: Pantheon, 1989.

Levine, Robert A. *The Poor Ye Need Not Have With You: Lessons from the War on Poverty*. Cambridge, MA: MIT Press, 1970.

Marris, Peter, and Martin Rein. *Dilemmas of Social Reform: Poverty and Community Action in the United States*. Harmondsworth, UK: Penguin, 1974.

Matusow, Allen J. *The Unravelling of America: A History of Liberalism in the 1960s*. London and New York: Harper & Row, 1986.

Moynihan, Daniel P. *On Understanding Poverty: Perspectives from the Social Sciences*. New York and London: Basic Books, 1968–1969.

Moynihan, Daniel P. *Maximum Feasible Misunderstanding: Community Action in the War on Poverty*. New York: Free Press, 1969.

Patterson, James T. *America's Struggle against Poverty 1900–1994*. Cambridge, MA, and London: Harvard University Press, 1994.

Schwarz, John E. *America's Hidden Success: A Reassessment of Public Policy from Kennedy to Reagan*. London and New York: W. W. Norton, 1988.

Skowronek, Stephen. *Building a New American State—The Expansion of National Administrative Capacities 1877–1920*. Cambridge, UK: Cambridge University Press, 1997.

Sundquist, James. *Politics and Policy: The Eisenhower, Kennedy, and Johnson Years*. Washington, DC: Brookings Institution, 1968.

Sundquist, James, ed. *On Fighting Poverty: Perspectives from Experience*. New York: Basic Books, 1969.

Trattner, Walter I. *From Poor Law to Welfare State: A History of Social Welfare in America*. New York: Macmillan, 1989.

Woods, Randall. *LBJ: Architect of American Ambition*. New York: Simon & Schuster, 2006.

NOTES

1. *The Economist*, Leader. "Is America Turning Left?" 11 August 2007.

2. Prominent critics have included Ronald Reagan, Newt Gingrich, D. P. Moynihan, Irving Kristol, and George W. Bush.

3. Charles Murray, *Losing Ground: American Social Policy 1950–1980* (New York: Basic Books, 1984), 9.

4. See: William Chafe, *The Unfinished Journey: America since World War II* (Oxford: Oxford University Press, 1991); Walter Trattner, *From Poor Law to Welfare State: A History of Social Welfare in America* (New York: Macmillan, 1989); Ira Katznelson, "Was the Great Society a Lost Opportunity," in *The Rise and Fall of the New Deal Order*, ed. Steve Fraser and Gary Gerstle (Princeton, NJ: Princeton University Press, 1989); Irving Bernstein, *Guns or Butter The Presidency of Lyndon Johnson* (Oxford: Oxford University Press, 1996); and Robert F. Caro, *The Years of Lyndon Johnson: The Path to Power* (London: Collins, 1982) and *The Years of Lyndon Johnson: Means of Ascent* (London: Bodley Head, 1990).

5. Chafe, *The Unfinished Journey*, 242; Allen J. Matusow, "The Great Society: A Twenty-Year Critique," in *Lyndon B. Johnson and American Liberalism: A Brief Biography with Documents*, ed. Bruce J. Schulman (Boston: Bedford Books, 1995), 186; and Judith Russell, *Economics, Bureaucracy, and Race: How Keynesians Misguided the War on*

Poverty (New York: Columbia University Press, 2004), 5–15.

6. See, for example, a January 5, 2014, *New York Times* article on the fifty-year anniversary of President Lyndon Johnson's launch of the War on Poverty. The *New York Times* asked a panel of opinion leaders a simple question: "Does the U.S. Need Another War on Poverty?" While the answers varied, all the invited debaters accepted the martial premise of the question. That a war on poverty had been fought and that eliminating poverty was a "fight" or a "battle" was not in doubt.

7. See, for example: National Public Radio "How America's Losing the War On Poverty," August 4, 2012; Robert Rector "How the War on Poverty Was Lost," *Wall Street Journal*, January 7, 2014; Erika Eichelberger, Jaeah Lee, and A. J. Vicens, "How We Won—and Lost—the War on Poverty, in 6 Charts," *Mother Jones*, January 8, 2014; and E. Porter, "The Measure of Our Poverty," *New York Times*, September 20, 2013.

8. C. DeNavas-Walt and D. Bernadette, US Census Bureau, Current Population Reports, P60–249, *Income and Poverty in the United States: 2013* (US Government Printing Office, Washington, DC, 2014), 12.

9. DeNavas-Walt and Bernadette, U.S. Census Bureau, Current Population Reports, P60–249.

10. Jeffrey Sachs, "The Social Welfare State, beyond Ideology," *Scientific American* (November 2006): 3.

11. Sachs, "The Social Welfare State, beyond Ideology."

12. A. Alesina, E. Glaeser, and B. Sacerdote, "Why Doesn't the US Have a European-Style Welfare State?" Harvard Institute of Economic Research, Discussion Paper Number 1933, Harvard 2001, 38–39.

13. Lyndon Johnson, Special Message to the Congress, March 15, 1965, Public Papers.

14. Richard Neustadt, *Presidential Power: The Politics of Leadership, with Reflections on Johnson and Nixon* (London and New York: Wiley, 1976), 34.

15. One of the biggest and most important differences between the Great Society and the New Deal was that the former was to be achieved by the harnessing of capitalism and free enterprise. See, for example, the importance attached to economic growth theory and tax cuts to LBJ's domestic program. On the contrary, the latter was justified as a consequence of the negative impact of the Great Depression and the perceived failures of unfettered capitalism.

16. Quoted in Woods, *LBJ*, 843.

17. Quoted in Woods, *LBJ*.

18. *Time*, "Poverty: Six-Star Sargent," March 18, 1966, *Time*, online archive.

19. Ronald Reagan, Remarks at a White House briefing for members of the American Legislative Exchange Council (http://www.reagan.utexas.edu/archives/speeches/1987/050187g.htm), May 1, 1987, *Public Papers of the President*.

20. George Packer, "The Fall of Conservatism: Have the Republicans Run Out of Ideas?" *New Yorker* (May 26, 2008): 47–54.

21. John Myles, "Postwar Capitalism and the Extension of Social Security into a Retirement Wage," in *The Politics of Social Policy in the United States*, ed. Margaret Weir, Ann Shola Orloff, and Theda Skocpol (Princeton, NJ: Princeton University Press), 268.

22. This was the version of Community Action that the Bureau of the Budget, Council of Economic Advisors, and President Johnson developed at the end of 1963 and early 1964. See D. P. Torstensson "The Politics of Failure, Community Action and the Meaning of Great Society Liberalism" (PhD diss., University of Oxford, 2009), chapter 2.

23. There did exist cases where the federal government gave money directly to individuals, bypassing state and local authorities. Examples of this were direct aid under the Office of Education, grants from the National Institute of Mental Health, programs administered by the Welfare Administration and Vocational Rehabilitation Agency, and the Federal Aviation Agency. For fiscal 1965 new obligations of these funds were $1.462 billion. See *War on Poverty Microfilm*, Part 1, WH Central Files, Reel 1, microfilm shot 389.

24. Sargent Shriver, Draft Document, "Charge to the Economic Opportunity Council," December 7, 1964, *War on Poverty Microfilm*, WH Central Files, Reel 1, microfilm shots 452–455.

25. Albert Quie, April 30, 1969, LBJ Oral History, Miller Center.

26. Michael Gillette, *Launching the War on Poverty: An Oral History* (New York: Twayne, 1996), 125. Other Congressman, such as Phil Landrum, supported the EOA in 1964 and while Landrum became an outspoken critic of the OEO and Community Action he nevertheless supported the re-authorization of the EOA in 1967 with the insertion of the Green amendment. See Torstensson, "The Politics of Failure," 231.

27. Only months after the first grants had been approved, Community Action was making the newspaper headlines for all the wrong reasons. In March 1965 the *Washington Post* ran a page 1 story entitled "Poverty-War Conflict Erupts over Local Control." This report detailed how the poverty program was generating conflict over the participation of the poor, particularly in the "most sensitive battle-ground" of Community Action. This was described as taking place all over the country, with the problem being particularly acute in Louisiana and Alabama, where there was the added issue of racial discrimination. On cue, national columnists and DC insiders Rowland Evans and Robert Novak published an *Inside Report*, "George Wallace vs. the Poor," a few days after this article detailing the local and national politics of Community Action. In this piece the duo argued that the "reliance on local leadership is the Achilles heel of the community action program" and the cause of so much of the trouble both in North and South: "In the big cities, patronage-hungry political bosses are muscling in…[and] Wallace-style segregationists are applying their deadening touch in the Deep South." By the end of March, a mere seven months after the passage of the Economic Opportunity Act, the *Washington Post* declared that "Civil War Goes on in Poverty Plans." See *Washington Post*, March 6, 11, and 22, 1965, ProQuest Historical Newspapers.

28. Lyndon Johnson, *The Vantage Point: Perspectives of the Presidency 1963–1969* (New York: Holt, Rinehart and Winston, 1971), 74.

29. Between 1965 and 1969 numerous management surveys of the OEO were carried out by the federal bureaucracy, private management consultants, independent groups, and the US Comptroller General. With remarkable consistency, they all pointed to a similar set of problems the agency faced and over time failed to come to terms with: the inability to agree on and define what the War on Poverty and Community Action actually desired to achieve and an incapacity to draw clear lines of responsibility and communication between the different levels of the agency.

30. Sargent Shriver, Draft Document, "Charge to the Economic Opportunity Council," December 7, 1964, *War on Poverty Microfilm*, WH Central Files, Reel 1, microfilm shots 452–455.

31. Norbert Schlei, May 15, 1980, LBJ Oral History, Miller Center.

32. Eric Tolmach, April 16, 1969, LBJ Oral History, Miller Center.

33. For example, in a bid to steer the political debate in a more liberal and for him personally more politically desirable direction, as member of the Kerner Commission Lindsay wrote the oft-cited report summary that gave a very polarizing view of the causes of rioting. The summary claimed baldly that America was moving toward two separate societies—one white, one black—and urgent, massive government action was required. From Gareth Davies, *From Opportunity to Entitlement: The Transformation and Decline of Great Society Liberalism* (Lawrence: University Press of Kansas, 1996), 204–205.

34. Ben Heinemann, April 16, 1970, LBJ Oral History, Miller Center.

35. Heinemann, LBJ Oral History, Miller Center.

36. Heinemann, LBJ Oral History, Miller Center.

37. Moynihan was fiercely critical of social scientists and sociologists whom he viewed as having played a key role in the poor performance of the War on Poverty. His criticism of the poverty program was part of a broader movement of former liberals moving away from the Democratic Party and the Great Society. By the late 1960s contemporary intellectuals and public policymakers were contributing to the popular chorus of critiques of the Great Society's social programs, the War on Poverty chief among them. Many liberals like Moynihan and sociologists Nathan Glazer and Daniel Bell became associated with Irving Kristol and Norman Podhoretz, founders of what would become labeled as neo-conservatism. Magazines such as *Public Interest* and *Commentary*— edited by Kristol and Podhoretz, respectively— began criticizing the Great Society and the very idea of transformative government social programs. Moynihan featured articles in both throughout the late 1960s in which he attacked the War on Poverty and Community Action.

38. Daniel P. Moynihan, "The Professors and the Poor," *Commentary* (August 1968): 28, ProQuest Historical Magazines.

39. Alice O'Connor, *Poverty Knowledge: Social Science, Social Policy, and the Poor in Twentieth-Century U.S. History* (Princeton, NJ: Princeton University Press, 2001), 170–172.

40. See "Memo From: Frederick Bohen, To: Members of the President's Task Force on Government Organization, Subject: The Attached Paper on the Poverty Program and the Office of Economic

Opportunity, November 30, 1966," *War on Poverty Microfilm*, WH Aides A-M, Reel 4, microfilm shot 634–675.

41. Letter from Ben Heinemann, December 15, 1966, with a summary statement and the full "Taskforce on Government Organization" report attached, *War on Poverty Microfilm*, WH Aides, A-M, Reel 6, microfilm shots 160–177.

42. Lyndon Johnson, State of the Union, January 10, 1967, Public Papers.

43. Only in the last few years has there been a sustained questioning of many of these negative policy conclusions. These newer studies are all of real importance precisely because they challenge established judgements about Community Action. See: Kent Germany, *New Orleans after the Promises: Poverty, Citizenship and the Search for the Great Society* (Athens, GA: University of Georgia Press, 2007); Robert Bauman, "The Black Power and Chicano Movements in the Poverty Wars in Los Angeles," *Journal of Urban History* 33 (January 2007): 277–295; Noel Cazenave, *Impossible Democracy: The Unlikely Success of the War on Poverty Community Action Programs* (Albany: State University of New York Press, 2007); Susan Youngblood Ashmore, *Carry It On: The War on Poverty and the Civil Rights Movement in Alabama, 1964–1972* (Athens, GA: University of Georgia Press, 2008); and Guian McKee, *The Problem of Jobs: Liberalism, Race, and Deindustrialization in Philadelphia* (Chicago: University of Chicago Press, 2008).

44. National Association for State Community Services Programs, *Community Services Block Grant Annual Report, Analysis and State-level Data* (http://www.acf.hhs.gov/programs/ocs/programs/csbg/about) (Washington, DC: NASCSP, 2014), 43–46.

45. National Association for State Community Services Programs.

46. See: US Department of Health and Human Services Administration for Children and Families (http://www.acf.hhs.gov/fact-sheets).

47. National Association of Community Action Agencies (http://www.communityactionpartnership.com/about/about_partnerships/fact_sheet), Community Action Partnership.

48. National Association of Community Action Agencies.

49. Marvin Olasky, *Compassionate Conservatism: What It Is, What It Does, and How It Can Transform America* (New York: Free Press, 2000), 6–7.

50. Olasky, *Compassionate Conservatism*, 2.

51. George W. Bush, "The Duty of Hope," July 22, 1999, in Olasky, *Compassionate Conservatism*, Appendix B, 219.

52. Bush, "The Duty of Hope," 218.

53. *New York Times*, "Republicans Stalk a Slogan, Hunting for Themselves," June 20, 1999, ProQuest Historical Newspapers.

54. George W. Bush, Remarks on Compassionate Conservatism in San Jose, California (http://www.presidency.ucsb.edu/), April 30, 2002, *Public Papers*.

55. Lester M. Salamon, *Partners in Public Service: Government-Nonprofit Relations in the Modern Welfare State* (Baltimore: Johns Hopkins University Press, 1995). See also Peter D. Hall's "The Welfare State and the Careers of Public and Private Institutions since 1945," in *Charity, Philanthropy, and Civility in American History*, ed. Lawrence J. Friedman and Mark D. McGarvie (Cambridge: Cambridge University Press, 2003), 380–381.

56. For details of the growth in the grants-in-aid system see Ben Canada's *Federal Grants to State and Local Government: A Brief History*, The Library of Congress, Report for Congress, Order Code RL30705.

57. S. Pettijohn, "Federal Government Contracts and Grants for Nonprofits," Urban Institute Washington DC, 2013, 1.

58. J. McGinnis et al., *Building Public Services through the Nonprofit Sector: Exploring the Risks of Rapid, Government Funded Growth in Human Service Organizations*, American University School of Public Affairs Research Paper No. 2014-0010, 2014, 1.

59. Hall, "The Welfare State and the Careers of Public and Private Institutions since 1945."

60. Gøsta Esping-Andersen, *The Three Worlds of Welfare Capitalism* (Princeton, NJ: Princeton University Press, 1990), 27.

61. Esping-Andersen, *The Three Worlds of Welfare Capitalism*.

62. See: A. Hicks and L. Kenworthy, "Varieties of Welfare Capitalism," *Socio-Economic Review* 1.1 (2003): 27–61; and Asian Development Bank, *The Social Protection Index Assessing Results for Asia and the Pacific*, ADB, 2013.

63. OECD, "Social Expenditure Update (November 2014)," OECD Social Expenditure database.

64. Jeremy Horpedahl and Harrison Searles, "The Tax Exemption of Employer-Provided Health Insurance," *Mercatus on Policy*, July 2013, George Mason University, 3.

65. M. Rae et al., "Tax Subsidies for Private Health Insurance," KFF, October 2014 Issue Brief. Federal budget numbers are from CBO (2014), "The Federal Budget in 2013: An Infographic," April 18, 2014.

66. OECD, Net total social expenditure, % of GDP, OECD Stat.

67. OECD, Net total social expenditure, % of GDP.

68. OECD, Public social expenditure, % of GDP, OECD Stat.

69. Jacob Hacker, *The Divided Welfare State The Battle over Public and Private Social Benefits in the United States* (New York: Cambridge University Press, 2002).

70. See Edwin Amenta and Theda Skocpol, "Redefining the New Deal: World War II and the Development of Social Provision in the United States," in Weir et al., *The Politics of Social Policy* (Princeton, NJ: Princeton University Press, 1988).

71. See, for example, Arnold Heidenhammer, Hugh Heclo, and Carolyn Teich Adams, *Comparative Public Policy: The Politics of Social Choice in America, Europe, and Japan*, (Basingstoke, UK: Macmillan, 1990); Meg Jacobs and Julian E. Zelizer, "The Democratic Experiment—New Directions in American Political History," in *The Democratic Experiment—New Directions in American Political History*, ed. Meg Jacobs, William J. Novak, and Julian E. Zelizer (Princeton, NJ: Princeton University Press, 2003), 1–19; and Julian E. Zelizer, "Clio's Lost Tribe: Public Policy History since 1978," *Journal of Policy History* 12.3 (2000): 369–394. Julian E. Zelizer, "Beyond the Presidential Synthesis: Reordering Political Time," in *A Companion to Post-1945 America*, ed. Jean-Christophe Agnew and Roy Rosenzweig (Oxford: Blackwell, 2002), 346–359; Theda Skocpol, *States and Social Revolutions* (Cambridge and New York: Cambridge University Press, 1980) (first published 1979); Stephen Skowronek, *Building a New American State: The Expansion of National Administrative Capacities, 1877–1920* (Cambridge: Cambridge University Press, 1997) (first published 1982); Esping-Andersen, *The Three Worlds*; Hicks and Kenworthy, "Varieties of Welfare Capitalism"; Trattner, *From Poor Law*; and Edward Berkowitz, *America's Welfare State* (Baltimore: Johns Hopkins University Press, 1991).

72. See Germany, *After the Promises*; Bauman, *Black Power and Chicano*; Cazenave, *Impossible Democracy*; Ashmore, *Carry It On*; and McKee, *The Problem of Jobs*.

73. See Robert Korstad and James Leloudis, *To Right These Wrongs: The North Carolina Fund and the Battle to End Poverty* (Chapel Hill: University of North Carolina Press, 2010); Thomas Kiffmeyer, *Reformers to Radicals: The Appalachian Volunteers and the War on Poverty* (Lexington: University Press of Kentucky, 2008); Greta de Jong, *A Different Day: African American Struggles for Justice in Rural Louisiana, 1900–1970* (Chapel Hill: University of North Carolina Press, 2002); William Clayson, *Freedom Is Not Enough: The War on Poverty and the Civil Rights Movement in Texas* (Austin: University of Texas Press, 2010); Françoise N. Hamlin, *Crossroads at Clarksdale: The Black Freedom Struggle in the Mississippi Delta after World War II* (Chapel Hill: University of North Carolina Press, 2012); and Annelise Orleck and Lisa Gayle Hazirjian, eds., *The War on Poverty: A New Grassroots History, 1964–1980* (Athens, GA: University of Georgia Press, 2011).

74. Papers of Bertrand Harding; LBJ, Papers, Confidential File, WE MC; Files of Marvin Watson; Files of Bill Moyers; Files of Frederick Panzer; Files of Harry McPherson; Files of Henry H. Wilson; Files of Charles H. Roche; Papers of Alfred H. Corbett; Papers of Bernard L. Boutin; LBJ Papers, Task Force Reports; Confidential Files, Agency Reports, OEO; Cabinet Papers; Legislative Background, Economic Opportunity Act.

75. Oral history interviews of key players in the War on Poverty and OEO housed at the Miller Center online collections include: Don Baker; John A. Baker; Ted Berry; Horace Busby; Edgar and Jean Cahn; William Cannon; Douglass Cater; Anthony Celebrezze; Jack T. Conway; James Gaither; Ronald Goldfarb; Kermit Gordon; Edith Green; Bertrand Harding; Ben W. Heinemann; Walter Heller; Harold W. Horowitz; Hubert Humphrey; Herbert Kramer; Frank Mankiewicz; Harry McPherson; Lawrence O'Brien; Ann Oppenheimer Hamilton; Robert C. Perrin; Albert Quie; Joseph Rauh; Norbert Schlei; Charles Schultze; Jule M. Sugarman; James Sundquist; Eric Tolmach; Jack Valenti; and Adam Yarmolinsky.

David Torstensson

SCHOOLS IN US CITIES

PERSISTENT QUESTIONS ABOUT US SCHOOLING

For Whom? Since the early 19th century, white advocates for publicly funded schooling in the United States adopted a language of universality. If dollars from the public coffer—pulling from everyone—were to sustain schools, then it was both logically and politically sensible to claim that schooling would benefit all young people as students as well as all others as their fellow citizens. In practice, though, schools rarely met this claim. Whole swaths of US citizens and residents were at various points—and until quite recently—wholly excluded from the enterprise of schooling. Categories of race, nationality, gender, dis/ability, class, religion, and language were deployed to constrain access to education and to condition the content and shape of schooling. Describing the US history of education for African Americans, historian James Anderson writes that schooling for first-class citizenship (with full political rights and economic power) and schooling for second-class citizenship (with curtailed rights and limited economic opportunity) are basic American traditions. An observation rooted in his careful study of the Reconstruction and Jim Crow South, Anderson's words demonstrate that inequality of various forms and across many categories was a purposeful rather than incidental outcome of schooling.[1]

Who Decides? During the 19th century, public schooling came to mean schooling provided by public dollars collected via taxation. Yet the provision of public funding did not answer the question of public governance. What defines public or democratic decision-making about schooling? What decisions are made by whom and how? For much of the 20th century, city residents elected or appointed school district-level bodies called school boards that performed this work. But at various moments across the history of public education in the United States, citizens imagined and advocated different configurations, with more or less power for popular or expert, corporate or individual, influence. Urban residents disagreed sharply over which arrangement they favored in various political and economic moments.

With What Meaning? Although they operate in cities shaped by the pursuit of profit, schools were never only that. In schools as in all other urban spaces, people built, created, and made meaning. Schools were at once sites of self-making, labor, cultural production and transmission, imagination, and even liberation, even as they were also places of governance and discipline, coercion and oppression.

THE INFORMAL EDUCATIONAL LANDSCAPE OF THE COLONIAL AND EARLY REPUBLICAN YEARS

Before the American Revolution, arrangements for educating children in urban contexts were as varied, as inconsistent, at times as haphazard, as those in towns and the countryside. Children learned at the knees of a local mother who brought youngsters into her kitchen (a "dame school"), or attended a tuition-charging private academy or a charity school run by a church or association serving black or white students, or in a few cases both. The school "year" may have only been a few months, or many more. Perhaps youngsters were taught to read, write, and calculate by a tradesperson completing his obligations to his apprentices. Enslaved children living in cities risked their safety to learn with family or community elders, or participated in classes offered by the Society for the Propagation of the Gospel up and down the Eastern Seaboard. Arrangements for girls' schooling were even more uncertain than those for boys in the colonial period, through explicit exclusion or via lack of regular provisions for girls. But girls' schooling became more stable in the early republican years. Access to education depended on race, class, religion, status—but the elite as well as the poor navigated this landscape of various informal arrangements.[2]

Despite colonial examples, such as the 1635 creation of the Boston Latin School for the sons of that city's elite white families, or the 1647 Massachusetts law requiring any settlement of more than 100 families to create a grammar school, colonial education often depended on borrowed infrastructure. Families, churches, and apprenticeships lent the physical and social structures in which instruction took place. Gradually, in the early republican decades, formal school structures expanded through the work of churches, charity groups, manumission societies, and other collections of citizens. These operated alongside the many independent masters, or teachers, who "kept school" funded by modest tuition payments for the children of workingmen's families and the middle and upper classes. Population density meant that cities often led the way in the making of formal educational institutions. New York was earlier than others in bringing public funding to support and expand schooling, in 1796. But even when tax dollars augmented private tuition dollars, the operation of these schools remained in private hands.[3]

MAKING THE PUBLIC SCHOOL IN THE 19TH CENTURY

Across US cities before the Civil War, schooling became an increasingly common experience. By the early 19th century, the majority of white US children attended school at some point during the year; between a quarter and two-fifths of free black students did. Girls were as likely to attend primary schools as boys, and they usually attended together. But many questions remained unresolved. White people, and in some contexts free people of color, were educated, but how, by whom, for how long, and at whose expense? In the mid-19th-century North and Midwest, multiple

arguments and organizing efforts coalesced into a broad commitment to publicly funded, publicly governed primary or elementary schooling. After the Civil War this commitment reached the South as well, but was soon undermined by Jim Crow violence and disfranchisement. In both regions, cities led in the growth of the idea of public education and the infrastructure that supported it, even as in both the nominal and legal commitment to public education was limited by segregation and inequality in many forms.

The idea of the "common school" took form and spread from 1820 to 1860. The notion drew sustenance from many currents in early 19th-century thought. Republican ideology provided one, especially as white male suffrage broadened when many states removed property-holding qualifications. But white peoples' thinking about citizenship had sharp limits—vividly captured by the 1820s push to disfranchise black Northerners and the *Dred Scott v. Sandford* (1857) US Supreme Court decision denying citizenship to people of African descent, enslaved or free. White Americans appealed to schooling to buttress their democratic citizenship, while seeing black peoples' exclusion from or segregation within schooling as a reinforcement of their position outside of the body politic.[4] Lawmakers in slave states, especially after a wave of antislavery activism in the 1830s, passed legislation to ban the education of enslaved people. Like Frederick Douglass and other abolitionists, slaveowners saw literacy as a threat to the institution.[5] Nonetheless, free black people in cities North and South built and sustained schools that aligned with their own views of citizenship and community.

Even with suffrage limited to men, ideas of democracy encouraged schooling for boys and girls alike. As of 1857, Boston's 213 primary schools were coeducational. Divisions in educational provision and access still held for later grades, there as in many other cities, but at the common school level ideas about women's participation in civic life through their influence in the home supported expenditures on girls' education as well as boys.[6]

Economic realities provided another prompt for public schooling. After the revolution, residents in cities such as Boston hoped that literacy and numeracy would stimulate commerce. Educators across many cities spoke about their hopes for students' abilities to support themselves as well as to function as citizens and moral actors in a new nation growing quickly via immigration. For those focused on new factories more than traditional crafts, industrial work required time and work habits of compliance that were cultivated inside the proto-industrial structure of the schoolhouse. The school bell and the factory bell had a similar ring. British educator Joseph Lancaster pioneered a method of schooling large numbers of young people for little money, using older students to teach younger ones. In the eyes of New York Governor Dewitt Clinton, the method was for education to be "what the neat finished machines for abridging labor and expense are in the mechanic arts."[7] Industrial analogies continued to grow in 19th- and 20th-century education.

Industrial production was a model, and a danger, in the eyes of common school proponents. Massachusetts's Horace Mann, Connecticut's Henry Barnard, and New York's Catharine Beecher returned time and again to claims that public education could ameliorate or even resolve social problems associated with mid-19th-century cities—many of which more than doubled in size from 1840 to 1860. Those who held to a Jeffersonian republican vision of a nation of yeoman farmers saw the growth of urban industrial production and landless industrial workers as a threat to the foundation on which they imagined (white, male) citizenship to rest. How could those without financial self-sufficiency via land become independent agents in a democracy rather than tools of their patrons or bosses? What could prevent the making of entrenched classes or castes, and the potential

radicalization of working people, evident in Europe's cities in the 1830s and 1840s?[8]

Horace Mann did not extend his worries about caste and citizenship to black people. Massachusetts abolished slavery and established, earlier than most cities, a public common school network. But black residents were barred from admission in various ways and thus turned to build their own institutions (even as they paid taxes to support the public schools). Later, when one of these became absorbed into the public system, all of Boston's black students were assigned to the same school. Baltimore offered a different mixture of common schooling, urban port economy, caste, and segregation. In the slave state of Maryland, Baltimore's sizeable free black population also supported public schools with their taxes. Black students were banned from these schools, but the profitability of black workers' literacy and numeracy opened spaces for African American education.[9] Baltimore did not fund education for its black residents, but unlike other southern states it did not legislate against their learning. Black educators operated schools and black craftspeople educated their apprentices. Yet in Baltimore as in the rest of the South, enslavement provided the most potent barrier to schooling. Enslaved people sought learning for themselves and their children, but had to do so in secret and informal spaces.[10]

With a mixture of civic and economic goals for common schooling, cities expanded the available public schools for their children and developed paradigmatic forms of schooling. Scale was the key variable. Where rural communities had small populations of students scattered inconsistently across ages and levels, cities with large populations made it a certainty that students would fill separate age-graded classes. City schools featured and helped spread "egg-crate" floor plans with classrooms on each side of a long corridor, predominantly female elementary school teaching forces, and mechanisms of testing and promotion from one level to another.

Growing European immigrant populations raised new questions about the content, and governance, of schools in cities. By 1855, more than half of all New Yorkers were foreign born. Religion, language, and culture all became terrain for conflict in city schools, and New York provided some of the most vivid examples. Many of the newest European immigrants to US cities were Catholic, and they perceived rampant anti-Catholicism in schooling at the time. Urban dioceses sought to meet the demand for education by expanding their own institutions—but their parishioners were often poor and the demand was greater than their resources. In New York, tax dollars already flowed to schools run by the quasi-public, historically elite Protestant Public School Society. New York Catholics asked, if universal schooling, or at least universal white schooling, was a public good, why not send tax dollars to schools that the Catholic Church would run, in ways amenable to Catholic families?[11]

New York City and state politicians wrestled over this question in dramatic conflict during the 1840s. The debate defined the ambitions as well as the limits of "common school" ideology. Advocates of publicly funded and publicly run schooling pressed for common-ness: the same structure, the same institution, the same curriculum to bind together students across different class, ethnic, linguistic, and previous national, if not racial, lines (as New York's schools were segregated by law). But Roman Catholic Bishop John Hughes, the lead spokesperson for the New York Catholic cause, rejected nonsectarian or even secular public schooling smoothed of its anti-Catholic edges. He wanted an affirmatively Catholic education, run by the Catholic Church, with the benefit of public funds—a model not unlike that taken by many other European nations in the 19th and 20th centuries. Some of Hughes's opponents suggested, as a threat, that if Catholics were granted this autonomy, black communities might want the same authority over their own schools. New York officials never gave

Hughes what he sought, but New York's Catholic schools continued to grow—serving as many as 100,000 students per year by the end of the century—as did the privately funded Catholic educational system in many other northeastern and midwestern cities. Hughes's proposal and its rejection helped solidify what public education meant in the later 19th and 20th centuries: schooling that was not only public in its stated purposes and its funding, but publicly governed by elected or local boards with some supervision by a state department or commission of education.

New York's "school wars" were one early and dramatic example of a struggle that recurred in many forms into the 20th and 21st centuries. Those who felt their beliefs, communities, and children were poorly served by public schools sought ways to access public funds but administer schooling in their own vision.

While New York Catholics faced one form of nativist sentiment, other immigrant groups experienced blunt exclusion at the nexus of nativism and racism. San Francisco schools excluded Chinese and Japanese students in the 1860s and 1870s; El Paso's schools admitted only English-speaking students, effectively barring the large Mexican population.[12]

For decades, historians saw the US South as an outlier in the story of common school development. They described a region that decided not to invest in public schooling because of the distortions of slavery—a hegemonic white planter elite schooled its own children privately, an agrarian white workforce saw little economic or political benefit from schooling, and black populations were separated from schooling by slavery and Jim Crow. The story of US public education was northern, and the South fell behind. Many southern states lagged behind the North, but in fact many southern cities moved quickly to establish common schools for white students in the mid-19th century. In New Orleans, local leaders built a system drawing directly on Horace Mann's counsel. And in New Orleans, black community leaders founded autonomous black schools to provide instruction for both material and civic gain. Even in Georgia, where no state system of education existed before the Civil War, networks of black educators in Savannah were immediately ready to establish an extensive network of weekday and Sabbath schools establishing schooling at the end of the war.[13] Southern cities came closer than did many rural areas, but the idea of public education for all remained not fully achieved in the South in the 19th century.

During the 19th century, the United States made the gradual, controversial, and still incomplete turn to publicly accessible, publicly funded, and publicly governed school systems. This turn was motivated significantly by the opportunities of, as well as worries about, US cities as growing, industrial, immigrant spaces. By the close of the century, when few other structures for social welfare were in place, schools were a core part of the urban infrastructure. As of 1910, nationally, 92.9 percent of US born white children under the age of 13 were enrolled in school. The rates were lower— 70.1, 72.1, and 62.9 percent, respectively—for African American, Native American, and Hispanic students. This variation reflected both racism and the related economic pressures families faced, but it also reflected the predominantly rural location of these groups in the United States.[14] While white Americans consolidated state mechanisms around common schools as one mechanism of exclusive white citizenship, black, Latino, and Asian American communities created their own spaces within or outside of public funding to demonstrate their view of their own citizenship and of education as a tool in its pursuit.

MAKING THE URBAN SCHOOL SYSTEM AT THE TURN OF THE 20TH CENTURY

A grand and massive building rose at the corner of Division and Sedgwick Streets on Chicago's North Side and opened for operation in the fall of 1908. The Albert Grannis Lane Manual Training High School, or "Lane Tech," symbolized many features and ambitions, as well as limitations, of US urban public education systems of the late 19th and early 20th centuries. In the eyes of the newly minted education experts who led schools such as Lane, and districts such as Chicago, the institutions were efficient as well as accessible, crucibles of both the city's economic and its civic future in an era of dramatic urban growth.

The US population grew by 30 million residents between 1900 and 1920; 14 million of them were new immigrants. Growth via immigration, as well as from southern African American migration to cities, meant that city classrooms swelled and schools expanded. But Lane Tech stood for a rapid expansion in the length of public schooling as well, not only its volume. The common school offered primary or elementary education. New kinds of skilled work emerging in the late 19th and early 20th centuries, in factories as well as offices, made secondary schooling seem appealing and worthwhile to more students and families. So, too, did the new idea of adolescence—a distinct life phase, best served in a distinct institution—and the slowly rising compulsory school age alongside tightening restrictions on child labor. An additional boost to high school enrollment came with the Great Depression—in which rising adult unemployment pushed younger workers out of the labor market and reduced previous opportunity costs for schooling. More US students chose to continue their schooling into high school than ever before, with girls attending at rates greater than or equal to boys.[15]

But if more people attended school for longer periods of time, what kind of schooling did they receive? When secondary schooling was an elite institution, enrolling fewer than 10 percent of the population, courses of study focused on preparation for college or for work as a teacher. With enrollment growing, educators increasingly linked high schooling to a broader economic landscape and a labor market marked by racial, ethnic, and gender segregation. School superintendents, principals, and university professors bearing new graduate degrees from recently created schools of education turned to business and industry for models of efficiency. Psychology—and particularly the pseudoscience of early intelligence testing—promised "social efficiency" via swift sorting of students by their future destination in the economy. Although claiming to measure innate capacity, in practice, tests reflected racist and cultural bias and worked to further inscribe social and political hierarchies. As more students entered secondary schooling, new divisions between types of schooling hardened. Names such as "technical," "manual," or "commercial" appeared in school titles—replacing or coexisting with academic offerings.

Early 20th-century high schools were microcosms of the economy and politics in which they operated. The industrial city created opportunities for economic mobility for those hired—recent immigrant arrivals alongside native-born white workers. With or without a high school diploma, employers often relegated black men to the lowest-paid and most unstable parts of this work. By contrast, white men and women with commercial or secretarial training found work in the expanding corporate offices and clerical pools of the day, but few black workers were hired into these positions until World War II. Formal education's emphasis on sorting students did not create the unequal labor market, but certainly reflected it. Surely many black students swam against the tide to access higher levels of schooling and employment. Despite then-powerful and universalizing messages of mobility through hard work and education, racism consistently pushed black students down or out in high school as in the workforce.

For the increasing numbers of women doing paid work outside of the home, early 20th-century high school curricula provided one preparatory route aligned to new kinds of employment—especially in the offices of growing corporations and government bureaucracies.[16] Working-class boys sought pathways to industrial and other employment via vocational and technical courses. For some among waves of European immigrant women, academic training in high school opened the path to careers as teachers, marking a first step into the middle class.[17] As relationships between schooling and the labor market were at once lauded and unstable, the crucial question was who decided. Did schools enable students and families to select their path, or did teachers or counselors make those decisions for them? Gendered, nativist, and racist stereotypes figured both in the shaping of the high school curriculum and school culture as well as in the assignment of individual students to courses.[18]

Segregated southern Jim Crow high schools for black students provided sharp examples of how schooling could simultaneously include and exclude. And they showed how communities, educators, and students resisted. High schools for black students remained rare in the South before World War II, but those that existed were overwhelmingly urban. Northern philanthropists encouraged black education, but on a model that constrained black students to the "Negro trades" of the segregated economy. Some black leaders such as Booker T. Washington supported this approach as a gradualist path to uplift. Others refused, most notably W. E. B. Du Bois and many black educators, who worked quietly to provide rigorous academic preparation even when their sponsors or supervisors thought they were doing otherwise. They worked in the context of Jim Crow disfranchisement, but they were guided by a vision of first-class citizenship. Presented with donations to support a new vocational school in New Orleans, black leaders rejected the proposal rather than accept it and its limitations.[19]

Within urban school systems, similar inclusions and exclusions coexisted as well. Chicago's schools—including Lane—not only sorted students by race between vocational and academic tracks or schools; educators

Figure 1. Grammar School No. 33, New York City, Assembled for morning exercises, c. 1880–1890. Photo courtesy of the Miriam and Ira D. Wallach Division of Art, Prints and Photographs, The New York Public Library, G91F216_059F.

were more likely to place black students in lower-skilled branches of the vocational curriculum than their white peers.[20] In the small California city of Oxnard, white board of education officials assigned Mexican students to separate classrooms, creating school-within-a-school segregation in the 1930s.[21] Meanwhile many cities, from Atlanta to New York to Kansas City, deployed a varied and adaptive set of technologies of racial segregation in schooling. These techniques built on and helped constitute the segregated residential landscape. On that terrain, though, black educators and community members turned segregated institutions into hubs of black community life and learning. Nashville's Pearl High School, Washington, DC's Paul Laurence Dunbar High School, and Atlanta's Booker T. Washington High School trained generations of local leaders and employed black teachers who anchored the local middle class. While buffeted by the storm of Jim Crow, these institutions served as shelters as well.

High schools such as Chicago's Lane Tech were not only markers of expanded participation in schooling. They were also capstones

Figure 2. Cooking class making salads, John Hay School, Chicago, Illinois, c. 1929. Meadville, PA, the Keystone View Company.
Photo courtesy of the Library of Congress, LC-DIG-stereo-1s12631.

of new, elaborate public school systems that developed at the turn of the century. Earlier, reformers such as Horace Mann intended high schools to push the widely varied and inconsistent landscape of common schooling toward standardization. Mann, hoping that educators would adopt uniform approaches to everything from student desk design to chalkboards to textbooks, believed that high schools would guide the larger school system, including the goals and methods of primary schools. He wanted crucial decisions—about what constituted a qualified teacher, for example—to be made by a centralized bureaucracy and not individual school administrators. By the early 20th century, high schools stood atop large and increasingly centralized school systems at a numeric and bureaucratic scale greater than what Mann ever imagined.[22]

Making and regulating urban schooling presented a perfect opportunity for turn-of-the-century social reformers. These new middle-class professionals and their elite allies celebrated university- or philanthropy-sanctioned expertise and professional decision-making over the street-level politics of the local ward, which they critiqued in ways that revealed anti-immigrant sentiment as well. New appointed boards that ran city systems pulled power away from (or replaced entirely) local ward boards, or gave more power to superintendents, in large cities such as New York as well as smaller ones including Cleveland and Kansas City. An "interlocking directorate" of local manufacturing and finance executives—celebrated for their managerial competence and their presumed political disinterest—and their favored education professionals claimed authority to make educational decisions for burgeoning city schools.[23] Leaders in these cities became nationally influential in education, bringing a distinctly urban perspective to the broader stage.[24] The managerial, professional, often northern elite inhabited a refined, urban milieu seemingly far from the blunt and brutal imagery of southern Jim Crow. Their aesthetics were different, and they worked with different tools, but many were equally comfortable advocating and instantiating segregation.[25]

Despite the centralizing agenda, crucial decisions remained in the hands of the teachers who saw students each day. The overwhelming majority of these teachers at the elementary school level were women (the 19th century saw a steady decline in the number of men in these roles, although most principals and district leaders were male). Female teachers faced a conflicting mix of external and internal expectations—that they were kind because of their inherent maternalism, that they were compliant cogs in a massive bureaucracy committed to tallying and ordering students, that they were employees in a public service occupation interested in shaping the terms and content of their work. Despite these fundamental and deeply gendered contradictions, teaching became a pathway to middle-class stability for European immigrant women, as well as for black and West Indian migrant women. Some men who negotiated often racist teacher hiring systems assumed positions in growing and segregated urban school systems.[26]

By 1900, the overwhelming majority of Americans attended a publicly operated primary school—if the duration and quality of that schooling still varied widely by region, and access and quality were both limited by racism and economic power. For Americans born between 1886 and 1890, 73 percent left school at or before eighth grade. For those born between 1926 and 1930, by contrast, more than 60 percent completed high school or beyond, and more than 80 percent attended at least some secondary school.[27] Not only did US urban school systems accommodate the radical increase in their number, but they expanded the reach of schooling into the secondary years. Fewer 20th-century Americans spoke of "common" schools than did their 19th-century forebears. Schooling was more extensive and more regularized in US cities of the day, but it was sharply divided and unequal.

CHALLENGING THE URBAN SCHOOL SYSTEM AFTER WORLD WAR II

The post-World War II urban school landscape saw nearly constant motion—from struggles over desegregation to school governance to increased federal pressure for testing. Most of these changes represented modifications to the existing structure of the school system. At the end of the 20th century, fundamental challenges to that structure were gathering strength. These reform efforts operate in the context of a wildly unequal economic landscape in the late 20th and early 21st centuries, with gaps in wealth and income by race widening since the 1970s. Weakened union protections and the loss of decently compensated work for those with a high school degree or less make the stakes of schooling greater than ever.[28]

The Great Depression catalyzed educational change by increasing high school enrollment. But the federal response to the Depression, in the form of the New Deal's housing policy, signaled a quieter but deeper transformation in the urban, and thus the urban educational, landscape. Federal dollars, in the form of mortgage guarantees for white residents purchasing homes in segregated white suburbs, eased the pathway of white families out of US cities and to the metropolitan collar.[29] And federal dollars, in the form of subsidized low-income housing, flowed to urban centers. These policies produced the massive demographic transformation of the mid-20th-century United States—white middle-class suburban outmigration alongside the concentration of working-class and poor African American and Latino communities in central cities. Previously loose or fluid patterns of segregation tightened. Schools played a part in this process, as municipal leaders planned, zoned, built, or moved schools in ways that reinforced residential segregation and privileged white suburban communities despite the activism of black and Latino urban communities for equitable and at times desegregated schools.

Urban school systems were locally funded entities. Therefore metropolitan demographic and economic shifts changed urban schooling substantially. Resources to fund city schools were constrained by a declining urban tax base (via the suburbanization of

manufacturing and corporate headquarters) as well as by tax policy that favored retaining or recruiting local businesses over funding services that residents needed. Resource scarcity resounded through schools, shaping how often—or rarely—classrooms were painted, windows replaced, or libraries stocked. It shaped teacher salary levels and thus competition for qualified teachers in metropolitan areas. And as rates of urban childhood poverty rose, cities struggled to provide social, medical, and welfare services to support their populations. Schools tried to serve students whose academic and personal needs were substantial.

Southern urban districts, like their rural counterparts, were formally and rigidly segregated by race until at least the 1960s. Segregation was equally evident—but depended on more veiled mechanisms—in urban districts outside of the South. Fully a decade after the Supreme Court's decision in *Brown v. Board of Education, Topeka, Kansas* (1954) finding school segregation unconstitutional, a tiny proportion of American students, North and South, attended schools that had sizeable proportions of both black and white students. (Hispanic students experienced sharp segregation, too, but this was often obscured in a bimodal categorization that identified them as black or white, as suited local segregationist purposes.)[30] Not until the combined leverage of the Civil Rights Act of 1964—which tied growing federal resources in education to some compliance with desegregation—and the acceleration of federal court pressure for desegregation in the late 1960s—with decisions calling for desegregation "now," undoing segregation "root and branch," and using affirmative measures including busing across school zone boundaries and neighborhood lines—did levels of segregation within school districts start to fall, reaching a national low around 1980. White families resisted desegregation mightily, however, and the number of white families willing to move to avoid schooling with black and brown children added to the federally funded outflow to the suburbs.[31] High levels of segregation operated increasingly across district lines, with urban systems (and some poorer suburban ones) isolated from relative suburban wealth.

Too many accounts of urban education in the post-World War II years essentially stop here. They equate segregation and financial struggle with the absence of educational ambition, innovation, or success. Or worse, they imply that rising proportions of students of color in urban school systems produced "decline," locating the difficulty in the bodies of the students rather than in the policy choices that erected barriers to schools' operations and to students' positive life chances.

In fact, many black and Latino communities reimagined schooling in the 1960s and

Figure 3. Flier from the 1964 New York City school boycott, in which nearly half a million students stayed home from school to protest segregation.

Photo courtesy of the City Wide Committee for Integrated Schools, "School Boycott! Flier," *Queens College Civil Rights Archives.*

1970s. Some conceptualized fully autonomous educational institutions aligned with nationalist or other political traditions.[32] Others took aim at the unresponsive bureaucracies in big-city school systems—ones that had sustained segregation within their districts and tolerated inequality in material and human resources for decades. Community control activists in New York City gained the support of the Ford Foundation and other philanthropists in launching an experiment in local democratic governance of education. New "demonstration districts" gathered together a handful of nearby schools and a locally elected school board, scaling down from the million-plus student district with its appointed board. Put differently, black and Latino city residents sought democratic governance of schools on the scale that most white suburbanites enjoyed as a matter of course. The New York City experiment foundered on the question of teacher hiring—whether it would be governed by the local board, or the recently won collective bargaining contract with the teachers' union. But it illustrated a partial reversal of the centralizing impulse of the turn-of-the-century school system.[33]

Spurred by decentralization, as well as by community activism and legal pressure for greater inclusion of students who spoke languages other than English, who had physical, mental, or emotional disabilities, or who had recently arrived in the United States with or without documentation, urban schools became sites of pedagogical innovation. In New York, Puerto Rican parents and student activists pressed for, and some allied educators helped develop, new approaches to bilingual and bicultural education to serve Spanish-speaking communities. In Los Angeles and Texas, Chicano communities did the same.[34] Teacher leaders created new alternative schools that rejected the massive feel of urban schools in favor of smaller, human-scale interaction.[35] Black educators worked through their own community networks to produce and share curricular materials that connected their students to black history. Students brought political movements of the day into schools in Chicago and Milwaukee, pressing for changes within schools and in their surrounding communities.[36]

While some innovations in urban education practice reflected black and Latino communities' best hopes for their children, others were guided by backlash politics of fear and racism. Deficit-minded ideas of communities and children scarred by a "culture of poverty" demeaned students' capacities. Austerity policies worsened fiscal strain on institutions and families. In the worst cases, community members and critics experienced public school systems as indifferent or malicious institutions, warehousing rather than supporting children. A disciplinary vise tightened around black and brown children as police began to patrol schools in the 1970s and disproportionate rates of school punishment became a step on the carceral continuum.[37]

City schools in the late 20th century sat at the intersection of two ideas of "crisis." The "urban crisis" notion met a crisis of educational achievement pronounced in the 1980s via statements such as the Reagan administration's *A Nation at Risk*. The 1983 report declared that US educational provision was so lacking that it left the nation vulnerable internationally. This announcement of crisis was national, not specifically urban. But it aligned with and reinforced popular cultural representations of urban schools in the 1980s and 1990s, portrayed as dysfunctional institutions that were home to troubled young people of color who could be reached and transformed only by the heroic efforts of maverick educators.[38]

Ideas of crisis opened the way to major changes in urban schooling. Many of these reforms operated nationally, but had more intense impact and visibility in urban contexts. Some offered new versions of centuries-old questions about how public dollars would flow to schooling and under what decision-making structures. Some attempted to bring ongoing inequality in education by race and class more to the fore. Together, these efforts revealed that the relatively stable century-long relationship between cities and public school systems was in question.

Ideas of crisis also set the stage for a more expansive federal role in education. The Elementary and Secondary Education Act of 1965 (ESEA) made a major federal investment in schooling as part of the War on Poverty. In the 1990s and 2000s, federal influence shifted to the idea of accountability—first, in setting and testing for achievement of academic standards, and then as of the 2000s in measuring how the achievement of students across categories of race, class, language, and disability compared. Mandates for frequent student testing, attached to funding and threats of closure, applied to all schools, but shaped urban schooling more intensively. The No Child Left Behind Act of 2001 (an amendment to the ESEA) and subsequent iterations created mandates for testing that pressed urban schools to narrow their curricula to focus on tested subjects, to accelerate opening new schools and closing old ones in efforts to generate higher achievement levels. Declarations of educational failure under these measures had various consequences—from loss of funding, to transfer opportunities for students, to catalyzing state takeovers of local city systems as in Newark, New Jersey, or groups of local schools, as in Tennessee's Achievement School District.

In the same years, states around the country adopted charter school legislation that allowed for the creation of new publicly funded schools authorized for a fixed period of years by a public entity (such as a school board, university, or state educational board) but managed and governed by private entities. Charter schools—like proposals for public vouchers that paid for individual students to attend private schools—appealed to those who saw public education as one example of many in which private rather than public management was more efficient, more flexible, and more effective. They also resonated with those community activists who for decades sought more autonomy from school district bureaucracy. In some states, legislation intentionally focused charter schools on city systems and, within city systems, on students who had attended low-performing schools. For much of the first two decades of charter school development, the strong majority of charters operated in city school systems. Early 21st-century cities became testing grounds for relationships between traditional public schools and growing numbers of charter schools, where the two compete for students, space, resources, and perceptions of educational success.

New institutions such as charters embodied a criticism of the urban school system as well as a shift from local democratic governance of schools to parental engagement in an educational marketplace as consumers. This appeal of the market and its supposed efficiencies and expertise helped support as well the 1990s and 2000s turn to reconfiguring urban school governance in many major cities away from an elected or appointed school board and to mayoral control. Chicago made this switch early, in 1995, and New York followed in 2002. Bringing school governance under the mayor's office, advocates claimed, meant more accountability for school performance in the office of a highly visible official. Opponents noted, however, that mayoral control meant many fewer points of leverage for parents and citizens interested in acting on or for schools. Centralized governance and privatizing education reforms coincided in a few dramatic cases, as when, as part of the Hurricane Katrina recovery, almost all of New Orleans's schools were reopened as charter schools.

Late 20th- and early 21st-century educational reforms were fueled both by frustrations with the urban school system and by impressions of failure. The historian Michael Katz noted the unusual consensus among both left- and right-leaning scholars that the

story of the 20th-century city was a story of failure. From the perspective of the beginning of the next century, nearly everyone agreed that segregation, deindustrialization, and concentrated poverty plagued cities, and that the state interventions to mitigate these ills proved insufficient, misguided, or ineffective. Urban historians had "naturalized public failure as the master narrative of urban history" for the 20th century.[39]

Education in the post-World War II years, as Katz well knew, fit tidily into this master narrative. But Katz urged his readers to recognize that "all of this is true, but it is not complete." Urban school systems indeed faced massive structural, political, and social challenges in the second half of World War II. Often they perpetuated or worsened inequalities by race and class. But this narrative was incomplete. Post-World War II urban schools were crucial parts of a multifaceted expansion of access to and achievement in public education in the United States. High school attendance became normative across all racial categories as well as previously excluded ability and linguistic categories. More than 80 percent of Americans born between 1946 and 1950 completed high school. Rates of white high school graduation, however, were separated from those of black high school graduation by a wide chasm: Only one-third as many black students graduated from high school as did white students in 1940. By 1980, the fissure narrowed: 78 percent of white students graduated, while 64 percent of black students did so.[40] These improvements were achieved even in the context of policy choices that sharply constrained cities' finances and political position. Simultaneously, individual and community action around education was robust, creative, and persistent—evidence of energy and vision that should not be obscured by discussions of failure.

Yet for many parents and community members, as well as teachers and educators who sought to serve them, the enduring question remained: Would public resources sufficiently support the education of black and Latino children residing in cities? And if so, would that education be for first- or second-class citizenship? Historians better understand the ways in which schools were historically linked to the search for profit in cities via land and labor, and how visions of citizenship in schooling were delimited by white supremacy. Educators and educational advocates face hard questions about what kind of lever for a more just and humane world schooling can be.

DISCUSSION OF THE LITERATURE

Urban history and the history of education grew up as scholarly subfields in the same decade—the 1960s—but operated largely on parallel tracks. Previous scholarly work on the historical origins and meaning of US public education, such as that of Stanford's Elwood Cubberley, was created within the education profession and often took a celebratory view. In the 1960s and 1970s, historians of education turned to urban cases to uncover the roots of US public education and the shaping of school systems. Scholars such as Michael Katz and David Tyack portrayed schools as expressions of social and economic hierarchy, rebutting earlier views of benevolence.

In the context of the 1980s United States, ideas about urban crisis and educational crisis shaped the questions historians asked and led many scholars of education to focus on urban spaces. Historian Jeffrey Mirel and others sought to explain the "rise and fall" of urban school systems, or to zoom in on the politics of white response to desegregation, as in the work of Kevin Kruse and Matthew Lassiter. Many of these interpretations left out the perspectives of black communities and educators or treated them as recipients of policies and conditions made by others.

As urban social history, and particularly African American urban history, developed

as a field, it inspired new views of the experience of schooling and the nature of community advocacy for education. James Anderson, Vanessa Siddle Walker, and Jack Dougherty, among others, trimmed the too-deterministic nature of earlier accounts, recognizing that parents, community members, and students have long pressed to shape education and schooling in the directions they sought.

A new wave of urban histories published in the last decade dig deeply into *how* schools and cities interact. Andrew Highsmith, Ansley Erickson, Walter Stern, and Emily Straus trace connections with urban planning, with housing markets, with labor markets, and with industrial development. They seek to recognize both the power of these structural connections with schooling in the context of racial capitalism and the diagnoses and strategies for change that communities of color deploy in contestation.[41] These accounts rest on detailed case studies, and there is no broad scholarly synthesis of urban educational history that works at national scale.

Many rich avenues beckon for further investigation, including social histories of education that work outside of the black–white binary, that consider schooling as one part of the historical experience of childhood (with connections to health, policing, social welfare policy, and criminalization and incarceration), and new considerations of the history of work, labor, and vocationalism in connection with schooling in shifting forms of capitalism.[42] And as historians of schooling have long noticed, but few have taken up the charge, a full history of urban education would be more than a history of schooling. There is much to do to understand how people have learned and been part of educational processes in all of their varied forms and meanings, well beyond schooling.

PRIMARY SOURCES

Scholars in the history of education often work across multiple archives, in search of individual as well as institutional perspectives on schooling. While schools generate copious amounts of paper, very little of it makes its way into the archive. The highly decentralized nature of US schooling marks the record as well—as what is archived depends on the varied choices of local school districts and municipalities.

Scholars seeking to understand the experience of children in schools, at any point in time, will find the search challenging. Children leave limited traces in most aspects of their lives, including in schools. Diaries of schoolgoing, discussion of school experiences in oral histories, published student writing, all can offer incomplete but useful views into what children experienced in school. Adults' experiences in schools are more likely to be captured, but often the best documented educational practices or experiences are those farthest from the classroom. Historians have made productive use of the individual manuscript collections of individual teachers or school leaders, as well as of their collective work in unions (including the extensive UFT and AFT collections at the Walter Reuther Library at Wayne State). Oral histories with educators have also provided a rich source of material.

Few schools have consistent mechanisms for archiving their work. Renovations result in old materials being thrown out, or school closures mean a whole building is emptied. Researchers are wise to check with schools to see what might be held—in the form of old yearbooks, diplomas, student prizes, or the like. (Some of these materials, alongside photographs of school buildings, can be found in digital repositories such as the Digital Public Library of America or the Library of Congress's digital collection, and in the digital collections of larger archives.) But unfortunately, much of what can be perceived about a particular school depends on the extent to which a school district made it visible within their records.

Archives of city school systems vary widely—some have their own dedicated archives, as in the Charles Sumner School Museum in Washington, DC, or the archives of the Atlanta Public School; some are established parts of city archives, as in New York; and some have neither. The depth of their collections varies tremendously as well. School board minutes, policy statements, enrollment data, and the like all convey important elements of the system's work, but do so behind a bureaucratic veneer.

More multifaceted views of what happened in schools—and how individuals and communities experienced this and made meaning of it—can be found in moments when schools became the locus of conflict. The papers of activists, community organizations, lawyers, and others can be rich sources on schools. Black and Latino archives are good sources for these materials. When this activism led to litigation, court records can be valuable sources not only for legal proceedings but also for the documentary record amassed in the process.

State and federal education agencies often hold quantitative reports on school systems, and at times have sources that offer qualitative views as well.

FURTHER READING

Anderson, James. *The Education of Blacks in the South, 1865–1930.* Chapel Hill: University of North Carolina Press, 1988.

Delmont, Matthew. *Why Busing Failed: Race, Media, and the National Resistance to School Desegregation.* Oakland: University of California Press, 2016.

Dougherty, Jack. *More Than One Struggle: The Evolution of Black School Reform in Milwaukee.* Chapel Hill: University of North Carolina Press, 2004.

Erickson, Ansley. *Making the Unequal Metropolis: School Desegregation and Its Limits.* Chicago: University of Chicago Press, 2016.

Garcia, David. *Strategies of Segregation: Race, Residence, and the Struggle for Educational Equality.* Oakland: University of California Press, 2018.

Kaestle, Carl. *Pillars of the Republic: Common Schools and American Society.* New York: Hill and Wang, 1983.

Moss, Hilary. *Schooling Citizens: The Struggle for African American Education in Antebellum America.* Chicago: University of Chicago Press, 2009.

Neckerman, Kathryn. *Schools Betrayed: Roots of Failure in Inner City Education.* Chicago: University of Chicago Press, 2008.

Neem, Johann. *Democracy's Schools.* Baltimore: Johns Hopkins University Press, 2018.

Ramsey, Sonya. *Reading, Writing, and Segregation: A Century of Black Women Teachers in Nashville.* Urbana: University of Illinois Press, 2008.

Ravitch, Diane. *The Great School Wars: A History of the New York City Public Schools.* Paperback edition. Baltimore: Johns Hopkins University Press, 2000. (First published 1974 by Basic Books.)

Reese, William. *America's Public Schools: From Common Schools to No Child Left Behind.* Baltimore: Johns Hopkins University Press, 2005.

Rickford, Russell. *We Are an African People: Independent Education, Black Power, and the Radical Imagination.* New York: Oxford University Press, 2016.

Rousmaniere, Kate. *City Teachers: Teaching and School Reform in Historical Perspective.* New York: Teachers College Press, 1997.

Steffes, Tracy. *School, State, and Society: A New Education to Govern Modern America, 1890–1940.* Chicago: University of Chicago Press, 2012.

Stern, Walter. *Race and Education in New Orleans: Creating the Segregated City, 1764–1960.* Baton Rouge: Louisiana State University Press, 2018.

Straus, Emily. *Death of the Suburban Dream: Race and Schools in Compton, California.* Philadelphia: University of Pennsylvania Press, 2014.

Todd-Breland, Elizabeth. *A Political Education: Black Politics and Education Reform in Chicago Since the 1960s.* Chapel Hill: University of North Carolina Press, 2018.

Tyack, David. *The One Best System: A History of American Urban Education.* Cambridge, MA: Harvard University Press, 1974.

NOTES

1. James Anderson, *The Education of Blacks in the South, 1865–1930* (Chapel Hill: University of North Carolina Press, 1988).

2. Carl Kaestle, "Common Schools Before the 'Common School Revival': New York Schooling in the 1790s," *History of Education Quarterly* 12.4 (Winter 1972): 465–500; Johann Neem,

Democracy's Schools: The Rise of Public Education in America (Baltimore: Johns Hopkins University Press, 2018); David Tyack and Elizabeth Hansot, *Learning Together: A History of Coeducation in American Public Schools* (New York: Russell Sage, 1990); Heather Williams, *Self-Taught: African American Education in Slavery and Freedom* (Chapel Hill: University of North Carolina Press, 2005); and Walter Stern, *Race and Education in New Orleans: Creating the Segregated City, 1764–1960* (Baton Rouge: Louisiana State University Press, 2018).

3. Kaestle, "Common Schools."

4. Hilary Moss, *Schooling Citizens: The Struggle for African American Education in Antebellum America* (Chicago: University of Chicago Press, 2009).

5. Williams, *Self-Taught.*

6. Tyack and Hansot, *Learning Together.*

7. Quoted in Neem, *Democracy's Schools.*

8. William Reese, *America's Public Schools: From Common Schools to No Child Left Behind* (Baltimore: Johns Hopkins University Press, 2005); "Report for 1848 (https://hdl.handle.net/2027/njp.32101068983400)," in Horace Mann, *Annual Reports on Education* (Boston: Lee and Shepard, 1872), via HathiTrust.

9. Moss, *Schooling Citizens.*

10. Williams, *Self-Taught.*

11. Diane Ravitch, *The Great School Wars: A History of the New York City Public Schools* (Baltimore: Johns Hopkins University Press, 2000); and Benjamin Justice, *The War That Wasn't: Religious Conflict and Compromise in the Common Schools of New York State, 1865–1900* (Albany: State University of New York Press, 2005).

12. Reese, *America's Public Schools.*

13. Anderson, *Education of Blacks in the South.*

14. Reese, *America's Public Schools.*

15. David Tyack, *The One Best System: A History of American Urban Education* (Cambridge, MA: Harvard University Press, 1974); and John Rury, *Female Schooling and the Division of Labor in Urban America, 1870–1930* (Albany: State University of New York Press, 1991).

16. David Angus and Jeffrey Mirel, *The Failed Promise of the American High School* (New York: Teachers College School, 1999); and Tyack, *One Best System.*

17. Kate Rousmaniere, *City Teachers: Teaching and School Reform in Historical Perspective* (New York: Teachers College Press, 1997).

18. Tyack, *One Best System*; Kathryn Neckerman, *Schools Betrayed: Roots of Failure in Inner City Education* (Chicago: University of Chicago Press, 2008); and Herbert Kliebard, *Schooled to Work: Vocationalism and the American Curriculum, 1876–1946* (New York: Teachers College Press, 1999).

19. Anderson, *Education of Blacks*.

20. Neckerman, *Schools Betrayed*.

21. David G. Garcia, *Strategies of Segregation: Race, Residence, and the Struggle for Educational Equality* (Berkeley: University of California Press, 2018).

22. Neem, *Democracy's Schools*.

23. Tyack, *One Best System*.

24. Reese, *America's Public Schools*.

25. For one example of progressive reformist segregation practices, see Ansley Erickson and Andrew Highsmith, "The Neighborhood Unit: Schools, Segregation, and the Shaping of the Modern Metropolitan Landscape," *Teachers College Record* 120.3 (2018).

26. Rousmaniere, *City Teachers*; Christina Collins, *Ethnically Qualified: Race, Merit, and the Selection of Urban Teachers* (New York: Teachers College Press, 2011); and Jack Dougherty, *More Than One Struggle: The Evolution of Black School Reform in Milwaukee* (Chapel Hill: University of North Carolina Press, 2004).

27. Claudia Goldin, "America's Graduation from High School," *Journal of Economic History* 58.2 (June 1998): 345–374, Table 1.

28. For a summary of these patterns, see Colin Gordon, *Growing Apart: A Political History of American Inequality*, 2018.

29. This is a short description of a process described in much more detail in the *Oxford Research Encyclopedia of American History* articles on "Suburbanization in the United States after 1945" and "Spatial Segregation and Neighborhoods".

30. For recent work on Latino segregation, see Garcia, *Strategies of Segregation*.

31. Desegregation is the most intensively studied element of 20th-century education policy. Many earlier works focused on white resistance. Those that take a different focus include Vanessa Siddle-Walker, *Their Highest Potential: An African American School Community in the Segregated South* (Chapel Hill: University of North Carolina Press, 1994); and Dougherty, *More Than One Struggle*. Michelle Purdy, *Transforming the Elite: Black Students and the Desegregation of Private Schools* (Chapel Hill: University of North Carolina Press, 2018) adds private schooling to the desegregation story.

32. Russell Rickford, *We Are an African People: Independent Education, Black Power, and the Radical Imagination* (New York: Oxford University Press, 2016).

33. Daniel Perlstein, *Justice, Justice: School Politics and the Eclipse of Liberalism* (New York: Peter Lang, 2006); and Jerold Podair, *The Strike That Changed New York: Blacks, Whites, and the Ocean Hill–Brownsville Crisis* (New Haven, CT: Yale University Press, 2004).

34. Adina Back, "'Parent Power': Evelina Antonetty, the United Bronx Parents, and the War on Poverty," in *The War on Poverty: A New Grassroots Perspective, 1964–1980*, ed. Annelise Orleck and Lisa Gayle Hazirjian (Athens, GA: University of Georgia Press, 2011), 184–208; Heather Lewis, *New York City Public Schools From Brownsville to Bloomberg* (New York: Teachers College, 2013); and Natalia Mehlman-Petrzela, *Classroom Wars: Language, Sex, and the Making of Modern Political Culture* (New York: Oxford University Press, 2015).

35. Deborah Meier, *The Power of Their Ideas: Lessons for America from a Small School in Harlem* (Boston: Beacon, 2015).

36. Dionne Danns, "Black Student Empowerment and Chicago: School Reform Efforts in 1968," *Urban Education* 37.5 (2002): 631–655; and Dougherty, *More Than One Struggle*.

37. Judith Kafka, *The History of "Zero Tolerance" in American Public Schooling* (New York: Palgrave, 2011); and Carla Shedd, *Unequal City: Race, Schools, and Perceptions of Injustice* (New York: Russell Sage, 2015).

38. National Commission on Excellence in Education, *A Nation at Risk: The Imperative for Educational Reform* (Washington, DC: US Government Printing Office, 1983).

39. Michael B. Katz, *Why Don't American Cities Burn?* (Philadelphia: University of Pennsylvania Press, 2012).

40. John L. Rury and Shirley A. Hill, *The African American Struggle for Secondary Schooling: Closing the Graduation Gap* (New York: Teachers College Press, 2012).

41. Ansley Erickson, *Making the Unequal Metropolis: School Desegregation and Its Limits* (Chicago: University of Chicago Press, 2016); Garcia,

Strategies of Segregation; Andrew Highsmith, *Demolition Means Progress: Flint, Michigan and the Fate of the American Metropolis* (Chicago: University of Chicago Press, 2015); and Stern, *Race and Education*; and Matthew Gardner Kelly, "The Tangled Roots of Real Estate Markets, the State, and Public Education," *Journal of Educational Administration and History* (2017).

42. On works that bridge childhood and history of education in cities, see Marcia Chatelain, *South Side Girls: Growing Up in the Great Migration* (Chapel Hill: University of North Carolina Press, 2014); and LaKisha Simmons, *Crescent City Girls: The Lives of Young Black Women in Segregated New Orleans* (Chapel Hill: University of North Carolina Press, 2015). On youth, criminality, and incarceration, see Elizabeth Kai Hinton, *From the War on Poverty to the War on Crime* (Cambridge, MA: Harvard University Press, 2016); and Carl Suddler, *Presumed Criminal: Youth, Race, and Justice in an American City* (NYU Press, 2019). On relationships between education and labor, see work in progress by Christina Groeger, *Paths to Work: The Political Economy of Education and Social Inequality in the United States, 1870–1940* (PhD dissertation, Harvard University, 2017); and Nick Juravich, *The Work of Education: Community-Based Educators in Schools, Freedom Struggles, and the Labor Movement* (PhD dissertation, Columbia University, 2017).

Ansley T. Erickson

NIGHTLIFE IN THE AMERICAN CITY

The term *nightlife* today typically refers to social activities in urban commercial spaces—particularly drinking, dancing, dining, and listening to live musical performances. In the 19th century, the term was often used more broadly to include all nocturnal activities outside the home, including working and walking the streets. The modern understanding of nightlife emerged in the early 20th century as commercial entertainment grew dramatically in scale and attracted wider participation. Now focused on recreational consumption, nightlife is viewed as an important component of urban economic life.

BEFORE 1830

Cities in colonial America and the early American Republic were typically quiet at night. Almost all work took place during daylight hours, and commercial entertainment options were few.

Colonial cities kept curfews, which began at an established hour in the early evening and were signaled by the ringing of bells, the beating of drums, or the firing of cannons. Pedestrians in the streets at night risked being challenged, questioned, and perhaps detained until morning by the city's night watchmen. Local laws prohibited juveniles, blacks, and Indians from being out after curfew. Women suspected of prostitution could be arrested for "night walking." Southern cities such as Charleston and New Orleans, where whites feared slave uprisings, had larger forces of military guards to police the nighttime streets. The curfews and patrols succeeded in forcing most law-abiding people indoors. Still, doctors, midwives, and servants ventured out on errands at the risk of being waylaid by muggers and rapists. Virtually no street lighting existed in the colonial era except for widely spaced oil lamps and candle lanterns on a few streets in the largest cities. Unable to see where they were going unless they carried lanterns, pedestrians stumbled into puddles, tripped over sidewalk obstructions, and collided with posts.

While curfews and dangers discouraged people from venturing into the dark streets, few attractions tempted them to go out anyway. Entertainment options consisted mostly of taverns and brothels, ensuring that most people out for an evening of pleasure were male. Taverns through the end of the 18th century drew a diverse clientele of men from different class backgrounds, who mingled somewhat uneasily within these shared spaces. Young men on drinking sprees enjoyed passing from tavern to tavern, singing as they went and occasionally getting in brawls with other carousers. The Christmas season was an especially popular time for drunken rowdiness at night: somewhat like 20th-century trick-or-treaters, young men in early 19th-century Philadelphia and New York knocked on doors demanding drinks or small gifts. They often retaliated against householders who refused.

The theater was the only major venue for night entertainment that drew large numbers of women as well as men in the late colonial and early national periods. Public performances were sporadic at best in most cities. Plays were banned in New England cities, forcing traveling troupes to bill their performances as "moral dialogues." Theatrical performances became more frequent in the early 19th century, particularly in New York and Philadelphia. An evening at the theater included a long series of diverse performances intended to appeal to every taste within a broad audience. With the house lights kept up, audiences paid as much attention to socializing and people-watching as to the performance. People felt free to talk through the performance. Bolder attendees even interrupted the performance by bantering with the actors, calling for encores of favorite songs, or booing weak performers off the stage.

1830–1880

Nightlife expanded in the middle decades of the 19th century. The growing size and diversity of the urban population contributed to this shift, as did changes in the nature of work, living arrangements, street lighting, and police protection.

Even during the early decades of industrialization, working hours for the vast number of urban Americans continued to follow the schedule of natural daylight. Oil and gas lamps allowed "lighting up" textile mills for a few

hours of evening production, but the expense and poor quality of the illumination discouraged round-the-clock industrial production until the coming of electricity in the 1880s. One effect of industrialization, though, was to encourage stricter work discipline that pushed leisure activities out of the day and into the night. Workers had once enjoyed the freedom to take unscheduled breaks for a round of drinks or to watch some interesting activity in the street. By the middle of the 19th century, factory owners and other employers insisted on keeping workers steadily on task during established hours of labor. Drinking and socializing now happened after work.

In an earlier era of household-based craft production, apprentices and journeymen often lived with the families of their employers, subject to the employer's discipline. Partly because of a shift toward larger-scale work units in the 19th century and a new middle-class desire for familial privacy, employees now increasingly lived on their own. In the booming canal port of Rochester in the late 1820s and 1830s, temperance-minded employers successfully stifled drinking in their workplaces but were powerless to suppress it in the burgeoning working-class neighborhoods. Thus, a hard-drinking culture flourished among working-class men after work, even as their employers grew increasingly devoted to self-discipline and sobriety. Growing numbers of middle-class young men, having left their families' supervision for urban jobs as clerks, joined in the hedonistic "sporting" culture of drinking, gambling, and whoring.

Holidays—notably Christmas, New Year's Eve, and Independence Day—continued to be marked by wild street celebrations that lasted well into the night. On Christmas Eve in 1833, according to one observer in Philadelphia, "Gangs of boys howled as if possessed by the demon of disorder." Affluent people responded by leaving town during the uproar or by celebrating quietly indoors. Working-class organizations that aspired to greater respectability held street parades on various holidays. Catholic religious societies, labor unions, and volunteer militias all marched in formation. These attempts at order were parodied in mock parades held by other groups of young men dressed in outrageous costumes and raising a racket with the discordant music of "callithumpian" bands. Political organizations from the mid- to late 19th century held torchlight parades during the weeks before elections. Election nights saw a chaotic mishmash of marches, street bonfires, and drunken revelry, drawing mostly men and boys.

The growing safety of public space encouraged street activity on ordinary nights as well. Gas lamps illuminated public streets starting in 1817 in Baltimore, and, by the 1850s, they could be found in most other significant cities. Gas lighting focused on streets in commercial districts, enticing pedestrians to stroll there in the evenings and encouraging shops to stay open later. Restaurants, ice cream parlors, and oyster saloons also clustered in the well-lit commercial districts. Almost simultaneously, cities created professional police forces to replace the poorly trained and unmotivated night watchmen who had once patrolled the city. Police concentrated in the commercial districts as well, reinforcing the perception that light meant safety.

Respectable evening entertainments expanded in the better-lit streets of antebellum America. Church events drew both men and women. Evening meetings were held by a growing number of charitable and moral reform groups. Lyceum associations were formed in the 1830s and 1840s in cities and towns throughout the northern states, particularly in New England. Lyceums offered entertaining lectures on a range of topics, in addition to musical performances. One observer called the lecture room "a kind of compromise between the theatre and the Church." Instrumental and vocal concerts were considered so respectable that they actually were sometimes held in churches. Evening hours

in public libraries offered men an opportunity to develop their knowledge and cultural capital.

Theatrical performances continued to be viewed with suspicion by moralists through the middle decades of the 19th century. Middle-class Americans grew less tolerant of the tumultuous atmosphere and mixed crowd of the theater, particularly the presence of prostitutes in the third tier of seats. Some impresarios worked to attract a more refined audience by suppressing the audience noise and social diversity that was once an inevitable feature of the theater. The elite Astor Place Opera-House in New York opened in 1847 with an interior design that lacked both the notorious third tier and the "pit" where rowdy men had traditionally sat or stood on benches near the stage. With high ticket prices and a schedule of events that reinforced its snob appeal, the Astor Place Opera-House drew the enmity of working-class New Yorkers. In May of 1849 a mob attacked the theater during a performance of *Macbeth*, drawing a lethal volley from the militia assigned to protect the building. More successfully, the popular museums of Moses Kimball in Boston and P. T. Barnum in New York provided sanitized plays and other performances for a family audience in what were euphemistically termed "lecture rooms." Theaters in big cities increasingly divided along class lines. Reformed theaters sought a genteel clientele by enforcing audience passivity and offering shorter evenings of tasteful performances. Working-class theaters continued to tolerate audience noise and provided a series of diverse amusements that continued as late as midnight. "Concert saloons" emerged as another popular performance space during the Civil War era, offering an almost exclusively male, mixed-class audience the chance to drink and flirt with waitresses while watching variety shows. Both of these unreformed spaces continued to provide opportunities for prostitution.

Late hours were controversial partly because they interfered with people's ability to rest up for the next day's work and partly because urban nightlife after midnight continued to be dominated by the least respectable activities: gambling, drinking, and whoring. More than five hundred gambling houses operated in Cincinnati in the early 1850s, declared a worried local clergyman. "Night after night they are thronged with a motley company of all ages, from all classes of society. Day and night the emissaries of the pit circulate around hotels, and restaurants, and stores, and boarding-houses, to entrap the stranger and the youth into these terrestrial hells." Taverns and houses of prostitution also proliferated in the middle decades of the century, as did flagrant streetwalking by prostitutes along commercial streets, including New York's Broadway. Clusters of brothels developed into early commercial sex districts in the major cities, which, combined with saloons, gave late-night entertainment a persistent reputation for immorality. Nonetheless, urban Americans of all classes enthusiastically attended balls that stretched on until long after midnight. Private balls proliferated despite disapproval by clergymen. Public dances drew large crowds in the mid-19th century, though with diminishing participation by the affluent.

Nightlife varied considerably from city to city. Cities in the South and West were slow to develop the refined cultural opportunities that could be found in eastern metropolitan centers. A Philadelphian visiting Baltimore in 1848 remarked: "The habits of the people are more social and primitive than with us, more villagelike. They go into each other's houses at all hours and in the evenings you see groups of gentlemen and ladies sitting on the steps at the street doors." People kept earlier hours in small cities such as Albany, Bangor, or New Bedford where members of the middle class remained hesitant to attend the theater. Those who did go out at night in small cities or in the South were reported to be cruder and more prone to drunkenness. In the theater at Terre Haute, wrote one British visitor in 1860,

"Although more than a third of the audience were ladies, the backwoods yells and shrieks of delight were indulged in with gusto, and did not seem to offend the fair sex."

In the larger cities of the Northeast and Midwest, a defined schedule of urban nightlife developed in the middle decades of the 19th century. Early evening marked the close of work and the beginning of leisure time for most urban Americans. A range of morally acceptable activities could be found through 10 p.m. Most concerts and reformed theatrical performances ended by 11 p.m. After midnight little remained but controversial "dissipations." Many cities even shut off the gas lamps after midnight to save money. This schedule of nightlife declined in the late 19th and early 20th centuries.

1880–1920

Hours of work and leisure grew less distinct in the late 19th century. Most jobs until then had stopped around dusk, though oil and gas lamps had allowed early evening work in some factories and in many retail stores. Only a small minority of men worked at night. Among these were the "nightmen" who cleaned privies, garbage collectors, watchmen, marketmen, longshoremen, railroad employees, newspaper printers, bakers, waiters, and bartenders. Little industrial production took place around the clock with the exception of ironmaking at blast furnaces. The ranks of night workers expanded in the late 19th century partly because of the adoption of new processes of continuous production in the iron, glass, paper, and petrochemical industries. These processes were enabled or facilitated by the availability of electric power after about 1880 and by the superiority of electric lighting. Night industry expanded in many small and medium-sized cities with paper mills and glass manufactories, such as Holyoke and Toledo, and was most conspicuous in heavily industrial Pittsburgh. Better lighting also encouraged additional night work on the docks and in the manufacturing of textiles and books. The rise in night work, along with the lower cost of running electric trolleys, encouraged streetcar companies to expand their "owl car" service late at night.

Electric lighting further encouraged the growth of commercial nightlife. In the "bright lights districts" of Chicago, Minneapolis, and many smaller cities, brilliant illumination made downtown streets seem safer and more exciting. Advertising signs, theater marquees, and glowing store windows added to the flood of illumination from arc and incandescent street lamps. New York's Broadway again led the trend, with the theater district in Times Square emerging as a famously bright urban node in the early 20th century. At the nexus of mass transit lines, and close to Grand Central Terminal, Times Square became the hub of nightlife not just for America's largest city but for the nation as a whole.

A gradual decline in hours of labor and a slow rise in income also contributed to the expansion of nightlife. Large numbers of young women entered wage labor during the late 19th and early 20th centuries, taking jobs in factories, retail stores, and offices. Ordinary urban Americans had more leisure time and disposable income than ever before. Cultural changes also contributed. Moral opposition to commercial entertainment dwindled away among middle-class Americans at the end of the 19th century; even clergymen now advocated amusements to relieve the effects of overwork.

Still, more men than women went out at night. Cities in the decades around 1900 attracted unusually large numbers of young bachelors, who patronized concert saloons, pool halls, burlesque shows, brothels, and gambling saloons as well as "taxi-dance" halls where they could pay to dance with a woman and perhaps arrange for further intimacies. Meetings of fraternal organizations also drew large numbers of men—single and married—out at night. The Masons, Odd Fellows, Knights of Pythias, and other societies

counted five a half million members by the 1890s. In every significant city, dozens or hundreds of lodges held ritual-filled meetings every week, sometimes two or three times.

Taverns remained by far the most numerous amusement places. At the end of the 19th century more than 200,000 licensed liquor dealers could be found in the United States, in addition to countless unlicensed ones. An 1895 survey of American cities found a licensed saloon for every 317 people. Saloons were typically long, narrow storefronts where men stood drinking along the bar. They contained few or no tables where groups of friends could cluster. Instead, the space encouraged a more open form of socializing where strangers could easily be brought into conversation, songs, or reciprocal rounds of "treating" to drinks. Saloons in downtown areas, and at junctions of streetcar lines, drew an eclectic and shifting clientele. Those in outlying neighborhoods drew many regulars and often developed the atmosphere of a social club. Some catered specifically to the needs of a particular ethnic group or to workers at a nearby factory. Political clubs and other neighborhood organizations used the saloons as meeting places; some saloons had semi-private back rooms for this purpose. Saloons were almost exclusively male places. Women could enter during the day to carry out buckets of beer, but the presence of women drinking in the saloon usually signaled prostitution. One exception was the German beer hall, which drew immigrant couples and families as well as groups of young men.

Nightlife at the very end of the 19th century began to shift decisively away from the all-male "homosociality" that had prevailed until then. Mixed-gender restaurants and increasingly lavish hotel dining rooms opened for business, supplementing the chophouses and oyster saloons that still catered to men. The elegant new restaurants attracted affluent dinner parties that once gathered in private homes. As in the days of the Astor Place Opera-House, elite city residents continued to enhance their status by attending exclusive, "high-brow" entertainments. Opera and classical music were commonly said to reflect a refined, feminine taste that had an uplifting effect on men. Affluent white citizens of Atlanta in the 1910s, for instance, arranged annual visits by New York's Metropolitan Opera; image-conscious men and women assiduously attended the performances as a way of demonstrating the sophistication to be found in Georgia's capital.

The theater had long been a mixed-gender venue. Theater owners successfully allayed fears about audience disorder and immoral plays, sanitizing the legitimate theater so thoroughly by 1900 that it even came to be seen as entertainment for women. High ticket prices limited theater attendance, but inexpensive melodrama and vaudeville had a broader reach. Starting in the 1880s, vaudeville houses operated by Benjamin Keith and Edward Albee succeeded in attracting a mixed-gender, mass audience to theaters in Boston and Providence; the inoffensive language of the variety acts, and the diligent policing by ushers, made sure that women felt secure. Vaudeville theaters held the interest of repeat customers by offering a constantly changing lineup of performers, who traveled on circuits from city to city throughout the United States. Vaudeville theaters were among the early venues showing short motion pictures.

After the turn of the 20th century, some new theaters showed only films. "Nickelodeons"—storefront movie theaters charging five-cent admission—exploded in popularity after 1905. These clustered in central business districts and on commercial streets in working-class neighborhoods; immigrants and native-born audiences of both genders and all ages enjoyed the silent films, often talking and cheering as they watched. Like vaudeville houses, nickelodeons offered continuous performances that allowed viewers to come and go as they pleased. Nickelodeons became known for diverse audiences of rowdy children, women with crying babies, amorous

couples, and men looking to pick up young women. Large, lavishly decorated "movie palaces" opened in the late 1910s and 1920s, with diligent ushers to impose stricter discipline on audiences. These succeeded in attracting more affluent visitors to what had been a working-class amusement. Movie palaces, claimed the architect George Rapp, became "shrines to democracy" where all classes mixed amicably. But this democracy was for whites only; even in northern cities, movie palaces discouraged attendance by blacks or confined them to inconspicuous corners and balconies. More than 20,000 movie theaters operated across the United States by the mid-1920s. Censorship efforts, including the formation of a National Board of Censorship in 1909, suppressed violent and salacious films that were thought unsuitable for general audiences.

Moral reformers in the 1910s made a determined effort to clean up all forms of public amusement. Until then, police, encouraged by bribes, turned a blind eye to brothels as long as they were unobtrusive and remained largely within immigrant, Chinese, and African American neighborhoods. Public officials tolerated "red light districts" as a necessary evil that protected innocent women and children by keeping prostitution away from residential neighborhoods. Moral reformers rejected this excuse, arguing that even discreet prostitution debauched men, exploited women, and spread venereal disease. Local "vice commissions" in Chicago, Portland, Charleston, Syracuse, Bridgeport, and many other cities published reports on the dangers of prostitution that successfully pressured city governments to close vice districts in the 1910s. Enforcement was strengthened during World War I and spread to additional cities in an effort to ensure that troops at training camps remained chaste. Even the famous Storyville district in New Orleans shut down in 1917. Prostitution continued in every city, of course, but it spread out to numerous locations or relocated deeper inside black neighborhoods.

Telephones and automobiles helped break down the geographical limits of prostitution. Rendezvous could be arranged by phone with call girls, while cars were used for discreet travel or as concealment for sexual acts.

Public dancing also drew the attention of moral reformers. Commercial dance halls proliferated during the first decades of the 20th century. Most of the commercial dance halls were in rooms adjoining saloons, or immediately upstairs. Social investigators warned that the halls threatened the morals of young people by encouraging them to drink and by bringing them into contact with disreputable men and prostitutes who solicited there. Some "dancing academies" sought a more refined atmosphere by screening the crowd, excluding alcohol, and banning suggestive "tough dances." Opulent new ballrooms opened on major commercial streets in the 1910s and 1920s. Dance palaces attended carefully to their reputation by policing the behavior of the audience and by discouraging jazz music that might stir up sexual feelings. The dance palaces succeeded in drawing a crowd from all classes.

Efforts to reform the theaters, cinemas, and dance halls persuaded more women to venture into mixed-sex amusement places. Cabarets, though, drew men and women together in a very different atmosphere. Cabarets in the 1910s escaped the confines of the vice districts to bring their mix of stage shows, dancing, dining, and drinking to a wider audience. Pretentious old "lobster palace" restaurants converted themselves into cabarets, while new venues opened in cellars and roof gardens. Performances included musical revues that featured attractive chorus girls. Cabarets allowed a greater feeling of freedom than what prevailed at many other mixed-sex venues. Performers and audiences interacted freely, much as theater audiences had done a century before. Well-dressed couples socialized not only with those in their own party, but also spontaneously with those at other tables. Cabarets found subterfuges, such as

claiming to be private clubs, to stay open past legal closing hours. Cultivating a moderately risqué reputation while discouraging prostitution and inappropriate dancing, cabarets succeeded in exciting adventurous men and women without repelling them.

Changes in patterns of courtship encouraged mixed-gender nightlife. Instead of courting young women in the latter's homes, men in the 20th century took them out on "dates" to public entertainment places such as restaurants, theaters, and dance halls. Dating freed young couples from parental supervision, a development much assisted by the advent of the automobile. Courtship became a more expensive process transacted partly in public space. Power shifted toward the man who paid the costs and provided transportation and protection. Young men and women typically went on numerous dates with many different partners, evaluating each carefully, before finally choosing one to marry. Though young women now participated more frequently in nightlife, older adults did not. Nightlife in the 20th century was shaped increasingly by the patronage and tastes of young adults and teenagers.

PROHIBITION

The passage of the Nineteenth Amendment and Volstead Act in 1920 largely shut down the saloon, the main institution of same-sex nightlife. Prohibition seemed at first a great victory for moral reformers, but it ultimately destroyed the remaining gender barriers that shielded women from the morally dubious nightlife of men.

Liquor law enforcement varied considerably from city to city. Illegal drinking thrived in large cities. Some smaller towns, such as Galveston also became notorious for being "wide open." Most urban saloons shut down immediately, though some saloonkeepers struggled to continue in business selling coffee, meals, or soft drinks. Restaurateurs and cabaret owners also suffered a drop in business, forcing many to close. Optimists had predicted that theaters would see a surge in business as people sought alternatives to the nightclub, but attendance stagnated; without the attraction of alcohol, nightlife and urban tourism declined.

Alcohol continued to be served illicitly in hotels, restaurants, and the remaining nightclubs, often with the involvement of organized crime. Speakeasies and illegal nightclubs were cheaply decorated, transient places that thrived briefly until a police raid, after which they reopened in a new location. Already in defiance of liquor laws, these venues ignored legal closing hours as well. Nightclub entertainment did not even begin until 10:30 or 11 p.m., after theaters closed, and then continued long after midnight. Nightclubs offered women a chance to socialize roughly as equals with men, in stark contrast with the old saloons. Nonetheless, the nightclubs decisively rejected the older model of attracting women customers through refined entertainment. Performances included jazz music and scantily clad young female dancers and singers.

Enhancing their aura of exciting naughtiness, nightclubs for whites opened in African American neighborhoods, most notably in Harlem in New York City. These nightclubs contributed to the vogue of "slumming" in racial ghettoes and immigrant neighborhoods, where affluent white visitors could imagine themselves freed from civilized constraints. White customers visited black prostitutes at "buffet flats" in Harlem, gawked at dark-skinned women in the clubs along Los Angeles's Central Avenue, and drank and danced with African Americans in the interracial "Black and Tan" clubs of Chicago's Bronzeville. Such neighborhoods attracted tourists from out of town as well as white visitors from other parts of the city. Some Harlem nightspots, such as the Cotton Club, tried to make risk-seeking slummers feel safe by excluding black patrons, while others found that an interracial clientele attracted white customers. Residents of racial ghettoes often resented the white slummers who came looking for "primitivism" and illicit

thrills in the neighborhoods where ordinary families made their homes. Conservative community leaders tried with little success to increase black support for Prohibition. They warned that the drinking culture and slumming contributed to racial exploitation and negative stereotypes. Nonetheless, the flourishing nightlife in Harlem, Memphis's Beale Street, and other African American neighborhoods contributed to the growth of black musical culture, supporting the early performers who developed blues and jazz.

Interracial clubs provided space for another violation of social taboos: homosexuality. Men seeking connections with other men, either of the same race or across the color line, found opportunities in the Black and Tans of the Southside of Chicago and the nightclubs of Harlem. Lesbians also found a tolerant atmosphere there. Some black speakeasies offered white male customers the choice of male or female prostitutes. The modern conception of a homosexual identity was largely undeveloped. As in the 19th century, same-sex acts continued to be viewed as sinful lapses rather than as indicators of one's essential nature; as long as a man did not adopt a feminine manner or perform a submissive role in sex, he was not seen as inherently deviant. This older understanding of sexuality made it easier for masculine men to take an interest in feminine "fairies" and "pansies." The culture of the pansy flourished in the nightclubs of the Prohibition era, as just another form of misbehavior that accompanied the virtual illegalization of nightlife. Flamboyantly gay men and transvestites were a common sight in the streets and clubs of Times Square and Greenwich Village as well as in Chicago's Near North Side. Observing the Chicago scene in 1930, *Variety* magazine claimed that "The world's toughest town is going pansy. And liking it."

1933–1965

Repeal of Prohibition shook up the institutions of American nightlife again. Many of the seedier speakeasies folded, while new taverns and nightclubs sprang up in their place. Repeal did not fully restore the old homosocial drinking culture of the saloon. The Prohibition-era pattern of men and women socializing together continued in many of the drinking places that opened (or became legal) after 1933. Taverns still featured bars, now lined with barstools, but customers often preferred to sit with friends around tables. Legal nightclubs continued to offer live music and dancing to a mixed-gender clientele.

A backlash against homosexuality and racial mixing accompanied Repeal. Once legalized, nightclubs became more open to official scrutiny. Club owners anxiously redrew the eroded lines of respectability, suppressing disorderly behavior and excluding stigmatized people. As early as 1931, police in New York began a campaign of harassment against clubs with pansy acts and against drag balls. In the later 1930s, nightclub owners sought to protect their licenses by omitting performances that might draw police intervention. Suppressing homosexual displays and prostitution, they limited sexual titillation to the less controversial form of skimpily dressed showgirls. Male homosexual culture retreated from mainstream nightclubs into specialized drinking spots that catered almost exclusively to gays. Gay bars in the 1930s, 1940s, and 1950s were typically short-lived places controlled by organized crime. Some nightclubs in black neighborhoods continued to offer drag performances for mixed-race audiences. However, white slumming in black neighborhoods declined; in New York, interest dropped off after a 1935 riot in Harlem.

Theaters struggled during the Great Depression. Most vaudeville theaters converted into movie houses and others began offering burlesque shows. Partial female nudity, usually involving flesh-colored tights, had been seen in theaters since the mid-19th century. Crudely humorous burlesque shows travelled through small towns or were performed in theaters in outlying commercial streets within the city. Starting in the 1930s and 1940s, however, burlesque occupied more prominent locations in entertainment hubs such as New York's Times Square and Boston's Scollay Square, attracting largely male crowds from diverse class backgrounds.

After a brief drop in admissions during the early years of the Depression, movie theaters thrived through the remainder of the 1930s and during World War II, especially with the new attractions of sound and color. Thereafter they saw a sharp fall in attendance. Television, which drew viewers to the communal setting of taverns in the 1940s, became pervasive in most private homes in the 1950s and early 1960s, reaching 90 percent of US households by 1962. Watching TV with one's family became a popular alternative to going out at night. As a significant proportion of the urban population moved to the suburbs, and as people relied more on automobiles than public transportation, a trip to view a movie in the congested downtown seemed inconvenient. Savvy entrepreneurs capitalized on suburbanization by opening drive-in theaters; by 1958, 5,000 of these establishments could be found nationwide. Total movie admissions plummeted from 4.1 billion in 1946 to 1.1 billion in 1962. Many struggling downtown theaters were demolished in the 1950s and 1960s to make way for office buildings or parking lots.

Jazz music, with its roots in black culture, flourished in the illegal nightclubs of the Prohibition era and the legalized ones after repeal. Big jazz bands dominated popular music in the late 1930s and early 1940s, synthesizing black and white influences into a swing music that was easy to dance to and commercially successful. Radio broadcasts and records accelerated the diffusion of musical innovation. Jukeboxes allowed young people to listen to the latest tunes, and sometimes dance, in new public venues such as soda fountains, candy shops, and pool halls. Whether played in ballrooms or less formal venues, swing encouraged young people to develop energetic new dancing styles, which disturbed older observers. Nightclubs along New York's 52nd Street became known for an atmosphere of racial mixing that some people found liberating and others frightening.

Bebop jazz combos flourished in smaller nightclubs in the late 1940s and 1950s, offering innovative but less danceable music. Young, white, bebop hipsters sneered at the conventionality of mainstream society, welcomed the sexuality they associated with black culture, and, in many cases, enhanced their listening experience by using marijuana and heroin. Blues, once heard mostly in black dance halls, spread into white popular music in the 1950s in the form of early rock-and-roll. The dance culture of young whites came to focus on rock, while bop fans preferred just to listen to this increasingly intellectual art form. Rock concerts brought new life and prosperity briefly to some downtown movie houses in the late 1950s, until they were halted by concerns about improper dancing and juvenile delinquency. After a minor riot took place outside the Boston Arena on the night of May 3, 1958, Boston banned rock concerts (and arrested concert promoter and disc jockey Alan Freed). City officials and theater owners in other cities followed suit. Adult organizers of teen dances at church halls and schools struggled to control the effects of rock by limiting the number of rock tunes and imposing rules about dancing and dress.

Even in northern cities, African Americans continued to face discrimination or exclusion in white-owned nightspots through the mid-20th century. Blacks often preferred to attend performances, dances, and music in primarily black venues within black neighborhoods; large cities had movie palaces and opulent ballrooms that catered mostly to blacks. African American nightlife in the mid-20th century also flourished in private social clubs; one observer estimated that more than 2,000 of these existed in Chicago alone, typically hosting parties and dances for their members and guests.

1965–PRESENT

Rising crime rates in the 1960s and 1970s discouraged urban nightlife. A soaring murder rate produced frightening headlines and television news reports, while mugging became a far more common danger in daily life. Urban riots from 1964 through 1968 contributed to a fear of public spaces. After outlying commercial streets in almost every major city were damaged by arson and looting, nightspots and other businesses shut their doors. Whites often conflated criminality with racial diversity, seeing the rising black population of cities as itself a cause for alarm. Downtown Detroit by the 1970s was nearly deserted after dark; most of the restaurants and nightclubs had already closed and the last two first-run movie houses soon joined them.

Amusement parks were among the biggest casualties of the 1960s. These parks had flourished in the early to mid-20th century, offering rides, games of chance, cheap food, and swimming. Typically located in outlying areas at the end of trolley lines, they did most of their business on weekends and evenings. Amusement parks resisted pressure for racial integration, claiming that it would deter white visitors. Park owners grudgingly opened their doors to African Americans in response to the Civil Rights Act of 1964, as did owners of bowling alleys and other segregated amusements. Continuing racial tension and discrimination exploded into riots at amusement parks near Newark, Washington, Oklahoma City, and Louisville. White attendance dropped sharply as owners neglected maintenance and the parks developed a reputation as hangouts for juvenile gangs. Most amusement parks shut down altogether in the late 1960s and 1970s.

The rise of rock-and-roll as the dominant popular music in the 1960s and 1970s stimulated the growth of nightclubs. The most prominent bands filled concert halls and sports arenas, some holding tens of thousands of teenagers and young adults. Earsplitting arena rock concerts were major events for surrounding downtown areas, where crowds spilled over into bars and dance halls afterward. Similar spill-over effects were seen in urban neighborhoods adjacent to ballparks and sports arenas. Introduced at major league ballparks in the late 1930s and 1940s, night baseball became the norm long before Wrigley Field, home of the Chicago Cubs, finally lit up in 1988. But a number of teams vacated central-city ballparks in the 1950s, 1960s, and 1970s for suburban locations that were more appealing to affluent, white fans.

One success story in urban nightlife in the 1960s and 1970s was the rise of the discotheque. Dance halls with continuous recorded music were cheaper to operate than those with live musicians, and they succeeded in attracting crowds of young adults. Struggling jazz clubs and dance palaces found a new lease on life. The loud amplification, light shows, and packed dance floors encouraged a frenetic level of activity. Drug use was common. Attendance by celebrities added cachet and drew overflow crowds to flashy clubs like Studio 54 in Midtown Manhattan and its downtown competitors. Lines waited eagerly outside for bouncers' permission to enter. Amid a liberalization of sexual mores, discos became centers for a new pick-up culture for young men and women, and for gay men. Most venues mixed gay and straight customers.

A New York nightspot was the site for a watershed moment in the history of the gay rights movement. In the early morning hours of June 28, 1969, New York police raided the Stonewall Inn, a gay bar and dance spot in Greenwich Village. Police were astonished when customers refused to submit to the abusive protocol of a raid; some resisted arrest and began fighting back. Police found themselves besieged inside the club as a growing, angry mob surrounded the place, barraged it with stones and bottles, and tried to set it on fire. Though police harassment of gay bars continued for years afterward, Stonewall encouraged gay men to defend their way of life.

Homosexuality became more open in New York, San Francisco, and other cities. Gay bathhouses and sex clubs offered men the chance for anonymous contact with strangers until the AIDS epidemic forced most of them to close in the 1980s.

Dance parties called "raves" drew thousands of young people in Chicago, New York, San Francisco, and other major cities in the late 1980s and 1990s. Often held in old warehouses, raves featured dazzling light shows, deafening electronic music, and rampant use of party drugs such as ecstasy. Unlike in the first half of the 20th century, when nightclubs drew customers from a broader age range, dancing became a form of nightlife heavily dominated by people under thirty years old. Older adults are more likely to spend evenings at restaurants.

THE NIGHTLIFE INDUSTRY IN URBAN ECONOMIES

Since the late 20th century, cities have increasingly promoted nightlife; the main goals have been to strengthen commercial districts and to encourage a sense of urban excitement that might persuade affluent people to live and do business in the commercial core. Though mainstream commercial amusements scattered to the suburbs in most metropolitan areas after 1960, highbrow entertainments, such as opera companies, dance troupes, and symphony orchestras, continued to be held downtown. Municipal governments and private foundations after 1970 developed performing arts centers in Detroit, San Francisco, Cleveland, Philadelphia, and Portland. Old movie palaces were converted to concert halls in New Orleans, St. Louis, and other cities. Some struggling smaller cities, such as Hartford, promote their surviving cultural institutions, nightclubs, and downtown restaurants as "arts and entertainment districts." Since the 1990s, formerly decrepit neighborhoods of obsolete, multistory warehouses and factories have been redeveloped into clusters of restaurants, nightclubs, and art galleries. These locales include Chicago's River North, Kansas City's Power & Light District, Baltimore's Station North, Milwaukee's Historic Third Ward, and areas simply called the "Warehouse District" in New Orleans, Austin, Cleveland, and Minneapolis. Blues bars are a Chicago specialty in River North and in outlying neighborhoods; largely white, young audiences, many of them tourists, visit the clubs to hear black musicians perform old standards.

The casino districts in Las Vegas are atypical, of course, but several other cities have permitted legalized gambling in an attempt to inject prosperity into tired downtowns. A strip of casinos emerged along Atlantic City's Boardwalk starting in the late 1970s; New Orleans and Detroit welcomed casinos in the late 1990s and Baltimore did so in 2014. Casinos are largely self-contained entertainment centers with limited spillover effects into surrounding areas, as seen in Atlantic City. Nonetheless, gambling in New Orleans strengthens the city's appeal to tourists, who also crowd the nearby French Quarter, where, mirroring its name, alcohol-serving establishments dominate the Bourbon Street nightlife district.

New York City remains the dominant center for nightlife tourism, with "Broadway" still used as a metonym for the theater business. The city's most ambitious effort to promote the entertainment economy was the makeover of the Times Square district in the 1990s. Observers began fretting about the decline of Times Square during the Great Depression, a period that saw an invasion by burlesque houses and chop suey joints. Throngs continued to attend movie houses and legitimate theaters there, but the area grew increasingly seedy. Commercial sex became flagrantly open in the 1960s after US Supreme Court decisions hobbled attempts to suppress pornography. Pornographic bookstores, massage parlors, X-rated movie houses, live sex shows, and streetwalking proliferated in or around the square. Feminist organizations targeted the district for protests, arguing that the sex trade fostered violence against women. Faced with concerns about the survival of the theater district, in the 1970s New York mayors began to crack down on prostitution and related crime in the Times Square area and to encourage redevelopment. The 42nd Street Development Project in the 1980s and 1990s succeeded in pushing most sex businesses out of Times Square and in attracting new theaters and theme restaurants. By the early 21st century, the square was transformed into a more family-friendly tourist attraction, though at the expense of what critics called "Disneyfication." In Boston, law enforcement and private redevelopment in the 1980s cleared out the old "Combat Zone," a downtown cluster of strip joints and pornographic movie theaters where the city had attempted to confine the sex trade. Home video and Internet sites in later decades took over most of the pornography business nationwide, while strip joints have scattered throughout metropolitan areas. Encounters with prostitutes are often arranged online rather than through meetings in public spaces.

Nightlife—defined as social activity in urban commercial spaces—is, of course, not the only way that people spend their evening leisure hours. As in earlier eras, urban Americans continue to go out for religious worship, visit with friends, and take recreational walks. Many men and women routinely devote their evenings to solitary exercise at health clubs. *Bowling Alone*, a 2000 study by the sociologist Robert Putnam, observed that people far more commonly spend an evening at a friend's home than going to a theater or ballpark. Putnam argued that social life of all forms declined after 1960, as a result of television, generational changes, suburban sprawl, and work pressures. He observed a decline in participation in social groups of all sorts, including bowling leagues, parent-teacher organizations and veterans' associations. Putnam's conclusions about a decline in public life have been challenged, but it is hard to deny that evening entertainment has retreated into the home since the mid-20th century. For instance, movie theater attendance has never recovered from the massive decline of the late 1940s through 1950s. Movie admissions for the United States and Canada totaled only 1.3 billion in 2013, a modest increase from the low point of the 1960s. Instead of going out at night, more Americans stay home and watch television or play games on their computers.

DISCUSSION OF THE LITERATURE

Since the 1990s, historians have produced an extensive scholarship on the social experience of nightlife in American cities. This work focuses heavily on the largest cities, especially New York, in the period from approximately 1880 to the 1960s.

Much of the literature on the era before electrification in the 1880s has considered the effects of social class formation on manners and gender relations. Overviews of nocturnal activity in the 19th century, focusing on the cities of the Northeast and Midwest and on drinking culture, attendance at performances, sexuality, and gambling are available.[1]

A large body of scholarship covers nightlife from 1880 through the 1960s. Early works considered the influence of "modernity" in breaking down Victorian culture or dealt with the frustrated efforts to impose various forms of social control. Works on women noted the liberating potential of consumer culture. Several works examine how concerns about race relations shaped recreation for whites as well as blacks, provide an overview of nightlife during these years, examine the importance of gender in urban environments, and treat subjects that include amusement parks, dancing, drinking, fraternal organizations, nightclubs and music, theater and concerts, and sexuality.[2]

Most scholarly work on the experience of urban nightlife in the period since 1965 is produced by sociologists or urban theorists, not historians. Several scholarly overviews consider the place of nightlife in urban cultures and economies.[3]

PRIMARY SOURCES

SPORTING CULTURE IN THE 19TH CENTURY

Disreputable urban amusements of the 19th century are well documented in the pages of the *Sporting Times*, the *National Police Gazette*, and the more obscure publications in the American Antiquarian Society's "Racy Newspapers" collection, available at http://www.americanantiquarian.org/

PERFORMING ARTS

Billy Rose Theater Division, New York Public Library, is a large archive devoted to theater history. It contains collections of playbills, photographs, and correspondence.

The New York Public Library also contains extensive collections devoted to the history of music and dance. These collections, like those in the theater division, focus on the art forms and the performance rather than on the audience experience.

The Harvard Theatre Collection, Harvard University. This is another extensive archive devoted to the history of theater and other performing arts.

SEXUALITY

American Social Health Association Records, 1905–2005, Elmer L. Andersen Library, University of Minnesota, Minneapolis. This large collection documents the organization's work, including its efforts to suppress prostitution in cities during the world wars.

"Blue Books," Williams Research Center, Historic New Orleans Collection, New Orleans. A collection of guides to the Storyville commercial sex district of New Orleans.

Committee of Fourteen Records, New York Public Library. This collection contains investigators' reports and other manuscripts of the Committee of Fourteen, which sought to document and suppress illicit sexuality in New York from 1905 to 1932. Contains material on dance halls.

Committee of Fifteen Records, New York Public Library. Contains the papers of a citizen's group founded in 1900 to fight prostitution and gambling in New York.

Committee of Fifteen Records, University of Chicago Libraries. Chicago followed New York in creating a Committee of Fifteen in 1908 to combat prostitution.

Women Against Pornography Records, 1979–1989, Schlesinger Library, Radcliffe Institute. Includes manuscripts and publications documenting the pornography business in various cities as well as material related to this organization's work.

MISCELLANEOUS

Ernest Watson Burgess papers, University of Chicago Libraries. This is a massive and eclectic collection of correspondence, reports, student papers, and notes by a leading sociologist of the early 20th century. It contains extensive material concerning life and social conditions in Chicago.

Juvenile Protective Association records, Richard J. Daley Library Special Collections and University Archives, University of Illinois at Chicago. Contains reports, manuscripts, and other material concerning juvenile delinquency in early-20th-century Chicago.

New York District Attorney Records of Cases, 1895–1971, New York City Department of Records. Includes records of criminal cases and scrapbooks with news clippings.

DIGITAL MATERIALS

- "Hip Hop Party and Event Flyer" collection (http://rmc.library.cornell.edu/hiphop/flyers.html), Cornell University.
- "African American Band Music and Recordings, 1883-1923 (http://lcweb2.loc.gov/diglib/ihas/html/stocks/stocks-home.html)," Library of Congress.
- "The American Ballroom Companion: Dance Instruction Manuals, 1490–1920 (http://memory.loc.gov/ammem/dihtml/dihome.html)," Library of Congress.
- Miss Frank E. Buttolph American Menu Collection, 1851–1930 (http://digitalgallery.nypl.org/nypldigital/explore/dgexplore.cfm?col_id=159), New York Public Library (online image collection of restaurant menus, mostly from the early 20th century).

FURTHER READING

Ahlquist, Karen. *Democracy at the Opera: Music, Theater, and Culture in New York City, 1815–1860*. Urbana: University of Illinois Press, 1997.

Allen, Robert C. *Horrible Prettiness: Burlesque and American Culture*. Chapel Hill: University of North Carolina Press, 1991.

Altschuler, Glenn. *All Shook Up: How Rock 'n' Roll Changed America*. New York: Oxford University Press, 2003.

Baldwin, Peter C. *In the Watches of the Night: Life in the Nocturnal City, 1820–1930*. Chicago: University of Chicago Press, 2012.

Bank, Rosemarie K. *Theatre Culture in America, 1825–1860*. Cambridge: Cambridge University Press, 1997.

Boyd, Nan Alamilla. *Wide-Open Town: A History of Queer San Francisco to 1965*. Berkeley: University of California Press, 2005.

Butsch, Richard. *The Making of American Audiences: From Stage to Television, 1750–1990*. Cambridge: Cambridge University Press, 2000.

Campbell, Gavin James. *Music and the Making of a New South*. Chapel Hill: University of North Carolina Press, 2004.

Carnes, Mark C. *Secret Ritual and Manhood in Victorian America*. New Haven, CT: Yale University Press, 1989.

Chatterton, Paul, and Robert Hollands, eds. *Urban Nightscapes: Youth Cultures, Pleasure Spaces and Corporate Power*. New York: Routledge, 2003.

Chauncey, George. *Gay New York: Gender, Urban Culture, and the Making of the Gay Male World, 1890–1940*. New York: Basic Books, 1994.

Chudacoff, Howard. *The Age of the Bachelor: Creating an American Subculture*. Princeton, NJ: Princeton University Press, 1999.

Clement, Elizabeth Alice. *Love for Sale: Courting, Treating, and Prostitution in New York City, 1900–1945*. Chapel Hill: University of North Carolina Press, 2006.

Cohen, Patricia Cline. *The Murder of Helen Jewitt: The Life and Death of a Prostitute in Nineteenth-Century New York*. New York: Alfred A. Knopf, 1999.

Currid, Elizabeth. *The Warhol Economy: How Fashion, Art and Music Drive New York City*. Princeton, NJ: Princeton University Press, 2007.

Duis, Peter R. *The Saloon: Public Drinking in Chicago and Boston, 1880–1920*. Urbana: University of Illinois Press, 1983.

Erenberg, Lewis A. *Steppin' Out: New York Nightlife and the Transformation of American Culture, 1890–1930*. Westport, CT: Greenwood, 1981.

Erenberg, Lewis A. *Swingin' the Dream: Big Band Jazz and the Rebirth of American Culture*. Chicago: University of Chicago Press, 1998.

Fabian, Ann. *Card Sharps and Bucket Shops: Gambling in Nineteenth-Century America*. New York: Routledge, 1999.

Fikentscher, Kai. *"You Better Work!" Underground Dance Music in New York City*. Hanover, NH: University Press of New England, 2000.

Garcia, Cindy. *Salsa Crossings: Dancing Latinidad in Los Angeles*. Durham, NC: Duke University Press, 2013.

Gilfoyle, Timothy J. *City of Eros: New York City, Prostitution, and the Commercialization of Sex, 1820–1920*. New York: W. W. Norton, 1992.

Gottdiener, Mark, Claudia Collins, and David R. Dickens. *Las Vegas: The Social Production of an All-American City*. Malden, MA: Blackwell, 1999.

Grazian, David. *Blue Chicago: The Search for Authenticity in Urban Blues Clubs*. Chicago: University of Chicago Press, 2003.

Hannigan, John. *Fantasy City: Pleasure and Profit in the Postmodern Metropolis*. New York: Routledge, 1998.

Heap, Chad. *Slumming: Sexual and Racial Encounters in American Nightlife, 1885–1940*. Chicago: University of Chicago Press, 2009.

Kasson, John F. *Amusing the Million: Coney Island at the Turn of the Century*. New York: Hill and Wang, 1978.

Lawrence, Tim. *Love Saves the Day: A History of American Dance Music Culture, 1970–1979*. Durham, NC: Duke University Press, 2003.

Lerner, Michael A. *Dry Manhattan: Prohibition in New York City*. Cambridge, MA: Harvard University Press, 2008.

Levine, Lawrence W. *Highbrow/Lowbrow: The Emergence of Cultural Hierarchy in America*. Cambridge, MA: Harvard University Press, 1988.

Lloyd, Richard. *Neo-Bohemia: Art and Commerce in the Postindustrial City*. New York: Routledge, 2006.

Long, Alecia P. *The Great Southern Babylon: Race, Sex, and Respectability in New Orleans, 1865–1920*. Baton Rouge: Louisiana State University Press, 2005.

Lott, Eric. *Love and Theft: Blackface Minstrelsy and the American Working Class*. New York: Oxford University Press, 1995.

Lyons, Clare A. *Sex among the Rabble: An Intimate History of Gender and Power in the Age of Revolution, Philadelphia, 1730–1830*. Chapel Hill: University of North Carolina Press, 2006.

Maginn, Paul J., and Christine Steinmetz, eds. *(Sub)Urban Sexscapes: Geographies and Regulation of the Sex Industry*. New York: Routledge, 2015.

McBee, Randy D. *Dance Hall Days: Intimacy and Leisure among Working Class Immigrants in the United States*. New York: New York University Press, 2000.

McConachie, Bruce A. *Melodramatic Formations: American Theatre and Society*. Iowa City: University of Iowa Press, 1992.

Nasaw, David. *Going Out: The Rise and Fall of Public Amusements*. New York: Basic Books, 1993.

Peiss, Kathy. *Cheap Amusements: Working Women and Leisure in Turn-of-the-Century New York*. Philadelphia: Temple University Press, 1986.

Peretti, Burton W. *The Creation of Jazz: Music, Race and Culture in Urban America*. Urbana: University of Illinois Press, 1992.

Peretti, Burton W. *Nightclub City: Politics and Amusement in Manhattan*. Philadelphia: University of Pennsylvania Press, 2007.

Powers, Madelon. *Faces along the Bar: Lore and Order in the Workingmen's Saloon, 1870–1920*. Chicago: University of Chicago Press, 1998.

Rabinovitz, Lauren. *For the Love of Pleasure: Women, Movies, and Culture in Turn-of-the-Century Chicago.* New Brunswick, NJ: Rutgers University Press, 1998.

Rabinovitz, Lauren. *Electric Dreamland: Amusement Parks, Movies, and American Modernity.* New York: Columbia University Press, 2012.

Reichl, Alexander J. *Reconstructing Times Square: Politics and Culture in Urban Development.* Lawrence: University Press of Kansas, 1999.

Sagalyn, Lynne B. *Times Square Roulette: Remaking the City Icon.* Cambridge, MA: MIT Press, 2001.

Schafer, Judith Kelleher. *Brothels, Depravity and Abandoned Women: Illegal Sex in Antebellum New Orleans.* Baton Rouge: Louisiana State University Press, 2009.

Schloss, Joseph G. *Foundation: B-Boys, B-Girls and Hip-Hop Culture in New York.* New York: Oxford University Press, 2009.

Sides, Josh. *Erotic City: Sexual Revolutions and the Making of Modern San Francisco.* New York: Oxford University Press, 2009.

Snyder, Robert W. *The Voice of the City: Vaudeville and Popular Culture in New York.* New York: Oxford University Press, 1991.

Stott, Richard. *Jolly Fellows: Male Milieus in Nineteenth-Century America.* Baltimore: Johns Hopkins University Press, 2009.

Thompson, Peter. *Rum, Punch & Revolution: Taverngoing & Public Life in Eighteenth-Century Philadelphia.* Philadelphia: University of Pennsylvania Press, 1999.

Waller, Gregory A. *Main Street Amusements: Movies and Commercial Entertainment in a Southern City, 1896–1930.* Washington, DC: Smithsonian Institution Press, 1995.

Wolcott, Victoria. *Race, Riots, and Roller Coasters: The Struggle over Segregated Recreation in America.* Philadelphia: University of Pennsylvania Press, 2012.

NOTES

1. For an overview of nocturnal activity in the 19th century, focusing on the cities of the Northeast and Midwest, see Peter C. Baldwin, *In the Watches of the Night: Life in the Nocturnal City, 1820–1930* (Chicago: University of Chicago Press, 2012). On drinking culture, see Peter Thompson, *Run Punch & Revolution: Taverngoing and Public Life in Eighteenth-Century Philadelphia* (Philadelphia: University of Pennsylvania Press, 1999); and Prichard Stott, *Jolly Fellows: Male Milieus in Nineteenth-Century America* (Baltimore: Johns Hopkins University Press, 2009). On attendance at performances, see Karen Ahlquist, *Democracy at the Opera: Music, Theater, and Culture in New York City, 1815–1860* (Urbana: University of Illinois Press, 1997); Rosemarie K. Bank, *Theatre Culture in America, 1825–1860* (Cambridge: Cambridge University Press, 1997); Richard Butsch, *The Making of American Audiences: From Stage to Television, 1750–1990* (Cambridge: Cambridge University Press); Lawrence W. Levine, *Highbrow/Lowbrow: The Emergence of Cultural Hierarchy in America* (Cambridge, MA: Harvard University Press, 1988); Eric Lott, *Love and Theft: Blackface Minstrelsy and the American Working Class* (New York: Oxford University Press, 1995); and Bruce A. McConachie, *Melodramatic Formations: American Theatre and Society* (Iowa City: University of Iowa Press, 1992). On sexuality, see Patricia Cline Cohen, *The Murder of Helen Jewitt: The Life and Death of a Prostitute in Nineteenth-Century New York* (New York: Alfred A. Knopf, 1999); Clare A. Lyons, *Sex among the Rabble: An Intimate History of Gender and Power in the Age of Revolution, Philadelphia, 1730–1830* (Chapel Hill: University of North Carolina Press, 2006); Timothy J. Gilfoyle, *City of Eros: New York City, Prostitution, and the Commercialization of Sex, 1820–1920* (New York: W. W. Norton, 1992); and Judith Kelleher Shafer, *Brothels, Depravity and Abandoned Women: Illegal Sex in Antebellum New Orleans* (Baton Rouge: Louisiana State University Press, 2009). On gambling, see Ann Fabian, *Card Sharps and Bucket Shops: Gambling in Nineteenth-Century America* (New York: Routledge, 1999).

2. For an overview of nightlife during these years, see David Nasaw, *Going Out: The Rise and Fall of Public Amusements* (New York: Basic Books, 1993). Works examining the importance of gender in urban amusements include Howard Chudacoff, *The Age of the Bachelor: Creating an American Subculture* (Princeton, NJ: Princeton University Press, 1999); and Kathy Peiss, *Cheap Amusements: Working Girls and Leisure in Turn-of-the-Century New York* (Philadelphia: Temple University Press, 1986). On amusement parks, see John F. Kasson, *Amusing the Million: Coney Island at the Turn of the Century* (New York: Hill and Wang, 1978);

Lauren Rabinowitz, *Electric Dreamland: Amusement Parks, Movies, and American Modernity* (New York: Columbia University Press, 2012); and Victoria Wolcott, *Race, Riots, and Roller Coasters: The Struggle over Segregated Recreation in America* (Philadelphia: University of Pennsylvania Press, 2012). On dancing, see Randy D. McBee, *Dance Hall Days, Intimacy and Leisure among Working-Class Immigrants in the United States* (New York: New York University Press, 2000). On drinking, see Perry R. Duis, *The Saloon: Public Drinking in Chicago and Boston, 1880–1920* (Urbana: University of Illinois Press, 1920); Madelon Powers, *Faces Along the Bar: Lore and Order in the Workingmen's Saloon, 1870–1920* (Chicago: University of Chicago Press, 1998); and Michael A. Lerner, *Dry Manhattan: Prohibition in New York City* (Cambridge, MA: Harvard University Press, 2008). On fraternal organizations, see Mark C. Carnes, *Secret Ritual and Manhood in Victorian America* (New Haven, CT: Yale University Press, 1989). On movies, see Lauren Rabinovitz, *For the Love of Pleasure: Women, Movies, and Culture in Turn-of-the-Century Chicago* (New Brunswick, NJ: Rutgers University Press, 1998); and Gregory A. Waller, *Main Street Amusements: Movies and Commercial Entertainment in a Southern Town, 1896–1930* (Washington, DC: Smithsonian Institution Press, 1995). On nightclubs and music, see Glenn Altschuler, *All Shook Up: How Rock 'n' Roll Changed America* (New York: Oxford University Press, 2003); Lewis A. Erenberg, *Steppin' Out: New York Nightlife and the Transformation of American Culture, 1890–1930* (Westport, CT: Greenwood, 1981); Lewis A. Erenberg, *Swingin' the Dream: Big Band Jazz and the Rebirth of American Culture* (Chicago: University of Chicago Press, 1998); Chad Heap, *Slumming: Sexual and Racial Encounters in American Nightlife, 1885–1940* (Chicago: University of Chicago Press, 2009); Burton W. Peretti, *The Creation of Jazz: Music, Race, and Culture in Urban America* (Urbana: University of Illinois Press, 1992); and Burton W. Peretti, *Nightclub City: Politics and Amusement in Manhattan* (Philadelphia: University of Pennsylvania Press, 2007). On theaters and concerts, see Robert C. Allen, *Horrible Prettiness: Burlesque and American Culture* (Chapel Hill: University of North Carolina Press, 1991); Richard Butsch, *The Making of American Audiences: From Stage to Television, 1750–1990*

(Cambridge: Cambridge University Press, 2000); Gavin James Campbell, *Music and the Making of a New South* (Chapel Hill: University of North Carolina Press, 2004); and Robert W. Snyder, *The Voice of the City: Vaudeville and Popular Culture in New York* (New York: Oxford University Press, 1991). On sexuality, see Nan Alamilla Boyd, *Wide-Open Town: A History of Queer San Francisco to 1965* (Berkeley: University of California Press, 2005); George Chauncey, *Gay New York: Gender, Urban Culture, and the Making of the Gay Male World, 1890–1940* (New York: Basic Books, 1994); Elizabeth Alice Clement, *Love for Sale: Courting, Treating, and Prostitution in New York City, 1900–1945* (Chapel Hill: University of North Carolina Press, 2006); and Alecia P. Long, *The Great Southern Babylon: Race, Sex, and Respectability in New Orleans, 1865–1920* (Baton Rouge: Louisiana State University Press, 2005).

3. For scholarly overviews, see Paul Chatterton and Robert Hollands, eds., *Urban Nightscapes: Youth Cultures, Pleasure Spaces and Corporate Power* (New York: Routledge, 2003); Elizabeth Currid, *The Warhol Economy: How Fashion, Art and Music Drive New York City* (Princeton, NJ: Princeton University Press, 2007); Mark Gottdiener, Claudia Collins, and David R. Dickens, *Las Vegas: The Social Production of an All-American City* (Malden, MA: Blackwell, 1999); John Hannigan, *Fantasy City: Pleasure and Profit in the Postmodern Metropolis* (New York: Routledge, 1998); Richard Lloyd, *Neo-Bohemia: Art and Commerce in the Post-industrial City* (New York: Routledge, 2006); Alexander J. Reichl, *Reconstructing Times Square: Politics and Culture in Urban Development* (Lawrence: University Press of Kansas, 1999); and Lynne B. Sagalyn, *Times Square Roulette: Remaking the City Icon* (Cambridge, MA: MIT Press, 2001). Additional scholarly and semi-scholarly works include Kai Fikentscher, *"You Better Work!" Underground Dance Music in New York City* (Hanover, NH: University Press of New England, 2000); Cindy Garcia, *Salsa Crossings: Dancing Latinidad in Los Angeles* (Durham, NC: Duke University Press, 2013); David Grazian, *Blue Chicago: The Search for Authenticity Urban Blues Clubs* (Chicago: University of Chicago Press, 2003); Tim Lawrence, *Love Saves the Day: A History of American Dance Music Culture, 1970–1979* (Durham, NC: Duke University Press,

2003); Joseph G. Schloss, *Foundation: B-Boys, B-Girls and Hip-Hop Culture in New York* (New York: Oxford University Press, 2009); and Josh Sides, *Erotic City: Sexual Revolutions and the Making of Urban San Francisco* (New York: Oxford University Press, 2009).

Peter C. Baldwin

JAZZ, BLUES, AND RAGTIME IN AMERICA, 1900–1945

In early 1938, the same year as Benny Goodman's Carnegie Hall success, Jelly Roll Morton, self-proclaimed "Originator of Jazz and Stomps," wrote a letter to the jazz magazine, *Down Beat*, announcing that "New Orleans is the cradle of jazz, and I, myself, happened to be the creator [of jazz] in the year 1902." Prematurely aged by bad health, Morton used the letter to center himself in the history of jazz music. By the Swing Era, countless articles had begun to sketch out the early years of jazz, and Morton was desperate to claim appropriate credit. "My contributions were many," Morton wrote, "first clown director, with witty sayings and flashily dressed, now called master of ceremonies; first glee club in orchestra; the first washboard was recorded by me; bass fiddle, drums—which were supposed to be impossible to record."[1] This letter inspired Alan Lomax to seek out the piano player for a series of interviews, which would soon develop into an extended oral history of the first years of jazz music. New Orleans—and Morton—figured prominently in this narrative, and the piano player posited the city as the essential element in the jazz story. With African, Caribbean, French, and Spanish connectors, New Orleans also had a complex demographic structure, with a racialized society fractured along white, black, and Creole lines. "I thought," Morton succinctly told Lomax, "New Orleans was the whole world."[2]

The musical culture discussed by Morton had its roots in the late 19th century, and two entertainment forms in particular—ragtime and the blues—would have a major impact on the development of jazz. In addition, the vaudeville stage, with its connections to minstrelsy and instrumental proficiency, would help foster a diverse network of theaters and musicians located across the nation. The broader context of these musical developments was the shift to modernism, as more and more Americans began to seek out new ways of connecting with one another. This cultural shift signaled a revolution in terms of crafting an integrated nation as technological innovations and mass production helped create a more singular American culture. As modernism—with its roots in urbanism, secularism, and industrialism—began to creep into American culture, it formed the framework for new modes of expression. Ragtime and the blues, then, developed within this fertile period as technological innovation, business expansion, and growing urbanization radically redefined the cultural landscape of America.

RAGTIME AND THE BLUES

In the 1890s, a series of events would underscore the dramatic changes beginning to emerge in American society.[3] The first was the largest economic catastrophe to that date as the stock market crash of 1893 called into question the economic stability of the nation. At the same time, the World's Columbian Exposition commemorated the four centuries that had passed since Europeans began to establish a foothold in the western hemisphere. These two moments underscored the vast array of experiences that came to define America in the late 19th century: the volatility of a modern economy and the convergent sense of newness and oldness that shaped the discussion of Columbus. In addition, Chicago (site of the fair) also hosted that year's annual meeting of the American Historical Association. There, historian Frederick Jackson Turner proposed the frontier as the fundamental element of the American character—the definitive aspect of American identity.[4]

Ragtime came of age within this context of upheaval and questioning, hopefulness and concern. This new music was a syncopated synthesis of a variety of earlier genres such as marches, popular dance songs, music from the black South, and music from the Caribbean. Despite this disparate collection of components, ragtime developed a coherent sound through the explicit use of a strongly syncopated beat. This pronounced, ragged beat gave ragtime its name as well as its attendant controversy. The rhythmic drive of the music—present in each of ragtime's various forms—spurred a national conversation about the alleged immoral nature of the music. A number of commentators argued that the music eroded the Victorian values of the nation, while others attacked it for being too raw, too untamed, too black. African American musicians played such a large role in the creation and diffusion of ragtime, that many white critics faulted the music for not being "American" enough.[5]

Ragtime peaked in the two decades before America entered World War I, and much of its popularity was made possible through new business practices that allowed for the mass production of pianos and the mass distribution of sheet music. These innovations helped link the localized, if widespread, world of vaudeville theaters to a national, mass-produced and distributed, culture.[6] Vaudeville theaters helped develop an audience for ragtime as well as provide for a repertoire. But vaudeville also brought with it certain elements from blackface minstrelsy.[7] Ragtime emerged from this complicated context of blackface caricature, racist comedic tropes, and a burgeoning entertainment market. African Americans negotiated this challenging landscape through a combination of playing to and fighting against expectations from audiences as well as businessmen. Ultimately, ragtime was defined by the racially coded world

built by Jim Crow, and the music's reception (if not the music itself) would be shaped explicitly by issues of race and racism. Still, ragtime, at least for a few years, was wildly popular with white audiences, many of whom enjoyed a particular lyrically driven subset of the genre known colloquially as "ragtime song." As ragtime became the popular music of the day, however, another musical form, rooted directly in the black experience, began to percolate out of the rural South.

Unlike ragtime, which had a fairly linear progression from a syncopated piano-based music to its popular lyrical incarnation, the story of the blues defies easy characterization. Ultimately, a raw form of what would come to be called the blues began to emerge in a variety of locations across the rural South. Connected to the work songs and spirituals of the slave community, the blues was a music intricately connected to the lives of black southerners. By the 20th century (as ragtime became popular), various forms of the blues helped define, musically, the experience of many black southerners. The blues was rooted rhythmically and lyrically to the work songs that served a multiplicity of roles within the enslaved plantation culture of the South.[8] Beyond the musicological connections, the blues was linked directly to black America. The origin and definition of the blues, James Cone has noted, "cannot be understood independent of the suffering that black people endured in the context of white racism and hate." "The blues," therefore, "tells us about black people's attempt to carve out a significant existence in a very trying situation. The purpose of the blues is to give structure to black existence in a context where color means rejection and humiliation."[9]

Far removed from the origins of the music, the most important person in the popularizing of the blues was W. C. Handy. Handy, a trained cornet player who had played in various dance and marching bands, saw firsthand the power of the blues (and its possible commercial appeal) when he saw a black guitar player in Tutwiler, Mississippi. The guitarist was improvising lyrics as he played, and something in that volatile mix of untrained musicianship and wordplay affected Handy. Nothing had prepared Handy for this type of folk music, so detached from the rules of the conservatory. "As he played," Handy later recalled, "he pressed a knife on the strings of the guitar in a manner popularized by Hawaiian guitarists who used steel bars." It was, simply, "the weirdest music I had ever heard."[10] On a subsequent tour of the area, this time in Cleveland, Mississippi, Handy listened to a band improvising a tune that was enthusiastically received by the local audience. "A rain of silver dollars began to fall around the outlandish, stomping feet," Handy wrote, "Dollars, quarters, halves—the shower grew heavier and continued so long I strained my neck to get a better look. There before the boys lay more money than my nine musicians were being paid for the entire engagement." "Then," Handy succinctly summarized, "I saw the beauty of primitive music."[11]

These Mississippi trips inspired Handy to begin experimenting with this new form. What Handy composed—in songs such as "St. Louis Blues," "Memphis Blues," and "Beale Street Blues"—was a particular type of the blues that coupled a 12-bar blues structure to a more uniform dance beat with a strong melody. Not the music of rural Mississippi, but a form that was still quite flexible in terms of form and format. What Handy helped craft was a stylized and more formal type of blues. Popular in several northern cities, especially New York City, this style of the blues would eventually add vaudeville and minstrel material into the mix to create a very distinctive, and popular, song-based genre. Performed and recorded usually with a small, almost exclusively male, band and often featuring a female singer—most notably Bessie Smith, Ma Rainey, and Mamie Smith—this form of blues (often labeled "classic blues") was part of a long line of black musical entertainment.

The blues, however, had many permutations during these years and reflected a wide array of influences. Musical and lyrical improvisation was central to this subgenre, as was the guitar. More portable than the piano and more harmonically open to invention than an ensemble, guitar-based blues (sometimes referred to as "country blues") allowed for a great deal of elasticity in terms of harmony and arrangement. In addition, this form of blues was primarily a masculine form, as most of the performers were men. More extemporaneous in sound than the classic blues and more fluid in its harmonic structure, the country blues would remain a vital link to its rural roots and would lead to a series of reinventions throughout the 20th century. Still, both of these iterations shared a distinctive verse and musical structure that gave the blues a specific identity. Most notably, the blues centered on several elements that defied easy transcription via sheet music: idiosyncratic rhythms and vocalizations as well as the pronounced use of "blue notes"—notes that fall between established pitches.[12] These elements were primordial in terms of human history and singing, but within the context of modern America, these sounds offered something novel and unique. More importantly—within an entertainment world centered on sheet music—the defining characteristic of the blues defied transcription. The blues arrived on a larger scene, however, just as recording technology began to coalesce. Thus, a music connected to musical techniques both ancient and not so ancient, as well as to the centuries-old history of American slavery, emerged as the key signifier to modern black life.

Together, ragtime and the blues anticipated the Jazz Age musically as well as culturally. The technological elements that helped spread ragtime and the blues helped provide a market for early jazz recordings. In addition, the various controversies connected to ragtime and the blues—especially in terms of race and morality—found fresh footing in jazz as a new expression of modernity materialized. This context helps explain the jazz era, too, as many of the same fears and arguments became attached to jazz. More than just musical antecedents, then, ragtime and the blues helped construct a national audience as well as a national conversation for jazz music. These genres underscored the interconnected society that began to shape American culture, but jazz, more than any previous music, came of age just as a national media network made possible the widespread transmission of live and recorded sound.

JAZZ ORIGINS

The history of jazz music is deeply linked to and embedded with the history of New Orleans. As ragtime and the blues began to circulate, New Orleans incubated music that would come to be called jazz, and the unique social construction of the city provided a cadre of musicians as well as an audience to support and sustain a particular form of musical expression. The key element to understanding the early development of jazz relates to its multi-dimensional role within New Orleans. The music existed within a fluid spectrum between folk and commerce, with neighbors performing for neighbors in and out of a formal entertainment world. Bars and honkytonks were settings, but so were private gatherings, funerals, dances, and a large array of other events. If the blues reflected a true folk heritage and ragtime connected to the commercial world of selling music, then jazz represented a middle way: a form that helped craft and preserve the identity of the local groups that created this new sound. Ultimately, within this unique multi-racial setting, jazz emerged from an unplanned collision of ragtime, the blues, minstrel shows, vaudeville routines, brass band repertoires, string band songs, dance music, marching music, and funeral music. The result was an improvised sound that, within a few years, would captivate the nation.[13]

A significant aspect as to why jazz emerged as it did in New Orleans concerned the city's unique social order with white, black, and Creole residents living in a landscape defined by French, Spanish, African, and Caribbean influences. Simultaneously the quintessential southern city, as well as a place unlike any other place in the South, New Orleans offered a racial and cultural dynamism few other urban areas in the United States shared. In New Orleans in the late 19th and early 20th centuries, Creole musicians like pianist Jelly Roll Morton and clarinetists Alphonse Picou and Sidney Bechet, white musicians such as brass band leader "Papa" Jack Laine and cornetist Nick LaRocca, and black cornetists Buddy Bolden and Joe "King" Oliver each contributed in different ways to a flourishing music scene defined by syncopation and improvisation. At the same time, the racial fluidity that had shaped much of the early history of the city had collapsed through a series of legislative, judicial, and violent acts. By the late 1890s—as *Plessy v. Ferguson* (a New Orleans case) made Jim Crow a national language—the city's Creole community, in particular, was broken down as various "One Drop" regulations destroyed the distinctive racial patterns that had long defined New Orleans life.[14] This combination of musical inventiveness and social upheaval provided early jazz a basic form as well as a cultural framework that would soon be disseminated across the entire nation.

DISSEMINATION

Although born in New Orleans, early jazz developed an identity elsewhere. The Great Migration of black southerners helped redefine the landscape of the urban Midwest and Northeast, and jazz music played into this transition. One of the central mythic images of the jazz story relates to a young Louis Armstrong clutching a fish sandwich and waiting for a Chicago-bound train. And yet, the transposition of many of the leading jazz players out of New Orleans had an immeasurable impact on American musical culture. Railroad networks were crucial here, and the train emerged as a potent symbol of change, opportunities, movement, and freedom. Steamboats, too, played an important role, especially in terms of bringing new music to the waterways of the Midwest and upper South. Jazz and jazz-related music found fertile soil in places like Kansas City and St. Louis, which developed unique music scenes concurrent to what was happening in the urban North. Chicago, though, stood at the center of so much of the musical evolution of jazz.

Chicago's vast transportation system and vibrant black neighborhoods made the city attractive to thousands of black southerners. Throughout the 1910s and 1920s the black population of Chicago grew exponentially, providing both an audience and a culture supportive of jazz music in its diverse forms.[15] More than providing a demographic shift, Chicago proved crucial to the transformation of jazz from a regional quasi-folk music to a national music reflective of modern America, by opening up midwestern recording studios to recently transplanted musicians. Studios such as Gennett Records—a train ride away in Richmond, Indiana—preserved the sounds of early jazz through the recording of King Oliver, Jelly Roll Morton, Louis Armstrong, and Bix Beiderbecke, among many others. Jazz had been recorded before, and the Original Dixieland Jazz Band recorded several sides for Columbia and Victor Records in New York City in 1917, but in the subsequent decade, recording technology eclipsed sheet music as the ideal way to transmit jazz music. Records, unlike sheet music, disseminated the significant aspects of jazz: the rhythmic pulse, the improvisational structure, and modern impulse to a growing national audience.

ASCENDENCY

Radio towers, not phonograph records, supplied the majority of jazz to Americans in the late 1920s, however, and the rapid increase in households with radios, coupled with the Great Depression, made radio the dominant mode of jazz transmission. As the center of the radio industry, as well as its thriving entertainment culture, New York City would eclipse Chicago as the center of the jazz world. For the next twenty years or so, New York would define the national jazz scene as larger bands and a more arranged type of jazz would entice a larger and (increasingly whiter) audience. Although the big band variant would become the most well known, New York City encompassed several distinct styles of jazz, from Fats Waller's solo stride piano to the polished arrangements of Fletcher Henderson to the exploratory ambitions of Duke Ellington. The Harlem Renaissance provided an intellectual context for this new music as the "New Negro" movement flourished.[16] At the same time, white audiences began to clamor for these new variations. Part of the reason for growing white acceptance was the commercialism at the heart of New York City jazz. Unlike New Orleans jazz—and in many regards the music of Chicago—New York City jazz never had overt folk roots; the music emerged in tandem with the flourishing music business. The music, especially the big band sounds that filled dancehalls, was arranged for entertaining large groups, and by the late 1920s this style of jazz found a national audience through radio broadcasts.

Beyond larger band arrangements, with multiple instruments per section and more stylized solo breaks, the jazz made in the late 1920s and early 1930s incorporated several new instrumental changes, too. The growing use of the saxophone (no longer used as a novelty break), the dominance of the guitar over the banjo, and the plucked string bass rather than tuba, allowed for a much more modern sound. These changes coalesced along with technological breakthroughs in microphones, radio transmitters, and electrical recording techniques that allowed the sounds heard live to be broadcast with greater clarity, attack, and fidelity. What had emerged were the building blocks of swing music: the dance-driven genre that would define American popular music throughout the 1930s and 1940s.[17]

SUMMARY

The large and diverse audience made possible through phonograph sales, radio broadcasts, and motion pictures produced a national musical culture. Within twenty years, jazz had left its folk music moorings of South Louisiana to become the quintessential marker of modern America. By the 1930s, much of the controversy that had shadowed jazz for years began to dissipate as a large number of Americans avidly listened to the many permutations of jazz music. Jazz, especially in its arranged big band form, defined modern America and, by World War II, was the popular music of the nation. In many ways, Benny Goodman served as the clearest expression of this new form, musically and through his biography. Born in Chicago in 1909 to a large, working-class Jewish family, Goodman soon became obsessed with the clarinet. With legitimate training from a premier tutor as well as a strong interest in hot jazz records, Goodman ably combined technical musicality with a keen ear for improvisation and rhythmic inventiveness to produce a long career of popular recordings, radio programs, and live performances. Goodman, aside from his musical innovations and attributes, connected directly to a developing youth culture and its identity based around the key concepts of modern America. Across four decades, a sea change in American attitudes and values had occurred due to urbanization and industrialization, demographic shifts, and technological innovations. Ragtime, the blues, and jazz each contributed to and mirrored these shifts, and the rise of a national popular culture centered on the mass production of swing music bridged the folk music of the South to the dynamic urban settings of the Midwest and to the commercially oriented centers on both coasts. No longer

regionally defined, jazz was simply American music.

DISCUSSION OF THE LITERATURE

Ragtime, the blues, and jazz have long interested scholars from various fields. Far from one-dimensional, these genres have encouraged a tremendous amount of creative and dynamic studies. Musicologists, of course, have been central to our understanding of the musical elements of these forms, but cultural historians, literary scholars, and others have exponentially increased our understanding of the origins of the musical forms as well as their connection to American life.

Ragtime has received comparatively less attention than the genres that followed. This relative lack of attention perhaps relates to the fact that the music came of age just before the technological revolutions that brought jazz to a national audience. Still, some strong recent work by scholars has shown the importance of ragtime both in terms of the black performer community and in terms of the way ragtime intersected business and cultural interests in the late 19th and early 20th century. David Gilbert, in particular, has pushed for ragtime to be seen as much more than simply an antecedent to the jazz age. Future avenues here should continue to contextualize ragtime in the black artistic society that helped give it vitality.[18]

Unlike ragtime, the blues has been the focus of numerous scholars from wildly diverse fields. From literary criticism, to cultural anthropology, to art history, to critical racial theory, to southern history, to musicologists, the blues has inspired complete libraries. The blues—with its lyrical richness, musical elasticity, and historical density—has inspired a great deal of strong interdisciplinary work. With its direct connections to black life and its reverberations across rural and urban America, the blues continues to serve as a rewarding subject of study. The historiography of the blues has for decades mined the lives of known and unknown musicians, the gendered and racial tropes embedded in the form, and the various ways in which the blues mirrored and drove American culture. Today, the blues history is a diverse and nuanced field with much of the mythology burnished from the story. Still, prospective studies that continue to synthesize these issues into compelling studies of the intersectionality of American life during this period would be welcomed.

The historiography of jazz is immense, with much of the work focused on the postwar period with the music at its most explosive (especially the bop/post-bop years and the Miles Davis and John Coltrane-fueled 1960s). Recently, comparable attention has been paid to the free jazz movement, especially in terms of its connection to the turbulent racial politics of the late 1960s and 1970s. The early decades of jazz, however, have received less attention. While Louis Armstrong and Jelly Roll Morton have garnered serious studies for decades, the actual history of the music was shrouded more often than not with the vagaries of myth and legend instead of solid historical work. In the late 1970s, Donald Marquis and others began to bolster the field with strong archival research. Still, unlike the blues, early jazz was relatively neglected by scholars of race, gender, and culture until the late 1990s and early 2000s. More recently, however, several groundbreaking studies have reshaped and reenergized this incredibly important and fertile area. Between critical analytically driven studies and more synthesis-centered ones, the early decades of the jazz story have proven to be a fertile ground for thoughtful and innovative scholarly work.[19]

PRIMARY SOURCES

New Orleans, not surprisingly, is the center for several important archives of early jazz including the phenomenally important Hogan Jazz Archive housed at Tulane University, as well as the William Russell Jazz Collection at the Historic New Orleans Collection. In addition, the Duke Ellington Collection and America's Jazz Heritage Collection at the Smithsonian are also good resources. Other necessary archives include the Institute of Jazz Studies at Rutgers University, the Chicago Jazz Archive at the University of Chicago, the National Ragtime and Jazz Archive at Southern Illinois University at Edwardsville, and the Jazz Archive at Duke University. In addition, websites such as Columbia University's Center for Jazz Studies offer an array of online resources for researchers.

For the blues, important repositories include the Blues Archive at the University of Mississippi, the Chicago Blues Archive in the Chicago Public Library, the Samuel and Ann Charters Archives of Blues and Vernacular African American Musical Culture at the University of Connecticut, the Delta Blues Museum in Clarksdale, Mississippi, and the Lomax Family Collections at the American Folklife Center at the Library of Congress.

DIGITAL MATERIALS

Original Dixieland Jass Band, "Livery Stable Blues" (1917). https://www.youtube.com/watch?v=5WojNaU4-kI.

Mamie Smith, "Crazy Blues" (1920). https://www.youtube.com/watch?v=qaz4Ziw_CfQ.

W. C. Handy, "St. Louis Blues" (1922). https://www.youtube.com/watch?v=Gpp75gQ-T6Y.

King Oliver and His Creole Jazz Band, "Snake Rag" (1923). https://www.youtube.com/watch?v=Nklm3JoAh3o.

Louis Armstrong and His Hot Five, "Heebie Jeebies" (1925). https://www.youtube.com/watch?v=ksmGt2U-xTE.

Louis Armstrong, "West End Blues" (1928). https://www.youtube.com/watch?v=W232OsTAMo8.

Duke Ellington & His Orchestra, "Mood Indigo" (1930). https://www.youtube.com/watch?v=ojamSYmjEs0.

George Gershwin, "Rhapsody in Blue" in King of Jazz (1930). http://americanhistory.oxfordre.com/view/10.1093/acrefore/9780199329175.001.0001/acrefore-9780199329175-e-13.

Paul Howard's Quality Serenaders, "Cuttin' Up" (1930). https://www.youtube.com/watch?v=OCtvINUVGTs.

Benny Goodman, "Don't Be That Way" (1938). https://www.youtube.com/watch?v=Bno2zhEuU0o.

FURTHER READING

Baraka, Amira. *Blues People: Negro Music in White America*. New York: Quill, 1963.

Brothers, Thomas. *Louis Armstrong's New Orleans*. New York: W. W. Norton, 2006.

Carney, Court. *Cuttin' Up: How Early Jazz Got America's Ear*. Lawrence: University Press of Kansas, 2009.

Collier, James Lincoln. *The Making of Jazz: A Comprehensive History*. Boston: Houghton Mifflin, 1978.

Davis, Angela Y. *Blues Legacies and Black Feminism: Gertrude "Ma" Rainey, Bessie Smith, and Billie Holliday*. New York: Pantheon, 1998.

Davis, Francis. *The History of the Blues: The Roots, The Music, The People from Charley Patton to Robert Cray*. New York: Hyperion, 1995.

Gilbert, David. *The Product of Our Souls: Ragtime, Race, and the Birth of the Manhattan Musical Marketplace*. Chapel Hill: University of North Carolina Press, 2015.

Gioia, Ted. *Delta Blues: The Life and Times of the Mississippi Masters Who Revolutionized American Music*. New York: W. W. Norton, 2008.

Hennessey, Thomas J. *From Jazz to Swing: African-American Jazz Musicians and Their Music*. Detroit: Wayne State University Press, 1994.

Hersch, Charles. *Subversive Sounds: Race and the Birth of Jazz in New Orleans*. Chicago: University of Chicago Press, 2007.

Kennedy, Rick. *Jelly Roll, Bix, and Hoagie: Gennett Records and the Birth of Recorded Jazz*. Bloomington: Indiana University Press, 1994.

Kenney, William H. *Chicago Jazz: A Cultural History, 1904–1930*. New York: Oxford University Press, 1993.

Leonard, Neil. *Jazz and the White Americans*. Chicago: University of Chicago Press, 1962.

Levine, Lawrence W. "Jazz and American Culture." *The Journal of American Folklore* 102.403 (January–March 1989): 6–22.

Marquis, Donald M. *In Search of Buddy Bolden: First Man of Jazz*. Baton Rouge: Louisiana State University Press, 1978.

Oakley, Giles. *The Devil's Music: A History of the Blues*. New York: Da Capo, 1997.

Ogren, Kathy J. *The Jazz Revolution: Twenties America and the Meaning of Jazz*. New York: Oxford University Press, 1989.

Peretti, Burton W. *The Creation of Jazz: Music, Race, and Culture in Urban America*. Urbana: University of Illinois Press, 1992.

Schuller, Gunther. *Early Jazz: Its Roots and Musical Development*. New York: Oxford University Press, 1968.

Wald, Elijah. *Escaping the Delta: Robert Johnson and the Invention of the Blues*. New York: HarperCollins, 2004.

NOTES

1. Jelly Roll Morton, "I Created Jazz in 1902," *Down Beat* (August 1938): 3. An early version of the letter is at the Historic New Orleans Collection. See MSS 507, "Jelly Roll Morton Correspondence," William Russell Collection, Folder 1, Historic New Orleans Collection, New Orleans, Louisiana.

2. Alan Lomax, *Mister Jelly Roll: The Fortunes of Jelly Roll Morton, New Orleans Creole and Inventor of Jazz* (Berkeley: University of California Press, 1973), 8. See also, Lawrence Gushee, *Pioneers of Jazz: The Story of the Creole Band* (Oxford: Oxford University Press, 2005), 4–7; 293–295.

3. Nell Irving Painter, *Standing at Armageddon: The United States, 1877–1919* (New York: W. W. Norton, 1987), 116–140.

4. Frederick Jackson Turner, "The Significance of the Frontier in American History," in *Rereading Frederick Jackson Turner: "The Significance of the Frontier in American History" and Other Essays*, ed. Frederick Jackson Turner and John Mack Faragher (New Haven, CT: Yale University Press, 1999), 31–60.

5. Edward A. Berlin, *Ragtime: A Musical and Cultural History* (Berkeley: University of California Press, 1980), 11–13, 26–29, 40–44.

6. David A. Jasen and Gene Jones, *That American Rag: The Story of Ragtime from Coast to Coast* (New York: Schirmer Books, 2000), xxxv.

7. Edward A. Berlin, *King of Ragtime* (New York: Oxford University Press, 1994), 11. See also Eric Lott, *Love & Theft: Blackface Minstrelsy and the American Working Class* (New York: Oxford University Press, 1995).

8. William Barlow, *"Looking Up At Down": The Emergence of Blues Culture* (Philadelphia: Temple University Press, 1989), 13.

9. Quoted in David Meltzer, ed., *Writing Jazz* (San Francisco: Mercury Press, 1999), 43.

10. Handy, *Father of the Blues* (New York: Macmillan, 1941), 74.

11. Handy, Father of the Blues, 77. See also Giles Oakley, *The Devil's Music: A History of the Blues* (New York: Da Capo, 1997), 40–41; and Francis Davis, *The History of the Blues: The Roots, The Music, The People from Charley Patton to Robert Cray* (New York: Hyperion, 1995), 23–28.

12. James Lincoln Collier, *The Making of Jazz: A Comprehensive History* (Boston: Houghton Mifflin, 1978), 27.

13. Bruce Raeburn has long argued the point that early jazz existed somewhere between folk tradition and commercialism. See Bruce Raeburn, "New Orleans Style: The Awakening of American Jazz Scholarship and Its Cultural Implications" (PhD diss., Tulane University, 1991), 25.

14. Virginia R. Dominguez, *White by Definition: Social Classification in Creole Louisiana* (New Brunswick, NJ: Rutgers University Press, 1986), 136.

15. Leroy Ostransky, *Jazz City: The Impact of Our Cities on the Development of Jazz* (Englewood Cliffs, NJ: Prentice-Hall, 1978), 83. See also Davarian L. Baldwin, *Chicago's New Negroes: Modernity, the Great Migration, and Black Urban Life* (Chapel Hill: University of North Carolina, 2007), 23–25; William Howland Kenney, *Chicago Jazz: A Cultural History, 1904–1930* (New York: Oxford University Press, 1993), xi–xv, 3–60; Baldwin, *Chicago's New Negroes*, 2–19, 21–52.

16. Houston A. Baker Jr. *Modernism and the Harlem Renaissance* (Chicago: University of Chicago Press, 1987), 9–14. See also Samuel A. Floyd, *The Power of Black Music: Interpreting Its History from Africa to the United States* (New York, Oxford University Press, 1995), 100–102; and Kathy J. Ogren, *The Jazz Revolution: Twenties America and the Meaning of Jazz* (New York: Oxford University Press, 1989), 116–120.

17. Joel Dinerstein, *Swinging the Machine: Modernity, Technology, and African American Culture Between the Wars* (Amherst: University of Massachusetts Press, 2003), 56–62.

18. David Gilbert, *The Product of Our Souls: Ragtime, Race, and the Birth of the Manhattan Musical Marketplace* (Chapel Hill: University of North Carolina Press, 2015).

19. Donald M. Marquis, *In Search of Buddy Bolden: First Man of Jazz* (Baton Rouge: Louisiana State University Press, 1978).

Court Carney

JAZZ IN AMERICA AFTER 1945

MODERNISTIC

In the years between the two world wars, jazz was nothing less than the pulse of American modernity. With its youthful dynamism, formal flexibility, emotional honesty, tolerant social norms, and racial mixing, jazz helped supplant entrenched Victorian ideals of hierarchy, purity, moral discipline, and cultural uplift. Jazz was the sound of an urban, industrial America humanized by the warmth, spontaneity, and expressiveness of African American culture. The music and its surrounding culture marked a shift in the United States from a largely traditional rural and small-town Anglo-German Protestant culture to a dynamic, forward-looking one centered in bustling metropolitan centers like Chicago, New York, Pittsburgh, and Detroit. There, African American migrants and southern and eastern European immigrants jostled and mingled, while the most forward-looking white intellectuals, artists, and bohemians went "slumming" among these lower classes as they absorbed ideas and energies unleashed by Darwinism, socialism, Freudianism, feminism, primitivism, Futurism, and other modern modes of thought and action. Jazz changed the way American bodies sounded, looked, and moved, in turn changing the shape of American imagination and desire. Jazz was modern energy and *movement*: it catalyzed the shift from old to new, field to factory, prim and proper social dancing to the revved-up vigor of the Lindy Hop, rigidly scored compositions to improvised hot solos. Throughout the Depression and World War II, millions of Americans danced to the big bands of Duke Ellington, Count Basie, Benny Goodman, Artie Shaw, Jimmie Lunceford, and a host of others. The hallmark of the swing big band, an American modernization of the Germanic symphonic orchestra, was a streamlined rhythmic groove that echoed the propulsive dynamism of the fast-moving railroad train.

By the end of World War II, then, jazz had already served for several decades along with the Hollywood cinema as a key herald of modern Americanism. But only in the years following the 1945 armistice did *modern jazz*—the progressive stylistic thrust within jazz itself—emerge as a full-blown movement. Jazz's own internal modernist revolution began to take shape in the early 1940s when a group of New York–based African American musicians started to hold informal, after-hours jam sessions in Harlem. These musicians—drummer Kenny Clarke, guitarist Charlie Christian, trumpeter John Birks "Dizzy" Gillespie, alto saxophonist Charlie "Bird" Parker, pianists Bud Powell, and Thelonious Monk foremost among them—had begun to rebel against the standardized and mechanized aspects of big band work. They hungered for the intimacy of small-group jazz and sparkled with new ideas about harmony, time, and texture. On up-tempo tunes, they wanted to swing even harder than the swing bands did; on slow ballads, they wanted the music to become more deeply expressive and personal.

Parker and Gillespie pioneered a new style of horn soloing full of virtuosic phrasing, blistering tempos, and agile, quicksilver runs through and over the tune's chord patterns. Clarke accented the horn players' fractured, serpentine phrasings with a new drumming approach featuring abstract, almost ironic snare drum riffs and—in place of the martial four-to-the-floor style of swing drumming— the deft dropping of bass drum "bombs" in odd corners of the meter. Monk hatched a

musical vision situated in the harmonic innovations of bebop but still firmly grounded in the older swing and stride piano traditions. He eschewed the runaway tempos and flashy technical displays that became bebop hallmarks in favor of medium tempo swing grooves and ballads tethered to the song's melody, even while waxing experimental and futuristic in his use of dissonant chord clusters, silences, hesitations, and disjointed phrasing.

Bebop's supporters found its angular and abstract musical grammar witty and highly engaging, its quality of intense rhythmic orality evident in the work of instrumentalists and singers (Sarah Vaughan, Betty Carter, Jon Hendricks) alike. Its legion of detractors— especially self-fashioned "moldy figs," who preferred older styles of jazz, especially the collective polyphony of New Orleans and Chicago small groups of the 1920s and 1930s which found new life in a "Dixieland Revival" of the late 1940s and early 1950s—heard and felt in the new music a cold, even neurotic affect that seemed antithetical to the soulfulness of blues-saturated early jazz. Jazz critics and fans, clamoring passionately in the established jazz magazines *Down Beat* and *Metronome* and newer specialized collector sheets like *Record Changer*, carried the traditionalist/modernist sectarian war deep into the 1950s. Among the musicians, meanwhile, *modern jazz* heralded a dramatic shift in style and attitude connected with broader currents in African American culture and politics. The young boppers, along with several leading swing performers, notably Lester Young and Billie Holiday from the Count Basie band, chafed at the minstrelsy-tinged dynamics of the music business, with its image of the musician as a happy-go-lucky servant-entertainer rather than a serious and challenging artist. A new performance persona and cultural style arrived, catalyzed by wartime demands for racial equality. Called *cool* (even when the music itself burned hot, as with bebop's fleet tempos and mercurial chord changes), it was defined by an ineffable charisma, an air of mystery, a relaxed intensity resulting in an ability to create excitement without showing excitement.

BIRTH OF THE COOL

The dominant popular symbol of cool (and its twin term *hip*) was trumpeter and bandleader Miles Davis, perhaps the leading stylistic innovator of modern jazz. Davis moved from East St. Louis, Illinois, to New York in 1944 to attend the Juilliard School of Music but soon shifted his focus to the Harlem club scene, where he forged relationships with Parker, Gillespie, Monk, and others from the original bebop circle. In the early 1950s, Davis emerged as a distinctive stylist whose lyrical, introspective sound—often abetted by his use of a Harmon mute—marked a sharp contrast with bebop's flashy pyrotechnics as well as the bravura virtuosity of Louis Armstrong. Davis was a seminal influence on the mostly white West Coast cool movement associated with trumpeter/singer Chet Baker, saxophonists Art Pepper, Gerry Mulligan, and New York–born Stan Getz, drummer Shelley Manne and others, even as he remained tightly aligned with the black East Coast hard bop school led by drummers Art Blakey and Max Roach, bassist Charles Mingus (a transplant from Los Angeles), trumpeter Clifford Brown, and saxophonists Dexter Gordon (also originally from Los Angeles), Sonny Rollins, John Coltrane, and Cannonball Adderley. In collaboration with arranger Gil Evans, Davis produced three albums from 1957 to 1960—*Miles Ahead, Porgy and Bess, Sketches of Spain*—that found a large popular audience for a lush, romantic orchestral jazz. In this same period, Davis began to use modes rather than chords as the harmonic foundation for improvised solos, an approach on display on *Kind of Blue* (1959), the best-selling jazz album in history.

Davis was more than an important musician; by the early 1960s he was a celebrity whose public persona combined romance, danger, and mystery. A shrewd real estate investor, connoisseur of luxury cars, and perennial on *Esquire's* list of best-dressed men in America, Davis was a black man who seemed liberated from conventional racial constraints. Davis's cool masculinity expressed the dignity, elegance, and sovereignty of an emancipated black identity. His razor tongue and signature on-stage gestures (wearing dark sunglasses, turning his back to the audience) became associated with a spirit of rebellion and anti-conformism in Cold War America.

Jazz cool arose as a survival technique used by black musicians to ward off the invasive white gaze, a mask of integrity and self-possession to resist Jim Crow indignities and replace the Uncle Tom minstrel mask, the ingenious but outdated survival technique of an earlier generation. The new style and attitude resonated strongly across the color line and permeated modern art and thought. The silence, mystery, and composure associated with jazz figures like Lester Young and Miles Davis informed the composed violence and molten sexual allure of Hollywood *film noir* actors Humphrey Bogart, Alan Ladd, and Robert Mitchum. This cool register deepened in the shadow side of Frank Sinatra's persona as the world-weary raconteur and in Marlon Brando's erotic menace and vulnerability. *Existential cool*—in the form of Albert Camus's figure of the metaphysical ethical rebel—arose in jazz-smitten France in the context of the Nazi occupation and the fallen promise of Soviet Communism, soon saturating US intellectual life and college student culture. *Beat cool* was a state of mind, an ideal of spiritual balance that writers Jack Kerouac and Allen Ginsberg pursued through a synthesis of jazz and Zen Buddhism. Though masculinity was hegemonic in overlapping jazz, '50s rebel cinema, Beat, and existentialist circles in Paris and New York, cool women—philosopher Simone de Beauvoir, jazz singers Billie Holiday, Anita O'Day, and Abbey Lincoln; writers Hettie Jones and Diane Di Prima; actresses Juliette Greco, Veronica

Lake, Barbara Stanwyck, Lauren Bacall, and Joanne Woodward—were vital threads in this cultural weave.[1]

Even as jazz connected with postwar discourses of anti-conformism, it also (and perhaps more strongly) aligned itself with narratives of cultural normalization, maturation, respectability, and "mainstream" accreditation. African American musicians such as the members of the Modern Jazz Quartet, composer and theorist George Russell, and bassist/composer Charles Mingus, as well as white "progressive" musicians like Lennie Tristano, Stan Kenton, Dave Brubeck (a former student of European émigré composer Darius Milhaud), Jimmy Giuffre, and Gunther Schuller championed a blending of jazz language and technique with theories and structures drawn from European concert music; Schuller and MJQ pianist John Lewis spearheaded a "Third Stream" movement devoted to the concept. Meanwhile, news of jazz's mounting middle-class adult appeal and artistic legitimacy flooded the US popular media. A burgeoning LP trade, college concert bookings, festivals (Newport, Monterey, and a host of smaller ones across the country), and educational initiatives (notably the Lenox School of Jazz in the Berkshires of western Massachusetts, helmed by John Lewis) gave the music a strutting, triumphal presence in the expanded postwar cultural marketplace. State Department–sponsored tours used the music as a tool of cultural diplomacy in Cold War hot spots across the globe. In lockstep with the consensus, end-of-ideology politics of the 1950s, jazz was evangelized as a force of racial harmony and bourgeois normalcy, cleansing the music of its affiliations with leftist radicalism and bohemian subcultures.

But jazz was much more complex, edgy, and enigmatic than this mainstreaming process acknowledged. Black pride sentiment in jazz was not an advent of the 1960s, but an integral feature of the entire history of the music—not least in the down-home blues singing of Dinah Washington and Joe Williams,

and in the *soul jazz* movement of the late 1950s in which pianists Bobby Timmons and Horace Silver and others developed a black roots–infused style redolent of churchy gospel. And white identification with jazz in this period was more complicated and variegated than the normalization narrative would suggest. The age of "Jazz at the Philharmonic," Dave Brubeck's LP *Jazz Goes to College*, and Chet Baker glamour photographs coincided with a period of widespread anguish over social conformity, standardization, the soul-deadening banality of mass culture, and the dangers of affluence. In the time of the hyperrepressed Organization Man, *Playboy*-reading bachelors, Beat writers, and Norman Mailer's White Negro continued to embrace jazz as a symbol of hip rebellion, transgression, instinct, ecstasy, eroticism, and authenticity. Psychiatrists who studied jazz audiences in the 1950s argued that the music held special appeal for three groups craving freedom and individuality: adolescents, intellectuals, and Negroes—the idea that African Americans might also be adolescents or intellectuals evidently eluding the researchers.

FREEDOM NOW

Jazz's multiple meanings and cultural tensions ramified from the late 1950s to the early 1970s, a period in which collisions between the Cold War, the black freedom movement, Third World internationalism, and the rock counterculture reverberated in the music's sound and convulsed its social and economic foundations.

In what might be regarded as jazz's transcendent moment of high modernism, four canonical LPs recorded in 1959 heralded the sound of the new and foreshadowed the music's forward-looking state of permanent diversity. Miles Davis's modal masterpiece *Kind of Blue* distilled an exquisitely hip melancholy out of each of its tune's shapely melodies. Davis's main pianist on the session, Bill Evans, would go on to become one of modern jazz's most affecting players, his chamber-like trio work striking in its gentle poignancy and tenderness at a time when the much of the music became more muscular and aggressive to suit the increasingly roiling political climate. The Dave Brubeck Quartet's *Time Out* featured time signatures unusual for jazz at the time (notably the 5/4 meter of the album's hit single "Take Five"), resulting from the band's assimilation of Turkish and Greek folk music on a State Department tour. John Coltrane, on *Giant Steps*, brought bebop harmonic complexity to an ecstatic peak, bobsledding with breathless technical skill through the title track's dense chordal maze. The commanding power of Coltrane's performance raised the stakes for other post-bop saxophonists, in particular Sonny Rollins, who would later emerge from a legendary two-year sabbatical to play with renewed vigor. Ornette Coleman's *The Shape of Jazz to Come* lived up to its title, meanwhile, bringing wide notice to the highly controversial work of jazz's most significant innovator since Charlie Parker.

The Texas-reared Coleman combined deep southern blues with a part-scholarly, part-bohemian iconoclasm. During the same months he was collaborating with John Lewis and Gunther Schuller on several of their highbrow Third Stream projects, Coleman galvanized audiences at the Five Spot, the clubhouse of the downtown New York avant-garde, with the keening sound of his plastic alto sax and the striking originality of his piano-less quartet. On "Lonely Woman," Coleman seemed to recover an ancient soulfulness in long skeins of haunting melody that sounded absolutely personal, nothing jazz had sounded like before and yet, because of its uncanny rural blues overtones, strangely familiar. On the other hand, there was nothing at all familiar about *Free Jazz*, Coleman's 1960 LP that used a double-quartet to experiment with extended form (the longest continuous jazz recording to date at 40 minutes on two album sides) using collective free improvisation on top of skeletal themes.

The musicians associated with the first wave of free jazz—Coleman, Coltrane, fellow saxophonists Jimmy Giuffre, Eric Dolphy, Archie Shepp, Albert Ayler, and Pharoah Sanders, trumpeters Don Cherry and Bill Dixon, pianists Cecil Taylor and Paul Bley, bassists Charlie Haden, Steve Swallow, and Henry Grimes, drummers Billy Higgins, Ed Blackwell, Andrew Cyrille, and Sunny Murray—disrupted such received notions of jazz musicianship as centered tonality, regular beat and tempo, bar divisions, conventional theme-and-variation structure, and improvisation based solely on chord changes. Their experiments with dissonant extremes of pitch falling outside of the American pop song and blues harmonic palette; their eschewal of a standard time feel in favor of oscillating pulses and bursts of rhythmic energy; and their solemn attitudes that were so different from the exuberant personae not just of earlier swing-era entertainers like Louis Armstrong but even certain beboppers like Dizzy Gillespie, led some critics to label the new music "anti-jazz." Other critics, even if ambivalent about the most discordant sounds, embraced the new jazz avant-garde as evidence of the progressive logic of the music and yet another sign of its ballyhooed artistic legitimacy.

The sign of "freedom" fairly defined the US Cold War political and cultural zeitgeist: while American foreign policy aimed to promote capitalist free enterprise, artistic movements like free jazz, Abstract Expressionism, Beat poetry, Method acting, and modern dance enshrined expressive freedom as their highest aesthetic ideal. Thelonious Monk once was quoted as saying "jazz and freedom go hand in hand," and the sound bite found its way into Cold War–era propaganda campaigns linking jazz to American ideals of liberty and democracy. This was a time, alas, when the publishers of *Down Beat* refused to put black jazz musicians on their magazine cover, and civil rights workers were showing up dead in backwoods Mississippi. While black musicians drew on the "freedom" discourse to signal their music's political urgency (e.g., Max Roach's "Freedom Now Suite"), they also sought to distance themselves from the term's association with unfettered choice and wanton artistic license. Some of the era's most innovative and challenging sounds came from jazz composers and auteurs—George Russell, Sun Ra, Cecil Taylor, Charles Mingus—who fashioned themselves heirs to the formal ambitions of Duke Ellington.

Still, some jazz of the early to mid-1960s was so superbly performed, so bracing in both imagination and execution, it could not help but be heard as the emblematic sound of its own historical moment. Miles Davis's quintet in this period stretched all post-bebop ideas to new and dizzying heights of intensity, each of his sidemen (bassist Ron Carter, drummer Tony Williams, pianist Herbie Hancock, saxophonist Wayne Shorter) unique stylists in their own right who would go on to become key innovators of modern jazz's second and third waves. John Coltrane emerged in this period not just as a canonical jazz figure but a cultural hero among black artists and intellectuals as well as the rock counterculture. His 1965 LP *A Love Supreme*, featuring the classic quartet with pianist McCoy Tyner, bassist Jimmy Garrison, and drummer Elvin Jones, synthesized hard bop, modal jazz, and free jazz while also moving jazz into the new expressive territory of spiritual awakening and purity ritual. By turns devotional and ecstatic, tender and frenzied, the album soon exerted widespread totemic influence from the Black Arts Movement to the rock guitar effusions of Jimi Hendrix and Carlos Santana.

The music of Davis, Coltrane, Coleman, Mingus, Roach, Rollins, and others churned with a potent feeling of struggle and yearning. Like the civil rights movement, the pan-African anti-colonial movement, and the Black Power movement, this jazz was driven by collective energy and collaborative action. While the new music continued to be performed, recorded, publicized, and critically evaluated within the same matrix of commercial institutions (nightclubs, festivals, magazines, etc.) that had governed jazz for decades, as the 1960s unfolded musicians went about creating new spaces and institutions where they could exercise greater control over their own creativity and connect it to grassroots community-building efforts in their own neighborhoods. Much of this activity converged with the activist efforts of poet, playwright, and jazz critic Amiri Baraka and other politically engaged African American artists and intellectuals who positioned jazz as a bulwark of the interdisciplinary Black Arts Movement. A great deal of the most compelling jazz of the late 1960s and 1970s found its origins in Black Arts institutions whose atmosphere was thick with colliding energies from the arts (music, dance, theater, painting, poetry), social activism, and black self-consciousness. This wave included The Association for the Advancement of Creative Musicians (AACM) in Chicago, which birthed the Art Ensemble of Chicago; the Black Arts Group in St. Louis (BAG), spawning ground for the World Saxophone Quartet; and the Union of God's Musicians and Artists Ascension (UGMAA), the Watts Writers Workshop, and other organizations in Los Angeles, where Stanley Crouch, Jayne Cortez, Arthur Blythe, David Murray, Butch Morris, and other vital contributors to the downtown New York scene in the 1970s first worked in a collaborative community setting.

By the late 1960s, jazz had grown into an even deeper state of permanent diversity, the music proliferating in an increasing variety of styles while expressing multiple, and often conflicting, values and ideals. While jazz "collectives" nurtured explicitly noncommercial projects and front-line innovators Taylor, Coleman, Sun Ra, and others continued to experiment with radical new sounds and performance norms, many West Coast jazz musicians found steady, remunerative work in the Hollywood studios, where various strains of modern jazz suffused the soundtracks of a number of films and TV show themes. From its inception, jazz was an international, multi-national music with roots in both African and European vernaculars, seasoned by what New Orleans jazz pianist Jelly Roll dubbed the "Latin tinge." In the Cold War period, as American jazz musicians became more culturally adventurous, and as the US government and media industries proselytized the music across the globe—United States Information Agency jazz disc jockey Willis Conover became one of the most famous Americans in the world—jazz's inherent cosmopolitanism escalated yet further. Afro-Cuban jazz already had been percolating in the work of trumpeter and arranger Mario Bauzá and singer and maracas player Machito when Dizzy Gillespie introduced clave rhythms into bebop in 1947, featuring the Cuban *conguero* Chano Pozo in a Carnegie Hall concert and on a subsequent European tour. Miles Davis's *Sketches of Spain* was rife with Andalusian passions. Sonny Rollins employed calypso rhythms on "St. Thomas," a signature tune reflecting his Virgin Island heritage. Stan Getz scored one of jazz's biggest popular hits with "The Girl from Ipanema," a collaboration with Brazilian bossa nova stars Antonio Carlos Jobim and Astrud Gilberto. Charles Mingus evoked the California/Mexico borderlands in *Tijuana Moods*. Duke Ellington's *Far East Suite* (which might have been more appropriately named "Far and Near East Suite") captured themes and moods his band developed during a mid-1960s tour of Beirut, Kabul, New Dehli, Tehran, Cairo, and Tokyo. John Coltrane nurtured an interest in raga's modal drones and rhythms and featured them explicitly on his tune "India." Rollins's "Airegin" (Nigeria spelled backwards), Coltrane's "Dahomey Dance" and "Africa," and pianist Randy Weston's "Uhuru Afrika (Freedom Africa)" expressed strong affinities between vanguard African American jazz and the African anti-colonial movement. Similarly, the Afro-Latin jazz of Tito Puente, Mongo Santamaria, Ray Barreto, Eddie Palmieri, and others became not just another layer of the US urban soundscape but a vivid expression of transnational, multicultural identity.

ROCKIT

By the late 1960s, this global cultural ambit reflected not just the musicians' cosmopolitan spirit but also their recognition that jazz, both its swing-bebop-cool mainstream and its various tributaries, had been eclipsed by rock music as the dominant force in modern American popular culture. Jazz and rock shared the same DNA, but as modern jazz developed into a more cerebral listening music, the blues and gospel legacy of stomping, hand-clapping, pleasure-centered music and dance fell to Ray Charles, Muddy Waters, B. B. King, Etta James, Elvis Presley, Little Richard, Chuck Berry, and other artists in the R&B (rhythm-and-blues) and rock n' roll orbit. 1960s British Invasion blues-based rock and its various US imitations, producer Phil Spector's "wall of sound," Motown pop, Memphis soul, and the first stirrings of hard rock gained massive cross-racial popularity among the exploding baby boomer youth demographic, leaving jazz with an aging and diminishing audience. In 1960, the look of music-world hipness was the cover of a Blue Note LP with a stylish chiaroscuro image of black jazz musicians working arduously at their craft. By 1970, that image seemed like an archival remnant suddenly supplanted by celebrity photographs of androgynous, libertine rock superstars.

This was the context in which Miles Davis found himself overshadowed in celebrity and youth idolatry by rock guitar deity Jimi Hendrix and soul luminaries like James Brown and Aretha Franklin. In one of the most controversial transformations in jazz history, Davis decided to shun established jazz norms and bourgeois African American culture alike. His clothing and persona now drew on counter-cultural sources such as Afrocentrism and psychodelia. His music—on albums like *Miles in the Sky* (1968), *Bitches Brew* (1969), and

On the Corner (1972), and in concerts held in huge rock venues—turned to heavily amplified electronics, Afro-Brazilian percussion, rock and funk rhythms, and open-ended forms. Some damned Davis as an apostate for moving away from acoustic instruments, swing rhythm, and standard song form; they struggled to hear Davis's melodic beauty and expressive finesse in the sonic maelstrom. Others embraced this move as a creative innovation in the spirit of jazz's history as an ever-changing art that moved forward by absorbing new styles and cultivating new audiences.

Davis's new sound was billed as a jazz-rock synthesis—not the first, vibraphonist Gary Burton and guitarist Larry Coryell having already explored the idea for a couple of years—but its concept was more ambitious than that: it was questioning whether jazz should be, or ever was, a pure and autonomous form. Black music had always troubled and defied conventional genre boundaries, and the exaltation of jazz as an elite and singular music had always been—in spite of the canonizing efforts of jazz critics, intellectuals, and modern musicians themselves—in dynamic tension with African American culture's strong impulse toward inclusive populism. The idea of jazz as part of a unified black music aesthetic and ethos—what critic Amiri Baraka famously called "the changing same"—gathered force through the influence of the Black Arts Movement. Far from being just fashionable nationalist propaganda, the idea was deeply rooted in practical musical experience: John Coltrane, Ornette Coleman, Eric Dolphy, and Albert Ayler started their careers in R&B bands, which was also true of the next generation of jazz innovators such as Oliver Lake, Hamiet Bluiett, Arthur Blythe, and Anthony Braxton. The one jazz style that garnered a growing popular audience during the 1960s was soul jazz, whose lean grooves, gospel-rich chords, and hip urban vibe became an ambient sound of black neighborhoods in cities all across the country. Jazz label recordings like Herbie Hancock's "Watermelon Man"

(and its Latin cover by Mongo Santamaria), Lee Morgan's "The Sidewinder," Ramsey Lewis's "The 'In' Crowd," and Cannonball Adderley's "Mercy, Mercy, Mercy" rose to the top of the R&B charts. Keyboardist Jimmy Smith pioneered the use of the Hammond B3 organ in a trio with drums and saxophone or guitar, a soul jazz offshoot that became a standard live format in urban neighborhood bars. Saxophonists Pharoah Sanders, Joe Henderson, and Gary Bartz popularized John Coltrane's spiritualism in a new Afrocentric style combining ethereal sonorities drawn from free jazz with danceable grooves augmented by African percussion. Herbie Hancock's 1973 LP *Head Hunters* found a mass cross-racial audience in both the older soul jazz cohort and among younger college students. With Hancock playing Fender Rhodes electric piano, synthesizers, and clavinet and modeling a Sly Stone–influenced Afro-futurist look, and with African percussion punctuating its deep R&B grooves, the album helped announce the arrival a new subgenre: *jazz-funk*. A decade later, Hancock again showed his facility with fresh styles and his desire to stay connected to a mass youth audience with his 1983 single "Rockit," a techno/dance club hit featuring synthesizers and programmed drum machine.

Various forms of hyphenated jazz (soul jazz, jazz-rock, jazz-funk, Latin jazz, and *fusion*) would gain popularity through the 1970s and early 1980s as major record labels—now fattened by profits from their rock acts into full-fledged corporate operations—abandoned most of their straight-ahead (i.e., acoustic post-bebop) jazz artists and looked for commercially viable niche markets among relatively sophisticated and adventurous consumers. Musicians highly skilled in post-bop styles (The Crusaders, Eddie Henderson, Donald Byrd, George Benson, The Brecker Brothers, and others) met mid-range popular success with material that featured jazz-quality chops and soul/funk grooves contoured for

FM radio–friendly popular formats. Weather Report, headed by saxophonist Wayne Shorter and Austrian émigré keyboardist Joe Zawinal, started as an avant-garde experimental spin-off from the Miles Davis electric band, then developed its own unique blend of African American, Latin, and world music styles deployed through shifting time signatures and richly layered sonic textures. The Tony Williams Lifetime, a power trio featuring Davis's virtuoso drummer, the British guitarist John McLaughlin, and jazz organist Larry Young, combined hard rock energy and volume with fierce improvisational agility. Pianist/keyboardist Chick Corea's electric group Return to Forever featured Brazilian and Latin rhythms and textures knit together by the deft fretless electric bass playing of Stanley Clarke.

An impressive level of technical proficiency—not just the leaders but sidemen like Clarke, fellow bassist Jaco Pastorius with Weather Report, guitarist Al Di Meola in Return to Forever—became a hallmark of this new music, though very few bands could match the musicality and conceptual innovation of these pioneering groups. Instrumental technique and cutting-edge electronic equipment often became fetishized in the broader fusion movement, resulting in a sound that struck many traditional jazz, soul, and American popular song fans as bereft of warmth, gracefulness, and conversational intimacy. At the same time, certain jazz-knowledgeable pop artists developed styles that valued tunefulness and groove over fusion-style pyrotechnics. These included Donald Fagen and Walter Becker of Steely Dan, who brought a deep grounding in Ellington, bebop, and soul to their rock/pop concept and used top-drawer jazz talent like saxophonists Wayne Shorter and Phil Woods on their studio recordings; Joni Mitchell, who moved from singer/songwriter-centered folk rock to a sophisticated jazz-seasoned sound when she hired Pastorius and other jazz/rock musicians into her group; Carlos Santana, who

crafted a hugely popular mix of guitar-centered arena rock, blues, jazz, and salsa into Coltrane-like sheets of sound; and Earth Wind & Fire, who synthesized R&B, funk, and Afro-Latin rhythmic textures under a modern big-band jazz-style horn section.

As traditional, straight-ahead jazz fought a losing battle in the music marketplace of the late 1970s and 1980s, the racial boundaries of the music shifted in several ways. From the 1920s to the mid-1960s, most European jazz had been a straightforward imitation of American jazz, with expatriate African American musicians such as Kenny Clarke, Bud Powell, Sidney Bechet, and Dexter Gordon serving as hallowed models of jazz authenticity. This pattern began to change in the late 1960s. European musicians like Peter Brotzmann, Derek Bailey, Evan Parker, and Willem Breuker both emulated and diverged from American jazz culture during the apogee of African American cultural nationalism, embracing the ethos of free improvisation associated with John Coltrane, Ornette Coleman, Albert Ayler, and others, but also embarking on an effort to cultivate a separate jazz aesthetic informed by a non-American cultural ethos. Even as members of the AACM and BAG and other African American musicians in the second wave of the jazz avant-garde relocated to Europe in the late 1960s, European musicians developed various nation-based free jazz scenes where the music often aligned with local countercultural and libertarian social movements.

Jazz had long been thought of as a primarily urban music, its high-affect sound and dynamic pulse associated with cities like New Orleans, Chicago, New York, and Kansas City. Historically, jazz was in large part music produced by urban migrants and immigrants—not just African Americans, but also Jews, Italians, Latinos, and Asians. The 1970s brought a shift in jazz's cultural and racial geography. The Munich-based ECM record label flourished in that decade with a signature sound evoking pastoral and rural landscapes, including a so-called "Nordic tone" among its Scandinavian artists. American pianist Keith Jarrett began an association with Norwegian saxophonist Jan Gabarek and drummer Jan Christensen and Swedish bassist Palle Danielsson (musicians earlier mentored by expatriate African American composer George Russell). Jarrett's ECM recordings with his European quartet, along with his 1975 live solo album *The Köln Concert,* were among the era's best-selling jazz records in the American market. ECM also recorded guitarist Pat Metheny, including his LPs *New Chautauqua* (1979) and *As Falls Witchita So Falls Wichita Falls* (1981), which strongly evoked a frontier sensibility redolent of the small-town Midwest plains. Missouri-reared Metheny cut the figure of a white post-hippie, blue jeans–clad land grant state university student playing jazz with overtones of bluegrass, country, and white church music. This made it all the more interesting when he began to collaborate regularly throughout the 1980s with Ornette Coleman and his circle (including bassist Charlie Haden and saxophonist Dewey Redman) and other venerable black modernists such as Chicago-reared Miles Davis alumni Herbie Hancock and drummer Jack DeJohnette. The musical vocabulary and sensibility shared by these musicians underscored how jazz resisted and scrambled conventional codes of race and geography as often as it buttressed them. Metheny's association with Ornette Coleman made it easier to hear in Coleman's classic free jazz quartet of the late 1950s the "country" sound of his own Texas and his bassist Haden's Iowa heartland heritage. And that made it easier to recall earlier jazz/country affinities such as Bob Wills and his Texas Playboy's Western swing, fiddler Vassar Clements's hillbilly jazz, and legendary Nashville studio guitarist Hank Garland's crossover projects with jazz modernists from Charlie Parker (known as "Bird," short for "Yardbird," as in barnyard chicken) to vibraphonist Gary Burton.

"AMERICA'S CLASSICAL MUSIC"

Partly as a response to the profusion of hyphenated styles and the constant, commercially driven pursuit of newness, partly as a matter of the natural aging process of the music and the need to memorialize its progenitors—Louis Armstrong died in 1971, Duke Ellington in 1974—prominent jazz musicians, critics, and other cultural mediators worked hard in this era to establish permanent forms of institutional recognition of jazz as an American national treasure, even as "America's classical music." Renowned critic Martin Williams, in his role as head of jazz programming at the Smithsonian Institution, curated a multi-LP set called *The Smithsonian Collection of Classic Jazz* (1973), which drew on his book *The Jazz Tradition* (1970) to present a canon of classic jazz recordings from Bessie Smith, King Oliver, Armstrong, and Ellington down to John Coltrane and Ornette Coleman. A number of new jazz history textbooks arrived on the market (many of them using the *Smithsonian Collection* for their listening examples) to service a growing number of courses at colleges and universities. Gunther Schuller, tribune of the jazz/classical Third Stream, president of the New England Conservatory of Music, and author of the groundbreaking study *Early Jazz* (1968), spearheaded a "jazz repertory" movement that later culminated in the advent of the Smithsonian Jazz Masterworks Orchestra. Billy Taylor, a pianist and composer who started his career on the 1940s New York bebop scene, now became widely known as "Dr. Billy Taylor"—not just for his University of Massachusetts doctorate and his multiple honorary degrees, but also for his extraordinary work as the public face of the jazz education movement. In 1961, Taylor had founded New York's Jazzmobile, a citywide program of arts enrichment workshops, master classes, and outdoor concerts. Over the next several decades, Taylor became a ubiquitous presence in radio and television jazz programming and served as the inaugural artistic director of jazz at the Kennedy Center in Washington, DC. Many other top-rank jazz performers who had come of age in the 1950s and 1960s (David Baker, Archie Shepp, Reggie Workman, Sam Gill, and Anthony Braxton among them) secured teaching posts at colleges and universities. Jazz became an increasingly integral part of US music performance and education at every level; rare, by the 1980s, was the American college, high school, or junior high school that did not have a jazz band, and whose music director did not struggle to get students interested in European classical music in addition to jazz. In 1998, the twenty-fifth annual convention of the International Association of Jazz Educators drew more than 7,000 participants.

Much of the allure of jazz throughout its history had to do with its radical individualism, its outsider stance, its renegade assault on musty conventions and proprieties. Many of its canonical figures were larger-than-life characters (Satchmo, Billie, Prez, Count, Duke, Bird, Monk, Miles, Mingus), American originals who became subjects of romantic legend and myth. On the face of it, the new preservationist mission ran against this current, emphasizing past accomplishment over present and future change, tradition over innovation, established authority over resistance and reinvention. What made jazz special and powerful, for many, was that it was an intrepid music with a heroic narrative full of audacious risk and arduous struggle. How could jazz maintain its verve and vigor if it became another music of the conservatory, the library, and the museum? How could it avoid being consumed by its past and continue to be a living and growing art form?

These questions began to dominate the conversation about jazz in the mid-1980s, generated to a very large degree by the persona of the music's most visible and controversial symbol and spokesperson during this period, trumpeter Wynton Marsalis. Marsalis hailed from a family of highly accomplished jazz musicians in New Orleans, including his father, pianist and educator Ellis Marsalis, and his brother, saxophonist Branford Marsalis. Marsalis swiftly gained notice in his first years in New York in the early 1980s for his technical excellence in both the jazz and classical idioms. After a stint with Art Blakey's Jazz Messengers, he emerged as a leader of his own group of fellow youthful African American musicians playing a style reminiscent of Miles Davis's 1960s modal/hard bop band, also performing with Herbie Hancock, Ron Carter, and Tony Williams in what was marketed as a reunion of Davis's classic group. Marsalis's facility with this music was remarkable, but what made him mainstream jazz's first popular crossover figure in years was less his musical performance than his persuasive self-fashioning as nothing less than jazz's savior. Fiercely outspoken and highly media-savvy, Marsalis claimed to be leading a holy mission to redeem true jazz from the apostasies of free jazz and fusion, a campaign for time-honored standards countering the preceding generation's misplaced emphasis on both unfettered creative freedom and pop culture relevance. Marsalis began to publicly castigate Miles Davis as jazz's premier heretic, venerating his pre-1968 acoustic work and scorning everything that came after his turn to electric instruments. As Davis, undeterred, reached out to the MTV generation with covers of Michael Jackson and Cindy Lauper pop tunes, Marsalis's jazz purism took on an increasingly pointed rearward focus, reaching back to King Oliver and Louis Armstrong for models of jazz greatness.

Marsalis's posture might have registered merely as a curious postmodern version of earlier moldy-fig and Dixieland Revival leanings, if not for the trumpeter's rising celebrity status among cultural elites, his adoption by key African American public intellectuals into a new stream of neoclassical thought, and his impressive abilities as a mover and shaker. This heady convergence made it possible for Marsalis to become the avatar of a new kind of jazz heroic narrative. Marsalis's putative heroism was ideally suited to the post–civil rights era moment—a heroism not in the mold of John Coltrane's transcendent spirituality or touched by the valor and grace of 1960s freedom riders, but the heroism of the arts world warrior fighting for African American representation and power in the key institutions of elite American culture. Marsalis became a blistering scourge of rap and hip-hop, aligning himself with conservative critiques of alleged American cultural decadence while also highlighting a widening class schism in black culture. He and fellow African American "young lions" of jazz (Roy Hargrove, Christian McBride, Cyrus Chestnut, and others) were held up as exemplars of bourgeois refinement, their fine tailoring noted as often as their music. Marsalis's image of dignified taste-fulness, coupled with his reverence for the blues-and-swing-centered jazz they loved, moved the eminent African American writers Ralph Ellison, Albert Murray, and Stanley Crouch to embrace the trumpeter as the new standard-bearer of a time-honored black masculine éclat crucial to the health of the entire American nation. The deep eloquence with which Murray, Crouch, and Marsalis himself voiced their jazz ethos helped convince the City of New York, major philanthropic organizations, and corporate underwriters to finance Jazz at Lincoln Center (JALC), a venerable performing arts center with a lavish new home in Columbus Circle, with Marsalis as artistic director. In 1994, Marsalis won jazz's first Pulitzer Prize for his oratorio "Blood on the Fields," a narrative of heroic black struggle set to a musical score of spirituals, blues, gospel, and swing played in reverentially traditional fashion.

As the first African American director of a major, well-funded, autonomous jazz institution, Marsalis found himself navigating tricky racial waters. Some accused Marsalis of reverse racism in his choices of which jazz master figures to honor in his programming, and in his alleged "Crow Jim" hiring practices for the JALC orchestra—the kind of charge that was never leveled at the almost completely white composition of the Metropolitan Opera, the New York Philharmonic, and other organizations under the Lincoln Center umbrella. A more enduring criticism of Marsalis focused on what was widely perceived (not least among a number of African American musicians) as the narrow and rigid neoclassical orthodoxy of his jazz canon. This critique intensified in the wake of Ken Burns's documentary film *Jazz*, which aired on PBS in 2000 and won public acclaim as a kind of official US national history of jazz. Many inside the jazz world saw Burns's film as unduly beholden to JALC scripture, its narrative giving the impression that jazz effectively died in the late 1960s, only to be resurrected by one Wynton Marsalis.

PLANET JAZZ

Over time, JALC's programming—and Marsalis's work in other projects—gradually opened up at its edges to a more pluralist, inclusive conception of the music, including efforts to feature Latin jazz and country/jazz parallels and crossovers. Meanwhile, the vast majority of jazz musicians built their careers caring little or not at all what Marsalis said or did—though perhaps resenting how little public and corporate funding and mass audience attention was left over after Marsalis took his lion's share. In the years when the "young lions" appeared on magazine covers and dominated PBS/NPR jazz coverage, living titans Sonny Rollins, Lee Konitz, Max Roach, Abbey Lincoln, Johnny Griffin, Cecil Taylor, Ornette Coleman, Hank Jones, Phil Woods, and Tommy Flanagan were playing some of the best music of their careers. Non-JALC traditionalists Scott Hamilton, Bob Wilber, and Kenny Davern were breathing new life into old-fashioned swing. Established avant-gardists (an oxymoron, but an accurate indication of the permanency of the genre) Anthony Braxton, James Blood Ulmer, Sonny Sharrock, Ronald Shannon Jackson, David Murray, Oliver Lake, Odean Pope, Marty Erlich, George Lewis,

William Parker, and Hamid Drake deepened their creative explorations. New waves of maverick experimentation spilled forth from Matthew Shipp, Steve Coleman, Myra Melford, Greg Osby, Kenny Garrett, Dave Douglas, Fred Hersch, Tim Berne, Uri Caine, and John Zorn. Both generations participated in vibrant multi-arts alternative scenes in "downtown" Manhattan (a euphemism for the East Village blocks where loft apartments and other spaces in repurposed industrial buildings served as performance sites) and Brooklyn (especially the Fort Greene and Clinton Hill neighborhoods where a "new black arts movement" flourished in the late 1980s and 1990s). Latin jazz players Jerry Gonzalez, Steve Turre, Arturo Sandoval, Hilton Ruiz, Ray Vega, Dave Valentin, and Chucho Valdez added new layers and flavors to their thriving genre. Veteran female musicians like the composer/bandleaders Carla Bley and Toshiko Akiyoshi continued to excel, while a new generation of women (composer/bandleader Maria Schneider, pianists Melford, Geri Allen, and Renee Rosnes, violinist Regina Carter, drummer Terri Lynn Carrington, among others) and openly gay men and women (Taylor, Hersch, Burton, singers Andy Bey and Patricia Barber) mounted a bold challenge to the dominance of jazz's presumptive hetero-masculinity (age-old and rearguard, but newly energized by the Marsalis neoconservative circle).

In spite of this creative ferment, by the beginning of the 21st century, jazz had become such a sweepingly global and diverse multicultural art form that many began to wonder if the United States was any longer the music's creative epicenter. In the years since the rock revolution wreaked havoc on jazz's stateside economy—sales of recorded jazz now made up less than 5 percent of the consumer market—American jazz musicians came to depend on bookings in Europe and Asia for most of their income. Outside of New York, Boston, Philadelphia, Chicago, and San Francisco, there were hardly any possibilities for steadily remunerative work other

than festivals, the biggest of which took place in Montreal, Rotterdam, and Perugia (Italy). This was true even for a new breed of well-publicized hip-nerd artists such as The Bad Plus (a trio of midwesterners who ingeniously drew on recent pop and alternative rock sources as improvisational material), Don Byron (a woodwind virtuoso whose wide-ranging eclecticism included jazz/klezmer crossover), and Vijay Iyer (a stunningly original pianist and composer who worked effortlessly across styles and genres). Even with such artists finding modest success among adventurous college-age listeners, earnest jazz jeremiahs continued to wonder whether the music's canonization—jazz education, repertory orchestras, documentary films, CD reissue programs, museum exhibits—had turned it into a historic relic: honored, appreciated, even revered, but nowhere near the thriving pulse of vanguard American culture as it had been from the 1920s through the 1960s.

Over that period, jazz had produced a remarkable succession of pioneering innovators, master figures whose conceptual originality changed people's understanding of what jazz could be and pointed the whole field in that new direction. No such master figure emerged after Miles Davis, John Coltrane, and Ornette Coleman. And yet American jazz continued to attract extraordinary talent, expand its language, insinuate itself in a variety of cultural contexts, and—most of all—surprise its listeners. This was the case with one of the more heralded musicians of the new millennium, the pianist, bandleader, and multimedia artist Jason Moran. Amiably hip with his Thelonious Monk–inspired penchant for rakishly stylish hats, Moran cut a figure emblematic not just of the jazz tradition but also of fresh, dynamic stirrings in hip hop-era African American cultural and intellectual life. Born in 1975 and raised in a middle-class Houston, Texas, family before moving to New York to attend the Manhattan School of Music, Moran became a central figure in the efflorescence of art and culture that some called the "New Harlem Renaissance."

Moran's 2002 solo CD *Modernistic* was a rare event for a jazz record in its having generated widespread enthusiasm from normally dissonant, conflicting corners of the US jazz criticism and jazz musician communities. It did so by positing contemporary jazz as a capacious cultural archive reaching from Schumann lieder to James P. Johnson stride to Muhal Richard Abrams post-free to hip-hop and electronica. Younger listeners especially prized Moran's wry cover of "Planet Rock," the early hip-hop anthem by Afrika Bambaataa and Soul Sonic Force. Moran—who found his way to jazz through hip-hop, discovering Monk and Horace Silver in De La Soul breakbeat samples—used the song's paint-by-the-numbers melody to evoke a spacy techno vibe on top of a delightfully cheesy synthesizer sample that sounds like something one might hear in an amusement park or bowling alley. "Planet Rock" said that jazz improvisation didn't have to remain tethered to popular standards from the 1940s and 1950s; it could also draw on the popular music and culture of the 1970s, 1980s, and 1990s.

In his role as artistic director of the San Francisco Jazz Center, Moran devised an event in which his trio, Bandwagon, improvised a funky version of "Blue Monk" to a crew of skateboarders careening around a ramp set up in front of the band. After succeeding Dr. Billy Taylor as jazz director at the Kennedy Center, Moran moved quickly to attract a new and younger audience. He curated events for which the center converted its atrium into a lounge-style club where multigenerational, multicultural audiences crowd the dance floor for, say, the jam band Medeski, Martin & Wood, the funk-jazzers Soulive, and the Afropop jazzer Lionel Loueke. Moran himself teamed up with neo-soul icon Meshell Ndegeocello for a project called the Fats Waller Dance Party. Moran playfully donned a huge papier mâché mask of Waller's fedora-topped head, and limned the melodies of "Honeysuckle Rose," "Jitterbug Waltz," and "Your Feet's Too Big" against funk vamps and hip-hop grooves. Dancers and musicians shared the stage in a spectacle that recalled the joyous revelry of Harlem rent parties.

Building on the foundation that took shape with pre–World War II blues and post–World War II bebop and spread in multiple directions over the next several decades, Moran and his contemporaries embraced changes in culture and technology that kept jazz pointed forward, ensuring that the music did not suffocate under the weight of its mighty tradition. Seventy years after Bird, Diz, and Monk insisted that jazz move ahead, a half-century after Miles Davis and John Coltrane moved it into previously unimagined territory, jazz was a memento of modern America's past that remained a beacon of its future.

DISCUSSION OF THE LITERATURE

In a clarion call to jazz scholars across academic disciplines, music historian Scott DeVeaux wrote in 1991 that "the time has come for an approach that is less invested in the ideology of jazz as an aesthetic object and more responsive to issues of historic particularity. Only in this way can the study of jazz break free from its self-imposed isolation, and participate with other disciplines in the exploration of meaning in American culture."[2] Contemporary jazz scholarship, whether affiliated with ethnomusicology, American Studies, cultural studies, or history, investigates the ways jazz has been imagined, defined, managed, and shaped within particular cultural contexts. It considers how jazz as an experience of sounds, movements, and states of feeling has always been mediated and complicated by broader cultural patterns, especially those of race and sexuality.

Often called "the new jazz studies," recent jazz scholarship aims to take the discussion of the music beyond the insider discourse of record collectors and aficionados, the sober formalism of traditional musicology, and the impressionistic treatments of popular journalism. Central to the new turn has been the recognition that jazz has never been just music—it has been a cornerstone of the modern cultural imagination, an archive of mythological images, an aesthetic model for new modes of seeing, moving, and writing. Across the spectrum of high, middlebrow, and low culture, from symphonies and modern dance to cartoons and advertising, jazz has been appropriated, remembered, dismembered, loved, and abused.

Jazz has loomed large in stories that individuals and groups like to tell about themselves. These stories—stories about freedom, oppression, democracy, dissent, individuality, conformity, communalism, improvisation, modernity, urbanity, mobility, hipness, soulfulness, struggle, authenticity, innovation, tradition—constitute an important field of meaning, not just in the United States but throughout the world. Recognizing this, scholars conceive jazz as a site of intense fascination, desire, anxiety, and scrutiny, with people looking to the music and its cultural milieu for models of expressivity, identity, and self-fashioning. Jazz musicians have been influential exemplars of style, speech, dress, and attitude—even when they have also served as symbols of tragedy and pathology. Seizing on an enormously rich corpus of sound, visual imagery, folklore, criticism, and literature, jazz studies has positioned itself as a leading interdisciplinary field at the intersection of race and ethnic studies, film and media studies, cultural history, and cultural studies. A notably rich vein of recent scholarship has concerned itself with jazz's gender and sexual dynamics—its tradition as a space of overtly normative hetero-masculinism as well as covert (until recently) expressions of non-normative (feminist, womanist, queer) sexualities and gender identities.

Jazz scholars who focus on the post-1945 period have been especially interested in the ways the music has intersected with social movements (black freedom, international anti-colonialism, feminism, multiculturalism, LGBT) and cultural/artistic formations (the Beats, abstract visual art, modern and postmodern dance and theater, Hollywood cinema, alternative cinema, the Black Arts Movement and other ethnicity-centered cultural programs, various countercultures, neoclassicism, American heritage). Following DeVeaux, many jazz scholars have endeavored to take a critical, analytical stance toward what might be called jazz exceptionalism: the assumption that jazz is a unique and singular art form that hovers in an exalted aesthetic space above the hurly-burly of politics and commerce. A central feature of recent scholarship is to regard jazz's deep anti-commercialism discourse as ideology rather than reality—and to explore exactly how jazz positions itself within the commercial institutions of art and entertainment, drawing boundaries between itself and other genres of music and cultural expression. This critical attitude carries over into a suspicion toward uses of jazz within an ideology of American exceptionalism. Increasingly, scholars question the assumption that jazz is an essentially American music. This takes the form of encouraging the investigation of jazz as a global culture—not just a projection of jazz as an American culture across the world, but the exploration of jazz trans-nationalism throughout its entire history.

PRIMARY SOURCES

The premier location for primary research in jazz is the Institute of Jazz Studies at Rutgers University/Newark. The Institute holds the world's largest collection of jazz recordings, scores, books, periodicals, photographs, business records, and oral histories.

The US Library of Congress (LOC) has vast holdings of jazz materials. The library's Music Division holds scores, sheet music, and copyright deposit lead sheets as well as the private papers of such major jazz figures as Ella Fitzgerald, Charles Mingus, Gerry Mulligan, and Dexter Gordon. Other LOC divisions (Motion Pictures, Broadcasting, and Recorded Sound;

Prints and Photographs; the American Folklife Center) contain extensive collections of recordings, moving and still images, artifacts, and oral histories.

The Hogan Jazz Archive at Tulane University contains a wealth of materials concerning the history of jazz and related styles (ragtime, gospel, blues, R&B) in New Orleans. These materials include local oral histories, sound recordings, films, photographs, sheet music, personal papers, and records of the American Federation of Musicians union local.

Jazzinstitut Darmstadt, in Darmstadt, Germany, Europe's largest public jazz archive, houses an extensive collection of jazz recordings, periodicals, books, and photographs. The institute's weekly e-newsletter, *Jazz News*, is a comprehensive digest of jazz coverage in general-interest newspapers and periodicals from around the world.

The Harry Ransom Research Center at the University of Texas, Austin, holds the private papers of Ross Russell, an important modern jazz record producer, critic, and historian.

The Center for Black Music Research at Columbia College, Chicago holds recordings, books, and periodicals and administers the Mark Tucker Fund for Jazz Research Materials.

FURTHER READING

Ake, David. *Jazz Matters: Sound, Place, and Time Since Bebop*. Berkeley: University of California Press, 2010.

Anderson, Iain. *This Is Our Music: Free Jazz, the Sixties, and American Culture*. Philadelphia: University of Pennsylvania Press, 2007.

Cawthra, Benjamin. *Blue Notes in Black and White: Photography and Jazz*. Chicago: University of Chicago Press, 2011.

DeVeaux, Scott. *The Birth of Bebop: A Social and Cultural History*. Berkeley: University of California Press, 1999.

Dinerstein, Joel. *The Origins of Cool in Postwar America*. Chicago: University of Chicago Press, 2016.

Early, Gerald, ed. *Miles Davis and American Culture*. St. Louis: Missouri Historical Society Press, 2001.

Gabbard, Krin. *Better Git It in Your Soul: An Interpretive Biography of Charles Mingus*. Berkeley: University of California Press, 2016.

Gennari, John. *Blowin' Hot and Cool: Jazz and Its Critics*. Chicago: University of Chicago Press, 2006.

Giddins, Gary. *Weather Bird: Jazz at the Dawn of Its Second Century*. New York: Oxford University Press, 2004.

Griffin, Farah Jasmine, and Salim Washington. *Clawing at the Limits of Cool: Miles Davis, John Coltrane, and the Greatest Jazz Collaboration*. New York: St. Martin's Press, 2008.

Kelley, Robin. *Thelonious Monk: The Life and Times of an American Original*. New York: Free Press, 2009.

Lewis, George. *A Power Stronger Than Itself: The AACM and American Experimental Music*. Chicago: University of Chicago Press, 2008.

Litweiler, John. *The Freedom Principle: Jazz After 1958*. New York: William Morrow, 1984.

Mandel, Howard. *Miles, Ornette, Cecil: Jazz Beyond Jazz*. New York: Routledge, 2007.

Monson, Ingrid. *Freedom Sounds: Civil Rights Call Out to Jazz and Africa*. New York: Oxford University Press, 2007.

Nicholson, Stuart. *Jazz-Rock: A History*. New York: Schirmer, 1998.

O'Meally, Robert, Brent Hayes Edwards, and Farah Jasmine Griffin, eds. *Uptown Conversation: The New Jazz Studies*. New York: Columbia University Press, 2004.

Ramsey, Guthrie. *The Amazing Bud Powell: Black Genius, Jazz History, and the Challenge of Bebop*. Berkeley: University of California Press, 2013.

Rosenthal, David. *Hard Bop: Jazz and Black Music, 1955–1965*. New York: Oxford University Press, 1992.

Rustin, Nichole, and Sherrie Tucker, eds. *Big Ears: Listening for Gender in Jazz Studies*. Durham, NC: Duke University Press, 2008.

Saul, Scott. *Freedom Is, Freedom Ain't: Jazz and the Making of the Sixties*. Cambridge, MA: Harvard University Press, 2005.

Szwed, John. *So What: The Life of Miles Davis*. New York: Simon & Schuster, 2002.

Taylor, Yuval, ed. *The Future of Jazz*. Chicago: Chicago Review Press, 2002.

Von Eschen, Penny. *Satchmo Blows Up the World: Jazz Ambassadors Play the Cold War*. Cambridge, MA: Harvard University Press, 2004.

Whyton, Tony. *Beyond a Love Supreme: John Coltrane and the Legacy of an Album.* New York: Oxford University Press, 2013.

NOTES

1. Joel Dinerstein, *The Origins of Cool in Postwar America* (Chicago: University of Chicago Press, 2016).
2. Scott DeVeaux, "Constructing the Jazz Tradition: Jazz Historiography," *Black American Literature Forum* (Fall 1991): 553.

John Gennari

ROCK AND ROLL

Every year, the Rock and Roll Hall of Fame and Museum in Cleveland announces nominees for induction and the debate begins again. What is rock and roll? Is it the same thing as rock? Why does the nominating committee repeatedly propose the disco band Chic, only to see them rejected by an electorate more inclined to vote for, as in 2015, hard rockers Deep Purple? How can the hip-hop group N.W.A have been voted in if hip-hop is outside rock and roll altogether?

Answers turn on how rock and roll has defined itself—or failed to. Even the spelling is in question: many prefer rock 'n' roll to emphasize, positively or negatively, its unlettered qualities. A prominent disc jockey, arriving in New York City in 1954 after success in Cleveland, called his radio show *Alan Freed's Rock and Roll Party*. The biggest hit since "White Christmas," providing the opening soundtrack to *Blackboard Jungle* in 1955, was Bill Haley's "(We're Gonna) Rock Around the Clock." And by 1956, there was a "king" of rock and roll: Elvis Presley, the biggest new pop star of the decade. Rock and roll's identity was intensely mediated: a DJ's slang, a movie tie-in, an overnight sensation.

Skip ahead fifteen years, to about 1970 and the publication of *The Sound of the City: The Rise of Rock and Roll*, by Charlie Gillett, the first historian of the form but also a young amateur who wrote early drafts for fanzines. Gillett's generation claimed discursive control over the music they had grown up on. As simply rock, this era spawned its own FM radio, a hippie vision where rock and roll had relied on Top 40. There were rock festivals and arena concerts, headlined in full sets by white male acts like the Rolling Stones, where the more diverse 1950s groups played package tours of short sets. And at rock magazines such as *Rolling Stone*, writers shared a background with musicians, replacing earlier press incredulity.

Make one more jump to the mid-1980s, when artists were first inducted into the Rock and Roll Hall of Fame and "classic rock" stations introduced. The best days of rock seemed behind it. The Rolling Stones became their own revivalists. *Rolling Stone* promised advertisers yuppie readers. Punk rebellion had failed. Spandexed hair metal bands screamed fecklessness to all but their millions of devotees. MTV made new pop icons like Madonna, with synth-driven hits and arguably more visual than musical cleverness—was that rock at all? Rap was emerging: the new leaders, Run-D.M.C., called themselves "Kings of Rock."

There would be further chapters in the story but the pattern was set. Rock and roll existed as an ideal—a note to hit, the invocation of an inclusive, pop-leaning American wildness. In its fragmentation, rock remained more identifiable, but compromised and in decline. Yet no forms of popular music, if you could put Humpty together again, were bigger in appeal or in influence on performers.

ROCK AND ROLL IS HERE TO STAY: THE 1950s

It took almost a decade for rock and roll's musical arrival to translate. The sound was fixed by 1947 Los Angeles, as Roy Brown, renaming the jump blues of Louis Jordan, wrote and performed "Good Rocking Tonight." Brown's small combo fused blues chords, jazz riffs, dance beats, and pop song structure into a party on wax that made the race records charts. Wynonie Harris's cover version topped those charts in 1948, as WDIA in Memphis became the first black-oriented radio station. In 1949, *Billboard* renamed race records rhythm and blues (R&B), the format that most birthed rock and roll. Elvis Presley, a teenage southern white and WDIA listener nonetheless, covered Harris's cover for Memphis independent Sun Records in 1954. When he sang "let's rock," rock and roll became an identity beyond music. Most Americans didn't register that, or Presley, until 1956.[1]

To bring that about, a few things happened in tandem as technology changed music, recording, and distribution. Instruments electrified, particularly guitar, with sounds that had been background now in lead roles. Magnetic recording made it easier to edit studio work and highlight, even exaggerate, effects, from guitar solos to the taunting twitches in Presley's vocals. Records increasingly came in two sizes, with 78 RPMs replaced by longer playing albums on 33 and the rock and roll and indie label choice, singles, on 45. Playing singles were radio stations that relied on disc jockeys spinning records, with network feeds increasingly lost to television.[2]

These developments brought prominence to styles and audiences long considered marginal. The music of black and white southerners, divided into separate categories by record companies, overlapped stylistically. In the postwar era, R&B found a counterpart in the electrified country of honky-tonk and western swing. "Rocket 88," a 1951 R&B chart-topper on Sun by Jackie Brenston and his Delta Cats (including Ike Turner and a "fuzz guitar" solo caused by a busted amp), was covered in a similar fashion by Bill Haley and the Saddlemen for country fans, as Haley began the merger popularized with "Rock Around the Clock." R&B and hillbilly boogie shared

more than songs. Each amplified the lives of working class people with loose bills and loosened rules, moving north and to urban or suburban streets in a Great Migration for white as much as black southerners. Each recorded for independents like Sun, proliferating in the postwar boom.[3]

If rock and roll rose on technological advances and the emboldened position of black and white working classes, its assimilation fed on changes in middle-class suburban America, where prosperity joined with Cold War fears in an era of domestic "containment"—younger marriages, a baby boom, and the nuclear family as resistance to communism.[4] Suburban sterility is often summed up in rock history through the most dreaded pop hit of all: Patti Page's 1953 "Doggie in the Window." Singing primly—though the contemporary tracking let her harmonize with herself—about a puppy, heard yipping in rhythm, Page was all rock and rollers opposed.

Listeners chose a different canine, Presley's "Hound Dog," whose roots and routes modeled rock and roll diversity. Songwriters Jerry Leiber and Mike Stoller were young Jews enthralled by black pop. The original R&B hit was produced by Johnny Otis, born Ioannis Alexandres Veliotesa to Greek immigrants, who "passed" in Los Angeles for black. Alabama-born singer Big Mama Thornton dressed as a man, presenting a transgressive sexuality. Houston record label, Peacock, was a black-owned independent. Presley's later version built on a comic parody; Freddie Bell and the Bellboys did white takes on R&B in Las Vegas lounges. But the joke was at first on Presley, a former truck driver, when rock and roll hating New York TV host Steve Allen had him don black tie to sing "Hound Dog" to an actual basset. Furious, Presley recorded "Hound Dog" the next day, turning Thornton's gender blur into class outrage: "you said you were high class, but *that* was just a lie." The result topped pop, R&B, and country charts alike.[5]

The gender, class, and regional contrasts between "Doggie in the Window" and "Hound

Dog" were less discussed than race and propriety in the "leerics" and "big beat" preoccupations of 1950s pop commentary. But they mattered, just as it did that older star Frank Sinatra, an Italian American steeped in jazz, Broadway standards, and leftist Popular Front culture, hated *both* songs as infantile, responding with adult pop albums and a dissolute Rat Pack persona. Swinging cosmopolitanism blended immigrant and Harlem New York hustle, jazz band brass, movie and radio star intimacy. But formations of American music moved away from this Tin Pan Alley and show business nexus. The rocking newcomers were younger, overtly southern and black in ways that registered as raw, less professional.[6]

To offer examples from the Rock Hall roster: Little Richard's falsetto-tinged, piano-banged, former gay bar anthem, "Tutti Frutti," defined rock and roll wildness, though Jerry Lee Lewis was a hillbilly (now "rockabilly") rival. The shrewd lyrics and guitar licks of Chuck Berry's "Maybellene" created the rock and roll singer-songwriter, as did Buddy Holly's younger, whiter, and nerdier anthems. Fats Domino gave a face to New Orleans rhythms, the roll in rock and roll. Ray Charles and Johnny Cash were genius synthesizers of Americana, Etta James the greatest female rocker of the period. The Drifters and Frankie Lymon's Teenagers were early boy bands, doo wop fashioning rock and roll of nonsense syllables and romantic hyperbole.[7]

Structurally, though, rock and roll was unsound. Its home was Top 40 radio, happy with hits of any kind: Pat Boone covering Little Richard, Fabian as teen pinup promoted on Dick Clark's afternoon TV show *American Bandstand*. Artists had little control over mercurial careers: Presley was drafted, steered by his manager; Little Richard left pop for religion; Berry found himself imprisoned on racist sex charges; Lewis became ostracized for marrying a young second cousin; Holly died in a plane crash on a flimsy package tour. In an era of burgeoning civil rights,

rock and roll embodied new racial freedoms more than it could articulate them explicitly. Many fans moved on as they hit college. Perhaps, some thought, it had all just been a fad.[8]

YOU SAY YOU WANT A REVOLUTION: ROCK IN THE 1960s

In 1964 the Beatles arrived in America, taking over Top 40 in a British Invasion. Much had happened earlier in the decade: a folk craze, girl groups and Beach Boys, Motown Records, the Twist. But Beatlemania was a rock and roll revival. "Nothing really affected me until Elvis," John Lennon said, and the Fab Four used an *Ed Sullivan* TV appearance to become iconic much as Presley had. "I Want to Hold Your Hand" was not the message: that transmitted when the music surged in pace and girls in Sullivan's audience screamed and took over the camera.[9]

Unlike before, this 1960s incarnation of rock and roll matured. Taking a critique of mass culture from the musical pilgrims assembled at the Newport Folk Festival, it became a rock counterculture gathered less earnestly at Monterey in 1967 and Woodstock in 1969. The Beatles no longer performed live; they made increasingly complex albums. Songs like "Strawberry Fields Forever," with its Indian instruments and backwards tape effects, used the multitrack recording studio—and unlimited budget—to produce a blockbuster product with an artsy feel, alluding to psychedelic drug experience without much concealment.[10]

Formal experimentation, social experimentation, and big business carved rock from rock and roll. The Rolling Stones, named for a Muddy Waters song, formed in London of shared kinship for blues, pursuing non-pop lineages. "Satisfaction" in 1965 poked fun at advertising even as it conquered commercial-laden US Top 40. "Street Fighting Man" answered Motown's "Dancing in the Streets," accompanying protests at the 1968 Democratic convention. In 1969, the Stones topped the charts with "Honky Tonk Women," which nodded to country and blues in its title and sound, then sex and drugs in a lyric allowed airplay: "she blew my nose and then she blew my mind." That year, the group toured America, propagating a rock culture built around communal yet commercial gathering.[11]

The most consequential rocker of the decade barely played rock and roll. Bob Dylan, whose early "Song to Woody," for folksinger Woody Guthrie, made the cross-generational claim the Stones did with Waters, was known for poetic anthems, both collective ("Blowin' in the Wind") and personal ("Mr. Tambourine Man"). But when the Beatles rekindled rock and roll he found "Tambourine Man" charting in a "folk-rock" version by the Byrds and readied his own electric reinvention, "Like a Rolling Stone." A number 2 hit despite exceeding six minutes, the anthem's influence was deregulatory: pop structures were optional, lyrics could be obscure, an unpolished voice had broad appeal. Dylan's persona redefined the singer-songwriter to represent the most college-educated cohort in American history.[12]

Rock differed from rock and roll because it meant albums alongside singles, counterculture over youth culture. By the 1967 triumphs of Jimi Hendrix and Janis Joplin at the Monterey Pop Festival, rare examples of alternatives to white men in lead roles, major record labels understood that rock's sales and status dwarfed other music. Finishing what Sinatra and adult pop from Ray Charles to *West Side Story* started, rockers demanded creative freedom. Rock, a mainstream commercial form, positioned itself as anti-commercial or at least "authentic": built around either the romantic authenticity of personal and communal experience or the modernist authenticity of newness and experiment. Whereas rock and roll's popularity in the 1950s led to the music becoming softer, rock's led to the music becoming louder: a response to violent times and the Vietnam draft, technology

letting city-sized audiences hear every sustained note.[13]

Rock and roll lacked structural support, but rock had foundations in radio, touring, media, and urban neighborhoods. FM radio became the home for rock channels that began as stoned sounding "underground" or "free form" stations. Woodstock and Altamont were poorly organized music festivals, but the crowds they drew demonstrated the commercial potential of more organized tours. And the underground press of the era was funded by record industry advertisements and other merchants participating in what became known as "Hip Capitalism." *Rolling Stone* magazine, in particular, a countercultural newspaper when it began in the hippie Bay Area, empowered a new creature, the rock critic, to argue over the meaning of the music, past and present. San Francisco itself, a bohemian haven earlier for the Beat poetry scene in North Beach, the most important of the Pacifica public radio stations (KPFA), and the writing of culture critics such as music's Ralph Gleason and film's Pauline Kael, became the American city that most defined the new rock sensibility, as the Haight-Ashbury district hosted the summer of love in 1967 and brought the Jefferson Airplane, Grateful Dead, and Joplin to prominence.[14]

Still, as the 1960s ended, rock's revolutionary moment passed. Star deaths from drug use (Hendrix, Joplin, Jim Morrison) proved the risks of new mores. Divides separated younger audiences who sought hard rock and former folkies who favored singer-songwriter messages. Undergrounds began to appear, with influential recordings like the Velvet Underground's "Heroin" set at the fringe. Black fans and performers used rock notions to redefine R&B as soul and funk—they had to, shut out from rock's definition as art even as James Brown's rhythmic changes were the decade's most revolutionary. This era dominates discussion of rock's peak, yet it was really only a few short years—the length, say, of a college education.[15]

ARENAS AND FORMATS: ROCK IN THE 1970s

Cultural memory of rock in the 1970s has been framed through movies. Cameron Crowe looked back on his youth profiling bands for *Rolling Stone* in *Almost Famous*. Richard Linklater recalled his Texas high school in *Dazed & Confused*. Both films show how widely rock values proliferated by the middle of the decade: high school as much as college, middle and working class, stoners and jocks, boys and girls, with the music supporting sex and drug uses that felt, somehow, innocent. Rock bands became akin to deities. Crowe recreates Led Zeppelin's leonine lead singer, Robert Plant, announcing "I am a golden God!" in a wasted moment.[16]

Rock was now an industry, fit for arenas and stadiums everywhere. Major label executives, notably David Geffen (who would become a billionaire in the process), made Southern California the geographic center for record labels and rock the core genre of pop. Rockers like Zeppelin and Grand Funk Railroad, criticized by critics and countercultural listeners as unprogressive, used the improved execution (stacked amplifiers, lighting to separate band from audience, reliable security) to showcase rock bigness as a triumph unto itself. "Cock rock," as some called it, rooted in the working-class masculinity that connected electrified R&B and honky-tonk country. But this version, the swagger and long guitar solos of anthems like "Whole Lotta Love," or ballads like "Stairway to Heaven" saluted with lit cigarette lighters, let a young, white, male-dominated counterculture cross class lines. Marketing it was the 18–34 year-old male-focused format of rock radio, AOR (album-oriented rock), geared to play arena rock's warhorses constantly, fetishistically.[17]

Singer-songwriters emerged as no less commercially dominant, especially in album sales, creating a middle of the road soft rock known on radio by 1980 as "adult contemporary." From Simon and Garfunkel's *Bridge over Troubled Water* and Carole King's *Tapestry*, the biggest albums ever to that point, to the mellow James Taylor and Jackson Browne or arena groups with akin sensibilities like Fleetwood Mac and the Eagles, singer-songwriters connected more to 1960s values than hard rockers. Their key subject, feminism and altered gender notions, used rock's literacy and middle-class formal address to normalize social change as new bourgeois identity: contemporary casual, laid-back but still wealthy.[18]

The decade was a golden age for the artistic LP: Neil Young, Joni Mitchell, Bruce Springsteen, and David Bowie, among others, explored changing taste and behavior in ways both intensely personal and commercially public, with supportive major labels. Those that critic Robert Christgau called "semipopular" performers, such as poet Leonard Cohen or sardonic balladeer Randy Newman, found stable perches too. Rock critics, who had emerged in underground publications at first, now held staff positions at daily newspapers and magazines; they reinforced the discourse that treated rock more as a new art form than an ephemeral commodity, with books from *The Sound of the City* to Greil Marcus's soon hallowed *Mystery Train* and the critical collection, *The Rolling Stone Illustrated History of Rock and Roll*, sealing in a narrative.[19]

In emphasizing artistic control, albums, splashy staging, and commercial anticommercialism, rock shaped other categories. Soul and funk musicians recorded landmark albums and staged concerts akin to arena rock; some, like Aretha Franklin and Stevie Wonder, reached rock fans, but most, like Maze or the Ohio Players, did not. Bob Marley, symbol of Third World Black Nationalism, was groomed to Dylan dimensions by label head Chris Blackwell. In country, outlaw figures like Willie Nelson, who rejected Nashville for more countercultural Austin, created a "redneck rock" hybrid; southern rockers Lynyrd Skynyrd and the Allman Brothers stressed regional pride. Salsa musicians, New Yorkers with roots from Puerto Rico to Panama, provocatively reinvented Latin music. Rock even affected newer classical: *Philip Glass's on the Beach* resembled the Who's rock opera *Tommy*.[20]

Ultimately, though, the corporate 1970s version of rock counterculture smashed up as the decade progressed, like the United States and United Kingdom overall. Competing for the title of the biggest rock album of the decade was Pink Floyd's *Dark Side of the Moon*, a stoned vision that new teens found endlessly fascinating, keeping it in *Billboard*'s charts for 741 weeks between 1973 and 1988. "Art rock," or "progressive rock," was rock quite distant from rock and roll. A revival movement, punk, started in New York around the nightclub CBGB, its most influential band the loud, fast, dumb acting Ramones, whose "Blitzkrieg Bop" compared arena shows to Nazi rallies. In London, an angry young man scrawled I Hate across his Pink Floyd shirt, took the name Johnny Rotten, and began British punk singing for the Sex Pistols. When Presley died in 1977, critic Lester Bangs eulogized not the King but rock and roll, now too fragmented to connect races, classes, regions, or tastes.[21]

If punk offered a backlash against mainstream rock, disco suffered a backlash led by mainstream rock. The dance craze, with its cross-racial appeal, Top 40 hits, and coded gay content (akin to Elton John in pop, Queen in arena rock, glam and Bowie as subculture), recalled earlier rock and roll. But not rock, whose AOR fans, outraged when heroes like the Rolling Stones "went disco" or radio stations switched to disco formats, gleefully destroyed disco records at a 1979 rally led by a rock DJ. Disco survived, as club music, as MTV pop, even as new wave in conjunction with rock. Mainstream rock, though, a caricature in punk attacks and its own disco attacks, never recovered its progressive image. Commercially successful rock now seemed compromised. The hallowed years of rock were behind it.[22]

THRILLER OR DESTRUCTION? POP AND ROCK IN THE 1980s

While Bruce Springsteen achieved global superstardom with his *Born in the U.S.A.* album, and Irish rockers U2 joined the select ranks of arena bands categorized as formally and politically progressive, most 1980s rock registered as a retread, too regressive or obscure. Boomer rockers sang for charity in "We Are the World" and Live Aid; fans like Tipper Gore started organizations like the PMRC (Parents' Music Resource Council) to decry youth trends. *Rolling Stone* founder Jann Wenner inaugurated a Rock and Roll Hall of Fame whose inductions, beginning in 1986 (the museum opened in Cleveland a decade later), ratified the rock view of pop history. Compact disc reissues enriched catalogs, promoted by classic rock radio stations.[23]

Yet the 1980s were also among the best for rock and roll, to use that rubric for diverse, challenging youth-pop. Cable channel MTV launched in 1981, playing music videos as a rock radio equivalent with few black artists. But quickly, British new wave bands like Duran Duran, Culture Club, and Eurythmics—style conscious, gender bending, postmodern, preferring synthesizer to guitar—supplied the visuals and spark MTV required. Next, Michael Jackson, followed by Prince and Madonna—none white men—built superstar personas on MTV, now Top 40. With videos, album promotions could stretch over years, each new short extending the performer's star text. Rockers Dire Straits had the blue-collar protagonist of "Money for Nothing" homophobically complain, as if protesting disco: "See the little faggot with the earring and the makeup...that ain't working." If, as with rock and roll in the 1950s, MTV encouraged a cross-racial youth culture, this Reagan-era iteration was no celebration of working-class culture, at least at first.[24]

Instead, the new superstars subsumed group identity as they rose. Jackson, once of Motown's Jackson 5, triumphed solo with *Thriller* on

Epic, validating major label R&B; the album made James Brown grooves central to Top 40, turned videos into blockbuster musical theater, and deployed rockers like Paul McCartney and Eddie Van Halen. Accused of abandoning blacks for crossover, Jackson more staged a coup: from Elvis as king of rock and roll to a new "King of Pop." Prince, his rival, connected R&B mastery to guitar chops and motorbike rebellion on the album/film *Purple Rain*, redefining rock virtuosity in the decade that saw a Black Rock Coalition form. Madonna, sonically disco and chart pop, used video's funhouse mirroring of original songs to insert third wave feminist comment on "Material Girl" gender assumptions. "Hound Dog" had touted liberation (working class, male, white-from-black sources) from the mainstream "Doggie in the Window." "Like a Prayer," "Thriller," and "When Doves Cry" presented racial and gender alternatives to the white-male rock posturing, now itself mainstream, of "Stairway to Heaven," "Dream On," and "Free Bird." Was this pop a new rock and roll? Superstar freedoms compensated for weakened group identity in the inequitable 1980s. Michael Jackson dominated alongside Michael Jordan but for African Americans as a whole, an "underclass" experience of crack epidemic, mass incarceration, and social separation later called the *New Jim Crow* locked in. Madonna's intimacies matched Oprah's but feminists experienced what Susan Faludi called a *Backlash*: the rejection of the Equal Rights Amendment and Moral Majority anti-feminism.[25]

From a new sounds perspective, rap was the decade's rock and roll: a radicalizing of the pop voice to favor rhythm and timbre over melody, upending taste yet again: "not bad meaning bad but bad meaning good," as Run-D.M.C. put it. Indie labels again led the way, notably Def Jam, operated by Run's brother Russell Simmons. Rappers came out of New York City to start but were national by the end of the decade, notably N.W.A in Los Angeles. Unlike rock and roll, whites

rarely coopted hip-hop, as its larger form was increasingly called. At its most idealistic, from the politics of Public Enemy to visionaries like rapper Rakim, it represented a new soul. At its most pragmatic, N.W.A's gangsta rap crime narratives, it had bullet-proof authenticity, rebranding the most disparaging word of all: to represent among Niggaz Wit Attitudes was to occupy an identity no white could claim.[26]

Still, white and black working-class experiences continued to parallel; N.W.A. found its Los Angeles counterpart in sexually confrontational ("turn around bitch") rock group Guns N' Roses. GNR was the last in a wave of Sunset Strip bands, from Van Halen to Mötley Crüe, mocked as hair metal by outsiders for their manes, make-up and spandex, yet belligerent in their partying, cartoonishly anti-authoritarian ("We're Not Gonna Take It"). For fans, metal extended arena rock's *Dazed & Confused* ethos. And the bands were pop savvy, slipping in synths and glossy production, using MTV more strategically than Dire Straits predicted. They needed cable: rock radio splintered over metal, which did not draw those advertisers preferred. Classic rock radio added few new songs. Modern rock radio, built on new wave, had a marginal audience share sold as more affluent.[27]

If rock in the 1970s had created space for adventurous albums, 1980s trends favored more postmodern blends: downtown art scene figures like Talking Heads, Paul Simon's NPR-friendly African music album *Graceland*, parodic television like *The Simpsons*, the rocker as director (David Lynch), computer programmer (Steve Jobs and Apple, named after the Beatles' holding company), or television host (David Letterman). Experimental rock from groups like Hüsker Dü, the Replacements, and Sonic Youth relied on independent labels, now not expecting to create Top 40 hits, establishing sustainable touring club-level networks in conjunction with college radio stations. Scene leaders R.E.M. compared their status to illicit "Radio Free Europe."

Metal aside, rock rarely enjoyed the crossover thrill of rock and roll.[28]

COMMODIFYING DISSENT IN THE 1990s

The blockbuster products of 1991 set the tone for the decade's reuniting of rock with rock and roll. Metallica's self-titled "black" album, the biggest of the bunch, joined metal and punk for working-class listeners who no longer believed in a utopic "Stairway to Heaven" or even hair metal glamour. Pearl Jam and Nirvana's albums, major label versions of a Seattle grunge scene centered on the indie label Sub Pop, worked the same punk-metal fusion for middle-class listeners within the creative capitalism that nurtured Microsoft, Amazon, and Starbucks. And the industry marveled at the first Lollapalooza tour, which revealed a new rock and roll hybrid: alternative rock and hip-hop acts sharing the stage for a pierced and tattooed post-boomer audience, dubbed Generation X.[29]

Grunge, gangsta rap, and New Country all claimed a large, engaged audience in the early 1990s, inheriting parts of rock's mantle. Top 40 declined, crossover less necessary given these expanded segments. It was the return of counterculture, if with blatant sponsorship and major labels that struck deals with Sub Pop or hip-hop's Death Row, incorporating indie and street marketing into global corporations: only one major was now American owned. Rock radio resumed playing new music. R&B incorporated hip-hop as figures like Dr. Dre and Snoop Dogg hosted a groupie-filled party that resembled hair metal. Garth Brooks sold more albums, collectively, than anybody in the decade with an arena country that included Billy Joel and Aerosmith covers but no pop hits. *Rolling Stone* had magazine rivals in *Spin* (for alt-rock) and *Vibe* (for hip-hop and R&B).[30]

Once again, the revolutionary period proved short-lived. Notably, in the 1990s commercial popularity became an issue to an extent not seen before. In 1994, Nirvana leader Kurt Cobain, a heroin addict, killed himself in a tragedy viewed as reflecting his struggles with popularity; Pearl Jam stopped making videos and scaled back their ambitions. The murders of rival West and East Coast rappers Tupac Shakur and Notorious B.I.G. in 1995 and 1996 raised similar questions about the commodified rebellion of hip-hop. Brooks, like actual crossover country figures Shania Twain and Billy Ray Cyrus, found his popularity raising hackles among fans used to stars not getting above their raising.[31]

A second key 1990s shift was that rock put women more front and center. If very male grunge claimed the spotlight, rock critiques launching from the riot grrrl scene just south in Olympia, Washington, were no less pivotal: Bikini Kill's Kathleen Hanna gave Cobain the phrase "Smells Like Teen Spirit" and he saw his breakout as a blend of the two movements; in a different blend, Sleater-Kinney, another riot grrrl band, and grunge's Pearl Jam became the region's most lasting rockers, if at different levels of popularity. Commercially, Alanis Morissette's *Jagged Little Pill* rivaled grunge and Metallica with an anthem, "You Oughta Know," whose lyrics ("Is she perverted like me?/Would she go down on you in a theater?") combined "Honky Tonk Women" and Madonna: a woman's rock not pop. Songwriter Diane Warren dominated adult contemporary, while performer Sheryl Crow had "Hot AC" hits; this younger category aimed at women as rock listeners supported Hootie and the Blowfish, Gin Blossoms, and others. New Country, from Twain to the Dixie Chicks, saw what one hit called "girls with guitars" chart higher than before or since. Lilith Fair offered a women's music version of Lollapalooza.[32]

All of this made the contrast to hard rock and hip-hop masculinity striking. New arena rock, as the 1990s ended, was still dominated by a metal-punk fusion that now added hip-hop elements, recognizing the working-class commonalities. This could take a radical form: Rage

Against the Machine played against the World Trade Organization protests of 1999. But the "nu-metal" of groups like Limp Bizkit and Korn was interpreted as a new low in rock's now long history of reactionary rage; Woodstock '99, an anniversary concert, saw male fans attacking female spectators in a spectacle that electronic rocker Moby dubbed "rape rock." Hip-hop success, meanwhile, centered on black street credibility that included referring to women as bitches and "hoes." Differing takes on these intersectional modalities were inevitable: academics started to rethink the narrative of rock and roll as deliverance from prejudice, reaching back to 19th-century blackface minstrelsy, viewing identity as performed, and contextualizing through cultural studies.[33]

Many who loved music recoiled from rock and rap altogether by the end of the 1990s. Pop resurged on MTV's afternoon program *Total Request Live*, where boy bands (Backstreet Boys, N'Sync) and pop princesses (Britney Spears, Christina Aguilera) vied for audience votes. Global fans awaited each release, with influential writer-producers coming out of Sweden, most prominently Max Martin, and a flurry of Latin superstars: Jennifer Lopez, Ricky Martin, and Shakira. Jive Records, home to many *TRL* acts, sold for $3 billion in 2002, the most ever paid for a label. Yet the performers seemed as tame as the manufactured stars Dick Clark once introduced on *American Bandstand*. Many had started on Disney's *New Mickey Mouse Club*. Could a Spears, asserting sexuality in ways that resembled Madonna, be viewed as third wave feminist when she seemed so much less in control of her career? Was Memphis's Justin Timberlake a new Elvis figure? Few said yes.[34]

Collegiate genres at decade's end also looked to get away from rock and rap. Electronica, extending the legacy of disco, gave rockers a non-guitar palette: bands big as Radiohead and Daft Punk explored this direction; arenas became sites for dancing. Rootsier sounds, sometimes called alt-country and eventually

Americana, kept the guitars but lost any connection to metal and almost any to punk. Even swing jazz enjoyed a momentary revival, alongside lounge exotica. Within hip-hop culture, a bohemian movement sometimes called neo-soul (Erykah Badu, D'Angelo, OutKast) questioned gangsta posturing. The most rock thing to do, as a half-century of rock and roll concluded, was often to not rock out at all.[35]

ROCK IN A NEW CENTURY: RECENT DEVELOPMENTS

Nothing defined rock and roll's legacy in the early 21st century better than the mash-up: two records, vocals from one with backing tracks of the other, merged on a home computer by an amateur producer who posted an MP3 for downloading. Beyond records, mash-ups combined genres and formats: early on, Top 40 singer Christina Aguilera's "Genie in a Bottle" and alt-rock band the Strokes' "Hard to Explain," became "A Stroke of Genius" by Freelance Hellraiser. If rock and roll had married R&B, country, and Top 40, mash-ups stitched a new hybridity. Technology dissolved requirements of production studios and distribution networks. Whether social boundaries would fade so easily was a harder question.[36]

This latter sense, that mash-ups mixed people as much as the genres that divided them in the rock era, informed *Glee*, which aired on Fox in the 2000s, often after *American Idol*. The glee club teacher used mash-ups to heal race, gender, class, and disability: "the big difference between them is what makes them great," he explained. *Glee* itself, like *Idol*, was a mash-up—the TV show and pop industry combined as part of what Henry Jenkins called "convergence culture," old media meeting new, like the video games *Guitar Hero* and *Rock Band* too, like making a vintage rock and roll jukebox or Top 40 playlist out of the shuffle button on one's brand new Apple iPod. *Glee*'s first anthem was a cover of Journey's

"Don't Stop Believin'," a power ballad that old school rockers might have dismissed as cheesy. In this century, it made as much sense as Barry Manilow covers on *Idol*. The older rock walls between types of music cultures had come down; not as rock and roll tearing them down but dissolved with a karaoke singer's grin.[37]

Crossover seemed vital again: if the 1990s were troubled that everything could be commodified, no matter how marginal, the 2000s worried that nothing could be sold, no matter how mainstream. Napster, the illicit file sharing technology, and successors like Bit Torrent, made it impossible to keep recordings proprietary: album sales collapsed, with only rare performers (Taylor Swift, Adele) subsequently able to enjoy big totals. The shattered model of the record industry prompted artists to become brands unto themselves, reliant on their own convergence culture—sponsorships, connections to other media. Reality television and tabloid celebrity nurtured aspects of pop. *Billboard* charts came to reflect songs streamed from YouTube, a video site that provided hits on demand and let fans upload their versions, which counted too. Records, as a distillation of culture, gave way to broader media exposure and overlapping social networks.[38]

To consider major figures of this century, with notions of rock and roll or rock in mind, shows how confusingly remixed they'd become. Rapper Jay-Z called himself "the new Sinatra," took swagger and Chairman of the Board savvy from rock into hip-hop. Kanye West emphasized the rocker as provocateur, making ambitious albums that intertwined bohemian neo-soul, indie experimentalism, hip-hop bravado, and synergistic promotion. Beyoncé calibrated her tabloid crossover, with "Single Ladies" a YouTube parody favorite. She also, one night on iTunes, with a single tweet as promotion, released an album of songs accompanied by videos, the artistry updating Prince's standard of virtuosity. Taylor Swift, a confessional singer-songwriter, moved from

country to Top 40, building working womanhood and a rock and roll echo of riot grrrl on 1990s paradigms. Adele, who after the death of Amy Winehouse inherited the British Invasion tradition, broke record sales records as an Adult Contemporary singer of relatable experience and a soulful tone.[39]

If the blockbuster performer as CEO was one pop response to shattered business models, another was a resurgence of Top 40 culture as catch-all, a global pop of mashed-up identities—Black Eyed Peas, Bruno Mars. The radio format itself boomed in the 2000s, as PPM (Portable People Meter) devices proved the popularity of eclectic hits presentations over ostensibly targeted approaches; the Jack format, an oldies blend impish about genre lines, was another version. What the 1970s had called disco, the 1980s house and techno, and the 1990s electronica was now EDM, or electronic dance music, which began registering hits that mashed up celebrity singers with influential live DJs. Critics started calling themselves poptimists and criticizing as rockism attempts to essentialize great music.[40]

At times, the results were unpredictable and exciting—a new rock and roll. A billion people globally checked out Psy's madcap video for "Gangnam Style" and contemplated the Motown-in-Asia spectacles of K-Pop. Lady Gaga drew upon MTV traditions of superstar spectacle to create post-postmodernism. Rappers making "rhythmic Top 40" dance hits fostered a half-decade of the blackest pop programming in years, perhaps ever. At other times, popular music's mash-up approach to history registered as too haphazard to create a lasting impact. *American Idol* fell into a rut of electing "WGWGs" (white guys with guitars) the winner. Top 40 stopped allowing R&B hits to cross to its top positions altogether. One tried to remember the last time a rocker had felt as central to the culture as Kurt Cobain. What were the collective stories of this new era?[41]

Yet the impact of rock and roll and rock, however reconstituted, remained massive. The biggest touring acts were rock derived, the subformats of rock on radio, added together, eclipsed other genres, and so did rock album sales—both new and catalog material. The indie networks of the 1980s that fed neoliberal creative corporations of the 1990s now remade neighborhoods in Brooklyn, East Nashville, or Portland around the hipster ethos of bands covered in *Pitchfork* or playing festivals like Coachella and Bonnaroo. As social networks went berserk rehashing Beyoncé or Kanye, the Black Lives Matter-inspired masterpiece by rapper Kendrick Lamar (*To Pimp a Butterfly*), or that goofy new Drake video, it seemed apparent, if largely unspoken, that the major inheritors of cultural ambitions distilled from rock and roll into rock were African Americans. This represented a shift three generations in the making, just as the boldest explorers of messy rock and roll were now women.[42]

For about a century, once, the minstrel songs and show business ethos that cast a spell from Stephen Foster to "White Christmas" ruled American music. It seems likely that we are in the tail end of a second century, from Elvis Presley and Top 40 to the Beatles and rock, from rock and roll to hip-hop and EDM, the double imperatives of crossover and authenticity structuring a dialectic with new chapters every decade or so. Rock and roll's revolution is too unstable; rock's far too stable; the players and issues change but the back and forth continues to fascinate.

DISCUSSION OF THE LITERATURE

The earliest writing on rock and roll, usually by figures unfamiliar with its musical lineages, hasn't aged well, though later studies by figures older than the first fans (Arnold Shaw, with his music business expertise; pioneering musicologist Charles Hamm, sociologists Philip Ennis and Richard Peterson) offer a useful, because distanced, perspective.[43] The first key contemporaneous studies came from England, Nik Cohn capturing the pop cultural mythos and then Gillett the facts (with an emphasis on independent labels) of the transition from R&B to rock and roll.[44] American rock critic views coalesced by the mid-1970s with *The Rolling Stone Illustrated History of Rock & Roll* (avoid the final 1992 edition), rock and roll epiphany collector (and rock mistruster) Greil Marcus's American studies treatise *Mystery Train*, and the mytho-historical efforts of Nick Tosches (an American Cohn) and Peter Guralnick (an American Gillett).[45] Other first-generation writers include feminist Ellen Willis, ecumenical canonizer Robert Christgau, protopunk Lester Bangs, Robert Palmer (the rare example of a musician-critic), working class identified Dave Marsh, white southern stalwart Stanley Booth, and conceptualist Richard Meltzer.[46]

In the next generation, from the 1980s to early 2000s, perspectives on rock and roll diversified considerably. Scenester extraordinaire Nelson George and Black Arts theorist Greg Tate's *Village Voice* writing established black critical perspectives, hard to find earlier beyond perhaps the soul writing of Phyl Garland.[47] As writers and editors, Ann Powers, Evelyn McDonnell, and Barbara O'Dair worked systematically to document, interpret, and increase women's voices.[48] Rap criticism, starting with maverick author David Toop's outsider perspective, became a discourse unto itself in the *Source*, *Vibe*, and so on, collected by Raquel Cepeda, with books too from hip-hop feminist Joan Morgan, the gonzo zine *Ego Trip*, an Experience Music Project oral history, and Jeff Chang and later Dan Charna's authoritative syntheses.[49] Alternative rock views emerged around *Spin* and the *Voice*, with new wave-identified Rob Sheffield, alternative-to-alternative Chuck Eddy, mainstream defender Chuck Klosterman, poet-of-singles Joshua Clover, worldly Will Hermes, and British spy Simon Reynolds among those expanding rock canons.[50] As classic rock flourished, uncritical hagiographies or equally uncritical exposes produced bestsellers; by contrast, David Ritz co-wrote memoirs by rock and roll types, often understudied African Americans, and Barney Hoskyns brought nuance to rock and soul storytelling.[51]

Over the same quarter-century, academic writing on rock became a growing field.[52] Popular music studies developed from the sociology merged with early pop (challenging rock) criticism of Simon Frith and the legacy of Birmingham Centre cultural studies, including minstrelsy rethinker Eric Lott, rock postmodernist Lawrence Grossberg, mod subculturalist Dick Hebdige, black diaspora theorist Paul Gilroy, pop modernist Iain Chambers, girls subculturalist Angela McRobbie, clubculturalist Sarah Thornton, and genre unpacker Keith Negus, with Keir Keightley's "Reconsidering Rock" exemplifying a new rock studies synthesis.[53] African American studies and ethnic studies intervened via rap subculturalist Tricia Rose, post-soul pioneer Mark Anthony Neal, race music redefiner Guthrie Ramsey Jr., aesthete Fred Moten, sage hip-hop judge Imani Perry, black rock scholar Maureen Mahon, subaltern roots rocker George Lipsitz, and audiotopian Josh Kun.[54] Musicologists (feminist Susan McClary, roots of power, and power chords, investigator Robert Walser, cross-categorizer David Brackett) and ethnomusicologists (Charles Keil and Steven Feld debating grooves, Joseph Schloss collecting beats, Daniel Cavicchi worshipping with Springsteen fans) belatedly explored rock and pop's working languages, with John Covach, Alan Moore, Susan Fast, and Albin Zak theorizing rock alongside philosopher Theodore Gracyk.[55] Academics like Will Straw, Barry Shank, Sara Cohen, Keith Kahn-Harris, Richard Lloyd, and Holly Kruse examined rock scenes differently than journalists had Beatlemania or grunge, as evolving urban cultural formations.[56]

Recent critical takes on rock and roll have turned toward confronting taste. Inspired by a Kelefa Sanneh essay reviving the critique of "rockism" from new wave days, critics developed "poptimism" to embrace commercial diversity. Key essays were collected in *Best*

Music Writing, published yearly by Da Capo from 2000 to 2011 with guest editors. Another new source for critical writing, the 33 ⅓ series of idiosyncratic music album monographs, included Carl Wilson's look at a much-dismissed Celine Dion album, *Let's Talk about Love*. Framing his study as a "journey to the end of taste," Wilson popularized Bourdieu's ideas of cultural capital; rock and roll's belated apology to Patti Page. Another much-noted book, Elijah Wald's *How the Beatles Destroyed Rock 'n' Roll*, went back to the 1920s in an effort to denounce rock's rejection of teen girls dancing to black pop in the name of art.[57]

Historical digging and textual reinterpretation, aided by new Internet access to archival material and growing academic hiring, has shaped recent scholarly work. Disco's underground links to rock counterculture were clarified by Tim Lawrence; Alice Echols complicated this to appreciate mainstream disco's identity moves. Diane Pecknold and other country scholars dismantled that genre's "hardcore" and soft-shell versions of rockism. The roots of rock and roll read differently as David Suisman, Karl Hagstrom Miller, Barry Mazor, Edward Comentale, and Marybeth Hamilton supplied new chapters and Michael Kramer historicized early rock. Questioning category, Hugh Barker and Yuval Taylor explored authenticity debates in multiple eras, Charles Hughes deconstructed mythologies of integrated soul, Steve Waksman removed the divide between punk and metal, and my study reframed rockism/poptimism around questions of genre and format. Mitchell Morris brought musicology to soft pop sounds; Loren Kajikawa an equal focus to the sonics of race in rap. And the expanded presence of popular music in the second edition of the *Grove Dictionary of American Music* demonstrated the growth of the field within music departments. Music made by US Latinos finally intersected the rock and roll story: Ned Sublette on Cuban inheritances, theorizing by Alexandra Vazquez, punk Latinos via Michelle

Habell-Pallán, Deborah Paredez and Deborah Vargas on Chicana divas, Dolores Inés Casillas on regional Mexican music and radio; the best overview to date comes from Deborah Pacini Hernandez.[58]

PRIMARY SOURCES

Rock and roll recordings have never been easier to access, through streams from services like Spotify, individual tracks from YouTube, downloads via iTunes, and albums mail-ordered from Amazon. The harder challenge is to winnow down and find trustworthy discographical information: All Music Guide, www.allmusic.com, is invaluable as a first, not final reference point. YouTube has also made much more available rock and roll's visual history: television appearances, music videos, concert footage. The proliferation in the 2000s of DVDs made it almost as likely that a full-length visual recording would exist of a performer as an audio recording.

Written material on rock and roll represents a second key growth area. For period critical writing, *Rock's Backpages* collects thousands of reviews and articles by leading British and American music press writers from the 1960s to 2000s. Databases preserve magazines and trade journal sources: notably, ProQuest's Entertainment Industry Magazine Archive documents *Billboard*, *Radio & Records*, *Melody Maker*, *New Music Express*, and *Spin*. Music memoir, a form adding stories to the record that were not told at the time, has flourished: examples include Chuck Berry, Ronnie Spector, Tommy James, Bob Dylan, Keith Richards, Pamela DesBarres's groupie memoir, Loretta Lynn, Gregg Allman, Steven Tyler, Patti Smith, the oral history *Please Kill Me*, Viv Albertine, Nile Rodgers, Kristin Hersh, Jay-Z, Questlove, the RZA, and Carrie Brownstein.[59]

The rock documentary, or rockumentary, offers another way to survey rock and roll, so long as one watches as much to see how the story is being framed as to learn a direct lesson. Among the most hallowed, including films that still document a pop moment: *Good Rockin' Tonight: The Legacy of Sun Records* and *Elvis: That's the Way It Is* (original rock and roll); *The Beatles: The First U.S. Visit* and *TAMI Show* (1960s rock and roll); *Don't Look Back*, *Monterey Pop*, *Woodstock*, and *Gimme Shelter* (1960s rock revolution); *Soul Power* and *Wattstax* (soul era); *The Song Remains the Same*, *Tommy*, *Ziggy Stardust and the Spiders from Mars*, and *The Last Waltz* (1970s arena rock); *The Blank Generation*, *The Filth & the Fury*, and *The Decline of Western Civilization* (punk); *Stop Making Sense*, *Purple Rain*, *Truth or Dare* (1980s new wave and MTV); *Decline of Western Civilization, Part II: The Metal Years* and *Heavy Metal Parking Lot* (hair metal); *Style Wars*, *Rhyme & Reason*, and *Planet Rock: The Story of Hip-Hop and the Crack Generation* (hip-hop); *1991: The Year Punk Broke*, *Hype*, *Meeting People Is Easy*, *Some Kind of Monster* (1990s rock); *The Punk Singer*, *Shut Up and Play the Hits*, and *I Am Trying to Break Your Heart* (21st-century indie).[60] Overview television histories include Time-Life's *The History of Rock 'n' Roll* and PBS's *Rock & Roll*, both of which run through the 1990s, the latter more critically insightful.[61] Different series focus on performers, with *Behind the Music* and *Unsung* emphasizing scandal and redemption, *Unplugged* and *VH1 Storytellers* the performers looking back at their repertoire.

There are a range of archives worth investigating, starting with The Rock and Roll Hall of Fame and Museum Library and Archives, but also: the New York City Public Library for the Performing Arts, ARChive of Contemporary Music, and Schomburg Center for Research in Black Culture in New York; The Paley Center for Media in New York and Los Angeles; the Country Music Hall of Fame and Museum in Nashville, a long-standing archive with many non-country holdings, and Center for Popular Music at Middle Tennessee State University in Murfreesboro, Tennessee, the Film

& Television Archive and other collections at University of California, Los Angeles; the Music Library and Sound Recording Archives at Bowling Green State University in Bowling Green, Ohio; the Southern Folklife Collection at the University of North Carolina; and the Center for Black Music Research at Columbia College in Chicago.

FURTHER READING

Bennett, Andy, Barry Shank, and Jason Toynbee, eds. *The Popular Music Studies Reader.* New York: Routledge, 2006.

Brackett, David, ed. *The Pop, Rock, and Soul Reader: Histories and Debates.* 3d ed. New York: Oxford University Press, 2013.

Cateforis, Theo, ed. *The Rock History Reader.* 2d ed. New York: Routledge, 2013.

Cepeda, Raquel, ed. *And It Don't Stop: The Best American Hip-Hop Journalism of the Past 25 Years.* New York: Faber and Faber, 2004.

Echols, Alice. *Hot Stuff: Disco and the Remaking of American Culture.* New York: W. W. Norton, 2010.

Forman, Murray, and Mark Anthony Neal, eds. *That's the Joint: The Hip-Hop Studies Reader.* 2d ed. New York: Routledge, 2012.

Frith, Simon. *Sound Effects: Youth, Leisure, and the Politics of Rock 'n' Roll.* New York: Pantheon, 1981.

Gillett, Charlie. *The Sound of the City: The Rise of Rock and Roll.* Rev. ed. New York: Pantheon, 1984. Originally published in 1970.

Guralnick, Peter. *Last Train to Memphis: The Rise of Elvis Presley.* New York: Little, Brown, 1994.

Hernandez, Deborah Pacini. *Oye Como Va! Hybridity and Identity in Latino Popular Music.* Philadelphia: Temple University Press, 2010.

Keightley, Keir. "Reconsidering Rock." In *The Cambridge Companion to Pop and Rock,* Edited by Simon Frith, Will Straw, and John Street, 109–142. Cambridge: Cambridge University Press, 2001.

Kramer, Michael J. *The Republic of Rock: Music and Citizenship in the Sixties Counterculture.* New York: Oxford University Press, 2013.

Lipsitz, George. *Time Passages: Collective Memory and American Popular Culture.* Minneapolis: University of Minnesota Press, 1990.

Marcus, Greil. *Mystery Train: Images of America in Rock 'n' Roll Music.* 6th ed. New York: Plume, 2015. Originally published in 1975.

Matos, Michaelangelo. *The Underground Is Massive: How Electronic Dance Music Conquered America.* New York: Dey Street Books, 2015.

McDonnell, Evelyn, and Ann Powers, eds. *Rock She Wrote: Women Write about Rock, Pop and Rap.* New York: Delta, 1995.

Miller, Jim, ed. *The Rolling Stone Illustrated History of Rock & Roll.* Rev. ed. New York: Rolling Stone Press/Random House, 1980.

Moore, Ryan. *Sells Like Teen Spirit: Music, Youth Culture, and Social Crisis.* New York: New York University Press, 2009.

Negus, Keith. *Music Genres and Corporate Cultures.* New York: Routledge, 1994.

Palmer, Robert. *Rock & Roll: An Unruly History.* New York: Harmony, 1995.

Savage, Jon. *England's Dreaming: Anarchy, Sex Pistols, Punk Rock and Beyond.* New York: St. Martin's Press, 1992.

Waksman, Steve. *This Ain't the Summer of Love: Conflict and Crossover in Heavy Metal and Punk.* Berkeley: University of California Press, 2009.

Wald, Elijah. *How the Beatles Destroyed Rock 'n' Roll: An Alternative History of American Popular Music.* New York: Oxford University Press, 2009.

Walser, Robert. *Running with the Devil: Power, Gender, and Madness in Heavy Metal Music.* Hanover, NH: Wesleyan University Press, 1993.

Weisbard, Eric. *Top 40 Democracy: The Rival Mainstreams of American Music.* Chicago: University of Chicago Press, 2014.

Willis, Ellen. *Out of the Vinyl Deeps: Ellen Willis on Rock Music.* Minneapolis: University of Minnesota Press, 2011.

Zak, Albin. *I Don't Sound Like Nobody: Remaking Music in 1950s America.* Ann Arbor: University of Michigan Press, 2010.

NOTES

1. Charlie Gillett, *The Sound of the City: The Rise of Rock and Roll,* expanded 2d ed. (New York: Pantheon, 1984); Richard Peterson, "Why 1955? Explaining the Advent of Rock Music," *Popular Music* 1.9 (1990): 97–116; Philip Ennis, *The Seventh Stream: The Emergence of Rocknroll in American Popular Music* (Hanover, NH: Wesleyan University

Press, 1992); Peter Guralnick, *Last Train to Memphis: The Rise of Elvis Presley* (New York: Little, Brown, 1994).

2. For guitar, see Robert Palmer, "Church of the Sonic Guitar," in *Present Tense: Rock & Roll and Culture*, ed. Anthony DeCurtis (Durham, NC: Duke University Press, 1992) and Steve Waksman, *Instruments of Desire: The Electric Guitar and the Shaping of Musical Experience* (Cambridge, MA: Harvard University Press, 1999). For Presley's vocalizing, see Edward Comentale, *Sweet Air: Modernism, Regionalism, and American Popular Song* (Urbana: University of Illinois Press, 2013). The best overview is Albin J. Zak III, *I Don't Sound Like Nobody: Remaking Music in 1950s America* (Ann Arbor: University of Michigan Press, 2010).

3. Karl Hagstrom Miller, *Segregating Sound: Inventing Folk and Pop Music in the Age of Jim Crow* (Durham, NC: Duke University Press, 2010); George Lipsitz, *Rainbow at Midnight: Labor and Culture in the 1940s* (Urbana: University of Illinois Press, 1994); James Gregory, *The Southern Diaspora: How The Great Migrations of Black and White Southerners Transformed America* (Chapel Hill: University of North Carolina Press, 2005); John Broven, *Record Makers and Breakers: Voices of the Independent Rock 'n' Roll Pioneers* (Urbana: University of Illinois Press, 2009).

4. Elaine Tyler May, *Homeward Bound: American Families in the Cold War* (New York: Basic Books, 1988); Leerom Medovoi, *Rebels: Youth and the Cold War Origins of Identity* (Durham, NC: Duke University Press, 2005).

5. Greil Marcus, *Mystery Train: Images of America in Rock 'n' Roll Music*, 6th ed. (1975; reprint New York: Plume, 2015); Robert Fink, "Elvis Everywhere: Musicology and Popular Music Studies at the Twilight of the Canon," *American Music* 16.2 (1998): 135–179; Maureen Mahon, "Listening for Willie Mae 'Big Mama' Thornton's Voice: The Sound of Race and Gender Transgressions in Rock and Roll," *Women and Music: A Journal of Gender and Culture* 15 (2011): 1–17.

6. Kerry Segrave and Linda Martin, *Anti-Rock: The Opposition to Rock 'n' Roll*, rev. ed. (New York: Da Capo, 1993); Keir Keightley, "You Keep Coming Back Like a Song: Adult Audiences, Taste Panics, and the Idea of the Standard," *Journal of Popular Music Studies* 13 (2001): 7–40; Michael Denning, *The Cultural Front: The Laboring of American Culture in the Twentieth Century* (New York: Verso, 1996).

7. Charles White, *The Life and Times of Little Richard: The Quasar of Rock* (New York: Harmony Books, 1985); W. T. Lhamon Jr., *Deliberate Speed: The Origins of a Cultural Style in the American 1950s* (Washington, DC: Smithsonian Institution Press, 1990); Nick Tosches, *Hellfire: The Jerry Lee Lewis Story* (New York: Delta, 1982); Craig Morrison, *Go Cat Go: Rockabilly Music and Its Makers* (Urbana: University of Illinois Press, 1996); Robert Christgau, "Chuck Berry," in *The Rolling Stone Illustrated History of Rock & Roll*, rev. and expanded ed., ed. Jim Miller (New York: Rolling Stone Press/Random House, 1980), 54–60; Chuck Berry, *The Autobiography* (New York: Fireside, 1986); for Holly, Comentale, *Sweet Air*; John Broven, *Rhythm and Blues in New Orleans*, 3d ed. (1988; reprint Gretna, LA: Pelican Publishing, 2016); Robert Palmer, *Rock & Roll: An Unruly History* (New York: Harmony, 1995) and "Liner Notes for *Ray Charles: The Birth of Soul* in *Blues & Chaos: The Music Writing of Robert Palmer*, ed. Anthony DeCurtis (New York: Scribner, 2009), 163–188; Ray Charles and David Ritz, *Brother Ray: Ray Charles' Own Story* (New York: Dial, 1978); Michael Streissguth, ed., *Ring of Fire: The Johnny Cash Reader* (New York: Da Capo, 2002); Alice Echols, "Smooth Sass and Raw Power: R&B's Ruth Brown and Etta James," in *Trouble Girls: The Rolling Stone Book of Women in Rock*, ed. Barbara O'Dair (New York: Random House, 1997); Etta James and David Ritz, *Rage to Survive: The Etta James Story* (New York: Villard, 1995); for doo wop, Brian Ward, *Just My Soul Responding: Rhythm and Blues, Black Consciousness and Race Relations* (Berkeley: University of California Press, 1998).

8. Matthew F. Belmont, *The Nicest Kids in Town: American Bandstand, Rock 'n' Roll, and the Struggle for Civil Rights in 1950s Philadelphia* (Berkeley: University of California Press, 2012); Michael Bertrand, *Race, Rock, and Elvis* (Urbana: University of Illinois Press, 2000).

9. Greil Marcus, "The Beatles," in *The Rolling Stone Illustrated History of Rock & Roll*, 177–189; Barbara Ehrenreich, Elizabeth Hess, and Gloria Jacobs, *Re-Making Love: The Feminization of Sex* (New York: Anchor Press/Doubleday, 1986); Devin McKinney, *Magic Circles: The Beatles in Dream and History* (Cambridge, MA: Harvard University Press, 2003).

10. Elijah Wald, *How the Beatles Destroyed Rock 'n' Roll: An Alternative History of American Popular Music* (New York: Oxford University Press, 2009).

11. Stanley Booth, *The True Adventures of the Rolling Stones* (1984; reprint Chicago: Chicago Review Press, 2000); Andrew Loog Oldham, *Stoned: A Memoir of London in the 1960s* (New York: St. Martin's Press, 2000); Keith Richards with James Fox, *Life* (New York: Little, Brown, 2010).

12. Ellen Willis, "Dylan," in *Out of the Vinyl Deeps: Ellen Willis on Rock Music* (Minneapolis: University of Minnesota Press, 2011); Bob Dylan, *Chronicles,* vol. 1 (New York: Simon & Schuster, 2004); Mike Marqusee, *Wicked Messenger: Bob Dylan and the 1960s,* rev. ed. (New York: Seven Stories Press, 2005); Lee Marshall, *Bob Dylan: The Never Ending Star* (Cambridge, U.K.: Polity Press, 2007); David Shumway, *Rock Star: The Making of Musical Icons from Elvis to Springsteen* (Baltimore: Johns Hopkins University Press, 2014).

13. Keir Keightley, "Reconsidering Rock," in *The Cambridge Companion to Pop and Rock,* ed. Simon Frith, Will Straw, and John Street (Cambridge: Cambridge University Press, 2001), 109–142; Grace Elizabeth Hale, *A Nation of Outsiders: How the White Middle Class Fell in Love with Rebellion in Postwar America* (New York: Oxford University Press, 2010).

14. Michael J. Kramer, *The Republic of Rock: Music and Citizenship in the Sixties Counterculture* (Oxford: Oxford University Press, 2013); Susan Krieger, *Hip Capitalism* (Beverly Hills, CA: SAGE, 1979); Devon Powers, *Writing the Record: The Village Voice and the Birth of Rock Criticism* (Amherst: University of Massachusetts Press, 2013); Charles Perry, *The Haight-Ashbury: A History* (New York: Random House, 1984).

15. Greil Marcus, "Rock-a-Hula, Clarified," *Creem,* June 1971, 36–52; Lester Bangs, "James Taylor Marked for Death," *Who Put the Bomp,* Winter-Spring 1971 and *Psychotic Reactions and Carburetor Dung,* ed. Greil Marcus (New York: Alfred A. Knopf, 1987), 53–81; David Browne, *Fire and Rain: The Beatles, Simon & Garfunkel, James Taylor, CSNY, and the Lost Story of 1970* (New York: Da Capo, 2011); Clinton Heylin, *From the Velvets to the Voidoids: The Birth of American Punk Rock,* 2d ed. (Chicago: Chicago Review Press, 2005); RJ Smith, *The One: The Life and Times of James Brown* (New York: Gotham, 2012).

16. *Almost Famous* (Universal City, CA: DreamWorks Home Entertainment, 2001), DVD; *Dazed & Confused* (1993; Universal City, CA: Universal Studios, 2004), DVD.

17. Fred Goodman, *The Mansion on the Hill: Dylan, Young, Geffen, Springsteen, and the Head-On Collision of Rock and Commerce* (New York: Times Books, 1997); Stephen Davis, *Hammer of the Gods: The Led Zeppelin Saga* (New York: William Morrow, 1985); Steve Waksman, "Heavy Music: Cock Rock, Colonialism, and Led Zeppelin," in *Instruments of Desire,* and *This Ain't the Summer of Love: Conflict and Crossover in Heavy Metal and Punk* (Berkeley: University of California Press, 2009); Susan Fast, *In the Houses of the Holy: Led Zeppelin and the Power of Rock Music* (New York: Oxford University Press, 2001); Eric Weisbard, *Top 40 Democracy: The Rival Mainstreams of American Music* (Chicago: University of Chicago Press, 2014).

18. Barney Hoskyns, *Waiting for the Sun: Strange Days, Weird Scenes, and the Sound of Los Angeles* (New York: St. Martin's Press, 1996) and *Hotel California: The True-Life Adventures of Crosby, Stills, Nash, Young, Mitchell, Taylor, Browne, Ronstadt, Geffen, the Eagles, and Their Many Friends* (Hoboken, NJ: Wiley, 2006); Sheila Weller, *Girls Like Us: Carole King, Joni Mitchell, Carly Simon—And the Journey of a Generation* (New York: Atria, 2008); Bruce J. Schulman, *The Seventies: The Great Shift in American Culture, Society, and Politics* (New York: Free Press, 2001).

19. Jimmy McDonough, *Shakey: Neil Young's Biography* (New York: Random House, 2002); Rolling Stone Magazine, *Neil Young: The Ultimate Compendium of Interviews, Articles, Facts, and Opinions from the Files of Rolling Stone* (New York: Macmillan, 1994); Stacey Luftig, *The Joni Mitchell Companion: Four Decades of Commentary* (New York: Schirmer Books, 2000); Michelle Mercer, *Will You Take Me as I Am: Joni Mitchell's Blue Period* (New York: Free Press, 2009); June Skinner Sawyers, ed., *Racing in the Street: The Bruce Springsteen Reader* (New York: Penguin, 2004); Paul Trynka, *David Bowie: Starman* (New York: Little, Brown, 2011); Peter Doggett, *The Man Who Sold the World: David Bowie and the 1970s* (New York: HarperCollins, 2012); Robert Christgau, *Christgau's Record Guide: Rock Albums of the '70s* (New Haven, CT: Ticknor &

Fields, 1981); Marcus, *Mystery Train*; Miller, *The Rolling Stone Illustrated History of Rock & Roll.*

20. Nelson George, *The Death of Rhythm & Blues* (New York: E. P. Dutton, 1988); Mark Anthony Neal, *What the Music Said: Black Popular Music and Black Public Culture* (New York: Routledge, 1999); Ward, *Just My Soul Responding*; Craig Werner, *Higher Ground: Stevie Wonder, Aretha Franklin, Curtis Mayfield, and the Rise and Fall of American Soul* (New York: Crown, 2004); Jason Toynbee, *Bob Marley: Herald of a Postcolonial World?* (Cambridge: Polity Press, 2007); Jan Reid, *The Improbable Rise of Redneck Rock* (1977; reprint Austin: University of Texas Press, 2004); Travis D. Stimeling, *Cosmic Cowboys and New Hicks: The Countercultural Sounds of Austin's Progressive Country Music Scene* (Oxford: Oxford University Press, 2011); Will Hermes, *Love Goes to Buildings on Fire: Five Years in New York That Changed Music Forever* (New York: Faber and Faber, 2011).

21. Jefferson Cowie, *Stayin' Alive: The 1970s and the Last Days of the Working Class* (New York: New Press, 2010); Edward Macan, *Rocking the Classics: English Progressive Rock and the Counterculture* (New York: Oxford University Press, 1997); Kevin Holm-Hudson, ed., *Progressive Rock Reconsidered* (New York: Routledge, 2002); Dick Hebdige, *Subculture: The Meaning of Style* (London: Methuen, 1979); Greil Marcus, *Lipstick Traces: A Secret History of the Twentieth Century* (Cambridge, MA: Harvard University Press, 1989); Jon Savage, *England's Dreaming: Anarchy, Sex Pistols, Punk Rock and Beyond* (New York: St. Martin's Press, 1992); Legs McNeil and Gillian McCain, *Please Kill Me: The Uncensored Oral History of Punk* (New York: Grove Press, 1996); Lester Bangs, "Where Were You When Elvis Died?," in *Village Voice*, August 29, 1977, and *Psychotic Reactions and Carburetor Dung*, 212–216.

22. Simon Frith, *Sound Effects: Youth, Leisure, and the Politics of Rock 'n' Roll* (New York: Pantheon, 1981); Alice Echols, *Shaky Ground: The Sixties and Its Aftershocks* (New York: Columbia University Press, 2002) and *Hot Stuff: Disco and the Remaking of American Culture* (New York: W. W. Norton, 2010); Tim Lawrence, *Love Saves the Day: A History of American Dance Music Culture, 1970–1979* (Durham, NC: Duke University Press, 2003); Peter Shapiro, *Turn the Beat Around: The Secret History of Disco* (New York: Faber & Faber, 2005); Theo Cateforis, *Are We Not New Wave? Modern Pop at the Turn of the 1980s* (Ann Arbor: University of Michigan Press, 2011).

23. Dave Marsh, *Glory Days: The Bruce Springsteen Story* (New York: Pantheon, 1987); Simon Frith, "The Real Thing—Bruce Springsteen," in *Music for Pleasure: Essays in the Sociology of Pop* (New York: Routledge, 1988), 94–101; Daniel Cavicchi, *Tramps Like Us: Music & Meaning among Springsteen Fans* (New York: Oxford University Press, 1998); Tipper Gore, *Raising PG Kids in an X-Rated Society* (New York: Bantam, 1988); Fredric Dannen, *Hit Men: Power Brokers and Fast Money Inside the Music Business* (New York: Times Books, 1990); Robert Walser, *Running with the Devil: Power, Gender, and Madness in Heavy Metal Music* (Hanover, NH: Wesleyan University Press, 1993); Chuck Klosterman, *Fargo Rock City: A Heavy Metal Odyssey in Rural North Dakota* (New York: Scribner, 2001).

24. Dave Rimmer, *Like Punk Never Happened: Culture Club and the New Pop* (London: Faber and Faber, 1985); Andrew Goodwin, *Dancing in the Distraction Factory: Music Television and Popular Culture* (Minneapolis: University of Minnesota Press, 1992); Carol Vernallis, *Experiencing Music Video: Aesthetics and Cultural Context* (New York: Columbia University Press, 2004); Rob Sheffield, *Talking to Girls about Duran Duran: One Young Man's Quest for True Love and a Cooler Haircut* (New York: Dutton, 2010); Craig Marks and Rob Tannenbaum, *I Want My MTV: The Uncensored Story of the Music Video Revolution* (New York: Dutton, 2011).

25. Kobena Mercer, "Monster Metaphors: Notes on Michael Jackson's 'Thriller,'" in *Sound and Vision: The Music Video Reader*, ed. Simon Frith, Andrew Goodwin, and Lawrence Grossberg (New York: Routledge, 1993), 93–108; Greg Tate, "I'm White!: What's Wrong with Michael Jackson," in *Flyboy in the Buttermilk: Essays on Contemporary America* (New York: Simon & Schuster, 1992), 95–99 and "Michael Jackson: The Man in Our Mirror," in *Best Music Writing 2010*, ed. Ann Powers (New York: Da Capo, 2010), 29–35; Jason King, "Michael Jackson: An Appreciation of His Talent," *Best Music Writing 2010*, 36–48; Susan Fast, *Michael Jackson's Dangerous* (New York: Bloomsbury, 2014); Michaelangelo Matos, *Sign "O" the Times* (New York: Continuum, 2004);

Touré, *I Would Die for You: Why Prince Became an Icon* (New York: Atria, 2013); Maureen Mahon, *Right to Rock: The Black Rock Coalition and the Cultural Politics of Race* (Durham, NC: Duke University Press, 2004); Susan McClary, "Living to Tell: Madonna's Resurrection of the Fleshly," in *Feminine Endings: Music, Gender, & Sexuality* (Minneapolis: University of Minnesota Press, 1991); Lisa Frank and Paul Smith, eds., *Madonnarama: Essays in Sex and Popular Culture* (Pittsburgh, PA: Cleis Press, 1993); Carol Benson and Allan Metz, eds., *The Madonna Companion: Two Decades of Commentary* (New York: Schirmer Books, 1999); Lucy O'Brien, *Madonna: Like an Icon* (New York: Bantam, 2007); Michele Alexander, *The New Jim Crow: Mass Incarceration in the Age of Colorblindness* (New York: New Press, 2010); Susan Faludi, *Backlash: The Undeclared War Against American Women* (New York: Crown, 1991); Gil Troy, *Morning in America: How Ronald Reagan Invented the 1980's* (Princeton, NJ: Princeton University Press, 2005).

26. David Toop, *The Rap Attack: African Jive to New York Hip Hop* (Boston: Serpent's Tail, 1984); Tricia Rose, *Black Noise: Rap Music and Black Culture in Contemporary America* (Hanover, NH: Wesleyan University Press, 1994); Raquel Cepeda, ed., *And It Don't Stop: The Best American Hip-Hop Journalism of the Past 25 Years* (New York: Faber and Faber, 2004); Jeff Chang, *Can't Stop Won't Stop: A History of the Hip-Hop Generation* (New York: St. Martin's Press, 2005); Dan Charnas, *The Big Payback: The History of the Business of Hip-Hop* (New York: New American Library, 2010); Murray Forman and Mark Anthony Neal, eds., *That's the Joint: The Hip-Hop Studies Reader*, 2d ed. (New York: Routledge, 2012).

27. Robert Duncan, *The Noise: Notes from a Rock 'n' Roll Era* (New York: Ticknor & Fields, 1984); Deena Weinstein, *Heavy Metal: A Cultural Sociology* (New York: Lexington Books, 1991); Chuck Eddy, *Stairway to Hell: The 500 Best Heavy Metal Albums in the Universe* (New York: Harmony, 1991); Donna Gaines, *Teenage Wasteland: Suburbia's Dead End Kids* (New York: Pantheon Books, 1991); Walser, *Running with the Devil*; Klosterman, *Fargo Rock City*; Waksman, *This Ain't the Summer of Love*; Weisbard, *Top 40 Democracy*.

28. Lawrence Grossberg, *Dancing in Spite of Myself: Essays on Popular Culture* (Durham, NC: Duke University Press, 1997); George Lipsitz, *Time Passages: Collective Memory and American Popular Culture* (Minneapolis: University of Minnesota Press, 1990); Bernard Gendron, *Between Montmartre and the Mudd Club: Popular Music and the Avant-Garde* (Chicago: University of Chicago Press, 2002); Gina Arnold, *Route 666: On the Road to Nirvana* (New York: St. Martin's Press, 1993); Michael Azerrad, *Our Band Could Be Your Life: Scenes from the American Indie Underground 1981–1991* (New York: Little, Brown), 2001.

29. Glenn Pillsbury, *Damage Incorporated: Metallica and the Production of Musical Identity* (New York: Routledge, 2006); Ryan Moore, *Sells Like Teen Spirit: Music, Youth Culture, and Social Crisis* (New York: New York University Press, 2009); Joshua Clover, *1989: Bob Dylan Didn't Have This to Sing About* (Berkeley: University of California Press, 2009); Rob Sheffield, *Love Is a Mix Tape: Life and Loss, One Song at a Time* (New York: Crown, 2007).

30. Alan Light, ed., *The Vibe History of Hip-Hop* (New York: Three Rivers Press, 1999); Eric Weisbard with Craig Marks, eds., *Spin Alternative Record Guide* (New York: Vintage, 1995); Will Hermes, ed., *Spin: 20 Years of Alternative Music: Original Writing on Rock, Hip-hop, Techno, and Beyond* (New York: Three Rivers Press, 2005); Bruce Feiler, *Dreaming Out Loud: Garth Brooks, Wynonna Judd, Wade Hayes, and the Changing Face of Nashville* (New York: Avon Books, 1998); David Hesmondhalgh, *The Cultural Industries*, 3d ed. (London: SAGE, 2012); Timothy Dowd, "Concentration and Diversity Revisited: Production Logic and the U.S. Mainstream Recording Market, 1940-1990," *Social Forces* 82 (2004): 1411–1455.

31. Wendy Fonarow, *Empire of Dirt: The Aesthetics and Rituals of British Indie Music* (Hanover, NH: Wesleyan University Press, 2006); Stephen Duncombe, *Notes from Underground: Zines and the Politics of Alternative Culture*, 2d ed. (Bloomington, IN: Microcosm Publishing, 2008); Eithne Quinn, *Nuthin' but a "G" Thang: The Culture and Commerce of Gangsta Rap* (New York: Columbia University Press, 2004); Keith Negus, *Music Genres and Corporate Cultures* (New York: Routledge, 1999).

32. Sara Marcus, *Girls to the Front: The True Story of the Riot Grrrl Revolution* (New York: Harper-Perennial, 2010); Carrie Brownstein, *Hunger Makes Me a Modern Girl: A Memoir* (New York:

Riverhead Books, 2015); O'Dair, *Trouble Girls*; Evelyn McDonnell and Ann Powers, eds., *Rock She Wrote: Women Write about Rock, Pop and Rap* (New York: Delta, 1995); Sheila Whitely, ed., *Sexing the Groove: Popular Music and Gender* (New York: Routledge, 1997); Mary A. Bufwack and Robert K. Oermann, *Finding Her Voice: Women in Country Music, 1800–2000* (Nashville, TN: Vanderbilt University Press, 2003); Pamela Fox, *Natural Acts: Gender, Race, and Rusticity in Country Music* (Ann Arbor: University of Michigan Press, 2009).

33. Moore, *Sells Like Teen Spirit*; V/A, "Special Report: Woodstock '99: How Three Days of Music Erupted into Fire, Rape and Riot," *Spin*, November 1999; Charles Aaron, "What the White Boy Means When He Says Yo," *Spin*, November 1998, and Cepeda, *And It Don't Stop*, 211–237; Joan Morgan, *When Chickenheads Come Home to Roost: A Hip-hop Feminist Breaks It Down* (New York: Simon & Schuster, 1999); Imani Perry, *Prophets of the Hood: Politics and Poetics in Hip-Hop* (Durham, NC: Duke University Press, 2004); Mark Anthony Neal, *Looking for Leroy: Illegible Black Masculinities* (New York: New York University Press, 2013); Eric Lott, *Love and Theft: Blackface Minstrelsy and the American Working Class* (New York: Oxford University Press, 1993); Simon Frith, *Performing Rites: On the Value of Popular Music* (Cambridge, MA: Harvard University Press, 1996).

34. Gayle Wald, "'I Want It That Way': Teenybopper Music and the Girling of Boy Bands," *Genders* 35 (Spring 2001); John Seabrook, *The Song Machine: Inside the Hit Factory* (W. W. Norton, 2015); Vanessa Grigoriadis, "The Tragedy of Britney Spears," *Rolling Stone*, February 21, 2008, and Greil Marcus, ed., *Best Music Writing 2009* (New York: Da Capo Press, 2009), 115–141.

35. Simon Reynolds, *Generation Ecstasy: Into the World of Techno and Rave* (Boston: Little, Brown, 1998); Sarah Thornton, *Club Cultures: Music, Media and Subcultural Capital* (Hanover, NH: Wesleyan University Press, 1996); for reception of Radiohead's shift away from rock, contrast Brent DiCrescenzo, 10.0/10 review of *Kid A*, *Pitchfork*, October 2, 2000, and Nick Hornby, "Beyond the Pale," *New Yorker*, October 30, 2000; Grant Alden and Peter Blackstock, eds., *The Best of No Depression: Writing about American Music* (Austin: University of Texas Press, 2005);

Richard A. Peterson and Bruce A. Beal, "Alternative Country: Origins, Music, Worldview, Fans, and Taste in Genre Formation," *Popular Music and Society* 25.1–2 (2001): 233–249; Barbara Ching, "Going Back to the Old Mainstream: *No Depression*, Robbie Fulks, and Alt.Country's Muddied Waters," in *A Boy Named Sue: Gender and Country Music*, ed. Kristine M. McCusker and Diane Pecknold (Jackson: University Press of Mississippi, 2004), 178–195; Degen Pener, *The Swing Book* (New York: Hachette, 1999); Bill Milkowski, *Swing It: An Annotated History of Jive* (New York: Billboard Books, 2001); Mark Anthony Neal, *Soul Babies: Black Popular Culture and the Post-Soul Aesthetic* (New York: Routledge, 2002).

36. Sasha Frere-Jones, "1+1+1+1=1: The New Math of Mashups," *New Yorker*, January 10, 2005, and Theo Cateforis, ed., *The Rock History Reader*, 2d ed. (New York: Routledge, 2013), 339–342; Aram Sinnreich, *Mashed Up: Music, Technology, and the Rise of Configurable Culture* (Amherst: University of Massachusetts Press, 2010); Simon Reynolds, *Retromania: Pop Culture's Addiction to Its Own Past* (New York: Faber & Faber, 2011).

37. Henry Jenkins, *Convergence Culture: Where Old and New Media Collide* (New York: New York University Press, 2006); Katherine Meizel, *Idolized: Music, Media, and Identity in American Idol* (Bloomington: Indiana University Press, 2011); Karen Tongson, "The Grain of Glee," *In Media Res*, April 5, 2010.

38. Stephen Witt, *How Music Became Free: The End of an Industry, the Turn of the Century, and the Patient Zero of Music Piracy* (New York: Viking, 2015); Anita Elberse, *Blockbusters: Hit-Making, Risk-Taking, and the Big Business of Entertainment* (New York: Henry Holt, 2013); Kiri Miller, *Playing Along: Digital Games, YouTube, and Virtual Performance* (New York: Oxford University Press, 2011).

39. Kelefa Sanneh, "Jay-Z and the Rise of Corporate Rap," *New Yorker*, August 20, 2001; Jay-Z, *Decoded* (New York: Spiegel & Grau, 2010); Jon Caramanica, "Behind Kanye's Mask," *New York Times*, June 11, 2013; Daphne A. Brooks, "'All That You Can't Leave Behind': Black Female Soul Singing and the Politics of Surrogation in the Age of Catastrophe," *Meridians: Feminism, Race, Transnationalism* 8.1 (2007): 180–204; Emily J. Lordi, "Beyoncé's Boundaries," *New*

Black Man, December 18, 2013; Rachel Kaadzi Ghansah, "How Sweet It Is to Be Loved by You: The BeyHive," *NPR: The Record*, March 1, 2014; Jody Rosen, "Platinum Underdog: Why Taylor Swift Is the Biggest Pop Star in the World," *New York Magazine*, November 17, 2013; Tavi Gevinson, "Just Kidding, Love Sucks: Notes on Taylor Swift," *The Believer*, July/August, 2013; Lindsay Zoladz, "On Adele's 25, Pop's Old Soul Goes Modern Enough to Keep Things Interesting," *Vulture.com*, November 20, 2015.

40. Gabriel Rossman, *Climbing the Charts: What Radio Airplay Tells Us about the Diffusion of Innovation* (Princeton, NJ: Princeton University Press, 2012); Michaelangelo Matos, *The Underground Is Massive: How Electronic Dance Music Conquered America* (New York: Dey Street Books, 2015); Kelefa Sanneh, "The Rap Against Rockism," *New York Times*, October 31, 2004.

41. JungBong Choi and Roald Maliangkay, eds., *K-pop: The International Rise of the Korean Music Industry* (New York: Routledge, 2015); Kyung Hyun Kim and Youngmin Choe, eds., *The Korean Popular Culture Reader* (Durham, NC: Duke University Press, 2014); Judith Halberstam, *Gaga Feminism: Sex, Gender, and the End of Normal* (Boston: Beacon, 2012); Charnas, *The Big Payback*; Raquel Rivera, Wayne Marshall, and Deborah Pacini Hernandez, eds., *Reggaeton* (Durham, NC: Duke University Press, 2009); Maura Johnston, "Wimpy White Dudes with Guitars Ruined American Idol," *The Concourse*, May 13, 2015, and "How This Summer's Monumentour Testifies to the Resilient Role of Rock 'n' Roll," *Indy Week*, July 16, 2014; Chris Molanphy, "100 & Single: The R&B/Hip-Hop Factor in the Music Business's Endless Slump," *Village Voice*, July 16, 2012.

42. Motti Regev, *Pop-Rock: Aesthetic Cosmopolitanism in Late Modernity* (Malden, MA: Polity Press, 2013); Scott Plagenhoef and Ryan Schreiber, eds., *The Pitchfork 500: Our Guide to the Greatest Songs from Punk to the Present* (New York: Simon & Schuster, 2008); Richard Lloyd, *Neo-Bohemia: Art and Commerce in the Postindustrial City* (New York: Routledge, 2005); Greg Tate, "How #BlackLivesMatter Changed Hip-Hop and R&B in 2015," *Rolling Stone*, December 16, 2015; Jon Caramanica, "Drake: Rapper, Actor, Meme," *New York Times*, October 23, 2015; Zandria F. Robinson, "Beyoncé's Black Southern Formation,"

Rolling Stone, February 8, 2016; Jessica Hopper, *The First Collection of Criticism by a Living Female Rock Critic* (Chicago: Featherproof Books, 2015).

43. For compendia of writing on rock and pop, including early accounts, see David Brackett, ed., *The Pop, Rock, and Soul Reader: Histories and Debates*, 3d ed. (New York: Oxford University Press, 2013); Cateforis, *The Rock History Reader*; Hanif Kureishi and Jon Savage, eds., *The Faber Book of Pop* (London: Faber and Faber, 1995); Arnold Shaw, *The Rockin' 50s: The Decade That Transformed the Pop Music Scene* (New York: Hawthorn, 1974); Charles Hamm, *Putting Popular Music in Its Place* (New York: Cambridge University Press, 1995); Ennis, *The Seventh Stream*; Peterson, "Why 1955?"

44. Nik Cohn, *Awopbopaloobop Alopbamboom: The Golden Age of Rock* (1969; reprint New York: Grove Press, 2001); Gillett, *The Sound of the City*.

45. Miller, *The Rolling Stone Illustrated History*; Marcus, *Mystery Train*; Nick Tosches, *Hellfire: The Jerry Lee Lewis Story* (New York: Dell, 1982) and Guralnick, *Last Train to Memphis*.

46. Willis, *Out of the Vinyl Deeps*; Christgau, *Christgau's Record Guide: Rock Albums of the '70s*; Bangs, *Psychotic Reactions*; DeCurtis, *Blues & Chaos: The Music Writing of Robert Palmer*; Dave Marsh, *The Heart of Rock & Soul: The 1001 Greatest Singles Ever Made* (New York: Plume, 1989); Booth, *The True Adventures of the Rolling Stones*; Richard Meltzer, *The Aesthetics of Rock* (1970; reprint New York: Da Capo, 1987). For collections, focused on earlier writers, see William McKeen, ed., *Rock and Roll Is Here to Stay: An Anthology* (New York: W. W. Norton, 2000); Clinton Heylin, ed., *The Penguin Book of Rock & Roll Writing* (New York: Penguin, 1992). For histories, Powers, *Writing the Record*; Gendron, *Between Montmartre and the Mudd Club*; DeRogatis, *Let It Blurt: The Life and Times of Lester Bangs, America's Greatest Rock Critic* (New York: Broadway Books, 2000); Robert Christgau, *Going into the City: Portrait of a Critic as a Young Man* (New York: Dey Street Books, 2015).

47. George, *The Death of Rhythm & Blues*; Tate, *Flyboy in the Buttermilk*; Phyl Garland, *The Sound of Soul* (Chicago: H. Regnery, 1969).

48. Powers and McDonnell, *Rock She Wrote*; O'Dair, *Trouble Girls*.

49. Toop, *The Rap Attack*; Light, *Vibe History of Hip-Hop*; Cepeda, *And It Don't Stop*; Morgan, *When*

Chickenheads Come Home to Roost; Sacha Jenkins et al., eds., *Ego Trip Book of Rap Lists* (New York: St. Martin's Griffin, 1999); Chang, *Can't Stop Won't Stop*; Charnas, *The Business of Hip-Hop*; Jim Fricke, *Yes Yes Y'All: The Experience Music Project Oral History of Hip-Hop's First Decade* (New York: Da Capo Press, 2002).

50. Weisbard, *Spin Alternative Record Guide*; Sheffield, *Love Is a Mix Tape*; Chuck Eddy, *Rock and Roll Always Forgets: A Quarter-Century of Music Criticism* (Durham, NC: Duke University Press, 2011); Klosterman, *Fargo Rock City*; Clover, *1989*; Hermes, *Love Goes to Buildings on Fire*; Reynolds, *Generation Ecstasy*.

51. Jerry Hopkins and Daniel Sugarman, *No One Here Gets Out Alive* (New York: Warner, 1980); Davis, *Hammer of the Gods*; Marsh, *Glory Days*; Dannen, *Hit Men*; Tommy Lee et al., with Neil Strauss, *The Dirt: Confessions of the World's Most Notorious Rock Band* (New York: Regan, 2001); David Ritz, *Divided Soul: The Life of Marvin Gaye* (New York: McGraw-Hill, 1985); James and Ritz, *Rage to Survive*.

52. For overviews, see Simon Frith and Andrew Goodwin, eds., *Rock, Pop, and the Written Word* (New York: Pantheon, 1990); David Hesmond-halgh and Keith Negus, eds., *Popular Music Studies* (London: Arnold, 2002); Simon Frith, ed., *Popular Music: Critical Concepts in Media and Cultural Studies* (New York: Routledge, 2004); Andy Bennett, Barry Shank, and Jason Toynbee, eds., *The Popular Music Studies Reader* (New York: Routledge, 2006).

53. Simon Frith, *Taking Popular Music Seriously: Selected Essays* (Burlington, VT: Ashgate, 2007); Lott, *Love and Theft*; Grossberg, *Dancing in Spite of Myself*; Hebdige, *Subculture*; Paul Gilroy, *The Black Atlantic: Modernity and Double Consciousness* (Cambridge, MA: Harvard University Press, 1993); Iain Chambers, *Urban Rhythms: Pop Music and Popular Culture* (New York: St. Martin's Press, 1985); Angela McRobbie, *Postmodernism and Popular Culture* (New York: Routledge, 1994); Thornton, *Club Cultures*; Negus, *Music Genres and Corporate Cultures*; Keightley, "Reconsidering Rock."

54. Rose, *Black Noise*; Neal, *What the Music Said*; Guthrie P. Ramsey Jr., *Race Music: Black Cultures from Bebop to Hip-Hop* (Berkeley: University of California Press, 2003); Fred Moten, *In the Break: The Aesthetics of the Black Radical Tradition*

(Minneapolis: University of Minnesota Press, 2003); Perry, *Prophets of the Hood*; Bakari Kitwana, *The Rap on Gangsta Rap* (Chicago: Third World Press, 1994); Lipsitz, *Time Passages*; Josh Kun, *Audiotopia: Music, Race, and America* (Berkeley: University of California Press, 2005).

55. McClary, *Feminine Endings*; Walser, *Running with the Devil*; David Brackett, *Interpreting Popular Music* (Berkeley: University of California Press, 2000); Charles Keil and Steven Feld, *Music Grooves: Essays and Dialogues* (Chicago: University of Chicago Press, 1994); Joseph G. Schloss, *Making Beats: The Art of Sample-Based Hip-Hop* (Middletown, CT: Wesleyan University Press, 2004); Cavicchi, *Tramps Like Us*; Susan D. Crafts et al., *My Music* (Hanover, NH: Wesleyan University Press, 1993); John Covach and Graeme M. Boone, *Understanding Rock: Essays in Musical Analysis* (New York: Oxford University Press, 1997); Allan Moore, *Rock, the Primary Text: Developing a Musicology of Rock* (Brookfield, VT: Ashgate, 2001); Fast, *Houses of the Holy*; Albin Zak, *The Poetics of Rock: Cutting Tracks, Making Records* (Berkeley: University of California Press, 2001); Theodore Gracyk, *Rhythm and Noise: An Aesthetics of Rock* (Durham, NC: Duke University Press, 1997).

56. Will Straw, "Systems of Articulation, Logics of Change: Scenes and Communities in Popular Music," *Cultural Studies* 5.3 (October 1991): 361–375; Barry Shank, *Dissonant Identities: The Rock 'n' Roll Scene in Austin, Texas* (Hanover, NH: Wesleyan University Press, 1994); Sara Cohen, *Rock Culture in Liverpool: Popular Music in the Making* (New York: Oxford University Press, 1991); Keith Kahn-Harris, *Extreme Metal: Music and Culture on the Edge* (New York: Berg, 2007); Lloyd, *Neo-Bohemia*; Holly Kruse, *Site and Sound: Understanding Independent Music Scenes* (New York: Peter Lang, 2003); Andy Bennett and Richard Peterson, eds., *Music Scenes: Local, Trans-local and Virtual* (Nashville, TN: Vanderbilt University Press, 2004).

57. Sanneh, "The Rap Against Rockism"; Douglas Wolk, "Thinking about Rockism," *Seattle Weekly*, May 4, 2005; Jody Rosen, "The Perils of Pop-timism," *Slate*, May 9, 2006; Daphne A. Brooks, "The Write to Rock: Racial Mythologies, Feminist Theory, and the Pleasures of Rock Music Criticism," *Women and Music: A Journal of Gender and Culture* 12 (2008): 54–62; Miles

Park Grier, "Said the Hooker to the Thief: 'Some Way Out' of Rockism," *Journal of Popular Music Studies* 25.1 (March 2013): 31–55; Carl Wilson, *Let's Talk about Love: A Journey to the End of Taste* (New York: Continuum, 2007); Wald, *How the Beatles Destroyed Rock 'n' Roll*. See also essays first presented at the EMP Pop Conference, collected in Eric Weisbard, ed., *This Is Pop: In Search of the Elusive at Experience Music Project* (Cambridge, MA: Harvard University Press, 2004); *Listen Again: A Momentary History of Pop Music* (Durham, NC: Duke University Press, 2007); and *Pop When the World Falls Apart: Music in the Shadow of Doubt* (Durham, NC: Duke University Press, 2012).

58. Lawrence, *Love Saves the Day*; Echols, *Hot Stuff*; Diane Pecknold, *The Selling Sound: The Rise of the Country Music Industry* (Durham, NC: Duke University Press, 2007) and McCusker and Pecknold, *A Boy Named Sue*; David Suisman, *Selling Sounds: The Commercial Revolution in American Music* (Cambridge, MA: Harvard University Press, 2009); Miller, *Segregating Sound*; Barry Mazor, *Ralph Peer and the Making of Popular Roots Music* (Chicago: Chicago Review Press, 2014); Comentale, *Sweet Air*; Marybeth Hamilton, *In Search of the Blues* (New York: Basic Books, 2008); Kramer, *The Republic of Rock*; Hugh Barker and Yuval Taylor, *Faking It: The Quest for Authenticity in Popular Music* (New York: W. W. Norton, 2007); Charles Hughes, *Country Soul: Making Music and Making Race in the American South* (Chapel Hill, NC: University of North Carolina Press, 2015); Waksman, *This Ain't the Summer of Love*; Mitchell Morris, *The Persistence of Sentiment: Display and Feeling in Popular Music of the 1970s* (Berkeley: University of California Press, 2013); Kajikawa, *Sounding Race in Rap*; Charles Hiroshi Garrett, ed., *The Grove Dictionary of American Music*, 2d ed. (New York: Oxford University Press, 2013); Ned Sublette, *Cuba and Its Music: From the First Drums to the Mambo* (Chicago: Chicago Review Press, 2004); Alexandra T. Vazquez, *Listening in Detail: Performances of Cuban Music* (Durham, NC: Duke University Press, 2013); Michelle Habell-Pallán, *Loca Motion: The Travels of Chicana and Latina Popular Culture* (New York: New York University Press, 2005); Deborah Paredez, *Selenidad: Selena, Latinos, and the Performance of Memory* (Durham, NC: Duke University Press,

2009); Deborah Vargas, *Dissonant Divas in Chicana Music: The Limits of La Onda* (Minneapolis: University of Minnesota Press, 2012); Dolores Inés Casillas, *Sounds of Belonging: U.S. Spanish-Language Radio and Public Advocacy* (New York: New York University Press, 2014); Deborah Pacini Hernandez, *Oye Como Va! Hybridity and Identity in Latino Popular Music* (Philadelphia: Temple University Press, 2010); see too George Lipsitz, *Footsteps in the Dark: The Hidden Histories of Popular Music* (Minneapolis: University of Minnesota Press, 2007).

59. Berry, *The Autobiography*; Ronnie Spector with Vince Waldren, *Be My Baby: How I Survived Mascara, Miniskirts, and Madness, or My Life as a Fabulous Ronette* (New York: Harmony Books, 1990); Tommy James with Martin Fitzpatrick, *Me, the Mob, and the Music: One Helluva Ride with Tommy James and the Shondelles* (New York: Scribner, 2010); Dylan, *Chronicles*; Richards, *Life*; Pamela DesBarres, *I'm with the Band: Confessions of a Groupie* (New York: William Morrow Company, 1987); Loretta Lynn with George Vecsey, *Coal Miner's Daughter* (Chicago: Regnery, 1976); Aerosmith with Stephen Davis, *Walk This Way: The Autobiography of Aerosmith* (New York: Avon, 1997); Patti Smith, *Just Kids* (New York: Ecco, 2010); McNeil and McCain, *Please Kill Me*; Viv Albertine, *Clothes, Clothes, Clothes: Music, Music, Music: Boys, Boys, Boys: A Memoir* (New York: Thomas Dunne, 2014); Nile Rodgers, *Le Freak: An Upside Down Story of Family, Disco, and Destiny* (New York: Spiegel & Grau, 2014); Kristin Hersh, *Rat Girl* (New York: Penguin, 2010); Jay-Z, *Decoded*; Questlove with Ben Greenman, *Mo' Meta Blues: The World According to Questlove* (New York: Grand Central Publishing, 2013); Brownstein, *Hunger Makes Me a Modern Girl*.

60. *Good Rockin' Tonight: The Legacy of Sun Records* (Chatsworth, CA: Image Entertainment, 2002), DVD; *Elvis: That's the Way It Is* (1970; Burbank, CA: Warner Home Video, 2007), DVD; *The Beatles: The First U.S. Visit* (1964; Hollywood, CA: Capitol Records, 2003), DVD; *TAMI Show* (1964; Los Angeles: Shout Factory, 2010), DVD; *Don't Look Back* (1967; New York: Docurama, 1999), DVD; *Monterey Pop* (1968; Santa Monica, CA: Criterion, 2006), DVD; *Woodstock* (1969; Burbank, CA: Warner Bros. Pictures, 2009), DVD; *Gimme Shelter* (1970;

Santa Monica, CA: Criterion, 2000), DVD; *Soul Power* (2008; Culver City, CA: Sony Pictures Home Entertainment, 2010), DVD; *Wattstax* (1974; Burbank, CA: Warner Home Video, 2004), DVD; *The Song Remains the Same* (1976; Burbank, CA: Warner Home Video, 1999), DVD; *Tommy* (1975; New York: Columbia TriStar Home Video, 2009), DVD; *Ziggy Stardust and the Spiders from Mars: The Motion Picture* (1973; New York: EMI Records, 2002), DVD; *The Last Waltz* (1978; Santa Monica, CA: MGM Home Entertainment, 2002), DVD; *The Blank Generation* (1976; Oaks, PA: MVD Visual, 2001), DVD; *The Filth and the Fury* (Los Angeles: New Line Home Video, 2000), DVD; *The Decline of Western Civilization* (1981; Los Angeles: Shout Factory, 2015), DVD; *Stop Making Sense* (1984; New York: Palm Pictures, 1999), DVD; *Purple Rain* (1984; Burbank, CA: Warner Home Video, 1997), DVD; *Madonna: Truth or Dare* (1991; Santa Monica, CA: Artisan Home Entertainment, Inc., 1999), DVD; *The Decline of Western Civilization, Part II: The Metal Years* (1988; Los Angeles: Shout Factory, 2015), DVD; *Heavy Metal Parking Lot* (1986: Factory 515, 2005), DVD; *Style Wars* (1983; Los Angeles: Public Art Films, 2003), DVD; *Rhyme & Reason* (1997; Burbank, CA: Buena Vista Home Entertainment, 2000), DVD; *Planet Rock: The Story of Hip-Hop and the Crack Generation* (New York: VH1 Docs, 2010), DVD; *1991: The Year Punk Broke* (1992; Santa Monica, CA: Universal Home Entertainment, 2011); *Hype!* (1996; Santa Monica, CA: Lions Gate Home Entertainment, 2004); *Meeting People Is Easy* (Hollywood, CA; Capitol, 1999), DVD; *Some Kind of Monster* (Hollywood, CA: Paramount, 2005), DVD; *The Punk Singer* (New York: IFC Films, 2014), DVD; *Shut Up and Play the Hits* (New York: Oscilloscope Laboratories, 2012), DVD; *I Am Trying to Break Your Heart* (New York, Plexigroup, 2003), DVD.

61. *The History of Rock 'n' Roll* (1995; Burbank, CA: Warner Home Video, 2004), DVD; WGBH's 1995 series *Rock & Roll* for PBS, produced in partnership with the BBC, with VHS tapes made available to educators, has not been issued on DVD—likely for licensing reasons. There is, however, a bootleg version, and full clips are available on YouTube to download. How rock and roll is that?

Eric Weisbard

RAP MUSIC

Rap is the musical practice of hip-hop culture that features a vocalist, or master of ceremony (MC), reciting lyrics over a beat. Rap music is an example of what scholars have called polyculturalism, which refers to the notion that various racial and ethnic groups have historically exchanged and borrowed ideas and cultural practices.[1] Black and Latinx youth in New York City, many of them Caribbean immigrants, responded to poverty, urban renewal, deindustrialization, and inner-city violence by creating their own cultural practices—throwing parties featuring DJs playing breakbeats, MCs rapping and regulating the crowd, dancers breaking to the beat, and graffiti artists tagging trains and walls.

Historically, rap music and hip hop culture have been a male-dominated realm. Much of rap music performed by men has raised questions about masculinity because of the prominence of sexist, homophobic, and misogynist lyrics. The rap industry also suffers from gender inequities as fewer women have been able to pursue a lengthy career rapping and producing. This has not stopped women from participating despite often vacillating between the margins and center of rap music. This process has led women artists not only to use rap to critique sexism within the culture, but also to contribute to the development of intersectional feminism. Other marginalized groups such as genderqueer people have remained on the margins of the rap industry.

Rap music sparked new conversations about race and authenticity, gender, sexuality, and respectability, social problems such as police brutality, as well as Black and Latinx youth's relationship to politics, technology, and the economy. In addition, rap music reflects a running conversation and commentary on authenticity. The questions of who is a "real nigga" and what is "real hip hop" often intersect with masculinity, place and space, and aesthetics.[2] Rap also illustrates how inner-city youth repurposed music technology such as record players, records, mixers, and samplers to create a new genre of music. Rappers have also commented on their geographic location and politics, often highlighting racial discrimination and state violence. Critics have raised questions about the violent and misogynistic lyrics contained in rap culture, even going as far as to censor it.

But despite censorship and controversy, rap music is positioned centrally within American popular culture. Rappers have earned Academy Awards and have entered into the Rock and Roll Hall of Fame. Corporations use rap to market products to customers. Rap is featured in movies, television, and on Broadway. Rappers have also leveraged their success into accumulating large amounts of wealth and influence. And since 1973, the culture has spread beyond New York to all regions of the United States and throughout the world. Oppressed youth in places like Ghana, the United Kingdom, and Paris have adopted the cultural form in response to their particular surroundings.

THE BIRTH OF HIP HOP CULTURE AND RAP MUSIC, 1973–1979

Hip hop culture was born in a first floor recreation room at 1520 Sedgwick Avenue on August 13, 1973, in the Bronx, New York City. Clive Campbell, also known as DJ Kool Herc, spun records for his sister's party. Staying true to his Jamaican roots, he was known in the Bronx for having the loudest sound system. While Herc played a number of dancehall and funk records, including selections from James Brown's live albums, his friend Coke LaRock served as the master of ceremony, or the MC. Little did the Campbells know that their party featured several elements—DJ'ing, MC'ing, and dancing—of a new innovative culture.[3]

While many rap artists and scholars locate the birth of hip hop culture in the United States, the origins of the burgeoning genre

was always diasporic and polycultural.[4] Hip hop, in part, was the product of the migration of people and culture. The first three prominent DJs were born either in the Caribbean or into an immigrant family. Campbell and the other DJs such as Afrika Bambaataa brought elements of Caribbean DJ culture, such as loud mobile sound systems and "toasting," which referred to deejays talking over music. Hip hop also drew from other musical genres such as funk, disco, soul, and electronica. DJs sampled this music, which entailed using parts of songs or reinterpreting them.

The breakbeat formed the sonic backbone of rap music. Kool Herc discovered the break while deejaying. Herc noticed dancers enjoyed grooving to the intermittent drum break found within particular songs.[5] Deejays also enlisted MCs to assist in regulating the crowd. Emcees engaged the crowd by screaming rhyming catch-phrases and leading chants. Grandmaster Flash discovered the "scratch," another vital deejay technique that turned the turntable into an instrument. Kool Herc and Afrika Bambaataa also featured break dancers, many of whom were Puerto Rican and Latino, in their performances.[6]

Hip hop culture emerged in the context of New York City's economic restructuring during the 1970s. In that decade, fiscal crisis, deindustrialization, white flight, and urban renewal decimated the Bronx. The South Bronx shed tens of thousands of manufacturing jobs. Forty percent of the industrial sector disappeared. The youth unemployment rate rose to 60 percent. Urban renewal projects and the construction of the Cross-Bronx Expressway displaced African Americans and Puerto Ricans. Around 60,000 Bronx homes were razed during the 1960s and 1970s.[7] The decline of the Black Power movement, the rise of drug markets, and street gangs provided the backdrop for young blacks and Puerto Ricans who sought to make sense of their lives artistically during the late 1970s and early 1980s.

Deejays formed the base of hip hop culture during the 1970s. They organized parties and served as the primary artists. By the mid-1970s, DJs Kool Herc, Grandmaster Flash, and Afrika Bambaataa dominated the burgeoning hip hop scene. Grandmaster Flash, Afrika Bambaataa, and Herc controlled sections of the Bronx.[8]

Herc played in the nightclubs in East Bronx and in neighborhoods in the West. Grandmaster Flash and his Casanova Crew controlled the South Bronx from 138th to 163rd streets. However, Bambaataa saw hip hop culture as a path out of gang violence and an instrument of black and brown unity.[9] Inspired by a trip abroad and the movie, *Zulu*, Bambaataa formed the Universal Zulu Nation, which would draw from black nationalism and pan-African themes and sought to use hip hop as an organizing tool against gang violence.[10]

The number of DJs proliferated after the July 1977 blackout in New York City. During the 24-hour power outage, residents looted hundreds of stores and committed almost a thousand acts of arson.[11] Stores selling music equipment represented prime targets for many New Yorkers. Consequently, the blackout provided more aspiring DJs and artists greater access to necessary expensive equipment. Even DJ Grandmaster Caz, who performed that evening, admitted to going to the store where he first bought his equipment and taking a mixer.[12]

Women also helped shape the culture's founding. In 1977, Sheri Sher and seven other women formed the first all-women rap group, The Mercedes Ladies (Figure 1).

The Mercedes Ladies emerged out of the all-female crews that roamed the Bronx.[13] The group featured several MCs and DJs: Ever Def, Zena Z, Tracey T, RD Smiley, Baby D, MC Smiley, and DJ La Spank. The group encountered sexist treatment in the industry. Promoters tried to book the group without paying them. The Mercedes Ladies' attempts to break into the rap industry and to be

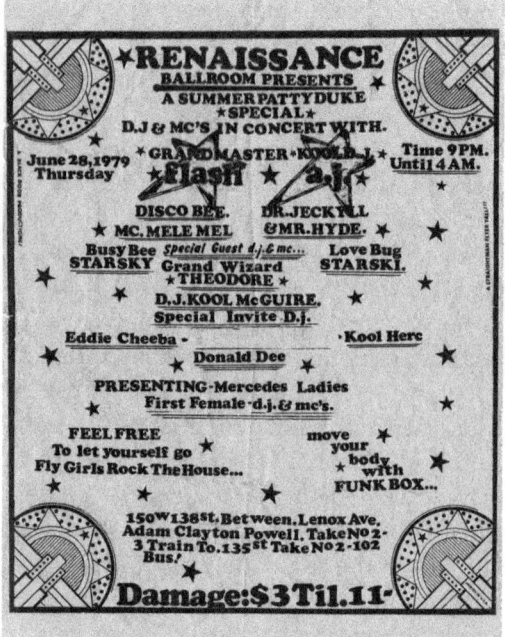

Figure 1. Event flier for a hip hop performance at the Renaissance Ballroom on June 28, 1979. The event featured several notable DJs and rappers, including Grandmaster Flash, Melle Mel, and the Mercedes Ladies, an all-woman hip hop group. Courtesy Cornell University Library Hip-Hop Collection. Hip Hop Party and Event Flyers. Ithaca, N.Y.: Cornell University Library, Division of Rare & Manuscript Collections, 2013.

compensated fairly anticipated the struggles that women artists generally faced.[14]

Rap music began its transition from moment to commodity in 1979. Before then, hip hop music was merely distributed through taped dance parties.[15] Former R&B singer-turned-record executive Sylvia Robinson released the genre's first record. With her career flailing, Robinson sought to capitalize on the growing rap phenomenon. She and her brother discovered Henry "Big Bank Hank" Jackson, a worker at a local pizzeria. Jackson then recruited two of his friends and formed the Sugar Hill Gang. Shortly after, Big Bank Hank, Wonder Mike, and Master Gee recorded the first rap song, "Rapper's Delight."

Rapping over Chic's "Good Times" instrumental, Sugar Hill Gang's "Rapper's Delight" put rap on record. Clocking in at over four-teen minutes, the song tried to capture the spirit of the original block parties. "Rapper's Delight" also introduced another tension in rap music that persisted—that of authentic-ity, what was "real" and what was not. To some DJs and MCs, hip hop could not be captured on record because it was a moment. Also, the Sugar Hill Gang was a manufac-tured group, while other collectives assem-bled out of prior relationships and in relation to specific conditions.

In the wake of the success of Sugar Hill Gang's "Rapper's Delight," Robinson signed three more rap groups to record singles, The Funky 4 + 1 (which included a woman, Sha Rock), The Treacherous Three, and an all-women rap group called The Sequence. Robinson's signings helped pave the way for women artists to record rap music. The Sequence included Cheryl Cook, also known as "Cheryl the Pearl," Gwendolyn Chisolm, known as "Blondie," and Angie Brown Stone, who went by "Angie B." The Sequence re-leased "Funk You Up" in December 1979. The Sequence challenged notions of rap as being thought of as an all-black male domain.[16]

Figure 2. Event flier for a hip hop performance at Walton High School on January 12, 1979. The event featured Grandmaster Flash and members of the Furious Five.

Courtesy Cornell University Library Hip-Hop Collection. Hip Hop Party and Event Flyers. Ithaca, N.Y.: Cornell University Library, Division of Rare & Manuscript Collections, 2013.

RAP MUSIC'S FIRST GOLDEN AGE, 1980–1991

While rap music's popularity increased among young African Americans, Latinxs, and whites, rap groups and solo rappers struggled to gain credibility among older black DJs and a skep-tical and discriminatory music industry. Yet, hip hop culture eventually expanded into other entertainment forms during the 1980s.

Rap was featured prominently in movies and documentaries throughout the 1980s. Released in 1983, *Style Wars* and *Wild Style* documented the lives of graffiti writers. *Krush Groove*, starring Blair Underwood as Russell Simmons, comically dramatized the found-ing of Def Jam Recordings. Rap music was on TV as well. For instance, *Yo! MTV Raps*

migrated from MTV Europe to the United States where it debuted in October 1987.[17]

Several releases in the early 1980s signaled the greater innovation of rap music. The DJ's influence decreased while the MC emerged as the focal point. Kurtis Blow's early success exemplified this development. His hit song, "The Breaks," was the first rap song to feature a chorus and a theme. The up-tempo disco rap track introduced wordplay as he used "the breaks" to list bad situations and decisions one makes in a daily basis.[18] Afrika Bambaataa and the Soul Sonic Force's "Planet Rock" and the rock band Blondie's "Rapture" illustrated the polyculturalism of rap music. "Rapture" included a rap verse from Debbie Harry, while the video featured her friend, graffiti artist Fred Brathwaite, also known as Fab 5 Freddy.[19] Afrika Bambaataa and the Soul Sonic Force sampled German electronic band Kraftwerk's "Trans Europa Express" in "Planet Rock," which tapped into afrofuturist themes.[20] Grandmaster Flash and the Furious Five's "The Message" illustrated how a socially conscious message could be expressed through rap. The first "reality" rap song, "The Message," captured the frustration of black and brown folks living in the midst of economic recession, inflation, urban divestment, and Reaganomics.

No group had a bigger impact on hip hop culture during this period than Run-DMC. The Queens-based group consisted of rappers Run, DMC, and DJ Jam Master Jay. Their first single, "It's Like That/Sucker MC's," sold 250,000 copies. Their 1987 *Raising Hell* sold three million albums. They distinguished themselves from other artists by wearing black leather jackets, black fedora hats, large gold chains, and Adidas sneakers. Run-DMC not only rapped over familiar breakbeats, but also they were the first rap artists to synthesize rap and rock music. Their third single from their 1984 self-titled debut album, "Rock Box," prominently featured riffs from guitarist Eddie Martinez. In 1986, Run-DMC's cover of Aerosmith's "Walk This Way" and the music video catapulted the group into the mainstream.[21]

In 1984, Russell Simmons, who also managed Run-DMC, and New York University (NYU) student and producer Rick Rubin, started Def Jam Recordings. They signed the first rap vocalist to cross over into mainstream stardom, a young Queens rapper who went by the name, LL Cool J. LL Cool J released his debut album, *Radio*, in November 1985. Simmons and Rubin also recruited a quartet of Jewish party-loving-punk rockers—Adam Horowitz, Adam Yauch, Michael Diamond, and drummer Kate Schellenbach—who called themselves the Beastie Boys.[22] The Beastie Boys' debut album, *Licensed to Ill*, sold more than a million records. Their early catalog featured punk-rock-influenced anthems such as "Fight for Your Right" and the frat boy humor featured in singles like "Hey Ladies." Despite

being one of the few Jewish, if not white, rap acts, the Beastie Boys illustrated how hip hop and punk rock emerged in the same historical, spatial, and political context.[23]

Some DJs such as Mr. Magic, Kool DJ Red Alert, and DJ Marley Marl became players in the industry. Mr. Magic and Marley Marl found themselves at the center of the genre's high-profile rap battles during the 1980s. The battle between MC Shan and Boogie Down Productions (BDP) vocalist, KRS One, centered on rap music's origins. MC Shan claimed in the song, "The Bridge," produced by Marley Marl, that hip hop began in Queens. KRS One pointed to Kool Herc and Coke LaRock's parties and Afrika Bambaataa's Zulu Nation as the progenitors of the culture in "South Bronx." KRS One effectively won the battle with "The Bridge Is Over" where he rapped over a dancehall track using a Jamaican accent, underlining the historical Caribbean–Bronx connection. Both songs appeared on BDP's debut album. *Criminal Minded*. While KRS One and Scot LaRock were the first to pose with guns on their album cover, Philadelphia's Schoolly D introduced listeners to "gangsta rap" with his song, "P.S.K.: What Does It Mean?"

It took longer for hip hop culture to take root in California than in New York. Many of the genre's stalwarts like Dr. Dre and Arabian Prince cut their teeth in Los Angeles's electronic DJ culture. Also, West Coast rap grew out of the decline of black social movements, street gangs such as the Crips and Bloods, the illicit drug economy, and the war on drugs. Producers such as Dr. Dre created a distinctive sound, which sampled 1970s funk and artists like Parliament Funkadelic. In 1986, Eric "Eazy-E" Wright founded Ruthless Records, which featured the group he and Dr. Dre founded, Niggaz Wit' Attitude (NWA). NWA included Eazy-E, Dr. Dre, Ice Cube, DJ Yella, and MC Ren. Ruthless Records also featured the all-woman group, J. J. Fad, whose platinum-selling album, Supersonic, provided the funding needed to release NWA's debut album, *Straight Outta Compton*. NWA's *Straight Outta Compton*, made NWA an instant cultural phenomenon. Their brash and vulgar gangsta style appealed not only to black youth, but also to young white men. The group generated controversy with their anti-police brutality song, "Fuck tha Police." The song prompted the FBI to send a letter demanding they stop performing the song. However, the Los Angeles Police Department's (LAPD's) killing of Eula Love in 1979 over a gas bill and their fifteen killings while using chokeholds during the early 1980s supported NWA's criticisms of policing.[24] Yet, while NWA appeared as another source of resistance against state violence, these songs appeared alongside others such as "A Bitch iz a Bitch" and "She Swallowed It," which contained sexist and misogynistic lyrics. Members of NWA lived out some of these lyrics. For instance, producer Dr. Dre physically assaulted rapper and journalist Dee Barnes in 1991.

During the 1980s, a few women rappers would move from the margins closer to the mainstream. Queensbridge's Roxanne Shante made a name for herself after confronting the rap group, U.T.F.O., for their song called "Roxanne, Roxanne," which was about a woman refusing their advances. She responded with "Roxanne's Revenge," where she claimed that she had better rap skills and that she would have "fired them" if they worked for her.[25] MC Lyte performed songs that captured the lived experiences of black women. The rap group, Salt-N-Pepa, was the first group of women performers to achieve mainstream success. The group included Salt, Pepa, and their DJ, Spinderella. Salt-n-Pepa's 1987 "Push It" was their breakout single. They commented on various issues of importance for many black women, notably sexism, relationships, and moral panics around sex and sexually transmitted diseases.[26]

Queen Latifah distinguished herself from other women rappers in the late 1980s by combining black nationalism and feminism in her lyrics. Latifah's and Monie Love's "Ladies First" represented the genre's first black feminist anthem.[27] Latifah also spoke out against domestic violence and sexism. Latifah and Salt-N-Pepa illustrated that black women could rap about a number of topics and could control their own image. Latifah's and Salt-N-Pepa's success did not preclude black women artists from being marginalized, however. The masculinism and corporatism of the rap industry represented a barrier of entry that many black women struggled to overcome.

RAP MUSIC, POLITICS, AND SAMPLING IN THE LATE 1980s

Like Queen Latifah, other rap artists and groups turned to black nationalism and racial solidarity as modes of expression. No group exemplified the adoption of Black Power iconography better than Def Jam signees, Public Enemy. The group ushered in a harder, more intellectual, black nationalistic, version of rap music. Public Enemy included Chuck D, the wacky Flavor Flav, DJ Terminator X, their version of the Fruit of Islam, the Security of the First World (S1W), and the production crew, the Bomb Squad. Their first four albums—*Yo! Bumrush the Show*, *It Takes a Nation of Millions to Hold Us Back*, *Fear of a Black Planet*, and *Apocalypse 91 ... The Enemy Strikes Black*—commented on a range of political issues, including black empowerment, racism in Hollywood, the history of minstrelsy, and police brutality. Public Enemy's "Fight the Power," which appeared on Spike Lee's *Do the Right Thing* soundtrack, is often recognized as one of the genre's iconic protest anthems. In the song, Chuck D took aim at America's cultural icons like Elvis and John Wayne and reminded listeners that those he admired were too radical to be mainstreamed by the media and the state.[28] Chuck D saw rap as more than just party and braggadocio music. It was a form through which African American artists could report on their surroundings and communicate politics. Rap music was "the Black CNN."[29]

The late 1980s also saw the rise of rap collectives such as the Juice Crew and the Native Tongues. The Native Tongues collective crafted and presented an aesthetic that departed drastically from dominant forms of hip hop masculinity and femininity. Rather than wearing large gold chains, Adidas sneakers, sweatsuits, or Los Angeles Raiders jackets, members of the collective often dressed in Afrocentric garb. The Native Tongues initially consisted of the Jungle Brothers, De La Soul, A Tribe Called Quest, Black Sheep, Monie Love, and Queen Latifah. A Tribe Called Quest's Q-Tip and Ali Shaheed Muhammad attended the same high school as Mike G and Afrika Baby Bam, members of the Jungle Brothers. Mike G's uncle, Kool DJ Red Alert, helped the Jungle Brothers and A Tribe Called Quest establish a foothold in the industry. The Native Tongues' rap style was playful, yet serious. Rather than the straightforwardness of Chuck D or the in-your-face style of NWA, the collective's songs often featured pro-black views, albeit subtly.[30]

Other rap acts, such as Houston's Geto Boys and the Miami-based 2 Live Crew, were ensnared in the culture wars during the early 1990s. Christian fundamentalist groups criticized the Geto Boys for their explicit lyrics detailing gruesome killings.[31] These groups also sought to pressure President George H. W. Bush to ban 2 Live Crew. Politician Jack Thompson claimed that 2 Live Crew violated obscenity laws. He successfully lobbied to get 2 Live Crew's album, *As Nasty As They Wanna Be*, banned in Broward County, Florida.[32] Luther Campbell and other members of 2 Live Crew were arrested in June 1990 in Hollywood, Florida, for performing songs on their album. They were eventually acquitted of the charges.[33] The dispute over obscenity raised the same questions about artistry and the first amendment as the FBI.'s dispute with NWA. Thompson continued his protests against Geto Boys.[34]

Sampling in hip hop changed as music technology transformed. Rather than just relying on techniques such as using two records and turntables to create a breakbeat, creating pause tapes, producers began using electronic samplers and beat machines such as the SK-1, SP-1200, and the Akai MPC. However, sampling became a point of contention among musicians, critics, and lawyers as artists sought to collect a share of profits. In 1991, Gilbert O'Sullivan sued Biz Markie over using a sample in "Alone Again." The 1960s rock group, The Turtles, settled with De La Soul for $1.7 million over the rap group sampling "You Showed Me."[35] Some musicians such as Mtume criticized rap producers' use of sampling. Stetasonic, rap's first act to perform with instrumentalists, responded by recording "Talking All That Jazz."[36] Disputes over different styles of sampling also generated debates around authenticity within the genre as producers such as Sean "Puff Daddy" Combs would rely more on samples recognized to the mainstream to craft songs.

HIP HOP GOES MAINSTREAM, 1990–1999

Rap music invaded American popular and political culture during the 1990s. By the end of the decade, rap simultaneously grew both more national and more regional. Publications such as *The Source*, *Vibe Magazine*, and *XXL*, as well as television shows such as *Yo! MTV Raps* and Black Entertainment Television's *Rap City*, helped construct what some have called the "hip hop nation."[37] At the same time, regionally based record labels and rap artists developed rap music that was distinct from New York's and California's sounds. This decade also saw the proliferation of black-run rap record labels, which were often subsidiaries of larger conglomerates.

Rap intersected with electoral politics during the early 1990s. For a politician such as Democratic presidential candidate Bill Clinton, confronting hip hop culture represented an opportunity to demonstrate that he would not back down in the face of racial politics.

In a conversation about the 1992 Los Angeles uprising with *Washington Post* journalist, David Mills, activist-rapper Lisa Williamson, also known as Sistah Souljah, wondered whether African Americans would be right to retaliate against white Americans in response to racism and police brutality. Clinton not only criticized Williamson's comments, but he equated her with white supremacist David Duke at a Rainbow Coalition gathering convened by Reverend Jesse Jackson in 1992. Many in politics labeled Clinton's criticism of Williamson as the "Sistah Souljah moment," an instance where a politician demonstrates "political courage" in the face of the excesses of racial politics. Clinton demonstrated that he was willing to stand up to rappers and Jesse Jackson while at a gathering Jackson organized.[38]

Ice-T's and Bodycount's "Cop Killer" thrust rap into debates about the First Amendment, censorship, and policing. In the recorded version of the song, Ice-T referenced the LAPD's beating of Rodney King. The song depicts Ice-T engaging in a revenge killing of a police officer in response to police violence against African Americans.[39] Police organizations, politicians, and other public figures protested Ice-T and Warner Brothers' refusal to censor the song. Vice President Dan Quayle, Tipper Gore, and Charlton Heston roundly criticized the song. Law enforcement organizations across the country protested.[40] The protests worked as stores pulled the record from their shelves. Ice-T took "Cop Killer" off the Bodycount record.[41] The response to "Cop Killer" produced a chilling effect on politically charged music as labels began to disinvest in promoting such music and forced artists such as Paris off of the label.[42]

The Staten Island, New York, group, Wu Tang Clan, revolutionized the rap industry. The nine-member group led by The RZA—GZA/Genius, Inspectah Deck, Raekwon, Ghostface Killa, Method Man, Ol' Dirty Bastard, U-God, and Masta Killa—announced themselves in October 1992 on the aggressive

single, "Protect Ya Neck."[43] The Wu Tang Clan's contractual arrangement with Loud Records altered the way rap groups interacted with record labels. Their contract allowed The Wu Tang Clan to sign as a collective while providing each member the freedom to sign individual deals with other record companies. The group's most charismatic member, Method Man, signed with Def Jam Records. Elektra Records signed Ol' Dirty Bastard, and GZA signed a deal with Geffen Records. Ghostface Killah signed with Epic Records, while Raekwon and Inspectah Deck stayed with Loud Records. The group released five solo albums between the Wu Tang Clan's first two releases, *Enter the Wu Tang (36 Chambers)* in 1993 and *Wu Tang Forever* in 1997. Each album not only showcased the individual artists' talents, but they continued to feature the rest of the group.

Lyricists and producers also innovated rap music. Dr. Dre unleashed his debut album, *The Chronic*, in 1992 after he left Ruthless Records for Suge Knight's Death Row Records. Songs like the Snoop Doggy Dogg-assisted "Nuthin' But a G Thang" exemplified the "G-Funk" sound. Dr. Dre and Snoop Doggy Dogg followed up The Chronic with his debut album, Doggystyle.

Queensbridge's Nasty Nas, released his debut album, *Illmatic* in 1994. Some critics refer to *Illmatic* as the greatest rap album of all time because of the combination of Nas's poetic rhymes and its sonic backdrop composed by multiple up-and-coming producers such as Main Source member Large Professor, DJ Premier from Gangstarr, A Tribe Called Quest's Q-Tip, and Pete Rock. Bad Boy Records also released Notorious BIG's debut album, *Ready to Die*, which put Notorious BIG and the label at the vanguard of East Coast and New York rap. The album marked the return of the use of blatant samples such as "Juicy," which sampled Mtume's "Juicy Fruit."[44]

The infamous rivalry between East and West Coast rappers, mainly between Death

Row and Bad Boy Records, consumed hip hop during the mid-1990s. The beef allegedly began the night of November 30, 1994, when several burglars ambushed, shot, and robbed Tupac Shakur at Quad Studios while the Notorious BIG recorded inside. Tupac was born in 1971 to Afeni Shakur, a member of the Black Panther Party. Shakur had garnered much notoriety for his rapping and acting before he was convicted of sexual assault. He released two albums, starred in movies *Above the Rim* and *Poetic Justice*, and appeared as a guest on *The Cosby Show*. Tupac was the wild card in the coastal dispute. In an interview with *Vibe Magazine* before his sentencing, Shakur implicated Sean Combs and the Notorious BIG in the robbery, charges they subsequently denied.[45]

Tensions between California and New York rappers spilled out in the open in 1995. While on stage at The Source Hip Hop Music Awards, Suge Knight called out Puff Daddy for overshadowing his artists in their videos.[46] Puff Daddy took a more conciliatory tone, stating that he was "proud" of Death Row.[47] Snoop Dogg's and Tha Dogg Pound's "NY, NY," escalated the rivalry. The song ridiculed New York City, and the video featured a giant Snoop Dogg kicking down the city's buildings. Queens-based Capone-n-Noreaga, Mobb Deep, and Tragedy Khadafi recorded a response, "L.A., L.A.," mocking Tha Dogg Pound's "New York, New York" song and video.

Tupac signed with Death Row Records after Suge Knight posted Tupac's $1.4 million bail. Soon after, Tupac released the double album, *All Eyez on Me*, which included the Dr. Dre-produced anthem, "California Love." He escalated the attacks, claiming to have slept with singer Faith Evans, Notorious BIG's wife, in the song, "Hit 'Em Up." Tupac also targeted other East Coast artists such as Mobb Deep, Nas, Jay-Z, Q-Tip, and De La Soul. The deaths of Tupac and Notorious BIG virtually ended the East Coast–West Coast rivalry. Tupac Shakur was gunned down in Las Vegas on September 7, 1996, and died of his wounds six days later. The Notorious B.I.G. met a similar fate in Los Angeles on March 9, 1997. He was shot while his vehicle was at a stoplight. Much mystery surrounded their deaths. It appeared that Shakur's death was related to a physical altercation with a gang member the night of his death. In Wallace's case, it is possible his killing was in retaliation for Shakur's death, although there is little substantiated evidence linking him, or Sean Combs, to it. Law enforcement failed to solve either murder.

Other rappers sought to position themselves as leading artists in the culture in the wake of Shakur's and the Notorious B.I.G.'s deaths. Rappers DMX, Jay Z, Nas, and Ja Rule were among those who sought to fill the void left by the two slain artists. Jay Z released a series of critically acclaimed albums on Roc-A-Fella Records, which he owned along with Damon "Dame" Dash and Kareem "Biggs" Burke. Jay Z earned a taste of the type of commercial success that he would enjoy later on his 1998 album, *Hard Knock Life*. DMX appeared to capture hip hop's zeitgeist on songs such as "Ruff Ryders Anthem" on his 1998 debut album, *It's Dark and Hell Is Hot*. DMX, like Shakur, rapped with intense emotion over dark beats crafted by producers like Swizz Beatz and Dame Grease. He mixed personal tales of hardship with momentary expressions of spirituality. In an unprecedented feat, DMX released his second platinum-selling album, *Flesh of My Flesh, Blood of My Blood*, in a single calendar year.

THE RESURGENCE OF THE UNDERGROUND, WOMEN RAPPERS, THE SOUTH, AND LATINX RAP, 1997–2001

The East Coast–West Coast beef provoked a critique from more "conscious" artists, revealing another division within the genre bubbling beneath the surface. These divisions revolved around long-standing debates over cultural authenticity—"real" hip hop versus "commercial" rap—which sporadically sprang up in rap music. Rap artists and groups such as Kool Keith, Xzibit, A Tribe Called Quest, The Roots, The Fugees, Common, Apani B. Fly Emcee, and Mos Def and Talib Kweli mocked and criticized mainstream artists such as the Notorious B.I.G. and Puff Daddy for their violent lyrics, materialism, and striving for more commercial success. De La Soul drew fire from Treach for Naughty By Nature and Tupac Shakur for "Ego Trippin'" and remarks they made on the 1996 album, *Stakes Is High*, which served as a rebuke of rap's gangsterism.

Latinx rappers continued to impact the culture as well. Cypress Hill, a West Coast rap group consisting of B Real, Sen Dog, and producer DJ Muggs, was the first Latino group to achieve mainstream success. In 1993, the group released its second album, Black Sunday, which sold more than 3 million albums. The album included their biggest hit single, "Insane in the Brain," which also sold more than 3 million records. The Queens-based group, The Beatnuts, comprising JuJu and Psycho Les, were fixtures in the East Coast rap underground. Bronx rapper Fat Joe also appealed to underground audiences in the first half of the 1990s, until he discovered another Latino rapper who would push Latinx rap further into the mainstream, Big Punisher (Big Pun). The Beatnuts helped thrust Big Pun into the mainstream when they featured him on their hit song, "Off the Books." Big Pun released his debut solo album, *Capital Punishment*, in 1998. The album went platinum, making Big Pun the first Latino solo artist to sell more than a million albums.

During the 1990s, a more diverse group of women rappers emerged, and some moved closer to the mainstream. Lil' Kim and Foxy Brown were affiliated with two of rap's burgeoning collectives, Notorious B.I.G.'s Junior Mafia and The Firm, which included Nas, AZ, and Nature. Lil' Kim's and Foxy Brown's lyricism and image on songs such as "Crush on You" and "Gotta Get You Home" embodied sexual freedom. The Fugees's Lauryn Hill,

however, presented a complex picture of black womanhood. She did not discard her sexual appeal, but her lyricism on her 1998 album, *The Miseducation of Lauryn Hill*, proved that she could comment on serious topics such as reproductive freedom while demonstrating that she could hold her own lyrically.[48] Hill's blending of rap, R&B, and soul music paved the way for artists such as Mos Def, Kid Cudi, and Drake to synthesize various musical genres. Missy "Misdemeanor" Elliot was another trailblazer in rap.

She, along with producer Timbaland, introduced and popularized "bounce," on her album, *Supa Dupa Fly*. This sound was characterized by frantic drums, inconspicuous samples, and other futuristic sounds. Elliot presented a black feminism distinct from that of Lil' Kim and Foxy Brown. She challenged beauty standards in her videos and performances, famously wearing a black inflatable body suit.[49]

Southern rap took off during the 1990s as well.[50] Jermaine Dupri's So So Def Records was among the first southern rap music labels to enjoy mainstream success. However, artists like Outkast and rap labels like No Limit Records created a permanent home for the "dirty south" in hip hop culture. Based in Atlanta, Andre Benjamin and Big Boi adopted the playa persona on their first album. Their name—Outkast—also underscored the group's outsider status. Outkast seemed to draw from various influences that included P-Funk, Afrika Bambaataa, black southern culture, and the Native Tongues. The group's style evolved to include lyrical content that extended to afrofuturist themes, black solidarity, spirituality, and mortality. The group also belonged to a collective called the Dungeon Family, named after the studio where they recorded their music, which consisted of the producers Organized Noize, Goodie Mob, Sleepy Brown, Big Rube, the Witchdoctor, and Cool Breeze.[51]

Master P's No Limit Records was one of the most successful black-owned and independent rap labels. The label originated from a record store called No Limit that he opened while living in Richmond, California.[52] Master P formed No Limit Records in 1994 and moved it to New Orleans. His label featured a small roster of performers in the beginning—him, his wife, Sonya Miller, his brother, Silkk the Shocker, rap producer E-A-Ski, and their group Tru. After selling around 150,000 albums across the South and on the West Coast, Master P and his partners at No Limit signed a distribution deal with Priority Records.[53] Backed by the production collective, Beats By the Pound, No Limit Records released fifty albums—selling over 30 million records—which included records from Master P and his brothers, Mia X, Mystikal, and Snoop Dogg, who signed with the label after leaving Death Row Records.

Debates regarding race and authenticity took a different turn during the late 1990s when Detroit's Marshall Mathers, also known as Eminem, released his debut album, *The Slim Shady LP* on Dr. Dre's struggling record label, Aftermath Entertainment. Eminem's single, "My Name Is" and album launched him and Aftermath into the stratosphere of rap and popular culture. A shock rapper, Eminem's over-the-top provocative lyrics often aimed at pop stars like Britney Spears and political figures like Tipper Gore and C. Delores Tucker. His violent and misogynistic lyrics attracted the ire of many critics. Eminem's success raised questions about race and whether or not he was a cultural interloper. Did he represent rap's version of Elvis Presley, a white performer who so successfully repackaged black cultural practices for mass audiences?[54] The answer to the question was more complex. Eminem's participation in local rap battles earned him the respect of black artists such as Royce da 5'9 and Proof. Eminem's class position also allowed him to traverse rap music's color line as well. He rapped about growing up in a single-parent household in an impoverished trailer park in Detroit.[55] Eminem built on the success of his

first two albums, which included *Marshall Mathers LP*, by releasing albums with his group of Detroit rappers, D12, and starting his own label, Shady Records. Eminem's movie, which was loosely based on his experiences seeking acceptance and success in local hip hop culture, *8 Mile*, and its soundtrack, propelled him further into the mainstream.

HIP HOP IN THE 21ST CENTURY: RAP TAKES CONTROL OF THE MAINSTREAM

Rap music further embedded itself in popular culture and in the record industry in the 21st century. Corporations such as McDonald's began using hip hop music as marketing tools. More rappers began partnering with corporations to endorse or create products.

By the end of the decade, television networks began investing more in rap-themed shows such as *Empire*, *The Breaks*, and *The Get Down*, and Marvel's *Luke Cage*. Rap even found audiences on Broadway. Scores of Americans, mostly white and wealthy, have packed the theater to watch Lin-Manuel Miranda's hip hop musical—*Hamilton*—dramatizing the life of founding father, Alexander Hamilton. Ed Piskor has released a critically acclaimed comic book series based on the history of rap, *Hip Hop Family Tree*. "Hybrid" artists, such Janelle Monae, Erykah Badu, Childish Gambino, and Kid Cudi blurred the boundaries between the genres as they sung and rapped on their projects.

Even though more women continued to rap, their influence in the genre waned during the 2000s. Lil' Kim, Missy Elliot, Trina, and the Ruff Ryders's Eve all recorded albums that enjoyed mainstream success. The Grammy Awards dropped the Best Female Rap category in 2005 due to a decline in the number of mainstream women recording artists. The restructuring of the music industry made women and men more disposable. Instead of investing in artist development, record labels now sought more polished artists who could sell more records at a lower cost. Women artists were disproportionately affected by this development. The cost for labels to not only record albums and produce videos, but to invest in a woman's upkeep, was more expensive, thus, making her more expendable.[56]

These struggles have not totally foreclosed success for women. Queen Latifah has successfully crossed over from rap to acting in television and movies. She has also served as a Covergirl model. Young Money's Nicki Minaj and former T.I. affiliate, Iggy Azalea entered the mainstream during the 2010s with songs like "Fancy." Like Lil' Kim, Missy Elliot, and Eve, both artists blended hip hop and catchy pop music. Both artists have endured criticisms over their authenticity, albeit for different reasons. At the 2012 Hot97 Summer Jam Concert, DJ Peter Rosenberg alleged that Nicki Minaj was not "real" hip hop because of her hit, "Starships." This sparked a controversy as Minaj pulled out of the event arguing that Rosenberg would not advance such claims if she were not a woman performer.[57] In 2014, rapper Azalea Banks accused white Australian rapper Iggy Azaelia of cultural appropriation.

Big Pun's sudden death in 2000 due to a heart attack and respiratory problems appeared to have left a void in Latinx rap. However, New York City radio DJ Angie Martinez embarked on a short, yet rather successful, rap career during the mid- to late 1990s that culminated in the release of two albums, *Up Close and Personal* in 2001 and *Animal House* in 2002. Big Pun's comrade, Fat Joe, enjoyed more mainstream success during this period. Rather than remaining in New York City, Fat Joe moved to Miami and began collaborating with singers, southern rappers, and DJs like R. Kelly, Ashanti, Lil' Wayne, Rick Ross, and Arab-American turntabalist DJ Khaled. Cuban American rapper, Pitbull, surpassed Big Pun in commercial success in the 2000s. Pitbull named his debut album after the city in which he was born and raised, *M.I.A.M.I.* Pitbull specialized in recording and performing fast-paced

dance music. He forged partnerships with products such as Kodak, Dr. Pepper, and Budweiser, and his music has been featured in NBA advertisements on the ESPN and ABC networks.

Jay-Z continued his mainstream success in the new century. He released *The Blueprint* in 2001, an album that many critics heralded a classic. The album also included the diss song aimed at Mobb Deep and Nas entitled "The Takeover." Tensions between Jay-Z and Nas bubbled beneath the surface after Notorious B.I.G.'s death with both artists trading subliminal disses. Jay Z's "The Takeover" represented the first high-profile rap battle since the East Coast–West Coast feud. Nas returned the favor with his response, "Ether," that appeared on his 2001 album, *Stillmatic*. Even though many in the hip hop world considered Nas the winner of the battle, both artists traded lyrical barbs on their follow-up albums. Jay Z announced his retirement from recording upon the release of *The Black Album* in 2004. Soon after, he parted ways with the other Roc-A-Fella co-owners. Then Def Jam changed ownership and leadership as it briefly employed Jay-Z as its president after the CEOs of his label. The decline of Roc-A-Fella reminded those in the music industry that even the most popular labels could dissolve under the weight of an executive's ambitions and internal tensions.

Kanye West emerged as one of the most important rap artists of the decade as Roc-A-Fella Records declined. West, a Chicagoan, made his mark with his production on Jay-Z's *The Blueprint*. Although West supplied beats for the likes of Roc-A-Fella artists such as Jay-Z and Beanie Sigel, as well as other artists such as Talib Kweli and Scarface, he saw himself as a vocalist. On his 2004 debut album, *The College Dropout*, West deemphasized tales of drug dealing and violent lyrics embedded in gangsta rap. Yet, West's lyrics remained materialistic and misogynistic. West also incorporated lyrics about dropping out of college, politics, spirituality, and his struggle to be taken seriously as a rapper. He also bridged generation and stylistic gaps in rap music. West became famous by reinvigorating sample-based production, often relying on soul samples that he chopped and sped up. Kanye's rap and beatmaking style also drew from the likes of Pete Rock and A Tribe Called Quest. West was the first prominent rapper and producer in the late 1990s and early 2000s to collaborate with both "commercial" and "underground" artists and groups such as Dilated Peoples, Jay-Z, Scarface, Common, and Talib Kweli.

West emerged alongside other producers and groups who took their musical cues from the Native Tongues and other producers such as Pete Rock. Even though Detroit-based producer J. Dilla's group, Slum Village, released their debut album, *Fantastic, Vol. 1*, in 2000. J. Dilla, Baatin, and T3 rapped over J. Dilla's sample-based beats. J. Dilla drew from various genres like soul, jazz, and electronica. Before he succumbed from complications from lupus, Dilla released *Donuts*, where he arranged loops of sampled beats in a manner that contemplated mortality.[58] North Carolina's Little Brother also represented a descendant of the Native Tongues. Rappers Big Pooh and Phonte traded rhymes of 9th Wonder's soul-laced tracks.

The 21st century has represented a golden age for Southern and non-New York City hip hop. In 2000, St. Louis rapper Nelly released *Country Grammar*, which featured the hit song by the same name. Nelly seemed to draw from Cleveland's Bone-Thugs-N-Harmony's melodic delivery. Three 6 Mafia earned the genre its first Academy Award in 2006 for its performance of "It's Hard Out Here for a Pimp" in the movie, *Hustle & Flow*.

The popularity of the South's "trap music" surged in the 21st century.[59] Atlanta's T.I. re-emphasized the subgenre during the 2000s. New Orleans's Lil' Wayne, and Miami's Rick Ross also emerged as the South's biggest solo artists during the 2000s. While T.I released his first album, *I'm Serious*, in 2001, he did not reach mainstream stardom until the

mid-2000s. Cash Money's Lil' Wayne released three albums before he was considered one of the genre's best rappers. Lil' Wayne solidified his position at the top of the rap industry with his *Tha Carter* series and his mixtapes. Rick Ross's persona and hit song, "Hustlin'," raised questions about authenticity in hip hop. Ross adopted the name of drug dealer Freeway Ricky Ross, who admonished the rapper for taking his name. Then, in 2008, evidence of Ross's past employment as a correctional officer surfaced, raising questions about his legitimacy. However, Ross's use of his imagination is what made his song, "Hustlin'" and his role as a performer significant.[60]

RAP MUSIC, TECHNOLOGY, MOGULS, AND POLITICS IN THE 21ST CENTURY

The maturation of .mp3 technology and the advent of digital music players such as Apple's iPod may have been the most consequential advances in the music industry in the 21st century. These developments reordered the industry as they changed the production, distribution, and consumption of rap, and music generally. Record labels and artists struggled to adapt to the burgeoning digital era. While many record labels continued to produce and distribute rap music on compact discs, the advent of the .mp3 and digital music players allowed for consumers to share music across disparate networks on platforms such as Napster. While rappers had to deal with bootleggers and album leaks as far back as the early 1990s, such practices increased as more people could copy compact discs and acquire music digitally.

This change in the market actually boosted the careers of some rappers like 50 Cent, who recorded numerous mixtapes with his group, G-Unit. 50 Cent's mixtapes were more advanced than those in the past that featured freestyle verses over other artists' songs. 50 Cent and G-Unit would rerecord other artists' songs, infusing them with their gangsta style. This method paved the way for artists to sidestep the traditional recording process through labels. They could record new music and release them via mixtapes on their own. 50 Cent's mixtape productivity launched him to the fore of the rap industry. He caught Eminem's ear, and Eminem eventually signed him to Shady-Aftermath where he released hit songs such as "In Da Club" and the overwhelmingly successful *Get Rich or Die Tryin'* and *The Massacre*. 50 Cent turned his mixtape hustle into a record label deal—G Unit Records—with Shady-Aftermath's parent company, Interscope Records.

Rap artists and executives also became moguls during the 21st century. Dr. Dre and Interscope Records' Jimmy Iovine invested in Beats headphones, which was subsequently bought by Apple. Jay-Z runs his own entertainment company, Roc Nation, which specializes in music, film, television, marketing, and talent representation. He is also a co-owner of the music streaming company, Tidal. In addition to running Bad Boy Records and a television network, Revolt TV, Combs has established lucrative partnerships with Ciroc Vodka. Dr. Dre's and Sean Combs's earnings have pushed northward of $800 million, making them the first rap artists and executives to possibly earn $1 billion.[61]

Rap groups and soloists emerged during the 2000s to speak out against racism, economic exploitation, mass incarceration, and the war in Iraq. Dead Prez's *Let's Get Free* criticized poverty, the education system, and policing. West Coast rapper Paris teamed up with Public Enemy to record an album calling for greater black solidarity called *Rebirth of a Nation*, which played upon D. W. Griffith's white supremacist movie, *Birth of a Nation*. The X-Clan returned in 2007 with *Return from Mecca*, which included one of the genre's most potent songs, simply called "Prison," which criticized mass incarceration. Latino rapper Immortal Technique spoke out against racism, the corporatization of rap, and the international drug trade on all of his albums: *Revolutionary, Vol. 1*, *Revolutionary, Vol. 2*, and

The 3rd World. White rapper Macklemore recorded songs about homophobia, white privilege, and police violence. However, the overwhelming success of his and Ryan Lewis's debut album, *The Heist*, raised questions about race and authenticity in hip hop. Women rappers like Angel Haze and Detroit-based rapper, Invincible, continued to speak out on political issues in song. Drawing from the city's history of deindustrialization, Invincible has spoken out against urban disinvestment and gentrification.

Between 2008 and 2016, rap drew inspiration from electoral politics and social movements. Will.I.Am, Jeezy, and Nas recorded songs praising Obama and encouraging Americans to vote. Obama also publicly exhibited his affinity with hip hop culture. In April 2008, he famously brushed his shoulder in response to a criticism from Hillary Clinton. The gesture referenced Jay-Z's song, "Dirt Off Your Shoulder," that appeared on *The Black Album*. Social movements such as Occupy Wall Street and Black Lives Matter also inspired hip hop artists during the Obama era. Talib Kweli supported Black Lives Matter by participating in the Ferguson October protest in 2015. Chicago rapper Lupe Fiasco has recorded songs criticizing the history of settler-colonialism, foreign policy, and mass incarceration. Kendrick Lamar's *To Pimp a Butterfly* features songs such as "The Blacker the Berry" confronting police killings, mass incarceration, and inner-city violence. One song, in particular, however, "Alright," has become a protest anthem for many Black Lives Matter activists.

DISCUSSION OF THE LITERATURE

Hip hop studies has expanded in the previous three decades despite academia's questions regarding its relevance and rigor.[62] The number of studies of hip hop culture increased during the 1990s and the 2000s. Tricia Rose's *Black Noise: Rap Music and Black Culture in Contemporary America* was among the first theoretical analyses of hip hop culture. Rose analyzed the relationship between technology, political economy, and space in the development of rap music. She also presented analyses of rap music's relationship between race, gender, and politics. Bakari Kitwana's *The Hip Hop Generation: Young Blacks and the Crisis in African-American Culture* analyzes the rise of what he defines as the "hip hop generation"—those born between 1965 and 1984—and its relationship to mass incarceration, film, unemployment, and sexism and the gender divide.[63] Murray Forman's and Mark Anthony Neal's *That's the Joint: The Hip Hop Studies Reader* and Jeff Chang's edited collection, *Total Chaos: The Art and Aesthetics of Hip-Hop* illustrate the breadth of the study of rap music as a field. Chang's edited collection features various articles on hip hop historiography, aesthetics, authenticity, space, gender, politics, and technology. Chang's collection also frames hip hop as a cultural movement in the vein of the Black Arts movement.

Many of the rap histories are journalistic. Jeff Chang's *Can't Stop, Won't Stop: A History of the Hip-Hop Generation* remains the best synthetic history of the genre. Chang contextualizes the emergence of the genre in the Jamaican diaspora and the political, economic, and spatial transformations of New York City. The author uses culture and politics to analyze the development of hip hop culture from 1973 until 2001, ending with an analysis of the corporatization and globalization of rap music at the end of the 20th century. Dan Charnas's *The Big Payback: The History of the Business of Hip-Hop* is the first economic history of the genre. In *The Big Payback*, music executives emerge as the prominent players in the genre's development alongside pioneering DJ's and rappers. Ben Westhoff's *Original Gangstas: The Untold Story of Dr. Dre, Eazy-E, Ice Cube, Tupac Shakur, and the Birth of West Coast Rap* and *Dirty South: Outkast, Lil Wayne, Souljah Boy and the Southern Rappers Who Reinvented Hip Hop* are the first journalistic

histories that shift the focus of rap's origins to places such as Compton, Los Angeles, the Bay Area, New Orleans, and Atlanta.

Many scholars have focused on analyzing the relationship between hip hop culture, rap music, feminism, and gender. Gwendolyn Pough builds upon black feminist scholars such as Tricia Rose in her book, *Check It While I Wreck It: Black Womanhood, Hip-Hop Culture, and the Public Sphere*. Pough illustrates how black women rappers had to "wreck it," demonstrating great lyrical skill, to carve a space in the predominantly black male rap counterpublic. Due to this struggle, according to Pough, this space becomes a launch point for black feminist thought, pedagogy, and politics. Sociologist Michael Jeffries concentrates on the relationship between rap music and masculinity in *Thug Life: Race, Gender, and the Meaning of Hip-Hop*. His method is notable because he focuses more on audience than on rappers and other performers.[64]

Many scholars have been interested in the political potential of rap music and the hip hop generation.[65] These texts specifically explore the intersections between hip hop culture and its relationship with traditional politics. The title of S. Craig's Watkins's book, *Hip Hop Matters: Politics, Pop Culture, and the Struggle for the Soul of the Movement* serves as a rebuke of those critics who claim that hip hop does not contain any politics. Political Scientist Cathy Cohen takes up questions regarding black youth participation in electoral politics and activism, moral panics and respectability politics, and their relationship with Barack Obama in *Democracy Remixed*. Political Scientist Lester Spence considers the development of hip hop culture in relation to the emergence of neoliberalism. Spence confronts critics of rap music and black culture who claim that it has no political significance. While analyzing the production, consumption, and circulation of rap music, the author identifies the points where rap artists and black culture transmit messages supporting neoliberal logic.

Music critics and journalists have published anthologies analyzing many of the genre's most notable albums.[66] Hip hop journalists Sasha Jenkins, Elliot Wilson, Chairman Mao, Gabriel Alvarez, and Brent Rollins put together *Ego Trip's Book of Rap Lists*. This 352-page book features scores of lists exploring the genre's greatest producers, the best DJs, the greatest rap groups of all time, and "twenty colorful songs about racism." Journalist Brian Coleman published two volumes of *Check the Technique: Liner Notes for Hip-Hop Junkies*, which has offered deep analyses of albums from the Beastie Boys, Diagable Planets, Raekwon, Black Star, Eric B. & Rakim, and Ice Cube. Shea Serrano's *The Rap Yearbook* analyzes the best rap songs from the Sugar Hill Gang's "Rapper's Delight," released in 1979 to Rich Gang's 2014 "Lifestyle." Michael Eric Dyson and Sohail Daulatzai edited a collection of essays analyzing every song from Nas's debut album, *Illmatic*.

Rappers have also published memoirs documenting their experiences in the hip hop industry.[67] Journalist Joan Morgan's memoir, *When Chickenheads Come Home to Roost: My Life as a Hip-Hop Feminist*, interrogates the nuances of black feminism and some of the problematic aspects of hip hop culture. The Roots' drummer, Questlove, mused about his musical influences and the story of his band's rise in *Mo' Meta Blues: The World According to Questlove*. He contextualizes The Roots' career in the development of hip hop culture during the 1980s and 1990s. Wu Tang Clan's The Rza frames his coming of age story within the lessons he gleaned from his various influences in *The Tao of Wu*. Jay-Z also published *Decoded*, which featured the artist's annotations of some of his most famous verses.

PRIMARY SOURCES

Harvard University and Cornell University have opened archives containing primary sources. The Cornell Hip-Hop Collection in Ithaca, New York, contains collections from Afrika Bambaataa, journalist Kevin Powell, and Def Jam music executive Bill Adler.[68] Harvard's Hip Hop Archive and Research Institute at the Hutchins Center, Harvard University, features profiles of several hip hop artists and contains 200 vinyl records in their Classic Crates Project. It also includes an extensive bibliography.[69] Adam Bradley and Andrew DuBois published a collection of rap lyrics in 2010, *The Anthology of Rap*. This compilation contains lyrics from rap artists from 1978 to 2010. Genius is an annotation website that stores rap verses from thousands of songs. The Original Hip Hop Lyrics Database also contains rap lyrics.[70]

DIGITAL MATERIALS

History of Rap Spotify Playlist. https://open.spotify .com/user/122428933/playlist/3B9Gvl9hOqNzo Wifo7AEkB.

FURTHER READING

Chang, Jeff. *Can't Stop, Won't Stop: A History of the Hip-Hop Generation*. New York: St. Martin's Press, 2005.

Charnas, Dan. *The Big Payback: The History of the Business of Hip Hop*. New York: New American Library, 2010.

Coleman, Brian. *Check the Technique: Liner Notes for Hip-Hop Junkies*. New York: Villard, 2007.

Coleman, Brian. *Check the Technique, Volume 2: More Liner Notes for Hip-Hop Junkies*. Everett, MA: Wax Facts Press, 2014.

Collins, Patricia Hill. *From Black Power to Hip Hop: Racism, Nationalism, and Feminism*. Philadelphia: Temple University Press, 2006.

Dyson, Michael Eric, and Sohail Daulatzai, eds. *Born to Use Mics: Reading Nas's Illmatic*. New York: Basic Civitas, 2010.

Forman, Murray, and Mark Anthony Neal. *That's the Joint! The Hip-Hop Studies Reader*. New York: Routledge, 2004.

Jeffries, Michael P. *Thug Life: Race, Gender, and the Meaning of Hip Hop*. Chicago: University of Chicago Press, 2011.

Jenkins, Sasha, Elliot Wilson, Chairman Mao, Gabriel Alvarez, and Brent Rollins, *Ego Trip's Book of Rap Lists*. New York: St. Martin's Griffin, 1999.

Kitwana, Bakari. *The Hip Hop Generation: Young Blacks and the Crisis in African American Culture*. New York: Basic Civitas, 2002.

Kitwana, Bakari. *Why White Kids Love Hip-Hop: Wankstas, Wiggers, Wannabees, and the New Reality of Race in America*. New York: Basic Civitas, 2005.

Lipsitz, George. *Dangerous Crossroads: Popular Music Postmodernism, and the Poetics of Place*. New York: Verso, 1994.

Morgan, Joan. *When Chickenheads Come Home to Roost: My Life as a Hip-Hop Feminist*. New York: Simon & Schuster, 1999.

Ogbar, Jeffrey O. G. *The Hip-Hop Revolution: The Culture and Politics of Rap*. Lawrence: University Press of Kansas, 2007.

Perry, Imani. *Prophets of the Hood: Politics and Poetics in Hip Hop*. Durham, N.C.: Duke University Press, 2004.

Piskor, Ed. *Hip Hop Family Tree*. Seattle, WA: Fantagraphics Books, 2013.

Pough, Gwendolyn. *Check It While I Wreck It: Black Womanhood, Hip-Hop Culture, and the Public Sphere*. Boston: Northeastern University Press, 2004.

Rose, Tricia. *Black Noise: Rap Music and Black Culture in Contemporary America*. Hanover, NH: University Press of New England, 2004.

The Rza. *The Tao of Wu*. New York: Riverhead, 2009.

Serrano, Shea. *The Rap Yearbook: The Most Important Rap Song From Every Year Since 1979, Discussed, Debated, and Deconstructed*. New York: Abrams Image, 2015.

Spence, Lester. *Stare in the Darkness: The Limits of Hip-Hop and Black Politics*. Minneapolis: University of Minnesota Press, 2011.

Thompson, Ahmir "Questlove," *Mo' Meta Blues: The World According to Questlove*. New York: Grand Central Publishing, 2013.

Vibe Magazine Staff, *Hip-Hop Divas*. New York: Three Rivers Press, 2001.

Watkins, S. Craig. *Hip Hop Matters: Politics, Pop Culture, and the Struggle for the Soul of the Movement*. Boston: Beacon, 2005.

Westoff, Ben. *Original Gangstas: The Untold Story of Dr. Dre, Eazy-E, Ice Cube, Tupac Shakur, and the Birth of West Coast Rap*. New York: Hachette, 2016.

NOTES

1. Robin Kelley, "Polycultural Me," *UTNE Reader*, September–October 1999.
2. Jeffrey O. G. Ogbar, *The Hip-Hop Revolution: The Culture and Politics of Rap* (Lawrence: University Press of Kansas, 2007): 5–7.
3. Jeff Chang, *Can't Stop, Won't Stop: A History of the Hip-Hop Generation* (New York: St. Martin's Press, 2005), 67–70; Angus Batey, "DJ Kool Herc DJs his first block party (his sister's birthday) at 1520 Sedgwick Avenue, Bronx, New York," *The Guardian*, June 12, 2011.
4. George Lipsitz, *Dangerous Crossroads: Popular Music, Postmodernism and the Politics of Place* (New York: Verso, 1994), 25.
5. Chang, 79.
6. Dan Charnas, *The Big Payback: The History of the Business of Hip-Hop* (New York: New American Library, 2010), 18.
7. Chang, 10–14.
8. Chang, 83.
9. Charnas, 19; Chang, 101.
10. In 2016, the leadership of the Zulu Nation marginalized Bambaataa after activist, politician, and music executive Ronald Savage accused him of sexual assault. The Zulu Nation issued a formal apology to Savage. See Marc Hogan, "Zulu Nation Apologizes to Afrika Bambaataa's Alleged Sexual Abuse Victims," *Pitchfork*, June 1, 2016.
11. Sewell Chan, "Remembering the '77 Blackout," *The New York Times*, July 9, 2007.
12. 99% Invisible and Delaney Hall, "Was the 1977 New York City Blackout a Catalyst for Hip Hop's Growth?," Slate.com, October 16, 2014; Chang, 84.
13. Vibe Magazine Staff, *Hip-Hop Divas* (New York: Three Rivers Press, 2001), 8–9.
14. Vibe Magazine Staff, 9.
15. Charnas, 15.
16. Sasha Jenkins, Elliot Wilson, Chairman Mao, Gabriel Alvarez, and Brent Rollins, *Ego Trip's Book of Rap Lists* (New York: St. Martin's Press, 1999), 30.
17. Charnas, 233.
18. Shea Serrano, *The Rap Year Book: The Most Important Rap Song Every Year Since 1979, Discussed, Debated, and Deconstructed* (New York: Abrams Image, 2015), 17–20.
19. Charnas, 57.
20. Chang, 92; J. S. Rafaeli, "We Spoke to Afrika Bambaataa about Hip-Hop, Afrofuturism, and 'Bewitched,'" Vice.com, October 2, 2014.

21. Chang, 203.

22. Schellenbach's was marginalized as Horowitz, Yauch, and Diamond concentrated more on producing rap music. Charnas, 134.

23. Austin McCoy, "Fight for Your Right to Party"?: The Politics of Hip Hop's 'Funky Ass Jews,'" *Another Level*, August 17, 2012.

24. Kelley, 184.

25. Adam Bradley and Andrew DuBois, eds., *The Anthology of Rap* (New Haven, CT: Yale University Press, 2010), 283.

26. Tricia Rose, *Black Noise: Rap Music and Black Culture in Contemporary America* (Middletown, CT: Wesleyan University Press, 1994), 151.

27. Chang, 445.

28. Bradley and DuBois, 257.

29. Chang, 251.

30. Eric Thurm, "A BEGINNER'S GUIDE TO HIP-HOP COLLECTIVE Native Tongues," THE AV CLUB, July 5, 2013.

31. David Mills, "The Geto Boys: Beating the Murder Rap," *The Washington Post*, December 15, 1991.

32. Mills, "The Geto Boys," 393.

33. Steve Hochman, "Two Members of 2 Live Crew Arrested," *Los Angeles Times*, June 11, 1990; "The Anatomy of a Crusade," *Los Angeles Times*, June 18, 1990 (http://articles.latimes.com/1990-06-18/entertainment/ca-92_1_live-crew).

34. Sara Rimer, "Obscenity or Art? Trial on Rap Lyrics Opens," *New York Times*, October 17, 1990.

35. Oliver Wang, "20 Years Ago Biz Markie Got the Las Laugh," NPR Music.

36. Jeff Mao, "Interview: Mtume on Miles Davis, Juicy Fruit and Donny Hathaway's Last Recording Session," *Red Bull Music Academy*, May 13, 2014.

37. Greg Tate, "Hip Hop Nation," *The Village Voice*, January 19, 1988.

38. Charnas, 381; Chang, 394–395; Matt Latimer, "Why There Are No More Sistah Souljah Moments," *Politico*, June 24, 2015.

39. Bodycount, "Out in the Parking Lot/Cop Killer Lyrics," Rap Genius (http://genius.com/Body-count-out-in-the-parking-lot-cop-killer-lyrics).

40. Chang, 396–399.

41. Charnas, 389.

42. Chang, 399.

43. The Rza, *The Tao of Wu* (New York: Riverhead Books, 2009), 107.

44. Serrano, 103.

45. Charnas, 474–475.

46. Nadirah Simmons, "Today in 1995: The 2nd Annual Source Awards Makes Hip Hop History," The Source.com, August 3, 2016.

47. Charnas, 475.

48. Lester Spence, *Stare into the Darkness: The Limits of Hip Hop and Black Politics* (Minneapolis: University of Minnesota Press, 2011), 1.

49. Noisey Staff, "The Evolution of Timbaland," *Noisey*, February 3, 2015; Kat George, "Why Missy Elliot's feminist legacy is criminally underrated," *Dazed* (January 2016).

50. David Mills, "The Geto Boys Beating the Murder Rap," *Washington Post*, December 15, 1991.

51. Pitchfork Staff, "Atlanta to Atlantis: An OutKast Retrospective," *Pitchfork*, November 5, 2013.

52. Ben Westhoff, *The Dirty South: Outkast, Lil Wayne, Soulja Boy, and the Southern Rappers Who Reinvented Hip-Hop* (Chicago: Chicago Review Press, 2011), 118.

53. Charnas, 516–157.

54. Charnas, 522.

55. Jonah Hahn, "The Politics of Race in Rap," *Harvard Political Review*, June 8, 2014; [another citation]

56. Austin McCoy, "In Between Cultural Appropriation, Racism, and Sexism: Azealia Banks and the Erasure of Black Women in Rap," *Nursing Clio*, January 29, 2015.

57. Austin McCoy, "Holding It Down for Women: Nicki Minaj and the Problem of Gender Inequity in Hip Hop," *Nursing Clio*, July 25, 2012.

58. Jordan Ferguson, *Donuts* (New York: Bloomsbury Academic, 2014).

59. Christina Lee, "Trap Kings: How the Hip-Hop Sub-genre Dominated the Decade," *The Guardian*, August 13, 2015.

60. Serrano, 177.

61. Zack O'Malley Greenberg, "Cash Kings 2016: Hip-Hop's Highest Earning Acts," *Forbes*, September 7, 2016.

62. For a comprehensive bibliography on the history of hip hop, see Andrew Leach, "'One Day It'll All Make Sense': Hip-Hop and Rap Resources for Librarians," *Notes*, 2d ser., 65.1 (September 2008): 9–37.

63. Bakari Kitwana, *The Hip Hop Generation: Young Blacks and the Crisis in African-American Culture* (New York: Basic Civitas, 2002), 3.

64. Gwendolyn Pough, *Check It While I Wreck It: Black Womanhood, Hip-Hop Culture, and the Public Sphere* (Boston: Northeastern University

Press, 2004); Michael P. Jeffries, *Thug Life: Race, Gender, and The Meaning of Hip-Hop* (Chicago: Chicago University Press, 2011). Also see Patricia Hill Collins, *From Black Power to Hip Hop: Racism, Nationalism, and Feminism* (Philadelphia: Temple University Press, 2006).

65. S. Craig Watkins, *Hip Hop Matters: Politics, Pop Culture, and the Struggle for the Soul of the Movement* (Boston: Beacon, 2005); Cathy J. Cohen, *Democracy Remixed: Black Youth and the Future of American Politics* (New York: Oxford University Press, 2010); Portia Hemphill, "Rebel Without a Pause: Discovering the Relationship Between Rap Music and the Political Attitudes and Participation of Black Youth" (PhD diss, University of Michigan, 2015).

66. Brian Coleman, *Check the Technique: Liner Notes for Hip-Hop Junkies* (New York: Villard, 2007); *Check the Technique, Volume 2: More Liner Notes for Hip-Hop Junkies* (Everett, MA: Wax Facts Press, 2014); Michael Eric Dyson and Sohail Daulatzai, eds., *Born to Use Mics: Reading Nas's Illmatic* (New York: Basic Civitas, 2010)

67. Jay Z, *Decoded* (New York: Spiegel & Grau, 2010); Ahmir "Questlove" Thompson, *Mo' Meta Blues: The World According to Questlove* (New York: Grand Central Publishing, 2015).

68. "Guide to the Cornell University Library Hip Hop Collection, circa 1975–2008," Division of Rare and Manuscript Collections Cornell University Library. Ithaca, New York.

69. "Bibliography," The Hip Hop Archive, Hip Hop Archive and Research Institute at the Hutchins Center, Harvard University, Cambridge, MA.

70. The Original Hip-Hop Lyrics Archive (http://ohhla.com/index.html).

Austin McCoy

Violence and Disorder

RIOTS AND RIOTING IN US CITIES, 1800–2000

INTRODUCTION

Rioting in the United States has historically had a ritual character. According to the sociologist Charles Tilly, participants in collective violence rely on repertoires of shared understandings, interests, and traditions. In the 17th- and 18th-century European mobs studied by Tilly and others, rioters used heavily stylized and restrained public violence as a way to regulate communal morality and dialogue with authorities.[1] Americans in the early 1800s adapted this purpose of rioting, as a means of self-rule and theatrical protest, to local conditions, establishing basic traditions for popular disorder in US history: to regulate

communal morality, defend community against outside threats, and protest government abuse of power. Yet American rioting became much more violent than its European predecessor. This largely owed to the historical evolution of racial slavery, western expansion, and local police departments.

This short historical overview of US rioting emphasizes the experience of cities and the role of power, ideology, and structural conditions. Between 1800 and 1840, the variety of antagonists in popular disorder was seemingly endless: rival fire-fighting companies, native born and foreign born, Protestant and Catholic, white and nonwhite. Rioting—like lynching and the civilian posse—was embedded in the institutions and culture of local communal policing. Rioting mobs could also be drunken, recreational, aimless. During the

1840s and 1850s, however, white Americans combined mass rioting and the lynch mob to create a lethal and effective instrument of white settler sovereignty to facilitate the conquest of the western territories and suppress dissent against slavery. In the decades after the Civil War and the emancipation of four million enslaved African Americans, white Americans, particularly in the South, conspired with local police to perpetrate racial massacres to assert white supremacy, seize political power, and enforce the strict racial regime of Jim Crow segregation. During the 20th century, the character of rioting changed, as millions of nonwhites migrated to cities. White-instigated disputes over segregated residential boundaries were common, but racial minorities also began to use rioting to defend communities from civilian and police violence.

NEW RITUALS OF RIOTING FROM COLONIAL TO JACKSONIAN AMERICA, 1800–1850

Scholars reference "the Anglo-American mob tradition" to describe rioting in the American colonies and the new United States.[2] This rioting was highly ritualized and focused on harming property rather than persons. Colonial and early US authorities frequently tolerated and on occasion condoned such restrained rioting as legitimate expressions of popular discontent. Knowing this, rioters were careful to act in ways that respected cultural norms and elite expectations. "These pressures of legitimacy," historian Wayne E. Lee has argued, "led early modern rioters to precede violence with petitions, to carefully select their targets, to favor proxies or even effigies as the focus for their anger."[3] Similarly, European historians of crowds, most notably E. P. Thompson, Eric Hobsbawm, George Rudé, and Natalie Zemon Davis, have argued that public group violence in 17th-century towns and villages in France and England was sanctioned by communal consensus but that

rioters also demonstrated restraint to retain public support and remain in good standing with elites.[4]

The Anglo-American mob that prevailed in the late 18th century used tightly scripted public violence to protest the perceived arbitrary power of the British Crown and federal government. The primary grievance was economic, specifically burdensome taxes. Colonial mobs marched on governors' mansions and destroyed consumer goods, famously dumping tea into Boston Harbor, to protest new import duties.[5] After the Revolution, violent protests against taxes continued, including Shays' Rebellion in 1787, and the Whiskey Rebellion in 1794. Rarely did mobs kill when their targets were other white Europeans. Rather, as Lee observes, early American rioters, like their European counterparts, used carefully staged violence because they "expected a paternalistic response" from public authorities.[6] The armed revolts against excise duties, some seeking to unseat local government, deviated from this script. Yet, in asserting communal rights against perceived government overreach, they, too, argues historian Thomas P. Slaughter, demonstrate "the degree of continuity from the Stamp Act crisis through and beyond the anti-excise disorders of the 1790s."[7]

Sometime in the second decade of the 19th century, American popular disorder shifted from the "careful riots" studied by Lee to the less-restrained violence that dominated the Jacksonian and pre-Civil War era. One key factor was the rapid urban growth of the first decades of the 19th century. Two population trends of the 1820s to 1840s are worth highlighting: the arrival of Irish Catholic immigrants fleeing hardship and finding unskilled work in new factories, displacing the longstanding craft system of primarily native-born artisans, and the growing number and prominence of African Americans in free northern cities like Philadelphia, as well as in border cities like Baltimore.[8] Both groups encountered frequent hostility and violence from native Protestants and whites, respectively.

Changing demographics and structural conditions meant crowds, and their grievances, looked different, too. In Lee's study of colonial North Carolina, riots were typically made up of white artisans and merchants of middling class with some participation by political elites.[9] As cities became larger and more stratified by race, religion, and class, the power of personal ties to cool and contain rebellion—the basis of reciprocal paternalism—grew weaker, while intercommunal divisions sharpened. As riots became less majoritarian and more sectarian, crowds abandoned political theater—mock trials of effigies or methodically leveling elite dwellings—and opened the floodgates of physical violence upon persons.

The historian Paul Gilje observes this "breakdown in the Anglo-American mob tradition" in the month-long Baltimore Riot during the War of 1812. After pro-war Republican mobs in late June tore down the *Federalist-Republican* building in protest of the newspaper's anti-war and possibly pro-British stance, crowds remained riotous for several weeks. The mayor and militia commander made repeated verbal pleas to no avail. By late July, rioters had not only destroyed and stripped another Federalist property, but violent offshoots had erupted that had little to do with the original complaint: whites attacked African Americans, Irish Protestants and Irish Catholics fought each other, and armed persons disabled Spanish grain ships suspected of trading with England. In a departure from past riot patterns, the mob invaded the jail holding Federalist prisoners and beat them, killing one.[10]

The decade between 1834 and 1844 was one of the most riotous periods in US history. The numbers tell a story of unrestrained violence to police racial and religious minorities, to enforce social mores against gambling and drinking, and to decide the outcome of political elections. In the most comprehensive summary published to date, the historian David Grimsted counted 147 riots in 1835, 107 between July and October alone. About sixty of these involved whites attacking abolitionists or African

Americans.[11] An estimated two dozen major riots took place in 1834 and at least three dozen in 1835, provoking President Andrew Jackson, not exactly known for even-tempered restraint, to denounce "mob-law." In 1838, one year after a mob murdered abolitionist editor Elijah Lovejoy in Illinois, Abraham Lincoln, a twenty-eight-year-old lawyer, warned that such "vicious" popular violence spelled doom for government. Grimsted contends that rioting claimed more than one thousand lives in the antebellum period.[12]

One is struck by the range of grievances during this era. Rival urban firefighter companies staged elaborate violent battles that sometimes lasted days. Anti-abolitionist fervor drove much of the violence. The Philadelphia mayor and his part-time constables were powerless to stop a crowd from burning to the ground Pennsylvania Hall in 1838 mere days after it opened, in response to rumors that the hall's abolitionist owners plotted to promote interracial sex in the city.[13] In 1842, a Rhode Island lawyer named Thomas Dorr led a makeshift brigade of residents angry over their disenfranchisement by the state's constitution in a failed attempt to commandeer the arsenal in the state capitol of Providence.[14] Mormons and Catholics faced frequent violent assaults, their places of worship torched or destroyed by native-born Protestants. In perhaps the most famous ethnic and religious riot of the era, intense controversy over the use of Catholic Bibles in Kensington schools, a suburb of Philadelphia, culminated in multiple gun battles between crowds and county militia over several weeks that resulted in up to twenty deaths of both nativists and Irish Catholics. Whig and Democratic partisans engaged in frequent rowdy free-for-alls on election day, motivated less by political or ideological differences than what historian Michael Feldberg has called "expressive rioting."[15] Twenty-two people died at the Astor Place Opera House in New York City on May 10, 1849, after the militia opened fire on rioting audience-members embroiled in a dispute over the perceived aristocratic leanings of a British actor.[16]

The 1830s to 1840s were pivotal decades, too, in the way local government responded to disorder. Examining court records in Lancaster County, Pennsylvania, between 1834 and 1854, the historian Thomas P. Slaughter found that the riot complaints tripled compared to any comparable previous period, even though the ratio of prosecutions to accusations changed little from the previous century. From this seemingly contradictory data, Slaughter concludes there was a "growing sensitivity to disorder," but rather than criminally prosecute offenders, authorities mainly used the riot charge as a catch-all offense to control working-class behavior. Lancaster judges, for example, imposed sizable bonds on defendants for one-to-two years as a sort of parole to enforce "good behavior."[17] In addition to the courts, local executives had a patchwork of control agents they deployed to the scene of trouble: sheriffs, constables, civilian posses, and volunteer county militias.[18]

Toward the close of what Feldberg called the "turbulent era," large US cities increasingly centralized control authority in unified municipal police departments. In Philadelphia, that process began after the 1844 riots. According to historian Allen Steinberg, after the horrific riots in suburban Kensington, Catholics made "one of the earliest pleas for a consolidated county police force." In 1850, the state legislature created a countywide sheriff's position and funded a small county force of one officer per 150 taxable residents. The 1854 Consolidation Act, joining city and county, officially established the Philadelphia Police Department, authorizing 820 full-time patrol positions salaried according to rank. As in Philadelphia, the new urban police departments were beholden to machine rule, with personnel and enforcement decisions controlled by patronage and party interests.[19]

MASS RIOTING IN THE INDUSTRIAL ERA

Urban police departments expanded the reach of state authority at the same time that Americans deployed extralegal violence on an increasingly industrial scale. The transformation of lynching from non-lethal public flogging in 1830 to racial terrorism in 1870 was a key factor motivating this change. Long before the mass spectacle of murders of racial minorities in the late 19th century, lynching—if the term was used at all—was one type among several of community-sanctioned extralegal punishment, especially common in frontier towns where formal criminal justice institutions were absent or weak.[20] The term "lynching" entered national vernacular in 1835 when an increasingly national press, abetted by faster transportation and communication networks, reported on a crowd's hanging of five gamblers in Vicksburg, Virginia, as punishment for killing a doctor during a local moral panic around gambling.[21]

Lynch mobs contained many of the qualities that defined rioting—public violence carried out by groups against selected targets—but their core aim was to punish alleged crime. According to historian Christopher Waldrep, lynching in this era meant "the work of a community or neighborhood united against outrageous crimes."[22] Lynching resembled the communal rough justice of colonial "careful riots," civilian posses, Southern slave patrols, and western vigilantism. Most famously, the Vigilance Committee in San Francisco in 1856 rose to power with a lynching. With mass support, they stormed a city jail, seized two Democratic officeholders who had murdered a newspaper editor and US Marshal, and hanged them, citing corrupt and ineffective law enforcement as justification. The Whig-allied nativists on the Vigilance Committee amassed a private army of six thousand and overthrew the Irish-Democratic machine, installing a new regime with a promise to rid the city of crime and corruption.[23]

The rise of racially sectarian lynching produced a deadlier variety of rioting. Historian Michael J. Pfeifer has argued that lynching became more regular in the mid-19th century, especially in rural, frontier, or Southern locales, to supplant non-existent criminal justice institutions or to preempt a growing emphasis in legal circles on due process for the accused. Behind this trend, Pfeifer argues, was an assertion of white male settler sovereignty, or the right to use communal violence as a check on the alleged criminality and deviance of nonwhite and marginal populations.[24] Nineteenth-century riots tended to follow a less linear and narrow path, but those that contained this punishment imperative—lynch riots—were the most lethal and destructive of the industrial era.

Western expansion in the 1840s and 1850s and the accompanying increase in sectional tensions created the conditions for a sharp rise in racial mob violence. In 1848, the modern boundaries of California were set with the Treaty of Guadeloupe-Hidalgo, ending the Mexican-American War. That year, miners discovered gold outside of San Francisco, bringing tens of thousands of settlers seeking fortune, many of them young men and immigrants, transforming San Francisco from frontier outpost to major population center in a few years.[25] In 1850, California was admitted to the Union as a free state as part of the Compromise of 1850, which enacted the Fugitive Slave Law, giving Southern slaveowners extraordinary power to coerce Northerners to assist in the recapture of allegedly escaped slaves. Michael Pfeifer has identified fifty-six "mob executions" of blacks in the South between 1824 and 1862. More than two-thirds took place after 1849. Forty-four victims were enslaved. Murder was the most common alleged crime. Forty victims were accused of murder, fifteen specifically for the murder or attempted murder of the master or members of his family. More than one-fourth of the cases involved an allegation of rape. Pfeifer notes that his data set omits the hundreds more African Americans indiscriminately killed by white Southerners in response to slave rebellions, real or imagined.[26]

Scholars have shown how lynching extended well beyond the South and the black-white binary. The artist Ken Gonzales-Day documented more than 350 lethal lynchings in California from 1850 to 1935. Just eight cases involved African American victims, whereas

210 were Native American, Asian, or Latino from North and South America and 120 were white European.[27] The historians William D. Carrigan and Clive Webb identified 597 Mexicans killed by lynch mobs between 1848 and 1928, mainly in Texas and the Southwest, the vast majority in the period before 1880, when popular histories typically date the start of the lynching era. In California, 163 Mexicans alone were lynched between 1848 and 1860. Carrigan and Webb calculated that in some states Mexicans faced a much higher risk of lethal mob violence than African Americans in the postbellum South. Carrigan and Webb conclude that the vast majority of victims in their data set were "summarily executed" without "even the semblance of a trial" by mobs who "acted less out of a rational interest in law and order than an irrational prejudice towards racial minorities."[28]

Racial minorities had little recourse against mobs before the Civil War but to defend themselves through violence, which carried great risk. Carrigan and Webb note that Anglo hostility toward Mexicans derived from economic competition, tense US-Mexico diplomatic relations, and racism. During the Gold Rush, lawmakers gave Anglos a systematic advantage over non-whites through the Foreign Miner's Tax of 1851 and the Anti-Vagrancy Act of 1855 targeting "all persons who are commonly known as Greasers or the issue of Spanish or Indian blood." These laws further conferred impunity on Anglo lynch mobs. Decades before founding legal defense organizations like the League of United Latin American Citizens, Mexicans tried to protect their communities and retaliate against lynching through physical violence. This strategy often "proved counter-productive," according to Carrigan and Webb, because Anglos had the power of law enforcement at their disposal, such as the Texas Rangers, whose tactics—which included lynching—were "tantamount to state-sanctioned terrorism."[29]

Despite its inadequacy, community defense provided a counterweight to not only white vigilantism but also state policies supporting white supremacy. Abolitionists in northern cities created Vigilance Committees in the 1830s to assist runaway and free African Americans. Yet, Paul Gilje observes that whites rarely participated in black community defense rioting until the passage of the Fugitive Slave Law.[30] The 1850 law enabled slaveowners to compel Northerners to join federal posses to recapture escaped slaves. Between 1850 and 1858, the Boston Vigilance Committee rescued four hundred fugitives from federal custody on the street, in courthouses, and from southbound ships.[31] Black resistance to the Fugitive Slave Law was violent on a few notable occasions. In 1851, African Americans in Lancaster, Pennsylvania, defended four runaways from a federal posse, in the process killing the Maryland slaveowner. In a trial that became a national sensation, heightening sectional tensions before the Civil War, thirty-eight men were charged with treason, yet all were acquitted.[32]

During the Civil War, as the Union took steps to end slavery and incorporate African Americans into US society, white Northerners helped reinvent lynching as a means of reasserting white supremacy. Pfeifer has argued that this phenomenon was an important precursor to the better-known racial lynching across the South from the 1880s to the 1930s. In September 1861, five dozen Irishmen in Milwaukee, Wisconsin, raided the city jail that was keeping two African American men who had fatally stabbed an Irishman during a street altercation over the black men's interactions with two white women. The mob dragged one of the men, Marshall Clark, to the firehouse and hanged him from a pile driver before a thousand spectators. Indicating prior coordination and planning, the fire companies rang their bells after the death of the Irishman and a firehouse served as the site of Clarke's mock trial; local law enforcement never interfered with the mob. Local press coverage blamed Republican support for abolitionism, racial equality, and violating the Fugitive Slave Law for inciting the violent extralegal response from the mostly Democratic Irish community.[33]

Mass urban racial lynching reached a devastating scale two years later in the anti-draft rioting in New York City, a terrifying harbinger of post-war violence and one of the most lethal popular rebellions of US history. In March 1863, Congress passed the Conscription Act to support the Union war effort. The law, however, provided two exemptions: a draftee could present an "acceptable substitute" or pay a $300 commutation fee. By allowing wealthier citizens to opt out, the law appeared to shift the burdens of war onto the working class and the poor. Additionally, in January, President Abraham Lincoln had made ending slavery a central war aim with the Emancipation Proclamation. Weeks after the law's passage, white rioters attacked African Americans and looted and burned their property after the draft lottery began in Detroit, lashing out at the group deemed responsible for conscription.[34]

On Saturday, July 11, the federal draft office opened in working-class districts of New York. After weekend meetings, on Monday, July 13, Irish industrial workers went on strike. Led by fire companies, they destroyed draft offices, attacked Republican officeholders, and chanted pro-Confederate slogans. Beginning on Tuesday, July 14, the riot shifted when Irish laborers began brutally assaulting Republican-identified city police officers and soldiers, torching provost marshal offices and police stations, tearing up railroad tracks and severing telegraph lines, and lynching African Americans in a ritual involving, variously, hanging, burning, genital mutilation, and drowning. Scholars have observed that many of the most violent rioters were too young for the draft but joined with older rioters after rioting began on Monday to seek out political enemies and reassert local white Democratic sovereignty. On Thursday, July 16, federal troops arrived from the battlefields of Gettysburg to put down the rebellion. By Friday, it was over. At least 105 people perished over the five days, including three police officers, eight soldiers, and eleven African Americans. Most riot fatalities were working-class whites; at least twenty-three were killed by the military. Anecdotal evidence suggests the total number of dead was likely higher, since bodies were dumped in the Hudson River.[35]

During the mass hardship, dislocation, and violence of the Civil War, urban white Southern women took the unusual step of leading riots. Historian Stephanie McCurry chronicles dozens of Confederate riots from March to April 1863 led by soldiers' wives to advance what she terms the "mass politics of subsistence." Typically, women organizers held mass meetings to select the targets, speculator merchants who charged more than government prices, and choreograph the violence to maximize public sympathy. The April 2 Richmond disturbance, which McCurry calls the "biggest civilian riot in Confederate history," began, according to plan, with a coterie of women entering a store and offering to pay government rates. When refused, they drew their weapons—the riot was on. More than three hundred women raided Richmond stores, carting off large quantities of foodstuffs and other necessities, before a crowd of one thousand men and women. As in colonial-era bread riots, white Confederate women emphasized their prescribed role as maternal guardians and soldiers' wives to retain popular support and overcome gendered strictures on women doing politics. The 1863 bread riots ultimately succeeded in pressuring public authorities to more strictly regulate the price of consumer goods and provide more generous social assistance to poor white families.[36]

URBAN LYNCH RIOTS AND INDUSTRIAL CONFLICT AFTER THE CIVIL WAR

The New York City draft riots helped to establish a new template of disorder: the urban lynch riot. From the 1860s to the 1920s, white Americans regularly used large-scale racial terror to subordinate racial minorities, particularly African Americans, in an era of intensifying industrial production, urbanization, and constant struggle over the rights and meaning of US

citizenship after the abolition of slavery. Urban police departments, almost entirely white and, in northern and western cities, predominantly Irish and Italian, frequently enabled racial terror either by directly helping white rioters or at least not trying to stop them. Additionally, violent labor conflict became more routine and deadly as the scale of production dramatically increased, especially in the coal, steel, and oil industries that rapidly expanded to support the effort to build a transcontinental railroad. Facing great danger and hardship on the job, workers used group violence as one strategy to fight their bosses and foreign-born competition.

Mob killings in the late 19th century served a more overtly political purpose after the war, especially in the South. In the 1860s, Christopher Waldrep observes, the murders committed by the Ku Klux Klan were rarely called "lynchings" because they lacked popular sanction from the white community. Also, Republicans in Congress and the US military occupying the former Confederacy made great efforts to arrest and prosecute white vigilantes. Nevertheless, the Klan and similar groups terrorized freedpeople after the war. In 1866 mobs of white civilians and police massacred scores of African Americans in Memphis, Tennessee, and New Orleans.[37] At the start of the 1870s, Republicans began to lose power in the South as white Democrats won office through fraud, terror, and violence. One of the worst racial massacres in US history arose from a contested election in Grant Parish, Louisiana, in April 1873. Black Republicans holed up in a Colfax courthouse to constitute the new government when a white militia mustered by Democrats opened fire on the occupants, hunting down the ones who fled into the nearby woods, ultimately killing an estimated 150 African Americans. Forty-eight black men were executed afterward as prisoners. Historian LeeAnna Keith has observed that subsequent generations of whites remembered the 1873 massacre as a "riot" to justify the violence as a police action to control disorderly blacks and overturn "carpetbag misrule."[38]

In the 1890s African American anti-lynching activists like Ida B. Wells and the *Chicago Tribune* began documenting and publicizing lynching as a specifically racial and Southern phenomenon. Waldrep notes that this activism changed the meaning of lynching, convincing many Americans, including black Americans, to view the practice as criminal and immoral rather than as a "sensible popular response to monstrous crime."[39] In the 1880s and 1890s, after major newspapers like the *New York Times* started denouncing lynching on due process grounds, white Southerners articulated a new racial rationale for the practice, as a necessary means of policing African American criminality, especially for rape and murder. Between 1877 and 1950, as many as 4,075 African Americans were murdered by mobs in the states of the former Confederacy. Scholars credit several factors for lynching's decline: national press coverage, more robust federal enforcement, the consciousness-raising activism of Wells and civil rights organizations like the National Association for the Advancement of Colored People, and the growing use of the death penalty in the South as a substitute method of retributive killing.[40]

During the demographic and political upheavals of the 1890s to the 1920s, whites used large-scale violent terror to enforce racial hierarchy and limit African American advancement. In these decades, especially after America's entry into World War I in 1917, one million African Americans migrated to northern and western cities, fleeing the strict caste system of the South and seeking economic opportunity in urban areas and wartime factories. Racial pogroms in this era typically began with a rumor of a black man's violent crime against a white woman. Starting as a police action, they morphed into wholesale massacres as law enforcement enabled the killing. Using the shorthand of "Black Uplift, White Fury," the historian William M. Tuttle Jr. has characterized 1917 to 1923 as "the bloodiest era of racial violence in the history of the United States." Tuttle offers the "conservative" estimate of 735 deaths from massacres and 387 deaths from lynch mobs, totaling 1,122 riot fatalities, nearly all of them African American.[41]

Southern lynch riots often had an overt political purpose, to consolidate one-party rule and establish *de jure* Jim Crow segregation, whereas many Northern pogroms arose during World War I to contain black mobility. The Southern massacres were an integral part of a political project known as Redemption, led by white planters and Democratic leaders like South Carolina US Senator Ben Tillman, who advocated white male dominion over African Americans as a natural right. In Wilmington, North Carolina, in 1898, where African Americans were the majority of the population and many held elected and appointed public office, white press, politicians, merchants, and common laborers orchestrated an armed political coup against the Fusionists—a racially liberal coalition of Republicans and Populists. The mob destroyed a prominent black printing press and drove black public officials from Wilmington. The massacre ended with a ceremony installing a new white Democratic government. Probably dozens of African Americans were slaughtered, their bodies never recovered.[42]

The Northern lynch riots, by contrast, were rooted in the experiences of the white urban industrial workforce facing new competition from black migrants. In many of these pogroms, white police officers, former antagonists in labor strife, joined with white laborers in ritualized acts of destruction and killing against a common foe. A protracted labor dispute preceded the pogrom in East St. Louis in 1917, after striking white workers at Aluminum Ore Company blamed African American migrants for their economic woes. Many of the strikebreakers used by the employer were black. Over two days in July, white mobs, assisted by police and National Guardsmen, killed thirty-nine African Americans by rope, fire, and gun. An additional nine whites died in the rioting.[43] In Chicago in July 1919, white gangs, workers, and police joined to violently crush African American protest after a white man killed a black boy for swimming to the "white side" of a city beach on Lake Michigan. This riot grew out of several years of intense boundary disputes over segregation in recreation and residence, including over two dozen bombings of black homes since 1917. The 1919 riot signaled more effective resistance from African Americans. Twenty-three of the thirty-eight dead were black. Fifteen were white.[44]

Chicago's violence was part of a cresting wave of post-emancipation racial mob killings. During the Red Summer of 1919, seventy-eight African Americans were lynched. Ten were military veterans. Eleven were burned alive. Twenty-six major riots took place between April and October, in the North and the South, in cities and the countryside. In Phillips County, Arkansas, African Americans outnumbered whites by three to one but made up 90 percent of the labor force in corn and cotton sharecropping. African American veterans returning from World War I helped to organize the community to assert their rights. After a shootout between black leaders and police resulted in an officer dead, white posses roamed the county killing black people at random. Up to two hundred African Americans died over two days.[45]

Black assertiveness and social mobility provoked large-scale killing and property destruction in the oil boomtown of Tulsa, Oklahoma, in 1921. After police arrested a black man accused of raping a young white woman, a white lynch mob came to the jail but were met by armed African Americans seeking to protect the accused. After a scuffle caused an errant gun shot, many in the original lynch mob were deputized by Tulsa police to attack the Greenwood district known as "Negro Wall Street." Armed black residents repelled some "special deputies" but were ultimately overpowered. White posses had superior numbers and firepower, including machine guns and private planes, with police escort, that dropped dynamite on Greenwood. White mobs torched more than one thousand homes and businesses, leveling the once-prospering black neighborhood.

Police arrested six thousand black Tulsans and confined them to three makeshift city internment camps for up to a week. Hundreds more fled the city for good. Historian Scott Ellsworth estimates between seventy-five and 175 died in the pogrom. Most of the dead were African American, but in a testament to black armed resistance, a sizable number were white.[46]

The Red Summers of 1917 to 1923 marked a turning point in US riot history. Thereafter, the dominant style of rioting was led by the downtrodden and the marginalized against the state and more powerful social groups. Racial violence and mob killings continued, of course, as in Beaumont, Texas, in 1943, and the national anti-desegregation violence of the 1950s and 1960s. But increasingly rioting and especially urban rioting attacked up the social hierarchy rather than down. The geography of riot violence also shifted. Between 1890 and 1970, more than six million African Americans left the South and resettled in northern and western cities. Mexican Americans and Puerto Ricans made a similar journey north as well, albeit on a smaller scale. During these Great Migrations, concentrated around World War I and World War II, racial minorities faced frequently violent hostility and discrimination from white residents and urban police departments. This confrontation set the stage for the urban rebellions of the 1960s.

Although racial mob killings from 1880 to 1930 inspired little reform among law enforcement agencies, the industrial strife of this era did inspire a movement to centralize and professionalize state-directed riot control. In the summer of 1877, hundreds of thousands of railroad workers went on strike after companies cut wages by 10 percent. Beginning in West Virginia, the Railroad Strike in two weeks affected "about two-thirds of the country's total rail mileage." Mobs ripped up railroad tracks, damaged company property, and with knives and guns fought state militias. In Pittsburgh, rioters destroyed the Pennsylvania Railroad Union Depot and Hotel, thirty-nine other buildings, more than one hundred trains, and more than two thousand cars. The estimated Pittsburgh dead ranged from twenty to forty. More than one hundred died nationally in two weeks, including as many as fifty in Chicago. The victims were mainly strikers, killed by militia. In a rare act, President Rutherford B. Hayes called out federal troops to put down the unrest.[47]

In the late 19th century, local governments could use local police, state militias, and federal troops to break strikes and suppress worker violence, but each of these methods had serious flaws. Local police often sympathized with striking workers and had no training in riot control. Federal troops were well trained and disciplined, but authorities were reluctant to use them due to public fears of military police and restrictions under the Posse Comitatus Act of 1878. The volunteer state militias were superior to local police but unreliable for similar reasons. In the Railroad Strike of 1877, militiamen in some cities set down their arms or gave them to rioters. In subsequent decades, many states reorganized their volunteer militias along military lines, provided new weapons and uniforms, offered training and pay, and renamed them the National Guard. In the labor violence from the 1880s to the 1920s, local governments dispatched the Guard at the behest of employers to put down strikes, often with ruthless and illegal tactics. In the first decades of the 20th century, many state governments created state police agencies, which also served as strike-breaking forces.[48]

RESCUE RIOTS, COMMUNITY DEFENSE, AND URBAN REBELLION IN THE 20TH CENTURY

During the 20th century, a notable shift in rioting took place: marginalized populations, especially people of color living in cities, used rioting to defend their communities against white civilian and police violence. In July 1900 Robert Charles, an itinerant African American laborer in New Orleans, rebuffed police manhandling during on-the-street questioning,

fled amid gunshots, killed two police officers during the manhunt, and fled again. Hunted by white posses and police, Charles holed up in an associate's house on Saratoga Street, where he died in a shootout with three hundred armed vigilantes surrounded by thousands of white onlookers, his corpse mutilated and carted to the city morgue, one week after the initial police stop. Historian William Ivy Hair has documented how at the time of his death Charles had embraced proto-black nationalism and was raising money to settle American blacks in Africa. In his act of resistance, Charles tapped into deep strains of armed self-defense within the African American community.[49] He also joined a tradition of mobbing the police dating to the postbellum period. In the 1870s and 1880s, as whites reclaimed their place in Southern urban police departments, white patrol officers faced increasingly hostile black crowds who issued taunts, threw rocks and bricks, and occasionally attempted to rescue the prisoner from official custody.[50]

Rescue riots aimed to protect the community from the state. For most of the 20th century, federal and state courts upheld this communitarian tradition as the individual's right to resist unlawful arrest, recognizing the supposedly natural inclination of people to react violently to state cruelty. Anti-police mobbing also derived from young men's desire to prove manhood and toughness. The historian Christopher Thale has chronicled how young Irish men and white patrolmen in New York City in the 1910s viewed street-corner scuffles as "not only a test of individual autonomy and authority, but of masculinity."[51] Likewise, researchers in Philadelphia in 1966 observed that both young men and white police viewed the "battle of the corner" as "challenges to their manhood."[52] Indeed, many of the urban riots of the 1960s began from this masculinist impulse, with African American or Latino crowds acting on a rumor of gendered state violence against a vulnerable member of the community, such as a pregnant woman or girl. Anti-police mobbing provided a means for rioters, typically young men, to protect their communities from frequently violent and racist mistreatment by police.[53]

During World War II, the largest internal migration in US history transformed America's racial geography and led to a round of major rioting. Wartime manufacturing drew millions of African American migrants from the Jim Crow South: one hundred thousand to Chicago, sixty thousand to Detroit, twenty-five thousand to Philadelphia and Harlem, and two hundred thousand to Los Angeles.[54] Residential segregation, enforced by federal law and street-level violence, created the conditions for intense boundary disputes when nonwhite migrants settled in or near white areas. As historian Victoria Wolcott documents, much urban rioting in the 1930s and 1940s arose from conflicts over access to segregated public recreation.[55] The historian Arnold S. Hirsch documents dozens of Chicago riots over public housing desegregation in the 1950s. Famously, Martin Luther King Jr. was pelted with rocks on a march through a segregated white neighborhood in Chicago in the summer of 1966. Similar street violence occurred in Detroit and Philadelphia.[56]

Summer 1943 seemed to complete the turn toward community defense begun during World War I as the dominant mode of rioting. In 1943, the Social Science Institute at Fisk University documented 242 incidents of interracial violence in forty-seven cities. Most were traditional white mob justice. In Los Angeles, in June, white servicemen and civilians roamed the city attacking young Mexican American men dressed in zoot suits—baggy, brightly colored suits tapering at the ankles, a subversive statement that violated wartime clothing rations and to many whites signaled gang affiliation—in lynch-mob rituals involving physical violence and public humiliation. A week earlier, in Detroit, white and black youths sparred in the parks of Belle Isle. Hours later, one of the largest disorders in US history started. Crowds of African Americans looted stores in Black Bottom on the city's eastside, and the following day, ten thousand whites amassed on Woodward Avenue, a main thoroughfare, and attacked black pedestrians at random. Detroit police did little to stop white brutality and instead heightened it. President Franklin Roosevelt had to send federal troops to restore order. Thirty-four people died during Detroit's riots. Twenty-five were African American, seventeen killed by police. Eighty-five percent of the arrested were black, in a city more than two-thirds white.[57]

The Harlem disorder in August 1943 spotlighted the new riot landscape. When a black serviceman tried to prevent the arrest of a black woman for prostitution, the white officer got off a shot. A false rumor of the soldier's death spread among Harlem residents, inflaming popular anger over the many black veterans lynched while in uniform in the South. Thousands began looting and burning stores and attacking police officers. City officials cordoned off the area to prevent interracial conflict, toured Harlem with notable African American activists to clear the streets, and instructed police to use restraint. Six people died. The 1943 disorder took place eight years after rioting by African Americans in Harlem in response to a rumor that a white police officer had killed a black boy for shoplifting at a department store. In both examples, rioters focused their fury on police and property.[58]

Demeaning, violent, and racist police tactics provoked a rise in rescue riots in the mid to late 1950s, heralding the larger rebellions to come. Crowd rescues became national news. The peak year of public interest was 1961 when the New York Police Department reported 2,525 individual assaults against 492 officers. More than two hundred were done by groups of civilians. A close analysis of 255 police assaults in San Francisco between 1962 and 1965 showed that the most common precipitating police action was either an order to "move on" or physical contact. In some instances, spectators chanted "Birmingham" or "Freedom Now," referencing famous Southern battles over Jim Crow and civil rights. Several spontaneous street protests became serious riots, as in Kinloch, Missouri, a St. Louis suburb, in September 1962; North Philadelphia in October 1963; and Des Moines, Iowa, in May 1964.[59]

During the 1960s, large-scale rioting in cities and suburbs became a routine and widespread summer phenomenon. The sociologist Seymour Spilerman has counted 820 "racial incidents" in 673 cities between 1961 and 1968 involving at least thirty people and characterized by "Negro aggression." Using thirty participants for 1964 to 1971, others have summarized the tally as follows: 752 uprisings, 1,802 days of riots, 228 deaths, 12,741 persons injured, 69,099 persons arrested, and 15,835 arson incidents. The more traditional shorter timeline with a higher participant threshold posits 221 deaths in 341 riots between 1963 and 1968. The National Advisory Commission on Civil Disorders, appointed in July 1967 and known as the Kerner Commission for its chair, Illinois Governor Otto Kerner, estimated eighty-three deaths in 164 disorders in 128 cities in the first nine months of 1967 alone.[60]

The urban riots of the 1960s are distinctive in US history for several reasons. Departing from tradition, they were mob justice from below against the state, rather than an attempt to preserve social hierarchies. Their scale was national, in cities of every size in every region of the country, and their duration lasted several years. Some disorders were among the most destructive and lethal in US history, in part because the state responded with overwhelming force, including lynching-style violence.[61] The urban rebellions also attained such scale because they belonged to a national insurgency against Jim Crow. As historian Malcolm McLaughlin has argued, to riot against white officialdom "was to make a political statement," forcing scores of towns and cities to reckon with apartheid.[62] According to sociologist Carol Mueller, most riots in the peak years of 1967 and 1968 took place in cities with populations below 250,000, and nearly half in cities with fewer than twenty-five thousand African American residents.[63]

Urban rioting in the 1960s took several forms and elicited a range of responses from authorities. In Rochester, New York, in July 1964, black teenagers, some of them in social clubs or gangs, helped lead and organize rioting on the second night, stockpiling Molotov cocktails and rocks on rooftops. In Hough, Cleveland, in July 1966, rioting started after a white bar-owner refused to serve a black patron a glass of water and police ignored the crowd's pleas. In a few dozen cities, especially after the rise of Black Power in 1966, black teenagers used rioting as a bargaining tactic to obtain meetings with the mayor and demand concessions, typically better recreation, more employment opportunities, and police reforms like civilian review and an end to investigative arrests.[64] Looting was a feature of most riots. In some cities, rioters targeted white merchants especially resented by the community for charging high prices for inferior goods and extending credit at high interest rates. Elsewhere, looters ignored "Soul Brother" signs and wrecked any store with desired merchandise.[65]

A handful of riots produced mass destruction and casualties. The six-day rebellion in Watts, Los Angeles, in August 1965, led to four thousand arrests, six hundred damaged buildings (two hundred from fire), and thirty-five deaths. Thirteen people were killed while looting, six shot in the back. Los Angeles Police killed nineteen civilians. Seventeen were black, one was Latino, and one was Japanese-American. The National Guard killed eight. The rebellions in Newark and Detroit in late July 1967 combined for sixty-six deaths, twenty-three and forty-three, respectively. Of the dead, fifty-four were African American. Twenty-two were looters, fourteen shot while fleeing. In both cities, police shot into people's homes. In vivid testimony to the Kerner Commission, victims described police torturing, humiliating, and viciously beating people on the street and at the station house. Some state violence resembled the emasculating rituals of lynching: white Detroit cops used rifle butts to bash black men in the genitals upon arrest. At the Algiers Motel,

Detroit police tortured and killed three black teenage boys and taunted their white female companions for socializing with black men.[66]

Scholars have documented a dramatic increase in rioting in other marginalized communities in the late 1960s and 1970s. Collective violence provided a means for invisible and beleaguered minorities to defy oppressive authority and take a public stand for their rights and dignity. Historian Aaron Fountain has found twelve Latino riots for all of 1966 to 1969 but seventeen in each of 1970 and 1971. Of the eighty-nine total Latino riots Fountain identified between 1966 and 2012, two-thirds involved Puerto Ricans and most took place in the Northeast—New Jersey had seventeen. Many Latino uprisings responded to police violence but tapped into familiar grievances over unequal education, housing, recreation, and employment. Gays and lesbians famously rioted at the Stonewall Inn in New York City in 1969 to protest police harassment, building upon prior activism to help launch the Gay Liberation Movement. Prison riots became more common at the height of Black Power, rising from five in 1967, to fifteen in 1968, twenty-seven in 1970, thirty-seven in 1971, and forty-two in 1972, the most in US history. In September 1971, more than two thousand prisoners rioted at Attica State Correctional Facility in upstate New York over appalling conditions and the recent killing of African American prison activist George Jackson at St. Quentin. Attica inmates seized control of a prison wing, took guards hostage, and negotiated for better conditions with prison officials. Governor Nelson Rockefeller instead dispatched state police who slaughtered forty-three people, including thirty-three inmates and ten guards.[67]

AN END TO RIOTING? THE STATE'S MONOPOLY ON VIOLENCE SINCE THE 1970S

In retrospect, the burst of rioting in the early 1970s was more of an end than a beginning.

Since 1975, rioting has declined overall and large-scale rebellions have almost entirely disappeared. The two major riots of this period—Miami in 1980 and Los Angeles in 1992—combined popular anger directed at the state and other racial groups. Miami had eighteen deaths and $80 million in property damage. In Los Angeles, the unrest spanned several dozen square miles, caused fifty-one deaths and cost more than $1 billion. In both cities, the spark was the jury acquittal of officers responsible for horrific violence—fatal in the case of Miami—against black men guilty of traffic violations. Yet most riot fatalities in both cities were caused by civilians not police. Both uprisings reflected the country's changing demographics since the Immigration Act of 1965 relaxed immigration restrictions on East Asia and the global South. As in past interracial riots, labor competition between native-born and foreign-born racial groups, long a source of tension, resulted in violent clashes between African Americans and Cubans in Miami and African Americans and South Koreans in Los Angeles. Also, journalist Mike Davis has argued that there were two Los Angeles riots: the more famous one led by African Americans in South Central and the lesser-known one in Mid-City, where 225,000 Mexican and Central American immigrants had settled in the previous decade, struggling to survive on meager earnings from manual labor and service work.[68]

For scholars puzzling over the relative absence of rioting since the 1970s, Miami and Los Angeles have provided glaring exceptions to a new norm. The historian Michael Katz has identified several factors for why urban unrest dissipated. The boundary disputes, a crucial catalyst for many 20th-century riots, subsided as millions of whites migrated to the suburbs. New immigrants after 1970 maintained a low profile in fear of native xenophobia. The Cuban and Korean populations in Miami and Los Angeles, respectively, were well established, and although many Latinos rioted in Los Angeles, immigrant fears were soon validated when Republicans and Democrats from Southern California proposed immediately deporting undocumented immigrants arrested during the unrest or depriving their US-born children of citizenship. Katz further argues that class stratification within the African American community, combined with greater black political representation, made rioting less feasible and desirable.[69]

A final factor in the decline of rioting was the dramatic expansion in state capacities to suppress mass civilian violence. In 1965, Congress created the Office of Law Enforcement Assistance to offer modest funds to local criminal justice agencies, including police. Three years later, after hundreds of riots and a sudden increase in criminal violence, a law-and-order Congress formally established the Law Enforcement Assistance Administration (LEAA). Between 1969 and 1980, the agency spent $7.5 billion on a wide range of initiatives. Local authorities used some on education and training and some to hire more police officers and guards, build more jails and prisons, and acquire more powerful weaponry. The federal money, although unprecedented, amounted to 5 percent of total spending on crime control. Local police budgets ballooned from $2 billion in 1965 to $58 billion in 1995 to more than $90 billion in 2015. State and local governments spent $17 billion on incarceration in 1980 and $71 billion in 2013. Rescue riots were perhaps a more tempting option against officers carrying only a baton and a pistol than against heavily armed SWAT (Special Weapons And Tactics) members riding in armored personnel carriers.[70]

Yet, aggressive urban policing has not only deterred potential disorder but has arguably provoked retaliatory violence from heavily policed populations. Rioting has thus ebbed but not disappeared, remaining in the early 21st century a communal check on state violence. Deaths of young black men at the hands of police has caused prolonged community defense unrest, mainly looting and burning stores, in a handful of cities since 2000: Cincinnati,

Ohio, in April 2001; Oakland, California, in January 2009; Ferguson, Missouri in August and November 2014; Baltimore, Maryland, in April 2015; and Milwaukee, Wisconsin in August 2016.

DISCUSSION OF THE LITERATURE

The state of US riot history in 2018 is sprawling, hardly a field in any real sense. Perhaps that is progress. In 1970, Richard Hofstadter proclaimed that "the rediscovery of our violence will undoubtedly be one of the most important intellectual legacies of the 1960s."[71] At that time of urban rebellion and political violence, US historians began to study more closely and systematically America's violent past. Many were inspired by European historians E. P. Thompson, George Rudé, Natalie Zemon Davis, and Eric Hobsbawm, whose signal contribution was to treat disorderly crowds and rioters as rational actors whose violence contained hidden clues to the desires and social worlds of ordinary people and the power relations that structured their lives.[72] Richard Maxwell Brown soon published his influential study arguing that American violence was rooted in a vigilante tradition that arose in frontier colonial South Carolina.[73] A wave of urban riot histories was published at this time, most notably by Dominic Capeci Jr. on Detroit, Capeci and Martha F. Wilkerson on Harlem, and William Tuttle Jr. on Chicago.[74] This work was greatly indebted to social scientific theories on "status deprivation" and crowd behavior innovated by sociologists.[75] It also followed the protocols of social history, with painstaking research documenting the lives of ordinary people who belonged to the universe of the riot event. Since the pioneering works of the 1970s, only a few have attempted a grand narrative. The historian Paul Gilje wrote perhaps the only recent synthetic historical monograph on US rioting, published in 1995.[76]

Perhaps the field's waning sense of mission represents progress, since America's violent past is no longer so arresting or surprising. Still, the scholarship to arrive after the initial wave has coalesced around a few lines of inquiry. Instead of deeply exploring the causes and consequences of single events, historians write about rioting as a practice of popular justice and how it relates to dominant political structures or conflicts of a particular moment, such as Wayne Lee on the colonial era, David Grimsted on the antebellum period, Victoria Wolcott on the 1910s to the 1960s, and Malcolm McLaughlin on the 1960s.[77] Similarly, the new lynching historiography has moved from case studies to regional or national histories and has mainly focused on uncovering patterns in violence linking crowds to social structures and ideology. Historians Christopher Waldrep and Michael Pfeifer in particular emphasize how lynching rose and fell in concert with changes in dominant legal practice and law enforcement.[78] Likewise, historian Alex Elkins encourages riot scholars to trace the historical development of rioting and policing as practices of popular justice that have moved in tandem.[79]

PRIMARY SOURCES

Some riots are better documented than others, but most leave a similar paper trail.

GOVERNMENT ARCHIVES

STATE AND LOCAL ARCHIVES

In the 19th and 20th century, it was common for local or state authorities to order an autopsy of a riot through some commission appointed for the purpose. These bodies produced reports that are often available at local public libraries or archives. Some have been digitized. More than a few commissions left behind substantial records. Court and police records, in addition to providing basic information about the event (number of arrests, property damage, etc.), will offer some detail on who the rioters were (residence, occupation, age, sex, race, etc.). City and state archives, including the papers of public officials, will offer background on

the participants in the conflict, the core grievances, and actions taken in the aftermath. For rioting after World War II, municipal human relations commissions closely documented intergroup tensions and conflict. Their papers are often stored in the special collections of public universities. For instance, the Detroit Commission on Community Relations has their complete papers at the Walter Reuther Library at Wayne State University.

NATIONAL ARCHIVES

Starting in the late 19th and early 20th centuries, when the federal government created new agencies in social services and law enforcement, national archives become more relevant and essential, such as the Freedmen's Bureau or the Federal Bureau of Investigation. Some rioting was serious enough to warrant federal attention. The East St. Louis Riot of 1917 crossed state lines and thus prompted the US House of Representatives to appoint a committee, whose records are now stored at the National Archives in College Park, Maryland. The 1960s urban rebellions led President Lyndon Johnson to create the National Advisory Commission on Civil Disorders. The records are kept at Johnson's presidential library in Austin, Texas.

PRIVATE COLLECTIONS

Private collections of activists, notables, or organizations will give additional insight into the issues that mattered most to contemporaries. If researching the 20th century, the National Association for the Advancement of Colored People made it a part of its core mission to document mob violence. Their papers are invaluable. The national papers are housed at the Library of Congress. Local branch papers are typically stored in special collections at universities. For the 19th century, riot historians rely on newspaper accounts—now digitized but also kept as microfilm at many university libraries or archives—and the letters, diaries, and memoirs of elite individuals, including persons directly involved in the riot.

FURTHER READING

Brown, Richard Maxwell. *Strain of Violence: Historical Studies of American Violence and Vigilantism*. New York: Oxford University Press, 1975.

Carrigan, William D., and Clive Webb. "The Lynching of Persons of Mexican Origin or Descent in the United States, 1848 to 1928." *Journal of Social History* 37, no. 2 (2003): 411–438.

Elkins, Alex. "Battle of the Corner: Urban Policing and Rioting in the United States, 1943–1971." PhD diss., Temple University, 2017.

Gilje, Paul. "The Baltimore Riots of 1812 and the Breakdown of the Anglo-American Mob Tradition." *Journal of Social History* 13, no. 4 (1980): 547–564.

Gilje, Paul. *Rioting in America*. Bloomington: Indiana University Press, 1995.

Maier, Pauline. "Popular Uprisings and Civil Authority in Eighteenth-Century America." *The William and Mary Quarterly* 27, no. 1 (1970): 3–35.

McLaughlin, Malcolm. *The Long, Hot Summer of 1967: Urban Rebellion in America*. New York: Palgrave MacMillan, 2014.

Pfeifer, Michael J. *The Roots of Rough Justice: Origins of American Lynching*. Urbana: University of Illinois Press, 2011.

Thompson, Heather Ann. *Blood in the Water: The Attica Prison Uprising of 1971 and Its Legacy*. New York: Pantheon, 2016.

Waldrep, Christopher. *The Many Faces of Judge Lynch: Extralegal Violence and Punishment in America*. New York: Palgrave Macmillan, 2002.

Wolcott, Victoria. *Race, Riots, and Roller Coasters: The Struggle over Segregated Recreation in America*. Philadelphia: University of Pennsylvania Press, 2012.

NOTES

1. Charles Tilly, *Contentious Performances* (New York: Cambridge University Press, 2008), 8–19.

2. Paul Gilje, "The Baltimore Riots of 1812 and the Breakdown of the Anglo-American Mob Tradition," *Journal of Social History* 13, no. 4 (1980): 547–564; and Gordon S. Wood, "A Note on Mobs in the American Revolution," *The William and Mary Quarterly* 23, no. 4 (1966): 637–638.

3. Wayne E. Lee, *Crowds and Soldiers in Revolutionary North Carolina: The Culture of Violence in Riot and War* (Gainesville: University Press of Florida, 2001), 3.

4. E. P. Thompson, "The Moral Economy of the English Crowd in the Eighteenth Century," *Past & Present* 50 (February 1971): 78; Eric J. Hobsbawm, *Bandits* (New York: Delacorte, 1969); George Rudé, *The Crowd in History: A Study of Popular Disturbances in France and England, 1730–1848* (New York: John Wiley & Sons, 1964); Natalie Zemon Davis, "The Rites of Violence: Religious Riot in Sixteenth-Century France," *Past & Present* 59 (May 1973): 51–91; and Natalie Zemon Davis, "Writing 'The Rites of Violence' and Afterward," *Past & Present* 214, no. S7 (2012): 8–29.

5. Pauline Maier, "Popular Uprisings and Civil Authority in Eighteenth-Century America," *The William and Mary Quarterly* 27, no. 1 (1970): 4–5.

6. Lee, *Crowds and Soldiers*, 18.

7. Thomas P. Slaughter, *The Whiskey Rebellion: Frontier Epilogue to the American Revolution* (New York: Oxford University Press, 1986), 227.

8. David Montgomery, "The Shuttle and the Cross: Weavers and Artisans in the Kensington Riots of 1844," *Journal of Social History* 5, no. 4 (1972): 414–421; and Paul Gilje, *Rioting in America* (Bloomington: Indiana University Press, 1995), 64–67.

9. Lee, *Crowds and Soldiers*, 43.

10. Gilje, "The Baltimore Riots of 1812," 548–557.

11. David Grimsted, *American Mobbing, 1828–1861* (New York: Oxford University Press, 1998), 4.

12. David Grimsted, "Rioting in Its Jacksonian Setting," *The American Historical Review* 77, no. 2 (1972): 364.

13. Beverly C. Tomek, *Pennsylvania Hall: A "Legal Lynching" in the Shadow of the Liberty Bell* (New York: Oxford University Press, 2013).

14. Grimsted, *American Mobbing*, 209–210.

15. Michael Feldberg, *The Turbulent Era: Riot and Disorder in Jacksonian America* (New York: Oxford University Press, 1980), chaps. 1–4; and Gilje, *Rioting in America*, 77–79

16. Gilje, *Rioting in America*, 74–75.

17. Thomas P. Slaughter, *Bloody Dawn: The Christiana Riot and Racial Violence in the Antebellum North* (New York: Oxford University Press, 1991), 144–146.

18. Allen Steinberg, *The Transformation of Criminal Justice: Philadelphia, 1800–1880* (Chapel Hill: University of North Carolina Press, 1989), chaps. 1, 2, and 6.

19. Steinberg, *Transformation of Criminal Justice*, 142; and Zachary M. Schrag, "Nativist Riots of 1844," *The Encyclopedia of Greater Philadelphia*, 2013.

20. Manfred Berg, *Popular Justice: A History of Lynching in America* (New York: Ivan R. Dee, 2011), 49–54.

21. Christopher Waldrep, *The Many Faces of Judge Lynch: Extralegal Violence and Punishment in America* (New York: Palgrave Macmillan, 2002), 27–35.

22. Waldrep, *The Many Faces*, 49–61.

23. Philip J. Ethington, "Vigilantes and the Police: The Creation of a Professional Police Bureaucracy in San Francisco, 1847–1900," *Journal of Social History* 21, no. 2 (1987): 202–203; Christopher Waldrep, "The Popular Sources of Political Authority in 1856 San Francisco: Lynching, Vigilance, and the Difference between Politics and Constitutionalism," in *Lynching beyond Dixie: American Mob Violence outside the South*, ed. Michael J. Pfeifer (Urbana: University of Illinois Press, 2013), 56–63; and William D. Carrigan, "The Strange Career of Judge Lynch: Why the Study of Lynching Needs to Be Refocused on the Mid-Nineteenth Century," *The Journal of the Civil War Era* 7, no. 2 (2017): 302.

24. Michael J. Pfeifer, *The Roots of Rough Justice: Origins of American Lynching* (Urbana: University of Illinois Press, 2011), 4–5.

25. Ken Gonzales-Day, *Lynching in the West, 1850–1935* (Durham: Duke University Press, 2006), 25.

26. Pfeifer, *Roots of Rough Justice*, 34, 38–39, 41.

27. Gonzales-Day, *Lynching in the West*, 9.

28. William D. Carrigan and Clive Webb, "The Lynching of Persons of Mexican Origin or Descent in the United States, 1848 to 1928," *Journal of Social History* 37, no. 2 (2003): 413–414, 416; Carrigan, "The Strange Career of Judge Lynch," 305; and William D. Carrigan and Clive Webb, "Muerto Por Unos Desconocidos (Killed by Persons Unknown): Mob Violence against African Americans and Mexican Americans," in *Beyond Black and White: Race, Ethnicity, and Gender in the U.S. South and Southwest*, ed. Stephanie Cole and Alison Parker (College Park: Texas A&M University Press, 2004), 49.

29. Carrigan and Webb, "The Lynching of Persons," 416–417, 425–426; and Gonzales-Day, *Lynching in the West*, 24–26.

30. Gilje, *Rioting in America*, 88.

31. Eric Foner, *Gateway to Freedom: The Hidden History of America's Fugitive Slaves* (New York: Oxford University Press, 2015), 147–150.

32. Slaughter, *Bloody Dawn*, 8–9, chap. 7.

33. Michael J. Pfeifer, "The Northern United States and the Genesis of Racial Lynching: The Lynching of African Americans in the Civil War Era," *The Journal of American History* 97, no. 3 (2010): 627–631; and Pfeifer, *Roots of Rough Justice*, 71–76.

34. Iver Bernstein, *The New York City Draft Riots: Their Significance for American Society and Politics in the Age of the Civil War* (New York: Oxford University Press, 1990), 7–11; and Gilje, *Rioting in America*, 91–92.

35. Bernstein, *New York City Draft Riots*, 5, 17–42, 288–289.

36. Stephanie McCurry, *Confederate Reckoning: Power and Politics in the Civil War South* (Cambridge, MA: Harvard University Press, 2012), 187, 191–203; and Gilje, *Rioting in America*, 25.

37. Waldrep, *The Many Faces*, chap. 4

38. LeeAnna Keith, *The Colfax Massacre: The Untold Story of Black Power, White Terror, and the Death of Reconstruction* (New York: Oxford University Press, 2008), xii–xiv.

39. Waldrep, *The Many Faces*, 86.

40. Waldrep, *The Many Faces*, chap. 6, 151–177; Pfeifer, *Roots of Rough Justice*, chap. 5; estimate comes from the Equal Justice Initiative, *Lynching in America: Confronting the Legacy of Racial Terror*, 2nd ed. (Montgomery, AL: Equal Justice Initiative, 2015), 5.

41. Ann V. Collins, *All Hell Broke Loose: American Race Riots from the Progressive Era through World War II* (Santa Barbara: Praeger, 2012), 5; and William M. Tuttle Jr., "Black Uplift, White Fury: The Shame of America's Red Summers, 1917–1923" (paper presented at the Mid-America Conference on History, Springfield, MO, October 1, 2004 [revised 2014]), 1.

42. Stephen Kantrowitz, "Ben Tillman and Hendrix McLane, Agrarian Rebels: White Manhood, 'The Farmers,' and the Limits of Southern Populism," *The Journal of Southern History* 66, no. 3 (2000): 499–500; Collins, *All Hell Broke Loose*, 36–41; and David S. Cecelski and Timothy B. Tyson, eds., *Democracy Betrayed: The Wilmington Race Riot of 1898 and Its Legacy* (Chapel Hill: University of North Carolina Press, 1998).

43. Malcolm McLaughlin, *Power, Community, and Racial Killing in East St. Louis* (New York:

Palgrave Macmillan, 2005); Charles L. Lumpkins, *American Pogrom: The East St. Louis Race Riot and Black Politics* (Athens, OH: Ohio University Press, 2008); and Elliot Rudwick, *Race Riot at East St. Louis, July 2, 1917* (Carbondale: Southern Illinois University Press, 1964).

44. Collins, *All Hell Broke Loose*, 95–99; William M. Tuttle Jr., *Race Riot: Chicago in the Red Summer of 1919* (New York: Atheneum, 1970); and Tuttle Jr., "Black Uplift, White Fury," 6, 25.

45. Collins, *All Hell Broke Loose*, 71, 107–112; Tuttle Jr., "Black Uplift, White Fury," 6–7; and Cameron McWhirter, *Red Summer: The Summer of 1919 and the Awakening of Black America* (New York: Henry Holt, 2011).

46. Scott Ellsworth, *Death in a Promised Land: The Tulsa Race Riot of 1921* (Baton Rouge: Louisiana University Press, 1982), chap. 3, 71–72.

47. Robert M. Fogelson, *America's Armories: Architecture, Society and Public Order* (Cambridge, MA: Harvard University Press, 1989), 20–21; and Philip Taft and Philip Ross, "American Labor Violence: Its Causes, Character, and Outcome," in *Violence in America: Historical and Comparative Perspectives; A Report to the National Commission on the Causes and Prevention of Violence*, vol. 2 (Washington, DC: Government Printing Office, 1969), 221–301.

48. Fogelson, *America's Armories*, 34–42; and P. O. Ray, "Metropolitan and State Police," *Journal of the American Institute of Criminal Law and Criminology* 11, no. 3 (1920): 453–467.

49. William Ivy Hair, *Carnival of Fury: Robert Charles and the New Orleans Race Riot of 1900*, 2nd ed. (Baton Rouge: Louisiana State University Press, 2008); Charles E. Cobb Jr., *This Nonviolent Stuff'll Get You Killed: How Guns Made the Civil Rights Movement Possible* (New York: Basic Books, 2014); Karlos K. Hill, "Black Vigilantism: The Rise and Decline of African American Lynch Mob Activity in the Mississippi and Arkansas Deltas, 1883–1923," *The Journal of African American History* 95 (2010): 26–43; Steven Hahn, *A Nation under Our Feet: Black Political Struggles in the Rural South, from Slavery to the Great Migration* (Cambridge, MA: Harvard University Press, 2003); Shannon King, "'Ready to Shoot and Do Shoot': Black Working-Class Self-Defense and Community Politics in Harlem, New York, during the 1920s," *Journal of Urban History* 37, no. 5 (2011): 757–774; Donna Murch, *Living for the City: Migration,*

Education, and the Rise of the Black Panther Party in Oakland, California (Chapel Hill: University of North Carolina Press, 2010); and Timothy Tyson, *Radio Free Dixie: Robert F. Williams and the Roots of Black Power* (Chapel Hill: University of North Carolina Press, 1999).

50. Howard N. Rabinowitz, "The Conflict between Blacks and the Police in the Urban South, 1865–1900," *The Historian* 39, no. 1 (1976): 62–76, 70–74.

51. Christopher P. Thale, "Civilizing New York City: Police Patrol, 1880–1935" (PhD diss., University of Chicago, 1995), 270.

52. Joseph D. Lohman and Gordon E. Misner, *The Police and the Community: The Dynamics of Their Relationship in a Changing Society*, Field Surveys IV, vol. 2 (Washington, DC: Government Printing Office, 1966), 156.

53. Alex Elkins, "Battle of the Corner: Urban Policing and Rioting in the United States, 1943–1971" (PhD diss., Temple University, 2017), 375–376.

54. Karl E. Johnson, "Black Philadelphia in Transition: The African American Struggle on the Homefront during World War II and the Cold War Period, 1941–1963" (PhD diss., Temple University, 2001), 28; Josh Sides, *L.A. City Limits: African American Los Angeles from the Great Depression to the Present* (Berkeley, CA: University of California Press, 2003), 43; Thomas J. Sugrue, *The Origins of the Urban Crisis: Race and Inequality in Postwar Detroit*, 2nd ed. (Princeton, NJ: Princeton University Press, 2005), 23, 41; and Dominic J. Capeci Jr. and Martha Wilkerson, "The Detroit Rioters of 1943: A Reinterpretation," *Michigan Historical Review* 16, no. 1 (1990): 52.

55. Victoria Wolcott, *Race, Riots, and Roller Coasters: The Struggle over Segregated Recreation in America* (Philadelphia: University of Pennsylvania Press, 2012).

56. Arnold R. Hirsch, "Massive Resistance in the Urban North: Trumbull Park, Chicago, 1953–1966," *The Journal of American History* 82, no. 2 (1995): 533–537, 547–548, 550; Hirsch, *Making the Second Ghetto*, chap. 2; Thomas J. Sugrue, "Crabgrass-Roots Politics: Race, Rights, and the Reaction against Liberalism in the Urban North, 1940–1964," *The Journal of American History* 82, no. 2 (1995): 560–562; and Elkins, "Battle of the Corner," 175–177.

57. Elkins, "Battle of the Corner," 109–112.

58. Elkins, "Battle of the Corner," 112–113; and Cheryl Greenberg, "The Politics of Disorder: Reexamining Harlem's Riots of 1935 and 1943," *Journal of Urban History* 18 (August 1992): 395–441.

59. Elkins, "Battle of the Corner," 275–277, 285–293, 306–363.

60. Seymour Spilerman, "The Causes of Racial Disturbances: A Comparison of Alternative Explanations," *American Sociological Review* 35, no. 4 (1970): 630; William J. Collins and Robert A. Margo, "The Economic Aftermath of the 1960s Riots in American Cities: Evidence from Property Values," *The Journal of Economic History* 67, no. 4 (2007): 853; Sidney Fine, *Violence in the Model City: The Cavanagh Administration, Race Relations, and the Detroit Riot of 1967*, 2nd ed. (East Lansing: Michigan State University Press, 2007), 299; and *Report of the National Advisory Commission on Civil Disorders* (Washington, DC: Government Printing Office, 1968), 65.

61. Elkins, "Battle of the Corner," 430–456.

62. Malcolm McLaughlin, *The Long, Hot Summer of 1967: Urban Rebellion in America* (New York: Palgrave MacMillan, 2014), 10; see also Max Arthur Herman, *Summer of Rage: An Oral History of the 1967 Newark and Detroit Riots* (New York: Peter Lang, 2017); and Mark Krasovic, *The Newark Frontier: Community Action in the Great Society* (Chicago: The University of Chicago Press, 2016).

63. Elkins, "Battle of the Corner," 402; and Carol Elizabeth Mueller, "Riot Negotiations: Conditions of Successful Bargaining in the Urban Riots of 1967 and 1968" (PhD diss., Cornell University, 1971), 132–138.

64. Elkins, "Battle of the Corner," 396–430; Todd M. Michney, *Surrogate Suburbs: Black Upward Mobility and Neighborhood Change* (Chapel Hill: University of North Carolina Press, 2017), 8–9; and Todd M. Michney, "Race, Violence, and Urban Territoriality: Cleveland's Little Italy and the 1966 Hough Uprising," *Journal of Urban History* 32, no. 3 (2006): 404–428

65. Malcolm McLaughlin, *The Long, Hot Summer,* 164–176.

66. Elkins, "Battle of the Corner," 436–437, 439–442, 448–452.

67. Aaron Fountain, "Forgotten Latino Urban Riots and Why They Can Happen Again," *Latino Rebels,* May 2, 2016; Pedro Amaury Regalado, "Urban Uprisings, 1960s–1970s," in *50 Events That Shaped Latino History: An Encyclopedia of the American Mosaic,* ed. Lilia Fernandez (Santa Barbara: Greenwood, 2018), 556–571; Gregg Lee Carter, "Hispanic Rioting During the Civil Rights Era," *Sociological Forum* 7, no. 2 (1992): 301–322; Lilia Fernandez, *Brown in the Windy City: Mexicans and Puerto Ricans in Postwar Chicago* (Chicago: University of Chicago Press, 2012), 159–167; Marie Gottschalk, *The Prison and the Gallows: The Politics of Mass Incarceration in America* (New York: Cambridge University Press, 2006), 178–179; Dan Berger, *Captive Nation: Black Prison Organizing in the Civil Rights Era* (Chapel Hill: The University of North Carolina Press, 2015), 93; and Heather Ann Thompson, *Blood in the Water: The Attica Prison Uprising of 1971 and Its Legacy* (New York: Pantheon, 2016).

68. Max Arthur Herman, *Fighting in the Streets: Ethnic Succession and Urban Unrest in Twentieth-Century America* (New York: Peter Lang, 2005), 114–156; Bruce Porter and Marvin Dunn, *The Miami Riot of 1980: Crossing the Bounds* (Lexington, MA: Lexington Books, 1984); Mike Davis, "Who Killed Los Angeles? Part Two: The Verdict is Given," *New Left Review* I, no. 199 (May–June 1993): 37–40; and Brenda E. Stevenson, *The Contested Murder of Latasha Harlins: Justice, Gender, and the Origins of the LA Riots* (New York: Oxford University Press, 2015), 279, 288–290.

69. Mike Davis, "In L.A., Burning All Illusions," *The Nation,* June 1, 1992, 744.

70. Michael B. Katz, *Why Don't American Cities Burn?* (Philadelphia: University of Pennsylvania Press, 2012), 91–92; "Police And Corrections Expenditures," *Urban Institute;* and "State and Local Expenditures on Corrections and Education," a brief from the US Department of Education, Policy and Program Studies Service, July 2016, 1.

71. Richard Hofstadter, "Introduction," in *American Violence: A Documentary History,* ed. Richard Hofstadter and Michael Wallace (New York: Vintage, 1970), 3.

72. Paul A. Gilje, "The Crowd in American History," *American Transcendental Quarterly* 17, no. 3 (2003): 146–157.

73. Richard Maxwell Brown, *Strain of Violence: Historical Studies of American Violence and Vigilantism* (New York: Oxford University Press, 1975).

74. Tuttle Jr., *Race Riot;* Domenic J. Capeci, *The Harlem Riot of 1943* (Philadelphia: Temple University Press, 1977); and Domenic J. Capeci and Martha Frances Wilkerson, *Layered Violence:*

The Detroit Rioters of 1943 (Jackson: University of Mississippi Press, 1991).

75. Domenic J. Capeci, "Race Riot Redux: William M. Tuttle, Jr. and the Study of Racial Violence," *Reviews in American History* 29, no. 1 (2001): 167; and Gilje, "The Crowd in American History," 148–151.

76. Gilje, *Rioting in America*.

77. Lee, *Crowds and Soldiers*; Grimsted, *American Mobbing*; Wolcott, *Race, Riots, and Roller Coasters*; and McLaughlin, *The Long, Hot Summer*.

78. Michael J. Pfeifer, "At the Hands of Parties Unknown? The State of the Field of Lynching Scholarship," *The Journal of American History* 101, no. 3 (2014): 832–846; and Carrigan, "The Strange Career of Judge Lynch."

79. Alex Elkins, "Stand Our Ground: The Street Justice of Urban American Riots, 1900–1968," *Journal of Urban History* 42, no. 2 (2016): 422–423.

Alex Elkins

THE ANTI-CHINESE MASSACRE IN LOS ANGELES AS A RECONSTRUCTION-ERA EVENT

On October 24, 1871, a gunfight broke out around 5:30 in the evening in Los Angeles, California. Over the next six hours, that isolated exchange of gunfire expanded beyond the confines of a localized feud and metastasized into a cataclysm of many parts: an unforeseen killing, a siege, a deliberately set fire, a mob run amuck, and the public life-taking of eighteen denizens of the "City of Angels." All who were killed by the mob were Chinese residents of Los Angeles. The perpetrators who hunted, shot, and lynched the Chinese were a multifarious lot that included men, women, and at least one child from a range of ethnicities and social backgrounds, all of them mobilized by a desire to obliterate members of Chinese Los Angeles, most energized by the need to assert the safety and dominance of white Los Angeles.

Long regarded as a violent outburst that only interested students of California history,

the anti-Chinese massacre should be understood for what it reveals about the Reconstruction era, the larger chapter in US history that shaped the mass killing in particular ways. Usually periodized as beginning in 1865 and ending in 1877, Reconstruction involved multitudinous changes created by the Union victory in the Civil War and the emancipation of four million persons once held in bondage. Put simply, Reconstruction involved a long effort to remake America without slavery. Given slavery's deep impress throughout the nation, it is not surprising that Reconstruction involved a struggle waged on a staggering number of fronts: constitutional, legal, social, economic, political, and racial. As a slaveholder's wife put it in January 1865, a Southern loss in the war would produce "a general remodeling of everything."[1]

To those desiring to make an America without slavery, this "general remodeling" promised a future of freedom and full citizenship. But to those whose lives and livelihoods directly benefited from American slavery, it threatened disruption, ruin, and "social equality" with those they had earlier ordered about as chattel property. For a number of white Southerners, this was intolerable. They sought to stem the revolutionary tide with the weapons of unfinished war: violence and terror.

Although the killings occurring in the former Confederacy had different aims and often were expressly political—to overthrow Reconstruction's revolution—the mass killings in Los Angeles resembled the Southern mobbings in one key particular. The 1871 massacre of the Chinese was an instance of racial disciplining during Reconstruction. In the South, former slaveholders and whites invested in the antebellum social regime believed that former slaves should be disciplined to know their place; they may now be freedmen before the law, but they should be subordinate to white order. In California, Chinese had to be disciplined because they were unruly as well, but in a different way. Chinese in the 1870s were increasingly characterized as "infusible," the postwar term that labeled "Asiatics" as incapable (and worse, unwilling) of incorporating into America. In addition, the postbellum Chinese were "unruly" because for a number of Americans, they were hard to categorize within the US racial order. Cast by some whites as bearing visual and character kinship with African Americans, the Chinese in California became a species of the trouble African Americans posed to white society.[2] It was not accidental that the Chinese killed on October 24, 1871, were culturally linked to the name of their neighborhood: Calle de los Negros, or as English-speaking Angelenos dubbed it, Negro Alley.

RECONSTRUCTION: THE SETTING FOR THE ANTI-CHINESE MASSACRE IN LOS ANGELES

The links between the anti-Chinese massacre in Los Angeles and Reconstruction were not causal; rather they were co-located within a discursive "field" of new controversies that debated the significance of race after the Civil War. Still, the relationship between the two has received little study, in part because of erroneous assumptions about California and the West being "cut off" from the national stage of events after the Civil War. Such a misunderstanding impoverishes our historical knowledge about Reconstruction. Moreover, decoupling the anti-Chinese massacre from the temporal context of Reconstruction, indeed, disassociating the history of Chinese in the United States from postwar developments, is unwarranted. The Chinese in California and freed blacks in the South both agitated white public concern about the character of the nation, producing violence in the 1870s and later, legislation restricting Asian immigration and the rise of Jim Crow laws in the 1880s.[3] The lynchings in Los Angeles marked the nadir of a decade of controversies over the "proper" place of African Americans and Chinese in the postbellum emancipationist social order. What happened in Southern California in 1871 was due in no small way to how Chinese were

already implicated in the numerous debates about the "general remodeling of everything." The tensions surrounding the Reconstruction era created the larger setting for the night of mobbing in a far-off town on the Pacific Coast.

Thus, the Chinese in the United States mattered at key points in the epochal developments after the war and were far from being mere bystanders to the era's turbulence. First in California and then in far-flung locales across the nation (including the South and strike-torn North Adams, Massachusetts, in 1870), the suddenly noticed presence of the Chinese in America sparked debates in Congress, informed Reconstruction-era civil rights efforts, inspired political artwork in notable print culture forums, and troubled public discourse about what lay ahead for America after the Civil War.

The new presence was graphically illustrated by Thomas Nast, the famed *Harper's Weekly* illustrator, who did his part to convey the sudden significance of Chinese in the United States when he captured the gamut of postbellum crises and anxieties through his drawings. During this period he drew more than forty scenes commenting on the Chinese and their plight. One year before the Los Angeles massacre, he characterized the Chinese (and more importantly, the new environment of public anxiety over them) in a telling illustration: in "The New Comet—A Phenomenon Visible in All Parts of the U.S." Nast showed white Americans visibly unnerved by what portended in the sky: a comet with a Chinese face auguring a future already shadowed by white unease over the freed African American.[4]

Other characterizations fueled economic desires in the South. The Chinese figured in the imaginations of many white Southerners as they faced a transformed labor predicament in their fields, having lost their enslaved labor source. The Chinese came to preoccupy many instances of Southern discourse and inspired commercial attempts to import them into agricultural fields in Louisiana and Mississippi. Looking at their fields after the war, white Southerners believed they found a new way to discipline African American farm hands, considered an ever-growing necessity since the freedmen were no longer as "tractable" as when they were slaves. The solution lay in importing Chinese agricultural laborers, an answer that first beckoned from Cuba, where Chinese laborers had worked during the Civil War, and then California, where Chinese had built growing communities since the 1840s. In 1869, the appeal of this labor force lay in "the cheapness" of their labor but also in what Southerners attributed to the Chinese as "the peculiar adaptedness of that race to the climate of the South and to the production of Southern staples, and in the cheap and convenient transportation afforded by the Pacific Railroad."[5]

Importing Chinese laborers would do more than augment the number of laborers in Southern fields. The obsession was to discipline the larger numbers of African Americans. Complaining that the "negro" was made "lazy, insubordinate and unreliable" by "too sudden [an] introduction to political rights and equality with the white race," many white Southerners believed the imported Chinese labor would constitute "the counteracting influence" of an "equally capable and far more docile and manageable race."[6] The vast majority of white Southerners, both men and women saw Chinese labor as a way to frighten African American freedmen and intimidate them into socially coercive labor situations. The journalist Whitelaw Reid reported that he heard "men of all ages and conditions" exclaim across the region: "We can drive the n[pejorative] out and import coolies [the term used for Chinese laborers] that will work better, at less expense, and relieve us from this cursed n[pejorative] impudence."[7] The grim accounting that white Southerners wanted done in the fields was labor discipline, the type that would make freedmen forget both political and social equality and instead cower before the harsh market-driven urgency of Chinese laborer competition. These gains were quickly summed up by

one Mississippian: "Give us five million Chinese laborers in the valley of the Mississippi and we can furnish the world with cotton and teach the negro his proper place."[8]

White Southerners not only wanted the Chinese laborers' bodies, but attributed to them the docility necessary for restoring traditional order amidst emancipation's repercussions. Southerners said Chinese workers subscribed to the "oriental philosophy of indifferentism," meaning indifference to politics, thus making them servile to the traditional racial social order.[9] In doing so, white Southerners conveniently ignored reports that Chinese laborers in Cuba had shown a capability to exhibit "refractory discontent" and "angry insubordination."[10] White Southerners continued these fantasies until political realities made them obsolete. With the suppression of Republican African American political officeholders and the retreat from Reconstruction that started in 1877, the perceived need for Chinese abated as the post-Reconstruction state legislatures inaugurated unopposed methods of controlling African Americans.

Both in the South and throughout the nation the political and commercial discourses acted upon the Chinese, but in California the Chinese saw the years after 1865 as a moment when they could act for themselves and speak on their own behalf. On the West Coast, Chinese Californians appraised the changes of Reconstruction and saw themselves participating in the era's legal transformations. In one key moment of federal civil rights lawmaking, they lobbied for legal protection and got it, although unfortunately, only to a limited extent. In 1870 and 1871 Congress passed two Enforcement Acts to enable federal redress of state-level deprivation of rights. The Enforcement Act of 1870 and the Ku Klux Klan Act of 1871 are textbook cases of the "military acts" that sought to remedy the actions of those whites who opposed Reconstruction and intimidated African Americans through violence and state denial of newly won civil rights. But buried inside the Enforcement Act of 1870 was a provision protecting Chinese from discriminatory taxes and local violence in California. Section 16 of the Enforcement Act of 1870 announced "That all persons within the jurisdiction of the United States…shall have the same right…in the United States to make and enforce contracts, to sue, be parties, give evidence, and to the full and equal benefit of all laws and proceedings for the security of person and property as is enjoyed by white citizens, and shall be subject to the like punishments, pains, penalties, taxes, licenses, and exactions of every kind, and none other."[11]

While mentioning neither the Chinese nor California, Section 16 dealt with both. The previous year, in June 1869, a Congressional delegation met with representatives of the Chinese community in San Francisco as part of a fact-finding expedition to the West Coast. The meeting proved to be an eye-opener for the legislators, as they heard about discriminatory tax laws that the California legislature had passed that targeted Chinese Californians. Worse, both the California State Supreme Court and the California legislature had banned the testimony of Chinese in the courts, thus leaving Chinese vulnerable to depredations and violence. The senator who sponsored the language that eventually became Section 16 made the legislative remedy for the Chinese clear when he spoke on May 20, 1870. "We are inviting to our shores…Asiatics. For twenty years every obligation of humanity, of justice, and of common decency toward these people has been violated by a certain class of men…It is as solemn a duty as can be devolved upon Congress to see that those people are protected."[12] For the anti-Chinese newspaper, the *San Francisco Examiner*, the provisions that would protect "any person" meant that Reconstruction's protections were being extended to persons such as the Chinese who were not citizens. Inferring correctly the legal import of the words of Section 16, the *Examiner* complained publicly that under the new law, "no State legislation can apply to a Chinaman which does not apply equally to all people."[13]

Unfortunately, the statutory victory in 1870 lacked the teeth of enforcement and implementation. Section 16 may have been a victory for the Chinese Californians, but it proved hard to vindicate. While it was a civil rights gain in the statute books, its provision for Chinese safety was muffled due to the lack of clear pronouncements, a failing that reflected the lukewarm commitment to Chinese civil rights by lawmakers and the increasing electoral costs of supporting such rights. Perhaps no better illustration of this dynamic can be found than in the career of a US senator from the West who supported Section 16 expressly as a measure to protect the Chinese from increasing hostility. Senator William Stewart of Nevada had served as the district attorney for Nevada County in California, where he prosecuted a murder case that led to the California Supreme Court in 1854 declaring Chinese incapable of testifying in cases involving white Californians. In 1870, Senator Stewart stood up for Section 16 and Chinese civil rights on the floor of Congress, congratulating his country and his colleagues for "provisions which extend the strong arm of Government to the protection of the Chinese." Unfortunately, eighteen years later, Stewart stood on the floor of Congress and pandered to the anti-Chinese movement that was roiling the nation in the 1880s. He urged immigration restriction of the Chinese because they were diseased and degraded.[14]

William Stewart was not the only public figure during the 1870s and 1880s to be inconsistent on Chinese rights, nor was he the only politician to twist emancipationist legacies into immigration restriction. That process showed itself early in California's history with Reconstruction and it disclosed precisely on the matter that William Stewart thought so unjust when he was the district attorney for Nevada County, California: that Chinese could not testify in cases involving whites and thus were made legally vulnerable to white violence. The ever-resonating and endlessly ramifying effect of California's way of limiting Reconstruction's gains made the link between the anti-Chinese massacre in Los Angeles and Reconstruction that much more intimate and that much more tragic.

RECONSTRUCTION'S PARADOXES: CHINESE CALIFORNIANS AS THE LIMIT TO RECONSTRUCTION-ERA CHANGES

California was indeed its own cauldron of change and opposition to change during the emancipationist spring of the mid-to-late 1860s. One recent study of California's relation to Reconstruction noted the complexity of the postwar environment in the Golden State, which "precluded any kind of straightforward transition from bondage to freedom."[15] The transition was complicated by the variety of unfree labor systems that exploited African Americans, California Indians, and Chinese, and an environment of bound labor that further exploited along lines of gender. "Emancipation and Reconstruction, uneven and incomplete processes across the United States, were especially complex in California."[16] This complexity ensured that "emancipation had radically divergent consequences for different groups of Californians" with emancipation having "especially contradictory outcomes for Chinese men and women."[17]

This proved especially true when it came to testimonial competence. For decades, California's lawmakers had refused to shield the Native Peoples and then Chinese from a disability to testify in law cases involving white persons, a disability common in the slaveholding South. In 1850, when California was the scarce-born thirty-first "free" state in the Union, its legislature mandated that no "Black or Mulatto or Indian" be allowed "to give evidence in favor or against" a "white man" in criminal cases, and that in civil cases, no "Indian or Negro" be allowed to testify in any action or proceeding "in which a White person is a party."[18] Four years later, the California Supreme Court ruled that the Chinese could be inferred to belong

to the abjected category of "Indian" and thus disabled from testifying in court in cases involving white persons.[19] This monolith of racial disabling cracked during the Civil War, but only a bit and not for all disabled by these legal actions. During the war, in a fit of wartime solidarity with the Lincoln administration, the state's coalition of Republicans and loyal Democrats in the "Union Party" acted on the President's Emancipation Proclamation in 1863 by freeing African Americans from the testimonial disability in the 1850, statutes and thus removing a badge of servitude that kept them servile and made them vulnerable to ever-present threats of white violence and predation.

The logic of the emancipationist spring in 1863 should have led to the same unfettering for Indians and Chinese, but California's legislature refused to endow testimonial competence on both. In a prefiguring of what would happen throughout Reconstruction, the California legislature said in effect that emancipation applied to liberated chattel slaves, but extending liberation from the badges of servitude to Chinese would be dangerous. As historian Stacey L. Smith has put it, "Radical Republicans in the Union Party successfully mobilized [the effort to repeal anti-black testimony laws that propped up the pro slavery regime and African American bondage] ... when these same [Radical Republicans] sought testimony rights for Indians and Chinese, they ran up against former Democrats in the Union Party who argued [such testimony] would collapse all racial hierarchies and degrade whites."[20] Hence, the Chinese and Indians constituted the outer limit for what could be imagined as Reconstruction's possibility to make new citizens in a revolutionizing America. The California legislature raised the ante on this deal when it passed a statute that expressly forbade Chinese from testifying in cases involving whites, and in 1870 the California Supreme Court effectively affirmed its earlier 1854 decision that included Chinese under the testimonial ban, declaring that the postwar

California statute did not raise constitutional issues as conflicting with the Reconstruction-era Fourteenth Amendment because California was a "sovereign state" and the federal government's Reconstruction amendment did not reach California.[21] In short, California was as unreconstructed and constitutionally obstinate at this point in postbellum American history as any Southern state that witnessed acts of white violence and white terror in 1870.

RECONSTRUCTION-ERA VIOLENCE

Federal legislation to empower African Americans as citizens during the emancipationist phase of the postbellum years met with violence from former Confederates in the South and preexisting political interests in the North and West, both fighting to limit the circle of those capable of being new public participants in the postwar world. The violence ranged from abusive political rhetoric against the Chinese in California to physical violence in the South that manifested as furious massacres. Eric Foner's sober historiographical judgment compares the violence of 1868 to the 1870s with that in other societies that underwent the change of emancipation. Foner writes, "In its pervasive impact and multiplicity of purposes, however, the wave of counter revolutionary terror that swept over large parts of the South between 1868 and 1871 lacks counterpart either in the American experience or in that of other Western Hemisphere societies that abolished slavery in the 19th century. It is a measure of how far change had progressed that the reaction against Reconstruction proved so extreme."[22]

That extreme reaction took its toll in the South, and the grim inventory includes these events. A Memphis riot between April 30 and May 2, 1866 took forty-six African American lives and wounded eighty. Violence in New Orleans on July 30, 1866 took thirty-four African American lives and injured more than 200. Two hundred eighty African Americans died during an Easter Sunday mobbing in Colfax, Louisiana in April 1873. The incidents expanded across the South: Camilla, Georgia in September 1868; Laurens, South Carolina and Eutaw, Alabama in October 1870; Meridian, Mississippi in March 1871; Vicksburg, Mississippi in December 1874; Clinton, Mississippi in September 1875; and Hamburg, South Carolina in July 1876.[23] This violence aimed to intimidate political activity by African Americans and white sympathizers of Reconstruction in the South. The mobbings and murders sought to discipline former slaves into formally emancipated racial subordinates. As one historian notes, "The purpose [of these violent acts], and to a great degree the result... was to demoralize and intimidate the freedmen."[24]

The 1871 Los Angeles anti-Chinese mobbing did not have the same electoral political stakes as raised in the Southern locations, but it exuded a strong anti-Asian disciplinary function. If African American freedmen had to be kept in place through violence in Meridian, Mississippi in March 1871, then Chinese Angelenos eight months later were likewise punished for threatening the stability of local white authority. Protection of white residents against the upstart threat of Chinese, who were rumored to be "killing the white men by wholesale" during an urban fracas, became a rallying cry. Unwarranted, but spreading like wildfire, the rumor mobilized white Angeleno anxieties about the Chinese, a pent-up hostility that took public form when some called to "clean the Chinese out of the city." This rhetoric of cleansing was made easier to express because Reconstruction-era California public officials had excluded the Chinese from political emancipation. To "clean the Chinese out of" Los Angeles meant a purge and a reversal. The purge would take the form of one night of violence. But the reversal sought to stem something that had been proceeding for at least thirty years, namely, increased Chinese immigration, which took new form during Reconstruction.

CHINESE IMMIGRANTS AND SETTLEMENT IN LOS ANGELES

The Chinese who lived in Los Angeles in 1871 participated in a larger flow of Chinese migration to the United States, a movement first witnessed in New York in the 1820s. Twenty years later, the migration flows from Asia to California established the more familiar history of Chinese settlements in San Francisco, Stockton, Sacramento, and northern and central California.

After the Civil War, these migration flows continued, but the surge of such migration during the middle 1860s happened under the aegis of Reconstruction-era innovations that forged new promises concerning rights and social benefits, matters that figured in new treaty relations between the United States and China in 1868.

That year, in the midst of Congressional debate about the Fourteenth Amendment, the postbellum legacy that made the Reconstruction a constitutional revolution, the US government negotiated the Burlingame Treaty with China. Named after Anson Burlingame, an American who mediated diplomatic relations between the two nations, the Burlingame Treaty declared that free emigration would mutually benefit both nations. It is not insignificant in the context of Reconstruction that the treaty described these rights in the same language used in the Fourteenth Amendment to signify new Reconstruction-era rights. The Treaty mentioned immigrant "privileges and immunities," the same undefined provisions stated in Section 1 of the Fourteenth Amendment that the Congress debated in the same year.

The Burlingame Treaty achieved its purpose. The number of Chinese entrants to the United States swelled from 6,707 in 1868 (the year the treaty was debated) to 12,874 in 1869 and 15,740 in 1870. In 1870, the number of Chinese in the United States was 63,199 with 49,277 in California, most of the Chinese having settled in San Francisco and northern and central California. Los Angeles' share of the Californian Chinese population was 234.[25] While most Chinese settlement concentrated for several decades in northern and central California, developments in the 1870s produced a substantial Chinese community in Los Angeles. Growing diversification in the Southern California economy to supplant a declining cattle business faltering through drought played a major role in luring Chinese to Los Angeles.[26]

Still, the small Los Angeles Chinese community in 1870 witnessed significant demographic distortions with some significant social consequences. Historical studies by Raymond Lou and Scott Zesch reveal that 80 percent of the city's 234 Chinese were male and that two-thirds of the thirty-four Chinese women were under the age of twenty. Although observers and even historians have assumed that many of the young women were sex workers or prostitutes, Lou and Zesch show cause for being skeptical about such blanket characterizations. The 1870 census, court records, and news accounts reveal two Chinese Angeleno women working in laundries, several prominent Asian men with wives, three Chinese households with one man and one woman, and "another nine mixed dwellings may have housed as many as fifteen couples." Zesch concluded that "more than half of the thirty-four Asian women living in Los Angeles may have been wives" or were living in some cohabiting male-female relationship.[27]

By reinterpreting the demographic profile of Chinese in Los Angeles in 1870, one moves beyond the stereotype that Chinese women occupied only one situation, that of prostitution. Unfortunately in 1870, the social institution of heteronormative marriage and the various kinds of male-female cohabitation created unbearable social tensions among the Chinese in Los Angeles and contributed to continued stereotyping of the Chinese by non Chinese Angelenos. This was especially the case on the eve of the 1871 massacre.

Indeed, traditional accounts often traced the lynchings that happened on October 24,

1871 to a precipitating fight between rival groups of Chinese males over possession of a Chinese female. Preceding that outburst, Southern California English-language newspapers delighted in reporting marriage conflicts within the Chinese community, reveling in the strange-sounding Chinese names and Chinese wranglings, fights, flights, and court proceedings. Later-19th-century American newspapers wallowed in this "comical" Chinese narrative. Yet the fights may have also represented Chinese immigrants' desire to establish the kinds of social roots actually legitimated by the white civic norms of Los Angeles, including marriage and the formation of communities, public and private aspirations that their non-Chinese neighbors were often not willing to acknowledge. Read against the grain in this way, it becomes both telling and ironic that the massacre of 1871 was told (and incessantly retold through the years thereafter) as caused by one of these relationship disputes.

THE FATAL NIGHT

The tragedy of October 24, 1871, began with an outburst among some Chinese Los Angelenos that may have been contained had it not been for the galvanizing power of anxiety over white lives, a stirring that accelerated matters into public revenge and then mass killing.[28] Prior to October 24, trouble brewed in the Chinese district situated in the Coronel Adobe on the Calle de los Negros, or "Negro Alley." Located near the Los Angeles Plaza, the street was notorious for vice and abjection and harboring the city's criminals. Most accounts of the massacre published since the 1880s cast the source of trouble within the Chinese district itself, namely, a feud between rival groups of Chinese Los Angelenos. In fact, subsequent historical investigation has uncovered a relatively brief gunfight between two Chinese that resulted in no casualties.[29] The bloodletting happened only when a self-appointed peacekeeper intervened.

The interference of a white rancher and former saloonkeeper, Robert Thompson, propelled matters into mass violence. Thompson was not a policeman but during the afternoon of October 24, 1871, possibly thinking he could successfully end the dispute between immigrants, he fired point-blank at Chinese Angelenos firing at him from behind a door. It was Thompson who was shot, and he died shortly thereafter.[30]

Thompson's killing was the available accelerant that turned fears and rumors about Chinese immigrants into demands for retribution. After Thompson's death, a crowd of white Angelenos lynched a Chinese resident named Wong Tuck. The crowd pummeled Tuck, whose life snapped at the end of a rope thrown over a makeshift hangman's scaffold at New High and Temple Streets.

News of Thompson's killing warmed passions aided by the flow of alcohol served in the saloons bordering the Calle de los Negros and the excitement of a three-hour gunfight. What happened in the hours after the Chinese fight was bitterly ironic. The original Chinese antagonists who started the altercation actually escaped during the melee, leaving many remaining Chinese at the mercy of white Angelenos. For example, two Chinese women, Cha Cha and Fan Cho, attempted to leave the besieged Chinese quarter but were met by a hail of fifteen to twenty shots; exactly what happened to them and other Chinese women in Los Angeles remains unknown.[31]

Press reports began detailing what would become a massacre. An Associated Press employee telegraphed his San Francisco counterpart that something terrible was happening. The first report sent out at 7 in the evening, and the next at 9 p.m., described "fears of a general slaughter" in Los Angeles. Fifteen minutes later, this general fear became graphic: "Eight Chinamen have been hung and more will be hung as soon as the ropes can be applied. There is intense excitement and a general riot is impending."[32]

The Los Angeles rioters acted efficiently, killing eighteen Chinese in about four hours. It was possible that the vengeance moved quickly because the mob knew that a garrison of federal troops in nearby Wilmington could be mustered to suppress further killing, a parallel to Reconstruction-era scenarios in the South where anti-black mobs acted in the shadow of nearby federal troops. In the South and California, anti-black and anti-Chinese violence took its license as an angry response to a crisis in post–Civil War era whiteness. In Los Angeles, the mob defended the racialized status quo upon hearing rumors that Chinese "were killing the white men...in Negro Alley," thus they rushed to punish such impertinence and insubordination.[33]

AFTERMATH AND CONSEQUENCES

The 1871 Los Angeles anti-Chinese massacre was not the first, nor would it be the last act of mass violence targeting Chinese immigrants in 19th-century America, but at that moment it was the most horrific and noticeable. Los Angeles itself was an old Spanish, Mexican, and Californio city, but it was young as an American municipality. Prior to the massacre, few in the eastern United States knew much about Los Angeles. After the massacre, newspapers in Chicago and New York could not help but harp on the ironic name of that faraway place where angels acted like devils.

The massacre was horrible enough for the Chinese in Los Angeles, and its disposition in the California courts evinced only cruel dismissiveness. A court decision convicted eight rioters, but they eventually had the last laugh. On May 21, 1873, the California Supreme Court reversed their convictions on the grounds that the original indictments were "fatally defective" because they failed to allege a crime. The state Supreme Court declared this in a two-paragraph opinion that the law-trained writer Scott Zesch noted "cited no statutes or judicial precedent."[34]

In the years after the massacre, members of the Los Angeles Chinese community did what they could to seek redress and bear witness. They largely remained in the city (a mind-boggling decision in many respects)

and contributed to the economic development of Southern California by helping construct the rail infrastructure that would link Los Angeles to the rest of the state. They also bore witness to what happened on October 24, 1871, to the best they could. One of the Chinese residents brought a lawsuit against the city of Los Angeles seeking damages against city officials for not having done more to prevent the death and destruction inflicted by the massacre. He lost.[35] A number of Chinese residents commemorated the massacre through annual observances performed in the city.

Unfortunately, the massacre was a harbinger of worse to come for Chinese in Los Angeles and throughout the United States. Violence increased rather than ended and anti-Chinese hostility took illegal, extra-legal, and legal forms, the last became national policy when Congress enacted the restrictive immigration regime known as the Chinese Exclusion system. Starting as a set of Congressional statutes, it grew to include judicial opinions and US Immigration Service administrative actions that worked together to inhibit and reduce Chinese immigration to the United States. Foreshadowed in 1875, enacted in 1882, reauthorized in 1892 and 1902, and finally established without need for renewal in 1904, the Chinese Exclusion system provided the template for immigration restrictions that targeted other communities of Asian migrants to the United States.

As Congress enacted and renewed the Chinese Exclusion system violence—shootings, forced exclusions, arson, mob action—against Chinese living in America increased. The 1880s witnessed ninety-one instances of anti-Chinese violence, the years 1885 and 1886 forming a midpoint apex with thirty and forty-three events apiece. Even Milwaukee, Wisconsin, heard the rallying cry of "The Chinese Must Go" when in 1889 it became the site of a citywide anti-Chinese urban disturbance, an example of how anti-Chinese sentiment could travel east of the Mississippi River.[36]

EPITAPHS

The night of horror in Los Angeles left few physical traces in the city's built environment. Today, a street that witnessed one of the murderous hunts fronts a housing complex catering to elderly Asians, most of whom lived in Chinatown for decades. Only recently has the city memorialized the massacre with a street placard that describes what happened, sketching the horror in a few words.

The victims of 1871, usually described as "the eighteen killed" are often as summarily noted as the official placard; their names and fates are rarely mentioned, but a brief roll call testifies to the violence they faced and the turbulent years that produced it. The two women, Cha Cha and Fan Cho, were shot, but we do not know their fates and they are usually not counted amongst the killed. Chee Long Ton, reputed to be a doctor and called by white Los Angelenos "Gene" Tong, was shot through the head, then hanged. Wa Sin Quai, "resident of Negro Alley," was shot in the abdomen and legs. Chang Wan, resident at Doctor Tong's house, was hanged, as was Long Quai. Joung Burrow was shot though the head and left wrist. Another with no name, but later thought to be the cigar manufacturer Won Yu Tuk, was hanged. Wong Chin was hanged; three cartridges were later found in his pocket. Tong Wan was shot, stabbed, and hanged. Ah Loo, Wan Foo, Day Kee, Ah Was, Ah Wen, Lo Hey, and Wing Chee all were hanged. Ah Cut, a liquor manufacturer, was shot in the abdomen and extremities. Fun Yu was shot in the head and died three days later. An unidentified Chinese male, probably Wong Tuck, was hanged and found in a cemetery.[37]

The Chinese caught in the October 1871 Los Angeles anti-Chinese massacre, like the African Americans murdered throughout the post–Civil War South, witnessed to the breadth of violence that forestalled changes in America's social and political order. That the Chinese were as much a part of the turmoil of revolution and counterrevolution of the 1870s was

not lost on men and women of the time. As a congressman put it when debating the first of the Chinese Exclusion laws, the act would be "the first break in the levee. I would deem the new country we will have after this bill becomes law as changed from the old country we have to-day as our country would have been changed if the rebellion of 1861 had succeeded."[38] Reconstruction, the era that saw far-reaching civil rights legislation simultaneously "became the era of Chinese exclusion," a development darkly realized on an October night in 1871 on a street called Calle de Los Negros in the heart of the City of the Angels.[39]

DISCUSSION OF THE LITERATURE

Reconstruction. At one time considered the "dark and bloody ground" of American historical writing, the historiography of Reconstruction is as eventful as Reconstruction itself, taking dramatic turns, each of which had far-reaching consequences for grappling with the American past. Put very simply, the contested ground of Reconstruction historiography can be mapped broadly with these landmarks. Beginning in the first years of the 20th century, graduate students under the tutelage of William Dunning at Columbia University produced dissertations, master's theses, and monographs that composed the interpretation known as "the Dunning School," a body of work about Reconstruction that interpreted postwar efforts to change the South as generally misguided, even "execrable" and "diabolical," because Reconstruction would empower former slaves. The adherents of this school built their interpretations on the cornerstone of their racial assumptions, which according to Eric Foner, stressed "negro incapacity." For the "Dunning School," efforts such as that pursued by Congressional Republicans under the aegis of "Radical Republicanism" not only were foolish but were doomed to fail and led to "the degradation of the South." In the 1930s, the countercurrent to the "Dunning School" was powerfully articulated by the African American sociologist W. E. B. Du Bois in *Black Reconstruction in America*, a study that not only resisted the racial assumptions of the Dunning School but argued for the agency of freedmen and white sympathizers to build a new social order that was both racially equal and equalitarian for working peoples. Running through Reconstruction historiography in the 1930s onward was the theme of how the postwar years witnessed yet another stage in the struggle over how capitalism was to take shape and to what extent the "Second American Revolution" of capitalism vs. agrarianism could have taken different directions. During the civil rights era of the 1960s, historians chipped away at the Dunning School and produced new studies of the efforts to remake the South by Radical Republicans and freedmen and how new freedom produced new forms of agency by African Americans. Culminating developments in the 1930s–1970s, Professor Eric Foner of Columbia University published a synthesis of the new Reconstruction historiography in 1988. *Reconstruction: America's Unfinished Revolution, 1863–1877* sought to tell the postbellum years in as sweeping and coherent a manner as the Dunning School but with an eye to replacing the center of the story. Instead of the "degraded South" and a cast of white protagonists, Foner placed African American agency at the center of his narrative, emphasizing how "blacks were active agents in the making of Reconstruction." That in place, Foner synthesized the many dimensions of Reconstruction that historians in the 1960s and 1970s showed: the political, the social, the local, the experiential, the gendered, and the cultural. Expansion of themes and consideration of different sites also marked *Reconstruction: America's Unfinished Revolution*, the latter taking form as "The Reconstruction of the North" and "The Politics of Depression," the depression being the economic crisis of the 1870s. Since 1988 and Foner's achievement, the movement by a number of recent historians of Reconstruction has been toward new broader frameworks

and even more sites of study, the West being very prominent. It is within this general terrain of scholarship that recent work on the anti-Chinese massacre of 1871 should be located.[40]

The history of the Chinese in postbellum America and the anti-Chinese massacre in 1871 are intimately linked with Reconstruction. Recognizing these connections owes much to the developments in Reconstruction historiography that have been forming since at least the 1980s. Within the general flow of scholarship that challenged the frankly racist outlook that dominated historical writing about slavery and the Civil War in the years prior to the end of the Second World War, a growing number of contemporary scholars have expanded the geographical scope of Reconstruction studies by balancing the traditional focus on Southern sites with studies of change in the North. A way to enhance this expanded perspective is to triangulate both the North and the South with a focus on the West during the postbellum years. One of those historians, Stacey L. Smith, has made the most recent arguments for moving beyond the traditional North-and-South view of Reconstruction. She wrote, "Reimagined as integral rather than peripheral to the story of American slavery and American freedom, the Far West becomes a starting point for rethinking this most turbulent era in U.S. history."[41]

Beginning in 1981 with Eugene Berwanger's pioneering study, *The West and Reconstruction*, a growing contingent of historians has examined the trans-Mississippi West and the Pacific Coast as places where Reconstruction mattered. Berwanger himself noted that mere lack of interest (and study) created the stunted impression that "postwar western politics operated in a vacuum," cut off from Washington, D.C. and events that happened north and south of the Mason-Dixon line. This was an oversight that stemmed from the limited conception of Reconstruction that many traditional historians had, often believing that "Reconstruction…applied strictly to the South [and] the West therefore could not have felt [its] impact."[42] Such a view relied on too narrow a view of Reconstruction, and Berwanger applied a broadened sense of the unfinished revolution after the Civil War, thus seeing how that famous chapter did have its echoes in Western debates about the changing structure of postbellum government and the changes in American race relations.

In 2006, Heather Cox Richardson, speaking from an interest in race and policy during the postbellum period, announced a new trend in Reconstruction historiography, one that could corral sites of study in the West and herd them alongside re-examinations of events in the North and the South. She wrote that America's half-finished revolution was not only a making (and remaking) of America without slavery, it was a public reimagining of a new nation, a process whereby the debates in the public sphere quarreled over "what America would stand for and who would be a welcome participant in that nation."[43] Such an all-consuming project encompassed all regions of the nation and its effect could be particularly vexing in the West, "the most racially mixed area of the nation."[44] Going so far as to suggest that Reconstruction can be fruitfully renamed as the "Era of Citizenship," when "Americans defined who would be citizens and what citizenship meant," her conceptualization not only ties the West with the North and South, it also makes room for thinking harder about the Chinese in the United States during this formative period.

The Anti-Chinese Massacre in Los Angeles.

Of the two topics considered, "the anti-Chinese massacre in Los Angeles" and "Reconstruction," the former has not received the scholarly attention bestowed on the latter, but developments since the 1970s have revived interest in the Los Angeles incident of 1871 and made it the inspiration for both new historical writing and cultural revisiting, the latter taking the form of journalism, websites, and a stage play that opened in 2011.

One can point to two broad developments that made the killings suddenly arresting: the growth in Asian American studies and the emergence of the "Los Angeles School" of urban cultural studies. Asian American studies has matured quickly since its early appearance on a few university campuses in the 1970s. In the subsequent four decades, historians working on Asian American topics have broadened approaches to the study of Asians in the United States to include transnationalism, borderlands dynamics, the study of empire, and racial governmentality as well as deepened work in the gendered dimensions of Asian American communities. In addition, the field has expanded the meaning of Asian America beyond the study of Chinese and Japanese in the United States to include the many ethnicities and identities that can be categorized under Southeast Asian and South Asian classifications. By doing so, by the 2010s Asian American studies had positioned itself to study the ever-proliferating diversity and multiplicity of Asian-derived communities. One signifier of this dimension was captured by the US census in 2010, when it counted nineteen different Asian-derived self-classifications just in the US Midwest.

Asian American studies has alerted a range of both scholarly and popular writers to incidents such as the anti-Chinese massacre because this violence can be transformed into an interpretive "window" into the dynamics of racial conflict, specifically as it involved a category such as "Asian American," which falls astride (and outside) the usual way "race" is talked about in America, that way being an exclusive focus on black and white relations.

The other major influence that made the Los Angeles massacre a lens is the formation and maturation of "the Los Angeles School" of urban cultural studies. First garnering widespread attention in the 1990s, the focus on Los Angeles and its contradictions has produced a far-ranging amount of work in a short spurt of twenty years. Historicizing has always been an imperative for practitioners across Los Angeles studies, because history in their hands is the active means to discover the contingencies whereby an unlikely metropolis came to be and continues to exert its influence. For historians, who take much pleasure in announcing history in a city that was notorious for denying or bulldozing its history, an event such as the anti-Chinese massacre motivates inquiry into race and the uneasy multiculturalism of a region that underwent American conquest in the 19th century. When seen in this light, the massacre of 1871 becomes more than a woeful and embarrassing blot on civic pride and a spur to recuperative boosterism. It was the social flashpoint that anticipated so many racialized social flashpoints and outbreaks that reflected deeper running conundrums that have characterized the "City of Angels" from the 1870s to the present.

PRIMARY SOURCES

Primary sources for further study of the Los Angeles anti-Chinese massacre can be found in published and unpublished form: the former were the newspapers in Los Angeles (as well as the newspapers familiar to scholars outside of Los Angeles such as the *Chicago Tribune* and the *New York Times*). The Los Angeles newspapers from 1871 to consult are the *Los Angeles Star* and the *Los Angeles News*. From October 26 through October 29, both newspapers published the eyewitness testimonies that were taken at the coroner's inquest. Scott Zesch skillfully wove a narrative drawn from seventy-nine of these eyewitness testimonies. Other papers to consult include the *Alta California*, the *San Francisco Chronicle*, and the *San Diego Bulletin*.

Official unpublished archival material can be found in the Los Angeles Area Court Records housed at Huntington Library in San Marino, California. Key cases to examine there include *Wing Chung Co. vs. Los Angeles City*, Case Number 1941, June 22, 1872, 17th Judicial District Court, Civil Cases; and *People vs. Richard Kerren*, Case Number 1101, January 5, 1872, Los Angeles County Court, Criminal Cases.

Papers of individuals who tried to account for the massacre can be found in archival depositories in the Los Angeles Area. An example is Joseph Mesmer, "Massacre of Chinamen in 1871" and "Massacre of Chinese" in the Joseph Mesmer Papers at the University of California, Los Angeles.

Primary sources on Reconstruction-Era violence that are accessible through published or digital versions depending on a library's holdings include the testimonies taken at Congressional hearings on Southern violence.

- 42nd Congress, 2nd Session, House Report 22: Testimony Taken by the Joint Committee to Enquire into the Condition of Affairs in the Late Insurrectionary States (Ku Klux Klan Hearings).
- 43rd Congress, 2nd Session, House Report 261: Condition of Affairs in the South (Louisiana).
- 43rd Congress, 2nd Session, House Report 262: Affairs in Alabama.
- 43rd Congress, 2nd Session, House Report 265: Vicksburg Troubles.
- 44th Congress, 1st Session, Senate Report 527: Mississippi in 1875.

FURTHER READING

ON THE 1871 MASSACRE

Zesch, Scott. *The Chinatown War: Chinese Los Angeles and the Massacre of 1871.* New York: Oxford University Press, 2012.

ON LOS ANGELES

Deverell, William, and Greg Hise, eds. *A Companion to Los Angeles.* Oxford: Wiley-Blackwell, 2010.

Faragher, John Mack. *Eternity Street: Violence and Justice in Frontier Los Angeles.* New York: W. W. Norton, 2016.

Torres-Rouff, David Samuel. *Before L.A.: Race, Space, and Municipal Power in Los Angeles, 1781–1894.* New Haven, CT: Yale University Press, 2013.

ON RECONSTRUCTION

Brown, Thomas J., ed. *Reconstructions: New Perspectives on the Postbellum United States.* New York: Oxford University Press, 2008.

Foner, Eric. *Reconstruction: America's Unfinished Revolution, 1863–1877.* New York: Harper and Row, 1988.

Jung, Moon-Ho. *Coolies and Cane: Race, Labor, and Sugar in the Age of Emancipation.* Baltimore: Johns Hopkins University Press, 2006.

Smith, Stacey L. *Freedom's Frontier: California and the Struggle over Unfree Labor, Emancipation, and Reconstruction.* Chapel Hill: University of North Carolina Press, 2013.

NOTES

1. Stephen A. West, "'A General Remodeling of Every Thing': Economy and Race in the Post-Emancipation South," in *Reconstructions: New Perspectives on the Postbellum United States,* ed. Thomas J. Brown (New York: Oxford University Press, 2008), 10.

2. Dan Caldwell, "The Negroization of the Chinese Stereotype in California," *Southern California Quarterly* 53 (1971): 123–131.

3. Rogers Smith, *Civic Ideals: Conflicting Visions of Citizenship in U.S. History* (New Haven, CT: Yale University Press, 1997). Smith referred to immigration as the "legal scaffolding" for the new restrictive Americanism that emerged after Reconstruction. "Only the subsequent and inter-linked construction of Jim Crow laws approached immigration in importance" (357).

4. Thomas Nast's Cartoons of Chinese Americans: Chinese Cartoons—Timeline. *Illustrating Chinese Exclusion* 2014. © Michele Walfred. An image of "The New Comet" can be found in Moon-Ho Jung, *Coolies and Cane: Race, Labor, and Sugar in the Age of Emancipation* (Baltimore: Johns Hopkins University Press, 2006), 112.

5. Jung, *Coolies and Cane,* 98.

6. Jung, *Coolies and Cane,* 98.

7. Jung, *Coolies and Cane,* 79.

8. Eric Foner, *Reconstruction: America's Unfinished Revolution, 1863–1877* (New York: Harper and Row, 1988), 419–420.

9. Jung, *Coolies and Cane,* 97.

10. Jung, *Coolies and Cane,* 89.

11. Najia Aarim-Heriot, *Chinese Immigrants, African Americans, and Racial Anxiety in the United States, 1848–82* (Urbana and Chicago: University of Illinois Press, 2003), 141.

12. Charles J. McClain, *In Search of Equality: The Chinese Struggle against Discrimination in Nineteenth-Century America* (Berkeley and Los Angeles: University of California Press, 1994), 39.

13. McClain, *In Search of Equality,* 40.

14. McClain, *In Search of Equality,* 345, n.6.

15. Stacey L. Smith, *Freedom's Frontier: California and the Struggle over Unfree Labor, Emancipation, and Reconstruction* (Chapel Hill: University of North Carolina Press, 2013), 205.

16. Smith, *Freedom's Frontier,* 175.

17. Smith, *Freedom's Frontier,* 175.

18. *People vs. Hall,* 4 Cal. 399; 1854 Cal. LEXIS 137. The California Supreme Court expanded the available categories proscribed from testifying in cases involving whites in the statutes. The wording of those statutes as set forth in *People vs. Hall* was as follows: "The 394th section of the Act Concerning Civil Cases, provides that no Indian or Negro shall be allowed to testify as a witness in any action or proceeding in which a White person is a party" and "The 14th section of the Act of April 16th, 1850, regulating Criminal Proceedings, provides that 'No Black or Mulatto person, or Indian, shall be allowed to give evidence in favor of, or against a white man.'" *People vs. Hall,* 4 Cal. 399.

19. *People vs. Hall,* 4 Cal. 405.

20. Smith, *Freedom's Frontier,* 175.

21. *People vs. Brady,* 40 Cal. 198.

22. Foner, *Reconstruction,* 425.

23. Allen W. Trelease, *White Terror: The Ku Klux Klan Conspiracy and Southern Reconstruction* (New York: Harper and Row, 1971), xliv. See Foner, *Reconstruction,* for the Colfax massacre as "the bloodiest single instance of racial carnage in the Reconstruction era" (437).

24. Trelease, *White Terror,* xliv.

25. Elmer Clarence Sandmeyer, *The Anti-Chinese Movement in California* (Urbana: University of Illinois Press, 1973), 16. Los Angeles figures are from Raymond Lou, *The Chinese American Community of Los Angeles, 1870–1900: A Case of Resistance, Organization, and Participation* (PhD diss., University of California, Irvine, 1982), 32.

26. William R. Locklear, "The Celestials and the Angels: A Study of the Anti-Chinese Movement in Los Angeles to 1882," *The Historical Society of Southern California Quarterly* 42 (1960): 241.

27. Lou, "Chinese American Community," 23–24. Scott Zesch, "Chinese Los Angeles in 1870–1871: The Makings of a Massacre," *Southern California Quarterly* 90 (Summer 2008): 117–118.

28. The most recent book-length study of the massacre is Scott Zesch, *The Chinatown War: Chinese Los Angeles and the Massacre of 1871* (New York: Oxford University Press, 2012).

29. This draws on the account of how matters both descended into mob violence and escalated into mass killing in Victor Jew, "The Anti-Chinese Massacre in Los Angeles and Its Strange Career," in *A Companion to Los Angeles*, ed. William Deverell and Greg Hise (Oxford: Wiley-Blackwell, 2010), 115–118. The account has been modified or updated at appropriate points.

30. Jew, "Anti-Chinese Massacre," 116.

31. See Zesch, *Chinatown War*, 133, for the names of Cha Cha and Fan Cho and their fate on October 24, 1871.

32. Jew, "Anti-Chinese Massacre," 117.

33. Jew, "Anti-Chinese Massacre," 117. See Zesch, *Chinatown War*, 132, for the quotation "killing the white men by wholesale."

34. Zesch, *Chinatown War*, 207.

35. Zesch, *Chinatown War*, 205–206, 210.

36. Victor Jew, "The Violent Articulation of Chinese Otherness and Interracial Sexuality in the U.S. Midwest, 1885–1889," *Journal of Social History* 37 (2003): 390. An overview of much of this violence can be found in Jean Pfaelzer, *Driven Out: The Forgotten War against Chinese Americans* (New York: Random House, 2007).

37. Jew, "Anti-Chinese Massacre," 122–123.

38. Andrew Gyory, *Closing the Gate: Race, Politics, and the Chinese Exclusion Act* (Chapel Hill: University of North Carolina Press, 1998), 2.

39. Smith, *Freedom's Frontier*, 230.

40. This fast overview of developments in Reconstruction historiography draws upon Foner, *Reconstruction*, xix–xxvii.

41. Smith, *Freedom's Frontier*, 234.

42. Eugene H. Berwanger, *The West and Reconstruction* (Urbana: University of Illinois Press, 1981), 7, 10.

43. Heather Cox Richardson, "North and West of Reconstruction: Studies in Political Economy," in *Reconstructions: New Perspectives on the Postbellum United States*, ed. Thomas J. Brown (New York: Oxford University Press, 2008), 84–90.

44. Richardson, "North and West," 85.

Victor Jew

ASIAN AMERICANS AND THE 1992 LOS ANGELES UPRISING

INTRODUCTION

The 1992 Los Angeles riots held immense significance for Asian Americans—immigrants and the US-born—especially Koreans, whose businesses were among the main targets of looting and arson. Commonly called the most deadly and costly race riot, as well as the largest civil uprising, in US history, the LA riots were also important in bringing unprecedented national attention to the Korean American population of Southern California. Members of this community, by and large the product of recent Asian immigration following the passage of the Immigration Act of 1965, had been forging a precarious existence in America against a backdrop of deindustrialization, socioeconomic inequality, and rising interracial tension. As their struggles before and during the riots came to the forefront of national attention, commentators used the figure of the Korean riot victim to express their lamentations about American life in the late 20th century. To some, the experience of Koreans powerfully encapsulated a modern immigrant nightmare—an American dream shattered—while to others it merely confirmed the violent pathology of the black underclass.

The visibility of Koreans (as well as Latinos) in the uprising, furthermore, forced Americans to acknowledge the stubborn reality of racism in the late 20th century and the fact that this was a complex problem that affected and implicated multiple—not merely two—racial and ethnic groups. For their part, the riots were a crucial turning point for Korean Americans—and other Asian Americans—that continues to resonate more than twenty years later. The crisis paved the way for the ascent of new leaders who could work with government agencies, speak to the media, and become deeply engaged with US race relations.

Additionally, new organizations that simultaneously promoted ethnic empowerment and broad civic engagement proliferated. Personal reflections from Korean Americans who experienced the riots directly and indirectly also shed light on a new, more critical mindset in Asian America that understood the need for a deeper interest in and engagement with the histories and struggles of others, and regarded with greater skepticism—or outright rejected—the ideology of the "American dream."

THE LOS ANGELES RIOTS

The Los Angeles riots of 1992 erupted after a judge announced not guilty verdicts for four police officers charged with using excessive force against the African American motorist Rodney King following a high-speed freeway chase. While the issue of police brutality against blacks was nothing new, King's beating, which occurred in March 1991, was different because it had been captured on amateur video. Although the footage was grainy, it unmistakably and disturbingly showed a lone unarmed black man being mercilessly beaten by a group of mostly white officers.[1] The video was subsequently seen widely and repeatedly around the world. Handed down against a backdrop of growing disfranchisement and despair in poor and working-class black communities, the verdict symbolized, for many, just the latest evidence of the systematic inequality and injustice they faced on a daily basis.

From April 29 to May 4, rioting and looting overtook much of South Central Los Angeles and nearby Koreatown. The LA riots inevitably became a major media event, disseminated jarring images worldwide, and culminated in a racialized controversy that held the nation's interest for more than a year. News footage showed youths of various races violently attacking passersby, setting fire to property, and ransacking stores. One of the most indelible and disturbing episodes, seen by the nation via helicopter camera, involved the driver Reginald

Denny being dragged out of his semi-truck to be beaten nearly to death. California governor Pete Wilson issued a state of emergency and called in about 6,000 National Guard troops. In the course of the five days, fifty-four people died, more than 2,300 were injured, and about 12,000 were arrested. In terms of property loss, about 4,500 businesses were looted, 1,100 buildings were destroyed, and 3,600 fires were set.[2]

As the last of the fires were extinguished in South Central Los Angeles, journalists, scholars, and other pundits sought to explain the meanings of the riots and place them within a broader historical understanding. Their interpretations varied widely. Commentators on the right drew on dated "culture of poverty" arguments to explain the behavior of the rioters and fuel the fears of readers about urban blacks and Latinos. For example, Harold Johnson of the *National Review* emphasized the "black and Hispanic" character of South Central and described the riots as a dystopian nightmare come to life, in which miscreants engaged in "party-like looting" and "murderous gangs did their worst."[3] Though such writings were drenched in racially charged language, conservative writers uniformly denied that anti-black racism played any role in either the uprising or the King verdict. Johnson furthermore intoned that if South Central were to rise from the ashes, the community must shed "the pathologies of the decimated black family."[4] Linking decades of socioeconomic decline in black communities to coddling and permissive liberal culture and policy, he continued, "After telegraphing a relativist ethic in a thousand ways, and devaluing the goal of internal discipline, should we be surprised when we move from social vertigo to social breakdown, one day turning on the tube to see armies of looters carting booty away, gleefully untroubled by conscience?"[5] In a similar vein, White House spokesman Marlin Fitzwater seized the opportunity to politicize the riots and indict the programs of the Great Society, which he blamed for creating the conditions that led to the unrest. "We believe," he said, "that many of the root problems that have resulted in inner city difficulties were started in the 60's and 70's and that they have failed."[6] Another common reaction from the right was to argue for even more militarization and policing in the daily lives of poor minorities deemed threatening to the public welfare.[7]

At the other end of the spectrum, a common interpretation of the events was that they were an *uprising* and not a random, senseless outbreak of violence. Indeed, that people in the streets could be heard chanting "No Justice No Peace," indicated the presence of a protest element among the throngs and echoed earlier uprisings in disenfranchised black communities in America.[8] A. T. Callinicos situated the riots against large-scale developments over the preceding decade and a half, saying they were a "reaction to the 15-year offensive on the economic condition of the majority of Americans… an offensive from which black people suffered with peculiar intensity."[9] South Central's longtime major employers in heavy industry had been declining since the 1960s and were virtually wiped out during the economic recession of 1979–1982. Furthermore, War on Poverty programs served the youth and poor, which had been lifelines in this community, suffered cut backs or elimination, with devastating social and economic effects. By the 1980s, Los Angeles embodied a remarkable paradox in which an "accumulation of misery" existed alongside "spectacular displays of wealth." It was in these conditions, which Callinicos argued were but a function of the "brutal, dynamic, and controlled" workings of late capitalism, that the seeds of the riots were laid. Because once effective intermediaries such as the labor movement were either wiped out or weakened: "The result is an alternation between periods… in which laissez-faire capitalism reigns supreme, and periods in which the discontent accumulated earlier on explode, because of the relative weakness of reformism, in a violent and uncontrolled form." The King verdict, then, which "epitomized the systematic bias of American legal and political structures against black people," was neither new nor unprecedented; rather, it came at a time of accumulated discontent.[10]

Other comentators on the left emphasized the degree to which the riots signaled a new era in America. Betty Sutton of the *Los Angeles Sentinel* rejected the parallels that had been drawn between the 1992 uprising and the Watts riot of 1965, saying, the "Watts riot isn't in the same hemisphere as the L. A. riot."[11] She conceded that both had been sparked by anti-black racism, but she insisted that a more salient takeaway was the fact that the more recent "disturbance was an international, multi-racial, equal opportunity riot in which Blacks participated in numbers proportionate to their dwindling percentage of the affected neighborhood's population."[12] Others similarly pointed to the multiethnic nature of the Los Angeles riots to argue for the need to think and talk about American race relations outside a black-white binary. In the course of the riots, businesses and property owned by members of many different ethnic groups were destroyed. The looters, furthermore, were of varied backgrounds. To approach the matter of race relations and rebuilding riot-damaged neighborhoods as an endeavor involving just blacks and whites would overlook the history and reality on the ground.

KOREAN LOS ANGELES

The Los Angeles riots cast an unprecedented national spotlight on Korean immigrants and Korean Americans. At the time, most Americans probably had been unaware that the city actually had the nation's largest Korean American population, but suddenly they were inundated with images of Korean people—men and women, young and old—in the urban unrest. As observers tried to understand them and situate their circumstances within a larger social and historical context, they often depicted Korean business owners as hard-working immigrants in the great American tradition, whose misfortune was being in the wrong place at the wrong time. Indeed, among the rioting victims, Koreans incurred the greatest losses; of the 4,500 stores destroyed, more than 2,300 were Korean-owned or run, and nearly every building in Koreatown was damaged.[13] In other words, tens of thousands instantly lost their livelihoods.

What had happened in the years leading up to the uprising? And what were the circumstances under which so many Korean merchants appeared in South Central and Koreatown? The Korean population in Los Angeles (and nationwide) underwent tremendous growth from the late 1960s. In Los Angeles, their numbers increased from 8,900 in 1970 to 145,431 in 1990.[14] Although many of these immigrants brought with them skills and capital (or had access to capital via ethnic networks such as *kye*), language and cultural barriers led a large number into self-employment and entrepreneurship.[15] Their expansion into business ownership was striking: by the time of the riots, in Los Angeles County, one in three Korean immigrants operated a small family business. According to a study by the Korean-American Grocers Association (KAGRO), a total of 3,320 Korean American–owned liquor stores and markets existed in Southern California with annual sales totaling $1.8 billion.[16] In South Central, the NAACP estimated that up to 70 percent of gas stations were owned by Koreans.

These markers of entrepreneurial success, however, obscured the daily hardships and sacrifices that merchants and their family members negotiated. Many of the businesses owned by Korean immigrants operated with few or no employees and relied heavily on unpaid family labor. And as middlemen they were resented by the customers to whom they sold goods while being exploited by the large companies whose products they peddled. Although they might have had enough money to open a business and live in a nice suburb, they usually did not have enough to run an establishment in a prime location. The only feasible option, then, was to start or acquire businesses in declining, less costly areas. Present-day Koreatown

emerged in such a location, growing around the Olympic Market purchased by Hi Duk Lee in 1971. Additionally, many Koreans opened commercial establishments in South Central Los Angeles, an area bordering Koreatown that had been all but abandoned by large-scale retailers.

KOREAN-BLACK RELATIONS

As the number of Korean-owned businesses grew while other retailers continued their exodus from the area, the mostly black residents of South Central came to rely greatly on the immigrant entrepreneurs for their daily needs. Los Angeles's black population, of course, had a long and storied history in the city, having expanded most markedly during the early and mid-20th century when jobs in manufacturing were abundant and offered a degree of economic security and mobility. With deindustrialization and white flight, which accelerated after the 1960s, their once vital, dynamic neighborhoods and secure jobs crumbled. Adding to these disruptive changes was the seemingly sudden appearance of Korean immigrant shopkeepers who were unfamiliar with the struggles of African Americans, had not witnessed the civil rights movement, and had little inkling of the histories of the neighborhoods in which they were establishing their businesses. As a larger group, Asians were not new to Los Angeles. Scholars, for instance, have noted the presence of Chinese in the city as early as the 19th century, Japanese Americans' history of interethnic relations with their black neighbors before World War II, and a small community of Koreans after the turn of the 20th century. By the early 1990s, however, this rich past was lost on many Angelenos, whether due to historical amnesia or to the simple fact that the post-1965 newcomers were an entirely different group from those who had settled before.

Though Korean merchants and black customers in South Central usually interacted peaceably and without incident, instances of misunderstanding and conflict eventually drew the attention of a media that highlighted the impression that black customers and Korean merchants clashed on a regular basis. During the 1970s and 1980s, a narrative of "Korean-black conflict" took hold, as news articles and editorials stressed the ways in which Koreans were seen as "taking over" the black community in Los Angeles.[17] The Korean population had grown very rapidly, making its presence near the city core of South Central seem as if it had occurred suddenly and out of nowhere. The vast majority were, furthermore, immigrants who had arrived after 1965. Just half had been in the United States for more than ten years.[18] As journalist Helen Zia has explained, "In their pursuit of the American dream, the new immigrants seemed oblivious to the African Americans' long history of struggle for their unfulfilled dreams. In Los Angeles as well as New York and other cities, black people bristled over incidents of disrespectful treatment and false accusations of shoplifting."[19]

Following a series of negative encounters between Korean shop owners and black customers, which the media gave copious attention to, African Americans' grievances against Koreans intensified during the 1980s. One major flashpoint was the eight-month boycott of Family Red Apple Market in New York City's Flatbush section in Brooklyn. The boycott was initiated in 1990 after a physical altercation between a black customer of Haitian descent and a Korean proprietor who had accused the former of stealing. Closer to home in South Central, a violent encounter that would prove pivotal in the events leading to the riots occurred in March 1991. A fifteen-year-old African American named Latasha Harlins entered Empire Liquor Market on South Figueroa Street. That day, Soon Ja Du, a middle-aged Korean immigrant, was working at the store. She was there because her son Joseph, who would have been working that day, stayed home. He did so because of threats that he had received by members of the Crips gang after agreeing to testify against them in the wake of a

robbery attempt. In the store, Du accused Harlins of stealing, and an altercation between the two led to Harlins punching Du and knocking her down, after which Du shot Harlins in the back of the head. Harlins was later found to have had juice from the store in her backpack and money in her hand.

The tensions escalated further following the death of Harlins, putting Korean-black community relations on the edge. Young Kyu Yi, a business owner of a store in South Central, called for calm and understanding, saying, "We should not lose our tempers over a bottle of orange juice."[20] Other co-ethnics rushed to defend Du, pointing out her Christian religiosity and involvement in her church. Reflecting the growing anger of blacks toward Koreans, a writer for the Los Angeles Sentinel called Korean business owners "poison pushing merchants who are apparently more outraged about being called names than they are about a dead Black child."[21] And after the Empire Liquor Store shut down following the shooting, the black organization Brotherhood Crusade placed a banner across its door, saying, "Closed for Murder and Disrespect of Black People."[22]

Through the second half of the 1980s and into the 1990s, these intergroup problems, to a large degree played up by the media, escalated until they reached a breaking point. It is important to note that, in addition to the run-ins during which Koreans displayed insensitivity toward African Americans, Korean immigrants were also feeling besieged and vulnerable against a backdrop of rising incidents that targeted them. The year 1986, for example, was an alarming one as four Korean storekeepers in Los Angeles were shot and killed by blacks in separate incidents. In 1991, Koreatown was the scene of forty-eight murders and 2,500 robberies. Koreans had been the number one target of anti-Asian hate crimes in the area.[23]

By the early 1990s, the discourse of "black-Korean conflict" had crystallized. An indication of this was the appearance of the Korean shop owner as a staple in mainstream popular culture. Spike Lee's groundbreaking 1989 film, *Do the Right Thing*, for instance, included a Korean shop owner couple as minor but pivotal characters. And in 1990, a year before the Harlins killing, the rapper Ice Cube released his track *Black Korea*, whose lyrics warned that if Korean storekeepers did not show respect to blacks, their businesses would be burned. In response, Korean Americans called for a boycott of the CD and members of the Korean American Grocers Association refused to sell the brand of malt liquor that Ice Cube had endorsed.[24]

Meanwhile, in other quarters, Koreans and blacks worked together to heal the rifts between their communities. In 1986, in the wake of the rash of killings of Korean merchants, community leaders, with the help of Los Angeles County Human Relations Commission, established the Black-Korean Alliance (BKA), whose objective was to maintain an ongoing dialogue between the two communities. It encountered problems from the start because Korean merchant groups were afraid of bringing negative attention to themselves after the killings, and many African Americans were hesitant to rally around the issue of interracial cooperation at the potential expense of justice and empowerment. However, the BKA did draw support from representatives in the NAACP and SCLC, as well as merchants and shopkeepers from the black and Korean communities. Chung Lee, the owner of Watts Market, was the first Korean merchant to join the BKA and expressed pride in his relationship with blacks in the neighborhood, hiring local workers and becoming involved in black community life. Other Korean merchants, however, disapproved of Lee's prominent role in the BKA and his willingness to talk to the media. Eventually, under their pressure, he resigned from the organization.[25]

The work of the BKA and Human Relations Commission in Los Angeles was further undermined by the publicity generated by the Latasha Harlins killing, particularly after police released the videotape of the altercation between Harlins and Soon Ja Du. In November 1991 Soon Ja Du was found guilty of manslaughter, but her sentence was suspended and she received five years' probation and was ordered to pay a fine ($500) and funeral costs for Harlins and perform community service. Asian American leaders were largely silent while many black leaders expressed outrage.[26]

SA-I-GU

A confluence of events including the Harlins-Du verdict, "Black Korea" fiasco, and Rodney King's beating, had greatly heightened tensions and tempers on the ground. Thirteen days after the Harlins shooting, the videotape of Rodney King's beating was released. A few months later, when the verdict was announced, the powder keg exploded.

Koreans called the Los Angeles riots *Sa-I-Gu*, or 4-2-9 (April 29). That they reserved a special name for it underscored how momentous they immediately recognized it to be. Jan Jung-Min Sunoo of the Los Angeles County Human Relations Commissions said *Sa-I-Gu* was "our worst nightmare come true," while Korean American journalist K. W. Lee called it an American pogrom: "For us it was like the Jewish last stand in Warsaw, or the internment of the Japanese Americans. Sa-i-gu was a convenient way for mainstream America to deflect black rage."[27, 28] Looking back twenty years later, Edward Chang said: "*Sa-i-gu* erupted after the acquittal of one Latino and three white police officers charged with the beating of Rodney King, a black motorist. Blacks, whites, Latinos, Asian Americans, Korean Americans and others were directly and indirectly affected—and involved—in *Sa-i-gu*. But it was Korean immigrant merchants who were, memorably, too often caught in the middle."[29]

Official responses to the riots brought a sharp focus on racial and class inequalities entrenched in American life and how they affected Koreans as well as blacks. Although their businesses were the most vulnerable to looting and damage, Korean merchants in South Central and Koreatown, along with everyone else in these neighborhoods, received virtually no police protection.[30] The low priority assigned to the areas was underscored when Chief Daryl Gates left the police headquarters to attend a political fund-raising event even though at that very time rioting and arson were escalating. He sought to justify his action as well as the lack of assistance and protection provided by his police force in saying: "There are going to be situations where people are going to go without assistance... That's just the facts of life. There are not enough of us to be everywhere."[31]

Without police protection, a number of Koreans took their security into their own hands, taking up arms and improvising security forces. The resulting stories and images, which underscored the "Bitter, Armed, and Determined" attitude of many Koreans, were especially surprising and unforgettable.[32] One of these, a photograph in *Newsweek* that became nicknamed the "vigilante Korean," showed a young Korean American man standing in front of a burning building while holding a semi-automatic gun and donning a Malcolm X t-shirt with the quote, "By any means necessary."[33] Also remarking on the armed Koreans, Seth Mydans of the *New York Times* noted, "One of the most gripping and, increasingly, controversial television images of the violence was a scene of two Korean merchants firing pistols repeatedly from a military stance. The image seemed to speak of race war, and of vigilantes taking the law into their own hands."[34]

As noted, property damage from the rioting was estimated to be between $785 million and $1 billion.[35] Of this, damage to Korean-owned property was between $350 million and $400 million. The establishments affected were diverse, including grocery stories, swap meet shops, clothing shops, liquor stores, dry cleaners, electronic shops, gas stations, jewelry shops, restaurants, beauty salons, auto shops, furniture shops, and video shops. Korean business owners faced a daunting, and for many impossible, recovery. Most of the businesses destroyed were uninsured at the time, and ten months after the riots, just a quarter of Korean

victims' establishments had reopened.[36] Sometimes the costs of rebuilding and moving on set people back even further. For instance, some turned to high interest loans to pay for their expenses and subsequently fell behind in their mortgages, leading to the loss of their homes. Rent and mortgage assistance were reported as the areas of greatest need.[37]

A survey conducted in the immediate aftermath shed light on the profound impact of the riots on people's livelihoods, psychology, and self-perceptions. Half of the respondents said they believed their chances of rebuilding their businesses were nil. Troublingly, most reported having symptoms of post-traumatic stress disorder, such as trouble sleeping, nightmares, ulcers, stress, depression, family conflict, and domestic violence.[38] The responses also underscored a drastic change in victims' self-image as a result of losing the self-confidence and respect that went along with their victimization and financial losses.

The modest and limited efforts at forging intercommunity understanding between Koreans and blacks collapsed in the months after the riots. Under siege and called "race traitors," the Black-Korean Alliance disbanded in December 1992. According to Helen Zia, the BKA's difficulties exposed some of the challenges of pan-Asian unity as well as the inadequacies of an "old style multiracial coalition" to improve black-Korean relations. Some members lamented that they never received sufficient support and resources from the mayor's office and other parties that they needed to improve multiracial relations. They also cited the limitations of relying on dialogue to solve what were very intransigent, complex problems. Finally, another issue was that member organizations and leaders were not always well connected to the people on the ground. As Marcia Choo of the Asian Pacific American Dispute Resolution Center reflected: "In our zeal to do the right things, we sometimes tried to fix things without consulting with the community."

Meanwhile, the faith of many Korean immigrants in American opportunity and the

"American dream" shattered as a result of their experience. As if securing a socioeconomic foothold as a business owner in South Central Los Angeles hadn't been challenging enough, the suddenness with which their already precarious livelihoods struggled was inexplicably cruel and unfair, particularly in light of the unshakeable belief that many had in the American system. "These feelings of betrayal have been intensified not just by the original harm inflicted by the minority local residents but also by the subsequent disappointing responses from various federal, state, and local government agencies."[39]

REFLECTING, REBUILDING, AND MOVING ON

The riots served as a wake-up call and turning point for the nation at large and Koreans in America in particular, becoming the regrettable vehicle through which many Americans first became aware of the nation's large Korean population. The riots also underscored the ways in which racism had many targets and was not simply something directed by whites toward nonwhites. Indeed, late-20th-century America was a much more complex nation socially and demographically than it had been some fifty years earlier. In this landscape, discussing race relations was pressing but difficult. Cornel West, for instance, criticized the "worn out vocabulary" used in the immediate responses to the riots that left people "morally disempowered," and he was also troubled that people seemed to stop reflecting on the events just months later. "The Los Angeles upheaval forced us to see not only that we are not connected in ways we would like to be but also," he said, "in a more profound sense, that this failure to connect binds us, even more tightly together. The paradox of race in America is that our common destiny is more pronounced and imperiled precisely when our divisions are deeper."[40]

Not only had the riots been a multiracial affair involving Asians, blacks, Latinos, and whites, but also, as historian George Sanchez pointed out, they "[offered] stark evidence of the way in which immigrants provided the perfect scapegoat for American populations frustrated with developments in their society."[41] Late-20th-century racism, he explained, was informed by a nativist streak that had resurged in American life during the 1980s and early 1990s, and it included both the left and the right. In the midst of the riots, Sanchez notes, young blacks were heard saying that Latinos and Asians had invaded their territory, and how they would let Latinos go but teach Koreans who it was who ruled. Thus, among the rioters were so-called new nativists who shared the broader feeling that the nation was in decline but who were additionally angered by the collapse of the inner-city economy. Amidst these struggles and concerns arose a Pacific Rim global economy that transformed parts of Los Angeles and accounted for at least some of the wealth of new Asian immigrants. In this context, Koreans stood out as an easy target.

Meanwhile, Korean Americans coped with their losses, reflected, and tried to move on. The practical aspects of moving on were, as noted, daunting, and, for many, the ability to do so proved impossible. Also difficult was the spiritual and emotional reckoning the riots compelled. As Edward Chang explained, many were pushed to reexamine critically "what it meant to be Korean American in relation to multicultural politics and race, economics, and ideology."[42] Some saw the experience as an extension of a narrative of trauma and displacement beginning in Korea and continuing in the United States. On the other hand, states Taeku Lee, *Sa-I-Gu* underlined in unmistakable terms "the geography of inequality, the nature of state power, and the paradoxes of inclusion and opportunity for immigrants of color in America."[43] Many blamed themselves for what they saw as their self-imposed isolation in their suffering, and, in turn, they decided to be more engaged with mainstream politics and affairs. Others felt demoralized and were pessimistic about the prospects for intergroup understanding; instead, they focused on the task of rebuilding Koreatown and forgetting the traumas of *Sa-I-Gu*. A large number of Korean Americans fled the city altogether, unwilling to rebuild in South Los Angeles. Since the riots, the Korean population around Koreatown has declined, while it has grown in places such as Orange County.

Within Korean American communities, the riots prompted a change in leadership, as the US born and those who had immigrated as children (1.5 generation) stepped up. Many from the immigrant generation had been reluctant to talk to the mainstream media about their hardships, leaving a gap for younger Korean Americans to fill. "Perhaps the second generation understands the importance of sharing such stories," said Angela Oh, "but the strong ethic of self-help and private struggle in the first generation prevented many important voices from being heard. Their view was too much shame, too much 'hahn,' fate had shown its hand, and help from the outside was an illusion."[44] The riots had also shown that the existing leadership structure in Los Angeles, which revolved around the Korea Federation, an organization whose legitimacy came from its ties to the South Korean government, could no longer meet the community's needs. In particular, language barriers, an absence of meaningful ties to local residents, its inability to gets its message outside the Korean American media, and its tendency to criticize black politicians especially undermined the Korean Federation's legitimacy and efficacy amidst the crisis.[45] In its place emerged younger, more media friendly and politically savvy figures such as Angela Oh, Marcia Choo, Roy Hong, Bong Hwan Kim, and Ryan Song. Angela Oh's groundbreaking moment came during her appearance on ABC's *Nightline*, during which she became a rare voice in the mainstream media for the concerns of Korean Americans.

A political reorientation that saw the Korean community become less consumed with homeland politics and more engaged with US politics typified the shift in generational leadership among Korean Americans. Taeku Lee believed the riot experience was pivotal in fostering a stronger civic-mindedness and pan-Asian awareness. He cited a 2008 National Asian American Survey, in which Korean Americans demonstrated the strongest belief among Asian groups that their fate was linked to other Asian Americans.[46] They also showed a stronger co-ethnic solidarity and feeling of commonality with African Americans and Latinos than did other Asians. Since the riots, Koreatown has also become more integrated as one political district, facilitating residents' political involvement and coalition work in Los Angeles. In the immediate months and years after 1992, Korean Americans focused their political activity on meeting urgent post-riot needs, such as accessing resources to rebuild. To achieve their goals, a flurry of new organizations, such as the Koreatown Youth and Community Center, Koreatown Immigrant Workers Alliance (KIWA), and National Korean American Service and Education Consortium, emerged.

Korean American community and political life in the post-riot era has been marked by philosophical and strategic disagreements over how best to work toward political and economic advancement. One new aspect of intra-ethnic politics since the riots, according to Edward Park, has been open partisanship. Leaders such as Angela Oh and Bong Hwan Kim, for example, aligned themselves with the Democratic Party, while Jay Kim, Michelle Park-Steel, and others embraced more conservative politics and identified as Republicans.[47] Liberal Korean Americans in organizations such as the Korean American Democratic Committee (KADA) argued that co-ethnics should align with the traditional civil rights coalition, that Koreans were victims of racial oppression, and that whatever rights they enjoyed were the results of the civil rights movement, in general, and the Hart-Celler Act in particular. Their best hope was to join other communities of color in recognition of their shared struggle and pursue strategies of incorporation. Conservative Koreans, by contrast, who tend to be driven by material interests, argued that the Republican Party was inclusive of minorities—citing Colin Powell, Ward Connerly, and others as examples. They rejected the contention of liberals that joining the civil rights coalition would help them and said minorities had been failed by it, as well as by the welfare state.[48]

A controversy over how to rebuild South Central Los Angeles illustrated the ideological and political terrain of post-riot Korean America. Local leaders had launched a "Campaign to Rebuild South Central without Liquor Stores." Koreans saw this as a cynical way to uplift black residents by scapegoating Korean merchants, as they had owned 175 of 200 liquor stores in the area.[49] To protect their interests, KAGRO, which represented Korean liquor storeowners, bypassed dealing with city hall by going to the state legislature and getting help from a Republican representative. Edward Park notes that the controversy hurt leaders like Angela Oh and Bong Hwan Kim, as it showed that their strategy of telling Koreans to work with blacks and Latinos was insufficient, and it helped the KARA (Korean American Republican Association) to become more influential. Jay Kim, a Korean American Republican, used the issue to get elected to the House of Representatives in November 1992.

Despite these differences in ideology, the heightened political activity and engagement has helped to elevate the visibility of Koreans as Asian Americans in general, both in Los Angeles and elsewhere. This heightened visibility and activism made clear the need for Asian American voices in local affairs and discussions about race relations. Angela Oh and Bong Hwan Kim, for example, played integral roles in the formation of the Multicultural Collaborative (MCC) and the Asian Pacific Americans for a New Los Angeles (APANLA). Cindy Choi was the founding director of MCC, an important progressive voice in Los Angeles politics. In other arenas, Korean Americans have made key strides. The *Los Angeles Times* hired K. Connie Kang as a writer and the Department of Commerce hired T. S. Chung.

Asian Americans also played a major and visible role in coalitional work. Official efforts by Los Angeles City Hall at ethnic consolidation after the riots came in the form of the Rebuild Los Angeles program. Although no Koreans held leadership positions, Asian Americans were prominent.[50]

The riots also increased interest among scholars in Los Angeles, the fate of post-industrial cities, multiethnic relations, and Korean Americans. For scholars of Korean ancestry who studied Korean Americans such as Edward Chang, the event brought a new urgency to and appreciation for their work. This scholarly research—Chang for instance conducted interviews with more than 100 Koreans in the Los Angeles area—also represented one of the few venues in which audiences could access the voices and perspectives of Korean Americans.[51] The riots and academic interest in Korean entrepreneurs also generated renewed appreciation for existing social science work by scholars such as Ivan Light and Edna Bonacich, who had theorized about the role of Korean business owners in the larger economy and have since greatly influenced how we understand late-20th-century post-industrial conditions more broadly. They discussed how the merchants brought down labor costs to keep prices low, but how doing so required working long hours. In turn, Korean entrepreneurs in Los Angeles represented what they called a "disguised form of cheap labor."[52]

CONCLUSION

About ten years after the riots, Angela Oh observed that many open wounds, traumas, and frustrations remained among Koreans in Los Angeles. "Politicians who had promised to help realized that once they got into office, helping Korea Americans was not politically viable."[53] The nation might have turned away its attention, but hardships were far from over. "[Virtual] silence on the deeper emotional, psychological, and cultural impact of the riots on Korean Americans."[54] Furthermore, Oh feared that important lessons initially drawn from the riots had been forgotten. "Their families did what many people naturally try to do in the face of tragedy—forget the past, bury the pain, ignore what cannot be changed."[55]

Ongoing demographic change in Los Angeles since 1992 has shown that the conversation with regard to America's multiethnic population is an evolving one. Twenty years after the riots, Korean Americans still dominated mom and pop stores in South Los Angeles, but "Korean-black conflict" no longer dominated the discussion on race relations in the area. Business ownership has become more diverse, with Latinos, Arabs, and Southeast Asians increasingly moving into South Los Angeles, which has also become less black and more Latino ("black flight"). Moreover, black-Latino tensions have become more acute in recent years.

As its legacy continues to evolve, the Los Angeles riots of 1992 will likely stand out as a watershed moment in the history of American race relations and Asian Americans. To close with an observation from Angela Oh, "For Korean Americans it was a blessing and a curse to be present at that particular moment in time and space for these realizations to surface. In some ways, Koreans were the emissaries for the rest of this nation to understand the significant change that had occurred in many of the large urban centers around the country."[56]

DISCUSSION OF THE LITERATURE

The Los Angeles riots (also known as the Los Angeles civil uprising, Rodney King riots, and other variations thereof) have spawned a rich literature across several disciplines and interdisciplinary fields since the 1990s. The earliest writings, which were both scholarly and editorial, and published as the dust from the riots were still settling, focused largely on African American poverty and disfranchisement, black-white conflict, and the ravages of late-20th-century capitalism.[57] On the heels of this initial spate of analysis emerged new

scholarship that considered the place of Asians, mainly Koreans, in the uprising. While social scientists in fields such as sociology and anthropology took the lead in building this literature and, thus, framing much of the scholarly discussion about Koreans and the riots, the last few years have seen a notable shift, with new historical work and perspectives seeking to situate the significance of the riots—and the experiences of those affected by them—in the context of broad developments over the 20th century.

Social science research during the 1990s focusing on the experiences of Koreans during the riots tended to be concerned with questions regarding how they ended up in the line of fire, whether they were perpetrators or victims, and the causes of "Korean-black conflict." This literature examines various facets of the lives of Korean immigrants leading up to the riots, including the circumstances that brought them to South Central, their struggles as business owners, and their relations with black customers. Because the scholarship was social science-heavy, it also placed great emphasis on developing and testing theories.[58] Importantly, the work coming out of this period renewed appreciation for existing scholarship in urban and immigration studies. Gaining particular attention was the work of Edna Bonacich and Ivan Light, who proposed the middleman minority thesis to explain the place of Korean merchants in Los Angeles.[59] Offering a layered understanding of Korean immigrant experiences since the 1960s, they argued that Korean immigration and entrepreneurship should be understood within the broader struggle of working-class and poor blacks in the post-industrial city.

After this initial spate of sociological work, the topics and approaches pursued by scholars interested in the riots have diversified. First person, journalistic, and creative works produced in the wake of the uprising, in turn, influenced interventions in fields such as literary studies and media criticism.[60] For example, Min Song's 2005 book, *Strange Future*, examined the ways in which the riots were significant as a "cultural-literary event."[61] Specifically, Song argues that the riots—vis-à-vis the numerous creative works produced about them—crystallized a narrative of national decline and social trauma particular to the late 20th century.

The scholarly literature has also shifted toward paying greater attention to the *impact* of the riots on Korean American individuals, communities, and subjectivities. The book *Blue Dreams* by anthropologists Nancy Abelmann and John Lie was pivotal in this regard.[62] Not only did the authors place Koreans at the center, but also they situated their struggle in Los Angeles in a transnational context and analyzed the meanings of the riots for their history and identity. Also playing a crucial role in developing the scholarly literature on the impact of the riots on Koreans and Asian Americans were the editors of *Amerasia*, a journal published by the UCLA Asian American Studies Center. The journal devoted several issues to the riots and has published a large number of articles over the years examining different aspects of Korean American and Asian American life, history, and identity in relation to the riots.[63] More recently, books such as Nadia Kim's *Imperial Citizens* and Angie Chung's *Legacies of Struggle* represent exciting advances in Korean American studies by taking on questions raised by the scholarship, such as the challenges of institution building, identity and racial politics, and intergroup relations.[64]

In the years following the riots, historians mainly sought to offer context and clarification, with particular care given to explaining why the populations affected were so diverse and why the 1992 uprising should not be interpreted as merely a replay of Watts. In an important intervention, George Sanchez argued in 1997 that the riots illustrated the rise of a "new nativism" in American life that was primarily directed at Asians and Latinos. "[At] its core," he stated, "the Los Angeles riots provide stark evidence of the way in which immigrants provided the perfect scapegoat for American populations frustrated with developments in

their society."[65] Important to people's overall understanding, Sanchez asserted, was that the riots occurred against the backdrop of the dissemination of newly published new anti-immigrant books and rising anti-immigrant sentiment in California, seen, for instance, in the movement to pass restrictive legislation that culminated in Proposition 187 in 1994.

After a relative lull in scholarly production, a recent revival of interest promises to bring new interpretations and understandings to the riots and their significance in Asian America. Give that more than twenty years have passed since the uprising, historians and other scholars are revisiting the events of 1992, less as an illustration of the current moment than as a salient historical episode in its own right. The editors of *Amerasia Journal* published a twenty-year anniversary issue in which several Korean American scholars reflected upon the events and reaffirmed their status in marking a turning point, both personally and collectively. Historian Brenda Stevenson's book, *The Contested Murder of Latasha Harlins*, takes a comparative and intersectional approach to analyzing the pivotal Harlins-Du episode as a precursor to the riots.[66] Shifting our view back to the origins and causes of the riots, while considering the ways in which immigration, race, and gender intersected both in the altercation and trial as well as in the broader social fabric of Los Angeles, Stevenson's book represents an innovation in the scholarship on the Los Angeles riots and may signal a new stage in historical inquiry that situates Asian immigration and Asian people at the center of some of the most significant developments in American racial and ethnic relations during the late 20th century.

PRIMARY SOURCES

An array of primary sources exist that shed light on Asian American experiences before, during, and after the Los Angeles riots. Because the riots occurred relatively recently and were widely covered by the media, many of these materials are easily accessible via online sources.

With regard to media coverage, newspapers, magazines, and other printed media constitute a rich base of material that can provide researchers a sense of how the riots were covered, the attention that was paid to Korean Americans, and the points of view of Asian American leaders and spokespersons. Major national newspapers such as the *Los Angeles Times* and *New York Times* covered the riots as well as ran articles focusing on the history of Koreans in Los Angeles and their struggles to move on. These can usually be accessed via databases such as Proquest Historical Newspapers and Lexis-Nexis. In addition, perspectives from the ethnic media, by way of publications such as the *Los Angeles Sentinel*, a black newspaper serving Los Angeles, and the *Korea Times*, the largest bilingual Korean newspaper in Los Angeles, can be found via Proquest.

Also readily accessible are various firsthand accounts and memoirs, which can be valuable for insights they provide on Korean American perspectives and experiences. Unfortunately, these sources are few in number. Angela Oh's *Open: One Woman's Journey* (2002) is an autobiography about a Korean American from Los Angeles who witnessed the riots and emerged to prominence as a spokesperson for the ethnic community. *East to America*, a compilation of Korean American life histories published in 1996, contains several accounts by individuals who lived through the riots and their aftermath. Documentaries have also served as an important format for Korean American representation and expression with regard to the riots and Korean American identity. Especially notable in this regard are *Another America* (1996) and *Sa-I-Gu* (1992). The former, by Michael Cho, explores urban violence and Korean-black relations against his own family's experience. The latter, produced by Dai Sil Kim-Gibson, Christine Choy, and Elaine Kim, sheds light on the riots from the perspective of Korean immigrant women.

In terms of manuscript collections, the amount of available material is also small but growing. Much of the manuscript material about Koreans in the Los Angeles riots can be found in collections relating to the history of Los Angeles. At Loyola Marymount University, the Rebuild LA Papers shed light on the role of Koreans in city efforts as well as the challenges that business owners faced in obtaining assistance to rebuild. Collections of former government officials who represented Koreans in Los Angeles give a sense of the community's main concerns and relationship to city leaders and agencies. Here the David Roberti Papers at Loyola Marymount, Tom Bradley Papers at UCLA, and Kenneth Hahn Papers at the Huntington Library are important. With regard to Korean American activism in the wake of the riots, the Southern California Library for Social Studies and Research in Los Angeles holds the papers of the Korean Immigrant Workers Alliance (KIWA), which is a good place to start.

FURTHER READING

Abelmann, Nancy, and John Lie. *Blue Dreams: Korean Americans and the Los Angeles Riots*. Cambridge, MA: Harvard University Press, 1997.

Abu-Lughod, Janet L. *Race, Space, and Riots in New York, Chicago, and Los Angeles*. Oxford: Oxford University Press, 2012.

Afary, Kamran. *Performance and Activism: Grassroots Discourse after the Los Angeles Rebellion of 1992*. Lanham, MD: Lexington, 2009.

Alan-Williams, Gregory. *A Gathering of Heroes: Reflections on Rage and Responsibility*. Chicago: Chicago Review Press, 2005.

Baldassare, Mark, ed. *The Los Angeles Riots: Lessons for the Urban Future*. Boulder, CO: Westview, 1994.

Cannon, Lou. *Official Negligence, How Rodney King and the Riots Changed Los Angeles and the LAPD*. New York: Basic Books, 1999.

Castuera, Ignacio, ed. *Dreams on Fire, Embers of Hope: From the Pulpits of Los Angeles after the Riots*. Saint Louis, MO: Chalice Press, 1992.

Chang, Edward. "'As Los Angeles Burned, Korean America Was Born': Community in the Twenty-First Century." *Amerasia Journal* 30, no. 1 (2004): vii–ix.

Chang, Edward T., and Russell C. Leong, eds. *Los Angeles: Struggles toward Multiethnic Community*. Seattle: University of Washington Press, 1994.

Chung, Angie Y. *Legacies of Struggle: Conflict and Cooperation in Korean American Politics.* Stanford, CA: Stanford University Press, 2007.

Cohen, Nathan, ed. *The Los Angeles Riots: A Socio-psychological Study.* New York: Praeger, 1970.

Davis, Mike. "The Rebellion That Rocked a Superpower." *Socialist Review* 152 (June 1992): 8–9.

Freer, Regina. "Black-Korean Conflict." In *The Los Angeles Riots: Lessons for the Urban Future*, edited by Mark Baldassare, 175–204. Boulder, CO: Westview, 1994.

Gooding-Williams, Robert. *Reading Rodney King/ Reading Urban Uprising.* New York: Routledge, 1993.

Hunt, Darnell, and David Yoo, eds. "Los Angeles since 1992: Commemorating the 20th Anniversary of the Uprisings." Special Issue, *Amerasia Journal* 38, no. 1 (Spring 2012).

Institute for Alternative Journalism. *Inside the L.A. Riots: What Really Happened, and Why It Will Happen Again.* New York: Institute for Alternative Journalism, 1992.

Kim, Kwang Chung, and Shin Kim. "The Multiracial Nature of Los Angeles Unrest in 1992." In *Koreans in the Hood: Conflict with African Americans.* Edited by Kwang Chung Kim, 17–38. Baltimore: Johns Hopkins University Press, 1999.

Kim, Shin. "Political Economy of Korean-African American Conflict." In *Korean Americans: Conflict and Harmony.* Edited by Ho-Youn Kwon. Chicago: North Park College and Theological Seminary, 1994.

Kim-Gibson, Dai Sil, dir. *Sa-I-Gu.* DVD. San Francisco: CrossCurrent Media, 1993.

Korean American Inter-Agency Council (KAIAC). Korean American Inter-Agency Council Announces Results of a Comprehensive Survey Assessing Situation of Korean American Victims Ten Months after the LA Riots. Unpublished report. Los Angeles: Korean American Inter-Agency Council, 1993.

Los Angeles Times. Understanding the Riots: Los Angeles before and after the Rodney King Case. Los Angeles: Los Angeles Times Syndicate Books, 1996.

Madhubuti, Haki R., ed. *Why L.A. Happened: Implications of the '92 Los Angeles Rebellion.* Chicago: Third World Press, 1993.

Marable, Manning. *Beyond Black and White: Transforming African American Politics.* New York: Verso, 1995.

Min, Pyong Gap. *Caught in the Middle: Korean Communities in New York and Los Angeles.* Berkeley: University of California Press, 1996.

Ong, Paul M., and Suzanne Hee. *Losses in the Los Angeles Civil Unrest, April 29–May 1, 1992: Lists of the Damaged Properties and Korean Merchants and the L. A. Riot Rebellion.* Los Angeles: University of California at Los Angeles, 1993.

Rivas, Jorge. "Two Decades Later, Children of the L.A. Riots Share Memories." Retrieved on May 07, 2014 from http://colorlines.com/archives /2012/04/two_decades_later_young_voices _on_the_la_riots.html.

Sanchez, George J. "Face the Nation: Race, Immigration, and the Rise of Nativism in Late Twentieth Century America." *International Migration Review* 31, no. 4 (Winter 1997): 1009–1030.

Smith, Deveare. *Twilight—Los Angeles, 1992.* New York: Dramatists Play Service, 2003.

Sonenshein, Raphael. *Politics in Black and White: Race and Power in Los Angeles.* Princeton, NJ: Princeton University Press, 1993.

Song, Min Hyoung. *Strange Future: Pessimism and the 1992 Los Angeles Riots.* Durham, NC: Duke University Press, 2005.

Stevenson, Brenda. *The Contested Murder of Latasha Harlins: Justice, Gender, and the Origins of the L.A. Riots.* New York: Oxford University Press, 2013.

Wall, Brenda. *The Rodney King Rebellion: A Psychopolitical Analysis of Racial Despair and Hope.* Chicago: African American Images, 1997.

Yu, Eui-Young. *Black-Korean Encounter: Toward Understanding and Alliance.* Los Angeles: California State University Press, 1994.

NOTES

1. The officers were Stacey Koon, Laurence Powell, Timothy Wind, and Theodore Briseno.
2. Brenda Stevenson, *The Contested Murder of Latasha Harlins: Justice, Gender, and the Origins of the LA Riots* (New York: Oxford University Press, 2013), xvii.
3. Harold Johnson, "The Fire this Time," *The National Review* May 25, 1992, 17.
4. Johnson, "The Fire this Time."
5. Johnson, "The Fire this Time," 18.
6. Michael Wines, "Riots in Los Angeles: The President, White House Links Riots to Welfare," *New York Times*, May 5, 1992.

7. Eugene Methvin, "How to Hold a Riot," *The National Review*, June 8, 1992, 32.
8. Stevenson, *Contested Murder*, xvii.
9. A. T. Callinicos, "Meaning of Los Angeles Riots," *Economic and Political Weekly* 27, no. 30 (July 25, 1992): 1605.
10. Callinicos, "Meaning of Los Angeles Riots."
11. Betty Sutton, "A Tale of Two Riots," *Los Angeles Sentinel*, May 13, 1992, A-1.
12. Sutton, "A Tale of Two Riots."
13. Stevenson, *Contested Murder*, xviii.
14. Helen Zia, *Asian American Dreams: The Emergence of an American People* (New York: Macmillan, 2001), 173.
15. Among Koreans in America, *kye* refers to ethnic rotating credit associations used to finance businesses. Originating in Korea and appearing in the U.S. West Coast and Hawaii as early as 1903, these organizations allowed for the establishment and success of many Korean-owned businesses after 1965. In the 1970s and 1980s *kye* pools could be as large as several hundred thousand dollars, or even a few million. See Kyeyoung Park, *The Korean American Dream: Immigrants and Small Business in New York City* (Ithaca, NY: Cornell University Press, 1997), 58–60.
16. Kyeyoung Park, "Use and Abuse of Race and Culture: Black-Korean Tension in America," in *Koreans in the Hood, Koreans in the Hood: Conflict with African Americans*, edited by Kwang Chung Kim, 64 (Baltimore: Johns Hopkins University, Press, 1999).
17. Zia, *Asian-American Dreams*, 173.
18. Zia, *Asian-American Dreams*, 174.
19. Zia, *Asian-American Dreams*.
20. Zia, *Asian-American Dreams*, 179.
21. Zia, *Asian-American Dreams*, 177.
22. Zia, *Asian-American Dreams*, 178.
23. Zia, *Asian-American Dreams*.
24. The liquor manufacturer persuaded him to apologize. Zia, *Asian-American Dreams*, 177.
25. Zia, *Asian-American Dreams*, 175.
26. Zia, *Asian-American Dreams*, 180.
27. Zia, *Asian-American Dreams*, 182.
28. Zia, *Asian-American Dreams*, 172.
29. Edward T. Chang, "Korean American Community Coalesces," *Los Angeles Times*, April 29, 2012.
30. Kwang Chung Kim and Shin Kim. "The Multiracial Nature of Los Angeles Unrest in 1992," in *Koreans in the Hood: Conflict with African Americans*, edited by Kwang Chung Kim, 34 (Baltimore: Johns Hopkins University Press, 1999).
31. Robert Reinhold, "Riots in Los Angeles," *Los Angeles Times*, May 5, 1992.
32. Seth Mydans, "A Target of Rioters, Koreatown Is Bitter, Armed, and Determined," *New York Times*, May 3, 1992, 2.
33. An analysis of this photograph can be found in David Palumbo-Liu, *Asian/America: Historical Crossings of a Racial Frontier* (Durham, NC: Duke University Press, 1999), 183–186.
34. Mydans, "A Target of Rioters, Koreatown Is Bitter, Armed, and Determined," 2.
35. Kim and Kim, "The Multiracial Nature of Los Angeles Unrest in 1992," 26.
36. Kim and Kim, "The Multiracial Nature of Los Angeles Unrest in 1992."
37. Kim and Kim, "The Multiracial Nature of Los Angeles Unrest in 1992."
38. Kim and Kim, "The Multiracial Nature of Los Angeles Unrest in 1992," 27.
39. Kim and Kim, "The Multiracial Nature of Los Angeles Unrest in 1992," 28.
40. Cornel West, "Learning to Talk of Race," *New York Times*, August 2, 1992, SM24.
41. George J. Sanchez, "Face the Nation: Race, Immigration, and the Rise of Nativism in Late Twentieth Century America," *International Migration Review* 31, no. 4 (Winter 1997): 1011.
42. Edward Chang, "'As Los Angeles Burned, Korean America Was Born': Community in the Twenty-First Century," *Amerasia Journal* 30, no. 1 (2004): xvii.
43. Taeku Lee, "Riot, Remembrance, and Rebuilding: Some Longer Term Aftereffects of Sa-I-Gu, *Amerasia Journal* 38, no. 1 (Spring 2012): 39–40.
44. Angela Oh, *Open: One Woman's Journey* (Los Angeles: UCLA Asian American Studies Center, 2002), 16.
45. Edward Park, "Competing Visions: Political Formation of Korean Americans, 1992–1997," *Amerasia Journal* 24, no. 1 (1998): 44.
46. Lee, "Riot, Remembrance, and Rebuilding," 40.
47. Park, "Competing Visions," 47.
48. Park, "Competing Visions," 54.
49. Park, "Competing Visions," 51.
50. Park, "Competing Visions," 46.
51. Edward Taehan Chang, "Remembering Saigu," *Amerasia Journal* 38, no.1 (2012): 32.
52. Kim and Kim, "The Multiracial Nature of Los Angeles Unrest in 1992," 32.
53. Oh, *Open: One Woman's Journey*, 15.

54. Oh, *Open*, 16.
55. Oh, *Open*, 17.
56. Oh, *Open*, 34.
57. Mike Davis, "The Rebellion That Rocked a Superpower," *Socialist Review*, June, 1992, 8–9; A. T. Callinicos, "Meaning of Los Angeles Riots," *Economic and Political Weekly* 26, no. 30 (July 25, 1992): 1603–1606.
58. Edward T. Chang. "New Urban Crisis: Korean-African American Relations," in Kim, *Koreans in the Hood*: 39–59; Kyeyoung Park, "Use and Abuse of Race and Culture: Black-Korean Tension in America," in Kim, *Koreans in the Hood*, 60–74.
59. Edna Bonacich and Ivan Light, *Immigrant Entrepreneurs: Koreans in Los Angeles, 1965–1982* (Berkeley: University of California Press, 1991).
60. Oh, *Open: One Woman's Journey*; Anna Deveare Smith, *Twilight—Los Angeles, 1992* (New York: Dramatists Play Service, 2003).
61. Min Hyoung Song, *Strange Future: Pessimism and the Los Angeles Riots* (Durham, NC: Duke University Press, 2005).
62. Nancy Abelmann and Joh Lie, *Blue Dreams: Korean Americans and the Los Angeles Riots* (Cambridge, MA: Harvard University Press, 1997).
63. Content from a 1993 issue was republished as Edward T. Chang and Russell C. Leong, eds., *Los Angeles: Struggles toward Multiethnic Community* (Seattle: University of Washington Press, 1994); Daryl Hunt and David Yoo, eds., "Los Angeles since 1992: Commemorating the 20th Anniversary of the Uprisings," Special issue, *Amerasia Journal* 38, no. 1 (Spring 2012).
64. Nadia Kim, *Imperial Citizens: Koreans and Race from Seoul to LA* (Stanford, CA: Stanford University Press, 2008); Angie Chung, *Legacies of Struggle: Conflict and Cooperation in Korean American Politics* (Stanford, CA: Stanford University Press, 2007).
65. George J. Sanchez, "Face the Nation: Race, Immigration, and the Rise of Nativism in Late Twentieth Century America," *International Migration Review* 31, no. 4 (Winter 1997): 1011.
66. Brenda Stevenson, *The Contested Murder of Latasha Harlins: Justice, Gender, and the Origins of the LA Riots* (New York: Oxford University Press, 2013).

Shelley Sang-Hee Lee

STREET GANGS IN THE 20TH-CENTURY AMERICAN CITY

STREET GANGS, RACE, AND AMERICANIZATION IN THE INTERWAR ERA

The sociologist Frederic Thrasher effectively launched academic inquiry into street gangs with his classic publication *The Gang: A Study of 1,313 Gangs in Chicago* (1927). Adhering to the Chicago School of sociology's social disorganization theory, Thrasher explained the emergence of gangs in Chicago as related primarily to a breakdown of social institutions—family, religious, educational—in the city's immigrant and low-income districts. "The gang," he wrote, "may be regarded as an interstitial element in the framework of society, and gangland as an interstitial region in the layout of the city." By *interstitial*, Thrasher referred to an "ecological" condition: the interstitial regions existed between industry and the "better residential districts" and between "immigrant or racial colonies."[1] Yet what Thrasher and other Chicago School sociologists ignored in an era long before scholars explored the unstable nature of race and ethnicity was that the primary ethnic groups of gangland were also "inbetween" in another sense.[2] A good number of their "territorial" conflicts were in many ways the struggles of young immigrants and second-generation ethnics to negotiate and define their place within the ethno-racial hierarchies that were determining their access to neighborhoods, jobs, and social standing within the interwar city. In the interwar years, when nativist anti-immigration debates circulating within the domains of politics and popular culture cast certain immigrant groups as foreign and even un-American "races," the meanings of *race* and *Americanism* were hard to separate out on the streets. The explosion of street gangs in Northeastern and mid-western cities witnessing massive influxes of Southern and Eastern European immigrants in the first two decades of the 20th century thus reflected a widespread collective will among working-class youths to form peer groups out on the streets to handle the uncertainties surrounding their respective communities.[3]

Thrasher's inattention to racial dynamics playing out in Chicago's low-income immigrant neighborhoods was, in part, a manifestation of the Chicago School's investment in a "race relations cycle" paradigm that envisioned all ethno-racial groups in the city—African Americans included—gradually shedding their Old World ways and integrating into the more prosperous zones of the city.[4] This minimization of race as an organizing force in Chicago's gangland was surprising in view of the fact that Thrasher began his research in a moment when gangs had gained great notoriety in Chicago and other cities of the industrial North for their role in mob attacks against African Americans. As blacks from the rural South migrated northward to take advantage of higher-paying industrial jobs available with the outbreak of World War I, racial violence erupted along the color lines in a number of cities witnessing rapid increases in their black populations. Bloody race riots struck East St. Louis in 1917, Philadelphia in 1918, and Chicago in 1919, with white street gangs identified as key provocateurs in each affair. In Chicago, in particular, a number of Irish "social athletic clubs"—street gangs with political ties—in the area around the city's stockyards were identified as primary instigators by city officials. "But for them," the twelve-member commission assembled to study the riot concluded, "it is doubtful if the riot would have gone beyond the first clash."[5]

Street gangs were not only active in enforcing and reinforcing the boundaries around black ghettos but also in patrolling the interfaces of different European American communities during the interwar years. Americanized Irish gangs, in particular, played leading roles in such activities, which, according to historians

David Roediger and James Barrett, imparted to recent immigrants "a racialized map of the city, a range of attitudes about African Americans, and a language of racial exclusion."[6] In fact, "white" gangs that were led and largely dominated by Irish ethnics also engaged in a pattern of aggression against the youths of "new immigrant" groups—mainly Jews, Italians, and to a lesser extent Poles—in cities like Boston, Buffalo, Chicago, and New York. Such activities worked to define certain groups as "racially inbetween" and to establish an informal pecking order in the parks and streets of such cities, an order enforced by the Irish and other older immigrants who dominated their police forces and political organizations.[7] By the mid-1920s, as new immigrant groups were better integrated into the fabric of city life and gained leverage in political, labor, and religious institutions, they increasingly mixed with the Irish and older immigrants in pan-ethnic "white" gangs. Thrasher's survey of Chicago's gangland, for example, revealed that 351 of the 880 gangs there were of mixed ethnicity or nationality.[8]

Such evidence suggests the importance of territorial circumstances and dynamics in the organization and activities of gangs. This did not mean, however, that space trumped race in the world of street gangs, as some historians have argued.[9] The fact is that the majority of gangs Thrasher observed were nonetheless ethno-racially homogeneous, a remarkable situation in view of the scarcity of neighborhoods in the interwar cities of the Northeast and Midwest in which a single ethnic group constituted a numerical majority of residents. Moreover, a significant number of those gangs that were not homogeneous were largely dominated by one ethnic group or another, and ethno-racial tensions within these "mixed" gangs persisted in ways that created status hierarchies along ethno-racial lines among the members. Indeed, the ambiguities and uncertainties surrounding race and Americanization were central preoccupations among the predominantly first- and second-generation ethnics who ran with gangs in the urban Northeast and Midwest.[10] This was because, as historian Arnold Hirsch argues, new immigrants occupied a "third tier" within the racial order of the interwar city. Editorials in the foreign-language newspapers of Chicago's Polish, Lithuanian, Jewish, and Italian communities alike frequently contrasted their respective group identity and social standing with those of "whites" and "Americans," a state of affairs that translated into fraught relations between these different groups out on the streets.[11]

Many street gangs were, to one extent or another, products of the rapidly shifting racial orders of cities in the Northeast and Midwest during the interwar years. Some of the more high-profile gangs were supported and protected by ward politicians and syndicate kingpins for the muscle and networks they mobilized on Election Day or in showdowns over turf. Observers in both Chicago and New York noted how well-connected social athletic clubs served as ladders of mobility for youths looking for jobs in the municipal workforce or underground economy.[12] Indeed, street gangs in the interwar cities of the Northeast and Midwest were central to a number of converging discourses about urban poverty, immigration, and citizenship. To the settlement house movement, ethnic gangs were critical targets of Americanization strategies.[13] To the alliances of reformers and government agencies that drove crusades against alcohol consumption, vice, organized crime, and political corruption, gangs were vital components of such scurrilous rackets. To Chicago sociologists, youth gangs were all this and more. As Robert Park wrote in 1925, "These gangs have exercised a considerably greater influence in forming the character of the boys who compose them than has the church, the school, or any other community agency outside of the families and homes in which the members of the gangs are reared."[14]

MAKING GHETTOS AND BARRIOS

The demographic, social, and cultural circumstances behind the explosion of street gangs in the urban Northeast and Midwest shifted during the 1930s with the dissipation of black migration from the South and the tapering off of white ethnic immigration after the passage of the restrictive immigration laws of 1921 and 1924. Racial violence along the boundaries of black ghettos declined in intensity from that witnessed around the riotous affairs of the previous decade, although the climate of hostility remained hot enough to spur the formation of a noticeable number of defensive-oriented African American youth gangs in cities like Chicago, New York, and Philadelphia. By the end of the decade, moreover, the forces of cultural and social assimilation began to weaken the "third tier" occupied by Southern and Eastern Europeans. Mexicans, by contrast, proved to be relatively "un-absorbable" and faced persistent discrimination in schools and public spaces—conditions that led to the emergence of youth gangs within Mexican communities in the 1930s, such as in Chicago, where Mexicans were recruited to work in the steel industry,[15] as well as in San Antonio, El Paso, and Los Angeles, where, despite the Depression-era drive for repatriation, Mexicans became the most important source of immigrant labor.

The entrance of the United States into World War II disrupted the stability of the urban social context in the early 1940s, especially in cities on the East and West Coasts and in the Midwest. Some 1.5 million African Americans left the South, seeking the relatively high wages of war production jobs in northern cities during the war years, and another 1.2 million made the same move during the first postwar decade. Between 1940 and 1960, the black population more than doubled in Chicago, Detroit, New York, and Philadelphia, while increasing more than six-fold in Los Angeles, nearly ten-fold in Oakland and some fifteen-fold in San Francisco. Black

migrants arriving in these and other war production centers were mostly forced into preexisting black ghetto areas whose boundaries
began to expand into long-standing working-
class white ethnic areas amid wartime housing
shortages and rent-gouging practices targeting
black families.

This historically momentous process of
racial transition that swept across industrial
centers of the urban North during the 1940s
and 1950s did not merely involve dynamics
of black ghettoization. In Los Angeles and
other cities in the Southwest witnessing a
surge in Mexican immigration due in part to
the Bracero Program, similar circumstances
also pushed Mexican migrants into *barrio*
neighborhoods. In New York and Chicago,
moreover, a wave of Puerto Rican migration
led to the development of Puerto Rican enclaves. On Chicago's Near West Side and in
New York's East Harlem neighborhood, communities of African Americans, Puerto Ricans,
and white ethnics lived in close proximity and
competed for housing, jobs, and resources
during the 1950s.[16]

As in the interwar years, street gangs developed and thrived in this shifting multiracial context, emerging as central actors on all
sides of the color lines in the postwar urban
North. In white ethnic neighborhoods, they
contributed muscle and energy to grassroots
resistance to racial integration, and in black,
Mexican, and Puerto Rican neighborhoods,
they defended the rights of their communities
to access city spaces and resources, against intimidation and violence. This resurgence of
youth gang formation and conflict took center
stage nationwide amid concerns about home-
front unity in 1943, when the Social Science
Institute at Fisk University reported hundreds
of racial battles in forty-seven cities, pitting
black against white youth gangs. Italian
American and African American teens fought
week-long battles in Newark and Philadelphia,
and recurrent clashes broke out between black
and Polish gangs in Buffalo and Chicago.[17] The
major race "riots" in Los Angeles, Detroit, and

Harlem that summer were all preceded by
rising tensions in spaces of youth leisure. In
Detroit, white gangs clashed repeatedly with
black youths clad in "zoot suits" in parks and
outside of dances. In Los Angeles, mobs of
white sailors, soldiers, and local youths
tracked down and beat Mexican zoot suiters
for several weeks in May and June. In Harlem,
moreover, observers noted the leading role
of young zoot suiters organized into gangs in
battling police.

If a good many of these wartime incidents
were more the work of loosely assembled
cliques and mobs than well-established, tightly
organized gangs, the collective actions being
carried out by youths increasingly found
more coherent institutional form out on the
streets in the postwar years. In Detroit and
Chicago, white neighborhood youth gangs
engaged in daily forms of harassment against
minority groups around schools, parks,
beaches, pools, and commercial venues and
joined campaigns spearheaded by parishes,
improvement organizations, and homeowners associations to hold off racial *invasion*
through acts of arson, physical aggression, intimidation, and verbal abuse between the
mid-1940s and late 1950s.[18] Such actions,
usually undertaken in the name of communities identified as "white," reinforced bonds of
whiteness between different ethnic groups
and contributed to the development of an
ideology of defensive localism in working-
class neighborhoods undergoing white flight
and racial transition in this era.[19]

Youth gangs in black and Latinx neighborhoods—male and female—put another variant of defensive localism into practice during
these years. Although some observers noted
the existence of African American and Mexican
gangs as far back as the 1920s and 1930s, the
wave of racial migration, conflict, and neighborhood transition occurring in the 1940s
and 1950s greatly increased their numbers.
Most scholars who trace the origins of such
gangs have viewed their formation as, at least
in part, a defensive response to the racial

aggression directed at the residents of their communities, both by white ethnics and other groups of color. East Harlem, for example, witnessed the outbreak of three-way race riots involving blacks, Puerto Ricans, and Italians in the 1940s.[20] Such circumstances of ethnic succession and conflict combined with demographic factors related to the high percentage of youths within black and Latinx communities in the first postwar decade. In New York, for example, black gangs proliferated along tense racial boundaries in Harlem, the Bronx, and Brooklyn in the 1940s.[21] A similar set of circumstances surrounded the emergence of black street gangs in West Philadelphia, the South Side of Chicago, and in South Central and East Los Angeles, where violence frequently erupted around racially mixed schools and parks.[22]

Mexican and Puerto Rican gang formation in this era also responded to the forces of racial discrimination in the context of everyday life, but the story was more varied and complicated for these groups. In Los Angeles, in particular, the growth of Mexican gangs in the Boyle Heights and Maravilla *barrios* of East Los Angeles occurred within the context of moral panics about Mexican juvenile delinquency fueled by the Sleepy Lagoon murder trial of 1942 and the Zoot Suit Riots of 1943. Stereotyped as "ratpacks" and "pachuco gangsters" in the press, and facing attacks in schools, the members of these gangs adopted a defiant style symbolized by the wearing of zoot suits that flaunted wartime rationing restrictions.[23] In Chicago, however, where racial boundaries were somewhat more porous for Mexicans, the story was quite different. Although sizable Mexican gangs grew out of the Mexican communities of the Near West Side and South Chicago by the 1950s, Mexican youths living in these ethno-racially heterogeneous areas also joined white ethnics in gangs largely preoccupied with defending neighborhood boundaries against black "invasion."[24] Moreover, social workers and other observers close to both Mexican and Puerto Rican gangs in Chicago

and New York noted strong tensions within these groups over color, with lighter-skinned youths at times disrespecting and even excluding darker-skinned ones.[25] Brown and white racism thus converged in the youth gang subcultures that spread through many US cities in the postwar decades, exacerbating racial tensions at the interfaces between ethno-racial communities in ways that pushed and pulled people into *barrios*, ghettos, and *colonias* in the postwar city.

HONOR, TERRITORY, AND YOUTH GANG SUBCULTURES IN THE POSTWAR CITY

The emergence of street gangs across the urban United States in the era of large-scale immigration and demographic change between the 1910s and late 1950s closely related to dynamics of racial formation, conflict, and succession; however, other factors explained the propensity of young men and, to a lesser extent, women, to join such organizations.[26] In the 1950s, a range of social programs aimed at gang prevention appeared in a number of cities, including New York, Boston, Philadelphia, Chicago, El Paso, San Antonio, Seattle, San Francisco, and Los Angeles. Following upon the "street work" model established by Chicago sociologist Clifford Shaw's Chicago Area Project (CAP), these programs sought to use indigenous leaders from working-class communities to "reach" gang members and steer them away from delinquent forms of behavior, including fighting, theft, and vandalism. They employed sociologists to better understand why youths engaged in risky behavior.[27] Around this same time, gangs entered into national discourse with a wave of "wild youth" exploitation movies following on the heels of blockbusters like *Blackboard Jungle* and *Rebel without a Cause*, the meteoric rise of rock 'n' roll, a juvenile delinquency panic stirred up by the hearings by the United States Senate Subcommittee on Juvenile Delinquency, and then the release of the enormously successful cinematic production of *West Side Story* in 1961. On the local level, newspapers in cities across the nation ran sensationalistic stories about "wolfpack complexes," "juvenile terrorism," and senseless gang feuds tearing up schools and neighborhoods.

If, in its tale of ethno-racial conflict between Italians and Puerto Ricans, *West Side Story* pointed to the lingering problem of race in postwar gang culture, by the early 1960s the forces of urban renewal, white migration, black ghettoization, and the clustering of Mexicans and Puerto Ricans in tight ethnic enclaves had greatly decreased the contentious interfaces between these groups. Massive black ghettoization and white flight virtually eliminated violence between black and white gangs in highly segregated cities like Chicago, St. Louis, and Milwaukee. Intraracial violence certainly existed prior to this time, but postwar deindustrialization, rising youth unemployment rates, and the transformation of working-class neighborhoods wrought by slum clearance and redevelopment projects led to conditions of social marginalization and community breakdown that, according to some sociologists, shaped violent fighting gang subcultures within African American and Latinx neighborhoods by the 1960s. In such areas, scholars and street workers observed youth gangs developing parallel structures of opportunity and empowerment to compensate for the lack of legitimate means of achieving status and mobility. Building on Albert Cohen's seminal 1955 work on the search for status and respect among socially marginalized gang youths, sociological studies by Richard Cloward, Lloyd Ohlin, and Irving Spergel described criminally oriented gangs engaging in turf battles and illegal activities to obtain social status and honor.[28] Spergel, in particular, viewed African American gangs as prone to fighting intraracial turf battles for *rep*, in contrast with Italian gangs, which were swayed by political and syndicate leaders in the Italian community to avoid infighting and direct their energy toward defending neighborhood boundaries against encroachments by Puerto Ricans and blacks.[29]

Hence, as forces of ethnic and racial succession dissipated across much of the urban landscape, lethal turf clashes among gangs increasingly turned on a search for masculine honor and respect, even if such battles involved an extra boost of adrenaline when waged against ethno-racial others. Gangs of all stripes exhibited a fierce attachment to place in the 1950s and 1960s, often identifying themselves after the streets and neighborhoods they occupied and emblazoning these place-based identities on jackets, walls, and even their own bodies in tattoo ink. Historian Eric Schneider argues that for young men running in gangs in New York during this era, this defense of place articulated an assertion of masculine prowess in a context of subordination at school and powerlessness in the expanding low-wage service sector of the postwar labor market. Similar labor conditions linked with postwar deindustrialization shaped the development of violent gang subcultures within segregated African American neighborhoods in Philadelphia, Cleveland, Detroit, St. Louis, and Milwaukee. In Los Angeles, fighting gangs sprang up around the Watts housing projects by the late 1950s.

Worsening the situation in a number of cities, moreover, was the loss of opportunities for black gangs in underground economies, as Italian syndicates took control of policy rackets that had provided livelihoods for African Americans in the past.[30] In Chicago, for instance, such circumstances compounded the loss of some 131,000 jobs (or 22%) between 1955 and 1963 as the number of potential jobseekers increased by some 300,000. By the early 1960s, fighting gangs with between twenty-five and one-hundred members were commonplace in white, African American, Mexican, and Puerto Rican neighborhoods on the city's West and South Sides and the stakes of their clashes were becoming increasingly lethal. In solidly black neighborhoods like

Lawndale on the West Side and Woodlawn on the South Side, some of the city's most notorious black fighting gangs—the Vice Lords, Egyptian Cobras, Devil's Disciples, and Blackstone Rangers—fought for dominance by incorporating groups of unaffiliated youths into their ranks. On the much more ethno-racially mixed Near West Side and Near North Sides of the city, however, racially charged conflicts were still frequent at the boundaries between communities of Mexicans, Puerto Ricans, Italians, and Poles, where they served to reinforce bonds of ethno-racial solidarity in a context of neighborhood transition due to urban renewal and migration.[31]

Teenage girls became much more active within the fighting gang subcultures of this era. In Chicago, many of the major male fighting gangs of the late 1950s and early 1960s affiliated themselves with female counterparts: for example, the Vice Lords with the Vice Ladies, the Egyptian Cobras with the Cobraettes, and the Italian Near West Side's Taylor Dukes with the Taylor Capris.[32] While much of the sociological literature on girl gangs in the 1960s and early 1970s cast them as mere auxiliaries or possessions of male gangs, a number of studies since that time demonstrate that female gangs often acted autonomously in their own rituals involving the fashioning of rebellious identities and the defense of community and place. Joan Moore's work on East Los Angeles *barrio* gangs, for example, reveals some female gangs forming as counterparts to male gangs and consisting largely of relatives of the male members, but others developing in the context of violent struggles over turf and status with rival female gangs from the *barrio*.[33] On Chicago's racially tense Near West Side in the late 1950s and 1960s, moreover, turf battles between Mexican and largely Italian female gangs grew out of racial tensions between the two communities. For example, in the midst of a wave of racial aggression around the Near West Side's Harrison High School in 1961, the city's

Mayor's Committee on Youth Welfare was forced to send a representative to head off a "rumble" at a nearby city beach between two girl groups—the Italian Taylor Capris and the Mexican Spanish Queens gang. For the young women in these gangs, like their male peers, such rituals involving the defense of neighborhood and community bestowed a sense of honor and respect.

GANG POLITICIZATION IN THE ERA OF CIVIL RIGHTS AND BLACK POWER

The tide of civil rights consciousness and activism that washed over the urban landscape in the early 1960s powerfully reshaped the political and ideological context of fighting gang subcultures in many cities. In the months following the momentous March on Washington in 1963, activists affiliated with the Student Nonviolent Coordinating Committee (SNCC) and the Congress of Racial Equality (CORE) organized school boycotts in Chicago, Boston, New York, Kansas City, Cleveland, and Milwaukee, actions that worked to reframe the injustices young African Americans—gang affiliated or not—were confronting not only in their schools but out on the streets. Around this same time civil rights leaders in the North consciously reached out to young people as the potential foot soldiers of the growing civil rights movement. In 1964, for example, Max Stanford, one of the founders of the radical group Revolutionary Action Movement (RAM), published an article in which he argued that working-class gang youths offered a potential rich source of oppositional energy. "Instead of fighting their brothers and sisters," he wrote, "they can be trained to fight 'Charlie.' They can be developed into a blood brotherhood (black youth army) that will serve as a liberation force in the black revolution."[34]

Such ideas inspired campaigns waged by civil rights activists to bring about truces between rival black gangs in order to turn them toward local protest politics. In Philadelphia, for example, the local branch of the National

Association for the Advancement of Colored People (NAACP), under the leadership of Cecil Moore, effectively recruited gang youths into its picketing campaign to desegregate a North Philadelphia boarding school for fatherless boys. Moore was able to do this because he tapped into the discourse of collective self-defense being articulated by Malcolm X and Robert F. Williams.[35] Indeed, even more than educational injustices, the cause that began to sway African American youths away from internecine gang conflicts and toward forms of collective action during these years was the need to respond to the aggressive policing of their neighborhoods. Around the same time as the wave of school boycotts, the CORE organized youth demonstrations against police misconduct in San Francisco, Syracuse, Cleveland, and Brooklyn, and the organization ACT led a protracted protest campaign on the West Side of Chicago, incorporating hundreds of gang youths.[36] In Harlem, moreover, the Blood Brotherhood and other so-called "anti-white" gangs battled police on a number of occasions in the spring and summer of 1964. According to a *New York Times* investigative report, such gangs took to the streets on their own in violent protest to the presence of Tactical Patrol Forces as well as the implementation of "no-knock" and "stop-and-frisk" practices.[37] Similar circumstances characterized the fighting gang subcultures of South Central Los Angeles, where widespread resistance to racist police practices exploded into the Watts rebellion of August 1965. Scholars and observers have described Watts as a key turning point in the politicization of South Central gangs, with notorious organizations like the Slausons and Gladiators declaring truces with rivals and directing their energies toward defending their communities against the police.[38]

That two former Slauson leaders, Alprentice "Bunchy" Carter and Jon Huggins, became the founding members of the Southern California chapter of the Black Panther Party (BPP) three years later reveals the extent to which black fighting gang subcultures became crucibles for black power politics in the mid-1960s. A range of black power activists have identified their gang experiences as critical to their turn toward the politics of community empowerment, such as Walter Palmer, a key leader of Philadelphia's Black People's Unity Movement (BPUM), who described making a natural transition from gang leader to community organizer.[39] In the late 1960s, the Black Panther Party engaged in aggressive recruiting campaigns among gang youths in Chicago and Los Angeles, capitalizing on growing anger about rampant police brutality and political repression directed at black power organizations. This was a moment, when, in many ghetto neighborhoods, gangs circulated among community activists, student protestors, and black studies groups within spaces shaped by the politics and culture of black power. Within this context, some of the era's emerging "super-gangs"—federations stretching across vast territories and incorporating thousands of youths—identified themselves with names that evoked black power sensibilities: for example, the Ghetto Brothers and Black Spades in the Bronx, and the Blackstone Ranger Nation on Chicago's South Side.

In Chicago, in particular, such circumstances produced the most striking examples of gang politicization of this era. In 1967, the Office of Economic Opportunity (OEO) granted the Blackstone Rangers and their rivals, the Disciples, $927,000 of Great Society antipoverty funds to work with The Woodlawn Organization (TWO) in running a job-training program on the South Side. That same year, Lawndale's Conservative Vice Lords gang incorporated as a business organization with the goal of uplifting themselves and their community, obtaining more than a quarter of a million dollars in private foundation grants in the years to follow. The Vice Lords, as was the case with a number of gangs seeking to make the turn toward legitimate activities in this moment, mixed political activism with community uplift and entrepreneurial ambitions, participating in tenant rights campaigns, cleaning rubbish from allies, and opening viable businesses.

These projects ended with mixed results. Although the Rangers managed to run a somewhat effective job-training program, put on a successful theatrical production, and reduce violence in their neighborhoods, their efforts were shrouded in scandal after a Senate investigation found members of the gang guilty of misuse of federal funds.[40] In the aftermath of major urban uprisings in Newark, Detroit, Chicago, and Baltimore, conservatives accused the Johnson administration of making payoffs to gangs for peace. The Vice Lords, for their part, stayed clear of any such charges and boasted a similar set of accomplishments, but their turn toward politics and community uplift was derailed by the inability of some of its members to leave behind their gangbanging ways.[41] Moreover, both the Rangers and Vice Lords, who provoked the ire of Mayor Richard J. Daley by marching with Martin Luther King Jr. in protest of Chicago's segregated housing market in 1966, were hampered by the subversive activities of the Chicago Police Department's Gang Intelligence Unit, which worked to foment tensions between rival gangs and to undermine the Illinois Panther Party's attempts to organize South and West Side gangs into a powerful coalition to challenge the Daley Machine.[42] In 1969, emboldened by the controversies surrounding the Rangers and Vice Lords, Daley brought his fight into the open, declaring a "War on Gangs"—an early example of the kind of local law-and-order campaign that proliferated in cities across the country in the coming decade.

Despite this wave of repression, the Conservative Vice Lords, Black P. Stone Nation, and Black Disciples merged to form the LSD (Lords, Stones, Disciples) coalition in 1969, working with a range of political organizations, including Operation Breadbasket, on a campaign to pressure the Chicago Building Trades Union Council to hire more African American youths, which continued into 1970. Another truce with similar consequences was concluded in New York's South Bronx in December of 1971, after Black Panther Joseph Mpa persuaded leaders of the Ghetto Brothers to meet with more than 100 other local gang leaders at a local Girls and Boys Club to discuss how to address the lack of jobs and social services in their neighborhoods. The following year, the Ghetto Brothers marched into a local job office to demand employment for blacks and Puerto Ricans in the area.[43] In Los Angeles as well, Black Panther organizing efforts brought about a reduction of intraracial gang violence and a turn toward politicization. But the murder of Bunchy Carter and John Huggins by members of rival nationalist group Organization US in 1969 and a fierce wave of repression directed at the Panthers by the Los Angeles Police Department put an end to the BPP's organizing efforts in South Central. With the withdrawal of the Panthers came a resurgence of homicidal gang violence, which in turn provoked the rapid fusion of gangs into opposing federations of Crips and Bloods in the early 1970s.[44]

Many of the same forces working to politicize black gangs also operated in both Puerto Rican and Mexican communities during the late 1960s and early 1970s. Chicago's Puerto Rican Young Lords gang formed in 1959 and spent the first seven years of its existence fighting with rivals and protecting the Puerto Rican community from white ethnic gang attacks on the city's Near North Side. But in the months following a violent three-day rebellion in the Humboldt Park *barrio* over the police shooting of an unarmed youth, the Young Lords gang, under the leadership of José "Cha-Cha" Jiménez and with the encouragement of Chicago BPP Chairman Fred Hampton, transformed itself into the Young Lords Organization (YLO) and began to move toward political activism. By 1967, the YLO negotiated a truce with the city's largest

Latino street gang, the Latin Kings, and in the years to follow it set up daycare centers and free breakfast programs, and led spirited campaigns to demand health care services and protest the displacement of working-class Puerto Rican residents from Lincoln Park because of gentrification. In 1969, a branch of the YLO was founded in East Harlem, with smaller branches springing up in Boston, New Haven, Philadelphia, and Newark in subsequent years. But, once again, these projects were disrupted by state-sponsored subversion and repression. Jiménez was forced underground in 1970, after being charged for a range of trumped-up felonies, and sentenced to a year in prison for the petty theft of lumber; and the pastors of the National Young Lords People's Church, who had provided valuable support to the YLO's campaigns in Lincoln Park, were murdered under suspicious circumstances.

In Mexican communities across the urban Southwest, Chicano nationalism provided the framework for the conversion of former gang members into activists affiliated with militant organizations like the Brown Berets. Founded in East Los Angeles after a case of police brutality in November of 1967, the Brown Berets attracted recruits from *barrio* gangs by emphasizing collective self-defense against racist policing and harassment. In San Antonio, in particular, gang members in the local chapter of the Brown Berets used the networks of gang life to build the organization, setting up police patrols and brokering truces between rival *barrio* gangs.[45] Such efforts, however, were short-lived. Like the Black Panthers and Young Lords, the Brown Berets were crippled by local police repression, including infiltration and other subversive activities, on the part of agents working for the Federal Bureau of Investigation's COINTELPRO (derived from COunter INTELligence PROgram) project.

Hence, by the mid-1970s, the interface between gangs and political activism was decisively ruptured by systematic repression and the law-and-order politics of the Great Society backlash. A sign of the times was the passage by a predominantly Democratic Congress of the Omnibus Crime Control and Safe Streets Act of 1968, which provided generous funding to municipalities to reinforce and equip police forces for quelling civil disturbances. Great Society liberals effectively accelerated the process of criminalizing urban spaces in minority communities at the very moment that these spaces were transformed into staging grounds for a youthful brand of contentious politics that helped to radicalize many gang members.[46] With the carceral state amping up operations, the forces of deindustrialization continuing to erode the urban job base, and massive super-gangs locked in increasingly deadly combat for control of emerging drug markets, gangs made "the transition from turf to profits."[47]

GANGS IN THE POSTINDUSTRIAL CITY IN AN ERA OF HYPERINCARCERATION

Prior to the mid-1970s, the "gang problem" in the United States was, geographically and demographically speaking, a fairly circumscribed phenomenon. Gangs largely developed and operated in African American, Mexican, Puerto Rican, and white working-class districts in the metropolises of the Northeast, mid-Atlantic, Midwest, Texas, and California. Major cities in these regions and states, to some extent, shared a set of historical circumstances between the 1900s and 1970s—migration, ethnic conflict and succession, ghetto and *barrio* formation, declining labor market conditions—that shaped the emergence of comparable gang subcultures. However, in the 1980s and 1990s, a number of cities falling somewhat outside these regions and this historical trajectory witnessed the rapid development of gangs in the midst of a perfect storm of economic restructuring, chronic unemployment for minority youths, hypersegregation, the meteoric rise of underground drug economies, and a new militarized police apparatus linked to the expansion of an increasingly punitive carceral state.[48]

The Sun Belt, in particular, saw a spectacular rise in gang activity in this period. Between 1970 and 1995, for example, the number of gang cities increased in Florida from 2 to 67, in South Carolina from 1 to 17, in Alabama from 2 to 22, in Texas from 7 to 95, in New Mexico from 1 to 21, and in Arizona from 3 to 20. Indeed, while gangs were on the rise nationwide during this period, with the number of counties reporting gang problems jumping ten-fold, the gang problem shifted markedly southward. Although the West possessed the highest number of cities reporting gang activities throughout the period between 1970 and 1998, the region saw an increase of a mere 4 percent compared with 33 percent for the South, which previously lagged far behind the rest of the nation but now moved into second place among the different regions, ahead of the Northeast and Midwest.[49] Three cities that emblematized the circumstances surrounding this explosion of gangs in the Sun Belt were Miami, Atlanta, and New Orleans, where, by the mid-1980s, gangs had developed around predominantly black housing projects to battle for control of the local crack cocaine market. In Miami, a major port of entry for drugs arriving in the United States, law enforcement officials estimated gangs in the city doubled in a three-year period between 1984 and 1987; in New Orleans, a rise in gang-related murders in the scramble over crack turf had made it the murder capital of the country by 1994.[50] Meanwhile, Los Angeles was the epicenter of gang activity in the Southwest, counting approximately 1,000 male gangs with 200,000 gang members by the turn of the 21st century.[51] Here as well, the battle for crack marketing territories culminated in a spike in gang-related drive-by murders in the mid-1980s, as Crips and Bloods integrated numerous subgroupings into hierarchical organizations with centralized leadership structures.[52]

The explosion of gangs in the 1980s and 1990s was also shaped, in part, by new migration patterns stemming from the Immigration and Nationality Act of 1965, which led to a rise in immigration from Latin America and Asia, creating a "rainbow of gangs" in cities like New York, Miami, Chicago, Houston, and Los Angeles.[53] Many of these new immigrants settled in New York and California, but Texas, Florida, Illinois, and New Jersey were also prominent receiving states. In New York and Chicago, Mexicans poured into Puerto Rican neighborhoods, provoking ethnic tensions between these groups. By the end of the 1990s, the Mexican population had clearly surpassed Puerto Ricans in the historic Puerto Rican *barrio* of Humboldt Park, where Puerto Rican and Mexican youths commonly hung their respective country's flags from rearview mirrors to avoid mistaken identity on the cruising strip of Western Avenue. Moreover, a range of new Latin American and Asian groups—Cubans, Dominicans, Cambodians, Filipinos, Chinese, Koreans, and Vietnamese, among others—moved in and around long-standing African American and Mexican neighborhoods in cities in California, Texas, Florida, and New York, leading, in some instances, to competition over jobs and housing, a situation revealed dramatically in the clashes between Koreans, Latin Americans, and African Americans during the Los Angeles uprising of 1992.

In comparison with the gangs of the interwar and postwar decades, however, gangs forming in Latin American and Asian immigrant communities in the 1980s and 1990s were generally less oriented around conflicts with rival youths from neighboring communities over identity, status, turf, and resources. The "immigrant experience" of this era, sociologist Martin Sánchez-Jankowski argues, "produced gangs that [were] primarily, although not exclusively, predatory on their community."[54] Such was the case with the Chinese and Vietnamese gangs that emerged within the Chinatowns of New York, Boston,

Los Angeles, and San Francisco in the late 1970s and early 1980s. Although hostile contacts with other ethnic groups provided the impetus to some early gang formation among Chinese immigrant youths in the early 1970s, the Chinese and Vietnamese street gangs that came to provide muscle for Chinese organized crime syndicates in the late 1970s and 1980s were pure products of the social order of Chinatown, where they engaged in racketeering, extortion, heroin trafficking, and human smuggling.[55] Vietnamese gangs, in particular, grabbed headlines in a number of cities for some high-profile grudge murders, which, according to observers and scholars, reflected the codes of a gang culture imported from Vietnam.[56] In 1990, for example, the *Los Angeles Times* reported on Vietnamese gang members fatally gunning down two diners in a Vietnamese restaurant because one had allegedly flirted with a gang member's date; two years later, covering a series of killings in Houston's Little Saigon, a journalist for the *Houston Chronicle* remarked that "retribution killings [had] brought an old-world style of justice and honor to the refugee-dominated cafes and pool halls where unemployed Vietnamese pass the hours."[57]

The story of Asian gangs in this era reveals a key dimension of contemporary gang history that was hardly specific to immigrant communities: as in the past, the "search for respect" continued to propel youths—white, black, Latino, and Asian alike—into deadly confrontations on the streets of the postindustrial city.[58] During the 1970s and 1980s, white ethnic gangs in Boston, Philadelphia, and Brooklyn achieved a sense of honor by defending the community against the perceived incursions of African Americans.[59] And in black and Latino communities witnessing rising numbers of gang-related killings perpetrated by gang "soldiers" and "lieutenants" fighting to monopolize drug markets, lethal gang violence also stemmed quite often from grudges, insults, and teenage bravado in a moment when youths had increasingly easy

access to handguns. Moreover, as sociologist Elijah Anderson's ethnographic work on black youths in Philadelphia demonstrated, aggressive police tactics in this era further reinforced "codes of the street" that valorized the use of violence—against the police or rival gang members—to attain respect.[60] This was a moment when the hysteria around gangs produced by the Reagan administration's War on Drugs in the 1980s, the proliferation of ruthless drug-trafficking gangsters in the dystopian inner-city landscapes of television and mainstream cinema, and the eruption of public outrage around the "nihilism" and obscenity of gangsta rap made gangs into the boogeyman for a range of urban problems—drugs, gun violence, concentrated poverty, unemployment, and deficient schools. Although this was certainly not the first time such problems were explained in cultural terms, this conjuncture was particularly propitious for the "culturalization" of urban problems, a process which in turn provided the rationale for the withdrawal of social services and the punitive turn in public policy. That the War on Drugs so pointedly targeted black and Latinx communities led to the conflation of hardened criminal gangbangers with ordinary black and Latinx youths (some affecting a gangsta style), a tendency that translated into draconian anti-gang policies, such as California's Street Terrorism and Enforcement Prevention (STEP) Act of 1988, which made participation in a street gang a criminal offense and provided for the prosecution of parents who did not exercise "reasonable care" in preventing their children's activities. Such blatantly racist policies were given justification by Nancy Reagan's "Just Say No" campaign, which frequently had the First Lady posing for photo ops surrounded by African American children or, on one occasion in Los Angeles, by SWAT operatives during a raid of a "crack house" in a black neighborhood.

Making matters worse, moreover, was the dearth of ethnographic research in the 1980s and early 1990s investigating the precise nature of the relationship between the expansion of the drug trade and the spread of gang violence, and challenging what sociologist Sudhir Venkatesh describes as "the public mythology of the morally reprehensible outlaw capitalist overtaking American inner cities."[61] Much of the sociological literature on gangs published during this period viewed gang activities as responses to unemployment and degrading experiences in low-paying service sector jobs.[62] Although this situation affected working-class white, Latino, and Asian youths as well, it was most severe in hypersegregated black communities witnessing high unemployment and the wholesale withdrawal of social services. Between 1970 and 1982, the number of unemployed or marginally employed African American men between ages 18 and 29 in the country's central cities increased from 24 to 54 percent.[63] Lofty unemployment rates were thus the backdrop for the worst outbreaks of gang violence during the prime years of the crack wars from the mid-1980s through the 1990s. In mid-1980s Los Angeles, for example, where the war between the Crips and Bloods increased the number of gang homicides by 87 percent in a single year, the unemployment rate for black youths stood at around 45 percent. In 1990s Chicago, when the mightiest African American gangs—the Gangster Disciples, Vice Lords, and Saints, among others—were setting up elaborate centralized, hierarchical organizations to administer crack distribution in their respective territories and engaging in a pattern of drive-by killings that pushed homicides in the city to historic highs, the local employment rate for black males over the age of 16 hovered near 50 percent.[64]

The increase in deadly gang violence during these moments in part reflected the fact that poor labor market conditions had blocked the transition of youths from the gang into stable adult lives, with older members in need of livelihoods turning toward the opportunities offered by the underground economy and at times pulling along impressionable younger members with them.[65] Such conditions, according to sociologists William Julius Wilson and Robert Sampson, contributed to the overall "disorganization" of black ghetto communities, which because of physical deterioration and a loss of social controls linked with the withdrawal of the state and flight of social capital, became fertile terrain for the development of criminally oriented gangs.[66] Under such circumstances, gangs headed by older members at times assumed the role of providing community services, making repairs in neglected housing projects, sponsoring barbecues and basketball tournaments, mediating disputes, and helping poor residents pay for bail bonds, rent, clothes, and groceries.[67]

While historians were slow to build upon the sociological literature dealing with the structure of gangs, their internal dynamics, their motivations, and their relationship to their communities, recent histories of the carceral state and the law-and-order politics surrounding it have made important interventions in the project of historicizing gangs in the American city over the last quarter of the 20th century.[68] The bipartisan crime control consensus that developed in the late 1960s led to a punitive turn in penal and urban policy, and by the mid-1970s drug enforcement was emerging as the new field of punishment. As a result of a wave of federal and state laws mandating harsher sentencing guidelines for drug offences, drug-related arrests soared from 322,300 to 1,375,600 between 1970 and 2000. Between the 1980s and the 1990s, moreover, "the chances of receiving a prison sentence following arrest increased by more than 50 percent" and "the average length of sentences served increas[ed] by nearly 40 percent."[69] In addition, the Anti-Drug Abuse Act of 1986 specifically targeted crack use and trafficking in minority communities by imposing mandatory minimum sentencing requirements for those convicted with a mere five grams of crack (compared with 500 grams of powder cocaine). Targeting the nexus between crack trafficking and minority street gangs, this legal framework unleashed a wave of stings and sweeps conducted by the increasingly militarized anti-gang tactical units that sprang up across the United States during the 1970s and 1980s. As a result, a breathtakingly high proportion of those incarcerated on drug convictions during these years were young men from black and Latinx communities—as many as 90 percent in some states.[70] Young African Americans, in particular, bore the brunt of such policies, with blacks constituting more than 50 percent of the prison population between the ages of 18 and 29 by the turn of the 21st century.

Hyperincarceration dramatically reshaped the world of street gangs between the mid-1970s and 1990s, as imprisoned gang leaders formed elaborate networks and alliances that extended beyond prison walls into the streets of US cities. On the one hand, prisoners readily integrated into such alliances for protection and support; on the other, prison wardens and guards used gang divisions to maintain order as prisons became overcrowded. In Chicago, in particular, hyperincarceration contributed to the development in the mid-1980s of the rival alliances of People and Folks, which, taken together, encompassed more than half of the city's gangs by the mid-1990s. These alliances extended across racial lines, with the Folks growing out of a merger between the Black Gangster Disciple Nation and the Latin Disciples, and the People out of an alliance between the Vice Lords and Latin Kings.[71] In Texas, Mexican prison gangs, such as Mexikanemi, Syndicato Tejano, and Puro Tango Blast, sprung up in the 1970s and 1980s, incorporating youths from Houston, Dallas, Fort Worth, El Paso, San Antonio, and Austin, and developing extensive drug-trafficking networks with ties to Mexican cartels. Mexikanemi, which became the largest of these rival gangs by the 1990s, promoted a brand of Chicano nationalism marked by a belief in a spiritual bond with the southwestern homeland of Aztlán. With white supremacist branches of the Aryan Brotherhood gang operating in prisons across the country, the nationalist politics of past years took on a new a life among black and Latino prison gangs in the 1980s and 1990s.

DISCUSSION OF THE LITERATURE

In view of the formidable presence of street gangs within the urban social fabric as well as within discourses about the most pressing urban problems throughout the 20th century, the very limited production of historical scholarship dealing specifically with their structure, dynamics, activities, and politics is striking. Fortunately, sociologists equipped with a range of investigative tools, from ethnography to neighborhood-level survey data, have helped to pick up the slack. Beginning with Frederic Thrasher's foundational 1927 classic, *The Gang*, a rich tradition of sociological inquiry on the causes of gang formation, the role of gangs as institutions within their neighborhoods and communities, and their impact on the behavior, identity, and mindsets of their members has provided the basis of historicizing gangs over the past century. Indeed, any discussion of the literature on street gangs must begin with Thrasher's work in *The Gang*, which, by extending the Chicago School's "disorganization theory" into the world of youths out on the streets, set the theoretical agenda for successive generations of gang scholars. Disorganization theory, as developed by Chicago sociologists Robert Park and Ernest Burgess, rested on the idea that weakened social institutions (family, church, schools, political organizations) and mechanisms of social control in the city's disadvantaged "slum" districts explained the development of deviant and criminal forms of behavior.[72] According to Thrasher, the gang emerged in this context of social disorganization to take the place of inadequate or malfunctioning social institutions—"as a substitute for what society fails to give."[73]

Although Thrasher's work would subsequently be criticized for its inattention to gender and racial dynamics and its overly reductive equation of urban poverty with social disorganization, his perspective on gangs as products of the ecological conditions of their disorganized neighborhoods guided street gang research throughout much of the 20th century. One of the first key interventions in the field to build upon this model was Clifford Shaw and Henry D. McKay's 1942 book, *Juvenile Delinquency and Urban Areas*, which, based on interviews with thousands of juvenile delinquents in Chicago, developed the theory of cultural transmission—the idea that socially disorganized neighborhoods facilitated the transmission of "a coherent system of values supporting delinquent acts" from one generation to the next.[74] In the 1950s and 1960s, with the proliferation of gang intervention programs and the emergence of a gang criminology field with increasing links to social policy, a wave of new studies emerging from these intervention efforts continued to explore the circumstances and conditions that gave rise to gangs and delinquent "subcultures" in lower-class communities.[75]

By the 1970s and 1980s, as streets gangs became increasingly correlated with minority communities mired in conditions of racial and social marginalization, scholars began focusing on race and ethnicity as key factors motivating individuals to join gangs and shaping their behavior as gang members. Some of the seminal studies of this kind came out of fieldwork with *barrio* youths revealing how gangs provide ethnically inflected forms of self-esteem and personal valor—honor and respect—to young men and women facing discrimination at school, in the labor market and in mainstream US society.[76] By the end of the 1980s, with the War on Drugs raging on the streets, many scholars were viewing such forms of racial and ethnic self-identification within gangs in relation to their drug-trafficking activities.[77] It was during this same moment, moreover, that scholars sought to address the

relative invisibility of female gang members by investigating how and why young women become involved in gangs.[78] Although all these approaches departed somewhat from the framework established by Thrasher and the sociological studies of the 1950s and 1960s, this did not, however, mean that social disorganization had been cast aside as a theoretical concept. Following upon the publication of William Julius Wilson's influential 1987 study, *The Truly Disadvantaged*, which demonstrated how the post-Fordist transformation of US cities from motors of production to low-wage service centers had decimated social and economic institutions in African American communities, a number of gang scholars described how such circumstances of increasing social disorganization were critical to the increase in gang formation, crime, and violence in the 1980s and 1990s.[79] And yet, this more recent variant of social disorganization theory was also challenged and complicated by a number of studies that have illuminated the ways in which gangs have integrated into community institutions and exerted various forms of social control.[80]

With a few notable exceptions, historians, for their part, have yet to exploit the resources offered by the abundant sociological research on gangs. Published in 1999, Eric Schneider's *Vampires, Dragons, and Egyptian Kings: Youth Gangs in Postwar New York* represented the first book-length analysis of gangs from a historian. In line with the strand of sociological gang literature focusing on how gangs provide their members with a sense of self-worth and status otherwise absent from their lives, Schneider argues that a lack of opportunity in New York's deindustrializing postwar labor market led white, African American, and Latino youths alike to turn toward the gang to help them define their masculinity.[81] The only other historical monograph dealing extensively with gangs in the 20th-century city over the *longue durée* appeared ten years later with the publication of Andrew Diamond's *Mean Streets: Chicago Youths and the Everyday*

Struggle for Empowerment in the Multiracial City. Challenging Schneider's emphasis on masculinity as the raison d'être of gang culture, Diamond argues that gangs at times played critical roles in negotiating the uncertainties of race and ethnicity out on the streets and in policing the racial and ethnic boundaries of communities, activities that made them key actors in political struggles for rights and empowerment in the postwar decades.[82]

PRIMARY SOURCES

The relative dearth of archival sources documenting the activities of street gangs explains, in part, why they have largely eluded the historical gaze as objects of study in their own right. Because of its centrality within the field of sociology, Chicago far and away possesses the richest body of primary resources for the period between the 1920s and the 1950s. The Chicago History Museum holds a number of manuscript collections that include the records, observations, reports, and diaries of settlement house and gang outreach workers.[83] Similar resources can be found in the Stephen Bubacz Papers in the Special Collections of the University Illinois at Chicago, which contain a particularly rich body of documentation on the dynamics of race, ethnicity, and Americanization in gangs of the 1930s. Privileged glimpses into such dynamics are also provided by the English-language translations of foreign-language newspapers gathered within the Foreign Language Press Survey collection at the Newberry Library. Invaluable ethnographic data on Chicago gangs in the interwar years can also be gleaned from Thrasher's *The Gang*.

As for research on street gangs outside the city of Chicago during these decades, the manuscript collections of settlement houses, social services agencies, and neighborhood associations remain the required starting points of any inquiry. A useful entry point for work on gangs in East Harlem is the Leonard Covello Papers at the Balch Institute for Ethnic Studies, which provides excellent documentation of Italian and Puerto Rican gangs from the 1940s through the 1960s. Because street gangs and their deeds were quite often the subjects of sensationalized press coverage, city and neighborhood newspapers are also vital resources. Oral histories detailing the activities of gangs in this period are scarce, so Brooklyn youth worker Vincent Ricco's interview in the Oral History Collection at Columbia University is especially useful. Sociologist Michael Tapia recorded a series of oral histories with former members of San Antonio *barrio* gangs, covering their experiences between the 1940s and 1960s, although these sources have not yet found a permanent home. Finally, the various municipal race relations organizations that emerged in many US cities in the 1940s also produced data on the racial violence perpetrated by white ethnic gangs in the postwar years.

For inquiries into the emergence of fighting gangs and their politicization between the late 1950s and early 1970s, Chicago once again offers unparalleled primary sources, thanks to the availability of a vast body of the surveillance files of the Gang Intelligence Unit in the Red Squad Collection at the Chicago History Museum. This collection provides a unique look at the political engagement of street gangs, but use of these resources is difficult because of restrictions on identifying people and organizations named in the reports without their written consent. The Kenneth Marshall Papers at the New York Public Library offer a rich body of sources on Harlem fighting gangs during this era. Another useful source is the New York City Youth Board's report entitled *Reaching the Fighting Gang*. An outpouring of policy studies on dealing with the "gang problem" occurred across the urban landscape between the 1970s and 1990s, most of which are easily accessible.

FURTHER READING

Adamson, Christopher. "Defensive Localism in White and Black: A Comparative History of

European-American and African-American Youth Gangs." *Ethnic and Racial Studies* 23, no. 2 (March 2000): 272–298.

Bourgois, Philippe. *In Search of Respect: Selling Crack in El Barrio*. Cambridge: Cambridge University Press, 2003.

Brotherton, David C., and Luis Barrios. *The Almighty Latin King and Queen Nation: Street Politics and the Transformation of a New York City Gang*. New York: Columbia University Press, 2004.

Campbell, Anne. *The Girls in the Gang*. Cambridge, MA: Blackwell, 1984.

Chin, Ko-Lin. *Chinatown Gangs: Extortion, Enterprise, and Ethnicity*. New York: Oxford University Press, 1996.

Coughlin, Brenda C., and Sudhir Alladi Venkatesh. "The Urban Street Gang after 1970." *Annual Review of Sociology* 29 (August 2003): 41–64.

Diamond, Andrew J. *Mean Streets: Chicago Youths and the Everyday Struggle for Empowerment in the Multiracial City, 1908–1969*. Berkeley: University of California Press, 2009.

Hagedorn, John M. *People and Folks: Gangs, Crime and the Underclass in a Rustbelt City*. Chicago: Lakeview Press, 1998.

Hinton, Elizabeth. *From the War on Poverty to the War on Crime: The Making of Mass Incarceration in America*. Cambridge, MA: Harvard University Press, 2016.

Horowitz, Ruth. *Honor and the American Dream: Culture and Identity in a Chicano Community*. New Brunswick, NJ: Rutgers University Press, 1978.

Huff, C. Ronald, ed. *Gangs in America* (Third Edition). Thousand Oaks, CA: SAGE.

Klein, Malcolm W. *The American Street Gang: Its Nature, Prevalence, and Control*. New York: Oxford University Press, 1995.

Moore, Joan W. *Homeboys: Gangs, Drugs and Prison in the Barrios of Los Angeles*. Philadelphia: Temple University Press, 1978.

Moore, Joan W. *Going Down to the Barrio: Homeboys and Homegirls in Change*. Philadelphia: Temple University Press, 1991.

Padilla, Felix M. *The Gang as an American Enterprise*. New Brunswick, NJ: Rutgers University Press, 1992.

Sánchez-Jankowski, Martin. *Islands in the Street: Gangs and American Urban Society*. Los Angeles: University of California Press, 1991.

Schatzberg, Rufus, and Robert J. Kelley. *African American Organized Crime: A Social History*. New Brunswick, NJ: Rutgers University Press, 1997.

Schneider, Eric. *Vampires, Dragons, and Egyptian Kings: Youth Gangs in Postwar New York*. Princeton, NJ: Princeton University Press, 1999.

Spergel, Irving A. *Racketville, Slumtown, Haulburg: An Exploratory Study of Delinquent Subcultures*. Chicago: University of Chicago Press, 1964.

Tapia, Mike. *The Barrio Gangs of San Antonio, 1915–2015*. Fort Worth: Texas Christian University Press, 2017.

Thrasher, Frederic M. *The Gang: A Study of 1,313 Gangs in Chicago*. Chicago: University of Chicago Press, 2013.

Venkatesh, Sudhir Alladi. *American Project: The Rise and Fall of a Modern Ghetto*. Cambridge, MA: Harvard University Press, 2000.

Venkatesh, Sudhir Alladi, and Steven Levitt. "'Are We a Family or a Business?' History and Disjuncture in the Urban American Street Gang." *Theory and Society* 29 (2000): 427–462.

Vigil, James Diego. *A Rainbow of Gangs: Street Cultures in the Mega-City*. Austin: University of Texas Press, 2002.

Whyte, William. *Street Corner Society: The Social Structure of an Italian Slum*. Chicago: University of Chicago Press, 1993.

NOTES

1. Frederic Thrasher, *The Gang: A Study of 1,313 Gangs in Chicago* (Chicago: University of Chicago Press, 2013), 20–22.

2. For a detailed discussion of how Southern and Eastern European immigrants and their children were racially "inbetween peoples," see James R. Barrett and David Roediger, "Inbetween Peoples: Race, Nationality and the 'New Immigrant' Working Class," *Journal of American Ethnic History* 16, no. 3 (Spring 1997): 3–44.

3. On the role of street gangs in the encounter of white ethnic youths with race and Americanization in the interwar years, see James R. Barrett, "Americanization from the Bottom Up: Immigration and the Remaking of the Working Class in the United States," *Journal of American History* 79 (December 1992): 996–1020; Andrew J. Diamond, *Mean Streets: Chicago Youths and the Everyday Struggle for Empowerment in the Multiracial City, 1908–1969* (Berkeley: University

of California Press, 2009); and Lizabeth Cohen, *Making a New Deal: Industrial Workers in Chicago, 1919–1939* (New York: Cambridge University Press, 1990).

4. John M. Hagedorn, "Race Not Space: A Revisionist History of Gangs in Chicago," *Journal of African American History* 91, no. 2 (Spring 2006): 194–196.

5. The Chicago Commission on Race Relations (CCRR), *The Negro in Chicago: A Study of Race Relations and a Race Riot* (Chicago: University of Chicago Press, 1922), 11.

6. James R. Barrett and David R. Roediger, "The Irish and the 'Americanization' of the 'New Immigrants' in the Streets and in the Churches of the Urban United States," *Journal of American Ethnic History* 24 (Summer 2005): 15.

7. Barrett and Roediger, "The Irish and the 'Americanization' of the 'New Immigrants' in the Streets and in the Churches of the Urban United States," 8–13.

8. Thrasher, *The Gang*, 191.

9. Eric Schneider, *Vampires, Dragons, and Egyptian Kings: Youth Gangs in Postwar New York* (Princeton, NJ: Princeton University Press, 1999); and Christopher Adamson, "Tribute, Turf, Honor and the American Street Gang: Patterns of Continuity and Change since 1820," *Theoretical Criminology* 2, no. 1 (1998): 57–84.

10. According to Thrasher's data, gangs of "foreign extraction" made up more than 87 percent of the total count: Thrasher, *The Gang*, 191.

11. Arnold R. Hirsch, "E Pluribus Duo: Thoughts on 'Whiteness' and Chicago's 'New' Immigration as a Transient Third Tier," *Journal of American Ethnic History* 23 (Summer 2004): 7–44.

12. Hagedorn, "Race Not Space," 196–198.

13. On the Americanization of youths within settlement houses, see Thomas Lee Philpott, *The Slum and the Ghetto: Immigrants, Blacks, and Reformers in Chicago, 1880–1930* (New York: Oxford University Press, 1978), 278–279.

14. Robert Park, "Community Organization and Juvenile Delinquency," in *The City: Suggestions for Investigation of Human Behavior in the Urban Environment*, ed. Robert Park, Ernest W. Burgess, and Roderick D. McKenzie (Chicago: University of Chicago Press, 1967), 112.

15. Gabriella F. Arredondo, *Mexican Chicago: Race, Identity, and Nation, 1916–39* (Urbana and Champaign, IL: University of Illinois Press, 2008), 401.

16. Diamond, *Mean Streets*, chapter 5; and Philippe Bourgois, *In Search of Respect: Selling Crack in El Barrio* (Cambridge: Cambridge University Press, 2003), chapter 2.

17. Harvard Sitkoff, "Racial Militancy and Interracial Violence in the Second World War," *Journal of American History* 58, no. 3 (December 1971): 671.

18. Thomas Sugrue, *The Origins of the Urban Crisis: Race and Inequality in Postwar Detroit* (Princeton, NJ: Princeton University Press, 2014); Arnold R. Hirsch, *Making the Second Ghetto: Race & Housing in Chicago, 1940–1960* (Chicago: University of Chicago Press, 1998); and Diamond, *Mean Streets*.

19. Margaret Weir originally coined the term *defensive localism* in her work on city-suburban relations, but Thomas Sugrue redefined it to describe the aggressive form of white grassroots mobilization that responded to perceived threats to neighborhood and property posed by racial integration in the postwar urban North: see Thomas J. Sugrue, "Crabgrass-Roots Politics: Race, Rights, and the Reaction against Liberalism in the. Urban North, 1940–1964," *Journal of American History* 82, no. 2 (September 1995): 551–578. For a study that specifically applies the term to street gangs, see Christopher Adamson, "Defensive Localism in White and Black: A Comparative History of European-American and African-American Youth Gangs," *Ethnic and Racial Studies* 23, no. 2 (2000): 272–298.

20. Bourgois, *In Search of Respect*, chapter 2.

21. Schneider, *Vampires, Dragons, and Egyptian Kings*, 35.

22. Walter B. Miller, "American Youth Gangs: Past and Present," in *Current Perspectives on Criminal Behavior*, ed. A. Blumberg (New York: Knopf, 1974), 210–239; Useni Eugene Perkins, *The Explosion of Chicago's Black Street Gangs: 1900 to the Present* (Chicago: Third World Press, 1987); and Mike Davis, *City of Quartz: Excavating the Future in Los Angeles* (New York: Verso, 2006).

23. Joan W. Moore, *Going Down to the Barrio: Homeboys and Homegirls in Change* (Philadelphia: Temple University Press, 1991), chapter 3.

24. Diamond, *Mean Streets*, 224–225.

25. Diamond, *Mean Streets*, 208–209; for an excellent description of tensions over color among

Puerto Rican youths in Harlem, see Piri Thomas, *Down These Mean Streets* (New York: Vintage Books, 1967).

26. Scholars have documented the emergence of rather small and loosely structured girl gangs in African American, Mexican, and white ethnic neighborhoods as early as the late 1930s and 1940s: see, Joan Moore, *Going Down to the Barrio*, 27–28; and Diamond, *Mean Streets*, 84–88.

27. George E. Tita and Andrew Papachristos, "The Evolution of Gang Policy: Balancing Intervention and Suppression," in *Youth Gangs and Community Intervention: Research, Practice, and Evidence*, ed. Robert J. Chaskin (New York: Columbia University Press, 2010), 26–27; and Solomon Kobrin, "The Chicago Area Project—A 25-Year Assessment," *Annals of the American Academy of Political and Social Science* 322 (March, 1959): 19–29.

28. Adamson, "Defensive Localism in White and Black," 284–286; Albert K. Cohen, *Delinquent Boys: The Culture of the Gang* (New York: Free Press, 1971 [1955]); Richard A. Cloward and L. E. Ohlin, *Delinquency and Opportunity: A Study of Delinquent Gangs* (New York: Routledge, 2013); and Irving A. Spergel, "Male Young Adult Criminality, Deviant Values, and Differential Opportunity in Two Lower-Class Neighborhoods," *Social Problems* 10, no. 3 (1963): 237–250.

29. Irving A. Spergel, *Racketville, Slumtown, Haulburg* (Chicago: University of Chicago Press, 1964).

30. Adamson, "Defensive Localism in White and Black," 284.

31. Diamond, *Mean Streets*, chapter 5.

32. Diamond, *Mean Streets*, 232.

33. Moore, *Going Down To The Barrio*, chapter 3.

34. Cited in Robin D. G. Kelley, *Freedom Dreams: The Black Radical Imagination* (Boston: Beacon Press, 2002), 85.

35. Matthew J. Countryman, *Up South: Civil Rights and Black Power in Philadelphia* (Philadelphia: University of Pennsylvania Press, 2006), 170–171.

36. Diamond, *Mean Streets*, 259–260.

37. *New York Times*, May 29, 1964.

38. Davis, *City of Quartz*, 297; and A. A. Alonso, "Racialized Identities and the Formation of Black Gangs in Los Angeles," *Urban Geography* 25, 668.

39. Countryman, *Up South*, 192.

40. For a detailed account of the activities of the Blackstone Rangers in the context of the OEO grant program, see John Hall Fish, *Black Power/White Control: The Struggle of the Woodlawn Organization in Chicago* (Princeton, NJ: Princeton University Press, 1973), 148–174.

41. For a first-hand narrative of the politicization of the Vice Lords during these years, see David Dawley, *A Nation of Lords: The Autobiography of the Vice Lords* (Prospect Heights: Waveland Press, 1992).

42. Diamond, *Mean Streets*, 278–283.

43. *New York Times*, July 16, 1972.

44. Davis, *City of Quartz*, 297–300.

45. Marc Simon Rodriguez, *Rethinking the Chicano Movement* (New York: Routledge, 2014), 75–77.

46. On the punitive turn of liberals and the Democratic Party and its political consequences, see Heather Thompson, "Why Mass Incarceration Matters: Rethinking Crisis, Decline, and Transformation in Postwar American History," *Journal of American History* 97, no. 3 (December 2010): 703–734.

47. John M. Hagedorn, *The In$ane Chicago Way: The Daring Plan of Chicago Gangs to Create a Spanish Mafia* (Chicago: University of Chicago Press, 2015).

48. For an excellent account of the rise of the carceral state amidst such conditions, see Elizabeth Hinton, *From the War on Poverty to the War on Crime: The Making of Mass Incarceration in America* (Cambridge: Harvard University Press, 2016).

49. Walter B. Miller, *The Growth of Youth Gang Problems in the United States: 1970–98* (Washington, DC: Office of Juvenile Justice and Delinquency Prevention, 2001), 2, 64.

50. James C. Howell, *The History of Street Gangs: Their Origins and Transformations* (Lanham, MD: Lexington Books, 2015), 42.

51. James Diego Vigil, *A Rainbow of Gangs: Street Cultures in the Mega-City* (Austin: University of Texas Press, 2002), 5. Estimates of the percentage of female gangs in the city range between 4 and 10 percent.

52. Martin Sanchez-Jankowski, *Islands in the Street: Gangs and American Urban Society* (Berkeley: University of California Press, 1991), 205.

53. Vigil, *A Rainbow of Gangs*.

54. Sanchez-Jankowski, "Gangs and Social Change," *Theoretical Criminology* 7, no. 2 (2003): 203.

55. Ko-Lin Chin, *Chinatown Gangs: Extortion, Enterprise, and Ethnicity* (New York: Oxford University Press, 1996).

56. James Diego Vigil and Steve Chong Yun, "Vietnamese Youth Gangs in Southern California," in *Gangs in America*, ed. C. Ronald Huff (Newbury Park, CA: SAGE, 1990), 146–162.

57. Quoted in Min Zhou and Carl Bankston, *Growing up American: How Vietnamese Children Adapt to Life in the United States* (New York: Russell Sage Foundation, 1999), 187.

58. Bourgois, *In Search of Respect.*

59. Adamson, "Defensive Localism in White and Black," 286–287; for an account of racial attacks perpetrated by white ethnic gangs in Boston in the 1970s, see Anthony J. Lukas, *Common Ground* (New York: Knopf, 1985), 157–158, 525; on white gangs engaging in racial violence in Philadelphia, see Wesley G. Skogan, *Disorder and Decline: Crime and the Spiral of Decay in American Neighborhoods* (New York: Free Press, 1990), 25; on white ethnic gangs in Brooklyn, see Jonathan Reider, *Canarsie: The Jews and Italians of Brooklyn Against Liberalism* (Cambridge, MA: Harvard University Press, 1985), 179.

60. Elijah Anderson, *Code of the Street: Decency, Violence, and the Moral Life of the Inner City* (New York: W. W. Norton, 1999).

61. Sudhir Alladi Venkatesh and Steven Levitt, "'Are We a Family or a Business?' History and Disjuncture in the Urban American Street Gang," *Theory and Society* 29 (2000): 431.

62. See, for example, Bourgois, *In Search of Respect*; and John M. Hagedorn, *People and Folks: Gangs, Crime and the Underclass in a Rustbelt City* (Chicago: Lakeview Press, 1998).

63. Daniel T. Lichter, "Racial Differences in Under-employment in American Cities," *American Journal of Sociology* 93, no. 4 (1988): 782.

64. Andrew J. Diamond, *Chicago on the Make: Power and Inequality in a Modern City* (Oakland: University of California Press, 2017), 266.

65. Hagedorn, *People and Folks*, 1988.

66. Robert J. Sampson and William Julius Wilson, "Toward a Theory of Race, Crime and Urban Inequality," in *Crime and Inequality*, ed. J. Hagan and R. D. Peterson (Stanford, CA: Stanford University Press, 1995), 37–54.

67. Sudhir A. Vankatesh, "The Social Organization of Street Gang Violence in an Urban Ghetto," *American Journal of Sociology* 103, no. 1 (1997): 101.

68. Max Felker-Kantor, "Politicizing Youth: Police, Politics, and Gangs in the Late-Twentieth-Century City," *Journal of Urban History* (2018).

69. Thompson, "Why Mass Incarceration Matters," 709.

70. Hinton, *From the War on Poverty to the War on Crime*, 317.

71. Carolyn Rebecca Block and Richard Block, *Street Gang Crime in Chicago: Research in Brief* (Washington, DC: US Department of Justice, National Institute of Justice, 1993).

72. Robert E. Park and Ernest W. Burgess, *Introduction to the Science of Sociology* (Chicago: University of Chicago Press, 1924).

73. Thrasher, *The Gang*, 13.

74. Clifford Shaw and Henry D. McKay, *Juvenile Delinquency and Urban Areas* (Chicago: University of Chicago Press, 1972).

75. See, for example, Albert K. Cohen, *Delinquent Boys: The Culture of the Gang* (Glencoe, IL: Free Press, 1955); Walter B. Miller, "Lower Class Culture as a Generating Milieu of Gang Delinquency," *Journal of Social Issues* 14 (Summer 1958): 5–19; Cloward and Ohlin, *Delinquency and Opportunity*; James F. Short, Jr., and Fred L. Strodtbeck, *Group Process and Gang Delinquency* (Chicago: University of Chicago Press, 1965); and Spergel, *Racketville, Slumtown, Haulburg*.

76. Moore, *Homeboys*; Ruth Horowitz, *Honor and the American Dream: Culture and Identity in a Chicano Community* (New Brunswick, NJ: Rutgers University Press, 1983); and James Diego Vigil, *Barrio Gangs: Street Life and Identity in Southern California* (Austin: University of Texas Press, 1988).

77. Felix Padilla, *The Gang as American Enterprise* (New Brunswick, NJ: Rutgers University Press, 1992); Bourgois, *In Search of Respect*; and Venkatesh and Levitt, "'Are We a Family or a Business?'"

78. Anne Campbell, *The Girls in the Gang* (Cambridge, MA: Blackwell, 1984); Moore, *Going Down to the Barrio*; and David C. Brotherton and Luis Barrios, *The Almighty Latin King and Queen Nation: Street Politics and the Transformation of a New York City Gang* (New York: Columbia University Press, 2004).

79. William Julius Wilson, *The Truly Disadvantaged: The Inner City, the Underclass, and Public Policy* (Chicago: University of Chicago Press, 2012); Hagedorn, *People and Folks*; Skogan, *Disorder and Decline*; Sampson and Wilson, "Toward a Theory of Race, Crime and Urban Inequality," 37–54; and Sudhir Alladi Venkatesh, "The Social Organization of Street Gang Activity in an Urban Ghetto," *American Journal of Sociology* 103 (July 1997): 82–111.

80. See, for example, Sanchez-Jankowski, *Islands in the Street*; and Venkatesh, "The Social Organization of Street Gang Activity in an Urban Ghetto." For earlier studies that cast white ethnic gangs in this light, see William Whyte, *Street Corner Society: The Social Structure of an Italian Slum* (Chicago: University of Chicago Press, 1993); and Gerald D. Suttles, *The Social Order of the Slum: Ethnicity and Territory in the Inner City* (Chicago: University of Chicago Press, 1968).

81. Schneider, *Vampires, Dragons, and Egyptian Kings*.

82. Diamond, *Mean Streets*. For an exchange between Eric Schneider and Andrew Diamond on the racial and political consciousness of gangs in the postwar city, see Timothy J. Gilfoyle, Eric Schneider, and Andrew Diamond, "Gangs in the Post-World War II North American City: A Forum," *Journal of Urban History* 28 (July 2002): 658–663.

83. See, for example, the Chicago Area Project Collection and the Hans Mattick Papers.

Andrew J. Diamond

JUVENILE JUSTICE IN THE UNITED STATES

The ideological origins of American juvenile justice predate the American Revolution. As the historian Holly Brewer has shown, the architects of modern democratic theory, including the political and educational theorist John Locke, argued that children lacked reason and thus should not be allowed to participate in self-government, have a voice in legal proceedings, or make binding contracts. Instead, it was the responsibility of their parents and/or the state to educate children so that they could later exercise the rights and obligations of citizenship. Children were entitled to custody, not liberty.[1]

Compilers of the common law, such as the treatise writer William Blackstone, incorporated this assumption about children's inability to reason into the criminal law. They codified a tripartite schema for handling the cases of minors who were accused of committing felonies. Children younger than seven years were immune to prosecution because they were deemed incapable of forming the intent to commit a crime (i.e., *mens rea* or a guilty mind). Children between seven and fourteen years of age were also presumed inculpable, but the state could seek to rebut this presumption. Once children reached fourteen years of age, they were tried and punished as adults.

The opening in the 1820s and 1830s of houses of refuge started the process of segregating children from adults for correctional purposes and downplayed potential differences between how the state should handle cases of child neglect and juvenile delinquency. The 1838 Pennsylvania Supreme Court decision in Ex Parte *Crouse* established the principle that a state could use indeterminate sentences to incarcerate children whose parents could or would not care for them.[2] The decision applied the concept of *parens patriae* (the state as a father or parent) to legitimize the community acting as a guardian for a child. The court asked, "May not the natural parents, when unequal to the task of education, or unworthy of it, be superseded by the *parens patriae*, or common guardian of the community?" *Crouse* also analogized the reformatory to a school, not a prison. By doing so, the opinion initiated the legal practice of confining neglected children with juvenile delinquents and of differentiating juvenile correctional institutions from adult prisons, even though houses of refuge and reform schools often became brutal mini-prisons for children.[3]

This antebellum decision was emblematic of the "common law vision of a well-regulated society" that emphasized the social nature of human beings and granted vast discretionary power to local officials to police individual behavior for the sake of the welfare of the entire community.[4] Although the common-law vision of a well-regulated society eventually gave way to the rise of a more individually based conception of constitutional law after the Civil War, state courts continued to use *Crouse* as a precedent into the 20th century.[5]

PROGRESSIVE JUVENILE JUSTICE

The leaders of the juvenile court movement at the end of the 19th century, popularly known as "the child savers," belonged to a new generation of progressive reformers that searched for sociological answers and governmental solutions to interrelated social problems such as poverty and crime.[6] They argued that treatment, not punishment, should serve as the rationale for a separate justice system for juveniles.[7] They worked with influential stakeholders to lobby state lawmakers to pass legislation that would divert children's cases from the criminal court. Their vision for a separate children's court became an institutional reality, when the world's first juvenile court, located in Chicago, Illinois, opened its doors on July 3, 1899.[8] Remarkably, within a generation, juvenile courts had become a basic feature of urban governance in the United States. By 1925, every state except for Maine and Wyoming had established juvenile courts, and the juvenile court idea had spread globally. Such courts now operate in almost every nation in the world.[9]

Juvenile courts have worked differently across time and space but share two critically important features. First, their jurisdiction is age-based. These courts hear only the cases

of persons below a prescribed age. Second, juvenile courts daily put into practice the theory that criminal charges for young offenders should be tried in a separate court. The architects of the Illinois Juvenile Court Act of 1899 purposefully designed the new court to be sensitive to the developmental needs of children. As the court's first probation officer, Timothy Hurley, emphasized, "a child should be treated as a child."[10] To create such an environment, its architects stripped away the distinguishing features of a criminal court, including its adversarial process. Juvenile court personnel made intake decisions, filed delinquency petitions, presented evidence in court, and supervised children on probation.[11] Until the late 1960s, defense and prosecuting attorneys appeared only occasionally in juvenile courts in the United States.[12]

Progressive-Era state lawmakers defined "delinquency" as a noncriminal act. Grace Abbott, the social-work pioneer and chief of the US Children's Bureau (1921–1934), explained why this legal definition mattered. Instead of classifying the child as a criminal offender who should be punished, the state now defined children as delinquents who were "misdirected and misguided and needing aid, encouragement, help, and assistance."[13] This approach, as she explained, turned the concept of equal justice on its head. "The old conception of evenhanded justice was that each offender should receive exactly the same treatment for an offense committed with the same intent. But equality of treatment," she added, "is not the test of justice in the juvenile court. A new conception of what constitutes justice for children was adopted by the state in the juvenile-court legislation. In the juvenile courts children are all treated alike only when each is treated in accordance with his needs."[14] Whereas criminals deserved punishment, juvenile delinquents required individualized treatment plans.

The first generation of juvenile court reformers envisioned that the court's personnel, especially presiding judges and probation officers, would incorporate scientific research on child development into the court's daily operations. The juvenile court would not only divert children from being destroyed by the criminal justice system but also "cure" them of their delinquency. They expected the judge to cultivate a courtroom environment focused on individualized treatment, relied upon probation instead of incarceration, and shielded children from unnecessary and stigmatizing publicity.[15]

Building on the paternalistic ideal of the state as a father, embodied in the legal concept of *parens patriae*, Julian Mack famously argued in the pages of the *Harvard Law Review* that juvenile courts should function as chancery courts that used their equity power to focus on the needs of their clientele.[16] Progressive juvenile justice rested on the foundational ideal that the juvenile court was the legal embodiment of the state acting as a kindly parent to reform, not punish, children. These courts heard the cases of abused, neglected, and delinquent children.

Juvenile courts, as Mack observed, were only one part of larger communities that relied primarily on private associations to provide social services to families in need. Mack and other leading reformers knew that some children, especially African Americans, were excluded from receiving services from these sources. As Grace Abbott later noted, "Thus, whether Negro children, for example, are receiving equal treatment in our juvenile courts depends upon whether the resources available for treatment of delinquent Negro children are as adequate and scientific as for white children."[17] Even though resources were scarce, black child-savers fought to have the cases of African American children tried in juvenile court instead of the more punitive criminal justice system.[18]

The idealized juvenile court that the first generation of child savers spoke about so glowingly existed more concretely in sociological

theory than in everyday practice. Even in Chicago's model court, conflicts erupted from the beginning. They ranged from individual disputes, such as an ill mother asking the governor to convince the court to release her incarcerated son, to political mobilization, such as that of Catholics seeking to remove a Jewish judge they accused of interfering in their community's affairs. These critics were challenging the underlying assumption that the interests of the child and the state were the same and questioned the reformers' motives for wanting to save *their* children.[19]

Others challenged the legal fiction that juvenile courts treated but did not punish children. In *Criminal Justice in America* (1930), Dean Roscoe Pound of Harvard Law School maintained that "our legal treatment of delinquents is not preventative but is punitive in its conception and administration."[20] Although numerous lawsuits questioned the constitutionality of depriving children of liberty without following the same due-process standards required in criminal courts, they were largely unsuccessful until the 1950s.[21] As a result, juvenile courts could be administered very differently from criminal courts.

The enormous diversity among juvenile courts both across the nation and even within states makes it difficult to write a comprehensive history of juvenile justice. This diversity stemmed from the fact that American juvenile courts are statutory creations. Not every state followed the Illinois model that granted juvenile courts equity jurisdiction over children who committed delinquent acts. In New York, Maryland, and New Jersey, for example, children's courts operated as separate sites within the criminal justice system and used more formal procedures than courts that followed Illinois's chancery model.[22]

It has also been difficult for lawmakers to establish juvenile courts in rural areas. Initially, many states did not create these courts in sparsely populated areas. Later in the 20th century, when statewide juvenile justice systems were in operation, the same judge in a rural area often presided over both the criminal and juvenile court sessions. The diversity of practices and terminology in American juvenile justice, which still exists, has complicated the efforts of researchers to provide national snapshots of juvenile justice at any particular moment in time.[23]

The clientele for juvenile courts, however, has largely comprised children from predominantly poor and marginalized ethnic and racial communities. During the Progressive Era, Poles and Italians were disproportionately represented in the juvenile justice system, and later the same was true for African Americans and Latinos. Scholars have used class as the primary analytical category with which to analyze the history of juvenile justice because of the concentration of children from poor families.

And, since the 1970s, scholars have drawn on feminist theories to explain why juvenile courts treated boys' and girls' antisocial behavior differently. Girls, who have constituted fewer than 20 percent of the cases in juvenile court, have historically been incarcerated at substantially higher rates than boys.[24] Adolescent girls exploring their sexuality or challenging their parents' authority risked confinement for noncriminal misbehavior or status offenses (i.e., behaviors that are illegal only because the offender is a minor). Policing girls for the so-called crime of precocious sexuality became an entrenched practice in juvenile courts across North America.[25]

Even though influential children's advocates, such as Grace Abbott, publicly admitted by the 1920s that the juvenile court had not lived up to its initial promise to treat and cure delinquency, they adamantly defended the decision to establish the specialized court. "No mistake was made," Abbott stressed, "in taking children and young persons out of the jurisdiction of the criminal courts and creating specialized courts for dealing with them."[26] The juvenile court, in her opinion, remained

a good idea because it recognized the developmental needs of children and kept them out of the criminal justice system.

Progressive juvenile justice did not establish a single system for all youth crime. Although many child welfare experts called for juvenile courts to have original and exclusive jurisdiction over all cases that involved crimes committed by people younger than eighteen, state legislatures rejected this approach. Instead, the majority of states developed a dual system in which juvenile courts tried most but not all cases involving offenders up to a legislatively prescribed age limit. By 1930, almost every state had created its own combination of a maximum age limit and legislatively excluded offenses, or had some version of concurrent jurisdiction. Concurrent jurisdiction meant that some cases were eligible to be tried in either juvenile or criminal court. In such a system, the prosecutor could choose to charge a child who committed a crime in either juvenile or adult court, based on the prosecutor's own discretion. Meanwhile, juvenile courts across the nation developed their own local cultures for trying cases that included transferring at least some adolescents to criminal court. Once a state settled on its structure for trying young offenders, the framework remained fairly stable into the 1970s.[27]

THE TRANSFORMATION OF THE JUVENILE COURT

The worlds of criminal and juvenile justice changed during the 1960s and 1970s. The appearance of the Model Penal Code in 1962 revitalized the study of substantive criminal law and inspired thirty-four states to revise their criminal codes in the coming years.[28] The American Law Institute developed the Model Penal Code to encourage state legislatures to create more up-to-date and uniform penal laws. Several states, including California and New York, also commissioned major studies of their juvenile justice systems.[29] What started out as an exercise in federalism (i.e., individual states experimenting with criminal and juvenile justice reform) quickly became nationalized during the Supreme Court's Due Process Revolution (1961–1972), which transformed first the criminal justice system and then juvenile justice.[30] The Supreme Court's 1967 landmark *In re Gault* decision, written by Justice Abe Fortas, rejected the traditional *parens patriae* justification for why juvenile courts did not need robust due-process safeguards. Fortas relied on extensive social-scientific research to demonstrate that the reality of juvenile justice in the 1960s often contradicted the benevolent rhetoric that had long justified its informal proceedings. In *Gault*, for the first time, the court held that fundamental due-process protections must be granted to children in juvenile court adjudicatory hearings, including the right to notice, counsel, confrontation, and cross-examination of witnesses, and the privilege against self-incrimination. Over the course of the next decade, the Supreme Court went further, holding that juvenile courts, like criminal courts, must use the "beyond a reasonable doubt standard" in determining innocence or guilt, and that the prohibition against "double jeopardy" attached to juvenile court hearings.[31]

As the Supreme Court's due-process revolution gradually wound down, the justices in *McKeiver v. Pennsylvania* (1971) stopped short of requiring juvenile courts to provide jury trials.[32] Justice Harry Blackmun, who had recently been appointed to the court by President Richard Nixon, explained that mandating jury trials would "remake the juvenile proceeding into a fully adversary process and put an effective end to what has been the idealistic prospect of an intimate, informal protective proceeding."[33] Thus, the Supreme Court did not require juvenile courts to provide juveniles with all the due-process protections required in criminal court, including the right to a jury trial and the right to appellate review.

Like the Supreme Court's landmark decision in *Brown v. Board of Education* (1954), which declared segregated schools unconstitutional, *Gault* also proved difficult to implement because of local resistance.[34] The lack of procedural due-process protections in many of the nation's juvenile courts, including notifying juveniles of their right to counsel, has continued into the 21st century.[35]

Moreover, scholars have argued that the Supreme Court's *Gault* and *Winship* decisions shook the ideological foundations of the juvenile justice system. As the political scientist Christopher Manfredi has contended, the court's decisions that made juvenile court proceedings more like criminal proceedings "articulated a new conception of childhood that embodied a broader understanding of children's capacity for independent judgment and action." He added, "This new perspective encouraged both reform advocates and state legislatures to shift the focus on juvenile court proceedings from identifying and eliminating the behavioral causes of delinquency to holding juveniles more directly accountable for the harm caused by their offenses."[36] Increasingly, during the late 1970s, the philosophy of "just deserts" became the rallying cry of crime control advocates who argued that adolescents who were accused of committing serious and violent crimes should be prosecuted and punished as adults.

During the 1970s, the federal government also began to play a more prominent role in juvenile justice. The passage of the Juvenile Justice and Delinquency Prevention Act of 1974 created the Office of Juvenile Justice and Delinquency Prevention (OJJDP), provided block grants to states, created advisory groups to assist state governors in the allocation of federal funds, and established the National Advisory Committee for Juvenile Justice and Delinquency Prevention to develop national standards for the administration of juvenile justice. The federal law required states participating in the program to remove all status offenders, such as truants or runaways, from secure detention and correctional facilities and ensure that all juvenile prisoners were separate from adult offenders in prisons. By the end of the 20th century, the cases of status offenders dropped to approximately 15 percent of the juvenile court caseload. Status offenders were also institutionalized much less frequently than they had been earlier in the 20th century.[37] The overall drop, however, masked how girls' cases were handled. Higher percentages of girls than boys were still incarcerated, although many were placed in private facilities.[38]

Although juvenile justice experts during the 1970s sought to reconcile the ideology of *parens patriae* with procedural due-process protection to create a juvenile court that would provide social services while simultaneously protecting children's constitutional rights, those policy experts ultimately lost control of the reform process in the 1980s.

THE RISE AND FALL OF THE "GET TOUGH" ERA

In response to a soaring rate of juvenile arrests and serious and violent crime in the late 1980s, including the doubling of the murder rate, most states passed laws during the early 1990s to make it easier to prosecute children's cases in the criminal court system.[39] By 1995, twenty-seven states allowed for the prosecution of a ten-year-old charged with murder as an adult.[40] The trend toward punishing adolescents more severely in both juvenile and criminal courts was part of the dramatic increase in the use of imprisonment in the United States during the late 20th century that led to a quintupling of the number of individuals in prison between the early 1970s and mid-1990s. Initially, the diversionary rationale of the juvenile justice system spared many children and adolescents from this "Get Tough" approach that was first adopted in the criminal justice system.[41]

But the juvenile court's success in diverting juveniles from the criminal justice system during the 1970s and 1980s contributed to the juvenile court itself becoming a target in the 1990s. Moreover, several prominent criminologists popularized the idea that children growing up in "moral poverty" had become a new breed of "super-predators." As the criminologist John DiIulio warned in 1995,

On the horizon, therefore, are tens of thousands of severely morally impoverished juvenile super-predators. They are perfectly capable of committing the most heinous acts of physical violence for the most trivial reasons (for example, a perception of slight disrespect or the accident of being in their path). They fear neither the stigma of arrest nor the pain of imprisonment. They live by the meanest code of the meanest streets, a code that reinforces rather than restrains their violent, hair-trigger mentality. In prison or out, the things that super-predators get by their criminal behavior—sex, drugs, money—are their own immediate rewards. Nothing else matters to them. So for as long as their youthful energies hold out, they will do what comes "naturally": murder, rape, rob, assault, burglarize, deal deadly drugs, and get high.[42]

The moral panic over super-predators contributed to federal and state lawmakers enacting laws to prosecute and punish more children as adults, and shifted the power to determine which children should be transferred from juvenile court to the adult criminal justice system from juvenile court judges to prosecutors.[43] Ironically, when juveniles were tried in criminal proceedings, they automatically received all the rights that the court had guaranteed them in juvenile proceedings and the right to a jury trial.

The punitive turn in American juvenile law raised troubling questions, especially as advancements in neuroscience highlighted significant differences between adolescent and adult brains.[44] This science reaffirmed longstanding ideas about the difference between children and adults and raised new questions about the competency of younger defendants to stand trial in criminal court and the related issue of the culpability of adolescents for their offenses. In addition, the disproportionate representation of minorities in the juvenile and criminal justice systems focused attention on the differential handling of cases of youth crime based on race and ethnicity.[45] Finally, policy experts criticized the economic costs and effectiveness of prosecuting and punishing juveniles as adult offenders.[46]

As the eminent criminologist Michael Tonry noted in his 2008 Presidential Address to the American Society for Criminology, Americans were now punishing their fellow citizens, including minors, in ways that were "unimaginable in most other Western countries."[47] These practices included "the prosecution of children as if they were adults." This state of affairs led scholars to search for answers in American history and culture to explain the widening divide between American and European approaches to criminal justice.[48]

Significantly, by the time that many "Get Tough" on juvenile crime laws were being adopted in the mid-1990s, the nation's rate of youth violence had already begun to drop dramatically.[49] This decline opened up the possibility of refocusing juvenile justice policies. The John T. and Catherine D. MacArthur Foundation, for example, spent $150 million to support research on adolescent development and juvenile justice in order to develop sound public policies and model programs that addressed the related issues of competency and culpability.[50]

Beginning in 2005, children's-rights advocates won a series of Supreme Court cases in which the court held unconstitutional the juvenile death penalty,[51] mandatory life sentences without the possibility of parole for minors for non-homicidal crime,[52] and mandatory life without the possibility of parole for minors even for the crime of homicide.[53] All these decisions reinforced the idea that children and adolescents are immature, vulnerable, and malleable.[54] These decisions symbolized the end of the "Get Tough" era and constitutionalized the idea that, at least for sentencing purposes, children had to be treated differently from adults. Yet much of the punitive legislation from the moral panic over super-predators during the 1990s is still part of American juvenile justice in the 21st century.[55]

DISCUSSION OF THE LITERATURE

There are three distinct traditions in the historical literature on American juvenile justice: the progressive mythmakers, the skeptics, and the liberal preservationists. All three traditions began with examinations of the creation of the juvenile court at the turn of the 20th century, and scholars working in the skeptical and liberal preservationist traditions have analyzed the subsequent evolution of American juvenile justice.

Progressive mythmakers, such as the prominent social-settlement leader Jane Addams, characterized the juvenile court movement as a revolutionary and humanitarian advancement in child protection. In 1935, Addams famously portrayed the beginnings of the juvenile court more than thirty years earlier as a radical departure from past practices.

She reminisced:

There was almost a change in *mores* when the Juvenile Court was established. The child was brought before the judge with no one to prosecute him and with no one to defend him—the judge and all concerned were merely trying to find out what could be done on his behalf.

The element of conflict was absolutely eliminated and with it, all notion of punishment as such with its curiously belated connotation.[56]

Similar characterizations of the juvenile court as a benevolent institution that sought to treat children, instead of punishing them as criminals, were commonplace. For example, Herbert Lou's *Juvenile Courts in the United States* (1927) announced that until a "better and finer agency may be evolved, the juvenile court will remain to serve as a fountain of mercy, truth, and justice to our handicapped children."[57] Until the late 1960s, non-historians used this framework to write the histories of juvenile justice for aspiring professionals who intended to work within the system.

In the 1960s, civil-rights lawyers and scholars questioned both the theory and practice of juvenile courts. Their scathing critiques helped form the skeptical tradition that challenged the assumptions of scholars like Lou and informed the Supreme Court's landmark decision in *In re Gault* (1967). The social and rights revolutions of the 1960s also provided the context for Anthony Platt's *The Child Savers* (1969), an instant classic in the field that used the sociological concept of social control to reinterpret the ideological origins of the juvenile court. According to Platt, powerful interest groups supported the expansion of state power and intervention into the lives of poor families in order to impose so-called middle-class values on them and their children. Since then, scholars in the skeptical tradition have analyzed how juvenile justice systems have perpetuated gender and racial hierarchies in American society.[58] A subset of this scholarship draws on case files from these court systems to complicate the social-control thesis. Instead of focusing solely on the role of reformers as historical actors, these more nuanced studies, such as Mary Odem's *Delinquent Daughters* (1996), emphasizes how children and their families exercised agency and negotiated with juvenile justice personnel.

The liberal preservationists accept many of the critiques offered by the skeptics but still emphasize the importance of the founding principle of the juvenile court that children should be treated as children and diverted from the criminal justice system.[59] Their histories argue that the founders of the juvenile court were largely well intentioned but that the concerns of the skeptics must be addressed including the need for due-process safeguards to ensure that children's rights are protected. Yet skeptics, such as Elizabeth Hinton, contend that liberals since the 1960s have been part of a bipartisan consensus that created crime-control policies that targeted black youth in highly segregated urban areas and set the stage for the rise of mass incarceration during the final decades of the 20th century.[60]

In addition to these three established traditions, scholars are beginning to write the history of juvenile justice in Indian country.[61] Historians have also begun to use a transnational perspective to understand the development and spread of juvenile justice ideas and practices across the world during the 20th century.[62] Future studies will also do more to examine the changing relationship over time between juvenile and criminal justice systems, as well as the changing power relationships within juvenile courts brought about by the *Gault* revolution. Historians will also need to explain the rise and fall of the "Get Tough" era and analyze the significance of the Supreme Court drawing on brain science in its decisions to constitutionalize the idea that children are different from adults in the context of sentencing decisions.[63]

PRIMARY SOURCES

Scholars of juvenile justice history have used a variety of qualitative and quantitative sources that include exposés of juvenile courts at work,[64] government publications such as reports by the Children's Bureau (1912–)[65] and the Office of Juvenile Justice and Delinquency Prevention (1974–),[66]

US Supreme Court decisions,[67] international reports and laws,[68] juvenile court case files and annual reports,[69] manuscript collections that include the papers of prominent reformers, private organizations, and human rights organizations,[70] newspapers,[71] oral histories,[72] popular-culture artifacts (such as film, television programming, and social media),[73] and state and national legislation.[74] Due to the longstanding interest in juvenile delinquency by many academic disciplines such as sociology, criminology, and law, historians have analyzed older MA theses, PhD dissertations, and law-review articles as primary sources. In addition, the reports of commissions in the United States that sought to reform juvenile justice policy during the 1970s and 1980s are valuable sources.[75] Finally, the MacArthur Foundation maintains a website devoted to juvenile justice issues that include useful sources for scholars interested in contemporary issues.

FURTHER READING

Bernstein, Nell. *Burning Down the House: The End of Juvenile Prison*. New York: The New Press, 2016.

Bush, William S. *Who Gets a Childhood: Race and Juvenile Justice in Twentieth-Century Texas*. Athens: University of Georgia Press, 2010.

Chávez-García, Miroslava. *States of Delinquency: Race and Science in the Making of California's Juvenile Justice System*. Oakland: University of California Press, 2012.

Feld, Barry C. *Bad Kids: Race and the Transformation of the Juvenile Court*. New York: Oxford University Press, 1999.

Feld, Barry C. *The Evolution of the Juvenile Court: Race, Politics, and the Criminalizing of Juvenile Justice*. New York: New York University Press, 2017.

Hinton, Elizabeth. *From the War on Poverty to the War on Crime: The Making of Mass Incarceration in America*. Cambridge, MA: Harvard University Press, 2016.

Kupchik, Aaron. *Judging Juveniles: Prosecuting Adolescents in Adult and Juvenile Court*. New York: New York University Press, 2006.

Lou, Herbert. *Juvenile Courts in the United States*. Chapel Hill: University of North Carolina Press, 1927.

Mack, Julian W. "The Juvenile Court." *Harvard Law Review* 23 (1909–1910): 104–122.

Odem, Mary E. *Delinquent Daughters: Protecting and Policing Adolescent Female Sexuality in the United States 1885–1920*. Chapel Hill: University of North Carolina, 1995.

Platt, Anthony M. *The Child Savers: The Invention of Delinquency*. Chicago: University of Chicago Press, 1969.

Rosenheim, Margaret K., Franklin E. Zimring, David S. Tanenhaus, and Bernardine Dohrn. *A Century of Juvenile Justice*. Chicago: University of Chicago Press, 2002.

Schlossman, Steven L. *Love and the American Delinquent: The Theory and Practice of "Progressive" Juvenile Justice, 1820–1920*. Chicago: University of Chicago Press, 1977.

Steinberg, Lawrence, and Elizabeth S. Scott. *Rethinking Juvenile Justice*. Cambridge, MA: Harvard University Press, 2010.

Tanenhaus, David S. *Juvenile Justice in the Making*. New York: Oxford University Press, 2004.

Ward, Geoff K. *The Black Child-Savers: Racial Democracy and Juvenile Justice*. Chicago: University of Chicago Press, 2012.

Zimring, Franklin E. *American Juvenile Justice*. New York: Oxford University Press, 2005.

NOTES

1. Holly Brewer, *By Birth or Consent: Children, Law, and the Anglo-American Revolution in Authority* (Chapel Hill: University of North Carolina Press, 2005).

2. Ex Parte Crouse, 4 Wharton 9 (Pa. 1838).

3. Steven L. Schlossman, "Delinquent Children: The Juvenile Reform School," in *Oxford History of the Prison: The Practice of Punishment in Western Society*, eds. Norval Morris and David J. Rothman (New York: Oxford University Press, 1993), 325–349.

4. William J. Novak, *The People's Welfare: Law and Regulation in Nineteenth-Century America* (Chapel Hill: University of North Carolina Press, 1996).

5. David S. Tanenhaus, "Between Dependency and Liberty: The Conundrum of Children's Rights in the Gilded Age," *Law and History Review* 23 (Summer 2005): 351–386.

6. Barry C. Feld, *Bad Kids: Race and the Transformation of the Juvenile Court* (New York: Oxford University Press, 1999); Michael Willrich, *City of Courts: Socializing Justice in Progressive Era Chicago* (New York: Cambridge University Press, 2003).

7. Julian W. Mack, "The Juvenile Court," *Harvard Law Review* 23 (1909–1910): 104–122.

8. David S. Tanenhaus, *Juvenile Justice in the Making* (New York: Oxford University Press, 2004), 23.

9. *Juvenile Justice in Global Perspective*, eds. Franklin E. Zimring, Maximo Langer, and David S. Tanenhaus (New York: New York University Press, 2015).

10. T. D. Hurley, "Development of the Juvenile-Court Idea," in *Children's Courts in the United States: Their Origin, Development, and Results* (New York: AMS, 1973), 8.

11. See, e.g., Steven L. Schlossman, *Transforming Juvenile Justice: Reform Ideals and Institutional Realities, 1825–1920* (DeKalb: Northern Illinois University Press, 2005).

12. M. Marvin Finkelstein, *Prosecution in the Juvenile Courts: Guidelines for the Future* (US Department of Justice, 1973), 12.

13. Grace Abbott, *The Child and the State*, vol. 2 (Chicago: University of Chicago Press, 1938), 332. Colorado, Missouri, and Tennessee used the language about "misdirected" children that Abbott quoted.

14. Abbott, *The Child and the State*, 332.

15. Bernard Flexner and Reuben Oppenheimer, *The Legal Aspect of the Juvenile Court* (Washington, DC: Government Printing Office, 1922), 1–42.

16. Julian W. Mack, "The Juvenile Court," *Harvard Law Review* 23 (1909–1910): 104–122.

17. Mack, "The Juvenile Court," 332.

18. Geoff K. Ward, *The Black Child-Savers: Racial Democracy and Juvenile Justice* (Chicago: University of Chicago Press, 2012), chs. 5 and 6; and William S. Bush, *Who Gets a Childhood: Race and Juvenile Justice in Twentieth-Century Texas* (Athens: University of Georgia Press, 2010).

19. David S. Tanenhaus, "The Evolution of Transfer out of the Juvenile Court," in *The Changing Borders of Juvenile Justice: Transfer of Adolescents to Criminal Court*, eds. Jeffrey Fagan and Franklin E. Zimring (Chicago: University of Chicago Press, 2000), 18.

20. Roscoe Pound, *Criminal Justice in America* (New York: Henry Holt, 1930), 33.

21. Chester James Antieau, "Constitutional Rights in Juvenile Court," *Cornell Law Quarterly* 46 (Spring 1961): 387–415.

22. Mack, "The Juvenile Court," 18–19.

23. For example, the Wickersham Committee's Report on the Child Offender in the Federal System (1931) noted that state "legislation is constantly changing and therefore no information is strictly up to date" (158).

24. Steven L. Schlossman and Stephanie Wallach, "The Crime of Precocious Sexuality: Female Juvenile Delinquency in the Progressive Era," *Harvard Educational Review* 48 (February 1978): 65–94.

25. Barry C. Feld, *The Evolution of the Juvenile Court: Race, Politics, and the Criminalizing of Juvenile Justice* (New York: New York University Press, 2017), ch. 6; and Jane B. Sprout and Anthony N. Doob, *Justice for Girls? Stability and Change in the Youth Justice Systems of the United States and Canada* (Chicago: University of Chicago Press, 2009).

26. Abbott, *Child and the State*, 338.

27. Abbott, *Child and the State*, 25.

28. Michael Willrich, "Criminal Justice in the United States," in *The Cambridge History of Law in America*, vol. 3, eds. Michael Grossberg and Christopher Tomlins (New York: Cambridge University Press, 2008), 214.

29. California Governor's Special Study Commission on Juvenile Justice Reports, pts. 1 and 2 (1960) and New York Joint Legislative Commission on Court Reorganization, report pt. 2, the Family Court Act (1962).

30. Willrich, "Criminal Justice in the United States," 212–222.

31. *In re Winship*, 397 US 358 (1970); *Breed v. Jones*, 421 US 519 (1975).

32. *McKeiver v. Pennsylvania*, 403 US 528 (1971).

33. *McKeiver v. Pennsylvania*, 403 US 528, 545 (1971).

34. Donald Horowitz, *The Courts and Social Policy* (Washington, DC: The Brookings Institution, 1977).

35. Barry C. Feld, *Bad Kids* and *Defend Children: A Blueprint for Effective Juvenile Defender Services* (Washington, DC: National Juvenile Defender Center, 2016).

36. Christopher P. Manfredi, *The Supreme Court and Juvenile Justice* (Lawrence, KS: University Press of Kansas, 1998), 159.

37. Lee Teitelbaum, "Status Offenses and Status Offenders," in *A Century of Juvenile Justice*, eds. Margaret K. Rosenheim, Franklin E. Zimring, David S. Tanenhaus, and Bernardine Dohrn (Chicago: University of Chicago Press, 2002), 158–176.

38. Kimberly Kempf-Leonard, "The Conundrum of Girls and Juvenile Justice Processing," in *The Oxford Handbook of Juvenile Crime and Juvenile Justice*, eds. Barry C. Feld and Donna M. Bishop (New York: Oxford University Press, 2012), 485–525.

39. Jeffrey Fagan and Franklin E. Zimring, eds., *The Changing Borders of Juvenile Justice: Transfer of Adolescents to the Criminal Court* (Chicago: University of Chicago Press, 2000).

40. *Juvenile Offenders and Victims: A National Report* (Washington, DC: US Government Printing Office, 1995), 86–87.

41. Franklin E. Zimring, *American Juvenile Justice* (New York: Oxford University Press, 2005), ch. 4.

42. John J. DiIulio Jr., "The Coming of the Super-predators," *Weekly Standard*, November 27, 1995.

43. Franklin E. Zimring, "The Power Politics of Juvenile Court Transfer in the 1990s," in *Choosing the Future for American Juvenile Justice*, eds. Franklin E. Zimring and David S. Tanenhaus (New York: New York University Press, 2014), 37–51.

44. Terry A. Maroney, "The Once and Future Juvenile Brain," in *Choosing the Future for American Juvenile Justice*, eds. Franklin E. Zimring and David S. Tanenhaus (New York: New York University Press, 2014), 189–2015.

45. Darnell F. Hawkins and Kimberly Kempf-Lenoard, eds., *Our Children, Their Children: Confronting Racial and Ethnic Differences in American Juvenile Justice* (Chicago: University of Chicago Press, 2005).

46. Steinberg and Scott, *Rethinking Juvenile Justice*.

47. Michael Tonry, "Crime and Human Rights—How Political Paranoia, Protestant Fundamentalism, and Constitutional Obsolescence Combined to Devastate Black America: The American Society of Criminology 2007 Presidential Address," *Criminology* 46 (2008): 3.

48. James Q. Whitman, *Harsh Justice: Criminal Punishment and the Widening Divide between America and Europe* (New York: Oxford University Press, 2003).

49. Franklin E. Zimring, "American Youth Violence: A Cautionary Tale," in *Choosing the Future for American Juvenile Justice*, eds. Franklin E. Zimring and David S. Tanenhaus (New York: New York University Press, 2014), 7–36.

50. See, e.g., Lawrence Steinberg and Elizabeth S. Scott, *Rethinking Juvenile Justice* (Cambridge, MA: Harvard University Press, 2010).

51. *Roper v. Simmons*, 543 US 551 (2005).

52. *Graham v. Florida*, 560 US 48 (2010).

53. *Miller v. Alabama*, 567 US (2012).

54. Ashley Nellis, *A Return to Justice: Rethinking Our Approach to Juveniles in the System* (Lanham, MD: Rowman & Littlefield, 2016), 83.

55. Zimring and Tanenhaus, *Choosing the Future for American Juvenile Justice*.

56. Jane Addams, *My Friend, Julia Lathrop* (New York: Macmillan, 1935), 137.

57. Herbert Lou, *Juvenile Courts in the United States* (Chapel Hill: University of North Carolina Press, 1927), 220.

58. See, e.g., the expanded fortieth-anniversary edition of Anthony Platt, *The Child Savers: The Invention of Delinquency*, with an introduction by Miroslava Chávez-García (Rutgers University Press, 2009).

59. Zimring and Tanenhaus, *Choosing the Future for American Juvenile Justice*, chs. 1 and 10.

60. Elizabeth Hinton, *From the War on Poverty to the War on Crime* (Cambridge, MA: Harvard University Press, 2016), ch. 6.

61. Addie Rolnick, "Untangling the Web: Juvenile Justice in Indian Country," 19 N.Y.U. J. Legis. & Pub. Pol'y 49 (2016).

62. See, e.g., Heather Ellis, ed., *Juvenile Delinquency and the Limits of Western Influence, 1850 to 2000* (London: Palgrave MacMillan, 2014); Franklin E. Zimring, Máximo Langer, and David S. Tanenhaus, eds., *Juvenile Justice in Global Perspective* (New York: New York Univeresity Press, 2015); and William S. Bush and David S. Tanenhaus, eds., *Ages of Anxiety: Historical and Transnational Perspectives on Juvenile Justice* (New York: New York University Press, July 2018).

63. See, e.g., Elizabeth S. Scott, "*Miller v. Alabama* and the (Past and) Future of Juvenile Crime Regulation," *Law and Inequality* 31 (2012–2013): 535–558.

64. See, e.g., Edward Humes, *No Matter How Loud I Shout: A Year in the Life of the Juvenile Court* (New York: Simon and Schuster, 1996).

65. See e.g., Helen Jeter, *The Chicago Juvenile Court* (Washington, DC: Government Printing Office, 1922).

66. See, e.g., Howard Snyder and Melissa Sickmund, *Juvenile Offenders and Juvenile Victims: 1999 National Report* (Washington, DC: US Department of Justice, 1999).

67. See, e.g., *In re Gault*, 1 US 387 (1967).

68. See, e.g., the United Nations Convention on the Rights of the Child.

69. In *Transforming Juvenile: Reform Ideals and Institutional Realities, 1825–1920* (DeKalb: Northern Illinois Press, 2005), Steven Schlossman discusses how social historians have used juvenile court case files.

70. These collections include the papers of the prominent Denver Juvenile Court Judge Benjamin B. Lindsey and the records of Illinois's Juvenile Protective Association.

71. See, e.g., Tanenhaus, *Juvenile Justice in the Making*, ch. 4.

72. See, e.g., James Bennett, *Oral History and Delinquency: The Rhetoric of Criminology* (Chicago: University of Chicago Press, 1988).

73. See, e.g., James Gilbert, *A Cycle of Outage: America's Reaction to the Juvenile Delinquent in 1950s* (New York: Oxford University Press, 1988).

74. See, e.g., Franklin E. Zimring, Gordon G. Hawkins, and Sam Kamin, *Punishment and Democracy: Three Strikes and You're Out in California* (New York: Oxford University Press, 2003).

75. See, e.g., Twentieth Century Fund, *Confronting Youth Crime: Sentencing Policy Toward Young Offenders* (New York: Holmes and Meier, 1978).

David S. Tanenhaus

UNITED STATES VAGRANCY LAWS

ORIGINS OF VAGRANCY LAWS

English colonists brought vagrancy laws with them to the New World. Centuries later, scholars and lawyers traced the laws' roots back to the mid-14th-century English Statutes of Laborers, which aimed to ensure that all able-bodied laborers worked after the Black Death.

The more direct antecedents of American vagrancy laws, however, were the English vagrancy laws of the 16th and 17th centuries, passed alongside laws instituting new methods of poverty relief, erecting houses of correction, and controlling wages. Though such laws were primarily economically motivated—untethered workers could exact high wages in a tight labor market and the wandering unemployed could try to obtain relief from local governments not obligated to support them—they served critical political purposes as well. The "sturdy rogues" and "masterless men" of the Elizabethan era were a problem for governance as well as the economy.[1]

In the colonies, vagrancy laws functioned much as they did in England: to exclude and regulate poor strangers while keeping poor locals in check. Vast differences in demographic, political, and economic context notwithstanding, the American colonies and then the states used vagrancy laws to control workers in a changing political economy. As aspiration if not reality, the description of one 19th-century English historian would have struck a chord on both sides of the Atlantic: "A man must work where he happened to be, and must take the wages offered to him on the spot, and if he went about, even to look for work, he became a vagrant and was regarded as a criminal."[2]

Vagrancy laws were also used to exclude and suppress racial and religious minorities. Race, racial identity, and a racialized sense of who belonged where had been part of vagrancy and related laws from their English origins. At times, vagrancy laws explicitly targeted certain groups. At other times the laws were used, though not written, to target them. At various moments, the Irish, whom the English accused of loose morals, "popery," and "filth," and the Roma (then called "gypsies" or "Egyptians"), who were itinerant and "masterless," each came in for special attention. Many of the specific behaviors in the English vagrancy statutes, such as prohibitions on "palmistry," or fortune telling, originated in concerns about the Roma.[3]

Colonies and then states and localities also targeted religious and racial outliers. The Massachusetts Bay Colony enacted a special vagrancy law applicable only to Quakers in 1658, and the town of Salem excluded Native Americans after dark. Many states aggressively passed vagrancy laws regulating the whereabouts, livelihoods, and lives of their minority residents over the following centuries. By Reconstruction, so-called sundown towns excluded minorities not only with vagrancy laws but also with signs that read "Whites Only within City Limits after Dark." In the West and Southwest, Latinos, Chinese Americans, Japanese Americans, and Native Americans were targets. In Hawaii, law enforcement targeted native Hawaiians and later Japanese Americans.[4]

Arrests of women for defying conventional mores of female sexuality, and for prostitution more specifically, were another mainstay of early vagrancy enforcement. In part because prostitution had not been a crime at common law, prostitutes had been treated as a kind of vagrant since the 15th century. By the early 17th century, the application of vagrancy laws to women leading a "lewd and idle" life was an established part of vagrancy regulation in the colonies. Colonial anxiety about individual morality and colonial suppression of sexual deviance frequently manifested themselves in vagrancy prosecutions. As cities grew after independence, local officials tended to use vagrancy laws more to maintain public order and morality than to regulate private conduct. Because separate statutory prohibitions against prostitution per se remained almost nonexistent, officials used vagrancy and disorderly conduct laws with particular force against the increasingly public and increasingly commercial sex trade. Vagrancy convictions fell disproportionately on urban women who could not afford to practice prostitution behind closed doors. In Boston, for example, women prosecuted as "nightwalkers" regularly faced several months in prison, while their male customers were merely fined a few dollars.[5]

THE 19TH CENTURY

From the very start, vagrancy laws were premised on the immorality of idle poverty and targeted those who failed to work or remain in their prescribed place. From 1837 on, the Supreme Court gave its imprimatur to this view. In *New York v. Miln*, the court stated, "We think it as competent and as necessary for a state to provide precautionary measures against the moral pestilence of paupers, vagabonds, and possibly convicts; as it is to guard against the physical pestilence [of] infectious disease." But with the 19th-century explosion of immigration to the United States, the Industrial Revolution, and the end of the Civil War, the image of the threatening stranger that had long justified restrictions on intra- and interstate movement began to change, and with it the nature of the vagrancy regime.[6]

Between 1820 and 1860 more than five million immigrants came to the United States. These immigrants quickly became identified with vagrancy, and they filled poorhouses in disproportionate numbers. Masters of vessels were required to report a list of passengers, to remove "undesirables," and to provide a bond for those who might become a public charge. Most coastal states passed laws expressly placing responsibility for vagrants on the shoulders of ship masters. Though some immigrants were subject to removal, they were more often sent as "state paupers" to workhouses as a cheaper alternative. And as immigrants flocked to the cities of the Atlantic and New England regions, the perception of transience became associated as well with a perception of vice. Reformers sounded the alarm about idleness, drunkenness, and licentiousness among the poor. Without colonial strictures, new forms of social control were needed. Vagrancy laws again, and even more extensively, filled that role.[7]

The end of the Civil War in 1865 further expanded the role of vagrancy laws in American life. Free African Americans had borne the brunt of vagrancy laws in the antebellum era. After the war, slave states expelled emancipated slaves and barred entry to free blacks from other states. With the end of slavery, Southern whites turned even more aggressively to vagrancy laws as a means of racial regulation. The so-called Black Codes of the South regulated African American economic and social interactions with whites and were designed to return African Americans to a position as close to slavery as legally possible. New laws authorized the hiring out of vagrancy convicts. Mississippi, for example, auctioned off vagrants "at public outcry, to any white person."[8]

With the beginning of military reconstruction and the passage of federal laws prohibiting explicit discrimination, Southern states rewrote their vagrancy statutes in race-neutral terms. But race neutrality went only so far. From citizen patrol to sheriff to judge to jury, the whites who enforced vagrancy laws knew they were aimed at African Americans, especially those African Americans who asserted their autonomy. When thousands of blacks moved from Mississippi to Kansas in 1879, for example, the leaders of the exodus were arrested for vagrancy.[9]

Northern states experienced change as well. In 1877 vagrancy arrests in New York City rose to more than one million, which was twice as many as the number of arrests in the prior year. The workers and veterans set adrift by the Civil War, the consolidation of industrial capitalism, with its attendant booms and busts, and the growth of the railroad across the continent led to a steep increase in labor mobility. Civil War veterans—injured physically and psychologically and accustomed to riding the rails and foraging for food as part of military life—often took to the road, as did workers who found themselves unemployed in one of the many postwar depressions or seasonally unemployed due to the nature of the work itself. Other travelers included those who resisted the new disciplines of industrial work and preferred to peddle their wares and services from house to house.[10]

As the problem of the transient unemployed exploded with the Industrial Revolution, the perceived moral failings of men marked by indolence, filled with radical ideas, or bitten by the bug of "the hobo life" captured the public imagination. Hoboes were seen as politically volatile, economically unstable, physically threatening, and culturally transgressive. The able-bodied young man who roamed the country in search of work was labeled a "tramp." Vagrancy laws and legislation targeting tramps imposed harsh penalties against those unemployed who wandered too far from home, and as the laws proliferated, so too did their uses. Tramps were often not only would-be workers; they were increasingly union men as well. With the spread of labor unions, employers and the propertied classes became concerned that workers posed political as well economic threats, and that their speech and wandering idleness required containment. Even when the union men were not tramps, employers and their allies called striking men "tramps, bummers, and vagrants." Union men protested, but vagrancy and tramp laws proved powerful weapons of "the employing class." From the mines of Telluride, Colorado, to the textile mills of South Carolina, the police used vagrancy laws to suppress both labor organizing and the free speech such organizing required. At times, union membership alone could lead to an arrest, which police justified by the lack of funds on "snared agitators" or their refusal to accept certain kinds of work.[11]

Those convicted of vagrancy in the 19th century challenged their convictions when they could. Occasionally sympathetic judges were troubled by the laws. One criminal court judge in Cook County, Illinois, found the 1877 Vagabond Act unconstitutional because of the lack of a jury trial for the accused. But such cases were rare. Judges and legal scholars treated vagrancy laws as presumptively valid both for regulating the poor and preventing crime. In part, this was because they did not think of vagrancy laws as criminal laws. Despite the penalties they carried, legal professionals viewed the laws as quintessential "police power regulations" that inhered in the state's comprehensive power to protect the public welfare and morals. As such, prohibitions on vagrancy were subject to fewer constitutional constraints and procedural protections than "criminal laws." The conceptual origin of vagrancy-as-crime-control was the belief that vagrants—who by definition lacked a livelihood—would be forced into a life of crime. Instrumentally, vagrancy laws enabled police to arrest suspicious persons where they would otherwise have been stymied by procedural restraints. The breadth and ambiguity of vagrancy laws made finding—or constructing—a violation easy. Even where police found no other evidence of criminality, vagrancy prosecutions often led to small fines and stints in jail that lasted anywhere from a few days to a few months or longer.[12]

EARLY 20TH CENTURY

Vagrancy enforcement as social policing peaked in the Progressive Era of the late 19th and early 20th centuries. The Progressive movement took a new "social crime" approach, in which crime became a symptom of other social problems and criminal law became a tool for social engineering, especially of immigrants, minorities, and the poor. Prominent legal scholar Roscoe Pound, settlement house leader Jane Addams, and other Progressives joined police officials, lawyers, and judges in embracing vagrancy and similar prohibitions on loitering or disturbing the peace because they thought, in Pound's words, that "preventive justice [was] the most effective agency of social control."[13]

Radical speech, especially by labor activists, was also a prime target of vagrancy laws. Across the country, police used such laws, as well as laws prohibiting loitering, obstructing traffic, holding parades, and making loud noises, to break strikes and suppress political dissidents. Perhaps more than any other group, the Industrial Workers of the World (IWW), also known as the Wobblies, ran afoul of the vagrancy regime. In response to their diverse

and often itinerant membership, their radical ideas, and their confrontational tactics and rhetoric, the Wobblies prompted law enforcement officers to raid their headquarters, seize books, and arrest anyone attending a meeting, often for vagrancy. A Kansas City, Missouri, ordinance enacted in 1918 explicitly expanded the definition of a vagrant to include anyone who was a member of any organization or association that "uttered seditious sentiments against the United States government" alongside anyone who "refused to accept and engage in some lawful trade or occupation," which could cover striking workers.[14] With less legal and public oversight, fewer procedural protections, and fewer evidentiary requirements, vagrancy laws were easier to use than other laws directly targeting radicals.

Political vagrancy arrests continued into the Depression decade of the 1930s, but the nature of the arrests and the persons arrested once again changed. Just as suppression of labor organizing and free speech had gone hand in hand for decades, protection of labor unions and free speech now ascended together. As both Congress and the executive branch came to embrace organized labor as part of the New Deal, so too the Supreme Court frequently protected free speech rights in the 1930s precisely because the speech was about labor. Two such cases in the 1940s, *Thornhill v. Alabama* and *Carlson v. California*, addressed the constitutionality of loitering laws that were directed at labor organizing.

In *Thornhill*, the court pointed out that the law "readily [lent] itself to harsh and discriminatory enforcement by local prosecuting officials, against particular groups deemed to merit their displeasure." The problem was not just that these loitering laws hindered free speech. It was that the laws hindered the speech of labor organizers, which was "indispensable to the effective and intelligent use of the processes of popular government to shape the destiny of modern industrial society." Vagrancy and loitering laws were more diffuse and multifaceted than the usual laws silencing unpopular speech, but government officials often wielded them for similar reasons. If such laws could encroach on newly protected spaces for free speech, then they might need to be reined in as well.[15]

At the same time that protection of free speech was increasing, the legal assumption that idle poverty was inherently immoral, dangerous, and appropriately criminal was in decline. In part, this change was due to the prevalence of forced joblessness during the Depression of the 1930s. The 1941 case of *Edwards v. California* reflected the new trend. When the Supreme Court struck down a law that made it a crime to bring an indigent person into California, it announced that "the theory of the Elizabethan poor laws no longer fits the facts." The court explicitly rejected the reasoning in *Miln*: "Whatever may have been the notion then prevailing, we do not think that it will now be seriously contended that, because a person is without employment and without funds, he constitutes a 'moral pestilence.' Poverty and immorality are not synonymous." *Edwards* did not involve a vagrancy law, but its rupture of centuries-old jurisprudential assumptions about regulating the poor readily applied to vagrancy laws. If poverty resulted from large-scale structural economic issues rather than the moral failings of individuals, punishment seemed anachronistic and unjust.[16]

The legal basis for vagrancy laws themselves began to erode as well. In 1939, in *Lanzetta v. New Jersey*, the Court reviewed a law stating that "any person not engaged in any lawful occupation, known to be a member of any gang consisting of two or more persons, who has been convicted at least three times of being a disorderly person, or who has been convicted of any crime . . . is declared to be a gangster." Though the law did not mention vagrancy per se, the case was closely related. *Lanzetta*'s law grew out of widespread attempts in the 1930s by state and local legislatures to apply vagrancy laws to organized criminals and other "public enemies."

Moreover, its constitutional infirmities were the same ones the court would later find in vagrancy laws. Though one might have read the law as both fairly specific and requiring some past unlawful conduct, the court concluded that it was vague and "condemned no act or omission." The justices did not clarify, however, whether the fact that the law created a status crime was part of what made the law vague or whether it represented a distinct constitutional infirmity. At least some justices began to describe vagrancy laws as "in a class by themselves," given that they were designed "to allow the net to be cast at large, to enable men to be caught who are vaguely undesirable in the eyes of police and prosecution, although not chargeable with any particular offense."[17]

These changes notwithstanding, vagrancy laws survived the first half of the 20th century intact. That the old rationales for arresting the unemployed poor had somewhat eroded led less to the discontinuation of vagrancy arrests than to the formulation of new rationales for them. Into the mid-century, judges upheld convictions on the theory that vagrancy laws were not subject to the usual conduct requirements (as other criminal laws were), and many scholars defended the legitimacy of such laws. According to the well-known treatise *Corpus Juris* in 1934, vagrancy laws were not intended "to punish [vagrants] for the doing of specific overt acts." As the Virginia Supreme Court put it: "The offense does not consist in particular affirmative acts of a person but of his mode of life, habits, and character." The unusual form of vagrancy laws was thus not a problem for the common law, for political legitimacy, for doctrinal frameworks, or for the constitutional community. Venerated for their longevity and their flexibility, vagrancy laws' exceptionalism was precisely their advantage.[18]

THE CONSTITUTIONAL CHALLENGE

Police put vagrancy laws to many uses, new and old, during the mid-20th century. By the

1960s, however, massive changes in law, politics, and culture enabled those targeted by vagrancy laws to challenge them. Though litigants claimed only a limited immunity from arrest on sight, that immunity was crucial to the central concerns of the era: racial equality, personal autonomy, sexual freedom, and political protest. By the early 1970s, vagrancy laws were deemed constitutionally invalid.

The Supreme Court began to reject the assumption of poverty's immorality in *Edwards v. California* in the early 1940s, but the 1960s saw all of American society rethink what it meant to be poor. Keynesian economic theory depicted unemployment as a structural necessity rather than a moral blight. The persistence of dire need among both whites and racial minorities inspired civil rights activists and then presidents John F. Kennedy and Lyndon B. Johnson to formulate a new breed of federal antipoverty policies. Johnson's "War on Poverty" created food stamps, Medicare, and Medicaid, and instituted reforms addressing education, jobs, voting, cities, and housing. With their emphasis on providing a "hand up" rather than a "hand out," these programs embodied a rights-bearing, rather than morally deficient and dependent, view of poor people. The poor also gained access to new legal resources. Though most states had already provided some indigent criminal defendants with lawyers, the Supreme Court's 1963 case *Gideon v. Wainwright* and the decisions that followed nationalized, constitutionalized, and expanded the Sixth Amendment's guarantee of "the assistance of counsel," requiring states to provide free lawyers to indigent defendants under certain circumstances. Meanwhile, the rise of legal aid services gave poor Americans substantial access to civil legal representation for the first time.[19]

Vagrancy laws had long been used against speakers, but as commitment to First Amendment values gained ground and political dissidents, especially peaceful civil rights protestors, garnered more sympathy, the use of vagrancy laws to silence such dissidents generated

increasing skepticism. The 1949 arrest of Isidore Edelman, a radical soapbox orator in Los Angeles, raised novel questions in the Supreme Court about speech-motivated vagrancy enforcement. Although the justices declined to rule on the validity of California's statute, Edelman's case drew attention to the political uses of vagrancy laws and suggested that laws previously too entrenched for constitutional scrutiny were now vulnerable to attack.

An all-out assault on political arrests soon followed with the African American civil rights movement. The army of lawyers who represented thousands of civil rights activists arrested for petty offenses now challenged the legality of vagrancy laws in order to defend clients that included everyone from grassroots organizers to the reverends Martin Luther King Jr., and Fred Shuttlesworth. Police arrested civil rights activists at sit-ins and other protests, as they paused on street corners to confer with colleagues, or in private homes. Although the Supreme Court did not explicitly invalidate vagrancy laws in the vagrancy-related civil rights cases it encountered, the escalation of the civil rights struggle both clarified and publicized the illegitimacy of vagrancy enforcement while marshaling new legal resources against it. The outbreak of anti-Vietnam War protests across the country, and the widespread use of vagrancy and loitering arrests to silence protestors, brought even more soldiers to the vagrancy battle.[20]

As politically unpopular speakers gained ever-greater constitutional protection, cultural changes also began to make room for other kinds of nonconformity. The Beat Generation and many of its prominent members ran afoul of vagrancy laws in the 1950s. Everything about the Beats—their dress, language, sex lives, drug use, and art—challenged the image of mid-century American complacence. A San Francisco police officer allegedly told a countercultural artist, "We're going to get you every week until you get a haircut, shave and put on a suit and tie." Though litigation rarely resulted from such encounters, some observers began to question the legitimacy of using vagrancy laws as a means of social control. The *San Francisco Chronicle* asked, "Are Beatniks Being Pushed Around Because They Are Non-conformists?" Similar questions arose as the American counterculture proliferated in the 1960s.

Hippies—with their long hair, odd clothing, and open sexuality—unnerved older and more conventional "straights," provoking intense conflict on streets and in parks. Throughout the politically intense summer and fall of 1968, police across the country raided hippie hangouts and gathering places and charged them with vagrancy. But the police had overreached. Arrests of hippies in their homes highlighted just how far the vagrancy laws could be pressed, and how out of place they increasingly seemed. Judicial resistance was enhanced by the fact that many of the hippies were privileged white youths. The social position of these "vagrants" made hippies familiar to lawyers, reporters, and judges, who might have had children, siblings, or other relatives making similar choices. Within a year of the 1968 raids, lower federal courts had struck down a number of vagrancy laws across the country. As one lawyer crowed, "Vagrancy laws are falling like ninepins, and 1969 is clearly the banner year."[21]

Legal efforts against the use of vagrancy laws to target sexual nonconformists were less successful. Until the late 1960s, many gay men and lesbians were charged under vagrancy laws that authorized the arrest of any "lewd or dissolute person." A woman could be arrested for a single instance of nude dancing or "roaming the country . . . with a man who was not her husband." As late as 1965, women were arrested under an ordinance making it a crime for a "woman of notorious character" to walk down the street. But as the "sexual revolution" blossomed—first with Beats and hippies challenging sexual norms and then with increasingly open discussion of previously taboo subjects, the advent of the

birth control pill, the women's liberation movement, and the beginnings of the gay rights movement—the landscape of American sexual and gender relations shifted dramatically. For example, by the late 1960s, judges had grown increasingly skeptical about law enforcement's insistence that vagrancy laws were necessary to combat prostitution and female promiscuity. In 1968, an alleged prostitute subject to repeated harassment by police persuaded a federal court in Washington, DC, to strike down sections of that city's vagrancy law as unconstitutionally vague. Advocates for gay men and lesbians faced greater opposition. Into the early 1970s, their vagrancy challenges achieved only occasional victories. Vagrancy laws could still constitutionally be used to harass and arrest sexual minorities.[22]

More generally, many still saw vagrancy laws as a legitimate tool in the efforts of the police to control crime. Social scientific studies revealed that law enforcement officers used vagrancy laws "to justify detention and interrogation of persons suspected of more serious crimes," as well as "dragnets" or "round-ups" of known criminals in the vicinity of a crime for which there were no apparent suspects. Vagrancy arrests gave the police the opportunity to search, fingerprint, investigate, identify, and interrogate individuals without a warrant. Officers assumed that vagrancy laws were "intended primarily as aids to investigation." The problem, though, was that it was not always clear whether officers made vagrancy arrests because they suspected "real" crimes were afoot, or whether they did so to regulate, harass, and control minorities and other marginalized groups. In 1968, the Supreme Court sidestepped these issues in three cases, declining to address the constitutionality of vagrancy laws in *Wainwright v. New Orleans* and *Johnson v. Florida*, while authorizing greater police discretion to stop and frisk suspects merely on the basis of reasonable suspicion in *Terry v. Ohio*.[23]

In 1971, however, the justices made important, although still incomplete, strides against vagrancy-related laws. In *Palmer v. City of Euclid*, the court invalidated a suspicious persons law "as applied" to a particular defendant—a black man sentenced to thirty days in jail after he dropped off a black woman at an all-white apartment complex late at night—but did not question the "facial" validity of the law itself. In *Coates v. Cincinnati*, the court held an ordinance prohibiting three or more people congregating on sidewalks who were "annoying to persons passing by" to be unconstitutionally vague. Although neither opinion said much about the larger question of the constitutionality of vagrancy laws generally, the press began to take up the issue. *The Washington Post* noted, for example, that "although loitering laws differ from city to city, the high court's broad condemnation of a Cincinnati ordinance raised fresh questions in Washington and other urban areas where loosely phrased laws have been challenged as weapons used chiefly against minorities and the poor." The vagrancy regime was poised to topple.[24]

The following year, *Papachristou v. Jacksonville* presented the justices with a comprehensive challenge to the constitutionality of the nation's vagrancy laws. Dogged Florida lawyer Sam Jacobson brought together a diverse group of litigants who had been arrested for vagrancy. Four were black, four were white. Three of the arrests were for crime control purposes. Another defendant was arrested for having "illegitimate" children and a part-time job with "a Negro political organization." Four were arrested together simply for being two white women and two black men out for a night on the town. After twenty years of false starts and hesitations, the Supreme Court unanimously held a traditional vagrancy law facially unconstitutional. In his opinion for the court, Justice William O. Douglas explained that the "ordinance [was] void for vagueness" because of both its lack of notice to ordinary people and its licensing of "arbitrary and erratic arrests and convictions." The constitutional rules for how the police could treat people, and especially people "out of place,"

had fundamentally changed. *Papachristou* reflected new understandings about the meaning of the Constitution in a new era of social and cultural pluralism, an era in which many thought that the Constitution should provide protection for difference and should constrain the authority of the police to treat difference as danger.[25]

POST-1972 DEVELOPMENTS

The Supreme Court's embrace of new constitutional rules in *Coates*, *Palmer*, and *Papachristou* was only one moment in a process of change that began long before and continued long after those decisions. The court's pronouncements did not initiate the destruction of the vagrancy law regime. Lawyers, scholars, judges, legislators, and executive officials had already substantially undermined the regime before the court offered its belated intervention. Nor did the court's decisions eradicate the effects of all vagrancy laws. Some government officials continued to enforce invalid laws. When they found themselves defending such laws in court, they at least occasionally convinced judges to let them stand. What the court's decisions did do, though, was constitutionalize a previously overlooked legal issue. They withdrew legal sanction for vagrancy laws, questioned the legitimacy of unfettered police discretion, reinterpreted the Constitution, and reframed debates going forward. People out of place gained an important constitutional resource in future conflicts over state authority.[26]

As state and local officials attempted to reconstitute some of the authority that had previously resided in vagrancy laws, they enacted more specific loitering statutes that were designed to address the vagueness concerns that had triggered the Supreme Court's intervention. Assessing these new laws, state and lower federal court judges came to differing conclusions about their validity. With the exception of laws governing loitering in or near schools, courts tended to invalidate general prohibitions on loitering in various public places, transportation facilities, parking lots, and gambling sites. They cited *Papachristou* as they struck down loitering laws used to target controversial groups such as abortion rights protesters. Many courts struck down laws that made it a crime to loiter with the intent to engage in or to solicit prostitution, or to loiter with the intent to engage in a drug transaction. Other courts, though, upheld laws that made it a crime to loiter with the intent to beg or to engage in aggressive panhandling.[27]

When the Supreme Court later addressed the constitutionality of this new generation of laws, advocates on all sides conceded that *Papachristou* meant that old-style, status-based, broad and ambiguous vagrancy laws were dead. Other things were different, too. New threats to public safety, such as the spread of crack cocaine and the related rise in gang violence, prompted the enactment of new types of crime-control laws. Moreover, at the very time that the court decided *Papachristou*, national politics shifted decisively to the right. Less than a year after the decision, President Richard Nixon was reelected in a landslide. Over the next two decades, existing fissures among liberals grew, and Republican appointees made the Supreme Court less hospitable to civil rights and civil liberties claims. Reigning ideas about criminal justice also embraced what has been dubbed a "retributive" model that endorsed broad laws, harsh sentences, and mass incarceration. The momentum for decriminalization of victimless crimes dissipated, while the demand for increased criminalization and broader law enforcement authority increased.[28]

Some things remained constant. When it came to crime control for example, African American men continued to be frequent victims of police discretion, too frequent in the eyes of many critics. In *Kolender v. Lawson*, an African American man repeatedly arrested in white neighborhoods challenged the disorderly conduct law that had replaced California's vagrancy statute in 1962. The Supreme Court struck down the new law in 1983, however, reaffirming *Papachristou*. Sixteen years later,

in *Morales v. Chicago*, the Court also invalidated a new kind of status offense, which prohibited "criminal street gang members" from "loitering" with other gang members or other people in public places.

But the demand for vagrancy-like laws persisted. Four years after *Morales*, in a sharply divided 5–4 decision, the Supreme Court in *Hiibel v. Nevada* upheld the constitutionality of a Nevada law authorizing the detention of any person under circumstances suggesting criminality "to ascertain his identity and the suspicious circumstances surrounding his presence." In doing so, the court validated a category of "stop and identify statutes," which "often combine elements of traditional vagrancy laws with provisions intended to regulate police behavior in the course of investigatory stops." Although the majority acknowledged the origins of stop and identify statutes in the longer history of vagrancy laws, it concluded that the provision in *Hiibel* was "narrower and more precise" than those it had invalidated in prior decisions.[29]

It was not just new laws that communities and police departments used to approximate the powers they had once exercised under traditional vagrancy laws. Police across the country turned increasingly to "*Terry* stops," as the stop and frisk sanctioned in *Terry v. Ohio* came to be known. State and local officials continued to use vague but more conduct-oriented disorderly conduct and breach of the peace laws to fill the vacuum. Officials also increasingly deployed stringent drug laws and trespass and housing infractions—conduct sometimes called "lingering" to distinguish it from the now-discredited but eerily similar "loitering." And with new forms of "broken windows" and "order maintenance" policing, officials once again embraced the centuries-old idea that vagrancy laws' challengers had largely rejected: because petty crime would lead to more serious crime, law enforcement should take aim at the former in order to prevent the latter. These neovagrancy-type justifications for the regulation of incipient crime mimicked the old vagrancy laws, but fell short of fully replicating them.[30]

These efforts notwithstanding, public officials were no longer able to rely on an infinitely elastic law to address new social problems. Almost simultaneous with the delegitimization of traditional vagrancy laws, and rising in part out of the same 1960s impulse toward liberty, autonomy, and nonconformity, state mental institutions began to discharge their patients on a massive scale. Officials faced with an increase in what they called "the derelict population" complained loudly about being hamstrung by the absence of vagrancy laws, and they blamed the Supreme Court. They turned instead to a variety of legal and nonlegal strategies for responding to the subsequent and enduring rise in homelessness. These ranged from laws prohibiting panhandling and sleeping on park benches and in cars, to technological changes (such as armrests dividing park benches), zoning regulations, and gated communities. The response to the homeless might come to mind most readily as evidence that coercive governmental power survived the end of vagrancy laws, albeit in new forms. After all, the homeless always best fit the popular label of "vagrants." They still do, even in the absence of constitutional vagrancy laws and the subsequent linguistic shift from "vagrants" and "bums" to "homeless" and "unhoused."[31]

For better or worse, the invalidation of traditional vagrancy laws made it harder for government to regulate a wide range of people: men whose children receive welfare because they do not provide for them; women and transgender women suspected of but not obviously engaged in prostitution; migrant farmworkers seeking legal or medical services; speakers occupying public parks; day laborers gathering in public spaces in the hope of finding work; minority teens whose sartorial choices are found offensive and symbolically dangerous, just as the hippies' choices once were. The absence of a freewheeling, always available, infinitely flexible law enforcement

tool serves as a reference point for all of these developments and then some. The traditional vagrancy law regime also serves as a reference point for the status regulation of everyone from sex offenders to juveniles to undocumented workers. Regulating such people, tackling such threats, was work that before 1972 would have been undertaken at least in part under the auspices of vagrancy enforcement. It has produced new forms of legal authority ever since.

DISCUSSION OF THE LITERATURE

Until recently, it was difficult to identify the history of vagrancy law as a subject in its own right. In part, the invisibility of that history mirrored the invisibility of the regime itself. In part, it was a product of the successful legal challenges. With vagrancy laws gone, the various groups that opposed them shifted their energies to resisting less universal legal strictures. That fragmentation has made it hard to see vagrancy law as a coherent category with its own history. Scholars who have examined discrete parts of the story have divvied up the cases by litigant (civil rights protestor, skid row drunk, soapbox orator), constitutional claim (free speech, due process, criminal procedure), or historical framework (race, labor, poverty, crime, sexuality, geography).

The various uses of vagrancy laws have accordingly been subsumed within, and viewed as adjuncts to, the specific contexts in which they arose. Vagrancy laws occasionally surfaced in histories of poverty and welfare from colonial times onward.[32] In the 1980s, labor historians became interested in vagrancy laws as tools the capitalist class used against rising labor unions and the working class, including prostitutes, in the late 19th and early 20th centuries.[33] Around the same time, and continuing for the next two decades, scholars of African American history identified vagrancy laws as among the web of laws used to subordinate African Americans socially, economically, and politically in the post-Civil War South.[34]

With the increased visibility of homelessness in the 1980s and 1990s, historians documenting that homelessness, the history of skid row, and poverty more generally included vagrancy laws in their ambit. So too did scholars exploring the many types of legal restriction used against gay men and lesbians in the mid-20th century. Legal scholars who began their inquiries with the seminal Supreme Court case of *Papachristou v. Jacksonville* (1972) understood the downfall of vagrancy laws within the related contexts of the Warren Court criminal procedure revolution and the 1960s civil rights movement. They have also explored the legal repercussions of that downfall in the years since. More recently, scholars have identified vagrancy laws as a subject in their own right, excavating the hidden history of vagrancy laws and the social and legal developments that made their downfall both possible and necessary.[35] More work remains to be done to explore the treatment of vagrancy-type laws after *Papachristou* and other types of laws that came to replace vagrancy law authority in greater detail.

PRIMARY SOURCES

Because of the wide range of uses to which vagrancy laws were put, primary source materials on the history of American vagrancy laws are widely dispersed. Traditional legal sources provide an excellent way into the material. Thousands of published opinions in state and federal courts enable scholars to trace the doctrinal history of vagrancy laws and their interpretation.[36] Insight into judicial views can also be found in the papers of specific judges, many of which are housed at the Library of Congress (https://www.loc.gov/rr/mss/f-aids/mssfa.html). Changes in the treatment of vagrancy laws in legal treatises, casebooks, and the Model Penal Code provide information about the changing views of scholars and other legal professionals, as do scholarly articles and books.[37] Information about arrests is more difficult to locate. The FBI compiles basic arrest information, though

scholars have criticized its methodology and incompleteness.[38] Local arrest records can sometimes be obtained from specific police departments. Because the American Civil Liberties Union and its affiliates were involved in vagrancy cases across the greatest number of contexts, their papers provide the broadest access to the attack on vagrancy laws.[39] The papers of the National Association for the Advancement of Colored People (https://www.loc.gov/loc/lcib/1003/collection.html) and its local chapters provide important insight into the relationship between vagrancy challenges and the civil rights movement. Newspapers and other popular media are also illuminating sources for the increasing visibility of vagrancy arrests and adjudication, and will be especially helpful in exploring post-1972 developments.

FURTHER READING

Adler, Jeffrey S. "A Historical Analysis of the Law of Vagrancy." *Criminology* 27, no. 2 (1989): 214–215.

Agee, Christopher Lowen. *The Streets of San Francisco.* Chicago: University of Chicago Press, 2014.

Cohen, William. *At Freedom's Edge: Black Mobility and the Southern White Quest for Racial Control 1861–1915.* Baton Rouge: Louisiana State University Press, 1991.

DePastino, Todd. *Citizen Hobo: How a Century of Homelessness Shaped America.* Chicago: University of Chicago Press, 2003.

Ellickson, Robert C. "Controlling Chronic Misconduct in City Spaces: Of Panhandlers, Skid Rows, and Public-Space Zoning." *Yale Law Journal* 105, no. 5 (1996): 1165–1248.

Eskridge, William N., Jr. *Gaylaw: Challenging the Apartheid of the Closet.* Cambridge, MA: Harvard University Press, 1999.

Goluboff, Risa. *Vagrant Nation: Police Power, Constitutional Change, and the Making of the 1960s.* New York: Oxford University Press, 2016.

Harring, Sidney. "Class Conflict and the Suppression of Tramps in Buffalo, 1892–1894." *Law and Society Review* 11, no. 5 (1977): 873–911.

Herndon, Ruth Wallis. *Unwelcome Americans: Living on the Margin in Early New England.* Philadelphia: University of Pennsylvania Press, 2001.

Jeffries, John C., Jr. "Legality, Vagueness, and the Construction of Penal Statutes." *Virginia Law Review* 71 (1985): 189–245.

Kahan, Dan M., and Tracey L. Meares. "The Coming Crisis in Criminal Procedure." *Georgetown Law Journal* 86, no. 2 (1998): 1153–1184.

Kerber, Linda K. *No Constitutional Right to Be Ladies: Women and the Obligations of Citizenship.* New York: Hill and Wang, 1998.

Kusmer, Kenneth L. *Down and Out, On the Road: The Homeless in American History.* New York: Oxford University Press, 2002.

Livingston, Debra. "Police Discretion and the Quality of Life in Public Places: Courts, Communities, and the New Policing." *Columbia Law Review* 97, no. 3 (1997): 551–672.

Monkkonen, Eric H., ed. *Walking to Work: Tramps in America, 1790–1935.* Lincoln: University of Nebraska Press, 1984.

Post, Robert C. "Reconceptualizing Vagueness: Legal Rules and Social Orders." *California Law Review* 82 (1994): 491–507.

Ribton-Turner, C. J. *A History of Vagrants and Vagrancy and Beggars and Begging.* London: Chapman and Hall, 1887.

Roberts, Dorothy E. "Foreword: Race, Vagueness, and the Social Meaning of Order-Maintenance Policing." *Journal of Criminal Law & Criminology* 89, no. 3 (1999): 775–836.

Rothman, David J. *The Discovery of the Asylum: Social Order and Disorder in the New Republic.* Rev ed. London: Routledge, 2002.

Schneider, John C. "The Police on Skid Row: A Historical Perspective." *Criminal Justice Review* 13, no. 2 (1988): 15–20.

Schragger, Richard C. "The Limits of Localism." *Michigan Law Review* 100, no. 2 (2001): 371–472.

Seo, Sarah A. "The New Public." *Yale Law Journal* 125, no. 6 (2016): 1548–1819. https://www.yale lawjournal.org/essay/the-new-public.

Stanley, Amy Dru. "Beggars Can't Be Choosers: Compulsion and Contract in Postbellum America." *Journal of American History* 78, no. 4 (1992): 1265–1293.

Stuntz, William J. "Local Policing after the Terror." *Yale Law Journal* 111, no. 8 (2002): 2137–2194.

White, Ahmed A. "A Different Kind of Labor Law: Vagrancy Law and the Regulation of Harvest Labor, 1913–1924." *University of Colorado Law Review* 75, no. 3 (2004): 667–744.

Willrich, Michael. *City of Courts: Socializing Justice in Progressive Era Chicago.* New York: Cambridge University Press, 2003.

NOTES

1. Statute of Labourers, 1350, 25 Edw. 3, stat. 2; 1350, 25 Edw. 3, stat. 7; Vagrancy Act of 1597 (An Act for Punishment of Rogues, Vagabonds, and Sturdy Beggars), 39 Eliz. 1, c. 4.

2. William P. Quigley, "Reluctant Charity: Poor Laws in the Original Thirteen States," *University of Richmond Law Review* 31, no. 1 (1997): 111–178; "The Quicksands of the Poor Law: Poor Relief Legislation in a Growing Nation, 1790–1820," *Northern Illinois University Law Review* 18, no. 1 (1997): 1–98; and Sir James Fitzjames Stephen, *A History of the Criminal Law of England*, vol. 3 (London: Macmillan, 1883), 267.

3. Paul A. Slack, "Vagrants and Vagrancy in England, 1598–1664," *Economic History Review* 27, no. 3 (August 1974): 365; Mark Netzloff, "'Counterfeit Egyptians' and Imagined Borders: Johnson's *The Gypsies Metamorphosed*," *ELH* 68, no. 4 (2001): 763–793; and A. L. Beier, *Masterless Men: The Vagrancy Problem in England, 1560–1640* (New York: Methuen, 1985), 58–62, 64–65.

4. Stefan A. Riesenfeld, "The Formative Era of American Public Assistance Law," *California Law Review* 43, no. 2 (1955): 207; Nathaniel B. Shurtleff, ed., *Records of the Governor and Company of the Massachusetts Bay in New England Printed by Order of the Legislature*, vol. 4, bk. 2: 1661–1674 (Boston: William White, 1854), 2–4; James W. Loewen, *Sundown Towns: A Hidden Dimension of American Racism* (New York: New Press, 2005); An Act for the Government and Protection of Indians, ch. 133, 1850 Cal. Stat. 408; An Act to Punish Vagrants, Vagabonds, and Dangerous and Suspicious Persons, ch. 175, 1855 Cal. Stat. 217; 1896 Haw. Sess. Laws 87 (Act 36); 1850 Penal Code of the Hawaiian Islands 91–92, ch. 38; Robert F. Heizer and Alan J. Almquist, *The Other Californians: Prejudice and Discrimination under Spain, Mexico, and the United States to 1920* (Berkeley: University of California Press, 1971), 48–49; and Gary Okihiro, *Cane Fires: The Anti-Japanese Movement in Hawaii, 1865–1945* (Philadelphia: Temple University Press, 1991), 239.

5. Barbara Meil Hobson, *Uneasy Virtue: The Politics of Prostitution and the American Reform Tradition*

(New York: Basic Books, 1987), 32–33; A. V. Judges, ed., *The Elizabethan Underworld* (London: G. Routledge & Sons, 1930), cited in A. L. Beier, *Masterless Men*, 7; and Tim Hitchcock, Adam Crymble, and Louise Falcini, "Loose, Idle and Disorderly: Vagrant Removal in Late Eighteenth-century Middlesex," *Social History* 39, no. 4 (2014): 509–510.

6. New York v. Miln, 36 U.S. 102, 142–143 (1837).

7. Michael B. Katz, *In the Shadow of the Poorhouse: A Social History of Welfare in America* (New York: Basic Books, 1996), 9; N.Y. Sess. Laws 1788, ch. 62; N.Y. Sess. Laws 1824, ch. 37; Quigley, "Quicksands of the Poor Law," 42; and Gerald L. Neuman, "The Lost Century of American Immigration Law (1776–1875)," *Columbia Law Review* 93, no. 8 (1993): 1852.

8. William Cohen, *At Freedom's Edge: Black Mobility and the Southern White Quest for Racial Control 1861–1915* (Baton Rouge: Louisiana State University Press, 1991), 28–31, 242–246.

9. Theodore B. Wilson, *The Black Codes of the South* (Tuscaloosa: University of Alabama Press, 1965), 68, 117; Eric Foner, *Reconstruction: America's Unfinished Revolution, 1863–1877*, updated ed. (New York: Harper Perennial, 2014), 199–201, 205, 363, 372, 593; Act of November 29, 1865, ch. 23 (1865) Miss. Laws 165, 167, quoted in Ahmed A. White, "A Different Kind of Labor Law: Vagrancy Law and the Regulation of Harvest Labor, 1913–1924," *University of Colorado Law Review* 75, no. 3 (2004): 680; Report and Testimony of the Select Committee of the United States Senate to Investigate the Causes of the Removal of the Negroes from the Southern States to the Northern States, 46th Cong., 2d Sess., Rpt. 693, Pt. 3 (1880), 500–501.

10. Paul T. Ringenbach, *Tramps and Reformers 1873–1916: The Discovery of Unemployment in New York* (Westport, CT: Greenwood Press, 1973), 11.

11. John J. McCook, "A Tramp Census and Its Revelations," *Forum* 15 (1893): 753; Katz, *In the Shadow of the Poorhouse*, 95; John C. Schneider, *Detroit and the Problem of Order, 1830–1880: A Geography of Crime, Riot, and Policing* (Lincoln: University of Nebraska Press, 1980), 109–110; See, e.g., "Miners' Trouble: Result of Arrest of Strikers in Colorado, Mining Town," *Evening News*, December 3, 1903, 5; "Strikes Still On at Carhartt," *Evening Herald*, June 17, 1920, 6.

12. Amy Dru Stanley, "Beggars Can't Be Choosers: Compulsion and Contract in Postbellum America," *Journal of American History* (March 1992): 1265–1293, esp. 1280; Marcus Dubber, *The Police Power* (New York: Columbia University Press, 2005), 130–138; and Ernst Freund, *The Police Power: Public Policy and Constitutional Rights* (1904; repr., New York: Arno Press, 1976), 99.

13. F. B. Sanborn, "The Year's Work in Administration and Legislation," in *Proceedings of the Sixth Annual Conference of Charities*, ed. F. B. Sanborn (Boston: A. Williams, 1879), 25; Francis Wayland and F. B. Sanborn, "Tramp Laws and Indeterminate Sentences," in *Proceedings of the Seventh Annual Conference of Charities and Correction*, ed. F. B. Sanborn, 277–281, cited in Kenneth L. Kusmer, *Down and Out, on the Road: The Homeless in American History* (New York: Oxford University Press, 2002), 53; Ringenbach, *Tramps and Reformers*, 23–24; and Roscoe Pound, "Introduction," in *A Selection of Cases on Criminal Law*, ed. Francis Bowes Sayre (Rochester: Lawyers Co-Operative Publishing, 1927), xxxvi.

14. Dennis E. Hoffman and Vincent J. Webb, "Police Response to Labor Radicalism in Portland and Seattle, 1913–19," *Oregon Historical Quarterly* 87, no. 4 (1986): 348–349; Kevin Starr, *Endangered Dreams: The Great Depression and California* (New York: Oxford University Press, 1996), 29; Melvin Dubofsky, *We Shall Be All: A History of the Industrial Workers of the World* (Chicago: Quadrangle Books, 1969), 349; Record of the Fight for Free Speech in 1923, p. 14, box 82, American Civil Liberties Union of Southern California Records (collection 900), Charles E. Young Research Library, UCLA Special Collections; "I.W.W. Ordered to Invade City," *Oregonian* (Portland, OR), October 25, 1922, 1; "I.W.W. Trial Set," *Oregonian* (Portland, OR), August 7, 1917, 12; Ex parte Clancy, 210 P. 487 (Kan. 1922); James Gray Pope, "Labor's Constitution of Freedom," *Yale Law Journal* 106, no. 4 (1997): 1009–1010; Ex parte Taft, 225 S.W. 457, 458 (Mo. 1920); and Zechariah Chafee Jr., *Free Speech in the United States* (Cambridge, MA: Harvard University Press, 1941), 100n107.

15. Hague v. CIO, 307 U.S. 496 (1939); Carlson v. California, 310 U.S. 106, 112 (1940); and Thornhill v. Alabama, 310 U.S. 88, 97–98, 100 (1940).

16. Edwards v. California, 314 U.S. 160, 174, 177 (1941); and Arthur H. Sherry, "Vagrants, Rogues

and Vagabonds—Old Concepts in Need of Revision," *California Law Review* 48, no. 4 (1960): 557–559.

17. Lanzetta v. New Jersey, 306 U.S. 451, 458 (1939); Jerome Hall, "The Law of Arrest in Relation to Social Problems," *University of Chicago Law Review* 3, no. 3 (1936): 369; Carl V. Eimbeck, "Some Recent Methods of Harassing the Habitual Criminal," *St. Louis Law Review* 16, no. 2 (1930–1931): 155; and Winters v. New York, 333 U.S. 507, 540 (Frankfurter, J., dissenting).

18. William A. Martin, "Vagrancy," in *Corpus Juris*, ed. William Mack and Donald J. Kiser (New York: American Law Book Co., 1934), 66:399; and Morgan v. Commonwealth, 191 S.E. 791, 794 (Va. 1937).

19. Martha F. Davis, *Brutal Need: Lawyers and the Welfare Rights Movement, 1960–1973* (New Haven, CT: Yale University Press, 1993); and Thomas Miguel Hilbink, "Constructing Cause Lawyering: Professionalism, Politics, and Social Change in 1960s America" (PhD diss., New York University, 2006).

20. Edelman v. California, 344 U.S. 357, 358–359 (1953); and Stephen L. Wasby, Anthony A. D'Amato, and Rosemary Metrailer, *Desegregation from Brown to Alexander* (Carbondale: Southern Illinois University Press, 1977), 343–359.

21. Ernest Besig to Thomas Cahill, April 7, 1959, MS 3580, carton 36, folder 781, California Historical Society ACLU Papers; handwritten notes, March 19, 1959, MS 3580, carton 36, folder 781, California Historical Society ACLU Papers (by Ernest Besig); "Are Beatniks Being Pushed Around Because They Are Nonconformists?" *San Francisco Chronicle*, July 29, 1958, MS 3580, carton 36, folder 782, California Historical Society ACLU Papers; Wheeler v. Goodman, 306 F.Supp. 58 (W.D. N.C. 1969) (No. Civ. 2431), box 1831, American Civil Liberties Union Records, Series 4, Subseries 4A, Department of Rare Books and Special Collections, Princeton University Library.

22. Joyce Murdoch and Deb Price, *Courting Justice: Gay Men and Lesbians v. The Supreme Court* (New York: Basic Books, 2001), 143–146; Coty R. Miller and Nuria Haltiwanger, "Prostitution and the Legalization/Decriminalization Debate," *Georgetown Journal of Gender and Law* 5, no. 1 (2004): 207; and Ricks v. District of Columbia, 414 F.2d 1097 (D.C. Cir. 1968).

23. Wayne R. LaFave, *Arrest: The Decision to Take a Suspect into Custody* (Boston: Little, Brown, 1965), 87–89, 151–152, 354–357; Wainwright v. City of New Orleans, 392 U.S. 598 (1968); Johnson v. Florida, 391 U.S. 596 (1968); and Terry v. Ohio, 392 U.S. 1 (1968).

24. Palmer v. City of Euclid, 402 U.S. 544 (1971); Coates v. City of Cincinnati, 402 U.S. 611 (1969); and John P. MacKenzie, "Loitering Law Upset by Court as Too Vague," *Washington Post*, June 2, 1971, A1.

25. Papachristou v. City of Jacksonville, 405 U.S. 156, 162 (1972).

26. On enforcing invalidated laws, see, e.g., William Glaberson, "Long Fight Ends over Arrests for Loitering," *New York Times*, February 7, 2012. On evading litigation, see, e.g., Govt. of the Canal Zone v. Castillo L., 568 F.2d 405 (5th Cir. 1978); People v. Solomon, 108 Cal. Rptr. 867 (Cal. Ct. App. 1973); State v. Williams, 315 So.2d 449 (Fla. Dist. Ct. App. 1975); Dinitz v. Christensen, 577 P.2d 873 (Nev. 1978); and State v. Jones, 511 P.2d 74 (Wash. Ct. App. 1973).

27. For lower court cases taking the doctrine seriously, see, e.g., State v. Rackle, 523 P.2d 299, 301 (1974). For lower court cases upholding ordinances prohibiting loitering around schools, see, e.g., McSherry v. Block, C.A.9 (Cal.) July 21, 1989, 880 F.2d 1049. For invalidations of loitering laws, see Ruff v. Marshall, M.D.Ga. October 5, 1977, 438 F.Supp. 303 (loitering in public places), People v. Velazquez; N.Y.City Crim.Ct. April 24, 1974, 77 Misc.2d 749 (loitering in transportation facilities), Switzer v. City of Tulsa, Okla.Crim.App. July 19, 1979, 598 P.2d 247 (loitering at gambling sites), Lytle v. Doyle, E.D.Va. December 17, 2001, 197 F.Supp.2d 481 (loitering on bridges), City of St. Louis v. Burton, Mo. April 10, 1972, 478 S.W.2d 320 (loitering by prostitutes). For lower court cases upholding ordinances prohibiting "aggressive" panhandling, see, e.g., State ex rel. Williams v. City Court of Tucson, Ariz.App. Div. 2 April 09, 1974 21 Ariz. App. 489.

28. On the 1970s generally, see, e.g., Edward D. Berkowitz, *Something Happened: A Political and Cultural Overview of the Seventies* (New York: Columbia University Press, 2006); Jefferson Cowie, *Stayin' Alive: The 1970s and the Last Days of the Working Class* (New York: New Press, 2010); Dan Berger, ed., *The Hidden 1970s: Histories of*

Radicalism (New Brunswick, NJ: Rutgers University Press, 2010). On changes in ideas about criminal justice, see, e.g., National Advisory Committee on Criminal Justice Standards and Goals, *Organized Crime: Report of the Task Force on Organized Crime* (Washington, DC: Government Printing Office, 1976), 65; "Shoot the Messenger," *Wall Street Journal*, November 13, 1978, 24.

29. Kolender v. Lawson, 461 U.S. 352 (1983); City of Chicago v. Morales, 527 U.S. 41, 47 (1999); Hiibel v. Sixth Judicial Dist. Court of Nevada, 542 U.S. 177, 184 (2004).

30. On displacement to disorderly conduct, see David Thatcher, "Policing after *Papachristou*: A Case Study of the Impact of Legal Change on the Police," paper presented at the Law and Society Association Annual Conference, Boston, Massachusetts, May 30, 2013. On lingering, see, e.g., J. David Goodman, "Police Patrols in New York Public Housing Draw Scrutiny," *New York Times*, December 15, 2014, A1; cf. Peter Ramsay, *The Insecurity State: Vulnerable Autonomy and the Right to Security in the Criminal Law* (Oxford: Oxford University Press, 2013).

31. On deinstitutionalization, see Erving Goffman, *Asylums: Essays on the Social Situation of Mental Patients and Other Inmates* (Garden City, NY: Anchor Books, 1961); Nicholas N. Kittrie, *The Right to Be Different: Deviance and Enforced Therapy* (Baltimore, MD: Johns Hopkins University Press, 1971); Thomas Szasz, *The Myth of Mental Illness: Foundations of a Theory of Personal Conduct* (New York: Hoeber-Harper, 1961). On officials' response, see, e.g., Richard Lamb, ed., *The Homeless Mentally Ill: A Task Force Report of the American Psychiatric Association* (Washington, DC: American Psychiatric Association, 1984); Andrew T. Scull, *Decarceration: Community Treatment and the Deviant: A Radical View* (Englewood Cliffs, NJ: Prentice-Hall, 1977). On new techniques of control, see, e.g., Katherine Beckett and Steve Herbert, *Banished: The New Social Control in Urban America* (Oxford: Oxford University Press, 2010); Teresa Gowan, *Hobos, Hustlers, and Backsliders: Homeless in San Francisco* (Minneapolis: University of Minnesota Press, 2010); and National Law Center on Homelessness and Poverty, *No Homeless People Allowed: A Report on Anti-Homeless Laws, Litigation, and Alternatives in 49 United States Cities* (Washington,

DC: National Law Center on Homelessness and Poverty, 1994), 10–12, 16–21, 36–39.

32. John K. Alexander, *Render Them Submissive: Responses to Poverty in Philadelphia, 1760–1800* (Amherst: University of Massachusetts, 1980); Margaret Creech, *Three Centuries of Poor Law Administration: A Study of Legislation in Rhode Island* (1936; repr. College Park: McGrath, 1969); Michael B. Katz, *The Undeserving Poor: From the War on Poverty to the War on Welfare* (New York: Pantheon Books, 1989); Benjamin J. Klebaner, *Public Poor Relief in America, 1790–1869* (New York: Arno Press, 1976); David M. Schneider, *The History of Public Welfare in New York State, 1609–1866* (Chicago: University of Chicago Press, 1938); Douglas Lamar Jones, "The Strolling Poor: Transiency in Eighteenth-Century Massachusetts," *Journal of Social History* 8, no. 3 (1975): 28–54; and William P. Quigley, "Work or Starve: Regulation of the Poor in Colonial America," *University of San Francisco Law Review* 31, no. 1 (1996): 40; "Reluctant Charity," 111–178; "The Quicksands of the Poor Law, 1–98.

33. Alexander Keyssar, *Out of Work: The First Century of Unemployment in Massachusetts* (New York: Cambridge University Press, 1986); Ringenbach, *Tramps and Reformers*; Schneider, *Detroit and the Problem of Order*; and Jeffrey S. Adler, "Streetwalkers, Degraded Outcasts, and Good-for-Nothing Huzzies: Women and the Dangerous Class in Antebellum St. Louis," *Journal of Social History* 25, no. 4 (1992): 737.

34. See, e.g., Foner, *Reconstruction*.

35. Risa Goluboff, *Vagrant Nation: Police Power, Constitutional Change, and the Making of the 1960s* (New York: Oxford University Press, 2016).

36. Prominent Supreme Court cases include: Papachristou v. City of Jacksonville, 405 U.S. 156 (1972); Coates v. City of Cincinnati, 402 U.S. 611 (1971); Palmer v. City of Euclid, 402 U.S. 544 (1971); Wainwright v. City of New Orleans, 392 U.S. 598 (1968); Johnson v. Florida, 391 U.S. 596, 615 (1968); Hicks v. District of Columbia, 383 U.S. 252 (1966); Shuttlesworth v. City of Birmingham, 382 U.S. 87, 89 (1965); Arceneaux v. Louisiana, 376 U.S. 336 (1964); Thompson v. Louisville, 362 U.S. 199 (1960); and Edelman v. California, 344 U.S. 357 (1953).

37. Paul Chevigny, *Police Power: Police Abuses in New York City* (New York: Pantheon Books, 1969); Anthony G. Amsterdam, "The Void-for-Vagueness

Doctrine in the Supreme Court," *University of Pennsylvania Law Review* 109 (1960): 67; "Federal Constitutional Restrictions on the Punishment of Crimes of Status, Crimes of General Obnoxiousness, Crimes of Displeasing Police Officers, and the Like," *Criminal Law Bulletin* 3, no. 4 (1967): 207; Egon Bittner, "The Police on Skid-Row: A Study of Peace Keeping," *American Sociological Review* 32, no. 5 (1967): 703; William O. Douglas, "Vagrancy and Arrest on Suspicion," *Yale Law Journal* 70, no. 1 (1960): 9; Caleb Foote, "Vagrancy-Type Law and Its Administration," *University of Pennsylvania Law Review* 104, no. 5 (1956): 603; and "Project: The Consenting Adult Homosexual and the Law: An Empirical Study of Enforcement and Administration in

Los Angeles County," *UCLA Law Review* 13, no. 3 (1966): 643.

38. US Department of Justice, Federal Bureau of Investigation, *Uniform Crime Reports* (Washington, DC: Government Printing Office).

39. Princeton University's Mudd Library contains the national ACLU papers. Affiliates are often locally held. See, e.g., Online Archive of California, Finding Aid for the American Civil Liberties Union of Southern California records, ca. 1935-; Online Archive of California, Finding Aid for the American Civil Liberties Union of Northern California records, 1900–2000; ACLU of Ohio.

Risa L. Goluboff and Adam Sorensen

The Postwar and Postindustrial Metropolis

THE BLACK FREEDOM STRUGGLE IN THE URBAN NORTH

Histories of racial inequality and the struggle for civil rights in the United States tend to focus on the South, with attention on the aftermath of slavery, the short-lived freedoms of Reconstruction, the rise of intensive state-sanctioned racial segregation, and the emergence of nonviolent protests against Jim Crow in the 1950s. The history of the black freedom struggle outside the South has generally remained in the shadows. The North had a long—if mostly forgotten—history of chattel slavery from the 17th through the early 19th centuries. Many fortunes in banking, textiles, and shipping up North were built on the backs of unfree African American labor. Cities such as Boston, New York, and Philadelphia rose to economic power because of the trade in slaves and the products of plantations in the South and Caribbean, particularly cotton.[1]

As slavery waned in the 19th-century North with gradual emancipation, racial inequality persisted and, in many places, hardened. In 1835 the French political theorist Alexis de Tocqueville observed that

> in the North the white no longer clearly perceives the barrier that is supposed to separate him from this debased race, and he shuns the Negro all the more assiduously for fear that he might one day become indistinguishable from him.

Even in those northern states that had abolished or prohibited slavery, Tocqueville observed that the Negro is free, but he cannot share the rights, pleasures, labors, or sorrows— not even the tomb of him whose equal he has been declared to be. There is no place where the two can come together, whether in life or death.[2]

In the decades preceding the Civil War, northern abolitionists worked to destroy slavery both in their own region and in the South. Black and white anti-slavery activists participated in the Underground Railroad, resisted Fugitive Slave Laws, and valiantly fought the Confederacy. In some states, under pressure by civil rights activists, legislatures abolished racially separate schools and extended voting rights to African American men during the decades preceding and immediately following the Civil War. During Reconstruction, several northern states passed laws forbidding discrimination by race in public education and public accommodations.[3]

THE GREAT MIGRATION

Questions of race and civil rights, however, remained minor issues in northern politics until the 20th century. As late as 1920, nearly nine out of ten African Americans still lived in the South, and large sections of states outside the old Confederacy had few, if any, nonwhites. Most northern blacks were concentrated in a handful of large cities, notably Philadelphia and New York. Those patterns changed profoundly with the Great Migration (1910–1970) of African Americans northward. More than six million African Americans left the South in search of economic opportunities in burgeoning northern industries. Some fled the declining southern agricultural economy. Others were refugees from widespread racial violence. Many migrants saw themselves as part of an exodus to a "promised land" or a "New Canaan," where they would be free from the indignities and dangers of southern racism.[4]

The Great Migration generated intense racial conflict in the North. During the first decades of the 20th century, dozens of race riots broke out in northern towns and cities, always instigated by whites threatened by growing black populations. Those riots peaked in times of social and economic instability. During World War I and its aftermath, whites attacked African Americans in East Saint Louis and Chicago.[5] During the 1920s, millions of northern whites joined the Ku Klux Klan, an organization committed to nativism, anti-Catholicism, and opposition to equality between African Americans and whites. Members of the Klan gained political power throughout the North. In Detroit, a Klansman lost the 1925 mayoral election on technicalities in a city riven by racial tensions. The same year as the near-KKK victory, whites attacked the house of Ossian Sweet, an African American doctor who moved into a white neighborhood.[6]

JIM CROW IN PUBLIC ACCOMMODATIONS

Few northern states had laws that required the segregation of blacks and whites in public spaces, but Jim Crow was commonly practiced north of the Mason-Dixon line. Movie theaters regularly turned away black customers or confined them to the balconies (colloquially called the "crow's nests"). Swimming pools, roller rinks, dance halls, bowling alleys, and amusement parks were strictly segregated by race.[7] The Young Women's and Young Men's Christian Associations (YWCA and YMCA) provided recreation, education, and social services to blacks and whites in racially separate buildings.[8] Public parks, beaches, and pools were rigorously segregated by race. In some cities, public swimming facilities sometimes admitted African Americans on a segregated basis, usually on the day before pools were emptied, cleaned, and refilled.[9] Few restaurants and hotels in the North that served white patrons allowed African Americans entry. Black travelers relied on *The Negro Motorist's Green Book* and on advertisements in African American newspapers to find hotels, campgrounds, and restaurants that were open to them.[10]

WORKPLACE DISCRIMINATION

During the Great Migration, most northern employers refused to hire African Americans at all. For the first third of the 20th century, most black men held service jobs, serving as janitors, maintenance men, barbers, and cooks. The vast majority of African American women in the paid workforce in the North through the Great Depression worked as domestics, cooks, or laundry workers. Others worked in informal jobs, ranging from prostitution to numbers running. Few blacks found work in the skilled building trades. Retail jobs that required interaction with white customers were closed to African Americans. Even fewer found white-collar positions. Even African Americans with professional degrees, including doctors, engineers, and lawyers, found it nearly impossible to find work in white-owned businesses or major corporations until the 1960s.[11]

Before World War II, African Americans sometimes found work in industry but nearly always in unskilled jobs, often in dangerous or unpleasant settings. In Chicago, black men found work on the killing floors of meatpacking plants. In major steel-producing cities, including Chicago, Gary, Cleveland, and Pittsburgh, black workers generally toiled in the unbearable heat of foundries, pouring molten iron and stoking furnaces with coke, a form of processed coal. In the auto industry, blacks were confined to maintenance jobs or hazardous jobs such as engine lifting and car-body painting. Many employers hired black workers to replace white workers who were on strike and in the process fueled racial resentment by whites who believed that African Americans were stealing their jobs. Other firms instituted a strict system of racial segregation on the shop floor or assembly line, refusing to place black workers in white jobs. Whether as

domestics and cooks or assembly line workers, African Americans were almost always paid less than their white counterparts. They were the first to be laid off during economic downturns and the last to be hired. Even companies that employed African American workers often did so as a last resort, particularly during periods of labor shortages, including World War I and World War II. Black workers regularly complained of being turned away when they applied for jobs, even as employers continued to hire whites.[12]

Labor unions had a mixed record of providing support for African American workers. Most unions in the American Federation of Labor (AFL), which was dominated by skilled labors, regularly endorsed racially discriminatory practices. Construction unions favored the sons, brothers, and relatives of their members, who were usually all white. But the AFL also included all-black unions, including the influential Brotherhood of Sleeping Car Porters, led by Asa Philip Randolph. The Sleeping Car Porters had an outsized role in civil rights organizing, in part because of Randolph's leadership, in part because as railway workers, porters carried black newspapers, pamphlets, and accounts of black resistance to nearly every town in the United States with a railroad depot and a black population.[13]

The Congress of Industrial Organizations (CIO), founded in 1935, which represented workers in some of the nation's largest manufacturers, tended to be more open to African American workers. During the Depression and World War II, as the CIO rapidly expanded, its leaders rallied workers around the slogan "black and white, unite and fight." This slogan was based on the argument that a unified workforce could more effectively challenge employers who profited from pitting the interests of black and white workers against each other. Still, many CIO unions did not challenge employers' use of racial classifications for assigning work. Even in some of the most racially progressive unions, such as the autoworkers, electrical workers, and steel-workers, blacks were trapped in unskilled jobs and seldom, if ever, were hired or promoted to well-paying skilled jobs.[14]

SYSTEMATIC HOUSING SEGREGATION

During the period of the Great Migration, northern whites, acting individually and collectively—and working through banks, real estate firms, and government—imposed a system of nearly complete segregation in the housing market. Racial segregation was not commonplace in the North before the Great Migration. In his pathbreaking study of Philadelphia (the northern city with the largest black population at the end of the 19th century), W. E. B. Du Bois found that blacks and whites lived close to each other. Later historians writing about Chicago, Cleveland, Detroit, and New York noted that African Americans tended to live in poor and working-class neighborhoods that were racially and ethnically heterogeneous.[15]

That pattern changed rapidly beginning in the 1920s. Nearly every new home built in white neighborhoods between 1920 and 1948 included racial restrictions in home titles, deeds, and rental agreements. Using the racial and ethnic classifications commonplace in the early 20th century, racially restrictive covenants forbade the occupancy or use of properties by groups other than "whites" or "Caucasians," and prevented the sale or rental of homes to "Negroes" (sometimes called Africans or Ethiopians) as well as Jews and sometimes Asians. Many northern municipalities became "sundown towns," posting signs forbidding the presence of African Americans after dark.[16]

Residential segregation took a more systematic form during the Great Depression. New government agencies (the Home Owners Loan Corporation, created in 1933; the Federal Housing Administration, in 1934, the Federal Home Loan Bank Board in 1937; and the Veterans Administration, in 1944), promoted home ownership by guaranteeing affordable home loans and mortgages. As a result of the loosening of credit, rates of homeownership skyrocketed in the United States. But federally backed loans and mortgages were generally unavailable to African Americans. The Home Owners Loan Corporation (HOLC), collaborating with local bankers and real estate brokers, prepared maps that ranked neighborhoods to determine the eligibility of properties for federally guaranteed mortgages and home loans. The HOLC designated neighborhoods as "the best" (A or green), "still desirable" (B or blue), "definitely declining" (C or yellow), and "hazardous" (D or red). Any neighborhood with even a handful of African Americans, unless they were live-in domestic servants, received a D rating.[17]

With access to affordable home mortgages and loans, whites moved in growing numbers to racially homogeneous suburbs, where banks refused to extend mortgages to African Americans. The result was the confinement of African Americans to what some at the time called "ghettos," including New York's Harlem, Chicago's Bronzeville, and Detroit's Paradise Valley, or in small black suburbs, mostly places with long-established black communities and self-built housing. Because African Americans did not have access to conventional mortgages, they had to resort to various forms of predatory lending, most commonly contract buying, which had high interest rates and substantial monthly charges. The majority of blacks in northern cities were trapped in rental housing, often in deteriorating neighborhoods. By the middle of the 20th century, the nation's most racially segregated metropolitan areas were all in the northeast and Midwest.[18]

EDUCATIONAL SEGREGATION

Many northern states had laws dating to the 19th century that forbade racial separation in schools; however, some states, including New York, New Jersey, and Indiana, permitted racially segregated public schools well into the 20th century. But even states where school segregation was forbidden by law, such statutes were seldom honored. In communities with small black populations, school districts built "colored" or "Negro" schools that all African American students were required to attend, regardless of where they lived. A traveler driving across the North could stop in nearly every town with a black population and find a school named after Abraham Lincoln, Thaddeus Stevens, or prominent black intellectuals such as Phyllis Wheatley or Arthur Dunbar and know by the school's name that it was segregated. If a town's black student population was not large enough to justify a separate school, districts regularly confined black students to their own classrooms. Some districts even required African Americans students to play in separate playgrounds. In bigger cities, school attendance zones tended to correspond with racially segregated neighborhoods. When the African American population expanded, school districts usually redrew or gerrymandered school boundaries to ensure that schools remained racially heterogeneous. Most districts also refused to hire African American teachers, except to teach African American students. Black teachers were almost always paid less than their white counterparts.[19]

VIOLENCE AND POLICING

In many African American neighborhoods in the North, the only whites present wore blue uniforms. Northern police forces were usually all white or nearly all white through the early 1970s. Urban African Americans were deeply distrustful of the police and mostly for good reason. White police officers regularly targeted blacks who ventured into white neighborhoods. They regularly harassed, threatened, and beat black suspects and arrestees. When whites attacked the homes of the first African Americans to move into formerly all-white neighborhoods, the police usually turned a

blind eye to window breaking, arson, and other vandalism. They seldom investigated racial incidents. And they usually refused to uphold laws that forbade racial discrimination in public places. Police regularly arrested African Americans who refused to give up their seats at white-only restaurants, even in states where such segregation was illegal. Instead, they often charged black protestors with disturbing the peace, trespassing, or resisting arrest. Even when the police were accused of negligence, harassment, or brutality, they were usually immune from discipline and seldom faced criminal charges. White judges and juries usually sympathized with the police and refused to convict uniformed officers of wrongdoing.[20]

COMMUNITY FORMATION AND POLITICAL MOBILIZATION

The Great Migration witnessed an intense period of community formation in African American neighborhoods throughout the north. Black-run institutions, including churches, civic clubs, fraternities and sororities, social service organizations, trade unions, and cultural organizations thrived in densely packed African American districts. So-called race businesses provided goods and services that whites would not provide to blacks. Migrant communities gave rise to the thriving culture of the "New Negro," particularly in Harlem and Chicago, where artists, poets, musicians, and authors used their work to celebrate black culture and challenge racial conventions. The concentration of population fostered a sense of community consciousness and became the basis for political organization and grassroots resistance to discrimination and segregation.[21]

As the northern African American population grew, the ranks of black elected officials swelled. Unlike in the South, where only a small percentage of blacks had the right to vote, northern blacks faced fewer obstacles to political participation. African Americans in northern cities used the power of the ballot box to gain patronage jobs and political recognition. In states where the electorate was closely divided between Democrats and Republicans, white politicians heeded the demands of their black constituents as a matter of political expediency. By the mid-1930s, however, urban blacks increasingly cast their political lot with the Democratic Party, largely because they benefited from New Deal social programs. Still, enough African American voters remained in the party of Lincoln through the 1960s to attract the attention of politicians of both parties. By mid-century, nearly all the largest northern cities, led by Chicago, had elected at least a few African Americans to office, including to school boards, city councils, state legislatures, and the US House of Representatives. They used their positions to pressure local, state, and federal governments to hire African Americans. The percentage of black public employees grew steadily in the decades following the New Deal, even if most of them worked in menial jobs, particularly janitorial and sanitation work. African Americans, especially in northern states with intense partisan competition, also pushed (often successfully) for the passage of local and state civil rights legislation, winning support from both parties.[22]

African Americans—still a small minority in most states—also pushed for social change through non-governmental organizations, most notably civil rights and racial advocacy organizations, many founded during the first wave of black migration northward. Some, like the United Negro Improvement Association, founded in 1919 and headquartered in Harlem, argued for black advancement through the creation of black-run businesses. Most northern cities also had vibrant chapters of the Booker T. Washington Business Association, a group that also promoted "race businesses." During the Depression, the Young Negroes' Co-Operative League, the Ladies Auxiliary of the Brotherhood of Sleeping Car Porters, and grassroots organizations in cities as diverse

as Buffalo, Chicago, Cleveland, Cincinnati, Gary, New York, Philadelphia, and Pittsburgh established cooperative grocery stores and cooperative credit unions to meet the needs of black consumers ill-served by white-dominated retailers and banks.[23]

Black women created a particularly extensive web of organizations committed to advancing the race, most of them particularly active in the North. The National Association of Colored Women's Clubs (founded in 1896), the Young Women's Christian Association, and various churchwomen's organizations promoted a politics of respectability among African American migrant women. African American sororities had an outsized influence in working to provide charitable assistance to black women. The National Council of Negro Women, founded in 1935, began as an organization promoting self-help and racial respectability but also grew increasingly active in protests and lobbied for local, state, and federal legislation to expand civil rights.[24]

Also committed to racial uplift was the National Urban League, founded in 1910. The Urban League conducted research on racial inequality in northern cities and provided social services and job training to black migrants as a vehicle for racial advancement. By the 1930s, the Urban League also joined efforts to challenge discrimination in housing, education, and employment. Urban League officials met with white employers to persuade them to hire black workers. In addition, the Urban League also collaborated with other civil rights organizations to advocate civil rights legislation on the local, state, and national levels, with special attention to laws forbidding workplace discrimination.[25]

The most influential civil rights organization in the 20th century was the National Association for the Advancement of Colored People (NAACP), founded in 1909. The largest secular African American–dominated mass membership organization in the country, the NAACP pushed for racial equality through anti-discrimination legislation, litigation, and grassroots protest. The NAACP energetically formed local branches in hundreds of cities and towns in the north. Grassroots NAACP activists supported national civil rights efforts, including anti-lynching legislation and the desegregation of the military, but also organized intensively on the local level against segregated housing, discrimination and unemployment, and separate and unequal public education. In the late 1930s, the NAACP took a leftward turn, in part prompted by the rise of the National Negro Congress (NNC), an umbrella organization that included socialists and Communists, churchwomen, and militant trade unionists. The NNC had large chapters in nearly every major northern city, but lost membership when it struggled with factional disputes between Communists and their critics, eventually collapsing during the Cold War. During the same period, the NAACP expanded its mission and grew rapidly. By the end of World War II, the NAACP had more than a half million members nationwide, with the largest share in the urban North. While the NAACP's central office dedicated its energy toward litigation around housing segregation, military desegregation, voting rights, labor discrimination, and especially southern school desegregation, its local branches, particularly in the North, directed much of their energy to local problems—full employment and fair employment in cities with major industrial unions; racially separate schools in smaller cities and suburbs; and anti-discrimination statutes in major cities—with little interference from the national office. Local branches varied in their base of support and tactics (some chapters were proudly proletarian and protest oriented, others were resolutely middle class and committed to fundraising and quiet lobbying. In large metropolitan areas, branches were always interracial; in smaller communities, they were often mostly black. Some branches were dominated by secular leftists, others closely associated with labor unions and still others tied to moderate religious leaders or black social clubs.[26]

CHALLENGING NORTHERN JIM CROW

As early as the 1920s, civil rights activists began to resist Jim Crow in northern public accommodations but only sporadically. Efforts to desegregate public accommodations intensified during World War II, particularly because of wartime anti-fascist rhetoric. How could America be fighting for victory against racist regimes abroad while African Americans faced second-class status at home? In Cincinnati, for example, civil rights activists fought to open up downtown movie theaters to black customers by slowing ticket lines. In Detroit, black activists, many affiliated with the United Automobile Workers, protested against racial exclusion in downtown restaurants, bars, and bowling alleys. The most influential group to challenge segregation in public accommodations was the Congress of Racial Equality (CORE), founded in Chicago in 1942. An interracial group, informed by Christian socialism and nonviolence, CORE held sit-ins at city restaurants that refused to serve African Americans. Sit-ins became one of the most successful tactics of the civil rights movement nationwide. CORE members engaged in wade-ins at swimming pools and similar protests at bowling alleys, roller rinks, and amusement parks throughout the North in the 1940s, 1950s, and early 1960s. Some of CORE's earliest members, among them Bayard Rustin and James Farmer, would travel southward in the 1950s, spreading the gospel of nonviolent resistance that they had honed in the North. Their efforts shaped the strategies of Reverend Martin Luther King Jr. and the Student Non-Violent Coordinating Committee, including lunch counter sit-ins and the Freedom Rides.[27]

Another tactic pioneered by northern activists was the use of paired black and white "testers," who visited restaurants and hotels demanding service. If whites were served and

1374 • THE BLACK FREEDOM STRUGGLE IN THE URBAN NORTH

blacks were not, activists filed discrimination complaints and publicized their efforts in the African American press. Slowly, these efforts succeeded in breaking down the barriers of segregation in the North and, at the same time, provided models for efforts to resist Jim Crow in commercial establishments south of the Mason-Dixon line. By the early 1960s, most northern restaurants and hotels served black customers, even if civil rights organizations fielded complaints about racial harassment, especially in dining establishments for decades more. But civil rights activists won pyrrhic victories against segregation in public pools, beaches, and amusement parks. Many cities closed pools rather than allowing blacks and whites to swim together. The 1960s witnessed a wave of urban amusement park closings as whites refused to send their children to integrated parks. In densely populated parts of the country, like the New Jersey shore and coastal Connecticut, municipalities restricted the use of beaches to local residents or required expensive beach passes—ostensibly color-blind measures designed to keep racial minorities out.[28]

OPENING THE WORKPLACE

Civil rights activists targeted workplaces, particularly during the Great Depression and World War II. One of the major grievances was the lack of jobs for African Americans in neighborhood stores. Some activists, particularly those associated with fledgling black nationalist organizations including the United Negro Improvement Association founded "race" businesses that hired black workers to sell to black customers. Many northern cities had chapters of the Booker T. Washington Business Association, a group founded to promote black business ownership. During the 1930s, black activists launched cooperatives in several cities. The most influential efforts in the 1930s involved "Don't Buy Where You Can't Work" campaigns, which boycotted white-owned businesses with no black employees.[29]

As African Americans migrated to northern cities in search of industrial employment, civil rights activists turned their attention to undermining workplace discrimination and in expanding job opportunities. Activist women, including Ella Baker and Anna Arnold Hedgeman, investigated and reported on the abysmal conditions of black women laundry workers and domestics who gathered in New York's infamous "slave market." The National Negro Congress teamed with labor organizers to promote the unionization of African American workers, particularly in the industrial North. The NAACP collaborated closely with the United Automobile Workers in the 1930s and early 1940s to organize at Ford and other auto and defense plants and fight workplace discrimination. In the late 1940s and early 1950s, the left-led National Negro Labor Council challenged workplace discrimination and led opposition to corporations that shut down plants in northern cities and moved production to suburbs, rural areas, and especially to the South, where workplace Jim Crow was nearly universal.[30]

As the United States mobilized industries for military production in 1940 and 1941, A. Philip Randolph launched the March on Washington Movement (MOWM), using the threat of a mass demonstration in the nation's capital to pressure President Franklin Delano Roosevelt to open employment in defense industries to black workers. In June 1941, in part to prevent the march, the president issued Executive Order 8802, which created the Fair Employment Practices Committee (FEPC) to investigate and prevent discrimination.[31] Supporters of the MOWM regrouped near the end of World War II to demand the creation of a permanent federal FEPC. At the state and local level, civil rights organizations, led by the NAACP, pushed for laws to forbid workplace discrimination. In California, one of the few states in the mid-20th century with a large multiracial population, labor and civil rights organizers attempted to build a coalition of African American, Mexican, and Asian workers, with mixed success, to challenge workplace discrimination and to expand employment opportunities. By 1964, twenty-four states, all of them in the North and West, had passed laws prohibiting workplace discrimination by race. Title VII of the 1964 Civil Rights Act, which forbade discrimination on the basis of race, as well as sex, national origin, and age, drew its language and legal frameworks from state laws.[32]

The passage of anti-discrimination laws did not, however, automatically break down workplace discrimination. Many state laws were relatively toothless. Rather than penalizing employers for the systematic exclusion of blacks, they required efforts to educate employers or put into place mediation programs to resolve discrimination cases on an individual basis. Likewise Title VII of the Civil Rights Act required expensive litigation. By the early 1960s, civil rights activists pushed for more aggressive efforts to open workplaces to African Americans. Increasingly, they turned their attention to the skilled trades, public employment, and the health-care sectors. During the mid- and late 1960s, protesters in Philadelphia, New York, Newark, St. Louis, Pittsburgh, and San Francisco mounted dramatic protests against discrimination in the building trades. In Philadelphia in 1963, protesters engaged in sit-ins at the mayor's office and picketed federally funded construction sites. That year and the next, in Queens, New York, black activists gathered outside a massive housing complex and a hospital, both under construction, and on one occasion chained themselves to a massive crane. In St. Louis, in 1965, demonstrators chained themselves atop the partially built Gateway Arch. All of them demanded more aggressive efforts to open lucrative construction jobs to blacks. In 1969, the Nixon administration, under pressure, required that all federal government contractors engage in affirmative action, setting aside jobs for minority workers.[33]

Under pressure from civil rights activists and litigators, local and state governments also instituted their own affirmative action programs, as did many colleges and universities. Anti-discrimination activists also targeted hospitals, usually located in or near urban African American neighborhoods, which provided a wide range of jobs, including janitorial and food service work, nursing, and surgery. In the aftermath of the urban uprisings of the 1960s, black protestors also targeted white-dominated police and fire departments, demanding jobs and usually facing fierce resistance. Although affirmative action was unpopular among whites, such policies led to dramatic increases in the number of black public employees, government-contracted workers, and students in selective colleges and universities. For the first time, big city police forces and fire departments opened their ranks to African American officers in significant numbers. Private employers, even those not bound by affirmative action requirements, also opened jobs to African Americans, especially women. Through the late 1950s, it was uncommon to see black women working in sales positions, or as secretaries, nurses, social workers, or clerks, except in black-owned firms. By the end of the 20th century, black women were well-represented in retail, clerical, health care, and social service professions.[34]

FAIR HOUSING

Civil rights activists in the North fought housing segregation, particularly during the World War II era, when segregation created a housing shortage, confining African Americans, especially wartime workers, to overcrowded and expensive housing. Lawyers, often working closely with local branches of the NAACP, filed suits challenging the legality of racially restrictive covenants in St. Louis, Chicago, and Detroit, among others. In California, where blacks, Mexican Americans, and Asian Americans experienced various degrees of discrimination in housing, civil rights activists and litigators attempted with mixed success to build interracial alliances to resist racial covenants and segregation. In a landmark 1948 case, *Shelley v. Kraemer*, the US Supreme Court ruled that racially restrictive covenants were legally unenforceable. Civil rights activists also charged private real estate developers with racial discrimination, including Metropolitan Life, which built large apartment complexes in New York, and builder Arthur Levitt, whose firm developed Levittowns in suburban New York, Pennsylvania, New Jersey, and elsewhere. Private racial discrimination proved more resistant to change. State and federal courts regularly ruled that the government could not interfere in private real estate transactions. [35]

Civil rights activists took two other tacks in the battle against housing segregation. In the 1940s, a coalition of religious groups and civil rights organizations launched fair or open housing campaigns, attempting to change the hearts and minds of white Americans about the desirability of black neighbors. Through films, pamphlets, and sermons, they made a case that housing discrimination was both immoral and economically irrational. At the same time, fair housing organizations lobbied local and state governments to enact laws that forbade racial discrimination in the sale or rental of housing. These campaigns bore fruit. By 1967, twenty-four states had enacted fair housing laws. Those laws become a model for the 1968 Fair Housing Act, passed by Congress in the aftermath of urban riots and the assassination of Rev. Martin Luther King Jr.[36]

Achieving the goal of fair housing proved to be difficult, however, even after the passage of anti-discrimination laws. Those laws were difficult and costly to enforce. Real estate brokers and lenders found all sorts of ways to avoid selling and renting homes to African Americans, including steering black homebuyers away from white neighborhoods and vice versa. Lenders continued to redline African American neighborhoods, leaving black homebuyers to the whims of the subprime and non-conventional lending market, with high interest rates, punitive fees, and a high risk of foreclosure. The federal Department of Housing and Urban Development faced protests and budget cuts, particularly during the 1970s and 1980s, after it attempted to subsidize public housing in suburbia. Many suburban communities enacted zoning laws or used ostensibly color-blind tools such as environmental impact laws to exclude affordable housing. And whites continued to vote with their feet, despite a liberalization of attitudes toward racial integration, picking up and leaving neighborhoods that attracted even a small percentage of African Americans. The result was that racial segregation lessened very slowly, especially in the northern metropolitan areas with large African American populations. In 2010, twenty-one of the nation's twenty-five most-segregated metropolitan areas were in the Northeast and Midwest.[37]

DESEGREGATING PUBLIC EDUCATION

The challenge to separate and unequal education also proceeded by fits and starts in the North. Throughout the 20th century, especially during World War II and the ensuing decade, grassroots activists in racially mixed suburbs and small towns in the North fought to abolish separate schools. Black mothers led school boycotts in dozens of towns, particularly in New York and New Jersey. The NAACP also went to state and federal court in support of parents in places as diverse as Hillburn, Hempstead, and New Rochelle, New York; Cairo, Illinois; and Trenton and Englewood, New Jersey. In the aftermath of the Supreme Court's landmark *Brown v. Board of Education* decision, activists increasingly turned their attention to big city school districts, leading massive student walkouts against overcrowded, underfunded, segregated schools in New York, Milwaukee, Cleveland, Chicago, Boston, and other cities throughout the first half of the 1960s.[38]

Civil rights attorneys, particularly the NAACP Legal Defense Fund, turned to federal courts in the 1960s and first half of the

1970s, backing parents and students who demanded quality, racially balanced schools for their children. Many early federal cases required intradistrict integration in districts that had a record of drawing school boundaries to maintain segregation, including New Rochelle, Pontiac, Michigan, and Denver, Colorado. Intradistrict plans could not, however, adequately deal with the fact that white families mostly avoided racial integration by moving outside of central city districts to majority or all-white suburban schools. As long as northern school district boundaries overlapped with segregated metropolitan housing patterns, it was impossible to create racial balance in public education. But metropolitan-wide desegregation ultimately fell with the Supreme Court's *Milliken v. Bradley* (1974) decision, which struck down a plan to bus children between the majority-black Detroit Public Schools and districts in dozens of surrounding all-white suburbs. The most prominent post-*Milliken* case involved Boston, where a federal court ordered intradistrict busing in lieu of a metropolitan-wide mandatory desegregation plan. Whites in Boston fiercely resisted school integration. Some majority-white suburban districts accepted African American students through a token, voluntary desegregation program; however, the pattern of racial imbalance across the metropolitan area was unchanged. As in Boston, big city school districts throughout the North, left to solve the problem of racial inequality in public education themselves without the option of regional solutions, experienced re-segregation, as whites continued to flee, leaving behind majority-minority public schools.[39]

While most African Americans supported racial integration, they put quality education at the top of their list. When big city districts did not integrate, they looked for alternatives. By the end of the 1960s, some activists, influenced by black power, called for community-controlled schools and, in some cities, pushed for Afrocentric education. Others pushed cities to create special interest or magnet schools

that would attract the most talented African American and white students. Some black activists embraced the idea of vouchers to send their children to private schools and school choice programs that would allow them to transfer to majority-white suburban schools. And by the 1990s, a wide interracial coalition of business and religious elites, foundations, and educational reformers advocated for the creation of charter schools, run by non-profits or businesses. From the late 1970s onward, black educational gains stagnated in most big city districts. And the emergence of large minority-dominated districts sapped political will in white-dominated state legislatures and in the US Congress for expanding funding for public education.[40]

RACE, POLICING, AND THE CARCERAL STATE

Racial disparities in policing and incarceration remained pressing and unresolved issues in the North. Throughout the 20th century (and beyond) civil rights organizations regularly fielded complaints from their constituents about police harassment and brutality. During the 1940s, left-leaning organizations, including the National Negro Congress and the Civil Rights Congress (CRC), publicized incidents of police brutality in both the North and the South. In its 1951 manifesto sent to the United Nations, "We Charge Genocide," the CRC charged that "the wanton killing of Negroes…is no longer a sectional phenomenon." Charges of police harassment mostly languished in the courts and were usually ignored by police departments. Police community relations worsened in the next few decades. Spurred by fears of juvenile delinquency and sensational accounts of gang violence in the 1950s, northern police departments stepped up activity, particularly on the borders of racially changing neighborhoods. Those efforts led to a full-blown crackdown on crime by the early 1960s. During the late 1950s and early 1960s, protests against police brutality intensified, often sparked by media coverage of the police beating and arresting civil rights protestors.

The fact that the vast majority of northern police were white greatly exacerbated tensions. Black newspapers regularly reported on police beatings, unwarranted arrests, and investigations and harassment of civil rights protestors. By 1963, in a period of intensifying civil rights protest and growing militancy nationwide, police departments began accumulating riot gear, preparing for what many saw as an impending race war. Those fears came to fruition in a series of long, hot summers. In 1964, African Americans angry about police violence took to the streets in Harlem, Rochester, and Philadelphia, looting stores and clashing with law enforcement officials. In 1965, the Watts neighborhood in Los Angeles exploded in the wake of rumors that police killed an unarmed black woman. In 1967, blacks rose up in 163 cities and towns, as small as Nyack, New York, and Plainfield, New Jersey, and as big as Detroit and Newark.

BLACK POWER

Many observers noted the coincidence of urban uprisings and the growing visibility of a movement demanding black power. The term "black power," popularized by Harlem-raised activist Stokely Carmichael in the fall of 1966, was less accurate as the description of a singular movement than as a name for a diverse impulse that had coursed through the black freedom struggle in the North at least since the Great Migration. Calls for black self-determination and self-defense waxed and waned in the period from the 1920s through the 1960s, but never fully disappeared. Groups like the Nation of Islam steadily expanded in the period following World War II, mostly without gaining media attention; the Universal Negro Improvement Association diminished in size but still had active chapters throughout the North; and black support for self-defense and racially separate institutions persisted. In the 1940s and

1950s, black activists in the United States drew inspiration from anticolonial struggles in Africa and Asia and increasingly adopted the language of self-determination. By the late 1950s, many black journalists and intellectuals increasingly argued that the plight of African Americans was like that of Africans yearning to free themselves from the yoke of colonization.[41]

In the early 1960s, newly formed black organizations, including the Deacons for Defense and the Revolutionary Action Movement argued that African Americans should take up arms against white oppression. Malcolm X and Robert F. Williams gained large followings in northern cities for their rejection of nonviolence. Calls for black power, self-defense, and separatism took fuel from the failures of civil rights in education, housing, and the workplace during the postwar years. And they drew inspiration from struggles against imperialism in Africa and the Caribbean. For most black power activists, the struggle for freedom in the United States was tied to resistance against apartheid in South Africa; independence movements in Algeria, Ghana, and the Congo; and revolutions in places as diverse as Cuba, Vietnam, and China.[42]

A growing cadre of black militants called for the celebration of African culture, the creation or reinvigoration of separate black institutions, and the unleashing of black economic power through black-owned businesses. One of the most enduring currents of black power celebrated African and African American cultures through art, music, clothing, and poetry. The Black Arts movement, which thrived in New York, Detroit, and Los Angeles, turned the visual arts, song, and verse into tools to create and reinforce a distinctive black communal ethos. Black power advocates adapted African dress (such as the dashiki), celebrated natural hairstyles, and created new celebrations and rituals (most notably the holiday of Kwanzaa) to create common identities.[43] Many of these efforts had analogues in the self-help, artistic, nationalist, and cooperative movements of the Great Migration era.

But black power was also shaped by distinctive features of postwar American culture. Many black militants called for the reassertion of a strong black masculinity, one that reinforced traditional notions of patriarchy. Some embraced the Second Amendment to the US Constitution, forming gun clubs and openly brandishing weapons on the streets. Others argued that white supremacy had psychologically damaged African Americans, drawing from postwar pop psychology. They argued that an emphasis on black pride and school curricula that valorized black heroes and black culture would bolster self-esteem and that African-influenced education would empower students who were marginalized by white teachers who used textbooks that denigrated people of African descent or ignored them altogether.[44]

Black power organizations were mostly small in membership and varied widely in their emphases. One observer hailed the rise of "cement-roots" organizations that promoted black advancement through community-run economic development and job training programs. The Black Panthers embraced Maoist ideas and also created community health and food distribution programs. The Revolutionary Union Movement pushed for black control on the shop floors of the auto industry. The Revolutionary Action Movement armed its small but ardent group of supporters for an upcoming race war. The Republic of New Afrika called for the United States to set aside land for an independent black nation. Nearly all of these organizations, for all of their different visions and strategies, faced intense repression by law enforcement officials, who infiltrated black radical organizations and introduced agents provocateurs who fueled intergroup rivalries and hatched violent schemes. Local police forces frequently raided black radical groups' offices and storefronts, regularly arrested and sometimes assassinated radical leaders, and charged them (often falsely) with petty and major crimes, including disorderly conduct, murder, and sedition.

The Federal Bureau of Investigation's COINTELPRO program infiltrated many black militant organizations, using agents to stir up factional rivalries and frame activists for conspiracies.[45]

LAW AND ORDER AND ITS DISCONTENTS

The combination of protest and rebellion led to urgent demands for a harsh new law-and-order politics. President Lyndon Johnson announced an ambitious "war on crime" and dramatically increased federal funding to police departments, which had long been supported by local tax revenue. Police departments purchased expensive military equipment and hired experienced military officials who were previously part of international counterinsurgency programs during the Cold War to provide training. The clamor for law and order became a central issue in local and national politics, leading big city majors to give license to harsh policing tactics and, increasingly, to state legislatures to pass laws that tightened sentencing. Alarmed by fears of a drug-infused counterculture that supposedly emanated from urban black culture, politicians launched a war on narcotics that led to stiffening sentences for the possession and sale of drugs. States also began expanding prison systems to accommodate those swept up in the anti-crime campaign—disproportionately African American men. The prison population expanded dramatically between the 1970s and the end of the first decade of the 21st century.[46]

In the 1970s, civil rights and black power activists turned their anger toward the prison system. Radical groups publicized the police and FBI infiltration of their organizations, and organized campaigns around the arrests or death of black activists. Mass prison uprisings in the 1970s, the most infamous at Attica in upstate New York, grew from prisoners' discontent at miserable conditions and everyday brutality behind bars. But prisoners' rights efforts were small in scale compared to what activists called the rise of the prison-industrial complex, a grim reality worsened by the long-term detention of arrestees and the emergence of long mandatory sentences for many crimes.[47]

The persistence of police brutality in the early 21st century, well documented by social media and on online news sources, fueled a new wave of outrage and grassroots organizing. In the early 2000s, activists complained of black motorists pulled over and harassed for "driving while black," leading to investigations of racial profiling. But nothing was more galvanizing than a wave of well-publicized police killings in Ferguson, Missouri; Chicago; Baltimore; New York; Minneapolis; and elsewhere. Beginning in 2014, protestors took to the streets in mass demonstrations on a larger scale than anything since the 1960s. Activists took to Twitter, using the hashtag Black Lives Matter, and sparking a new national movement working—as had past northern protests—through protest, litigation, and legislation, to resist ongoing racial injustice.[48]

DISCUSSION OF THE LITERATURE

Until recently, the history of civil rights in the South overshadowed the history of the African American freedom struggle in the North.[49] The North usually appeared as a tragic coda to the southern freedom struggle, usually in accounts of "the movement moving North" through protests led by the Reverend Martin Luther King Jr. in Chicago (1966) and accounts of racial conflicts that generated mass media attention, including the rise of the Black Panthers, debates about black power and community control in public education, and battles over school busing.[50] Journalists and historians paid disproportionate attention to the supposed backlash of northern working-class whites against black power and liberalism in the 1960s and 1970s, with special attention to just a few places, namely Brooklyn, where black power advocates and

urban Jews clashed over public education and affirmative action, and Boston, where blue-collar Irish and Italian Americans fiercely resisted racially integrated schools. Other accounts argued that well-meaning whites were alienated by black radicalism, urban riots, and skyrocketing rates of violent crime in northern cities. With few exceptions, influential accounts of race and politics in the North paid little heed to the deep roots of northern white opposition to racial equality, the long history of official and market-based segregation and discrimination in the North, or to the strategies, motivations, and ideology of black activists who fought for equality and rights.[51]

Conventional narratives of the civil rights movement rest also on a binary distinction between the South and North. They emphasize exceptional nature of southern racism, rooted in slavery, secession, racial terrorism, and systemic Jim Crow. Racism in the South, the conventional argument goes, was de jure—that is, legally mandated. Segregation in the North, by contrast, was de facto, the result of individual actions and prejudices or of ostensibly race-neutral market processes supposedly individualized and subtle. Histories of the freedom struggle in the South focused largely on non-violent struggles against violent, virulent white racism. Scholars downplayed the long history of black militancy and self-defense in the region, largely treating black militancy and black power as northern phenomena.[52]

Since the early 2000s, however, a slew of local and regional case studies of the black politics and activism outside the South and a handful of synthetic accounts, have reoriented our understandings of the black freedom struggle.[53] The most influential books and articles built on decades of work on urban and suburban history, on African American community life, and more generally on social and cultural, labor, and gender history, as well as on innovative work on grassroots politics. African American historiography laid the groundwork.

In the aftermath of the urban uprisings of the 1960s, urbanists focused on the rise of segregated black ghettos through detailed case studies of Harlem, Chicago, Cleveland, and Detroit.[54] Beginning in the 1980s, many African American historians challenged the paradigm of ghettoization, instead emphasizing community formation, with special attention to the role of black churches, fraternal organizations, and businesses in creating a common racial consciousness.[55] In the 1990s and 2000s, urban and political historians turned their attention to the racialization of public space, housing, and labor in the period following the New Deal, in what one historian called "the spatial turn" in American political history. These histories, for all of their strengths, usually gave only scant attention to institutional and grassroots efforts to battle against northern racial inequality.[56]

By the early 2000s, Jacqueline Dowd Hall made a strong case for revisionist histories of "the long civil rights movement," pushing the movement's chronology backward in time and rejecting "the myth of southern exceptionalism," thus expanding its geography northward and westward.[57] Rather than focusing on the "classic period" of civil rights history in the South from the Montgomery Bus Boycott through the assassination of Rev. King, long civil rights historians researched black-led grassroots social movements in Boston, Chicago, Detroit, Indianapolis, Los Angeles, Milwaukee, Newark, New York City, Oakland, Seattle, and St. Louis. Other historians wrote case studies of the black freedom struggle in smaller places such as Grand Rapids, Michigan; coastal Connecticut; and Wichita, Kansas. Many of these books emphasized radical politics and challenged conventional distinctions between civil rights and black power.[58]

A significant subset of newer northern civil rights histories focused on the origins of northern black activism during the Great Migration, turning their attention to groups that were underrepresented in earlier civil rights historiography, including black women activists and the politics of respectability and black girls and activism, and grassroots black internationalism.[59] An explosion of work on black radicalism, nationalism, and militancy, focusing on activism from the interwar years through the 1960s uncovered a history of demands for black self-determination, anti-colonialism, self-defense, and community control that long predated black power.[60] Historians of black leftism have offered fresh perspectives on the relationship of socialists and leftists to civil rights politics, including a spectrum of organizations ranging from the National Negro Congress, the Socialist Workers, the Brotherhood of Sleeping Car Porters, and the Communist Party. They have engaged in a robust debate about Communism and anti-Communism and whether or not the Cold War opened possibilities for civil rights activists or channeled civil rights demands away from a critique of capitalism and toward notions of individual rights.[61]

Scholars of civil rights in the North have also opened up new perspectives on civil rights litigation and legislation. For decades following the civil rights revolution, legal historians focused on key Supreme Court decisions and offered top-down histories of the NAACP's litigation strategies, usually through biographies of nationally known attorneys and close analyses of legal arguments, briefs, and opinions. Many influential legal scholars treated the NAACP's litigation strategy as tailored toward the black elite and narrowly focused on integration. Recently, however, a handful of scholars have turned their attention to local and state courts and to lesser-known attorneys, in the process shedding new light on the rich, variegated, and often contradictory history of civil rights lawyering. The history of civil rights law from below, still underdeveloped, has uncovered local cases dealing with restrictive covenants, criminal law, and educational segregation and neighborhood schooling that were often at odds with or irrelevant to the NAACP's southern-oriented litigation strategy. Recent books on anti-discrimination laws and their enforcement have also fruitfully explored intergroup conflict and collaboration, particularly around affirmative action.[62]

Recent years have seen an outpouring of scholarship on black power organizations, dominated by work on the Black Panther Party (BPP). The best of the new work on the BPP moves beyond polarized debates about the efficacy of its strategies of self-defense and its leaders' fiery rhetoric to rich accounts of its health and free breakfast programs, its relationship to a long history of black anticolonialism, its gender politics, and the political and strategic diversity of its many local chapters. Other black power groups, many of which received less media attention than the Panthers and, as a result have received far less scholarly attention, including CORE (after its shift to black nationalism), Maulana Karenga's US, the Revolutionary Action Movement, various Revolutionary Union Movements, the Young Lords, and the Republic of New Afrika.[63] Revisionists have shed fresh light on black power's gender politics, business and black power, black power and urban electoral politics, and the relationship of black power to conservatism.[64] Biographies of activists who spent much of their lives in the North have greatly enriched our understanding of the connections between civil rights and black power movements, among them Grace Lee Boggs and James Boggs, Stokely Carmichael, Amiri Baraka, Rosa Parks, and Malcolm X.[65]

Several pathbreaking works turned attention to what historian Lisa Levenstein has called "a movement without marches" largely led by black women, to improve public housing, challenge punitive welfare laws, and champion the rights of poor people. Recent books and articles have moved the history of the welfare rights and anti-poverty movements from the margins to the center of the field.[66] A topic that long received scant attention from urban, political, and African American historians—racially disparate policing and

incarceration—has sparked the rise of a new and rich subfield of books and articles about law and order politics, police brutality, the disparate racial impact of the war on drugs, and prison unrest and prisoner rights movements.[67]

A growing body of work has focused on connections between religion and the black freedom struggle. African American religious history is a booming subfield, incorporating work on black nationalist sects, including the early Nation of Islam, black churchwomen, and black liberation theology.[68] Several studies devoted attention to Roman Catholics who fought against the racial integration of their parishes and neighborhoods, and a small but vocal group of Catholics who supported civil rights.[69] Histories of black-Jewish relations have largely moved beyond the bitter debates about black power and allegations of anti-Semitism dating to the late 1960s to explore the complicated relationship between Jewish institutions and leaders who were often staunchly pro-civil rights and Jewish business leaders and ordinary urban Jews, who were frequently indifferent or hostile to racial integration.[70] The role of liberal white Protestants as allies of the civil rights movement has also attracted new attention.[71]

The scholarship on the black freedom struggle in the North—for all of the sweeping syntheses and detailed local case studies that have been published in recent years—remains incomplete. There are potentially hundreds of local studies to be written because nearly every city and town in the United States has its own, largely untold, civil rights and black power histories, with abundant materials in local archives, in the news media, in the records of national civil rights organizations with local chapters, and in still-to-be conducted oral histories of grassroots activists. Few historians have ventured deeply into the history of civil rights struggles after the 1970s (often misleadingly described as the "post-civil rights" era). Some recent historians have begun considering the legacy of the northern freedom struggle on early 21st-century politics, especially the election of Barack Obama and rise of the Black Lives Matter movement. As long as racial inequality persists, as long as the struggle for justice continues, the history of the northern freedom struggle will remain urgent.[72]

PRIMARY SOURCES

Any study of civil rights in the North must rely on the papers of the nation's leading civil rights organizations, which had national offices and local and state affiliates that challenged racial discrimination and segregation in the courts, lobbied city halls and the federal and state governments, and mobilized grassroots activists to fundraise and protest racial inequalities. The largest mass membership civil rights organization, the National Association for the Advancement for Colored People, has archives available in the Library of Congress and on microfilm. Most NAACP branches sent material to the national office, making the national records an indispensable source for state and local research. The National Urban League records, also on deposit at the Library of Congress, document the organization's investigations of discrimination and contain abundant material on topics as diverse as social services, employment discrimination, and federal and state civil rights legislation. The short-lived but influential National Negro Congress and Civil Rights Congress have papers on deposit at the Schomburg Center for Research in Black Culture and on microfilm. One of the largest repositories of civil rights records in the United States, the Schomburg Center includes the papers of many local activists and organizations in New York, as well as national organizations. The Schomburg's extraordinary vertical files, which include ephemeral pamphlets, posters, brochures, and publications are available at the library and on microfiche. The Mary McLeod Bethune Council House National Historic Site holds the National Archives for Black Women's History (https://www.nps.gov/mamc/learn/historyculture /nabwh_collections.htm), a collection that includes the records of The National Council of Negro Women and its affiliates. The Congress of Racial Equality papers, at the Wisconsin Historical Society, also digitized and on microfilm, span the period from World War II through the late 1960s, offering insight into grassroots protests and civil disobedience in many northern cities and on college campuses. They also illustrate the connections between the struggles for racial equality on both sides of the Mason-Dixon line. More and more archival collections are now digitized and available online, including the African American Studies collection of Gale's Archives Unbound (https://www.gale.com/primary-sources /archives-unbound-african-american-studies), which includes the records of many key civil rights organizations, individual activists, and Federal Bureau of Investigation dossiers on black radical groups.

The history of racial discrimination in the North may be documented in a number of important archives. For the federal role in housing segregation, the collections of the Federal Home Finance Board are held by the National Archives in Suitland, Maryland. Redlining maps, prepared by the Home Owners' Loan Corporation, are available online at *Mapping Inequality* (https://dsl.richmond .edu/panorama/redlining/#loc=4/36.71 /-96.93&opacity=0.8). The United States Civil Rights Commission published reports documenting segregation and discrimination in public education, housing, and policing. Its publications are available in government documents collections at major research libraries nationwide. The research papers of the National Advisory Commission on Civil Disorders, also known as the Kerner Commission, are available in full at the Lyndon Baines Johnson Library in Austin, Texas, and have been digitized by University Publications of America.

No history of the African American freedom struggle can be written without use of black newspapers and periodicals, many of which are fully digitized. Most African American newspapers circulated widely, well outside their cities of publication, and as a result often covered protests and organizations throughout the North. Of particular value because of the breadth of their readership are the *Baltimore Afro-American*, *Chicago Defender*, *Michigan Chronicle*, *New York Amsterdam News*, *Philadelphia Tribune*, and *Pittsburgh Courier*. Many incidents of racial discrimination and protests against them were never reported by white-owned newspapers, making the black press particularly important. In addition, researchers will find valuable material in *The Crisis*, the NAACP's monthly magazine, *Liberator Magazine* (1960–1971), and in scholarly periodicals, including the *Journal of Negro Education* and *Phylon*. These publications are widely available in research libraries.

FURTHER READING

Biondi, Martha. *To Stand and Fight: The Struggle for Civil Rights in Postwar New York City*. Cambridge, MA: Harvard University Press, 2003.

Countryman, Matthew. *Up South: Civil Rights and Black Power in Philadelphia*. Philadelphia: University of Pennsylvania Press, 2005.

Delmont, Matthew F. *Why Busing Failed: Race, Media, and the National Resistance to School Segregation*. Berkeley and Los Angeles: University of California Press, 2016.

Douglas, Davison M. *Jim Crow Moves North: The Battle Over Northern School Segregation, 1865–1954*. New York: Cambridge University Press, 2005.

Farmer, Ashley D. *Remaking Black Power: How Black Women Transformed an Era*. Chapel Hill: University of North Carolina Press, 2017.

Joseph, Peniel. *Waiting 'til the Midnight Hour: A Narrative History of Black Power*. New York: Henry Holt, 2006.

Meier, August, and Elliott Rudwick. *Along the Color Line: Explorations in the Black Experience*. Urbana: University of Illinois Press, 1976.

Nadesen, Premilla. *Welfare Warriors: The Welfare Rights Movement in the United States*. New York: Routledge, 2005.

Sokol, Jason. *All Eyes Are Upon Us: Race and Politics from Boston to Brooklyn*. New York: Basic Books, 2014.

Speltz, Mark. *North of Dixie: Civil Rights Photography Beyond the South*. Los Angeles: The J. Paul Getty Museum, 2015.

Sugrue, Thomas J. *Sweet Land of Liberty: The Forgotten Struggle for Civil Rights in the North*. New York: Random House, 2008.

Taylor, Keeanga-Yahmatta. *From #BlackLivesMatter to Black Liberation*. Chicago: Haymarket Books, 2016.

Theoharis, Jeanne F., and Komozi Woodard, eds. *Freedom North: Black Freedom Struggles Outside the South, 1940–1980*. New York: Palgrave, 2003.

Williams, Rhonda Y. *Concrete Demands: The Search for Black Power in the 20th Century*. New York: Routledge, 2015.

NOTES

1. Leon F. Litwack, *North of Slavery: The Negro in the Free States, 1790–1860* (Chicago: University of Chicago Press, 1961); Leslie Harris and Ira Berlin, eds., *Slavery in New York* (New York, NY: New Press, 2005); Sven Beckert, *The Empire of Cotton* (New York: Alfred A. Knopf, 2014); and Tiya Miles, *The Dawn of Detroit: A Chronicle of Slavery and Freedom in the City of the Straits* (New York: New Press, 2017).

2. Alexis de Tocqueville, *Democracy in America*, vol. 1 [1835], trans. Arthur Goldhammer, ed. Olivier Zunz (New York: Library of America, 2004), 396.

3. James Oliver Horton and Lois E. Horton, *In Hope of Liberty: Culture, Community, and Protest Among Northern Free Blacks, 1600–1860* (New York: Oxford University Press, 1997); Gary B. Nash and Jean R. Soderlund, *Freedom by Degrees: Emancipation in Pennsylvania and Its Aftermath* (New York: Oxford University Press, 1991); Litwack, *North of Slavery*; and Pauli Murray, ed., *States' Laws on Race and Color* [1951], reprint (Athens, GA: University of Georgia Press, 1997).

4. James N. Gregory, *Southern Diaspora: How the Great Migrations of Black and White Southerners Changed America* (Chapel Hill: University of North Carolina Press, 2005); James R. Grossman, *Land of Hope: Chicago, Black Southerners, and the Great Migration* (Chicago: University of

Chicago Press, 1989); Joe W. Trotter Jr., ed., *The Great Migration in Historical Perspective* (Bloomington: Indiana University Press, 1991); and Isabel Wilkerson, *The Warmth of Other Suns: The Epic Story of America's Great Migration* (New York: Random House, 2010).

5. Roberta Senechal, *The Sociogenesis of a Race Riot: Springfield Illinois in 1908* (Urbana: University of Illinois Press, 1990); William Tuttle, *Race Riot: Chicago in the Red Summer of 1919* (New York: Athenaeum, 1970); August Meier and Elliott Rudwick, *Along the Color Line: Explorations in the Black Experience* (Urbana: University of Illinois Press, 1976); David Allan Levine, *Internal Combustion: The Races in Detroit, 1915–1926* (Westport, CT: Greenwood Press, 1976); Domenic J. Capeci Jr., *The Harlem Riot of 1943* (Philadelphia: Temple University Press, 1977); and Elliott Rudwick, *Race Riot at East Saint Louis, July 2, 1917* (Urbana: University of Illinois Press, 1982).

6. Kenneth T. Jackson, *The Ku Klux Klan in the City* (New York: Oxford University Press, 1968); Leonard J. Moore, *Citizen Klansmen: The Ku Klux Klan in Indiana, 1921–1928* (Chapel Hill: University of North Carolina Press, 1991). Linda Gordon, *The Second Coming of the KKK: The Ku Klux Klan of the 1920s and the American Political Tradition* (New York: W. W. Norton, 2017); and Kevin M. Boyle, *Arc of Justice: A Saga of Race, Civil Rights, and Murder in the Jazz Age* (New York: Henry Holt, 2005).

7. Victoria Wolcott. *Race, Riots, and Roller Coasters: The Struggle over Segregated Recreation in America* (Philadelphia: University of Pennsylvania Press, 2012); for a general overview of patterns of Jim Crow in the North, see Sugrue, *Sweet Land*, chap. 5.

8. Nina Mjagkij, *Light in the Darkness: African Americans and the YMCA, 1852–1946* (Lexington: University Press of Kentucky, 2003); Nina Mjagkij and Margaret Pratt, eds. *Men and Women Adrift: The YMCA and YWCA in the City* (New York: New York University Press, 1997), see especially chapters 4 and 6–9; and Judith Weisenfeld, *African American Women and Christian Activism: New York's Black YWCA, 1905–45* (Cambridge, MA: Harvard University Press, 1997).

9. Jeff Wiltse, *Contested Waters: A Social History of Swimming Pools in America* (Chapel Hill: University of North Carolina Press, 2007); Wolcott, *Race, Riots, and Roller Coasters*; and

Bryant Simon, *Boardwalk of Dreams: Atlantic City and the Fate of Urban America* (New York: Oxford University Press, 2004).

10. Sugrue, *Sweet Land of Liberty*, chap. 3.

11. Robert H. Zieger, *For Jobs and Freedom: Race and Labor in America since 1865* (Lexington: University Press of Kentucky, 2010); Jacqueline Jones, *Labor of Love, Labor of Sorrow: Black Women, Work, and the Family from the Civil War to the Present* (New York: Basic Books, 1985); and Eric Arnesen, ed., *The Black Worker: Race. Labor, and Civil Rights Since Emancipation* (Urbana: University of Illinois Press, 2007), chapters 5, 8, 9, 11. The best overview of labor patterns for African American workers remains Robert C. Weaver, *Negro Labor: A National Problem* (New York: Harcourt, Brace, 1946).

12. David R. Roediger and Elizabeth D. Esch, *The Production of Difference: Race and the Management of Labor in U.S. History* (New York: Oxford University Press, 2012); Michael Reich, *Racial Inequality: A Political-Economic Analysis* (Princeton, NJ: Princeton University Press, 1981); David M. Gordon, Richard Edwards, and Michael Reich, *Segmented Work, Divided Workers: The Historical Transformation of Labor in the United States* (Cambridge: Cambridge University Press, 1982); Herbert Northrup et al., *Negro Employment in Basic Industry: A Study of Racial Policies in Six Industries* (Philadelphia: Wharton School, University of Pennsylvania, 1970); Beth Tompkins Bates, *The Making of Black Detroit in the Age of Henry Ford* (Chapel Hill: University of North Carolina Press, 2013); and Thomas J. Sugrue, *The Origins of the Urban Crisis: Race and Inequality in Postwar Detroit* (Princeton, NJ: Princeton University Press, 2014).

13. Beth Tompkins Bates, *Pullman Porters and the Rise of Protest Politics in Black America, 1925–1945* (Chapel Hill: University of North Carolina Press, 2001); Eric Arnesen, *Brotherhoods of Color: Black Railroad Workers and the Struggle for Equality* (Cambridge, MA, 2001), 84–115; and Melinda Chateauvert, *Marching Together: Women of the Brotherhood of Sleeping Car Porters* (Urbana: University of Illinois Press, 1998).

14. Robert H. Zieger, *The CIO, 1935–1955* (Chapel Hill: University of North Carolina Press, 2006); Robert Korstad and Nelson Lichtenstein, "Opportunities Found and Lost: Labor Radicals and the Early Civil Rights Movement," *Journal of*

American History 75 (1988): 786–811; Michael Goldfield, *Race and the CIO: The Possibilities for Racial. Egalitarianism During the 1930s and 1940s* (New York: Cambridge University Press, 1993). On the CIO, labor, and race generally, see Eric Shickler, *Racial Realignment: The Transformation of American Liberalism, 1932–1965* (Princeton, NJ: Princeton University Press, 2016); and Reuel Schiller, *Forging Rivals: Race, Class, Law, and the Collapse of Postwar Liberalism* (New York: Cambridge University Press, 2015).

15. W. E. B. Du Bois, *The Philadelphia Negro* (Philadelphia: University of Pennsylvania Press, 1899); and David M. Katzman, *Before the Ghetto: Black Detroit in the Nineteenth Century* (Urbana: University of Illinois Press, 1974).

16. Robert M. Fogelson, *Bourgeois Nightmares: Suburbia, 1870–1930* (New Haven, CT: Yale University Press, 2005); and James Loewen, *Sundown Towns: A Hidden Dimension of American Racism* (New York: New Press, 2005).

17. Louis Lee Woods II, "The Federal Home Loan Bank Board, Redlining, and the National Proliferation of Racial Lending Discrimination, 1921–1950," *Journal of Urban History* 38 (2012): 1036–1059; Kenneth T. Jackson, "Race, Ethnicity, and Real Estate Appraisal: The Home Owners' Loan Corporation and the Federal Housing Administration," *Journal of Urban History* 6 (1980): 419–452; and Robert K. Nelson et al., "Mapping Inequality", in *American Panorama*, ed. Robert K. Nelson and Edward L. Ayers (Richmond, VA: University of Richmond Digital Processing Lab, 2016). This site includes digitized HOLC appraisal maps for dozens of cities.

18. Arnold R. Hirsch, "With or Without Jim Crow: Black Residential Segregation in the United States," in *Urban Policy in Twentieth-Century America*, ed. Arnold R. Hirsch and Raymond A. Mohl (New Brunswick, NJ: Rutgers University Press, 1993), 65–99; Stephen Grant Meyer, *As Long As They Don't Move Next Door: Segregation and Racial Conflict in American Neighborhoods* (Lanham, MD: Rowman & Littlefield, 2000); Andrew Wiese, *Places of Their Own: African American Suburbanization in the Twentieth Century* (Chicago: University of Chicago Press, 2004); Beryl Satter, *Family Properties: Race, Real Estate, and the Exploitation of Black Urban America* (New York: Metropolitan Books, 2009); Douglas S. Massey and Nancy A. Denton,

American Apartheid: Segregation and the Making of the Urban Underclass (Cambridge, MA: Harvard University Press, 1993). Key case studies of ghetto formation include Gilbert Osofsky, *Harlem: The Making of a Ghetto, 1890–1930* (New York: Harper and Row, 1966); Gilbert Osofsky, "The Enduring Ghetto," *Journal of American History* 55 (1968): 243–255; Kenneth T. Kusmer, *A Ghetto Takes Shape: Black Cleveland, 1870–1930* (Urbana: University of Illinois Press, 1976); Thomas L. Philpott, *The Slum and the Ghetto: Neighborhood Deterioration and Reform, Chicago, 1880–1930* (New York: Oxford University Press, 1978); Allan H. Spear, *Black Chicago: The Making of a Negro Ghetto* (Chicago: University of Chicago Press, 1967); and Kenneth L. Kusmer, "The Black Urban Experience in American History," in *The State of Afro-American History: Past, Present, and Future*, ed. Darlene Clark Hine (Baton Rouge: Louisiana State University Press, 1986), 91–122. For a long view of history, see Mitchell Duneier, *Ghetto: The Invention of a Place, the History of an Idea* (New York: Farrar, Straus & Giroux, 2016).

19. Davison M. Douglas, *Jim Crow Moves North: The Battle over Northern School Segregation, 1865–1954* (New York: Cambridge University Press, 2005); Sugrue, *Sweet Land of Liberty*, chapters 6 and 13; Matthew D. Lassiter, "De Jure/De Facto Segregation: The Long Shadow of a National Myth," in *The Myth of Southern Exceptionalism*, ed. Lassiter and Joseph Crespino (New York: Oxford University Press, 2009), 25–48; for case studies, see Emily E. Straus, *Death of a Suburban Dream: Race and Schools in Compton, California* (Philadelphia: University of Pennsylvania Press, 2014); Jack Dougherty, *More than One Struggle: The Evolution of Black School Reform in Milwaukee* (Chapel Hill: University of North Carolina Press, 2004); Vincent P. Franklin, *The Education of Black Philadelphia: The Social and Educational History of a Minority Community, 1900–1950* (Philadelphia: University of Pennsylvania Press, 1979); Michael W. Homel, *Down From Equality: Black Chicagoans and the Public Schools, 1920–41* (Urbana: University of Illinois Press, 1984); and August Meier and Elliott Rudwick, *Along the Color Line: Explorations in the Black Experience* (Urbana: University of Illinois Press, 1976), 312–314, 359–362, 376–377.

20. *Report of the National Advisory Commission on Civil Disorder* (Washington, DC: US Government Printing Office, 1968); Marilynn Johnson, *Street Justice: A History of Police Violence in New York City* (Boston: Beacon Press, 2003); Clarence Taylor, *Fight the Power: African Americans and the Long History of Police in New York* City (New York: New York University Press, 2018); and Andrew J. Diamond, *Mean Streets: Chicago Youths and the Everyday Struggle for Empowerment in the Multiracial City, 1908–1969* (Berkeley and Los Angeles: University of California Press, 2009), includes an extensive discussion of police and black youth. More generally, see "Special Issue: African Americans, Police Brutality, and the U.S. Criminal Justice System: Historical Perspectives," *Journal of African American History* 98, no. 2 (2013): 197–303.

21. Eric Arnesen, *Black Protest and the Great Migration: A Brief History with Documents* (Boston: Bedford Books, 2002); Grossman, *Land of Hope*; Robert S. Gregg, *Sparks from the Anvil of Oppression: Philadelphia's African Methodists and Southern Migrants, 1890–1940* (Philadelphia: Temple University Press, 1993); Joe William Trotter, *Black Milwaukee: The Making of an Industrial Proletariat, 1915–1945* (Urbana: University of Illinois Press, 1985), 123–124, 127–129; Richard Walter Thomas, *Life for Us Is What We Make It: Building Black Community in Detroit, 1915–1945* (Bloomington: Indiana University Press, 1992); Richard B. Pierce, *Polite Protest: The Political Economy of Race in Indianapolis, 1920–1970* (Bloomington: Indiana University Press, 2005); Kimberley L. Phillips, *AlabamaNorth: African American Migrants, Community, and Working-Class Activism in Cleveland, 1915–45* (Urbana: University of Illinois Press, 2009); Nathan Irvin Huggins, *Harlem Renaissance* (New York: Oxford University Press, 1971); David Levering Lewis, *When Harlem Was in Vogue* (New York: Alfred A. Knopf, 1981); Cheryl Lynn Greenberg, *Or Does It Explode? Black Harlem in the Great Depression* (New York: Oxford University Press, 1991); Shannon King, *Whose Harlem Is This, Anyway? Community Politics and Grassroots Activism During the New Negro Era* (New York: New York University Press, 2015); Davarian Baldwin, *Chicago's New Negroes: Modernity, the Great Migration, and Black Urban Life* (Chapel Hill: University of North Carolina

Press, 2007); and Darlene Clark Hine and John McCluskey Jr., eds., *The Black Chicago Renaissance* (Urbana: University of Illinois Press, 2012); and Adam Green, *Selling the Race: Culture and Community in Black Chicago, 1940–55* (Chicago: University of Chicago Press, 2007).

22. Harvard Sitkoff, *A New Deal for Blacks: The Emergence of Civil Rights as a National Issue: The Depression Decade* (New York: Oxford University Press, 1978); Nancy Weiss, *Farewell to the Party of Lincoln: Black Politics in the Age of FDR* (Princeton, NJ: Princeton University Press, 1983); James Wolfinger, *Philadelphia Divided: Race and Politics in the City of Brotherly Love* (Chapel Hill: University of North Carolina Press, 2011); Jeffrey Helgeson, *Crucible of Black Empowerment: Chicago's Neighborhood Politics from the New Deal to Harold Washington* (Chicago: University of Chicago Press, 2014); Jason Sokol, *All Eyes Are Upon Us: Race and Politics from Boston to Brooklyn* (New York: Basic Books, 2014); Leah Wright Rigeur, *The Loneliness of the Black Republican: Pragmatic Politics and the Pursuit of Power* (Princeton, NJ: Princeton University Press, 2015); and Joshua D. Farrington, *Black Republicans and the Transformation of the GOP* (Philadelphia: University of Pennsylvania Press, 2016).

23. Robert E. Weems Jr., *Desegregating the Dollar: African American Consumerism in the Twentieth Century* (New York: NYU Press, 1998); and Jessica Gordon Nembhard, *Collective Courage: A History of African American Cooperative Economic Thought and Practice* (University Park: Pennsylvania State University Press, 2014).

24. Darlene Clark Hine, "Black Migration to the Urban Midwest: The Gender Dimension, 1915–1945," in Trotter, *The Great Migration*, 127–146; and Hine, "'We Specialize in the Wholly Impossible' The Philanthropic Work of Black Women," in *Lady Bountiful Revisited: Women, Philanthropy, and Power*, ed. Kathleen D. McCarthy (New Brunswick, NJ: Rutgers University Press, 1990), 70–93; Elsa Barkley Brown, "Womanist Consciousness," *Signs* 14 (1989): 610–633; Dorothy Salem, *To Better Our World: Black Women in Organized Reform, 1890–1920* (New York: Carlson, 1990); Paula Giddings, *When and Where I Enter: The Impact of Black Women on Race and Sex in America* (New York: Viking,

1984); Deborah Gray White, *Too Heavy a Load: Black Women in Defense of Themselves, 1894–1994* (New York: W. W. Norton, 1999); V. P. Franklin and Bettye Collier-Thomas, "For the Race in General and Black Women in Particular: The Civil Rights Activities of African American Women's Organizations, 1915–1950," in *Sisters in the Struggle*, ed. Collier-Thomas and Franklin, 21–41; Victoria Wolcott, *Remaking Respectability: African American Women in Interwar Detroit* (Chapel Hill: University of North Carolina Press, 2001); Gretchen Lemke-Santangelo, *Abiding Courage: African American Migrant Women and the East Bay Community* (Chapel Hill: University of North Carolina Press, 1996); Anne Meis Knupfer, *The Chicago Black Renaissance and Women's Activism* (Urbana: University of Illinois Press, 2006); and Lisa Krissoff Boehm, *Making a Way Out of No Way: African American Women and the Second Great Migration* (Jackson: University Press of Mississippi, 2009).

25. Touré F. Reed, *Not Alms But Opportunity: The Urban League and the Politics of Racial Uplift, 1910–1950* (Chapel Hill: University of North Carolina Press, 2008); Nancy J. Weiss, *The National Urban League, 1910–1940* (New York: Oxford University Press, 1974): Nancy J. Weiss, *Whitney M. Young, Jr. and the Struggle for Civil Rights* (Princeton, NJ: Princeton University Press, 1989); and Dennis C. Dickerson, *Militant Mediator: Whitney M. Young, Jr.* (Lexington: University Press of Kentucky, 1998).

26. Gilbert Jonas, *Freedom's Sword: The NAACP and the Struggle Against Racism in America, 1909–1969* (New York: New Press, 2004); Manfred Berg, *The Ticket to Freedom: The NAACP and the Struggle for Black Political Integration* (Gainesville: University Press of Florida, 2005); Christopher Robert Reed, *The Chicago NAACP and the Rise of Black Professional Leadership* (Bloomington: Indiana University Press, 1997); Patricia A. Sullivan, *Lift Every Voice: The NAACP and the Making of the Civil Rights Movement* (New York: New Press, 2009); Kenneth Janken, *White: The Biography of Walter White, Mr. NAACP* (New York: New Press, 2003); and Beth Tompkins Bates, "A New Crowd Challenges the Agenda of the Old Guard in the NAACP, 1933–1941," *American Historical Review* 102 (1997): 340–377.

27. Meier and Rudwick, *CORE*; James Tracy, *Direct Action: Radical Pacifism from the Union Seven to the Chicago Eight* (Chicago: University of Chicago Press, 1996), 14–15; and John D'Emilio, *Lost Prophet: The Life and Times of Bayard Rustin* (New York: Free Press, 2003).

28. Sugrue, *Sweet Land*, chap. 5; Wolcott, *Race, Riots and Roller Coasters*, Simon, *Boardwalk of Dreams*; and Andrew W. Kahrl, *Free the Beaches: The Story of Ned Coll and the and the Battle for America's Most Exclusive Shoreline* (New Haven, CT: Yale University Press, 2018).

29. Meier and Rudwick, *Along the Color Line*, 314–332; Trotter, *Black Milwaukee*, 125–127, 134–135; Richard W. Thomas, *Life for Us Is What We Make It: Building the Black Community in Detroit, 1915–45* (Bloomington: Indiana University Press, 1992), 194–201; Andor Skotnes, "'Buy Where You Can Work:' Boycotting for Jobs in African-American Baltimore, 1933–34," *Journal of Social History* 27 (1994): 735–762; and Jeffrey Helgeson, "'Don't Buy Where You Can't Work' Campaigns," in *Encyclopedia of U.S. Labor and Working-Class History*, vol. 1, ed. Eric Arnesen (New York: Routledge, 2006), 380–382.

30. Barbara Ransby, *Ella Baker and the Black Freedom Movement: A Radical Democratic Vision* (Chapel Hill: University of North Carolina Press, 2003); Sugrue, *Sweet Land of Liberty*, chaps. 1 and 2; Meier and Rudwick, *Black Detroit and the Rise of the UAW*; Bates, *Making of Black Detroit*; Kevin Boyle, "There Are No Sorrows the Union Cannot Heal": The Struggle for Racial Equality in the UAW, 1940–60, *Labor History* 36 (1995): 5–23; Bruce Nelson, *Divided We Stand: American Workers and the Struggle for Black Equality* (Princeton, NJ: Princeton University Press, 2001); Rick Halpern, *Down on the Killing Floor: Black and White Workers in Chicago's Packinghouses, 1904–1954* (Urbana: University of Illinois Press, 1997); Roger Horowitz, "*Negro and White, Unite and Fight!*": *A Social History of Industrial Unionism in Meatpacking, 1930–90* (Urbana: University of Illinois Press, 1997); Ruth Needleman, *Black Freedom Fighters in Steel: The Struggle for Democratic Unionism* (Ithaca, NY: ILR Press, 2003); Megan Taylor Shockley, *We, Too, Are Americans: African American Women in Detroit and Richmond, 1940–54* (Urbana: University of Illinois Press, 2003) and generally, Robert H. Zieger, *For Jobs and Freedom: Race*

and *Labor in America since 1865* (Lexington: University Press of Kentucky, 2010); and Paul Moreno, *Black Americans and Organized Labor: A New History* (Baton Rouge: Louisiana State University Press, 2006).

31. William P. Jones, *The March on Washington: Jobs, Freedom, and the Forgotten History of Civil Rights* (New York: W. W. Norton, 2013), chaps. 1 and 2; Bates, *Pullman Porters and the Rise of Black Protest*; Paula E. Pfeffer, *A. Philip Randolph: Pioneer of the Civil Rights Movement* (Baton Rouge: Louisiana State University Press, 1990); and Herbert Garfinkel, *When Negroes March* (Glencoe, IL: Free Press, 1959).

32. Merl Reed, *Seedtime for the Modern Civil Rights Movement: The President's Committee on Fair Employment Practice, 1941–46* (Baton Rouge: Louisiana State University Press,1991); Andrew Edmund Kersten, *Race, Jobs, and the War: The FEPC in the Midwest, 1941–46* (Urbana: University of Illinois Press, 2000); Anthony Chen, *The Fifth Freedom: Jobs, Politics, and Civil Rights in the United States, 1941–1972* (Princeton, NJ: Princeton University Press, 2009); Duane Lockard, *Toward Equal Opportunity: A Study of State and Local Antidiscrimination Laws* (London: Macmillan, 1968); and Hugh Davis Graham, *The Civil Rights Era: Origins and Development of National Policy* (New York: Oxford University Press, 1990). On interracial organizing efforts in California, see Mark Brilliant, *The Color of America Has Changed: How Racial Diversity Shaped Civil Rights Reform in California, 1941–1978* (New York: Oxford University Press, 2010).

33. John David Skrentny, *The Ironies of Affirmative Action* (Chicago: University of Chicago Press 1996); Nancy MacLean, *Freedom Is Not Enough: The Opening of the American Workplace* (Cambridge, MA: Harvard University Press, 2006); Thomas J. Sugrue, "Affirmative Action From Below: Civil Rights, the Building Trades, and the Politics of Racial Equality in the North, 1945–1969," *Journal of American History* 91 (2004): 145–173; Stacy Kinlock Sewell, "The 'Not-Buying Power' of the Black Community: Equal Employment Opportunity in the Civil Rights Movement, 1960-1964," *Journal of African American History* 89, no. 2 (2004): 135–151; and David Goldberg and Trevor Griffey, eds., *Black Power at Work: Community Control, Affirmative Action, and the Construction Industry* (Ithaca, NY: Cornell University Press, 2010).

34. Francis P. Ryan, *AFSCME's Philadelphia Story: Municipal Workers and Urban Power in the Twentieth Century* (Philadelphia: Temple University Press, 2011); Dennis Deslippe, *Protesting Affirmative Action: The Struggle over Equality after the Civil Rights Revolution* (Baltimore: Johns Hopkins University Press, 2012); David Goldberg, *Black Firefighters and the FDNY: The Struggle for Jobs, Justice, and Equity in New York City* (Chapel Hill: University of North Carolina Press, 2017); and Thomas J. Sugrue, "'The Largest Civil Rights Organization Today': Title VII and the Transformation of the Public Sector," *Labor: Studies in Working Class History of the Americas* 11, no. 3 (2014): 25–29.

35. Clement Vose, *Caucasians Only: The Supreme Court, the NAACP, and the Restrictive Covenant Cases* (Berkeley: University of California Press, 1959); and Jeffrey D. Gonda, *Unjust Deeds: The Restrictive Covenant Cases and the Making of the Civil Rights Movement* (Chapel Hill: University of North Carolina Press, 2015). On California, see Scott Kursashige, *The Shifting Grounds of Race: Black and Japanese Americans in the Making of Multiethnic Los Angeles* (Princeton, NJ: Princeton University Press, 2008); Shana Bernstein, *Bridges of Reform: Interracial Civil Rights Activism in Twentieth-Century Los Angeles* (New York: Oxford University Press, 2011); Martha Biondi, *To Stand and Fight: The Struggle for Civil Rights in Postwar New York City* (Cambridge, MA: Harvard University Press, 2003); Sugrue, *Sweet Land of Liberty*; and Dianne Harris, ed., *Second Suburb: Levittown, Pennsylvania* (Pittsburgh, PA: University of Pittsburgh Press, 2010).

36. See generally, Juliet Saltman, *Open Housing as a Social Movement* (Lexington, MA: Heath, 1971); Sugrue, *Sweet Land of Liberty*, chapters 7 and 12; for case studies, see Abigail Perkiss, *Making Good Neighbors: Civil Rights, Liberalism, and Integration in Postwar Philadelphia* (Ithaca, NY: Cornell University Press, 2014); Lily Geismer, *Don't Blame Us: Suburban Liberals and the Transformation of the Democratic Party* (Princeton, NJ: Princeton University Press, 2015), chapter 2; and Sidney M. Fine, "Michigan and Housing Discrimination, 1949–1968," *Michigan Historical Review* 23, no. 2 (1997): 81–114;

data on state laws from Lockard, *Toward Equal Opportunity*.

37. Christopher Bonastia, *Knocking on the Door: The Federal Government's Attempt to Desegregate the Suburbs* (Princeton, NJ: Princeton University Press, 2006); Gregory D. Squires, ed., *The Fight for Fair Housing: Causes, Consequences and Future Implications of the 1968 Federal Fair Housing Act* (New York: Routledge, 2018).

38. For a discussion of many of these cases, see Sugrue, *Sweet Land of Liberty*, chap. 13; see also Jack Dougherty, *More than One Struggle: The Evolution of Black School Reform in Milwaukee* (Chapel Hill: University of North Carolina Press, 2004); and Clarence Taylor, *Milton A. Galamison and the Struggle to Integrate New York City's Public Schools* (New York: Columbia University Press, 1997).

39. *Milliken v. Bradley*, 418 U.S. 717 (1974); 188–189, 192–193, 258–259, 261; Paul R. Dimond, *Beyond Busing: Inside the Challenge to Urban Segregation* (Ann Arbor: University of Michigan Press, 1985); Jeffrey Mirel, *The Rise and Fall of an Urban School System: Detroit, 1907–1981* (Ann Arbor: University of Michigan Press, 1993). Anthony Lukas, *Common Ground: A Turbulent Decade in the Lives of Three American Families* (New York: Knopf, Alfred A. 1986); Ronald Formisano, *Boston Against Busing: Race, Class, and Ethnicity in the 1960s and 1970s* (Chapel Hill: University of North Carolina Press, 1991); Jeanne Theoharis, "'We Saved the City: Black Struggles Against Educational Inequality in Boston, 1960–76," *Radical History Review* 81 (2001): 61–93; Jeanne Theoharis and Matthew Delmont, eds., "Special Section: Rethinking the Boston Busing Crisis," *Journal of Urban History* 43 (2017): 191–293; and Geismer, *Don't Blame Us*, chap. 3.

40. Jennifer Hochschild and Nathan Skovronick, *The American Dream and the Public Schools* (New York: Oxford University Press, 2003); Gary Orfield, Susan Eaton, and the Harvard Project on School Desegregation, *Dismantling Desegregation: The Quiet Reversal of Brown v. Board of Education* (New York: The New Press, 1996); Michael B. Katz and Mike Rose, eds., *Public Education Under Siege* (Philadelphia: University of Pennsylvania Press, 2013); and Dougherty, *More Than One Struggle*; and Straus, *Death of a Suburban Dream*.

41. Rhonda Y. Williams, *Concrete Demands: The Search for Black Power in the 20th Century* (New York: Routledge, 2015); Peniel Joseph, *Waiting Til the Midnight Hour: A Narrative History of Black Power in America* (New York: Henry Holt, 2006); Keisha Blain, *Set the World on Fire: Black Nationalist Women and the Global Struggle for Freedom* (Philadelphia: University of Pennsylvania Press, 2018); Dayo F. Gore, *Radicalism at the Crossroads: African American Women Activists in the Cold War* (New York: NYU Press, 2011); Penny von Eschen, *Race Against Empire: Black Americans and Anticolonialism, 1937–57* (Ithaca, NY: Cornell University Press, 1997); Brenda Gayle Plummer, *In Search of Power: African Americans in the Era of Decolonization, 1956–1974* (New York: Cambridge University Press, 2013); Robin D. G. Kelley, *Freedom Dreams: The Black Radical Imagination* (Boston: Beacon Press, 2002); Peniel Joseph, ed., *The Black Power Movement: Rethinking the Civil Rights-Black Power Era* (New York: Routledge, 2005); Dean E. Robinson, *Black Nationalism in American Politics and Thought* (Cambridge: Cambridge University Press, 2001); and Rod Bush, *We Are Not What We Seem: Black Nationalism and Class Struggle in the American Century* (New York: New York University Press, 1999).

42. Simon Wendt, *The Spirit and the Shotgun: Armed Resistance and the Struggle for Civil Rights* (Gainesville: University Press of Florida, 2017); Timothy Tyson, *Radio Free Dixie: Robert F. Williams and the Roots of Black Power* (Chapel Hill: University of North Carolina Press, 1999); Joshua Bloom and Waldo E. Martin Jr., *Black Against Empire: The History and Politics of the Black Panther Party* (Berkeley and Los Angeles: University of California Press, 2013); Sean L. Malloy, *Out of Oakland: Black Panther Party Internationalism during the Cold War* (Ithaca, NY: Cornell University Press, 2017); and Nico Slate, ed., *Black Power beyond Borders: The Global Dimensions of the Black Power Movement* (New York: Palgrave Macmillan, 2012).

43. Tanisha C. Ford, *Liberated Threads: Black Women, Style, and the Global Politics of Soul* (Chapel Hill: University of North Carolina Press, 2015); James Smethurst, *The Black Arts Movement: Literary Nationalism in the 1960s and 1970s* (Chapel Hill: University of North Carolina Press, 2005); Scot

Brown. *Fighting for Us: Maulana Karenga, the US Organization, and Black Cultural Nationalism* (New York: New York University Press, 2003); William Van Deburg, *New Day in Babylon: The Black Power Movement in American Culture, 1965–1975* (Chicago: University of Chicago Press, 1992); and Laura Warren Hill and Julia Rabig, eds., *The Business of Black Power: Corporate Responsibility, Community Development, and Capitalism in Post-War America* (Rochester, NY: University of Rochester Press, 2012).

44. Jeffrey O. G. Ogbar, *Black Power: Radical Politics and African American Identity* (Baltimore: Johns Hopkins University Press, 2004); William L. Van Deburg, *Black Camelot: African American Culture Heroes in their Times, 1960–1980* (Chicago: University of Chicago Press, 1997), Daryl M. Scott, *Contempt and Pity: Social Policy and the Image of the Damaged Black Psyche, 1880–1996* (Chapel Hill: University of North Carolina Press, 2004), chapter 9; and Russell Rickford, *We Are an African People: Independent Education, Black Power, and the Radical Imagination* (New York: Oxford University Press, 2016).

45. Sugrue, *Sweet Land*, chap. 10;

46. Heather Ann Thompson, "Why Mass Incarceration Matters: Rethinking Crisis, Decline, and Transformation in Postwar American History," *Journal of American History* 97 (2010): 703–734; Naomi Murakawa, *The First Civil Right: How Liberals Built Prison America* (New York: Oxford University Press, 2014); Michael Flamm, *Law and Order: Street Crime, Civil Unrest, and the Crisis of Liberalism in the 1960s* (New York: Columbia University Press, 2005); Marie Gottschalk, *Caught: The Prison State and the Lockdown of American Politics* (Princeton, NJ: Princeton University Press, 2014); Ruth Wilson Gilmore, *Golden Gulag: Prisons, Surplus, Crisis and Opposition in Globalizing California* (Berkeley: University of California Press, 2007); and Heather Ann Thompson and Donna Murch, eds., "Special Section: Urban America and the Carceral State," *Journal of Urban History* 41 (2015): 751–824.

47. Dan Berger, *Captive Nation: Black Prison Organizing in the Civil Rights Era* (Chapel Hill: University of North Carolina Press, 2014); Heather Ann Thompson, *Blood in the Water: The Attica Prison Uprising of 1971 and Its Legacy* (New York: Pantheon Books, 2017); Dan Berger and Toussaint Losier, *Rethinking the American Prison Movement* (New York: Routledge, 2017); Michelle Alexander, *The New Jim Crow: Mass Incarceration in an Era of Colorblindness* (New York: New Press, 2010); and John F. Pfaff, *Locked In: The True Causes of Mass Incarceration and How to Achieve Real Reform* (New York: Basic Books, 2017).

48. Christopher J. Lebron, *The Making of Black Lives Matter: A Brief History of an Idea* (New York: Oxford University Press, 2017); and Keeanga-Yahmatta Taylor, *From #BlackLivesMatter to Black Liberation* (Chicago: Haymarket Books, 2016).

49. For exceptions, see the work of August Meier and Elliot Rudwick, particularly *CORE: A Study in the Civil Rights Movement, 1942–1968* (New York: Oxford University Press, 1973); *Along the Color Line: Explorations in the Black Experience* (Urbana: University of Illinois Press, 1976); and *Black Detroit and the Rise of the UAW*.

50. Alan B. Anderson and George W. Pickering, *Confronting the Color Line: The Broken Promise of the Civil Rights Movement in Chicago* (Athens, GA: University of Georgia Press, 1986); Martin Mayer, *The Teachers Strike, New York, 1968* (New York: Harper and Row, 1969); Marilyn Gittell and Maurice Berube, eds., *Confrontation at Ocean Hlll-Brownsville* (New York: Praeger, 1969); Daniel H. Perlstein, *Justice, Justice: School Politics and the Eclipse of Liberalism* (New York: Peter Lang, 2004); Richard Kahlenberg, *Tough Liberal: Albert Shanker and the Battle Over Schools, Unions, Race, and Democracy* (New York: Columbia University Press, 2007); Jonathan Rieder, *Canarsie: The Jews and Italians of Brooklyn against Liberalism* (Cambridge, MA: Harvard University Press, 1985); J. Anthony Lukas, *Common Ground: A Turbulent Decade in the Lives of Three American Families* (New York: Knopf, 1986); Ronald Formisano, *Boston Against Busing: Race and Ethnicity in the 1960s and 1970s* (Chapel Hill: University of North Carolina Press, 1991). Important early correctives to this scholarship include James Ralph, *Northern Protest: Martin Luther King, Jr., Chicago, and the Civil Rights Movement* (Cambridge, MA: Harvard University Press, 1993); and Jerald Podair, *The Strike that Changed New York: Blacks, Whites, and the Ocean Hill-Brownsville Crisis* (New Haven, CT: Yale University Press, 2002).

51. Synthetic accounts that solidified the conventional wisdom about white backlash and black radical excesses include Allen Matusow, *The Unraveling of America: A History of Liberalism in the 1960s* (New York, NY: Harper and Row, 1984); Jonathan Rieder, "The Rise of the 'Silent Majority,'" in *The Rise and Fall of the New Deal Order*, ed. Steve Fraser and Gary Gerstle (Princeton, NJ: Princeton University Press, 1989); Jim Sleeper, *The Closest of Strangers: Liberalism and the Politics of Race in New York* (New York, NY: Norton, 1990); Thomas and Mary Edsall, *Chain Reaction: The Impact of Race, Rights, and Taxes on American Politics* (New York, NY: Basic Books, 1991); Stephan Thernstrom and Abigail Thernstrom, *America in Black and White: One Nation, Indivisible* (New York, NY: Simon & Schuster, 1997); Fred Siegel, *The Future Once Happened Here: New York, DC, LA, and the Future of America's Big Cities* (New York, NY: Free Press, 2000); and Tamar Jacoby, *Someone Else's House: America's Unfinished Struggle for Integration* (New York, NY: Free Press, 2000).

52. Lassiter, "De Jure/De Facto Segregation;" Jeanne Theoharis, "Hidden in Plain Sight: The Civil Rights Movement Outside the South," in *Myth of Southern Exceptionalism*, ed. Lassiter and Crespino, 49–73; Sugrue, *Sweet Land of Liberty*, xiii–xxviii; and Jeanne Theoharis, *A More Beautiful and Terrible History: The Uses and Misuses of Civil Rights History* (Boston, MA: Beacon, 2018).

53. Useful synthetic accounts include Quintard Taylor, In *Search Of The Racial Frontier: African Americans in the American West, 1528-1990* (New York, NY: W. W. Norton, 1998); Theoharis and Woodard, *Freedom North*; Sugrue, *Sweet Land of Liberty*; Sokol, *All Eyes are Upon Us*; Mark Speltz, *North of Dixie: Civil Rights Photography Beyond the South* (Los Angeles, CA: The J. Paul Getty Museum, 2015). Few synthetic overviews of civil rights history nationwide have thoroughly integrated the history of the North. One noteworthy exception is Caroline Rolland-Diamond, *Black America: Une histoire des luttes pour l'égalité et la justice* (Paris, France: La Découverte, 2016).

54. Osofsky, *Black Harlem*; Kusmer, *A Ghetto Takes Shape*; Philpott, *Slum and the Ghetto*; Spear, *Black Chicago*; Katzmann, *Before the Ghetto*.

55. See Grossman, *Land of Hope*; Trotter, *Black Milwaukee*; Thomas, *Life is for Us What We Make It*; and Quintard Taylor, *The Forging of a Black Community: Seattle's Central District from 1870 through the Civil Rights Era* (Seattle: University of Washington Press, 1994).

56. The term "spatial turn" was coined by Matthew Lassiter, *The Silent Majority: Suburban Politics in the Sunbelt South* (Princeton, NJ: Princeton University Press, 2007), 7. For examples concerning race and metropolitan areas outside the South, see Arnold Hirsch, *Making the Second Ghetto: Race and Housing in Chicago, 1940–1960* (Cambridge, UK: Cambridge University Press, 1983); Sugrue, *Origins of the Urban Crisis*; Robert O. Self, *American Babylon: Race and the Struggle for Postwar Oakland* (Princeton, NJ: Princeton University Press, 2003); Lizabeth Cohen, *A Consumers' Republic: The Politics of Mass Consumption in Postwar America* (New York, NY: Knopf, 2003); Amanda R. Seligman, *Block by Block: Neighborhoods and Public Policy on Chicago's West Side* (Chicago, IL: University of Chicago Press, 2005); David M. P. Freund, *Colored Property: State Policy and White Racial Politics in Suburban America* (Chicago, IL: University of Chicago Press, 2007); Colin Gordon, *Mapping Decline: St. Louis and the Fate of the American City* (Philadelphia: University of Pennsylvania Press, 2008); Andrew Highsmith, *Demolition Means Progress: Flint, Michigan, and the Fate of the American Metropolis* (Chicago, IL: University of Chicago Press, 2015); Geismer, *Don't Blame Us*; and Andrew J. Diamond, *Chicago on the Make: Power and Inequality in an American City* (Berkeley and Los Angeles: University of California Press, 2017).

57. Jacqueline Dowd Hall, "The Long Civil Rights Movement and the Political Uses of the Past," *Journal of American History* 90, no. 4 (2005): 1233–1263; Sugrue, *Sweet Land*; Lassiter and Crespino, *The Myth of Southern Exceptionalism*. For a critique of the long civil rights framework, see Sundiata Keita Cha-Jua and Clarence Lang, "The 'Long Movement' as Vampire: Temporal and Spatial Fallacies in Recent Black Freedom Studies," *Journal of African American History* 92, no. 2 (2007): 265–288.

58. Many case studies can be found in edited collections, including Jeanne Theoharis and Komozi Woodard, eds., *Groundwork: Local Black Freedom Movements in America* (New York: New York University Press, 2005); Theoharis and Woodard,

Freedom North; Peniel Joseph, ed., *The Black Power Movement: Rethinking the Civil Rights-Black Power Era* (New York: Routledge, 2006); and Yohuru Williams and Jama Lazerow, eds., *Liberated Territory: Untold Local Perspectives on the Black Panther Party* (Durham, NC: Duke University Press, 2008). For book-length case studies by city see Chicago: Ralph, *Northern Protest*; Diamond, *Chicago on the Make*; Helgeson, *Crucible of Black Empowerment*; Green, *Selling the Race*; Seligman, *Block by Block*; Detroit: Karen R. Miller, *Managing Inequality: Northern Racial Liberalism in Interwar Detroit* (New York: New York University Press, 2014); Meier and Rudwick, *Black Detroit*; Bates, *Making of Black Detroit*; Heather Ann Thompson, *Whose Detroit? Politics, Labor, and Race in a Modern American City* (Ithaca, NY: Cornell University Press, 2001); Los Angeles: Josh Sides. *L.A. City Limits: African American Los Angeles from the Great Depression to the Present* (Berkeley: University of California Press, 2003); Kurashige, *Shifting Grounds of Race*; Bernstein, *Bridges of Reform*; Newark Kevin Mumford, *Newark: A History of Race, Rights, and Riots in America* (New York: New York University Press, 2008); Julia Rabig, *The Fixers: Devolution, Development and Civil Society in Newark, 1960–1990* (Chicago: University of Chicago Press, 2016); Mark Krasovic, *The Newark Frontier: Community Action in the Great Society* (Chicago: University of Chicago Press, 2016); Biondi, *To Stand and Fight*; Craig Wilder, *A Covenant with Color: Race and Social Power in Brooklyn* (New York: Columbia University Press, 2000); Clarence Taylor, ed., *Civil Rights in New York City from World War II to the Giuliani Era* (New York: Fordham University Press, 2011); Brian Purnell, *Fighting Jim Crow in the County of Kings: The Congress of Racial Equality in Brooklyn* (Lexington: University Press of Kentucky, 2013); Oakland: Self, *American Babylon*; Donna Jean Murch, *Living for the City: Migration, Education, and the Rise of the Black Panther Party in Oakland, California* (Chapel Hill: University of North Carolina Press, 2010); Philadelphia: Levenstein, *Movement Without Marches*; Countryman, *Up South*; Matthew F. Delmont, *The Nicest Kids in Town: American Bandstand, Rock 'n' Roll, and the Struggle for Civil Rights in 1950s Philadelphia* (Berkeley and Los Angeles: University of California Press, 2014); Stanley Arnold, *Building*

the Beloved Community: Philadelphia's Interracial Civil Rights Organizations and Race Relations, 1930–1970 (Jackson: University Press of Mississippi, 2014); St. Louis: Clarence Lang, *Grassroots at the Gateway: Class Politics and Black Freedom Struggle in St. Louis* (Ann Arbor: University of Michigan Press, 2009); Kenneth Jolly, *Black Liberation in the Midwest: The Struggle in St. Louis, Missouri, 1964–1970* (New York: Routledge, 2006); Other places: Patrick Jones, *The Selma of the North: Civil Rights Insurgency in Milwaukee* (Cambridge, MA: Harvard University Press, 2009); Randal Jelks, *African Americans in the Furniture City: The Struggle for Civil Rights in Grand Rapids* (Urbana: University of Illinois Press, 2006); Kahrl, *Free the Beaches*; and Gretchen Cassel Eick, *Dissent in Wichita: The Civil Rights Movement in the Midwest, 1954–1972* (Urbana: University of Illinois Press, 2001).

59. Marcia Chatelain, *South Side Girls: Growing up in the Great Migration* (Durham, NC: Duke University Press, 2015); Victoria Wolcott, *Remaking Respectability: African-American Women in Interwar Detroit* (Chapel Hill: University of North Carolina Press, 2001); Cheryl D. Hicks, *Talk with You Like a Woman: African American Women, Justice, and Reform in New York, 1890–1935* (Chapel Hill: University of North Carolina Press, 2015); and Keona K. Ervin, *Gateway to Equality: Black Women and the Struggle for Economic Justice in St. Louis* (Lexington: University Press of Kentucky, 2018).

60. Winston James, *Holding Aloft the Banner of Ethiopia: Caribbean Radicalism in Early Twentieth Century America* (New York: Verso, 1998); Minkah Makalani, *In the Cause of Freedom: Radical Black Internationalism from Harlem to London, 1917–1939* (Chapel Hill: University of North Carolina Press, 2011); Blain, *Set the World on Fire*; William R. Scott, *The Sons of Sheba's Race: African-Americans and the Italo-Ethiopian War, 1935–41* (Bloomington: Indiana University Press, 1993); and Von Eschen, *Race Against Empire*; Gerald Horne, *Red Seas: Ferdinand Smith and Radical Black Sailors in the United States and Jamaica* (New York: New York University Press, 2005); and more generally, Kelley, *Freedom Dreams*; and Joseph, *Waiting Til the Midnight Hour*.

61. Mark Naison, *Communists in Harlem During the Great Depression* (Urbana: University of Illinois

Press 1983); Eric Gellman, *Death Blow to Jim Crow: The National Negro Congress and the Rise of Militant Civil Rights* (Chapel Hill: University of North Carolina Press, 2012); Biondi, *To Stand and Fight*; Gerald Horne, *Communist Front? The Civil Rights Congress, 1946–1956* (Rutherford, NJ: Fairleigh Dickinson University Press, 1988); Gerald Horne, *Black Liberation/Red Scare: Ben Davis and the Communist Party* (Newark: University of Delaware Press, 1994); Carol Anderson, *Eyes Off the Prize*; Brenda Gayle Plummer, *Rising Wind: Black Americans and U.S. Foreign Affairs, 1935–1960* (Chapel Hill: University of North Carolina Press, 1996); Mary Dudziak, *Cold War Civil Rights: Race and the Image of American Democracy* (Princeton, NJ: Princeton University Press, 2000); Thomas Borstelmann, *The Cold War and the Color Line: American Race Relations in the Global Arena* (Cambridge, MA: Harvard University Press, 2001); Eric Arnesen, "No 'Graver Danger:' Black Anticommunism, the Communist Party, and the Race Question," *Labor* 3 (2006): 13–52; Gore, *Radicalism at the Crossroads*; Erik McDuffie, *Sojourning for Freedom: Black Women, American Communism, and the Making of Black Left Feminism* (Durham, NC: Duke University Press, 2011); and Carol Anderson, "Bleached Souls and Red Negroes: The NAACP and Black Communists in the Early Cold War, 1948–52," in *Window on Freedom*, ed. Brenda Gayle Plummer (Chapel Hill: University of North Carolina Press, 2003), 93–113.

62. Richard Kluger, *Simple Justice: The History of Brown v. Board of Education and Black America's Struggle for Equality* (New York: Alfred A. Knopf, 1975); Mark V. Tushnet, *The NAACP's Legal Strategy against Segregated Education, 1925–1950* (Chapel Hill: University of North Carolina Press, 1987); Mark V. Tushnet, *Making Civil Rights Law: Thurgood Marshall and the Supreme Court, 1936–1961* (New York: Oxford University Press, 1994); Michael Klarman, *From Jim Crow to Civil Rights: The Supreme Court and the Struggle for Racial Equality* (New York: Oxford University Press, 2004); for newer work see Kenneth W. Mack, "Bringing the Law Back into the History of the Civil Rights Movement," *Law and History Review* 27, no. 3 (Fall 2009): 657–670; Kenneth W. Mack, "Rethinking Civil Rights Lawyering and Politics in the Era Before

Brown," *Yale Law Journal* 115 (2005): 256–354. Kenneth W. Mack, "Law and Mass Politics in the Making of the Civil Rights Lawyer, 1931–1941," *Journal of American History* 93, no. 1 (June 2006): 37–62; Kenneth W. Mack, *Representing the Race: The Creation of the Civil Rights Lawyer* (Cambridge, MA: Harvard University Press, 2012); David Canton, *Raymond Pace Alexander: A New Negro Lawyer Fights for Civil Rights in Philadelphia* (Jackson: University Press of Mississippi, 2010); Risa Goluboff, "'Let Economic Equality Take Care of Itself': The NAACP, Labor Litigation, and the Making of Civil Rights in the 1940s," *UCLA Law Review* 52 (2005): 1393–1486. For a bottom-up history of housing cases, see Gonda, *Unjust Deeds*; for a grassroots history of education protests and litigation, see Sugrue, *Sweet Land of Liberty*, 163–199. An excellent model for a bottom-up history of civil rights litigation that could be applied to a northern city is Tomiko Brown-Nagin, *Courage to Dissent: Atlanta and the Long History of the Civil Rights Movement* (New York: Oxford University Press, 2011). For three quite different legal histories of interracial collaboration and conflict, see Brilliant, *The Color of America Has Changed*; MacLean, *Freedom Is Not Enough*; and John David Skrentny, *The Minority Rights Revolution* (Cambridge, MA: Harvard University Press, 2002).

63. Useful overviews of black power history include Ogbar, *Black Power* and Joseph, *Waiting 'til the Midnight Hour*. On the Black Panthers, see Joshua Bloom and Waldo E. Martin Jr., *Black Against Empire: The History and Politics of the Black Panther Party* (Berkeley and Los Angeles: University of California Press, 2013); Sean L. Malloy, *Out of Oakland: Black Panther Party Internationalism during the Cold War* (Ithaca, NY: Cornell University Press, 2017); Murch, *Living for the City*; Yohuru Williams, *Black Politics/White Power: Civil Rights, Black Power, and the Black Panthers in New Haven* (New York: Wiley, 2000); Jakobi Williams, *From the Bullet to the Ballot: The Illinois Chapter of the Black Panther Party and Racial Coalition Politics in Chicago* (Chapel Hill: University of North Carolina Press, 2013); Williams and Lazerow, eds., *Liberated Territory*; Judson L. Jeffries, *On the Ground: The Black Panther Party in Communities across America* (Oxford: University Press of Mississippi, 2010); Lucas N. N. Burke and Judson L. Jeffries, *The*

Portland Black Panthers: Empowering Albina and Remaking a City (Seattle: University of Washington Press, 2016); Robyn C. Spencer, *The Revolution Has Come: Black Power, Gender, and the Black Panther Party in Oakland* (Durham, NC: Duke University Press, 2016); Alondra Nelson, *Body and Soul: The Black Panther Party and the Fight Against Medical Discrimination* (Minneapolis: University of Minnesota Press, 2011); and Charles E. Jones, ed., *The Black Panther Party Reconsidered* (Oakland, CA: Black Classic Press, 1998). For other organizations, see various essays in Joseph, *Black Power*; Muhammad Ahmad, *We Will Return in the Whirlwind: Black Radical Organizations. 1960–1975* (Chicago: Charles Kerr, 2008); Brown, *Fighting for US*; Nishani Frazier, *Harambee City: The Congress of Racial Equality in Cleveland and the Rise of Black Power Populism* (Fayetteville: University of Arkansas Press, 2017); William W. Sales Jr., *From Civil Rights to Black Liberation: Malcolm X and the Organization of Afro-American Unity* (Boston: South End Press, 1994); and James A. Geschwender, *Class, Race. and Worker Insurgency: The League of Revolutionary Black Workers* (Cambridge: Cambridge University Press, 1977).

64. Tracye Matthews, "No One Ever Asks What a Man's Role in the Revolution Is": Gender and the Politics of the Black Panther Party, 1966–1971," in *Black Panther Party Reconsidered*, ed. Jones, 267–304; Kimberley Springer, *Living for the Revolution: Black Feminist Organizations, 1968–80* (Durham, NC: Duke University Press, 2006); Steve Estes, *I Am a Man: Race, Manhood, and the Civil Rights Movement* (Chapel Hill: University of North Carolina Press, 2005), Bettye Collier Thomas and V. P. Franklin, eds., *Sisters in the Struggle: African American Women in the Civil Rights-Black Power Movement* (New York: New York University Press, 2001); Ashley D. Farmer, *Remaking Black Power: How Black Women Transformed an Era* (Chapel Hill: University of North Carolina Press, 2017); Trevor Griffey and David Goldberg, eds., *Black Power at Work* (Ithaca, NY: Cornell University Press, 2010); Rabig and Warren, *The Business of Black Power*; Rabig, *The Fixers*; Martha Biondi, *The Black Revolution on Campus* (Berkeley: University of California Press, 2012); on black power and electoral politics, see Self, *American Babylon*;

Countryman, *Up South*; Williams, *From the Bullet to the Ballot*; David R. Colburn and Jeffrey S. Adler, eds., *African American Mayors: Race, Politics, and the American City* (Urbana: University of Illinois Press, 2001); and Leonard N. Moore, *The Defeat of Black Power: Civil Rights and the National Black Political Convention of 1972* (Baton Rouge: Louisiana State University Press, 2018).

65. Steven M. Ward, *In Love and Struggle: The Revolutionary Lives of James and Grace Lee Boggs* (Chapel Hill: University of North Carolina Press, 2016); Jeanne F. Theoharis, *The Rebellious Life of Mrs. Rosa Parks* (Boston: Beacon Press, 2013); Peniel Joseph, *Stokely: A Life* (New York: Basic Books, 2014); Komozi Woodard, *A Nation Within a Nation: Amiri Baraka (LeRoi Jones) and Black Power Politics* (Chapel Hill: University of North Carolina Press, 1999); and Manning Marable, *Malcolm X: A Life of Reinvention* (New York: Henry Holt, 2010).

66. Lisa Levenstein, *A Movement Without Marches: African American Women and the Politics of Poverty in Postwar Philadelphia* (Chapel Hill: University of North Carolina Press, 2009); Rhonda Y. Williams, *The Politics of Public Housing: Black Women's Struggles Against Urban Inequality* (New York: Oxford University Press, 2004); Premilla Nadasen, *Welfare Warriors: The Welfare Rights Movement in the United States* (New York: Routledge, 2005); Felicia Kornbluh, *The Battle Over Welfare Rights* (Philadelphia: University of Pennsylvania Press, 2009); Annelise Orleck, *Storming Caesar's Palace: How Black Mothers Fought Their Own War on Poverty* (Boston: Beacon Press, 2006); and Gordon Mantler, *Power to the Poor: Black-Brown Coalition and the Fight for Economic Justice, 1960–1974* (Chapel Hill: University of North Carolina Press, 2013).

67. Thompson, "Why Mass Incarceration Matters;" Murakawa, *First Civil Right*; Flamm, *Law and Order*; Gottschalk, *Caught*; Gilmore, *Golden Gulag*; Thompson and Murch, "Special Section: Urban America and the Carceral State"; Berger, *Captive Nation*; Berger and Losier, *Rethinking the American Prison Movement*; Alexander, *New Jim Crow*; Elizabeth Hinton, *From the War on Poverty to the War on Crime: The Making of Mass Incarceration in America* (Cambridge, MA: Harvard University Press, 2016); Michael Javen Fortner,

The Black Silent Majority: The Rockefeller Drug Laws and the Politics of Punishment (Cambridge, MA: Harvard University Press, 2015); James Forman Jr., *Locking Up Our Own: Crime and Punishment in Black America* (New York: Farrar Straus Giroux, 2017); and Julilly Kohler-Hausmann, *Getting Tough: Welfare and Imprisonment in 1970s America* (Princeton, NJ: Princeton University Press, 2017).

68. Michael A. Gomez, *Black Crescent: The Experience and Legacy of African Muslims in the Americas* (New York: Cambridge University Press, 2005); Claude Clegg, *An Original Man: The Life and Times of Elijah Muhammad* (New York: St. Martin's Press, 1997); Ula Yvette Taylor, *The Promise of Patriarchy: Women and the Nation of Islam* (Chapel Hill: University of North Carolina Press, 2017); Manning Marable, *Malcolm X: A Life of Reinvention* (New York: Henry Holt, 2010); Judith Weisenfeld, *New World A-Coming: Black Religion and Racial Identity during the Great Migration* (New York: New York University Press, 2017); Bettye Collier-Thomas, *Jesus, Jobs, and Justice: African American Women and Religion* (New York: Alfred A. Knopf, 2010); Clarence Taylor, *The Black Churches of Brooklyn* (New York: Columbia University Press, 1994); Clarence Taylor, *Black Religious Radicals: The Fight for Equality from Jim Crow to the Twenty First Century* (New York: Routledge, 2002); Angela Dillard, *Faith in the City: Preaching Radical Social Change in Detroit* (Ann Arbor: University of Michigan Press, 2007); Nick Salvatore, *Singing in a Strange Land: C.L Franklin, the Black Church, and the Transformation of America* (New York: Alfred A. Knopf, 2005); and Kerry Pimblott, *Faith in Black Power: Religion, Race, and Resistance in Cairo, Illinois* (Lexington: University Press of Kentucky, 2017).

69. John T. McGreevy, *Parish Boundaries: The Catholic Encounter with Race in the Twentieth Century Urban North* (Chicago: University of Chicago Press, 1996); Gerald Gamm, *Urban Exodus: Why the Jews Left Boston and the Catholics Stayed* (Cambridge, MA: Harvard University Press, 1999); Eileen McMahon, *Which Parish Are You From? A Chicago Irish Community and Race Relations* (Lexington: University Press of Kentucky, 1995); and Timothy B. Neary, *Crossing Parish Boundaries: Race, Sports, and Catholic Youth in Chicago, 1914–1954* (Chicago: University of Chicago Press, 2017).

70. Murray Friedman, *What Went Wrong: The Creation and Collapse of the Black-Jewish Alliance* (New York: Free Press, 1995); Maurianne Adams and John Bracey, eds., *Strangers and Neighbors: Relations Between Blacks and Jews in the United States* (Amherst: University of Massachusetts Press, 1999); Gamm, *Urban Exodus*; Wendell Pritchett, *Brownsville, Brooklyn: Blacks, Jews, and the Changing Face of the Ghetto* (Chicago: University of Chicago Press, 2002); Podair, *Strike that Changed New York*; and Cheryl Greenberg, *Troubling the Waters: Black-Jewish Relations in the American Century* (Princeton, NJ: Princeton University Press, 2006).

71. James F. Finlay, *Church People in the Struggle: The National Council of Churches and the Black Freedom Movement, 1950–1970* (New York: Oxford University Press, 1997); and David A. Hollinger, *Protestants Abroad: How Missionaries Tried to Change the World but Changed America* (Princeton, NJ: Princeton University Press, 2017).

72. William Jelani Cobb, *The Substance of Hope: Barack Obama and the Paradox of Progress* (New York: Walker, 2010): Peniel Joseph, *Dark Days, Bright Nights: From Black Power to Barack Obama* (New York: Basic Books, 2010); Thomas J. Sugrue, *Not Even Past: Barack Obama and the Burden of Race* (Princeton, NJ: Princeton University Press, 2010); and Taylor, *From #BlackLivesMatter to Black Liberation*.

Thomas J. Sugrue

THE BLACK FREEDOM STRUGGLE IN THE URBAN SOUTH

A week after Republican Senator Warren G. Harding won the 1920 presidential election in a landslide victory over Governor James M. Cox of Ohio, the New York headquarters of the National Association for the Advancement of Colored People (NAACP) received a disturbing letter from Dr. Charles A. McPherson, a resident of Birmingham, Alabama, who served as the general secretary of the local NAACP chapter. The disgruntled activist detailed how registrars had altered their office hours without notice, subjected civil rights organizers to verbal assault and threats of violence, and expunged voter registration applications filed by African Americans. "It seems to be the policy of those in authority," McPherson raged, "to discourage registration and voting among our people."[1] Of the many civil rights violations endured by African Americans during the 1920 election season, the discriminatory treatment of newly franchised African American women troubled McPherson the most. Five thousand black women in Birmingham applied for voter registration cards in the weeks preceding the election, but only one hundred had their applications approved. In the coming weeks, McPherson assisted the national office of the NAACP in its efforts to reapportion southern representation in Congress.

Over the next two decades, McPherson remained a fearless champion of African Americans' civil rights. Well respected among blacks within and beyond Birmingham, McPherson tackled a wide range of political issues, including racial discrimination in the labor arena and police brutality. His most profiled activity involved the legal defense of Willie Peterson, a World War I veteran accused of the murder of two white women, and this was also his most courageous. On August 4, 1931, a gunman fatally shot two white women, Jennie Wood and Augustus Williams, and wounded another, Nell Williams, near the woods of Shades Mountain. Even though the lone survivor, Nell Williams, initially described the suspect as a large, light-complexioned African American man, she would later identify Peterson, a dark-skinned man barely 125 pounds, as the assailant. Peterson was arrested and tried for murder. The first trial, which included testimonies from witnesses who confirmed Peterson's alibi that he was home at the time of the murders, ended in a mistrial as jurors failed to reach a verdict. The prosecution's case at the second trial was equally weak, yet the jury found the

defendant guilty. Peterson was sentenced to death, but Governor Benjamin M. Muller commuted his sentence to life in prison. Throughout his trial and sentencing, Peterson found an invaluable ally in McPherson, who spearheaded the local NAACP's legal strategy and raised funds for retaining one of the state's most respected lawyers, John Altman. To intimidate McPherson and the local black community, the Ku Klux Klan paraded through Peterson's neighborhood. The determined activist pressed ahead in his goal of securing justice for Peterson. "We are not deterred by anything they may do," McPherson informed the *Norfolk Journal and Guide*. For his efforts in the Peterson case, the NAACP awarded McPherson the Madame C. J. Walker gold award for demonstrating "exceptional loyalty, devotion, and courage in the face of prejudices, handicaps, and dangers of a southern city."[2] Thanks to his arduous efforts, the Birmingham chapter boasted a membership of more than one thousand in 1940, no easy feat for a city in the deep South.[3]

The national office of the NAACP depended heavily on McPherson, who remained a faithful servant of the organization well into his sixties. Unfortunately, on December 9, 1948, McPherson died in a car accident. Four days after his death, mourners packed St. Paul Episcopal Church to pay their respects to the courageous activist who had been at the forefront of the local civil rights struggle for nearly three decades.[4]

The same year local blacks mourned the death of McPherson, the newly formed States Rights Democratic Party, also known as the Dixiecrats, convened in Birmingham for its first convention. On July 17, six thousand people poured into the Birmingham Municipal Auditorium to pledge their allegiance to the Dixiecrats as well as voice their outrage with the Democratic National Party (DNP). At its nominating convention in Philadelphia, the DNP put forth a platform endorsing the abolition of the poll-tax, the passage of anti-lynching legislation, and a fair employment practices bill. Under the leadership of South Carolina Governor Strom Thurmond and Governor Fielding Lewis Wright of Mississippi, the Dixiecrats stated in unequivocal terms their opposition to civil rights:

> We stand for the segregation of the races and the racial integrity of each race; the constitutional right to choose one's associates; to accept private employment without governmental interference, and to earn one's living in any lawful way. We oppose the elimination of segregation employment by federal bureaucrats called for by the misnamed civil rights program. We favor home rule, local self-government and a minimum interference with individual rights.[5]

Pledging to defend their way of life, Dixiecrats predicted that the civil rights platform of the DNC "would be utterly destructive of the social, economic and political life of the Southern people." Their activism reflected not just their frustration with the direction of the Democratic Party but also their fear of the growing militancy of African Americans during and immediately after World War II. With the entry of the United States into war, African Americans intensified their struggle for freedom, justice, and equality in all areas of public life. "Double Victory" emerged as a central rally cry from African American communities across the nation as blacks insisted that the US government commit itself to the defeat of not only Nazism abroad but also stringent white racism within its borders, particularly in the Jim Crow South. The slogan "Double V" also encompassed the anticolonial perspectives of African American activists, along with those of black newspapers like the *Chicago Defender* and the *Pittsburgh Courier*, who were committed to the decolonization struggles led by oppressed groups in India, Asia, and Africa.[6] The rising militancy of African Americans was not lost on many high-ranking officials in the Democratic Party,

which had become increasingly dependent on the black vote.

A year before the DNC convention, President Harry Truman appeared on the verge of pushing the nation closer to its democratic ideals. "It is my deep conviction that we have reached a turning point in the long history of our country's efforts to guarantee freedom and equality to all of our citizens," noted Truman in his historic address at the NAACP's 1947 convention. "Our immediate task is to remove the last remnants of the barriers which stand between millions of our citizens and their birth right. There is no justifiable reason for discrimination because of ancestry, or religion, or race or color."

Notwithstanding Truman's optimistic outlook, as well as his landmark executive orders that outlawed segregation in the armed forces and federal employment, African Americans faced an uphill battle in their struggle for racial and social justice. Nowhere was this battle more visible than in the urban South, where courageous women and men not only challenged the legal, political, and economic underpinnings of Jim Crow segregation and racial exclusion but also provided the nation and the larger world with alternative visions of justice, freedom, and human possibility.

No analysis of the civil rights movement's dismantling of the Jim Crow system would be complete without serious engagement in broader regional trends, particularly the growing power of white racial moderates. As historian Matthew Lassiter argues in his seminal study, *Silent Majority: Suburban Politics in the Sunbelt South*, "While civil rights activism and federal intervention proved to be necessary ingredients in the process of dismantling Jim Crow, the actions of white moderates were critical in undermining the defiant politics of white supremacy and constructing a grassroots alternative to the racial caste system." These racial moderates played a significant role in the fall of Jim Crow, but they also contributed to the erection of new racial barriers. As Lassiter rightly points out: "The political economies of southern metropolises such as Atlanta and Charlotte and Richmond increasingly resembled their sprawling counterparts in the North and West, with pervasive structures of racial and class segregation imbedded in the built environment rather than enforced by Jim crow legislation."[7] The successes and failures of the civil rights movement in the urban South not only represent one of the most important social revolutions in 20th-century history but also explain many of the social and political inequalities of our contemporary moment.

THE URGENCY OF NOW: THE MONTGOMERY BUS BOYCOTT

If we embrace historian Vincent Harding's metaphoric rendering of the black freedom struggle as a river, then 1955 was a year in which its tributaries roared with renewed intensity. On the heels of the Supreme Court's historic *Brown v. Board of Education* decision (1954) declaring the separate but equal segregationist doctrine unconstitutional, thousands of black southerners launched individual and collective challenges against the racial status quo. Across the urban South, African Americans confronted city officials to desegregate the public-school system, demanded an end to discriminatory hiring practices, and challenged Jim Crow practices on public and private conveyances. One place in which local whites definitely noticed an upsurge in black activism was Montgomery, Alabama. A destination spot for thousands of black Alabamians migrating from the countryside to the city, Montgomery witnessed a substantial increase in its African American population in the postwar period. Many of these migrants performed critical roles in one of the most impressive campaigns in modern US history: the Montgomery Bus Boycott.

On Thursday afternoon, December 1, 1955, Rosa Louise McCauley Parks, a seamstress at Montgomery Fair department store, boarded the Cleveland Avenue bus with plans for a quiet evening dinner with her husband, Raymond, and her mother, Leora McCauley, who lived with the couple. During the previous months, public transportation had been a site of political protest as several African Americans had refused orders to vacate their seats for white passengers. In fact, local civil rights leaders had contemplated using two of the protesters, Claudette Colvin and Mary Louise Smith, as possible test cases in challenging the constitutionality of the city's segregation laws. Like most African Americans in the city, Rosa Parks detested the treatment of African Americans on the city buses. Moreover, the seasoned activist, who was actively involved in the local National Association for the Advancement of Colored People (NAACP), had experienced her share of run-ins with local bus drivers. Even though African Americans constituted 75 percent of the Montgomery Bus Line's customers, they were subjected to the draconian regulations of Alabama's segregation laws as well as the whims of white bus drivers, who had been granted police power to arrest anyone in violation of the law.

One bus driver who readily exercised his police powers was James Blake. On December 1, he demanded that Rosa Parks and three other black passengers relinquish their seats after the white section had filled to capacity. Seated in the middle section of the bus, the four African American passengers occupied what historian Jeanne Theoharris refers to as liminal space.[8] The passengers initially ignored Blake's orders, but after he repeated his demands three of the riders exited their seats. Forty-two-year-old activist Rosa Parks, however, remained seated in a moving act of political defiance and self-determination. "Are you going to stand up?" Blake queried Parks as she remained in her seat. To his query, the determined seamstress replied, "No."[9]

Angered by her defiance, Blake exited the bus and called his supervisor, who recommended throwing Parks off the bus. Instead of simply discharging her from the bus, Blake pushed for her arrest by summoning nearby police. Upon their arrival on the scene, police officers F. B. Day and D. W. Mixon consulted with Blake and then arrested Parks. Once fingerprinted and booked at the city jail, Parks phoned home and informed her mother of her arrest. Her mother relayed the news to her husband, who rushed immediately to the jail. Within a matter of minutes, civil rights activist and labor leader E. D. Nixon, who served as president of the local chapter of the Brotherhood of Sleeping Car Porters, received word of Parks's arrest. So, too, did JoAnn Robinson, head of the Women's Political Council and longtime opponent of Montgomery's segregated bus policies. Once they secured Parks's release from jail, Robinson, Nixon, and other local activists put in motion a plan to challenge the city's segregation laws.

Robinson, a professor at Alabama State University, immediately sprang to action, enlisting students to distribute thirty thousand leaflets informing the black community of Parks's arrest and requesting them to stay off the buses Monday morning.

> Don't ride the buses to work, to town, to school, or anywhere on Monday. You can afford to stay out of school for one day if you have no other way to go except by bus. You can also afford to stay out of town for one day. If you work, take a cab, or walk. But please, children and grown-ups, don't ride the bus at all on Monday. Please stay off all buses Monday.

The leaders created the Montgomery Improvement Association (MIA) to better coordinate their efforts. They appointed as president a recently arrived minister from Atlanta: Dr. Martin Luther King Jr. At the boycott's outset, the MIA did not call for an end to segregated seating but simply improved and more courteous service for black passengers, the hiring of African American drivers on black routes, and a first come, first served

seating policy. Over time, however, the movement's goals included the total elimination of segregated accommodations.

Lawyer Fred Gray soon filed a suit against Mayor William Gayle on behalf of Aurelius Browder, challenging the constitutionality of the city's segregation ordinance. As the case made its way through the courts, black Montgomery continued the boycott of public buses. To ensure the movement's success, local leaders held public meetings filled with dynamic singing and preaching, as well as powerful speeches on what their movement meant for not just the local community but all of black America.

The personal sacrifices of black working women and men were as deeply moving as the fiery speeches delivered by the well-known leaders of the boycott. For more than a year, black laborers endured long walks to work, economic reprisals from their employers, and the general inconveniences experienced by all protesters during a boycott. Their sacrifices would not be in vain, as the Supreme Court declared Montgomery's segregation law unconstitutional. On November 13, 1956, the Supreme Court upheld the District Court's ruling in *Browder v. Gayle* and mandated that Alabama and Montgomery desegregate their buses. Five weeks after the ruling, on December 20, the Montgomery buses were desegregated. A monumental event in US political history, the Montgomery Bus Boycott demonstrated the political potency of nonviolent direction action, catapulted Martin Luther King Jr. into the national spotlight, and inspired a new generation of civil rights activists to fundamentally transform the political and economic structures of the country.

Among those deeply inspired by the Montgomery Bus Boycott was a courageous minister who pastored Bethel Baptist Church in Birmingham, Alabama: Fred Shuttlesworth. Fiercely independent, strong in his Christian faith, and unwavering in his commitment to redeem the soul of the nation, Shuttlesworth emerged from his humble beginnings in Mount

Mergs, Alabama, to become one of the movement's most prophetic voices. At the age of three, he moved with his family to Birmingham, where he experienced the sting of second-class citizenship, honed his leadership skills within the institutional matrix of the black church, and eventually graduated from Rosedale High in 1940. The valedictorian of his class, Shuttlesworth worked briefly as a handyman at a local doctor's office, converted from Methodist to Baptist, and moved around the state in search of his vocation. Widening economic opportunities in the defense industry brought him to Mobile in 1943. Five years later, he moved to Dallas County, where he enrolled at Selma University and served as pastor of the First Baptist Church of Selma.

A year before the *Brown v. Board* decision, Shuttlesworth returned to Birmingham, where he accepted an offer to pastor Bethel Baptist Church. Sensing that the political moment was ripe for radical change, he sought to build on the political momentum created by *Brown* and later the Montgomery Bus Boycott. On June 5, 1956, Shuttlesworth and a group of local ministers formed the Alabama Christian Movement for Human Rights with the twin objectives of desegregating the city and ending racial discrimination in employment. On December 26, a day after the bombing of Shuttlesworth's home, he and two hundred African Americans engaged in civil disobedience by sitting in the white section of the public buses. For their actions, they were arrested for violating the city's segregation law, despite the recent Supreme Court decision in *Gayle v. Browder.*

Concurrent with the upsurge in protest among African Americans was the growing visibility of white racial moderates based largely in the metropolitan Sunbelt. Tempting as it might be to portray the white South as a political monolith, this was not the case. According to historian Matthew Lassiter, "the metropolitan Sunbelt replaced the rural Black Belt as the center of political power in the South, and a two-party system dominated by the interests of large corporations and the priorities of white-collar suburbs supplanted the traditional culture of white supremacy that governed the Jim Crow era."[10] One arena in which racial moderates most clearly articulated their vision was public education. The late 1950s witnessed the growing power of groups like the Southern Regional Council, which, after the passage of the *Brown v. Board* decision, fought against massive resistance with the hopes of building a moderate South. Unlike their massive resisters, who denounced the *Brown* decision and promoted the closing of public schools, politically liberal and moderate suburban white residents countered with a class-based desegregation compromise that emphasized "freedom of choice" and "neighborhood schools," a formula that was described as "race-neutral."[11] The organizational vehicles through which racial moderates sought to implement their vision of civil rights included the Virginia Committee for Public Schools, the Southern Regional Council, the New Orleans–based Save Our Schools, the Women's Emergency Committee in Arkansas, and Help Our Public Education in Georgia.[12]

White racial moderates may have been a thorn in the side of the ultra-segregationists in the South. Yet, they were hardly ally material for many African American civil rights activists calling for immediate change. In fact, the political limitations of white racial moderates became a topic of increasing concern as African Americans embarked on another phase of the black freedom struggle.

A NEW DAY IS COMING: THE 1960 SIT-INS AND THE BIRTH OF THE STUDENT NONVIOLENT COORDINATING COMMITTEE

Sit-ins were a potent political weapon for labor activists during the late 1930s. The civil rights movement, however, did not fully embrace this strategy until February 1, 1960. On this historic day, at approximately 4:30 p.m., four college students from North Carolina A&T conducted a sit-in at the F. W. Woolworth store in downtown Greensboro. With anything but haste in their efforts to segregate the lunch counter, Joseph McNeil, Franklin McCain, Ezell Blair, and David Richmond had frequently discussed civil rights issues during their heated debates in their dorm room at Scott Hall. Convinced that the black freedom struggle mandated courageous action against the white power structure, the four students decided to launch their own campaign against segregation on February 1. That day, the young men entered the Woolworth, sat down at the "whites only" lunch counters, and placed an order for coffee. The shocked waitress denied their request and ordered them to leave immediately. Nervous but determined, McNeil, McCain, Blair, and Richmond remained seated until the store closed at 5 p.m.

News of their actions emboldened twenty-five other students, who converged on Woolworth's segregated lunch counter the next day, asking to be served. The students remained at Woolworth from 11 a.m. to 3 p.m., despite the presence of rowdy white hecklers threatening bodily harm on the orderly protesters. Their campaign quickly attracted the attention of local media, which struggled to make sense of the protest. On the third day, the sit-in campaign expanded to include students from nearby Bennett College as well as Dudley High School. Not even the presence of the local Ku Klux Klan undermined their protests, which by the fourth day had three white supporters, Eugenia Seaman, Marilyn Lott, and Ann Dearsley. By this time students were also targeting the Kress chain store, which, like Woolworth, had segregated lunch counters. White officials pressured college administrators to put an end to the protests, to no avail. Early Saturday morning, more than 1,400 students assembled in North Carolina A&T's Harrison Auditorium to reiterate their opposition to Jim Crow segregation and racial exclusion as well as their commitment to direct-action protest. Later that day, more than one thousand protesters packed Woolworth as angry whites pledged to defend their way of life.

The Greensboro sit-in quickly sparked demonstrations in nearby Winston-Salem and Durham. On Monday, February 8, students in these cities conducted sit-ins at their local Woolworth and Kress stores. Shortly thereafter, protests erupted in Charlotte, Raleigh, and Fayetteville. By the third week of February, the sit-in wave had spread to cities in South Carolina, Florida, Tennessee, Virginia, and Georgia. On February 5, in Nashville, Tennessee, nearly five thousand volunteers packed First Baptist Church to launch their own sit-in movement. Theologian James Lawson provided crash courses on nonviolence. "White Nashville," writes historian Taylor Branch, "awoke slowly to a kind of invasion force it never had encountered before, as rows of neatly dressed college students filed into the downtown stores to wait for food service."[13] College students in Atlanta were also impressive. On March 15, campus activists from Morehouse, Spellman, and Clark Atlanta launched several sit-ins at segregated eating establishments in the capital city. The protesters faced opposition not just from hostile whites but black conservatives who questioned their emphasis. The black weekly, *The Daily World*, advised students to focus their attention on voter registration, school desegregation, and civil rights legislation rather than desegregating lunch counters. Undeterred by their critics, students in Atlanta and elsewhere pressed ahead in their goals.[14]

To build on the momentum of the student sit-ins, Ella Baker called a meeting at Shaw University on April 1 to institutionalize already developing networks among young black activists across the South, map out a plan by which students could have a greater degree of autonomy from established groups like the National Association for the Advancement of Colored People (NAACP) and Dr. Martin Luther King's Southern Christian Leadership Conference (SCLC), and discuss the best strategies for particular local conditions. Few, if any, were more qualified to assist the students in their democratic endeavors than Baker. The Norfolk-born organizer was a human rights activist whose political work brought her into leadership roles with most of the major civil rights organizations, including the NAACP, the SCLC, and the Student Nonviolent Coordinating Committee (SNCC). These experiences proved critical as she shepherded the SCLC during its formative stages in the 1950s and shaped the organizing philosophy of the organization that emerged at the Shaw meeting: the Student Nonviolent Coordinating Committee. Under the influence of Baker and Bob Moses, among others, the SNCC initiated direct action protests and voter registration drives throughout the deep South, catapulted local leaders like Fannie Hamer into the national spotlight, and influenced the political development of future politicians like Julian Bond, John Lewis, and Marion Berry.

The historic gathering at Shaw injected a great deal of confidence and energy into student activists as they returned to their communities and commenced their protests. Slowly but surely, African American students began to win concessions. In May, Nashville businesses agreed to integrate lunch counters and other public arenas. Then on July 21, 1960, the launching pad for the sit-ins, F. W. Woolworth in Greensboro, ended its segregated policy and agreed to serve all customers regardless of race.

This was but one victory in an ongoing war. Across the South, African Americans maintained their pressure on the white establishment as they fought against the policies of racial segregation and exclusion. Though Jim Crow remained the way of life for many, the legal edifice of white supremacy had noticeable cracks. The sit-ins desegregated lunch counters in several major centers of the urban South. Then on December 5, 1960, the Supreme Court ruled in *Boynton v. Virginia* that racial segregation in bus terminals violated the Interstate Commerce Act. This decision effectively banned segregation on interstate buses and at the terminals servicing such buses, setting in motion one of the most dramatic dramas of the civil rights movement: the Freedom Rides of 1961.

THE FREEDOM HIGHWAY

On May 4, 1961, an interracial coalition of six whites and seven blacks departed from the nation's capital for New Orleans. Organized by CORE, the group aimed to challenge segregated interstate travel, which was outlawed by the Supreme Court. On their travels, "Freedom Riders" defied the South's Jim Crow laws and customs by attempting to use "whites-only" restrooms and lunch counters at bus stations and terminals.

The original thirteen riders split into two groups. One group traveled with Greyhound and the other with Trailways. The possibility of death lingered in the minds of the Freedom riders, and on Mother's Day, the courageous activists teetered dangerously close to a tragic end. That day, a white mob converged on the Trailways bus station in Birmingham, anxiously awaiting the arrival of a bus from Atlanta carrying Freedom riders James Peck, Walter and Frances Bergman, Charles Person, and Ike Reynold. Upon leaving Atlanta, Klansmen began an endless round of verbal assaults on the riders. "You niggers will be taken care of once you get in Alabama," one Klansman promised. On their stop in Anniston, the civil rights activists received news that the Greyhound bus carrying their comrades had been burned and that the injured parties were hospitalized. Fearful but determined, the Freedom riders commenced with their tradition of ignoring Jim Crow custom and sitting wherever they pleased. Their actions enraged the Klansmen on the bus, who then roughed up Person and Peck. Even amid the violence, the driver proceeded on his route to Birmingham. By the time the bus arrived at the Trailways bus station in downtown

Birmingham, "the Klansmen and their police were all in place, armed and ready" to do what had to be done to protect the southern way of life.[15] With the approval of the Commissioner of Public Safety, Bull Connor, and the knowledge of the Federal Bureau of Investigation (FBI), law enforcement officials cleared the target area for fifteen minutes to allow the local Klan to inflict as much physical terror as possible within the agreed-upon amount of time. Upon the bus's arrival, the white supremacists wasted no time in attacking the freedom fighters along with innocent bystanders. Within moments of entering the waiting room and approaching the lunch counter, Peck and Pearson met a steady round of blows from the white supremacists. "Get that son of a bitch," Edward Fields yelled as "several burly men" pummeled Person with their fists. Their violence would not be limited to the African American riders. When Peck came to his comrade's rescue, an enraged group of whites, armed with pipes and oversized key rings, violently punched and kicked him.[16] The next day, photos of the bloodied face of Peck and the ransacked bus station appeared in newspapers across the country.

Even with the brutal images coming out of Birmingham and the recalcitrance of white supremacists across the South, President John Kennedy and his administration refused to commit themselves fully to the civil rights causes. Throughout 1961 and 1962, Dr. King and other civil rights leaders' demands for an executive of all public facilities fell on deaf ears. Thus, black southerners and their small army of white allies had no choice but to press ahead in their massive demonstrations and acts of civil disobedience.

WHY WE CAN'T WAIT: THE BATTLE AGAINST JIM CROW CONTINUES

One city where the protests continued was Durham. National Association for the Advancement of Colored People (NAACP) youth chapters and CORE organizers launched a series of attacks against segregated lunch counters in 1962. Belying its image as a progressive southern city, Durham was racist to its core. In fact, even when the white power structure appeared to bend in favor of African Americans, its actions proved more symbolic than substantive. The conflict between the city's racial moderates and more direct-action oriented activists reached a fever pitch in the summer of 1962. Late in July, CORE and the NAACP picketed Eckerd's Drug Store and Howard Johnson's Ice Cream Parlor. Eckerd's had refused to hire African American clerks, despite the fact that blacks constituted half of its customers. Howard Johnson's, similarly, opposed hiring African Americans in clerical positions. It had also refused to desegregate its lunch counter, even after the sit-ins of 1960 led other stores to reverse their segregation policies. Taking the lead in the fight against Howard Johnson's were black students from North Carolina Central, who endured verbal assaults from whites and arrest in their fight to implement change. For their refusal to pay a trespass fine for protesting Howard Johnson's, students Guytana Horton and Joycelyn McKissick would be sentenced to thirty days in jail.

The arrest and subsequent jailing of Horton and McKissick galvanized the community. A large rally was held at one of the city's movement centers, St. Joseph African Methodist Episcopal Church. Shortly after the rally, 1,500 African Americans headed to Howard Johnson's to continue their protests. These protests continued throughout the summer as part of the "Freedom Highways project," a CORE-directed campaign that extended from Maryland to Florida, which eventually forced Howard Johnson's to desegregate more than half of their lunch counters in North Carolina. One holdout was the Howard Johnson's restaurant in Durham; in 1963 it became the site of one of the largest demonstrations in North Carolina.

Frustration gripped the black South as protesters lost patience with whites and African

Americans who counseled against acts of civil disobedience and encouraged backroom negotiations with the power structure. "Go slow—go slow—go slow," said Miles College student Frank Dukes, after many unsuccessful attempts to break the back of Jim Crow in Birmingham. "That's what you all advise us to do," he lamented to conservative black leaders who embraced the philosophy of gradualism. No longer could African Americans place their faith in the promises of white liberals or sit and wait for God to intervene on their behalf. "God helps those who help themselves. You pray to God but when you get off your knees, you got to go out and work if you want to eat. God will help you start if you start off things yourself."

In 1961, Dukes and his colleagues were involved in numerous demonstrations to desegregate the city's public accommodations and expand African Americans' employment opportunities. Students at Miles issued "This We Believe," a statement on their principles and their political demands in which students vowed to "use every legal and nonviolent" weapon at their disposal to "secure for ourselves and our unborn children these God-given rights guaranteed by the Constitution of the United States." A month later, Dukes and his colleagues organized the Anti-Injustice Movement, which launched a boycott of selective downtown stores. In their view, African Americans were foolish to patronize businesses in which they were treated like second-class citizens. Concerned about loss in sales and outside interference, a few businesses voluntarily desegregated temporarily, but for the most part Jim Crow remained the order of the day in the city.

BUT FOR BIRMINGHAM: THE SOUTH'S MOST SEGREGATED CITY

To push the movement forward, the Reverend Fred Shuttlesworth solicited the assistance of the Southern Christian Leadership Conference (SCLC) and Dr. Martin Luther King. Still reeling from its losses in Albany, Georgia, the SCLC exercised caution in deciding whether to launch a desegregation campaign in what many regarded as the most dangerous city in the country. After much deliberation and planning, King arrived in Birmingham on April 3. Over the next week, the movement held a series of mass meetings and hundreds engaged in acts of civil disobedience and protests. To stymie the protests, Bull Connor and the Chief of Police, Jamie Moore, secured a temporary injunction from state circuit court Judge William A. Jenkins prohibiting civil rights protesters from engaging in any demonstration or activity that would cause a breach of peace. On April 12, two days after the injunction, King and other activists decided to participate in a march in clear violation of Judge Jenkins's orders. King was quickly arrested and sent to the city jail. During his confinement, he wrote one of the most important documents in civil rights and 20th-century history, "Letter from Birmingham Jail." The document laid out the distinction between a just law and an unjust law, insisted that civil rights activists had a Christian duty to challenge and overthrow Jim Crow, and challenged the silence of white moderates, particularly white clergymen. As religious studies scholar Jonathan Rieder notes, "Letter from Birmingham Jail" brilliantly showcased King the preacher, the prophet, and the activist:

He took aim at the core of American culture, the vast universe of people who imagined themselves to be decent but never dwelled on the shame of American racism. He was not naïve about the power of soaring moral rhetoric to change hearts. King did not rest his optimism on faith in the American dream or the ordained nature of freedom in America. Instead, he found solace in his deep love of black people and the exceptional spirit of the slave ancestors. In all these ways, the "Letter" anticipates the King of the later years who thundered against poverty, racism, and war before he was assassinated in 1968.[17]

King resumed his activities upon his release from jail. But despite the release of the civil rights movement's most recognized leader, the Birmingham campaign appeared to be on the road to the same dead end as the Albany protest of 1962. Problems included a severe shortage of volunteers, low morale among the faithful few, and declining media interest. "The image of Martin Luther King had failed to attract the needed new blood to keep the campaign in the public's eye," explained historian Glenn Askew. Moreover, "a divided black community further complicated matters as the traditional Negro leadership class publicly repudiated the authority of King and Fred Shuttlesworth." To maintain the movement, James Bevel and Ike Reynolds called for the recruitment of African American school children. Their suggestion met firm resistance from many local leaders, including Authur G. Gaston. Notwithstanding opposition to the idea, the Alabama Christina Movement for Civil Rights ACMHR and the SCLC prepared to enlist more school children, several of whom were already involved in the movement. Details were still in the works, but a decision was made to have the students march downtown on Thursday, May 2.

Much like the college students of 1960, the young people of Birmingham willingly embraced their role as foot soldiers in the movement, ready to put their bodies on the line for freedom. On the morning of the scheduled march, thousands of black students headed for 16th Street Baptist Church rather than school to register their discontent with the status quo and push the movement for racial justice forward. As scheduled, the students headed toward downtown a little after noon. Freedom songs pierced the air as the students marched toward City Hall. Anger engulfed Connor, who ordered fire engines to the intersection of 4th Avenue and 17th Street to impede the students' path. By rush hour, the

number of children arrested exceeded one thousand. With pride and determination, they willfully submitted to arrest without protest or violence. Moved by the students' courage, two thousand African Americans packed 6th Avenue Baptist Church to salute the children's courage as well as prepare for the next day's protest.

The next morning, Connor prepared for his showdown with the protesters. Determined to put an end to the protest, he stationed the local police on the eastern side of Kelly Ingram Park while deploying fire trucks at several major thoroughfares downtown. Not long after taking instructions from Dr. King and other leaders, the nonviolent protesters filed out of their meeting place and commenced with their march for freedom. Shortly thereafter, Connor unleashed a reign of terror on the children. Within minutes of the march's start, he ordered the Fire Department to turn its hoses on the children. "Disperse or you'll get wet," police chief Glenn Evans shouted to the young protesters. When they refused to obey his orders, the firemen aimed their high-powered hoses at the children. "The sheer force of the water sent students spinning down the streets, dreadfully skinning exposed flesh," historian Glenn Eskew writes.[18]

The harrowing image of firemen assaulting African American children with high-powered firehoses circulated throughout the national and international media. So, too, did photographs of Connor's canine team of German Shepherds dogs attacking African American children. If civil rights leaders were waiting for the perfect picture of racial hatred and violence in an American city, Connor and his team of safety officials readily supplied it.

The spectacle of Birmingham shook the nation. The Birmingham protests also elicited a great deal of outrage from the international community of human rights activists. Fearful of the implications for the city, racial moderates begged for an end to the protests and invited civil rights leaders to the bargaining table. On May 8, civil rights leaders struck a compromise agreement with city leaders. "We must now move from protest to reconciliation," King told the African American community, which included some who were disappointed with the deal.

MISSISSIPPI GODDAMN: A SEASON OF VIOLENCE

A month after the Children's Crusade in Birmingham, the civil rights movement suffered a devastating loss. On June 12, 1963, white supremacist Byron De La Beckwith assassinated the Jackson, Mississippi-based civil rights activist Medgar Evers, whose wife, Myrlie, heard the gunfire and dashed out of their house. To her horror, she found her badly wounded husband staggering to reach the front door. An hour later, he was pronounced dead at the University Hospital. One of the nation's most dynamic organizers, Evers galvanized thousands of blacks in Mississippi with his indefatigable work ethic, his fearlessness, and his unwavering commitment to racial justice. His death dealt a devastating blow to his family and the civil rights movement. "We all knew the danger was increasing," Myrlie Evers wrote in a moving tribute published in *Life Magazine*. "Threats came daily, cruel and cold and constant, against us and the children. But we had lived with this hatred for years and we did not let it corrode us."[19] Evers's death weighed heavily on the minds of civil rights activists as they prepared for the imminent March on Washington for Freedom and Jobs. The planned march was designed to pressure President Kennedy into passing a civil rights bill to end Jim Crow. Across the South, black women and men made preparations for the historic march. Two hundred miles from the nation's capital in the city of Norfolk, the local National Association for the Advancement of Colored People (NAACP) branch and the Youth Council secured six air-conditioned, restroom-equipped buses for the trip to Washington. On the day of the march, at approximately 5 a.m., the DC-bound caravan buses departed Norfolk with hundreds of elated African Americans. The highlight of the day-long event was Martin Luther King's dynamic "I Have a Dream" speech, in which he fused the prophetic vision of the black church with hardcore political analysis to not only inspire the 250,000 attendees but also to remind the nation's leaders of what he called the "urgency of now." "This is no time to engage in the luxury of cooling off or to take the tranquilizing drug of gradualism. Now is the time to make real the promise of democracy. Now is the time to rise from the dark and desolate valley of segregation to the unlit path of racial justice."[20]

Moved by the day's events, Kennedy issued a statement praising the "deep fervor and the quiet dignity that characterizes the thousands who gathered in the Nation's Capital from across the country to demonstrate their faith and confidence in our democratic form of government." Though noting that "this summer has seen remarkable progress in translating civil rights from principles into practices," the president admitted that the nation had "a very long way yet to travel." Ignoring the integration of public facilities, Kennedy focused his attention on economics:

The executive branch of the Federal Government will continue its efforts to obtain increased employment and to eliminate discrimination in employment practices, two of the prime goals of the March. In addition, our efforts to secure enactment of the legislative proposals made to the Congress will be maintained, including not only the civil rights bill, but also proposals to broaden and strengthen the manpower development and training program, the youth employment bill, amendments to the vocational education program, the establishment of a work-study program for high school age youth, strengthening of the adult basic education provisions in the administration's education program, and the amendments proposed to the public welfare work-relief and training program.[21]

Kennedy concluded on an optimistic note. In the coming weeks, however, it would be hard for many in the civil rights movement to remain optimistic.

Eighteen days after the historic March on Washington, a bomb rocked the 16th Street Baptist Church in Birmingham, killing four school-aged girls, Denise McNair, Carole Robertson, Addie Collins, and Cynthia Wesley. Outraged gripped the nation as white supremacists proved that African Americans were not safe in even the most sacred of spaces. "Those four children did not die in vain," the Reverend Edward Gardner told a crowd of 1,500 blacks gathered at a rally about one mile from the site of the bombing. "There will be a better tomorrow." Taking a page from the prophet Jeremiah, Gardner promised divine retribution for the evils of segregation and racism. "Birmingham is going to pay for every evil deed because God is watching what is going on down here."[22]

More violence rocked the nation in November when President Kennedy was assassinated in Dallas, Texas. Weary but determined, millions of African Americans joined the nation in mourning the death of its beloved leader. Noting that Kennedy's assassination "killed not only a man but a complex of illusions," Martin Luther King situated the president's death within the larger context of the nation's violent culture. "Negroes tragically know political assassination well. In the life of Negro civil-rights leaders, the whine of the bullet from ambush, the roar of the bomb have all too often broken the night's silence.... Nineteen sixty-three was a year of assassinations. Medgar Evers in Jackson, Mississippi, William Moore in Alabama, six Negro children in Birmingham—and who could doubt that these too were political assassinations?"[23]

In the wake of Kennedy's assassination, calls for national civil rights intensified among activists, who hoped the slain leader's successor, Lyndon Baines Johnson, would move the nation closer to its democratic ideas. The degree to which Johnson responded to the needs of African Americans garnered serious attention in the January 1964 issue of the black community's premier monthly, *Ebony*. Under a full-sized picture of Johnson read the title of Lerone Bennett's insightful article: "What Can Negroes Expect from President Lyndon Johnson? America's First Southern Born President since Wilson." "There will be differences in pace, style, and touch," Bennett predicted when discussing the shift from Kennedy to Johnson. Though maintaining a healthy degree of skepticism, Bennett delicately suggested that Johnson might be better on civil rights than his predecessor. "The new president has been talking for several years about civil rights. As he climbed the rungs of power—from the House to the Senate to the Vice-Presidency—he became increasingly militant."[24]

THE PASSAGE OF THE CIVIL RIGHTS AND VOTING RIGHTS ACTS

A decade after the *Brown v. Board* decision, a Democratic-controlled Congress with guidance from the president passed the Civil Rights Act (CRA). On July 2, 1964, Lyndon Johnson signed the act into law. Immediately affecting the fields of education, health care, and labor, the CRA outlawed discrimination on the basis of race, sex, religion, and national origin in public accommodations and employment.

A year after the passage of the CRA, Johnson signed the Voting Rights Act of 1965 (VRA), sweeping legislation that outlawed educational requirements for voting in states and counties where less than half of the voting population were registered on November 1, 1964. The law also empowered the Civil Rights Commission to assign federal registrars to enroll voters. The bill passed in the Senate by a vote of seventy-five to nineteen.

The two most immediate results were the expansion in the black electorate in the South and the growing number of African Americans on local city councils and school boards. The election of Moon Landrieu as the first black mayor of New Orleans was a watershed event in the history of not just the "Crescent City" but throughout the urban South. In keeping with his campaign promise, the percentage of African Americans working in the city government jumped from 10 percent to 40 percent during his two terms. Two years after Landrieu, Atlanta elected Maynard Jackson as mayor. His election, according to Robert Bullard, "marked the coming of age of black Atlanta, in that nine of the eighteen city council members were black and five of the nine school board members were black."[25]

The passage of the civil rights and voting acts were watershed events in the nation's history. These legislative decrees, however, hardly marked the culmination of the black freedom struggle. Instead, African Americans' historic quest for racial justice entered a new phase as black women and men tackled such complex issues as housing, deindustrialization, underemployment and unemployment, voter dilution and annexation, and school desegregation. In many parts of the South, the civil rights movement moved decidedly to the left as African Americans intensified their critique of the maldistribution of wealth in US society, the shortcomings of President Johnson's Great Society programs, and the failure of the state to respond to the social maladies caused by the intransigence and persistence of white supremacy.

INNER-CITY BLUES: AFRICAN AMERICANS AND THE URBAN CRISIS

One issue of great importance for many African Americans who called the urban South home was the deleterious effects of urban renewal and downtown revitalization programs on African American families. Throughout the region, urban renewal exacted a heavy toll on

African Americans as the nation's bulldozer revolution uprooted families, razed historic neighborhoods, destroyed or compromised historic landscapes within the African American community, and contributed to greater levels of wealth disparities across racial lines. The case of Richmond was particularly instructive. Here, the city government, with financial backing from the federal government, engaged in what landscape architect Ian Grandison refers to as "punitive planning." Shortly after the passage of the Federal Housing Act of 1949, the city of Richmond and the Richmond Redevelopment and Housing Authority (RRHA) applied for a $1.3 million grant for slum clearance and an additional $33,000 to survey prospective land for public housing units. During the 1950s, officials commenced the process of relocating poorer African Americans from tenements to public housing units. The RRAA demolished hundreds of dilapidated homes, displaced more than seven thousand of the city's most economically vulnerable citizens, and intensified patterns of racial segregation. To advance its modernization agenda and meet the needs of white suburbanites, the city completed the construction of the /I-64-95 freeway in 1958. The I-95/I-64 connector sliced through two of the largest and most historically rich neighborhoods in the city—Jackson Ward and Navy Hill. One of the major casualties of the interstate was Virginia Union University, a center of black intellectual life that claimed such distinguished alums as Charles Johnson, Abram Harris, Spottswood Robinson, and Douglass Wilder. It had also been a central training ground for many civil rights activists in the city. The highway's construction through the heart of Richmond was part of the city's larger political agenda. "The freeway," Ian Grandison argues, "not only blocked, physically and symbolically, Virginia Union University's access to Richmond's official civic and commercial centers; it also devalued sites of other important black institutions—schools, churches, banks, funeral homes, fraternal lodges—by razing them or razing their surroundings, their fronts and backs up against the highway." Simply put, this was another manifestation of the punitive planning that characterized urban renewal in the South. "The freeway was used as a racial weapon to put African Americans, and their dreams for inclusive citizenship, back in their proper place. Either obliterated by the freeway, or pressed up against it, through the glaring disrespect for their homes and institutions, African Americans were being told in the most flagrant way imaginable that, despite hopeful new interpretations of civil rights law, they still did not belong on the right side of tracks."[26] Urban renewal not only compromised historically black institutions, but it also worsened the city's severe housing shortage.

The situation was equally bleak in the city of Atlanta, where urban renewal devastated the predominantly black neighborhoods of Vine City, Summerhill, and Dixie Hills. Due to years of governmental neglect, the predominance of slumlords, and racist lending policies of the Federal Housing Authority, these inner-city neighborhoods were plagued by overcrowding, substandard housing, and rodent infestations. The construction of the Atlanta Stadium in 1965 on the site of the old Washington Rawson neighborhood ravished the adjacent community of Summerhill. The razing of slums in Summerhill displaced ten to twelve thousand residents. One hundred and twenty miles south of Atlanta, Birmingham witnessed the clearance of several downtown residential neighborhoods surrounding the rapidly expanding Medical Center. The southside neighborhoods slated for demolition had a population of 2,750, of which 2,000 were African Americans. A remarkably similar pattern of downtown rehabilitation and massive black displacement also characterized the housing situation in New Orleans, where between 1957 and 1967 urban renewal projects led to the demolition of 21,000 housing units.

Clashes over housing rocked Durham in 1967 and 1968. In 1966, when the Redevelopment Commission announced plans for the construction of the East-West Expressway, two hundred predominantly black and low-income families were threatened with eviction. That same year, black working women in Durham formed the United Organizations for Community Improvement (UOCI), a federation of low-income neighborhoods. By 1967, the UOCI had grown to sixteen neighborhood councils. A year later, the organization had one thousand members. The founding of the UOCI proved critical in mobilizing low-income and other African Americans: the neighborhood federation was soon identified as the major protest organization in the city.[27] Shunning the politics of backroom negotiations, the organization and its leaders confronted the city's powerbrokers in the most dramatic fashion. On July 17, 1967, for example, 150 African Americans stormed a city council meeting in a moving display of political solidarity and self-determination. Their purpose was to oppose a public housing project and to demand that the city enforce its housing codes.

Concurrent with their efforts to address the problem of housing, African Americans in the urban South also turned their attention to the labor arena. Long-standing practices of racial discrimination in the public and private sectors had excluded African American women and men from clerical and administrative positions, confined them to the lowest paying and most physically grueling jobs, and rendered them more subjected to the vicissitudes of the capitalist system. To make matters worse, deindustrialization dealt a devastating blow to many blue-collar workers in cities like Durham and Birmingham. Small surprise given these realities, African Americans intensified their battle against employment discrimination, pushed for greater access to skilled and clerical positions in the service sector, and sought to empower themselves through unionization.

This rising militancy of black workers was especially visible in the city of Memphis, where the death of two sanitation workers, Robert Walker and Echol Cole, fueled one of the most impressive labor campaigns of the late 1960s: the Memphis Sanitation Strike of 1968. This three-month strike fused the social-movement ethos of the civil rights revolution with the bread-and-butter concerns of organized labor. Subpar pay, terrible working conditions, and the anti-union impulses of the local government had long been a concern for African Americans. In February 1968, when supervisors ordered black workers home during a rainstorm without pay while whites remained on the job, 1,300 African Americans declared themselves on strike. Aligning themselves with the American Federation of State, County, and Municipal Employees, the workers called for wages starting at $2.35 an hour, safety programs, overtime pay, and union recognition. Several weeks into the strike, the sanitation workers successfully convinced Dr. Martin Luther King to come to the city as a way to draw national attention to their plight. As labor historian Peter Levy explains in his coverage of the strike, King's presence had three important benefits: (1) it drew national attention to the problems of black sanitation workers; (2) it helped AFSCME in mobilizing more of black Memphis behind the strike; and (3) it provided traditional civil rights organizations with the opportunity to galvanize around a central concern of black communities across the nation: improving the life chances and experiences of African American blue-collar workers. The success of the strike galvanized not just sanitation workers in other parts of the South but public employees in other occupations.

CONCLUSION

The 20th-century civil rights movement inaugurated a new era in American public life and paved the way for an expansion in African American political power and influence. The post–civil rights era witnessed African Americans rise to the highest offices in such southern cities as Atlanta, Birmingham, New Orleans, Richmond, Charlotte, Dallas, and Memphis. Then in 2008, with heavy support from African Americans and liberal whites, Barack Hussein Obama became the 44th president of the United States. His election, particularly his success in the states of Florida, Virginia, and North Carolina, occasioned critical debate in some circles over whether the United States was a post-racial society. His political rise signaled for some that race no longer determined an individual's social, economic, or political status. To such claims, opponents of the idea of a post-racial society pointed to the racial disparities in health and wealth, the problem of mass incarceration, and the disproportionate number of African Americans and Latinos represented in the criminal justice system. As has long been the case, the US South will be a key battleground in the ongoing quest for racial justice.

DISCUSSION OF THE LITERATURE

The scholarly literature on the civil rights movement in the urban South has expanded tremendously over since the mid-1990s as historians have challenged conventional chronological frames, focused more attention on the ideological diversity within the black freedom struggle, adopted a more transnational perspective on African Americans' fight for racial justice, shifted focus more to the critical contributions of black women, and explored the links between the civil rights movement and the black power movement.

Four foundational studies, published in the 1980s, include: Clayborne Carson's *SNCC and the Awakening of the 1960s*, William Chafe's *Civilities and Civil Rights: Greensboro and the Black Struggle for Freedom*, David Garrow's *Bearing the Cross: Martin Luther King and the Southern Christian Leadership Conference*, and Taylor Branch's *Parting the*

Waters: America in the King Years 1954–1963.[28] Each, in their own distinctive fashion, broadened our understanding of key individuals, events, organizations, and phases of the civil rights movement. Carson's book provided the first comprehensive study of the Student Nonviolent Coordinating Committee (SNCC), which in recent years has received detailed attention from historians Wesley C. Hogan, Cheryl L. Greenberg, and Emilye Crosby. Taking a more local approach, Chafe's *Civilities and Civil Rights* did much more than illuminate the importance of the Greensboro sit-in to the success of the larger movement; it added a more nuanced perspective on the regional differences within the South and the ways in which the polite racism of the upper South could be as debilitating to the freedom struggle as the vitriolic racism of the deep southern states of Alabama and Mississippi. The sweeping narratives of Branch and Garrow added complexity to the dominant image of Dr. Martin Luther King and offered a broader and more national view of the civil rights movement.

The next decade witnessed more interventions within the field of civil rights historiography as Charles Payne's *I've Got the Light of Freedom* and John Dittmer's *Local People: The Struggle for Civil Rights in Mississippi* embraced a more bottom-up approach to the study of the black freedom struggle.[29] With their rich archival research and elegant writing styles, Payne and Dittmer challenged scholars to focus more on grassroots organizing and the centrality of ordinary people in the movement's success. Their work coincided with and fueled the development of more locally oriented studies that focused on one specific city or state. With regards to the urban South, some of the most valuable of those studies include Glenn T. Eskew's *But for Birmingham: The Local and National Movements in the Civil Rights Struggle*, Winston A. Grady-Willis's *Challenging U.S. Apartheid: Atlanta and Black Struggles for Human Rights, 1960–1977*, Christina Greene's *Our Separate Ways: Women*

and the Black Freedom Movement in Durham, North Carolina, and more recently Julian Maxwell Hayter's *The Dream Is Lost: Voting Rights and the Politics of Race in Richmond, Virginia.*[30]

Not all but many of these local studies embrace the "long civil rights" framework, a concept coined and popularized by historian Jacquelyn Dowd Hall in 2005. This framework both complicates and challenges conventional narratives of the black freedom struggle in three significant ways: (1) it emphasizes the connections between the civil rights insurgencies of the 1950s and 1960s and the labor activism of the 1930s and 1940s; (2) it includes movements and activists whose political goals extended beyond the desegregation of public schools and public accommodations; and (3) it accentuates the ideological continuities between the civil rights revolution and the black power movement without ignoring important distinctions in terms of political ideas and goals. More recently, several scholars, most notably Clarence Lang and Sundiata Cha-Jui, have criticized the "long civil rights" perspective for exaggerating the continuities in African American social movement history and overlooking important differences in the black power and civil rights movements.[31]

A growing body of scholarship on the civil rights movement has also broadened our understanding of the contributions of women. Fortunately, the vibrant field of black women's history along with new directions in civil rights historiography have deepened our knowledge of the lives, politics, and intellectual labors of key figures like Rosa Parks, Ella Baker, and Fannie Lou Hamer; the critical work of local chapters of the National Welfare Rights Organization; and the intense debates around gender between black women, white women, and black men. Barbara Ransby's landmark study, *Ella Baker and the Black Freedom Movement: A Radical Democratic Vision*, is a tour de force that traces Baker from her early upbringing in Virginia and

North Carolina to her education at Shaw, to her intellectual maturation within the institutional matrix of 1930s Harlem, to her organizing work with the National Association for the Advancement of Colored People (NAACP) and the Southern Christian Leadership Conference (SCLC) in the 1940s and 1950s, and to her critical guidance of the Student Nonviolent Coordinating Committee (SNCC) in the 1960s.[32] Through the life and political legacy of Baker, Ransby forces her readers to grapple with the complex intersections of race, class, and gender in American public life, the meaning of democracy and integration, and the limitations of charismatic leadership. Important questions regarding the gender politics of the civil rights movement also emerge from such studies as Jeanne Theoharris's *The Rebellious Life of Mrs. Rosa Parks*, Danielle McGuire's *At the Dark End of the Street: Black Women, Rape and Resistance; A New History of the Civil Rights Movement from Rosa Parks to the Rise of Black Power*, and Chana Lee's *For Freedom's Sake: The Life of Fannie Lou Hamer*.[33]

Increasingly, scholars of civil rights history have also sought to examine the movement within the context of the rise and fall of liberalism and the major transformations within the nation's political economy. These works include Adolph Reed's *Stirring in the Jug*, which includes incisive critiques on Atlanta's civil rights politicians and urban regime politics, Nathan Matthew Lassiter's *Silent Majority: Suburban Politics in the Sunbelt South*, and Devin Fergus's *Liberalism, Black Power, and the Making of American Politics, 1965–1980*, which centers primarily on urban North Carolina.[34]

PRIMARY SOURCES

Valuable information on the civil rights movement in the urban South can be gleaned from the personal papers and autobiographies of the key participants; the administrative papers of the National Association for the

Advancement of Colored People (NAACP), CORE, and other activist organizations; black newspapers and monthlies; and oral histories. Housed at the Library of Congress and digitized by ProQuest, the papers of the NAACP, for example, provide detailed accounts of the major legal battles, judicial decisions, and protests during the civil rights movement, as well as extensive information on litigation and organizing around housing discrimination, urban renewal, employment discrimination, and the entrenched racism within the criminal justice system.

To gain a day-to-day perspective on the movement, it is also important to engage the major black newspapers, weeklies, and monthlies of the era: the *Atlanta Daily World*, the *Norfolk Journal and Guide*, the *Pittsburgh Courier*, the *Chicago Defender*, the *Florida Star*, and the *Birmingham World*, among others. Other critical sources are the Johnson publications, *Jet* and *Ebony*, which often sent their reporters and photographers to the South.

If seeking to gain a deeper understanding of the civil rights movement's most recognized leader, Martin Luther King Jr., as well as the battles he waged in the urban South, the *Martin Luther King, Jr. Papers*, edited by Clayborne Carson, and which now consist of fourteen volumes, should be consulted.[35] These papers contain correspondence, newspaper clippings, his sermons and speeches, and his writings. Equally important are the books King published during his lifetime, most notably, *Why We Can't Wait, Stride for Freedom*, and *Where Do We Go from Here: Chaos or Community?*[36] These readings provide the reader with his unique perspective on such highly publicized events as the Montgomery Boycott, the Children's Crusade in Birmingham in 1963, and the March on Washington, as well as his philosophy on the social responsibilities of the clergy, his views on black power, and his firm belief in the inextricable connection between economic injustice and racial injustice.

DIGITAL SOURCES

Civil Rights Digital Library (http://crdl.usg.edu /events/).

SNCC Legacy Project (http://www.sncclegacyproject .org/).

King Papers (https://kinginstitute.stanford.edu/king -papers/about-papers-project).

FURTHER READING

Branch, Taylor. *Parting the Waters: America in the King Years, 1954–63.* New York: Simon and Schuster, 1988.

Brown-Nagin, Tomiko. *Courage to Dissent: Atlanta and the Long History of the Civil Rights Movement.* Oxford: Oxford University Press, 2011.

Chafe, William H. *Civilities and Civil Rights: Greensboro, North Carolina, and the Black Struggle for Freedom.* New York: Oxford University Press, 1980.

Collier-Thomas, Bettye, and V. P. Franklin, eds. *Sisters in the Struggle: African American Women in the Civil Rights-Black Power Movement.* New York: New York University Press, 2001.

Dittmer, John. *Local People: The Struggle for Civil Rights in Mississippi.* Urbana: University of Illinois Press, 1995.

Eskew, Glenn T. *But for Birmingham: The Local and National Movements in the Civil Rights Struggle.* Chapel Hill: University of North Carolina Press, 1997.

Fergus, Devin. *Liberalism, Black Power, and the Making of American Politics, 1965–1980.* Athens, GA: University of Georgia Press, 2009.

Grady-Willis, Winston A. *Challenging U.S. Apartheid: Atlanta and Black Struggles for Human Rights, 1960–1977.* Durham, NC: Duke University Press, 2006.

Greene, Christina. *Our Separate Ways: Women and the Black Freedom Movement in Durham, North Carolina.* Chapel Hill: University of North Carolina Press, 2005.

Hayter, Julian Maxwell. *The Dream Is Lost: Voting Rights and the Politics of Race in Richmond, Virginia.* Lexington: University Press of Kentucky, 2017.

Hogan, Wesley. *Many Minds, One Heart: SNCC's Dream for a New America.* Chapel Hill: University of North Carolina Press, 2007.

Jackson, Thomas F. *From Civil Rights to Human Rights: Martin Luther King, Jr., and the Struggle for Economic Justice.* Philadelphia: University of Pennsylvania Press, 2007.

Lassiter, Matthew D. *The Silent Majority: Suburban Politics in the Sunbelt South.* Princeton, NJ: Princeton University Press, 2006.

Lawson, Steven F. *Black Ballots: Voting Rights in the South, 1944–1969.* New York: Columbia University Press, 1976.

Payne, Charles M. *I've Got the Light of Freedom: The Organizing Tradition and the Mississippi Freedom Struggle.* Berkeley: University of California Press, 1995.

Ransby, Barbara. *Ella Baker and the Black Freedom Movement: A Radical Democratic Vision.* Chapel Hill: University of North Carolina Press, 2003.

NOTES

1. Charles A. J. McPherson to the NAACP on November 9, 1920, in: *NAACP Papers* (Bethesda: University Publications of America), Part 4, Reel 1.
2. *Norfolk Journal and Guide*, January 21, 1933.
3. *Chicago Defender*, June 1, 1940.
4. *Norfolk Journal and Guide*, December 18, 1948.
5. "Platform of the States Rights Democratic Party," in *The American Presidency Project*, ed. Gerhard Peters and John T. Woolley, August 14, 1948.
6. Matthew Lassiter, *Silent Majority: Suburban Politics in the Sunbelt South* (Princeton, NJ: Princeton University Press, 2006), 41.
7. Lassiter, *Silent Majority*, 41.
8. Jeanne Theoharris, *The Rebellious Life of Mrs. Rosa Parks* (Boston: Beacon Press, 2013), 62.
9. Theoharris, *Rebellious Life*, 63.
10. Lassiter, *Silent Majority*, 3.
11. Lassiter, *Silent Majority*, 13–14.
12. Lassiter, *Silent Majority*, 40.
13. Taylor Branch, *Parting the Waters: America in the King Years 1954–1963* (New York: Simon and Schuster, 1988), 274.
14. Winston A. Grady-Willis, *Challenging U.S. Apartheid: Atlanta and Black Struggles for Human Rights, 1960–1977* (Durham, NC: Duke University Press, 2006).
15. Raymond Arsenault, *Freedom Riders*, 103.
16. Arsenault, *Freedom Riders*, 107.
17. Jonathan Rieder, *Gospel of Freedom: Martin Luther King, Jr.'s Letter from Birmingham Jail and the Struggle that Changed A Nation* (New York: Bloomsbury Press, 2013), xvi.

18. Glenn T. Eskew, *But for Birmingham: The Local and National Movements in the Civil Rights Struggle* (Chapel Hill: University of North Carolina Press, 1997), 268.

19. Myrlie Evers, "He Said He Wouldn't Mind Dying—If...," *Life*, June 28, 1963, 35.

20. Martin Luther King Jr., "I Have a Dream," 1963.

21. John F. Kennedy, "Statement by the President on the March on Washington for Jobs and Freedom," in *The American Presidency Project*, ed. Gerhard Peters and John T. Woolley, 2018.

22. "Birmingham Still Seething," *Chicago Defender*, September 18, 1963, AI.

23. Martin Luther King Jr., *Why We Can't Wait* (New York: Penguin Books, 1964), 144–145.

24. Lerone Bennett, "What Negroes Can Expect from President Lyndon Johnson," *Ebony*, January, 1964, 82.

25. Robert D. Bullard and E. Kiki Thomas, "Atlanta: Mecca of the Southeast," in *In Search of the New South: The Black Urban Experience in the 1970s and 1980s*, ed. Robert Bullard (Tuscaloosa: University of Alabama Press, 1991), 94.

26. Ian Grandison, "Other Side of the 'Free' Way," 221.

27. Christina Greene, *Our Separate Ways: Women and the Black Freedom Movement in Durham, North Carolina* (Chapel Hill: University of North Carolina Press, 2005), 11.

28. Clayborne Carson, *SNCC and the Awakening of the 1960s*; William H. Chafe, *Civilities and Civil Rights: Greensboro, North Carolina, and the Black Struggle for Freedom* (New York: Oxford University Press, 1980); David Garrow, *Bearing the Cross: Martin Luther King and the Southern Christian Leadership Conference* (New York: William Morrow, 1986); and Taylor Branch, *Parting the Waters: America in the King Years, 1954–63* (New York: Simon and Schuster, 1988).

29. Charles M. Payne, *I've Got the Light of Freedom: The Organizing Tradition and the Mississippi Freedom Struggle* (Berkeley: University of California Press, 1995); and John Dittmer, *Local People: The Struggle for Civil Rights in Mississippi* (Urbana: University of Illinois Press, 1995).

30. Eskew, *But for Birmingham*; Grady-Willis, *Challenging U.S. Apartheid*; Greene, *Our Separate Ways*; and Julian Maxwell Hayter, *The Dream Is Lost: Voting Rights and the Politics of Race in Richmond, Virginia* (Lexington: University Press of Kentucky, 2017).

31. Sundiata Keita Cha-Jua and Clarence Lang, "The 'Long Movement' as Vampire: Temporal and Spatial Fallacies in Recent Black Freedom Studies," *Journal of African American History* 92, no. 2 (2007): 265–288.

32. Barbara Ransby, *Ella Baker and the Black Freedom Movement: A Radical Democratic Vision* (Chapel Hill: University of North Carolina Press, 2003).

33. Theoharris, *Rebellious Life*; Danielle McGuire, *At the Dark End of the Street: Black Women, Rape and Resistance; A New History of the Civil Rights Movement from Rosa Parks to the Rise of Black Power* (Boston: Beacon Press, 2013); and Chana Lee, *For Freedom's Sake: The Life of Fannie Lou Hamer* (Urbana: University of Illinois Press, 1999).

34. Adolph Reed *Stirring in the Jug: Black Politics in the Post-Segregation Era* (Minneapolis: University of Minneosta Press, 1999); and Lassiter, *Silent Majority*; and Devin Fergus, *Liberalism, Black Power, and the Making of American Politics, 1965–1980* (Athens, GA: University of Georgia Press, 2009).

35. Clayborne Carson, ed., *Martin Luther King, Jr. Papers* (Berkeley: University of California Press, 2000).

36. King Jr., *Why We Can't Wait* (New York: New American Library, 1964); Martin Luther King Jr., *Stride for Freedom: The Montgomery Story* (New York: Harper &Brothers, 1958); and Martin Luther King Jr., *Where Do We Go from Here: Chaos or Community?* (New York: Harper & Row, 1967).

Claudrena N. Harold

THE SIT-IN MOVEMENT

WHAT WAS THE SIT-IN MOVEMENT?

When the lunch counter sit-in movement of 1960 "ripped through Dixie with the speed of a rocket and the contagion of the old plague" (as a writer for the *Chicago Defender* put it), many were left wondering where this all came from.[1] The students who led the movement emphasized the spontaneous elements of the sit-ins. The protests, they insisted over and

over again, were nothing more than a necessary, commonsense response to this particular racial injustice.[2] Civil rights groups, however, emphasized connections between the
1960 sit-ins and earlier protest campaigns.[3]
Both explanations contain seeds of truth. Even
as the sit-in movement was a bold and largely
unplanned venture into uncharted waters, established civil rights organizations played a
critical role in its success. A movement this decentralized built upon thousands of individual
and small-group decisions and cannot be captured by any single explanation. It was spontaneous and independent. It was also a product
of a complex network of communication between protest communities and the result of
years of careful organization and planning.[4]

Precursors. Sporadic sit-in protests at
lunch counters and restaurants took place in
the two decades preceding the 1960 sit-in
movement. The Congress of Racial Equality
(CORE) initiated sit-in protests at restaurants
in Chicago in the early 1940s and then led a
successful challenge to lunch counter segregation in St. Louis variety stores between
1949 and 1953. In the 1950s, CORE organized more sit-ins across the upper South and
border states through the 1950s; in 1959, its
activists organized sit-in protests in Miami.[5]

In the late 1950s, members of the Oklahoma
City Youth Council branch of the National
Association for the Advancement of Colored
People (NAACP), led by Clara Luper, a
high school teacher and advisor to the Youth
Council, organized a series of lunch counter
sit-in protests. Luper took a group of black
children, ages seven to fifteen, into a downtown Oklahoma City chain store where, after
being refused service, they sat until closing
time. After several days of protests, the store's
management decided to desegregate lunch
counters at its nearly forty stores in Oklahoma,
Missouri, Kansas, and Iowa. Between 1957
and 1960, NAACP Youth Councils followed
Oklahoma City's lead and organized sit-ins at
lunch counters in sixteen cities in the Midwest.[6]

Although some scholars have emphasized
the importance of these protests, even insisting that these sit-ins mark the true beginning
of the sit-in movement, it is important to
recognize the limitations of these campaigns.
The press gave them little coverage. The scattered protests never coalesced in a way that
would force the white media to pay attention.
The desegregation that occurred did not necessarily stand out at a time when segregation
practices in the region already were breaking
down. Protest victories could be frustratingly
uneven, as lunch counter operators would desegregate and then sometimes quietly revert
back to their old policies. The NAACP national office made no effort to publicize the
actions of their youth branches and sometimes
even urged local leaders to stop the protests.[7]
There is also little evidence that the students
who initiated the 1960 sit-in movement knew
much, if anything, about these earlier protests.[8]

Greensboro. When Ezell Blair Jr., Franklin
McCain, Joseph McNeil, and David Richmond
walked into the Greensboro Woolworth's on
the afternoon of February 1, 1960, their protest could very well have followed the pattern
of these earlier sit-ins. The first-year students
at North Carolina Agricultural and Technical
College could have gotten some local attention. They could have convinced a local restaurant operator to stop discriminating. Maybe,
as in Oklahoma, they could have even inspired
some others to follow. But this time, to everyone's surprise, including the four who started
it all, it all turned out quite differently. The four
became twenty on day two of the Greensboro
protest and within a week some two hundred
protesters were demonstrating at downtown
lunch counters.[9] The manager of the Woolworth
knew that if he chose to press trespassing
charges against the students, the police would
arrest them. But he chose not to. "Let them
sit there," he told his employees. "Don't say
anything to them."[10]

Students rejected a proposal from city
leaders for a two-week moratorium on

protests to explore whether local custom would allow for integrated seating, and the next day an estimated 600 people—integrationists, segregationists, and onlookers—crammed into the Woolworth eating area. The Ku Klux Klan arrived, joining forces with what one reporter described as "[g]angs of shoving, shouting [white] teenagers." Police removed a number of whites who were verbally abusing the protesters and arrested three white men.[11] Someone called in a bomb threat, and police emptied the store. "The Negro students set up a wild round of cheering as the announcement of closing was made and carried their leaders out on their shoulders," reported the local newspaper. They moved on to the nearby Kress store, which promptly shut down. Then they marched back to campus, chanting "It's all over" and "We whipped Woolworth." That night the students held another mass meeting where they agreed to hold off on further sit-ins to allow time for "negotiation and study."[12]

The Spark Catches. Events in Greensboro attracted not just local but also national press attention and inspired college students in other North Carolina cities to start their own sit-ins. On February 8, students in Durham and Winston-Salem sat in at their local lunch counters. In the following days, students in Charlotte, Raleigh, Fayetteville, Elizabeth City, High Point, and Concord joined what quickly became a statewide movement.

This first wave of North Carolina sit-ins followed the Greensboro model. They often began with a bold, spontaneous act. The Winston-Salem sit-ins began when Carl Matthews, a graduate of the Winston-Salem Teachers College who worked in a local factory, sat down at the lunch counter of the Kress store in the middle of the lunch rush. Later that afternoon, six other African Americans, several of them students at the Teachers College, joined him—and the movement grew from there.[13] In Raleigh, protests were sparked by a local radio announcer who confidently predicted that area college students would not follow

Greensboro's lead. Intent on proving him wrong, a group of students went downtown the following morning and began the Raleigh sit-ins.[14]

As in Greensboro, segregationists hovered around the demonstrations, bringing intimidation, sporadic acts of violence, and threats of more serious retribution. When white youths threw eggs at black students seated at the Raleigh Woolworth's lunch counter, the protesters "gave no reaction either to this or to jeers and catcalls thrown at them," noted a reporter.[15] Bomb threats became a common tactic for disrupting sit-ins.

There were also variations from the template established in Greensboro. In High Point, high school rather than college students initiated the sit-ins, and they received close guidance from adult civil rights leaders. The High Point protests also ran into some new obstacles. The day after sit-in protests led to a shutdown of two variety store lunch counters, a local merchant paid a group of white high school students to arrive early and occupy all the lunch counter stools at the Woolworth's so the black protesters had nowhere to sit. When they came back the next day, the store had converted its lunch counter into a display counter, each stool adorned with a box of Valentine chocolates. The students converted their sit-in to a stand-in and forced the manager to shut down the store.[16]

On February 11, students in Hampton, Virginia, brought the sit-in movement beyond North Carolina. The next day, students in two more Virginia cities, Norfolk and Portsmouth, joined. Sit-ins continued to spread to new cities in North Carolina: Salisbury on February 16; Shelby on the 18th; Henderson on the 25th; and Chapel Hill on the 28th.[17]

The first student arrests took place on February 12 when the manager of a Raleigh shopping center brought trespassing charges against forty-one students who had gathered outside a Woolworth whose lunch counter they had just forced to shut down. Fined $10 each, their convictions were quickly overturned on appeal.[18] (The fact that they were arrested on the sidewalk and not inside the business itself meant they could claim the arrest violated their rights under the First Amendment.) On the same day, the movement spread deeper into the South, reaching Florida and South Carolina. In Rock Hill, South Carolina, white youths knocked a black protester from his stool, someone threw a bottle of ammonia into a store, setting off fumes that stung the eyes of the demonstrators inside, and then bomb threats cleared two targeted stores. The *New York Times* covered the Rock Hill protest on its front page—another first for the sit-in movement.[19]

Nashville. No group of students was more ready for the sit-in movement than those in Nashville, where they had been preparing a sit-in campaign months before the Greensboro Four took their seats.[20] Reverend James Lawson, an African American divinity student at Vanderbilt University and devoted follower of the nonviolent principles espoused by Mahatma Gandhi, had been leading workshops on nonviolent protest techniques for several years. Lawson organized small-scale test sit-ins of local lunch counters in late 1959, with the goal of starting sit-in protests after the holidays.

News of the Greensboro protests spurred students in Nashville to follow through on their plans. On February 13, over one hundred students sat at lunch counters in three Nashville variety stores. The next sit-in, five days later, brought out 200 students; almost double that number came out two days later. The protests were carefully organized, orderly, and, as far as the sit-ins went, rather uneventful. The same could not be said about the next wave of protests, in late February. At the Nashville Woolworth store, one of five stores targeted, hundreds of people—reporters, supporters, opponents, and curious onlookers—crammed in to watch the sit-in demonstration, "like spectators at a boxing match," according to one account. After more than an hour of escalating assaults against the students seated at the lunch counter, some white teenagers dragged three protesters from their stools and started beating them. "The three Negroes did not fight back, but stumbled and ran out of the store; the whites, their faces red with anger, screamed at them to stop and fight, to please goddam stop and fight. None of the other Negroes at the counter ever looked around. It was over in a minute."[21] Only then did the police step in, arresting eighty-one of the sit-in protesters (but none of the white assailants) on disorderly conduct charges.

Atlanta. Despite having many of the ingredients that would seem to predict robust sit-in movement activism, including a number of African American colleges and a group of committed activist students, the Atlanta movement was slow to get going. Atlanta students would not launch their own movement until the following fall, after the larger lunch counter sit-in movement had run its course.[22]

After Greensboro, Atlanta student leaders sought the counsel of older black community leaders who urged them to direct their energies toward supporting ongoing negotiation and litigation efforts. Then, in early March, as students were preparing a series of downtown sit-in protests, university leaders persuaded them to postpone their protests once again, suggesting they first prepare a statement of principles. Published in Atlanta newspapers on March 9, "An Appeal for Human Rights" was a forceful denunciation of Jim Crow and a declaration of support for the sit-in movement. "We do not intend to wait placidly for those which are already legally and morally ours to be meted out to us one at a time," proclaimed the student leaders. "Today's youth will not sit by submissively, while being denied all of the rights, privileges, and joys of life."[23]

After several more false starts, delays, and bickering among factions within the civil rights community, Atlanta's students finally joined the sit-in movement. Lawyers had advised the students to focus their protests on publicly owned facilities and facilities that were involved in interstate transportation (and thus subject to federal nondiscrimination rules). At precisely 11:30 a.m. on March 15, after placing an anonymous phone call to the United Press International detailing their plans, Atlanta students launched a coordinated series of sit-in demonstrations at ten eating establishments.[24] According to one news account, "[n]early everyone concerned, demonstrators, arresting police, onlookers, behaved quietly, unemotionally, as though in the performance of a ritual."[25] Police arrested seventy-seven demonstrators at cafeterias in the capitol, the county courthouse, city hall, and several bus terminals and train stations, charging them under a newly passed state antitrespassing law. Georgia Governor Ernest Vandiver personally ordered the arrest of the students who targeted the state capitol cafeteria and then issued a statement that described "these mass violations of State law and private property rights" as "subversive in character."[26]

The day after the mass arrests, Donald Hollowell, a prominent African American lawyer who was representing the arrested students, persuaded the students to stop their protests until they received a "final judgment" in the pending court cases. The students turned their efforts to organizing a boycott of downtown department stores. An organized lunch counter sit-in campaign would not return to Atlanta until the following fall.[27]

Violence in a Nonviolent Movement.
White segregationist attacks on sit-in protesters escalated as the protests drew more participants, spread farther south, and, in some instances, as student protesters decided to fight back when abused. An increase in violent confrontations between protesters and counterprotesters was a cost of success for the sit-in movement.

More violence was all but inevitable when the movement reached the Deep South. On February 25, thirty-five students sat in at the courthouse cafeteria in Montgomery, Alabama. The governor demanded that Alabama State College, an all-black institution, expel students who took part in the protests. In an expression of solidarity with those threatened with expulsion, 1,200 students from the college marched to the state capital. Montgomery police did nothing when Ku Klux Klan members arrived, armed with baseball bats, and attacked the marchers.[28]

By mid-March, one reporter noted "increasing racial hostility—a belligerence on both sides that goes beyond the immediate issue of whether Negroes should be served, while they're sitting down, at segregated lunch counters."[29] In Savannah, a white youth was arrested after punching a black sit-in demonstrator and breaking his jaw. The police hooked up fire hoses, ready to break up the crowds of whites and blacks.[30] In late March, following a KKK meeting in Anniston, Alabama, members went around town setting up burning crosses and someone threw a fire bomb in the yard of the home of a lawyer representing sit-in protesters.[31] The segregationist backlash took a sadistic turn in Houston. Two days after sit-ins began there, a group of segregationist vigilantes captured and tortured a young African American man, carving the letters "KKK" across his chest.[32]

Although participants in the first wave of sit-in protests professed a commitment to nonviolence, this commitment weakened as the movement grew. Most sit-in demonstrators recognized nonviolent resistance to oppression as a strategically effective approach, but they did not necessarily embrace it as a way of life. As the sit-in movement swept more and more people into its orbit, a growing number of participants came to the demonstrations without a strong commitment to nonviolence, either as an ideology or a strategy. The violence that accompanied the sit-ins was overwhelmingly white brutality against African Americans and their white allies. But in some instances African Americans did not turn the other cheek.[33]

After two weeks of rising tension and scattered white attacks on demonstrators, the first incident of black youths fighting back took place in High Point, North Carolina on February 15. School had been canceled because of a snowstorm, and a group of white youths took advantage of the day off to head down to the Woolworth's that had been the target of several days of sit-in protests. They taunted and threw snowballs at the protesters, most of whom were high school students. When police stood by doing nothing, local NAACP leader Elton Cox declared, "We will not undergo embarrassment and assault again without fighting back."[34] After whites started punching black protesters leaving the local Woolworth store, some blacks returned their punches. The police stepped in, arresting two African Americans and one white. White abuse of the peaceful protesters was news; responding in kind was bigger news. "Negroes Fight Back in the South" was the headline the next day in the *Amsterdam News*, a New York-based black newspaper.[35] The *Atlanta Constitution* ran the story under the headline, "Race Brawl Erupts at Restaurant."[36]

The next days brought more violence, this time in Portsmouth, Virginia, where, as in High Point, high school students led the local sit-in effort. After whites attempted to block a protest by arriving at a targeted lunch counter ahead of the demonstrators and occupying all the stools, several hundred black and white youths collected in the parking lot outside the store, some armed with hammers, wrenches, chains, and razors. A fight erupted. A black student leader attributed the violence to "this other element" of local blacks who were not part of the planned demonstration. A CORE field officer soon arrived in Portsmouth to conduct workshops in nonviolence for the students.[37]

In late February, sit-ins in Chattanooga, Tennessee, led to two days of rioting. When police ordered a Kress lunch counter cleared after the store shut it down in the face of a sit-in demonstration, a brawl erupted involving about fifty black protesters and 150 white segregationists. Seven whites were arrested; there were no reported black arrests. The next day over one thousand whites were gathered in the downtown business district when demonstrators arrived. Police created a barrier to keep the two groups apart. Some threw bottles and rocks. Eleven blacks and nine whites were arrested. To break up those who refused to disperse, police turned fire hoses on both blacks and whites. When whites turned out in force the following day, the students decided to hold off on further protests.[38]

These events illustrate how as the sit-in movement expanded its ranks, it attracted more people who had little or no connection with the coordination efforts and nonviolence training used in Greensboro, Nashville, and other places where the movement was most organized. The discipline and commitment to nonviolence that defined the first wave of protests remained evident in many locations, but not everywhere.

Policing Jim Crow. Along with the increase in extralegal violence, white segregationists responded to the sit-ins with legal action. The legal options available to defenders of lunch counter segregation were somewhat different from other battles of the civil rights movement. When civil rights protests took place on public property, as most did, since protesters usually targeted southern local and state governments, government officials were the ones who decided whether to arrest the protesters or not. But lunch counter sit-ins typically took place on private property, so the initial choice of whether to call the police was in the hands of the operators of these businesses. Their typical reaction was not to call the police. Most of these men (they were almost always men) saw themselves as businessmen first and foremost, and sending potential paying customers to jail for doing nothing more than asking to spend money at their lunch counters was not good business. They wanted the protests to stop, and their most common approach to dealing with them was to just ignore the protesters or, if that did not work, to shut down their lunch counters.[39]

But some did call the police, and by the end of the spring thousands of young men and women would be arrested for taking part in sit-in protests. Arrests sometimes came quickly. In Atlanta and Montgomery, for example, police and lunch counter managers met coordinated sit-in protest campaigns with immediate arrests. Elsewhere, arrests only occurred after weeks of protest. In Greensboro, where protests began at the beginning of February 1960, the first arrests of sit-in protests did not happen until April. Sometimes the arrests came in ones and twos; sometimes there were mass arrests of protesters.

At a trial of seventy-five Nashville protesters, the judge promptly found protesters guilty of disorderly conduct and sentenced them to a fine of $50 or thirty days in jail. The students chose jail. The following day, four more Nashville students were found guilty of disorderly conduct and also chose to spend thirty-three days in jail rather than pay their fines. Three thousand supporters gathered outside the courthouse singing hymns and the National Anthem.[40] Later that month, in Little Rock, a group of college students went straight from the city court, where they watched their classmates convicted on charges of breaching the peace for taking part in a sit-in protest, to a new round of downtown sit-ins. After they shut down several downtown lunch counters, they gathered at the state capital and sang "God Bless America" and "The Star-Spangled Banner."[41] Students thus demonstrated a new tactic that would become an integral part of the sit-in movement: transforming judicial proceedings into a new protest platform.[42]

In Tallahassee, Florida, a local judge found eleven demonstrators guilty of disturbing the peace and chastised the students for their "complete disregard for private property rights" and for following "preachers, professors and organizations" who were using the students for "publicity purposes." Three of the students chose to pay $300 fines; eight chose sixty-day jail sentences instead.[43] The biggest single arrest of the sit-in movement took place in Orangeburg, South Carolina. When students heading toward a protest refused to turn back when ordered by police, they turned fire hoses on them. Since the jail could not contain the hundreds arrested, students were herded into a pen normally used as a chicken coop.[44] In Baton Rouge, Louisiana, a group of sit-in protesters were arrested on charges of disturbing the peace. ("How were they disturbing the peace?" the students' lawyer asked the arresting officer at the subsequent trial. "By sitting there," he answered.[45]) After finding them guilty, a judge doled out sentences of thirty days in jail plus a $100 fine. Administrators at Southern University also expelled eighteen students who took part in the sit-ins, leading to a mass student boycott of classes.[46]

The NAACP reported that by June almost 2,000 students had been arrested for taking part in the demonstrations, with more than $44,000 paid in fines and $100,000 put up for bail.[47]

Summer of 1960 and Beyond.

When the spring term came to an end and many of the leaders and troops of the sit-in movement left campus, the lunch counter sit-in campaign, at least as a regionwide phenomenon, dissipated. Even before the end of the school year, there had been signs that the movement was slowing. The feverish excitement of those opening months was impossible to sustain. Much of the early energy of the protests was channeled into more organized forms, such as coordinated boycotts and negotiations. Protest leaders began to complain about lagging support among their classmates. With the end of the term, these challenges only increased.[48]

With most college students scattered to hometowns and summer jobs, the work of the sit-ins was left to others. High school students took over the protests in some cities.[49] In Knoxville, where students had difficulty mobilizing an effective sit-in campaign, a group of black and white professionals (some of whom had criticized the student movement) formed a group they called the Associated Council for Full Citizenship and launched their own sit-ins.

Their carefully orchestrated campaign was far more effective than the halting student protests that had preceded it, and in just over a month they convinced Knoxville's merchants to provide nondiscriminatory service.[50]

By the summer of 1960, the lunch counter sit-in movement had fractured into countless local protest campaigns. The sit-in, as its own distinctive movement, had run its course. The sit-in as a protest tactic, however, had not. It would remain one of the most powerful weapons of the larger civil rights movement for years to come.

WHAT CAUSED THE SIT-IN MOVEMENT?

Frustration and Hope. What led this generation of young African Americans to this stunning act of collective defiance? When the reporters who rushed to cover the sit-ins asked this very question, the answers they received were a seemingly paradoxical mix of disillusionment and hopefulness. Sources of frustration were twofold. The students were deeply frustrated, of course, with the persistent inequities and indignities of life in the Jim Crow South. But they were also frustrated with the older generation of African Americans who they felt were not doing enough to challenge the status quo. Some chastised their parents for their apparent willingness to accept unjust racial practices. "Our adults are too worried about security to do anything," complained a North Carolina student. "They are too afraid of their jobs. We've got to do it. And we're not afraid."[51] Some expressed frustration with the tactics favored by older activists. "The legal redress, the civil-rights redress, are far too slow for the demands of our time," declared James Lawson. "The sit-in is a break with the accepted tradition of change, of legislation and the courts. It is the use of a dramatic act to gain redress."[52]

Intertwined with this frustration and disillusionment, the students also demonstrated a powerful strain of optimism. Early in their lives, President Truman had ended segregation in the military and Jackie Robinson had broken major league baseball's color line. The United States Supreme Court had struck down state-mandated segregation policies in public schools in the landmark 1954 *Brown v. Board of Education* decision. In 1957, Congress passed the first federal civil rights law since Reconstruction. Those who followed overseas events in the late 1950s saw African nations freeing themselves from European colonial control. Around the world, the black freedom struggle was making unprecedented gains. Many of these students were also the first in their family to attend college, and practically all experienced more economic security than their parents had growing up.

Yet despite dramatic victories in the Supreme Court and despite the passage of a new federal civil rights act, the daily lives of young black men and women in the South had not been transformed. Because they had reason to believe their lives would and should be better than those of their parents, the generation of African Americans who joined the sit-in movement in 1960 felt continued racial exclusion as more of an affront to their dignity than had their parents.

These interlocking strands of hope and frustration created a potent blend of emotions for African American college students at the dawn of the 1960s. Optimism that there was a better world in the offing, and that they had it in their power to bring it about, allowed them to turn frustration into mobilization.

Why Lunch Counters? To understand why this generation of students was ready to do something does not answer another central question of the sit-in movement: Why, considering all the racial injustices they experienced on a daily basis in the Jim Crow South, did the students target lunch counters?

Martin Luther King Jr. eloquently summarized the "tragic inconveniences" of this particular form of racial oppression. "The answer," he wrote, "lies in the fact that here the Negro has suffered indignities and injustices that cannot be justified or explained . . . . In a real sense the 'sit-ins' represent more than a demand for service; they represent a demand for respect."[53] "Sitting at a lunch counter may seem like a small thing to some," explained one participant, "but the right to do so is so inextricably bound up with the American idea of equality for all."[54] The fact that most department stores accepted their money everywhere else in the store, but then refused to let African American customers sit and eat at the lunch counter made this particular form of racism especially offensive. The raw, personal experience of exclusion from department store lunch counters pulled the student protesters toward this particular target.

Another factor also played a role in pulling the students toward this protest target: availability. As African American journalist Louis Lomax explained, the protesters "wanted to get into the fight and they chose the market place, the great center of American egalitarianism, not because it had any overwhelming significance for them but because it was there— accessible and segregated."[55] The department store lunch counter was a target of opportunity.

The legal situation in 1960 also shaped the students' choice of target. Racial discrimination at lunch counters and other public accommodations was not a central concern for racial justice groups prior to 1960, in part because civil rights lawyers saw other targets as more vulnerable to legal challenge. They recognized the distinctively difficult legal dilemmas raised by privately operated businesses that served the public and focused their energies elsewhere.[56] Few of the students appreciated these concerns about constitutional doctrine. What they knew was that this was an offensive practice and no one seemed to be doing anything about it. Among the students themselves and among outside sympathizers, the sit-ins resonated in large part because it was clear that this was the students' protest and that it was not being orchestrated by far-away civil rights strategists or radical ideologues.[57]

Creating a Movement. To understand why students were ready to act and why they selected lunch counters still leaves one more key question: Why did these protests spread so quickly and so far? In other words, why did a series of protests turn into a movement?

The simplicity of the sit-in protest was critical to its success. As a protest tactic, the genius of the lunch counter sit-in was its ability to convey a clear, powerful message through such a simple act. The protests were easily replicated. New groups of students could be readily drawn into the movement. A phone call from a friend or family member, a picture in a newspaper, a report on the radio was often all that was needed to plant the spark in another city. Through the winter and spring of 1960, students across the South performed the same basic routines again and again. Put on nice clothes. Gather for a discussion of logistics, some final words of inspiration, perhaps a prayer. Then walk into a local drugstore or department store, sit down at the lunch counter, and request service. Staging a sit-in protest did not require elaborate planning (although as the sit-in movement unfolded, civil rights organizations and lawyers played an increasingly significant role). Just a handful of people could initiate one, as the Greensboro Four showed the world. The remarkable spread of the sit-in protest across the South was made possible by the accessibility and replicability of the protest action itself.[58]

The tactic of the sit-in protests allowed for an immediate sense of accomplishment for the students. Many different outcomes could be seen as an achievement. Being part of this new, defiant movement was an achievement. Creating student-run organizations that would strategize and coordinate sit-in protests might be cited as a victory for the movement. According to one observer, the sit-in "workshop" not only trained students on the mechanism of a lunch counter protest, it also functioned as a "cohesive, morale-building mechanism which served to infuse an ideology into the Negro student participants."[59] Students even saw going to jail as a critically important experience.

When arrested, some defiantly refused to pay bail, electing instead to sit in jail until their trials; when convicted, some chose jail sentences over paying a fine. The students thus transformed the very response that segregationists saw as their greatest weapon against the protesters—the police officer, the paddy wagon, and the jail cell—into a victory for the protesters.[60] Tangible, small-scale goals—forcing a lunch counter to shut down, pressuring city leaders to create a committee to discuss the issue, perhaps even persuading a lunch counter manager to serve the protesters—had the tremendous advantage that they held the possibility of immediate attainment.

Also critical to the spread of the sit-in movement were communication networks. Most people learned of the protests through radio and newspapers. The sit-ins were a major news story across the South, particularly when the protests brought out the white counterprotests and sporadic episodes of violence. News accounts were not only an inspiration and a challenge to African American students in cities where protests had yet to happen, they also sometimes provided quite detailed operating instructions for those planning their own protests. When asked what moved them to act, one early protester answered simply, "Well, we read the papers."[61]

The sit-in movement also drew on existing organizational networks within the African American community, particularly those that linked black colleges and churches. "Students, faculties and college presidents testified that after the Greensboro incident a strange fever swept across the campuses of the country's 120 Negro colleges," reported a journalist. "Within a week of Greensboro there was scarcely another topic of conversation on Negro campuses."[62] In many southern communities, the black church provided the essential tools for protest mobilization. It was a place where students met and organized. Activist church leaders regularly played key roles in organizing sit-in protests. And relationships among church leaders provided valuable communication networks

that helped spread the reports that fueled the sit-in movement.[63]

Although the students themselves proclaimed over and over that they were acting on their own and that they were not following the lead of adults or "outside" civil rights organizations, adult activists were never far from the scene of the sit-ins. In some places, they played a minimal role in spreading and supporting the protests, but in other places their role was essential. Particularly important were the local chapters, youth councils, and college chapters of the NAACP and activists associated with the Southern Christian Leadership Conference (SCLC). Although the role of established civil rights organizations was sporadic in the early weeks of the movement, it increased in significance as the movement progressed through the spring of 1960.[64]

The success of the sit-in movement was also a product of the ability of the lunch counter protest to effectively communicate a message to various audiences. From the white store operator standing across the lunch counter, to other customers, to those who saw photographs and read about the events in the newspapers, the core message the students sought to convey was clear. As one student protester explained in a documentary NBC aired on the protests, the goal of the movement was to "project the idea that here sits beside me another human being."[65] Racial discrimination in public life was wrong. African Americans were not going to accept being treated as "second-class citizens." They were willing to risk abuse and possible arrest to make their point. The students also sought to send a message to their parents' generation and to established civil rights organizations: they had a new method of protest. It would not wait for permission from lawyers or organizations. By the simple act of taking a seat at a lunch counter, young African Americans were able to convey to a wide, diverse audience all of this: the fundamental wrongness of racial segregation; the depth of their commitment to challenging racial injustice; and their impatience with established modes of civil rights reform.[66]

Before February 1960, no one could have predicted that this many people would risk arrest and physical attack to protest this particular facet of life in Jim Crow America. Even the people who took part in the protests often seemed surprised at the acts of courage and sacrifice they were witnessing all around them.

WHAT DID THE SIT-IN MOVEMENT ACHIEVE?

The student sit-in movement of 1960 reshaped and reinvigorated the struggle for racial equality. It marked a new phase of the civil rights movement, one in which mass participatory direct-action protest would become the leading edge of the movement's demand for social and political change. Activists who were younger, less patient, and less willing to compromise than the older generation of civil rights activists led this wave of assaults against Jim Crow. As the historian and movement participant Howard Zinn wrote in 1964, "[T]he great social upsurge of post-war America is the Negro revolt, and this revolt has gotten its most powerful impetus from young people, who gave it a new turn in 1960 and today, as anonymous as infantrymen everywhere, form the first rank in a nonviolent but ferocious war against the old order."[67] The sit-ins elevated the role of women in the civil rights movement. In contrast to the male-dominated established civil rights organizations, the decentralized mass protest movement offered opportunities for women not only to participate but often to assume leadership roles. Ella Baker, the executive director of the Southern Christian Leadership Conference, played a critical role in helping to organize the student movement. Diane Nash became a leading spokesperson for the Nashville student movement, and Patricia and Priscilla Stephens did the same for the Tallahassee movement. The sit-in movement also led to the creation of an influential new civil rights organization, the Student Nonviolent Coordinating Committee (SNCC), whose challenge to the established

ways of civil rights reform and the established civil rights organizations initiated a cycle of tensions, breaks, and alliances between the youth activists and the older generation that energized and challenged the larger civil rights movement throughout the 1960s.

SNCC. Two months into the sit-in movement, Ella Baker took the lead in organizing a conference for student activists. The "Youth Leadership Meeting" was held at Shaw University in Raleigh, North Carolina, in mid-April. Baker assured the students that this was not a ploy by older civil rights activists to take over the student movement. She worked throughout the meeting and afterward to ensure that the students remained in control of the movement they had started. The students, she wrote proudly in her summary of the meeting, "were intolerant of anything that smacked of manipulation or domination."[68]

The meeting brought together 142 student leaders from across the South.[69] After listening to King encourage the students to "consider training a group of volunteers who willingly go to jail rather than pay bail or fines," the students issued a statement urging protesters to do just that. (Some had already chosen this path.[70]) James Lawson gave an electrifying address at the opening of the conference in which he defined the student movement in sharp opposition to established civil rights organizations such as the NAACP, which he criticized for failing to appreciate the value of mass protest.[71]

Perhaps most consequentially, the conference led to the creation of the Student Nonviolent Coordinating Committee. It was initially conceived of as a temporary organization that would help guide the local student protest movements that were already under way around the South. SNCC would soon become one of the most consequential organizations of the civil rights movement. Its founders, many of whom were drawn from the dedicated Nashville group of student activists, created a decentralized community-based organization, based on consensus building among smaller groups, and direct-action protest tactics. Among its achievements in the coming years were organizing the Freedom Rides in 1961 and the Freedom Summer voter registration campaign in 1964.[72]

Local Victories. At first the breakthroughs were small and uncertain: a lunch counter shut down or, in a few cases, the quiet desegregation of service. The first negotiated citywide lunch counter desegregation brought about by the movement took place in San Antonio, Texas, where, on March 15, 1960, before the protests actually hit their stores, local business leaders agreed to end their segregation policies. Galveston, Texas, soon followed San Antonio's lead. By late spring, lunch counters in eleven cities had desegregated under pressure from sit-in protests.[73]

The most dramatic breakthrough of the sit-in movement occurred in Nashville. After weeks of sit-ins and failed negotiations, segregationists struck back, bombing the home of Z. Alexander Looby, an African American member of the Nashville city council and attorney who was representing the students. (Looby and his wife escaped injury.) Nearly 4,000 students marched to City Hall to confront Mayor Ben West about the escalating violence. When asked if he believed the lunch counters in Nashville should be desegregated, West, for the first time, publicly sided with the students. The mayor's dramatic statement helped pressure storeowners, already hurting from the combined effects of protests and boycotts, to desegregate their lunch counters.[74]

Nashville's carefully orchestrated integration affair served as a model for subsequent lunch counter desegregation agreements. At 3:00 p.m. on May 10, after the lunch crowds had cleared, a group of African Americans, "carefully chosen, middle-class, well-dressed, well-mannered," according to one news account, entered six downtown stores, sat down, and were served. One reason for the prosaic nature of the event was that the agreement under which the lunch counters desegregated included a news blackout: local radio and television stations and newspapers did not publicize the event in advance. Most of the other people in the store were plainclothes policemen. During the three-day interim period, the agreement required blacks to only sit with other blacks, and no blacks would ask for service on the first Saturday of desegregated service (since this was the day "country people" came into the city to shop). Although the event lacked the tense drama of the protests that had shaken the city in the previous months ("How much can you write about a mother and a child eating a hamburger?" complained one reporter), it did, for a moment at least, symbolize something of an achievement for a city whose citizens prided themselves on being better than their southern neighbors when it came to race relations.[75]

The trickle of desegregation victories strengthened in the coming months. Operators of targeted stores took advantage of the slowing of protests during the summer to make changes as inconspicuously as possible. By midsummer, twenty-seven southern cities had desegregated lunch counters in response to sit-ins.[76] On July 25, the Woolworth and Kress stores in Greensboro served their first black customers at the lunch counter. "What began quietly at a Greensboro variety store lunch counter six months ago—and then mushroomed into the South's most explosive issue—ended quietly at the same location," wrote the editors of the *Greensboro Daily News*.[77] "Sit-Ins Victorious Where They Began" ran the front-page headline in the *New York Times*.[78]

Legal Change. In addition to changing service policies on the local level, the sit-ins also set in motion a national debate over racial discrimination in public accommodations. The protest movement took an issue that was not at the top of the agendas of civil rights activists or liberal policy makers and transformed it into one of the most pressing issues for the nation, debated in town councils, corporate board rooms, editorial pages, courtrooms, on the presidential campaign trail, and on the floor of Congress. This national debate culminated with the passage of the Civil Rights Act of 1964, which included a provision that outlawed racial discrimination in eating facilities across the nation.

In the Courts. The courts, particularly the United States Supreme Court, struggled with the sit-ins. Thousands of students were arrested for their involvement with the lunch counter sit-ins and were charged with crimes such as vagrancy, loitering, disturbing the peace, and trespassing. Hundreds of the resulting convictions were appealed and, between 1961 and 1964, the justices of the Supreme Court faced round after round of these "sit-in cases."[79]

As an act of social protest, one of the great strengths of the sit-in was its ability to clearly display the fundamental wrongness of Jim Crow. Yet this moral clarity became considerably less clear when translated into a legal claim. Supreme Court justices whose sympathies lay on the side of the students and the cause of civil rights generally had difficulty dealing with these cases. A majority was always able to find a way to overturn the students' convictions, but the justices fractured over the legal rationale for doing so. They overturned protester convictions on narrow grounds, concluding that there was insufficient evidence to support a conviction or that there was direct state encouragement of or involvement in the lunch counter manager's decision to discriminate.

The looming question in the sit-in cases had to do with the reach of the equal protection clause of the Fourteenth Amendment, which provides that "no state shall deny to any person . . . the equal protection of the laws." The central constitutional question for the sit-ins was whether the *government* was responsible for the racial discrimination in these cases. This area of constitutional law is known as the "state action doctrine."

Judges had to determine whether the operator of a "public accommodation," a private business whose very purpose was to serve the public and who received a license from the state for this purpose, violated the equal protection requirement of the Constitution when he refused to serve African American customers. (This kind of racial discrimination, if practiced by a state-operated facility, such as a town beach, municipal golf course, or courthouse cafeteria, would have been held unconstitutional.) If one accepted that the restaurant operator's discriminatory choice was a "private" one, like selecting guests to one's home or membership in a private club, and thus was not constrained by the Constitution, judges still had to consider the fact that the police arrested the protesters and judges then convicted them for violating state law. Were southern states denying African Americans equal protection of the laws when they enforced the discriminatory policies of private business owners?

As a result of the sit-ins, these complexities of constitutional law, which for years had been puzzling the courts, lawyers, and legal scholars in other contexts, suddenly became one of the most urgent issues facing the nation.[80] The Supreme Court, which ruled unanimously in all the cases involving school desegregation it faced in the decade following *Brown*, fractured in the sit-in cases. Although the justices found ways to overturn the convictions of those who took part in the sit-ins, they remained divided on the core constitutional question the sit-ins raised. As a matter of constitutional law, it remains the case today that a business owner who refuses service to a customer because of that customer's race does not violate the Constitution, nor does the state violate the Constitution if its officials use criminal prosecutions to protect the property rights of the discriminating business owner.

In Congress. The ultimate legal victory of the sit-in movement came not from the Supreme Court but from Congress, and it came more than four years after the movement began.

When the sit-ins first spread across the South in 1960, the possibility of a nationwide public accommodations law was, in the words of one observer, "so remote that a discussion of it is largely academic."[81] Not only was the constitutional foundation for such a law unclear, the very idea of a federal nondiscrimination requirement in public accommodations was highly controversial and, considering the power held by long-serving southern Senators and their ability to use the filibuster, unlikely to pass. Yet the sit-in movement, and the series of civil right protests that erupted across the South in its wake, would transform the political landscape.

Title II of the Civil Rights Act of 1964 outlawed racial discrimination in public accommodations across the nation. The Supreme Court not only quickly upheld the law, it used the law as a justification to throw out the thousands of pending convictions of sit-in protesters. "The law the sit-inners had helped to create had protected them," civil rights lawyer Jack Greenberg noted with satisfaction.[82]

DISCUSSION OF THE LITERATURE

Although historians have frequently written about the sit-in movement, the only book dedicated entirely to the subject is Christopher Schmidt's *The Sit-Ins: Protest and Legal Change in the Civil Rights Era*.[83] This book, which gives particular attention to legal issues related to the sit-ins, examines the sit-in movement and its impact from various perspectives: the student protesters themselves, the civil rights lawyers who defended the students in court, people who did not participate in the movement but sympathized with its goals, business operators and southern politicians who defended segregation, the justices of the US Supreme Court who decided the sit-in cases, and the government officials and elected representatives who drafted and debated the 1964 Civil Rights Act.

Many of the best historical accounts of the sit-ins center on particular communities where students organized protests. William H. Chafe includes an excellent chapter on the Greensboro sit-in movement in *Civilities and Civil Rights: Greensboro, North Carolina, and the Black Struggle for Freedom*.[84] Tomiko Brown-Nagin offers two deeply researched chapters on the student movement in Atlanta in *Courage to Dissent: Atlanta and the Long History of the Civil Rights Movement*; she is particularly insightful on the often tense relationship between the students, older leaders of the black community, and civil rights lawyers.[85] In *The Children*, David Halberstam drew on his own experiences as a young reporter in Nashville, Tennessee, in the spring of 1960 to construct a portrait of the leaders of the Nashville sit-in movement and their subsequent lives.[86] John Kirk has insightfully explored the sit-in movement in Little Rock, Arkansas.[87]

Historical profiles of various civil rights organizations often include valuable material on the sit-in movement. Clayborne Carson's classic account of SNCC includes material on the sit-ins, as does August Meier and Elliot Rudwick's history of CORE.[88] Thomas Bynum has written on the NAACP and the sit-ins.[89]

Sociologist Aldon D. Morris's account of the organizational dynamics of the sit-in movement in *The Origins of the Civil Rights Movement*, which emphasizes the importance of the black church and civil rights organizations, has been particularly influential.[90] Sociologist Francesca Polletta has examined the ways in which student demonstrators described their actions, particularly their insistence on the spontaneous nature of their movement.[91]

Legal scholars have long debated the connection between the Supreme Court, particularly its *Brown* decision, and subsequent civil rights developments.[92] In his essential *From Jim Crow to Civil Rights*, Michael Klarman argues that legal scholars and civil rights lawyers tend to exaggerate *Brown*'s role in sparking civil rights protests, concluding that the linkages between the Court's decision and the sit-ins were, at best, "indirect."[93] Schmidt builds on Klarman's revisionist account, emphasizing the importance of these link-ages—and, more generally, legal factors historians have tended to overlook—in making the sit-ins possible.[94]

Recent historical accounts have given more attention to those who stood opposed to the sit-in protests. George Lewis and Clive Webb have written insightful essays on segregationist reactions to the sit-ins, and Schmidt's *Sit-Ins* includes a chapter on defenders of segregation.[95] Economic historian Gavin Wright's *Sharing the Prize* analyzes the factors that contributed to the demise of racial discrimination in public accommodations.[96]

PRIMARY SOURCES

Primary sources on the sit-ins can be divided into four groupings. One group is first-person accounts of people involved in the protests. CORE published a collection of reports of student activists.[97] There have also been many oral histories of those who were involved in the sit-in movement, and some participants have written memoirs.[98] Various scholars studied the sit-ins as they were occurring, and their master's theses, dissertations, and published works often include firsthand insights on the protests.[99]

Second, there are the papers of civil rights organizations that played a role in the sit-ins. Although SNCC is the organization most closely identified with the sit-in movement, the organization's papers include relatively little on the critical opening months of the sit-ins, since it was not founded until April 1960, midway through the sit-in movement.[100] CORE's papers are valuable for not only the 1960 movement but also other sit-in protests with which the group was involved.[101]

The best single manuscript collection for studying the sit-ins is the NAACP papers.[102] Although the organization often was not at the forefront of the sit-in movement, its national office and field offices closely monitored the unfolding events. The papers also include fascinating material on the struggles

of the national office to identify a place for itself in this new phase of direct-action protest. Also closely monitoring the sit-in movement was the Southern Regional Council, a prominent voice of southern liberalism and a strong supporter of the sit-ins, as reflected in the research reports the group issued.[103] Martin Luther King Jr.'s papers are also an excellent source of material on the sit-ins.[104]

A third group of primary materials are archives connected with business operators and public officials who confronted the sit-in protests. These sources can be found in every state in which sit-ins took place. The papers of Luther Hodges, North Carolina's governor during the sit-ins, are particularly valuable.[105] The papers of the manager of the Greensboro Woolworth's also include some fascinating material.[106]

A fourth grouping of source materials are media accounts.[107] The sit-ins were a major news event, attracting not only local newspaper reporters, but also the national wires, press, and television networks. Among local newspapers, the *Greensboro Daily News* provided particularly thorough coverage of the North Carolina protests from the start.[108] The *New York Times* had reporters on the scene of many of the major sit-in campaigns, as did the *Chicago Defender*, the nation's leading black newspaper. Some of the best contemporary accounts of the sit-ins were by journalists writing for periodicals.[109] Also valuable is a documentary NBC aired in December 1960, which profiled the Nashville protests.[110]

DIGITAL MATERIALS

Civil Rights Digital Library. http://crdl.usg.edu /events/.

Civil Rights Greensboro, Martha Blakeney Hodges Special Collections and University Archives, UNCG University Libraries, Greensboro, North Carolina. http://libcdm1.uncg.edu/cdm/subjects /collection/CivilRights.

Civil Rights Movement Veterans. http://www .crmvet.org/.

Eyes on the Prize Interviews. http://digital.wustl
.edu/e/eop/index.html.

Global Nonviolent Action Database. http://
nvdatabase.swarthmore.edu/.

The King Center Archives. http://www.thekingcenter
.org/archive/.

Southern Oral History Program, Center for the Study
of the American South, University of North
Carolina at Chapel Hill. http://sohp.org/.

FURTHER READING

Branch, Taylor. *Parting the Waters: America in the
King Years, 1954–1963*. New York: Simon &
Schuster, 1988.

Brown-Nagin, Tomiko. *Courage to Dissent: Atlanta
and the Long History of the Civil Rights Movement*.
New York: Oxford University Press, 2011.

Carson, Clayborne. *In Struggle: SNCC and the Black
Awakening of the 1960s*. 2nd ed. Cambridge, MA:
Harvard University Press, 1995.

Chafe, William H. *Civilities and Civil Rights:
Greensboro, North Carolina, and the Black Struggle
for Freedom*. New York: Oxford University Press,
1980.

Halberstam, David. *The Children*. New York:
Random House, 1998.

Klarman, Michael J. *From Jim Crow to Civil Rights:
The Supreme Court and the Struggle for Racial
Equality*. New York: Oxford University Press,
2004.

Morgan, Iwan, and Philip Davies, eds. *From Sit-Ins to
SNCC: The Student Movement in the 1960s*.
Gainesville: University Press of Florida, 2012.

Morris, Aldon D. *The Origins of the Civil Rights
Movement: Black Communities Organizing for
Change*. New York: Free Press, 1984.

Schmidt, Christopher W. "Divided by Law: The Sit-
Ins and the Role of the Courts in the Civil Rights
Movement." *Law and History Review* 33 (2015):
93–149.

Schmidt, Christopher W. *The Sit-Ins: Protest and
Legal Change in the Civil Rights Era*. Chicago:
University of Chicago Press, 2018.

Wolff, Miles. *Lunch at the 5 & 10*. [1970] rev. ed.
Chicago: Ivan Dee, 1990.

Wright, Gavin. *Sharing the Prize: The Economics of the
Civil Rights Revolution in the American South*.
Cambridge, MA: Harvard University Press, 2013.

NOTES

1. L. F. Palmer, "New Face of Young Negro
America," *Chicago Defender*, March 21, 1960, 1,
9, 11.

2. See Francesca Polletta, *It Was Like a Fever:
Storytelling in Protest and Politics* (Chicago:
University of Chicago Press, 2006), chap. 2.

3. Aldon D. Morris, *The Origins of the Civil Rights
Movement: Black Communities Organizing for
Change* (New York: Free Press, 1984), 188–215.

4. Christopher W. Schmidt, *The Sit-Ins: Protest and
Legal Change in the Civil Rights Era* (Chicago:
University of Chicago Press, 2018), chap. 1.

5. August Meier and Elliot Rudwick, *CORE: A Study
of the Civil Rights Movement, 1942–1968* (New
York: Oxford University Press, 1973), 3–14, 91,
102; and Morris, *Origins of the Civil Rights
Movement*, 188–192.

6. Clara Luper, *Behold the Walls* (Oklahoma City,
OK: Jim Wire, 1979); Morris, *Origins of the
Civil Rights Movement*, 192–193; Ronald
Walters, "The Great Plains Sit-In Movement,
1958–1960," *Great Plains Quarterly* 16 (Spring
1996): 85–94; Gretchen Cassel Eick, *Dissent
in Wichita: The Civil Rights Movement in the
Midwest, 1954–72* (Urbana: University of
Illinois Press, 2001), 1–11; and Thomas Bynum,
*NAACP Youth and the Fight for Black Freedom,
1936–1965* (Knoxville: University of Tennessee
Press, 2013), 95–99.

7. Martin Oppenheimer, "The Southern Student
Movement: Year 1," *Journal of Negro Education* 33
(1964): 396–403, at 397; and Morris, *Origins of
the Civil Rights Movement*, 124–125.

8. Paul Ernest Wehr, "The Sit-Down Protests: A
Study of a Passive Resistance Movement in
North Carolina" (master's thesis, University of
North Carolina, Chapel Hill, 1960), 19–20; and
James H. Laue, *Direct Action and Desegregation,
1960–1962: Toward a Theory of Rationalization
of Protest* (Brooklyn, NY: Carlson, 1989) (reprint of PhD diss., Harvard University, 1965),
147.

9. On the Greensboro sit-ins, see Miles Wolff, *Lunch
at the 5 & 10* (1970; rev. ed., Chicago: Ivan Dee,
1990); and William H. Chafe, *Civilities and Civil
Rights: Greensboro, North Carolina, and the Black
Struggle for Freedom* (New York: Oxford University
Press, 1980), 112–120.

10. Wolff, *Lunch at the 5 & 10*, 15; Schmidt, *Sit-Ins*, 93–97.

11. "White Men Arrested at Sitdown," *Greensboro Daily News*, February 6, 1960, B1; and "Bomb Scares Halt Negro Sitdown," *Atlanta Constitution*, February 7, 1960, 18A.

12. "A&T Students Call Two-Week Recess In Protest Here," *Greensboro Daily News*, February 7, 1960, A1.

13. "Demonstration Grows," *Greensboro Daily News*, February 9, 1960, A3; and Clarence H. Patrick, *Lunch Counter Desegregation in Winston-Salem, North Carolina* (Pamphlet distributed by the Southern Regional Council, 1960), 4.

14. "Resistance Move to Continue," *Greensboro Daily News*, February 12, 1960, A10; and Helen Fuller, "'We Are All So Happy'," *New Republic*, April 25, 1960, 13–16, at 14.

15. "Eggs Spray Negro in Cafe Flareup," *Atlanta Constitution*, February 11, 1960, 12.

16. "Lunch Counter Strikes Spread to High Point," *Greensboro Daily News*, February 12, 1960, A1, A6; Almetta C. Brooks, "White Patrons Balk Negro Sitdowners," *Greensboro Daily News*, February 13, 1960, A3; and "Negro Pupils Crowd Store; It Closes," *Greensboro Daily News*, February 14, 1960, A1.

17. Southern Regional Council, "A Chronological Listing of the Cities in Which Demonstrations Have Occurred, February 1–March 31, 1960 (http://www.crmvet.org/docs/6004_sitin-list.pdf)."

18. "43 Negroes Fined in Raleigh Court," *New York Times*, March 29, 1960, 28.

19. Claude Sitton, "Negroes' Protest Spreads in South," *New York Times*, February 13, 1960, 1, 6.

20. On the Nashville sit-ins, see Paul Laprad, "Nashville: A Community Struggle," in *Sit-Ins: The Students Report*, ed. James Peck (New York: Congress of Racial Equality, 1960), 6–8; Morris, *Origins of the Civil Rights Movement*, 205–212; Taylor Branch, *Parting the Waters: America in the King Years, 1954–1963* (New York: Simon & Schuster, 1988), 272–280; and David Halberstam, *The Children* (New York: Random House, 1998), 25–92.

21. David Halberstam, "A Good City Gone Ugly," *Reporter*, March 31, 1960, 17–19, at 19.

22. On the Atlanta student movement, the best source is Tomiko Brown-Nagin, *Courage to Dissent: Atlanta and the Long History of the Civil Rights Movement* (New York: Oxford University Press, 2011), chaps. 6 and 7.

23. "An Appeal for Human Rights," *Atlanta Constitution*, March 9, 1960, 13.

24. Howard Raines, *My Soul Is Rested: The Story of the Civil Rights Movement in the Deep South* (New York: Putnam, 1977), 86 (interview with Julian Bond).

25. Pat Watters, "Headline Makers," *Atlanta Constitution*, March 20, 1960, 2C.

26. John Britton, "Students Bound Over to a Higher Court After Food Service Appeal," *Atlanta Daily World*, March 16, 1960, 1; "77 Negroes Arrested Here As Cafeteria Sitdowns Start," *Atlanta Constitution*, March 16, 1960, 1; and "Governor Pledges Aide if Needed," *Atlanta Constitution*, March 16, 1960, 1.

27. Ted Lippman, "No More Sitdowns Now, Students Say," *Atlanta Constitution*, March 17, 1960, 1, 12; and Maurice C. Daniels, *Saving the Soul of Georgia: Donald L. Hollowell and the Struggle for Civil Rights* (Athens, GA: University of Georgia Press, 2013), 107.

28. Julius Duscha, "1200 Negroes March to Capitol, Pray, Sing Anthem in Alabama," *Washington Post*, March 2, 1960, B6; and J. Mills Thornton III, *Dividing Lines: Municipal Politics and the Struggle for Civil Rights in Montgomery, Birmingham, and Selma* (Tuscaloosa: University of Alabama Press, 2002), 113–114.

29. "Violence Sweeps Dixie in Negro Sitdowns," *Boston Globe*, February 28, 1960, 8.

30. "Savannah Sitdowner Hit As Tension Flares," *Atlanta Constitution*, April 17, 1960, 20A; "Blast Home of Sit-In Lawyer," *Chicago Defender*, April 30, 1960, 12.

31. "KKK on Rampage Against Sit-Ins," *Daily Defender*, March 29, 1960, 3.

32. Southern Regional Council, "A Follow-Up Report on the Student Protest Movement After Two Months," North Carolina Council on Human Relations Records 4880, Folder 757, Southern Historical Collection, The Wilson Library, University of North Carolina at Chapel Hill.

33. On the limits of a commitment to nonviolence in the sit-in movement, see Martin Oppenheimer, *The Sit-In Movement of 1960* (Brooklyn, NY: Carlson, 1989) (PhD diss., University of

Pennsylvania, 1963), 47; Ted Dienstfrey, "A Conference on the Sit-Ins," *Commentary* 30 (June 1960): 524–528, at 526; and Clayborne Carson, *In Struggle: SNCC and the Black Awakening of the 1960s*, 2nd. ed. (Cambridge, MA: Harvard University Press, 1995), 19, 22–23.

34. "Negroes Fight Back in the South," *New York Amsterdam News*, February 16, 1960, 1.

35. "Negroes Fight Back in the South."

36. "Race Brawl Erupts at Restaurant," *Atlanta Constitution*, February 16, 1960, 2.

37. Edward Rodman, "Portsmouth: A Lesson in Nonviolence," in *Sit-Ins: The Students Report*, ed. James Peck (New York: CORE, 1960), 4–6; "Lunch Counter Sitdown Erupts into Racial Melee," *Atlanta Constitution*, February 17, 1960, 1; and "500 Are Dispersed at Racial Dispute," *New York Times*, February 18, 1960, 14.

38. Claude Sitton, "Chattanooga Quiet," *New York Times*, February 26, 1960, 8; "Violence in Chattanooga," *Southern School News*, March 1960, 1.

39. Schmidt, *Sit-Ins*, chap. 4.

40. "Negroes Throng Sitdown Trials," *New York Times*, March 1, 1960, 20; "N.Y. Coeds Describe Sit-Down," *Amsterdam News*, March 12, 1960, 26; and Halberstam, "Good City Gone Ugly," 17–19.

41. John Kirk, "Another Side of the Sit-Ins: Nonviolent Direct Action, the Courts, and the Constitution," in *From Sit-Ins to SNCC: The Student Movement in the 1960s*, ed. Iwan Morgan and Philip Davies (Gainesville: University Press of Florida, 2012), 23–40, at 26.

42. Christopher W. Schmidt, "Divided by Law: The Sit-Ins and the Role of the Courts in the Civil Rights Movement," *Law and History Review* 33 (2015): 93–149.

43. "Eight Negroes Chose Jail in Sitdown Case," *Chicago Tribune*, March 19, 1960, 12; "Tallahassee Sitdowners Convicted," *Atlanta Constitution*, May 8, 1960, 12D; "Judge Convicts 11 in Sitdown," *Washington Post*, May 8, 1960, B6; and Patricia Stephens, "Tallahassee: Through Jail to Freedom," in *Sit-Ins: The Students Report*, ed. James Peck (New York: CORE, 1960), 2–4.

44. Thomas Gaither, "Orangeburg: Behind the Carolina Stockade," in Peck, *Sit-Ins*, 9–11.

45. Brief for the United States as Amicus Curiae, 9, *Garner v. Louisiana*, Nos. 26, 27, 28, October Term, 1961, September 11, 1961.

46. "Hundreds Seek to Quit Negro College That Expelled Demonstrators," *New York Times*, April 1, 1960, 1, 25; Major Johns, "Baton Rouge: Higher Education—Southern Style," in Peck, *Sit-Ins*, 11-13; and Adam Fairclough, *Race and Democracy: The Civil Rights Struggle in Louisiana, 1915–1972* (Athens, GA: University of Georgia Press, 1995), 266–271.

47. Elsie Carper, "Youths in Rally For Civil Rights," *Washington Post*, June 23, 1960, B9.

48. Wehr, "Sit-Down Protests," 44; Doug McAdam, "Tactical Innovation and the Pace of Insurgency," *American Sociological Review* 48 (1983): 735–754, at 744.

49. "Children in Sit-In," *New York Times*, June 18, 1960, 11; Oppenheimer, "Southern Student Movement," 401.

50. Merrill Proudfoot, *Diary of a Sit-In* (Chapel Hill: University of North Carolina Press, 1962); and Cynthia Griggs Fleming, "White Lunch Counters and Black Consciousness: The Story of the Knoxville Sit-ins," *Tennessee Historical Quarterly* 49 (1990): 40–52.

51. L. F. Palmer, "Uprising for Freedom," *Chicago Defender*, March 22, 1960, 9.

52. Halberstam, "Good City Gone Ugly," 18.

53. Martin Luther King Jr., "The Burning Truth in the South," *Progressive* 24 (May 1960): 8.

54. Major Johns, "Baton Rouge: Higher Education—Southern Style," in *Sit-Ins: The Students Report*, 13.

55. Louis E. Lomax, "The Negro Revolt Against 'The Negro Leaders,'" *Harper's* (June 1960): 41–48, at 48.

56. Christopher W. Schmidt, "The Sit-Ins and the State Action Doctrine," *William & Mary Bill of Rights Journal* 18 (2010): 767–829.

57. See Schmidt, "Divided by Law"; Schmidt, *Sit-Ins*, chap. 3.

58. McAdam, "Tactical Innovation and the Pace of Insurgency."

59. Oppenheimer, "The Southern Student Movement," 399.

60. Schmidt, "Divided by Law," 127–129.

61. "Cafe Push Spreads to Tennessee," *Atlanta Constitution*, February 20, 1960, 2.

62. Ben H. Bagdikian, "Negro Youth's New March on Dixie," *Saturday Evening Post*, September 8, 1962, 15–19, at 16.

63. Morris, *Origins of the Civil Rights Movement*, 196–203.

64. Morris, *Origins of the Civil Rights Movement*, 188–215; and Doug McAdam, *Political Process and the Development of Black Insurgency, 1930–1970*, 2nd ed. (Chicago: University of Chicago Press, 1999), chap. 6.

65. "Sit-In," NBC White Paper, No. 2, aired on December 20, 1960, at 9:45 p.m.

66. See Schmidt, *Sit-Ins*, chap. 3.

67. Howard Zinn, *SNCC: The New Abolitionists* (Boston: Beacon Press, 1964), 4.

68. Ella Baker, "Bigger Than a Hamburger," *Southern Patriot* 18 (June 1960): 4. See also Barbara Ransby, *Ella Baker and the Black Freedom Movement: A Radical Democratic Vision* (Chapel Hill: University of North Carolina Press, 2003), 239–247.

69. "Delegates to Youth Leadership Conference," April 21, 1960; "142 Students Push Integration Drive," *Atlanta Constitution*, April 18, 1960, 5; and Dienstfrey, "Conference on the Sit-Ins."

70. Claude Sitton, "Racial Problems Put to President," *New York Times*, April 18, 1960, 21; and Helen Fuller, "Southern Students Take Over," *New Republic*, May 2, 1960, 14–16.

71. Claude Sitton, "Negro Criticizes N.A.A.C.P. Tactics," *New York Times*, April 17, 1960, 32; James Lawson, "From a Lunch-Counter Stool," April 1960, reprinted in August Meier, Elliott Rudwick, and Francis Broderick, eds., *Black Protest Thought in the Twentieth Century*, 2nd ed. (Indianapolis, IN: Bobbs-Merrill, 1971), 308–315.

72. See Carson, *In Struggle*; and Wesley C. Hogan, *Many Minds, One Heart: SNCC's Dream for a New America* (Chapel Hill: University of North Carolina Press, 2007).

73. "Some Negroes Served," *New York Times*, March 8, 1960, 23; "Freeze & Thaw," *Time*, March 28, 1960, 26; "Galveston Becomes Second Texas City to Desegregate Its Lunch Counters," *Washington Post*, April 6, 1960, A14; and Laue, *Direct Action and Desegregation*, 77.

74. "Bombing Rips House, Hosp. In Nashville," *Atlanta Daily World*, April 20, 1960, 1; "Blast Home of Sit-In Lawyer," *Chicago Defender*, April 20, 1960, 12. "Sit-In," NBC White Paper; and Oppenheimer, *Sit-In Movement*, 124–130.

75. "Negroes Win Dining Rights in Nashville," *Chicago Tribune*, May 11, 1960, A1; Robert S. Bird, "Local Eating Going Well in Nashville," *New York Herald Tribune*, May 12, 1960, 24;

"The Nashville Story," *Chicago Tribune*, May 13, 1960, 12; and "It Happened in Nashville," *Reporter*, May 26, 1960, 2–4.

76. Margaret Price, "Why Some Areas Solve 'Sit-Ins,'" *Chicago Defender*, July 2, 1960, 8.

77. Editorial, "A Quiet Denouement," *Greensboro Daily News*, July 27, 1960, A8.

78. "Sit-Ins Victorious Where They Began," *New York Times*, July 26, 1960, 1, 19.

79. See Schmidt, *Sit-Ins*, chap. 5.

80. Schmidt, "The Sit-Ins and the State Action Doctrine."

81. Earl Lawrence Carl, "Reflections on the 'Sit-Ins,'" *Cornell Law Quarterly* 46 (1961): 444–457, at 455.

82. Jack Greenberg, "The Supreme Court, Civil Rights and Civil Dissonance," *Yale Law Journal* 77 (1968): 1520–1544, at 1532.

83. Schmidt, *Sit-Ins*. Prior to the publication of this book, the only book-length accounts of the sit-ins were two sociology dissertations written in the 1960s: Martin Oppenheimer, "Genesis of the Southern Negro Student Movement" (PhD diss., University of Pennsylvania, 1963), reprinted as *The Sit-In Movement of 1960* (Brooklyn, NY: Carlson, 1989); and James H. Laue, "Direct Action and Desegregation, 1960–1962: Toward a Theory of Rationalization of Protest" (PhD diss., Harvard University, 1965; reprint Brooklyn, NY: Carlson, 1989).

84. Chafe, *Civilities and Civil Rights*, chap. 3.

85. Brown-Nagin *Courage to Dissent*, chaps. 6 and 7.

86. Halberstam, *The Children*.

87. Kirk, "Another Side of the Sit-Ins"; and John A. Kirk, *Redefining the Color Line: Black Activism in Little Rock, Arkansas, 1940–1970* (Gainesville: University Press of Florida, 2002), 143–146.

88. Carson, *In Struggle*, chap. 1; Meier and Rudwick, *CORE*, chap. 2. See also Hogan, *Many Minds, One Heart*, chap. 1; and Howard Zinn, *SNCC: The New Abolitionists* (Boston: Beacon Press, 1964), chap. 2.

89. Thomas Bynum, *NAACP Youth and the Fight for Black Freedom, 1936–1965* (Knoxville: University of Tennessee Press, 2013), 95–106.

90. Morris, *Origins of the Civil Rights Movement*, 188–215. Additional analysis of the organizational dynamics of the sit-ins can be found in Lewis M. Killian, "Organization, Rationality and Spontaneity in the Civil Rights Movement," *American Sociological Review* 49 (1984): 770–783;

McAdam, *Political Process and the Development of Black Insurgency*, chap. 6; Kenneth T. Andrews and Michael Biggs, "The Dynamics of Protest Diffusion: Movement Organizations, Social Networks, and News Media in the 1960 Sit-Ins," *American Sociological Review* 71 (2006): 752–777; and Michael Biggs, "Who Joined the Sit-ins and Why: Southern Black Students in the Early 1960s," *Mobilization: An International Journal* 11 (2006): 321–336.

91. Polletta, *It Was Like a Fever*, chap. 2.

92. See, for example, Gerald N. Rosenberg, *The Hollow Hope: Can Courts Bring About Social Change?* (Chicago: University of Chicago Press, 1991), 39–169; and Michael W. McCann, "Reform Litigation on Trial," *Law & Social Inquiry* 17 (1992): 715–743.

93. Michael J. Klarman, *From Jim Crow to Civil Rights: The Supreme Court and the Struggle for Racial Equality* (New York: Oxford University Press, 2004), chap. 7.

94. Schmidt, "Divided by Law"; Schmidt, *Sit-Ins*.

95. George Lewis, "'Complicated Hospitality': The Impact of the Sit-Ins on the Ideology of Southern Segregationists," in *From Sit-Ins to SNCC*, 41–57; Clive Webb, "Breaching the Wall of Resistance: White Southern Reactions to the Sit-Ins," in *From Sit-Ins to SNCC*, 58–80; and Schmidt, *Sit-Ins*, chap. 4.

96. Gavin Wright, *Sharing the Prize: The Economics of the Civil Rights Revolution in the American South* (Cambridge, MA: Harvard University Press, 2013), chap. 3.

97. Peck, *Sit-Ins*. See also Diane Nash, "Inside the Sit-ins and Freedom Rides: Testimony of a Southern Student," in *The New Negro*, ed. Mathew H. Ahmann (Notre Dame, IN: Fides, 1961), 43–62.

98. Published collections include Raines, *My Soul Is Rested*; Henry Hampton and Steve Fraser, *Voices of Freedom: An Oral History of the Civil Rights Movement from the 1950s through the 1980s* (New York: Bantam, 1990). Recordings and transcripts can be found at Oral Histories: Southern Oral History Program, Center for the Study of the American South, University of North Carolina at Chapel Hill; William Henry Chafe Oral History Collection, David M. Rubenstein Rare Book & Manuscript Library, Duke University; Greensboro Voices/ Greensboro Public Library Oral History Project;

Bluford Library, North Carolina Agricultural and Technical College. See also John Lewis with Michael D'Orso, *Walking with the Wind: A Memoir of the Movement* (New York: Simon & Schuster, 1998).

99. See, for example, Wehr, "Sit-Down Protests"; Oppenheimer, *Sit-In Movement*; Laue, *Direct Action and Desegregation*; and Fredric Solomon and Jacob R. Fishman, "Action and Identity Formation in the First Student Demonstration," *Journal of Social Issues* 20 (April 1964): 36–45.

100. SNCC Papers, 1959–1972 (microfilm) (Bethesda, MD: University Publications of America). See also the volumes of the SNCC newsletter, *The Student Voice*, which began in June 1960.

101. Congress of Racial Equality Papers, 1941–1967 (microfilm) (Bethesda, MD: University Publications of America).

102. NAACP Papers, Library of Congress, Washington, DC, Manuscript Division; NAACP Papers, (digitized), ProQuest.

103. Southern Regional Council Papers, 1944–1968 (microfilm) (Bethesda, MD: University Publications of America). Some of the SRC reports are online (http://www.crmvet .org).

104. *The Papers of Martin Luther King, Jr.*, vol. 5, ed. Clayborne Carson (Berkeley: University of California Press, 1992).

105. Governor's Papers: Luther Hartwell Hodges, North Carolina State Archives, Raleigh, NC.

106. Clarence Lee Harris Papers, Martha Blakeney Hodges Special Collections and University Archives, UNCG University Libraries, Greensboro, NC.

107. On press coverage of the civil rights movement, see Gene Roberts and Hank Klibanoff, *The Race Beat: The Press, the Civil Rights Struggle, and the Awakening of a Nation* (New York: Knopf, 2006).

108. Many *Greensboro Daily News* articles relating to the sit-ins are available online at Civil Rights Greensboro, Martha Blakeney Hodges Special Collections and University Archives (http:// libcdm1.uncg.edu/cdm/subjects/collection /CivilRights), UNCG University Libraries, Greensboro, NC.

109. See, for example, Michael Walzer, "A Cup of Coffee and a Seat," *Dissent* 7 (Spring 1960):

111–120; Dienstfrey, "Conference on the Sit-Ins"; Louis E. Lomax, "The Negro Revolt Against 'The Negro Leaders'"; Howard Zinn, "Finishing School for Pickets," *Nation*, August 6, 1960, 72; and Nat Hentoff, "A Peaceful Army," *Commonweal*, June 10, 1960, 275–278.
110. "Sit-In," NBC White Paper.

Christopher W. Schmidt

THE SIXTIES

A NARRATIVE OF THE DECADE

The historical groundwork for the 1960s was laid in the mid-1950s. In 1954, urged by the National Association for the Advancement of Colored People (NAACP) lead attorney Thurgood Marshall and headed, as its chief justice, by a little known former California governor named Earl Warren, the Supreme Court issued its ruling in *Brown v. Board of Education of Topeka*. The *Brown* decision closed the door on fifty-eight years of the "separate but equal" legal doctrine of racial subjugation and opened a new era in American constitutional law. *Brown* in itself did far less for racial equality than either its defenders or critics claimed, but between 1955 and 1969 the Warren Court built on *Brown's* foundation, under constant pressure from a generation of activist lawyers who believed that the law should be a lever of social justice, to expand the rights and civil liberties of American citizens. The Warren Court defined the legal contours of the sixties, and for the first time since the 1930s the Court decisively shaped national political debate.

In the year after the first *Brown* decision, 1955, the Montgomery bus boycott, led by a 26-year-old Baptist minister named Martin Luther King Jr., opened a new phase in the centuries-long struggle of African Americans for social and political equality. Following on the heels of the brutal murder by white supremacists of fourteen-year-old Emmett Till,

a black youth visiting Mississippi from Chicago, the Montgomery movement seemed to answer tragedy with hope. The tactic of Gandhian nonviolent resistance employed in Montgomery, which had been imported to the United States in the 1930s and 1940s by Quaker pacifists in the Fellowship of Reconciliation, shocked a nation in which most white Americans blithely assumed, whatever else divided them, their superiority to black Americans. In that same year, a continent away, Ngo Dinh Diem, a Catholic from an elite Vietnamese family who had spent three years living in exile in New Jersey, became president of South Vietnam with the support of the US Central Intelligence Agency (CIA) and State Department. Emboldened by US sponsorship, in 1956 Diem violated the Geneva Agreements calling for open elections to unify Vietnam and began building a right-wing anticommunist dictatorship.

These events occurred long before our decade, but the 1960s unfolded in their considerable shadow. *Brown* and the Warren Court, King and insurgent black protest, and anticommunism and the US war in Vietnam decisively shaped the course of the 1960s. Rights, activism, and war—these were the crucibles of action and change that marked this distinct era.

The dawning events of the 1960s came in quick succession. In February 1960 four black college students from North Carolina A&T staged a direct action, a "sit-in" at a white-only lunch counter at a Woolworth's drugstore in Greensboro, North Carolina. The Greensboro Four inspired a wave of student-led sit-ins and direct actions, involving some seventy thousand people, that swept across the South over the course of the year. In the midst of that wave, Ella Baker, an official of the Southern Christian Leadership Conference (SCLC), brought hundreds of those students together to found the Student Nonviolent Coordinating Committee (SNCC), among the decade's most important dramatis personae. Then in May, inspired by the southern sit-ins, college students in San Francisco sat in to protest the House Un-American Activities Committee

(HUAC), among the chief institutions of domestic Cold War anticommunism, which had convened in the city to investigate local teachers, professors, and labor leaders. The students were dragged down the hard marble steps of City Hall, assaulted by fire hoses, and tossed into waiting police vans. That same year, taking SNCC as their model, left-wing student activists at the University of Michigan founded Students for a Democratic Society (SDS) and committed themselves to social justice. By the end of 1960, a small but vocal collection of college-age Americans, black and white, had registered their refusal to accept the basic terms of Cold War American life.

John F. Kennedy, a member of the World War II generation and scion of a prominent American family, both inspired and constrained these emerging social forces. His election to the presidency in November 1960 emboldened young left-wing and liberal activists, who saw in his youthful optimism a mirror of their own. The new president projected glamour and a certain liberal style, and many Americans were galvanized by his invocation of the "New Frontier" and his call to "ask what you can do for your country." Beneath the lofty rhetoric, Kennedy was a conventional Cold War politician whose administration became embroiled in escalating tensions with the Soviet Union in the developing world. In the failed Bay of Pigs invasion of communist Cuba in 1961 and in the tension packed Cuban Missile Crisis of 1962, Kennedy demonstrated first brash overconfidence and then great aplomb in navigating superpower tensions. In Southeast Asia, having inherited US sponsorship of the Diem regime, Kennedy reluctantly committed increasing numbers of American military personnel to advise, and ultimate to fight alongside, Diem's army in its war against the communist insurgents in South Vietnam, known as the National Liberation Front (NLF) and sponsored by the Viet Minh regime in North Vietnam. Domestically, Kennedy was cautious and pragmatic when it came to the emerging black freedom struggle. Like Democratic presidents

Roosevelt and Truman before him, Kennedy feared losing the support of white southern Democrats and was therefore reluctant to issue even pro forma calls for racial equality. He offered little federal protection, for instance, to the black and white activists engaged in the "freedom rides" implementing the Supreme Court's desegregation of interstate bus lines in 1961, even when they were brutally attacked by white mobs. The movement forced his hand, however. He submitted a civil rights bill to Congress in June 1963, and delivered a major speech endorsing racial equality, but only after photographs of police dogs and fire hoses being turned on peaceful black marchers in Birmingham, Alabama, had sped around the world, embarrassing both the president and the United States. Cautious and pragmatic, Kennedy was more a symbol than an agent of change.

In the eighteen months that followed Kennedy's announcement of the civil rights bill, like so many sequences of time in the decade, dramatic, even stunning, events followed fast on one another, and the country seemed to age a generation in less than two years. The day after Kennedy's speech, a white supremacist murdered Medgar Evers, the head of the Mississippi NAACP, in cold blood. In August, four African American girls were murdered in the 16th Street Baptist Church bombing in Birmingham. The country had barely reckoned with this act of domestic terrorism when, in early November, in a US–supported coup, Diem was assassinated by his own military, sending South Vietnam into chaos. Three weeks later, on November 22, 1963, Kennedy himself was himself the victim of an assassination, bringing Lyndon Johnson to the presidency. Domestically, the new president faced a rapidly radicalizing black freedom movement and an equally radicalizing backlash, evident in the Evers assassination and the 16th Street Church bombing. Following Diem's death, South Vietnam became nearly ungovernable, making victory for communist-led insurgents there increasingly likely. In the face of mounting crises, Johnson pursued two lines of action. Domestically, he showed increasing support for the legislative aims of the black freedom movement, playing an essential role, alongside King, Roy Wilkins, Whitney Young, and other black leaders, in the passage of the Civil Rights Act in June 1964. Overseas, to prevent the collapse of South Vietnam's anticommunist government, Johnson escalated the war against the NLF, a commitment he hid from the American public during the 1964 presidential election.

That year Johnson faced Republican Barry Goldwater, a conservative senator from Arizona, who publically denounced the Civil Rights Act as an assault on personal liberty and castigated Democrats and liberal Republicans alike for showing insufficient resolve in the battle against global communism. As Kennedy had inspired left-wing and liberal youth in 1960, Goldwater inspired their right-wing counterparts in 1964, helping to lay the groundwork for the emergence of the New Right by the end of the decade. Indeed, four years earlier, in 1960, right-wing student activists and followers of Goldwater had founded Young Americans for Freedom (YAF), which would in time claim a larger membership than SDS. The organization adopted as its call to arms the "Sharon Statement," which defended the principle of absolute economic liberty, named "international communism" as the chief threat to global liberty, and asserted that when government exceeds its minimal functions "it accumulates power, which tends to diminish order and liberty." It was a testament to the growing divide in American life that left-wing activists believed that the United States had taken anticommunism too far while right-wing activists believed that the country's leaders had not taken it far enough. Conservatives were not influential enough, or possessed of a compelling enough political message, to see their candidate to victory in 1964, however. In the shadow cast by Kennedy's assassination, Johnson defeated Goldwater in a historic landslide. Undaunted in the face of defeat, Goldwater conservatives established the organizational basis for later insurgent conservative activism.

The militancy of the black freedom movement, combined with Johnson's landslide victory over Goldwater, ushered in a liberal government that undertook reforms on a scale not seen since the New Deal. Even before that electoral victory, in the spring of 1964, Congress had passed major War on Poverty legislation and the Civil Rights Act and Johnson had announced his Great Society legislative agenda. Overall, between 1964 and 1966, Congress passed, and Johnson signed, the Civil Rights and Voting Rights Acts, legislation creating Medicare and Medicaid, major education, highway, housing, and wilderness preservation laws, era-defining immigration legislation, and a host of other laws addressing water and air quality, illiteracy, arts and humanities, and economic development. Seeing himself as a New Deal liberal in the Roosevelt mold, Johnson believed that the Democratic Party could mobilize government to improve the lives of American citizens and bring forth what he called the Great Society. (This burst of government action, accomplished with the support of many liberal Republicans, would encourage Goldwater's followers to redouble their efforts to win control of the Republican Party. They saw the Great Society as a package of overweening government programs that threatened personal liberty.) Johnson astutely linked his fate with the black freedom movement, and the result was the short-lived but undeniable high point of American liberalism's confidence in the possibility of a genuine, universal equality.

Even as he took bold progressive action domestically, Johnson broadened and intensified the war in Vietnam, which spurred the rise of the most militant antiwar movement in American history. Having told the public before the 1964 election that he would not widen the war in Vietnam (when US soldiers there numbered about 23,000), by 1968 Johnson had committed more than half a million US troops to Southeast Asia. In 1965, a series of college and university teach-ins, organized by students and professors, and a 25,000-person march in Washington, DC, questioned the war's legitimacy, morality, and necessity. Loosely organized but passionate and media-savvy, the antiwar movement expanded quickly beyond the initial teach-ins, staging major protests in Washington, New York, Chicago, San Francisco, and other major cities and college towns between 1965 and 1971. Antiwar activists fomented opposition to the draft, accused the United States of prosecuting a deeply immoral war, and hounded politicians, from the president and senators to local elected officials. Marches and protests occurred in hundreds of cities, but four in the nation's capital loom large in the movement's history: the 100,000-strong March on the Pentagon in 1967; the Moratorium march in October 1969 (which also featured local marches nationwide of 2 million–3 million Americans); a second, 500,000-strong, Moratorium march, known as "Mobe" for the New Mobilization Committee to End the War in Vietnam, in November 1969; and the intense and spirited 1971 Vietnam Veterans Against the War demonstrations, officially called Dewey Canyon III.

American debates about the war, democracy, and the rights of citizens were part of a larger global uprising of a transnational "new left" in the 1960s. Around the world, citizens of many nations interpreted the US war in Vietnam through a distinct lens: Vietnamese resistance to US power. Those who cheered that resistance, especially in the European left and in various anti-colonial struggles in Africa, Asia, and Latin America, saw the NLF as heroic guerrilla fighters battling Western imperialism. The NLF joined Che Guevara, the Argentine Marxist who fought in revolutionary struggles throughout Latin America, as iconic symbols of this resistance. Vietnam was a potent issue worldwide, but young people, especially students, in many societies also took to the streets against incumbent governing regimes, whether liberal-capitalist,

communist, military oligarchies, or autocracies (or some combination thereof). In societies as diverse as Mexico, France, West Germany, Brazil, Czechoslovakia, Japan, and Italy, student-led or youth movements of one sort or another sought greater citizen-level democracy. Many had peaceful origins and intentions, but resistance and provocations by authorities produced street scenes of pitched violence: students barricaded themselves in an encampment on the Left Bank in Paris; in the Tlatelolco Massacre in Mexico City, authorities shot into crowds of students, killing or injuring hundreds; in Prague, Soviet tanks swept into the city and ended the flowering of democratic reform politics known as the "Prague Spring." Each movement was unique, but each, too, shared the American black freedom and antiwar movements' sense that Cold War–era governments were authoritarian, unresponsive, immoral, and only vaguely interested in their citizens' welfare.

In the United States, fights over civil rights and the war in Vietnam shook the Democratic Party to its foundation. Passing the Civil Rights and Voting Rights Acts had required open warfare between the party's liberal wing and its more conservative, and historically white supremacist, southern wing. By 1968, the year Martin Luther King Jr. was assassinated, southern Democrats were in open revolt against the liberals. Vietnam made matters worse. As hawks (supporters) and doves (opponents) took sides in the American public square, Johnson held the party together only through 1968, when things began to fall apart. More and more Democratic politicians became doves, and Johnson faced primary challenges that year from two antiwar candidates, Eugene McCarthy and Robert F. Kennedy. To avoid an embarrassing battle for his party's nomination, and probably to avoid a direct confrontation with Kennedy, with whom he had an unfriendly rivalry, Johnson announced that he would not seek a second full presidential term—a stunning announcement by a sitting president, which a wan and tired-looking Johnson made on national television. No matter, even without Johnson's presence the 1968 Democratic Convention in Chicago was spared neither controversy nor disruption. Kennedy had been assassinated in June, just after winning the California primary, deepening the sense that the nation had descended into a kind of incomprehensible madness and leaving the antiwar movement without a viable candidate. In August, thousands of antiwar activists descended on Chicago, where the police forces of the city's Democratic political boss, and Vietnam hawk, Mayor Richard M. Daley, showed little restraint. The police harassed antiwar activists throughout the convention, and, sensing that the moment was ripe to challenge what they regarded as a fascist state, some of the protesters themselves provoked further confrontations. On the convention's final night, when the presidential nominee would be chosen, clashes erupted between police and protesters in what some called "The Battle for Michigan Avenue" and a subsequent federal report called a "police riot." Network cameras switched back and forth between the chaotic convention floor and scenes of tanks and police in riot gear assaulting protesters in the streets of Chicago. Dominant in national politics since the 1930s, the Democratic Party had come undone before a national television audience. Republican Richard Nixon won the presidency, though narrowly, in November.

Black freedom and antiwar activists were far from alone in seeking a transformative rupture in the status quo. In the second half of the 1960s, a new generation of American women both reignited and greatly expanded demands for equality and social justice that stretched back to the 19th century. Having secured "sex" as a prohibited category of discrimination, alongside race, color, national origin, and religion, in Title VII of the 1964 Civil Rights Act, women took to the streets, courts, and legislatures to democratize American life. Born in demands for economic equality with men, the women's movements that erupted in the 1960s were never about

economics alone. African American and Chicana women brought renewed attention to their economic and sexual exploitation, while also defending the respectability of motherhood and family. Women organized to secure reproductive self-determination by fighting to legalize contraception and abortion and to end the practice of forced sterilization. They demanded subsidized child care, reform of punitive government welfare programs, an end to rape and sexual harassment, and the full inclusion of women in the educational, governing, business, and commercial institutions of the nation in these years. Emanating from within the black freedom, antiwar, labor, and progressive religious movements of the 1960s, where women encountered both condescending patriarchy and ideological inspiration, the fight for women's equality in the 1960s was more a movement of movements than a single entity. That movement would reach its high point in the early 1970s, but its initial momentum was generated in the second half of the 1960s, as women of various class and racial backgrounds pushed for gender equity and greater social justice for women and families.

Another movement whose greatest impact came in the 1970s but that nonetheless played a crucial role in 1960s insurgencies was the homophile and later gay liberation movement. Homophiles, as gay rights activists called themselves until 1969, had formed key organizations in major cities and staged the first national protest demonstrations—in Philadelphia and Washington, DC—in 1965. Their voices were muted by both the late-sixties cacophony on the left and the relentless heterosexual bias of all but a handful of left-wing activists. But in the Stonewall Riot of July 1969, in New York City, when dozens of LGBT youth—most of them working class, many of them African American and Puerto Rican—fought back against police harassment, a new generation of activists, calling themselves "gay liberationists" seized on the radical energies surging around them and advanced the movement into the consciousness of ordinary Americans and, most important, the political class.

The insurgent social forces that arose in the 1960s, from the black freedom and anti-war movements to various feminisms and gay liberation, ignited a backlash. Fueled by politicians and opinion-makers who cast demands for equality and inclusion as dangerous extremism, and labeled criticism of the war in Vietnam unpatriotic and even pro-communist, the backlash was evident in the bombings and assassinations of black activists in the Deep South, Goldwater's campaign against the 1964 Civil Rights Act, and Ronald Reagan's election as governor of California in 1966. Some chose extreme actions, others extreme rhetoric, but as the avatars of the backlash saw it, extremism was nothing more than what left-liberal activists had long practiced. In his inaugural address as Alabama governor in 1963, George Wallace famously declared his support for "segregation now, segregation tomorrow, segregation forever." Running for California governor in 1966, Reagan told an approving crowd that the "ring leaders" of the Berkeley free speech movement of 1964, "who have no appreciation for freedom," should have been "taken by the scruff of the neck and thrown out of the university once and for all."[1] Backlash politicians held to the twin convictions that the status quo in American life was just fine as it was and that young left-liberal activists, of whatever variety, were undisciplined troublemakers who needed nothing more than the strong hand of a tough parent.

Stymied by a political backlash on one hand and the slow pace of institutional change on the other, left-liberal movements radicalized after 1966. Radical voices had been present all along, but 1960s movements had predominantly sought either greater inclusion and fairness in American social and political life or, in the case of the antiwar movement, to end the war in Vietnam through peaceful protest. They sought, as the SNCC Statement of Purpose put it, "a social order of justice permeated by love."[2] Between 1966 and 1969,

however, many activists began to speak not of liberal inclusion or democratic persuasion, and certainly not of love, but of a total revolution in American values and institutions. Black power advocates, following the example set by Stokely Carmichael's "black power" speech in Greenwood, Mississippi, in 1966, charged that racism went to the core of the nation's institutions—from city councils and school boards to housing markets and the prison system—and could not be vanquished with minor reforms like the Civil Rights Act. It would take, Carmichael later wrote, "the creation of a society where human misery and poverty are repugnant to that society."[3] Radical feminists argued that patriarchy, like racism, had to be torn from American life, root and branch, rather than ameliorated with well-intentioned legislation. Many antiwar activists, under the banner "bring the war home," believed they had to shut the country down to end the war. For others, nothing short of a full revolution at home would do—at the far reaches of that leftist radicalism, defined by the SDS off-shoot known as the Weathermen, even bombings and guerrilla warfare tactics were justified. Some searched for usable doctrines in Maoism—revolution through violence—others in separatism or consciousness raising or Marxist feminism. Not much united the various radicalisms of the late sixties, other than a conviction that traditional American institutions, from corporations to political parties, from the media to Congress, were incapable of producing basic social justice, at home or abroad.

Radicalisms on the left were matched on the political right by the emergence of a diffuse and broadly appealing conservative populism. Wallace, the segregationist governor of Alabama, ran for the Democratic presidential nomination in 1964 and for president in 1968 on the American Independent Party ticket. His platform was devoted to resisting racial desegregation and protecting "regular" Americans from the predations of civil rights activists, feminists, and "hippies." Both times he surprised observers by winning large numbers of white voters, not just in the South but in northern states like Wisconsin, including 13 percent of the total electorate in 1968. Richard Nixon built on Wallace's foundation and helped to engineer one of the great reversals of political rhetoric in the 20th century. New Deal liberals had once spoken on behalf of ordinary Americans against the interests of corporations, employers, and the wealthy. Those liberals were populists in the 1930s. Wallace and Nixon now cast liberals themselves—whom they represented as intellectuals, wealthy "limousine liberals," and overwrought activists on the diffuse liberal-left—as the overweening and powerful big interests, who would use government to impinge on the ambitions and opportunities of modest, ordinary, white Americans. Conservatives now claimed the populist banner. Nixon enshrined the latter as the "silent majority," a brilliantly effective political phrase that captured the new center-right populism. As the decade came to a close, the "silent majority" seemed on the ascent as much or perhaps now more than the left-liberal social movements of earlier in the decade.

The 1960s are best known as a decade of great social change and political fracturing. But protests and rage were far from the decade's only products. These years witnessed the strongest period of economic growth since World War II—until inflation, hastened by government spending on the war in Vietnam, began to climb after 1968—which enlarged the middle class and led to a vast suburban housing boom. That boom contrasted sharply with its paired twin: large-scale government programs, including "urban renewal" and interstate highway construction, that demolished whole swaths of older central cities, deepening racial inequality and hastening what became known as the "death of downtowns" in America. In an entirely different register, a new creative impulse, limned with anti-authoritarianism, reshaped the music, literary production, and filmmaking of the decade. Driven by a vast new consumer market composed of the coming-of-age "baby boom" generation, popular artists of all sorts—the British invasion bands, the New Journalists, and a young generation of Hollywood filmmakers, to name just a few—upended existing genres and infused their work with a spirit of rebellion. These original and defiant creative impulses overlapped with and fed a wider and more diffuse counterculture, in which the pursuit of authenticity, a more intense sense of personhood and self, and, often, consciousness-altering drugs blended into a mélange of invented, eclectic spirituality.

Like any ten-year period, the 1960s had its share of both change and continuity with the past. Few decades in the 20th century, however, witnessed the sixties' combination of social and political ruptures and its cascade of dramatic, violent, and consequential events.

COLLAPSE OF THE VITAL CENTER

Few developments in the 1960s were more definitive than the collapse of the centrist consensus that had organized national political life since the late 1940s. In 1949, the Harvard historian, and later adviser to President Kennedy, Arthur Schlesinger Jr., called this consensus the "Vital Center," by which he meant New Deal liberalism combined with anticommunism. Liberals, Schlesinger argued, had to defend the New Deal at home, spare no expense in containing communism abroad, and drive radicalisms of all sorts from American political life. This was a practical ideology, meant to insulate liberals against the charge that they had been "soft" on communism in the 1930s and remained so. But Schlesinger and liberals of his persuasion were also convinced that communism threatened the global market economy on which American affluence rested. This political stance is also known as "Cold War liberalism," because of the close connection between domestic and foreign affairs that was a hallmark of the postwar decades in the United States.

Above all, Vital Center liberalism was wedded to the containment policy, under which the United States pledged to "contain" communism within the geographic borders of the Soviet Union and Eastern Europe (and, after 1949, China). Once the United States replaced Great Britain as the West's chief global superpower in the years following World War II, its military and its spy and covert action agency, the CIA, expanded its reach ever further across the globe. The United States avoided direct military conflict with the Soviet Union by supporting anticommunist forces in what became known as "proxy wars," and in some cases simply coups d'état, in Greece, Turkey, Iran, Guatemala, Cuba, Israel, Malaysia, and Southeast Asia, among other places. The Korean War, in which Americans battled communist forces directly, was the principal exception until escalation in Vietnam in the early 1960s. Domestically, Vital Center liberals supported the growth of both the military-industrial complex and the national security state. The latter, launched by Congress and President Truman with the National Security Act of 1947, made "disloyalty" and "subversion" into household words. In the name of preventing communist influence in the United States, politicians, corporate and education leaders, and opinion-makers of all sorts fomented a red scare in the late 1940s and 1950s—known colloquially as McCarthyism—that discredited radicalism and cast suspicion on nonconformities of all kinds, political, social, and sexual.

Vital Center liberalism defined the main current of national politics for roughly two decades, and a majority of both Democratic and Republican politicians swam with rather than against it. Liberalism became at once more stable and accepted but also more technical and bureaucratic: the aim of social justice, associated with communism, was replaced by economic management in the service of an ever-growing consumer economy. Labor unions, though never fully tolerated by the nation's business class, won considerable social benefits for workers, including wage increases,

pensions, and health care, in their collectively bargained contracts. Expansions of national government programs came with Cold War rationales. Most prominently, the Highway Act of 1956 (officially the National Interstate and Defense Highway Act), which built the interstate highway system, was cast as a measure to speed the evacuation of cities in the event of a nuclear attack; the National Defense Education Act, the largest federal education program when it was passed in 1958, was a reaction to the Soviet Union's successful launch of the *Sputnik* satellite. The latter helped bring into being the Cold War university, where science, engineering, language study, social science, and foreign policy studies were well funded as Cold War imperatives. Politicians of all stripes supported such programs, and Congress seamlessly grafted Cold War military expenditures onto "pork barrel politics," in which members won funding for projects in their states or districts. The region stretching from southern California through Arizona, Texas, and Florida, and into upper South states like Virginia and North Carolina (what became known as the Sunbelt), benefited from military contracts, military bases, and other defense-related federal spending. This, too, was part of Vital Center, or Cold War, liberalism.

Vital Center liberalism came undone in the 1960s. It could not withstand pressure from the left, especially from the black freedom, antiwar, and women's movements, and from the right, symbolized by Barry Goldwater and the backlash against civil rights. Centrist political commitments to a moderate welfare state, anticommunism, and projecting US power abroad did not disappear—far from it. But the social eruptions of the 1960s profoundly destabilized American politics for more than a generation. Indeed, the events of the decade made many question whether there had actually been a "vital center" in the first place.

Despite the constant threat they would be labeled "subversive" or "communist," a variety of groups on the political left came together to oppose the Cold War verities of Vital Center liberalism. In the late 1950s, peace and antinuclear organizations objected to the US–Soviet arms race, the threat of nuclear annihilation, and what seemed to them a dangerous militarization of global affairs. The National Committee for a Sane Nuclear Policy (SANE), the Fellowship of Reconciliation (FOR), and the Student Peace Union (SPU) had all, by 1960, registered their vocal objections to US nuclear and foreign policy. In 1960, SDS emerged from the League for Industrial Democracy, a socialist organization, with a powerful, if inchoate, critique of the American military-industrial complex and the persistence of domestic racism and poverty. These groups opposed both US militarism abroad and Cold War anticommunism at home, and they would in time form the core of the sixties antiwar movement. In their own way, the Southern Christian Leadership Conference (SCLC), Student Nonviolent Coordinating Committee (SNCC), the Congress of Racial Equality (CORE), and other black freedom organizations also challenged the assumptions of Vital Center liberalism. Often accused of being "communistic" by their opponents, black freedom groups adopted a tactic, direct action against unjust laws and social norms, and pursued an objective, equality and social justice for nonwhite Americans, that challenged the Cold War verity that the United States was a global beacon of liberty.

These and other activist organizations constituted a "New Left," a term that came into prominence in the early 1960s. Journalists and academics reserved the term for students and other young activists, largely white and male, who emerged within and around Students for a Democratic Society (SDS) and other campus-based and peace organizations in the first half of the decade. Basic New Left ideas were consolidated in the Port Huron Statement, drafted by SDS members in 1962 and based on the teachings of Ella Baker, Herbert Marcuse, and C. Wright Mills, among others, and were on full display in the Mississippi Freedom Summer and the Free Speech

Movement in Berkeley, California, in 1964. The New Left embraced a radical notion of participatory democracy in contrast to what it considered the sclerotic, racist, and corporate-dominated American political system. New Left activists saw Cold War containment as a cover for US global hegemony and criticized the institutions that embraced it, especially the Democratic Party, urban political machines, and labor unions, which a generation earlier had built the American welfare state. The latter was now, in the New Left's view, a massive welfare-warfare bureaucracy. Black activists such as Stokely Carmichael, Huey Newton, and Angela Davis are generally associated more with Black Power than the New Left, but the two camps enjoyed considerable overlap, and black radicals delivered their own blistering critiques of US foreign and domestic policy.

The New Left's most concerted action in the decade was opposition to the Vietnam War. SDS, the Berkeley Free Speech Movement, and other student groups organized the first Vietnam teach-ins, protests, and marches in 1965. The campuses of the University of Wisconsin, Madison, the University of California, Berkeley, the University of Michigan, Columbia University, and Harvard University (Cold War universities all) were centers of this activism. New organizations emerged between 1965 and 1967: the Vietnam Day Committee, the National Mobilization Committee to End the War in Vietnam (MOBE), and Stop the Draft Week and other draft resistance groups. Between 1967 and 1970, the antiwar movement cycled through thousands of local and national protests, the latter including the 1967 March on the Pentagon and the 1969 Vietnam Moratorium. SNCC activists, such as Carmichael and Julian Bond, were outspoken opponents of the war, as was the Black Panther Party, founded in 1966. In 1967, Martin Luther King Jr., delivered a major speech against the war in New York, which symbolized the confluence of the black freedom and antiwar causes. By 1971, a new organization, Vietnam Veterans Against the War (VVAW), asserted moral leadership of the antiwar cause. With its emphasis on stemming both US imperialism overseas and racism at home, the antiwar movement produced a sustained attack on the assumptions of Vital Center liberalism.

Centrist Cold War liberalism held little appeal for American conservatives, and they too resisted its strictures in the 1960s. Right-wing Americans staged fewer marches and protests than the left but registered their dissatisfaction with the Vital Center in no uncertain terms. Nationally, the key figure was Goldwater, whose ghost-written 1960 polemic, *The Conscience of a Conservative*, and 1962 manifesto, *Why Not Victory? A Fresh Look at American Foreign Policy*, set forth the basic ideology of the New Right. Joined by the anticommunist activist Phyllis Schlafly (whose 1964 book, *A Choice Not an Echo*, became a conservative classic), Goldwater issued three fundamental indictments of the political center. First, he argued, liberalism stifled individual initiative and compromised property rights; the welfare state and civil rights should be resisted at every turn. Second, American foreign policy should be committed to the *defeat*, not simply containment, of global communism. Finally, the Republican Party, as both Goldwater and Schlafly saw it, had reflexively adopted Democratic policies under the leadership of Dwight Eisenhower rather than articulating clear ideological alternatives. Conservative groups like the Young Americans for Freedom (YAF), Americans for Goldwater, the John Birch Society, and the Orange County School of Anti-Communism, among many others, rallied behind this message. The Republican Party establishment, based in the Northeast and Midwest, was slow to comprehend that Goldwater's followers, whose strength lay in the Sunbelt, represented not a passing political eruption but a well-organized movement determined to capture control of the party.

Richard M. Nixon had been Eisenhower's vice president and had made his political career as a Joseph McCarthy–like communist hunter and red baiter in the early years of the Cold War. An unlikely inheritor of the Goldwater movement, because of his association with Ike, Nixon served as a bridge figure between centrist and conservative Republicans. He was the third outsized president of the decade, a politician best known for his survival instinct and his canny ability to adapt to the exigencies of the moment. Nixon coined the terms *forgotten Americans* in 1968 and *silent majority* in 1969 to describe the "non shouters, the non demonstrators," an open-ended political appeal to working- and middle-class white Americans alienated or threatened by the insurgent social forces on the left. Nixon's "silent majority" political strategy depended on carefully cultivating a sense that people who identified as "ordinary" Americans were under siege by a lawless and hyperactive left, an appeal that by 1968 was not difficult to make. Throughout his first term as president, Nixon expertly waged a populist campaign to retake the initiative on virtually every major issue of the decade: black freedom and civil rights, school desegregation, the Vietnam War, feminism, the Warren Court's civil liberties decisions, welfare, and many others. The New Right was never simply a reaction to the New Left. Much of the organizing on the right, especially the Goldwater movement, predated the full emergence of the New Left. However, the New Right gained considerable traction in the second half of the 1960s, as the backlash against civil rights, the antiwar movement, feminism, and the counterculture gained momentum. Nixon was never the Right's favorite political son (that honor went to Ronald Reagan), but he helped to consolidate an enduring center-right political ideology.

One of Nixon's signature contributions to national political life, and to the fracturing of the Vital Center, was the southern strategy. Captured in the 1969 book by Kevin Phillips, *The Emerging Republican Majority*, the southern strategy's objective was to drive anti–civil rights southern Democrats into the Republican fold and to remake the once Democratic solid South into a Republican stronghold. As Phillips saw it, the southern strategy was part of a larger national effort to join Sunbelt Goldwater conservatives, midwestern and Mid-Atlantic white working-class Catholic "ethnics," and southern opponents of black rights into a new Republican presidential majority. In fact, Nixon's political team developed multiple electoral strategies: a national strategy based on associating civil rights with violence and crime, a suburban strategy based on appeals to moderate, middle-class whites who believed in a race-blind meritocracy, and a southern strategy based on Nixon's promise to slow federal enforcement of civil rights laws. Debates raged within Nixon's close political circle about whether pursuing centrist or right-wing voters constituted the best electoral strategy, and to this day historians, too, debate whether the "silent majority" was a harbinger of a new centrism or a new conservatism in American politics. Whatever the case, Nixon mapped the route to the post-sixties Republican political coalition, a path followed by Ronald Reagan and subsequent national Republican political leaders.

With both major political parties consumed by internal factionalism of the center, left, and right, the foundation of the Vital Center, and the Cold War consensus, had eroded to the point that it no longer seemed to offer a cohesive framework for national political life.

AFRICAN AMERICAN POLITICAL INSURGENCY

The black freedom movement, or insurgency ("civil rights movement" is a less appropriate term, because black political objectives in the decade were never limited to a narrow set of civil rights, as crucial as those were), reawakened the American protest tradition, transformed the Constitution, and played a critical role in reconstituting American liberalism and national politics writ large. Civil rights lawyers taught a generation of constitutional outsiders, including women, other people of color,

and LGBT people, how to make successful arguments in court, and insurgent organizations, such as the Southern Christian Leadership Conference (SCLC), the Student Nonviolent Coordinating Committee (SNCC), and the Congress of Racial Equality (CORE), taught a generation of dissidents how to make their case in the streets. Every subsequent insurgent social movement of the decade, especially the antiwar, womens', and homophile/gay liberation movements, owed its greatest debt to the black organizing tradition.

There are many possible ways to characterize the black freedom insurgency. Historians of late have adopted the notion of a "long civil rights movement," to denote the period between the 1941 March on Washington Movement and the 1972 Black Political Convention in Gary, Indiana. Analyzing the movement in terms of that thirty-year sequence is more productive in many respects than isolating the decade of the 1960s. Nevertheless, within the ten-year boundary of the sixties, five crucial dimensions of the black organizing tradition can be identified: legal, direct action, legislative, nationalist, and radical. The first three were tactics, the second two ideological orientations. Different segments of the black insurgency of the decade mixed these elements in distinct ways.

The legal dimension of that tradition was two decades old by 1960. Founded in 1940 under the leadership of Thurgood Marshall, the NAACP Legal Defense and Education Fund (LDF) challenged Jim Crow segregation in court. Building on a few successful cases the NAACP had already waged in the 1930s, Marshall and the LDF set about systematically testing the constitutionality of the legal foundations of black subjugation in the United States: the "white primary," poll taxes, and other vote-suppression techniques in the South, instruments of housing segregation, such as "covenants" preventing home sales to black buyers, and the segregation of public facilities, from parks and playgrounds to law and medical schools, universities, and K–12 education. These efforts were remarkably successful in a strictly legal sense, and included victories in *Smith v. Allright* (1944), *Brown v. Board of Education I* (1954) and *II* (1955), and *Cooper v. Aaron* (1958), among many other landmark decisions by the Warren Court. Legal victories made little immediate change in the lives of ordinary people, but they were the necessary preconditions for racial equality and social justice, and they produced a powerful backlash. In 1956, under the banner of "massive resistance," Senator Harry F. Byrd Sr. of Virginia issued the "Southern Manifesto," a document signed by more than one hundred southern congressional representatives declaring their absolute determination to resist implementation of *Brown*.

The insurgent direct action protest that became so crucial in and emblematic of the 1960s emerged in the shadow of massive white resistance. The legal work of the LDF continued on its own trajectory, but a generation of African Americans was determined to push for more fundamental changes to the nation's racial order. Predominant in these efforts were three organizations: CORE, founded in 1942 in Chicago by James Farmer and other members of the Fellowship of Reconciliation influenced by the teachings of Mahatma Gandhi; the SCLC, founded in 1957 by Marin Luther King Jr. and other black southern ministers following the success of the Montgomery bus boycott; and SNCC, founded in 1960 by Ella Baker and college students involved in the massive sit-in campaigns of that year. As important as they were, national organizations such as CORE, SCLC, and SNCC, alongside the NAACP, were only one dimension of black organizing in the 1960s. Most such organizing took place locally and rarely received national notoriety. From Little Rock and Atlanta to Philadelphia, Detroit, and Oakland—and dozens and dozens of places in between—religious, secular, liberal, nationalist, and radical black organizations thrived in the 1960s, working to desegregate employment, housing, politics, and government, and on behalf of justice in policing and against poverty, among a wide range of other causes.

Early in the decade, following the 1960 wave of sit-ins, black insurgency gained momentum in the South. Local organizations, such as the Alabama Christian Movement for Human Rights, based in Birmingham, drew on religious and labor leaders, black women's organizations, high school and college students, and other diverse segments of the black community. They focused on local conditions, especially employment and educational inequities, but in the first half of the 1960s an important strategy developed. It actually had roots in the 1950s, when the push for equal education in places like Little Rock (1957) forced the national government to override local white resistance. In the Freedom Rides through numerous states in 1961, in Birmingham in 1963, throughout Mississippi in the summer of 1964, and in Selma, Alabama, in 1965 what began as local organizing and direct action developed into a national strategy. That strategy was to dramatize white resistance, brutality, and injustice in order to force the federal government—either the executive branch or Congress—into decisive action. Events in Birmingham and Selma, in particular, were instrumental in the passage of the 1964 Civil Rights Act and the 1965 Voting Rights Act. So, too, was the 1963 March on Washington, organized by Bayard Rustin and A. Philip Randolph, an original version of which had been planned in 1941. In these instances, direct action and the legislative strategy complemented, and depended on, one another. Only a new national legal framework of racial justice offered the possibility of overcoming local resistance and entrenched white power.

As critical as the local-national dynamic proved to be, the heart of the direct action insurgency remained rooted at the city, county, and state levels. Insurgents focused overwhelmingly on the economic subordination and police brutality that African Americans endured across the country, North and South. Local CORE branches, for instance, campaigned in many cities against employment discrimination and the banishment of black workers from entire categories of the best-paying jobs. Between 1963 and 1968, local groups staged protests at white-only construction sites in nearly a dozen major cities, demanding the fair and equal employment of black workers on skyscraper, housing, stadium, and highway projects. Activists demanded less oppressive policing, community review boards to track police misconduct, and the employment of more black officers. Other groups took aim at the ferocious housing discrimination practiced by the real estate industry and mandated by federal mortgage programs. Often a combination of protest and political coalition building proved decisive. In California, for instance, the 1963 Rumford Fair Housing Act was passed after years of both protest and political lobbying. Instances of such local organizing numbered in the hundreds, perhaps thousands, in the 1960s. They do not often receive their due in public memory, but they were instrumental to the process of forging a more equal, if still deeply segregated and unjust, society.

In one of the more remarkable essays of the 20th century, long-time pacifist and racial justice advocate Bayard Rustin summed up the movement at the decade's midpoint. Writing in 1965, Rustin called the years between 1954 and 1964 "the period in which the legal foundations of racism in America were destroyed."[4] But, Rustin quickly added, desegregating lunch counters and hotels would not fundamentally change the economic foundations of racial subjugation. Second-class social and economic citizenship could not be ameliorated by a civil rights law. An equally challenging problem, he wrote, was "the failure of many whites of good will to understand the nature of our problem." The black freedom movement, Rustin argued, must turn "from protest to politics" and reconstitute the liberal political tradition on a new footing. This would necessitate reorganizing the Democratic Party, a revolution "whose logic is the displacement of Dixiecrat power," and the building of a new, multiracial agenda of economic and social justice. Rustin underestimated the extent of the white backlash, missed the crucial role of suburban whites in resisting fundamental reform, and was overly optimistic about the capacity of the American political system to serve as a vehicle for racial justice. Nevertheless, his summation expertly captured the successes of the movement by 1965 as well as its ongoing dilemmas.

The nationalist and radical dimensions of the black organizing tradition were interwoven into all the strategies discussed. Nationalism and radicalism were less strategies than ideological or conceptual orientations. Nevertheless, it is useful to separate out the two because doing so allows an appreciation of the full scope of African American life and politics in the 1960s. The speeches and writings of Malcolm X, for instance, helped to build the Nation of Islam (NOI), a nationalist church that emphasized black pride and self-determination. Malcolm X often disdained SCLC and CORE protests and marches, seeing in them an older pattern of black supplication before whites—though he always reserved his sharpest criticisms for white society. Meaningful black power, not the petitioning of white institutions, interested him. Malcolm X's example inspired other nationalists and radicals, groups like the Black Panther Party, founded in 1966 in Oakland, California. Many radicals shared the black self-help tradition of nationalists, but in addition they drew on various ideologies of liberation, from Marxism to Maoism, and sought a wider web of alliances with left-wing organizations. Taking aim at police brutality and highlighting the racialized poverty that decades of Jim Crow had produced, as revolutionary black nationalists the Panthers refused to recognize a distinction between the militarization of urban streets by city police and the militarization of the globe by the United States.

Any such distinction was further complicated by the burst of urban uprisings between 1964 and 1968 and the literal militarization of entire cityscapes in response. In Rochester,

New York, and in Harlem in 1964, in Watts, south of Los Angeles, in 1965, in Newark and Detroit in 1967, and in over one hundred cities after the assassination of Martin Luther King Jr. in 1968, African Americans engaged in uprisings against police and property. Virtually every incident began in a similar fashion: a local episode of heavy-handed policing sparked outrage and then violence. In all, between 1964 and 1968, tens of thousands of people were arrested, hundreds were killed (both residents and police), and hundreds of millions of dollars in property was damaged or destroyed. In 1968, one of the most forthright government documents ever released, the Kerner Commission Report, pointed the finger at decades of housing segregation and job discrimination against African Americans and declared that the country was "moving toward two societies, one black, one white—separate and unequal."[5] But the report made clear who bore responsibility. "[W]hite society is deeply implicated in the ghetto," the report read. "White institutions created it, white institutions maintain, and white society condones it." Some black activists, notably H. Rap Brown, encouraged the burning of cities as a justified response to lack of meaningful white action on racial equality. But most black leaders condemned the violence and saw it as an unfortunate, if understandable, symptom of the total marginalization of many black people from the larger society.

Inspired by the black freedom insurgency, but equally grounded in their own long-term organizing traditions, other Americans of color demanded equality and justice during the decade. Latina/o Americans, particularly those of Mexican and Puerto Rican heritage, forged prominent activist organizations. The Puerto Rican Young Lords Party issued a thirteen-point platform calling for, among other things, self-determination for Puerto Rico and for Latina/o in the United States, liberation of all Third World people, and community control of institutions and land. Among Mexican

Americans, a host of groups and causes defined the sixties-era struggle. The Community Services Organization (CSO), based in Los Angeles, trained Cesar Chavez and Dolores Huerta, who went on to found the United Farm Workers of America (UFW), whose series of boycotts and strikes in the early 1960s inspired many Mexican Americans. Calling themselves Chicana/o, young Mexican Americans formed student, antiwar, feminist, and nationalist organizations, many of which were local or regional, such as Denver's Crusade for Justice or Los Angeles's Brown Berets. In 1967, the Mexican American Youth Organization (MAYO) was founded in San Antonio, which in turn helped to found La Raza Unida in 1970, a major political party that advanced the social and political cause of Mexican Americans. Native American activists founded the American Indian Movement (AIM) in Minneapolis in 1968 and staged a series of direct action protests, including the occupation of Alcatraz Island between 1969 and 1971, and the cross-country trail of broken treaties march in 1972. By the early 1970s, groups like the Young Lords and AIM, alongside black radicals and nationalists, called not for inclusion in a putatively liberal polity but for an international solidarity of colonized people.

In the 1960s, people of color in the United States, long constitutional, social, and political outsiders, called for an end to racism and began to imagine a new kind of multiracial nation. That project began with the resurgence, after decades of brutal Jim Crow laws and practices, of African American political agency, but it was also part of the global 1960s, particularly the wave of decolonization movements across Africa and Asia that had begun in the years after World War II. The African American freedom insurgency inspired and drew inspiration from, in equal measure, those decolonization movements, as domestically the resurgence of black cultural and political voices in the 1960s recast the narrative of national life more fundamentally than at any time since Reconstruction.

RIGHTS POLITICS: WELFARE LIBERALISM AND RIGHTS LIBERALISM

That recasting had broader implications for the nature and content of the American liberal tradition. In the first half of the 20th century, rich industrialized nations, including the United States, constructed welfare regimes of various kinds designed to empower and protect their citizens. The timing of the major welfare initiatives varied by nation, and in the United States the central innovations came during the New Deal of the 1930s. Those innovations, including the Social Security and National Labor Relations Acts of 1935, were designed and sponsored by the Democratic Party in the spirit of what President Roosevelt later called "freedom from want" and "freedom from fear." Thereafter, American liberalism came to be associated with the social welfare paradigm: that government owed citizens a minimum standard of economic security and protection alongside the opportunity to improve wages and working conditions through collective bargaining by organized labor. This "welfare liberalism," which was at the heart of the Vital Center discussed previously, commanded the loyalty of a generation of Democratic, as well as many Republican, politicians, officials, and voters.

During the decade of the 1960s, a new generation of activists, attorneys, and politicians transformed American liberalism. They forged an altogether new "rights liberalism" based on the concept of invidious discrimination and the rights of individuals found in amendments to the Constitution and enumerated in such major legislation as the Civil Rights and Voting Rights Acts. Thereafter, American liberalism embraced both the welfare and rights paradigms, though the political emphasis on one or the other varied over time and among political constituencies. The embrace of the rights paradigm by liberals, as noted previously, was forged by the black freedom movement's legal and legislative assault on African Americans' second-class citizenship. All subsequent efforts in the rights field drew on that movement's legal argumentation and techniques and endeavored to frame the case for legal change in relationship to the civil rights paradigm. Indeed, one way of thinking about the post-1960s history of liberalism is that it struggled *internally* to reconcile the welfare and rights paradigms and it struggled *externally* against a growing political opposition mounted by the New Right.

Johnson's Great Society endeavored to link the civil rights and welfare paradigms. In the rights field, the Civil Rights Acts of 1964 and 1968 and the Voting Rights Act of 1965 extended protections against discrimination to citizens on the basis of race, color, religion, sex, and national origin and erected a bulwark against political oppression. The Immigration and Nationality Act of 1965 undid much, though not all, of the race- and religion-based chauvinism of the reigning 1924 immigration legislation. In these and other measures, the national government promised to safeguard the capacity of citizens to participate fully in the social and political life of the nation. In the welfare field, Great Society liberals also forged new national health insurance for older and low-income Americans (Medicare and Medicaid). The two measures fell short of universal national health insurance, an objective of liberals since the 1930s, but they represented the most aggressive and optimistic expansion of welfare liberalism since the New Deal. Johnson also took a step toward universal pre-kindergarten childhood education with the Head Start program, created under the Economic Opportunity Act of 1964, the foundation of the War on Poverty. At the same time and in contrast, Great Society liberals sought to reduce the income support component of Aid to Families with Dependent Children (AFDC), actions that Johnson's critics saw as a short-sighted abandonment of a key anti-poverty program that itself dated to the 1930s.

Despite the Great Society's advancements, the welfare liberalism of the New Deal bequeathed to the 1960s deep gender and racial biases—in the form of what we might call "breadwinner liberalism." Welfare policy had long been based on a male breadwinner model of economic and family life, in which women were conceived primarily as dependents of men and heterosexuality was both presumed and valorized. Moreover, New Deal housing, labor, and social security programs began their life with powerful racial exclusions embedded in them. Thus, 1930s welfare liberalism had legislated gender and racial hierarchies—and perpetuated inequalities—and created a fractured social safety net that covered only a portion of the citizenry.

Advocates of the rights paradigm in the 1960s sought to address these and other forms of legal and social exclusion and oppression. In the Civil Rights Acts of 1964 and 1968, for instance, the black freedom movement won what it had long sought: legal protection against labor and housing market discrimination. In the 1964 legislation, women, too, gained protection against gender-based discrimination in employment. At the state and municipal level, African Americans, Mexican Americans and other Latina/o, women, and gay men and lesbians lobbied for laws and ordinances that prohibited labor and housing market discrimination. Hard-won legislative victories came, but those seeking redress also turned to the courts. When they did, the Fourteenth Amendment played a defining role. Since the 1930s, the NAACP Legal Defense Fund (LDF) had argued that the "equal protection" and "due process" clauses of that amendment rendered most forms of racial discrimination illegal. Using such arguments, for instance, the LDF chipped away at discrimination in educational institutions, culminating in the *Brown* decision of 1954 (and *Brown II* in 1955). By the late 1960s, the Warren Court had developed the "strict scrutiny" standard for laws and public policies that made distinctions on the basis of race, rendering virtually all such distinctions unconstitutional (in *Loving v. Virginia*, in 1967,

for example, the Court declared laws prohibiting interracial marriage unconstitutional). In a series of decisions in the 1970s, the Court applied "intermediate scrutiny" to laws employing gender distinctions, a slightly lower burden.

In addition to responding to petitioners on questions of race and gender, the Warren Court expanded First Amendment rights, particularly in the arena of publishing, filmmaking, and other forms of artistic expression. In many instances the Court's rulings permitted greater sexual content in art and public discourse (what had traditionally been called "obscenity"), which engendered a reaction among moral conservatives. The group Citizens for Decent Literature, for instance, produced the 1965 film *Perversion for Profit*, an expose about the pornography industry and, as the group saw it, the Court's culpability in its growth. The Warren Court also expanded the rights of people arrested, in the 1966 *Miranda v. Arizona* ruling; acknowledged the right of low-income Americans in criminal trials to a government-appointed attorney, in the 1963 *Gideon v. Wainwright* ruling; and completed the long process of applying the Bill of Rights to state as well as federal law in the 1969 *Benton v. Maryland* ruling. During these same years, the Warren Court ruled that mandatory school prayer and Bible reading in public schools were unconstitutional violations of the separation of church and state—decisions that deeply offended many Christians. Together, the Warren Court's rulings over more than a decade produced a powerful conservative movement calling for "judicial restraint." The John Birch Society, in this spirit, notably declared, "Save Our Republic: Impeach Earl Warren."

No Warren Court development was more influential, or became more politically charged, than the emergence of the "right of privacy." Drawing on concepts that dated to the 1890s, but had entered Supreme Court rulings only in footnotes, the Warren Court first enunciated a "marital" right of privacy in the 1965

Griswold v. Connecticut decision, in a case involving access to birth control. Warren left the bench in 1969, but in the 1972 ruling in *Eisenstadt v. Baird*, and, most famously, in the 1973 *Roe v. Wade* decision, the Court extended the logic of privacy—that is, freedom of choice—to individual women seeking either birth control or an abortion. No one loved the *Roe* decision. Conservatives claimed it was blatant judicial overreach, and a vast political movement arose against it. Feminists thought it too weak but learned to live with and defiantly defend it. Gay men and lesbians argued that privacy ought to be extended to people's choice of sexual partners, which the Court adamantly refused to do until 2004. The right of privacy was, in the end, the product of feminists organizing for both social and legal change and a Court seeking ways to cautiously extend individual liberty. It was as much evolution as revolution.

The rights paradigm developed alongside the welfare paradigm, and the two have lived, sometimes comfortably sometimes awkwardly, together in liberal thought and politics since the 1960s. The 1972 Equal Rights Amendment (which was never ratified by the requisite number of states), the development of equal employment and sexual harassment law in the 1970s and 1980s, and the 1990 Americans with Disabilities Act are examples of the legacy of the rights paradigm. The limits of the rights paradigm, too, have been in evidence since the 1960s. There are three such limitations worth noting here. First, a rights claim often invokes a counter rights claim, as has been evident in affirmative action and reproductive politics, and thus rights become less absolute than subject to negotiation. Second, rights have proved to be highly wealth and status sensitive—that is, people who already have resources tend to benefit more from rights than those without such resources. And third, rights-based legislation and court decisions have eliminated many formal legal distinctions (such as race, color, and gender) in ways that have benefited individuals but have proved

less able to ameliorate broad patterns of group disadvantage. Even with these substantial limitations, the "rights revolution" that began in the 1960s was among the most divisive developments of the decade and set the terms of political debate, and conflict, in ways eminently recognizable today.

ANTI-AUTHORITARIANISM

In his 1956 book, *Growing Up Absurd*, which became a cult classic in the 1960s, Paul Goodman wrote about, and in many ways for, the "disaffected youth" he saw around him. "Their main topic is the 'system,' with which they refuse to cooperate,"[6] he explained. A decade later, in their manifesto *Black Power*, Kwame Ture (formerly Stokely Carmichael) and Charles Hamilton rejected assimilation into the white middle class "because the values of that class are in themselves anti-humanist." They too wrote of a "system," by which they meant "the entire American complex of basic institutions, values, beliefs, etc." For 1960s dissidents, "the system" could mean many things: corporations, the war in Vietnam, the military, politicians and government, patriarchy, the middle class, anyone belonging to the World War II generation, racism, sexism, and much else. "The system" looked different depending on where one stood. But its authority, especially its authority over the individual, was widely, often seriously, sometimes mockingly, derided. The spirit of dissent embodied in the social insurgencies of the decade both fed on and helped produce a larger climate of anti-authoritarianism, the fourth and final development of the decade considered here.

"I am an orphan of America," Abbie Hoffman scoffed during his trial for conspiracy to riot at the 1968 Democratic National Convention. When asked where he resided, Hoffman declared, "I live in Woodstock nation," and when asked, for the record of the court, when he was born, Hoffman replied, "Psychologically, 1960." The transcript of Hoffman's testimony in the trial of the Chicago Seven is replete with sarcasm and disdain for the government's case against him and the six other defendants, among whose number was Black Panther Party co-founder Bobby Seale and Students for a Democratic Society (SDS) co-founder Tom Hayden. Hoffman, a founder of the "Yippies" (Youth International Party), was among the most anarchic anti-authoritarian troublemakers of the sixties; he refused to take any official institution in American society seriously. Hoffman may have been an extreme case, but he was nonetheless representative of a much broader pattern of anti-authoritarian sentiment, behavior, and thinking that reached a kind of crescendo in the late 1960s.

Virtually no arena of national life remained untouched by the anti-authoritarian ethos: family, church, government, law, and cultural norms were all deeply challenged. Measuring the precise valence, or the full extent, of anti-authoritarian attitudes is difficult, but a wide variety of evidence can be assembled to represent the landscape of those attitudes. The various feminisms of the decade, for instance, challenged male prerogative, the sexual double standard, and even the organization of the nuclear family. Beginning with Betty Friedan's *The Feminine Mystique* and continuing through the far more radical *Sexual Politics* (1969), by Kate Millett, and *Abortion Rap* (1971), by Diane Schulder and Florynce Kennedy, feminist writings, manifestos, and speeches mocked and derided the assumed cultural authority of men. With regard to race, black freedom advocates openly questioned the integrity of the major churches (and especially their southern congregations), white social, economic, and educational institutions, and virtually all levels of government. In his "Letter from Birmingham Jail," Martin Luther King Jr. challenged the Christian integrity of his colleagues among the white pastorate. The antiwar movement deeply questioned the motives of national elected officials, including Presidents Johnson and Nixon, and accused many in the government of lying

about the war in Vietnam. By the later years of the decade, few in the antiwar movement believed anything that government officials said about the war, and the long history of official deceit was laid bare when the Pentagon Papers were published in 1971 by the *New York Times*, the *Washington Post*, and other major newspapers. Across virtually every sector of American life in the 1960s, the authority of basic institutions was not simply called into question but often openly disbelieved and publically ridiculed.

The anti-authoritarian ethos extended beyond the social movement insurgencies of the decade into media, culture, and art. The broad movement known as New Journalism upended facile distinctions between fact and fiction by inserting the reporter into reportage and crafting a subjective point of view about modern life. Practitioners such as Gay Talese, Tom Wolfe, and Joan Didion wrote in a variety of genres, from the traditional newspaper profile piece to long-form and deeply personal essays. In *The Armies of the Night* (1968) and *Miami and the Siege of Chicago* (1968), Norman Mailer, and in *Hell's Angels* (1967), *Fear and Loathing in Las Vegas* (1971), and *Fear and Loathing on the Campaign Trail* (1972), Hunter S. Thompson explored the depths of subjectivity, irony, and personalization, in the process showing how journalism could capture the essence of an event without strict adherence to "facts." In film, the vertically integrated Hollywood studio system in place since the 1930s was imploding. Freed from its confines, and the genre formulas it imposed, a new generation of film school graduates and other "auteurs" began making more thematically ambitious films that romanticized outlaws: including, among others, the monstrously biting send-up of the Cold War, *Dr. Strangelove* (1964); the two major films of white middle-class rebel-fantasy of 1967, *The Graduate* and *Bonnie and Clyde*; the dark story of urban eroticism, *Midnight Cowboy* (1969); the decade's signature dreamscape of male rebellion, *Butch Cassidy and the Sundance*

Kid (1969); the anti-Vietnam film, *M.A.S.H.* (1970); and the genre-busting, bleak view of America in *McCabe and Mrs. Miller* (1971). Late-sixties cinema, inspired by the European New Wave, gave those who would buck convention and object to traditional sources of authority new role models and new license.

Most of the anti-authoritarian rebels who made it to the big screen or found themselves lionized by the counterculture were men. Narratives of male rebellion exerted a powerful gravitational pull in the 1960s. Even the counterculture, a shifting mélange of styles and attitudes more than a definitive "culture," took its cues from male-centered forms of rebellion. "If man and wife in a suburban split-level was a symbol of all that was wrong with plastic, bourgeois America," the feminist Susan Brownmiller wrote, "'man and chick' in a Lower East Side tenement flat was hardly the new order [women] had dreamed of."[7] The counterculture's embrace of a new, and as they saw it more authentic, way of living did not necessarily dislodge male prerogative. Nevertheless, the counterculture's basic argument, that individuals ought to be free to experience pleasure and purpose, love and spirituality, on their own terms unfettered by prevailing institutions and norms, inspired Americans of all genders and sexualities. Nowhere was this more evident than in the growing use of marijuana, along with hallucinatory drugs such as LSD, among wide segments of the population.

Sixties anti-authoritarianism was part of an ecstatic celebration of youth, an elevation of young people of the baby boom generation to an unprecedented vantage from which to shape American society. Long after the protests died down, drug use declined, and the politics of rebellion dissipated, the validation of youth remained a potent social and cultural force, particularly in consumer culture. It is part of the irony of the 1960s that youthful rebellion, so meaningful at times in the decade, acquired such a prosaic meaning within consumer capitalism in later decades, used to sell everything from cars to shoes. Youthful styles, milestones, patterns of consumption, attitudes, and slang have enjoyed a popularity since the 1960s rooted in the idea that young people should set the cultural tone for the society as a whole, and particularly that their general disdain for older traditions and older adults is worthy of emulation.

Sixties anti-authoritarianism was also part of the long-standing tension in American life between the celebration of individualism and the valuing of hierarchy and order. As a white settler colony lacking a landed aristocracy and founded on principles of economic liberty, the United States has long regarded "freedom" as the hallmark of its national character. Yet religious principles—particularly strains of puritan Christian theology and various kinds of Christian evangelicalism—moral traditionalisms of various sorts, and respect for generational, particularly patriarchal, continuity have also played central roles in ordering national life. Just how far "liberty" ought to extend into the realm of personal behavior has been an unsettled, controversial question since the 18th century. Sixties' anti-authoritarianism raised anew debates over the degree to which individuals should regulate their own behavior rather than relying on parents, families, religion, neighbors, or government. The counterculture popularized rock music, drug use, unconventional spirituality, sartorial flamboyance, and personal authenticity and community solidarity, among other things, as totems of a new pathway to personal freedom. The counterculture led the way, but a more general anti-authoritarian spirit suffused American life during the 1960s.

When the decade of the 1960s closed, the Cold War had not ended, the Vietnam War raged on, the most politically rightward-leaning president in more than a generation occupied the White House, and racial-. gender-, and sexuality-based inequalities remained woven into the fabric of national life. Despite such continuities with earlier decades and the failure of insurgencies to immediately transform the country, the 1960s nonetheless marks a fundamental break in the 20th century. A post-1960s world dawned, and the developments, conflicts, and terms of debate etched in the decade would come to define much of the next half century.

DISCUSSION OF THE LITERATURE

The historical literature on the 1960s, as with most decades, falls into specific topics and subfields. Among the richest is the historiography on the black freedom movement and African American politics, protest, and organizing. A classic, fine-grained and readable study of the Mississippi Summer project of 1964 is *I've Got the Light of Freedom: The Organizing Tradition and the Mississippi Freedom Struggle*, by Charles M. Payne.[8] Foundational studies include *The Origins of the Civil Rights Movement: Black Communities Organizing for Change*, by Aldon D. Morris, and *Race, Reform, and Rebellion: The Second Reconstruction in Black America, 1945–1990*, by Manning Marable.[9] There are compelling reasons not to reflexively divide the movement into "southern" and "northern," though the literature has largely developed along these lines. Terrific, award-winning books on the southern movement include *Ella Baker and the Black Freedom Movement: A Radical Democratic Vision*, by Barbara Ransby, and *Crossroads at Clarksdale: The Black Freedom Struggle in the Mississippi Delta after World War II*, by Francoise Hamlin.[10] An important overview of the northern movement is *Sweet Land of Liberty: The Forgotten Struggle for Civil Rights in the North*, by Thomas J. Sugrue.[11] Engaging topical and city-based studies include *To Stand and Fight: The Struggle for Civil Rights in New York City*, by Martha Biondi; *American Babylon: Race and the Struggle for Postwar Oakland*, by Robert O. Self; and *Up South: Civil Rights and Black Power in Philadelphia*, by Matthew J. Countryman.[12]

Historians have intensely debated the various political transformations of the decade. Taking on the long-held view that Richard Nixon pursued a "southern strategy" of political realignment, Matthew Lassiter argues instead for a "convergence" of North and South along an axis defined by a middle-class white suburban politics. That book is *The Silent Majority: Suburban Politics in the Sunbelt South*.[13] Two other Sunbelt books that make an argument for a distinctly regional conservatism are *Suburban Warriors: The Origins of the New American Right*, by Lisa McGirr, and *From Bible Belt to Sunbelt: Plain-Folk Religion, Grassroots Politics, and the Rise of Evangelical Conservatism*, by Darren Dochuk.[14] Rick Perlstein makes a provocative argument about the centrality of Richard Nixon in the political realignment than began in the 1960s in *Nixonland: The Rise of a President and the Fracturing of a Nation*.[15] Looking beyond the black freedom struggle, historians have documented the complex and multivalent racial politics of the decade. See, for instance, *Racism on Trial: The Chicano Fight for Justice*, by Ian F. Haney López; *The Color of America Has Changed: How Racial Diversity Shaped Civil Rights Reform in California, 1941–1978*, by Mark Brilliant; *Youth, Identity, Power: The Chicano Movement*, by Carlos Muñoz; and *The American Indian Occupation of Alcatraz Island: Red Power and Self-Determination*, by Troy R. Johnson.[16]

The historical literature on rights politics, social movements, and the law in the 1960s is also critical to understanding the decade. See, for example, *Reasoning from Race: Feminism, Law, and the Civil Rights Revolution*, by Serena Mayeri, and *The Lost Promise of Civil Rights*, by Lisa L. Goluboff.[17] On the many feminisms of the 1960s, see *Finding the Movement: Sexuality, Contested Space, and Feminist Activism*, by Anne Enke; *Radical Sisters: Second-Wave Feminism and Black Liberation in Washington, D.C.*, by Anne M. Valk; and *Living for the Revolution: Black Feminist Organizing*, by Kimberly Springer.[18] On homophile and early gay liberation and gay rights movements, the classic reference remains *Sexual Politics, Sexual Communities: The Making of a Homosexual Minority in the United States, 1940–1970*, by John D'Emilio, but newer work, such as *Wide*

Open Town: A History of Queer San Francisco to 1965, by Nan Alamilla Boyd, and Timothy Stewart-Winter's *Queer Clout: Chicago and the Rise of Gay Politics*, have deepened and enriched the narrative of 1960s queer history.[19]

The literature on Vietnam, too, is vast and deep, and only a few titles can be cited here. For a terrific overview, see *The Vietnam Wars, 1945–1990*, by Marilyn B. Young, and *Embers of War: The Fall of an Empire and the Making of America's Vietnam*, by Fredrik Logevall,[20] the latter of which won the Pulitzer Prize. For three unique and different portraits of aspects of the war, see Tom Wells, *The War Within: America's Battle over Vietnam*, *Dear Dr. Spock: Letters about the Vietnam War to America's Favorite Baby Doctor*, edited by Michael S. Foley, and *Pay Any Price: Lyndon Jonson and the Wars in Vietnam*, by Lloyd Gardner.[21]

PRIMARY SOURCES

Because so much of the history of the 1960s can be told through social movements, the decade's archive is spread across the country. The papers of Martin Luther King Jr. are located at the King Center in Atlanta, as are the SNCC papers. The King papers are being edited and published in a fourteen-volume set, seven of which have so far been published, by The Martin Luther King, Jr. Research and Education Institute at Stanford University, a cooperative venture with the King Center. The Stanford Library also has the papers of the Black Panther Party. The Schlesinger Library at the Radcliffe Institute for Advanced Study at Harvard University houses one of the nation's best collections of American women's history, including the papers of the National Organization for Women (NOW), the National Abortion Rights Action League (NARAL), Betty Friedan, Pauli Murray, and many other notable organizations and individuals. No history of American women in the 1960s is possible without visiting the Schlesinger. The vast alternative press created

by feminists and women's advocates in the 1960s and 1970s has been preserved on ninety reels of microfilm under the title *Herstory*.[22] Primary sources for the homophile movement can be found in many archives across the country, among them the GLBT Historical Society in San Francisco, the Lesbian Herstory Archives in Brooklyn, New York, and the Human Sexuality Collection at the Cornell University Library.

As with any period in the 20th century, a great deal of the history of the 1960s can be told through materials held at presidential libraries. Presidential papers in this era are not merely the dry ephemera of high politics and power brokerage but vast assemblages of documents collected by presidents, agencies, advisers, and other White House officials. These papers are especially critical to understanding the Vietnam War. The John F. Kennedy Presidential Library and Museum in Boston, the LBJ Presidential Library in Austin, Texas, and the Nixon Presidential Library and Museum in Yorba Linda, California, have remarkable holdings on the politics and social movements of the decade. For the history of the New Right, the Barry Goldwater Papers are held at the Arizona Historical Foundation at Arizona State University.

DIGITAL MATERIALS

The Public Papers of the Presidents are available at The American Presidency Project (http://www.presidency.ucsb.edu/). Access to the collection of the National Security Archive (http://nsarchive.gwu.edu/) is also available online. A vast and important collection is the Vietnam Center and Archive (http://www.vietnam.ttu.edu/) at Texas Tech University, but the Zinn Education Project (http://zinnedproject.org/materials/teaching -vietnam-war/) also has a wealth of materials and references for teaching the Vietnam War. The Pentagon Papers (http://www.archives .gov/research/pentagon-papers/) are the federal government's self-study of the history of US involvement in Southeast Asia. The Gilder Lehrman Institute of American History (http://www.gilderlehrman.org /history-by-era/1945-present/civil-rights -movement) boasts a terrific civil rights website, and the Voices of Feminism Oral History Project (https://www.smith.edu/library/libs /ssc/vof/vof-intro.html) at Smith College is another useful source. A terrific site for civil rights (http://www.crmvet.org/) has been put together by movement veterans themselves. The Miller Center (http://millercenter .org/president/speeches) at the University of Virginia has made available many presidential speeches, many of which address key issues of the 1960s.

FURTHER READING

Brick, Howard. *Age of Contradiction: American Thought and Culture in the 1960s.* New York: Twayne, 1998.

Cobble, Dorothy Sue. *The Other Women's Movement: Workplace Justice and Social Rights in Modern America.* Princeton, NJ: Princeton University Press, 2005.

Countryman, Matthew. *Up South: Civil Rights and Black Power in Philadelphia.* Philadelphia: University of Pennsylvania Press, 2007.

Foley, Michael Stewart. *Confronting the War Machine: Draft Resistance during the Vietnam War.* Chapel Hill: University of North Carolina Press, 2003.

Joseph, Peniel. *Waiting 'til the Midnight Hour: A Narrative History of Black Power in America.* New York: Henry Holt, 2006.

Lewis, Penny. *Hardhats, Hippies, and Hawks: The Vietnam Antiwar Movement as Myth and Memory.* Ithaca, NY: ILR Press, 2013.

Miller, James. *Democracy Is in the Streets: From Port Huron to the Siege of Chicago.* New York: Simon & Schuster, 1987.

Payne, Charles M. *I've Got the Light of Freedom: The Organizing Tradition and the Mississippi Freedom Struggle.* Berkeley: University of California Press, 1995.

Ransby, Barbara. *Ella Baker and the Black Freedom Movement: A Radical Democratic Vision.* Chapel Hill: University of North Carolina Press, 2005.

Rosen, Ruth. *The World Split Open: How the Modern Women's Movement Changed America.* New York: Viking, 2000.

Self, Robert. *All in the Family: The Realignment of American Democracy since the 1960s.* New York: Hill and Wang, 2013.

Stein, Marc. *Rethinking the Gay and Lesbian Movement.* New York: Routledge, 2012.

Young, Marilyn. *Vietnam Wars, 1945–1990.* New York: Harper Collins, 1991.

NOTES

1. Source: Matthew Dallek, *The Right Moment: Ronald Reagan's First Victory and the Decisive Turning Point in American Politics* (Oxford, 2000), 102.

2. Jonathan Birnbaum and Clarence Taylor, eds. *Civil Rights Since 1787: A Reader on the Black Struggle* (NYU, 2000), 474.

3. Source: Kwame Ture and Charles Hamilton, *Black Power: The Politics of Liberation* (orig. 1967, Vintage edition, 1992), 41.

4. Source: Bayard Rustin, *Down the Line: The Collected Writings of Bayard Rustin* (Quadrangle, 1971), 111.

5. Source: *Report of the United States National Advisory Commission On Civil Disorders* (U.S Govt. Printing Office, 1968), 2.

6. Source: Paul Goodman, *Growing up Absurd: Problems of Youth in the Organized Society* (orig. 1960, New York Review Books Classics, 2012), 5.

7. Source: Robert O. Self, *All in the Family: The Realignment of American Democracy Since the 1960s* (Hill and Wang, 2012), 191.

8. Charles M. Payne, *I've Got the Light of Freedom: The Organizing Tradition and the Mississippi Freedom Struggle* (Berkeley: University of California Press, 1995).

9. Aldon D. Morris, *The Origins of the Civil Rights Movement: Black Communities Organizing for Change* (New York: The Free Press, 1984); and Manning Marable, *Race, Reform, and Rebellion: The Second Reconstruction in Black America, 1945–1990* (Jackson: University of Mississippi Press, 1991).

10. Barbara Ransby, *Ella Baker and the Black Freedom Movement: A Radical Democratic Vision* (Chapel Hill: University of North Carolina Press, 2003); and Francoise Hamlin, *Crossroads*

at Clarksdale: The Black Freedom Struggle in the Mississippi Delta after World War II (Chapel Hill: University of North Carolina Press, 2012).

11. Thomas J. Sugrue, Sweet Land of Liberty: The Forgotten Struggle for Civil Rights in the North (New York: Random House, 2008).

12. Martha Biondi, To Stand and Fight: The Struggle for Civil Rights in New York City (Cambridge, MA: Harvard University Press, 2003); Robert O. Self, American Babylon: Race and the Struggle for Postwar Oakland (Princeton, NJ: Princeton University Press, 2003); and Matthew J. Countryman, Up South: Civil Rights and Black Power in Philadelphia (Philadelphia: University of Pennsylvania Press, 2006).

13. Matthew Lassiter, The Silent Majority: Suburban Politics in the Sunbelt South (Princeton, NJ: Princeton University Press, 2006).

14. Lisa McGirr, Suburban Warriors: The Origins of the New American Right (Princeton, NJ: Princeton University Press, 2001); and Darren Dochuk, From Bible Belt to Sunbelt: Plain-Folk Religion, Grassroots Politics, and the Rise of Evangelical Conservatism (New York: W. W. Norton, 2011).

15. Rick Perlstein, Nixonland: The Rise of a President and the Fracturing of a Nation (New York: Scribner, 2008).

16. Ian F. Haney López, Racism on Trial: The Chicano Fight for Justice (Cambridge, MA: Harvard University Press, 2003); Mark Brilliant, The Color of America Has Changed: How Racial Diversity Shaped Civil Rights Reform in California, 1941-1978 (New York: Oxford University Press, 2010); Carlos Muñoz, Youth, Identity, Power: The Chicano Movement (London: Verso, 2007); and Troy R. Johnson, The American Indian Occupation of Alcatraz Island: Red Power and Self-Determination (Lincoln: University of Nebraska Press, 1996).

17. Serena Mayeri, Reasoning from Race: Feminism, Law, and the Civil Rights Revolution (Cambridge, MA: Harvard University Press, 2011); and Lisa L. Goluboff, The Lost Promise of Civil Rights (Cambridge, MA: Harvard University Press, 2007).

18. Anne Enke, Finding the Movement: Sexuality, Contested Space, and Feminist Activism (Durham, NC: Duke University Press, 2007); Anne M. Valk, Radical Sisters: Second-Wave Feminism and Black Liberation in Washington, D.C. (Urbana: University of Illinois Press, 2008); and Kimberly Springer, Living for the Revolution: Black Feminist Organizing (Durham, NC: Duke University Press, 2005).

19. John D'Emilio, Sexual Politics, Sexual Communities: The Making of a Homosexual Minority in the United States, 1940-1970 (Chicago: University of Chicago Press, 1983); Nan Alamilla Boyd, Wide Open Town: A History of Queer San Francisco to 1965 (Berkeley: University of California Press, 2003); and Timothy Stewart-Winter, Queer Clout: Chicago and the Rise of Gay Politics (Philadelphia: University of Pennsylvania Press, 2016).

20. Marilyn B. Young, The Vietnam Wars, 1945-1990 (New York: Harper Collins, 1991); and Fredrik Logevall, Embers of War: The Fall of an Empire and the Making of America's Vietnam (New York: Random House, 2012).

21. Tom Wells, The War Within: America's Battle over Vietnam (Berkeley: University of California Press, 1994); Michael S. Foley, ed., Dear Dr. Spock: Letters about the Vietnam War to America's Favorite Baby Doctor (New York: New York University Press, 2005); and Lloyd Gardner, Pay Any Price: Lyndon Jonson and the Wars in Vietnam (Chicago: I. R. Dee, 1995).

22. Herstory (Wooster, OH: Micro Photo Division, Bell & Howell, 1972).

Robert O. Self

SUBURBANIZATION IN AMERICA AFTER 1945

1945–1970: ERA OF MASS-SUBURBANIZATION

Postwar Real Estate Development. Postwar suburbia was built upon a prewar metropolitan landscape characterized by "segregated diversity," a heterogeneous mix of landscapes, functions, and populations that emerged in the late 19th century. Prewar commuter suburbs with lush landscaping and large houses abutted farms and orchards, modest streetcar suburbs, and Main Street shopping districts. Elsewhere, smokestacks broke the rural skyline alongside worker housing. As geographers Richard Harris and Robert Lewis conclude, "Prewar suburbs were as socially diverse as the cities that they surrounded."[1] Ironically, this heterogeneous landscape, and especially the open spaces lying between and beyond it, was the setting for a massive wave of postwar suburbanization that was characterized by similarity and standardization.[2]

This history originated in the chaotic transition to peacetime society after 1945. World War II migrations, military deployment, and demobilization compounded a housing shortage that dated back to the Depression. In 1945, experts estimated a shortage of 5 million homes nationwide. Veterans returned to "no vacancy" signs and high rents. As late as 1947, one-third were still living doubled up with relatives, friends, and strangers. American family life was on hold.[3]

The solution to this crisis emerged from a partnership between government and private enterprise that exemplified the mixed Keynesian political economy of the postwar era. The federal government provided a critical stimulus to suburbanization through policies that revolutionized home building and lending, subsidized home ownership, and built critical suburban infrastructure, such as the new interstate highway system.[4] Private enterprise, for its part, applied new mass production techniques and technologies tested during the war to ramp up home building. Key to this partnership was a New Deal–era agency, the Federal Housing Administration (FHA). At the heart of FHA policy was a mortgage insurance program that took the risk out of home lending and made the long-term (25–30 years), low-interest home mortgage the national standard. The FHA also granted low-interest construction loans to builders and established basic construction guidelines that set new nationwide building standards. Along with a companion program in the Veterans' Administration (VA) created by the 1944 GI Bill, the FHA stimulated a flood of new construction that brought the price of

home ownership within the reach of millions of families. "Quite simply," concludes historian Kenneth Jackson, "it often became cheaper to buy than to rent."[5] Jackson also notes that these programs had a pro-suburban bias. FHA and VA requirements for standard setbacks, building materials, lot sizes, and other features ruled out loans to large sections of urban America while giving preference to new homes on the suburban fringe. By the 1950s, as many as one-third of home buyers in the United States received support from the FHA and VA programs, and home ownership rates rose from four in ten US households in 1940 to more than six in ten by the 1960s. The vast majority of these new homes were in the suburbs.[6]

Equally important to the postwar boom was a revolution in construction. In response to pent-up demand and new federal supports, a cohort of builder-developers modernized home building to achieve mass production. The new builders were young, bold, and creative; many were the children of immigrants. Using techniques pioneered by prewar builders, such as Fritz Burns of Los Angeles, and refined through work on large war construction projects, contractors streamlined home building, employing standardized parts and floor-plans, subassembly of doors and windows, and subdivision of labor to minimize the need for skilled or unionized workers.[7] The scale of building took off. Whereas "large builders" in prewar America might have built 25 homes per year, by the late 1940s, large firms were building several hundred homes per year. Annual housing starts leaped upward from 142,000 in 1944 to an average of 1.5 million per year in the 1950s.[8]

Emblematic of the new builders was William J. Levitt, who joined his immigrant father in the construction business in the 1930s. After experimenting with mass production during WWII, in the late 1940s the Levitts built what would become the most famous housing development of the age, the 17,000-home Levittown on Long Island, New

York. By the mid-1950s, Levitt was the nation's largest builder, with an annual production of more than 2,000 houses.[9] While large-scale builders such as Levitt attracted the lion's share of media attention, more typical were smaller-volume and custom builders who constructed fewer than 250 homes per year, but they too turned out homes uniform in appearance and amenities, reflecting the broad standardization of the industry and the landscapes it was producing.[10]

The typical postwar home of the late 1940s was the "minimum house," a reference to the FHA's minimum building standards. They were small, often cramped for families in the midst of a baby boom, but they were considered entirely modern with their up-to-date appliances, mechanical systems and utilities (with costs for everything neatly rolled into a 25-year mortgage). The average home in 1950 was 983 square feet (down from 1,140 in 1940). It had 5 to 6 rooms—typically two bedrooms, one bathroom, a living room and kitchen on a single floor.[11] The size and simple construction of these homes encouraged owners to remodel as their families changed. At Levittown, Long Island, the "Cape Cod" house model included a half-story "expansion attic" upstairs. By the mid-1950s and 1960s, as consumers demanded more space, builders increased home sizes, introducing open floor plans and new designs such as split-levels and expansive, horizontal ranch homes for buyers at different price points. By the mid-1950s, mass suburbs that had started out with a mix of incomes were sorting out into neighborhoods and communities that were increasingly homogenous in terms of class.[12]

The media hailed developers like Levitt as "community builders" because they not only subdivided land and built houses but created whole communities from scratch. Despite these accolades, historian Dolores Hayden points out that the drive for profit pushed community planning to the back burner in much of postwar suburbia. Developers often

set aside space for civic facilities, but local taxpayers were responsible for the cost of parks, playgrounds, libraries, and other public amenities. Levittown, Long Island, for example, was built without public sewers or even adequate septic tanks, forcing homeowner/taxpayers to make expensive upgrades after the Levitts moved on. Smaller builders were often even more frugal. Thus, for many new suburbanites, the companion to low housing prices was a high tax bill. The ongoing struggle of many suburbanites to build a sense of community in the unfinished civic landscape of mass suburbia was a legacy of this era.

New residential suburbs represented just one element of the postwar suburban trend. By the early 1950s, commercial developers, corporate headquarters, big retailers and other businesses, were also migrating to the suburban fringe, setting the stage for a wholesale reorganization of metropolitan economies by the end of the century. Aided by federal tax policies such as accelerated depreciation that subsidized new buildings over the maintenance of existing ones, retailers like Macy's and Allied Stores opened new suburban branches to capture consumer dollars that traditionally flowed to their downtown stores. Architect-developers like Victor Gruen—who designed many early suburban shopping centers, including the nation's first indoor shopping mall, the Southdale Center in suburban Minneapolis, 1956—evangelized the new shopping center as a modern civic center, a privately-built "public" space that would replace the traditional downtown.[13] Corporate headquarters and other offices also began a slow shift to suburban locations. Attracted by the prestige value of elite suburbia, *Fortune* 500 companies such as General Foods, Reader's Digest, and Connecticut General Life Insurance built landscaped campus "estates" in suburbs such as Westchester County, New York, and Bloomfield, Connecticut, during the 1950s, signaling a trend that peaked in the 1980s.[14] In the Washington, DC, area, government agencies also shifted to suburbia, led by the Central Intelligence Agency, which broke ground on its new campus headquarters in Langley, Virginia, in 1957.[15]

The City-Suburb Divide: Urban–Suburban Inequality in the Postwar Era.

At the metropolitan scale, the suburban shift in population and investment shaped divergent futures for US cities and suburbs—a drain of people and resources from cities to their suburbs that the columnist William Laas labeled simply, "suburbitis."[16] Older industrial centers, especially, faced serious challenges. The relocation of factories to suburbs and other lower cost locations sapped resources that had sustained city neighborhoods since the 19th century. Urban job losses stoked unemployment and poverty. Declining tax revenues forced cut-backs on infrastructure, schools and other services, which reinforced the cycle of suburbanization. By the 1960s, commentators pointed to a full-fledged "urban crisis." Meanwhile, the suburbs boomed.[17]

The metropolitan political structure of the United States played a hand in this divergence. As independent political entities, urban and suburban municipalities competed for business, people, and tax dollars. Cities and suburbs both used municipal powers such as land use and tax policy to maximize economic advantages within the town limits, but in the postwar period, suburbs held a clear advantage. In California's East Bay region, for instance, the historian Robert Self shows that suburban civic leaders shaped zoning policies, infrastructure spending, and tax rates to capture flows of people and capital. They attracted new factories and other investment and bolstered services for local residents, while excluding unwanted groups such as blue-collar workers, African Americans, and other people of color. By contrast, the city of Oakland faced waves of capital flight, job losses, and growing tax and service burdens for a population that included rising numbers of African Americans and Latinos, who were prevented from moving by racial barriers in the suburban housing market.[18] The fortunes of cities and suburbs remained linked throughout the postwar decades, but the balance of prestige and power within metropolitan regions had clearly shifted.

Race, Ethnicity, and Exclusion.

Mass suburbanization had equally dramatic consequences for race in postwar America. Suburbia beckoned with opportunity for millions of whites, but it remained rigidly segregated and broadly exclusive throughout the postwar decades. Mass suburbs supported ethnic and racial assimilation, where Italians, Poles, Greeks, Jews, and other European-Americans found a common social ground that solidified their identity as "whites."[19] The beneficiaries of racially structured federal policies, millions of "not yet white ethnics" (as historian, Thomas Sugrue described them) attained symbols of white, middle-class status, such as college educations, pensions, small businesses, and homes of their own.[20] Mass suburbia tied these benefits together in a coherent spatial package, providing a setting for common experiences, aspirations, and interests. And because these communities were prefaced on the principle of racial exclusion, the new suburbs reinforced solidarities of race while downplaying the significance of ethnic, religious, and occupational differences. Further reinforcing this merger of race and suburbia were the ever-present images in the national media of happy, white families celebrating the postwar suburban dream.

At the same time, African American, Asian American, and Latino families battled for access to the suburbs, challenging not only the presumed whiteness of suburbia but the ideology of white supremacy implicit in postwar suburban ideology. In response, white suburbanites in concert with other crucial players—including government—created a web of discrimination that secured links between race, social advantage, and metropolitan space.

Mechanisms of segregation included collusion by real estate brokers, homebuilders and lenders, discriminatory federal housing guidelines, local neighborhood associations, municipal land use controls, and the threat of violence. FHA underwriting guidelines, for example, explicitly required racial segregation until the early 1950s. In most cases, that spelled exclusion from a program that did so much to lift millions of whites into the middle class. By 1960, African Americans and other people of color had received just 2 percent of FHA-insured mortgages.[21] Added to the barriers of institutional racism, recent historical studies suggest that acts of violence and intimidation against nonwhite neighbors—including arson, bombings, death threats, and mob assaults—numbered in the hundreds during the decades after World War II. In the Chicago suburb of Cicero, for instance, rumors that a black family had rented a local apartment in 1951 provoked a mob to ransack the building. This bleak side of postwar urban history led historian Arnold Hirsch to refer to the 1940s and 1950s as "an era of hidden violence."[22] African Americans were targeted in most of these attacks, but discrimination also affected Asian Americans and Latinos, albeit in less predictable and capricious ways. In one well-publicized instance, a Chinese American couple, Grace and Sing Sheng, responded to the objections of white neighbors, who opposed their purchase of a house in suburban San Francisco in 1952, by suggesting a vote. Opponents prevailed 174–28 in the informal canvas, and the disillusioned Shengs decided to move elsewhere.[23]

Despite such obstacles, growing numbers of minority families found footholds in postwar suburbia. Between 1940 and 1960, the number of African American suburbanites increased by 1 million, amounting to 2.5 million by 1960—approximately 5 percent of the total suburban population. Regional variations typified this movement. In the South, where African Americans had lived on the metropolitan fringes for decades, developers built more than 200,000 new homes and apartments by 1960. In many cities, explicit planning for "Negro expansion areas" preserved access to places where blacks could move without upsetting segregation or provoking violence. Developments such as Collier Heights in west Atlanta, Washington Shores near Orlando, and Hamilton Park in north Dallas created suburban-style footholds for a growing black middle class.[24] Outside the South the proliferation of new suburban municipalities, each with control over local land use, limited construction for minority families. As a result, African Americans and other nonwhites struggled to find housing in existing city and suburban neighborhoods. Older black communities in suburbs such as Evanston, Illinois, Pasadena, California, and Mount Vernon, New York, welcomed new residents. In every region, most of these new suburbanites settled near existing minority communities, with the result that racial segregation expanded in metropolitan America even as court decisions and mass mobilization for civil rights upset the legal structures of Jim Crow. Movement into white neighborhoods was fiercely contested. And communities of color—in suburbs and cities alike—faced ongoing pressures such as school segregation, poor services, redlining, lax zoning enforcement, and reckless "slum clearance" that forced residents to organize politically as racial communities, sharpening the connection between race and place of residence. For whites and nonwhites alike, race emerged as part of the physical structure of the metropolis, reinforced by the separate and unequal spaces that they occupied.[25]

Social Life of Postwar Suburbanites.

The social history of postwar suburbia remains a fairly understudied area by historians. It is defined as much by sociologists and journalists observing suburbanites at the time, as by historians who have produced case studies of individual suburbs. Such studies offer useful starting points, especially the detailed accounts of social life that focused on the iconic mass-produced suburbs of the Levittowns and Park Forest, Illinois. Although they were hardly typical postwar subdivisions, they attracted a lion's share of scrutiny.[26]

Demographics established an important basic context. Right after World War II, new suburbs attracted a remarkably homogenous population, composed of relatively young, white married couples with kids. Heterosexual families with distinct roles for men and women were the accepted norm. In 1953, just 9 percent of suburban women worked outside the home, compared to 27 percent nationally.[27] In the era's best known development, Levittown, New York, residents were all white, ranged from 25 to 35 years old, were married less than seven years, and had an average of three children. The husband was employed and the wife was a homemaker.[28] There was notable religious and ethnic diversity, however, with a mix of Protestants, Catholics, and Jews, while approximately 15 percent were foreign born.[29] Suburbs like Levittown attracted both white- and blue-collar workers, who together, through their capacity to buy homes and the consumer goods of suburban life, defined the expanding American middle class.[30] Approximately 41 percent of men and 38 percent of women had some college education; many of the men were veterans.[31] Over time, however, suburbanites of different incomes sorted into different communities, creating greater socioeconomic homogeneity within suburbs, but growing class stratification and inequality across suburbia as a whole. As historian Lizabeth Cohen points out, the rising trend toward "hierarchy and exclusion" meant that residents by the 1960s "participated in more homogeneous, stratified communities [and] the contact they did have with neighbors connected them to less diverse publics."[32]

The mass-produced suburb became the subject of intense public scrutiny, representing a proliferating built form that appeared to present a new, untested social canvas. Observers wondered, was this setting producing new patterns of life and behavior? Under this microscope, certain salient themes emerged about suburban social life. For one, postwar suburbanites were active participants in their neighborhoods. A number of accounts documented this pattern, but perhaps the most influential portrait was by *Fortune* editor William H. Whyte in his 1956 bestseller *The Organization Man*. The final third of that book provided a detailed portrait of Park Forest, Illinois, which he dubbed the "dormitory" of the organization man, and characterized as a "hotbed of Participation" with a capital "P."[33] Whyte was one among many journalists from mass circulation magazines like *Harpers*, *Fortune*, and *Look* who delved into social experience on the new suburban frontier.

Whyte found neighbors who were closely connected, and immersed in a culture of borrowing and lending, participation in local clubs and civic groups, and social intimacy. Neighbors were not merely acquainted. They bonded on multiple levels—in the minutiae of the everyday demands of child raising and running homes, in mutual concerns about local civic issues, and even in intellectual and spiritual life.[34] Suburbia seemed to encourage a habit of joining. Similarly, studies of the Levittowns reveal that early residents relied upon one another, especially the many isolated, carless housewives. Neighbors gave each other rides, formed babysitter co-ops, gathered regularly for television viewing parties, and created a nurturing social environment.[35] Even yard work became a socializing experience, as neighbors shared tips with one another.[36] Without fences to separate neighbors, children freely circulated from one backyard to the next, and acted as a kind of social "glue" for their parents.[37] As a child in Levittown, New York, Martha Mordin later recalled, "Living here was like being in an extended family. There were lots of mothers. If you couldn't talk to your own mother, you could talk to someone else's mother."[38] One Levittowner concluded simply, "Had we stayed in the city, I never would have joined anything."[39] Even sociologist Herbert Gans, whose participant-observer study of Levittown, Pennsylvania, was meant to challenge an emerging suburban critique of hyperactive socializing and conformity, conceded that suburbanites engaged in high levels of community engagement.[40]

The centrality of women was another feature of postwar suburban social history. In these dormitory suburbs, husbands typically commuted to work during the day leaving their wives at home to dominate daily life in the community. The postwar return to domesticity was driven by powerful media imagery and platitudes by national leaders that valorized the housewife, infusing her role as household consumer and manager with patriotic overtones in the context of the Cold War.[41] Popular magazines schooled suburban women in the ways of scientific housekeeping, pushing products and the latest techniques for cleaning, entertaining, and child rearing. Yet despite this image of quiescent domesticity, women were active community participants in suburbia—as the "telephoners, organizers, and arrangers of community life."[42] They built social networks, joined clubs, and engaged in politics. Although suburban men tended to dominate positions of local leadership, women did much of the everyday work to keep social and civic life vibrant.[43]

"Culture Wars" over the Postwar Suburbs. The spread of mass suburbs touched off a virtual "culture war" in America between suburbia's boosters and its critics. This debate pulled in a range of participants, from advertisers, real estate developers, and politicians to journalists, academics, and filmmakers. In the course of debating the relative merits of mass suburbia, each side put forth vivid—if often distorted—images of suburban life, swinging wildly between the extremes of utopia and dystopia. The suburban portrayals and images they generated had deep and lasting impact on the ways that many

Americans came to view the suburbs, even up to our own day.

On one side were the boosters—business interests and politicians with a stake in selling suburban homes and the consumer goods to fill them. To them, the suburbs represented the fulfillment of the postwar "American dream"—a warm, happy place filled with healthy families and friendly neighbors, living cozy lives in homes brimming with the latest products and appliances. Magazines, television commercials, and real-estate developers peddled this image tirelessly, depicting contented white families thriving in suburbia. A logical collusion infused their efforts. Real-estate interests plugged the homes themselves, while shelter magazines ran articles on suburban living alongside vivid advertisements for refrigerators, range-tops, television sets, cleaning products, and other household goods. These ads invariably depicted happy homemakers set against a backdrop of gleaming, modern suburban interiors. The picture came full circle on television sitcoms like *Leave It to Beaver* and *Father Knows Best*, which offered benign, family-centered stories of generational quarrels and reconciliation, all sponsored by advertisers eager to tap into the lucrative suburban market. The result was a reinforcing web of suburban salesmanship.[44] Political leaders, too, celebrated suburban living, linking suburban consumption to the health of the republic itself. And they elevated the suburban home to a gleaming symbol of American superiority during the Cold War. In the so-called "Kitchen Debates" of 1959, which took place at an exposition of US products in Moscow, Vice President Richard Nixon sparred with Soviet Premier Nikita Khrushchev over the merits of capitalism versus communism, while standing in a six-room $14,000 ranch house assembled by a Long Island sub-divider and furnished by Macy's Nixon used this slice of everyday suburban life as the ultimate Cold War propaganda weapon.[45]

On the other side were the critics, who believed suburbia was inflicting profound damage on the American character. Academics, novelists, filmmakers, and designer-planners, among others, blamed mass suburbia for some of the most disturbing social trends of the era. Homogeneous suburban landscapes, they believed, spawned homogenous people, who followed the dictates of blind conformity. Bland, monotonous, isolating landscapes oppressed women and pushed bored kids toward juvenile delinquency. Female-centric suburban life distorted gender relations and left men emaciated. And the list went on. Not only did suburbia trivialize life, as Lewis Mumford wrote, but it fostered "the temptation to retreat from unpleasant realities, to shirk public duties, and to find the whole meaning of life in the most elemental social group, the family, or even in the still more isolated and self-centered individual. What was properly a beginning was treated as an end."[46] The final result was a devastating turn away from civic obligation. Even suburban family life was lambasted, portrayed as the polar opposite of the carefree innocence depicted on popular television sitcoms. Novelists and filmmakers in particular depicted all manner of suburban domestic dysfunction: alcoholism, adultery, inept parenting, wounding anxieties, deeply troubled marriages, and fraught sexuality, all concealed beneath a smiling public face. These themes animated such classic postwar films as *Mildred Pierce* (1945), *Rebel Without a Cause* (1955), *Man in the Gray Flannel Suit* (1956), and *The Graduate* (1967), and the fiction of Richard Yates, John Cheever, and John Updike.[47]

Several social scientists in the 1960s set out to challenge what they called "the myth of suburbia" created by this polemical discourse. Sociologists like Bennett Berger, Herbert Gans, and William Dobriner found that moving to suburbia did not actually change people, as both the critics and boosters suggested. Instead, suburbanites continued to make life choices based upon such factors as class, ethnicity, religion, and personal preference.[48] Their scholarship challenged the notion that environments shape human behavior (or environmental determinism).[49] Yet for the most part, their voices were drowned out by the shriller, more lurid suburban depictions filling the bookstores, airwaves, and movie houses.

Political Life. Scholars have examined the political culture of postwar suburbia since the mass suburban boom began, tracing critical trends that have shaped US politics at large, including ideals of localism, meritocratic individualism, home owner entitlement, and aversion to general taxation. In the 1950s, political scientist Robert Wood explored the fragmented municipal landscape of suburbia and the localism that characterized its political culture much as it had since the 19th century. This ideal of localism manifested in campaigns around municipal incorporation and zoning controls, annexation, taxation, school policy, and local services from potholes to public swimming pools. Other political identities blossomed at the local level. Many suburbanites derived their core political identity—as white middle-class, taxpaying homeowners—within the context of their suburban neighborhoods, often politically independent municipalities. Suburbanites made a direct connection between their role as taxpayers and their right to a particular quality of life, delivered through services like good schools and safe streets. They developed a sense of entitlement to these advantages, which they perceived as the just rewards of their individual efforts to achieve home ownership. Historians, in turn, have exposed the limitations in this thinking by underscoring the broad web of governmental policies that subsidized and privileged white suburban homeowners.[50] Nevertheless, the notion of homeowner entitlement based on meritocratic individualism remained as a core element of postwar suburban political culture, one that transcended party lines and mobilized suburbanites against an array of perceived threats, ranging from communists to free-spending liberals, the urban poor, excluded minorities, and inefficient government.[51] Their local efforts in the postwar years came to influence national politics and the political parties. The rich scholarship on suburban politics produced by historians in recent years challenges an earlier image of suburban civic banality painted by some postwar critics, and highlights the national importance of suburban politics.

Recent scholarship has documented the crucial role suburbia played in the rise of postwar conservatism, while newer studies linked suburbs to centrist and liberal politics. Two important works on suburban conservatism centered on California. Historian Lisa McGirr's study of Orange County demonstrated how this prosperous region—characterized by high-tech defense industry, an all-white well-educated populace, and Christian evangelicalism—was a potent breeding ground for modern-day conservatism. In the late 1950s and 1960s, these "suburban warriors" coalesced into a remarkable grassroots movement that attacked communism locally and globally, opposed big government, and supported the protection of property rights and Christian morality. Michelle Nickerson's study of Los Angeles documented a similar movement of suburban women who rallied against communism and racial integration, particularly in public education. The infrastructure they created—study groups, newsletters, bookstores, and clubs—represented a crucial formative aspect of a maturing Republican Party. Both studies argued that localized suburban politics in this era deeply shaped conservatism at the national scale.[52] Another cluster of studies highlighted racial politics in postwar suburbia, and the dogged efforts of suburbanites to resist federal civil rights mandates to integrate neighborhoods and public schools. Evoking the language of "white rights," colorblind meritocratic individualism, and homeowner entitlement, suburbanites across the nation—and across the partisan spectrum—resisted school desegregation, court-ordered busing, open housing laws, and public housing, in battles that began locally but ultimately influenced federal policy and the national parties. As Matthew Lassiter and others have shown, this bipartisan suburban movement elevated the issues of metropolitan politics onto the national stage by asserting the interests of suburban taxpayers, etching deeply entrenched patterns of inequality across metropolitan areas. The Republican Party was first to connect with this voting bloc at the national level, using it to win electoral majorities in seven of the ten Presidential elections from 1968 to 2004, but Democrats likewise supported suburban political mandates during the postwar years.[53]

Recent scholarship has also explored the presence of liberal and progressive politics in postwar suburbs, through grassroots movements for affordable housing, pacifism, and desegregation in housing and schools. Sylvie Murray's study of families in the suburban fringe of eastern Queens, New York, for instance, shows that women played critical roles in liberal political causes. Residents like a young Betty Friedan mobilized to enhance their quality of life, which included a vision of integrated schools and multicultural neighbors, and they sought the active hand of government to achieve these ends. Lily Geismer's study of Boston reveals the strength, and also the limits, of liberal activism in suburbia. White liberals in suburbs like Brookline and Newton actively supported a racially open housing market, but they rarely challenged the high economic hurdles that ensured that most people of color could not afford these neighborhoods.[54]

Local politics in the first two Levittowns exemplified these and other themes. In the 1950s, conflicts over the Levittown, New York, schools broke out between advocates of progressive versus traditional education, refracting larger differences between liberals and conservatives.[55]

More dramatic was the race riot that erupted in 1957 when the first black family moved into Levittown, Pennsylvania. Their arrival was facilitated by a small, dedicated group of local activists, mainly leftists and Quakers, who were committed to civil rights. When William and Daisy Myers stepped forward to become black pioneers in Levittown, their arrival sparked massive grassroots resistance. For several weeks, hundreds of white residents gathered in the evenings, hurling rocks and yelling epithets. They burned a cross and sprayed "KKK" on the property of Myers supporters. Yet other white residents stepped up to support the Myers family. As the conflict turned Levittown into a "civil rights battleground," the event illustrated the presence of both pro- and anti-integrationists in the suburb. Eventually, emotions simmered down. Yet as Tom Sugrue shows, the end result signaled the limits of racial liberalism in places like Levittown where blacks remained a minuscule percentage of the population for decades, as well as in other metro areas where sharp class and race inequality persisted.[56]

Suburbanites played key roles in other political movements as well. Levittowners engaged in environmental activism by the late 1960s, part of a broader push among suburbanites nationally.[57] As ironic as this may have appeared to those who saw Levittown as the epitome of denuded nature, many Levittowners in fact had a discernible connection to their natural environment, fostered both by the developers and their own labors in yards and gardens. When Levittown began feeling the effects of local factory pollutants and encroaching overdevelopment, residents united in action. This new politics coalesced around Earth Day in 1970, then fanned out into a range of grassroots activities. Residents gathered for garbage clean-up days, opposed a proposed nuclear power plant, held environmental teach-ins, circulated petitions, and picketed the nearby US Steel plant over industrial pollutants.[58] Suburban politics in the postwar years, thus, encompassed a range of political players who embraced such wide-ranging impulses as environmentalism, racial liberalism, and feminism.

1970–PRESENT: GROWTH AND DIVERSIFICATION

Land Development and Real Estate. Changing economic conditions in the United States after 1970 reshaped suburbia, as they did much of American life. The decline of manufacturing across the industrial heartland, the rise of service employment, high-tech growth, deregulation, and globalization altered the context for metropolitan life, resulting in regional shifts, growing economic volatility, polarization of wealth and income, and unstable futures for cities and suburbs alike.

New trends in the housing market set the tone for events that affected American suburbs through the following decades. New patterns of real estate investment in the 1960s and 1970s, for example, foreshadowed the coming merger of real-estate development and global financial markets that triggered recurrent housing volatility, including the global financial crisis of 2008. After 1960 new real estate investment trusts (REITs), investment banks, major pension and insurance funds, and *Fortune* 500 corporations poured capital into metropolitan real-estate development.[59] Financial deregulation at the state and federal levels opened up additional sources of investment for real-estate lending, and government sponsored financial entities, such as FNMA (colloquially known as "Fannie Mae") facilitated the flow of money to real estate through the sale of mortgage-backed securities to investors worldwide. By 2015, mortgage-backed securities were valued at almost $9 trillion, representing almost two-thirds of funds invested in the US mortgage market.[60]

Flush with new capital, real-estate firms dramatically increased the scale and scope of development after 1960. In places like California, development schemes reached gargantuan proportions that made even postwar developments like Levittown look small by comparison. Miles of pristine coastline and 10,000-acre cattle ranches succumbed to the bulldozer, giving birth to future suburban cities such as Irvine, Thousand Oaks, Temecula, and Mission Viejo, and laying the template for the pervasive sprawl that characterized modern suburban life (see Figure 1). The period saw the rise of the first truly national development firms, corporate real-estate enterprises such as Ryan and Pulte Homes, Kaufman and Broad, and Levitt, which had operations in multiple US—and even international—markets. By the early 21st century, firms such as these and their successors were building tens of thousands of units per year, replicating standardized architecture and community planning across the United States. By the peak of the housing bubble in 2005, the top five largest builders each closed on more than 30,000 houses for the year.[61] Their robust activity symbolized the

dramatic expansion of suburban areas and rise in the suburban population in the US with a majority of Americans living in suburbia by 2010 (see Table 1).

The scale and scope of real-estate investment and development ushered in new levels of volatility in US real-estate markets after 1970 that had been subdued in the long postwar boom. The early 1970s witnessed the first in a series of modern boom-and-bust cycles that rocked the housing market through the 21st century. Builders reached the all-time record in US housing starts of 2.36 million in 1972 and the largest three-year total in US history between 1971 and 1973. The bust, when it came, in 1974, sparked widespread bankruptcies and job losses, helping to drag the US economy into recession. With frightening regularity, housing market crises returned in the early 1980s, the early 1990s, and late 2000s, creating a nauseating series of economic roller-coaster rides for homeowners and renters alike. Across these same decades, the United States

Figure 1. Irvine, California, exemplified the massive scale of suburban developments after 1960, as well as their multiple functions—including suburban housing, offices, retail, and industry. Irvine housed more than 60,000 people by 1980, and 212,000 by 2010.
Photograph by Andrew Wiese, 2005.

Table 1. The Growth of Metropolitan and Suburban Areas in the United States, 1940–2010

		Population in Thousands			
Date	US Population	Metropolitan Area Population (includes city and suburbs)	% of US Population	Suburban Area Population	% of US Population
1940	131,669	60,293	45.8	17,666	13.4
1970	203,302[a]	139,500	68.6	75,500	37.1
2010	308,746	258,318	83.7	157,575	51.0

Metropolitan areas for 1970 and 2010 defined according to Census definitions for 1970 and 2010 (urbanized counties adjacent a central city(ies) of 50,000 or more). See US Bureau of the Census, Census of Population and Housing: 2000, vol. I, *Summary of Population and Housing Characteristics*, pt. 1 (Washington: Government Printing Office, 2002), Appendix A-1; Office of Management and Budget, 2010 Standards for Delineating Metropolitan and Micropolitan Statistical Areas; Notice, *Federal Register*, vol. 25.123 (June 28, 2010), 37249–37252.

Sources: US Census Bureau, *2010 Census, Summary File 1*, American FactFinder; US Bureau of the Census, Census of Population: 1970, vol. I, *Characteristics of the Population*, pt. 1, *U.S. Summary*, section 1 (Washington: Government Printing Office, 1973), 258.

witnessed a generalized rise in housing prices. Driven by growing suburban land-use restrictions, a shortage of buildable land in many metro areas, and increased supplies of mortgage capital, the long upward price spiral was a boon to property owners who hung on for the long term, but it produced a burden of rising property taxes and a growing crisis in affordability. Aspiring homeowners faced outsized home prices, pushing them to work more hours, drive greater distances, and take on greater loads of debt to purchase a suburban home. By 2013, nearly 40 million American households were paying more than 30 percent of their income for housing, and as many as 10 percent of homeowners were paying upwards of 50 percent.[62] In booming suburban markets, such as Orange County, California, Long Island and Westchester County, New York, and Fairfax County, Virginia, children were priced out of the suburban areas where they grew up. Public and private efforts to expand home ownership in the 1990s and 2000s met this reality with increasingly risky credit arrangements—interest-only and stated income loans, and ballooning adjustable-rate mortgages that were almost unheard of in postwar suburbia. These arrangements were at the

center of the housing meltdown and global economic crisis in 2008–2010. For households left out of the market—blue-collar families, singles, young couples, many people of color—the spiral in housing prices was an obstacle to building wealth and a continuing source of economic disparity in America's post-civil rights era.

Metropolitanism. After 1970, the economic ascendancy of suburbia that had been building since 1945 reached maturity. In a landmark, 1976 study, Geographer Peter Muller explored the rise of the "Outer City," his term for the hubs of retail activity, office parks, super-regional shopping malls, and gleaming business headquarters that clustered along the nation's metropolitan highway exchanges. Muller concluded that "suburbia," was now the "essence of the contemporary American city," no longer "sub" to the "urb."[63] By the early 1970s, suburban employment outnumbered city jobs for first time, and suburban "edge cities," such as the Washington, DC, Beltway; Schaumburg, Illinois; Boston's Route 128 corridor; Seattle's high-tech suburbs such as Redmond and Bellevue; and California's Silicon Valley played a central role in the nation's economy. By the 1990s, fewer than one in five metropolitan area jobs was located within three miles of the old central business district, whereas almost half were located ten or more miles from that center.[64] While many central cities rebounded in the 2000s with new high-tech and innovation clusters of their own, they now represented just one part of the complex and poly-nucleated metropolitan economies that Muller explored in the 1970s. Analysts increasingly recognized these metropolitan economies as the drivers of the nation's economy, competing independently in the global marketplace against other metro areas worldwide. By 2010, this metropolitan ascendance was evident: the 100 largest metro areas in the United States were responsible for three-quarters of the nation's gross domestic product (GDP).[65]

After 1970, these trends played out across a pervasive physical pattern of suburban sprawl. Between 1982 and 2012, metropolitan regions ballooned in area, with real-estate development consuming 43 million acres of rural land, an area larger than Washington State. By 2002, according to one estimate, the United States was losing two acres of farmland per minute to suburban development.[66] Low-density, auto-dependent development characterized fast-growing regions such as Atlanta and Los Angeles, where residents endured multi-hour commutes from new "drive 'til you qualify" subdivisions in the rural fringe. Even in comparatively slow-growing metro areas such as Pittsburgh and Detroit, rates of suburban sprawl outpaced population growth.[67] By the early 21st century, Americans were driving more miles, spending more time in the car, and using more energy than ever before. Per-capita automobile miles driven tripled between 1960 and 2003, resulting in gridlock, taxi-parenting, and hectic patterns of family life on the road that became common features of modern suburbia.[68] The fiscal costs of sprawl were equally significant. As US suburban areas spent billions on new infrastructure, existing urban systems deteriorated, resulting in

continued disparities between growing suburbs and declining urban and inner suburban places. Even on the fringe, however, low-density sprawl frequently failed to pay for itself. As Myron Orfield shows, fast growing "exurban" areas were among the most fiscally stressed metropolitan communities, with major imbalances in tax revenue versus needs for service.[69] To make ends meet, thousands of suburban governments employed "fiscal zoning," restricting apartments, raising lot sizes, and setting aside large areas for big box retailers to boost tax revenues. As many Americans looked forward to more sustainable ways of living, the sprawling landscapes of modern suburbia represented a major policy challenge.[70]

In contrast to the era of postwar "sitcom suburbs," recent decades witnessed the construction of more varied types of suburban housing. In response to rising home prices, land shortages, and the growing crisis in affordability, corporate real-estate firms built millions of new suburban condominiums, attached homes, and apartments after 1970. Many of these were built as part of common interest developments (CIDs), and planned neighborhoods governed by homeowners' associations, which were ruled according to strict covenants, conditions, and restrictions (CC&Rs). Home to fewer than 1 percent of the population in 1970, by 2015 as many as one in five Americans lived in a community governed by a private association, and homeowners' associations dominated the market for new construction. In 2014, for example, 72 percent of new single-family homes were built as part of a homeowners' association.[71] For builders, CIDs squeezed more units (and dollars) out of finite acreage. Suburban municipalities, for their part, welcomed CIDs—despite higher densities and more affordable housing types—because private amenities such as pools, parks, and playgrounds reduced public expenditures. Finally, in a context of rising home prices, townhome and condo developments were among the few affordable housing options for many families. For first-time homebuyers, retirees, empty nesters, and families without children, condominiums and townhomes provided flexibility lacking in postwar "sitcom suburbs." At the same time, the rise of CIDs signaled a shift away from the suburban dream of a single-family home in communion with nature. While average house sizes grew (2,450 square feet in 2014), lot sizes shrank.[72]

The proliferation of gated CIDs after 1990 raised additional debates about privacy, exclusivity, and social division across metro America. Research by anthropologist Setha Low suggested that rather than making residents safer, gated communities tended to intensify fears of crime and social distrust.[73] Such concerns were brought into deadly focus in 2012 by the shooting of Trayvon Martin, an unarmed black teenager killed by a neighborhood watch volunteer in the gated enclave where he lived near Orlando, Florida.

Social Diversification. One of the most striking features of American suburbs since 1970 has been rapid social diversification, marking a return to suburbia's historic diversity.[74] After 1970, a wide cross-section of Americans settled the suburbs, including singles, divorced adults, gays, lesbians, the elderly, the poor, and perhaps most significantly an array of ethnic and racial groups. The proportion of working women also rose substantially, shattering earlier images of suburban housewives trapped at home. As more Americans settled in the suburbs, suburbia looked increasingly like America itself.

A confluence of forces underlay these changes. Trends affecting suburban women and families included the aging of baby boomers, the rise in feminism, economic slumps, and soaring inflation of the 1970s that pushed many women into the labor force. The suburban influx of racial and ethnic groups was spurred by new waves of immigration from Asia and Latin America in the wake of the 1965 Hart-Celler Act, and the

passage of the federal Civil Rights Act of 1964 and Fair Housing Act of 1968, which improved minority job prospects and curbed housing discrimination. These factors created new demographic realities, while policy changes opened suburban areas—growing at a fast clip—to groups that were once fervently excluded.

One change was the suburban family, earlier typified by a working husband, homemaker wife, and the requisite two or three children. By 1970, scholars noted an increase in divorced, separated, and single adults living in the suburbs, as well as an uptick in working women. One study of the suburbs of Nassau County, New York, found that these trends accelerated from 1960 to 1980. By 1980, two of every five adults lived in a non-nuclear family arrangement (single, separated, divorced, or widowed). Families were having fewer children, and more than half of married women with children aged six to seven years worked outside the home. The author attributed the changes to an aging population, liberalized divorce laws, and the 1970s economic downturn which "propelled more married women into the labor market."[75] These trends continued over the next decades. By 2000, the suburbs contained more nonfamily households (29%)—mostly young singles and elderly people living alone—than married couples with children (27%). There were also substantial proportions of married couples with no kids under 18 (29%), and rising numbers of single parents, divorced, unmarried partners, and adult relatives living in suburban homes.[76] By 2010, 75 percent of suburban homes did *not* contain a married-couple family with kids, exploding the older image of the "Leave it to Beaver" domicile.[77] And while statistical data on the social geography of LGBTQ (lesbian, gay, bisexual, transgender, queer/questioning) are elusive, a range of evidence suggests that gays and lesbians also migrated to suburbia.[78] One catalyst was a shift in federal housing housing/borrowing eligibility guidelines by the US Department of Housing and Urban Development (HUD), which altered its definition of family away from heterosexual "marital or biological attachments" toward a more pluralist concept that would include "any stable family relationship," including LGBTQ households.[79] The powerful image of heterosexual "married with children" families in suburbia was giving way to the more complex family structures that mirrored national social change.

Ethnic and racial diversification was also significant. While African Americans, Latinos, and Asian Americans comprised just less than 10 percent of the suburban population in 1970, by 2010 they represented 28 percent. Minorities have propelled the bulk of recent suburban population gains in the 100 largest metropolitan areas, as demographer William Frey has noted.[80] Even more striking are data on specific population groups. For example, from 1970 to 2010 the number of black suburbanites climbed from 3.5 to nearly 15 million, comprising 39 percent of all African Americans. Even faster growth occurred among Latinos and Asians, who endured less severe housing discrimination than blacks. By 2010, 46 percent of Latinos and 48 percent of Asians nationally resided in the suburbs. And in the largest 100 metro areas, the proportions were even higher—62 percent of Asian Americans and 59 percent of Latinos. Immigrants comprised a significant portion of new suburbanites as well. By 2013, suburbia housed 50 percent of foreign-born residents in the United States, and numbers were even greater in the biggest metropolitan areas, where most immigrants lived.[81]

Even the iconic postwar suburbs reflected these changes, though in different ways. In Park Forest, the site where William Whyte documented social conformity in his 1956 best-seller *The Organization Man*, liberal activists initiated a program of "managed integration" in the 1960s and 1970s to recruit African American neighbors gradually. As a strategy designed to stave off white flight, the approach seemed to work at first: from 1970 to 1990, the proportion of blacks rose from just 2.3 percent to 24.4 percent of the local populace. From 2000 to 2010, however, a process of racial resegregation accelerated; large numbers of whites left the suburb and the proportion of African Americans rose from 39.4 to 59.8 percent.[82] Lakewood, a postwar mass-produced suburb in southern Los Angeles, drew national attention in the 1950s when it became the largest development in the country with 17,500 homes, surpassing even Levittown. Lakewood eventually became a site of robust multiethnic diversity: by 2010, the population was 40.9 percent white, 30.1 percent Latino, 16 percent Asian, and 8.3 percent black, making it one of Los Angeles's most racially balanced cities.[83] The irony was thick. The very suburbs once reviled for their monotonous landscapes—which supposedly churned out monotonous, conforming people—became the staging ground for racial and ethnic diversity. In some ways, this was no surprise because these communities, which were originally built to be affordable, maintained that quality once nonwhite buyers gained the economic wherewithal to become suburban homeowners and the barriers to racial segregation fell. In Levittown, New York, by contrast, whites maintained an overwhelming majority, composing more than 80 percent of the population as late as 2010.[84] All three places illustrate trends in suburbia since 1970—growing diversity alongside persistent racial segregation.

Another notable trend was the rise of class inequality across suburbia, with growth in both poor and rich suburbs. While poor people had long resided in the periphery, after 1970 a different set of pressures accelerated the trend. A crucial factor was economic restructuring, which created an "hourglass economy" characterized by high- and low-paying jobs, a shrinking middle class, and falling income levels for most Americans. The effects of these structural changes reverberated across suburban space. Many inner-ring suburbs contended with aging housing and infrastructure and high service needs from a growingly poor, immigrant populace. Deindustrialization in the 1970s and 1980s, in turn, devastated older industrial suburbs, which suffered a difficult combination of job loss, white flight, and environmental degradation in the wake of industry's departure.[85] Suburban poverty accelerated after 2000, as Elizabeth Kneebone and Alan Berube have shown, driven by two economic recessions and the continued effects of restructuring and globalization.[86]

In addition to these economic forces, public policy also played a role. Reversing years of policies that protected the rights of suburbs to exclude the poor, the federal government gradually promoted the dispersal of low-income families into suburban areas through policies such as the 1974 Section 8 voucher program, which granted a housing allowance to people with qualified incomes who could then choose their own housing on the open market—thus untethering them from public housing projects concentrated in poor urban areas. Fair-share housing initiatives and modest inclusionary zoning and affordable housing programs also helped open the suburbs to poorer people.[87] As a result, the number of poor people in the suburbs climbed. In the 1980s and 1990s, poor populations increased in *both* cities and suburbs; however, in the 1990s and 2000s, the rate of increase in suburbs was twice that of cities. During the 2000s, moreover, for the first time more poor people lived in suburbs than in cities—signaling that metropolitan America had "crossed an economic Rubicon." By 2010, 55 percent of the metropolitan poor lived in the suburbs, while one in three poor Americans overall lived in the suburbs, "making them home to the largest and fastest-growing poor population in the country."[88]

At the same time, affluent suburbs proliferated, especially around high-tech and financial hubs like the Silicon Valley, California, Boston's Route 128, and Fairfield County, Connecticut.

Wealthy executives, tech workers, and professionals clustered in these upscale areas, their outsized salaries driving real estate prices to stratospheric levels. Despite the much-heralded return to the city by millennials and the "creative class" (i.e., workers in "knowledge intensive industries" such as computer science, medicine, the arts, and education) as late as 2014, the super-rich concentrated in tony suburbs of the bicoastal economy in places like Greenwich, Connecticut, Coral Gables, Florida, and Newport Beach, California.[89] The middle class, meanwhile, faced mixed prospects in suburbia.[90]

In the 21st century, American suburbs have come to house a cross section of America itself, including the poor, the rich, and a broad array of racial and ethnic groups and family types. Inequality was reproduced across suburbia, while ethno-racial diversity set the stage for emerging forms of suburban lifeways and politics.

Social Life. Suburban variations led to disparate social experiences, yielding a mosaic of suburban social histories after 1970. While it is impossible to offer a synthesis of this history due to wide variations among suburbanites themselves as well as the nascent nature of the scholarship, certain salient themes have emerged on social life and suburban ideals in the post-1970 era.

One group of scholars has emphasized a trend of social disconnection, especially among whites. After the intensive sociability of the 1950s and 1960s, suburbanites after 1970 appeared to swing to the other extreme—social alienation and detachment. This was apparent in ethnographer M. P. Baumgartner's book *The Moral Order of a Suburb*. Conducting field work in a suburb of New York City in the late 1970s, Baumgartner was interested in exploring how people handled conflict in their town. What she found was a culture of tolerance and avoidance. The suburb lacked "social integration," and instead was defined by a sense of indifference between neighbors. Avoidance as a strategy was thus logical: "It is easy to end a relationship that hardly exists."[91] She attributed this lack of neighborhood connectedness to the privatism of families; the high mobility of homeowners, making it hard for them to form lasting bonds; and the compartmentalizing of social life (at work, at church and synagogue, and at school). Other scholars extended this theme in exploring fear and privatism in suburbia, characterized in the extreme by the rise of privatized, gated neighborhoods.[92] By 2000, observers from political scientist Robert Putman in his landmark book *Bowling Alone* to proponents of the New Urbanism agreed that suburbs fostered social and civic disconnection.[93] It was no coincidence that this change occurred at the moment many suburbs were diversifying. One study of Pasadena, California, over this time period found that racial integration in the 1970s had variable effects on community engagement among suburbanites, pushing some whites into their own insular social communities, reorienting the nature and purpose of local clubs and organization as they saw their numbers decline, and creating some pockets of multiracial social vibrancy.[94] This comports roughly with the findings of some political and social scientists, who observed decreased levels of "social capital" in communities experiencing ethno-racial diversification.[95]

At the same time some suburbanites were retreating, others created new cultures and lifeways in the suburbs. Scholarship on ethnic suburbia, in particular, documented this from several angles. Anthropologist Sarah Mahler investigated the lives of working-poor Salvadoran immigrants living in substandard housing in Long Island, New York. The enormous economic pressures they faced, from the challenge to survive on low wages while also supporting families in El Salvador, altered the social dynamic in the Salvadoran community, away from co-ethnic reciprocity toward more individualistic survival. "Burdened with debt

and remittance responsibilities," Mahler writes, immigrant suburbanites "frequently must wring this surplus out of their own deprivation, forgoing everything but an ascetic existence."[96] A more robust ethnic culture developed in the middle-class suburbs of the west San Gabriel Valley, California, where Asian and Latino residents fostered community life and values around ideals of racial inclusivity. Wendy Cheng describes this as a "moral geography of differentiated space ... a world view that challenged and opposed whiteness as property."[97] Remaining in these communities as white residents fled, Asian American and Mexican American residents valued the comfort and familiarity of interracial spaces. Groups like the Boy Scouts reflected this multiethnic sensibility, which in turn stimulated high levels of participation both by boys and their parents.[98]

Robust displays of ethnic culture and identity were strongest in what geographer Wei Li described as "ethnoburbs," defined as "suburban ethnic clusters of residential and business districts ... [that] are multiracial/multiethnic, multicultural, multilingual, and often multinational communities."[99] In ethnoburbs,

Figure 2. Suburban childhood, 1989. Mark Padoongpatt, age 6, the son of Thai immigrants, stands in front of his suburban home in Arleta, a neighborhood in Los Angeles's San Fernando Valley inhabited by Mexican Americans, Salvadorans, Filipinos, Vietnamese, Thais, African Americans, and Anglos.
Photograph by Victor Chalermki used by permission of Mark Padoongpatt.

ethnic culture is constantly refreshed by the transnational flow of immigrants, capital, and businesses. In contrast to older sociological models that considered the suburbs a site of Americanization, ethnoburbs reinforced and sustained ethnicity within suburbia.

Ethnoburbs appeared across the country, in places like the San Gabriel Valley and Silicon Valley, California, Langley Park, Maryland, Palisades Park, New Jersey, Upper Darby, Pennsylvania, and Chamblee, Georgia. In ethnic suburbs, some residents forged new suburban ideals around such values as robust public life, defying long-standing suburban traditions of privatism. For example, Thai residents of the east San Fernando Valley, California, held lively weekend food festivals at the Wat Thai Buddhist Temple, a quasi-public community space. Asian Indian residents of Woodbridge, New Jersey, celebrated days-long Navrati festivals under enormous tents, with music, dancing, and vendors selling traditional Indian food and dress. Along Whittier Boulevard—which traversed the suburbs of Montebello, Pico Rivera, and Whittier, outside of Los Angeles, Mexican American youth developed a cruising culture tied to the use of suburban public space.[100] These practices helped cultivate community, and as Mark Padoongpatt writes of the Wat Thai festivals, "fostered a public sociability that went against dominant and even legal definitions of suburbia."[101]

Politics across Diverse Suburbia. Suburban politics after 1970 came to reflect these differences as well, revealing political leanings as varied as suburbanites themselves. One powerful strand worked to sustain suburban privilege. The solid tradition of tax-averse homeowner politics remained strong, and in the post-civil rights era, white suburbanites, especially, increasingly deployed a discourse of colorblind meritocratic individualism to defend their rights, claiming that suburbs were open equally to all and race and class played no role in who lived where. In general, this politics worked to protect suburbanites'

fiscal resources, to defend their quality of life, and to maintain class and racial segregation. Suburban citizens framed these efforts in terms of their hard-earned rights as taxpaying homeowners, which they felt were under siege by free-spending liberals, minorities, the urban poor, inefficient government, and even drug pushers. This political agenda manifested in several ways. One was a full-fledged tax revolt movement. In 1978, California taxpayers resoundingly passed Proposition 13, a measure that placed severe limits on property tax rates. This campaign led the way for similar tax revolts in other states and helped propel former California governor Ronald Reagan, a fervent supporter of Prop 13, to the White House in 1980. Reagan embraced many of the core principles of this campaign—cutting taxes and government power—suggesting the national resonance of suburban political ideals.[102] Second, many suburbanites opposed initiatives seeking to close the gap between cities and suburbs in terms of wealth, opportunity, and race. Across the country, suburbanites mobilized against busing for school integration, open housing, affordable housing, and Section 8 tenants.[103] In a similar way, nonpartisan suburban NIMBY (Not In My Back Yard) campaigns proliferated against public and nonprofit projects such as group homes, AIDS clinics, daycare centers, garbage dumps, and nuclear power plants.[104] Their actions suggested that suburbanites sought to reap the benefits of metropolitan belonging while minimizing its burdens. A third manifestation was suburbia's role in the war on drugs. As recent work by Matt Lassiter shows, it created a policy approach that perceived a binary of "white suburban addict-victims and minority ghetto predator-criminals." This construct reinforced in American political culture a tendency to demonize urban minorities while rendering white suburbanites as innocent victims, an oversimplification that belied more complex realities.[105] The cumulative effect of these efforts, many of them successful, was to reinforce inequality across metropolitan space. Moreover, these efforts attracted the attention of politicians at the national level, who increasingly cultivated these voters' support through federal policies and judicial appointments that supported suburban prerogatives. During the Richard Nixon presidency, for instance, the federal government limited its support for fair housing, metropolitan school integration, and the dispersal of affordable housing.[106]

In the wake of civil rights laws that broke down explicit racial barriers in the housing market, suburban exclusion increasingly pivoted on class, fueling class segregation since 1980.[107] Local governments played a crucial role in this. Some suburbanites withdrew into privately owned and governed residential enclaves, known as Common Interest Developments (CIDs) or what Evan McKenzie labelled "privatopias" for their capacity to concentrate local resources under tight local control.[108] In CIDs, civic and social belonging was restricted to select groups defined by ownership as opposed to citizenship. Suburbanites also used local zoning and building regulations as colorblind tools to exclude low-income residents through tactics like "exclusionary"—or "snob"—zoning, environmental protection codes, land trusts, historic preservation, and no-growth activism, which effectively shut out affordable housing. "Snob" zoning, for example, required large lots and floor areas and limited construction to single-family homes while prohibiting apartments and other multifamily dwellings. While housing and civil rights activists recognized this trend as early as the 1960s, it intensified over the following decades. These local initiatives were pushed not only by whites, but also some affluent Asian Americans who recognized value in suburban exclusivity.[109] During the 1970s, the US Supreme Court in two cases upheld these broad municipal powers, defining "general welfare" in terms of the existing residents of a community, making it impossible for new, poorer residents to enter in and have a civic voice. As race disappeared from the rhetoric of suburban exclusion, it was replaced by a class-oriented discourse of property values, landscape aesthetics, tax rates,

congestion, and environmental protection, often captured by the catchall phrase "quality of life." One result was a crisis in affordable housing, with deep ramifications for African Americans, Latinos, and other minorities who generally earned less money than whites. By harnessing the power of local government, suburbanites maintained exclusionary practices using new tools and approaches.[110]

This suburban outlook continued to influence the political parties and their agendas at the national level. The Republicans remained aligned with this suburban worldview, and by the 1990s the Democrats too—traditionally a city-based party—recognized the importance of the "suburban vote" and altered its ideology and platforms to win over this critical bloc. For the Democrats, this adjustment was enormous, forcing the party to recalibrate its traditional commitment to the urban poor, minorities, and labor (and their demand for public programs), with a new commitment to middle-class suburban voters (and their aversion to taxes and social welfare spending, and their reluctance to imperil their own property values). Some saw this adjustment—known variously as the "third way" or the "New Democrats"—as the effective death of liberalism; others saw it as a realistic shift toward the political center. In either case, the influence of suburban political culture on the party's shifting values was enormous.[111] In her study of Boston's Route 128 suburbs, Lily Geismer described a hierarchical set of values among suburban liberals that justified their support of progressive causes like racially open housing while simultaneously opposing affordable housing. As progressive citizens who lived in suburbia, they viewed themselves as somehow apart, as "separate from, and not responsible for, many of the consequences of suburban growth and the forms of inequality and segregation that suburban development fortified."[112] This captured a central dilemma of suburban Democrats.

Parallel to this suburban politics of defensive self-interest, a contrasting strand of progressive, social justice politics grew in the suburbs, particularly those experiencing ethno-racial change. As social diversification increased, so did new political agendas and forms of political organization, revealing "progressive potential in places once dismissed as reactionary."[113] Progressive organizations included the Suburban Action Institute, established in 1969 to wage legal battles against exclusionary zoning, and Long Island's Workplace Project and the Southwest Suburban Immigrant Project of Chicago, which campaigned to secure better education, workplace rights, and immigration reform. One study deployed Henri Lefebvre's concept of "right to the city" to analyze progressive suburban activism. It focused on Maywood, California, southeast of Los Angeles, a suburb of working-class Latino immigrants (including the undocumented) who claimed rights by virtue of inhabitance in particular places. They mobilized around the issue of immigrant rights, challenging the local police practice of using DUI (driving under the influence of alcohol) checkpoints to identify and criminalize undocumented immigrants, who were charged high fees for towing, impounding, and fines, which amounted to "a municipal tax on immigrants."[114] A grassroots movement successfully challenged this policy, and went on to win seats on the city council which ultimately declared Maywood a "sanctuary city."[115] Maywood and neighboring Latino suburbs also waged environmental justice campaigns.[116] Other progressive initiatives were launched in places like Alviso and Richmond, California Silver Spring, Maryland Shaker Heights, Ohio, and suburbs around Cincinnati and Chicago.[117]

Reforming Suburbia. The cumulative effects of suburban expansion since 1970 ranged from the toll on the environment, to the fiscal drain on both cities and outer suburbs, to the stubborn persistence of class and race segregation, to the everyday burdens of long commutes and social isolation and stimulated a wave of reform. Initiatives were wide ranging, some winning more public favor than others. All of these efforts sought to mitigate the effects of suburban sprawl through more equitable, diverse, and sustainable forms of metropolitan development.

Some of these initiatives stemmed from the growing recognition that metropolitan areas had become the drivers of the national—and global—economy. As such, they held more importance than ever as the fulcrum of the nation's economic health. Scholars like Bruce Katz, Mark Muro, and Jennifer Bradley argue that the stakes are high when it comes to metropolitan well-being because they compete against other global metropolises in a race for capital and investment. Only those with "future growth plans that minimize traffic gridlock, pollution, ugly sprawl, and environmental devastation" can hope to succeed. Because the national economy hinges on vibrant, high-functioning metros, they contend, the federal government must reorient its economic development policies toward enhancing their power and resources (e.g., by funneling infrastructure money directly to metro areas instead of the states).[118]

Other regional reformers extend this logic, arguing that metro-wide equity is crucial to metropolitan health and competitiveness in the global marketplace. Recognizing the negative effects of suburban political balkanization, which gives individual suburban municipalities the powers to act in their own narrow self-interest and veto wider social obligations, these reformers sought ways to overcome this suburban intransigence. They crafted programs that operated on a regional scale and emphasized the mutual benefits to all metropolitan players, suburban and urban alike, with regional equity and prosperity as the intertwined end goals. Urban analysts such as David Rusk, Myron Orfield, Peter Dreier, Manuel Pastor, and Chris Benner argued that metropolitan regions work best when class disparities are lessened, poverty is reduced, and communities across the board share both the benefits (like jobs) and obligations (like affordable housing) of metropolitan citizenship. As one study noted, "[C]ities and suburbs have become interdependent parts of shared regional economies. A number of recent studies have indicated that problem-ridden cities and declining suburbs go hand in hand. In other words, suburban islands of prosperity cannot exist in a sea of poverty."[119] Poverty and inequality, they contend, drag down an entire metro region. For the good of all metropolitan players (e.g., rich, poor, businessmen, and workers) equity is a prerequisite if a metropolis stands any chance in the global economic race.[120]

One plan to level the metropolitan playing field was proposed by legislator and legal scholar Myron Orfield, based on initiatives he spearheaded in Minneapolis–St. Paul during his term in the Minnesota State Legislature (1991–2003). Orfield's approach was predicated on his detailed demographic analysis of American suburbs, which showed a wide range from prosperous to severely fiscally stressed. All suburbs, he argued, served to benefit from greater regional equity. To achieve this, he called for regional tax-base sharing that would lessen wasteful competition among suburbs and gradually equalize their resources, provide regionally coordinated planning of housing and infrastructure, and facilitate the formation of strong, accountable regional governing bodies. Orfield couched this as a "win–win" for cities and all suburbs based on their shared interests in metropolitan success.[121]

A related reform movement is known as "Smart Growth." This approach calls for the close coordination of metropolitan land-use planning to support efficient and environmentally friendly development. Seeking to stop the relentless push of outward sprawl, it supports higher-density, mixed-use developments closer to existing communities and job centers, metro growth boundaries, the preservation of open space for parks, farmland, and native habitat, and in-fill projects. The rationale is to move away from wasteful and environmentally draining sprawl toward denser, more environmentally sustainable development.[122] Oregon was a pioneer in the Smart Growth movement, passing the nation's first statewide land use act in 1973, which established growth boundaries for metro areas

such as Portland. Other regions followed with similar legislation, including Minneapolis–St. Paul in 1994, Maryland (which passed a Smart Growth Act in 1997) as well as Florida, Arizona, New Jersey, and Pennsylvania. In 1998 alone, 240 state and local ballot initiatives related to land use and growth, with voters approving more than 70 percent of these initiatives; by 2000, more than 550 growth-related initiatives appeared on ballots, 72 percent of which passed.[123]

An influential off-shoot of Smart Growth is New Urbanism, a movement of designers, architects, developers, and planners which coalesced in the late 1980s.[124] In 1993, they founded the Congress for New Urbanism to promote the principles of compact, mixed-used, walkable developments—tenets that completely inverted the design of post-WWII suburbs. As their charter states, "We advocate the restructuring of public policy and development practices to support the following principles: neighborhoods should be diverse in use and population; communities should be designed for the pedestrian and transit as well as the car; cities and towns should be shaped by physically defined and universally accessible public spaces and community institutions; urban places should be framed by architecture and landscape design that celebrate local history, climate, ecology, and building practice."[125]

Smart Growth and New Urbanism are not without their critics. Some decry their tendency to promote gentrification, drive housing prices upward, and insufficiently provide for low-income residents. Because Smart Growth often limits the amount of developable land, it tends to help established homeowners by driving up their property values, while locking everyone else out. Describing Smart Growth in Los Angeles, Mike Davis characterized it as homeowner exclusivism, "whether the immediate issue is apartment construction, commercial encroachment, school busing, crime, taxes, or simply community designation," with only the flimsiest link to environmentalism.[126] The same squeeze on land can promote gentrification. Smart Growth

Figure 3. The Del Mar Station project in Pasadena, Ca., exemplifies New Urbanism principles. It is a transit-oriented development that combines apartments (including 15 percent affordable units), retail, restaurants, and a plaza, all adjacent to a Metro station. In 2003, it won a Congress for New Urbanism Charter Award.
Photograph courtesy of Moule and Polyzoides Architects and Urbanists.

pioneer Portland, Oregon, for example, landed at the top of recent lists on metro areas with accelerating gentrification. Ringed by strict growth boundaries, the city became denser and housing prices and rents spiked, fueling gentrification. The trend hit the African American community especially hard. The city's core lost 10,000 blacks from 2000 to 2010; historically black neighborhoods like King, Woodlawn, and Boise-Eliot transitioned to majority white. The result is what one account dubbed "the racial failure of New Urbanism."[127]

SUBURBAN CRISIS, SUBURBAN REGENERATION

In recent years, the suburbs came under a new round of criticism, this time perhaps the harshest yet. While bands like Green Day and Arcade Fire wailed on the suburbs for killing youthful freedom and joy, echoing generations of suburban critics, writers like *Fortune magazine's* Leigh Gallagher took it a step further by declaring "The End of the Suburbs" in her 2013 best-selling book. The alarm was justifiably stoked by the Great Recession of 2007–2009, which devastated millions of American families who lost their homes to foreclosure, or saw their suburban home values plummet. Many questioned the wisdom of home ownership, which in turn cast doubt on the viability of suburbia altogether. These concerns, along with worries over sprawl's negative impacts on climate change and millennials' desires for more urban styles of living, fueled a back-to-the-city movement. Writers like Gallagher contended this was the end of the line for the suburbs. Americans were finally turning their backs on the form, reversing a long history of sprawling development. "Speaking simply," she wrote, "more and more Americans don't want to live there anymore."[128]

Yet different trends suggested otherwise. Immigrants, young families, seniors emotionally attached to their homes, and others continued gravitating toward suburban homeplaces, for a host of reasons—whether good schools, nostalgia, ethnic familiarity, jobs, or few good alternatives. Recent data suggest a return of suburban growth, after a post-recession slowdown.[129] In turn, contemporary suburbia is showing signs of change, adaptation, and stasis—all at once. As Manuel Pastor noted at a recent roundtable discussion on Suburban Crisis, Suburban Regeneration (https://icwblog.wordpress.com/2015/11/18/suburban-crisis-suburban-regeneration/) "the suburbs have a future, but the future ain't what it used to be." Some suburbs have transformed into ethnoburbs that support the values and needs of new immigrants, some have spawned social justice movements, others are adapting to aging populations through innovative retrofitting, while still others persist seemingly untouched, clinging to deeply entrenched traditions.[130] The discourse of suburbia's demise may have attracted much public attention, but it masks the fascinating ways that the nation's suburbs continue to claim a central, dynamic place in American life.

DISCUSSION OF THE LITERATURE

The historical scholarship of post-1945 suburbia has flourished in recent decades, pushing the boundaries of urban history scholarship. As suburbia's role in postwar American life has grown stronger and broader, historians have responded by exploring multiple angles of this influence.

A foundational text is Kenneth T. Jackson's *Crabgrass Frontier: The Suburbanization of the United States* (1985), which provided the first comprehensive overview of American suburban history. Adopting a definition of suburbia that emphasized their white, affluent, and middle-class character, Jackson surveyed the major stages of suburban development, starting with the elite 19th-century romantic suburbs, then tracing the gradual democratization

of the form from streetcar and automobile suburbs to postwar mass-produced suburbs. While Jackson identified the broad forces that underlay this evolution, his emphasis on federal policy was a seminal contribution, outlining how Washington, DC, not only subsidized massive postwar suburbanization but created racial/class exclusion in the process. The results were devastating for cities and the minorities and poor left behind. Along with Robert Fishman in *Bourgeois Utopias* (1986), Jackson established a normative portrait of suburbs as residential spaces of affluent white privilege. In a 30-year retrospective (https://tropicsofmeta.wordpress.com/2014/10/15/the-magic-of-crabgrass-thirty-years-later-an-appraisal-of-kenneth-jacksons-crabgrass-frontier/) on *Crabgrass Frontier*, Dianne Harris noted that because the book established a clear set of characteristics for the suburbs (i.e., racial and economic homogeneity, gender roles, and architectural similarity), historians since had "a template with which to compare and contrast, and yes, to push back against."[131] Working around the same time as Jackson and Fishman, historians Carol O'Connor, John Archer, Mary Corbin Sies, and Michael Ebner traced the roots of elite and socially exclusive suburbs and their subsequent trajectories into the 20th century.[132]

Iconic postwar suburbs like Levittown were the focus of a cluster of studies that followed, including Barbara Kelley's analysis of quotidian architectural practices in Levittown, Long Island; Dianne Harris's edited collection on Levittown, Pennsylvania; and Elizabeth Ewen and Rosalyn Baxandall's historical survey of Long Island's suburbs. Like others before them, these works often took a local focus, digging deeply into the culture, architecture, politics, and institutions of specific suburban sites.[133]

Other scholars pushed the boundaries of analysis, both geographically and demographically. One important current has been dubbed "the metropolitan turn." Scholars in this school analyzed suburbs not in isolation but as fully embedded in the metropolitan political economy. These works pulled the lens back to explore not only "the ideological, political, and economic issues that bound city and suburb together in the postwar world" but also the "tensions that divided suburbs as they competed for business, development, and investment in the politically and socioeconomically fragmented metropolis."[134] Jon Teaford's pioneering work analyzed the politics and governance of metropolitan fragmentation. Since 1990, Thomas Sugrue, Robert Self, Matthew Lassiter, and Kevin Kruse have produced influential works that investigated the ways suburbs proactively created and protected advantage—in the realms of business growth, politics (from conservative to centrist), wealth, and infrastructure—establishing enduring patterns of metropolitan inequality.[135] The "metropolitan turn" is also exemplified in recent scholarship by Lily Geismer, Andrew Highsmith, Ansley Erickson, Andrew Needham, Allan Dietrich-Ward, and Lila Berman, among others, who explored suburbs within a metropolitan scale of analysis, around issues such as liberalism, schooling, environmentalism, and religion.[136]

Scholars have also explored the role of metropolitan spaces producing social distinctions such as race, gender, and sexuality. From the early postwar years, activist scholars such as Robert Weaver, Charles Abrams, and Clement Vose pioneered a large body of literature documenting discrimination in housing and the disadvantages of racial segregation in US metro areas. In the 1980s and 1990s, scholars extended these insights, exploring the social and spatial production of inequality in metropolitan contexts. Feminist scholars such as Dolores Hayden illuminated the ways that separate and unequal assumptions about gender were built into the spaces of postwar suburbia.[137] Arnold Hirsch, George Lipsitz, and Thomas Sugrue revealed how biased federal housing policies, unequal access to homeownership, and suburbanization helped to forge an enlarged sense of white racial identity in postwar America that was attached to distinct social advantages—what Lipsitz called "a possessive investment in whiteness."[138] Scholars such as David Freund, Eric

Avila, and Robert Self show that ideas about race and white supremacy became inscribed in spaces ranging from suburban property markets to municipalities to popular culture and to the metropolis as a whole.[139]

Another current of analysis pushed demographic boundaries, challenging the assumption that suburbs were white, middle class by definition. They argued for a more expansive profile that incorporated class, race, and ethnic diversity. Revisionist scholars such as Bruce Haynes, Andrew Wiese, Emily Straus, Matthew Garcia, Jerry Gonzalez, and Becky Nicolaides explored histories of African Americans, Mexican Americans, and white working-class suburbs. They identified distinct lifeways, cultures, and politics that in some cases stood apart from mainstream white suburbs, though in others replicated their class-driven concerns in the postwar period.[140]

This focus on diverse suburbia carried forward in studies of the post-1970 era. This work offers some of the most robust challenges to the trope of suburbia as the domain of white middle-class privilege. This approach reflects not only a revisionist analytical perspective but also the changing realities of life in suburbs where immigrants, ethnic groups, racial minorities, and the poor have had time to settle in. Geographers and demographers began by mapping out changing demographic patterns in metropolitan areas, establishing a critical baseline for qualitative scholarship.[141] Subsequent scholars explored the internal dynamics and histories of these communities. An early focus was on ethnic suburbs. Pioneering studies by Timothy Fong, Leland Saito, and John Horton explored the explosive racial politics that erupted in Monterey Park, California, when it transitioned from all-white to multiethnic, while scholars like Wei Li and Min Zhou theorized new models of race and space around processes of ethnic suburban settlement. Asian American suburbanization, in fact, emerged as a particularly robust field of inquiry perhaps because Asians gained an early foothold in postwar suburbs and became the "most suburban" of all ethnic groups. These studies explored the nature and implication of settlement patterns, spatial practices, transnational connections, political and cultural practices, and internal community dynamics.[142] More recently, historians have explored social justice politics in suburbia, some such as Lily Geismer emphasizing the limits of racial liberalism, others identifying vigorous progressive activism around issues like immigrant rights. This latest wave of scholarship, perhaps more than any, offers bold alternatives to the orthodox narrative, recognizing in suburbia multiple politics, culture, lifeways, and values which reflect the outlook of their diverse inhabitants.[143]

PRIMARY SOURCES

Historical sources on postwar suburbia exist in multiple locales, depending on the scale of analysis. For localized research on individual suburbs, sources often exist in local libraries, historical societies, or state historical societies. Materials may include local newspapers, clip files, real-estate promotional material, oral histories, and records of local institutions. Because local newspapers are rarely digitized, most are available on microfilm or in original paper form. Municipal city halls may contain city council and planning department records, local ordinances, design review board minutes, mayoral papers, and the records of other local governing bodies, though some local public documents have been deposited in local or state archives. Some university libraries also hold material relating to suburban neighborhoods, while some specialized archives—such as the Huntington Library in Los Angeles, the Chicago Historical Society, and Detroit's Walter P. Reuther Library of Labor and Urban Affairs—contain a wealth of local history materials, maps, booklets, real-estate ephemera, and private and public organization records. For the Levittowns, no intact corporate archive exists according to Dianne Harris.[144] For Park Forest, Illinois, and Lakewood, California, good holdings exist at the local public libraries.

At the county and metropolitan level, records may be available in county government offices—including property records such as building, deed, and mortgage records, which are indispensable to histories of real-estate development. Regional governing and planning bodies and university libraries may also hold regional reports on metropolitan transit, infrastructure, housing, planning, and the like. On the history of metro-wide politics, around issues such as busing, redevelopment, public housing, and environmentalism, university archives often hold the papers of key individuals, agencies, or advocacy groups. It is worth exploring the special collections in local universities of the metro area under study.

The National Archives holds a number of important collections that reflect federal policies on metropolitan areas such as the Housing and Home Finance Agency/Department of Housing and Urban Development, which includes the Home Owners Loan Corporation (e.g., individual city survey files and maps; a growing body of this material has been digitized on a few websites), the Federal Housing Administration and the Public Housing Administration.

The built landscape itself is an excellent source for exploring the history of post 1945-suburbia, since much of this landscape is still intact. Homes, commercial districts, parks, streetscapes, job clusters, and physical barriers between segregated suburbs, as well as New Urbanist complexes and physical growth boundaries in Smart Growth cities, are all important markers of the suburban past. In 2002, the National Park Service also issued its own standards for historic preservation of America's suburbs, called "Historic Residential Suburbs: Guidelines for Evaluation and Documentation for the National Register of Historic Places (https://www.nps.gov/Nr /publications/bulletins/suburbs/index .htm)." Although somewhat outdated, it reflects the preservation field's understanding of America's suburban past.

DIGITAL MATERIALS AND ARCHIVES

National Center for Suburban Studies at Hofstra University. http://www.hofstra.edu/academics/css/ncss_research_objectives.html.

Culture of the Suburbs: International Research Network—This international network of institutions devoted to suburban studies began in 2011. Its website has good links to resources across the globe. http://suburbs.exeter.ac.uk/.

Bill Owens Photographs of Suburbia—From Bill Owens's book *Suburbia*, a compilation of photos of everyday life in Livermore, California, in 1972. This website is based on an exhibition of these photographs at UC Riverside in 2000. http://138.23.124.165/exhibitions/suburbia/.

Park Forest House Museum & Archive—A museum and archive relating to the development of Park Forest, Illinois, a key postwar mass-produced suburb, and the site of William Whyte's suburban research for the seminal work, *The Organization Man*. http://www.parkforesthistory.org/museum-home.html.

Levittown, Pennsylvania: "Levittown Links." http://www.levittowners.com/links.htm.

Levittown, Pennsylvania: Our Home Town. A promotional film for Levittown, Pennsylvania. https://archive.org/details/OurHomeT1954_2.

Johnson County Museum, Kansas—The mission of this museum is "to be nationally recognized for presenting the past and exploring the future of one of America's leading suburban counties." http://www.jocogov.org/dept/museum/home.

"In the Suburbs" (1957)—This promotional film produced by *Redbook* magazine offers an optimistic view of postwar suburban life as a world of mass consumption. https://archive.org/details/IntheSub1957.

"Crisis in Levittown" (1957)—A documentary produced in 1957 on the integration "crisis" in Levittown, Pennsylvania. https://www.youtube.com/watch?v=ZwJeJfZzcaE.

LINKS ON METROPOLITAN INEQUALITY, RACIAL, CLASS, AND ETHNIC GEOGRAPHIES

HOLC Maps—This collection is produced by Professor LaDale Winling of Virginia Tech. It shows the color-coded residential security maps produced by the HOLC in the late 1930s, which became the basis of "redlining.", http://www.urbanoasis.org/projects/holc-fha/digital-holc-maps.

Center for Metropolitan Opportunity, University of Minnesota, School of Law—This website explores the diverse fiscal conditions and disparities across metropolitan America. https://www1.law.umn.edu/metro/index.html.

Brookings Metropolitan Policy Program—This program provides timely trend analysis, cutting-edge research and policy ideas for improving the health and prosperity of cities and metropolitan areas. The site includes events, media reports, research and commentary, projects, news and blogs. https://www.brookings.edu/program/metropolitan-policy-program/.

Mapping Decline: St. Louis and the American City—Professor Colin Gordon's excellent website mapping white flight, race and property, municipal zoning, and urban renewal. Offers rich context for the Ferguson crisis. http://mappingdecline.lib.uiowa.edu/map/.

American Panorama: An Atlas of the Historical Geography of the United States—This online map collection is created by the Digital Scholarship Lab at the University of Richmond, edited by Robert K. Nelson and Edward L. Ayers. It contains maps on foreign-born populations over time, and will include maps on redlining during the Depression and urban renewal. http://dsl.richmond.edu/panorama/.

LINKS ON THE CONTEMPORARY CHALLENGES AND FUTURE OF SUBURBIA

The Atlantic CityLab—Up-to-date reporting and analysis on cities, suburbs, and metros. http://www.citylab.com/.

Calthorpe Associates—Innovators in urban planning and design. http://www.calthorpe.com/.

Congress for the New Urbanism—Main website for the national organization advocating for denser, more sustainable designs. https://www.cnu.org/who-we-are/charter-new-urbanism.

Sprawl Costs—New Urbanism's overview of the multifaceted costs of sprawl. http://www.newurbanism.org/sprawlcosts.html.

Statistics on Sprawl, by the American Farmland Trust. https://www.farmland.org/initiatives/state-of-americas-farm-and-ranch-land.

Sustainable Cities Collective—This independently moderated community is a clearinghouse of information on sustainable urbanism. "Looking at issues such as transportation, building practices, community planning and development, education, water, health and infrastructure, we hope to create a community where people can get involved and learn about the advances in how cities are becoming smarter and greener in the 21st century." http://www.sustainablecitiescollective.com/about?ref=navbar.

Streetsblog—A website devoted to sustainable urbanism, it provides daily news feeds on "Sustainable transportation and livable communities." http://www.streetsblog.net/about/.

Planetizen.com—This site bills itself as "The independent resource for people passionate about planning and related fields." It is a public-interest website that deals with multiple aspects of metro planning. http://www.planetizen.com/.

The Urban Reinventors—An open-source online urban journal offering global perspectives on pressing issues facing metro areas. http://www.urbanreinventors.net/.

FURTHER READING

Archer, John, Paul Sandul, and Katherine Solomonson, eds. *Making Suburbia: New Histories of Everyday America*. Minneapolis: University of Minnesota Press, 2015.

Cheng, Wendy. *The Changs Next Door to the Díazes: Remapping Race in Suburban California*. Minneapolis: University of Minnesota Press, 2013.

Duaney, Andres, Elizabeth Plater-Zyberk, and Jeff Speck. *Suburban Nation: The Rise of Sprawl and the Decline of the American Dream*. New York: North Point Press, 2000.

Harris, Dianne, ed. *Second Suburb: Levittown, Pennsylvania*. Pittsburgh: University of Pittsburgh Press, 2010.

Hayden, Dolores. *Building Suburbia: Green Fields and Urban Growth, 1820–2000*. New York: Vintage, 2003.

Jackson, Kenneth T. *Crabgrass Frontier: The Suburbanization of the United States*. New York: Oxford University Press, 1985.

Kruse, Kevin M., and Thomas J. Sugrue, eds. *The New Suburban History*. Chicago: University of Chicago Press, 2006.

Lassiter, Matthew. *Silent Majority: Suburban Politics in the Sunbelt South*. Princeton, NJ: Princeton University Press, 2006.

McGirr, Lisa. *Suburban Warriors: The Origins of the New American Right*. Princeton, NJ: Princeton University Press, 2001.

Nicolaides, Becky. *My Blue Heaven: Life and Politics in the Working-Class Suburbs of Los Angeles, 1920–1965*. Chicago: University of Chicago Press, 2002.

Nicolaides, Becky, and Andrew Wiese, eds. *The Suburb Reader*. 2d ed. New York: Routledge, 2016.

Orfield, Myron. *American Metropolitics: The New Suburban Reality*. Washington, DC: Brookings Institution Press, 2002.

Self, Robert. *American Babylon: Race and the Struggle for Postwar Oakland*. Princeton, NJ: Princeton University Press, 2003.

Singer, Audrey, Susan W. Hardwick, and Caroline B. Brettell, eds. *Twenty-First Century Gateways: Immigrant Incorporation in Suburban America*. Washington, DC: Brookings Institution Press, 2008.

Teaford, Jon. *The American Suburb: The Basics*. New York: Routledge, 2008.

Wiese, Andrew. *Places of Their Own: African American Suburbanization in the Twentieth Century*. Chicago: University of Chicago Press, 2004.

NOTES

1. Richard Harris and Robert Lewis, "The Geography of North American Cities and Suburbs," *Journal of Urban History* 27.3 (March 2001): 263.

2. See Ann Durkin Keating, "Suburbanization Before 1945," in *Oxford Research Encyclopedia of American History*, ed. Jon Butler (New York: Oxford University Press, 2015).

3. Kenneth T. Jackson, *Crabgrass Frontier: The Suburbanization of the United States* (New York: Oxford University Press, 1985).

4. Dolores Hayden, *Building Suburbia: Greenfields and Urban Growth, 1820–2000* (New York: Pantheon Books, 2003); Thomas Hanchett, "U.S. Tax Policy and the Shopping Center Boom of the 1950s and 1960s," *American Historical Review* 101.4 (October 1996): 1082–1110; Owen Gutfreund, *Twentieth Century Sprawl: Highways*

and the Reshaping of the American Landscape (New York: Oxford University Press, 2005).

5. Jackson, Crabgrass Frontier, 205.

6. Jackson, Crabgrass Frontier, 203–208.

7. Hayden, Building Suburbia, 133.

8. Nonfarm Housing Starts, 1889–1958, Bulletin No. 1260, US Department of Labor, US Government Printing Office, 1960, 15–16. "Revised Estimates of New Nonfarm Housing Units Started, 1945–1958, U.S. Department of Commerce, Construction Reports: Housing Starts, C20–60, Issued June, 1964, p. 9. Documents accessed at http://www.michaelcarliner.com/Arch-Data.html.

9. Hayden, Building Suburbia, 133–135.

10. James J. Jacobs, Detached America: Building Houses in Postwar Suburbia (Charlottesville: University of Virginia Press, 2015), 20–21; Marion Clawson, Suburban Land Conversion in the U.S.: An Economic and Governmental Process (Baltimore: Johns Hopkins University Press, 1971), 89–90.

11. Jacobs, Detached America, 109–110.

12. Jacobs, Detached America, chapters 4–5.

13. Lizabeth Cohen, A Consumer's Republic: The Politics of Mass Consumption in Postwar America (New York: Vintage, 2004), 260–278; David Smiley, Pedestrian Modern: Shopping and American Architecture, 1925–1956 (Minneapolis: University of Minnesota, 2013); Richard Longstreth, City Center to Regional Mall: Architecture, the Automobile, and Retailing in Los Angeles, 1920–1950 (Boston: MIT Press, 1997). https://mitpress.mit.edu/books/city-center-regional-mall.

14. Louise Mozingo, Pastoral Capitalism: A History of Suburban Corporate Landscapes (Boston: MIT Press, 2011).

15. Andrew Friedman, Covert Capital: Landscapes of Denial and the Making of US Empire in the Suburbs of Northern Virginia (Berkeley: University of California Press, 2013).

16. William Laas, "The Suburbs Are Strangling the City," New York Times Magazine, June 18, 1950, 22, 52–53.

17. Thomas Sugrue, Origins of the Urban Crisis: Race and Inequality in Postwar Detroit (Princeton, NJ: Princeton University Press, 1996).

18. Robert Self, American Babylon: Race and the Struggle for Postwar Oakland (Princeton, NJ: Princeton University Press, 2003).

19. Deborah Dash Moore, To the Golden Cities: Pursuing the American Jewish Dream in Miami and L.A. (Cambridge, MA: Harvard University Press, 1994); Karen Brodkin, How Jews Became White Folks and What That Says About Race in America (New Brunswick, NJ: Rutgers University Press, 1998); David Roediger, Working Toward Whiteness: How America's Immigrants Became White: The Strange Journey from Ellis Island to the Suburbs (New York: Basic Books, 2006).

20. Thomas J. Sugrue, Origins of the Urban Crisis: Race and Inequality in Postwar Detroit (Princeton, NJ: Princeton University Press, 1996), 9.

21. Jackson, Crabgrass Frontier; Andrew Wiese, Places of Their Own: African American Suburbanization in the 20th Century (Chicago: University of Chicago Press, 2004).

22. Arnold Hirsch, Making the Second Ghetto: Race and Housing in Chicago, 1940–1960 (Chicago: University of Chicago Press, 1978); Raymond Mohl, "Making the Second Ghetto in Metropolitan Miami, 1940–1960," Journal of Urban History 21 (March, 1995): 395–427; Charles Abrams, Forbidden Neighbors: A Study of Prejudice in Housing (New York: Harpers, 1955).

23. Charlotte Brooks, Alien Neighbors, Foreign Friends: Asian Americans, Housing, and the Transformation of Urban California (Chicago: University of Chicago Press, 2009). http://www.amazon.com/exec/obidos/ASIN/0226075974.

24. Wiese, Places of Their Own; William H. Wilson, Hamilton Park: A Planned Black Community in Dallas (Baltimore: Johns Hopkins University Press, 1998).

25. Wiese, Places of Their Own.

26. Key works on the Levittowns include Herbert Gans, The Levittowners: Ways of Life and Politics in the New Suburban Community (New York: Columbia University Press, 1982 ed.); William Dobriner, Class in Suburbia (Englewood Cliffs, NJ: Prentice-Hall, 1963); Dianne Harris, ed., Second Suburb: Levittown, Pennsylvania (Pittsburgh: University of Pittsburgh Press, 2010); Barbara Kelley, Expanding the American Dream: Building and Rebuilding Levittown (New York: State University of New York Press, 1993); Rosalyn Baxandall and Elizabeth Ewen, Picture Windows: How The Suburbs Happened (New York: Basic Books, 2000). On Park Forest, Illinois, see William H. Whyte Jr., The Organization Man (New York: Simon & Schuster, 1956).

27. Otis Dudley Duncan and Albert J Reiss Jr., "Suburbs and Urban Fringe," in The Suburban Community, ed. William M. Dobriner (New York:

G. P. Putnam's Sons, 1958), 48–61; Hugh A. Wilson, "The Family in Suburbia: From Tradition to Pluralism," in *Suburbia Re-examined*, ed. Barbara M. Kelly (New York: Greenwood, 1989), 85–86; Gwendolyn Wright, *Building the Dream: A Social History of Housing in America* (Cambridge, MA: MIT Press, 1988), 256; Clayton Howard, "Building a 'Family Friendly' Metropolis: Sexuality, the State, and Postwar Housing Policy," *Journal of Urban History* 39.5 (September 2013): 933–955.

28. Ernest Mowrer, "The Family in Suburbia," in *The Suburban Community*, ed. William M. Dobriner (New York: G. P. Putnam Sons, 1958), 158.

29. Harris, ed., *Second Suburb*, 4–5; Gans, *The Levittowners*.

30. Harris, ed., *Second Suburb*, 5–6; Jackson, *Crabgrass Frontier*, chapter 13; Becky Nicolaides, *My Blue Heaven: Life and Politics in the Working-Class Suburbs of Los Angeles, 1920–1965* (Chicago: University of Chicago Press, 2002), chapters 5–6.

31. Baxandall and Ewen, *How the Suburbs Happened*, 144.

32. Cohen, *A Consumers Republic*, chapter 5, quote at 255.

33. Whyte, *Organization Man*, 287.

34. Whyte, *Organization Man*, 280–298. Although Whyte went on to critique this way of life, he nonetheless depicted in detail a culture of vibrant neighborhood life.

35. Baxandall and Ewen, *How the Suburbs Happened*, 146–156.

36. Christopher Sellers, "Suburban Nature, Class, and Environmentalism in Levittown," in *Second Suburb: Levittown, Pennsylvania*, ed. Dianne Harris (Pittsburgh: University of Pittsburgh Press, 2010), 294–295.

37. Chad M. Kimmel, "Revealing the History of Levittown, One Voice at a Time," in *Second Suburb: Levittown, Pennsylvania*, ed. Dianne Harris (Pittsburgh: University of Pittsburgh Press, 2010), 30–31, 36.

38. Baxandall and Ewen, *How the Suburbs Happened*, 154.

39. Baxandall and Ewen, *How the Suburbs Happened*, 156.

40. Gans, *Levittowners*, 154–155. Other works documenting strong social and civic engagement in suburbia in the 1950–1960s include John R. Seeley, R. Alexander Sim, and Elizabeth W. Loosley, *Crestwood Heights* (New York: Basic Books, 1956); Sylvia Fleis Fava, "Contrasts in Neighboring,"

in *The Suburban Community*, ed. William M. Dobriner (New York: G. P. Putnam's Sons, 1958); S. F. Fava, "Suburbanism as a Way of Life," *American Sociological Review* 21 (February 1956): 34–38; Robert C. Wood, *Suburbia: Its People and Their Politics* (Boston: Houghton Mifflin, 1959); Claude S. Fischer and Robert Max Jackson, "Suburbanism and Localism," in *Networks and Places*, eds., Fischer et. al. (New York: Free Press, 1977); Sylvie Murray, *The Progressive Housewife: Community Activism in Suburban Queens, 1945–1965* (Philadelphia: University of Pennsylvania Press, 2003), chapter 4.

41. Elaine Tyler May, *Homeward Bound: American Families in the Cold War Era* (New York: Basic Books, 1988); Nancy Rubin, *The New Suburban Woman: Beyond Myth and Motherhood* (New York: Coward, McCann & Geoghegan, 1982), 58–59.

42. Baxandall and Ewen, *How the Suburbs Happened*, 152.

43. Baxandall and Ewen, *How the Suburbs Happened*, 156; Joanne Meyerowitz, ed., *Not June Cleaver: Women and Gender in Postwar America, 1945–1960* (Philadelphia: Temple University Press, 1994); Rubin, *New Suburban Woman*, 64–65. On women's pivotal role in suburban politics, see Murray, *Progressive Housewife*: Michelle Nickerson, *Mothers of Conservatism: Women and the Postwar Right* (Princeton, NJ: Princeton University Press, 2012).

44. On the television industry's market-driven approach to depicting postwar suburban family life, see Nina C. Liebman, *Living Room Lectures: The Fifties Family in Film and Television* (Austin: University of Texas Press, 1995).

45. Karal Ann Marling, *As Seen on TV: The Visual Culture of Everyday Life in the 1950s* (Cambridge, MA: Harvard University Press, 1994), 243–246; Cohen, *Consumers' Republic*. Scholars have recently explored how suburban elements such as home ownership and detached housing were an integral part of housing initiatives overseas during the Cold War. For the global reach of American suburban ideals in this period, see: Nancy Kwak, *Homeownership for All: American Power and the Politics of Housing Aid Post-1945* (Chicago: University of Chicago Press, 2015); Lauren Hirschberg, "Nuclear Families: (Re)producing 1950s Suburban America in the Marshall Islands," *OAH Magazine of History* 26.4 (2012): 39–43.

46. Lewis Mumford, *The City in History: Its Origin, Its Transformation, and Its Prospects* (New York: Houghton Mifflin, 1961), 494.

47. Becky Nicolaides and Andrew Wiese, eds., *The Suburb Reader*, 2d ed. (New York: Routledge, 2016), chapter 10; Catherine Jurca, *White Diaspora: The Suburb and the Twentieth-Century American Novel* (Princeton, NJ: Princeton University Press, 2001); Robert Beuka, *SuburbiaNation: Reading Suburban Landscape in Twentieth-Century American Fiction and Film* (New York: Palgrave, 2004); Martin Dines and Timotheus Vermeulen, eds., *New Suburban Stories* (London: Bloomsbury Academic, 2013).

48. Gans, *The Levittowners*; Bennett M. Berger, "The Myth of Suburbia," *Journal of Social Issues* 17 (1961); William Dobriner, *Class in Suburbia* (Englewood Cliffs, NJ: Prentice-Hall, 1963); Bennett M. Berger, *Working-Class Suburb: A Study of Autoworkers in Suburbia* (Berkeley: University of California Press, 1969).

49. For elaboration of this argument, see J. John Palen, *The Suburbs* (New York: McGraw-Hill, 1995), 82–84.

50. Matthew Lassiter, *Silent Majority: Suburban Politics in the Sunbelt South* (Princeton, NJ: Princeton University Press, 2006); Jackson, *Crabgrass Frontier*; David M.P. Freund , *Colored Property: State Policy and White Racial Politics in Suburban America* (Chicago: University of Chicago Press, 2007); Kevin Kruse, *White Flight: Atlanta and the Making of Modern Conservatism* (Princeton, NJ: Princeton University Press, 2005), and see the authors in Kevin M. Kruse and Thomas J. Sugrue, eds., *The New Suburban History* (Chicago: University of Chicago Press, 2006).

51. Lassiter, *Silent Majority*; Kruse, *White Flight*; Nicolaides, *My Blue Heaven*.

52. Lisa McGirr, *Suburban Warrior* (Princeton, NJ: Princeton University Press, 2001); Michelle Nickerson, *Mothers of Conservatism: Women and the Postwar Right* (Princeton, NJ: Princeton University Press, 2012).

53. Of this extensive literature, key works include: Arnold Hirsch, *Making the Second Ghetto: Race and Housing in Chicago, 1940–1960* (Cambridge: Cambridge University Press, 1983); Jonathan Rieder, *Canarsie: The Jews and Italians of New York against Liberalism* (Cambridge, MA: Harvard University Press, 1987); Sugrue, *Origins of the Urban Crisis*; Lassiter, *Silent Majority*;

Nicolaides, *My Blue Heaven*; Robert Self, *American Babylon: Race and the Struggle for Postwar Oakland* (Princeton, NJ: Princeton University Press, 2003); Kruse, *White Flight*; Freund, *Colored Property*; Thomas Sugrue, *Sweet Land of Liberty: The Forgotten Struggle for Civil Rights in the North* (New York: Random House, 2009); Kenneth D. Durr, *Behind the Backlash: White Working-Class Politics in Baltimore, 1940–1980* (Chapel Hill: University of North Carolina Press, 2007); Darren Dochuk, *From Bible Belt to Sunbelt: Plain Folk Religion, Grassroots Politics, and the Rise of Evangelical Conservatism* (New York: W. W. Norton, 2010); Andrew Highsmith, *Demolition Means Progress: Flint, Michigan, and the Fate of the American Metropolis* (Chicago: University of Chicago Press, 2015); Ansley Erickson, *Making the Unequal Metropolis: School Desegregation and Its Limits* (Chicago: University of Chicago Press, 2016).

54. Murray, *Progressive Housewife*, chapter 3; Daniel Martinez HoSang, *Racial Propositions: Ballot Initiatives and the Making of Postwar California* (Berkeley: University of California Press, 2010); Lily Geismer, *Don't Blame Us: Suburban Liberals and the Transformation of the Democratic Party* (Princeton, NJ: Princeton University Press, 2014).

55. Baxandall and Ewen, *How the Suburbs Happened*, 155.

56. Thomas J. Sugrue, "Jim Crow's Last Stand: The Struggle to Integrate Levittown," in Dianne Harris, ed., *Second Suburb*, 175–199, quote at 175; Daisy D. Myers, "Reflections on Levittown," in Harris, ed., *Second Suburb*, 41–59.

57. Adam Rome, *The Bulldozer in the Countryside: Suburban Sprawl and the Rise of American Environmentalism* (Cambridge: Cambridge University Press, 2001); Andrew Wiese, "'The Giddy Rise of the Environmentalists': Corporate Real Estate Development and Environmental Politics in San Diego, California, 1968–73," *Environmental History* 19 (January 2014): 28–54; Christopher C. Sellers, *Crabgrass Crucible: Suburban Nature and the Rise of Environmentalism in Twentieth-Century America* (Chapel Hill: University of North Carolina Press, 2015).

58. Christopher Sellers, "Suburban Nature, Class, and Environmentalism in Levittown," in Dianne Harris, ed., *Second Suburb*, 281–313.

59. Mike Davis, *City of Quartz: Excavating the Future in Los Angeles* (London: Verso Books, 1990), 120–159; Elizabeth Blackmar, "Of REITS

and Rights: Absentee Ownership at the Periphery" in *City, Country, Empire: Landscapes in Environmental History* (Pittsburgh: University of Pittsburgh Press, 2005); Kevin Fox Gotham, "The Secondary Circuit of Capital Reconsidered: Globalization and the U.S. Real Estate Sector," *American Journal of Sociology*, 112.1 (July 2006); Wiese, "'The Giddy Rise of the Environmentalists.'"

60. Vladimir Atanasov and John J. Merrick Jr., "Liquidity and Value in the Deep vs. Shallow Ends of Mortgage-Backed Securities Pool," July 11, 2012, https://www.sec.gov/divisions/riskfin/seminar/atanasov071912.pdf, Working Paper, Securities and Exchange Commission, 2012; Gotham, "The Secondary Circuit of Capital Reconsidered," 231–275; Freddie Mac Update, http://www.freddiemac.com/investors/pdffiles/investor-presentation.pdf), February, 2016.

61. "2006 Builder 100," *Builder Magazine*; "2015 Housing Giants Ranking," *Professional Builder*.

62. Joint Center for Housing Studies of Harvard University, The State of the Nation's Housing, 2015.

63. Peter Muller, *The Outer City: The Geographical Consequences of the Urbanization of the Suburbs* (Washington, DC: American Association of Geographers, 1976).

64. Edward Glaeser and Mathew Kahn, "Decentralized Employment and the Transformation of the American City." Brookings-Wharton Papers on Urban Affairs 2 (2001). http://www.nber.org/papers/w8117.

65. Joel Garreau, *Edge City: Life on the New Frontier* (New York: Anchor Books, 1992); Jennifer Bradley, Bruce Katz, and Mark Muro, "Miracle Mets: How U.S. Metros Propel America's Economy and Might Drive Its Recovery," *Democracy Journal* (Spring, 2009).

66. American Farmland Trust, Farmland Information Center; Elizabeth Becker, "2 Farm Acres Lost per Minute, Study Says," *New York Times*, Oct. 4, 2002.

67. Sierra Club, "Population Growth and Suburban Sprawl: A Complex Relationship."

68. Hayden, *Building Suburbia*, Sierra Club, Sprawl Costs Us All: How Your Taxes Fuel Suburban Sprawl, Report Spring 2000.

69. Myron Orfield, *American Metropolitics: The New Suburban Reality* (Washington, DC: Brookings Institution Press, 2002).

70. Peter Calthorpe, *Urbanism in the Age of Climate Change* (Washington, DC: Island Press, 2010)

71. Ernie Smith, "Study, Homeowners Associations Hit New Populations Peak," *Associations Now*, May 15, 2015; Teresa Mears, "How to Successfully Live Under a Home Owners' Association," *U.S. News and World Report*, April 27, 2015, http://money.usnews.com/money/personal-finance/articles/2015/04/27/how-to-successfully-live-under-a-homeowners-association; US Bureau of the Census, Census of Housing, Characteristics of New Housing, 2014.

72. Joel Aschbrenner, "Report Shows Trend toward Bigger Homes, Smaller Lots," *Des Moines Register*, June 20, 2015. http://www.desmoinesregister.com/story/money/business/development/2015/06/20/bigger-homes-smaller-lots-prairie-trail/29010087/. See also, US Bureau of the Census, Census of Housing, Characteristics of New Housing, 2014.

73. Setha Low, *Behind the Gates: Life, Security and the Pursuit of Happiness in Fortress America* (New York: Routledge, 2003).

74. See Ann Durkin Keating, "Suburbanization Before 1945," *Oxford Research Encyclopedia of American History*. From a historical perspective, the suburban periphery was long marked by diversity—ethnic, class, and even racial—yet the postwar period represented something of an interruption to that trend with young, white nuclear families predominating in new suburban tracts. For a fine discussion of the *longue durée* of suburban diversity, see Matthew Lassiter and Christopher Niedt, "Suburban Diversity in Postwar America," *Journal of Urban History* 39.1 (January 2013): 3–14.

75. Wilson, "The Family in Suburbia," 85–93, quote at 90–91.

76. William H. Frey and Alan Berube, "City Families and Suburban Singles: An Emerging Household Story from Census 2000," Center on Urban & Metropolitan Policy, Brookings Institution, February 2002. Their study analyzes census data from the 102 most populous metropolitan areas between 1990 and 2000.

77. Nancy A. Denton and Joseph R. Gibbons, "Twenty-First Century Suburban Demography," in *Social Justice in Diverse Suburbs: History, Politics, and Prospects*, ed. Christopher Niedt (Philadelphia: Temple University Press, 2013), 22.

78. Gary J. Gates, "Geographic Trends Among Same-Sex Couples in the U.S. Census and the American Community Survey," Williams Institute, UCLA School of Law, November 2007; Karen Tongson,

Relocations: Queer Suburban Imaginaries (New York: New York University Press, 2011); Katrin B. Anacker, "Queering the Suburbs: Analyzing Property Values in Male and Female Same-Sex Suburbs in the United States," in *Queering Planning: Challenging Heteronormative Assumptions and Reframing Planning Practice*, ed. Petra L. Doan (Farnham, UK: Ashgate, 2011), 107–125.

79. Ian Baldwin, "Family, Housing, and the Political Geography of Gay Liberation in Los Angeles County, 1960–1986" (PhD diss., University of Nevada Las Vegas, 2016). While this definition initially applied to low-income families seeking housing aid, it set the tone for a broader federal housing policy that "opened the door to queer recognition." In conversation, Baldwin suggested that this also likely created a shifted climate for gay suburban access as well. (Conversation with Becky Nicolaides, Los Angeles, Nov. 2015).

80. William H. Frey, "Melting Pot Cities and Suburbs: Racial and Ethnic Change in Metro America in the 2000s," State of Metropolitan America series, no. 30, Brookings Institution, May 4, 2011.

81. US Census Bureau, 2010 Census, Summary File 1; Frey, "Melting Pot Cities and Suburbs," 1; Audrey Singer and Jill H. Wilson, "Immigrants in 2010 Metropolitan America: A Decade of Change," State of Metropolitan America series, no. 41, Brookings Institution, October 13, 2011, 8–11.

82. US Census Bureau statistics from 1970–2010. Also see June Williamson, "Retrofitting Levittown," *Places* 17. 2 (2005). https://placesjournal.org/article/retrofitting-levittown/.

83. Linda Lou, Hyojung Lee, Anthony Guardado, and Dowell Myers, "Racially Balanced Cities in Southern California, 1990 to 2010," USC Price Center, Population Dynamics Research Group (February 2012), 6.

84. Data from 2010 US Census, General Population and Housing Characteristics. Statistics are for "non-Hispanic whites," "non-Hispanic blacks," "non-Hispanic Asians," and "Hispanics." The Levittowns themselves illustrated these variations. While two of the three Levittowns remained mostly white, the third Levittown—Willingboro, NJ—was 72.7 percent African American in 2010.

85. Orfield, *American Metropolitics.*

86. Elizabeth Kneebone and Alan Berube, *Confronting Suburban Poverty in America* (Washington, DC: Brookings Institution Press, 2013), 9.

87. Edward G. Goetz, "Housing Dispersal Programs," *Journal of Planning Literature* 18.1 (August 2003), 3–16. Expanded "housing choice vouchers" and "mobility programs" in the 1990s bolstered Section 8, through services like mobility counseling for tenants and active recruitment of landlords.

Among the most notable housing dispersal efforts was Illinois' Gautreaux Program. Formed in the wake of two lawsuits, it involved 6,000 African American Section 8 tenants who moved into white suburbs around the Chicago area. The story is recounted in Leonard Rubinowitz and James E. Rosenbaum, *Crossing the Class and Color Lines: From Public Housing to White Suburbia* (Chicago: University of Chicago Press, 2001).

88. Kneebone and Berube, *Confronting Suburban Poverty*, 17–18. Their data was drawn from the 100 most populous metropolitan areas in the United States.

89. Richard Florida, "The Creative Class and Economic Development," *Economic Development Quarterly*, 28.3 (2014): 197; Richard Florida, "America's 1,000 Richest Neighborhoods," *Atlantic CityLab*, March 13, 2014. http://www.citylab.com/housing/2014/03/americas-1000-richest-neighborhoods/8610/.

90. Nicolaides and Wiese, eds., *The Suburb Reader*, chapter 15.

91. M. P. Baumgartner, *The Moral Order of a Suburb* (New York: Oxford University Press, 1988), 11, 13.

92. Several examples of this large literature include: Jackson, *Crabgrass Frontier*, chapter 15; Low, *Behind the Gates*; Evan McKenzie, *Privatopia: Homeowner Associations and the Rise of Residential Private Government* (New Haven, CT: Yale University Press, 1994); Davis, *City of Quartz*; James Howard Kunstler, *Geography of Nowhere* (New York: Simon & Schuster, 1993); Christopher Caldwell, "Levittown to Littleton," *National Review* (May 31, 1999); Andres Duany, Elizabeth Plater-Zyberk, and Jeff Speck, *Suburban Nation: The Rise of Sprawl and the Decline of the American Dream* (New York: North Point Press, 2000), especially chapter 7.

93. Robert D. Putnam, *Bowling Alone: The Collapse and Revival of American Community* (New York: Simon & Schuster, 2000), chapter 12; Duany et al., *Suburban Nation*, chapter 7.

94. Becky Nicolaides, "The Social Fallout of Racial Politics: Civic Engagement in Suburban Pasadena, 1950–2000," in *Making Suburbia: New Histories of Everyday America*, eds., John Archer, Paul Sandul, and Katherine Solomonson (Minneapolis: University of Minnesota Press, 2015), 10–16.

95. J. Eric Oliver, *The Paradoxes of Integration: Race, Neighborhood, and Civic Life in Multiethnic America* (Chicago: University of Chicago Press, 2010). Other studies have explored this dilemma, by examining different scales and proposing scenarios for overcoming these tendencies: Robert D. Putnam and Lewis M. Feldstein, *Better Together: Restoring the American Community* (New York: Simon & Schuster, 2003); Zachary Neal and Jennifer Watling Neal, "The (In)compatibility of Diversity and Sense of Community," *American Journal of Community Psychology* 53 (2014): 1–12; Richard Florida, "The Missing Link Between Diversity and Community," *Atlantic City Lab*, November 4, 2015.

96. Sarah J. Mahler, *American Dreaming: Immigrant Life on the Margins* (Princeton, NJ: Princeton University Press, 1995), 98.

97. Wendy Cheng, *The Changs Next Door to the Díazes: Remapping Race in Suburban California* (Minneapolis: University of Minnesota Press, 2013), 60.

98. Cheng, *Changs Next Door*, 104. The Boy Scout troops that Cheng analyzed included a mix of later-generation Chinese American and Japanese Americans, more recent ethnic Chinese immigrants, Mexican Americans, and kids with mixed backgrounds (including Anglo).

99. Wei Li, *Ethnoburb: The New Ethnic Community in Urban America* (Honolulu: University of Hawai'i Press, 2009), 29.

100. Nicolaides and Wiese, *The Suburb Reader*, 2d ed., chapter 14; Tanachai Mark Padoongpatt, "'A Landmark for Sun Valley': Wat Thai of Los Angeles and Thai American Suburban Culture in 1980s San Fernando Valley," *Journal of American Ethnic History* 34.2 (Winter 2015): 83–114; S. Mitra Kalita, *Suburban Sahibs: Three Immigrant Families and Their Passage from India to America* (New Brunswick, NJ: Rutgers University Press, 2003), 15–31; Jerry Gonzalez, "'A Place in the Sun': Mexican Americans, Race, and the Suburbanization of Los Angeles,

1940–1980" (PhD diss., University of Southern California, 2009), 195–204. Asian malls represent a quasi-public venue for ethnic community building. See Willow Lung-Amam, "Malls of Meaning: Building Asian America in Silicon Valley Suburbia," *Journal of American Ethnic History* 34.2 (Winter 2015), 18–53.

101. Padoongpatt, "A Landmark for Sun Valley," 104.

102. Peter Schrag, *Paradise Lost: California's Experience, America's Future* (New York: New Press, 1998).

103. Lassiter, *Silent Majority*; Kruse, *White Flight*; Erickson, *Making the Unequal Metropolis*; L. Owen Kirkpatrick and Casey Gallagher, "The Suburban Geography of Moral Panic: Low-Income Housing and the Revanchist Fringe," in *Social Justice in Diverse Suburbs*, ed. Christopher Niedt (Philadelphia: Temple University Press, 2013), 31–53. Opposition was often strongest in suburbs on the geographic front lines of these issues.

104. Kyle Riismandel, "Under Siege: The Discursive Production of Embattled Suburbs and Empowered Suburbanites in America, 1976–1992" (PhD diss., George Washington University, 2010), 29.

105. Matthew Lassiter, "Impossible Criminals: The Suburban Imperatives of America's War on Drugs," *Journal of American History* 102.1 (June 2015), 126–140; Matthew Lassiter, "Pushers, Victims, and the Lost Innocence of White Suburbia: California's War on Narcotics during the 1950s," *Journal of Urban History* 41.5 (2015): 787–807.

106. Lassiter, *Silent Majority*; C. Michael Henry, *Race, Poverty, and Domestic Policy* (New Haven, CT: Yale University Press, 2008); Charles Lamb, *Housing Segregation in Suburban America since 1960: Presidential and Judicial Politics* (Cambridge: Cambridge University Press, 2005).

107. Richard Fry and Paul Taylor, "The Rise of Residential Segregation by Income," Pew Research Social and Demographic Trends, August 1, 2012. http://www.pewsocialtrends .org/2012/08/01/the-rise-of-residential -segregation-by-income/.

108. McKenzie, *Privatopia*. By 2014, according to an estimate by the Community Associations Institute, 66.7 million Americans lived in CIDs—most of them in the suburbs.

109. Becky M. Nicolaides and James Zarsadiaz, "Design Assimilation in Suburbia: Asian

Americans, Built Landscapes, and Suburban Advantage in Los Angeles's San Gabriel Valley since 1970," *Journal of Urban History* (online first, November 2015).

110. James S. Duncan and Nancy G. Duncan, *Landscapes of Privilege: The Politics of the Aesthetic in an American Suburb* (New York: Routledge, 2004); Nicolaides and Weise, eds., *Suburb Reader*, 2d ed., 526; Wim Wiewel and Joseph Persky, eds, *Suburban Sprawl: Private Decisions and Public Policy* (New York: Routledge, 2015).

111. William Schneider, "The Suburban Century Begins: The Real Meaning of the 1992 Election," *Atlantic Monthly* (July 1992): 33–44; Nicolaides and Wiese, eds., *Suburb Reader*, 2d ed., 406.

112. Geismer, *Don't Blame Us*, 20.

113. Niedt, *Social Justice in Diverse Suburbs*, 4.

114. In 2002, 1,800 cars were impounded in Maywood, only 7 of these for drunk driving.

115. Genevieve Carpio, Clara Irazábal, and Laura Pulido, "Right to the Suburb? Rethinking Lefebvre and Immigrant Activism," *Journal of Urban Affairs* 33.2 (2011): 185–208.

116. Laura Pulido, "Rethinking Environmental Racism: White Privilege and Urban Development in Southern California," *Annals of the Association of American Geographers* 90 (2000): 12–40; Karen Brodkin, *Power Politics: Environmental Activism in South Los Angeles* (New York: Rutgers University Press, 2009).

117. Niedt, *Social Justice in Diverse Suburbs*, passim; also see Audrey Singer, Susan W. Hardwick, and Caroline B. Brettell, eds., *Twenty-First Century Gateways: Immigrant Incorporation in Suburban America* (Washington, DC: Brookings Institution Press, 2008).

118. Bruce Katz, Mark Munro, and Jennifer Bradley, "Miracle Mets: Our Fifty States Matter a Lot Less Than Our 100 Largest Metro Areas," *Democracy: A Journal of Ideas*, 12 (Spring 2009): 22–35. Also see William Barnes and Larry C. Ledebur, *The New Regional Economies: The U.S. Common Market and the Global Economy* (Thousand Oaks, CA: Sage Publications, 1998); Neal R. Peirce, *Citistates: How Urban America Can Prosper in a Competitive World* (Washington, DC: Seven Locks Press, 1993).

119. Manuel Pastor Jr., Peter Dreier, J. Eugene Grigsby III, and Marta Lopez-Garza, *Regions that Work: How Cities and Suburbs Can Grow Together* (Minneapolis: University of Minnesota Press, 2000), 3.

120. For examples of this work, see Pastor et al., *Regions that Work*; David Rusk, *Inside Game/Outside Game: Winning Strategies for Saving Urban America* (Washington, DC: Brookings Institution, 2001); Peter Dreier, John Mollenkopf, and Todd Swanstrom, *Place Matters: Metropolitics for the Twenty-First Century*, 3d ed. (Lawrence: University Press of Kansas, 2014); Chris Benner and Manuel Pastor, *Just Growth: Inclusion and Prosperity in America's Metropolitan Regions* (New York: Routledge, 2012); Chris Benner and Manuel Pastor, *Equity, Growth, and Community: What the Nation Can Learn from America's Metro Areas* (Berkeley: University of California Press, 2015).

121. Orfield, *American Metropolitics*.

122. From "Smart Growth Principles," from the Maryland Department of Planning's Smart Growth Website.

123. Orfield, *American Metropolitics*, 111.

124. The Del Mar Station Project in Pasadena, California, exemplifies New Urbanism principles. It is a transit-oriented development that combines apartments (including 15 percent affordable units), retail, restaurants, and a plaza, all adjacent to a Metro station. In 2003, it won a Congress for New Urbanism Charter Award.

125. The Charter of the New Urbanism.

126. Davis, *City of Quartz*, 159.

127. Mike Maciag, "Gentrification in America Report," *Governing: The States and Localities*, February 2015; Abigail Savitch-Lew, "Gentrification Spotlight: How Portland Is Pushing Out Its Black Residents," *Colorlines*, Apr 18, 2016. http://www.colorlines.com/articles/gentrification-spotlight-how-portland-pushing-out-its-black-residents.

128. Leigh Gallagher, *The End of the Suburbs* (New York: Penguin, 2014), 5. Also see Thomas J. Sugrue, "The New American Dream: Renting," *Wall Street Journal*, August 14, 2009.

129. Jed Kolko, "2015 U.S. Population Winners: The Suburbs and the Sunbelt," *Atlantic CityLab*, March 24, 2016. http://www.citylab.com/housing/2016/03/2015-us-population-winners-the-suburbs-and-the-sunbelt/475251/.

130. On retrofitting, see June Williamson, "Retrofitting Levittown," *Places* 17.2 (2005); on spatial stasis in the midst of demographic

change, see Nicolaides and Zarsadiaz, "Design Assimilation in Suburbia.

131. "The Magic of Crabgrass: Thirty Years Later, An Appraisal of Kenneth Jackson's Crabgrass Frontier (Best of UHA 2014, Part 2)," Tropics of Meta blogsite, October 15, 2014.

132. Carol O'Connor, *A Sort of Utopia: Scarsdale, New York, 1891–1981* (Albany: State University of New York Press, 1983); John Archer, *Architecture and Suburbia: From English Villa to American Dream House, 1690–2000* (Minneapolis: University of Minnesota Press, 2005); Mary Corbin Sies, "Paradise Retained: An Analysis of Persistence in Planned, Exclusive Suburbs, 1880–1980," *Planning Perspectives* 12 (1997): 165–191; Michael Ebner, *Creating Chicago's North Shore: A Suburban History* (Chicago: University of Chicago Press, 1988). Also see Keating, "Suburbanization Before 1945," *Oxford Research Encyclopedia of American History*, for more works on the early period.

133. Barbara M. Kelly, *Expanding the American Dream: Building and Rebuilding Levittown* (Albany: State University of New York Press, 1993); Dianne Harris, ed., *Second Suburb: Levittown, Pennsylvania* (Pittsburgh: University of Pittsburgh Press, 2010); Baxandall and Ewen, *Picture Windows*.

134. Kruse and Sugrue, *New Suburban History*, 6.

135. Jon Teaford, *City and Suburb: The Political Fragmentation of Metropolitan America, 1850–1970* (Baltimore: Johns Hopkins University Press, 1979); Jon Teaford, *Post-Suburbia: Government and Politics in the Edge Cities* (Baltimore: Johns Hopkins University Press, 1997). Robert Self, *American Babylon: Race and the Struggle for Postwar Oakland* (Princeton NJ: Princeton University Press, 2003); Matthew Lassiter, *The Silent Majority: Suburban Politics in the Sunbelt South* (Princeton NJ: Princeton University Press, 2006); Kevin Kruse, *White Flight: Atlanta and Making of Modern Conservatism* (Princeton NJ: Princeton University Press, 2007).

136. Geismer, *Don't Blame Us*; Andrew Highsmith, *Demolition Means Progress: Flint, Michigan, and the Fate of the American Metropolis* (Chicago: University of Chicago Press, 2015); Ansley Erickson, *Making the Unequal Metropolis: School Desegregation and its Limits* (Chicago: University of Chicago Press, 2015); Andrew

Needham and Allen Dieterich-Ward, "Beyond the Metropolis: Metropolitan Growth and Regional Transformation in Postwar America," *Journal of Urban History* 35.7 (2009): 943–969; Allen Dieterich-Ward, *Beyond Rust: Metropolitan Pittsburgh and the Fate of Industrial America*, Politics and Culture in Modern America (Philadelphia: University of Pennsylvania Press, 2015); Lila Berman, *Metropolitan Jews: Politics, Race, and Religion in Postwar Detroit* (Chicago: University of Chicago Press, 2015).

137. Dolores Hayden, *Redesigning the American Dream: The Future of Housing, Work, and Family Life* (New York: W. W. Norton, 1984).

138. Arnold Hirsch, *Making the Second Ghetto*; Thomas Sugrue, *Origins of the Urban Crisis*; George Lipsitz, *The Possessive Investment in Whiteness: How White People Profit from Identity Politics* (Philadelphia: Temple University Press, 1998).

139. David Freund, *Colored Property: State Policy and White Racial Politics in Suburban America* (Chicago: University of Chicago Press, 2007); Robert Self, *American Babylon*; Eric Avila, *Popular Culture in the Age of White Flight: Fear and Fantasy in Suburban Los Angeles* (Berkeley: University of California Press, 2004). On the production of heteronormativity in postwar suburbia, see Clayton Howard, "Building a 'Family Friendly' Metropolis: Sexuality, the State, and Postwar Housing Policy," *Journal of Urban History* 2013.

140. Andrew Wiese, *Places of Their Own: African American Suburbanization in the Twentieth Century* (Chicago: University of Chicago Press, 2004); Emily Straus, *Death of a Suburban Dream: Race and Schools in Compton, California* (Philadelphia: University of Pennsylvania Press, 2014); Matthew Garcia, *A World of Its Own: Race, Labor, and Citrus in the Making of Greater Los Angeles, 1900–1970* (Chapel Hill: University of North Carolina Press, 2002); Jerry Gonzalez, "'A Place in the Sun': Mexican Americans, Race, and the Suburbanization of Los Angeles, 1940–1980" (PhD diss., University of Southern California, 2009), Nicolaides, *My Blue Heaven*. Also see Kruse and Sugrue, eds., *The New Suburban History*; Matthew D. Lassiter and Christopher Niedt, "Suburban Diversity in Postwar America," *Journal of Urban History* 39.1 (January 2013): 3–14; Nicolaides and Wiese, eds., *The Suburb Reader*, 2d ed., especially chapters 7 and 14.

141. Key works included William H. Frey, "Melting Pot Cities and Suburbs: Racial and Ethnic Change in Metro America in the 2000s," Brookings Institution *State of Metropolitan America* series 30 (May 4, 2011), Audrey Singer, Susan W. Hardwick, and Caroline B. Brettell, eds., *Twenty-First Century Gateways: Immigrant Incorporation in Suburban America* (Washington, DC: Brookings Institution Press, 2008); Michael B. Katz, Matthew J. Creighton, Daniel Amsterdam, and Merlin Chowkwanyun, "Immigration and the New Metropolitan Geography," *Journal of Urban Affairs* 32.5 (2010): 523–547.

142. "Most suburban" quote is from Susan Hardwick, "Toward a Suburban Immigrant Nation," in Audrey Singer, Susan W. Hardwick, and Caroline B. Brettell, eds., *Twenty-First Century Gateways: Immigrant Incorporation in Suburban America* (Washington, DC, 2008), 45. On Asian American suburban historiography, see Becky M. Nicolaides, "Introduction: Asian American Suburban History," *Journal of American Ethnic History* 34.2 (Winter 2015): 5–17. For example, see Min Zhou, Yen-Fen Tseng, and Rebecca Y. Kim, "Rethinking Residential Assimilation: The Case of a Chinese Ethnoburb in the San Gabriel Valley, California," *Amerasia Journal* 34.3 (2008): 55–83; Wei Li, *Ethnoburb: The New Ethnic Community in Urban America* (Honolulu: University of Hawaii, 2009); Charlotte Brooks, *Alien Neighbors, Foreign Friends: Asian Americans, Housing, and the Transformation of Urban California* (Chicago: University of Chicago Press, 2009).

143. Geismer, *Don't Blame Us*; Niedt, ed., *Social Justice in Diverse Suburbs*; Carpio et al. "Right to the Suburb."

144. Harris, ed., *Second Suburb*, 363 n3.

Becky Nicolaides and Andrew Wiese

ASIAN AMERICAN SUBURBAN CULTURE SINCE WORLD WAR II

COLD WAR ASIAN AMERICAN SUBURBAN PIONEERS, 1945–1968

Before World War II, Asian immigrants and Asian Americans were largely restricted to living in urban slums with decrepit housing and infrastructure, poor amenities, overcrowding, and disease. However, significant numbers—especially Japanese, Filipino, and South Asians—worked and settled in neighborhoods and small towns in the rural fringes and unincorporated areas of metropolitan industrial centers, dating back to the mid-1800s.[1] While some purchased homes in these "suburbs," by the early 20th century a formidable combination of white supremacist laws, policies, and practices were codified to effectively exclude Asians from homeownership. Japanese immigrants in the western United States, for instance, faced Alien Land Laws that barred "aliens ineligible for citizenship" from purchasing and owning property. In addition, racially restrictive covenants—private contractual agreements in deeds that prohibit the purchase, lease, or occupation of a property by a particular racial group widely accepted by the housing industry and enforced by developers and real estate professionals—excluded Asian Americans from new suburban housing markets.[2]

The end of World War II was a watershed in Asian American suburbanization. A series of events, including challenges to housing discrimination that involved legal and court battles as well as a bit of ingenuity and law breaking, pried open the door for Asian Americans to enter suburban neighborhoods. Asian American veterans, many of whom fought for the United States in segregated ranks, were among the first to settle. They returned from the war hoping for racial equality and the American Dream. For many, this meant a new home in the suburbs with plentiful space, good schools, and rising property values.[3] By 1947, many had successfully seized that dream, usually by purchasing covenanted homes from white sellers.[4] Tommy Amer, a 24-year-old Chinese American World War II veteran, bought a covenanted home in South Los Angeles in 1946, fully aware it was in an area limited to "persons of the white or Caucasian race."[5] Nearby, Korean American Yin Kim and his wife also purchased a home in the racially restricted neighborhood of Arlington Heights, where they quietly moved into the home in the middle of the night to avoid detection by neighbors and having an injunction filed against them to prevent them from physically occupying their new home.[6]

This strategic process of succession and housing integration incited the wrath of white neighbors. A plethora of lawsuits to remove Asian Americans from their homes for violating racially restrictive covenants ensued. Asian Americans, more out of necessity than for racial justice, responded by engaging in legal battles against race-based housing restrictions. Thus, they were key participants in the struggle for housing desegregation. Interracial community organizations and alliances played a major role, especially in Los Angeles. Multiracial groups like the Wilshire Defense Committee and the Los Angeles Committee Against Restrictive Covenants provided legal counsel and fought for nonwhite families desperate to keep their covenanted homes.[7] These organizations and the individuals they represented, which included Amer and Kim, quickly gained national significance and became part of a larger movement to dismantle racially restrictive covenants and push for racial desegregation around the country. Both the Amer and Kim cases were among the seven lawsuits admitted for review by the US Supreme Court that, despite the Court's opting not to hear them, ultimately informed the Court's landmark *Shelley v. Kraemer* ruling in 1948 that banned the state from enforcing restrictive covenants.[8]

While the *Kraemer* decision opened up new housing opportunities for Asian Americans in the 1950s, the decision did not allow them to buy anywhere they desired. Since a majority of Asian American suburban "pioneers" did not move into exclusively white neighborhoods but ones that were in racial transition (yet still restricted), the ruling simply expanded neighborhoods in which they and other nonwhites already lived. Moreover, the decision did not

bring down racial barriers in housing. It only forbade state enforcement of restrictive covenants—not housing discrimination itself. With this loophole, private builders and developers as well as public agencies and laws, such as the Federal Housing Administration and the Servicemen's Readjustment Act of 1944 (better known as the GI Bill), engaged in and encouraged practices to maintain all-white suburban residences and kept them off limits to Asian Americans.[9] White homeowners also turned to a wide range of extra-legal tactics—realtor discrimination and steering, intimidation, vandalism, and threats of violence—to "protect" neighborhoods from nonwhite infiltration. Others simply sold their homes and left. Even though, as historian Charlotte Brooks argues, white homeowners viewed Asian Americans as more acceptable neighbors than African Americans, they remained steadfast in their opposition to live next to Asian Americans.[10]

In the 1960s a confluence of factors shifted views of Asian Americans in ways that accelerated their suburbanization. US Cold War racial liberalism and postwar expansion into Asia and the Pacific refashioned Asian Americans from racially unassimilable "aliens ineligible for citizenship" to ethnically assimilable "model minorities." As the new global leader, America's desire to build strategic alliances with Asian nations and peoples to achieve foreign policy objectives in the region generated a "mood of greater acceptance" of Asian Americans as "foreign friends."[11] This eased their entry into white suburban neighborhoods, albeit in a liminal status between integrated and marginalized.[12] As model minorities, Asian Americans were characterized as having the right cultural values to be good suburbanites, namely a commitment to the heterosexual nuclear family and traditional gender roles rooted in Confucian and patriarchal values, which white Americans recognized and commended because they conformed to their suburban norms.[13]

Meanwhile, a seismic political, economic, and spatial transformation was taking place in the United States, as residential developments, jobs, resources and amenities relocated from urban cores to outer fringes of sprawling metropolitan areas. This shift, what historian Robert Self describes as the "overdevelopment of suburbs and the underdevelopment of cities," made suburban living not only more attractive but in many ways a necessity for the American Dream.[14] In addition, the federal Fair Housing Act of 1968 made suburban housing available to more nonwhites by closing loopholes in the *Shelley v. Kraemer* (1948) ruling and prohibiting discriminatory housing practices based on race, religion, and national origin.

Moreover, "new" Asian immigration also fueled the movement of Asian Americans into suburbia. The number of Asian Americans grew dramatically from 490,000 in 1940 to approximately 18.2 million in 2010 (5.8 percent of the population).[15] Postwar US capitalist intervention, militarization, and war in Asia and the Pacific induced an influx of migrants, refugees, and war brides from "new" countries—Thailand, Vietnam, Cambodia, Laos, Korea, and India—as well as familiar ones—China, Japan, and the Philippines. At the same time, the Immigration Act of 1965 generated increased immigration and demographic diversity that changed not only the makeup of Asian America but also its settlement patterns. The federal legislation dismantled Asian exclusion by effectively eliminating the 1924 national origins quota system based on a hierarchy of racial desirability that had favored Northern Europeans and banned Asians.[16] The law also established a preference for family reunification and individuals with educational or job skills, which resulted in a leveling of gender ratios and stark class bifurcation (well-educated, middle-class entrepreneurs, managers, and professionals on one end; low-wage, service-sector, and manufacturing laborers on the other). More importantly, it led to settlement in not just central cities but also suburbs.[17]

POPULATING AND SETTLING THE VARIEGATED SUBURBS, 1968–2018

From the 1970s onward, Asian Americans emerged as "the most suburban" of all nonwhite groups in the United States.[18] By 2010, a majority of Asians—62 percent, roughly 10.7 million people—lived in the suburbs, with South Asian Indian Americans and Korean Americans ranking at the top. In addition to attracting many US-born Asians, they also became the preferred gateway communities for Asian newcomers who bypassed immigrant enclaves in central cities and opted instead for the suburbs upon arrival. Asian American suburbanization reflected a much larger explosion in the diversification of suburbia after the 1970s that included more Latinos and African Americans as well as young singles, one-parent families, retirees, and gays and lesbians.[19] For example, in 1970 racial and ethnic minorities made up only 10 percent of the suburban population; by 2010 they grew to 35 percent.[20] In 2000, for the first time ever, a majority (52 percent) of foreign-born residents in the United States called the suburbs home. And in some metropolitan areas—Atlanta, Dallas, Orlando, Las Vegas—up to 75 percent of immigrants lived in suburban neighborhoods.[21]

While an overwhelming majority of Asian Americans settled first in the suburbs of California and the West, by 2000 they had also suburbanized in other regions and nearly all major metropolitan areas. In 1950s California, they gained entry into middle-class white suburbs like Crenshaw, Gardena, and Monterey Park in Los Angeles and Menlo Park, Palo Alto, and San Jose in the San Francisco Bay Area. A couple of decades later, many found suburban residence in Pacoima in the San Fernando Valley, Alhambra, Arcadia, San Marino, and other cities across the San Gabriel Valley, and Garden Grove and Westminster in Orange County in Southern California. In Northern California, the number of Asian

Americans in Milpitas, Cupertino, and Sunnyvale in Silicon Valley, Fremont and Union City in Alameda County, and Daly City in south San Francisco increased significantly since the 1980s. This pattern also played out during this period in other major cities like Chicago and New York City. A sizable number of Taiwanese immigrants, for instance, moved to Flushing in Queens, New York, and by the early 1990s, Edison and Iselin in Middlesex County, New Jersey became hubs for "suburban sahibs," while Fort Lee and Palisades Park in Bergen County witnessed their Korean populations explode. By the early 21st century, Asian Americans had moved most rapidly into the suburbs of Detroit, Washington, DC, Phoenix, and Las Vegas as well as of the southern and southeastern cities of Houston, Dallas, Atlanta, Orlando, and Tampa.

Asian Americans lived in, and helped shape, different types of suburbs with varying degrees and patterns of ethnic expression. Many, no doubt, dispersed into predominantly white suburban neighborhoods. Others, meanwhile, scattered into multiracial, multiethnic ones. Some resided in, as with Indians in Phoenix, what geographer Emily Skop calls "invisiburbs"—suburban spaces in which all external traces of their ethnicity are muted, effectively "invisible," and therefore unidentifiable in the homes, businesses, and institutions that represent them.[22] In contrast, a significant number, such as the Chinese in Monterey Park, clustered together and generated heavily immigrant, transnational suburbs with assertive, highly visible ethnic expression in the built landscape of the neighborhood itself—which Wei Li has dubbed as "ethnoburbs." They also resided in all sorts of suburban types in the spectrum between invisiburbs and ethnoburbs, including majority-Asian suburbs like Daly City, Milpitas, Monterey Park, and Rosemead in California, and "cosmoburbs"—rapidly growing, heavily populated (more than 100,000) large suburban municipalities where a vast number of residents are homeowners, highly educated high-tech and white-collar professionals—such as Silicon Valley's Cupertino; Plano, Texas; and Bellevue, Washington.[23]

The suburbs inhabited by Asian Americans also were not created equal: They expressed a sharply growing class inequality among Asian Americans and embodied the class heterogeneity of American suburbs as a whole. In the 1970s, a combination of economic factors and public policies accelerated class inequality across suburbia, evidenced by the rapid growth of both poorer, deprived suburbs and more affluent, upscale suburban communities. Asian Americans could be found, as historian Becky Nicolaides points out, in every type of suburb across this gamut, a pattern that registered the incredible class and ethnic diversity of post-1965 Asian America itself (a diversity that remapped onto suburban spaces).[24] In California, wealthy Asians lived in opulent and well-gated suburban residences like Cupertino, Palo Alto, San Marino, and Palos Verdes where they enjoyed the privileges of high-quality schools, sound infrastructure, and fiscal isolation. Houston's Sugarland and John's Creek of Atlanta also became home to affluent South Asian Indians, Chinese, and Koreans. Middle-class Asians settled in Bellevue, Washington; Plano, Texas; Chicago's Schaumberg; Edison, New Jersey; Flushing, New York; Phoenix's East Valley; and Cerritos, Diamond Bar, Irvine, Walnut, San Mateo, and Fremont in California. On the other hand, the Korean suburbanites in Fort Lee and Palisades Park, New Jersey, and Garden Grove, California, were lower-middle and working class. Vietnamese residents, too, found homes in the lower-middle-class suburbs of San Jose and Westminster in California and in northern Virginia. And in the working-class suburbs of Pacoima, El Monte, and Rosemead in California, various ethnic Asian groups enjoyed their versions of the suburban good life as they struggled to find jobs and fought for resources to improve schools alongside mostly other people of color, especially Latinos.

These multifaceted, ever-changing suburban types, many of which were 21st-century formations, captured the broader spatial transformations of American suburbs themselves as a whole, especially their urbanization. As metropolitan areas witnessed the acceleration in the suburban periphery of attributes typically associated with urban centers—jobs, factories, shopping centers, entertainment, class heterogeneity, racial and ethnic diversity, immigrants, gangs, and crime—suburbia itself became an increasingly complex place that scholars have tried to define with designations like "postsuburbia," "outer city," "urban village," "edge city," and "exopolis," to list a few.[25]

To be sure, much of our knowledge is weighted to the West Coast, especially California. This is primarily because of the region's heavy concentration of Asian Americans dating back to late 19th- and early 20th-century migration and settlement patterns. The West Coast was also where some of the first Asian American struggles and victories for suburban housing took place. Furthermore, major metropolitan areas in the region, namely Los Angeles and the San Francisco Bay Area, are representative sites of post-1945 mass suburbanization and turn-of-the-21st-century suburban transformations.

California and the West, however, were hardly a stand-in for understanding the formation of Asian American suburbs and experiences of Asian American suburbanites as a whole. Asian American suburban culture differed by region and location. In fact, Asian American suburbs and suburban lives throughout the West Coast, including even within a single city, were quite different depending on location and neighborhood. Regionally and locally specific histories and contexts—of racial formation, race relations, immigration, class structures, gender conventions, political activism, environment, design, and land use, to

name only a few—made Asian American suburbs, to a degree, unique from one place to the next.

Relatedly, political jurisdiction also shaped Asian American suburban culture in meaningful ways. A majority of the suburbs occupied by Asian Americans were independently incorporated cities with locally elected officials (typically a mayor and city councilmembers) and municipal services, such as Monterey Park, Arcadia, San Marino, Torrance, Westminster, Fremont, Falls Church, Plano, and Sugarland. Others were similarly structured and governed suburban townships (Edison), villages (Schaumberg), and boroughs (Fort Lee, Palisades Park). Some were neighborhoods and communities, including unincorporated towns, inside much larger metropolitan areas. The political structure of these suburbs was important to postwar Asian American suburban culture because it influenced engagement in local politics and political representation. In addition, politics shaped the size and scope of design and architecture through planning commissions and the creation and enforcement of zoning laws. It also determined school districts and educational curriculum. Moreover, it affected attempts to seize tax dollars and flows of capital, capture services, and attract businesses and industry.

One thing is clear: During the second half of the 20th century, American suburbs were shaken and transformed by increased racial, ethnic, and class diversification—and Asian Americans played a lead role. The middle-class white neighborhood with nuclear families consisting of a male breadwinner and stay-at-home mom—the archetype of 1950s suburbia—proved to be more of an ideal (yet still a very powerful one) than a reality. By the turn of the 21st century, the suburbs were multifaceted, heterogeneous, and elaborate places not entirely rooted in white suburban homeowner culture and politics characterized by hostile privatism, individualism, defensive localism, and private property values.

CLAIMING A "RIGHT TO THE SUBURB": ASIAN AMERICAN SUBURBAN CULTURE

The settlement of Asians from different ethnic, national, and class backgrounds into suburban neighborhoods profoundly impacted their communities and identities as well as suburbia as a whole. In essence, they did not simply inhabit the suburbs—they reshaped them and themselves through a range of social and cultural practices. Some reinforced suburban norms; some recrafted and changed the function of spaces; others resisted and challenged them altogether. Asian suburban settlement was a complicated process that cannot be understood simply as assimilation into whiteness. Rather, they merged their dynamic ethnic practices and proclivities with those of dominant American culture and society, blended the local with the national and global, and articulated all of this in physical places. In the process, they made claims on suburban space and tried to assert themselves as full-fledged participants in suburban culture and life.

These claims did not go uncontested. They resulted from hard-fought struggles as Asian American social and cultural practices led to conflicts with other suburbanites that often erupted into heated, racialized battles over immigration, assimilation, and multiculturalism. Significantly, these battles coincided with (and fueled) the rise of Asian American political culture in the suburbs. By the 1980s, Asian American political engagement flourished in suburbia, which included a number of Asian Americans and Asian immigrants who ran for and were elected to local office. Some elected officials, like Chinese American Judy Chu from Monterey Park, even moved on to positions at the state and federal level.[26] Formal political organizations, groups, and networks—both pan-ethnic and ethnic-specific— with views and commitments that spanned the political spectrum exploded and gained influence, too. This activity contributed to the growth of suburbs as "incubators for ethnic politics" in ways that informed Asian American politics in the United States more broadly.[27] Above all, navigating and making inroads into suburban politics allowed Asian American suburbanites to not only establish more of a presence but also the ability to shape and define suburbia more effectively. This was a critical part of the story of Asian American suburban culture.

Offering a synthesis of Asian American suburban culture and how it grew out of struggle and contention is daunting given the sheer complexity and diversity of Asian America, coupled with the fact that suburbs themselves are kaleidoscopic and ever-changing places. However, a few significant overlapping and interrelated themes and patterns emerge from existing scholarship that provide a glimpse into this rich history.

Everyday Life. From the outset, domestic life was a meaningful site of Asian American cultural citizenship in suburbia. Some of the first Asian American suburban families during the Cold War comported, at least in public, to the era's prevailing white middle-class heteronormative domesticity centered squarely on the nuclear family to prove that they were assimilated Americans with the right values to live in the suburbs. Driven by the need to project the superiority of American democracy and racial equality abroad to secure Asian allies, many whites began describing and representing Asian Americans positively as sharing the same attributes with white Americans. As Charlotte Brooks writes, Asians were "people who shared the kinds of values that whites usually identified exclusively with themselves and their neighborhoods," which formed the basis for the model minority myth.[28] When Sing Sheng, a foreign-born Chinese World War II veteran who served in the Chinese Nationalist Army, and his American-born wife and son became embroiled in a widely publicized fight to purchase a home in the restricted white suburban neighborhood of Southwood in San Francisco in the early 1950s, local newspapers featured him properly performing his assigned gender role as father, husband, and more importantly, head of a heterosexual nuclear family.[29] As historian Cindy I-Fen Cheng contends, doing so constructed Sheng and his family as "fully assimilated into the American way of life" and "facilitated a cultural enfranchisement" into the nation's suburbs more than Sheng's identity as a middle-class, college-educated veteran did alone.[30]

Asian Americans also immersed themselves in their neighborhoods outside the home. They participated in an array of social activities, community events, and everyday socializing and bonding. In postwar Crenshaw, Japanese Americans were active in school clubs, such as the Japanese American club at Dorsey High School, formed street gangs, went to Centenary church and Senshin temple, strolled the promenade and enjoyed summer Obon festivals at Crenshaw Plaza, grabbed a bite and knocked over pins at the 24-hour Holiday Bowl, and received fresh fish, tofu, and nori from door-to-door delivery "fish man" Chiharu Ikeda.[31] Throughout the 1980s, Vietnamese in Orange County attended *ao dai* pageants to raise funds for refugees and orphans of the Vietnam war, listened to the latest Vietnamese songs and watched music videos—recorded and produced locally in hi-tech studios—and strutted onto nightclub dance floors in Little Saigon.[32] In northern Virginia, just outside the greater Washington, DC, area, their fellow countrywomen and men spent their days shopping and eating in Clarendon's Little Saigon, which grew into a hub of Vietnamese American suburban social and cultural life on the East Coast.[33]

While this engagement was often mono-ethnic, Asian Americans also interacted frequently with African Americans and Latinos, engaging in high levels of social intimacy—deep friendships, romantic relationships, and marriages—in ways that profoundly shaped their identities. In 1960s Los Angeles, Japanese Americans and African Americans on the Westside developed strong relationships as they shared the same streets, shopping centers, and recreational spaces. The Holiday Bowl, for instance, was an especially vibrant site of multiracial interaction and integration that brought Asian and Black suburbanites together for decades. The Bowl, fondly remembered by patrons as a hub of the black and Japanese communities in Crenshaw, housed a popular coffee shop that served Chinese food and later Japanese dishes and black soul food, which drew in large late-night and Sunday brunch crowds.[34] Some Japanese American and black youth, in addition, were part of the same street gang out of Dorsey High, the Ministers.[35] On the Eastside, meanwhile, Asian Americans experienced similar kinds of interracial and cross-cultural interactions and relationships but mostly with Latinos. As Wendy Cheng's work on San Gabriel Valley suburbs uncovered, they spent time in each other's homes, dated, married, and started families.[36] The influence of interactions with African Americans and Latinos on Asian American identities in the 1960s, particularly for youth, came through at the annual Nisei Week Carnival in Little Tokyo, where, as Evelyn Yoshimura remembered, one could clearly tell the difference between young Japanese American men from the Westside and the Eastside: Crenshaw boys sported bellbottoms and a "pimp walk," while the Chicano-influenced kids from Boyle Heights and Monterey Park wore vato-style chinos and T-shirts.[37]

Queer identity-making was another feature of Asian American suburban life. Finding themselves pushed outside of suburbia's heteronormative culture of conformity rooted in the nuclear family, queer Asian Americans constructed, negotiated, and affirmed their identities through an array of consumer-based practices in the margins. Karen Tongson's pathbreaking work has excavated the way immigrant and working-class Asian American queer youth in Orange County turned the

Studio K dance club at the hyperconservative Knott's Berry Farm into a world that, while not overtly "queer" or Asian American, fostered nascent desires, identities, and affinities between queer Asian American teens, even if brief and fleeting.[38] In these kinds of space they not only built community and a sense of belonging, but also used them to survive suburbia's deeply ingrained cultural structure and imaginary that rendered queerness non-normative, unfit, and abject.

Foodways were also an integral part of postwar Asian American suburban culture. Asian grocery stores, restaurants, and other food establishments sustained Asian American suburban life with "authentic" ingredients, foodstuffs, and cuisine. In addition to the crossing of racial and ethnic boundaries, they were also places for face-to-face interactions among co-ethnics across class, generational, and citizenship lines. They preserved and recreated cultural heritage and a tangible sense of ethnic, diasporic, and transnational identity that made Asian American experiences and acculturation into highly racialized suburban spaces a bit less unsettling.[39] Grocery stores small and large triggered nostalgia for the homeland and alleviated feelings of displacement while also making the "work" of shopping in the suburbs a much more communal and social activity.[40] Rick Bonus's ethnography of Filipino-owned "Oriental" grocery stores in suburban strip malls across Los Angeles and San Diego in the early 1990s revealed the way these small retail shops acted as key sites where the "collective pleasurable practices" of Filipino American suburbanites constructed, imagined, and articulated Filipinoness in particular and "Otherness" more broadly through the consumption of commodities from the Philippines, odors, and magazines and newspapers.

Inside restaurants, Asian American restaurateurs and patrons forged racialized ethnic, national, and regional culinary identities. Asian cuisine was not new to the postwar suburbs. It was introduced in the 1950s and 1960s by several Polynesian restaurants along with white American suburban housewives via "Oriental" cookbooks, themed dinner parties, and cooking classes. However, the number of Asian restaurants in the suburbs owned and operated by Asians catering to Asians exploded in the 1980s. This expansion involved not only the sheer quantity of eateries but also more diversity, complexity, and depth of tastes and flavors. More culinary styles and types of cuisines from "new" countries and regions from Asia and the Pacific enhanced the typical Cantonese-dominated suburban Asian food scene. In fact, some of the top Asian restaurants in metropolitan areas were found in suburban strip malls. For example, Wonder Seafood in Monterey Park, which opened in 1988 to join the roughly fifty Chinese restaurants in the area, served up dishes like abalone and duck hot pot, ground pigeon glazed with plum sauce, a house special three-snake soup featuring cobra, and "Fo Tiao Qiang"—a stew-style dish originating from China's Fujian province that consisted of abalone, fish maw, sea cucumber, conch, soft-shell turtle, and a variety of other ingredients, and a favorite among Taiwanese in the area.[41]

Across town in the San Fernando Valley, Thai chef Mongkorn Kaiswai brought regional diversity to Los Angeles's Thai restaurants by cooking "searingly hot" Isaan dishes with "a fascinating balance of tastes from ingredients traditionally used in his native northeastern Thailand" that gave "distinction to the familiar."[42] As head chef at Thai Gourmet in Northridge, he earned a prestigious Gault-Millau award as the highest-rated ethnic restaurant in Los Angeles. Later, as owner and chef of Rama Thai in Van Nuys, he received rave reviews from not only his Thai clientele but also esteemed food critic Jonathan Gold, who praised Kaiswai as "perhaps the most celebrated of local Thai chefs" for giving Thai cuisine a boost beyond "the Malaysian-influenced Bangkok cooking that you might be sick of by now."[43] In the early 21st century, specialty shops serving desserts and drinks, such as boba milk tea or Vietnamese coffee, also delivered a taste of ethnic identity in all its varied forms as well as transnational spaces for suburban Asian American youth to socialize, gossip, study, or simply hang out.[44]

Cultural festivals showcasing food, music, dance, and other performances and rituals were also a key part of Asian American suburban food cultures. While Asian Americans had organized and participated in ethnic festivals for decades in urban cores, they reproduced these kinds of events in suburbia almost immediately upon arrival. At Crenshaw Square in Los Angeles, Japanese Americans put on summer Obon festivals with food booths and bon dori—traditional Japanese line dancing—"reminiscent of Nisei Week in Little Tokyo."[45] By the 1980s, days-long festivals, especially those celebrating holidays like Lunar New Year, were happening regularly at quasi-public spaces. Some were held indoors—inside high school gyms, for instance. Most, however, were so popular that they had to be held in parking lots of shopping plazas and religious centers to accommodate festivalgoers. For example, tens of thousands of Indians from the Northeast descended upon Edison, New Jersey, every year to join each other under massive tents to celebrate Navratri, a nine-day long Hindu festival filled with food, music, and dancing.[46]

As purveyors of racial and ethnic difference, food festivals were more than just entertaining exhibitions of ethnicity and cultural heritage; they were sites of conflict and debates within communities over what it meant to be Indian, Thai, or Vietnamese and how to articulate and represent such complex identities. In addition to crafting a sense of community in local neighborhoods and beyond, festivals allowed Asian Americans to announce their presence in suburban spaces. At one level, they brought new sights, sounds, aromas, and tastes to what were imagined historically to be quiet, odorless spaces.[47] At another level, as commercialized celebrations of multiculturalism that attracted many non-Asians seeking to indulge in cultures different from their own, festivals contributed to, at some level, a recognition and appreciation of Asians as members of suburbia and US society.[48]

Thus, beyond constructing and affirming identities, food sites allowed Asian American grocery store owners, restaurateurs, chefs, and food vendors to emerge as "place-makers" who brought members of their respective communities together and profoundly influenced the cultural and physical landscapes of suburbia and broader metropolitan identity. They did so not only visually with signs and decor but also by way of smells, tastes, and sounds, which helped mark suburban neighborhoods as "Asian." At the same time, however, food establishments also generated and reinforced ethnic divisions. Cuisine served as a powerful, pleasurable way for Asian Americans to distinguish themselves from others within and outside of their racial and ethnic group. As sites of labor and work, the food industry also exacerbated class and gender divisions within communities that were often masked by the homogenous face of ethnic solidarity. Thai restaurants, for example, relied heavily on the low or unpaid labor of family and friends, especially children. When Thai restaurant owners did compensate workers, they often paid low wages well below minimum wage (and under the table) and offered little to no benefits. Many also took advantage of the labor of undocumented Thais and other immigrants. Thus, even as Asian restaurants preserved cultural heritage and fostered ethnic identities, they were simultaneously places rife with exploitation, human rights violations, poor working conditions, and sexism.

Asian American everyday practices in the suburbs produced new identities and cultures, albeit in the context of increased privatization of public space and capitalist consumption. They reflected both a certain level of mobility within and through physical suburban landscapes as well as a navigation of the dominant cultural conventions that structure suburbia.

Community Spaces and Institutions.

A wide range of community organizations and institutions provided important cultural and social outlets that brought Asian American suburbanites together, lubricated social relationships, and fostered friendships. Religious centers in particular allowed Asian Americans to practice, redefine, and put on full display their respective religious traditions in an ideal physical setting of a suburban landscape. They were, however, more than places of worship. They not only nurtured robust religious cultures but also served as community centers, hosting festivals and offering language classes and other services. For recently arrived migrants, these spaces connected them with co-ethnics and forged transnational ties as they built lives in a new country; for US-born Asian Americans, they provided places to learn about their cultural heritage and foster ethnic identity and community. In Phoenix, Arizona, for instance, gatherings at permanent sites like the Indo-American Cultural and Religious Center and the Hindu Temple of Arizona as well as meetings at "transitory" religious spaces brought together members of a heterogeneous Indian community dispersed in suburban neighborhoods throughout Phoenix to recreate a sense of Indian-ness.[49] Nestled on a scenic mountaintop in Hacienda Heights, California, the Hsi Lai Temple, an enormous Taiwanese Buddhist monastery, held meditation classes and educational programs open to all. The Wat Thai of Los Angeles in the east San Fernando Valley, California, the first and largest Thai Buddhist temple in the nation when it opened in 1979, served local Thai residents and drew thousands across Southern California and from Thailand. They visited the temple (a quasi-public space) to meditate and pray but also for the lively weekend festivals.

While many supported these events in the name of religious freedom and multiculturalism, the events also frustrated local residents and led to fierce, lengthy battles. While the negative reactions toward the function of Asian religious centers were intertwined with anti-Asian sentiment, the conflicts were more complex than just anti-Asian racism alone. They stemmed from a wide range of issues and concerns: land use, property values, the character and compatibility of Asian religious practices, the infiltration of urban ills, noise, parking, and other "quality of life" issues. The festivals at Wat Thai, for example, sparked complaints of noise, trash, and parking problems from neighborhood residents who tried using zoning law to shut them down. Though framed as a "culture clash," this particular conflict was rooted in competing visions over the use and meaning of suburban space. The opposition was fueled not entirely by personal bigotry toward Thais but could instead be seen as an attempt to reclaim a 1950s suburban ideal rooted in white middle-class values and the sanctity of private property. Thai immigrants, on the other hand, believed that a central public space, rather than the home itself, should serve as the heart and focal point of suburban life.[50]

Overt racism and xenophobia, however, surfaced in similar cases elsewhere. At around the same time, Wat Thai Buddhanusorn in Fremont, California, also dealt with intense opposition from local residents who harassed monks and the laity and tried to petition the city to stop temple construction, citing traffic, illegal parking, and violation of single-family use.[51] Anthropologist Jiemin Bao has documented that Thais were not welcomed because they were "misrecognized as poor immigrants or 'boat people,' although they were predominantly urban, affluent, well-educated professionals."[52] Temple officials were convinced that racial prejudices were "being hidden behind some legitimate claims" since the residents expressed fears that "Thai cooking smells would be offensive," "a Buddhist 'cult' would be their midst," and that Thais would "ruin the neighborhood."[53] The Hsi Lai Temple in Hacienda Heights, too, faced strong resistance from local residents. Over the course of roughly a hundred public meetings and six major zoning hearings, the residents vocalized concerns over traffic and parking, claiming that the temple was too big for the neighborhood of single-family homes, and that the "traditional" Chinese architectural style would not fit in. They also made unfounded assumptions that Hsi Lai was a religious cult that would kidnap their children, perform animal sacrifices, wake up residents with pre-dawn gongs and chanting, and disrupt peace and quiet with firecrackers.[54] Even as they admitted to being worried about the influx of Asian Americans into their majority-white suburb, most denied they were racists.

Debates over supposedly race-neutral issues like zoning and "quality of life" developed into some of the most critical political battles for Asian Americans in the suburbs during the 1980s. Asian religious centers were frequently in the middle of such debates. In these conflicts, Asian American suburbanites successfully recreated "home," built community, and affirmed ethnic identity. At the same time, they also claimed a rightful place in suburbia based on an alternative suburban ideal centered on public sociability that went against both dominant racialized imaginings of suburban life as well as zoning law and other ordinances regulating suburban space.

By the 1980s, shopping centers also emerged as premier community spaces for Asian American suburbanites. Though private enterprises, they functioned as public spaces that breathed life into communities and vibrant, multilayered suburban lives and identities. The popularity of "Asian malls" embodied the way increased privatization of public spaces and the erosion of public services in the United States blurred the line between private property and public facilities, as people treated commercial and private places—shopping malls, bookstores, coffee shops—more and more as public community centers for relaxation, socializing, and even protest.

Although shopping centers providing ethnic-specific and mainstream goods to Asian Americans existed in the 1950s, Asian malls proliferated in commercial strips around the country in the 1990s (by 2003 an estimated 140 of such complexes existed).[55] They refashioned and revived the shopping mall—the archetype of post-war suburban culture—into an even more robust social and cultural space for a wide cross section of Asian suburbanites. Many grew into one-stop destinations where Asian Americans completed their everyday errands—shopped for groceries, deposited money at a bank, visited the dentist—and pursued leisure and entertainment in restaurants, food courts, karaoke bars, beauty salons, bookstores, and music and video shops. Willow Lung-Amam's exploration of Asian malls in Silicon Valley illustrates that they also functioned as places of comfort and acceptance where Asian Americans spoke their native language and reinforced other everyday cultural practices without shame or strange looks, interacted with non-Asians, experimented with new cuisines, strengthened family bonds, met friends, discussed politics, and dressed to "see and be seen." Perhaps most important, as central hubs for Asian American suburbanites from different ethnic, national, class, and generational backgrounds, these malls served, according to Aihwa Ong, as "common ground" where "different streams of Asians become Asian-American."[56]

The importance of Asian malls extended beyond their local neighborhoods. They were transnational spaces that linked Asian migrants in real and imagined ways to their respective homelands and other members of the diaspora via capital and consumption. Often developed or revitalized with money from Asia and the Pacific, the malls not only reflected the multidirectional, complex nature of Asian American lives but became key settings for the forging of Asian American identities and communities that spanned nation-state boundaries. Southern California's Little Saigon, with its copious mini-malls and mega-mall, Phước Lộc Thọ (Asian Garden Mall), marketed and sold ethnic identity and delivered nostalgia to Vietnamese refugees searching for a bridge to loved ones. The music, videos, food, and fashion inside stores transported Vietnamese Americans, for a time, to an imagined, idealized version of "what Saigon would have been like if the South had won" as they built new lives in Orange County.[57]

Like religious centers, Asian malls generated a great deal of conflict and controversy. In a number of suburbs, local officials and residents—which, in Asian American suburbs often consisted of not just whites but people of color—deemed them nonnormative, undesirable, and foreign, rendering them out of place in the retail landscape of middle-class suburbia. Some longtime residents believed Asian shopping centers to be racially and ethnically segregated and therefore unwelcoming and uncomfortable places that, because of their "Asian" way of doing business, had destroyed their cherished tight-knit American community, charm, and way of life. The growth of Asian shopping plazas in Monterey Park in the 1980s, for instance, triggered resentment from whites, Latinos, and even Asian American residents. An older white resident reported having her day-to-day activities transformed from pleasant, warm encounters with friendly shopkeepers who said hello and tried to help—"the American way"—to being treated rudely by new Chinese storeowners who only seemed interested in customers' money.[58]

In addition, the type of shops in Asian malls became hotly debated. In several cases, city officials and residents felt their neighborhoods had too many Asian-oriented retail establishments. In response, they demanded more "traditional" retail shops, including major chain stores that appealed to "typical" middle- and upper-class suburbanites. The disputes over redevelopment in Monterey Park, according to the fieldwork of sociologist Leland Saito, included a discussion about "good" restaurants at a design review meeting in which a white woman exclaimed, "At Atlantic and Garvey [a major intersection in a commercial area] they were supposed to put in nice restaurants like the Velvet Turtle, but it ended up being totally

Oriental."[59] Moreover, others took issue with the poor quality of Asian shopping centers— their bad structural maintenance, "excessive" signage of lower quality, and "poor tenant mix."[60]

Yet, despite the resistance and pushback, Asian malls were simultaneously celebrated and shaped by the rhetoric of multiculturalism. Recognizing their political and economic value, local leaders strategically promoted Asian shopping centers in ways that showcased them as exemplars of suburban cosmopolitanism. These careful, concerted efforts flipped the racialization of Asian malls as foreign and exotic, which were used to justify their marginalization in the suburban landscape, to construct, package, and market them as destinations where suburbanites interacted with racial and cultural others and thus experienced "authentic" Asian culture via the consumption of food and entertainment. Scholars like Willow Lung-Amam and Wendy Cheng have found that local officials and developers also mobilized the notion of pluralist multiculturalism to promote diversity and inclusion in suburban redevelopment campaigns.[61] On one hand, this consumer-based "decontextualized multiculturalism" strengthened ties to the global capitalist economy to attract foreign investment that increased capital flow, a fiscal lifeline, into struggling suburbs. On the other hand, it glossed over the heated racialized conflicts about culture, identity, and use of space ignited by the malls themselves and ignored how they were effectively marginalized as out of place in the suburban cultural landscape.

Asian American everyday practices at malls and the identities they embodied and produced challenged conventional ideas of suburban public life and the purpose and function of private space, thereby allowing them to establish a place in suburbia. Yet the framing of Asian malls in the context of multiculturalism meant that they were not necessarily— by default—resistant. Instead, they sometimes functioned in service of neoliberalism and elided structural racism.

Architecture and Design. The design of private residences was important for Asian American suburbanites. Through architecture, they conformed to but also reshaped suburbia through one of the most iconic, sacred, and fiercely regulated parts of suburban life: the single-family home. For Asian American suburban pioneers in the 1950s, keeping home exterior aesthetic and landscaping in line with dominant postwar suburban design norms was key to demonstrating that they were acceptable neighbors who valued private property and were thus good Americans and good suburbanites.[62] Images of Nisei, for example, painting a picket fence or standing proudly on nicely manicured front lawns of their mass produced suburban tract homes became common postwar depictions of Asian Americans as typical suburbanites.

Asian Americans conceded to hegemonic white American landscape aesthetics and muffling Asian design elements, both willingly and through coercion, in their communities well into the later 20th century for various reasons and to different ends. This phenomenon, what Becky Nicolaides and James Zarsadiaz refer to as "design assimilation," was especially at play in middle-class "invisiburbs" and wealthy neighborhoods where, despite rapid demographic changes, Anglo architectural customs persisted.[63] For instance, after 1980 Chinese residents in San Marino, California, in spite of their growing numbers, embraced established Euro-American tastes and design principles—Tudor, Spanish Colonial Revival, Mediterranean/Italian Renaissance, and plentiful trees—because they upheld property values as well as provided an elevated class position and social distinction over fellow Chinese in "ugly" ethnoburbs such as adjacent Monterey Park.[64] Above all, this afforded a semblance of full-fledged membership into affluent suburbia locally and cultural capital in the Asian diaspora globally.

While far less common, Asian Americans expressed their ethnic identities and aesthetic precepts in subtle ways on their suburban properties. In the 1980s some of San Marino's Chinese residents removed large, healthy trees near their homes because they attracted insects and generated bad feng shui that blocked good energy from flowing into their households.[65] In high-end Arcadia, California, several Chinese homeowners increased the size and square-footage of their homes to create monster "McMansions" that towered over older, smaller existing homes. This included the home of Japanese martial artist and actor Sho Kosugi, who built an unabashed blue tile-roofed Japanese-style three-story mansion with a red bridge and a Buddhist shrine.[66] The upscale Mission Ranch neighborhood in Silicon Valley also experienced Asian "mansionization" during its mid-1990s development boom. Though not overtly "Asian" in motif, McMansions became synonymous with Asian immigrants, emanating in part from a desire among many Asian homeowners to meet what they saw as Asian cultural needs, namely more space to house and take care of parents, grandparents, and other family members.[67] With these design choices, Asian Americans perhaps unintentionally and unknowingly prioritized a commitment to their versions of ethnic culture over dominant and even legal Euro-American suburban aesthetic customs. Moreover, they asserted their right, as property owners, to make their homes in their own vision.

Both design assimilation and ethnic expressiveness extended beyond private residences into commercial areas, though unevenly. Asian ethnic culture hardly materialized on the main streets and shopping centers of design-assimilated places like San Marino. Despite having sizable Asian American populations, the businesses, shops, and signage in these suburbs had no visible trace of "Asian," save a Chinese restaurant or two. But a kaleidoscope of ethnic cultures and identities was on full display in a number of other suburbs. Even in the immediate post-war years, Asian Americans left visible ethnic imprints on commercial spaces. Historian Scott Kurashige

documents the way 1950s Los Angeles suburbs "took on a Japanese American identity in
Crenshaw," particularly with the construction
of the Crenshaw Square shopping center—a
$7-million development, located in the neigh-
borhood's main thoroughfare, that catered to
the area's growing Nisei population.[68] More
importantly, the Square "consciously promoted
ethnic character" by showcasing "Oriental"
style architecture and landscaping as distinguishing features unlike the typical whitebread "American" design of virtually every
other suburb at the time.

The display of ethnic culture and identity
intensified with the rise of ethnoburbs in the
1980s. The transnational flow of goods, peoples, capital, and businesses from Asia and the
Pacific infused and revitalized suburban commercial spaces like Monterey Park's Atlantic
Square; Bolsa Avenue of Little Saigon in
Westminster, California; the countless strip
malls of Silicon Valley; Plano, Texas's Park
Pavilion Center; northern Virginia's Eden
Center; and Broad Avenue in the heart of
Palisades Park, New Jersey, with ethnic character and design elements. These places became
lined with noticeably Asian shops and businesses speckled with multilingual signs.

This ethnic assertiveness was highly contested. Asian Americans defended it in the
face of fierce opposition. Local officials and
residents often worked to pass measures regulating design, landscaping, and structure at
the whiff of potential Asian "foreign" aesthetic encroachment into "their" neighborhoods. In the 1980s, white San Marino residents, with support from Chinese community
leaders, spearheaded a "discreet, preemptive
campaign" to shut down any possibility of
having the neighborhood's physical appearance transformed by Asian immigrants, an
effort informed by what they saw happening
next door in Monterey Park.[69] In 1987, the
city council codified Euro-American design
precepts in a plethora of detailed measures—
including an anti-mansionization ordinance and
the creation of a Design Review Committee

to enforce taste. A nastier dispute over mansionization happened in Fremont's Mission
Ranch where the mostly Asian American supporters and white opponents came out, according to one city planner, "in full force at planning commission and city council meetings"
to argue impassionedly about the impact of
large homes on aesthetic ideals, private property rights, the neighborhood's character and
"way of life," and its sense of community.[70]
New design regulations were implemented to
encourage large home owners to conform to
Mission Ranch's existing home and neighborhood character. Couched as race-neutral,
suburban design regulations in upper-class
neighborhoods like San Marino and Mission
Ranch not only laid out what residents did not
want but, at the same time, privileged, normalized, and protected Euro-American character
to set themselves apart from more visibly
ethnic suburbs.

Tensions also erupted over the expressly
Asian design of businesses and commercial
plazas. The redevelopment of Monterey Park's
Atlantic Square shopping center, a deteriorated strip mall, in the 1980s sparked heated
confrontations as white, Latino, and Asian
residents tried to select an architectural theme
and business tenants for the center. The city
council approved a "Mediterranean" style over
Chinese influences.[71] Long-term residents of
Monterey Park also became outraged over
the proliferation of Chinese signage on businesses and strip mall signs, which they saw as
a clear example of Asians' refusal to assimilate. This outrage was part of a broader movement led by a group of white residents to promote "slow growth" and make English the
city's official language. However, in the late
1980s a new coalition of Asian American and
Latino elected officials emerged who, together
with liberal whites, mobilized under the banner
of multiculturalism and civil rights to combat
and ultimately defeat anti-immigrant policies,
like English-only measures, and the officials
who supported them.[72] Decades later, Asian
Americans in Fremont, California, also fought

against city officials who implemented zoning and other regulations to coerce Asian-themed shopping malls to look and feel more like other mainstream suburban strip malls.[73] Asian American residents and developers responded mainly by claiming that city assessments were inherently biased and that city officials were out of touch with the needs and desires of the growing number of Fremont's Asian residents, which, for them, dictated the development of more Asian-themed malls, not less.

For Asian American suburbanites, push-back and regulation led to many outcomes on ethnic expressiveness in suburban residential and commercial architectural design. Some capitulated, while others compromised. Still others resisted. Even in cases where Asian Americans participated and supported design assimilation, they did not do so entirely by choice, evidenced by the fact that while many may have suppressed and veiled Asian ethnic motifs on the public faces of their homes and storefronts to present a "façade of assimilation," they also "retained robust ethnic identity in private spatial realms," according to Nicolaides and Zarsadiaz.[74] What's clear is that these decisions were made in the arena of local political institutions within the context of the power of coercion, regulation, enforcement, and policing that sought to privilege seemingly neutral, common-sense Euro-American aesthetic ideals in the suburban built environment.

Education and Schools. Education, too, emerged as a critical arena for Asian American social and cultural life in suburbia. For parents and youth, particularly middle- and upper-class Chinese and Indian Americans, educational values and "good" schools played a prominent role in their decisions concerning which neighborhoods in which to reside, in their aspirations for upward mobility and social status, and in their achieving the suburban dream. It is also where they emphatically asserted a right to the suburb.

After 1980, Asian Americans participated in the transformation of academic culture in suburbs across the country by valorizing high educational performance, especially in high schools. Though not solely responsible, Asian American parents and students altered school curriculums by raising the demand and increasing the number of honors and Advanced Placement (AP) courses, mainly in math and sciences. Asian American students helped raise school test scores, rankings, and graduation and college acceptance rates. They joined and created school clubs to pad college applications. They also took community college courses on weekends and during summers. They even shifted the culture of high school sports, avoiding quintessential "All-American" sports like football and cheerleading to compete in badminton, tennis, and chess and debate teams.[75] Mission High in San Jose, California, reflected this shift. The school, which changed from majority-white "Little Scandinavia" in the 1970s to majority Asian in 2014, became internationally renowned for high academic achievement with the arrival of Asian American and Asian immigrant students who boosted performance in nearly all measurable categories and were also accepted into the nation's most prestigious colleges and universities.[76] Asian American families not only amped up studying, rigor, and competitiveness, but in doing so also reshaped the cultural and social landscape and built environment of suburbia. The proliferation of education-centered businesses in suburban neighborhoods registered the transformation, as standardized test prep courses, after-school programs, tutors, academic summer camps, and a range of other services capitalized on the phenomenon.[77]

In suburbia, Asian Americans became associated with academic overachievement, rigor, and hyper-competitiveness. In the 1980s, Asian American academic prowess turned into a nationwide fixation that reinforced the racialization of Asian Americans as the model minority. A number of media outlets and academics applauded Asian Americans and became fascinated by the "achievement gap" between Asian Americans and non-Asian students, which fueled debates over whether their high achievement was a product of genetic superiority and higher IQs or cultural differences and values.[78] Avoiding structural explanations altogether, such as preferences in US immigration law that favored highly educated professionals, the cultural argument ultimately gained the most traction, with Asian parents deemed responsible for instilling Confucian values of education, family, and filial piety in their children that pushed them to work harder than other students.[79] Research and news reports describing strict Asian parents with high expectations pressuring obedient kids to study harder for higher grades and test scores abounded.[80] These stories turned education into a main pillar of the model minority image and positioned Asian Americans above other nonwhite groups along the US racial hierarchy because they reinforced conservative ideals of self-reliance and hard work (as opposed to demanding structural change, government assistance, and social programs). At the same time, it also framed Asian Americans and Asian immigrants together as distinctly different culturally from white Americans. The notion of academic competitiveness and "super achievement" as an "Asian" trait that was diametrically opposed to American educational culture persisted well into the 21st century. Annie Liu, a second-generation Chinese-Korean American who attended San Gabriel Valley's predominantly Asian and Latino Alhambra High School in 2013, recalled that Asian American students a few years behind her were "even more competitive" with perfect SAT scores, straight As, and involvement in countless extracurricular activities that made them "further 'Asianized' or whatever you want to call it . . . working their butts off to get into a good college."[81] She added, "whenever I encounter parents who were like, 'oh, as long as they're doing their best,' I think to myself, that's such a Westernized kind of thought, you know?"[82]

While academic prowess afforded Asian Americans a certain level of acceptance in suburbia because they elevated the rankings and success of schools (and thus increased the value of what has historically been a highly coveted suburban amenity), it also triggered resistance and backlash that reinforced racial divisions by marginalizing Asian American families as foreign and abnormal. Whites and even other Asian Americans found the dedication to educational success among Asian American families as unhealthy, inappropriate, and out of place in American suburbs. Many blamed Asian immigrant parents for not assimilating to American educational norms, expectations, and practices. At Mission High, both white and Asian American parents were critical of an academic culture increasingly driven by wealthy, elitist Asian immigrant values that was not "normal" or agreeable with typical American high school students. They responded by demanding a more "well-rounded" and "balanced" education and more active social lives they believed were "regular" and "appropriate." For example, one Mission High teacher revealed the sentiment of several disgruntled parents, saying, "There are no electives available for the White students that the parents felt were appropriate. All you're doing is upping the advanced placement this, advanced placement that. This is no longer a traditional, regular high school that is amenable to a regular kid."[83] Many responded by simply leaving schools (and neighborhoods) altogether, triggering a new wave of white flight.

Education played a profound role in Asian American identity formation and lived experiences in the suburbs. For Asian American youth especially, the model minority stereotype impacted the way they thought of themselves and what it meant to be Asian American. Many invested in and played up to the model minority image in ways that naturalized educational values and the academic achievement gap by referring to biological notions of racial differences, which reinforced and maintained racial thinking and divisions as well as intraracial and interethnic rifts. As a result, racial stereotypes of Asian Americans as "nerds" and "curve busters" impacted social dynamics in schools, influencing who Asian Americans became friends with and how they interacted with other students. As "exceptional" students who occupied a position of "racialized privilege" in both predominantly white and multiracial, multiethnic schools, not only were Asian Americans in the same classes where they socialized mostly with other Asian Americans, but they were also valorized by school officials and peers. At the same time, the high standards that came with being perceived as model minorities, coupled with parents' demands, also generated tremendous pressure and stress. Asian American students often walked a "tightrope" between striving for perfect GPAs and test scores and their desire to go out with friends and be "normal" American teens.[84] This led to resistance and rebellion that spawned oppositional suburban Asian American youth cultures that negotiated, undermined, and outright challenged model minority expectations, a phenomenon that became so commonplace it was adopted and portrayed in Justin Lin's 2003 film *Better Luck Tomorrow*.

DISCUSSION OF THE LITERATURE

Numerous scholars—historians, sociologists, anthropologists, geographers—and journalists have unearthed and documented the social and cultural practices of Asian Americans in suburbia after World War II. As part of the growing body of literature on the increased racial and ethnic diversification of American suburbs, their research has expanded the fields of metropolitan history, Asian American studies, and immigration history, charting exciting new directions for exploration. The attention to the social, cultural, and spatial practices of Asian American suburbanites has provided significant insight into the everyday life, identities, and place-making practices within various Asian American communities to highlight the way suburbs eclipsed urban cores as the primary backdrop for Asian American experiences and emerged as preferred gateway neighborhoods for Asian newcomers.

Research examining the way Asian American social and cultural life reshaped and transformed

suburbia emerged in the 1990s. Foundational works like Timothy Fong's *The First Suburban Chinatown* (1994), Leland Saito's *Race and Politics* (1998), and Joseph Wood's "Vietnamese American Place Making in Northern Virginia" were among the first to chart Asian American suburban settlement and community formation and their impact on built and cultural landscapes, politics, economies, and networks and flows within and through specific suburban spaces.[85] Since then, a new wave of scholars like Wei Li, Min Zhou, Wendy Cheng, Becky Nicolaides, James Zarsadiaz, Emily Skop, and Jennifer Fang have made generative contributions that expand and deepen our understanding of the agency of Asian American suburbanites and their struggles to assert a "right to the suburb."[86] Going beyond internal community dynamics, they established that Asian Americans have reinforced, built off, and challenged long-standing hegemonic suburban cultures in a range of social and cultural arenas, which developed new identities, places, and what George Lipsitz calls "spatial imaginaries."[87] Together, these studies stand as the cornerstone of scholarship on Asian American suburban cultures.

One major theme and analytic approach has been explorations of racialized conflicts and antagonisms between Asian American and white suburbanites over control of suburban life. Willow Lung-Amam's *Trespassers?* (2017) offers one of the more recent and comprehensive treatments of these complex "battles for suburbia." She analyzes the way Chinese, Taiwanese, and Indian suburbanites in Silicon Valley actively fought against longtime white residents, who sought to maintain suburban norms in the face of demographic changes via race-neutral mechanisms of exclusion, in quintessential suburban sites—architectural design, shopping malls, and schools—to establish a sense of belonging and create places centered on their needs, desires, and values. Alongside Lung-Amam, the work of Wei Li, Jiemin Bao, Becky Nicolaides, and James Zarsadiaz offer further insight into the way Asian American suburbanites turned not only to formal politics, legal tactics, and protests but also to myriad cultural, social, and discursive practices to combat racial segregation, attacks on public space, and other forms of exclusion that marginalized them from full-fledged suburban citizenship, and thereby claim space and make place.[88]

Studies examining the transnational dimensions of Asian American suburban cultures have been another main thread and important trend. This approach reflects a critical diasporic and transnational perspective that interrogates the nexus between the local and the global, specifically the impact of US foreign policy, war, and the expansion of capitalism around the world on migration and social and cultural phenomena in the United States.[89] A number of scholars have recently shed light on the multidirectional, transnational lives of Asian American suburbanites by showing how they forged identities, communities, and cultures around practices and symbols across and within nation-state boundaries. This includes Nhi Lieu's exploration of the role of music, beauty pageants, websites, and other forms of leisure and entertainment in the construction of Vietnamese diasporic cultural identities in Orange County's Little Saigon; Andrew Friedman's analysis of Vietnamese lives, communities, and spaces in the deeply transnational suburbs of northern Virginia structured and underpinned by US imperialism; Jiemin Bao's work on the transnational making and maintenance of a Thai Buddhist temple in Silicon Valley; Hillary Jenks's study of Japanese Americans in Los Angeles who tapped into transnational ties to Japan during the 1960s and 1970s to develop the suburb of Gardena; and Haiming Liu and LianLian Lin's work on food, restaurants, and the formation of transnational culinary identities among Chinese immigrants in San Gabriel Valley.[90] These works illuminate how Asian American suburban cultures were transnational to the core, and show that they allowed Asian Americans to negotiate domestic US racism and America's global power in ways that facilitated their integration into and transformation of suburbia.

Scholars have also extended their analysis of Asian American suburban lifeways beyond middle- and upper-class white suburbs to working-class, multiracial and multiethnic ones. As part of the surge of studies on diverse suburbia, the work of Karen Tongson, S. Mitra Kalita, Leland Saito, Wendy Cheng, and Jean-Paul de-Guzman has exploded the conventional suburban narrative by uncovering the everyday, locally specific practices of new actors, such as cash-strapped Asian immigrant families in New Jersey and queer working-class Asian American youth in California's Inland Empire.[91] Also influenced by the comparative turn in ethnic studies, this line of inquiry also underscores how the Asian-white binary framework is too narrow and shortsighted for understanding the formation of Asian American suburban identities and cultures, especially as people of color, immigrants, and poor people moved into suburbs in greater numbers. Wendy Cheng's *The Changs Next Door to the Díazes* stands out among the more recent scholarship. She deftly illustrates the way the everyday, often shared, practices of Asian American and Latino suburbanites that occurred "beneath the public radar" in the San Gabriel Valley generated a view and experience of suburbia that embraced, to an extent, a multiracial and multiethnic sensibility.[92] This growing body of research counters the dominant notion of suburbia as white middle-class spaces of conformity and privilege. It decenters white suburbanites (but not whiteness or white supremacy) as the main actors and creators of suburban culture and, more importantly, treats the formation of Asian American suburban cultures in relation to other non-white groups as stories worth being told in their own right. Moreover, it illustrates how processes of racial formation take place on the suburban stage.

As the scholarship continues to develop, there is still much to be learned about Asian American suburban cultures in the period between 1945 and 1965. The social and cultural worlds of Cold War Asian American suburban pioneers are intriguing because they might tell us more about the impact that the era's positive sentiment toward Asia and the Pacific—"Cold War Orientalism"—had on not just easing access to suburban housing but also the daily practices and ethnic expressions of some of the first Asian Americans to navigate suburbia.[93] It is also important to continue to push demographic and geographic boundaries beyond the well-studied middle- and upper-class Chinese, Taiwanese, and Indian American suburbanites of California's San Gabriel Valley and Silicon Valley. Plenty of practices need to be explored further—foodways, schools, interior design—and others that are ripe for exploration. For example, an analysis of Asian American suburban sporting cultures, from spelling bees and golf to figure skating and import car racing, can generate valuable insights into the history of Asian American suburbanization, especially regarding the role of gender and the making of gender identities. Such investigations intersect with broader gender history as well as the budding fields of sports history and sports studies.

The goal of pushing these boundaries is more than just diversifying the cast of historical actors and suburban settings and tacking them onto the existing suburban narrative. Rather, it is to boost interrogations of the particular histories of racialization and how they inform the meaning of suburban practices for specific groups; the role of race, class, gender, sexuality, and citizenship in suburban formations in regional and local contexts; and intra-Asian ethnic interactions, antagonisms, and solidarities. Doing so will reveal what Asian Americans did after they moved into the suburbs and how that transformed suburban culture, life, and ideals.

PRIMARY SOURCES

Researchers will find it challenging to track down historical sources and materials on Asian American suburban cultures, but they do exist. Oral histories are a critical source of evidence related to the everyday lifeways of Asian Americans in suburbia. They provide important details about the inner workings and meanings of social and cultural practices not captured in the written record. However, very few interviews were created specifically to document the history of Asian American suburban cultures. Thus, researchers need to rely on portions of oral histories found in published works focused on other aspects of Asian American suburbanization and then reinterpret them under theoretical frameworks concerning race, space, and place. Furthermore, given that few scholars have made their interviews available to the public, researchers should conduct oral histories with as many Asian American suburbanites as possible, being careful to document their everyday practices and what these practices meant to them, especially with Cold War-era pioneers who are approaching their 80s and 90s.

Published articles, dissertations, and books are also valuable. Coupled with the growing number of historical works on Asian American suburbs, studies by sociologists, geographers, and anthropologists include useful data, from interviews to thick descriptions (which, too, must be reinterpreted in the context of suburban cultures). National and local newspapers and magazines, many of which have been digitized and made available electronically, are helpful as well. Outlets like *The New York Times, Los Angeles Times, AsianWeek, U.S. News & World Report,* and *Time* delivered coverage of settlement patterns, people, family dynamics, restaurants, events, activities, and conflicts between Asian American suburbanites and long-standing residents.

Researchers will have to think expansively and be creative in their approach to sources to shed light on this history. This includes having to mine for clues dispersed and scattered in archives, collections, community centers, offices, and homes across the country. General collections on Asian Americans can be found at the University of California Berkeley's Bancroft and Ethnic Studies libraries, University of California Los Angeles's

Asian American Studies Center, University of California Riverside's Special Collections, and University of California Irvine's Southeast Asian Archive. The Smithsonian Asian Pacific American Center (Washington, DC) and Museum of Chinese in America (New York) also collects historical sources on Asian Americans and Pacific Islanders and presents them via physical exhibits and digital programs. At the municipal level, it might be fruitful to excavate city planning department records, corporate archives, and police reports. At the neighborhood level, residential design guidelines and builder and developer plans can also provide insight into Asian American struggles for and claims to suburban space. In addition, local libraries, historical societies, community centers, and private collections typically contain a range of materials and ephemera. Lastly, cultural production—novels, films, music—offer useful glimpses into Asian American suburban life. While a few of these collections provide enough sources and materials to build an article or perhaps a monograph, a significant exploration into the history of Asian American suburban cultures will demand multi-site research.

FURTHER READING

Bao, Jiemin. *Creating a Buddhist Community: A Thai Temple in Silicon Valley*. Philadelphia: Temple University Press, 2015.

Brooks, Charlotte. *Alien Neighbors, Foreign Friends: Asian Americans, Housing, and the Transformation of Urban California*. Chicago: University of Chicago Press, 2009.

Cheng, Cindy I-Fen. *Citizens of Asian America: Democracy and Race during the Cold War*. New York: New York University Press, 2013.

Cheng, Wendy. *The Changs Next Door to the Díazes: Remapping Race in Suburban California*. Minneapolis: University of Minnesota Press, 2013.

Chowkwanyun, Merlin, and Jordan Segall. "The Rise of the Majority-Asian Suburb." The Atlantic City Lab, August 24, 2012. https://www.citylab.com/equity/2012/08/rise-majority-asian-suburb/3044/.

deGuzman, Jean-Paul. "Beyond 'Living 'La Vida Boba': Social Space and Transnational, Hybrid Asian American Youth Culture." *Amerasia Journal* 32, no. 2 (2006): 89–102.

deGuzman, Jean-Paul. "'And Make the San Fernando Valley My Home': Contested Spaces, Identities, and Activism on the Edge of Los Angeles." PhD diss., University of California Los Angeles, 2014.

Fang, Jennifer Y. "'To Cultivate Our Children to Be of East and West': Contesting Ethnic Heritage Language in Suburban Chinese Schools." *Journal of American Ethnic History* 34, no. 2 (2015): 54–82.

Fong, Timothy P. *The First Suburban Chinatown: The Remaking of Monterey Park, California*. Asian American History and Culture. Philadelphia: Temple University Press, 1994.

Friedman, Andrew. *Covert Capital Landscapes of Denial and the Making of U.S. Empire in the Suburbs of Northern Virginia*. Berkeley: University of California Press, 2013.

Hsu, Becky. "(Un)settling Suburbia: Asian American Suburban Narratives in the Nineties." PhD diss., University of California Berkeley, 2009.

Jenks, Hillary. "Seasoned Long Enough in Concentration: Suburbanization and Transnational Citizenship in Southern California's South Bay." *Journal of Urban History* 40, no. 1 (2014): 6–30.

Kalita, S. Mitra. *Suburban Sahibs Three Immigrant Families and Their Passage from India to America*. New Brunswick, NJ: Rutgers University Press, 2003.

Kurashige, Scott. *The Shifting Grounds of Race: Black and Japanese Americans in the Making of Multiethnic Los Angeles*. Princeton, NJ: Princeton University Press, 2008.

Lang, Robert, and Jennifer B. LeFurgy. *Boomburbs: The Rise of America's Accidental Cities*. Washington, DC: Brookings Institution Press, 2007.

Li, Wei. *Ethnoburb: The New Ethnic Community in Urban America*. Honolulu: University of Hawai'i Press, 2009.

Lieu, Nhi T. *The American Dream in Vietnamese*. Minneapolis: University of Minnesota Press, 2011.

Liu, Haiming, and Lianlian Lin. "Food, Culinary Identity, and Transnational Culture: Chinese Restaurant Business in Southern California." *Journal of Asian American Studies* 12, no. 2 (2009): 135–162.

Lung-Amam, Willow S. *Trespassers?: Asian Americans and the Battle for Suburbia*. Oakland: University of California, 2017.

Meyers, Jessica. "Pho and Apple Pie: Eden Center as a Representation of Vietnamese American Ethnic Identity in the Washington, D.C. Metropolitan Area, 1975–2005." *Journal of Asian American Studies* 9, no. 1 (2006): 55–85.

Nicolaides, Becky M. "Introduction: Asian American Suburban History." *Journal of American Ethnic History* 34, no. 2 (2015): 5–17.

Nicolaides, Becky M., and James Zarsadiaz. "Design Assimilation in Suburbia: Asian Americans, Built Landscapes, and Suburban Advantage in Los Angeles's San Gabriel Valley since 1970." *Journal of Urban History* 43, no. 2 (2017): 332–371.

Numrich, Paul David. "How the Swans Came to Lake Michigan: The Social Organization of Buddhist Chicago." *Journal for the Scientific Study of Religion* 39, no. 2 (2000): 189–203.

Padoongpatt, Tanachai Mark. "'A Landmark for Sun Valley': Wat Thai of Los Angeles and Thai American Suburban Culture in 1980s San Fernando Valley." *Journal of American Ethnic History* 34, no. 2 (2015): 83–114.

Saito, Leland T. *Race and Politics: Asian Americans, Latinos, and Whites in a Los Angeles Suburb.* Urbana: University of Illinois Press, 1998.

Skop, Emily. "Saffron Suburbs: Indian Immigrant Community Formation in Phoenix." PhD diss., Arizona State University, 2002.

Skop, Emily. *The Immigration and Settlement of Asian Indians in Phoenix, Arizona 1965–2011: Ethnic Pride vs. Racial Discrimination in the Suburbs.* Lewiston, NY: Edwin Mellen Press, 2012.

Skop, Emily and Wei Li. "Asians in America's Suburbs: Patterns and Consequences of Settlement." *The Geographical Review* 95, no. 2 (2005): 167–188.

Small, Cathy. *Voyages: From Tongan Villages to American Suburbs.* Ithaca, NY: Cornell University Press, 2011.

Tongson, Karen. *Relocations: Queer Suburban Imaginaries.* New York: New York University Press, 2011.

Wood, Joseph. "Vietnamese American Place Making in Northern Virginia." *American Geographical Society* 87, no. 1 (1997): 58–72.

Zarsadiaz, James. "Where the Wild Things Are: 'Country Living': Asian American Suburbanization, and the Politics of Space in Los Angeles's East San Gabriel Valley, 1945–2005." PhD diss., Northwestern University, 2014.

Zhou, Min, Yen-Fen Tseng, and Rebecca Kim. "Rethinking Residential Assimilation: The Case of a Chinese Ethnoburb in the San Gabriel Valley, California." *Amerasia Journal* 34, no. 3 (2008): 53–83.

NOTES

1. Hillary Jenks, "Seasoned Long Enough in Concentration: Suburbanization and Transnational Citizenship in Southern California's South Bay," *Journal of Urban History* 40, no. 1 (2014): 8–9.

2. Scott Kurashige, *The Shifting Grounds of Race: Black and Japanese Americans in the Making of Multiethnic Los Angeles* (Princeton, NJ: Princeton University Press, 2008), 26–29; Charlotte Brooks, *Alien Neighbors, Foreign Friends: Asian Americans, Housing, and the Transformation of Urban California* (Chicago: University of Chicago Press, 2009), 60–61; and Cindy I-Fen Cheng, *Citizens of Asian America: Democracy and Race during the Cold War* (New York: New York University Press, 2013), 21–22.

3. Jenks, "Seasoned Long Enough in Concentration," 9.

4. On the west coast, although most whites remained steadfast in maintaining housing segregation, by 1946 a number of white homeowners in areas bordering "the racially and unrestricted neighborhoods of San Francisco and Los Angeles began to sell to nonwhite buyers." Brooks, *Alien Neighbors, Foreign Friends*, 176.

5. Cheng, *Citizens of Asian America*, 21.

6. Cheng, *Citizens of Asian America*, 39–40.

7. Brooks, *Alien Neighbors, Foreign Friends*, 179.

8. Cheng, *Citizens of Asian America*, 21–24.

9. Brooks, *Alien Neighbors, Foreign Friends*, 184.

10. Brooks, *Alien Neighbors, Foreign Friends*, 187.

11. Becky M. Nicolaides, "Introduction: Asian American Suburban History," *Journal of American Ethnic History* 34, no. 2 (2015): 5–17.

12. According to Brooks, the fight against racially restrictive covenants in San Francisco and Los Angeles earned some partial victories, but it did not lead to full integration and open housing. In other words, it simply expanded areas where Asian Americans and people of color already lived, rather than making it possible for Asian Americans to live wherever they pleased. Also, Brooks writes, "The inclusion of Asian Americans in the suburban good life was never on equal basis, however, nor was it complete: stereotypes, rather than a belief in racial equality, created this

integration." Brooks, *Alien Neighbors, Foreign Friends*, 236.

13. Cheng, *Citizens of Asian America*, 78–79; and Brooks, *Alien Neighbors, Foreign Friends*, 221.

14. Robert Self, *American Babylon: Race and the Struggle for Postwar Oakland* (Princeton, NJ: Princeton University Press, 2003), 1.

15. Pew Research Center, "The Rise of Asian Americans," 2; and Elizabeth M. Hoeffel et al., "The Asian Population: 2010" (Washington, DC: US Department of Commerce, Economics, and Statistics Administration, US Census Bureau, 2012).

16. For an in-depth examination of the Immigration Act of 1924, see Mae Ngai, *Impossible Subjects: Illegal Aliens and the Making of Modern America* (Princeton, NJ: Princeton University Press, 2004), chap. 1. See also chapter 7 for an excellent discussion of the 1965 Immigration Act.

17. Paul M. Ong, Edna Bonacich, and Lucie Cheng, *The New Asian Immigration in Los Angeles and Global Economic Restructuring* (Philadelphia: Temple University Press, 1994); Rhacel Salazar Parrenas, "Asian Immigrant Women and Global Restructuring," in *Asian/Pacific Islander American Women: A Historical Anthology*, ed. Shirley Hune and Gail M. Nomura (New York: New York University Press, 2003), 271–285; and Roger Daniels, "Immigration," in *A Companion to 20th Century America*, ed. Stephen J. Whitfield (Malden, MA: Blackwell, 2007), 215–232.

18. The phrase "most suburban" is borrowed from Susan Hardwick, "Toward a Suburban Immigrant Nation," in *Twenty-First Century Gateways: Immigrant Incorporation in Suburban America*, ed. Audrey Singer, Susan W. Hardwick, and Caroline B. Brettell (Washington, DC, 2008), 45.

19. Becky M. Nicolaides and Andrew Weise, *The Suburb Reader* (New York: Routledge, 2016), 439.

20. Nicolaides, "Introduction: Asian American Suburban History," 6.

21. Nicolaides and Weise, *The Suburb Reader*, 440.

22. Emily Skop and Wei Li, "From the Ghetto to the Invisiburb: Shifting Patterns of Immigrant Settlement in Contemporary America," in *Multiracial Geographies: The Changing Racial/Ethnic Patterns of the United States*, ed. John W. Frazier and Florence M. Margai (New York: State University of New York Press, 2010), 120.

23. Robert E. Lang and Jennifer B. LeFurgy, *Boomburbs: The Rise of America's Accidental Cities* (Washington, DC: Brookings Institution Press, 2007), 66.

24. Nicolaides, "Introduction: Asian American Suburban History," 8.

25. Jack Rosenthal, "The Outer City: US in Suburban Turmoil," *New York Times*, May 30, 1971; Rob Kling, Spencer C. Olin Jr., and Mark Poster, *Postsuburban California: The Transformation of Orange County since World War II* (Berkeley: University of California Press, 1995); Christopher B. Leinberger and Charles Lockwood, "How Business Is Reshaping America," *Atlantic Monthly* 258, no. 10 (1986): 43–52; Joel Garreau, *Edge City: Life on the New Frontier* (Norwell, MA: Anchor Press, 2011); and Edward W. Soja, "Inside Exopolis: Scenes from Orange County," in *Variations on a Theme Park: The New American City and the End of Public Space*, ed. Michael Sorkin (New York: Hill and Wang, 1992): 94–122.

26. Leland T. Saito, *Race and Politics: Asian Americans, Latinos, and Whites in a Los Angeles Suburb* (Urbana: University of Illinois Press, 1998), 64.

27. Saito, *Race and Politics*, 10.

28. Brooks, *Alien Neighbors, Foreign Friends*, 221.

29. Cheng, *Citizens of Asian America*, 78.

30. Cheng, *Citizens of Asian America*, 78.

31. Jenks, "Seasoned Long Enough in Concentration," 12; and Kurashige, *The Shifting Grounds of Race*, 253.

32. Nhi T. Lieu, *The American Dream in Vietnamese* (Minneapolis: University of Minnesota Press, 2011), 51, 63; and Zan Dubin and Rick Vanderknyff, "From Isolation to Mainstream: After an Embryonic 20 Years, the Influence of Vietnamese Artists, Musicians, and Writers in Orange County is Exploding," *Los Angeles Times*, March 12, 1995.

33. Joseph Wood, "Vietnamese American Place Making in Northern Virginia" *American Geographical Society* 87, no. 1 (1997): 65–66.

34. Jenks, "Seasoned Long Enough in Concentration," 12; Kurashige, *The Shifting Grounds of Race*, 257, 293; and Sharon Sekhon, The Holiday Bowl History Project.

35. Jenks, "Seasoned Long Enough in Concentration," 11; and Kurashige, *The Shifting Grounds of Race*, 253–254.

36. Wendy Cheng, *The Changs Next Door to the Díazes: Remapping Race in Suburban California*

(Minneapolis: University of Minnesota Press, 2013), chap. 5.

37. Quoted in Jenks, "Seasoned Long Enough in Concentration," 11.

38. Karen Tongson, *Relocations: Queer Suburban Imaginaries* (New York: New York University Press, 2011), 108–109.

39. Focusing on the "culinary identity" of Chinese immigrants in Los Angeles's San Gabriel Valley, Haiming Liu and Lianlian Lin argue that rather than "wholesale assimilation, post-1965 Chinese immigrants have selectively maintained some of their native cultural traditions such as food" to make transnational identity a tangible reality. Liu and Lin, "Food, Culinary Identity, and Transnational Culture: Chinese Restaurant Business in Southern California," *Journal of Asian American Studies* 12, no. 2 (2009): 136.

40. Rick Bonus, *Locating Filipino Americans: Ethnicity and the Cultural Politics of Space* (Philadelphia: Temple University Press, 2000), 64–65.

41. Liu and Lin, "Food, Culinary Identity," 143.

42. Jonathan Gold, "Mongkorn Kawasai's Searingly Hot Thai Food Is Flavorful, but Not for the Meek," *Los Angeles Times*, April 15, 1988.

43. Gold, "Mongkorn Kawasai's Searingly Hot Thai Food."

44. Jean-Paul deGuzman, "Beyond 'Living La Vida Boba': Social Space and Transnational, Hybrid Asian American Youth Culture," *Amerasia Journal* 32, no. 2 (2006): 89–102.

45. Kurashige, *The Shifting Grounds of Race*, 256.

46. S. Mitra Kalita, *Suburban Sahibs Three Immigrant Families and Their Passage from India to America* (New Brunswick, NJ: Rutgers University Press, 2003), 15, 17, 19.

47. For excellent discussions on racialized and classed discourses of smell and the relationship between food, smell, and place, see Martin F. Manalansan, "The Empire of Food: Place, Memory and Asian Ethnic Cuisines," in *Gastropolis: Food and New York City*, ed. Jonathan Deutch and Annie Hauck-Lawson (New York: Columbia University Press, 2009), 93–107, and "Immigrant Lives and the Politics of Olfaction in the Global City," in *The Smell Culture Reader*, ed. Jim Drobnick (Oxford: Berg, 2006), 41–52.

48. Uma Narayan contends that ethnic food festivals are "one of the rare public events where one is visually, viscerally, and positively conscious of the range of diverse ethnicities and identities that in fact constitute us as a community." *Dislocating Cultures: Identities, Traditions, and Third-World Feminism* (New York: Routledge, 1997), 184.

49. Emily Skop, *The Immigration and Settlement of Asian Indians in Phoenix, Arizona, 1965–2011: Ethnic Pride vs. Racial Discrimination in the Suburbs* (Lewiston, NY: Edwin Mellen Press, 2012), chaps. 4–5.

50. Tanachai Mark Padoongpatt, "'A Landmark for Sun Valley': Wat Thai of Los Angeles and Thai American Suburban Culture in 1980s San Fernando Valley," *Journal of American Ethnic History* 34, no. 2 (2015): 83–114.

51. The vice president of the board tried to reassure the neighbors, but the police had to intervene. The temple laypeople were issued parking tickets, even when other residents parked the same way but did not receive tickets. Jiemin Bao, *Creating a Buddhist Community: A Thai Temple in Silicon Valley* (Philadelphia: Temple University Press, 2015), 61; and Jiemin Bao, "From Wandering to Wat: Creating a Thai Temple and Inventing New Space in the United States," *Amerasia Journal* 34, no. 3 (2006): 6.

52. Bao, "From Wandering to Wat," 6.

53. Bao, *Creating a Buddhist Community*, 61; and Bao, "From Wandering to Wat," 6.

54. Philip P. Pan, "Good Neighbor: Hemisphere's Largest Buddhist Temple Wins Over Residents," *Los Angeles Times*, August 8, 1993.

55. Jenks, "Seasoned Long Enough in Concentration," 15; and Patricia Leigh Brown, "The New Chinatown? Try the Asian Mall," *New York Times*, March 24, 2004.

56. Brown, "The New Chinatown? Try the Asian Mall."

57. Lieu, *The American Dream in Vietnamese*, 50.

58. Saito, *Race and Politics*, 35.

59. Saito, *Race and Politics*, 48.

60. Willow S. Lung-Amam, *Trespassers?: Asian Americans and the Battle for Suburbia* (Oakland: University of California, 2017), 115–122.

61. Lung-Amam, *Trespassers?*, 128–134; Wendy Cheng, *The Changs Next Door to the Díazes: Remapping Race in Suburban California* (Minneapolis: University of Minnesota Press, 2013), chap. 4; see also Jessica Meyers, "Pho and Apple Pie: Eden Center as a Representation of Vietnamese

American Ethnic Identity in the Washington, D.C. Metropolitan Area, 1975–2005," *Journal of Asian American Studies* 9, no. 1 (2006): 55–85.

62. In Los Angeles, Asian Americans were restricted to older houses that were already ten years old or in need of repair. New homes were only made available to whites. Kurashige, *The Shifting Grounds of Race*, 244.

63. Becky Nicolaides and James Zarsadiaz, "Design Assimilation in Suburbia: Asian Americans, Built Landscapes, and Suburban Advantage in Los Angeles's San Gabriel Valley since 1970," *Journal of Urban History* 43, no. 2 (2017): 332–371.

64. Nicolaides and Zarsadiaz, "Design Assimilation in Suburbia," 345.

65. Nicolaides and Zarsadiaz, "Design Assimilation in Suburbia," 346.

66. Nicolaides and Zarsadiaz, "Design Assimilation in Suburbia," 344–345; and Mark Arax, "San Gabriel Valley Asian Influx Alters Life in Suburbia," *Los Angeles Times*, April 5, 1987.

67. Nicolaides and Zarsadiaz, "Design Assimilation in Suburbia," 346; and Lung-Amam, *Trespassers?* 153.

68. Kurashige, *The Shifting Grounds of Race*, 256.

69. Nicolaides and Zarsadiaz, "Design Assimilation in Suburbia," 344–345.

70. Lung-Amam, *Trespassers?* 161.

71. Saito, *Race and Politics*, 46–48.

72. Saito, *Race and Politics*, 72–73.

73. Lung-Amam, *Trespassers?* 100.

74. Nicolaides and Zarsadiaz, "Design Assimilation in Suburbia," 115.

75. Lung-Amam, *Trespassers?* 69.

76. Lung-Amam, *Trespassers?* 57, 67.

77. Lung-Amam, *Trespassers?* 68.

78. Edgar Poma, "More on Asian American Success: U.S. Publications Continue Their Adulation," *Asian Week*, December 5, 1986.

79. David Brand, "The New Whiz Kids: Why Asian-Americans Are Doing So Well, and What It Costs Them," *Time*, August 31, 1987.

80. To list just a few examples: Poma, "More on Asian American Success"; Brand, "The New Whiz Kids"; Fox Butterfield, "Why Asians Are Going 'To the Head of the Class,'" *New York Times*, August 3, 1986; "Phenomenal Success of Asian Students in U.S.," *Asian Week*, March 31, 1983; and "Family Credited for Success of Asian American Students," *Asian Week*, July 27, 1984.

81. Quoted in Cheng, *The Changs Next Door to the Díazes*, 72.

82. Quoted in Cheng, *The Changs Next Door to the Díazes*, 72.

83. Lung-Amam, *Trespassers?* 83.

84. "Report Lauds Asians' Success but Bemoans Pressure on Students," *Asian Week*, January 03, 1986; and Lung-Amam, *Trespassers?* 69–73.

85. Timothy P. Fong, *The First Suburban Chinatown: The Remaking of Monterey Park, California. Asian American History and Culture* (Philadelphia: Temple University Press, 1994); Leland Saito, *Race and Politics*; and Wood, "Vietnamese American Place Making in Northern Virginia."

86. Nicolaides and Zarsadiaz, "Design Assimilation in Suburbia"; Lung-Amam, *Trespassers?*; Cheng, *The Changs Next Door to the Díazes*; Jennifer Y. Fang, "'To Cultivate Our Children to Be of East and West': Contesting Ethnic Heritage Language in Suburban Chinese Schools," *Journal of American Ethnic History* 34, no. 2 (2015): 54–82; Wei Li, *Ethnoburb: The New Ethnic Community in Urban America* (Honolulu: University of Hawai'i Press, 2009); James Zarsadiaz, "Where the Wild Things Are: 'Country Living': Asian American Suburbanization, and the Politics of Space in Los Angeles's East San Gabriel Valley, 1945–2005" (PhD diss., Northwestern University, 2014); and Min Zhou, Yen-Fen Tseng, and Rebecca Kim, "Rethinking Residential Assimilation: The Case of a Chinese Ethnoburb in the San Gabriel Valley, California," *Amerasia Journal* 34, no. 3 (2008): 53–83.

87. George Lipsitz, *How Racism Takes Place* (Philadelphia: Temple University Press, 2011), introduction; and George Lipsitz, "The Racialization of Space and the Spatialization of Race: Theorizing the Hidden Architecture of Landscape," *Landscape Journal* 26, no. 1 (2007): 10–23.

88. Jiemin Bao, *Creating a Buddhist Community*; Wei Li, *Ethnoburb*; and Nicolaides and Zarsadiaz, "Design Assimilation in Suburbia."

89. See Yen Le Espiritu, *Home Bound: Filipino American Lives Across Cultures, Communities, and Countries* (Berkeley: University of California Press, 2003); Stephen Castles, "Migration and Community Formation under Conditions of Globalization," *International Migration Review* 36, no. 4 (December 2002): 1143–1168; Paul Ong, Edna Bonacich, and Lucie Cheng, eds., *The New Asian Immigration in Los Angeles and*

Global Restructuring (Philadelphia: Temple University Press, 1994); Lisa Lowe, *Immigrant Acts: On Asian American Cultural Politics* (Durham, NC: Duke University Press, 1996), chap. 7; Aihwa Ong, *Buddha Is Hiding: Refugees, Citizenship, the New America* (Berkeley: University of California Press, 2003); Saskia Sassen, *The Mobility of Labor and Capital: A Study of International Investment and Labor Flows* (New York: Cambridge University Press, 1988); and Linda Basch, Nina Glick Schiller, and Cristina Blanc, *Nations Unbound: Transnational Projects, Postcolonial Predicaments, and Deterritorialized Nation-States* (New York: Gordon and Breach, 1994).

90. Lieu, *The American Dream in Vietnamese*; Andrew Freidman, *Covert Capital Landscapes of Denial and the Making of U.S. Empire in the Suburbs of Northern Virginia* (Berkeley: University of California Press, 2013); Bao, *Creating a Buddhist Community*; Jenks, "Seasoned Long Enough in Concentration"; and Liu and Lin, "Food, Culinary Identity."

91. Tongson, *Relocations*; Kalita, *Suburban Sahibs*; Saito, *Race and Politics*; Cheng, *Changs Next Door to the Díazes*; and Jean-Paul deGuzman, "'And Make the San Fernando Valley My Home': Contested Spaces, Identities, and Activism on the Edge of Los Angeles" (PhD diss., University of California, Los Angeles, 2014).

92. Cheng, *Changs Next Door to the Díazes*, 10.

93. Christina Klein, *Cold War Orientalism: Asia in the Middlebrow Imagination, 1945–1961* (Berkeley: University of California Press, 2003).

Mark Padoongpatt

ZONING IN 20TH-CENTURY AMERICAN CITIES

Zoning is the exercise of public control over private property through a legal instrument available to local government to regulate real property, including buildings and structures, by designating districts according the nature and extent of their use. Zoning is intended to enable orderly growth of a city, town, village, or county according to a framework for development that seeks to ensure that incompatible uses do not undermine the quality or value of real property. Local governments determine the character of the real property within their jurisdictions and its fitness for particular uses in accordance with a master plan. The comprehensive approach to designating districts as residential, commercial, and industrial avoids the problem of arbitrary exercise of government power. Zoning emerged early in the 20th century as the most widely used land planning tool to correct problems associated with random land development, especially in cities where the incursion of certain environmentally harmful industrial uses jeopardized property values in areas of predominantly residential and commercial uses. The greatest impact of zoning was in determining the form of new development in the suburbs surrounding the urban core, which became the primary site of urban growth beginning after 1920. The Supreme Court decision *Euclid v. Ambler Realty* (1926) cleared the way for zoning to be upheld as a legitimate exercise of the police power. Subsequently, nearly all states adopted some form of zoning regulation.

The relatively simple zoning schemes legitimized under the *Euclid* decision exerted a powerful influence over land use changes in localities throughout the United States after 1940. Zoning classifications became substantially more refined, thereby ensuring even more segregated patterns of land use and development. This was largely in response to the perception that sustaining property values was best accomplished by preserving strict separation of different land uses according to size and density. This also generated new criticism of the rigidity and unintended consequences of conventional zoning schemes. New zoning techniques were introduced to create more flexibility in zoning systems, including planned unit developments (PUD), transfer of development rights (TDR), zoning overlay districts, and traditional neighborhood development (TND). More recently, some have argued that the whole system of structured land use districts for city and suburbs should be eliminated in favor of a system known as form-based codes.

19TH-CENTURY PRECEDENTS FOR ZONING

Defining the power of municipalities to regulate public health, park construction, transportation networks, and water and sewer systems were key challenges of expanding 19th-century cities. This required a public intervention into land use regulation that provided the legal foundations to support zoning.[1] As Schultz noted, the expanded scope of authority of the municipal corporation provided the legal basis upon which city planning and zoning eventually rested.[2] The application of Dillion's rule—that cities only had powers granted by states—impeded full development of land use regulations. A precedent-setting case was *Vanderbilt v. Adam*, 7 Cowen 349 (NY 1827).[3] It concerned the ability of the City of New York to regulate ship docking at private wharves and the concept that it was in the interest of public welfare to deal with urban densities, and it justified public exercise of the police power. The case was widely cited in support of urban policing of property uses.[4] The Massachusetts Supreme Court in 1899 upheld a Boston ordinance regulating the height and mode of building construction as a proper use of the police power.[5] University of Chicago professor of law Ernest Freund, in *The Police Power: Public Policy and Constitutional Rights*, (Chicago: Callaghan, 1904) defended the inalienable character of the police power, and argued that it be exercised "flexibly to effect the greatest good for the greatest number of people." He accentuated the positive characteristics of policing power to promote the general welfare that was increasingly embraced by courts.

A major push for zoning occurred in conjunction with work of the Committee on Congestion of Population in New York City.

New York City settlement house leaders hired Benjamin C. Marsh as the Committee's first Executive Director in 1907. After travelling to Europe to study British, French, and German approaches to house and city planning, the Committee staged an exhibition in 1908, at the American Museum of Natural History, which graphically depicted the problems of overcrowding. The exhibition moved on to Washington in 1909, and prompted the first National Conference on City Planning and Congestion,[6] and led to the publication of *An Introduction to City Planning: Democracy's Challenge & the American City* (1909). Frankfurt, Germany was celebrated as an ideal model, convincing Marsh that "the most important part of City Planning, as far as the future health of the city is concerned, is the districting of the city into zones."[7] Although Marsh initially pushed the innovative notion of German-style zoning, he devoted more energy to the radical "single tax" scheme of Henry George and the efforts to relieve congestion by taxing property being held for speculative purposes. This put him at odds with others in the mainstream of the nascent US planning movement, which quickly embraced zoning as the most effective tool to ensure that planning would result in desired changes on the ground.[8] New York City real estate interests resisted Marsh's cheap land strategies, but acknowledged that zoning could stabilize uncertain real estate conditions. Thus, they backed the nation's first comprehensive zoning law in New York City in 1916.[9]

The German model that Marsh highlighted in Frankfurt-on-the-Main was advanced by Frankfurt's reform-minded Mayor Franz Adickes in 1891. This model, based upon a concept first advanced in 1876 by Reinhart Baumeister of the Technical University in Karlsruhrwhich, created six zones, two for residential uses, two for mixed uses, and two for factories, and set density and building bulk requirements.[10] Similar ordinances emerged in various German cities (Berlin, 1892; Hamburg, 1896; Stuttgart, 1897; Mannheim, 1901;

Hanover, 1902; Nuremberg, 1903; and Munich, 1903) during the next decade. Contemporaneous zoning initiatives in the United States started with controlling building heights in business districts, largely to ensure access to light and air. The other zoning focus was on regulating the location of certain undesired businesses, such as Chinese-run laundries.[11] San Francisco and Modesto, California, ordinances in the 1880s regulated commercial laundries to certain areas and were upheld as legal; Los Angeles had similar ordinances. As Logan noted, "Between 1909 and 1915, Los Angeles established 27 industrial districts and about 100 residence exception districts and about 100 exception districts," which allowed all but heavy and objectionable industries.[12] In 1898, a Massachusetts state statute limited the height of buildings in central Boston around Copley Square and the State House on Beacon Hill. Although the New York City building zone resolution passed by the Board of Estimate and Apportionment in 1916 is commonly cited as the first comprehensive zoning ordinance, other city-wide zoning schemes—one in Baltimore, Maryland, and the other in Richmond, Virginia—created city-wide zoning based upon racial occupancy.

One of the key distinctions between the German and US approaches to zoning was the separation of uses, which was not a central objective in German zoning.[13] In contrast to the German model, the US version of zoning consistently sought to regulate land use in terms of the likely population those uses served, and for the express purpose of separating the undesirable classes from the more affluent.[14] German zoning rarely utilized exclusively single family zones. But it is significant to note that "the overzealous separation of homes from commercial services and places of employment was not present in the early applications of zoning in either Germany or the United States."[15] Eventually, the separation of uses zoning became the end in itself, which differed from the original intent.

Conflicts between the existing and future land use needs generated efforts to regulate growth as urban communities expanded in the early 20th century. In Los Angeles, the Hadacheck Brickworks opened in an unannexed fringe of the city in 1902. When the city annexed the area and residential development began in the neighborhood, the city passed an ordinance to shut down the brickworks. Hadacheck claimed that this amounted to an unlawful taking of his property. In *Hadacheck v. Sebastian* (1915), the US Supreme Court ruled that the nuisance created and continued by the business would preclude proper development of the city. Thus, the exercise of the police power to remove the brickworks nuisance was warranted and legal. Overturning the city's ordinance would "preclude development and fix a city forever in its primitive condition," in the Court's opinion. "There must be progress, and if in its march private interests are in the way, they must yield to the good of the community."[16]

THE 1916 NEW YORK CITY BUILDING ZONE PLAN RESOLUTION

The 1916 New York City Building Zone Plan is commonly and incorrectly regarded as the nation's first zoning ordinance in an American city. The Plan was based upon a comprehensive assessment of land use conditions and was instrumental in advancing the approach, legality, and popularity of zoning as a land development regulating tool. In response to unregulated growth of tall buildings in the city's commercial heart, the widely held belief that blocking natural air and light generated harmful health effects, and the perception that unregulated design of new buildings created congestion on the ground, Manhattan Borough President George McAneny proposed in 1913 that the concept of zoning districts be explored. This was two years after the deadly Triangle Shirtwaist Factory fire, an event that was blamed on unregulated building construction. Edward M. Bassett chaired the

Heights of Building Commission that produced a detailed report that identified various problems with unregulated tall buildings, and that posited that using zoning to regulate building was constitutional. Like Marsh, Bassett had traveled to Europe and drew upon the German model in drafting the New York City resolution. Other advocates for devising ways to reduce urban densities and congestion included New York housing reformer and author of the New York State Tenement Act of 1901 Lawrence Veiller; attorney Robert H. Whitten, who would later participate in defending the Town of Euclid, Ohio, in the landmark *Euclid* case; and planner George B. Ford, worked with Bassett on the New York Building Commission. The New York ordinance was the first that applied both use and bulk restrictions to the entire municipality.[17]

The New York zone system had only three categories of uses: residential, commercial and unrestricted. The latter was intended to accommodate industrial uses that were excluded from the other two. The use of the unrestricted use district was common in early zoning schemes but disappeared as localities sought to more explicitly identify industrial districts and incorporated finer gradations in the residential and commercial categories. The intent of the 1916 regulation was simply to prevent further incursions by the garment industry into the Fifth Avenue commercial district. The regulation, however, failed to remove those that already existed in the area. These *nonconforming* uses could not be expanded or replicated if they ceased to operate for any reason. Because zoning did not constitute the power to remove existing uses, it took considerable time for the removal and disappearance of nonconforming uses. Usually, such uses were removed because of decisions by the property owners to relocate or close down for business reasons. Over time, however, the zoning scheme enabled to district to take on the character of a predominantly commercial district.[18]

THE *EUCLID* CASE LEGITIMIZES ZONING

The US Supreme Court decision in *Village of Euclid v. Ambler Realty Co.* (1926) authorized municipal police power to direct and control private land uses in the United States. Cities only had to demonstrate with "reasonable" evidence that the decision promoted the health, safety, and comfort of the general public.[19] The Court agreed to review the decision of Judge David C. Westenhaven of the US District Court for the Northern District of Ohio in January 1924, which declared the Euclid ordinance null and void. Interestingly, Ambler Realty counsel argued that the effort of the Village of Euclid to create residential zones provided the affluent with the larger area for light and air, while it called for those who were in congested two-family residences and apartments to be put in the low-lying areas adjacent to construction areas. To maintain the community aesthetic, the plaintiff argued, their zoning ordinance not only "deprived honest businessmen of their due profits; worse they had literally denied the honest working people of the community their place in the sun."[20]

Writing for the majority of the Court, the strict constructionist Justice George Sutherland contended that the growing complexities of urban life, with great increases and concentrations of population, required additional restrictions in the use and occupation of private lands in urban communities. The arguments of *Euclid* were prepared by Alfred Bettman of Cincinnati and Edward Bassett, author of New York City's 1916 Zoning Resolution. The *Euclid* defense of zoning was argued by James F. Metzenbaum, a village resident and Cleveland lawyer, who had headed the commission that drafted the village ordinance following passage of the state enabling act. Unlike the three-district New York City scheme, Euclid was divided into six height, area, and use districts that restricted the location of businesses, industries, and residences (including the type of housing).

The *Euclid* case focused on the power of local government to determine how it wanted to develop without reference to any existing nuisance. Unlike in the *Hadacheck* case, which relied upon proof of a nuisance to uphold the city's expulsion of the brickyard, *Euclid* allowed the village to prohibit shops, industries, and apartments from single-family districts on the grounds that these uses had a deleterious effect on the community, much like the nuisance created by the brickyard in Los Angeles. But the argument to exclude these uses, as set forth by Charles Henry Cheney, a prominent national planning consultant, in a *National Municipal Review* article in 1920, captured the prevailing view of the incompatibility of different housing types existing side-by-side. As Cheney put it: "Once a block of homes is invaded by flats and apartments, few new single family dwellings ever go up afterwards. It is marked for change, and the land adjoining is forever held on a speculative basis in the hope that it may all become commercially remunerative generally, without thought for the great majority of adjoining owners who have invested for a home and home neighborhood only."[21] The linkage between zoning and the separation of commercial and industrial uses from residential districts was vividly demonstrated in the case of Los Angeles. With the power to regulate land use through zoning from the 1920s onward, a group of large community builders in the Los Angeles area developed planned neighborhood units of single family homes in the green fields around the city to form what became the modern bedroom suburb.[22] Yet shortly after the *Euclid* decision, Justice Sutherland issued a very different verdict in the case of *Nectow v. City of Cambridge* (1928). Cambridge, Massachusetts had a zoning scheme similar to that considered in *Euclid* and was conceded to be constitutional based upon that decision. But Sutherland found that the ways the three districts were drawn put one portion of Nectow's property in an industrial zone and one portion, which previously but no

longer was in residential use, in the residential zone that did not permit any industrial use. The result was that the potential purchaser of the property refused to comply with the contract to buy because of the zoning restrictions. Sutherland's judgment was that the specific zoning plan did not support the health, safety, convenience, and general welfare of the inhabitants of that part of the city, that the plaintiff was seriously injured financially, and that it violated the due process provisions of the Fourteenth Amendment.[23]

STANDARD STATE ZONING ENABLING ACT (SSZEA) AND BEYOND

The Standard State Zoning Enabling Act, disseminated by the US Department of Commerce after 1924, demonstrated that zoning was a national movement even before the *Euclid* decision. Most states, however, needed to enact enabling legislation in order for their local governments to use it. The first edition of the Act sold 55,000 copies; within two years all but five of the forty-eight states had adopted enabling legislation. This accounted for the 420 local governments that adopted zoning ordinances and many more that were preparing them. By 1929, according to Hubbard and Hubbard, 753 local governments had enacted zoning systems.[24]

The stated objectives of the zoning system that the SSZEA advanced focused on how zoning lessened congestion caused by overcrowding of land, ensured access in communities to the health and welfare benefits of sufficient light and air (as advanced with the New York zoning scheme of 1916), mitigated against the dangers of fire and disease (also associated with congestion of structures and population), and facilitated the provision of transportation, water, sewerage, schools, parks, and other public requirements by predetermining the scale and intensity of growth. Two other motivating factors behind zoning, "to exclude unwanted people or uses" and to protect property values, were not explicitly mentioned in the act, but were definitely part of public discourse that propelled zoning into a national movement.[25] The SSZEA provided the basis for granting power to local governments to zone through a local ordinance. It emphasized that the zone plan needed to be comprehensive rather than piecemeal, that the ordinance would be vetted through a public input process, and that a zoning commission of citizens would oversee the public input process. A separate citizen body would be needed to consider appeals of actions of the zoning commission. This model was closely replicated nationwide because this was seen as the best way to ensure that zoning would stand up to legal scrutiny.

SSZEA ordinances remained the norm throughout the 20th century, relatively consistent with what the Hoover Commission proposed in the 1920s. The SSZEA format consisted of two parts: a text providing the regulations and a map delineating the locations of the various districts or zones. The text included verbal descriptions of the zoning district standards, administrative provisions for changes (such as amendments, variations, and special uses), and nonconformities (that is, uses existing at the time of the zoning ordinances that did not conform to the zone scheme). The map delineated in spatial terms the various use districts in the locality, typically grouped into the general categories of residential, commercial, and industrial. Over time, the basic components of the zoning ordinance remained relatively static, but the complexity and the prescriptive character of the ordinance increased. As planner Walter Blucher noted, in 1955, "the early zoning ordinances were simple and crude, but to a very considerable extent they told a property owner what he might do with his property. Current zoning ordinances are no longer simple: they are terribly complicated and to an increasing extent fail to tell a property owner what he might do with his property as a matter of right."[26]

The text of the zoning ordinance set forth a list of permitted uses for each district, along with permitted accessory uses and requirements (such as garage. carport, outbuildings, etc.) and allowable temporary uses. The text also identified parking and space loading zone requirements. Finally, it specified the land intensity or "bulk" standards, such as height, side-front-rear yards, lot coverage, and floor-to-area ratios. Typically, zoning schemes included buffers, which sought to shield higher order uses from lower order uses. So a single-family zone would likely be buffered by a multifamily or apartment zone from either an industrial or commercial zone. In addition, the SSZEA required creation of a body or commission, a board of adjustment, and a process to address amendments to the zoning scheme, special exceptions, and appeals.

RACIAL ORIGINS OF ZONING

The prevailing focus of zoning history scholarship and relevant court cases on its use to regulate and shape the built environment and to protect property values obscures past prevailing social objectives. According to legal scholar Yale Rabin, the post-*Euclid* legacy of zoning expanded from "a means of improving the blighted physical environment in which people lived and worked to a mechanism for protecting property values and excluding the undesirables."[27] In the early 20th century, two groups regarded as undesirables were newly arrived immigrants and African Americans. The first comprehensive racial zoning ordinance in the United States appeared in Baltimore in 1910, before either the New York City or Euclid plans, although several California cities had for decades employed "police power" to control the spread of Chinese laundries outside Chinese neighborhoods. Local white attorney Milton Dashiel fashioned Baltimore's racial zoning plan immediately following the momentous decision of black attorney, George W. F. McMechen, to move into the fashionable Eutaw Place neighborhood. Dashiel's plan moved methodically through both branches of city council despite immediate protests from black residents. Mayor J. Barry Mahool, a nationally recognized member of the "social justice" wing of the national Progressive movement, supported this pioneering racial zoning ordinance and signed it into law in December 1910. Mahool subscribed to the position that "Blacks should be quarantined in isolated slums in order to reduce the incidents of civil disturbance, to prevent the spread of communicable disease into nearby White neighborhoods, and to protect property values among the White majority."[28]

Passage of the Baltimore ordinance drew national attention and unleashed a flood of similar laws in southern cities. In Virginia, Richmond, Norfolk, Portsmouth, Roanoke, and Ashland enacted modified versions of the Baltimore ordinance. Atlanta, Georgia, Greenville, South Carolina; Asheville, and Winston-Salem, North Carolina; Birmingham, Alabama; and Madisonville and Louisville, Kentucky, joined in the racial zoning movement. Other cities, including Charlotte, North Carolina; Charleston, South Carolina; Meridian, Mississippi; and New Orleans, Louisiana, considered, but did not immediately enact, racial zoning ordinances. In Richmond, for example, the racial zoning ordinance followed immediately after the Virginia Supreme Court of Appeals decision, in 1910, to approve Richmond's 1908 ordinance regulating the height and arrangement of building (a decision later used also in support of the New York City zoning resolution). Virginia's enabling legislation allowed cities to zone their entire area according to race, whereas the original Baltimore plan applied only to all-white or all-black blocks. In contrast, the Richmond ordinance stipulated that a "block is White where a majority of residents are White and colored where a majority... are colored."[29] Richmond's residential segregation ordinance received the blessing of the state's highest court in *Hopkins v. City of Richmond* (1915), where two individuals, one white and one black, moved together into a house in a designated "White zone" and violated the law. The court ruled there was no taking of rights or value from the owner without just compensation since this act occurred after passage of the act, and would have been allowed under the grandfather provision of the act had it taken place prior to the act, since it also designated "mixed neighborhoods." Atlanta's residential segregation ordinance (1913) initially failed in court for violating state and federal protection of "rights in property acquired previous to its enactment." A revised version exempted residences acquired before passage of the ordinance, and the Georgia high court sustained the city's racial zoning plan in 1917.[30]

The euphoria of segregationists faded quickly, however, when the Supreme Court unanimously struck down the Louisville, Kentucky, racial zoning ordinance. In *Buchanan v. Warley* (1917), the Court ruled unanimously that the denial of full use of property "from a feeling of race hostility" constituted inadequate grounds to uphold the Louisville racial zoning ordinance.[31] The immediate impact of the Court's unequivocal rejection of racial zoning was to vacate existing racial zoning schemes. But it did not end the movement to use zoning to maintain residential racial segregation.[32] A law review publication in 1927 contended that preserving social order, not racial hostility, was the overarching objective, since "the comingling of the homes and places of abode of White men and Black men gives unnecessary provocation for miscegenation, race riots, lynching, and other forms of social malaise, existent when a childlike undisciplined, inferior race is living in close contact with a people of more mature civilization." So long as zoning did not deprive owners of property previously acquired, pro-racial zoning advocates believed that it would be upheld as constitutional even when it involved racial motives.[33] The *Buchanan* ruling proved to be narrow in scope, because it focused just on the matter of denying property rights and was silent on the 14th Amendment's equal protection clause. Thus Holt concluded that, so long as zoning did not result in a taking of property from minorities, it could stand. But, with later efforts to utilize various tools of exclusion under the guise of protecting property values, the effect of denial of equal protection raised new challenges to the system.

Throughout the 1920s, revised racial zoning plans emerged in Atlanta, Georgia; Charleston, South Carolina; Roanoke, Virginia; Kingsport, Tennessee; and New Orleans, Louisiana, although all ran afoul of the *Buchanan* decision.[34] By the 1930s, the racial zoning movement had run its course, but not so the interest in the racial imperatives of land use regulations. The 1930s and 1940s constituted an important period in local planning, since many cities that had previously devised plans that called for separate black sections of the cities found new ways to accomplish this goal. Public housing and slum clearance provided new resources to reconstruct the social landscape to achieve racial separation, and southern and non-southern cities eagerly participated in these efforts. Exclusionary zoning practices with the effect of racial separation represented another strategy that withstood both legal and political challenges.

ZONING COMES OF AGE

Between the *Euclid* decision (1926) and the mid-1970s, the US Supreme Court was largely silent on zoning. Instead, state courts served as arbiters of what had become the most widely used instrument to control land development. With explicitly race-defined zones no longer a legally sustainable option, but with race and ethnicity issues still alive in the United States, a variety of tools were used to maintain the color line. These included restrictive covenants that prohibited blacks and other minorities from owning property, manipulation of the real estate market to deny access to property, restricting the location of multi-family properties (including public housing) to safeguard single-family homeowners from the introduction of low-income populations, and setting high minimum building,

lot size, and setback requirements within zoning regulations to ensure that the mixed-income neighborhoods of the 19th century would not be possible in the newly created urban and suburban communities. While cities typically enacted zoning ordinances that allowed for some mixing, at least in adjacent districts of different land uses, the long term effect of city zoning schemes was to eliminate mixed-use districts. As a result, many remaining vestiges of residences in the core areas were pushed out as property converted to commercial uses. Where zoning had its most noticeable impact was in creating the single-family home suburbs. As land use attorneys Clifford Weaver and Richard Babcock note in *City Zoning: The Once and Future Frontier*, "the history of zoning in [the] past half-century [since 1926] has been largely written in the suburbs"[35] More than 10,000 zoning cases were decided between 1926 and 1976, the overwhelming majority involving zoning issues in the suburbs, not cities. Issues such as the legality of planned developments, the introduction of flexible zoning, and the wide array of exclusionary devices kept the courts busy refining the increasingly more complex zoning system.

An inventory of city and county land use regulations compiled and released in 1937 by the National Resources Planning Board indicated that 1,390 cities and counties had zoning ordinances, and there were 517 subdivision ordinances, the other legal tool to control development.[36] Generally, the courts sustained broad authority for local government to regulate land use both through zoning and subdivision controls. The American Society of Planning Officials noted in 1938 that many of the earlier ordinances were in the process of scaling down the size of commercial, industrial, and multifamily districts to more closely link to the community needs, but were also beginning to exclude new residences from industrial districts, except for the newly popular manufactured homes that were assigned to commercial and industrial zones, and adjusting parking requirements to keep the vehicles off streets in new developments.[37] Only during World War II was there pressure to relax zoning restrictions in order to allow war-demanded multifamily housing and industrial facilities in places where the existing zoning disallowed these uses. More often, local zoning was increasingly restrictive regarding the location of uses. But they were also more firmly grounded in data derived from land use surveys and economic assessments that helped to determine both the size and location needed for industrial and commercial zones. The planned unit development concept was introduced to allow diversified uses within newly created communities, and in large cities revised zoning regulations more precisely distinguished between types of commercial uses.[38]

The reshaping of urban land and the consolidation of commercial and industrial zones was facilitated through the federally sponsored urban renewal, which kicked off in the 1949 Housing Act and expanded through the 1954 Urban Redevelopment Act. Urban renewal enabled the acquisition and reformation of urban land uses, a process made possible either through direct purchase of blighted areas or, if necessary, with condemnation under police powers available through eminent domain. *Berman v. Parker* (1954) established the authority of local government to take private property through eminent domain and, in this case, property that the owner claimed was not in a blighted condition but which the public needed to reconstruct the area. The *Berman* decision substantiated that the public purpose of eliminating blighted conditions did not violate the Fifth Amendment protection against private property being taken for public purpose without just compensation. The decision sanctioned the use of police power to achieve aesthetic objectives as well as to remove blighted conditions to facilitate rebuilding.[39] Urban renewal projects across the United States cleared and rebuilt the inner areas of cities based upon the conceptions of the modern city contained in the general plans required to secure federal financing. The situation in the suburbs was very different, driven by the federal mortgage insurance program of the Federal Housing Administration, which propagated new development based almost exclusively upon single-family construction in large planned communities.

RECASTING LAND USE REGULATIONS

The onset of a sustained critique of the Euclidian zoning can be traced to the publication of Jane Jacobs's *Death and Life of Great American Cities*. Her iconoclastic critique of the principle tools of planning, including zoning, urban renewal, and transportation planning aimed at facilitating widespread reliance on the automobile transformed urban planning in general and zoning in particular. Drawing upon her experiences living in New York City's Greenwich Village, Jacobs challenged city planners who had "branded whole areas substandard, zoned cities into dull, single-use districts, delighted in divisive freeways, and created dangerous open spaces in which hoodlums lurked and attacked."[40] Jacobs was not fundamentally opposed to the objectives of zoning to achieve some desirable order, but rather disturbed that this powerful land regulation tool eliminated the diversity of places that make cities so vibrant. As she put it, "City districts will be economically and socially congenial places for diversity to generate itself and reach its best potential if the districts possess good mixtures of primary uses, frequent streets, a close-grained mingling of different ages in their buildings, and a high concentration of people."[41] These typically were land use traits that zoning plans often sought to eliminate. As Jacobs pointed out, trying to preserve small neighborhood commercial business in a residential neighborhood was incompatible with the existing zoning theory that sought to separate them. Although the residences might remain if part of the district was changed to a commercial designation, this might also invite other less neighborhood-friendly enterprises that would undermine the diversity that was being sought. But if there was no change, the existing small businesses were there only by exemption or in violation of zoning. So the question was "what kind of categories in the new zoning will be least at odds with the needs of real life?"[42]

That became the quest among many planners and urban reformers like Jacobs for the last portion of the 20th century, but without doing away with zoning or other public approaches to land use regulation. One innovation to offset some of the limitations of more rigid zoning and to achieve the diversity that Jacobs advocated was the use of overlay districts, a regulatory tool that created special zoning districts, placed over existing base zones, and identified special provisions in addition to those in the underlying base zone. The overlay district shared common boundaries with the base zone or cut across base zone boundaries. Regulations or incentives were attached to the overlay district to protect a specific resource or guide development within a special area. Overlay districts were and have been used to protect natural resources or to deal with site limitations not covered by the underlying zone such as steep slopes, unsuitable soils, flood hazards, or protection of vulnerable places. It was also used to acknowledge and address the needs of cultural resources such as historic assets in historic districts or to create neighborhood commercial districts.

The use of form-based codes was another of the alternatives (or additions) to Euclidian zoning, by substituting the two-dimensional approach of assigning land uses to properties for one that is based upon a three-dimensional vision of how spaces should be ordered. Form-based codes did not entirely do away with conventional zones but added to the zoning scheme attention to the design of the buildings, their relationship to streets and open spaces, and to patterns of intensity from the less dense of the fringe to the more intense of the inner city. These and other innovations in land development control regulations will forge the basis for the 21st century of urban and regional development and planning.[43]

DISCUSSION OF LITERATURE

An abundant literature exists on the development of zoning in the United States, beginning with the 19th-century precedents thoroughly covered in Stanley K. Schultz, *Constructing Urban Culture: American Cities and City Planning, 1800–1920*. Also valuable is an article by Jon C. Teaford, "Special Legislation and the Cities, 1865–1900." The classic text overview of zoning development in the United States is Seymour I. Toll, *Zoned America*. The key case law from the 19th century is treated in Ernest Freund, *The Police Power: Public Policy and Constitutional Rights*. This is supplemented by Norman Williams, *American Planning Law*.[44]

The publication that helped spur the zoning movement in the United States is Benjamin C. Marsh, *An Introduction to City Planning: Democracy's Challenge & the American City*. The influence of European approaches to land use regulation which the Marsh publication advanced is analyzed thoroughly in Sonia A. Hirt, *Zoned in the USA: The Origins and Implications of American Land-Use Regulation* and Thomas H. Logan, "The Americanization of German Zoning," *Journal of the American Institute of Planners*.[45]

The basics of the New York City Zoning Resolution of 1916 and the *Euclid* case can be found in most planning and zoning histories, such as Mel Scott, *American City Planning Since 1890* and Charles M. Haar and Jerome S. Kayden, *Zoning and the American Dream*. The most thorough assessment is Michael Allan Wolf, *The Zoning of America: Euclid v. Ambler*. Also useful is Edward M. Bassett, *Zoning: The Laws, Administration, and Court Decisions During the First Twenty Years*, given Bassett's role in presenting a brief in support of zoning for the Village of Ambler. How the early zoning schemes shaped suburban development is explored in Marc A. Weiss, *The Rise of the Community Builders: The American Real Estate Industry and Urban Land Development*. The growth of the zoning movement in US cities and suburbs in the 1920s is documented in Theodora K. Hubbard and Henry V. Hubbard, *Our Cities of Today and Tomorrow: A Survey of Planning and Zoning Progress in the United States.*[46]

The use of zoning to achieve residential segregation by race has been the subject of writings both during the period prior to and after the US Supreme Court decision in *Buchanan v. Warley* (1917). See Gilbert T. Stephenson, "The Segregation of the White and Negro Races in Cities," *South Atlantic Quarterly*; Christopher Silver, "The Racial Origins of Zoning in American Cities," June Manning Thomas and Marsha Ritzdorf, *Urban Planning and the African American Community: In the Shadows*; Garret Power, "Apartheid Baltimore Style: The Residential Segregation Ordinance of 1910–1913," *Maryland Law Review* 42 (1983): 296–301; and Roger L. Rice, "Residential Segregation by Law, 1910–1917," in the *Journal of Southern History*. The ongoing efforts to use zoning to advance exclusionary objectives aimed at blacks, other minorities, and the poor is the focus of Yale Rabin, "Expulsive Zoning: The Inequitable Legacy of Euclid," in Haar and Kayden, *Zoning and the American Dream*; and Marsha Ritzdorf, "Locked Out of Paradise: Contemporary Exclusionary Zoning, the Supreme court, and African Americans, 1970 to the Present," in Thomas and Ritzdorf, *Urban Planning and the African American Community.*[47]

The development of zoning into one of the key tools by communities to advance implementation of the plans, and to offset some of the limitations of Euclidian zoning through innovative strategies such as planning unit developments, overlay zones, and more recently form-based codes is discussed thoroughly in Barry Cullingworth and Roger W. Caves, *Planning in the USA: Policies, Issues,*

and Processes. The most widely cited critique of zoning's impact on urban vitality is presented forcefully in Jane Jacobs, *The Death and Life of Great American Cities*. The best recent assessment of how land use regulations have influenced urban form that includes a discussion of form-based codes, see Emily Talen, *City Rules: How Regulations Affect Urban Form.*[48]

NOTES

1. Stanley K. Schultz, *Constructing Urban Culture: American Cities and City Planning, 1800–1920.* (Philadelphia: Temple University Press, 1989), 59.
2. Schultz, *Constructing Urban Culture,* 62.
3. Schultz, 77.
4. Schultz, 54–55.
5. *Attorney General v. Henry B. Williams and others,* 174 Mass. 476 (1899).
6. Harvey A. Kantor, "Benjamin C. Marsh and the Fight over Population Congestion," *Journal of the American Institute of Planners* 40 (November 1974): 423–427.
7. Benjamin C. Marsh, *An Introduction to City Planning: Democracy's Challenge & the American City.* (New York: Privately Published, 1908), 28.
8. Kantor, "Benjamin C. Marsh and the Fight," 428.
9. Kantor., 428.
10. Thomas H. Logan, "The Americanization of German Zoning," *Journal of the American Institute of Planners* 42 (October 1976): 379. Also see, Sonia A. Hirt, *Zoned in the USA: The Origins and Implications of American Land-Use Regulation* (Ithaca, NY: Cornell University Press, 2014).
11. Logan, "The Americanization of German Zoning," 381.
12. Logan.
13. Logan, "The Americanization of German Zoning," 383.
14. Logan, 383.
15. Logan, "The Americanization of German Zoning," 383–384.
16. Cited in Barry Cullingworth and Roger W. Caves, *Planning in the USA: Policies, Issues, and Processes,* 3d ed. (London and New York: Routledge, 2009), 67; and Ernest Freund, *The Police Power: Public Policy and Constitutional Rights* (Chicago, 1904).
17. Michael Allan Wolf, *The Zoning of America: Euclid v. Ambler* (Lawrence: University Press of

Kansas, 2008), 26–28; and Raphael Fischler, "The Metropolitan Dimension of Early Zoning: Revisiting the 1916 New York City Ordinance," *Journal of the American Planning Association* 64 (1998): 170–188.

18. Cullingworth and Caves, 69.

19. Schultz, *Constructing Urban Culture*, 80.

20. Schultz, 87; *Zoning Ordinance No. 2812 and Amending Ordinance No. 5421; Village of Euclid, November 13, 1922; Village of Euclid v. Ambler Realty Co.,* 272 U.S. 365 (1926).

21. Edward M. Bassett, *Zoning: The Laws, Administration, and Court Decisions During the First Twenty Years* (New York: Russell Sage Foundation, 1936); and C. H. Cheney, "Zoning in Practice," *National Municipal Review* 9 (1920): 31–43, quoted in Cullingworth and Caves, p. 74.

22. Weiss, Marc A., *The Rise of the Community Builders: The American Real Estate Industry and Urban Land Development* (New York: Columbia University Press, 1987), 105–106.

23. David L. Callies and Robert H. Freilich, *Cases and Materials on Land Use* (St. Paul, MN: West Publishing, 1986), 42–45; and *Nectow v. City of Cambridge,* 277 U.S. 183, 48 S. Ct. 447, 72 L.Ed. 842 (1928).

24. Theodora K. Hubbard and Henry V. Hubbard, *Our Cities of Today and Tomorrow: A Survey of Planning and Zoning Progress in the United States* (Cambridge, MA: Harvard University Press, 1929).

25. Cullingworth and Caves, 72.

26. Blucher quoted in Callies and Freilich, *Cases and Materials,* 47.

27. Yale Rabin, "Expulsive Zoning: The Inequitable Legacy of Euclid," in *Zoning and the American Dream,* ed. Charles M. Haar and Jerome S. Kayden (Washington, DC: American Planning Association, 1989), 105.

28. Garret Power, "Apartheid Baltimore Style: The Residential Segregation Ordinance of 1910–1913," *Maryland Law Review* 42 (1983): 301.

29. Christopher Silver, "The Racial Origins of Zoning in American Cities," in *Urban Planning and the African American Community: In the Shadows,* ed. June Manning Thomas and Marsha Ritzdorf (Thousand Oaks, CA: SAGE, 1997), 27–28; Gilbert T. Stephenson, "The Segregation of the White and Negro Races in Cities," *South Atlantic Quarterly* 13 (1914): 1–18; and Stanislaw J. Makielski, *Local Planning in Virginia: Development,* *Politics and Prospects* (Charlottesville: University of Virginia Institute of Government, 1964), 17.

30. *Hopkins v. City of Richmond,* 117 Va. 692, 86 S.E. 139–148 (1915); *Carey v. City of Atlanta,* 143 Ga. 192, 84 S.E. 456 (1915); and *Harden v. City of Atlanta,* 147 Ga. 248, 93 S.E. 401 (1917).

31. *Buchanan v. Warley,* 245 U.S. 60 (1917); Power, 312–313; and Roger L. Rice, "Residential Segregation by Law, 1910–1917," *Journal of Southern History* 64 (1968): 179–199.

32. George D. Hott, "Constitutionality of Municipal Zoning and Segregation Ordinances," *West Virginia Quarterly* 33 (1927): 344–345.

33. Hott, "Constitutionality of Municipal Zoning," 348–349.

34. Major Gardner, "Race Segregation in Cities," *Kentucky Law Journal* 29 (1941): 213–219.

35. Clifford L. Weaver and Richard Babcock, *City Zoning: The Once and Future Frontier* (Chicago: American Planning Association Press, 1979), 13–14.

36. Weiss, *The Rise of the Community Builders,* 5.

37. Mel Scott, *American City Planning Since 1890* (Berkeley: University of California Press, 1971), 349–350.

38. Scott, *American City Planning,* 483.

39. *Berman v. Parker,* 348 U.S. 26 (1954).

40. Scott, *American City Planning,* 592.

41. Jane Jacobs, *The Death and Life of Great American Cities.* New York: Random House, 1961), 242.

42. Jacobs, *The Death and Life,* 235.

43. See online (http://codesproject.asu.edu/sites/default/files/1922%20Zoning%20Ord%20_1.pdf) for a pdf of the Zoning Ordinance No. 2812 and Amending Ordinance No. 5421, Village of Euclid.

44. For zoning precedents in the 19th century, see Stanley K. Schultz, *Constructing Urban Culture: American Cities and City Planning, 1800–1920* (Philadelphia: Temple University Press, 1989); also Jon C. Teaford, "Special Legislation and the Cities, 1865–1900," *American Journal of Legal History* 23 (1979): 189–212. The classic overview is Seymour I. Toll, *Zoned America* (New York: Grossman, 1969). The key case law from the 19th century is in Freund, *The Police Power* (Chicago, 1904), supplemented by Norman Williams, *American Planning Law* (Chicago: Callaghan, 1975).

45. See Marsh, *An Introduction to City Planning* (1908) for the beginnings of the zoning movement,

while European approaches are described in Hirt, *Zoned in the USA*; also Logan, "The Americanization of German Zoning."

46. For the basics, see Scott, *American City Planning Since 1890*; and Haar and Kayden, ed., *Zoning and the American Dream*. Allan Wolf, *The Zoning of America* is the most thorough assessment, and Bassett, *Zoning: The Laws,* is quite useful. Early zoning schemes are described in Weiss, *The Rise of the Community Builders*. Hubbard and Hubbard treat zoning in the United States in *Our Cities of Today and Tomorrow*.

47. On the topic of zoning to achieve racial segregation, see the Supreme Court decision in *Buchanan v. Warley* (1917); Stephenson, "The Segregation of the White and Negro Races in Cities"; Silver, "The Racial Origins of Zoning in American Cities"; Thomas and Ritzdorf, *Urban Planning and the African American Community*, 23–42; Power, "Apartheid Baltimore Style"; Rice, "Residential Segregation by Law"; Rabin, "Expulsive Zoning"; and Ritzdorf, "Locked Out of Paradise: Contemporary Exclusionary Zoning, the Supreme court, and African Americans, 1970 to the Present," in Thomas and Ritzdorf, eds., *Urban Planning and the African American Community*, 43–57.

48. For discussion of zoning use to advance community planning, see Cullingworth and Caves, *Planning in the USA*. For a look at the impact of zoning and regulation on urban areas, see Jacobs, *The Death and Life of Great American Cities*; and Emily Talen, *City Rules: How Regulations Affect Urban Form* (Washington, DC: Island Press, 2012).

Christopher Silver

URBAN RENEWAL

Urban renewal, in its narrowest sense, emerged as a term recommended by President Eisenhower's Advisory Committee on Housing, and then incorporated into the ensuing Housing Act of 1954, to encourage "a broader and more comprehensive approach to prevent the growth of slums."[1] More commonly, urban renewal refers to a broad raft of interrelated national and local policies, programs, and projects, implemented in the vast majority of American cities between 1949 and 1973, which typically entailed major redevelopment of existing areas with a view to the modernization of housing, highway infrastructure, commercial, and business districts, as well as other large-scale constructions. Construed broadly, urban renewal also incorporated the (often frustrated) ambitions of generations of reformers, from the Progressive Era through the Great Society, to ameliorate the conditions of poverty and inequality in American cities by focusing primarily on physical transformation of the urban built environment.

To the extent that there has been a national urban policy in the United States, it has generally been concerned with the renewal of cities. Urban renewal scholarship overlaps and intersects with the separable histories of public housing, city planning, and transportation (especially highway building). Any examination of urban renewal, like any public policy, should consider the program's goals, processes, and effects, each of which entails its own potentially distinct history and scholarly approaches. Nor are policy studies separable from the surrounding societal and cultural contexts: Urban policies in particular are inextricably tied up with attitudes toward cities, the associations with their inhabitants and lifestyles, and the social or economic effects thereof. The story of urban renewal thus reflects the dynamic, tumultuous course of American urban life over the 20th century. As a set of evolving public policies it embodies a national consciousness and an extended political conversation about the meaning of the United States as an urban society.

LOCAL ANTECEDENTS AND PROGRESSIVE REFORMERS

As the United States developed an industrial capitalist economy, with its attendant urbanizing populations, voices soon called for refashioning the industrial cityscape in order to redress its social, aesthetic, and environmental shortcomings. Even the earliest experiments in large-scale American manufacturing were conceived in deliberate response to the failings of British industrial cities. Notably, within a generation Lowell, Massachusetts, proved a spectacular failure (if a financial success) with regard to the epidemics, pollution, and proletarianization the enterprising Boston Associates designed the mill town expressly to avert. Similarly, the Pullman railcar manufacturer's eponymous company town in Illinois, far from ameliorating labor militancy through paternalistic city planning, was consumed in a bloody strike with workers in 1894.[2]

Nineteenth-century experiments by the private sector in urban mitigation via urban reorganization—literally, to re-*form* the industrial city—were eventually taken up by public authorities at the dawn of the 20th century. For its part, the federal government took virtually no hand in the building or rebuilding of US cities until decades later. Instead, local city governments paved the way toward urban redevelopment in North America. But many of their urban policy prescriptions, like many urbanites in the period of mass immigration to American cities, had transatlantic roots. These included socialistic programs such as the municipalization of services and utilities: for example, transforming mass transit to public transit, as borrowed from established models in Britain and Germany.[3]

Around the turn of the 20th century, "muckrakers" such as Danish immigrant Jacob Riis published reformist (if sensationalist) photographic and journalistic *exposées* on the conditions in poor urban neighborhoods, defining and elevating the issue of "how the other half lives." The emergent fields of social work and social science added data collection to this cause of pathologizing and diagnosing urban ills. Charles and Eugenia Weller compiled an exhaustive survey, *Neglected Neighbors: Stories of Life in the Alleys, Tenements and Shanties of the National Capital* (1909). Lawrence Veiller and other Progressive Era reformers

successfully lobbied the New York legislature, during the governorship of Theodore Roosevelt, to pass new laws regulating Manhattan's tenement conditions.[4]

At a time when women were still legally disenfranchised, elite women employed their social and economic clout for urban reform. First Lady Ellen Wilson toured DC's inhabited alleys and helped convince President Woodrow Wilson to endorse "the great task of clearing away the slums" by 1913. Such affluent figures were matched by working-class women leading urban labor movements, such as Elizabeth Gurley Flynn, Clara Lemlich, and Emma Goldman. These two strata sometimes even collaborated, particularly in the context of the urban Settlement House movement (with prominent female advocates such as Jane Addams and Florence Kelley) and of neighborhood reform generally. Out of this context, Edith Elmer Wood and Mary Kingsbury Simkhovitch became two of the most vocal exponents for government intervention into urban affairs, particularly housing provision.[5]

Perhaps the most potent influence of all on the impulse toward urban redevelopment, directly and indirectly, was the example of Paris. During the 1850s and 1860s, that city was aggressively reconstructed by under Napoleon III by city prefect Georges-Eugène Haussmann. That vision of a forcibly modernized cityscape, with its harmonious bourgeois boulevards and (not incidentally) marginalized industrial workers and workplaces, inspired generations of urban reformers on both sides of the Atlantic. The Paris model was promulgated via architectural designs following the École des Beaux-Arts, and then under the banner of the City Beautiful movement more broadly. The *locus classicus* for the importation and popularization of this pattern into the American scene was the World's Columbian Exposition in Chicago in 1893, especially the impressive, if temporary, "White City" that it presented to 27 million visitors.[6]

Architect Daniel Burnham, a key designer for the Exposition, was unable to convince his fellow Chicagoans with his plan to redevelop their civic center along City Beautiful lines. Yet such proposals garnered Burnham and other City Beautiful proponents the attention of a far more powerful patron: Washington, DC. Burnham was invited to join a commission convened by Senator James McMillan of Michigan, who oversaw affairs of the US capital at a time when the District of Columbia was administered directly by the federal government, rather more like a colonial territory than a self-governing city. Burnham and the McMillan commission produced a 1902 plan to transform Washington into a White City, calling for extensive redevelopment of central neighborhoods in order to produce a monumental core. A linchpin of the plan was the creation of an administrative district just north of this expanded National Mall corridor, stretching from the Capitol to the White House. The so-called Federal Triangle was predicated on the eradication of a twenty-block neighborhood associated with illicit activities and marginalized groups (prostitutes, Chinese immigrants, African Americans). Redevelopment of the area began in the 1920s and continued for decades thereafter, with much of the area's new character as an official bureaucratic corridor taking shape during the Franklin Roosevelt administration.

The Federal Triangle's redevelopment into perhaps the greatest achievement of the City Beautiful movement reveals an integral goal of creating a "white city." In another sense, however, that process often included the displacement of undesirable social—especially racial—groups. Early 20th-century experiments in government-sponsored urban redevelopment coincided with the "nadir of race relations" in the United States, and thus racist attitudes were incorporated into many policies. While southern communities became notorious for violently enforcing an elaborate Jim Crow legal regime in public spaces, formal and informal systems of racial segregation were actually implemented nationwide. Some took

the form of half-hidden private sector practices, particularly in the real estate industry, such as "covenants" in contracts that excluded property transfer to non-white (even non-Christian) buyers. But far more enduring was the imposition of zoning, a key policy innovation for land-use control. An urban regulatory mechanism (again) incubated at the local level, the earliest Supreme Court challenges to the constitutionality of such unprecedented restriction of property rights made clear that zoning was a tool for exclusion of undesirable groups and activities from sanitized cityscapes.[7]

Meanwhile, however, marginalized groups staked their own claims to shape a renewed urban life through redevelopment. Industrial labor unions that organized primarily working-class immigrants, the very populations enduring substandard urban slum conditions, executed several pioneering redevelopment projects to create cooperative housing. Adapting models from some older Victorian-era housing philanthropies, the Amalgamated Clothing Workers Union and other labor organizations cleared several tenement blocks from the Lower East Side to the Bronx and redeveloped those sites into garden-style cooperative apartments, particularly after the New York state legislature provided incentives via its Limited Dividend Housing Companies Law of 1926. Between 1932 and 1935, a federation of hosiery workers in Philadelphia commissioned the Carl Mackley Houses, the first to receive federal financing from the Housing Division of the Public Works Administration. They were also among the first to feature the kind of European avant-garde designs that eventually came to connote public housing nationwide. This iconoclastic modernist architecture initially reflected the leftist politics that united the architects with their union clients, eschewing the Beaux Arts–influenced neoclassicism that still dominated public and private building through the Second World War.[8]

NEW DEAL URBAN RENEWAL THROUGH DEPRESSION AND WAR

During the 1930s, global economic collapse catalyzed the various local trends and fused them into a national strategy for urban renewal by the 1940s. In economic and social terms, the Great Depression proved a harrowing experience for American cities. And in a nation that was predominantly urban, at least since the 1920 census, the federal government could hardly ignore the distress in these quarters. Federal urban policy during the Great Depression was initially devoted to the question of reviving the real estate and construction sectors in American cities. President Roosevelt's alphabet soup of New Deal programs included the Federal Housing Authority (FHA), Home Owners Loan Corporation (HOLC), and eventually, the Veterans Administration (VA). Such agencies and the funds they disbursed primed the pump of mortgage lending and private housing construction, greatly expanding access to home ownership in the process. But they also gave an official federal imprimatur while simultaneously exacerbating patterns of discrimination and segregation by favoring new, racially homogenous suburban developments while neglecting older, diverse inner-city neighborhoods. This exclusion of certain groups and areas from such relief came to be known as "redlining," in reference to the maps used by banks and government agencies. Redlining essentially sentenced to decline those districts marked out of bounds for private lending and public guarantees.[9]

While federal subsidies for new private construction was directed disproportionately toward private builders on the suburban periphery, other kinds of federal funding became available for public works projects in declining central cities. In that realm, the pioneering public entrepreneur was Robert Moses, a legendary New York official with unrivaled talents for marshalling federal funding and local authorities. With roots sunk deep in the Progressive Era (his 1913 Columbia doctoral thesis examined British civil service reform), Moses became a role model and prominent lobbyist for urban renewal from the 1920s through the 1960s. His earliest notoriety was gained from building parks, pools, and other public leisure amenities for the urban masses, as well as later automobile infrastructure projects including bridges, tunnels, and highways. And over three decades he also enabled the construction of thousands of units of public and private housing, from low-income to high-end redevelopments.[10]

The federal government began providing for direct redress of urban housing conditions during the Depression years. New York City's Housing Authority was created in 1934 to qualify for federal financing and was then used to demolish every third tenement on East Third Street and renovate the remaining structures, for the aptly named "First Houses" project. Atlanta was arguably the first city to commit to an aggressive program of slum clearance and public housing construction. And in pattern that was sadly replicated by programs nationwide, and despite a rhetoric of colorblindness that was espoused by officials as high up as US Secretary of the Interior Harold Ickes, these government-sponsored projects helped reinforce segregation in Atlanta. During 1937 racial fault lines in the nation's capital placed Washington's Alley Dwelling Authority in an untenable position between whites—who refused to admit blacks into the first federally financed public housing in St. Mary's Court—and advocates of racial equality who complained that the authority was destroying more housing than they were providing. Similar patterns of conflict persisted over the coming decades.[11]

Despite being fought thousands of miles overseas, World War II transformed American cities, particularly in terms of the US government's engagement with urban affairs. Enormous industrial sectors of the American urban economy came under federal coordination for the war effort. Meanwhile, millions of men and women migrated across regions and into cities to meet wartime mobilization and manpower demands. These (and many other) abrupt shifts, especially coming after a decade of economic stagnation, created new patterns of thought and action in urban planning. Under the initial rationale of civil defense, namely the protection of patriotic shrines from the American Revolution such as Independence Hall, the first urban national park was created in Philadelphia beginning in 1941. This act of 18th-century historic preservation, however, also entailed clearing acres of structures from the intervening centuries, many of them historic or architecturally significant in their own right, in the interest of creating a firebreak.[12]

World War II's unprecedented augmentation of national administrative capacities, together with the brazen destruction of cities around the globe, prepared the way for tabula rasa proposals (not to mention the exile of many European modernist architects and planners) that envisioned a radical transformation of city life. In 1943, the editors of *Architectural Forum* encouraged urbanists to imagine planning the postwar American city upon the cessation of hostilities. That this would entail profound shifts in both the form and process of urban development seemed as assured as it was desirable.[13]

THE POSTWAR URBAN RENEWAL ORDER

In the late 1940s, the United States segued into an atomic Cold War. The strategically charged comparisons between two competing political and economic systems gave new urgency to tackling potentially embarrassing slum conditions and helped ensure a federal interest in such questions. Many city planners, housing reformers, and modernist architects called for rational, comprehensive, centralized planning. Yet a United States political culture of paranoid anti-Communism also dictated that the American system be distinguished from the top-down planning of the Soviet Union. Within this context, a hybrid, even fluid model emerged, with partnerships between local and national authorities, and the public and private sectors.

A regular series of national legislative acts built up the resources and momentum for urban renewal between the late 1940s and early 1970s. The opening shot came with the Housing Act of 1949, with an equally important sequel passed in 1954. Each of these laws (as well as major housing bills in 1965 and 1968) reflected successive shifts—in party strength, ideology, and goals. They also reinforced, however, some consistent patterns: urban programs would reflect the three-ply complexities of American federalism, whereby national funding and mandates had to be dispensed to authorities that the individual states chartered with jurisdiction to act within local municipalities. Federal financing, for example, could underwrite a state-chartered redevelopment authority that would demolish areas in a particular city, under the coordination of a local planning agency. In addition to appropriations running well into the billions over the ensuing decades, urban renewal legislation authorized these agencies with far-reaching powers of compulsory purchase of private property, so-called eminent domain under Title I of the 1949 legislation. Such forced expropriation technically required an inspector's survey and designation of properties as "blighted" and thus suitable for redevelopment.[14]

Even after clearing the US Congress and obtaining presidential approval, the ambitious urban renewal program still faced a final hurdle in the courts. The sweeping legislation entailed a significant shift away from constitutional protections of private property vis-a-vis public aims. The test case emerged right in Uncle Sam's backyard. The run-down, southwest neighborhood on Washington's waterfront also boasted some of the oldest buildings in the capital. But it was designated as an urban renewal area slated for nearly total demolition. The residents were primarily poor African Americans, though many business proprietors were Jewish. Among the latter, one family that owned a retail store filed suit challenging the constitutionality of their dispossession for mere beautification. When the Supreme Court ruled against their claim in the landmark *Berman v. Parker* case (1954), citing the legitimacy of aesthetic improvement as a government aim, the decision thereby provided a broad interpretation of the law, expanded to permit large-scale application of eminent domain under justification well beyond the traditional bounds of the Fifth Amendment's public use clause.[15]

Just as dramatic as Title I's transformation of the status quo was Title III of the Housing Act of 1949, which authorized appropriations for more than 800,000 units of public housing. Robert Moses was well positioned to lay claim to nearly one-sixth of these for New York alone. In addition to modest-scale, interwar housing experiments such as the First Houses, or even the ambitious multiblock Rockefeller Center project, New York City boasted many large-scale residential redevelopments by the 1940s: Metropolitan Life Insurance Company's Parkchester in the Bronx, the eighty-acre Stuyvesant Town project, and the neighboring Peter Cooper Village, on Manhattan's Lower East Side. But even those enormous privately financed projects paled in comparison with the vast stretches of the city redeveloped for public housing after 1949.[16]

Postwar urban renewal also took a page from the turn-of-the-century City Beautiful movement by emphasizing showpiece civic and cultural centers, from the Carnegie complex of museums and libraries in Pittsburgh to the National Mall in Washington, DC. This predilection for concentrating cultural institutions into large building ensembles found their most high profile expression in two performing arts hubs: New York's Lincoln Center (1955–1969) and Washington's Kennedy

Center (1958–1971). Each invoked eminent domain to raze many city blocks in order to assemble a single giant parcel. Multiple cultural organizations then came to be housed on the same campus or even, in the Washington, DC case, under one massive roof. For Lincoln Center these included the New York Philharmonic (relocating from no less storied an address than Carnegie Hall), the Metropolitan Opera, the New York City Ballet, and the Juilliard School of Music, among others; the Kennedy Center would host domestic and international touring performers, as well as the Washington Opera, the National Symphony, and the American Ballet Theatre. No other communities undertook cultural construction on such a scale, but during the 1950s and 1960s almost every American city utilized urban renewal funds and authorities to enact civic projects, including auditoriums, sports stadiums, hotels, convention centers, fairgrounds, museums, archives, and libraries.[17]

Cultural institutions were modest organizations compared with two other major players in the urban renewal drama: medicine and higher education. Both of these actors expanded dramatically at the time thanks to federal insurance, research, and tuition programs. In the postwar era of suburbanization and deindustrialization, private disinvestment from cities contrasted with city hospitals and universities that were then growing into major urban employers. Areas around such institutions were commonly designated for urban renewal, to accommodate their expanding physical plants that demanded an everlarger real estate footprint, to permit the modernization of their image and operations, and to "renew" deteriorating urban neighborhoods and populations deemed undesirable by their white-collar stakeholders. The knock-on effects of these "meds and eds" anchors extended well beyond their campuses, as affluent employees participated in the rehabilitation or redevelopment of private housing stock in surrounding neighborhoods, a process that was eventually termed "gentrification." One example from the earliest period occurred in the Hyde Park near the University of Chicago, where college officials and resident faculty deliberately insulated the neighborhood from a poor black enclave to the east. Nationwide, the combined impact of large-scale official campus redevelopment along with the cumulative pressures of many individual homebuyers served to displace enormous numbers of poor and usually minority residents near hospitals and universities. The result was a new and often racially charged version of the town-gown rivalry in the urban renewal era. The most dramatic of these erupted in 1968 when Columbia University officials attempted to build a gymnasium between its campus and Harlem in Morningside Park.[18]

It was not only nonprofit, tax-exempt organizations (whether cultural, educational, or medical) that became substantial beneficiaries of government-orchestrated urban renewal. In fact, the for-profit, private sector—at least its largest actors—intervened vigorously throughout the period. An important inter-war prototype for large-scale urban redevelopment was provided by Rockefeller Center, certainly one of the most ambitious private real estate developments during its period of construction from 1931 to 1939. John D. Rockefeller Jr. rebuilt twenty-two acres of midtown Manhattan into a unified ensemble of art deco towers, indoor concourses, and outdoor open spaces for offices, theaters, soundstages, dining, shopping, and leisure. All this heralded a new city-within-a-city paradigm, one oriented inward, shunning the conventional sidewalks and avenues of metropolitan street life. Then, during the 1940s, Pittsburgh's business elite executed a dramatic private sector urban renewal initiative involving multiple corporate stakeholders and extending across a much larger site. Mellon Bank, Union Steel, Aluminum Company of America, Pittsburgh Plate Glass, and others conspired to transform the entire "golden triangle," a sooty industrial district at the confluence of the city's major rivers, into a Gateway Center

that portended the area's renaissance into a cleansed, modernist office district.[19]

Urban retailers had struggled through the Great Depression and World War II rationing only to be hit hard by the suburban migration of consumers of the postwar years. While many commercial enterprises folded and others reoriented from downtown flagship stores to outlying shopping malls, some made use of urban renewal approaches to reinvent their urban footprint. Rochester provided the first opportunity for shopping mall architect Victor Gruen to bring the format he pioneered for "green field" settings into an older urban core. With the backing of city hall officials and two established department stores, Midtown Plaza (1958–1962) redeveloped fourteen blocks into an enclosed shopping mall with parking, a hotel, office tower, even an auditorium. On a smaller scale, municipal and business leaders split the cost of converting Kalamazoo's Burdick Street in 1958–1959 into the first permanent pedestrian mall in North America.[20]

Urban renewal worked dramatic transformations on every major US city and many smaller ones. The cities and projects noted here are representative (or in some cases highlights) but hardly exhaustive. Comparable examples exist across the country, from Rochester to Miami, Milwaukee to Denver, Seattle to San Diego. New Haven became an important laboratory for the collaboration between the reformist mayor Richard Lee, the public entrepreneur Ed Logue, and key stakeholders in the nonprofit sector such as Yale University and the business community.[21]

Similarly (and again with a hand from Ed Logue), Boston was the setting for a number of key redevelopment projects, particularly given the influence of nearby architects, planners, and urban social scientists at Harvard University and the Massachusetts Institute of Technology. Incorporating the earlier corporate urban renewal models from Pittsburgh's golden triangle and New York's Rockefeller Center, the Prudential Insurance Company redeveloped the Back Bay's railyards into an iconic modernist office tower after 1957. Boston's West End, site of an expanding Massachusetts General Hospital, became equally iconic for entirely different reasons, intensely studied as an example of the effects of neighborhood demolition. And at the city's ancient core—"the hub"—extensive redevelopment produced a redoubtable government center and cut off the North End with a major highway artery.[22]

St. Louis initially focused urban renewal on Plaza Square, then the Mansion House area, in hopes of redeveloping upscale housing near city hall. Industrial districts including Mill Creek Valley and Kosciusko were then targeted, followed by plans for a civic center and stadium. Once again, government housing and urban renewal projects after 1937, particularly the massive postwar Cochran Gardens, Pruitt-Igoe, and Mill Creek complexes, only served to further entrench residential segregation in St. Louis.[23]

A nationally prominent role model for its distinctive brand of urban renewal was Philadelphia.

That city's recipe included a number of key ingredients. A political reform movement, led by a young generation of white-collar professionals, unseated the established political machine by the 1950s. Notably, this initiative placed modern city planning at the center of its bid to voters, exhibiting elaborate models (including in a popular department store) to illustrate the promise of a redeveloped center city. Planning commission director Edmund Bacon literally became a poster boy for urban renewal (he was featured on the cover of *Time* magazine in 1964). Like New York's Robert Moses, Bacon coordinated a full portfolio of project types: clearance of unfavored residential and industrial sites, low- and high-income housing redevelopments (public and private respectively), urban expressways, a new civic center, and even a downtown shopping mall. Unlike Moses, who disdained both electoral politics and academic planners, Bacon styled himself as a visionary artist in the tradition of baroque European city builders. And particularly with his selective demolition in the historic colonial areas around Independence Park, Bacon also displayed the most restrained renewal approach during a period otherwise characterized by clear-cutting of neighborhoods. None of this made Philadelphia immune from mass dislocations, with disparate impacts on poor and minority communities, or, eventually, a sharp backlash against urban renewal.[24]

The highwater mark for US federal engagement with urban affairs came during the Lyndon B. Johnson administration (1963–1969). Urban renewal programs dovetailed with his larger agenda for the Great Society, including "war on poverty" initiatives of the Office of Economic Opportunity. This period culminated with the creation of the first cabinet level agency for coordinating urban policy in 1965: the Department of Housing and Urban Development (HUD). At the same time, despite clearing political and legal hurdles in Washington, urban renewal projects faced constant challenges before, during, and after implementation. Given that they were enacted in the midst of civil rights mobilization, it is unsurprising that these disputes often turned on the issue of race. Demands for greater empowerment of poor, minority communities in the face of so many massive urban renewal projects led to the Model Cities initiative, launched in 1966 with the expressed goal of "maximum feasible participation" by citizens during the urban planning process. While radically democratic in its conception, Model Cities ultimately stoked complicated power struggles among community organizers, municipal elites, and federal officials. The conflicts often proved irreconcilable, particularly when overlain with racial fault lines. The Johnson administration thus oversaw not only the high-water mark of urban renewal as implemented over the previous two decades but also the beginning of its end.[25]

COLLAPSE OF THE URBAN RENEWAL ORDER AND AFTERMATH

Urban renewal was in many ways the consummate domestic policy initiative of American liberals between the late 1940s and 1960s. Together with Cold War anti-Communism, urban renewal was one of the few clear expressions of a consensus that transcended partisan affiliations or even the ideological poles within the major parties. The various programs entailed sustained federal government appropriations matched by few civilian programs in US history. Nevertheless, urban renewal unquestionably reinforced private capitalism, in keeping with the main thrust of liberal programs since the New Deal, with large-scale urban business interests—from builders to retailers—among its prime beneficiaries. Proponents of urban renewal relied upon the aggressive exercise of executive authority, particularly through widespread use of eminent domain and condemnation. Yet these powers resided primarily in municipal jurisdictions and in most cases reflected American federalism in terms of local agency control.

Given its many inherent tensions, like those of midcentury American liberalism generally, urban renewal was subjected to unanswerable critiques and unsustainable pressures from both sides of the political spectrum and all sectors of US society during the fractious 1960s. Some of the earliest, and in many ways most trenchant critiques originated from policy-oriented intellectuals within the establishment who hitherto advocated, and in some cases even crafted, the urban renewal programs in question. Arguably the first to cry foul, already by the late 1950s, was Catherine Bauer, disappointed with the "dreary deadlock" that beset the public housing programs she vigorously promoted after 1920. Others who began to swing into an opposition posture focused on the pain of dislocations imposed by slum clearance, highway construction, and urban redevelopment projects, which was being borne disproportionately by poor, minority, and otherwise disempowered groups within urban society.[26]

Social scientists in the early 1960s homed in on the human issues of forced uprooting, including mental health impacts, such as Marc Fried's evocative 1963 study, "Grieving for a Lost Home: Psychological Costs of Relocation." Herbert Gans's *The Urban Villagers* (1962) proved to be an influential (at least in academic policy debates) examination of residents in Boston's West End before, during, and after redevelopment. Gans pointedly questioned the destruction of traditional working-class neighborhood communities. Meanwhile, Jane Jacobs advanced a less academic but consequently much more widely read version of such arguments against slum clearance in *The Death and Life of Great American Cities* (1961).[27]

By the mid-1960s, political scientists began posing difficult questions regarding the policy rationales for urban renewal. The floodgates were opened by Martin Anderson's "critical analysis of urban renewal" covering the decade and a half since the Housing Act of 1949, a censorious tone encapsulated by its ominous title: *The Federal Bulldozer*. James Q. Wilson, Edward Banfield, and Daniel Patrick Moynihan, among other critical policy advisors with prestigious academic posts, soon began circling unsympathetically. Urban problems, they concluded, were either inexorably cultural (citing a "culture of poverty" theory, ideas of "social pathologies," or instability in African American family patterns) or else they were politically intractable (and hence not soluble by the technocratic expertise of urban social reformers or city planners). Whereas urban renewal stood as a centerpiece for midcentury American liberalism, the critiques and critics of it became foundational for a countervailing policy regime. By the late 1960s, these critics emerged under the banner of "neoconservatism." Thus, Daniel Patrick Moynihan counseled three successive presidents (Kennedy, Johnson, Nixon) with a decidedly rightward trend in his evolving policy positions, culminating in 1970 when he recommended a "period of benign neglect" as Nixon's urban affairs adviser. Martin Anderson would also advise Nixon from his 1968 campaign through the ensuing administration, laying the groundwork for a long career serving under Republican presidents Ford, Reagan, and Bush.[28]

Such intellectual critiques reflected mounting grassroots dissatisfaction with urban renewal, while also anticipating a more forceful popular backlash as the 1960s unfolded. Public opposition to redevelopment that entailed extensive demolition first coalesced against urban highway projects. Such so-called freeway revolts occurred across the country from the 1950s through the 1970s and succeeded in halting roads including San Francisco's Embarcadero Freeway, New York's Lower Manhattan Expressway, Washington's Three Sisters Bridge, Baltimore's Franklin-Mulberry corridor, Chicago's Crosstown Expressway, and Philadelphia's Crosstown Expressway. And such temporary movements had lasting effects: few new urban highway routes were constructed in older cities thereafter. Ad hoc citizens' groups also formed to defeat other kinds of redevelopment proposals, notably the community organization Jane Jacobs led from 1963 to 1968 against an urban renewal plan to demolish her own West Village neighborhood in Manhattan. These neighborhood defense impulses converged with an older historic preservation movement to yield blanket protections of the urban fabric through the designation of historic districts, beginning with Brooklyn Heights in 1965. Most other cities witnessed a similar progression from redevelopment toward preservation in the wake of public outcry.[29]

Urban renewal again proved most contentious when it intersected with US racial inequalities and prejudices. Each of the aforementioned fault lines proved particularly treacherous in the era of an assertive civil rights movement and an attendant white backlash. Consider the issue of resident relocation:

"Urban renewal means negro removal, and the federal government is an accomplice to this fact," author James Baldwin provocatively declared in 1963, thereby suggesting that minority dislocations were neither unintended consequences nor unfortunate byproducts. Rather, Baldwin asserted, they were primary and deliberate goals of the program. Similarly, Student Non-violent Coordinating Committee leader (and future Washington, DC, mayor) Marion Barry recast freeway revolts in the nation's capital as a question of racial justice with the slogan: "No white man's roads thru black men's homes!" Opponents to Philadelphia's proposed inner ring of highways accused planners of fashioning a "race moat" around the center city. And in the wake of Columbia University's controversial and unsuccessful attempt to expand its campus into Morningside Park in 1968, politicized black urbanists formed the Architects' Renewal Committee in Harlem (ARCH). The organization's leaders drew up and published documents, such as the East Harlem Triangle Plan, intended to reflect the African American community's own goals and visions for a revitalized neighborhood.[30]

For the most part, however, the impact of urban renewal projects—as well as the struggles to oppose or even improve them, ironically—produced a record of shameful, nearly unmitigated failure with respect to the conditions of poor African Americans in US cities. Nowhere was this more disastrous than in the case of low-income housing. First, the situation was structurally exacerbated because vastly more housing units were demolished under the auspices of slum clearance and other redevelopment programs than were ever to be created through public housing projects. Second, much of the public housing that was actually constructed proved so inadequate or ill-conceived that these projects were soon decried as a constituting a "second ghetto." Some even proved so unacceptable in terms of segregation, stigma, social disorder, and other deleterious effects—worse even than the private slums they had replaced—that officials quickly began contemplating their abandonment, beginning with the notorious demolition of St. Louis's Pruitt-Igoe housing project in 1972. Finally, the advent of violent, destructive mass uprisings (labeled riots at the time) in African American urban neighborhoods—beginning in Harlem and North Philadelphia during the summer of 1964, and growing more widespread and intense through the wake of Martin Luther King's assassination in 1968—dramatized black grassroots dissatisfaction with what was increasingly described as America's "urban crisis." Simultaneously, a suburban white "silent majority" (as President Richard Nixon styled his supporters) turned against Great Society liberalism and toward racial and economic conservatism. In such a context, the days of a public policy consensus around urban renewal were clearly numbered.[31]

If by the early 1970s Washington's increasingly conservative policymakers agreed with Harvard University's Edward Banfield that "government cannot solve the urban problem," the only question left was what should replace the urban renewal order. In 1973 Richard Nixon declared a moratorium on many of the federal housing and urban renewal programs administered by HUD and related agencies and initiated a comprehensive review. At the same time, Democrats in Congress began preparing legislation that would provide the policy framework for a post-urban renewal era. When it was finally signed by President Gerald Ford, the Housing and Community Development Act of 1974 devolved funding and authority into "community development block grants" (CDBG) for state and local governments, which were disbursed to non-profit development corporations instead of public agencies. Section 8 of the law shifted away from government provision of low-income housing toward a voucher system that subsidized rentals in the private real estate market. The CDBG system remained in effect as the dominant paradigm for the federal government's engagement—or relative

disengagement—with urban affairs for the rest of the 20th century, aside from some comparatively minor interventions such as "superfund" industrial site remediation, economic "empowerment zones," and the Hope VI program to demolish public housing constructed during the foregoing period. Meanwhile, despite enormous economic and physical growth by the beginning of the 21st century, racial and class disparities across American urban regions remained as stark as they were at the dawn of the Progressive Era.[32]

DISCUSSION OF THE LITERATURE

In addition to the myriad of excellent studies focused on urban renewal in specific cities, cited throughout this essay, several scholarly surveys of national urban policy, or of the fate of cities viewed nationally, should be considered. These include Mark Gelfand, *A Nation of Cities: The Federal Government and Urban America, 1933–1965* (1975); Jon Teaford, *Rough Road to Renaissance: Urban Revitalization in America* (1990); Raymond Mohl, "Shifting Patterns of American Urban Policy since 1900," in *Urban Policy in Twentieth-Century America* (1993). Kenneth Jackson, *Crabgrass Frontier: The Suburbanization of the United States* (1985) ranges widely but remains essential reading for many major debates, the most recent of which can be gleaned in a special issue of the *Journal of Urban History* (May 2013) dedicated to "thinking through urban renewal" (see also the scholarly responses published in *Journal of Urban History* [July 2014]). Christopher Klemek, *Transatlantic Collapse of Urban Renewal: Postwar Urbanism from New York to Berlin* (2011) charts the rise and fall of the urban renewal order, and places the US experience in comparative, transnational context.

Many key texts on urban renewal straddle the line between primary and secondary sources but remain of great interest, including: J. L. Sert, *Can Our Cities Survive? An ABC of Urban Problems, Their Analysis, Their Solutions,*

Based on the Proposals Formulated by the CIAM (1942); *Urban Renewal: People, Politics and Planning* (1967); and *Urban Renewal: The Record and the Controversy* (1966).

PRIMARY SOURCES

Researchers interested in urban renewal in a particular city will almost certainly find useful materials in the respective municipal archives. These are complemented by the records of national agencies that supported local authorities, such as the Department of Housing and Urban Development (or its predecessors) that generally can be accessed at the National Archives in Washington, DC. Private archives, particularly those affiliated with urban universities, also house many excellent primary source collections within their research libraries, notably the Temple University Urban Archives, Loeb Library at the Harvard Graduate School of Design, George Washington University Special Collections, the Regenstein Library at the University of Chicago, Bancroft Library at the University of California Berkeley, or the Jane Jacobs Papers at Boston College's Burns Library.

FURTHER READING

Ballon, Hilary, and Kenneth Jackson, eds. *Robert Moses and the Modern City: The Transformation of New York*. London: W. W. Norton, 2007.

Bellush, Jewel, and Murray Hausknecht, eds. *Urban Renewal: People, Politics and Planning*. Garden City, NY: Doubleday, 1967.

Gelfand, Mark. *A Nation of Cities: The Federal Government and Urban America, 1933–1965*. New York: Oxford University Press, 1975.

Hirsch, Arnold. *Making the Second Ghetto: Race and Housing in Chicago, 1940–1960*. Cambridge: Cambridge University Press, 1983.

Jackson, Kenneth. *Crabgrass Frontier: The Suburbanization of the United States*. New York: Oxford University Press, 1985.

Klemek, Christopher. *Transatlantic Collapse of Urban Renewal: Postwar Urbanism from New York to Berlin*. Chicago: University of Chicago Press, 2011.

Mohl, Raymond. "Shifting Patterns of American Urban Policy Since 1900." In *Urban Policy in Twentieth-Century America*, edited by Arnold Hirsch and Raymond Mohl, 1–45. New Brunswick, NJ: Rutgers University Press, 1993.

Teaford, Jon. *Rough Road to Renaissance: Urban Revitalization in America*. Baltimore: Johns Hopkins University Press, 1990.

von Hoffman, Alexander. "Forum: Urban Renewal." *Journal of Urban History* 40, no. 4 (July 2014): 631–647.

Wilson, James, ed. *Urban Renewal: The Record and the Controversy*. Cambridge, MA: Joint Center for Urban Studies, 1966.

NOTES

1. Jewel Bellush and Murray Hausknecht, eds., *Urban Renewal: People, Politics and Planning* (Garden City, NY: Doubleday, 1967), 15; on the evolving term and policy concept, see also Alexander von Hoffman, "The Lost History of Urban Renewal," *Journal of Urbanism* 1, no. 3 (2008): 281–301.

2. Thomas Bender, *Toward an Urban Vision: Ideas and Institutions in Nineteenth-Century America* (Lexington: University Press of Kentucky, 1975); Ted Steinberg, *Nature Incorporated: Industrialization and the Waters of New England* (Boston: University of Massachusetts Press, 1994); and Stanley Buder, *Pullman: An Experiment in Industrial Order and Community Planning, 1880–1930* (Oxford: Oxford University Press, 1970).

3. Daniel Rodgers, *Atlantic Crossings: Social Politics in a Progressive Age* (Cambridge, MA: Harvard University Press, 1998), ch. 4.

4. Roy Lubove, *The Progressives and the Slums: Tenement House Reform in New York City, 1890–1917* (Pittsburgh, PA: University of Pittsburgh Press, 1963); Lawrence Friedman, *Government and Slum Housing: A Century of Frustration* (Chicago: Rand McNally, 1968); and James Borchert, *Alley Life in Washington: Family, Community, Religion, and Folklife in the City, 1850–1970* (Urbana: University of Illinois Press, 1980). See also Jacob Riis, *How the Other Half Lives: Studies Among the Tenements of New York* (New York: Scribner's, 1890), as well as Charles and Eugenia Weller, *Neglected Neighbors: Stories of Life in the Alleys, Tenements and Shanties of the National Capital* (Philadelphia: Winston, 1909).

5. Howard Gillette, *Between Justice and Beauty: Race, Planning, and the Failure of Urban Policy in Washington* (Baltimore: Johns Hopkins, 1995), 121; Eugenie L. Birch, "Edith Elmer Wood and the Genesis of Liberal Housing Thought: 1910–1942" (PhD diss., Columbia University, 1976); and Birch, "Woman-Made America: The Case of Early Public Housing Policy," *Journal of the American Institute of Planners* 44 (April 1978): 130–144.

6. David Harvey, *Paris, Capital of Modernity* (London: Routledge, 2004).

7. Keith D. Revell, *Building Gotham: Civic Culture and Public Policy in New York City, 1898–1938* (Baltimore: Johns Hopkins University Press, 2002), chap. 5; Patricia Burgess, *Planning for the Private Interest: Land-Use Controls and Residential Patterns in Columbus, Ohio, 1900–1970* (Columbus: Ohio State University Press, 1994); and Stanislaw J. Makielski Jr., *The Politics of Zoning: The New York Experience* (New York: Columbia University Press, 1966).

8. Gail Radford, *Modern Housing for America: Policy Struggles in the New Deal Era* (Chicago: University of Chicago Press, 1997), 141–143; and Richard Plunz, *A History of Housing in New York City* (New York: Columbia University Press, 1990), 149–163.

9. Mark Gelfand, *A Nation of Cities: The Federal Government and Urban America, 1933–1965* (New York: Oxford University Press, 1975); Kenneth Jackson, *Crabgrass Frontier: The Suburbanization of the United States* (Oxford: Oxford University Press, 1985) ch. 11; and Amy Hillier, "Redlining and the Home Owners' Loan Corporation," *Journal of Urban History* 29, no. 4 (2003).

10. Joel Schwartz, *The New York Approach: Robert Moses, Urban Liberals, and Redevelopment of the Inner City* (Columbus: Ohio State University Press, 1993); and Hilary Ballon and Kenneth T. Jackson, eds., *Robert Moses and the Modern City: The Transformation of New York* (New York: W. W. Norton, 2007).

11. Katie Schank, "Producing the Projects: Atlanta and the Cultural Creation of Public Housing, 1933–2011" (PhD diss., George Washington University, 2016); and Gillette, *Between Justice & Beauty*, 142–143.

12. Constance M. Greiff, *Independence: The Creation of a National Park* (Philadelphia: University of Pennsylvania Press, 1987).

13. Andrew Shanken, 194X: *Architecture, Planning, and Consumer Culture on the American Home Front* (Minneapolis: University of Minnesota Press, 2009); and Eric Mumford, *The CIAM Discourse on Urbanism, 1928–1960* (Cambridge, MA: MIT Press, 2002).

14. Jewel Bellush and Murray Hausknecht, eds., *Urban Renewal: People, Politics and Planning* (Garden City, NY: Doubleday, 1967).

15. Gillette, *Justice and Beauty*, 160–165; and Wendell Pritchett, "The 'Public Menace' of Blight: Urban Renewal and the Private Uses of Eminent Domain," *Yale Law & Policy Review* 21, no. 1 (2003).

16. Plunz, *History of Housing*, 253–259; and Nicholas Dagen Bloom, *Public Housing That Worked: New York in the Twentieth Century* (Philadelphia: University of Pennsylvania Press, 2009).

17. Samuel Zipp, *Manhattan Projects: The Rise and Fall of Urban Renewal in Cold War New York* (Oxford: Oxford University Press, 2012).

18. Arnold Hirsch, *Making the Second Ghetto: Race and Housing in Chicago, 1940–1960* (Cambridge: Cambridge University Press 1983); and Brian Goldstein, *The Roots of Urban Renaissance: Gentrification and the Struggle over Harlem* (Cambridge, MA: Harvard University Press, 2017).

19. Alan Balfour, *Rockefeller Center: Architecture as Theater* (New York: McGraw Hill, 1978); and Roy Lubove, *Twentieth-Century Pittsburgh: Government, Business, and Environmental Change* (Pittsburgh: University of Pittsburgh Press, 1996).

20. M. Jeffrey Hardwick, *Mall Maker: Victor Gruen, Architect of an American Dream* (Philadelphia: University of Pennsylvania Press, 2010); and Alison Isenberg, *Downtown America: A History of the Place and the People Who Made It* (Chicago: University of Chicago Press, 2004).

21. Robert Dahl, *Who Governs? Democracy and Power in the American City* (New Haven, CT: Yale University Press, 1961); Jeanne Lowe, *Cities in a Race with Time: Progress and Poverty in America's Renewing Cities* (New York: Random House, 1967); and Lizabeth Cohen, *Saving America's Cities: Ed Logue and the Struggle to Renew Urban America in the Suburban Age* (New York: Farrar, Straus & Giroux, forthcoming).

22. Thomas O'Connor, *Building a New Boston: Politics and Urban Renewal, 1950–1970* (Boston: Northeastern University Press, 1993); Lawrence Kennedy, *Planning the City Upon a Hill: Boston Since 1630* (Amherst: University of Massachusetts Press; 1994); Elihu Rubin, *Insuring the City: The Prudential Center and the Postwar Urban Landscape* (New Haven, CT: Yale University Press, 2012); and Lawrence Vale, *From the Puritans to the Projects: Public Housing and Public Neighbors* (Cambridge, MA: Harvard University Press, 2000).

23. Colin Gordon, *Mapping Decline: St. Louis and the Fate of the American City* (Philadelphia: University of Pennsylvania Press, 2008); and Joseph Heathcott, Máire Agnes Murphy, "Corridors of Flight, Zones of Renewal," *Journal of Urban History* 3, no. 2 (2005): 151–189.

24. Edmund Bacon, *Image of the City*; John F. Bauman, *Public Housing, Race, and Renewal: Urban Planning in Philadelphia, 1920–1974* (Philadelphia: Temple University Press, 1987); Madeline L. Cohen, "Postwar City Planning in Philadelphia: Edmund N. Bacon and the Design of Washington Square East" (PhD diss., University of Pennsylvania, 1991); Valerie Sue Halverson Pace, "Society Hill, Philadelphia: Historic Preservation and Urban Renewal in Washington Square East" (PhD diss., University of Minnesota, 1976); Guian A. McKee, "Liberal Ends Through Illiberal Means: Race, Urban Renewal, and Community in the Eastwick Section of Philadelphia, 1949–1990," *Journal of Urban History* 27, no. 5 (July 2001): 547–583; and Nancy Kleniewski, "Neighborhood Decline and Downtown Renewal: The Politics of Redevelopment in Philadelphia, 1952–1962" (PhD diss., Temple University, 1982).

25. Bell Julian Clement, "Creative Federalism and Urban Policy: Placing the City in the Great Society" (PhD diss., George Washington University, 2014); Wendell E. Pritchett, *Robert Clifton Weaver and the American City: The Life and Times of an Urban Reformer* (Chicago: University of Chicago Press, 2008); Robert C. Wood, *Whatever Possessed the President? Academic Experts and Presidential Policy, 1960–88* (Amherst: University of Massachusetts Press, 1993); and Bret A. Weber, and Amanda Wallace, "Revealing the Empowerment Revolution: A Literature Review of the Model Cities Program," *Journal of Urban History* 38, no. 1 (2012): 173–192.

26. Catherine Bauer, "The Dreary Deadlock of Public Housing," *Architectural Forum* 106, no. 5 (May 1957): 140–142, 219–221; and A. Scott Henderson, *Housing and the Democratic Ideal: The Life and Thought of Charles Abrams* (New York: Columbia University Press, 2000), 198–203.

27. Herbert Gans, *The Urban Villagers* (New York: Free Press, 1962). See also Gans, "The Human Implications of Current Redevelopment and Relocation Planning," *Journal of the American Institute of Planners* 25 (February 1959): 15–25; *The Last Tenement: Confronting Community and Urban Renewal in Boston's West End*, ed. Sean M. Fisher and Carolyn Hughes (Boston: Bostonian Society, 1992), including Gans's essay, "The Urban Village Revisited." Chester Hartman, "Social Values and Housing Orientations," *Journal of Social Issues* 19 (April 1963): 113–131; Hartman, "The Limitations of Public Housing: Relocation Choices in a Working-Class Community," *Journal of the American Institute of Planners* 29 (November 1963): 283–296. Chester Hartman, "The Housing of Relocated Families," *Journal of the American Institute of Planners* 30, no. 4 (November 1964): 266–286. M. Fried and P. Gleicher, "Some Sources of Residential Satisfaction in an Urban Slum," *Journal of the American Institute of Planners* 27 (1961): 305–315; Marc Fried, "Grieving for a Lost Home: Psychological Costs of Relocation," in *The Urban Condition: People and Policy in the Metropolis*, ed. Leonard J. Duhl (New York: Basic Books, 1963); and Fried, "Social Change and Working Class Orientations: The Case of Forced Relocation," in *Mobility and Mental Health*, ed. Mildred Kantor (New York: D. Van Nostrand, 1964).

28. Martin Anderson, *Federal Bulldozer: A Critical Analysis of Urban Renewal, 1949–1962* (Cambridge, MA: Joint Center for Urban Studies, 1964); James Q. Wilson, ed., *Urban Renewal: The Record and the Controversy* (Cambridge, MA: Joint Center for Urban Studies, 1966); and James T. Patterson, *Freedom Is Not Enough: The Moynihan Report and America's Struggle Over Black Family Life—from LBJ to Obama* (New York: Basic Books, 2010).

29. Christopher Klemek, *Transatlantic Collapse of Urban Renewal: Postwar Urbanism from New York to Berlin* (Chicago: University of Chicago, 2011); Zachary M. Schrag, "The Freeway Fight in Washington, DC: The Three Sisters Bridge in Three Administrations"; Raymond A. Mohl, "Stop the Road: Freeway Revolts in American Cities," *Journal of Urban History* 30, no. 5 (July 1, 2004): 674–706; and Eric Avila, *The Folklore of the Freeway: Race and Revolt in the Modernist City* (Minneapolis: University of Minnesota Press, 2014).

30. Klemek, *Transatlantic Collapse of Urban Renewal*; Goldstein, *Roots of Urban Renaissance*; and Robert Self, *American Babylon: Race and the Struggle for Postwar Oakland* (Princeton, NJ: Princeton University Press, 2004).

31. Arnold Hirsch, *Making the Second Ghetto*; Sudhir Venkatesh, *American Project. The Rise and Fall of a Modern Ghetto* (Cambridge, MA: Harvard University Press, 2000); Amy Howard, *More Than Shelter: Activism and Community in San Francisco Public Housing* (Minneapolis: University of Minnesota Press, 2014); Rhonda Williams, *The Politics of Public Housing: Black Women's Struggles Against Urban Inequality* (New York: Oxford University Press, 2008); Raymond Vernon, *The Myth and Reality of Our Urban Problems* (Cambridge, MA: Harvard University Press, 1966); John K. Meyer, *Bibliography of the Urban Crisis: The Behavioral, Psychological, and Sociological Aspects of the Urban Crisis* (Chevy Chase, MD: National Institute of Mental Health, 1969); and Edward Banfield, *The Unheavenly City: The Nature and Future of Our Urban Crisis* (Boston: Little, Brown, 1970).

32. Edward Banfield, *Why Government Cannot Solve the Urban Problem* (Cambridge, MA: Joint Center for Urban Studies, 1968); Frieden, Bernard J., and Marshall Kaplan, eds., *The Politics of Neglect: Urban Aid from Model Cities to Revenue Sharing* (Cambridge, MA: MIT Press, 1975); Alexander von Hoffman, *House by House, Block by Block: The Rebirth of America's Urban Neighborhoods* (Oxford: Oxford University Press, 2003); and Lawrence Vale, *Purging the Poorest: Public Housing and the Design Politics of Twice-Cleared Communities* (Chicago: University of Chicago Press, 2013).

Christopher Klemek

JAPANTOWN AND THE SAN FRANCISCO FILLMORE DISTRICT

CONTEXTUALIZING CONTEMPORARY DISPLACEMENT IN ASIAN AMERICAN NEIGHBORHOODS

Today Asian American urban neighborhoods face severe displacement pressures from gentrification. In 2013, for example, a multiracial coalition of residents, small business owners, and community organizers formed Chinatown Community for Equitable Development (CCED) to prevent the opening of a Walmart in Los Angeles Chinatown: CCED opposed the retail giant, citing Walmart's poor labor practices, the deleterious effect that the chain store would have on Chinatown's predominantly mom-and-pop stores, and the gentrification pressures that would lead to displacement of the neighborhood's working-class Latino and Asian immigrant renters. Similar examples of gentrification and displacement can be found in East Coast Chinatowns where, for example, former New York City Mayor Bloomberg encouraged economic development–friendly rezoning. Philadelphia officials supported the expansion of luxury condominiums, and Boston-area universities have expanded their facilities—all of which have reduced the size of those cities' Chinatowns and encouraged the displacement of residents and businesses.[1]

These examples illustrate the widespread threat that working-class Asian American urban neighborhoods are currently facing due to corporate- and private-developer-sponsored, municipally backed gentrification.[2] This threat is very real, but it is also a threat that is not new, but rather has broader historical antecedents. Understanding these antecedents helps us contextualize the recent threats to Asian American spaces and neighborhoods and leads us to a broad history of Asian American geographies. These antecedents include the larger history of the racialization of Asian American spaces, historical attempts to displace Asian

American ethnic enclaves, and the long struggle of Asian Americans to prevent their displacement and claim a "right to the city."[3] Such struggles around space and place include mob violence and municipal attempts to eliminate Asian American ethnic enclaves in the late 19th and early 20th centuries. They also include the World War II incarceration of Japanese Americans, the fight to save the International Hotel between the late 1960s and 1970s, and the large-scale, federally funded attempts to redevelop so-called blighted areas and slums after World War II.[4] This last example, redevelopment, bears greater attention. Because of its widespread impact, particularly on the US West Coast, redevelopment is a key historical moment when Asian American urban neighborhoods faced elimination. Following World War II, city governments utilized federal law to target so-called slums and blighted neighborhoods for demolition and subsequent rebuilding in conjunction with private developers that included Asian American communities in Stockton, California; Seattle, Washington; Sacramento, California; Los Angeles, California; and San Francisco, California.

The attempts to redevelop San Francisco's Japantown, located approximately a mile northwest of the downtown central business district (CBD) and part of a larger multiracial and multiethnic neighborhood known as the "Fillmore District" or the "Western Addition," offers an illustrative example of urban renewal's impact on Asian American enclaves. It was redeveloped between the 1950s and 1980s. Arguably, the Fillmore was targeted, in part, because of the longer history connecting racism and space in the city: that is, the "racialization of space," which resulted in attempts to contain, surveil, police, and sometimes eliminate Asian American and multiracial spaces. The Fillmore was also targeted because urban elites believed that existing communities in proposed redevelopment project areas did not fit their plans for postwar development and urban restructuring. Careful attention, then, needs to be paid to these redevelopment plans and the language that diverse elites utilized to promote urban renewal in the Fillmore and in other contemporaneous locations where Asian Americans and other communities of color faced urban renewal. In the end, Fillmore's two redevelopment phases displaced approximately 20,000 individuals (with nearly 2 million people being displaced nationally by urban renewal and interstate construction). The loss of home and community, with their strong sense of place, caused residents to mobilize against displacement, resulting in changes in redevelopment policy toward building rehabilitation (rather than demolition) and nominally greater community consultation. This resistance was mirrored in locations across the United States.

Racialization of Space. Urban renewal policy pathologized urban space as a slum or as afflicted with urban blight, both socially constructed conditions that redevelopment proponents argued could spread throughout a city and infect additional spaces. As such, this intersectional discourse of urban crisis was not only heavily racialized but, in turn, highlighted the social construction of race as an inherently spatial process that relies on spatial metaphors, spatial relations, and the use of space to produce racial difference; it 'otherizes' social groups and the spaces they inhabit and traverse. This complex process of racializing space is nothing new, as it began occurring even before the mid-20th century's urban renewal heyday. In the 19th and early 20th centuries, white portrayals of Asian American neighborhoods discursively painted the residents, homes, and businesses in these districts as filthy, crime- and disease-ridden, dangerous zones of potential racial intermixture. These zones were also portrayed as heteronormative-non and as evidence of Asian immigrants' inability to assimilate rather than a product of structural racism and discursive alchemy.[5]

Why were Asian immigrants and their spaces racialized? Some have argued that Chinese immigrants were the "indispensable enemy" for resurrecting the fortunes of both the Democratic Party and also of the white labor movement in the US West after the Civil War, as both groups deployed anti-Chinese nativism to draw supporters and material resources.[6] Asian immigrants were also the "indispensable enemy" or discursive foil for the formation of the white race—a process that was spatialized where Asian ethnic enclaves directly and indirectly helped define the nation as white, the boundaries of propriety, and the privileges and protections of heteronormative whiteness.[7] Thus, the racialization of space drew upon and intersected with processes of foreigner racialization and Orientalist discourse that were, in turn, enmeshed within practices of empire and nation building.[8]

Given the racialization of Asian American urban spaces, municipalities attempted to police and contain enclave space and their inhabitants, sanctioned white attempts to drive out enclave residents, and sponsored efforts to displace and/or relocate enclaves. Starting in the late 19th century, municipal police and public health departments cited the supposed vice and filth threat of Asian enclaves to investigate them, write reports on their supposed dangers, arrest individuals for allegedly endangering the public good, and attempt to shut down businesses. In short, portraying Asian American neighborhoods as a threat justified the expansion of municipal police powers over public health and proved formative in the development of modern-day zoning and nuisance law in West Coast cities.[9] This surveillance, harassment, and potential arrest also policed the behavior of whites who might be led astray by the proximity of alleged vice—in other words, the intimate relations of whites and non-whites were being surveilled and policed.[10] The state also sanctioned white resident attempts to eliminate Asian American enclaves. Nightly Workingmen's Party rallies in the late 1860s and 1870s called for elimination of Chinatowns and the forced repatriation of

Chinese immigrants and led not only to the 1871 massacre and lynching of as many as twenty of Los Angeles's Chinatown residents but also drove Chinese residents out of rural areas and smaller towns and cities along the West Coast in the 1870s and 1880s, among them Tacoma, Washington.[11] Some municipalities attempted to relocate Asian American enclaves by force. Although their efforts were overturned in federal court, San Francisco's supervisors passed a racial zoning ordinance, the 1890 Bingham Ordinance, which declared the city's Chinatown a public nuisance and attempted to relocate it and its residents to the Bayview neighborhood, approximately five miles south, where the city had zoned for "offensive trades."[12] Similarly, eminent domain was used in the 1930s to remove a Japanese American community in San Francisco's South Park neighborhood to construct the Bay Bridge, while Los Angeles's Old Chinatown was removed for the construction of Union Station, which displaced Chinese Americans, Latinos and Latinas, and working-class whites from a neighborhood regularly portrayed as a dangerous "eyesore."[13]

The previous examples of threatened displacement and outright removal were precursors to post–World War II redevelopment and relied on socio-spatial processes that racialized space. These processes, in turn, manufactured and trafficked in discourses of racialized and spatialized danger and decay, making residents of ethnic enclaves and multiracial neighborhoods susceptible to harassment and the neighborhoods themselves vulnerable to containment and removal.[14] The neighborhoods were viewed as foreign, or as external to the larger body politic—the spatial manifestation of foreigner racialization—and hence, as disposable. In addition, while the vulnerability of Asian American spaces to displacement reflects the West Coast's particular historical racial formation, the processes of displacement were built on a foundation of prior racialized expropriation and dispossession that justified attacks on and elimination of indigenous and Mexican communities, made the land alienable, and protected white male property ownership.[15] In short, displacement was predicated on and sanctioned by prior dispossessions—its discourses, logics, techniques, accrued privileges—and its ghosts.

REDEVELOPMENT POLICY

The end of World War II brought renewed state attempts to displace communities of color. Here key legislative changes and the strategic use of spatial language sanctioned this displacement. While many prewar interests had decried poor housing conditions in neighborhoods of color, lack of legislation with budgeted funding, as well as Asian American resistance, impeded the wholesale demolition of these so-called eyesores. Ironically such criticism recognized poor conditions in racialized communities while overlooking their root causes, including denial of municipal services, landlord neglect, and the Great Depression, which together produced declining conditions. In this sense, urban decline was rooted in material conditions of racial capitalism and their intersection with asymmetrical power relations rooted in economic disparities and entrenched structural and institutional racism.[16] Starting in the 1930s, different interests called on state and federal governments to address urban decay, in the process creating a discourse known as "urban crisis." It portrayed cities as beset by spreading socio-spatial ills and as dangers to white heteronormative society, a discourse that was highly racialized, classed, and gendered as well.[17] Although the discourse has been described in terms of its impact on African Americans, on the West Coast, racist portrayals of Asian Americans and their spaces helped define and manufacture notions of urban crisis.[18] These West Coast neighborhoods, thus, became singled out for postwar state intervention, and redevelopment policy can be interpreted as

the culmination of decades of the racialization of space.

The United States victory in the war changed approaches to urban problems, as newfound global hegemony and a modernist sense of purpose emboldened the state to tackle urban crisis directly via rebuilding infrastructure and vigorously attacking urban decay through redevelopment. As such, the policy's proponents believed that any displacement and destruction resulting from redevelopment was justified in the name of a universal "public good."

To this end, Congress passed two laws that directly stimulated neighborhood redevelopment, the 1949 Housing Act and the 1956 Interstate and Defense Highways Act. Although the 1956 Highways Act impacted many of the same communities affected by urban renewal, the Housing Act had a particularly dramatic effect on communities like the Fillmore. This Act laid out three main provisions. The first continued the government's support for suburbanization, which effectively subsidized the creation of suburbia and the middle-class as largely white by underwriting mortgages and sanctioning racially restrictive covenants and mortgage redlining. The second provision authorized urban renewal to clear slums and blighted areas with the federal government covering two-thirds of redevelopment project costs, which paid for building condemnation and clearance, municipalities covering the final third, and private developers implementing actual development. The third provision funded public housing construction for those displaced by urban renewal, although conservatives found such housing anathema and undermined this provision.[19]

Given the historical racialization of Asian American spaces and the postwar association of these spaces with urban crisis, municipalities began employing the 1949 Housing Act to designate these neighborhoods as slums and blighted areas to procure funding under the law. The notion of urban blight was a crucial element in postwar urban crisis discourse. Its usage likened blighted areas to diseased plants in a crop that needed to be eliminated to prevent the spread of illness. Afflicted neighborhoods were to be amputated from the urban body to save the remaining city from this social-spatial disease. Urban blight's definition was broad: it included physical manifestations such as dilapidated housing, economic manifestations such as excessive public service costs, and social manifestations such as presence of juvenile delinquency and crime. While any one of these aspects was sufficient to designate blight, in the Fillmore's case (as in other locations) blight was portrayed as a multi-vectored threat that elided the economic, physical, and social.[20] For example, when the postwar redevelopment coalition characterized the Fillmore as severely blighted, they rearticulated prior discourses of racialized and spatialized disorder. For example, the 1930s Homeowner Loan Corporation's (HOLC) "residential security maps" for the Fillmore described the neighborhood as San Francisco's "slum," specifically pointing to the presence of African Americans, Japanese, and other "hazardous infiltrating subversive groups."[21] Similarly, in 1947 the San Francisco Planning and Housing Association, made up of local business, political, and social welfare elites, published *Blight and Taxes*, which characterized the Fillmore as a drain on public resources, including policing and fire protection, and decried the neighborhood's dangerous diversity.[22]

In declaring the Fillmore blighted in 1948, pro-redevelopment elites utilized existing discourses and built upon previous displacement attempts of racialized neighborhoods. Together the pre- and postwar racialization of Asian American spaces and their intersection with foreigner racialization suggest that the discursive and spatial incorporation of Asian Americans within a notion of the "public" has been conditional at best and in practice often nonexistent. Thus, post–World War II urban renewal in the Fillmore and in other locations, such as Los Angeles's Little Tokyo/Bronzeville or Sacramento's West End, can be interpreted as the culmination and confluence of processes of foreigner racialization, racial triangulation, and the racialization of space.[23]

In practice, urban renewal projects resulted in the expansion of central business districts (CBDs) rather than rebuilding targeted areas for existing residents. The interests that supported CBD-focused urban renewal, also known as pro-redevelopment coalitions, represented a contradictory amalgamation of different interests, including corporate leaders, real estate investors, local politicians, and social reformers. Propertied interests in these coalitions redirected urban renewal toward expanding downtown office building space, building new upscale housing for white-collar workers, and constructing luxury hotels, instead of supporting more general urban reform and renovation of existing structures with local community input.[24] The policy also was typified early on by "total clearance," which meant that the community had little voice in the redevelopment process. Little assistance was offered to help relocate the displaced, and the displaced had little recourse to return, resulting in eventual resistance against redevelopment.

In addition to remaking downtown, redevelopment had far wider impacts. It spurred developers to engage in development outside designated project areas, which impacted Asian American neighborhoods. For example, the Asian American Movement's fight to save the International Hotel in San Francisco's Manilatown and Chinatown area, which was not a formal redevelopment project area, began when the owner attempted to evict a hundred largely senior Filipino and Chinese American tenants to build a parking lot for downtown commuters.[25] In turn, urban renewal projects in the city's South of Market Area, its Embarcadero, and the Fillmore, increased pressure for privately funded development in other parts of the city.

Because business interests dominated the redevelopment process, many residents and small businesses in project areas had little substantive say in shaping the renewal process, particularly in the first twenty years. Thus, by the mid-1960s communities began organizing actively and in large numbers against the destructive effects of displacement, loss of community, and dispossession. Eventually these mobilizations forced authorities to alter redevelopment policy and include greater community voice within the process. This voice was merely symbolic in some locations. But in others, community groups attempted to control the redevelopment process. Thus, resistance to redevelopment helped stall the renewal process and occasionally saved key sites from destruction or won concessions from authorities. Although President Richard Nixon formally ended redevelopment in the late 1960s, the policy had already shattered affected communities with the effects being felt most heavily on vulnerable seniors, monolingual immigrants, the working class, small business proprietors, renters, and people of color, who were displaced by the thousands.

These deleterious effects were not limited to urban renewal. Highway construction also resulted in substantial neighborhood destruction and dispossession. The 1956 Interstate Act funded the construction of $27 billion of interstate highways but also demolished thousands of homes, businesses, and community spaces to make way for freeway construction. In practice, the sites for proposed interstate construction tended to be locations already identified as blighted. Thus, the 1956 law functioned as a form of redevelopment.[26]

This highway construction affected many Asian American neighborhoods. For example, the construction of the Crosstown Freeway and Interstate 5 eviscerated Stockton's Little Manila and Chinatown between 1961 and 1975.[27] Similarly, I-5 dislocated residents and businesses in Seattle's panethnic International District and multiracial Central District in the early 1960s and in Sacramento's West End

neighborhood, which housed Asian Americans, African Americans, and working-class whites. In Los Angeles, freeway construction destroyed parts of the Japanese American Sawtelle district in West Los Angeles and many parts of the multiracial and multiethnic East Los Angeles.[28] Thus, displacement (whether caused by urban renewal, freeway construction, or private development) was a more generalized experience for postwar Asian Americans neighborhoods and other vulnerable communities.

SAN FRANCISCO'S REDEVELOPMENT COALITION AND THE FILLMORE

San Francisco's urban renewal and redevelopment proponents included CEO's of downtown corporations, such as Macy's department store, William Randolph Hearst, the editor of the *San Francisco Examiner*, local and state politicians, urban planners, real estate developers, and social welfare advocates. Later, as the Fillmore redevelopment plan unfolded, the pro-growth coalition would be joined by representatives of Japanese corporations, which helped develop and manage a Japanese-themed mall in the Fillmore.[29]

Members of this coalition had long declaimed that the Fillmore was among the city's most rundown neighborhoods, a sentiment that dated from the 1906 San Francisco Earthquake that destroyed much of the downtown area but left the Fillmore, to the West of downtown, intact. As a result, the neighborhood became inundated with earthquake survivors fleeing the destruction of homes and businesses. Buildings in the former white middle-class Fillmore District became subdivided into apartments to house the new residents and their businesses. Land uses became a mix of residential, commercial, and industrial, and the neighborhood's racial and ethnic makeup became equally diverse. The neighborhood's Japantown dates from this period. When the city's previous Japanese ethnic enclave, which was located within San Francisco's Chinatown, burned to the ground with the downtown's destruction, Japanese immigrants and their families eventually built up a 5,000-resident enclave in the Fillmore neighborhood, located next to and among working-class ethnic whites (Jews and Russians), Latinos, other Asian American ethnic groups (namely Filipino and Chinese), and African Americans. Later the neighborhood became the heart of the city's African American community during World War II when more than forty thousand African Americans from the South came in search of wartime jobs. Like Japanese Americans before them, these new migrants were barred from living in many parts of the city and were forced to cram into already segregated neighborhoods such as the Fillmore, whose Japanese Americans had been evacuated and imprisoned in concentration camps within the US interior, a process that dispossessed Japanese American citizens and immigrants alike.[30] For expediency's sake, city authorities allowed African Americans to move into the vacated Japantown spaces, turning the Fillmore into a predominantly African American community, the cultural and social heart of this new community replete with blues and jazz clubs, and key faith-based and social institutions. The neighborhood became known as the "Harlem of the West," much like Los Angeles's Little Tokyo, where African American wartime migration resulted in the neighborhood becoming known as "Bronzeville." In response to this new influx, Fillmore landlords further subdivided apartments. In short, the densely diverse, multiracial, and multiethnic Fillmore District that had been the immediate target of postwar redevelopment was produced out of the needs of wartime capitalism, of dispossession, and of intense segregation, all of which thrived on the exploitation of racialized vulnerability.

Urban renewal in the Fillmore was part of a larger plan to reshape the entire Bay Area regional political economy. Beginning during World War II, Bay Area economic and political leaders saw the need for greater regional economic coordination and planning. With the war's end, this elite, through organizations such as the Bay Area Council, envisioned the South Bay as the center for technology, the East Bay as the center of light industry and oil refining, and San Francisco as the center for tourism and white-collar professional services, shifting away from shipping and blue-collar manufacturing.[31] Given its relative proximity to the downtown area, this elite saw the Fillmore as a site to house employees in this new service-based economy and as a potential tourist attraction. Consequently, instead of apartments and modest homes housing seniors, the white working-class, and people of color, this elite envisioned new upscale apartments and condominiums for white-collar professionals in the Fillmore, and instead of a Japanese American and multiracial space, this elite saw the neighborhood as a site to promote ties to the Pacific Rim and to generate Asian-themed tourism. Here the pro-growth coalition's interests in tourism dovetailed with postwar Orientalism: San Francisco, like Seattle and Los Angeles, desired to become the West Coast's gateway to the Pacific Rim after the United States victory against Japan and thus saw part of the Fillmore's redevelopment as an opportunity to promote the city's and the region's ties to Japan and Asia.

To these ends, the Fillmore was redeveloped in two phases: the first project, Western Addition Project Area 1 (WA-1), redeveloped twenty-eight city blocks between 1956 to 1973, affecting a core section of the city's Japantown through the construction of new luxury housing and roadway improvements, and the second, Western Addition Project Area 2 (WA-2), redeveloped seventy blocks between 1966 to 2008, affecting part of Japantown and a large section of the neighborhood's African American community for the construction of the Nihonmachi Mall, more new housing, and a failed mall development known as the Fillmore Center.[32]

Significantly, WA-1 included the widening of Geary Boulevard into an eight-lane expressway within the Fillmore to help facilitate the downtown commute for new residents in the Fillmore and for commuters

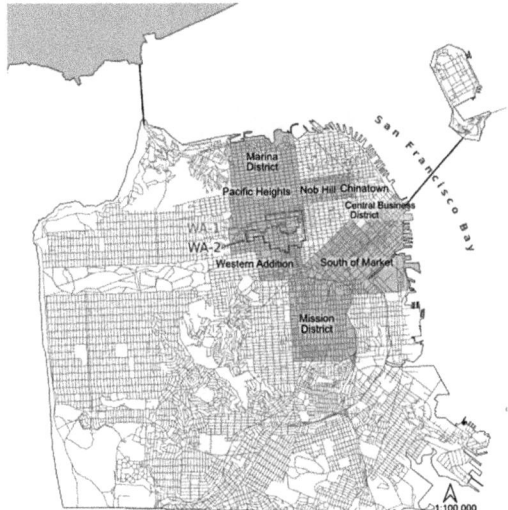

Figure 1. Map of the redevelopment project's location in San Francisco.
Map drawn by Dr. Sheryl-Ann Simpson.

Figure 2. The Buchanan Mall development looking north at the Japanese Cultural and Trade Center's Peace Pagoda.
Photograph courtesy of Dr. Kelly N. Fong.

living across the Golden Gate Bridge in posh Marin County and along the Avenues in San Francisco's middle-class Richmond District. This roadway project, the new housing construction, and the building of a four-block-long mall and entertainment complex along Geary between Laguna and Steiner, known as the Japanese Cultural and Trade Center (JCTC), ended up displacing eight thousand individuals and destroying significant numbers of low-income housing units in the WA-1 project area. Tellingly, the JCTC was WA-1's cornerstone development, which redevelopment proponents hoped would promote both tourism and also economic and symbolic ties to Asia. In other words, the Center was "imagineered" as a gateway to the Pacific Rim, a symbol of San Francisco's supposed love for Japan and for the Japanese people.[33] Such a sentiment reflected changing postwar international relations in which Japan shifted from being depicted as a demonized and racialized enemy to being portrayed as a bulwark ally in Asia against the Soviet threat. These geopolitical shifts subsequently affected views of Asian Americans who were still subject to foreigner racialization but no longer viewed primarily as enemy aliens.[34] It should be emphasized that San Francisco's redevelopment imagineers seemed unable to distinguish the city's Japantown space from Japan and its Japanese Americans from Japanese, the result of both foreigner racialization as well as postwar Orientalism and its consequent desires for Asian riches. Developed in conjunction with transnational Japanese capital, Hawaii-based but Issei-run National-Braemer Incorporated, and the Kintetsu Corporation (a subsidiary of the Kenki-Nippon Railway Corporation), the JCTC opened to great fanfare on the pro-growth coalition's part in 1968. It included space for the Japanese Consulate, a Japanese-themed luxury hotel, the Miyako, a Japanese-designed concrete Peace Pagoda and Peace Plaza commemorating the friendship between Japan and San Francisco, a thousand-seat theater to stage kabuki and other variety shows,

Figure 3. The Japanese Cultural and Trade Center looking east at the Miyako Hotel (currently known as the Hotel Kabuki) and Peace Plaza.
Photograph courtesy of Dr. Kelly N. Fong.

and a three-building mall that housed offices to promote trade and tourism with Japan, branches of Japanese restaurants and retail stores, and spaces to demonstrate Japanese culture and exhibit the latest Japanese exports. The JCTC was indeed ambitious, but the project proved to be an economic failure, and various business, including its kabuki theater, went out of business within three years.

Planning for WA-2 began in the late 1950s, but a federal lawsuit contesting the use of eminent domain for redevelopment and mass resident mobilization against the project delayed demolition. Regarding the latter, Fillmore residents, like residents in many redevelopment project areas, found the lack of consultation, blanket displacement, and dispossession of total clearance to be insufferable. In response, a multiracial and multiethnic group of renters, homeowners, progressive clergy, students, and community organizers mobilized through an umbrella organization called the Western Addition Community Organization (WACO) against WA-2, utilizing grassroots organizing, direct action, and eventually a lawsuit that won a short-lived injunction against

the project in 1968. Planning for WA-2 and subsequent demolition resumed by early 1969. However, in response to mobilization in multiple locations, the federal government began moving away from total clearance toward supposedly greater community consultation and collaboration in the redevelopment process. Thus, WA-2 included numerous low-income housing units for seniors that were developed with area African American and Japanese American churches, and the Nihonmachi Mall, which was developed in the mid-1970s with Japanese American business owners and leaders along with the transnational Kintetsu Corporation. Despite the involvement of mostly Nisei business owners in this open-air mall's development, members of the local Asian American Movement and a multiracial group of renters and small business owners, who were being displaced by the four-block project, organized the Committee Against Nihonmachi Eviction (CANE) to resist this development. They felt that the efforts of the Nisei business group, the RDA, and the Kintetsu Corporation promoted tourism and self-interest to the detriment of the most vulnerable renters and small business owners. However, despite spirited resistance, CANE, WACO, and WACO's successor, the Western Addition Project Area Committee (WAPAC), failed to stop the WA-2 redevelopment. The RDA proved particularly resistant to WAPAC's efforts to become the community's oversight body for the A-2 process, despite a Housing and Urban Development directive that redevelopment projects needed to have community input. In addition to resident mobilization, the pace of redevelopment began slowing by the late 1970s and 1980s because the RDA was having difficulty finding developers for cleared A-2 plots, which spoke to the changing political economic climate and to the racialization of the Fillmore's space and the association of parts of the neighborhood with blackness. The absence of developers was one of the reasons why the RDA turned increasingly to church groups to build senior housing in A-2. But redevelopment also slowed because federal urban policy changed. Lack of investment meant that some plots of land remained empty for years, becoming their own eyesores, a symbol of failure in Keynesian urban liberalism and the overreach of top-down planning.[35] Thus, little development occurred in WA-2 during the 1990s and early 2000s until a development group proposed a jazz heritage center and theater in the African American portion of the neighborhood, whose completion allowed the RDA to officially sunset WA-2 in 2008. By this time, WA-2 had eventually displaced 13,500 individuals, some for the second or third time, and destroyed another 5,000 low-rent units, arguably levelling the remaining heart of the Fillmore.[36]

Despite redevelopment, many of the Fillmore's diverse members remained in parts of the neighborhood, several key institutions remained or were relocated, and new spaces developed community significance: one example is the Japanese Cultural and Community Center of Northern California, a hard-won concession from the RDA and a testament to the creativity of local knowledge.[37] Yet the integument, the complex layer of historical associations and experiences that had been community, was badly frayed and for some sundered. Urban renewal's devastation lay well beyond the numbers of individuals displaced or buildings destroyed. Rather, it embodied the cumulative impact that the loss of home, loss of neighborhood ties, and loss of sense of place wrought on the displaced and on those who managed to stay. In other words, dispossession and its concomitant community-wide shock produced far deeper wounds.[38]

THE BROADER IMPACT OF URBAN RENEWAL ON ASIAN AMERICAN COMMUNITIES

In conclusion, the Fillmore's redevelopment was not isolated. Total clearance typified displacement in Los Angeles's Little Tokyo/Bronzeville neighborhood in the 1950s, when eminent domain was used to build a new police headquarters, and in Sacramento's West End in the late 1950s and early 1960s, when that city redeveloped its downtown for the Capitol Mall project. Each of these projects displaced over a thousand residents, community businesses, and the Sacramento project entirely obliterated that city's Japantown and the core of its African American community.[39] Likewise, in the mid-1970s the Los Angeles Community Redevelopment Agency pursued a new Japanese-themed renewal project in Little Tokyo and worked with a Japanese corporation, the Kajima Corporation, to build a mall and luxury hotel, the New Otani, that like San Francisco's JCTC, would promote tourism and ties with Asia.[40] This project was opposed by the Little Tokyo People's Rights Organization (LTPRO), which, like CANE, comprised AAM organizers, residents, older activists, and merchants, and sought to defend the neighborhood's most vulnerable residents (immigrants and seniors) in single-room occupancy hotels (SROs).[41]

Seattle's International District Improvement Association (Inter*Im) also mobilized to defend Asian American seniors in the Milwaukee Hotel in 1977, which was threatened with closure because it did not meet the city's building code.[42] Finally, Asian Americans and Pacific Islanders in other cities mobilized against displacement from expanding tourism. Seattle's Inter*Im opposed building a new baseball stadium in the late 1960s, and Honolulu organizers fought eviction from expansion of luxury hotels and upscale condominiums in Kalama Valley and the Waiahole-Waikane Valleys during the 1970s.[43] Arguably, many of these struggles drew inspiration from the Asian American Movement and its place-based struggles, e.g., over the Fillmore or Manilatown's International Hotel.

Figure 4. The Benkyo-Do dinner and Japanese confection shop. It was a neighborhood institution and threatened with displacement.
Photograph courtesy of Dr. Kelly N. Fong.

There are many more examples of late 20th-century displacement in Asian America and in other structurally vulnerable places due to redevelopment, freeway construction, property speculation, and gentrification that have resulted in loss of home, sense of place, and community. These struggles, along with contemporary 21st-century gentrification are genealogically linked to these prior displacements through the racialization of space and techniques of dispossession.

DISCUSSION OF THE LITERATURE

For a history of the African American Fillmore see Broussard , Daniels, Pepin and Watts, and Oaks.[44] For Japantown's history, see Okazaki, Wong , and the Japantown Taskforce.[45] As of now, no single scholarly study focuses on these racialized communities together: see Kurashige for an analysis of the African American and Japanese American struggle for housing in postwar Los Angeles.[46]

See Hartman with Carnochan for a comprehensive discussion of the history of postwar planning in San Francisco.[47] Read also Mollenkopf for an analysis of San Francisco's pro-growth coalition.[48] A more general discussion of urban blight discourse and how it was racialized and deployed to justify redevelopment can be found in Beauregard and in Sugrue, but see also Anderson and Shah for discursive analyses of Chinatown and of the racialization of space.[49] Also reference Thomas and Thomas and Ritzdorf to understand the devastating effects of urban renewal on African American communities.[50]

For an analysis of redevelopment in Japantown, reference Seigel, Tatsuno, Morozumi, Okazaki, Oda, and Lai.[51] Personal accounts of resistance against redevelopment in Japantown can be found in Ho et al. and in Louie and Omatsu.[52] Academic accounts of resistance against redevelopment in Japantown can be found in Okita; Geron; Yoshikawa; Liu, Geron, and Lai; and Lai.[53] For African American mobilization against redevelopment, please read Biondi and Crowe.[54]

PRIMARY SOURCES

One of the first primary sources to consult on the Fillmore's urban renewal is San Francisco Redevelopment Agency (RDA) and San Francisco Planning Department reports on the Fillmore District or Western Addition. In 1945, the then San Francisco Planning Commission published *The Master Plan of San Francisco: The Redevelopment of Blighted Areas*, which identified San Francisco's key blighted neighborhoods in need of slum clearance or "blight removal." Two years later planner Mel Scott wrote *Western Addition District: An Exploration of the Possibilities of Replanning and Rebuilding One of San Francisco's Largest Blighted Districts Under the California Community Redevelopment Act of 1945* for the Planning Commission. Along with the San Francisco Planning and Housing Association's (1947) *Blight and Taxes* and the City and County of San Francisco Supervisors' (1948) report, *Public Hearing on Redevelopment of the Western Addition*, the hearing that officially declared the Fillmore blighted, these reports articulated both the city's and local development elites' views of the multiracial and multiethnic Fillmore District and their hopes for the neighborhood's remaking.

One should also reference the RDA's (1956) *The Redevelopment Plan for the Western Addition Approved Redevelopment Project Area A-1* and planner Aaron Levine's (1959) SFRA-commissioned *The Urban Renewal of San Francisco* report, both of which rearticulated the Fillmore's blighted status and outline redevelopment plans for this neighborhood. Another primary source is the RDA's annual reports, which summarize demolition, clearance, and rebuilding progress in its redevelopment project areas, including Western Addition A-1 and A-2. These annual reports name key developers and community partners

for specific development projects, and occasionally they offer a glimpse into opposition to redevelopment.

The RDA and Planning Department reports are readily accessible at the UC Berkeley Environmental Design Library as well as in the Archives Room at the San Francisco Public Library. The Environmental Design Library also holds meeting minutes from the SFRA Board, which adds additional information about redevelopment plans, opposition to redevelopment, and the varied interests behind urban renewal. The Public Library's Archive Room includes papers, reports, and correspondence regarding the JCTC's construction and opening; correspondence regarding the RDA and specific projects such as the Martin Luther King Jr. Square development; copies of *Freedom House*, an organization that opposed A-2; papers on WACO, including copies of its newsletter *The WACO Organizer*; and the papers for relevant mayoral administrations. The Public Library also holds primary source documents related to Jim Jones's Peoples' Temple, whose membership included many Fillmore residents who had lost their homes due to redevelopment and whose main San Francisco church was based in the Fillmore. In addition to the public library, one can reference RDA materials through the city's Office on Community Investment and Infrastructure (OCII). Prior to its disbanding in 2011, the SFRA kept papers, newspaper clippings, photographs, and reports in its Records Room on Van Ness Avenue. The OCII has relocated to a new site.

Local newspapers are also excellent primary sources to understand redevelopment in the Fillmore. Mainstream newspapers include the *San Francisco Examiner* and the *San Francisco Chronicle*. In addition, one should reference community-based newspapers, including Carlton Goodlett's *The Fillmore Sun* for coverage of the neighborhood's African American community. In the Japanese American community, read articles and editorials in the now-defunct *Hokubei Mainichi*, and *Nichibei Times*.

Lastly, primary source material on redevelopment resistance includes newsletters, flyers, photographs, and meeting minutes kept by activists and organizations, including Freedom House, Western Addition Community Organization, Western Addition Project Area Committee, and Committee Against Nihonmachi Evictions. These can be found in the Japanese American National Library, the San Francisco Library's Archives Room, and the San Francisco Archdiocese's archives room.

FURTHER READING

Avila, Eric. *Popular Culture in the Age of White Flight: Fear and Fantasy in Suburban Los Angeles*. Berkeley: University of California Press, 2006.

Avila, Eric. *The Folklore of the Freeway: Race and Revolt in the Modernist City*. Minneapolis: University of Minnesota Press, 2014.

Beauregard, Robert. *Voices of Decline: The Postwar Fate of US Cities*. New York: Routledge, 2003.

Crowe, Daniel. *Prophets of Rage: The Black Freedom Struggle in San Francisco, 1945–1969*. New York: Garland, 2000.

Daniels, Douglas Henry. *Pioneer Urbanites: A Social and Cultural History of Black San Francisco*. Berkeley: University of California Press, 1990.

Dong, Harvey. "The Origins and Trajectory of the Asian American Movement in the San Francisco Bay Area, 1868–1978," PhD dissertation, University of California, Berkeley, 2002.

Geron, Kim. "Serve the People: An Exploration of the Asian American Movement," In *Asian American Politics: Law, Participation, and Policy*, edited by Don Nakanishi and James Lai, 163–79. New York: Rowman & Littlefield, 2003.

Hartman, Chester, with Sarah Carnochan. *City for Sale: The Transformation of San Francisco*. Berkeley: University of California Press, 2002.

Horiuchi, Lynne. "Object Lessons in Home Building: Racialized Real Estate Marketing in San Francisco." *Landscape Journal* 26.1 (2007): 61–82.

Kurashige, Scott. *The Shifting Grounds of Race: Black and Japanese Americans in the Making of Multiethnic Los Angeles*. Princeton, NJ: Princeton University Press, 2008.

Lai, Clement. "The Racial Triangulation of Space: The Case of Urban Renewal in San Francisco's Fillmore District." *Annals of the Association of American Geographers* 102.1 (2012): 151–170.

Lai, Clement. "Saving Japantown, Serving the People: The Scalar Politics of the Asian American Movement." *Environment and Planning D: Society and Space* 31.3 (2013): 467–484.

Liu, Michael, and Kim Geron. "Changing Neighborhood: Ethnic Enclaves and the Struggle for Social Justice." *Social Justice* 35.2 (2008): 18–35.

Liu, Michael, Kim Geron, and Tracy Lai. *The Snake Dance of Asian American Activism: Community, Vision, and Power*. Lanham, MD: Lexington, 2008.

Mollenkopf, John H. *The Contested City*. Princeton, NJ: Princeton University Press, 1983.

Oda, Meredith. "Remaking the 'Gateway to the Pacific': Urban, Economic, and Racial Redevelopment in San Francisco, 1945–1970," PhD dissertation, University of Chicago, 2010.

Oda, Meredith. "Rebuilding Japantown: Japanese Americans in Transpacific San Francisco during the Cold War." *Pacific Historical Review* 83 (2014): 57–91.

Okazaki, Suzie. *Nihonmachi: A Story of San Francisco's Japantown*. SKO Studios, 1985.

Okita, David. "Redevelopment of San Francisco Japantown," Master's thesis, California State University, Hayward, 1980.

Santos, Bob. *Hum Bows, Not Hot Dogs*. Seattle: International Examiner, 2002.

Seigel, Shizue. "Nihonmachi and Urban Renewal." *Nikkei Heritage* 12–13.4 (2000): 6.

Sugrue, Thomas J. *The Origins of the Urban Crisis: Race and Inequality in Postwar Detroit*. Princeton, NJ: Princeton University Press, 1996.

Tatsuno, Sheridan. "The Political and Economic Effects of Urban Renewal on Ethnic Communities: A Case Study of San Francisco's Japantown." *Amerasia Journal* 1.1 (1971): 33–51.

Thomas, June Manning. *Redevelopment and Race: Planning a Finer City in Postwar Detroit*. Baltimore: Johns Hopkins University Press, 1997.

Wildie, Kevin. *Sacramento's Historic Japantown: Legacy of a Lost Neighborhood*. Charleston, SC: History Press, 2013.

Yoshikawa, Ernest. "Japanese Community Politics: A Case Study of the Evolution of Political Style," Master's thesis, San Francisco State University, 2005.

NOTES

1. Bethany Li et al., *Chinatown Then and Now: Gentrification in Boston, New York, and Philadelphia* (New York: Asian American Legal Defense and Education Fund [AALDEF]), 2013.
2. Neil Smith, "New Globalism, New Urbanism: Gentrification as Global Urban Strategy," *Antipode* 34.3 (2002): 427–450.
3. Henri Lefebvre, "The Right to the City" in *Writings on Cities*, ed. and trans. Eleonore Kofman and Elizabeth Lebas (Malden, MA: Blackwell, 1997), 147–159.
4. Harvey Dong, "The Origins and Trajectory of the Asian American Movement in the San Francisco Bay Area, 1868–1978" (PhD dissertation, University of California, Berkeley, 2002); and Estella Habal, *San Francisco's International Hotel: Mobilizing the Filipino American Community in the Anti-Eviction Movement* (Philadelphia: Temple University Press, 2007).
5. Kay Anderson, *Vancouver's Chinatown: Racial Discourse in Canada, 1875–1980* (Kingston, ON: McGill-Queen's University Press, 1991); Nayan Shah, *Contagious Divide: Epidemics and Race in San Francisco's Chinatown*, (Berkeley: University of California Press, 2001); and Nayan Shah, *Stranger Intimacy: Contesting Race, Sexuality, and the Law in the North American West* (Berkeley: University of California Press, 2011).
6. Alexander Saxton, *The Indispensable Enemy: Labor and the Anti-Chinese Movement in California* (Berkeley: University of California Press, 1995).
7. Anderson, *Vancouver's Chinatown*; Shah, *Contagious Divides*; Lisa Lowe, *Immigrant Acts: On Asian American Cultural Politics* (Durham, NC: Duke University Press, 1996).
8. Edward Said, *Orientalism* (London: Penguin, 2003); Angelo Ancheta, *Race, Rights, and the Asian American Experience* (New Brunswick, NJ: Rutgers University Press, 2006); Andrea Smith, "Heteropatriarchy and the Three Pillars of White Supremacy," in *The Color of Violence: The Incite! Anthology*, eds. Andrea Smith, Beth Richie, Julia Sudbury, Janelle White, and Incite! Women of Color Against Violence (Boston: South End, 2006), 66–73.
9. Shah, *Contagious Divides*; Paul Ong, "The Chinese and the Laundry Laws, the Use and Control of Urban Space," (PhD dissertation, University of

Washington, 1975); and Charles McClain, *In Search of Equality: The Chinese Struggle Against Discrimination in Nineteenth-Century America* (Berkeley: University of California Press, 1994).
10. Shah, *Stranger Intimacy*.
11. Ronald Takaki, *Strangers from a Different Shore: A History of Asian Americans* (Boston: Little, Brown, 1998); and Jean Pfaelzer, *Driven Out: The Forgotten War Against Chinese Americans* (Berkeley: University of California Press, 2008).
12. McClain, *In Search*, 223–233.
13. Suzie Okazaki, *Nihonmachi: A Story of San Francisco's Japantown* (SKO Studios, 1985); Isabela Quintana, "Shaken as by an Earthquake: Chinese Americans, Segregation and Displacement in Los Angeles, 1870–1938," *Gum Saan Journal* 32.1 (2010): 3–23; and Mark Wild, *Street Meeting: Multiethnic Neighborhoods in Early Twentieth-Century Los Angeles*, (Berkeley: University of California Press, 2005).
14. Ruth Wilson Gilmore, "Race and Globalization," in *Geographies of Global Change*, eds. P. J. Taylor, R. L. Johnstone, and M.J. Watts, (Malden, MA: Blackwell, 2002), 261–274. Gilmore defines racism as vulnerability to premature death.
15. Andrea Smith, "Three Pillars"; and Shah, *Stranger Intimacy*.
16. Cedric Robinson, *Black Marxism: The Making of the Black Radical Tradition* (Chapel Hill: University of North Carolina Press, 2000).
17. Thomas Sugrue, *The Origins of the Urban Crisis: Race and Inequality in Postwar Detroit* (Princeton, NJ: Princeton University Press, 1996); and Robert Beauregard, *Voices of Decline: The Postwar Fate of US Cities* (New York: Routledge, 2003).
18. Scott. Kurashige, *The Shifting Grounds of Race: Black and Japanese Americans in the Making of Multiethnic Los Angeles* (Princeton, NJ: Princeton University Press, 2008).
19. Kenneth Jackson, *Crabgrass Frontier: The Suburbanization of the United States* (New York: Oxford University Press, 1985); Eric Avila, *Popular Culture in the Age of White Flight: Fear and Fantasy in Suburban Los Angeles* (Berkeley: University of California Press, 2006); Laura Pulido, "Rethinking Environmental Racism: White Privilege and Urban Development in Southern California," *Annals of the Association of American Geographers* 90.1 (2000): 12–40; Ruth Wilson Gilmore, "Globalisation and US

Prison Growth: From Military Keynesianism to Post-Keynesian Militarism," *Race & Class* 40.2–3 (1998): 171–188; and Donald Parson, *Making a Better World: Public Housing, the Red Scare, and the Direction of Modern Los Angeles* (Minneapolis: University of Minnesota Press, 2005).

20. Lai, "Racial Triangulation of Space."

21. "San Francisco D-3," Testbed for the Redlining Archives of California's Exclusionary Spaces (http://salt.umd.edu/T-RACES/data/sf/ad /ad0093.pdf) (T-RACES).

22. San Francisco Planning and Housing Association. *Blight and Taxes* (San Francisco: San Francisco Planning and Housing Association, 1947).

23. Claire Kim, "The Racial Triangulation of Asian Americans," *Politics and Society* 27.1 (1999): 105–138; Kurashige, *Shifting Grounds*; Clement Lai, "The Racial Triangulation of Space: The Case of Urban Renewal in San Francisco's Fillmore District," *Annals of the Association of American Geographers* 102.1 (2012): 151–170; and KVIE, "Replacing the Past: Sacramento's Redevelopment History (http://vids.kvie.org /video/2365719790/)," *ViewFinder*.

24. Chester Hartman with Sarah Carnochan, *City for Sale: The Transformation of San Francisco* (Berkeley: University of California Press, 2002).

25. Dong, "The Origins and Trajectory of the Asian American Movement in the San Francisco Bay Area, 1868–1978"; and Habal, *San Francisco's International Hotel: Mobilizing the Filipino American Community in the Anti-Eviction Movement.*

26. Avila, *Popular Culture*; and Eric Avila, *The Folklore of the Freeway: Race and Revolt in the Modernist City* (Minneapolis: University of Minnesota Press, 2014).

27. Dawn Mabalon, *Little Manila Is in the Heart: The Making of the Filipina/o American Community in Stockton, California* (Durham, NC: Duke University Press, 2013).

28. Avila, *Popular Culture.*

29. John Mollenkopf, *The Contested City,* (Princeton, NJ: Princeton University Press, 1983).

30. Newsletters of the Committee Against Nihonmachi Eviction, Japanese American National Library, San Francisco, CA; Keith Aoki, "No Right to Own? The Early Twentieth-Century 'Alien Land Laws' as a Prelude to Internment," *Boston College Law Review* 40 (1998): 37–72.

31. Hartman and Carnochan, *City for Sale.*

32. Shizue Seigel, "Nihonmachi and Urban Renewal," *Nikkei Heritage* 12/13, no. 4/1 (2000): 6–9 and 20–24.

33. Lai, "Racial Triangulation of Space."

34. John Dower, *War Without Mercy: Race and Power in the Pacific War* (New York: Pantheon, 1993); and Charlotte Brooks, *Alien Neighbors, Foreign Friends: Asian Americans, Housing, and the Transformation of Urban California* (Chicago: University of Chicago Press, 2009).

35. James Scott, *Seeing Like a State: How Certain Schemes to Improve the Human Condition Have Failed* (New Haven, CT: Yale University Press, 1998).

36. Seigel, "Nihonmachi."

37. Scott, *Seeing Like a State.*

38. Mindy Fullilove, *Root Shock: How Tearing Up City Neighborhoods Hurts America, and What We Can Do About It,* (New York: One World/ Ballantine, 2004); and Gilmore, "Globalisation."

39. Kurashige, *Shifting Grounds*; Kelly Simpson, "Three Waves of Little Tokyo Redevelopment," KCET: Departures, July 31, 2012; Ellen Endo, "Stakeholders: 'Return Site to Little Tokyo'": LA Conservancy, JA Community At Odds Over Parker Center's Fate" (http://www.rafu .com/2017/01/stakeholders-return-site-to -little-tokyo/), *Rafu Shimpo*; Kevin Wildie, *Sacramento's Historic Japantown: Legacy of a Lost Neighborhood* (Charleston, SC: The History Press, 2013); and KVIE, "Replacing the Past."

40. Michael Liu, Kim Geron, and Tracy Lai. *The Snake Dance of Asian American Activism: Community, Vision, and Power* (Lanham, MD: Lexington, 2008).

41. Liu, Geron, and Lai, *Snake Dance*; Karen Ishizuka, *Serve the People: Making Asian America in the Long Sixties* (New York: Verso, 2016).

42. Bob Santos, *Hum Bows, Not Hot Dogs* (Seattle: International Examiner, 2002); Doug Chin, *Seattle's International District: The Making of a Pan-Asian American Community* (2d ed.) (Seattle: International Examiner, 2009); Quintard Taylor, *The Forging of a Black Community: Seattle's Central District From 1870 Through the Civil Rights Era* (Seattle: University of Washington Press, 1994); and Jeffrey Sanders, *Seattle and the Roots of Urban Sustainability: Inventing Ecotopia* (Pittsburgh: University of Pittsburgh Press, 2010).

43. Santos, *Hum Bows*; Chin, *Seattle's International District*; Liu, Geron, and Lai, *Snake Dance*; and Noelani Goodyear-Ka'opua, *The Seeds We Planted: Portraits of a Native Hawaiian Charter School* (Minneapolis: University of Minnesota Press, 2013).

44. Albert Broussard, *Black San Francisco: The Struggle for Racial Equality in the West, 1900–1954* (Lawrence: University of Kansas Press, 1993); Douglas Daniels, *Pioneer Urbanites: A Social and Cultural History of Black San Francisco* (Berkeley: University of California Press, 1990); Elizabeth Pepin and Lewis Watts. *Harlem of the West: The San Francisco Fillmore Jazz Era* (San Francisco: Chronicle, 2005); and Robert Oaks, *San Francisco's Fillmore District*, (Charleston, SC: Arcadia, 2005).

45. Suzie Okazaki, *Nihonmachi: A Story of San Francisco's Japantown* (SKO Studios, 1985); Diane Wong, ed., *Generations: A Japanese American Community Portrait*, (San Francisco: Japanese Cultural and Community Center of Northern California, 2000); and Japantown Taskforce, Inc., *San Francisco's Japantown* (Charleston, SC: Arcadia, 2005).

46. Scott Kurashige, *The Shifting Grounds of Race: Black and Japanese Americans in the Making of Multiethnic Los Angeles* (Princeton, NJ: Princeton University Press, 2008).

47. Chester Hartman and Sarah Carnochan, *City for Sale: The Transformation of San Francisco* (Berkeley: University of California Press, 2002).

48. John Mollenkopf, *The Contested City* (Princeton, NJ: Princeton University Press, 1983).

49. Robert Beauregard, *Voices of Decline: The Postwar Fate of US Cities* (New York: Routledge, 2003); Thomas Sugrue, *The Origins of the Urban Crisis: Race and Inequality in Postwar Detroit* (Princeton, NJ: Princeton University Press, 1996); Kay Anderson, *Vancouver's Chinatown: Racial Discourse in Canada, 1875–1980* (Kingston, ON: McGill-Queen's University Press, 1991); and Nayan Shah, *Contagious Divide: Epidemics and Race in San Francisco's Chinatown*, (Berkeley: University of California Press, 2001).

50. June Manning Thomas, *Redevelopment and Race: Planning a Finer City in Postwar Detroit* (Baltimore: Johns Hopkins University Press, 1997); and June Manning Thomas and Marsha Ritzdorf, eds. *Urban Planning and the African American Community: In the Shadows* (Thousand Oaks, CA: SAGE, 1997).

51. Shizue Seigel, "Nihonmachi and Urban Renewal," *Nikkei Heritage* 12/13.4 (2000): 6–9 and 20–24; Sheridan Tatsuno, "The Political and Economic Effects of Urban Renewal on Ethnic Communities: A Case Study of San Francisco's Japantown," *Amerasia Journal* 1.1 (1971): 33–51; Toni Morozumi, "San Francisco's Nihonmachi," unpublished undergraduate paper (Asian American Studies Department, University of California, Berkeley, 1977); Okazaki, *Nihonmachi*; Meredith Oda, "Remaking the 'Gateway to the Pacific': Urban, Economic, and Racial Redevelopment in San Francisco, 1945–1970," PhD dissertation, University of Chicago, 2010; and Clement Lai, "The Racial Triangulation of Space: The Case of Urban Renewal in San Francisco's Fillmore District," *Annals of the Association of American Geographers* 102.1 (2012): 151–170.

52. Ray Tasaki, "New Dawn Rising: History and Summary of the Japan Town Collective," eds. Fred Ho, Carolyn Antonio, Diane Fujino, and Steve Yip, 53–57 (San Francisco: AK, 2000).

53. David Okita, "Redevelopment of San Francisco Japantown," Master's thesis, California State University, Hayward, 1980; Kim Geron, "Serve the People: An Exploration of the Asian American Movement," in *Asian American Politics: Law, Participation, and Policy*, eds. Don Nakanishi, and James Lai, 163–179 (New York: Rowman & Littlefield, 2003); Ernest Yoshikawa, "Japanese Community Politics: A Case Study of the Evolution of Political Style," Master's thesis (San Francisco State University, 2005); Michael Liu, Kim Geron, and Tracy Lai, *The Snake Dance of Asian American Activism: Community, Vision, and Power* (Lanham, MD: Lexington, 2008); and Clement Lai, "Saving Japantown, Serving the People: The Scalar Politics of the Asian American Movement," *Environment and Planning D: Society and Space* 31.3 (2013): 467–484.

54. Martha Biondi, *The Black Revolution on Campus* (Berkeley: University of California Press, 2012); and Daniel Crowe, *Prophets of Rage: The Black Freedom Struggle in San Francisco, 1945–1969* (New York: Garland, 2000).

Clement Lai

GENTRIFICATION IN THE UNITED STATES

Gentrification is one of the most controversial issues in American cities today. But it also remains one of the least understood. Few agree how to define it or whether it is a boon or curse for cities. Gentrification historically has had a smaller demographic impact on American cities than suburbanization or immigration. But since the late 1970s, gentrification has dramatically reshaped cities like Seattle, San Francisco, and Boston. Furthermore districts such as New Orleans's French Quarter, New York City's Greenwich Village and Washington DC's Georgetown, have had an outsized influence on the political, cultural, and architectural history of cities. Gentrification thus must be placed alongside suburbanization as one of the major historical trends shaping the 20th-century American metropolis.

WHAT IS GENTRIFICATION?

Gentrification is difficult to define. Scholars are divided between those who advocate strict and broad definitions. English sociologist Ruth Glass coined the term in 1964 to describe a specific phenomenon she noticed in East London.[1] Middle-class pioneers were migrating into older working-class districts, purchasing and renovating run-down buildings, and eventually displacing longtime poorer residents. Social scientists in the United States first borrowed her term in the late 1970s to describe a similar trend in American cities.

"Gentrification," according to this strict definition, was distinct from "urban redevelopment." Urban redevelopment referred to the large-scale demolition of slum areas, the erection of new structures, and government subsidies. Gentrification, in contrast, involved the gradual and private rehabilitation of the existing housing stock. Redevelopment was planned by government officials and large developers. Gentrification began at a grassroots level and was largely unplanned. Where urban redevelopment was subsidized by public funds, young white middle-class "pioneers" mostly used their own private savings and sweat equity. Urban redevelopment conjured the bulldozers of Robert Moses. Gentrification was an outgrowth of organic "unslumming" championed by his nemesis Jane Jacobs.

Since the late 1970s, when city planners and developers turned from modernist slum clearance to postmodern festival markets and the adaptive reuse of older buildings, the distinction between gentrification and urban redevelopment has blurred. Today the public uses "gentrification" quite liberally to describe any shift of urban space from poor to wealthy, whether through rehabilitation or slum clearance. Some scholars thus have called for a broader and more flexible definition that captures a wider set of processes in cities as they become postindustrial, neoliberal, and globalized. Leading gentrification scholars Loretta Lees, Tom Slater, and Elvin Wyly, for example, have called for a more multifaceted and flexible term that still includes Glass's "classical gentrification" but allows for newer variants such as "retail gentrification," "new-build gentrification," and "studentification."[2]

Historians are wary of the abstract categories and models used by social scientists. But a historian of gentrification does need a workable definition that is narrow enough to distinguish from other processes yet broad enough to allow for change over time.[3] From the earliest small-scale renovation of townhouses in Charleston, South Carolina, in the 1910s to the large mixed-use waterfront development projects in Brooklyn of the 2000s, gentrification has consistently displayed two features to varying degrees that when combined distinguish it from other types of urban change.

1. A class shift in a given area in which wealthier residents and consumers replace poorer residents and consumers, or in which

residents and consumers with more cultural and/or financial capital replace residents and consumers with less cultural and/or financial capital.

2. The restoration, rehabilitation, or adaptive reuse of existing buildings rather than large-scale slum clearance and redevelopment.

Three additional features have very often characterized gentrification in the United States. But they have not been omnipresent. Historians thus would be advised not to include them in a definition of gentrification.

3. A transformation that results in the direct or indirect displacement of longtime residents.

4. A racial transformation of an area in which white residents replace African American, Latino, or other nonwhite residents.

5. A market-driven, gradual, and unplanned process rather than a planned process funded by the state.

Features 3, 4, and 5 deserve more explanation.

Whether gentrification causes displacement is a heated debate among scholars. Residential displacement is nearly impossible to measure as it requires locating thousands of departed residents to determine their reasons for leaving. Some argue that gentrification historically has caused minimal displacement when compared to the more devastating counter-trend of disinvestment and housing abandonment. Others have even argued that by improving services and attracting more amenities, gentrification actually provides the poor with *more* incentive to stay in inner-city districts. From a historical perspective, on the other hand, plenty of archival evidence demonstrates that gentrification has often caused displacement, particularly in eras when the state had few protections for tenants. Other scholars point to political or cultural displacement that may be difficult to quantify. Rather than trying to develop a universal rule, historians are better equipped to research the

varying impacts gentrification has had on the poor in different locations over time. To write a comprehensive political, cultural, and social history of gentrification, historians need not be handcuffed by the displacement debate.[4]

The relationship between race and gentrification is also complex. Although gentrification has transformed cities from Amsterdam to Tokyo, in the United States the public today often uses the word as a euphemism for a type of "reverse white flight" in which wealthy whites migrate into poorer African American neighborhoods. While African Americans have been disproportionately displaced, the history of race and gentrification differs somewhat from conventional wisdom. "Gentrifiers" in the United States have since the early 1910s indeed been overwhelmingly white. The racial composition of the neighborhoods that they migrated into, however, has changed over time and reflects the shifting landscape of urban poverty. From the 1910s through the 1940s, gentrification occurred in older inner-city districts that were often home to a mix of impoverished European immigrants, African Americans, Puerto Ricans, and "old money" white families. From the 1950s to the mid-1970s, gentrification was almost exclusively limited to poor and working-class white inner-city areas. As many of these districts also underwent racial transition, white urban professionals often displaced African Americans from individual rooming houses and apartments. Yet, the number of African Americans in many gentrifying districts actually rose during this period. By the 1980s, as many cities became stratified "dual cities," white urban professionals began to push into neighboring blocks that in the 1960s had become home to poorer African Americans and Latinos. In the 1990s, white middle-class residents began to move into historically African American districts such as New York's Harlem and Bedford-Stuyvesant, sparking a new set of tensions. Recent studies have pointed to the migration of a new African American middle class into the inner city, which further complicates the racial dynamics of gentrification.[5]

The role of the state in promoting gentrification is also a contentious issue in the scholarship. Scholars all agree that the state has taken a stronger role since the 1970s in directing the process. What in 1960s was a small-scale renovation fad led by "pioneers" using personal savings and sweat equity transformed by the 2000s into a central growth strategy for cities eager to attract a "creative class" to the city center. Yet while they concur that the role of the state has expanded over time, scholars are divided as to whether the public sector has primarily fueled gentrification or regulated it to protect the poor.[6]

Where sociologists once debated about "production-side" and "consumption-side" explanations, scholars today concur about the historical causes of gentrification. As city economies shifted from manufacturing to services, white-collar, college-educated workers employed in finance, law, administration, government, and the arts migrated to housing in convenient access to central business districts. While many looked to the suburbs or new high-rise apartment towers rising downtown, a small number moved into and repurposed older buildings from previous economic eras that still remained at the core of many cities.

Several factors led this group to choose older housing. Nineteenth-century townhouses, lofts, alley dwellings, and stables in the center city suffered decades of disinvestment and were cheap. They also offered convenient access to the central business district. Gentrification also reflected the changing cultural tastes of a new postindustrial middle class. Young white-collar professionals moving to older inner-city districts described themselves as rejecting modern suburbs and postwar high-rise apartment towers that they described as alienating and sources of anomie. They championed a new urban ideal that celebrated the 19th-century built environment for being mixed-use, walkable, historic, and, most importantly, authentic. Many of the white-collar workers moving into this older housing also belonged to key subgroups that looked to the center city as a refuge from suburbs they described as conformist and intolerant: "bohemian" artists and writers, childless couples and divorcees, single women, gays and lesbians. Some scholars in contrast point to an angry, revanchist, and even colonial impulse that underlay gentrification. Having left in previous decades for the suburbs, white middle-class arrivals described themselves as returning to take back inner-city neighborhoods that were rightfully theirs and had been stolen by minority groups.[7]

When American social scientists first began to study gentrification in the late 1970s, they theorized that gentrification occurred in "stages." Young and risk-taking artists, bohemians, and historic preservationists "pioneered" poorer areas. Risk-averse yuppies, real estate speculators, and developers soon followed. Today scholars have largely abandoned these rigid stages and emphasize instead that gentrification is a historical process that evolved over time. Geographers and sociologists have begun to periodize gentrification, although more from a theoretical perspective. Neil Smith and Jason Hackworth, for example, split gentrification into several "waves" that remain the most useful framework for examining gentrification historically.[8]

THE SEED STAGE: GENTRIFICATION IN THE 1910S AND 1920S

In the first decades of the 20th century, American cities experienced an early wave of gentrification. Sixty years before the word "gentrifiers" came into existence, a new middle class migrated into and renovated the dilapidated 19th-century tenements, townhouses, horse stables, wooden piers, and industrial lofts that hugged the central business districts of cities ranging from New York to Charleston, South Carolina. Chicago School sociologists at the time labeled this inner-city belt of ramshackle buildings the "Zone of Transition." Local residents often used names like "Old" or "Little" to describe districts that sat in the shadow of new skyscrapers and had some of the oldest housing in the city. Built during a previous century, the Zone of Transition was walkable and mixed-use *avant la lettre*. Industrial lofts and tenements near the waterfront sat steps away from the decaying mansions and townhouses of declining urban aristocracies of a previous economic era: the "Brahmins" of Boston, the "Creoles" of New Orleans, the "Cave Dwellers" of Georgetown, and the former merchant-planter families of Charleston, for example. In the North and Midwest and on the West Coast, poorer residents were largely immigrants from southern and eastern Europe. In southern cities like Washington, DC, and Charleston, alley dwellings and tenements home to African Americans sat cheek by jowl with the homes of wealthy whites.[9]

One reason for this early burst of gentrification was the rapid growth of white-collar workers in American cities. In 1870, less than 1 percent of American laborers performed clerical work. By 1930, that number had risen to 10 percent of the population. By mid-century, clerical workers, along with sales employees, managers, and professionals made up 37 percent of all American workers. This new white-collar labor force looked hungrily for housing in convenient access to the new skyscrapers and department stores of the central business district.[10]

The vast majority of white-collar workers, however, moved to the urban periphery. Housing in the Zone of Transition was in dismal shape in the 1910s and 1920s. Townhouses in elite districts like Beacon Hill lacked modern electrical wiring and plumbing. Decaying mansions were regarded by the descendants of old aristocratic families as "white elephants" requiring endless repairs and an army of full-time domestic staff. Tenements were in even worse shape: disease-ridden fire traps with shared toilets, thin walls,

and no ventilation. Industrial lofts and working waterfronts exposed residents to noise and pollution. Many middle-class city workers felt an antipathy about sharing space with impoverished immigrants and African Americans.

Some white-collar workers, however, found suburban living unappealing. Many were young singles or childless couples who sought cheap rent within walking distance to the new office buildings and the entertainment districts of the center city. Young women were particularly important in this regard. In the 19th century, clerical work was done almost entirely by men with women working primarily as teachers, domestics, and unskilled farm or factory workers. By 1900, however, a quarter of clerical jobs were held by women. By 1960, the number rose to 62 percent. The number of professional women in business rose in the United States from 100,000 to 450,000 in the 1920s alone. These new "white-collar girls," often single and working in new skyscrapers, moved into center-city apartments or boarding houses with roommates. Gay men and lesbians were also an important group who also eschewed the suburbs for the center city. Artists, writers, and musicians also migrated to affordable rentals in older buildings.[11]

Gentrification began with little support from city "growth machines." Downtown business leaders and city planners in the 1910s and 1920s saw little potential in areas like New Orleans's Vieux Carré and hoped to build new skyscrapers, parking facilities, modern auditoriums, and other tourist attractions. Developers responded to new white-collar demand by demolishing older buildings to erect the first apartment towers. In the 1880s, the earliest high-rise apartments purposefully built for the middle class appeared in Manhattan. By the end of the 1920s, areas like Manhattan's West Side, Philadelphia's Rittenhouse Square, and Chicago's Gold Coast district had transformed from blocks of small row houses and mansions to upper-income apartment buildings.[12]

Gentrification instead was spearheaded on the local level by individual architects, preservationists, and small-time entrepreneurs, many of whom were women. Young architects were among the first to gentrify working-class row houses, first for themselves and then for clients. In 1908, New York City architect Frederick Sterner became perhaps the first "gentrifier" in the city when he renovated an East 19th Street rooming house that he had purchased in the Gramercy Park neighborhood and from which he had evicted the residents. Sterner's renovation was so successful that architects began to emulate him by remodeling run-down row houses in Gramercy Park, Murray Hill, East Midtown, Treadwell Farm, and Lenox Hill. The row house renovation trend soon spread across the river to Brooklyn Heights. By the end of the 1920s, most of the row houses of Manhattan's East Side once home to the poor and working class now housed wealthy owners and renters.[13]

Other cities saw a similar trend. Boston's Brahmin families began to leave Beacon Hill as early as the 1880s. By 1905 only 242 families listed in the *Social Register* remained in the neighborhood, and most of its townhouses were subdivided into rooming houses. That year, a young architect, Frank A. Bourne, moved to the area and renovated a deteriorated colonial townhouse. Joined by William Coombs Codman, a Brahmin whose family lived in Beacon Hill for generations, Bourne recruited friends and business acquaintances to purchase and renovate properties both for themselves and to sell on the market. Although their efforts were small-scale and not publicized in major newspapers or realtor publications, their efforts sparked a renovation movement that continued into the 1950s. In Philadelphia's Rittenhouse Square, architects such as William B. Koelle similarly renovated smaller buildings in rear alleys like Panama Street.[14]

Renovators did not only "make over" old buildings for new white-collar professional residents. In new bohemian districts like Chicago's Towertown, landlords converted tenements and rooming houses into apartments and studios for artists, musicians, and writers. In New York's Greenwich Village, contractors cut large, north-facing windows in townhouses and former horse stables to emulate the studios of the West Bank of Paris. Writers and artists like DuBose Heyward and Elizabeth O'Neill Verner bought property on and around Tradd Street in Charleston, South Carolina, and soon became known as a "Charleston Renaissance." Sherwood Anderson, William Faulkner, Edmund Wilson, and Alberta Kinsey were among the number of creative minds, many with connections to Tulane University, who moved into New Orleans's struggling Vieux Carré. Along with paying higher rents, bohemian residents acted as countercultural boosters for downtrodden inner-city districts by writing and painting romantic portraits of poor residents and celebrating the charm and history of the architecture. DuBose Heyward's novel *Porgy and Bess*, for example, brought national attention to "Catfish Row," a pseudonym for Cabbage Row, a collection of African American tenements near his home. Shortly after the novel's publication, Cabbage Row was renovated for wealthier white residents and its tenants evicted.[15]

Foreshadowing activists like Jane Jacobs in the 1960s, women in the 1910s and 1920s played a particularly important role in initiating gentrification. Shunned by real estate developers and city planners, dilapidated housing in the inner-city offered entrepreneurial opportunities and financial independence for ambitious middle-class women. Preservation and home restoration also dovetailed with other Progressive urban reform causes championed by women's civic groups. In Charleston, Susan Pringle Frost, the daughter of one of the city's declining aristocratic families, used her experience from working as a secretary for a prominent architect to purchase old homes in the city's historic southern tip. Using ironworks and artifacts she had salvaged over the years from demolished buildings and with the hired assistance of Thomas Pinckney, an African American craftsman, she restored buildings, often evicting their African American tenants, and sold them at a small profit. She later helped found the Society for the Preservation of Old Buildings, which pushed the city to pass one of the nation's first zoning ordinances in 1931 protecting historic architecture in "Old and Historic Charleston District." In New Orleans's Vieux Carré, Elizabeth Werlein and other middle-class women founded the Quartier Club, which initiated preservation efforts and lobbied middle-class residents to purchase property in the area. Along with writing one of the first architectural studies of the area, *The Wrought Iron Railings of the Vieux Carré New Orleans*, Werlein founded and led the Vieux Carré Commission and the Vieux Carré Property Owners Association, which advocated protecting the area from redevelopment.[16]

Local ethnic entrepreneurs also played an important role in marketing poorer areas to a new wealthier clientele. In New York's Greenwich Village, Italian American immigrant realtor Vincente Pepe was an avid booster of his impoverished neighborhood, who after renovating several townhomes began to promote the area's bohemian ambience in New York City newspapers as well as writing the influential 1914 guide *How Would You Like to Open One of These Doors in Greenwich Village?* "It was Vincent Pepe who conceived of the idea of having artists and scribes colonize a slum and then gradually improve the district by crowding out the wicked, vicious and slovenly tenants," complained Robert Edward, publisher of the Greenwich Village monthly *The Quill* in 1924.[17]

In the late 1920s, cities saw the first public outcries against gentrification. New neighborhood associations lobbied for the first zoning laws to stop the encroachment of high-rise apartment buildings. Newspapers criticized home renovators for displacing the poor.

Groups like the American League of Artists and the Authors' League of America complained that white-collar professionals were coopting *la vie bohéme*. "Pseudo-artists" and "poseurs" were pouring into Greenwich Village and the French Quarter, driving up rent prices and displacing real artists from their workspaces. By the 1930s, former enthusiasts lamented that bohemian districts had become tourist traps. "As in Greenwich Village," wrote the *New York Times* in 1922, "the most ardent of the poseurs [in the French Quarter], the youths with the longest and girls with the shortest hair, hail from Peoria and Oshkosh. Someday a patient sociologist will chart the invisible watershed which turns some of these acolytes of art toward New York Bay and some toward the Gulf. ... The French Quarter has suffered the fate of such quarters. It has become a fad."[18]

THE FORMATIVE STAGE: GENTRIFICATION IN THE 1960s AND 1970S

During the Depression and World War II, gentrification in most cities stalled. One exception was Washington, DC, where the New Deal brought thousands of new federal office workers to the city, a prominent group of whom restored 19th-century homes in Georgetown. But starting in the 1950s gentrification took off again. Gentrified districts from the 1910s and 1920s, such as Brooklyn Heights, Rittenhouse Square, and Beacon Hill, became springboards for renters who fanned outward in search of cheaper rents and affordable homes to purchase. By the 1970s, gentrification had expanded from a small renovation trend in a few cities to a national phenomenon.

Because gentrification remained largely private, grassroots, and unplanned during these decades, scholars have referred to this period alternatively as the "pioneer stage," "R and D stage," or "first wave" of gentrification. In an era of experimentation and grassroots activism, new middle-class "pioneers" moved into poorer districts and rehabilitated homes. They coined new names for enclaves, started new block and neighborhood associations, planted trees, led home tours, and wrote newsletters and guides about home restoration. New historic preservation groups researched the history of their enclaves. Frustrated that realtors were steering white homebuyers from their revitalizing enclaves, some residents founded small real estate agencies that specialized in purchasing, restoring, and selling Victorian housing. A "heritage industry" of small businesses produced stonework, stained glass windows, and faux gaslights for restored townhouses. Journalists and writers who moved into poorer areas penned articles about their up-and-coming districts. By the early 1970s, major newspapers around the country began to describe a "brownstone revitalization movement" or "back-to-the-city" movement that was transforming American cities. Newspapers in different cities used a variety of names for middle-class renovation efforts: "brownstoning," "townhousing," "whitepainting," "sandblasting," and "rehabilitation." The term "gentrification" didn't enter the popular lexicon until the late 1970s.[19]

Most new middle-class renovators were drawn to Victorian townhouses and homes in inner-city neighborhoods such as Atlanta's Inman Park, Columbus Ohio's German Village, and San Antonio's King William. But in other districts, gentrifiers converted industrial lofts, warehouses, horse stables, and other 19th- and early 20th-century structures for residential uses. In New York City, for example, artists began in the 1950s to move illegally into manufacturing lofts in the Cast Iron district. By the 1970s, New Yorkers began to refer to the loft district as SoHo.[20]

In absolute numbers, gentrification remained limited. From 1974 to 1976, according to a Department of Housing and Urban Development study, gentrification and condominium conversions affected only between 519,000 and 541,000 people, or less than 4 percent of the nation's population who moved. But the phenomenon was widespread, with a majority of the nation's cities experiencing some degree of gentrification. One 1975 study showed that 48 percent of the nation's 143 cities with populations over 50,000 were "experiencing some degree of private-market, nonsubsidized housing renovation in older deteriorating areas." By January 1979, the Urban Land Institute found that 86 percent of cities with more than 150,000 residents had at least one gentrifying district. Gentrification was present primarily in older cities in the East, Midwest, and South. San Francisco, Denver, and Seattle also had experienced significant gentrification. A 1976–1979 study of the nation's 30 largest cities found that Washington, DC, San Francisco, and Seattle were experiencing the most private renovation. Detroit, Newark, New Jersey, and Cleveland sat at the bottom of the list.[21]

Gentrification during this era largely occurred in white working-class neighborhoods undergoing the early stages of racial transition and white flight. According to a 1979 study of 967 gentrifying tracts, new middle-class arrivals were moving not to "ghettoes" but to areas with fewer vacant units, more owner-occupied units, and some professional households already. Out-movers from gentrifying districts according to studies from the late 1970s were 96 percent white in Washington, DC, 90 percent in St. Louis, 92 percent in Seattle, and 93 percent in St. Paul. African Americans, Puerto Ricans, and other minorities, however, were moving to many of these areas and formed a significant subpopulation. The result was gentrifying neighborhoods in which African Americans were disproportionately displaced but also growing as a percentage of the overall population. By the 1980s, many districts had transformed from industrial white working-class neighborhoods to sharply stratified postindustrial neighborhoods with wealthy white professionals living blocks away from poorer minorities.[22]

The new urban middle class of the 1960s and 1970s shared many of the characteristics of their earlier counterparts from the 1910s and 1920s. Studies of cities like St. Paul, Boston, and New Orleans in the 1970s showed that new arrivals in revitalizing districts were overwhelmingly young, white, and employed in white-collar professions and the arts. Two-thirds of renovators had bachelor's degrees, and in some districts even up to 90 percent had completed some graduate school. Many new arrivals were single or couples without children. Gay men and lesbians were represented in disproportionate numbers.[23]

As in the previous wave of gentrification, new middle-class residents were drawn to inner-city areas for economic reasons. Outpriced from the enclaves of the 1910s and 1920s, new arrivals looked elsewhere for cheap housing with historic architecture and convenient access to new office towers in the central business district. During the 1970s, runaway inflation and skyrocketing fuel prices drove up the cost of constructing and purchasing new homes, making it comparatively cheaper to "recycle" older buildings. High interest rates made refinancing difficult, leading many landlords to sell their buildings or convert them to condominiums.

Like their predecessors, gentrifiers also moved to older districts because of changing cultural tastes. Inspired by the counterculture and other social movements of the 1960s, new arrivals described themselves as rejecting modernist downtown skyscrapers, institutional university campuses, and suburban tract homes, which they regarded as dehumanizing and inauthentic. Older inner-city districts, in contrast, had historic housing that seemingly rooted residents in the past. Immigrant urban villages offered an imagined ethnic authenticity and face-to-face community that gentrifiers felt was lost in new suburban shopping malls.

Gentrification during this period continued to be a grassroots phenomenon not yet supported by the finance, insurance, and real estate sector. Most banks in the 1960s refused to grant loans in redlined inner-city districts.

Home and fire insurance was difficult to procure. Realtors steered white home buyers away from areas with African American, Puerto Rican, or Mexican American residents. To purchase a townhouse in a poorer district, many middle-class gentrifiers drew from private savings or paid expensive mortgage brokers to cobble together financing from a hodgepodge of lenders. Others turned to purchase-money mortgages in which they borrowed directly from the seller. Perhaps most striking about this wave of gentrification was how many renovators relied on sweat equity and restored homes themselves.

Gentrifying districts began to develop a political identity during these decades. New middle-class residents founded the first Reform Democratic clubs in the 1950s, in many cases out of frustration that regular Democrats failed to support Adlai Stevenson's two presidential runs. By the late 1960s, gentrifying districts were hotbeds of political activism, with many college-educated home renovators like Jane Jacobs drawn to new social movements like the environmental, antiwar, and women's movement. A new activist and left-leaning white middle class in districts such as New York's West Village, Washington, DC's Adams-Morgan, and Atlanta's Inman Park joined with poorer neighbors to fight urban redevelopment, new expressways, and redlining. A wave of new reform politicians with roots in gentrifying districts formed part of a "neighborhood movement" that in the 1970s challenged city growth machines in cities like San Francisco and Boston.[24]

Gentrification during this period was largely unsupported by the public sector. Local and federal officials, as well as developers and downtown business leaders, remained convinced until the early 1970s that urban redevelopment was the only viable strategy for attracting white middle-class residents back to center cities. While the 1954 and 1968 Housing Acts had more support for rehabilitation than the 1949 version, federal grants and loans had income requirements that limited their use by middle-class renovators. "Conservation districts" were largely aimed to encourage incumbent upgrading and prevent white flight rather than attract new upper-income whites to older districts. A handful of cities launched pilot urban renewal projects in the 1960s that rehabilitated older townhouses and tenements for middle- and upper-income residents: Philadelphia's Society Hill, New York City's Upper West Side Renewal Area, Baltimore's Bolton Hill, Providence's College Hill, and Chicago's Lincoln Park, for example. Yet while they gained a lot of publicity, these pilot projects represented only a tiny fraction of each city's larger urban redevelopment program.

In the mid-1970s, city and state governments began to take a limited but more active role in promoting gentrification. Faced with citizen protests against demolition, a federal moratorium on public housing funding, thousands of abandoned buildings, and crippling budget shortfalls, many cities in the mid-1970s halted their urban redevelopment programs and shifted to offering grants and tax incentives for private rehabilitation and adaptive reuse of old buildings. Quite small in number and bound by strict income guidelines, this mix of homesteading programs, tax abatements, and loans for rehabbing did not really constitute a "pro-gentrification" policy. But in practice, public funds were sometimes used to subsidize middle-class displacement of low-income residents. Section 312 federal funds for rehabilitation, for example, only had rent control requirements for five years. Some cities, such as Jersey City, New Jersey, and Columbus, Ohio, funneled grants into "Neighborhood Strategy Areas" that were already being revitalized by middle-class home renovators. Enacted in 1955 to help landlords improve tenement conditions, New York City's J-51 law offered property tax abatements and exemptions to owners who rehabilitated rental buildings. In 1975, the law was expanded to include the conversion of nonresidential buildings like manufacturing and commercial buildings into multiple-dwelling apartment buildings. In Manhattan's SoHo, owners converted cast iron industrial lofts into expensive apartments, displacing small manufacturing firms as well as artists who since the 1950s had illegally lived and worked there.[25]

Federal anti-redlining legislation passed in the 1970s also helped fuel gentrification by "greenlining" poor neighborhoods once shunned by lending institutions. In 1975, due to pressure from activists around the country, Congress adopted the Home Mortgage Disclosure Act. In 1977, Congress passed the Community Reinvestment Act, which allowed bank regulators to monitor whether federally supervised lending institutions were extending credit to homebuyers in low and moderate income urban areas.

New historic preservation legislation in the 1970s also provided indirect state support for gentrification. The National Historic Preservation Act of 1966 established the National Registry of Historic Places. During the late 1960s and 1970s, middle-class gentrifiers in cities nationwide lobbied to have their revitalizing enclaves placed on the Registry. According to a 1975 study, around two-thirds of the nation's gentrifying enclaves were historic districts. The Tax Reform Act of 1976, along with several state and local programs, provided tax incentives for the rehabilitation of historic buildings with no income requirements or protection against displacement. The tax policy complained that National Commission of Neighborhoods in 1979, "created incentives for historic district restoration...often...at the expense of low and moderate income residents of those newly discovered historic neighborhoods, many of whom have been displaced by more affluent homeowners."[26]

The "formative stage" of gentrification lasted until the mid-1970s and was largely celebrated by newspapers and public officials as a welcome countertrend to white flight, deindustrialization, and heavy-handed government-led slum clearance. Gentrification was not a word yet used by Americans. Protests by poorer residents against middle-class rehabilitation efforts in the 1950s and 1960s were sporadic. In 1950, for example, African American residents in Washington, DC's Georgetown testified at Congress against the passage of the Old Georgetown Act, an early historic preservation ordinance. But until the late 1970s, state-sponsored redevelopment, suburban flight, deindustrialization, and urban expressways were regarded by most as the primary threat to poorer inner-city communities.

"THE SPECULATIVE STAGE"— GENTRIFICATION IN THE 1980S AND 1990S

At the start of the 1980s, many older American cities continued to struggle as their industrial economies contracted and residents migrated to the suburbs or Sunbelt. Cities like San Francisco, New York, Boston, and Seattle, however experienced dramatic economic revivals as they transformed into postindustrial financial and administrative centers for regional, national, and international trade. While manufacturing jobs continued to plummet from 1976 to 1985, Boston saw employment in professional services increase by 62 percent, business services by 55 percent, and the FIRE sector by 32 percent. New York City saw an increase of 272,000 jobs in corporate services in the same period.[27]

As cities emerged from the fiscal crisis of the 1970s, gentrification transformed from a grassroots renovation movement led by cash-strapped "pioneers" to a process spearheaded by developers, speculators, and city planners. Real estate investors drove up rents in the former countercultural districts of the 1960s and 1970s. The cost of Victorian homes in inner-city historic districts skyrocketed. In manufacturing areas where artists once illegally worked and lived, developers now converted industrial lofts into luxury apartment complexes. Along Brooklyn's waterfront, for example, developer David Walentas in the early 1980s bought and converted an entire district of industrial warehouses into apartments and art galleries, hoping his planned version of DUMBO (or Down Under the Manhattan Bridge Overpass) would match the artsy aesthetic and popularity of Manhattan's SoHo. In cities from Baltimore to San Francisco, new festival marketplaces tried to capture the feel of gentrified districts by mimicking their historic architecture, ethnic culture, small shops, and imagined authenticity. Architectural critics celebrated and derided a new "postmodern" era of urban architecture and planning.[28]

Although gentrification continued to be driven largely by the private sector, the state in the 1980s began to more aggressively subsidize gentrification. Much of this support was initially unintended. Developers and speculators abused tax incentives and abatements created during the financially desperate 1970s to help subsidize the conversion of older buildings to luxury apartments. New York City's J-51 tax incentive, for example, came under fire from critics in the 1980s for giving tax breaks to developers for projects in wealthy Manhattan districts that they would have completed anyway. Others complained that speculators used J-51 abatements to convert single-room-occupancy hotels to luxury apartment buildings at great cost to the poor. In the 1990s, the federal government offered its first direct public funding for gentrification with the federal HOPE VI program, which provided cities with funding to demolish distressed high-rise public housing and replace them with mixed-income projects. Lauded by most housing reformers, a growing group of skeptics accused cities of subsidizing "gentrification by stealth." Enterprise zones in the 1990s were criticized by some scholars as catalysts for gentrification.[29]

But the state was not only a booster of gentrification. City, state, and federal governments starting in the late 1970s also intervened to protect the poor from private rehabilitation and restoration. Much of this was the result of pressure from the first anti-gentrification groups that emerged in the late 1970s. On the federal level, for example, Congress in 1978 responded to public outcry with a Housing and Community Development Amendment, which required HUD to commission a study of displacement in US communities. In 1980, faced with widespread complaints about a wave of condo conversions and speculation in cities, Congress passed the Condominium and Cooperative Conversion Protection and Abuse Act Relief Act. On the local level, 54 cities in the late 1970s and 1980s passed ordinances regulating speculation and condominium conversions.[30]

In the 1980s and 1990s, gentrifying cities became highly stratified "dual cities" divided between white-collar professionals and non-white service workers. Gentrification became a highly racialized issue as white-collar professionals who were largely white migrated into and drove up rents in predominantly African American and Latino working-class and poor areas. At the start of the 1980s, gentrification still largely occurred in areas that were either white, racially mixed, or home to immigrants. In the 1990s, white middle-class renters and home buyers began to move into highly segregated African American neighborhoods like Bedford-Stuyvesant and Harlem in New York and Bronzeville in Chicago, to the surprise of many scholars who had considered these areas "gentrification proof."

Not all new middle-class arrivals were white. A small African American middle class also moved into areas such as Harlem in New York City, Bronzeville in Chicago, and Auburn Avenue in Atlanta. A new Latino middle class similarly sought homes in poorer Mexican American areas like Chicago's Pilsen. Scholars debate about whether this migration marked the beginnings of "black gentrification," "Latino gentrification," or "nonwhite gentrification" or represented a different type of process altogether.[31]

"THE GLOBAL STAGE": GENTRIFICATION IN THE 2000s

In the 2000s, cities like New York City had districts that were so high-priced that some pointed to a new trend they called "super-gentrification." Rather than wealthy home-buyers or local entrepreneurs, global investment firms now used Manhattan and Brooklyn real estate as piggy banks to store capital. Property values in some districts rose to levels that even displaced the wealthy arrivals from the 1980s and 1990s. "Zombie" high-rise apartment buildings sat half empty with uninhabited units owned by foreign firms. During the 2000s, the Michael Bloomberg administration in New York City encouraged this new wave of investment by upzoning manufacturing districts along the waterfront and on the periphery of gentrified areas.[32]

DISCUSSION OF THE LITERATURE

Historians researching gentrification should familiarize themselves with the extensive social scientific literature covering the subject. The first wave of scholarship on gentrification in the United States consisted of empirical studies in the late 1970s and early 1980s that remain invaluable resources. Shirley Bradway Laska and Daphne Spain's *Back to the City: Issues in Neighborhood Renovation*, Neil Smith and Peter William's *Gentrification of the City*, and Dennis E. Gale's *Neighborhood Revitalization and the Postindustrial City* are three of the most important and offer a good starting point.

In the 1980s and 1990s, social scientists developed sophisticated theories about gentrification. "Production-side" theories offered by neo-classical economists and Marxist geographers focused on the housing supply and uneven development of cities. Gentrification, according to these theorists, was the result of a cycle of disinvestment and economic restructuring that lowered the cost of inner-city property in comparison to suburbs. Neil Smith's *The New Urban Frontier* is a seminal "production-side" work that presented his influential "rent-gap" hypothesis. "Consumption-side" theories were developed by cultural and humanistic geographers like David Ley and emphasized the changing cultural tastes of a "new middle class." Ley and others linked gentrification to the counterculture, the women's movement, the gay liberation movement, and other social movements of the 1960s and 1970s. Postindustrial baby boomers looked to older inner-city districts for a sense of authenticity and freedom they felt was lacking in postwar mass suburbia and modernist high-rise apartment towers. Although his focus is on Canadian cities, Ley's *The New Urban Middle Class* is a must-read for historians.

Historians need not worry about choosing between production- or consumption-side explanations as social scientists since the 1990s have largely accepted both. Newer scholarship has turned to transnational studies of gentrification, subsets of gentrification such as "rural gentrification," as well as gentrification in former Eastern-bloc countries and the developing world. Scholars also have begun to pay more attention to the role of the state and neoliberal policy in shaping the trajectory of gentrification. Most importantly for historians, social scientists have begun to examine gentrification historically and theorize how to periodize the phenomenon. For a good overview of the social scientific scholarship, one can consult several readers. Loretta Lees, Tom Slater, and Elvin Wyly's *The Gentrification Reader* and Japonica Brown-Saracino's *The Gentrification Debates* have seminal articles by Ruth Glass, Robert Beauregard, Sharon Zukin, Neil Smith, and others. Lees, Slater, and Wyly's *Gentrification* also provides a comprehensive overview of the subject.

Historical works on gentrification are few. The most extensive history of gentrification in the 1910s and 1920s is Andrew Dolkart's *The Row House Reborn: Architecture and Neighborhoods in New York City*. Although they never or rarely use the term "gentrification," many informative case studies exist about early restoration efforts and historic preservation in cities like New Orleans, Charleston, Annapolis, Boston, and New York City. Historians should also consult the many histories of bohemian districts in the early 20th century ranging from Caroline Ware's *Greenwich Village* to Chad Heap's *Slumming*. The historical literature on gentrification after World War II is similarly limited. Jon Teaford's *The Metropolitan Revolution* offers a good national overview. Several new books are forthcoming: Aaron Shkuda's *Lofts and the Origins of Gentrification: Artists and Industry in SoHo, New York, 1950–1980* and Brian Goldstein's *The Roots of Urban Renaissance: Gentrification and the Struggle over Harlem*. Historians should also draw from histories of the counterculture, women's history, gay and lesbian history, histories of historic preservation, the history of urban environmentalist activism, and the history of the antiwar movement.

PRIMARY SOURCES

The history of gentrification has yet to be fully examined by historians. An abundance of case studies around the country deserve more attention. Historians should examine the collections of neighborhood civic groups, block associations, and local historical societies. City and state archives should have vertical files about specific neighborhoods as well as records about city planning, housing, and redevelopment. More research needs to be done about how federal policy has shaped gentrification over time. Researchers should start with the papers of former secretaries of the Department of Housing and Urban Development such as Robert Weaver, George Romney Patricia Harris, and Jack Kemp. Before the late 1970s, the term "gentrification" will likely not appear in the archives, so researchers should look for other terms in finding aids: "rehabilitation, historic preservation, revitalization, private restoration, and brownstoning," among others. As many were employed in media and arts, new middle-class residents of gentrifying districts produced a cornucopia of newsletters, alternative newspapers, articles in city newspapers and magazines, studies and reports, novels and films. As a result, most histories of gentrification tend to focus on the experiences of new middle-class arrivals. For the perspective of the poor in gentrifying districts, historians need to be creative. Edited by Joseph Barry and John Derevlany, *Yuppies Invade My House at Dinnertime* is an interesting collection of letters to the *Hoboken Reporter* about gentrification and captures much of the tension in that city during the 1980s. DW Gibson *The Edge Becomes the Center: An Oral History of Gentrification in the 21st Century* is a rich collection of interviews about gentrification with a wide range of New York City residents.

FURTHER READING

Dolkart, Andrew. *The Row House Reborn: Architecture and Neighborhoods in New York City, 1908–1929*. Baltimore: Johns Hopkins Press, 2009.

Freeman, Lance. *There Goes the 'Hood: Views of Gentrification from the Ground Up*. Philadelphia: Temple University Press, 2006.

Gale, Dennis E. *Neighborhood Revitalization and the Postindustrial City: A Multinational Perspective*. Lexington, MA: Lexington Books, 1984.

Gibson, D. W. *The Edge Becomes the Center: An Oral History of Gentrification in the 21st Century*. New York: Overlook Press, 2015.

Hartman, Chester, Dennis Keating, and Richard LeGates. *Displacement: How to Fight It*. Berkeley, CA: National Housing Law Project, 1982.

Hyra, Derek. *The New Urban Renewal: The Transformation of Harlem and Bronzeville*. Chicago: University of Chicago Press, 2008.

Laska, Shirley Bradway, and Daphne Spain. *Back to the City: Issues in Neighborhood Revitalization*. New York: Pergamon Press, 1980.

Lees, Loretta, Tom Slater, and Elvin Wyly, eds. *The Gentrification Reader*. London: Routledge, 2010.

Osman, Suleiman. *The Invention of Brownstone Brooklyn: Gentrification and the Search for Authenticity in Postwar New York*. New York: Oxford University Press, 2011.

Smith, Neil, and Peter Williams. *Gentrification of the City*. New York: Allen & Unwin, 1986.

Von Hoffman, Nicholas. *House by House, Block by Block: The Rebirth of America's Urban Neighborhoods*. New York: Oxford University Press, 2004.

NOTES

1. Ruth Glass, "Introduction," in *London: Aspects of Change*, ed. Centre of Urban Studies (London: MacGibbon & Kee, 1964), xviii. Cited in Japonica Brown-Saracino, ed., *The Gentrification Debates* (New York: Routledge, 2010).

2. For an overview of the debate over how to define gentrification, see Loretta Lees, Tom Slater, and Elvin Wyly, eds. "Introduction," in *The Gentrification Reader* (London and New York: Routledge, 2010), xv–xvi, 3–6. See also Robert A. Beauregard, "The Chaos and Complexity of Gentrification," in *Gentrification of the City*, ed. Neil Smith and Peter Williams (Boston: Allen & Unwin, 1986), 35–55; and Eric Clark, "The Order and Simplicity of Gentrification," in *Gentrification in a Global Context: The New Urban Colonialism*, ed. Rowland Atkinson and Gary Bridge (London and New York: Routledge, 2005), 256–264. Both articles are also excerpted in *The Gentrification Reader*.

3. Clark, "The Order and Simplicity of Gentrification."

4. This article argues that displacement *should not* be a required part of a historical definition of gentrification. For a convincing counterargument that displacement *should* be a key part of any definition of the term, see Tom Slater, "The Eviction of Critical Perspectives from Gentrification Research," *International Journal of Urban and Regional Research* 30.4 (December 2006); for a balanced analysis of the displacement debate, see Lance Freeman, *There Goes the 'Hood: Views of Gentrification from the Ground Up* (Philadelphia: Temple University Press, 2006); for a nuanced analysis of political and cultural displacement and gentrification, see Japonica Brown-Saracino, *A Neighborhood That Never Changes: Gentrification, Social Preservation and the Search for Authenticity* (Chicago: University of Chicago Press, 2010).

5. For an analysis of the new black middle-class migration to New York's Harlem and Chicago's Bronzeville, see Derek Hyra, *The New Urban Renewal: The Economic Transformation of Harlem and Bronzeville* (Chicago: University of Chicago Press, 2008); Michelle R. Boyd, *Jim Crow Nostalgia: Reconstructing Race in Bronzeville* (Minneapolis: University of Minnesota Press, 2008); and Lance Freeman, *There Goes the 'Hood: Views of Gentrification from the Ground Up* (Philadelphia: Temple University Press, 2006).

6. Richard Florida, *The Rise of the Creative Class: And How It's Transforming Work, Leisure, Community and Everyday Life* (New York: Basic Books, 2002); and Loretta Lees and David Ley, "Introduction to Special Issue on Gentrification and Public Policy," *Urban Studies* 45.12 (November 2008): 2379–2384.

7. For an analysis of the countercultural roots of gentrification, see David Ley, *The New Middle Class and the Remaking of the Central City* (New York: Oxford University Press, 1996); for an analysis of gentrification as a rejection of urban modernism, see Jon Caufield, *City Form and Everyday Life: Toronto's Gentrification and Critical Social Practice* (Toronto: University of Toronto Press, 1994); for an analysis of gentrification and discourses about authenticity, see Japonica Brown-Saracino, *A Neighborhood that Never Changes: Gentrification, Social Preservation and the Search for Authenticity* (Chicago: University of Chicago Press, 2009); for a critique of revanchist ideology and frontier imagery in gentrifying districts, see Neil Smith, *The New Urban Frontier: Gentrification and the Revanchist City* (New York: Routledge, 1996); for an analysis of gentrification as a "new urban colonialism," see Roland Atkinson and Gary Bridge, "Introduction," in *Gentrification in a Global Context*, 1–17.

8. Jason Hackworth and Neil Smith, "The Changing State of Gentrification," *Tijdschrift voor economische en sociale geografie* 92 (2001): 464–477; also cited in Lees, Slater, and Wyly, *Gentrification*.

9. The "Zone of Transition" was coined by Ernst W. Burgess, "The Growth of a City: An Introduction to a Research Project," in *The City*, ed. Robert E. Park, Ernst W. Burgess, and Robert E. McKenzie (Chicago: University of Chicago Press, 1925); Harvey Warren Zorbaugh, *The Gold Coast and the Slum: A Sociological Study of Chicago's Near North Side* (Chicago:

University of Chicago Press, 1929); Dennis E. Gale, "Restoration in Georgetown, Washington, D.C., 1915–65 (PhD Diss., George Washington University, 1982), 92–93; and Richard O. Baumbach Jr. and William E. Borah, *The Second Battle of New Orleans: A History of Vieux Carré Riverfront-Expressway Controversy* (Tuscaloosa: University of Alabama Press, 1981), 17–23.

10. C. Wright Mills, *White Collar: The American Middle Classes* (New York: Oxford University Press, 1956), 63–66; and Oliver Zunz, *Making America Corporate 1870–1920* (Chicago: University of Chicago Press, 1990), 126.

11. Mills, 198–204; and Zunz, 126.

12. Andrew Dolkart, *The Row House Reborn: Architecture and Neighborhoods in New York City, 1908–1929* (Baltimore: Johns Hopkins Press, 2009), 11; Anthony J. Stanonis, *Creating the Big Easy: New Orleans and the Emergence of Modern Tourism, 1918–1945* (Athens, GA: University of Georgia Press, 2006), 28–69; Bobbye Burke, "History and Development," in *Historic Rittenhouse: A Philadelphia Neighborhood*, ed. Trina Vaux (Philadelphia: University of Pennsylvania Press, 1985), 30–33; and Homer Hoyt, *One Hundred Years of Land Values in Chicago: The Relationship of the Growth of Chicago to the Rise of its Land Value, 1830–1933* (1933; reprint. Washington, DC: Beard Books, 2000), 237–245.

13. Andrew Dolkart, *The Row House Reborn*. Dolkart's book is the most detailed and groundbreaking study to date of gentrification during this period.

14. Dolkart, *The Row House*, 180; and Walter Firey, *Land Use in Central Boston* (New York: Greenwood Press, 1968), 117–121.

15. Chad Heap, *Slumming: Sexual Encounters in American Nightlife, 1885–1940* (Chicago: University of Chicago Press, 2008), 59–62; Dolkart, *The Row House*, 114–123; Baumbauch and Borah, *The Second Battle of New Orleans*, 22–23; Robert R. Weyeneth, "Ancestral Architecture: The Early Preservation Movement in Charleston," in *Giving Preservation a History: Histories of Historic Preservation in the United States*, ed. Max Page and Randall Mason (New York: Routledge, 2004).

16. Sidney R. Bland, *Preserving Charleston's Past, Shaping It's Future: The Life and Times of Susan Pringle Frost* (Westport, CT: Greenwood Press, 1994); and Anthony J. Stanonis, *Creating the Big Easy: New Orleans and the Emergence of Modern*

Tourism, 1918–1945 (Athens, GA: University of Georgia Press, 2006), 129, 141–169.

17. Dolkart, *The Row House*, 123, 169–173.

18. Dolkart, *The Row House*; "Greenwich Village on Royal Street," *New York Times*, July 23, 1922; also cited in John Shelton Reed, *Dixie Bohemia: A French Quarter Circle in the 1920s* (Baton Rouge: Louisiana State University Press, 2012), 91.

19. Hackworth and Smith, "The Changing State of Gentrification"; David Ley response to Suleiman Osman, "Gentrification and the Death and Life of Great American Cities: Was Jane Jacobs a 'Gentrifier'?" public lecture, Gentrification and the City series, Simon Fraser University, Vancouver, Canada, November 20, 2013; Tom Slater, "Gentrification in Canada's Cities: From Social Mix to 'Social Tectonics,'" in *Gentrification in a Global Context: The New Urban Colonialism*, 41; and Suleiman Osman, *The Invention of Brownstone Brooklyn: Gentrification and the Search for Autheniticity in Postwar New York* (New York: Oxford University Press, 2011), 8, 12.

20. Dennis E. Gale, "Restoration in Georgetown, Washington, D.C., 1915–65" (PhD Diss., George Washington University, 1982).

21. Dennis E. Gale, *Neighborhood Revitalization and the Postindustrial City: A Multinational Perspective* (Lexington, MA: Lexington Books, 1984), 9–10, 22; and J. Thomas Black, "Private-Market Housing Renovation in Central Cities: An Urban Land Institute Survey," in *Back to the City: Issues in Neighborhood Revitalization*, ed. Shirley Bradway Laska and Daphne Spain (New York: Pergamon Press, 1980), 11.

22. Richard T. Legates and Chester Hartman, "The Anatomy of Displacement in the United States," in *Gentrification of the City*, ed. Neil Smith and Peter Williams (Boston: Allen & Unwin, 1986), 185–186;

23. Gale, *Neighborhood Revitalization*, 11.

24. Shirley Bradway Laska and Daphne Spain, "Anticipating Renovators' Demands: New Orleans," in *Back to the City*, 131–132.

25. Chester Hartman, Dennis Keating, and Richard LeGates, *Displacement: How to Fight It* (Berkeley, CA: National Housing Law Project, 1982), 154–162.

26. Gale, *Neighborhood Revitalization*, 4, 9; and Hartman, Keating, and LeGates, *Displacement*, 162–165.

27. Jon Teaford, *The Metropolitan Revolution: The Rise of Post-Urban America* (New York: Columbia University Press, 2006), 168–169.

28. Jason Hackworth, *The Neoliberal City: Governance, Ideology, and Development in American Urbanism* (Ithaca, NY: Cornell University Press, 2007), 144–149.

29. Gary Bridge, Tim Butlee, and Loretta Lees, eds., *Mixed Communities: Gentrification by Stealth?* (Chicago: Policy Press, 2012).

30. Hartman, Keating, and LeGates, *Displacement*, 33, 45–48; and Matthew Lasner, *High Life: Condo Living in the Suburban Century* (New Haven, CT: Yale University Press, 2012).

31. Matthew B. Anderson and Carolina Sternberg, "'Non-White' Gentrification in Chicago's Bronzeville and Pilsen: Racial Economy and the Intraurban Contigency of Urban Redevelopment," *Urban Affairs Review* 49 (2013): 442; and Kesha S. Moore, "Gentrification in Black Face?: The Return of the Black Middle Class to Urban Neighborhoods," *Urban Geography* 30.2 (2009): 118–142.

32. Loretta Lees, "Super-Gentrification: The Case of Brooklyn Heights," *Urban Studies* 40.12 (2003): 2487–2509; Julian Brash, *Bloomberg's New York: Class and Governance in the Luxury City* (Athens, GA: University of Georgia Press, 2011); and "Stream of Foreign Wealth Flows to New York City Real Estate," *New York Times*, Feburary 7, 2015; "Has Zombie Urbanism Gripped the Global City," KCRW, accessed October 17, 2015.

Suleiman Osman

Directory of Contributors

Peter C. Baldwin
University of Connecticut

Betsy A. Beasley
University of Texas, Austin

Brian D. Behnken
Iowa State University

Chad Berry
Berea College

David Blanke
Texas A&M University, Corpus Christi

Charlotte Brooks
Baruch College, City University of New York

David Brundage
University of California, Santa Cruz

Vincent J. Cannato
University of Massachusetts, Boston

Christopher D. Cantwell
University of Wisconsin, Milwaukee

Court Carney
Stephen F. Austin State University

James J. Connolly
Ball State University

Jean-Paul R. deGuzman
University of California, Los Angeles

Andrew J. Diamond
Université Paris-Sorbonne

Chris Elcock
Université Jean Moulin Lyon 3

Alex Elkins
University of Michigan, Ann Arbor

Ansley T. Erickson
Columbia University

Robbie Ethridge
University of Mississippi

John D. Fairfield
Xavier University

Maureen A. Flanagan
Illinois Institute of Technology

Margaret Garb
Washington University in St. Louis

Lily Geismer
Claremont McKenna College

Erik S. Gellman
University of North Carolina, Chapel Hill

John Gennari
University of Vermont

Robert R. Gioielli
University of Cincinnati

David Goldfield
University of North Carolina, Charlotte

Risa L. Goluboff
University of Virginia

Hardy Green
Stony Brook University, State University of New York

Claudrena N. Harold
University of Virginia

Leslie M. Harris
Northwestern University

Emma Hart
University of St. Andrews

Jeffrey Helgeson
Texas State University

Hidetaka Hirota
Institute for Advanced Study, Waseda University, Tokyo, Japan

Emily K. Hobson
University of Nevada, Reno

Ella Howard
Wentworth Institute of Technology

Joseph E. Hower
Southwestern University

D. Bradford Hunt
Newberry Library, Chicago

Andrew Hurley
University of Missouri, St. Louis

Victor Jew
University of Wisconsin, Madison

Ann Durkin Keating
North Central College

Christopher Klemek
George Washington University

Clement Lai
California State University, Northridge

Erika Lee
University of Minnesota

Shelley Sang-Hee Lee
Oberlin College

Cindy Lobel
Lehman College, City University of New York

Daryl Joji Maeda
University of Colorado, Boulder

Brian McCammack
Lake Forest College

Austin McCoy
Auburn University

Megan Kate Nelson
Writer and historian based in Lincoln, Massachusetts

Phuong Nguyen
California State University, Monterey Bay

Becky Nicolaides
University of California, Los Angeles

Carl Nightingale
University at Buffalo, State University of New York

Peter Norton
University of Virginia

Suleiman Osman
George Washington University

Dominic Pacyga
Columbia College Chicago

Mark Padoongpatt
University of Nevada, Las Vegas

Harold L. Platt
Loyola University Chicago

Jessica Pliley
Texas State University

Gail Radford
University at Buffalo, State University of New York

Christopher R. Reed
Roosevelt University

Jonathan Rees
Colorado State University, Pueblo

Emily Remus
University of Notre Dame

Steven A. Riess
Northeastern Illinois University

Kyle B. Roberts
Loyola University Chicago

Nicolas G. Rosenthal
Loyola Marymount University

Elihu Rubin
Yale University

Margaret Rung
Roosevelt University

A. K. Sandoval-Strausz
Pennsylvania State University

David Schley
Hong Kong Baptist University

Christopher W. Schmidt
Illinois Institute of Technology

David Schuyler
Franklin and Marshall College

Robert O. Self
Brown University

Jessica Sewell
University of Virginia

Adam Shprintzen
Marywood University

Christopher Silver
University of Florida

Adam Sorensen
University of Virginia

Jordan Stanger-Ross
University of Victoria

Tyina Steptoe
University of Arizona

Thomas J. Sugrue
New York University

Kristin M. Szylvian
St. John's University

Chloe E. Taft
Independent Scholar

David S. Tanenhaus
University of Nevada, Las Vegas

Joel A. Tarr
Carnegie Mellon University

Lorrin Thomas
Rutgers University, Camden

H. Paul Thompson Jr.
North Greenville University

David Torstensson
Pugatch Consilium

Matthew Vaz
City College of New York, City University of New York

Patrick Vitale
Eastern Connecticut State University

Wendy L. Wall
Binghamton University, State University of New York

Eric Weisbard
University of Alabama

Andrew Wiese
San Diego State University

Daniel Wilson
Muhlenberg College

LaDale Winling
Virginia Tech

Jay Young
Archives of Ontario

Judy Yung
University of California, Santa Cruz

Xiaojian Zhao
University of California, Santa Barbara

Index

Note: Page numbers printed in boldface indicate a major discussion, those followed by "*f*" indicate figures and illustrations, "*t*" indicates tables. Page numbers followed by "n" indicate a note and the note number follows.

AAA. *See* Agricultural Adjustment Act; Automobile Association of America
AALL. *See* American Association of Labor Legislation
AAPA. *See* Asian American Political Alliance
Aaron, Hank, 370
Abbott, Edith, 185, 343
Abbott, Grace, 188, 1340–1342
Abelmann, Nancy, 1315
Abernathy, Ralph, 738
abolitionists. *See also* antislavery movements; manumission societies
    violence against, 50
Abortion Rap (Schulder, D., and Kennedy, F.), 1452
Above World, 2, 4
Abrams, Charles, 839
abstinence
    evangelical support of, 415
    temperance movement and, 410

accelerated depreciation policy, 324
Ackerman, Frederick, 906
ACLU. *See* American Civil Liberties Union
ACMHR. *See* Alabama Christian Movement for Civil Rights
activist women, in machine politics, 125
ACT UP. *See* AIDS Coalition to Unleash Power
Adams, Henry C., 184, 341
Adams, John, 432
adaptive reuse, in cities, 330
Addams, Jane, 125, 127, 129, 185–186, 188–192, 1342–1346, 1353
    as environmental pollution activist, 1032
    as housing reform activist, 805
    as settlement house activist, 891, 1141
    on solid waste pollution, 1033–1034
    on urban environments, 1012–1013, 1016
Adderley, Cannonball, 1216
addiction, to drugs, 471–472

Adickes, Franz, 1517
Adler, Polly, 441
AFDC. *See* Aid to Families with Dependent Children
affirmative action, 1375
AFL. *See* American Federation of Labor
Africa, immigration from, 555, 558
African Americans. *See also* Black Freedom movement;
    black middle class; Great Migration; interracial
    marriage; slave economies; slavery; slavery
    markets; slaves
    AFSCME and, 278
    BKA and, 1309
    Black Arts Movement, 1219, 1221
    as black power activists, 137–138
    Black Power movement and, 407–408, 1282–1283
    in BPP, 1326–1327
    BSCP and, 263–264, 1369, 1372
    as city mayors, 138
    civil rights organizations by, 257
    community organizations for, 1372–1373
    Cuban Americans and, relationship with, 737–738
    deindustrialization as influence on, 324
    in Democratic Party, 1372, 1397–1398
    economic success of, globalization as influence on, 105
    Emancipation Proclamation and, 1294
    gambling industry and, 392–394
    gentrification and, 1559–1560
    during the Great Depression, 201
    Harlem Renaissance, 257
    incomes of, in early cities, 44
    International Labor Defense Fund for, 262–263
    in Japantown, in San Francisco, 758–759, 1548
    jazz music and, 573–574, 1214–1215
    in juvenile justice system, unequal treatment of,
        1341, 1345
    Korean-Americans and, conflicted relationships with,
        1307–1311, 1313–1314, 1318n15
    labor strikes by, 255
    in labor unions, 257, 262–263, 1369–1370
    Latino Americans and, relationships with, **730–744**.
        See also specific groups
    lynch mobs against, 1277–1279
    in major league baseball, 370
    Mexican Americans and, 732–735
    as middle-class, 75
    migration to urban American South, 73–75
    mobility restrictions for, 44
    music culture of, 573–574
    NAACP, 189, 257, 1326, 1372–1376
    "New Negro" movement, 1210
    in NNC, 209, 264, 1373, 1377
    in NNL, 370
    passing for white, 582
    police brutality against, 145
    political power of, 149n20, 1219, 1221, 1371–1373

population distribution of (1890), 74*f*
in postindustrial cities, 331
poverty for, 1146
in PPC, 731, 738–739
during prohibition movement, 417–418
protest politics by, 209
in public housing, 820, 824
in public schools, 1174–1175, 1181–1183
public sector unions and, 279
Puerto Ricans and, relationship with, 735–737
racialized progressivism for, 189
in Rainbow Coalition, 736
religion of, in US cities, 1109–1110, 1126–1127
residential segregation of, 636–637
in Richmond, Virginia, 1409–1410
rioting against, 1272–1273, 1276, 1278–1283
Scottsboro Boys case, 206, 263
as slaves in cities, 153
soul food, 1095
in street gangs, 1324–1325
suburbanization and, 792–793
in "sundown towns," 1370
in temperance movement, 409, 415
tourism promotion by, 362
unemployment rates for, during Great Depression, 201
urban crisis for, in urban South, 1409–1411
urban neighborhoods for, 257
urban planning and, neighborhoods displaced
    during, 908
urban redevelopment and, 135–136
vagrancy laws and, unequal application of, 1352,
    1356, 1358
African American women
    in American South, 75–76
    in beauty culture, 572
    community organizations for, 1372–1373
    as consumer market, discrimination against, 171
    during Great Migration, 571–572
    in ILGWU, 735
    as laundry workers, 1374
    National Association of Colored Women, 75
    Neighborhood Union and, 182
    prostitution and, 442, 446
    as teachers, 75–76, 1371
Afro-Cuban jazz music, 1220
AFSCME. *See* American Federation of State, County
    and Municipal Employees
AFT. *See* American Federation of Teachers
Age of Industrial Conflict, 249
age of mass tourism, 358–360
Agricultural Adjustment Act (AAA), US (1938), 200,
    231, 261, 1095
agriculture. *See also* urban agriculture; *specific crops*
    in Cahokia, declining outputs of, 5
Ah Loo, 1299. *See also* anti-Chinese massacre

Ah Was, 1299. *See also* anti-Chinese massacre
Ah Wen, 1299. *See also* anti-Chinese massacre
AIDS Coalition to Unleash Power (ACT UP), 676
Aid to Families with Dependent Children (AFDC), 261,
    723, 1146, 1449
AIM. *See* American Indian Movement
air pollution, 1034–1035, 1038–1041
    from automobile use, 971–972, 972f
    under Clean Air Act, 972, 1040
    under Motor Vehicle Air Pollution Act, 972
    smog, 972f, 975
air traffic controllers
    public sector unions for, 279
    Reagan, R., and, 280
Alabama
    Black Warrior River, 5–6
    cotton mills in, 61
    industrialization of industry in, 61
    Montgomery bus boycott, 77, 940, 1399–1401
Alabama Christian Movement for Civil Rights
    (ACMHR), 1406
Alarcón, Rafael, 563
Albee, Edward, 1194
Alciatore, Antoine, 1084
alcohol production, 406–407
alcohol use. *See also* prohibition; temperance
    movement
    abstinence and, 410
    consumption patterns of, 406–407
    dry counties, 415–416
    historical use of, 406–407
    under Maine Liquor Law, 412
    religious response to, 407–409
    during Revolutionary War, 407
    social context for, 406
Alcott, William, 390
Alexandria, Virginia, 157
Alfaro Sisquieros, David, 701
Alien Land Laws, US, 757, 763, 1492
Alinsky, Saul, 1158
Allen, Richard, 1109–1110
Altman, John, 1397
Altschuler, Glenn, 226
Amalgamated Association of Steel and Iron
    Works, 90–91
Amalgamated Clothing Workers of America, 253
Amer, Tommy, 1492
American Association of Labor Legislation (AALL),
    184–185
American Bandstand, 1232, 1238
American Bar Association, 278
American Bottoms, 17n12
    Cohokia and, 6
    during middle Mississippi period, 5
American Civil Liberties Union (ACLU), 255, 278

*An American Dilemma: The Negro Problem and Modern
    Democracy* (Myrdal), 1144
American Exodus (Lange), 210–211
The American Family Home: Principles of Domestic Science
    (Stowe, H. B., and Beecher, C.), 804
American Federation of Labor (AFL), 186–187,
    203–204, 236
    African Americans in, 1369
    failures of, 260
    membership of, 251–252
    opposition to public sector unions, 273
    U.S. immigration and, 486
American Federation of State, County and Municipal
    Employees (AFSCME), 276–278, 280, 284n39
    Black Freedom movement and, 278
American Federation of Teachers (AFT), 273
American Football League, 374
American Indian Movement (AIM), 1448
Americanism, 190
    street gangs and, 1319–1320
American Medical Association, 181
"American Plan," 258
American Protective Association, 487
American Psychiatric Association, classification of
    homosexuality, 671, 680n3
American Public Health Association, 804–805
American Revolution
    early seaport cities during, 29–31
    New York City occupation during, 31
American Social Hygiene Association (ASHA), 443–445
American Society of Planning Officials, 1523–1524
Americans with Disabilities Act (1990), 1451
American System of Manufactures, 47
American Temperance Society (ATS), 410–412
American Temperance Union (ATU), 141
American Tobacco Company, 67
American Tract Society, 410
American Union Against Militarism, 188
amphetamine use, 469
amusement and theme parks, 359–360. *See also* Walt
    Disney World
amusement parks, 1198
Anasazi people, 685–686
Anderson, Elijah, 1330
Anderson, James, 1173
Anderson, Martin, 1536–1537
Anderson, Nels, 815
Andrews, John B., 184
And the Soul Shall Dance (Yamauchi), 753
Angel Island Immigration Station, **526–541**
    Chinese immigrants at, 527–529, 531
    civic organizations' role in, 536
    comparison of immigration experiences, 532–535
    construction and development of, 527–529
    contagious diseases and, 530

Angel Island Immigration Station (*Continued*)
corruption at, 531–532
deportation rates from, 527, 534
detention policies at, 527–529, 535–537
exclusion policies at, 527, 530
female arrivals at, 534–535
food quality issues at, 535–536
interrogation procedures at, 530–532
law enforcement at, 529
legacy of, 537–538
medical examinations at, 529–530
as National Historic Landmark, 537
racial discrimination at, 530–532, 535
rejection rates at, 532
South Asian immigrants at, 532–533
Annenberg, Moe, 396
Anslinger, Henry, 421
antebellum era
Judaism during, 1112–1113
juvenile justice during, 1340
municipal housing in, 802–803
religion during, 1110–1113
slavery debate during, 72–73
urban American South during, 72–73
anti-authoritarianism
amongst American youth, 1453
in films, 1452
individualism and, 1453
in literature, 1452
national expression of, 1452
during 1960s, 1451–1454
antibiotic development, for contagious diseases, 1057–1058
anti-Chinese massacre, in Los Angeles, **1290–1304**
aftermath of, 1298
fatalities in, 1297–1298
historical legacy of, 1299
legal prosecution after, 1298
press reports on, 1297–1298
anticommunist movements
HUAC and, 277
public sector unions and, 278
Red Scare and, 190, 274
Anti-Drug Abuse Act, US (1986), 1331
anti-gambling movements, 389–391
anti-lynching movements, 1278
anti-machine organizations, 121
antimonopoly progressivism, 185
anti-noise campaigns, 1035
Anti-Saloon League (ASL), 418–420, 422
antislavery movements, 161–162
Anti-Vagrancy Act (1855), 1275
anti-Vietnam War movement, 1438–1441
Asian Americans in, 744, 750–752
Democratic Party and, 1438

Dewey Canyon III, 1438
King, M. L., Jr., and, 1443–1444
March on the Pentagon, 1438
New Left response to, 1443
during 1968 Democratic National Convention, 1438–1439
student protests as part of, 1438
VVAW and, 1444
Anzaldúa, Gloria, 674
Apalachee (chiefdom), 8
apartment building and houses, 65
the Dakota, 805–806
as municipal housing, 805–806
as public housing, 820
skyscrapers as, 859, 870–871
Appleton, Nathan, 87
April 29. *See* Sai-I-Gu
aqueducts, 920
archsegregationist societies, 640–642
arena rock, 1237–1238
Armed Forces of National Liberation (FALN), 723
Armfield, John, 159
Armour, Philip Danforth, 1079
Armstrong, Louis, 1210, 1218
Army, US, prostitution regulated by, 447–448
Arnold, Bion J., 889
Aron, Cindy, 363
Arthur, T. S., 413
artisanal production, 48
artisans. *See tabaqueros*
artist interventions, in postindustrial cities, 330
art rock, 1235
arts and entertainment districts, 1199–1200
ASHA. *See* American Social Hygiene Association
Ashcroft, John, 1161
Asia, immigration from, 553–555. *See also specific countries*
Asian American neighborhoods
for Chinese, 657–658
displacement pressures on, 1542–1545
for Japanese Americans, 758–759
Japantown, in San Francisco, **1542–1557**
racialization of space in, 1543–1545
redevelopment policies for, after World War II, 1545–1547
in Seattle, 1552
urban renewal in, long-term impact of, 1551–1552
Asian American Political Alliance (AAPA), 745
Asian American political movements, **744–757**
anti-Vietnam War movement and, 744, 750–752
Basement Workshop and, 752–753
Black Power movement as influence on, 744–745
civil rights movement and, 744
on college campuses, 746–747
community-based arts organizations and, 752–753

cultural expression as result of, 752–753
on East Coast, 745–746, 749
Free Speech Movement and, 744, 747
gender discrimination in, 751–752
in Hawai'i, 747–748
internationalism and, 750–751
in Los Angeles, 749
in New York City, 749
origins of, 745–746
political organizations for, 745–748
Red Guard Party, 745, 748–749
in San Francisco, 745–749
in Seattle, 747–748
for self-determination, 748–750
student strikes, 746–747
through theater, 753
US-Philippines War and, 750
Women's Liberation Movement and, 751–752
Asian Americans. *See also* Chinese; interracial marriage;
    Japanese immigration; Japanese resettlement;
    Korean Americans; Korean-Americans
academic studies on, 1301–1302
as model minority, 766, 1497
during 1992 riots, **1304–1319**
rioting against, 1275
in street gangs, 1329–1330
Asian American suburban culture, **1492–1516**
academic scholarship on, 1508–1510
under Alien Land Laws, 1492
architecture and design in, 1504–1506
in California, 1494–1496, 1515n62
during Cold War, 1493–1494
culinary identity of, 1514n39
cultural festivals as part of, 1500
daily life in, 1497–1500
education and schools in, 1506–1508
ethnic expressiveness in, 1504–1505
under Fair Housing Act of 1968, 1494
food in, 1499–1500
under GI Bill, 1493
Indian Americans, 1494–1496
LGBTQ and, 1498–1499
in Monterey Park, 1502–1503, 1505–1506
from 1945–1968, 1492–1494
from 1968–2018, 1494–1496
Nisei population, 1504–1505
political expression in, 1496
racially restrictive covenants and, 1512n12
racism and, 1501–1502
residential segregation of, 1493, 1512n4, 1515n62
Shelley v. Kraemer and, 1493–1494
shopping centers and, 1502–1503
Asiatic Barred Zone, 488, 496
Asiatic Exclusion League, 533
Askew, Reubin, 78

ASL. *See* Anti-Saloon League
assassinations, political
of Kennedy, R. F., 1438
of King, M. L., Jr., 278, 822, 1438
assembly lines, 60
in automobile industry, 65–66
Ford, H., and, 65–66, 250
welfare capitalism and, 105
Atlanta, Georgia
after Civil War, 73
destruction of, during Civil War, 846–848
diversity issues in, 80
League of Neighborhoods in, 139
Neighborhood Union in, 182
public segregation in, 77
residential segregation in, 137
sit-in movement in, 1418–1419
urban planning for, 911
urban redevelopment and renewal in, 139, 1410–1411
urban redevelopment in, 139
zoning laws in, 1522
"Atlanta Blueprint," for public housing, 825
"Atlanta Compromise," 76
Atlantic Creoles, 156
atmospheric pollution, 1034–1035, 1039–1041
ATS. *See* American Temperance Society
ATU. *See* American Temperance Union
Auerbach, Red, 377
Austin, Minnesota, 95–97
Austin, Texas
as creative capital, 346
healthcare strategies in, 348–349
universities in, 344–347
authoritarianism, racial discrimination through, 646
automats, 1098
Automobile Association of America (AAA), 891–955
automobile industry. *See also* Ford, Henry
assembly line construction in, 65–66
car culture and, development of, 359
central business districts and, 174
deindustrialization of, 324
automobile use, in cities, **964–993**
air pollution as result of, 971–972, 972f
during bicycle craze, 967
car manufacturers and, 968, 970–971
in Central Park, 1004–1006
City Beautiful movement and, 968–969
by commuters, 967
as conceptual relationship, 964–965, 964f
driver and passenger safety issues, 972–973, 976
drivers' role in, 965–969
in "edge cities," 974–975, 982n33
gasoline taxes, 955
during the Great Depression, 969
as lived experience, 964

automobile use, in cities (*Continued*)
  MacDonald and, 969–971
  mass automobility, 966–969
  mass transit and, 941–942, 971, 975–976
  Model A, 67
  Model T, 65
  as modern revolution, 967–969
  Moses and, 969–971
  under Motor Vehicle Air Pollution Act, 972
  in MSA, 971
  NACC and, 954–955
  national trends in, 974
  smog, 972*f*, 975
  on streets, roads, and highways, 952–958
  suburbanization influenced by, 792–793
  technology as influence on, 967–969
  in urban parks, 1004–1006
  urban planning for, 965–971
  urban sprawl as result of, 974–975, 975*f*
  white flight and, 970
Avery Index, 876
Avila, Eric, 960, 1025
Ayler, Albert, 1222
Azalea, Iggy, 1263

Babbitt (Lewis, S.), 874
Babcock, Richard, 642, 1523
"baby boom" generation, 1441
baby boom population, 907–908
Bacon, Edmund, 134, 1535
Bacon's Rebellion, 22
bacteriological theory, 1032–1033
  antibiotic development, 1058
  vaccine development, 1057–1058
Baer, Christopher, 959
Bailyn, Bernard, 32
Baker, Chet, 1216–1217
Baker, Dean, 215
Baker, Ella, 1374, 1402–1403, 1425, 1435, 1443
Baker, Frank, 850
Baldwin, James, 1537
Baldwin, Peter, 959
Ballinger, Richard, 186
Ballon, Hilary, 959
Balogh, Brian, 959
Baltimore, Maryland, 103
  early populations of, 37–38
  planned development in, 104–105
  public-private enterprise in, 40
  slavery in, 157, 159
Baltimore Riot, 1273
Bambaataa, Afrika, 1254, 1256
Bands of Hope, 411
Banfield, Edward, 1536
bank holidays, 199–200, 227

Banking Act of 1935, US, 228
banking industry
  Bank of England, 48
  First Bank of the United States, 43, 48, 288
  Second Bank of the United States, 43
banking systems, under New Deal, 228
Bank of England, 48
Bank of the United States (BUS), dissolution of, 48
bank panics, 199
bankruptcy, of New York City, 109
Bảo Nguyễn, 778
Baraka, Amiri, 1221
Barber, Alice, 364
Barnard, George N., 851, 852*f*
Barnard, Henry, 1175
Barnes, Clifford, 443
Barnett, Claude, 586
Barnett, George, 202
Barnum, P. T., 1191
Barrett, James, 630, 1320
Barrett, Paul, 941, 945, 959
El Barrio, 735
barrios. *See* ghettoes and barrios
Barry, David, 372
Barry, Kathleen, 452
Barry, Marion, 1537
bars. *See* taverns and saloons
BART. *See* Bay Area Rapid Transit
Bartholomew, Harland, 184, 808
Basch, Norma, 815
baseball. *See* major league baseball
Basement Workshop, 752–753
Basie, Count, 1215
basketball. *See* professional basketball
Bass, Charlotte, 149n20
Bassett, Edward M., 1518–1519
Bauer, Catherine, 810, 818–819, 839
Baumeister, Reinhart, 1517
Baumgartner, M. P., 1472
Bay Area Rapid Transit (BART), 943–944, 946
Bayh, Birch, 348
Bayh-Dole Act, US (1980), 347–348
Baylor, Elgin, 377
Beam, Joseph, 674
Beard, Charles, 191
Beard, Mary, 191
Beasley, Betsy, 316
Beastie Boys, 1256
Beat Generation, 1129
The Beatles, 1232
Beauregard, Robert, 333
beauty culture, African American women in, 572
bebop jazz, 1215
Bechet, Sidney, 1222
Beck, Ulrich, 974

Becker, Walter, 1222
Becket, Sven, 53
Beecher, Catherine, 804, 1175
Beecher, Henry Ward, 390
Beecher, Lyman, 408
Beiderbeck, Bix, 1210
Belasco, Warren, 959
Bel Geddes, Norman, 956
Bell, Daniel, 316, 324, 333, 401, 1170n37
Bell, Tom, 90
Bellamy, Edward, 882
Bellamy, Robert V., Jr., 379
Below World, 2, 4
Beman, Solon S., 791–792
Bemis, Edward W., 183
Benjamin, Andre, 1261
Benner, Chris, 1476
Bennett, Bill, 1161
Bennett, Edward, 172–173, 184, 356, 862, 889–891,
    1004–1005, 1016
Bennett, Lerone, 583, 1408
Bennett, William James, 44f
Ben-Shalom, Miriam, 673
Bentley, Gladys, 574
Benton, Thomas Hart, 211–212
Benzedrine, 469–470
Berg, Vernon, 673
Berger, Bennett, 1464
Berger, Victor, 255
Bergman, Frances, 1403
Bergman, Walter, 1403
Berkman, Alexander, 516
Berkowitz, Richard, 675
Berlin, Ira, 156
Berman v. Parker, 1524, 1533
Bernstein, Barton, 240
Berry, Carrie, 847–848
Berry, Chuck, 1220, 1232
Berry, Marion, 1403
Berwanger, Eugene, 1300
Bessemer steel, 64
The Best Years of Our Lives, 833
Bethune, Divine, 1106
Bethune, Mary McLeod, 575
Better Communities Act, US (1972), 836
Better Luck Tomorrow, 1508
Bettman, Alfred, 1519
Bettman, Gary, 376
Bevel, James, 1406
Beveridge, Albert, 187–188
Beyond the Melting Pot (Glazer and Moynihan),
    654, 661
Bhaktivedanta, A. C., 1132
bicycling, 951–952
    as popular craze, 967

BIDs. *See* business improvement districts
Biehler, Dawn, 1024
Bierstadt, Albert, 353
Big Band era, 1211, 1215
Bigott, Joseph, 791, 796
Bilandic, Michael, 1070
Binford, Henry, 786, 795
Bird, Larry, 378
Birmingham, Alabama
    ACMHR and, 1406
    conflicts within African American leadership in, 1406
    Connor, B., in, 1405
    King, M. L., Jr. in, 1405–1407
    racial segregation in, 1405–1407
    SCLC in, 1405–1407
birth control, right to access, 1451
birth rates, during the Great Depression, 202
BKA. *See* Black-Korean Alliance
Black, Julian, 394
Black and Tans, 1196
Black Arts Movement
    Black Power movement and, 1378
    jazz as part of, 1219, 1221, 1226
black churches
    in sit-in movement, 1424
    in urban American South, 75
Black Codes, 1352
black convention movement, 409
"Black Ecology" (Hare), 1021
blackface minstrelsy, 1207
Black Freedom movement, 278–279. *See also*
    specific organizations
    AFSCME and, 278
    Freedom Rides as part of, 1403–1404,
        1426, 1446
    Great Migration as influence on, 1368
    historical approach to, 1380–1383
    Jim Crow laws and, 1368–1369
    Ku Klux Klan and, 1368
    as political insurgency movement, 1445–1448
    after slavery, 1367–1368
    social justice movements influenced by, 1448
    Supreme Court challenges during, 1446
    in urban North, **1367–1396**
    in urban South, **1396–1415**
    urban uprisings as part of, 1447–1448
Black Hawk War, 40
Black-Korean Alliance (BKA), 1309
Black Lives Matter movement, 145, 1265
Blackmar, Elizabeth, 54, 800, 815, 984
Black Metropolis, 585
black middle-class, development of, 75
Blackmun, Harry (Justice), 1343
black nationalism, 1257
black-owned newspapers, 570, 584

Black Panther Party (BPP), 1326–1327, 1379, 1447
  academic scholarship on, 1382–1383
  establishment of, 745
  Gay Liberation Movement and, 670
  Mexican American immigrants and, 734–735
  Puerto Ricans and, 721, 736
Black Political Convention, 1445
black politics, 575–576, 587–588
Black Power (Ture), 1451
Black Power movement. *See also* Black Freedom
    movement; Carmichael, Stokely; Cleaver,
    Eldridge; X, Malcolm; *specific organizations*
  academic scholarship on, 1382–1383
  Asian American political movements influenced
    by, 744–745
  Black Art movement and, 1378
  black organizations created as result of, 1378
  FBI response to, 1379
  patriarchal foundations of, 1379
  political activism in, 407–408
  RAM, 1325
  rap music from, 1253
  riots and, 1282–1283
  Second Amendment and, 1379
  street gangs and, 1325–1328
  in urban North, 1378–1379
Black Sox scandal, 396
Blackstone, William, 1339
Black Warrior River, 5–6
Blackwell, Chris, 1234
Blair, Ezell, Jr., 1402, 1416–1417
Blair, Karen, 129
Blake, Eubie, 573
Blake, James, 1399
Blake, Nelson, 929
blexting, 329
Blocker, Jack S., Sr., 424
Bloods street gang, 1331
Bloom, Nicholas Dagen, 827
Bloomberg, Michael, 839, 958, 1568
Blucher, Walter, 1521
Blue, Rupert, 1054
blue-collar workers
  as census category, 318n5
  in postindustrial service economies, 308–309,
    309t, 312
blues music. *See* ragtime and blues music
Bluestone, Barry, 332
Blum, Fred, 97
Blumin, Stuart, 226
Blythe, Arthur, 1219
Boernstein, Heinrich, 656
Bogart, Michelle, 896
Bogle, Robert, 1086
Bombeck, Erma, 834

Bonacich, Edna, 1313–1314
Bonaparte, Napoleon, 45
Bond, Julian, 1403, 1443
Bong Hwan Kim, 1312–1313
Bonilla, Frank, 719
Bonsack, James, 67
"Bonus Army" camps, 259
Bonus Expeditionary Force, 205–206
bookmaking, 394–397
Borgwardt, Elizabeth, 226
"Boss Tweed." *See* Tweed, William Magear
Boston, Massachusetts
  central business districts in, 169
  early populations of, 37–38
  Knowles Riots in, 29
  municipal reform in, 123
  police unions in, 274
  public buildings in, 28
  public parks in, 1000–1001, 1007
  recreation plans in, 21
  slavery in, 154, 157
  urban redevelopment in, 138–139
Bottle Creek (chiefdom), 5, 8
Bottles, Scott, 945, 959
Bourke-White, Margaret, 875
Bourne, Frank A., 1562
Bourne, Randolph, 190
Bouton, Edward H., 807
Bowers v. Hardwick, 676
Bowery Gals, 986
Bowie, David, 1234
Bowling Alone (Putnam), 1200, 1473
Boyce, Edward, 626
boycotts
  against employment discrimination, 1374–1375
  Montgomery bus boycott, 77, 940, 1399–1401, 1403
Boydston, Jeanne, 815
Boyer, Louis, 908
Boyer, M. Christine, 896
Boyer, Paul S., 896
Boylston, Zabdiel, 1050, 1057
Boynton v. Virginia, 1403
BPP. *See* Black Panther Party
Bracero Program, 499, 541–542, 551–552, 700–701
Bradley, Jennifer, 145, 1476
Bradley, Tom, 133, 138, 143–144
Brady, Matthew, 851
Branch, Taylor, 1402
Brandeis, Louis (Justice), 180, 187
Bras, Juan Mari, 721
Braun, Charles, 445
Braverman, Harry, 309
"Bread and Roses Strike," 254
bread riots, 1277
Breckenridge, Sophonisba, 185, 189, 815

Breedlove, Sarah, 572
Bretton Woods system, 102
Breugmann, Robert, 786, 795
Brewer, Holly, 1339
Bridenbaugh, Carl, 31, 815
Bridges, Amy, 127
bridges, Tilikum Crossing, 958
Bridgetown, Connecticut, recreation plans in, 21
Brier, Jennifer, 675
Briggs, John, 670–671
Briggs Initiative. *See* Proposition 6, in California
Bright, Josefina Fierro de, 734
Brinkley, Alan, 240
Briseno, Theodore, 1317n1
Bristol, Katherine, 827
Bristow, Nancy, 1054
Broadway theaters, 1200
    rap music in, 1262
Brody, David, 255
Bronzeville neighborhood, 758–759, 1548
Brooke, Edward, 823, 836
Brooks, Charlotte, 107, 763, 1497
Brophy, John, 627–628
brothels, 432
    abolishment of, 444–448
    call houses and, 446
    madams in, 441
    police and, interactions with, 441–442
    during Progressive Era, 441–444
    public visibility of, 435
    racial segregation for, 442
    in residential neighborhoods, integration of, 435
    riots between, 435
Brotherhood of Sleeping Car Porters (BSCP), 263–264,
    1369, 1372
Browder, Aurelius, 1400
Browder v. Gayle, 1400–1401
Brower, Abraham, 934
Brown, Adrienne, 876
Brown, Glenn, 886
Brown, H. Rap, 745
Brown, James, 1220, 1236
Brown, Richard Maxwell, 1284
Brown, William "Box," 162
Brown Berets, 734–735
Brownell, Herbert, 518
Brownlee, W. Elliot, 258
Brownmiller, Susan, 449, 1453
Brown v. Board of Education, 821, 1181, 1343, 1422
    desegregation of public schools, 1377
Brubeck, Dave, 1217–1218
Bryan, John N., 1007
Bryan, William Jennings, 188
Bryant, Anita, 672–673
Bryant, William Cullen, 52, 996

BSCP. *See* Brotherhood of Sleeping Car Porters
Buchanan v. Warley, 808, 1522–1523
Buchoz, Kathy, 775, 778
Buckley, Christopher, 120
Buenker, John, 191
Buffalo, New York, 999–1000
buffer zones, in chiefdoms, 2
Buffington, Eugene, 91
Bulfinch, Charles, 801
Bull, Marijoan, 839
Bullard, Robert, 1022
"Bulldozer Revolution," 78
"bungalow belts," 793
Bunshaft, Gordon, 869
Burgee, John, 873
Burgess, Ernest, 175, 653–654, 661, 815, 1332
Burgos, Adrian, 380
burial practices, in Cahokia, 4
Burlingame, Anson, 1296
Burlingame Treaty (1868), 1296
Burnham, Daniel, 138, 172–173, 356, 862–864, 882,
    889–891, 904, 1002, 1004–1005, 1529–1530
    Columbian Exposition and, 883–884
    landscape design by, 968
Burns, Fritz, 813, 1458
Burns, Ken, 1225
Burroughs, Nannie Helen, 189
Burroughs, William, 470
Burrows, Edwin, 54
BUS. *See* Bank of the United States
buses, 941–942
    Montgomery bus boycott, 77, 940
Bush, George H. W., 472, 614, 824
    housing policies under, 838
    LGBTQ populations under, 677
Bush, George W., 280, 298, 836–837, 1156, 1161–1162
Bushman, Richard, 32
"business decade," 257–258
    labor strikes during, 258, 258f
business districts. *See* central business districts
business improvement districts (BIDs), 315
busing policies, 79. *See also* desegregation
    desegregation of schools as goal of, 1377
    Milliken v. Bradley, 1377
    in urban North, 1377
Busse, Fred, 891
Butler, Benjamin, 437
Butler, Jon, 655
Butler, Nicholas Murray, 511
Byrd, Harry, 1446

CAAs. *See* Community Action Agencies
cabarets, 1195
cable cars, 936–937
Caesar's Columns (Donnelly, I.), 882

Cahokia
  agricultural outputs in, decline of, 5
  American Bottoms and, 6, 17n12
  Below World and, 4
  building of, 4
  burial practices in, 4
  climate change and, 5
  decline of, 5
  geographic size of, 4
  Monks Mound, 4
  Mound 72 in, 4
  regional influence of, 4
  as religious movement, 17n12
  religious ordering in, 4
  This World and, 4
  Above World and, 4
Cain, Louis, 930
Cairo, Illinois, 42
Calder, Alexander, 871
California. *See also specific cities*
  Angel Island Immigration Station, 526–540
  Anti-Vagrancy Act, 1275
  Asian American suburban culture in, 1494–1496, 1515n62
  Chinese migration to, 1296–1297
  climate change in, 1064
  emancipation movement in, 1294–1295
  Enforcement Act in, 1292–1293
  Foreign Miner's Tax of 1951, 1275
  Gold Rush era in, 430, 438–439, 1275
  lettuce pickers in, 203f
  Little Saigon, 770–780
  People v. Hall, 1303n18
  Proposition 6 in, 670–671
  Proposition 13, 1474
  Proposition 15, 763
  Proposition 22, 734
  Proposition 87, 560
  public authorities in, 303n23
  public sector unions in, 284n39
  during Reconstruction era, 1290–1295
  treatment of Native Americans in, 1294–1295
  Vietnamese immigrants in, settlement patterns for, 774–776
Callen, Richard, 675
call houses, 446
Callinicos, A. T., 1306
Call Off Your Old Tired Ethics (COYOTE), 450–451
Calloway, Cab, 573
Cameron, Simon, 851
Campbell, Allen, 850
Campbell, Clive "DJ Kool Herc," 1253
Canada
  immigrants from, 496
  immigration from, 551
  Jewish segregation in, 664n36

Canaday, Margot, 665–666
candy production, company towns for, 89
CAP. *See* Chicago Area Project; Community Action Program
Capeci, Dominic, Jr., 1284
capital flight, globalization as influence on, 107–108
capital investment, deindustrialization and, 323–324
capital investments
  in China, 111
  in electrical grid development, 62
  during the Great Depression, declines in, 201
  in postindustrial cities, 315
capitalism
  monopolistic, 185
  under New Deal, stabilization strategies of, 237
  progressives on, 180
capital markets, 294–295
capital towns, in chiefdoms, 5
Capote, Truman, 470
Carbo, Frankie, 396
car culture, development of, 359
card games, 388
"careful" riots, 1272
Carey, James, 625, 628
Caribbean, immigration from, 553
Carlson, Douglas W., 423
Carmichael, Stokely, 721, 1378, 1440, 1443. *See also* Black Power movement
Carnegie, Andrew, 249, 342
Caro, Robert A., 286–287, 1005–1006
Carr, Joe, 372, 376
Carrier, Willis Haviland, 1069
Carrigan, William D., 1275
Carroll, John M., 380
Carson, Ben, 839
Carson, Rachel, 1036
Carswell, Andrew, 839
Carter, Alprentice "Bunchy," 1326–1327
Carter, Jimmy, 78, 545, 1159, 1164
car traffic, in central business districts, 171–173
Cartwright, Peter, 410
Cash, Johnny, 1232
casinos, 327, 1200
Castle Garden Immigration Station, 508–509
Catawbas tribe, 11
catering industry, 1086
Catholic Church
  anti-Catholic sentiment and, 482
  immigrants and, 480–481. *See also* Irish immigrants; Polish immigration
  Irish immigrants as, 620–622, 629
  in machine politics, 123–124
  from 1900–1929, 1123–1126
  PNCC, 604–606
  in suburbs, 1128–1131

Caudill, Harry M., 95
Cayton, Horace, 401, 584, 588
CCC. *See* Civilian Conservation Corps
CCED. *See* Chinatown Community for Equitable
    Development
CC&Rs. *See* covenants, conditions, and restrictions
CDBGs. *See* community development block grants
CDCs. *See* community development corporations
Celebration, Florida, as planned community, 914*f*
Census Bureau, US, 318n5
    Mexican American immigrants and, racial
        categorization of, 733
censuses
    postindustrial service economies and, data collection
        on, 308, 318n5
    public authorities in, data on, 302n7
    of urban populations, 39*f*, 60. *See also specific cities*
    US, 37, 318n5, 733
Central America
    immigration from, 553
    Latino urbanism in US influenced by, 704–705
    prostitution in, 444
central business districts, **169–179**
    automobile ownership and, 174
    in Boston, 169
    in Chicago, 172
    city layouts and, 170
    conflicting public opinions on, 171–173
    consumer capitalism and, 170–171
    decline of, 173–174
    department stores in, 170–172
    evolution of, 170–171
    industrial growth in, 169–170
    in Japantown, 1546
    in Jim Crow South, 171
    mixed-use space in, 169
    in New York City, 169–170, 173
    pedestrian malls in, 175
    pedestrian safety in, 172–173
    private residences in, 169
    public transportation improvements as influence
        on, 169–170
    restaurant chains in, 174
    restaurants in, 174, 1097–1098
    shopping districts in, 170
    sidewalks and city streets in, 984–985
    skyscrapers in, 173
    streetcars in, 938–939
    suburbanization as influence on, 173–174
    tourism to, 357–358, 361
    traffic in, 171–173
    urban planning of, 911
    urban renewal of, 174–175
    women in, 170–171
    yuppies in, as consumer market for, 175

Central Park, in New York City, 988–989
    automobiles in, 1004–1006
    Conservancy for, 1006
    construction costs of, 997
    crime in, 1006
    early design plans for, 996–997
    establishment of, 996
    national influence of, 998–1001
    Olmsted, F. L., and, 902, 988–989, 996–1001, 1014
    political control of, 998
    as public works project, 997
    site choice for, 997
    urban planning for, 902*f*
    Vaux and, 902, 988–989, 996–1001, 1014
A Century of New Migration (Woodson), 582
CERCLA. *See* Comprehensive Environmental Response,
    Compensation, and Liability Act
Cernak, Anton, 127
Cha Cha, 1297, 1299. *See also* anti-Chinese massacre
Chadwick, Edwin, 922
Chafin, Don, 93
chain migration
    for African Americans, 569–571
    to urban neighborhoods, 654–655
The Challenge of Liberty (Hoover), 215
Chamberlain, Wilt, 377
Chamberlain-Kahn Act, US, 445
Champion v. Ames, 389
Chandler, William, 510
Chang, Edward, 1309, 1311
Chang Wan, 1299. *See also* anti-Chinese massacre
Chapin, Edwin Hubbell, 118
Chapman, Carrie, 189
Charity Organization Society, 1147
Charles, Ray, 1127, 1220, 1232–1233
Charles, Robert, 1280
Charles II (King), 800
Charleston, South Carolina
    early populations of, 37
    gentrification in, 1558
    libraries in, 28
    public buildings in, 28
    recreation plans in, 21
    as slave port, 156
    slavery-based markets in, 40
    slavery in, 159
    urban planning of, 22
    Vesey rebellion in, 160, 162
Charlotte, North Carolina
    public segregation in, 77
    residential segregation in, 137
Charlotte Thompson mound site, 10
charter reform, 183
charter schools, 1183–1184
Chávez, Cesar, 733–734, 738, 1448

Chávez, Linda, 723–724
chemical industries, mass production and, 66–67
Chen, Roger, 774
Cheney, Charles Henry, 1520
Cheng, Cindy I-Fen, 1497
Cheng, Wendy, 1503
Chernow, Ron, 68
Cherokee nation, 11
    relocation of, for cotton production, 45
Cherrington, Ernest, 419
Chesapeake region, seaport cities in, 22
Chesebrough, Ellis, 1030
Chetro Ketl, 685–686
Cheyenne Nation, 52
Chicago, Illinois
    African American neighborhoods in, 257
    Black and Tans in, 1196
    central business districts in, 172
    Columbian Exposition in, 356, 883–884, 884f, 952
    Commercial Club in, 172
    department stores in, 170
    environmental movements in, 1013–1015
    establishment of, 40–42
    gambling houses in, 388, 393
    Great Migration to, **581–592**
    Hull House in, 182
    industrialization in, 61
    interracial clubs in, 1196
    investment in, 42
    jazz music in, 1210, 1215
    juvenile courts in, 181, 1340–1341
    Latino urbanism in, 700, 703–704, 703f
    Little Village Environmental Justice
        Organization, 1023
    lynch mobs in, 1279
    machine politics in, 126–127
    map of, 41f
    municipal reform in, 122
    1968 Democratic National Convention in, 1438–1439
    Plan of Chicago, 172–173, 184, 356
    Polish immigration in, 603–604
    public parks in, 1000, 1007
    public sector unions in, 273
    Puerto Ricans in, 718, 721
    rapid urban growth of, 60–61
    residential segregation in, 642–643
    rioting in, 576, 1279
    Riverside commuter suburb, 787–788
    sewerage systems in, 880–881
    skyscrapers in, 861–864
    street gangs in, 1319–1321, 1324–1329, 1332
    suburbanization of, 787–788, 791–792
    suburbs of, 787–788, 791–792
    as "White City," 356, 883–884, 884f
Chicago Area Project (CAP), 1323

Chicago School of Sociology, 175
    disorganization theory of, 1332
    on ethnicity, 661
    gentrification and, 1560–1561
Chicago Seven, 1452
Chicago Teachers Federation (CTF), 273
Chicano nationalism, 1332
Chicaza nation, 12
Chickasaw society, 11–12
Chickencoop Chinaman (Chin), 753
chiefdoms, during Mississippi period
    Apalachee, 8
    Bottle Creek, 5, 8
    buffer zones in, 5
    capital towns and, 5
    Cofitachequi, 8–11
    commoner housing, 5
    complex, 2
    as concept, academic debate over, 16n2
    Coosa, 10, 12
    craftspeople in, 5
    Etowah, 5–7
    Guatari, 10
    Irene, 5, 8
    Joara, 10
    Lake George, 5
    during late period, 7–11
    length of, 4–6
    Mabila, 10, 12
    micos in, 2
    during middle period, 5–8
    mixed economies in, 6
    Moundville, 5–6
    Mulberry site, 8
    paramount, 2
    Piachi, 10, 12
    Piedmont, 12
    Rembert, 5
    simple, 2
    in the South, 6
    Spiro, 5
    Talisi, 10
    Tascalusa, 8, 10–12
    Town Creek, 5
    Winterville, 5
chiefs. *See* micos
chieftainess. *See* micos
child custody, for LGBTQ populations, 671–672
child laborers
    in company towns, 93f
    constitutional amendments about, 181
    Irish immigrants as, 623f
children, in temperance movement, 411
Children's Bureau, US, 1340
children's rights, in juvenile justice system, 1339, 1345

child welfare, under Sheppard-Towner Maternity and
    Infant Welfare bill, 181
Chin, Frank, 753
China
    capital investment in, 111
    opium trade in, 48
    Taiping Rebellion in, 483
    in World Trade Organization, 102
Chinatown Community for Equitable Development
    (CCED), in San Francisco, 1542
Chinese Exclusion Act, US (1882), 189, 526–527,
    533–534, 757, 1298
    repeal of, 500, 537–538, 542–544
Chinese food, 1093
Chinese immigrants, in America
    at Angel Island Immigration Station, 527–529, 531
    anti-Chinese massacre, in Los Angeles, **1290–1304**
    anti-Chinese racism, 483–484
    Asian American studies on, 1301–1302
    under Burlingame Treaty, 1296
    in California, during Reconstruction era, 1290–1295
    under Chinese Exclusion Act, 189, 500, 526–527, 1298
    during Civil War, 1292
    displacement from neighborhoods, 1544
    under Enforcement Act, 1292–1293
    exclusion laws against, 488
    food traditions, 1093
    in gambling industry, 391–392, 392f
    under Geary Act of 1892, 484
    as imported labor force, 1292
    Irish immigrants and, racism towards, 624
    legislative statutes against, 1294–1295
    in Los Angeles, 1296–1297
    lynching of, 1296–1297
    migration patterns for, 1296–1297
    opiates and, 465–466
    under Page Act of 1875, 484
    People v. Hall, 1303n18
    racial discrimination against, 1290–1293
    under Scott Act of 1888, 484
    in sex markets, 440
    social equality for, 1290
    social status of, 1291–1292
    in the South, 1292–1293
    Taiping Rebellion and, 483
    in urban neighborhoods, 657–658
Chisolm, Shirley, 576
chlorination, in water supply systems, 925
"chocolate cities," 637
Choi, Cindy, 1313
cholera outbreaks, 1051, 1056
Choo, Marcia, 1310, 1312
Christgau, Robert, 1234, 1240
Christian evangelicalism. *See* evangelical Christianity
Christie, Chris, 281

Chung, Angie, 1315
Chung, T. S., 1313
Chung Lee, 1309
Church, Frederic, 353
churches. *See* black churches
CIDs. *See* common interest developments
Cincotta, Gale, 139
Cincotta, Simone, 1099
CIO. *See* Congress of Industrial Organizations
Ciosek, William, 615
Cisneros, Henry, 825, 838–839
cities. *See also* slavery; *specific cities*
    industrialization in, 49–51
    working-class neighborhoods in, development of,
        50, 135–136
citizenship, 1173
    for Cuban Americans, expedited approach to, 737
    for Puerto Ricans, 713–714, 728n11
citizens' movements, 139
The City (Burgess), 653–654, 661
City Beautiful movement, **880–901**, 1016, 1033
    automobile use and, 968–969
    civic art in, 885
    civic organizations in, 885
    contagious diseases and, 880–881
    democratic process as influence on, 891–893
    design professionals in, 888
    development of, 881
    dirty cities as foundation for, 880–881
    germ theory of disease and, 881
    long-term legacy of, 895
    miasma theory and, 880–881
    motivations in, 887–889
    municipal housekeeping in, 893
    New Urbanism and, 895
    Plan of Chicago, 889–891
    playgrounds in, 887
    processional boulevards in, 888
    publicity campaigns for, 891–892
    public parks in, 881–883, 888
    as social reform, 894
    streets, roads, and highways during, 951
    transitional art of, 887–889
    urban destruction and, 881–883
    urbanization as influence on, 883
    urban renewal in, 1530, 1533
    Utopian visions of, 880–881
    in Washington DC, 884–887
    women in, 893–895
city charters, 134
city expositions, 356, 358, 359f
    Columbian Exposition, 883–884, 884f
city mayors, tourism influenced by, 360–361
City of Eros (Gilfoyle), 355
"city of knowledge," 107

city parks. *See* parks
City Reform League, 120
city streets. *See* sidewalks and city streets
city-suburb divide, 1460
City Zoning: The Once and Future Frontier (Babcock, R. and Weaver, C.), 1523
ciudades (Spanish cities), 696–697
civic art, in City Beautiful movement, 885
civic federations, 183
civic organizations, in City Beautiful movement, 885
civic pride, 985
Civil Aeronautics Act, US (1938), 200
Civilian Conservation Corps (CCC), 200, 228–229
civil rights. *See also* children's rights; voting rights
    BPP as response to, 1326–1327
    CORE, 1325
    employment discrimination and, 1374–1375
    for housing segregation, 1375–1376
    under Kennedy, J. F., 1404, 1407–1408
    rioting for, 1281–1283
    sit-in movement for, **1415–1435**
    SNCC, 1325
    street gangs and, 1325–1328
    in urban American South, 77–78
Civil Rights Act, US (1964), 77, 1408–1409, 1437, 1449–1450
Civil Rights Congress (CRC), 1377
civil rights movement. *See also* Black Freedom movement
    Asian American political movements influenced by, 744
    "Black Lives Matter" movement, 145
    Black Power movement, 407–408, 1282–1283
    Gay Liberation Movement, 140–141, 668–671, 1283
    jazz music during, 1217–1220
    Native Americans during, 691
    Polish immigration during, 614
    residential segregation and, 643–645
civil rights organizations, run by African Americans, 257
civil service associations. *See* independent civil service associations
civil service protections, through public sector unions, 273
civil society, purpose of, 187–188
civil unrest. *See also* riots; social uprisings
    urban planning influences by, 910
Civil War, US. *See also* antebellum era; postbellum period; Reconstruction era; urban destruction
    Chinese during, 1292
    Conscription Act, 1276
    gender roles during, 73
    horse racing after, increased popularity of, 390
    immigration before, 479–481, 485–486
    industrialization during, 51
    Judaism during, 1112–1113
    Lowell, Massachusetts during, 88

machine politics after, 120
patriotism during, 73
politics in urban areas after, 118
prostitution after, 438
public health departments during, 1055–1056
railroad industry during, 52
reconstruction of southern cities after, 73
religion after, 1110–1113
rioting during and after, 1276–1280
sex markets influenced by, 437–448
skyscrapers after, 858
slavery in cities and, 163
temperance movement during, 413–414
universities and colleges during, 340
urban American South after, 73
urban destruction during, **844–858**
urban tourism after, 355
vagrancy laws after, 1351–1352
Civil Works Administration (CWA), 200, 229
    sewage treatment and, 926
clandestine prostitution, 444–448
The Clansman (Dixon), 1105
Clardy, Lucille, 598
Clark, Dick, 1232, 1238
Clark, Jonas Gilman, 342
Clark, Kenneth, 717
Clark, Norman, 424
Clark-Pujara, Cristy, 164
Clarkson, Matthew, 1051
Clay, Lucius, 957
Clayton Antitrust Act, US (1914), 186, 256
Clean Air Act, US (1970), 972, 1040
Clean Water Act, US (1972), 927–928, 1037
Clean Water and How to Get It (Hazen), 925
Cleaver, Eldridge, 137–138, 751
Clemente Orozco, José, 701
clergy, in temperance movement, 411
Cleveland, Grover, 90
Cleveland, H. W. S., 1277
Cleveland, Ohio, as postindustrial city, 315
Cleveland, William Shaler, 1000, 1009
The Cliff Dwellers (Fuller, H. B.), 861
Clifton, Nat, 377
climate change, **1063–1077**. *See also* environmental justice movements
    in American Southwest, 1064
    Cahokia influenced by, 5
    in California, 1064
    as concept, 1063
    disaster planning and, 1069–1070
    extreme temperatures, 1067–1069
    flooding, 1065–1067
    global urban patterns and, 1064
    in New Orleans, 1064–1065
    in Phoenix, 1064

resilience planning and, 1070–1072
storms and, 1065–1067, 1070–1072
urbanization as influence on, 1063–1065
urban tourism influenced by, 358
US Weather Bureau and, establishment of, 1069–1070
Clinton, Bill, 78, 779
on hip-hop culture, 1258–1259
housing policies under, 836, 838
LGBTQ populations under, 677
public authorities under, 299
Clinton, Dewitt, 1175
Cloward, Richard, 1324
Club of Rome, 912
coal-mining company towns, 89, 93–95, 94f
decline of, 95
in Harlan County, Kentucky, 94
labor agents in, 94–95
labor unions in, 94
under New Deal policies, 94
under NIRA, 94
outbreaks of violence in, 94
United Mine Workers in, 94
Coates, Samuel, 431
Coats, Dan, 1161
Cobain, Kurt, 1237, 1239
Cobb, Henry Ives, 886
Cobb, Ty, 369
Cobo, Albery, 20
cocaine use, 466–468, 472
crime and, 468
Cocks, Catherine, 355, 364
Codman, Henry Sargent, 1009
Codman, William Coombs, 1562
Cody, William "Buffalo Bill," 689
Coe, Andrew, 1099
Cofitachequi (chiefdom), 8–11
introduction of disease in, 10
"Lady of Cofitachequi," 8
Cohen, Alfred, 1324
Cohen, Julius Henry, 292
Cohen, Leonard, 1234
Cohen, Lizabeth, 128–129, 236, 1462
Cohen, Lizbeth, 1462
Cohen, Patricia Cline, 435, 453
Cohen, Ruth Schwartz, 1099–1100
Cohn, Nik, 1240
COINTELPRO project. See Counter Intelligence
Program project
Cold War
Asian Americans during, 1493–1494
globalization influenced by, 102, 106–108
immigration during, 545, 550–551
jazz music during, 1218–1219
"Kitchen Debate," 107–108
Puerto Ricans during, 716–718

universities and colleges during, 340
Vital Center Liberalism during, 1442–1443
Cold War liberalism, 1441–1442. See also Vital Center
Liberalism
Cole, Albert, 833
Cole, Echol, 1411
Cole, Thomas, 353
Coleman, Ornette, 1218, 1221–1223, 1225
collective bargaining
by labor unions, 261
by public sector unions, 283n9
colleges. See universities and colleges
Collins, Addie, 1408
Cólon, Jesús, 735
colonial era. See also European colonists
education during, 1173–1174
ethnicity during, 655
Latino urbanism during, 696–698
municipal housing and, 800
Native Americans in urban environments during,
686–687
in Northern states, 71
religion during, 1106–1108
residential segregation during, 638
sex markets during, 430–433
streets, roads, and highways during, 949–950
temperance movement and, 406
vagrancy laws in, 1351
Colored Seamen's Act, South Carolina (1822), 160
Colten, Craig, 1041, 1073
Coltrane, John, 1212, 1216, 1218–1219, 1221–1223
spirituality of, 1225
Columbia, South Carolina, after Civil War, 73
Columbian Exposition, 356, 883–884, 884f.
See also "White City"
religion at, 1122–1123
street design for, 952
Colvin, Claudette, 1399
Comanches, 155
comic books, as popular culture, 212
The Coming of Post-Industrial Society (Bell, D.), 324, 333
Comiskey, Charles, 396
commerce, early (1790–1870), **37–60**.
See also industrialization
First Bank of the United States, 43
industrialization of production, 45–49
in New York City, 43
Panic of 1837, 40, 48–49, 57n38
slavery markets, 40
commerce, post Civil-War (1880–1929), **60–70**
assembly lines, 65–66
electrical grid development, 60–63
mass production techniques, 65–67
structural steel development and, construction
with, 63–65

Commercial Club, 172
commercial ice production, 1078–1079
commercial public schools, 1178
commodity chains, 103
Commoner, Barry, 1035, 1040
commoners, housing for, 5
common interest developments (CIDs),
    1469–1470, 1475
Commons, John R., 184, 266, 272
common schools, 1174
Commons School, 266
communism. See also anticommunist movements
    HUAC and, 277
    Polish immigration influenced by, 612–613
    Red Scare and, 190, 274
    in Vietnam, 1436–1437
Communist Party of the United States (CPUSA).
    See also anticommunist movements
    during the Great Depression, 207–208
    HUAC and, 277
    labor unions and, 262
    Scottsboro Boys case and, 206
Community Action Agencies (CAAs), 1159–1161
Community Action Program (CAP), 1157–1161, 1170n27
community activism, 136
community-based arts organizations, for Asian
    Americans, 752–753
community building, suburbanization and, 1459
community development block grants (CDBGs), 1538
community development corporations (CDCs), 645, 812
Community Redevelopment Act, US (1974), 1538
Community Reinvestment Act, US (1975), 1566
Community Reinvestment Act, US (1977), 327–328,
    645, 835
Community Service Block Grants (CSBGs), 1160–1161
commuter suburbs, 788
commuting
    automobile use and, 967
    through ride-sharing systems, 958
    slugging system, 958
company towns, 86–102
    Austin, Minnesota, 95–97
    for candy production, 89
    child laborers in, 93f
    for coal-mining, 89, 93–95, 94f
    for copper mining, 89
    Corning, New York, 97f, 98
    country towns' expansion into, 95–97
    defined, 86
    development of, impetus for, 89
    economic development through, 86
    factory expansion in, 88
    founders of, 87
    housing in, 93
    immigrant populations in, 87–88

labor shortages in, 89
    for manufacturing, 89
    for meatpacking, 89, 96–97
    Menlo Park, California, 98
    Mountain View, California, 98
    for munitions production, 89
    in New England, 86–88. See also Lowell,
        Massachusetts
    Newton, Iowa, 95–96
    problems in, 90–91
    purpose of, 86
    in Rhode Island, 86
    social development through, 86
    for steel production, 89–90
    as suburbs, 791–792
    suburbs as, 791–792
    for textile production, 93, 93f, 95
    for timber industry, 89
    in 21st century, 97–98
    in Upper South, 92–95
    Vandegrift, Texas, 90–91
    welfare programs in, 96
    during World War II, 96
compassionate conservatism, 1161–1162
complex chiefdoms, 2
Comprehensive Environmental Response,
    Compensation, and Liability Act (CERCLA), US
    (1980), 332, 1038
compulsory work laws, during postbellum period, 51
Comstock, Anthony, 390
Cone, James, 1207
Confederate monuments, controversy over, 82
Congress of Industrial Organizations (CIO), 204–205,
    275–276
    African Americans in, 1369–1370
    formation of, 208, 236, 247n62
    immigration and, 498
Congress of Racial Equality (CORE), 1325, 1373,
    1445–1447
    Freedom Highways project, 1403–1404
    sit-in movement and, 1416
Conkin, Paul, 240
Connerly, Ward, 1313
Connolly, James, 128, 129
Connor, Bull, 81–82, 1404–1406
The Conscience of a Conservative (Goldwater, B.),
    1444
Conscription Act (1863), 1276–1277
conservation movements, 1012–1029
    City Beautiful movement and, 1016
    Earth Day, 1018, 1021
    open spaces in, preservation of, 1018–1019
    urban renewal as factor in, 1020
Consolidation Act, US (1854), 1274
Constitution, US

banning of child labor under, 181
Eighteenth Amendment, 419–422
Fourteenth Amendment, 180
Jim Crow laws and, unconstitutionality of, 905
Nineteenth Amendment, 189, 257, 419–420, 422, 1195
Second Amendment, 1379
Seventeenth Amendment, 186
Sixteenth Amendment, 186
state action doctrine under, 1427
Constitutional Convention, 31
construction industry
    of apartment houses, 65
    during the Great Depression, 67
    public housing, 65
    structural steel and, development of, 63–65
consumer markets
    in central business districts, 170–171
    Latino American women in, discrimination
        against, 170
    non-white women and, 171
    in postindustrial cities, 325–326
    white women and, 170–171
    yuppies in, 175
contagious diseases, **1049–1063**
    18th century quarantines, 1050–1051
    19th century quarantines, 1051–1052
    20th century quarantines, 1052–1054
    at Angel Island Immigration Station, 530
    antibiotic development for, 1057–1058
    cholera, 1051, 1056
    City Beautiful movement and, 880–881
    at Ellis Island Immigration Station, 510, 514
    germ theory of disease, 881
    HIV/AIDS, 1058
    influenza, 1054
    in municipal housing, 803–804
    under New York Metropolitan Health Act, 1056
    penicillin and, 1058
    plague, 1052–1053
    polio, 1053
    public health department responses to, 1052
    public health issues from, 1049, 1058–1059
    during quarantine era, from 1700–1920, 1049–1054
    SARS, 1058
    smallpox, 1050
    vaccines for, 1057–1058
    viral, 1058–1059
    yellow fever, 23, 1029–1030, 1050–1051
Continental Army soldiers, 431–432
Contract Labor Law, US (1885), 509
convention centers, development of, 359
convergence culture, 1238–1239
Coolidge, Calvin, 274, 496
cool jazz, 1215–1217
cool jazz music, 1215–1217. *See also* Davis, Miles

Cooper, Campbell, 875
Cooper, Chuck, 377
Coosa (chiefdom), 10, 12
copper mining company towns, 89
Corbett, Harvey Wiley, 968
Corcoran, W. W., 996
CORE. *See* Congress of Racial Equality
Corea, Chick, 1222
corn, as agricultural crop, during Mississippi period, 6
Corning, New York, 98, 98f
corporate America, rise of, 249–251
    Age of Industrial Conflict, 249
    Gilded Age and, 250
    labor violence and, 249
    during Progressive Era, 250
    Social Darwinism and, 250
corporate rock, 1235
corporations
    government, as public authorities, 293, 295–298
    under Government Corporation Control Act, 298
corruption
    at Angel Island Immigration Station, 531–532
    public authorities and, 288
Cortes, Hernán, 685
Cortez, Jayne, 1219
cosmos, as concept, 2–3
    Below World, 2, 4
    Middle World, 2
    Above World, 2, 4
Costello, Frank, 395f
Cotton Club, 573–574, 1196
cotton famine, 88
cotton gin, 45
cotton mills, 61, 88f
cotton production
    in Alabama, 61
    cotton gin, 45
    after Haitian Revolution of 1791–1804, 45
    industrialization of, 45–46
    after Louisiana Purchase, 45
    in Lowell, Massachusetts, 46, 46f, 88f
    New Orleans and, 45–46
    New York City and, 45–46
    relocation of Cherokees for, 45
    relocation of slaves for, 45
    in textile mills, 46–47
Couch, Harvey, 291
Coughlin, Charles, 209, 209f, 261
Coughlin, John, 891
Counter Intelligence Program (COINTELPRO)
        project, 1328
country music, 1237
court systems. *See also* Supreme Court
    public authorities in, 294–295
Courtwright, David, 472

covenants. *See* restrictive covenants
covenants, conditions, and restrictions
  (CC&Rs), 1469
Cowan, Aaron, 364
Cowie, Jefferson, 108, 241, 333
Cox, Elton, 1420
Cox, George, 119–120
Cox, James M., 1396
COYOTE. *See* Call Off Your Old Tired Ethics
CPUSA. *See* Communist Party of the United States
crack cocaine use, 472
Craft, Ellen, 162
Craft, William, 162
craftspeople, in chiefdoms, 5
Cranz, Galen, 991
CRC. *See* Civil Rights Congress
creative classes, 325
Creek Confederacy, 11–12
Creel, George, 892
Creole communities. *See also* Atlantic Creoles
  jazz music and, 1209
Creole community, jazz music and, 1209
Crimes Without Victims (Schur), 449
Criminal Justice of America (Pound), 1341
Crips street gang, 1331
The Crisis, 582
Croker, Richard, 120, 127, 390
Croly, Herbert, 187, 188, 888–889
Cronon, William, 53, 68, 959, 1042
Crouch, Stanley, 1219, 1225
CSBGs. *See* Community Service Block Grants
CTF. *See* Chicago Teachers Federation
Cuba
  immigration from, 552
  US invasion of, 187
Cuban Americans
  African Americans and, relationship with, 737–738
  expedited citizenship for, 737
  integration into public school system, 737–738
  in Miami, 737–738
Cudahy, Brian J., 937, 944
cultural assimilation, during 1960s, 1451–1452
cultural festivals, in Asian American suburban
  culture, 1500
"culture of clearance," 327
culture of poverty, 1148, 1305–1306, 1536
  public schools and, 1183
culture wars, 363, 1258, 1463–1464
Cumming, Kate, 73
Cupper, Dan, 959
Curley, James Michael, 123, 126
Curran, Joseph, 628
Curry, Leonard P., 164
Curtis, Edwin, 274
CWA. *See* Civil Works Administration

Czitrom, Daniel, 391, 398
Czolgosz, Leon, 249

Daft, Leo, 937
Dakota (apartment building), 805–806
Daley, Richard J., 644
Daley, Richard M., 361, 1007, 1070, 1327
  during 1968 Democratic National Convention, 1439
Daniels, Howard, 998
Daniels, Josephus, 445
Dannnenbaum, Jed, 424
DAR. *See* Daughters of the American Revolution
Darrow, Clarence, 514
Daughters of Bilitis, 668
Daughters of Temperance, 411
Daughters of the American Revolution (DAR), 536
Davenport, John, 1106
Davis, Angela, 1443
Davis, Gherardi, 1008
Davis, Gordon, 1006
Davis, Katherine, 185
Davis, Mike, 1073, 1283, 1477
Davis, Miles, 1212, 1216–1219, 1223–1224
  as civil right symbol, 1217–1218
  cultural influence of, 1216–1217
  rock-and-roll influences on, 1220–1221
Davis, Natalie Zemon, 1272, 1284
Davis, Sylvester, 732
Davis-Bacon Act, US (1931), 256
Dawson, William L., 393
Day Key, 1299. *See also* anti-Chinese massacre
Dayton, Abram, 1083
DDT, as environmental pollutant, 1036
Dearsley, Ann, 1402
The Death and Life of Great American Cities (Jacobs, J.),
  134–135, 705, 822, 834, 908, 915, 1524–1525, 1536
De Blasio, Bill, 839, 958
DeBlois, Natalie, 869
Debs, Eugene, 186, 252, 254–255. *See also* Socialist Party
  of America
debt. *See* public debt
debtor nations, 198
decriminalization, of prostitution, 450
defense riots, in African American communities, 1276,
  1280–1283
defensive burning, during Civil War, 850–851
defensive localism, 1336n19
deflationary cycles, during the Great Depression,
  199, 201
Degler, Carl, 239
DeGriek, Jerry, 672
deindustrialization, **322–340**. *See also* postindustrial
  cities; postindustrialization
  accelerated depreciation policy and, 324
  acceleration of, 323

African Americans influenced by, 324
of automobile industry, 324
capital investment migration and, 323–324
causes of, 323
of cities, 322
at community level, 323–324
as concept, 322
definition of, 322–324
of Detroit, 322
Polish immigration influenced by, 614
postindustrial service economies and, 311–312
Puerto Rican economic status influenced by, 718–720
regional, 322–323
rightsizing and, 322, 328–329
riots and, 324
in Rust Belt, 322
in "shrinking cities," 322–323
in the South, 323
stagflation and, 323
suburbanization and, 105
tax policies as influence on, 324
as urban process, 322
urban redevelopment and, 321
white flight and, 324
De La Beckwith, Byron, 1407
Dell, Michael, 346
democracy
City Beautiful movement and, 891–893
industrial, 257–258
international progressivism and, 188–189
NCL and, 182
political progressivism and, 182–183
progressivism as influence on, 181–182
Democratic National Convention (1968), 1438–1439
police response to, 1439
Democratic Party
African Americans in, 1372, 1397–1398
anti-Vietnam War movement and, 1438
Dixiecrats, 238, 1397–1398
Irish immigrants and, 50
Korean-Americans in, 1312
machine politics within, 119–120, 126–127
New Democrats, 267, 1475
1968 Democratic National Convention, 1438–1439
Populist Party and, 180
Puerto Ricans in, 714–715
Reagan Democrats, 146
"Redeemer" Democrats in, 417
Roosevelt, F. D., as presidential candidate, 225
in the South, 235, 247n74
temperance movement and, 415
women in, 238
WPA and, 230
demolition, in postindustrial cities, 329
demonstration districts, 1182

Denny, Reginald, 1305
Denton, Nancy, 649
Department of Homeland Security (DHS), 560
department stores
in Boston, 170
in central business districts, 170–172
female staff in, 170
in New York City, 170
in Philadelphia, 170
in suburban locations, 173
window designs in, 172
deportation rates, at Angel Island Immigration Station, 527, 534
De Priest, Oscar, 575
desegregation, of schools, 138, 1181–1182, 1188n31
through *Brown v. Board of Education*, 1377
through busing, 1377
in urban North, 1376–1377
De Silva, Cara, 1099
detentions
at Angel Island Immigration Station, 527–529, 535–537
at Ellis Island Immigration Station, 517–518
Detroit, Michigan. *See also* automobile industry
African American neighborhoods in, 257
deindustrialization of, 322
economic decline of, 110–111
economic resurgence in, 145
as Fordist city, 108
Native American slaves in, 156
rioting in, 1282–1283
social uprisings in, 138
urban planning in, 329
white ethnic neighborhood associations in, 135–136
Deukmejian, George, 775
DeVos, Betsy, 678
Dewey, John, 185, 188, 881
Dewey, Thomas, 396–397, 446
Dewey Canyon III, 1438
De Witt, Benjamin, 191
De Witt, John, 759
Deyle, Steven, 53
DHS. *See* Department of Homeland Security
Diamond, Andrew, 1333–1334, 1339n82
Diaz, Manny, 736
Dickens, Charles, 42, 87
Didion, Joan, 1452
Dieterich-Ward, Allen, 333
diets, of urban populations, 1085–1086
Diggs, Charles, 575
DiIulio, John, 1344
Dillingham, William P., 488
DiMento, Joseph, 960, 968
Diner, Hasia, 630, 1099
Dirksen, Everett, 644

disaster planning
   climate change and, 1069–1070
   under Federal Disaster Relief Act, 1070
   FEMA and, 1070
   Hurricane Betsy and, 1070
   Red Cross and, 1070
   for storms, 1069–1070
disaster tourism, 363
discotheques, 1199
discrimination. *See* racial discrimination
disease, introduction of
   in Cofitachequi, 10
   germ theory of disease and, 881, 903–904, 923
   in Mississippian world, 11
   in North American seaport cities (1600–1800), 23–24
disorganization theory, 1332
distribution centers, 326
distribution networks, for food, 1079–1080
diversity. *See also* interracial social networks; interracial
      trade networks
   in Atlanta, 80
   in New Orleans, 80
diversity visas, 560
The Divided Welfare State (Hacker), 1166
divorce rates, during the Great Depression, 202
Dixiecrats, 238, 1397–1398
Dixon, Thomas, Jr., 1105
Dobriner, William, 813, 1464
Dodd, Jill Siegel, 424
Dodd-Frank Wall Street Reform and Consumer
      Protection Act, US (2012), 838
Doerflinger, Thomas, 32
Doig, Jameson W., 295–296
Dole, Robert, 348, 1161
Dollar Diplomacy, 187
domestic service, Irish immigrants in, 623
Dominican Republic, 552–553
Donahue, Thomas R., 629
Donnelly, Ignatius, 882
Donnelly, Joseph, 628
Don't Ask, Don't Tell policy, 677
Dornan, Bod, 778
Dorr, Thomas, 1273
Dorsey, Thomas A., 1127
Do the Right Thing, 1309
Douglas, Paul, 839
Douglass, Frederick, 49, 72, 162, 1174
Douglass, Harlan Paul, 795
Douglass, William O. (Justice), 1357
Dow, Neal, 412, 414
Downing, Andrew Jackson, 802, 882, 996
Downing, George, 1086
Downing, Thomas, 1086
downtowns. *See* central business districts
Doyle, David, 630

draft riots, 882, 1276–1277
   Irish immigrants in, 624
Drake, St. Claire, 401, 584, 588–589
Dreier, Peter, 1476
Dreiser, Theodore, 170
Drew, Thomas, 1127
drinking water, water supply systems for, 924
drive-in movie theaters, 1197
droughts, during Mississippi period, 7, 17n24
Drucker, Peter, 316
drug subcultures, **465–477**
   addiction to drugs in, 471–472
   amphetamine use, 469
   Benzadrine, 469–470
   cocaine use, 466–468, 472
   crack cocaine use, 472
   distribution networks for, 471–472
   under Harrison Narcotic Act, 468
   heroin use, 466, 469–470
   LSD use, 470–472
   marijuana use, 469
   MDMA use, 470–472
   from 1914–1960, 468–470
   from 1960–2018, 470–472
   during 19th century, 465–466
   opiate consumption, 465–466
   organized crime involvement in, 472
   during Progressive Era, 467
   psychedelic drugs, 470–471
   rock-and-roll music and, 1233
   during World War II, 469
dry counties, 415–416
"dual cities," gentrification and, 1559, 1568
dual labor markets, 312–313
Duane, William, 620
Dubinsky, David, 262
Dubofsky, Melvyn, 266
Du Bois, W. E. B., 189, 574, 582, 584, 815,
      1178, 1300, 1370
Duck, James "Buck," 67
Dudley, Kathryn, 332
Duffy, John, 930, 959, 1055–1056
Duke, David, 1259
Dukes, Frank, Jr., 1405
dumbell tenement, 65
Dunbar, Erica Armstrong, 164
Duncan, John H., 1002
Duneier, Mitchell, 984
Dunning, William, 1299
Durand, Jorge, 563
Durkheim, Emile, 1148
Dust Bowl, 206, 207f
   extreme temperatures as result, 1068
   Okies and, 207
Dutch West India Company, 154

Dyck, Erika, 473
Dylan, Bob, 1233

Eagleson, Alan, 375–376
Early, Jubal, 849
early Mississippi period, 4
early skyscrapers, 858–859
early suburbs, 786
early urban parks, 995–996
Earth Day, 912, 1018, 1021, 1036, 1466
Eastern Europe, immigration from, 485. *See also*
        specific countries
East West Players theater company, 753
Ebner, Michael, 796
economic Bill of Rights, 344
economic inequality, in postindustrial cities, 330–332
economic markets. *See specific markets*
Economic Opportunity Act, US (1964), 1145, 1158, 1160
economic progressivism, 185–189
    antimonopoly progressivism as aspect of, 185
    through legislative acts, 185
    monopolistic capitalism and, 185
    municipal ownership as part of, 187
    presidential progressivism as aspect of, 186
    trade union progressivism as aspect of, 186–187
economic recessions
    Great Recession of 2007, 1478
    under Roosevelt, F. D., 200, 237, 261
    in US, 198, 200
Economy Act, US (1932), 200
Edelman, Isidore, 1355
Edelson, Max, 32
"edge cities," 910, 974–975, 982n33
Edison, Thomas, 61–63. *See also* electrical grid
Edison Electric Company, 61
education. *See also* public schools
    Asian American suburban culture and, 1506–1508
    Brown v. Board of Education, 821, 1181, 1343
    during colonial era, 1173–1174
    for girls, 1173–1174
    for Native Americans, increased access for, 691–693
    in postindustrial cities, 325
    in postindustrial service economies, 311
    for Puerto Ricans, 736
educational segregation
    of African American teachers, 1371
    after Great Migration, 1370–1371
    of public schools, 1178–1180
    in urban North, 1370–1371
Eggertsson, Gauti, 215
Eichengreen, Barry, 214, 219n15
Eighteenth Amendment, 419–422
    repeal of, 422
Eight-Point Agreement of 1940, 447
Einhorn, Robin L., 921

Eisenhower, Dwight, 226, 259, 833–834, 942, 1444
    Executive Order 10450, 666
    housing policies under, 834
    interstate highways under, 956–957
    urban renewal under, 1528
electoral processes
    political progressivism and, 182–183
    redistricting schemes and, 246n34
    for Senate seats, 246n34
electrical grid, development of, 60–63
    capital investment in, 62
    early dangers of, 62
    Edison Electric Company, 61
    in factory settings, 62–63
    light bulbs, creation of, 61
    mass production and, 66–67
    mass transit and, 937–940
    under New Deal, 233
    in New York City, development of, 62
    nightlife influenced by, 1193
    public transportation and, 63
    railroad industry expansion through, 63
    transportation improvements influenced by, 61–63
    for urban workplaces, 62
electric elevator, 64
electric streetcars, 63, 937–940
Elementary and Secondary Education Act of 1965,
        US, 1183
elevated railroads, 936
elevators. *See* electric elevator
Elias, Megan, 1099–1100
Eliot, Charles, 1009, 1277
elite priests, in Moundville, 6
elite sex markets, 446
Elkins, Alex, 1285
Elkins Act, US (1903), 185
Ellington, Edward "Duke," 573, 1210, 1215, 1223
Ellington, George, 434
Elliot, Missy, 1261
Elliott, Beth, 674
Ellis, Cliff, 960, 968
Ellis, Frank C., 96
Ellis Island Immigration Station, 488
    abandonment of, 518–520
    congressional role in, 508–509
    contagious disease issues at, 510, 514
    detentions at, 517–518
    exclusion policies, 512–515
    immigrant runners, 508–509
    inspection procedures, 512–515
    IRL and, 512
    moral turpitude clauses and, 514
    national quotas at, 515–517
    origins of, 508–510
    peak years at, 510–512

Ellis Island Immigration Station (*Continued*)
  public criticism of, 511–512
  quarantines on, 510
  Red Scare and, 516
  renovation and revitalization of, 518–520
  Statue of Liberty and, 519
  steamship companies at, 513
  undesirables category at, 514
  during World War I, 515–517
  during World War II, 517–518
Ely, Richard T., 184, 266, 642, 815
emancipation, of slaves. *See also* free African Americans
  in northern colonies, 158
emancipation movement
  in California, 1294–1295
  violence as result of, 1295
Emancipation Proclamation, 1294
Emergency Banking Act, US, 227
Emergency Quota Acts, US, 516, 526–527
emergency quotas, in immigration, 496
Emergency Relief and Construction Act (ERCA), US
  (1932), 290–291, 303n24
The Emerging Republican Majority (Phillips, K.),
  1444–1445
Emery, John J., 867–868
Eminem. *See* Mathers, Marshall
eminent domain, 1524, 1533
employment
  of Japanese Americans, after resettlement in Los
    Angeles, 761–763
  in postindustrial service economies, for
    manufacturing, 308–311
employment discrimination
  boycotts against, 1374–1375
  as civil rights focus, 1374–1375
  in police forces, 1375
  in urban South, 1410–1411
Employment Non-Discrimination Act (ENDA), US, 678
employment rates, data collection on, 247n68
  manufacturing, 308–311
  in postindustrial service economies, for government
    employees, 312
ENDA. *See* Employment Non-Discrimination Act
Enforcement Act, US (1870), 1292–1293
Engelmann, Larry, 424
English Poor Law, 1139
Eno, William Phelps, 979
entertainment industry. *See also* casinos; films; television;
    vice industries
  in postindustrial cities, 325–326
entrepreneurialism. *See* urban entrepreneurialism
environmental activism, in suburbs, 1466
environmental crises, 1013–1016
environmental justice movements, 332
  African Americans and, 1022

  in Chicago, 1023
  Latino Americans and, 1022
  Little Village Environmental Justice Organization, 1023
environmental movements, **1012–1029**
  in Chicago, 1013–1015
  City Beautiful movement and, 1016
  Earth Day, 1018, 1021
  environmental crisis as influence on, 1013–1016
  industrialization as influence on, 1013–1014
  mainstream, 1022
  metropolitan inequality and, 1016–1018
  modern, 1035–1041
  municipal housekeeping, 1015
  National Forest systems and, establishment of, 1014
  National Park systems and, establishment of, 1014
  during New Deal, 1016
  open spaces in, preservation of, 1018–1019
  polluting industries and, 1017
  during Progressive Era, 1014–1017, 1020–1021
  substandard housing and, 1021
  suburbanization and, 1018–1020, 1022
  tract-home developments and, 1018–1019
  urban crisis for, 1019–1022
  urban renewal as factor in, 1020
  urban sprawl, 1018–1019
  women in, 1015
environmental pollution. *See* pollution
Environmental Protection Agency (EPA), 928,
  1036, 1038
Equal Rights Amendment, 189, 1451
ERCA. *See* Emergency Relief and Construction Act
Erickson, Frank, 395
Erie, Steven, 128
Erie Canal, 40, 42f, 43, 353
  food transport through, 1078
Erskine, Albert Russel, 979
Erving, Julius, 377
Eskew, Glenn, 1406
Esping-Anderson, Gøsta, 1163
Espinosa, Joe, 733
Estrada, Pascual, 1087
ethical consumption of food, 1096–1097
ethnic cuisines, 1084
ethnicity, **653–665**. *See also specific ethnic populations*
  Chicago School on, 661
  through collective practices, 654
  during colonial era, 655
  defined, 653–654
  environmental pollution and, 1031
  ethnoburbs, 908
  food cuisines by, 1084
  gambling industry and, 391–392
  rioting through ethnic conflict, 1272
  suburbanization and, 791–792, 1460–1461, 1471,
    1473–1474

suburbs influenced by, 660–661, 791–792
urban neighborhoods and, 654–659
white ethnic neighborhood associations and, 135–136
ethnic neighborhoods. *See also* urban neighborhoods
Native Americans in, 689
white ethnic neighborhood associations and, 135–136
ethnoburbs, 908, 1473–1474, 1505
Etowah (chiefdom)
abandonment of, 6
decline of, 6
elite hierarchy in, 5–7
political re-ordering in, 6
social re-ordering in, 6
Euclid v. Ambler Realty, 1516, 1519–1520
Europe. *See also specific countries*
immigration from, 547
European colonists
during Mississippi period, 4–5, 11
in urban American South, 70–72
European currencies, during the Great Depression, 199
evangelical Christianity, 1109, 1453
abstinence and, 415
on industrialization, 47
in Protestant Church, 1124–1125
Evans, Bill, 1217–1218
Evans, Gil, 1216
Evans, Glenn, 1406
Evans, Rowland, 1170n27
Evers, Medgar, 1407–1408, 1436
Evers, Myrlie, 1407
exclusion policies, in immigration
at Angel Island Immigration Station, 527, 530
at Ellis Island Immigration Station, 512–515
Executive Order 10450, 666
experimental rock, 1236–1237
extreme temperatures
Dust Bowl, 1068
heatwaves, 1067–1068
mechanical air conditioning use and, 1068–1069
mortality rates from, 1068

Fabian, Ann, 57n38, 388, 401
factories
in company towns, expansion of, 88
electrical grid development and, 62–63
in postindustrial cities, closures of, 331
Fagen, Donald, 1222
Fahler, Paul, 424
The Failure of Protestantism in New York and Its Causes (Dixon), 1105
Fairfield, John D., 896, 959
Fair Housing Act, US (1968), 647, 811, 1376
Asian Americans under, 1494
urban planning under, 910
Fair Labor Standards Act, US (1938), 214, 236, 239

fair lending practices, in housing policies, 837–838
Fairmount Gardens, 995–996, 998
FALN. *See* Armed Forces of National Liberation
Faludi, Susan, 1236
Fan Cho, 1297, 1299. *See also* anti-Chinese massacre
"fancy girl" trade, 458n54, 458n56
Fannie Mae. *See* Federal Home Mortgage Guarantor Association
Fard, Wallace, 1127
Farfan, Francisco, 435
farm auctions, 198, 198f
Farm Credit Administration (FCA), 231
Farmer, Fanny, 1100
Farmer, James, 1446
farmers, under New Deal programs, 230–233
under Agricultural Adjustment Act, 200, 231
conservation programs, 232–233
FCA and, 231
FSA and, 210, 232
industrial policies for, 233–234
regional applications of, 232–233
under TVA, 200, 226, 232–233, 239, 261
farm incomes, during the Great Depression, 201–202
farming communities, 788–789
Farm Security Administration (FSA), 210, 232
Farnsley, Charles, 344–345
fast food restaurants, 1098
Fauset, Jessie, 574
FBI. *See* Federal Bureau of Investigation
FCA. *See* Farm Credit Administration
FDIC. *See* Federal Deposit Insurance Program
Federal Aid Highway Act, US (1956), 134, 942, 956f, 957
Federal Aid Road Act, US (1916), 969
Federal Arts Project, 229–230
the Federal Bulldozer (Wilson, J.), 1536
Federal Bureau of Indian Affairs, 691
Federal Bureau of Investigation (FBI)
Black Power movement and, 1379
Freedom Rides and, 1404
PPC and, 739
Federal Deposit Insurance Program (FDIC), 200, 228, 297
Federal Disaster Relief Act, US (1950), 1070
Federal Emergency Management Agency (FEMA), 1070
Federal Emergency Relief Administration (FERA), 229
Federal Home Loan Bank Act, US (1931), 809
Federal Home Mortgage Guarantor Association (Fannie Mae), 837–838, 1017
suburbanization through, 1466
Federal Housing Act, US (1949), 1409
Federal Housing Authority (FHA), 200, 1017, 1531
home ownership and, 809–810
as housing policy, 831–833
municipal housing under, 809–810
residential segregation and, 642–643
suburbanization and, 794, 1458

federalism. *See* new federalism
Federal League, 369–370
Federally Funded Research and Development Centers
    (FFRDCs), 298
Federal Reserve, 200
Federal Reserve Act, US (1913), 186
federal tax codes, for postindustrial service economies,
    313–314
Federal Trade Commission, US, 186
Federal Transient Program (FTP), 1147
Federal Transient Service (FTS), 206
Feldberg, Michael, 1273–1274
Feldman, Roberta, 827
Felton, Rebecca Latimer, 189
FEMA. *See* Federal Emergency Management Agency
Female Sexual Slavery (Barry, K.), 452
The Feminine Mystique (Friedan), 1452
feminism
    lesbian, 668–671. *See also* lesbian, gay, bisexual,
        transgender and queer populations
    postwar sexual politics and, 449–452
    prostitution and, 449–452
    radical, 1440
    rap music and, 1257
    rock-and-roll music and, 1236
    sex work and, 449–452
FERA. *See* Federal Emergency Relief Administration
Ferrall, John, 620
Ferriss, Hugh, 867, 968
ferry boats, 934–935
FFRDCs. *See* Federally Funded Research and
    Development Centers
FHA. *See* Federal Housing Authority
Field, Alexander, 219n18
Fields, Edward, 1404
Fields, Mamie Garvin, 76
50 Cent, 1264–1265
Figone, Albert, 396
Filene, Edward, 67, 170
Filene, Peter, 191
Fillmore, Millard, 996
film industry, Native Americans in, 689
films
    anti-authoritarianism in, 1452
    housing policies in, 833
    LGBTQ characters in, 666
    Nickelodeons, 1194
    as popular culture, 212
    rap music in, 1255
    rock-and-roll music in, 1234
    skyscrapers in, 875
    streetcars in, 941
    suburbanization in, 1464
filtration systems, in water supply systems, 924–925
finance industries. *See also* tax increment financing

in postindustrial cities, 325, 327–328
    postindustrial service economies and, 308–311
Financial Institutions Reform, Recovery, and
    Enforcement Act, US (1989), 837
Fink, James, 959
Fink, Leon, 128, 267
Finley, James B., 410
firefighters
    public sector unions for, 276
    rioting by, 1273
First Bank of the United States, 43, 48, 288
First Great Migration, 567–579
First Houses, 907, 1531
First New Deal, 227, 260
Fisher, Colin, 1068
Fishman, Robert, 787, 795, 816, 975
Fiske, Haley, 864
Fitchie, Thomas, 511
Fitzgerald, Albert, 628
Fitzgerald, John, 123
Fitzwater, Marlin, 1305
Flagg, Ernest, 862, 864
Flanagan, Maureen, 129, 896
Fleming, Alexander, 1058
Flexner, Abraham, 343
Flink, James, 970
Flood, Curt, 380
flooding, 1065–1067
    Great Mississippi River Flood, 1066–1067
    Johnstown Flood, 1073
Florida. *See also* Spanish Florida
    postindustrial cities in, 325
Florida, Richard, 325, 331, 334, 349–350
Flynn, Elizabeth Gurley, 252, 626, 1529
Fogelson, Robert M., 175, 793, 796
Follett, Mary Parker, 125, 182
Follis, Charles W., 373
Foner, Eric, 1299–1300
food, **1077–1103**
    at Angel Island Immigration Station, 535–536
    in Asian American suburban culture, 1499–1500
    catering industry, 1086
    Chinese food, 1093
    commercial ice production and, 1078–1079
    commercial opportunities through, 1093–1094
    distribution networks for, 1079–1080
    Erie Canal and, economic impact of, 1078
    ethical consumption of, 1096–1097
    ethnic cuisines, 1084
    in food cooperatives, 1096
    Great Migration as influence on, 1092
    in grocery stores, 1080
    hucksters and, 1082
    immigrant influences on, 1086–1088, 1092–1094
    industrialization of, 1079, 1092

mechanical refrigeration of, 1092
Mexican food, 1094
in 19th Century Amercian cities, **1077–1092**
in North American seaport cities, 26
in private food shops, 1080–1081
protests over, 1094–1095
public dining and, 1082–1085
public health crusades through, 1097
in public markets, 1080–1081, 1097
purchasing of, 1095–1097
railroad transport of, expansion of, 1078–1080, 1092
restaurant industry, 1082–1085, 1097–1098
safety issues for, 1079
selling of, 1095–1097
social opportunities through, 1093–1095
soul food, 1095
street vendors, 1081–1082
in supermarkets, 1096
technological changes and, 1092
technological developments for, 1077–1080, 1092
in 20th Century Amercian cities, **1092–1103**
urban diets, 1085–1086
waterway transport for, development of, 1077–1078
food cooperatives, 1096
food safety issues, 1079
food services, 1086
food shops. *See* private food shops
football. *See* professional football
Foraker Act, US (1900), 713
For Bread. *See Za Chlebem*
Ford, Arnold Josiah, 1127
Ford, George, 184, 1519
Ford, Gerald, 328, 545, 836, 838, 1160, 1538
Ford, Henry, 60, 258, 417, 792
   assembly lines and, early development of, 65–66, 250
   global economies and, 105–106
   Model A, 67
   Model T, 65
Ford, Melbourne, 509
Ford, Paul Leicester, 127
Fordist systems and cities, 105–106, 108. *See also*
     Ford, Henry
   postindustrial service economies and, 312
Foreign Miner's Tax of 1951, 1275
foreign-trade zones (FTZs), 105
Foreign-Trade Zones Act, US (1934), 105
Fortas, Abe (Justice), 1343
forts. *See* presidios
Foster, George, 1083–1084
Foster, Maggie, 445
Foster, Mark, 959, 969
Foster, Norman, 874
Foster, Rube, 370
Fountain, Aaron, 1283
Fourteenth Amendment, 180

Fox, Billy, 396
Fox, Cybelle, 241
Franklin, Aretha, 1127, 1234
Franklin, Benjamin, 28, 30, 655
Franklin, Isaac, 159
Franklin, Nobia, 572
Fraser, Steve, 240
fraternal lodges, 411
fraternal organizations, 1193
Frazier, Franklin, 585, 592n20
Frazier, Latoya Ruby, 334
Frederick, Christine, 173
Fredericksburg, Virginia, destruction of, 844–846, 845*f*
free African Americans
   riots against, 161
   urban communities for, 161
   violence against, 50
   wage inequality for, 51
Freedman, Estelle, 129
Freedom Highways project, 1403–1404
"freedom of contract," 180
Freedom Rides, 1403–1404, 1446
   sit-in movement as influence on, 1426
free jazz, 1224
Freeman, Joshua, 630
Free Speech Movement, Asian American political
     movements influenced by, 744, 747
free speech protections, vagrancy laws and, 1353–1356
freeway revolts, 1537
French, Joseph Nathaniel, 866
French colonies, slavery in, 154
Freund, Ernest, 1517
Frick, Henry Clay, 90
Fried, Marc, 1536
Friedan, Betty, 910, 1452, 1465
Friedel, Frank, 239
Frieden, Bernard, 333
Friedman, Andrew, 316
Friedman, Milton, 214
Friedrich v. California Teachers Association, 281
Friss, Evan, 967
Frost, Susan Pringle, 1562
Frum, David, 1156
Fry, Frank, 779
FSA. *See* Farm Security Administration
FTP. *See* Federal Transient Program
FTS. *See* Federal Transient Service
FTZ. *See* foreign-trade zones
Fuentas, Marisa J., 437
Fuerst, J. S., 839
Fugitive Slave Law, US (1850), 163, 850, 1276
fugitive slaves, 850–851
Fuller, George A., 861
Fuller, George W., 925
Fuller, Henry B., 861

Fuller, Robert, 473
Fulton, Robert, 353, 934. *See also* steam power
furniture production, mass techniques in, 67

GAA. *See* Gay Activists Alliance
Gabbaccia, Donna, 1088, 1099
Gadsden, Christopher, 25
Gaebler, Ted, 298
Gallagher, Leigh, 1478
Galveston Hurricane of 1900, 1070
gambling houses
    in Chicago, 388, 393
    in New York City, 388
gambling industry, **387–406**. *See also* Las Vegas, Nevada
    African Americans and, 392–394
    anti-gambling movements, 389–391
    bookmaking and, 394–397
    card games, 388
    Champion v. Ames, 389
    Chinese and, 391–392, 392*f*
    early development of, 387
    ethnicity and, 391–392
    gambling houses, 388–389
    during Gilded Age, 391–392
    horse racing, 390, 393–397
    Indian Game Regulatory Act, 401
    Kefauver Committee on, 398–399
    lotteries, 388–390, 399–401
    machine politics and, 393–395
    Mapp v. Ohio, 399
    moral arguments against, 390–391
    Native Americans and, 693–694
    New York Society for the Suppression of
        Gambling, 388
    in 19th century, 387–392
    numbers games, 392–393
    organized crime syndicate involvement in, 388,
        393–394, 395*f*, 398–399
    point spreads in, 396–397
    police response to, 394*f*, 397–399, 398*f*
    in poolrooms, 390
    during Progressive Era, 389–391
    public condemnation of, 388–390
    race and, 391–392
    sports and, 394–397
    table games, 388
    in 20th century, 392–401
    urban development as influence on, 387–388
games and leisure, as popular culture, 212
    table games, 388
Gandhi, Mahatma, 1418, 1446
The Gang: A Study of 1,313 Gangs in Chicago (Thrasher),
    610, 1319, 1332
gang prevention strategies, 1323
gangs. *See* street gangs

gangsta rap, 1237
Gans, Herbert, 795, 1463–1464, 1536
Garcia, Inez, 671
Garcia Rivera, Oscar, 716
Gardner, Alexander, 851
Gardner, Edward, 1408
garment workers
    Amalgamated Clothing Workers of America for, 253
    ILGWU, 209, 253
    organization of, 253
    radicalism of, 253–254, 253*f*
    Triangle Shirtwaist factory fire and, 182, 253, 253*f*,
        256, 1518
Garreau, Joel, 975, 982n33
Garton, Stephen, 392, 401
Garvey, Ed, 374
Garvey, Marcus, 257, 1127
Gary, Indiana, steel production in, 91, 92*f*
gasoline taxes, 955
Gassan, Richard, 354
Gaston, Arthur, 1406
Gates, Daryl, 1300
Gay Activists Alliance (GAA), 671
"gayborhoods," 674
Gayle, William, 1400
Gay Liberation Front (GLF), 669–670
Gay Liberation Movement, 140–141, 668–671, 1283
    AIDS epidemic and, 1199
    BPP and, 670
    early start of, 1439–1440
    nightlife and, 1199
    Stonewall Inn riot and, 1199, 1439
"A Gay Manifesto" (Wittman), 669
Gay Men's Health Crisis, 675
GDP. *See* gross domestic product
Geary Act of 1892, US, 484
Gee, Emma, 745
Geffen, David, 1234
Gehry, Frank, 98, 874, 1007
Geismer, Lily, 1024, 1475
gender discrimination, in Asian American political
        movements, 751–752
gender ideology, sex markets and, 433
gender roles
    rock-and-roll music and, 1231–1232
    during US Civil War, 73
General Electric, 67
General Federation of Women's Clubs, 181, 185, 190
genteel class, in early seaport cities, 27–28
Gentlemen's Agreement, between Japan and US, 188,
        488, 533–534
gentrification, **1558–1572**
    African Americans and, 1559–1560
    artists' role in, 1560, 1562
    in Charleston, 1558, 1562

Chicago School and, 1560–1561
through conservation districts, 1560, 1562
defined, 1558–1560
"dual cities" and, 1559, 1568
features of, 1559
formative stage of, 1566–1567
globalization as influence on, 113
global stage of, 1568
Latino urbanism and, 707
of New York City, 110
from 1910–1929, 1560–1563
from 1960–1979, 1563–1567
from 1980–1999, 1567–1568
political identity as result of, 1565
in postindustrial cities, 331
public protests against, 1563
race and, 1559–1560
row house renovations as part of, 1562
of sidewalks and city streets, 985–986
speculative stage of, 1567–1568
state role in, 1560
from 2000–2018, 1568
by urban middle-class, 1564–1565
urban redevelopment and, 145
white-collar workers influence on, 1561
women's role in, 1562–1563
George, Henry, 124, 626, 1517
Georgia. *See also specific cities*
as colony, 157
Oconee River, 8
slavery in, 157
Gerhard, Charles, 448
German immigrants, 480–481
from 1850–1920, 655–656
religion for, 1112
Germany
hyperinflation in, 198
Nuremberg laws in, 213
germ theory of disease, 881
sewer systems and, 923
urban planning and, 903–904
Gerstle, Gary, 240
"Get Tough" era, 1344–1345
Getz, Stan, 1216, 1220
Gey, George, 347
ghettoes and barrios, 701
Great Migration and, 1370
street gangs in, 1321–1323, 1327–1328
GI Bill
Asian Americans under, 1493
home ownership under, 499–500, 810, 1143
loans after, 107
New Deal and, 226, 245n8
university attendance under, 344–346
urban planning and, 907

Gibson, Josh, 370
Gideon v. Wainwright, 1450
Giedion, Sigfried, 863, 865
Gilbert, Benjamin, 432
Gilbert, Cass, 865
Gilbert, Dan, 874
Gilberto, Astrud, 1220
Gilbreth, Frank, 250
Gilbreth, Lillian, 250
Gilded Age. *See also* Long Gilded Age
corporate America during, 250
gambling industry during, 391–392
immigration during, 484–486, 488
Judaism during, 1114–1115
machine politics during, 120–121
religion during, 1113–1116
universities and colleges during, 340
urban planning during, 904
Gilfoyle, Timothy, 355, 435, 453
Gilje, Paul, 1273, 1276, 1284
Gillespie, John Birks "Dizzy," 1215, 1218
Gillett, Charlie, 1230
Gillette, Howard, 333
Gilman, Charlotte Perkins, 805
Gilman, Daniel Coit, 342
Ginsberg, Allen, 470, 1129, 1216
Gioielli, Robert, 1042
girls
early education for, 1173–1174
in street gangs, 1325, 1337n26
Glass, Ruth, 1558
Glass-Steagall Act, US (1932), 228
Glazer, Nathan, 654, 661, 1170n37
Glee, 1238–1239
GLF. *See* Gay Liberation Front
global cities
Los Angeles as, 111, 143
low wages in, 110
New York City as, 102
San Francisco as, 111
as service cities, 109–110
globalization, **102–116**
African-American economic success and, 105
capital flight influenced by, 107–108
Cold War as influence on, 102, 106–108
commodity chains and, 103
definition of, 102–103
deindustrialization and, 108–109
Fordist systems and, 105–106, 108
under Foreign-Trade Zones Act, 105
in FTZs, in US, 105
gentrification influenced by, 113
during global wars, 106–107
hypersegregation from, 103
immigration influenced by, 103, 111–112

globalization (*Continued*)
   impact on US cities, 103
   industrialization of US cities as influence on, 105–106
   investment patterns and, 103
   of jazz music, 1225–1227
   labor trends influenced by, 111–112
   Latino-American economic success and, 105
   of monetary regimes, 102
   NAFTA and, 111
   under New Deal policies, 105
   of New York City, 102
   offshore production and, 108
   after Reconstruction, 104
   of religion, in US cities, 1131–1133
   service economies through, expansion of, 109–111
   transatlantic slave trade and, 103
   before 20th century, 103–105
   urban segregation from, 104
   in Western cities, 104
global money supply, during the Great Depression, 223n102. *See also* European currencies
Global South, 310, 312
Glotzer, Paige, 104
Glover, Melvin, 528
Goddard, Henry, 514
Gold, Jonathan, 1499
Goldberg, Bertrand, 871
Goldin, Claudia, 163–164
Goldman, Emma, 516, 1529
Goldman, Eric, 239
Goldman, Joanne Abel, 930
Goldmark, Josephine, 180, 188
Gold Rush era, in California, 430, 438–439
   Foreign Miner's Tax of 1951, 1275
   immigration during, 483–484
   riots during, 1275
gold standard, 198, 228
Goldwater, Barry, 1159, 1437, 1444
Goldwater, Julius, 758
Goloboy, Jennifer, 32
Gompers, Samuel, 186–187, 253, 255–256, 625
Gone With the Wind (film), 212
Gone With the Wind (Mitchell, Margaret), 73
Gonzales, Rodolfo "Corky," 738
Gonzales-Day, Ken, 1275
González, Humberto, 563
Goode, Wilson, 138
Goodenow, Bob, 376
Goodhue, Bertram, 865
Goodman, Benny, 1211, 1215
Goodman, Paul, 1451
Good Neighbor Policy, 547
Goodnow, Frank, 122
"good roads" movement, 951–953
Google, 98

Gordon, Colin, 333, 816
Gordon, Linda, 241
Gordon-Reed, Annette, 164
Gore, Albert, 299
Gore, Tipper, 1262
Gottlieb, Robert, 1024, 1031
Gough, John B., 412–413
Gould, Jay, 936
Government Corporation Control Act, US (1945), 298
government corporations
   under Government Corporation Control Act, 298
   as public authorities, 293, 295–298
   RFC, 290, 303n23
governments
   employees, in postindustrial service economies, 312
   municipal, 291–292
   in postindustrial cities, 315–316, 327–328
   postindustrial service economies and, 313
   public authorities as distinct from, 286
government services, in postindustrial cities, 314–315
Graham, Billy, 1129
Grandison, Ian, 1409
les grands, in New Orleans, 24
Grange, Harold "Red," 372–373, 380
Granger, R. S., 438
Grant, Madison, 516, 610
Grant, Ulysses S., 847
The Grapes of Wrath (book) (Steinbeck), 207, 210, 212, 232
The Grapes of Wrath (film), 210, 212
The Grass is Always Greener Over the Septic Tank (Bombeck), 834
Graves, Michael, 873
Grayson, Fred, 1400
Great Britain
   return to gold standard, 198
   US suburbanization influenced by, 787
Great Compression, 331
the Great Depression, **197–225**
   African Americans during, 201
   automobile use during, 969
   bank holidays during, 199–200, 219n16
   bank panics and, 199
   birth rates during, 202
   Bonus Expeditionary Force and, 205–206
   causes of, 197–200, 225
   Communist Party during, 207
   concentration of wealth prior to, 198
   construction industry during, 67
   data collection for, 200–202, 220n22
   deflationary cycles during, 199, 201
   divorce rates during, 202
   Dust Bowl during, 206–207, 207f
   European currencies during, 199
   farm auctions during, 198, 198f

farm incomes during, 201–202
flood refugees during, 206f
foreclosures during, 201
FTS established during, 206
GDP during, 200–201
global money supply during, 223n102
Great Migration during, of African Americans, 205
"hobo jungles" during, 205f
homelessness during, 205–207
Hoovervilles, 205, 259, 813, 907
horse racing during, 395
immigration during, 497–498
investment declines during, 201
iron scrappers during, 201f
labor rates during, 202–205, 220n28
labor strikes during, 204f
labor unions during, 203–205
Lowell, Massachusetts during, 88
major league baseball during, 370
marriage rates during, 202
migration patterns during, 205–207
municipal housing during, 799, 808–809
Musteites during, 207
New Deal as response to, 226–236
nightlife during, 1197
Okies during, 207
popular culture during, 210–213
Popular Front during, 210
poverty during, 1139, 1145, 1147
professional football during, 373
prostitution during, 446–447
protest politics during, 207–209
public authorities during, 297
public housing during, 818–820
public schools during, 1177, 1181
public sector unions during, 274
Puerto Ricans during, 715–716
Socialist Party of America during, 207
speculative markets and, 199
suburbanization during, 792–794
suicide rates during, 202
theater attendance during, 1197
transience during, 205–207
unemployment rates during, 200–202
urban planning during, 905–906
urban renewal during, 1531–1532
urban tourism during, 358
vagrancy laws during, 1352–1354
Wagner Act during, 203
World War I and, 197–198
Great Famine, 622–624
Great Migration, of African Americans, 76, **567–**
African American women during, 571–572
Black Metropolis and, 585
black-owned newspapers as influence on, 570, 584

black politics and, 575–576, 587–588
to black urban communities, 571–573
as chain migration, 569–571
to Chicago, **581–592**
community formation as result of, 1371–1373
consequences of, 588
in *The Crisis*, 582
economic change as factor for, 567–569
educational segregation after, 1370–1371
First, 567–579
food styles influenced by, 1092
ghettoes as result of, 1370
during the Great Depression, 205
Great Mississippi Flood and, 568
housing competition as result of, 587
housing discrimination after, 1370
jazz music influenced by, 1209–1210
Jim Crow laws and, 569
Juneteenth holiday and, 572
music culture influenced by, 574
The Negro Motorist's Green Book and, 1368–1369
to northern cities, 568–569
origins of, 583–584
political mobilization as result of, 1371–1373
popular culture influenced by, 573–575
during prohibition movement, 572
Pullman porters and, 586–587
race riots as result of, 1368
by rail travel, 569–570
during Reconstruction Era, 582
religion in US cities influenced by, 1126
residential segregation after, 640, 1370
restrictive covenants and, 1370
rioting as response to, 1279, 1281
Second, 581
social networks as influence on, 570
street gangs and, 1321–1322
suburbanization influenced by, 792, 794
Urban League and, 570–571
to urban North, 1368
urban violence and, 576–577
wage labor and, 567
workplace discrimination during, 1369–1370
during World War I, 257, 567–569
Great Mississippi River Flood, 1066–1067
Great Railroad Strike of 1894, 92f
Great Recession of 2007, 1478
Great Society, 226, 1155–1157, 1437, 1449–1450
CAAs, 1159–1161
CAP, 1157–1161
criticisms of, 1154
CSBGs, 1160–1161
failures of, 1153–1154
housing policies in, 834–835
modern social policies through, 1162–1163

Great Society (*Continued*)
  New Deal compared to, 1169n15
  poverty and, 1144–1145
  university attendance and, 347
  urban renewal as part of, 1528
  welfare state and, 1154
Greeley, Horace, 997
Greenbelt towns, 907
Greenberg, Dolores, 1023
Greenberg, Jack, 1428
Greene, Emily, 188
Greene, Julie, 251
Greene, Victor, 616
green infrastructure, 928–929
Greenlee, Gus, 394
Greensboro, North Carolina, 1416–1417
Greenwald, Herbert, 871
Gregory, James N., 593, 594–595, 600
Griffin-Gracy, Major, 669, 669f
Grimsted, David, 1272–1273, 1285
grocery stores, 1080. *See also* private food shops; supermarkets
Gropius, Walter, 833, 871
Groppi, James, 1131
Gross, Alina, 839
Gross, Samuel E., 788, 807
gross domestic product (GDP), during the Great
    Depression, 200–201
Grossman, James R., 586
Group Areas Act of 1950, South Africa, 641
Growing Up Absurd (Goodman, P.), 1451
Gruen, J. Philip, 364
Gruen, Victor, 1459
grunge music, 1237
Guatari (chiefdom), 10
Guerin, Jules, 862, 890f, 891
Guevara, Che, 1438
Guha, Ramachandra, 1022
Guiney, Patrick, 624
Gunn, L. Ray, 53
Gusfield, Joseph, 423–424
Guthrie, Woody, 1233
Gutman, Herbert, 266, 585
Guzik, Jake, 395–396

Habermas, Jurgen, 128, 992
Hacker, Jacob, 1166
Hadacheck v. Sebastian, 1518
Hague, Frank, 395
Haiman, Miecislaus, 615
Haiming Liu, 1514n39
Hair, William Ivy, 1280
Haitian Fairness Refugee Act, US (1990), 553
Haitian Revolution of 1791–1804, 45
Hale, Sarah Josepha, 802
Hale, William, 575

Haley, Alex, 519
Haley, Andrew, 1087
Haley, Heather, 442
Haley, Margaret, 273, 626
Hall, William Hammond, 1009, 1277
Halleck, Henry, 849
Hallenburg, Józef von, 609
Haller, Mark, 388, 399, 401
Hallidie, Andrew, 936–937
Hamer, Fannie, 1403
Hamilton, Alexander, 43, 86, 89
Hamilton, Alice, 1032
Hamilton, Charles, 1451
Hammitee, Jim, 595–596
Hampton, Fred, 736, 1327
Hancock, Herbie, 1221, 1223–1224
Handlin, Oscar, 630
Handy, W. C., 1207–1208
Hardesty, Jared Ross, 32, 164
Harding, Vincent, 1399
Harding, Warren G., 1396
Hardy, Stephen, 379
Hare, Nathan, 1021
Harlan County, Kentucky, 94
Harlem neighborhood, in New York City
    Cotton Club, 573–574, 1196
    Renaissance of, 257, 574–575, 1210
    riots in, 1281
    urban tourism and, 357
Harlins, Latasha, 1308–1309
Harrington, Michael, 1144
Harris, Abram, 1409
Harris, Jessica B., 1082
Harris, LaShawn, 393, 401–402
Harris, Leslie, 53
Harris, Neil, 363
Harris, Richard, 796, 806, 1458
Harrison, Benjamin, 389
Harrison, Bennett, 332
Harrison, Carter, 124
Harrison, Hubert, 257
Harrison, Wallace K., 868, 871
Harrison Narcotic Act, US (1914), 468
Hart, Emma, 32
Hart-Cellar Immigration Act. *See* Immigration and
    Naturalization Act of 1965
Harvard University, 341
Harvey, David, 112, 350
Haskell, Llewellyn, 812
Hassam, Childe, 875
Hatch Act, US (1939), 277
Hatcher, Richard, 138
hate crimes. *See also* lynch mobs
    against Asian Americans, 502–503
    against Korean-Americans, 1308–1309

Haussmann, Georges-Eugène, 1529
Havermeyer, William, 119
Hawai'i
    annexation of, 187
    Asian American political movements in, 747–748
    plague in, 1052
Hawkins, Augustus, 576
Hawkins, Connie, 378
Hawkins, John Henry Willis, 412
Hay, Harry, 667–668
Hayden, Delores, 815
Hayden, Tom, 1452
Hayek, Friedrich, 223n100, 347
Hayes, Rutherford B., 1280
Haynes, Edmund, 570
Hays, Barbara, 1023
Hays, Samuel, 191, 1023
Haywood, "Big" Bill, 252
Haywood, Harry, 588
Hazen, Allen, 925
HCV. *See* Housing Choice Voucher
Head, John, 27
healthcare. *See also* contagious diseases
    in postindustrial cities, 325
    in postindustrial service economies, 311
    urban strategies for, 348–349
Heap, Chad, 356
Hearst, William Randolph, 1547
Heathcott, Joseph, 333
Hedgeman, Anna Arnold, 1374
Heffelfinger, William, 372
Hefner, Hugh, 449
Heinemann, Ben, 1159
Heller, Walter, 1157
Helms, Jesse, 676
Hempel, Robert, 424
Hemphill, Essex, 674
Henderson, Charles R., 184
Henderson, Fletcher, 1210
Henderson v. Mayor of New York, 509
Hendrix, Jimi, 1233
Henkin, David, 992
Henry, Joseph, 996
Henry, Thomas P., 954
Herberg, Will, 1128
Hering, Rudolf, 923
heritage streetcar lines, 944
Herman, Bernard, 32
Hernandez, Pete, 733
Hernandez v. Texas, 733
heroin use, 466, 469–470
Herr, Henry, 91
Herrera-Duran, Pat, 1021
Herrold, George, 970
Hershey, Milton, 89, 91

Hestnes, Harold, 296
Hewitt, Abraham, 124
Heyrman, Christine Leigh, 32
Heyward, DuBose, 1562
HFA. *See* Housing Finance Authority
Hickok, Lorena, 231
Hicks, Louise Day, 138–139
Hi Duk Lee, 1307
Highsmith, Andrew, 333
Highway Act, US (1956), 1442
highway and freeway construction
    under Highway Act, 1442
    under Interstate and Defense Highways Act,
        1545–1547
    in urban renewal projects, 1410
highways. *See* streets, roads, and highways
Highway Trust Fund, 957, 969
Hilberseimer, Ludwig, 871
Hill, Lauryn, 1261
Hillman, Sidney, 262
Hillquit, Morris, 188, 255
Hills v. Gautreaux, 824
Hillyer, Reiko, 364
Hinduism, 1122–1123, 1131–1132
Hine, Lewis, 875
Hines, Gerald, 873
Hines, Thomas S., 896
Hing, Alex, 745, 751
Hinton, Elizabeth, 1346
hip-hop music, 1255f
    academic studies on, 1265–1267
    Black Lives Matter movement and, 1265
    Clinton, B., on, 1258–1259
    crossover appeal of, 1262–1263
    economic moguls in, 1265
    Jay-Z, 1239, 1260, 1263
    mainstream popularity of, 1258–1260, 1262–1264
    as male-dominated, 1252
    neo-soul and, 1238
    political activism through, 1264–1265
    rap music as foundation for, 1237
    in the South, 1261–1262, 1264
    technological influences on, 1264
    trap music, 1264
    from 2001–2018, 1262–1264
    West, K., and, 1239, 1263–1264
    women in, 1254–1255, 1257, 1260–1262
hippies, vagrancy laws and, 1356
Hirabayashi, Lane, 759
Hirsch, Arnold S., 815, 821, 826, 1143, 1281, 1321, 1461
Hispanic Young Adult Association (HYAA), 719
Hitler, Adolf, 212–213
HIV/AIDS epidemic, 1199
    ACT UP and, 676
    antiretroviral drug therapies, 676–677

HIV/AIDS epidemic (*Continued*)
  federal response to, 673
  Gay Men's Health Crisis and, 675
  LGBTQ political activism during, 675–677
  under Reagan, R., 676
  safe sex strategy during, 675–676
"hobo jungles," 205*f*
Hobsbawm, Eric, 1272, 1284
Hobson, Richard, 421
Ho Chi Minh City, 778
Ho-Chunk Nation, 694
Hoffman, Abbie, 910, 1451–1452
Hofstadter, Richard, 191, 239, 1284
Hogan, Frank, 397
Hokanson, Drake, 959
HOLC. *See* Home Owners Loan Corporation
Hollowell, Donald, 1419
Holman, Nat, 397
Holstein, Casper, 392
home construction industry, 807. *See also* self-built
    private homes
homelessness. *See also* vagrancy laws
  causes of, 1148
  FTP for, 1147
  during the Great Depression, 205–207
  Skid Rows and, demolition of, 1148
  temporary housing programs, 1148
Home Loan Bank Act, US (1932), 831
home mortgage crisis, 837–838
Home Mortgage Disclosure Act, US (1975), 1566
Home Mortgage Disclosure Act, US (1976), 645
Home Mortgage Urban Development Act,
    US (1968), 835
home ownership. *See also* private homes
  credit default schemes for, 648
  discriminatory practices for, 136. *See also* residential
    segregation
  domestication of, 800–802
  expansion of, 806–808
  FHA and, 809–810
  under GI Bill, 499–500, 810, 1143
  home mortgage crisis, 837–838
  municipal housing and, 799
  under New Deal programs, 810
  subprime loans for, 648
  suburbanization influenced by, 793
Home Ownership and Opportunity for People
    Everywhere (HOPE) program, 838
Home Owners Loan Corporation (HOLC), 200,
    237–238, 794, 809, 831–832, 1017, 1531, 1546
  racial elements of, 1142
  residential segregation and, 642–643, 1370
home rule, political progressivism and, 183
homonationalism, 678
homophile movement, 667–668

homosexuality. *See* lesbian, gay, bisexual, transgender and
    queer populations
Hong, Roy, 1312
honor, street gangs and, 1323–1325
Hood, Clifton, 946
Hood, John Bell, 848
Hood, Raymond, 865, 868
Hooker, Evelyn, 668
Hoover, Herbert, 199, 215, 226
  municipal housing policies under, 809
  prohibition movement and, 421
  public authorities under, 290
  public opinion on, 259–260
  residential segregation under, 642
Hoovervilles, 205, 259, 813, 907
Hope, Lugenia, 182
H. O. people, 778–779
HOPE program. *See* Home Ownership and Opportunity
    for People Everywhere program
Hopkins, Harry, 229, 275–276, 497, 1147
Hopkins, Johns, 342
Hopkins v. City of Richmond, 1522
Hormel, George A., 96–97. *See also* meatpacking
    company towns
Hormel, Jay, 96
Horner, Henry, 395
horsecars, 935–937
  during Industrial Revolution, 936
  in New York City, 935
  technology transfer and, 935
  urbanization influenced by, 935
horse racing, 393–397
  after Civil War, 390
  during the Great Depression, 395
  off-track betting for, 390, 394, 399–401
Horton, Guytana, 1404–1405
hotels
  SRO, 813
  urban tourism and, 355–356, 356*f*, 358–359
  women and, 170
Hounshell, David, 67
House Committee on Un-American Activities
    (HUAC), 277
housing. *See* municipal housing
Housing Act of 1937, US, 819, 826, 1143
  urban planning under, 907
Housing Act of 1949, US, 134, 327, 810, 820, 833,
    1532–1533, 1545–1546
  urban planning under, 907
  zoning laws under, 1524
Housing Act of 1954, US, 134, 327, 1532–1533
Housing Act of 1961, US, 836
Housing and Community Development Act,
    US (1974), 1143
Housing and Economic Recovery Act, US (2008), 838

Housing and Urban Development (HUD) Act, US
    (1968), 811, 822, 835–837, 838, 1535
Housing Choice Voucher (HCV), 836
Housing Finance Authority (HFA), 293–295
housing policies, **831–844**. *See also* Federal Housing
    Authority; Home Owners Loan Corporation;
    public housing; *specific legislation*
    under Bush, G. H. W., 838
    under Clinton, B., 836, 838
    under Eisenhower, 834
    fair lending practices as part of, 837–838
    fair-share, 1472
    Fannie Mae, 837–838
    federal aid for affordable housing in, 838–839
    under Ford, G., 836, 838
    GI Bill and, 833
    in Great Society, 834–835
    under HOLC, 831–832
    during home mortgage crisis, 837–838
    HOPE program, 838
    Japanese resettlement and, 761–763
    under Johnson, L. B., 644, 834–835
    under Kennedy, J. F. K., 644, 835–836
    King, M. L., on, 644, 835
    Model Cities program, 811, 834–835, 1145, 1535
    for municipal housing, 808–812
    under Nixon, R., 834–835, 838, 1475
    under Obama, 837
    in popular films, 833
    during postwar years, 833–834
    privatization of, 835–837
    under PWA, 832
    under Roosevelt, F. D., 831–833
    Section 8 program, 823–824, 836, 1472
housing reform. *See also* public housing; residential
    segregation
    Addams and, 805
housing segregation. *See also* housing policies; redlining;
    residential segregation
    as civil rights focus, 1375–1376
    after Great Migration, 1370
    in Levittowns, 1376
    against Puerto Ricans, 719
    through residential segregation, 635–636
    Shelley v. Kraemer, 644, 764, 833, 1144, 1376,
        1493–1494
    in urban North, 1370, 1375–1376
Howard, Amy, 827
Howard, Ebenezer, 915
Howe, Daniel Walker, 52
Howe, Frederic, 125, 182–183, 185, 188, 190, 515–516
Howe, George, 868
Howells, John Mead, 865
How the Other Half Lives (Riis), 391, 881–882, 1013, 1141
Hoy, Suellen M., 896

Hoyt, Homer, 642–643
HUAC. *See* House Committee on Un-American
    Activities
hucksters, 1082
HUD Act. *See* Housing and Urban Development Act
Huerta, Dolores, 1448
Huggins, John, 1326–1327
Hughes, John, 621–622, 1176
Hughes, Langston, 574
Hughes, Thomas P., 959
Hull, Bobby, 375
Hull House, 182, 1141
human immunodeficiency virus/acquired immune
    deficiency syndrome (HIV/AIDS), 1058
Hunt, D. Brad, 839
Hunt, Richard Morris, 805, 859, 1002
Hunter, David, 849
Hunter, Phyllis Whitman, 32
Hunter, Robert, 805, 1140
Hurley, Andrew, 333, 1024, 1042
Hurley, Timothy, 1340
Hurricane Andrew, 1071
Hurricane Betsy, 1070
Hurricane Camille, 1070–1071
Hurricane Harvey, 1072
Hurricane Katrina, 79, 1071–1072
    urban tourism after, 363
Hurston, Zora Neale, 210–211, 574
Huxtable, Ada Louise, 875
HYAA. *See* Hispanic Young Adult Association
hyperincarceration, of street gangs, 1328–1332
hyperinflation, in Germany, 198
hypersegregation, 103

Iacocca, Lee, 519
IBM. *See* International Business Machines
Ice-T, 1259
Ichioka, Yuji, 745
Ickes, Harold, 291, 303n24, 1531
"ideal woman," prostitutes compared to, 433–434
If Christ Came to Chicago (Stead), 1116
"If We Must Die" (McKay), 577
Igoe, William, 1143
"I Have a Dream" (King, M. L., Jr.), 1407
Iijima, Kazu, 745
Ikeda, Chiharu, 1497
ILGWU. *See* International Ladies Garment Workers Union
Illinois Juvenile Court Act, US (1899), 1340
IMF. *See* International Monetary Fund
immigrant runners, 508–509
immigrants. *See also specific ethnic groups*
    from Canada, 496
    Catholic, 480–481
    in company towns, 87–88
    in ethnic neighborhoods, 502–503

immigrants (*Continued*)
food influenced by, 1086–1088, 1092–1094
globalization as influence on, 103, 111–112
Korean-American experience, 1307–1308
in machine politics, 123
New Deal and, 238–239
political activism by, 144–145
during prohibition movement, 416–417
under Refugee Relief Act, 500
rioting by, 1272
in street gangs, 1319–1323
undesirables category for, 514
undocumented, 111
in urban American South, 72–73, 76
urban redevelopment and, 144–145
vagrancy laws and, 1351
voting rights for, 50
immigration, to US, **479–567**. *See also specific ethnic groups; specific Immigration Acts*
AFL and, 486
from Africa, 555, 558
American Protective Association, 487
Angel Island Immigration Station, **526–541**
anti-Catholic sentiment and, 482
anti-Chinese racism, 483–484
from Asia, 553–555
Asiatic Barred Zone and, 488, 496
Bracero Program, 499, 541–542, 551–552
from Canada, 551
from Caribbean, 553
Castle Garden Immigration Station, 508–509
from Central America, 553
CIO and, 498
before Civil War, 479–481, 485–486
during Cold War, 545, 550–551
congressional regulation of, 508–509
under Contract Labor Law, 509
from Cuba, 552
demographic changes in, 659
diversity visas and, 560
from Dominican Republic, 552–553
from Eastern Europe, 485
from 1820–1924, by country, **479–495**, 480t
from 1850–1920, by country, 484t
Ellis Island Immigration Station and, 488, **508–526**
under Emergency Quota Act, 516, 526–527
emergency quotas in, 496
from Europe, 547
foreign-born populations from, in 1850, 481t
under Geary Act of 1892, 484
under Gentlemen's Agreement, 188, 488, 533–534
in Gilded Age, 484–486, 488
during Gold Rush era, 483–484
during the Great Depression, 497–498
under Hart-Cellar Immigration Act, 111
Henderson v. Mayor of New York, 509
under Immigration and Naturalization Act of 1965, 496
increased rates of, 111
IRL, 189, 487, 512
Japanese, 486–488
Japanese and Korean Exclusion League and, 488
under Johnson, L. B., 519, 546
under Johnson-Reed Act, 489, 516
Knights of Labor and, 486
Know Nothing movement and, 482–483
Ku Klux Klan as response to, 497
labor issues and, 487
Mexican, 486, 499, 541–542, 551–552
national origins quotas, abolishment of, 545–546
nativism movement as response to, 481–483, 487–489, 496–497
under New Deal programs, 498
in New York, 482
from 1901–1910, by country, 485t
from 1924–2017, **495–508**
after 1945, **541–567**
from 1950–2009, by country, 548t, 551t, 552f
"Operation Wetback," 542
under Page Act of 1875, 484
pauperism and, 482
political effects of, 502
poverty as result of, 481
during Progressive Era, 484–486, 488
racial categorization and, 498
racialized progressivism and, restrictions through, 189–190
racial segregation as result of, 497–498
refugee policies, 544–545
residential segregation as result of, 497
sanctuary cities and, 504
under Scott Act of 1888, 484
during second Industrial Revolution, 485
after September 11th attacks, 504, 559–560
Social Darwinism and, 487
social effects of, 502
from Southern Europe, 485
suburbanization influenced by, 499–501, 658–659
to suburbs, 503–504
Taiping Rebellion and, 483
under Trump administration, 504
from 2001–2003, 556t
from 2001–2013, 558t
"urban crisis" and, 501–503
VOLAGS, 544
from Western Hemisphere, 547, 550–553
white flight as response to, 496
Workingmen's Party and, 483
during World War II, 499

Immigration Act of 1882, US, 488
Immigration Act of 1891, US, 488, 512
Immigration Act of 1907, US, 190, 515
Immigration Act of 1917, US, 190, 496, 526, 530
Immigration Act of 1924, US, 111, 495, 496–497
Immigration Act of 1990, US, 546, 560
Immigration and Nationality Act, US (1952), 666
Immigration and Naturalization Act of 1965, US, 111,
     496, 501–503, 546, 702, 1131, 1494
Immigration Reform and Control Act (IRCA), US
     (1986), 560–561, 705
Immigration Restriction League (IRL), 189, 487, 512
incarceration rates. *See also* prisons
     racial disparities in, 1377–1378
     in urban North, racial inequities with, 1377–1378
incarceration theory. *See also* prisons
     hyperincarceration, 1328–1332
     for juvenile justice, 1344–1345
incinerators. *See* landfills and incinerators
income levels
     of African Americans, in early cities, 44
     for farm, during the Great Depression, 201–202
     of Puerto Ricans, 722
     in the South, 599–600
     of women, in early cities, 44
incorporation laws, 789–790
independent civil service associations, 274
Independent Order of Good Samaritans, 411
Independent Order of Good Templars, 411
Independent Union of All Workers, 96
India, residential segregation in, 639
Indian Americans, 1494–1496
Indian Game Regulatory Act, 401
individualism, anti-authoritarianism and, 1453
industrial democracy, 257–258
industrialization
     American System of Manufactures, 47
     assembly lines as influence on, 60, 65–66
     in Chicago, 61
     in cities, 49–51
     of cotton production, 45–46
     from 1880–1929, 60–69
     electrical grid and, development of, 60–63
     environmental movements influenced by, 1013–1014
     environmental pollution and, 1031–1035
     evangelical Christianity on, 47
     of food preparation, 1079, 1092
     globalization influenced by, 105–106
     inflation as result of, 48
     labor activism and, 48
     through large-scale mechanized factories, 51–52
     through mass production, 66–67
     of municipal housing, 801
     in New South, 76
     during postbellum period, 51–52

prohibition movement influenced by, 417
prostitution influenced by, 434
public transportation improvements and, 47
riots and, 1274–1280
from 1790–1870, 37–55
sex markets influenced by, 434
in the South, 61
structural steel and, construction with, 63–65
suburbanization influenced by, 787–788
of tailoring, 48
transportation infrastructure improvements
     through, 61–63
during the US Civil War, 51
of US production, 45–49
wage labor and, 49
wage slavery and, 49
of water-power mechanization, 45
industrial parks, 326
Industrial Revolution
     immigration during, 485
     Second, 485
     vagrancy laws during, 1351–1352
industrial suburbs, 788–789
Industrial Workers of the World (IWW), 96, 254–255
     vagrancy laws and, 1353
inflation
     hyperinflation, 198
     industrialization as influence on, 48
influenza epidemics, 1054
information centers, in cities, **340–353**. *See also* universities
Inouye, Kazuo K., 764
institutional centers, suburbs as, 788–789
insurance industry, in postindustrial cities, 325
integration. *See also* racial segregation; residential
     segregation
     of major league baseball, 370
     of professional basketball, 377
     of professional football, 373
International Business Machines (IBM), 98
internationalism, 750–751
International Labor Defense Fund, 262–263
International Ladies Garment Workers Union (ILGWU),
     209, 253, 715, 735
International Monetary Fund (IMF), 226
international progressivism
     civil society as goal of, 187–188
     democracy as result of, 188–189
     economic progress as goal of, 187
     international cooperation as part of, 188–189
internment camp incarceration, of Japanese immigrants,
     499, 758–759. *See also* Asian American
     neighborhoods
interracial marriage, legal restrictions against
     Loving v. Virginia, 732
     Perez v. Sharp, 732

interracial sex, 441–442

interracial social networks, in early seaport cities, 29

interracial trade networks, in early seaport cities, 29

interrogation procedures, at Angel Island Immigration Station, 530–532

Interstate and Defense Highways Act, US (1956), 1545–1547

Interstate Commerce Act, US (1887), 185

interstate highways

congestion issues, 958

during Eisenhower administration, 956–957

Highway Trust Fund for, 957

public critics of, 957

ride-sharing systems, 958

safety issues, 958

slugging system, 958

toll roads, 956, 958

"White Flight" and, 957

In the Heights, 707

invisiburbs, 1495

IRCA. *See* Immigration Reform and Control Act

Ireland, John, 1126

Irene (chiefdom), 5, 8

Irish immigrants, 50, 480–481, 484–485, **620–634**

anti-Chinese racism of, 624

Catholic Church as influence on, 620–622, 629

as child laborers, 623*f*

Democratic Party and, 50

in domestic service, 623

in draft riots, 624

from 1845–1880, 622–624

from 1880–1925, 624–627

female, 626

Great Famine and, 622–624

industrial growth and, 622–624

in Knights of Labor, 625–627

in labor movement, 620–621, 625–628

in labor unions, 624–630

Long Strike of 1875 and, 624

Molly Maguires and, 624

multiethnic relationships with, 624–627

in national labor movements, 623–630

under National Origins Act, 627

from 1926–2018, 627–630

political influence of, 622

in popular culture, 629–630

Protestant Church as influence on, 620–622

racial segregation practiced by, 627

religion in US cities influenced by, 1112

settlement patterns for, 621

from 1790–1845, 620–622

in textile mills, 623, 623*f*

voting rights for, 50

IRL. *See* Immigration Restriction League

iron scrappers, 201*f*

Iroquois people, 40

Irvine, California, 1467–1468, 1467*f*

Isaac, Paul, 424

Isenberg, Alison, 175, 991

Islam, 1122–1123. *See also* Nation of Islam

Issei generation, of Japanese Americans, 758

I Wor Kuen, 748

IWW. *See* Industrial Workers of the World

Jack, Hulan, 716

The Jack-Roller (Shaw, C.), 610

Jackson, Andrew, 43, 271, 363, 1273

Jackson, George, 1283

Jackson, Jesse, 1259

Jackson, Kenneth T., 68, 787, 793, 795, 809, 816, 937, 959, 1458

Jackson, Mahalia, 1127

Jackson, Maynard, 138, 146, 1409

Jackson, Michael, 1235–1236

Jackson, Patrick Tracy, 87

JACL. *See* Japanese American Citizens League

Jacobs, Harriet, 162

Jacobs, Jane, 134–135, 705, 822, 834, 908, 915, 957, 973, 1524–1525, 1536, 1562, 1565

Jacobson, Max, 470

Jacobson, Sam, 1357

Jaffee, David, 59n58

Jahn, Helmut, 873

JALC. *See* Jazz at Lincoln Center

Jamaica, earthquakes in, 23

James, Etta, 1220, 1232

Jameson, Frederic, 873

James River, 71

Jamestown, Virginia, 23

English settlements in, 71

recreation plans in, 21

slavery in, 153

Jang, Lindsey, 779

Jao, Frank, 774

Japanese American Citizens League (JACL), 762–763

Japanese and Korean Exclusion League, 488

Japanese immigration, to US, 486–488

under Alien Land Laws, 757, 763

under Chinese Exclusion Act, 757

under Gentlemen's Agreement, 188, 488, 533–534

internment camp incarceration as response to, 499, 758–759

as model minority, 766

racial discrimination against, 760–761

during World War II, 499, 758

Japanese resettlement, in Los Angeles, **757–770**

activist organizations' role in, 765–766

architecture of, 759–761

economic losses as result of, 760

employment opportunities after, 761–763

geographic area of, 758–759
in hostels, 761
housing discrimination during, 763
housing policies and, 761–763
Issei generation and, 758
JACL and, 762–763
Kibei generation and, 758
in local news media, 760–761
long-term legacy of, 765–766
of Nikkei generation, 757–759, 766
from 1950–1969, 763–765
Nisei generation and, 765
under Proposition 15, 763
Sansei generation and, 765
Shelley v. Kraemer, 764
social impact of, 761–763
in temporary camps, 761–762
WRA and, 759, 761–762
Japantown, in San Francisco, **1542–1557**, 1549*f*
African Americans in, 758–759, 1548
Bronzeville neighborhood and, 758–759, 1548
CCED and, 1542
development phases for, 1548–1551
displacement pressures in, 1542–1545
expansion of central business districts, 1546
HOLC and, 1546
JCTC in, 1549–1550, 1549*f*, 1550*f*
land use in, 1546–1548
public protests against development of, 1550–1551
redevelopment coalition for, 1547–1551
Jay-Z, 1239, 1260, 1263
Jazz (documentary), 1225
Jazz at Lincoln Center (JALC), 1225
jazz music, **1206–1230**. *See also* Coltrane, John;
    Davis, Miles
academic studies of, 1227–1228
African American culture as influence on, 573–574,
    1214–1215
Afro-Cuban, 1220
as America's classical music, 1223–1225
anti-conformism and, 1217
bebop, 1215
in Big Band era, 1211, 1215
Black Arts Movement and, 1219, 1221, 1226
in Chicago, 1210, 1215
during civil rights movement, 1217–1220
during Cold War, 1218–1219
cool, 1215–1217
in Creole community, 1209
dissemination of, 1209–1210
female vocalists, 1215
free, 1224
funk music with, 1221
globalization of, 1225–1227
Great Migration as influence on, 1209–1210

growing popularity of, 1210–1211
during Harlem Renaissance, 1210
Latin influences on, 1220, 1226
modernistic, 1214–1216
in New Orleans, 1209–1210, 1215
in New York City, 1210
nightlife and, 1197–1198
after 1945, **1214–1230**
origins of, 1209
in performing arts centers, 1225
radicalization of, 1219–1220
ragtime and blues music and, 1208–1209
repertory movement in, 1223
rock-and-roll music and, 1220–1223
subsets of, 1221–1222
after World War II, 1215
Jeanneret, Charles-Édouard. *See* Le Corbusier
Jefferson, Thomas, 86, 118, 164, 250, 1030
on property ownership, 799, 801
Jenkins, Henry, 1238–1239
Jenks, Hillary, 761
Jenner, Edward, 1057
Jenney, William Le Baron, 860, 1000
Jennings, Dale, 667–668
Jensen, Jens, 1005
Jewett, Helen, 453
Jewish neighborhoods
in Canada, segregation of, 664n36
in New York City, 656–659, 657*f*
Jim Crow laws
central business districts during, 171
Great Migration during, 569
Ku Klux Klan and, 80
Latino Americans during, 731–732
mass transit during, 940. *See also* Montgomery bus
    boycott
NAACP response to, 1404
poverty during, 1142
prohibition movement during, 417
public schools, 1178
riots during, 1282
sit-in movement during, 1420–1421
unconstitutionality of, 905
in urban North, 1368–1369, 1373–1374
urban planning during, 905
in urban South, 75–76, 1404–1405
Jiménez, José "Cha Cha," 721, 736, 1327–1328
jitneys, 941
Joara (chiefdom), 10
Jobim, Antonio Carlos, 1220
John, Richard R., 68
Johns Hopkins University, 342
Johnson, Charles S., 583, 585–586, 592n20, 1409
Johnson, Earvin "Magic," 378
Johnson, Ellsworth Raymond, 572

Johnson, Harold, 1305
Johnson, Ken, 473
Johnson, Lillian, 445
    poverty programs under, 1144–1145
Johnson, Lyndon B., 107, 345, 943–944, 1153, 1155–1157,
        1355. *See also* Great Society
    Civil Rights Act (1964), 77, 1408–1409, 1437
    housing policies under, 644, 834–835
    immigration policy under, 519, 546
    law-and-order policies under, 1379–1380
    Model Cities program, 811, 834–835, 1145, 1535
    public housing under, 811
    refusal of second presidential term by, 1438–1439
    urban renewal under, 1535
    Vietnam War under, expansion of, 1437–1438
    Voting Rights Act (1965), 77, 718, 722–723,
        1408–1409, 1437
    War on Poverty, 328
Johnson, Marsha P., 669
Johnson, Paul E., 424
Johnson, Philip, 519, 869, 873
Johnson, Rashauna, 53
Johnson, Susan Lee, 430
Johnson, Tom, 183, 187
Johnson, Walter, 53
Johnson-Reed Act, US, 489, 516
Johnston, Robert D., 129, 191
Johnstown Flood, 1073
Jones, Christopher, 1042
Jones, Doug, 81
Jones, Maggie, 569
Jones, Mary Harris "Mother," 252, 252*f*, 626, 626*f*
Jones, Quincy, 574
Jones Act, US (1917), 713
Jones-Miller Act, US (1922), 421
Joplin, Janis, 1233
Jordan, Barbara, 576
Jordan, June, 674
Jordan, Michael, 378, 1236
Jordy, William, 875
Judaism
    during antebellum era, 1112–1113
    during Civil War, 1112
    in colonial cities, 1107–1108
    during Gilded Age, 1114–1115
    Reform, 1125–1126
    in suburbs, 1128–1131
Judd, Dennis, 150n81, 361, 363–364
Judd, Donald, 331
Juneteenth holiday, 572
The Jungle (Sinclair), 837
Jung-Min Sunoo, 1309
jurisdiction, of juvenile courts, 1340
juvenile courts
    in Chicago, 181, 1340–1341

development of, 1339–1342
diversity of, in national court system, 1341–1342
Due Process Revolution and, 1343
early failures of, 1342
function of, 1341
under Illinois Juvenile Court Act, 1340
jurisdiction of, 1340
Model Penal Code and, 1342–1343
personnel in, 1340
private associations' role in, 1341
during Progressive Era, 1340
transformation of, 1342–1344
US Children's Bureau, 1340
juvenile delinquency, Polish immigration and, 610–611
juvenile justice, **1339–1350**
    African American children in, treatment
        of, 1341, 1345
    during antebellum era, 1340
    children's rights and, 1339, 1345
    federal government role in, 1343
    in "Get Tough" era, 1344–1345
    ideological origins of, 1339–1340
    incarceration philosophy for, 1344–1345
    legal development of, 1339–1340
    moral poverty approach to, 1344
    parens patriae tradition in, 1342–1344
    progressive, 1340–1342
    during Progressive Era, 1340
    racial discrimination in, 1345
    re Gault case, 1342–1343, 1346
    sentencing reform in, 1345
    "super-predators" and, 1344
    in Supreme Court cases, 1343, 1345
    US Children's Bureau, 1340
Juvenile Justice and Delinquency Prevention Act,
        US (1974), 1343

Kahn, Albert, 866
Kahn, Ely Jacques, 866
Kain, John, 944
Kaneko, Josephine, 187
Kang, K. Connie, 1313
Kannapolis, North Carolina, 93, 95
Kapoor, Anish, 1007
Karvonen, Andrew, 930
Kasich, John, 281
Kasson, John, 363
Katz, Bruce, 145, 1476
Katz, Michael, 1184, 1283
Katznelson, Ira, 226, 241, 247n74
Kaufman Index, 706
Kearney, Denis, 624
Keating, Ann Durkin, 796
Keating-Owen Child Labor Act, US (1916), 181
Keats, John, 973

Keefe, Daniel, 533, 625
Keenan, John C., 773
Kefauver, Estes, 398–399
Keith, Benjamin, 1194
Keith, LeeAnna, 1277
Keith, Nathaniel, 839
Kelley, Florence, 180, 182, 184, 188, 894
Kelley, Robin, 940, 946
Kellogg, Clarence W., 439
Kellogg, Paul, 188, 574
Kellor, Frances, 185, 186, 190
Kelly, Ed (Mayor), 395
Kelly, Edward, 127, 667
Kelly, John, 120
Kelly, Joseph, 813
Kelman, Ari, 1073
Kemp, Jack, 824, 838, 1161
Kemp, Ray, 373
Kenna, Mike "Hinky Dink," 891
Kennedy, David, 225, 227, 241
Kennedy, Edward, 629
Kennedy, Florynce, 1452
Kennedy, John F., 278, 470, 629, 1355
    civil rights under, 1404, 1407–1408
    election of, 1436
    housing policies under, 644, 835–836
Kennedy, Robert F., 373, 1159
    assassination of, 1438
Kennedy, Rose Fitzgerald, 1007
Kern, Maximilian G., 1277
Kerner, Otto, 1282
Kerouac, Jack, 470, 1129, 1216
Kerr, Clark, 345, 349–350
Kessler, George, 1009, 1277
Kessler-Harris, Alice, 241
Key, V. O., Jr., 78
Keynes, John Maynard, 213–214
Keyserling, Leon, 819
Kibei generation, of Japanese Americans, 758
Kiechle, Melanie, 1041
Kieft's War, 157
Kilbride, Daniel, 354
Kim, Jay, 1312–1313
Kim, Lester, 772
Kim, Nadia, 1315
Kimball, Moses, 1191
Kindleberger, Charles, 214
King, B. B., 1220
King, Martin Luther, Jr., 78, 82, 1281, 1327, 1355, 1373,
    1405–1407
    anti-Vietnam War speech by, 1443–1444
    assassination of, 278, 822, 1438, 1448
    on assassination of Kennedy, J. F., 1408
    in Birmingham, Alabama, 1405–1407
    "Letter from Birmingham Jail," 1405–1406, 1452

    in Memphis, Tennessee, 1411
    on national housing policies, 644, 835
    political ascension of, 1435
    Poor People's Campaign, 1156
    on sit-in movement, 1422–1423
    social activism of, 1130
King, Rodney, 1305, 1309
King Philip's War, 22, 153
Kirk, Edward Norris, 410
Kirkland, Edward Chase, 92
"Kitchen Debate," 107–108
Kitchen Debates, 1463
Klein, Daniel, 959
Klingle, Matthew, 1041
Kloppenberg, James T., 241
Knapp, Whitman, 399
Knauff, Ellen, 517–518
Knauff, Kurt, 518
Kneeland, George, 441
Knight, Suge, 1259–1260
Knights of Labor, 124, 180, 250, 272
    immigration and, 486
    Irish immigrants in, 625–627
    public sector unions and, 273
Knoll, Florence, 869
"knowledge worker," 316
Knowles, Charles, 29
Knowles, Scott, 1073
Knowles Riots, 29
Know Nothing movement, 482–483
Koch, Ed, 133, 142–143, 361
Koch, Robert, 923
Koelle, William B., 1562
Koeppel, Gerald, 930
Kolko, Gabriel, 191
Koolhaas, Rem, 98
Koon, Stacey, 1317n1
Koop, C. Everett, 676
Korean-Americans
    African Americans and, conflicted relationship with,
        1307–1311, 1313–1314, 1318n15
    BKA and, 1309
    in Democratic Party, 1312
    under Hart-Cellar Immigration Act, 1312
    hate crimes against, 1308–1309
    immigrant experience for, 1307–1308
    as merchants, in African American neighborhoods,
        1308–1309, 1318n15
    in New York City, 1308
    1992 riots and, impact on, 1304, 1306–1314
    Sai-I-Gu for, 1309–1312
Kosugi, Sho, 1504
Kristol, Irving, 1170n37
Krugman, Paul, 215
Kruse, Kevin M., 241

Krushchev, Nikita, 107–108
    Kitchen Debates and, 1463
Kruszka, Waclaw, 615
Ku, Robert Ji-Song, 1099
Ku Klux Klan, 80
    Freedom Rides and, 1403–1404
    lynch mobs by, 1277
    during prohibition movement, revival of, 420
    response to immigration, 497
    sit-in movement and, 1417, 1419
    in urban South, 1397
Ku Klux Klan Act, US (1871), 1292
Kurashige, Scott, 763, 766
Kwak, Nancy, 833

Laas, William, 1460
labor, **249–271**. *See also* employment rates; labor strikes;
        labor unions; public sector unions; unemployment
        rates; *specific industries*
    "American Plan," 258
    during "business decade," 257–258
    Chinese imported as, 1292
    globalization as influence on, 111–112
    from Global South, 310, 312
    during the Great Depression, 202–205, 220n28
    Irish immigrants as, 620–621, 625–628
    IWW and, 96, 254–255
    National War Labor Board, 264–265
    under New Deal programs, 235–236, 259–261
    under NIRA, 94, 200, 203, 235–236
    organizing of, as political movement, 251–252
    radicalism of, 252–254
    self-employment rates, 250
    in "sick industries," 258
    Socialist Party of America and, 252
    unskilled, 47
    workday hour limitations for, 256
    during World War I, 257
    during World War II, 264–266
labor activism, industrialization and, 48
labor markets. *See* dual labor markets
labor shortages, in company towns, 89
labor strikes
    by African Americans, 255
    by Amalgamated Association of Steel and Iron
        Works, 91
    "Bread and Roses Strike," 254
    during "business decade," 258, 258f
    during the Great Depression, 204f
    Great Railroad Strike of 1894, 92f
    Long Strike of 1875, 624
    in Memphis, 1411
    New Deal and, 236, 260–261
    in Pittsburgh, 258f
    by police, 274

    Polish immigration and, 508–509
    by public sector unions, 277
    rioting and, 1278–1280
    under Taft-Hartley Act, 277
    by textile workers, 252f
labor unions. *See also* public sector unions; working
        hours; *specific unions*
    African Americans in, 257, 262–263, 1369–1370
    in coal-mining company towns, 94
    collective bargaining by, 261
    CPUSA and, 262
    decline of, 258
    during the Great Depression, 203–205
    Irish immigrants in, 624–630
    Knights of Labor, 124, 180, 250, 272
    machine politics and, 124–125
    for major league baseball players, 371–372
    mass production and, 67
    New Industrial Union movement, 262–264
    for NHL players, 375–376
    Polish immigration and, 607–609, 611
    for professional football players, 374
    during Progressive Era, 254–256
    Proposition 22 and, 734
    Puerto Ricans' exclusion from, 714–716
    racial discrimination in, 263
    under Roosevelt, T., 272
    for steel industry, 262
    under Wagner Act, 203
    white, 49–50
    during World War I, 257
    "yellow dog" contracts and, 203
labor violence, 249. *See also* labor strikes
La Cava, Gregory, 212
Lacks, Henrietta, 347
Lacy, Adolph, 597
Ladies' Health Protective Association (LHPA), 1033
"Lady of Cofitachequi," 8
La Follette, Belle Case, 188
La Follette, Robert, 182–183, 186, 188
LaGuardia, Fiorello, 126, 517, 1094
Laite, Julia, 452
Lake George (chiefdom), 5
"Lakewood Plan," 908
Lâm, Tony, 777
Lama, Alfred J., 304n33
Lamar, Kendrick, 1240, 1265
LaMotta, Jake, 396
Lanctot, Neil, 380
land banks, 329
land development, suburbanization through, 1466–1468
landfills and incinerators, 326–327
land grants
    property rights through, 800
    for universities and colleges, 341–342

Landis, Kenesaw M., 380, 396
Land Ordinance of 1785, 40, 949
Land Ordinance of 1785, US, 949, 950*f*
Landrieu, Mitch, 363
Landrieu, Moon, 360, 1409
Landron, Maggie, 972
Landrum, Phil, 1169n26
Lands, LeeAnn, 796
landscape architects, for urban parks, 1001
land surveying, for municipal housing, 800
land use regulations, 1524–1525
    in Japantown, 1546–1548
Lane, Barbara Miller, 840
Lange, Dorothea, 210–211, 211*f*
Langston, Nancy, 1042
Larsen, Nella, 574
Larson, John Lauritz, 52–53
Lassiter, Matthew, 1398–1399, 1401, 1465, 1474
Las Vegas, Nevada
    casinos, 327, 1200
    nightlife in, 1200
    urban tourism to, 359
late Mississippi period
    chiefdoms during, 7–11
    collapse of, 11–13
    de Soto and, 7–10
    Spanish contact in, 11–13
Lathrop, Julia, 181, 188
Latina American women
    as consumer market, 170
    in ILGWU, 735
Latino Americans, **730–744**. *See also* interracial
    marriage; Mexican American immigrants; Puerto
    Ricans
    African Americans and, relationships between,
        730–744. *See also specific groups*
    Chicano nationalism, 1332
    economic success of, globalization as influence on, 105
    jazz music influenced by, 1220, 1226
    under Jim Crow segregation, 731–732
    police brutality against, 145, 503
    population growth for, 705–707
    in public schools, 1181–1183
    racial discrimination against, 731–732
    rap music influenced by, 1260–1262
    residential segregation of, 636–637, 731
    rioting against, 1281
    in street gangs, 1324–1325, 1331–1332
Latino urbanism, **696–712**
    in barrios, 701
    Bracero Program and, 700–701
    Central American political instability as influence on,
        704–705
    in Chicago, 700, 703–704, 703*f*
    in ciudades, 696–697

during colonial era, 696–698
commercial development areas influenced by,
    703–704
community organization and, 702
ethnic diversity and, 705
gentrification and, 707
historical study of, 708–709
under Immigration and Naturalization
    Act of 1965, 702
under IRCA, 705
in Kaufman Index, 706
under *Laws of the Indies*, 697
in Los Angeles, 699–701
mass migration trends for, 702–704
along Mexico-U.S. border, 698–700
in Miami, 705
in Midwest cities, 699–700
missions and, 696–697, 697*f*
muralismo movement and, 701–702
under National Origins Act of 1924, 702
from 1995–2018, 706–708
origins of, 696–698
in Philadelphia, 701
in presidios, 697
in pueblos, 696–697, 697*f*
Puerto Rico as US territory and, 699
railway development and, 698
Revolution of 1910 in Mexico and, 698–699
in San Antonio, 699
in San Diego, 701–702
in Southwest region, 698–700
Spanish-American War as influence on, 699
Spanish colonialism and, 696–698
in Teotihuacán, 696
in theatrical musicals, 707
urban renewal and, 700–702
in villas, 696–697
during wartime, 700–702
Latrobe, Benjamin, 1029–1030
Lavender Scare, 666–667
Lawrence, Jacob, 211
Lawrence v. Texas, 677
Laws of the Indies, 697
Lawson, James, 1402, 1418, 1425
LDF. *See* Legal Defense and Education Fund
League of Neighborhoods, 139
Lears, Jackson, 392
Le Corbusier, 867
Lee, K. W., 1309
Lee, Robert E., 845
Lee, Spike, 1309
Lee, Wayne E., 1272, 1285
Lees, Loretta, 1558
Lefebvre, Henri, 316, 350, 1476
Legal Defense and Education Fund (LDF), 1445–1446, 1450

Leisler's Rebellion, 22, 29
leisure centers, suburbs as, 788–789
Lemlich, Clara, 253, 1529
Lenape people, 157
L'Enfant, Pierre Charles, 885, 996, 1002–1003
Lennon, John, 1232
Leonard, Buck, 370
Lepler, Jessica, 53
lesbian, gay, bisexual, transgender and queer (LGBTQ)
    populations, **665–684**. *See also* HIV/AIDS
    epidemic
  American Psychiatric Association's classification of,
    671, 680n3
  Asian American suburban culture and, 1498–1499
  Bowers v. Hardwick case, 676
  during Bush, G. H. W., administration, 677
  child custody for, 671–672
  during Clinton administration, 677
  Daughters of Bilitis, 668
  early publications by, 668
  economic class and, 673–675
  electoral politics of, 671–673
  under ENDA, 678
  under Executive Order 10450, 666
  in federal government, restrictions of, 666
  in films, 666
  GAA, 671
  Gay Liberation Movement, 140–141, 668–671, 1283
  gender expression and, 673–675
  GLF, 669–670
  homonationalism, 678
  homophile movement for, 667–668
  under Immigration and Nationality Act, 666
  Lavender Scare, 666–667
  Lawrence v. Texas case, 677
  legal successes of, 671–673
  lesbian feminism, 668–671
  marriage rights, 677–678
  Mattachine Society, 667–668
  in military, 666, 677–678
  in New Left, 668–671
  New Right response to, 672
  nightlife for, 1196–1197
  normativity of sexuality for, 677–678
  "pink-washing," 678
  police harassment of, 1197
  political activism of, 669, 671–673, 672f, 674
  postwar context for, 665
  as public school teachers, 666–667
  race and, 673–675
  under Reagan, R., 677
  rioting by, for civil rights, 1283
  Romer v. Evans case, 677
  in San Francisco, 668–669
  SIR group, 670

Stonewall riots, 669
  "straight state" response to, 665–668
  in suburbs, 1470–1471, 1488n79
  urban neighborhoods for, 674
  urban tourism for, 362–363
Lescaze, William, 868
Leslie, Stuart W., 349
Lessoff, Alan, 129
"Letter from Birmingham Jail" (King, M. L., Jr.),
    1405–1406, 1452
Leuchtenburg, William E., 200, 215, 240
Levenstein, Lisa, 827
Levi, Julian, 344
Levine, Peter, 379
Levine Museum of the New South, 82
Levitt, Alfred, 813
Levitt, Arthur, 1376
Levitt, William, 813, 908, 1018, 1458–1459
Levittowns, 908, 1128, 1458
  housing segregation in, 1376
  political life in, 1465–1466
  race riots in, 1466
Levy, Peter, 1411
Lewis, Jan, 815
Lewis, John, 1403
Lewis, John L., 203, 235–236, 247n62, 262, 276
Lewis, Oscar, 1144
Lewis, Robert, 796, 1458
Lewis, Sinclair, 874
LGBTQ populations. *See* lesbian, gay, bisexual,
    transgender and queer populations
LHAs. *See* local housing authorities
LHPA. *See* Ladies' Health Protective Association
Lianlian Lin, 1514n39
liberalism. *See also* Cold War liberalism;
    neoliberalization; rollout liberalization; Vital
    Center Liberalism
  rights, 1449–1451
  in universities and colleges, 343–347
  urban, machine politics and, 124, 343–347
  welfare, 1449–1451
"liberty tree," 30
Libeskind, Daniel, 873–874
libraries, in early seaport cities, 28
licensed prostitution, origins of, 459n74
Lichtenstein, Nelson, 240
Lie, John, 1315
Light, Ivan, 1313
light bulbs, creation of, 61
light rail transit (LRT) systems, 944–945
LIHTC. *See* Low Income Housing Tax Credit
Lillard, Joe, 373
liminal space, racial discrimination and, 1399
Limited Nuclear Test Ban Treaty, 1039
Lin, Justin, 1508

Lincoln, Abraham, 208, 238, 1273, 1276
  Emancipation Proclamation, 1294
Lindsay, John, 400, 1159, 1170n33
Linklater, Richard, 346
Lippmann, Walter, 189
literature, as popular culture, 210–211
Little, Joanne, 671
Little Ice Age, 17n24
Little Red Songbook, 254
"Little Richard." *See* Penniman, Richard "Little Richard"
Little Saigon, California
  cultural institutions in, 776
  early community spaces in, 773–774
  electoral successes of, 777–778
  expansion of, 774–776
  faith-based organizations in, 772–773
  Ho Chi Minh City and, 778
  H. O. people in, 778–779
  in mainstream media, 779
  music culture in, 776
  in Orange County, 772–779
  political activism in, 776–778
  population of, 770–771, 775
  as Special Tourist Zone, 775
  Vietnamese-owned businesses in, 775–776
  Vietnam War refugees in, 771–773
"Little Steel," 262
Little Village Environmental Justice Organization, 1023
Litwack, Leon F., 582
Living Newspapers, 230
living wages, 187
LL Cool J, 1256
Lloyd, Earl, 377
Lloyd-LaFollette Act, US (1912), 273
local housing authorities (LHAs), 821
Lochner v. New York, 180, 256
Locke, John, 22, 1339
Logan, William, 431
Logue, Edward, 134, 1534
Lo Hey, 1299. *See also* anti-Chinese massacre
loitering laws, 1353, 1357–1358
Lomasney, Martin, 120, 123
Lomax, Alan, 1206
Lomax, Louis, 1423
Lomax, Michael, 380
London, England, 21
Long, Huey, 209, 261
Longfellow, Julia D., 940
Long Gilded Age, 267
Long Quai, 1299. *See also* anti-Chinese massacre
Long Strike of 1875, 624
Looby, Z. Alexander, 1426
Looking Backward (Bellamy, E.), 882
looting, 1282
Lorde, Audre, 674

Los Angeles, California. *See also* Japanese resettlement
  Asian American political movements in, 749
  Chinese immigrants in, 1296–1297
  Korean-American experience in, 1307–1311, 1313–1314
  Latino urbanism in, 699–701
  lynching in, 1296–1297
  Native Americans in, 691
  1992 riots in, 1283–1284, 1304–1314
  public health nursing programs in, 181
  uprisings in, 144
  urban redevelopment in, 135, 143–144
  Watts riots, 1282
  as world city, 111, 143
  Zoot Suit riots in, 1323
Losing Ground (Murray, C.), 1153–1154
Lotchin, Roger, 349
Lott, Marilyn, 1402
lotteries, state, 388–390
  banning of, 388
  expansion of, 401
  under Indian Game Regulatory Act, 401
  in Louisiana, 389
  national adoption of, 399–400
  technical purpose of, 400
Lou, Herbert, 1346
Lou, Raymond, 1296
Louis, Joe, 212, 370, 394
Louisiana. *See also specific cities*
  lotteries in, 389
Louisiana Purchase, 1109
  cotton production after, 45
Lovejoy, Elijah, 1273
Loving v. Virginia, 732
Low, Setha, 1470
Lowell, Francis Cabot, 46, 87, 89
Lowell, Massachusetts
  during Civil War, 88
  as company town, 86–88
  cotton famine in, 88
  cotton mills in, 88f
  cotton production in, 46, 46f, 88f
  during Great Depression, 88
  textile production in, 88–89
  urban national park in, 88
Lowell Scientific School, 341
Lowen, Rebecca, 349
Low Income Housing Tax Credit (LIHTC), 818, 824
LSD use, 470–472
Lubove, Roy, 795
Luciano, Charles "Lucky," 446
Luckman, Charles, 869
Luna, Tristán de, 7
Lunceford, Jimmie, 573, 1215
Lung-Aman, Willow, 1503

Luper, Clara, 1416
Luytens, Edwin, 639
lyceum associations, 1191
Lyles, Aubrey, 573
lynch mobs, 1272, 1274–1275, 1277–1280
  against African Americans, 1277–1279
  anti-lynching movements, 1278
  in Chicago, 1279
  against Chinese, 1296–1297
  Ku Klux Klan and, 1277
  in Los Angeles, 1296–1297
  in Northern states, 1278–1279
  in the South, 1278
Lyons, Clare A., 432
Lyson, Thomas A., 600

Mabila (chiefdom), 10, 12
MacChesney, Nathan William, 642
MacDonald, Thomas, 960, 969–971
machine politics, 117–121
  activist women in, 125
  alternatives to, 123–126
  anti-machine organizations, 121
  business interests and, 118–119
  Catholics in, 123–124
  challenges to, 123–126
  in Chicago, 126–127
  after Civil War, 120
  definition of, 121
  within Democratic Party, 119–120,
    126–127
  exclusionary practices of, 127
  gambling industry and, 393–395
  during Gilded Age, 120–121
  immigrants' role in, 123
  labor unions and, 124–125
  under New Deal, 125
  during Progressive Era, 123–125
  public sector unions and, 272
  religious conflicts and, 118–119
  Tammany Hall and, 119–121
  urbanization as influence on, 118
  urban liberalism and, 124
  urban populations and, 118
  workingmen's movement, 119
  WPA and, 126
Mack, Julian, 1341
MacKaye, Benton, 906
madams, in brothels, 441
Madonna, 1236–1237
Magnuson, Warren G., 543
Magnuson Act, US (1943), 543
Magruder, John B., 851
Mahler, Sarah, 1473
Mahool, J. Barry, 1522

Mai Cong, 773–774
Maier, Pauline, 31
Mailer, Norman, 1217
Maine Liquor Law, 412
mainstream environmental movements, 1022
maize, as agricultural crop, during Mississippi period, 6.
    See also corn
Majewski, John, 959
major league baseball
  African Americans in, 370
  attendance growth for, 372
  Black Sox scandal and, 396
  classic ballpark era, 369
  development of, 369
  expansion teams in, 371
  Federal League and, 369–370
  franchise relocations, 371
  during the Great Depression, 370
  integration of, 370
  during interwar years, 370
  NNL and, 370
  players unions in, 371–372
  publicly-financed ballparks, 371
  racial segregation in, 370
  "retro fields," 371
  salary increases in, 372
  television contracts for, 371
  after World War II, 371
Making the Second Ghetto (Hirsch), 1143
malaria, 23
Malcher, Fritz, 968
males
  as prostitutes, 430
  suburban experiences for, 787
Mallon, Mary, 1054, 1097
Mallory, Shepard, 850
Manfredi, Christopher, 1343
Mann, Horace, 1175–1177, 1179–1180
Manning, Timothy, 629
manufacturing company towns, 89
manufacturing employment, in postindustrial service
    economies, 308–311
manumission societies, 161
Mapp, Dollree, 399
Mapplethorpe, Robert, 674
Mapp v. Ohio, 399
maquiladoras, 108, 111
Marcantonio, Vito, 716
Marchand, Yves, 334
March on the Pentagon, 1438
March on Washington (1965), 729n21
March on Washington Movement (MOWM),
    1374–1375, 1445
Marcus, Greil, 1234, 1240
Marcuse, Herbert, 1443

marijuana use, 469
  legalization of, 473
Markel, Howard, 1050, 1052
market societies, 39–45
  slavery-based, 40
Marley, Bob, 1234
marriage rates, during the Great Depression, 202
marriage rights, for LGBTQ populations, 677–678
Marsalis, Branford, 1224
Marsalis, Ellis, 1224
Marsalis, Wynton, 1224–1225
Marsh, Benjamin, 1517–1518
Marsh, John, Jr., 141
Marsh, Margaret, 796
Marshall, George Preston, 373
Marshall, Thurgood, 644, 734, 1435, 1445
Martin, Emma, 596–597
Martin Chuzzlewit (Dickens), 42
Martínez, Elizabeth, 733
Martinez Alier, Juan, 1022
Mason, Louis C., Jr., 362
Massachusetts. *See also specific cities*
  founding of cities in, ideological forces in, 22
  public authorities in, 286
Massachusetts Bay Colony, 70
Massey, Douglas, 563, 648–649
mass production
  through assembly lines, 60, 65–66
  chemical industries and, 66–67
  electrical grid development and, 66–67
  of furniture, 67
  industrialization through, 66–67
  labor unions and, 67
  origins of, 66–67
  reorganization of, 67
mass transit, **933–949**. *See also* public transportation;
   specific cities
  automobile use influenced by, 941–942, 971, 975–976
  buses, 941–942
  cable cars, 936–937
  conceptual development of, 933–934
  decline of, 940–942
  electricity in, 937–940
  elevated railroads, 936
  federal funding of, 942–945
  ferry boats, 934–935
  historical development of, 933–934
  horsecars, 935–937
  during Jim Crow era, 940
  jitneys, 941
  LRT systems, 944–945
  in 19th century, 934–935
  omnibuses, 934–935
  public ownership of, 943
  ridership stability for, 942–945

  in San Francisco, 943–944, 946
  sexual harassment on, 940
  through steam power, 936
  streetcars, 793, 937–940
  in 20th century, 940–942
  under UMTA, 943–944
  underground railways, 938
  in Washington DC, 943–944
  during World War II, 942
Masuda, Minn, 745
Mather, Cotton, 1050, 1057
Mathers, Marshall (Eminem), 1262
Mathewson, Christy, 369
Matlovich, Leonard, 673
Matson, Cathy, 32
Matsumoto, Valerie, 762
Mattachine Society, 667–668
Matthew, Thomas, 519
Matthews, Robert, 1112–1113
Mattson, Kevin, 129
Maurer, Katharine, 536
May Act, US, 447
Mayer, Holly A., 432
Mayhew, Jonathan, 1108
Mayo, Elton, 250
mayors. *See* city mayors
Mays, Willie, 370
Maytag, Elmer, 96
Maytag, Frederick, 95–96
McAneny, George, 1518
McCain, Franklin, 1402, 1416–1417
McCain, John, 778
McCammack, Brian, 1025
McCarran-Walter Act, US (1952), 543, 547
McCarthur, Douglas, 259
McCarthy, Charles, 186
McCarthy, Eugene, 1438
McCarthy, Joseph, 628
McCarthyism, 1442
McCartin, Joseph, 280–281
McCartney, Paul, 1236
McCauley, Leora, 1399
McCausland, John, 849
McClintock, Miller, 979
McCormick, Robert, 865
McCullough, David, 1073
McCurry, Stephanie, 1277
McDonald, Charles, 396
McDonald, Mike, 388–390
McDonald, Terence, 128
McDougal, Alexander, 431
McDowell, Mary, 1015
McGinnis, George, 377
McGirr, Lisa, 422, 424, 1465
McGovern, George, 1156, 1159

McKay, Claude, 393, 576–577
McKay, Henry D., 1333
McKee, Guian, 349
McKelvey, Blake, 1073
McKenzie, Evan, 1475
McKenzie, Roderick D., 795
McKim, Charles Follen, 886, 1002
McKinistry, Marshal, 437
McKinley, William, 187, 249, 510
McKissick, Jocelyn, 1404–1405
McLaughlin, Allan J., 512
McLaughlin, Hugh, 119
McLaughlin, Malcolm, 1282, 1285
McManes, Jim, 967
McMansions, 145
McMechen, George W. F., 1521
McMillan, James, 885–887, 1002
McMillan Plan, for Washington DC, 885–887
    streets, roads, and highways in, 952
McMurty, George Gibson, 90
McNair, Denise, 1408
McNeal, A. Clement, 583
McNeil, Joseph, 1402, 1416–1417
McNeur, Catherine, 54, 1041
McPherson, Aimee Semple, 1124–1125, 1127
McPherson, Carlos, 689
McPherson, Charles A., 1396–1397
McShane, Clay, 935, 939, 945, 959, 966
McSweeney, Edward F., 510–511
MDMA use, 470–472
M'Donald, Preston, 852
The M'Donalds; or, the Ashes of Southern Homes: A Tale of
    Sherman's March (Peck, W. H.), 852
Meany, George, 629
Meat Inspection Act, US (1906), 185
meatpacking company towns, 89, 96–97
    labor strikes in, 97
mechanization, in postindustrial service economies, 310
Medicaid program, expansion of, 1154
Medicare program, expansion of, 1154
Medieval Warm Period, 17n24
Meffre, Romain, 334
Meinig, D. W., 959
Mellon, Andrew, 259
Mellon, Richard King, 870
Melosi, Martin, 930, 1041, 1074
Melton, A. P., 91
memorial museums
    Confederate monuments and, 82
    in urban American South, 81–82
Memphis, Tennessee
    King, M. L., Jr., in, 1411
    Sanitation Strike of 1968, 1411
    slavery in, 159
Mencken, H. L., 422, 1126

Menlo Park, California, 98
Mergen, Bernard, 1073
Merton, Robert, 127
Mesoamerica, 684–685
Metheny, Pat, 1223
Metropolis of Tomorrow (Ferriss), 867
metropolitanism, 1468–1470
metropolitanization, 599–601
The Metropolitan Revolution (Katz, B., and Bradley, J.), 145
Metropolitan Statistical Area (MSA), 971
Mettler, Suzanne, 241
Metzenbaum, James F., 1519
Mexican American immigrants, 486
    African Americans and, 732–735
    BPP and, 734–735
    Bracero Program, 499, 541–542, 551–552
    Brown Berets and, 734–735
    food styles influenced by, 1094
    "Operation Wetback" and, 542
    in PPC, 731, 738–739
    Puerto Ricans compared to, 717–718
    racial categorization of, in US censuses, 733
    rioting against, 1275
    in SNCC, 733–734
    in street gangs, 1321–1323, 1332
    UFW and, 734–735
    Zoot Suit riots, 499, 1323
Mexico
    African Americans and, 731
    border crossings from, Latino urbanism through,
        698–700
    maquiladoras in, 108, 111
    Revolution of 1910 in, 698–699
    Spanish-American War and, 699
    Teotihuacán, 684–685, 696
    US war with, 40
Meyer, John, 944
Meyer, Sabine N., 423
Meyer, William, 1073
Mezei, Ignatz, 518
MIA. See Montgomery Improvement Association
Miami, Florida
    Cuban Americans in, 737–738
    Latino urbanism in, 705
miasma theory
    City Beautiful movement and, 880–881
    environmental pollution and, 1029–1031
    urban planning and, 903–904
micos (chiefs/chieftainess), 2
middle-class
    black, development of, 75
    early development of, 50
    gentrification by, 1564–1565
    in postindustrial service economies, 313
    prostitution and, 434

in suburbs, 790
in temperance movement, 411
in universities and colleges, 340
middle Mississippi period
American Bottoms during, 5
chiefdoms in, 5–8
drought during, 7
Middle World, 2
migration patterns. *See also* Great Migration; white migration
for Chinese, in Los Angeles, 1296–1297
during the Great Depression, 205–207
for Native Americans, to urban environments, 687–690
Mikan, George, 377
Miles, Tiya, 164, 168n31
military. *See also* Army
Continental Army, 431–432
Don't Ask, Don't Tell policy, 677
LGBTQ in, 666, 677–678
Native Americans in, 691
prostitution and, 445, 459n67
public authorities and, 298
spending, in postindustrial service economies, 312
military veterans
"Bonus Army" camps, 259
protest marches by, 259
Milk, Harvey, 133, 140–141, 672
Milkman, Ruth, 332
Miller, Donald L., 68
Miller, Flournoy, 573
Miller, Kerby, 630
Miller, Margaret, 432
Miller, Marvin, 372, 379
Miller, Zane, 796
Millet, Kate, 450, 1452
Milliken v. Bradley, 1377
Mills, C. Wright, 316, 1443
Mills, David, 1259
Mills, Ethel, 689
Mills, Joseph, 689
Minaj, Nicki, 1263
Miner, Craig, 53
Mingus, Charles, 1217, 1220
"minimum houses," 1459
Minimum Wage Law, US (1961), 1144
mining. *See* coal-mining company towns; copper mining company towns
Mink, Gwendolyn, 241
Min Song, 1314–1315
Miranda, Lin-Manuel, 707
Miranda v. Arizona, 1450
Misa, Thomas, 68
Mises, Ludwig von, 347
misogyny, in rap music, 1257, 1262

missionary societies, 1111
missions. *See* Spanish missions
Mississippi, racial segregation in, 1407–1408
NAACP in, 1407
Mississippi period/world, **1–21**
archaeological evidence of, 4
Cahokia, 6–5
chiefdoms, 4–11, 16n2
corn agriculture during, 6
cosmos concept, 2–3
disease in, introduction of, 11
drought during, 17n24
early, 4
elite authorities in, 6
European colonists during, 4–5, 11
late, 7–13
during Little Ice Age, 17n24
maize agriculture during, 6
during Medieval Warm Period, 17n24
middle, 5–7
political iconography during, 2
religious iconography during, 2
shatter zone in, 11
source material on, 14–15
war iconography during, 2
Mitchell, Arthur, 575
Mitchell, Bobby, 373
Mitchell, John, 293
Mitchell, Joni, 1222, 1234
Mitchell, MacNeil, 304n33
Mitchell, Margaret, 73, 212
Mitchell-Lama program, 304n33
mixed economies, in chiefdoms, 6
mixed-use space, in central business districts, 169
mob killings, 1277
Model A automobile, 67
Model Cities program, 811, 834–835, 1145, 1535
model minority, Asian Americans as, 766, 1497
Model Penal Code, 1342–1343
Model T automobile, 65
Modern Civic Art; or, The City Made Beautiful (Robinson, C. M.), 887
modern environmentalism movements, 1035–1041
Modern Housing (Bauer), 818–819
modernist theory, skyscrapers in, 868–869
Moehring, Eugene P., 363
Mohl, Raymond, 960
Moley, Raymond, 228
Molly Maguires, 624
Molony, Joseph P., 628
Molotch, Andrew, 333
Mondale, Walter, 1156
Mongkorn, Kaiswai, 1499–
Monk, Thelonious, 1215
Monks Mound, in Cahokia, 4

monopolistic capitalism, 185
Monroe, Sarah, 48
Monroe Doctrine, 187
Monterey Park, California, 1502–1503
Montgomery, David, 266, 424, 630
Montgomery bus boycott, 77, 940
    Boynton v. Virginia, 1403
    Browder v. Gayle, 1400–1401
    King, M. L., Jr., and, 1400
    liminal space and, 1399
    NAACP and, 1399
Montgomery Improvement Association (MIA), 1400
Moody, Dwight, 1115
Moody's rating agencies, 293
Mooney, Walter D., 891
Moore, Annie, 510
Moore, Cecil, 1326
Moore, Charles, 882
Moore, Joan, 1325
Moore, Roy, 81
Moore, William, 1408
Moorefield, Storey, 643–644
Moraga, Cherríe, 674
Morales, Iris, 721
moral geography, 357
morality
    of gambling industry, 390–391
    moral turpitude clauses, 514
    prostitution and, 443
    rioting and, as regulatory strategy, 1271
moral obligation bonds, 293
The Moral Order of a Suburb (Baumgartner), 1472
moral poverty, 1344
moral reform movements, nightlife and, 1194–1196
moral turpitude clauses, 514
Mordin, Martha, 1462–1463
Moreno, Luisa, 734
Morgan, Robin, 674
Morone, James, 422, 424
Morrill Land Grant Acts, US (1862), 341
Morris, Butch, 1219
Morris, Charles S., 214
Morrisette, Alanis, 1237
Morrison, Gayle, 773–774
Morton, Jelly Roll, 1206, 1209–1210
Moscone, George, 672
Moses, Robert, 106, 134–135, 146, 286, 969–971, 1403,
    1535, 1558
    park design by, 1005–1006
Mothers' Aid, 1145
Motley, Marion, 373
Motor Vehicle Air Pollution Act, US (1965), 972
Mound 72, in Cahokia, 4
Moundville (chiefdom), 5–6
    elite priests in, 6

Mound B, 6
    social shifts in, 6
Mountain View, California, 98
movie theaters
    drive-in, 1197
    Nickelodeons, 1194
MOWM. See March on Washington Movement
Mowry, George, 191
Moynihan, Daniel Patrick, 341, 654, 661, 1146, 1159,
    1170n37, 1536
Mpa, Joseph, 1327
MSA. See Metropolitan Statistical Area
MTV. See Music Television
Mueller, Carol, 1282
Mugwump faction, of Republican Party, 180
Muhammad, Elijah Poole, 1127–1128
Mulberry site (chiefdom site), 8
Muller, Benjamin, 1397
Muller, Peter, 1468–1469
Muller v. Oregon, 180, 256
multiracial political alliances, 136
Mumford, Lewis, 793, 906, 957, 970, 1006, 1464
Munchow, Helen, 815
Muncy, Robyn, 191
Mundelein, George, 1126
municipal governments, public authorities and, 291–292
municipal housekeeping, 1015
    in City Beautiful movement, 893
    for sidewalks and city streets, 985
municipal housing, 798–817. See also home ownership;
        public housing
    in antebellum era, 802–803
    in apartment buildings, 805–806
    CDCs for, 645, 812
    during colonial period, 800
    contagious diseases in, 803–804
    design planning for, 801
    economic class and, 804
    under Federal Home Loan Bank Act, 809
    federal policy for, 808–812
    FHA and, 809–810
    during the Great Depression, 799, 808–809
    grid development for, 800
    HOLC and, 809
    home ownership goals, 799
    under Hoover, 809
    under Housing Act of 1949, 810
    housing developers and, 807–808
    industrialization of, 801
    land surveying for, 800
    markets for, 800
    mass production of, 801–802, 807–808
    NAACP response to, 812
    under New Deal programs, 799
    political purpose of, 804

public health and, 803–806
real estate industry and, 799–800
residential segregation in, 808
under Roosevelt, F. D., 809
row houses, 802–803
sanitation technology in, 803–805
suburbanization and, 808
in suburbs, 812–814
Supreme Court cases on, 808
tenements, 804, 806
under Wagner-Steagall Housing Act, 810
workingmen's associations and, 802–803
municipal ownership, economic progressivism and, 187
municipal reform
    anti-machine organizations, 121
    bossism and, growth of, 120
    in Boston, 123
    in Chicago, 122
    City Reform League and, 120
    National Municipal League and, 121–122
    through political consolidation, 126–127
    during Progressive Era, 122
    Republican Party and, 120
    under Roosevelt, F. D., 291
    Union Leagues and, 120–121
    Whig Party and, 120
municipal sanitary systems, 1029–1030
munitions production, in company towns, 89
Muñoz Marín, Luis, 717
muralismo movement, 701–702
Muro, Mark, 1476
Murphy, Michael J., 400
Murphy, Patrick V., 399
Murray, Charles, 1146, 1153–1154
Murray, David, 1219
Murray, Elizabeth, 25
Murray, Philip, 262, 628
museums
    as civic attractions, 989–990
    memorial, 81–82
music culture. See also hip-hop music; jazz music;
    ragtime and blues music; rap music; rock-and-roll
    music
    in Little Saigon, 776
Music Television (MTV), 1235, 1238, 1255
Muskie, Edmund, 927
Muste, A. J., 207
Musteites, 207
Mydans, Seth, 1300
Myer, Dillon, 759
Myers, Daisy, 1466
Myers, William, 1466
Myles, John, 1157
My Man Godfrey, 212
Myrdal, Gunnar, 1144

NAACP. See National Association for the Advancement
    of Colored People
NACC. See National Automobile Chamber of
    Commerce
NAFTA. See North American Free Trade Agreement
Nagourney, Adam, 1162
Naismith, James, 376
Nam Lộc Nguyễn, 773–774
NAPRCR. See National Association of Puerto Rican
    Civil Rights
Napster technology, 1239
Narayan, Uma, 1514n48
NASA. See National Aeronautics and Space
    Administration
Nasaw, David, 363
Nash, John, 787
Nash, Pat, 127
Nashville, Tennessee
    public segregation in, 77
    sit-in movement in, 1426
Nast, Thomas, 121, 1291
Natchez nation, 12–13
Natchez Trace trail, 949
National Aeronautics and Space Administration
    (NASA), 98
National Affordable Housing Act, US (1990), 836, 838
National Association for the Advancement of Colored
    People (NAACP), 189, 257, 1326, 1372–1376,
    1396, 1435
    LDF, 1445–1446, 1450
    in Mississippi, 1407
    Montgomery bus boycott and, 1399
    on municipal housing, 812
    sit-in movement and, 1402–1403, 1416, 1421, 1424
National Association of Colored Women, 75, 189, 190
National Association of Puerto Rican Civil Rights
    (NAPRCR), 720
National Automobile Chamber of Commerce (NACC),
    954–955
National Baptist Convention, 189
National Basketball Association (NBA), 377–378
National Basketball League (NBL), 376–378
National Board of Censorship, 1194
National Civic Federation, 251
National Civil Rights Museum, 82
National Conference on City Planning, 184
National Consumers League (NCL), 182
National Defense Housing Act, US, 833
National Federation of Federal Employees (NFFE), 274
National Flood Insurance Act, US (1968), 1070
National Football League (NFL), 372–374
National Forest systems, 1014
national historic landmarks
    Angel Island Immigration Station as, 537
    Statue of Liberty, 519

National Historic Preservation Act, US (1966), 360, 1566

National Hockey League (NHL)

  establishment of, 375

  expansion teams in, 375

  labor unions in, for players, 375–376

  salary caps in, 376

  television contracts for, 376

national immigration quotas

  abolishment of, 545–546

  at Ellis Island Immigration Station, 515–517

National Industrial Recovery act (NIRA), 200, 203

  coal-mining company towns under, 94

  nullification of, by Supreme Court, 236

  Puerto Ricans under, 715

  Section 7a, 235–236, 260

National Interstate and Defense Highway Act.
    See Highway Act

nationalism, among Puerto Ricans, 718, 723

Nationality Act, US (1965), 1329

National Labor Relations Act (NLRA), US (1935), 236,
    256, 261, 1449. See also Wagner Act

National League of Women Voters, 190

National Liberation Front (NLF), 1436

National Mall, in Washington DC, 1003

National Municipal League, 121–122, 183

National Negro Congress (NNC), 209, 264, 1373, 1377

National Organization of Women (NOW), 450

National Origins Act, US (1924), 627, 702

national origins quotas, abolishment of, 545–546

National Park systems, 1014

National Performance Review (NPR), 299, 306n51

National Prohibition Act. See Volstead Act

National Recovery Administration (NRA),
    233–234, 260

  Section 7a, 235–236

National Security Act, US (1947), 1442

National Urban League, 1372

National War Labor Board, 264–265

National Woman's Party, 189

National Women's Trade Union League (NWTUL), 182

Nation of Islam (NOI), 1127–1128, 1447

Native (Urban Areas) Act of 1923, South Africa, 641

Native Americans, **684–696**. See also chiefdoms; specific
    nations; specific societies; specific tribes

  academic scholarship on, in colleges and universities,
    693–695

  AIM and, 1448

  ancestry as evidence for freedom, 155

  Black Hawk War, 40

  during civil rights movement, 691

  college attendance for, 691–693

  educational access for, 691–693

  in film industry, 689

  in gambling industry, 693–694

  in military, 691

  in New England colonies, 686–687

  religion for, 1106–1108

  return to reservations for, 690

  rioting against, 1275

  roads and trails for, 949–950

  "second Native diaspora," 153

  as slaves, 156

  US wars against, 40

  in "Wild West" shows, 689

Native Americans, in urban environments

  Anasazi and, 685–686

  in Cahokia, 685. See also Cahokia

  Chetro Ketl, 685–686

  during colonial era, 686–687

  cultural organizations for, 691–692

  educational access for, 691–693

  in ethnic neighborhoods, 689

  Federal Bureau of Indian Affairs, 691

  in Los Angeles, 691

  in Mesoamerica, 684–685

  from 1900–1949, 687–691

  from 1950–1999, 691–694

  pre-Columbian era, 684–686

  of Pueblo peoples, 686

  in railroad industry, 688–689

  through Relocation Program, 691

  Seattle and, 687

  in Southwest region, 688

  Teotihuacán, 684–685

  urban migration of, 687–690

  during War on Poverty, 692

  during World War II, 690

Native Location Laws, South Africa, 641

Native Son (Wright, R.), 210

nativism, as response to immigration, 481–483, 487–489,
    496–497

natural disasters, urban tourism after, 363

Navajos, 155

NBA. See National Basketball Association

NBL. See National Basketball League

NCL. See National Consumers League

Nectow v. City of Cambridge, 1520

Needham, Andrew, 1042, 1073

Neglected Neighbors: Stories of Life in the Alleys, Tenements
    and Shanties of the National Capital (Weller, C., and
    Weller, E.), 1529

negro expansion areas, suburbanization and, 792–793

The Negro Motorist's Green Book, 1368–1369

Negro National League (NNL), 370

neighborhood activism. See also ghettoes and barrios

  anti-government emphasis of, 139–140

  against urban redevelopment, 137–140

neighborhood associations, for white ethnic populations

  in Detroit, 135–136

  in San Francisco, 140

neighborhoods. *See* Asian American neighborhoods; Harlem neighborhood; urban neighborhoods
Neighborhood Union, 182
neighborhood units, in suburbs, 792
Nelson, Gaylord, 1036
Nelson, Stevie, 1234
neo-conservatism, 1170n37
neoliberalization
    postindustrial cities and, 314–315
    public housing and, as political approach, 823–825
Neptune, Jessica, 473
Nettleton, Asahel, 410
Neumann, Tracy, 328, 333
Neutra, Richard J., 833
New Amsterdam. *See also* New York City
    recreation plans in, 21
    as slave port, 153–154
    slavery in, 154
Newark, New Jersey, riots in, 1282
New Deal, **225–248**. *See also specific programs*
    bank holidays as part of, 199–200, 227
    banking systems under, 228
    capitalism under, stabilization of, 237
    definition of, 225–226
    electric grid development under, 233
    under Emergency Banking Act, 227
    environmental movement and, 1016
    Fair Deal and, 226
    farmers' aid under, 230–233
    financial systems under, stabilization of, 227–228
    First, 227, 260
    GI Bill and, 226, 245n8
    globalization under, 105
    Great Society and, 226
    Great Society compared to, 1169n15
    immigrants' response to, 238–239
    immigration and, 498
    infrastructure programs in, 200
    investment systems under, 228
    labor strikes and, 236, 260–261
    labor under, 235–236, 259–261
    limitations of, 237–239
    machine politics under, 125
    municipal housing in, 799
    political coalition for, 226–227
    political legacy of, 237–239
    public authorities and, 286, 292–294, 303n24
    public housing under, 812
    public sector unions and, 275
    Puerto Ricans under, 715–716
    purpose of, 227
    redlining in, 1142
    as response to the Great Depression, 226–236
    Second, 227, 261–262
    securities markets under, 228

sewage treatment under, 926
Square Deal and, 225
unemployment relief under, 228–230
urban parks under, 1006
urban planning under, 906–907
urban renewal under, 1531–1532
New Democrats, 267, 1475
Newell, Margaret, 153–154
New England. *See also specific states*
    company towns in, 86–88
    Native Americans in, 686–687
New Federalism, 141–142
New Freedom platform, 186
New Industrial Union movement, 262–264
    Second New Deal, 262
New Left
    in anti-Vietnam War movement, 1443
    LGBTQ in, 668–671
    Vital Center Liberalism and, 1443
Newman, Harvey K., 364
"New Negro," 1371
"New Negro" movement, 1210
New Orleans, Louisiana
    bureaucrats in, 24
    after Civil War, 73
    climate change in, 1064–1065
    cotton production in, 45–46
    Creole community in, 1209
    diversity in, 80
    global trade in, 103–104
    les grands in, 24
    Hurricane Katrina in, 79, 363, 1071–1072
    jazz music in, 1209–1210, 1215
    les petits in, 24
    population of, 38, 60
    promotion of urban growth in, 21
    restaurants in, 1084
    sex markets in, 436
    slavery in, 154, 159
    urban tourism to, 360
    "Vieux Carée" in, 24
Newport, Rhode Island, as slave port, 156
New Public Management Movement, 298
New Republic, 188, 190
New Right, 645–647
    creation of, in 1960s, 1437
    election of Nixon, R., and, 1439, 1441
    LGBTQ and, 672
    in 1960s, foundations of, 1437, 1440, 1444
    Reagan and, 1440
    "silent majority" and, 1441, 1444–1445
New South, 73–76. *See also specific states*
    industrialization in, 76
    reconstruction of southern cities in, 73
    urbanization in, 76

newspapers. *See* black-owned newspapers; Living
     Newspapers
The New State (Follett), 125
Newton, Huey, 670, 745, 1443. *See also* Black Panther
     Party
Newton, Iowa, 95–96
New Urbanism, 913, 1473, 1478*f*
     City Beautiful movement and, 895
     "Smart Growth" movement and, 1477–1478
New York (state). *See also specific cities*
     Bacon's Rebellion in, 22
     Ellis Island Immigration Station, 488, 508–520
     immigration in, 482
     Iroquois people evicted from, 40
     Port Authority of New York, 286–287, 293–295,
          304n27, 307
     public authorities in, 286–287, 293–295, 304n27,
          304n33
     rap music beginnings in, 1253–1255
New York City
     African American neighborhoods in, 257.
          See also Harlem neighborhood
     Asian American political movements in, 749
     bankruptcy of, 109, 142, 279, 328
     central business districts in, 169–170, 173
     Central Park, 902, 988–989, 996–1001,
          1004–1006, 1014
     Chinese neighborhoods in, 657–658
     cholera outbreak in, 1056
     cotton production in, 45–46
     department stores in, 170
     draft riots in, 882, 1276–1277
     early grid development of, 800
     early populations of, 37–38
     electrical grid development in, 62
     as epicenter of early US commerce, 43
     ferry boats in, 934
     Five Points neighborhood, 50
     gambling houses in, 388
     gentrification of, 110
     as global cultural capital, 102
     horsecars in, 935
     jazz music in, 1210
     Jewish neighborhoods in, 656–659, 657*f*
     Korean-Americans in, 1308
     Leisler's Rebellion, 22, 29
     manufacturing in, 306–307
     New York Metropolitan Health Act, 1056
     occupation during Revolutionary era, 31
     off-track betting in, 400
     omnibuses in, 934
     as postindustrial city, 315
     private home construction in, 64
     Prospect Park, 998–1000
     public buildings in, 28

     public dining in, 1083
     public housing in, 823
     public schools in, 1174–1176, 1179*f*, 1182
     restaurants in, 1083
     Rockefeller Center, 868, 1533
     service economies in, 306–307
     skyscrapers in, 861–864
     as slave port, 153–154
     slavery-based markets in, 40
     Tammany Hall, 119–121
     Times Square, 1193, 1200
     Triangle Shirtwaist factory fire in, 182, 253, 253*f*,
          256, 1518
     urban redevelopment in, 142–143
     urban tourism to, 354–357
     urban zoning laws in, 1032
     Women's Municipal League, 125
     as world city, 111
     World Trade Center in, 871, 873–875
     zoning laws in, 1517–1519
New York City Housing Authority (NYCHA), 823
New York Metropolitan Health Act (1866), 1056
New York Society for the Suppression of Gambling, 388
New York State Tenement Act of 1901, 1519
New York v. Miln, 1351
NFFE. *See* National Federation of Federal Employees
NFL. *See* National Football League
NHL. *See* National Hockey League
Nichols, Jesse Clyde, 793, 807
Nickerson, Michelle, 1465
Nicolaides, Becky, 796, 1495, 1504
Niggaz With Attitude (NWA), 1257
Night Comes to the Cumberlands (Caudill), 95
Nightengale, Carl, 104
nightlife, **1189–1206**
     before 1830, 1189–1190
     in African American neighborhoods, 1196
     AIDS epidemic and, 1199
     amusement parks, 1198
     in arts and entertainment districts, 1199–1200
     cabarets, 1195
     casinos, 1200
     discotheques, 1199
     from 1830–1880, 1190–1192
     from 1880–1920, 1192–1195
     electric lighting as influence on, 1193
     fraternal organizations and, 1193
     gay rights movement, 1199
     during the Great Depression, 1197
     holidays and, 1190–1191
     interracial clubs, 1196
     jazz music and, 1197–1198
     in Las Vegas, 1200
     late working hours as influence on, 1192–1193
     LGBTQ and, 1196–1197

lyceum associations, 1191
mixed-gender socializing, 1193–1194, 1197
moral reform movement and, 1194–1196
Nickelodeons, 1194
from 1933–1965, 1196–1198
from 1965–2018, 1198–1199
performing arts centers, 1199
during prohibition, 1195–1196
prostitution and, 1189, 1194–1195
public dancing, 1195
racial segregation in clubs, 1198
rock-and-roll music and, 1198–1199
in the South, 1192
suburbanization and, 1197
taverns and saloons, 1189–1190, 1193
during temperance movement, 1190
theaters, 1190–1192, 1194, 1197, 1200
in Times Square, 1193, 1200
in urban economies, 1199–1201
vice commissions, 1194
in the West, 1192
Nikkei generation, of Japanese Americans, 757–759, 766
Niles, Hezekiah, 44
NIMBY protests. *See* "Not in My Backyard" protests
1960s, urban America during, **1435–1457**. *See also* Black
    Freedom movement; civil rights; civil rights
    movement; Great Society; Vietnam War; War on
    Poverty; *specific legislation; specific liberation
    movements; specific presidents*
anti-authoritarianism during, 1451–1454
anti-Vietnam War movement during, 744, 750–752,
    1438–1441
"baby boom" generation and, 1441
Civil Rights Act (1964), 77, 1408–1409, 1437,
    1449–1450
cultural assimilation during, 1451–1452
narrative of, 1435–1441
New Right during, foundations of, 1437, 1440, 1444
1968 as year of violence, 1438–1439
1968 Democratic National Convention, 1438–1439
political radicalism during, 1436, 1439–1441
presidential elections in, 1436
rights liberalism, 1449–1451
SDS and, 1436, 1440, 1443
sociocultural context for, 1435–1436
Vital Center Liberalism, 1441–1445
Voting Rights Act (1965), 77, 718, 722–723,
    1408–1409, 1437
Weathermen and, 1440
welfare liberalism, 1449–1451
1992 riots, in Los Angeles, **1304–1319**
anti-black racism and, 1305
culture of poverty and, 1305–1306
Harlins' death and, 1308–1309
Korean-Americans during, 1304, 1306–1314

media coverage of, 1305–1306, 1308, 1312
police brutality as foundation for, 1305–1306
politicization of, 1305–1306
property damage costs, 1310
root causes of, 1305–1306
as Sai-I-Gu, 1309–1312
social context for, 1304–1306
social legacy after, 1310–1313
Soon Ja Du and, 1308–1309
War on Poverty and, 1306
Nineteenth Amendment, 189, 257, 419–420, 422, 1195
NIRA. *See* National Industrial Recovery act
Nisei generation, of Japanese Americans, 765
Nix, Robert N. C., Sr., 575
Nixon, E. D., 1400
Nixon, Richard, 107–108, 226, 240, 293, 614, 645–646,
    1159, 1343, 1444
election of, 1439
housing policies under, 834–835, 838, 1475
Kitchen Debates and, 1463
New Federalism under, 141–142
vagrancy laws under, 1358
NLF. *See* National Liberation Front
NLRA. *See* National Labor Relations Act
NNC. *See* National Negro Congress
NNL. *See* Negro National League
Noble, Elaine, 672
No Child Left Behind Act, US (2001), 1183
Noguchi, Isamu, 871
NOI. *See* Nation of Islam
Nolen, John, 184, 189
Norfolk, Virgina, 157
Norris, Frank, 190
Norris, Isaac, Jr., 27–28
Norris, John, 27–28
Norris-LaGuardia Act, US (1932), 203, 256
North America. *See* Central America; Mexico; United
    States
North American Free Trade Agreement (NAFTA), 111
North Carolina. *See also specific cities*
    cotton mills in, 61
North Carolina Mutual Insurance Company, 75
Northern states. *See also* urban North; *specific states*
    colonialism in, 71
    lynch mobs in, 1278–1279
    racial segregation in, 75, 78–79
    vagrancy laws in, 1352
Northwest Laundry v. Des Moines, 183
Northwest Ordinance of 1787, US, 949
Norton, Peter, 941, 945
"Not in My Backyard" (NIMBY) protests, 1039
    against urban planning, 913, 1474
Novak, Michael, 654
Novak, Robert, 1170n27
NOW. *See* National Organization of Women

NPR. *See* National Performance Review
NRA. *See* National Recovery Administration
nuclear proliferation, 1443
numbers games, 392–393
Nuremberg Trials, 226
NWA. *See* Niggaz With Attitude
NWTUL. *See* National Women's Trade Union League
NYCHA. *See* New York City Housing Authority
Nye, David, 939, 946

Obama, Barack, 648, 837, 1411
Object Orange (Williams, A.), 330
O'Brien, Ambrose, 375
O'Brien, Michael J., 375
O'Connell, James, 625
O'Connor, Alice, 1160
O'Connor, Ellen Hartigan, 32
Odem, Mary, 1346
O'Dwyer, William, 397–398
OECD. *See* Organisation for Economic Co-operation
    and Development
Oertel, Max, 656
Oestreicher, Richard, 128
office space, in skyscrapers, 860–861
off-track betting
    for horse racing, 390, 394, 399–401
    legalization of, 394, 399–401
    in New York City, 400
Ogle, Maureen, 930
Oglethorpe, James, 155, 995
Oh, Angela, 1312–1314
Ohlin, Lloyd, 1324
O'Keefe, Georgia, 875
Okrent, Daniel, 424
Olasky, Marvin, 1161
Olds, Ransom, 968
Olmsted, Frederick Law, 787, 882–883, 968
    Central Park and, 902, 988–989, 996–1001, 1014
    Columbian Exposition and, 883–884
    park designs by, 996–1004, 1008
    Prospect Park and, 998–1000
    suburban planning design by, 902
    Washington DC park system and, 1001–1004
Olmsted, Frederick Law, Jr., 807, 886, 892, 895, 905,
    1002–1004
Olmsted, John Charles, 1004, 1009
Olmsted, Kathryn, 215
O'Mara, Margaret Pugh, 107, 316, 349
Omnibus Crime Control and Safe Streets Act, US
    (1968), 1328
omnibuses, 934–935
O'Neill, John, 626
open urban spaces, preservation of, 1018–1019
"Operation Wetback," 542
opiate consumption

by Chinese Americans, 465–466
    legal ordinances for regulation of, 466
    in San Francisco, 466
opium trade, in China, 48
O'Ree, Willie, 375
Orenstein, Dara, 105–106
Orfield, Myron, 1469, 1476–1477
"Organic City," 904–906, 908–909
Organisation for Economic Co-operation and
    Development (OECD), 1163–1166, 1165*t*
Organization Man (Whyte), 1462, 1471
organized crime
    drug subcultures and, 472
    gambling industry and, involvement in, 388, 393–394,
        395*f*, 398–399
    mob killings, 1277
    during prohibition movement, 421
    prostitution and, 446
Oriard, Michael, 379
Orsi, Jared, 1073
Orsi, Robert, 1106, 1123
Osborne, David, 298
Osman, Suleiman, 146
O'Sullivan, Timothy, 851
The Other America (Harrington), 1144
Otis, Elisha Graves, 64
Out of the Barrio (Chávez, L.), 723–724
Out of This Furnace (Bell, T.), 90
overlay districts, 1525
Owens, Jesse, 212, 370

Pace, David, 1094
Padoongpatt, Mark, 1473*f*
Paige, Satchel, 370
Palermo, Blinky, 396
Palermo Protocol, 452
palliative urban planning, 329
Palmer, Walter, 1326
Panama Canal Zone, 296–297
Panic of 1837, 40, 48–49, 57n38
Pantoja, Antonia, 719–720
"paper cities," 40
parades, 987
paramount chiefdoms, 2
Pardo, Juan, 7–10
parens patriae tradition, 1342–1344
Park, Edward, 1312–1313
Park, Robert, 815, 1321
Parker, Abraham, 437
Parker, Charlie, 1215, 1218, 1223
Parkhurst, Charles, 390
parkomania trend, 1000
parks, in urban settings, **995–1012**. *See also* National
    Park systems
    automobiles in, 1004–1006

in Boston, 1000–1001, 1007
in Buffalo, 999–1000
Central Park, 996–1001, 1004–1006
in Chicago, 1000, 1007
in City Beautiful movement, 881–883, 888
civic attractions in, 989–990
early, 995–996
European influences on, 996
Fairmount Gardens, 995–996, 998
landscape architects for, 1001
in Lowell, Massachusetts, 88
Moses and, 1005–1006
museums in, 989–990
national mall, in Washington DC, 1003
under New Deal, 1006
in new Millennium, 1006–1007
in New York City, 996–1001, 1004–1006
Olmsted, F. L., and, 996–1004, 1008
parkomania trend, 1000
parkways in, 1004–1006
picturesque, 988–990
in *Plan of Chicago*, 1004–1005
Prospect Park, 998–1000
public-private partnerships for, 1008
public promotion of, 996
Riis on, 1277
in seaport cities, 995–996
under Small Parks Act, 1277
in 20th century, 1004–1006
in urban planning, 905
urban renewal and, 1008
Vaux and, 996–1001
in Washington DC, 1001–1004
during World War II, 1006
Parks, Rosa, 940, 1399–1401
Park-Steel, Michelle, 1312
parkways, design of, 1004–1006
Parnell, Charles Stewart, 626
parochial schools, Polish immigrants in, 610
Parsons, Lucy, 252
passing for white, by African Americans, 582
The Passing of the Great Race (Grant, M.), 516, 610
Pasteur, Louis, 904, 923
Pastor, Manuel, 1476, 1479
PATCO. *See* Professional Air Traffic Controllers
    Organization
Patel, Kiran Klaus, 226
Patrick, Frank, 375
Patrick, Lester, 375
patriotism, during US Civil War, 73
patronage politics, political progressivism and, 183
Patterson, James T., 1139
Patterson, Joseph, 865
Patterson, Martha, 433
Patton, George, 259

Paul, Alice, 189
pauperism
    immigration and, 482
    outlawing of, 51
Payne-Aldrich Tariff Act, US (1909), 186
Peck, James, 1403
Peck, William Henry, 852
pedestrian malls, 175
pedestrian safety, in central business districts, 172–173
Pei, I. M., 870
Peiss, Kathy, 363
Pelli, Cesar, 873
Pellow, David, 1041
Pendergast, Jim, 120
penicillin, 1058
Penn, William, 22, 800, 987, 995
Penniman, Richard "Little Richard," 575, 1220, 1232
Pennington, Will, 598–599
Pennsylvania. *See specific cities*
Pentacostalism, 1126–1127
Pentagon Papers, 1452
People's Council for America, 188
People v. Hall, 1303n18
Pepper, Art, 1216
Pequot wars, 22
Perez, Andrea, 732
Perez v. Sharp, 732
performing arts centers, 1199
    JALC, 1225
    jazz music in, 1225
Perkins, Carl, 1157
Perkins, Francis, 236, 238, 497
Perkins, George, 186
Perkins, Napoleon, 846
Perlman, Selig, 266
Perry, Clarence, 792
Perry, Matthew, 542
Person, Charles, 1403
Personal Responsibility and Work Opportunity
    Reconciliation Act, US (1996), 1146, 1154
Peterson, Jon A., 896
Peterson, Willie, 1397
les petits, in New Orleans, 24
Petty, Audrey, 839
Pfeifer, Michael, 1274–1275, 1285
Philadelphia, Pennsylvania
    department stores in, 170
    Fairmount Gardens in, 995–996, 998
    Latino urbanism in, 701
    libraries in, 28
    merchant class in, 40
    population of, 37–38, 60
    public buildings in, 28
    Quakers in, 27
    recreation plans in, 21

Philadelphia, Pennsylvania (*Continued*)
  slavery in, 154, 157
  streets, roads, and highways in, 950–951, 951*f*
  urban planning of, 22
  urban redevelopment in, 138
  urban tourism to, 353–354
philanthropy, at universities and colleges, 342
Philippines, US-Philippines War, 750
Philips, Eliza, 437
Phillips, Kevin, 1444–1445
Phillips, Sarah, 226, 232
Phillips-Fein, Kim, 215, 241
Phoenix, Arizona, climate change in, 1064
photojournalism, 210–211
  of Civil War destruction, 851–853
Piachi (chiefdom), 10, 12
Picquet, Louisa, 436, 458n54
picturesque parks, 988–990
Piedmont chiefdoms, 12
Pilcher, Jeffrey, 1099
"pink-washing," 678
Pinza, Ezio, 517
Pitti, Stephen, 350
Pittsburgh, Pennsylvania
  labor strikes in, 258*f*
  as postindustrial city, 315, 328
  redlining in, 909*f*
  Renaissance of, 328
plague outbreaks, 1052–1053
plank roads, 950
planned unit developments (PUDs), 1516
Plan of Chicago (Burnham and Bennett, E.), 172–173,
      184, 356, 904, 905*f*, 1016
  City Beautiful movement in, 889–891
  skyscraper design in, 862
  urban park design in, 1004–1005
Platt, Anthony, 1346
Platt, Harold, 1023
Playboy magazine, 449
playgrounds
  in City Beautiful movement, 887
  as public spaces, 887, 990–991
plazas, as public spaces, 990–991
Pleasant, Mary Ellen, 1086
Plessy v. Ferguson, 75, 641, 940
Plunkett, Harriet, 805
Plunkitt, George Washington, 120
PNCC. *See* Polish National Catholic Church
Podhoretz, Norman, 1170n37
Point Four program, 226
point spreads, 396–397
police brutality, against minorities, 145
  Latino Americans, 503
  against LGBTQ, 1197
  1992 riots and, 1305–1306

riots as response to, 1280–1281
  in urban neighborhoods, 1371
  in urban North, 1371, 1377–1378
police corruption
  brothels and, 441–442
  gambling industry and, 394*f*, 397–399, 398*f*
police forces
  employment discrimination in, 1375
  riot responses by, 1284
  vagrancy laws and, over-application of, 1358–1359
The Police Power: Public Policy and Constitutional Rights
      (Freund), 1517
police unions
  in Boston, 274
  labor strikes by, 274
  as public sector unions, 273–274
polio outbreaks, 1053
  vaccine development for, 1057–1058
Polish immigration, **603–619**
  in Chicago, 603–604
  during Civil Rights Movement, 614
  communal response to, 604–609
  communism as influence on, 612–613
  deindustrialization as influence on, 614
  extra-communal response to, 604–609
  family dynamics in, role of, 607
  juvenile delinquency and, 610–611
  labor strikes and, 508–509
  labor unions and, 607–609, 611
  to Midwest, 604
  neighborhood system and, 613
  origins of, 603–604
  parochial schools and, 610
  PNCC parishes and, establishment of, 604–606
  Polishness and, 605–606
  Polish Women's Alliance and, 606–607
  Railroad Strike of 1877 and, 508
  Socialist Labor Party and, 609
  welfare agencies created through, 611
  women and, 606–609
  as working class population, 614–615
  during World War I, 609–611
  after World War II, 613–615
  during World War II, 611–613
  Za Chlebem and, 603
Polish National Catholic Church (PNCC), 604–606
Polishness, 605
Polish Women's Alliance, 606–607
political activism. *See also* labor activism; neighborhood
      activism
  of Asian Americans, **744–757**
  for black power, 137–138
  community activism, 136
  through hip-hop music, 1264–1265
  during HIV/AIDS epidemic, 675–677

by immigrants, 144–145
by LGBTQ population, 669, 671–673, 672f, 674, 675–677
in Little Saigon, 776–778
neighborhood activism, 137–140
1965 March on Washington, 729n21
through rap music, 1257–1258, 1264–1265
through rock-and-roll, 1237–1238
of Vietnamese immigrants, 776–778
of women, in machine politics, 125
political assassinations. *See* assassinations
political bosses, 117, 119–120
development of, 120
political iconography, during Mississippi period, 2
political parties. *See* Democratic Party; Republican Party; Whig Party
political progressivism
charter reform and, 183
civic federations in, 183
democratic mechanisms and, 182–183
electoral processes and, 182–183
experts on government and, 183–184
government regulation and, 183–184
home rule and, 183
National Municipal League and, 183
patronage politics and, 183
social science and, expertise in, 184–185
Wisconsin Idea and, 182–183
politics in urban areas, before 1940
after Civil War, 118
machine politics, 117–121
municipal reform, 120–123
political bosses in, 117, 119–120
urban growth as factor in, 118
politics in urban areas, after 1945
after the Great Depression, 133
urban redevelopment and, 133–135
through white ethnic neighborhood associations, 133
after World War II, 133
Pollard, Fritz, 373
polluting industries, environmental movements and, 1017
pollution, environmental, **1029–1049**
Addams on, 1032
anti-noise campaigns, 1035
atmospheric, 1034–1035, 1039–1041
bacteriological theory and, 1032–1033
CERCLA and, 1038
City Beautiful movement and, 1033
under Clean Air Act, 972, 1040–1041
under Clean Water Act, 1037
DDT and, 1036
EPA and, establishment of, 1036, 1038, 1040
in ethnic neighborhoods, 1031
industrialization and, 1031–1035

LHPA and, 1033
miasma theory and, 1029–1031
modern environmentalism movements, 1035–1041
under Motor Vehicle Air Pollution Act, 972
municipal sanitary systems, 1029–1030
NIMBY protests, 1039
in postwar era, 1035–1041
during Progressive Era, 1031
regulatory mechanisms for, 1035–1041
residential segregation and, 1032
under Resource Conservation and Recovery Act, 1038
under Safe Drinking Water Act, 1037
sewerage and water networks and, treatment of, 923–925
sewerage networks and, 1033
smoke density, 1034–1035
soil pollution, 1033–1034
solid waste, 1033–1034
suburbanization and, 1030, 1035–1036
in Sunbelt cities, 1036
toxic waste, 1038–1039
urban density influenced by, 1029
urbanization and, 1031–1035
urban zoning laws and, 1032
water pollution, 1032–1033, 1037–1038
under Water Quality Act, 1037
of waterways, 925
yellow fever and, 1029–1030
Poole, Mary, 241
poolrooms, gambling in, 390
Poor People's Campaign (PPC), 731, 738–739, 1156
FBI response to, 739
pop music, 1235–1238
POPS. *See* privately-owned public spaces
popular culture
comic books, 212
films, 212
games and leisure, 212
during the Great Depression, 210–213
Great Migration as influence on, 573–575
Irish immigrants in, 629–630
literature, 210–211
photojournalism, 210–211
sports, 212–213
temperance in, 412–413
World's Fairs, 213
Popular Front, 210
population censuses. *See also specific cities*
of African Americans, distribution of (1890), 74f
for Latino Americans, 705–707
for US, 37
Populist Party, 180
Port Authority of New York, 286–287, 293–295, 304n27, 307
port cities. *See* seaport cities

Portland, Oregon, 1477–1478
Portman, John, 873
Port Royal, South Carolina, 23
    recreation plans in, 21
Posse Comitatus Act, US (1878), 1280
Post, George, 859
postal employees, public sector unions for, 272–273
postbellum period
    compulsory work laws during, 51
    fall of slavery during, 51
    industrialization during, 51–52
    large-scale mechanized factories during, 51–52
    temperance movement during, 414–416
    vagrancy laws during, 51
postindustrial cities
    adaptive reuse in, 330
    African Americans in, 331
    artist interventions in, 330
    BIDs in, 315
    capital investment in, external sources of, 315
    casinos in, 327
    CERCLA in, 332
    Cleveland as, 315
    under Community Reinvestment Act, 327–328
    consumption in, 325–326
    creative classes in, 325
    "culture of clearance" in, 327
    demolition in, 329
    distribution centers in, 326
    economic inequality in, 330–332
    education in, 325
    entertainment industry in, 325–326
    environmental justice movements in, 332
    factory closures in, 331
    federal government role in, 327–328
    finance industries in, 325
    financial development in, 327–328
    in Florida, 325
    future of, 315–316
    gentrification cycles in, 331
    government services in, 314–315
    Great Compression in, 331
    healthcare industry in, 325
    industrial parks in, 326
    insurance industry in, 325
    land banks in, 329
    landfills and incinerators in, 326–327
    neoliberalization and, 314–315
    new economies in, 324–327
    New York City as, 315
    Pittsburgh as, 315, 328
    prisons in, 327
    professional class in, 324
    public-private partnerships in, 315, 328
    real estate industries in, 325

    redevelopment planning in, 331
    rightsizing in, 322, 328–329, 331
    rollout liberalization in, 315
    ruin gardens in, 329
    ruin porn in, 329–330, 332
    service economies in, 306–308, 314–316
    speculative markets in, 315
    technical class in, 324
    TIF in, 328
    tourism in, 325–326
    "tourist bubbles" in, 331–332
    urban agriculture in, 330
    "urban crisis" in, 328
    urban entrepreneurialism in, 315
    urban exploration in, 329–330
    urban planning in, 328–330
    urban tourism to, 325–326
    vice industries in, 327
    warehousing in, 326
    War on Poverty in, 328
postindustrialism, 328
postindustrialization
    new economies after, 324–327
    service economies and, 308–311
postindustrial service economies, **306–321**
    blue-collar workers in, 308–309, 309t, 312
    census data on, 308
    in cities, 308
    conceptualization of, 309–310
    deindustrialization and, 311–312
    dual labor markets in, 312–313
    economic development of, 308–311
    education in, 311
    execution of, 309–310
    expansion of, 311–312, 324–325
    federal tax code for, 313–314
    finance industries and, 308–311
    Fordist systems and, 312
    government employment in, 312
    growth of, 308
    healthcare in, 311
    local governments' response to, 313
    manufacturing employment and, 308–311
    mechanization and, 310
    middle class in, 313
    military spending in, 312
    sectors in, 308
    service industries and, 308–311
    space planning in, 313–314
    suburbanization and, 314
    warfare and, 312
    white-collar workers in, 308–309, 309t, 312
    women in, 311
    World War II and, 310, 313
Potowatomis people, 40

Potter, Hugh, 807
Pound, Dean Roscoe, 1341, 1353
poverty, **1139-1172**. *See also* War on Poverty
    for African Americans, 1146
    culture of poverty, 1148, 1305-1306
    definition of, 1139-1140
    English Poor Law and, 1139
    during the Great Depression, 1139, 1145, 1147
    Great Society approach to, 1144-1145
    from immigration, 481
    in Jim Crow South, 1142
    under Johnson, L. B., 1144-1145
    moral, 1344
    Mothers' Aid and, 1145
    during Progressive Era, 1140-1141
    public assistance programs, 1145-1146. *See also specific*
        programs
    public housing and, 1142-1144
    for Puerto Ricans, 723-724
    racial segregation and, 1141-1142
    Reagan, R., on, 1156
    redlining and, 1141-1142
    Salvation Army and, 1140, 1147
    settlement house movement and, 1141
    social organizations for, 1139-1140
    social reform movements against, 1139
    suburbanization and, 1142-1144
    urban growth as factor for, 1140-1141
    urban renewal and, 1142-1144
    women and, 1145-1146
    WPA and, 1147
Poverty (Hunter, R.), 1140
Powderley, Terrence, 124, 510-511, 625, 625*f*
Powell, Adam Clayton, Jr., 575
Powell, Bud, 1215
Powell, Colin, 1313
Powell, Laurence, 1317n1
Powers, John, 120, 125
power sources. *See also* electrical grid
    water wheels, 61
PPC. *See* Poor People's Campaign
PRACA. *See* Puerto Rican Association for Community
    Affairs
Pratt, William W., 413
La Prensa, 715-716
presidential progressivism, 186
presidios (Spanish forts), 697
Presley, Elvis, 1220, 1230-1232, 1240
priests. *See* elite priests
Prince, 1236
prisons, 327. *See also* hyperincarceration; incarceration
    theory
    mass uprisings in, 1379-1380
    racial disparities in, 1377-1378
    riots in, 1283

privacy rights, 1450-1451
private food shops, 1080-1081
private homes
    in central business districts, 169
    construction of, 64
    McMansions, 145
    in New York City, 64
    self-built, 806-807
privately-owned public spaces (POPS), 991
private schools, vouchers for, 1377
private sewerage and water networks, 920-921
Professional Air Traffic Controllers Organization
    (PATCO), 279
professional basketball
    development of, 376
    integration of, 377
    invention of, 376
    league mergers within, 378
    NBA, 377-378
    NBL, 376-378
    rule changes for, 377
    television contracts for, 378
    women and, 378
professional class, in postindustrial cities, 324
professional football
    American Football League and, 374
    early development of, 372
    expansion teams in, 374
    during the Great Depression, 373
    integration of, 373
    medical risks as result of, 374
    NFL and, 372-374
    player unions, 374
    racial segregation in, 373
    salary caps in, 374
    Super Bowl and, 374
    on television, 374
professional sports. *See* sports
Progressive Era, **179-197**. *See also* progressivism
    brothels during, 441-444
    corporate America during, 250
    drug subcultures during, 467
    environmental movements during, 1014-1017,
        1020-1021
    environmental pollution during, 1031
    gambling industry during, 389-391
    immigration during, 484-486, 488
    juvenile courts during, 1340
    juvenile justice during, 1340
    labor radicalism during, 252-254
    labor union organization during, 254-256
    machine politics during, 123-125
    municipal reform during, 122
    poverty during, 1140-1141
    progressivism after, 190

Progressive Era (*Continued*)
    prohibition movement during, 416–422
    public sector unions during, 272–274
    Socialist Party of America during, 254–255
    universities and colleges during, 340, 342
    urban planning during, 901, 905
    urban renewal during, 1528–1530
    vagrancy laws during, 1353
progressive juvenile justice, 1340–1342
Progressive Party, platform of, 187
progressive rock, 1235
Progressives, **179–197**. *See also* Progressive Era
    on capitalism, 180
Progressivism, **179–197**. *See also* Progressive Era
    democratic practices influenced by, 181–182
    economic, 185–189
    international, 187–189
    political, 182–185
    after Progressive Era, 190
    purpose of, 180
    racialized, 189–190
    social justice, 180–181
    in universities and colleges, 342–343
prohibition movement, **406–430**
    African Americans during, 417–418
    ASL, 418–420, 422
    dry counties and, 415–416
    economic class conflict and, 417
    under Eighteenth Amendment, 419–422
    expansion of, 415
    Great Migration during, 572
    Hoover and, 421
    immigrant populations and, 416–417
    industrialization as influence on, 417
    Jim Crow laws and, 417
    KKK revival as result of, 420
    national expansion of, 418–419
    nightlife during, 1195–1196
    under Nineteenth Amendment, 189, 257, 419–420,
        422, 1195
    as noble experiment, 422
    organized crime during, 421
    during Progressive Era, 416–422
    racial discrimination and, 417
    "Redeemer" Democrats and, 417
    Red Summer of 1919, 421–422
    religious doctrine and, 417
    Roosevelt, F. D., and, 422
    in the South, 417–418
    statewide referenda on, 417–418
    urbanization as influence on, 417–419
    under Volstead Act, 189, 257, 419–420, 422, 1195
    WCTU and, 415–416, 420–422
Prohibition Party, 414–415, 420
Project Head Start, 1157

promotional organizations, for urban tourism, 357
property damage, from 1992 riots, 1310
property rights and ownership
    Jefferson on, 799, 801
    through land grants, 800
    as legal tradition, 799–800
Proposition 6, in California, 670–671
Proposition 13, in California, 1474
Proposition 15, in California, 763
Proposition 22, California, 734
Proposition 87, in California, 560
Prospect Park, in New York City, 998–1000
Prost, Henri, 639
prostitution, prostitutes and, **430–465**. *See also* brothels;
    sex markets
    African American women and, 442, 446
    ASHA guidelines on, 443–445
    in Central America, 444
    under Chamberlain-Kahn Act, 445
    after Civil War, 438
    clandestine, 444–448
    COYOTE and, 450–451
    crimes related to, 436
    criminal organization of, 441
    criminal prosecution of, 433, 443–444
    decriminalization of, 450
    demographics of, 434
    earnings from, 441
    economic impact of, 441
    under Eight-Point Agreement of 1940, 447
    emerging visibility of, 430
    as exploitative, 452
    feminism and, 449–452
    in Gold Rush California, 430, 438–439
    during the Great Depression, 446–447
    "ideal woman" and, 433–434
    industrialization as influence on, 434
    interracial sex through, 441–442
    as intimate labor, 430
    licensed, origins of, 459n74
    male, 430
    under May Act, 447
    middle-class ideology and, 434
    military and, 445, 459n67
    morality arguments against, 443
    municipal regulation of, 440
    near military bases, 445
    nightlife and, 1189, 1194–1195
    for occupying military forces, 437–438
    organized crime and, 446
    under Palermo Protocol, 452
    public tolerance of, 434, 440–441
    racial segregation and, 442
    "red light" neighborhoods, 442
    sex trafficking and, 439–440, 452

as social evil, 441
social justification of, 436, 445
social reform movements and, 443
on urban streets, 446
US Army regulation of, 447–448
in US territories, 444, 448
under vagrancy laws, 432, 437
as "victimless crime," 463n180
white slavery and, 442–443
under White Slave Traffic Act, 443
WHO, 450
under Woman Order, 437
during World War I, 444–447
during World War II, 447–448
Protestant, Catholic, Jew (Herberg), 1128
Protestant Church, 620–622, 1110–1111
evangelicals in, 1124–1125
from 1900–1929, 1123–1126
in suburbs, 1128–1131
Protestant Public School Society, 1176
protest politics
by African Americans, 209
during the Great Depression, 207–209
Montgomery bus boycott, 77, 940, 1399–1401
by NNC, 209
over food, 1094–1095
rioting and, 1273–1274
by sharecroppers, through demonstrations, 208f
unemployment demonstrations, 208
urban planning and, 909–911, 910
Providence, Rhode Island, as slave port, 153, 156
Pruitt, Wendell O., 1143
Pryor, Elizabeth Stordeur, 53
psychedelic drugs, 470–471
Puar, Jasbir, 678
public assistance programs, 1145–1146
public authorities, **285–306**. *See also specific public authorities*
in California, 303n23
capital markets and, 294–295
census data on, 302n7
during Clinton administration, 299
corruption and, 288
in court systems, 294–295
defined, 285–287, 302n7
as distinct from government, 286
features of, 286
as federal level, 296–299
financing of, 295
First Bank of the United States and, 43, 48, 288
under Government Corporation Control Act, 298
government corporations as, 293, 295–298
during the Great Depression, 297
HFA, 293–295
under Hoover, 290

leadership of, 286
legislative responses to, 290–291
in Massachusetts, 286
through military, 298
Moody's rating agencies, 293
moral obligation bonds and, 293
municipal governments and, 291–292
national expansion of, 290–292
New Deal and, 286, 292–294, 303n24
during New Public Management Movement, 298
in New York, 286–287, 293–295, 304n27, 304n33, 307
NPR for, 299, 306n51
Panama Canal Zone and, 296–297
political opposition to, 290–291, 297–298
public controversies on, 295–296
public debt and, 287–289, 287f, 305n37
for public housing, 304n33
purpose of, 288
revenue bonds and, 286, 291–292
RFC, 290, 303n23
Roosevelt, F. D., and, 291–292
roots of, 288–290
self-funding of, 285–286
special funds and, 289
special taxing districts and, 289
in Spokane, 289
tax-exempt bond markets and, 294
traditional, 293
for transportation infrastructure, 292, 294
during World War I, 297
World War II and, 292–294, 297
public buildings, in early seaport cities, 28
public celebrations, on sidewalks and city streets, 987
public dancing, 1195
public debt, public authorities and, 287–289, 287f, 305n37
public dining, 1082–1085. *See also* restaurants; street vendors
Public Enemy, 1257–1258
public food markets, 1080–1081, 1097
public health crises, from contagious diseases, 1049
AIDS epidemic, 1199
residential segregation justified through, 638–639
public health departments
American Public Health Association, 804–805
during Civil War, 1055–1056
contagious diseases and, 1052
from 1800–1899, 1055–1056
food diets and, 1097
municipal housing and, 803–806
under New York Metropolitan Health Act, 1056
from 1900–1999, 1056–1057
sanitary reforms by, 1054–1057
from 1700–1799, 1055
sewerage and water networks and, 924
streetcars and, 939

public health nursing programs, in Los Angeles, 181
public housing, **817–831**
    African Americans in, 820, 824
    in apartment buildings, 820
    "Atlanta Blueprint" for, 825
    in company towns, 93
    construction of, 65, 93
    decline of, 822–823
    early development of, 149, 817–818
    economic diversity in, 811
    under Fair Housing Act, 811
    First Houses, 907
    during the Great Depression, 818–820
    high-rise design for, 822–823
    Hills v. Gautreaux, 824
    under Housing Act of 1937, 819, 826
    under Housing Act of 1949, 820
    under HUD Act, 811, 822–823, 826
    LHAs and, 821
    LIHTC, 818, 824–825
    mixed-income approach to, 825–826
    Model Cities program, 811, 834–835, 1145, 1535
    neoliberal approaches to, 823–825
    in New York City, 823
    from 1933–1945, 818–820
    from 1945–1960, 820–822
    from 1965–1992, 823–825
    from 1992–2018, 825–826
    NYCHA and, 823
    population demographics for, 818
    poverty and, 1142–1144
    public authorities for, 304n33
    under PWA, 819
    racial segregation in, 811, 821
    under Roosevelt, F. D., 818–819
    Section 8 housing, 823–824, 836
    slum clearances for, 819
    in the South, 821
    Techwood Homes, 907
    temporary, for homeless, 1148
    tenements, 65
    in urban planning, 907
    USHA and, 819–820
    Vanport, Oregon, 820
    after World War II, 811
    during World War II, 820
Public Law 600, US, 718
public-private enterprise
    in Baltimore, 40
    in postindustrial cities, 315, 328
    in suburbanization, 1458
    for urban parks, 1008
    in urban planning, 910
public schools, **1173–1189**
    African American students in, 1174–1175, 1181–1183

Asian American suburban culture and, 1506–1508
Boston Latin School, 1174
boycott of, 1182f
Brown v. Board of Education, 821, 1181, 1343
centralized regulation of, 1179–1180
charter schools compared to, 1183–1184
citizenship and, 1173
as coeducational, 1174–1175
commercial, 1178
as common schools, 1174
conceptual approach to, 1173
Cuban Americans in, integration into, 737–738
culture of poverty and, 1183
demonstration districts, 1182
desegregation of, 1181–1182, 1188n31, 1376–1377
domestic sciences in, 1179f
Du Bois on, 1178
economic factors for, 1175
educational reforms for, 1184
from 1800–1899, 1174–1177
floor plans for, 1175–1176
during the Great Depression, 1177, 1181
intelligence testing in, 1178
in Jim Crow South, 1178
Latino American students in, 1181–1183
LGBTQ teachers in, criticisms of, 666–667
municipal funding of, 1177, 1181
in New York City, 1174–1176, 1179f, 1182
from 1900–1920, 1177–1180
under No Child Left Behind Act, 1183
Protestant Public School Society, 1176
racism in, 1175–1176
segregation of, 1178–1180
slavery and, 1174
suburbanization and, 792
teachers in, 1182–1183
technical schools, 1177
trade schools, 1178
urban crisis in, 1183
vouchers and, 1377
War on Poverty and, 1183
Washington, B. T., on, 1178
after World War II, 1180–1185
public sector unions, **271–285**. *See also specific unions*
    AFL opposition to public sector unions, 273
    African American responses to, 279
    anticommunist movements and, 278
    in California, 284n39
    in Chicago, 273
    civil service protections through, 273
    collective bargaining by, 283n9
    for firefighters, 276
    during the Great Depression, 274
    independent civil service associations and, 274
    Knights of Labor and, 273

labor strikes by, 277
in late 20th century, 279–281
legal uncertainty and, 274–277
long-term resilience of, 280
under New Deal programs, 275
origins of, 271–272
for police, 273–274
political attacks against, 280–281
for postal employees, 272–273
postwar growth of, 277–279
during Progressive Era, 272–274
public reaction to, 279–281
for public transportation workers, 283n32
under Taft-Hartley Act, 277
for teachers, 273
urban political machines and, 272
before World War I, 272–274
under WPA, 275–276
public segregation. *See also* educational segregation;
    housing segregation; residential segregation
in urban American South, 77
public spaces, **983–994**
picturesque parks as, 988–990
playgrounds as, 887, 990–991
plazas as, 990–991
POPS, 991
public squares, 987–988
sidewalks and city streets as, 983–987
public sphere, as concept, 128
public squares, 987–988
shopping districts near, 988
public transportation
central business districts influenced by, 169–170
electrical grid development as influence on, 63
electric streetcars, 63
industrialization improved by, 47
public sector unions for, 283n32
suburbanization and, 793
urbanization influenced by, 50
Public Works Administration (PWA), 233–234, 290
housing policies under, 832
public housing under, 819
sewage treatment and, 926
transportation infrastructure under, 234
universities and, 343
university and college attendance under, 343
urban planning and, 907
PUD. *See* planned unit developments
Pueblo Indians, 686, 1106–1107
Pueblo Revolt, 155, 162
pueblos, 696–697, 697f
Puerto Rican Association for Community Affairs
    (PRACA), 719
A Puerto Rican in New York (Cólon), 735
"Puerto Rican problem," 716–717

Puerto Ricans, **713–730**
academic studies programs for, 721–722
African Americans and, relationship with, 735–737
in El Barrio, 735
BPP and, 721, 736
in Chicago, 718, 721
citizenship for, 713–714, 728n11
during Cold War, 716–718
colonia, 715–716
community organizations for, 719
deindustrialization as influence on, 718–720
in Democratic Party, 714–715
educational access for, 736
from 1890–1930, 713–715
electoral impact of, 713
electoral successes of, 716
ethnic conflicts with, 715
government benefits for, 723
during the Great Depression, 715–716
housing discrimination against, 719
HYAA and, 719
income levels of, 722
under Jones Act, 713–714
labor unions and, exclusion from, 714–716
Mexican immigrants compared to, 717–718
NAPRCR and, 720
nationalism among, 718
under New Deal programs, 715–716
from 1960–1969, 720–721
from 1970–1999, 722–724
under NIRA, 715
poverty rates for, 723–724
in PPC, 738–739
PRACA and, 719
La Prensa, 715–716
racial discrimination against, 715, 717–718
in Rainbow Coalition, 736
scholarly study on, 724–726
second-generation, 718–720
self-determination movements among, 720–721
in street gangs, 721, 736, 1322–1323, 1327–1329, 1448
as *tabaqueros*, 713
from 2000–2018, 724
unemployment for, 728n5
urban migration of, 716–718
Voting Rights Act and, 718, 722–723
in *West Side Story*, 719, 1324
Puerto Rico
FALN in, 723
under Foraker Act, 713
Latino urbanism and, 699
nationalist movement in, 718, 723
under Public Law 600, 718
under Treaty of Paris, 713
as US possession, 187, 713

Pulido, Laura, 1022
Pulitzer, Joseph, 859
Pullman, George, 90, 791–792
Pullman porters, 586–587
punitive planning, in urban planning, 1409
punk rock, 1235
Pure Food and Drug Act, US (1906), 180, 185
Putnam, Robert, 1200, 1473
PWA. *See* Public Works Administration
Pyle, C. C., 373

Quakers, 1108
Quality Housing and Work Responsibility Act, US, 836
Quapaw nation, 12–13, 20n46
quarantine era, from 1700–1920, 1049–1054
    18th century quarantines, 1050–1051
    19th century quarantines, 1051–1052
    20th century quarantines, 1052–1054
    Ellis Island Immigration Station during, 510
Queen Latifah, 1257, 1263
Quevedo, Eduardo, 734
Quie, Albert, 1157
Quill, Mike, 628
Quincy, Josiah, 119, 440
quotas. *See* national immigration quotas

Rabin, Yale, 1521
race riots, 1322–1323
    Great Migration and, 1368
    in Levittowns, 1466
racial categorization, with immigration, 498
racial discrimination
    at Angel Island Immigration Station, 530–532, 535
    against Asian Americans in suburbia, 1501–1502
    through authoritarianism, 646
    against Chinese, 1290–1293
    against Chinese immigrants, 483–484
    through HOLC, 1142
    against Japanese immigrants, 760–761
    in juvenile justice system, 1345
    in labor unions, 263
    against Latino Americans, 731–732
    in liminal space, 1399
    1992 riots as response to, 1305
    prohibition movement and, 417
    in public schools, 1175–1176
    against Puerto Ricans, 715, 717–718
    rioting and, 1272–1273, 1278–1279
    Scottsboro Boys case and, 206, 263
    street gangs and, 1319–1320, 1323
    in vagrancy laws, 1351, 1356, 1358
racial hierarchies, riots and, 1278
racialized progressivism
    African Americans and, 189
    Americanism and, 190

    immigration restrictions and, 189–190
racial segregation
    brothels and, 442
    Buchanan v. Warley, 808
    "color blind" politics and, 645–648
    through immigration, 497–498
    by Irish immigrants, 627
    in major league baseball, 370
    in Mississippi, 1407–1408
    New Right and, 645–646
    in nightclubs, 1198
    in Northern states, 75, 78–79
    poverty and, 1141–1142
    in professional football, 373
    prostitution and, 442
    in public housing, 811, 821
    on streetcars, 940
    through suburbanization, 645, 791–792, 1460
    in suburbs, 791–792
    in Supreme Court cases, 808
    through urban renewal, 144, 1142–1144
    by YMCA, 1368
    by YWCA, 1368
    through zoning laws, 794
Radburn, New Jersey, as designed suburb, 906, 906f
Radde, Bruce, 959
Rader, Benjamin, 379
Rader, Ralph, 973
Radford, Gail, 812, 819
radical feminism, 1440
radicalism
    of garment workers, 253–254, 253f
    of labor, 252–254
    during 1960s, 1436, 1439–1441
ragtime and blues music, **1206–1230**
    academic study on, 1211–1212
    female singers, 1208
    jazz music and, 1208–1209
    regional influences on, 1208
    slave influences on, 1207
    before World War I, 1207
railroad industry. *See also* light rail transit systems
    BSCP and, 263–264, 1369, 1372
    development of, 52
    early history of, 59n64
    electrical grid development as influence on, 63
    elevated railroads, 936
    employee wages in, 52
    food transport through, 1078–1080, 1092
    Great Migration and, 569–570
    Latino urbanism and, 698
    Native Americans in, 688–689
    Pullman porters, 586–587
    under Railway Labor Act, 256, 264
    suburbanization influenced by, 788–789

underground rail cars, 938
    urban tourism influenced by, 353–354, 355
    during US Civil War, 52
Railroad Strike of 1877, 1279–1280
    Polish immigrants in, 508
Railway Labor Act, US (1926), 256, 264
Rainbow Coalition, 736
Rainbow's End (Erie), 128
Rainey, Gertrude "Ma," 572–573
Rainey, Ma, 1208
Raitz, Karl, 959
RAM. *See* Revolutionary Action Movement
Randolph, Asa Philip, 209, 257, 263, 263f, 1369, 1446
    March on Washington Movement and,
        1374–1375, 1445
rap music, **1252–1270**. *See also* hip-hop music
    academic studies on, 1265–1267
    Beastie Boys, 1256
    birth of, 1253–1255
    Black Lives Matter movement and, 1265
    black nationalism in, 1257
    Black Power movement and, decline of, 1253
    breakbeat in, 1253
    on Broadway, 1262
    collectives in, 1258
    culture wars and, 1258
    deejays, 1253–1256
    East Coast-West Coast rivalry within, 1237, 1259–1260
    economic crises as foundation of, 1253
    economic moguls in, 1265
    from 1980–1991, 1255–1257
    Eminem, 1262
    feminist influences in, 1257
    in films, 1255
    foundations of, 1253–1254
    gangsta rap, 1237
    Latin influences in, 1260–1262
    LL Cool J, 1256
    as male-dominated, 1252
    Master P, 1261–1262
    misogyny in, 1257, 1262
    on MTV, 1255
    in New York City, 1253–1255
    from 1973–1979, 1253–1255
    NWA, 1257
    political activism through, 1257–1258, 1264–1265
    polyculturalism of, 1255
    Public Enemy, 1257–1258
    racial authenticity through, 1252–1253, 1262
    rock-and-roll music and, 1236, 1255–1256
    Run-DMC, 1256
    sampling in, 1257–1258
    in the South, 1261–1262, 1264
    Sugar Hill Gang and, 1254–1255
    technological influences on, 1264

    on television, 1262
    2 Live Crew, 1258
    underground movement in, 1260–1262
    on West Coast, 1256–1257
    women in, 1254–1255, 1257, 1260–1262
Rapp, George, 1194
Rappahannock River, 71
"Rapper's Delight," 1255
Rasmussen, Nicolas, 470
Rauchway, Eric, 215, 246n34
Rawson, Michael, 930
REA. *See* Rural Electrification Administration
Reagan, Nancy, 1330
Reagan, Ronald, 241, 280, 472, 614, 645, 928, 1146, 1160
    as California governor, 1440
    HIV/AIDS epidemic under, 676
    LGBTQ populations under, 677
    on poverty, 1156
    Proposition 13 and, 1474
    student strikes and, political response to, 747
Reagan Democrats, 146
real estate industry
    municipal housing and, 799–800, 807–808
    in postindustrial cities, 325
    suburbanization and, 789, 793, 813, 1457–1460
    suburbs developed by, 789, 793, 813
    urban planning and, 905
real estate investment trusts (REITs), 1466
recessions. *See* economic recessions
Reconstruction era
    African Americans during, violence against, 1295
    anti-Chinese massacre during, 1291–1294, 1296–1299
    California during, 1290–1295
    emancipation movement during, 1294–1295
    globalization after, 104
    Great Migration during, 582
    southern cities during, 73
    violence during, 1295–1296
Reconstruction Finance Corporation (RFC), 290, 303n23
Red Cross, 1070
"Redeemer" Democrats, 417
redevelopment agencies, 134
redevelopment planning, in postindustrial cities, 331
Red Guard Party, 745, 748–749
"red light" neighborhoods, 442
redlining
    in New Deal, 1142
    poverty and, 1141–1142
    residential segregation through, 642–643, 1376
    reverse, 647
    as unconstitutional, 1142
    through urban planning, 908, 909f
Red Scare, 190, 274
    Ellis Island Immigration Station and, 516
    HUAC and, 277

Red Summer of 1919, 421–422
Red Summers, rioting and, 1279
Reed, James, 420
Reed, Ralph, 1161
refrigeration, of food, 1092
refugee policies, immigration and, 544–545
Refugee Relief Act, US (1953), 500, 544–545
Regalado, Samuel, 380
re Gault case, 1342–1343, 1346
regional deindustrialization, 322–323. See also
    specific cities
"Regulator" movements, 31
Reid, Whitelaw, 1292
Reinventing Government (Gaebler and Osborne), 298
Reiss, Steven, 378, 391, 401
REITs. See real estate investment trusts
religion, in US cities, **1105–1139**. See also Catholic
    Church; Protestant Church
  for African Americans, 1109–1110, 1126–1127
  during antebellum era, 1110–1113
  for Beat Generation, 1129
  after Civil War, 1110–1113
  in colonial cities, 1106–1108
  at Columbian Exposition, 1122–1123
  diversification of, 1114
  in early seaport cities, 1108–1109
  from 1830–1870, 1110–1113
  from 1870–1900, 1113–1116
  evangelical denominations, 1109
  German immigrants' influence on, 1112
  during Gilded Age, 1113–1116
  globalization of, 1131–1133
  Great Migration as influence on, 1126
  Hinduism, 1122–1123, 1131–1132
  Irish immigrants' influence on, 1112
  Islam, 1122–1123
  Judaism, 1107–1108, 1112–1115, 1125–1126, 1128–1131
  Louisiana Purchase as influence on, 1109
  missionary societies, 1111
  Nation of Islam, 1127–1128
  of Native Americans, 1106–1108
  from 1900–1929, 1123–1126
  from 1900–2000, **1122–1139**
  from 1929–1949, 1126–1128
  from 1949–1969, 1128–1131
  from 1970–2018, 1131–1133
  from 1050–1780, 1106–1108
  Pentacostalism, 1126–1127
  postwar urbanization as influence on, 1115
  Quakers, 1108
  Republicanism and, 1110
  in Rust Belt, 1131
  Salvation Army and, 1115
  from 1780–1830, 1108–1110
  Sikhs, 1131

  from 1600–1900, **1105–1122**
  social activism through, 1130–1131
  Social Gospel, 1123
  in social reform movements, 1111–1112
  in suburbs, 1128–1131
religious doctrine
  alcohol use and, 407–409
  prohibition movement and, 417
  during temperance movement, 411
religious iconography, during Mississippi period, 2
religious ordering, in Cahokia, 4
religious segregation, through zoning laws, 794
Relocation Program, for Native Americans, 691
Relph, Edward, 973
reluctant suburbs, 813
Rembert (chiefdom), 5
Reno, Janet, 677
Reps, John W., 896
Republicanism, 408, 1110
Republican Party
  Knights of Labor and, 180
  Mugwump faction of, 180
  municipal reform and, 120
  New Right, 645–647, 1439–1441
  during 1920s, ascendancy of, 255
  suburbs as voting block for, 1465
  in "Sunbelt" region, 78
  temperance movement and, 414
Republic of New Afrika, 1379
Republic of Texas, 49
rescue riots, 1280–1283
reservations, for Native Americans, 690
Resettlement Administration, 232
residential segregation, **635–653**. See also redlining
  in archsegregationist societies, 640–642
  of Asian Americans, 1493, 1512n4, 1515n62
  in Atlanta, 137
  in Charlotte, 137
  in Chicago, 642–643
  civil rights challenges to, 643–645
  during colonial era, 638
  environmental pollution and, 1032
  FHA and, 642–643
  first surge of, 639
  as form of social inequity, 635–637
  fourth surge of, 640
  after Great Migration, 640, 1370
  historical development of, 637–640
  HOLC and, 642–643, 1370
  under Hoover, 642
  through housing discrimination, 635–636
  in India, 639
  of Latino Americans, 636–637, 731
  in municipal housing, 808
  paradoxes of, 637–638, 648–649

under *Plessy v. Ferguson*, 641
political power through, 638
for public health reasons, 638–639
through public planning, 639–640
through racially restrictive covenants, 643–644, 794
riots against, 1281
under Roosevelt, F. D., 642
second surge of, 639
Shelley v. Kraemer, 644, 764, 833, 1144, 1376, 1493–1494
in South Africa, compared to US, 640–642
suburbanization as influence on, 791–792
third surge of, 640
through tract-home development, 1019
in urban American South, 75
through urban redevelopment, 137
vestibule neighborhoods, 636
through zoning laws, 794
resilience planning, 1070–1072. *See also* disaster planning
Resource Conservation and Recovery Act, US (1976), 1038
restaurants, 1082–1085
automats, 1098
in central business districts, 174, 1097–1098
chains, 174
for fast food, 1098
in New Orleans, 1084
in New York City, 1083
as social culture, 1097–1098
restrictive covenants, by race
against Asian Americans, in suburbia, 1512n12
CC&Rs, 1469
Great Migration and, 1370
residential segregation through, 643–644, 794
in *Shelley v. Kraemer*, 644, 764, 833, 1144, 1376, 1493–1494
in suburbs, 794
retail shops. *See also* department stores; shopping districts
in early seaport cities, 25–26
"retro fields," for major league baseball, 371
Revenue Act, US (1954), 1164
revenue bonds, 286, 291–292
reverse redlining, 647
Revolutionary Action Movement (RAM), 1325
Revolutionary Union Movement, 1379
Revolutionary War
alcohol use during, 407
slavery in cities during, 158–163
streets, roads, and highways after, 949
Revolution of 1910, 698–699
Reynolds, Ike, 1403, 1406
RFC. *See* Reconstruction Finance Corporation
Rhode Island. *See also specific cities*
company towns in, 86
Rice, Margie, 779

Rich, Robert M., 463n180
Richards, Ellen, 895
Richardson, Heather Cox, 1301
Richardson, Henry Hobson, 859
Richmond, David, 1402, 1416–1417
Richmond, Virginia
African Americans in, 1409–1410
after Civil War, 73
early public transportation in, 63
Hopkins v. City of Richmond, 1522
riots in, 1277
slum clearance in, 1409
Richter, Amy, 53
Rickey, Branch, 370, 380
ride-sharing systems, 958
Rieder, Jonathan, 1405–1406
Riess, Steven A., 390
Riggs, Marlon, 674
rightsizing, 322, 328–329, 331
rights liberalism, 1449–1451
Americans with Disabilities Act, 1451
birth control access, 1451
Equal Rights Amendment, 1451
privacy rights, 1450–1451
"right to the city," 1476
Riis, Jacob, 391–392, 881–882, 1013, 1529
on need for public parks, 1277
on poverty, 1141
riots, rioting and, **1271–1290**
against African Americans, 1272–1273, 1276, 1278–1283
against Asian Americans, 1275
Baltimore Riot, 1273
Black Power movement and, 1282–1283
bread riots, 1277
between brothels, 435
"careful," 1272
in Chicago, 576, 1279
for civil rights, 1281–1283
after Civil War, 1277–1280
during Civil War, 1276–1277
congressional response to, 1284
under Consolidation Act, 1274
as defense, in African American communities, 1276, 1280–1283
deindustrialization and, 324
in Detroit, 1282–1283
draft riots, 882, 1276–1277
from 1800–1850, 1271–1274
ethnic conflicts as factor in, 1272
against free African Americans, 161
during Gold Rush era, 1275
during Great Migration, 1279, 1281
Harlem disorder, 1281
immigrants and, 1272

riots, rioting and (*Continued*)
  in industrial era, 1274–1280
  against Jim Crow laws, 1282
  labor strikes and, 1278–1280
  against Latino Americans, 1281
  by LGBTQ persons, 1283
  local state government responses to, 1274, 1280, 1283–1284
  looting during, 1282
  by lynch mobs, 1272, 1274–1275, 1277–1280
  against Mexicans, 1275
  in Miami, 1283
  mob killings and, 1277
  national political response to, 1273
  against Native Americans, 1275
  in Newark, 1282
  in New York City, 882, 1276–1277
  1992 riots, in Los Angeles, **1304–1319**. *See also* 1992 riots
  police response to, 1284
  as political protest, 1273–1274
  in prisons, 1283
  purpose of, 1271
  race riots, 1322–1323, 1368, 1466
  racial hierarchy enforced by, 1278
  as racial violence, 1272–1273, 1278–1279
  Railroad Strike of 1877 and, 1279–1280
  during Red Summers, 1279
  regulation of communal morality through, 1271
  rescue riots, 1280–1283
  against residential segregation, 1281
  in Richmond, 1277
  as ritual, 1271–1272
  Shays' Rebellion, 1272
  after Stamp Act, 1272
  Stonewall Inn riot, 1199, 1439
  Stonewall riots, 669
  in 20th century, 1280–1283
  by urban firefighters, 1273
  urbanization as influence on, 1272
  against urban police actions, 1280–1281
  as urban rebellion, 1280–1283
  from urban redevelopment, 137
  in Watts, 1282
  Western expansion and, 1275
  Whiskey Rebellion, 1272
  by white Americans, 1272, 1275–1276, 1280–1283
  white vigilantism and, 1275–1276
  during World War II, 1281
  Zoot Suit riots, 499, 1323
The Rise of the Unmeltable Ethnic (Novak, M.), 654
Ritchie v. People, 180
Rivera, Diego, 701
Rivera, Sylvia, 669, 674
Riverside, Illinois, as designed suburb, 902
Rizzo, Frank, 133, 138

Roach, Max, 1216, 1225
roads. *See* streets, roads, and highways
road safety, 958
  driver and passenger issues, 972–973, 976
  on interstate highways, 955–956
Robertson, Carole, 1408
Robertson, Oscar, 377
Robertson, Stephen, 392, 401
Robeson, Paul, 373
Robins, Margaret Dreier, 187
Robinson, Charles Mumford, 884, 887–888
Robinson, Jackie, 370, 380
Robinson, JoAnn, 1400
Robinson, Spottswood, 1409
Robinson, Sylvia, 1254–1255
Roche, Josephine, 191
rock-and-roll music, 1198–1199, **1230–1252**
  American Bandstand, 1232, 1238
  arena rock, 1237–1238
  art rock, 1235
  British invasion, 1232–1233
  class contrasts in, 1231–1232
  convergence culture and, 1238–1239
  corporate, 1235
  crossover styles, 1239
  Davis, M., influenced by, 1220–1221
  drug use and, 1233
  experimental rock, 1236–1237
  feminist influences on, 1236
  in films, 1234
  gender contrasts in, 1231–1232
  grunge music, 1237
  historians of, 1230
  jazz music influenced by, 1220–1223
  in literature, 1234
  mash-ups, 1238–1239
  MTV channel, 1235, 1238
  Napster technology and, 1239
  from 1951–1959, 1230–1232
  from 1960–1969, 1232–1233
  from 1970–1979, 1234–1235
  from 1990–1999, 1237–1238
  pop music and, 1235–1238
  Presley and, 1220, 1230–1232, 1240
  progressive rock, 1235
  punk rock, 1235
  rap music and, 1236, 1255–1256
  regional contrasts in, 1231–1232
  Rolling Stone magazine, 1230, 1233–1234
  singer-songwriters, 1234
  as social dissent, 1237–1238
  from 2000–2018, 1238–1240
  women in, 1237
Rockefeller, David, 871
Rockefeller, John D., 342, 417

Rockefeller, John D., Jr., 868, 1534
Rockefeller, Nelson, 293–294, 400, 473, 871, 1283
Rockefeller Center, 868, 1533
Rockman, Seth, 54, 103
Rodgers, Daniel T., 191
Roebling, Emily Warren, 903
Roebling, John Augustus, 903
Roebling, Washington, 903
Roediger, David, 1320
Rogers, Elisabeth Barlow, 626, 1006
Rogers, Naomi, 1053
Rolling Stone magazine, 1230, 1233–1234
The Rolling Stones, 1232–1233
Rollins, Sonny, 1216, 1218, 1220, 1225
rollout liberalization, 315
Rome, Adam, 1023–1024, 1042
Romer, Christina, 200, 215, 223n102
Romer v. Evans, 677
Roney, Frank, 624
Roosevelt, Eleanor, 230, 238, 575
Roosevelt, Franklin Delano. *See also* New Deal
  bank holidays under, 199–200, 219n16, 227
  as Democratic Party candidate, 225
  economic Bill of Rights under, 344
  economic recession under, 200, 237, 261
  Good Neighbor Policy, 547
  housing policies under, 831–833
  immigration policy under, 497–498
  Magnuson Act under, 543
  municipal housing policies under, 809
  municipal reform under, 291
  polio and, 1058
  prohibition movement and, 422
  public authorities under, 291–292
  public housing under, 818–819
  public opinion on, 260
  residential segregation under, 642
  response to urban rioting, 1281
  on Tammany Hall, 126
Roosevelt, Theodore, 124, 185–186, 188–190, 251,
    511–512, 887, 1529
  Gentlemen's Agreement with Japan, 188, 488, 533–534
  labor unions under, legislative limitations of, 272
  promotion of Americanism, 190
  Square Deal, 225
Root, Elihu, 187
Roots: The Saga of an American Family (Haley, Alex), 519
Root-Takahira Agreement, 187
Rorabaugh, William, 424
Rose, Mark, 959
Rosen, Elliot, 215
Rosenberg, Barbara Gutman, 930
Rosenberg, Charles, 1051–1052
Rosenwald, Julius, 583
"Rosie the Riveter," 265

Ross, J. Andrew, 379
Rosskam, Edwin, 211
Rothman, Hal K., 364
Rothstein, Arnold, 396
Rouse, James, 325–326, 912
row houses, 802–803
row houses, renovations of, 1562
Rowland, Wirt C., 866
Roxborough, John, 394
Roybal, Edward, 136
Royce, Ed, 777–778
Rozario, Kevin, 1073
Rozelle, Pete, 373–374, 397, 400
Rubin, Rick, 1256
Rudé, George, 1272, 1284
Ruggles, David, 161
Rugh, Jacob S., 648
ruin gardens, 329
ruin porn, in postindustrial cities, 329–330, 332
Run-DMC, 1256
Rung, Arnold, 276
Rural Electrification Administration (REA), 233
rural life, urban life and, boundaries between, 49
rural regions, in US, early population trends in, 38f
rural roads, 952
Rush, Benjamin, 407–408
Rusk, David, 1476
Russell, Bill, 377
Russell, Howard H., 418
Rust Belt cities. *See also specific cities*
    deindustrialization in, 322
    religion in, 1131
    urban planning in, 907
    urban redevelopment in, 143
    white migration from, 593–594
Rustin, Bayard, 667, 729n21, 1446–1447
Ruth, Babe, 370, 380
Ryan, Brent, 329
Ryan, John, 187
Ryan, Mary, 54, 992

Saarinen, Eero, 98
Sabin, Albert, 1057
Sachs, Jeffrey, 1154
Sadik-Khan, Janette, 958
Safe Drinking Water Act, US (1974), 1037
safe sex strategy, 675–676
Sagalyn, Lynne, 333
Sai-I-Gu (April 29), 1309–1312
Saint-Méry, Moreau de, 432
Saito, Leland, 1503
salaries. *See also* income levels
    in major league baseball, 372
    in NHL, 376
    in professional football, 374

Salk, Jonas, 1057–1058
Salt-N-Pepa, 1257
Salvation Army, 1115, 1140, 1147
Sampson, Robert, 1331
Samuels, Howard, 400
San Antonio, Texas, 699
Sanchez, George, 1311, 1315
Sánchez-Jankowski, Martin, 1329
sanctuary cities, 504
Sanders, Jeffrey Craig, 1024
San Diego, California, 701–702
San Francisco, California. *See also* Angel Island
    Immigration Station
  Asian American political movements in, 745–749
  BART in, 943–944, 946
  Bronzeville neighborhood in, 758–759, 1548
  CCED in, 1542
  Chinese neighborhoods in, 658
  Japantown in, **1542–1557**
  LGBTQ populations in, 668–669. *See also* lesbian, gay,
    bisexual, transgender and queer populations
  mass transit in, 943–944, 946
  Milk in, 133, 140–141
  neighborhood associations in, 140
  plague in, 1052–1053
  Proposition 6 in, 670–671
  Red Guard Party, 745, 748–749
  as world city, 111
Sanger, William, 434–435
sanitary engineers. *See also* sewerage and water networks
  sewage treatment by, 925
sanitary reforms, by public health departments,
  1054–1057
sanitation technology, in municipal housing, 803–805
Sankey, Ira, 1115
Sansei generation, of Japanese Americans, 765
Santorum, Rick, 81
Saperstein, Abe, 377
Sarracino, Etta, 689
SARS. *See* Sudden Acute Respiratory Syndrome
Sassen, Saskia, 109–110, 112, 333
Savannah, Georgia
  after Civil War, 73
  slavery in, 153, 159–160
Saxe, Susan, 671
Saxenian, Annalee, 349
Sbragia, Alberta M., 296
scale houses, in early seaport cities, 25
Schaefer, William Donald, 360
Schermerhorn, Calvin, 53
Schlafly, Phyllis, 1444
Schlei, Norbert, 1158
Schlesinger, Arthur M., Jr., 215, 235, 239, 1441
Schlesinger, Arthur M., Sr., 31, 915
Schmeling, Max, 212

Schmidt, Laura, 423
Schmidt, Richard, 864
Schneider, Eric, 472, 1324, 1333, 1339n82
Schneirov, Richard, 128
Schomburg, Arturo Alonso, 574, 713
schools. *See* public schools
Schrag, Zachary, 942, 943, 946, 960
Schulder, Diane, 1452
Schultz, Dutch, 393
Schultz, Stanley K., 896
Schultze, Charles, 1157
Schumpeter, Joseph, 347
Schur, Edwin, 449
Schuyler, Montgomery, 862
Schwartz, David, 388, 401
Schwarzmann, H. J., 1277
SCLC. *See* Southern Christian Leadership Conference
Scobey, David, 54, 128
Scott, Emmett J., 583
Scott, Joan Wallach, 266–267
Scott, Mel, 896, 915
Scott Act of 1888, US, 484
Scottsboro Boys, 206, 263
Screvane, Paul, 400
SCS. *See* Soil Conservation Service
Scully, Vincent, 875
Scutt, Der, 873
SDS. *See* Students for a Democratic Society
Seabury, Samuel, 398
Seale, Bobby, 735, 745, 1452. *See also* Black Panther Party
Seaman, Eugenia, 1402
seaport cities, in North America, **21–37**. *See also specific*
    cities and towns
  in Chesapeake region, 22
  disease in, from European colonists, 23–24
  as economic anchors, 24–26
  economic functions of, 24–25
  as electric transformers, 24
  elite neighborhoods in, 28–29
  failures in, 23–24
  food markets in, 26
  genteel class in, 27–28
  interracial social networks in, 29
  interracial trade networks in, 29
  "liberty tree" in, 30
  libraries in, 28
  motivation for construction of, 21–22
  Native American threats to, 22
  as political capitals, 30
  primary sources for, 33–34
  public buildings in, 28
  "Regulator" movements in, 31
  religion in, 1108–1109
  retail shops in, 25–26
  role in American Revolution, 29–31

scale houses, 25
security of urban life in, 22–23
sewerage and water networks in, 920
sex markets in, 431, 437
slavery in, 153–154, 156–157
slaves in, 26
socioeconomic class in, 27–28
Sons of Liberty in, 30
success of, 23–24
as transference of European urbanism, 21
urban culture in, 26–29
urban merchants in, 26
urban parks in, 995–996
as "walking cities," 28
wharf activity in, 25
Sears, John F., 355
Seattle, Washington
    Asian American neighborhoods in, 1552
    Asian American political movements in, 747–748
    Native Americans in, 687
Second Bank of the United States, 43
Second Continental Congress, 31
second-generation Puerto Ricans, 718–720
Second Great Awakening, 407, 410, 423
Second Great Migration, 581
Second Industrial Revolution, 485
"second Native diaspora," 153
Second New Deal, 227, 261
    New Industrial Union movement and, 262
Section 7a, of NIRA, 235–236, 260
Section 8 housing program, 823–824, 836, 1472,
    1488n87
Securities and Exchange Commission, 239
securities markets, under New Deal, 228
Sedgwick, William T., 924
Seely, Bruce, 960
segregated diversity, in suburbs, 1457
segregation. See also civil rights; educational segregation;
    public segregation; racial segregation; residential
    segregation
    hypersegregation, 103
    as political term, 639
Seiler, Cotton, 959
SEIU. See Service Employees International Union
Self, Robert, 323
self-built private homes, 806–807
self-employment rates, 250
Sellers, Charles, 52
Sellers, Christopher, 1024, 1042
Seminole tribe, 693
sentencing reform, in juvenile justice system, 1345
September 11 attacks, immigration after, 504, 559–560
Serrano, Andres, 674
service economies, 109–111, **306–321**. See also
    postindustrial service economies

historical development of, after 1950, 306–308
    in New York City, 306–307
    in postindustrial cities, 306–308, 314–316
    postindustrialization and, 308–311
Service Employees International Union (SEIU), 112,
    276, 280
service industries. See also hotels
    in postindustrial service economies, 308–311
Servicemen's Readjustment Act. See GI Bill
Sessions, Kate Olivia, 1004
settlement house movement
    Addams as activist for, 891, 1141
    Hull House, 182, 1141
    poverty and, 1141
    purposes of, 1141
Settlement House movement, 1529
Seventeenth Amendment, 186
sewage treatment, 925–928
    CWA and, 926
    in New Deal programs, 926
    PWA and, 926
    sanitary engineers, 925
    technology for, 926
    USPHS guidelines for, 925
    under Water Pollution Control Act, 925–926
    waterway pollution, 925
Sewell, Jessica, 992
sewerage and water networks, development of,
    919–933, 1033
    aqueducts, 920
    in Chicago, 880–881
    in early seaport cities, 920
    EPA framework for, 928
    green infrastructure for, 928–929
    national legislation on, 924
    pollution treatment in, 923–925
    privately-owned, 920–921
    under Reagan, R., 928
    sewage treatment in, 925–928
    sewer systems, 921–923
    urban health issues with, 924
    water supply systems, 920–921
sewer systems, 921–923
    construction of, 923
    germ theory of disease and, 923
    for storm water management, 923
sexism, in Asian American political movements, 751–752
sex markets
    Chinese women in, 440
    Civil War as influence on, 437–448
    during colonial era, 430–433
    for Continental Army soldiers, 431–432
    economic class stratification for, 439
    from 1820–1920, 433–441
    during 18th century, 430–433

sex markets (*Continued*)
  elite, 446
  gender ideology and, 433
  industrialization as influence on, 434
  labor opportunities in, for young women, 434
  location of, 435
  in New Orleans, 436
  in post-Revolutionary era, 432
  during postwar era, 448–451
  racial stratification for, 439–440
  in seaport cities, 431, 437
  sex trafficking for, 439–440
  slavery markets as, 436–437, 458n54, 458n56
  social justification of, 436, 445
  in the South, 436
  transnational, 439–440
  under vagrancy laws, 432, 437
sex trafficking, 439–440
  under Palermo Protocol, 452
  white slavery and, 442–443
sexual harassment, on mass transit systems, 940
Sexual Politics (Millet), 1452
sexual politics, postwar, 448–452
  feminism and, 449–452
  interracial sex and, 441–442
  Playboy magazine, 449
sex workers, 51. *See also* brothels; prostitution
  COYOTE, 450–451
  feminism and, 449–452
  organizations for, 451
  WHO, 450
  workers' rights for, 451–452
Seymour, Dorothy, 379
Seymour, Harold, 379
Seymour, William J., 1126
Shakur, Tupac, 1260
Shales, Amy, 247n82
The Shame of the Cities (Steffens), 122
Shapiro, Laura, 1100
sharecroppers, 567
  demonstrations by, 208f
"Sharon Statement," 1437
Shaw, Albert, 122
Shaw, Artie, 1215
Shaw, Clifford, 610, 1323, 1333
Shays' Rebellion, 1272
Shelley v. Kraemer, 644, 764, 833, 1144, 1376, 1493–1494
Shelton, Jon, 279
Shelton, Robert, 437
Sheng, Grace, 1461
Shepherd, Alexander, 1002
Shepherd, Jack, 597
Sheppard-Towner Maternity and Infant Welfare bill, US (1921), 181

Sherman, Rachel, 109
Sherman, William T., 73, 846
Sherman Antitrust Act, US (1890), 185, 256
Shermer, Elizabeth Tandy, 599
Shipley, Morgan, 473
Shkuda, Aaron, 112
shopping districts
  in central business districts, 170
  near public squares, 988
  pedestrian malls and, 175
Shorter, Wayne, 1221–1222
"shrinking cities," 322–323
Shriver, Sargent, 1158–1159
Shuttlesworth, Fred, 1130, 1355, 1400–1401, 1406
"sick industries," 258
sidewalks and city streets
  in central business districts, 984–985
  civic pride and, 985
  as commercial space, 984–986
  gentrification of, 985–986
  main streets, 985
  municipal housekeeping for, 985
  in 19 century, 983–984
  parades on, 987
  public celebrations on, 987
  as social space, 986–987
  suburbanization and, 985
  white flight and, 985
Sikhs, 1131
silent majority, 1441, 1444–1445
Silent Majority: Suburban Politics in the Sunbelt South (Lassiter), 1398–1399
Silent Spring (Carson, R.), 1036
Silicon Valley, 107, 109
Simkhovitch, Mary Kingsbury, 184–185, 818, 894, 1529
Simmons, Russell, 1236, 1256. *See also* Run-DMC
Simon, Bryant, 361
simple chiefdoms, 2
Sinclair, Upton, 190, 209, 837, 1099
Siney, John, 624
single-room occupancy (SRO) hotels, 813
Sing Sheng, 1461, 1497
Sioux Nation, 52
SIR group. *See* Society for Individual Rights group
Sissle, Noble, 573
Sister Souljah. *See* Williamson, Lisa
sit-in movement, **1415–1435**
  in Atlanta, 1418–1419
  black churches as part of, 1424
  causes of, 1422–1425
  for civil rights, 77, 1401–1403
  communication networks as part of, 1424
  CORE and, 1416
  creation of, 1423–1425
  defined, 1415–1422

expansion of, 1402, 1417–1418
Freedom Rides influenced by, 1426
Gandhi as influence on, 1418
in Greensboro, North Carolina, 1416–1417
historical accounts of, 1418–1419
Jim Crow laws and, 1420–1421
King, M. L., Jr. on, 1422–1423
Ku Klux Klan response to, 1417, 1419
legal defense strategies during, 1420–1421
legal effects of, 1426–1428
local victories as result of, 1426
long-term legacy of, 1425–1428
lunch counter strategy in, 1422–1423
NAACP and, 1402–1403, 1416, 1421, 1424
in Nashville, 1426
non-violent principles as foundation of, 1418–1420
precursors to, 1416
SCLC and, 1402–1403, 1424
SNCC and, 1403, 1425–1426
student arrests during, 1417–1419, 1421
during summer of 1960, 1421–1422
Supreme Court cases influenced by, 1427
in urban South, 1401–1403
US Congress influenced by, 1427–1428
violence during, 1417, 1419–1420
Six Sermons on the Nature, Occasions, Signs, Evils, and Remedy of Intemperance (Beecher, L.), 408
Sixteenth Amendment, 186
Skid Rows, demolition of, 1148
Skop, Emily, 1495
skyscrapers, 63–65, **858–880**, 858*f*, 862*f*, 864*f*, 866*f*, 869*f*, 870*f*, 872*f*, 873*f*
as apartment buildings, 859, 870–871
architects for, 865–869
Art Deco styles for, 865–867
in Avery Index, 876
building technology for, 860–861
in central business districts, 173
in Chicago, 861–864
after Civil War, 858
decentralization of, away from city centers, 870–872
design for, 859, 862–865
early, 858–859
economic activity in, benefits of, 64
electric elevators and, 64
in films, 875
in modernist theory, 868–869
municipal regulation of, 862–865
as new urban form, 872–874
in New York City, 861–864
office space in, 860–861
as popular term, 859–860
postwar construction of, 870–872
regional planning for, 867–868
Rockefeller Center, 868

as sociocultural concept, 874–875
as speculative industry, 859–861
as symbol of economic expansion, 858–859
urban morphology and, 862–865
World Trade Center, 871, 873–875
under zoning laws, 865–867
Slacker, 346
Slater, Joseph E., 273
Slater, Samuel, 86
Slater, Tom, 1558
Slaughter, Thomas P., 1272, 1274
slave economies. *See also specific cities*
expansion of, 158–159
plantation geography as factor in, 158–159
slave housing, in cities, 160–161
slave rebellions. *See also* Vesey, Denmark
in cities, 162
slavery, in cities, **152–169**
of African Americans, 153. *See also* free African Americans
antislavery movements and, 161–162
Civil War and, 163
colonial urban culture and, 156–158
establishment of, 152–158
European involvement in, 152–153
expansion of, during post-revolutionary period, 158–160
in French settlements, 154
under Fugitive Slave Law, 163, 850, 1276
in Jamestown, 153
manumission societies, 161
of Native Americans, 153, 156
political responses to, 161
public schools and, 1174
Revolutionary War and, 158–163
in Savannah, 153
in seaport cities, 153–154, 156–157
slave housing, 160–161
slave rebellions, 162
in Spanish settlements, 154
slavery markets
in Charleston, 40
economic considerations in, 188n56
"fancy girl" trade, 458n54, 458n56
globalization of, 103
in New York City, 40
during postbellum period, decline in, 51
as sex markets, 188n54, 436–437, 458n56
slaves. *See also* free African Americans; Native Americans
early emancipation of, in northern colonies, 158
in early seaport cities, 26
fugitive, 850–851
Pueblo Revolt and, 155, 162
punishment of, 160–161
ragtime and blues music influenced by, 1207
sexual abuse of, 154

slugging system, 958
Slum Acts of 1935, South Africa, 641
slum clearances, 819. *See also* tenements
　in Richmond, Virginia, 1409
　in urban planning, 908, 910
Small Parks Act, US (1887), 1277
smallpox epidemics, 23, 1050
Smalls, Biggie, 1260
"Smart Growth" movement, 1477–1478
Smelser, Marshall, 380
Smith, Al, 422, 497
Smith, Andrew W., 1099
Smith, Bessie, 1208, 1223
Smith, Carl, 896, 930
Smith, Charles Sprague, 182
Smith, Chuck, 775, 777–778
Smith, Gerrit, 411
Smith, L. C., 864
Smith, Mamie, 1208
Smith, Mary Louise, 1399
Smith, Stacey, 1294, 1300
smog, 972f, 975
smoke density, 1034–1035
smoke pollution, in cities, 184
SNCC. *See* Student Nonviolent Coordinating
　　Committee
Snell, Bradford, 941
Snyder, Brad, 380
soccer, 378
social activism, through religion, 1130–1131
Social Darwinism, 250, 487
social equality, for Chinese, 1290
Social Gospel, 1105, 1123
Socialist Labor Party, 609
Socialist Party of America
　during the Great Depression, 207
　labor and, 252
　during Progressive Era, 254–255
Social Justice, 209f
social justice progressivism
　legal precedents and, 180–181
　social realism and, 180–181
　state role in, 181
　women's suffrage rights and, 181
The Social Life of Small Urban Spaces (Whyte), 316
social networks, interracial, in early seaport cities, 29
social realism, 180–181
social reform movements. *See also* prohibition
　　movement; temperance movement
　against poverty, 1139
　prostitution and, 443
Social Security Act, US (1935), 182, 234–235, 261,
　　1163, 1449
　passage of, 207–208, 1147
Social Security Acts of 1965, US, 1145

social uprisings. *See also* riots
　in Black Freedom movement, 1447–1448
　in Detroit, 138
　in Los Angeles, 144
Society for Individual Rights (SIR) group, 670
Soil Conservation Service (SCS), 207
soil pollution, 1033–1034
Solazzo, Salvatore, 397
Soleri, Paolo, 974
solid waste, as pollution, 1033–1034
Somers, Margaret, 728n11
Song, Ryan, 1312
Sons of Liberty, 30
Sons of Temperance, 411, 414
Soon Ja Du, 1308–1309
Sorkin, Michael, 992
Soto, Hernando de, 7–10
　route of, 9f
soul food, 1095
The Sound of the City: The Rise of Rock and Roll (Gillett), 1230
the South. *See also* New South; urban South; *specific states*
　antebellum era, 72–73
　Chinese in, 1292–1293
　company towns in, 92–95
　deindustrialization in, 323
　Democratic Party in, 235, 247n74
　Dixiecrats in, 238
　European colonization in, 70–72
　hip-hop music from, 1261–1262, 1264
　industrialization in, 61
　lynch mobs in, 1278
　maize agriculture in, 6
　Mississippi chiefdoms in, 6
　The Negro Motorist's Green Book, 1368–1369
　nightlife in, 1192
　per capita income levels in, 599–600
　prohibition movement in, 417–418
　public housing in, 821
　rap music from, 1261–1262, 1264
　sex markets in, 436
　Spanish settlers in, 70–71
　urban exceptionalism in, **70–86**
　vagrancy laws in, 1352
　white laborers in, 49
South Africa
　as archsegregationist society, 640–642
　Group Areas Act of 1950, 641
　Native (Urban Areas) Act of 1923, 641
　Native Location Laws in, 641
　residential segregation in, compared to US, 640–642
　Slum Acts of 1935, 641
South Asian immigrants, at Angel Island Immigration
　　Station, 532–533
South Carolina. *See also specific cities*
　Colored Seamen's Act, 160

cotton mills in, 61
Stono Rebellion in, 29
Souther, Mark, 364
Southern Christian Leadership Conference (SCLC),
1130, 1435, 1445
in Birmingham, Alabama, 1405–1407
sit-in movement and, 1402–1403, 1424
Southern Europe, immigration from, 485. *See also specific*
countries
Southern Manifesto, 1446
Southern Tenant Farmers' Union (STFU), 208
Soviet Union, fall of, 102. *See also* Cold War
SPA. *See* Springfield Parking Authority
Spanish-American War, 699, 905
Spanish Florida
native communities in, 11. *See also specific native tribes*
St. Augustine, 11, 71
Spanish missions, 696–697, 697f
Spanish settlements. *See also* Spanish Florida
slavery in, 154
Spartan Association, 119
Spears, Ellen Griffith, 1042
special taxing districts, 289
Special Tourist Zones, 775
Spector, Phil, 1220
speculative markets
the Great Depression and, 199
in postindustrial cities, 315
Spellman, Francis J., 629
Spergel, Irving, 1324
Spero, Sterling, 274
Spilerman, Seymour, 1282
Spillane, Joseph, 468, 472
Spiro (chiefdom), 5
Spokane, Washington, public authorities in, 289
sports, professional teams and, **368–385**
gambling industry and, 394–397
major league baseball, 369–372
National Hockey League, 375–376
as popular culture, 212–213
professional basketball, 376–378
professional football, 372–374
soccer, 378
Sprague, Frank, 63, 937–938
Springfield Parking Authority (SPA), 286
Springsteen, Bruce, 1234
SRO hotels. *See* single-room occupancy hotels
SSZEA. *See* Standard State Zoning Enabling Act
stagflation, 323
Stall, Susan, 827
Stallmeyer, John, 350
Stamp Act, US (1765), 30
riots after, 1272
Standard State Zoning Enabling Act (SSZEA), US
(1924), 1520–1521

Stanford, Leland, 342, 345
Stanford, Max, 1325
Stanford University, 342
Stansell, Christine, 54, 815
Starr, Ellen Gates, 1141
Starrett, Paul, 875
Starrett, William A., 875
state action doctrine, 1427
States Rights Democratic Party. *See* Dixiecrats
Statue of Liberty, 519
St. Augustine, Florida, 11, 71
Stead, William T., 1116
steam power, 936
Stearns, J. N., 414
Steele, C. K., 1130
steel production
Amalgamated Association of Steel and Iron Works,
90–91
in company towns, 89–90
in Gary, Indiana, 91, 92f
labor unions for, 262
"Little Steel," 262
of structural steel, 63–65
United States Steel Corporation, 91
Steffens, Lincoln, 122, 127
Steichen, Edward, 875
Stein, Clarence, 793, 906
Stein, Gil, 376
Steinbeck, John, 207, 210, 212, 246n33
Steinberg, Ted, 1073
STEP Act. *See* Street Terrorism and Enforcement
Prevention Act
Stephens, Priscilla, 1425
Stern, David, 378
Sterne, Evelyn, 128
Sterner, Frederick, 1561
Stevenson, Adlai, 1565
Stevenson, Brenda, 188n56, 1315
Steward, Luther C., 275
Stewart, Bruce, 424
Stewart, William, 1293
STFU. *See* Southern Tenant Farmers' Union
Stilgoe, John, 787
Stimson, Henry, 447
St. James, Margo, 450–451. *See also* sex workers
St. Louis, Missouri, urban zoning laws in, 1032
Stokes, Carl, 138
Stonewall Inn riot, 1199, 1439
Stonewall riots, 669
Stono Rebellion, 29
storms, 1065–1067
disaster planning for, 1069–1070
Galveston Hurricane of 1900, 1070
Hurricane Andrew, 1071
Hurricane Betsy, 1070

storms (*Continued*)
  Hurricane Camille, 1070–1071
  Hurricane Harvey, 1072
  Hurricane Katrina, 79, 363, 1071–1072
  resilience planning for, 1070–1072
  Superstorm Sandy, 1071
storm water management, 923
Stover, John, 59n64
Stowe, Harriet Beecher, 408, 804
Stradling, David, 1023–1024, 1041–1042
Stradling, Richard, 1024, 1042
"straight state," LGBTQ populations in, 665–668
Stranahan, James T., 998
Strange Future (Min Song), 1314–1315
Straus, Nathan, 819–820, 839
Straus, Oscar, 511
streetcars. *See also* horsecars
  in central business districts, 938–939
  electric, 937–940
  expansion of, 939
  in films, 941
  heritage lines, 944
  public health issues with, 939
  racial segregation on, 940
  suburbanization and, 793, 938–939
  women on, 940
streetcar suburbs, 790, 813
street gangs, **1319–1339**
  in African American neighborhoods, 1324–1325
  Americanism and, 1319–1320
  Asian immigrants in, 1329–1330
  Black Power movement and, 1325–1328
  BPP and, 1326–1327
  CAP and, 1323
  in Chicago, 1319–1321, 1324–1329, 1332
  Chicago School of Sociology and, 1319
  Chicano nationalism and, 1332
  civil rights movement and, 1325–1328
  COINTELPRO project, 1328
  Crips and Bloods, conflicts between, 1331
  defensive localism and, 1336n19
  female, 1325, 1337n26
  as form of defense, 1326
  gang prevention strategies, 1323
  Great Migration and, 1321–1322
  for honor, 1323–1325
  hyperincarceration strategies for, 1328–1332
  immigrants as part of, 1319–1323
  during interwar era, 1319–1321
  in Latino American neighborhoods, 1324–1325, 1331–1332
  Mexicans in, 1321–1323, 1332
  under Nationality Act, 1329
  under Omnibus Crime Control and Safe Streets Act, 1328

  organized crime protection of, 1321
  police protection of, 1321
  political activism through, 1326–1328, 1339n82
  politicization of, 1325–1328
  in popular films, 1323–1324
  in postindustrial cities, 1328–1332
  postwar industrialization as social factor, 1324
  in prisons, 1332
  Puerto Ricans in, 721, 736, 1322–1323, 1327–1329, 1448
  in race riots, 1322–1323
  racial discrimination and, 1319–1320, 1323
  in racial ghettoes and barrios, 1321–1323, 1327–1328
  socioeconomic context for formation of, 1328–1329
  under STEP Act, 1330
  subcultures within, 1323–1325
  in Sunbelt region, 1329
  super-gangs, 1326
  territorial protection by, 1323–1325
  unemployment rates and, 1331
  urban migration patterns as influence on, 1329
  U.S. government response to, 1327–1328
  during World War II, 1321–1322
  Zoot Suit riots, 1323
streets, roads, and highways, **949–963**. *See also* highway and freeway construction
  automobile use and, 952–958
  bicycling on, 951–952
  bridge crossings, 958
  during City Beautiful movement, 951
  during colonial era, 949–950
  for Columbian Exposition, 952
  congestion on, 954–956, 958
  congressional funding of, 949
  from 1890–1910, 951–953
  European influences on, 952
  under Federal Aid Highway Act, 134, 942, 956f, 957
  under Federal Aid Road Act, 969
  "good roads" movement and, 951–953
  highway safety issues and, 955–956
  Highway Trust Fund, 957, 969
  horsecars on, 951
  interstate highways, 956–958
  under Land Ordinance of 1785, 949, 950f
  in McMillan Plan, 952
  municipal distinctions between, 950
  Natchez Trace trail, 949
  for Native Americans, 949–950
  from 1920–1940, 954–956
  during 19th century, 950–951, 952f
  under Northwest Ordinance of 1787, 949
  in Philadelphia, 950–951, 951f
  plank roads, 950
  after Revolutionary War, 949
  rural roads, 952

superhighways, 968
turnpikes, 956
in urban planning, 950–951, 951*f*
for "White City," 952
Street Terrorism and Enforcement Prevention (STEP)
    Act, US (1988), 1330
street vendors, for food, 1081–1082
strikes. *See* labor strikes
Strode, Woody, 373
Strong, Josiah, 1123–1124
structural steel, construction with
    Bessemer steel and, 64
    skyscrapers, 63–65
Student Nonviolent Coordinating Committee (SNCC),
    733–734, 1325, 1373, 1435, 1445
    sit-in movement and, 1403, 1425–1426
student protests, against Vietnam War, 1438
Students for a Democratic Society (SDS), 1436
    Weathermen and, 1440
student strikes. *See also* sit-in movement
    Asian American political movements and, 746–747
    Reagan, R., and, political response to, 747
Studio 54, 1199
substandard housing, 1021
suburbanization, **785–798, 1457–1492**. *See also*
        white flight
    before 1945, **785–798**
    automobile ownership as influence on, 792–793
    central business districts and, 173–174
    of Chicago, 787–788, 791–792
    city-suburb divide, 1460
    as community building, 1459
    crisis of, 1478–1479
    cultural symbolism of, 1463
    culture wars and, 1463–1464
    defined, 786–787
    deindustrialization and, 105
    early forms of, 786–787
    economic class and, 791–792
    English influences on, 787
    environmental movements influenced
        by, 1018–1020, 1022
    environmental pollution influenced by, 1030,
        1035–1036
    ethnicity and, 791–792, 1460–1461, 1471, 1473–1474
    Fannie Mae and, 1466
    farming communities and, 788–789
    female experiences with, 787
    FHA role in, 794, 1458
    in films, 1464
    during the Great Depression, 792–794
    Great Migration as influence on, 792, 794
    growth rates of, from 1940–2010, 1468*t*
    HOLC and, 794
    home ownership as factor for, 793

immigration as influence on, 499–501, 658–659
    improved rail service as influence on, 788–789
    incorporation laws and, 789–790
    in industrial age, 787–788
    infrastructure issues with, 789–790
    institutional centers and, 788–789
    land development and, 1466–1468
    leisure centers and, 788–789
    Levittowns and, 908, 1128, 1376, 1458, 1465–1466
    local governance and, 789–792
    male experiences with, 787
    metropolitanism and, 1468–1470
    "minimum houses" and, 1459
    municipal housing and, 808
    myth of, 1464
    in negro expansion areas, 792–793
    neighborhood diversity in, 788
    New Urbanism and, 1473, 1478*f*
    nightlife and, 1197
    from 1945–1970, 1457–1466, 1487n74
    from 1970–2018, 1466–1478
    political conservatism and, 1465
    political life influenced by, 1464–1466, 1474–1476
    postindustrial service economies and, 314
    postwar real estate development, 1457–1460
    poverty and, 1142–1144
    public-private enterprise and, 1458
    public schools and, 792
    public transportation and, 793
    racial residential patterns with, 791–792
    racial segregation through, 645, 791–792, 1460–1461
    real estate development and, 789, 793
    reformation of, 1476–1478
    REITs and, 1466
    Riverside commuter suburb, 787–788
    sidewalks and city streets and, 985
    "Smart Growth" movement, 1477–1478
    social diversification through, 1470–1472
    social life and, 1461–1463, 1472–1474
    streetcars as influence on, 793, 938–939
    technology as influence on, 789–792
    transportation technology development and, 787, 793
    of urban American South, 79–80
    urban sprawl and, 786, 1018–1019, 1467
    VA and, 1458
    after War of 1812, 787
    women and, social life influenced by, 787, 1463
    World War I and, 792–795
suburbs. *See also* white flight
    Asian Americans in, **1492–1516, 1492–1517**
    boundaries with cities, 790–791
    as "bungalow belts," 793
    Catholicism in, 1128–1131
    CC&Rs in, 1469
    of Chicago, 787–788, 791–792

suburbs (*Continued*)
  CIDs in, 1469–1470, 1475
  commuter, 788
  company towns as, 791–792
  consolidation of, 790
  department stores in, 173
  early, 786
  economic class distinctions in, 791–792
  environmental activism in, 1466
  ethnicity as influence on, 660–661, 791–792,
    1460–1461, 1471, 1473–1474
  ethnoburbs, 908, 1473–1474, 1505
  farming communities as, 788–789
  growth rates for, 1940–2010, 1468*t*
  immigration to, 503–504
  incorporation laws for, 789–790
  industrial, 788–789
  infrastructure issues in, 789–790
  as institutional centers, 788–789
  invisiburbs, 1495
  Judaism in, 1128–1131
  as leisure centers, 788–789
  Levittowns and, 908
  LGBTQ in, 1470–1471, 1488n79
  local governance of, 789–792
  middle-class in, 790
  municipal annexation of, 790
  municipal housing in, 812–814
  neighborhood units in, 792
  planning design for, 902
  Protestantism in, 1128–1131
  in public schools, 792
  racially restrictive covenants in, 794
  racial segregation in, 791–792
  real estate development and, 789, 793, 813
  regeneration of, 1478–1479
  regional shopping centers in, 173–174
  religion in, 1128–1131
  reluctant, 813
  Republican Party and, as voting block for, 1465
  Riverside commuter suburb, 787–788
  segregated diversity in, 1457
  streetcar, 790, 813
  technology in, 789–792
  tourism to, 360
  urban planning for, 902, 906, 906*f*, 912, 914*f*
  urban tourism to, 360
  "vanilla," 637
  zoning laws in, 793–794
Sudden Acute Respiratory Syndrome (SARS), 1058
suffrage rights. *See* voting rights
Sugar Hill Gang, 1254–1255
Sugiyama, Alan, 747
Sugrue, Thomas, 138, 332–333, 1336n19, 1460
suicide rates, during the Great Depression, 202

Sullivan, "Big" Tim, 390
Sullivan, Louis, 63–64, 863, 875
Sumi, Pat, 751
Summers, Nancy, 432
sumptuary laws, 415
Sunbelt region, 78–79
  environmental pollution in, 1036
  Republican Party strength in, 78
  street gangs in, 1329
  urban redevelopment in, 136–137
  white migration to, 594
"sundown towns," 1370
Super Bowl, 374
super-gangs, 1326
superhighways, 968
supermarkets, 1096
"super-predators," 1344
Superstorm Sandy, 1071
Supreme Court, US
  Berman v. Parker, 1524, 1533
  Black Freedom movement and, legal challenges
    during, 1446
  Bowers v. Hardwick, 676
  Boynton v. Virginia, 1403
  Browder v. Gayle, 1400–1401
  Brown v. Board of Education, 821, 1181, 1343, 1376,
    1422
  Buchanan v. Warley, 808, 1522–1523
  Champion v. Ames, 389
  Due Process Revolution for, 1343
  Euclid v. Ambler Realty, 1516, 1519–1520
  Friedrich v. California Teachers Association, 281
  Gideon v. Wainwright, 1450
  Hadacheck v. Sebastian, 1518
  Henderson v. Mayor of New York, 509
  Hills v. Gautreaux, 824
  Hopkins v. City of Richmond, 1522
  juvenile justice cases, 1343, 1345
  Lawrence v. Texas, 677
  Lochner v. New York, 180, 256
  Loving v. Virginia, 732
  Mapp v. Ohio, 399
  Milliken v. Bradley, 1377
  Miranda v. Arizona, 1450
  Muller v. Oregon, 180
  municipal housing cases, 808
  Nectow v. City of Cambridge, 1520
  New York v. Miln, 1351
  NIRA nullified by, 236
  Northwest Laundry v. Des Moines, 183
  People v. Hall, 1303n18
  Perez v. Sharp, 732
  Plessy v. Ferguson, 75, 641, 940
  re Gault case, 1342–1343, 1346
  residential segregation cases, 808

Ritchie v. People, 180
Romer v. Evans, 677
Shelley v. Kraemer, 644, 764, 833, 1144, 1376, 1493–1494
   sit-in movement as influence on, 1427
   state action doctrine and, 1427
   vagrancy law cases, 1353–1359
Vanderbilt v. Adam, 1517
   zoning law cases, 808, 1516–1520, 1522–1524
Sutherland, George, 1519
Sutter, Paul, 959
Sutton, Betty, 1306
Swanstrom, Todd, 150n81
Sweeney, John, 629
Sweeney, Vincent, 628
Sweet, Ossian, 1368
Swift, Gustavus, 1079
Sze, Julia, 1024

tabaqueros (Puerto Rican artisans), 713
table games, 388
Taeku Lee, 1311–1312
Taft, Chloe, 112
Taft, William Howard, 186, 272
Taft-Ellender-Wagner Housing Act, US. *See* Housing Act of 1949
Taft-Hartley Act, US (1947), 277
Tagawa, Mike, 747
tailoring, industrialization of, 48
Taiping Rebellion, 483
Takei, George, 761
Talent, Jim, 1161
Talese, Gay, 1452
Talisi (chiefdom), 10
Tammany Hall, political controversy and, 119–121.
   See also Tweed, William Magear
   public response to, 121
   Roosevelt, Franklin Delano, on, 126
Tanaka, Janice, 765
TANF. *See* Temporary Assistance for Needy Families
Tangires, Helen, 1080
Taper, Mark, 908
Tarbell, Ida, 190
Tarr, Joel, 930, 935, 945, 959, 1041, 1074
Tascalusa (chiefdom), 8, 10–12
taverns and saloons, 1189–1190, 1193
taxation
   deindustrialization and, 324
   in postindustrial service economies, 313–314
tax codes. *See* federal tax codes
tax-exempt bond markets, 294
tax increment financing (TIF), 328
taxing districts. *See* special taxing districts
Tax Reform Act, US (1966), 1566
Taylor, Billy, 1223–1224, 1227

Taylor, Dorcetta, 1024, 1042
Taylor, Frederick Winslow, 250
Taylor, Graham Romeyn, 91, 795
Taylor, Joseph S., 996
Taylor, Paul, 211
Taylor, William R., 357
TDRs. *See* transfer of development rights
teachers
   African American women as, 75–76, 1371
   in public schools, 1182–1183
   public sector unions for, 273
   segregation of, by race, 1371
   training for, at universities and colleges, 343
Teaford, John, 333, 790, 796
Tea Party, 30
technical class, 324
technical schools, 1177
Techwood Homes, 907
television
   major league baseball on, contracts for, 371
   MTV channel, 1235, 1238, 1255
   NHL on, 376
   professional basketball on, 378
   professional football on, 374
   rap music on, 1262
Temin, Peter, 214
temperance, **406–430**
   defined, 407–408
   literature on, 409
   in popular culture, 412–413
temperance movement, **406–430**
   abstinence and, 410
   African Americans as part of, 409, 415
   American Tract Society and, 410
   ATS, 410
   Beecher, L., and, 408
   black convention movement and, 409
   children in, 411
   during Civil War, 413–414
   as class-based movement, 408
   clergy as part of, 411
   during colonial period, 406
   conflicts within, 410–411
   Democratic Party and, 415
   dry counties and, 415–416
   from 1836–1893, 410–416
   fraternal lodges in, 411
   ideology of, 406
   in individual states, 412
   legal backlash against, 412
   methodology of, 409–410
   middle-class in, 411
   motivations of, 408
   nightlife during, 1190
   organizations in, 409–411, 414–416

temperance movement (*Continued*)
  political impact of, 411–412, 415–416
  in popular literature, 413
  during postbellum period, 414–416
  Prohibition Party and, 414–415
  purpose of, 408–409
  under Republicanism, 408
  Republican Party and, 414
  Second Great Awakening and, 407, 410, 423
  from 1784–1836, 406–410
  sumptuary laws and, 415
  in theater productions, 413
  ultraists and, 408
  Washingtonians in, 411–413
  women as part of, 409, 414–415
  Young Men's Christian Association, 413–414
temperance societies, 409–411. *See also specific societies*
Temporary Assistance for Needy Families (TANF), 1146
temporary housing programs, 1148
tenements, 65
  as municipal housing, 804, 806
Tennessee Valley Authority (TVA), 200, 226, 232–233, 239, 261, 286, 297, 299
Teotihuacán, Mexico, 684–685, 696
Terrell, Mary Church, 75
territories, US. *See also* Puerto Rico
  prostitution in, 444, 448
terrorism, urban tourism influenced by, 363
Texas. *See* Republic of Texas; *specific cities*
textile mills. *See also* cotton mills
  Cannon Mills factories, 93
  cotton production and, 46–47
  Irish immigrants in, 623, 623*f*
textile production. *See also* cotton production
  in company towns, 93, 93*f*, 95
  in Kannapolis, North Carolina, 93, 95
  in Lowell, Massachusetts, 88–89
textile workers, labor strikes by, 252*f*
Thale, Christopher, 1280
Thatcher, Margaret, 298
theaters, 1190–1192
  Asian American political movements through, 753
  Broadway, 1200, 1262
  during the Great Depression, 1197
  Latino urbanism in, 707
  temperance movement and, 413
  vaudeville, 1194
  women as patrons of, 170
theme parks. *See* amusement and theme parks
Theoharris, Jeanne, 1399
Thernstrom, Stephen, 815
Third World movements, 750
This World, 4
Thomas, Alice, 431
Thomas, Lynnell, 364

Thomas, William I., 610, 615
Thompson, David, 377–378
Thompson, E. P., 266, 1272, 1284
Thompson, Heather, 137
Thompson, Hunter S., 1452
Thompson, Jack, 1258
Thompson, James, 400–401
Thompson, Robert, 1297. *See also* anti-Chinese massacre
Thompson, Thomas, 1146
Thompson, William "Big Bill," 126, 575
Thompson, William Hale, 123
Thoreau, Henry David, 88
Thorpe, Jim, 372
Thrasher, Frederic, 610, 1319, 1332
Thurmond, Strom, 78, 1398
TIF. *See* tax increment financing
Tilikum Crossing, 958
Tillman, Ben, 1278
Tilly, Charles, 1271
timber industry, in company towns, 89
Times Square, 1193, 1200
Timothy, Peter, 28
TND. *See* traditional neighborhood development
Tobin, John, 625
Tocqueville, Alexis de, 1367–1368
toll roads, 956, 958
Tong, "Gene," 1299. *See also* anti-Chinese massacre
Tongson, Karen, 1498
Tong Wan, 1299. *See also* anti-Chinese massacre
Tonry, Michael, 1345
Torres, Felipe, 718
tour companies, 356
tourism, in cities, **353–368**
  African American promotion of, 362
  in age of mass tourism, 358–360
  amusement and theme parks and, 359–360
  car culture and, development of, 359
  to central business districts, 357–358, 361
  for city expositions, 356, 358, 359*f*
  city mayors' role in, 360–361
  after Civil War, 355
  climate change and, 358
  convention center development and, 359
  culture wars and, 363
  disaster, 363
  early reasons for, 354
  from 1800–1870, 353–355, 354*f*
  from 1870–1930, 355–358, 356*f*, 357*f*
  through expositions, 359*f*
  during the Great Depression, 358
  to Harlem, 357
  for historical attractions and resources, 360–361
  hotels and, 355–356, 356*f*, 358–359
  after Hurricane Katrina, 363
  to Las Vegas, 359

for LGBTQ populations, 362–363
moral geography and, 357
after National Historic Preservation Act, 360
after natural disasters, 363
to New Orleans, 360
to New York City, 354–357
from 1930–1970, 358–360
from 1970–2018, 360–363
to Philadelphia, 353–354
in postindustrial cities, 325–326
promotional organizations for, 357
publications for, 356–357
railroad expansion as influence on, 353–354, 355
to specific ethnic neighborhoods, 357
suburbs and, 360
terrorism as influence on, 363
tour companies, 356
tourist bubbles, 361–364
transportation infrastructure as factor for, 359
urban planning for, 912
urban renewal and, 362
after World War II, 360
WPA and, 358
"tourist bubbles," 331–332, 361–364
Town Creek (chiefdom), 5
Townsend, Francis, 209
Townshend, James, 850
toxic waste pollution, 1038–1039
tract-home development
environmental impact of, 1018–1019
residential segregation in, 1019
trade networks, interracial, in early seaport cities, 29
trade schools, 1178
trade union progressivism, 186–187
traditional neighborhood development (TND), 1516
traditional public authorities, 293
traffic congestion, 958
on streets, roads, and highways, 954–956
The Tragedy of American Compassion (Olasky), 1161
transfer of development rights (TDRs), 1516
transience, during the Great Depression, 205–207
transnational sex markets, 439–440
transportation infrastructure. *See also* highway and
    freeway construction; public transportation;
    railroad industry
electrical grid development as influence on, 61–63
under Highway Act of 1956, 134
public authorities for, 292, 294
under PWA, 234
suburbanization influenced by, 787, 793
urban tourism influenced by, 359
Transport Workers Union (TWU), 283n32
trap music, 1264
Treaty of Amity and Commerce, 542
Treaty of Kanagawa, 542

Treaty of Nanjing, 542
Treaty of Paris, 40, 713
Treaty of Wanghia, 542
Triangle Shirtwaist factory fire, 182, 253, 253f, 256, 1518
Trollope, Frances, 801, 1084
Trouble in Mind: Black Southerners in The Age of Jim Crow
    (Litwack), 582
Trounstine, Jessica, 127
Trowbridge, John T., 850–851
Truman, Harry, 277, 544, 629, 1398
    Fair Deal, 226
Trump, Donald, 111, 615
    immigration policy under, 504
Tucker, C. Delores, 1262
Tugwell, Rexford G., 832, 907
Tunicas nation, 12
Ture, Kwame, 1451. *See also* Carmichael, Stokely
Turnbo-Malone, Annie, 572
Turner, Eliza, 437
Turner, Frederick Jackson, 1206–1207
Turner, George Kibbe, 443
Turner, John, 514
turnpikes, 956
Tuttle, William M., Jr., 1278, 1284
TVA. *See* Tennessee Valley Authority
Tweed, William Magear ("Boss Tweed"), 120–121
Twelve Million Black Voices (Wright, R.), 211
2 Live Crew, 1258
TWU. *See* Transport Workers Union
Tydings-McDuffie Act, US (1934), 543
Tygiel, Jules, 380
"Typhoid" Mary. *See* Mallon, Mary

UCAPAWA. *See* United Cannery, Agricultural, Packing,
    and Allied Workers Union
Udall, Stewart, 373
UFW. *See* United Farm Workers
ultraists, 408
Umbach, Fritz, 827
UMTA. *See* Urban Mass Transportation Act
Uncle Tom's Children (Wright, R.), 210
underground railways, 938
undesirables, as immigrant category, 514
undocumented immigrants, 111
unemployment rates. *See also* employment rates
    for African Americans, during the Great
        Depression, 201
    during the Great Depression, 200–202
    for Puerto Ricans, 728n5
    street gangs and, 1331
unemployment relief, under New Deal, 228–230
Union Leagues, 120–121
unions. *See* labor unions; public sector unions
United Cannery, Agricultural, Packing, and Allied
    Workers Union (UCAPAWA), 208

United Farm Workers (UFW), 733–734
United Mine Workers, 94, 203, 235–236
United Nations, 226
    on sex trafficking, 452
United Negro Improvement Association, 1372, 1374
United Public Workers of America (UPWA), 277–278,
    284n39
United States (US). *See also* Cold War; Constitution;
    immigration; Supreme Court; *specific regions;*
    specific states
    as archsegregationist society, 640–642
    border crossings from Mexico, Latino urbanism
        through, 698–700
    DHS in, 560
    Dollar Diplomacy of, 187
    early censuses, on population, 37
    early rural populations, 38, 38*f*
    early urban populations, 38, 38*f*
    economic development in, after World War II, 1419
    economic recessions in, 198, 200, 237
    Federal Reserve in, 200
    First Bank of the United States, 43, 48, 288
    FTZs in, 105
    gold standard in, 198, 228
    as immigrant nation, 558–560
    international migration to, 198–201, 561*t*, 562*f*
    invasion of Cuba by, 187
    Puerto Rico as US possession, 187, 713
    Red Scare in, 190
    residential segregation in, compared to South Africa,
        640–642
    Second Bank of the United States, 43
    self-employment rates in, 250
    Spanish-American War and, 699
    Third World movements in, 750
    US-Philippines War, 750
    wars against Native Americans, 40
    war with Mexico, 40
United States Housing Authority (USHA), 819–820
United States Steel Corporation, 91
Universal Negro Improvement Association, 257
universities and colleges, in cities, **340–353**. *See also*
        specific universities and colleges
    Asian American political movements in, 746–747
    in Austin, Texas, 344–347
    under Bayh-Dole Act, 347–348
    during Civil War, 340
    during Cold War, 340
    as economic investment, 341–342
    educational ideology in, 341
    federal investment in, 344–347
    GI Bill and, 344–346
    during Gilded Age, 340
    in Great Society program, 347
    historical phases of, 340

    as information centers, 341
    land grants for, 341–342
    liberalism in, during mid-century, 343–347
    marketing of, 347–349
    middle-class and, 340
    under Morrill Land Grant Acts, 341
    Native American attendance, 691–693
    philanthropic investment in, 342
    for postgraduate studies, 340
    postwar expansion of, 344–347
    during Progressive Era, 340, 342
    progressive reform in, 342–343
    under PWA, 343
    research collaborations in, 347–349
    teacher training for, 343
    urban growth and, 341
    urban renewal supported by, 344
    white-collar class and, 340
    under WPA, 343
University of Chicago, 342–343
unskilled labor, 47
uprisings. *See* riots; social uprisings
Upshaw, Gene, 374
Upton, Dell, 32, 54, 986, 992
UPWA. *See* United Public Workers of America
urban agriculture, in postindustrial cities, 330
"urban crisis," immigration and, 501–503
urban destruction, during Civil War, **844–858**
    aesthetics of, 851–853
    Atlanta, 846–848
    cities as military targets, 844
    civilian morale as result of, 844
    through defensive burning, 850–851
    Fredericksburg, Virginia, 844–846, 845*f*
    fugitive slaves and, 850–851
    photography of, 851–853
    as revenge and retaliation, 848–850
    by soldiers, 848–850
    Vicksburg, Mississippi, 846
urban entrepreneurialism, 315
urban exceptionalism, in American South, **70–86**
    African American migration and, 73–75
    for African American women, 75–76
    during antebellum era, 72–73
    "Atlanta Compromise," 76
    black churches and, 75
    black middle class and, 75
    "Bulldozer Revolution," 78
    busing policies and, 79
    civil rights and, 77–78
    during Civil War, 73
    Confederate monuments and, controversy over, 82
    diversity issues, 80
    European colonialism and, 70–72
    evangelical churches and, 79–80

immigrants in, 72–73, 76
during Jim Crow era, 75–76
memorial museums and, 81–82
in New South, 73–76
northern migration and, 79
Plessy v. Ferguson and, 75, 940
public segregation and, 77
residential segregation and, 75
rural-urban divisions, 81
suburbanization and, 79–80
in Sunbelt region, 78–79
urban planning discrimination and, 79
urban renewal and, 79
voting rights and, 77
during World War II, 77
urbanization, in US, **37–70**. *See also* suburbanization;
   urban regions; *specific cities*
in censuses, 37, 39f, 60
City Beautiful movement influenced by, 883
climate change influenced by, 1063–1065
early rural population trends, 38f
early urban population trends, 38f
environmental pollution influenced by, 1029,
   1031–1035
gambling industry influenced by, 387–388
machine politics influenced by, 118
market societies and, 39–45
in New South, 76
"paper cities," 40
politics in urban areas after 1945, **133–152**
politics in urban areas before 1940, **117–132**
poverty influenced by, 1140–1141
prohibition movement influenced by, 417–419
public transportation as influence on, 50
religion in US cities influenced by, 1115
rioting influenced by, 1272
small villages influenced by, 43
Urban League, 570–571
urban liberalism, machine politics and, 124
urban life. *See also* urban North; urban South
rural life and, boundaries between, 49
Urban Mass Transportation Act (UMTA), US (1964),
   943–944
urban migration
Latino urbanism and, 702–704
of Native Americans, 687–690
of Puerto Ricans, 716–718
urban neighborhoods. *See also* Asian American
   neighborhoods; ghettoes and barrios; Harlem
   neighborhood; working-class neighborhoods
for African Americans, 257, 571–573, 1324–1325
El Barrio, 735
Bronzeville, in San Francisco, 758–759, 1548
chain migration to, 654–655
in Chicago, 257

Chinese, 657–658
city-suburb divide, 1460
in Detroit, 257
displacement of, through urban planning, 908
elite, in seaport cities, 28–29
ethnicity and, 654–659
ethnoburbia, 659–661
Great Migration to, 571–573
immigrants in, 502–503
for Japanese Americans, 758–759
Jewish, 656–659, 657f, 664n36
for Latino Americans, 1324–1325, 1331–1332
for LGBTQ, 674
police abuse in, of African Americans, 1371
Polish immigrants in, 613
for Puerto Ricans, 735
"red light" neighborhoods, 442
street gangs in, 1324–1325
tourism in, 357
white ethnic neighborhood associations in, 135–136
urban North. *See also* Great Migration; *specific cities;*
   specific states
Black Freedom movement in, **1367–1396**
Black Power movement in, 1378–1379
busing policies in, 1377
community formation in, 1371–1373
desegregation of public schools in, 1376–1377
educational segregation in, 1370–1371
Great Migration as influence on, 1368
housing segregation in, 1370, 1375–1376
incarceration polices in, inequities of, 1377–1378
Jim Crow laws in, 1368–1369, 1373–1374
law-and-order policies in, 1379–1380
police abuse in, 1371, 1377–1378
political mobilization in, of African Americans,
   1371–1373
racial violence in, 1371
workplace discrimination in, 1369–1370
urban parks. *See* parks
urban planning, **901–919**
before 1850, 901–902
African American neighborhoods and, displacement
   of, 908
in Atlanta, 911
for automobile use, 965–971
baby boom population as consideration of, 907–908
central business districts and, 170
for Central Park, 902f
of Charleston, 22
civil unrest as factor for, 910
Club of Rome and, 912
in Detroit, 329
discrimination and, in urban American South, 79.
   See also residential segregation
downtown regeneration as part of, 911

urban planning (*Continued*)
  Earth Day and, 912
  in "edge cities," 910
  from 1850–1909, 903–904
  ethnoburbs and, 908
  under Fair Housing Act, 910
  germ theory of disease and, 903–904
  GI Bill and, 907
  during Gilded Age, 904
  during the Great Depression, 905–906
  in Greenbelt towns, 907
  under Housing Act of 1937, 907
  under Housing Act of 1949, 907
  infrastructural technology development for, 901–902
  during Jim Crow era, 905
  as key to civilization, 22
  "Lakewood Plan," 908
  Levittowns, 908
  local funding of, 906
  miasma theory and, 903–904
  modern definition of, 901
  National Conference on City Planning, 184
  under New Deal, 906–907
  in New Orleans, promotion of, 21
  New Urbanism through, 913
  NIMBY responses to, 913, 1474
  from 1909–1945, 904–907
  from 1945–1965, 907–908
  from 1965–1989, 909–911
  from 1989–2018, 911–913
  for "Organic City," 904–906, 908–909
  palliative, 329
  parks as part of, 905
  of Philadelphia, 22
  in postindustrial cities, 328–330
  during Progressive Era, 901, 905
  public housing as part of, 907
  public-private enterprise in, 910
  public revolt against, 909–911
  punitive planning strategies, 1409
  PWA and, 907
  by real estate developers, 905
  reclamation of nature as part of, 912
  redlining with, 908, 909*f*
  residential segregation through, 639–640
  in Rust Belt region, 907
  slum clearance as part of, 908, 910, 1409
  streets, roads, and highways in, 950–951, 951*f*
  of suburban communities, 902, 906, 906*f*, 912, 914*f*
  tourism as result of, 912
  in urban renewal and redevelopment, 134, 907
  urban sprawl and, 903
  zoning codes and laws in, 905
Urban Redevelopment Act, US (1954), 1524
urban redevelopment and renewal, **1528–1542**

African Americans and, 135–136
agencies for, 135
in Asian American neighborhoods, long-term impact
    of, 1551–1552
in Atlanta, 139, 1410–1411
black power activists and, 137–138
in Boston, 138–139
CDBGs, 1538
in central business districts, 174–175
citizen rebellions against, 137
citizens' movements and, 139
in City Beautiful movement, 1530, 1533
through city charters, 134
during Cold War, 1536
collapse of, 1536–1538
for communities of color, 1545
community activism in, 136
under Community Redevelopment Act, 1538
conservation movements and, 1020
through cultural institutions, 1533
deindustrialization and, 321
desegregation of schools and, 138
discriminatory practices for home ownership, 136
through economic restructuring, 144
under Eisenhower, 1528
electoral trends and, 145
through eminent domain, 1533
environmental movement and, 1020
federal government role in, 1538
federal urban policy and, 141
under Ford, Gerald, 1538
freeway construction as part of, 1410
freeway revolts, 1537
gay rights movement and, 140–141
gentrification and, 145, 1533–1534
during the Great Depression, 1531–1532
Great Society and, 1528
under Highway Act of 1956, 134
under Housing Act of 1949, 134, 1532–1533,
    1545–1546
under Housing Act of 1954, 134, 1532–1533
under HUD, 1535
immigrant activism and, 144–145
immigrant settlement patterns, 144–145
Japantown, in San Francisco, 1542–1552
under Johnson, L. B., 1535
Latino urbanism and, 700–702
local antecedents for, 1528–1530
in Los Angeles, 135, 143–144
minority populations and, 135–137
Model Cities program and, 811, 834–835, 1145, 1535
multiracial political alliances and, 136
national political trends as result of, 145
neighborhood activism as result of, 137–140
under New Deal, 1531–1532

in New York City, 142–143
under Nixon R., 1538
opposition against, 134–135
Paris model for, 1529–1530
in Philadelphia, 138
through planning programs, 134
police brutality issues and, 145, 1280–1281
in postwar period, 1532–1535
poverty influenced by, 1142–1144
during Progressive Era, 1528–1530
racial considerations in, 1537
racial segregation as result of, 144, 1142–1144,
    1308–1310
through redevelopment agencies, 134
residential segregation and, 137
riots as result of, 137
Rockefeller Center and, 1533
in Rust Belt cities, 143
in the South, 79
in Sunbelt region, 136–137
universities' role in, 344
urban parks and, 1008
urban planning in, 134, 907
in urban South, 1409–1410
urban tourism influenced by, 362
of Washington DC, 1530
white ethnic neighborhood associations and, 135–136
white flight to suburbs and, 141–142
working-class populations and, 135–136
during World War II, 1531–1532
urban regions, in US. *See also* politics in urban areas;
    specific cities
early population trends in, 38*f*
urban renewal. *See* urban redevelopment and renewal
urban segregation, from globalization, 104
urban South. *See also specific cities*
Black Freedom movement in, **1396–1415**
Civil Rights Act (1965) and, 1408–1409
employment discrimination in, 1410–1411
Freedom Rides in, 1403–1404
during Jim Crow era, 75–76, 1404–1405
Ku Klux Klan in, 1397
Montgomery bus boycott, 77, 940, 1399–1401
opposition to civil rights in, 1398
sit-in movement in, 1401–1403
urban crisis in, for African Americans, 1409–1411
urban renewal and development in, 1409–1410
Voting Rights Act (1965) and, 1408–1409
urban sprawl
from automobile use, 974–975, 975*f*
through suburbanization, 786, 1018–1019, 1467
urban planning for, 903
urban tourism. *See* tourism
The Urban Transportation Problem (Meyer, J., Kain, J., and
    Wohl, M.), 944

The Urban Villagers (Gans), 1536
US. *See* United States
US Congress, sit-in movement and, 1427–1428
The Uses of the University (Kerr), 345, 349–350
USHA. *See* United States Housing Authority
Usner, Daniel, 164, 169n31
US-Philippines War, 750
US Public Health Service (USPHS), 925
US territories. *See* territories, US
Utes, 155

VA. *See* Veterans Administration
vaccine development
    for contagious diseases, 1057–1058
    for polio, 1057–1058
Vagabond Act, US (1877), 1352
vagrancy laws, **1350–1365**
    African Americans and, 1352, 1356, 1358
    Black Codes and, 1352
    after Civil War, 1351–1352
    during colonial era, 1351
    constitutional challenges to, 1354–1357
    convictions for, 1352–1353
    enforcement of, 1353
    free speech protections and, 1353–1356
    during the Great Depression, 1352–1354
    hippies and, 1356
    immigrants and, 1351
    during Industrial Revolution, 1351–1352
    IWW and, 1353
    loitering laws and, 1353, 1357–1358
    New York v. Miln, 1351
    during 19th century, 1351–1353
    after 1972, 1357–1359
    during 1960s, 1355–1356
    during Nixon presidency, 1358
    in Northern States, 1352
    origins of, 1350–1351, 1353
    police abuse of, 1358–1359
    during Progressive Era, 1353
    purpose of, 1350
    racial discrimination in, 1351, 1356, 1358
    socioeconomic context for, 1355–1356
    in the South, 1352
    in Supreme Court cases, 1353–1359
    during 20th century, 1353–1359
    under Vagabond Act, 1352
    in War on Poverty and, 1355
    women and, 1351
Vale, Lawrence, 820, 827
Van Alen, William, 866
Van Buren, Martin, 271
Vandegrift, Texas, 90–91
van Depoele, Charles, 937
Vanderbilt, Cornelius, 342

van der Rohe, Ludwig Mies, 869, 871
Vandiver, Ernest, 1419
Van Halen, Eddie, 1236
"vanilla" suburbs, 637
Vanport, Oregon, 820
Van Valkenburgh, Michael, 1007
Varela, María, 733
vaudeville theaters, 1194
    blackface minstrelsy in, 1207
Vaux, Calvert, 787
    Central Park and, 902, 988–989, 996–1001, 1014
    Prospect Park and, 998–1000
    suburban planning design by, 902
Vaux, Richard, 119
Veiller, Lawrence, 805, 1519, 1529
Venkatesh, Sudhir, 827
Vergara, Camilo José, 874
Verner, Elizabeth O'Neill, 1562
Vesey, Denmark, 160, 162
vestibule neighborhoods, 636
veterans. See military veterans
Veteran's Administration (VA), 1458, 1531
vice commissions, 1194
vice industries, 327. See also casinos; prostitution;
        sex markets
Vicksburg, Mississippi, destruction of, 846
"victimless crimes," prostitution as, 463n180
Viele, Egbert L., 996
Vietnam, communist-led insurgencies in, 1436–1437
Vietnamese immigrants, 545, **770–783**. See also Little
        Saigon
    businesses owned by, 775–776
    community spaces for, 773–774
    cultural institutions for, 776
    in Little Saigon, 770–780
    political activism of, 776–778
    during post-cold war era, 778–779
    settlement in Orange County, California, 774–776
Vietnam Veterans Against the War (VVAW), 1444
Vietnam War. See also anti-Vietnam War movement
    foundations of, 1435
    Johnson, L. B., and, expansion of, 1437–1438
    NLF and, 1436
    refugees after, 771–773
"Vieux Carée," 24
View of South Street, from Maiden Lane (Bennett, W. J.), 44f
villas, 696–697
Villier, Laurence, 815
violence. See also hate crimes; riots; specific topics
    emancipation movement and, 1295
    during Reconstruction era, 1295–1296
viral contagious diseases, 1058–1059. See also human
        immunodeficiency virus/acquired immune
        deficiency syndrome; Sudden Acute Respiratory
        Syndrome

Virginia. See also specific cities
    James River, 71
    Rappahannock River, 71
    tobacco port settlements, 71, 71f
Vital Center Liberalism, 1441–1445
    during Cold War, 1442–1443
    New Left and, 1443
    nuclear proliferation and, 1443
VOLAGS. See voluntary social service networks
Volck, Adalbert John, 847f
Vollmer, Joan, 470
Volstead, Andrew, 419
Volstead Act, US (1919), 189, 257, 419–420, 422, 1195
voluntary social service networks (VOLAGS), 544
voting rights
    for Irish immigrants, 50
    social justice progressivism and, 181
    in urban American South, 77
    for women, 181, 190
Voting Rights Act, US (1965), 77, 718, 722–723,
        1408–1409
vouchers, for private schools, 1377
VVAW. See Vietnam Veterans Against the War

Wacker, Charles, 891
Wade, Richard, 53, 163
wage inequality
    for free African Americans, 51
    in global cities, 110
    for women, 48
wage labor
    Great Migration and, 567
    industrialization and, 49
wages. See also income levels; salaries
    living, 187
    under Minimum Wage Law, 1144
    from prostitution, 441
    in railroad industry, 52
wage slavery, industrialization and, 49
Wagner, Robert F., 203, 236, 290, 400, 718, 810–811.
        See also Wagner-Steagall Housing Act
    public housing programs and, 819
Wagner Act, US (1935), 203
Wagner-Steagall Housing Act, US (1937), 810, 834
Wald, Lillian, 188, 190
Waldrep, Christopher, 1274, 1277–1278, 1285
Walentas, David, 1567
Walker, C. J. (Madame), 572
Walker, James R., 379
Walker, Ralph, 866
Walker, Robert, 1411
Walker, Scott, 281
"walking cities," early seaport cities as, 28
Walkowitz, Judith, 453
Wallace, George, 645, 1159, 1440–1441

Wallace, Henry, 231–232
Wallace, Mike, 54
Wallach, Jennifer, 1099
Waller, Fats, 1210
Wall Street Crash of 1929
    automobile industry after, 259
    Hoover's response to, 259
    immediate aftermath of, 258–259
    industrial production after, 259
Walsh, Annmarie Hauck, 296
Walsh, Mike, 119, 621–622
Walt Disney World, 359–360
Walters, Ronald G., 424
Wan Foo, 1299. *See also* anti-Chinese massacre
War Brides Act, US (1945), 544
Ward, Edward, 125
Ward, Henry Ward, 408
Ward, John M., 369
warehousing, 326
warfare, postindustrial service economies and, 312
Warhol, Andy, 470, 910
war iconography, during Mississippi period, 2
Waring, George E., 272, 881, 1033
Waring, George E., Jr., 923
Warner, Sam Bass, Jr., 68, 790, 795, 816
War of 1812, 787
War on Poverty, 328, 1144–1145, **1153–1172**, 1155–1157,
    1306, 1437
    Native Americans and, 692
    programs in, 1156
    public schools and, 1183
    vagrancy laws and, 1355
    welfare state and, 1154, 1163–1165
War Relocation Authority (WRA), 759, 761–762
Warren, Diane, 1237
Warren, Earl, 1435
Washington, Booker T., 76, 189, 583
    on segregation in public schools, 1178
Washington, Dinah, 1217
Washington, Forrester B., 570
Washington, George, 164
Washington, Harold, 138, 141
Washington, Kenny, 373
Washington DC
    City Beautiful movement in, 884–887
    civic organizations in, 885
    L'Enfant and, 996, 1002–1003
    mass transit in, 943–944
    McMillan Plan for, 885–887, 952
    National Mall as memorial park, 1003
    urban parks in, 1001–1004
    urban renewal in, 1530
Washingtonians, in temperance movement, 411–413
Wa Sin Quai, 1299. *See also* anti-Chinese massacre
Watchorn, Robert, 511, 513

water carrier technology, 922
    aqueducts, 920
Waterhouse, Benjamin, 1057
water networks. *See* sewerage and water networks; water
    supply systems
water pollution, 1037–1038
    bacteriological theory and, 1032–1033
    under Clean Water Act, 927–928, 1037
    under Safe Drinking Water Act, 1037
    sewerage networks and, 1033
    under Water Quality Act, 927–928, 1037
Water Pollution Control Act, US (1948), 925–926
water-power mechanization, 45
Water Quality Act, US (1965), 927–928, 1037
Waters, Muddy, 1220
water supply systems, **919–933**
    aqueducts, 920
    chlorination in, 925
    for drinking water, 924
    filtration systems in, 924–925
    wastewater flow and disposal, 921, 927*f*
    water carrier technology for, 922
    water sources, 921
waterway pollution, 925
waterway transport. *See also* Erie Canal; Panama Canal
    Zone
    of food products, 1077–1078
water wheels, 61
Watts riots, 1282
WCTU. *See* Women's Christian Temperance Union
Weather Bureau, US, 1069–1070
Weathermen, 1440
Weaver, Clifford, 1523
Weaver, Robert, 834, 839
Web, Del, 813
Webb, Clive, 1275
Weber, Adna Ferrin, 795
Weber, Max, 109–110
Wei Li, 1473–1474
Wei Min She, 748–749
Weingart, Ben, 908
Weir, Margaret, 1336n19
Weiss, Alexander, 1329
Weiss, Mark, 793–794, 840
welfare liberalism, 1449–1451
welfare programs, **1153–1172**. *See also* child welfare;
    Social Security Act
    abuse of, 1146
    AFDC, 261, 1146
    in company towns, 96
    funding of, 1163
    Great Society and, 1154
    modern social policies, 1162–1163
    Polish immigration as influence on, 611
    Project Head Start, 1157

welfare programs (*Continued*)
   for public assistance, 1145–1146
   public social expenditures for, 1165*t*
   reform of, 1146
   TANF, 1146
   War on Poverty and, 1154
"welfare queens," 1146
Weller, Charles, 1529
Weller, Eugenia, 1529
Welles, Orson, 230
Wells, Christopher, 942, 959, 964, 969
Wells, Ida B., 1278
Wells-Barnett, Ida B., 189, 583
Wenner, Jann, 1235
Weschler, Nancy, 672
Wesley, Cynthia, 1408
West, Kanye, 1239, 1263–1264
Westerhaven, David C., 1519
Westhoff, Laura, 129
West Side Story, 719, 1324
wharf activity, in early seaport cities, 25
Wheeler, Wayne, 419, 421–422
When You're Smiling: The Deadly Legacy of Internment, 765
Whig Party, 120
Whiskey Rebellion, 1272
White, Dan, 141, 672
White, E. B., 1039
White, George, 394
White, Graham, 392
White, Kevin, 360
White, Shane, 53, 392, 401
White, Sherman, 397
White, Stanford, 1002
"White City," Chicago as, 356, 883–884, 884*f*
white-collar cities, 106–107
white-collar workers
   as census category, 318n5
   gentrification influenced by, 1561
   in postindustrial service economies, 308–309, 309*t*, 312
   universities and, 340
white flight, to suburbs, 141–142, 648
   automobile use and, 970
   deindustrialization and, 324
   immigration and, 496
   interstate highways and, 957
   sidewalks and city streets and, 985
white laborers, in urban South, 49
white migration, **593–603**
   demographics of, 593–595
   map of, 593–595
   metropolitanization and, 599–601
   during postwar era, 597–599
   from Rust Belt, 593–594

   to Sunbelt region, 594
   to Western states, 593
   of women, 594–595
   during World War II, 595–597
   WPA and, 595
White Negro, 1217
white slavery, 49, 442–443
White Slave Traffic Act, US (1910), 443
white vigilantism
   through Ku Klux Klan, 80, 420, 1277
   through rioting, 1275–1276
Whitman, Walt, 996
Whitney, Eli, 45
Whores, Housewives, and Others (WHO), 450
Why Not Victory? A Fresh Look at American Foreign Policy (Goldwater, B.), 1444
Whyte, William H., 98, 316, 957, 1462, 1471
Wickensham, George, 421
Wiebe, Robert, 191
Wiese, Andrew, 792, 794, 796
The Wild Boys of the Road, 228
Wilder, Douglass, 1409
Wilentz, Sean, 54, 128
Wilkerson, Isabell, 589
Wilkerson, Martha F., 1284
Wilkins, Roy, 1437
Willard, Frances, 414–415
William, Raymond, 915
Williams, Amanda, 330
Williams, Augusta, 1397
Williams, Eugene, 576
Williams, Joe, 1217
Williams, John, 436
Williams, Nell, 1397
Williams, Rhonda, 824, 827, 839
Williams, Robert F., 1326, 1378
Williams, William, 511–513
Williamson, Lisa, 1259
Willis, Bill, 373
Willis, Carol, 860, 866–867
Willis, Lee L., 423
Willis, Winston E., 362
Wilson, Ellen, 1529
Wilson, James, 574, 1536
Wilson, Lionel, 138
Wilson, Pete, 777–778
Wilson, William, 272, 896
Wilson, William Julius, 1331, 1333
Wilson, Woodrow, 186, 189, 419, 515, 1529
Wind, Timothy, 1317n1
Wing Chee, 1299. *See also* anti-Chinese massacre
Winn, Robert, 779
Winterville (chiefdom), 5
Winthrop, John, 1107
Wirka, Susan Marie, 896

Wisconsin Idea, 182–183
Wise, Isaac Mayer, 1112
Wittman, Carl, 669, 673
Wobblies. *See* Industrial Workers of the World
Wohl, Martin, 944
Wolcott, Victoria, 572, 1285
Wolfe, Tom, 1452
Woman Order, 437
women. *See also* gender discrimination; gender ideology; gender roles; girls; prostitution; sex markets; sexual harassment; sex work
  at Angel Island Immigration Station, 534–535
  in artisanal production, 48
  in central business districts, 170–171
  in City Beautiful movement, 893–895
  clubs and organizations, 170, 181. *See also specific clubs and organizations*
  as consumer market, 170–171
  in environmental movements, 1015
  gentrification and, 1562–1563
  in hip-hop music, 1254–1255, 1257, 1260–1262
  as hotel patrons, 170
  incomes of, in early cities, 44
  Irish immigrants, 626
  as laborers, during World War II, 265
  migration of, for white women, 594–595
  in Polish immigration community, 606–609
  as political activists, 125
  in postindustrial service economies, 311
  poverty and, 1145–1146
  in professional basketball, 378
  in rap music, 1254–1255, 1257, 1260–1262
  "Rosie the Riveter," 265
  on streetcars, 940
  in street gangs, 1325, 1337n26
  suburbanization and, 787, 1463
  in temperance movement, 409, 414–415
  as theater patrons, 170
  during US Civil War, southern attitudes of, 73
  vagrancy laws and, 1351
  voting rights for, 181, 190
  wage inequality for, 48
  working-class, 50, 170
Women's Christian Temperance Union (WCTU), 415–416, 420–422
Women's Liberation Movement
  Asian American political movements and, 751–752
  early foundations of, 1439
Women's Municipal League, 125
Women's Peace Party, 188
Women's Trade Union League, 124
Wonder, Stevie, 1234
Wong Chin, 1299
Wong Tuck, 1297
Won Tu Tuk, 1299. *See also* anti-Chinese massacre

Wood, Edith Elmer, 815, 818, 1529
Wood, Elizabeth, 821
Wood, Fernando, 119, 440, 996
Wood, Jennie, 1397
Wood, Robert, 1464
Woods, Henry, 413
Woods, Sylvia, 1095
Woodson, Carter G., 582, 586
Woodward, C. Vann, 78
Woolfolk, Austin, 45, 159
Woolworth, Frank, 865
Work, Monroe Nathan, 592n20
working class. *See also* blue-collar workers
  Polish immigrants as, 614–615
  women in, 50, 170
working-class neighborhoods. *See also* blue-collar workers
  development of, 50
  Five Points, 50
  urban redevelopment as influence on, 135–136
  women in, 50
working hours, limitations of. *See also* "yellow dog" contracts
  for federal laborers, 271
  Lochner v. New York, 180, 256
  Muller v. Oregon and, 180, 256
workingmen's associations, 802–803
workingmen's movement, 119
Workingmen's Party, 483
workplace discrimination. *See* employment discrimination
Works Progress Administration (WPA), 200, 229–230
  criticism of, 230
  as Democratic Party machine, 230
  machine politics and, 126
  poverty and, 1147
  public sector unions under, 275–276
  universities and, 343
  urban tourism and, 358
  Writers' Project, 211
World Bank, 226
World's Fairs, 213. *See also* city expositions
World Trade Center, 871, 873–875
World Trade Organization, China in, 102
World War I
  crop production declines during, 246n31
  Ellis Island Immigration Station during, 515–517
  the Great Depression and, 197–198
  Great Migration during, 257, 567–569
  labor improvements during, 257
  labor unions during, 257
  Polish immigration during, 609–611
  prostitution during, 444–447
  public authorities during, 297
  suburbanization during and after, 792–795
  US entry into, 188

World War II. *See also* Cold War
    Asian American neighborhoods after, redevelopment
        policies for, 1545–1547
    company towns during, 96
    drug subcultures during, 469
    Ellis Island Immigration Station during,
        517–518
    GI Bill loans after, 107
    immigration during, 499
    internment camps during, 499
    Japanese immigration to US during, 499, 758
    jazz music after, 1215
    labor during, 264–266
    major league baseball after, 371
    mass transit during, 942
    National War Labor Board and, 264–265
    Native Americans during, 690
    Point Four program after, 226
    Polish immigration during and after, 611–615
    postindustrial service economies during and
        after, 310, 313
    prostitution during, 447–448
    public authorities during and after, 292–294
    public housing during and after, 811, 820
    public schools after, 1180–1185
    public sector unions after, growth of, 277–279
    riots during, 1281
    "Rosie the Riveter," 265
    skyscraper construction after, 870–872
    street gangs during, 1321–1322
    urban American South during, 77
    urban renewal during, 1531–1532
    urban tourism after, 360
    US economic development after, 1419
    white migration during, 595–597
    WRA, 759, 761–762
WPA. *See* Works Progress Administration
WRA. *See* War Relocation Authority
Wright, Carroll, 435
Wright, Fielding Lewis, 1398
Wright, Frank Lloyd, 867, 1065
Wright, Gwendolyn, 803, 815, 839
Wright, Harry, 369
Wright, Henry, 793, 906
Wright, Jane, 436
Wright, Richard, 211
Wright, Richard R., Jr., 592n20
Writers' Project, 211
Wu Tang Clan, 1259
Wyly, Elvin, 1558
Wyman, Walter, 1052
Wytrwal, Joseph A., 615

X, Malcolm, 746, 1130, 1326, 1378
    NOI and, 1127–1128, 1447

YAF. *See* Young Americans for Freedom
Yale Scientific School, 341
Yamasaki, Minoru, 822
Yamasee War, 22–23
Yamauchi, Wakako, 753
"yellow dog" contracts, 203, 256
yellow fever epidemics, 23, 1050–1051
    from environmental pollution, 1029–1030
Yến Đỗ, 774
Yin Kim, 1492–1493
YMCA. *See* Young Men's Christian Association
Yoshimura, Evelyn, 751, 1497
Young, Alfred, 31
Young, Andrew, 146
Young, Coleman, 133, 138, 143, 146
Young, Neil, 1234
Young, Whitney, 1437
Young Americans for Freedom (YAF), 1437, 1444
Young Kyu Yi, 1308
Young Men's Christian Association (YMCA),
        413–414, 536
    racial segregation by, 1368
Young Women's Christian Association (YWCA), 536
    racial segregation by, 1368
yuppies, as consumer market, 175
YWCA. *See* Young Women's Christian Association

Za Chlebem (For Bread), 603
Zander, Arnold, 276
Zarsadiaz, James, 1504
Zeckendorf, William, 868, 870
Zeiler, Thomas, 102–103
Zesch, Scott, 1296
Zia, Helen, 1300, 1308
Zieger, Robert, 239
Ziegler, John, 376
Zinn, Howard, 240, 1425
Zipp, Samuel, 106, 316
Zitello, Gemma, 516
Znaniecki, Florian, 610, 615
zoning laws, **1516–1528**
    American Society of Planning Officials and,
        1523–1524
    in Atlanta, 1522
    Berman v. Parker, 1524
    Buchanan v. Warley, 808, 1522–1523
    eminent domain and, 1524
    environmental pollution and, 1032
    Euclid v. Ambler Realty, 1516, 1519–1520
    form-based codes in, 1525
    German models for, 1517–1518
    Hadacheck v. Sebastian, 1518
    Hopkins v. City of Richmond, 1522
    under Housing Act of 1949, 1524
    land use regulations, recasting of, 1524–1525

Marsh, B., and, 1517–1518
Nectow v. City of Cambridge, 1520
in New York City, 1032, 1517–1519
in 19th Century, 1517–1518
nonconforming uses in, 1519
overlay districts and, 1525
PUDs and, 1516
purpose of, 1516
racial origins of, 1521–1523
racial segregation influenced by, 794
religious segregation through, 794
residential segregation through, 794
skyscrapers under, 865–867
SSZEA, 1520–1521

in St. Louis, 1032
in suburbs, 793–794
in Supreme Court cases, 808, 1516–1520, 1522–1524
TDRs and, 1516
TND and, 1516
in 20th Century American cities, 1516–1525
in urban planning, 905
under Urban Redevelopment Act, 1524
urban reform of, 1525
Vanderbilt v. Adam, 1517
Zoot Suit riots, 499, 1323
Zueblin, Charles, 892
Zukin, Sharon, 112, 360, 364
Zweig, Michael, 281